Major British Writers

CHAUCER

SPENSER

SHAKESPEARE

BACON

DONNE

MILTON

DRYDEN

SWIFT

POPE

JOHNSON

BOSWELL

ENLARGED EDITION

I

HARCOURT, BRACE & WORLD, INC. *New York Burlingame*

COPYRIGHTS AND ACKNOWLEDGMENTS

Selections from the Manly-Rickert text of *The Canterbury Tales* (1940) used by permission of the publishers, the University of Chicago Press.

A NOTE ON THE COVER: The coat of arms reproduced on the cover of this book is that of the Worshipful Company of Stationers and Papermakers of London. This ancient City Company was originally a guild of stationers and craftsmen who made and dealt in parchment, paper, quill pens, and materials for binding books. In 1557 (eighty-one years after printing was first introduced into England) the Stationers were granted a charter which gave them the monopoly of the "Art or Mystery of Printing." At the same time they received their coat of arms from the College of Heralds. For many years it was the custom for the titles of books to be printed by members of the Company to be entered in the Stationers' Register, which is thus a record of the first printing of most of the famous works known to students of the literature of the sixteenth and seventeenth centuries.

To W. A. B.

To W.A.B.

CONTENTS

WILLIAM SHAKESPEARE   *Edited by* G. B. HARRISON

FRANCIS BACON   *Edited by* BASIL WILLEY

JOHN DONNE   *Edited by* BASIL WILLEY

JOHN MILTON   Edited by DOUGLAS BUSH

JOHN DRYDEN   *Edited by* MARK VAN DOREN

PREFACE

Great literature can be studied mainly in two ways. It can be regarded as part of the history and culture of a people; and if so, the student should become acquainted with an extensive collection of many samples and varieties. It can also be regarded as the product of fine minds; and if so, it is better to study the works of great writers with greater intensity.

Either approach has its advantages — and disadvantages. The wide survey gives a nodding acquaintance with many writers and a little of the best of each, but the selections must inevitably be too few and too brief for full understanding of any one author. The study in depth necessitates selection and concentration — certain favorite writers and certain fashionable movements must inevitably be left out. Those who still prefer the study in breadth are well supplied with several good and well-known anthologies, but there is no adequate text for the more intensive study. To supply this need is the aim of *Major British Writers*.

In planning this collection we determined as a first, basic principle that each author should be *fully* represented, preferably by complete works, or, whenever that was physically impossible, by large sections. *Major British Writers* thus offers, within its two volumes, a significant proportion, averaging 75,000 words, of the best writing of twenty-two great authors.

The first — and most difficult — editorial problem in planning these volumes was to select the authors to be represented. Our principle was threefold: the author must be great in himself, representative of his age, and, not least important, significant to the modern reader. In any collection of " major writers," Chaucer, Spenser, Shakespeare, and Milton will first be chosen; but thereafter selection becomes more difficult.

With our principles before us we have chosen Donne to represent the Elizabethan and Jacobean poets because of his great influence on modern poets and critics. Bacon as the father of the modern scientific method and as a master of English prose in his own right was picked as the prose writer of the first half of the seventeenth century rather than Thomas Browne. Dryden, Pope, and Swift represent the " Augustans," though we omitted Addison with regret. Dr. Johnson represents his own inimitable self, but, especially since the discovery of the Boswell Papers, he is inseparable from his biographer, James Boswell. Of the great writers of the early nineteenth century the pre-eminence of Wordsworth, Coleridge, Byron, Shelley, and Keats is hardly disputable. Choice in the Victorian period was far more difficult. While we selected Tennyson, Browning, and Arnold, we realize that some would have substituted for one or another of our preferences Carlyle, Ruskin, Newman, or Mill.

We determined also to include some of the moderns, that is, authors who have been writing during the past half century. Here the choice is embarrassingly difficult. While we doubt whether any reader would reject from the company of the "great moderns" the names of Shaw, Yeats, or Eliot, we realize that every reader would wish to include also at least half a dozen of his own favorites — and thereby have made the second volume of *Major British Writers* impossibly bulky.

The next problem was to plan the editing. We felt that the intensive selections would require equally intensive editing — each writer should be introduced by a full critical essay and should be well annotated. While uniformity was desirable, we regarded the quality of the editing as far more important. We therefore decided to invite a different scholar and critic of well-established reputation to edit each section with the hope that the diversity of gifts of each editor would be fully used. We believe that this hope has been realized and that the critical essays in *Major British Writers* will be recognized as notable contributions to English literary criticism.

Certain general principles were suggested to each editor. Wherever it seemed suitable, they were asked to include in their introductions a biographical sketch of the author, an appreciation of his work as a whole, and a more detailed consideration of some chosen examples of his work. In this way we hoped to meet the differing interests of teachers and students. Further, editors were made aware of what their colleagues were doing, and the selections were correlated. Thus the passages chosen from John Dryden include the remarkable appreciation of Chaucer from the Preface to *Fables, Ancient and Modern* and those from Samuel Johnson include the famous criticism of the "Metaphysical poets" from the *Life of Cowley,* as well as large excerpts from the Preface to Shakespeare and the *Lives of Milton* and *Pope.* Similarly in selecting from the Coleridge lectures on Shakespeare, those on *Hamlet* and *The Tempest* were chosen. The section given to Matthew Arnold includes his essays on Wordsworth and Keats, while Shakespeare and Donne are again illustrated by Mr. Eliot's essays on "*Hamlet*" and "The Metaphysical Poets."

In technical matters it should be noted that while the spelling of Chaucer, Spenser, Byron, Shelley, Keats (in his letters), Tennyson, Shaw, Yeats, and Eliot (the last two in their poetry) has been kept, in general, spelling, use of capitals, punctuation, and other typographical matters conform with modern American usage. In poetry the final *-ed,* when accented, is marked with a diacritical mark and the earlier practice, never consistent, of omitting the silent *e* has been dropped; thus we print *determinèd* and *determined,* and not *determinéd* and *determin'd.* In the first volume (but not in the second) the sign ° has been used in verse passages to call attention to a word or passage annotated; in prose a superior numeral has been used.

In such a project as this contributors and organizers become acutely aware of each other's personalities. Publisher and General Editor wish to thank the several editors for their patience and forbearance, and for their exceptional, friendly, and ready co-operation at all times.

G. B. H.

Ann Arbor, Michigan
January 10, 1959

Major British Writers

Geoffrey Chaucer

1343?–1400

In his lifetime Geoffrey Chaucer was hailed as the greatest poet of his age. And today, after more than five and a half centuries, during which the warmth, color, humor, and humanity of his poetry have endeared him to his readers, his name stands in the annals of English literature second only to that of Shakespeare.

There are few poets who have so strongly impressed their personalities upon what they wrote as Chaucer, and there are fewer still whose writings suggest such an engaging personality as his. To every age he seems perennially new. His comments on life, despite the lapse of years, are the comments we would like to make. His tone is immediate, modern, and companionable. He speaks not as a forefather but as a brother. It would therefore be a matter of unusual interest to know what sort of man he was, but the answer is not easily found.

In his *Canterbury Tales* the poet supplies a glimpse of himself. "What sort of man are you?" the jovial Host of the Tabard Inn asks him as they ride together on a pilgrimage. "You look as if you were trying to find a hare, for I see you keep staring at the ground." Then, without waiting for an answer from the preoccupied poet, the corpulent Host exclaims to the other pilgrims, "Let this man have room! He's as well shaped in the waist as I am! He'd make quite a puppet for any slim and fair-faced woman to gather in her arms!" But, feeling perhaps that his sally has missed its mark, he adds, "To judge by his bearing, he seems like an elf, for he pays no attention to anyone." [1]

[1] Here and elsewhere throughout the Introduction medi-

But Chaucer's Host obviously saw only the externals; the elflike and elusive poet had no intention of revealing the depths of his character through an interpreter of this sort. And the other occasions on which Chaucer portrays himself in his writings are equally inconclusive, so that we are forced to turn in our quest for further clues to the records of his life, though these are fragmentary and impersonal and leave much to surmise.

I. CHAUCER'S CIVIL CAREER

Chaucer was by instinct a poet, but he was also a practical man of affairs and earned his living chiefly in what we would now call the civil service. He was born about 1343 of a wealthy bourgeois family and was comfortably reared in London. He probably did not attend either Oxford or Cambridge, though he may have studied civil law and business procedure in London at the law school known as the Inner Temple. Certainly, whatever the source of his education, he acquired a sound knowledge of Latin, French, and Italian and a wide familiarity with the world of letters; and his career gave him an acquaintance with the world of people such as has fallen to the lot of few poets.

He gained his first practical experience by serving variously as page boy, valet, and esquire in the household of Elizabeth of Ulster, a daughter-in-law of King Edward III. His duties were

eval sources have when convenient been quoted in modernized form.

at first humble, including probably such mundane jobs as making beds and looking after clothing, but he had the compensations of traveling in Elizabeth's retinue throughout England and perhaps in Ireland and enjoying a valet's-eye view of the ruling aristocracy of his age. He also served as a soldier against the French under Elizabeth and subsequently under King Edward's influential son, John of Gaunt, and thus learned at first hand something of the mingled chivalry and sordidness of the Hundred Years' War. On one occasion, in company with several of Elizabeth's officers, he was captured by the French but returned by one of those ransoms which Froissart tells us the French and English always arranged so amicably.

In 1366 he married Philippa Roet, who was lady in waiting to her Flemish compatriot Queen Philippa, King Edward's wife, and later to Constance of Castile, John of Gaunt's second wife. By this marriage Chaucer apparently had two sons and a daughter. Both he and his wife throughout their lifetime seem to have found warm friends among the members of the reigning house.

From 1368 on he served occasionally as a royal diplomatic agent in France and, at least twice, in Italy—a duty for which his linguistic ability and his tact suited him and which in turn certainly contributed most profitably to his own literary development. For the most part, however, he lived a settled life in London. In 1374 he was appointed by King Edward as Controller of Customs and Subsidy of Wools, Skins, and Hides. This was a responsible position, for wool was one of England's most valuable dutiable exports. He discharged his duties personally until 1385 and through a deputy until 1386, when his appointment lapsed.

In 1385 he moved temporarily outside the city of London into the neighboring county of Kent, where he held the office of Justice of the Peace; and in 1386 he represented the county for one session as member of parliament. His wife apparently died in 1387, and in 1389 he returned to London as Clerk of the Works, to supervise such important matters as construction and repairs around Westminster Abbey, the Tower of London, Windsor Castle, the royal manor at West Sheen (now Richmond on the Thames), and the south bank of the Thames between Greenwich and Woolwich. By 1391 he had been re-

moved, probably at his own request, from this strenuous responsibility and appointed to a less onerous charge as Subforester of the King's forest at North Petherton, 130 miles west of London.

In 1399 he rented a house in the gardens of Westminster Abbey, and in 1400 he died and was buried in the section of the south transept of the Abbey which later came to be known as the Poets' Corner.

Other isolated records of Chaucer's civil career have survived, but they do not add much to our understanding of him, and even those details that have been mentioned are open to various interpretations. In general, however, it may be said that Chaucer lived a busy and comparatively prosperous life throughout a stormy period of English history. In his lifetime the warrior King Edward III died in his dotage (in 1377), the boy King Richard II succeeded his grandfather on the throne, and the bold Henry IV in 1399 deposed the ineffectual Richard. (See Additional Note D below, p. 197.) When Richard ascended the throne, Chaucer was apparently on familiar terms with the ten-year-old boy and his mother, the Fair Maid of Kent, for he addressed a fatherly poem of personal advice to the new monarch; and even after Richard had been deposed, his position at court remained sufficiently privileged that he felt free to address a playful request for the replenishment of his purse to the new King Henry.

Both Chaucer and his wife were granted annuities and other perquisites by royal employers and patrons. Chaucer received from King Edward at least two lucrative wardships of heirs who had become orphans while not yet of age. He was awarded by Edward a lifetime gift of a daily pitcher of Gascon wine, and by Richard an annual butt of wine—a gift which was renewed by Henry, who also presented him with a scarlet robe trimmed with fur.

Since other civil servants received similar rewards, these may have been bestowed on Chaucer for his usefulness in public affairs, not for his literary achievements. Even his burial in Westminster Abbey may not have been intended as a special honor accorded to a national poet, for Chaucer was living on the grounds and may have been entitled to burial in the Abbey as a tenant. But there can be no doubt that Chaucer was widely acclaimed as a writer in his lifetime, and nowhere more enthusiastically than at the brilliant court of his royal employers.

His works circulated universally in manuscript while he was alive, and after his death new copies continued to appear in profusion until the introduction of printing. Eighty-four different manuscripts of the *Canterbury Tales* actually survive to the present time. And among the first works to appear from Caxton's press in the fifteenth century were the writings of Chaucer, whom England's first printer saluted as " the worshipful father and first founder and embellisher of ornate eloquence in our English " and as a writer who " ought eternally to be remembered."

II. CHAUCER'S LITERARY CAREER

Chaucer was, like Spenser and Milton, a writer who possessed the energy and inspiration to live laborious days and produce great poetry in the midst of an active career. We know that he had already turned to poetry in his twenties, and there is every indication that he was still at work when he died in his fifties.

His early work is conventional and strongly influenced by contemporary French verse, though even then its voice bears the individuality of Chaucer. His earliest extant poem is a prayer to the Virgin Mary translated freely from Guillaume Deguilleville's *Pilgrimage of the Human Life,* and it is remarkable both for its religious sensitivity and its metrical skill. A comparison of even one stanza of Chaucer's flowing verse with the abrupt and inverted phrasing of the Old French original will suffice to foreshadow the greatness to come.

> *A toi du monde le refui,*
> *Vierge glorieuse, m'en fui*
> *Tout confus. Ne puis miex faire.*
> *A toi me tien, a toi m'apui.*
> *Relieve moi! Abatu sui.*
> *Vaincu m'a mon aversaire.*
> *Puis qu'en toi ont tous repaire,*
> *Bien me doi vers toi retraire*
> *Avant que j'aie plus d'annui.*
> *N'est pas luite necessaire*
> *A moi, se tu, debonnaire,*
> *Ne me sequeurs comme a autrui.*[1]

[1] To thee, the refuge of the world, glorious Virgin, I flee all confounded. Better I cannot do. To thee I hold, on thee I rest. Relieve me! I am stricken. My adversary has conquered me. Since all have resort to thee, I may well retreat to thee before I suffer more distress. No strife is necessary for me, if thou, O gracious one, succor me as thou hast others.

Almighty and al merciable quene,
To whom that al this world fleeth for socour
To have relees of sinne, sorwe, and tene,
Glorious virgine, of alle floures flour,
To thee I flee, confounded in errour!
Help and releve, thou mighty debonaire!
Have mercy on my perilous langour!
Venquisshed me hath my cruel adversaire.

Chaucer's other early works include some love lyrics in which he expresses his complete devotion to his beloved lady in the conventionally plaintive tone which was first affected by courtly European poets in the twelfth century and remained popular in England until the appearance of John Donne. " The more I love, the more she makes me smart," he cries in a typically exaggerated passage. " Through which I see that, without remedy, from death I can in no way escape."

His first extensive and original poem, the graceful *Book of the Duchess,* was composed as a tribute to the memory of the charming young Duchess Blanche, John of Gaunt's first wife, who died in 1369. Here too Chaucer imitates his French contemporaries in features such as the conventional description of the lady, but the tone and conception of the work are original; and though some of its phrases may have been borrowed, Chaucer has adapted them ideally to the pathetic circumstances which occasioned its composition.

In comparison with his final achievements, however, his earlier poetry savors more of artifice than of art, perhaps because of the influence of his sophisticated and quite un-English models. From the first he showed a particularly marked affection for his three famous French contemporaries, the court musician and poet Machaut, Machaut's disciple Deschamps, and the aristocratic chronicler and poet Froissart — all of whom were courtly writers, brilliant in style, witty, mordant, and graceful, but with none of the unassuming geniality of the later Chaucer.

Early in his career, also, Chaucer read, absorbed, and in part translated the French *Romance of the Rose.* The first part of this vast poem, left unfinished in the 1230's by Guillaume de Lorris, portrays allegorically the difficulties experienced by a young lover in attaining the love of the Rose, a maiden withheld from him by all the restraints imposed by the conventions of courtly love. In contrast, the panoramic completion supplied by Jean de Meun in the 1270's argues that neither faintness of heart nor the dictates of reason, nor false modesty, nor the contemplation of impending old age, nor the dissimulation, avarice, and malice of society can blight the beneficent processes of Nature and the generative forces of Love. Under the influence of such an exhaustive and suggestive treatment, it is hardly surprising that Chaucer always showed a lively awareness of the many-sided problems of love.

Later, the great Italian poets of his own century exercised their spell. His uncompleted *House of Fame* was evidently written after his appointment to the Customs (1374), for in it he reports that after doing his daily reckonings he has sat up at his books at home each night, reading till he is dazed and writing till his head aches. This poem proves that Chaucer had already made an acquaintance with Italian literature, perhaps as the result of his diplomatic journeys in Italy. In the poem he dreams that a garrulous eagle has carried him off to show him whether those in the service of Love are really glad or not; and the eagle (whose mission Chaucer unfortunately left unfulfilled) is modeled upon a more modest eagle guide in Dante's *Divine Comedy* (1307–21).

As Chaucer matured, he turned his attention to philosophy and (*c.* 1380) translated the *Consolation of Philosophy* into English prose. This influential work was written by Boethius, a Roman nobleman, statesman, and scholar unjustly condemned to death in 524 by the Emperor Theodoric. In it the author, imprisoned and awaiting execution, laments that Fortune continually turns her whirling wheel, indifferently changing the lowest to the highest and the highest to the lowest; and Philosophy replies that God, providently aware of man's vicissitudes, makes even adverse Fortune work towards the ultimate good of man. The subtle interplay of argument obviously appealed to Chaucer, in whose later works the words, phrases, and ideas of Boethius reappear in many contexts.

At about the same time Chaucer may have prepared the first draft of the Clerk's Tale, later included in the *Canterbury Tales*. This tale he translated from the Latin prose version of the story of Griseldis as told by the Italian poet Petrarch, who in turn had derived the story from Boccaccio's Italian collection of tales, the famous *Decameron* (1353).

In this same period Chaucer assured himself of lasting greatness by writing his brilliant tragic romance, *Troilus and Criseyde,* a masterly reinterpretation of the material used by Boccaccio in his poem, the *Filostrato.* Chaucer was invited to recite his poem in public before the most distinguished members of the English court — an event memorialized in an appropriately splendid illuminated picture on the frontispiece of one of the *Troilus* manuscripts. His fame was now secure. He was hailed by Deschamps in a French eulogy as a Socrates in philosophy, a Seneca in morality, an Aulus Gellius [1] in practical affairs, and an Ovid in poetry. The literary apprentice had become the master of his art and the model for posterity.

In the year 1387 Chaucer began to compile materials for the *Canterbury Tales,* his most original and most characteristically English work. The framework of this collection of tales was provided by a familiar English scene, the journey to Canterbury of a group of pilgrims, whom Chaucer describes in a general prologue and in links connecting the tales.

According to Chaucer's ambitious plan, each of the thirty or more pilgrims was to tell two tales on the road to Canterbury and two on the road back to London. He died before he had completed the poem, but he did write twenty-four tales, consisting of more than two thousand lines of prose and seventeen thousand lines of verse, most of them linked together by animated conversations between the pilgrims and their master of ceremonies, the Host of the Tabard Inn; and in so doing won for himself an unchallenged position, in the words of Spenser, " on Fame's eternal beed-roll."

III. CHAUCER'S WORLD

The differences between the age of the Canterbury pilgrimages and our own technological era are considerable, though some of the more obvious dissimilarities are superficial. Travel, for example, was slower and more painful than it is today. Thus, while it took Chaucer's pilgrims two or three days of rough riding on horseback over indifferent roads to travel the

---

[1] A Roman philosopher who was respected not only as a writer but also as a judge.

sixty miles from London to Canterbury, leisurely sight-seers now ride the distance by bus in two or three hours. But the vital differences of social and political structure and of religious life, which are much more important in determining the quality of man's behavior, are far from obvious to the casual reader of Chaucer.

In the fourteenth century the government of England was aristocratic rather than democratic, and the efficacy of the monarch's rule depended largely on the strength of his character and on the power of the nobles whom he could rally to his support. Hence the fate of the country was determined by the personality of the king in a manner now quite undreamed of.

Next to the king, the richest and most influential people in England were those, such as John of Gaunt, who controlled vast agricultural areas. These privileged few had feudal possession of the land, in return for which they supplied manpower, equipment, and money for the wars of their overlord. Inevitably their views played a large part in the administration of the internal and external affairs of the realm. A number of lesser landlords of various ranks were dependent upon them. And, at the bottom of the feudal order, the unprivileged many were virtual serfs who worked the land for their masters. Feudal custom varied from locality to locality, and the social structure was not completely fixed. The king might grant lands and title to a commoner, or a needy knight might marry off his aristocratic son to the plebian daughter of a farmer, provided the farmer was wealthy. But, in general, the people of England accepted as inevitable the rank, whether high or low, to which they were born and the feudal privileges and duties accompanying it.

The workings of the system are mirrored in seven of the Canterbury pilgrims. The Knight held land and in return for it served in the wars of his overlord, the king, and when necessary supplied trained fighting men; his son, the Squire, was learning to follow in his father's footsteps; and the Knight's Yeoman was a family servant trained to uphold the way of life of his master. The Franklin was an independent gentleman farmer who probably supplied military assistance to the country, when necessary, by a payment of some kind rather than by personal service. The Miller by feudal right milled all the grains grown in an area assigned to him and charged a toll for his service. (Chaucer tells us that his Miller contrived to exact a triple toll!) The Reeve managed a large country estate, and the Plowman was a serf bound to employment under the owner of the land on which he was born.

But in Chaucer's day feudalism did not embrace the entire population, for urban life with its greater social freedom was beginning to play an important role in England. Thirteen of the pilgrims are dependent on the economy of the town, much as they would be today—the Manciple (a purchasing agent), the Merchant (a wholesale importer-exporter), the Shipman (the owner of a merchant ship), the Haberdasher, the Carpenter, the Weaver, the Dyer, the Tapestry Maker, the Cook, the Clothmaker (the Wife of Bath), the Innkeeper, and, to some extent, the two professional men, the Physician and the Sergeant of the Law.

The influences of religion were, in contrast to our own day, much more nearly omnipresent in human affairs, whether spiritual or secular, rural or urban. There was only one church, and everyone was a Catholic. People might, and did, disobey the teachings of Holy Church, but no one could ignore it. It controlled all education and, in addition to its regular services of worship, played a daily part among all ranks of society and at all stages of a person's life, from the time of baptism through confirmation and marriage to the funeral rites at burial. It held vast areas of land throughout England, and its complex organization included not merely the regular clergy attached to churches but also a great number of other religious, such as monks and nuns dedicated to the contemplative life and friars devoted to an active life of service to mankind.

Consequently the reader should not be surprised to discover that no less than thirteen of Chaucer's pilgrims depend in some manner upon the church—the Parson, the Summoner (a sort of church policeman), the Monk, the Prioress with her accompanying Nun and three Priests, the Friar, the Pardoner, the Clerk (an ecclesiastical university student), and the Canon and his Yeoman who later join the pilgrimage.

The deeply religious undercurrent of medieval life is clearly apparent in Chaucer's Canterbury pilgrimage. It springs to birth in a common meeting place at the crossroads of England under the inspiration of a worldly innkeeper and commences with a courtly romance told by a knight. But the pilgrims, worldly and unworldly alike, regardless of rank or of wealth, are all directed towards a holy shrine in a solemn cathedral. The last tale they hear is a sermon by a godly parson who points their thoughts towards the "perfect glorious pilgrimage called heavenly Jerusalem"; and this tale is concluded by Chaucer with a repudiation of all that is sinful in his writing and a prayer that he "may be one of them at the Day of Judgment that shall be saved."

In one important respect, however, Chaucer's age was closely akin to ours, for just as much as our own it was a prey to all the ills that flesh is heir to. It was troubled by disease, political insecurity, international animosity, religious dissension, social unrest, and economic disasters.

The Black Plague, which ravaged Europe in 1348, entered England and, like "the privy thief called Death" alluded to in the Pardoner's Tale, slew in every town and village "both man and woman, child, and hind, and page." At its first onslaught it is said to have wiped out perhaps half the population of England. In succeeding years it recurred with appalling severity. It bereft parishes of priests, farms of laborers, and towns of workmen and enriched no one with the possible exception of fortunate doctors such as Chaucer's shrewd Physician, who "kept what he gained in the pestilence." It spared neither the talented nor the great, killing a profound scholar like Archbishop Bradwardine of Canterbury, yet it passed by corrupt men like Chaucer's Friar and Pardoner, who were enabled by the death of honest churchmen to climb unchecked to power and wealth.

The Black Death affected England's economy more disastrously than did World War II. Surviving laborers were so scarce that they refused to work unless granted excessive wages. Commodities also became scarce and prices high. Under the unfortunate young Richard II the attempts of the king's council to control the economy failed, and the "stormy people, unstable and ever untrue" rebelled. During the Peasant's Revolt of 1381 an unruly mob broke into London and murdered those whom they considered to be their exploiters, including some unhappy Flemish weavers (referred to by the Nun's Priest) whose competition they resented.

Political life was a dangerous struggle for power. Chaucer's Man of Law remarks in his tale that an observer can always recognize the "pale face, among a crowd, of one that is lead toward his death." And Chaucer had every reason to share this disquieting knowledge, for in 1388 Nicholas Brembre, one of his superiors in the Customs, and Thomas Usk, one of his literary disciples, were executed, along with several others, because of their ill-advised support of King Richard during the temporary ascendancy of the Duke of Gloucester's party.

During the reign of King Richard, the Hundred Years' War between France and England took on a less promising complexion than it had in the happy days of Edward III's victories at Crécy and Poitiers. As the French rallied, England began to fear invasion. English merchant ships had to be impressed for naval service; shore defenses were prepared; and everyone experienced at least some kind of inconvenience, including Chaucer's self-interested Merchant, who feared that his shipping lanes between England and Holland would be cut off.

Not even the great power and influence of the Church were able to bring peace between the two most cultured nations of western Europe, for the Church itself suffered the weakness of division. During the Great Schism from 1378 to 1417 the papacy lay divided. The pope at Rome was supported by the allegiance of the Holy Roman Empire and England, while the antipope at Avignon was supported by France, Scotland, and other nations. It is not surprising, therefore, that in England during this period of disorganization many abuses were committed against religion by fraudulent pardoners, mercenary friars, and worldly monks, whom Chaucer and other contemporary writers such as Gower and the author of *Piers Plowman* condemned, or that Wycliffe and his Lollard preachers went to the heretical length of questioning the very structure of the Church itself.

Despite these tribulations, however, England reached a cultural peak in the latter part of the fourteenth century. The English were warmly sympathetic to the cultural influences of the Continent. French art, architecture, and music, and — as we have seen in the sketch of Chaucer's own literary career — French and Italian literature were widely appreciated in courtly circles. England, moreover, had a distinguished literature of her own. The anonymous *Sir Gawain and the Green Knight,* for instance, represents the acme of the medieval Arthurian romance; and Langland's *Piers Plowman* is a remarkable and powerful satirical vision almost unique of its kind. Chaucer's supreme achievements were, in fact, a glory superadded to the already great attainments of his countrymen.

IV. CHAUCER'S TECHNIQUE

When we turn from an appraisal of Chaucer's era to the actual reading of his poetry, the distance of time, the differences of material culture, and the divergencies of human belief, custom, and behavior which separate his world from ours seem miraculously to disappear. The only barrier to our appreciation is one of language, and even that can no more hinder us from relishing his work than a foreign accent can prevent us from enjoying a talented actor on the stage or screen. Besides, our unfamiliarity with Chaucer's language is not his fault.

Chaucer, quaintly clad in antique guise,
With unfamiliar mien scares modern eyes.
No doubt he well invented, nobly felt,
But, O ye powers, how monstrously he spelt!

So wrote Hartley Coleridge, but he added an important injunction:

Yet, thou true poet, let no judgment wrong
Thy rich, spontaneous, many-colored song!

Fortunately for the judgment of Chaucer's song, modern readers soon grow accustomed to his antique guise, which was after all the living language of his day, and a language which he used with the most effortless grace. And, having once accustomed their ears to its melody, they will readily realize that in the control of meter, rhyme, and verse form Chaucer equals any of the great English poets of later times, just as he immeasurably excels his own contemporaries.

Chaucer developed a repertoire of meters hitherto unparalleled in English poetry. His especial forte lay in the five-beat line, which he evolved into various rhyming stanzas never used before in English, including the six-line stanza of the song at the end of the Clerk's Tale, the seven-line stanza (later known as the rhyme royal) of the Clerk's and Prioress's Tales, and the eight-line stanza of the Monk's Tale. But the verse form which he used most widely in the *Canterbury Tales* is the most famous, the five-beat couplet, later known in the age of Dryden and Pope as the heroic couplet.

Even a random inspection of the verse included in this volume will reveal Chaucer's ease and accuracy in rhyming and the sureness of his control over metrical regularity and variation. The rapid phrasing of the comic lines in the Nun's Priest's Tale (ll. 555–57) describing a widow's pursuit of a fox who has stolen her rooster may be compared, for instance, with the measured slowness of the tragic lines in the Prioress's Tale (ll. 134–35) describing a widow's vain search for her missing son:

The sely widw(e) and eek hir(e) doghtres two
Herden this(e) hennes cry(e) and maken wo,
And out att(e) dores stirten they anon, . . .

This poure wydw(e) awaiteth al that nyght
After her litel child, ‖ but he cam noght; . . .

In an attempt to explain the difference of effect in the two passages, one might point out that in the first extract the first two lines are run on and thus increase the impression of speed, while in the second extract the painful conclusion of the last line is delayed by a caesura. (Notice that, as in classical French poetry, final -*e*'s are pronounced unless elided with a following vowel.) But the total effect is, of course, determined by the context, for the real secret of poetry lies not in mere technique but in qualities which transcend all technicalities.

What then are the chief sources of Chaucer's greatness? The answers are numerous and interlinked, for literary effects are not attributable to a neat set of isolated features. Four of Chaucer's characteristics, however, may be said to be particularly important: namely, his affectionate understanding of mankind, his comic spirit, his narrative skill, and — surprisingly enough in an author who seems so spontaneous — his bookishness.

Perhaps one of the most deeply seated reasons for Chaucer's age-long popularity lies in his understanding portrayal of the character of people, young and old, rich and poor, saintly and sinful. Consider the individuality of his characterizations. In the General Prologue and links of the *Canterbury Tales,* for instance, we meet the ever-amorous Wife of Bath, the degenerate Pardoner who cheerfully confesses his own depraved and avaricious deceptions, the drunken and irreverent Miller, the courtly Prioress, the pious Parson who taught Christ's teaching but first followed it himself. " I see . . . all the pilgrims," said Dryden, " as distinctly as if I had supped with them at the Tabard in Southwark."

And the characters in the tales are equally memorable: the mysterious old man in the Pardoner's Tale who longs for death but cannot die; the tender little schoolboy in the Prioress's Tale who directs his whole being to the adoration of the Virgin Mary; Dorigen, the warmly affectionate and faithful wife in the Franklin's Tale; Griseldis, the pathetically submissive wife in the Clerk's Tale. From the way in which they are portrayed it is obvious that Chaucer enjoyed the contemplation of humanity.

In part Chaucer's characters seem eminently real because he has the power — intensified no doubt by travel — of fully visualizing them in his imagination and of then bringing them to life by depicting the salient and memorable features of their lineaments and gestures and the precise details of their clothing and equipment, even down to such minute externals as the lanyard on which the Shipman wears his dagger, the Yeoman's peacock arrows bright and sharp, the Franklin's daisy-white beard, the tuft of hairs crowning the Miller's wart as red as the bristles on a sow's ears.

Yet Chaucer also understands the inner qualities of mankind. We still can find men as boorish as the Miller or as devoted as the Parson, and ladies as dainty as the Prioress. As William Blake with his poet's wisdom and artist's perceptivity remarked after making a painting of the pilgrims, " Every age is a Canterbury Pilgrimage; we all pass on, each sustaining one or other of these characters."

A second reason for Chaucer's popularity undoubtedly is his comic spirit. This quality is easily exemplified but eludes precise definition. It makes Chaucer akin to Aristophanes, Cervantes, Molière, or Shakespeare. But essentially it arises from the deep underlying religious faith characteristic of many medieval artists, for it is ultimately founded upon the view that in the sight of eternity all human joys and sorrows are equally laughable.

The manifestations of the comic spirit are many and varied. At its simplest level it leads Chaucer to describe, for instance, in the Miller's Tale, the preposterous scheme by which an ardent lover deceives a gullible husband and persuades him to drop himself in a tub from the roof of his house. At its most exalted level it leads Chaucer to transport Troilus to heaven after his tragic death, there to laugh at those below in " this little spot of earth " who weep for his unhappy fate.

The devices of Chaucer's comedy include puns, burlesque, the mock-heroic, parody, innuendo, irony, and satire. In the General Prologue he turns his laughter against the social and religious abuses of his day. Sometimes his innuendo is gentle and conceals the implied reproof. The Prioress, for instance, feeds her small hounds on roasted meat and white wheat bread. Chaucer merely reports the fact and generously remarks that she was all " conscience and tender heart." But on reflection his contemporaries would have realized that a nun was, in the first place, officially forbidden to keep pets; and some of the less sentimental among them, moreover, would have agreed with those social reformers who condemned the feeding of fat pets in an age when the poor were kept lean by recurrent famines.

Sometimes he is playfully facetious, as when he remarks that the Merchant was so stately in his dealings that no one would ever suspect he might actually be in debt. Sometimes he is deliberately ironic, as when he pretends to agree with the Monk's objections to the rules of his order. On occasions, but only rarely, he betrays a more bitter tone, as when he portrays the vicious and cynical Summoner with his leprous face and his garlic-laden breath.

By comparison with his own English contemporaries, however, Chaucer is remarkably restrained about the corruptions of his age. Compare with his view of the pilgrims, for instance, an extract from Langland's vision of a similar scene in *Piers Plowman:*

Pilgrims and palmers pledged each other
To seek Santiago and the saints at Rome,
Went forth on their way with many wise tales,
And, all their life after, had leave to tell lies.

Heaps of hermits with hooked staves
Went to Walsingham, and their wenches after
    them.
Great lubbers and long, who were loath to toil,
Clothed themselves in copes to be known from
    others,
Shaped themselves as hermits, to have their ease.

Now Chaucer does not really like hypocrites and scoundrels any more than Langland does, but his comic spirit wears a genial air. His Friar, for instance, is obviously no better than the feigned hermits condemned in *Piers Plowman,* but the modes of portrayal are poles apart. "He had arranged many a marriage for young women at his own cost," Chaucer blandly remarks, leaving the spicy details of the Friar's misbehavior to our imagination, and leaving to us also the right to draw whatever moral judgment we will.

In short, he seems to believe that laughter, not loathing, is the best and most practical response to the errors of mankind and the conflicts of this world.

A third reason for Chaucer's popularity lies in the fact that he excels in the most universally enjoyed of all literary genres, namely storytelling.

Apart from some brief experiments, Chaucer did not attempt to weave the plots of his *Canterbury Tales* around actual current events and famous contemporary figures. It would no more have occurred to him to have King Richard II, for instance, play a part in a story (though he does refer to actual contemporaries in his lyric poetry) than it would have occurred to Shakespeare to introduce Elizabeth and Essex on the stage. His plots are, like many of Shakespeare's, derived largely from fictions invented in the past, though his sympathetic understanding of the ways of the world enabled him to convert the inherited materials into lively realities.

Chaucer had a rare instinct for discovering good story material. The basic plots of the seven widely varying tales included in the present anthology, though their *immediate* sources are sometimes literary, can all be traced back to an *ultimate* origin in the folk tale, and they thus possess an inherent dramatic economy and neatness of pattern imposed upon them by the skill of generations of storytellers and by the demands of generations of listeners. The extraordinary perfection of the plot of the Pardoner's Tale, which can be traced back to analogues recorded a thousand years before Chaucer wrote, is an excellent example of the artist's debt to the common people.

But Chaucer is obviously not just a popular raconteur of folk tales. He remolds the theme, content, characterization, and setting of the material he borrows according to his own understanding of life and his own artistic principles. Sometimes he feels that not much need be done, as, for instance, when he retells the popular story of the tested wife in the Clerk's Tale from a version which had already been reworked by a master craftsman. Here his chief task is to turn into English verse a literary work available to him in Latin prose. But even in this tale, which was probably one of his earlier works, he adds little touches of characterization lacking in his original.

In the Franklin's Tale he reworks the folk tale of the rash promise, known to him also in a literary version, but here he introduces extensive alterations. He transfers the setting to the seacoast of Brittany, with which he must have been acquainted, to judge from the vividness of his description, and he endows its savage black rocks with the importance of a principal protagonist in the tale.

Even when his plots hinge on the supernatural, as in the Franklin's Tale, his characters always seem real and vital. To be sure, he is as fond as De Maupassant or O. Henry of a flawless plot, but he never overlooks any suitable opportunity to amplify a favorite character. Thus, in the narration of the Pardoner's Tale, which actually occupies only 256 lines (1–22, 199–432), Chaucer still finds room for individualizing touches. When, for instance, the youngest of the three scoundrels buys poison from the apothecary with which to kill his two friends, he casually explains that he wishes to rid his hedge of a weasel which has been attacking his poultry. His grimly ironic excuse is not necessary for the actual development of the plot, but it affords the reader such a sudden and alarming glimpse into the mind of the abandoned young criminal that the effect of the narration is strongly intensified.

The plot of the Nun's Priest's Tale, which is likewise derived from folklore, is fundamentally a fable concerning a rash rooster who is captured by the flattery of a fox, but by subtle characterization Chaucer transforms the story into a brilliant satire on human behavior. In a most lifelike scene, for instance, Chauntecleer argues affectionately but vigorously with his wife. He tells her he has dreamed that his life has been threatened by a savage beast. Pertelote is skeptical, however, and ridicules his forebodings. But when with truly feminine scorn she ascribes the dream to indigestion and recommends a laxative, the stubborn male indignantly retorts, " I set no store on laxatives, for they are venomous. . . . I defy them! I love them not at all! "

Furthermore, in amplifying his narrative materials, Chaucer adapts the tale to the character of the teller. He knows that the effect of a story is dependent not only on plot and characterization but also on the attitude of the narrator towards the conflict. The happy device of the framework in the *Canterbury Tales* enables us to enjoy a lively story told to a critical audience by a speaker who projects his own interests and prejudices into the telling. Thus, in recounting the advice given by Pertelote to Chauntecleer, the Nun's Priest, who presumably serves as father confessor in the Prioress's convent, says, " Women's counsels are often fatal," but hastily adds with a whimsical innocence, " These are the cock's words and not mine. *I* can't imagine harm in any woman! "

Hence each tale differs from the others in its dominant tone. The mock-heroic exaggeration of incidents in the Nun's Priest's Tale is playfully learned and quietly satiric, while the pathetic tale told by the Prioress is deeply religious; the Wife of Bath's Tale is entwined with argumentation, while the Miller's raffish tale is hilariously comic. Thus the tales and the connecting links form a brilliant tapestry, unique in kind, in which Chaucer has woven together the multicolored warp of narrative with the subtle woof of drama.

Finally, a fourth reason for Chaucer's appeal arises from his refreshingly unpedantic love of books, for the fruits of his wide reading greatly enriched his writing. In an age when books were, by modern standards, scarce and inaccessible, he read prodigiously. In the *Legend of Good Women* he writes:

We must give credence . . . to the books we find, through which old things are recalled, and to the teaching of the sages of old, and trust in the old

approved stories of holiness, of reigns, of victories, of love, of hate, and various other things. . . . And if old books were away, the key of memory would be lost. . . .

And, as for me, though I know but little, I delight in reading books and hold them in reverence in my heart.

And knowing what we do of Chaucer, we may be sure that the driving force behind his reading was not any mere antiquarianism but a genuine curiosity about people of all ages and climes.

The influence of his reading on his poetry is manifested in many ways, some obvious and at times — at least for the modern reader — even obtrusive, some so elusive as to be perceptible only to a scholarly specialist.

From his reading, for instance, he culls catalogues of illustrative example, for Jankin's entertaining recitation of evil women (Wife of Bath's Prologue, ll. 719-77), and the Nun's Priest's mock-heroic list (in his tale, ll. 535-53) of ladies who have bewailed the loss of husbands, and Dorigen's somewhat excessive catalogue (in the Franklin's Tale, ll. 660-748) of women who have taken their own lives to preserve their chastity. He also quotes illustrative anecdotes such as the two examples of a dream's fulfillment narrated by Chauntecleer (ll. 164-284).

Inspired by his reading, he embarks upon philosophical disquisition in the Nun's Priest's comments on God's foreknowledge (ll. 414-30), scientific commentaries in the complicated astrological reckonings described throughout the Franklin's Tale, and religious sermonizings in the Pardoner's condemnations of gluttony.

In such borrowings, no matter how completely he may have integrated them into the narrative, the author's indebtedness is obvious, but there are occasions when the reader would never suspect any source behind Chaucer's brilliance other than his unaided creative imagination. A most striking example is afforded by the Wife of Bath. No one could seem more real. The circumstantial details of her life are all easily corroborated. She has prudently acquired for herself a weaving business at a time when wool provided one of England's most prosperous industries. She lives " beside Bath "; that is, she must have lived in the suburb known as St. Michael's Without, which was in fact a center of weaving. She could very well be a portrait drawn from life of someone whom Chaucer actually knew.

Chaucer is partially indebted to his reading, however, even for the Wife of Bath. Original though she is, she bears a distinct family resemblance to the figure of the Crone (*la Vieille*), who plays an important and dramatic part in the great French poem, the *Romance of the Rose,* which Chaucer so much admired. Like the Wife, the Crone boasts that she need not rely on scholarly authorities, for she can speak about love from experience.

When she thinks of her former successes, the Crone ruefully remarks, "It is useless to regret it; what is gone cannot return. I shall never again be able to hold a man, for my face is so wrinkled that they have no further care for any threat of mine."

"But," she continues resolutely, "it still pleases me when I think back on it. Greatly do my thoughts delight and my members rejoice when I recall my good times and the jolly life which my heart now envies so."

Similarly the Wife of Bath (in her Prologue,

ll. 475–81) exclaims, "Heavens! When I look back on my youth and my jollity, it tickles me to the root of my heart. To this day it does my heart good that I have had my world in my time. But age, alas, which will envenom all, has robbed me of my beauty and my pith."

The aged and embittered hag in the *Romance,* however, is a schematic personification of the last odious stage in the career of a self-seeking and avaricious woman who has perverted the true nature of love. The eternally buoyant Wife, on the other hand, has not been created to illustrate an argument. "I'll still try to be merry," she cheerfully asserts; and, like Shakespeare's Falstaff, she *is* the very embodiment of human mirth. She is a creature of breath and life, real, human, and unique.

Chaucer, the lover of letters and the practical man of affairs, learned of life from two great teachers — his wide reading and his rich personal experience; and so memorably did he combine the wit and wisdom he had gleaned from the past with his own vital knowledge of the present that his vanished world still survives today, alive perennially in his poetry.

NOTE ON CHAUCER'S LANGUAGE

SOUNDS

The written record of Chaucer's language does not, of course, now tell us precisely how Chaucer would have pronounced what he wrote, but scholars have succeeded in working out what is probably a close approximation. In particular, the quality of certain long stressed vowels has changed considerably between the fourteenth century and the present, even though the spelling of many of the words in which they occur has not changed at all. Details may be found in the editions referred to in the bibliography, but the reader who applies even the following three rules will be able to recapture something of the melody of Chaucer's poetry.

(1) *Pronounce all written consonants as we do those in modern English.* Also, pronounce the sound (now foreign to English) represented by *gh* in *night* somewhat as we now pronounce the *h* sound in *how* but with a stronger breathing. (It is like the *ch* in the Scottish pronunciation of *loch* or in the German pronunciation of *Bach.*)

(2) *Pronounce all final syllables,* even those represented by a final -*e* (here written with a dot over it) and no longer pronounced in modern English. Thus,

pronounce Chaucer's *damė* with two syllables as *dah-meh,* and his *damės* as *dah-mess.* (The sound of the final -*e* was probably the same as that of the modern English final unstressed vowel, when unemphatic, in words such as *Stella* and *raven.*)

(3) *Give all written vowels (both short and long) their so-called "Continental" sounds,* such as they would receive, for instance, in modern French or Italian or in our modern pronunciation of Latin.

Thus, pronounce the long vowel spelled *a* in Chaucer's *damė* as the *ah* sound of modern French *dame* or modern English *father,* not as the *ay* sound of modern English *dame.* Other instances are *barė, carė, famė, gamė, hatė, lamė, makė, namė, pagė, ragė, savė, takė, wakė.*

Pronounce the long vowel spelled *e* or *ee* in Chaucer's *regioun* as the *ay* sound of modern French *région* or modern English *rage,* not as the *ee* sound of modern English *region.* Other instances are Chaucer's *be, he, me, she, thee.* For simplicity's sake the reader may ignore the set of words in which the *e* or *ee* as in Chaucer's *heeth* (modern *heath*) represented a distinctive vowel sound like that in modern English *ebb,* only lengthened.

Pronounce the long vowel spelled *i* or *y* in Chaucer's

finė as the *ee* sound in modern French *fine* or modern English *machine*, not as the *eye* sound in modern English *fine*. Other instances are Chaucer's *bitė, glidė, kyndė, minė, primė, ridė, strivė, thinė, wyn* (modern *wine*).

Pronounce the long vowel *u* spelled *ou* or *ow* in Chaucer's *doute* as the *ou* sound in modern French *doute* or modern English *soup*, not as the *ow* sound in modern English *doubt*. Instances are *bour* (modern *bower*), *doute* (modern *doubt*), *flour* (modern *flower*), *foul, hous, licour, mous, out, tour* (modern *tower*).

The other long vowels and diphthongs and all the short vowels have passed down into modern English with less notable change, and the reader may therefore rely on his instinct for their pronunciation.

To illustrate the application of these rules, the first four lines of the General Prologue are here represented in a roughly phonetic transcription, in which all long vowels and diphthongs have been marked with a sign of length.

Whan that Aprill with his shoures soote
The droghte of March hath perced to the roote
And bathed every veyne in swich licour
Of which vertu engendred is the flour, . . .

Whan that Ahpril with his shoures sohte
The drocht(e) of March hath perced to the rohte
And bahthed ev(e)ry veyn(e) in swich licour
Of which vertu engendred is the flour, . . .

FORMS

All obscure words and idioms in the following selections have been interpreted in the footnotes, but a recognition of certain frequently recurring forms and constructions will facilitate the reading of Chaucer's language.

Pronouns are the same as in modern English with the chief exception of two ambiguities which have now disappeared. The word variously spelt *her, here, hir, hire* is Chaucer's equivalent not only of the modern *her* but also of the modern *their*. Similarly Chaucer's *his* is the equivalent not only of modern *his* but also *its*.

Most verb forms resemble their modern counterparts, but the following peculiarities should be noted. Chaucer normally uses the form (*he, she, it*) *lovėth* rather than the modern verb form *loves*. Verbs with stem ending in *-d* or *-t*, however, regularly contract the ending *-eth*, thus appearing as *he bit* (for *biddeth*), *fint* (*findeth*), *holt* (*holdeth*), *rit* (*rideth*), *stant* (*standeth*). Notice also that *hym lest* (for *lesteth*) means "*it pleases him*" and has a past tense *hym leste*, "it pleased him." (In all three forms the root is variously spelled *lest-, list-, lust-.*)

Many verb endings had a final *-n*, now gone, which might be dropped. Thus *we* (*ye, they*) *lovė* and *lovėn* are used interchangeably for modern *we love; we lovėdė(n)* for modern *we loved;* and *to lovė(n)* for modern *to love*. Also optional was the prefix *y-* as a sign of the past participle, so that the modern *I have loved* appears as *I havė lovėd* or *y-loved*, and modern *I have drunk* as *I havė dronkė(n)* or *y-dronkė(n)*.

One sign of the negative was the still familiar *not* or its variants *noght* and *naught*. Another sign, now gone, was *ne* or *n'*, which was often accompanied by other negative words. "He nevere yet no vileynye *ne* sayde / In al his lyf unto no maner wight" (Gen. Prol., ll. 70-71) means literally, "he never yet no villainy didn't say to no kind of person"; i. e., "he never yet spoke any villainy to any kind of person." *Ne* combines with the following word in the frequently occurring collocations *nadde* (*ne hadde*, "hadn't"), *nere* ("weren't"), *nolde* ("wouldn't"), *noot* (*ne woot*, "know not"), *nyl* ("will not"), *nyste* (*ne wiste*, "knew not").

A variant form of the past tense was provided by the verb *gan*, which was used sometimes with its literal meaning "began" but often conveyed no more than the modern English *did* in a phrase such as *did go*. Thus it is equivalent to "began" in the sentence (Franklin's Tale, l. 428): "Anon for joye his herte gan to daunce." But it is merely a sign of the past in the sentence (Wife's Tale, l. 398): "A thousand tyme . . . he gan hir kisse"; i. e., "a thousand times . . . he kissed her."

The text of the following selections is based, with the kind permission of the University of Chicago Press, upon *The Text of the Canterbury Tales Studied on the Basis of All Known Manuscripts*, 8 vols. (1940), edited by John M. Manly and Edith Rickert. Punctuation has been added, capitalization has been normalized, and a few preferable readings have been selected from the recorded variants. Readers should notice that the spelling of Chaucer's scribes, which has been left unaltered, is not consistent. After only a little practice in reading, however, it becomes easy to recognize, for instance, that *heigh, heighe, hey, heye, hy*, and *hye* are simply variant spellings of our modern *high*. (Here and elsewhere there is generally a grammatical reason for the appearance of the final *-e*. For details, consult the editions by Manly or Robinson listed below.)

Reading Suggestions

EDITIONS

J. M. Manly, editor, *Canterbury Tales by Geoffrey Chaucer* (1928). The introductory summary of Chaucer's grammar is particularly useful.

F. N. Robinson, editor, *Complete Works of Geoffrey Chaucer* (1933). An indispensable edition containing a definitive text, exhaustive notes, and excellent literary appraisals of each of Chaucer's works.

CRITICISM

G. L. Kittredge, *Chaucer and His Poetry* (1915).

R. K. Root, *The Poetry of Chaucer* (revised edition, 1922).

Caroline F. E. Spurgeon, *Five Hundred Years of Chaucer Criticism and Allusion, 1357-1900*, 3 vols. (1925). The introduction contains a most important discussion of changes in literary taste.

J. L. Lowes, *The Art of Geoffrey Chaucer* (1930).

G. K. Chesterton, *Chaucer* (1932). An entertaining, though sometimes unreliable, study.

H. S. Bennett, *Chaucer and the Fifteenth Century* (1947). Contains a useful bibliographical guide to Chaucerian studies.

R. D. French, *Chaucer Handbook* (2nd edition, 1947).

A. C. Baugh, "Middle English Literature," in *A Literary History of England* edited by A. C. Baugh *et al.* (1948). An excellent account of the literature before and contemporary with Chaucer.

Muriel A. Bowden, *Commentary on the General Prologue to the Canterbury Tales* (1948).

Nevill Coghill, *The Poet Chaucer* (1949).

W. W. Lawrence, *Chaucer and the Canterbury Tales* (1950).

J. S. P. Tatlock, *The Mind and Art of Chaucer* (1950).

Kemp Malone, *Chapters on Chaucer* (1951).

HISTORICAL BACKGROUND

Marchette Chute, *Geoffrey Chaucer of England* (1946). A readable, popular account of Chaucer's life and work.

Edith Rickert, compiler, *Chaucer's World* (1948).

G. M. Trevelyan, *Illustrated English Social History*, vol. i, *Chaucer's England and the Early Tudors* (1949).

G. G. Coulton, *Chaucer and His England*, 7th edition (1950).

RECORDINGS OF READINGS IN CHAUCERIAN ENGLISH

Harry Morgan Ayres, *Selections from General Prologue and Nun's Priest's Tale*, Historical Poets, I. National Council of Teachers of English. 78 rpm (no date).

Kemp Malone, *Nun's Priest's Tale*, English Classics, E. Chatain, Baltimore. XTV 17216/7. 33 1/3 rpm (no date).

Fred Norris Robinson, *Selections from Pardoner's Tale*, Harvard University Phonograph Records. SS 5028/9. 78 rpm (no date).

THE CANTERBURY TALES

THE GENERAL PROLOGUE

The opening scene of the General Prologue is set in the Tabard Inn "beside the Bell" at Southwark on the south side of the River Thames opposite London; the date, to judge from subsequent astronomical allusions, is mid-April, 1387, and the innkeeper's name, we later learn, is Harry Bailly. In these details, as in others, the framework which encloses the *Canterbury Tales* presents a faithful portrait of real life in fourteenth-century England; for, in Chaucer's day, there actually was an inn known as the Tabard in Southwark, and another known as the Bell, and an innkeeper (or possibly more than one) by the name of Henry Bailly.

Chaucer joins up with a group of people numbering "a good nine-and-twenty" (according to l. 24, though the General Prologue in fact describes thirty characters, not counting Chaucer and the innkeeper), who are to ride as pilgrims the sixty miles of much-traveled road to the shrine of St. Thomas Becket at Canterbury Cathedral. The famous "holy, blissful martyr," Archbishop Becket, had been murdered in 1170 because he championed the Church against the secular power of King Henry II. In 1172 he was canonized as a saint; in 1174 the king did penance at his tomb; and in 1220 his remains were translated to the splendid shrine which became the most popular of all the religious resorts in England. Pilgrims sought there inspiration for their faith, remission of penalties due for their sins, extra merits, healing for their bodies, and incidentally — in some cases — satisfaction for their wanderlust.

Whan that° Aprill with his shoures soote°
The droghte of March hath perced to the roote
And bathed every veyne in swich licour°
Of which vertu° engendred is the flour,
Whan Zephirus° eek° with his sweete breeth
Inspired hath in every holt° and heeth°
The tendre croppes,° and the yonge sonne
Hath in the Ram his half cours y-ronne,°
And smale foweles maken° melodye
That slepen al the nyght with open eye,   10
So priketh hem Nature in hir corages,°
Than longen folk to goon° on pilgrymages,

GENERAL PROLOGUE.   1. **Whan that:** when.   **soote:** sweet.
3. **swich licour:** such liquid.   4. **Of ... vertu:** by power of
which.   5. **Zephirus:** the west wind.   **eek:** also.   6. **holt:** wood.
heeth: heath.   7. **croppes:** shoots.   7-8. **yonge ... y-ronne:**
The young sun of spring has run its second half-course through
the zodiacal sign of the Ram (April 11). (See Note A, p. 195.)
9. **foweles maken:** birds make.   11. **So ... corages:** Nature so
stirs them in their hearts.   12. **Than ... goon:** Then people
long to go.

And palmeres for to seken straunge strondes,°
To ferne halwes kouthe° in sondry londes.
And specially, from every shires ende
Of Engelond, to Caunterbury they wende,
The holy, blisful martir° for to seke
That hem hath holpen° whan that they were seeke°
  Bifel° that in that sesoun on a day
In Southwerk at the Tabard, as I lay   20
Redy to wenden on my pilgrymage
To Caunterbury with ful devout corage,°
At nyght was come into that hostelrye
Wel nyne-and-twenty in a compaignye
Of sondry folk by aventure y-falle°
In felaweshipe, and pilgrymes were they alle
That toward Caunterbury wolden° ryde.
The chambres and the stables weren wyde,°
And wel we weren esed atte beste;°
And shortly, whan the sonne was to reste,   30
So hadde I spoken with hem everichon°
That I was of hir° felaweshipe anon;
And made forward° erly for to ryse
To take oure wey ther-as° I yow devyse.°
  But, nathelees,° whil I have tyme and space,
Er that° I ferther in this tale pace,°
Me thynketh it° acordant to resoun
To telle yow al the condicioun
Of ech of hem° so as it semed me,
And whiche they weren, and of what degree,   40
And eek in what array that they were inne;
And at a knyght than wol I first bigynne.

  A KNYGHT ther was, and that a worthy man,
That, fro the tyme that he first bigan
To riden out,° he loved chivalrye,
Trouthe and honour, fredom and curteisye.
Ful worthy was he in his lordes werre,°
And ther-to hadde he riden, no man ferre,°
As wel in Cristendom as in hethenesse,°
And evere honoured for his worthyness.   50
  At Alisaundre° he was whan it was wonne.

Ful ofte tyme he hadde the bord bigonne°
Aboven alle nacions in Pruce.°
In Lettow° hadde he reysed,° and in Ruce,°
No Cristen man so ofte of his degree.
In Gernade° at the seege eek° hadde he be°
Of Algezir,° and riden in Belmarye.°
At Lyeys° was he and at Satalye°
Whan they were wonne; and in the Grete° See
At many a noble armee° hadde he be.   60
At mortal batailles hadde he been fiftene,
And foghten for oure feith at Tramyssene°
In lystes thries,° and ay° slayn his foo.
This ilke° worthy Knyght hadde been also
Som tyme with the lord of Palatye°
Agayn° another hethen in Turkye.
  And evere moore° he hadde a sovereyn prys,°
And, though that he were worthy, he was wys
And of his port° as meke as is a mayde.
He nevere yet no vileynye ne sayde°   70
In al his lyf unto no maner wight.°
He was a verray,° parfit, gentil knyght.
  But for to tellen yow of his array,
Hise hors° were goode, but he was nat gay.
Of fustian° he wered a gypoun°
Al bismotered° with his habergeoun,°
For he was late y-come from his viage°
And wente for to doon his pilgrymage.

  With hym ther was his sone, a yong SQUYER,
A lovere and a lusty bacheler,°   80
With lokkes crulle as° they were leyd in presse.°
Of twenty yeer of age he was, I gesse.
  Of his stature he was of evene° lengthe,
And wonderly delyvere,° and of greet strengthe;
And he hadde been som tyme in chivachye°
In Flaundres, in Artoys, and Picardye,°
And born° hym wel, as of so litel space,°
In hope to stonden° in his lady° grace.
  Embrouded° was he as it were a meede°

13. palmeres ... strondes: pilgrims (long) to seek unfamiliar strands. 14. ferne ... kouthe: distant shrines known. 17. martir: Thomas Becket. See headnote. 18. holpen: helped. seeke: sick. 19. Bifel: it befell. 22. corage: heart. 25. by ... y-falle: by chance fallen. 27. wolden: intended to. 28. wyde: spacious. 29. esed ... beste: entertained at the best. 31. everichon: everyone. 32. hir: their. 33. made forward: (we) made agreement. 34. ther-as: where. devyse: tell. 35. nathelees: nevertheless. 36. Er that: before. pace: pass. 37. Me ... it: it seems to me. 39. hem: them. 45. riden out: ride in expeditions. 47. werre: war. As a feudal duty to his overlord, the king, he had fought in "his lord's war," a term presumably referring to the campaigns of the Hundred Years' War between England and France. The subsequent allusions indicate that the Knight must have been a veteran of more than forty years' service, for he had also enlisted voluntarily against the pagan hordes of northeastern Europe and against the Mohammedans in the Moorish realms of the western Mediterranean and in the Turkish realms of the eastern Mediterranean. 48. ferre: farther. 49. hethenesse: heathendom. 51. Alisaundre: Alexandria (Egypt).

52. bord bigonne: table headed. 53. Pruce: Prussia. 54. Lettow: Lithuania. reysed: campaigned. Ruce: Russia. 56. Gernade: Granada (Spain). eek: also. be: been. 57. Algezir: Algeciras. Belmarye: Benmarin (Morocco). 58. Lyeys: Ayas (Armenia). Satalye: Adalia (Turkey). 59. Grete: Mediterranean. 60. armee: sea-borne expedition. 62. Tramyssene: Tlemcen (Algeria). 63. lystes thries: single combats thrice. ay: always. 64. ilke: same. 65. Palatye: Balat (Turkey). 66. Agayn: against. 67. evere moore: always. prys: reputation. 69. port: deportment. 70. no ... sayde: said anything boorish. 71. unto ... wight: to any kind of person. 72. verray: true. 74. hors: horses. 75. fustian: rough cotton. gypoun: blouse. 76. bismotered: stained. habergeoun: coat of mail. 77. viage: journey. 80. bacheler: As a "bachelor" or candidate for knighthood, the Squire was an apprentice both in military training and in courtly love. 81. crulle as: curled as if. presse: curlers. 83. evene: medium. 84. delyvere: agile. 85. in chivachye: on a raid. 86. In ... Picardye: Under the pretext of aiding the Pope against the rival claimant supported by the French, an English force raided Flanders, Artois, and Picardy in 1383 without opposition. 87. born: conducted. space: time. 88. stonden: stand. lady: lady's. 89. Embrouded: embroidered. meede: meadow.

Al ful of fresshe floures white and reede.　90
Syngynge he was or floytynge° al the day.
He was as fressh as is the monthe of May.
Short was his gowne with sleves longe and wyde.
Wel koude he sitte on hors and faire° ryde.
He koude songes make and wel endite,°
Juste,° and eek daunce, and wel purtreye,° and
　　write.
So hoote he lovede that by nyghtertale°
He slepte namoore than dooth a nyghtyngale.
　Curteys he was, lowely, and servysable,
And carf° biforn his fader at the table.　100
　A YEMAN° hadde he° and servantz namo°
At that tyme, for hym liste° ryde so,
And he was clad in coote and hood of grene.
A sheef of pecok arwes° bright and kene
Under his belt he bar° ful thriftily.°
Wel koude he dresse° his takel° yemanly;
His arwes drouped noght with fetheres lowe.
And in his hand he bar a myghty bowe.
A not° heed hadde he, with a broun visage.
Of wodecraft wel koude° he al the usage.　110
Upon his arm he bar a gay bracer,°
And by his syde a swerd° and a bokeler,°
And on that° oother syde a gay daggere,
Harneysed° wel, and sharp as poynt of spere,
A Cristofre° on his brest of silver shene.°
An horn he bar, the bawdryk° was of grene.
A forster° was he soothly,° as I gesse.
　Ther was also a nonne, a PRIORESSE,
That of hir smylyng was ful symple° and coy.°
Hir gretteste ooth was but " By Seint Loy! "°　120
And she was cleped° Madame Eglentyne.
Ful wel she soong° the servyce dyvyne,
Entuned° in hir nose ful semely,°
And Frenssh she spak ful faire and fetisly°
After the scole of Stratford atte Bowe,°
For Frenssh of Parys was to hire unknowe.°
　At mete° wel y-taught was she with alle;
She leet° no morsel from hir lippes falle,
Ne wette hir fyngres in hir sauce depe;

Wel koude she carie a morsel, and wel kepe°　130
That no drope ne fille° upon hir brest.
In curteisie was set ful muchel° hir lest.°
Hir over lippe wyped she so clene
That in hir coppe ther was no ferthyng° sene
Of grece whan she dronken hadde hir draughte.
Ful semely after hir mete she raughte,°
And sikerly° she was of greet desport,°
And ful plesaunt and amyable of port,°
And peyned hire to countrefete cheere°
Of court, and to been estalich° of manere,　140
And to been holden digne° of reverence.
　But for to speken of hir conscience,
She was so charitable and so pitous,°
She wolde wepe if that she sawe a mous
Caught in a trappe, if it were deed or bledde.
Of smale houndes hadde she that she fedde
With rosted flessh, or mylk and wastel° breed;
But soore wepte she if oon of hem were deed,
Or if men° smoot it with a yerde smerte.°
And al was conscience and tendre herte.　150
　Ful semely° hir wympel pynched° was,
Hir nose tretys,° hir eyen° greye° as glas,
Hir mouth ful smal, and there-to softe and reed,
But sikerly she hadde a fair forheed;
It was almoost a spanne° brood, I trowe,°
For hardily° she was nat undergrowe.
Ful fetys° was hir cloke, as I was war;°
Of smal coral aboute hir arm she bar°
A peyre of bedes, gauded al with grene,°
And ther-on heng a brooch of gold ful shene,°　160
On which ther was first writen a crowned A,
And after *Amor vincit omnia.*°

　Another NONNE with hire hadde she,
That was hir chapeleyne, and PREESTES thre.

　A MONK ther was, a fair for the maistrye,°
An outridere° that lovede venerye,°
A manly man, to been an abbot able.
Ful many a deyntee° hors hadde he in stable,
And whanne he rood, men myghte° his brydel
　heere
Gynglen° in a whistlynge wynd as cleere　170

And eek° as loude as dooth the chapel belle
Ther-as° this lord was kepere of the celle.°

    The reule of Seint Maure or of Seint Beneit,°
Bycause that it was old and somdel streit,° —
This ilke Monk leet olde thynges pace°
And heeld after the newe world, the space.°
He yaf° nat of that text a pulled° hen
That seith that hunters been° nat holy men,
Ne that a monk, whan he is recchelees,°
Is likned til° a fissh that is waterlees,   180
This is to seyn,° a monk out of his cloystre.
But thilke° text heeld he nat worth an oystre;
And I seyde his opinioun was good.
What° sholde he studie and make hymselven
    wood°
Upon a book in cloystre alwey to poure,°
Or swynken° with his handes and laboure
As Austyn bit?° How shal the world be served?°
Lat Austyn have his swynk° to hym reserved.
Therfore he was a prikasour° aright.
Grehoundes he hadde as swift as fowel° in flight.
Of prikyng° and of huntyng for the hare   191
Was al his lust,° for no cost wolde he spare.

    I seigh° his sleves y-purfiled° at the hond
With grys,°and that the fyneste of a lond;
And for to festne his hood under his chyn
He hadde of gold wroght a ful curious pyn;
A love knotte in the gretter° ende ther was.
His heed was balled,° that shoon as any glas,
And eek his face as° he hadde been enoynt.°
He was a lord ful fat and in good poynt,°   200
Hise eyen stepe° and rollynge in his heed,
That stemed° as a forneys° of a leed,°
His bootes souple, his hors in greet estat.°

    Now certeynly he was a fair prelat.
He was nat pale as a forpyned goost.°
A fat swan loved he best of any roost.
His palfrey was as broun as is a berye.

    A FRERE° ther was, a wantowne° and a merye,
A lymytour,° a ful solempne° man.
In alle the ordres foure° is noon that kan°   210
So muche of daliaunce° and fair langage.
He hadde maad° ful many a mariage
Of yonge wommen at his owene cost.

    Unto his ordre he was a noble post.°
Ful wel biloved and famulier was he
With frankeleyns over-al° in his contree
And with worthy wommen of the toun,
For he hadde power of confessioun,
As seyde hymself, moore than a curat,°
For of his ordre he was licenciat.   220
Ful swetely herde he confessioun,
And plesaunt was his absolucioun.
He was an esy man to yeve° penaunce
Ther-as he wiste° to have a good pitaunce.°
For unto a poure ordre for to yive°
Is signe that a man is wel y-shryve;°
For if he yaf, he dorste make avaunt,°
He wiste that a man was repentaunt;
For many a man so hard is of his herte,
He may not wepe, althogh hym° soore smerte.°
Therfore, in stede of wepynge and preyeres,   231
Men moote° yeve silver to the poure freres.

    His typet° was ay farsed° ful of knyves
And pynnes for to yeven faire wyves.

    And certeynly he hadde a murye note.
Wel koude he synge and pleyen on a rote;°
Of yeddynges° he bar outrely° the prys.
His nekke whit was as the flour de lys;°
Ther-to° he strong was as a champioun.

    He knew the tavernes wel in every toun   24°
And every hostiler° and tappestere°
Bet° than a lazar° or a beggestere,°
For unto swich° a worthy man as he
Acorded nat,° as by his facultee,°
To have with sike° lazars aqueyntaunce.

---

171. eek: also. 172. Ther-as: where. celle: group. 173. The
. . . Beneit: The originator of the Benedictine order, St. Benedict
(Beneit), formulated the rule of behavior in Italy in the sixth century, and his disciple St. Maur brought it to France. 174. somdel streit: somewhat strict. 175. pace: pass by. 176. the
space: for the meanwhile. 177. yaf: gave. pulled: plucked.
178. been: are. 179. recchelees: without a care. 180. likned
til: comparable to. 181. seyn: say. 182. thilke: that same.
184. What: why. hymselven wood: himself insane. 185. poure:
pore. 186. swynken: work. 187. Austyn bit: Augustine commands (biddeth). The widely followed monastic rule established
by St. Augustine of Hippo in the fifth century warned monks
against sloth. How . . . served?: Who else will perform the
many worldly services which require a cleric's education if monks
withdraw themselves from the world to the life of spiritual contemplation required of them? (Suitably educated laymen were
not sufficiently numerous.) 188. swynk: work. 189. prika-
sour: fast rider. 190. fowel: bird. 191. prikyng: tracking
(the hare). 192. lust: pleasure. 193. seigh: saw. y-pur-
filed: trimmed. 194. grys: gray fur. 197. gretter: larger.
198. balled: bald. 199. as: as if. enoynt: anointed. 200. poynt:
condition. 201. eyen stepe: eyes prominent. 202. stemed:
glowed. forneys: furnace. leed: boiler. 203. greet estat:
splendid condition. 205. forpyned goost: tormented spirit.

208. Frere: friar. wantowne: gay. 209. lymytour: limiter,
one allotted a limit or district. Unlike monks, friars followed an
active life of preaching and teaching rather than a contemplative
life. When first organized in the thirteenth century, they earned
any necessary money by manual labor. By Chaucer's time, however, they had become mendicants who begged for alms and were
licensed to raise funds within local limits by hearing confessions
and granting absolutions. solempne: splendid. 210. ordres
foure: The four orders were Carmelites, Augustinians, Francis-
cans, and Dominicans. kan: knows. 211. daliaunce: flirtation.
212. maad: arranged. 214. post: pillar. 216. frankeleyns
over-al: rich landholders everywhere. 219. curat: parish priest.
223. yeve: give. 224. wiste: knew. pitaunce: gift. 225. yive:
give. 226. is . . . y-shryve: has made a good confession.
227. if . . . avaunt: if he (the man) gave, he (the Friar) dared
to avow. 230. hym: he. smerte: smart. 232. Men
moote: one ought to. 233. typet: cape. ay farsed: always
stuffed. 236. rote: stringed instrument. 237. yeddynges:
ballads. bar outrely: carried off completely. 238. flour de
lys: fleur-de-lis. 239. Ther-to: in addition. 241. hostiler:
innkeeper. tappestere: barmaid. 242. Bet: better. lazar:
leper. beggestere: female beggar. 243. swich: such.
244. Acorded nat: It was not suitable. facultee: capacity.
245. sike: sick.

It is nat honeste,° it may nat avaunce,°
For to deelen with no swich poraille°
But al with riche and selleres of vitaille.°
And, over-al° ther-as profit sholde arise,
Curteys he was and lowely of servyse.   250
Ther was no man nowher so vertuous.°
He was the beste beggere in his hous,°
For thogh a wydwe° hadde noght a sho,°
So plesant was his *In principio,*°
Yet wolde he have a ferthyng er° he wente.
His purchas was wel bettre than his rente.°
And rage° he koude as it were right° a whelpe.
In lovedayes° ther koude he muchel° helpe,
For ther he was nat lyk a cloysterer
With a thredbare cope,° as is a poure scoler,   260
But he was lyk a maister° or a pope;
Of double worstede was his semycope,°
That rounded as a belle out of the presse.
  Somwhat he lipsed° for his wantownesse°
To make his Englissh sweete upon his tonge;
And in his harpyng, whan that he hadde songe,
Hise eyen° twynkled in his heed aright
As doon the sterres in the frosty nyght.
This worthy lymytour was cleped° Huberd.

  A MARCHANT° was ther with a forked berd,
In motlee,° and hye on hors he sat,   271
Upon his heed a Flaundryssh° bever hat,
His bootes clasped faire and fetisly.°
  Hise resons° he spak ful solempnely,°
Sownynge° alwey the encrees of his wynnyng.°
He wolde the see were kept° for any thyng
Bitwixe Middelburgh° and Orewelle.°
Wel koude he in eschaunge sheeldes selle.°
  This worthy man ful wel his wit bisette.°
Ther wiste° no wight° that he was in dette,   280
So estatly was he of his governaunce
With his bargaynes and with his chevysaunce.°

For sothe,° he was a worthy man with alle,
But, sooth to seyn,° I noot° how men hym calle.

  A CLERK° ther was of Oxenford° also
That unto logyk hadde longe y-go.°
  As leene was his hors as is a rake,
And he was nat right° fat, I undertake,°
But looked holwe° and ther-to sobrely.
Ful thredbare was his overeste courtepy,°   290
For he hadde geten hym yet no benefice,°
Ne was so worldly for to have office,°
For hym was levere° have at his beddes heed
Twenty bookes clad in blak or reed
Of Aristotle and his philosophie
Than robes riche or fithele° or gay sautrie.°
  But, al be that he was a philosophre,
Yet hadde he but litel gold in cofre,°
But al that he myghte of his frendes hente,°
On bookes and on lernynge he it spente,   301
And bisily gan for the soules preye°
Of hem that yaf° hym wher-with to scoleye.°
  Of studie took he moost cure° and moost heede,
Noght oo° word spak he moore than was neede,
And that was seid in forme and reverence°
And short and quyk and ful of heigh sentence.°
Sownynge in° moral vertu was his speche,
And gladly wolde he lerne and gladly teche.

  A SERGEANT OF THE LAWE, war° and wys,
That often hadde been at the Parvys,°   310
Ther was also, ful riche of excellence.
Discreet he was and of greet reverence —
He semed swich,° hise wordes weren° so wyse.
  Justice he was ful often in assise°
By patente° and by pleyn° commissioun.
For° his science° and for his heigh renoun,
Of fees and robes hadde he many oon.°
So greet a purchasour° was nowher noon;

246. honeste: proper. avaunce: benefit. 247. swich poraille: such poor folk. 248. vitaille: victuals. 249. over-al: everywhere. 251. vertuous: gifted. 252. hous: friary. 253. wydwe: widow. sho: shoe. 254. *In principio:* "In the beginning" — the first words of St. John's Gospel, used in the Middle Ages as a religious and even magic formula. 255. ferthyng er: farthing before. 256. purchas . . . rente: pickings were much better than his regular income. 257. rage: frolic. as . . . right: just like. 258. lovedayes: arbitration days for settling disputes, especially financial disputes. muchel: much. 260. cope: cloak. 261. maister: Master of Arts. 262. semycope: short cloak. 264. lipsed: lisped. wantownesse: playfulness. 267. eyen: eyes. 269. cleped: called. 270. Marchant: merchant, probably a large wholesale importer-exporter. 271. motlee: figured cloth. 272. Flaundryssh: Flemish. 273. fetisly: elegantly. 274. resons: views. solempnely: impressively. 275. Sownynge: relating. wynnyng: profit. 276. wolde . . . kept: wished the sea were guarded, especially against French pirates. 277. Middelburgh: Middelburg in Holland, where English wool was sold. Orewelle: Orwell Harbor in England, through which the Merchant presumably shipped his wares. 278. Wel . . . selle: He knew well how to sell écus (shields) in exchange. Legally, only the royal money-changers were permitted to exchange French funds. 279. bisette: applied. 280. wiste: knew. wight: person. 282. chevysaunce: manipulation.

283. For sothe: truly. 284. seyn: say. noot: don't know. 285. Clerk: student. Oxenford: Oxford. 286. That . . . y-go: who had long since started on the study of logic, one of the subjects required for a B.A. 288. right: particularly. undertake: vow. 289. holwe: hollow. 290. overeste courtepy: outer short coat. 291. benefice: ecclesiastical appointment. 292. office: secular position. 293. hym . . . levere: he would rather. 296. fithele: fiddle. sautrie: psaltery (harp). 298. cofre: coffer. The Clerk was obviously a student of moral philosophy rather than of natural philosophy or science, which included alchemy. Students of the latter hoped to discover how to transmute base metals into gold. 299. hente: get. 301. gan preye: prayed. 302. yaf: gave. scoleye: study. 303. cure: care. 304. oo: one. 305. in . . . reverence: formally and respectfully. 306. sentence: significance. 307. Sownynge in: tending toward. 309. war: wary. 310. Parvys: the place in London where clients consulted their lawyers. From what follows we learn that the Sergeant of the Law, one of a select group of lawyers appointed by the King, has served not only as a legal counsel but also as a judge in circuit courts outside London. 313. swich: such. weren: were. 314. assise: local assize court. 315. patente: royal appointment. pleyn: full. 316. For: in reward for. science: knowledge. 317. oon: a one. 318. purchasour: buyer of land.

Al was fee symple° to hym in effect.
His purchasyng myghte° nat been infect.°   320
  Nowher so bisy a man as he ther nas,°
And yet he semed bisier than he was.
  In termes° hadde he caas° and doomes° alle
That from the tyme of Kyng William° were falle.
Ther-to° he koude endite° and make a thyng;°
Ther koude no wight pynchen° at his writyng.
And every statut koude° he pleyn by roote.°
  He rood but hoomly° in a medlee° coote,
Girt with a ceynt° of silk with barres smale.
Of his array telle I no lenger tale.   330

  A FRANKELEYN° was in his compaignye.
Whit was his berd as is the dayesye;°
Of his complexioun he was sangwyn.°
Wel loved he by the morwe° a sop° in wyn.
To lyven in delyt was evere his wone,°
For he was Epicurus owene sone,
That heeld opynyoun that pleyn° delit
Was verray° felicitee parfit.°
  An housholdere, and that a greet,° was he;
Seint Julyan he was in his contree.°   340
His breed, his ale, was alweys after oon.°
A bettre envyned° man was nevere noon.
Withoute bake-mete° was nevere his hous
Of fissh and flessh,° and that so plentevous°
It snewed° in his hous of mete° and drynke,
Of alle deyntees that men koude thynke,
After° the sondry sesons of the yeer,
So chaunged° he his mete and his soper.°
Ful many a fat partrich hadde he in muwe,°
And many a breem and many a luce° in stuwe.°
Wo was his cook but if° his sauce were   351
Poynaunt° and sharp, and redy al his geere.°
His table dormaunt in his halle° alway
Stood redy covered al the longe day.
  At sessions ther he was lord and sire;°

Ful ofte tyme he was knyght of the shire.°
An anlaas° and a gipser° al of silk
Heeng° at his girdel whit as morne° mylk.
A shirreve° hadde he been and a countour;°
Was nowher swich a worthy vavasour.°   360

  An HABERDASSHERE and a CARPENTER,
A WEBBE,° a DYERE, and a TAPYCER° —
And they were clothed alle in oo° lyveree
Of a solempne° and a greet fraternytee.°
Ful fressh and newe hir geere apiked was;°
Hir knyves were chaped° noght with bras
But al with silver; wroght ful clene and wel
Hir girdles and hir pouches everydel.°
Wel semed ech of hem a fair burgeys°
To sitten in a yeldehalle° on a deys.°   370
Everych° for the wisdom that he kan°
Was shaply° for to been an alderman,
For catel° hadde they ynogh and rente,°
And eek hir wyves wolde it wel assente,°
And elles° certeyn they were to blame.
It is ful fair to been y-cleped° " madame "
And goon to vigilies° al bifore
And have a mantel roialliche y-bore.°

  A COOK they hadde with hem for the nones°
To boille the chiknes° with the marybones,°   380
And poudre-marchaunt° tart, and galyngale.°
Wel koude he knowe° a draughte of Londoun ale.
He koude rooste and sethe° and broille and frye,
Maken mortreux,° and wel bake a pye.
But greet harm was it, as it thoughte° me,
That on his shyne° a mormal° hadde he.
For blankmanger° that made he with the beste.

  A SHIPMAN° was ther wonyng fer by° weste;
For aught I woot,° he was of Dertemouthe.°
He rood upon a rouncy as he kouthe°   390
In a gowne of faldyng° to the knee.
A daggere hangynge on a laas° hadde he

319. fee symple: unrestricted possession.   320. myghte: could.
infect: invalidated.   321. nas: was.   323. In termes: precisely.
caas: cases.   doomes: judgments.   324. William: William I
(1066–87).   325. Ther-to: in addition.   endite: compose.
make a thyng: draw up a document.   326. wight pynchen: person find fault.   327. koude: knew.   pleyn . . . roote: fully by
memory.   328. hoomly: plainly.   medlee: striped.   329. ceynt:
belt.   331. Frankeleyn: a rich landowner and householder.
332. dayesye: daisy.   333. sangwyn: blood-red (see Note B,
p. 196).   334. morwe: morning.   sop: piece of bread.   335. wone:
custom.   337. pleyn: complete.   338. verray: true.   parfit:
perfect.   339. greet: great (one).   340. Seint . . . contree: He
was the local counterpart of St. Julian, the traditional patron saint
of hospitality.   341. after oon: consistently good.   342. en-
vyned: wined.   343. bake-mete: pie.   344. flessh: meat.
plentevous: plentiful.   345. snewed: snowed.   mete: food.
347. After: according to.   348. chaunged: varied.   soper:
supper.   349. muwe: coop.   350. luce: pike.   stuwe: pond.
351. but if: unless.   352. Poynaunt: pungent.   geere: utensils.
353. His . . . halle: his permanent (dormaunt) table (rather than
a removable board and trestles) in the main room of his house
(halle).   355. At . . . sire: He presided at sessions of the local
justices of the peace. (More serious cases would be brought
before assize courts conducted by justices such as his companion
the Sergeant of the Law.)

356. knyght . . . shire: member of parliament.   357. an-
laas: dagger.   gipser: purse.   358. Heeng: hung.   morne:
morning.   359. shirreve: sheriff.   countour: auditor.
360. vavasour: squire.   362. Webbe: weaver.   Tapycer: tapestry maker.   363. oo: one.   364. solempne: important.   fraternytee: religious guild.   365. hir . . . was: their accessories
were trimmed.   366. chaped: decorated.   368. everydel: altogether.   369. burgeys: citizen.   370. yeldehalle: guildhall.
deys: platform.   371. Everych: each one.   kan: knows.
372. shaply: suited.   373. catel: property.   rente: income.
374. assente: agree to.   375. elles: otherwise.   376. y-cleped:
called.   377. vigilies: festivals on eves of saints' days.   378. roialliche y-bore: royally carried.   379. nones: occasion.   380. chik-
nes: chickens.   marybones: marrowbones.   381. poudre-
marchaunt: flavoring.   galyngale: spice.   382. knowe:
judge.   383. sethe: boil.   384. Maken mortreux: make stews.
385. thoughte: seemed to.   386. shyne: shin.   mormal: ulcer.
387. blankmanger: sweet creamed fowl.   388. Shipman: mer-
chant-ship owner.   wonyng . . . by: living far to the.   389. woot:
know.   Dertemouthe: Dartmouth (in Devon).   390. rouncy
. . . . kouthe: nag as best he could.   391. faldyng: serge.
392. laas: lanyard.

Aboute his nekke, under his arm adoun.
The hoote somer had maad his hewe al broun.
　And certeynly he was a good felawe.°
Ful many a draughte of wyn hadde he drawe
Fro Burdeuxward° whil that the chapman sleep.°
Of nyce° conscience took he no keep;°
If that he faught and had the hyer hond,
By water he sente hem hoom° to every lond.　400
　But of his craft to rekene wel his tydes,
His stremes,° and his daungers hym bisydes,°
His herberwe,° and his moone, his lodemenage,°
Ther nas noon swich° from Hulle to Cartage.°
Hardy he was and wys to undertake.°
With many a tempest hadde his berd been shake.
He knew alle the havenes as they were
Fro Gootland° to the cape of Fynystere°
And every cryke° in Britaigne° and in Spayne.
His barge y-cleped was the Mawdelayne.　410

　With us ther was a DOCTOUR OF PHISIK;°
In al this world ne was ther noon hym lyk,
To speke of phisik and of surgerye,
For he was grounded in astronomye.°
He kepte° his pacient a ful greet deel
In houres° by his magik natureel.°
Wel koude he fortunen the ascendent°
Of hise ymages° for his pacient.
He knew the cause of every maladye,
Were it of hoot or coold or moyste or drye,　420
And where engendred, and of what humour.°
He was a verray,° parfit practisour.°
　The cause y-knowe° and of his harm the roote,
Anon° he yaf° the sike man his boote.°
Ful redy hadde he hise apothecaries
To sende hym drogges and his letuaries,°
For ech of hem made oother for to wynne;°
Hir° friendshipe nas nat° newe to begynne.

Wel° knew he the olde Esculapius,
And Deiscorides, and eek Rufus,　430
Old Ypocras, Haly, and Galyen,
Serapion, Razis, and Avycen,
Averrois, Damascien, and Constantyn,
Bernard, and Gatesden, and Gilbertyn.
Of his diete mesurable° was he,
For it was of no superfluitee
But of greet norissynge° and digestible.
His studie was but litel on the Bible.
　In sangwyn° and in pers° he clad was al,
Lyned with taffata and with sendal,°　440
And yet he was but esy° of dispence.°
He kepte that he wan in pestilence.°
For° gold in phisik is a cordial,°
Therfore he loved gold in special.

A good WYF was ther of biside BATHE,
But she was somdel° deef, and that was scathe.°
　Of clooth-makyng she hadde swich an haunt,°
She passed hem° of Ypres and of Gaunt.°
In al the parisshe, wyf ne was ther noon
That to the offrynge bifore hire sholde goon;°　450
And if ther dide, certeyn, so wrooth was she
That she was out of alle charitee.
Hir coverchiefs° ful fyne were of ground;°
I dorste° swere they weyeden ten pound
That on a Sonday weren upon hir heed.
Hir hosen weren of fyn scarlet reed,
Ful streite y-teyd,° and shoes ful moyste and
　newe.
Boold was hir face and fair and reed of hewe,
She was a worthy womman al hir lyve.
Housbondes at chirche dore° she hadde fyve,　460
Withouten° oother compaignye in youthe —
But ther-of nedeth nat to speke as nouthe.°
　And thries° hadde she been at Jerusalem.
She hadde passed many a straunge° strem.
At Rome she hadde been, and at Boloyne,°

395. **good felawe:** rascal.　397. **Fro Burdeuxward:** from Bordeaux (which was the exporting center of the French wine trade and was, in Chaucer's day, held by England).　**chapman sleep:** dealer slept.　398. **nyce:** tender.　**keep:** heed.　400. **hem hoom:** them home (overboard).　402. **stremes:** currents.　**bisydes:** around.　403. **herberwe:** harbor.　**lodemenage:** pilotage.　404. **nas . . . swich:** was none such.　**Hulle to Cartage:** Hull (northern England) to Cartagena (in Spain).　405. **undertake:** conduct an enterprise.　408. **Gootland:** Gottland (off Sweden).　**Fynystere:** Finisterre (in Spain).　409. **cryke:** creek. **Britaigne:** Brittany.　411. **Phisik:** medicine.　414. **astronomye:** astrology, or the study of the influence of the planets on the human body. (See Note A, p. 195.)　415. **kepte:** watched. 416. **houres:** astrologically important hours, when appropriate conjunctions of the planets might favor his recovery.　**magik natureel:** natural (not black) magic, by means of which he counteracted malignant influences.　417. **fortunen . . . ascendent:** determine the correct point of the zodiac.　418. **ymages:** representations either of the patient or of his astrological circumstances, made in order to study and cure his malady. 421. **humour:** See Note B, p. 196.　422. **verray:** true. **practisour:** practitioner.　423. **y-knowe:** known.　424. **Anon:** immediately.　**yaf:** gave.　**boote:** remedy.　426. **letuaries:** remedies.　427. **wynne:** gain.　428. **Hir:** their.　**nas nat:** was not.

429–34. **Wel . . . Gilbertyn:** He knew all the standard authorities, including five Greek writers (ll. 429–31), from the legendary Aesculapius through Hippocrates, Dioscorides, and Rufus, to Galen in the second century A.D.; seven Arabic writers (ll. 431–33) from the ninth to the twelfth century; and three British writers (l. 434) from the mid-thirteenth century up to Gaddesden of Oxford, who died in 1361.　435. **mesurable:** moderate.　437. **norissynge:** nourishment.　439. **sangwyn:** red.　**pers:** Persian blue.　440. **sendal:** silk.　441. **esy:** cautious.　**dispence:** spending.　442. **that . . . pestilence:** what he gained in time of plagues, which ravaged England in the second half of the fourteenth century.　443. **For:** because.　**cordial:** heart remedy. 446. **somdel:** somewhat.　**scathe:** a pity.　447. **swich an haunt:** such a skill.　448. **passed hem:** surpassed them (the Flemish weavers).　**Gaunt:** Ghent.　450. **goon:** go.　453. **coverchiefs:** head coverings.　**ground:** texture.　454. **dorste:** would dare. 457. **streite y-teyd:** tightly tied.　460. **dore:** Medieval marriages took place at the church door, preceding nuptial mass at the altar.　461. **Withouten:** not to mention.　462. **as nouthe:** now. 463. **thries:** thrice.　464. **straunge:** foreign.　465. **Boloyne:** Boulogne (France).

In Galice° at Seint Jame,° and at Coloyne.°
She koude° muche of wandrynge by the weye.
Gat-tothed° was she, soothly° for to seye.
  Upon an amblere esily she sat,
Y-wympled wel,° and on hir heed an hat   470
As brood as is a bokeler° or a targe,°
A foot-mantel° aboute hir hipes large,
And on hir feet a peyre of spores° sharpe.
  In felawshipe wel koude she laughe and carpe;°
Of remedies° of love she knew par chaunce,°
For she koude° of that art the olde daunce.

  A good man was ther of religioun
And was a poure PERSOUN° of a toun,
But riche he was of holy thoght and werk.
He was also a lerned man, a clerk,°   480
That Cristes gospel trewely° wolde preche.
His parisshens° devoutly wolde he teche.
Benygne he was and wonder° diligent,
And in adversitee ful pacient,
And swich he was preved° ofte sithes.°
Ful looth were hym° to cursen° for his tithes,°
But rather wolde he yeven out of doute°
Unto his poure parisshens aboute
Of his offrynge° and eek of his substaunce.°
He koude in litel thyng have suffisaunce.   490
Wyd was his parisshe and houses fer asonder,
But he ne lafte° nat for reyn ne° thonder,
In siknesse nor in meschief,° to visite
The ferreste° in his parisshe, muche° and lite,°
Upon his feet, and in his hond a staf.
This noble ensample° to his sheep he yaf,°
That first he wroghte, and afterward he taughte.
Out of the gospel he tho° wordes caughte.°
And this figure° he added eek ther-to,
That if gold ruste, what sholde iren do?   500
For if a preest be foule on whom we truste,
No wonder is a lewed° man to ruste.
And shame it is, if a preest take keep,°
A shiten° shepherde and a clene sheep.
Wel oghte a preest ensample for to yive°
By his clennesse how that his sheep sholde lyve.
He sette nat his benefice to hyre

And leet° his sheep encombred in the myre
And ran to Londoun unto Seint Poules°
To seken° hym a chauntrye° for soules,   510
Or with a bretherhede° to been withholde,°
But dwelte at hoom and kepte° wel his folde
So that the wolf ne made it nat myscarye.
He was a shepherde and noght a mercenarye.
  And thogh he hooly were and vertuous,
He was noght to synful men despitous,°
Ne° of his speche daungerous ne digne,°
But in his techyng discreet and benigne.
To drawen folk to hevene by fairnesse,
By good ensample, this was his bisynesse.°   520
But it° were any persone obstinat,
What so° he were of heigh or lowe estat,
Hym wolde he snybben° sharply for the nonys.°
  A bettre preest I trowe° that nowher noon ys.
He wayted after° no pompe and reverence,
Ne maked hym a spiced° conscience,
But Cristes loore° and his apostles twelve
He taughte, but first he folwed it hymselve.

  With hym ther was a PLOWMAN, was his brother,
That hadde y-lad° of donge° ful many a fother.°
A trewe swynkere° and a good was he,   531
Lyvynge in pees and parfit charitee.
God loved he best with al his hoole herte
At alle tymes, thogh hym gamed or smerte,°
And thanne his neighebore right° as hymselve.
He wolde thresshe and ther-to dyke° and delve°
For Cristes sake for every poure wight
Withouten hire,° if it lay in his myght.
His tithes payde he ful faire and wel
Bothe of his propre swynk° and his catel.°   540
In a tabard° he rood, upon a mere.°

  Ther was also a REVE° and a MILLERE,
A SOMNOUR° and a PARDONER also,
A MAUNCIPLE° and myself; ther were namo.°
  The MILLER was a stout carl for the nones.°
Ful big he was of brawn and eek of bones.

508. leet: left. As the result of the Great Plague priests were scarce, and rural charges were deserted in favor of urban. 509. Seint Poules: St. Paul's (Cathedral). 510. seken: secure. chauntrye: endowment established by a donor to pay for the singing of masses for the repose of his own or some other soul. 511. bretherhede: religious guild such as that alluded to in l. 364. withholde: retained (as chaplain). 512. kepte: watched. 516. despitous: scornful. 517. Ne: nor. daungerous ne digne: domineering or pompous. 520. bisynesse: concern. 521. it: if there. 522. What so: whether. 523. snybben: reprove. nonys: occasion. 524. trowe: believe. 525. wayted after: expected. 526. Ne . . . spiced: nor assumed an overscrupulous. 527. loore: teaching. 530. y-lad: hauled. donge: manure. fother: load. 531. swynkere: laborer. 534. hym . . . smerte: he rejoiced or grieved. 535. right: just as much. 536. dyke: ditch. delve: dig. 538. hire: payment. 540. propre swynk: own work. catel: property. 541. tabard: smock. mere: mare (an unfashionable mount). 542. Reve: reeve. 543. Somnour: summoner. 544. Maunciple: manciple. namo: no more. 545. a . . . nones: an especially stout fellow.

466. Galice: Galicia, a region in Spain.   Jame: James of Compostela.   Coloyne: Cologne.   467. koude: knew.   468. Gat-tothed: gap-toothed.   soothly: truly.   470. Y-wympled wel: well hooded.   471. bokeler: buckler.   targe: shield.   472. foot-mantel: outer skirt.   473. spores: spurs (because she rode astride).   474. carpe: talk.   475. remedies: restoratives.   par chaunce: perchance.   476. koude: knew.   478. Persoun: parson.   480. clerk: scholar.   481. trewely: faithfully.   482. parisshens: parishioners.   483. wonder: remarkably.   485. preved: proved.   sithes: times.   486. were hym: was he.   cursen: excommunicate.   tithes: church dues.   487. yeven . . . doute: give without doubt.   489. offrynge: voluntary gifts.   substaunce: income.   492. lafte: neglected.   ne: nor.   493. meschief: misfortune.   494. ferreste: furthest (members).   muche: great.   lite: small.   496. ensample: example.   yaf: gave.   498. tho: those.   caughte: took.   499. figure: parallel.   502. lewed: unlearned.   503. keep: heed.   504. shiten: defiled.   505. yive: give.

That proved wel, for over-al ther° he cam,
At wrastlyng he wolde have alwey the ram.°
He was short-sholdred, brood, a thikke knarre.°
Ther was no dore that he nolde° heve of harre°
Or breke it at a rennyng with his heed.   551
His berd as any sowe or fox was reed°
And ther-to brood° as though it were a spade.
Upon the cop right° of his nose he hade
A werte,° and ther-on stood a tuft of herys,°
Reed as the bristles of a sowes erys.°
His nosethirles° blake were and wyde.
A swerd and a bokeler bar° he by his syde.
   His mouth as greet was as a greet fourneys.°
He was a jangler° and a goliardeys.°   560
And that was moost of synne and harlotries.°
   Wel koude he stelen corn and tollen thries,°
And yet he hadde a thombe of gold,° pardee.°
   A whit cote and a blew hood wered° hee.
A baggepipe wel koude he blowe and sowne,°
And ther-with-al he broghte us out of towne.

   A gentil MAUNCIPLE° was ther of a temple°
Of which achatours° myghte take exemple
For to be wys in byynge of vitaille,°
For wheither that he payde or took by taille,°   570
Algate he wayted so in his achaat°
That he was ay biforn° and in good staat.
   Now, is nat that of God a ful fair grace
That swich a lewed° mannes wit shal pace°
The wisdom of an heep of lerned men!
Of maistres hadde he mo° than thries ten
That weren of° lawe expert and curious,°
Of whiche° ther were a dozeyne in that hous
Worthy to been stywardes° of rente° and lond
Of any lord that is in Engelond,   580
To make hym lyve by his propre good°
In honour detteles, but if° he were wood,°
Or lyve as scarsly° as hym list° desire;
And able for to helpen° al a shire

In any caas that myghte falle or happe.
And yet this Maunciple sette hir aller cappe.°

   The REVE° was a sclendre, colerik man.
His berd was shave as neigh° as ever he kan;
His heer was by his erys° ful round y-shorn;
His top was dokked° lyk a preest byforn.   590
Ful longe were his legges and ful lene;
Ylik a staf,° ther was no calf y-sene.
   Wel koude he kepe a gerner° and a bynne;
Ther was noon auditour koude on hym wynne.
Wel wiste° he by the droghte and by the reyn
The yeldynge of his seed and of his greyn.
His lordes sheep, his neet,° his dayerye,
His swyn, his hors, his stoor,° and his pultrye
Was hoolly in this Reves governynge,
And by his covenant yaf° the rekenynge   600
Syn° that his lord was twenty yeer of age.
Ther koude no man brynge hym in arrerage.°
Ther nas baillif,° ne hierde,° ne oother hyne°
That he ne knew his sleighte° and his covyne.°
They were adrad° of hym as of the deeth.
   His wonyng° was ful faire upon an heeth;
With grene trees shadwed was his place.
He koude bettre than his lord purchace;
Ful riche he was astored pryvely.°
His lord wel koude he plesen subtilly   610
To yeve° and lene° hym of his owene good°
And have a thank and yet° a coote and hood.
   In youthe he hadde lerned a good myster:°
He was a wel good wrighte, a carpenter.
   This Reve sat upon a ful good stot,°
That was al pomely° grey and highte° Scot.
A long surcote of pers° upon he hade,
And by his syde he baar° a rusty blade.
Of Northfolk° was this Reve of which I telle,
Biside a toun men clepen Baldeswelle.°   620
Tukked he was as is a frere° aboute;
And evere he rood the hyndreste° of oure route.°

   A SOMNOUR° was ther with us in that place,
That hadde a fyr-reed cherubynnes face,°

For saucefleem° he was, with eyen narwe.
As hoot he was and lecherous as a sparwe,°
With scaled° browes blake and piled° berd.
Of his visage children were aferd.°
Ther nas quyksilver, lytarge,° ne brymstoon,
Boras,° ceruce,° ne oille° of tartre noon,   630
Ne oynement that wolde clense and byte,
That hym myghte helpen° of his whelkes° white,
Nor of the knobbes sittynge on his chekes.
    Wel loved he garlek, oynons, and eek lekes,
And for to drynke strong wyn reed as blood;
Thanne wolde he speke and crye as° he were
          wood;°
And whan that he wel dronken hadde the wyn,
Thanne wolde he speke no word but Latyn.
    A fewe termes hadde he, two or thre,
That he had lerned out of som decre.   640
No wonder is! He herde it al the day;
And eek ye knowen wel how that a jay
Kan clepen "Watte"° as wel as kan the Pope.
But who so koude in oother thyng hym grope,°
Thanne hadde he spent al his philosophie.
Ay° " Questio, quid juris?"° wolde he crie.
    He was a gentil harlot° and a kynde;
A bettre felawe sholde men noght fynde.
He wolde suffre,° for a quart of wyn,
A good felawe° to have his concubyn°   650
A twelf monthe and excuse hym atte fulle.°
Ful pryvely a fynch eek koude he pulle;°
And if he foond owher° a good felawe,
He wolde techen hym to have noon awe
In swich caas of the ercedekenes curs°
But if° a mannes soule were in his purs,
For in his purs he sholde y-punysshed be.
"Purs is the ercedekenes helle," seyde he.
But wel I woot° he lyed right in dede;
Of cursyng oghte ech gilty man drede —   660
For curs wol slee,° right as assoillyng° savith —
And also war hym of° a significavit.°
    In daunger° hadde he at° his owene gyse°
The yonge gerles° of the diocise,
And knew hir counseil,° and was al hir reed.°

625. saucefleem: pimpled.   626. sparwe: sparrow.   627. scaled:
scabby.   piled: scanty.   628. aferd: afraid.   629. lytarge:
lead ointment.   630. Boras: borax.   ceruce: white lead.
oille: cream.   632. helpen: rid.   whelkes: (leprous) sores.
636. as: as if.   wood: mad.   643. clepen "Watte": call out
"Walter" (as a parrot calls out "Polly").   644. grope: examine.   646. Ay: always.   " Questio . . . juris?": "Query, what
of the law (here)?"   647. gentil harlot: obliging rascal.   649. suffre: allow.   650. good
felawe: rascal.   concubyn: mistress.   651. atte fulle: fully.
652. Ful . . . pulle: He also knew how to fornicate very secretively.   653. foond owher: found anywhere.   655. ercedekenes
curs: archdeacon's curse (of excommunication).   656. But if:
unless.   659. woot: know.   661. slee: slay.   assoillyng: absolution.   662. war . . . of: beware.   significavit: writ for arrest.
663. daunger: subjection.   at: in.   gyse: way.   664. gerles:
people (male and female).   665. hir counseil: their secrets.
al . . . reed: adviser of all of them.

A gerland° hadde he set upon his heed,
As greet as it were for an ale stake;°
A bokeler° hadde he maad hym of a cake.
    With hym ther rood a gentil PARDONER
Of Rouncival, his freend and his comper,°   670
That streight was comen fro the court of Rome.°
Ful loude he soong,° " Com hider,° love, to me."
This Somnour bar° to hym a stif burdoun,°
Was nevere trompe° of half so greet a soun.°
    This Pardoner hadde heer° as yelow as wex,°
But smothe it heeng° as dooth a strike of flex.°
By ounces° henge his lokkes that he hadde,
And ther-with he his shuldres overspradde,
But thynne it lay by colpons oon and oon.°
But hood, for jolitee,° wered° he noon,   680
For it was trussed up in his walet.
Hym thoughte he rood al of the newe jet.°
Dischevelee,° save his cappe he rood al bare.
Swiche glarynge eyen hadden he as an hare.
    A vernycle° hadde he sowed upon his cappe,
His walet biforn hym in his lappe,
Bret° ful of pardoun comen from Rome al hoot.°
    A voys he hadde as smal as hath a goot.°
No berd° hadde he, ne nevere sholde have;
As smothe it was as it were late y-shave.°   690
I trowe he were a geldyng° or a mare.
    But of his craft fro Berwyk into Ware
Ne was ther swich another pardoner,
For in his male° he hadde a pilwe-beer°
Which that he seyde was Oure Lady veyl.°
He seyde he hadde a gobet° of the seyl°
That Seint Peter hadde whan that he wente°
Upon the see til Jesu Crist hym hente.°
He hadde a croys of latoun° ful of stones,
And in a glas he hadde pigges bones.   700
But with thise relikes, whan that he fond

666. gerland: garland.   667. ale stake: alehouse sign.   668. bokeler: buckler (small shield).   670. comper: comrade.   671. That
. . . Rome: Special indulgences (remissions of the temporal punishment still due after a sinner has been absolved) were issued
by the Pope through pardoners, who were entitled to collect
money for some pious object from penitents who chose to work
off the remaining temporal punishment by this additional act of
penance. In Chaucer's time, however, some unlicensed swindlers
such as the Pardoner of Rouncivalle (a religious hospital near
London) took notorious advantage of the system for their own
profit.   672. soong: sang.   hider: hither.   673. bar: carried.
stif burdoun: strong accompaniment.   674. trompe: trumpet.
soun: sound.   675. heer: hair.   wex: wax.   676. heeng:
hung.   strike of flex: hank of flax.   677. By ounces: in wisps.
679. by . . . oon: in single strands.   680. jolitee: jauntiness.
wered: wore.   681. walet: traveling bag.   682. jet: style.
683. Dischevelee: with loose hair.   685. vernycle: a copy of
St. Veronica's handkerchief, which, according to legend, was miraculously imprinted with the image of Christ's face.   687. Bret:
cram.   hoot: hot.   688. goot: goat.   689. berd: beard.
690. late y-shave: newly shaved.   691. trowe . . . geldyng: believe he must have been a gelding.   694. male: bag.   pilwe-
beer: pillowcase.   695. Oure Lady veyl: Our Lady's veil.
696. gobet: piece.   seyl: sail.   697. wente: walked.   698. hente:
caught. See Matt. 14:29.   699. latoun: copper alloy.

A poure persoun° dwellyng upon lond,°
Upon a° day he gat hym moore moneye
Than that the persoun gat in monthes tweye.
And thus with feyned flaterye and japes°
He made the persoun and the peple his apes.°

But trewely to tellen, atte laste,
He was in chirche a noble ecclesiaste.
Wel koude he rede a lessoun or a storie,°
But alderbest° he song° an offertorie,   710
For wel he wiste° whan that song was songe,
He moste° preche and wel affile° his tonge
To wynne silver, as he ful wel koude.
Ther-fore he song the murierly° and loude.

Now have I told yow soothly in a clause°
Th' estaat, th' array, the nombre, and eek the cause
Why that assembled was this compaignye
In Southwerk at this gentil hostelrye,
That highte° the Tabard, faste° by the Belle.°
But now is tyme to yow for to telle   720
How that we baren us° that ilke° nyght
Whan we were in that hostelrie alyght;°
And after wol I telle of oure viage°
And al the remenant of oure pilgrymage.

But first I pray yow of youre curteisye
That ye n' arette it nat my vileynye°
Thogh that° I pleynly speke in this matere
To telle yow hir° wordes and hir cheere°
Ne thogh I speke° hir wordes proprely.°
For this ye knowen also° wel as I,   730
Who so shal telle° a tale after a man,
He moot reherce° as neigh° as evere he kan
Everich a° word if it be in his charge,
Al° speke he nevere so rudeliche° and large,°
Or ellis° he moot telle his tale untrewe,
Or feyne thyng,° or fynde wordes newe.
He may nat spare° al thogh he were his brother;
He moot° as wel seye o° word as another.
Crist spak hymself ful brode° in Holy Writ,
And wel ye woot,° no vileynye is it.   740
Eek° Plato seith, who so kan hym rede,
The wordes mote° be cosyn° to the dede.

Also, I pray yow to foryeve° it me,
Al° have I nat set folk in hir degree°
Here in this tale as that° they sholde stonde.°
My wit is short, ye may° wel understonde.

Greet cheere made oure HOOST us everichon,°
And to the soper sette he us anon.°
He served us with vitaille° at the beste.
Strong was the wyn, and wel to drynke us
          leste.°   750
A semely° man oure Hoost was with alle
For to been a marchal° in an halle.°
A large man he was, with eyen stepe.°
A fairer burgeys° was ther noon in Chepe,°
Boold of his speche, and wys, and wel y-taught,
And of manhode hym° lakked right naught.
Eke ther-to he was right° a murye man,
And after soper pleyen° he bigan
And spak of myrthe,° amonges othere thynges,
Whan that we hadde maad° oure rekenynges,° 760
And seyde thus, "Now, lordynges,° trewely,
Ye been° to me right welcome, hertely,
For by my trouthe, if that I shal not lye,
I saugh nat this yeer so murye a compaignye
At ones° in this herberwe° as is now.
Fayn° wolde I doon° yow myrthe, wiste I° how.
And of a myrthe I am right now bythoght
To doon yow ese,° and it shal coste noght.
"Ye goon° to Canterbury, God yow spede!
The blisful martir quyte° yow youre mede!°   770
And wel I woot as ye goon by the weye,
Ye shapen yow to talen° and to pleye,
For trewely confort ne° myrthe is noon°
To ryde by the weye domb as a stoon.
And ther-fore wol I maken yow disport,°
As I seyde erst,° and doon yow som confort.
And if yow liketh alle by oon° assent
For to stonden at° my juggement
And for to werken° as I shall yow seye,
Tomorwe, whan ye riden by the weye,   780
Now, by my fader° soule, that is deed,
But° ye be murye, I wol yeve yow myn heed.°
Hoold up youre hondes withouten moore speche."
Oure conseil was nat longe for to seche.°

702. persoun: parson (who would introduce him to the parish). lond: the country.   703. a: one.   705. japes: tricks.   706. apes: fools.   709. storie: Bible story or saint's life.   710. alderbest: best of all.   song: sang.   711. wiste: knew.   712. moste: must.   affile: make smooth.   714. murierly: more merrily.   715. soothly . . . clause: truly in brief.   719. highte: was called.   faste: close.   Belle: Bell (Inn).   721. baren us: conducted ourselves.   ilke: same.   722. alyght: alighted.   723. viage: journey.   726. n' arette . . . vileynye: won't blame it on my boorishness.   727. Thogh that: even if.   728. hir: their.   cheere: behavior.   729. Ne . . . speke: and if I repeat.   proprely: literally.   730. also: as.   731. telle: retell.   732. moot reherce: must repeat.   neigh: closely.   733. Everich a: every single.   734. Al: even though.   rudeliche: rudely.   large: broadly.   735. ellis: else.   736. feyne thyng: invent something.   737. spare: hold back.   738. moot: must.   o: one.   739. brode: freely.   740. woot: know.   741. Eek: also.   742. mote: must.   cosyn: cousin.

743. foryeve: forgive.   744. Al: even if.   hir degree: their order of rank.   745. as that: just as.   stonde: stand.   746. may: can.   747. us everichon: for each of us.   748. anon: immediately.   749. vitaille: victuals.   750. leste: it pleased.   751. semely: suitable.   752. marchal: marshal to arrange ceremonies.   halle: banquet hall.   753. stepe: prominent.   754. burgeys: citizen.   Chepe: Cheapside (London).   756. hym: he.   757. right: truly.   758. pleyen: to joke.   759. myrthe: amusement.   760. maad: paid.   rekenynges: bills.   761. lordynges: sirs.   762. been: are.   765. ones: once.   herberwe: lodging.   766. Fayn: gladly.   doon: provide.   wiste I: if I knew.   768. ese: comfort.   769. goon: are going.   770. quyte: grant.   mede: reward.   772. shapen . . . talen: intend to tell tales.   773. ne: nor.   noon: none.   775. disport: amusement.   776. erst: before.   777. oon: one.   778. stonden at: abide by.   779. werken: do.   781. fader: father's.   782. But: unless.   heed: head.   784. seche: seek.

Us thoughte it was nat worth to make it wys,°
And graunted° hym withouten moore avys°
And bad hym seye his voirdit° as hym leste.°
　"Lordynges," quod° he, "now herkneth° for the beste,
But taketh it not, I pray yow, in desdeyn.°
This is the poynt, to speken short and pleyn,　790
That ech of yow, to shorte with oure weye,°
In this viage° shal telle tales tweye,° —
To Caunterburyward° I mene it so, —
And homward he shal tellen othere two
Of aventures that whilom° have bifalle.
And which° of yow that bereth° hym best of alle,
That is to seyn, that telleth in this caas
Tales of best sentence° and moost solaas,°
Shal have a soper at oure aller cost°
Here in this place, sittyng by this post,　800
Whan that we come agayn fro Caunterbury.
And, for to make yow the moore mury,
I wol myself goodly with yow ryde
Right at myn owene cost and be your gyde;
And who so° wol my juggement withseye°
Shal paye al that we spende by the weye.
And if ye vouchesauf that it be so,
Tel me anoon° withouten wordes mo,°
And I wol erly shape me° ther-fore."
　This thyng was graunted, and oure othes swore°
With ful glad herte, and preyden° hym also　811
That he wolde vouchesauf for to do so,
And that he wolde been oure governour,
And of oure tales juge and reportour,°
And sette a soper at a certeyn prys,
And we wol reuled been at his devys°
In heigh and lough.° And thus by oon assent
We been acorded to his juggement;
And ther-upon the wyn was fet° anoon.
We dronken,° and to reste wente echon °　820
Withouten any lenger taryynge.
　A morwe,° whan that day bigan to sprynge,
Up roos oure Hoost and was oure aller cok°
And gadred° us togidre° in a flok,
And forth we riden,° a° litel moore than pas,°
Unto the wateryng° of Seint Thomas,

And there oure Hoost bigan his hors areste°
And seyde, "Lordynges, herkneth,° if yow leste.°
Ye woot youre forward° and it yow recorde.°
If evensong and morwesong acorde,°　830
Lat se° now who shal telle the firste tale.
As evere moot° I drynke wyn or ale,
Who so be rebel to my juggement
Shal paye for al that by the wey is spent.
Now draweth cut er that we ferrer twynne.°
He which that hath the shorteste shal bigynne.
Sire Knyght," quod he, "my mayster and my lord,
Now draweth° cut, for that is myn acord.°
Cometh neer," quod he, "my lady Prioresse,
And ye, sire Clerk, lat be° your shamefastnesse,°
Ne studieth noght. Ley hond to, every man."　841
　Anoon° to drawen every wight bigan,
And shortly for to tellen as it was,
Were it by aventure° or sort° or cas,°
The sothe° is this: the cut fil° to the Knyght,
Of which ful blithe and glad was every wight,°
And telle he moste° his tale, as was resoun°
By forward and by composicioun,°
As ye han° herd. What nedeth wordes mo?
　And whan this goode man saugh that it was so,
As he that wys was and obedient　851
To kepe his forward by his free assent,
He seyde, "Syn° I shal bigynne the game,
What,° welcome be the cut, a° Goddes name!
Now lat us ryde, and herkneth what I seye."
And with that word we ryden forth oure weye,
And he bigan with right a murye° cheere
His tale anoon and seyde as ye may heere.

THE PARDONER'S PROLOGUE

　The allegorical figure known as False Semblance in the *Romance of the Rose* may in part have inspired the self-confessions of Chaucer's avaricious and hypocritical Pardoner, just as the Crone in the *Romance* may have suggested the self-confessions of the Wife of Bath. But False Semblance is a composite figure allegorizing all the deceits that may lurk under the cloak of true religion. He is "sometimes knight, sometimes monk, . . . sometimes clerk, or sometimes priest, . . . sometimes maiden, sometimes lady, . . . sometimes nun, sometimes abbess." Chaucer's Pardoner, on the other hand, is intensely real and individual. He practices the sin of avarice, which he confesses so cheerfully, in the manner of the impostors who were widely condemned in Chau-

785. wys: difficult.　786. graunted: (we) yielded to.　avys: consideration.　787. voirdit: verdict.　leste: it pleased. 788. quod: said.　herkneth: listen.　789. in desdeyn: contemptuously.　791. shorte . . . weye: cut short our way with. 792. viage: journey.　tweye: two.　793. To Caunterburyward: toward Canterbury.　795. whilom: once upon a time. 796. which: whichever.　bereth: conducts.　798. sentence: significance.　solaas: delight.　799. oure . . . cost: the expense of all of us.　805. who so: whosoever.　withseye: resist. 808. anoon: immediately.　mo: more.　809. shape me: prepare.　810. swore: sworn.　811. preyden: (we) begged. 814. reportour: critic.　816. devys: discretion.　817. In . . . lough: in all matters.　819. fet: fetched.　820. dronken: drank. echon: each one.　822. A morwe: the next morning.　823. oure . . . cok: the cock (who crowed) for us all.　824. gadred: gathered.　togidre: together.　825. riden: rode.　a: at a.　pas: footpace.　826. wateryng: watering place (two miles from Southwark).

827. areste: to halt.　828. herkneth: listen.　leste: it pleases. 829. woot . . . forward: know your agreement.　it . . . recorde: remember it.　830. morwesong acorde: morning song agree. 831. Lat se: let's see.　832. moot: may.　835. cut . . . twynne: lots before we further depart.　838. draweth: draw a.　acord: agreement.　840. lat be: lay aside.　shamefastnesse: modesty. 842. Anoon: immediately.　844. aventure: chance.　sort: lot. cas: destiny.　845. sothe: truth.　fil: fell.　846. wight: person. 847. moste: must.　resoun: right.　848. composicioun: compact.　849. han: have.　853. Syn: since.　854. What: why. a: in.　857. right a murye: a very merry.

cer's England, but his character differentiates him from all others of his kind. He is a pardoner extraordinary, not just the common butt of satirists and reformers.

From the General Prologue we gather that he is what medieval physicians would have called a eunuch from birth; that is, he is sexless. And, among the pilgrims, he is apparently the friend of none except the repulsive Summoner. Yet, as he tells his captive audience of pilgrims in his Prologue and proves to them in his Tale, he is a brilliant preacher, for all his faults and failings.

"Lordynges," quod° he, "in chirches whan I preche,
I peyne me° to han an hauteyn° speche
And rynge it out as round as gooth a belle,
For I kan° al by rote that I telle.
My theme is alwey oon,° and ever was —
Radix malorum est cupiditas.°
"First I pronounce whennes that° I come,
And thanne my bulles° shewe I alle and some.°
Oure lige lordes° seel on my patente,
That shewe I first, my body to warante,° 10
That no man be so bold, ne° preest ne° clerk,
Me to destourbe of Cristes holy werk.
And after that thanne telle I forth my tales.
Bulles of popes and of cardynales,
Of patriarkes and bisshopes I shewe,
And in Latyn I speke a wordes fewe
To saffron with my predicacioun,°
And for to stire hem to devocioun.
Thanne shewe I forth my longe cristal stones°
Y-crammed ful of cloutes° and of bones; 20
Relikes been° they, as wenen° they echon.°
Thanne have I in latoun° a shulder-bon
Which that was of an holy Jewes sheep.°
'Goode men,' I seye, 'tak of my wordes keep.°
If that this boon be wasshe° in any welle,
If cow, or calf, or sheep, or oxe swelle,
That any worm hath ete or worm y-stonge,°
Taak water of that welle, and wassh his° tonge,
And it is hool anoon.° And forther moor,
Of pokkes,° and of scabbe, and every soor 30
Shal every sheep be hool that of this welle

Drynketh a draughte. Taak kepe, eek, what° I telle:
If that the goode man that the bestes oweth°
Wol every wyke,° er that the cok hym croweth,°
Fastynge, drynken of this welle a draughte,
As thilke° holy Jew oure eldres taughte,
Hise bestes and his stoor° shal multiplie.
"'And, sire, also it heeleth jalousie,
For thogh a man be falle in jalous rage,
Lat maken° with this water his potage, 40
And nevere shal he moore his wyf mystriste,°
Thogh he the soothe° of hir defaute wiste,°
Al° hadde she taken preestes two or thre.
"'Heere is a miteyn,° eek,° that ye may se.
He that his hand wol putte in this mitayn,
He shal have multiplyyng of his grayn
Whan he hath sowen, be it whete or otes,
So that° he offre pens or ellis grotes.°
"'Goode men and wommen, o° thyng warne I yow,
If any wight° be in this chirche now 50
That hath doon synne horrible, that he
Dar° nat for shame of it y-shryven° be,
Or any womman, be she yong or old,
That hath y-maked hir housbond cokewold,°
Swich° folk shal have no power, ne no grace,
To offren to my relikes in this place.
And whoso° fyndeth hym° out of swich blame,
They wol come up and offre, a° Goddes name,
And I assoille° hym by the auctoritee°
Which that by bulle y-graunted was to me.' 60
"By this gaude° have I wonne yeer by yeer
An hundred mark° sith° I was pardoner.
I stonde° lyk a clerk° in my pulpet,
And whan the lewed° peple is doun y-set,
I preche so as ye han° herd bifore,
And telle an hundred false japes° more.
Thanne peyne I me° to strecche forth the nekke,
And est and west upon the peple I bekke,°
As dooth a dowve° sittyng on a berne.°
Myne handes and my tonge goon° so yerne° 70
That it is joye to se my bisynesse.°
Of avarice and of swich cursednesse
Is al my prechyng, for to make hem free

PARDONER'S PROLOGUE. 1. quod: said. 2. peyne me: take pains. hauteyn: dominating. 4. kan: know. 5. alwey oon: always one. 6. *Radix . . . cupiditas*: The root of evils is avarice. 7. whennes that: whence. 8. bulles: grants issued by the pope. alle . . . some: one and all. 9. lige lordes: liege lord's (bishop's). 10. my . . . warante: to safeguard my person. 11. ne . . . ne: neither . . . nor. 17. saffron . . . predicacioun: flavor my preaching with. 19. cristal stones: glass cases (reliquaries). 20. cloutes: rags. 21. been: are. wenen: believe. echon: each one. 22. in latoun: (set) in copper alloy. 23. Which . . . sheep: which was taken from the sheep of a holy Jew (that is, some Old Testament hero). The ancient practice of divination by the shape of a shoulder bone survived among the credulous in the Middle Ages. 24. keep: heed. 25. wasshe: washed. 27. That . . . y-stonge: which has eaten any worm (i.e., injurious serpent), or which any worm has stung. 28. his: its. 29. hool anoon: cured at once. 30. pokkes: pocks.

32. kepe . . . what: heed, also, of what. 33. oweth: owns. 34. wyke: week. er . . . croweth: before the cock crows. 36. thilke: that same. 37. stoor: stock. 40. Lat maken: have made. 41. mystriste: mistrust. 42. soothe: truth. defaute wiste: fault should know. 43. Al: even if. 44. miteyn: mitten. eek: also. 48. So that: provided that. ellis grotes: else groats (fourpennies). 49. o: one. 50. wight: person. 52. Dar: dare. y-shryven: confessed and absolved. 54. cokewold: cuckold. 55. Swich: such. 57. whoso: whoever. hym: himself. 58. a: in. 59. assoille: absolve. auctoritee: authority. 61. gaude: trick. 62. mark: marks (13s. 4d.). sith: since. 63. stonde: stand. clerk: ecclesiastical scholar. 64. lewed: ignorant. 65. han: have. 66. japes: frauds. 67. peyne I me: I take pains. 68. bekke: nod. 69. dowve: dove. berne: barn. 70. goon: go. yerne: eagerly. 71. bisynesse: industriousness.

To yeven hir° pens, and namely° unto me.
For myn entente is nat but for to wynne,°
And nothyng° for correccioun of synne.
I rekke° nevere, whan that° they been beryed,°
Thogh that hir soules goon a-blakeberyed.°
For certes° many a predicacioun°
Comth ofte tyme of yvel entencioun,   80
Som for plesance° of folk and flaterye,
To been avanced by ypocrisye,
And some for veyne glorie, and som for hate.
For whan I dar noon oother weyes debate,°
Thanne wol I stynge hym with my tonge smerte°
In prechyng, so that he shal nat asterte°
To been defamed falsly, if that he
Hath trespased to° my bretheren or to me.
For thogh I telle noght his propre name,
Men shal wel knowe that it is the same   90
By signes and by othere circumstances.
Thus quyte° I folk that doon° us displesances;
Thus spitte I out my venym under hewe°
Of holynesse, to seme holy and trewe.
   "But shortly myn entente I wol devyse:°
I preche of no thyng but for coveityse.°
Therfore my theme is yet, and evere was,
Radix malorum est cupiditas.
Thus kan I preche agayn° that same vice
Which that I use, and that is avarice.   100
But though myself be gilty in that synne,
Yet kan I maken oother folk to twynne°
From avarice, and soore° to repente.
But that is nat my principal entente.
I preche no thyng but for coveitise.
Of this matere it oghte ynow° suffise.
   "Thanne telle I hem ensamples° many oon°
Of olde stories longe tyme agoon,°
For lewed peple loven tales olde.
Swiche thynges kan they wel reporte° and holde.°
What! Trowe° ye that, whiles I may preche, 111
And wynne gold and silver for° I teche,
That I wol lyve in poverte wilfully?°
Nay, nay! I thoghte it nevere, trewely.
For I wol preche and begge in sondry landes;
I wol nat do no labour with myne handes,
Ne make baskettes and lyve ther-by,
Bycause I wol nat beggen ydelly.°

I wol noon of the apostles countrefete.°
I wol have moneye, wolle,° chese, and whete,   120
Al° were it yeven° of the poureste° page,
Or of the poureste widwe° in a village,
Al sholde hir children sterve° for famyne.
Nay, I wol drynke licour of the vyne
And have a joly wenche in every toun.
   "But herkneth, lordynges, in conclusioun.
Youre likyng is that I shal telle a tale.
Now have I dronke a draghte of corny° ale,
By God, I hope I shal yow telle a thyng
That shal by resoun been at youre likyng.   130
For, thogh myself be a ful vicious man,
A moral tale yet I yow telle kan,
Which I am wont° to preche for to wynne.°
Now, holde youre pees.° My tale I wol bigynne."

THE PARDONER'S TALE

   The source of the Pardoner's Tale is a widely known
folk tale, versions of which had been employed by
pagan and Christian alike for purposes of edification
or entertainment long before Chaucer wrote the *Canterbury Tales*. The Pardoner, however, uses it as the
exemplum or illustrative story for a sermon on the text
from I Timothy 6:10: "For the love of money is the
root of all evil: which while some coveted after, they
have erred from the faith, and pierced themselves
through with many sorrows." And then, having demonstrated his manner of preaching, he brazenly turns
(l. 453) to the pilgrims and applies his appeal to them.

   In Flaundres whilom° was a compaignye
Of yonge folk that haunteden° folye,
As° riot, hasard,° stewes,° and tavernes
Where-as° with haipes, lutes, and gyternes°
They daunce and pleyen at dees° bothe day and
      nyght,
And ete also and drynke over hir myght,°
Thurgh which they doon the devel sacrifise
Withinne that develes temple in cursed wise
By superfluytee abhomynable.
Hir othes been° so grete and so dampnable   10
That it is grisly for to heere hem swere;
Oure blissed Lordes body they to-tere;°
Hem thoughte° that Jewes rente hym noght
      ynough!

74. **yeven hir**: give their.   **namely**: particularly.   75. **but . . .
wynne**: only to gain.   76. **nothyng**: in no way.   77. **rekke**:
care.   **whan that**: when.   **been beryed**: are buried.   78. **Thogh
. . . a-blakeberyed**: though their souls go blackberrying (that is,
go wandering without direction).   79. **certes**: certainly.   **predicacioun**: sermon.   81. **plesance**: the satisfying.   84. **weyes
debate**: way contend.   85. **smerte**: sharp.   86. **asterte**: avoid.
88. **trespased to**: wronged.   92. **quyte**: repay.   **doon**: cause.
93. **hewe**: pretext.   95. **devyse**: explain.   96. **coveityse**:
covetousness.   99. **agayn**: against.   102. **twynne**: depart.
103. **soore**: sorely.   106. **ynow**: enough.   107. **ensamples**:
(illustrative) examples.   **oon**: a one.   108. **agoon**: past.
110. **report**: repeat.   **holde**: remember.   111. **Trowe**: believe.
112. **for**: because.   113. **wilfully**: willingly.   118. **ydelly**: in
vain.

119. **countrefete**: imitate.   120. **wolle**: wool.   121. **Al**: though.
yeven: given.   **poureste**: poorest.   122. **widwe**: widow.
123. **sterve**: perish.   128. **corny**: tasting strongly of malt.
133. **wont**: accustomed.   **wynne**: gain.   134. **pees**: peace.
PARDONER'S TALE.   1. **Flaundres whilom**: Flanders once.
2. **haunteden**: practiced.   3. **As**: such as.   **hasard**: dicing.
stewes: brothels.   4. **Where-as**: where.   **gyternes**: gitterns, a
type of guitar.   5. **dees**: dice.   6. **over . . . myght**: beyond
their capacity.   10. **Hir . . . been**: their oaths are.   12. **to-
tere**: tear apart, i.e., when they swear by parts of Christ's body.
13. **Hem thoughte**: It seemed to them.

And ech° of hem at otheres synne lough.°
And right anon thanne comen tombesteres,°
Fetys° and smale,° and yonge frutesteres,°
Syngeres with harpes, baudes,° wafereres,°
Whiche been the verray develes officeres,
To kyndle and blowe the fyr of lecherye,
That is annexed unto glotonye.   20
The Holy Writ take I to my witnesse
That luxurie° is in wyn and dronkenesse.
   Lo how that dronken Loth° unkyndely°
Lay by his doghtres two unwityngly.°
So dronke he was, he nyste° what he wroghte.°
Herodes,° whoso° wel the stories soghte,
Whan he of wyn was replet° at his feste,
Right at his owene table he yaf° his heste°
To sleen° the Baptist John ful giltelees.
Senec° seith a good word, doutelees.   30
He seith he kan no difference fynde
Bitwix a man that is out of his mynde
And a man which that is dronkelewe,°
But° that woodnesse y-fallen° in a shrewe
Persevereth lenger than dooth dronkenesse.
O glotonye, ful of cursednesse,
O cause first of oure confusioun!°
O original of oure dampnacioun,
Til Crist hadde boght us with his blood agayn!°
Lo how deere,° shortly for to sayn,°   40
Aboght° was thilke° cursed vileynye.
Corrupt was al this world for glotonye.
   Adam oure fader, and his wyf also,
Fro° Paradys to labour and to wo
Were dryven for that vice, it is no drede.°
For whil that Adam fasted, as I rede,
He was in Paradys; and whan that he
Eet of the fruyt defended° on the tree,
Anon° he was out cast to wo and peyne.
O glotonye, on thee wel oghte us pleyne.°   50
O, wiste° a man how manye maladies
Folwen of° excesse and of glotonyes,
He wolde been the moore mesurable°
Of his diete, sittyng at his table.
Allas, the shorte throte, the tendre mouth,
Maketh that, est and west and north and south,
In erthe, in eyr, in water, men to swynke°
To gete a glotoun deyntee mete and drynke.

Of this matere, O Paul, wel kanstow° trete.
"Mete unto wombe,° and wombe eek° unto mete,
Shal God destroyen bothe," as Paulus seith.   61
Allas, a foul thyng is it, by my feith,
To seye this word, and fouler is the dede,
Whan man so drynketh of the white and rede°
That of his throte he maketh his pryvee°
Thurgh thilke cursed superfluitee.
   The apostle° wepyng seith ful pitously,
"There walken manye of whiche yow toold have I, —
I seye it now wepyng with pitous voys —
They been enemys of Cristes croys,   70
Of whiche° the ende is deth; wombe is hir° God."
O wombe, O bely, O stynkyng cod,°
Fulfilled of donge and of corrupcioun,
At either ende of thee foul is the soun!°
How greet labour and cost is thee to fynde!°
Thise cokes,° how they stampe, and streyne, and grynde,
And turnen substaunce into accident,°
To fulfillen° al thy likerous talent.°
Out of the harde bones knokke they
The mary,° for they caste noght awey   80
That may go thurgh the golet° softe and soote.°
Of spicerie of leef, and bark, and roote
Shal been his sauce y-maked, by delit°
To make hym yet a newer appetit.
But, certes,° he that haunteth swiche delices°
Is deed whil that° he lyveth in tho° vices.
   A lecherous thyng is wyn, and dronkenesse
Is ful of stryvyng° and of wrecchednesse.
O dronke man, disfigured is thy face,
Sour is thy breeth, foul artow° to embrace,   90
And thurgh thy dronke nose semeth the soun
As thogh thou seydest ay,° "Sampsoun, Sampsoun."
And yet, God woot,° Sampsoun° drank nevere no wyn.
Thou fallest as it were a stiked swyn,°
Thy tonge is lost, and al thyn honeste cure.°
For dronkenesse is verray sepulture°
Of mannes wit° and his discrecioun.
In whom that drynke hath dominacioun,
He kan no conseil kepe, it is no drede.

14. ech: each.   lough: laughed.   15. tombesteres: dancing girls.   16. Fetys: trim.   smale: slender.   frutesteres: fruit sellers.   17. baudes: bawds.   wafereres: confectioners.   22. luxurie: excess.   23. Loth: Lot (Gen. 19:33, 35).   unkyndely: unnaturally.   24. unwityngly: unknowingly.   25. nyste: didn't know.   wroghte: was doing.   26. Herodes: Herod (Matt. 14).   whoso: as one would know who.   27. replet: overfilled.   28. yaf: gave.   heste: order.   29. sleen: slay.   30. Senec: Seneca.   33. dronkelewe: drunken.   34. But: except.   woodnesse y-fallen: madness occurring.   37. confusioun: ruin.   39. boght agayn: redeemed.   40. deere: dearly.   sayn: say.   41. Aboght: paid for.   thilke: that same.   44. Fro: from.   45. drede: doubt.   48. defended: forbidden.   49. Anon: at once.   50. oghte us pleyne: should we complain.   51. wiste: knew.   52. Folwen of: follow.   53. mesurable: moderate.   57. swynke: toil.

59. kanstow: can you.   60. wombe: belly.   eek: also.   64. rede: red (wine).   65. pryvee: privy.   67. apostle: Paul.   71. whiche: whom.   hir: their.   72. cod: paunch.   74. soun: sound.   75. fynde: provide for.   76. cokes: cooks.   77. turnen ... accident: turn substance into accident — a facetious allusion to the philosophical theory that "substance" only becomes apparent when it takes on the "accidents" of some particular shape, size, color, etc.   78. fulfillen: satisfy.   likerous talent: unrestrained appetite.   80. mary: marrow.   81. golet: gullet.   soote: sweet.   83. delit: delight.   85. certes: certainly.   haunteth ... delices: pursues such delights.   86. deed ... that: dead while.   tho: those.   88. stryvyng: strife.   90. artow: are you.   92. ay: always.   93. woot: knows.   Sampsoun: Samson, who was bound by his vow as a Nazarite never to drink wine.   94. as ... swyn: like a stuck pig.   95. honeste cure: care for honor.   96. verray sepulture: the very burial.   97. wit: understanding.

Now kepe yow fro the white and fro the rede,   100
And namely° fro the white wyn of Lepe°
That is to selle in Fisshstrete° or in Chepe.°
This wyn of Spaigne crepeth subtilly
In othere wynes growynge faste by,°
Of which ther riseth swich fumositee°
That, whan a man hath dronken draghtes thre,
And weneth° that he be at hoom in Chepe,
He is in Spaigne right at the toune of Lepe,
Nat at the Rochel° ne at Burdeux° toun.   109
And thanne wol he seyn, " Sampsoun, Sampsoun."

But herkneth, lordynges, o° word, I yow preye,
That alle the sovereyn actes, dar I seye,
Of victories in the Olde Testament,
Thurgh verray God, that is omnipotent,
Were doon in abstinence and in prayere.
Looketh° the Bible, and ther ye may it leere.°

Looke, Attila,° the grete conquerour,
Deyde in his sleep with shame and dishonour,
Bledyng at his nose in dronkenesse.
A capitayn sholde lyve in sobrenesse.   120
And over al this, avyseth yow° right wel
What was comaunded unto Lamwel° —
Nat Samuel but Lamwel, seye I.
Redeth the Bible, and fynd it expresly
Of wyn-yevyng° to hem that han justise.
Namoore of this, for it may wel suffise.

And now that I have spoken of glotonye,
Now wol I yow defenden hasardrye.°
Hasard is verray moder of lesynges,°
And of deceite, and cursed forswerynges,°   130
Blaspheme° of Crist, manslaughtre, and wast° also
Of catel° and of tyme; and forther mo
It is repreve° and contrarie of honour
For to ben holde° a commune hasardour.
And evere the hyer he is of estaat,
The moore is he holden desolat.
If that a prynce useth hasardrye,
In alle governaunce and policye
He is, as by° commune opynyoun,
Y-holde the lasse in reputacioun.   140
Stilbon, that was a wys embassadour,
Was sent to Corynthe in ful gret honour
Fro Lacedomye° to make hire alliaunce;

101. namely: particularly.   Lepe: in Spain.   102. Fisshstrete:
Fish Street (London).   Chepe: Cheapside.   104. faste by: near
by, that is, the more expensive vintages of France, which were
evidently adulterated in England with coarser Spanish wines.
105. swich fumositee: such spirituous vapors.   107. weneth:
believes.   109. the Rochel: La Rochelle.   Burdeux: Bordeaux
(in France).   111. o: one.   116. Looketh: look at.   leere:
learn.   117. Attila: the invader of Rome, who, according to tradition, died of drunkenness on his wedding night.   121. avyseth
yow: consider.   122. Lamwel: Lemuel, an otherwise unknown king enjoined in Prov. 31:4–7 to avoid wine.   125. wyn-
yevyng: wine-giving.   128. defenden hasardrye: forbid dicing.   129. verray . . . lesynges: the very mother of falsehood.
130. forswerynges: perjuries.   131. Blaspheme: blasphemy.
wast: waste.   132. catel: substance.   133. repreve: reproach.
134. For . . . holde: to be considered.   139. as by: by.
143. Lacedomye: Lacedaemon (Sparta).

And whan he cam, hym happed° par chaunce
That alle the gretteste that were of that lond
Pleiynge atte hasard he hem fond.°
For which, as soone as it myghte be,
He stal° hym hoom agayn to his contree,
And seyde, " Ther wol I nat lese° my name,
N' I wol nat° take on me so greet defame   150
Yow for to allie unto none hasardours.
Sendeth othere wise embassadours,
For, by my trouthe, me were levere° dye
Than I yow sholde to hasardours allye.
For ye that been so glorious in honours
Shal nat allye yow with hasardours
As by my wyl ne as by my tretee."°
This wise philosophre thus seyde he.

Looke eek that to the kyng Demetrius
The kyng of Parthes,° as the book seith us,   160
Sente hym a paire of dees° of gold in scorn,
For° he hadde used hasard ther-biforn;°
For which he heeld his glorie or his renoun
At no value or reputacioun.
Lordes may fynden oother manere° pley
Honeste ynow° to dryve the day awey.

Now wol I speke of oothes false and grete
A word or two, as olde bokes trete.
Greet sweryng is a thyng abhomynable,
And fals sweryng is yet moore reprevable.°   170
The heighe God forbad sweryng at al.
Witnesse on Mathew; but in special
Of sweryng seith the holy Jeremye,°
" Thow shalt swere sooth° thyne othes and nat lye,
And swere in doom° and eek in rightwisnesse."°
But ydel° sweryng is a cursednesse.
Bihoold and se that, in the firste table
Of heighe Goddes Hestes° honurable,
How that the Seconde Heste of hym is this:
" Take nat my name in ydel° or amys."   180
Lo, rather he forbedeth swich sweryng
Than homycide or many a cursed thyng.
I seye that, as by ordre,° thus it standeth;
This knowen, that hise Hestes understandeth,
How that the Seconde Heste of God is that.
And forther over, I wol thee telle al plat°
That vengeance shal nat parten° from his hous
That of hise othes is to° outrageous.
" By Goddes precious herte," and " By his nayles,"
And " By the blood of Crist that is in Hayles,°   190

144. hym happed: it happened to him.   146. fond: found.
148. stal: stole.   149. lese: lose.   150. N' . . . nat: nor will I.
153. me . . . levere: I would rather.   157. tretee: agreement.
160. Parthes: Parthia.   161. dees: dice.   162. For: because.
ther-biforn: previously.   165. manere: sort of.   166. ynow:
enough.   170. reprevable: reprovable.   173. Jeremye: Jere-
miah.   174. sooth: truthfully.   175. doom: judgment.   rightwisnesse: righteousness.   176. ydel: vain.   178. Hestes: (Ten)
Commandments.   180. in ydel: in vain.   183. as by ordre: in
order.   186. plat: plainly.   187. parten: depart.   188. to: too.
190. in Hayles: (preserved) at Hayles, Gloucestershire.

Sevene is my chaunce, and thyn is cynk° and
    treye,"°
"By Goddes armes, if thow falsly pleye,
This daggere shal thurgh out thyn herte go," —
This fruyt cometh of the bicched bones° two,
Forsweryng, ire, falsnesse, homycide.
Now, for the love of Crist, that for us dyde,
Lete° youre othes, bothe grete and smale.
But, sires, now wol I telle forth my tale.

    Thise riotoures° thre of whiche I telle,
Longe erst er pryme rong° of any belle,   200
Were set hem° in a taverne to drynke;
And, as they sat, they herde a belle clynke°
Biforn a cors° was caried to his grave.
That oon° of hem gan callen to his knave:°
"Go bet,"° quod he, "and axe° redily
What cors is this that passeth heer forby.
And looke that thow reporte his name wel."
    "Sire," quod this boy, "it nedeth° never a del.°
It was me told er ye cam here two houres.
He was, pardee,° an old felawe° of youres,   210
And sodeynly he was y-slayn to-nyght,°
Fordronke,° as he sat on his bench upright.
Ther cam a pryvee° theef, men clepeth° Deeth,
That in this contree al the peple sleeth,°
And with his spere he smoot his herte a-two,°
And wente his wey withouten wordes mo.
He hath a thousand slayn, this pestilence.
And, maister, er ye come in his presence,
Me thynketh that it were necessarie
For to be war of swich an adversarie.   220
Beth° redy for to meete hym evere moore.°
Thus taughte me my dame.° I sey namoore."
    "By seinte Marie," seyde this taverner,°
"The chiid seith sooth, for he hath slayn this yer,
Henne over a myle,° withinne a greet village,
Bothe man and womman, child, and hyne° and
        page.
I trowe° his habitacioun be there.
To been avysed° greet wisdom it were,
Er that he dide a man a dishonour."
    "Ye,° Goddes armes!" quod this riotour.   230
"Is it swich peril with hym for to meete?
I shal hym seke by wey and eek by strete,
I make avow to Goddes digne° bones.
Herkneth, felawes. We thre been al ones.°

Lat ech of us holde up his hand til° oother,
And ech of us bicome otheres brother,°
And we wol sleen this false traytour Deeth.
He shal be slayn, he that so manye sleeth,
By Goddes dignytee, er it be nyght."
    Togidres° han thise thre hir trouthes plight°   240
To lyve and dyen ech of hem for oother,
As thogh he were his owene y-bore° brother.
And up they stirte,° al dronken in this rage,
And forth they goon towardes that village
Of which the taverner hadde spoke biforn.
And many a grisly ooth thanne han they sworn,
And Cristes blessed body they to-rente.°
Deeth shal be deed, if that they may hym hente!°
    Whan they han goon nat fully half a myle,
Right° as they wolde han treden° over a stile,   250
An old man and a poure° with hem mette.
This olde man ful mekely hem grette°
And seyde thus, "Now, lordes, God yow se."°
    The proudeste of thise riotoures thre
Answerde agayn,° "What, carl!° With sory grace!°
Why artow° al forwrapped° save thy face?
Why lyvestow° so longe in so greet age?"
    This olde man gan looke° in his visage
And seyde thus: "For I ne kan nat fynde
A man, thogh that I walked into Inde,°   260
Neither in citee ne in no village,
That wolde chaunge his youthe for myn age.
And, therefore, moot I han° myn age stille,
As longe tyme as it is Goddes wille.
    "Ne Deeth, allas, ne wol nat han my lyf.
Thus walke I lyk a restelees caytyf,°
And on the ground, which is my modres° gate,
I knokke with my staf bothe erly and late,
And seye, 'Leeve° moder, leet me in.
Lo, how I vanysshe, flessh, and blood, and skyn.   270
Allas, whan shul my bones been at reste?
Moder, with yow wolde I chaunge my cheste,°
That in my chambre longe tyme hath be,°
Ye, for an heyre clowt° to wrappe me!'
But yet to me she wol nat do that grace,
For which full pale and welked° is my face.
    "But, sires, to yow it is no curteisye
To speken to an old man vileynye
But° he trespase in word or elles° in dede.
In Holy Writ ye may yourself wel rede,   280

---

191. cynk: five. treye: three. 194. bicched bones: cursed dice.
197. Lete: restrain. 199. riotoures: profligates. 200. erst . . .
rong: before prime (9 A.M.) rang. 201. set hem: seated.
202. clynke: clang. 203. cors: corpse (which). 204. That oon:
one. knave: boy. 205. Go bet: go faster, i.e., hurry. quod:
said. axe: ask. 208. nedeth: is necessary. a del: one bit.
210. pardee: certainly. felawe: companion. 211. to-nyght:
last night. 212. Fordronke: very drunk. 213. pryvee: secretive. men clepeth: (whom) they call. 214. sleeth: slays.
215. a-two: in two. 221. Beth: be. evere moore: always.
222. dame: mother. 223. taverner: innkeeper. 225. Henne
. . . myle: within a mile hence. 226. hyne: servant. 227. trowe:
believe. 228. been avysed: be prepared. 230. Ye: yes.
233. digne: worthy. 234. ones: one.

235. til: to. 236. otheres brother: the other's sworn brother.
240. Togidres: together. hir . . . plight: pledged their faith.
242. y-bore: born. 243. stirte: sprang. 247. to-rente: tore
to pieces. 248. hente: catch. 250. Right: just. han
treden: have stepped. 251. poure: poor. 252. grette:
greeted. 253. se: save. 255. agayn: back. carl: churl.
With . . . grace: curse you. 256. artow: are you. for-
wrapped: wrapped up. 257. lyvestow: live you. 258. gan
looke: looked. 260. Inde: India. 263. moot I han: must I have.
266. caytyf: wretch. 267. modres: mother's. 269. Leeve:
dear. 272. cheste: clothes chest. 273. be: been. 274. heyre
clowt: hair rag. 276. welked: withered. 279. But: unless.
elles: else.

' Agayns° an old man, hoor° upon his heed,
Ye sholde arise.' Wherefore I yeve° yow reed:°
Ne dooth° unto an old man noon harm now,
Namoore than that ye wolde men dide to yow
In age, if that ye so longe abyde.
And God be with yow, wher° ye go° or ryde.
I moot° go thider as° I have to go."
   "Nay, olde cherl. By God, thow shalt nat so,"
Seyde this oother hasardour° anon.
"Thow partest° nat so lightly,° by seint John. 290
Thow spak right now of thilke° traytour Deeth,
That in this contree alle oure freendes sleeth.
Have here my trouthe,° as thow art his espye,°
Telle wher he is, or thow shalt it abye,°
By God and by the holy sacrament!
For soothly thow art oon of his assent°
To sleen us yonge folk, thow false theef! "
   "Now, sires," quod he, "if that yow be so leef°
To fynde Deeth, turn up this croked wey.
For in that grove I lafte° hym, by my fey,° 300
Under a tree, and ther he wol abyde.
Nat for youre boost he wol hym° nothyng hyde.
Se ye that ook?° Right ther ye shal hym fynde.
God save yow, that boghte agayn° mankynde,
And yow amende." Thus seyde this olde man.
And everich° of thise riotoures ran
Til they came to that tree, and ther they founde
Of floryns° fyne of gold y-coyned rounde
Wel ny an eighte° busshels, as hem thoughte.°
No lenger thanne after Deeth they soughte; 310
But ech of hem so glad was of the sighte,
For that the floryns been so faire and brighte,
That doun they sette hem° by this precious hoord.
The worste of hem he spak the firste word.
   "Brethren," quod he, "taak kepe° what I seye.
My wit° is greet, thogh that I bourde° and pleye.
This tresor hath fortune unto us yeven,°
In myrthe and jolitee oure lyf to lyven.
And lightly as it cometh, so wol we spende.
By Goddes precious dignytee, who wende° 320
Today that we sholde han so fair a grace?
But, myghte this gold be caried fro this place
Hoom to myn hous, or ellis unto youres —
For wel ye woot° that al this gold is oures —
Thanne were we in heigh felicitee.
But, trewely, by daye it may nat be.

Men wolde seyn° that we were theves stronge°
And for oure owene tresor doon us honge.°
This tresor moste y-caried be by nyghte
As wisly° and as slyly as it myghte. 330
Wherfore I rede° that cut° among us alle
Be drawe, and lat se° wher the cut wol falle.
And he that hath the cut, with herte blithe
Shal renne° to the toune, and that ful swithe,°
And brynge us breed and wyn ful pryvely.
And two of us shul kepen subtilly°
This tresor wel; and if he wol nat tarie,
Whan it is nyght, we wol this tresor carie
By oon assent wher-as us thynketh° best."
   That oon° of hem the cut broghte in his fest,° 340
And bad hem drawe and looke wher it wol falle,
And it fil on the youngeste of hem alle,
And forth toward the toun he wente anon.
And also° soone as that he was agon,°
That oon of hem spak thus unto that oother:
" Thow knowest wel, thow art my sworn brother.
Thy profit wol I telle thee anon.
Thow woost° wel that oure felawe is agon,
And heere is gold, and that ful greet plentee,
That shall departed° been among us thre. 350
But, nathelees,° if I kan shape it so
That it departed were among us two,
Hadde I nat doon a freendes torn° to thee? "
   That oother answerde, " I noot° how that may be.
He woot that the gold is with us tweye.°
What shal we doon? What shall we to hym seye? "
   " Shal it be conseil? "° seyde the firste shrewe.°
" And I shal tellen in a wordes fewe
What we shul doon, and brynge it wel aboute."
   " I graunte," quod that oother, " out of doute, 360
That, by my trouthe, I wol thee nat biwreye."°
   " Now," quod the firste, " thow woost wel we be tweye,
And two of us shul strenger be than oon.
Looke, whan that he is set, that right anoon
Arys as though thow woldest with hym pleye,
And I shall ryve° hym thurgh the sydes tweye,
Whil that thow strogelest with him as in game,
And with thy daggere looke thow do the same,
And thanne shal al this gold departed be,
My deere freend, bitwixe me and thee. 370
Thanne may we bothe oure lustes al fulfille,
And pleye at dees° right at oure owene wille."
And thus acorded been thise shrewes tweye

281. **Agayns**: before. **hoor**: hoar. 282. **yeve**: give. **reed**: advice. 283. **Ne dooth**: don't do. 286. **wher**: whether. **go**: walk. 287. **moot**: must. **as**: where. 289. **hasardour**: gambler. 290. **partest**: depart. **lightly**: easily. 291. **thilke**: that same. 293. **trouthe**: oath. **espye**: spy. 294. **abye**: pay for. 296. **of . . . assent**: in agreement with him. 298. **leef**: eager. 300. **lafte**: left. **fey**: faith. 302. **hym**: himself. 303. **ook**: oak. 304. **boghte agayn**: redeemed. 306. **everich**: each. 308. **floryns**: florins (coins). 309. **Wel . . . eighte**: very nearly eight. **hem thoughte**: it seemed to them. 313. **hem**: themselves. 315. **kepe**: heed to. 316. **wit**: understanding. **bourde**: jest. 317. **yeven**: given. 320. **wende**: would have believed. 324. **woot**: know.

327. **seyn**: say. **stronge**: violent. 328. **doon us honge**: have us hanged. 330. **wisly**: cautiously. 331. **rede**: advise. **cut**: cuts. 332. **lat se**: let see. 334. **renne**: run. **swithe**: quickly. 336. **kepen subtilly**: guard craftily. 339. **wher-as us thynketh**: where it seems to us. 340. **That oon**: the one. **fest**: fist. 344. **also**: as. **agon**: gone. 348. **woost**: know. 350. **departed**: divided. 351. **nathelees**: nevertheless. 353. **torn**: turn. 354. **noot**: don't know. 355. **tweye**: two. 357. **conseil**: secret. **shrewe**: wretch. 361. **biwreye**: betray. 366. **ryve**: stab. 372. **dees**: dice.

To sleen° the thridde, as ye han herd me seye.
This youngeste, which that wente to the toun,
Ful ofte in herte he rolleth up and doun
The beautee of thise floryns newe and brighte.
"O Lord," quod he, "if so were that I myghte
Have al this tresor to myself allone,
Ther is no man that lyveth under the trone   380
Of God that sholde lyve so myrie as I!"
And atte laste the feend,° oure enemy,
Putte in his thoght that he sholde poyson beye,°
With which he myghte sleen his felawes tweye,
For-why° the feend foond° hym in swich lyvynge
That he hadde leve° hym to sorwe brynge.
For this was outrely° his full entente,
To sleen hem bothe and nevere to repente.
And forth he goth — no lenger wolde he tarie —
Into the toun unto a pothecarie,°   390
And preyed hym that he hym wolde selle
Som poysoun that he myghte his rattes quelle,°
And eek ther was a polcat° in his hawe,°
That, as he seyde, his capouns° hadde y-slawe,°
And fayn° he wolde wreke hym,° if he myghte,
On vermyn that destroyed° hym by nyghte.
The pothecarie answerde, "And thow shalt have
A thyng that, also° God my soule save,
In al this world ther is no creature
That ete° or dronke hath of this confiture°   400
Nat but the montaunce° of a corn° of whete,
That he ne shal his lyf anoon forlete.°
Ye,° sterve° he shal, and that in lasse while
Than thow wolt goon a paas° nat but a myle,
The poysoun is so strong and violent."
This cursed man hath in his hond y-hent°
This poysoun in a box, and sith° he ran
Into the nexte strete unto a man
And borwed of hym large botels thre,
And in the two his poyson poured he.   410
The thridde he kepte clene for his drynke,
For al the nyght he shoop hym for to swynke°
In cariyng of the gold out of that place.
And whan this riotour — with sory grace!° —
Hadde filled with wyn hise grete botels thre,
To hise felawes agayn repaireth he.
What nedeth it to sermone of it moore?
For right as they hadde cast° his deeth bifore,
Right so they han hym slayn, and that anon.   419
And whan that this was doon, thus spak that oon:

"Now lat us sitte, and drynke, and make us merye,
And afterward we wol his body berye."
And with that word it happed hym par cas°
To take the botel ther° the poysoun was,
And drank, and yaf° his felawe drynke also,
For which anon they storven° bothe two.
But, certes,° I suppose that Avycen
Wroot nevere in no canon ne in no fen°
Mo wonder signes° of empoysonyng   429
Than hadde thise wrecches two er hir° endyng.
Thus ended been thise homicides two,
And eek the false empoysonere also.
O cursed synne of alle cursednesse!
O traytours homicide! O wikkednesse!
O glotonye, luxurie,° and hasardrye!
Thou blasphemour of Crist with vileynye
And othes grete of usage° and of pryde!°
Allas, mankynde, how may it bityde
That to thy Creatour, which that thee wroghte°
And with his precious herte-blood thee boghte,   440
Thow art so fals and so unkynde,° allas?
Now, goode men, God foryeve° yow youre trespas,
And ware yow fro° the synne of avarice.
Myn holy pardoun may yow alle warice,°
So° that ye offre nobles° or sterlynges,°
Or elles silver broches, spones, rynges.
Boweth youre heed under this holy bulle!
Cometh up, ye wyves! Offreth of youre wolle!°
Youre name I entre here in my rolle anon;
Into the blisse of hevene shul ye gon.   450
I yow assoille,° by myn heigh power,
Yow that wol offre, as clene and eek as cler
As ye were born. — And lo, sires, thus I preche.
And Jesu Crist, that is oure soules leche,°
So graunte yow his pardoun to receyve,
For that is best. I wol yow nat deceyve.

EPILOGUE

"But, sires, o° word forgat I in my tale.
I have relikes and pardon in my male°
As faire as any man in Engelond,
Whiche were me yeven by the Popes hond.   460
If any of yow wol, of° devocioun,
Offren and han myn absolucioun,
Com forth anon, and kneleth here adoun,

And mekely receyveth my pardoun;
Or ellis taketh pardoun, as ye wende,°
Al newe and fressh at every myles ende,
So that ye offren, alwey newe and newe,°
Nobles or pens whiche that been goode and trewe.
It is an honour to everich° that is heer
That ye mowe° have a suffisant° pardoner   470
T' assoille yow, in contree as ye ryde,
For aventures° whiche that may bityde.
Peraventure ther may falle oon or two
Doun of° his hors, and breke his nekke atwo.
Looke which° a seuretee° is it to yow alle
That I am in youre felaweship y-falle,°
That may assoille yow, bothe moore° and lasse,°
Whan that the soule shal fro the body passe.
I rede° that oure Hoost shal bigynne,
For he is moost envoluped° in synne.   480
Com forth, sire Hoost, and offre first anon,
And thow shalt kisse the relikes everychon,°
Ye, for a grote.° Unbokele anon thy purs."
  "Nay, nay!" quod he. "Thanne have I Cristes
    curs!
Lat be!" quod he. "It shal nat be, so thee'ch.°
Thow woldest make me kisse thyn olde breech,
And swere it were a relyk of a seint,
Thogh it were with thy fundement depeynt.°
But, by the croys which that Seint Eleyne fond,°
I wolde I hadde thy coylons° in myn hond   490
In stede of relikes or of seintuarie.°
Lat kutte hem of!° I wol thee helpe hem carie.
They shul be shryned — in an hogges toord!"°
  This Pardoner answerde nat a word;
So wrooth he was, no word ne wolde he seye.
  "Now," quod oure Hoost, "I wol no lenger
    pleye
With thee, ne with noon oother angry man."
But right anon the worthy Knyght bigan,
Whan that he saugh that al the peple lough,
"Namoore of this, for it is right ynough.   500
Sire Pardoner, be glad and murye° of cheere.
And ye, sire Hoost, that been to me so deere,
I pray yow that ye kisse the Pardoner.
And, Pardoner, I pray thee, drawe thee neer.
And, as we diden, lat us laughe and pleye."
Anon they kiste, and ryden° forth hir weye.

THE PRIORESS'S TALE

The Prioress recites one of the many miracles ascribed in the Middle Ages to the Virgin Mary, which were narrated in prose from the pulpit and sung in verse by minstrels throughout western Europe.

The Prioress's intense religious devotion to the Virgin and her human affection for the engaging little scholar who suffers martyrdom because of his adoration of the Virgin are eminently suited to her character. "The fierce bigotry of the Prioress" toward the Jews, who are the villains of the tale, surprised Wordsworth, and it is possible that Chaucer himself disapproved of it. Actually, however, there were no Jews in Chaucer's England. The story the Prioress tells and the legend of Hugh of Lincoln to which she refers (l. 232) both originated in anti-Jewish libels circulating in England prior to the expulsion of the Jews from the country in 1290.

But, no matter how we interpret Chaucer's somewhat ambiguous characterization of the Prioress, the dominant tone of the narration certainly voices her "conscience and tendre herte," and we are not surprised to learn in the following link that for once all the pilgrims were reduced to a sober silence by the tale.

PROLOGUE

  "O° Lord, oure Lord, thy name how merveil-
    lous°
Is in this large worlde y-sprad,"° quod° she;
"For nat oonly thy laude° precious
Parfourned° is by men of dignytee,
But by the mouth of children thy bountee
Parfourned is, for on the brest soukynge°
Som tyme shewen° they thyn heriynge.°

"Wher-fore in laude, as I best kan or may,
Of thee and of the white lilye flour°
Which that° thee bar,° and is a mayde° alway,
To telle a storie I wol do my labour,   11
Nat that I may encressen hir honour,
For she hirself is honour and the roote°
Of bountee, next hir Sone, and soules boote.°

"O moder Mayde, O mayde Moder free!°
O bussh unbrent, brennyng in Moyses sighte,°
That ravysedest° doun fro the Deitee,

465. wende: travel.   467. newe . . . newe: again and again.
469. everich: each one.   470. mowe: can.   suffisant: adequate.   472. aventures: incidents.   474. of: off.   475. which: what.   seuretee: security.   476. y-falle: fallen.   477. moore: high.   lasse: low.   479. rede: advise.   480. envoluped: enveloped.   482. everychon: each one.   483. grote: groat (4d.). 485. thee'ch: may I prosper.   488. depeynt: discolored. 489. which . . . fond: which St. Helena found. Helena, the Emperor Constantine's mother, who was believed to have rediscovered the true Cross, was especially revered in England, since legend claimed her to be of British origin.   490. coylons: testicles.   491. seintuarie: holy objects.   492. Lat . . . of: have them cut off.   493. toord: turd.   501. murye: merry. 506. ryden: rode.

PRIORESS'S TALE. 1–7. O . . . heriynge: The first stanza is derived from Ps. 7:1–2, which would have been particularly familiar to the Prioress, since it forms part of the Office of the Blessed Virgin.   1. merveillous: marvelously.   2. y-sprad: spread. quod: said.   3. laude: praise.   4. Parfourned: celebrated. 6. soukynge: suckling.   7. shewen: show forth.   heriynge: praise.   9. flour: flower. The image, derived from the Song of Sol. 2:2, here symbolizes the Virgin.   10. Which that: who. bar: bore.   mayde: virgin.   13. roote: source.   14. boote: salvation.   15. free: gracious.   16. O . . . sighte: O bush unburnt, burning in Moses's sight. The bush from which God spoke to Moses (Exod. 3:2) here symbolizes the Virgin, upon whom the Holy Ghost descended.   17. ravysedest: drew.

Thurgh thyn humblesse, the Goost° that in th'
   alighte,°
Of whos vertu, whan he thyn herte lighte,°
Conceyved was the Fadres sapience,°   20
Help me to telle it in thy reverence!

"Lady, thy bountee, thy magnificence,
Thy vertu, and thy grete humylitee
Ther may° no tonge expresse in no science.°
For somtyme, Lady, er° men praye to thee,
Thow goost biforn,° of thy benygnytee,
And getest us the light of thy prayere
To gyden us unto thy Sone so deere.

"My konnyng° is so wayk,° O blisful Queene,
For to declare thy grete worthynesse   30
That I ne may the weighte nat sustene.
But as a child of twelf month old or lesse,
That kan unnethe° any word expresse,
Right so fare I, and therfore, I yow preye,
Gydeth° my song that I shal of yow seye."

THE PRIORESS'S TALE

Ther was in Asye,° in a greet citee,
Amonges Cristen folk a Jewerye,°
Sustened by a lord of that contree
For foul usure° and lucre of vileynye,°
Hateful to Crist and to his compaignye.   40
And thurgh this strete° men myghte ryde and
   wende,°
For it was free and open at eyther ende.

A litel scole of Cristen folk ther stood
Doun at the ferther ende, in which ther were
Children an heep,° y-comen of Cristen blood,
That lerned in that scole yeer by yere
Swich manere doctrine° as men used there,
This is to seyn,° to syngen and to rede
As smale children doon in hir° childhede.

Among thise children was a wydwes° sone,   50
A litel clergeoun,° seven yeer of age,
That day by day to scole was his wone;°
And eek also, wher-as he say° th'ymage
Of Cristes moder, hadde he in usage,°

As hym was taught, to knele adoun and seye
His *Ave Marie* as he goth by the weye.

Thus hath this wydwe hir litel sone y-taught
Oure blisful Lady, Cristes moder deere,
To worshipe ay,° and he forgat it naught,
For sely° child wol alwey° soone lere.°   60
But ay whan I remembre on this matere,
Seint Nicholas stant° evere in my presence,
For he so yong to Crist dide reverence.°

This litel child, his litel book lernynge,
As he sat in the scole at his prymer,°
He *Alma redemptoris*° herde synge
As children lerned hir Antiphoner,°
And, as he dorste,° he drow hym ner° and ner
And herkned ay the wordes and the note
Til he the firste vers koude° al by rote.   70

Noght wiste° he what this Latyn was to seye,°
For he so yong and tendre was of age,
But on a day his felawe gan he preye°
T'expounden hym this song in his langage
Or telle hym why this song was in usage.
This preyde he hym to construen and declare
Ful ofte tyme upon his knowes° bare.

His felawe, which that elder was than he,
Answerde hym thus: "This song, I have herd seye,
Was maked of° oure blisful Lady free,   80
Hire to salue° and eek hire for to preye
To been oure help and socour° whan we deye.
I kan namoore expounde in this matere.
I lerne song, I kan° but smal gramere."

"And is this song maked in reverence
Of Cristes moder?" seyde this innocent.
"Now, certes,° I wol do my diligence
To konne° it al er° Cristemasse be went.
Thogh that I for my prymer shal be shent°
And shal be beten thries° in an houre,   90
I wol it konne, oure Lady for to honoure."

His felawe taughte hym homward° pryvely
Fro day to day til he koude it by rote,
And thanne he song° it wel and boldely

18. Goost: (Holy) Ghost. **in . . . alighte:** in you alighted. **19.** lighte: lightened. **20.** the . . . sapience: the Father's sapience — Christ, whom Paul calls "the wisdom of God." **24.** may: can. **in . . . science:** in any learned manner. **25.** er: before. **26.** goost biforn: precede. **29.** konnyng: skill. **wayk:** weak. **33.** unnethe: hardly. **35.** Gydeth: guide. **36.** Asye: Asia. **37.** Jewerye: ghetto. **39.** usure: interest. Church law prohibited Christians from charging interest but, in order to facilitate loans necessary for business, exempted Jewish moneylenders from the restriction. **lucre of vileynye:** filthy lucre. **41.** strete: street. **wende:** go. **45.** an heep: a lot. **47.** Swich . . . doctrine: such kind of teaching. **48.** seyn: say. **49.** hir: their. **50.** wydwes: widow's. **51.** clergeoun: pupil. **52.** wone: custom. **53.** wher-as . . . say: where he saw. **54.** hadde . . . usage: he was accustomed.

59. ay: ever. **60.** sely: a good. **alwey:** always. **lere:** learn. **62.** stant: stands. **63.** reverence: St. Nicholas, the patron saint of children, was said as an infant to have abstained voluntarily from suckling more than once on each fast day. **65.** prymer: Latin prayer book studied at school. **66.** *Alma redemptoris:* an anthem in the breviary beginning "Blessed Mother of the Redeemer." **67.** Antiphoner: any book of psalms, hymns, or prayers sung responsively. **68.** dorste: dared. **drow . . . ner:** drew nearer. **70.** koude: knew. **71.** wiste: knew. **was to seye:** meant. **73.** felawe . . . preye: companion he begged. **77.** knowes: knees. **80.** maked of: made for. **81.** salue: salute. **82.** socour: succor. **84.** kan: know. **87.** certes: certainly. **88.** konne: know. **er:** before. **89.** shent: scolded. **90.** thries: thrice. **92.** homward: on the way home. **94.** song: sang.

Fro word to word acordyng with the note.
Twyes a day it passed thurgh his throte,
To scoleward° and homward whan he wente.
On Cristes moder set was his entente.

As I have seyd, thurghout the Juerye
This litel child as he cam to and fro   100
Ful murily wolde he synge and crye
O Alma redemptoris everemo.
The swetnesse his herte perced so
Of Cristes moder that, to hire to preye,
He kan nat stynte of° syngyng by the weye.

Oure firste foo,° the serpent Sathanas,
That hath in Jewes herte his waspes nest,
Up swal° and seyde, "O Hebrayk peple, allas!
Is this to yow a thyng that is honest°
That swich° a boy shal walken as hym lest,°   110
In youre despit,° and synge of swich sentence,°
Which is agayns oure lawes reverence? "

Fro thennes forth the Jewes han° conspired
This innocent out of the world to chace.
An homycide° therto han they hired,
That in an aleye° hadde a pryvee place.
And as the child gan° forby for to pace°
This cursed Jew hym hente,° and heeld hym faste,
And kitte° his throte, and in a pit hym caste.

I seye that in a wardrobe° they hym threwe,   120
Wher-as° thise Jewes purgen hir entraille.
O cursed folk of Herodes al newe,°
What may youre yvel entente yow availle?
Mordre° wol out, certeyn, it wol nat faille,
And namely ther-as° th'onour of God shal sprede.
The blood out crieth on youre cursed dede.

O martir, souded° to virginitee,
Now maystow° syngen, folwyng evere in oon°
The white Lamb celestial — quod she —
Of which the grete evangelist seint John   130
In Pathmos° wroot, which° seith that they that
      gon
Biforn this Lamb and synge a song al newe,
That nevere, flesshly,° wommen they ne knewe.

This poure wydwe awaiteth al that nyght
After hir litel child, but he cam noght;
For which, as soone as it was dayes lyght,
With face pale of drede and bisy thoght,
She hath at scole and elleswhere hym soght
Til fynally she gan so fer espie°
That he last seyn was in the Jewerie.   140

With modres pitee in hir brest enclosed
She goth as° she were half out of hir mynde
To every place wher she hath supposed
By liklyhede° hir litel child to fynde,
And evere on Cristes moder meke and kynde
She cryde, and at the laste thus she wroghte,°
Among the cursed Jewes she hym soghte.

She frayneth,° and she preyeth pitously
To every Jew that dwelte in thilke° place
To telle hire if hir child wente oght forby.°   150
They seyde "Nay," but Jesu of his grace
Yaf in hir thought,° inwith° a litel space,
That° in that place after hir sone she cryde
Wher he was casten in a pit bisyde.°

O grete God, that parfournest° thy laude
By mouth of innocentz, lo, here thy myght!
This gemme of chastitee, this emeraude°
And eek° of martirdom the ruby bright,
Ther° he with throte y-korven° lay upright,°
He Alma redemptoris gan to synge   160
So loude that al the place gan to rynge.

The Cristen folk that thurgh the strete wente
In coomen° for to wondre upon this thyng,
And hastily they for the provost° sente.
He cam anon withouten tariyng,
And herieth° Crist, that is of hevene kyng,
And eek his Moder, honour of mankynde,
And after that the Jewes leet he bynde.°

This child with pitous lamentacioun
Up taken was, syngynge his song alway,   170
And with honour of greet processioun
They carien hym unto the nexte° abbay.
His moder swownyng by his beere° lay.
Unnethe° myghte the peple that was there
This newe Rachel° bryngen fro his beere.

97. To scoleward: toward school. 105. stynte of: stop from.
106. foo: foe. 108. swal: swelled. 109. honest: honorable.
110. swich: such. lest: it pleases. 111. youre despit: scorn
of you. sentence: theme. 113. han: have. 115. homycide:
murderer. 116. aleye: alley. 117. gan: began. pace: pass.
118. hente: seized. 119. kitte: cut. 120. wardrobe: privy.
121. Wher-as: where. 122. cursed . . . newe: The "folk of
Herod cursed anew" are the Jews. King Herod the Great had
the infants of Bethlehem killed; his son had John the Baptist
beheaded and assented to the crucifixion of Christ; and his
grandson killed the apostle James. 124. Mordre: murder.
125. namely ther-as: particularly where. 127. souded: attached. 128. maystow: you can. in oon: consistently.
131. Pathmos: Patmos. which: who. 133. flesshly: carnally.
According to Revelation, those who sang a new song are "they
which were not defiled with women."

139. gan . . . espie: so far discovered. 142. as: as if. 144. liklyhede: likelihood. 146. wroghte: did. 148. frayneth: inquires. 149. thilke: that same. 150. wente . . . forby: went
past at all. 152. Yaf . . . thought: gave her insight. inwith:
within. 153. That: so that. 154. bisyde: nearby. 155. par-
fournest: celebrate. 157. emeraude: emerald. 158. eek: also.
159. Ther: where. y-korven: cut. upright: face upward.
163. In coomen: gathered. 164. provost: magistrate. 166. he-
rieth: praises. 168. leet he bynde: he caused to be bound.
172. nexte: nearest. 173. beere: bier. 174. Unnethe: hardly.
175. Rachel: the mother of Joseph and Benjamin, referred to
here figuratively, as in Jer. 31:15 and Matt. 2:18.

With torment and with shameful deth echon°
This provost dooth° thise Jewes for to sterve°
That of this mordre wiste,° and that anon.
He nolde no swich° cursednesse observe.°
Yvel shal have that° yvel wol deserve.   180
Therfore with wilde hors he dide hem drawe,°
And after that he heng° hem by the lawe.

Upon this beere ay lith° this innocent
Biforn the chief auter° whil the masse laste.
And after that, the abbot with his covent°
Han sped hem° for to burien hym ful faste;
And whan they holy water on hym caste,
Yet° spak this child, whan spreynd° was holy
     water,
And song° O Alma redemptoris mater.

This abbot, which that was an holy man,   190
As monkes ben, or elles oghten° be,
This yonge child to conjure° he bigan
And seyde, "O deere child, I halsen° thee
In vertu of the holy Trinitee,
Tel me what is thy cause for to synge
Sith that° thy throte is kit° to my semynge? "°

"My throte is kit unto my nekke boon,"
Seyde this child, "and, as by wey of kynde,°
I sholde have dyed, ye,° longe tyme agoon.
But Jesu Crist, as ye in bokes fynde,   200
Wol° that his glorie laste and be in mynde,°
And for the worship of his Moder deere
Yet may° I synge O Alma loude and clere.

"This welle of mercy, Cristes moder swete,
I loved alwey, as after my konnynge,°
And whan that I my lyf sholde forlete,°
To me she cam and bad me for to synge
This anteme,° verraily,° in my deiynge,
As ye han herd; and whan that I had songe,   209
Me thoughte she leyde a greyn° upon my tonge.

"Wher-fore I synge, and synge moot,° certeyn,
In honour of that blisful Mayden free,
Til fro my tonge of° taken is the greyn.
And, after that, thus seyde she to me:

' My litel child, now wol I fecche thee
Whan that the greyn is fro thy tonge y-take.
Be nat agast. I wol thee nat forsake.' "

This holy monk, this abbot, hym mene I,
His tonge out caughte and took awey the greyn,
And he yaf° up the goost ful softely.   220
And whan this abbot hadde this wonder seyn,
His salte teerys° trikled doun as reyn,
And gruf° he fil al plat° upon the grounde,
And stille he lay as he hadde been y-bounde.

The covent eek lay on the pavement,
Wepynge and herying° Cristes moder deere.
And after that they ryse, and forth been went,°
And toke awey this martir from his beere,
And in a tombe of marbil stones cleere
Enclosen they this litel body swete.   230
Ther° he is now, God leve° us for to meete.

EPILOGUE

O yonge Hugh° of Lyncoln, slayn also
With° cursed Jewes, as it is notable,
For it is but a litel while ago,
Preye eek for us, we synful folk unstable,
That, of his mercy, God so merciable
On us his grete mercy multiplie
For reverence of his moder Marie. Amen.

THE MILLER'S TALE

From the General Prologue it is clear that there is a
difference in temperament between the Miller and the
Reeve. When the pilgrims set out from Southwark, the
stout and rubicund Miller rides at their head, playing
the bagpipes, while the lean and choleric Reeve, we
are told, rides always the hindermost. From the link
preceding the Miller's Tale we gather that there is
some personal reason for their violent dislike of each
other.

The Miller tells a tale, possibly derived through
English oral tradition from a French comic narrative
poem, or fabliau, about the seduction of a carpenter's
wife by an Oxford student. Neither the Carpenter nor
the Clerk of Oxford raises any objections against it;
but the Reeve, who is also a carpenter by training, takes
violent offense at it for reasons which Chaucer leaves
to the reader to guess.

Whilom ther was dwellyng in Oxenford°
A riche gnof that gestes held to bord,°
And of his craft he was a carpenter.

176. echon: each one.   177. dooth: causes.   sterve: die
178. mordre wiste: murder knew.   179. nolde no swich:
wouldn't any such.   observe: tolerate.   180. that: who.
181. hors . . . drawe: horses he had them drawn.   182. heng:
hung.   183. ay lith: ever lies.   184. auter: altar.   185. covent:
convent.   186. Han . . . hem: have hastened.   188. Yet: still.
spreynd: sprinkled.   189. song: sang.   191. elles oghten: else
ought to.   192. conjure: beseech.   193. halsen: implore.
196. Sith that: since.   kit: cut.   to my semynge: apparently.
198. kynde: nature.   199. ye: yea.   201. Wol: wishes.   in
mynde: remembered.   203. Yet may: still can.   205. as . . .
konnynge: according to my ability.   206. sholde forlete: was to
give up.   208. anteme: anthem.   verraily: truly.   210. greyn:
pearl.   211. synge moot: must sing.   213. of: off.

220. yaf: gave.   222. teerys: tears.   223. gruf: face down.
plat: flat.   226. herying: praising.   227. been went: have
gone.   231. Ther: where.   leve: grant.   232. Hugh: In 1255
a boy named Hugh was found dead in a well in Lincoln. Local
Jews were blamed, and Hugh's shrine became a pilgrimage
resort.   233. With: by.   MILLER'S TALE.   1. Oxenford: Oxford.
2. gnof . . . hord: fellow who boarded guests.

With hym ther was dwellynge a poure scoler
Had lerned art,° but al his fantasie°
Was turned for to lerne astrologye,
And koude a certeyn of conclusions
To demen by interrogacions,°
If that men axed° hym in certein houres
Whan that men sholde have droghte or ellis°
    shoures,°   10
Of if men axed hym what sholde bifalle
Of everythyng — I may nat rekene hem° alle.
    This clerk was cleped hende° Nicholas.
Of derne° love he koude° and of solas,°
And therto he was sleigh° and ful pryvee°
And lyk a mayden meke for to see.
A chambre hadde he in that hostelrye,
Allone withouten° any compaignye,
Ful fetisly dight° with herbes swoote,°
And he hymself as swete as is the roote   20
Of licorys° or any cetewale.°
    His *Almageste,*° and bokes grete and smale,
His astrelabye° longynge for° his art,
His augrym stones,° layen faire apart
On shelves couched at his beddes heed,°
His presse° y-covered with a faldyng reed.°
And al above ther lay a gay sautrye,°
On which he made anyghtes° melodie
So swetely that al the chambre rong,°
And *Angelus ad Virginem*° he song,   30
And after that he song the Kynges Note.°
Ful often blessed was his murye° throte.
And thus this swete clerk his tyme spente,
After his frendes fyndyng and his rente.°
    This carpenter had wedded newe° a wyf
Which that° he loved moore than his lyf.
Of eighteteene yeer she was of age.
Jalous he was and heeld hire narwe° in
    cage,
For she was wilde and yong, and he was old
And demed hymself been° lyk a cokewold.°   40

He knew nat Catoun,° for his wit was rude,
That bad men° sholde wedde his similitude.°
Men sholde wedden after hir estaat,°
For youthe and elde° is often at debaat.
But, sith that° he was fallen in the snare,
He moste° endure as oother folk his care.
    Fair was this yonge wyf, and therwithal
As any wesele° hir body gent° and smal.°
A ceynt° she wered barred° al of silk,
A barmcloth° as whit as morne° mylk   50
Upon hir lendes,° ful of many a goore;°
Whit was hir smok,° and broyden° al bifore
And eek° bihynde, on hir coler° aboute,
Of col-blak silk withinne and eek withoute;
The tapes of hir white voluper°
Were of the same sute of° hir coler,
Hir filet brood° of silk and set ful hye.
    And sikerly° she hadde a likerous° eye.
Ful smale y-pulled° were hir browes two,
And tho° were bent° and blake° as any slo.°   60
She was ful moore blisful on to see°
Than is the newe perjonette° tree,
And softer than the wolle° is of a wether,°
And by hir girdel heng a purs of lether,
Tasseled with silk and perled with latoun.°
In al this world to seken up and doun,
Ther nys° no man so wys that koude thenche°
So gay a popelote° or swich° a wenche.
Ful brighter was the shynyng of hir hewe°
Than in the Tour the noble y-forged newe.°   70
But of hir song, it was as loude and yerne°
As any swalwe° sittyng on a berne.°
Therto° she koude skippe and make game
As any kyde or calf folwynge his dame.°
Hir mouth was swete as bragot,° or the meeth,°
Or hoord of apples leyd° in hey or heeth.°
Wynsyng° she was as is a joly colt,
Long as a mast, and upright as a bolt.
A broche she bar° upon hir lowe coler
As brood as is the boos° of a bokeler.°   80

---

5. Had . . . art: (who) had studied (the liberal) arts. fantasie:
fancy. 7–8. koude . . . interrogacions: (he) knew a certain
number of operations by which to determine (the future) through
investigations (of the position of the planets). See Note A, p. 195.
9. axed: asked. 10. ellis: else. shoures: showers. 12. may
. . . hem: cannot recount them. 13. cleped hende: called
gentle. 14. derne: secret. koude: knew. solas: fun.
15. sleigh: sly. pryvee: secretive. 18. withouten: without.
19. fetisly dight: daintily scented. swoote: sweet. 21. lico-
rys: licorice. cetewale: zedoary. 22. *Almageste:* the second-
century treatise by Ptolemy of Alexandria, which was still the
standard textbook on astronomy. 23. astrelabye: astrolabe, an
instrument once used for measuring the altitude of planets and
stars. longynge for: belonging to. 24. augrym stones: algo-
rism counters (for counting on an abacus). 25. heed:
head. 26. presse: clothespress. faldyng reed: red cloth.
27. sautrye: psaltery (stringed instrument). 28. anyghtes: at
night. 29. rong: rang. 30. *Angelus ad Virginem:* "The
Angel to the Virgin," an Annunciation hymn. song: sang.
31. Kynges Note: a popular song. 32. murye: merry. 34. After . . . rente: with the support of his friends and his own income.
35. newe: newly. 36. Which that: whom. 38. narwe: strictly.
40. been: to be. cokewold: cuckold.

41. Catoun: Dionysius Cato, the reputed author of a collection
of proverbs. 42. bad men: ordered one that he. similitude:
equal. 43. after . . . estaat: according to their status. 44. elde:
old age. 45. sith that: since. 46. moste: must. 48. wesele:
weasel. gent: graceful. smal: slim. 49. ceynt: belt. wered
barred: wore striped. 50. barmcloth: apron. morne: morning. 51. lendes: loins. goore: fold. 52. smok: smock.
broyden: embroidered. 53. eek: also. coler: collar. 55. vo-
luper: cap. 56. sute of: kind as. 57. filet brood: headband
broad. 58. sikerly: certainly. likerous: lecherous. 59. smale
y-pulled: finely plucked. 60. tho: those. bent: arched.
blake: black. slo: sloe (the plumlike fruit of the blackthorn).
61. on to see: to look on. 62. perjonette: pear. 63. wolle:
wool. wether: bellwether. 65. perled . . . latoun: with buttons made of copper alloy. 67. nys: is. thenche: imagine.
68. popelote: doll. swich: such. 69. hewe: hue. 70. in . . .
newe: the noble (a gold coin) newly minted in the Tower (of
London). 71. yerne: lively. 72. swalwe: swallow. berne:
barn. 73. Therto: moreover. 74. his dame: its mother.
75. bragot: honey ale. meeth: mead. 76. leyd: stored.
heeth: heather. 77. Wynsyng: skittish. 79. bar: wore.
80. boos: boss. bokeler: buckler (small shield).

Hir shoes were laced on hir legges hye.
She was a prymerole,° a piggesnye,°
For any lord to leggen° in his bedde,
Or yet for any good yeman° to wedde.

Now, sire, and eft,° sire, so bifel the cas°
That on a day this hende° Nicholas
Fil° with this yonge wyf to rage° and pleye,
Whil that hir housbonde was at Oseneye,°
As clerkes° been ful subtil and ful queynte,°
And pryvely° he caughte hire by the queynte°   90
And seyde, " Ywis, but if ich° have my wille,
For derne love of thee, lemman,° I spille,"°
And heeld hire harde by the haunche bones
And seyde, " Lemman, love me al atones,°
Or I wol dyen, also° God me save! "

And she sprong° as a colt doth in the trave,°
And with hir heed she wryed° faste awey.
She seyde, " I wol nat kisse thee, by my fey.°
Wy, lat be, quod ich.° Lat be, Nicholas,
Or I wol crye ' Out, harrow '° and ' Allas.'   100
Do wey° youre handes, for youre curteisye."

This Nicholas gan° mercy for to crye,
And spak so faire and profred hym° so faste
That she hir love hym graunted atte° laste,
And swoor hir ooth by Seint Thomas° of Kent
That she wolde been at his comaundement
Whan that she may hir leyser° wel espie.
" Myn housbonde is so ful of jalousie
That, but° ye wayte wel and be pryvee,
I woot° right wel I nam but deed,"° quod° she.
" Ye moste been ful derne as in this cas."°   111

" Nay, thereof care thee noght," quod Nicholas.
" A clerk had litherly biset his while°
But if° he koude a carpenter bigyle."

And thus they been acorded° and y-sworn
To waite a tyme as I have told biforn.°

Whan Nicholas had doon thus everydel°
And thakked° hire aboute the lendes° wel,
He kiste hir swete, and taketh his sautrye°
And pleyeth faste and maketh melodye.   120

Thanne fil° it thus that to the parissh chirche,
Cristes owene werkes for to wirche,°

This goode wyf wente on an haliday.°
Hir forheed shoon as bright as any day,
So was it wasshen whan she leet° hir werk.

Now, was ther of that chirche a parissh clerk°
The which that was y-cleped° Absolon.
Crul° was his heer, and as the gold it shoon
And strouted° as a fanne large and brode;
Ful streight and evene lay his joly shode.°   130
His rode° was reed,° his eyen greye° as goos.

With Poules wyndow corven° on his shoos,
In hoses° rede he wente fetisly.°
Y-clad he was ful smal° and proprely
Al in a kirtel of a light waget;°
Ful faire and thikke been the poyntes set;°
And therupon he hadde a gay surplys
As whit as is the blosme° upon the rys.°
A mery child° he was, so God me save.
Wel koude he laten° blood, and clippe, and shave,
And maken a chartre of lond or aquitaunce.°   141
In twenty manere° koude he trippe and daunce,
After the scole of Oxenforde, tho,°
And with his legges casten° to and fro,
And pleyen songes on a smal rubible.°
Therto he song somtyme a loud quynyble,°
And as wel koude he pleye on a gyterne.°
In al the toun nas° brewhous ne taverne
That he ne visited with his solas,°
Ther° any gaylard tappestere° was.   150
But, sooth to seyn,° he was somdel squaymous°
Of fartyng, and of speche daungerous.°

This Absolon, that joly was and gay,
Goth° with a sencer° on the haliday,
Sensynge° the wyves of the parisshe faste,
And many a lovely look on hem° he caste,
And namely° on this carpenteres wyf.
To loke on hire hym thoughte° a mery lyf.
She was so propre° and swete and likerous,°
I dar wel seyn, if she had been a mous   160
And he a cat, he wolde hir hente anon.°

123. haliday: holy day.   125. leet: left.   126. clerk: As parish clerk Absalom serves at mass and collects the offering on holy days, but on weekdays he does odd jobs such as barbering.   127. The . . . y-cleped: who was called.   128. Crul: curly.   129. strouted: spread out.   130. shode: parting.   131. rode: complexion.   reed: red.   greye: blue.   132. With . . . corven: carved with a design like the tracery in the windows of St. Paul's Cathedral.   133. hoses: leggings.   fetisly: daintily.   134. smal: trimly.   135. waget: blue.   136. been . . . set: are the decorative tags set (on the kirtle).   138. blosme: blossom.   rys: branch.   139. child: young man.   140. laten: let.   141. aquitaunce: written receipt.   142. manere: manners, ways.   143. After . . . tho: according to the mode of Oxford, though.   144. casten: leap.   145. rubible: a two-stringed fiddle.   146. quynyble: falsetto.   147. gyterne: gittern, a kind of guitar.   148. nas: was no.   149. solas: entertaining.   150. Ther: where.   gaylard tappestere: merry barmaid.   151. sooth to seyn: truth to tell.   somdel squaymous: somewhat censorious.   152. daungerous: fastidious.   154. Goth: goes.   sencer: censer (incense burner).   155. Sensynge: censing, swinging the censer (during the church service) at.   156. hem: them.   157. namely: particularly.   158. hym thoughte: seemed to him.   159. propre: trim.   likerous: lascivious.   161. wolde . . . anon: would at once have seized her.

82. prymerole: primrose.   piggesnye: darling (lit., the pigsney flower).   83. leggen: lay.   84. yeman: yeoman.   85. eft: again.   cas: case.   86. hende: gentle.   87. Fil: fell.   rage: sport.   88. Oseneye: Osney, just west of Oxford.   89. clerkes: scholars.   queynte: ingenious.   90. pryvely: stealthily.   queynte: genitals.   91. Ywis . . . ich: indeed, unless I.   92. lemman: sweetheart.   spille: shall perish.   94. al atones: right now.   95. also: so.   96. sprong: sprang.   trave: enclosure for handling a wild horse.   97. wryed: twisted.   98. fey: faith.   99. quod ich: I said.   100. harrow: help.   101. Do wey: take away.   102. gan: began.   103. profred hym: offered himself.   104. atte: at (the).   105. Thomas: Becket.   107. leyser: opportunity.   109. but: unless.   110. woot: know.   nam . . . deed: am no better than dead.   quod: said.   111. moste . . . cas: must be very stealthy in this matter.   113. litherly: ill, while: spent his time poorly.   114. But if: unless.   115. been acorded: have agreed.   116. biforn: before.   117. everydel: every bit.   118. thakked: stroked.   lendes: loins.   119. sautrye: psaltery.   121. fil: befell.   122. for to wirche: to perform.

This parisshe clerk, this joly Absolon,
Hath in his herte swich a love-longynge
That of no wyf took he noon offrynge.
For° curteisye, he seyde, he wolde noon!°
　　The moone, whan it was nyght, ful brighte
　　　　shoon,°
And Absolon his gyterne hath y-take.
For paramours° he thoghte for to wake.°
And forth he goth, jolyf and amorous,
Til he cam to the carpenteres hous　　　170
A litel after cokkes hadde y-crowe,
And dressed hym° up by a shot-wyndowe°
That was upon the carpenteres wal.
He syngeth in his voys gentil and smal,
" Now dere lady, if thy wille be,
I preye yow that ye wol rewe° on me,"
Ful wel acordant to° his giternynge.
　　This carpenter awook and herde hym synge,
And spak unto his wyf and seyde anon,
" What, Alison! Herestow noght° Absolon　180
That chaunteth thus under oure boures° wal? "
　　And she answered hir housbonde therwithal,
" Yis,° God wot,° John. I here it everydel."°
　　This passeth forth. What wol ye bet° than wel?
Fro day to day this joly Absolon
So woweth° hire that hym° is wo bigon;
He waketh al the nyght and al the day.
He kembeth° his lokkes brode and made hym gay;
He woweth hire by menes° and brocage,°
And swoor he wolde been hir owene page;　190
He syngeth brokkyng° as a nyghtyngale,
He sente hir pyment,° meeth,° and spiced ale,
And wafres° pipyng hoot out of the glede;°
And, for° she was of towne, he profred mede,°
For som folk wol be wonnen° for richesse,°
And som for strokes, and som for gentilesse.°
Som tyme, to shewe his lightnesse° and maistrye,°
He pleyeth Herodes° upon a scaffold° hye.
　　But what availleth hym as in this cas?
She loveth so this hende Nicholas　　　200
That Absolon may blowe the bukkes horn.°
He ne had for his labour but° a scorn,

And thus she maketh Absolon hir ape,°
And al his ernest turneth til a jape.°
Ful sooth is this proverb, it is no lye;
Men seith right thus, " Alwey the nye slye
Maketh the ferre leeve to be looth."°
For, thogh that Absolon be wood° or wrooth,°
Bycause that he fer was from hir sighte,
This nye° Nicholas stood in his lighte.　　210
　　Now bere thee° wel, thow hende Nicholas,
For Absolon may waille and synge " Allas."
　　And so bifel it on a Saterday,
This carpenter was goon til° Osenay,
And hende Nicholas and Alisoun
Acorded been° to this conclusioun
That Nicholas shal shapen hem a wyle°
This sely,° jalous housbonde to bigyle,
And if so be the game wente aright
She sholde slepen in his arm al nyght,　　220
For this was hir desir and his also.
　　And right anoon, withouten wordes mo,°
This Nicholas no lenger wolde tarie
But doth ful softe unto his chambre carie
Bothe mete° and drynke for a day or tweye,°
And to hir housbonde bad° hir for to seye,
If that he axed after Nicholas,
She sholde seye she nyste° wher he was;
Of al that day she seigh° hym noght with eye;
She trowed° that he was in maladye,　　230
For, for no cry, hir mayde koude hym calle;
He nolde° answere for nothyng that myghte falle.°
　　This passeth forth al thilke° Saterday
That Nicholas stille in his chambre lay,
And eet and sleep, or dide what hym leste,°
Til Sonday that° the sonne gooth to reste.
This sely carpenter hath greet mervaille°
Of Nicholas, or what thyng myghte hym aille,
And seyde, " I am adrad,° by seint Thomas,
It stondeth nat aright with Nicholas.　　240
God shilde° that he deyde° sodeynly.
This world is now ful tikel,° sikerly.°
I saugh° today a corps y-born to chirche
That now on Monday last I saugh hym wirche.°
Go up " quod he, " unto his knave° anoon.
Clepe° at his dore, or knokke with a stoon.
Loke how it is, and tel me boldely."

165. For: because of. **noon:** none. **166. shoon:** shone.
168. paramours: the cause of love. **thoghte...wake:** intended
to keep watch. **172. dressed hym:** took his stance. **shot-
wyndowe:** hinged window. **176. rewe:** take pity. **177. acordant to:** harmonizing with. **180. Herestow noght:** don't you
hear. **181. boures:** bedroom's. **183. Yis:** yes, indeed. **wot:**
knows. **everydel:** every bit. **184. bet:** better. **186. woweth:**
woos. **hym:** he. **188. kembeth:** combs. **189. menes:** go-
betweens. **brocage:** agency. **191. brokkyng:** quavering.
192. pyment: spiced wine. **meeth:** mead. **193. wafres:** wafer
cakes. **glede:** coal fire. **194. for:** because. **mede:** money
(which a townswoman might have accepted, though a courtly
lady would not). **195. wonnen:** won. **for richesse:** by riches.
196. gentilesse: courtliness. **197. lightnesse:** dexterity. **maistrye:** skill. **198. Herodes:** the violent role of Herod in the local
production of a miracle play. **scaffold:** a pageant or platform
used for the outdoor staging of a play. **201. blowe...horn:**
blow the buck's horn, that is, waste his efforts. **202. ne had
but:** had nothing but.

203. ape: fool. **204. til a jape:** into a joke. **206-07. Alwey
...looth:** Always the sly one who is near makes the distant
dear one loathsome. (That is, "out of sight, out of mind.")
208. wood: mad. **wrooth:** wrathful. **210. nye:** near. **211. bere
thee:** conduct yourself. **214. goon til:** gone to. **216. Acorded
been:** have agreed. **217. shapen...wyle:** plan a scheme for
them. **218. sely:** simple. **222. mo:** more. **225. mete:** food.
tweye: two. **226. bad:** told. **228. nyste:** didn't know.
229. seigh: saw. **230. trowed:** supposed. **232. nolde:** would
(not). **falle:** befall. **233. thilke:** that same. **235. hym
leste:** he wished. **236. that:** when. **237. mervaille:** marvel.
239. adrad: afraid. **241. shilde:** forbid. **deyde:** should die.
242. tikel: unstable. **sikerly:** certainly. **243. saugh:** saw.
y-born: carried. **244. That...wirche:** whom (*that hym*)...
I saw working. **245. knave:** boy servant. **246. Clepe:** call.

This knave gooth hym° up ful sturdily,
And, at the chambre dore whil that he stood,
He cride and knokked as that° he were wood,°
"What! How! What do ye, maister Nicholay? 251
How may ye slepen al the longe day?"

But al for noght. He herde nat a word.
An hole he fond° ful lowe upon a bord
Ther-as° the cat was wont in for to crepe,
And at that hole he looked in ful depe,
And atte laste he hadde of hym a sighte.
This Nicholas sat evere capyng uprighte°
As° he had kiked° on the newe moone.

Adoun° he gooth and tolde his maister soone°
In what array he saugh this ilke° man, 261
This carpenter to blessen hym° bigan
And seyde, "Help us, Seinte Frideswyde.°
A man woot° litel what hym shal bityde.
This man is falle° with his astromye°
In som woodnesse or in som agonye.
I thoghte ay° wel how that it sholde be!
Men sholde noght knowe of Goddes pryvetee.°
Ye,° blessed be alwey a lewed° man
That noght but oonly his bileve kan.° 270
So ferde° another clerk with astromye.
He walked in the feeldes for to prye
Upon the sterres what ther sholde bifalle,
Til he was in a marle° pit y-falle.
He saw nat that. But yet, by Seinte Thomas,
Me reweth sore of° hende Nicholas.
He shal be rated of° his studiyng,
If that I may,° by Jesus hevene° kyng!
Get me a staf that I may underspore,°
Whil that thow, Robyn, hevest up the dore. 280
He shal out of his studiyng, as I gesse."

And to the chambre dore he gan hym dresse.°
His knave was a strong carl for the nones,°
And by the haspe he haf° it up atones.°
Into the floor the dore fil anoon.
This Nicholas sat ay as stille as stoon
And evere caped upward into the eyr.
This carpenter wende° he were in despeyr,
And hente° hym by the shuldres myghtily,
And shook hym harde, and cride spitously,° 290

"What, Nicholay! What! How! Loke adoun.
Awake, and thenk on Cristes passioun.
I crouche° thee from elves and fro wightes."°
Therwith the nyght-spel° seyde he anon rightes°
On foure halves° of the hous aboute
And on the thresshfold on the dore withoute:
"Jesu Crist and Seint Benedight,°
Blesse this hous from every wikked wight.
For the nyghtes verye,° the white Pater-noster.°
Where wentestow,° Seint Petres soster?"° 300
And at the laste this hende Nicholas
Gan for to sike° soore and seyde, "Allas!
Shal al the world be lost eftsones° now?"

This carpenter answerde, "What seistow?°
What! Thenk on God, as we doon, men that
swynke."°
This Nicholas answerde, "Fecche me drynke,
And after wol I speke in pryvetee
Of certein thyng that toucheth me and thee.
I wol telle it noon oother man, certayn."

This carpenter gooth doun and comth agayn, 310
And broghte of myghty ale a large quart,
And whan that ech of hem had dronke his part,
This Nicholas his dore faste shette,°
And doun the carpenter by hym he sette
And seyde, "John, myn hoost lief° and deere,
Thou shalt upon thy trouthe swere me heere
That to no wight thou shalt this counseil wreye,°
For it is Cristes counseil that I seye,
And, if thou telle it man, thou art forlore,°
For this vengeaunce thow shalt have therfore, 320
That, if thow wreye me, thow shalt be wood."°

"Nay, Crist forbede it, for his holy blood,"
Quod tho° this sely man. "I nam no labbe,°
Ne, thogh I seye,° I nam nat lief to gabbe.°
Sey what thow wolt,° I shal it nevere telle
To child ne wyf, by hym that harwed° helle."

"Now John," quod Nicholas, "I wol noght lye.
I have y-founde in myn astrologye,
As I have looked in the moone bright,
That now a° Monday next, at quarter-nyght,°

248. gooth hym: goes. 250. that: if. wood: mad. 254. fond: found. 255. Ther-as: where. 258. capyng uprighte: gaping face-upwards. 259. As: as if. kiked: stared. 260. Adoun: down. soone: at once. 261. ilke: same. 262. blessen hym: cross himself. 263. Frideswyde: Frideswide, a local heroine enshrined in what later became the cathedral at Oxford. 264. woot: knows. 265. is falle: has fallen. astromye: the unlearned carpenter's mispronunciation of the word "astronomy." 267. thoghte ay: always expected. 268. pryvetee: secrecy. 269. Ye: yes. lewed: ignorant. 270. noght . . . kan: knows nothing but his creed (alone). 271. ferde: fared. 274. marle: marl. 276. Me . . . of: I sorely pity. 277. rated of: scolded for. 278. If . . . may: if I can do anything about it. hevene: Heaven's. 279. underspore: pry underneath. 282. gan . . . dresse: betook himself. 283. a . . . nones: an exceptionally strong fellow. 284. haf: heaved. atones: at once. 288. wende: supposed. 289. hente: seized. 290. spitously: defiantly.

293. crouche: protect by marking with the sign of the cross. wightes: (other) creatures. 294. nyght-spel: charm against the dangers of the night, recorded here in an intentionally ludicrous form. anon rightes: right away. 295. halves: corners. 297. Benedight: Benedict. 299. verye: evil spirits. white Pater-noster: the name of a charm of this kind, presumably derived from some version of "Our Father" intended to effect white (legitimate) magic. 300. wentestow: did you go? soster: sister. 302. sike: sigh. 303. eftsones: very soon. 304. seistow: do you say? 305. swynke: work. 313. shette: shut. 315. lief: beloved. 317. counseil wreye: secret betray. 319. forlore: lost. 321. be wood: become insane (as a punishment). 323. tho: then. labbe: babbler. 324. seye: say (it myself). nam . . . gabbe: don't like to blab. 325. wolt: will. 326. harwed: harrowed (harassed). According to an apocryphal gospel, Christ after his crucifixion routed the evil spirits in Hell and removed the souls of the patriarchs to Heaven — a favorite episode in miracle plays. 330. a: on. quarter-nyght: the end of the first quarter of the night (9 P.M.).

Shal falle a reyn, and that so wilde and wood,   331
That half so greet was nevere Noes° flood.
This world," he seyde, " in lasse than in an hour
Shal al be dreynt,° so hidous is the shour.
Thus shal mankynde drenche° and lese hir° lif."
    This carpenter answerde, " Allas, my wyf!
And shal she drenche! Allas, myn Alisoun!"
    For sorwe of this he fil almoost adoun
And seyde, " Is ther no remedie in this cas?"
    " Why, yis, for Gode," quod hende Nicholas,   340
" If thow wolt werken after loore and reed.°
Thow mayst noght werken after thyn owene heed,°
For thus seith Salomon° that was ful trewe,
' Werk al by conseil, and thow shalt noght rewe.'°
And if thow werken wolt by good consayl,
I undertake, withouten mast or sayl,
Yit° shal I save hire and thee and me.
Hastow° nat herd how saved was Noe
Whan that Oure Lord had warned hym biforn°
That al the world with water sholde be lorn?"°
    " Yis," quod this carpenter, " ful yore° ago."
    " Hastow nat herd," quod Nicholas, " also   352
The sorwe of Noe with his felaweshipe°
Er that° he myghte gete his wyf to shipe.
Hym had levere,° I dar wel undertake,°
At thilke tyme than al hise wetheres blake°
That she hadde had a ship hirself allone!
And therfore wostow° what is best to done?°
This axeth° haste, and of an hastyf° thyng
Men may noght preche or maken tariyng.   360
Anon,° go gete us faste into this in°
A knedyng trogh, or ellis° a kemelyn°
For ech° of us, but looke that they be large
In which we mowen swymme° as in a barge,
And han therinne vitaille suffisaunt°
But for a day. Fy on the remenaunt.°
The water shal aslake° and goon away
Aboute pryme° upon the nexte day.
But Robyn may nat wite° of this, thy knave,°
Ne eek thy mayde Gille I may nat save.   370
Axe noght why, for thogh thou axe me,
I wol noght tellen Goddes pryvetee.°
Suffiseth thee, but if° thy wittes madde,°
To han as greet a grace as Noe hadde.

Thy wyf shal I wel saven, out of° doute!
Go now thy wey and speed thee heer-aboute.°
But whan thou hast, for hire and thee and me,
Y-geten° us thise knedyng tubbes thre,
Thanne shaltow hange hem in the roof ful hye
That no man of oure purveiaunce espye;°   380
And whan thow thus hast doon as I have seyd,
And hast oure vitaille faire in hem y-leyd,°
And eek an ax to smyte the corde atwo,°
Whan that the water cometh, that we may go
And breke an hole an heigh° upon the gable
Unto the gardynward° over the stable
That we may frely passen° forth oure wey
Whan that the grete shour is goon awey.
Thanne shaltow swymme as murye, I undertake,
As doth the white doke° after his° drake.   390
Thanne wol I clepe,° ' How, Alison! How, John!
Be murye, for the flood wol passe anon.'
And thou wolt seyn, ' Hail, maister Nicholay!
Good morwe. I see thee wel, for it is day.'
    " And thanne shal we be lordes al oure lyf
Of al the world, as Noe and his wyf.
But of o° thyng I warne thee ful right.
Be wel avysed° on that ilke nyght
That we been° entred into shippes bord
That noon of us ne speke noght a word,   400
Ne clepe ne crye, but been in° his preyere,
For it is Goddes owene heste deere.°
Thy wyf and thow mote° hange fer atwynne°
For that bitwixe yow shal be no synne
Namoore in lookyng than ther shal in dede.
This ordinaunce is seyd. Go, God thee spede!
Tomorwe at nyght, when men been alle aslepe,
Into oure knedyng tubbes wol we crepe
And sitten ther, abidyng° Goddes grace.
Go now thy wey. I have no lenger space°   410
To make of this no lenger sermonyng.
Men seyn thus, ' Send the wise, and sey no thyng.'
Thow art so wys, it nedeth nat teche.°
Go save oure lyf, and that I thee biseche."°
    This sely carpenter gooth forth his wey.
Ful ofte he seyde " Allas and weylawey." °
And to his wyf he tolde his pryvetee,
And she was war° and knew it bet° than he
What al this queynte cast was for to seye,°
But nathelees° she ferde as° she wolde deye   420

332. Noes: Noah's.   **334. dreynt:** drowned.   **335. drenche:** drown.   **lese hir:** lose their.   **341. werken . . . reed:** act according to teaching and advice.   **342. heed:** mind.   **343. Salomon:** Solomon (the saying is actually from Ecclus. 32:19).   **344. rewe:** rue.   **347. Yit:** still.   **348. Hastow:** have you.   **349. biforn:** beforehand.   **350. lorn:** lost.   **351. yore:** long.   **353. felaweshipe:** company. In the miracle plays Noah's wife provided comic relief by her obstreperousness.   **354. Er that:** before.   **355. Hym . . . levere:** he had sooner.   **undertake:** assert.   **356. wetheres blake:** black sheep.   **358. wostow:** do you know.   **done:** do.   **359. axeth:** demands.   **hastyf:** hasty.   **361. Anon:** at once.   **in:** house.   **362. ellis:** else.   **kemelyn:** tub.   **363. ech:** each.   **364. mowen swymme:** can float.   **365. vitaille suffisaunt:** sufficient victuals.   **366. Fy . . . remenaunt:** Never mind the remainder.   **367. aslake:** slacken.   **368. pryme:** prime (9 A.M.).   **369. wite:** know.   **knave:** servant boy.   **372. pryvetee:** secret.   **373. but if:** unless.   **madde:** become mad.

375. out of: without.   **376. speed . . . heer-aboute:** hurry about this business.   **378. Y-geten:** gotten.   **380. no . . . espye:** no one may discover our preparation.   **382. y-leyd:** laid.   **383. atwo:** in two.   **385. an heigh:** on high.   **386. Unto . . . gardynward:** on the gardenward side of the house. The same roof evidently runs over both house and stable.   **387. frely passen:** freely pass.   **390. doke:** duck.   **his:** its.   **391. clepe:** call out.   **397. o:** one.   **398. avysed:** advised.   **399. That we been:** when we have.   **401. in:** at.   **402. heste deere:** commandment precious.   **403. mote:** must.   **fer atwynne:** far apart.   **409. abidyng:** awaiting.   **410. space:** time.   **413. nedeth . . . teche:** it is not necessary to teach *you*.   **414. biseche:** beseech.   **416. weylawey:** woe.   **418. war:** aware.   **bet:** better.   **419. queynte . . . seye:** ingenious plan meant.   **420. nathelees:** nevertheless.   **ferde as:** acted as if.

And seyde, "Allas! Go forth thy wey anon.
Help us to scape, or we been dede echon.°
I am thy trewe, verray° wedded wyf.
Go, deere spouse, and help to save oure lyf."
Lo, which° a greet thyng is affeccioun!°
Men may dye of ymaginacioun,
So depe may impressioun be take.°
This sely carpenter bigynneth quake.
Hym thynketh verrailiche° that he may se
Noes flood come walwyng° as the see   430
To drenchen° Alison, his hony deere.
He wepeth, waileth, maketh sory cheere.
He siketh° with ful many a sory swogh,°
And gooth and geteth hym a knedyng trogh,
And after a tubbe and a kymelyn,°
And pryvely he sente hem to his in,°
And heeng hem in the roof in pryvetee.
His° owene hand he made laddres thre
To clymben by the ronges and the stalkes°
Unto the tubbes hangyng in the balkes°   440
And hem vitailled,° bothe trogh and tubbe,
With breed and chese and good ale in a jubbe,°
Suffisynge right ynogh as for a day.
But er that he had maad al this array,
He sente his knave and eek his wenche also
Upon his nede° to Londoun for to go,
And on the Monday, whan it drogh° to nyght,
He shette his dore withouten candel lyght
And dressed° alle thyng as it sholde be,
And, shortly up they clomben alle thre.   450
They seten° stille wel a furlong-way.°
"Now Pater-noster, clum!"° seyde Nicholay.
And "Clum," quod John, and "Clum," seyde
      Alisoun.
This carpenter seyde his devocioun,
And stille he sit° and biddeth° his prayere,
Awaitynge on the reyn if he it heere.
The dede sleep for wery bisynesse°
Fil on this carpenter right as I gesse
Aboute corfew° tyme or litel moore.
For travaille° of his goost° he groneth soore,   460
And eft° he routeth,° for his heed myslay.°
Doun of the laddre stalketh Nicholay,
And Alisoun ful softe adoun she spedde.
Withouten wordes mo, they goon to bedde.
Theras° the carpenter is wont to lye,

Ther was the revel and the melodye!
And thus lyth° Alison and Nicholas
In bisynesse of myrthe and in solas°
Til that the belle of laudes° gan to rynge
And freres° in the chauncel gonne synge.   470
This parissh clerk, this amorous Absolon,
That is for love alwey so wo-bigon,
Upon the Monday was at Oseneye
With compaignye hym to disporte and pleye,
And axed upon cas a cloisterer°
Ful pryvely after John the carpenter,
And he drogh hym apart out of the cherche°
And seyde, "I noot.° I saugh hym here noght
      werche°
Sith Saterday. I trowe° that he be went°
For tymber ther° oure abbot hath hym sent,   480
For he is wont for tymber for to go
And dwellen at the graunge° a day or two,
Or ellis he is at his hous certeyn.
Wher that he be, I kan noght soothly° seyn."
This Absolon ful joly was and lyght
And thoughte, "Now is tyme to wake al nyght,
For sikerly° I saugh hym noght stirynge
Aboute his dore syn day bigan to sprynge.
So mote° I thryve, I shal at cokkes crowe°
Ful pryvely knokken at his wyndowe   490
That stant ful lowe upon his boures wal.
To Alison now wol I tellen al
My love longyng, for yit I shal nat mysse
That at the leeste wey° I shal hir kisse.
Som maner° confort shal I have, parfay!°
My mouth hath icched° al this longe day.
That is a signe of kissyng, atte leeste.
Al nyght me mette eek° I was at a feeste.
Therfore, I wol go slepe an houre or tweye,
And al the nyght than wol I wake and pleye!"   500
Whan that the firste cok hath crowe, anon
Up rist° this joly lovere Absolon
And hym° arrayeth gay at poynt devys,°
But first he cheweth greyn° and likorys
To smellen swete, er° he hadde kembd° his heer.
Under his tonge a trewe-love° he beer,°
For therby wende° he to be gracious.
He rometh to the carpenteres hous,
And stille he stant under the shot-wyndowe —

422. been . . . echon: shall be dead each one.   423. trewe, verray: faithful, true.   425. which: what.   affeccioun: a mental
impression.   427. take: received.   429. verrailiche: truly.
430. walwyng: welling.   431. drenchen: drown.   433. siketh:
sighs.   swogh: groan.   435. kymelyn: tub.   436. in: house.
438. His: with his.   439. stalkes: uprights.   440. in . . .
balkes: on the roof beams.   441. hem vitailled: supplied them.
442. jubbe: jug.   446. nede: errand.   447. drogh: drew.
449. dressed: prepared.   451. seten: sat.   a furlong-way: a
few minutes (lit., as long as it takes to walk a furlong).   452. Pater-noster, clum: (say) a paternoster, and then mum's the word!
455. sit: sits.   biddeth: prays.   457. wery bisynesse: wearying activity.   459. corfew: curfew (about 8 P.M.).   460. travaille: disturbance.   goost: spirit.   461. eft: in turn.   routeth:
snores.   myslay: lay in the wrong position.   465. Theras: where.

467. lyth: lie.   468. solas: delight.   469. laudes: the first service
after midnight.   470. freres: friars.   475. upon . . . cloisterer:
by chance a cloisterer (of Osney Abbey).   477. cherche: church
(of the abbey).   478. noot: don't know.   saugh . . . werche:
haven't seen him work here.   479. trowe: suppose.   be went:
has gone.   480. ther: where.   482. graunge: (abbey's) farmhouse.   484. soothly: truly.   487. sikerly: certainly.   489. mote:
may.   crowe: presumably at the *first* crow (as in l. 501), which
was thought to occur at midnight.   494. at . . . wey: at least.
495. maner: sort of.   parfay: in faith.   496. icched: Itching
was commonly interpreted as an omen.   498. me . . . eek: I
dreamed also.   502. rist: rises.   503. hym: himself.   gay . . .
devys: gaily to perfection.   504. greyn: grain of paradise (an
aromatic seed).   505. er: before.   kembd: combed.   506. trewe-
love: leaf of herb Paris, a medicinal herb growing in the shape
of a truelove knot.   beer: carried.   507. wende: expected.

Unto his brest it raughte,° it was so lowe — 510
And softe he cougheth with a semysoun.°
"What do ye, honycomb, swete Alisoun,
My faire bryd,° my swete cynamome?
Awaketh, lemman° myn, and speketh to me.
Wel litel thynken ye upon my wo,
That for youre love I swete ther° I go.
No wonder is thogh that I swelte° and swete.
I moorne as dooth a lamb after the tete.°
Ywis,° lemman, I have swich love-longyng
That lyk a turtel° trewe is my moornyng.   520
I may nat ete namoore than a mayde."
    "Go fro the wyndow, Jakke fool,"° she sayde.
"As help me God, it wol nat be 'com pa° me.'
I love another — and ellis I were to blame° —
Wel bet than thee, by Jesu, Absolon.
Go forth thy wey, or I wol caste a stoon,
And lat me slepe, a twenty develwey."°
    "Allas," quod Absolon, "and weilawey
That trewe love was evere so yvel biset.°
Thanne kys me, syn it may be no bet,°   530
For Jesus love, and for the love of me."
    "Woltow thanne go thy wey therwith?" quod
    she.
    "Ye, certes, lemman," quod this Absolon.
    "Thanne make thee redy," quod she. "I come
anon."
    And unto Nicholas she seyde stille,°
"Now hust,° and thou shalt laughen al thy fille."
    This Absolon doun sette hym on his knees
And seyde, "I am a lord at alle degrees,
For, after this, I hope ther cometh moore.
Lemman, thy grace, and, swete bryd, thyn oore."°
    The wyndow she undoth, and that in haste.   541
"Have do,"° quod she. "Com of, and speed thee
faste
Lest that oure neighebores thee espye."
    This Absolon gan wipe his mouth ful drye.
Derk was the nyght as pych° or as the cole,°
And at the wyndow out she putte hir hole,
And Absolon hym fil° no bet ne wers°
But with his mouth he kiste hir naked ers°
Ful savourly° er he were war° of this.
    Abak he sterte° and thoghte it was amys,   550
For wel he wiste° a womman hath no berd.°
He felte a thyng al rogh and long y-herd,°
And seyde, "Fy, allas! What have I do?"
    "Tehee," quod she, and clapte the wyndow to,

And Absolon gooth forth a sory paas.°
    "A berd, a berd!" quod hende Nicholas.
    "By Goddes corpus!° This gooth faire and wel!"
    This sely Absolon herde every del,°
And on his lippe he gan for anger byte,   559
And to hymself he seyde, "I shal thee quyte."°
Who rubbeth now, who froteth°now his lippes
With dust, with sond,° with straw, with clooth,
    with chippes
But Absolon, that seith ful ofte, "Allas!
My soule bitake° I unto Sathanas,
But me were levere° than al this toun," quod he,
"Of this despit awreken for to be.°
Allas," quod he, "allas, I ne hadde y-bleynt!"°
    His hote love was coold and al y-queynt,°
For, fro that tyme that he had kist hir ers,
Of paramours° he sette noght a kers,°   570
For he was heeled° of his maladye.
Ful ofte paramours he gan defye°
And weep° as dooth a child that is y-bete.
    A softe paas° he wente over the strete
Until° a smyth men clepen daun° Gerveys,
That in his forge smythed plough harneys.
He sharpeth shaar° and cultour° bisily.
    This Absolon knokketh al esily°
And seyde, "Undo, Gerveys, and that anon!"
    "What? Who artow?"° "It am I, Absolon."   580
    "What, Absolon! What, Cristes swete tree,°
Why rise ye so rathe,° ey, benedicitee?°
What eyleth yow? Som gay gerl, God it woot,
Hath broght yow thus upon the viritoot°—
By Seint Note, ye woot wel what I mene!"
    This Absolon ne roghte nat a bene°
Of al his pley; no word agayn he yaf.°
He hadde moore tow° on his distaf
Then Gerveys knew and seyde, "Freend so deere,
That hoote cultour in the chymenee heere,   590
As lene° it me. I have therwith to doone.°
I wol brynge it thee agayn ful soone."
    Gerveys answerde, "Certes, were it gold,
Or in a poke nobles al untold,°
Thow sholdest have, as I am trewe smyth.
Ey, Cristes foo!° What wol ye do therwith?"
    "Therof," quod Absolon, "be as be may.
I shal wel telle it thee tomorwe day,"

555. a . . . paas: at a sorry pace.   557. corpus: body.   558. del:
part.   560. quyte: pay back.   561. froteth: rub.   562. sond:
sand.   564. bitake: commit.   565. me . . . levere: I would
sooner.   566. despit . . . be: insult be avenged.   567. I . . .
y-bleynt: that I didn't turn aside!   568. y-queynt: quenched.
570. paramours: lovers.   kers: curse.   571. heeled: cured.
572. gan defye: renounced.   573. weep: wept.   574. A . . .
paas: quietly.   575. Until: to.   clepen daun: called Master.
577. shaar: share.   cultour: plow colter.   578. esily: gently.
580. artow: are you.   581. swete tree: precious cross.   582. rathe:
early.   benedicitee: God bless you.   584. upon . . . viritoot: on
the move.   586. ne . . . bene: didn't care a bean.   587. agayn
he yaf: he replied.   588. tow: tow (to spin).   591. As lene:
lend.   therwith to doone: something to do with it.   594. in
. . . untold: nobles (gold coins worth 6s. 8d.) all uncounted in a
bag.   596. foo: foot.

510. raughte: reached.   511. semysoun: half-sound.   513. bryd:
bird.   514. lemman: sweetheart.   516. swete ther: sweat where.
517. swelte: faint.   518. tete: teat.   519. Ywis: indeed.
520. turtel: turtledove.   522. Jakke fool: jackass.   523. pa:
kiss.   524. were to blame: would be blameworthy.   527. a
. . . develwey: the Devil away with you, twenty times over.
529. yvel biset: poorly bestowed.   530. bet: better.   535. stille:
quietly.   536. hust: hush.   540. oore: mercy.   542. do: done.
545. pych: pitch.   the cole: coal.   547. hym fil: to him befell.
ne wers: nor worse.   548. ers: bottom.   549. savourly: de-
lightedly.   war: aware.   550. sterte: started.   551. wiste:
knew.   berd: beard.   552. y-herd: haired.

And caughte° the cultour by the colde stele.°
Ful softe out at the dore he gan to stele   600
And wente unto the carpenteres wal.
He cogheth first, and knokketh therwithal
Upon the wyndowe right as he dide er.°
This Alison answerde, "Who is ther
That knokketh so? I warante it a theef!"
"Why, nay," quod he. "God woot, my swete
    lief,°
I am thyn Absolon, thy derelyng.°
Of gold," quod he, "I have thee broght a ryng.
My moder yaf° it me, so God me save.
Ful fyn it is, and therto° wel y-grave.°   610
This wol I yeven° thee if thow me kisse."
This Nicholas was risen for to pisse
And thoghte he wolde amenden° al the jape;°
He sholde kisse his ers er that he scape;°
And up the wyndow dide° he hastily,
And out his ers he putteth pryvely°
Over the buttok to the haunche bon.
And therwith spak this clerk, this Absolon:
"Spek, swete brid,° I noot noght° wher thow art."
This Nicholas anoon leet fle a fart   620
As greet as it hadde been a thonder dent,°
That with the strook he was almoost y-blent,°
And he was redy with his iren hoot,
And Nicholas in the ers he smoot.°
Of° gooth the skyn an hand brede° aboute;
The hoote cultour brende° so his toute°
That for the smert° he wende° for to dye.
As he were wood, for wo he gan to crye,
"Help! Water! Water! Help, for Goddes herte!"
This carpenter out of his slomber sterte   630
And herde oon° cryen, "Water!" as he were wood
And thoghte, "Allas, now cometh Nowelys°
    flood."
He sette hym° up withoute wordes mo,
And with his ax he smoot the corde atwo,
And doun gooth al. He fond° neither to selle
Ne breed ne ale til he cam to the celle°
Upon the floor, and there aswoone° he lay.
Up stirte hire° Alison and Nicholay
And criden, "Out!" and "Harrow!"° in the
    strete.
The neighebores bothe smale and grete   640
In ronnen for to gauren° on this man
That aswowne lay bothe pale and wan,

For with the fal he brosten° hadde his arm.
But stonde he moste° unto his owene harm,
For whan he spak, he was anon bore doun°
With° hende Nicholas and Alisoun.
They tolden every man that he was wood;
He was agast° so of "Nowelys flood"
Thurgh fantasie that, of his vanytee,
He hadde y-boght hym knedyng tubbes thre   650
And hadde hem hanged in the roof above;
And that he preyed hem° for Goddes love
To sitten in the roof par compaignye.°
The folk gan laughen at his fantasye.
Into the roof they kiken° and they cape°
And turned al his harm unto a jape,
For, what so that this carpenter answerde,
It was for noght; no man his reson° herde.
With othes° grete he was so sworn adoun
That he was holden° wood in al the toun,   660
For every clerk anon right heeld° with oother.
They seyde, "The man is wood, my leve brother."
And every wight gan laughen at this stryf.
Thus swyved° was the carpenteres wyf
For al his kepyng° and his jalousye,
And Absolon hath kist hir nether eye,
And Nicholas is scalded in the toute.
This tale is doon, and God save al the route.°

THE WIFE OF BATH'S PROLOGUE

Chaucer evidently did not live long enough to prepare an introductory link for the Wife of Bath's Prologue and Tale, but he did link together the ensuing sequence of tales elicited by the Wife's views. This group of seven tales — the Wife of Bath's, the Friar's, the Summoner's, the Clerk's, the Merchant's, the Squire's, and the Franklin's — has in fact been labeled the Marriage Group.

The Wife's Prologue is a most unusual defense of womankind against the view widely held in the Middle Ages that Eve was responsible for Adam's fall and hence for Christ's crucifixion and that the daughters of Eve have ever since wrought mischief among men.

In elaborating the Wife's spirited argument against this preconception Chaucer has made an ingenious selection from his extensive reading on the subject. The Wife, for instance, repeats the views advanced in the fifth century by the heretical Jovinian, who, despite the religious prestige of the hermits' way of life, had maintained that marriage was not inferior to celibacy. And she indignantly repudiates St. Jerome's authoritative refutations of Jovinian which her fifth husband had dared to mention.

599. caughte: took.   stele: handle.   603. er: before.   606. lief: dear.   607. derelyng: darling.   609. yaf: gave.   610. therto: besides.   y-grave: carved.   611. yeven: give.   613. amenden: improve upon.   jape: joke.   614. scape: escaped.   615. dide: put.   616. pryvely: stealthily.   619. brid: bird.   noot noght: don't know.   621. dent: dint.   622. y-blent: blinded. 624. smoot: struck.   625. Of: off.   brede: breadth.   626. brende: burned.   toute: bottom.   627. smert: pain.   wende: expected.   631. oon: someone.   632. Nowelys: Noel's (the Carpenter confuses the name of Noah with that of Christmas). 633. sette hym: sat.   635. fond: found (the opportunity). 636. celle: sill.   637. aswowne: aswoon.   638. stirte hire: sprang.   639. Harrow!: help.   641. gauren: stare.

643. brosten: broken.   644. stonde he moste: he must attest. 645. bore doun: borne down.   646. With: by.   648. agast: afraid.   652. hem: them (Nicholas and Alisoun).   653. par compaignye: by way of company.   655. kiken: peer.   cape: gape.   658. reson: argument.   659. othes: oaths.   660. holden: considered.   661. heeld: agreed.   664. swyved: lain with. 665. kepyng: watching.   668. route: company.

She carries the war into the enemy's camp by charging that, if women emulated the writings of ecclesiastical scholars, they could write more wickedness of men that all the sons of Adam could redress. She appeals to her own experience rather than the conventional authorities and insists that marriage is an honorable estate and that it need not be woeful — provided that the wife holds the mastery.

"Experience, thogh noon auctoritee°
Were in this world, is right ynogh for me
To speke of wo that is in mariage,
For, lordynges, sith° I twelve yeer was of age,
Thonked be God, that is eterne on lyve,°
Housbondes at chirche dore I have had fyve,
If I so ofte myghte han wedded be,°
And alle were worthy men in hir° degree.
But me was told, certeyn, noght longe agon° is,
That, sith that° Crist ne wente nevere but onys° 10
To weddyng in the Cane° of Galilee,
That by the same ensemple taughte he me
That I ne sholde wedded be but ones.°
Herke eek,° lo, which° a sharp word for the nones°
Bisyde a welle Jesus, God and man,
Spak in repreeve° of the Samaritan.
"'Thow hast y-had fyve housbondes,' quod he,
'And that ilke° man that now hath thee
Is nat thyn housbonde.' Thus he seyde, certeyn.
What that he mente ther-by, I kan nat seyn, 20
But° that I axe° why that the fifthe man
Was noon housbonde to the Samaritan.
How manye myghte she have in mariage?
Yet herde I nevere tellen in myn age
Upon this nombre diffinicioun.
Men may dyvyne° and glosen° up and doun,
But wel I woot,° expres,° withouten lye,
God bad us for to wexe° and multiplye.
That gentil text kan I wel understonde.
Eek wel I woot, he seyde myn housbonde 30
Sholde lete° fader and moder and take to me,
But of no nombre mencioun made he,
Of bigamye or of octogamye.°
Why sholde men thanne° speke of it vileynye?°

"Lo, here the wise kyng daun Salomon,ˇ
I trowe° he hadde wyves mo° than oon.°
As wolde° God it leveful° were to me
To be refresshed half so ofte as he!
Which yifte° of God hadde he for alle his wyvys!
No man hath swich° that in this world alyve is. 40
God woot, this noble kyng, as to my wit,°
The firste nyght had many a murye° fit
With ech of hem, so wel° was hym on lyve.°
Blessed be God that I have wedded fyve,
Of whiche I have pyked out the beste
Bothe of here nether purs° and of here cheste.°
Diverse scoles maken parfyt clerkes,°
And diverse practyk° in many sondry werkes
Maken° the werkman parfit, sekirly.°
Of fyve husbondes scoleiyng° am I. 50
Welcome the sixte whan that evere he shal;
For sith I wol nat kepe me chaast° in al,
Whan myn housbonde is fro the world y-gon,
Som Cristen man shal wedde me anon,°
For thanne th' apostle° seith that I am free
To wedde, a Goddes half,° wher it liketh me.
He seith that to be wedded is no synne;
Bet° is to be wedded than to brynne.°
What rekketh me theigh° folk seye vileynye
Of shrewed Lameth° and his bigamye? 60
I woot wel Abraham was an holy man,
And Jacob eek, as fer as evere I kan,°
And ech of hem hadde wyves mo than two,
And many another holy man also.
Where kan ye seye,° in any maner° age,
That heighe God defended° mariage
By expres word? I pray yow, telleth me.
Or where comanded he virginitee?
I woot as wel as ye, it is no drede,°
Th' apostle, whan he speketh of maydenhede,° 70
He seyde that precept thereof hadde he noon.
Men may conseille a womman to be oon,°
But conseillyng is no comandement.
He put it in oure owene juggement,
For hadde God comanded maydenhede,
Thanne hadde he dampned° weddyng with the dede.°

WIFE OF BATH'S PROLOGUE. 1. noon auctoritee: no (scholarly) authority. 4. sith: since. 5. eterne on lyve: eternally alive. 7. If . . . be: if I might (lawfully) have been married so often. The Wife has been married five times "at the church door" (see Gen. Prol., l. 460n.), but some canonists condemned *bigamy* (that is, not "double marriage" but "remarriage," as in ll. 33, 92, 102) as unlawful. 8. hir: their. 9. agon: ago. 10. sith that: since. onys: once. 11. the Cane: Cana. 13. ones: once. That is, since the New Testament mentions Christ's attendance at only one wedding, only one marriage is therefore lawful, as St. Jerome had argued in the book quoted by the Wife's fifth husband (ll. 679 ff.). 14. eek: also. which: what. nones: occasion. 16. repreeve: reproof (John 4:18). 18. ilke: same. 21. But: except. axe: ask. 26. dyvyne: guess. glosen: interpret. 27. woot: know. expres: expressly. 28. wexe: increase. 31. lete: leave. 33. octogamye: eighth marriage. 34. thanne: then. vileynye: reproach.

35. daun Salomon: Lord Solomon (who had seven hundred wives and three hundred concubines). 36. trowe: believe. mo: more. oon: one. 37. As wolde: would to. leveful: allowable. 39. Which yifte: what a gift. 40. swich: such. 41. wit: judgment. 42. murye: merry. 43. wel: well off. hym on lyve: he in his time. 46. here . . . purs: their lower purse (genitals). cheste: money chest. 47. clerkes: scholars. 48. practyk: practice. 49. Maken: make(s). sekirly: certainly. 50. scoleiyng: schooling. 52. chaast: chaste. 54. anon: forthwith. 55. apostle: Paul, whose views the Wife quotes enthusiastically in her own defense (ll. 55–58, 70–71, 109–10, 135–36, 160–67) except in ll. 348–51, where she repudiates the text quoted against her. 56. a . . . half: in God's name. 58. Bet: better. brynne: burn. 59. rekketh me theigh: care I though. 60. shrewed Lameth: cursed Lamech (Gen. 4:19). 62. kan: know. 65. seye: say. maner: kind of. 66. defended: forbade. 69. drede: doubt. 70. maydenhede: virginity. 72. oon: one (a virgin). 76. dampned: condemned. dede: marital act.

And certes, if ther were no seed y-sowe,°
Virginitee thanne, whereof sholde it growe?
Poul dorste° nat comanden, at the leeste,
A thyng of which his maister yaf noon heeste.°   80
The dart° is set up for virginitee.
Cacche who so may, who renneth best lat se.
"But this word is noght take of° every wight°
But ther-as° God list yeve° it, of his myght.
I woot wel that th' apostle was a mayde;°
But nathelees,° thogh that he wroot and sayde
He wolde° that every wight were swich as he,
Al nys but° conseil to virginitee;
And for to been a wyf he yaf° me leve
Of indulgence. So° is it no repreve   90
To wedde me, if that my make dye,
Withoute excepcioun of bigamye.
Al° were it good no womman for to touche, —
He mente as in his bed or in his couche,
For peril is bothe fyr and tow t' assemble;°
Ye knowe what this ensample may resemble.
This al and som,° he heeld virginitee
Moore parfit than weddyng in freletee.°
Freletee clepe° I but if that° he and she
Wolde leden al hir° lyf in chastitee.   100
"I graunte it wel I have noon envye
Thogh maydenhede preferre° bigamye.
It liketh hem° to be clene in body and goost.°
Of myn estat ne wol I make no boost.
For wel ye knowe, a lord in his houshold
Ne hath nat every vessel al of gold;
Somme been° of tree° and doon hir lord servyse.
God clepeth folk to hym in sondry wyse,°
And everich° hath of God a propre yifte,°
Som this, som that, as hym liketh shifte.°   110
"Virginitee is greet perfeccioun,
And continence eek with devocioun;
But Crist, that of perfeccioun is welle,°
Bad nat every wight he sholde go selle
Al that he hadde, and yeve it to the poore,
And in swich wise folwe° hym and his foore;°
He spak to hem° that wolde lyve parfitly.
And, lordynges, by youre leve, that am nat I!
I wol bistowe the flour of al myn age
In th' actes and in fruyt of mariage.   120

"Telle me also, to what conclusioun°
Were membres maad° of generacioun
And of so parfit wys a wight y-wrought?°
Trusteth right wel, they were nat maad for noght.
Glose° who so wole, and seye bothe up and doun
That they were maad for purgacioun
Of uryne, and oure bothe thynges° smale
Were eek to knowe a femele from a male,
And for noon oother cause! Sey ye no?
Th' experience woot° wel it is noght so.   130
So that° the clerkes be nat with me wrothe,
I sey this, that they maked been° for bothe,
That is to seye, for office,° and for ese°
Of engendrure,° ther° we nat God displese.
Why sholde men ellis° in hir° bokes sette
That man shal yelde° to his wyf hir dette?°
Now, wher-with sholde he make his paiement,
If he ne° used his sely° instrument?
Thanne° were they maad upon a creature
To purge uryne and eek for engendrure.   140
"But I seye noght that every wight is holde,°
That hath swich harneys° as I to yow tolde,
To goon and usen hem° in engendrure.
Thanne sholde men take of chastitee no cure.°
Crist was a mayde and shapen as a man,
And many a seynt sith that° the world bigan,
Yet lyved they evere in parfit chastitee.
I nyl° envye no virginitee.
Lat hem° be breed° of pured whete° seed,
And lat us wyves hote° barly breed.   150
And yet with barly breed, Mark° telle kan,
Oure lord Jesu refresshed many a man.
In swich estat as God hath cleped us
I wol persevere. I nam nat precius.°
In wyfhode wol I use myn instrument
As frely as my makere hath it sent.
If I be daungerous,° God yeve me sorwe.
Myn housbonde shal it have bothe eve and morwe°
Whan that hym list° com forth and paye his dette.
An housbonde wol I have, I wol nat lette,°   160
Which shal be bothe my dettour and my thral°
And have his tribulacioun withal°
Upon his flessh while that I am his wyf.

77. y-sowe: sown.   **79. Poul dorste:** Paul dared.   **80. yaf . . .
heeste:** gave no order.   **81. dart:** race prize.   **83. take of:**
applied to.   **wight:** person.   **84. ther-as:** where.   **list yeve:**
wishes to give.   **85. mayde:** virgin.   **86. nathelees:** nevertheless.   **87. wolde:** wished.   **88. nys but:** is no more than.
89. yaf: gave.   **90–92. So . . . bigamye:** So there is no reproach
in marrying (again), if my mate die, not excepting the reproach
directed against remarriage (bigamy).   **93. Al:** although.
95. tow t' assemble: tow (tinder) to bring together.   **97. This
. . . som:** all in all.   **98. freletee:** frailty.   **99. clepe:** call.
but if that:** unless.   **100. leden al hir:** lead all their.   **102. pre-
ferre:** be exalted over.   **103. liketh hem:** pleases them.   **goost:**
spirit.   **107. been:** are.   **tree:** wood.   **108. sondry wyse:** various ways.   **109. everich:** each.   **propre yifte:** individual gift.
110. shifte: to ordain.   **113. welle:** the source.   **116. folwe:**
follow.   **foore:** way.   **117. hem:** those.

121. conclusioun: purpose.   **122. maad:** made.   **123. wys . . .
y-wrought:** manner a person constructed.   **125. Glose:** interpret.   **127. oure . . . thynges:** the organs of us both.   **130. woot:**
knows.   **131. So that:** as long as.   **132. maked been:** are made.
133. office: function.   **ese:** assistance.   **134. engendrure:** procreation.   **ther:** wherein.   **135. ellis:** otherwise.   **hir:** their.
136. yelde: pay.   **dette:** debt.   **138. ne:** not.   **sely:** good.
139. Thanne: therefore.   **141. holde:** required.   **142. swich
harneys:** such equipment.   **143. hem:** them (it).   **144. cure:**
heed.   **146. sith that:** since.   **148. nyl:** will (not).   **149. hem:**
them (virgins).   **breed:** bread.   **pured whete:** finest wheat.
150. hote: be called.   **151. Mark:** It is actually John who specifically mentions barley loaves (6:9) in the miracle of the loaves
and fishes.   **154. nam . . . precius:** am not fastidious.   **157. daungerous:** unyielding.   **158. morwe:** morning.   **159. Whan . . .
list:** when it pleases him to.   **160. lette:** desist.   **161. thral:**
slave.   **162. withal:** besides.

I have the power duryng al my lyf
Upon his propre° body, and nat he.
Right thus th' apostle tolde it unto me
And bad oure housbondes for to love us wel.
Al this sentence° me liketh every del."°

Up stirte° the Pardoner, and that anon.
"Now dame," quod he, "by God and by Seint
John,   170
Ye been° a noble prechour in this cas.
I was aboute to wedde a wyf. Allas,
What° sholde I bye° it on my flessh so deere?°
Yet hadde I levere° wedde no wyf to-yeere."°

"Abyde," quod she. "My tale is nat bigonne.
Nay, thow shalt drynken on another tonne,°
Er that° I go, shal savoure° wors than ale.
And whan that I have toold thee forth my tale
Of tribulacioun in mariage,
Of which I am expert in al myn age, —   180
This is to seye, myself hath been the whippe,° —
Thanne maystow chese° whether thow wolt sippe
Of thilke° tonne that I shal abroche.°
Be war of it er thow to neigh° approche,
For I shal telle ensamples mo than ten.
'Who so that nyl° be war° by othere men,
By hym shal othere men corrected be.'
Thise same wordes writeth Ptholome.°
Rede in his *Almageste,* and take it there."

"Dame, I wolde praye yow, if youre wil were,"
Seyde this Pardoner, "as ye bigan,   191
Telle forth youre tale, spareth° for no man,
And teche us yonge men of youre praktyke."°

"Gladly," quod she, "sith° it may yow lyke.°
But that I praye to al this compaignye,
If that I speke after my fantasye,°
As taketh nat agrief of that° I seye,
For myn entente nys but° for to pleye.

"Now, sire, thanne wol I telle yow forth my tale.
As evere moot° I drynke wyn and ale,   200
I shal seye sooth,° tho° housbondes that I hadde,
As three° of hem were goode, and two were badde.
The thre were goode men, and riche, and olde.
Unnethe myghte° they the statut holde°
In which that they were bounden unto me.
Ye woot° wel what I mene of this, pardee.°
As help me God, I laughe whan I thynke

How pitously° a° nyght I made hem swynke°
And, by my fey,° I tolde° of it no stoor.°
They hadde me yeven° hir land and hir tresoor.
Me neded nat do lenger diligence   211
To wynne hir love or doon hem reverence.
They loved me so wel, by God above,
That I ne tolde no deyntee of hir° love.
A wys womman wol bisye hire evere in oon°
To gete hir love, ye,° ther-as° she hath noon.
But sith I hadde hem hoolly in myn hond,°
And sith they hadde yeven me al hir lond,
What° sholde I take kepe° hem for to plese
But it were° for my profit and myn ese?   220
I sette hem so awerke,° by my fey,
That many a nyght they songen 'Weylawey!'°
The bacon was nat fet° for hem, I trowe,°
That som men han° in Essex at Donmowe.°
I governed hem so wel after my lawe
That ech of hem ful blisful was and fawe°
To brynge me gaye thynges fro the feyre.°
They were ful glad whan I spak to hem feyre,°
For, God it woot, I chidde° hem spitously.°

"Now herkneth how I bar° me properly,   230
Ye wise wyves that konne° understonde.

"Thus sholde ye speke and bere hem wrong on
honde,°
For half so boldely kan ther no man
Swere and lyen° as a womman kan.
I sey nat this by° wyves that ben wyse
But if it be° whan they hem mysavyse.°
A wys wyf, if that she kan hir° good,
Shal beren hym on hond° the cow° is wood°
And take witnesse of hir owene mayde
Of hir assent.° But herkneth how I sayde: 240
"'Sire olde kaynard,° is this thyn array?
Why is my neighebores wyf so gay?
She is honoured over al ther° she goth.
I sitte at hoom, I have no thrifty cloth.°
What dostow° at my neighebores hous?

165. propre: own.   168. sentence: verdict.   del: part.
169. stirte: started.   171. been: are.   173. What: why.   bye:
pay for.   deere: dearly.   174. levere: rather.   to-yeere: this
year.   176. tonne: cask.   177. Er that: before.   shal savoure:
(which) will taste.   181. myself . . . whippe: I have been the whip.
182. maystow chese: may you choose.   183. thilke: that same.
abroche: broach.   184. to neigh: too near.   186. nyl: will not.
war: warned.   188. Pthitholeme: Ptolemy of Alexandria, the
author of an astronomical treatise known as the *Almagest,* to
whom the sayings here and in ll. 332–33 were apocryphally
attributed.   192. spareth: hold back.   193. praktyke: practice.
194. sith: since.   lyke: please.   196. after my fantasye: according to my notions.   197. As . . . that: take no offense at what.
198. nys but: is only.   200. moot: may.   201. sooth: truly.
tho: those.   202. As three: three.   204. Unnethe myghte:
hardly could.   holde: obey.   206. woot: know.   pardee: certainly.

208. pitously: pitifully.   a: at.   swynke: toil.   209. fey: faith.
tolde: took.   stoor: account.   210. me yeven: given me.
214. ne . . . hir: set no value on their.   215. bisye . . . oon:
exert herself continually.   216. ye: certainly.   ther-as: where.
217. hond: control.   219. What: why.   kepe: heed.   220. But
it were: except.   221. awerke: to work.   222. 'Weylawey!':
'Alas!'   223. fet: fat.   trowe: believe.   224. han: have.
Donmowe: The Dunmow Priory awarded a flitch of bacon to
any married couple who could swear that they had enjoyed a
whole year of marriage in complete contentment.   226. fawe:
glad.   227. feyre: fair.   228. feyre: graciously.   229. chidde:
chid.   spitously: spitefully.   230. bar: conducted.   231. konne:
can.   232. bere . . . honde: deceive them.   234. lyen: lie.
235. by: about.   236. But . . . be: except.   hem mysavyse:
fall in error.   237. kan hir: knows her own.   238. Shal . . . hond:
will maintain to him that.   cow: chough (jackdaw).   wood:
mad.   According to a folk tale, the chough told its master
that his wife was unfaithful, but the wife was able to persuade
him that the bird was insane, and so the husband killed it.
240. assent: agreement (that it was mad).   241. kaynard:
dotard. In ll. 241–384 the Wife provides a sample of the kind of
argument she used against all of her first three old husbands.
243. over al ther: everywhere.   244. thrifty cloth: good dress.
245. dostow: do you do.

Is she so fair? Artow so amorous?
What rowne° ye with oure mayde? *Benedicite,°*
Sire olde lechour, lat thy japes° be!
And if I have a gossib° or a freend
Withouten gilt,° ye chiden as a feend   250
If that I walke or pleye unto his hous.
Thow comest hoom as dronken as a mous
And prechest on thy bench, with yvel preef!°
Thow seyst to me it is a greet meschief
To wedde a poure womman, for costage;°
And if that she be riche, of heigh parage,°
Thanne sei·tow° that it is a tormentrye°
To suffre hir pryde and hir malencolye;
And if that she be fair, thow verray knave,
Thow seist that every holour° wol hire have;   260
She may no while in chastitee abyde
That is assayled upon ech a° syde.

  "'Thow seyst som folk desire us for richesse,
Somme for oure shap,° and somme for oure fair-
  nesse,
And somme for° she kan either synge or daunce,
And somme for gentillesse° and daliaunce,°
Somme for hir handes and hir armes smale.°
Thus goth° al to the devel, by thy tale.°
Thow seyst men may nat kepe a castel wal,
It may so longe assailled been over al.°   270

  "'And if that she be foul, thow seyst that she
Coveiteth every man that she may se,
For as a spanyel she wol on hym lepe
Til that she fynde som man hir to chepe.°
Ne noon so grey goos° goth ther in the lake
As, seistow, wol be withoute make,°
And seyst° it is an hard thyng for to welde
A thyng that no man wol, his thankes,° helde.°
Thus seistow, lorel,° whan thow goost to bedde,
And that no wys man nedeth for to wedde   280
Ne no man that entendeth° unto hevene.
With wilde thonder dynt° and firy levene°
Moote° thy welked° nekke be to-broke.°

  "'Thow seyst that droppyng° houses, and eek
  smoke,
And chidyng wyves maken men to flee
Out of hir owene houses. A! *Benedicitee!*
What eyleth° swich an old man for to chide?

  "'Thow seyst we wyves will oure vices hide
Til we be fast,° and thanne we wol hem shewe!°

Wel may that be a proverbe of a shrewe!   290
  "'Thow seist that oxen, asses, hors,° and
  houndes,
They been assayed° at diverse stoundes,°
Bacynes,° lavours,° er that men hem bye,°
Spoones, stooles, and al swich housbondrye,
And so be pottes, clothes, and array;
But folk of wyves maken noon assay
Til they be wedded, olde dotard shrewe!
And thanne, seistow, we wil oure vices shewe!

  "'Thow seist also that it displeseth me
But if that° thow wolt preise my beautee,   300
And but thow poure° alwey upon my face
And clepe° me "faire dame" in every place,
And but thow make a feeste° on thilke° day
That I was born, and make me fressh and gay,
And but thow do to my norice° honour,
And to my chambrere° withinne my bour,°
And to my fadres° folk and his allyes.°
Thus seistow, olde barel ful of lyes!

  "'And yet of oure apprentice Jankyn,
For his crisp heer° shynyng as gold so fyn,   310
And for he squyereth me bothe up and doun,
Yet hastow caught a fals suspecioun.
I wil° hym nat, thogh thow were deed tomorwe.

  "'But tel me this. Why hidestow,° with sorwe,°
The keyes of thy cheste awey fro me?
It is my good° as wel as thyn, pardee.
What? Wenestow° make an ydiot of oure dame?°
Now, by that lord that called is Seint Jame,°
Thou shalt noght bothe, thogh thow were wood,
Be maister of my body and of my good.°   320
That oon° thow shalt forgo, maugree° thyne eyen.
What helpeth it of me enquere° and spyen?°
I trowe thow woldest loke° me in thy chiste.°
Thow sholdest seye, "Wyf, go wher thee liste.°
Taak youre disport. I nyl nat leve no talys.°
I knowe yow for a trewe wyf, dame Alys."
We love no man that taketh kepe° or charge°
Wher that we goon. We wol been at oure large.°

  "'Of alle men y-blessed moot he be,
The wise astrologen,° daun Ptholome,°   330
That seith this proverbe in his *Almageste:*
"Of alle men his wisdom is hyeste
That rekketh° nat who hath the world in honde."°

---

247. rowne: whisper.   *Benedicite:* God bless you.   248. japes:
tricks.   249. gossib: companion.   250. Withouten gilt: innocently.   253. with . . . preef!: bad luck to you!   255. for costage: because of expense.   256. heigh parage: noble extraction.
257. seistow: you say.   tormentrye: torment.   260. holour:
adulterer.   262. ech a: every.   264. shap: shape.   265. for:
because.   266. gentillesse: gentleness.   daliaunce: flirtation.   267. smale: slender.   268. goth: goes.   tale: account.
270. over al: at all points.   274. hir to chepe: to traffic with
her.   275. Ne . . . goos: and no goose so gray.   276. make: mate.
277. seyst: (you) say.   welde: control.   278. his thankes:
willingly.   helde: hold.   279. lorel: wretch.   281. entendeth: aims.   282. dynt: stroke.   levene: lightning.   283. Moote:
may.   welked: withered.   to-broke: broken.   284. droppyng:
leaking.   287. eyleth: ails.   289. fast: wed.   shewe: show.

291. hors: horses.   292. assayed: tested.   stoundes: times
293. Bacynes: basins.   lavours: washbowls.   bye: buy.
300. But if that: unless.   301. poure: pore.   302. clepe: call.
303. feeste: celebration.   thilke: the same.   305. norice:
nurse.   306. chambrere: chambermaid.   bour: room.   307. fadres:
father's.   allyes: connections.   310. crisp heer: curly hair.
313. wil: wish.   314. hidestow: do you hide.   with sorwe: grief
upon it.   316. good: property.   317. Wenestow: do you
expect to.   of . . . dame: of me.   318. Jame: James (of Compostela).   320. good: wealth.   321. That oon: the one (or other).
maugree: despite.   322. enquere: to inquire.   spyen: spy
323. loke: lock.   chiste: chest.   324. liste: it pleases.   325. nyl . . .
talys: won't believe any tales.   327. kepe: note.   charge: heed
328. oure large: liberty.   330. astrologen: astrologer.   daun
Ptholome: Master Ptolemy (see l. 188n.).   333. rekketh: cares.
hath in honde: owns.

By this proverbe thow shalt understonde,
"Have thow ynogh. What thar thee° rekke or care
How myrily that othere folkes fare?"
For certes, olde dotard, by youre leve,
Ye shal han queynte° right ynogh at eve.
He is to° greet a nygard that wil werne°
A man to lighte a candel at his lanterne;   340
He shal han never the lasse light, pardee.
Have thow ynogh! Thee thar nat pleyne thee.°
    "'Thow seist also that if we make us gay
With clothyng and with precious array,
That it is peril of oure chastitee;
And yet, with sorwe,° thow most enforce thee°
And seye thise wordes in th' apostles name:
"In habit° maad with chastitee and shame°
Ye wommen shal apparaille yow," quod he,
"And nat in tressed heer° and gay perree°   350
As° perles, ne with gold, ne clothes riche."
After° thy text, ne after thy rubriche,°
I wol nat werke as muchel° as a gnat.
    "'Thow seydest this, that I was lyk a cat.
For who so wolde senge° a cattes skyn,
Than wolde the cat wel dwellen in his in;°
And if the cattes skyn be slyk° and gay,
She wol nat dwelle in house half a day,
But forth she wole er° any day be dawed°
To shewe hir skyn and goon a-caterwawed.°   360
This is to seye, if I be gay, sire shrewe,
I wol renne° out, my borel° for to shewe.
    "'Sire olde fool, what helpeth° thee t' espyen?°
Thogh thow preye Argus with his hundred eyen
To be my warde-corps,° as he kan best,
In feith, he shal nat kepe me but me lest.°
Yet koude I make his berd,° so moot I thee!°
    "'Thow seydest eek that ther ben thynges three,
The whiche thynges troublen al this erthe,
And that no wight° may endure the ferthe.°   370
O leeve° sire shrewe, Jesu shorte° thy lyf!
Yet prechestow and seist° an hateful wyf
Y-rekened is for oon of thise myschaunces.
Been ther noone othere resemblaunces
That ye may likne youre parables to
But if° a sely° wyf be oon of tho?°
    "'Thow liknest eek wommanes love to helle,

To bareyne lond ther° water may nat dwelle.
    "'Thow liknest it also to wilde fyr,
The moore it brenneth,° the moore it hath
        desyr   380
To consume every thyng that brent wol be.
Thow seist, right° as wormes shende° a tree,
Right so a wyf destroyeth hir housbonde;
This knowen they that been to wyves bonde.'°
    "Lordynges, right thus, as ye han understonde,
Bar I stifly° myne olde housbondes on honde°
That thus they seyden in hir° dronkenesse,
And al was fals, but° that I took witnesse
On Jankyn, and on my nece also.
O Lord, the peyne I dide hem and the wo   390
Ful giltlees, by Goddes swete pyne!°
For as an hors I koude byte° and whyne.°
I koude pleyne and° I was in the gilt,
Or elles often tyme I hadde been spilt.°
Who so that first to mille comth, first grynt.°
I pleyned first; so was oure werre stynt.°
They were ful glad to excusen hem ful blyve°
Of thyng° of which they nevere agilte hir lyve.°
    "Of wenches wolde I beren hem on honde
Whan that for syk° they myghte unnethe° stonde.
Yet tikled I his herte, for that he   401
Wende° that I hadde of hym so greet chiertee.°
I swoor that al my walkyng out by nyghte
Was for to espye wenches that he dighte.°
Under that colour° hadde I many a myrthe.
For al swich wit° is yeven° us in oure birthe;
Deceite, wepyng, spynnyng God hath yeve
To wommen kyndely° whil they may lyve.
And thus of o° thyng I avaunte me:°
Atte° ende I hadde the bet° in each degree,   410
By sleighte, or force, or by som maner° thyng,
As° by continuel murmur or grucchyng.°
Namely° abedde hadden they meschaunce;
Ther wolde I chide and do° hem no plesaunce;°
I wolde no lenger in the bed abyde
If that I felte his arm over my syde
Til he hadde maad his raunceon° unto me.
Thanne wolde I suffre° hym do his nycetee.°
And ther-fore every man this tale I telle,
Wynne who so may, for al is for to selle.°   420

335. What . . . thee: why need you.   338. han queynte: have intercourse.   339. to: too.   werne: refuse.   342. Thee . . . thee: you need not complain.   346. with sorwe: grief upon it! enforce thee: reinforce yourself.   348. habit: clothing.   shame: modesty.   350. tressed heer: braided hair.   perree: jewelry. 351. As: such as.   352. After: according to.   rubriche: rubric (direction).   353. muchel: much.   355. senge: singe.   356. wel . . . in: willingly stay in its home.   357. slyk: sleek.   359. er: before.   dawed: dawned.   360. goon a-caterwawed: go cater-wauling.   362. renne: run.   borel: clothing.   363. helpeth: does it help.   t' espyen: to spy.   365. warde-corps: guardian. 366. but me lest: unless it pleases me.   367. make . . . berd: outwit him.   moot I thee: may I prosper.   370. wight: one. ferthe: fourth. According to Prov. 30:21-23, one of four intolerable misfortunes is "an odious woman when she is married." 371. leeve: dear.   shorte: shorten.   372. seist: say.   376. But if: unless.   sely: poor.   tho: those.

378. ther: where.   380. brenneth: burns.   382. right: just. shende: destroy.   384. bonde: bound.   386. Bar on honde: accused.   stifly: boldly.   387. hir: their.   388. but: except. 391. swete pyne: precious suffering.   392. byte: bite (crossly). whyne: whinny (nicely).   393. pleyne and: complain if. 394. spilt: ruined.   395. grynt: grinds.   396. werre stynt: war stopped.   397. blyve: speedily.   398. thyng: something.   agilte . . . lyve: were guilty in their lives.   400. syk: sickness.   myghte unnethe: could hardly.   402. Wende: believed.   chiertee: affection.   404. dighte: lay with.   405. colour: pretext.   406. wit: ingenuity.   yeven: given.   408. kyndely: by nature. 409. o: one.   avaunte me: boast.   410. Atte: at the.   bet: better. 411. maner: sort of.   412. As: such as.   grucchyng: grumbling. 413. Namely: particularly.   414. do: show.   plesaunce: affection.   417. raunceon: ransom.   418. suffre: allow.   nycetee: will.   420. Wynne . . . selle: gain whoever can (from this tale), for all things are for sale (in love).

With empty hond men may none haukes lure.
For wynnyng wolde I al his lust endure
And make me a feyned appetit,
And yet in bacoun° hadde I nevere delit.
That made me that evere I wolde hem chyde,
For, though the Pope had seten hem bisyde,°
I wolde noght spare hem at hir owene bord,
For, by my trouthe, I quytte° hem word for word.
As help me verray God omnipotent,
Thogh I right now sholde make my testament, 430
I ne owe hem nat a word that it nys quyt.°
I broghte it so aboute by my wit
That they moste yeve it up as for the beste,
Or elles hadde we nevere been in reste.
For thogh he looked as a wood leoun,°
Yet sholde he faille of his conclusioun.°
   "Thanne wolde I seye, 'Good lief,° taak keep°
How mekely looketh Wilkyn oure sheep.
Com neer, my spouse. Lat me ba° thy cheke.
Ye sholden be al pacient and meke 440
And han a swete, spiced° conscience,
Sith° ye so preche of Jobes pacience.
Suffreth alwey, syn° ye so wel kan preche.
And, but° ye do, certeyn we shal yow teche
That it is fair to han a wyf in pees.
Oon of us two moste bowen,° doutelees.
And, sith a man is moore reasonable
Than womman is, ye mosten° been suffrable.°
What eyleth° yow to grucche thus and grone?
Is it for° ye wolde have my queynte° allone? 450
Wy!° Taak it al! Lo, have it every del.°
Peter!° I shrewe° yow but ye love it wel!
For if I wolde selle my *bele chose*,°
I koude walke as fressh as is a rose.
But I wol kepe it for youre owene tooth.
Ye be to blame, by God. I sey yow sooth.'°
   "Swiche manere° wordes hadde we on honde.
Now wol I speke of my ferthe° housbonde.
   "My ferthe housbonde was a revelour,°—
This is to seyn, he hadde a paramour°— 460
And I was yong and ful of ragerye,°
Stibourne and strong, and joly as a pye.°
How koude I daunce to an harpe smale
And syng, ywys,° as any nyghtyngale
Whan I had dronke a draughte of swete wyn!
Metellius, the foule cherl, the swyn,
That with a staf birafte° his wyf hir lyf

For she drank wyn, though° I hadde been his wyf,
Ne sholde nat han daunted me fro drynke!
And after wyn, on Venus moste° I thynke, 470
For also siker° as coold engendreth hayl,
A likerous° mouth moste han a likerous tayl.
In womman vynolent° is no defence°—
This knowen lechours by experience.
   "But, Lord Crist, whan that it remembreth me°
Upon my youthe and on my jolytee,
It tikeleth me aboute myn herte roote.°
Unto this day it dooth myn herte boote°
That I have had my world as in my tyme.
But age, allas, that al wole envenyme,° 480
Hath me biraft my beautee and my pith.
Lat go! Far well! The devel go ther-with!
The flour° is goon; ther is namoore to telle.
The bren° as I best kan now moste I selle.
But yet to be right murye wol I fonde.°
Now wol I tellen of my ferthe housbonde.
   "I seye, I hadde in herte gret despit°
That he of any oother had delit.
But he was quyt,° by God and by Seint Joce!°
I made hym of the same wode° a croce.° 490
Nat of my body, in no foul manere,
But certeynly I made folk swich cheere°
That in his owene grece I made hym frye
For angre and for verray jalousye.
By God, in erthe I was his purgatorie,
For which I hope his soule be in glorie.
For God it woot, he sat ful ofte and song°
Whan that his shoo ful bitterly hym wrong.°
Ther was no wight save God and he that wiste,°
In many wise,° how soore I hym twiste.° 500
He deyde whan I cam from Jerusalem
And lyth y-grave° under the roode beem,°
Al° is his toumbe noght so curyous°
As was the sepulcre of hym Daryus°
Which that Appelles° wroghte subtilly.
It nys but wast° to burye hym preciously.°
Lat hym fare wel, God gyve his soule reste.
He is now in his grave and in his cheste.
   "Now of my fifthe housbonde wol I telle,
God lat his soule nevere come in helle! 510
And yet was he to me the mooste shrewe.°

424. **bacoun:** old meat.   426. **seten . . . bisyde:** sat beside them.
428. **quyt:** requited.   431. **it . . . quyt:** isn't requited (already).
435. **wood leoun:** mad lion.   436. **conclusioun:** purpose.
437. **lief:** dear.   **taak keep:** take notice.   439. **ba:** kiss.
441. **spiced:** scrupulous.   442. **Sith:** since.   443. **syn:** since.
444. **but:** unless.   446. **bowen:** yield.   448. **mosten:** must.
suffrable: patient.   449. **eyleth:** ails.   450. **for:** because.
queynte: genitals.   451. **Wy:** why.   **del:** part.   452. **Peter!:**
by St. Peter.   **shrewe:** curse.   453. *bele chose:* genitals.
456. **sooth:** truth.   457. **manere:** kind of.   458. **ferthe:** fourth.
459. **revelour:** playboy.   460. **paramour:** mistress.   461. **ragerye:** wildness.   462. **pye:** magpie.   464. **ywys:** indeed.
467. **birafte:** bereft.

468. **though:** if.   470. **moste:** must.   471. **also siker:** as surely.
472. **likerous:** lecherous.   473. **vynolent:** wine-filled.   **defence:**
resistance.   475. **whan . . . me:** when I look back.   477. **herte
roote:** heart's root.   478. **boote:** good.   480. **al . . . envenyme:**
will envenom all.   483. **flour:** flower.   484. **bren:** bran.
485. **fonde:** try.   487. **despit:** spite.   489. **quyt:** paid back.
Seint Joce: a Breton saint.   490. **wode:** wood.   **croce:** stick
(to beat him with).   492. **made . . . cheere:** behaved to people
so.   497. **song:** sang.   498. **wrong:** pinched.   499. **wiste:**
knew.   500. **wise:** ways.   **twiste:** tortured.   502. **lyth y-grave:**
lies buried.   **roode beem:** crucifix beam between the nave and
chancel.   (Wealthy people were often buried inside the church.)
503. **Al:** even if.   **curyous:** intricate.   504. **hym Daryus:**
(King) Darius III, who was buried by his conqueror, Alexander.
505. **Appelles:** Apelles, the celebrated Greek artist and friend
of Alexander.   506. **nys . . . wast:** is only a waste.   **preciously:**
expensively.   511. **mooste shrewe:** greatest scold.

That feele I on my ribbes al by rewe°
And evere shal unto myn endyng day.
But in oure bed he was so fressh and gay,
And ther-with-al so wel koude he me glose,°
Whan that he wolde han my *bele chose,*
That, thogh he hadde me bet° on every bon,°
He koude wynne agayn my love anon.°
I trowe I loved hym best for that° he
Was of his love daungerous° to me.   520
We wommen han, if that I shal nat lye,
In this matere a queynte fantasye.°
Wayte-what° thyng we may nat lightly° have,
Ther-after wol we crye al day and crave.
Forbede us thyng,° and that desiren we.
Presse on us faste, and thanne wol we fle.°
With daunger oute° we al oure chaffare;°
Greet prees° at market maketh deere ware,
And to° greet cheep° is holde at litel prys.°
This knoweth every womman that is wys.   530
  "My fifthe housbonde, God his soule blesse,
Which that I took for love and no richesse,
He som tyme was a clerk of Oxenford°
And hadde laft scole and wente at hom° to bord
With my gossyb° dwellyng in oure toun;
God have hir soule, hir name was Alisoun.
She knew myn herte and eek my pryvetee°
Bet° than oure parissh preest, so mote I thee!°
To hire biwreyed° I my conseil al,
For hadde myn housbonde pissed on a wal   540
Or doon a thyng that sholde have cost his lyf,
To hire and to another worthy wyf
And to my nece, which that I loved wel,
I wolde han toold his conseil every del°
And so I dide ful often, God it woot,
That made his face often reed° and hoot
For verray shame, and blamed° hymself for he
Hadde toold to me so greet a pryvetee.
  "And so bifel that ones in a Lente —
So often tymes I to my gossyb wente,   550
For evere yet I loved to be gay
And for to walke in March, Aprill, and May
From hous to hous to here sondry tales —
That Jankyn clerk, and my gossyb dame Alys,
And I myself into the feeldes wente.
Myn housbonde was at Londoun al that Lente;
I hadde the bettre leyser° for to pleye,
And for to se, and eek for to be seye,°

Of lusty° folk. What wiste° I wher my grace°
Was shapen for to be,° or in what place?   560
Ther-fore I made my visitacions
To vigilies° and to processions,
To prechyng eek, and to thise pilgrymages,
To pleyes of myracles and mariages,
And wered upon° my gaye scarlet gytes.°
Thise wormes, ne thise moththes, ne thise mytes,
Upon° my peril, frete° hem nevere a del.
And wostow° why? For they were used wel!
  "Now wol I tellen forth what happed° me.
I seye that in the feeldes walked we   570
Til trewely we hadde swich daliaunce,
This clerk and I, that, of my purveiaunce,°
I spak to hym and seyde hym how that he,
If I were wydewe,° sholde wedde me.
For certeynly, I seye for no bobaunce,°
Yet was I nevere withouten purveiaunce
Of mariage n' of° othere thynges eek.
I holde a mouses herte nat worth a leek
That hath but oon hole for to sterte° to,
And if that faille, thanne is al y-do.°   580
  "I bar hym on honde° he hadde enchanted
        me, —
My dame° taughte me that soutiltee —
And eek I seyde I mette° of hym al nyght,
He wolde han slayn me as I lay upright,°
And al my bed was ful of verray° blood:
'But yet I hope that ye shal do me good,
For blood bitokeneth° gold, as me was taught.'
And al was fals. I dremed of it right naught,
But as I folwed ay my dames loore°
As wel of that as of othere thynges moore.   590
  "But now, sire, lat me se. What shal I seyn?°
A ha, by God, I have my tale ageyn!
  "Whan that my fourthe housbonde was on
        beere,°
I weep algate° and made sory cheere,
As wyves mooten,° for it is usage,°
And with my coverchief° covered my visage.
But, for that I was purveyed° of a make,°
I wepte but smal, and that I undertake.°
  "To chirche was myn housbonde born amorwe°
With neghebores that for hym maden sorwe,   600
And Jankyn oure clerk was oon of tho.°
As help me God, whan that I saw hym go

512. al by rewe: each in order. 515. glose: interpret. 517. bet:
beaten. bon: bone. 518. anon: immediately. 519. for that:
because. 520. daungerous: reluctant. 522. queynte fantasye:
quaint fancy. 523. Wayte-what: whatever. lightly: easily.
525. thyng: something. 526. fle: flee. 527. daunger oute:
(apparent) reluctance offer. chaffare: wares. 528. prees:
demand. 529. to: too. cheep: cheapness. prys: esteem.
533. a . . . Oxenford: an Oxford student. 534. at hom: in a
private home. 535. gossyb: friend. 537. pryvetee: secrets.
538. Bet: better. mote I thee!: may I prosper. 539. biwreyed:
revealed. 544. del: part. 546. reed: red. 547. blamed: (he)
blamed. 557. leyser: leisure. 558. seye: seen.

559. lusty: pleasure-loving. What wiste: how knew. grace:
favor. 560. shapen . . . be: destined to be granted. 562. vigilies: festivals on eves of saints' days. 565. wered upon: wore.
gytes: gowns. 567. Upon: at. frete: ate. 568. wostow: do
you know. 569. happed: happened to. 572. of my purveiaunce: out of foresight. 574. wydewe: widow. 575. bobaunce:
boast. 577. n' of: nor of. 579. sterte: run. 580. is al y-do:
all is up. 581. bar . . . honde: made him think. 582. dame:
mother. 583. mette: dreamed. 584. upright: face-up.
585. verray: real. 587. bitokeneth: signifies (in dreams).
589. loore: teaching. 591. shal I seyn?: am I about to say?
593. beere: his bier. 594. algate: constantly. 595. mooten:
must. usage: the custom. 596. coverchief: kerchief. 597. purveyed: provided. make: mate. 598. undertake: vouch for.
599. amorwe: the next morning. 601. tho: those.

After the beere, me thoughte he hadde a paire
Of legges and of feet so clene and faire
That al myn herte I yaf° unto his hoold.
He was, I trowe, twenty wynter oold,
And I was fourty, if I shal seye sooth;°
But yet I hadde alwey a coltes° tooth.
Gat-tothed° I was, and that bicam° me weel.
I hadde the preente° of seynt Venus seel.°   610
As help me God, I was a lusty oon,
And fair and riche and yong and wel bigoon,°
And trewely, as myne housbondes tolde me,
I hadde the beste *quonyam* mighte° be.
For certes I am al Venerien°
In feelyng, and myn herte is Marcien.°
Venus me yaf my lust, my likerousnesse,°
And Mars yaf me my sturdy hardynesse.°
Myn ascendent° was Taur,° and Mars ther-inne.
Allas, allas, that evere love was synne!   620
I folwed ay myn inclinacioun
By vertu° of my constellacioun,
That made me I koude noght withdrawe
My chambre of Venus from a good felawe;
Yet have I Martes° mark upon my face
And also in another pryvee° place.
For God so wysely be my savacioun,°
I loved nevere by no° discrecioun
But evere folwed myn appetit
Al were he° short, long, blak, or whit.   630
I took no kepe,° so that° he liked° me,
How poure he was, ne eek of what degree.°
    "What sholde I seye, but at the monthes ende
This joly clerk Jankyn that was so hende°
Hath wedded me with greet solempnytee!°
And to hym yaf I al the lond and fee°
That evere was me yeven° ther bifore,
But afterward repented me ful sore.
He nolde suffre° nothyng of my list.°
By God, he smoot me ones° on the lyst,°   640
For that I rente out of his book a leef,
That of the strook myn ere wex° al deef.
Stibourne° I was as is a leonesse
And of my tonge a verray jangleresse,°
And walke I wolde as I hadde doon biforn
From hous to hous, al thogh he hadde it sworn;°

For which he often tymes wolde preche,
And me of olde Romayn gestes° teche,
How he Symplicius Gallus lafte his wif
And hire forsook for terme° of al his lif   650
Noght but for open-heveded° he hir say°
Lokyng out at his dore upon a day.
    "Another Romayn tolde he me by name
That, for his wyf was at a someres° game
Withouten his wityng,° he forsook hire eke.
And thanne wolde he upon his Bible seke
That ilke° proverbe of Ecclesiaste°
Where he comandeth, and forbedeth faste,°
Man shal nat suffre his wyf go roule° aboute.   659
Thanne wolde he seye right thus, withouten doute,
    "'Who so that buyldeth his hous al of salwes,°
And priketh° his blynde hors over the falwes,°
And suffreth his wyf to go seken halwes°
Is worthy to ben hanged on the galwes.'°
But al for noght. I sette° noght an hawe°
Of° his proverbes n' of his olde sawe,°
Ne I wolde nat of° hym corrected be.
I hate hym that my vices telleth me,
And so doo mo,° God woot, of us than I.
This made hym with me wood al outrely.°   670
I nolde noght forbere° hym in no cas.
    "Now wol I sey yow sooth, by Seint Thomas,
Why that I rente° out of his book a leef,
For which he smoot me so that I was deef.
    "He hadde a book that gladly nyght and day
For his disport° he wolde rede alway;
He cleped° it *Valerie and Theofraste,*°
At which book he lough° alwey ful faste.°
And eek ther was som tyme a clerk at Rome,
A cardynal that highte° Seint Jerome,   680
That made a book agayn Jovinian,°
In which book eek ther was Tertulan,°
Crisippus, Trotula,° and Helowys,°
That was abbesse nat fer fro Parys,

648. **Romayn gestes:** Roman stories.   650. **terme:** the remainder.   651. **Noght . . . open-heveded:** only because bareheaded. **say:** saw.   654. **someres:** summer's.   655. **wityng:** knowledge.   657. **ilke:** same.   **Ecclesiaste:** Ecclus. 25:25.   658. **faste:** strictly.   659. **roule:** gad.   661. **salwes:** willow twigs.   662. **priketh:** spurs.   **falwes:** fallow ground.   663. **seken halwes:** seeking pilgrim shrines.   664. **galwes:** gallows.   665. **sette:** cared. **hawe:** haw (hawthorn fruit).   666. **Of:** for.   **sawe:** lore. 667. **of:** by.   669. **mo:** more.   670. **wood al outrely:** utterly furious.   671. **nolde . . . forbere:** would not forgive.   673. **rente:** tore.   676. **disport:** amusement.   677. **cleped:** called.   *Valerie . . . Theofraste:* the title of Jankin's book is derived from Walter Map's *Letter of Valerius Against Marriage* (twelfth century) and Theophrastus's *Golden Book on Marriage* (third century B.C., known only in later translation). Like other medieval manuscript volumes, it contained a miscellaneous collection of texts and excerpts.   678. **lough:** laughed.   **faste:** hard.   680. **highte:** was called.   681. **Jovinian:** Jerome (fifth century) refuted the heretical Jovinian, who held that marriage was not inferior to celibacy.   682. **Tertulan:** Tertullian (third century).   683. **Crisippus, Trotula:** two unidentified authors.   **Helowys:** Héloïse, Abélard's mistress (twelfth century), who later became a nun. (See Pope's *Eloïsa to Abelard,* below, p. 784).

605. **yaf:** gave.   607. **sooth:** truth.   608. **coltes:** colt's, i.e., frisky.   609. **Gat-tothed:** gap-toothed (see *Gen. Prol.,* l. 468). **bicam:** suited.   610. **preente:** imprint.   **seel:** birthmark, i.e., I was born for love.   612. **bigoon:** contented.   614. *quonyam* **mighte:** genitals (that) could.   615. **Venerien:** influenced by Venus. (See Note A, p. 195.)   616. **Marcien:** influenced by Mars.   617. **likerousnesse:** lecherousness.   618. **hardynesse:** boldness.   619. **ascendent:** sign at birth.   **Taur:** Taurus (Venus's mansion).   622. **vertu:** influence.   625. **Martes:** Mars's. 626. **pryvee:** private.   627. **savacioun:** salvation.   628. **by no:** according to any.   630. **Al . . . he:** whether he were.   631. **kepe:** heed.   **so that:** as long as.   **liked:** pleased.   632. **degree:** rank. 634. **hende:** fine.   635. **solempnytee:** splendor.   636. **fee:** property.   637. **yeven:** given.   639. **nolde suffre:** would (not) allow. **list:** pleasure.   640. **ones:** once.   **lyst:** ear.   642. **wex:** grew. 643. **Stibourne:** stubborn.   644. **verray jangleresse:** real prattler.   646. **it sworn:** sworn against it.

And eek the Parables° of Salomon,
Ovydes *Art*,° and bokes many on;°
And alle thise were bounden in o° volume.
And every nyght and day was his custume,
Whan he hadde leyser and vacacioun
From oother worldly occupacioun,   690
To reden in this book of wikked wyves.
He knew of hem mo legendes and lyves
Than been of good wyves in the Bible.
For trusteth wel, it is an inpossible°
That any clerk wol speke good of wyves
But if° it be of holy seintes lyves,
N' of noon° oother woman never the mo.
Who peynted the leoun? Tel me who?°
By God, if wommen hadde writen stories
As clerkes han withinne hir oratories,   700
They wolde han writen of men moore wikkednesse
Than al the mark° of Adam may redresse.
The children of Mercurie and Venus
Been in hir wirkyng° ful contrarius.°
Mercurie loveth wysdam and science,°
And Venus loveth riot and dispence.°
And, for° hir diverse disposicioun,
Ech falleth in otheres exaltacioun;
And thus, God woot, Mercurie is desolat
In Pisces, wher Venus is exaltat,   710
And Venus falleth ther° Mercurie is reysed.
Ther-fore no womman of no clerk is preysed.
The clerk, whan he is old and may noght do
Of Venus werkes worth his olde sho,
Thanne sit he doun and writ in his dotage
That wommen kan nat kepe hir mariage.
  " But now, to purpos why I tolde thee
That I was beten for a book, pardee.
Upon a nyght Jankyn, that was oure sire,°
Redde on his book as he sat by the fire   720
Of Eva° first, that for hir° wikkednesse
Was al mankynde broght to wrecchednesse,
For which that Jesu Crist hymself was slayn,
That boghte us with his herte blood agayn.
Lo, here expres of° wymmen may ye fynde
That womman was the los of al mankynde.
  " Tho° redde he me how Sampson loste his
        heres;°
Slepynge, his lemman kitte° it with hir sheres,

Thurgh which tresoun loste he bothe his eyen.
  " Tho redde he me, if that I shal nat lyen,   730
Of Hercules and of his Dianyre,°
That caused hym to sette hymself afyre.°
  " Nothyng° forgat he the care and the wo
That Socrates hadde with his wyves two,
How Xantippa° caste pisse upon his heed.
This sely° man sat stille as he were deed;
He wipte his heed; namoore dorste° he seyn
But ' Er that thonder stynte,° comth a reyn.'
  " Of Phasipha,° that was the queene of Crete,
For shrewednesse hym thoughte° the tale swete.
Fy! Spek namoore — it is a grisly thyng —   741
Of hir horrible lust and hir likyng.
  " Of Clitermystra,° for hir lecherye,
That falsly made hir housbonde for to dye,
He redde it with ful good devocioun.
  " He tolde me eek for what occasioun
Amphiorax° at Thebes loste his lyf.
Myn housbonde hadde a legende of his wyf,
Eriphilem,° that for an ouche° of gold
Hath pryvely° unto the Grekes told   750
Wher that hir housbonde hidde hym in a place,
For which he hadde at Thebes sory grace.
  " Of Lyvia° tolde he me and of Lucye.°
They bothe made hir housbondes for to dye;
That oon for love, that oother was for hate.
Lyvia hir housbonde on an even late
Empoysoned hath, for that she was his fo.
Lucya, likerous,° loved hir housbonde so
That, for he sholde alwey upon hir thynke,
She yaf hym swich a maner° love-drynke   760
That he was deed er it were by the morwe.
And thus algates° housbondes han sorwe.
  " Thanne tolde he me how oon Latumyus
Compleyned unto his felawe° Arrius
That in his gardyn growed° swich a tree
On which he seyde how that his wyves thre
Honged hemself for° herte despitus.°
  " ' O leeve° brother,' quod this Arrius,
' Yif° me a plante of thilke blessed tree,
And in my gardyn planted shal it be.'   770
  " Of latter date of wyves hath he red
That somme han slayn hir housbondes in hir bed,
And lete hir lechour dighte° hire al the nyght

685. Parables: Proverbs.   686. Ovydes *Art*: Ovid's *Art of Love*.
on: a one.   687. o: one.   694. inpossible: impossibility.
696. But if: unless.   697. N' of noon: nor of any.   698. Accord-
ing to fable, a lion reminded an artist who had portrayed a man
overcoming a lion that lions had also overcome men.   702. mark:
(male) descendants.   704. hir wirkyng: their behavior.   con-
trarius: contrary.   705. science: knowledge.   706. dispence:
extravagance.   707-10. for . . . exaltat: Because of their con-
trary positions (as planets), each falls (in the belt of the zodiac)
during the rising of the other. And thus, God knows, Mercury is
depressed in Pisces (a sign of the zodiac), where Venus reaches
the highest ascendance. (Hence, a scholar, under the influence
of Mercury, is antipathetic to anyone influenced by Venus.)
711. ther: where.   719. oure sire: my husband.   721. Eva:
Eve.   that . . . hir: because of whose.   725. expres of: ex-
pressly concerning.   727. Tho: then.   heres: hair.   728. lem-
man kitte: lover cut.

731. Dianyre: Dejaneira.   732. afyre: afire (with a poisoned
shirt).   733. Nothyng: in no way.   735. Xantippa: Xantippe,
a notorious shrew.   736. sely: innocent.   737. dorste: dared.
738. stynte: stops.   739. Phasipha: Pasiphaë, who became the
mother of the Minotaur by a bull.   740. hym thoughte: seemed
to him.   743. Clitermystra: Clytemnestra, who in league with
her lover Aegisthus slew her husband Agamemnon.   747. Am-
phiorax: Amphiaraus.   749. Eriphilem: Eriphyle, who betrayed
Amphiaraus into fighting against Thebes, though he foresaw that
he would die there.   ouche: brooch.   750. pryvely: secretly.
753. Lyvia: Livia, who in league with Sejanus killed her
husband Drusus.   Lucye: Lucilia, wife of the great Roman poet
Lucretius, the real cause of whose death is unknown.   758. liker-
ous: lustful.   760. maner: kind of.   762. algates: always.
764. felawe: friend.   765. growed: grew.   767. for: out of.
despitus: angry.   768. leeve: dear.   769. Yif: give.   773. dighte:
lie with.

Whan that the corps lay in the floor upright.°
And somme han dryven nayles in hir brayn
Whil that they sleep, and thus they han hem slayn.
Somme han hem yeven poysoun in hir drynke.
He spak moore harm than herte may bithynke,°
And ther-with-al he knew of mo proverbes°
Than in this world ther growen gras or herbes.
'Bet° is,' quod he, 'thyn habitacioun   781
Be with a leoun or a foul dragoun
Than with a womman usyng° for to chide.'
'Bet is,' quod he, 'hye in the roof abyde°
Than with an angry wyf doun in the hous.
They been so wikked and contrarious,
They haten that° hir housbondes loveth ay.'°
He seyde, 'A womman cast° hir shame away
Whan she cast of° hir smok';° and forther mo,
'A fair womman, but° she be chaast° also,   790
Is lyk a gold ryng in a sowes nose.'
Who wolde wene° or who wolde suppose
The wo that in myn herte was and pyne?°
 "And whan I say° he wolde nevere fyne°
To reden on this cursed book al nyght,
Al sodeynly thre leves have I plyght°
Out of his book right as he radde,° and eke
I with my fist so took hym on the cheke
That in oure fyr he fil bakward adoun.
And he up stirte° as dooth a wood leoun,   800
And with his fest he smoot me on the heed
That in the floor I lay as I were deed.
And whan he saugh how stille that I lay,
He was agast and wolde han fled his way
Til atte laste out of my swough° I brayde.°
'O hastow slayn me, false theef,' I sayde,
'And for my land thus hastow mordred me?
Er I be deed, yet wol I kisse thee.'
 "And neer he cam and kneled faire adoun
And seyde, 'Deere suster° Alisoun,   810
As help me God, I shal thee nevere smyte.
That I have doon, it is thyself to wyte.°
Foryeve it me, and that I thee biseke.'°
And yet eft-soones° I hitte hym on the cheke
And seyde, 'Theef, thus muchel° am I wreke.°
Now wol I dye. I may no lenger speke.'
But at the laste, with muchel care and wo,
We fille acorded° by us-selven° two.
He yaf me al the brydel in myn hond
To han the governaunce° of hous and lond,   820

And of his tonge, and of his hond also,
And made hym brenne° his book anon right tho;°
And whan that I hadde geten unto me
By maistrye al the soveraynetee,
And that° he seyde, 'Myn owene trewe wyf,
Do as thee lust° the terme of al thy lyf;
Keep thyn honour, and keep eek myn estaat,'—
After that day we hadden nevere debaat.
God help me so, I was to hym as kynde
As any wyf from Denmark unto Inde°   830
And also° trewe, and so was he to me.
I pray to God, that sit in magestee,
So blesse his soule for his mercy deere.
Now wol I seye my tale, if ye wol here."
 The Frere logh° whan he hadde herd al this.
"Now dame," quod he, "so have I joye or blis,
This is a long preamble of a tale!"
And whan the Somnour herde the Frere gale,°
"Lo," quod the Somnour, "Goddes armes two!
A frere wol entremette hym evere mo.°   840
Loo, goode men, a flye and eek a frere
Wol falle in every dyssh and matere.
What spekestow° of preambulacioun?
What, amble, or trotte, or pees,° or go sit doun!
Thow lettest° oure disport in this manere."
 "Ye!° Woltow° so, sir Somnour?" quod the
    Frere.
"Now, by my feith, I shal, er that° I go,
Telle of a somnour swich a tale or two
That al the folk shal laughen in this place."
 "Now, elles,° Frere, I wol bishrewe° thy face,"
Quod this Somnour, "and I bishrewe me   851
But if° I telle tales two or three
Of freres, er I come to Sydyngborne,°
That I shal make thyn herte for to morne,
For wel I woot thy pacience is gon."
 Oure Hoost cride, "Pees, and that anon,"
And seyde, "Lat the womman telle hir tale.
Ye fare as folk that dronken ben of ale.
Do, dame, tel forth youre tale, and that is best."
 "Al redy, sire," quod she, "right as yow lest,°
If I have licence of this worthy Frere."   861
 "Yis,° dame," quod he. "Tel forth, and I wol
    here."

THE WIFE OF BATH'S TALE

The Wife's Tale is ultimately derived from an in-
ternationally disseminated folk tale, perhaps known to
Chaucer from oral recitation. The tale was familiar in

---

774. upright: face-up. 778. bithynke: imagine. 779. mo proverbes: more proverbs. (Those following [ll. 781–91] are from
Ecclesiasticus and Proverbs.) 781. Bet: better. 783. usyng:
accustomed. 784. abyde: to stay. 787. haten that: hate what.
ay: always. 788. cast: casts. 789. of: off. smok: smock.
790. but: unless. chaast: chaste. 792. wene: guess. 793. pyne:
pain. 794. say: saw. fyne: finish. 796. plyght: plucked.
797. radde: was reading. 800. stirte: jumped. 805. swough:
swoon. brayde: revived. 810. suster: sweetheart. 812. wyte:
blame. 813. biseke: beseech. 814. eft-soones: once again.
815. muchel: much. wreke: avenged. 818. fille acorded:
fell into accord. us-selven: ourselves. 820. governaunce:
control.

822. brenne: burn. tho: then. 825. that: when. 826. lust:
it pleases. 830. Inde: India. 831. also: as. 835. logh:
laughed. 838. gale: exclaim. 840. wol . . . mo: will always
meddle. 843. What spekestow: why do you speak. 844. pees:
peace. 845. lettest: hinder. 846. Ye: yes. Woltow: will
you. 847. er that: before. 850. elles: otherwise. bishrewe:
curse. 852. But if: unless. 853. Sydyngborne: Sittingbourne.
860. right . . . lest: just as it pleases you. 862. Yis: yes, indeed.

England and was used by Chaucer's friend John Gower
in his *Lover's Confession,* but Chaucer has adapted it
particularly to the context and narrator. The sly mockery of friars at the opening, the proud admission of
woman's lack of secretiveness in the digression on
Midas's wife, the fierce lecture on true gentility delivered by the Hag — a debater as formidable as the
Wife herself — and the underlying theme of woman's
mastery in marriage are all contrived by Chaucer himself.

In th' olde dayes of the Kyng Arthour,
Of which that Britons speken greet honour,
Al was this land fulfild of fairye.°
The elf queene with hir joly compaignye
Daunced ful ofte in many a grene mede.°
This was the olde opynyoun,° as I rede;
I speke of many hundred yeres ago.
But now kan no man se none elves mo,°
For now the grete charitee and prayeres
Of lymytours° and othere holy freres,   10
That serchen° every lond and every streem,
As thikke as motes in the sonne beem,
Blessynge halles, chambres, kichenes, boures,°
Citees, burghes, castels, hye toures,
Thropes,° bernes,° shipnes,° dayeryes —
This maketh° that ther been no fairyes.
For, ther-as wont° to walken was an elf,
Ther walketh now the lymytour hymself
In undermeles° and in morwenynges,
And seith his matyns and his holy thynges   20
As he gooth° in his lymytacioun.
Wommen may go saufly up and doun
In every bussh or under every tree.
Ther is noon oother incubus° but he,
And he ne wol doon hem but° dishonour.
    And so bifel that this Kyng Arthour
Hadde in his hous a lusty bacheler
That on a day cam ridyng fro ryver;°
And happed° that, allone as he was born,
He say° a mayde walkynge hym biforn   30
Of which mayde anoon,° maugree hir hed,°
By verray force he rafte° hir maydenhed;°
For which oppressioun was swich° clamour
And swich pursuyte unto the Kyng Arthour
That dampned° was this knyght for to be deed
By cours of lawe and sholde han° lost his heed —

Paraventure° swich was the statut tho° —
But° that the queene and othere ladyes mo
So longe preyden° the kyng of° grace
Til he his lyf hym graunted in the place   40
And yaf° hym to the queene, al at hir wille,
To chese° wheither she wolde hym save or spille.°
    The queene thanked the kyng with al hir myght,
And after this thus spak she to the knyght
Whan that she saugh° hir tyme upon a day:
"Thow standest yet," quod she, "in swich array°
That of thy lyf yet hastow° no suretee.
I graunte thee lyf if thow kanst tellen me
What thyng is it that wommen moost desiren.
Be war,° and keep thy nekke boon° from iren.°
And if thow kanst nat tellen it me anon,   51
Yet wol I yeve thee leve for to gon
A twelf monthe and a day to seche° and lere°
An answere suffisant in this matere.
And suretee wol I han er that° thow pace,°
Thy body for to yelden° in this place."
    Wo° was this knyght, and sorwefully he siketh,°
But what! He may nat doon al as hym liketh.°
And atte laste he chees hym for to wende°
And come agayn right at the yeres ende   60
With swich answere as God wolde hym purveye,°
And taketh his leve and wendeth forth his weye.
    He seketh every hous and every place
Where-as° he hopeth for to fynde grace
To lerne what thyng wommen loven moost,
But he ne koude arryven in no coost°
Where-as he myghte° fynde in this matere
Two creatures acordyng in feere.°
    Somme seyden wommen loven best richesse,
Somme seyde honour, somme seyde jolynesse,   70
Somme riche array, somme seyden lust a-bedde,
And ofte tyme to be wydwe° and wedde.°
    Somme seyde that oure herte is moost esed°
Whan that we been° y-flatered and y-plesed.
He gooth ful ny° the sothe,° I wol nat lye.
A man shal wynne us best with flaterye;
And with attendaunce and with bisynesse°
Been we y-lymed,° bothe moore° and lesse.°
And somme seyn that we loven best
For to be free and do right as us lest,°   80
And that no man repreve° us of oure vice

But seye that we be wise and nothyng nyce.°
For trewely ther is noon of us alle,
If any wight° wol clawe us on the galle,°
That we nyl kike for° he seith us sooth.°
Assay,° and he shal fynde it that so dooth,
For, be we nevere so vicious withinne,
We wol be holden° wise and clene° of synne.

    And somme seyn that greet delit han° we
For to be holden stable and eek secree,°   90
And in o purpos stedefastly to dwelle,
And nat biwreye° thyng that men us telle;
But that tale is nat worth a rake-stele.°
Pardee,° we wommen konne nothyng hele.°
Witnesse on Mida,° wol ye heere the tale.
Ovyde,° amonges othere thynges smale,
Seyde Mida hadde under his longe heres°
Growynge upon his heed two asses eres,°
The whiche vice° he hidde as he best myghte
Ful sotilly° from every mannes sighte   100
That, save his wyf, ther wiste° of it namo.°
He loved hire moost and trusted hire also.
He preyed hire that to no creature
She sholde tellen of his disfigure.
She swoor hym, "Nay." For al this world to
    wynne,°
She nolde° do that vileynye or synne
To make hir housbonde han so foul a name.
She nolde nat telle it for hir owene shame.
But, natheless,° hir thoughte° that she dyde°
That she so longe sholde a conseil° hyde.   110
Hir thoughte it swal° so soore aboute hir herte,
That nedely° som word hir moste asterte;°
And, sith° she dorste° telle it to no man,
Doun to a marys faste by° she ran.
Til she cam there, hir herte was afyre.
And, as a bitore bombleth in the myre,°
She leyde hir mouth unto the water doun.
"Biwrey° me nat, thow water, with thy soun,"°
Quod she. "To thee I telle it and namo.
Myn housbonde hath longe asses erys° two!   120
Now is myn herte al hool.° Now is it oute.
I myghte° no lenger kepe° it, out of doute."
Heere may ye see, thogh we a tyme abyde,
Yet out it moot.° We kan no conseil hyde.

The remenant of the tale if ye wol heere,
Redeth Ovyde, and ther ye may it leere.°
    This knyght of which my tale is specially,
Whan that he say° he myghte nat come
    ther-by,° —
This is to seye, what wommen loven moost —
Withinne his brest ful sorweful was the goost;°
But hom he gooth. He myghte nat sojourne.°   131
The day was come that homward moste he torne;°
And in his wey it happed hym° to ryde,
In al this care, under a forest syde,
Wher-as he say upon a daunce go
Of ladyes foure-and-twenty and yet mo,
Toward the whiche daunce he drow° ful yerne°
In hope that som wisdom sholde he lerne.
But certeynly, er° he cam fully there,
Vanysshed was this daunce, he nyste° where.   140
No creature saugh he that bar° lyf,
Save on the grene he say sittynge a wyf.
A fouler wight ther may no man devyse.°
Agayn° the knyght this olde wyf gan ryse°
And seyde, "Sire knyght, heer° forth ne lyth° no
    wey.
Tel me what that ye seken, by your fey.°
Paraventure,° it may the bettre be.
Thise olde folk konne muchel° thyng," quod she.
    "My leeve moder,"° quod this knyght, "certeyn
I nam but deed but if that° I kan seyn   150
What thyng it is that wommen moost desire.
Koude ye me wisse,° I wolde wel quyte° youre
    hyre."
    "Plight° me thy trouthe,° here in myn hand,"°
    quod she,
"The nexte thyng that I requere thee,
Thow shalt it do, if it lye in thy myght,
And I wol telle it yow er it be nyght."
    "Have here my trouthe," quod the knyght, "I
    graunte."°
    "Thanne," quod she, "I dar me wel avaunte,°
Thy lyf is sauf,° for I wole stonde ther-by,°
Upon my lyf, the queene wol seye as I.   160
Lat see which is the proudeste of hem alle
That wereth on a coverchief° or a calle°
That dar seye 'Nay' of that° I shal thee teche.
Lat us go forth withouten lenger speche."

---

82. nothyng nyce: in no way foolish. 84. wight: person. clawe
. . . galle: scratch us on the sore spot. 85. That . . . for: that
won't kick because. sooth: truth. 86. Assay: try. 88. holden: considered. clene: pure. 89. han: have. 90. eek
secree: also secretive. 92. biwreye: betray. 93. rake-stele:
rake handle. 94. Pardee: certainly. hele: conceal. 95. Mida:
Midas. 96. Ovyde: Ovid. 97. heres: hair. 98. eres: ears.
99. vice: defect. 100. sotilly: skillfully. 101. wiste: knew.
namo: no other. 105. wynne: gain. 106. nolde: wouldn't.
109. nathelees: nevertheless. thoughte: it seemed to. dyde:
would die. 110. conseil: secret. 111. swal: swelled.
112. nedely: necessarily. moste asterte: escape from. 113. sith:
since. dorste: dared. 114. marys . . . by: marsh nearby.
116. bitore . . . myre: bittern drones in the swamp. 118. Bi-
wrey: betray. soun: sound. 120. erys: ears. 121. hool:
whole. 122. myghte: could. kepe: conceal. 124. moot: must.

126. leere: learn. 128. say: saw. come ther-by: discover it
130. goost: spirit. 131. sojourne: stay. 132. torne: turn.
133. it . . . hym: he happened. 137. drow: drew. yerne:
eagerly. 139. er: before. 140. nyste: knew not. 141. bar:
bore. 143. devyse: imagine. 144. Agayn: toward. gan ryse:
arose. 145. heer: here. lyth: lies. 146. fey: faith. 147. Paraventure: perchance. 148. konne muchel: know many a.
149. leeve moder: dear mother. 150. nam . . . that: am but
dead unless. 152. wisse: inform. quyte: reward. 153. Plight:
give. trouthe: promise. in . . . hand: by a handshake.
157. graunte: consent. 158. dar . . . avaunte: dare well boast.
159. sauf: safe. stonde ther-by: guarantee. 162. wereth . . .
coverchief: has on a kerchief. calle: cap. 163. that: that
which.

Tho rowned° she a pistel° in his ere
And bad hym to be glad and have no fere.
   Whan they be comen to the court, this knyght
Seyde he hadde holde° his day as he had hight,°
And redy was his answere, as he sayde.
Ful many a noble wyf, and many a mayde,   170
And many a widwe, for that° they ben wise,
The queene hirself sittyng as justise,
Assembled been,° his answere for to here.
And afterward this knyght was bode° appere.
   To every wight comanded was silence,
And that the knyght sholde telle in audience
What thyng that worldly wommen loven best.
This knyght ne stood nat stille as dooth a best°
But to his questioun anon answerde
With manly voys that al the court it herde.   180
   "My lige lady, generally," quod he,
"Wommen desiren to have sovereynte
As wel over hir housbonde as hir love
And for to been in maistrie° hym above.
This is youre mooste° desir, thogh ye me kille.
Dooth as yow list.° I am here at youre wille."
   In al the court ne was ther wyf, ne mayde,
Ne wydwe that contraried that° he sayde
But seyden he was worthy han° his lyf.   189
   And with that word up stirte° that olde wyf
Which that the knyght say° sittyng on the grene.
"Mercy," quod she, " my sovereyn lady queene,
Er that youre court departe, do me right.
I taughte this answere unto the knyght,
For which he plighte me his trouthe there,
The firste thyng I wolde hym requere,
He wolde it do, if it laye in his myght.
Bifore the court thanne preye I thee, sire knyght,"
Quod she, "that thow me take unto° thy wyf.
For wel thow woost° that I have kept° thy lyf.
If I seye fals, sey 'Nay,' upon thy fey."   201
   This knyght answered, "Allas and weylawey,°
I woot right wel that swich was my biheste.
For Goddes love, as chees° a newe requeste!
Taak al my good,° and lat my body go."
   "Nay, thanne," quod she. "I shrewe° us bothe
      two.
For, thogh that I be foul, old, and poore,
I nolde,° for al the metal ne for oore°
That under erthe is grave° or lith° above,
But if thy wyf I were and eek thy love."   210
   "My love!" quod he. " Nay, my dampnacioun!°
Allas that any of my nacioun°

Sholde evere so foule° disparaged be!"
But al for noght! Th' ende is this that he
Constreyned was, he nedes moste° hir wedde,
And taketh his olde wyf, and goth to bedde.
   Now wolden som men seye, paraventure,
That for my necligence I do no cure°
To tellen yow the joye and al th' array
That at the feste was that ilke° day;   220
To which thyng shortly answere I shal.
I seye, ther nas° no joye ne° feste at al!
Ther nas but hevynesse° and muche sorwe,
For pryvely° he wedded hire on morwe,°
And al day after hidde hym° as an owle,
So wo was hym,° his wyf looked so foule.
   Greet was the wo the knyght hadde in his thoght
Whan he was with his wyf a-bedde y-broght.
He walweth,° and he turneth to and fro.
His olde wyf lay smylyng evere mo°   230
And seyde, " O deere housbonde, benedicite!°
Fareth° every knyght thus with his wyf as ye?
Is this the lawe of Kyng Arthures hous?
Is every knyght of his thus daungerous?°
I am youre owene love and youre wyf.
I am she which that saved hath youre lyf.
And certes yet ne dide I yow nevere unright.
Why fare ye thus with me this firste nyght?
Ye faren° lyk a man hadde° lost his wit.
What is my gilt? For Goddes love, tel it,   240
And it shal ben amended, if I may."°
   "Amended!" quod this knyght. "Allas, nay,
      nay.
It wol nat ben amended nevere mo.°
Thow art so loothly, and so old also,
And ther-to comen of° so lowe a kynde°
That litel wonder is thogh I walwe and wynde.°
So wolde God, myn herte wolde breste!"°
   "Is this," quod she, " the cause of youre un-
      reste? "
   "Ye, certeynly," quod he. "No wonder is."
   "Now sire," quod she, "I koude amende al
      this,
If that me liste, er it were dayes thre,   251
So wel ye myghte bere yow unto me.
   "But, for° ye speken of swich gentilesse°
As is descended out of old richesse,°
That therfore sholden ye be gentil men,
Swich arrogance is nat worth an hen.
Looke-who-that° is moost vertuous alway,

165. Tho rowned: then whispered.   pistel: lesson.   168. holde:
kept.   hight: promised.   171. for that: because.   173. been:
are.   174. bode: ordered to.   178. best: beast.   184. maistrie:
mastery.   185. mooste: greatest.   186. list: it pleases.   188. contraried that: contradicted what.   189. han: to have.   190. stirte:
sprang.   191. say: saw.   199. unto: to be.   200. woost: know.
kept: saved.   202. weylawey: woe.   204. as chees: choose.
205. good: goods.   206. shrewe: curse.   208. nolde: wouldn't
wish (anything else).   oore: ore.   209. grave: buried.   lith:
lies.   211. dampnacioun: ruination.   212. nacioun: birth.

213. foule: foully.   215. nedes moste: needs must.   218. do
no cure: take no care.   220. ilke: same.   222. nas: was.
ne: nor.   223. hevynesse: gloom.   224. pryvely: privately.
morwe: the morrow.   225. hym: himself.   226. wo . . . hym:
woeful was he.   229. walweth: wallows.   230. evere mo: all the
while.   231. benedicite!: God bless you!   232. Fareth: behaves.
234. daungerous: reluctant.   239. faren: act.   hadde: (who)
had.   241. may: can.   243. nevere mo: ever after.   245. comen
of: descended from.   kynde: nature.   246. wynde: twist.
247. breste: burst.   253. for: since.   gentilesse: gentility.
254. richesse: wealth.   257. Looke-who-that: whoever.

Pryvee° and apert,° and moost entendeth ay°
To do the gentil dedes that he kan;
Taak hym for the gretteste gentil man.   260
Crist wol,° we clayme of hym oure gentillesse,
Nat of oure eldres for hir° old richesse,
For, thogh they yeve us al hir heritage
For which we clayme to been of heigh parage,°
Yet may° they nat biquethe, for nothyng,
To noon of us hir vertuous lyvyng
That made hem gentil men y-called be
And bad° us folwen hem in swich degree.
   "Wel kan the wise poete of Florence
That highte Dant° speken in this sentence.°   270
Lo, in swich maner° rym is Dantes tale:°
'Ful selde° up riseth by his braunches smale
Prowesse° of man, for God of his prowesse
Wol° that of hym we clayme oure gentillesse.'
For of oure eldres may we nothyng clayme
But temporel thyng that man may hurte and
      mayme.
   "Eek every wight woot this as wel as I,
If gentillesse were planted naturelly°
Unto° a certeyn lynage doun the lyne,
Pryvee and apert, thanne wolde they nevere fyne°
To doon of gentilesse the faire office;   281
They myghte° do no vileynye or vice.
   "Taak fyr, and bere° it in the derkeste hous
Bitwix this and the mount Kaukasous,°
And lat men shette° the dores and go thenne,°
Yet wol the fyr as faire lye° and brenne°
As° twenty thousand men myghte it biholde.
His office° naturel ay wol it holde,°
Up° peril of my lyf, til that it dye.
   "Here may ye se wel how that genterye°   290
Is nat annexed to possessioun,
Sith folk ne doon hir operacioun°
Alwey as dooth the fyr, lo, in his kynde.
For, God it woot, men may wel often fynde
A lordes sone do shame and vileynye.
And he that wol han prys of° his gentrye,
For he was born of a gentil hous
And hadde his eldres noble and vertuous,
And nyl° hymselven do no gentil dedis°
Ne folwen his gentil auncestre that deed° is,   300
He nys° nat gentil, be he duc or erl,

For vileyns synful dedes make a cherl.
For gentilesse nys but renomee°
Of thyn auncestres for hir hye bountee,
Which is a straunge° thyng for thy persone.
Thy gentilesse cometh fro God allone.
Thanne comth oure verray° gentilesse of grace;
It was nothyng biquethe° us with oure place.
   "Thenketh how noble, as seith Valerius,°
Was thilke° Tullius Hostillius   310
That out of poverte roos to heigh noblesse.
Redeth Senek,° and redeth eek Boece.°
Ther shul ye seen expres° that no drede° is
That he is gentil that dooth gentil dedis.
And therfore, leve° housbonde, I thus conclude,
Al° were it that myne auncestres were rude,
Yet may the hye God, and so hope I,
Graunte me grace to lyven vertuously.
Thanne am I gentil, whan that I bigynne
To lyven vertuously and weyve° synne.   320
   "And ther-as° ye of poverte me repreve,°
The hye God, on whom that we bileve,
In wilful° poverte chees° to lyve his lyf.
And certes every man, mayden, or wyf
May understonde that Jesus, hevene° Kyng,
Ne wolde nat chese° a vicious lyvyng.
Glad° poverte is an honeste thyng, certeyn;
This wol Senek and othere clerkes° seyn.
Who so that halt hym payd of° his poverte,
I holde hym riche, al hadde he nat a sherte.   330
He that coveiteth is a poure wight,
For he wolde han that is nat in his myght;
But he that noght hath ne coveiteth to have
Is riche, althogh ye holde hym but a knave.
   "Verray poverte, it syngeth properly.
Juvenal seith of poverte myrily:°
'The poure man, whan he gooth by the weye,
Biforn° the theves he may synge and pleye.'
Poverte is hateful good and, as I gesse,
A ful greet bryngere out of bisynesse,°   340
A greet amendere eek° of sapience,°
To hym that taketh° it in pacience.
Poverte is this, althogh it seme alenge,°
Possessioun that no wight wol chalenge.
Poverte ful often, whan a man is lowe,
Maketh° his God and eek hymself to knowe.

258. Pryvee: inwardly. apert: outwardly. entendeth ay: strives always. 261. wol: desires (that). 262. hir: their. 264. parage: lineage. 265. may: can. 268. bad: required. 270. highte Dant: is called Dante. sentence: opinion. 271. maner: sort of. tale: saying. 272. selde: seldom. 273. Prowesse: excellence. 274. Wol: wishes. 278. planted naturelly: implanted by nature. 279. Unto: within. 280. fyne: cease. 282. myghte: could. If the quality of gentility could be naturally inherited, the heirs could never be unworthy of their rank. 283. bere: bring. 284. Kaukasous: Caucasus. 285. shette: shut. thenne: thence. 286. lye: blaze. brenne: burn. 287. As: as if. 288. His office: its function. holde: retain. 289. Up: on. 290. genterye: gentility. 292. ne . . . operacioun: don't behave. 296. han . . . of: have esteem for. 299. nyl: will (not). dedis: deeds. 300. deed: dead. 301. nys: is (not).

303. renomee: renown. 305. straunge: alien, i.e., the "high goodness" of your ancestors cannot descend into *your* character. 307. verray: true. 308. nothyng biquethe: in no way bequeathed to. 309. Valerius: Valerius Maximus, a Roman moralist and historian. 310. thilke: that same. 312. Senek: Seneca, a Roman author. Boece: Boethius, the author of the *Consolation of Philosophy* (see Intro., p. 4.). 313. expres: expressly. drede: doubt. 315. leve: dear. 316. Al: even if. 320. weyve: shun. 321. ther-as: whereas. repreve: reproach. 323. wilful: willing. chees: chose. 325. hevene: heaven's. 326. chese: choose. 327. Glad: willing. 328. clerkes: scholars. 329. halt . . . of: considers himself rewarded by. 336. myrily: merrily. 338. Biforn: in front of. 340. bisynesse: care. 341. amendere eek: improver also. sapience: wisdom. 342. taketh: receives. 343. alenge: miserable. 346. Maketh: causes (him).

Poverte a spectacle° is, as thynketh° me,
Thurgh which he may his verray freendes se.
And therfore, sire, syn that° I noght yow greve,°
Of my poverte namoore ye me repreve.°   350

"Now, sire, of elde° ye repreve me;
And certes, sire, thogh noon auctoritee°
Were in no book, ye gentils of honour
Seyn° that men sholde an old wight doon favour
And clepe° hym fader, for youre gentilesse;
And auctours° shal I fynden,° as I gesse.

"Now, ther° ye seye that I am foul and old,
Thanne drede yow noght to been a cokewold,°
For filthe and elde, also mote I thee,°
Been grete wardeyns° upon chastitee.   360
But, nathelees,° syn I knowe youre delit,
I shal fulfille youre worldly appetit.

"Chees now," quod she, "oon of thise thynges
          tweye:°
To han me foul and old til that I deye,
And be to yow a trewe, humble wyf,
And nevere yow displese in al my lyf;
Or elles ye wol han me yong and fair
And take youre aventure° of the repair°
That shal be to youre hous bycause of me,
Or in som oother place, may wel be.   370
Now chees yourselven wheither that yow liketh."°

This knyght avyseth hym° and soore siketh,°
But atte laste he seyde in this manere:
"My lady, and my love and wyf so deere,
I putte me in youre wise governaunce.
Cheseth° yourself which may be moost plesaunce
And moost honour to yow and me also.
I do no fors the wheither° of the two,
For as yow liketh, it suffiseth me."

"Thanne have I gete° of yow maistrye," quod
          she,   380
"Syn I may chese and governe as me lest? "°
"Ye, certes, wyf," quod he. "I holde it best."
"Kys me," quod she. "We be no lenger wrothe,
For, by my trouthe,° I wol be to yow bothe —
This is to seyn, ye,° bothe fair and good.
I pray to God that I mote sterven wood°
But° I to yow be also° good and trewe
As evere was wyf syn that the world was newe.
And but I be to-morn as fair to sene°
As any lady, emperice, or queene   390

That is bitwix the est and eek the west,
Do with my lyf and deth right as yow lest.
Cast up the curtyn. Looke how that it is."
And whan the knyght sey° verraily al this,
That she so fair was and so yong ther-to,
For joye he hente° hire in his armes two.
His herte bathed in a bath of blisse,
A thousand tyme a rewe he gan hir kisse,°
And she obeyed hym in every thyng
That myghte do hym plesance° or likyng.   400
And thus they lyve unto hir° lyves ende
In parfit joye, and Jesu Crist us sende
Housbondes meke, yonge, and fressh a-bedde,
And grace t' overbyde hem° that we wedde.
And eek I praye Jesu shorte hir lyves
That noght wol be governed by hir wyves;°
And olde and angry nygardes of dispence,°
God sende hem soone verray pestilence.

THE CLERK'S TALE

The source of the Clerk's Tale is one of the stories
in Boccaccio's famous Italian prose work, the *Decameron* (1353), but Chaucer followed a Latin prose
translation made by Petrarch and, side by side, a
French translation of the Latin. So closely, in fact, did
he follow these two versions that it is frequently possible to tell which he was looking at when he wrote
particular passages.

The story had circulated as an unpretentious folk
tale before Boccaccio made his literary adaptation, and
Chaucer instinctively preserved the remoteness and un-
reality inherent in the folk tale which make it so
ideally suited to the otherworldly Clerk. But the predominant tone of the tale has been subtly adapted to
the character of the narrator, and the theme has acquired a new and amusing significance through its
juxtaposition to the Wife of Bath's Tale. And Chaucer's
version is further original in its graceful rhyme-royal
stanzas and in the extraordinary tour de force at the
end, where the same set of rhymes (*ababcb*) runs
through six stanzas.

I

Ther is at the west syde of Ytaille,°
Doun at the roote of Vesulus° the colde,
A lusty° playne habundant of vitaille,°
Wher many a tour° and toun thow mayst biholde
That founded were in tyme of fadres° olde,
And many another delitable° sighte,
And Saluces° this noble contree highte.°

347. spectacle: eyeglass.   thynketh: it seems to.   349. syn
that: since.   greve: harm.   350. repreve: reproach.   351. elde:
old age.   352. noon auctoritee: no authoritative decision.
354. Seyn: say.   355. clepe: call.   356. auctours: authors.
fynden: find (as authorities).   357. ther: whereas.   358. cokewold: cuckold.   359. also . . . thee: as I may prosper.   360. war-
deyns: guards.   361. nathelees: nevertheless.   363. tweye: two.
368. aventure: chance.   repair: resort.   371. wheither . . . liketh:
whichever pleases you better.   372. avyseth hym: ponders.
siketh: sighs.   376. Cheseth: choose.   378. do . . . wheither:
don't care which.   380. gete: gotten.   381. lest: it pleases.
384. trouthe: faith.   385. ye: indeed.   386. mote . . . wood:
may die mad.   387. But: unless.   also: as.   389. sene: see.

394. sey: saw.   396. hente: seized.   398. a rewe . . . kisse:
in a row he kissed her.   400. plesance: pleasure.   401. hir:
their.   404. t' overbyde hem: to overrule them.   407. nygardes
of dispence: niggardly spenders.   CLERK'S TALE.   1. Ytaille:
Italy.   2. Vesulus: Monte Viso.   3. lusty: pleasant.   habundant of vitaille: abundant in food.   4. tour: tower.   5. fadres:
ancestors.   6. delitable: delightful.   7. Saluces: Saluzzo.
highte: is called.

A markys whilom° lord was of that lond,
As were his worthy eldres hym bifore,
And obeisant ay° redy to his hond   10
Were alle his liges° bothe lasse and moore.
Thus in delit he lyveth and hath doon yoore,°
Biloved and drad° thurgh favour of Fortune
Bothe of his lordes and of his commune.°

Therwith he was, to speke as of lynage,°
The gentileste y-born of Lumbardye,°
A fair persone, and strong and yong of age,
And ful of honour and of curteisye,
Discret ynogh° his contree for to gye,°
Save° in somme thynges that he was to blame;   20
And Walter was this yonge lordes name.

I blame hym thus that he considered noght
In tyme comynge what myghte hym bityde,°
But on his lust° present was al his thoght,
As for to hauke and hunte on every syde.
Wel neigh alle oothere cures leet° he slyde;
And eek° he nolde° — and that was worst of
    alle —
Wedde no wyf for noght that may bifalle.

Oonly that point his peple bar so soore°
That flokmele° on a day they to hym wente;   30
And oon of hem° that wisest was of loore° —
Or ellis° that the lord best wolde assente
That he sholde telle hym what his peple mente,°
Or ellis koude he shewe° wel swich° matere —
He to the markys seyde as ye shal heere:

"O noble markys, youre humanitee
Assureth us and yeveth° us hardynesse,°
As ofte as tyme is of necessitee,
That we to yow mowe° telle oure hevynesse.
Accepteth,° lord, now of youre gentillesse°   40
That° we with pitous° herte unto yow pleyne,°
And lat° youre erys° noght my voys desdeyne.

"Al° have I noght to doone° in this matere
Moore than another man hath in this place,
Yet, for as muche as ye, my lord so deere,
Han° alwey shewed me favour and grace,

I dar° the bettre aske of yow a space°
Of audience to shewen oure requeste,
And ye, my lord, to doon right as yow leste.°

"For certes,° lord, so wel us liketh° yow   50
And al youre werk, and evere han doon, that we
Ne kouden nat usself devysen° how
We myghte lyven in moore felicitee,
Save o° thyng, lord, if it youre wille be,
That for to been a wedded man yow leste.°
Thanne were youre peple in sovereyn° hertes reste.

"Boweth youre nekke under that blisful yok
Of sovereynetee, noght of servyse,°
Which that men clepe spousaille° or wedlok;
And thenketh, lord, among youre thoghtes wyse
How that oure dayes passe in sondry wyse,°   61
For, thogh we slepe or wake or rome° or ryde,
Ay° fleeth the tyme; it nyl° no man abyde.

"And thogh youre grene youthe floure as yit,
In crepeth age alwey as stille as stoon,
And deth manaceth° every age and smyt°
In ech estat,° for ther escapeth noon;°
And, also° certeyn as we knowe echon°
That we shul dye, as uncerteyn we alle
Been° of that day whan deth shal on us falle.   70

"Accepteth thanne of us the trewe entente
That° nevere yet refuseden youre heste,°
And we wol, lord, if that ye wol assente,
Chese° yow a wyf, in short tyme at the leeste,
Born of the gentileste° and of the meeste°
Of al this lond, so that it oghte seme°
Honour to God and yow, as° we kan deme.°

"Delyvere us out of al this bisy drede,°
And tak a wyf, for hye° Goddes sake,
For if it so bifelle — as God forbede!° —   80
That thurgh youre deeth youre lyne sholde slake,°
And that a straunge° successour sholde take
Youre heritage, O wo were us° alyve!
Wherfore we pray yow hastily to wyve."°

Hir° meke prayere and hir pitous cheere°
Made the markys herte han pitee.

" Ye wol,"° quod° he, " myn owene peple deere,
To that° I nevere erst° thoghte streyne° me.
I me rejoysed of° my libertee,
That selde tyme° is founde in mariage.   90
Ther° I was free, I moot° been in servage.

" But, nathelees,° I se youre trewe entente,
And truste upon youre wit, and have doon ay.
Wherfore of my free wyl I wol assente
To wedde me as soone as evere I may.
But, theras° ye han profred me today
To chese me a wyf, I yow relesse
That choys and pray yow of that profre cesse.°

" For God it woot that children ofte ben
Unlyk hir worthy eldres hem bifore.   100
Bountee° comth al of God, nat of the stren°
Of which they been° engendred and y-bore.°
I truste in Goddes bountee, and therfore
My mariage and myn estat and reste°
I hym bitake;° he may doon as hym leste.°

" Lat me allone in chesyng of my wyf;
That charge upon my bak I wol endure.
But I yow pray and charge, upon youre lyf,
What° wyf that I take, ye me assure
To worshipe hire whil that hir lyf may dure°   110
In word and werk, bothe here and everywhere,
As° she an emperoures doghter were.

" And ferthermoore this shal ye swere, that ye
Agayn° my choys shal neither grucche° ne stryve,
For, sith° I shal forgoon° my libertee
At your requeste, as evere mote° I thryve,
Theras° myn herte is set, ther wol I wyve;
And, but° ye wol assente in swich manere,   118
I pray yow, speketh namoore° of this matere."

With hertly° wyl they sworen and assenten, —
To al this thyng ther seyde no wight° "nay" —
Bisekynge hym of grace, er that° they wenten,
That he wolde graunten hem a certein day
Of his spousaille as soone as evere he may,
For yet alwey the peple somwhat dredde°
Lest that the markys no wyf wolde wedde.

He graunted hem a day swich as hym leste°
On which he wolde be wedded sikerly,°
And seyde he dide al this at hir requeste;
And they with humble entente buxomly°   130
Knelynge upon hir knees ful reverently
Hym thanken alle, and thus they han an ende
Of hir entente, and hom agayn they wende.

And herupon he to his officers
Comaundeth for the feste to purveye,°
And to his pryvee° knyghtes and squyers
Swich charge yaf° as hym liste on hem leye,
And they to his comandement obeye,
And ech of hem dooth al his diligence
To doon unto the feste reverence.   140

II

Noght fer fro thilke° paleys honurable
Wheras this markys shoop° his mariage,
Ther stood a throop° of site delitable°
In which that poure folk of that village
Hadden hir bestes° and hir herbergage°
And of° hir labour toke° hir sustenance
After that° the erthe yaf hem habundance.

Among thise poure folk ther dwelte a man
Which that° was holden° pourest of hem alle,
But hye God somtyme sende can   150
His grace into a litel oxes stalle.
Janicula men of that throop hym calle.
A doghter hadde he fair ynogh to sighte,
And Grisildis this yonge mayden highte.°

But, for to speke of vertuous beautee,°
Thanne was she oon° the faireste under sonne,
For poureliche y-fostred up° was she.
No likerous° lust was thurgh hir herte y-ronne.°
Wel ofter° of the welle than of the tonne°
She drank, and, for she wolde vertu plese,   160
She knew wel labour, but noon ydel ese.

But thogh this mayde tendre were of age,
Yet in the brest of hir virginitee
Ther was enclosed rype and sad corage,°
And in greet reverence and charitee

---

87. wol: will. quod: said. 88. that: what. erst: before. streyne:
constrain. 89. me . . . of: rejoiced in. 90. selde tyme: seldom.
91. Ther: where. moot: must. 92. nathelees: nevertheless.
96. theras: whereas. 98. cesse: (to) cease. 101. Bountee:
goodness. stren: strain. 102. been: are. y-bore: born.
104. reste: repose. 105. hym bitake: commit to him. hym
leste: pleases him. 109. What: whatever. 110. dure: endure. 112. As: as if. 114. Agayn: against. grucche: grum-
ble. 115. sith: since. forgoon: forgo. 116. mote: may.
117. Theras: where. 118. but: unless. 119. speketh namoore:
say no more. 120. hertly: cordial. 121. wight: person. 122. er
that: before. 125. dredde: feared.

127. swich . . . leste: such as suited him. 128. sikerly: certainly. 130. buxomly: submissively. 135. purveye: provide.
136. pryvee: personal. 137. yaf: gave. 141. fer . . . thilke:
far from that same. 142. shoop: prepared. 143. throop: village. delitable: delightful. 145. bestes: animals. herbergage: shelter. 146. of: by. toke: won. 147. After that:
according as. 149. Which that: who. holden: considered.
154. highte: was called. 155. vertuous beautee: the beauty of
virtue (rather than the mere beauty of sight). 156. oon: one
of. 157. poureliche y-fostred up: poorly nurtured. 158. likerous: lecherous. y-ronne: run. 159. Wel ofter: much more
often. tonne: barrel. 164. sad corage: serious heart.

Hir olde, poure fader fostred she.
A fewe sheep, spynnynge on feld,° she kepte;°
She wolde noght been ydel til she slepte.

And whan she homward cam, she wolde brynge
Wortes° or othere herbes tymes ofte,   170
The whiche she shredde° and seeth° for hir
     lyvynge,°
And made hir bed ful hard and nothyng softe,
And ay she kepte hir fadres lyf on lofte°
With every obeisance° and diligence
That child may doon to fadres reverence.

   Upon Grisilde, this poure creature,
Ful ofte sithe° this markys sette his eye
As he on huntyng rood paraventure,°
And whan it fil° that he myghte hire espye,
He noght with wantowne lookyng of folye   180
His eyen caste on hire, but in sad° wyse
Upon hir cheere° he wolde hym ofte avyse,°

Commendynge in his herte hir wommanhede
And eek hir vertu passyng° any wight
Of so yong age as wel in cheere as dede,
For, thogh the peple have no greet insight
In vertue, he considered ful right
Hir bountee and disposed° that he wolde
Wedde hire oonly, if evere he wedden sholde.

   The day of weddyng cam, but no wight kan
Telle what womman that it sholde be,   191
For which merveille wondred many a man
And seyden, whan they were in pryvetee,
"Wol nat oure lord yet leve his vanytee?°
Wol he nat wedde? Allas, allas, the while!
Why wol he thus hymself and us bigyle?"

   But nathelees this markys hath doon make,°
Of gemmes set in gold and in asure,°
Broches and rynges, for Grisildis sake;
And of hir clothyng took he the mesure   200
Of a mayde lyk to hir stature,
And eek of othere ornamentes alle
That unto swich a weddyng sholde falle.

The tyme of undren° of the same day
Approcheth that this weddyng sholde be,
And al the paleys put was in array,
Bothe halle and chambres ech in his° degree.

Houses of office° stuffed with plentee
Ther maystow° seen of deyntevous° vitaille
That may be founde as fer as last° Ytaille.   210

This roial markys, richely arrayed,
Lordes and ladyes in his compaignye
The whiche that to the feste were y-prayed,°
And of his retenue the bachelrye°
With many a soun of sondry melodye
Unto the village of the which I tolde
In this array the righte wey han holde.

   Grisilde, of this, God woot, ful innocent°
That for hire shapen° was al this array,
To fecchen water at a welle is went,   220
And cometh hoom as soone as ever she may,
For wel she hadde herd seyd that thilke day
The markys sholde wedde; and, if she myghte,
She wolde fayn han seyn° som of that sighte.

She thoghte, "I wole with othere maydens stonde°
That been my felawes° in oure dore and se
The markisesse,° and therfore wol I fonde°
To doon at hoom as soone as it may be
The labour which that longeth° unto me,
And thanne I may at leyser° hir biholde   230
If she this wey unto the castel holde."

And as she wolde over hir thresshfold gon,
The markys cam and gan hire for to calle,°
And she sette doun hir water pot anon
Bisyde the thresshfold in an oxes stalle,
And doun upon hir knees she gan to falle,
And with sad contenance kneleth stille
Til she hadde herd what was the lordes wille.

   This thoghtful markys spak unto this mayde
Ful sobrely and seyde in this manere: 240
"Where is youre fader, O Grisildis," he sayde;
And she with reverence in humble cheere
Answerde, "Lord, he is alredy heere."
And in she goth withouten lenger lette,°
And to the markys she hir fader fette.°

He by the hand than took this olde man
And seyde thus, whan he hym hadde asyde,
"Janicula, I neither may ne kan
Lenger the plesance° of myn herte hyde.
If that thow vouchesauf, what so bityde,   250

167. spynnynge on feld: (while) spinning (by hand with a spindle) on the field. kepte: tended. 170. Wortes: roots. 171. shredde: shredded. seeth: boiled. lyvynge: sustenance. 173. kepte on lofte: sustained. 174. obeisance: obedience. 177. sithe: time. 178. rood paraventure: rode perchance. 179. fil: befell. 181. sad: sober. 182. cheere: appearance. hym avyse: consider. 184. passyng: surpassing. 188. disposed: determined. 194. vanytee: folly. 197. doon make: caused to be made. 198. asure: azure. 204. undren: 9 A.M. 207. his: its.

208. Houses of office: household storerooms. 209. maystow: you may. deyntevous: the most dainty. 210. last: extends. 213. y-prayed: invited. 214. bachelrye: bachelor band. 218. innocent: unsuspecting. 219. shapen: prepared. 224. wolde . . . seyn: would very much like to see. 225. stonde: stand. 226. felawes: companions. 227. markisesse: marchioness. fonde: try. 229. longeth: belongs. 230. leyser: leisure. 233. gan . . . calle: called her. 244. lenger lette: longer delay. 245. fette: fetched. 249. plesance: inclination.

Thy doghter wol I take er that I wende°
As for° my wyf unto my lyves ende.

"Thow lovest me, I woot it wel certeyn,
And art my feithful lige° man y-bore,°
And al that liketh° me, I dar wel seyn,
It liketh thee, and specially therfore
Tel me that point that I have seyd bifore,
If that thow wolt unto that purpos drawe°
To take me as for thy sone-in-lawe."

The sodeyn cas° this man astoneyd° so   260
That reed° he wax;° abayst° and al quakyng
He stood; unnethe° seyde he wordes mo°
But oonly thus, "Lord," quod he, "my willyng
Is as ye wole, ne ayeins youre likyng
I wol no thyng, ye be my lord so deere.
Right as yow list, governeth this matere."

"Yet wol I," quod this markys softely,
"That in thy chambre I and thow and she
Have a collacioun,° and wostow° why?
For I wol aske if it hir wille be   270
To be my wyf and rule hire after me,°
And al this shal be doon in thy presence.
I wol noght speke out of thyn audience."°

And in the chambre whil they were aboute
Hir tretys,° which as ye shal after heere,
The peple cam unto the hous withoute
And wondred hem° in how honeste° manere
And tentifly° she kepte hir fader deere.
But outrely° Grisildis wondre myghte,
For nevere erst ne saw she swich a sighte.   280

No wonder is thogh that she were astoned
To see so greet a gest° come in that place.
She nevere was to swiche gestes woned,°
For which she looked with ful pale face.
But, shortly forth this matere for to chace,°
Thise arn° the wordes that the markys sayde
To this benygne, verray,° feithful mayde.

"Grisilde," he seyde, "ye shal wel understonde
It liketh to° youre fader and to me
That I yow wedde, and eek it may so stonde,   290
As I suppose, ye wol that it so be.

But thise demandes aske I first," quod he,
"That sith it shal be doon in hastif° wyse,
Wol ye assente or ellis yow avyse?°

"I sey this. Be ye redy with good herte
To al my lust,° and that I frely may,
As me best thynketh, do yow laughe or smerte,°
And nevere ye to grucche it nyght ne day;
And eek, whan I sey 'ye,' ne sey nat 'nay,'
Neither by word ne frownyng contenance?   300
Swere this, and here I swere oure alliance."

Wondrynge upon this word, quakyng for drede,
She seyde, "Lord, undigne° and unworthy
I am to thilke honour that ye me bede,°
But, as ye wol yourself, right so wol I.
And heere I swere that nevere willyngly
In werk ne thoght I nyl yow disobeye
For to be deed,° thogh me were looth° to deye."

"This is ynogh, Grisilde myn," quod he;
And forth he goth with a ful sobre cheere   310
Out at the dore, and after that cam she;
And to the peple he seyde in this manere:
"This is my wyf," quod he, "that standeth
     heere.
Honureth hire, and loveth hire, I preye,
Whoso me loveth. Ther is namoore to seye."

And, for that nothyng of hir olde gere°
She sholde brynge into his hous, he bad
That wommen sholde dispoylen° hir right there,
Of which thise ladyes were noght right glad
To handle hir clothes wherinne she was clad;   320
But nathelees this mayde bright of hewe
Fro foot to heed they clothed han al newe.

Hir herys° han they kembd° that laye untressed
Ful rudely, and with hir fyngres smale°
A corone° on hir heed they han y-dressed,°
And sette hire ful of nowches° grete and smale.
Of hir array what° sholde I make a tale?
Unnethe° the peple hir knew for hir fairnesse
Whan she translated was in swich richesse.

This markys hath hire spoused with a ryng   330
Broght for the same cause, and thanne° hir sette
Upon an hors snow-whit and wel amblyng,
And to his paleys, er he lenger lette,°

251. wende: leave.   252. As for: for.   254. lige: liege.   y-bore:
born.   255. liketh: pleases.   258. wolt drawe: will agree.
260. sodeyn cas: sudden outcome.   astoneyd: astonished.
261. reed: red.   wax: grew.   abayst: abashed.   262. unnethe:
hardly.   mo: more.   269. collacioun: conference.   wostow:
do you know.   271. rule . . . me: conduct herself according to
my will.   273. audience: hearing.   275. tretys: agreement.
277. wondred hem: marveled.   honeste: honorable a.   278. ten-
tifly: attentively.   279. outrely: utterly.   282. gest: guest.
283. woned: accustomed.   285. chace: pursue.   286. arn: are.
287. verray: true.   289. liketh to: pleases.

293. hastif: hasty.   294. yow avyse: consider.   296. lust:
pleasure.   297. As . . . smerte: as seems best to me, make you
laugh or grieve.   303. undigne: unequal.   304. bede: offer.
308. For . . . deed: on pain of death.   me . . . looth: I should
be loath to die.   316. gere: clothing.   318. dispoylen: undress.
323. herys: hair.   kembd: combed.   324. smale: slim.   325. co-
rone: coronet.   y-dressed: arranged.   326. nowches: jewelry.
327. what: why.   328. Unnethe: hardly.   331. thanne: then.
333. lette: delayed.

With joyful peple that hir ladde° and mette
Conveyed hire; and thus the day they spende
In revel til the sonne gan descende.

And shortly forth this tale for to chace,
I seye that to this newe markysesse
God hath swich favour sent hire of his grace
That it ne semed nat by liklynesse° 340
That she was born and fed in rudenesse
As in a cote° or in an oxe stalle
But norissed° in an emperoures halle.

To every wight she woxen° is so deere
And worshipful that folk ther she was bore
And from hir birthe knewe hire yeer by yeere
Unnethe trowed° they — but dorste han swore° —
That to Janicle, of which I spak bifore,
She doghter were, for as by conjecture
Hem thoughte° she was another creature. 350

For, thogh that evere vertuous was she,
She was encressed° in swich excellence
Of thewes° goode y-set in heigh bountee,
And so discreet and fair of eloquence,
So benygne and so digne° of reverence,
And koude so the peples herte embrace
That ech hir lovede that looked on hir face.

Noght oonly of Saluces° in the toun
Publissed° was the bountee of hir name,
But eek bisyde° in many a regioun, 360
If oon seyde wel, another seyde the same.
So spradde° of hir heighe bountee the fame
That men and wommen as wel yonge as olde
Goon to Saluce upon hire to biholde.

Thus Walter, lowely — nay! but roially —
Wedded with fortunat honestetee,°
In Goddes pees lyveth ful esily
At hom, and outward grace ynow° hadde he;
And, for he saugh° that under lowe degree
Was ofte vertu hid, the peple hym helde 370
A prudent man, and that is seyn ful selde.°

Noght oonly this Grisildis thurgh hir wit
Koude al the feet° of wyfly humblenesse,
But eek, whan that the cas required it,
The commune profit° koude she redresse.

Ther nas discord, rancour, ne hevynesse°
In al that land that she ne koude apese°
And wisly brynge hem alle in reste and ese.

Thogh that hir housbond absent were anon,
If gentilmen or othere of hir contree 380
Were wrothe, she wolde bryngen hem aton.°
So wise and rype° wordes hadde she,
And juggementz of so greet equytee,
That she from Hevene sent was, as men wende,°
Peple to save and every wrong t' amende.

Nat longe tyme after that this Grisild
Was wedded, she a doghter hath y-bore.
Al had hir levere° have born a knave° child,
Glad was the markys and the folk therfore,
For, thogh a mayde child coome al bifore,° 390
She may unto a knave child atteyne
By liklyhede syn she nys nat bareyne.

III

Ther fil, as it bifalleth tymes mo,
Whan that this child had souked° but a throwe,°
This markys in his herte longeth so
To tempte° his wyf hir sadnesse° for to knowe
That he ne myghte out of his herte throwe
This merveillous desir his wyf t' assaye.
Nedelees,° God woot, he thoghte hire for
  t' affraye.°

He hadde assayed hire ynow bifore 400
And fond° hire evere good. What neded it
Hir for to tempte and alwey moore and moore,
Thogh som men preyse it for a subtil wit?
But, as for me, I seye that yvele it sit°
T' assaye a wyf whan that it is no nede
And putten hire in angwyssh and in drede.

For which this markys wroghte in this manere:
He cam allone a nyght ther as° she lay
With steerne face and with ful trouble cheere°
And seyde thus: " Grisilde," quod he, " that day
That I yow took out of youre poure array 411
And putte yow in estat of heigh noblesse,
Ye have nat that forgeten, as I gesse.

" I seye, Grisilde, this present dignitee
In which that I have put yow, as I trowe,
Maketh yow nat foryetful for to be
That I yow took in poure estat ful lowe

---

334. ladde: led. 340. by liklynesse: in likelihood. 342. cote: hut. 343. norissed: nurtured. 344. woxen: grown. 347. trowed: believed. dorste . . . swore: would have sworn the contrary. 350. Hem thoughte: it seemed to them. 352. encressed: increased. 353. thewes: customs. 355. digne: worthy. 358. Saluces: Saluzzo, the town. 359. publissed: made known. 360. bisyde: besides. 362. spradde: spread. 366. honestetee: distinction. 368. ynow: enough. 369. saugh: saw. 371. selde: seldom. 373. feet: art. 375. profit: interest.

376. hevynesse: oppression. 377. apese: appease. 381. aton: into accord. 382. rype: mature. 384. wende: believed. 388. Al . . . levere: though she would sooner. knave: boy. 390. coome al bifore: came first. 394. souked: suckled. throwe: while. 396. tempte: test. sadnesse: stability. 399. Nedelees: needlessly. thoghte . . . t' affraye: decided to alarm her. 401. fond: found. 404. yvele it sit: ill it sits. 408. ther as: where. 409. trouble cheere: troubled countenance.

For any wele° ye mote° yourselven knowe.
Tak hede of every word that I yow seye.
Ther is no wight that hereth it but we tweye. 420

"Ye woot yourself wel how that ye cam heere
Into this hous, it is nat longe ago,
And, thogh to me that ye be lief° and deere,
Unto my gentils° ye be nothyng so.
They seyn, to hem it is greet shame and wo
For to be subgetz° and been in servage°
To thee that born art of a smal village.

"And namely sith° thy doghter was y-bore,
Thise wordes han they spoken, doutelees.
But I desire, as I have doon bifore, 430
To lyve my lyf with hem in reste and pees.
I may nat in this cas be recchelees.°
I moot° doon with thy doghter for the beste,
Nat as I wolde, but as my peple leste.°

"And yet, God woot, this is ful looth to me.
But, nathelees,° withouten youre wityng°
I wol nat doon.° But this wol I," quod he,
"That ye to me assente as in this thyng.
Shewe now youre pacience in youre wirkyng°
That ye me highte° and swore in youre village
That day that maked was oure mariage." 441

Whan she hadde herd al this, she noght ameved°
Neither in word or cheere or contenaunce,
For, as it semed, she was nat agreved.°
She seyde, "Lord, al lith° in youre plesance.
My child and I with hertly obeisance°
Been youres al, and ye mowe° save or spille°
Youre owene thyng. Werketh after° youre wille.

"Ther may nothyng, God so my soule save,
Liken to° yow that may displese me, 450
Ne I desire nothyng for to have
Ne drede for to lese° save oonly ye.
This wyl is in myn herte and ay shal be.
No lengthe of tyme or deth may this deface,
Ne chaunge my corage° to another place."

Glad was this markys of hir answeryng,
But yet he feyned as° he were nat so.
Al drery° was his cheere and his lookyng

Whan that he sholde out of the chambre go.
Soone after this a furlong wey or two° 460
He pryvely hath told al his entente
Unto a man and to his wyf hym sente.

A maner sergeant° was this pryvee° man
The which that° feithful ofte he founden hadde
In thynges grete, and eek swich folk wel kan
Doon execucioun in thynges badde.
The lord knew wel that he hym loved and dradde.
And whan this sergeant wiste° his lordes wille,
Into the chambre he stalked hym ful stille.

"Madame," he seyde, "ye mote° foryeve it me
Thogh I do thyng to which I am constreyned. 471
Ye ben so wys that ful wel knowe ye
That lordes hestes° mowe nat ben y-feyned.
They mowe wel been biwailled or compleyned,
But men mote nede° unto hir lust° obeye,
And so wol I. Ther is namoore to seye.

"This child I am comaunded for to take";
And spak namoore, but out the child he hente°
Despitously° and gan a cheere make°
As thogh he wolde han slayn it er he wente. 480
Grisildis moot al suffren and al consente,
And as a lamb she sitteth meke and stille
And leet this cruel sergeant doon his wille.

Suspecious° was the diffame° of this man,
Suspect his face, suspect his word also,
Suspect the tyme in which he this bigan.
Allas, hir doghter that she loved so,
She wende he wolde han slawen° it right tho.°
But nathelees she neither weep ne syked,°
Conformynge hire to that the markys liked. 490

But at the laste speken she bigan,
And mekely she to the sergeant preyde,
So as he was a worthy, gentil man,
That she moste kisse hir child er that it deyde;
And in hir barm° this litel child she leyde
With ful sad face, and gan the child to blisse,°
And lulled it, and after gan it kisse.

And thus she seyde in hir benygne voys,
"Farewel, my child. I shal thee nevere see,
But, sith I thee have marked with the croys° 500
Of thilke° Fader — blessed mote he be —

That for us deyde upon a croys of tree,°
Thy soule, litel child, I hym bitake,°
For this nyght shaltow dyen for my sake."

    I trowe that to a norice° in this cas
It hadde been hard this routhe° for to se;
Wel myghte a moder than han cryd "allas"!
But nathelees, so sad° stedefast was she
That she endured al adversitee,
And to the sergeant mekely she sayde,   510
"Have here agayn youre litel yonge mayde.

    "Goth° now," quod she, "and doth my lordes
      heste.
But o thyng wol I pray yow, of youre grace,
That, but° my lord forbad yow, at the leste
Burieth this litel body in som place
That bestes° ne no briddes° it to-race."°
But he no word wol to that purpos seye,
But took the child, and wente upon his weye.

    This sergeant cam unto his lord agayn,
And of Grisildis wordes and hir cheere   520
He tolde hym poynt for poynt in short and playn,
And hym presenteth with his doghter deere.
Somwhat this lord hath routhe° in his manere;
But, nathelees, his purpos held he stille,
As lordes doon whan they wol han hir wille,

    And bad this sergeant that he pryvely
Sholde this child softe wynde° and wrappe,
With alle circumstances tendrely,
And carie it in a cofre° or in a lappe,°
But, upon peyne his heed of for to swappe,°   530
That no man sholde knowe of his entente,
Ne whennes° he cam, ne whider that he wente,

    But at Boloigne° to his suster deere,
That thilke tyme of Panyk° was countesse,
He sholde it take and shewe° hire this matere,
Bisekynge hire to doon hir bisynesse°
This child to fostre in al gentilesse,
And whos child that it was, he bad hire hyde
From every wight for aught that may bityde.

    The sergeant goth and hath fulfild this thyng.
But to this markys now retourne we,   541
For now goth he ful faste ymagynyng°
If by his wyves cheere he myghte se,

Or by hir word aperceyve, that she
Were chaunged, but he nevere hir koude fynde
But evere in oon° ylike sad° and kynde.

    As glad, as humble, as bisy in servyse
And eek in love as she was wont to be
Was she to hym in every maner wise,°
Ne of hir doghter noght a word spak she.   550
Noon accident,° for noon adversitee,°
Was seyn in hire, ne nevere hir doghter° name
Ne nempned° she in ernest ne in game.

IV

    In this estat ther passed ben foure yeer
Er she with childe was, but, as God wolde,
A knave child she bar by this Walter,
Ful gracious and fair for to biholde;
And, whan that folk it to his fader tolde,
Nat oonly he but al his contree merye
Was for this child, and God they thanke and
      herye.°   560

    Whan it was two yeer old, and fro the brest
Departed° of his norice, on a day
This markys caughte yet another lest°
To tempte his wyf yet ofter° if he may.
O nedelees was she tempted in assay,
But wedded men ne knowe no mesure
Whan that they fynde a pacient creature!

    "Wyf," quod this markys, "ye han herd er this
My peple sikly berth° oure mariage,
And, namely sith° my sone y-born is,   570
Now is it worse than evere in al oure age.
The murmur sleeth° myn herte and my corage,°
For to myn erys comth the voys so smerte°
That it wel neigh destroyed hath myn herte.

    "Now sey they thus, 'Whan Walter is agon,°
Thanne shal the blood of Janicle succede
And been oure lord, for oother have we noon.'
Swiche wordes seith my peple out of drede.°
Wel oghte I of swich murmur taken hede,
For certeinly I drede swich sentence,°   580
Though they nat pleyn speke in myn audience.°

    "I wolde lyve in pees, if that I myghte;
Wherfore I am disposed outrely,°

---

502. tree: wood.   503. hym bitake: to him commit.   505. norice: nurse. 506. routhe: sorrow. 508. sad: soberly. 512. Goth: go. 514. but: unless. 516. bestes: beasts. briddes: birds. to-race: may (not) destroy. 523. routhe: pity. 527. wynde: swathe. 529. cofre: chest. lappe: wrapper. 530. upon . . . swappe: on pain of having his head cut off. 532. whennes: whence. 533. Boloigne: Bologna. 534. Panyk: Panico. 535. shewe: explain to. 536. doon . . . bisynesse: exercise her diligence. 542. ymagynyng: wondering.

546. in oon: consistently. sad: steadfast. 549. maner wise: sort of way. 551. Noon accident: no disturbance. for . . . adversitee: no matter what the adversity. 552. doghter: daughter's. 553. nempned: named. 560. herye: praise. 562. Departed: taken. 563. caughte . . . lest: was again seized with another desire. 564. ofter: once more. 569. sikly berth: are dissatisfied with. 570. namely sith: particularly since. 572. sleeth: pierces. corage: spirit. 573. smerte: bitterly. 575. agon: gone. 578. out of drede: without a doubt. 580. sentence: opinion. 581. audience: hearing. 583. outrely: utterly.

As I his suster served by nyghte,
Right so thenke I to serve hym pryvely.
This warne I yow that ye nat sodeynly
Out of yourself for no wo sholde outraye.°
Beth pacient, and therof I yow praye."

"I have," quod she, "seyd thus and evere
    shal:
I wol nothyng, ne nyl° nothyng, certeyn,   590
But as yow list. Noght greveth me at al
Thogh that my doghter and my sone be sleyn —
At youre comandement, this is to seyn.
I have nat had no part of children tweyne°
But first siknesse, and after wo and peyne.

"Ye ben oure lord. Dooth with youre owene thyng
Right as yow list. Axeth no reed° of me,
For, as I lefte at hom al my clothyng
Whan I first cam to yow, right so," quod she,
"Lefte I my wyl and al my libertee   600
And took youre clothyng; wherfore, I yow preye,
Dooth youre plesance. I wol youre lust° obeye.

"And certes if I hadde prescience°
Youre wyl to knowe, er ye youre lust me tolde,
I wolde it doon withouten necligence.
But now I woot° youre lust and what ye wolde,
Al youre plesance° ferme and stable I holde,
For wiste I° that my deeth wolde doon yow ese,°
Right gladly wolde I dyen yow to plese.

"Deeth may nat make no comparisoun   610
Unto youre loue." And whan this markys say°
The constance of his wyf, he caste adoun
His eyen two and wondreth that she may
In pacience suffre al this array;
And forth he goth with drery contenance,
But to his herte it was ful gret plesance.

    This ugly sergeant, in the same wyse
That he hir doghter caughte,° right so he —
Or worse, if men kan worse devyse° —
Hath hent° hir sone that ful was of beautee;   620
And evere in oon so pacient was she
That she no cheere made of hevynesse,
But kiste hir sone and after gan it blesse,

Save this: she preyde hym that, if he myghte,
Hir litel sone he wolde in erthe grave,°
His tendre lymes delicat to sighte
Fro foweles and fro bestes for to save.
But she noon answere of hym mighte have.

He wente his wey as hym nothyng ne roghte,°
But to Boloigne he tendrely it broghte.   630

This markys wondreth ever lenger° the moore
Upon hir pacience; and, if that he
Ne hadde soothly knowen ther bifoore
That parfitly hir children loved she,
He wolde have wend° that of som subtiltee
And of malice or of cruel corage
That she hadde suffred this with sad visage.

But wel he knew that, next hymself, certayn,
She loved hir children best in every wise.
But now of wommen wolde I asken fayn°   640
If thise assayes myghte nat suffise.
What koude a sturdy housbond moore devyse
To preve° hir wifhod and hir stedfastnesse,
And he contynuynge evere in sturdynesse?°

But ther ben folk of swich condicioun
That, whan they have a certeyn purpos take,
They kan nat stynte of hir entencioun,
But, right as° they were bounden to that stake,
They wol nat of that firste purpos slake.°
Right so this markys fulliche° hath purposed   650
To tempte his wyf as he was first disposed.

He wayteth if by word or contenance
That she to hym was chaunged of corage,
But nevere koude he fynde variance.
She was ay oon in herte and in visage,
And ay the ferther that she was in age,
The moore trewe, if that it were possible,
She was to hym in love and moore penyble.°

For which it semed thus that of hem two
Ther nas but o° wyl, for as Walter leste,   660
The same lust was hir plesance also;
And, God be thanked, al fil° for the beste.
She shewed wel for no° worldly unreste
A wif as of hirself nothyng ne sholde
Wille in effect but as hir housbond wolde.

    The sclaundre° of Walter ofte and wyde spradde
That of a cruel herte he wikkedly,
For° he a poure womman wedded hadde,
Hath mordred bothe his children pryvely.
Swich murmur was among hem comunly.   670
No wonder is,° for to the peples ere
Ther cam no word but that they mordred were.

---

587. outraye: become overwhelmed. 590. nyl: shall (I) wish.
594. tweyne: two. 597. reed: advice. 602. lust: pleasure.
603. prescience: foreknowledge. 606. woot: know. 607. plesance: pleasure. 608. wiste I: if I knew. doon yow ese:
satisfy you. 611. say: saw. 618. caughte: seized. 619. devyse: imagine. 620. hent: taken. 625. grave: bury.

629. as . . . roghte: as if he did not care at all. 631. lenger:
the longer. 635. wend: supposed. 640. wolde fayn: would
like to. 643. preve: test. 644. sturdynesse: sternness.
648. right as: just as if. 649. slake: desist. 650. fulliche:
fully. 658. penyble: sacrificing. 660. o: one. 662. fil: befell.
663. for no: despite any 666. sclaundre: slander. 668. For:
because. 671. is: it is.

For which, wheras his peple ther bifore
Hadde loved hym wel, the sclaundre of his diffame
Made hem that they hym hated therfore.
To ben a mordrere is an hateful name.
But, nathelees, for ernest ne for game
He of his cruel purpos nolde stente.°
To tempte his wyf was set al his entente

Whan that his doghter twelve yeer was of age,
He to the court of Rome, in subtil° wise   681
Enformed of his wil, sente his message,°
Comaundynge hem swiche bulles° to devyse
As to his cruel purpos may suffise
How that the pope as for his peples reste°
Bad hym to wedde another if hym leste.

I seye, he bad they sholde contrefete°
The popes bulles, makyng mencioun
That he hath leve his firste wyf to lete°
As by the popes dispensacioun   690
To stynte rancour and dissencioun
Bitwixe his peple and hym; thus seyde the bulle
The which they han publissed at the fulle.°

The rude peple, as it no wonder is,
Wenden ful wel that it hadde ben right so.
But whan thise tidynges cam to Grisildis,
I deme that hir herte was ful wo,
But she, ylike sad° for evere mo,
Disposed was this humble creature
Th' adversitee of fortune al t' endure,   700

Abidynge evere his lust and his plesance
To whom that she was yeven herte and al
As to hir verray worldly suffisance.
But, shortly if this storie telle I shal,
This markys writen hath in special
A lettre in which he sheweth his entente,
And secrely he to Boloigne it sente.

To the erl of Panyk which that hadde tho°
Wedded his suster, preyde he specially
To bryngen hom agayn his children two   710
In honurable estat al openly;
But o thyng he hym prayde outrely
That he to no wight, thogh men wolde enquere,
Sholde nat telle whos children that they were,

But seye the mayden sholde y-wedded be
Unto the markys of Saluce anon.
And as this erl was preyed, so dide he,
For at day set, he on his wey is gon

Toward Saluce, and lordes many oon
In riche array, this mayden for to gyde,   720
Hir yonge brother ridyng hir bisyde.

Arrayed was toward hir mariage
This fresshe mayde ful of gemmes clere,°
Hir brother, which that seven yeer was of age,
Arrayed eek ful fressh in his manere.
And thus in gret noblesse and with glad cheere
Toward Saluces shapyng hir journey,
Fro day to day they ryden in hir wey.

V

Among° al this, after his wikke usage,°
This markys, yet his wif to tempte moore   730
To the outreste preve° of hir corage,
Fully to han experience and loore°
If that she were as stedefast as bifore,
He on a day in open audience
Ful boistously° hath seyd hire this sentence:

"Certes,° Grisilde, I hadde ynogh plesance
To han yow to my wyf for youre goodnesse,
As for youre trouthe and for youre obeisance,
Noght for youre lynage ne for youre richesse;
But now knowe I in verray sothfastnesse°   740
That in gret lordshipe, if I wel avyse,°
Ther is gret servitute in sondry wyse.

"I may nat do as every plowman may.
My peple me constreyneth for to take
Another wyf, and crien day by day;
And eek the pope, rancour for to slake,
Consenteth it, that dar I undertake.°
And, trewely, thus muche I wol yow seye,
My newe wyf is comynge by the weye.

"Be strong of herte, and voyde° anon hir place,
And thilke dowere that ye broghten me   751
Tak it agayn, I graunte it of my grace.
Retourneth to youre fadres hous," quod he.
"No man may alwey han prosperitee.
With evene° herte I rede° yow t' endure
The strook of fortune or of aventure."°

And she agayn answerde in pacience.
"My lord," quod she, "I woot and wiste°
     alway
How that bitwixen youre magnificence
And my poverte no wight kan ne may   760
Maken comparisoun; it is no nay.°

---

678. nolde stente: wouldn't desist.   681. subtil: secret.   682. message: messengers.   683. bulles: papal bulls.   685. as . . . reste: for the pacification of his (Walter's) people.   687. contrefete: counterfeit.   689. lete: leave.   693. at the fulle: in full.   698. ylike sad: consistently steadfast.   708. tho: then.

723. clere: brilliant.   729. Among: during.   wikke usage: cruel custom.   731. outreste preve: uttermost proof.   732. loore: knowledge.   735. boistously: roughly.   736. Certes: certainly. 740. sothfastnesse: truth.   741. avyse: consider.   747. undertake: vow.   750. voyde: vacate.   755. evene: steady.   rede: advise.   756. aventure: chance.   758. wiste: knew.   761. it . . . nay: there's no denying.

I ne heeld° me nevere digne° in no manere
To be youre wyf, no, ne youre chambrere.°

"And in this hous ther° ye me lady made,
The heighe God take I for my witnesse —
And also wisly he my soule glade° —
I nevere heeld me lady ne maistresse
But humble servant to youre worthynesse,
And evere shal, whil that my lyf may dure,°
Aboven every worldly creature.   770

"That ye so longe of youre benygnytee
Han holden° me in honour and nobleye°
Whereas I was noght worthy for to be,
That thonke I God — and yow — to whom I
        preye,
Foryelde° it yow. Ther is namoore to seye.
Unto my fader gladly wol I wende
And with hym dwelle unto my lyves ende.

"Ther I was fostred of a child ful smal,
Til I be deed, my lyf ther wol I lede,
A wydewe clene in body, herte, and al;   780
For, sith I yaf° to yow my maydenhede°
And am youre trewe wyf, it is no drede,°
God shilde° swich a lordes wyf to take
Another man to housbond or to make.°

"And of youre newe wyf, God of his grace
So graunte yow wele° and prosperitee,
For I wol gladly yelden hire my place
In which that I was blisful wont to be;
For, sith it liketh yow, my lord," quod she,
"That whilom° weren al myn hertes reste,   790
That I shal goon, I wol goon whan yow leste.

"But, theras ye me profre swich dowaire
As I first broghte, it is wel in my mynde,
It were my wrecched clothes nothyng faire,
The whiche to me were hard now for to fynde.
O goode God, how gentil and how kynde
Ye semed by youre speche and youre visage
The day that maked was oure mariage.

"But sooth is seyd — algate° I fynde it trewe,
For in effect it proved is on me —   800
Love is noght old° as whan that it is newe.
But certes, lord, for noon° adversitee,
To dyen in the cas,° it shal nat be

That evere in word or werk I shal repente
That I yow yaf myn herte in hool° entente.

"My lord, ye woot that in my fadres place
Ye dide me strepe° out of my poure wede°
And richely me cladden of youre grace.
To yow broght I noght ellis, out of drede,°
But feith° and nakednesse and maydenhede.   810
And here agayn my clothyng I restore,
And eek my weddyng ryng for evere moore.

"The remenant of youre jewels redy be
Inwith youre chambre, dar I saufly sayn.
Naked out of my fadres hous," quod she,
"I cam, and naked moot I turne agayn.
Al youre plesance wol I folwen fayn.
But yet I hope it be nat youre entente
That I smoklees° out of youre paleys wente.

"Ye koude nat doon so dishoneste a thyng   820
That thilke wombe in which youre children leye
Sholde biforn the peple in my walkyng
Be seyn° al bare. Wherfore, I yow preye,
Lat me nat lyk a worm go by the weye.
Remembre yow, myn owene lord so deere,
I was youre wyf, thogh I unworthy weere.

"Wherfore, in gerdoun° of my maydenhede
Which that I broghte and noght agayn I bere,
As voucheth sauf° to yeve me to my mede°
But swich a smok as I was wont to were,   830
That I therwith may wrye° the wombe of here°
That was youre wyf, and here I take my leve
Of yow, myn owene lord, lest I yow greve."

"The smok," quod he, "that thow hast on thy
        bak,
Lat it be stille, and bere it forth with thee."
But wel unnethes° thilke word he spak
But wente his wey for routhe and for pitee.
Biforn the folk hirselven strepeth she,
And in hir smok with heed and foot al bare
Toward hir fader hous forth is she fare.   840

The folk hir folwen wepynge in hir weye,
And Fortune ay they cursen as they goon,
But she fro wepyng kepte hir eyen dreye,
Ne in this tyme word ne spak she noon.
Hir fader, that this tidynge herd anon.
Curseth the day and tyme that nature
Shoop° hym to be a lyves° creature.

---

762. heeld: considered.   digne: worthy.   763. chambrere:
chambermaid.   764. ther: where.   766. also . . . glade: may
he truly comfort my soul.   769. dure: last.   772. holden: maintained.   nobleye: nobility.   775. Foryelde: repay.   781. yaf:
gave.   maydenhede: maidenhood.   782. drede: doubt.
783. shilde: forbid.   784. make: mate.   786. wele: welfare.
790. whilom: once.   799. algate: at least.   801. noght old: not
the same when it is old.   802. for noon: no matter what the.
803. To . . . cas: (even) in case of death.

805. hool: whole.   807. dide me strepe: had me stripped.
wede: clothing.   809. out of drede: without doubt.   810. feith:
fidelity.   819. smoklees: without a smock.   823. seyn: seen.
827. gerdoun: reward.   829. As . . . sauf: vouchsafe.   mede:
reward.   831. wrye: conceal.   here: her.   836. unnethes:
hardly.   847. Shoop: shaped.   lyves: living.

For, out of doute, this olde poure man
Was evere in suspect° of hir mariage,
For evere he demed sith that it bigan   850
That, whan the lord fulfild hadde his corage,°
Hym wolde thynke it were a disparage°
To his estat so lowe for t' alighte,°
And voyden° hire as soone as evere he myghte.

Agayns° his doghter hastiliche goth he,
For he by noyse of folk knew hir comynge,
And with hir olde cote as° it myghte be
He covered hire, ful sorwefully wepynge.
But on hir body myghte° he it nat brynge,
For rude was the clooth and she moore of age 860
By dayes fele° than at hir mariage.

Thus with hir fader for a certein space
Dwelleth this flour° of wifly pacience,
That neither by hir wordes ne hir face
Biforn the folk, ne eek in hir absence,
Ne shewed she that hir was doon° offence,
Ne of hir heighe estat no remembrance
Ne hadde she, as by° hir contenance.

No wonder is, for in hir grete estat
Hir goost° was evere in pleyn humylitee.   870
No tendre mouth, noon herte delicat,
No pompe, no semblant° of realtee,°
But ful of pacient benygnytee,
Discreet and pridelees, ay honurable,
And to hir housbonde evere meke and stable.

Men speke of Job, and moost for his humblesse,
As clerkes, whan hem lest,° kan wel endite,°
Namely of men; but as in soothfastnesse,°
Thogh clerkes preyse wommen but a lite,°
Ther kan no man in humblesse hym acquite   880
As wommen kan, ne kan be half so trewe
As wommen been, but it be falle of newe.°

VI

Fro Boloigne is this erl of Panyk come,
Of which the fame up sprong to moore and lesse,
And to the peples eres° alle and some
Was kouth° eek that a newe markisesse
He with hym broghte in swich pompe and richesse
That nevere was ther seyn with mannes eye
So noble array in al West Lumbardye.

The markys which that shoop and knew al
      this,
Er that this erl was come, sente his message   891
For thilke sely° poure Grisildis,
And she with humble herte and glad visage,
Nat with no swollen thoght in hir corage,
Cam at his heste° and on hir knees hir sette,
And reverently and wysly she hym grette.°

"Grisilde," quod he, "my wille is outrely°
This mayden that shal wedded been to me
Receyved be tomorwe as really°
As it possible is in myn hous to be,   900
And eek that every wight in his degree°
Have his estat in sittyng° and servyse
And heigh plesance as I kan best devyse.

"I have no wommen suffisant, certayn,
The chambres for t' arraye in ordynance°
After my lust,° and therfore wolde I fayn
That thyn were al swich manere governance.°
Thow knowest eek of old al my plesance.
Though thyn array be badde and yvel biseye,°
Do thow thy devoir at the leeste weye."°   910

"Nat oonly, lord, that I am glad," quod she,
"To doon youre lust, but I desire also
Yow for to serve and plese in my degree
Withouten feyntyng° and shal evere mo,
Ne nevere for no wele ne no wo
Ne shal the goost withinne myn herte stente°
To love yow best with al my trewe entente."

And with that word she gan the hous to dighte,°
And tables for to sette, and beddes make,
And peyned hire° to doon al that she myghte,   920
Preyynge the chambreres, for Goddes sake,
To hasten hem and faste swepe and shake.
And she, the mooste servysable of alle,
Hath every chambre arrayed and his halle.

Abouten undren° gan this erl alighte,°
That with hym broghte thise noble children tweye,
For which the peple ran to seen the sighte
Of hire array so richely biseye;
And thanne at erst° amonges hem° they seye°
That Walter was no fool thogh that hym leste 930
To chaunge his wyf, for it was for the beste.

For she is fairer, as they demen alle,
Than is Grisilde and moore tendre of age,
And fairer fruyt bitwene hem sholde falle
And moore plesant for° hire heigh lynage;
Hir brother eek so fair was of visage,
That hem to seen the peple hath caught plesance,
Commendynge now the markys governance.°

"O stormy peple, unsad° and evere untrewe,
Ay undiscreet and chaungynge as a vane,°   940
Delitynge evere in rumbul° that is newe,
For lyk the moone ay wexe ye and wane,
Ay ful of clappyng deere ynow a jane!°
Youre doom° is fals, youre constance yvele
    preveth.°
A ful greet fool is he that on yow leveth."°

Thus seyden sadde° folk in that citee,
Whan that the peple gazed up and doun
For they were glad right° for the noveltee
To han a newe lady of hir toun.
Namoore of this make I now mencioun,   950
But to Grisilde agayn wol I me dresse°
And telle hir constance and hir bisynesse.°

Ful bisy was Grisilde in every thyng
That to the feste was apertinent.
Right noght was she abayst° of hir clothyng
Thogh it were rude and somdel eek to-rent,°
But with glad cheere she to the yate is went
With oother folk to greete the markysesse,
And after that dooth forth hir bisynesse.

With so glad cheere his gestes she receyveth,   960
And so konnyngly everich° in his degree,
That no defaute° no man aperceyveth,
But ay they wondren what she myghte be
That in so poure array was for to se
And koude° swich honour and reverence,
And worthily they preysen hir prudence.

In al this menewhile she ne stente°
This mayde and eek hir brother to commende
With al hir herte in ful benygne entente
So wel that no man koude hir pris amende.°   970
But at the laste, whan that thise lordes wende
To sitten doun to mete, he gan to calle
Grisilde as she was bisy in his halle.

"Grisilde," quod he, as it were in his pley,
"How liketh thee my wyf and hir beautee?"
"Right wel," quod she, "my lord, for, in good fey,°
A fairer saw I nevere noon than she.
I prey to God, yeve hire prosperitee,
And so hope I that he wol to yow sende
Plesance ynogh unto youre lyves ende.   980

"O thyng biseke° I yow, and warne also,
That ye ne prike° with no tormentynge
This tendre mayden as ye han don mo,°
For she is fostred in hir norissynge°
Moore tendrely, and, to my supposynge,
She koude nat adversitee endure
As koude a poure fostred creature."

And whan this Walter saw hir pacience,
Hir glade cheere, and no malice at al,
And he so ofte had doon to hire offence,   990
And she ay sad and constant as a wal,
Continuynge evere hir innocence over al,
This sturdy markys gan his herte dresse°
To rewen° upon hir wifly stedfastnesse.

"This is ynogh, Grisilde myn," quod he.
"Be now namoore agast ne yvele apayed.°
I have thy feith and thy benygnytee,
As wel as evere womman was, assayed
In greet estat and poureliche arrayed.
Now knowe I, deere wyf, thy stedfastnesse";   1000
And hire in armes took and gan hir kesse.

And she for wonder took of it no keep.°
She herde nat what thyng he to hir seyde.
She ferde as° she hadde stirt out of a sleep,
Til she out of hir mazednesse abreyde.°
"Grisilde," quod he, "by God that for us deyde,
Thow art my wyf, ne noon oother I have,
Ne nevere hadde, as God my soule save.

"This is thy doghter which thow hast supposed
To be my wyf; that oother, feithfully,   1010
Shal be myn heir, as I have ay disposed.
Thow bare hym in thy body, trewely.
At Boloigne have I kept hem pryvely.
Tak hem agayn, for now maistow° nat seye
That thow hast lorn noon° of thy children tweye.

"And folk that oother weys° han seyd of me,
I warne hem wel that I have doon this dede
For no malice ne for no crueltee
But for t' assaye in thee thy wommanhede,

---

935. plesant for: satisfactory because of.   938. governance:
planning.   939. unsad: unstable.   940. vane: weathervane.
941. rumbul: rumor.   943. clappyng . . . jane: chatter, dearly
bought at any price.   944. doom: judgment.   constance . . .
preveth: constancy meets the test poorly.   945. leveth: believes.
946. sadde: sober.   948. right: just.   951. me dresse: address
myself.   952. bisynesse: diligence.   955. abayst: abashed.
956. somdel . . . to-rent: also somewhat tattered.   961. konnyngly
everich: adeptly each one.   962. defaute: fault.   965. koude:
was familiar with, i.e., behaved with such dignity.   967. stente:
ceased.   970. hir . . . amende: improve upon her excellence.

976. fey: faith.   981. biseke: beseech.   982. prike: goad.
983. mo: others.   984. norissynge: nurture.   993. dresse: to
change.   994. rewen: rue.   996. agast . . . apayed: afraid or
grieved.   1002. keep: heed.   1004. ferde as: acted as if.
1005. mazednesse abreyde: daze was aroused.   1014. maistow:
you may.   1015. lorn noon: lost any.   1016. oother weys:
otherwise.

And nat to sleen my children, God forbede, 1020
But for to kepe hem pryvely and stille
Til I thy purpos knewe and al thy wille."

Whan she this herde, aswowne° doun she falleth
For pitous joye, and after hir swownynge
She bothe hir yonge children to hire calleth,
And in hir armes pitously wepynge
Embraceth hem, and tendrely kissynge
Ful lyk a moder with hir salte teres
She bathed both hir visage and hir heres.°

O which° a pitous thyng it was to se 1030
Hir swownyng, and hir humble voys to heere!
"Graunt mercy,° lord. God thanke it yow," quod
    she,
"That ye han saved me my children deere.
Now rekke I nevere to been ded° right heere.
Sith I stonde in youre love and in youre grace,
No fors of° deeth, ne whan my spirit pace.°

"O tendre, o deere, o yonge children myne!
Youre woful moder wende° stedfastly
That cruel houndes or som foul vermyne
Hadde eten yow, but God of his mercy 1040
And youre benygne fader tendrely
Hath doon yow kept."° And in that same stounde°
Al sodeynly she swapte° adoun to grounde.

And in hir swough,° so sadly° holdeth she
Hir children two whan she gan hem t' embrace
That with greet sleighte° and greet difficultee
The children from hir arm they gonne arace.°
O, many a teer on many a pitous face
Doun ran of hem that stoden hir bisyde.
Unnethe° abouten hire myghte they abyde.° 1050

Walter hir gladeth and hir sorwe slaketh.
She riseth up abaysed° from hir traunce,
And every wight hir° joye and feste° maketh
Til she hath caught agayn° hir contenaunce.
Walter hir dooth so feithfully plesaunce
That it was deyntee° for to seen the cheere
Bitwix hem to, now they ben met y-feere.°

Thise ladies, whan that they hir tyme say,°
Han taken hire, and into chambre goon,
And strepen hire out of hir rude array; 1060
And in a clooth of gold that brighte shoon,°

1023. aswowne: in a swoon. 1029. both . . . heres: the face
and hair of both of them. 1030. which: what. 1032. Graunt
mercy: much thanks. 1034. rekke . . . ded: I care never even
if I were dead. 1036. No . . . of: no matter for. pace: pass on.
1038. wende: believed. 1042. doon . . . kept: caused you to be
saved. stounde: moment. 1043. swapte: sank. 1044. swough:
swoon. sadly: firmly. 1046. sleighte: care. 1047. gonne
arace: removed. 1050. Unnethe: hardly. abyde: remain.
1052. abaysed: abashed. 1053. hir: for her. feste: happiness.
1054. caught agayn: recovered. 1056. deyntee: a delight.
1057. y-feere: together. 1058. hir . . . say: their opportunity
saw. 1061. shoon: shone.

With a coroune° of many a riche stoon
Upon hir hed, they into halle hir broghte,
And ther she was honured as hir oghte.

Thus hath this pitous day a blisful ende,
For every man and womman dooth his myght
This day in murthe and revel to dispende,
Til on the welkne° shoon the sterres lyght,
For moore solempne° in every mannes syght
This feste was and gretter of costage° 1070
Than was the revel of hir mariage.

Ful many a yeer in heigh prosperitee
Lyven thise two in concord and in reste;
And richely his doghter maried he
Unto a lord, oon of the worthieste
Of al Ytaille; and thanne in pees and reste
His wyves fader in his court he kepeth
Til that the soule out of his body crepeth.

His sone succedeth in his heritage
In reste and pees after his fader day, 1080
And fortunat was eek in mariage,
Al° putte he nat his wyf in gret assay.
This world is nat so strong — it is no nay —
As it hath been in olde tymes yore.
And herkneth what this auctour° seith therfore:

This storie is seyd, nat for that wyves sholde
Folwen° Grisilde as in humylitee,
For it were inportable° thogh they wolde,
But for that every wight in his degree
Sholde be constant in adversitee 1090
As was Grisilde; therfore Petrak writeth
This storie, which with heigh stile he enditeth.

For, sith a womman was so pacient
Unto a mortal man, wel moore us oghte
Receyven al in gree° that God us sent.°
For greet skile is,° he preve that he wroghte;°
But he ne tempteth no man that he boghte,°
As seith Seint Jame, if ye his Pistel° rede.
He preveth folk al day, it is no drede,°

And suffreth us as for oure excercise 1100
With sharpe scourges of adversitee
Ful ofte to be bete° in sondry wise,
Nat for to knowe oure wyl, for certes he,

1062. coroune: coronet. 1068. welkne: heavens. 1069. solempne: magnificent. 1070. costage: expense. 1082. Al:
even if. 1085. auctour: author (Petrarch). 1087. Folwen:
follow. 1088. inportable: intolerable. 1095. in gree: submissively. sent: sends. 1096. skile is: reason (there) is.
preve . . . wroghte: test what he has made. 1097. boghte: redeemed. 1098. Pistel: St. James's Epistle. 1099. drede:
doubt. 1102. bete: beaten.

Er we were born, knew al oure freletee,°
And for oure beste is al his governance.
Lat us thanne lyve in vertuous suffrance.°

EPILOGUE

"But o word, lordynges, herkneth er I go.
It were ful hard to fynde now-a-dayes
In al a toun Grisildis thre or two,
For, if that they were put to swiche assayes,   1110
The gold of hem hath now so badde alayes°
With bras that, thogh the coyne be fair at eye,
It wolde rather breste° a-two than plye.°

"For which heere, for the Wyves love of Bathe,°
Whos lyf and al hir secte God mayntene
In heigh maistrie° — and elles° were it scathe° —
I wol with lusty herte fressh and grene
Seye yow a song to glade yow, I wene.
And lat us stynte of ernestful matere.
Herkneth my song, that seith in this manere: 1120

"Grisilde is deed, and eek hir pacience,
And bothe atones° buryed in Ytaille,
For which I crie in open audience,
No wedded man so hardy be t' assaille°
His wyves pacience in trust° to fynde
Grisildis, for in certein he shal faille.

"O noble wyves, ful of heigh prudence,
Lat noon humilitee youre tonge nayle,
Ne lat no clerk have cause or diligence
To write of yow a storie of swich mervaille   1130
As of Grisildis, pacient and kynde,
Lest Chichivache° yow swelwe° in hir entraille.

"Folweth Ekko, that holdeth no silence
But evere answereth at the countretaille.°
Beth nat bidaffed° for youre innocence,
But sharply tak on yow the governaille.°
Emprenteth° wel this lessoun in youre mynde,
For commune profit sith it may availle.

"Ye archewyves,° stondeth at defense,
Syn ye be strong as is a greet camaille,°   1140
Ne suffreth nat° that men yow doon offense.

And sklendre° wyves, fieble as in bataille,
Beth egre° as a tigre yond in Ynde.°
Ay clappeth° as a mille, I yow consaille.

"Ne dreed hem nat, dooth hem no reverence,
For thogh thyn housbond armed be in maille,
The arwes° of thy crabbed eloquence
Shal perce his brest and eek his aventaille.°
In jalousie I rede° eek thow hym bynde,
And thow shalt make hym couche° as dooth a
        quaille.   1150

"If thow be fair, ther folk ben in presence,°
Shewe thow thy visage and thyn apparaille.
If thow be foul, be fre of thy dispence.°
To gete thee freendes ay do thy travaille.°
Be ay of cheere as light as leef on lynde,°
And lat hym care, and wepe, and wrynge, and
        waille!"

THE FRANKLIN'S TALE

The Franklin's Tale stems ultimately from the common folklore motif known as the Rash Promise. A literary adaptation of it in Boccaccio's Italian prose work, the *Filocolo*, probably provided Chaucer with the skeleton of his own tale. But Chaucer remolds his material considerably, as has been pointed out in the Introduction, giving it the appearance of a Breton poetic short story or lay. (Actually there are no lays extant in the Breton language, but Marie de France in the twelfth century made the genre famous by claiming that her French lays had been translated from Breton.)

For Boccaccio, the interest of the plot lay in the question as to which of the three men — the husband of the compromised lady, the lady's lover, or the magician who assisted the lover — was the most generous in setting aside his own interests. For the Franklin, the interest lies in the fact that the story serves as an appropriate reply to the Wife of Bath. In it he is able to show that the marriage of Arveragus and Dorigen was a happy one, not because either one had mastery over the other, but because both of them submitted to the dictates of gentilesse, a medieval concept embracing the two virtues of gentleness and gentility.

Thise olde, gentil Britons° in hir° dayes
Of diverse aventures maden layes,°
Rymeyed° in hir firste Briton tonge,°
Whiche layes with hir instrumentz they songe,

1104. freletee: frailty. 1106. suffrance: submission. 1111. badde
alayes: badly alloyed. 1113. breste: break.   plye: bend.
1114. the . . . Bathe: love of the Wife of Bath. 1116. maistrie:
sovereignty.   elles: else.   scathe: a pity. 1122. atones: at
once. 1124. so . . . assaille: be so bold as to assail. 1125. trust:
expectation.   1132. Chichivache: a legendary creature who
fed only on patient wives and was therefore, as the name implies in French, a lean cow.   swelwe: swallow. 1134. at . . .
countretaille: in retort. 1135. Beth . . . bidaffed: don't be outwitted. 1136. governaille: control. 1137. Emprenteth: imprint.
1139. archewyves: archwives ("superwomen"). 1140. camaille:
camel. 1141. Ne . . . nat: and don't allow.

1142. sklendre: slender. 1143. egre: fierce.   yond in Ynde:
in distant India. 1144. clappeth: clatter. 1147. arwes: arrows. 1148. aventaille: helmet's faceplate. 1149. rede: advise.
1150. couche: cower. 1151. ben in presence: are present.
1153. dispence: spending. 1154. do . . . travaille: strive.
1155. lynde: linden. FRANKLIN'S TALE. 1. Britons: Bretons.
hir: their. 2. maden layes: made lays. 3. Rymeyed: rhymed.
firste . . . tonge: original Breton language.

Or elles redden° hem for hir plesaunce.°
And oon° of hem have I in remembraunce,
Which I shal seyn° with good wyl as° I kan.
   But, sires, bycause I am a burel° man,
At my bigynnyng first I yow biseche,
Have me excused of my rude speche.   10
I lerned nevere rethorik,° certeyn.°
Thyng that I speke, it moot° be bare and pleyn.
I sleep° nevere on the mount of Parnaso,°
Ne lerned Marcus Tullius Scithero.°
Colours° ne knowe I none, withouten drede,°
But swich° colours as growen in the mede,°
Or ellis° swiche as men dye or peynte.
Colours of rethoryk ben to queynte;°
My spirit feeleth nat of swich matere.
But, if yow list,° my tale shul ye heere.   20
   In Armorik,° that called is Britayne,°
Ther was a knyght that loved and dide his payne°
To serve a lady in his beste wise;°
And many a labour, many a gret emprise,°
He for his lady wroghte er° she were wonne,
For she was oon° the faireste under sonne,
And eek° ther-to come of so heigh kynrede°
That wel unnethes dorste° this knyght for drede°
Telle hire his wo, his peyne, and his distresse.
But atte laste she for his worthynesse,   30
And namely° for his meke obeysaunce,°
Hath swich a pitee caught° of his penaunce°
That pryvely° she fel of° his acord
To take hym for hir housbonde and hir lord,
Of swich lordshipe as men han° over hir wyves.
And, for to lede the moore in blisse hir lyves,
Of his fre wyl he swoor hire° as a knyght
That nevere in al his lyf he day ne° nyght
Ne sholde upon hym take no maistrye°
Agayn° hir wyl, ne kithe° hire jalousye,   40
But hire obeye, and folwe° hir wyl in al,
As any lovere to his lady shal,°
Save that the name of soveraynetee,
That wolde he have for shame of his degree.°
   She thanked hym and with ful gret humblesse
She seyde, "Sire, sith° of youre gentilesse°
Ye profre me to have so large a reyne,°

Ne wolde nevere God° bitwix us tweyne,
As in my gilt,° were outher werre° or stryf.
Sire, I wol be youre humble, trewe° wyf.   50
Have heer my trouthe° til that myn herte breste."°
Thus been they bothe in quiete and in reste.
   For o° thyng, sires, saufly° dar I seye,
That freendes everich° oother moot obeye
If they wol longe holden compaignye.
Love wol nat be constreyned by maistrye.
Whan maistrie comth, the god of love anon°
Beteth hise wynges, and farwel, he is gon.
Love is a thyng as any spirit free.
Wommen of kynde° desiren libertee   60
And nat to been constreyned as a thral,°
And so doon° men, if I sooth seyn° shal.
Looke-who-that° is moost pacient in love,
He is at his avantage al above.
Pacience is an heigh vertu, certeyn,
For it venquysseth,° as thise clerkes° seyn,
Thynges that rigour sholde° nevere atteyne.
For every word men may° nat chide or pleyne.°
Lerneth to suffre, or elles, so moot I gon,°
Ye shul it lerne wher° so ye wole or non.   70
For in this world, certeyn, ther no wight° is
That he ne dooth or seith som tyme amys.°
Ire, siknesse, or constellacioun,°
Wyn,° wo, or chaungyng of complexioun,°
Causeth ful ofte to doon amys or speken.
On every wrong a man may nat be wreken.°
After the tyme moste be temperaunce
To every wight that kan on governaunce.°
And therfore hath this wise worthy knyght
To lyve in ese suffraunce° hire bihight,°   80
And she to hym ful wisly gan to swere°
That nevere sholde ther be default in here.°
   Here may men seen an humble, wys acord.
Thus hath she take hir servant and hir lord,
Servant in love, and lord in mariage.
Thanne was he bothe in lordshipe and servage.°
Servage? Nay, but in lordshipe above,
Sith he hath bothe his lady and his love;
His lady, certes,° and his wyf also,
The which that lawe of love acordeth to.   90

---

5. elles redden: else read.   plesaunce: pleasure.   **6.** oon: one.
7. seyn: tell.   as: as best.   **8.** burel: unlearned.   **11.** rethorik:
rhetoric.   certeyn: certainly.   **12.** moot: must.   **13.** sleep:
slept.   Parnaso: Parnassus.   **14.** Scithero: Cicero.   **15.** Colours: ornaments of speech.   drede: doubt.   **16.** swich: such.
mede: meadow.   **17.** ellis: else.   **18.** ben to queynte: are too
intricate.   **20.** list: it pleases.   **21.** Armorik: Armorica.   Britayne: Brittany.   **22.** dide . . . payne: took pains.   **23.** wise:
manner.   **24.** emprise: undertaking.   **25.** er: before.   **26.** oon:
one (of).   **27.** eek: also.   so . . . kynrede: such high lineage.   **28.** unnethes dorste: hardly dared.   drede: timidity.
31. namely: particularly.   obeysaunce: obedience.   **32.** caught:
taken.   penaunce: voluntary suffering.   **33.** pryvely: secretly.
of: into.   **35.** han: have.   **37.** hire: to her.   **38.** ne: or.
39. maistrye: domination.   **40.** Agayn: against.   ne kithe: nor
show.   **41.** folwe: follow.   **42.** shal: should.   **44.** for . . . degree: out of regard for his status.   **46.** sith: since.   gentilesse:
gentility.   **47.** large a reyne: free a rein.

48. Ne . . . God: would to God that never.   **49.** As . . . gilt: on
my account.   outher werre: either war.   **50.** trewe: faithful.
51. trouthe: promise.   breste: burst.   **53.** o: one.   saufly:
safely.   **54.** everich: each.   **57.** anon: at once.   **60.** of kynde:
by nature.   **61.** thral: slave.   **62.** doon: do.   sooth seyn:
truth say.   **63.** Looke-who-that: whoever.   **66.** venquysseth:
vanquishes.   clerkes: scholars.   **67.** sholde: could.   **68.** may:
can.   pleyne: complain.   **69.** moot I gon: may I prosper.
70. wher: whether.   **71.** wight: person.   **72.** amys: amiss.
73. constellacioun: combination of astrological forces believed
to influence human affairs. (See Note A, p. 195.)   **74.** Wyn:
wine.   complexioun: temperament. (See Note B, p. 196.)
76. wreken: avenged.   **78.** kan on governaunce: understands
self-control.   **80.** suffraunce: permission.   bihight: promised.
81. gan to swere: swore.   **82.** here: her.   **86.** servage: servitude.
89. certes: certainly.

And whan he was in this prosperitee,
Hom with his wyf he gooth to his contree.
Nat fer fro Pedmark° ther his dwellyng was,
Wher-as° he lyveth in blisse and in solas.°
  Who koude telle but he hadde wedded be°
The joye, the ese, and the prosperitee
That is bitwix an housbonde and his wyf?
A yeer and moore lasted this blisful lyf,
Til that the knyght of which I speke of thus,
That of Kairrud° was cleped° Arveragus,   100
Shoop hym° to goon and dwelle a yeer or twayne
In Engelond, that cleped was eek Britayne,
To seke in armes worship° and honour,
For al his lust° he sette in swich labour;
And dwelled ther two yeer, the book seith thus.
  Now wol I stynte of° this Arveragus,
And speke I wole of Dorigene his wyf,
That loveth hir housbonde as hir hertes lyf.
For his absence wepeth she and siketh,°
As doon thise noble wyves whan hem liketh.°   110
She moorneth, waketh,° waileth, fasteth, pleyneth.°
Desir of his presence hir so destreyneth°
That al this wide world she set° at noght.
Hir freendes, whiche that° knewe hir hevy thoght,
Conforten hire in al that ever they may.
They prechen° hire, they telle hire nyght and day
That causelees she sleeth° hirself, allas.
And every confort possible in this cas
They doon to hire with al hir bisynesse,°
Al for to make hire leve° hir hevynesse.   120
  By proces, as ye knowen everichoon,°
Men may so longe graven° in a stoon
Til som figure therinne emprented be;
So longe han they conforted hire til she
Receyved hath by hope and by resoun
The emprentyng of hir consolacioun,
Thurgh which hir grete sorwe gan aswage.°
She may nat alwey duren° in swich rage.°
  And eek Arveragus in al this care
Hath sent hire lettres hom of his welfare,   130
And that he wol come hastily agayn,
Or ellis hadde this sorwe hir herte slayn.
  Hir freendes sawe hir sorwe gan to slake°
And preyde hire on knees, for Goddes sake,
To come and romen hire° in compaignye,
Awey to dryve hir derke fantasye;
And finally she graunted that requeste,

For wel she saw that it was for the beste.
  Now stood hir castel faste° by the see,
And often with hir freendes walketh she   140
Hir to disporte° upon the bank an-heigh,°
Wher-as she many a ship and barge seigh°
Seillynge hir cours° wher-as hem liste° go.
But thanne was that a parcel of hir wo,
For to hirself ful ofte, "Allas," seith she,
"Is ther no ship, of so manye as I se,
Wol bryngen hom my lord? Thanne were myn
    herte
Al warisshed° of hise° bittre peynes smerte."°
  Another tyme there wolde she sitte and thynke,
And caste hir eyen dounward fro the brynke;
But whan she seigh the grisly rokkes blake,°   151
For verray fere° so wolde hir herte quake
That on hir feet she myghte hir noght sustene.
Thanne wolde she sitte adoun upon the grene,
And pitously into the see biholde,
And seyn° right thus, with sorweful sikes° colde:
"Eterne God, that thurgh thy purveiance°
Ledest the world by certeyn governance,°
In ydel,° as men seyn, ye nothyng make.
But, Lord, thise grisly, feendly° rokkes blake, 160
That semen° rather a foul confusioun
Of werk than any fair creacioun
Of swich a parfit, wys God and a stable,
Why han ye wroght this werk unresonable,
For by this werk south, north, ne west, ne est
Ther nys° y-fostred man, ne bryd,° ne beest?
It doth no good, to my wit,° but anoyeth.°
Se ye nat, Lord, how mankynde it destroyeth?
An hundred thousand bodies of mankynde
Han rokkes slayn, al° be they nat in mynde;°   170
Which mankynde is so fair part of thy werk
That thow it madest lyk to thyn owene merk.°
  "Thanne° semed it ye hadde a greet chiertee°
Toward mankynde, but how thanne may it be
That ye swiche menes° make, it to destroyen,
Whiche menes do no good but evere anoyen?
I woot° wel, clerkes wol seyn as hem leste,°
By argumentz, that al is for the beste,
Thogh I ne kan the causes nat y-knowe.
But thilke° God that made wynd to blowe,   180
As kepe° my lord! This is my conclusioun.
To clerkes lete° I al disputisoun;°

But wolde God that alle thise rokkes blake
Were sonken into helle for his sake.
Thise rokkes sleen° myn herte for the feere."°
Thus wolde she seyn with many a pitous teere.

Hir freendes sawe that it was no disport
To romen° by the see, but disconfort,
And shopen° for to pleyen somwher elles.
They leden° hire by ryvers, and by welles,   190
And eek in othere places delitables.°
They dauncen, and they pleyen at ches and tables.°

So on a day, right in the morwe-tyde,°
Unto a gardyn that was ther bisyde,
In which that they hadde maad hir ordinance°
Of vitaille° and of oother purveiance,°
They goon and pleye hem al the longe day.
And this was on the sixte morwe of May,
Which May hadde peynted with his softe shoures°
This gardyn ful of leves and of floures;   200
And craft of mannes hond° so curiously°
Arrayed hadde this gardyn, trewely,
That nevere was ther gardyn of swich prys,°
But if° it were the verray Paradys.
The odour of floures and the fresshe sighte
Wolde han maked any herte lighte
That evere was born, but if to° greet siknesse
Or to greet sorwe helde it in distresse,
So ful it was of beautee with plesaunce.°
At after-dyner gonne° they to daunce   210
And synge also, save Dorigen allone,
Which made alwey hir compleynt and hir mone,
For° she ne saugh° hym on the daunce go
That was hir housbonde and hir love also.
But, nathelees,° she moste a tyme abyde°
And with good hope lete hir sorwe slyde.

Upon this daunce, amonges othere men,
Daunced a squier bifore Dorigen
That fressher was and jolyer of array,
As to my doom,° than is the monthe of May.   220
He syngeth, daunceth, passyng° any man
That is, or was, sith that the world bigan.
Ther-with he was, if men sholde hym discryve,°
Oon of the beste farynge man on lyve,°
Yong, strong, right vertuous, and riche, and wys,
And wel biloved, and holden in gret prys.°
And shortly, if the sothe° I tellen shal,
Unwityng of this Dorigen at al,
This lusty squier, servant to Venus,

Which that y-cleped° was Aurelius,   230
Hadde loved hire best of any creature
Two yeer and moore, as was his aventure,°
But nevere dorste° he tellen hire his grevance.
Withouten coppe° he drank al his penance.
He was despeyred; nothyng dorste he seye,
Save in his songes somwhat wolde he wreye°
His wo, as in a general compleynyng;
He seyde he lovede, and was biloved nothyng.°
Of swich matere made he many layes,°
Songes, compleyntes,° roundels, virelayes,°   240
How that he dorste nat his sorwe telle,
But langwissheth as a Furye dooth in helle.
And dye he moste, he seyde, as dide Ekko°
For Narcisus, that dorste nat telle hir wo.
In oother manere than ye heere me seye,
Ne dorste he nat to hire his wo biwreye,°
Save that, paraventure,° som tyme at daunces
Ther° yong folk kepen hir observaunces,°
It may wel be he looked on hir face
In swich a wise° as man° that asketh grace.   250
But nothyng wiste° she of his entente.
Nathelees,° it happed er they thennes wente,
Bycause that he was hir neighebour
And was a man of worship and honour,
And hadde° y-knowen hym of tyme yoore,°
They fille° in speche; and forth,° moore and moore,
Unto his purpos drough° Aurelius.
And whan he saugh his tyme, he seyde thus:
"Madame," quod° he, "by God that this world
       made,
So that I wiste it myghte youre herte glade,°   260
I wolde, that day that youre Arveragus
Wente over the see, that I Aurelius
Hadde went ther nevere I sholde have come
       agayn,
For wel I woot° my servyce is in vayn.
My gerdon° is but brestyng° of myn herte.
Madame, reweth° upon my peynes smerte,
For with a word ye may me sleen or save.
Here at youre feet, God wolde that I were grave!°
I ne have as now no leyser° moore to seye.
Have mercy, swete, or ye wol do° me deye."   270
She gan to looke upon Aurelius.
"Is this youre wil," quod she, "and sey ye thus?

185. sleen: slay.   for . . . feere: for fear.   189. shopen:
decided.   190. leden: lead.   191. delitables: delightful.   192. tables: backgammon.   193. morwe-tyde: morning
time.   195. ordinance: preparation.   196. vitaille: victuals.
purveiance: provisions.   199. shoures: showers.   201. hond:
hand.   curiously: ingeniously.   203. prys: excellence.   204. But
if: unless.   207. to: too.   209. plesaunce: delight.   210. gonne:
began.   213. For: because.   ne saugh: did not see.   215. nathelees: nevertheless.   abyde: endure.   220. doom: judgment.
221. passyng: surpassing.   223. discryve: describe.   224. beste
. . . lyve: handsomest men alive.   226. prys: esteem.   227. sothe:
truth.

230. y-cleped: called.   232. aventure: fate.   233. dorste: dared.
234. Withouten coppe: without cup, i.e., he drank his penance
in full measure without the aid of a cup.   236. wreye: reveal.
238. nothyng: in no way.   239. layes: lays, lyrics.   240. compleyntes: love laments.   roundels, virelayes: lyrics with intricate rhyming patterns.   243. Ekko: Echo, who pined away for
Narcissus till only her voice remained.   246. biwreye: disclose.
247. paraventure: perchance.   248. Ther: where.   kepen . . .
observaunces: hold celebrations.   250. wise: manner.   man:
one.   251. wiste: knew.   252. Nathelees: nevertheless.
255. hadde: (she) had.   of . . . yoore: of old.   256. fille:
fell.   forth: forward.   257. drough: drew.   259. quod: said.
260. glade: gladden.   264. woot: know.   265. gerdon: reward.
brestyng: breaking.   266. reweth: have pity.   268. grave:
buried.   269. leyser: leisure.   270. do: make.

Nevere erst,"° quod she, "ne wiste I what ye
  mente,
But now, Aurelie, I knowe youre entente.
By thilke God that yaf° me soule and lyf,
Ne shal I nevere been untrewe wyf
In word ne werk, as fer as I have wit.°
I wol been his to whom that I am knyt.
Taak this for fynal answere as of me."
But after that, in pleye, thus seyde she: 280
  "Aurelie," quod she, "by heighe God above,
Yet wolde I graunte yow to been youre love,
Syn° I yow se so pitously complayne,
Looke-what° day that endelong° Britayne
Ye remoeve alle the rokkes, stoon by stoon,
That they ne lette° ship ne boot to goon.
I seye, whan ye han maad the coost° so clene
Of rokkes that ther nys no stoon y-sene,
Thanne wol I love yow best of any man.
Have heer my trouthe° in al that evere I kan."   290
  "Is ther noon oother grace in yow?" quod
  he.
  "No, by that Lord," quod she, "that maked me.
For wel I woot that it shal nevere bityde.°
Lat swiche folies out of youre herte slyde.
What deyntee° sholde a man han in his lyf
For to go love another mannes wyf
That° hath hir body whan so that hym liketh?"
  Aurelius ful ofte soore siketh.°
Wo was Aurelie whan that he this herde,
And with a sorweful herte he thus answerde: 300
  "Madame," quod he, "this were an inpossible.°
Thanne moot I dye of sodeyn° deth horrible."
And with that word he turned hym anon.°
Tho coome hir° othere freendes many oon,°
And in the aleyes° romeden up and doun,
And nothyng wiste of this conclusioun,
But sodeynly bigonne revel newe
Til that the brighte sonne loste his hewe°
For th' orisonte° hath reft° the sonne his light.
This is as muche to seye as °it was nyght!   310
And hoom they goon in joye and in solas,
Save oonly wrecched Aurelius, allas.
He to his hous is goon with sorweful herte.
He seeth he may nat from his deeth asterte.°
Hym semed that he felte his herte colde.°
Up to the hevene his handes he gan holde,°
And on his knowes° bare he sette hym doun,
And in his ravyng seyde his orisoun.°

For verray wo out of his wit° he breyde.°
He nyste° what he spak, but thus he seyde.   320
With pitous herte his pleynt hath he bigonne
Unto the goddes,° and first unto the sonne.
  He° seyde, "Appollo, god and governour
Of every plaunte, herbe, tree, and flour,
That yevest,° after thy declynacioun,°
To ech of hem his° tyme and his sesoun
As theyn herberwe° chaungeth, lowe or heighe,
Lord Phebus, cast thy merciable eighe°
On wrecche° Aurelie, which that am but lorn.°
Lo, lord, my lady hath my deeth y-sworn   330
Withouten gilt,° but° thy benygnytee
Upon my dedly° herte have som pitee.
For wel I woot,° lord Phebus, if yow lest,°
Ye may me helpen, save° my lady, best.
Now voucheth sauf° that I may yow devyse°
How that I may been holpen, and in what wyse.
  "Youre blisful suster, Lucyna the shene,°
That of the see is chief goddesse and queene, —
Thogh Neptunus have deitee° in the see,
Yet emperesse aboven° hym is she, —   340
Ye knowen wel, lord, that right° as hir desir
Is to be quyked° and lighted of youre fyr,
For which she folweth° yow ful bisily,°
Right so the see desireth naturelly
To folwen° hire as she that is goddesse
Bothe in the see and ryvers moore and lesse.°
Wher-fore, lord Phebus, this is my requeste:
Do this myracle, or do° myn herte breste,
That now next at this opposicioun,°
Which in the signe shal be of the Leoun,°   350
As preyeth° hire so greet a flood to brynge
That fyve fadme° at the leeste it oversprynge
The hyeste rok in Armoryk Britayne;
And lat this flood endure yeres twayne.
Thanne, certes,° to my lady may I seye,
'Holdeth youre heste.° The rokkes been aweye.'
  "Lord Phebus, dooth this myracle for me.
Prey hire, she go no faster cours than ye.

319. wit: mind.   breyde: went.   320. nyste: didn't know.
322. goddes: goddess (Lucina).   323–371. Aurelius prays to
Phoebus Apollo (the sun) that he will cooperate with Lucina
(the moon) to cause a high tide which will cover the rocks for
two years.   325. yevest: give.   after . . . declynacioun: according to your height in the sky.   326. his: its.   327. herberwe:
position.   328. merciable eighe: merciful eye.   329. wrecche:
wretched.   lorn: lost.   331. Withouten gilt: without any guilt
on my part.   but: unless.   332. dedly: dying.   333. woot:
know.   lest: it pleases.   334. save: apart from.   335. voucheth sauf: vouchsafe.   devyse: explain to.   337. shene: beautiful.   339. deitee: godship.   340. aboven: over.   341. right:
just.   342. quyked: enlivened.   343. folweth: follows.   bisily:
diligently.   345. folwen: follow (in its ebb and flow).   346. moore
. . . lesse: greater and smaller.   348. do: make.   349. next . . .
opposicioun: at this next opposition (of the sun and moon, when
the two bodies will pull the waters from opposite sides of the
earth and cause high tides).   350. Leoun: the zodiacal sign of
the Lion (mid-July to mid-August). See Note A, p. 195.   351. As
preyeth: pray.   352. fadme: fathom.   355. certes: certainly.
356. Holdeth . . . heste: keep your promise.

273. erst: before.   275. yaf: gave.   277. wit: knowledge.
283. Syn: since.   284. Looke-what: on whatever.   endelong:
all along.   286. ne lette: prevent neither.   287. coost: coast.
290. trouthe: promise.   293. bityde: happen.   295. deyntee:
respect.   297. That: who (the husband).   298. soore siketh:
sorely sighs.   301. inpossible: impossibility.   302. sodeyn:
sudden.   303. turned . . . anon: turned away at once.   304. Tho
. . . hir: then came her.   oon: a one.   305. aleyes: paths.
308. hewe: color.   309. orisonte: horizon.   reft: taken away
from.   310. to . . . as: as to say that.   314. asterte: escape.
315. colde: grow cold.   316. gan holde: held.   317. knowes:
knees.   318. orisoun: prayer.

I seye, thus preyeth youre suster that she go
No faster cours than ye thise yeres two;   360
Thanne shal she been evene at the fulle alway,
And spryng flood lasten bothe nyght and day.
And, but she vouchesauf in swich manere
To graunte me my sovereyn lady deere,
Pray hire to synken every rok adoun
Into hir owene dirke° regioun
Under the ground ther Pluto dwelleth inne,
Or nevere mo shal I my lady wynne.
Thy temple in Delphos° wol I barfoot seke.
Lord Phebus, se the teerys° on my cheke,   370
And of my peyne have som compassioun."
And with that word in swowne° he fil adoun,
And longe tyme he lay forth in a traunce.
    His brother, which that knew of his penaunce,
Up caughte hym, and to bedde he hath hym
        broght.
Dispeired in this torment and this thoght,
Lete° I this woful creature lye.
Chese he, for me, wher° he wol lyve or dye.
    Arveragus with heele° and greet honour,
As he that was of chivalrie the flour,   380
Is comen hom, and othere worthy men.
O blisful artow° now, thow Dorigen,
That hast thy lusty housbonde in thyn armes,
The fresshe knyght, the worthy man of armes,
That loveth thee as his owene hertes lyf.
Nothyng list hym to been ymagynatyf°
If any wight hadde spoke, whil he was oute,
To hire of love. He hadde of it no doute.°
He noght entendeth to no swich° matere,
But daunceth, justeth,° maketh hir good cheere,
And thus in joye and blisse I lete hem dwelle,   391
And of the syke° Aurelius wol I telle.
    In langour and in torment furyus
Two yeer and moore lay wrecche Aurelius
Er any foot he myghte on erthe gon,°
Ne confort in this tyme hadde he noon,
Save of° his brother, which that was a clerk.
He knew of al this wo and al this werk,
For to noon oother creature, certeyn,
Of this matere he dorste no word seyn.   400
Under his brest he baar it moore secree°·
Than evere dide Pamphilus for Galathee.°
His brest was hool, withoute for to sene,°
But in his herte ay° was the arwe kene,°
And wel ye knowe that of a sursanure°

In surgerye is perilous the cure,
But° men myghte touche the arwe or come
        ther-by.°
His brother weep° and wayled pryvely°
Til at the laste hym fil in remembraunce°
That, whiles he was at Orliens° in Fraunce,   410
As yonge clerkes that been lykerous°
To reden artes° that been curious°
Seken in every halke° and every herne°
Particuler sciences for to lerne —
He hym remembred that, upon a day
At Orliens in studie, a book he say°
Of magyk naturel,° which his felawe,°
That was that tyme a bacheler of lawe,
Al° were he ther to lerne another craft,
Hadde pryvely upon his desk y-laft,°   420
Which book spak muchel° of the operaciouns
Touchynge the eighte-and-twenty mansiouns°
That longen° to the moone, and swich folye,
As in oure dayes is nat worth a flye,
For Holy Chirches feith, in oure bileve,°
Ne suffreth° noon illusioun us to greve.
And whan this book was in his remembraunce,
Anon for joye his herte gan to daunce,
And to hymself he seyde pryvely,
" My brother shal be warisshed° hastily,   430
For I am siker° that ther be sciences
By whiche men make diverse apparences,°
Swiche as thise subtile tregetours° pleye;
For ofte at festes, have I wel herd seye,
That tregetours withinne an halle large
Have maad come in, a water and a barge,
And in the halle rowen° up and doun.
Som tyme hath semed come a grym leoun,
And som tyme floures sprynge as in a mede,°
Som tyme a vyne and grapes white and rede,   44?
Som tyme a castel al of lym° and stoon;
And whan hem lyked, voyded° it anoon.
Thus semed it to every mannes sighte.
    " Now thanne, conclude I thus, that, if I myghte
At Orliens som old felawe y-fynde
That hadde thise moones mansions in mynde,°
Or oother magyk naturel above,
He sholde wel make my brother han his love.
For with an apparence a clerk may make
To mannes sighte that alle the rokkes blake   450

366. dirke: dark.   369. Delphos: Delphi.   370. teerys: tears.
372. swowne: a swoon.   377. Lete: leave.   378. Chese . . . wher:
let him choose, as far as I'm concerned, whether.   379. heele:
prosperity.   382. artow: are you.   386. Nothyng . . . ymagy-
natyf: in no way does he wish to be curious.   388. doute: fear.
389. noght . . . swich: doesn't care about such a.   390. justeth:
jousts.   392. syke: sick.   395. gon: walk.   397. Save of:
except from.   401. secree: secretively.   402. Galathee: Gala-
tea, the heroine of a medieval romance.   403. hool . . . sene:
whole, outwardly to be seen.   404. ay: ever.   arwe kene:
arrow sharp.   405. sursanure: wound healed only on the
surface.

407. But: unless.   come ther-by: reach it.   408. weep: wept.
pryvely: in private.   409. hym . . . remembraunce: he remembered.   410. Orliens: Orléans (University).   411. lykerous:
eager.   412. reden artes: study arts.   curious: obscure.
413. halke: nook.   herne: corner.   416. say: saw.   417. magyk
naturel: natural (or legitimate) magic, such as the Doctor (Gen.
Prol., l. 416) studied for professional reasons, and not black
magic.   felawe: companion.   419. Al: though.   420. y-laft:
left.   421. muchel: much.   422. mansiouns: daily stations.
423. longen: belong.   425. bileve: belief.   426. Ne suffreth:
allows.   430. warisshed: cured.   431. siker: sure.   432. apparences: apparitions.   433. tregetours: jugglers.   437. rowen:
(have) rowed.   439. mede: meadow.   441. lym: lime.
442. voyded: (they have) removed.   446. in mynde: in his
memory.

Of Britaigne were y-voyded everichon,°
And shippes by the brynke comen and gon,
And in swich forme enduren a day or two.
Thanne were my brother warisshed of his wo.
Thanne moste she nedes holden hir biheste,
Or ellis he shal shame hire, at the leeste."

What° sholde I make a lenger tale of this?
Unto his brotheres bed he comen is,
And swich confort° he yaf° hym for to gon
To Orliens that he up stirte° anon,   460
And on his wey forthward thanne is he fare°
In hope for to been lissed° of his care.

Whan they were come almoost to that citee,
But if it were° a two furlong or thre,
A yong clerk romyng by hymself they mette,
Which that in Latyn thriftily° hem grette,°
And after that he seyde a wonder thyng.
"I knowe," quod he, "the cause of youre comyng."
And er they ferther any foote wente,
He tolde hem al that was in hir entente.   470

This Britoun° clerk hym asked of felawes
The whiche that he hadde knowe in olde dawes,°
And he answerde hym that they dede were,
For which he weep ful ofte many a teere.

Doun of° his hors Aurelius lighte° anon,
And with this magicien forth is he gon
Hom to his hous, and maden hem° wel at ese.
Hem lakked no vitaille that myghte hem plese;
So wel arrayed hous as ther was oon,°
Aurelius in his lyf saw nevere noon.   480

He shewed hym, er he wente to sopeer,
Forestes, parkes ful of wilde deer.°
Ther saw he hertes° with hir hornes hye,
The gretteste that evere were seyn with eye;
He saw of hem an hundred slayn with houndes,
And somme with arwes blede of bittre woundes.

He saw, whan voyded were thise wilde deer,
Thise fauconers° upon a fair ryver,°
That with hir haukes han the heron slayn.

Tho° saugh he knyghtes justyng° in a playn,
And after this he dide hym swich plesaunce   491
That he hym shewed his lady on a daunce,
On which hymself he daunced, as hym thoughte.
And whan this maister that this magyk wroughte
Saugh it was tyme, he clapte his handes two,
And farwel, al oure revel was ago.°
And yet remoeved° they nevere out of the hous
Whil they saugh al this sighte merveillous,
But in his studie, ther-as his bookes be,

They seten stille, and no wight° but they thre.   50c
To hym this maister called his squyer
And seide hym thus, "Is redy oure soper?
Almoost an hour it is, I undertake,°
Sith I yow bad oure soper for to make,
Whan that thise worthy men wenten with me
Into my studie, ther as my bookes be."
"Sire," quod this squyer, "whan it liketh yow,
It is al redy, thogh ye wol right now."
"Go we thanne soupe,"° quod he, "as for the
    beste.
This amorous folk som tyme mote han hir° reste."

At after-soper fille° they in tretee°   511
What somme° sholde this maistres gerdoun° be
To remoeven alle the rokkes of Britayne,
And eek from Gerounde° to the mouth of Sayne.°

He made it straunge° and swoor, so God hym
    save,
Lasse than a thousand pound he wolde nat have,
Ne gladly for that somme he wolde nat gon.

Aurelius with blisful herte anon
Answerde thus: "Fy on a thousand pound!
This wyde world, which that men seye is round,
I wolde it yeve if I were lord of it.   521
This bargayn is ful dryve,° for we ben knyt.°
Ye shal be payed trewely,° by my trouthe,°
But looketh° now, for no necligence or slouthe
Ye tarie° us heer no lenger than tomorwe."
"Nay," quod this clerk, "have heer my feith to
    borwe."°

To bedde is goon Aurelius whan hym leste,
And wel neigh al that nyght he hadde his reste.
What for his labour and his hope of blisse,°
His woful herte of penaunce hadde a lisse.°   530

Upon the morwe, whan that it was day,
To Britayne tooke they the righte° way,
Aurelius and this magicien bisyde,
And been descended° ther they wolde abyde.
And this was, as thise bookes me remembre,°
The colde, frosty seson of Decembre.

Phebus wax° old and hewed lyk latoun,°
That in his hote declynacioun°
Shoon as the burned° gold with stremes° brighte;
But now in Capricorn adoun he lighte,°   540
Wher-as° he shoon ful pale, I dar wel seyn.
The bittre frostes with the sleet and reyn
Destruyed hath the grene in every yerd.

500. wight: person.   503. undertake: am sure.   509. soupe:
sup.   510. mote . . . hir: must have their.   511. fille: fell.
in tretee: into discussion.   512. somme: amount.   gerdoun:
reward.   514. Gerounde: the Gironde.   Sayne: the Seine.
515. straunge: difficult.   522. ful dryve: fully driven.   knyt:
agreed.   523. trewely: faithfully.   trouthe: promise.   524. looketh: see to it.   525. tarie: delay.   526. to borwe: in pledge.
530. lisse: relief.   532. righte: direct.   534. descended: dismounted.   535. remembre: remind.   537. wax: grew.   hewed
. . . latoun: copper-colored.   538. declynacioun: declination (in
Cancer, mid-June to mid-July).   539. burned: burnished.
stremes: beams.   540. lighte: descended.   541. Wher-as: where.
In summer the sun (Phoebus) has been hot, but in Capricorn

451. everichon: everyone.   457. What: why.   459. confort:
encouragement.   yaf: gave.   460. stirte: sprang.   461. is he
fare: he has fared.   462. lissed: relieved.   464. But . . . were:
except for.   466. thriftily: fluently.   grette: greeted.   471. Bri-
toun: Breton.   472. dawes: days.   475. of: off.   lighte: alit.
477. hem: themselves.   479. as . . . oon: as that.   482. deer:
animals.   483. hertes: harts.   488. Thise fauconers: some
falconers.   ryver: river bank.   490. Tho: then.   justyng:
jousting.   496. ago: gone.   497. remoeved: moved.

Janus° sit by the fyr with double berd
And drynketh of his bugle-horn° the wyn;
Biforn hym stant brawen° of the tusked swyn;
And "Nowel"° crieth every lusty man.
     Aurelius, in al that evere he kan,
Dooth to this maister cheere and reverence,
And preyeth hym to doon his diligence   550
To bryngen hym out of his peynes smerte,
Or with a swerd that he wolde slitte his herte.
     This° subtil clerk swich routhe° hadde of this man
That, nyght and day, he spedde hym that°
     he kan
To wayten° a tyme of° his conclusioun,
This is to seyn, to make illusioun
By swich an apparence or jogelrye —
I ne kan° no termes of astrologye —
That she and every wight sholde wene° and seye
That of Britayne the rokkes were aweye,   560
Or ellis they were sonken under grounde.
So at the laste he hath his tyme y-founde
To maken his japes° and his wrecchednesse°
Of swich a supersticious cursednesse.
His tables Tolletanes° forth he broght
Ful wel corrected, ne ther lakked noght,
Neither his collect° ne his expans yeris,°
Ne hise rootes,° ne hise othere geris,°
As been° his centris,° and hise argumentz,°
And hise proporcionels convenientz°   570
For hise equacions° in every thyng.
And by his eighte speere in his wirkyng,
He knew ful wel how fer Alnath was shove
Fro the heed of thilke fixe Aries° above,
That in the nynthe speere considered is.
Ful subtilly he kalkuled° al this.
     Whan he hadde founde his firste mansioun,°

He knew the remenaunt by proporcioun,
And knew the arisyng of his moone wel
And in whos face,° and terme,° and everydel;°
And knew ful wel the moones mansioun   581
Acordaunt to his operacioun,
And knew also hise othere observaunces
For swiche illusiouns and swiche meschaunces°
As hethen folk useden° in thilke° dayes.
For which no lenger maked he delayes,
But thurgh his magyk, for a wyke° or tweye,
It semed that alle the rokkes were aweye.
     Aurelius, which that yet despeired is
Wher° he shal han his love or fare amys,°   590
Awaiteth nyght and day on this myracle;
And whan he knew that ther was noon obstacle,
That voyded were thise rokkes everichon,
Doun to his maistres feet he fil anon
And seyde, "I, woful wrecche, Aurelius,
Thank yow, lord, and lady myn, Venus,
That me han holpen fro my cares colde."
And to the temple his wey forth hath he holde,
Wher-as he knew he sholde his lady se.
And whan he saugh his tyme, anon right he,   600
With dredful° herte and with ful humble cheere,°
Salued° hath his soverayn lady deere.
     "My righte lady," quod this woful man,
"Whom I moost drede, and love as I best kan,
An lothest were of al this world displese,°
Nere it° that I for yow have swich disese°
That I moste dyen heer at youre foot anon,
Noght wolde I telle how me is° wo bigon,
But, certes, outher° moste I dye or pleyne.°
Ye sleen me, giltlees, for verray peyne.   610
But of my deeth thogh that ye have no routhe,°
Avyseth yow er that° ye breke youre trouthe.
Repenteth yow, for thilke° God above,
Er ye me sleen bycause that I yow love.
For, madame, wel ye woot what ye han hight,°
Nat that I chalange° anythyng of° right
Of yow, my sovereyn lady, but youre grace.°
But in a gardyn yond,° at swich a place,
Ye woot right wel what ye bihighten° me;
And in myn hand youre trouthe plighten° ye   620
To love me best. God woot, ye seyde so,
Al be that° I unworthy am ther-to.
Madame, I speke it for the honour of yow
Moore than to save myn hertes lyf right now.
I have do° so as ye comaunded me;

(mid-December to mid-January) it becomes pale.   544. January is the month of Janus, the two-faced Roman god who looks
back on the past year and forward to the new year.   545. bugle-
horn: an ox horn used as a drinking vessel.   546. stant brawen:
stands brawn, flesh.   547. Nowel: Noël.   553–88. The magician first calculated a suitable time in the moon's monthly course
when he could make it seem that the rocks were gone, and he
then brought about the illusion for a week or two. Though the
Franklin does not understand astrology, he mentions by name
numerous astronomical instruments, tables, and calculations
actually used by medieval astronomers, but he does not
attempt to explain how the magic operated.   553. routhe: compassion.   554. that: as best.   555. wayten: find.   of: for.
558. kan: know.   559. wene: believe.   563. japes: tricks.
wrecchednesse: mischief.   565. tables Tolletanes: astronomical
tables prepared in Toledo (Spain).   567. collect: collected.   expans yeris: expanded yearly tables.   568. rootes: data.   geris:
equipment.   569. As been: such as.   centris: astrolabe centers.
argumentz: tabular guides.   570. proporcionels convenientz:
relevant proportional tables.   571. equacions: astrological divisions.   572–74. by . . . Aries: By his eighth sphere (of fixed
stars) . . . he knew . . . how far Alnath (a star in the constellation Aries) was removed from the (theoretical) head of that
same fixed constellation Aries; i.e., he took into account the precession of the equinoxes.   576. kalkuled: calculated.   577. mansioun: station (of the moon).

580. face: zodiacal part.   terme: section.   everydel: every bit.
584. meschaunces: misdeeds.   585. useden: practiced.   thilke:
those.   587. wyke: week.   590. Wher: whether.   amys: amiss.
601. dredful: timid.   cheere: countenance.   602. Salued: saluted.
605. lothest . . . displese: most loath would be . . . to displese.
606. Nere it: were it not.   disese: misery.   608. me is: I am.   609.
outher: either.   pleyne: complain.   611. routhe: compassion.   612.
Avyseth . . . that: consider before.   613. thilke: that.   615. hight:
promised.   616. chalange: demand.   of: by.   617. grace: undeserved kindness.   618. yond: there.   619. bihighten: promised.   620. plighten: pledged.   622. Al be that: even if.
625. do: done.

And, if ye vouchesauf, ye may go se.
Dooth as yow list; have youre biheste in mynde.
For, quyk° or deed, right ther ye shal me fynde;
In yow lyth° al to do° me lyve or deye.
But wel I woot, the rokkes been aweye! "   630
  He taketh his leve, and she astoned° stood;
In al hir face nas° a drope of blood.
She wende° nevere have come in swich a trappe.
"Allas," quod she, "that evere this sholde happe,
For wende I nevere by possibilitee
That swich a monstre° or merveille myghte be.
It is agayns the proces of nature."
And hom she gooth a sorweful creature;
For verray feere unnethe° may she go.
She wepeth, wayleth, al a day or two,   640
And swowneth,° that it routhe° was to se.
But why it was, to no wight tolde she,
For out of towne was goon Arveragus.
But to hirself she spak and seyde thus,
With face pale and with ful sorweful cheere,
In hir compleinte, as ye shal after heere.
  "Allas," quod she, "on thee, Fortune, I pleyne,°
That, unwar,° wrapped hast me in thy cheyne,
For which t' escape woot I no socour
Save oonly deeth or dishonour.   650
Oon of thise two bihoveth me to chese.°
But, nathelees, yet have I levere to lese°
My lyf than of my body to have a shame,
Or knowe myselven° fals, or lese my name.
And with my deeth I may be quyt,° ywis.°
Hath ther nat many a noble wyf er this,
And many a mayde, y-slayn hirself, allas,
Rather than with hir body doon trespas.°
  "Yis, certes. Lo, thise stories beren witnesse:
Whan thritty tirauntz° ful of cursednesse   660
Hadde slayn Phidon in Atthenes atte feste,
They comaunded his doghtren for t' areste°
And bryngen hem biforn hem in despit,
Al naked, to fulfille hir foul delit,
And in hir fadres blood they made hem daunce
Upon the pavement, God yeve hem myschaunce!
For which thise woful maydens ful of drede,
Rather than they wolde lese hir maydenhede,
They pryvely been stirt° into a welle
And dreynte° hemselven, as the bokes telle.   670
  "They of Mecene leete enquere° and seke
Of Lacedomye° fifty maydens, eke,°

On whiche they wolden doon hir lecherye,
But was ther noon of al that compaignye
That she nas° slayn, and with a good entente
Chees rather for to dye than assente
To been oppressed° of hir maydenhede.
Why sholde I, thanne, to dye been in drede?
  "Lo, eek, the tiraunt Aristoclides,°
That loved a mayden heet Stymphalides;°   680
Whan that hir fader slayn was on a nyght,
Unto Dianes° temple gooth she right
And hente° the ymage in hir handes two,
Fro which ymage wolde she nevere go;
No wight° ne myghte hir handes of it arace,°
Til she was slayn right in the selve° place.
Now, sith that maydens hadden swich despit°
To been defouled with mannes foul delit,
Wel oghte a wyf rather hirselven slee
Than be defouled, as it thynketh me.   690
  "What shal I seyn of Hasdrubales wyf,
That at Cartage birafte° hirself hir lyf?
For whan she saw that Romayns wan° the
   toun,
She took hir children alle, and skipte° adoun
Into the fyr, and chees rather to dye
Than° any Romayn dide hire vileynye.
Hath nat Lucresse° y-slayn hirself, allas,
At Rome whan that she oppressed° was
Of° Tarquyn, for hir thoughte it was a shame
To lyven whan she hadde lost hir name?   700
The sevene maydens of Milesie° also
Han slayn hemself for verray drede and wo
Rather than folk of Gawle hem sholde oppresse.
Mo than a thousand stories, as I gesse,
Koude I now telle as touchyng this matere.
  "Whan Habradate° was slayn, his wyf so
   deere
Hirselven slow,° and leet° hir blood to glyde
In Habradates woundes depe and wyde,
And seyde, 'My body, at the leeste way,°
Ther shal no wight defoulen, if I may.'°   710
  "What° sholde I mo ensamples herof sayn,°
Sith that so many han hemselven slayn,
Wel rather than they wolde defouled be?
I wol conclude that it is bet° for me
To sleen myself than ben defouled thus.
I wol be trewe unto Arveragus,
Or rather sle myself in som manere,

---

628. quyk: alive.   629. lyth: lies.   do: make.   631. astoned: astounded.   632. nas: was not.   633. wende: expected. 636. monstre: prodigy.   639. unnethe: hardly.   641. swowneth: swoons.   routhe: pity.   647. pleyne: complain.   648. unwar: unaware.   651. chese: choose.   652. have . . . lese: I would sooner lose.   654. myselven: myself.   655. quyt: freed. ywis: indeed.   658. trespas: transgression.   660. thritty tirauntz: the Thirty Tyrants (of Athens).   662. doghtren . . . areste: daughters to be seized.   669. pryvely . . . stirt: secretly have leapt.   670. dreynte: drowned.   671. Mecene . . . enquere: Messene (in Greece) caused to find.   672. Lacedomye: Lacedaemon (Sparta).   eke: also.

675. That . . . nas: who was not.   677. oppressed: violated. 679. Aristoclides: tyrant of Orchomenus (Greece).   680. heet Stymphalides: named Stymphalis.   682. Dianes: Diana's (the goddess of chastity).   683. hente: seized.   685. No wight: no one.   of . . . arace: from it pull.   686. the selve: that very. 687. despit: aversion.   692. Cartage birafte: Carthage bereft. 693. wan: won.   694. skipte: leapt.   696. Than: than that. 697. Lucresse: Lucretia.   698. oppressed: violated.   699. Of: by.   701. Milesie: Miletus (when it was sacked by the Gauls). 706. Habradate: Abradates, King of the Susi (in Persia). 707. slow: slew.   leet: allowed.   709. at . . . way: at least. 710. may: can help it.   711. What: why.   sayn: tell.   714. bet: better.

As dide Democionis doghter° deere,
Bycause that she wolde nat defouled be." . . .°

Thus pleyned Dorigene a day or tweye,
Purposynge evere that she wolde deye. 750
But, nathelees, upon the thridde nyght
Hoom cam Arveragus, this worthy knyght,
And asked hire why that she weep so soore;
And she gan wepen ever lenger° the moore.
 "Allas," quod she, "that evere was I born!
Thus have I seyd," quod she, "thus have I sworn."
And tolde hym al as ye han herd bifore;
It nedeth nat reherce° it yow namoore.
 This housbond with glad cheere, in frendly wise,
Answerde and seyde, as I shal yow devyse,° 760
"Is ther oght ellis, Dorigen, but this?"
 "Nay, nay," quod she, "God help me so as wys!°
This is to°muche, and° it were Goddes wille."
 "Ye, wyf," quod he. "Lat slepen that° is stille.
It may be wel, paraventure,° yet today.
Ye shul youre trouthe holden, by my fay,°
For, God so wisly° have mercy upon me,
I hadde wel levere y-stiked for to be,°
For verray love which that I to yow have,
But if ye sholde youre trouthe kepe and save. 770
Trouthe is the hyeste thyng that man may kepe."
But with that word he brast° anon to wepe
And seyde, "I yow forbede, up° peyne of deeth,
That nevere, whil thee lasteth lyf ne breeth,
To no wight tel thow of this aventure.
As I may best, I wol my wo endure
Ne make no contenance° of hevynesse
That folk of yow may demen° harm or gesse."
 And forth he cleped° a squyer and a mayde.
"Goth° forth anon with Dorigen," he sayde, 780
"And bryngeth hire to swich° a place anon."
They take hir leve, and on hir wey they gon,
But they ne wiste why she thider wente.
He nolde° no wight tellen his entente.
 Paraventure an heep° of yow, ywis,
Wol holden hym a lewed° man in this,
That he wol putte his wyf in jupartie.°
Herkneth the tale er ye upon hire crie;
She may have bettre fortune than yow semeth;°
And, whan that ye han herd the tale, demeth.°

This squyer, which that highte° Aurelius, 791
On Dorigen that was so amorus,
Of aventure happed° hir to meete
Amydde the toun, right in the quykkest° strete,
As she was boun° to goon the wey forth right
Toward the gardyn ther-as she had hight,°
And he was to the gardynward° also,
For wel he spyed whan she wolde go
Out of hir hous to any maner° place.
But thus they mette of aventure or grace, 800
And he salueth° hire with glad entente
And asked of hire whiderward° she wente.
 And she answerde, half as she were mad,
"Unto the gardyn, as myn housbond bad,°
My trouthe for to holde, allas, allas."
 Aurelius gan wondren on this cas,
And in his herte hadde greet compassioun
Of hire and of hir lamentacioun,
And of Arveragus the worthy knyght,
That bad hir holden al that she had hight, 810
So looth hym was his wyf sholde breke hir trouthe.
And in his herte he caughte of this° greet routhe,
Considerynge the beste on every syde,
That fro his lust yet were hym levere abyde°
Than doon so heigh a cherlyssh wrecchednesse
Agayns franchise° and alle gentilesse.
For which in fewe wordes seyde he thus:
 "Madame, seyeth to youre lord Arveragus
That, sith I se his grete gentilesse
To yow, and eek I se wel youre distresse, 820
That hym were levere han° shame — and that
  were routhe —
Than ye to me sholde breke thus youre trouthe,
I have wel levere° evere to suffre wo
Than I departe° the love bitwix yow two.
I yow relesse, madame, into youre hond,
Quyt,° every serement° and every bond
That ye han maad to me as heer biforn°
Sith thilke tyme which that° ye were born.
My trouthe I plighte, I shal yow nevere repreve°
Of no biheeste. And here I take my leve 830
As of the treweste and the beste wyf
That evere yet I knew in al my lyf.
 "But every wyf be war of hir biheste.
On Dorigene remembreth, at the leste.
Thus kan a squyer doon a gentil dede,
As wel as kan a knyght, withouten drede."°
 She thonketh hym upon hir knees al bare,

718. Democionis doghter: Demotion's daughter, who slew herself when her fiancé died lest she should have to marry any other man and thus prove untrue to the one she had already married in intention if not in fact.   719. Lines 720–48, which merely extend Dorigen's catalogue of chastity defended, have been omitted.   754. lenger: the longer.   758. reherce: repeat.   760. devyse: tell.   762. so as wys: certainly.   763. to: too. and: if.   764. that: what.   765. paraventure: perchance. 766. fay: faith.   767. wisly: wisely.   768. wel . . . be: much rather be stabbed.   772. brast: burst out.   773. up: on. 777. contenance: appearance.   778. demen: judge.   779. cleped: called.   780. Goth: go.   781. swich: such and such.   784. nolde: would not.   785. an heep: a lot.   786. lewed: stupid.   787. jupartie: jeopardy.   789. semeth: it seems to.   790. demeth: judge.

791. which . . . highte: who was called.   793. Of . . . happed: by chance happened.   794. quykkest: busiest.   795. boun: bound.   796. hight: promised.   797. to . . . gardynward: (headed) toward the garden.   799. maner: kind of.   801. salueth: greets.   802. whiderward: where.   804. bad: ordered. 812. caughte of this: conceived from this.   814. were . . . abyde: he would rather desist.   816. franchise: the code of a free man. 821. hym . . . han: he would sooner have.   823. have . . . levere: would much rather.   824. Than I departe: than sever. 826. Quyt: discharged.   serement: oath.   827. as . . . biforn: hitherto.   828. Sith . . . that: since that time when.   829. repreve: reproach.   836. drede: doubt.

And hom unto hir housbond is she fare,
And tolde hym al as ye han herd me sayd.
And be ye siker,° he was so wel apayd°　　840
That it were inpossible me° to write.
What sholde I lenger of this cas endite?°

　　Arveragus and Dorigene his wyf
In sovereyn blisse leden° forth hir lyf.
Nevere eft° ne was ther angre hem bitwene.
He cherisseth hire as thogh she were a queene,
And she was to hym trewe for evere moore.
Of thise two folk ye gete of me namoore.

　　Aurelius, that his cost° hath al forlorn,°
Curseth the tyme that evere he was born.　　850
" Allas," quod he, " allas that I bihighte°
Of pured° gold a thousand pound of wighte°
Unto this philosophre. How shal I do?
I se namoore but that I am fordo.°
Myn heritage moot I nedes selle
And been a beggere. Here may I nat dwelle
And shamen al my kynrede in this place,
But° I of hym may gete bettre grace.
But, nathelees, I wol of hym assaye°
At certeyn dayes yeer by yeer to paye,　　860
And thonke hym of his grete curteisye.
My trouthe wol I kepe. I wol nat lye."

　　With herte soor, he gooth unto his cofre°
And broghte gold unto this philosophre
The value of fyve hundred pound, I gesse,
And hym bischeth of his gentillesse
To graunte hym dayes of the remenant,°
And seyde, " Maister, I dar wel make avant,°
I failled nevere of my trouthe as yit,
For sikerly my dette shal be quyt　　870
Towardes yow, however that I fare,
To goon abegged° in my kirtel° bare.
But, wolde ye vouchesauf, upon seuretee,°
Two yeer or thre for to respiten me,
Thanne were I wel, for ellis moot I selle
Myn heritage. Ther is namoore to telle."
This philosophre sobrely answerde,
And seyde thus, whan he thise wordes herde:
' Have I nat holden covenant unto thee? "

　　" Yis, certes, wel and trewely," quod he.　　880
" Hastow° nat had thy lady as thee liketh? "
" No, no," quod he, and sorwefully he siketh.°
" What was the cause? Tel me, if thow kan."
　　Aurelius his tale anon bigan,
And tolde hym al, as ye han herd bifore.
It nedeth nat to yow reherce it moore.

　　He seyde Arveragus, of° gentillesse,

Hadde levere° dye in sorwe and in distresse
Than that his wyf were of hir trouthe° fals.
The sorwe of Dorigen he tolde hym, als,°　　890
How looth hir was to ben a wikked wyf,
And that she levere had lost that day hir lyf,
And that hir trouthe she swoor thurgh innocence;
She nevere erst° hadde herd speke of apparence.°
" That made me han of hire so greet pitee;
And right° as freely as he sente hir me,
As frely sente I hire to hym agayn.
This al and som.° Ther is namoore to sayn."

　　This philosophre answerde, " Leeve° brother,
Everich of yow dide gentilly til oother.　　900
Thow art a squyer, and he is a knyght;
But God forbede, for his blisful myght,
But if a clerk° koude doon a gentil dede
As wel as any of yow, it is no drede.°
　　" Sire, I relesse° thee thy thousand pound,
As° thow right now were cropen° out of the
　　　ground,
Ne nevere er° now ne haddest knowen me.
For, sire, I wol nat take a peny of thee
For al my craft, ne noght° for my travaille.
Thow hast y-payed wel for my vitaille.°　　910
It is ynogh, and fare wel. Have good day."
And took his hors, and forth he goth his way.

　　Lordynges, this questioun than wol I aske now,
Which was the mooste free,° as thynketh° yow?
Now, telleth me, er that ye ferther wende.
I kan° namoore. My tale is at an ende.

THE NUN'S PRIEST'S TALE

　　In the General Prologue Chaucer did not develop
the character of the three priests riding in the Prioress's
retinue, perhaps because he felt that their quietness
would lend emphasis to the aristocratic stateliness of
the Prioress. But, in any case, the one priest for whom
Chaucer supplied a tale, though he is not described in
the Prologue, amply expresses his personality now.

　　He tells an ancient animal fable which in France
and Germany had been incorporated into the poetic
treatment of the life of the wily Reynard the Fox, a
popular folk character. But, with a subtlety of wit
which foreshadows the poetry of Pope four centuries
later, he elevates the fate of Chauntecleer to a mock-
heroic level, turning barnyard creatures into caricatures of human beings and their discussions of the
validity of dreams into a satire of scientific thought.

840. siker: sure.　apayd: satisfied.　841. me: for me.　842. endite: narrate.　844. leden: lead.　845. eft: again.　849. cost: expenditure.　forlorn: lost.　851. bihighte: promised.　852. pured:
pure.　wighte: weight.　854. fordo: destroyed.　858. But:
unless.　859. assaye: try.　863. cofre: money box.　867. dayes
. . . remenant: time for the remainder.　868. make avant:
boast.　872. abegged: begging.　kirtel: frock.　873. seuretee:
surety.　881. Hastow: have you.　882. siketh: sighs.　887. of:
out of.

888. levere: rather.　889. trouthe: promise.　890. als: also.
894. erst: before.　apparence: illusion.　896. right: just.
898. This . . . som: This is part and all.　899. Leeve: dear.
903. But . . . clerk: unless a scholar.　904. drede: doubt.
905. relesse: release.　906. As: just as if.　right . . . cropen:
only now had crept.　907. Ne . . . er: and never before.　909. ne
noght: nor anything.　910. vitaille: victuals.　914. free: generous.　thynketh: it seems to.　916. kan: can say.

As narrator the Priest plays the part of an unpretentious and unlearned man, but his allusions and judgments suggest that of all the pilgrims he is one of the best informed. He is well-read in both secular and religious subjects. He knows the theories of literary composition advocated by Geoffrey de Vinsauf, and he is equally familiar with the authorities on the theological problem of God's foreknowledge and man's freedom of will. And underneath his playful tone, there runs a note of seriousness, for tactfully but firmly he turns his tale at its conclusion into a sermon.

A poure widwe, somdel stape° in age,
Was whilom° dwellynge in a narwe° cotage
Biside a grove, stondyng in a dale.
This widwe of which I telle yow my tale,
Syn thilke° day that she was last a wyf,
In pacience ladde a ful symple lyf,
For litel was hire catel° and hire rente.°
By housbondrye of swich° as God hire sente
She foond° hireself and eek° hire doghtren° two.
Thre large sowes hadde she and namo,°   10
Thre kyn,° and eek a sheep that highte° Malle.
Ful sooty was hire bour° and eek hire halle,
In which she eet ful many a sklendre° meel.
Of poynaunt° sauce hir neded° never a deel.°
No deyntee morsel passed thurgh hir throte;
Hir diete was acordant to hir cote.°
Repleccioun ne made hire nevere syk;
Attempree° diete was al hir phisyk,
And excercise, and hertes suffisaunce.°
The goute lette° hire nothyng° for to daunce,   20
N' apoplexie shente nat hir heed.°
No wyn ne drank she, neither whit ne reed.
Hir bord° was served moost with whit and blak,
Milk and broun breed, in which she foond no lak,°
Seynd° bacoun, and som tyme an ey° or tweye,
For she was, as it were, a maner deye.°
A yeerd she hadde, enclosed al aboute
With stikkes, and a drye dych° withoute,
In which she hadde a cok heet° Chauntecleer.
In al the land of crowyng nas° his peer.   30
His voys was murier° than the myrie orgon
On massedayes that in the chirche gon.°
Wel sikerer° was his crowyng in his logge°
Than is a clokke or any abbey orlogge.°

By° nature° he knew ech ascensioun
Of the equinoxial in thilke toun,
For whan degrees fiftene were ascended,
Thanne krew he that it myghte nat ben amended.°
His comb was redder than the fyn coral
And batailled as° it were a castel wal.   40
His byle° was blak, and as the jeet° it shoon.
Lyk asure° were hise legges and his toon,°
Hise nayles whitter than the lylye flour,
And lyk the burned° gold was his colour.
This gentil cok hadde in his governaunce°
Sevene hennes for to doon al his plesaunce,°
Whiche were hise sustres° and his paramours,
And wonder° lyke to hym as of colours,
Of whiche the faireste hewed on hire throte
Was cleped° faire damoysele Pertelote.   50
Curteys she was, discreet, and debonaire,
And compaignable, and bar° hirself so faire
Syn thilke day that she was seven nyght oold
That, trewely, she hath the herte in hoold
Of Chauntecleer, loken° in every lith.°
He loved hire so that wel was hym ther-with.°
But swich a joye was it to here hem° synge,
Whan that the brighte sonne gan to sprynge,°
In swete acord " My leef is faren in londe."°
For thilke° tyme, as I have understonde,   60
Beestes and briddes° koude speke and synge.
And so bifel that in a dawenynge,°
As Chauntecleer among hise wyves alle
Sat on his perche, that was in the halle,
And next hym sat this faire Pertelote,
This Chauntecleer gan gronen° in his throte
As man that in his dreem is drecched° soore.
And whan that° Pertelote thus herde hym rore,
She was agast and seyde, " Herte deere,
What eyleth yow to grone in this manere?   70
Ye ben a verray° slepere. Fy, for shame! "
And he answerde and seyde thus: " Madame,
I prey yow that ye take it nat agrief.°
By God, me mette° I was in swich meschief
Right now that yet myn herte is soore afright.
Now God," quod° he, " my swevene recche°
    aright,
And kepe my body out of foul prisoun.

35-37. The sphere of the stars was thought of as rotating 360 degrees every twenty-four hours around the earth's equator. The equinoctial circle of the heaven thus turns or "ascends" 15 degrees every hour. (See Note A, p. 195.) **35. nature:** instinct. **38. that . . . amended:** so that it couldn't be bettered. **40. batailled as:** battlemented as if. **41. byle:** bill. **jeet:** jet. **42. asure:** azure. **toon:** toes. **44. burned:** burnished. **45. governaunce:** control. **46. plesaunce:** pleasure. **47. sustres:** sisters (sweethearts). **48. wonder:** wonderfully. **50. cleped:** called. **52. bar:** conducted. **55. loken:** locked. **lith:** limb. **56. wel . . . ther-with:** he was well contented. **57. hem:** them. **58. gan to sprynge:** began to rise. **59. leef . . . londe:** sweetheart has gone to the country. **60. thilke:** (at) that. **61. briddes:** birds. **62. in a dawenynge:** one dawn. **66. gan gronen:** began to groan. **67. drecched:** tormented. **68. whan that:** when. **71. verray:** sound. **73. agrief:** ill. **74. me mette:** I dreamed. **76. quod:** said. **my . . . recche:** may my dream work out.

NUN'S PRIEST'S TALE. **1. widwe . . . stape:** widow somewhat advanced. **2. whilom:** once. **narwe:** small. **5. Syn thilke:** since that same. **7. catel:** property. **rente:** income. **8. swich:** such. **9. foond:** supported. **eek:** also. **doghtren:** daughters. **10. namo:** no more. **11. kyn:** cows. **highte:** was called. **12. bour:** bedroom. **13. sklendre:** slender. **14. poynaunt:** pungent. **hir neded:** she needed. **deel:** bit. **16. cote:** means. **18. Attempree:** temperate. **19. suffisaunce:** sufficiency. **20. lette:** hindered. **nothyng:** in no way. **21. N' apoplexie . . . heed:** nor did apoplexy trouble her head. **23. bord:** table. **24. foond . . . lak:** found no fault. **25. Seynd:** broiled. **ey:** egg. **26. maner deye:** sort of dairywoman. **28. dych:** ditch. **29. heet:** named. **30. nas:** (there) was not. **31. murier:** merrier. **32. gon:** plays. **33. Wel sikerer:** much more accurate. **logge:** lodge. **34. orlogge:** horologe (clock).

Me mette how that I romed up and doun
Withinne oure yeerd, where-as I say° a beest,
Was lyk an hound and wolde han maad areest°   80
Upon my body and han° had me deed.
His colour was bitwixe yelow and reed,
And tipped was his tayl and bothe hise erys°
With blak unlik the remenaunt° of hise herys,°
His snowte smal, with glowyng eyen° tweye.
Yet of his look for fere almoost I deye.
This caused me my gronyng, doutelees."
    "Avoy! "° quod she. "Fy on yow, hertelees!°
Allas," quod she, "for, by that God above,
Now han ye lost myn herte and al my love.   90
I kan nat love a coward, by my feith!
For, certes,° what so° any womman seith,
We alle desiren, if it myghte be,
To han housbondes hardy, wise, and fre,°
And secree,° and no nygard, ne no fool,
Ne hym that is agast of every tool,°
Ne noon avauntour,° by that God above.
How dorste° ye seyn, for shame, unto youre love
That any thyng myghte make yow aferd?
Have ye no mannes herte and han a berd?   100
    "Allas, and konne ye ben agast° of swevenys!°
Nothyng, God woot,° but vanytee in swevene is.
Swevenes engendren of replexions,°
And ofte of fume° and of complexions,°
Whan humours ben to habundant in a wight.°
    "Certes, this dreem which ye han met to-nyght°
Comth of the grete superfluytee
Of youre rede colera,° pardee,°
Which causeth folk to dreden° in hir° dremes
Of arwes,° and of fyr with rede lemes,°   110
Of rede bestes that they wol hem byte,
Of contek,° and of whelpes grete and lyte,
Right° as the humour of malencolie
Causeth ful many a man in sleep to crie
For fere of blake beres,° or boles° blake,
Or elles blake develes, wol hem° take.
Of othere humours koude I telle also
That werken° many a man in sleep ful wo,°
But I wol passe as lightly as I kan.
Lo Catoun,° which that was so wys a man,   120

Seyde he nat thus: 'Ne do no fors of° dremes'?
    "Now sire," quod she, "whan we fle° fro the
        bemes,
For Goddes love, as taak° som laxatif.
Up° peril of my soule and of my lif,
I conseille yow the beste, I wol nat lye,
That bothe of colere and of malencolye
Ye purge yow. And, for° ye shal nat tarye,
Thogh in this toun is noon° apothecarye,
I shal myself to herbes techen° yow
That shul ben for youre heele° and for youre
        prow.°   130
And in oure yerd tho° herbes shal I fynde
The whiche han° of hire propretee by kynde°
To purge yow bynethe and eek° above.
Foryet nat this, for Goddes owene love:
Ye ben ful colerik of complexioun.
Ware° the sonne in his ascensioun,
Ne fynde yow nat replet of° humours hote,
And, if it do, I dar wel leye a grote°
That ye shul have a fevere terciane°
Or an agu that may be youre bane.°   140
A day or two ye shul have digestyves
Of wormes er° ye take youre laxatyves
Of lauriol,° centaure,° and fumetere,°
Or elles of ellebor° that groweth there,
Of katapuce,° or of gaitrys beryis,°
Of herbe yve° growyng in oure yerd, ther merye
        is.°
Pekke hem up right as they growe, and ete hem in.
Be myrie, housbonde, for youre fader kyn!°
Dredeth no dreem. I kan sey yow namoore."
    "Madame," quod he, "graunt mercy of youre
        loore.°   150
But nathelees, as touchyng daun Catoun,°
That hath of wisdom swich° a gret renoun,
Thogh that he bad no dremes for to drede,
By God, men may in olde bokes rede
Of many a man moore of auctoritee
Than evere Catoun was, so mote I thee,°
That al the revers° seyn of his sentence°
And han wel founden by experience
That dremes ben° significaciouns
As wel of joye as of tribulaciouns   160
That folk enduren in this lyf present.

79. where-as . . . say: where I saw.   **80. han . . . areest:** have seized.   **81. han:** have.   **83. erys:** ears.   **84. remenaunt:** rest.   **herys:** hair.   **85. eyen:** eyes.   **88. Avoy:** shame.   **hertelees:** faintheart.   **92. certes:** certainly.   **what so:** whatever.   **94. fre:** generous.   **95. secree:** discreet.   **96. tool:** weapon.   **97. avauntour:** boaster.   **98. dorste:** dared.   **101. agast:** afraid.   **swevenys:** dreams.   **102. woot:** knows.   **103. engendren . . . replexions:** are engendered from repletion.   **104. fume:** vapor.   **complexions:** temperaments.   **105. humours . . . wight:** humors are too abundant in a person. A superabundance of any one of the four humors affected the temperament. See Note B, p. 196.   **106. han . . . to-nyght:** have dreamed this night.   **108. rede colera:** red choler.   **pardee:** certainly.   **109. dreden:** be frightened.   **hir:** their.   **110. arwes:** arrows.   **lemes:** flames.   **112. contek:** strife.   **113. Right:** just.   **115. beres:** bears.   **boles:** bulls.   **116. wol hem:** (which) will them.   **118. werken:** make.   **wo:** woeful.   **120. Catoun:** Dionysius Cato, to whom a well-known collection of Latin maxims was ascribed.

121. Ne . . . of: pay no attention to.   **122. fle:** fly down.   **123. as taak:** take.   **124. Up:** upon.   **127. for:** in order that.   **128. noon:** no.   **129. techen:** direct.   **130. heele:** healing.   **prow:** well-being.   **131. tho:** those.   **132. The . . . han:** which have.   **kynde:** nature.   **133. eek:** also.   **136. Ware:** beware that.   **137. replet of:** overfilled with.   **138. grote:** groat (4*d.*).   **139. terciane:** tertian (recurring every other day).   **140. bane:** destruction.   **142. er:** before.   **143. lauriol:** spurge laurel.   **centaure:** centaury.   **fumetere:** fumitory.   **144. ellebor:** hellebore.   **145. katapuce:** caper spurge.   **gaitrys beryis:** gaiter-tree berries (dogwood).   **146. herbe yve:** ground ivy.   **ther . . . is:** where it is pleasant.   **148. fader kyn:** father's kin.   **150. graunt . . . loore:** much thanks for your instruction.   **151. daun Catoun:** Master Cato.   **152. swich:** such.   **156. mote I thee:** may I prosper.   **157. revers:** contrary.   **sentence:** opinion.   **159. ben:** are.

Ther nedeth° make of this noon argument;
The verray preeve° sheweth it in dede.
  " Oon° of the gretteste auctor° that men rede
Seith thus, that whilom° two felawes° wente
On pilgrymage in a ful good entente,
And happed so they coomen in a toun
Where-as ther was swich congregacioun
Of peple and eek so streit of herbergage°
That they ne founde as muche as a cotage 170
In which they bothe myghte y-logged° be.
Wherfore they mosten° of necessitee,
As for° that nyght, departen° compaignye,
And ech of hem gooth to his hostelrye
And took his loggyng as it wolde falle.
That oon of hem was logged in a stalle
Fer in a yeerd° with oxen of the plow.
That oother man was logged wel ynow°
As was his aventure° or his fortune,
That us governeth alle as in commune.° 180
  " And so bifel that, longe er it were day,
This man mette° in his bed ther-as° he lay
How that his felawe gan upon hym calle
And seyde, ' Allas, for in an oxes stalle
This nyght I shal be mordred ther° I lye.
Now help me, deere brother, or I dye.
In alle haste com to me,' he sayde.
  " This man out of his sleep for feere
    abrayde,°
But whan that he was wakned of his sleep,
He turned hym and took of this no keep.° 190
Hym thoughte° his dreem nas but° a vanytee.
Thus twies° in his slepyng dremed he,
And atte thridde tyme yet his felawe
Cam, as hym thoughte, and seyde, ' I am now
    slawe.°
Bihoold my blody woundes, depe and wyde.
Arys up erly in the morwe tyde,°
And at the west gate of the toun,' quod he,
' A carte ful of donge ther shaltow se,°
In which my body is hid ful pryvely.°
Do thilke° carte aresten° boldely. 200
My gold caused my mordre, sooth to seyn ';°
And tolde hym every poynt how he was slayn
With a ful pitous face pale of hewe.
And truste wel his dreem he fond° ful trewe,
For on the morwe, as soone as it was day,

To his felawes in° he took the way,
And whan that he cam to this oxes stalle,
After° his felawe he bigan to calle.
  " The hostiler answerde hym anon°
And seyde, ' Sire, youre felawe is agon. 210
As soone as day he wente out of the toun.'
  " This man gan fallen in suspecioun,
Remembrynge on hise dremes that he mette,
And forth he gooth, no lenger wolde he lette,°
Unto the west gate of the toun and fond
A dong carte, wente° as it were to donge° lond,
That was arrayed in the same wise
As ye han herd the dede man devyse,°
And with an hardy herte he gan to crye
Vengeaunce and justice of this felonye. 220
' My felawe mordred is this same nyght,
And in this carte heere he lyth gapyng
    upright.°
I crye out on the mynystres,'° quod he,
' That sholden kepe and reulen this citee.
Harrow,° allas! Heere lyth my felawe slayn!'
What sholde I moore unto this tale sayn?
The peple out sterte° and caste the cart to grounde,
And in the myddel of the dong they founde
The dede man, that mordred was al newe.°
  " O blisful God, that art so just and trewe, 230
Lo how that thow biwreyest° mordre alway.
Mordre wol out, that se° we day by day.
Mordre is so wlatsom° and abhomynable
To God, that is so just and resonable,
That he ne wol nat suffre it heled° be,
Thogh it abyde° a yeer, or two, or thre.
Mordre wol out, this is my conclusioun.
And right anon ministres of that toun
Han hent° the cartere and so soore hym pyned°
And eek the hostiler so soore engyned° 240
That they biknewe° hir wikkednesse anon
And were an-hanged by the nekke bon.°
  " Heere may men seen that dremes ben to
    drede.°
And, certes, in the same book I rede,
Right in the nexte chapitre after this—
I gabbe° nat, so have I° joye or blys—
Two men that wolde han passed over see
For certeyn cause into a fer contree,
If that the wynd ne hadde ben contrarie,
That made hem in a citee for to tarie, 250
That stood ful myrie° upon an haven° syde.
But on a day, agayn the even tyde,°

162. Ther nedeth: there is (no) need to.   163. verray preeve: very proof.   164. Oon: one.   auctor: author(s).   165. whilom: once.   felawes: companions.   169. streit of herbergage: short of lodgings.   171. y-logged: lodged.   172. mosten: must. 173. As for: for.   departen: part.   177. Fer . . . yeerd: far off in a courtyard.   178. ynow: enough.   179. aventure: lot. 180. alle . . . commune: all in common.   182. mette: dreamed. ther-as: where.   185. ther: where.   188. abrayde: awoke. 190. keep: heed.   191. Hym thoughte: it seemed to him. nas but: was only.   192. twies: twice.   194. slawe: slain. 196. morwe tyde: morning time.   198. shaltow: you will see. 199. ful pryvely: very secretly.   200. Do thilke: have that same.   aresten: stopped.   201. sooth to seyn: truth to tell. 204. fond: found.

206. felawes in: companion's lodging.   208. After: for.   209. anon: at once.   214. lette: stay.   216. wente: (which) went.   donge: manure, fertilize.   218. devyse: describe.   222. upright: face-upward.   223. mynystres: officers.   225. Harrow: help. 227. sterte: sprang.   229. al newe: just recently.   231. biwrey-est: dost reveal.   232. se: see.   233. wlatsom: foul.   235. heled: concealed.   236. abyde: await.   239. hent: seized.   pyned: tortured.   240. engyned: racked.   241. biknewe: confessed. 242. bon: bone.   243. ben to drede: are to be feared.   246. gabbe: exaggerate.   have I: may I have.   251. myrie: pleasant. haven: harbor.   252. agayn . . . tyde: towards evening time.

The wynd gan chaunge and blew right as hem
    leste.°
Jolif° and glad they wente unto hir° reste
And casten hem° ful erly for to saille.
  "But herkneth! To that o° man fil° a greet
    mervaille,
That oon of hem, in slepyng as he lay,
Hym mette a wonder° dreem agayn° the day.
Hym thoughte a man stood by his beddes syde,
And hym comanded that he sholde abyde,   260
And seyde hym thus: 'If thow tomorwe wende,°
Thow shalt be dreynt.° My tale is at an ende.'
He wook, and tolde his felawe what he mette,
And preyde hym his viage° to lette.°
As for that day, he preyde hym to abyde.
His felawe, that lay by his beddes syde,
Gan for to laughe and scorned hym ful faste.
'No dreem,' quod he, 'may so myn herte agaste°
That I wol lette for to do my thynges.°
I sette nat a straw by thy dremynges,   270
For swevenes ben but owtes and japes.°
Men dreme alday° of owles and of apes
And of many a maze° therwithal;
Men dreme of thyng that nevere was ne shal.°
But, sith I see that thow wolt here abyde,
And thus forslewthen wilfully° thy tyde,°
God woot,° it reweth me,° and have good day!'
And thus he took his leve and wente his way,
But er that° he hadde half his cours y-seyled,
Noot I° nat why ne° what meschaunce it eyled,°
But casuelly° the shippes botme rente,°   281
And ship and man under the water wente
In sighte of othere shippes it bisyde°
That with hem seyled at the same tyde.
And therfore, faire Pertelote so deere,
By swiche ensamples° olde maystow leere°
That no man sholde been to recchelees°
Of dremes, for I sey thee, doutelees,
That many a dreem ful soore is for to dred.°
  "Lo, in the lyf of Seint Kenelm I rede,   290
That was Kenulphus sone,° the noble kyng
Of Mercenrike,° how Kenelm mette a thyng.
A lite er° he was mordred on a day,
His mordre in his avysioun° he say.°

His norice° hym expowned every del°
His swevene, and bad hym for to kepe hym° wel
For° traisoun, but he nas but° sevene yeer old,
And therfore litel tale° hath he told°
Of any dreem, so holy was his herte.
By God, I hadde levere° than my sherte   300
That ye hadde rad° his legende as have I.
Dame Pertelote, I sey yow trewely,
Macrobeus,° that writ° the avysioun
In Affrike of the worthy Cipioun,°
Affermeth dremes and seith that they ben
Warnynge of thynges that men after sen.°
And forther-moore, I pray yow, looketh wel
In the Olde Testament, of Daniel,°
If he heeld dremes any vanytee.
Rede eek of Joseph, and there shul ye see   310
Wher° dremes be somtyme, I sey nat alle,
Warnynge of thynges that shul after falle.
Looke of Egipte the kyng, daun Pharao,°
His bakere, and his butiller also,
Wher they ne felte noon effect in dremes.
Who-so° wol seke actes of sondry remes°
May rede of dremes many a wonder thyng.
Lo Cresus,° which that was of Lyde kyng,
Mette he nat° that he sat upon a tree,
Which signified he sholde an-hanged be?   320
Lo heere Andromacha,° Ectores° wyf,
That day that Ector sholde lese° his lyf,
She dremed on the same nyght biforn
How that the lyf of Ector sholde be lorn°
If thilke° day he wente in to bataille.
She warned hym, but it myghte nat availle;
He wente for to fighte, nathelees.°
But he was slayn anon of° Achilles.
But thilke tale is al to° long to telle,
And eek it is ny° day. I may nat dwelle.   330
  "Shortly I seye, as for conclusioun,
That I shal han of this avysioun
Adversitee, and I seye forther-moor
That I ne telle of laxatyves no stoor,°
For they ben venymes,° I woot it wel.

---

253. hem leste: they wished. 254. Jolif: jolly. hir: their.
255. casten hem: decided. 256. o: one. fil: befell. 258. Hym
. . . wonder: dreamed a wonderful. agayn: before. 261. wende:
travel. 262. dreynt: drowned. 264. viage: voyage. lette:
delay. 268. agaste: frighten. 269. lette . . . thynges: stop
doing my business. 271. japes: follies. 272. alday: every
day. 273. maze: wonder. 274. ne shal: nor shall (be).
276. forslewthen wilfully: squander willingly. tyde: time.
277. woot: knows. it . . . me: I rue it. 279. er that: before.
280. Noot I: I don't know. ne: nor. eyled: ailed. 281. cas-
uelly: by chance. rente: burst. 283. it bisyde: beside it.
286. ensamples: examples. maystow leere: you may learn.
287. to recchelees: too heedless. 289. soore . . . dred: sorely
is to be feared. 291. Kenulphus sone: Kenulphus' son. Kenelm
dreamed that he had to fly to Heaven; subsequently he was
murdered by his aunt. 292. Mercenrike: Mercia (central
England). 293. lite er: little before. 294. avysioun: vision.
say: saw.

295. norice: nurse. expowned . . . del: expounded completely.
296. for . . . hym: to guard himself. 297. For: against. nas
but: was only. 298. tale: heed. told: paid. 300. levere:
rather. 301. rad: read. 303. Macrobeus: The commentary
by Macrobius on Cicero's account of the dream of Scipio Africanus Minor was regarded as a standard authority on dream
lore. writ: writes. 304. Cipioun: Scipio. 306. after sen:
afterwards see. 308. Daniel: The book of Daniel consists almost
entirely of dreams and their interpretations. 311. Wher:
whether. 313. daun Pharao: Lord Pharaoh. Joseph correctly
predicted the meaning of dreams both for him and for his
butler and baker (Gen. 37, 40, and 41). 316. Who-so: whoever. seke . . . remes: search the history of various realms.
318. Cresus: Croesus of Lydia, who according to legend was
proud of his dream till his daughter told him that the tree
signified the gallows. 319. nat: not. 321. Andromacha: Andromache. Ectores: Hector's. 322. lese: lose. 324. lorn:
lost. 325. thilke: that same. 327. nathelees: nevertheless.
328. anon of: immediately by. 329. to: too. 330. ny: near.
334. ne . . . stoor: set no store on laxatives. 335. ben venymes:
are venomous.

I hem deffye! I love hem never a del!°
"Now lat us speke of myrthe and stynte° al this.
Madame Pertelote, so have I° blis,
Of o thyng God hath sent me large grace,
For whan I se the beautee of youre face,   340
Ye ben so scarlet reed aboute youre eyen,
It maketh al my drede for to dyen,
For, also siker as In principio,°
'Mulier est hominis confusio.'°
"Madame, the sentence° of this Latyn is,
'Womman is mannes joye and al his blis.'
For whan I feele a-nyght youre softe syde,
Al be it that I may nat on yow ryde
For that° oure perche is maad° so narwe,° allas,
I am so ful of joye and of solas°   350
That I deffye bothe swevene° and dreem."
And with that word he fley° doun fro the beem,
For it was day, and eke hise hennes alle.
And with a chuk he gan hem for to calle,
For he hadde founde a corn,° lay° in the yerd.
Real° he was; he was na moore aferd.°
He fethered Pertelote twenty tyme
And trad° as ofte er that it was pryme.°
He looketh as it were° a grym leoun,°
And on hise toos he rometh up and doun.   360
Hym deyned° nat to sette his foot to grounde.
He chukketh whan he hath a corn y-founde,
And to hym rennen thanne hise wyves alle.
Thus real as a prince is in his halle
Leve I this Chauntecleer in his pasture,
And after wol I telle his aventure.
Whan that the monthe in which the world bigan,
That highte° March, whan God first maked man,
Was complet, and passed were also,
Syn March bigan, thritty dayes and two,   370
Bifel° that Chauntecler in al his pryde,
Hise sevene wyves walkyng hym bisyde,
Caste up hise eyen to the brighte sonne,
That in the signe of Taurus° hadde y-ronne
Twenty degrees and oon, and som-what moore,
And knew by kynde° and by noon oother loore
That it was pryme, and krew with blisful stevene.°
"The sonne," he seyde, "is clomben upon hevene
Fourty degrees and oon, and moore ywis.°

Madame Pertelote, my worldes blis,   380
Herkneth° thise blisful briddes, how they synge,
And se the fresshe floures how they sprynge.
Ful is myn herte of revel and solas."
But sodeynly hym fil° a sorweful cas,°
For evere the latter ende of joye is wo.
God woot that worldly joye is soone ago,°
And if a rethor° koude faire endite,°
He in a cronycle saufly myghte it write
As for a sovereyn notabilitee.°
Now every wys man, lat hym herkne° me;   390
This storie is also° trewe, I undertake,°
As is the book of Launcelot de Lake,°
That wommen holde in ful gret reverence.
Now wol I torne agayn to my sentence.°
A colfox° ful of sly iniquitee,
That in the grove hadde woned° yeres three,
By heigh ymaginacioun forncast,°
The same nyght thurgh-out the hegges brast°
Into the yerd ther Chauntecleer the faire
Was wont, and eek hise wyves, to repaire,   400
And in a bed of wortes° stille he lay
Til it was passed undren° of the day,
Waitynge his tyme on Chauntecleer to falle,
As gladly doon° thise homycides° alle
That in awayt liggen° to mordre men.
O false mordrour, lurkynge in thy den,
O newe Scariot,° newe Genyloun,°
False dissimilour,° O Greek Synoun,°
That broghtest Troye al outrely° to sorwe!
O Chauntecleer, acursed be that morwe°   410
That thow into the yerd flaugh° fro the bemes.
Thow were ful wel y-warned by thy dremes
That thilke day was perilous to thee.
But what that God forwoot moot nedes° be
After° the opynyoun of certeyn clerkis.°
Witnesse on hym that any parfit clerk is,
That in scole is greet altercacioun
In this matere and greet disputisoun,°
And hath ben of an hundred thousand men.
But I ne kan nat bulte it to the bren°   420

---

336. hem ... del: them not at all. 337. stynte: stop. 338. have I: may I have. 343. also ... principio: as surely as "In the beginning (was the Word)," i.e., as surely as the Gospel. (See Gen. Prol., l. 254.) 344. 'Mulier ... confusio': "Woman is man's ruin," a widely known Latin proverb carefully mistranslated by Chauntecleer in l. 346. 345. sentence: meaning. 349. For that: because. maad: made. narwe: narrow. 350. solas: pleasure. 351. swevene: vision. 352. fley: flew. 355. corn: grain of corn. lay: (which) lay. 356. Real: regal. na ... aferd: no more afraid. 358. trad: trod (her). pryme: prime (9 A.M.). 359. looketh ... were: looks like. leoun: lion. 361. Hym deyned: he deigned. 368. highte: is called. It was believed that the world was created in March. 371. Bifel: it befell. 374. Taurus: See Note A, p. 195. The date is May 3. (March, thirty days of April, and two days of May had passed.) 376. kynde: nature. 377. stevene: voice. 379. ywis: indeed.

381. Herkneth: listen to. 384. hym fil: befell him. cas: happening. 386. ago: gone. 387. rethor: rhetorician. endite: compose. 389. As ... notabilitee: as a supreme observation. 390. herkne: hearken to. 391. also: as. undertake: vow. 392. Launcelot de Lake: an entirely fictitious romance concerning Lancelot, the lover of Guinevere, King Arthur's wife. 394. sentence: subject. 395. colfox: coal fox. 396. woned: lived. 397. heigh ... forncast: divine knowledge foreordained. 398. hegges brast: hedges burst. 401. wortes: herbs. 402. undren: midmorning. 404. gladly doon: usually do. homycides: murderers. 405. in ... liggen: lie in waiting. 407. Scariot: Judas Iscariot, who betrayed Christ. Genyloun: Ganelon, who betrayed Charlemagne's nephew Roland. 408. dissimilour: deceiver. Synoun: Sinon, who persuaded the Trojans to take the Greeks' wooden horse into Troy. 409. al outrely: utterly. 410. morwe: morning. 411. flaugh: flew. 414. forwoot ... nedes: foreknows must needs. 415. After: according to. clerkis: scholars. 418. disputisoun: disputation. 420. I ... bren: I can't sift it to the bran; i.e., I can't reach certainty in this much-disputed theological problem. (If God foreknows the future, to what extent has man free will?)

As kan the holy doctour Augustyn,°
Or Boece,° or the bisshop Bradwardyn,°
Wheither that Goddes worthy forewityng°
Streyneth° me nedely° for to doon a thyng —
"Nedely " clepe° I symple necessitee —
Or ellis if fre choys be graunted me
To do that same thyng or do it noght,
Though God forwoot° it er that it was wroght;
Or if his wityng streyneth never a del°
But° by necessitee condicionel.   430
I wol nat han° to do of swich° matere.
My tale is of a cok, as ye may heere,
That took his conseil of his wyf with sorwe
To walken in the yerd upon that morwe
That he hadde met° the dreem that I yow tolde.
Wommens conseils ben ful ofte colde.°
Wommanes conseil broghte us first to wo
And made Adam fro Paradys to go,
Ther-as he was ful myrie and wel at ese.
But, for I noot° to whom it myghte displese   440
If I conseil of wommen wolde blame,
Passe over, for I seyde it in my game.°
Rede auctours° where they trete of swich matere,
And what they seyn° of wommen ye may heere.
Thise ben the cokkes wordes and nat myne;
I kan noon harm of no womman devyne.°
   Faire in the sond° to bathe hire myrily
Lith° Pertelote, and alle hir sustres by,
Agayn the sonne;° and Chauntecleer so free
Song myrier than the mermayde in the see,   450
For Phisiologus seithe sikerly°
How that they syngen wel and myrily.
   And so bifel that, as he caste his eye
Among the wortes° on a boterflye,
He was war° of this fox that lay ful lowe.
Nothyng ne liste hym thanne° for to crowe,
But cryde anon " Cok, cok," and up he sterte°
As man° that was affrayed° in his herte,

For naturelly° a beest desireth flee
Fro his contrarie,° if he may it see,   460
Though he nevere erst° hadde syn° it with his eye.
   This Chauntecleer, whan he gan hym espye,°
He wolde han fled but that the fox anon
Seyde, " Gentil sire, allas! Wher wol ye gon?
Be ye affrayed of me that am youre freend?
Now, certes, I were worse than a feend
If I to yow wolde° harm or vileynye.
I am nat come youre conseil for t' espye,°
But trewely the cause of my comynge
Was oonly for to herkne how that ye synge,   470
For trewely ye han as myrie a stevene°
As any aungel hath that is in hevene.
Ther-with ye han in musyk moore feelynge
Than hadde Boece° or any that kan synge.
My lord, youre fader — God his soule blesse! —
And eek youre moder, of hire gentillesse,°
Han in myn hous y-ben° to my greet ese.°
And, certes, sire, ful fayn° wolde I yow plese.
   " But, for° men speke of syngynge, I wol seye —
So mote I brouke° wel myne eyen tweye! —   480
Save yow I herde nevere man so synge
As dide youre fader in the morwenynge.
Certes, it was of herte,° al that he song.
And for to make his voys the moore strong,
He wolde so peyne hym° that with bothe hise eyen
He moste wynke,° so loude he wolde cryen,
And stonden on his tiptoon ther-with-al,
And strecche forth his nekke long and smal.
And eek he was of swich discrecioun
That ther nas no° man in no regioun   490
That hym in song or wisdom myghte passe.
I have wel rad° in *Daun*° *Burnel the Asse,*
Among his vers, how that ther was a cok,
For° a preestes sone yaf° hym a knok
Upon his leg, whil he was yong and nyce,°
He made hym for to lese° his benefice.
But, certeyn, ther nys no comparisoun
Bitwix the wisdom and discrecioun
Of youre fader and of his subtiltee.
Now syngeth, sire, for seinte° charitee!   500
Lat se, konne ye youre fader countrefete? "°

---

421. **Augustyn:** St. Augustine of Hippo, who discussed the likelihood that man has "free choice" (l. 426) of action despite the infallibility of God's foreknowledge of future events.   422. **Boece:** Boethius, the author of the *Consolation of Philosophy*, who distinguished between the simple (l. 425) and the conditional (l. 430) necessity of man's actions.   **Bradwardyn:** Archbishop Bradwardine of Canterbury (d. 1349), who lectured at Oxford on God's foreknowledge.   423. **worthy forewityng:** excellent foreknowing.   424. **Streyneth:** constrains.   **nedely:** necessarily.   425. **clepe:** call.   428. **forwoot:** foreknows.   429. **wityng . . . del:** knowing constrains not at all.   430. **But:** except.   431. **han:** have (anything).   **of swich:** with such.   435. **met:** dreamed.   436. **colde:** fatal.   440. **for I noot:** since I don't know.   442. **in my game:** in jest.   443. **auctours:** authors.   444. **seyn:** say.   446. **devyne:** imagine.   447. **sond:** sand.   448. **Lith:** lies.   449. **Agayn . . . sonne:** in the sun.   451. **Phisiologus . . . sikerly:** Physiologus says certainly. He was reputed to be the author of the first *Bestiary*, a compendium of lore about certain natural and supernatural creatures, including mermaids. The extreme popularity of its numerous adaptations arose less from the appended morals than from the fabulous marvels it recounted.   454. **wortes:** plants.   455. **war:** aware.   456. **Nothyng . . . thanne:** not at all did he wish then.   457. **sterte:** sprang.   458. **As man:** like someone.   **affrayed:** frightened.

459. **naturelly:** by nature.   460. **contrarie:** opposite. Each thing and being was believed to have its contrary and to feel a natural antipathy to it.   461. **erst:** before.   **syn:** seen.   462. **gan . . . espye:** noticed him.   467. **wolde:** intended.   468. **conseil . . . espye:** secret to discover.   471. **stevene:** voice.   474. **Boece:** Boethius also wrote a work entitled *On Music*.   476. **gentillesse:** gentility.   477. **y-ben:** been.   **ese:** satisfaction.   478. **fayn:** gladly.   479. **for:** since.   480. **mote I brouke:** may I use.   483. **of herte:** hearty.   485. **peyne hym:** strive.   486. **moste wynke:** must shut (his eyes).   490. **nas no:** was no.   492. **rad:** read.   *Daun: Master.* According to the twelfth-century poem, *Burnellus the Ass,* a young man threw a stone at a cock and broke its leg. Later, when he was to have been appointed to a benefice, the cock avenged itself by failing to crow in time to awaken him for the ordination.   494. **For:** because.   **yaf:** gave.   495. **nyce:** foolish.   496. **lese:** lose.   500. **seinte:** holy.   501. **countrefete:** imitate.

This Chauntecleer hise wynges gan to bete
As man that koude his traysoun nat espie,°
So was he ravysshed with° his flaterie.
   Allas, ye lordes, many a fals flatour°
Is in youre court, and many a losengeour,°
That plesen° yow wel moore, by my feith,
Than he that soothfastnesse° unto yow seith.
Redeth Ecclesiaste of° flaterye.
Beth war,° ye lordes, of hir trecherye.   510
This Chauntecler stood hye upon his toos,
Strecchynge his nekke, and heeld hise eyen cloos,°
And gan to crowe loude for the nones.°
And daun Russell the fox stirte up atones,°
And by the gargat hente° Chauntecleer,
And on his bak toward the wode° hym beer,°
For yet ne was ther no man that hym sewed.°
   O destynee, that mayst nat ben eschewed!°
Allas that Chauntecler fleigh° fro the bemes!
Allas, his wif ne roghte nat° of dremes!   520
And on a Friday fil al this meschaunce.
   O Venus, that art goddesse of plesaunce,°
Syn that thy servant was this Chauntecleer,
And in thy servyce dide al his power
Moore for delit° than world to multiplie,
Why woldestow suffre° hym on thy day° to dye?
   O Gaufred,° deere maister soverayn,
That, whan thy worthy kyng Richard was slayn
With shot, compleynedest° his deth so soore,
Why ne hadde I now thy sentence° and thy loore°
The Friday for to chide, as diden ye?   531
For on a Friday, soothly,° slayn was he.
Thanne wolde I shewe yow how that I koude
      pleyne°
For Chauntecleres drede and for his peyne.
   Certes, swich cry ne lamentacioun
Was nevere of ladyes maad° whan Ylioun°
Was wonne, and Pirrus° with his streite swerd°
Whanne he hadde hent° kyng Priam by the berd
And slayn hym, as seith us *Eneydos,*°
As maden alle the hennes in the cloos°   540
Whan they hadde seyn° of Chauntecleer the sighte.

But sovereynly° dame Pertelote shrighte°
Ful louder than dide Hasdrubales° wyf
Whan that hire housbonde hadde lost his lyf
And that the Romayns hadden brend Cartage.°
She was so ful of torment and of rage
That wilfully° into the fyr she sterte°
And brende hirselven° with a stedefast herte.
   O woful hennes, right so cryden ye
As, whan that Nero brende the citee   550
Of Rome, cryden senatours wyves
For that° hir housbondes losten alle hire° lyves.
Withouten gilt this Nero hath hem slayn.
Now wol I turne to my tale agayn.
   The sely° widwe and eek hire doghtres two
Herden thise hennes crye and maken wo,
And out atte dores stirten they anon,
And syen° the fox toward the grove gon,
And bar° upon his bak the cok away,
And criden " Out! Harrow! " and " Weilaway!°   560
Ha, ha, the fox! " And after hym they ran,   561
And eek with staves° many another man.
Ran Colle oure dogge, and Talbot, and Gerland,
And Malkyn, with a distaf in hire hand.
Ran cow, and calf, and eek the verray hogges,
So fered° for the berkyng of the dogges
And showtynge° of the men and wommen eek.
They ronne so, hem thoughte hir herte breek.°
They yelleden as fendes doon° in helle.
The dokes° cryden as men wolde hem quelle.°   570
The gees for feere flowen° over the trees.
Out of the hyve cam the swarm of bees.
So hydous° was the noyse, A, *benedicitee,*
Certes, he Jakke Straw and his meynee°
Ne made nevere shoutes half so shrille
Whan that they wolden any Flemyng kille
As thilke day was maad upon the fox.
Of bras they broghten bemes,° and of box,°
Of horn, of boon,° in whiche they blewe and
      powped,°
And ther-with-al they skryked,° and they howped.°
It semed as that° hevene sholde falle.   581
Now goode men, I prey yow, herkneth alle.
   Low, how Fortune turneth° sodeynly
The hope and pryde eek of hire enemy.

---

503. espie: perceive.   504. ravysshed with: overwhelmed by.
505. flatour: flatterer.   506. losengeour: deceiver.   507. plesen:
please.   508. soothfastnesse: truth.   509. Ecclesiaste of: Ecclesiasticus on.   510. Beth war: beware.   512. cloos: closed.
513. nones: occasion.   514. stirte . . . atones: sprang up at
once.   515. gargat hente: throat seized.   516. wode: wood.
beer: bore.   517. sewed: pursued.   518. eschewed: avoided.
519. fleigh: flew.   520. ne . . . nat: took no heed.   522. plesaunce: pleasure.   525. delit: delight.   526. woldestow suffre: would you allow.   thy day: Friday, the day of Venus.
527. Gaufred: Geoffrey de Vinsauf, who in his treatise on the
composition of poetry offers as a sample of his highly rhetorical
techniques an elegy for King Richard I, who was mortally
wounded on a Friday.   529. compleynedest: lamented.   530. sentence: erudition.   loore: learning.   532. soothly: truly.
533. pleyne: lament.   536. maad: made.   Ylioun: Ilium
(Troy).   537. Pirrus: Pyrrhus.   streite swerd: drawn sword.
538. hent: seized.   539. seith . . . Eneydos: (the) Aeneid tells
us.   540. cloos: enclosure.   541. seyn: seen.

542. sovereynly: especially.   shrighte: shrieked.   543. Hasdrubales: Hasdrubal's.   545. brend Cartage: burned Carthage.
547. wilfully: voluntarily.   sterte: leapt.   548. brende hirselven: burned herself.   552. For that: because.   losten . . .
hire: all lost their.   555. sely: poor.   558. syen: saw.   559. bar:
carry (*lit.,* carried).   560. Weilaway: alas.   562. staves: sticks.
566. fered: frightened.   567. showtynge: shouting.   568. hem
. . . breek: they thought their heart would break.   569. fendes
doon: fiends do.   570. dokes: ducks.   quelle: kill.   571. flowen:
flew.   573. hydous: hideous.   574. meynee: company. During
the Peasants' Revolt of 1381 Jack Straw led a group of rioters
into London, where they murdered a number of clothmakers from
Flanders who had kept their technique secret from the native
workers. (See Intro., p. 6.)   578. bemes: trumpets.   box:
boxwood.   579. boon: bone.   powped: puffed.   580. skryked:
shrieked.   howped: whooped.   581. as that: as if.   583. turneth: overturns.

This cok that lay upon the foxes bak
In al his drede unto the fox he spak
And seyde, "Sire, if that I were as ye,
Yit sholde I seyn,° as wys God helpe me,
'Turneth agayn,° ye proude cherles° alle.
A verray pestilence upon yow falle.   590
Now I am come unto this wodes syde,
Maugree youre heed,° the cok shal here abyde.
I wol hym ete, in feith, and that anon.' "
    The fox answerde, "In feith, it shal be don."
And as he spak that word, al sodeynly
This cok brak° from his mouth delyverly,°
And hye upon a tree he fley anon.
And whan the fox say° that he was gon,
"Allas," quod he, "O Chauntecleer, allas!
I have to yow," quod he, "y-doon trespas°   600
In as muche as I maked yow aferd
Whan I yow hente and broghte out the
    yerd.
But, sire, I dide it in no wikke° entente.
Com doun, and I shal telle yow what I mente.
I shal seye sooth to yow, God help me so."
    "Nay thanne," quod he, "I shrewe° us bothe
    two.
And first I shrewe myself, bothe blood and bones,
If thow bigile me any ofter° than ones.
Thow shalt namoore thurgh° thy flaterye
Do° me to synge and wynke with° myn eye,   610
For he that wynketh, whan he sholde see,
Al wilfully,° God lat hym nevere thee."°
    "Nay," quod the fox, "but God yeve° hym
    meschaunce°
That is so undiscreet of governaunce°
That jangleth° whan he sholde holde his pees."
    Lo, swich it is for to be recchelees,°
And necligent, and truste on flaterye.
    But ye that holden this tale a folye°
As of° a fox, or of a cok and hen,
Taketh the moralitee, goode men.   620
For Seint Poul° seith that al that writen is,
To oure doctryne° it is y-write,° ywis.°
Taketh the fruyt, and lat the chaf be stille.
Now goode God, if that it be thy wille,
As seith my lord, so make us alle goode men,
And brynge us to his heye blisse. Amen.

---

588. seyn: say.   **589. Turneth agayn:** turn back.   **cherles:** churls.   **592. Maugree . . . heed:** despite all you can do.   **596. brak:** broke.   **delyverly:** nimbly.   **598. say:** saw.   **600. trespas:** offense.   **603. wikke:** evil.   **606. shrewe:** curse.   **608. ofter:** more often.   **609. namoore thurgh:** no more through.   **610. Do:** persuade.   **wynke with:** close.   **612. wilfully:** voluntarily.   **thee:** prosper.   **613. yeve:** give.   **meschaunce:** misfortune.   **614. governaunce:** self-control.   **615. jangleth:** chatters.   **616. recchelees:** careless.   **619. folye:** idle tale.   **As of:** concerning.   **621. Poul:** Paul (Rom. 15:4).   **622. doctryne:** instruction.   **y-write:** written.   **ywis:** indeed.

CHAUCER'S PRAYER

Although Chaucer did not live to complete the entire plan of his *Canterbury Tales,* he evidently intended to use the Parson's Tale as his conclusion. At the end of this "little treatise," as Chaucer calls the Parson's Sermon on Penitence and the Seven Deadly Sins, he added the following prayer. His piety compels him to renounce his secular works and express satisfaction only with those writings pertaining to morality and devotion.

Now preye I to hem alle that herkne [1] this litel tretys or rede [2] that, if ther be any thing in it that liketh [3] hem, that therof they thanken oure Lord Jesu Crist, of whom precedeth al wit [4] and al goodnesse. And if ther be any thing that displese hem, I preye hem also that they arrette [5] it to the defaute of myn unkonninge [6] and nat to my wil, that wolde fayn have seyd bettre if I hadde had konninge. For oure Book [7] seith, "Al that is writen is writen for our doctrine," and that is myn entente.

Wherfore I beseke [8] yow mekely, for the mercy of God, that ye preye for me that Crist have mercy on me and foryeve [9] me my giltes; and namely [10] of my translacions and enditinges [11] of worldly vanitees, the which I revoke in my retracciouns, as is the *Book of Troilus,* the *Book* also *of Fame,* the *Book of the Five and Twenty Ladies,*[12] the *Book of the Duchesse,* the *Book of Seint Valentines Day of the Parlement of Briddes,* the *Tales of Caunterbury,* thilke [13] that sownen into [14] synne, the *Book of the Leoun,*[15] and many another book, if they were in my remembrance, and many a song and many a leccherous lay, that Crist for his grete mercy foryeve me the sinne.

But of the translacion of Boece [16] *De Consolacione,* and othere bookes of legendes of seintes [17] and omelies [18] and moralitee and devocioun, that thanke I oure Lord Jesu Crist and his blisful Moder, and all the seintes of Hevene, besekinge hem that they from hennesforth unto my lives ende sende me grace to bewaile my giltes, and to studie to the salvacioun of my soule, and graunte me grace of verray penitence, confessioun, and satisfaccioun to doon in this present lif, thurgh the benigne grace of him that is King of Kinges and Preest of alle Preestes, that boghte us with the precious blood of his herte, so that I may been oon of hem at the day of doom that shulle be saved. *Qui cum Patre et Spiritu Sancto vivit et regnat in secula seculorum.*[19] Amen.

PRAYER.   1. herkne: listen to.   **2. rede:** read (it).   **3. liketh:** pleases.   **4. wit:** understanding.   **5. arrette:** ascribe.   **6. unkonninge:** inability.   **7. Book:** the Bible (II Tim. 3:16).   **8. beseke:** beseech.   **9. foryeve:** forgive.   **10. namely:** especially.   **11. enditinges:** compositions.   **12. Book . . . Ladies:** *Legend of Good Women.*   **13. thilke:** those.   **14. sownen into:** pertain to.   **15. Book . . . Leoun:** probably a lost poem based on Machaut.   **16. Boece:** Boethius.   **17. legendes of seintes:** such as the Second Nun's Tale.   **18. omelies:** homilies, such as the Parson's Tale.   **19. Qui . . . seculorum:** "He who with the Father and Holy Spirit liveth and reigneth through all generations."

Edmund Spenser

1552–1599

EDMUND SPENSER, born in 1552, was (like most great English writers) a member of the middle class, the son of a Londoner. He was sent to the Merchant Taylors' School, where he learned, and doubtless suffered, under the famous Richard Mulcaster. There is some evidence that Mulcaster, even by the ferocious standards of that age, was a cruel teacher, but he was an interesting man whose views on education can still be studied in his *Positions* (1581) and *Elementary* (1582). Though long and very serious, they hardly go further than the theory of spelling, and if Mulcaster had completed a system of education on the same scale it would have been about as long as the Bible; a fact which might possibly have some bearing on the gigantic project (only a quarter of it was carried out) of *The Faerie Queene*. In 1569 Spenser entered Pembroke Hall at Cambridge. The most interesting thing about his university career is that he passed through it without becoming attached to either of the two intellectual movements by which Cambridge was then agitated.

We can hardly help calling them " Puritanism " and " humanism," but neither word meant the same as it does in modern America. By purity the Elizabethan Puritan meant not chastity but " pure " theology and, still more, " pure " church discipline. That is, he wanted an all-powerful Presbyterian Church, a church stronger than the state, set up in England, on the model of Calvin's church at Geneva. Knox in Scotland loudly demanded, and at least one English Puritan hinted, that this should be done by armed revolution. Calvin, the great successful

doctrinaire who had actually set up the " new order," was the man who had dazzled them all. We must picture these Puritans as the very opposite of those who bear that name today: as young, fierce, progressive intellectuals, very fashionable and up-to-date. They were not teetotalers; bishops, not beer, were their special aversion. And humanists in this context means simply " classicists " — men very interested in Greek, but more interested in Latin, and far more interested in the " correct " or " classical " style of Latin than in what the Latin authors said. They wanted English drama to observe the (supposedly) Aristotelian " unities," and some of them wanted English poets to abandon rhyme — a nasty, " barbarous " or " Gothic " affair — and use classical meters in English. There was no necessary enmity between Puritans and humanists. They were often the same people, and nearly always the same sort of people: the young men " in the Movement," the impatient progressives demanding a " clean sweep." And they were united by a common (and usually ignorant) hatred for everything medieval: for Scholastic philosophy, medieval Latin, romance, fairies, and chivalry.

There are some possible signs (but all ambiguous) in Spenser's *Shepheards Calendar* (1579) that he was once or twice nearly captured by the Puritans, but it certainly did not last long. What is more remarkable is that he never surrendered to humanism, though he clearly lived in a humanistic circle of the narrowest sort. His friend Gabriel Harvey — a very grotesque creature and, to judge from his surviving records, a textbook case of the Inferiority Complex — disapproved of the whole design of *The Faerie Queene*. He complained that in it " Hobgoblin " was stealing the garland from " Apollo ": in other words, that medieval romance was winning the day against classicism. Another member of the circle, the rather fatuous young man who contributed a commentary to *The Shepheards Calendar* over the signature E. K., could not let Spenser's references to fairies pass without adding, " to roote that rancke opinion of Elfes out of mens hearts, the truth is, that there be no such thinges." Nothing is more impressive about Spenser than his reaction to these humanist friends. He did neither of the two things we should expect. He never quarreled with them; and he never took the slightest notice of their advice. He remained a faithful friend to Harvey (who had few friends); and he devoted his whole poetical career to a revival, or prolongation, of those medieval motifs which humanism wished to abolish.

Spenser had taken his M.A. in 1576, and in 1578 had found temporary employment as secretary to the Bishop of Rochester. In 1579 he had been at Leicester House and enjoyed the very exciting experience of being noticed (and even used with some " familiarity ") by Philip Sidney himself. It must have seemed to the young poet that the world was opening to him. There was, of course, no question of living by his pen. In the 90's it was possible to live (precariously) by pamphleteering or (rather better) by writing and acting for the new companies of players, but this was hardly so in the 70's; nor would such a Bohemian and " rake-helly " career have been at all to Spenser's mind. On the other hand, we must not picture him choosing a profession or looking for a business opening as a young man might do today. Literary distinction could still lead to employment in the service of one of those great nobles who carried on the work of government. Such a reward fell to Spenser when he became secretary to Lord Grey of Wilton in 1580. Doubtless, it was not the kind of post Spenser had hoped for. It meant " foreign service," for Lord Grey had just been appointed Deputy of Ireland, and Spenser arrived in Dublin in August, 1580. He thus became (for life, had he known it) an instrument of the English domination in a hostile and incompletely conquered country. He had already begun *The Faerie Queene.*

Conquest is an evil productive of almost every other evil both to those who commit and to those who suffer it, and we should look in vain for any fruitful or pleasant relations between Spenser and the Irish. Nothing of that sort was possible. They were to him merely " natives," rebels, and Papists; he to them, a vile heretic and alien Sassenach. The plans which he propounded for their subjugation in his *View of the Present State of Ireland* (never printed in his lifetime, but written in 1596) are harsh and even cynical; and if some scholars have pleaded, not without success, that they are excusable, this of itself admits that they require excuse. But that, as we shall presently see, is not the whole story about Spenser's relations to Ireland.

In 1589, after receiving a visit from Raleigh, Spenser returned to England, bringing with him the manuscript of the first three Books of *The Faerie Queene,* which were published in the following year. They brought him fame, but not the post in England for which, no doubt, he had been hoping, and he returned to his house at Kilcolman in the county Cork. In 1594 he married Elizabeth Boyle: the sonnets (*Amoretti*) and the *Epithalamion,* both published in 1595, poetize his courtship and its conclusion. *Epithalamion* is his happiest poem. But happiness did not last long. There was another visit to England in 1595, and the second installment of *The Faerie Queene* was printed in 1596. Then came his doom. In 1598 the Irish rose under the Earl of Tyrone, defeated the English near Armagh, and flung a force into Munster. What they would do when they reached Kilcolman, every reader of Irish history knows in advance. It was, after all, the old seat of the Desmonds: the heretic, foreigner, and upstart had usurped it long enough. It is said (by Ben Jonson) that Spenser's third child, a baby, died in the flames. By December Spenser had contrived to reach London, carrying dispatches about the late rising. He died, certainly in poverty, as some say actually of hunger, in January, 1599.

II

Though Spenser seldom made poetry out of his own life in the direct fashion of Wordsworth's *Prelude,* the pattern of his biography and that of his poetical output are nevertheless interlocked in an interesting way. On the biographical side we have the long years of residence in Ireland punctuated by brief visits to England: that is, to civilization, safety, the court, patrons, and the hope of social success. On the poetical side, we have the single great work, certainly begun very early and perhaps begun even before the appearance of *The Shepheards Calendar,* obstinately adhered to in the teeth of criticism, worked at all his life and left unfinished; its composition punctuated, or interrupted, by the minor poems, all of them (except the *Epithalamion*) inferior to it. They usually came out just after a visit to England. It is not hard to guess what was happening. Whenever Spenser can reach England — whenever, in our language, he "goes on leave" — he brings with him some more *Faerie Queene* to be published. That is what he cares about. But of course the publisher urges him to "follow it up." Spenser gets together a volume of odds and ends, some of them not very recent work. Thus we get the *Complaints* volume of 1591 and the *Colin Clouts Come Home Againe* volume of '95. However their contents were written, they were published, we feel, less by Spenser the poet than by Spenser the man; Spenser the man, seizing an opportunity of reminding the patrons and the public that he was still in existence. For of course a great work slowly growing, stanza by stanza, through a lifetime, is a thing that people easily overlook. It thus comes about that the many years in Ireland lie behind Spenser's greatest poetry, and the few years in England behind his minor poetry. It is hard to resist the conviction that his prolonged exile was a great gain to English literature. It removed him perforce from the rapid changes of fashion, the ephemeral hopes and fears, the petty intrigues, and the time-wasting attendance upon great persons, which would almost certainly have been the portion of a literary man hanging upon the fringes of the court: it forced him to sink deeper and deeper into the world he was creating. To that extent, we can call *The Faerie Queene* an Irish product.

We can perhaps say a little more. Spenser could not love the people, but, surprisingly, he loved the country. He chose an Irish hill, Arlo, for his assembly of gods (Book VII, the "Mutability" Cantos, vi and vii). He introduced a poetic catalogue of Irish rivers (Book IV, Canto xi)

into one of his most highly wrought passages. In prose (*View of the Present State*) he pronounced Ulster "a most beautifull and sweete countrie as any is under heaven." He delighted in Irish history and antiquities and hoped to write a book about them. What is even stranger (and helps to show his freedom from the narrowness of humanistic taste), he had listened to Irish poetry in translation and thought that it "savored of sweete witt and good invencion." Most interesting from this point of view is the poem *Colin Clouts Come Home Againe,* not published until 1595 but written to celebrate Colin Clout's (that is, Spenser's) return from his first English visit in 1590 — his return to an Ireland which, as the title shows, has now become "home." It is a curiously broken-backed poem. It starts out with the view that we should expect. The visit to England has been wonderful because there Colin Clout saw the "blessed eye" of "that Angel" Queen Elizabeth, because her realm is all "fruitful corne, faire trees, fresh herbage," because (unlike Ireland) it has no "raging sword," "no ravenous wolves" nor "outlawes," and because the court is full of exquisite ladies and admirable poets. This, I say, is what we should expect: a compliment to the queen and the possible patrons and an appeal for an English job. But then Colin goes on in the latter part of the poem to paint a wholly different picture. His Anglo-Irish friends ask him why he ever returned from such a delightful country to "this barren soil" of Ireland "where cold and care and penury do dwell." Colin replies; one glance at the "enormities" of the English court convinced him that it would be a great mistake to "abandon quiet home" for court life and far wiser "back to his sheep to turne." For now it appears that court is full of "malice and strife," lying, backbiting, treachery, and dissimulation, no place "for any gentle wit," and that the love which courtiers incessantly talk of is a lewd, faithless affair quite unlike the high mystery of love as "we poore shepheards" know it. All this rings true. Spenser's visit to England had been a disappointment. He was not made for the fashionable world. This contrast between the "vain shows" of court and the simplicities of rustic life recurs increasingly in the later parts of *The Faerie Queene.* Shepherds, hermits, satyrs, even the Savage, become types to which he turns with love. It is difficult not to conclude that this represents his growing (though perhaps unadmitted) reconciliation to what had once been his place of exile but had now become home. He was coming to need that Irish life: the freedom, the informality, the old clothes, the hunting, farming, and fishing (he was proud of the superexcellent trout in his own river at Kilcolman). He may, as a poet, have needed the very country. There is a real affinity between his *Faerie Queene,* a poem of quests and wanderings and inextinguishable desires, and Ireland itself — the soft, wet air, the loneliness, the muffled shapes of the hills, the heart-rending sunsets. It was of course a different Ireland from ours, an Ireland without potatoes, whitewashed cottages, or bottled stout: but it must already have been "the land of longing." *The Faerie Queene* should perhaps be regarded as the work of one who is turning into an Irishman. For Ireland shares with China the power of assimilating all her invaders. It is an old complaint that all who go there — Danes, Normans, English, Scotch, very Firbolgs — rapidly become "more Irish than the Irish themselves." With Spenser the process was perhaps beginning. It is true he hated the Irish and they him: but, as an Irishman myself, I take leave to doubt whether that is a very un-Irish trait. ("The Irish, sir," said Dr. Johnson, "are an honest people. They never speak well of one another.")

III

When Spenser and Sidney began writing, English poetry was in a deplorable condition. Short histories of literature sometimes give the impression that the "Revival of Learning" began from the first to exercise a quickening influence upon our literature. I find no evidence that this was so. Nearly all the good poetry of the sixteenth century is crowded into its last twenty years (except in Scotland, where it comes at the beginning of the century and is overwhelmingly medieval in character). In England, until Sidney and Spenser arose, the last poet of real importance had been Sir Thomas Wyatt, who died in 1542: and his poetry, at its best, owes at least as much to the Middle Ages as to the Revival of Learning. Between Wyatt and Spenser there extends a period in which it looks as though English poetry were never going to rise again even half so high as it had already risen in the Middle Ages. The best product of this dull period had been the *Songs and Sonnets* (1557), usually called *Tottel's Miscellany* from the name of its publisher, which had contained, along with a very large body of wooden and clumsy verse, Wyatt's lyrics and some graceful (though rather tame) pieces by Surrey and others. Far worse and more characteristic was the huge *Mirror for Magistrates* which came out, repeatedly added to, at various dates from 1555 to 1587. In it the ghosts of various historical characters appeared to tell their stories or, as the *Mirror* calls them, their "tragedies." Apart from a good "induction" by Thomas Sackville and one goodish "tragedie" by John Dolman, the *Mirror* is about as bad as it could be. But it was fatally popular and thus important for its bad influence on later poets and as an index of the depths to which taste had sunk. In it, as in the work of Googe, Brooke, Turberville, or the truly appalling translators of Seneca, we see a total loss of that feeling for style which seems to have come so easily to most medieval poets. It is against this background that we can best understand the value, for their own age, of Spenser's minor works and most easily pardon the fact that even in his greatest poetry he was seldom safe from a relapse into the bad manner of his predecessors. He was not a man laying the coping stone on an edifice of good poetry already half-built; he was a man struggling by his own exertions out of a horrible swamp of dull verbiage, ruthlessly overemphatic meter, and screaming rhetoric.

Thus *The Shepheards Calendar* is not, at this distance of time, a very attractive work. Even if we can reacquire (and if we are to study English literature, we must try) a taste for the pastoral, we shall still find that Spenser's shepherds fall between two stools. They are not realistic enough to give us the pleasure we get from the rustics of Hardy or of *Huckleberry Finn:* yet they are far too realistic to waft us away into the purely poetic pastoral world of Drayton's *Muses Elizium* or Milton's "Lycidas." This happened, I believe, because Spenser was hesitating between two incompatible models: the wholly idealized *Arcadia* of Sannazaro and the more realistic (but poetically negligible) *Eclogues* (1515 and 1521) of Alexander Barclay. But if we had come to the *Calendar,* as its first readers did, from verse like that of the *Mirror,* we should feel as if we were passing from winter to spring. We should read

The simple ayre, the gentling warbling wynde,
So calme, so coole, as nowhere else I fynde:
The grassye ground with daintye Daysies dight,
The Bramble bush, where Byrds of every kynde,
To the waters fall their tunes attemper right.

Calendar, " June," 4

and we should perceive that poetry, which for nearly forty years had been able only to shout or mumble, was now once more beginning to sing. There are moments in literary history at which to achieve a manner and a music is more important than to deliver any " message," however profound or prophetic. The message can wait; it will have to wait forever unless the manner and music are found. It is idle to talk about a great ballet until people have, in the crudest and simplest sense, learned to dance, learned the steps. In the *Calendar* Spenser is learning — in its best passages has already learned — the steps.

Three poems which were not printed till they appeared in the *Complaints* of 1591 may have been written shortly after the *Calendar.* One of them is merely a translation from the difficult and very minor poem of Virgil's called the " Culex," or " Gnat," but the other two are interesting because they are so different from each other and from *The Faerie Queene,* thus warning us not to suppose that a great poet can write only the sort of poetry which he chooses to write chiefly. *Muiopotmos* is about the adventures of a butterfly, a poem full of flowers and sunshine written with great enjoyment in a lighter and swifter stanza than the famous " Spenserian." In it, as nowhere else, we see Spenser at play. Many critics believe that it is a veiled account of some affair at court, but I do not think this is certain. The third poem is *Mother Hubberds Tale,* a satire, modeled not (as Spenser's humanist friends would doubtless have wished) on the formal satire of the Romans but on the great medieval beast fable *Reynard the Fox.* The Ape and the Fox go into partnership and play all manner of tricks on the other beasts, even stealing the Lion's crown and scepter. The tale is, of course, full of allusions to contemporary politics which cannot be discussed here. In this poem we find none of the slow, stately pace which is characteristic of *The Fa-*erie Queene. Spenser writes in couplets, uses a homely style, and gets over the ground briskly.

Colin Clouts Come Home Againe has already been mentioned; the " ambivalence " which makes it so interesting as a personal document spoils its unity of effect as a poem. *Daphnaida* (1591), an elegy on the death of a noble lady, is perhaps the worst poem Spenser ever wrote. It is modeled on Chaucer's *Book of the Duchess* but entirely loses the charm of its original by exaggeration and straining after effect. The Elizabethans, even at their best, seem to lack that effortless good taste — one might almost say, that good breeding — which we nearly always find in the work of the Middle Ages. The Renaissance did not make men, in all senses, more *civilized.*

In the years '95 and '96 Spenser published a body of poetry about love which perhaps marks the summit of his achievement outside *The Faerie Queene.* The sonnets, or *Amoretti* (1595) are not among our greatest sonnets. We shall not find in them the almost divine selflessness and evocative power of Shakespeare's sonnets nor the immediacy of Drayton's " Since there's no help, come let us kiss and part." Yet if we go to them for what they have to give, for grace and harmony, we can read them with enjoyment. But the *Epithalamion* which was added to them belongs to a different world, and indeed there is no poem in English at all like it. It traces the whole bridal day and night from the moment at which the bride is awaked to the moment at which the tired lovers fall asleep and the stars pour down good influences on the child they have engendered and on all their descendants yet to be. Into this buoyant poem Spenser has worked all the diverse associations of marriage, actual and poetic, pagan and Christian: summer, landscape, neighbors, pageantry, religion, riotous eating and drinking, sensuality, moonlight — are all harmonized. The meter is a very long stanza with varying line lengths and a refrain, modeled, in fact, on the Italian *canzone* but filled with such festal pomp and jollity, such sustained exuberance of the whole man (spiritual, imaginative, and animal) that the effect is much closer to that of some great ode by Pindar than to any Italian poem. Those who have attempted to write poetry will know how very much easier it is to express sorrow than joy. That is what makes the *Epithalamion* matchless. Music has often reached that jocundity; poetry, seldom.

The *Foure Hymnes* (of Love and Beauty) which followed in 1596 are not on the same level. It would be hopeless, in the space at my disposal, to attempt to unravel their very learned and curious blend of scriptural, Platonic, and medieval ideas. They contain good poetry, but poetry hardly great enough for the arduous, and indeed overwhelming, themes that Spenser has chosen. The same year saw the publication of the *Prothalamion* in which Spenser, now writing on someone else's marriage, tries to repeat the splendors of his own marriage song: I think, with very imperfect success.

But it is high time that we turned to the life work by which Spenser's name really lives.

Like most of his contemporaries Spenser believed that English literature could never hold up its head in the world until it had produced a great epic, and that a poet ought to be a moral teacher; unlike some of his contemporaries, he also felt a strong impulse to continue and develop the medieval tradition of chivalrous romance. He did not in fact know very much medieval literature. Much of it was inaccessible in his time and, anyway, too hard for him in language: he makes little use of Malory; what he called "Chaucer" included many un-Chaucerian works and was so textually corrupt that Spenser could not have read it metrically even if he had understood Middle English meter (which he did not). The English poem which probably influenced him most was the late, allegorical romance *The Pastime of Pleasure* by Stephen Hawes, who wrote in the reign of Henry VII. This lack of medieval scholarship in Spenser was, however, far from being such a disadvantage as we might suppose. In the first place it set him free to embody, almost unconsciously, those elements of the Middle Ages which were still alive all round him in tournament and heraldry, pageant and symbolical pictures, whereas accurate knowledge might have made him merely a pedant and an antiquarian. In the second place, he could find a great deal of the method and temper of medieval romance, already refashioned, already, as it were, predigested and made more available for his purpose, in three great Italian poems: the *Orlando Innamorato* of Boiardo, the *Orlando Furioso* of Ariosto, and the *Gerusalemme Liberata* of Tas-

so. The first two of these deal with the adventures of Charlemagne and his paladins at war with the Saracens, and admit large comic elements; they are sometimes laughing at the marvels and high-flown sentiments of romance, but then at other times seriously enjoying these very same things. It is not absolutely certain that, in their comic passages, Spenser always saw the joke. The third is about the capture of Jerusalem by Godfrey of Bouillon and his crusaders: it is as serious and religious a poem as Spenser's own. All three together constitute such a varied, vigorous, unflagging body of poetical storytelling as is hardly equaled anywhere in European literature. They are Spenser's chief models.

By turning to them he turned his back on the strict humanists, who would have wished him to write a pseudoclassical epic, closely modeled on Virgil, like Ronsard's *Françiade*. By making Arthur the hero, or at least the nominal hero, of his poem he nevertheless attempted to gratify the humanists' wish, and his own, that the great poem should be, in some sort, a national epic. But in order to fulfill the demand that the poet should be a moral teacher he decided that he would follow Hawes as well as the Italians. His poem was to be a romance of chivalry, but it was also to have a secondary meaning throughout: to be, as he said, "a continued allegory." He decided, further, to introduce a new meter. All the Italians had used what is called *ottava rima,* the stanza which rhymes *abababcc,* best known to English readers in Byron's *Don Juan* or Shelley's *Witch of Atlas*. It is a beautifully light, rapid medium, excellently adapted for describing a breathless chase on horseback or telling an amusing anecdote with a dash of impropriety in it. Spenser himself had used it very well in *Muiopotmos*. But for *The Faerie Queene* he invented his new nine-line stanza which has wholly different qualities. The more complex interlacing of the rhymes and, still more, the concluding alexandrine, which gives to each stanza the effect of a wave falling on a beach, combine to make it slower, weightier, more stately. Of all Spenser's innovations his stanza is perhaps the most important. It makes all his resemblances to the Italians merely superficial. It dictates the peculiar tone of *The Faerie Queene*. Milton, who knew and loved both Spenser and Spenser's models, described it as "sage and solemn tunes." A brooding solemnity — now deeply joyful, now sensuous, now melancholy, now loaded with dread — is characteristic of the poem at its best.

This brief account of the genesis of *The Faerie Queene* is needed in order to explain some features of it which may deter modern readers. The necessity is, of course, to be deplored; and it is of very recent growth. From the time of its publication down to about 1914 it was everyone's poem — the book in which many and many a boy first discovered that he liked poetry; a book which spoke at once, like Homer or Shakespeare or Dickens, to every reader's imagination. Spenser did not rank as a hard poet like Pindar, Donne, or Browning. How we have lost that approach I do not know. And unfortunately *The Faerie Queene* suffers even more than most great works from being approached through the medium of commentaries and " literary history." These all demand from us a sophisticated, self-conscious frame of mind. But then, when we have used all these aids, we discover that the poem itself demands exactly the opposite response. Its primary appeal is to the most naïve and innocent tastes: to that level of our consciousness which is divided only by the thinnest veil from the immemorial lights and glooms of the collective Unconscious itself. It demands of us a child's love of marvels and dread of bogies, a boy's thirst for adventures, a young man's passion for physical beauty. If you have lost or cannot re-arouse these attitudes, all the commentaries, all your scholarship about " the Renaissance " or " Platonism " or Elizabeth's Irish policy will not avail. The poem is a great palace, but the door into it is so low that you must stoop to go in. No prig can be a Spenserian. It is of course much more than a fairy tale, but unless we can enjoy it as a fairy tale first of all, we shall not really care for it.

Those features in the poem which might deter a reader are: (1) its narrative technique; (2) its allegory; and (3) the texture of its language.

(1) The narrative technique, especially after the first two Books, consists in constantly shifting from one story and one set of characters to another, but with a " dovetail " or liaison at the point where we change. Thus in Book III, Canto i, we start out on a journey with Sir Guyon, Prince Arthur, and Prince Arthur's squire, Tim-

ias. Presently a strange knight appears riding toward them and tries a course of the lance with Guyon, who is unhorsed. Guyon's annoyance at this reverse is soothed down by the others, and the strange knight now joins the party. They are all proceeding quietly together when suddenly an unknown lady on a milk-white horse flashes past, obviously in flight. A moment later her pursuer, a forester, is seen galloping after her. Arthur, Guyon, and Timias give chase, but the strange knight does not. And Spenser, instead of telling us what happened to the lady and the forester and Arthur and Guyon and Timias, now proceeds to relate the further adventures of the strange knight, which are quite irrelevant to the story we began with. We have thus got rid of all the characters we started with (not to meet Arthur again till Canto iv, or Timias till v) and, in effect, changed trains.

The uninstructed reader would get the impression that Spenser was merely rambling, drifting at the mercy of his own imagination, as a man does in a dream. But the reader who knows a little more would remember that he had met exactly the same technique in Malory; and that it is also the technique of Boiardo, Ariosto, and Tasso. It is, I think, ultimately derived from Ovid's *Metamorphoses,* and may be called the " interwoven " or " polyphonic " narrative. Spenser is obeying a method as well established as the fugue. To what I have previously said about the naïve or childlike appeal of the stories he tells, we must now add the opposite truth that his method of disposing them is highly formal and sophisticated. (This contrast of naïve matter and sophisticated arrangement will seem less paradoxical if we remember how a composer can weave into a most learned symphonic whole the materials which he has derived from simple folk songs.) Now of course to explain that a certain method had a long history behind it does not, of itself, prove that it is a good one. Polyphonic narrative might be a vicious form, however many people had used it. But when we know that this technique dominated European fiction both in prose and verse from the thirteenth to the seventeenth century, that civilized audiences in so many different countries went on demanding it, and that Tasso's father (also a poet) lost all his popularity when he wrote a narrative poem without it, common sense will surely make us pause before we assume that it was simply wrong and that the technique of modern fiction is simply right. The old polyphonic story, after all, enjoyed a longer success than the modern novel has enjoyed yet. We do not know which will seem the more considerable literary phenomenon to a critic looking back from the year 2500. Such reflections should induce us to give the old technique, at least, a fair trial. Perhaps, if we have patience, it will begin to charm us as it charmed our ancestors.

Obviously, it produces great variety. In a polyphonic narrative the weird, the voluptuous, the exciting, the melancholy scenes can succeed one another not where the exigencies of a single rigid "plot" permit but wherever artistic fitness demands them. To that extent it is more like the technique of music than like that of modern literature. Obviously, too, the interruption of one story by another, often at a critical moment, has something in common with the technique of the serial story: the adventures of Arthur in pursuit of the fugitive lady are left "to be continued in our next." If we reply that this kind of suspense is lost on us because our bad memories frustrate it and when we get back to Arthur we have forgotten all about him, then, since our ancestors made no such objection, it would seem that we differ from them by an inferiority, not by a superiority. And no doubt we do. Cheap paper, typewriters, notebooks, and indexes have impaired our memories just as automobiles have made some people almost incapable of walking. (One of the great uses of literary history is to keep on reminding us that while man is constantly acquiring new powers he is also constantly losing old ones.) It behooves us therefore to be humble and do our best. The obstacle is not, in fact, insurmountable: growing familiarity with this kind of poetry will presently enable us to hold the different, and constantly suspended, stories in our heads, just as growing familiarity enables us to follow complex music. And even if we sometimes lose our way, I think we shall find, as we go on reading, that the polyphonic technique has a far more important effect than those two which I have already mentioned, although it is one very difficult to describe. It is an effect particularly suitable to a tale of strange adventures.

It adds to the poem what might be called depth, or thickness, or density. Because the (improbable) adventure which we are following is liable at any moment to be interrupted by some quite different (improbable) adventure, there steals upon us unawares the conviction that adventures of this sort are going on all round us, that in this vast forest (we are nearly always in a forest) this is the sort of thing that goes on all the time, that it was going on before we arrived and will continue after we have left. We lose the feeling that the stories we are shown were arbitrarily made up by the poet. On the contrary, we are sure there are plenty more which he has not time to show us. We are being given mere selections, specimens: instances of the normal life of that wooded, faerie world. The result of this is an astonishing sense of reality.

The young student should here be warned that the word "lifelike" as applied to literature is ambiguous. It may mean "like life as we know it in the real world"; in that sense the dullest character in a realistic novel may be "lifelike"; i.e., he is very like some real people and as lifeless as they. On the other hand "lifelike" may mean "seeming to have a life of its own"; in that sense Captain Ahab, old Karamazov, Caliban, Br'er Rabbit, and the giant who says "fee-fi-fo-fum" in *Jack the Giant-Killer,* are all lifelike. Whether we have met anything like them in the real world is irrelevant. Now Spenser's "faerie lond" is very unlike life in the first sense, but the polyphonic technique makes it extremely lifelike in the second. It is lifelike by its consistency—all the adventures bear the stamp of the world that produced them, have the right flavor, make each other probable; in its apparent planlessness—they collide, and get mixed up with one another and drift apart, just as events would in a real world; in its infinity—we can, so obviously, never get to the end of them, there are so obviously more and more, round the next corner. That is why Keats in his sonnet "To Spenser" (see Vol. II) speaks of one who loved *The Faerie Queene* as "a forester deep in thy midmost trees." There is forest, and more forest, wherever you look: you cannot see out of that world, just as you cannot see out of this.

(2) The allegory or "inner meaning" of *The Faerie Queene* is generally regarded as twofold: a "moral" or "philosophical" allegory, and a "historical" or "political" allegory. The first is clear, certain, essential; the second obscure, of-

ten doubtful, and poetically of little importance. Spenser himself in his prefatory " Letter " to Raleigh has told us that Gloriana, the Faerie Queene, means (in a certain sense) Queen Elizabeth; James I complained that Duessa was obviously Mary Queen of Scots; and there are places, in the worst parts of the worst Book (V), where the allegory about foreign affairs becomes unmistakable. Apart from these few equivalences, interpretation of the historical allegory is controversial and speculative. I myself (here differing from many scholars whom I respect) regard it with a good deal of skepticism. Some published fantasies of my own have had foisted on them (often by the kindliest critics) so many admirable allegorical meanings that I never dreamed of as to throw me into doubt whether it is possible for the wit of man to devise anything in which the wit of some other man cannot find, and plausibly find, an allegory. I do not believe that a consistent and detailed historical allegory (such as we find, say, in Dryden's *Absalom and Achitophel,* p. 574) runs through *The Faerie Queene.* Particular scenes contain, in addition to their moral or philosophical meaning, a parallel to some contemporary event. Probably it does not last beyond the scene in which it occurs: when we meet the same characters in a different scene we need not expect them to have the same (or, necessarily, any) historical meaning. How lightly the whole thing should be taken may be judged from the way in which Spenser himself speaks of it. Gloriana at some points and for some purposes symbolizes Elizabeth, but Elizabeth is also at other points and for other purposes, Belphoebe. But in his " generall intention " Gloriana is " Glory "; that is her permanent and essential meaning in the poem. The many generations who have read and reread *The Faerie Queene* with delight paid very little attention to the historical allegory; the modern student, at his first reading, will be well advised to pay it none at all.

The moral or philosophical meaning is, on the other hand, essential; and fortunately in approaching this we have an advantage which the nineteenth century lacked. Our grandfathers might regard allegory as an arbitrary literary device, a " figure " listed in the books on rhetoric. The work of Jung and Freud, and the practice of many modern poets and prose writers, has taught us an entirely different view. We now know that symbols are the natural speech of the soul, a language older and more universal than words. This truth, if not understood exactly as modern psychology would understand it, was accepted and acted upon by the ancient and medieval world, and had not yet been lost in Spenser's day. He came, in fact, just in time, just before the birth of that new outward-looking, rationalizing spirit which was going to give us victory over the inanimate while cutting us off from the depths of our own nature. After Spenser allegory became, till quite modern times, merely a sort of literary toy, as it is in Addison's or Johnson's essays. Spenser was the last poet who could use the old language seriously and who had an audience that understood it.

They understood it because they had been brought up to it. We shall understand it best (though this may seem paradoxical) by not trying too hard to understand it. Many things — such as loving, going to sleep, or behaving unaffectedly — are done worst when we try hardest to do them. Allegory is not a puzzle. As each place or person is presented to us in *The Faerie Queene* we must not sit down to examine it detail by detail for clues to its meaning as if we were trying to work out a cipher. That is the very worst thing we can do. We must surrender ourselves with childlike attention to the mood of the story. The broad outlines of the allegory are quite unmistakable. Spenser himself tells us that the six knights who are the heroes of the six Books are six virtues; and each therefore fights against, or is endangered by, the vices particularly opposed to the virtue he represents.[1] Thus in Book I Holiness encounters the various obstacles to the religious life — error, heresy, pride, despair, and so forth; in Book II Temperance encounters anger, avarice, and lust; in V Justice encounters graft or bribery (Lady Munera), egalitarianism, and the giantess who represents the domination of women over men. At a first glance, indeed, the reader might complain not so much of obscurity as of copybook platitude.

But he would be mistaken. In the first place, what looks like a platitude when it is set out in the abstract may become a different sort of thing when it puts on flesh and blood in the story; ac-

---

[1] Unity was to be secured by the overriding role of Arthur, who appears in every Book and helps minor champions out of difficulties. Unfortunately his own story remains unfinished in the fragment we have. On his quest for Gloriana, see below.

cording to the theory which Sidney set out in his *Defence of Poesie,* the poetic art existed for the precise purpose of thus turning dead truism into vital experience. Secondly, ideas have changed since the sixteenth century, and much of Spenser's thought is now not platitudinous but highly controversial. Not many readers of this book have been brought up to think either equality or feminism a form of injustice. On these points, therefore, *The Faerie Queene* can now do us one of the services for the sake of which (among other things) we read old literature. It can readmit us to bygone modes of thought and enable us to imagine what they felt like, to see the world through our ancestors' eyes. After we have done that, our rejection of those modes of thought (if we still reject them) will have some value. There is a great difference between rejecting something you have known from the inside and rejecting something (as uneducated people tend to do) simply because it happens to be out of fashion in your own time. It is like the difference between a mature and traveled man's love for his own country and the cocksure conviction of an ignorant adolescent that his own village (which is the only one he knows) is the hub of the universe and does everything in the Only Right Way. For our own age, with all its accepted ideas, stands to the vast extent of historical time much as one village stands to the whole world.

And thirdly, Spenser's moral thought is not in itself so platitudinous as we might at first suppose.[1] Guyon, the knight of Book II who represents Temperance, comes to the Bower of Acrasia, obviously a place of sexual temptation. But then the female knight of Book III, Britomart, represents Chastity. Obviously she too must be brought through a place of sexual temptation; and so she is, in the House of Busirane. If we were writing an allegory instead of reading one, we should at once see that we were coming to a difficulty. What are we to do with these two places? How are we to prevent the second from being merely a repetition of the first? But in Spenser there is no resemblance between them and no trace (which would have been just as bad) of a faked or forced difference between

them. The Bower of Acrasia is a luscious garden, genuinely luscious but in rather bad taste (they have metal ivy, painted to look like real, round a fountain); two naked girls are playing the fool in a bathing pond to attract Guyon's attention; Acrasia herself, in a beautiful "creation" of transparent lingerie, lies on a bed of roses leaning over the last young man she has captured. This is all plain sailing: the simplest reader cannot fail to understand it. But the House of Busirane is a vast building, hard to get into and hard to get out of when you are in. Britomart is there for hours. One empty room leads endlessly into another empty room: all silent, all blazing with an almost sickly splendor of intricate decoration. It is only at midnight, in the last room of all, that a little iron door opens, and out of it comes a strange procession, like a masque, of silent people who ignore Britomart, intent upon their own strange ceremonial. Behind that iron door the girl whom Britomart has come to rescue is being tortured.

As I have said before, we must not look for clues as if we were solving a puzzle. We must, if need be, reread both passages and soak ourselves in their differing atmospheres; the obvious, provocative, even garish sensuality of Acrasia's Bower, which is the foe to "temperance," to mere self-control and moderation, and the monotonous glitter, the claustrophobia, the costliness, loneliness, anguish of Busirane's House, which is the foe to "chastity" (Spenser makes quite clear that "chastity" for him includes faithful love, married, or hoping to be married). To a man tempted by the Bower, one would say, "Pull yourself together," but to a man tempted by Busirane, one would say, "Can you not *come out?* Out into the free air and sunlight? Can you never break this lifelong obsession?" It will dawn on every reader in the end that the difference between Acrasia and Busirane is that between Lust (appetite) and Love, bad love. Many moderns have been brought up to think that the difference between good and evil in sexual matters simply coincides with that between Love and Lust, that every *affaire* becomes "good" just insofar as it concerns the heart and not merely the senses. If that is our view, then Spenser is here offering us not (as we feared) platitude but full paradox. For he thinks there may be Loves quite distinct from Lust, but evil, miserable, poisoning a whole life;

---

[1] It is, for example, worth considering why the ludicrous and disgusting figure of Malbecco (Jealousy) comes in the Book on Chastity. If Hellenore's wantonness (see Selection XVI) sets a man in a rage, he must not assume that his rage results from a disinterested love of virtue.

illicit, secret loves that break up homes and lead to divorce courts, suicide pacts, and murders. They are expensive; the House of Busirane is ablaze with gold. They take a long time; the House of Busirane goes on and on. After fully comprehending Acrasia and Busirane (not as I have here given them in abstract but as they really live in the poem), the reader may of course still disagree with Spenser. He may think that the solemnity and grandeur of Busirane's House make it obviously superior to any establishment Acrasia could ever run. Or he may agree with Spenser and feel that he has learned something about human life which will stand him in very good stead. But whichever way he decides, his decision will be a more informed one than any he could have made without reading *The Faerie Queene*. Even that is not the whole story. A poet inventing with such energy as Spenser produces things that mean more than he knew or intended. The House of Busirane may become, to this or that reader, a symbol of (hence, partly a liberation from) some other psychic imprisonment which has nothing to do with love. This kind of poetry, if receptively read, has psychotherapeutic powers.

Another factor which saves Spenser's moral allegory from platitude is his method of hinting in each Book at what may be called " the virtue behind the virtue," the inner shrine. Book VI is about Courtesy (which in those days meant much more than etiquette or good manners, and included what we should call " chivalry ") and is, of course, full of examples of courteous behavior. But then in Canto x we discover that our attempts at courtesy, however laudable and necessary, will never make us perfectly courteous men. We shall still be clumsy, unless the Graces come and dance with us, unless a beauty which no man can achieve by effort flows into our daily acts of its own will. So in Book IV we discover that Justice can never be perfect while it remains mere Justice: it must go into the temple of Isis and learn better things from " clemence " or " equity." So in Book I, all the Redcrosse Knight's struggles with Error and Pride will not make him holy until he has been in the House of Cælia. This may be cold comfort to most of us, but it is hardly a copy-book platitude; and it might be true.

Three obstacles may prevent a receptive reading of Spenser's allegory. The first great obstacle for the reader of this volume is that he is being given only selections from it, not the poem itself. I have found it impossible to select in such a way that the pieces I included required no support from those I left out — if not support in respect of the " plot " or sequence of events, yet support from contrasting or harmonizing moods. Far from wishing to conceal this defect, I wish to emphasize it as much as possible. In that way I may possibly convince a reader what selections are for. Except for some (poetically irrelevant) purpose such as passing an examination, the only use of selections is to deter those readers who will never appreciate the original, and thus to save them from wasting their time on it, and to send all the others on to the original as quickly as possible. The sooner you toss my selections impatiently aside and go out to buy a copy of *The Faerie Queene,* the better I shall have succeeded. If I lead anyone to imagine, twenty years hence, that he has really read the poem, when in fact he has read only these shreds and patches, I shall have done him (but not without his own assistance) a grave injury.

The second obstacle is this. The picture-language of allegory is ultimately derived, as I have said, from the unconscious. But by Spenser's time allegory (both literary and pictorial) had been practiced so long that certain symbols had an agreed meaning which everyone could understand directly, without plunging into the depths. Many of these are lost on the modern reader who does not know the Bible, the classics, astrology, or the old emblem books. A simple example (still, we may hope, intelligible to many) would be the silver anchor which lay on Speranza's arm (I.x.14). The text in Hebrews 6:19 explains it. Similarly in I.iv.24 not all readers will now know why Lechery should be riding a goat: all Elizabethans knew that the goat was the sign of Lust. Again, Spenser's readers, comparing the Bower of Acrasia with the House of Busirane, would have noticed at the very outset a difference which I never mentioned (because I did not think it would help the modern student). Cupid is absent from the Bower and very much present in the House. Now in medieval allegory Cupid regularly meant Love (humanized, sentimental, refined, but not necessarily innocent); when they wanted to symbolize the mere sexual appetite they usually represented it by Cupid's mother, Venus.

Finally, an obstacle may arise from our own preconceptions. We may be so certain in advance what a word or an image ought to mean that we omit to notice what it really does mean in the poem. A ludicrous example would be if anyone took "Temperance" (the subject of Book II) to mean "not getting drunk," instead of control and moderation of all our passions, including our desire for wealth. A much more serious preconception occurs about the significance of beautiful, naked women in *The Faerie Queene*. A man may have a "puritan obsession" (in the modern, not the Elizabethan sense of the word "puritan") which leads him to assume that these will all be images of sin. Much more probably in our days he will have an anti-puritan obsession and assume that they are all to be welcomed as fruits of Spenser's "Renaissance" or "pagan" liberty. Both obsessions, if uncorrected, will lead to false reading. In the poem (as perhaps also in dreams and myths) this image may mean quite different things. And there is no need at all to be puzzled. If read without preconceptions the poem itself will make this perfectly clear. Everyone will see that the two young women in Acrasia's swimming pool are images of Sin; and that the Graces who dance round Colin Clout (VI.x) are nothing of the sort. They are the "virtue behind the virtue" of Courtesy, what Burke called "the unbought grace of life."

(3) The general quality of *The Faerie Queene* is so highly poetic that it has earned Spenser the name of "the poet's poet." But if we examine the texture of the language line by line we may think that it is sometimes flat and very often little distinguished from that of prose. There are, no doubt, some stanzas which, even in isolation, anyone would acclaim as high poetry. But usually we shall look in vain for anything like the phrase-by-phrase deliciousness of Shakespeare's sonnets, the "gigantic loftiness" of Milton's epic style, or the point and subtlety and pressure of Donne or the modern poets. The truth is that Spenser belongs to an older school. In the earliest times theology, science, history, fiction, singing, instrumental music, and dancing were all a single activity. Traces of this can still be found in Greek poetry. Then the different arts which had once all been elements of *poesis* developed and became more different from one another, and drew apart (the enor-

mous gains and losses of this process perhaps equal one another). Poetry became more and more unlike prose. It is now so unlike it that the number of those who can read it is hardly greater than the number of those who write it. Spenser is of course a long way from the ancient Greeks, but he belongs to an older school than Shakespeare. He is about midway between Shakespeare and Boiardo. Boiardo is first and foremost a storyteller, not a "poet" in the more specialized modern sense. As far as language is concerned, his poetry might be improvised— the phrases could be made up as one goes along. Spenser's style is richer, more elaborated than that. But it still has in view an audience who have settled down to hear a long story and do not want to savor each line as a separate work of art. Much of *The Faerie Queene* will therefore seem thin or overobvious if judged by modern standards. The "thickness" or "density" which I have claimed for it do not come from its language. They come from its polyphonic narrative, from its different layers of meaning, and from the high degree in which Spenser's symbols embody not simply his own experience, nor that of his characters at a given moment, but the experience of ages. In one sense a passage of Spenser is childishly simple compared with a poem by Donne, but in another sense this is not so. Donne wrote from his vivid consciousness of his own situation at a particular moment. He knew what he was putting into his poem, and we cannot get out of it more than he knew he was putting in. But Spenser, with his conscious mind, knew only the least part of what he was doing, and we are never sure that we have got to the end of his significance. The water is very clear, but we cannot see to the bottom. That is one of the delights of the older kind of poetry: "thoughts beyond their thoughts to those high bards were given." I do not mean by this that we should prefer the older kind. Their difference is a reason for reading both. There is no one right or absolute kind of poetry.

Spenser wrote primarily as a (Protestant) Christian and secondarily as a Platonist. Both systems are united with one another and cut off from some—not all—modern thought by their conviction that Nature, the totality of phenomena in space and time, is not the only thing that exists: is, indeed, the least important thing. Christians and Platonists both believe in an "other" world. They differ, at least in emphasis, when they describe the relations between that other world and Nature. For a Platonist the contrast is usually that between an original and a copy, between the real and the merely apparent, between the clear and the confused: for a Christian, between the eternal and the temporary, or the perfect and the partially spoiled. The essential attitude of Platonism is aspiration or longing: the human soul, imprisoned in the shadowy, unreal world of Nature stretches out its hands and struggles toward the beauty and reality of that which lies (as Plato says) "on the other side of existence." Shelley's phrase "the desire of the moth for the star" sums it up. In Christianity, however, the human soul is not the seeker but the sought: it is God who seeks, who descends from the other world to find and heal Man: the parable about the Good Shepherd looking for and finding the lost sheep sums it up. Whether in the long run there is any flat contradiction between the two pictures need not be discussed here. It is certainly possible to combine and interchange them for a considerable time without finding a contradiction, and this is what Spenser does. The Christian picture dominates the first two Books: divine grace, in the person of Una, is constantly helping St. George out of his difficulties, and an angel is sent down to preserve Guyon. On the other hand the central story of the whole poem was to have been Platonic: I say "was to have been" because Spenser did not live to finish it. In the fragment that we have, Prince Arthur is always seeking for "Gloriana." He knows almost nothing about her. When the beautiful Florimel flashes past him in the forest, he at once pursues her: she might be Gloriana (III.iv.54). He has seen the real Gloriana only in a dream (I.ix.13 ff.). This is a picture of the soul, as in Platonism, endlessly seeking that perfect beauty of which it has some dim premonition but which cannot be found — only shadows and blurred images of it — in the realm of Nature. This enables us to see what Spenser means when he says that Gloriana is "Glory." In his many-leveled poetry "Glory" is the divine glory or splendor which the Christian soul will not only see but share in Heaven; it is the glory of that real and perfect world which the Platonist

is seeking; it is also, insofar as Arthur is a knight-errant in a romance of chivalry, "Glory" in the sense of fame or honor. To add that it is also in some sense and at some moments Queen Elizabeth seems to us a profane and silly anticlimax. But we are not to suppose that Elizabeth appeared to Spenser as she does to us or even as she did to contemporaries who really knew her; and we must understand that her royal office had an importance for him which it could have for no modern. For monarchy, like everything else in this world, had its chief value in being the shadow or reflection of something in that other and more real world. Every earthly court was an imitation, however imperfect, of the Divine Court. Its splendor and order had a poetic, religious, and metaphysical appeal which had nothing to do with snobbery — a ritual appeal. Spenser would have understood the ancient Chinese idea that the function of the Emperor was to reproduce on earth the "Order of Heaven." His view was consistent, as we have seen, with the clearest insight into the corruptions of actual court life.

In these selections a grave accent indicates that a vowel which would be mute in modern English is to be pronounced; e.g., *prayèd, arrivèd*. An acute accent indicates that stress falls on a syllable which would now be unstressed, as in *massácre* (probably pronounced by Spenser so as to rhyme with *packer*), *meláncholy, trespás*, and so on. The termination *-ion* (as in *motion, affection*) could be sounded either as one or as two syllables in Spenser's time; some of his lines require the one pronunciation, and some the other. Words which recur continually in *The Faerie Queene* are explained in my notes on many occasions but not every time they recur.

It will be noticed that the spelling of Spenser's printer (as, doubtless, that of Spenser himself) did not attempt regularity.

Reading Suggestions

The body of critical and scholarly work on Spenser is enormous; a great deal of it will be found in the magnificent 10-volume Variorum Edition by Edwin Greenlaw, Charles G. Osgood, Frederick Morgan Padelford, and Roy Heffner (1932–45).

B. E. C. Davis, *Edmund Spenser* (1933). A useful biographical and critical study.

W. L. Renwick, *Edmund Spenser* (1925). An earlier

and shorter book than Davis's, by a great Spenserian.

Janet Spens, *Spenser's Faerie Queene* (1934). This book is partly concerned with theories about the composition of the poem which a beginner may neglect, but its critical chapters are full of insight.

C. H. Whitman, *A Subject-Index to the Poems of Edmund Spenser* (1918). Those who are likely to become lifelong readers of *The Faerie Queene* will find this book a great convenience.

EPITHALAMION

This poem is printed in its entirety. The modern reader should note (1) that Spenser lived in a world not of easy divorces, but of "endlesse matrimony" (l. 217); (2) that the dangers mentioned in lines 322–23 were only too real in the Ireland he knew; (3) that those in lines 341–44 were believed to be equally real; (4) that he is thinking a long way beyond the bridal night, about children and even remote descendants (ll. 390–403); (5) that the position of the planets at the moment of the child's begetting was really believed to be momentous (ll. 409–17) and is no mere "poetical fancy"; (6) that Spenser thinks of all his descendants as immortal souls who will outlive the whole physical universe (ll. 418–23). It is against this civil, cosmic, and theological (as well as erotic) background that the ceremonial and triumphal qualities of the poem can best be understood. (See also Introduction, p. 95.)

Ye learnèd sisters° which have oftentimes
Beene to me ayding, others to adorne:°
Whom ye thought worthy of your gracefull rymes,
That even the greatest did not greatly scorne
To heare theyr names sung in your simple layes,
But joyèd° in theyr prayse.
And when ye list° your owne mishaps to mourne,
Which death, or love, or fortunes wreck did rayse,
Your string could soone to sadder tenor° turne,
And teach the woods and waters to lament   10
Your dolefull dreriment.°
Now lay those sorrowfull complaints aside,
And having all your heads with girland° crownd,°
Helpe me mine owne loves prayses to resound,
Ne° let the same of any be envide:°
So Orpheus° did for his owne bride,
So I unto my selfe alone will sing,
The woods shall to me answer and my Eccho ring.

Early before the worlds light giving lampe,
His golden beame upon the hils doth spred,   20
Having disperst° the nights unchearefull dampe,
Doe ye awake, and with fresh lusty hed,°

Go to the bowre° of my belovèd love,
My truest turtle dove,
Bid her awake; for Hymen° is awake,
And long since ready forth his maske° to move,
With his bright Tead° that flames with many a flake,°
And many a bachelor to waite on him,
In theyr fresh garments trim.
Bid her awake therefore and soone her dight,°   30
For lo the wishèd day is come at last,
That shall for al the paynes and sorrowes past,
Pay to her usury° of long delight:
And whylest° she doth her dight,
Doe ye to her of joy and solace° sing,
That all the woods may answer and your eccho ring.

Bring with you all the Nymphes° that you can heare°
Both of the rivers and the forrests greene:
And of the sea that neighbours to her neare,
Al with gay girlands goodly wel beseene.°   40
And let them also with them bring in hand,
Another gay girlánd
For my fayre love of lillyes and of roses,
Bound truelove wize° with a blew silke ribánd.
And let them make great store of bridale poses,°
And let them eeke° bring store of other flowers
To deck the bridale bowers.
And let the ground whereas her foot shall tread,
For feare the stones her tender foot should wrong
Be strewed with fragrant flowers all along,   50
And diapred° lyke the discolored mead.°
Which done, doe at her chamber dore° awayt,
For she will waken strayt,°
The whiles doe ye this song unto her sing,
The woods shall to you answer and your Eccho ring.

EPITHALAMION. **1. learned sisters:** the nine Muses, inspirers of all poetry, daughters of Phoebus Apollo. **2. Beene . . . adorne:** helped me to adorn others. **6. joyed:** rejoiced. **7. list:** chose. **9. tenor:** tone. **11. dreriment:** sadness. **13. girland:** garland, wreath. **crownd:** crowned. **15. Ne:** nor. **envide:** envied. **16. Orpheus:** (two syllables only) the Greek singer who charmed beasts and even trees and stones with his music so that they followed him. His wife was Eurydice. **21. disperst:** dispersed. **22. lusty hed:** lustyhead, cheerfulness, jollity.

23. bowre: bower, bedroom. **25. Hymen:** the god of marriage. **26. maske:** masque, solemn procession of people in unusual costumes. **27. Tead:** torch (one of Hymen's regular "properties"). **flake:** spark, or piece of burning stuff thrown off as the torch is waved. **30. her dight:** dress herself. **33. usury:** "interest," "a dividend." **34. whylest:** whilst, while. **35. solace:** delight. **37. Nymphes:** minor goddesses. **heare:** hear of, know of. **40. beseene:** adorned. **44. truelove wize:** truelove-wise, in the manner of a "truelove knot." **45. bridale:** bridal. **poses:** posies, bouquets. **46. eeke:** also. **51. diapred:** diapered, having a diversified surface. **discolored mead:** variegated (i.e., dotted with wild flowers) field. **52. dore:** door. **53. strayt:** straightway, right now.

Ye Nymphes of Mulla° which with carefull heed,
The silver scaly trouts° doe tend full well,
And greedy pikes° which use therein to feed,
(Those trouts and pikes all others doo excell)
And ye likewise which keepe the rushy lake,°   60
Where none doo fishes take,
Bynd up the locks the which hang scatterd light,
And in his waters which your mirror make,
Behold your faces as the christall bright,
That when you come whereas my love doth lie,
No blemish she may spie.
And eke ye lightfoot mayds which keepe the
    deere,°
That on the hoary mountayne use to towre,°
And the wylde wolves which seeke them to de-
    voure,
With your steele darts doo chace° from comming
    neer   70
Be also present heere,
To helpe to decke° her and to help to sing,
That all the woods may answer and your eccho
    ring.

Wake, now my love, awake; for it is time,
The Rosy Morne long since left Tithones° bed,
All ready to her silver coche° to clyme,°
And Phœbus° gins° to shew his glorious hed.°
Hark how the cheerefull birds do chaunt theyr
    laies°
And carroll° of loves praise.
The merry Larke hir mattins° sings aloft,   80
The thrush replyes, the Mavis° descant° playes,
The Ouzell° shrills, the Ruddock° warbles soft,
So goodly all agree with sweet consent,
To this dayes merriment.
Ah my deere love why doe ye sleepe thus long,
When meeter were° that ye should now awake,
T' awayt the comming of your joyous make,°
And hearken to the birds lovelearnèd song,
The deawy° leaves among.

For they of joy and pleasance to you sing,   90
That all the woods them answer and theyr eccho
    ring.

My love is now awake out of her dreame,
And her fayre eyes like stars that dimmèd were
With darksome cloud, now shew theyr goodly
    beams
More bright then Hesperus° his head doth rere.°
Come now ye damzels,° daughters of delight,
Helpe quickly her to dight,
But first come ye fayre houres° which were begot
In Joves sweet paradice, of Day and Night,
Which doe the seasons of the yeare allot,   100
And al that ever in this world is fayre
Doe make and still repayre.
And ye three handmayds° of the Cyprian Queene,°
The which doe still adorne her beauties pride,
Helpe to addorne my beautifullest bride:
And as ye her array, still throw betweene
Some graces° to be seene,
And as ye use° to Venus, to her sing,
The whiles the woods shal answer and your eccho
    ring.

Now is my love all ready forth to come,   110
Let all the virgins therefore well awayt,
And ye fresh boyes that tend upon her groome°
Prepare your selves; for he is comming strayt.
Set all your things in seemely good aray
Fit for so joyfull day,
The joyfulst day that ever sunne did see.
Faire Sun, shew forth thy favourable ray,
And let thy lifull° heat not fervent be
For feare of burning her sunshyny° face,
Her beauty to disgrace.°   120
O fayrest Phœbus, father of the Muse,
If ever I did honour thee aright,
Or sing the thing, that mote° thy mind delight,
Doe not thy servants simple boone° refuse,
But let this day let this one day be myne,
Let all the rest be thine.
Then I thy soverayne prayses loud wil sing,
That all the woods shal answer and theyr eccho ring.

---

56. Mulla: a poetic name, probably of Spenser's invention, for
the river Awbeg near his house at Kilcolman. Professor Renwick
says it still provides good trout. **57. trouts:** the modern
plural is *trout.* **58. pikes:** modern plural, *pike;* a freshwater
fish. **60. rushy lake:** This is still to be seen in the neighborhood of Kilcolman. **67. keepe . . . deere:** look after the deer.
68. towre: to climb(?). **70. chace:** chase. **72. decke:** adorn.
75. Tithones: or Tithonus. A mortal loved by the dawn goddess,
who married him and persuaded the other gods to grant him immortality. But she forgot to ask perpetual youth for him, so that
he is now very senile. See Tennyson's *Tithonus.* **76. coche:**
coach, chariot. **clyme:** climb. **77. Phoebus:** Apollo, the sun
god. **gins:** begins. **hed:** head. **78. laies:** lays, songs.
79. carroll: sing. **80. mattins:** morning "service" (in ecclesiastical sense). **81. Mavis:** the song thrush (*Turdus musicus*).
descant: here used vaguely for "accompaniment." For the
precise sense, which cannot be given in a note, see musical dictionaries. **82. Ouzell:** blackbird (*Turdus merula*). **Ruddock:**
the robin redbreast. **86. meeter were:** It would be fitter, more
appropriate. **87. make:** mate. **89. deawy:** dewy.

95. Hesperus: the evening star, Venus. **rere:** rear, raise.
96. ye damzels: i.e., the damsels acting as bridesmaids.
98. houres: The Hours are daughters of Jove, but no one, so
far as I know, can tell us anything about Spenser's story of their
begetting. **103. three handmayds:** the three Graces (see below l. 257). **Cyprian Queene:** Venus, whose worship was especially associated with Cyprus. **107. graces:** The Graces
are to add "graces," extra beauties, to the bride. **108. use:**
are used or accustomed. **112. groome:** bridegroom, Spenser
himself. **118. lifull:** lifeful, vital. **119. sunshyny:** This does
not of course refer to the sort of "shine" that modern women
use powder to avoid, but to the general impression of brightness
given by eyes, teeth, and a joyous expression. The halo of saints
and the "battle light" attributed to warriors in some legends
possibly spring from the same effect. **120. disgrace:** disfigure.
123. mote: could, might. **124. boone:** prayer.

Harke how the Minstrels gin to shrill aloud
Their merry Musick that resounds from far,   130
The pipe, the tabor,° and the trembling Croud,°
That well agree withouten breach or jar.°
But most of all the Damzels doe delite,
When they their tymbrels° smyte,
And thereunto doe daunce and carrol sweet,
That all the sences they doe ravish quite,
The whyles° the boyes run up and downe the
    street,
Crying aloud with strong confusèd noyce,
As if it were one voyce.
Hymen io Hymen,° Hymen they do shout,   140
That even to the heavens theyr shouting shrill
Doth reach, and all the firmament° doth fill,
To which the people standing all about,
As in approvance° doe thereto applaud
And loud advaunce her laud,°
And evermore they Hymen Hymen sing,
That al the woods them answer and theyr eccho
    ring.

Loe where she comes along with portly° pace
Lyke Phœbè° from her chamber of the East,°
Arysing forth to run her mighty race,   150
Clad all in white, that seemes° a virgin best.
So well it her beseemes that ye would weene°
Some angell she had beene.
Her long loose yellow locks lyke golden wyre,
Sprinckled with perle,° and perling flowres° a
    tweene,
Doe lyke a golden mantle her attyre,
And being crownèd with a girland greene,
Seeme lyke some mayden Queene.
Her modest eyes abashèd to behold
So many gazers, as on her do stare,   160
Upon the lowly ground affixèd are.
Ne dare lift up her countenance too bold,
But blush to heare her prayses sung so loud,
So farre from being proud.
Nathlesse doe ye still loud her prayses sing.
That all the woods may answer and your eccho
    ring.

Tell me ye merchants daughters did ye see
So fayre a creature in your towne before,

So sweet, so lovely, and so mild as she,   169
Adorned with beautyes grace and vertues store,
Her goodly eyes lyke Saphyres shining bright,
Her forehead yvory white,
Her cheekes lyke apples which the sun hath rud-
    ded,°
Her lips lyke cherryes charming men to byte,
Her brest like to a bowle of creame uncrudded,°
Her paps lyke lyllies budded,
Her snowie necke lyke to a marble towre,
And all her body like a pallace fayre,
Ascending uppe with many a stately stayre,
To honors seat and chastities sweet bowre.°   180
Why stand ye still ye virgins in amaze,
Upon her so to gaze,
Whiles ye forget your former lay to sing,
To which the woods did answer and your eccho
    ring.

But if ye saw that which no eyes can see,
The inward beauty of her lively spright,°
Garnisht° with heavenly guifts of high degree,
Much more then would ye wonder at that sight,
And stand astonisht lyke to those which red°
Medusaes mazeful hed.°   190
There dwels sweet love and constant chastity,
Unspotted fayth and comely womanhood,°
Regard of honour and mild modesty,
There vertue raynes° as Queene in royal throne,
And giveth lawes alone.
The which the base° affections° doe obay,
And yeeld theyr services unto her will,
Ne thought of thing uncomely ever may
Thereto° approch to tempt her mind to ill.
Had ye once seene these her celestial threasures,°
And unrevealèd pleasures,   201
Then would ye wonder and her prayses sing,
That al the woods should answer and your echo
    ring.

Open the temple gates unto my love,
Open them wide that she may enter in,
And all the postes° adorne as doth behove,°
And all the pillours deck with girlands trim,

For to recyve° this Saynt with honour dew,
That commeth in to you.
With trembling steps and humble reverence,   210
She commeth in, before th' almighties vew,
Of her ye virgins learne obedience,
When so ye come into those holy places,
To humble your proud faces:
Bring her up to th' high altar, that she may
The sacred ceremonies there partake,
The which do endlesse matrimony make,
And let the roring Organs° loudly play
The praises of the Lord in lively notes,
The whiles with hollow throates   220
The Choristers the joyous Antheme° sing,
That al the woods may answere and their eccho
    ring.

Behold whiles she before the altar stands
Hearing the holy priest that to her speakes
And blesseth her with his two happy hands,
How the red roses flush up in her cheekes,
And the pure snow with goodly vermill° stayne,°
Like crimsin dyde in grayne,°
That even th' Angels which continually,
About the sacred Altare doe remaine,   230
Forget their service and about her fly,
Ofte peeping in her face that seemes more fayre,
The more they on it stare.
But her sad° eyes still fastened on the ground,
Are governèd with goodly modesty,
That suffers not one looke to glaunce awry,
Which may let in a little thought unsownd.°
Why blush ye love to give to me your hand,
The pledge of all our band?°
Sing ye sweet Angels, Alleluya sing,   240
That all the woods may answere and your eccho
    ring.

Now al is done; bring home the bride againe,
Bring home the triumph of our victory,
Bring home with you the glory of her gaine,°
With joyance° bring her and with jollity.
Never had man more joyfull day then° this,
Whom heaven would heape with blis.
Make feast therefore now all this live long day,
This day for ever to me holy is,
Poure out the wine without restraint or stay,°   250
Poure not by cups, but by the belly full,
Poure out to all that wull,°
And sprinkle all the postes and wals° with wine,

That they may sweat, and drunken be withall.°
Crowne ye God Bacchus° with a coronall,
And Hymen also crowne with wreathes of vine,
And let the Graces° daunce unto the rest;
For they can doo it best:
The whiles the maydens doe theyr carroll sing,
To which the woods shal answer and theyr eccho
    ring.   260

Ring ye the bels, ye yong men of the towne,
And leave your wonted° labors for this day:
This day is holy; doe ye write it downe,
That ye for ever it remember may.
This day the sunne is in his chiefest hight,°
With Barnaby° the bright,
From whence declining daily by degrees,
He° somewhat loseth of his heat and light,
When once the Crab behind his back he sees.°
But for this time it ill ordainèd was,   270
To chose the longest day in all the yeare,
And shortest night, when longest fitter weare:°
Yet never day so long, but late° would passe.
Ring ye the bels, to make it weare° away,
And bonefiers° make all day,
And daunce about them, and about them sing:
That all the woods may answer, and your eccho
    ring.

Ah when will this long weary day have end,
And lende° me leave to come unto my love?   279
How slowly do the houres theyr numbers spend?°
How slowly does sad° Time his feathers move?
Hast thee O fayrest Planet° to thy home
Within the Westerne fome:°
Thy tyrèd steedes° long since have need of rest.
Long though it be, at last I see it gloome,
And the bright evening star° with golden creast
Appeare out of the East.
Fayre childe of beauty, glorious lampe of love

208. recyve: receive.   218. Organs: i.e., probably the whole set of pipes and so forth which we now call one "organ." But the word could still in Spenser's time be used vaguely to mean musical instruments in general.   221. Antheme: anthem.
227. vermill: vermilion.   stayne: stain (verb).   228. grayne: cochineal.   234. sad: grave, steady.   237. unsownd: unsound, frail, wanton.   239. band: bond.   244. her gaine: our having gained her.   245. joyance: rejoicing.   246. then: than.
250. stay: pause, stoppage.   252. wull: will.   253. wals: walls.

254. withall: withal, as well as the rest of us.   255. Bacchus: the god of wine and drunkenness.   257. Graces: These were three, Euphrosyne, Aglaia, and Thalia (to rhyme with Sophia), daughters of Jove, ladies in waiting to Venus. See *FQ*, Sel. XXVI.   262. wonted: usual.   265. hight: height.   266. Barnaby: St. Barnabas' Day is now June 11, but in Spenser's time was June 22 (on change of calendar see *FQ*, Sel. XXVII. 552n.) and is of course called "bright" because it falls in high summer.   268. He: i.e., the sun.   269. Crab . . . sees: The sun moves into the house of Leo in mid-June and out of the house of Cancer, which he then sees at his back.   272. weare: were, would be.
273. late: (adverb) at last.   274. weare: wear.   275. bonefiers: bonfires, a regular part of the midsummer festivities.
279. lende: give.   280. theyr . . . spend: get through, dispose of, their quantity.   281. sad: nearer to the modern sense than in l. 234, but not quite there; grave, sedate, heavy.
282. Planet: the sun, which was of course one of the "planets" in Ptolemaic astronomy.   283. fome: foam, hence sea.
284. steedes: The chariot of the sun (or sun god) is pictured as horse-drawn.   286. evening star: Venus, "lampe of love" (l. 288) because she is the planet and goddess of love, and leading the host of heaven (l. 289) because she is usually visible in the evening before any other stars.

That all the host of heaven in rankes doost lead,
And guydest lovers through the nightès° dread,
How chearefully thou lookest from above,   291
And seemst to laugh atweene° thy twinkling light
As joying° in the sight
Of these glad many which for joy doe sing,
That all the woods them answer and their echo
    ring.

Now ceasse ye damsels your delights forepast;°
Enough is it, that all the day was youres:
Now day is doen,° and night is nighing° fast:
Now bring the Bryde into the brydall boures.°
Now night is come, now soone her disaray,°   300
And in her bed her lay;
Lay her in lillies and in violets,
And silken courteins over her display,
And odourd° sheetes, and Arras° coverlets.
Behold how goodly my faire love does ly
In proud humility;
Like unto Maia,° when as Jove her tooke,
In Tempè, lying on the flowry gras,
Twixt sleepe and wake, after she weary was,
With bathing in the Acidalian brooke.   310
Now it is night, ye damsels may be gon,
And leave my love alone,
And leave likewise your former lay to sing:
The woods no more shal answere, nor your echo
    ring.

Now welcome night, thou night so long expected,
That long daies labour doest at last defray,°
And all my cares, which cruell love collected,
Hast sumd° in one, and cancellèd for aye:°
Spread thy broad wing over my love and me,
That no man may us see,   320
And in thy sable mantle us enwrap,
From feare of perrill° and foule horror free.
Let no false treason seeke us to entrap,
Nor any dread disquiet once annoy
The safety of our joy:
But let the night be calme and quietsome,

Without tempestuous storms or sad afray:°
Lyke as when Jove with fayre Alcmena lay,
When he begot the great Tirynthian groome:°
Or lyke as when he with thy selfe did lie,   330
And begot Majesty.°
And let the mayds and yongmen° cease to sing:
Ne let the woods them answer, nor theyr eccho
    ring.

Let no lamenting cryes, nor dolefull teares,
Be heard all night within nor yet without:
Ne let false whispers, breeding hidden feares,
Breake gentle sleepe with misconceivèd dout.°
Let no deluding dreames, nor dreadful sights
Make sudden sad affrights;
Ne let housefyres, nor lightnings helpelesse° harmes,
Ne let the Pouke,° nor other evill sprights,   341
Ne let mischívous° witches with theyr charmes,
Ne let hob Goblins, names whose sence we see not,
Fray us with things that be not.
Let not the shriech Oule,° nor the Storke° be
    heard:
Nor the night Raven that still deadly yels,
Nor damnèd ghosts cald up with mighty spels,
Nor griesly° vultures make us once affeard:°
Ne let th' unpleasant Quyre° of Frogs still croking
Make us to wish theyr choking.   350
Let none of these theyr drery accents sing;
Ne let the woods them answer, nor theyr eccho
    ring.

But let stil Silence trew night watches keepe,
That sacred peace may in assurance rayne,°
And tymely sleep, when it is tyme to sleepe,
May poure his limbs forth on your° pleasant
    playne,
The whiles an hundred little wingèd loves,
Like divers fethered doves,
Shall fly and flutter round about your bed,
And in the secret darke, that none reproves,   360
Their prety stealthes shal worke, and snares shal
    spread
To filch away sweet snatches of delight,
Conceald through covert night.

290. nightes: two syllables. Spenser never sounds final -e as Chaucer does but sometimes makes the -es of plurals and possessive singulars a syllable.   292. atweene: amidst.   293. As joying: as if rejoicing.   296. forepast: passed, ended.   298. doen: done.   nighing: approaching.   299. boures: bedchamber (the plural is, I presume, merely poetical. There would hardly have been a bridal "suite" at Kilcolman).   300. disaray: undress.   304. odourd: perfumed.   Arras: ordinarily a rich tapestry used for hangings on interior walls. Perhaps here it only means "figured, having patterns and pictures on it like an arras."   307-10. Maia . . . Acidalian brooke: It was really in a cave on Mt. Cyllene in Arcadia that Jove lay with Maia, daughter of Atlas, and begat Mercury. The love affair usually associated with the vale of Tempe is that of Apollo and Daphne. Spenser, perhaps intentionally, often mixes his myths.   316. defray: pay for.   318. sumd: summed up, made a grand total of.   aye: ever.   322. perrill: peril. This prayer was by no means merely poetical; in Spenser's Ireland "peril," "horror," and "treason" might even have broken in on the lovers that very night. See Intro., p. 92.

327. afray: alarm, disturbance.   328-29. Jove . . . groome: When Jove lay with Alcmena, the wife of Amphitryon, the night was miraculously prolonged. The fruit of this amour was Hercules, called Tirynthian because he was born at the city of Tiryns.   330-31. with . . . Majesty: The story of Jove's begetting Majesty on the Night Goddess is so far unknown to commentators.   332. yongmen: young men.   337. misconceived dout: false alarm, fear (or doubt) based on a misconception.   340. helpelesse: irremediable, unavoidable.   341. Pouke: Puck. Shakespeare is largely responsible for making this once formidable spirit into a comic figure.   342. mischivous: a spelling of "mischievous," but the word had a much stronger meaning in Spenser's time: "disastrous, malignant."   345. shriech Oule: the "screech owl" or "barn owl."   Storke: the German legend of its bringing the babies was unknown to Spenser.   348. griesly: grisly, frightful.   affeard: frightened.   349. Quyre: choir.   354. rayne: reign.   356. your: Night's.

Ye sonnes of Venus, play your sports at will,
For greedy pleasure, carelesse of your toyes,°
Thinks more upon her paradise of joyes,
Then what ye do, albe° it good or ill.
All night therefore attend° your merry play,
For it will soone be day:
Now none doth hinder you, that say or sing, 370
Ne will the woods now answer, nor your Eccho
    ring.

Who is the same, which at my window peepes?
Or whose is that faire face, that shines so bright,
Is it not Cinthia,° she that never sleepes,
But walkes about high heaven al the night?
O fayrest goddesse, do thou not envý
My love with me to spy:
For thou likewise didst love, though now un-
    thought,°
And for a fleece of woll,° which privily,
The Latmian shephard° once unto thee brought,
His pleasures with thee wrought. 381
Therefore to us be favorable now;
And sith of wemens labours° thou hast charge,
And generation goodly dost enlarge,°
Encline thy will t' effect our wishfull vow,°
And the chast wombe informe with timely seed,
That may our comfort breed:
Till which we cease our hopefull hap° to sing,
Ne let the woods us answere, nor our Eccho ring.

And thou great Juno,° which with awful° might
The lawes of wedlock still dost patronize,° 391
And the religion of the faith first plight
With sacred rites hast taught to solemnize:°
And eeke for comfort often callèd art
Of women in their smart,°
Eternally bind thou this lovely band,
And all thy blessings unto us impart.

And thou glad Genius,° in whose gentle hand,
The bridale bowre and geniall° bed remaine,
Without blemish or staine, 400
And the sweet pleasures of theyr loves delight
With secret ayde doest succour and supply,
Till they bring forth the fruitfull progeny,
Send us the timely fruit of this same night.
And thou fayre Hebè,° and thou Hymen free,°
Grant that it may so be.
Til which we cease your further prayse to sing,
Ne any woods shal answer, nor your Eccho ring.

And ye high heavens, the temple of the gods,°
In which a thousand torches flaming bright 410
Doe burne, that to us wretched earthly clods,
In dreadfull darknesse lend desirèd light;
And all ye powers which in the same remayne,
More then we men can fayne,°
Poure out your blessing on us plentiously,
And happy influence° upon us raine,
That we may raise a large posterity,
Which from the earth, which they may long pos-
    sesse,
With lasting happinesse,
Up to your haughty pallaces may mount, 420
And for the guerdon of theyr glorious merit
May heavenly tabernacles there inherit,
Of blessed Saints for to increase the count.°
So let us rest, sweet love, in hope of this,
And cease till then our tymely joyes to sing,
The woods no more us answer, nor our eccho ring.

Song made in lieu° of many ornaments,
With which my love should duly have bene dect,°
Which cutting off through hasty accidents,
Ye would not stay your dew time to expect, 430
But promist both to recompens,°
Be unto her a goodly ornament,
And for short time an endlesse moniment.°

---

365. toyes: pranks, frivolities. 367. albe: albeit, although.
368. attend: attend to, mind. 374. Cinthia: Cynthia, another
name for Diana the moon goddess. 378. though . . . unthought:
though nobody now suspects it. 379. woll: wool. 380. Latmian shephard: Endymion, the mortal lover of the moon goddess,
whose story can be read in Keats's *Endymion* in Vol. II. But
Spenser once more mixes his myths; it was the god Pan who gave
Diana a fleece. 383. wemens labours: women's labors (in ob-
stetrical sense). The moon goddess, for obvious reasons, was the
goddess of childbirth. 384. generation . . . enlarge: dost favorably set free (at birth) what has been engendered. 385. wishfull vow: ardent prayer. *Wishful* had, of course, none of its
modern sneering implications. 388. hopefull hap: event that
we hope for. 390. Juno: wife of Jove and queen of heaven,
the patroness of marriage and therefore connected with childbirth
in its social aspect as Diana was in its biological. awful: venerable, deserving of awe. Cf. *Tempest*, IV. i. 103 ff. 391. dost
patronize: art patroness of. Again, the word has none of its
modern sneering implication. 392-93. And . . . solemnize: and
hast taught us to celebrate with religious (*sacred*) ceremony the
sanctity (*religion*) of the conjugal fidelity which we previously
promised. (Latin *religio* often has this sense.) 395. smart: then
meant pain in general and was not, as now, restricted to stinging,
superficial pains.

398. Genius: The god of reproduction, heredity, embryology,
etc., not to be confused with Venus (sexual appetite) nor with
"genius" in the modern sense of immense talent; the word in
that sense has a quite different history. 399. geniall: pertaining
to genius in the sense just described. The modern meaning (festive
or jocular) is quite absent. 405. Hebe: goddess of youth.
free: noble. 409. gods: stars and planets conceived (not merely
poetically, Spenser believed it) as conscious beings exercising
astrological influence on terrestrial affairs. 414. fayne: feign,
imagine. 416. happy influence: The temperament and fortunes
of the child begotten that night depend on stellar "influences."
423. Of . . . count: to increase the number of souls in bliss.
427. lieu: place, stead. 428. dect: decked, adorned. 429-
31. Which . . . recompens: The general meaning is that the poem
is offered instead of some jewelry or other adornments which
Spenser, or someone else, had intended to give the bride in time
for her wedding; but the construction is very obscure. Professor
Renwick thinks "cutting off" means "having been cut off."
Perhaps "cutting" is an active participle agreeing with "song"
(of course personified) — "omitting which, through accidental
circumstances which caused the date of the wedding to be advanced, you would not await their arrival." "Both" is also
obscure. 433. moniment: memorial.

THE FAERIE QUEENE

SELECTION I

The Redcrosse Knight (whom Spenser elsewhere identifies with St. George) is traveling with the Princess Una (Truth) to deliver her parents from a dragon. St. George, the hero of Book I, is the Knight of Holinesse rather in the sense that he finally achieves it than in the sense that he is a personification of it from the outset. This selection, from the opening of the poem, at once creates the atmosphere of Spenser's " faerie lond," remote (yet somehow familiar), beautiful, voluptuous, and troubled with the sense of hidden dangers. Archimago symbolizes, in general, Hypocrisy; in the historical allegory, the Church of Rome.

I

A gentle° Knight was pricking° on the plaine,
Ycladd° in mightie armes and silver shielde,
Wherein old dints of deepe woundes did remaine,
The cruell markes of many a bloody fielde;
Yet armes till that time did he never wield.
His angry steede did chide his foming° bitt,
As much disdayning to the curbe to yield:
Full jolly° knight he seemed, and faire did sitt,
As one for knightly giusts° and fierce encounters fitt.

2

And on his brest a bloodie Crosse he bore,   10
The deare remembrance of his dying Lord,
For whose sweete sake that glorious badge he wore,
And dead, as living, ever him ador'd:
Upon his shield the like was also scor'd,°
For soveraine hope which in his helpe he had.
Right faithfull true he was in deede and word,
But of his cheere° did seeme too solemne sad;°
Yet nothing did he dread, but ever was ydrad.°

4

A lovely Ladie rode him faire beside,
Upon a lowly Asse more white then snow,   20
Yet she much whiter; but the same did hide
Under a vele, that wimpled° was full low;
And over all a blacke stole° shee did throw
As one that inly mournd, so was she sad,
And heavie sate upon her palfrey slow;
Seemèd in heart some hidden care she had,
And by her, in a line, a milkewhite lambe she lad.

29

At length they chaunst° to meet upon the way
An aged Sire, in long blacke weedes° yclad,
His feete all bare, his beard all hoarie gray,   30
And by his belt his booke he hanging had:
Sober he seemde, and very sagely sad,
And to the ground his eyes were lowly bent,
Simple in shew,° and voide of malice bad;
And all the way he prayèd as he went,
And often knockt his breast, as one that did repent.

30

He faire the knight saluted, louting° low,
Who faire him quited,° as that courteous was;°
And after askèd him, if he did know
Of straunge adventures, which abroad did pas.   40
"Ah! my dear sonne," (quoth he) " how should, alas!
Silly° old man, that lives in hidden cell,
Bidding his beades° all day for his trespás,
Tydings of warre and worldly trouble tell?
With holy father sits not° with such thinges to mell.°

31

" But if of daunger, which hereby doth dwell,
And homebredd evil ye desire to heare,
Of a straunge man I can you tidings tell,
That wasteth all this countrie, farre and neare."
" Of such," (saide he) " I chiefly doe inquere,   50
And shall thee well rewarde to shew the place,
In which that wicked wight° his dayes doth weare;
For to all knighthood it is foule disgrace,
That such a cursèd creature lives so long a space."

32

" Far hence " (quoth he) " in wastfull wildernesse
His dwelling is, by which no living wight
May ever passe, but thorough° great distresse."
" Now," (saide the Ladie) " draweth toward night,
And well I wote,° that of your later° fight
Ye all forwearied be; for what so strong,   60
But, wanting rest, will also want of might?
The Sunne, that measures heaven all day long,
At night doth baite° his steedes the Ocean waves emong.

Sel. I: from *FQ*, I. i–ii.   **1. gentle**: originally, wellborn: hence, having the spirit and courtesy of a gentleman.   **pricking**: riding.   **2. Ycladd**: clothed.   **6. foming**: foaming.   **8. jolly**: confident.   **9. giusts**: jousts, combats on horseback.   **14. scor'd**: engraved, or perhaps merely depicted.   **17. cheere**: countenance, facial expression.   **sad**: grave.   **18. ydrad**: dreaded.   **22. wimpled**: falling in folds.   **23. stole**: a long robe.   **28. chaunst**: chanced, happened.   **29. weedes**: clothes.   **34. shew**: show (noun), appearance.   **37. louting**: bowing.   **38. quited**: requited.   **as . . . was**: like the courteous man he was.   **42. Silly**: simple.   **43. Bidding . . . beads**: saying his prayers.   **45. sits not**: is unsuitable.   **mell**: mingle.   **52. wight**: creature.   **57. thorough**: through.   **59. wote**: know.   **later**: recent.   **63. baite**: to feed (horses), to stop in order to feed horses on a journey.

33

"Then with the Sunne take, Sir, your timely rest,
And with new day new worke at once begin:
Untroubled night, they say, gives counsell best."
"Right well, Sir knight, ye have advisèd bin,"°
Quoth then that agèd man: "the way to win
Is wisely to advise; now day is spent:
Therefore with me ye may take up your In°   70
For this same night." The knight was well content;
So with that godly father to his home they went.

34

A litle lowly Hermitage it was,
Downe in a dale, hard by a forests side,
Far from resort of people that did pas
In traveill to and froe: a litle wyde°
There was an holy chappell edifyde,°
Wherein the Hermite dewly wont to say
His holy thinges each morne and eventyde:
Thereby a christall streame did gently play,   80
Which form a sacred fountaine wellèd forth alway.

35

Arrivèd there, the litle house they fill,
Ne° looke for entertainement where none was;
Rest is their feast, and all things at their will:
The noblest mind the best contentment has.
With faire discourse the evening so they pas;
For that olde man of pleasing wordes has store,
And well could file his tongue as smooth as glas:°
He told of Saintes and Popes, and evermore
He strowd an *Ave-Mary* after and before.   90

36

The drouping night thus creepeth on them fast;
And the sad humor° loading their eyeliddes,
As messenger of Morpheus,° on them cast
Sweet slombring deaw, the which to sleep them
   biddes.
Unto their lodgings then his guestes he riddes:°
Where when all drownd in deadly sleepe he findes,
He to his studie goes; and there amiddes
His magick bookes, and artes of sundrie kindes,
He seekes out mighty charmes to trouble sleepy
   minds.

37

Then choosing out few words most horrible,   100
(Let none them read) thereof did verses frame;
With which, and other spelles like terrible,
He bad awake blacke Plutoes° griesly Dame;

And cursèd heven; and spake reprochful shame
Of highest God, the Lord of life and light:
A bold bad man, that dar'd to call by name
Great Gorgon, prince of darkness and dead night;
At which Coctytus quakes, and Styx° is put to
   flight.

38

And forth he cald out of deepe darknes dredd
Legions of Sprights,° the which, like litle flyes   110
Fluttring about his ever-damnèd hedd,
Awaite whereto their service he applyes,
To aide his friendes, or fray° his enimies.
Of those he chose out two, the falsest twoo,
And fittest for to forge true-seeming lyes:
The one of them he gave a message too,°
The other by him selfe staide, other worke to doo.

39

He, making speedy way through spersèd° ayre,
And through the world of waters wide and deepe,
To Morpheus house doth hastily repaire.   120
Amid the bowels of the earth full steepe,
And low, where dawning day doth never peepe,
His dwelling is; there Tethys° his wet bed
Doth ever wash, and Cynthia° still doth steepe
In silver deaw his ever-drouping hed,
Whiles sad Night over him her mantle black doth
   spred.

40

Whose double gates he findeth lockèd fast,
The one faire fram'd of burnisht Yvory,
The other all with silver overcast;
And wakeful dogges before them farre doe lye,
Watching to banish Care their enimy,   131
Who oft is wont to trouble gentle Sleepe.
By them the Sprite doth passe in quietly,
And unto Morpheus comes, whom drownèd deepe
In drowsie fit he findes: of nothing he takes keepe.°

41

And more to lulle him in his slumber soft,
A trickling streame from high rock tumbling
   downe,
And ever-drizling raine upon the loft,
Mixt with a murmuring winde, much like the
   sowne°
Of swarming Bees, did cast him in a swowne.°   140
No other noyse, nor peoples troublous cryes,
As still° are wont t' annoy the wallèd towne,

---

67. bin: been.   70. In: inn, lodging.   76. wyde: distance away
from it.   77. edifyde: built.   83. Ne: nor.   88. file . . . glas:
make his words very plausible.   92. humor: moisture.
93. Morpheus: the god of sleep.   95. riddes: dispatches.
103. Plutoes: Pluto is the god of the underworld, the land of the
dead. His Dame, or wife, is Proserpina.

108. Cocytus . . . Styx: rivers in the world of the dead.
110. Sprights: spirits.   113. fray: frighten.   116. too: to.
118. spersed: dispersed, widespread.   123. Tethys: principal
goddess of the sea.   124. Cynthia: the moon goddess.
135. keepe: heed.   139. sowne: sound.   140. swowne: swoon.
142. still: always.

Might there be heard; but carelesse Quiet lyes
Wrapt in eternall silence farre from enimyes.

43

The Sprite then gan more boldly him to wake,
And threatned unto him the dreaded name
Of Hecatè:° whereat he gan to quake,
And, lifting up his lompish° head, with blame
Halfe angrie askèd him, for what he came.
"Hither" (quoth he) "me Archimago sent,   150
He that the Stubborne Sprites can wisely tame,
He bids thee to him send for his intent
A fit false dreame, that can delude the sleepers
    sent."°

44

The God obayde; and, calling forth straight way
A diverse Dreame out of his prison darke,
Delivered it to him, and downe did lay
His heavie head, devoide of careful carke;°
Whose sences all were straight benumbd and
    starke.
He,° backe returning by the Yvorie dore,
Remounted up as light as chearefull Larke;   160
And on his litle winges the dreame he bore
In hast unto his Lord, where he him left afore.

45

Who all this while, with charmes and hidden artes,
Had made a Lady of that other Spright,
And fram'd of liquid ayre her tender partes,
So lively and so like in all mens sight,
That weaker sence it could have ravisht quight:
The maker selfe, for all his wondrous witt,
Was nigh beguilèd with so goodly sight.
Her all in white he clad, and over it   170
Cast a black stole, most like to seeme for Una fit.

46

Now, when that ydle dreame was to him brought,
Unto that Elfin knight° he bad him fly,
Where he slept soundly void of evil thought,
And with false shewes abuse his fantasy,
In sort° as he him schoolèd privily:
And that new creature, borne without her dew,°
Full of the makers guyle, with usage sly
He taught to imitate that Lady trew,
Whose semblance she did carrie under feignèd
    hew.   180

47

Thus, well instructed, to their worke they haste;
And, comming where the knight in slomber lay,

The one upon his hardie head him plaste,
And made him dreame of loves and lustfull play,
That nigh his manly hart did melt away,
Bathèd in wanton blis and wicked joy.
Then seemèd him° his Lady by him lay,
And to him playnd, how that false wingèd boy°
Her chaste hart had subdewd to learne Dame Pleas-
    ures toy.

48

And she her selfe, of beautie soveraigne Queene,
Fayre Venus, seemde unto his bed to bring   191
Her, whom he, waking, evermore did weene°
To bee the chastest flowre that aye° did spring
On earthly braunch, the daughter of a king,
Now a loose Leman° to vile service bound:
And eke the Graces seemèd all to sing,
Hymen° Iö Hymen! dauncing all around;
Whylst freshest Flora her with Yvie° girlond
    crownd.

49

In this great passion of unwonted lust,
Or wonted feare of doing ought amis,   200
He starteth up, as seeming to mistrust
Some secret ill, or hidden foe of his.
Lo! there before his face his Ladie is,
Under blacke stole hyding her bayted hooke;
And as halfe blushing offred him to kis,
With gentle blandishment and lovely looke,
Most like that virgin true which for her knight him
    took.

53

"Love of your selfe," she saide, "and deare con-
    straint,
Lets me not sleepe, but waste the wearie night
In secret anguish and unpittied plaint,   210
Whiles you in carelesse sleepe are drownèd quight."
Her doubtfull words made that redoubted° knight
Suspect her truth: yet since no' untruth he knew,
Her fawning love with foule disdainefull spight
He would not shend;° but said, "Deare dame, I
    rew,
That for my sake unknowne such griefe unto you
    grew.

54

"Assure your selfe, it fell not all to ground;
For all so deare as life is to my hart,
I deeme your love, and hold me to you bound:
Ne° let vaine feares procure your needlesse smart,
Where cause is none; but to your rest depart."   221
Not all content, yet seemd she to appease

---

147. Hecate: goddess of the dead and of magic. See *Hamlet*, III.ii.266–71. 148. lompish: dull, heavy. 152. sent: sense perception. 157. carke: burden, trouble. 159. He: the sprite. 173. that . . . knight: i.e., St. George. 176. In sort: in such manner. 177. her dew: her due (of natural generation). 187. him: to him. 188. winged boy: Cupid. 192. weene: think. 193. aye: ever. 195. Leman: mistress, sweetheart. 197. *Hymen:* god of marriage. 198. Yvie: ivy. 212. redoubted: dreaded. 215. shend: put to shame. 220. Ne: nor.

Her mournefull plaintes, beguilèd of her art,
And fed with words that could not chose but please:
So, slyding softly forth, she turnd as to her ease.

55

Long after lay he musing at her mood,
Much griev'd to thinke that gentle Dame so light,
For whose defence he was to shed his blood.
At last, dull wearines of former fight
Having yrockt° asleepe his irkesome spright,°   230
That troublous dreame gan° freshly tosse his braine
With bowres,° and beds, and ladies deare delight:
But, when he° saw his labour all was vaine,
With that misformèd spright he backe returnd
  againe.

1

By this° the Northerne wagoner° had set
His sevenfold teme behind the stedfast starre°
That was in Ocean waves yet never wet,
But firme is fixt, and sendeth light from farre
To al that in the wide deepe wandring arre;
And chearefull Chaunticlere° with his note shrill
Had warnèd once, that Phœbus° fiery carre   241
In hast was climbing up the Easterne hill,
Full envious that night so long his roome did fill:

2

When those accursèd messengers of hell,
That feigning dreame, and that faire-forgèd
  Spright,
Came to their wicked maister, and gan tel
Their bootelesse° paines, and ill succeeding night:
Who, all in rage to see his skilfull might
Deluded so, gan threaten hellish paine,
And sad Prosérpines° wrath, them to affright: 250
But, when he saw his threatning was but vaine,
He cast about, and searcht his baleful bookes
  againe.

3

Eftsoones° he tooke that miscreated faire,
And that false other Spright, on whom he spred
A seeming body of the subtile aire,
Like a young Squire, in loves and lusty-hed°
His wanton daies that ever loosely led,
Without regard of armes and dreaded fight:
Those twoo he tooke, and in a secrete bed,   259
Covered with darkenes and misdeeming° night,
Them both together laid to joy in vaine delight.

230. **yrockt:** rocked.   **irkesome spright:** restless mind.
231. **gan:** began.   232. **bowres:** bedrooms.   233. **he:** the dream.
235. **By this:** by this time, by now.   **Northerne wagoner:** the
constellation called the Plow or Charles's Wain.   236. **the . . .
starre:** the Pole Star.   240. **Chaunticlere:** the cock.   241. **Phoebus:** the sun god.   247. **bootelesse:** unavailing.   250. **Proserpine:** the Queen of the dead. See l. 103n.   253. **Eftsoones:** then.   256. **lusty-hed:** jollity.   260. **misdeeming:**
literally, judging amiss; hence, leading to misjudgment.

4

Forthwith he runnes with feignèd faithfull hast
Unto his guest, who, after troublous sights
And dreames, gan now to take more sound repast;°
Whom suddenly he wakes with fearful frights,
As one aghast with feends or damnèd sprights,
And to him cals; " Rise, rise! unhappy Swaine,
That here wex° old in sleepe, whiles wicked wights
Have knit themselves in Venus shameful chaine:
Come, see where your false Lady doth her honor
  staine."   270

5

All in amaze he suddenly up start
With sword in hand, and with the old man went;
Who soone him brought into a secret part,
Where that false couple were full closely ment°
In wanton lust and leud embracèment:
Which when he saw, he burnt with gealous fire;
The eie of reason was with rage yblent,°
And would have slaine them in his furious ire,
But hardly was restreinèd of that aged sire.

6

Retourning to his bed in torment great,   280
And bitter anguish of his guilty sight,
He could not rest; but did his stout heart eat,
And wast his inward gall with deepe despight,°
Yrkesome of life, and too long lingring night.
At last faire Hesperus° in highest skie
Had spent his lampe, and brought forth dawning
  light;
Then up he rose, and clad him hastily:
The dwarfe° him brought his steed; so both away
  do fly.

SELECTION II

Parted from Una, the Redcrosse Knight is soon traveling with the false witch Duessa ("Double, two-
faced") in complete ignorance of her true character.
In this passage he hears a story which would have enlightened him if he had known her real name, but she
has told him it is Fidessa (Faithful). The bleeding and
talking tree is an image borrowed from Virgil.

28

Long time they thus together travailèd;
Til, weary of their way, they came at last
Where grew two goodly trees, that faire did spred
Their armes abroad, with gray mosse overcast;

264. **repast:** repose.   268. **wex:** wax, grow.   274. **ment:** mingled.   277. **yblent:** blinded.   283. **despight:** resentment.
285. **Hesperus:** Venus; here, as morning star.   288. **The
dwarfe:** This very minor character has been mentioned in an
omitted passage. He was the servant of Una and St. George.

And their greene leaves, trembling with every blast,
Made a calme shadowe far in compasse round:
The fearefull shepheard, often there aghast,
Under them never sat, ne wont° there sound
His mery oaten pipe, but shund th' unlucky ground.

29

But this good knight, soone as he them can spie,
For the coole shade him thither hastly got: 11
For golden Phœbus, now ymounted hie,
From fiery wheeles of his faire chariot
Hurlèd his beame so scorching cruell hot,
That living creature mote° it not abide;
And his new Lady it endurèd not.
There they alight, in hope themselves to hide
From the fierce heat, and rest their weary limbs a
      tide.°

30

Faire seemely pleasaunce° each to other makes,
With goodly purposes,° there as they sit;   20
And in his falsèd fancy he her takes
To be the fairest wight that livèd yit;°
Which to expresse he bends his gentle wit:
And, thinking of those braunches greene to frame
A girlond for her dainty forehead fit,
He pluckt a bough; out of whose rifte there came
Smal drops of gory bloud, that trickled down the
      same.

31

Therewith a piteous yelling voice was heard,
Crying, " O! spare with guilty hands to teare
My tender sides in this rough rynd embard;°   30
But fly, ah! fly far hence away, for feare
Least to you hap that happened to me heare,°
And to this wretched Lady, my deare love;
O, too deare love, love bought with death too
      deare! "
Astond° he stood, and up his heare did hove;°
And with that suddein horror could no member
move.

32

At last whenas the dreadfull passion°
Was overpast, and manhood well awake,
Yet musing at the straunge occasion,°
And doubting much his sence, he thus bespake: 40
" What voice of damnèd Ghost from Limbo° lake,

Or guilefull spright wandring in empty aire,
Both which fraile men doe oftentimes mistake,
Sends to my doubtful eares these speaches rare,
And ruefull plaints, me bidding guiltlesse blood to
      spare? "

33

Then, groning deep; " Nor damnèd Ghost," (quoth
      he)
" Nor guileful sprite to thee these words doth
      speake;
But once a man, Fradubio, now a tree;
Wretched man, wretched tree! whose nature weake
A cruell witch, her cursèd will to wreake,   50
Hath thus transformd, and plast° in open plaines,
Where Boreas° doth blow full bitter bleake,
And scorching Sunne does dry my secret vaines;
For though a tree I seme, yet cold and heat me
      paines."

34

" Say on, Fradubio, then, or man or tree."
Quoth then the Knight; " by whose mischiévous
      arts
Art thou misshapèd thus, as now I see?
He oft finds med'cine who his griefe imparts,
But double griefs afflict concealing harts,
As raging flames who striveth to suppresse."   60
" The author then," (said he) " of all my smarts,
Is one Duessa, a false sorceresse,
That many errant knights hath broght to wretched-
      nesse.

35

" In prime of youthly yeares, when corage hott
The fire of love, and joy of chevalree,°
First kindled in my brest, it was my lott
To love this gentle Lady, whome ye see
Now not a Lady, but a seeming tree;
With whome, as once I rode accompanyde,
Me chauncèd of a knight encountred bee,°   70
That had a like faire Lady by his syde;
Lyke a faire Lady, but did fowle Duessa hyde.

36

" Whose forgèd beauty he did take in hand
All other Dames to have exceeded farre:
I in defence of mine did likewise stand,
Mine, that did then shine as the Morning starre.
So both to batteill fierce arraungèd arre,
In which his harder fortune was to fall
Under my speare: such is the dye of warre.
His Lady, left as a prise martiall,°   80
Did yield her comely person to be at my call.

Sel. II: from *FQ*, I. ii.   **8. wont:** was used or accustomed to.
15. mote: might, could.   **18. tide:** time, space of time.
19. seemely pleasaunce: befitting entertainment.   **20. purposes:** speeches, remarks.   **22. yit:** yet.   **30. embard:** imprisoned.   **32. Least ... heare:** lest to you that should happen
which happened to me here.   **35. Astond:** astonished.   **hove:**
rise.   **37. passion:** three syllables.   **39. occasion:** four syllables.
41. Limbo: Originally a painless department of hell, inhabited by
those who have lost Heaven not through actual sins but through
lack of baptism. Spenser probably uses it vaguely to mean
"the abyss," "the unknown."

51. plast: placed.   **52. Boreas:** the north wind.   **65. chevalree:**
deeds of arms, knightly adventures.   **70. Me . . . bee:** I happened to meet a knight.   **80. prise martiall:** prize of battle.

37

" So doubly lov'd of ladies, unlike faire,
Th' one seeming such, the other such indeede,
One day in doubt I cast for° to compare
Whether° in beauties glorie did exceede:
A Rosy girlond was the victors meede.°
Both seemde to win, and both seemed won to bee,
So hard the discord was to be agreede.
Frælissa was as faire as faire mote bee,
And ever false Duessa seemde as faire as shee. 90

38

" The wicked witch, now seeing all this while
The doubtfull ballaunce equally to sway,
What not by right° she cast° to win by guile;
And by her hellish science raisd streight way
A foggy mist that overcast the day,
And a dull blast, that breathing on her° face
Dimmèd her former beauties shining ray,
And with foule ugly forme did her disgrace:
Then was she° fayre alone, when none was faire in
place. 99

39

" Then cride she out, ' Fye, fye! deformèd wight,
Whose borrowed beautie now appeareth plaine
To have before bewitchèd all mens sight:
O! leave her soone, or let her soone be slaine.'
Her loathly visage viewing with disdaine,
Eftsoones° I thought her such as she me told,
And would have kild her; but with faignèd paine
The false witch did my wrathful hand withhold:
So left her, where she now is turnd to trèen°
mould.

40

" Thensforth I tooke Duessa for my Dame,
And in the witch unweeting° joyd long time, 110
Ne ever wist° but that she was the same;°
Till on a day (that day is everie Prime,°
When Witches wont° do penance for their crime,)
I chaunst to see her in her proper hew,
Bathing her selfe in origane° and thyme:
A filthy foule old woman I did vew,
That ever to have toucht her I did deadly rew.

41

" Her neather partes misshapen, monstruous,
Were hidd in water, that I could not see;
But they did seeme more foule and hideous, 120

Then° womans shape man would beleeve to bee.
Thensforth from her most beastly companie
I gan refraine, in minde to slipp away,
Soone as appeard safe opportunitie:
For danger great, if not assured decay,
I saw before mine eyes, if I were knowne to stray.

42

" The divelish hag by chaunges of my cheare°
Perceiv'd my thought; and, drownd in sleepie night,
With wicked herbes and oyntments did besmeare
My body all, through charmes and magicke might,
That all my senses were bereavèd quight: 131
Then brought she me into this desert waste,
And by my wretched lovers side me pight;°
Where now, enclosed in wooden wals full faste,
Banisht from living wights, our wearie daies we
waste."

43

" But how long time," said then the Elfin knight,
" Are you in this misformèd hous to dwell? "
" We may not chaunge," (quoth he) " this evill
plight,
Till we be bathèd in a living well:
That is the terme prescribèd by the spell." 140
" O! how," sayd he, "mote° I that well out find,
That may restore you to your wonted well? "°
" Time and suffisèd fates° to former kynd
Shall us restore; none else from hence may us un·
bynd."

44

The false Duessa, now Fidessa hight,°
Heard how in vaine Fradubio did lament,
And knew well all was true. But the good knight,
Full of sad feare and ghastly dreriment,°
When all this speech the living tree had spent,
The bleeding bough did thrust into the ground,
That from the blood he might be innocent, 151
And with fresh clay did close the wooden wound:
Then, turning to his Lady, dead with feare her
fownd.

45

Her seeming dead he fownd with feignèd feare,
As all unweeting of that well she knew;°
And paynd himselfe with busie care to reare
Her out of carelesse swowne. Her eyelids blew,
And dimmèd sight, with pale and deadly hew,
At last she up gan lift: with trembling cheare
Her up he tooke, (too simple and too trew) 160

84. cast for: proposed, decided. 85. Whether: which of the two.
86. meede: reward. 93. What . . . right: what she could not
win by right. cast: resolved. 96. her: Fraelissa's. 99. she:
Duessa. 105. Eftsoones: then. 108. treen: wooden. 110. unweeting: unknowing. 111. wist: knew. the same: i.e., as she
appeared to be. 112. Prime: here, spring. (It more often means
morning.) 113. wont: are used or accustomed. 115. origane:
origan, an herb.

121. Then: than. 127. cheare: countenance, facial expression.
133. pight: pitched, fixed. 141. mote: might. 142. well: welfare. 143. suffised fates: accomplished destiny 145. hight:
called. 148. dreriment: dismay. 155. As . . . knew: as if
ignorant of what she knew well.

And oft her kist. At length, all passèd feare,
He set her on her steede, and forward forth did
    beare.

SELECTION III

Una, who was deserted by the Redcrosse Knight at
the end of Selection I, is now wandering alone in
search of him and has a strange adventure. This passage illustrates that co-existence of different levels which
is characteristic of Spenser's poetry: in stanzas 1 and 7
Una is a very human, forsaken girl, in stanza 5 her
divine character is hinted, and in 4 (where we are
shown Truth laying aside her veil) it is predominant.

1

Nought is there under heav'ns wide hollownesse,
That moves more deare compassion of mind,
Then° beautie brought t'unworthie wretchednesse
Through envies snares, or fortunes freakes unkind.
I, whether lately through her brightnes blynd,
Or through alleageance, and fast fealty,
Which I do owe unto all womankynd,
Feele my hart perst with so great agony,
When such I see, that all for pitty I could dy.

2

And now it is empassionèd so deepe,   10
For fairest Unaes sake, of whom I sing,
That my frayle eies these lines with teares do steepe,
To thinke how she through guylefull handèling,
Though true as touch,° though daughter of a
    king,
Though faire as ever living wight was fayre,
Though nor in word nor deede ill meriting,
Is from her knight divorcèd° in despayre,
And her dew loves deryv'd to that vile witches
    shayre.

3

Yet she, most faithfull Ladie, all this while
Forsaken, wofull, solitarie mayd,   20
Far from all peoples preace,° as in exíle,
In wildernesse and wastfull deserts strayd,
To seeke her knight; who, subtily betrayd
Through that late vision which th' Enchaunter
    wrought,
Had her abandoned. She, of nought affrayd,
Through woods and wastnes wide him daily
    sought;
Yet wishèd tydinges none of him unto her brought.

4

One day, nigh wearie of the yrkesome way,
From her unhastie beast she did alight;
And on the grasse her dainty limbs did lay   30
In secrete shadow, far from all mens sight:
From her fayre head her fillet° she undight,
And layd her stole aside. Her angels face,
As the great eye of heaven, shynèd bright,
And made a sunshine in the shady place;
Did ever mortall eye behold such heavenly grace?

5

It fortunèd, out of the thickest wood
A ramping° Lyon rushèd suddeinly,
Hunting full greedy after salvage° blood.
Soone as the royall virgin he did spy,   40
With gaping mouth at her ran greedily,
To have attonce° devourd her tender corse;°
But to the pray when as he drew more ny,
His bloody rage aswagèd with remorse,°
And, with the sight, amazd, forgat his furious
    forse.

6

In stead thereof he kist her wearie feet,
And lickt her lilly hands with fawning tong,
As° he her wrongèd innocence did weet.°
O, how can beautie maister the most strong,
And simple truth subdue avenging wrong!   50
Whose yielded pryde and proud submission,
Still dreading death, when she had markèd long,
Her hart gan melt in great compassion;
And drizling teares did shed for pure affection.

7

"The Lyon, Lord of everie beast in field,"
Quoth she, "his princely puissance doth abate,
And mightie proud to humble weake does yield,
Forgetfull of the hungry rage, which late
Him prickt, in pittie of my sad estate:
But he, my Lyon, and my noble Lord,   60
How does he find in cruell hart to hate
Her, that him lov'd, and ever most adord
As the God of my life? why hath he me abhord?"

SELECTION IV

Una, now protected by the Lion, has had several
more adventures and has finally met the Saracen Sansloy (Lawless). The Lion, enraged at his attempted fa-
miliarities with Una, attacks him and is killed. Una
flies, and this selection opens at the moment when the

---

32. fillet: headband.   **38. ramping:** standing on the hind legs
and extending the forepaws, threatening.   **39. salvage:** savage.
42. attonce: at once.   **corse:** body.   **44. remorse:** pity.
48. As: as if.   **weet:** know.

Sel. III: from *FQ*, I. iii.   **3. then:** than.   **14. touch:** touchstone.   **17. divorced:** divided.   **21. preace:** press, crowd.

Saracen overtakes her. The arrival of the wood gods shows Spenser in his more riotous and frolicsome vein; it is a scene Titian would have loved to paint. The wood gods represent untaught nature, which will, after its ignorant fashion, reverence the celestial beauty that Sansloy, corrupt nature, merely wants to possess.

4

With fawning wordes he courted her a while;
And, looking lovely and oft sighing sore,
Her constant hart did tempt with diverse guile:
But wordes, and lookes, and sighes she did abhore;
As rock of Diamond stedfast evermore.
Yet for to feed his fyrie lustfull eye,
He snatcht the vele that hong her face before:
Then gan her beautie shyne as brightest skye,
And burnt his beastly hart t'efforce her chastitye.

6

The pitteous mayden, carefull,° comfortlesse,   10
Does throw out thrilling shriekes, and shrieking
          cryes,
The last vaine helpe of womens great distresse,
And with loud plaintes importuneth the skyes,
That molten starres doe drop like weeping eyes;
And Phœbus, flying so most shameful sight,
His blushing face in foggy cloud implyes,°
And hydes for shame. What witt of mortal wight
Can now devise to quitt a thrall° from such a
          plight?

7

Eternall providence, exceeding thought,
Where none appeares can make her° selfe a way.
A wondrous way it for this Lady wrought,   21
From Lyons clawes to pluck the grypèd pray.
Her shrill outcryes and shrieks so loud did bray,
That all the woodes and forestes did resownd:
A troupe of Faunes and Satyres far away
Within the wood were dauncing in a rownd,
Whiles old Sylvanus° slept in shady arber sownd:

8

Who, when they heard that pitteous strainèd voice,
In haste forsooke their rurall meriment,
And ran towardes the far rebownded noyce,   30
To weet° what wight so loudly did lament.
Unto the place they come incontinent:°
Whom when the raging Sarazin espyde,
A rude, mishapen, monstrous rablement,°
Whose like he never saw, he durst not byde,
But got his ready steed, and fast away gan ryde.

10

She, more amazd, in double dread doth dwell;
And every tender part for feare does shake.
As when a greedy Wolfe, through honger fell,
A seely° Lamb far from the flock does take,   40
Of whom he meanes his bloody feast to make,
A Lyon spyes fast running towards him,
The innocent pray in hast he does forsake;
Which, quitt from death, yet quakes in every lim
With chaunge of feare, to see the Lyon looke so
          grim.

11

Such fearefull fitt assaid her trembling hart,
Ne word to speake, ne joynt to move, she had;
The salvage° nation feele her secret smart,
And read her sorrow in her count'nance sad;
Their frowning forheades, with rough hornes yclad,
And rustick horror, all asyde doe lay;   51
And, gently grenning,° shew a semblance glad
To comfort her; and, feare to put away,
Their backward bent° knees teach° her humbly to
          obay.

12

The doubtfull Damzell dare not yet committ
Her single person to their barbarous truth;
But still twixt feare and hope amazd does sitt,
Late learnd what harme to hasty trust ensu'th.°
They, in compassion of her tender youth,
And wonder of her beautie soverayne,   60
Are wonne with pitty and unwonted ruth;
And, all prostrate upon the lowly playne,
Doe kisse her feete, and fawne on her with count'-
          nance fayne.°

13

Their harts she ghesseth by their humble guise,
And yieldes her to extremitie of time:°
So from the ground she fearelesse doth arise,
And walketh forth without suspect of crime.
They, all as glad as birdes of joyous Pryme,°
Thence lead her forth, about her dauncing round,
Shouting, and singing all a shepheards ryme;   70
And with greene braunches strowing all the
          ground,
Do worship her as Queene with olive girlond
          cround.

14

And all the way their merry pipes they sound,
That all the woods with doubled Eccho ring;

Sel. IV: from *FQ*, I. vi.   10. **carefull**: full of care (anguish, anxiety).   16. **implyes**: wraps up.   18. **quitt a thrall**: to liberate a wretch or captive.   20. **her**: Providence is treated as feminine.   27. **Sylvanus**: god of the woods.   31. **weet**: know.   32. **incontinent**: headlong.   34. **rablement**: rabble.

40. **seely**: simple.   38. **salvage**: savage.   52. **grenning**: grinning.   54. **backward bent**: because they have goats' legs.   **teach**: i.e., teach their knees.   58. **ensu'th**: follows.   63. **fayne**: glad.   65. **extremitie of time**: the present emergency.   68. **Pryme**: from 6 to 9 A.M., hence, in general, "morning."

And with their hornèd feet doe weare the ground,
Leaping like wanton kids in pleasant Spring.
So towards old Sylvanus they her bring;
Who, with the noyse awakèd, commeth out
To weet the cause, his weake steps governing
And agèd limbs on cypresse stadle° stout;   80
And with an yvie twyne his waste is girt about.

16

The woodborne people fall before her flat,
And worship her as Goddesse of the wood;
And old Sylvanus selfe bethinkes not what
To thinke of wight so fayre, but gazing stood
In doubt to deeme her borne of earthly brood:
Sometimes Dame Venus selfe he seemes to see;
But Venus never had so sober mood:
Sometimes Diana he her takes to be,
But misseth bow and shaftes, and buskins° to her
     knee.   90

18

The wooddy nymphes, faire Hamadryadès,°
Her to behold do thither runne apace;
And all the troupe of light-foot Naiadès°
Flocke all about to see her lovely face;
But, when they vewèd have her heavenly grace,
They envy her in their malitious mind,
And fly away for feare of fowle disgrace:
But all the Satyres scorne their woody kind,
And henceforth nothing faire but her on earth they
     find.

19

Glad of such lucke, the luckelesse lucky mayd   100
Did her content to please their feeble eyes,
And long time with that salvage people stayd,
To gather breath in many miseryes.
During which time her gentle wit she plyes
To teach them truth, which worshipt her in vaine,
And made her th' Image of Idolatryes;
But when their bootlesse° zeale she did restrayne
From her own worship, they her Asse would wor-
     ship fayn.

SELECTION V

We return to the Redcrosse Knight, who is still with
Duessa. At the worst possible moment, when he has
just drunk of an enchanted well that drains away all
strength, he has a horrible surprise. One of Spenser's
nightmare passages.

7

Yet goodly court he made still to his Dame,
Pourd out in loosenesse° on the grassy grownd,
Both careless of his health, and of his fame;
Till at the last he heard a dreadfull sownd,
Which through the wood loud bellowing did re-
     bownd,
That all the earth for terror seemd to shake,
And trees did tremble. Th' Elfe,° therewith
     astownd,
Upstarted lightly from his looser make,°
And his unready weapons gan in hand to take.

8

But ere he could his armour on him dight,°   10
Or gett his shield, his monstrous enimy
With sturdie steps came stalking in his sight,
An hideous Geaunt, horrible and hye,
That with his tallnesse seemd to threat the skye;
The ground eke° gronèd under him for dreed:
His living like saw never living eye,
Ne durst behold: his stature did exceed
The hight of three the tallest sonnes of mortall
     seed.

9

The greatest Earth his uncouth mother was,
And blustring Æolus° his boasted syre;   20
Who with his breath, which through the world
     doth pas,
Her hollow womb did secretly inspyre,
And fild her hidden caves with stormie yre,
That she conceiv'd; and trebling the dew time
In which the wombes of wemen doe expyre,
Brought forth this monstrous masse of earthly
     slyme,°
Puft up with emptie wynd, and fild with sinfull
     cryme.

10

So growèn great, through arrogant delight
Of th' high descent whereof he was yborne,   29
And through presumption of his matchlesse might,
All other powres and knighthood he did scorne.
Such now he marcheth to this man forlorne,
And left to losse; his stalking steps are stayde
Upon a snaggy° Oke, which he had torne
Out of his mothers bowelles, and it made
His mortall mace, wherewith his foemen he dis-
     mayde.

Sel. V: from *FQ*, I. vii.   **2. Pourd . . . loosenesse:** spread out
and relaxed.   **7. Th' Elfe:** St. George.   **8. make:** mate, companion.   **10. dight:** put, arrange.   **15. eke:** also.   **20. Aeolus:**
god of the winds.   **26. slyme:** seed.   **34. snaggy:** jagged
knotty.

80. stadle: trunk.   **90. buskins:** high boots coming up to the
calves.   **92. Hamadryades:** wood nymphs.   **93. Naiades:**
nymphs of wells, brooks, etc.   **107. bootlesse:** unavailing.

11

That, when the knight he spyde he gan advaunce
With huge force and insúpportáble mayne,
And towardes him with dreadfull fury praunce;
Who haplesse, and eke hopelesse, all in vaine   40
Did to him pace sad battaile to darrayne,°
Disarmd, disgraste, and inwardly dismayde;
And eke so faint in every joynt and vayne,
Through that fraile fountain which him feeble
    made,
That scarsely could he weeld his bootlesse single
    blade.

12

The Geaunt strooke so maynly mercilesse,°
That could have overthrowne a stony towre;
And, were not hevenly grace that did him blesse,
He had beene pouldred° all as thin as flowre:°
But he was wary of that deadly stowre,°   50
And lightly lept from underneath the blow:
Yet so exceeding was the villeins powre,
That with the winde it did him overthrow,
And all his sences stound° that still he lay full
    low.

14

So daunted when the Geaunt saw the knight,
His heavie hand he heavèd up on hye,
And him to dust thought to have battred quight,
Untill Duessa loud to him gan crye,
" O great Orgoglio!° greatest under skye,
O! hold thy mortall hand for Ladies sake;   60
Hold for my sake, and doe him not to dye,
But vanquisht thine eternall bondslave make,
And me, thy worthy meed, unto thy Leman°
    take."

15

He hearkned, and did stay from further harmes,
To gayne so goodly guerdon° as she spake:
So willingly she came into his armes,
Who her as willingly to grace did take,
And was possessèd of his newfound make,°
Then up he tooke the slombred sencelesse corse,
And, ere he could out of his swowne awake,   70
Him to his castle brought with hastie forse,
And in a Dongeon deepe him threw without re-
    morse.

41. darrayne: Originally meant "to vindicate by battle."
Spenser apparently means by it only "to fight." **46. maynly
mercilesse:** mightily merciless. **49. pouldred:** pulverized.
flowre: flour. **50. stowre:** crisis. **54. stound:** stunned.
59. Orgoglio: Etymologically the name means Pride. The giant's
castle (see Sel. VII) suggests the prisons of the Spanish Inquisition, and he himself probably symbolizes Persecution. **63. Leman:** mistress, sweetheart. **65. guerdon:** reward. **68. make:**
mate.

SELECTION VI

Una, still seeking the Redcrosse Knight, now meets
Prince Arthur, who would have been the hero of the
whole poem if it had been finished. I have had to short-
en the description of his armor and equipment which
is very long in the original; such things as clothes are
not, for Spenser, mere externals but an expression of
the wearer's nature. From Una's narrative to Arthur
we first learn why she was traveling with the Redcrosse
Knight in Selection I. This practice of beginning a story
in the middle and then giving us the earlier stages in a
" flashback " is one that Spenser took over from Virgil
and Homer.

29

At last she chauncèd by good hap to meet
A goodly knight, faire marching by the way,
Together with his Squyre, arayèd meet:
His glitterand° armour shinèd far away,
Like glauncing light of Phœbus brightest ray;
From top to toe no place appearèd bare,
That deadly dint of steele endanger may.
Athwart his brest a bauldrick° brave he ware,
That shind, like twinkling stars, with stones most
    pretious rare.

30

And in the midst thereof one pretious stone   10
Of wondrous worth, and eke of wondrous mights,
Shapt like a Ladies head, exceeding shone,
Like Hesperus emongst the lesser lights,
And strove for to amaze the weaker sights:
Thereby his mortall blade full comely hong
In yvory sheath, ycarv'd° with curious slights,°
Whose hilts were burnisht gold, and handle
    strong
Of mother perle; and buckled with a golden tong.°

31

His haughtie Helmet, horrid° all with gold,
Both glorious brightnesse and great terrour
    bredd:
For all the crest a Dragon did enfold   21
With greedie pawes, and over all did spredd
His golden winges: his dreadfull hideous hedd,
Close couchèd on the bever,° seemd to throw
From flaming mouth bright sparckles fiery redd,
That suddeine horrour to faint hartes did show;
And scaly tayle was stretcht adowne his back full
    low.

Sel. VI: from *FQ*, I. vii.   **4. glitterand:** glittering.   **8. bauld-
rick:** sword belt, worn across the right shoulder.   **16. ycarv'd:**
carved.   **slights:** subtleties, intricate decorations.   **18. tong:**
tongue.   **19. horrid:** rough.   **24. bever:** visor, the part of the
helmet covering the face.

32

Upon the top of all his loftie crest,
A bounch of heares° discoloured díversely,
With sprincled pearle and gold full richly drest,   30
Did shake, and seemd to daunce for jollity,
Like to an almond tree ymounted° hye
On top of greene Selinis° all alone,
With blossoms brave bedeckèd daintily;
Whose tender locks do tremble every one
At everie little breath that under heaven is blowne.

38

Whenas this knight nigh to the Lady drew,
With lovely court he gan her entertaine;
But, when he heard her answers loth, he knew
Some secret sorrow did her heart distraine;   40
Which to allay, and calme her storming paine,
Faire feeling words he wisely gan display,
And for her humor fitting purpose° faine,°
To tempt the cause it selfe for to bewray,°
Wherewith enmovd, these bleeding words she gan
    to say:

43

" The forlorne Maiden, whom your eies have seene
The laughing stocke of fortunes mockeries,
Am th' onely daughter of a King and Queene.
Whose parents deare, whiles equal° destinies
Did ronne about,° and their felicities   50
The favourable heavens did not envý,
Did spred their rule through all the territories,
Which Phison and Euphrates floweth by,
And Gehons golden waves doe wash continually:

44

" Till that their cruell cursèd enemy,
An huge great Dragon, horrible in sight,
Bred in the loathly lakes of Tartary,
With murdrous ravine, and devouring might,
Their kingdome spoild, and countrey wasted
    quight:
Themselves, for feare into his jawes to fall,   60
He forst to castle strong to take their flight;
Where, fast embard° in mighty brasen wall,
He has them now fowr years besieged to make
    them thrall.

45

" Full many knights, adventurous and stout,
Have enterpriz'd that Monster to subdew:
From every coast that heaven walks about
Have thither come the noble Martial crew.

That famous harde atchievements still pursew;
Yet never any could that girlond win,
But all still shronke, and still he greater grew: 70
All they, for want of faith, or guilt of sin,
The pitteous pray of his fiers cruelty have bin.

46

" At last, yled° with far reported praise,
Which flying fame throughout the world had
    spred,
Of doughty knights, whom Faery land did raise,
That noble order hight° of maidenhed,
Forthwith to court of Gloriane° I sped,
Of Gloriane, great Queene of glory bright,
Whose kingdomes seat Cleopolis is red;°
There to obtaine some such redoubted knight,   80
That Parents deare from tyrants powre deliver
    might.

47

" Yt was my chaunce (my chaunce was faire and
    good)
There for to find a fresh unprovèd° knight;
Whose manly hands imbrewd in guilty blood
Had never beene, ne ever by his might
Had throwne to ground the unregarded right:
Yet of his prowesse proofe he since hath made
(I witnes am) in many a cruell fight;
The groning ghosts of many one dismaide
Have felt the bitter dent of his avenging blade.   90

49

" Well hopèd I, and faire beginnings had,
That he my captive langour should redeeme:
Till, all unweeting,° an Enchaunter bad
His sence abused, and made him to misdeeme
My loyalty, not such as it did seeme,
That rather death desire then such despight.
Be judge, ye heavens, that all things right esteeme,
How I him lov'd, and love with all my might.
So thought I eke of him, and think I thought
    aright."

SELECTION VII

Una has now come with Arthur to the castle in
which the giant Orgoglio imprisoned the Redcrosse
Knight at the end of Selection V. Arthur has killed the
giant and captured Duessa. I omit the fight (Spenser,
like all the Elizabethan poets, is bad at fights) and begin when Arthur enters the castle. The silence and ambiguity of the place, its mingled horror and splendor,

---

29. heares: hairs.   32. ymounted: mounted.   33. Selinis:
probably meant for Selinus, a city famous for its palms.
44. purpose: speeches.   faine: devise.   44. bewray: betray.
49. equal: kindly.   50. ronne about: run their course.
62. embard: imprisoned.

73. yled: led.   76. hight: called.   77. Gloriane: Gloriana, the
Faerie Queene: see Intro., p. 103.   79. red: read, mentioned,
known as.   83. unproved: untested.   93. unweeting: unknowing, i.e., without the Knight's knowledge.

the emphasis on humility in stanza 40, and the ruthless realism (I have omitted some of it) seen in 46, are all highly characteristic of Spenser's imagination.

29

Forthwith he gave in charge unto his Squyre,
That scarlot whore° to keepen carefully;
Whyles he himselfe with greedie great desyre
Into the Castle entred forcibly,
Where living creature none he did espye.
Then gan he lowdly through the house to call,
But no man car'd to answere to his crye:
There raignd a solemne silence over all:
Nor voice was heard, nor wight was seene in bowre
    or hall.

30

At last, with creeping crooked pace forth came   10
An old old man, with beard as white as snow,
That on a staffe his feeble steps did frame,
And guyde his wearie gate° both too and fro,
For his eye sight him faylèd long ygo;
And on his arme a bounch of keyes he bore,
The which unusèd rust did overgrow:
Those were the keyes of every inner dore;
But he could not them use, but kept them still in
    store.

31

But very uncouth sight was to behold,
How he did fashion his untoward pace;   20
For as he forward moovd his footing old,
So backward still was turnd his wrincled face:
Unlike to men, who ever, as they trace,
Both feet and face one way are wont to lead.
This was the auncient keeper of that place,
And foster father of the Gyaunt dead;
His name Ignaro° did his nature right aread.°

32

His reverend heares and holy gravitee
The knight much honord, as beseemèd° well;
And gently askt, where all the people bee,   30
Which in that stately building wont to dwell:
Who answerd him full soft, *he could not tell.*
Again he askt, where that same knight was layd,
Whom great Orgoglio with his puissaunce fell
Had made his caytive thrall: againe, he sayde,
He could not tell; ne ever other answere made.

33

Then askèd he, which way he in might pas?
He could not tell, againe he answerèd.

34

His answere likewise was, *he could not tell:*
Whose sencelesse speach, and doted ignorance,
Whenas the noble Prince had markèd well,
He ghest° his nature by his countenance,
And calmd his wrath with goodly temperance.   50
Then, to him stepping, from his arme did reach
Those keyes, and made himselfe free enterance.
Each dore he opened without any breach,°
There was no barre to stop, nor foe him to em-
    peach.°

35

There all within full rich arayd he found,
With royall arras, and resplendent gold,
And did with store of every thing abound,
That greatest Princes presence might behold.
But all the floore (too filthy to be told)   59
With blood of guiltlesse babes, and innocents° trew,
Which there were slaine as sheepe out of the fold,
Defilèd was, that dreadfull was to vew;
And sacred ashes over it was strowèd new.

36

And there beside of marble stone was built
An Altare, carv'd with cunning ymagery,
On which trew Christians blood was often spilt,
And holy Martyres often doen to dye
With cruell malice and strong tyranny:
Whose blessèd sprites, from underneath the stone,
To God for vengeance cryde continually;   70
And with great griefe were often heard to grone,
That hardest heart would bleede to hear their pite-
    ous mone.

37

Through every rowme he sought, and everie bowr,
But no where could he find that wofull thrall:
At last he came unto an yron doore,
That fast was lockt, but key found not at all
Emongst that bounch to open it withall;
But in the same a little grate was pight,°
Through which he sent his voyce, and lowd did
    call

---

43. pourtrahed: portrayed, drawn.   **49. ghest:** guessed.
53. without . . . breach: either (1) without having to break any of them down, or (2) without any break or interval between the unlocking of one and the unlocking of the next.   **54. empeach:** hinder.   **60. innocents:** a trisyllabic foot, rare but not un-paralleled in Spenser.   **78. pight:** fixed.

Sel. VII: from *FQ*, I. viii.   **2. that . . . whore:** i.e., Duessa.
13. gate: gait.   **27. Ignaro:** ignorant.   **aread:** interpret.
29. beseemed: was fitting.

With all his powre, to weet if living wight   80
Were housèd therewithin, whom he enlargen°
    might.

38

Therewith an hollow, dreary, murmuring voyce
These pitteous plaintes and dolours did resound:
"O! who is that, which bringes me happy choyce
Of death, that here lye dying every stound,°
Yet live perforce in balefull darkenesse bound?
For now three Moones have changèd thrice their
    hew,
And have been thrice hid underneath the ground,
Since I the heavens chearefull face did vew.
O! welcome thou, that doest of death bring tydings
    trew."   90

39

Which when that Champion heard, with percing
    point
Of pitty deare his hart was thrillèd sore;
And trembling horrour ran through every joynt,
For ruth° of gentle knight so fowle forlore;°
Which shaking off, he rent that yron dore
With furious force and indignation fell;
Where entred in, his foot could find no flore,
But all a deepe descent, as darke as hell,
That breathèd ever forth a filthie banefull smell.

40

But nether darkenesse fowle, nor filthy bands,   100
Nor noyous° smell, his purpose could withhold,
(Entire affection hateth nicer° hands)
But that with constant zele and corage bold,
After long paines and labors manifold,
He found the meanes that Prisoner up to reare;
Whose feeble thighes, unable to uphold
His pinèd corse, him scarse to light could beare;
A ruefull spectacle of death and ghastly drere.

41

His sad dull eies, deepe sunck in hollow pits,   109
Could not endure th' unwonted sunne to view;
His bare thin cheekes for want of better bits,°
And empty sides deceivèd of their dew,
Could make a stony hart his hap to rew;
His rawbone armes, whose mighty brawned
    bowrs°
Were wont to rive steele plates, and helmets hew,
Were clene consum'd; and all his vitall powres
Decayd, and all his flesh shronk up like withered
    flowers.

42

Whome when his Lady saw, to him she ran
With hasty joy: to see him made her glad,
And sad to view his visage pale and wan,   120
Who earst in flowres of freshest youth was clad.
Tho, when her well of teares she wasted° had,
She said; "Ah dearest Lord! what evill starre
On you hath frownd, and pourd his influence bad,
That of your selfe ye thus berobbèd arre,
And this misseeming° hew your manly looks doth
    marre? "

44

"Faire Lady," then said that victorious knight,
"The things, that grievous were to doe, or beare,
Them to renew, I wote,° breeds no delight;
Best musicke breeds delight in loathing eare: 130
But th' only good that growes of passèd feare
Is to be wise, and ware of like agein.
This daies ensample hath this lesson deare
Deepe written in my heart with yron pen,
That blisse may not abide in state of mortall men.

45

"Henceforth, Sir knight, take to you wonted
    strength,
And maister these mishaps with patient might.
Loe! where your foe lies stretcht in monstrous
    length;
And loe! that wicked woman in your sight,
The roote of all your care and wretched plight,
Now in your powre, to let her live, or die."   141
"To doe° her die," (quoth Una) "were despight,°
And shame t'avenge so weake an enimy;
But spoile her of her scarlot robe, and let her fly."

46

So, as she bad, that witch they disaraid,
And robd of roiall robes, and purple pall,°
And ornaments that richly were displaid;
Ne sparèd they to strip her naked all.
Then, when they had despoyld her tire and call,°
Such as she was their eies might her behold,   150
That her misshapèd parts did them appall:
A loathly, wrinckled hag, ill favoured, old,
Whose secret filth good manners biddeth not be
    told.

49

Which when the knights beheld amazd they were,
And wondred at so fowle deformèd wight.
"Such then," (said Una) "as she seemeth here,

---

81. enlargen: liberate.   85. stound: hour.   94. ruth: pity.
forlore: forlorn, abandoned.   101. noyous: offensive.
102. nicer: fastidious.   111. bits: bites, meals.   114. bowrs:
muscles.

122. wasted: exhausted.   126. misseeming: unbecoming (with
perhaps the implication of "discreditable").   129. wote: know.
142. doe: make, cause.   were despight: would be vindictive.
146. pall: mantle.   149. call: caul, headdress.

Such is the face of falshood: such the sight
Of fowle Duessa, when her borrowed light
Is laid away, and counterfesaunce° knowne."
Thus when they had the witch disrobèd quight,
And all her filthy feature° open showne,   161
They let her goe at will, and wander waies un-
   knowne.

50

Shee, flying fast from heavens hated face,
And from the world that her discovered wide,
Fled to the wastfull wildernesse apace,
From living eies her open shame to hide,
And lurkt in rocks and caves, long unespide.
But that faire crew of knights, and Una faire,
Did in that castle afterwards abide,
To rest them selves, and weary powres repaire;
Where store they fownd of al that dainty was and
   rare.   171

SELECTION VIII

The Redcrosse Knight is now free and reunited to
Una, but the effects of his long imprisonment remain.
It is therefore inevitable that he should soon meet the
deadliest of sins, Despair (the death wish). The deli-
ciously seductive quality in the closing lines of stanza
40 means, of course, not that Spenser agrees with Despair but that he regards him as an infinitely plausible
enemy (compare Selection X). I omit the rest of Book
I for lack of space. The Redcrosse Knight, after a spiritual re-education in the House of Holinesse, kills the
dragon and is betrothed to Una.

21

So as they traveild, lo! they gan espy
An armèd knight towards them gallop fast,
That seemèd from some fearèd foe to fly,
Or other griesly thing that him aghast.°
Still as he fledd his eye was backward cast,
As if his feare still followed him behynd:
Als° flew his steed as he his bandes had brast,°
And with his wingèd heeles did tread the wynd,
As he had beene a fole of Pegasus his kynd.°

22

Nigh as he drew, they might perceive his head   10
To bee unarmd, and curld uncombèd heares
Upstaring stiffe, dismaid with uncouth dread:
Nor drop of blood in all his face appeares,

Nor life in limbe; and, to increase his feares,
In fowle reproch of knighthoodes fayre degree,
About his neck an hempen rope he weares,
That with his glistring armes does ill agree;
But he of rope or armes has now no memoree.

23

The Redcrosse knight toward him crossèd fast,
To weet what mister wight° was so dismayd.   20
There him he findes all sencelesse and aghast,
That of him selfe he seemd to be afrayd;
Whom hardly he from flying forward stayd,
Till he these wordes to him deliver might:
"Sir knight, aread° who hath ye thus arayd,
And eke from whom make ye this hasty flight?
For never knight I saw in such misseeming plight."

24

He answered nought at all; but adding new
Feare to his first amazement, staring wyde
With stony eyes and hartlesse hollow hew,   30
Astonisht stood, as one that had aspyde
Infernall furies with their chaines untyde.
Him yett againe, and yett againe, bespake
The gentle knight; who nought to him replyde;
But, trembling every joynt, did inly quake,
And foltring tongue, at last, these words seemd
   forth to shake;

25

"For Gods deare love, Sir knight, doe me not
   stay;°
For loe! he comes, he comes fast after mee."
Eft° looking back would faine have runne away;
But he him forst to stay, and tellen free   40
The secrete cause of his perplexitie:
Yet nathèmore° by his bold hartie speach
Could his blood-frosen hart emboldened bee,
But through his boldnes rather feare did reach;
Yett, forst, at last he made through silence suddein
   breach.

27

"I lately chaunst (Would I had never chaunst!)
With a fayre knight to keepen companee,
Sir Terwin hight, that well himselfe advaunst
In all affayres, and was both bold and free;°
But not so happy as mote happy bee: 50
He lov'd, as was his lot, a Lady gent°
That him againe lov'd in the least degree;
For she was proud, and of too high intent,
And joyd to see her lover languish and lament:

28

"From whom retourning sad and comfortlesse,
As on the way together we did fare,
We met that villen, (God from him me blesse!°)
That cursèd wight, from whom I scapt whyleare,°
A man of hell that calls himselfe Despayre:
Who first us greets, and after fayre areedes°   60
Of tydinges straunge, and of adventures rare:
So creeping close, as Snake in hidden weedes,
Inquireth of our states, and of our knightly deedes.

29

"Which when he knew, and felt our feeble harts
Embost° with bale,° and bitter byting griefe,
Which love had launchèd° with his deadly darts,
With wounding words, and termes of foule re-
      priefe,
He pluckt from us all hope of dew reliefe,
That earst us held in love of lingring life;
Then hopelesse, hartlesse, gan the cunning thiefe
Perswade us dye, to stint all further strife: 71
To me he lent this rope, to him a rusty knife.

30

"With which sad instrument of hasty death,
That wofull lover, loathing lenger° light,
A wyde way made to let forth living breath:
But I, more fearefull or more lucky wight,
Dismayd with that deformèd dismall sight,
Fledd fast away, halfe dead with dying feare;
Ne yet assur'd of life by you, Sir knight,
Whose like infirmity like chaunce may beare;   80
But God you never let his charmèd speaches
      heare!"

32

"Certès,"° (sayd he) "hence shall I never rest,
Till I that treachours art have heard and tryde;
And you, Sir knight, whose name mote I request,
Of grace do me unto his cabin guyde."
"I, that hight° Trevisan," (quoth he) "will ryde
Against my liking backe to doe you grace:
But nor for gold nor glee° will I abyde
By you, when ye arrive in that same place;
For lever° had I die then see his deadly face."   90

33

Ere long they come where that same wicked wight
His dwelling has, low in an hollow cave,
Far underneath a craggy cliff ypight,°
Darke, dolefull, dreary, like a greedy grave,

That still for carrion carcases doth crave:
On top whereof ay dwelt the ghastly Owle,
Shrieking his balefull note, which ever drave°
Far from that haunt all other chearefull fowle;°
And all about it wandring ghostes did wayle and
      howle.

34

And all about old stockes and stubs of trees,   100
Whereon nor fruit nor leafe was ever seene,
Did hang upon the ragged rocky knees;
On which had many wretches hangèd beene,
Whose carcases were scattred on the greene,
And throwne about the cliffs. Arrivèd there,
That bare-head knight, for dread and dolefull
      teene,°
Would faine have fled, ne durst approchen neare;
But th' other forst him staye, and comforted in
      feare.

35

That darkesome cave they enter, where they find
That cursèd man, low sitting on the ground,   110
Musing full sadly in his sullein mind:
His griesie° lockes, long growèn and unbound,
Disordred hong about his shoulders round,
And hid his face, through which his hollow eyne°
Lookt deadly dull, and starèd as astound;°
His raw-bone cheekes, through penurie and pine,
Were shronke into his jawes, as° he did never
      dyne.

36

His garment, nought but many raggèd clouts,
With thornes together pind and patchèd was,
The which his naked sides he wrapt abouts;   120
And him beside there lay upon the gras
A dreary corse, whose life away did pas,
All wallowd in his own yet luke-warme blood,
That from his wound yet wellèd fresh, alas!
In which a rusty knife fast fixèd stood,
And made an open passage for the gushing flood.

37

Which piteous spectacle, approving trew
The wofull tale that Trevisan had told,
Whenas the gentle Redcrosse knight did vew,
With firie zeale he burnt in courage bold   130
Him to avenge before his blood were cold,
And to the villein sayd; "Thou damnèd wight,
The authour of this fact° we here behold,
What justice can but judge against thee right,
With thine owne blood to price his blood, here shed
      in sight?"

---

57. **blesse:** guard by this blessing.   58. **whyleare:** of late, just
now.   60. **areedes:** talks.   65. **Embost:** driven to bay, exhausted.   **bale:** woe.   66. **launched:** lanced.   74. **lenger:**
longer.   82. **Certes:** certainly.   86. **hight:** am called.   88. **glee:**
entertainment, play, hence perhaps here flattering persuasion.
90. **lever:** rather.   93. **ypight:** placed.

97. **drave:** drove.   98. **fowle:** birds.   106. **teene:** anguish.
112. **griesie:** greasy.   114. **eyne:** eyes.   115. **astound:** astonished.   117. **as:** as if.   133. **fact:** deed.

38

"What franticke fit," (quoth he) "hath thus dis-
    traught
Thee, foolish man, so rash a doome to give?
What justice ever other judgement taught,
But he should dye who merites not to live?
None els to death this man despayring drive   140
But his owne guiltie mind, deserving death.
Is then° unjust to each his dew° to give?
Or let him dye, that loatheth living breath,
Or let him die at ease, that liveth here uneath?°

39

"Who travailes by the wearie wandring way,
To come unto his wishèd home in haste,
And meetes a flood that doth his passage stay,
Is not great grace to helpe him over past,
Or free his feet that in the myre sticke fast?
Most envious man, that grieves at neighbours good;
And fond,° that joyest in the woe thou hast!   151
Why wilt not let him passe, that long hath stood
Upon the bancke, yet wilt thy selfe not pas the
    flood?

40

"He there does now enjoy eternall rest
And happy ease, which thou doest want and crave,
And further from it daily wanderest:
What if some little payne the passage have,
That makes frayle flesh to feare the bitter wave,
Is not short payne well borne, that bringes long
    ease,
And layes the soul to sleepe in quiet grave?   160
Sleepe after toyle, port after stormie seas,
Ease after warre, death after life, does greatly
    please.

45

"Thou, wretched man, of death hast greatest need,
If in true ballaunce thou wilt weigh thy state;
For never knight, that darèd warlike deed,
More luckless dissaventures did amate:°
Witnes the dungeon deepe, wherein of late
Thy life shutt up for death so oft did call;   168
And though good lucke prolongèd hath thy date,
Yet death then would the like mishaps forestall,
Into the which hereafter thou maist happen fall.

46

"Why then doest thou, O man of sin! desire
To draw thy dayes forth to their last degree?
Is not the measure of thy sinfull hire°
High heapèd up with huge iniquitee,

Against the day of wrath to burden thee?
Is not enough, that to this Lady mild
Thou falsèd hast thy faith with perjuree,
And sold thy selfe to serve Duessa vild,°   179
With whom in al abuse thou hast thy selfe defild?"

48

The knight was much enmovèd with his speach,
That as a swords poynt through his hart did perse,
And in his conscience made a secrete breach,
Well knowing trew all that he did reherse,
And to his fresh remembraunce did reverse°
The ugly vew of his deformèd crimes;
That all his manly powres it did disperse,
As he were charmèd with inchaunted rimes;
That oftentimes he quakt, and fainted oftentimes.

49

In which amazement when the Miscreaunt   190
Perceivèd him to waver, weake and fraile,
Whiles trembling horror did his conscience daunt,
And hellish anguish did his soule assaile;
To drive him to despaire, and quite to quaile,
Hee shewd him, painted in a table° plaine,
The damnèd ghosts that doe in torments waile,
And thousand feends that doe them endlesse paine
With fire and brimstone, which for ever shall re-
    maine.

50

The sight whereof so throughly him dismaid,
That nought but death before his eies he saw,   200
And ever burning wrath before him laid,
By righteous sentence of th' Almighties law.
Then gan the villein him to overcraw,°
And brought unto him swords, ropes, poison, fire,
And all that might him to perdition draw;
And bad him choose what death he would desire;
For death was dew to him that had provokt Gods
    ire.

51

But, whenas none of them he saw him take,
He to him raught° a dagger sharpe and keene,
And gave it him in hand: his hand did quake   210
And tremble like a leafe of Aspin greene,
And troubled blood through his pale face was seene
To come and goe with tidings from the heart,
As it a ronning messenger had beene.
At last, resolv'd to work his finall smart,
He lifted up his hand, that backe againe did start.

52

Which whenas Una saw, through every vaine
The crudled° cold ran to her well of life,

---

142. is then: is it then?   dew: due.   144. uneath: uneasily.
151. fond: foolish.   166. amate: cast down, overwhelm.
174. thy . . . hire: the wages of thy sin.

179. vild: vile.   185. reverse: return.   195. table: picture.
203. overcraw: crow over (like a winning cock).   209. raught:
reached, handed.   218. crudled: curdled.

As in a swowne: but, soone reliv'd againe,
Out of his hand she snatcht the cursèd knife,   220
And threw it to the ground, enragèd rife,°
And to him said; " Fie, fie, faint hearted Knight!
What meanest thou by this reprochfull strife?
Is this the battaile which thou vauntst to fight
With that fire-mouthèd Dragon, horrible and
    bright?

53

" Come; come away, fraile, feeble, fleshly wight,
Ne let vaine words bewitch thy manly hart,
Ne divelish thoughts dismay thy constant spright:
In heavenly mercies hast thou not a part?   229
Why shouldst thou then despeire, that chosen art?
Where justice growes, there grows eke greater
    grace,
The which doth quench the brond of hellish smart,
And that accurst hand-writing doth deface.°
Arise, sir Knight; arise, and leave this cursèd place."

54

So up he rose, and thence amounted streight.
Which when the carle° beheld, and saw his guest
Would safe depart, for all his subtile sleight,
He chose an halter from among the rest,
And with it hong him selfe, unbid, unblest.   239
But death he could not worke himselfe thereby;
For thousand times he so him selfe had drest,°
Yet nathèlesse it could not doe him die,
Till he should die his last, that is, eternally.

SELECTION IX

We are now in Book II with Guyon the Knight of
Temperance (Moderation, Self-Control). This is a
more humdrum virtue than Holinesse; hence Guyon is
accompanied not by a radiant figure like Una but by a
" Palmer . . . a sage and sober syre." The Selection
opens at the moment when one Atin (Mischief-Maker)
has just seen Guyon defeat the fiery and raging paynim
Pyrochles and runs with the news to his brother Cymochles. He finds him in the Bower of Acrasia (Excess,
Debauchery). As Guyon's final exploit is going to be
the destruction of that Bower, this episode serves as the
first hint of a theme which will later be taken up by
the whole orchestra. Notice that we are shown no love-
making, even no straightforward animalism, in the
Bower — only " *still* waves of deepe delight," immobile
titillation.

221. enraged rife: abundantly angry.   233. And . . . deface:
The explanation, which can hardly be given in a note, will be
found in the Bible. "Blotting out the handwriting of ordinances
that was against us, . . . and nailing it to his cross" (Col. 2:14).
236. carle: another form of *churl*, peasant, hence simply "man"
with some implication of disparagement. American "guy" or
English "fellow" might be roughly equivalent.   241. drest:
treated.

28

There Atin fownd Cymochles sojourning,
To serve his Lemans love: for he by kynd°
Was given all to lust and loose living,
When ever his fiers handes he free mote fynd:
And now he has pourd out his ydle mynd
In daintie délices, and lavish joyes,
Having his warlike weapons cast behynd,
And flowes in pleasures and vaine pleasing toyes,°
Mingled emongst loose Ladies and lascivious boyes.

29

And over him art, stryving to compayre   10
With nature, did an Arber greene dispred,
Framèd of wanton Yvie, flouring fayre,
Through which the fragrant Eglantine did spred
His prickling armes, entrayld with roses red,
Which daintie odours round about them threw:
And all within with flowres was garnishèd,
That, when myld Zephyrus° emongst them blew,
Did breath out bounteous smels, and painted colors
    shew.

30

And fast beside there trickled softly downe
A gentle streame, whose murmuring wave did play
Emongst the pumy° stones, and made a sowne,   21
To lull him soft asleepe that by it lay:
The wearie Traveiler, wandring that way,
Therein did often quench his thristy° heat,
And then by it his wearie limbes display,
Whiles creeping slomber made him to forget
His former payne, and wypt° away his toilsom
    sweat.

31

And on the other syde a pleasaunt grove
Was shott up high, full of the stately tree°
That dedicated is t' Olympick Jove,   30
And to his sonne Alcidès,° whenas hee
In Nemus gaynèd goodly victoree:
Therein the mery birdes of every sorte
Chaunted alowd their chearefull harmonee,
And made emongst them selves a sweete consórt,°
That quickned the dull spright with musicall com-
    fórt.

32

There he him found all carelessly displaid,
In secrete shadow from the sunny ray,

Sel. IX: from *FQ*, II. v.   2. kynd: nature.   8. toyes: frivolities.
17. Zephyrus: the west wind.   21. pumy: pumice (porous obsid-
ian).   24. thristy: thirsty.   27. wypt: wiped.   29. the . . .
tree: the oak.   31. Alcides: Hercules, though really the son of
Jove, was so called because his supposed father Amphitryon was
the son of Alceus. The first of his famous Twelve Labors was the
killing of a lion in the Vale of Nemea. Spenser's "Nemus" is a
mistake.   35. consort: partnership, hence partnership in music,
harmony.

On a sweet bed of lillies softly laid,
Amidst a flock of Damzelles fresh and gay,   40
That rownd about him dissolute did play
Their wanton follies and light meriments:
Every of which did loosely disaray
Her upper partes of meet habiliments,
And shewd them naked, deckt with many ornaments.

33

And every of them strove with most delights
Him to aggrate,° and greatest pleasures shew:
Some framd faire lookes, glancing like evening
   lights;
Others sweet wordes, dropping like honny dew;
Some bathèd kisses, and did soft embrew°   50
The sugred licour through his melting lips:
One boastes her beautie, and does yield to vew
Her dainty limbes above her tender hips;
Another her out boastes, and all for tryall strips.

34

He, like an Adder lurking in the weedes,
His wandring thought in deepe desire does steepe,
And his frayle eye with spoyle of beauty feedes:
Sometimes he falsely faines himselfe to sleepe,
Whiles through their lids his wanton eies do peepe
To steale a snatch of amorous conceipt,°   60
Whereby close fire into his heart does creepe:
So he them deceives, deceivd in his deceipt,
Made dronke with drugs of deare voluptuous receipt.

35

Atin, arriving there, when him he spyde
Thus in still waves of deepe delight to wade
Fiercely approaching to him lowdly cryde,
"Cymochles; oh! no, but Cymochles shade,
In which that manly person late did fade.
What is become of great Acratès° sonne?
Or where hath he hong up his mortall blade,   70
That hath so many haughty conquests wonne?
Is all his force forlorne, and all his glory donne?"

37

Suddeinly out of his delightfull dreame
The man awoke, and would have questiond more;
But he would not endure that wofull theame
For to dilate at large, but urgèd sore,
With percing wordes and pittifull implore,°
Him hasty to arise. As one affright
With hellish feends, or Furies mad uprore,
He then uprose, inflamd with fell despight,   80
And callèd for his armes, for he would algates°
   fight.

47. aggrate: please.   50. embrew: moisten.   60. conceipt:
thought.   69. Acrates: For the family history, see II.iv.41.
77. implore: entreaty.   81. algates: by all means, anyhow.

SELECTION X

We continue the story of Cymochles, who is no more
effective as an avenger than as a lover. The lady by
whom he is sidetracked in stanza 3 is Phaedria. Spenser
describes her elsewhere as "immodest Mirth," but in
her actual behavior the emphasis is less on immodesty
than on mere idleness, frivolity, the relaxed will. The
seduction in stanzas 15 and 16 should be compared with
Despair's speech in Selection VIII. There we had the
death wish in the key of melancholy; here, the death
wish in the key of the voluptuous.

2

Whom° bold Cymochles traveiling to finde,
With cruell purpose bent to wreake on him
The wrath which Atin kindled in his mind,
Came to a river, by whose utmost brim
Wayting to passe, he saw whereas did swim
Along the shore, as swift as glaunce of eye,
A litle Gondelay,° bedeckèd trim
With boughes and arbours woven cunningly,
That like a litle forrest seemèd outwardly.

3

And therein sate a Lady fresh and fayre,   10
Making sweet solace to herselfe alone:
Sometimes she song as lowd as larke in ayre,
Sometimes she laught, that nigh her breth was
   gone;
Yet was there not with her else any one,
That to her might move cause of meriment:
Matter of merth enough, though there were none,
She could devise; and thousand waies invent
To feede her foolish humour and vaine jolliment.

4

Which when far off Cymochles heard and saw,
He lowdly cald to such as were abord   20
The little barke unto the shore to draw,
And him to ferry over that deepe ford.
The merry mariner unto his word
Soone hearkned, and her painted bote streightway
Turnd to the shore, where that same warlike Lord
She in receiv'd; but Atin by no way
She would admit, albe° the knight her much did
   pray.

5

Eftsoones her shallow ship away did slide,
More swift than swallow sheres the liquid skye,
Withouten oare or Pilot it to guide,   30
Or wingèd canvas with the wind to fly:

Sel. X: from FQ, II. vi.   1. Whom: i.e., Guyon.   7. Gondelay:
gondola, originally a light boat used on the Venetian canals,
hence a light boat in general.   27. albe: though.

Onely she turnd a pin, and by and by
It cut away upon the yielding wave,
Ne carèd she her course for to apply;
For it was taught the way which she would have,
And both from rocks and flats it selfe could wisely
    save.

6

And all the way the wanton Damsell found
New merth her passenger to entertaine;
For she in pleasant purpose° did abound,
And greatly joyèd merry tales to faine,   40
Of which a store-house did with her remaine:
Yet seemèd, nothing well they her became;
For all her wordes she drownd with laughter
    vaine,
And wanted grace in utt'ring of the same,
That turnèd all her pleasaunce to a scoffing game.

7

And other whiles vaine toyes she would devize,
As her fantasticke wit did most delight:
Sometimes her head she fondly would aguize°
With gaudy girlonds, or fresh flowrets dight
About her necke, or rings of rushes plight: 50
Sometimes, to do him laugh, she would assay
To laugh at shaking of the leavès light
Or to behold the water worke and play
About her little frigot, therein making way.

11

Whiles thus she talkèd, and whiles thus she toyd,
They were far past the passage which he spake,
And come unto an Island waste and voyd,
That floted in the midst of that great lake;
There her small Gondelay her port did make,
And that gay payre, issewing on the shore,   60
Disburdned her.° Their way they forward take
Into the land that lay them faire before,
Whose pleasaunce she him shewd, and plentifull
    great store.

12

It was a chosen plott of fertile land,
Emongst wide waves sett, like a litle nest,
As if it had by Natures cunning hand
Bene choycely pickèd out from all the rest,
And laid forth for ensample of the best:
No daintie flowre or herbe that growes on grownd,
No arborett with painted blossomes drest   70
And smelling sweete, but there it might be
    fownd
To bud out faire, and throwe her sweete smels al
    arownd.

13

No tree whose braunches did not bravely spring;
No braunch whereon a fine bird did not sitt;
No bird but did her shrill notes sweetely sing;
No song but did containe a lovely ditt.°
Trees, braunches, birds, and songs, were framèd fitt
For to allure fraile mind to carelesse ease:
Carelesse the man soone woxe, and his weake witt
Was overcome of thing that did him please;   80
So pleasèd did his wrathfull purpose faire appease.

14

Thus when shee had his eyes and sences fed
With false delights, and fild with pleasures vayn,
Into a shady dale she soft him led,
And layd him downe upon a grassy playn;
And her sweete selfe without dread or disdayn
She sett beside, laying his head disarmd
In her loose lap, it softly to sustayn,
Where soone he slumbred fearing not be harmd:
The whiles with a love lay she thus him sweetly
    charmd.   90

15

"Behold, O man! that toilesome paines doest take,
The flowrs, the fields, and all that pleasaunt growes,
How they them selves doe thine ensample make,
Whiles nothing-envious nature them forth throwes
Out of her fruitfull lap; how no man knowes,
They spring, they bud, they blossome fresh and
    faire,
And decke the world with their rich pompous
    showes;
Yet no man for them taketh paines or care,
Yet no man to them can his carefull paines com-
    pare.

16

"The lilly, Lady of the flowring field,   100
The flowre-deluce, her lovely Paramoure,
Bid thee to them thy fruitlesse labors yield,
And soone leave off this toylsome weary stoure:°
Loe, loe! how brave she decks her bounteous boure,
With silkin curtens and gold coverletts,
Therein to shrowd her sumptuous Belamoure;°
Yet nether spinnes nor cardes,° ne cares nor fretts,
But to her mother Nature all her care she letts.

17

"Why then doest thou, O man! that of them all
Art Lord, and eke of nature Soveraine,   110
Wilfully make thyselfe a wretched thrall,
And waste thy joyous howres in needlesse paine,
Seeking for daunger and adventures vaine?

---

39. purpose: speech.   48. aguize: array.   61. her: i.e., the
boat.

76. ditt: ditty.   103. stoure: conflict.   106. Belamoure: lover.
107. cardes: prepares for spinning with the toothed instrument
called a "card."

What bootes° it al to have, and nothing use?
Who shall him rew that swimming in the maine
Will die for thrist,° and water doth refuse?
Refuse such fruitlesse toile, and present pleasures
    chuse."

SELECTION XI

Guyon also had unwarily taken a passage by Phaedria's skiff and had thus been parted from his Palmer
(whom Phaedria refused to take aboard). He now
meets Mammon (financial greed). In the description of
his gnomelike fiend's underground home, Spenser mingles material from Scripture, classical mythology, and
folklore. It illustrates the sense in which he can properly be called "dreamlike": the poetry has not the
vagueness of daydream but the vividness and irresistible concreteness of things seen in a dream proper. Note
especially stanzas 3, 26, 35–37, 57.

3

At last he came unto a gloomy glade,
Cover'd with boughes and shrubs from heavens
    light,
Whereas he sitting found in secret shade
An uncouth, salvage,° and uncivile wight,
Of griesly hew and fowle ill favour'd sight;
His face with smoke was tand,° and eies were
    bleard,
His head and beard with sout were ill bedight,
His cole-blacke hands did seeme to have ben seard
In smythes fire-spitting forge, and nayles like
    clawes appeard.

4

His yron cote, all overgrowne with rust,   10
Was underneath envelopèd with gold;
Whose glistring glosse, darkned with filthy dust,
Well yet appearèd to have beene of old
A worke of rich entayle° and curious mould,
Woven with antickes and wyld ymagery;
And in his lap a masse of coyne he told,
And turnèd upside downe, to feede his eye
And covetous desire with his huge threasury.

5

And round about him lay on every side
Great heapes of gold that never could be spent;
Of which some were rude owre,° not purifide 21
Of Mulcibers° devouring element;
Some others were new driven, and distent

Into great Ingowes° and to wedges square;
Some in round plates withouten moniment;°
But most were stampt, and in their metal bare
The antique shapes of kinges and kesars straunge
    and rare.

6

Soone as he Guyon saw, in great affright
And haste he rose for to remove aside   29
Those pretious hils from straungers envious sight,
And downe them pourèd through an hole full
    wide
Into the hollow earth, them there to hide.
But Guyon, lightly to him leaping, stayd
His hand that trembled as one terrifyde;
And though himselfe were at the sight dismayd,
Yet him perforce restraynd, and to him doubtfull
    sayd:

7

"What art thou, man, (if man at all thou art)
That here in desert hast thine habitaunce,
And these rich hils of welth doest hide apart
From the worldes eye, and from her right
    usaúnce?"°   40
Thereat, with staring eyes fixèd askaunce,
In great disdaine he answerd: "Hardy Elfe,
That darest view my direfull countenaunce,
I read thee rash and heedelesse of thy selfe,
To trouble my still seate, and heapes of pretious
    pelfe.

8

"God of the world and worldlings I me call,
Great Mammon, greatest god below the skye,
That of my plenty poure out unto all,
And unto none my graces do envýe:
Riches, renowme, and principality,   50
Honour, estate, and all this worldès good,
For which men swinck° and sweat incessantly,
Fro me do flow into an ample flood,
And in the hollow earth have their eternal brood.

20

"What secret place" (quoth he) "can safely hold
So huge a masse, and hide from heavens eie?
Or where hast thou thy wonne,° that so much gold
Thou canst preserve from wrong and robbery?"
"Come thou," (quoth he) "and see." So by and by
Through that thick covert he him led, and fownd
A darkesome way, which no man could descry, 61
That deep descended through the hollow grownd,
And was with dread and horror compassèd
    arownd.

---

114. bootes: avails.   116. thrist: thirst.   Sel. XI: from *FQ*,
II. vii. 4. salvage: savage.   6. tand: tanned.   14. entayle:
cut, fashion.   21. owre: ore.   22. Mulcibers: Vulcan's. Cf.
Milton, *PL*, I. 740, below.

24. Ingowes: ingots.   25. moniment: device; a token.
40. usaunce: use.   52. swinck: toil.   57. wonne: dwelling.

21

At length they came into a larger space,
That stretcht itselfe into an ample playne;
Through which a beaten broad high way did trace,
That streight did lead to Plutoes griesly rayne.°
By that wayes side there sate internall Payne,
And fast beside him sat tumultuous Strife:
The one in hand an yron whip did strayne,   70
The other brandishèd a bloody knife;
And both did gnash their teeth, and both did threten
     life.

23

And over them sad horror with grim hew
Did alwaies sore, beating his yron wings;
And after him Owles and Night-ravens flew,
The hatefull messengers of heavy things,
Of death and dolor telling sad tidíngs;
Whiles sad Celeno,° sitting on a clifte,
A song of bale and bitter sorrow sings,
That hart of flint asonder could have rifte;   80
Which having ended after him she flyeth swifte.

24

All these before the gates of Pluto lay,
By whom they passing spake unto them nought;
But th' Elfin knight with wonder all the way
Did feed his eyes, and fild his inner thought.
At last him to a litle dore he brought,
That to the gate of Hell, which gapèd wide,
Was next adjoyning, ne them parted ought:
Betwixt them both was but a litle stride,
That did the house of Richesse from hel-mouth
     divide.   90

25

Before the dore sat selfe-consuming Care,
Day and night keeping wary watch and ward,
For feare least Force or Fraud should unaware
Breake in, and spoile the treasure there in gard:
Ne would he suffer Sleepe once thither-ward
Approch, albe° his drowsy den were next;
For next to death is Sleepe to be compard;
Therefore his house is unto his annext:
Here Sleep, ther Richesse, and Hel-gate them both
     betwext.

26

So soon as Mammon there arrivd, the dore   100
To him did open and affoorded way:
Him followed eke Sir Guyon evermore,
Ne darkenesse him, ne daunger might dismay.
Soone as he entred was, the dore streight way
Did shutt, and from behind it forth there lept
An ugly feend, more fowle than dismall day,

The which with monstrous stalke behind him
     stept,
And ever as he went dew watch upon him kept.

27

Well hopèd hee, ere long that hardy guest,
If ever covetous hand, or lustfull eye,   110
Or lips he layd on thing that likte° him best,
Or ever sleepe his eie-strings° did untye,
Should be his pray. And therefore still on hye
He over him did hold his cruell clawes,
Threatning with greedy gripe to doe him dye,
And rend in peeces with his ravenous pawes,
If ever he transgrest the fatall Stygian lawes.

28

That houses forme within was rude and strong,
Lyke an huge cave hewne out of rocky clifte,
From whose rough vaut° the ragged breaches°
     hong
Embost with massy gold of glorious guifte,   121
And with rich metall loaded every rifte,
That heavy ruine they did seeme to threatt;
And over them Arachnè° high did lifte
Her cunning web, and spred her subtile nett,
Enwrappèd in fowle smoke and clouds more black
     than Jett.

29

Both roofe, and floore, and walls, were all of gold,
But overgrowne with dust and old decay,
And hid in darkenes, that none could behold
The hew thereof; for vew of cherefull day   130
Did never in that house it selfe display,
But a faint shadow of uncertein light:
Such as a lamp, whose life does fade away,
Or as the Moone, cloathèd with clowdy night,
Does show to him that walkes in feare and sad
     affright.

31

They forward passe; ne Guyon yet spoke word,
Till that they came unto an yron dore,
Which to them opened of his° owne accord,
And shewd of richesse such exceeding store,
As eie of man did never see before,   140
Ne ever could within one place be fownd,
Though all the wealth which is, or was of yore,
Could gathered be through all the world arownd,
And that above were added to that under grownd.

32

The charge thereof unto a covetous Spright
Commaunded was, who thereby did attend,

---

67. **griesly rayne:** grisly realm.   78. **Celeno:** one of the Harpies.
96. **albe:** though.   111. **likte:** liked, pleased.   112. **eie-strings:** tendons of the eye.
120. **vaut:** vault.   **breaches:** fissures.   124. **Arachne:** the
spider.   138. **his:** its.

And warily awaited day and night,
From other covetous feends it to defend,
Who it to rob and ransacke did intend. 149
Then Mammon, turning to that warriour, said:
" Loe! here the worldès blis: loe! here the end,
To which al men doe ayme, rich to be made:
Such grace now to be happy is before thee laid."

33

" Certès,"° (sayd he) " I n'ill° thine offred grace,
Ne to be made so happy doe intend:
Another blis before mine eyes I place,
Another happines, another end.
To them that list these base regardes I lend:
But I in armes, and in atchievements brave,
Do rather choose my flitting houres to spend, 160
And to be Lord of those that riches have,
Then them to have my selfe, and be their servile
sclave."

34

Thereat the feend his gnashing teeth did grate,
And griev'd so long to lacke his greedie pray;
For well he weenèd that so glorious bayte
Would tempt his guest to take thereof assay;°
Had he so doen, he had him snatcht away,
More light then Culver° in the Faulcons fist.
Eternall God thee save from such decay!
But, whenas Mammon saw his purpose mist, 170
Him to entrap unwares another way he wist.

35

Thence forward he him ledd, and shortly brought
Unto another rowme, whose dore forthright
To him did open, as° it had been taught.
Therein an hundred raunges weren pight,
And hundred fournaces all burning bright:
By every fournace many feendes did byde,
Deformèd creatures, horrible in sight;
And every feend his busie paines applyde
To melt the golden metall, ready to be tryde. 180

36

One with great bellowes gathered filling ayre,
And with forst wind the fewell did inflame;
Another did the dying bronds repayre
With yron tongs, and sprinckled ofte the same
With liquid waves, fiers Vulcans rage to tame,
Who, maystring° them, renewd his former heat:
Some scumd the drosse that from the metall came;
Some stird the molten owre with ladles great;
And every one did swincke,° and every one did
sweat.

37

But, when an earthly wight they present saw 190
Glistring in armes and battailous aray,
From their whot° work they did themselves with-
draw
To wonder at the sight; for till that day
They never creature saw that cam that way:
Their staring eyes sparckling with fervent fyre
And ugly shapes did nigh the man dismay,
That, were it not for shame, he would retyre;
Till that him thus bespake their soveraine Lord and
syre:

38

" Behold, thou Faeries sonne, with mortall eye,
That living eye before did never see. 200
The thing, that thou didst crave so earnestly,
To weet° whence all the wealth late shewd by mee
Proceeded, lo! now is reveald to thee.
Here is the fountaine of the worldès good:
Now, therefore, if thou wilt enrichèd bee,
Avise thee well, and chaunge thy wilfull mood,
Least thou perhaps hereafter wish, and be with-
stood."

39

" Suffise it then, thou Money God," (quoth hee)
" That all thine ydle offers I refuse.
All that I need I have: what needeth mee 210
To covet more than I have cause to use?
With such vaine shewes thy worldlinges vyle abuse;
But give me leave to follow mine emprise." °
Mammon was much displeasd, yet no'te he chuse°
But beare the rigour of his bold mesprise;°
And thence him forward ledd him further to entise.

40

He brought him, through a darksom narrow strayt,
To a broad gate all built of beaten gold:
The gate was open; but therein did wayt
A sturdie villein, stryding stiffe and bold, 220
As if the highest God defy he would:
In his right hand an yron club he held,
But he himselfe was all of golden mould,
Yet had both life and sence, and well could weld
That cursèd weapon, when his cruell foes he queld.

42

Soone as those glitterand° armes he did espye,
That with their brightnesse made that darknes
light,
His harmefull club he gan to hurtle hye,
And threaten batteill to the Faery knight;

---

154. Certes: certainly. n'ill: do not desire. 166. take . . .
assay: to make trial thereof. 168. Culver: dove. 174. as:
as if. 186. maystring: mastering. 189. swincke: toil.

192. whot: hot. 202. weet: know. 213. emprise: enterprise.
214. n'ote he chuse: he had no choice. 215. mesprise: contempt. 226. glitterand: glittering.

Who likewise gan himselfe to batteill dight,   230
Till Mammon did his hasty hand withhold,
And counseld him abstaine from perilous fight;
For nothing might abash the villein bold,
Ne mortall steele emperce his miscreated mould.

43

So having him with reason pacifyde
And that fiers Carle commaunding to forbeare,
He brought him in. The rowme was large and
    wyde,
As it some Gyeld° or solemne Temple weare.
Many great golden pillours did upbeare
The massy roofe, and riches huge sustayne;   240
And every pillour deckèd was full deare
With crownes, and Diademes, and titles vaine,
Which mortall Princes wore whiles they on earth
    did rayne.

44

A route° of people there assembled were,
Of every sort and nation under skye,
Which with great uprore preacèd° to draw nere
To th' upper part, where was advauncèd hye
A stately siege° of soveraine majestye;
And thereon satt a woman, gorgeous gay
And richly cladd in robes of royaltye,   250
That never earthly Prince in such array
His glory did enhaunce, and pompous pryde dis-
    play.

46

There, as in glistring glory she did sitt,
She held a great gold chaine ylinckèd well,
Whose upper end to highest heven was knitt,
And lower part did reach to lowest Hell;
And all that preace° did rownd about her swell
To catchen hold of that long chaine, thereby
To climbe aloft, and others to excell:
That was Ambition, rash desire to sty,°   260
And every linck thereof a step of dignity.

47

Some thought to raise themselves to high degree
By riches and unrightèous reward;
Some by close shouldring; some by flatteree;
Others through friendes; others for base regard,°
And all by wrong waies for themselves prepard:
Those that were up themselves kept others low;
Those that were low themselves held others hard,°
Ne suffred them to ryse or greater grow;
But every one did strive his fellow downe to throw.

48

Which whenas Guyon saw, he gan inquire,   271
What meant that preace about that Ladies
    throne,
And what she was that did so high aspyre?
Him Mammon answerèd; " That goodly one,
Whom all that folke with such contention
Doe flock about, my deare, my daughter is:
Honour and dignitie from her alone
Derivèd are, and all this worldès blis,
For which ye men doe strive; few gett, but many
    mis:

49

" And fayre Philótimè° she rightly hight,   280
The fairest wight that wonneth° under skie,
But that this darksom neather world her light
Doth dim with horror and deformity;
Worthie of heven and hye felicitie,
From whence the gods have her for envy thrust:
But, sith thou hast found favour in mine eye,
Thy spouse I will her make, if that thou lust,
That she may thee advance for works and merits
    just."

50

" Gramercy, Mammon," (said the gentle knight)
" For so great grace and offred high estate;   290
But I, that am fraile flesh and earthly wight,
Unworthy match for such immortall mate
My selfe well wote,° and mine unequall fate:
And were I not, yet is my trouth yplight,
And love avowd to other Lady late,
That to remove the same I have no might:
To chaunge love causelesse is reproch to warlike
    knight."

51

Mammon emmovèd was with inward wrath;
Yet, forcing it to fayne,° him forth thence ledd,
Through griesly shadowes by a beaten path,   300
Into a gardin goodly garnishèd
With hearbs and fruits, whose kinds mote not be
    redd:
Not such as earth out of her fruitfull woomb
Throwes forth to men, sweet and well savorèd,
But direfull deadly black, both leafe and bloom,
Fitt to adorne the dead, and deck the drery toombe.

52

There mournfull Cypresse grew in greatest store,
And trees of bitter Gall, and Heben° sad;
Dead sleeping Poppy, and black Hellebore;

238. Gyeld: guild hall. Cf. Chaucer Prol. l. 370, above.
244. route: crowd. 246. preaced: pressed, crowded. 248. siege:
seat, throne. 260. sty: ascend. 265. for . . . regard: by vile
services. 268. held . . . hard: gave them as little freedom as
they could.

280. Philotime: ambition. 281. wonneth: dwells. 293. wote:
know. 299. forcing . . . fayne: forcing himself to dissimulate.
308. Heben: ebony.

Cold Coloquintida,° and Tetra° mad;   310
Mortall Samnitis,° and Cicuta° bad,
With which th' unjust Atheniens° made to dy
Wise Socrates; who, thereof quaffing glad,
Pourd out his life and last Philosophy
To the fayre Critias, his dearest Belamy!°

53

The Gardin of Prosérpina° this hight;
And in the midst thereof a silver seat,
With a thick Arber goodly over-dight,
In which she often usd from open heat
Her selfe to shroud, and pleasures to entreat: 320
Next thereunto did grow a goodly tree,
With braunches broad dispredd and body great,
Clothèd with leaves, that non the wood mote see,
And loaden all with fruit as thick as it might bee.

54

Their fruit were golden apples glistring bright,
That goodly was their glory to behold;
On earth like never grew, ne living wight
Like ever saw, but they from hence were sold;
For those which° Hercules, with conquest bold
Got from great Atlas daughters, hence began,   330
And planted there did bring forth fruit of gold;
And those with which th' Eubœan young man°
      wan°
Swift Atalanta, when through craft he her out ran.

56

The warlike Elfe much wondred at this tree,
So fayre and great that shadowed all the ground,
And his broad braunches, laden with rich fee,°
Did stretcht themselves without the utmost bound
Of this great gardin, compast with a mound;
Which over-hanging, they themselves did steepe
In a blacke flood, which flow'd about it round.
That is the river of Cocytus deepe,   341
In which full many soules do endlesse wayle and
      weepe.

57

Which to behold he clomb up to the bancke,
And looking downe saw many damnèd wightes
In those sad waves, which direfull deadly stancke,

310. Coloquintida: *Citrullus Colocynthis.*   Tetra: perhaps *taetrum solanum* (deadly nightshade).   311. Samnitis: perhaps *Juniperus Sabina.*   Cicuta: hemlock.   312–15. Atheniens . . . Critias: Spenser appears confused. For the real story of Socrates' last hours, read Plato's *Phaedo.*   315. Belamy: *bel ami,* fair friend.   316. Proserpina: See Sel. I, l. 103n.   329. those which: i.e., the apples of the Hesperides. The theft of these apples and killing the dragon which guarded them was one of the Labors of Hercules.   332. Euboean . . . man: Atalanta refused to marry anyone who could not beat her in a foot race. Milanion (or in some versions Hippomenes) brought some of the golden apples of the Hesperides and threw them down, one by one, during the race. Atalanta stooped to pick them up, and this delay cost her the race. See Morris's *Earthly Paradise.* wan: won.   336. fee: treasure.

Plongèd continually of cruell Sprightes,
That with their piteous cryes, and yelling
      shrightes,°
They made the further shore resounden wide.
Emongst the rest of those same ruefull sightes,
One cursèd creature he by chaunce espide,   350
That drenchèd lay full deepe under the Garden
      side.

58

Deepe was he drenchèd to the upmost chin,
Yet gapèd still as coveting to drinke
Of the cold liquor which he waded in;
And stretching forth his hand did often thinke
To reach the fruit which grew upon the brincke;
But both the fruit from hand, and flood from
      mouth,
Did fly abacke, and made him vainely swincke;
The whiles he sterv'd with hunger, and with
      drouth,
He daily dyde, yet never throughly dyen couth.°

61

He lookt a litle further, and espyde   361
Another wretch, whose carcas deepe was drent
Within the river, which the same did hyde;
But both his handes, most filthy feculent,°
Above the water were on high extent,°
And faynd to wash themselves incessantly,
Yet nothing cleaner were for such intent,
But rather fowler seemèd to the eye;
So lost his labour vaine and ydle industry.

62

The knight him calling askèd who he was?   370
Who, lifting up his head, him answered thus:
"I Pilate am, the falsest Judge, alas!
And most unjust; that, by unrightèous
And wicked doome, to Jewes despitèous
Delivered up the Lord of life to dye,
And did acquite a murdrer felonous;
The whiles my handes I washt in purity,
The whiles my soule was soyld with fowle iniquity."

63

Infinite moe tormented in like paine
He there beheld, too long here to be told: 380
Ne Mammon would there let him long remayne,
For terrour of the tortures manifold,
In which the damnèd soules he did behold,
But roughly him bespake: "Thou fearefull foole,
Why takest not of that same fruite of gold?
Ne sittest downe on that same silver stoole,
To rest thy weary person in the shadow coole?"

347. shrightes: shrieks.   360. couth: could.   364. feculent: defiled.   365. extent: extended.

64

All which he did to do him deadly fall
In frayle intemperaunce through sinfull bayt;
To which if he inclynèd had at all,   390
That dreadfull feend, which did behinde him wayt,
Would him have rent in thousand peeces strayt:
But he was wary wise in all his way,
And well perceivèd his deceiptfull sleight,
Ne suffred lust his safety to betray.
So goodly did beguile the Guyler of his pray.

65

And now he has so long remainèd theare,
That vitall powres gan wexe both weake and wan
For want of food and sleepe, which two upbeare,
Like mightie pillours, this frayle life of man,   400
That none without the same enduren can:
For now three dayes of men were full out-wrought,
Since he this hardy enterprize began:
Forthy great Mammon fayrely he besought
Into the world to guyde him backe, as he him
    brought.

SELECTION XII

Guyon, now once more accompanied by his Palmer,
arrives by boat at the Bower of Acrasia, surveys all its
lavishness of cold sensuality, and surprises Acrasia with
her latest captive. My selection breaks off at that point;
in what follows, Acrasia is bound "in chaines of adamant," the Bower destroyed, and the captive (still unwilling) rescued.

30

And now they nigh approchèd to the sted°
Whereas those Mermayds dwelt: it was a still
And calmy bay, on th' one side shelterèd
With the brode shadow of an hoarie hill;
On th'other side an high rocke tourèd° still,
That twixt them both a pleasaunt port they made,
And did like an halfe Theatre fulfill:
There those five sisters had continuall trade,°
And used to bath themselves in that deceiptfull
    shade.

32

So now to Guyon, as he passèd by,   10
Their pleasaunt tunes they sweetly thus applyde:
"O thou fayre sonne of gentle Faèry,
That art in mightie armes most magnifyde
Above all knights that ever batteill tryde,
O! turne thy rudder hitherward awhile
Here may thy storme-bett vessell safely ryde,
This is the Port of rest from troublous toyle,

The worldes sweet In° from paine and wearisome
    turmoyle."

33

With that the rolling sea, resounding soft,
In his big base them fitly answerèd;   20
And on the rocke the waves breaking aloft
A solemne Meane° unto them measurèd;
The whiles sweet Zephyrus° lowd whistelèd
His treble, a straunge kinde of harmony,
Which Guyons senses softly tickelèd,
That he the boteman bad row easily,
And let him heare some part of their rare melody.

42

Thence passing forth, they shortly doe arryve
Whereas the Bowre of Blisse was situate;
A place pickt out by choyce of best alyve,   30
That natures worke by art can imitate:
In which whatever in this worldly state
Is sweete and pleasing unto living sense,
Or that may dayntest fantasy aggrate,°
Was pourèd forth with plentifull dispence,
And made there to abound with lavish affluence.

50

Thus being entred, they behold arownd
A large and spacious plaine, on every side
Strowèd with pleasauns;° whose fayre grassy
    grownd
Mantled with greene, and goodly beautifide   40
With all the ornaments of Floraes pride,
Wherewith her mother Art, as halfe in scorne
Of niggard Nature, like a pompous bride
Did decke her, and too lavishly adorne,
When forth from virgin bowre she comes in th'
    early morne.

51

Therewith the Heavens always joviall
Lookte on them lovely, still in stedfast state,
Ne suffred storme nor frost on them to fall,
Their tender buds or leaves to violate;
Nor scorching heat, nor cold intemperate,   50
T' afflict the creatures which therein did dwell;
But the milde ayre with season moderate
Gently attempred, and disposd so well,
That still it breathèd forth sweet spirit and holesom
    smell:

52

More sweet and holesome then the pleasant hill
Of Rhodopè, on which the Nimphe° that bore

---

18. **In:** inn, resting place.   22. **Meane:** middle part (in the
musical sense).   23. **Zephyrus:** the west wind.   34. **aggrate:**
please.   39. **pleasauns:** delight.   56. **the Nimphe:** the nymph
Rhodope on whom Neptune begot the giant Athos.

Sel. XII: from *FQ*, II. xii.   1. **sted:** place.   5. **toured:** towered.
8. **trade:** way of life ("had . . . trade" equals "always lived").

A gyaunt babe herselfe for griefe did kill;
Or the Thessalian Tempè, where of yore
Fayre Daphne Phœbus hart with love did gore;
Or Ida, where the Gods lov'd to repayre,   60
When ever they their heavenly bowres forlore;
Or sweet Parnasse, the haunt of Muses fayre;
Or Eden selfe, if ought with Eden mote compayre.

53

Much wondred Guyon at the fayre aspéct
Of that sweet place, yet suffred no delight
To sincke into his sence, nor mind affect,
But passèd forth, and lookt still forward right,
Brydling his will and maystering his might,
Till that he came unto another gate;
No gate, but like one, being goodly dight   70
With bowes° and braunches, which did broad di-
late°
Their clasping armes in wanton wreathings intri-
cate:

54

So fashionèd a Porch with rare device.
Archt over head with an embracing vine,
Whose bounches hanging downe seemd to entice
All passers by to taste their lushious wine,
And did them selves into their hands incline,
As freely offering to be gatherèd;
Some deepe empurpled as the Hyacine,
Some as the Rubine laughing sweetely red,   80
Some like faire Emeraudes, not yet well ripenèd.

55

And them amongst some were of burnisht gold,
So made by art to beautify the rest,
Which did themselves emongst the leaves enfold,
As lurking from the vew of covetous guest,
That the weake boughes, with so rich load opprest
Did bow adowne as overburdenèd.
Under that Porch a comely dame did rest
Clad in fayre weedes° but fowle disorderèd,
And garments loose that seemd unmeet for woman-
hed.   90

56

In her left hand a Cup of gold she held,
And with her right the riper fruit did reach,
Whose sappy liquor, that with fulnesse sweld,
Into her cup she scruzd° with daintie breach
Of her fine fingers,° without fowle empeach,°
That so faire winepresse made the wine more sweet:
Thereof she usd to give to drinke to each,
Whom passing by she happenèd to meet:
It was her guise all Straungers goodly so to greet.

57

So she to Guyon offred it to tast,   100
Who, taking it out of her tender hond,
The cup to ground did violently cast,
That all in peeces it was broken fond,°
And with the liquor stainèd all the lond:
Whereat Excesse° exceedingly was wroth,
Yet no'te° the same amend, ne yet withstond,
But suffered him to passe, all° were she loth;
Who, nought regarding her displeasure, forward
goth.

58

There the most dainte Paradise on ground
It selfe doth offer to his sober eye,   110
In which all pleasures plenteously abownd,
And none does others happiness envýe;
The painted flowres, the trees upshooting hye,
The dales for shade, the hilles for breathing space,
The trembling groves, the christall running by,
And, that which all faire workes doth most aggrace,
The art which all that wrought appearèd in no
place.

60

And in the midst of all a fountaine stood,
Of richest substance that on earth might bee,
So pure and shiny that the silver flood   120
Through every channell running one might see;
Most goodly it with curious ymageree
Was overwrought, and shapes of naked boyes,
Of which some seemd with lively jollitee
To fly about, playing their wanton toyes,
Whylest others did them selves embay° in liquid
joyes.

61

And over all of purest gold was spred
A trayle of yvie in his native hew;
For the rich metall was so colourèd,
That wight who did not well avis'd it vew   130
Would surely deeme it to bee yvie trew:
Low his° lascivious armes adown did creepe,
That themselves dipping in the silver dew
Their fleecy flowres they fearefully did steepe,
Which drops of Christall seemd for wantonès° to
weep.

62

Infinit streames continually did well
Out of this fountaine, sweet and faire to see,
The which into an ample laver° fell,
And shortly grew to so great quantitie,
That like a litle lake it seemed to bee;   140

71. bowes: boughs.   dilate: extend.   89. weedes: clothes.
94. scruzd: squeezed.   94–95. breach . . . fingers: puncture (of
the grapeskins) made by her fingers.   95. empeach: hindrance.

103. fond: found.   105. Excesse: the woman's name.
106. no'te: could not.   107. all: although.   126. embay:
bathe.   132. his: its.   135. wantones: wantonness.   138. laver:
basin.

Whose depth exceeded not three cubits hight,
That through the waves one might the bottom see,
All pav'd beneath with Jaspar shining bright,
That seemd the fountaine in that sea did sayle up-
right.

63

And all the margent round about was sett
With shady Laurell trees, thence to defend
The sunny beames which on the billowes bett,
And those which therein bathèd mote offend.
As Guyon hapned by the same to wend,
Two naked Damzelles° he therein espyde,   150
Which therein bathing seemèd to contend
And wrestle wantonly, ne car'd to hyde
Their dainty partes from vew of any which them
eyd.

64

Sometimes the one would lift the other quight
Above the waters, and then downe againe
Her plong, as over-maysterèd by might,
Where both awhile would coverèd remaine,
And each the other from to rise restraine;   158
The whiles their snowy limbes, as through a vele,
So through the christall waves appearèd plaine:
Then suddeinly both would themselves unhele,°
And th' amorous sweet spoiles to greedy eyes re-
vele.

65

As that faire Starre, the messenger of morne,
His deawy face out of the sea doth reare;
Or as the Cyprian goddesse,° newly borne
Of th' Ocean's fruitfull froth, did first appeare:
Such seemèd they, and so their yellow heare
Christalline humor° droppèd downe apace.
Whom such when Guyon saw, he drew him neare,
And somewhat gan relent his earnest pace;   170
His stubborne brest gan secret pleasaunce to em-
brace.

66

The wanton Maidens, him espying, stood
Gazing awhile at his unwonted guise;
Then th' one her selfe low duckèd in the flood,
Abasht that her a straunger did avise;°
But thother rather higher did arise,
And her two lilly paps aloft displayd,
And all that might his melting hart entyse
To her delights she unto him bewrayd;
The rest hidd underneath him more desirous made.

67

With that the other likewise up arose,   181
And her faire lockes, which formerly were bownd

Up in one knott, she low adowne did lose,
Which flowing low and thick her cloth'd arownd,
And th' yvorie in golden mantle gownd:
So that faire spectacle from him was reft,
Yet that which reft it no lesse faire was fownd.
So hidd in lockes and waves from lookers theft,
Nought but her lovely face she for his looking left

68

Withall she laughèd, and she blusht withall,°   190
That blushing to her laughter gave more grace,
And laughter to her blushing, as did fall.
Now when they spyde the knight to slacke his
pace
Them to behold, and in his sparkling face
The secrete signes of kindled lust appeare,
Their wanton meriments they did encreace,
And to him beckned to approch more neare,
And shewd him many sights that corage cold could
reare.°

69

On which when gazing him the Palmer° saw,
He much rebukt those wandring eyes of his,   200
And counseld well him forward thence did draw.
Now are they come nigh to the Bowre of blis,
Of her fond favorites so nam'd amis,
When thus the Palmer: "Now, Sir, well avise;
For here the end of all our traveill is:
Here wonnes Acrasia, whom we must surprise,
Els she will slip away, and all our drift despise."

70

Eftsoones they heard a most melodious sound,
Of all that mote delight a daintie eare,
Such as attonce might not on living ground,   210
Save in this Paradise, be heard elsewhere:
Right hard it was for wight which did it heare,
To read what manner musicke that mote bee;
For all that pleasing is to living eare
Was there consorted in one harmonee;
Birdes, voices, instruments, windes, waters, all
agree:

71

The joyous birdes, shrouded in chearefull shade
Their notes unto the voice attempred sweet;
Th' Angelicall soft trembling voyces made
To th' instruments divine respondence meet;°   220
The silver sounding instruments did meet
With the base murmure of the waters fall;
The waters fall with difference discreet,
Now soft, now loud, unto the wind did call;
The gentle warbling wind low answerèd to all.

---

150. **naked Damzelles:** See Intro., p. 102.   161. **unhele:** uncover.   165. **Cyprian goddesse:** Venus.   168. **Christalline humor:** transparent moisture.   175. **avise:** look at.

190. **withall:** therewithal, at the same time.   198. **corage . . .
reare:** arouse quiescent lust.   199. **the Palmer:** a pilgrim who
has attended Guyon throughout.   220. **meet:** fitting.

72

There, whence that Musick seemèd heard to bee,
Was the faire Witch° her selfe now solacing
With a new Lover, whom, through sorceree
And witchcraft, she from farre did thither bring:
There she had him now laid aslombering   230
In secret shade after long wanton joyes;
Whilst round about them pleasauntly did sing
Many faire Ladies and lascivious boyes,
That ever mixt their song with light licentious
     toyes.°

73

And all that while right over him she hong
With her false eyes fast fixèd in his sight,
As seeking medicine whence she was stong,°
Or greedily depasturing delight;
And oft inclining downe, with kisses light
For feare of waking him, his lips bedewd,   240
And through his humid eyes did sucke his spright,
Quite molten into lust and pleasure lewd;
Wherewith she sighèd soft, as if his case she rewd.

74

The whiles some one did chaunt this lovely lay:
"Ah! see, whoso fayre thing doest faine to see,
In springing flowre the image of thy day.
Ah! see the Virgin Rose, how sweetly shee
Doth first peepe foorth with bashfull modestee,
That fairer seemes the lesse ye see her may.
Lo! see soone after how more bold and free   250
Her barèd bosome she doth broad display;
Lo! see soone after how she fades and falls away.

75

"So passeth, in the passing of a day,
Of mortall life the leafe, the bud, the flowre;
Ne more doth florish after first decay,
That earst° was sought to deck both bed and bowre
Of many a lady, and many a Paramowre.
Gather therefore the Rose whilest yet is prime,
For soone comes age that will her pride deflowre;
Gather the Rose of love whilest yet is time,   260
Whilest loving thou mayst lovèd be with equall
     crime."°

76

He ceast; and then gan all the quire of birdes
Their diverse notes t'attune unto his lay,
As in approvaunce of his pleasing wordes,
The constant payre° heard all that he did say,
Yet swarvèd not, but kept their forward way

Through many covert groves and thickets close,
In which they creeping did at last display
That wanton Lady with her lover lose,°
Whose sleepie head she in her lap did soft dis-
     pose.

77

Upon a bed of Roses she was layd,   271
As faint through heat, or dight to° pleasant sin;
And was arayd, or rather disarayd,
All in a vele of silke and silver thin,
That hid no whit her alablaster skin,
But rather shewd more white, if more might bee:
More subtile web Arachnè° cannot spin;
Nor the fine nets, which oft we woven see
Of scorched deaw, do not in th' ayre more lightly
     flee.

78

Her snowy brest was bare to ready spoyle   280
Of hungry eies, which n'ote° therewith be fild;
And yet, through languour of her late sweet toyle,
Few drops, more cleare then Nectar, forth distild,
That like pure Orient perles adowne it trild;
And her faire eyes, sweet smyling in delight,
Moystened their fierie beames, with which she
     thrild
Fraile harts, yet quenchèd not; like starry light,
Which, sparckling on the silent waves, does seeme
     more bright.

79

The young man, sleeping by her, seemd to be
Some goodly swayne° of honorable place,   290
That certès it great pitty was to see
Him his nobility so fowle deface:
A sweet regard and amiable grace,
Mixèd with manly sternesse, did appeare,
Yet sleeping, in his well proportiond face;
And on his tender lips the downy heare
Did now but freshly spring, and silken blossoms
     beare.

80

His warlike Armes, the ydle instruments
Of sleeping praise, were hong upon a tree;
And his brave shield, full of old moniments,   300
Was fowly ras't,° that none the signes might see:
Ne for them ne for honour carèd hee,
Ne ought that did to his advauncement tend;
But in lewd loves, and wastefull luxuree,
His dayes, his goods, his bodie, he did spend:
O horrible enchantment, that him so did blend!°

---

227. faire Witch: Acrasia.   **234. toyes:** frivolities, wanton acts.
237. stong: stung.   **256. earst:** first, formerly.   **261. crime:**
sin, fault ("Be lewd while you can find someone equally ready
to be lewd with you").   **265. payre:** Guyon and the Palmer.

269. lose: loose.   **272. dight to:** prepared for.   **277. Arachne:**
the spider.   **281. n'ote:** could not.   **290. swayne:** young man.
301. ras't: scraped (so as to erase the device).   **306. blend:**
blind.

81

The noble Elfe and carefull Palmer drew
So nigh them, minding nought but lustfull game,
That suddein forth they on them rusht, and threw
A subtile net, which only for that same   310
The skilfull Palmer formally° did frame:
So held them under fast; the whiles the rest
Fled all away for feare of fowler shame.
The faire Enchauntresse, so unwares opprest,
Tryde all her arts and all her sleights thence out to
    wrest.

SELECTION XIII

Our first glimpse of Florimel. We have now passed
from the severer allegory of the first two Books into
the pathless forest of the third. The appearance of
Florimel is as abrupt and unexplained (at this point)
in the original as in my selection. Only later do we
learn who she is and that she has left the faerie court
to seek the sea nymph's son Marinell, whom she vainly
loves. Unexplained entrances of new characters are deliberate strokes of art in Spenser. (Compare also headnote to Selection VI on the practice of beginning stories in the middle.)

14

Long they thus traveilèd in friendly wise,
Through countreyes waste, and eke well edifyde,°
Seeking adventures hard, to exercise
Their puissaunce,° whylome full dernly° tryde.
At length they came into a forest wyde,
Whose hideous horror and sad trembling sownd,
Full griesly seemd: Therein they long did ryde,
Yet tract of living creature none they fownd,
Save Beares, Lyons, and Buls, which romèd them
    arownd.

15

All suddenly out of the thickest brush,   10
Upon a milkwhite Palfrey all alone,
A goodly Lady did foreby them rush,
Whose face did seeme as cleare as Christall stone,
And eke, through feare, as white as whalès bone:
Her garments all were wrought of beaten gold,°
And all her steed with tinsell trappings shone,
Which fledd so fast that nothing mote him hold,
And scarse them leasure gave her passing to behold.

16

Still as she fledd her eye she backward threw,
As fearing evill that poursewd her fast;   20
And her faire yellow locks behind her flew,

Loosely disperst with puff of every blast:
All as a blazing starre° doth farre outcast
His hearie beames, and flaming lockes dispredd,
At sight whereof the people stand aghast;
But the sage wisard telles, as he has redd,
That it importunes° death and doleful dreryhedd.

17

So as they gazèd after her a whyle,
Lo! where a griesly foster° forth did rush,
Breathing out beastly lust her to defyle: 30
His tyreling° Jade he fiersly forth did push
Through thicke and thin, both over banck and
    bush,
In hope her to attaine by hooke or crooke,
That from his gory sydes the blood did gush.
Large were his limbes, and terrible his looke,
And in his clownish hand a sharp bore speare he
    shooke.

SELECTION XIV

Britomart, the female Knight of Chastity, has just
overthrown Marinell (see headnote to Selection XIII)
on the Rich Strand. The subsequent appearance of the
sea nymphs may be regarded as a rich Renaissance variation on a theme taken from Homer's *Iliad*, Book I.

18

The martiall Mayd stayd not him to lament,
But forward rode, and kept her ready way
Along the strond;° which, as she over-went,
She saw bestrowèd all with rich aray
Of pearles and pretious stones of great assay,°
And all the gravell mixt with golden owre:°
Whereat she wondred much, but would not stay
For gold, or perles, or pretious stones, an howre,
But them despisèd all; for all was in her powre.

19

Whiles thus he lay in deadly stonishment,   10
Tydings hereof came to his mothers eare:
His mother was the blacke-browd Cymoënt,
The daughter of great Nereus, which° did beare
This warlike sonne unto an earthly peare,°
The famous Dumarin; who, on a day
Finding the Nymph asleepe in secret wheare,
As he by chaunce did wander the same way,
Was taken with her love, and by her closely lay.

23. starre: i.e., comet. Cf. *I Henry IV*, III. i. 12, and Milton, *PL*, II. 708 below.   **27. importunes:** imports. means.   **29. foster:** forester.   **31. tyreling:** tireling, tired.   **Sel. XIV:** from *FQ*, III. iv.   **3. strond:** strand, sea beach.   **5. of . . . assay:** which, if subjected to the test or "assay" would be found very valuable.   **6. owre:** ore.   **13. which:** who.   **14. peare:** peer, probably in the sense of "mate" rather than "nobleman."

311. formally: skillfully.   **Sel. XIII:** from *FQ*, III. i.   **2. edifyde:** cultivated, civilized.   **4. puissaunce:** three syllables.   **dernly:** really means "secretly," but Spenser seems to think it means "grimly," "sternly," or something of the sort.   **15. beaten gold:** cloth of gold embroidery.

20

There he this knight of her begot, whom borne
She, of his father, Marinell did name;   20
And in a rocky cave, as wight forlorne,
Long time she fostred up, till he became
A mighty man at armes, and mickle° fame
Did get through great adventures by him donne:
For never man he suffred by that same
Rich strond to travell, whereas he did wonne,
But that he must do battail with the Sea-nymphes
    sonne.

25

And, for his more assuraunce, she inquir'd
One day of Proteus° by his mighty spell
(For Proteus was with prophecy inspir'd)   30
Her deare sonnes destiny to her to tell,
And the sad end of her sweet Marinell:
Who, through foresight of his eternall skill,
Bad her from womankind to keepe him well,
For of a woman he should have much ill;
A virgin straunge and stout him should dismay or
    kill.

29

Too trew the famous Marinell it fownd,
Who, through late triall, on that wealthy Strond
Inglorious now lies in sencelesse swound,
Through heavy stroke of Britomartis hond.   40
Which when his mother deare did understond,
And heavy tidings heard, whereas she playd
Amongst her watry sisters by a pond,
Gathering sweete daffadillyes, to have made
Gay girlonds from the Sun their forheads fayr to
    shade;

30

Eftesoones both flowres and girlonds far away
Shee flong, and her faire deawy lockes yrent;°
To sorrow huge she turnd her former play,
And gamesom merth to grievous dreriment:
Shee threw her selfe downe on the Continent,°   50
Ne word did speake, but lay as in a swowne,
Whiles all her sisters did for her lament
With yelling outcries, and with shrieking sowne;
And every one did teare her girlond from her
    crowne.

31

Soone as shee up out of her deadly fitt
Arose, shee bad her charett to be brought;
And all her sisters that with her did sitt
Bad eke attonce their charetts to be sought:

Tho,° full of bitter griefe and pensife thought,
She to her wagon clombe; clombe all the rest,   60
And forth together went with sorrow fraught.
The waves, obedient to theyr beheast,
Them yielded ready passage, and their rage sur-
    ceast.

32

Great Neptune stoode amazèd at their sight,
Whiles on his broad rownd backe they softly
    slid,
And eke him selfe mournd at their mournful
    plight,
Yet wist not what their wailing ment; yet did,
For great compassion of their sorrow, bid
His mighty waters to them buxome° bee
Eftesoones the roaring billowes still abid,   70
And all the griesly Monsters of the See
Stood gaping at their gate,° and wondred them to
    see.

33

A teme of Dolphins raungèd in aray
Drew the smooth charett of sad Cymoënt:
They were all taught by Triton° to obay
To the long raynes at her commaundèment:
As swifte as swallowes on the waves they went,
That their brode flaggy finnes no fome did reare
Ne bubling rowndell° they behinde them sent.
The rest, of other fishes drawen weare,   80
Which with their finny oars the swelling sea did
    sheare.

34

Soone as they bene arriv'd upon the brim
Of the Rich Strond, their charets they forlore,
And let their temèd° fishes softly swim
Along the margent of the fomy shore,
Least they their finnes should bruze, and surbate°
    sore°
Their tender feete upon the stony grownd:
And comming to the place, where all in gore
And cruddy° blood enwallowèd they fownd   89
The lucklesse Marinell lying in deadly swownd,

35

His mother swownèd thrise, and the third time
Could scarce recovered bee out of her paine:
Had she not beene devoide of mortall slime,°
Shee should not then have bene relyv'd againe;
But, soone as life recovered had the raine,°
Shee made so piteous mone and deare waymént,°
That the hard rocks could scarse from tears re-
    fraine;

23. mickle: much.   29. Proteus: a sea god, shepherd to the seals,
who could change himself into any shape.   47. yrent: tore.
50. Continent: shore.   59. Tho: then.   69. buxome: yielding, obedient.   72. gate:
gait, movement.   75. Triton: Cf. Wordsworth's sonnet, "The
World Is Too Much with us," in Vol. II.   79. rowndell: circle.
84. temed: harnessed.   86. surbate: hurt.   sore: grievously.
89. cruddy: curdled.   93. slime: seed.   95. raine: rein.
96. wayment: lamentation.

And all her sister Nymphes with one consent
Supplide her sobbing breaches° with sad comple-
    ment.

40

Thus when they all had sorowèd their fill,   100
They softly gan to search his griesly wownd:
And, that they might him handle more at will,
They him disarmd; and, spredding on the grownd
Their watchet° mantles frindgd with silver rownd,
They softly wipt away the gelly blood
From th' orifice; which having well upbownd,
They pourd in soveraine balme and Nectar good,
Good both for erthly med'cine and for hevenly
    food.

41

Tho° when the lilly handed Liagore
(This Liagore whilome had learnèd skill   110
In leaches° craft, by great Apolloes lore,
Sith her whilome upon high Pindus hill
He lovèd, and at last her wombe did fill
With hevenly seed, whereof wise Pæon sprong)
Did feele his pulse, shee knew there staièd still
Some litle life his feeble sprites emong;
Which to his mother told, despeyre she from her
    flong.

42

Tho, up him taking in their tender hands,
They easely unto her charett beare:
Her teme at her commaundement quiet stands,
Whiles they the corse into her wagon reare,   121
And strowe with flowres the lamentable beare.
Then all the rest into their coches clim,°
And through the brackish° waves their passage
    sheare;
Upon great Neptunes necke they softly swim,
And to her watry chamber swiftly carry him.

43

Deepe in the bottome of the sea her bowre
Is built of hollow billowes heapèd hye,
Like to thicke clouds that threat a stormy showre,
And vauted° all within, like to the Skye,   130
In which the Gods doe dwell eternally;
There they him laide in easy couch well dight,
And sent in haste for Tryphon, to apply
Salves to his wounds, and medicines of might,
For Tryphon of sea gods the soveraine leach is
    hight.

SELECTION XV

We return to Florimel, whom we left in flight at the
end of Selection XIII. This passage brings her to lodge
with a witch, records the making of the False Florimel,
carries the true one out to sea, and finally leaves her as
the prisoner of the minor sea god Proteus. The element
of fairy tale is here predominant, as in many parts of
Ariosto.

I

Like as an Hynd forth singled from the heard,
That hath escapèd from a ravenous beast,
Yet flyes away of her owne feete afeard,
And every leafe, that shaketh with the least
Murmure of winde, her terror hath encreast;
So fledd fayre Florimell from her vaine feare,
Long after she from perill was releast:
Each shade she saw, and each noyse she did
    heare,
Did seeme to be the same which she escapt while-
    are.°

2

All that same evening she in flying spent,   10
And all that night her course continewèd;
Ne did she let dull sleepe once to relent,
Nor weariness to slack her hast, but fled
Ever alike, as if her former dred
Were hard behind, her ready to arrest;
And her white Palfrey, having conquerèd
The maistring raines out of her weary wrest,°
Perforce her carrièd where ever he thought best.

3

So long as breath and hable puìssaunce°
Did native corage unto him supply,   20
His pace he freshly forward did advaunce,
And carried her beyond all jeopardy;
But nought that wanteth rest can long aby:°
He, having through incessant traveill spent
His force, at last perforce adowne did ly,
Ne foot could further move. The Lady gent°
Thereat was suddein strook with great astonish-
    ment;

4

And, forst t' alight, on foote mote algates fare
A traveiler unwonted to such way:
Need teacheth her this lesson hard and rare,   30
That fortune all in equall launce° doth sway,

---

99. sobbing breaches: intervals of sobbing which interrupted
her lament.   104. watchet: light blue.   109. Tho: then.
111. leaches: healer's.   123. clim: climb.   124. brackish: salt.
130. vauted: vaulted.

Sel. XV: from *FQ*, III. vii, viii.   9. whileare: whilom, formerly.   17. wrest: wrist.   19. hable puissaunce: able power.
23. aby: wrongly used by Spenser to mean "abide, endure."
26. gent: noble.   31. launce: balance.

And mortall miseries doth make her play.
So long she traveild, till at length she came
To an hilles side, which did to her bewray
A litle valley subject to the same,
All coverd with thick woodes that quite it over-
      came.

5

Through the tops of the high trees she did descry
A litle smoke, whose vapour thin and light
Reeking° aloft uprollèd to the sky:
Which chearefull signe did send unto her sight   40
That in the same did wonne some living wight.
Eftsoones her steps she thereunto applyd,
And came at last in weary wretched plight
Unto the place, to which her hope did guyde,
To finde some refuge there, and rest her wearie
      syde.

6

There in a gloomy hollow glen she found
A little cottage, built of stickes and reedes
In homely wize, and wald with sods around;
In which a witch did dwell, in loathly weedes°
And wilfull want, all carelesse of her needes;   50
So choosing solitairie to abide
Far from all neighbours, that her divelish deedes
And hellish arts from people she might hide,
And hurt far off unknowne whom ever she en-
      víde.

7

The Damzell there arriving entred in;
Where sitting on the flore the Hag she found
Busie (as seem'd) about some wicked gin:°
Who, soone as she beheld that suddein stound,°
Lightly upstarted from the dustie ground,
And with fell looke and hollow deadly gaze   60
Starèd on her awhile, as one astound,
Ne had one word to speake for great amaze,
But shewd by outward signes that dread her sence
      did daze.

8

At last, turning her feare to foolish wrath,
She askt, what devill had her thither brought,
And who she was, and what unwonted path
Had guided her, unwelcomèd, unsought?
To which the Damzell, full of doubtfull thought,
Her mildly answer'd: "Beldame,° be not wroth   70
With silly° Virgin, by adventure brought
Unto your dwelling, ignorant and loth,
That crave but rowme to rest while tempest over-
      blo'th."

9

With that adowne out of her christall eyne
Few trickling teares she softly forth let fall,
That like two orient perles did purely shyne
Upon her snowy cheeke; and therewithall
She sighèd soft, that none so bestiall
Nor salvage hart, but ruth of her sad plight
Would make to melt, or pitteously appall;
And that vile Hag, all were her whole delight   80
In mischiefe, was much movèd at so pitteous
      sight;

10

And gan recomfort her in her rude wyse,
With womanish compassion of her plaint,
Wiping the teares from her suffusèd eyes,
And bidding her sit downe, to rest her faint
And wearie limbes awhile. She, nothing quaint°
Nor 'sdeignfull of so homely fashion,
Sith brought she was now to so hard constraint,
Sate downe upon the dusty ground anon;
As glad of that small rest as Bird of tempest gon.

11

Tho gan she gather up her garments rent,   91
And her loose lockes to dight in order dew
With golden wreath and gorgeous ornament;
Whom such whenas the wicked Hag did vew,
She was astonisht at her heavenly hew,
And doubted her to deeme an earthly wight,
But or some Goddesse, or of Dianes crew,
And thought her to adore with humble spright:
T' adore thing so divine as beauty were but right.

12

This wicked woman had a wicked sonne,   100
The comfort of her age and weary dayes,
A laesy loord,° for nothing good to donne,
But stretchèd forth in ydlenesse alwayes,
Ne ever cast his mind to covet prayse,
Or ply himselfe to any honest trade,
But all the day before the sunny rayes
He us'd to slug, or sleepe in slothfull shade:
Such laesinesse both lewd and poore attonce him
      made.

13

He, comming home at undertime,° there found
The fayrest creature that he ever saw   110
Sitting beside his mother on the ground;
The sight whereof did greatly him adaw,°
And his base thought with terrour and with aw
So inly smot, that as one, which hath gaz'd
On the bright Sunne unwares, doth soone with-
      draw

---

39. Reeking: smoking.   **49. weedes:** clothes.   **57. gin:** device.
58. stound: emergency.   **69. Beldame:** good dame, good wife,
"goody."   **70. silly:** simple.

86. quaint: fastidious.   **102. loord:** lout, oaf.   **109. undertime:**
afternoon.   **112. adaw:** overawe, daunt.

His feeble eyne, with too much brightnes daz'd,
So starèd he on her, and stood long while amaz'd.

14

Softly at last he gan his mother aske,
What mister wight° that was, and whence deriv'd,
That in so straunge disguizement there did maske,
And by what accident she there arriv'd?   121
But she, as one nigh of her wits depriv'd,
With nought but ghastly lookes him answerèd;
Like to a ghost, that lately is reviv'd
From Stygian shores where late it wanderèd:
So both at her, and each at other wonderèd.

15

But the fayre Virgin was so meeke and myld,
That she to them vouchsafèd to embace°
Her goodly port,° and to their senses vyld
Her gentle speach applyde, that in short space   130
She grew familiare in that desert place.
During which time the Chorle,° through her so
      kind
And courteise use, conceiv'd affection bace,
And cast° to love her in his brutish mind:
No love, but brutish lust, that was so beastly tind.°

16

Closely the wicked flame his bowels brent,
And shortly grew into outrageous fire;
Yet had he not the hart, nor hardiment,
As unto her to utter his desire;
His caytive thought durst not so high aspire: 140
But with soft sighes and lovely semblaunces
He ween'd that his affection entire
She should aread;° many resemblaunces°
To her he made, and many kinde remembraunces.

17

Oft from the forrest wildings° he did bring,
Whose sides empurpled were with smyling red;
And oft young birds, which he had taught to sing,
His maistresse praises sweetly carolèd:
Girlonds of flowres sometimes for her faire hed
He fine would dight; sometimes the squirrell wild
He brought to her in bands, as conquerèd   151
To be her thrall, his fellow-servant vild:°
All which she of him tooke with countenance
      meeke and mild.

18

But, past a while, when she fit season saw
To leave that desert mansion, she cast°
In secret wize herselfe thence to withdraw,

For feare of mischiefe, which she did forecast
Might be by the witch or that her sonne compast.°
Her wearie Palfrey, closely as she might,
Now well recovered after long repast,   160
In his proud furnitures° she freshly dight,
His late miswandred wayes now to remeasure
      right.

19

And earely, ere the dawning day appear'd,
She forth issèwed, and on her journey went:
She went in perill, of each noyse affeard,
And of each shade that did it selfe present;
For still she fearèd to be overhent
Of that vile hag, or her uncivile sonne;
Who when, too late awaking, well they kent°
That their fayre guest was gone, they both be-
      gonne   170
To make exceeding mone, as they had been un-
      donne.

20

But that lewd lover did the most lament
For her depart, that ever man did heare:
He knockt his brest with desperate intent,
And scratcht his face, and with his teeth did teare
His rugged flesh, and rent his ragged heare;
That his sad mother, seeing his sore plight,
Was greatly woe begon, and gan to feare
Least his fraile senses were emperisht quight,
And love to frenzy turnd, sith love is franticke
      hight.°   180

21

All wayes shee sought him to restore to plight,
With herbs, with charms, with counsel, and with
      teares;
But tears, nor charms, nor herbs, nor counsell,
      might
Asswage the fury which his entrails teares:
So strong is passion that no reason heares.
Tho when all other helpes she saw to faile,
She turnd her selfe backe to her wicked leares;°
And by her divelish arts thought to prevaile
To bringe her backe againe, or worke her finall
      bale.°

22

Eftesoones out of her hidden cave she cald   190
An hideous beast of horrible aspect,
That could the stoutest corage have appald;
Monstrous, mishapt, and all his backe was spect
With thousand spots of colours queint elect,
Thereto so swifte that it all beasts did pas:
Like never yet did living eie detect;

---

119. **mister wight**: kind of creature.   128. **embace**: lower.
129. **port**: behavior.   132. **Chorle**: churl (i.e., the Witch's son).
134. **cast**: resolved, determined.   135. **tind**: kindled.
143. **aread**: interpret.   **resemblaunces**: similes.   145. **wildings**:
wild fruit.   152. **vild**: vile, abject.   155. **cast**: resolved.

158. **compast**: compassed, brought about.   161. **furnitures**:
harness, appurtenances.   169. **kent**: knew.   180. **hight**: called.
187. **leares**: sciences (i.e., her magic).   189. **bale**: destruction.

But likest it to an Hyena was,
That feeds on wemens flesh as others feede on gras.

23

It forth she cald, and gave it streight in charge
Through thicke and thin her to poursew apace,
Ne once to stay to rest, or breath at large,   201
Till her he had attaind and brought in place,
Or quite devourd her beauties scornefull grace.
The Monster, swifte as word that from her went,
Went forth in haste, and did her footing trace
So sure and swiftly, through his perfect sent
And passing speede, that shortly he her overhent.°

24

Whom when the fearefull Damzell nigh espide,
No need to bid her fast away to flie:
That ugly shape so sore her terrifide,   210
That it she shund no lesse then dread to die;
And her flitt° palfrey did so well apply
His nimble feet to her conceivèd feare,
That whilest his breath did strength to him supply,
From peril free he her away did beare;
But when his force gan faile his pace gan wex
   areare.°

25

Which whenas she perceiv'd, she was dismayd
At the same last extremity ful sore,
And of her safety greatly grew afrayd.
And now she gan approch to the sea shore,   220
As it befell, that she could flie no more,
But yield herselfe to spoile of greedinesse:
Lightly she leapèd, as a wight forlore,
From her dull horse, in desperate distresse,
And to her feet betooke her doubtfull sickernesse.°

27

It fortunèd (high God did so ordaine)
As shee arrivèd on the roring shore,
In minde to leape into the mighty maine,
A little bote lay hoving her before,
In which there slept a fisher old and pore,   230
The whiles his nets were drying on the sand.
Into the same shee lept, and with the ore
Did thrust the shallop from the floting° strand:
So safety fownd at sea which she fownd not at land.

2

But that accursèd Hag, her hostesse late,
Had so enranckled her malitious hart,
That she desyrd th' abridgement of her fate,
Or long enlargement of her painefull smart.
Now when the Beast, which by her wicked art

Late foorth she sent, she backe retourning spyde
Tyde with her golden girdle;° it a part   241
Of her rich spoyles whom he had earst° destroyd
She weend,° and wondrous gladnes to her hart ap-
   plyde.

3

And, with it ronning hast'ly to her sonne,
Thought with that sight him much to have reliv'd
Who, thereby deeming sure the thing as donne,
His former griefe with furie fresh reviv'd
Much more than earst, and would have algates
   riv'd
The hart out of his brest: for sith her dedd
He surely dempt,° himselfe he thought depriv'd
Quite of all hope wherewith he long had fedd   251
His foolish malady, and long time had misledd.

4

With thought whereof exceeding mad he grew,
And in his rage his mother would have slaine,
Had she not fled into a secret mew,°
Where she was wont her Sprightes to entertaine,
The maisters of her art: there was she faine
To call them all in order to her ayde,
And them conjúre, upon eternall paine,
To counsell her, so carefully dismayd,   260
How she might heale her sonne whose senses were
   decayd.

5

By their advice, and her owne wicked wit,
She there deviz'd a wondrous worke to frame,
Whose like on earth was never framèd yit;°
That even Nature selfe envíde the same,
And grudg'd to see the counterfet should shame
The thing it selfe: In hand she boldly tooke
To make another like the former Dame,
Another Florimell, in shape and looke
So lively and so like, that many it mistooke.   270

6

The substance, whereof she the body made,
Was purest snow in massy mould congeald,
Which she had gathered in a shady glade
Of the Riphœan hils,° to her reveald
By errant Sprights, but from all men conceald:
The same she tempred with fine mercury
And virgin wex that never yet was seald,
And mingled them with perfect vermily;°
That like a lively sanguine it seemd to the eye.

---

241. Tyde . . . girdle: Florimel had lost her girdle as she jumped
into the boat. In an omitted passage a knight had captured the
hyena and used the girdle as a leash, but the creature soon
escaped.   242. earst: first, formerly.   243. weend: weened,
thought.   250. dempt: deemed.   255. mew: den, hiding place.
264. yit: yet.   274. Riphoean hils: mountains in Scythia.
278. vermily: vermilion.

207. overhent: overtook.   212. flitt: fleet, swift.   216. wex
areare: get behindhand, fail to maintain the pace.   225. sickernesse: safety.   233. floting: wet.

7

Instead of eyes two burning lampes she set   280
In silver sockets, shyning like the skyes,
And a quicke moving Spirit did arret°
To stirre and roll them like to womens eyes:
Instead of yellow lockes she did devyse
With golden wyre to weave her curlèd head;
Yet golden wyre was not so yellow thryse
As Florimells fayre heare: and, in the stead
Of life, she put a Spright to rule the carcas dead;

8

A wicked Spright, yfraught with fawning guyle
And fayre resemblance above all the rest,   290
Which with the Prince of Darkenes fell some-
    whyle°
From heavens blis and everlasting rest:
Him needed not instruct which way were best
Him selfe to fashion likest Florimell,
Ne how to speake, ne how to use his gest;°
For he in counterfesaunce did excell,
And all the wyles of wemens wits knew passing
    well.

9

Him shapèd thus she deckt in garments gay,
Which Florimell had left behind her late;
That who so° then her saw would surely say   300
It was her selfe whom it did imitate,
Or fayrer then her selfe, if ought algate°
Might fayrer be. And then she forth her brought
Unto her sonne that lay in feeble state;
Who seeing her gan streight upstart, and thought
She was the Lady selfe whom he so long had
    sought.

20

But Florimell her selfe was far away,
Driven to great distresse by fortune straunge,
And taught the carefull Mariner to play,
Sith late mischaunce had her compeld to chaunge
The land for sea, at randon there to raunge: 311
Yett there that cruell Queene° avengeresse,
Not satisfyde so far her to estraunge
From courtly blis and wonted happinesse,
Did heape on her new waves of weary wretched-
    nesse.

21

For being fled into the fishers bote
For refuge from the Monsters cruelty,
Long so she on the mighty maine did flote,
And with the tide drove forward carelesly;
For th' ayre was milde and clearèd was the skie,

And all his windes Dan° Æolus° did keepe   321
From stirring up their stormy enmity,
As° pittying to see her waile and weepe:
But all the while the fisher did securely sleepe.

22

At last when droncke with drowsinesse he woke,
And saw his drover° drive along the streame,°
He was dismayd; and thrise his brest he stroke,
For marveill of that accident extreame:
But when he saw that blazing beauties beame,
Which with rare light his bote did beautifye,   330
He marveild more, and thought he yet did dreame
Not well awakte; or that some extasye
Assotted had his sence, or dazèd was his eye.

23

But when her well avizing hee perceiv'd
To be no vision nor fantasticke sight,
Great comfort of her presence he conceiv'd,
And felt in his old corage new delight
To gin awake, and stir his frosen spright:
Tho rudely askte her, how she thither came?   339
"Ah!" (sayd she) "father, I note° read° aright
What hard misfortune brought me to this same;
Yet am I glad that here I now in safety ame.

24

"But thou, good man, sith far in sea we bee,
And the great waters gin apace to swell,
That now no more we can the mayn-land see,
Have care, I pray, to guide the cock-bote well,
Least worse on sea then us on land befell."
Thereat th' old man did nought but fondly grin,
And saide his boat the way could wisely tell;
But his deceiptfull eyes did never lin°   350
To looke on her faire face and marke her snowy
    skin.

25

The sight whereof in his congealèd flesh
Infixt such secrete sting of greedy lust,
That the drie withered stocke it gan refresh,
And kindled heat that soone in flame forth brust:°
The driest wood is soonest burnt to dust.
Rudely to her he lept, and his rough hond
Where ill became him rashly would have thrust;
But she with angry scorne did him withstond,
And shamefully reprovèd for his rudenes fond.°

26

But he, that never good nor maners knew,   361
Her sharpe rebuke full litle did esteeme;

---

282. **arret:** appoint.   291. **somewhyle:** once upon a time.
295. **gest:** gestures.   300. **who so:** whoever.   302. **algate:** by
any means.   312. **that ... Queene:** Fortune.

321. **Dan:** "don," "master."   **Aeolus:** god of the winds.
323. **As:** as if.   326. **drover:** a kind of fishing boat.   **streame:**
tide, current.   340. **note:** know not how to, can't.   **read:** dis-
entangle.   350. **lin:** cease.   355. **brust:** burst.   360. **fond:**
foolish.

Hard is to teach an old horse amble trew:
The inward smoke, that did before but steeme,
Broke into open fire and rage extreme;
And now he strength gan adde unto his will,
Forcyng to doe that° did him fowle misseeme.
Beastly he threwe her downe, ne car'd° to spill°
Her garments gay with scales of fish that all did fill.

27

The silly virgin strove him to withstand   370
All that she might, and him in vaine revild:
Shee strugled strongly both with foote and hand
To save her honor from that villaine vilde,°
And cride to heven, from humane help exild.
O! ye brave knights, that boast this Ladies love,
Where be ye now, when she is nigh defild
Of filthy wretch? well may she you reprove
Of falsehood or of slouth, when most it may be-
    hove.

29

But sith that none of all her knights is nye,
See how the heavens, of voluntary grace   380
And soveraine favor towards chastity,
Doe succor send to her distressèd cace;
So much high God doth innocence embrace.
It fortunèd, whilest thus she stifly strove,
And the wide sea importunèd long space
With shrilling shriekes, Proteus abrode did rove,
Along the fomy waves driving his finny drove.

30

Proteus° is Shepheard of the seas of yore,
And hath the charge of Neptunes mighty heard;
An agèd sire with head all frory hore,°   390
And sprinckled frost upon his deawy beard:
Who when those pittifull outcries he heard
Through all the seas so ruefully resownd,
His charett swifte in hast he thither steard,
Which with a teeme of scaly Phocas° bownd
Was drawne upon the waves that fomèd him
    arownd.

31

And comming to that Fishers wandring bote,
That went at will withouten card° or sayle,
He therein saw that yrkesome sight, which smote
Deepe indignation and compassion frayle   400
Into his hart attonce: streight did he hayle°
The greedy villein from his hopèd pray,
Of which he now did very litle fayle,
And with his staffe, that drives his heard astray,
Him bett so sore, that life and sence did much dis-
    may.

32

The whiles the pitteous Lady up did ryse,
Ruffled and fowly raid° with filthy soyle,
And blubbred° face with teares of her faire eyes:
Her heart nigh broken was with weary toyle,
To save her selfe from that outrageous spoyle;   410
But when she lookèd up, to weet what wight
Had her from so infámous fact° assoyld,°
For shame, but more for feare of his grim sight,
Downe in her lap she hid her face, and lowdly
    shright.°

34

But he endeverèd with speaches milde
Her to recomfort, and accourage bold,
Bidding her feare no more her foemen vilde,
Nor doubt himselfe; and who he was her told:
Yet all that could not from affright her hold,
Ne to recomfort her at all prevayld;   420
For her faint hart was with the frosen cold
Benumbd so inly, that her wits nigh fayld,
And all her sences with abashment quite were
    quayld.

35

Her up betwixt his rugged hands he reard,
And with his frory° lips full softly kist,
Whiles the cold ysickles from his rough beard
Droppèd adowne upon her yvory brest:
Yet he him selfe so busily addrest,
That her out of astonishment° he wrought;
And out of that same fishers filthy nest   430
Removing her, into his charet brought,
And there with many gentle termes her faire be-
    sought.

36

But that old leachour, which with bold assault
That beautie durst presume to violate,
He cast to punish for his hainous fault:
Then tooke he him, yet trembling sith of late,°
And tyde behind his charet, to aggrate°
The virgin whom he had abusde so sore;
So drag'd him through the waves in scornfull state,
And after cast him up upon the shore;   440
But Florimell with him unto his bowre he bore.

37

His bowre is in the bottom of the maine,
Under a mightie rocke, gainst which doe rave
The roring billowes in their proud disdaine,
That with the angry working of the wave
Therein is eaten out an hollow cave,

---

367. that: what.   368. car'd: cared (i.e., he didn't mind).
spill: spoil.   373. vilde: vile.   388. Proteus: See Sel. XIV, l. 29n,
above.   390. frory hore: frosty gray.   395. Phocas: seals.
398. card: chart, or possibly a compass.   401. hayle: haul, pull.

407. raid: arrayed.   408. blubbred: tear-stained.   412. fact:
deed.   assoyld: set free.   414. shright: shrieked.   425. frory:
frosty.   429. astonishment: stupor.   436. sith of late: since
his recent beating.   437. aggrate: please.

That seemes rough Masons hand with engines°
    keene
Had long while labourèd it to engrave:
There was his wonne;° ne living wight was seene
Save one old Nymph, hight Panopè, to keepe it
    cleane.   450

38

Thither he brought the sory Florimell,
And entertainèd her the best he might,
And Panopè her entertaind eke well,
As an immortall mote a mortall wight,
To winne her liking unto his delight:
With flattering wordes he sweetly wooèd her,
And offerèd faire guiftes t' allure her sight;
But she both offers and the offerer
Despysde, and all the fawning of the flatterer.

41

To dreadfull shapes he did him selfe transforme;
Now like a Gyaunt; now like to a feend;   461
Then like a Centaure; then like to a storme
Raging within the waves: thereby he weend
Her will to win unto his wishèd eend;
But when with feare, nor favour, nor with all
He els could doe, he saw him selfe esteemd,
Downe in a Dongeon deepe he let her fall,
And threatned there to make her his eternall thrall.

SELECTION XVI

We abandon Florimel for a time to tell how a jealous
husband, Malbecco, pursued his runaway wife Hellenore. The selection begins with Malbecco hidden in a
thicket and watching Hellenore romping with the
satyrs. It ends with his horrible transformation, which
some moralists find undeserved. Spenser, however, symbolizes those results of jealousy which he has actually
seen. It is yet another of his nightmare passages.

45

The silly° man that in the thickett lay
Saw all this goodly sport, and grievèd sore;
Yet durst he not against it doe or say,
But did his hart with bitter thoughts engore,
To see th' unkindnes of his Hellenore.
All day they dauncèd with great lusty-hedd,
And with their hornèd feet the greene gras wore,
The whiles their Gotes upon the brouzes° fedd,
Till drouping Phœbus gan to hyde his golden
    hedd.

46

Tho° up they gan their mery pypes to trusse,   10
And all their goodly heardes did gather rownd;

But every Satyre first did give a busse°
To Hellenore; so busses did abound.
Now gan the humid vapour shed the grownd
With perly deaw, and th' Earthès gloomy shade
Did dim the brightnesse of the welkin° rownd,
That every bird and beast awarnèd made
To shrowd themselves, whiles sleepe their sences
    did invade.

47

Which when Malbecco saw, out of the bush
Upon his handes and feete he crept full light,   20
And like a Gote emongst the Gotes did rush;
That, through the helpe of his faire hornes° on
    hight,
And misty dampe of misconceyving night,
And eke through likenesse of his gotish beard,
He did the better counterfeite aright:
So home he marcht emongst the hornèd heard,
That none of all the Satyres him espyde or heard.

48

At night, when all they went to sleepe, he vewd
Whereas his lovely wife emongst them lay,
Embracèd of a Satyre rough and rude,   30
Who all the night did minde his joyous play:
Nine times he heard him come aloft ere day,
That all his hart with gealosy did swell;
But yet that nights ensample did bewray
That not for nought his wife them loved so well,
When one so oft a night did ring his matins bell.

49

So closely as he could he to them crept,
When wearie of their sport to sleepe they fell,
And to his wife, that now full soundly slept,
He whispered in her eare, and did her tell   40
That it was he which by her side did dwell;
And therefore prayd her wake to heare him plaine.
As one out of a dreame not wakèd well
She turnd her, and returnèd back againe;
Yet her for to awake he did the more constraine.

50

At last with irkesom trouble she abrayd;°
And then perceiving that it was indeed
Her old Malbecco, which did her upbrayd
With loosenesse of her love and loathly deed,
She was astonisht with exceeding dreed,   50
And would have wakt the Satyre by her syde;
But he her prayd, for mercy or for meed,
To save his life, ne let him be descryde,
But hearken to his lore, and all his counsell hyde.

---

447. **engines:** instruments.   449. **wonne:** dwelling.   **Sel. XVI:**
from *FQ*, III. x.   1. **silly:** simple.   8. **brouzes:** young shoots
and twigs of shrubs.   10. **Tho:** then.

12. **busse:** kiss.   16. **welkin:** sky.   22. **hornes:** In Elizabethan
slang an adulterous wife was said to have "horned" her husband,
or "given him horns." Origin unknown.   46. **abrayed:** woke
with a start.

51

Tho gan he her perswade to leave that lewd
And loathsom life, of God and man abhord,
And home returne, where all should be renewd
With perfect peace and bandes of fresh accord,
And she receivd againe to bed and bord,   60
As if no trespas ever had beene donne:
But she it all refusèd at one word,
And by no meanes would to his will be wonne,
But chose emongst the jolly Satyres still to wonne.

52

He wooèd her till day-spring he espyde,
But all in vaine; and then turnd to the heard,
Who butted him with hornes on every syde,
And trode downe in the durt, where his hore°
      beard
Was fowly dight,° and he of death afeard.
Early, before the heavens fairest light
Out of the ruddy East was fully reard,   70
The heardes out of their foldes were loosèd quight,°
And he emongst the rest crept forth in sory plight.

55

High over hilles and over dales he fledd,
As if the wind him on his winges had borne;
Ne banck nor bush could stay him, when he spedd
His nimble feet, as treading still° on thorne:
Grief, and despight, and gealosy, and scorne,
Did all the way him follow hard behynd;
And he himselfe himselfe loath'd so forlorne,
So shamefully forlorne of womankynd,   80
That, as a Snake, still lurkèd in his wounded mynd.

56

Still fled he forward, looking backward still;
Ne stayd his flight nor fearefull agony,
Till that he came unto a rocky hill
Over the sea suspended dreadfully,
That living creature it would terrify
To looke adowne, or upward to the hight:
From thence he threw him selfe despiteously,°
All desperate of his fore-damnèd° spright,°
That seemed no help for him was left in living
      sight.

57

But through long anguish and selfe-murdring
      thought   91
He was so wasted and forpinèd quight,°
That all his substance was consum'd to nought,

And nothing left but like an aery Spright,
That on the rockes he fell so flit° and light,
That he thereby receiv'd no hurt at all;
But chauncèd on a craggy cliff to light,
Whence he with crooked clawes so long did crall,
That at the last he found a cave with entrance
      small.

58

Into the same he creepes, and thenceforth there
Resolv'd to build his balefull mansion   101
In drery darkenes and continuall feare
Of that rocks fall, which ever and anon
Threates with huge ruine him to fall upon,
That he dare never sleepe, but that one eye
Still ope he keepes for that occasion;
Ne ever rests he in tranquillity,
The roring billowes beat his bowre so boystrously.

59

Ne ever is he wont on ought to feed
But todes and frogs, his pasture poysonous,   110
Which in his cold complexion° doe breed
A filthy blood, or humour rancorous,
Matter of doubt and dread suspitious,
That doth with curelesse care consume the hart,
Corrupts the stomacke with gall vitious,
Cros-cuts the liver with internall smart,
And doth transfixe the soule with deathes eternall
      dart.

60

Yet can he never dye, but dying lives,
And doth himselfe with sorrow new sustaine,
That death and life attonce unto him gives,   120
And painefull pleasure turnes to pleasing paine.
There dwels he ever, miserable swaine,
Hatefull both to him selfe and every wight;
Where he, through privy° griefe and horrour vaine,
Is woxen° so deform'd that he has quight
Forgot he was a man, and Gelosy is hight.

SELECTION XVII

Florimel's story is still left in suspense, and we reach
the climax of Book III. A knight called Scudamour has
enlisted Britomart's aid for the rescue of his beloved
Amoret, from the House of Busirane (lawless and ob-
sessive Love; see Introduction, p. 100). This passage,
like Selections XI and XII, shows Spenser's art at the
point where it differs most from that of the dramatist
or lyrist. An atmosphere which expresses a mood or
spiritual condition rather than a passion is created by
the slow, and increasingly disquieting, series of images.

---

67. hore: gray.   68. fowly dight: brought into a foul or filthy
condition.   71. quight: probably "quit," free; possibly "quite,"
completely.   76. still: always.   88. despiteously: mercilessly.
89. fore-damned: the *fore* might mean "already, previously,
damned" (cf. *fore*-see) or merely "utterly damned" (cf. *for*-
wearied).   spright: soul.   92. quight: quite.

95. flit: airy, volatile.   111. complexion: temperament, constitution.   124. privy: private, secret.   125. woxen: waxed,
grown.

21

There they dismounting drew their weapons bold,
And stoutly came unto the Castle gate,
Whereas no gate they found them to withhold,
Nor ward to waite at morne and evening late;
But in the Porch, that did them sore amate,°
A flaming fire, ymixt with smouldry smoke
And stinking sulphure, that with griesly hate
And dreadfull horror did all entraunce choke,
Enforcèd them their forward footing to revoke.

22

Greatly thereat was Britomart dismayd,   10
Ne in that stownd° wist how her selfe to beare;
For daunger vaine it were to have assayd
That cruell element, which all things feare,
Ne none can suffer to approchen neare:
And, turning backe to Scudamour, thus sayd:
"What monstrous enmity provoke we heare?
Foolhardy as th' Earthes children, the which made
Batteill against the Gods, so we a God invade."

25

Therewith, resolv'd to prove her utmost might,
Her ample shield she threw before her face,   20
And her swords point directing forward right
Assayld the flame; the which eftesoones gave place,
And did it selfe divide with equall space,
That through she passèd, as a thonder bolt
Perceth the yielding ayre, and doth displace
The soring clouds into sad showres ymolt;°
So to her yold° the flames, and did their force re-
volt.°

26

Whom whenas Scudamour saw past the fire
Safe and untoucht, he likewise gan assay
With greedy will and envious desire,   30
And bad the stubborne flames to yield him way:
But cruell Mulciber° would not obay
His threatfull pride, but did the more augment
His mighty rage, and with imperious sway
Him forst, (maulgre°) his fercenes to relent,
And backe retire, all scorcht and pittifully brent.

27

With huge impatience he inly swelt,°
More for great sorrow that he could not pas
Then° for the burning torment which he felt;
That with fell woodnes° he effiercèd° was,   40
And wilfully him° throwing on the gras
Did beat and bounse his head and brest ful sore:
The whiles the Championesse now entred has

The utmost rowme, and past the foremost dore;
The utmost rowme abounding with all precious
store:

28

For round about the walls yclothèd were
With goodly arras° of great majesty,
Woven with gold and silke, so close and nere
That the rich metall lurked privily,
As° faining to be hidd from envious eye;   50
Yet here, and there, and every where, unwares
It shewd it selfe and shone unwillingly;
Like a discoloured Snake, whose hidden snares
Through the greene gras his long bright burnisht
back declares.

29

And in those Tapets° weren fashionèd
Many faire pourtraicts, and many a faire feate;
And all of love, and al of lusty-hed,
As seemèd by their semblaunt, did entreat:
And eke all Cupids warres they did repeate,
And cruell battailes, which he whilome fought   60
Gainst all the Gods to make his empire great;
Besides the huge massácres, which he wrought
On mighty kings and kesars into thraldome
brought.

30

Therein was writt° how often thondring Jove
Had felt the point of his hart-percing dart,
And, leaving heavens kingdome, here did rove
In straunge disguize, to slake his scalding smart;
Now, like a Ram, faire Hellè to pervart,
Now, like a Bull, Europa to withdraw:
Ah! how the fearefull Ladies tender hart   70
Did lively seeme to tremble, when she saw
The huge seas under her t' obay her servaunts°
law.

32

Then was he turnd into a snowy Swan,
To win faire Leda° to his lovely trade:°
O wondrous skill! and sweet wit of the man,
That her in daffadillies sleeping made
From scorching heat her daintie limbes to shade;
Whiles the proud Bird, ruffing° his fethers wyde
And brushing his faire brest, did her invade:
She slept; yet twixt her eielids closely spyde   80
How towards her he rusht, and smilèd at his pryde.

34

Twise was he seene in soaring Eagles shape,
And with wide winges to beat the buxome° ayre:

Sel. XVII: from *FQ*, III. xi, xii.   5. amate: deject.   11. stownd:
crisis.   26. ymolt: melted.   27. yold: yielded.   revolt: draw
back.   32. Mulciber: Vulcan, god of fire.   35. maulgre: against
his will.   37. swelt: boiled.   39. Then: than.   40. woodnes:
madness.   effierced: enraged.   41. him: himself.

47. arras: hangings.   50. as: as if.   55. Tapets: tapestries.
64. writt: pictured.   72. servaunts: lover's.   74. Leda: Cf.
Yeats, "Leda and the Swan," in Vol. II.   his . . . trade: his
amorous transaction, the "dealings" he hoped to have with her.
78. ruffing: ruffling.   83. buxome: yielding.

Once, when he with Asteriè° did scape;
Againe, when as the Trojane boy° so fayre
He snatcht from Ida hill, and with him bare:
Wondrous delight it was there to behould
How the rude Shepheards after him did stare,
Trembling through feare least down he fallen
   should,
And often to him calling to take surer hould. 90

36

And thou, faire Phœbus, in thy colours bright
Wast there enwoven, and the sad distresse
In which that boy° thee plongèd, for despight
That thou bewray'dst his mothers wantonnesse,
When she with Mars was meynt° in joyfulnesse:
Forthy he thrild° thee with a leaden dart
To love faire Daphne, which thee lovèd lesse;
Lesse she thee lov'd then was thy just desart,°
Yet was thy love her death, and her death was thy
   smart.

37

So lovedst thou the lusty Hyacinct;° 100
So lovedst thou the faire Coronis° deare;
Yet both are of thy haplesse hand extinct,
Yet both in flowres doe live, and love thee beare,
The one a Paunce,° the other a sweet-breare:
For griefe whereof, ye mote have lively seene
The God himselfe rending his golden heare,
And breaking quite his garlond ever greene,
With other signes of sorrow and impatient teene.°

40

Next unto him was Neptune picturèd,
In his divine resemblance wondrous lyke: 110
His face was rugged, and his hoarie hed
Droppèd with brackish deaw: his threeforkt Pyke
He stearnly shooke, and therewith fierce did stryke
The raging billowes, that on every syde
They trembling stood, and made a long broad dyke,
That his swift charet might have passage wyde
Which foure great Hippodames° did draw in teme-
   wise tyde.

41

His seahorses did seeme to snort amayne,°
And from their nosethrilles blow the brynie
   streame, 119

That made the sparckling waves to smoke agayne,
And flame with gold; but the white fomy creame
Did shine with silver, and shoot forth his beame.
The God himselfe did pensive seeme and sad,
And hong adowne his head as he did dreame;
For privy love his brest empiercèd had,
Ne ought but deare Bisaltis° ay could make him
   glad.

46

Kings, Queenes, Lords, Ladies, knights and Dam-
   sels gent,°
Were heap'd together with the vulgar sort,
And mingled with the raskall rablement,°
Without respect of person or of port 130
To shew Dan Cupids powre and great effórt:°
And round about a border was entrayld°
Of broken bowes and arrowes shivered short;
And a long bloody river through them rayld,°
So lively and so like that living sence it fayld.°

47

And at the upper end of that faire rowme
There was an Altar built of pretious stone
Of passing valew and of great renowme,
On which there stood an Image all alone
Of massy gold, which with his owne light shone;
And winges it had with sondry colours dight, 141
More sondry colours then the proud Pavone°
Beares in his boasted fan, or Iris° bright,
When her discolourd bow she spreds through
   hevens hight.

48

Blyndfold he was; and in his cruell fist
A mortall bow and arrowes keene did hold,
With which he shot at randon, when him list,°
Some headed with sad lead, some with pure gold;
(Ah man! beware how thou those dartes behold.)
A wounded Dragon under him did ly, 150
Whose hideous tayle his lefte foot did enfold,
And with a shaft was shot through either eye,
That no man forth might draw, ne no man
   remedye.

49

And underneath his feet was written thus,
Unto the Victor of the Gods° this bee:
And all the people in that ample hous
Did to that image bowe their humble knee,
And oft committed fowle Idolatree.
That wondrous sight faire Britomart amazd,

84. Asterie: daughter of the Titan Coeus, one of Jove's innumerable mistresses. 85. Trojane boy: Ganymede. 93. that
boy: Cupid. 95. meynt: mingled. 96. thrild: pierced.
98. desart: desert. 100. Hyacinct: Hyacinthus, a boy loved
by Apollo who accidentally killed him at quoits. A flower was
formed from his blood, probably not that now known as the
hyacinth. 101. Coronis: Apollo begot on her the famous
physician Asclepius, but afterwards killed her in a fit of jealousy.
104. Paunce: pansy. 108. teene: anguish. 117. Hippodames:
probably a mistake for "Hippocamps" (sea monsters with the
hindparts of dolphins and the foreparts of horses). 118. amayne:
amain, strongly.

126. Bisaltis: i.e., the daughter of Bisaltus, Theophane.
127. gent: gentle, of gentle birth. 129. raskall rablement: the
canaille, the vulgar crowd. 131. effort: strength. 132. entrayld: entwined. 134. rayld: flowed. 135. fayld: deceived.
142. Pavone: peacock. 143. Iris: the rainbow goddess.
147. him list: he pleased. 155. Victor . . . Gods: i.e., Cupid.

Ne seeing could her wonder satisfie,   160
But ever more and more upon it gazd,
The whiles the passing brightnes her fraile sences
    dazd.

50

Tho,° as she backward cast her busie eye
To search each secrete of that goodly sted,
Over the dore thus written she did spye,
Bee bold: she oft and oft it over-red,
Yet could not find what sence it figurèd:
But what so were therein or writ or ment,
She was no whit thereby discouragèd
From prosecuting of her first intent,   170
But forward with bold steps into the next roome
    went.

51

Much fayrer then the former was that roome,
And richlier by many partes arayd;
For not with arras made in painefull° loome,
But with pure gold it all was overlayd,
Wrought with wilde Antickes, which their follies
    playd
In the rich metal as they living were.
A thousand monstrous formes therein were made,
Such as false love doth oft upon him weare;
For love in thousand monstrous formes doth oft
    appeare.   180

52

And all about the glistring walles were hong
With warlike spoiles and with victorious prayes
Of mightie Conquerours and Captaines strong,
Which were whilome captivèd in their dayes
To cruell love, and wrought their owne decayes.
Their swerds and speres were broke, and hauber-
    ques° rent,
And their proud girlonds of tryumphant bayes
Troden in dust with fury insolent,
To shew the victors might and mercilesse intent.

53

The warlike Mayd, beholding earnestly   190
The goodly ordinaunce of this rich Place,
Did greatly wonder; ne could satisfy
Her greedy eyes with gazing a long space:
But more she mervaild that no footings trace
Nor wight appeard, but wastefull emptinesse
And solemne silence over all that place:
Straunge thing it seem'd, that none was to possesse
So rich purveyaunce,° ne them keepe with careful-
    nesse.

54

And, as she lookt about, she did behold
How over that same dore was likewise writ,   200
Be bolde, be bolde, and every where, *Be bold;*
That much she muz'd, yet could not construe it
By any ridling skill, or commune wit.
At last she spyde at that rowmes upper end
Another yron dore, on which was writ,
Be not too bold; whereto though she did bend
Her earnest minde, yet wist not what it might in-
    tend.

55

Thus she there wayted untill eventyde,
Yet living creature none she saw appeare,
And now sad shadowes gan the world to hyde   210
From mortall vew, and wrap'n darkenes dreare;
Yet nould° she d'off her weary armes, for feare
Of secret daunger, ne let sleepe oppresse
Her heavy eyes with natures burdein deare,
But drew her selfe aside in sickernesse,°
And her wel-pointed wepons did about her dresse.

1

Tho, whenas chearelesse Night ycovered had
Fayre heaven with an universall clowd,
That every wight dismayd with darkenes sad
In silence and in sleepe themselves did shrowd, 220
She heard a shrilling Trompet sound alowd,
Signe of nigh battaill, or got victory:
Nought therewith daunted was her courage prowd,
But rather stird to cruell enmity,
Expecting ever when some foe she might descry.

2

With that an hideous storme of winde arose,
With dreadful thunder and lightning atwixt,°
And an earthquake, as if it streight would lose
The worlds foundations from his centre fixt:
A direful stench of smoke and sulphure mixt   230
Ensewd, whose noyaunce° fild the fearefull sted°
From the fourth howre of night untill the sixt;
Yet the bold Britonesse was nought ydred,
Though much emmov'd, but stedfast still per-
    severèd.

3

All suddeinly a stormy whirlwind blew
Throughout the house, that clappèd every dore,
With which that yron wicket open flew,
As it with mighty levers had bene tore;
And forth yssèwd, as on the readie flore
Of some Theatre, a grave personage   240

That in his hand a braunch of laurell bore,
With comely haveour and count'nance sage,
Yclad in costly garments fit for tragicke Stage.

4

Proceeding to the midst he stil did stand,
As if in minde he somewhat had to say;
And to the vulgare° beckning with his hand,
In signe of silence, as to heare a play,
By lively actions he gan bewray
Some argument of matter passionèd:
Which doen, he backe retyrèd soft away,   250
And, passing by, his name discoverèd,
Ease, on his robe in golden letters cypherèd.

5

' he noble Mayd still standing all this vewd,
And merveild at his straunge intendiment.°
With that a joyous fellowship isséwd
Of Minstrales making goodly meriment,
With wanton Bardes, and Rymers impudent;°
All which together song full chearefully
A lay of loves delight with sweet concent:
After whom marcht a jolly company,   260
In manner of a maske,° enrangèd orderly.

6

The whiles a most delitious harmony
In full straunge notes was sweetly heard to sound,
That the rare sweetnesse of the melody
The feeble sences wholly did confound,
And the frayle soule in deepe delight nigh drownd:
And, when it ceast, shrill trompets lowd did bray,
That their report did far away rebound;
And, when they ceast, it gan againe to play,
The whiles the maskers marchèd forth in trim
    aray.   270

7

The first was Fansy,° like a lovely Boy
Of rare aspéct, and beautie without peare,
Matchable ether to that ympe° of Troy,
Whom Jove did love and choose his cup to beare;
Or that same daintie lad, which was so deare
To great Alcidès,° that, when as he dyde,
He wailèd womanlike with many a teare,
And every wood and every valley wyde
He filled with Hylas° name; the Nymphes eke
    Hylas cryde.

246. the vulgare: the people, audience.   254. intendiment:
purpose.   257. impudent: shameless.   261. maske: a masque
or entertainment (later of a semidramatic nature) in which the
performers, who were normally amateurs, wore masks or other
disguises.   271. Fansy: an amorous liking or "fancy" for a
particular person.   273. ympe: scion, offshot. Ganymede is
meant. He was loved by Jove, carried up to heaven by an eagle,
and made the gods' cupbearer.   276. Alcides: Hercules.
279. Hylas: a youth loved by Hercules when they both sailed
under Jason on the Argo. At one landing place Hylas was kid-

8

His garment nether° was of silke nor say,°   280
But paynted plumes in goodly order dight,
Like as the sunburnt Indians do aray
Their tawney bodies in their proudest plight:
As those same plumes so seemd he vaine and light,
That by his gate° might easily appeare;
For still he far'd as dauncing in delight,
And in his hand a windy fan did beare,
That in the ydle ayre he mov'd still here and theare.

9

And him beside marcht amorous Desyre,
Who seemd of ryper yeares then th' other Swayne,
Yet was that other swayne this elders syre,   291
And gave him being, commune to them twayne:
His garment was disguysèd° very vayne,
And his embrodered Bonet sat awry:
Twixt both his hands few sparks he close did
    strayne,
Which still he blew and kindled busily,
That soone they life conceiv'd, and forth in flames
    did fly.

10

Next after him went Doubt, who was yclad
In a discolour'd cote of straunge disguyse,
That at his backe a brode Capuccio° had,   300
And sleeves dependaunt Albanesè-wyse:°
He lookt askew with his mistrustfull eyes,
And nycely trode, as thornes lay in his way,
Or that the flore to shrinke he did avyse;°
And on a broken reed he still did stay
His feeble steps, which shrunck when hard thereon
    he lay.

11

With him went Daunger, cloth'd in ragged weed
Made of Beares skin, that him more dreadfull made;
Yet his owne face was dreadfull, ne did need
Straunge horrour to deforme his griesly shade:
A net in th' one hand, and a rusty blade   311
In th' other was; this Mischiefe, that Mishap:
With th' one his foes he threatned to invade,
With th' other he his friends ment to enwrap;
For whom he could not kill he practizd° to entrap.

12

Next him was Feare, all arm'd from top to toe,
Yet thought himselfe not safe enough thereby,
But feard each shadow moving too or froe;
And, his owne armes when glittering he did spy

naped by water nymphs and never seen again. Hercules lamented his loss, as described in the text.   280. nether: neither.
say: a cloth rather like serge.   285. gate: gait.   293. disguysed:
oddly made or arranged.   300. Capuccio: hood.   301. Al-
banese-wyse: in the Albanian manner (?).   304. avyse: perceive.   315. practizd: plotted, maneuvered.

Or clashing heard, he fast away did fly,   320
As ashes pale of hew, and wingèd heeld,°
And evermore on Daunger fixt his eye,
Gainst whom he alwayes bent a brasen shield,
Which his right hand unarmèd fearefully° did
    wield.

13

With him went Hope in rancke, a handsome Mayd,
Of chearefull looke and lovely to behold:
In silken samite° she was light arayd,
And her fayre lockes were woven up in gold:
She alway smyld, and in her hand did hold
An holy-water-sprinckle, dipt in deowe,   330
With which she sprinckled favours manifold
On whom she list, and did great liking sheowe,
Great liking unto many, but true love to feowe.

14

And after them Dissemblaunce and Suspect
Marcht in one rancke, yet an unequall paire;
For she was gentle and of milde aspéct,
Courteous to all and seeming debonaire,
Goodly adornèd and exceeding faire:
Yet was that all but paynted and pourloynd,
And her bright browes were deckt with borrowed
    haire;   340
Her deeds were forgèd, and her words false coynd,
And alwaies in her hand two clewes of silke she
    twynd.

15

But he was fowle, ill favourèd, and grim,
Under his eiebrowes looking still askaunce;
And ever, as Dissemblaunce laught on him,
He lowrd on her with daungerous eyeglaunce,
Shewing his nature in his countenaunce:
His rolling eies did never rest in place,
But walkte each where for feare of hid mischaunce,
Holding a lattis° still before his face,   350
Through which he stil did peep as forward he did
    pace.

16

Next him went Griefe and Fury, matcht yfere;°
Griefe all in sable sorrowfully clad,
Downe hanging his dull head with heavy chere,
Yet inly being more then seeming sad:
A paire of Pincers in his hand he had,
With which he pinchèd people to the hart,
That from thenceforth a wretched life they ladd;°
In wilfull languor and consuming smart,
Dying each day with inward wounds of dolours
    dart.   360

17

But Fury was full ill appareilèd
In rags, that naked nigh she did appeare,
With ghastly looks and dreadfull drerihed;
And from her backe her garments she did teare,
And from her head ofte rente her snarlèd° heare:
In her right hand a firebrand shee did tosse
About her head, still roming here and there;
As a dismayèd Deare in chace embost,
Forgetfull of his safety, hath his right way lost.

18

After them went Displeasure and Pleasaúnce,   370
He looking lompish° and full sullein sad,
And hanging downe his heavy countenaunce;
She chearfull, fresh, and full of joyaunce glad,
As if no sorrow she ne felt ne drad;°
That evill matchèd paire they seemd to bee:
An angry Waspe th' one in a viall had,
Th' other in hers an hony-laden Bee.
Thus marchèd these six couples forth in faire de-
    gree.

19

After all these there marcht a most faire Dame,
Led of two grysie Villeins, th' one Despight,°   380
The other clepèd° Cruelty by name:
She, dolefull Lady, like a dreary Spright
Cald by strong charmes out of eternall night,
Had Deathes owne ymage figurd in her face,
Full of sad signes, fearfull to living sight;
Yet in that horror shewd a seemely grace,
And with her feeble feete did move a comely pace.

20

Her brest all naked, as nett° yvory
Without adorne of gold or silver bright,
Wherewith the Craftesman wonts it beautify,   390
Of her dew honour was despoylèd quight;
And a wide wound therein (O ruefull sight!)
Entrenchèd deep with knyfe accursèd keene,
Yet freshly bleeding forth her fainting spright,
(The worke of cruell hand) was to be seene,
That dyde in sanguine red her skin all snowy
    cleene.

21

At that wide orifice her trembling hart
Was drawne forth, and in silver basin layd,
Quite through transfixèd with a deadly dart,
And in her blood yet steeming fresh embayd:°   400
And those two villeins, which her steps upstayd,
When her weake feete could scarcely her sustaine,
And fading vitall powres gan to fade,

321. heeld: heeled.   324. fearefully: timidly.   327. samite:
silk fabric sometimes interwoven with gold.   350. lattis: lattice.
352. yfere: together.   358. ladd: led.

365 snarled: tangled.   371. lompish: lumpish, dull and heavy
looking.   374. drad: dreaded.   380. Despight: spitefulness,
malice.   381. cleped: called.   388. nett: pure.   400. embayd:
bathed.

Her forward still with torture did constraine,
And evermore encreasèd her consuming paine.

22

Next after her, the wingèd God° him selfe
Came riding on a Lion ravenous,
Taught to obay the menage of that Elfe
That man and beast with powre imperious
Subdeweth to his kingdome tyrannous.   410
His blindfold eies he bad awhile unbinde,
That his proud spoile of that same dolorous
Faire Dame he might behold in perfect kinde;
Which seene, he much rejoycèd in his cruell minde.

23

Of which ful prowd, him selfe up rearing hye
He lookèd round about with sterne disdayne,
And did survay his goodly company;
And, marshalling the evill-ordered trayne,
With that the darts which his right hand did
          straine
Full dreadfully he shooke, that all did quake,   420
And clapt on hye his coulourd wingès twaine,
That all his many° it affraide did make:
Tho, blinding him againe, his way he forth did
          take.

24

Behinde him was Reproch, Repentaunce, Shame;
Reproch the first, Shame next, Repent behinde:
Repentaunce feeble, sorrowful, and lame;
Reproch despightfull, carelesse, and unkinde;
Shame most ill-favourd, bestiall, and blinde:
Shame lowrd, Repentaunce sighd, Reproch did
          scould;
Reproch sharpe stings, Repentaunce whips en-
          twinde,   430
Shame burning brond-yrons in her hand did hold:
All three to each unlike, yet all made in one mould.

25

And after them a rude confusèd rout
Of persons flockt, whose names is hard to read:
Emongst them was sterne Strife, and Anger stout;
Unquiet Care, and fond Unthriftyhead;
Lewd Losse of Time, and Sorrow seeming dead;
Inconstant Chaunge, and false Disloyalty;
Consuming Riotise, and guilty Dread
Of heavenly vengeaunce; faint Infirmity;   440
Vile Poverty; and, lastly, Death with infamy.

26

There were full many moe like maladies,
Whose names and natures I note° readen well;
So many moe, as there be phantasies

In wavering wemens witt, that none can tell,
Or paines in love, or punishments in hell:
All which disguizèd marcht in masking wise
About the chamber by the Damozell;
And then returnèd, having marched thrise,
Into the inner rowme from whence they first did
          rise.   450

27

So soone as they were in, the dore streightway
Fast lockèd, driven with that stormy blast
Which first it opened, and bore all away.
Then the brave Maid, which al this while was plast
In secret shade, and saw both first and last,
Issewèd forth, and went unto the dore
To enter in, but fownd it lockèd fast:
It vaine she thought with rigorous uprore
For to efforce, when charmes had closèd it afore.

28

Where force might not availe, there sleights and
          art   460
She cast to use, both fitt for hard emprize:
Forthy from that same rowme not to depart
Till morrow next shee did her selfe avize,
When that same Maske againe should forth arize.
The morrowe nexte appeard with joyous cheare,
Calling men to their daily exercize:
Then she, as morrow fresh, her selfe did reare
Out of her secret stand that day for to outweare.

29

All that day she outwore in wandering
And gazing on that Chambers ornament,   470
Till that againe the second evèning
Her covered with her sable vestiment,
Wherewith the worlds faire beautie she hath blent:°
Then, when the second watch was almost past,
That brasen dore flew open, and in went
Bold Britomart, as she had late forecast,°
Nether of ydle showes, nor of false charmes
          aghast.

30

So soone as she was entred, rowned about
Shee cast her eies to see what was become
Of all those persons which she saw without: 480
But lo! they streight were vanisht all and some;
Ne living wight she saw in all that roome,
Save that same woefull Lady, both whose hands
Were bounden fast, that did her ill become,
And her small waste girt rownd with yron bands
Upon a brasen pillour, by the which she stands.

---

406. winged God: Cupid.   422. many: household, retinue.
443. note: cannot.

473. blent: blinded (i.e., made invisible).   476. forecast: pre-
determined.

31

And her before the vile Enchaunter° sate,
Figuring straunge charácters° of his art:
With living blood he those charácters wrate,°
Dreadfully dropping from her dying hart,   490
Seeming transfixèd with a cruell dart;
And all perforce to make her him to love.
Ah! who can love the worker of her smart?
A thousand charmes he formerly did prove,°
Yet thousand charmes could not her stedfast hart
    remove.

32

Soone as that virgin knight he saw in place,
His wicked bookes in hast he overthrew,
Not caring his long labours to deface;
And, fiercely running to that Lady trew,
A murdrous knife out of his pocket drew,   500
The which he thought, for villeinous despight,
In her tormented bodie to embrew:°
But the stout Damzell, to him leaping light,
His cursèd hand withheld, and maisterèd his
    might.

33

From her, to whom his fury first he ment,
The wicked weapon rashly he did wrest,
And, turning to herselfe, his fell intent,
Unwares it strooke into her° snowie chest,
That litle drops empurpled her faire brest.
Exceeding wroth therewith the virgin grew,   510
Albe° the wound were nothing deepe imprest,
And fiercely forth her mortall blade she drew,
To give him the reward for such vile outrage dew.

34

So mightily she smote him, that to ground
He fell halfe dead: next stroke him should have
    slaine,
Had not the Lady, which by him stood bound,
Dernly° unto her callèd to abstaine
From doing him to dy. For else her paine
Should be remedilesse; sith none but hee   519
Which wrought it could the same recure againe.
Therewith she stayed her hand, loth stayd to bee;
For life she him envýde, and long'd revenge to see:

35

And to him said: "Thou wicked man, whose meed
For so huge mischiefe and vile villany
Is death, or if that ought doe death exceed;
Be sure that nought may save thee from to dy

But if that thou this Dame do presently°
Restore unto her health and former state:
This doe, and live, els dye undoubtedly."
He, glad of life, that lookt for death but late,   530
Did yield him selfe right willing to prolong his
    date:

36

And, rising up, gan streight to over-looke
Those cursed leaves, his charmes back to reverse.
Full dreadfull thinges out of that balefull booke
He red, and measur'd many a sad° verse,
That horrour gan the virgins hart to perse,
And her faire locks up starèd stiffe on end,
Hearing him those same bloody lynes reherse;
And, all the while he red, she did extend
Her sword high over him, if ought he did° offend.

37

Anon she gan perceive the house to quake,   541
And all the dores to rattle round about:
Yet all that did not her dismaièd make,
Nor slack her threatfull hand for daungers dout:°
But still with stedfast eye and courage stout
Abode, to weet° what end would come of all.
At last that mightie chaine, which round about
Her tender waste was wound, adowne gan fall,
And that great brasen pillour broke in peeces small.

38

The cruell steele, which thrild° her dying hart,   550
Fell softly forth, as of his° owne accord,
And the wyde wound, which lately did dispart
Her bleeding brest, and riven bowels gor'd,
Was closèd up, as it had not beene bor'd,
And every part to safèty full sownd,
As° she were never hurt, was soone restored.
Tho, when she felt her selfe to be unbownd
And perfect hole,° prostrate she fell unto the
    grownd.

39

Before faire Britomart she fell prostráte,
Saying; "Ah noble knight! what worthy meede°
Can wretched Lady, quitt from wofull state,   561
Yield you in lieu of this your gracious deed?
Your vertue selfe her owne reward shall breed,
Even immortal prayse and glory wyde,
Which I your vassall, by your prowesse freed,
Shall through the world make to be notifyde,
And goodly well advaunce that goodly well was
    tryde."

---

487. vile Enchaunter: Busirane.   488. characters: letters or
other symbolic shapes.   489. wrate: wrote.   494. prove: try
out.   502. embrew: moisten.   503. her: Britomart's.
511. Albe: though.   517. Dernly: really means "secretly."
Spenser perhaps thought it meant "grimly." See Sel. XIII, l. 4n.

527. presently: immediately.   535. sad: in the sense of the
Latin *tristis*, grisly, ill-omened.   540. if . . . did: lest . . . should.
544. dout: fear.   546. weet: know.   550. thrild: thrilled, i.e.,
pierced.   551. his: its.   556. As: as if.   558. hole: whole,
sound.   560. meede: reward.

40

But Britomart, uprearing her from grownd,
Said: " Gentle Dame, reward enough I weene,
For many labours more then I have found,   570
This, that in safetie now I have you seene,
And meane° of your deliverance have beene.
Henceforth, faire Lady, comfort to you take,
And put away remembrance of late teene;
Insted thereof, know that your loving Make°
Hath no lesse griefe endurèd for your gentle sake."

41

She much was cheard to heare him mentiond,
Whom of all living wightes she lovèd best.
Then laid the noble Championesse strong hond
Upon th' enchaunter which had her distrest   580
So sore, and with foule outrages opprest.
With that great chaine, wherewith not long ygoe
He bound that pitteous Lady prisoner, now relest,
Himselfe she bound, more worthy to be so,
And captive with her led to wretchednesse and
    wo.

42

Returning back, those goodly rowmes, which erst°
She saw so rich and royally arayd,
Now vanisht utterly and cleane subverst
She found, and all their glory quite decayd;
That sight of such a chaunge her much dismayd
Thence forth descending to that perlous porch   591
Those dreadfull flames she also found delayd°
And quenchèd quite like a consumèd torch,
That erst all entrers wont so cruelly to scorch.

SELECTION XVIII

Scudamour, who was left behind when Britomart
passed through the fire into Busirane's House in the
preceding Selection, has since then been traveling with
Britomart's female attendant, Old Glaucè. He is looking for Amoret and Britomart; never having seen Britomart except in full armor, Scudamour believes her to
be a man and is jealously suspicious of her association
with Amoret. The symbolical meaning of the cottage
at which he arrives in this passage needs no explanation.

32

So as they travellèd, the drouping night,
Covered with cloudie storme and bitter showre,
That dreadfull seem'd to every living wight,
Upon them fell, before her timely howre;
That forcèd them to seeke some covert bowre,
Where they might hide their heads in quiet rest,

And shrowd their persons from that stormie
    stowre.°
Not farre away, not meet for any guest,
They spide a little cottage, like some poore mans
    nest.

33

Under a steepe hilles side it placèd was,   10
There where the mouldred earth had cav'd the
    banke;
And fast beside a little brooke did pas
Of muddie water, that like puddle stanke,
By which few crooked sallowes° grew in ranke:
Whereto approaching nigh they heard the sound
Of many yron hammers beating ranke,
And answering their wearie turnes around,
That seemèd some blacksmith dwelt in that desert
    ground.

34

There entring in, they found the goodman selfe
Full busily unto his worke ybent;   20
Who was to weet a wretched wearish° elfe,
With hollow eyes and rawbone cheekes forspent,
As if he had in prison long bene pent:
Full blacke and griesly did his face appeare,
Besmeard with smoke that nigh his eye-sight
    blent;°
With rugged beard, and hoarie shagged heare,
The which he never wont to combe, or comely
    sheare.

35

Rude was his garment, and to rags all rent,
Ne better had he, ne for better cared:
With blistred hands emongst the cinders brent,   30
And fingers filthie with long nayles unpared,
Right fit to rend the food on which he fared.
His name was Care; a blacksmith by his trade,
That neither day nor night from working spared,
But to small purpose yron wedges made;
Those be unquiet thoughts that carefull minds in-
    vade.

36

In which his worke he had six servants prest,°
About the Andvile standing evermore
With huge great hammers, that did never rest   39
From heaping stroakes which thereon sousèd°
    sore:
All six strong groomes, but one then other more;
For by degrees they all were disagreed,
So likewise did the hammers which they bore,

---

572. meane: means.   575. Make: mate, lover (i.e., Scudamour).
586. erst: previously.   592. delayd: mitigated.

Sel. XVIII: from *FQ*, IV. v.   7. stowre: originally "fight, conflict"; by Spenser's time meant little more than "occasion."
14. sallowes: willows.   21. wearish: pale and shriveled.
25. blent: blinded.   37. prest: ready at hand.   40. soused:
struck.

Like belles in greatnesse orderly succeed,
That he which was the last the first did farre exceede.

38

Sir Scudamour there entring much admired°
The manner of their worke and wearie paine;
And, having long beheld, at last enquired
The cause and end thereof, but all in vaine;
For they for nought would from their worke re-
fraine,   50
Ne let his speeches come unto their eare.
And eke the breathfull bellowes blew amaine,
Like to the Northern winde, that none could heare:
Those Pensifenesse did move; and Sighes the bel-
lowes weare.

39

Which when that warriour saw, he said no more,
But in his armour layd him down to rest:
To rest he layd him downe upon the flore,
(Whylome for ventrous Knights the bedding best)
And thought his wearie limbs to have redrest.
And that old aged Dame,° his faithfull Squire,
Her feeble joynts layd eke adowne to rest;   61
That needed much her weake age to desire,
After so long a travell which them both did tire.

40

There lay Sir Scudamour long while expecting
When° gentle sleepe his heavie eyes would close;
Oft chaunging sides, and oft new place electing,
Where better seem'd he mote himselfe repose;
And oft in wrath he thence againe uprose,
And oft in wrath he layd him downe againe.
But wheresoever he did himselfe, dispose,   70
He by no meanes could wishèd ease obtaine:
So every place seem'd painefull, and each changing
vaine.

41

And evermore, when he to sleepe did thinke,
The hammers sound his senses did molest,
And evermore, when he began to winke,
The bellowes noyse disturb'd his quiet rest,
Ne suffred sleepe to settle in his brest:
And all the night the dogs did barke and howle
About the house, at sent of stranger guest: 79
And now the crowing Cocke, and now the Owle
Lowde shriking, him afflicted to the very sowle.

42

And, if by fortune any litle hap
Upon his heavie eye-lids chaunst to fall,

Eftsoones one of those villeins him did rap
Upon his headpeece with his yron mall;°
That he was soone awakèd therewithall,
And lightly started up as one affrayd,
Or as if one him suddenly did call:
So oftentimes he out of sleepe abrayd,°
And then lay musing long on that him ill apayd.°

43

So long he muzèd, and so long he lay,   91
That at the last his wearie sprite, opprest
With fleshly weaknesse, which no creature may
Long time resist, gave place to kindly rest,
That all his senses did full soone arrest:
Yet in his soundest sleepe his dayly feare
His ydle braine gan busily molest,
And made him dreame those two° disloyall were:
The things, that day most minds, at night doe most
appeare.

44

With that the wicked carle, the maister Smith,
A paire of red-whot yron tongs did take   101
Out of the burning cinders, and therewith
Under his side him nipt; that, forst to wake,
He felt his hart for very paine to quake,
And started up avengèd for to be
On him the which his quiet slomber brake:
Yet, looking round about him, none could see;
Yet did the smart remaine, though he himselfe did
flee.

45

In such disquiet and hart-fretting payne
He all that night, that too long night, did passe
And now the day out of the Ocean mayne   111
Began to peepe above this earthly masse,
With pearly dew sprinkling the morning grasse:
Then up he rose, like heavie lumpe of lead,
That in his face, as in a looking glasse,
The signes of anguish one mote plainely read,
And ghesse the man to be dismayd with gealous
dread.

SELECTION XIX

We return to Florimel, who has been languishing in
Proteus' dungeon ever since the end of Selection XV.
Meanwhile Spenser describes the marriage of two English river deities (Thames and Medway); their wedding, which of course represents their confluence, is
celebrated in Proteus' house. The decorative purpose
of this episode is to introduce the great processional
pageant of aquatic deities: its purpose in the plot is to
bring Marinell within earshot of Florimel and thus produce the happy ending.

---

46. admired: wondered at.   60. aged Dame: Britomart's attendant. See headnote.   64-65. expecting When: waiting till.

85. mall: hammer.   89. abrayd: woke with a start.   90. on . . .
apayd: on what pleased him ill.   98. those two: Britomart and
Amoret.

3

Deepe in the bottome of an huge great rocke
The dongeon was, in which her bound he left,
That neither yron barres, nor brasen locke,
Did neede to gard from force, or secret theft
Of all her lovers which would her have reft:
For wall'd it was with waves, which rag'd and ror'd
As they the cliffe in peeces would have cleft;
Besides ten thousand monsters foule abhor'd
Did waite about it, gaping griesly, all begor'd.

4

And in the midst thereof did horror dwell,   10
And darkenesse dredd that never viewèd day,
Like to the balefull house of lowest hell,
In which old Styx° her aged bones alway,
Old Styx the Grandame of the Gods, doth lay.
There did this lucklesse mayd seven months abide,
Ne ever evening saw, ne mornings ray,
Ne ever from the day the night describe,
But thought it all one night that did no houres divide.

5

And all this was for love of Marinell,
Who her despysd (ah! who would her despyse?)
And wemens love did from his hart expell,   21
And all those joyes that weake mankind entyse.
Nathlesse his pride full dearely he did pryse;
For of a womans hand it was ywroke,°
That of the wound he yet in languor lyes,
Ne can be curèd of that cruell stroke
Which Britomart him gave, when he did her provoke.

6

Yet farre and neare the Nymph his mother sought,
And many salves did to his sore applie,
And many herbes did use. But when as nought,
She saw, could ease his rankling maladie,   31
At last to Tryphon she for helpe did hie,
(This Tryphon is the Sea-gods surgeon hight,°)
Whom she besought to find some remedie,
And for his paines a whistle him behight,°
That of a fishes shell was wrought with rare delight.

7

So well that Leach° did hearke to her request,
And did so well employ his carefull paine,
That in short space his hurts he had redrest,
And him restor'd to healthfull state againe: 40
In which he long time after did remaine
There with the Nymph his mother, like her thrall:

Sel. XIX: from *FQ*, IV. xi, xii.   **13.** Styx: river goddess of the
lower world.   **24.** ywroke: avenged.   **33.** hight: called.   **35.** behight: promised.   **37.** Leach: healer.

Who sore against his will did him retaine,
For feare of perill which to him mote fall
Through his too ventrous prowesse provèd over
all.

8

It fortun'd then, a solemne feast was there
To all the Sea-gods and their fruitfull seede,
In honour of the spousalls which then were
Betwixt the Medway° and the Thames agreed.
Long had the Thames (as we in records reed)   50
Before that day her wooèd to his bed,
But the proud Nymph would for no worldly meed,
Nor no entreatie, to his love be led;
Till now, at last relenting, she to him was wed.

9

So both agreed that this their bridale feast
Should for the Gods in Proteus house be made;
To which they all repayr'd, both most and least,
As well which in the mightie Ocean trade,°
As that in rivers swim, or brookes doe wade;
All which, not if an hundred tongues to tell,   60
And hundred mouthes, and voice of brasse I had,
And endlesse memorie that mote excell,
In order as they came could I recount them well.

11

First came great Neptune, with his threeforkt
mace,
That rules the Seas and makes them rise or fall;
His dewy lockes did drop with brine apace
Under his Diademe imperiall:
And by his side his Queene with coronall,
Faire Amphitritè, most divinely faire,
Whose yvorie shoulders weren covered all,   70
As with a robe, with her owne silver haire,
And deckt with pearles which th' Indian seas for
her prepaire.

12

These marchèd farre afore the other crew:
And all the way before them, as they went,
Triton his trompet shrill before them blew,
For goodly triumph and great jollyment,
That made the rockes to roare as they were rent.
And after them the royall issue came,
Which of them sprung by lineall descent: 79
First the Sea-gods, which to themselves doe clame
The powre to rule the billowes, and the waves to
tame.

18

Next came the aged Ocean and his Dame
Old Tethys, th' oldest two of all the rest;

49. Medway: an English river.   **58.** trade: live.

For all the rest of those two parents came,
Which afterward both sea and land possest;
Of all which Nereus, th' eldest and the best,
Did first proceed, then which none more upright,
Ne more sincere in word and deed profest;
Most voide of guile, most free from fowle despight,
Doing him selfe, and teaching others to doe right.

20

And after him the famous rivers came,   91
Which doe the earth enrich and beautifie:
The fertile Nile, which creatures new doth
    frame;°
Long Rhodanus,° whose sourse springs from the
    skie;
Faire Ister,° flowing from the mountaines hie:
Divine Scamander,° purpled yet with blood
Of Greeks and Trojans which therein did die;
Pactolus° glistring with his golden flood;
And Tygris fierce, whose streames of none may be
    withstood;

23

Then was there heard a most celestiall sound   100
Of dainty musicke, which did next ensew
Before the spouse: that was Aríon° crownd;
Who, playing on his harpe, unto him drew
The eares and hearts of all that goodly crew,
That even yet the Dolphin, which him bore
Through the Agæan seas from Pirates vew,
Stood still by him astonisht at his lore,
And all the raging seas for joy forgot to rore.

24

So went he playing on the watery plaine;
Soone after whom the lovely Bridegroome came,
The noble Thamis,° with all his goodly traine; 111
But him before there went, as best became,
His auncient parents, namely th' auncient Thame.°
But much more aged was his wife then he,
The Ouze, whom men doe Isis rightly name;
Full weake and crooked creature seemèd shee,
And almost blind through eld, that scarce her way
    could see.

93. which . . . frame: It was widely believed that the Nile mud
spontaneously engendered various low animal forms.   94. Rhodanus: the river Rhone, in France, which rises in the Alps.
95. Ister: the river Danube.   96. Scamander: a Trojan river.
98. Pactolus: a river in Lydia, from which gold was washed.
102. Arion: a famous Greek harp player and poet. Once, when
he had been captured by pirates, he jumped overboard and was
carried home by a music-loving dolphin.   111. Thamis: the
river god of the Thames. Throughout this passage the personal
relations between the river deities of course represent geographi-
cal relations between the rivers. Thus Isis (the Thames at Oxford)
and the river Thame flow into the Thames proper and are thus
his parents. Those who are interested should consult a map of
England.   113. Thame: another English river.

45

Then came the Bride, the lovely Medua° came,
Clad in a vesture of unknowen geare
And uncouth fashion, yet her well became,   120
That seem'd like silver, sprinckled here and theare
With glittering spangs° that did like starres ap-
    peare,
And wav'd upon, like water Chamelot,°
To hide the metall, which yet every where
Bewrayd it selfe, to let men plainely wot
It was no mortall worke, that seem'd and yet was
    not.

46

Her goodly lockes adowne her backe did flow
Unto her waste, with flowres bescatterèd,
The which ambrosiall odours forth did throw
To all about, and all her shoulders spred   130
As a new spring; and likewise on her hed
A Chapèlet of sundry flowers she wore,
From under which the deawy humour° shed
Did tricle downe her haire, like to the hore°
Congealèd litle drops which doe the morne adore.

3

All those were there, and many other more,
Whose names and nations were too long to tell
That Proteus house they fild even to the dore;
Yet were they all in order, as befell,
According their degrees disposèd well.   140
Amongst the rest was faire Cymodocè,
The mother of unlucky Marinell,
Who thither with her came, to learne and see
The manner of the Gods when they at banquet be.

4

But for he was halfe mortall, being bred
Of mortall sire, though of immortall wombe,
He might not with immortall food be fed,
Ne with th' eternall Gods to bancket come;
But walkt abrode, and round about did rome
To view the building of that uncouth place,   150
That seem'd unlike unto his earthly home:
Where, as he to and fro by chaunce did trace,
There unto him betid a disaventrous case.°

5

Under the hanging of an hideous clieffe
He heard the lamentable voice of one,
That piteously complaind her carefull grieffe
Which never she before disclosd to none,
But to her selfe her sorrow did bemone:

118. Medua: Medway, a Kentish river.   122. spangs: spangles,
small bright ornaments.   123. water Chamelot: camlet (a rich
fabric, originally Oriental) which has been given a wavy, lustrous
finish by the process technically known as "watering."
133. humour: moisture.   134. hore: gray.   153. disaventrous
case: unfortunate happening.

So feelingly her case she did complaine,
That ruth it movèd in the rocky stone,   160
And made it seeme to feele her grievous paine,
And oft to grone with billowes beating from the
    maine:

9

"Ye Gods of seas, if any Gods at all
Have care of right, or ruth° of wretches wrong,
By one or other way me, woefull thrall,
Deliver hence out of this dungeon strong,
In which I daily dying am too long:
And if ye deeme° me death for loving one
That loves not me, then doe it not prolong,
But let me die and end my daies attone,°   170
And let him live unlov'd, or love him selfe alone.

11

"But O vaine judgement, and conditions vaine,
The which the prisoner points unto the free!
The whiles I him condemne, and deeme his paine,°
He where he list goes loose, and laughes at me.
So ever loose, so ever happy be!
But where so loose or happy that thou art,
Know, Marinell, that all this is for thee."
With that she wept and wail'd, as if her hart
Would quite have burst through great abundance
    of her smart.   180

12

All which complaint when Marinell had heard,
And understood the cause of all her care
To come of him for using her so hard,
His stubborne heart, that never felt misfare,
Was toucht with soft remorse and pitty rare;
That even for griefe of minde he oft did grone,
And inly wish that in his powre it weare
Her to redresse: but since he meanes found none,
He could no more but her great misery bemone.

13

Thus whilst his stony heart with tender ruth
Was toucht, and mighty courage mollifide,   191
Dame Venus sonne, that tameth stubborne youth
With iron bit, and maketh him abide
Till like a victor on his backe he ride,
Into his mouth his maystring° bridle threw,
That made him stoupe, till he did him bestride:
Then gan he make him tread his steps anew,
And learne to love by learning lovers paines to rew.

18

And now by this the feast was throughly ended,
And every one gan homeward to resort: 200
Which seeing, Marinell was sore offended

That his departure thence should be so short,
And leave his love in that sea-wallèd fort.
Yet durst he not his mother disobay,
But her attending in full seemly sort,
Did march amongst the many° all the way,
And all the way did inly mourne, like one astray.

20

That in short space his wonted chearefull hew
Gan fade, and lively spirits deaded quight: 209
His cheeke-bones raw, and eie-pits hollow grew,
And brawney armes had lost their knowen might,
That nothing like himselfe he seem'd in sight.
Ere long so weake of limbe, and sicke of love
He woxe, that lenger he note° stand upright,
But to his bed was brought, and layd above,
Like ruefull ghost, unable once to stirre or move.

21

Which when his mother saw, she in her mind
Was troubled sore, ne wist well what to weene;
Ne could by search nor any meanes out find
The secret cause and nature of his teene,°   220
Whereby she might apply some medicine;
But weeping day and night did him attend,
And mourn'd to see her losse before her eyne,°
Which griev'd her more that she it could not
    mend:
To see an helplesse evill double griefe doth lend.

25

Nathlesse she rested not so satisfide;
But leaving watry gods, as booting° nought,
Unto the shinie heaven in haste she hide,°
And thence Apollo, King of Leaches, brought.
Apollo came; who, soone as he had sought   230
Through his disease, did by and by out find
That he did languish of some inward thought,
The which afflicted his engrievèd mind;
Which love he red to be, that leads each living
    kind.

26

Which when he had unto his mother told,
She gan thereat to fret and greatly grieve;
And, comming to her sonne, gan first to scold
And chyde at him that made her misbelieve:
But afterwards she gan him soft to shrieve,°
And wooe with fair intreatie, to disclose   240
Which of the Nymphes his heart so sore did mieve;°
For sure she weend it was some one of those,
Which he had lately seene, that for his love he
    chose.

---

164. ruth: pity.   168. deeme: adjudge.   170. attone: at once.
174. deeme . . . paine: decide on his penalty.   195. maystring:
mastering.

206. many: retinue.   214. note: could not.   220. teene:
anguish.   223. eyne: eyes.   227. booting: availing.   228. hide:
hied.   239. him . . . shrieve: hear his confession.   241. mieve:
move.

27

Now lesse she fearèd that same fatall read,°
That warnèd him of womens love beware,
Which being ment of mortall creatures sead,°
For love of Nymphes she thought she need not care,
But promist him, what ever wight she weare,
That she her love to him would shortly gaine.
So he her told: but soone as she did heare   250
That Florimell it was which wrought his paine,
She gan afresh to chafe, and grieve in every vaine.

28

Yet since she saw the streight extremitie,
In which his life unluckily was layd,
It was no time to scan the prophecie,
Whether old Proteus true or false had sayd,
That his decay should happen by a mayd.
It's late in death of daunger to advize,
Or love forbid him, that is life denayd;
But rather gan in troubled mind devize   260
How she that Ladies libertie might enterprize.

29

To Proteus selfe to sew° she thought it vaine,
Who was the root and worker of her woe,
Nor unto any meaner to complaine;
But unto great king Neptune selfe did goe,
And, on her knee before him falling lowe,
Made humble suit unto his Majestie
To graunt to her her sonnes life, which his foe,
A cruell Tyrant, had presumpteouslie
By wicked doome condemn'd a wretched death to
    die.   270

30

To whom God Neptune, softly smyling, thus:
"Daughter, me seemes of double wrong ye plaine,
Gainst one that hath both wrongèd you and us;
For death t' adward I ween'd did appertaine
To none but to the seas sole Soveraine.
Read therefore who it is which this hath wrought,
And for what cause; the truth discover plaine,
For never wight so evill did or thought,
But would some rightfull cause pretend, though
    rightly nought."   279

31

To whom she answer'd: "Then, it is by name
Proteus, that hath ordayn'd my sonne to die;
For that a waift,° the which by fortune came
Upon your seas, he claym'd as propertie:
And yet nor his, nor his in equitie,
But yours the waift by high prerogative.
Therefore I humbly crave your Majestie

It to replevie,° and my sonne reprive.
So shall you by one gift save all us three alive."

32

He graunted it: and streight his warrant made,
Under the Sea-gods seale autenticall,   290
Commaunding Proteus straight t' enlarge° the
    mayd,
Which wandring on his seas imperiall
He lately tooke, and sithence kept as thrall.
Which she receiving with meete thankefulnesse,
Departed straight to Proteus therewithall;
Who, reading it with inward loathfulnesse,
Was grievèd to restore the pledge he did possesse.

33

Yet durst he not the warrant to withstand,
But unto her delivered Florimell:
Whom she receiving by the lilly hand,   300
Admyr'd her beautie much, as she mote well,
For she all living creatures did excell;
And was right joyous that she gotten had
So faire a wife for her sonne Marinell.
So home with her she streight the virgin lad,
And shewèd her to him, then being sore bestad.°

34

Who soone as he beheld that angels face
Adorn'd with all divine perfection,
His che*rèd heart eftsoones away gan chace
Sad death, revivèd with her sweet inspection,   310
And feeble spirit inly felt refection:
As withered weed through cruell winters time,
That feeles the warmth of sunny beames reflec-
    tion,
Liftes up his head that did before decline,
And gins to spread his leafe before the faire sun-
    shine.

SELECTION XX

Britomart, wandering in search of her lover Artegall
(the Knight of Justice) comes to the Temple of Isis.
Notice here again the presence of different levels. The
dream, merely on psychological grounds, is suitable to
an enamoured but virtuous woman (given the place
and time), but it has two further significances: (a) that
Britomart, by Artegall, will become an ancestress of the
British royal house, and (b) that Justice (Artegall-
Osiris) must be subordinated to "clemence," equity or
mercy (Isis).

---

244. read: counsel.   246. sead: seed.   262. sew°: sue.
282. waift: something found straying and ownerless, a waif.

287. replevie: command to be restored.   291. enlarge: liberate.
306. sore bestad: in sorry plight.

13

Her seem'd,° as° she was doing sacrifize
To Isis,° deckt with Mitre on her hed
And linnen stole after those Priestès guize
All sodainely she saw transfigurèd
Her linnen stole to robe of scarlet red,
And Moone-like Mitre to a Crowne of gold;
That even she her selfe much wonderèd
At such a chaunge, and joyèd to behold
Her selfe adorn'd with gems and jewels manifold.

14

And, in the midst of her felicity,   10
An hideous tempest seemèd from below
To rise through all the Temple sodainely,
That from the Altar all about did blow
The holy fire, and all the embers strow
Uppon the ground; which, kindled privily,
Into outragious flames unwares did grow,
That all the Temple put in jeopardy
Of flaming, and her selfe in great perplexity.

15

With that the Crocodile, which sleeping lay
Under the Idols feete in fearelesse bowre,   20
Seem'd to awake in horrible dismay,
As being troubled with that stormy stowre;
And gaping greedy wide did streight devoure
Both flames and tempest: with which growen great,
And swolne with pride of his owne peerelesse
      powre.
He gan to threaten her likewise to eat,
But that the Goddesse with her rod him backe did
      beat.

16

Tho turning all his pride to humblesse meeke,
Him selfe before her feete he lowly threw,
And gan for grace and love of her to seeke;   30
Which she accepting, he so neare her drew
That of his game she soone enwombèd grew,
And forth did bring a Lion of great might,
That shortly did all other beasts subdew,
With that she wakèd full of fearefull fright,
And doubtfully dismayd through that so uncouth
      sight.

17

So thereupon long while she musing lay,
With thousand thoughts feeding her fantasie,
Untill she spide the lampe of lightsome day
Up-lifted in the porch of heaven hie: 40
Then up she rose fraught with meláncholy,
And forth into the lower parts did pas,

Whereas the Priestes she found full busily
About their holy things for morrow Mas;
Whom she saluting faire, faire resaluted was:

20

Then gan she to declare the whole discourse
Of all that vision which to her appeard,
As well as to her minde it had recourse.
All which when he unto the end had heard,
Like to a weake faint-hearted man he fared   50
Through great astonishment of that strange sight;
And, with long locks up-standing, stifly stared
Like one adawèd° with some dreadfull spright:
So, fild with heavenly fury, thus he her behight.°

21

"Magnificke Virgin, that in queint° disguise
Of British armes doest maske thy royall blood,
So to pursue a perillous emprize,
How couldst thou weene, through that disguizèd
      hood,
To hide thy state from being understood?
Can from th' immortall Gods ought hidden bee?
They doe thy linage, and thy Lordly brood,   61
They doe thy sire lamenting sore for thee,
They doe thy love forlorne in womens thraldome°
      see.

22

"The end whereof, and all the long event,
They do to thee in this same dreame discover;
For that same Crocodile doth represent
The righteous Knight that is thy faithfull lover,
Like to Osyris in all just endever:
For that same Crocodile Osyris is,
That under Isis feete doth sleepe for ever;   70
To shew that clemence oft, in things amis,
Restraines those sterne behests and cruell doomes
      of his.

23

"That Knight shall all the troublous stormes
      asswage
And raging flames, that many foes shall reare
To hinder thee from the just heritage
Of thy sires Crowne, and from thy countrey
      deare:
Then shalt thou take him to thy lovèd fere,°
And joyne in equall portion of thy realme;
And afterwards a sonne to him shalt beare,
That Lion-like shall shew his powre extreame.   80
So blesse thee God, and give thee joyance of thy
      dreame!"

Sel. XX: from *FQ*, V. vii. 1. Her seem'd: it seemed to her.
as: as if. 2. Isis: the Egyptian goddess. In Spenser she symbolizes Clemency.

53. adawed: overawed.   54. behight: promised.   55. queint:
subtle.   63. love . . . thraldome: Britomart's lover Artegall was
at this time the prisoner of the giantess Radigund.   77. fere:
mate.

SELECTION XXI

Spenser tells us what it felt like to be writing *The Faerie Queene*. From Book VI, Proem.

I

The waies, through which my weary steps I guyde
In this delightful land of Faèry,
Are so exceeding spacíous and wyde,
And sprinckled with such sweet variety
Of all that pleasant is to eare or eye,
That I, nigh ravisht with rare thoughts delight,
My tedious travell doe forget thereby;
And, when I gin to feele decay of might,
It strength to me supplies, and chears my dullèd
    spright.

SELECTION XXII

As untaught nature in the person of the wood gods
(see Selection IV) helped Una, so here, in the person
of the Savage it helps two lovers, Sir Calepine, who has
just been wounded by another knight, and Serena, who
has been bitten by the Blatant Beast. This creature
(possibly derived from Malory's Questing Beast) symbolizes Slander, the enemy whom Sir Calidore, the
Knight of Courtesy, is pursuing throughout this Book
(VI). Its appearance here has the same anticipatory
function as our first glimpse of Acrasia's Bower in Selection IX. Book VI is softer than any preceding Book,
more sylvan and rustic; note the freshness and simplicity at the opening of stanza 17. (I cannot here give
the end of the bear-and-baby story: the baby was saved.)

II

But the wyld man, contrarie to her feare,
Came to her creeping like a fawning hound,
And by rude tokens made to her appeare
His deepe compassion of her doleful stound,°
Kissing his hands, and crouching to the ground;
For° other language had he none, nor speach,
But a soft murmure and confusèd sound
Of senselesse words, which nature did him teach
T' expresse his passions, which his reason did em-
    peach.

12

And, comming likewise to the wounded knight,
When he beheld the streames of purple blood   11
Yet flowing fresh, as movèd with the sight,
He made great mone after his salvage mood;

And, running streight into the thickest wood,
A certaine herbe from thence unto him brought,
Whose vertue he by use well understood;
The juyce whereof into his wound he wrought,
And stopt the bleeding straight, ere he it staunchèd
    thought.

13

Then taking up that Recreants° shield and speare,
Which earst he left, he signes unto them made   20
With him to wend unto his wonning neare;
To which he easily did them perswade.
Farre in the forrest, by a hollow glade
Covered with mossie shrubs, which spredding brode
Did underneath them make a gloomy shade,
Where foot of living creature never trode,
Ne scarse wyld beasts durst come, there was this
    wights abode.

14

Thether he brought these unacquainted guests,
To whom faire semblance, as he could, he shewed
By signes, by lookes, and all his other gests;°   30
But the bare ground with hoarie mosse bestrowed
Must be their bed; their pillow was unsowed:°
And the frutes of the forest was their feast;
For their bad° Stuard neither plough'd nor sowed,
Ne fed on flesh, ne ever of wyld beast
Did taste the bloud, obaying natures first beheast.

15

Yet, howsoever base and meane it were,
They tooke it well, and thankèd God for all,
Which had them freèd from that deadly feare,
And sav'd from being to that caytive thrall,   40
Here they of force (as fortune now did fall)
Compellèd were themselves awhile to rest,
Glad of that easement, though it were but small;
That having there their wounds awhile redrest,
They mote the abler be to passe unto the rest.

16

During which time that wyld man did apply
His best endevour and his daily paine
In seeking all the woods both farre and nye
For herbes to dresse their wounds; still seeming
    faine
When ought he did, that did their lyking gaine.
So as ere long he had that knightès wound   51
Recurèd well, and made him whole againe;
But that same Ladies hurt no herbe he found
Which could redresse, for it was inwardly unsound.

Sel. XXII: from *FQ*, VI. iv. 4. stound: emergency, disaster.
6–9. For . . . empeach: obscure. What hindered (*empeached*) his
season may be either "his passions" or the fact that he could
not speak.

19. Recreants: coward's: reference to the knight who has
wounded Calepine. 30. gests: behavior. 32. pillow . . . unsowed: They had no sewn (i.e., proper) pillow, only moss.
34. bad: unskillful.

17

Now when as Calepine was woxen° strong,
Upon a day he cast° abrode to wend,
To take the ayre and heare the thrushes song,
Unarm'd, as fearing neither foe nor frend,
And without sword his person to defend:
There him befell, unlookèd for before,   60
An hard adventure with unhappie end,
A cruell Beare, the which an infant bore
Betwixt his bloodie jawes, besprinckled all with
    gore.

SELECTION XXIII

Serena, separated from Calepine, has now met Arthur and his squire, Timias, who has also been bitten
by the Blatant Beast. Arthur here leaves them both in
the care of a Hermit. Note that this good Hermit is in
externals very like the wicked Hermit in Selection I.
Spenser's symbols are not ready-made labels.

35

And nigh thereto a little Chappell stoode,
Which being all with Yvy overspred
Deckt all the roofe, and, shadowing the roode,
Seem'd like a grove faire braunchèd over-hed:
Therein the Hermite, which his life here led
In streight observaunce of religious vow,
Was wont his howres and holy things to bed;°
And therein he likewise was praying now,
Whenas these Knights arriv'd, they wist not where
    nor how.

36

They stayd not there, but streightway in did pas:
Whom when the Hermite present saw in place,   11
From his devotion streight he troubled was;
Which breaking off he toward them did pace
With stayèd steps and grave beseeming grace:
For well it seem'd that whilome he had beene
Some goodly person, and of gentle race,
That could his good° to all; and well did weene
How each to entertaine with curt'sie well beseene.

37

And soothly° it was sayd by common fame,
So long as age enabled him thereto,   20
That he had beene a man of mickle° name,
Renowmèd much in armes and derring doe;°
But being agèd now, and weary to

Of warres delight and worlds contentious toyle,
The name of knighthood he did disavow;
And, hanging up his armes and warlike spoyle,
From all this worlds incombraunce did himselfe
    assoyle.°

38

He thence them led into his Hermitage,
Letting their steedes to graze upon the greene.
Small was his house, and like a little cage,   30
For his owne turne, yet inly neate and clene,
Deckt with greene boughes and flowers gay beseene:
Therein he them full faire did entertaine
Not with such forgèd showes, as fitter beene
For courting fooles that curtesies would faine,
But with entire affection and appearaunce plaine.

39

Yet was their fare but homely, such as hee
Did use his feeble body to sustaine,
The which full gladly they did take in gree,°
Such as it was, ne did of want complaine,   40
But being well suffiz'd them rested faine.
But fair Serene all night could take no rest,
Ne yet that gentle Squire, for grievous paine
Of their late woundes, the which the Blatant Beast
Had given them, whose griefe through suffraunce
    sore increast.

40

So all that night they past in great disease,
Till that the morning, bringing earely light
To guide mens labours, brought them also ease,
And some asswagement of their painefull plight.
Then up they rose, and gan them selves to dight
Unto their journey; but that Squire and Dame   51
So faint and feeble were, that they ne might
Endure to travell, nor one foote to frame:
Their hearts were sicke; their sides were sore; their
    feete were lame.

2

Such were the wounds the which that Blatant
    Beast
Made in the bodies of that Squire and Dame;
And, being such, were now much more increast
For want of taking heede unto the same,
That now corrupt and curelesse they became:
Howbe° that carefull Hermite did his best,   60
With many kindes of medicines meete, to tame
The poysnous humour which did most infest
Their ranckling wounds, and every day them duely
    drest.

---

55. **woxen:** grown. 56. **cast:** resolved. **Sel. XXIII:** from *FQ*,
VI. v, vi. 7. **bed:** pray. 17. **could . . . good:** knew how to behave, had good manners. 19. **soothly:** truly. 21. **mickle:**
great. 22. **derring doe:** Spenser (mistakenly) thought this
meant "valor." (In Chaucer it really means "daring to do"
and has no sense unless a grammatical object follows.)

27. **assoyle:** to absolve, pardon; hence (as here) to set free.
39. **in gree:** contentedly. 60. **Howbe:** though.

3

For he right well in Leaches craft was seene;
And through the long experience of his dayes,
Which had in many fortunes tossèd beene
And past through many perillous assayes,
He knew the diverse went° of mortall wayes,
And in the mindes of men had great insíght;
Which with sage counsell, when they went astray,
He could enforme, and them reduce aright,   71
And all the passions heale which wound the weak-
er spright.

4

For whylome he had been a doughty Knight,
As any one that livèd in his daies,
And provèd oft in many perillous fight,
Of which he grace and glory wonne alwaies,
And in all battels bore away the baies:°
But being now attacht° with timely age,
And weary of this worlds unquiet waies,
He tooke him selfe unto this Hermitage,   80
In which he liv'd alone, like carelesse bird in cage.

5

One day, as he was searching of their wounds,
He found that they had festered privily;
Andranckling inward with unruly stounds,
The inner parts now gan to putrify,
That quite they seem'd past helpe of surgery;
And rather needed to be disciplinde
With holesome reede of sad sobriety,
To rule the stubborne rage of passion blinde:
Give salves to every sore, but counsell to the minde.

6

So, taking them apart into his cell,   91
He to that point fit speeches gan to frame,
As he the art of words knew wondrous well,
And eke could doe as well as say the same;
And thus he to them sayd: "Faire daughter Dame,
And you, faire Sonne, which here thus long now lie
In piteous languor since ye hither came,
In vaine of me ye hope for remedie,
And I likewise in vaine doe salves to you applie:

7

"For in your selfe your onely helpe doth lie   100
To heale your selves, and must proceed alone
From your owne will to cure your maladie,
Who can him cure that will be cur'd of none?
If therefore health ye seeke, observe this one:
First learne your outward senses to refraine
From things that stirre up fraile affection;
Your eies, your eares, your tongue, your talk re-
straine

From that they most affect,° and in due termes°
containe.

8

"For from those outward sences, ill affected,
The seede of all this evill first doth spring,   110
Which at the first, before it had infected,
Mote easie be supprest with little thing;
But being growen strong it forth doth bring
Sorrow, and anguish, and impatient paine,
In th' inner parts; and lastly, scattering
Contagious poyson close through every vaine,
It never rests till it have wrought his finall bane.

13

"In vaine therefore it were with medicine
To goe about to salve such kynd of sore,
That rather needes wise read° and discipline,   120
Then outward salves that may augment it more."
"Aye me!" (sayd then Serena, sighing sore)
"What hope of helpe doth then for us remaine,
If that no salves may us to health restore?"
"But sith we need good counsell," (sayd the
swaine)
"Aread, good Sire, some counsell that may us sus-
taine."

14

"The best" (sayd he) "that I can you advize,
Is to avoide the occasion of the ill:
For when the cause, whence evill doth arize,
Removèd is, th' effect surceaseth still.   130
Abstaine from pleasure, and restraine your will;
Subdue desire, and bridle loose delight;
Use scanted diet, and forbeare your fill;
Shun secresie, and talke in open sight:
So shall you soone repaire your present evill plight."

15

Thus having sayd, his sickely patients
Did gladly hearken to his grave beheast,
And kept so well his wise commaundèments,
That in short space their malady was ceast,
And eke the biting of that harmeful Beast   140
Was throughly heal'd. Tho when they did per-
ceave
Their wounds recur'd, and forces reincreast,
Of that good Hermite both they tooke their leave,
And went both on their way, ne ech would other
leave.

SELECTION XXIV

Serena, having left the hermitage with Timias, loses
him when he is captured by a Giant. She now falls

---

68. went: course.   77. baies: laurels (i.e., victory).   78. at-
tacht: arrested, confined.

108. affect: are attracted to.   termes: limits.   120. read:
counsel.

among Cannibals. The passage well illustrates Spenser's ruthless handling of horrors (stanzas 38, 39), his frank sensuality (42, 43), and his power of ominous suggestion (44).

35

In these wylde deserts where she now abode,
There dwelt a salvage nation, which did live
Of stealth and spoile, and making nightly rode°
Into their neighbours borders; ne did give
Them selves to any trade, (as for to drive
The painefull plough, or cattell for to breed,
Or by adventrous marchandize to thrive,)
But on the labours of poore men to feed,
And serve their owne necessities with others need.

36

Thereto they usde one most accursed order,   10
To eate the flesh of men whom they mote fynde,
And straungers to devoure, which on their border
Were brought by errour or by wreckfull wynde;
A monstrous cruelty gainst course of kynde!°
They, towards evening wandering every way
To seeke for booty, came by fortune blynde
Whereas this Lady, like a sheepe astray,
Now drownèd in the depth of sleepe all fearelesse lay.

37

Soone as they spide her, Lord! what gladfull glee
They made amongst them selves; but when her face
Like the faire yvory shining they did see,   21
Each gan his fellow solace and embrace
For joy of such good hap by heavenly grace.
Then gan they to devize what course to take;
Whether to slay her there upon the place,
Or suffer her out of her sleepe to wake,
And then her eate attonce, or many meales to make.

38

The best advizement was, of bad, to let her
Sleepe out her fill without encomberment;
For sleepe, they sayd, would make her battill° better: 30
Then when she wakt they all gave one consent
That, since by grace of God she there was sent,
Unto their God they would her sacrifize,
Whose share, her guiltlesse bloud, they would present;
But of her dainty flesh they did devize
To make a common feast, and feed with gurmandize.°

39

So round about her they them selves did place
Upon the grasse, and diversely dispose
As each thought best to spend the lingring space.
Some with their eyes the daintest morsels chose;
Some praise her paps; some praise her lips and nose;   41
Some whet their knives, and strip their elboes bare:
The Priest° him selfe a garland doth compose
Of finest flowers, and with full busie care
His bloudy vessels wash, and holy fire prepare.

40

The Damzell wakes; then all attonce upstart,
And round about her flocke, like many flies,
Whooping and hallowing on every part,
As if they would have rent the brasen skies.
Which when she sees with ghastly grieffull eies,   50
Her heart does quake, and deadly pallied hew
Benumbes her cheekes: Then out aloud she cries,
Where none is nigh to heare that will her rew,
And rends her golden locks, and snowy brests embrew.°

41

But all bootes° not; they hands upon her lay:
And first they spoile her of her jewels deare,
And afterwards of all her rich array;
The which amongst them they in peeces teare,
And of the pray each one a part doth beare.
Now being naked, to their sordid eyes   60
The goodly threasures of natúre appeare:
Which as they view with lustfull fantasyes,
Each wisheth to him selfe, and to the rest envýes: —

42

Her yvorie neck; her alablaster brest;
Her paps, which like white silken pillowes were
For love in soft delight thereon to rest;
Her tender sides; her bellie white and clere,
Which like an Altar did itselfe uprere
To offer sarifice divine thereon;
Her goodly thighes, whose glorie did appeare   70
Like a triumphal Arch, and thereupon
The spoiles of Princes hang'd which were in battel won.

43

Those daintie parts, the dearlings of delight,
Which mote not be prophan'd of common eyes,
Those villeins view'd with loose lascivious sight,
And closely tempted° with their craftie spyes;°

---

43. The Priest: i.e., the priest or medicine man of the Cannibals. 54. embrew: stain (with blood, by tearing them) or wet (with tears). Syntax demands "embrews"; Spenser perhaps forgot to make some necessary alteration. 55. bootes: avails. 76. tempted: explored.   spyes: eyes.

Sel. XXIV: from FQ, VI. viii.   3. rode: raid.   14. course of kynde: the order of nature.   30. battill: fatten.   36. gurmandize: gluttony.

And some of them gan mongst themselves devize
Thereof by force to take their beastly pleasure:
But them the Priest rebuking did avize
To dare not to pollute so sacred threasure   80
Vow'd to the gods: religion held even theeves in
      measure.

44

So, being stayd, they her from thence directed
Unto a litle grove not farre asyde,
In which an altar shortly they erected
To slay her on. And now the Eventyde
His brode black wings had through the heavens
      wyde
By this dispred, that was the tyme ordayned
For such a dismall deed, their guilt to tyde:
Of few green turfes an altar soone they fayned,
And deckt it all with flowres which they nigh hand
      obtayned.   90

45

Tho, when as all things readie were aright,
The Damzell was before the altar set,
Being alreadie dead with fearefull fright:
To whom the Priest with naked armes full net°
Approching nigh, and murdrous knife well whet,
Gan mutter close a certaine secret charme,
With other divelish ceremonies met:°
Which doen, he gan aloft t' advance his arme,
Whereat they shouted all, and made a loud alarme.

46

Then gan the bagpypes and the hornes to shrill
And shrieke aloud, that, with the peoples voyce
Confusèd, did the ayre with terror fill,   102
And made the wood to tremble at the noyce:
The whyles she wayld, the more they did rejoyce.
Now mote ye understand that to this grove
Sir Calepine, by chaunce more then by choyce,
The selfe same evening fortune hether drove,
As he to seeke Serena through the woods did rove.

47

Long had he sought her and through many a
      soyle
Had traveld still on foot in heavie armes,   110
Ne ought was tyrèd with his endlesse toyle,
Ne ought was fearèd of his certaine harmes:
And now, all weetlesse° of the wretched stormes,
In which his love was lost, he slept full fast;
Till, being wakèd with these loud alarmes,
He lightly started up like one aghast,
And, catching up his arms, streight to the noise
      forth past.

48

There by th' uncertaine glims of starry night,
And, by the twinkling of their sacred fire,
He mote perceive a little dawning sight   120
Of all which there was doing in that quire:°
Mongst whom a woman spoyld of all attire
He spyde lamenting her unluckie strife,
And groning sore from grievèd hart entire.
Eftsoones he saw one with a naked knife
Readie to launch° her brest, and let out lovèd life.

49

With that he thrusts into the thickest throng
And, even as his right hand adowne descends,
He him preventing layes on earth along,
And sacrifizeth to th' infernal feends: 130
Then to the rest his wrathful hand he bends;
Of whom he makes such havocke and such hew,°
That swarmes of damnèd soules to hell he sends:
The rest, that scape his sword and death eschew,
Fly like a flocke of doves before a Faulcons vew.

SELECTION XXV

Here at last we meet Calidore himself. The passage
shows Spenser in his last phase (see Introduction, p.
93), never less a courtier, never more ready to believe
that true courtesy is most likely to be found among simple, unambitious countryfolk. Latin and Italian pastoral
poetry and Stoic maxims about the life "according to
nature" have, no doubt, helped him to write thus.

2

Great travell hath the gentle Calidore
And toyle endurèd, sith I left him last
Sewing° the Blatant Beast; which I forbore
To finish then, for other present hast.
Full many pathes and perils he hath past,
Through hills, through dales, through forests, and
      through plaines,
In that same quest which fortune on him cast,
Which he atchievèd to his owne great gaines,
Reaping eternall glorie of his restlesse paines.

3

So sharpely he the Monster did pursew,   10
That day nor night he suffred him to rest,
Ne rested he himselfe, but natures dew,°
For dread of daunger not to be redrest,
If he for slouth forslackt so famous quest.
Him first from court he to the cities coursed,

---

94. net: clean (for ritual considerations).   97. met: meet,
fitting.   113. weetlesse: ignorant.

121. quire: company.   126. launch: lance, pierce.   132. hew:
slaughter.   Sel. XXV: from *FQ*, VI. ix.   3. Sewing: pursuing.
12. but . . . dew: save for what nature needed.

And from the citties to the townes him prest,
And from the townes into the countrie forsed,
And from the country back to private farmes he
    scorsed.°

4

From thence into the open fields he fled,   19
Whereas the Heardes were keeping of their neat,°
And shepherds singing to their flockes (that fed)
Layes of sweete love and youthes delightful heat:
Him thether eke, for all his fearefull threat,
He followed fast, and chacèd him so nie,
That to the folds, where sheepe at night doe seat,
And to the litle cots,° where shepherds lie
In winters wrathfull time, he forcèd him to flie.

5

There on a day, as he pursew'd the chace,
He chaunst to spy a sort° of shepheard groomes,
Playing on pipes and caroling apace,   30
The whyles their beasts there in the budded
    broomes°
Beside them fed, and nipt the tender bloomes;
For other worldly wealth they carèd nought.
To whom Sir Calidore yet sweating comes,
And them to tell him courteously besought,
If such a beast they saw, which he had thether
    brought.

6

They answer'd him that no such beast they saw,
Nor any wicked feend that mote offend
Their happie flockes, nor daunger to them draw;
But if that such there were (as none they kend°)
They prayd high God them farre from them to
    send.   41
Then one of them, him seeing so to sweat,
After his rusticke wise,° that well he weend,°
Offred him drinke to quench his thirstie heat,
And, if he hungry were, him offred eke to eat.

7

The knight was nothing nice,° where was no need,
And tooke their gentle offer: so adowne
They prayd him sit, and gave him for to feed
Such homely what° as serves the simple clowne,°
That doth despise the dainties of the towne.   50
Tho,° having fed his fill, he there besyde
Saw a faire damzell, which did weare a crowne
Of sundry flowres with silken ribbands tyde,
Yclad in home-made greene that her owne hands
    had dyde.

18. scorsed: perhaps "forced him to change" (*scorse* usually means "to exchange"). **20. neat:** cattle. **26. cots:** cottages, small houses. **29. sort:** group. **31. broomes:** shrubs. **40. kend:** knew. **43. wise:** fashion, way. **that . . . weend:** as he thought well (?). **46. nice:** fastidious. **49. what:** matter, things. **clowne:** rustic, peasant. **51. Tho:** then.

8

Upon a litle hillocke she was placed
Higher then all the rest, and round about
Environ'd with a girland, goodly graced,
Of lovely lasses; and them all without
The lustie shepheard swaynes sate in a rout,°
The which did pype and sing her prayses dew,   60
And oft rejoyce, and oft for wonder shout,
As if some miracle of heavenly hew
Were downe to them descended in that earthly vew.

9

And soothly sure she was full fayre of face,
And perfectly well shapt in every lim,
Which she did more augment with modest grace
And comely carriage of her count'nance trim,
That all the rest like lesser lamps did dim:
Who, her admiring as some heavenly wight,
Did for their soveraine goddesse her esteeme,   70
And, caroling her name both day and night,
The fayrest Pastorella her by name did hight.

11

Her whyles Sir Calidore there vewèd well,
And markt her rare demeanure, which him seemed
So farre the meane of shepheards to excell,
As that he in his mind her worthy deemed
To be a Princes Paragone° esteemed,
He was unwares surprisd in subtile bands
Of the blynd boy;° ne thence could be redeemed
By any skill out of his cruell hands;   80
Caught like the bird which gazing still on others
    stands.

13

By this the moystie night approching fast
Her deawy humour gan on th' earth to shed,
That warn'd the shepheards to their homes to hast
Their tender flocks, now being fully fed,
For feare of wetting them before their bed.
Then came to them a good old agèd syre,
Whose silver lockes bedeckt his beard and hed,
With shepheards hooke in hand, and fit attyre,
That wild° the damzell rise; the day did now ex-
    pyre.   90

15

She at his bidding meekely did arise,
And streight unto her litle flocke did fare:
Then all the rest about her rose likewise,
And each his sundrie sheepe with severall care
Gathered together, and them homeward bare:
Whylest everie one with helping hands did strive,
Amongst themselves, and did their labours share,

59. rout: crowd. **77. Paragone:** pattern, or rival. **79. blynd boy:** Cupid. **90. wild:** willed, desired.

To helpe faire Pastorella home to drive
Her fleecie flocke; but Coridon most helpe did
    give.

16

But Melibœe (so hight that good old man)   100
Now seeing Calidore left all alone,
And night arrivèd hard at hand, began
Him to invite unto his simple home;
Which though it were a cottage clad with lome,°
And all things therein meane, yet better so
To lodge then in the salvage fields to rome.
The knight full gladly soone agreed thereto,
(Being his harts owne wish,) and home with him
    did go.

17

There he was welcom'd of that honest syre
And of his agèd Beldame homely well;   110
Who him besought himselfe to disattyre,
And rest himselfe till supper time befell;
By which home came the fayrest Pastorell,
After her flocke she in their fold had tyde:
And supper readie dight° they to it fell
With small adoe, and nature satisfyde,
The which doth litle crave contented to abyde.

18

Tho when they had their hunger slakèd well,
And the fayre mayd the table ta'ne away,
The gentle knight, as he that did excell   120
In courtesie and well could doe and say,
For so great kindnesse as he found that day
Gan greatly thanke his host and his good wife;
And drawing thence his speach another way,
Gan highly to commend the happie life
Which Shepheards lead, without debate or bitter
    strife.

19

"How much " (sayd he) "more happie is the state
In which ye, father, here doe dwell at ease,
Leading a life so free and fortunate
From all the tempests of these worldly seas,   130
Which tosse the rest in daungerous disease;
Where warres, and wreckes and wicked enmitie
Doe them afflict, which no man can appease,
That certès I your happinesse envíe,
And wish my lot were plast in such felicitie."

20

"Surely, my sonne," (then answer'd he againe)
"If happie, then it is in this intent,
That having small yet doe I not complaine
Of want, ne wish for more it to augment,
But doe my selfe with that I have content;   140

So taught of nature, which doth litle need
Of forreine helpes to lifes due nourishment:
The fields my food, my flocke my rayment breed;
No better doe I weare, no better doe I feed.

21

" Therefore I doe not any one envý,
Nor am envýde of any one therefore:
They that have much, feare much to loose thereby,
And store of cares doth follow riches store.
The litle that I have growes dayly more
Without my care, but onely to attend it;   150
My lambes doe every yeare increase their score,
And my flockes father daily doth amend it.
What have I, but to praise th' Almighty that doth
    send it!

22

" To them that list the worlds gay showes I leave,
And to great ones such follies doe forgive;
Which oft through pride do their owne perill
    weave,
And through ambition downe themselves doe drive
To sad decay, that might contented live.
Me no such cares nor combrous thoughts offend,
Ne once my minds unmovèd quiet grieve;   160
But all the night in silver sleepe I spend,
And all the day to what I list I doe attend.

23

" Sometimes I hunt the Fox, the vowèd foe
Unto my Lambes, and him dislodge away;
Sometime the fawne I practise° from the Doe,
Or from the Goat her kidde, how to convay:
Another while I baytes and nets display
The birds to catch, or fishes to beguyle;
And when I wearie am, I downe doe lay
My limbes in every shade to rest from toyle,   170
And drinke of every brooke when thirst my throte
    doth boyle.

24

" The time was once, in my first prime of yeares,
When pride of youth forth prickèd my desire,
That I disdain'd amongst mine equall peares°
To follow sheepe and shepheards base attire:
For further fortune then I would inquire;
And, leaving home, to roiall court I sought,
Where I did sell my selfe for yearely hire,
And in the Princes gardin daily wrought:
There I beheld such vainenesse as I never thought.

25

" With sight whereof soone cloyd, and long de-
    luded   181

---

104. lome: clay.   115. dight: prepared.

165. practise: contrive.   174. peares: mates, fellows.

With idle hopes which them doe entertaine,
After I had ten yeares my selfe excluded
From native home, and spent my youth in vaine,
I gan my follies to my selfe to plaine,
And this sweet peace, whose lacke did then appeare:
Tho, backe returning to my sheepe againe,
I from thenceforth have learn'd to love more deare
This lowly quiet life which I inherite here."

26

Whylest thus he talkt, the knight with greedy eare
Hong still upon his melting mouth attent;   191
Whose sensefull words empierst his hart so neare,
That he was rapt with double ravishment,
Both of his speach, that wrought him great content,
And also of the object of his vew,
On which his hungry eye was alwayes bent;
That twixt his pleasing tongue, and her faire hew,
He lost himselfe, and like one halfe entrauncèd
   grew.

27

Yet to occasion meanes to worke his mind,
And to insinuate his harts desire,   200
He thus replyde: "Now surely, syre, I find,
That all this worlds gay showes, which we admire,
Be but vaine shadowes to this safe retyre
Of life, which here in lowlinesse ye lead,
Fearelesse of foes, or fortunes wrackfull° yre
Which tosseth states,° and under foot doth tread
The mightie ones, affrayd of every chaunges dread."

29

"In vaine" (said then old Meliboe) "doe men
The heavens of their fortunes fault accuse,
Sith they know best what is the best for them;   210
For they to each such fortune doe diffuse,
As they doe know each can most aptly use:
For not that which men covet most is best,
Nor that thing worst which men do most refuse;
But fittest is, that all contented rest
With that they hold: each hath his fortune in his
   brest.

30

"It is the mynd that maketh good or ill,
That maketh wretch or happie, rich or poore;
For some, that hath abundance at his will,
Hath not enough, but wants in greatest store,   220
And other, that hath litle, askes no more,
But in that litle is both rich and wise;
For wisedome is most riches: fooles therefore
They are which fortunes doe by vowes devize,
Sith each unto himselfe his life may fortunize."°

SELECTION XXVI

Calidore, still among the shepherds, climbs a hill and sees the Graces dancing. Note the totally different imaginative value of these nudes and those we had in Selections IX and XII, and compare headnote to XXIII on the two Hermits.

6

It was an hill plaste in an open plaine,
That round about was bordered with a wood
Of matchlesse hight, that seem'd th' earth to dis-
   daine
In which all trees of honour stately stood,
And did all winter as in summer bud,
Spredding pavilions° for the birds to bowre,
Which in their lower braunches sung aloud;
And in their tops the soring hauke did towre,
Sitting like King of fowles in majesty and powre:

7

And at the foote thereof a gentle flud   10
His silver waves did softly tumble downe,
Unmard with ragged mosse or filthy mud;
Ne mote° wylde beastes, ne mote the ruder clowne,
Thereto approch; ne filth mote therein drowne:
But Nymphes and Faeries by the bancks did sit
In the woods shade which did the waters crowne,
Keeping all noysome things away from it,
And to the waters fall tuning their accents fit.

8

And on the top thereof a spacious plaine
Did spred it selfe, to serve to all delight,   10
Either to daunce, when they to daunce would faiᵣe,
Or else to course about their bases° light;
Ne ought there wanted which for pleasure might
Desirèd be, or thence to banish bale,
So pleasauntly the hill with equall hight
Did seeme to overlooke the lowly vale;
Therefore it rightly cleepèd° was mount Acidale.°

10

Unto this place when as the Elfin Knight°
Approcht, him seemèd that the merry sound
Of a shrill pipe he playing heard on hight,   30
And many feete fast thumping th' hollow ground,
That through the woods their Eccho did rebound.
He nigher drew to weete what mote it be:
There he a troupe of Ladies dauncing found
Full merrily, and making gladfull glee,
And in the midst a Shepheard piping he did see.

Sel. XXVI: from *FQ*, VI. x.   6. **pavilions**: literally, tents.
13. **mote**: could.   22. **bases**: probably the game called "prisoners' base."   27. **cleeped**: called.   **Acidale**: Acidalia was a
surname of Venus.   28. **Elfin Knight**: Calidore.

205. **wrackfull**: devastating.   206. **states**: people in high positions.   225. **fortunize**: make fortunate.

11

He durst not enter into th' open greene,
For dread of them unwares to be descryde,
For breaking of their daunce, if he were seene;
But in the covert of the wood did byde,   40
Beholding all, yet of them unespyde.
There he did see that pleasèd much his sight,
That even he him selfe his eyes envýde,
An hundred naked maidens lilly white
All raungèd in a ring and dauncing in delight.

12

All they without were raungèd in a ring,
And dauncèd round; but in the midst of them
Three other Ladies did both daunce and sing,
The whilest the rest them round about did hemme,
And like a girlond did in compasse stemme:°   50
And in the middest of those same three was placed
Another Damzell, as a precious gemme
Amidst a ring most richly well enchaced,°
That with her goodly presence all the rest much
     graced.

13

Looke! how the crowne, which Ariadne° wore
Upon her yvory forehead, that same day
That Theseus her unto his bridale bore,
When the bold Centaures made that bloudy fray
With the fierce Lapithes which did them dismay,
Being now placèd in the firmament,°   60
Through the bright heaven doth her beames display,
And is unto the starres an ornament,
Which round about her move in order excellent.

14

Such was the beauty of this goodly band,
Whose sundry parts were here too long to tell;
But she that in the midst of them did stand
Seem'd all the rest in beauty to excell,
Crownd with a rosie girlond that right well
Did her beseeme: And ever, as the crew
About her daunst, sweet flowres that far did smell
And fragrant odours they uppon her threw;   71
But most of all those three did her with gifts en-
     dew.

15

Those were the Graces, daughters of delight,
Handmaides of Venus, which are wont to haunt
Uppon this hill, and daunce there day and night:
Those three to men all gifts of grace do graunt;

And all that Venus in her selfe doth vaunt
Is borrowèd of them. But that faire one,
That in the midst was placèd paravaunt,°
Was she to whom that shepheard pypt alone;   80
That made him pipe so merrily, as never none.

16

She was, to weete,° that jolly Shepheards lasse,
Which pipèd there unto that merry rout;
That jolly shepheard, which there pipèd, was
Poore Colin Clout,° (who knowes not Colin
     Clout?)
He pypt apace, whilest they him daunst about.
Pype, jolly shepheard, pype thou now apace
Unto thy love that made thee low to lout:°
Thy love is present there with thee in place;
Thy love is there advaunst to be another Grace.   90

17

Much wondred Calidore at this straunge sight,
Whose like before his eye had never seene;
And standing long astonishèd in spright,
And rapt with pleasaunce, wist° not what to
     weene;
Whether it were the traine of beauties Queene,
Or Nymphes, or Faeries, or enchaunted show,
With which his eyes mote have deluded beene.
Therefore, resolving what it was to know,
Out of the wood he rose, and toward them did
     go.

18

But, soone as he appearèd to their vew,   100
They vanisht all away out of his sight,
And cleane were gone, which way he never knew:
All save the shepheard, who, for fell despight
Of that displeasure, broke his bag-pipe quight,
And made great mone for that unhappy turne:
But Calidore, though no lesse sory wight
For that mishap, yet seeing him to mourne,
Drew neare, that he he the truth of all by him mote
     learne.

19

And, first him greeting, thus unto him spake:
"Haile, jolly shepheard, which thy joyous dayes
Hear leadest in this goodly merry-make,   111
Frequented of these gentle Nymphes alwayes,
Which to thee flocke to heare thy lovely layes!
Tell me, what mote these dainty Damzels be,
Which here with thee doe make their pleasant
     playes?

---

50. in . . . stemme: confine (surround) in a circle. 53. enchaced: "set" (in the jeweler's sense). 55. Ariadne: daughter
of Minos; she saved the Athenian prince Theseus from her
father's labyrinth (or maze) by a thread or "clue," and afterward escaped with him. The rest of the story as given by Spenser
is unlike all other versions, and the fight of the tribe called
Lapithae against the Centaurs occurred at quite a different
wedding. 60. firmament: It has become the constellation
Corona Borealis.

79. paravaunt: pre-eminent. 82. to weete: "to wit," i.e., if
you want to know. 85. Colin Clout: i.e., Spenser himself, who
had already given himself this name in *The Shepheards Calendar*.
It is derived from the character in the poet Skelton (1460?–1529),
but the Skeltonic use of it throws little light on the Spenserian.
88. lout: bow. 94. wist: knew.

Right happy thou that mayst them freely see!
But why, when I them saw, fled they away from
me? "

20

" Not I so happy," answered then that swaine,
" As thou unhappy, which them thence didst
chace,
Whom by no meanes thou canst recall againe;   120
For, being gone, none can them bring in place,
But whom they of them selves list so to grace."
" Right sory I," (said then Sir Calidore)
" That my ill fortune did them hence displace;
But since things passèd none may now restore,
Tell me what were they all, whose lacke thee grieves
so sore? "

21

Tho gan that shepheard thus for to dilate:
" Then wote,° thou shepheard, whatsoever thou
bee,
That all those Ladies, which thou sawest late,
Are Venus Damzels, all within her fee,°   130
But differing in honour and degree:
They all are Graces which on her depend,
Besides a thousand more which ready bee
Her to adorne, when so she forth doth wend
But those three in the midst doe chiefe on her at-
tend.

22

" They are the daughters of sky-ruling Jove,
By him begot of faire Eurynomè,
The Oceans daughter, in this pleasant grove,
As he, this way comming from feastfull glee
Of Thetis wedding with Æacidee,°   140
In sommers shade him selfe here rested weary:
The first of them hight mylde Euphrosynè,
Next faire Aglaia, last Thalia merry;
Sweete Goddesses all three, which me in mirth do
cherry!°

23

" These three on men all gracious gifts bestow,
Which decke the body or adorne the mynde,
To make them lovely or well-favoured show;
As comely carriage, entertainement kynde,
Sweete semblaunt, friendly offices that bynde,
And all the complements of curtesie: 150
They teach us how to each degree and kynde
We should our selves demeane, to low, to hie,
To friends, to foes; which skill men call Civility."

---

128. wote: know.   **130. fee:** a hereditary estate held by feudal
tenure. Hence "within her fee" means "among her vassals."
They are followers of Venus.   **140. Aeacidee:** Peleus, the son
of Aeacus and father of Achilles.   **144. cherry:** cheer.

SELECTION XXVII

This selection is from the unfinished Book (usually
known as "the Mutability Cantos "), and we do not
know what its narrative context would have been. With
an immense wealth of processional detail (we must remember that this is the age of the vanished arts of
masque and pageant) Spenser asserts that Change has
almost (but not quite) the supreme power in the universe.

1

What man that sees the ever-whirling wheele,
Of Change, the which all mortall things doth sway,
But that therby doth find, and plainly feele,
How Mutability in them doth play
Her cruell sports to many mens decay?
Which that to all may better yet appeare,
I will rehearse that whylome I heard say,
How she at first her selfe began to reare
Gainst all the Gods, and th' empire sought from
them to beare.

2

But first, here falleth fittest to unfold   10
Her antique race and linage ancient,
As I have found it registred of old
In Faery Land mongst records permanent.
She was, to weet, a daughter by descent
Of those old Titans° that did whylome strive
With Saturnes sonne° for heavens regiment;°
Whom though high Jove of kingdome did deprive,
Yet many of their stemme long after did survive:

3

And many of them afterwards obtain'd
Great power of Jove, and high authority: 20
As Hecatè, in whose almighty hand
He plac't all rule and principalitie,
To be by her disposèd diversly
To Gods and men, as she them list divide;
And drad Bellona,° that doth sound on hie
Warres and allarums unto Nations wide,
That makes both heaven and earth to tremble at
her pride.

4

So likewise did this Titanesse aspire
Rule and dominion to her selfe to gaine;
That as a Goddesse men might her admire,°   30
And heavenly honors yield, as to them twaine:
And first, on earth she sought it to obtaine;
Where shee such proofe and sad examples shewed

Sel. XXVII: from *FQ*, the unfinished Book, vi, vii.   **15. Titans:**
an earlier dynasty of gods who preceded, or were overthrown by,
the Olympians under Jove. See, of course, Keats's *Hyperion*.
16. Saturnes sonne: Jove.   **regiment:** rule.   **25. Bellona:** the
war goddess.   **30. admire:** wonder at.

Of her great power, to many ones great paine,
That not men onely (whom she soone subdewed)
But eke all other creatures her bad dooings rewed.

5

For she the face of earthly things so changed,
That all which Nature had establisht first
In good estate, and in meet order ranged,
She did pervert, and all their statutes burst: 40
And all the worlds faire frame (which none yet
    durst
Of Gods or men to alter or misguide)
She alter'd quite; and made them all accurst
That God had blest, and did at first provide
In that still happy state for ever to abide.

6

Ne shee the lawes of Nature onely brake,
But eke of Justice, and of Policie;
And wrong of right, and bad of good did make
And death for life exchangèd foolishlie:
Since which all living wights have learn'd to die,
And all this world is woxen° daily worse.   51
O pittious worke of Mutability,
By which we all are subject to that curse,
And death, instead of life, have suckèd from our
    Nurse!

7

And now, when all the earth she thus had brought
To her behest, and thrallèd to her might,
She gan to cast° in her ambitious thought
T' attempt the empire of the heavens hight,
And Jove himselfe to shoulder from his right.
At first, she past the region of the ayre   60
And of the fire, whose substance thin and slight
Made no resistance, ne could her contraire,
But ready passage to her pleasure did prepaire.

8

Thence to the Circle of the Moone she clambe,
Where Cynthia° raignes in everlasting glory,
To whose bright shining palace straight she came,
All fairely deckt with heavens goodly storie;
Whose silver gates (by which there sate an hory
Old agèd Sire, with hower-glasse in hand,
Hight Time,) she entred, were he liefe° or sory;
Ne staide till she the highest stage had scand,°   71
Where Cynthia did sit, that never still did stand.

9

Her sitting on an Ivory throne shee found,
Drawne of two steeds, th' one black, the other
    white,

Environd with tenne thousand starres around
That duly her attended day and night;
And by her side there ran her Page, that hight
Vesper, whom we the Evening-starre intend;°
That with his Torche, still twinkling like twylight,
Her lightened all the way where she should wend,
And joy to weary wandring travailers did lend: 81

11

Boldly she bid the Goddesse downe descend,
And let her selfe into that Ivory throne;
For she her selfe more worthy thereof wend,°
And better able it to guide alone;
Whether to men, whose falls she did bemone,
Or unto Gods, whose state she did maligne,
Or to th' infernall Powers her need give lone°
Of her faire light and bounty most benigne,
Her selfe of all that rule she deemèd most con-
    digne.°   90

12

But she, that had to her that soveraigne seat
By highest Jove assign'd, therein to beare
Nights burning lamp, regarded not her threat,
Ne yielded ought for favour or for feare;
But with sterne count'naunce and disdainfull cheare,
Bending her hornèd browes, did put her back;
And, boldly blaming her for comming there,
Bade her attonce from heavens coast to pack,
Or at her perill bide the wrathfull Thunders wrack.

13

Yet nathèmore° the Giantesse forbare,   100
But boldly preacing-on° raught forth her hand
To pluck her downe perforce from off her chaire;
And, there-with lifting up her golden wand,
Threatned to strike her if she did with-stand:
Where-at the starres, which round about her
    blazed,
And eke the Moones bright wagon still did stand,
All beeing with so bold attempt amazed,
And on her uncouth habit and sterne looke still
    gazed.

14

Mean-while the lower World, which nothing knew
Of all that chauncèd heere, was darkned quite;
And eke the heavens, and all the heavenly crew
Of happy wights, now unpurvaid of° light,   112
Were much afraid, and wondred at that sight;
Fearing least Chaos° broken had his chaine,
And brought againe on them eternall night;

---

51. woxen: grown.   57. cast: resolve.   65. Cynthia: Diana, the moon goddess.   70. were he liefe: whether he were glad.   71. scand: scanned, inspected. (But it is just possible that Spenser, Latinizing, means "climbed.")

78. whom . . . intend: by whom . . . we mean.   84. wend: weened.   88. lone: loan.   90. condigne: worthy.   100. nathemore: none the more.   101. preacing-on: pressing on, advancing.   112. unpurvaid of: unprovided with, lacking.   114. Chaos: The confusion or Chaos which existed before the world is pictured here as a monster who has been chained since the Creation.

But chiefely Mercury, that next doth raigne,
Ran forth in haste unto the king of Gods to plaine.

15

All ran together with a great out-cry
To Joves faire palace fixt in heavens hight;
And, beating at his gates full earnestly,   120
Gan call to him aloud with all their might
To know what meant that suddaine lacke of light.
The father of the Gods, when this he heard,
Was troubled much at their so strange affright,
Doubting least Typhon° were againe uprear'd,
Or other his old foes that once him sorely fear'd.°

16

Eftsoones the sonne of Maia° forth he sent
Downe to the Circle of the Moone, to knowe
The cause of this so strange astonishment,
And why she did her wonted course forslowe;°
And if that any were on earth belowe   131
That did with charmes or Magick her molest,
Him to attache,° and downe to hell to throwe;
But if from heaven it were, then to arrest
The Author, and him bring before his presence
    prest.°

17

The wingd-foot God so fast his plumes did beat,
That soone he came where-as the Titanesse
Was striving with faire Cynthia for her seat;
At whose strange sight and haughty hardinesse
He wondred much, and feared her no lesse: 140
Yet laying feare aside to doe his charge,
At last he bade her (with bold stedfastnesse)
Ceasse to molest the Moone to walke at large,
Or come before high Jove her dooings to dis-
    charge.°

18

And there-with-all he on her shoulder laid
His snaky-wreathèd Mace, whose awfull power
Doth make both Gods and hellish fiends affraid:
Where-at the Titanesse did sternly lower,
And stoutly answer'd, that in evill hower
He from his Jove such message to her brought,
To bid her leave faire Cynthia's silver bower;   151
Sith shee his Jove and him esteemèd nought,
No more then Cynthia's selfe; but all their king-
    doms sought.

19

The Heavens Herald staid not to reply,
But past away, his doings to relate

Unto his Lord; who now, in th' highest sky,
Was placèd in his principall Estate,°
With all the Gods about him congregate:
To whom when Hermès° had his message told,
It did them all exceedingly amate,°   160
Save Jove; who, changing nought his count'nance
    bold,
Did unto them at length these speeches wise un-
    fold:

20

"Harken to mee awhile, yee heavenly Powers!
Ye may remember since th' Earths cursèd seed°
Sought to assaile the heavens eternall towers,
And to us all exceeding feare did breed,
But, how we then defeated all their deed,
Yee all do knowe, and them destroyèd quite;
Yet not so quite, but that there did succeed
An off-spring of their bloud, which did alite   170
Upon the fruitfull earth, which doth us yet despite.

21

"Of that bad seed is this bold woman bred,
That now with bold presumption doth aspire
To thrust faire Phœbè° from her silver bed,
And eke our selves from heavens high Empíre,
If that her might were match to her desire.
Wherefore it now behoves us to advise
What way is best to drive her to retire,
Whether by open force, or counsell wise: 179
Areed, ye sonnes of God, as best ye can devise."

22

So having said, he ceast; and with his brow
(His black eye-brow, whose doomefull dreaded
    beck
Is wont to wield the world unto his vow,°
And even the highest Powers of heaven to check)
Made signe to them in their degrees to speake,
Who straight gan cast their counsell grave and
    wise.
Mean-while th' Earths daughter,° thogh she nought
    did reck
Of Hermès message, yet gan now advise
What course were best to take in this hot bold em-
    prize.

23

Eftsoones she thus resolv'd; that whil'st the Gods
(After returne of Hermès Embassie)   191
Were troubled, and amongst themselves at ods,

---

125. **Typhon:** a fire-breathing, hundred-headed giant.
126. **fear'd:** frightened.   127. **sonne of Maia:** Mercury. Cf.
Keats's "Ode to Maia" in Vol. II.   130. **forslowe:** slow up, retard.   133. **attache:** arrest.   135. **prest:** instantly.   144. **discharge:** exculpate, give a satisfactory account of.

157. **Estate:** assembly of persons exercising political power in
virtue of their status (cf. "the three estates of the realm").
"Senate" would be a tolerable translation of "principall Estate."
159. **Hermes:** Greek name for Mercury. Spenser usually prefers
the Latin names of the gods.   160. **amate:** dismay.   164. **Earths
. . . seed:** the Giants.   174. **Phoebe:** Diana, the Moon.
183. **vow:** wish.   187. **th' Earths daughter:** Mutability. Earth
was the mother of the Titans.

Before they could new counsels re-allie,°
To set upon them in that extasie,°
And take what fortune, time, and place would
    lend.
So forth she rose, and through the purest sky
To Joves high Palace straight cast to ascend,
To prosecute her plot. Good on-set boads good end.

24

Shee there arriving boldly in did pass;   199
Where all the Gods she found in counsell close,
All quite unarm'd, as then their manner was.
At sight of her they suddaine all arose
In great amaze, ne wist what way to chose:
But Jove, all fearlesse, forc't them to aby;°
And in his soveraine throne gan straight dispose
Himselfe, more full of grace and Majestie,
That mote encheare his friends, and foes mote ter-
    rifie.

25

That when the haughty Titanesse beheld,
All were she° fraught with pride and impudence,
Yet with the sight thereof was almost queld;   210
And, inly quaking, seem'd as reft of sense
And voyd of speech in that drad audience,
Until that Jove himselfe her selfe bespake:
"Speake, thou fraile woman, speake with con-
    fidence;
Whence art thou, and what doost thou here now
    make?
What idle errand hast thou earths mansion to for-
    sake?"

26

She, halfe confusèd with his great commaund,
Yet gathering spirit of her natures pride,
Him boldly answer'd thus to his demaund:
"I am a daughter, by the mothers side,   220
Of her that is Grand-mother magnifíde
Of all the Gods, great Earth, great Chaos' child;
But by the fathers, (be it not envíde)
I greater am in bloud (whereon I build)
Then all the Gods, though wrongfully from heaven
    exil'd.

27

"For Titan (as ye all acknowledge must)
Was Saturnes elder brother by birth-right,
Both sonnes of Uranus; but by unjust
And guilefull meanes, through Corybantès slight,°
The younger thrust the elder from his right: 230

Since which thou, Jove, injuriously hast held
The Heavens rule from Titans sonnes by might,
And them to hellish dungeons downe hast feld.°
Witnesse, ye Heavens, the truth of all that I have
    teld!"

28

Whil'st she thus spake, the Gods, that gave good
    eare
To her bold words, and markèd well her grace,
(Beeing of stature tall as any there
Of all the Gods, and beautifull of face
As any of the Goddesses in place,)
Stood all astonied; like a sort of steeres,°   240
Mongst whom some beast of strange and forraine
    race
Unwares is chaunc't, far straying from his peeres:
So did their ghastly gaze bewray their hidden
    feares.

29

Till, having pauz'd awhile, Jove thus bespake:
"Will never mortall thoughts ceasse to aspire
In this bold sort to Heaven claime to make,
And touch celestiall seats with earthly mire?
I would have thought that bold Procrustès° hire,°
Or Typhons° fall, or proud Ixions° paine,
Or great Prometheus° tasting of our ire,   250
Would have suffiz'd the rest for to restraine
And warn'd all men by their example to refraine.

30

"But now this off-scum of that cursèd fry°
Dare to renew the like bold enterprize,
And chalenge th' heritage of this our skie;
Whom what should hinder, but that we likewise
Should handle as the rest of her allies,
And thunder-drive to hell?" With that, he shooke
His Nectar-deawèd locks, with which the skyes
And all the world beneath for terror quooke,   260
And eft his burning levin°-brond in hand he
    tooke.

31

But when he lookèd on her lovely face,
In which faire beames of beauty did appeare

233. **feld:** felled, thrown down.   240. **sort . . . steeres:** group
of oxen.   248. **Procrustes:** the punishment of Procrustes, who
fitted victims to a bed by stretching the short or cutting
off the feet of the tall.   **hire:** wages, i.e., punishment.
249. **Typhon:** Typhon was a hundred-handed, fire-breathing
giant who attacked Jove and was buried under Mt. Etna.
Ixion: Ixion attempted (unsuccessfully) to rape Jove's queen,
Juno, and is now tied to a revolving wheel in the underworld.
(Jove substituted a cloud for Juno and on it Ixion begot the
Centaurs).   250. **Prometheus:** (only three syllables). He stole
fire from the gods and gave it to man, and was tied to a rock
in the Caucasus where an eagle daily eats out his liver. Read
Shelley's *Prometheus Unbound*.   253. **fry:** brood.   261. **levin:**
lightning.

193. **re-allie:** form anew.   194. **extasie:** state of being "beside
oneself."   204. **aby:** remain.   209. **All . . . she:** though she
were.   229. **Corybantes slight:** the trick of the Corybantes.
By dancing and clashing their weapons these noisy people
drowned the cries of the infant Jove when his father Saturn
(whom he afterward dethroned) was looking for him. They thus
saved his life.

That could the greatest wrath soone turne to
    grace,
(Such sway doth beauty even in Heaven beare)
He staid his hand; and, having chang'd his cheare,
He thus againe in milder wise began:
"But ah! if Gods should strive with flesh yfere,°
Then shortly should the progeny of man   269
Be rooted out, if Jove should do still° what he can.

32

"But thee, faire Titans child, I rather weene,
Through some vaine errour, or inducement light,
To see that° mortall eyes have never seene;
Or through ensample of thy sisters might,
Bellona, whose great glory thou doost spight,
Since thou hast seene her dreadfull power belowe,
Mongst wretched men (dismaide with her affright)
To bandie Crownes, and Kingdoms to bestowe:
And sure thy worth no lesse then hers doth seem to
    showe.

33

"But wote thou this, thou hardy Titanesse,   280
That not the worth of any living wight
May challenge ought in Heavens interesse;
Much lesse the Title of old Titans Right:
For we by conquest, of our soveraine might,
And by eternal doome of Fates decree,
Have wonne the Empire of the Heavens bright;
Which to our selves we hold, and to whom wee
Shall worthy deeme partakers of our blisse to bee.

34

"Then ceasse thy idle claime, thou foolish gerle;
And seeke by grace and goodnesse to obtaine   290
That place, from which by folly Titan fell:
There to thou maist perhaps, if so thou faine°
Have Jove thy gracious Lord and Soveraine."
So having said, she thus to him replide:
"Ceasse, Saturnes sonne, to seeke by proffers vaine
Of idle hopes t' allure me to thy side,
For to betray my Right before I have it tride.

35

"But thee, O Jove! no equall Judge I deeme
Of my desert, or of my dewfull Right;   299
That in thine owne behalfe maist partiall seeme:
But to the highest him, that is behight
Father of Gods and men by equall might,
To weet, the God of Nature, I appeale."
There-at Jove wexèd wroth, and in his spright
Did inly grudge, yet did it well conceale;
And bade Dan Phœbus scribe her Appellation
    seale.°

36

Eftsoones the time and place appointed were,
Where all, both heavenly Powers and earthly
    wights,
Before great Natures presence should appeare,
For triall of their Titles and best Rights: 310
That was, to weet, upon the highest hights
Of Arlo Hill° (Who knowes not Arlo Hill?)
That is the highest head (in all mens sights)
Of my old father Mole,° whom Shepheards quill
Renowmèd hath with hymnes fit for a rurall skill.

3

Now, at the time that was before agreed,
The gods assembled all on Arlo Hill;
As well those that are sprung of heavenly seed
As those that all the other world do fill,
And rule both sea and land unto their will: 320
Onely th' infernall Powers might not appeare;
As well for horror of their count'naunce ill,
As for th' unruly fiends which they did feare;
Yet Pluto and Prosérpina were present there.

4

And thither also came all other creatures,
What-ever life or motion do retaine,
According to their sundry kinds of features,
That Arlo scarsly could them all containe,
So full they fillèd every hill and Plaine;   329
And had not Natures Sergeant (that is Order)
Them well disposèd by his busie paine,
And raungèd farre abroad in every border,
They would have causèd much confusion and dis-
    order.

5

Then forth issewed (great goddesse) great dame
    Nature
With goodly port and gracious Majesty,
Being far greater and more tall of stature
Then any of the gods or Powers on hie:
Yet certès by her face and physnomy,°
Whether she man or woman inly were,
That could not any creature well descry;   340
For with a veile, that wimpled every where,
Her head and face was hid that mote to none ap-
    peare.

6

That, some do say, was so by skill devized,
To hide the terror of her uncouth hew
From mortall eyes that should be sore agrized;°
For that her face did like a Lion shew,
That eye of wight could not indure to view:
But others tell that it so beautious was,

---

268. yfere: together.   270. still: always.   273. that: what.
292. faine: wish.   306. bade ... seale: bade the secretary of
Lord (Dan) Phoebus (i.e., Apollo) seal her appeal.

312. Arlo hill: in Ireland.   314. Mole: an Irish mountain.
338. physnomy: physiognomy, countenance.   345. agrized: horrified.

And round about such beames of splendor threw,
That it the Sunne a thousand times did pass,   350
Ne could be seene but like an image in a glass.

8

In a fayre Plaine upon an equall Hill
She placèd was in a pavilion;
Not such as Craftes-men by their idle skill
Are wont for Princes states to fashion;
But th' Earth herselfe, of her owne motion,
Out of her fruitfull bosome made to growe
Most dainty trees, that, shooting up anon,
Did seeme to bow their bloosming heads full lowe
For homage unto her, and like a throne did showe.

10

And all the earth far underneath her feete   361
Was dight with flowers that voluntary grew
Out of the ground, and sent forth odours sweet;
Tenne thousand mores° of sundry sent and hew,
That might delight the smell, or please the view,
The which the Nymphes from all the brooks
    thereby
Had gatherèd, they at her foot-stoole threw;
That richer seem'd then any tapestry,
That Princes bowres adorne with painted imagery.

12

Was never so great joyance since the day   370
That all the gods whylome assembled were
On Hæmus hill in their divine array,
To celebrate the solemne bridall cheare
Twixt Peleus and Dame Thetis° pointed° there;
Where Phœbus selfe, that god of Poets hight,°
They say, did sing the spousall hymne full cleere,
That all the gods were ravisht with delight
Of his celestiall song, and Musicks wondrous
    might.

13

This great Grandmother of all creatures bred,
Great Nature, ever young, yet full of eld;°   380
Still mooving, yet unmovèd from her sted;
Unseene of any, yet of all beheld;
Thus sitting in her throne, as I have teld,
Before her came dame Mutability;
And, being lowe before her presence feld°
With meek obaysance and humilitie,
Thus gan her plaintif Plea with words to amplifie:

14

" To thee, O greatest Goddesse, onely great!
An humble suppliant loe! I lowely fly,
Seeking for Right, which I of thee entreat,   390

Who Right to all dost deale indifferently,
Damning all Wrong and tortious° Injurie,
Which any of thy creatures do to other
(Oppressing them with power unequally,)
Sith of them all thou art the equall mother,
And knittest each to each, as brother unto brother.

15

" To thee therefore of this same Jove I plaine,
And of his fellow gods that faine° to be,
That challenge to themselves the whole worlds
    raign,
Of which the greatest part is due to me,   400
And heaven it selfe by heritage in Fee:°
For heaven and earth I both alike do deeme,
Sith heaven and earth are both alike to thee,
And gods no more then men thou doest esteeme;
For even the gods to thee, as men to gods, do seeme.

16

" Then weigh, O soveraigne goddesse! by what
    right
These gods do claime the worlds whole soveraint-y,
And that° is onely dew unto thy might
Arrogate to themselves ambitiously:
As for the gods owne principality,   410
Which Jove usurpes unjustly, that to be
My heritage Jove's selfe cannot denie,
From my great Grandsire Titan unto mee
Deriv'd by dew descent; as is well knowen to
    thee.

17

" Yet mauger° Jove, and all his gods beside,
I do possesse the worlds most regiment;°
As if ye please it into parts divide,
And every parts inholders° to convent,°
Shall to your eyes appeare incontinent.°
And, first, the Earth (great mother of us all)   420
That only seemes unmov'd and permanent,
And unto Mutabilitie not thrall,
Yet is she chang'd in part, and eeke in generall.

18

" For all that from her springs, and is ybredde,
How-ever faire it flourish for a time,
Yet see we soone decay; and, being dead,
To turne againe unto their earthly slime:
Yet, out of their decay and mortall crime,°
We daily see new creatures to arize,
And of their Winter spring another Prime,°   430

---

364. mores: roots.   374. Peleus . . . Thetis: The mortal king
Peleus married the sea goddess Thetis (short *e*, rhyming with
lettuce), and begot Achilles.   pointed: appointed.   375. hight:
is called.   380. eld: age.   385. feld: prostrated

392. tortious: wrongful, involving what lawyers call a "tort."
398. faine: feign, pretend.   401. in Fee: as a hereditary estate.
408. that: what, that which.   415. mauger: despite.   416. regiment: rule.   418. inholders: occupants.   convent: assemble.
419. incontinent: instantly.   428. crime: I think Spenser, going
back to the earliest sense of the Latin *crimen*, means judgment,
doom, or sentence.   430. Prime: spring.

Unlike in forme, and chang'd by strange disguise:
So turne they still about, and change in restlesse
    wise.

19

"As for her tenants, that is, man and beasts,
The beasts we daily see massácred dy
As thralls and vassals unto mens beheasts;
And men themselves do change continually,
From youth to eld, from wealth to poverty,
From good to bad, from bad to worst of all:
Ne doe their bodies only flit and fly,   439
But eeke their minds (which they immortall call)
Still change and vary thoughts, as new occasions
    fall.

20

"Ne is the water in more constant case,
Whether those same on high, or these belowe;
For th' Ocean moveth still from place to place,
And every River still doth ebbe and flowe;
Ne any Lake, that seems most still and slowe,
Ne Poole so small, that can his smoothnesse holde
When any winde doth under heaven blowe;
With which the clouds are also tost and roll'd,
Now like great Hills, and streight like sluces them
    unfold,   450

21

"So likewise are all watry living wights
Still tost and turnèd with continuall change,
Never abiding in their stedfast plights:
The fish, still floting, doe at random range,
And never rest, but evermore exchange
Their dwelling places, as the streames them carrie:
Ne have the watry foules a certaine grange°
Wherein to rest, ne in one stead do tarry;
But flitting still doe flie, and still their places vary.

22

"Next is the Ayre; which who feeles not by sense
(For of all sense it is the middle meane°)   461
To flit still, and with subtill influence
Of his thin spirit all creatures to maintaine
In state of life? O weake life! that does leane
On thing so tickle° as th' unsteady ayre,
Which every howre is chang'd and altred cleane
With every blast that bloweth, fowle or faire:
The faire doth it prolong: the fowle doth it im-
    paire.

23

"Therein the changes infinite beholde,
Which to her creatures every minute chaunce;   470
Now boyling hot, streight friezing deadly cold;

457. grange: dwelling.   461. middle meane: medium, conductor.
465. tickle: mobile.

Now faire sun-shine, that makes all skip and
    daunce;
Streight bitter stormes, and balefull countenance
That makes them all to shiver and to shake:
Rayne, haile, and snowe do pay them sad penánce,
And dreadfull thunder-claps (that make them
    quake)
With flames and flashing lights that thousand
    changes make.

24

"Last is the fire; which, though it live for ever,
Ne can be quenchèd quite, yet every day
We see his parts, so soone as they do sever,   480
To lose their heat and shortly to decay;
So makes himself his owne consuming pray;
Ne any living creatures doth he breed,
But all that are of others bredd doth slay;
And with their death his cruell life dooth feed;
Nought leaving but their barren ashes without
    seede.

25

"Thus all these fower° (the which the ground
    work bee
Of all the world and of all living wights)
To thousand sorts of Change we subject see: 489
Yet are they chang'd (by other wondrous slights)
Into themselves, and lose their native mights;
The Fire to Ayre, and th' Ayre to Water sheere,°
And Water into Earth; yet Water fights
With Fire, and Ayre with Earth, approaching
    neere:
Yet all are in one body, and as one appeare.

26

"So in them all raignes Mutabilitie;
How-ever these, that Gods themselves do call,
Of them do claime the rule and soverianty;
As Vesta,° of the fire æthereall;
Vulcan, of this with us so usuall;°   500
Ops,° of the earth; and Juno, of the ayre;
Neptune, of seas; and Nymphes, of Rivers all:
For all those Rivers to me subject are,
And all the rest, which they usurp, be all my share.

27

"Which to approven true, as I have told,
Vouchsafe, O Goddesse! to thy presence call
The rest which doe the world in being hold;
As times and seasons of the yeare that fall:
Of all the which demand in generall,

487. fower: four.   492. sheere: bright.   499. Vesta: Roman
goddess of the family hearth.   500. this . . . usuall: The fire
we know on this earth as distinct from the elemental or ethereal
fire (see previous line) which was above the air.   501. Ops:
Roman goddess of agriculture.

Or judge thyselfe, by verdit of thine eye,   510
Whether to me they are not subject all."
Nature did yeeld thereto; and by-and-by
Bade Order call them all before her Majesty.

28

So forth isséw'd the Seasons of the yeare.
First, lusty Spring, all dight in leaves of flowres
That freshly budded and new bloosmes did beare,
(In which a thousand birds had built their bowres
That sweetly sung to call forth Paramours)
And in his hand a javelin he did beare,
And on his head (as fit for warlike stoures)   520
A guilt engraven morion° he did weare;
That as some did him love, so others did him feare.

29

Then came the jolly Sommer, being dight
In a thin silken cassock° coloured greene,
That was unlynèd all, to be more light;
And on his head a girlond well beseene
He wore, from which, as he had chauffèd° been,
The sweat did drop; and in his hand he bore
A boawe and shaftes, as he in forrest greene
Had hunted late the Libbard° or the Bore,   530
And now would bathe his limbes with labor heated
sore.

30

Then came the Autumne all in yellow clad,
As though he joyèd in his plentious store,
Laden with fruits that made him laugh, full glad
That he had banisht hunger, which to-fore
Had by the belly oft him pinchèd sore:
Upon his head a wreath, that was enrold
With ears of corne of every sort, he bore;
And in his hand a sickle he did holde,
To reape the ripened fruits the which the earth had
yold.°   540

31

Lastly, came Winter cloathèd all in frize,°
Chattering his teeth for cold that did him chill;
Whil'st on his hoary beard his breath did freese,
And the dull drops, that from his purpled bill
As from a limbeck° did adown distill.
In his right hand a tippèd staffe he held,
With which his feeble steps he stayèd still;
For he was faint with cold, and weak with eld,
That scarse his loosèd limbes he hable was to weld.

32

These, marching softly, thus in order went;   550
And after them the Monthes all riding came.

521. morion: helmet.   524. cassock: gown.   527. chauffed:
heated.   530. Libbard: leopard.   540. yold: yielded.
541. frize: coarse woolen cloth.   545. limbeck: alembic, vessel
used in distilling.

First, sturdy March,° with brows full sternly bent
And armèd strongly, rode upon a Ram,°
The same which over Hellespontus swam;
Yet in his hand a spade he also hent,
And in a bag all sorts of seeds ysame,°
Which on the earth he strowèd as he went,
And fild her wombe with fruitfull hope of nourish-
ment.

33

Next came fresh Aprill, full of lustyhed,
And wanton as a Kid whose horne new buds: 560
Upon a Bull he rode, the same which led
Europa° floting through th' Argolick fluds:
His hornes were gilden all with golden studs,
And garnishèd with garlonds goodly dight
Of all the fairest flowres and freshest buds
Which th' earth brings forth; and wet he seem'd in
sight
With waves, through which he waded for his loves
delight.

34

Then came faire May, the fayrest mayd on ground,
Deckt all with dainties of her seasons pryde,
And throwing flowres out of her lap around: 570
Upon two brethrens shoulders she did ride,
The twinnes of Leda: which on eyther side
Supported her like to their soveraigne Queene:
Lord! how all creatures laught when her they spide
And leapt and daunc't as they had ravisht beene!
And Cupid selfe about her fluttred all in greene.

35

And after her came jolly June, arrayd
All in greene leaves, as he a Player were;
Yet in his time he wrought as well as playd,   579
That by his plough-yrons mote right well appeare.
Upon a Crab he rode, that him did beare
With crooked crawling steps an uncouth pase,
And backward yode,° as Bargeman wont to fare
Bending their force contrary to their face;
Like that ungracious crew° which faines demurest
grace.

36

Then came hot Júly boyling like to fire,
That all his garments he had cast away.
Upon a Lyon raging yet with ire
He boldly rode, and made him to obay:
It was the beast that whylome did forray   590

552. March: Before 1751, when the Gregorian calendar was
officially adopted in Great Britain, the year began on March 25.
553. Ram: The creatures on which the Months ride, May's
twins, August's "mayd," and September's scales, are
their appropriate zodiacal signs.   556. ysame: together.
562. Europa: Jove, for love of this lady, transformed himself
into a bull and, inducing her to ride on his back, transported
her over the sea.   583. yode: went.   585. that . . . crew:
hypocrites.

The Nemæan forrest, till th' Amphytrionide°
Him slew, and with his hide did him array.
Behinde his back a sithe,° and by his side
Under his belt he bore a sickle circling wide.

37

The sixt was August, being rich arrayd
In garment all of gold downe to the ground;
Yet rode he not, but led a lovely Mayd
Forth by the lilly hand, the which was cround
With eares of corne, and full her hand was found:
That was the righteous Virgin,° which of old   600
Liv'd here on earth, and plenty made abound;
But after Wrong was lov'd, and Justice solde,
She left th' unrighteous world, and was to heaven
    extold.°

38

Next him September marchèd, eeke on foote,
Yet was he heavy laden with the spoyle
Of harvests riches, which he made his boot,°
And him enricht with bounty of the soyle:
In his one hand, as fit for harvests toyle,
He held a knife-hook; and in th' other hand   609
A paire of waights, with which he did assoyle°
Both more and lesse, where it in doubt did stand,
And equall gave to each as Justice duly scann'd.

39

Then came October full of merry glee;
For yet his noule° was totty° of the must,°
Which he was treading in the wine-fats see,°
And of the joyous oyle, whose gentle gust°
Made him so frollick and so full of lust:°
Upon a dreadfull Scorpion he did ride,
The same which by Dianaes doom unjust
Slew great Orion;° and eeke by his side   620
He had his ploughing-share and coulter° ready
    tyde.

40

Next was November; he full grosse and fat
As fed with lard, and that right well might seeme;
For he had been a fatting hogs of late,
That yet his browes with sweat did reek and
    steem,
And yet the season was full sharp and breem:°

591. Amphytrionide: Hercules.   593. sithe: scythe.   600. Virgin: Astraea, a goddess who lived on the earth while the golden age lasted and then withdrew to heaven: a symbol of Justice. 603. extold: raised.   606. boot: prize, wealth.   610. assoyle: solve, hence "determine."   614. noule: head.   totty: unsteady. must: new wine.   615. wine-fats see: the "sea" of wine in the vats.   616. gust: taste.   617. lust: pleasure.   619–20. Dianaes . . . Orion: The great hunter Orion is in some versions killed by Diana with an arrow for attempting to ravish her, or killed by Earth with a scorpion for boasting that he would exterminate all wild beasts. I do not know what version Spenser is following.   621. coulter: blade in front of a plowshare. 626. breem: rough (?).

In planting eeke he took no small delight.
Whereon he rode not easie was to deeme;
For it a dreadfull Centaure was in sight,
The seed of Saturne and faire Naìs, Chiron
    hight.   630

41

And after him came next the chill December:
Yet he, through merry feasting which he made
And great bonfires, did not the cold remember;
His Saviour's birth his mind so much did glad.
Upon a shaggy-bearded Goat he rode,
The same wherewith Dan Jove in tender yeares,
They say, was nourisht by th' Idæan mayd;°
And in his hand a broad deepe boawle he beares,
Of which he freely drinks an health to all his
    peeres.°

42

Then came old January, wrappèd well   640
In many weeds° to keep the cold away;
Yet did he quake and quiver, like to quell,°
And blowe his nayles to warme them if he may;
For they were numbd with holding all the day
An hatchet keene, with which he fellèd wood
And from the trees did lop the needlesse spray:
Upon an huge great Earth-pot steane° he stood,
From whose wide mouth there flowèd forth the
    Romane Flood.°

43

And lastly came cold February, sitting
In an old wagon, for he could not ride,   650
Drawne of two fishes, for the season fitting,
Which through the flood before did softly slyde
And swim away: yet had he by his side
His plough and harnesse fit to till the ground,
And tooles to prune the trees, before the pride
Of hasting Prime did make them burgein° round.
So past the twelve Months forth, and their dew
    places found.

44

And after these there came the Day and Night,
Riding together both with equall pase,
Th' one on a Palfrey blacke, the other white;   660
But Night had covered her uncomely face
With a blacke veile, and held in hand a mace,
On top whereof the moon and stars were pight;
And sleep and darknesse round about did trace:
But Day did beare upon his scepters hight
The goodly Sun encompast all with beamès
    bright.

637. Idaean mayd: Amalthea, a nymph, daughter of Ocean, brought up the infant Jove on goat's milk.   639. peeres: mates. 641. weeds: clothes.   642. quell: quail, faint.   647. Earth-pot steane: earthen jar or urn.   648. Romane Flood: the river Tiber.   656. burgein: bud.

45

Then came the Howres,° faire daughters of high
    Jove
And timely Night; the which were all endewed
With wondrous beauty fit to kindle love;
But they were virgins all, and love eschewed   670
That might forslack the charge to them foreshewed
By mighty Jove; who did them porters make
Of heavens gate (whence all the gods issúed)
Which they did daily watch, and nightly wake
By even turnes, ne ever did their charge forsake.

46

And after all came Life, and lastly Death;
Death with most grim and griesly visage seene,
Yet is he nought but parting of the breath;
Ne ought to see, but like a shade to weene,
Unbodièd, unsoul'd, unheard, unseene: 680
But Life was like a faire young lusty boy,
Such as they faine Dan Cupid to have beene,
Full of delightfull health and lively joy,
Deckt all with flowres, and wings of gold fit to em-
    ploy.

47

When these were past, thus gan the Titanesse:
" Lo! mighty mother, now be judge, and say
Whether in all thy creatures more or lesse
Change doth not raign and bear the greatest sway;
For who sees not that Time on all doth pray?
But Times do change and move continually: 690
So nothing heere long standeth in one stay:
Wherefore this lower world who can deny
But to be subject still to Mutability? "

48

Then thus gan Jove: " Right true it is, that these
And all things else that under heaven dwell
Are chaung'd of Time, who doth them all disseise°
Of being: But who is it (to me tell)
That Time himselfe doth move, and still compell
To keepe his course? Is not that namely wee   699
Which poure that vertue from our heavenly cell
That moves them all, and makes them changèd
    be?
So them we gods do rule, and in them also thee."

49

To whom thus Mutability: " The° things,
Which we see not how they are mov'd and swayd
Ye may attribute to your selves as Kings,
And say, they by your secret powre are made:
But what we see not, who shall us perswade?
But were they so, as ye them faine to be,

Mov'd by your might and ordered by your ayde.
Yet what if I can prove, that even yee   710
Your selves are likewise chang'd and subject unto
    mee?

50

" And first, concerning her that is the first,
Even you, faire Cynthia; whom so much ye make
Joves dearest darling, she was bred and nurst
On Cynthus hill, whence she her name did take;
Then is she mortall borne, how-so° ye crake:°
Besides, her face and countenance every day
We changèd see and sundry formes partake,
Now hornd, now round, now bright, now browne
    and gray;
So that ' as changefull as the Moone ' men use to
    say.   720

51

" Next Mercury; who though he lesse appeare
To change his hew, and alwayes seeme as one,
Yet he his course doth alter every yeare,
And is of late far out of order gone.
So Venus eeke, that goodly Paragone,°
Though faire all night, yet is she darke all day:
And Phœbus selfe, who lightsome is alone,
Yet is he oft eclipsèd by the way,
And fills the darkned world with terror and dis-
    may.

52

" Now Mars, that valiant man, is changèd most;
For he sometimes so far runnes out of square,   731
That he his way doth seem quite to have lost,
And cleane without his usuall spheere to fare;
That even these Star-gazers stonisht are
At sight thereof, and damne their lying bookes:
So likewise grim Sir Saturne oft doth spare
His sterne aspect, and calme his crabbed lookes.
So many turning cranks° these have, so many
    crookes.°

53

" But you, Dan° Jove, that only constant are,
And King of all the rest, as ye doe clame,   740
Are you not subject eeke to this misfare?
Then, let me aske you this withouten blame;
Where were ye borne? Some say in Crete by
    name,
Others in Thebes, and others other-where;
But, wheresoever they commént° the same,
They all consent that ye begotten were
And borne here in this world; ne other can ap-
    peare.

---

567. the Howres: Hours. 696. disseise: dispossess. 703–07. The
... perswade: Cf. Milton, *Paradise Lost,* IX.718–22, below.

716. how-so: howsoever. crake: boast. 725. Paragone: pattern, that which deserves imitation. 738. cranks: twists.
crookes: bends. 739. Dan: Lord. Cf. Chaucer, Nun's Priest's
Tale, l. 492, above. 745. comment: devise.

54

" Then are ye mortall borne, and thrall to me
Unlesse the kingdome of the sky yee make
Immortall and unchangeable to be: 750
Besides,° that power and vertue which ye spake,
That ye here worke, doth many changes take,
And your owne natures change; for each of you,
That vertue have or this or that to make,
Is checkt and changèd from his nature trew,
By others opposition or obliquid view.

55

" Besides, the sundry motions of your Spheares,
So sundry wayes and fashions as clerkes° faine,
Some in short space, and some in longer yeares,
What is the same but alteration plaine? 760
Onely the starry skie doth still remaine:
Yet do the Starres and Signes therein still move,
And even itselfe is mov'd, as wizards° saine:°
But all that moveth doth mutation love;
Therefore both you and them to me I subject prove.

56

" Then, since within this wide great Universe
Nothing doth firme and permanent appeare,
But all things tost and turnèd by transverse,°
What then should let,° but I aloft should reare
My Trophee, and from all the triumph beare? 770
Now judge then, (O thou greatest goddesse trew)
According as thy selfe doest see and heare,
And unto me addoom° that° is my dew;
That is, the rule of all, all being rul'd by you."

57

So having ended, silence long ensewed;
Ne Nature to or fro spake for a space,
But with firme eyes affixt the ground still viewed.
Meane-while all creatures, looking in her face,
Expecting th' end of this so doubtfull case, 779
Did hang in long suspence what would ensew,
To whether side should fall the soveraine place:
At length she, looking up with chearefull view,
The silence brake, and gave her doome° in speeches
 few.

58

" I well consider all that ye have said,
And find that all things stedfastnesse do hate
And changèd be; yet, being rightly wayd,

They are not changèd from their first estate;
But by their change their being do dilate,°
And turning to themselves at length againe,
Do worke their owne perfection so by fate: 790
Then over them Change doth not rule and raigne,
But they raigne over Change, and do their states
 maintaine.

59

" Cease therefore, daughter, further to aspire,
And thee content thus to be rul'd by mee,
For thy decay thou seekst by thy desire;
But time shall come that all shall changèd bee,
And from thenceforth none no more change shal
 see."
So was the Titanesse put downe and whist,°
And Jove confirm'd in his imperial see.°
Then was that whole assembly quite dismist, 800
And Natur's selfe did vanish, whither no man
 wist.

SELECTION XXVIII

The last word.

When I bethinke me on that speech whyleare°
Of Mutabilitie, and well it way,°
Me seemes, that though she all unworthy were
Of the Heav'ns Rule; yet, very sooth to say,
In all things else she beares the greatest sway:
Which makes me loath this state of life so tickle,ᶜ
And love of things so vaine to cast away;
Whose flowring pride, so fading and so fickle,
Short Time shall soon cut down with his consuming
 sickle.

2

Then gin I thinke on that which Nature sayd, 10
Of that same time when no more Change shall be,
But stedfast rest of all things, firmely stayd
Upon the pillours of Eternity,
That is contrayr to Mutabilitie;
For all that moveth doth in Change delight:
But thence-forth all shall rest eternally
With Him that is the God of Sabaoth hight:
O! that great Saboath God, grant me that Sabaoths
 sight.

751–56. Besides . . . view: The astrological influence of each
planet changes according to its position and is modified by the
others. 758. clerkes: learned men. 763. wizards: wise men,
scientists. saine: say. 768. by transverse: crosswise,
athwart. 769. let: hinder. 773. addoom: adjudge. that:
what. 783. doome: judgment.

788. dilate: extend. 798. whist: hushed. 799. see: seat.
Sel. XXVIII: from FQ, the unfinished Book, viii. 1. whyleare:
of old. 2. way: weigh. 6. tickle: precarious.

William Shakespeare

1564–1616

SHAKESPEARE'S LIFE

Every generation approaches Shakespeare in a somewhat different way. His contemporaries first admired him as the author of the poems *Venus and Adonis* and *Lucrece,* and then as a writer of first-rate plays for the stage. In the latter half of the seventeenth century and in the eighteenth century, he was esteemed rather as a genius who wrote irregular poetic dramas. The romantic poets and critics of the early nineteenth century, especially Coleridge, Lamb, and De Quincey, elevated him almost into the Genius of the English Race. Critics of the Victorian period admired his skill in creating character. In the first third of the twentieth century he was regarded as the greatest of all writers for the stage, while the mid-century critics have been more interested in his poetic techniques and ethical undertones. It is a sign of Shakespeare's perennial greatness that he can provide fresh literary experiences for such a diversity of readers and ages.

William Shakespeare was born in April, 1564, at Stratford-on-Avon, a small country town in the county of Warwickshire. He was the third child, and eldest son, of John Shakespeare and Mary Arden. His father was one of the most prosperous men of Stratford, and held in turn the chief offices in the town. His mother was of gentle birth, the daughter of Robert Arden of Wilmcote.

Stratford-on-Avon at that time was a little town of less than 2000 inhabitants, but its community life was vigorous. It had a grammar school, with a succession of competent schoolmasters who provided a good education for the boys of the town. Elizabethan education, though it might appear narrow by modern standards, was thorough in its disciplines of mind and body. Latin was the main subject of instruction. By the time a boy had finished his course, he had read widely in such authors as Cicero, Ovid, Virgil, and Seneca; he had also received considerable training in the use and structure of the Latin language, in rhetoric, and in the making of Latin verses.

Little is known of Shakespeare's early life; but it is unlikely that a writer who dramatized such a wide range and variety of human kinds and experiences should have spent his early manhood entirely in placid pursuits in a country town. There are various traditions about his early manhood which cannot be finally proved or denied. The most persistent is that he fled from Stratford because he was in trouble for deerstealing, and had fallen foul of Sir Thomas Lucy, the local magnate; another tradition declares that he was for some time a schoolmaster. In December, 1582, Shakespeare married Anne Hathaway, daughter of a farmer of Shottery, near Stratford. The records in the church at Stratford note that their first child, Susanna, was baptized on May 6, 1583, and twins, Hamnet and Judith, on February 22, 1585.

From 1592 onward the records are much fuller. In March, 1592, the Lord Strange's players produced a new play at the Rose Theater called *Harry the Sixth,* which was very successful, and was probably the First Part of Shakespeare's *Henry VI.* In August, 1592, Robert Greene, the best known of the professional writers, as he was dying wrote a letter to three fellow writers in which he warned them against the ingratitude of players in general, and in particular against an "upstart crow" who "supposes he is as well able to bombast out a blank verse as the best of you: and being an absolute Johannes Factotum [Johnny Do-All] is in his own conceit the only Shake-scene in a country." This is the first known reference to Shakespeare, and the whole passage suggests that to Greene's disgust Shakespeare had become suddenly famous as a playwright. At this time Shakespeare was brought into touch with Edward Alleyn, the great tragedian, and Christopher Marlowe, the poet and dramatist. Alleyn was then acting the thundering parts of Marlowe's Tamburlaine, the Jew of Malta, and Dr. Faustus, as well as Hieronimo, the hero of Kyd's *Spanish Tragedy,* which was the most popular of all Elizabethan plays.

In April, 1593, Shakespeare published his poem *Venus and Adonis,* which was dedicated to the young Earl of Southampton. It was a great and lasting success, and was reprinted nine times in the next few years. In May, 1594, his second poem, *The Rape of Lucrece,* was also dedicated to Southampton; it was almost as popular as *Venus and Adonis.*

There was little playing in 1593, for the theaters were shut during a severe outbreak of the plague, and the players went on tour in the country. But in the autumn of 1594, when the plague ceased, the playing companies were reorganized, and Shakespeare became a sharer in the company patronized by the Lord Chamberlain. This company, the Chamberlain's Men, went to play in the Theater in Shoreditch, north of the city of London. During these months Marlowe and Kyd died, and Shakespeare was thus for a time without a rival. He had already written the three parts of *Henry VI, Richard III, Titus Andronicus, Two Gentlemen of Verona, Love's Labor's Lost, the Comedy of Errors,* and *The Taming of the Shrew.* Soon afterward he wrote the first of his greater plays, *Romeo and Juliet,* and he followed this success in the next three years with *A Midsummer Night's Dream, Richard II,* and *The Merchant of Venice.* The two parts of *Henry IV,* introducing Falstaff, the most popular of all his comic characters, were probably written in 1597-98.

The company left the Theater in 1597 owing to disputes with the landlord over a renewal of the lease, and went to play at the Curtain in the same neighborhood. These wranglings continued throughout 1598, but during the Christmas holidays the players settled the matter by demolishing the old Theater and erecting a new playhouse on the south bank of the Thames, near London Bridge. This playhouse was named the Globe. The expenses of the new building were shared by the chief members of the company, including Shakespeare, who was now a man of some means. In 1596 he had bought New Place, a large house in the center of Stratford, and through his father purchased a coat of arms from the Heralds, which was official recognition that he and his family were gentlefolk.

By the summer of 1598 Shakespeare was recognized as the greatest of English dramatists. Booksellers were printing his more popular plays, at times even in pirated or stolen versions, and he received a remarkable tribute from a young writer named Francis Meres. In a long catalogue of English authors in his book *Palladis Tamia,* Meres gave Shakespeare more prominence than any other writer, and mentioned by name twelve of his plays.

Shortly before the Globe was opened, Shakespeare had completed a cycle of plays dealing with the story of the Wars of the Roses. The final play in this series was *Henry V.* It was followed by *As You Like It* and by *Julius Caesar,* the first of the maturer tragedies. In the next three years (1599-1602) he wrote *Troilus and Cressida, The Merry Wives of Windsor, Hamlet* (in its present form), and *Twelfth Night.*

On March 24, 1603, Queen Elizabeth died. Shakespeare's company had often performed before her, but they found her successor a far more enthusiastic patron. One of the first acts of King James I was to take over the company and to promote the players to be his own servants; the Lord Chamberlain's Company was henceforward known as the King's Men. They now acted very frequently at court, and prospered accordingly. In the early years of the reign Shakespeare wrote the more somber comedies, *All's Well That Ends Well* and *Measure for Measure,* which were followed by *Othello, King Lear,* and *Macbeth.* Then he returned to Roman themes with *Antony and Cleopatra* and *Coriolanus.*

Since 1601 Shakespeare had been writing fewer plays each year, and there were now a number of rival dramatists who were introducing new styles of drama, particularly Ben Jonson (whose first successful comedy, *Every Man in his Humor,* was acted by Shakespeare's company in 1598), Chapman, Dekker, Marston, and also Beaumont and Fletcher, who began to write in 1607. In 1608 the King's Men acquired a second playhouse, a private theater in the fashionable quarter of the Blackfriars in the city of London, and again Shakespeare was a sharer in the expenses. At private theaters, plays were performed indoors; the prices charged were higher than in the public playhouses, and the audience consequently was more select. Shakespeare seems to have retired from the stage about this time; his name does not occur in the various lists of players after 1607. Henceforward he lived for the most part at Stratford, where he was regarded as one of the most important citizens. He still wrote a few plays, and he tried his hand at the new form of tragicomedy — a play with tragic incidents but a happy ending — which Beaumont and Fletcher had popularized. He wrote four of these, *Pericles, Cymbeline, The Winter's Tale,* and *The Tempest;* the last two were acted at court in 1611. For the remaining years of his life Shakespeare lived in retirement. His son Hamnet had died in 1596; his two daughters were now married.

Shakespeare died at Stratford-on-Avon on April 23, 1616, and was buried in the chancel of the church, before the high altar. Shortly afterward a memorial tablet, with a portrait bust, was set up on the north wall. His wife survived him till 1623. The known facts of Shakespeare's life are thus considerable; unfortunately they tell us little of his personality.

SHAKESPEARE'S THEATER

All forms of art pass through three stages: naïveté, maturity, and decadence. Until the principles of a new form have been perfected, much experiment is needed. Although plays of one kind or another had been acted for many generations, no permanent theater had been established in England until a playhouse, designed solely for the presentation of plays and called the Theater, was built in 1576. Two other playhouses were built in the next four years, so that, when

Shakespeare began to write for the stage, actors and dramatists had been experimenting with stage techniques for fifteen years. During that time they had discovered most of the possibilities of the medium but had not as yet reached any kind of perfection. Shakespeare was thus fortunate in his times. He came to the theater at a point between the crudities of early Elizabethan drama and the decadence of the later Jacobean.

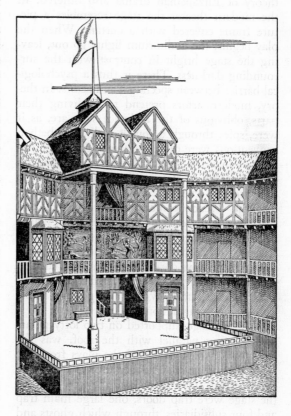

The Elizabethan playhouse was small by modern standards. The Globe, the most famous of all Elizabethan theaters (built in 1599 when Shakespeare was reaching the middle period of his activity) was an octagonal building. On the outside each of the eight sides measured approximately thirty-six feet; and the diameter of the whole was eighty-four feet. It was a frame structure, standing on low brick supports, and the roof was thatched with straw. It was about thirty-three feet high to the eaves. Inside ran three galleries, one above the other, surrounding the yard, which was fifty-six feet in diameter. The galleries looked down upon the stage, which occupied about a third of the yard at one end.

Three sections of the octagon were used for backstage; the remaining five were used for the spectators. The yard was open to the sky, and the stage was lit by daylight.

The Shakespearean stage differed considerably from the modern stage in its arrangements and in its conventions, and as a result the whole theory of Elizabethan drama also differed. In the modern theater the stage resembles a picture frame covered with a curtain. When the play begins, the auditorium lights go out, leaving the stage bright in contrast with the surrounding darkness. There is thus a psychological barrier between spectators and actors. In theory, modern actors pretend to be living their parts, oblivious of the audience who are, as it were, spies through a fourth wall. Elizabethan conventions were quite different. The stage jutted out into the yard and was surrounded on three sides by spectators. There was no curtain to conceal or reveal the main stage, no light but daylight. Hence contact between actors and spectators was close and intimate; both shared in one experience. As there was little attempt at scenery, so there was no realistic setting. All the illusion nowadays created by the electrician and the scene painter had to be effected by the dramatist and the actors. Words and gestures alone kindled the imagination.

Over the stage, supported on two lofty pillars and running parallel with the roof, was the "shadow," which protected the plays from the rain. The pillars had further utility: they were often used as trees, masts, and the like. Beneath the stage were trap doors, one large main trap and four subsidiaries, through which ghosts and spirits appeared.

Behind the main stage was an inner stage or recess, sometimes called the "tiring house" or "the place behind the stage" or the "study." It occupied one section of the octagon. Within this inner stage, which was frequently used, were played indoor scenes requiring properties, such as a court scene with a throne; a council chamber with a table and stools; a tavern; a tomb; a cave; a prison; or a study. When not in use, the inner stage was hidden by curtains, and so it was a natural place to conceal eavesdroppers. When Claudius and Polonius retired to over-

hear Hamlet's conversation with Ophelia, they stepped through these curtains and stood behind them. At the back of the inner stage was a door, and behind this door a staircase which led up to the second level.

On this second level, parallel with the second gallery and part of it, was the "chamber" or upper stage. When not required, this also was covered with a curtain. In front of it there jutted out a balcony which was used to represent the walls of a castle or town. The upper stage itself was the same size as the recess and could be used for a bedchamber or the living room in a house or for any occasion when the dramatist required characters on the upper level. On either side of the chamber there were windows. From one of these Romeo descended from Juliet's bedchamber. The upper stage was also useful as a part of the main stage. Since it jutted out, it provided a roof of sorts, which could become the eaves of a house, or a lean-to.

On the third level there was another chamber, normally used by the musicians, but available occasionally for scenes.

On the fourth level was the turret. It contained a bell frequently used to ring an alarm or to toll a knell. Here also were created the sound effects. Cannon balls were rolled on boards to imitate thunder, and the noises of "alarums and excursions" were produced with drums and trumpets.

The Elizabethan acting company was a "fellowship." It consisted of ten to fifteen sharers, three or four boys who would ultimately become full sharers, and perhaps another ten or a dozen extras — money gatherers (who were sometimes women), stagehands, and the like. The boys took the parts of girls or young women, for as yet there were no professional actresses on the English stage.

With the "groundlings," who stood in the yard because they could not afford to pay for a seat, the most popular member of the company was the clown. He was the low comedian, and most plays gave him a chance to play a comic servant or a watchman or a gravedigger or to indulge in some business of his own. In fact, the clown was so important a member of the cast that in stage directions in early texts he is usually designated as "Clown" regardless of the part which he represents. When the Chamberlain's Men were formed in the autumn of

1594, their first clown was Will Kempe. Kempe, who was older than the other chief sharers of the company, had already won a great reputation. He was an individualist and a great favorite. He was particularly famous for his jigs, which he performed after the play was over. But Kempe fell foul of his fellows, and left the company in 1599. Shakespeare's severe remarks on the clown in *Hamlet,* written after Kempe joined a rival company, were clearly directed against him. After Kempe's departure, a more intelligent and refined kind of clown is noticeable in Shakespeare's plays — Touchstone in *As You Like It,* Feste in *Twelfth Night,* and Lear's singing fool. These parts were taken by Robert Armin.

The chief member of the Chamberlain's Men was Richard Burbage, the youngest son of the James Burbage who had built the Theater. Burbage first made his name in the part of Richard III, and his rendering of Richard's cry of despair,

> A horse! A horse! My kingdom for a horse!

was particularly famous. He also is known to have taken the parts of Hamlet, Lear, and Othello. Shakespeare first worked in partnership with Richard Burbage in 1594. In 1616, when he made his will, Shakespeare left to Burbage and two others of his surviving fellows twenty-six shillings and eightpence to buy rings as mementos. Of Burbage's style as an actor we know little, but we can guess much from Hamlet's advice to the players. Shakespeare could hardly have been so severe a critic of robustious playing had Burbage been a " ham " actor.

If by some miracle we could be transplanted to a holiday performance at the Globe, we should be surprised in many ways. The playhouse would strike us as small, uncomfortably crowded, and far more intimate than any modern theater. The presentation would at first seem noisy and crude, but we should soon become used to the trumpet calls and the lack of scenery. The acting would appear embarrassingly emotional, but very slick and competent. Shakespeare is not the only dramatist to speak of the " two hours' traffic of the stage." Since the average play contains from sixteen thousand to twenty thousand words, there can have been little dawdling; the rate of speech must have

been very rapid, and such pace is only possible when the audience is sensitive, keen, and alert. Indeed, the greatest contrast to our modern theater would be in the spectators, who responded quickly and violently, unashamedly demonstrating their grief, pleasure, or amusement, and at times — if dissatisfied with the performance or the play — their anger. Shakespeare was lucky in having to write for the simple conditions of the Elizabethan playhouse. He would doubtless have succeeded even in Hollywood, but, as it happened, the kind of play which best suited his theater and his audiences needed also the highest kind of poetry.

SHAKESPEARE'S PLAYS

PUBLICATION. By the time Shakespeare died, fourteen of his plays had been separately published in booklets of the kind known as quartos.[1] In 1623 his surviving fellow actors, John Heming and Henry Condell, with the co-operation of a number of printers, published a collected edition of thirty-six plays in one folio volume — the famous First Folio — with an engraved portrait, memorial verses by Ben Jonson and others, and an Epistle to the Reader in which Heming and Condell make the interesting note that Shakespeare's " hand and mind went together, and what he thought, he uttered with that easiness that we have scarce received from him a blot in his papers."

The full list of Shakespeare's plays is:

APPROXIMATE DATE OF WRITING	FIRST PRINTED
1590–1594	
Henry VI (three parts)	1623 (folio)
Richard III	1597
Titus Andronicus	1594
Love's Labor's Lost	1598
The Two Gentlemen of Verona	1623 (folio)
The Comedy of Errors	1623 (folio)
The Taming of the Shrew	1623 (folio)
1594–1597	
Romeo and Juliet (pirated 1597)	1599
A Midsummer Night's Dream	1600
Richard II	1597

[1] The terms " quarto " and " folio," used to describe books, denote the foldings in the sheet of paper. The size of the standard piece of paper was about 14 x 18 inches. In a folio the sheet was folded once, thus giving two leaves (or four pages) each of about 14 x 9. In a quarto the sheet was folded again, thus giving four leaves (or eight pages) each of about 9 x 7 inches.

King John	1623	(folio)
The Merchant of Venice	1600	
1597–1600		
Henry IV, Part I	1598	
Henry IV, Part II	1600	
Henry V	1623	(folio)
(pirated 1600)		
Much Ado about Nothing	1600	
The Merry Wives of Windsor	1623	(folio)
(pirated 1602)		
As You Like It	1623	(folio)
Julius Caesar	1623	(folio)
Troilus and Cressida	1609	
1601–1608		
Hamlet	1604	
(pirated 1603)		
Twelfth Night	1623	(folio)
Measure for Measure	1623	(folio)
All's Well That Ends Well	1623	(folio)
Othello	1622	
King Lear	1608	
Macbeth	1623	(folio)
Timon of Athens	1623	(folio)
Antony and Cleopatra	1623	(folio)
Coriolanus	1623	(folio)
After 1608		
Pericles	1609	
(omitted from the Folio)		
Cymbeline	1623	(folio)
The Winter's Tale	1623	(folio)
The Tempest	1623	(folio)
Henry VIII	1623	(folio)

COMEDIES. In the Folio, Shakespeare's plays are divided into Comedies, Histories, and Tragedies. The division is simple and drastic, and yet it denotes certain general princples which he followed.

The main purpose of Shakespearean Comedy is entertainment; "our true intent," as Quince in *A Midsummer Night's Dream* reminds the spectators, "is all for your delight"; and, as Shakespeare knew well enough, the theme which always delights is a love story ending in a wedding. At the end of *Love's Labor's Lost,* which differs from the usual pattern because the ladies leave their lovers to a year's probation, Berowne sighs:

> Our wooing doth not end like an old play.
> Jack hath not Jill. These ladies' courtesy
> Might well have made our sport a comedy.

So the usual theme for Shakespearean comedy is how Jack woos Jill, or — as commonly — how Jill wins Jack.

The common pattern for a Shakespearean comedy — to be found in *Two Gentlemen of*

Verona, The Taming of the Shrew, A Midsummer Night's Dream, The Merchant of Venice, Much Ado about Nothing, As You Like It, Twelfth Night, and *The Tempest* — is a story which involves two or three sets of characters. In the main plot of each play the two principal lovers, after various adventures, are happily paired at the end of Act V. A second plot brings together two friends of the principals; and, to add change of mood to the whole mixture, a comic underplot gives the professional clowns a chance for lower but good-humored laughter.

The surprising fact is that after three hundred and fifty years these comedies should still be so actable and delightful. It shows that Shakespeare had a shrewder instinct for what is permanently pleasing than those grimmer playwrights and critics who demand that comedy as well as tragedy shall always present some moral, social, or psychological problem. Most of Shakespeare's comedies are romantic fantasies — stories of pleasant people in impossible situations.

HISTORIES. In writing his Histories Shakespeare had a more serious purpose. The study of history was popular, for it was regarded as useful and essential knowledge for any intelligent man. History recorded the fall of princes and great men who offended against divine and moral law, and it warned those who would follow such evil examples. Besides, Englishmen had every reason to observe the lessons of history. For more than a century before Shakespeare's time England had been in a state of recurring anarchy and civil war because of the crimes committed by and against ambitious princes. Shakespeare amply illustrated the moral lessons of history in a series of five early plays: the three parts of *Henry VI, Richard III,* and, after an interval, *Richard II.* They showed how the crime committed by Henry Bolingbroke, when he deposed Richard II and usurped the crown, ultimately led to the long and bloody civil Wars of the Roses. These first history plays are wordy and earnest. A little later, in rewriting an old play, by another hand, on the troublesome reign of King John, Shakespeare encountered the amusing but unhistorical character of the Bastard Falconbridge; the earthy humanity with which he endowed Falconbridge enlivens a dull Shakespearean play.

Thereafter Shakespeare mingled the high notes of sober history with scenes of lively low comedy. In writing *I* and *II Henry IV* he created Falstaff. Falstaff is a wholly fictitious character, and his vast bulk so overshadows the more important persons of real history that in the two plays the Falstaff scenes occupy more space than the historical episodes. *Henry V,* the last play of this series, lacks Falstaff in person — he dies offstage — but the heroics of the siege of Harfleur and the battle of Agincourt are balanced by the "humors" of Ancient Pistol and Henry's bluff wooing of French Kate.

At the end of his career Shakespeare wrote one more history play, *Henry VIII,* in which he presented in a series of pageant-like scenes some episodes of English history which culminated in the birth of the princess who afterward became Queen Elizabeth.

TRAGEDIES. Tragedy to an Elizabethan playgoer denoted a play ending with violent death for most of the principal persons. In his tragedies, Shakespeare usually followed the common pattern; there are three dead in the last scene of *Romeo and Juliet* and *Othello,* four in *Hamlet,* five in *Lear*. But to justify such carnage, tragedy also demanded that the disaster should be caused by some breach of fundamental moral law.

Shakespeare's greatest tragedies all show how the breaking of moral law leads inevitably to destruction. In *Hamlet,* Claudius' original sin of lust for Gertrude leads to the murder of Gertrude's husband, and ultimately to the deaths of Claudius, Gertrude, Laertes, and Hamlet. In *Othello,* Iago, for the basest of motives, persuades Othello to a mad passion of jealousy against his wife Desdemona, which results in the deaths of Othello, Desdemona, and incidentally of Emilia, Iago's wife. In *Lear,* the old king's foolish pride leads him to discard his faithful daughter Cordelia, while the ruthless ambition of the bastard Edmund prompts him to betray his brother Edgar and then his father Gloucester. As a direct result of pride and ambition, Lear, Gloucester, Edmund, Cordelia, and her two sisters Goneril and Regan all perish. In *Macbeth,* the ambition of Macbeth and his wife brings about the murder of Duncan and a whole series of disasters until Macbeth himself is killed in battle. Shakespeare's greatest tragedies reach down to the depths of emotion because his sense of moral law was as acute as his skill in portraying the pathos of human suffering.

SHAKESPEARE'S DRAMATIC TECHNIQUE

PLOT. It is a fashion nowadays with some critics to declare that Shakespeare's plays are "dramatic poems," and should therefore be subjected to the same kinds of minute dissection, analysis, and symbolical interpretation as modern poetry. There is, however, an elementary distinction to be made between a poem (or even a dramatic poem) and a play. A poem is intended primarily as an experience which first comes to us through the *sound* of the words; the *sight* of what is being done as well as the sound of the words is needed by the spectator of a drama. And Shakespeare wrote his plays to be acted on the stage, not to be analyzed in a laboratory nor even to be read privately.

A drama — and the original Greek word means a "doing" or an "acting" — is thus an artistic experience to be shared among dramatist, actors, and spectators. For that experience to be fully achieved, many different elements, including action, movement, speech, and sometimes music must be fused into a unity. Of these the script which the dramatist contributes is the most important, and for the reader all that remains of the original experience.

A good play needs four component parts: theme, plot, character, and speech or language. Many dramatists begin with the theme and then construct a play to illustrate it. This is not Shakespeare's usual method. Instead, he takes an existing and often familiar story and turns it into a play, and in so doing — no matter how improbable the original tale — he makes the people come alive and their adventures credible.

Shakespeare's plots are not always properly appreciated because his construction is apparently so free and artless, but a closer look will soon show that Shakespeare was an expert plot maker who devised his play so that it would not only convey the complete emotional effect he desired but would also keep the audience interested and attentive from beginning to end. *Hamlet* is a good example of subtle and elaborate plotting.

Hamlet opens with a scene intended to create the atmosphere of dread and impending evil. The Ghost appears and by its very silence arouses our curiosity. We sense that however outwardly serene the Danish court, there is something very rotten within. In Scene ii, the new King holds his first court, and in his opening speech tells us quite naturally of recent events: on the death of the late king, his brother, he has succeeded to the throne and married his brother's widow. He also dispatches ambassadors to Norway to deal with the threat of young Fortinbras, gives permission to Laertes to return to his studies in Paris, and, finally, persuades Hamlet not to return to Wittenberg. These actions are all so lifelike that unless we stop to think critically we do not realize that the purpose of this scene is to feed us with the information that we need to understand what follows.

This business being concluded, King, Queen, and courtiers withdraw, and Hamlet at last occupies our full attention. His first soliloquy reveals his frustrated disgust, and when Horatio and the others arrive to tell him of the midnight apparition, we sense that the Ghost will indeed have something to impart. Meanwhile, to increase our interest by delay, Shakespeare next gives us an intimate picture of the Polonius family at home: Laertes, the impetuous and somewhat priggish son; Ophelia, his sister, inexperienced in the intrigues of court life; and the old statesman himself — cunning, experienced, pompous, wordy, and worldly wise. From this delicious comedy, we are taken back to the battlements where Hamlet encounters the Ghost and is told the dread secret of his uncle's crime.

The whole play is planned with a masterly ease, each scene leading into or contrasting with the next, so that we are kept continuously alert and never allowed to tire with too much of the same emotion or the same situation.

One small detail will illustrate the concealed artistry of the whole design. At the end of the play Fortinbras, Prince of Norway, is needed to take over command and restore order to Denmark. Fortinbras's part is small — less than twenty-five lines in all — and yet at the end he dominates the stage as the most important character. Quietly and subtly Fortinbras has been built up throughout the play. His ambitions are the theme of Horatio's talk in I.i. His suspicious actions cause the sending of the ambassadors in I.ii. In II.ii the ambassadors report on their mission, and Claudius agrees that Fortinbras and his army may have passage through Denmark. In IV.iv Fortinbras himself appears very briefly so that we may see him and remember where he is. Finally, when he reappears just after Hamlet's death, his entrance is entirely natural and needs neither introduction nor explanation.

CHARACTER. Shakespeare's skill in creating character has been recognized from the first. The word "character" originally meant a letter in the Greek alphabet; thence "handwriting"; and so the nature of a man as written in his face. A living person is a compound of many qualities: his past history, his strength and weakness, his habits, morals, and beliefs, his loyalties, friendships, loves, and hates, and this amalgam is revealed most immediately to others in his face, bearing, gestures, clothes, and manner of speech. We learn to understand him further from the attitude and comments of his friends, his critics, and his enemies, from his own behavior in different situations, from the thoughts which he utters, and not less from the way in which he utters them, and even from his vocabulary. In drama, the bodily expressions and manner of speech are conveyed by the actor; the mind is revealed through the words supplied by the dramatist.

A good example of Shakespeare's methods in characterization is Harry Percy, the "Hotspur of the North," in I Henry IV. We first hear of young Hotspur in I.i, when Henry IV tells of Hotspur's victory over the Scots and his insolence in keeping the prisoners whom he has captured. Indeed, the weary King laments the contrast between his own son and this dashing Harry. Hotspur himself first appears in I.iii and at once reveals his fiery, impatient mind, darting away as a new thought appears, obsessed with a zeal for military honor which is not far from vanity, roused at a word, and so an easy victim for the unscrupulous King and his crafty uncle, Worcester. Having drawn this side of his nature, Shakespeare next shows Hotspur (II. iii) in a charming little episode at home with his young wife; and to give added point to this episode, Prince Hal in the next scene briefly sums him up:

. . . the Hotspur of the North, he that kills me some six or seven dozen of Scots at a breakfast, washes his hands, and says to his wife, "Fie upon this quiet life! I want work." "O my sweet Harry," says she, "how many hast thou killed today?" "Give my roan horse a drench," says he, and answers, "Some fourteen," an hour after — "a trifle, a trifle."

It is cruel parody, but a sign that Shakespeare was sure of himself, for only an artist who has complete self-confidence dares to make fun of his own serious efforts.

Hotspur is next shown in conference with Glendower, Worcester, and Mortimer, and the contrast between these four very different characters is cleverly drawn. Hotspur has no patience with the Welshman's solemn claims to be extraordinary, is too impetuous to conceal his boredom, and mocks him beyond endurance; it is a tribute to Hotspur's personality, and a piece of subtle artistry, that such a man as Glendower should twice swallow his anger and give way. Hotspur is a blunt and practical young man with no use for poetry or art, natural or supernatural, insisting on his own way until he gets it, and then yielding at once, and very fond of his wife in his own bluff way. He is a perfect specimen of the romantic soldier who filled Shakespeare with admiration and amusement, for he was careful to set Falstaff beside Hotspur. Falstaff's brief catechism on honor is a mocking echo of Hotspur's heroics. Hotspur dies at the hands of the Prince whom he had despised, lamenting not so much the loss of his hopes as of his honor as a soldier, and when he is dead his body is dishonorably prodded by the live Falstaff.

SPEECH. Shakespeare, as all Elizabethan dramatists, used four kinds of speech in his plays: blank verse, rhymed verse, prose, and song. Each kind has its uses, and the whole play, especially in his maturity, is conceived as a kind of verbal symphony, each scene or episode being composed as part of a complete harmony. *The Tempest* in its poetical scenes is the finest example of the musical use of words in all Shakespeare's plays.

Blank verse — in the form of unrhymed lines each having five stresses — is the normal form of speech in Shakespearean drama for all scenes and persons whose appeal is mainly through the emotions of the spectator or reader. English blank verse is a very versatile meter, and can be used with great variety of mood and "pressure" — for conversation of all kinds, serious or gay; for description, as in Hotspur's account of the foppish messenger (*I Hen IV*, I.iii.30–68); for exhortation or rebuke, as when Henry IV chides his erring son (III.ii); for passionate denunciation, as when Hamlet chastises his mother (*Haml*, III.iv); for garrulous volubility, as in Polonius' lecture to Reynaldo (II.i); for meditation and introspection, as when Hamlet rebukes himself for inaction or meditates on suicide (II.ii.575–632, III.i.55–88.)

Shakespeare is so subtle in the variation of rhythms, stresses, pauses, and tones in his blank verse that he can convey not only every mood but even the personal peculiarities of the speaker. In the passage between Hotspur and Glendower (*I Hen IV*, IV.i), the Welsh Prince's speeches, with their pompous insistence on his supernatural origin, almost demand to be spoken with a Welsh accent. Again, when Caliban mutters his grievances against Prospero and Miranda, the stress falls naturally on the snarling words:

> I must eat my dinner.
> This island's *mine*, by *Sycorax* my mother,
> Which thou takest from me. When thou camest first,
> Thou strokedst me, and madest much of me, wouldst give me
> Water with berries in't. And teach me how
> To name the bigger light, and how the less,
> That burn by day and night. And then I loved thee,
> And showed thee all the qualities o' th' isle,
> The fresh springs, brine pits, barren place and fertile.
> *Cursèd* be I that did so! All the charms
> Of Sycorax, *toads, beetles, bats,* light on you!
> For I am all the subjects that you have,
> Which first was mine own king. And here you *sty* me
> In this *hard* rock whiles you do keep from me
> The rest o' th' island.

The rhythm and tone are very different when Prospero, saddened and angered by the conspiracy against his life, in musing and visionary mood, comments on the pageant which has just disappeared:

> Be cheerful, sir.
> Our revels now are ended. These our actors,
> As I foretold you, were all spirits, and
> Are melted into air, into thin air.

And, like the baseless fabric of this vision,
The cloud-capped towers, the gorgeous palaces,
The solemn temples, the great globe itself —
Yea, all which it inherit — shall dissolve
And, like this insubstantial pageant faded,
Leave not a rack behind. We are such stuff
As dreams are made on, and our little life
Is rounded with a sleep.

Here rhythm and sound compel the speaker to go slowly and solemnly until he reaches the climax at " rounded with a sleep."

Rhymed verse in five-stress lines, usually in couplets, is common in Shakespeare's early plays, but in the middle period, to which *I Henry IV* and *Hamlet* belong, he was more sparing and used it for definite effects. The commonest use is in the form of a couplet at the end of a scene or episode. Here the rhyme has sometimes the practical purpose of warning those behind the stage of a change — a curtain to be drawn or an entrance to be made; but a couplet also rounds out the dialogue aesthetically and brings it to an effective close before the actors make their exit. Thus at the end of I.ii, Hamlet, before following Horatio and Marcellus off stage, turns to the audience to comment:

My father's spirit in arms! All is not well.
I doubt some foul play. Would the night were
    come!
Till then sit still, my soul. Foul deeds will rise,
Though all the earth o'erwhelm them, to men's
    eyes.

The rhyme effectively shows us that this episode is ended and that a new set of characters is about to enter.

Rhymed verse in or after a passage of blank verse or prose has also the effect of stiffening the dialogue and heightening the emotion. Thus in *Twelfth Night* (III.i.161), when Olivia can no longer control her feelings for the disguised Viola, whom she supposes to be " Cesario," she breaks out:

Cesario, by the roses of the spring,
By maidhood, honor, truth, and everything,
I love thee so, that, mauger all thy pride,
Nor wit nor reason can my passion hide.
Do not extort thy reasons from this clause,
For that I woo, thou therefore hast no cause,
But rather reason thus with reason fetter,
Love sought is good, but given unsought is better.

And Viola, whose complex emotions are in an even greater turmoil, retorts, also in rhyme:

By innocence I swear, and by my youth,
I have one heart, one bosom, and one truth,
And that no woman has; nor never none
Shall mistress be of it, save I alone.
And so adieu, good madam. Nevermore
Will I my master's tears to you deplore.
OLIVIA. Yet come again, for thou perhaps mayst
    move
That heart which now abhors to like his love.

In his later plays, end rhymes are less common, but Shakespeare will often use a single speech in rhyme for the definite purpose of underlining, as it were, a particularly significant moment or situation. Thus Coriolanus, writhing under the indignity of having to beg for the votes of the despised plebeians, comments:

Better it is to die, better to starve,
Than crave the hire which first we do deserve.
Why in this woolvish toge should I stand here,
To beg of Hob and Dick that do appear
Their needless vouches? Custom calls me to 't.
What custom wills, in all things should we do
The dust on ántique time would lie unswept,
And mountainous error to be too highly heaped
For truth to o'erpeer. Rather than fool it so,
Let the high office and the honor go
To one that would do thus. I am half-through.
The one part suffered, the other will I do.

The rhyme stresses the resentment which will soon lead Coriolanus to his destruction.

Another use of rhyme is to effect contrast. In *The Tempest,* Shakespeare inserts the little masque of Ceres (IV.i.61). The speeches of the goddesses are all in rhyme, and in a somewhat artificial diction which distinguishes the vision from the reality of Miranda and Ferdinand. Similarly in the play scene in *Hamlet* (III.ii.165–271), the Player King and Player Queen speak in a stilted rhymed verse while the talk of Hamlet at this moment is notably naturalistic.

Just as rhyme will stiffen the tension, so a passage of *prose* in a play which is mainly in verse inevitably lowers the emotional pitch and increases the pace; it is appropriate for passages of comedy, farce, and repartee. A Shakespearean character usually laughs in prose but he weeps in verse. Prose, too, is the natural speech for lower and more comic persons; verse would be unnatural on the lips of Falstaff, Osric, the gravediggers, Stephano, or Trinculo. Versatile characters will use all forms of speech; Prince Hal talks prose to Falstaff but verse when in the presence of the King. Hamlet addressing the King or his mother, or alone with his own emotions, will normally use blank verse; but he lapses naturally into prose when mocking Polonius, conversing with Guildenstern and Rosencrantz, instructing the players, or questioning the gravedigger.

Songs in Shakespeare's plays are usually intended to create a particular mood. Thus Ophelia's snatches of song emphasize her madness, and the bawdy little song which she sings to the horrified Queen adds greatly to the pathos of her end. In *The Tempest* there is considerable variety in the use of song. Ariel (who is invisible to all except to his master Prospero) conveys his messages by means of song appropriate to such a fairy creature; he deceives Ferdinand into believing that his father is dead by the song "Full fathom five," and when at last promised his freedom he breaks out into the airy excitement of "Where the bee sucks, there suck I." By contrast Stephano, Trinculo, and Caliban, as the drink takes hold of them, lapse into such raucous ditties as "The master, the swabber, the boatswain, and I" or "Flout 'em and scout 'em."

SHAKESPEARE'S POETRY

Poetry, being in the main a means of evoking emotion in the reader, achieves many of its effects indirectly. By the sounds of individual words and the rhythms of words in combination, the poet works through the ears of his hearers; by metaphor, simile, and the broader use of "imagery" he recalls their memories and associations and charms them to respond to his own mood.

Imagery is of many kinds, and Shakespeare's use of it was continually changing and maturing. In his earliest plays, the imagery is direct and simple, intended only to bring out the immediate meaning of a word or passage; later he uses imagery with constantly increasing subtlety. Thus Henry IV expresses and conveys his contempt for Richard II, whom he has supplanted, in these words:

The skipping King, he ambled up and down,

With shallow jesters and rash bavin wits,
Soon kindled and soon burnt; . . .

"Skipping" connotes childishness; "ambling" the aimless shuffling of a fool; "bavin" means brushwood for kindling — worthless and soon consumed. All these images are used directly, and they combine to form a general picture of the essential frivolity of Richard.

In the later plays there is a far more elaborate and indirect use of imagery, when the same kind of image is constantly repeated so that the hearer is almost compelled to feel in a certain way toward the persons and events throughout the play. Thus *Hamlet*[1] contains a number of images of corruption and bodily disorder, of ulcers, tumors, and foul diseases, of weeds and rankness: "Something is rotten in the state of Denmark" . . . "the fat weed / That roots itself in ease on Lethe wharf" . . . "So Lust . . . will sate itself in a celestial bed / And prey on garbage" . . . "your husband, like a mildewed ear, / Blasting his wholesome brother" . . . "do not spread the compost on the weeds / To make them ranker." These images in themselves form a very small part of the whole play, but by repetition they create, maintain, and convey the feeling of general rottenness pervading the court of Denmark; it is as if from time to time we smell whiffs of putrefaction.

In *The Tempest* the imagery is less patterned but far subtler; image, sound, and idea are welded into one. In Prospero's great speech, "These our actors," the rise and fall of the word music is blended inseparably with the images of solid magnificence: "cloud-capped towers, . . . gorgeous palaces, . . . solemn temples . . . ," which will dissolve into a nothingness less even than a wisp of cloud. Similarly Alonso's remorse (III.iii.95) is expressed as much in its deep music as in its images of thunder, of the bass notes of a great organ, and of muddy death:

Oh, it is monstrous, monstrous!
Methought the billows spoke, and told me of it,
The winds did sing it to me, and the thunder,
That deep and dreadful organ pipe, pronounced
The name of Prosper. It did bass my trespass.
Therefore my son i' th' ooze is bedded, and
I'll seek him deeper than e'er plummet sounded,
And with him there lie mudded.

[1] See Caroline Spurgeon, *Shakespeare's Imagery* (1935), pp. 316–17.

SHAKESPEARE'S UNIVERSALITY

There have been many attempts to analyze Shakespeare's peculiar genius, but none can be final because the mark of genius in a writer is that in some undefinable way he evokes individual responses from each reader, who is made to feel that he has a kind of kinship with the author as if both had shared their secret experiences. This quality exists to some degree in all great writers. Shakespeare differs from the rest because he makes a wider appeal to a greater number of readers of different ages and of different environments; he is more universal. This power of universality is unpredictable, for it is seldom if ever possible to say of any new work that it will be permanent. Yet when an author's popularity still endures after three and a half centuries, at least some of the marks of his genius can be isolated. Dr. Johnson, in his own sonorous way, thus expressed it:

Shakespeare is, above all writers, at least above all modern writers, the poet of nature; the poet that holds up to his readers a faithful mirror of manners and of life. His characters are not modified by the customs of particular places, unpracticed by the rest of the world; by the peculiarities of studies or professions, which can operate but upon small numbers; or by the accidents of transient fashions or temporary opinion; they are the genuine progeny of common humanity, such as the world will always supply, and observation will always find.[1]

Shakespeare has not only an instinctive understanding of humanity but he has also the power of expressing this understanding in such a way that his creatures — Hamlet, for instance, or Falstaff or Polonius — are more real to us than any person of history. They speak, think, and act not only as Elizabethans but as human beings always have thought, spoken, and acted. This requires a most sensitive and sympathetic power of observation. Shakespeare was fascinated by the infinite varieties of the human species; and Hamlet thus expresses it:

What a piece of work is a man! How noble in reason! How infinite in faculty! In form and moving how express and admirable! In action how like an angel! In apprehension how like a god! The beauty of the world! The paragon of animals!

But Shakespeare did not always look upon man

[1] For this essay, see p. 937, below.

with such enthusiasm or optimism. In another mood, Lear, at the beginning of his madness as he contemplates the naked beggar exclaims,

Consider him well. Thou owest the worm no silk, the beast no hide, the sheep no wool, the cat no perfume. Ha! Here's three on 's are sophisticated. Thou art the thing itself. Unaccommodated man [i.e., man without his trappings] is no more but such a poor, bare, forked animal as thou art.

Another of Shakespeare's qualities is his power to record what he perceived in language that cannot be bettered, and the range of experience expressed is so vast that one can find a quotation from Shakespeare to fit almost any occasion and mood. Indeed we seldom realize how often, instinctively or deliberately, we turn to Shakespeare to express our thoughts for us:

There are more things in Heaven and earth, Horatio,
Than are dreamt of in your philosophy.

All the world's a stage,
And all the men and women merely players.

Dost thou think because thou art virtuous, there shall be no more cakes and ale?

A little water clears us of this deed.
How easy is it then!

Mark you this, Bassanio,
The Devil can cite Scripture for his purpose.

Yond Cassius has a lean and hungry look.
He thinks too much, such men are dangerous.

And my poor fool is hanged! No, no, no life!
Why should a dog, a horse, a rat have life
And thou no breath at all? Thou'lt come no more,
Never, never, never, never, never!

We are such stuff
As dreams are made on, and our little life
Is rounded with a sleep.

There are hundreds of these incomparable lines which have been woven into the English language.

Above all, Shakespeare's plays have durability. One can read and reread them year after year, and at every reading they reveal new depths and understanding. No author in the English tongue wears so well or lasts so long.

Reading Suggestions

G. B. Harrison, editor, *Shakespeare: The Complete Works* (1952). Includes a full introduction to such matters as the records of Shakespeare's life, Shakespeare's England, the history of Elizabethan drama, Shakespearean criticism, and a reading list. The texts and notes of the three plays below are taken from this edition.

Andrew Cecil Bradley, *Shakespearean Tragedy* (1904). The most famous and best example of Victorian criticism. In the essays on *Hamlet,* Bradley minutely examined Hamlet's character to discover the reasons for his delay.

Walter Raleigh, *Shakespeare* (1907). A lively and human general introduction to the enjoyment of Shakespeare's plays.

Andrew Cecil Bradley, *Oxford Lectures on Poetry* (1909). The volume includes "The Rejection of Falstaff," an essay which has greatly influenced modern critics and is largely responsible for the tendency to romanticize Falstaff.

D. Nichol Smith, *Shakespeare Criticism: From the Beginnings to Carlyle* (1916). A useful selection of the earlier critical pronouncements. It includes Maurice Morgann's "An Essay on the Dramatic Character of Sir John Falstaff," the first major example of a "romantic" criticism of Shakespeare. Morgann defended Falstaff against the charge of cowardice.

Arthur Quiller-Couch, *Shakespeare's Workmanship* (1918). A good example of common-sense (though at times sentimental) criticism. Includes essays on *Hamlet* and *The Tempest.*

Edgar Elmer Stoll, *Hamlet: An Historical and Comparative Study* (1919). Deals with *Hamlet* from the point of view of an Elizabethan scholar; a valuable antidote to too much romantic or modern criticism.

T. M. Raysor, editor, *Coleridge's Shakespearean Criticism (1811–1834)*, 2 vols. (1930). Coleridge was the most influential of the critics of the "Romantic Revival," and his remarks on Hamlet have been mainly responsible for the idea of the hypersensitive prince. His lectures on *The Tempest* are also worth studying.

G. Wilson Knight, *The Shakespearean "Tempest"* (1931). One of the first attempts to examine one of Shakespeare's plays by the methods which have since been called the "new criticism." Wilson Knight also wrote on *Hamlet* in *The Wheel of Fire* (1930) ("Hamlet's Melancholia" and "The Embassy of Death: An Essay on *Hamlet*") and in *The Imperial Theme* (1931) ("Rose of May: An Essay on Life Themes in *Hamlet*").

John Dover Wilson, *What Happens in "Hamlet"* (1935). An interesting attempt to reconstruct Shakespeare's purposes in *Hamlet.*

Harley Granville-Barker, "*Hamlet,*" in *Prefaces to Shakespeare,* vol. i (originally published in 1936). A lively, valuable study from the point of view of an experienced producer of plays on the stage, looking "at Shakespeare's dramatic art in the light of the effect which he, surmisedly, meant to make by it."

John Dover Wilson, *The Fortunes of Falstaff* (1943). A study of Shakespeare's intentions in creating Falstaff, arising out of the author's editing of the texts of *I* and *II Henry IV.* A corrective to Bradley's essay.

See also in Vol. II of the present text: Johnson's Preface to Shakespeare, and T. S. Eliot's essay on *Hamlet.*

ADDITIONAL NOTES

A. THE ELIZABETHAN IDEA OF THE UNIVERSE

Although Copernicus' *De revolutionibus orbum Coelestium,* which first appeared in 1543, may be said to have revolutionized modern ideas about the physical structure of the universe, in Shakespeare's day the book was hardly known. Most Elizabethans still believed that the earth was the center of the universe and immovable, and that all matter on the earth was naturally drawn to its center, which was thus the absolute center of everything.

Around the earth moved the seven planets, each in its sphere, thus forming a series of concentric circles. Nearest was the moon; then came Mercury, Venus, Sol (the Sun), Mars, Jupiter, and Saturn. In an eighth circle were the fixed stars, which remained constant in their relationships to each other, and outside there was a ninth circle known as the *Primum Mobile,* or the First Mover. The *Primum Mobile* had the power to turn all the other circles around the earth from east to west once every twenty-four hours; yet each sphere had, at the same time, its own contrary motion as it moved from west to east in its own orbit.

The moon took twenty-eight days to complete its circle; Sol, Venus, and Mercury moved in a year; Mars in two years; Jupiter in twelve years; and Saturn in thirty. It was believed that the planets in their motion each made a musical note, the whole forming a perfect harmony of sound. Since the planets moved at different paces, their relationship to each other was constantly changing, and certain conjunctions of the planets were regarded as lucky, others as unlucky.

Planets were believed to give out a kind of ethereal fluid or "influence" (*influentia*), which greatly affected human beings. The moon, as the nearest and most easily observed, was known to affect the ebb and flow of tides and was believed to be peculiarly powerful. The other planets also were considered to have a direct bearing on the weather, and indeed on all earthly affairs. Accordingly, astrologers believed that as a result of their accumulation of observations they could by the pattern of the heavens decide what was likely to happen at any time. In the same way, by observing the various conjunctions of the heavenly bodies at the moment of a person's birth, a horoscope could be drawn up which would indicate the future course of his life. A man's fate was thus determined by the stars.

Although the pre-Copernican view of the universe was fallacious, astronomers had carefully recorded the positions of the fixed stars and the motions of the planets in compilations such as the Toledo Tables mentioned in Chaucer's Franklin's Tale, and for astrological purposes they could calculate fairly accurately what the position of any heavenly body would be for any given place and time. The position of the planets relative to the earth was measured against the background of stars before which they appeared to move. The sun by day and the planets by night seemed to trace approximately the same path around the earth against the background of fixed stars. This broad path was called the zodiac, and for purposes of measurement it was divided into twelve sectors of thirty degrees each, named after the constellations which lay in the background.

Thus, the sun on the first day of spring (at the vernal equinox) was said to enter Aries, the first house of the zodiac. That is, behind the sun lay the sign of the zodiac named Aries. It was, of course, invisible by day, but its neighboring sign could be seen at sunset. In twenty-four hours, the sun was seen to rotate once around the earth, but the stars which also seemed to rotate daily around the earth appeared to travel approximately one degree farther than the sun each day. Hence, in thirty days the sun appeared to lose thirty degrees against the signs of the zodiac, and on the thirty-first day it was said to enter Taurus, the second sign. (Its apparent motion may be compared to that of a ticket collector — the sun — on a merry-go-round, who walks slowly back from horse to horse — the signs of the zodiac — always rotating with the horses but eventually traversing the entire circuit past each horse.) The motion of the moon and other planets was more easily perceived, since they shone at night against a visible background of fixed stars.

Before the introduction of the Gregorian calendar (in 1752 in England), the sun entered each sign approximately on the eleventh, twelfth, or thirteenth day of each month; now it enters approximately on the twentieth, twenty-first, or twenty-second. Thus, the sun entered Aries (the Ram) on March 12, Taurus (the Bull) in April, Gemini (the Twins) in May, Cancer (the Crab) in June, Leo (the Lion) in July, Virgo (the Virgin) in August, Libra (the Scales) in September, Scorpio (the Scorpion) in October, Sagittarius (the Archer) in November, Capricornus (the Goat) in De-

cember, Aquarius (the Water Carrier) in January, and Pisces (the Fish) in February.

Abnormal events in the heavens, and especially the appearance of a comet or an eclipse, though sometimes predicted by astronomers, were popularly regarded as alarming portents of disaster.

B. THE HUMORS

It was believed that all matter consisted of the four elements of earth, fire, air, and water. In the human body these elements, called *humors* — humor literally means dampness — were identified with black bile (*earth*), blood (*air*), bile (*fire*), and phlegm (*water*). Each element produced a corresponding *temperament* which was outwardly indicated by a man's *complexion*. Too much earth produced the *melancholic* humor, air the *sanguine,* fire the *choleric,* water the *phlegmatic*. In a healthy body the humors counterbalanced each other, but if one humor was deficient or excessive the individual became mentally and physically unbalanced. The word "humor" is often used as a psychological term, but it bears a wide range of meanings. It may be used literally to denote moisture, or to imply one of the four humors, or more vaguely to denote whim, obsession, temperament, mood, temper, or inclination.

C. THE FENCING MATCH IN *HAMLET* (V.ii.171–77, 290–316.)

Laertes fancies himself an expert fencer and is therefore prepared to give Hamlet a handicap. He has bet the King that he will hit Hamlet twelve times before Hamlet hits him nine times. Hamlet's handicap is, then, plus three in twelve hits. The contest is with rapier (right hand) and dagger (left hand).

Hamlet scores the first two hits and is thus two up. Laertes then presses his attack and scores a hit with his pointed foil. Hamlet, realizing from his wound that Laertes is fighting with a pointed foil, carries out a textbook movement to exchange rapiers. In the maneuver, Laertes makes a short thrust. Hamlet parries, drawing back his left foot; then with his foil he pushes Laertes' blade to one side. Whereupon, bringing up his left foot, he swings round, drops his dagger, and with his left hand grasps the hilt of his opponent's foil and twists it backward. If Laertes holds onto his own foil, it will be twisted out of his hand, and his fingers broken as well. His only answer to this movement is to drop his own foil and retaliate by similarly grasping Hamlet's hilt with his left hand and twisting it out of his grasp. Each opponent now has the other's foil in his left hand. Each steps back, transfers the exchanged foil to the right hand, and resumes the contest.

Hamlet, having thus exchanged rapiers, now presses home the attack and scores his third hit with Laertes' pointed (and poisoned) rapier. At this moment the Queen swoons and the contest is broken off.

The stage direction in Q1 is "*They catch one another's Rapiers, and both are wounded.*" F1 reads "*In scuffling they change Rapiers.*" There is no stage direction in Q2.

D. THE HISTORY BEHIND
I HENRY IV

Except for *King John* and *Henry VIII*, Shakespeare's ten history plays are concerned with one central theme — the rise and fall of the House of Lancaster. They cover a period of nearly a century of complex events.

Edward III reigned fifty years (1327–77). He had seven sons, of whom the eldest was Edward, the Black Prince. Both Edwards were passionately devoted to war and were constantly campaigning in France or Spain. In his later days, Edward III became senile, but he outlived his eldest son; the Black Prince died in 1376, Edward III a few months later, in 1377. Thereupon the king's eleven-year-old grandson, Richard II, son of the Black Prince, became king, under the regency of John of Gaunt, Duke of Lancaster, the eldest surviving son of Edward III. In 1381 occurred the Peasants' Revolt. The boy king behaved with great bravery and pacified the rebels by promises of redress of their grievances, promises which were afterward broken by his advisers. In 1382, at the age of sixteen, Richard married Anne of Bohemia. By this time, Gaunt had left the country and was warring in Spain; the control of the kingdom had passed to Thomas of Woodstock, Duke of Gloucester, sixth son of Edward III.

Richard was now growing up; to Gloucester's alarm, he formed a court party of his own friends. Gloucester and his supporters (called the Lords Appellant), who included Henry Bolingbroke, Duke of Hereford (son of John of Gaunt), and Thomas Mowbray (Earl of Nottingham and afterward Duke of Norfolk), seized Richard's friends by force and executed them. In 1389, Richard suddenly declared that he was now of age, and Gloucester was obliged to resign his regency. Thereafter for some years Richard ruled competently and moderately; he even seemed to be reconciled with the Lords Appellant; but when Gloucester again began his intrigues he was arrested, sent to Calais (then an English possession), and there murdered.

Richard meanwhile had lost his first wife and had married again. His character changed. He became reckless and extravagant, and his court was filled with favorites and parasites. As a result he was constantly in need of money, which he raised by forced loans, benevolences ("voluntary" gifts from wealthy men), and by farming out the taxes; that is, in return for cash down he granted some financier the right to collect the taxes — a system of raising money which led to great abuses.

In 1398, Bolingbroke and Norfolk quarreled. At this point, Shakespeare's *Richard II* begins. Richard banished both noblemen — Norfolk for life and Bolingbroke for six years — but with the promise that the great estates which should come to Bolingbroke on the death of his father (John of Gaunt, Duke of Lancaster), should not be violated. Nevertheless, when Gaunt died a few months later, Richard broke his promise and seized the Lancaster estates to pay for his expedition to subdue a rebellion in Ireland. While Richard was away, Bolingbroke landed in Yorkshire, declaring that he had come to recover his rights as Duke of Lancaster. The Percies of Northumberland — the greatest and most powerful family in the northern parts — joined him, together with all Richard's enemies. When Richard returned to England, he found himself deserted. Bolingbroke now claimed the throne, and Richard was obliged to abdicate in favor of Bolingbroke, who became king as Henry IV. Plotting against the new king began almost at once. In 1400 Richard II was murdered. Here the play of *Richard II* ends.

The First Part of Henry IV is the sequel to *Richard II;* it covers the period of the next two and a half years, that is, 1400–03.

Richard II left no children. The line of the Black Prince being thus extinct, the next heir to the throne by right of birth was therefore the senior surviving descendant of Lionel, Duke of Clarence (second son of Edward III). Lionel's daughter Phillipa had married Edmund Mortimer, third Earl of March. She had three children, Roger (who became fourth Earl of March), Elizabeth (who married Henry Percy, called "Hotspur," son of the Earl of Northumberland, and who is Lady Percy in the play), and Edmund. Roger had died in Ireland in 1398 and *his* son Edmund, fifth Earl of March, was thus the legal heir to the throne.

The reign of Henry IV was full of troubles. The first serious rebellion occurred in 1403 when Owen Glendower, a Welsh chieftain, led a national rising against the English. King Henry went against him, but without success. He therefore left the command to Hotspur and Edmund Mortimer (uncle of Edmund, Earl of March) [1] and returned to London. Mortimer was captured by Glendower, but the two men became friends, and Mortimer married Glendower's daughter. Hotspur went back to the North, where at Holmedon Hill he defeated a large army of invading Scots under Douglas.

---

[1] Shakespeare confused the two Edmunds. The Edmund who married the Welsh lady was *not* heir to the throne. See Genealogical Table below.

Soon afterward the Percies quarreled with the king. The chief members of the family were Henry, Earl of Northumberland, Henry "Hotspur" (his son), and Thomas Percy, Earl of Worcester (his brother). When the king demanded that the Percies should hand over the valuable ransoms exacted from the prisoners taken at Holmedon, the Percies refused and rebelled. They planned to gather a combined force to meet the king, their allies being Mortimer, Glendower, and Douglas with his Scots. Hotspur and Douglas marched south to join with Glendower. The issue was decided at the Battle of Shrewsbury (1403). Hotspur was killed, Worcester captured and beheaded, and Douglas captured and ransomed; Northumberland, who was not present at the battle, submitted.

It is difficult nowadays to realize the vast power of these great nobles, most of whom were related by marriage to the royal family. Moreover, by their various intermarriages and alliances they amassed great wealth and owned much land, which meant also the services of those who lived and worked on the land. Their castles were fortified palaces, and it was easy for a nobleman to raise and maintain a private army of retainers from his estates, especially in days when a soldier needed little further equipment than a sword, a helmet, a bow, and a bundle of arrows.

The First Part of Henry IV comes to an end with the Battle of Shrewsbury.

GENEALOGICAL TABLE

THE HOUSE OF LANCASTER

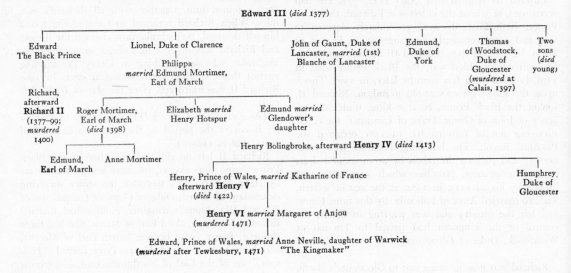

Edward III (*died* 1377)

Edward The Black Prince

Lionel, Duke of Clarence

Philippa *married* Edmund Mortimer, Earl of March

John of Gaunt, Duke of Lancaster, *married* (1st) Blanche of Lancaster

Edmund, Duke of York

Thomas of Woodstock, Duke of Gloucester (*murdered* at Calais, 1397)

Two sons (*died* young)

Richard, afterward **Richard II** (1377–99; *murdered* 1400)

Roger Mortimer, Earl of March (*died* 1398)

Elizabeth *married* Henry Hotspur

Edmund *married* Glendower's daughter

Henry Bolingbroke, afterward **Henry IV** (*died* 1413)

Edmund, **Earl** of March

Anne Mortimer

Henry, Prince of Wales, *married* Katharine of France afterward **Henry V** (*died* 1422)

Humphrey, Duke of Gloucester

Henry VI *married* Margaret of Anjou (*murdered* 1471)

Edward, Prince of Wales, *married* Anne Neville, daughter of **Warwick** (**murdered** after Tewkesbury, 1471)   "The Kingmaker"

The First Part of KING HENRY THE FOURTH

2 Henry IV

The First Part of King Henry IV is the best of Shakespeare's history plays, and the first in which he reached full maturity as a dramatist. The serious scenes are complete in themselves and tell a coherent and moving story — how the unscrupulous king forced the Percies into rebellion so that he might destroy dangerous rivals. The comic scenes of Sir John Falstaff and his disreputable gang contrast and enhance the lessons of sober history. All the persons are alive from the first, for Shakespeare took elaborate care in creating his characters, as has already been suggested in the analysis of Hotspur on pp. 190–91.

But the most notable person in the play is the fat knight, Sir John Falstaff, the supreme comic character in all drama. In creating Falstaff, Shakespeare used principally his own eyes and ears. Falstaff is the gross incarnation of a type of soldier found in any army, and there were many such — though on a lower level of greatness — swarming in London when the play was first written, spending the profits of the last campaign in taverns, brothels, and playhouses, while they intrigued for a new command in the next season's campaign. Some of these captains were of good background and education, younger sons of good family who preferred the excitements and loot of the wars to a quiet, drab life of country pursuits. Many of them were rogues who cheated the government and their own men on all occasions.

There is no need to debate whether Falstaff was a coward. His philosophy, like that of many a better man, was simple: " The better part of valor is discretion " (V.iv.120), and " Honor is a mere scutcheon " (V.i.142–43). " Give me life," he comments over the dead Blunt, " which if I can save, so; if not, honor comes unlooked-for, and there's an end." (V.iii.63–64). Nor can much be said in defense of Falstaff's morals. Though he can quote Scripture on occasion, he is a liar, a drunkard, and a cheat; he robs the poor and flouts every civic virtue; but on the stage at least he redeems his vices by his incomparable wit and his skill in escaping from every tight corner. It is as well not to regard Falstaff too solemnly, for in his own words (*II Hen IV*, I.ii.10–12) " I am not only witty in myself, but the cause that wit is in other men " — which is justification enough.

As for Prince Henry, he is shown as a young man who is deliberately posing as a waster so that when the time comes he may the more effectively confound the gloomy prophets and begin his reign by surprising his subjects. Herein he is as politic and crafty as his father. Henry IV had deliberately affected modesty, humility, and sobriety in contrast to his cousin, the shallow, pleasure-loving Richard II. Prince Hal purposely mixes with low company to contrast with his father; if his companions in riot do not realize their subordinate parts, the misfortune is theirs. In battle he shows himself the superior of young Harry Hotspur, not only as a soldier but in his far clearer understanding of men and of himself. This calculating self-control in all companies may not make Prince Hal an amiable man, but it is preparing him to become a ruthlessly efficient ruler.

DATE AND SOURCE OF THE PLAY. *I Henry IV* was probably written in the autumn of 1597. The play was entered for printing on February 26, 1598, and a quarto (Q1) was issued soon afterward; this quarto was reprinted in 1599, and in 1604, 1608, 1613, and 1622. Falstaff was the most popular of all Shakespeare's characters and was more often mentioned and quoted than any other. The source of the historical scenes was Raphael Holinshed's *Chronicles of England*. When Shakespeare first wrote the play, the fat knight was called Sir John Oldcastle. The original Oldcastle, sometimes called Lord Cobham, lived in the time of Henry IV and Henry V and was burned for heresy. The name Oldcastle caused Shakespeare considerable trouble. In 1597 the title of Lord Cobham had recently passed to a nobleman called Henry Brooke, who was so greatly offended that his predecessor should be presented on a public stage in such a disreputable guise that Shakespeare was obliged to alter the name. The fat knight was therefore renamed Falstaff, after Sir John Fastolfe, who had already made a brief but discreditable appearance in *I Henry VI*.

The adventures of Sir John Falstaff and Prince Hal are wholly fictitious and mostly Shakespeare's own inventing, though the Prince's wild behavior had long become a stage tradition and had been shown in at least one play which still survives in print. This was a crude piece called *The Famous Victories of Henry the Fifth*, which crams into a succession of short scenes the more popular episodes of the king's life.

Henry IV, Part I

DRAMATIS PERSONAE

KING HENRY *the Fourth*
HENRY, *Prince of Wales* ⎫
JOHN *of Lancaster* ⎬ *sons to the King*
EARL OF WESTMORELAND
SIR WALTER BLUNT
THOMAS PERCY, *Earl of Worcester*
HENRY PERCY, *Earl of Northumberland*
HENRY PERCY, *surnamed* HOTSPUR, *his son*
EDMUND MORTIMER, *Earl of March*
RICHARD SCROOP, *Archbishop of York*
ARCHIBALD, *Earl of Douglas*
OWEN GLENDOWER
SIR RICHARD VERNON
SIR JOHN FALSTAFF
SIR MICHAEL, *a friend to the Archbishop of York*

POINS
GADSHILL
PETO
BARDOLPH

LADY PERCY, *wife to Hotspur and sister to Mortimer*
LADY MORTIMER, *daughter to Glendower and wife to Mortimer*
MISTRESS QUICKLY, *hostess of a tavern in Eastcheap*

LORDS, OFFICERS, SHERIFF, VINTNER, CHAMBERLAIN, DRAWERS, *two* CARRIERS, TRAVELERS, *and* ATTENDANTS

SCENE — *England and Wales.*

Act I

SCENE I. *London. The palace.*

[*Enter* KING HENRY, LORD JOHN OF LANCASTER, *the* EARL OF WESTMORELAND, SIR WALTER BLUNT, *and others.*]

KING. So shaken as we are, so wan with care,
Find we° a time for frighted peace to pant,
And breathe short-winded accents of new broils
To be commenced in stronds° afar remote.
No more the thirsty entrance of this soil   5
Shall daub her lips with her own children's blood.
No more shall trenching war° channel her fields,
Nor bruise her flowerets° with the arméd hoofs
Of hostile paces. Those opposéd eyes,
Which, like the meteors° of a troubled heaven,   10
All of one nature, of one substance bred,
Did lately meet in the intestine shock°
And furious close° of civil butchery,
Shall now, in mutual well-beseeming° ranks,
March all one way, and be no more opposed   15
Against acquaintance, kindred, and allies.
The edge of war, like an ill-sheathéd knife,
No more shall cut his master. Therefore, friends,
As far as to the sepulcher of Christ,
Whose soldier now, under whose blesséd cross   20
We are impresséd° and engaged to fight,

Forthwith a power of English shall we levy,
Whose arms were molded in their mothers' womb
To chase these pagans in those holy fields
Over whose acres walked those blessed feet   25
Which fourteen hundred years ago were nailed
For our advantage on the bitter cross.
But this our purpose now is twelvemonth old,
And bootless 'tis to tell you we will go.
Therefore we meet not now.° Then let me hear   30
Of you, my gentle cousin° Westmoreland,
What yesternight our Council did decree
In forwarding this dear expedience.°
WEST. My liege, this haste was hot in question,°
And many limits of the charge° set down   35
But yesternight, when all athwart° there came
A post° from Wales loaden° with heavy news,
Whose worst was that the noble Mortimer,°
Leading the men of Herefordshire to fight
Against the irregular° and wild Glendower,   40
Was by the rude hands of that Welshman taken,
A thousand of his people butchered.
Upon whose dead corpse there was such misuse,
Such beastly shameless transformation,
By those Welshwomen done as may not be   45
Without much shame retold or spoken of.
KING. It seems then that the tidings of this broil
Brake off our business for the Holy Land.

Act I, Sc. i: **2. Find we:** let us find. **4. stronds:** strands, shores. **7. trenching war:** trench warfare. **8. flowerets:** little flowers. **10. meteors:** comets or shooting stars, regarded as terrifying omens. **12. intestine shock:** clash of civil war. **13. close:** hand-to-hand battle. **14. well-beseeming:** seemly. **21. impressed:** enlisted.

29–30. bootless . . . now: i.e., there is no need to tell you of my decision, which has long been made. Our present meeting is to consider the details. **bootless:** vain. **31. cousin:** kinsman, used of any near relation. **33. dear expedience:** urgent enterprise, dear to me. **34. hot in question:** under eager discussion. **35. limits . . . charge:** estimates of the cost. **36. athwart:** cutting across. **37. post:** messenger. **loaden:** laden. **38. Mortimer:** See headnote and Genealogical Table, p. 198. **40. irregular:** unruly.

WEST. This matched with other did, my gracious
    lord;
For more uneven° and unwelcome news   50
Came from the north and thus it did import:
On Holyrood Day,° the gallant Hotspur there,
Young Harry Percy, and brave Archibald,
That ever valiant and approvèd° Scot,
At Holmedon° met,   55
Where they did spend a sad and bloody hour,
As by discharge of their artillery,
And shape of likelihood,° the news was told.
For he that brought them, in the very heat
And pride of their contention° did take horse,   60
Uncertain of the issue° any way.
    KING. Here is a dear, a true industrious friend,
Sir Walter Blunt, new-lighted from his horse,
Stained with the variation of each soil
Betwixt that Holmedon and this seat of ours,   65
And he hath brought us smooth and welcome news.
The Earl of Douglas is discomfited.
Ten thousand bold Scots, two and twenty knights,
Balked° in their own blood did Sir Walter see
On Holmedon's plains. Of prisoners, Hotspur took
Mordake the Earl of Fife, and eldest son   71
To beaten Douglas; and the Earl of Athol,
Of Murray, Angus, and Menteith.
And is not this an honorable spoil?
A gallant prize? Ha, Cousin, is it not?   75
    WEST. In faith,
It is a conquest for a prince to boast of.
    KING. Yea, there thou makest me sad and makest
    me sin
In envy that my Lord Northumberland
Should be the father to so blest a son —   80
A son who is the theme of honor's tongue,
Amongst a grove, the very straightest plant,
Who is sweet Fortune's minion° and her pride —
Whilst I, by looking on the praise of him,
See riot and dishonor stain the brow   85
Of my young Harry. Oh, that it could be proved
That some night-tripping fairy° had exchanged
In cradle clothes our children where they lay,
And called mine Percy, his Plantagenet!
Then would I have his Harry, and he mine.   90
But let him from my thoughts. What think you,
    Coz,°
Of this young Percy's° pride? The prisoners
Which he in this adventure hath surprised

To his own use he keeps, and sends me word
I shall have none but Mordake Earl of Fife.   95
    WEST. This is his uncle's teaching. This is Wor-
    cester,
Malevolent° to you in all aspécts,
Which makes him prune° himself, and bristle up
The crest of youth against your dignity.
    KING. But I have sent for him to answer this,   100
And for this cause awhile we must neglect
Our holy purpose to Jerusalem.
Cousin, on Wednesday next our Council we
Will hold at Windsor. So inform the lords,
But come yourself with speed to us again,   105
For more is to be said and to be done
Than out of anger° can be uttered.
    WEST. I will, my liege.   [Exeunt.]

SCENE II. *London. An apartment of the
Prince's.*

[*Enter the* PRINCE OF WALES *and* FALSTAFF.]
    FAL. Now, Hal, what time of day is it, lad?
    PRINCE. Thou art so fat-witted, with drinking of
old sack° and unbuttoning thee after supper and
sleeping upon benches after noon, that thou hast forgotten to demand that truly which thou wouldst   5
truly know. What a devil hast thou to do with the
time of the day? Unless hours were cups of sack, and
minutes capons, and clocks the tongues of bawds,
and dials the signs of leaping houses,° and the
blessed sun himself a fair hot wench in flame-colored
taffeta,° I see no reason why thou shouldst be so
superfluous to demand the time of the day.   13
    FAL. Indeed, you come near me now, Hal; for we
that take purses go by the moon and the seven stars,
and not by Phoebus,° he, " that wandering knight so
fair." And I prithee, sweet wag, when thou art King,
as, God save thy Grace — Majesty I should say, for
grace thou wilt have none ——   20
    PRINCE. What, none?
    FAL. No, by my troth,° not so much as will serve
to be prologue to an egg and butter.   24
    PRINCE. Well, how then? Come, roundly, roundly.
    FAL. Marry, then, sweet wag, when thou art King,
let not us that are squires of the night's body be
called thieves of the day's beauty.° Let us be Diana's

---

50. uneven: rough. 52. Holyrood Day: September 14. 54. approved: tried. 55. Holmedon: in Northumberland, near the
Scottish border. 58. shape of likelihood: what was likely to
happen. 60. pride . . . contention: height of battle. 61. issue:
result. 69. Balked: laid in ridges. 83. minion: darling. 87. night-
tripping fairy: a fairy coming by night. The fairies, so some
believed, used sometimes to steal a beautiful child and to leave
a changeling in its place. 91. Coz: cousin. 92. young Percy:
Shakespeare depicts Hotspur as a rash youth of about the same
age as Prince Hal. Actually at the battle of Shrewsbury (1403)
the Prince was barely 14 years old and Percy was 39.

97. Malevolent: boding evil, like a planet that brings disaster.
98. prune: preen, like a hawk in good condition trimming its
feathers. 107. out of anger: from an angry heart.
Sc. ii: 3. sack: Spanish dry white wine. 10. leaping houses:
brothels. 11–12. flame-colored taffeta: bright red silk — the color
flaunted by harlots. 16. Phoebus: the sun, with a pun on the
Knight of the Sun, hero of a chivalric romance. 22. troth: truth.
27–28. let . . . beauty: i.e., do not let us who are gentlemen of the
dark (i.e., highwaymen) be called *thieves of the day's beauty* (i.e.,
loafers) — with a pun on "beauty" and "booty."

foresters,° gentlemen of the shade, minions of the moon. And let men say we be men of good government,° being governed, as the sea is, by our noble and chaste mistress the moon, under whose countenance we steal. 33

PRINCE. Thou sayest well, and it holds well too; for the fortune of us that are the moon's men doth ebb and flow like the sea, being governed, as the sea is, by the moon. As for proof, now — a purse of gold most resolutely snatched on Monday night and 39 most dissolutely spent on Tuesday morning; got with swearing "Lay by"° and spent with crying "Bring in"° — now in as low an ebb as the foot of the ladder,° and by and by in as high a flow as the ridge of the gallows.

FAL. By the Lord, thou sayest true, lad. And is not my hostess of the tavern a most sweet wench? 46

PRINCE. As the honey of Hybla,° my old lad of the castle.° And is not a buff jerkin° a most sweet robe of durance?°

FAL. How now, how now, mad wag! What, in thy quips° and thy quiddities?° What a plague have I to do with a buff jerkin? 52

PRINCE. Why, what a pox have I to do with my hostess of the tavern?

FAL. Well, thou hast called her to a reckoning many a time and oft.

PRINCE. Did I ever call for thee to pay thy part?

FAL. No. I'll give thee thy due, thou hast paid all there. 60

PRINCE. Yea, and elsewhere, so far as my coin would stretch. And where it would not, I have used my credit. 63

FAL. Yea, and so used it that, were it not here apparent that thou art heir° apparent —— But I prithee, sweet wag, shall there be gallows standing in England when thou art King? And resolution° thus fobbed° as it is with the rusty curb of old Father Antic° the law? Do not thou, when thou art King, hang a thief. 70

PRINCE. No, thou shalt.

FAL. Shall I? Oh, rare! By the Lord, I'll be a brave judge.

PRINCE. Thou judgest false already. I mean thou shalt have the hanging of the thieves and so become a rare hangman. 76

FAL. Well, Hal, well, and in some sort it jumps° with my humor° as well as waiting in the court, I can tell you.

PRINCE. For obtaining of suits? 80

FAL. Yea, for obtaining of suits,° whereof the hangman° hath no lean wardrobe. 'Sblood,° I am as melancholy as a gib-cat° or a lugged bear.°

PRINCE. Or an old lion, or a lover's lute. 84

FAL. Yea, or the drone of a Lincolnshire bagpipe.

PRINCE. What sayest thou to a hare,° or the melancholy of Moorditch?° 88

FAL. Thou hast the most unsavory similes, and art indeed the most comparative,° rascaliest, sweet young Prince. But, Hal, I prithee trouble me no more with vanity. I would to God thou and I knew where a commodity° of good names were to be bought. An old lord of the Council rated° me the other day 94 in the street about you, sir, but I marked him not; and yet he talked very wisely, but I regarded him not; and yet he talked wisely, and in the street too.

PRINCE. Thou didst well, for wisdom cries out in the streets, and no man regards it.° 100

FAL. Oh, thou hast damnable iteration,° and art indeed able to corrupt a saint. Thou hast done much harm upon me, Hal. God forgive thee for it! Before I knew thee, Hal, I knew nothing; and now am I, if a man should speak truly, little better than one 105 of the wicked. I must give over this life, and I will give it over. By the Lord, an° I do not, I am a villain. I'll be damned for never a king's son in Christendom.

PRINCE. Where shall we take a purse tomorrow, Jack? 111

FAL. 'Zounds,° where thou wilt, lad. I'll make one. An I do not, call me villain and baffle° me.

PRINCE. I see a good amendment of life in thee — from praying to purse-taking.

FAL. Why, Hal, 'tis my vocation, Hal. 'Tis no sin for a man to labor in his vocation. 117

[Enter POINS.] Poins! Now shall we know if Gadshill have set a match.° Oh, if men were to be saved by merit, what hole in Hell were hot enough for him? This is the most omnipotent villain that ever cried "Stand" to a true man.

PRINCE. Good morrow, Ned. 123

POINS. Good morrow, sweet Hal. What says Mon-

28–29. Diana's foresters: thieves who rob by night, Diana being the goddess of the moon. 30–31. good government: well-behaved. 41. Lay by: i.e., "stick 'em up." 42. Bring in: i.e., the drink. 43. ladder: from which a condemned man was thrust off the gallows into space. 47. Hybla: in Sicily, famous for its honey. 47–48. old . . . castle: roisterer, with a pun on Falstaff's original name of Oldcastle. 48. buff jerkin: leather coat worn by the sheriff's sergeant. 49. robe of durance: coat that endures (wears well) and that takes you to *durance* (prison). 51. quips: wisecracks. quiddities: quibbles. 64–65. heir . . . heir: a pun, *heir* being pronounced as "hair." 67. resolution: a stout heart. 68. fobbed: fubbed, cheated. 69. Father Antic: i.e., Daddy Buffoon.

77. jumps: agrees. 78. humor: whim. 81. obtaining of suits: with a pun on *suit*— "petitions to the sovereign for favor" and "clothes." 82. hangman: The clothes of the executed were the hangman's perquisite. 'Sblood: by God's blood. 83. gib-cat: tom-cat. lugged bear: a bear mauled in bearbaiting. 87. hare: regarded as a melancholy creature. 88. melancholy of Moorditch: Moorditch was one of the open sewers of the City of London, proverbial for its stink. 90. comparative: quick at making comparisons. 93. commodity: parcel. 94. rated: rebuked. 90–100. wisdom . . . it: quoted loosely from Proverbs 1:20–24. 101. iteration: ability to quote. 107. an: if. 112. 'Zounds: by God's Wounds. 113. baffle: disgrace; lit., degrade me from my knighthood. 119. set a match: "framed a holdup."

sieur Remorse? What says Sir John Sack and Sugar? Jack! How agrees the Devil and thee about thy soul, that thou soldest him on Good Friday last for a cup of Madeira and a cold capon's leg?°   129

PRINCE. Sir John stands to his word, the Devil shall have his bargain, for he was never yet a breaker of proverbs.° He will give the Devil his due.

POINS. Then art thou damned for keeping thy word with the Devil.   135

PRINCE. Else he had been damned for cozening° the Devil.

POINS. But, my lads, my lads, tomorrow morning, by four o'clock, early at Gadshill!° There are pilgrims going to Canterbury with rich offer- 140 ings,° and traders riding to London with fat purses. I have vizards° for you all, you have horses for yourselves. Gadshill lies tonight in Rochester. I have bespoke° supper tomorrow night in Eastcheap. We may do it as secure as sleep. If you will go, I 145 will stuff your purses full of crowns. If you will not, tarry at home and be hanged.

FAL. Hear ye, Yedward,° if I tarry at home and go not, I'll hang you for going.   150

POINS. You will, chops?

FAL. Hal, wilt thou make one?

PRINCE. Who, I rob? I a thief? Not I, by my faith.

FAL. There's neither honesty, manhood, nor good fellowship in thee, nor thou camest not of the blood royal, if thou darest not stand for ten shillings.°

PRINCE. Well then, once in my days I'll be a madcap.   160

FAL. Why, that's well said.

PRINCE. Well, come what will, I'll tarry at home.

FAL. By the Lord, I'll be a traitor then, when thou art King.   165

PRINCE. I care not.

POINS. Sir John, I prithee, leave the Prince and me alone. I will lay him down such reasons for this adventure that he shall go.   169

FAL. Well, God give thee the spirit of persuasion and him the ears of profiting, that what thou speakest may move and what he hears may be believed,° that the true Prince may, for recreation sake, prove a false thief; for the poor abuses of the time want countenance.° Farewell. You shall find me in Eastcheap.   176

PRINCE. Farewell, thou latter spring!° Farewell, Allhallown summer!°   [Exit FALSTAFF.]

POINS. Now, my good sweet honey lord, ride with us tomorrow. I have a jest to execute that I can- 180 not manage alone. Falstaff, Bardolph, Peto, and Gadshill shall rob those men that we have already waylaid. Yourself and I will not be there, and when they have the booty, if you and I do not rob them, cut this head off from my shoulders.

PRINCE. How shall we part with them in setting forth?   188

POINS. Why, we will set forth before or after them, and appoint them a place of meeting, wherein it is at our pleasure to fail, and then will they adventure upon the exploit themselves; which they shall have no sooner achieved but we'll set upon them.   194

PRINCE. Yea, but 'tis like that they will know us by our horses, by our habits,° and by every other appointment,° to be ourselves.

POINS. Tut! Our horses they shall not see, I'll tie them in the wood. Our vizards we will change after we leave them. And, sirrah, I have cases of buckram° for the nonce,° to immask our noted outward garments.   202

PRINCE. Yea, but I doubt they will be too hard for us.

POINS. Well, for two of them, I know them to be as true-bred cowards as ever turned back; and for the third, if he fight longer than he sees rea- 207 son,° I'll forswear arms. The virtue of this jest will be the incomprehensible lies that this same fat rogue will tell us when we meet at supper — how thirty, at least, he fought with; what wards,° what blows, what extremities he endured. And in the reproof° of this lies the jest.   213

PRINCE. Well, I'll go with thee. Provide us all things necessary and meet me tomorrow night in Eastcheap. There I'll sup. Farewell.

POINS. Farewell, my lord.   [Exit.]

PRINCE. I know you all,° and will a while uphold° The unyoked humor° of your idleness.
Yet herein will I imitate the sun,   220
Who doth permit the base contagious° clouds
To smother up his beauty from the world,
That, when he please again to be himself,
Being wanted, he may be more wondered at
By breaking through the foul and ugly mists   225
Of vapors that did seem to strangle him.

128–29. Good . . . leg: Good Friday being the Church's most solemn fast day, to drink Madeira and eat chicken was a damnable sin.   131–32. breaker of proverbs: one to prove proverbs false.   136. cozening: cheating.   139. Gadshill: near Rochester in Kent. Some slight confusion is caused as the same name is used for one of the gang. See l. 118, and II.i. 36–106.   140–41. rich offerings: i.e., for the shrine of Saint Thomas à Becket at Canterbury.   142. vizards: masks.   144. bespoke: ordered.   149. Yedward: a form of Edward, Poins's first name.   157–58. blood . . . shillings: pun on royal, a coin worth 10s.   170–72. God . . . believed: Falstaff constantly drops into the pious jargon of professional preachers.   174–75. want countenance: need encouragement.

177. latter spring: late spring; i.e., green autumn.   178. Allhallown summer: Indian summer. Allhallown (All Saints' Day) is on November 1.   196. habits: clothes.   197. appointment: accouterment.   200–01. cases of buckram: overalls of coarse linen.   201. nonce: occasion.   207–08. fight . . . reason: This is Falstaff's avowed rule of life. See later V.iv.120.   211. wards: defense. See II.iv.215.   212. reproof: rebuttal.   218. I . . . all: This soliloquy is important for the understanding of the Prince's later treatment of Falstaff and the gang. uphold: tolerate.   219. unyoked humor: unrestrained behavior.   221. contagious: poisonous.

If all the year were playing holidays,
To sport would be as tedious as to work.
But when they seldom come, they wished-for come,
And nothing pleaseth but rare accidents.   230
So, when this loose behavior I throw off
And pay the debt I never promisèd,
By how much better than my word I am,
By so much shall I falsify men's hopes.
And like bright metal on a sullen° ground,   235
My reformation, glittering o'er my fault,
Shall show more goodly and attract more eyes
Than that which hath no foil° to set it off.
I'll so offend, to make offense a skill,°
Redeeming time° when men think least I will.   240
                                        [Exit.]

SCENE III. *London. The palace.*

[*Enter the* KING, NORTHUMBERLAND, WORCESTER,
    HOTSPUR, SIR WALTER BLUNT, *with others.*]
  KING. My blood hath been too cold and temperate,
Unapt to stir at these indignities,
And you have found me;° for accordingly
You tread upon my patience. But be sure
I will from henceforth rather be myself,°   5
Mighty and to be feared, than my condition,°
Which hath been smooth as oil, soft as young down,
And therefore lost that title of respect°
Which the proud soul ne'er pays but to the proud.
  WOR. Our house, my sovereign liege, little de-
    serves   10
The scourge of greatness to be used on it,
And that same greatness too which our own hands
Have holp° to make so portly.°
  NORTH. My lord ——
  KING. Worcester, get thee gone, for I do see   15
Danger and disobedience in thine eye.
O sir, your presence is too bold and peremptory,
And Majesty might never yet endure
The moody frontier of a servant brow.°
You have good leave to leave us.° When we need
Your use and counsel, we shall send for you.   21
                              [*Exit* WORCESTER.]
[*To* NORTHUMBERLAND] You were about to speak.
  NORTH.   Yea, my good lord.
Those prisoners in your Highness' name demanded,°

Which Harry Percy here at Holmedon took,
Were, as he says, not with such strength denied   25
As is delivered to your Majesty.
Either envy,° therefore, or misprision°
Is guilty of this fault, and not my son.
  HOT. My liege, I did deny no prisoners.
But I remember, when the fight was done,   30
When I was dry with rage and éxtreme toil,
Breathless and faint, leaning upon my sword,
Came there a certain lord, neat, and trimly dressed,
Fresh as a bridegroom, and his chin new-reaped°
Showed like a stubble land at harvest home.   35
He was perfumèd like a milliner,
And 'twixt his finger and his thumb he held
A pouncet box,° which ever and anon
He gave his nose and took 't away again;
Who therewith angry, when it next came there,   40
Took it in snuff.° And still he smiled and talked,
And as the soldiers bore dead bodies by,
He called them untaught knaves, unmannerly,
To bring a slovenly unhandsome corse°
Betwixt the wind and his nobility.   45
With many holiday and lady terms°
He questioned me, amongst the rest, demanded
My prisoners in your Majesty's behalf.
I then, all smarting with my wounds being cold,
To be so pestered with a popinjay,°   50
Out of my grief° and my impatience
Answered neglectingly I know not what,
He should, or he should not; for he made me mad
To see him shine so brisk, and smell so sweet,
And talk so like a waiting gentlewoman°   55
Of guns and drums and wounds — God save the
    mark! —°
And telling me the sovereign'st° thing on earth
Was parmaceti° for an inward bruise;
And that it was great pity, so it was,
This villainous saltpeter should be digged   60
Out of the bowels of the harmless earth,
Which many a good tall° fellow had destroyed
So cowardly; and but for these vile guns,
He would himself have been a soldier.
This bald unjointed chat° of his, my lord,   65
I answered indirectly, as I said.
And I beseech you, let not his report
Come current° for an accusation

Betwixt my love and your high Majesty.

BLUNT. The circumstance considered, good my
lord,   70
Whate'er Lord Harry Percy then had said
To such a person and in such a place,
At such a time, with all the rest retold,
May reasonably die and never rise
To do him wrong, or any way impeach°   75
What then he said, so he unsay it now.

KING. Why, yet° he doth deny his prisoners,
But with proviso° and exception,
That we at our own charge shall ransom straight
His brother-in-law, the foolish Mortimer,   80
Who, on my soul, hath willfully betrayed
The lives of those that he did lead to fight
Against that great magician,° damned Glendower,
Whose daughter, as we hear, the Earl of March
Hath lately married. Shall our coffers, then,   85
Be emptied to redeem a traitor home?
Shall we buy treason, and indent° with fears,
When they have lost and forfeited themselves?
No, on the barren mountains let him starve.
For I shall never hold that man my friend   90
Whose tongue shall ask me for one penny cost
To ransom home revolted Mortimer.

HOT. Revolted Mortimer!
He never did fall off,° my sovereign liege,
But by the chance of war. To prove that true   95
Needs no more but one tongue for all those wounds,
Those mouthèd° wounds, which valiantly he took
When on the gentle Severn's sedgy° bank,
In single opposition, hand to hand,
He did confound° the best part of an hour   100
In changing hardiment° with great Glendower.
Three times they breathed and three times did they
drink,
Upon agreement, of swift Severn's flood;
Who then, affrighted with their bloody looks,
Ran fearfully among the trembling reeds,   105
And hid his crisp head in the hollow bank
Bloodstainèd with these valiant combatants.
Never did base and rotten policy°
Color her working° with such deadly wounds;
Nor never could the noble Mortimer   110
Receive so many, and all willingly.
Then let not him be slandered with revolt.

KING. Thou dost belie him,° Percy, thou dost belie
him.
He never did encounter with Glendower.
I tell thee,   115
He durst as well have met the Devil alone

As Owen Glendower for an enemy.
Art thou not ashamed? But, sirrah,° henceforth
Let me not hear you speak of Mortimer.
Send me your prisoners with the speediest means,
Or you shall hear in such a kind from me   121
As will displease you. My Lord Northumberland,
We license your departure with your son.
Send us your prisoners, or you will hear of it.

[*Exeunt* KING HENRY, BLUNT, *and train.*]

HOT. An if the Devil come and roar for them,
I will not send them. I will after straight   126
And tell him so, for I will ease my heart,
Albeit I make a hazard° of my head.

NORTH. What, drunk with choler?° Stay and
pause awhile.
Here comes your uncle.

[*Re-enter* WORCESTER.]

HOT.   Speak of Mortimer!   130
'Zounds, I will speak of him, and let my soul
Want mercy if I do not join with him.
Yea, on his part I'll empty all these veins,
And shed my dear blood drop by drop in the dust,
But I will lift the downtrod Mortimer   135
As high in the air as this unthankful King,
As this ingrate and cankered° Bolingbroke.

NORTH. Brother, the King hath made your nephew
mad.

WOR. Who struck this heat up after I was gone?

HOT. He will, forsooth, have all my prisoners.
And when I urged the ransom once again   141
Of my wife's brother, then his cheek looked pale,
And on my face he turned an eye of death,
Trembling even at the name of Mortimer.

WOR. I cannot blame him. Was not he proclaimed
By Richard that dead is the next of blood?   146

NORTH. He was, I heard the proclamation.
And then it was when the unhappy King —
Whose wrongs in us God pardon!° — did set forth
Upon his Irish expedition,   150
From whence he intercepted° did return
To be deposed and shortly° murdered.

WOR. And for whose death we in the world's wide
mouth
Live scandalized and foully spoken of.

HOT. But, soft, I pray you. Did King Richard
then   155
Proclaim my brother° Edmund Mortimer
Heir to the crown?

NORTH.   He did, myself did hear it.

HOT. Nay, then I cannot blame his cousin King,
That wished him on the barren mountains starve.
But shall it be that you, that set the crown   160

---

75. impeach: accuse, call in question.   77. yet: still, after all.
78. proviso: stipulation.   83. magician: See III.i.36–49.   87. indent: make a legal agreement.   94. fall off: fall away, desert.
97. mouthed: looking like a mouth.   98. sedgy: reedy.   100. confound: consume.   101. changing hardiment: exchanging blows.
108. policy: cunning.   109. Color . . . working: disguise its real
intention.   113. belie him: lie about him.

118. sirrah: a form of address used to an inferior, here deliberately
insulting.   128. hazard: risk.   129. choler: wrath.   137. cankered: malignant.   149. Whose . . . pardon: may God forgive
the wrongs committed by us against him.   151. intercepted:
being hindered.   152. shortly: in a short time.   156. brother:
brother-in-law.

Upon the head of this forgetful man,
And for his sake wear the detested blot
Of murderous subornation,° shall it be
That you a world of curses undergo,
Being the agents, or base second means,°   165
The cords, the ladder, or the hangman rather?
Oh, pardon me that I descend so low,
To show the line° and the predicament°
Wherein you range° under this subtle King.
Shall it for shame be spoken in these days,   170
Or fill up chronicles in time to come,
That men of your nobility and power
Did gage° them both in an unjust behalf,
As both of you — God pardon it! — have done,
To put down Richard, that sweet lovely rose,   175
And plant this thorn, this canker,° Bolingbroke?
And shall it in more shame be further spoken,
That you are fooled, discarded, and shook off
By him for whom these shames ye underwent?
No, yet time serves wherein you may redeem   180
Your banished honors, and restore yourselves
Into the good thoughts of the world again,
Revenge the jeering and disdained° contempt
Of this proud King, who studies day and night
To answer all the debt he owes to you   185
Even with the bloody payment of your deaths.
Therefore, I say ——
    WOR.   Peace, Cousin, say no more.
And now I will unclasp a secret book,
And to your quick-conceiving° discontents
I'll read you matter deep and dangerous,   190
As full of peril and adventurous spirit
As to o'erwalk a current roaring loud
On the unsteadfast footing of a spear.°
    HOT. If he fall in, good night! Or sink or swim.
Send danger from the east unto the west,   195
So honor cross it from the north to south,
And let them grapple. Oh, the blood more stirs
To rouse a lion than to start a hare!
    NORTH. Imagination of some great exploit
Drives him beyond the bounds of patience.°   200
    HOT. By Heaven, methinks it were an easy leap,
To pluck bright honor from the pale-faced moon,
Or dive into the bottom of the deep,
Where fathom line could never touch the ground,
And pluck up drownèd honor by the locks,   205
So he that doth redeem her thence might wear
Without corrival° all her dignities.
But out upon this half-faced fellowship!°

    WOR. He apprehends a world of figures here,°
But not the form of what he should attend.   210
Good Cousin, give me audience for a while.
    HOT. I cry you mercy.
    WOR.   Those same noble Scots
That are your prisoners ——
    HOT.   I'll keep them all.
By God, he shall not have a Scot of them.
No, if a Scot would save his soul, he shall not.   215
I'll keep them, by this hand.
    WOR.   You start away
And lend no ear unto my purposes.
Those prisoners you shall keep.
    HOT.   Nay, I will, that's flat.
He said he would not ransom Mortimer,
Forbade my tongue to speak of Mortimer.   220
But I will find him when he lies asleep,
And in his ear I'll holloa " Mortimer! "
Nay,
I'll have a starling° shall be taught to speak
Nothing but " Mortimer," and give it him,   225
To keep his anger still in motion.
    WOR. Hear you, Cousin, a word.
    HOT. All studies here I solemnly defy,
Save how to gall° and pinch this Bolingbroke.
And that same sword-and-buckler° Prince of
    Wales,
But that I think his father loves him not   231
And would be glad he met with some mischance,
I would have him poisoned with a pot of ale.
    WOR. Farewell, kinsman. I'll talk to you
When you are better tempered to attend.   235
    NORTH. Why, what a wasp-stung and impatient
    fool
Art thou to break into this woman's mood,
Tying thine ear to no tongue but thine own!
    HOT. Why, look you, I am whipped and scourged
    with rods,
Nettled,° and stung with pismires,° when I hear
Of this vile politician,° Bolingbroke.   24i
In Richard's time — what do you call the place? —
A plague upon it, it is in Gloucestershire,
'Twas where the madcap Duke his uncle kept,
His uncle York, where I first bowed my knee   245
Unto this king of smiles, this Bolingbroke —
'Sblood! —
When you and he came back from Ravenspurgh.
    NORTH. At Berkeley Castle.°
    HOT. You say true.   250
Why, what a candy deal° of courtesy

162–63. wear . . . subornation: wear the mark of shame as accessories to murder. subornation: procuring someone to commit a crime. 165. second means: assistants. 168. line: disgrace. predicament: class, category. 169. range: rank. 173. gage: pledge, engage. 176. canker: wild rose, contrasted with the garden rose. 183. disdained: disdainful. 189. quick-conceiving: quick-witted. 193. unsteadfast . . . spear: with a spear as unsteady bridge. 200. patience: self-control. 207. corrival: partner. 208. half-faced fellowship: starving partnership; i.e., sharing of honor which is insufficient for two to share.

209. apprehends . . . here: i.e., he is entirely carried away by his imagination. figures: shapes, fantasies. 224. starling: The starling, like the jackdaw and the parrot, can be taught to mimic sound. 229. gall: make sore. 230. sword-and-buckler: swashbuckler. 240. Nettled: whipped with nettles. pismires: ants. 241. politician: schemer. 249. Berkeley Castle: For this episode see *Rich II*, II.iii.41–50. 251. candy deal: deal of candy; i.e., hypocritical.

This fawning greyhound then did proffer me!
Look, "when his infant fortune came to age,"
And "gentle Harry Percy," and "kind Cousin."
Oh, the devil take such cozeners! God forgive me!
Good Uncle, tell your tale, I have done.   256
    WOR. Nay, if you have not, to it again.
We will stay° your leisure.
    HOT.   I have done, i' faith.
    WOR. Then once more to your Scottish prisoners.
Deliver them up without their ransom straight,   260
And make the Douglas' son your only mean°
For powers° in Scotland; which, for divers reasons
Which I shall send you written, be assured
Will easily be granted. [To NORTHUMBERLAND] You,
    my lord,
Your son in Scotland being thus employed,   265
Shall secretly into the bosom creep
Of that same noble prelate, well beloved,
The Archbishop.
    HOT. Of York, is it not?
    WOR. True, who bears hard°   270
His brother's death at Bristol, the Lord Scroop.
I speak not this in estimation,°
As what I think might be, but what I know
Is ruminated,° plotted, and set down,
And only stays but to behold the face   275
Of that occasion that shall bring it on.
    HOT. I smell it. Upon my life, it will do well.
    NORTH. Before the game is afoot, thou still° let'st
    slip.°
    HOT. Why, it cannot choose but be a noble plot.
And then the power of Scotland and of York,   280
To join with Mortimer, ha?
    WOR.   And so they shall.
    HOT. In faith, it is exceedingly well aimed.
    WOR. And 'tis no little reason bids us speed,
To save our heads by raising of a head;°
For, bear ourselves as even as we can,°   285
The King will always think him in our debt,
And think we think ourselves unsatisfied,
Till he hath found a time to pay us home.
And see already how he doth begin
To make us strangers to his looks of love.   290
    HOT. He does, he does. We'll be revenged on him.
    WOR. Cousin, farewell. No further go in this
Than I by letters shall direct your course.
When time is ripe, which will be suddenly,
I'll steal to Glendower and Lord Mortimer,   295
Where you and Douglas and our powers at once,
As I will fashion° it, shall happily meet,
To bear our fortunes in our own strong arms,

Which now we hold at much uncertainty.
    NORTH. Farewell, good Brother. We shall thrive,
    I trust.   300
    HOT. Uncle, adieu. Oh, let the hours be short
Till fields and blows and groans applaud our sport!
                                        [*Exeunt.*]

Act II

SCENE I. *Rochester. An innyard.*

[*Enter a* CARRIER *with a lantern in his hand.*]
    1. CAR. Heigh-ho! An it be not four by the day, I'll
be hanged. Charles's Wain° is over the new chimney, and yet our horse not packed.° What, ostler! 4
    OSTLER. [*Within*] Anon, anon.
    1. CAR. I prithee, Tom, beat° Cut's° saddle, put a
few flocks° in the point.° Poor jade,° is wrung° in
the withers° out of all cess.°   8
            [*Enter another* CARRIER.]
    2. CAR. Peas and beans are as dank here as a dog,
and that is the next way to give poor jades the bots.°
This house is turned upside down since Robin Ostler
died.
    1. CAR. Poor fellow, never joyed since the price of
oats rose. It was the death of him.   14
    2. CAR. I think this be the most villainous house in
all London road for fleas. I am stung like a tench.°
    1. CAR. Like a tench! By the mass, there is ne'er a
king Christen° could be better bit than I have been
since the first cock.   20
    2. CAR. Why, they will allow us ne'er a jordan,°
and then we leak in your chimney, and your chamber lye° breeds fleas like a loach.
    1. CAR. What, ostler! Come away and be hanged!
Come away.   25
    2. CAR. I have a gammon of bacon° and two razes°
of ginger, to be delivered as far as Charing Cross.
    1. CAR. God's body! The turkeys in my pannier°
are quite starved. What, ostler! A plague on thee!
Hast thou never an eye in thy head? Canst not hear?
An 'twere not as good deed as drink to break the pate

---

258. stay: await.   261. mean: means.   262. powers: forces, armies.   270. bears hard: takes hardly.   272. in estimation:
as a guess.   274. ruminated: considered.   278. still: continuously. let'st slip: let loose the greyhound.   284. head: armed
force.   285. bear . . . can: however discreetly we may behave.
297. fashion: contrive.

Act II, Sc. i: 2. Charles's Wain: Charles's Wagon, the constellation of the Great Bear, called also the Great Dipper.
4. horse . . . packed: Carriers at this time used pack horses for
transport.   6. beat: i.e., to make the padding more even. Cut:
name of a horse with a docked tail. 7. flocks: tufts of wool. point:
pommel. jade: horse in poor condition. wrung: galled. 8. withers:
point of the shoulder. out . . . cess: excessively.   10. bots: worms.
16. tench: The tench and the loach (fresh-water fish) are sometimes infested with a form of louse.   19. Christen: Christian.
21. jordan: chamber pot.   23. chamber lye: urine. Elizabethan
sanitary arrangements and domestic habits were crude.   26. gam-
mon of bacon: cured ham. razes: roots.   28. pannier: basket.

on thee, I am a very villain. Come, and be hanged!
Hast no faith in thee? 35

[*Enter* GADSHILL.]

GADS. Good morrow, carriers. What's o'clock?

1. CAR. I think it be two o'clock.

GADS. I prithee lend me thy lantern, to see my gelding in the stable. 39

1. CAR. Nay, by God, soft,° I know a trick worth
two of that, i' faith.

GADS. I pray thee, lend me thine.

2. CAR. Aye, when? Canst tell?° Lend me thy lantern, quoth he? Marry, I'll see thee hanged first.

GADS. Sirrah carrier, what time do you mean to
come to London? 46

2. CAR. Time enough to go to bed with a candle, I
warrant thee. Come, Neighbor Mugs, we'll call up
the gentlemen. They will along with company, for
they have great charge.° [*Exeunt* CARRIERS.]

GADS. What ho! Chamberlain!° 52

CHAM. [*Within*] At hand, quoth pickpurse.

GADS. That's even as fair as — at hand, quoth the
chamberlain; for thou variest no more from picking
of purses than giving direction doth from laboring.
Thou layest the plot° how. 57

[*Enter* CHAMBERLAIN.]

CHAM. Good morrow, Master Gadshill. It holds
current that I told you yesternight. There's a frank-
lin° in the wild° of Kent hath brought three hundred marks° with him in gold. I heard him tell it to
one of his company last night at supper — a kind of
auditor, one that hath abundance of charge too, God
knows what. They are up already, and call for eggs
and butter. They will away presently. 66

GADS. Sirrah, if they meet not with Saint Nicholas'
clerks,° I'll give thee this neck.

CHAM. No, I'll none of it. I pray thee, keep that for
the hangman, for I know thou worshipest Saint
Nicholas as truly as a man of falsehood may. 72

GADS. What talkest thou to me of the hangman?
If I hang, I'll make a fat pair of gallows; for if I hang,
old Sir John hangs with me, and thou knowest he is
no starveling. Tut! There are other Trojans° that
thou dreamest not of, the which for sport sake 77
are content to do the profession some grace; that
would, if matters should be looked into, for their
own credit sake, make all whole. I am joined with no
foot landrakers,° no long-staff sixpenny strikers,°

none of these mad mustachio purple-hued maltworms;° but with nobility and tranquility, burgomasters and great oneyers,° such as can hold in,°
such as will strike sooner than speak, and speak 85
sooner than drink, and drink sooner than pray. And
yet, 'zounds, I lie; for they pray continually to their
saint, the commonwealth; or rather, not pray to her,
but prey on her, for they ride up and down on her
and make her their boots.° 91

CHAM. What, the commonwealth their boots? Will
she hold out water in foul way?

GADS. She will, she will — justice hath liquored°
her. We steal as in a castle, cocksure. We have the
receipt° of fern seed,° we walk invisible. 96

CHAM. Nay, by my faith, I think you are more
beholding to the night than to fern seed for your
walking invisible.

GADS. Give me thy hand. Thou shalt have a share
in our purchase,° as I am a true man. 101

CHAM. Nay, rather let me have it, as you are a
false thief.

GADS. Go to. "Homo" is a common name to all
men. Bid the ostler bring my gelding out of 105
the stable. Farewell, you muddy° knave. [*Exeunt.*]

SCENE II. *The highway, near* GADSHILL.

[*Enter* PRINCE HENRY *and* POINS.]

POINS. Come, shelter, shelter. I have removed Falstaff's horse, and he frets like a gummed velvet.°

PRINCE. Stand close.

[*Enter* FALSTAFF.]

FAL. Poins! Poins, and be hanged! Poins! 4

PRINCE. Peace, ye fat-kidneyed rascal! What a
brawling dost thou keep!

FAL. Where's Poins, Hal?

PRINCE. He is walked up to the top of the hill. I'll
go seek him. 9

FAL. I am accursed to rob in that thief's company.
The rascal hath removed my horse, and tied him I
know not where. If I travel but four foot by the
squier° further afoot, I shall break my wind. Well, I
doubt not but to die a fair death for all this, if I 'scape
hanging for killing that rogue. I have forsworn° 16
his company hourly any time this two and twenty
years, and yet I am bewitched with the rogue's

---

40. soft: go easy. 43. Canst tell: i.e., "says you!" 51. great
charge: much money. 52. Chamberlain: man in charge of the
bedrooms at an inn. 57. layest . . . plot: It was a common complaint that the chamberlains of inns were in league with highwaymen. 60. franklin: rich farmer. wild: weald; the hilly district
in Kent and adjoining counties. 61. mark: 13s 4d (two-thirds of
an English pound). 67–68. Saint Nicholas' clerks: thieves,
Saint Nicholas being their patron saint. 76. Trojans: good
lads. 81. foot landrakers: roving footpads; i.e., thieves so poor
that they go on foot. long-staff . . . strikers: robbers who use a
long staff and will hold a man up for a pittance.

82–83. mustachio . . . maltworms: red-faced tipplers with great
mustaches. 84. oneyers: ones. hold in: keep their mouths shut.
91. boots: booty. The chamberlain caps his remark with a pun
on leather boots. 94. liquored: greased. 96. receipt: directions
for using, recipe. fern seed: The seed of the fern is so small that
it was said to be invisible, and if found on Saint John's Day, to
confer invisibility on the finder. 101. purchase: in thieves' language, plunder. 106. muddy: muddleheaded.
Sc. ii: 2. gummed velvet: Cheap velvet (as well as taffeta) was sometimes treated with gum to give it stiffening,
but it frayed sooner. 13. squier: square, rule. 16. forsworn:
sworn off.

company. If the rascal have not given me medicines°
to make me love him, I'll be hanged; it could not be
else, I have drunk medicines. Poins! Hal! A   21
plague upon you both! Bardolph! Peto! I'll starve ere
I'll rob a foot further. An 'twere not as good a deed
as drink, to turn true man and to leave these rogues,
I am the veriest varlet° that ever chewed with a   25
tooth. Eight yards of uneven ground is threescore
and ten miles afoot with me, and the stony-hearted
villains know it well enough. A plague upon it when
thieves cannot be true one to another! [*They*   30
whistle.] Whew! A plague upon you all! Give me
my horse, you rogues, give me my horse, and be
hanged!

PRINCE. Peace, ye fat-guts! Lie down, lay thine ear
close to the ground and list if thou canst hear the
tread of travelers.   35

FAL. Have you any levers to lift me up again,
being down? 'Sblood, I'll not bear mine own flesh so
far afoot again for all the coin in thy father's exchequer. What a plague mean ye to colt° me thus?

PRINCE. Thou liest. Thou art not colted, thou art
uncolted.   42

FAL. I prithee, good Prince Hal, help me to my
horse, good king's son.

PRINCE. Out, ye rogue! Shall I be your ostler?   45

FAL. Go hang thyself in thine own heir-apparent
garters! If I be ta'en, I'll peach for this. An I have
not ballads° made on you all and sung to filthy tunes,
let a cup of sack be my poison. When a jest is so forward, and afoot too! I hate it.   50

[*Enter* GADSHILL, BARDOLPH *and* PETO *with him.*]

GADS. Stand.

FAL. So I do, against my will.

POINS. Oh, 'tis our setter.° I know his voice. Bardolph, what news?   54

BARD. Case° ye, case ye, on with your vizards.
There's money of the King's coming down the hill,
'tis going to the King's exchequer.

FAL. You lie, ye rogue, 'tis going to the King's
tavern.

GADS. There's enough to make us all.   60

FAL. To be hanged.

PRINCE. Sirs, you four shall front them in the narrow lane, Ned Poins and I will walk lower. If they
'scape from your encounter, then they light on us.

PETO. How many be there of them?   66

GADS. Some eight or ten.

FAL. 'Zounds, will they not rob us?

PRINCE. What, a coward, Sir John Paunch?

FAL. Indeed I am not John of Gaunt, your grandfather, but yet no coward, Hal.   71

PRINCE. Well, we leave that to the proof.

POINS. Sirrah Jack, thy horse stands behind the

hedge. When thou needest him, there thou shalt find
him. Farewell, and stand fast.   75

FAL. Now cannot I strike him, if I should be
hanged.

PRINCE. Ned, where are our disguises?

POINS. Here, hard by. Stand close.

[*Exeunt* PRINCE *and* POINS.]

FAL. Now, my masters, happy man be his dole,°
say I. Every man to his business.   81

[*Enter the* TRAVELERS.]

1. TRAV. Come, neighbor. The boy shall lead our
horses down the hill. We'll walk afoot awhile, and
ease our legs.

THIEVES. Stand!

TRAVS. Jesus bless us!   86

FAL. Strike, down with them, cut the villains'
throats! Ah, whoreson° caterpillars,° bacon-fed
knaves! They hate us youth. Down with them, fleece
them.

TRAVS. Oh, we are undone, both we and ours forever!   92

FAL. Hang ye, gorbellied° knaves, are ye undone?
No, ye fat chuffs,° I would your store were here!°
On, bacons,° on! What, ye knaves! Young men must
live. You are grand jurors,° are ye? We'll jure ye,
'faith.   97

[*Here they rob them and bind them. Exeunt.*]

[*Re-enter* PRINCE HENRY *and* POINS *disguised.*]

PRINCE. The thieves have bound the true men.
Now could thou and I rob the thieves and go merrily to London, it would be argument° for a week,
laughter for a month, and a good jest forever.

POINS. Stand close. I hear them coming.   103

[*Enter the* THIEVES *again.*]

FAL. Come, my masters, let us share, and then to
horse before day. An the Prince and Poins be not
two arrant° cowards, there's no equity stirring.°
There's no more valor in that Poins than in a wild
duck.   108

PRINCE. Your money!

POINS. Villains! [*As they are sharing, the* PRINCE
and POINS *set upon them; they all run away; and* FAL-
STAFF, *after a blow or two, runs away too, leaving the
booty behind them.*]

PRINCE. Got with much ease. Now merrily to
horse.

The thieves are all scattered and possessed with fear
So strongly that they dare not meet each other.
Each takes his fellow for an officer.
Away, good Ned. Falstaff sweats to death,   115
And lards the lean earth as he walks along.

---

80. **happy . . . dole:** i.e., here's luck; lit., may the lucky man have
his reward.   88. **whoreson:** bastard. **caterpillars:** parasites
on the public.   93. **gorbellied:** big-bellied.   94. **chuffs:** mean
misers. **were here:** i.e., in your bellies.   95. **bacons:** fat pigs.
96. **grand jurors:** i.e., men of highest respectability.   101. **argument:** matter for talk.   106. **arrant:** complete. **no . . . stirring:**
no sound judgment in the world.

19. **medicines:** love potions.   25. **varlet:** knave.   40. **colt:** trick.
48. **ballads:** popular songs.   53. **setter:** the accomplice who
brings the victim in.   55. **Case:** mask.

Were't not for laughing, I should pity him.

POINS. How the rogue roared!   [*Exeunt.*]

SCENE III. *Warkworth Castle.*

[*Enter* HOTSPUR *alone, reading a letter.*]

HOT. "But, for mine own part, my lord, I could
be well contented to be there, in respect of the love I
bear your house." He could be contented. Why is he
not, then? In respect of the love he bears our house.
He shows in this he loves his own barn better 5
than he loves our house. Let me see some more.
"The purpose you undertake is dangerous" — why,
that's certain. 'Tis dangerous to take a cold, to sleep,
to drink; but I tell you, my lord fool, out of this nettle danger we pluck this flower safety. "The purpose
you undertake is dangerous; the friends you 10
have named uncertain; the time itself unsorted;° and
your whole plot too light for the counterpoise of so
great an opposition." Say you so, say you so? I say
unto you again, you are a shallow cowardly 15
hind,° and you lie. What a lackbrain is this! By the
Lord, our plot is a good plot as ever was laid, our
friends true and constant — a good plot, good
friends, and full of expectation. An excellent plot,
very good friends. What a frosty-spirited rogue 20
is this! Why, my Lord of York° commends the plot
and the general course of the action. 'Zounds, an I
were now by this rascal, I could brain him with his
lady's fan. Is there not my father, my uncle, and
myself? Lord Edmund Mortimer, my Lord of 25
York, and Owen Glendower? Is there not besides
the Douglas? Have I not all their letters to meet me
in arms by the ninth of the next month? And are
they not some of them set forward already? What a
pagan rascal is this, an infidel! Ha! You shall see 30
now in very sincerity of fear and cold heart, will he
to the King, and lay open all our proceedings. Oh, I
could divide myself, and go to buffets,° for moving°
such a dish of skim milk with so honorable an 35
action! Hang him! Let him tell the King. We are
prepared. I will set forward tonight.

[*Enter* LADY PERCY.] How now, Kate! I must leave
you within these two hours.

LADY P. O my good lord, why are you thus alone?
For what offense have I this fortnight been 41
A banished woman from my Harry's bed?
Tell me, sweet lord, what is't that takes from thee
Thy stomach,° pleasure, and thy golden sleep?
Why dost thou bend thine eyes upon the earth, 45
And start so often when thou sit'st alone?
Why hast thou lost the fresh blood in thy cheeks,

And given my treasures° and my rights of thee
To thick-eyed° musing and cursed melancholy?
In thy faint slumbers I by thee have watched, 50
And heard thee murmur tales of iron wars,
Speak terms of manage° to thy bounding steed,
Cry "Courage! To the field!" And thou hast talked
Of sallies and retires,° of trenches, tents,
Of palisadoes,° frontiers,° parapets, 55
Of basilisks, of cannon, culverin,°
Of prisoners' ransom, and of soldiers slain,
And all the currents° of a heady° fight.
Thy spirit within thee hath been so at war
And thus hath so bestirred thee in thy sleep 60
That beads of sweat have stood upon thy brow,
Like bubbles in a late-disturbèd stream.
And in thy face strange motions have appeared,
Such as we see when men restrain their breath
On some great sudden hest.° Oh, what portènts are
these? 65
Some heavy business hath my lord in hand,
And I must know it, else he loves me not.

HOT. What ho! [*Enter* SERVANT.] Is Gilliams with
the packet gone?

SERV. He is, my lord, an hour ago.

HOT. Hath Butler brought those horses from the
sheriff? 70

SERV. One horse, my lord, he brought even now.

HOT. What horse? A roan, a crop-ear,° is it not?

SERV. It is, my lord.

HOT.   That roan shall be my throne.
Well, I will back him straight. Oh, Esperance!°
Bid Butler lead him forth into the park. 75

[*Exit* SERVANT.]

LADY P. But hear you, my lord.

HOT. What say'st thou, my lady?

LADY P. What is it carries you away?

HOT. Why, my horse, my love, my horse.

LADY P. Out, you mad-headed ape! 80
A weasel hath not such a deal of spleen°
As you are tossed with. In faith,
I'll know your business, Harry, that I will.
I fear my brother Mortimer doth stir
About his title, and hath sent for you 85
To line° his enterprise. But if you go ——

HOT. So far afoot, I shall be weary, love.

LADY P. Come, come, you paraquito,° answer me

---

48. treasures: i.e., that ought to be mine. 49. thick-eyed: dull-
sighted, because he sees nothing. 52. manage: horsemanship.
54. sallies . . . retires: raids and retreats. 55 palisadoes: defensive protection made of pointed stakes. frontiers: barricades.
56. basilisks . . . culverin: the heavier pieces of artillery. The
basilisk was of 5-inch caliber and fired a shot of 15½ lbs., the
cannon of 8-inch caliber with a 60-lb. shot, the culverin of 5½-inch
caliber with a 17-lb. shot. Shakespeare is thinking of Elizabethan
ordnance rather than the cannon used in 1400. 58. currents:
courses, rapid movement. heady: fierce. 65. hest: command,
action. 72. crop-ear: with short ears. 74. Esperance: hope—
the battle cry of the Percies. 81. spleen: anger, passion. 86. line:
strengthen. 88. paraquito: parrot.

Sc. iii: 11. unsorted: ill-chosen. 16. hind: female deer, the
essence of timidity. 21. Lord of York: Richard Scroop, Archbishop of York. 34. go to buffets: come to blows. moving: trying
to move. 44. stomach: appetite.

Directly unto this question that I ask.
In faith, I'll break thy little finger, Harry, 90
An if thou wilt not tell me all things true.
  HOT. Away,
Away, you trifler! Love! I love thee not,
I care not for thee, Kate. This is no world
To play with mammets° and to tilt with lips.° 95
We must have bloody noses and cracked crowns,
And pass them current° too. God's me, my horse!
What say'st thou, Kate? What wouldst thou have
  with me?
  LADY P. Do you not love me? Do you not, indeed?
Well, do not, then, for since you love me not, 100
I will not love myself. Do you not love me?
Nay, tell me if you speak in jest or no.
  HOT. Come, wilt thou see me ride?
And when I am o' horseback, I will swear
I love thee infinitely. But hark you, Kate, 105
I must not have you henceforth question me
Whither I go, nor reason whereabout.
Whither I must, I must. And, to conclude,
This evening must I leave you, gentle Kate.
I know you wise, but yet no farther wise 110
Than Harry Percy's wife. Constant you are,
But yet a woman. And for secrecy,
No lady closer, for I well believe
Thou wilt not utter what thou dost not know,
And so far will I trust thee, gentle Kate. 115
  LADY P. How! So far?
  HOT. Not an inch further. But hark you, Kate,
Whither I go, thither shall you go too;
Today will I set forth, tomorrow you. 119
Will this content you, Kate?
  LADY P.   It must of force. [*Exeunt.*]

SCENE IV. *The Boar's Head Tavern in Eastcheap.*

[*Enter the* PRINCE, *and* POINS.]
  PRINCE. Ned, prithee come out of that fat° room,
and lend me thy hand to laugh a little.
  POINS. Where hast been, Hal?
  PRINCE. With three or four loggerheads° amongst
three or fourscore hogsheads.° I have sounded 5
the very base string of humility.° Sirrah, I am sworn
brother to a leash° of drawers, and can call them all
by their Christen names, as Tom, Dick, and Francis.
They take it already upon their salvation that though
I be but Prince of Wales, yet I am the king of 10
courtesy; and tell me flatly I am no proud Jack, like

Falstaff, but a Corinthian,° a lad of mettle, a good
boy, by the Lord, so they call me, and when I am
King of England, I shall command all the good lads
in Eastcheap. They call drinking deep, dyeing 15
scarlet, and when you breathe in your watering,°
they cry "hem!"° and bid you play it off.° To conclude, I am so good a proficient in one quarter of an
hour that I can drink with any tinker in his own 20
language during my life. I tell thee, Ned, thou hast
lost much honor that thou wert not with me in this
action. But, sweet Ned — to sweeten which name of
Ned, I give thee this pennyworth of sugar, clapped
even now into my hand by an underskinker,° 25
one that never spake other English in his life than
"Eight shillings and sixpence," and "You are welcome," with this shrill addition, "Anon,° anon, sir!
Score° a pint of bastard° in the Half-Moon,"° or so.
But, Ned, to drive away the time till Falstaff 30
come, I prithee do thou stand in some by-room while
I question my puny° drawer to what end he gave me
the sugar. And do thou never leave calling "Fran-
cis," that his tale to me may be nothing but 35
"Anon." Step aside, and I'll show thee a precedent.°
  POINS. Francis!
  PRINCE. Thou art perfect.
  POINS. Francis!   [*Exit* POINS.]
         [*Enter* FRANCIS.]
  FRAN. Anon, anon, sir. Look down into the Pom-
garnet,° Ralph.
  PRINCE. Come hither, Francis.
  FRAN. My lord?   44
  PRINCE. How long hast thou to serve, Francis?°
  FRAN. Forsooth, five years, and as much as to ——
  POINS. [*Within*] Francis!
  FRAN. Anon, anon, sir.   49
  PRINCE. Five year! By'r Lady, a long lease for the
clinking of pewter. But, Francis, darest thou be so
valiant as to play the coward with thy indenture°
and show it a fair pair of heels and run from it? 54
  FRAN. Oh, Lord, sir, I'll be sworn upon all the
books in England I could find in my heart.°
  POINS. [*Within*] Francis!
  FRAN. Anon, sir.
  PRINCE. How old art thou, Francis?
  FRAN. Let me see — about Michaelmas next I shall
be ——   61

---

95. mammets: dolls. tilt . . . lips: kiss. 97. current: with a pun
on *cracked crowns;* i.e., broken heads, and crown pieces, cracked
and so not current.
  Sc. iv: 1. fat: stuffy. 4. loggerheads: blockheads. 5. hogsheads: casks. 5–6. sounded . . . humility: i.e., have sunk to
the lowest depth. 7. leash: set of three, properly used of a
leash of greyhounds.

12. Corinthian: a gay lad. 16. watering: drinking. 17. cry
"hem": one of those exclamations made by topers, like "Here's
how." play it off: get it down. 25. underskinker: assistant bar-
tender. 28. Anon: at once or by and by, the drawer's cry,
"Coming, sir." 29. Score: chalk up, the method of recording
a debt for drink still used in English public houses. bastard:
a sweet white wine. Half-Moon: Each room in an inn or a tavern had its own name. 32. puny: freshman. 36. precedent:
specimen. 42. Pomgarnet: Pomegranate — another room.
45. How . . . Francis: i.e., how many years of your apprenticeship still remain. As Francis has only served two of his seven
years, he is sixteen. 53. indenture: agreement of apprenticeship.
56. could . . . heart: i.e., very willingly.

POINS. [*Within*] Francis!

FRAN. Anon, sir. Pray stay a little, my lord.

PRINCE. Nay, but hark you, Francis. For the sugar thou gavest me, 'twas a pennyworth, was't not?   66

FRAN. Oh, Lord, I would it had been two!

PRINCE. I will give thee for it a thousand pound. Ask me when thou wilt, and thou shalt have it.   70

POINS. [*Within*] Francis!

FRAN. Anon, anon.

PRINCE. Anon, Francis? No, Francis, but tomorrow, Francis; or, Francis, o' Thursday; or indeed, Francis, when thou wilt. But Francis!

FRAN. My lord?   76

PRINCE. Wilt thou rob this leathern-jerkin, crystal-button, not-pated, agate-ring, puke-stocking, caddis-garter, smooth-tongue, Spanish-pouch ——°   80

FRAN. Oh, Lord, sir, who do you mean?

PRINCE. Why, then, your brown bastard is your only drink, for look you, Francis, your white canvas doublet will sully. In Barbary,° sir, it cannot come to so much.

FRAN. What, sir?   86

POINS. [*Within*] Francis!

PRINCE. Away, you rogue! Dost thou not hear them call? [*Here they both call him; the* DRAWER *stands amazed, not knowing which way to go.*]
[*Enter* VINTNER.]

VINT. What, standest thou still, and hearest such a calling? Look to the guests within. [*Exit* FRANCIS.] My lord, old Sir John, with half-a-dozen more, are at the door. Shall I let them in?   94

PRINCE. Let them alone awhile, and then open the door. [*Exit* VINTNER.] Poins!
[*Re-enter* POINS.]

POINS. Anon, anon, sir.

PRINCE. Sirrah, Falstaff and the rest of the thieves are at the door. Shall we be merry?   99

POINS. As merry as crickets, my lad. But hark ye, what cunning match° have you made with this jest of the drawer? Come, what's the issue?°   103

PRINCE. I am now of all humors° that have showed themselves humors since the old days of Goodman Adam to the pupilage° of this present twelve o'clock at midnight.
[*Re-enter* FRANCIS.] What's o'clock, Francis?   108

FRAN. Anon, anon, sir.   [*Exit.*]

PRINCE. That ever this fellow should have fewer words than a parrot, and yet the son of a woman! His industry is upstairs and downstairs, his elo-

quence the parcel° of a reckoning. I am not yet of Percy's mind, the Hotspur of the North, he that kills me some six or seven dozen of Scots at a break-   115 fast, washes his hands, and says to his wife, "Fie upon this quiet life! I want work." "O my sweet Harry," says she, "how many hast thou killed to-day?" "Give my roan horse a drench,"° says he, and answers "Some fourteen" an hour after   120 —"a trifle, a trifle." I prithee call in Falstaff. I'll play Percy, and that damned brawn° shall play Dame Mortimer his wife. "Rivo!"° says the drunkard. Call in ribs, call in tallow.   125
[*Enter* FALSTAFF, GADSHILL, BARDOLPH, *and* PETO; FRANCIS *following with wine.*]

POINS. Welcome, Jack. Where hast thou been?

FAL. A plague of all cowards, I say, and a vengeance too! Marry, and amen! Give me a cup of sack, boy. Ere I lead this life long, I'll sew netherstocks° and mend them and foot them too. A plague of all cowards! Give me a cup of sack, rogue. Is there   131 no virtue extant?°   [*He drinks.*]

PRINCE. Didst thou never see Titan° kiss a dish of butter? Pitiful-hearted Titan, that melted° at the sweet tale of the sun's! If thou didst, then behold that compound.   136

FAL. You rogue, here's lime° in this sack too. There is nothing but roguery to be found in villainous man. Yet a coward is worse than a cup of sack with lime in it. A villainous coward! Go thy   140 ways, old Jack, die when thou wilt. If manhood, good manhood, be not forgot upon the face of the earth, then am I a shotten° herring. There live not three good men unhanged in England, and one of them is fat, and grows old. God help the while!° A bad world, I say. I would I were a weaver, I   146 could sing psalms° or anything. A plague of all cowards, I say still.

PRINCE. How now, woolsack! What mutter you?

FAL. A king's son! If I do not beat thee out of thy kingdom with a dagger of lath,° and drive all thy subjects afore thee like a flock of wild geese, I'll never wear hair on my face more. You Prince of Wales!   154

PRINCE. Why, you whoreson round man, what's the matter?

FAL. Are not you a coward? Answer me to that. And Poins there?

POINS. 'Zounds, ye fat paunch, an ye call me coward, by the Lord, I'll stab thee.   160

77-80. leathern-jerkin . . . Spanish-pouch: This list gives the outward characteristics of a prosperous innkeeper: leather coat (*jerkin*) with crystal buttons, close-cropped head (*not-pated*), large ring, gray (*puke*) stockings, worsted (*caddis*) garters, a *smooth tongue*, and a *pouch* of *Spanish* leather. 84. In Barbary: in North Africa — but the Prince's words have passed beyond location. 101. what . . . match: what is the game. 103. issue: result. 104. of . . . humors: i.e., will match my mood with any man's. 106. pupilage: boyhood.

113. parcel: items. 119. drench: purge. 122. brawn: fat pig. 124. Rivo: another drinkers' exclamation. See l. 17. 129. netherstocks: stockings, which at this time were usually cut out of material and sewed, not knitted. 132. virtue extant: manhood in existence. 133. Titan: the sun. 134. that melted: i.e., the butter. 137. lime: used to adulterate wine by giving it a better color and taste. 143. shotten: without its roe. 145. God . . . while: God help these times. 146-47. weaver . . . psalms: Protestant weavers were noted psalm-singers. 151. lath: wood.

FAL. I call thee coward! I'll see thee damned ere I call thee coward. But I would give a thousand pound I could run as fast as thou canst. You are straight enough in the shoulders, you care not who sees your back. Call you that backing of your friends? A plague upon such backing! Give me them that will face me. Give me a cup of sack. I am a rogue if I drunk today.   169

PRINCE. O villain! Thy lips are scarce wiped since thou drunkest last.

FAL. All's one for that. [*He drinks.*] A plague of all cowards, still say I.

PRINCE. What's the matter?   174

FAL. What's the matter! There be four of us here have ta'en a thousand pound this day morning.

PRINCE. Where is it, Jack? Where is it?

FAL. Where is it! Taken from us it is — a hundred upon poor four of us.   180

PRINCE. What, a hundred, man?

FAL. I am a rogue if I were not at half-sword° with a dozen of them two hours together. I have 'scaped by miracle. I am eight times thrust through the doublet,° four through the hose;° my buckler°   185 cut through and through; my sword hacked like a handsaw — *ecce signum!*° I never dealt° better since I was a man. All would not do. A plague of all cowards! Let them speak. If they speak more or less than truth, they are villains and the sons of darkness.   191

PRINCE. Speak, sirs, how was it?

GADS. We four set upon some dozen ——

FAL. Sixteen at least, my lord.

GADS. And bound them.   195

PETO. No, no, they were not bound.

FAL. You rogue, they were bound, every man of them, or I am a Jew else, an Ebrew° Jew.

GADS. As we were sharing, some six or seven fresh men set upon us ——   200

FAL. And unbound the rest, and then come in the other.

PRINCE. What, fought you with them all?   203

FAL. All! I know not what you call all, but if I fought not with fifty of them, I am a bunch of radish. If there were not two or three and fifty upon poor old Jack, then am I no two-legged creature.

PRINCE. Pray God you have not murdered some of them.   210

FAL. Nay, that's past praying for. I have peppered two of them — two I am sure I have paid,° two rogues in buckram suits. I tell thee what, Hal, if I tell thee a lie, spit in my face, call me horse.° Thou knowest my old ward.° Here I lay, and thus I bore

my point. Four rogues in buckram let drive at me ——   217

PRINCE. What, four? Thou saidst but two even now.

FAL. Four, Hal, I told thee four.

POINS. Aye, aye, he said four.   221

FAL. These four came all afront, and mainly° thrust at me. I made me no more ado, but took all their seven points in my target, thus.

PRINCE. Seven? Why, there were but four even now.   226

FAL. In buckram?

POINS. Aye, four, in buckram suits.

FAL. Seven, by these hilts,° or I am a villain else.

PRINCE. Prithee let him alone. We shall have more anon.

FAL. Dost thou hear me, Hal?

PRINCE. Aye, and mark thee too, Jack.   234

FAL. Do so, for it is worth the listening to. These nine in buckram that I told thee of ——

PRINCE. So, two more already.

FAL. Their points being broken ——

POINS. Down fell their hose.°   239

FAL. Began to give me ground. But I followed me close, came in foot and hand, and with a thought seven of the eleven I paid.

PRINCE. Oh, monstrous! Eleven buckram men grown out of two!   244

FAL. But, as the Devil would have it, three misbegotten knaves in Kendal green° came at my back and let drive at me; for it was so dark, Hal, that thou couldst not see thy hand.   248

PRINCE. These lies are like their father that begets them — gross as a mountain, open, palpable. Why, thou clay-brained guts, thou knotty-pated° fool, thou whoreson, obscene, greasy tallow catch ——°   253

FAL. What, art thou mad? Art thou mad? Is not the truth the truth?

PRINCE. Why, how couldst thou know these men in Kendal green when it was so dark thou couldst not see thy hand? Come, tell us your reason. What sayest thou to this?   259

POINS. Come, your reason, Jack, your reason.

FAL. What, upon compulsion? 'Zounds, an I were at the strappado, or all the racks° in the world, I would not tell you on compulsion. Give you a reason

---

182. at half-sword: within half a sword's length. A cautious fighter kept at greater distance.   185. doublet: coat. hose: breeches. buckler: small shield.   187. ecce signum: behold the sign. Here Falstaff displays the dents on his sword. dealt: fought.   198. Ebrew: Hebrew.   212. paid: paid home, done for.   214. horse: Like the ass, the horse was regarded as stupid. 215. ward: stance, position of guard. Here Falstaff re-enacts his heroic exploit.   222. mainly: violently.   229. hilts: sword hilt.   238-39. Their . . . hose: Poins puns on the other meaning of *points*, the laces used for tying the hose to the doublet.   246. Kendal green: cloth made (originally at Kendal in Westmoreland) of the poorest-quality wool, and used by woodmen and servants. 252. knotty-pated: blockhead.   253. tallow catch: the word is variously emended and interpreted. Johnson suggested "keech" — a lump of fat prepared by the butcher for the candlemaker. A *tallow catch* would naturally be "a thing for catching tallow"; i.e., the rim on the candlestick which, when piled up with the drippings of wax, is no bad image for Falstaff.   262. strappado . . . racks: forms of torture.

on compulsion! If reasons were as plentiful as   264
blackberries, I would give no man a reason upon
compulsion, I.

PRINCE. I'll be no longer guilty of this sin — this
sanguine° coward, this bed-presser, this horseback-
breaker, this huge hill of flesh ——   269

FAL. 'Sblood, you starveling,° you elf skin,° you
dried neat's tongue,° you bull's pizzle,° you stockfish!° Oh, for breath to utter what is like thee! You
tailor's yard, you sheath, you bow case, you vile
standing tuck ——°   274

PRINCE. Well, breathe a while, and then to it
again, and when thou hast tired thyself in base comparisons, hear me speak but this.

POINS. Mark, Jack.   278

PRINCE. We two saw you four set on four and
bound them, and were masters of their wealth. Mark
now, how a plain tale shall put you down. Then did
we two set on you four; and, with a word, outfaced
you from your prize, and have it, yea, and can show
it you here in the house. And, Falstaff, you carried
your guts away as nimbly, with as quick dex-   285
terity, and roared for mercy, and still run and roared,
as ever I heard bull calf. What a slave art thou, to
hack thy sword as thou hast done, and then say it
was in fight! What trick, what device, what starting
hole,° canst thou now find out to hide thee from this
open and apparent shame?   292

POINS. Come, let's hear, Jack. What trick hast thou
now?

FAL. By the Lord, I knew ye as well as he that
made ye. Why, hear you, my masters. Was it for me
to kill the heir apparent? Should I turn upon the true
Prince? Why, thou knowest I am as valiant as Hercules. But beware instinct, the lion will not touch the
true prince.° Instinct is a great matter, I was now a
coward on instinct. I shall think the better of   300
myself and thee during my life, I for a valiant lion,
and thou for a true Prince. But, by the Lord, lads, I
am glad you have the money. Hostess, clap to the
doors. Watch tonight, pray tomorrow. Gal-   305
lants, lads, boys, hearts of gold, all the titles of good
fellowship come to you! What, shall we be merry?
Shall we have a play extempore?

PRINCE. Content, and the argument° shall be thy
running away.   311

FAL. Ah, no more of that, Hal, an thou lovest me!

[Enter HOSTESS.]

HOSTESS. O Jesu, my lord the Prince!

PRINCE. How now, my lady the hostess! What sayest thou to me?   316

HOSTESS. Marry, my lord, there is a nobleman of
the Court at door would speak with you. He says he
comes from your father.

PRINCE. Give him as much as will make him a
royal man,° and send him back again to my mother.

FAL. What manner of man is he?   323

HOSTESS. An old man.

FAL. What doth gravity out of his bed at midnight? Shall I give him his answer?   326

PRINCE. Prithee do, Jack.

FAL. Faith, and I'll send him packing.   [Exit.]

PRINCE. Now, sirs. By'r Lady, you fought fair; so
did you, Peto; so did you, Bardolph. You are lions
too, you ran away upon instinct, you will not touch
the true prince — no, fie!   332

BARD. Faith, I ran when I saw others run.

PRINCE. Faith, tell me now in earnest, how came
Falstaff's sword so hacked?

PETO. Why, he hacked it with his dagger, and said
he would swear truth out of England but he would
make you believe it was done in fight, and persuaded
us to do the like.   339

BARD. Yea, and to tickle our noses with speargrass
to make them bleed, and then to beslubber° our garments with it and swear it was the blood of true
men. I did that I did not this seven year before, I
blushed to hear his monstrous devices.   344

PRINCE. O villain, thou stolest a cup of sack eighteen years ago, and wert taken with the manner,° and
ever since thou hast blushed° extempore. Thou hadst
fire and sword on thy side, and yet thou rannest
away. What instinct hadst thou for it?   350

BARD. My lord, do you see these meteors? Do you
behold these exhalations?°

PRINCE. I do.

BARD. What think you they portend?

PRINCE. Hot livers and cold purses.   355

BARD. Choler,° my lord, if rightly taken.

PRINCE. No, if rightly taken, halter.

[Re-enter FALSTAFF.] Here comes lean Jack, here
comes barebone. How now, my sweet creature of
bombast!° How long is't ago, Jack, since thou sawest
thine own knee?   361

---

268. sanguine: one suffering from an excess of the sanguine
humor. See Note B, p. 196.   270. you starveling: Falstaff,
thoroughly roused, retorts with a string of images expressing
the thinness of the Prince. elf skin: sometimes emended to
eelskin, but probably it meant snakeskin, which, as Oberon observed, was "Weed wide enough to wrap a fairy in." (MND,
II.i.256.)   271. neat's tongue: ox tongue. bull's pizzle: This
portion of the bull's anatomy was dried and used as a whip.
272. stockfish: dried codfish.   274. standing tuck: a rapier stuck
in the ground.   290–91. starting hole: a hole into which a rabbit
bolts for safety.   298–99. lion . . . prince: This was very generally believed.   310. argument: plot.

321–22. as . . . man: i.e., 3s 4d, which is the difference between
a royal (10s) and a noble (6s 8d). It is a manifest sign of Prince
Hal's low behavior that he should make such jokes about
a nobleman of the Court.   341. beslubber: smear.   346. with
. . . manner: in the act.   347. blushed: For Bardolph's permanent blush see III.iii.27–55 and Hen V, III.vi.108.   351–52. meteors . . . exhalations: Bardolph indicates his own fiery face
which, he claims, is proof that he is a man of wrath. exhalations: meteors.   356. Choler: anger; pronounced in the same
way as "collar," and so puns on the two words are common.
See T. Night, I.v.6,n.   360. bombast: cotton batting, used to
stuff garments to make them appear baggy.

FAL. My own knee! When I was about thy years, Hal, I was not an eagle's talon in the waist, I could have crept into any alderman's thumb ring.° A plague of sighing and grief! It blows a man up like a bladder. There's villainous news abroad. Here 366 was Sir John Bracy from your father; you must to the Court in the morning. That same mad fellow of the North, Percy, and he of Wales, that gave Amamon° the bastinado° and made Lucifer cuckold,° and swore the Devil his true liegeman° upon the cross of a Welsh hook — what a plague call you him? 372

POINS. O, Glendower.°

FAL. Owen, Owen, the same. And his son-in-law Mortimer, and old Northumberland, and that sprightly Scot of Scots, Douglas, that runs o' horseback up a hill perpendicular——

PRINCE. He that rides at high speed and with his pistol kills a sparrow flying. 380

FAL. You have hit it.

PRINCE. So did he never the sparrow.

FAL. Well, that rascal hath good mettle° in him. He will not run. 384

PRINCE. Why, what a rascal art thou then, to praise him so for running!

FAL. O' horseback, ye cuckoo, but afoot he will not budge a foot.

PRINCE. Yes, Jack, upon instinct. 389

FAL. I grant ye, upon instinct. Well, he is there too, and one Mordake, and a thousand bluecaps° more. Worcester is stolen away tonight; thy father's beard is turned white with the news. You may buy land now as cheap as stinking mackerel. 395

PRINCE. Why, then, it is like, if there come a hot June and this civil buffeting hold, we shall buy maidenheads as they buy hobnails, by the hundreds.

FAL. By the mass, lad, thou sayest true; it is like we shall have good trading that way. But tell me, Hal, art not thou horrible afeard? Thou being heir apparent, could the world pick thee out three such enemies again as that fiend Douglas, that spirit Percy, and that devil Glendower? Art thou not horribly afraid? Doth not thy blood thrill at it? 407

PRINCE. Not a whit, i' faith. I lack some of thy instinct.

FAL. Well, thou wilt be horribly chid tomorrow when thou comest to thy father. If thou love me, practice an answer. 412

PRINCE. Do thou stand for° my father, and examine me upon the particulars of my life.

FAL. Shall I? Content. This chair shall be my state,° this dagger my scepter, and this cushion my crown. 417

PRINCE. Thy state is taken for a joined stool,° thy golden scepter for a leaden° dagger, and thy precious rich crown for a pitiful bald crown! 420

FAL. Well, an the fire of grace be not quite out of thee, now shalt thou be moved. Give me a cup of sack to make my eyes look red, that it may be thought I have wept; for I must speak in passion, and I will do it in King Cambyses'° vein. 426

PRINCE. Well, here is my leg.°

FAL. And here is my speech. Stand aside, nobility.

HOSTESS. Oh Jesu, this is excellent sport, i' faith!

FAL. Weep° not, sweet queen, for trickling tears are vain. 430

HOSTESS. Oh, the father,° how he holds his countenance!°

FAL. For God's sake, lords, convey my tristful° queen,
For tears do stop the floodgates of her eyes. 435

HOSTESS. Oh Jesu, he doth it as like one of these harlotry players° as ever I see!

FAL. Peace, good pint pot; peace, good ticklebrain. Harry, I do not only marvel where thou spendest thy time, but also how thou art accompanied.° For 440 though the camomile,° the more it is trodden on, the faster it grows, yet youth, the more it is wasted, the sooner it wears. That thou art my son, I have partly thy mother's word, partly my own opinion, but chiefly a villainous trick° of thine eye, and a 445 foolish hanging of thy nether° lip, that doth warrant° me. If then thou be son to me, here lies the point; why, being son to me, art thou so pointed at? Shall the blessed sun of heaven prove a micher° 450 and eat blackberries? A question not to be asked. Shall the son of England prove a thief and take purses? A question to be asked. There is a thing, Harry, which thou hast often heard of, and it is known to many in our land by the name of pitch. This pitch, as ancient writers do report, doth 455 defile; so doth the company thou keepest. For, Harry, now I do not speak to thee in drink but in tears, not in pleasure but in passion, not in words only, but in

416. state: throne. 418. joined stool: wooden stool made by a joiner. 419. leaden: blunt. 426. King Cambyses': the chief character in an early drama which still survives; it is a marvelous specimen of ridiculous rant. 427. my leg: my curtsy. 430–35: Weep . . . eyes: Falstaff begins in the ranting and exaggerated style of earlier plays, of the kind still being acted by the rival company at the Rose playhouse. 431. Oh . . . father: by God the Father. holds . . . countenance: keeps a straight face. 434. tristful: sad, a poetical word. 437. harlotry players: worthless players. As the Admiral's Men were the only other company then playing in London, the parody of their heavy style was obvious. 440. how . . . accompanied: what company you keep. 441. For . . . camomile: The whole of this passage is a parody of the elaborate style of Lyly's *Euphues*. The *camomile* is a small creeping aromatic plant with a flower like a daisy. 445. trick: habit. 446. nether: lower. 447. warrant: guarantee. 450. micher: a truant.

364. thumb ring: large seal ring, especially common on the thumbs of businessmen. 369. Amamon: the name of a fiend. 370. bastinado: thrashing. cuckold: a man deceived by his wife. 371. liegeman: loyal subject. 373. O, Glendower: probably Shakespeare wrote *O* in his manuscript as abbreviation for Owen, which the printer mistook for an exclamation. 383. mettle: matter, material. 391. bluecaps: Scots. 413. stand for: represent.

woes also. And yet there is a virtuous man whom I have often noted in thy company, but I know not his name.   461

PRINCE. What manner of man, an it like your Majesty?

FAL. A goodly portly° man, i' faith, and a corpulent; of a cheerful look, a pleasing eye, and a   465
most noble carriage. And, as I think, his age some fifty, or, by'r Lady, inclining to threescore. And now I remember me, his name is Falstaff. If that man should be lewdly given, he deceiveth me, for, Harry, I see virtue in his looks. If then the tree may be   470
known by the fruit, as the fruit by the tree, then, peremptorily° I speak it, there is virtue in that Falstaff. Him keep with, the rest banish. And tell me now, thou naughty varlet, tell me, where hast thou been this month?   475

PRINCE. Dost thou speak like a king? Do thou stand for me, and I'll play my father.

FAL. Depose me? If thou dost it half so gravely, so majestically, both in word and matter, hang me up by the heels for a rabbit-sucker° or a poulter's° hare.

PRINCE. Well, here I am set.   482

FAL. And here I stand. Judge, my masters.

PRINCE. Now, Harry, whence come you?

FAL. My noble lord, from Eastcheap.   485

PRINCE. The complaints I hear of thee are grievous.

FAL. 'Sblood, my lord, they are false. Nay, I'll tickle ye° for a young Prince, i' faith.   489

PRINCE. Swearest thou, ungracious° boy? Henceforth ne'er look on me. Thou art violently carried away from grace. There is a devil haunts thee in the likeness of an old fat man, a tun° of man is thy companion. Why dost thou converse with that trunk of humors,° that bolting hutch° of beastliness,   495
that swollen parcel of dropsies, that huge bombard° of sack, that stuffed cloak bag° of guts, that roasted Manningtree° ox with the pudding in his belly, that reverend vice,° that gray iniquity, that father ruffian, that vanity in years? Wherein is he good,   500
but to taste sack and drink it? Wherein neat and cleanly,° but to carve a capon and eat it? Wherein cunning,° but in craft? Wherein crafty,° but in villainy? Wherein villainous, but in all things? Wherein worthy, but in nothing?   505

FAL. I would your Grace would take me with you.° Whom means your Grace?

PRINCE. That villainous abominable misleader of youth, Falstaff, that old white-bearded Satan.

FAL. My lord, the man I know.   510

PRINCE. I know thou dost.

FAL. But to say I know more harm in him than in myself were to say more than I know. That he is old, the more the pity, his white hairs do witness it; but that he is, saving your reverence, a whore-   515
master, that I utterly deny. If sack and sugar be a fault, God help the wicked! If to be old and merry be a sin, then many an old host that I know is damned. If to be fat be to be hated, then Pharaoh's lean kine are to be loved. No, my good lord. Banish Peto,   520
banish Bardolph, banish Poins. But for sweet Jack Falstaff, kind Jack Falstaff, true Jack Falstaff, valiant Jack Falstaff, and therefore more valiant, being, as he is, old Jack Falstaff, banish not him thy Harry's company, banish not him thy Harry's company.   525
Banish plump Jack, and banish all the world.

PRINCE. I do, I will.   [A knocking heard.
          Exeunt HOSTESS, FRANCIS, and BARDOLPH.]
          [Re-enter BARDOLPH, running.]

BARD. Oh, my lord, my lord! The sheriff with a most monstrous watch° is at the door.   530

FAL. Out, ye rogue! Play out the play. I have much to say in the behalf of that Falstaff.

          [Re-enter the HOSTESS.]

HOSTESS. Oh Jesu, my lord, my lord! —

PRINCE. Heigh, heigh! The Devil rides upon a fiddlestick.° What's the matter?   535

HOSTESS. The sheriff and all the watch are at the door. They are come to search the house. Shall I let them in?

FAL. Dost thou hear, Hal? Never call a true piece of gold a counterfeit. Thou art essentially mad, without seeming so.   541

PRINCE. And thou a natural coward, without instinct.

FAL. I deny your major.° If you will deny the sheriff, so; if not, let him enter. If I become not a cart° as well as another man, a plague on my bringing up! I hope I shall as soon be strangled with a halter as another.   548

PRINCE. Go, hide thee behind the arras,° the rest walk up above. Now, my masters, for a true face and good conscience.

FAL. Both which I have had; but their date is out,° and therefore I'll hide me.   553

PRINCE. Call in the sheriff.

          [Exeunt all except the PRINCE and PETO.]

464. portly: dignified.   472. peremptorily: conclusively.   481. rabbit-sucker: young rabbit.   poulter: poulterer.   489. I'll . . . ye: I'll show you how to do it.   490. ungracious: graceless.   493. tun: large barrel.   494-95. trunk of humors: great collection of diseases.   495. bolting hutch: round bin into which flour was sifted.   496. bombard: large leather jug used for carrying liquor.   497. cloak bag: for carrying cloaks.   498. Manningtree: a town in Essex where there was a famous cattle market. At fairs it was often a custom to roast an ox whole.   499. vice: the Devil in the old Morality Plays.   502. cleanly: clever.   503. cunning: skillful.   crafty: a craftsman.   506-07. take . . . you: explain yourself.

530. watch: citizen police force.   534-35. Devil . . . fiddlestick: what's all the fuss about?   544. I . . . major: I deny your major premise, i.e., the main argument on which your conclusion is based; a phrase used in academic arguments. Falstaff puns also on "mayor." "Major" and "mayor" were pronounced alike.   546. cart: which will take him to execution.   549. arras: curtain.   552. date is out: time is expired.

[*Enter* SHERIFF *and the* CARRIER.]

Now, Master Sheriff, what is your will with me?

SHER. First, pardon me, my lord. A hue and
cry°

Hath followed certain men unto this house.

PRINCE. What men?

SHER. One of them is well known, my gracious
lord,

A gross fat man.

CAR.   As fat as butter.   560

PRINCE. The man, I do assure you, is not here,

For I myself at this time have employed him.

And, sheriff, I will engage my word to thee

That I will, by tomorrow dinnertime,

Send him to answer thee, or any man,   565

For anything he shall be charged withal.

And so let me entreat you leave the house.

SHER. I will, my lord. There are two gentlemen

Have in this robbery lost three hundred marks.

PRINCE. It may be so. If he have robbed these
men,   570

He shall be answerable. And so farewell.

SHER. Good night, my noble lord.

PRINCE. I think it is good morrow, is it not?

SHER. Indeed, my lord, I think it be two o'clock.

[*Exeunt* SHERIFF *and* CARRIER.]

PRINCE. This oily rascal is known as well as   575
Paul's.° Go, call him forth.

PETO. Falstaff! — Fast asleep behind the arras, and
snorting like a horse.

PRINCE. Hark how hard he fetches breath. Search
his pockets. [*He searcheth his pockets, and findeth
certain papers.*] What hast thou found?   582

PETO. Nothing but papers, my lord.

PRINCE. Let's see what they be. Read them.

PETO. [*Reads.*]

" Item, A capon, ... *2s. 2d.*
  Item, Sauce, ...   *4d.*
  Item, Sack, two gallons, ... *5s. 8d.*
  Item, Anchovies and sack after supper, *2s. 6d.*
  Item, Bread, ...   *ob.*°"

PRINCE. Oh, monstrous! But one halfpenny-   591
worth of bread to this intolerable deal of sack! What
there is else, keep close, we'll read it at more advantage. There let him sleep till day. I'll to the Court in
the morning. We must all to the wars, and thy   595
place shall be honorable. I'll procure this fat rogue a
charge of foot,° and I know his death will be a march
of twelvescore.° The money shall be paid back again
with advantage.° Be with me betimes in the morning. And so good morrow, Peto.   600

PETO. Good morrow, good my lord.   [*Exeunt.*]

---

556. hue . . . cry: pursuit of a thief.   576. Paul's: St. Paul's,
the largest church in London.   590. ob: one halfpenny.
597. charge of foot: commission as commander of a company
of infantry.   598. twelvescore: i.e., paces. The pace was 60 inches.
599. advantage: interest.

Act III

SCENE I. *Bangor. The* ARCHDEACON'S *house.*

[*Enter* HOTSPUR, WORCESTER, MORTIMER, *and*
GLENDOWER.]

MORT. These promises are fair, the parties sure,

And our induction° full of prosperous hope.

HOT. Lord Mortimer, and Cousin Glendower,

Will you sit down?

And Uncle Worcester. A plague upon it!   5

I have forgot the map.

GLEND.   No, here it is.

Sit, Cousin Percy. Sit, good Cousin Hotspur,

For by that name as oft as Lancaster

Doth speak of you, his cheek looks pale, and with

A rising sigh he wisheth you in Heaven.   10

HOT. And you in Hell, as oft as he hears Owen
Glendower spoke of.

GLEND. I cannot blame him. At my nativity°

The front° of heaven was full of fiery shapes,

Of burning cressets;° and at my birth   15

The frame and huge foundation of the earth

Shaked like a coward.

HOT. Why, so it would have done at the same season if your mother's cat had but kittened, though
yourself had never been born.   20

GLEND. I say the earth did shake when I was born.

HOT. And I say the earth was not of my mind

If you suppose as fearing you it shook.

GLEND. The heavens were all on fire, the earth did
tremble.

HOT. Oh, then the earth shook to see the heavens
on fire,   25

And not in fear of your nativity.

Diseasèd nature oftentimes breaks forth

In strange eruptions; oft the teeming° earth

Is with a kind of colic pinched and vexed

By the imprisoning of unruly wind   30

Within her womb; which, for enlargement striving,

Shakes the old beldam° earth and topples down

Steeples and moss-grown towers. At your birth

Our grandam earth, having this distemperature,°

In passion° shook.

GLEND.   Cousin,° of many men   35

I do not bear these crossings.° Give me leave

To tell you once again that at my birth

The front of heaven was full of fiery shapes,

The goats ran from the mountains, and the herds

Act III, Sc. i: 2. induction: opening.   12. nativity: astrological
moment of birth.   14. front: forehead.   15. cressets: stars
blazing like beacons.   28. teeming: pregnant. This theory of
earthquakes — that they were caused by the expulsion of wind
from within the earth — was generally believed.   32. beldam:
grandmother.   34. distemperature: disorder.   35. passion:
agitation. Cousin: kinsman; used of any relation. Hotspur
is remotely related to Glendower through Lady Percy. See
Genealogical Table, p. 198.   36. crossings: opposition.

Were strangely clamorous to the frighted fields.   40
These signs have marked me extraordinary,
And all the courses of my life do show
I am not in the roll of common men.
Where is he living, clipped in° with the sea
That chides° the banks of England, Scotland, Wales,
Which calls me pupil,° or hath read to me?°   46
And bring him out that is but woman's son
Can trace° me in the tedious ways of art,°
And hold me pace° in deep experiments.
 HOT. I think there's no man speaks better Welsh.
I'll to dinner.   51
 MORT. Peace, Cousin Percy, you will make him
  mad.
 GLEND. I can call spirits from the vasty deep.
 HOT. Why, so can I, or so can any man;
But will they come when you do call for them?   55
 GLEND. Why, I can teach you, Cousin, to command
The Devil.
 HOT. And I can teach thee, Coz, to shame the
  Devil°
By telling truth. Tell truth, and shame the Devil.   59
If thou have power to raise him, bring him hither,
And I'll be sworn I have power to shame him hence.
Oh, while you live, tell truth, and shame the Devil!
 MORT. Come, come, no more of this unprofitable
  chat.
 GLEND. Three times hath Henry Bolingbroke
  made head°
Against my power. Thrice from the banks of Wye
And sandy-bottomed Severn have I sent him   66
Bootless° home and weather-beaten back.
 HOT. Home without boots, and in foul weather
  too!
How 'scapes he agues,° in the Devil's name?
 GLEND. Come, here's the map. Shall we divide our
  right   70
According to our threefold order° ta'en?
 MORT. The Archdeacon hath divided it
Into three limits° very equally.
England, from Trent and Severn hitherto,
By south and east is to my part assigned.   75
All westward, Wales beyond the Severn shore,
And all the fertile land within that bound,
To Owen Glendower. And, dear Coz, to you
The remnant northward, lying off from Trent.
And our indentures tripartite° are drawn;   80
Which being sealed interchangeably,°
A business that this night may execute,

Tomorrow, Cousin Percy, you and I
And my good Lord of Worcester will set forth
To meet your father and the Scottish power,   85
As is appointed us, at Shrewsbury.
My father° Glendower is not ready yet,
Nor shall we need his help these fourteen days.
Within that space you may have drawn together   89
Your tenants, friends, and neighboring gentlemen.
 GLEND. A shorter time shall send me to you, lords.
And in my conduct shall your ladies come,
From whom you now must steal and take no leave;
For there will be a world of water shed
Upon the parting of your wives and you.   95
 HOT. Methinks my moiety,° north from Burton
  here,
In quantity equals not one of yours.
See how this river comes me cranking in,°
And cuts me from the best of all my land
A huge half-moon, a monstrous cantle° out.   100
I'll have the current in this place dammed up,
And here the smug° and silver Trent shall run
In a new channel, fair and evenly.
It shall not wind with such a deep indent,°
To rob me of so rich a bottom° here.   105
 GLEND. Not wind? It shall, it must. You see it
  doth.
 MORT. Yea, but
Mark how he bears his course, and runs me up
With like advantage on the other side,
Gelding the opposèd continent° as much   110
As on the other side it takes from you.
 WOR. Yea, but a little charge° will trench him
  here
And on this north side win this cape of land,
And then he runs straight and even.
 HOT. I'll have it so. A little charge will do it.   115
 GLEND. I'll not have it altered.
 HOT.   Will not you?
 GLEND. No, nor you shall not.
 HOT.   Who shall say me nay?
 GLEND. Why, that will I.
 HOT. Let me not understand you, then. Speak it in
  Welsh.   120
 GLEND. I can speak English, lord, as well as you;
For I was trained up in the English Court,
Where, being but young, I framèd to the harp
Many an English ditty lovely well,
And gave the tongue a helpful ornament,°   125
A virtue that was never seen in you.
 HOT. Marry,°
And I am glad of it with all my heart.

---

44. clipped in: encircled. 45. chides: roars against. 46. calls me pupil: i.e., is my master. hath . . . me: has been my tutor. 48. trace: follow. tedious . . . art: difficult course of magic. 49. hold me pace: keep pace with me. 58. shame . . . Devil: because he is the father of lies. 64. made head: advanced. 67. Bootless: profitless. 69. agues: fever. 71. our . . . order: agreement made between us three. 73. limits: divisions. 80. indentures tripartite: agreement between three parties. 81. interchangeably: each party sealing each copy of the agreement.

87. father: i.e., father-in-law. 96. moiety: share. 98. me . . . in: comes winding into my part. 100. cantle: slice. 102. smug: smooth. 104. indent: indentation. 105. bottom: valley. 110. opposed continent: opposite bank. 112. charge: cost. 125. helpful ornament: i.e., musical accompaniment. 127. Marry: Mary, by the Virgin.

I had rather be a kitten and cry mew
Than one of these same meter balladmongers.° 130
I had rather hear a brazen canstick turned,°
Or a dry wheel grate on the axletree;
And that would set my teeth nothing on edge,
Nothing so much as mincing poetry.
'Tis like the forced gait of a shuffling nag. 135
   GLEND. Come, you shall have Trent turned.
   HOT. I do not care. I'll give thrice so much
     land
To any well-deserving friend.
But in the way of bargain, mark ye me,
I'll cavil° on the ninth part of a hair. 140
Are the indentures drawn? Shall we be gone?
   GLEND. The moon shines fair, you may away by
     night.
I'll haste the writer, and withal
Break with° your wives of your departure hence.
I am afraid my daughter will run mad, 145
So much she doteth on her Mortimer.   [*Exit.*]
   MORT. Fie, Cousin Percy! How you cross my
     father!
   HOT. I cannot choose. Sometime he angers me
With telling me of the moldwarp° and the ant,
Of the dreamer Merlin° and his prophecies, 150
And° of a dragon and a finless fish,
A clip-winged griffin° and a molten raven,
A couching lion and a ramping° cat,
And such a deal of skimble-skamble° stuff
As puts me from my faith. I tell you what— 155
He held me last night at least nine hours
In reckoning up the several° devils' names
That were his lackeys. I cried " hum," and " well, go
to,"
But marked him not a word. Oh, he is as tedious
As a tired horse, a railing wife, 160
Worse than a smoky house. I had rather live
With cheese and garlic in a windmill, far,
Than feed on cates° and have him talk to me
In any summerhouse° in Christendom.
   MORT. In faith, he is a worthy gentleman, 165
Exceedingly well read, and profited
In strange concealments;° valiant as a lion,
And wondrous affable, and as bountiful
As mines of India. Shall I tell you, Cousin?
He holds your temper° in a high respect, 170
And curbs himself even of his natural scope

---

130. meter balladmongers: doggerel rhymesters. 131. brazen . . .
turned: brass candlestick being cut out on the lathe. 140. cavil:
raise objections. 144. Break with: break the news to. 149. mold-
warp: mole. 150. Merlin: the old magician at King Arthur's
Court. As the Welsh were (more or less) descendants of Arthur's
British countrymen, Merlin's prophecies would appeal to Glendower. 151–53. And . . . cat: These beasts occur as symbols in
ancient prophecies. griffin: fabulous beast — half lion, half eagle.
153. ramping: on its hind legs. 154. skimble-skamble: rambling.
157. several: separate, different. 163. cates: delicacies. 164. summerhouse: country house. 166–67. profited . . . concealments:
expert in strange mysteries. 170. temper: character.

When you come 'cross his humor; faith, he does.
I warrant you that man is not alive
Might so have tempted him as you have done
Without the taste of danger and reproof. 175
But do not use it oft, let me entreat you.
   WOR. In faith, my lord, you are too willful-
     blame;°
And since your coming hither have done enough
To put him quite beside his patience.
You must needs learn, lord, to amend this fault. 180
Though sometimes it show greatness, courage,
     blood —
And that's the dearest° grace it renders you —
Yet oftentimes it doth present harsh rage,
Defect of manners, want of government,°
Pride, haughtiness, opinion,° and disdain; 185
The least of which haunting a nobleman
Loseth men's hearts, and leaves behind a stain
Upon the beauty of all parts besides,
Beguiling° them of commendation.
   HOT. Well, I am schooled. Good manners be your
     speed!° 190
Here come our wives, and let us take our leave.
   [*Re-enter* GLENDOWER *with the* LADIES.]
   MORT. This is the deadly spite° that angers me —
My wife can speak no English, I no Welsh.
   GLEND. My daughter weeps. She will not part with
     you.
She'll be a soldier too, she'll to the wars. 195
   MORT. Good Father, tell her that she and my aunt
     Percy
Shall follow in your conduct speedily.
   [GLENDOWER *speaks to* LADY MORTIMER *in Welsh,*
        and she answers him in the same.]
   GLEND. She is desperate here, a peevish self-willed
harlotry,° one that no persuasion can do good 199
upon.
        [LADY MORTIMER *speaks in Welsh.*]
   MORT. I understand thy looks. That pretty Welsh°
Which thou pour'st down from these swelling
     heavens°
I am too perfect in; and but for shame,
In such a parley° should I answer thee.
      [LADY MORTIMER *speaks again in Welsh.*]
I understand thy kisses and thou mine, 205
And that's a feeling disputation.°
But I will never be a truant, love,
Till I have learned thy language; for thy tongue
Makes Welsh as sweet as ditties highly penned,
Sung by a fair queen in a summer's bower, 210

---

177. willful-blame: to be blamed for willfulness. 182. dearest:
most valuable. 184. government: self-control. 185. opinion:
conceit. 189. Beguiling: causing to lose. 190. Good . . . speed:
may good manners bring you luck. 192. spite: vexation.
199. harlotry: silly girl. 201. pretty Welsh: i.e., tears.
202. swelling heavens: i.e., eyes full of tears. 204. parley:
manner of speech. 206. feeling disputation: conversation by
touch.

With ravishing division,° to her lute.

GLEND. Nay, if you melt, then will she run mad.
[LADY MORTIMER *speaks again in Welsh.*]

MORT. Oh, I am ignorance itself in this!

GLEND. She bids you on the wanton° rushes° lay
you down
And rest your gentle head upon her lap,   215
And she will sing the song that pleaseth you
And on your eyelids crown the god of sleep,
Charming your blood with pleasing heaviness,°
Making such difference 'twixt wake and sleep
As is the difference betwixt day and night   220
The hour before the heavenly-harnessed team°
Begins his golden progress in the east.

MORT. With all my heart I'll sit and hear her sing.
By that time will our book,° I think, be drawn.

GLEND. Do so,   225
And those musicians that shall play to you
Hang in the air a thousand leagues from hence,
And straight they shall be here. Sit, and attend.

HOT. Come, Kate, thou art perfect in lying down.
Come, quick, quick, that I may lay my head in thy
lap.   231

LADY P. Go, ye giddy goose.   [*The music plays.*]

HOT. Now I perceive the Devil understands
Welsh,
And 'tis no marvel he is so humorous.°
By'r Lady, he is a good musician.   235

LADY P. Then should you be nothing but musical,
for you are altogether governed by humors. Lie still,
ye thief, and hear the lady sing in Welsh.

HOT. I had rather hear Lady, my brach,° howl in
Irish.   241

LADY P. Wouldst thou have thy head broken?

HOT. No.

LADY P. Then be still.

HOT. Neither — 'tis a woman's fault.   245

LADY P. Now God help thee!

HOT. To the Welsh lady's bed.

LADY P. What's that?

HOT. Peace! She sings.
[*Here* LADY MORTIMER *sings a Welsh song.*]
Come, Kate, I'll have your song too.   250

LADY P. Not mine, in good sooth.°

HOT. Not yours, in good sooth! Heart! You swear
like a comfit-maker's° wife. "Not you, in good
sooth," and "as true as I live," and "as God shall
mend me," and "as sure as day,"   255
And givest such sarcenet surety for thy oaths°
As if thou never walk'st further than Finsbury.°
Swear me, Kate, like a lady as thou art,

A good mouth-filling oath, and leave "in sooth"
And such protest of pepper gingerbread°   260
To velvet guards° and Sunday citizens.°
Come, sing.

LADY P. I will not sing.

HOT. 'Tis the next way to turn tailor,° or be redbreast teacher.° An the indentures be drawn,   265
I'll away within these two hours, and so come in
when ye will.   [*Exit.*]

GLEND. Come, come, Lord Mortimer, you are as
slow
As hot Lord Percy is on fire to go.
By this our book is drawn. We'll but seal,   270
And then to horse immediately.

MORT.   With all my heart.   [*Exeunt.*]

SCENE II. *London. The palace.*

[*Enter the* KING, PRINCE OF WALES, *and others.*]

KING. Lords, give us leave. The Prince of Wales
and I
Must have some private conference. But be near at
hand,
For we shall presently have need of you.
[*Exeunt* LORDS.]
I know not whether God will have it so,
For some displeasing service I have done,   5
That, in his secret doom,° out of my blood°
He'll breed revengement and a scourge for me;
But thou dost in thy passages of life
Make me believe that thou art only marked
For the hot vengeance and the rod of Heaven   10
To punish my mistreadings. Tell me else,
Could such inordinate° and low desires,
Such poor, such bare, such lewd,° such mean at-
tempts,
Such barren pleasures, rude society,
As thou art matched withal and grafted to,   15
Accompany the greatness of thy blood,
And hold their level with thy princely heart?

PRINCE. So please your Majesty, I would I could
Quit° all offenses with as clear excuse
As well as I am doubtless I can purge   20
Myself of many I am charged withal.
Yet such extenuation let me beg
As, in reproof° of many tales devised,
Which oft the ear of greatness needs must hear,

260. **pepper gingerbread:** a very mild form of heat.   261. **velvet guards:** literally bands of velvet used to ornament a gown (and still used on the gown of a Ph.D.); so "peaceful, timid tradesmen." **Sunday citizens:** citizens in their Sunday best.   264. **turn tailor:** Tailors (before the invention of the sewing machine) used to sing at their work as they sat cross-legged.   265. **redbreast teacher:** one who teaches caged birds to sing. The little English robin was highly valued as a songbird.
Sc. ii: 6. **doom:** judgment. **out . . . blood:** through one of my children.   12. **inordinate:** intemperate.   13. **lewd:** low.   19. **Quit:** acquit myself of.   23. **reproof:** rebuttal.

211. **division:** melody.   214. **wanton:** luxuriant. **rushes:** used to cover floors.   218. **heaviness:** drowsiness.   221. **team:** i.e., the horses of the sun.   224. **book:** agreement.   234. **humorous:** full of whims.   240. **brach:** bitch.   251. **sooth:** truth.   253. **comfit-maker:** candymaker.   256. **sarcenet . . . oaths:** you swear by such soft things. **sarcenet:** fine silk.   257. **Finsbury:** Finsbury fields, whither London citizens took their Sunday-afternoon walk.

By smiling pickthanks° and base newsmongers, 25
I may for some things true wherein my youth
Hath faulty wandered and irregular
Find pardon on my true submission.
    KING. God pardon thee! Yet let me wonder,
      Harry,
At thy affections, which do hold a wing 30
Quite from the flight° of all thy ancestors.
Thy place in Council thou hast rudely lost,
Which by thy younger brother is supplied,
And art almost an alien to the hearts
Of all the Court and princes of my blood. 35
The hope and expectation of thy time°
Is ruined, and the soul of every man
Prophetically doth forethink thy fall.
Had I so lavish of my presence been,
So common-hackneyed° in the eyes of men, 40
So stale and cheap to vulgar company,
Opinion,° that did help me to the crown,
Had still kept loyal to possession,°
And left me in reputeless banishment,
A fellow of no mark nor likelihood. 45
By being seldom seen, I could not stir
But like a comet I was wondered at,
That men would tell their children "This is he."
Others would say, "Where, which is Bolingbroke?"
And then I stole all courtesy from Heaven, 50
And dressed myself in such humility
That I did pluck allegiance from men's hearts,
Loud shouts and salutations from their mouths,
Even in the presence of the crownèd King.
Thus did I keep my person fresh and new, 55
My presence, like a robe pontifical,°
Ne'er seen but wondered at. And so my state,
Seldom but sumptuous, showed like a feast,
And won by rareness such solemnity.
The skipping° King, he ambled up and down, 60
With shallow jesters and rash bavin° wits,
Soon kindled and soon burnt; carded° his state,
Mingled his royalty with capering fools,
Had his great name profanèd with their scorns,
And gave his countenance, against his name,° 65
To laugh at gibing° boys and stand the push°
Of every beardless vain comparative,°
Grew a companion to the common streets,
Enfeoffed° himself to popularity,°

25. pickthanks: men who curry favor by telling tales. 30–31. affections . . . flight: desires, natural inclinations . . . fly a different course. 36. time: lifetime. 40. common-hackneyed: at every
man's call. A hackney is a hired horse. 42. Opinion: popular
opinion. 43. loyal to possession: loyal to the possessor; i.e.,
Richard II. 56. robe pontifical: a bishop's robe. 60. skipping:
frivolous. 61. bavin: brushwood for kindling, worthless and
easily broken. 62. carded: adulterated. 65. against . . . name:
contrary to the interest of his reputation. 66. gibing: mocking.
stand . . . push: endure the sallies of. 67. beardless . . . comparative: every boy who cared to make jokes at his expense.
69. Enfeoffed: conveyed, made himself over to. popularity: low
company, common people.

That, being daily swallowed by men's eyes, 70
They surfeited with honey and began
To loathe the taste of sweetness, whereof a little
More than a little is by much too much.
So when he had occasion to be seen,
He was but as the cuckoo is in June, 75
Heard, not regarded; seen, but with such eyes
As, sick and blunted with community,°
Afford no extraordinary gaze,
Such as is bent on sunlike majesty
When it shines seldom in admiring eyes; 80
But rather drowsed and hung their eyelids down,
Slept in his face° and rendered such aspèct°
As cloudy° men use to their adversaries,
Being with his presence glutted, gorged, and full.
And in that very line,° Harry, standest thou; 85
For thou hast lost thy princely privilege
With vile participation.° Not an eye
But is aweary of thy common sight,
Save mine, which hath desired to see thee more,
Which now doth that I would not have it do — 90
Make blind itself with foolish tenderness.
    PRINCE. I shall hereafter, my thrice gracious
      lord,
Be more myself.
    KING.   For all the world
As thou art to this hour° was Richard then
When I from France set foot at Ravenspurgh, 95
And even as I was then is Percy now.
Now, by my scepter and my soul to boot,
He hath more worthy interest to the state
Than thou the shadow of succession;°
For of no right,° nor color like to right, 100
He doth fill fields with harness° in the realm,
Turns head against the lion's armèd jaws,
And being no more in debt to years than thou,°
Leads ancient lords and reverend bishops on
To bloody battles and to bruising arms. 105
What never-dying honor hath he got
Against renownèd Douglas! — whose high deeds,
Whose hot incursions° and great name in arms
Holds from all soldiers chief majority
And military title capital° 110
Through all the kingdoms that acknowledge Christ.
Thrice hath this Hotspur, Mars in swathling°
      clothes,
This infant warrior, in his enterprises
Discomfited great Douglas, ta'en him once,
Enlarged him, and made a friend of him, 115

77. blunted . . . community: satiated by that which is
common. 82. in . . . face: in his presence — a gross insult.
aspect: look. 83. cloudy: sullen. 85. line: class. 87. vile participation: mixing with low company. 94. to . . . hour: up to now.
99. shadow of succession: shadowy right of succession. 100. of
no right: with no right. 101. harness: armor. 103. no . . . thou:
See I.i.92,n. 108. incursions: raids. 109–10. Holds . . . capital:
keeps from all other soldiers the claim to be considered the greatest. 112. swathling: swaddling.

To fill the mouth of deep defiance up°
And shake the peace and safety of our throne.
And what say you to this? Percy, Northumberland,
The Archbishop's Grace of York, Douglas, Morti-
    mer,
Capitulate° against us and are up.   120
But wherefore do I tell these news to thee?
Why, Harry, do I tell thee of my foes,
Which art my near'st and dearest enemy?
Thou that art like enough through vassal° fear,
Base inclination, and the start of spleen°   125
To fight against me under Percy's pay,
To dog his heels and curtsy at his frowns,
To show how much thou art degenerate.
    PRINCE. Do not think so, you shall not find it so.
And God forgive them that so much have swayed
Your Majesty's good thoughts away from me!   131
I will redeem all this on Percy's head,
And in the closing of some glorious day
Be bold to tell you that I am your son;
When I will wear a garment all of blood,   135
And stain my favors° in a bloody mask
Which, washed away, shall scour my shame with it.
And that shall be the day, whene'er it lights,
That this same child of honor and renown,
This gallant Hotspur, this all-praisèd knight, 140
And your unthought-of Harry chance to meet.
For every honor sitting on his helm,
Would they were multitudes, and on my head
My shames redoubled! For the time will come
That I shall make this Northern youth exchange
His glorious deeds for my indignities.   146
Percy is but my factor,° good my lord,
To engross° up glorious deeds on my behalf.
And I will call him to so strict account
That he shall render every glory up —   150
Yea, even the slightest worship° of his time —
Or I will tear the reckoning from his heart.
This, in the name of God, I promise here.
The which if He be pleased I shall perform,
I do beseech your Majesty may salve°   155
The long-grown wounds of my intemperance.
If not, the end of life cancels all bands,°
And I will die a hundred thousand deaths
Ere break the smallest parcel° of this vow.
    KING. A hundred thousand rebels die in this. 160
Thou shalt have charge and sovereign trust herein.
[Enter BLUNT.] How now, good Blunt? Thy looks
    are full of speed.
    BLUNT. So hath the business that I come to speak
    of.
Lord Mortimer of Scotland hath sent word

That Douglas and the English rebels met   165
The eleventh of this month at Shrewsbury.
A mighty and a fearful head° they are,
If promises be kept on every hand,
As ever offered foul play in a state.
    KING. The Earl of Westmoreland set forth today,
With him my son, Lord John of Lancaster;   171
For this advértisement is five days old.
On Wednesday next, Harry, you shall set forward,
On Thursday we ourselves will march. Our meeting
Is Bridgenorth. And, Harry, you shall march   175
Through Gloucestershire, by which account,
Our business valued,° some twelve days hence
Our general forces at Bridgenorth shall meet.
Our hands are full of business. Let's away.
Advantage feeds him fat° while men delay.   180
                                    [Exeunt.]

SCENE III. *Boar's Head Tavern in Eastcheap.*

[*Enter* FALSTAFF *and* BARDOLPH.]
    FAL. Bardolph, am I not fallen away vilely since
this last action?° Do I not bate?° Do I not dwindle?
Why, my skin hangs about me like an old lady's
loose gown, I am withered like an old applejohn.°
Well, I'll repent, and that suddenly, while I am in 5
some liking.° I shall be out of heart° shortly, and
then I shall have no strength to repent. An I have not
forgotten what the inside of a church is made of, I
am a peppercorn, a brewer's horse° — the inside of a
church! Company, villainous company, hath been
the spoil of me.   11
    BARD. Sir John, you are so fretful you cannot live
long.
    FAL. Why, there is it. Come sing me a bawdy song,
make me merry. I was as virtuously given as a gentleman need to be — virtuous enough; swore little;
diced not above seven times a week; went to a
bawdyhouse not above once in a quarter — of an
hour; paid money that I borrowed, three or four   20
times; lived well, and in good compass.° And now I
live out of all order, out of all compass.
    BARD. Why, you are so fat, Sir John, that you must
needs be out of all compass, out of all reasonable
compass, Sir John.   26
    FAL. Do thou amend thy face, and I'll amend my
life. Thou art our admiral,° thou bearest the lantern

---

116. To . . . up: so that defiance may speak with a loud mouth.
120. Capitulate: make agreement. 124. vassal: slavish. 125. start
of spleen: impulse of bad temper. 136. favors: features, face.
147. factor: agent, buyer. 148. engross: buy up wholesale.
151. worship: honor. 155. salve: heal. 157. bands: bonds,
debts. 159. parcel: portion.

167. head: force. 177. Our . . . valued: considering how much
we have to do. 180. Advantage . . . fat: advantage makes the
most of his opportunities.
Sc. iii: 2. last action: i.e., the Gadshill affair. bate: grow thin.
applejohn: withered apple, long kept. 6. in . . . liking: in good
condition. out of heart: have no heart for it. 9. brewer's
horse: i.e., old and decrepit. 21. compass: (lit., circumference)
limits, with a pun on Falstaff's girth. 28. admiral: the admiral's ship, which led the way and carried a lighted lantern by
night so that the fleet should keep together.

in the poop,° but 'tis in the nose of thee. Thou art
the Knight of the Burning Lamp. 30

BARD. Why, Sir John, my face does you no harm.

FAL. No, I'll be sworn, I make as good use of it as
many a man doth of a death's-head° or a memento
mori.° I never see thy face but I think upon 35
Hell-fire and Dives° that lived in purple, for there he
is in his robes, burning, burning. If thou wert anyway given to virtue, I would swear by thy face; my
oath should be "By this fire, that's God's angel."°
But thou art altogether given over, and wert in- 40
deed, but for the light in thy face, the son of utter
darkness. When thou rannest up Gadshill in the
night to catch my horse, if I did not think thou hadst
been an ignis fatuus° or a ball of wildfire,° there's no
purchase in money. Oh, thou art a perpetual tri- 45
umph,° an everlasting bonfire light! Thou hast
saved me a thousand marks in links° and torches,
walking with thee in the night betwixt tavern and
tavern. But the sack that thou hast drunk me would
have bought me lights as good cheap at the dear- 51
est chandler's° in Europe. I have maintained that
salamander° of yours with fire any time this two and
thirty years, God reward me for it! 55

BARD. 'Sblood, I would my face were in your
belly!

FAL. God-a-mercy! So should I be sure to be heart-
burned. [Enter HOSTESS.] How now, Dame Partlet
the hen!° Have you inquired yet who picked my
pocket? 61

HOSTESS. Why, Sir John, what do you think, Sir
John? Do you think I keep thieves in my house? I
have searched, I have inquired, so has my husband,
man by man, boy by boy, servant by servant. 65
The tithe° of a hair was never lost in my house
before.

FAL. Ye lie, hostess. Bardolph was shaved° and
lost many a hair, and I'll be sworn my pocket was
picked. Go to, you are a woman, go. 70

HOSTESS. Who, I? No, I defy thee. God's light, I
was never called so in mine own house before!

FAL. Go to, I know you well enough.

HOSTESS. No, Sir John, you do not know me, Sir
John. I know you, Sir John. You owe me money, 75
Sir John, and now you pick a quarrel to beguile me
of it. I bought you a dozen of shirts to your back.

FAL. Dowlas,° filthy dowlas. I have given them

away to bakers' wives, and they have made bolters°
of them. 81

HOSTESS. Now, as I am a true woman, holland° of
eight shillings an ell.° You owe money here besides,
Sir John, for your diet and by-drinkings,° and
money lent you, four and twenty pound. 86

FAL. He had his part of it. Let him pay.

HOSTESS. He? Alas, he is poor, he hath nothing.

FAL. How! Poor? Look upon his face — what call
you rich? Let them coin his nose, let them coin 90
his cheeks. I'll not pay a denier.° What, will you
make a younker° of me? Shall I not take mine ease
in mine inn but I shall have my pocket picked? I
have lost a seal ring of my grandfather's worth forty
mark. 95

HOSTESS. Oh Jesu, I have heard the Prince tell
him, I know not how oft, that that ring was copper!°

FAL. How! The Prince is a Jack,° a sneak-cup.°
'Sblood, an he were here, I would cudgel him like a
dog if he would say so. 101

[Enter the PRINCE and PETO, marching, and FALSTAFF
meets them playing on his truncheon like a fife.]

How now, lad! Is the wind in that door, i' faith?
Must we all march?

BARD. Yea, two and two, Newgate fashion.°

HOSTESS. My lord, I pray you hear me. 105

PRINCE. What sayest thou, Mistress Quickly? How
doth thy husband? I love him well, he is an honest
man.

HOSTESS. Good my lord, hear me.

FAL. Prithee let her alone, and list to me. 110

PRINCE. What sayest thou, Jack?

FAL. The other night I fell asleep here behind the
arras, and had my pocket picked. This house is
turned bawdyhouse; they pick pockets.

PRINCE. What didst thou lose, Jack? 115

FAL. Wilt thou believe me, Hal? Three or four
bonds of forty pound apiece, and a seal ring of my
grandfather's.

PRINCE. A trifle, some eightpenny matter.

HOSTESS. So I told him, my lord, and I said I 120
heard your Grace say so. And, my lord, he speaks
most vilely of you, like a foul-mouthed man as he is,
and said he would cudgel° you.

PRINCE. What! He did not?

HOSTESS. There's neither faith, truth, nor womanhood in me else. 126

FAL. There's no more faith in thee than in a
stewed prune, nor no more truth in thee than in a

---

29. poop: stern.   **34. death's-head:** skull.   **34–35. memento
mori:** reminder of death.   **36. Dives:** the rich man in the parable of Dives and Lazarus. See Luke 16:19–31.   **39. By . . .
angel:** a parody of a line in Chapman's *Blind Beggar of
Alexandria,* a recent and popular play at the Rose Theater.
44. ignis fatuus: will-o'-the-wisp. **wildfire:** firework. **46. triumph:** rejoicing, celebrated with torches and bonfires. **47. links:**
torches used to light the way on a dark night. **52. chandler:**
seller of candles. **54. salamander:** a kind of lizard, believed to
enjoy fire. **59–60. Dame . . . hen:** the wife of Chanticleer the
cock in the story of Reynard the Fox. **66. tithe:** tenth part.
68. shaved: caught venereal disease. **78. Dowlas:** coarse linen.

80. bolters: sieves for sifting flour from bran. **82. holland:** fine
linen. **83. ell:** 45 inches. **85. by-drinkings:** drinks between
meals. **91. denier:** the smallest English coin, worth 1/10d.
92. younker: "sucker." **97. copper:** copper-gilt was the cheap-
est kind of imitation gold. **99. Jack:** knave. **sneak-cup:** one
who steals cups from taverns, the lowest kind of theft.
104. Newgate fashion: i.e., like the chain gang. **Newgate:** the
London prison for felons. **123. cudgel:** beat.

drawn fox,° and for womanhood, Maid Marian may be the deputy's wife of the ward to thee.° Go, you thing, go.   131

HOSTESS. Say, what thing? What thing?

FAL. What thing! Why, a thing to thank God on.

HOSTESS. I am no thing to thank God on, I 135 would thou shouldst know it. I am an honest man's wife. And, setting thy knighthood aside, thou art a knave to call me so.

FAL. Setting thy womanhood aside, thou art a beast to say otherwise.   140

HOSTESS. Say, what beast, thou knave, thou?

FAL. What beast! Why, an otter.

PRINCE. An otter, Sir John! Why an otter?

FAL. Why, she's neither fish nor flesh. A man knows not where to have her.   145

HOSTESS. Thou art an unjust man in saying so. Thou or any man knows where to have me, thou knave, thou!

PRINCE. Thou sayest true, hostess, and he slanders thee most grossly.   150

HOSTESS. So he doth you, my lord, and said this other day you ought° him a thousand pound.

PRINCE. Sirrah, do I owe you a thousand pound?

FAL. A thousand pound, Hal! A million! 155 Thy love is worth a million. Thou owest me thy love.

HOSTESS. Nay, my lord, he called you Jack, and said he would cudgel you.

FAL. Did I, Bardolph?   160

BARD. Indeed, Sir John, you said so.

FAL. Yea, if he said° my ring was copper.

PRINCE. I say 'tis copper.° Darest thou be as good as thy word now?   164

FAL. Why, Hal, thou knowest, as thou art but man, I dare; but as thou art Prince, I fear thee as I fear the roaring of the lion's whelp.

PRINCE. And why not as the lion?

FAL. The King himself is to be feared as the lion. Dost thou think I'll fear thee as I fear thy 170 father? Nay, an I do, I pray God my girdle break.

PRINCE. Oh, if it should, how would thy guts fall about thy knees! But, sirrah, there's no room for faith, truth, nor honesty in this bosom of thine; it is all filled up with guts and midriff. Charge an 175 honest woman with picking thy pocket! Why, thou whoreson, impudent, embossed° rascal, if there were anything in thy pocket but tavern reckonings, memorandums of bawdyhouses, and one poor penny-

worth of sugar candy to make thee long- 180 winded, if thy pocket were enriched with any other injuries° but these, I am a villain. And yet you will stand to it, you will not pocket up wrong. Art thou not ashamed?   184

FAL. Dost thou hear, Hal? Thou knowest in the state of innocency Adam fell, and what should poor Jack Falstaff do in the days of villainy?° Thou seest I have more flesh than another man, and therefore more frailty. You confess, then, you picked my pocket?   190

PRINCE. It appears so by the story.

FAL. Hostess, I forgive thee. Go, make ready breakfast. Love thy husband, look to thy servants, cherish thy guests. Thou shalt find me tractable° to any honest reason. Thou seest I am pacified 195 still.° Nay, prithee be gone. [*Exit* HOSTESS.] Now, Hal, to the news at Court. For the robbery, lad, how is that answered?

PRINCE. Oh, my sweet beef,° I must still be good angel to thee. The money is paid back again. 200

FAL. Oh, I do not like that paying back. 'Tis a double labor.

PRINCE. I am good friends with my father, and may do anything.   204

FAL. Rob me the exchequer the first thing thou doest, and do it with unwashed hands° too.

BARD. Do, my lord.

PRINCE. I have procured thee, Jack, a charge of foot.   209

FAL. I would it had been of horse. Where shall I find one that can steal well? Oh for a fine thief, of the age of two and twenty or thereabouts! I am heinously° unprovided. Well, God be thanked for these rebels, they offend none but the virtuous. I laud them, I praise them.   215

PRINCE. Bardolph!

BARD. My lord?

PRINCE. Go bear this letter to Lord John of Lancaster, to my brother John; this to my Lord of Westmoreland. [*Exit* BARDOLPH.] Go, Peto, to horse, 220 to horse, for thou and I have thirty miles to ride yet ere dinnertime. [*Exit* PETO.] Jack, meet me tomorrow in the Temple Hall at two o'clock in the afternoon.
There shalt thou know thy charge, and there receive Money and order for their furniture.°   226
The land is burning, Percy stands on high,
And either we or they must lower lie.   [*Exit.*]

FAL. Rare words! Brave world! Hostess, my breakfast, come!
Oh, I could wish this tavern were my drum! [*Exit.*]

---

129. **drawn fox:** fox driven out from cover, and so cunning. 129–30. **Maid . . . thee:** Maid Marian, the woman in Robin Hood's gang, was a character in a Whitsun morris dance. She was played by a man as lumpish and awkward. The wife of the deputy of the ward was likely to give herself airs of dignity. Falstaff means "you are more lumpish than Maid Marian compared with a most stately matron." 152. **ought:** owed. 162. **if he said:** See Touchstone on the virtue of "if" as a means of making a safe threat (*AYLI*, V.iv.100–08). 163. **I . . . copper:** Here Falstaff gets the "lie direct." 177. **embossed:** swollen.

181–82. **pocket . . . injuries:** a pun on the phrase "to pocket up injuries." 187. **days of villainy:** these wicked times. 194. **tractable:** agreeable. 196. **still:** always. 199. **beef:** ox. 206. **unwashed hands:** without stopping to wash your hands. 212. **heinously:** atrociously. 226. **furniture:** equipment.

Act IV

SCENE I. *The rebel camp near Shrewsbury.*

[*Enter* HOTSPUR, WORCESTER, *and* DOUGLAS.]

HOT. Well said, my noble Scot. If speaking truth
In this fine age were not thought flattery,
Such attribution° should the Douglas have
As not a soldier of this season's stamp°
Should go so general current through the world. 5
By God, I cannot flatter, I do defy
The tongues of soothers;° but a braver place
In my heart's love hath no man than yourself.
Nay, task me to my word.° Approve° me, lord.

DOUG. Thou art the king of honor. 10
No man so potent breathes upon the ground
But I will beard° him.

HOT.   Do so, and 'tis well.

[*Enter a* MESSENGER *with letters.*]

What letters hast thou there? — I can but thank
    you.

MESS. These letters come from your father.

HOT. Letters from him! Why comes he not him-
    self? 15

MESS. He cannot come, my lord, he is grievous
    sick.

HOT. 'Zounds! How has he the leisure to be sick
In such a justling° time? Who leads his power?
Under whose government come they along?

MESS. His letters bear his mind, not I, my lord.

WOR. I prithee tell me, doth he keep his bed? 21

MESS. He did, my lord, four days ere I set forth,
And at the time of my departure thence
He was much feared by his physicians.

WOR. I would the state of time had first been
    whole° 25
Ere he by sickness had been visited.
His health was never better worth° than now.

HOT. Sick now! Droop now! This sickness doth
    infect
The very lifeblood of our enterprise.
'Tis catching hither, even to our camp. 30
He writes me here that inward sickness —
And that his friends by deputation° could not
So soon be drawn,° nor did he think it meet
To lay so dangerous and dear° a trust
On any soul removed but on his own. 35

Yet doth he give us bold advértisement°
That with our small conjunction° we should on,
To see how fortune is disposed to us;
For, as he writes, there is no quailing now,
Because the King is certainly possessed° 40
Of all our purposes. What say you to it?

WOR. Your father's sickness is a maim to us.

HOT. A perilous gash, a very limb lopped off.
And yet, in faith, it is not; his present want°
Seems more than we shall find it. Were it good 45
To set° the exact° wealth of all our states
All at one cast?° To set so rich a main°
On the nice hazard° of one doubtful hour?
It were not good, for therein should we read
The very bottom and the soul of hope,
The very list,° the very utmost bound° 50
Of all our fortunes.

DOUG.   Faith, and so we should,
Where now remains a sweet reversion.°
We may boldly spend upon the hope of what
Is to come in. 55
A comfort of retirement° lives in this.

HOT. A rendezvous, a home to fly unto,
If that the Devil and mischance look big°
Upon the maidenhead of our affairs.

WOR. But yet I would your father had been here.
The quality and hair° of our attempt 61
Brooks no division. It will be thought
By some, that know not why he is away,
That wisdom, loyalty, and mere dislike
Of our proceedings kept the Earl from hence. 65
And think how such an apprehension
May turn the tide of fearful faction,°
And breed a kind of question in our cause;
For well you know we of the offering° side
Must keep aloof from strict arbitrament,° 70
And stop all sight holes, every loop from whence
The eye of reason may pry in upon us.
This absence of your father's draws° a curtain
That shows the ignorant a kind of fear
Before not dreamed of.

HOT.   You strain too far. 75
I rather of his absence make this use.
It lends a luster and more great opinion,
A larger dare to our great enterprise,
Than if the Earl were here; for men must think
If we without his help can make a head° 80
To push against a kingdom, with his help

Act IV, Sc. i: **3. attribution:** citation of merits. **4. season's stamp:** of this year's minting. The idea is that Douglas is like a new coin, acceptable (*current*) everywhere as valuable. **7. soothers:** flatterers. **9. task . . . word:** cause me to make my word good. **Approve:** put to the proof. **12. beard:** dare; lit., pull by the beard. **18. justling:** jostling, disturbed. **25. I . . . whole:** I wish the times themselves had first been healthy. **27. better worth:** worth more. **32. deputation:** deputy; i.e., he could not send anyone else. **33. drawn:** drawn together. **34. dear:** important.

36. advertisement: advice. **37. conjunction:** forces that have joined. **40. possessed:** informed. **44. his . . . want:** the need of him at this present time. **46. set:** hazard. **exact:** entire. **47. cast:** throw of the dice. **main:** stake. **48. nice hazard:** delicate chance. **51. list:** limit. **bound:** boundary. **53. reversion:** portion yet to come. **56. comfort of retirement:** a place to which we can retire for comfort. **58. look big:** threaten. **61. hair:** nature. **67. fearful faction:** timid rebellion. **69. offering:** challenging. **70. strict arbitrament:** exact judgment. **73. draws:** draws back. **80. make a head:** raise an army. See I.iii.284.

We shall o'erturn it topsy-turvy down.
Yet all goes well, yet all our joints are whole.
  DOUG. As heart can think. There is not such a word
Spoke of in Scotland as this term of fear.   85
        [*Enter* SIR RICHARD VERNON.]
  HOT. My cousin Vernon! Welcome, by my soul.
  VER. Pray God my news be worth a welcome, lord.
The Earl of Westmoreland, seven thousand strong,
Is marching hitherward; with him Prince John.
  HOT. No harm. What more?
  VER.   And further, I have learned,   90
The King himself in person is set forth,
Or hitherward intended speedily,
With strong and mighty preparation.
  HOT. He shall be welcome too. Where is his son,
The nimble-footed madcap Prince of Wales,   95
And his comrades, that daffed° the world aside
And bid it pass?°
  VER.   All furnished,° all in arms;
All plumed like estridges that with the wind
Bated like eagles having lately bathed;°
Glittering in golden coats, like images;°   100
As full of spirit as the month of May,
And gorgeous as the sun at midsummer;
Wanton° as youthful goats, wild as young bulls.
I saw young Harry, with his beaver° on,
His cuisses° on his thighs, gallantly armed,   105
Rise from the ground like feathered Mercury,°
And vaulted with such ease into his seat
As if an angel dropped down from the clouds
To turn and wind a fiery Pegasus,°   109
And witch° the world with noble horsemanship.
  HOT. No more, no more. Worse than the sun in
    March,
This praise doth nourish agues. Let them come.
They come like sacrifices in their trim,°
And to the fire-eyed maid of smoky war
All hot and bleeding will we offer them.   115
The mailèd Mars° shall on his altar sit
Up to the ears in blood. I am on fire
To hear this rich reprisal° is so nigh
And yet not ours. Come, let me taste my horse,
Who is to bear me like a thunderbolt   120
Against the bosom of the Prince of Wales.
Harry to Harry shall, hot horse to horse,

Meet and ne'er part till one drop down a corse.
Oh that Glendower were come!
  VER.   There is more news.
I learned in Worcester, as I rode along,   125
He cannot draw his power this fourteen days.
  DOUG. That's the worst tidings that I hear of yet.
  WOR. Aye, by my faith, that bears a frosty sound.
  HOT. What may the King's whole battle° reach
    unto?
  VER. To thirty thousand.
  HOT.   Forty let it be.   130
My father and Glendower being both away,
The powers of us may serve so great a day.
Come, let us take a muster speedily.
Doomsday is near. Die all, die merrily.
  DOUG. Talk not of dying. I am out of° fear   135
Of death or death's hand for this one half-year.
                                       [*Exeunt.*]

SCENE II. *A public road near Coventry.*

        [*Enter* FALSTAFF *and* BARDOLPH.]
  FAL. Bardolph, get thee before to Coventry, fill me
a bottle of sack. Our soldiers shall march through,
we'll to Sutton Co'fil'° tonight.
  BARD. Will you give me money, Captain?
  FAL. Lay out,° lay out.   5
  BARD. This bottle makes an angel.°
  FAL. An if it do, take it for thy labor. And if it
make twenty, take them all, I'll answer the coinage.°
Bid my Lieutenant Peto meet me at town's end.   10
  BARD. I will, Captain. Farewell.   [*Exit.*]
  FAL. If I be not ashamed of my soldiers,° I am a
soused gurnet.° I have misused the King's press°
damnably. I have got, in exchange of a hundred and
fifty soldiers, three hundred and odd pounds. I   15
press me none but good householders, yeomen's°
sons; inquire me out contracted bachelors,° such as
had been asked twice on the banns; such a commod-
ity° of warm slaves as had as lieve° hear the Devil as
a drum; such as fear the report of a caliver°   20
worse than a struck fowl or a hurt wild duck. I
pressed me none but such toasts-and-butter, with

129. **battle:** main army.   135. **out of:** free from.
  Sc. ii: 3. Sutton Co'fil': Sutton Coldfield, a town in Warwickshire.   5. **Lay out:** pay for it.   6. **makes an angel:** comes
to an angel (10s) which you owe me.   7–9. **take . . . coinage:**
Falstaff deliberately misunderstands Bardolph's "make" — "if
the bottle will make angels, I'll guarantee the coins."   12. **If . . .
soldiers:** Falstaff (see following to l. 52) was typical of many
dishonest captains in the 1590's. His methods of levying recruits (and releasing the best men for bribes) are further shown in
II Hen IV, III.ii.   13. **soused gurnet** (sea
fish with a large head). **King's press:** the right to conscript
soldiers granted by the King's commission.   16. **yeomen:** wealthy
farmers.   17. **contracted bachelors:** bachelors engaged to be
married in a short time.   19. **commodity:** parcel. **lieve:** soon.
20. **caliver:** lighter form of musket or harquebus, used by the
infantry.

96. **daffed:** waved.   97. **bid it pass:** cried "let the world pass";
i.e., "who cares a damn?" **furnished:** in full armor.   97–99. **All
. . . bathed:** These lines are much annotated. As they stand they
mean: "All wearing plumes like ostriches that flap their wings
(*bate*) in the wind like eagles that have lately bathed." But the
comparison seems hardly apt. Either a line has been omitted
after *wind*, or *with* is a misprint of some such verb as
"wing."   100. **images:** i.e., of the saints in a Catholic church
103. **Wanton:** lusty.   104. **beaver:** hinged visor of the helmet.
105. **cuisses:** thigh pieces.   106. **feathered Mercury:** Mercury,
the messenger of the gods, wore winged sandals.   109. **Pegasus:**
Perseus's winged horse.   110. **witch:** bewitch.   113. **in . . . trim:**
dressed up.   116. **mailed Mars:** the god of war in his armor.
118. **reprisal:** prize.

hearts in their bellies no bigger than pins' heads, and they have bought out their services. And now my whole charge consists of ancients, corporals, 25 lieutenants, gentlemen of companies,° slaves as ragged as Lazarus in the painted cloth° where the glutton's dogs licked his sores; and such as indeed were never soldiers, but discarded unjust serv- 30 ingmen,° younger sons to younger brothers,° revolted tapsters, and ostlers trade-fallen;° the cankers of a calm world and a long peace, ten times more dishonorable ragged than an old-faced ancient. And such have I to fill up the rooms of them that 35 have bought out their services that you would think that I had a hundred and fifty tattered prodigals lately come from swine-keeping, from eating draff and husks.° A mad fellow° met me on the way and told me I had unloaded all the gibbets° and 40 pressed the dead bodies. No eye hath seen such scarecrows. I'll not march through Coventry with them, that's flat. Nay, and the villains march wide betwixt the legs, as if they had gyves° on, for indeed I had the most of them out of prison. There's but a shirt and a half in all my company; and the half- 46 shirt is two napkins tacked together and thrown over the shoulders like a herald's coat° without sleeves; and the shirt, to say the truth, stolen from my host at St. Alban's, or the red-nose innkeeper of Daven- 50 try. But that's all one. They'll find linen enough on every hedge.°

[*Enter the* PRINCE *and* WESTMORELAND.]

PRINCE. How now, blown° Jack! How now, quilt! 54

FAL. What, Hal! How now, mad wag! What a devil dost thou in Warwickshire? My good Lord of Westmoreland, I cry you mercy. I thought your honor had already been at Shrewsbury. 59

WEST. Faith, Sir John, 'tis more than time that I were there, and you too; but my powers are there already. The King, I can tell you, looks for us all. We must away all night.

FAL. Tut, never fear me. I am as vigilant as a cat to steal cream. 65

25–26. **charge . . . companies:** Falstaff has picked up a selection of veterans of various ranks. **ancients:** ensigns, second lieutenants. **gentlemen of companies:** gentlemen of good family who served in the ranks of the companies of noblemen. 27. **Lazarus . . . cloth:** In taverns and less wealthy houses painted cloths showing scenes from Scripture and classical legend were hung on the walls instead of the more costly imported tapestry. 31. **servingmen:** upper-class servants from some great household. **younger . . . brothers:** young gentlemen who had no hope of an allowance or a legacy. 39. **draff . . . husks:** offal and husks, like the Prodigal Son in the parable who "would fain have filled his belly with the husks that the swine did eat" (Luke, 15:11–32). **mad fellow:** wit. 40. **unloaded . . . gibbets:** The bodies of executed felons were often hung up in iron cages near the scene of the crime until they rotted. 44. **gyves:** fetters on the legs. 48. **herald's coat:** a sleeveless coat embroidered with the royal coat of arms. 51–52. **linen . . . hedge:** The washing was laid on the hedges to dry and air. See *W Tale,* IV.iii.23–24. 53. **blown:** inflated.

PRINCE. I think to steal cream indeed, for thy theft hath already made thee butter. But tell me, Jack, whose fellows are these that come after?

FAL. Mine, Hal, mine.

PRINCE. I did never see such pitiful rascals. 70

FAL. Tut, tut, good enough to toss,° food for powder, food for powder. They'll fill a pit as well as better. Tush, man, mortal men, mortal men.

WEST. Aye, but, Sir John, methinks they are exceeding poor and bare, too beggarly. 75

FAL. Faith, for their poverty, I know not where they had that; and for their bareness, I am sure they never learned that of me.

PRINCE. No, I'll be sworn, unless you call three fingers° on the ribs bare. But, sirrah, make haste. Percy is already in the field. 81

FAL. What, is the King encamped?

WEST. He is, Sir John. I fear we shall stay too long.

FAL. Well,
To the latter end of a fray and the beginning of a
    feast 85
Fits a dull fighter and a keen guest.   [*Exeunt.*]

SCENE III. *The rebel camp near Shrewsbury.*

[*Enter* HOTSPUR, WORCESTER, DOUGLAS, *and* VERNON.]

HOT. We'll fight with him tonight.

WOR.   It may not be.

DOUG. You give him then advantage.

VER.   Not a whit.

HOT. Why say you so? Looks he not for supply?°

VER. So do we.

HOT.   His is certain, ours is doubtful.

WOR. Good Cousin, be advised, stir not tonight. 5

VER. Do not, my lord.

DOUG.   You do not counsel well.
You speak it out of fear and cold heart.

VER. Do me no slander, Douglas. By my life,
And I dare well maintain it with my life,
If well-respected° honor bid me on, 10
I hold as little counsel with weak fear
As you, my lord, or any Scot that this day lives.
Let it be seen tomorrow in the battle
Which of us fears.

DOUG.   Yea, or tonight.

VER.   Content.

HOT. Tonight, say I. 15

VER. Come, come, it may not be. I wonder much,
Being men of such great leading° as you are,
That you foresee not what impediments
Drag back our expedition.° Certain horse°
Of my cousin Vernon's are not yet come up. 20

---

71. **good . . . toss:** i.e., on pikes; "good enough for cannon fodder." 79–80. **three fingers:** i.e., three fingers' thickness of fat.

    Sc. iii: 3. **supply:** reinforcements. 10. **well-respected:** well-considered (not foolhardy). 17. **leading:** experience in leadership. 19. **expedition:** haste. **horse:** cavalry.

Your uncle Worcester's horse came but today,
And now their pride and mettle° is asleep,
Their courage with hard labor tame and dull,
That not a horse is half the half of himself.

HOT. So are the horses of the enemy   25
In general, journey-bated° and brought low.
The better part of ours are full of rest.

WOR. The number of the King exceedeth ours.
For God's sake, Cousin, stay till all come in.

          [*The trumpet sounds a parley.*]
       [*Enter* SIR WALTER BLUNT.]

BLUNT. I come with gracious offers from the King,
If you vouchsafe me hearing and respect.   31

HOT. Welcome, Sir Walter Blunt, and would to
    God
You were of our determination!°
Some of us love you well, and even those some
Envy your great deservings and good name   35
Because you are not of our quality,°
But stand against us like an enemy.

BLUNT. And God defend° but still I should stand
    so
So long as out of limit and true rule
You stand against anointed Majesty.   40
But to my charge.° The King hath sent to know
The nature of your griefs, and whereupon
You conjure from the breast of civil peace
Such bold hostility, teaching his duteous land
Audacious cruelty. If that the King   45
Have any way your good deserts forgot,
Which he confesseth to be manifold,
He bids you name your griefs, and with all speed
You shall have your desires with interest,
And pardon absolute for yourself and these   50
Herein misled by your suggestion.°

HOT. The King is kind, and well we know the
    King
Knows at what time to promise, when to pay.
My father and my uncle and myself
Did give him that same royalty he wears.   55
And when he was not six and twenty strong,
Sick in the world's regard,° wretched and low,
A poor unminded outlaw sneaking home,
My father gave him welcome to the shore.
And when he heard him swear and vow to God   60
He came but to be Duke of Lancaster,
To sue his livery° and beg his peace
With tears of innocency and terms of zeal,°
My father, in kind heart and pity moved,
Swore him assistance, and performed it too.   65
Now when the lords and barons of the realm

Perceived Northumberland did lean to him,
The more and less came in with cap and knee —
Met him in boroughs, cities, villages,
Attended him on bridges, stood in lanes,   70
Laid gifts before him, proffered him their oaths,
Gave him their heirs as pages, followed him
Even at the heels in golden° multitudes.
He presently, as greatness knows itself,
Steps me a little higher than his vow   75
Made to my father while his blood was poor,
Upon the naked shore at Ravenspurgh;
And now, forsooth, takes on him to reform
Some certain edicts and some strait° decrees
That lie too heavy on the commonwealth,   80
Cries out upon abuses, seems to weep
Over his country's wrongs. And by this face,
This seeming brow of justice, did he win
The hearts of all that he did angle for —
Proceeded further, cut me off the heads   85
Of all the favorites that the absent King
In deputation° left behind him here
When he was personal° in the Irish war.

BLUNT. Tut, I came not to hear this.

HOT.   Then to the point.
In short time after, he deposed the King,   90
Soon after that, deprived him of his life.
And in the neck° of that, tasked° the whole state.
To make that worse, suffered his kinsman March,
Who is, if every owner were well placed,
Indeed his king, to be engaged° in Wales,   95
There without ransom to lie forfeited;
Disgraced me in my happy victories,
Sought to entrap me by intelligence;°
Rated° mine uncle from the Council board,
In rage dismissed my father from the Court;   100
Broke oath on oath, committed wrong on wrong;
And in conclusion drove us to seek out
This head of safety,° and withal to pry
Into his title, the which we find
Too indirect° for long continuance.   105

BLUNT. Shall I return this answer to the King?

HOT. Not so, Sir Walter. We'll withdraw a
    while.
Go to the King, and let there be impawned°
Some surety for a safe return again,
And in the morning early shall mine uncle   110
Bring him our purposes. And so farewell.

BLUNT. I would you would accept of grace and
    love.

HOT. And maybe so we shall.

BLUNT.   Pray God you do. [*Exeunt.*]

---

22. mettle: ardor.   26. journey-bated: tired by the journey.
33. determination: mind.   36. quality: fellowship, party.   38. defend: forbid.   41. my charge: what I have been instructed
(*charged*) to say.   51. suggestion: temptation.   57. Sick . . .
regard: poorly regarded by the world.   62. sue . . . livery: claim
his inheritance. See *Rich II*, II.i.203; II.iii.129.   63. terms of
zeal: protestations of loyalty.

73. golden: wearing their richest clothes.   79. strait: strict.
87. In deputation: as his deputies.   88. was personal: went in
person.   92. in . . . neck: on top of. tasked: taxed.   95. engaged:
held as pledge, hostage.   98. intelligence: spies.   99. Rated:
dismissed with abuse.   103. head of safety: armed force to keep
us safe.   105. indirect: not in the straight line of descent
108. impawned: kept as hostage.

SCENE IV. *York. The* ARCHBISHOP'S *palace.*

[*Enter the* ARCHBISHOP OF YORK *and* SIR MICHAEL.°]

ARCH. Hie, good Sir Michael, bear this sealèd
    brief°
With wingèd haste to the Lord Marshal,
This to my cousin Scroop, and all the rest
To whom they are directed. If you knew   4
How much they do import, you would make haste.
    SIR M. My good lord,
I guess their tenor.°
    ARCH.   Like enough you do.
Tomorrow, good Sir Michael, is a day
Wherein the fortune of ten thousand men
Must bide the touch;° for, sir, at Shrewsbury,   10
As I am truly given to understand,
The King with mighty and quick-raisèd power
Meets with Lord Harry. And I fear, Sir Michael —
What with the sickness of Northumberland,
Whose power was in the first proportion,°   15
And what with Owen Glendower's absence thence,
Who with them was a rated sinew° too
And comes not in, o'er-ruled by prophecies —
I fear the power of Percy is too weak
To wage an instant° trial with the King.   20
    SIR M. Why, my good lord, you need not fear.
There is Douglas and Lord Mortimer.
    ARCH. No, Mortimer is not there.
    SIR M. But there is Mordake, Vernon, Lord Harry
    Percy,
And there is my Lord of Worcester and a head   25
Of gallant warriors, noble gentlemen.
    ARCH. And so there is. But yet the King hath
    drawn
The special head° of all the land together —
The Prince of Wales, Lord John of Lancaster,
The noble Westmoreland and warlike Blunt,   30
And many mo° corrivals° and dear men
Of estimation° and command in arms.
    SIR M. Doubt not, my lord, they shall be well op-
    posed.
    ARCH. I hope no less, yet needful 'tis to fear,
And, to prevent° the worst, Sir Michael, speed.   35
For if Lord Percy thrive not ere the King
Dismiss his power, he means to visit us,°
For he hath heard of our confederacy,°
And 'tis but wisdom to make strong against him.
Therefore make haste. I must go write again   40
To other friends. And so farewell, Sir Michael.
                      [*Exeunt.*]

Act V

SCENE I. *The* KING'S *camp near Shrewsbury.*

[*Enter the* KING, PRINCE OF WALES, LORD JOHN OF
    LANCASTER, SIR WALTER BLUNT, *and* FALSTAFF.°]

KING. How bloodily the sun begins to peer
Above yon busky° hill! The day looks pale
At his distemperature.°
    PRINCE.   The southern wind
Doth play the trumpet° to his purposes,
And by his hollow whistling in the leaves   5
Foretells a tempest and a blustering day.
    KING. Then with the losers let it sympathize,
For nothing can seem foul to those that win.
    [*The trumpet sounds. Enter* WORCESTER
             and VERNON.]
How now, my Lord of Worcester! 'Tis not well
That you and I should meet upon such terms   10
As now we meet. You have deceived our trust,
And made us doff our easy robes of peace
To crush our old'limbs in ungentle steel.
This is not well, my lord, this is not well.
What say you to it? Will you again unknit   15
This churlish knot° of all-abhorrèd war?
And move in that obedient orb° again
Where you did give a fair and natural light,
And be no more an exhaled meteor,°
A prodigy of fear,° and a portent   20
Of broachèd° mischief to the unborn times?
    WOR. Hear me, my liege.
For mine own part, I could be well content
To entertain the lag end of my life
With quiet hours, for I do protest   25
I have not sought the day of this dislike.
    KING. You have not sought it! How comes it,
    then?
    FAL. Rebellion lay in his way, and he found it.
    PRINCE. Peace, chewet,° peace!
    WOR. It pleased your Majesty to turn your looks
Of favor from myself and all our house.   31
And yet I must remember° you, my lord,
We were the first and dearest of your friends.
For you my staff of office° did I break
In Richard's time, and posted° day and night   35
To meet you on the way, and kiss your hand,
When yet you were in place and in account

Sc. iv: s.d., Sir Michael: He has not been identified, presumably a priest or knight in the Archbishop's service. 1. brief:
letter. 7. tenor: import. 10. bide . . . touch: be put to the
test. 15. in . . . proportion: the largest part. 17. rated sinew:
strength highly valued. 20. instant: immediate. 28. special
head: crack troops, "shock troops." 31. mo: more. corrivals:
supporters. 31–32. dear . . . estimation: men highly regarded.
35. prevent: forestall. 37. visit us: come our way. 38. confederacy: conspiracy.

Act V, Sc. i: s.d., Falstaff: It is worth noting that Shakespeare
places Falstaff in immediate attendance on the King. 2. busky:
bushy. 3. distemperature: sickness. 4. play . . . trumpet: like
the trumpeter blowing an introductory flourish. 16. churlish
knot: knot which unites men for a brutal purpose. 17. obedient
orb: sphere of obedience, like a planet taking its natural course.
19. meteor: Meteors were believed to be made of vapors drawn
up by the sun. 20. prodigy of fear: a fearful sign of disaster.
21. broached: set loose; lit., tapped (like a cask). 29. chewet:
jackdaw. 32. remember: remind. 34. staff of office: See *Rich
II*, II.iii.26–28. 35. posted: rode hastily.

Nothing so strong and fortunate as I.
It was myself, my brother, and his son
That brought you home, and boldly did outdare   40
The dangers of the time. You swore to us,
And you did swear that oath at Doncaster,
That you did nothing purpose 'gainst the state,
Nor claim no further than your new-fall'n right,°
The seat of Gaunt, Dukedom of Lancaster.   45
To this we swore our aid. But in short space
It rained down fortune showering on your head;
And such a flood of greatness fell on you,
What with our help, what with the absent King,
What with the injuries of a wanton° time,   50
The seeming sufferances° that you had borne,
And the contrarious winds that held the King
So long in his unlucky Irish wars
That all in England did repute him dead.
And from this swarm of fair advantages   55
You took occasion to be quickly wooed
To gripe° the general sway° into your hand;
Forgot your oath to us at Doncaster;
And being fed by us you used us so
As that ungentle gull,° the cuckoo's bird,°   60
Useth the sparrow — did oppress our nest;
Grew by our feeding to so great a bulk
That even our love durst not come near your sight
For fear of swallowing, but with nimble wing
We were enforced, for safety sake, to fly   65
Out of your sight and raise this present head.
Whereby we stand opposèd by such means
As you yourself have forged against yourself,
By unkind usage, dangerous countenance,°
And violation of all faith and troth°   70
Sworn to us in your younger enterprise.
    KING. These things indeed you have articulate,°
Proclaimed at market crosses, read in churches,
To face° the garment of rebellion
With some fine color that may please the eye   75
Of fickle changelings° and poor discontents,
Which gape and rub the elbow at the news
Of hurly-burly innovation.°
And never yet did insurrection want
Such water colors to impaint his cause,   80
Nor moody beggars, starving for a time
Of pell-mell havoc° and confusion.
    PRINCE. In both your armies there is many a soul
Shall pay full dearly for this encounter
If once they join in trial. Tell your nephew,   85
The Prince of Wales doth join with all the world
In praise of Henry Percy. By my hopes,

This present enterprise set off his head,°
I do not think a braver gentleman,
More active-valiant or more valiant-young,   90
More daring or more bold, is now alive
To grace this latter age with noble deeds.
For my part, I may speak it to my shame,
I have a truant been to chivalry,°
And so I hear he doth account me too.   95
Yet this before my father's majesty —
I am content that he shall take the odds°
Of his great name and estimation,
And will, to save the blood on either side,
Try fortune with him in a single fight.   100
    KING. And, Prince of Wales, so dare we venture
        thee,
Albeit considerations infinite
Do make against it. No, good Worcester, no,
We love our people well, even those we love
That are misled upon your cousin's part.   105
And, will they take the offer of our grace,
Both he and they and you — yea, every man —
Shall be my friend again and I'll be his.
So tell your cousin, and bring me word
What he will do. But if he will not yield,   110
Rebuke and dread correction wait on us°
And they shall do their office. So, be gone.
We will not now be troubled with reply.
We offer fair, take it advisedly.
        [Exeunt WORCESTER and VERNON.]
    PRINCE. It will not be accepted, on my life.   115
The Douglas and the Hotspur both together
Are confident against the world in arms.
    KING. Hence, therefore, every leader to his
        charge,°
For on their answer will we set on them.
And God befriend us as our cause is just!   120
[Exeunt all but the PRINCE OF WALES and FALSTAFF.]
    FAL. Hal, if thou see me down in the battle, and
bestride me so, 'tis a point of friendship.
    PRINCE. Nothing but a colossus° can do thee that
friendship. Say thy prayers, and farewell.   124
    FAL. I would 'twere bedtime, Hal, and all well.
    PRINCE. Why, thou owest God a death.   [Exit.]
    FAL. 'Tis not due yet, I would be loath to pay Him
before his day. What need I be so forward with him
that calls not on me? Well, 'tis no matter.   130
Honor pricks me on.° Yea, but how if honor prick
me off° when I come on? How then? Can honor set
to° a leg? No. Or an arm? No. Or take away the
grief of a wound? No. Honor hath no skill in surgery, then? No. What is honor? A word. What   135
is in that word honor? What is that honor? Air. A

44. new-fall'n right: inheritance which had recently come.
50. wanton: wild.   51. sufferances: injuries.   57. gripe: grip.
general sway: rule of the whole state.   60. gull: nestling.
cuckoo's bird: The cuckoo lays its eggs in the nest of another bird.
69. dangerous countenance: threatening looks.   70. troth:
truth.   72. articulate: drawn up in schedules.   74. face: trim.
76. changelings: turncoats.   78. hurly-burly innovation: confusion and revolution.   82. havoc: slaughter.

88. set . . . head: being excepted.   94. chivalry: knightly deeds.
97. take . . . odds: have the advantage.   111. wait on us: are
our servants.   118. charge: command.   123. colossus: See
Caesar, I.ii.135–38.   131. Honor . . . on: honor spurs me forward
to heroism.   131–32. prick me off: mark me down on the casualty list.   132–33. set to: mend.

trim° reckoning! Who hath it? He that died o' Wednesday. Doth he feel it? No. Doth he hear it? No.
'Tis insensible, then? Yea, to the dead. But will   140
it not live with the living? No. Why? Detraction°
will not suffer it. Therefore I'll none of it. Honor is
a mere scutcheon.° And so ends my catechism.

                                        [*Exit.*]

SCENE II. *The rebel camp.*

[*Enter* WORCESTER *and* VERNON.]

WOR. Oh, no, my nephew must not know, Sir
  Richard,
The liberal and kind offer of the King.
VER. 'Twere best he did.
WOR.   Then are we all undone.
It is not possible, it cannot be
The King should keep his word in loving us.   5
He will suspect us still, and find a time
To punish this offense in other faults.
Suspicion all our lives shall be stuck full of eyes;
For treason is but trusted like the fox,
Who, ne'er so tame, so cherished and locked up, 10
Will have a wild trick° of his ancestors.
Look how we can, or° sad or merrily,
Interpretation will misquote° our looks,
And we shall feed like oxen at a stall,
The better cherished, still the nearer death.   15
My nephew's trespass may be well forgot.
It hath the excuse of youth and heat of blood,
And an adopted name of privilege,°
A harebrained Hotspur, governed by a spleen.°
All his offenses live upon my head   20
And on his father's. We did train° him on,
And, his corruption being ta'en from us,
We, as the spring of all, shall pay for all.
Therefore, good Cousin, let not Harry know,
In any case, the offer of the King.   25
VER. Deliver° what you will, I'll say 'tis so.
Here comes your cousin.

[*Enter* HOTSPUR *and* DOUGLAS.]

HOT. My uncle is returned.
Deliver up° my Lord of Westmoreland.
Uncle, what news?   30
WOR. The King will bid you battle presently.°
DOUG. Defy him by the Lord of Westmoreland.
HOT. Lord Douglas, go you and tell him so.
DOUG. Marry, and shall, and very willingly.

                                        [*Exit.*]

WOR. There is no seeming mercy in the King.   35
HOT. Did you beg any? God forbid!
WOR. I told him gently of our grievances,
Of his oath-breaking, which he mended thus,
By now forswearing° that he is forsworn.
He calls us rebels, traitors, and will scourge 40
With haughty arms this hateful name in us.

[*Re-enter* DOUGLAS.]

DOUG. Arm, gentlemen, to arms! For I have
  thrown
A brave defiance in King Henry's teeth —
And Westmoreland, that was engaged,° did bear
  it —
Which cannot choose but bring him quickly on. 45
WOR. The Prince of Wales stepped forth before
  the King
And, Nephew, challenged you to single fight.
HOT. Oh, would the quarrel lay upon our heads,
And that no man might draw short breath° today
But I and Harry Monmouth! Tell me, tell me,   50
How showed his tasking?° Seem'd it in contempt?
VER. No, by my soul. I never in my life
Did hear a challenge urged° more modestly,
Unless a brother should a brother dare
To gentle exercise and proof of arms.   55
He gave you all the duties of° a man,
Trimmed up your praises with a princely tongue,
Spoke your deservings like a chronicle,
Making you ever better than his praise
By still dispraising praise valued with you.°   60
And, which became him like a prince indeed,
He made a blushing cital° of himself,
And chid his truant youth with such a grace
As if he mastered there a double spirit
Of teaching and of learning instantly.   65
There did he pause. But let me tell the world,
If he outlive the envy° of this day,
England did never owe° so sweet a hope,
So much misconstrued in his wantonness.
HOT. Cousin, I think thou art enamored   70
On his follies. Never did I hear
Of any prince so wild a libertine.
But be he as he will, yet once ere night
I will embrace him with a soldier's arm,
That he shall shrink under my courtesy.   75
Arm, arm with speed. And, fellows, soldiers, friends,
Better consider what you have to do
Than I, that have not well the gift of tongue,
Can lift your blood up with persuasion.

[*Enter a* MESSENGER.]

MESS. My lord, here are letters for you.   80
HOT. I cannot read them now.
O gentlemen, the time of life is short!

---

137. trim: neat. **141. Detraction:** slander. **143. scutcheon:** coat
of arms, painted on boards or cloth, carried in the funeral of a
gentleman and afterward hung up in the church.
  Sc. ii: 11. wild trick: wild habits. **12. or:** either. **13. Interpretation ... misquote:** men will deliberately misinterpret.
18. adopted ... privilege: his nickname Hotspur will be his
excuse. **19. spleen:** impetuosity. **21. train:** lure. **26. Deliver:**
report. **29. Deliver up:** release. Westmoreland had been hostage
for Worcester's safe return. **31. presently:** immediately.

39. forswearing: falsely denying an oath. **44. engaged:** pledged
as hostage. **49. draw ... breath:** i.e., in fighting. **51. tasking:**
challenge. **53. urged:** put forward. **56. duties of:** respect due to.
60. By ... you: by continuously saying that your praise was
undervalued. **62. cital:** recital. **68. envy:** malice. **69. owe:** own.

To spend that shortness basely were too long
If life did ride upon a dial's point,°
Still° ending at the arrival of an hour.   85
An if we live, we live to tread on kings;
If die, brave death when princes die with us!
Now, for our consciences, the arms are fair
When the intent° of bearing them is just.
      [*Enter another* MESSENGER.]
  MESS. My lord, prepare. The King comes on
    apace.   90
  HOT. I thank him, that he cuts me from my tale,
For I profess not talking, only this —
Let each man do his best. And here draw I
A sword whose temper° I intend to stain
With the best blood that I can meet withal   95
In the adventure of this perilous day.
Now, Esperance! Percy! and set on.
Sound all the lofty instruments of war,
And by that music let us all embrace;
For, heaven to earth, some of us never shall   100
A second time do such a courtesy.
    [*The trumpets sound. They embrace, and exeunt.*]

SCENE III. *Plain between the camps.*

[*The* KING *enters with his power. Alarum to the bat-
tle.*° *Then enter* DOUGLAS *and* SIR WALTER BLUNT.]
  BLUNT. What is thy name, that in the battle thus
Thou crossest me? What honor dost thou seek
Upon my head?
  DOUG.   Know then, my name is Douglas,
And I do haunt thee in the battle thus
Because some tell me that thou art a King.   5
  BLUNT. They tell thee true.
  DOUG. The Lord of Stafford dear today hath
    bought
Thy likeness; for instead of thee, King Harry,°
This sword hath ended him. So shall it thee
Unless thou yield thee as my prisoner.   10
  BLUNT. I was not born a yielder, thou proud Scot,
And thou shalt find a King that will revenge
Lord Stafford's death.
  [*They fight.* DOUGLAS *kills* BLUNT. *Enter* HOTSPUR.]
  HOT. O Douglas, hadst thou fought at Holmedon
    thus,   15
I never had triumphed upon a Scot.
  DOUG. All's done, all's won. Here breathless lies
    the King.
  HOT. Where?
  DOUG. Here.
  HOT. This, Douglas? No. I know this face full
    well.

---

84. **dial's point:** hand of a clock. 85. **Still:** always. 89. **intent:** cause. 94. **temper:** lit., hardness, quality.

Sc. iii: **s.d.,** Alarum . . . battle: battle noises. 8. **thee . . . Harry:** Blunt is wearing the King's coat of arms and not his own, and so is mistaken by Douglas for the King.

A gallant knight he was, his name was Blunt,   20
Semblably furnished° like the King himself.
  DOUG. A fool go with thy soul° whither it goes!
A borrowed title hast thou bought too dear.
Why didst thou tell me that thou wert a king?   24
  HOT. The King hath many marching in his coats.°
  DOUG. Now, by my sword, I will kill all his coats.
I'll murder all his wardrobe, piece by piece,
Until I meet the King.
  HOT.   Up, and away!   28
Our soldiers stand full fairly for the day.° [*Exeunt.*]
    [*Alarum. Enter* FALSTAFF, *alone.*]
  FAL. Though I could 'scape shot-free° at London,
I fear the shot here. Here's no scoring but upon the
pate. Soft! Who are you? Sir Walter Blunt. There's
honor for you! Here's no vanity!° I am as hot as
molten lead, and as heavy too. God keep lead out of
me! I need no more weight than mine own   35
bowels. I have led my ragamuffins where they are
peppered.° There's not three of my hundred and
fifty left alive, and they are for the town's end, to beg
during life. But who comes here?   40
    [*Enter the* PRINCE.]
  PRINCE. What, stand'st thou idle here? Lend me
    thy sword.
Many a nobleman lies stark and stiff
Under the hoofs of vaunting enemies
Whose deaths are yet unrevenged. I prithee lend me
    thy sword.   44
  FAL. O Hal, I prithee give me leave to breathe a
while. Turk Gregory° never did such deeds in arms
as I have done this day. I have paid Percy, I have
made him sure.
  PRINCE. He is, indeed, and living to kill thee. I
prithee lend me thy sword.   50
  FAL. Nay, before God, Hal, if Percy be alive, thou
get'st not my sword. But take my pistol, if thou wilt.
  PRINCE. Give it me. What, is it in the case?
  FAL. Aye, Hal, 'tis hot, 'tis hot. There's that will
sack a city.   56
    [*The* PRINCE *draws it out, and finds it
    to be a bottle of sack.*]
  PRINCE. What, is it a time to jest and dally now?
    [*He throws the bottle at him. Exit.*]
  FAL. Well, if Percy be alive, I'll pierce° him. If he
do come in my way, so. If he do not, if I come in   60
his willingly, let him make a carbonado° of me. I

---

21. **Semblably furnished:** wearing similar armor. 22. **A . . . soul:** a proverbial phrase, "you foolish soul." 25. **coats:** coats of arms. 29. **full . . . day:** i.e., are full of fight. 30. **shot-free:** without paying the *shot* (the tavern bill) which had been scored up against him. 33. **no vanity:** spoken ironically. "Who said honor was not a vain thing?" 36–37. **where . . . peppered:** Falstaff's heroism has a base motive. Until the army is remustered he will pocket the pay of his dead soldiers. 46. **Turk Gregory:** Pope Gregory VII, who had a reputation for ferocity. The Turk was proverbial for cruelty. 59. **pierce:** pronounced "perse," a pun on "Percy." 61. **carbonado:** piece of meat slashed for broiling.

like not such grinning honor as Sir Walter hath.
Give me life, which if I can save, so; if not, honor
comes unlooked-for, and there's an end.   [*Exit.*]

SCENE IV. *Another part of the field.*

[*Alarum. Excursions.*° *Enter the* KING, *the* PRINCE,
LORD JOHN OF LANCASTER, *and*
EARL OF WESTMORELAND.]

KING. I prithee
Harry, withdraw thyself, thou bleed'st too much.
Lord John of Lancaster, go you with him.
LANC. Not I, my lord, unless I did bleed too.
PRINCE. I beseech your Majesty, make up,°   5
Lest your retirement do amaze° your friends.
KING. I will do so.
My Lord of Westmoreland, lead him to his tent.
WEST. Come, my lord, I'll lead you to your tent.
PRINCE. Lead me, my lord? I do not need your
help.   10
And God forbid a shallow scratch should drive
The Prince of Wales from such a field as this,
Where stained° nobility lies trodden on
And rebels' arms triumph in massacres!
LANC. We breathe° too long. Come, Cousin West-
moreland,   15
Our duty this way lies. For God's sake, come.
        [*Exeunt* PRINCE JOHN *and* WESTMORELAND.]
PRINCE. By God, thou hast deceived me, Lan-
caster,
I did not think thee lord of such a spirit.
Before, I loved thee as a brother, John,
But now I do respect thee as my soul.   20
KING. I saw him hold Lord Percy at the point
With lustier maintenance than I did look for
Of such an ungrown warrior.
PRINCE.   Oh, this boy
Lends mettle° to us all!   [*Exit.*]
        [*Enter* DOUGLAS.]
DOUG. Another King! They grow like Hydra's
heads.°   25
I am the Douglas, fatal to all those
That wear those colors on them. What art thou,
That counterfeit'st the person of a king?
KING. The King himself, who, Douglas, grieves at
heart
So many of his shadows° thou hast met   30
And not the very King. I have two boys
Seek Percy and thyself about the field.
But, seeing thou fall'st on me so luckily,

I will assay° thee. So defend thyself.
DOUG. I fear thou art another counterfeit,   35
And yet, in faith, thou bear'st thee like a king.
But mine I am sure thou art, whoe'er thou be,
And thus I win thee.
[*They fight; the* KING *being in danger, re-enter*
PRINCE OF WALES.]
PRINCE. Hold up thy head, vile Scot, or thou art
like
Never to hold it up again! The spirits   40
Of valiant Shirley, Stafford, Blunt,° are in my arms.
It is the Prince of Wales that threatens thee,
Who never promiseth but he means to pay.
              [*They fight:* DOUGLAS *flies.*]
Cheerly, my lord. How fares your Grace?
Sir Nicholas Gawsey hath for succor sent,   45
And so hath Clifton. I'll to Clifton straight.
KING. Stay, and breathe a while.
Thou hast redeemed thy lost opinion,°
And showed thou makest some tender° of my life,
In this fair rescue thou hast brought to me.   50
PRINCE. Oh God! They did me too much injury
That ever said I hearkened for° your death.
If it were so, I might have let alone
The insulting° hand of Douglas over you,
Which would have been as speedy in your end   55
As all the poisonous potions in the world,
And saved the treacherous labor of your son.
KING. Make up to Clifton. I'll to Sir Nicholas
Gawsey.   [*Exit.*]
        [*Enter* HOTSPUR.]
HOT. If I mistake not, thou art Harry Monmouth.
PRINCE. Thou speak'st as if I would deny my
name.   60
HOT. My name is Harry Percy.
PRINCE.   Why, then I see
A very valiant rebel of the name.
I am the Prince of Wales. And think not, Percy,
To share with me in glory any more.
Two stars keep not their motion in one sphere,   65
Nor can one England brook a double reign
Of Harry Percy and the Prince of Wales.
HOT. Nor shall it, Harry, for the hour is come
To end the one of us. And would to God
Thy name in arms were now as great as mine!   70
PRINCE. I'll make it greater ere I part from thee,
And all the budding honors on thy crest
I'll crop, to make a garland for my head.
HOT. I can no longer brook thy vanities.
                              [*They fight.*]
        [*Enter* FALSTAFF.]
FAL. Well said, Hal! To it, Hal! Nay, you shall
find no boy's play here, I can tell you.   76

Sc. iv: s.d., **Excursions:** noises to indicate rapid movements
in battle.   **5. make up:** go up to the front line.   **6. amaze:** fill
with dismay.   **13. stained:** bloodstained.   **15. breathe:** rest.
24. mettle: courage.   **25. Hydra's heads:** Hydra was a many-
headed monster slain by Hercules. As soon as one head was cut
off, two others grew in its place.   **30. shadows:** imitations.

34. assay: challenge.   **41. Shirley . . . Blunt:** who have all fallen
in the battle.   **48. opinion:** reputation.   **49. makest . . . tender:**
hast some regard for.   **52. hearkened for:** desired.   **54. insulting:** triumphing.

[Re-enter DOUGLAS; *he fights with* FALSTAFF, *who falls down as if he were dead, and exit* DOUGLAS. HOTSPUR *is wounded, and falls.]*

HOT. O Harry, thou hast robbed me of my youth!
I better brook the loss of brittle life
Than those proud titles thou hast won of me.
They wound my thoughts worse than thy sword my
    flesh.   80
But thought's the slave of life, and life Time's fool,
And Time, that takes survèy of all the world,
Must have a stop.° Oh, I could prophesy,
But that the earthy and cold hand of death
Lies on my tongue. No, Percy, thou art dust,   85
And food for ——   *[Dies.]*
PRINCE. For worms, brave Percy. Fare thee well,
    great heart!
Ill-weaved ambition, how much art thou shrunk!
When that this body did contain a spirit,
A kingdom for it was too small a bound,°   90
But now two paces of the vilest earth
Is room enough. This earth that bears thee dead
Bears not alive so stout a gentleman.
If thou wert sensible° of courtesy,
I should not make so dear a show of zeal.°   95
But let my favors° hide thy mangled face,
And, even in thy behalf, I'll thank myself
For doing these fair rites of tenderness.
Adieu, and take thy praise with thee to Heaven!
Thy ignominy sleep with thee in the grave,   100
But not remembered in thy epitaph!
       [He spieth FALSTAFF *on the ground.]*
What, old acquaintance! Could not all this flesh
Keep in a little life? Poor Jack, farewell!
I could have better spared a better man.
Oh, I should have a heavy miss of thee   105
If I were much in love with vanity!°
Death hath not struck so fat a deer today,
Though many dearer, in this bloody fray.
Emboweled° will I see thee by and by.   109
Till then in blood by noble Percy lie.   *[Exit.]*
FAL. *[Rising up]* Emboweled! If thou embowel
me today, I'll give you leave to powder° me and eat
me too tomorrow. 'Sblood, 'twas time to counterfeit,
or that hot termagant° Scot had paid me scot and
lot° too. Counterfeit? I lie, I am no counterfeit. 115
To die is to be a counterfeit, for he is but the counterfeit of a man who hath not the life of a man. But to
counterfeit dying when a man thereby liveth is to be

no counterfeit, but the true and perfect image of life
indeed. The better part of valor is discretion, in   120
the which better part I have saved my life. 'Zounds,
I am afraid of this gunpowder Percy, though he be
dead. How if he should counterfeit too, and rise? By
my faith, I am afraid he would prove the better   125
counterfeit. Therefore I'll make him sure. Yea, and
I'll swear I killed him. Why may he not rise as well
as I? Nothing confutes me but eyes, and nobody sees
me. Therefore, sirrah *[Stabbing him]*, with a   130
new wound in your thigh, come you along with me.
       [Takes up HOTSPUR *on his back.]*
[Re-enter the PRINCE OF WALES *and* LORD JOHN
       OF LANCASTER.]*
PRINCE. Come, Brother John, full bravely hast
    thou fleshed
Thy maiden sword.°
LANC.   But, soft! Whom have we here?
Did you not tell me this fat man was dead?   135
PRINCE. I did, I saw him dead,
Breathless and bleeding on the ground. Art thou
    alive?
Or is it fantasy° that plays upon our eyesight?
I prithee, speak, we will not trust our eyes   139
Without our ears. Thou art not what thou seem'st.
FAL. No, that's certain, I am not a double° man.
But if I be not Jack Falstaff, then am I a Jack. There
is Percy *[Throwing the body down]*. If your father
will do me any honor, so; if not, let him kill the next
Percy himself. I look to be either earl or duke, I can
assure you.   146
PRINCE. Why, Percy I killed myself, and saw thee
    dead.
FAL. Didst thou? Lord, Lord, how this world is
given to lying! I grant you I was down and out of
breath, and so was he. But we rose both at an   150
instant, and fought a long hour by Shrewsbury
clock. If I may be believed, so; if not, let them that
should reward valor bear the sin upon their own
heads. I'll take it upon my death, I gave him this
wound in the thigh. If the man were alive, and   155
would deny it, 'zounds, I would make him eat a
piece of my sword.
LANC. This is the strangest tale that ever I heard.
PRINCE. This is the strangest fellow, Brother John.
Come, bring your luggage nobly on your back.   160
For my part, if a lie may do thee grace,
I'll gild it with the happiest terms° I have.
       [A retreat is sounded.]
The trumpet sounds retreat,° the day is ours.
Come, Brother, let us to the highest° of the field,
To see what friends are living, who are dead.   165
    [Exeunt PRINCE OF WALES *and* LANCASTER.]

81–83. thought's ... stop: thought can only exist while there is
life, but life is treated like a fool by Time, and Time itself will
end — a thought in one form or another constantly recurring in
Shakespeare's plays. 90. bound: boundary. 94. sensible: able
to feel. 95. show of zeal: mark of respect. 96. favors: scarf or
handkerchief given to a knight by his lady. 106. vanity: folly.
109. Emboweled: disemboweled. He carries on the metaphor and
pun of deer (l. 107), for the last act in the hunt was the disem-
boweling of the slain deer. 112. powder: pickle. 114. termagant: ferocious. 114–15. paid ... lot: paid all dues.

133–34. fleshed ... sword: you have fought bravely in your
first action. 138. fantasy: imagination, illusion. 141. double:
i.e., a double of myself. 162. happiest terms: best phrases.
163. trumpet ... retreat: i.e., to recall the troops from the
pursuit. 164. highest: i.e., ground.

FAL. I'll follow, as they say, for reward. He that rewards me, God reward him! If I do grow great, I'll grow less; for I'll purge, and leave sack, and live cleanly as a nobleman should do.   [*Exit.*]

SCENE V. *Another part of the field.*

[*The trumpets sound. Enter the* KING, PRINCE OF WALES, LORD JOHN OF LANCASTER, EARL OF WESTMORELAND, *with* WORCESTER *and* VERNON *prisoners.*]

KING. Thus ever did rebellion find rebuke.
Ill-spirited° Worcester! Did not we send grace,
Pardon, and terms of love to all of you?
And wouldst thou turn our offers contrary,
Misuse the tenor of thy kinsman's trust?   5
Three knights upon our party slain today,
A noble Earl and many a creature else
Had been alive this hour
If like a Christian thou hadst truly borne
Betwixt our armies true intelligence.   10
WOR. What I have done my safety urged me to.
And I embrace this fortune patiently,
Since not to be avoided it falls on me.
KING. Bear Worcester to the death, and Vernon too.
Other offenders we will pause upon.   15
          [*Exeunt* WORCESTER *and* VERNON, *guarded.*]
How goes the field?
PRINCE. The noble Scot, Lord Douglas, when he saw

Sc. v: 2. Ill-spirited: evil-spirited.

The fortune of the day quite turned from him,
The noble Percy slain, and all his men
Upon the foot of fear, fled with the rest;   20
And falling from a hill, he was so bruised
That the pursuers took him. At my tent
The Douglas is, and I beseech your Grace
I may dispose of him.
KING.   With all my heart.
PRINCE. Then, Brother John of Lancaster, to you
This honorable bounty shall belong.   26
Go to the Douglas, and deliver him
Up to his pleasure, ransomless and free.
His valor shown upon our crests today
Hath taught us how to cherish such high deeds   30
Even in the bosom of our adversaries.
LANC. I thank your Grace for this high courtesy,
Which I shall give away immediately.
KING. Then this remains, that we divide our power.
You, Son John, and my cousin Westmoreland   35
Toward York shall bend you with your dearest° speed,
To meet Northumberland and the prelate Scroop,
Who, as we hear, are busily in arms.
Myself and you, Son Harry, will toward Wales,
To fight with Glendower and the Earl of March.   40
Rebellion in this land shall lose his sway,
Meeting the check° of such another day.
And since this business so fair is done,
Let us not leave till all our own be won.   [*Exeunt.*]

36. dearest: best.   42. Meeting . . . check: incurring such a disaster.

The Tragedy of HAMLET, PRINCE OF DENMARK

Hamlet is the most controverted play ever written; even its bibliography fills a large volume. As a drama, its history is long and intricate; the text is full of problems for the scholar; and for the last hundred and fifty years critics of all kinds have competed in offering their key to the heart of Hamlet's mystery. It is the topmost ambition of every serious actor to play the part; and even the doctors, especially the psychiatrists, have taken Hamlet into the clinic to examine his inhibitions.

As for the interpretations of *Hamlet,* discussion is endless, particularly of the problem of why Hamlet delayed in exacting vengeance for his father's death after the Ghost's revelation (I.v) and again when Claudius so clearly revealed his guilt after the play scene (III.ii.276).

There are many answers, none of them wholly satisfactory.

Dr. Johnson, whose comments are always worth pondering, was less puzzled by the play than were many of his successors. He summed it up thus:

If the dramas of Shakespeare were to be characterized, each by the particular excellence which distinguishes it from the rest, we must allow to the tragedy of *Hamlet* the praise of variety. The incidents are so numerous, that the argument of the play would make a long tale. The scenes are interchangeably diversified with merriment and solemnity; with merriment that includes judicious and instructive observations, and solemnity, not strained by poetical violence above the natural sentiments of man. New characters appear from time to time in continual succession, exhibiting various forms of life and particular modes of conversation. The pretended madness of Hamlet causes much mirth, and the mournful distraction of Ophelia fills the heart with tenderness, and every personage produces the effect intended, from the apparition that in the first act chills the blood with horror, to the fop in the last, that exposes affectation to just contempt.

The conduct is perhaps not wholly secure against objections. The action is indeed for the most part incontinual progression, but there are some scenes which neither forward nor retard it. Of the feigned madness of Hamlet there appears no adequate cause, for he does nothing which he might not have done with the reputation of sanity. He plays the madman most, when he treats Ophelia with so much rudeness, which seems to be useless and wanton cruelty.

Hamlet is, through the whole play, rather an instrument than an agent. After he has, by the stratagem of the play, convicted the king, he makes no attempt to punish him, and his death is at last effected by an incident which Hamlet has no part in producing.

The catastrophe is not very happily produced; the exchange of weapons is rather an expedient of necessity, than a stroke of art. A scheme might easily have been found to kill Hamlet with the dagger, and Laertes with the bowl.

The poet is accused of having shown little regard to poetical justice, and may be charged with equal neglect of poetical probability. The apparition left the regions of the dead to little purpose; the revenge which he demands is not obtained but by the death of him that was required to take it; and the gratification which would arise from the destruction of an usurper and a murderer, is abated by the untimely death of Ophelia, the young, the beautiful, the harmless, and the pious.

Dr. Johnsons' rational analysis of the play was more than compensated for by Goethe's enthusiasm:

To me it is clear that Shakespeare meant, in the present case, to represent the effects of a great action laid upon a soul unfit for the performance of it. In this view the whole piece seems to me to be composed. There is an oak tree planted in a costly jar, which should have borne only pleasant flowers in its bosom; the roots expand, the jar shivered.

A lovely, pure, noble and most moral nature, without the strength of nerve which forms a hero, sinks beneath a burden which it cannot bear and must not cast away. All duties are holy for him; the present is too hard. Impossibilities have been required of him; not in themselves impossibilities, but such for him. He winds, and turns, and torments himself; he advances and recoils; is ever put in mind, ever puts himself in mind; at last does all but lose his purpose from his thoughts; yet still without recovering his peace of mind.

Goethe's judgment has been much quoted, but we may prefer to follow Coleridge, who declared that Shakespeare

intended to portray a person, in whose view the external world, and all its incidents and objects, were comparatively dim, and of no interest in themselves, and which began to interest only, when they were reflected in the mirror of his mind. Hamlet beheld external things in the same way that a man of vivid imagination, who shuts his eyes, sees what has previously made an impression on his organs.

The poet places him in the most stimulating circumstances that a human being can be placed in. He is the heir apparent of a throne; his father dies suspiciously; his mother excludes her son from his throne by marrying his uncle. This is not enough; but the Ghost of the murdered father is introduced, to assure the son that he was put to death by his own brother. What is the effect upon the son? instant action and pursuit of revenge? No: endless reasoning and hesitating — constant urging and solicitation of the mind to act, and as constant an escape from action; ceaseless reproaches of himself for sloth and negligence, while the whole energy of his resolution evaporates in these reproaches. This, too, not from cowardice, for he is drawn as one of the bravest of his time — not from want of forethought or slowness of apprehension, for he sees through the very souls of all who surround him, but merely from that aversion to action, which prevails among such as have a world in themselves.

Or we may accept the opinion of Bradley, who saw Hamlet rather as a "tragedy of moral idealism," for he regarded Hamlet as a young man of the highest ideals who has received a shock so terrible that he is driven into a state of utter melancholy which deprives him of all initiative.

Or we may take the more practical view that Hamlet never has any chance of killing his uncle because he is always closely guarded, except for the brief episode after the play scene when Hamlet comes on him at prayer; and the moment is not suitable for revenge.

Or we may apply modern psychological theories to Hamlet's case and brood over the Oedipus complex, and Hamlet's feelings toward his mother.

Or we may follow the scholars who argue about Elizabethan melancholy and ghost lore and remind us that Hamlet is one of many Elizabethan revenge plays which have their regular pattern; and that in most of them the plot is unfolded in stages: (1) the crime, (2) the difficulty in identifying the murderer, (3) the impediments to revenge, and (4) the final bloody slaughter.

No answer is wholly satisfactory; each has some element of truth; and the problem is the more interesting because insoluble. Perhaps Hazlitt has summed it up most neatly: "Hamlet is a name; his speeches and sayings but the ideal coinage of the poet's brain. What then, are they not real? They are as real as our own thoughts. Their reality is in the reader's mind. It is we who are Hamlet."

And we may also reflect that when we watch a good performance of Hamlet or read the play uncritically, we are so absorbed that we forget all about the problems!

But, problems apart, most readers will agree that Hamlet is the most fascinating of all plays; indeed it seems also to have been Shakespeare's favorite, for he revised it more than once. When he wrote it he was, with all the thinking men of his generation, in a period of profound disillusionment and pessimism; and he made Hamlet the vessel into which he poured his thoughts on all kinds of topics: on fathers and children, on sex, on drunkenness, on suicide, on loyalty, on acting, on glory and honor, on handwriting even, on fate, on man and the universe. There is more of Shakespeare himself in Hamlet than in any other play which he created.

DATE AND SOURCE OF THE PLAY. Hamlet in its present form was probably written about 1600 or 1601. A earlier play was being acted in London in 1594, and perhaps in 1589. Shakespeare's play was first printed in a garbled and pirated quarto (Q1) in 1603; a second quarto (Q2), probably set up from Shakespeare's own manuscript, was published in 1604; the version in the first folio omits more than 200 lines to be found in Q2 and adds some new passages of its own. The immediate source was probably the old lost play of 1594, but the Hamlet story goes back in European literature to the twelfth century. The version in François de Belleforest's Histoires Tragiques, published in Paris in 1576, was probably the original for English plays on Hamlet.

Hamlet

DRAMATIS PERSONAE

CLAUDIUS, *King of Denmark*
HAMLET, *son to the late, and nephew to the present King*
POLONIUS, *Lord Chamberlain*
HORATIO, *friend to Hamlet*
LAERTES, *son to Polonius*
VOLTIMAND ⎫
CORNELIUS ⎪
ROSENCRANTZ ⎬ *courtiers*
GUILDENSTERN ⎪
OSRIC ⎪
A GENTLEMAN ⎭
A PRIEST
MARCELLUS ⎫ *officers*
BERNARDO ⎬
FRANCISCO, *a soldier*

REYNALDO, *servant to Polonius*
PLAYERS
TWO CLOWNS, *gravediggers*
FORTINBRAS, *Prince of Norway*
A CAPTAIN
ENGLISH AMBASSADORS

GERTRUDE, *Queen of Denmark, and mother to Hamlet*

OPHELIA, *daughter to Polonius*
LORDS, LADIES, OFFICERS, SOLDIERS, SAILORS, MESSENGERS, *and other* ATTENDANTS

GHOST *of Hamlet's father*

SCENE — *Denmark.*

Act I

SCENE I. *Elsinore. A platform° before the castle.*

[FRANCISCO *at his post. Enter to him* BERNARDO.]
BER. Who's there?
FRAN. Nay, answer me. Stand, and unfold yourself.°
BER. Long live the King!°
FRAN. Bernardo?
BER. He.   5
FRAN. You come most carefully upon your hour.
BER. 'Tis now struck twelve. Get thee to bed, Francisco.
FRAN. For this relief much thanks. 'Tis bitter cold,
And I am sick at heart.
BER. Have you had quiet guard?
FRAN.   Not a mouse stirring.   10
BER. Well, good night.
If you do meet Horatio and Marcellus,
The rivals° of my watch, bid them make haste.
FRAN. I think I hear them. Stand, ho! Who is there?
          [*Enter* HORATIO *and* MARCELLUS.]
HOR. Friends to this ground.
MAR.   And liegemen° to the Dane.   15
FRAN. Give you good night.

MAR.   Oh, farewell, honest soldier.
Who hath relieved you?
FRAN.   Bernardo hath my place.
Give you good night.   [*Exit.*]
MAR.   Holloa! Bernardo!
BER.   Say,
What, is Horatio there?
HOR.   A piece of him.
BER. Welcome, Horatio. Welcome, good Marcellus.   20
MAR. What, has this thing appeared again tonight?
BER. I have seen nothing.
MAR. Horatio says 'tis but our fantasy,°
And will not let belief take hold of him
Touching this dreaded sight twice seen of us.   25
Therefore I have entreated him along
With us to watch the minutes of this night,
That if again this apparition come,
He may approve our eyes° and speak to it.
HOR. Tush, tush, 'twill not appear.
BER.   Sit down awhile,   30
And let us once again assail your ears,
That are so fortified against our story,
What we have two nights seen.
HOR.   Well, sit we down,
And let us hear Bernardo speak of this.
BER. Last night of all,   35
When yond same star that's westward from the pole°
Had made his course to illume° that part of heaven

Act I, Sc. i: **s.d., platform:** the level place on the ramparts where the cannon were mounted.   **2. unfold yourself:** reveal who you are.   **3. Long . . . King:** probably the password for the night.   **13. rivals:** partners.   **15. liegemen:** loyal subjects.

23. fantasy: imagination.   **29. approve our eyes:** verify what we have seen.   **36. pole:** Polestar.   **37. illume:** light.

Where now it burns, Marcellus and myself,
The bell then beating one ——
        [Enter GHOST.]
MAR. Peace, break thee off. Look where it comes
   again!   40
BER. In the same figure, like the King that's
   dead.
MAR. Thou art a scholar.° Speak to it, Horatio.
BER. Looks it not like the King? Mark it, Horatio.
HOR. Most like. It harrows° me with fear and
   wonder.
BER. It would be spoke to.
MAR.   Question it, Horatio.   45
HOR. What art thou that usurp'st this time of
   night,
Together with° that fair and warlike form
In which the majesty of buried Denmark°
Did sometimes march? By Heaven I charge thee,
   speak!
MAR. It is offended.
BER.   See, it stalks away!   50
HOR. Stay! Speak, speak! I charge thee, speak!
                 [Exit GHOST.]
MAR. 'Tis gone, and will not answer.
BER. How now, Horatio! You tremble and look
   pale.
Is not this something more than fantasy?
What think you on 't?   55
HOR. Before my God, I might not this believe
Without the sensible and true avouch
Of mine own eyes.°
MAR.   Is it not like the King?
HOR. As thou art to thyself.
Such was the very armor he had on   60
When he the ambitious Norway combated.
So frowned he once when, in an angry parle,°
He smote the sledded Polacks° on the ice.
'Tis strange.
MAR. Thus twice before, and jump at this dead
   hour,°   65
With martial stalk hath he gone by our watch.
HOR. In what particular thought to work I know
   not,
But in the gross and scope° of my opinion
This bodes some strange eruption° to our state.

MAR. Good now, sit down and tell me, he that
   knows,   70
Why this same strict and most observant watch
So nightly toils° the subject° of the land;
And why such daily cast of brazen cannon
And foreign mart° for implements of war;
Why° such impress° of shipwrights, whose sore
   task   75
Does not divide the Sunday from the week;
What might be toward,° that this sweaty haste
Doth make the night joint laborer with the day.
Who is 't that can inform me?
HOR.   That can I,
At least the whisper goes so. Our last King,   80
Whose image even but now appeared to us,
Was, as you know, by Fortinbras of Norway,
Thereto pricked° on by a most emulate° pride,
Dared to the combat, in which our valiant Ham-
   let —
For so this side of our known world esteemed
   him —   85
Did slay this Fortinbras. Who° by a sealed com-
   pact,°
Well ratified by law and heraldry,°
Did forfeit, with his life, all those his lands
Which he stood seized of° to the conqueror.
Against the which, a moiety competent°   90
Was gagèd° by our King, which had returned
To the inheritance of Fortinbras
Had he been vanquisher, as by the same covenant
And carriage of the article designed°
His fell to Hamlet. Now, sir, young Fortinbras, 95
Of unimprovèd mettle° hot and full,
Hath in the skirts° of Norway here and there
Sharked° up a list of lawless resolutes,°
For food and diet,° to some enterprise   99
That hath a stomach° in 't. Which is no other —
As it doth well appear unto our state —
But to recover of us, by strong hand
And terms compulsatory,° those foresaid lands
So by his father lost. And this, I take it,
Is the main motive of our preparations,   105
The source of this our watch and the chief head°

---

72. toils: wearies. **subject:** subjects.   **74. foreign mart:** purchase abroad.   **75–78. Why . . . day:** i.e., workers in shipyards and munition factories are working night shifts and Sundays. **impress:** conscription. **toward:** in preparation.   **83. pricked:** spurred. **emulate:** jealous.   **86–95. Who . . . Hamlet:** i.e., before the combat it was agreed that the victor should win the lands of the vanquished.   **86. sealed compact:** formal agreement. **87. heraldry:** The heralds were responsible for arranging formal personal combats.   **89. seized of:** possessed of, a legal term. **90. moiety competent:** adequate portion.   **91. gaged:** pledged. **94. carriage . . . designed:** fulfillment of the clause in the agreement.   **96. unimproved mettle:** untutored, wild material, nature.   **97. skirts:** outlying parts. **98. Sharked:** collected indiscriminately, as a shark bolts its prey. **lawless resolutes:** gangsters.   **99. diet:** maintenance.   **100. stomach:** resolution. **103. terms compulsatory:** force.   **106. chief head:** main purpose.

42. scholar: As Latin was the proper language in which to address and exorcise evil spirits, a scholar was necessary.   **44. harrows:** distresses; lit., plows up.   **47. Together with:** i.e., appearing in.   **48. majesty . . . Denmark:** the dead King. **57–58. Without . . . eyes:** unless my own eyes had vouched for it. **sensible:** perceived by my senses. **62. parle:** parley. **63. sledded Polacks:** There has been much controversy about this phrase. Q1 and Q2 read "sleaded Pollax," F1 reads "sledded Pollax." Either the late King smote his heavy (leaded) poleax on the ice, or else he attacked the Poles in their sledges. There is no further reference to this incident.   **65. jump . . . hour:** just at deep midnight.   **68. gross . . . scope:** general conclusion.   **69. eruption:** violent disturbance.

Of this posthaste and romage° in the land.
BER. I think it be no other but e'en so.
Well may it sort° that this portentous figure   109
Comes armèd through our watch, so like the King
That was and is the question of these wars.
HOR. A mote° it is to trouble the mind's eye.
In the most high and palmy° state of Rome,
A little ere the mightiest Julius fell,   114
The graves stood tenantless, and the sheeted° dead
Did squeak and gibber° in the Roman streets.
As stars° with trains of fire and dews of blood,
Disasters° in the sun, and the moist star°
Upon whose influence Neptune's empire stands
Was sick almost to doomsday with eclipse.   120
And even the like precurse° of fierce events,
As harbingers° preceding still the fates
And prologue to the omen° coming on,
Have Heaven and earth together demonstrated
Unto our climatures° and countrymen.   125
[Re-enter GHOST.] But soft, behold! Lo where it
      comes again!
I'll cross it,° though it blast me. Stay, illusion!
If thou hast any sound, or use of voice,
Speak to me.
If° there be any good thing to be done   130
That may to thee do ease and grace to me,°
Speak to me.
If thou art privy to° thy country's fate,
Which, happily,° foreknowing may avoid,
Oh, speak!   135
Or if thou hast uphoarded in thy life
Extorted° treasure in the womb of earth,
For which, they say, you spirits oft walk in death,
Speak of it. Stay, and speak! [The cock crows.°]
      Stop it, Marcellus.
MAR. Shall I strike at it with my partisan?°   140
HOR. Do, if it will not stand.
BER.   'Tis here!
HOR.   'Tis here!
MAR. 'Tis gone!   [Exit GHOST.]

107. posthaste . . . romage: urgency and bustle.   109. Well . . .
sort: it would be a natural reason.   112. mote: speck of dust.
113. palmy: flourishing, like a palm.   115. sheeted: in their
shrouds.   116. gibber: utter strange sounds.   117. As stars:
The sense of the passage is here broken; possibly a line has been
omitted after l. 116.   118. Disasters: unlucky signs. moist star:
the moon, which influences the tides.   121. precurse: forewarn-
ing.   122. harbingers: forerunners. The harbinger was an officer of the Court who was sent ahead to make the arrangements
when the Court went on progress.   123. omen: disaster.
125. climatures: regions.   127. cross it: stand in its way.
130–39. If . . . speak: In popular belief there were four reasons
why the spirit of a dead man should walk: (a) to reveal a secret,
(b) to utter a warning, (c) to reveal concealed treasure, (d) to
reveal the manner of its death. Horatio thus adjures the ghost
by three potent reasons, but before he can utter the fourth the
cock crows.   131. grace to me: bring me into a state of spiritual
grace.   133. privy to: have secret knowledge of.   134. happily:
by good luck.   137. Extorted: evilly acquired.   139. s.d., cock
crows: i.e., a sign that dawn is at hand. See ll. 147–64.   140. partisan: type of spear, used by palace guards.

We do it wrong, being so majestical,
To offer it the show of violence,
For it is as the air invulnerable,   145
And our vain blows malicious mockery.
BER. It was about to speak when the cock crew.
HOR. And then it started like a guilty thing
Upon a fearful° summons. I have heard
The cock, that is the trumpet to the morn,   150
Doth with his lofty and shrill-sounding throat
Awake the god of day, and at his warning,
Whether in sea or fire, in earth or air,
The extravagant and erring° spirit hies
To his confine.° And of the truth herein   155
This present object made probation.°
MAR. It faded on the crowing of the cock.
Some say that ever 'gainst° that season comes
Wherein Our Saviour's birth is celebrated,
The bird of dawning singeth all night long.   160
And then, they say, no spirit dare stir abroad,
The nights are wholesome, then no planets° strike,
No fairy takes° nor witch hath power to charm,
So hallowed and so gracious is the time.   164
HOR. So have I heard and do in part believe it.
But look, the morn, in russet mantle clad,
Walks o'er the dew of yon high eastward hill.
Break we our watch up, and by my advice
Let us impart what we have seen tonight
Unto young Hamlet, for upon my life,   170
This spirit, dumb to us, will speak to him.
Do you consent we shall acquaint him with it,
As needful in our loves, fitting our duty?
MAR. Let's do 't, I pray. And I this morning know
Where we shall find him most conveniently.   175
                                       [Exeunt.]

SCENE II. A room of state in the castle.

[Flourish.° Enter the KING, QUEEN, HAMLET,
  POLONIUS, LAERTES, VOLTIMAND, CORNELIUS,
        LORDS, and ATTENDANTS.]

KING. Though yet of Hamlet our dear brother's
      death
The memory be green,° and that it us befitted
To bear our hearts in grief and our whole kingdom
To be contracted in one brow of woe,°
Yet so far hath discretion° fought with nature°   5
That we with wisest sorrow think on him,

149. fearful: causing fear.   154. extravagant . . . erring: both
words mean "wandering."   155. confine: place of confinement.   156. probation: proof.   158. 'gainst: in anticipation of.
162. planets: Planets were supposed to bring disaster. See
Note A, p. 195.   163. takes: bewitches.
Sc. ii: s.d., Flourish: fanfare of trumpets.   2. green: fresh.
4. contracted . . . woe: i.e., every subject's forehead should be
puckered with grief.   5. discretion: common sense. nature:
natural sorrow.

Together with remembrance of ourselves.
Therefore our sometime sister,° now our Queen,
The imperial jointress° to this warlike state,
Have we, as 'twere with a defeated joy —   10
With an auspicious and a dropping eye,°
With mirth in funeral and with dirge in marriage,
In equal scale weighing delight and dole° —
Taken to wife. Nor have we herein barred
Your better wisdoms,° which have freely gone   15
With this affair along. For all, our thanks.
Now follows that you know. Young Fortinbras,
Holding a weak supposal° of our worth,
Or thinking by our late dear brother's death
Our state to be disjoint and out of frame,   20
Colleagued with the dream of his advantage,°
He hath not failed to pester us with message
Importing the surrender of those lands
Lost by his father, with all bonds of law,°
To our most valiant brother. So much for him.   25
Now for ourself, and for this time of meeting.
Thus much the business is: We have here writ
To Norway, uncle of young Fortinbras —
Who, impotent and bedrid, scarcely hears
Of this his nephew's purpose — to suppress   30
His further gait° herein, in that the levies,
The lists° and full proportions,° are all made
Out of his subject.° And we here dispatch
You, good Cornelius, and you, Voltimand,
For bearers of this greeting to old Norway,   35
Giving to you no further personal power
To business with the King more than the scope°
Of these delated articles° allow.
Farewell, and let your haste commend° your duty.
   COR. & VOLT. In that and all things will we show
     our duty.   40
   KING. We doubt it nothing. Heartily farewell.
          [Exeunt VOLTIMAND *and* CORNELIUS.]
And now, Laertes, what's the news with you?
You told us of some suit° — what is 't, Laertes?
You cannot speak of reason to the Dane
And lose your voice. What wouldst thou beg,
    Laertes,
That shall not be my offer, not thy asking?   45

The head is not more native° to the heart,
The hand more instrumental° to the mouth,
Than is the throne of Denmark to thy father.
What wouldst thou have, Laertes?
   LAER.   My dread° lord, 50
Your leave and favor to return to France,
From whence though willingly I came to Denmark
To show my duty in your coronation,
Yet now, I must confess, that duty done,   54
My thoughts and wishes bend again toward France
And bow them to your gracious leave and pardon.
   KING. Have you your father's leave? What says
    Polonius?
   POL. He hath, my lord, wrung from me my slow
    leave
By laborsome petition, and at last
Upon his will° I sealed my hard consent.°   60
I do beseech you give him leave to go.
   KING. Take thy fair hour, Laertes, time be thine,
And thy best graces spend° it at thy will!
But now, my cousin° Hamlet, and my son ——
   HAML. *[Aside]* A little more than kin and less
    than kind.°   65
   KING. How is it that the clouds still hang on you?
   HAML. Not so, my lord. I am too much i' the
    sun.
   QUEEN. Good Hamlet, cast thy nighted color° off,
And let thine eye look like a friend on Denmark.
Do not forever with thy vailèd lids°   70
Seek for thy noble father in the dust.
Thou know'st 'tis common — all that lives must die,
Passing through nature to eternity.
   HAML. Aye, madam, it is common.
   QUEEN.   If it be,
Why seems it so particular with thee?   75
   HAML. Seems, madam! Nay, it is. I know not
    " seems."
'Tis not alone my inky cloak, good Mother,
Nor customary suits of solemn black,
Nor windy suspiration of forced breath —
No, nor the fruitful river° in the eye,   80
Nor the dejected havior of the visage,°
Together with all forms, moods, shapes of grief —
That can denote me truly. These indeed seem,
For they are actions that a man might play.°
But I have that within which passeth show,   85
These but the trappings° and the suits of woe.

---

3. **sister:** i.e., our former sister-in-law. 9. **jointress:** partner
by marriage. 11. **auspicious . . . eye:** an eye at the same time
full of joy and of tears. 13. **dole:** grief. 14–15. **barred . . .
wisdoms:** i.e., in taking this step we have not shut out your
advice. As is obvious throughout the play, the Danes chose
their King by election and not by right of birth. See V.ii.65,
366. 18. **weak supposal:** poor opinion. 21. **Colleagued . . .
advantage:** uniting himself with this dream that here was a
good opportunity. 24. **with . . . law:** legally binding, as already explained in ll. 80–95 above. 31. **gait:** progress. 32. **lists:**
rosters. **proportions:** military establishments. 33. **subject:** subjects. 37. **scope:** limit. 38. **delated articles:** detailed instructions. Claudius is following usual diplomatic procedure. Ambassadors sent on a special mission carried with them a letter
of introduction and greeting to the King of the foreign Court
and detailed instructions to guide them in the negotiations.
39. commend: display; lit., recommend. 43. **suit:** petition.

---

47. **native:** closely related. 48. **instrumental:** serviceable.
50. **dread:** dreaded, much respected. 60. **will:** desire. **sealed
. . . consent:** agreed to, but with great reluctance. 63. **best . . .
spend:** i.e., use your time well. 64. **cousin:** kinsman. The word
was used for any near relation. 65. **A . . . kind:** too near a relation (uncle-father) and too little natural affection. **kind:** affectionate. 68. **nighted color:** black. Hamlet alone is in deep
mourning; the rest of the Court wear gay clothes. 70. **vailed
lids:** lowered eyelids. 80. **fruitful river:** stream of tears.
81. **dejected . . . visage:** downcast countenance. 84. **play:**
act, as in a play. 86. **trappings:** ornaments.

KING. 'Tis sweet and commendable in your
  nature, Hamlet,
To give these mourning duties to your father.
But you must know your father lost a father,
That father lost, lost his, and the survivor bound   90
In filial obligation for some term
To do obsequious sorrow.° But to perséver
In obstinate condolement° is a course
Of impious stubbornness, 'tis unmanly grief.
It shows a will most incorrect to Heaven,   95
A heart unfortified,° a mind impatient,
An understanding simple and unschooled.
For what we know must be and is as common
As any the most vulgar° thing to sense,
Why should we in our peevish opposition   100
Take it to heart? Fie! 'Tis a fault to Heaven,
A fault against the dead, a fault to nature,
To reason most absurd, whose common theme
Is death of fathers, and who still hath cried,
From the first corse° till he that died today,   105
" This must be so." We pray you throw to earth
This unprevailing° woe, and think of us
As of a father. For let the world take note,
You are the most immediate° to our throne,
And with no less nobility of love   110
Than that which dearest father bears his son
Do I impart toward you. For your intent
In going back to school° in Wittenberg,
It is most retrograde° to our desire.
And we beseech you bend you° to remain   115
Here in the cheer and comfort of our eye,
Our chiefest courtier, cousin, and our son.
  QUEEN. Let not thy mother lose her prayers,
    Hamlet.
I pray thee, stay with us, go not to Wittenberg.   119
  HAML. I shall in all my best obey you, madam.
  KING. Why, 'tis a loving and a fair reply.
Be as ourself in Denmark. Madam, come,
This gentle and unforced accord of Hamlet
Sits smiling to my heart. In grace whereof,
No jocund health that Denmark drinks today   125
But the great cannon° to the clouds shall tell,
And the King's rouse° the Heaven shall bruit°
    again,
Respeaking earthly thunder. Come away.
    [*Flourish. Exeunt all but* HAMLET.]
  HAML. Oh, that this too too solid flesh would melt,
Thaw, and resolve itself into a dew!   130

Or that the Everlasting had not fixed
His canon° 'gainst self-slaughter! Oh, God! God!
How weary, stale, flat, and unprofitable
Seem to me all the uses° of this world!
Fie on 't, ah, fie! 'Tis an unweeded garden,   135
That grows to seed, things rank° and gross in
    nature
Possess it merely.° That it should come to this!
But two months dead! Nay, not so much, not two.
So excellent a King, that was, to this,
Hyperion° to a satyr.° So loving to my mother   140
That he might not beteem° the winds of heaven
Visit her face too roughly. Heaven and earth!
Must I remember? Why, she would hang on him
As if increase of appetite had grown   144
By what it fed on. And yet within a month ——
Let me not think on 't. — Frailty, thy name is
    woman! —
A little month, or ere those shoes were old
With which she followed my poor father's body,
Like Niobe° all tears. — Why she, even she —   149
Oh, God! A beast that wants discourse of reason°
Would have mourned longer — married with my
    uncle,
My father's brother, but no more like my father
Than I to Hercules. Within a month,
Ere yet the salt of most unrighteous tears
Had left the flushing in her gallèd° eyes,   155
She married. Oh, most wicked speed, to post°
With such dexterity° to incestuous sheets!
It is not, nor it cannot, come to good.
But break, my heart, for I must hold my tongue!
    [*Enter* HORATIO, MARCELLUS, *and* BERNARDO.]
  HOR. Hail to your lordship!
  HAML.   I am glad to see you well.   160
Horatio — or I do forget myself.
  HOR. The same, my lord, and your poor servant
    ever.
  HAML. Sir, my good friend — I'll change that
    name° with you.
And what make you from Wittenberg, Horatio?
Marcellus?   165
  MAR. My good lord?
  HAML. I am very glad to see you. [*To* BERNARDO]
    Good even, sir.
But what, in faith, make you from Wittenberg?
  HOR. A truant disposition, good my lord.
  HAML. I would not hear your enemy say so,   170
Nor shall you do my ear that violence

92. obsequious sorrow: the sorrow usual at funerals.   93. obstinate condolement: lamentation disregarding the will of God.
96. unfortified: not strengthened with the consolation of religion.
99. vulgar: common.   105. corse: corpse. There is unconscious
irony in this remark, for the first corpse was that of Abel, also
slain by his brother.   107. unprevailing: futile.   109. most immediate: next heir.   113. school: university.   114. retrograde:
contrary.   115. bend you: incline.   126. great cannon: This
Danish custom of discharging cannon when the King proposed
a toast was much noted by Englishmen.   127. rouse: deep
drink. bruit: sound loudly, echo.

132. canon: rule, law.   134. uses: ways.   136. rank: coarse.
137. merely: entirely.   140. Hyperion: the sun god. satyr: a
creature half man, half goat — ugly and lecherous.   141. be-
teem: allow.   149. Niobe: She boasted of her children, to the
annoyance of the goddess Artemis, who slew them all. Thereafter
Niobe became so sorrowful that she changed into a rock everlast-
ingly dripping water.   150. wants . . . reason: is without ability
to reason.   155. galled: sore.   156. post: hasten.   157. dexterity: nimbleness.   164. that name: i.e., friend.

To make it truster of your own report
Against yourself. I know you are no truant.
But what is your affair in Elsinore?
We'll teach you to drink deep° ere you depart.   175
    HOR. My lord, I came to see your father's funeral.
    HAML. I pray thee do not mock me, fellow student.
I think it was to see my mother's wedding.
    HOR. Indeed, my lord, it followed hard upon.
    HAML. Thrift, thrift, Horatio! The funeral baked
       meats   180
Did coldly furnish forth the marriage tables.°
Would I had met my dearest° foe in Heaven
Or ever I had seen that day, Horatio!
My father! — Methinks I see my father.
    HOR. Oh, where, my lord?
    HAML.   In my mind's eye, Horatio.   185
    HOR. I saw him once. He was a goodly King.
    HAML. He was a man, take him for all in all.
I shall not look upon his like again.
    HOR. My lord, I think I saw him yesternight.
    HAML. Saw? Who?   190
    HOR. My lord, the King your father.
    HAML.   The King my father!
    HOR. Season your admiration° for a while
With an attent° ear till I may deliver,
Upon the witness of these gentlemen,
This marvel to you.
    HAML.   For God's love, let me hear.   195
    HOR. Two nights together had these gentlemen,
Marcellus and Bernardo, on their watch
In the dead vast and middle of the night,°
Been thus encountered. A figure like your father,
Armed at point exactly, cap-a-pie,°   200
Appears before them and with solemn march
Goes slow and stately by them. Thrice he walked
By their oppressed and fear-surprisèd eyes
Within his truncheon's° length, whilst they, dis-
     tilled°
Almost to jelly with the act of fear,   205
Stand dumb, and speak not to him. This to me
In dreadful secrecy impart they did,
And I with them the third night kept the watch.
Where, as they had delivered, both in time,   209
Form of the thing, each word made true and good,
The apparition comes. I knew your father.
These hands are not more like.
    HAML.   But where was this?
    MAR. My lord, upon the platform where we
      watched.
    HAML. Did you not speak to it?

---

175. **drink deep:** For more on the drunken habits of the Danes,
see I.iv.8–38.   180–81. **Thrift . . . tables:** they hurried on the
wedding for economy's sake, so that the remains of food served
at the funeral might be used cold for the wedding. **baked meats:**
feast.   182. **dearest:** best-hated.   192. **Season . . . admiration:**
moderate your wonder.   193. **attent:** attentive.   198. **dead . . .
night:** deep, silent midnight.   200. **at . . . cap-a-pie:** complete
in every detail, head to foot.   204. **truncheon:** a general's staff.
distilled: melted.

    HOR.   My lord, I did,
But answer made it none. Yet once methought   215
It lifted up it° head and did address
Itself to motion, like as it would speak.
But even then the morning cock crew loud,
And at the sound it shrunk in haste away
And vanished from our sight.
    HAML.   'Tis very strange.   220
    HOR. As I do live, my honored lord, 'tis true,
And we did think it writ down in our duty
To let you know of it.
    HAML. Indeed, indeed, sirs, but this troubles me.
Hold you the watch tonight?
    MAR. & BER.   We do, my lord.   225
    HAML. Armed, say you?
    MAR. & BER.   Armed, my lord.
    HAML.   From top to toe?
    MAR. & BER. My lord, from head to foot.
    HAML. Then saw you not his face?
    HOR. Oh yes, my lord, he wore his beaver° up.
    HAML. What, looked he frowningly?   230
    HOR. A countenance more in sorrow than in an-
      ger.
    HAML. Pale, or red?
    HOR. Nay, very pale.
    HAML.   And fixed his eyes upon you?
    HOR. Most constantly.
    HAML.   I would I had been there.   235
    HOR. It would have much amazed you.
    HAML. Very like, very like. Stayed it long?
    HOR. While one with moderate haste might tell°
      a hundred.
    MAR. & BER. Longer, longer.
    HOR. Not when I saw 't.
    HAML.   His beard was grizzled?° No?   240
    HOR. It was as I have seen it in his life,
A sable silvered.°
    HAML.   I will watch tonight.
Perchance 'twill walk again.
    HOR.   I warrant it will.
    HAML. If it assume my noble father's person,
I'll speak to it though Hell itself should gape   245
And bid me hold my peace. I pray you all,
If you have hitherto concealed this sight,
Let it be tenable° in your silence still,
And whatsoever else shall hap tonight,
Give it an understanding, but no tongue.   250
I will requite° your loves. So fare you well.
Upon the platform, 'twixt eleven and twelve,
I'll visit you.
    ALL.   Our duty to your Honor.
    HAML. Your loves, as mine to you. Farewell.
                 [*Exeunt all but* HAMLET.]
My father's spirit in arms! All is not well.   255

216. **it:** its.   229. **beaver:** front part of the helmet, which could
be raised.   238. **tell:** count.   240. **grizzled:** gray.   242. **sable
silvered:** black mingled with white.   248. **tenable:** held fast.
251. **requite:** repay.

I doubt° some foul play. Would the night were
   come!
Till then sit still, my soul. Foul deeds will rise,
Though all the earth o'erwhelm them, to men's
   eyes.   [*Exit.*]

SCENE III. *A room in* POLONIUS'S *house.*

[*Enter* LAERTES *and* OPHELIA.]

LAER. My necessaries° are embarked. Farewell.
And, Sister, as the winds give benefit
And convoy is assistant,° do not sleep,
But let me hear from you.

OPH.   Do you doubt that?

LAER. For Hamlet, and the trifling of his favor,°
Hold it a fashion and a toy in blood,°
A violet in the youth of primy° nature,
Forward, not permanent, sweet, not lasting,
The perfume and suppliance of a minute° —
No more.

OPH. No more but so?

LAER.   Think it no more.   10
For Nature crescent does not grow alone
In thews and bulk,° but as this temple° waxes
The inward service of the mind and soul
Grows wide withal. Perhaps he loves you now,
And now no soil nor cautel° doth besmirch   15
The virtue of his will.° But you must fear,
His greatness weighed,° his will is not his own,
For he himself is subject to his birth.
He may not, as unvalued persons do,
Carve° for himself, for on his choice depends   20
The safety and health of this whole state,
And therefore must his choice be circumscribed°
Unto the voice and yielding of that body
Whereof he is the head. Then if he says he loves you,
It fits your wisdom so far to believe it   25
As he in his particular act and place
May give his saying deed, which is no further
Than the main voice of Denmark goes withal.
Then weigh what loss your honor may sustain
If with too credent° ear you list his songs,   30
Or lose your heart, or your chaste treasure° open
To his unmastered importunity.
Fear it, Ophelia, fear it, my dear sister,
And keep you in the rear° of your affection,
Out of the shot and danger of desire.   35

The chariest maid is prodigal enough
If she unmask her beauty to the moon.
Virtue itself 'scapes not calumnious strokes.
The canker galls the infants° of the spring
Too oft before their buttons° be disclosed,   40
And in the morn and liquid dew of youth
Contagious blastments° are most imminent.
Be wary, then, best safety lies in fear.
Youth to itself rebels, though none else near.°

OPH. I shall the effect of this good lesson keep   45
As watchman to my heart. But, good my brother,
Do not, as some ungracious pastors do,
Show me the steep and thorny way to Heaven
Whilst, like a puffed° and reckless libertine,
Himself the primrose path of dalliance° treads   50
And recks not his own rede.°

LAER.   Oh, fear me not.
I stay too long. But here my father comes.
[*Enter* POLONIUS.] A double blessing is a double
   grace,
Occasion smiles° upon a second leave.

POL. Yet here, Laertes! Aboard, aboard, for
   shame!   55
The wind sits in the shoulder of your sail
And you are stayed° for. There, my blessing with
   thee!
And these few precepts in thy memory
Look thou chárácter.° Give thy thoughts no tongue,
Nor any unproportioned° thought his act.   60
Be thou familiar, but by no means vulgar.
Those friends thou hast, and their adoption tried,°
Grapple them to thy soul with hoops of steel,
But do not dull thy palm with entertainment°   64
Of each new-hatched unfledged° comrade. Beware
Of entrance to a quarrel, but being in,
Bear 't that the opposèd may beware of thee.
Give every man thy ear, but few thy voice.°
Take each man's censure,° but reserve thy judg-
   ment.
Costly thy habit° as thy purse can buy,   70
But not expressed in fancy° — rich, not gaudy.
For the apparel oft proclaims the man,
And they in France of the best rank and station
Are of a most select and generous chief in that.°

256. doubt: suspect.

Sc. iii: 1. necessaries: baggage.   3. convoy . . . assistant:
means of conveyance is available.   5. favor: i.e., toward you.
6. toy in blood: trifling impulse.   7. primy: springtime; i.e.,
youthful.   8. perfume . . . minute: perfume which lasts only
for a minute.   11-12. For . . . bulk: for natural growth is not
only in bodily bulk.   12. temple: i.e., the body.   15. cautel:
deceit.   16. will: desire.   17. His . . . weighed: when you
consider his high position.   20. Carve: choose.   22. circumscribed: restricted.   30. credent: credulous.   31. chaste treasure: the treasure of your chastity.   34. in . . . rear: i.e., farthest from danger.

39. canker . . . infants: maggot harms the unopened buds.
40. buttons: buds.   42. Contagious blastments: infectious blasts.
44. though . . . near: without anyone else to encourage it.
49. puffed: panting.   50. primrose . . . dalliance: i.e., the pleasant way of love-making.   51. recks . . . rede: takes no heed of
his own advice.   54. Occasion smiles: i.e., here is a happy
chance.   57. stayed: waited.   59. character: inscribe.   60. un-
proportioned: unsuitable.   62. adoption tried: friendship tested
by experience.   64. dull . . . entertainment: let your hand grow
callous with welcome.   65. unfledged: lit., newly out of the egg,
immature.   68. Give . . . voice: listen to everyone but commit
yourself to few.   69. censure: opinion.   70. habit: dress.
71. expressed in fancy: fantastic.   74. Are . . . that: A disputed
line; this is the F1 reading. Q2 reads "Or of the most select and
generous, chief in that"; i.e., the best noble and gentle families
are very particular in their dress. generous: of gentle birth.

Neither a borrower nor a lender be,   75
For loan oft loses both itself and friend
And borrowing dulls the edge of husbandry.°
This above all: To thine own self be true,
And it must follow, as the night the day,
Thou canst not then be false to any man.   80
Farewell. My blessing season° this in thee!
    LAER. Most humbly do I take my leave, my lord.
    POL. The time invites you. Go, your servants
    tend.°
    LAER. Farewell, Ophelia, and remember well
What I have said to you.
    OPH.   'Tis in my memory locked,   85
And you yourself shall keep the key of it.
    LAER. Farewell.   [*Exit.*]
    POL. What is 't, Ophelia, he hath said to you?
    OPH. So please you, something touching the Lord
Hamlet.
    POL. Marry,° well bethought.°   90
'Tis told me he hath very oft of late
Given private time to you, and you yourself
Have of your audience been most free and bounte-
ous.
If it be so — as so 'tis put on me,
And that in way of caution — I must tell you   95
You do not understand yourself so clearly
As it behooves° my daughter and your honor.
What is between you? Give me up the truth.
    OPH. He hath, my lord, of late made many ten-
ders°
Of his affection to me.   100
    POL. Affection! Pooh! You speak like a green girl,
Unsifted° in such perilous circumstance.
Do you believe his tenders, as you call them?   103
    OPH. I do not know, my lord, what I should think.
    POL. Marry, I'll teach you. Think yourself a baby
That you have ta'en these tenders° for true pay,
Which are not sterling.° Tender yourself more
    dearly,
Or — not to crack the wind of° the poor phrase,
Running it thus — you'll tender me a fool.   109
    OPH. My lord, he hath importuned me with love
In honorable fashion.
    POL. Aye, fashion° you may call it. Go to, go to.
    OPH. And hath given countenance to his speech,°
    my lord,
With almost all the holy vows of Heaven.
    POL. Aye, springes° to catch woodcocks.° I do
    know,   115
When the blood burns, how prodigal° the soul

Lends the tongue vows. These blazes,° daughter,
Giving more light than heat, extinct in both,
Even in their promise as it is a-making,
You must not take for fire. From this time   120
Be something scanter of your maiden presence,
Set your entreatments at a higher rate
Than a command to parley.° For Lord Hamlet,
Believe so much in him, that he is young,
And with a larger tether° may he walk   125
Than may be given you. In few,° Ophelia,
Do not believe his vows, for they are brokers,°
Not of that dye which their investments° show,
But mere implorators° of unholy suits,
Breathing like sanctified and pious bawds°   130
The better to beguile. This is for all.
I would not, in plain terms, from this time forth
Have you so slander any moment leisure°
As to give words or talk with the Lord Hamlet.
Look to 't, I charge you. Come your ways.   135
    OPH. I shall obey, my lord.   [*Exeunt.*]

SCENE IV. *The platform*

[*Enter* HAMLET, HORATIO, *and* MARCELLUS.]
    HAML. The air bites shrewdly.° It is very cold.
    HOR. It is a nipping and an eager° air.
    HAML. What hour now?
    HOR.   I thinks it lacks of twelve.
    MAR. No, it is struck.
    HOR. Indeed? I heard it not. It then draws near
    the season   5
Wherein the spirit held his wont to walk.
         [*A flourish of trumpets, and ordnance*
                         shot off within.°]
What doth this mean, my lord?
    HAML. The King doth wake° tonight and takes
    his rouse,°
Keeps wassail,° and the swaggering upspring reels.°
And as he drains his draughts of Rhenish° down,
The kettledrum and trumpet thus bray out   11
The triumph of his pledge.
    HOR.   Is it a custom?
    HAML. Aye, marry, is 't.

---

117. **blazes:** flashes, quickly extinguished (*extinct*).   122–23. **Set ... parley:** when you are asked to see him do not regard it as a command to negotiate. **parley:** meeting to discuss terms.   125. **tether:** rope by which a grazing animal is fastened to its peg.   126. **In few:** in short.   127. **brokers:** traveling salesmen.   128. **investments:** garments.   129. **implorators:** men who solicit.   130. **bawds:** keepers of brothels. F1 and Q2 read "bond," an easy misprint for "baud" — the Elizabethan spelling of "bawd."   133. **slander ... leisure:** misuse any moment of leisure.

Sc. iv: 1. **shrewdly:** bitterly.   2. **eager:** sharp.   6. **s.d., within:** off stage.   8. **wake:** "makes a night of it." **rouse:** See I.ii.127,n.   9. **wassail:** revelry. **swaggering ... reels:** reel in a riotous dance.   10. **Rhenish:** Rhine wine.

---

77. **husbandry:** economy.   81. **season:** bring to fruit.   83. **tend:** attend.   90. **Marry:** Mary, by the Virgin Mary. **well bethought:** well remembered.   97. **behooves:** is the duty of.   99. **tenders:** offers.   102. **Unsifted:** untried.   106–09. **tenders ... tender:** Polonius puns on "tenders," counters (used for money in games); "tender," value; "tender," show.   107. **sterling:** true currency. 108. **crack ... of:** i.e., ride to death.   112. **fashion:** mere show. 113. **given ... speech:** confirmed his words.   115. **springes:** snares. **woodcocks:** foolish birds.   116. **prodigal:** extravagantly.

But to my mind, though I am native here
And to the manner born, it is a custom   15
More honored in the breach than the observance.
This heavy-headed revel° east and west
Makes us traduced and taxed of° other nations.
They clepe° us drunkards, and with swinish phrase
Soil our addition,° and indeed it takes   20
From our achievements, though performed at
    height,°
The pith and marrow of our attribute.°
So oft it chances in particular men,
That for some vicious mole° of nature in them,
As in their birth — wherein they are not guilty, 25
Since nature cannot choose his origin —
By the o'ergrowth of some complexion,°
Oft breaking down the pales° and forts of reason,
Or by some habit that too much o'erleavens°   29
The form of plausive° manners, that these men —
Carrying, I say, the stamp of one defect,
Being Nature's livery,° or Fortune's star° —
Their virtues else — be they as pure as grace,
As infinite as man may undergo —
Shall in the general censure take corruption   35
From that particular fault. The dram of eale
Doth all the noble substance of a doubt
To his own scandal.°

              [*Enter* GHOST.]

HOR.   Look, my lord, it comes!
HAML. Angels and ministers of grace defend us!
Be thou a spirit of health or goblin damned,°   40
Bring with thee airs from Heaven or blasts from
    Hell,
Be thy intents wicked or charitable,
Thou comest in such a questionable° shape

---

17. **heavy-headed revel:** drinking which produces a thick head.
18. **traduced . . . of:** disgraced and censured by. 19. **clepe:**
call. 20. **soil . . . addition:** smirch our honor. **addition:** lit.,
title of honor added to a man's name. 21. **though . . . height:**
though of the highest merit. 22. **pith . . . attribute:** essential
part of our honor; i.e., we lose the honor due to our achievements
because of our reputation for drunkenness. 24. **mole:** blemish.
27. **o'ergrowth . . . complexion:** some quality allowed to overbalance the rest. See Note B, p. 196. 28. **pales:** defenses. 29. **o'er-**
leavens: mixes with. 30. **plausive:** agreeable. 32. **Nature's**
livery: i.e., inborn. **Fortune's star:** caused by some external misfortune. 36–38. **The . . . scandal:** This is the most famous of
all disputed passages in Shakespeare's plays. The general meaning is clear: "a small portion of evil brings scandal on the whole
substance, however noble." "Eale" is an Elizabethan spelling
and pronunciation of "evil," as later in Q2 (II.ii.628); "deale"
is the spelling and pronunciation of "Devil." The difficulty lies
in "of a doubt," which is obviously a misprint for some such
word as "corrupt"; but to be satisfactory it must fit the meter
and be a plausible misprint. So far, although many guesses have
been made, none is wholly convincing. The best is perhaps "often
dout" — often put out. 40. **spirit . . . damned:** a holy spirit
or damned fiend. Hamlet, until convinced at the end of the play
scene (III.ii.298), is perpetually in doubt whether the ghost
which he sees is a good spirit sent to warn him, a devil sent to
tempt him into some damnable action, or a hallucination created
by his own diseased imagination. See II.ii.627–32. 43. **ques-**
tionable: inviting question.

That I will speak to thee. I'll call thee Hamlet,
King, Father, royal Dane. Oh, answer me!   45
Let me not burst in ignorance, but tell
Why thy canónized° bones, hearsèd° in death,
Have burst their cerements,° why the sepulcher
Wherein we saw thee quietly inurned°
Hath oped his ponderous and marble jaws   50
To cast thee up again. What may this mean,
That thou, dead corse, again, in complete steel,°
Revisit'st thus the glimpses of the moon,
Making night hideous, and we fools° of nature
So horridly to shake our disposition°   55
With thoughts beyond the reaches of our souls?
Say, why is this? Wherefore? What should we do?
           [GHOST *beckons* HAMLET.]
  HOR. It beckons you to go away with it,
As if it some impartment° did desire
To you alone.
  MAR.   Look with what courteous action 60
It waves you to a more removèd ground.
But do not go with it.
  HOR.   No, by no means.
  HAML. It will not speak. Then I will follow it.
  HOR. Do not, my lord.
  HAML.   Why, what should be the fear?
I do not set my life at a pin's fee,°   65
And for my soul, what can it do to that,
Being a thing immortal as itself?
It waves me forth again. I'll follow it.
  HOR. What if it tempt you toward the flood, my
    lord,
Or to the dreadful summit of the cliff   70
That beetles o'er° his base into the sea,
And there assume some other horrible form
Which might deprive your sovereignty of reason°
And draw you into madness? Think of it.
The very place puts toys of desperation,°   75
Without more motive, into every brain
That looks so many fathoms to the sea
And hears it roar beneath.
  HAML.   It waves me still.
Go on. I'll follow thee.
  MAR. You shall not go, my lord.
  HAML.   Hold off your hands. 80
  HOR. Be ruled. You shall not go.
  HAML.   My fate cries out,
And makes each petty artery in this body
As hardy as the Nemean lion's nerve.°
Still am I called. Unhand me, gentlemen.   84

---

47. **canonized:** buried with full rites according to the canon of
the Church. **hearsed:** buried. 48. **cerements:** waxen shroud,
used to wrap the bodies of the illustrious dead. 49. **inurned:**
buried. 52. **complete steel:** full armor. 54. **fools:** dupes.
55. **disposition:** nature. 59. **impartment:** communication.
65. **fee:** value. 71. **beetles o'er:** juts out over. 73. **sover-**
eignty of reason: control of your reason over your actions.
75. **toys of desperation:** desperate fancies. 83. **Nemean . . .**
nerve: sinew of a fierce beast slain by Hercules.

By Heaven, I'll make a ghost of him that lets° me!
I say, away! Go on. I'll follow thee.
                      [*Exeunt* GHOST *and* HAMLET.]
HOR. He waxes desperate with imagination.
MAR. Let's follow. 'Tis not fit thus to obey him.
HOR. Have after. To what issue will this come?
MAR. Something is rotten in the state of Den-
    mark.   90
HOR. Heaven will direct it.
MAR.   Nay, let's follow him.   [*Exeunt.*]

SCENE V. *Another part of the platform.*

[*Enter* GHOST *and* HAMLET.]
HAML. Whither wilt thou lead me? Speak. I'll go
    no further.
GHOST. Mark me.
HAML.   I will.
GHOST.   My hour is almost come
When I to sulphurous and tormenting flames
Must render up myself.
HAML.   Alas, poor ghost!   4
GHOST. Pity me not, but lend thy serious hearing
To what I shall unfold.
HAML.   Speak. I am bound to hear.
GHOST. So art thou to revenge, when thou shalt
    hear.
HAML. What?
GHOST. I am thy father's spirit,
Doomed for a certain term to walk the night   10
And for the day confined to fast in fires
Till the foul crimes done in my days of nature
Are burnt and purged away. But that I am forbid
To tell the secrets of my prison house,
I could a tale unfold whose lightest word   15
Would harrow up thy soul, freeze thy young blood,
Make thy two eyes, like stars, start from their
    spheres,°
Thy knotted and combinèd° locks to part
And each particular° hair to stand an° end
Like quills upon the fretful porpentine.°   20
But this eternal blazon° must not be
To ears of flesh and blood. List, list, oh, list!
If thou didst ever thy dear father love ——
HAML. Oh, God!
GHOST. Revenge his foul and most unnatural mur-
    der.   25
HAML. Murder!
GHOST. Murder most foul, as in the best° it is,
But this most foul, strange, and unnatural.

HAML. Haste me to know 't, that I, with wings as
    swift
As meditation or the thoughts of love,   30
May sweep to my revenge.
GHOST.   I find thee apt,
And duller shouldst thou be than the fat° weed
That roots itself in ease° on Lethe wharf°
Wouldst thou not stir in this. Now, Hamlet, hear.
'Tis given out that, sleeping in my orchard,   35
A serpent stung me — so the whole ear of Denmark
Is by a forgèd process° of my death
Rankly abused. But know, thou noble youth,
The serpent that did sting thy father's life
Now wears his crown.
HAML.   Oh, my prophetic soul!   40
My uncle!
GHOST. Aye, that incestuous, that adulterate beast,
With witchcraft of his wit, with traitorous gifts —
O wicked wit and gifts, that have the power
So to seduce! — won to his shameful lust   45
The will of my most seeming-virtuous Queen.
O Hamlet, what a falling-off was there!
From me, whose love was of that dignity
That it went hand in hand even with the vow
I made to her in marriage, and to decline   50
Upon a wretch whose natural gifts were poor
To those of mine!
But virtue, as it never will be moved
Though lewdness court it in a shape of Heaven,°
So Lust, though to a radiant angel linked,   55
Will sate itself° in a celestial bed
And prey on garbage.
But soft! Methinks I scent the morning air.
Brief let me be. Sleeping within my orchard,
My custom always of the afternoon,   60
Upon my secure hour° thy uncle stole
With juice of cursèd hebenon° in a vial,
And in the porches° of my ears did pour
The leperous distillment,° whose effect
Holds such an enmity with blood of man   65
That swift as quicksilver it courses through
The natural gates and alleys of the body,
And with a sudden vigor it doth posset°
And curd, like eager° droppings into milk,
The thin and wholesome blood. So did it mine,   70
And a most instant tetter barked° about,
Most lazarlike,° with vile and loathsome crust,
All my smooth body.
Thus was I, sleeping, by a brother's hand

---

85. lets: hinders.
   Sc. v: 17. spheres: See Note A, p. 195.   18. knotted . . . combined: the hair that lies together in a mass.   19. particular: individual. an: on.   20. porpentine: porcupine.   21. eternal blazon:
description of eternity.   27. in . . . best: i.e., murder is foul even
when there is a good excuse.

32. fat: thick, slimy, motionless.   33. in ease: undisturbed.
Lethe wharf: the bank of Lethe, the river of forgetfulness in the
underworld.   37. forged process: false account.   54. lewdness
. . . Heaven: though wooed by Lust disguised as an angel.
56. sate itself: gorge.   61. secure hour: time of relaxation.
62. hebenon: probably henbane, a poisonous plant.   63. porches:
entrances.   64. leperous distillment: distillation causing leprosy.
68. posset: curdle.   69. eager: acid.   71. tetter barked: eruption formed a bark.   72. lazarlike: like leprosy.

Of life, of crown, of Queen, at once dispatched —
Cut off even in the blossoms of my sin,°   76
Unhouseled, disappointed, unaneled,°
No reckoning made, but sent to my account
With all my imperfections on my head.
Oh, horrible! Oh, horrible, most horrible!   80
If thou hast nature° in thee, bear it not.
Let not the royal bed of Denmark be
A couch for luxury° and damned incest.
But, howsoever thou pursuest this act,
Taint not thy mind, nor let thy soul contrive   85
Against thy mother aught. Leave her to Heaven
And to those thorns that in her bosom lodge
To prick and sting her. Fare thee well at once!
The glowworm shows the matin° to be near,
And 'gins to pale his uneffectual° fire.   90
Adieu, adieu, adieu! Remember me.   [*Exit.*]
   HAML. O all you host of Heaven! O earth! What
       else?
And shall I couple Hell? Oh, fie! Hold, hold, my
       heart,
And you, my sinews, grow not instant old
But bear me stiffly up. Remember thee!   95
Aye, thou poor ghost, while memory holds a seat
In this distracted globe.° Remember thee!
Yea, from the table° of my memory
I'll wipe away all trivial fond° recórds,
All saws° of books, all forms,° all pressures° past,
That youth and observation copied there,   101
And thy commandment all alone shall live
Within the book and volume of my brain,
Unmixed with baser matter. Yes, by Heaven!
O most pernicious woman!   105
O villain, villain, smiling, damnèd villain!
My tables — meet it is I set it down
[*Writing*] That one may smile, and smile, and be a
       villain.
At least I'm sure it may be so in Denmark.
So, Uncle, there you are. Now to my word.°   110
It is "Adieu, adieu! Remember me."
I have sworn 't.
   HOR. & MAR. [*Within*] My lord, my lord!
       [*Enter* HORATIO *and* MARCELLUS.]
   MAR.   Lord Hamlet!
   HOR.   Heaven secure him!
   HAML. So be it!
   MAR. Illo, ho, ho,° my lord!   115
   HAML. Hillo, ho, ho, boy! Come, bird, come.

   MAR. How is 't, my noble lord?
   HOR.   What news, my lord?
   HAML. Oh, wonderful!
   HOR. Good my lord, tell it.
   HAML.   No, you will reveal it.
   HOR. Not I, my lord, by Heaven.
   MAR.   Nor I, my lord.   120
   HAML. How say you, then, would heart of man
       once think it?
But you'll be secret?
   HOR. & MAR.   Aye, by Heaven, my lord.
   HAML. There's ne'er a villain dwelling in all Den-
       mark
But he's an arrant° knave.
   HOR. There needs no ghost, my lord, come from
       the grave   125
To tell us this.
   HAML.   Why, right, you are i' the right.
And so, without more circumstance° at all,
I hold it fit that we shake hands and part —
You as your business and desire shall point you,
For every man hath business and desire,   130
Such as it is. And for my own poor part,
Look you, I'll go pray.
   HOR. These are but wild and whirling° words, my
       lord.
   HAML. I'm sorry they offend you, heartily,
Yes, faith, heartily.
   HOR.   There's no offense, my lord.   135
   HAML. Yes, by Saint Patrick, but there is, Horatio,
And much offense too. Touching this vision here,
It is an honest° ghost, that let me tell you.
For your desire to know what is between us,
O'ermaster 't as you may. And now, good friends,
As you are friends, scholars, and soldiers,   141
Give me one poor request.
   HOR. What is 't, my lord? We will.
   HAML. Never make known what you have seen
       tonight.
   HOR. & MAR. My lord, we will not.
   HAML.   Nay, but swear 't.
   HOR.   In faith,   145
My lord, not I.
   MAR.   Nor I, my lord, in faith.
   HAML. Upon my sword.
   MAR.   We have sworn, my lord, already.
   HAML. Indeed, upon my sword,° indeed.
   GHOST. [*Beneath*] Swear.
   HAML. Ah, ha, boy! Say'st thou so? Art thou
       there, truepenny?°   150
Come on. You hear this fellow in the cellarage.
Consent to swear.

---

76. Cut . . . sin: cut off in a state of sin and so in danger of damnation. See III.iii.80–86.   77. Unhouseled . . . unaneled: without receiving the sacrament, not properly prepared, unanointed — without extreme unction.   81. nature: natural feelings. 83. luxury: lust.   89. matin: morning.   90. uneffectual: made ineffectual by daylight.   97. globe: i.e., head.   98. table: notebook. Intellectual young men carried notebooks in which they recorded good sayings and notable observations. See III.ii.42,n. 99. fond: trifling.   100. saws: wise sayings. forms: images in the mind. pressures: impressions.   110. word: cue.   115. Illo . . . ho: the falconer's cry to recall the hawk.

124. arrant: out-and-out.   127. circumstance: ceremony. 133. whirling: violent.   138. honest: true. See I.iv.40,n. 148. upon . . . sword: on the cross made by the hilt of the sword; but for soldiers the sword itself was a sacred object. 150. truepenny: old boy.

HOR.   Propose the oath, my lord.

HAML. Never to speak of this that you have seen,
Swear by my sword.

GHOST. [*Beneath*] Swear.   155

HAML. *Hic et ubique?*° Then we'll shift our
  ground.
Come hither, gentlemen,
And lay your hands again upon my sword.
Never to speak of this that you have heard,
Swear by my sword.   160

GHOST. [*Beneath*] Swear.

HAML. Well said, old mole! Canst work i' the
  earth so fast?
A worthy pioner!° Once more remove,° good
  friends.

HOR. Oh, day and night, but this is wondrous
  strange!

HAML. And therefore as a stranger give it wel-
  come.   165
There are more things in Heaven and earth, Hora-
  tio,
Than are dreamt of in your philosophy.
But come,
Here, as before, never, so help you mercy,
How strange or odd soe'er I bear myself,   170
As I perchance hereafter shall think meet
To put an antic disposition° on,
That you, at such times seeing me, never shall,
With arms encumbered° thus, or this headshake,
Or by pronouncing of some doubtful phrase,   175
As "Well, well, we know," or "We could an if we
  would,"
Or "If we list to speak," or "There be, an if they
  might,"
Or such ambiguous giving out, to note
That you know aught of me. This not to do,
So grace and mercy at your most need help you,   180
Swear.

GHOST. [*Beneath*] Swear.

HAML. Rest, rest, perturbèd spirit! [*They swear.*]
So, gentlemen,
With all my love I do commend me to you.
And what so poor a man as Hamlet is   185
May do to express his love and friending° to you,
God willing, shall not lack. Let us go in together.
And still your fingers on your lips, I pray.
The time is out of joint. Oh, cursèd spite
That ever I was born to set it right!   190
Nay, come, let's go together.   [*Exeunt.*]

---

156. Hic et ubique: here and everywhere.   163. pioner: miner.
remove: move.   172. antic disposition: mad behavior.   174. encumbered: folded.   186. friending: friendship.

Act II

SCENE I. *A room in* POLONIUS's *house.*

[*Enter* POLONIUS *and* REYNALDO.]

POL. Give him this money and these notes, Reynaldo.

REY. I will, my lord.

POL. You shall do marvelous wisely, good Rey-
  naldo,
Before you visit him, to make inquire
Of his behavior.

REY.   My lord, I did intend it.   5

POL. Marry, well said, very well said. Look you,
  sir,
Inquire me first what Danskers° are in Paris,
And how, and who, what means,° and where they
  keep,°
What company, at what expense, and finding
By this encompassment and drift of question°   10
That they do know my son, come you more nearer
Than your particular demands will touch it.°
Take you, as 'twere, some distant knowledge of him,
As thus, "I know his father and his friends,
And in part him." Do you mark this, Reynaldo?   15

REY. Aye, very well, my lord.

POL. "And in part him, but," you may say, "not
  well.
But if 't be he I mean, he's very wild,
Addicted so and so" — and there put on him
What forgeries° you please. Marry, none so rank°
As may dishonor him, take heed of that,   21
But, sir, such wanton, wild, and usual slips
As are companions noted and most known
To youth and liberty.

REY.   As gaming, my lord.

POL. Aye, or drinking, fencing,° swearing, quarreling,   25
Drabbing.° You may go so far.

REY. My lord, that would dishonor him.

POL. Faith, no, as you may season° it in the charge.
You must not put another scandal on him,
That he is open to incontinency.°   30
That's not my meaning. But breathe his faults so
  quaintly°
That they may seem the taints of liberty,
The flash and outbreak of a fiery mind,
A savageness in unreclaimèd° blood,

Act II, Sc. i: 7. Danskers: Danes.   8. what means: what their
income is.   keep: live.   10. encompassment . . . question:
roundabout method of questioning.   12. your . . . it: i.e., you
won't get at the truth by straight questions.   20. forgeries:
inventions. rank: gross.   25. fencing: A young man who
haunted fencing schools would be regarded as quarrelsome and
likely to belong to the sporting set.   26. Drabbing: whoring.
28. season: qualify.   30. open . . . incontinency: So long as
Laertes does his drabbing inconspicuously Polonius would not
be disturbed.   31. quaintly: skillfully.   34. unreclaimed:
naturally wild.

Of general assault.°

REY.   But, my good lord——   35
POL. Wherefore should you do this?
REY.   Aye, my lord,
I would know that.
POL.   Marry, sir, here's my drift,°
And I believe it is a fetch of warrant.°
You laying these slight sullies° on my son,
As 'twere a thing a little soiled i' the working,   40
Mark you,
Your party in converse, him you would sound,
Having ever seen° in the prenominate° crimes
The youth you breathe of guilty, be assured
He closes with you in this consequence° —   45
"Good sir," or so, or "friend," or "gentleman,"
According to the phrase or the addition°
Of man and country.
REY.   Very good, my lord.   49
POL. And then, sir, does he this — he does——
What was I about to say? By the mass, I was about
to say something. Where did I leave?
REY. At "closes in the consequence," at "friend or
so," and "gentleman."
POL. At "closes in the consequence," aye, marry,
He closes with you thus: "I know the gentleman.
I saw him yesterday, or t'other day,   56
Or then, or then, with such, or such, and, as you
     say,
There was a' gaming, there o'ertook in 's rouse,
There falling out at tennis."° Or perchance,
"I saw him enter such a house of sale,"   60
Videlicet,° a brothel, or so forth.
See you now,
Your bait of falsehood takes this carp of truth.
And thus do we of wisdom and of reach,°
With windlasses° and with assays of bias,°   65
By indirections find directions out.°
So, by my former lecture and advice,
Shall you my son. You have me, have you not?
REY. My lord, I have.
POL.   God be wi' ye, fare ye well.
REY. Good my lord!   70
POL. Observe his inclination in° yourself.
REY. I shall, my lord.
POL. And let him ply his music.
REY.   Well, my lord.
POL. Farewell!   [Exit REYNALDO.]

35. Of . . . assault: common to all men.   37. drift: intention.
38. fetch . . . warrant: trick warranted to work.   39. sullies:
blemishes.   43. Having . . . seen: if ever he has seen. prenom-
inate: aforementioned.   45. closes . . . consequence: follows
up with this reply.   47. addition: title. See I.iv.20.   59. tennis: Visitors to France were much impressed by the enthusiasm of all classes of Frenchmen for tennis, which in England
was mainly a courtier's game.   61. Videlicet: namely, "viz."
64. wisdom . . . reach: of far-reaching wisdom.   65. windlasses:
roundabout methods. assays of bias: making our bowl (ball) take
a roundabout course.   66. indirections . . . out: by indirect
means come at the direct truth.   71. in: for.

[Enter OPHELIA.] How now, Ophelia! What's the
     matter?
OPH. Oh, my lord, my lord, I have been so af-
     frighted!   75
POL. With what, i' the name of God?
OPH. My lord, as I was sewing in my closet,°
Lord Hamlet, with his doublet° all unbraced,
No hat upon his head, his stockings fouled,
Ungartered and down-gyved° to his ankle,   80
Pale as his shirt, his knees knocking each other,
And with a look so piteous in purport
As if he had been loosèd out of Hell
To speak of horrors, he comes before me.
POL. Mad for thy love?
OPH.   My lord, I do not know,
But truly I do fear it.   86
POL.   What said he?
OPH. He took me by the wrist and held me hard.
Then goes he to the length of all his arm,
And with his other hand thus o'er his brow,
He falls to such perusal of my face   90
As he would draw it. Long stayed he so.
At last, a little shaking of mine arm,
And thrice his head thus waving up and down,
He raised a sigh so piteous and profound
As it did seem to shatter all his bulk   95
And end his being. That done, he lets me go.
And with his head over his shoulder turned,
He seemed to find his way without his eyes;
For out o' doors he went without their helps,
And to the last bended their light on me.   100
POL. Come, go with me. I will go seek the King.
This is the very ecstasy° of love,
Whose violent property fordoes° itself
And leads the will to desperate undertakings
As oft as any passion under heaven   105
That does afflict our natures. I am sorry.
What, have you given him any hard words of late?
OPH. No, my good lord, but, as you did command,
I did repel his letters and denied
His access to me.
POL.   That hath made him mad.   110
I am sorry that with better heed and judgment
I had not quoted° him. I feared he did but trifle
And meant to wreck thee, but beshrew° my jeal-
     ousy!
By Heaven, it is as proper° to our age
To cast beyond ourselves° in our opinions   115
As it is common for the younger sort
To lack discretion. Come, go we to the King.

77. closet: private room.   78. doublet: the short close-fitting
coat which was braced to the hose by laces. When a man was relaxing or careless of appearance, he unbraced, as a modern man
takes off his coat or unbuttons his waistcoat. Hamlet behaves like
a melancholic lover.   80. down-gyved: hanging around his ankles
like fetters.   102. ecstasy: frenzy.   103. property fordoes:
natural quality destroys.   112. quoted: observed carefully.
113. beshrew: a plague on.   114. proper: natural.   115. cast
. . . ourselves: be too clever.

This must be known, which, being kept close, might
  move
More grief to hide than hate to utter love.° 119
Come.   [*Exeunt.*]

SCENE II. *A room in the castle.*

[*Flourish. Enter* KING, QUEEN, ROSENCRANTZ,
  GUILDENSTERN, *and* ATTENDANTS.]

KING. Welcome, dear Rosencrantz and Guilden-
  stern!
Moreover° that we much did long to see you,
The need we have to use you did provoke
Our hasty sending. Something have you heard
Of Hamlet's transformation — so call it,   5
Sith° nor the exterior nor the inward man
Resembles that it was. What it should be,
More than his father's death, that thus hath put him
So much from the understanding of himself
I cannot dream of. I entreat you both   10
That, being of so young days brought up with him
And sith so neighbored to his youth and havior°
That you vouchsafe your rest° here in our Court
Some little time, so by your companies
To draw him on to pleasures, and to gather   15
So much as from occasion you may glean,
Whether aught to us unknown afflicts him thus
That opened lies within our remedy.°
QUEEN. Good gentlemen, he hath much talked of
  you,
And sure I am two men there art not living   20
To whom he more adheres.° If it will please you
To show us so much gentry° and goodwill
As to expend your time with us a while
For the supply and profit of our hope,°
Your visitation shall receive such thanks   25
As fits a king's remembrance.
ROS.   Both your Majesties
Might, by the sovereign power you have of us,
Put your dread pleasures more into command
Than to entreaty.
GUIL.   But we both obey,
And here give up ourselves, in the full bent°   30
To lay our service freely at your feet,
To be commanded.
KING. Thanks, Rosencrantz and gentle Guilden-
  stern.

QUEEN. Thanks, Guildenstern and gentle Rosen-
  crantz.
And I beseech you instantly to visit   35
My too-much-changèd son. Go, some of you,
And bring these gentlemen where Hamlet is.
GUIL. Heavens make our presence and our prac-
  tices
Pleasant and helpful to him!
QUEEN.   Aye, amen! [*Exeunt* ROSENCRANTZ,
  GUILDENSTERN, *and some* ATTENDANTS.]
                         [*Enter* POLONIUS.]
POL. The ambassadors from Norway, my good
  lord,   40
Are joyfully returned.
KING. Thou still° hast been the father of good
  news.
POL. Have I, my lord? I assure my good liege
I hold my duty as I hold my soul,
Both to my God and to my gracious King.   45
And I do think, or else this brain of mine
Hunts not the trail of policy so sure
As it hath used to do,° that I have found
The very cause of Hamlet's lunacy.   49
KING. Oh, speak of that. That do I long to hear.
POL. Give first admittance to the ambassadors.
My news shall be the fruit° to that great feast.
KING. Thyself do grace° to them and bring them
  in.   [*Exit* POLONIUS.]
He tells me, my dear Gertrude, he hath found   54
The head and source of all your son's distemper.°
QUEEN. I doubt it is no other but the main,°
His father's death and our o'erhasty marriage.
KING. Well, we shall sift him.
         [*Re-enter* POLONIUS, *with* VOLTIMAND
                   and CORNELIUS.]
                         Welcome, my good friends!
Say, Voltimand, what from our brother Norway?
VOLT. Most fair return of greetings and desires.
Upon our first,° he sent out to suppress   61
His nephew's levies, which to him appeared
To be a preparation 'gainst the Polack,
But better looked into, he truly found
It was against your Highness, whereat, grieved   65
That so his sickness, age, and impotence
Was falsely borne in hand,° sends out arrests
On Fortinbras; which he, in brief, obeys,
Receives rebuke from Norway, and in fine°
Makes vow before his uncle never more   70
To give the assay of arms° against your Majesty.
Whereon old Norway, overcome with joy,
Gives him three thousand crowns in annual fee

118-19. which . . . love: by being kept secret it may cause more
sorrow than it will cause anger by being revealed; i.e., the King
and Queen may be angry at the thought of the Prince's marrying
beneath his proper rank.
   Sc. ii: 2. Moreover: in addition to the fact that. 6. Sith:
since. 12. neighbored . . . havior: so near to his youthful
manner of living. 13. vouchsafe . . . rest: consent to stay.
18. opened . . . remedy: if revealed, might be put right by us.
21. To . . . adheres: whom he regards more highly. 22. gentry: courtesy. 24. supply . . . hope: to bring a profitable conclusion to our hope. 30. in . . . bent: stretched to our uttermost.

42. still: always. 47-48. Hunts . . . do: is not so good at following the scent of political events as it used to be. 52. fruit:
the dessert, which comes at the end of the feast. 53. do grace:
honor; i.e., by escorting them into the royal presence. 55. distemper: mental disturbance. 56. main: principal cause.
61. first: i.e., audience. 67. borne in hand: imposed upon.
69. in fine: in the end. 71. give . . . arms: make an attack.

And his commission to employ those soldiers,
So levied as before, against the Polack.   75
With an entreaty, herein further shown,
     [*Giving a paper*]
That it might please you to give quiet pass°
Through your dominions for this enterprise,
On such regards of safety and allowance°
As therein are set down.

KING.   It likes° us well,   80
And at our more considered time we'll read,
Answer, and think upon this business.
Meantime we thank you for your well-took labor.
Go to your rest. At night we'll feast together.
Most welcome home!
     [*Exeunt* VOLTIMAND *and* CORNELIUS.]
POL.   This business is well ended.   85
My liege, and madam, to expostulate°
What majesty should be, what duty is,
Why day is day, night night, and time is time,
Were nothing but to waste night, day, and time.
Therefore, since brevity is the soul of wit   90
And tediousness the limbs and outward flourishes,°
I will be brief. Your noble son is mad.
Mad call I it, for to define true madness,
What is 't but to be nothing else but mad?
But let that go.

QUEEN.   More matter, with less art.°
POL. Madam, I swear I use no art at all.
That he is mad, 'tis true. 'Tis true 'tis pity,
And pity 'tis 'tis true—a foolish figure,°
But farewell it, for I will use no art.
Mad let us grant him, then. And now remains   100
That we find out the cause of this effect,
Or rather say the cause of this defect,
For this effect defective comes by cause.
Thus it remains and the remainder thus.
Perpend.°   105
I have a daughter—have while she is mine—
Who in her duty and obedience, mark,
Hath given me this. Now gather and surmise.°
[*Reads.*]
"To the celestial, and my soul's idol, the most beau-
     tified° Ophelia—"
That's an ill phrase, a vile phrase, "beautified" is a
vile phrase. But you shall hear. Thus: [*Reads.*]
"In her excellent white bosom, these," and so forth.
QUEEN. Came this from Hamlet to her?   114
POL. Good madam, stay awhile, I will be faithful.
[*Reads.*] "Doubt thou the stars are fire,
          Doubt that the sun doth move,
          Doubt truth to be a liar,
          But never doubt I love.   119

"O dear Ophelia, I am ill at these numbers,° I
have not art to reckon my groans, but that I love thee
best, O most best, believe it. Adieu.
     "Thine evermore, most dear lady, whilst this
               machine° is to him, HAMLET."
This in obedience hath my daughter shown me,
And more above, hath his solicitings,   126
As they fell out by time, by means and place,
All given to mine ear.

KING.   But how hath she
Received his love?
POL.   What do you think of me?
KING. As of a man faithful and honorable.   130
POL. I would fain prove so. But what might you
think,
When I had seen this hot love on the wing—
As I perceived it, I must tell you that,
Before my daughter told me—what might you
Or my dear Majesty your Queen here think   135
If I had played the desk or table book,°
Or given my heart awinking, mute and dumb,
Or looked upon this love with idle sight—
What might you think? No, I went round° to work,
And my young mistress thus I did bespeak:°   140
"Lord Hamlet is a Prince, out of thy star.°
This must not be." And then I prescripts° gave her
That she should lock herself from his resort,
Admit no messengers, receive no tokens.
Which done, she took the fruits of my advice.   145
And he, repulsèd, a short tale to make,
Fell into a sadness, then into a fast,
Thence to a watch, thence into a weakness,
Thence to a lightness,° and by this declension°
Into the madness wherein now he raves   150
And all we mourn for.
KING. Do you think this?
QUEEN.   It may be, very like.
POL. Hath there been such a time, I'd fain know
that,
That I have positively said " 'Tis so"
When it proved otherwise?
KING.   Not that I know.   155
POL. [*Pointing to his head and shoulder.*] Take
this from this, if this be otherwise.
If circumstances lead me, I will find
Where truth is hid, though it were hid indeed
Within the center.°

---

77. quiet pass: unmolested passage.   79. regards . . . allowance: safeguard and conditions.   80. likes: pleases.   86. expostulate: indulge in an academic discussion.   91. flourishes: ornaments.   95. art: ornament.   98. figure: i.e., a figure of speech.   105. Perpend: note carefully.   108. surmise: guess the meaning.   110. beautified: beautiful.

120. numbers: verses.   124. machine: i.e., body, an affected phrase.   136. desk . . . book: i.e., acted as silent go-between (desks and books being natural post offices for a love letter), or been a recipient of secrets but took no action (as desks and notebooks are the natural but inanimate places for keeping secrets).   139. round: straight.   140. bespeak: address.   141. out . . . star: above your destiny.   142. prescripts: instructions.   147-49. Fell . . . lightness: Hamlet's case history, according to Polonius, develops by stages—melancholy, loss of appetite, sleeplessness, physical weakness, mental instability, and finally madness.   149. declension: decline.   159. center: i.e., of the earth. See Note A, p. 195.

KING.   How may we try it further?

POL. You know sometimes he walks four hours
together   160
Here in the lobby.

QUEEN.   So he does indeed.

POL. At such a time I'll loose° my daughter to
him.
Be you and I behind an arras° then.
Mark the encounter. If he love her not,
And be not from his reason fall'n thereon,   165
Let me be no assistant for a state,
But keep a farm and carters.°

KING.   We will try it.

QUEEN. But look where sadly the poor wretch
comes reading.

POL. Away, I do beseech you, both away.   169
I'll board° him presently.   [*Exeunt* KING, QUEEN,
                                          and ATTENDANTS.]

[*Enter* HAMLET, *reading.*] Oh, give me leave. How
does my good Lord Hamlet?

HAML. Well, God-a-mercy.

POL. Do you know me, my lord?

HAML. Excellent well. You are a fishmonger.°

POL. Not I, my lord.   175

HAML. Then I would you were so honest a man.

POL. Honest, my lord!

HAML. Aye, sir, to be honest, as this world goes, is
to be one man picked out of ten thousand.

POL. That's very true, my lord.   180

HAML. For if the sun breed maggots° in a dead
dog, being a god° kissing carrion° —— Have you a
daughter?

POL. I have, my lord.   184

HAML. Let her not walk i' the sun. Conception is
a blessing, but not as your daughter may conceive —
friend, look to 't.

POL. [*Aside*] How say you by that? Still harping
on my daughter. Yet he knew me not at first, he said
I was a fishmonger. He is far gone, far gone. And
truly in my youth I suffered much extremity for
love, very near this. I'll speak to him again. — What
do you read, my lord?   193

HAML. Words, words, words.

POL. What is the matter, my lord?

HAML. Between who?   196

POL. I mean the matter that you read, my lord.

HAML. Slanders, sir. For the satirical rogue says
here that old men have gray beards, that their faces
are wrinkled, their eyes purging thick amber and
plum-tree gum, and that they have a plentiful lack
of wit, together with most weak hams.° All which,

sir, though I most powerfully and potently believe,
yet I hold it not honesty to have it thus set down;
for yourself, sir, should be old as I am if like a crab
you could go backward.   206

POL. [*Aside*] Though this be madness, yet there
is method° in 't. — Will you walk out of the air, my
lord?

HAML. Into my grave.   210

POL. Indeed, that's out of the air. [*Aside*] How
pregnant° sometimes his replies are! A happiness°
that often madness hits on, which reason and sanity
could not so prosperously be delivered of. I will
leave him, and suddenly contrive the means of
meeting between him and my daughter. — My
honorable lord, I will most humbly take my leave
of you.   218

HAML. You cannot, sir, take from me anything
that I will more willingly part withal — except my
life, except my life, except my life.

POL. Fare you well, my lord.

HAML. These tedious old fools!

[*Enter* ROSENCRANTZ *and* GUILDENSTERN.]

POL. You go to seek the Lord Hamlet. There he is.

ROS. [*To* POLONIUS] God save you, sir!   225
                                          [*Exit* POLONIUS.]

GUIL. My honored lord!

ROS. My most dear lord!

HAML. My excellent good friends!° How dost
thou, Guildenstern? Ah, Rosencrantz! Good lads,
how do you both?   230

ROS. As the indifferent° children of the earth.

GUIL. Happy in that we are not overhappy.
On Fortune's cap we are not the very button.°

HAML. Nor the soles of her shoe?

ROS. Neither, my lord.   235

HAML. Then you live about her waist, or in the
middle of her favors?

GUIL. Faith, her privates° we.

HAML. In the secret parts of Fortune? Oh, most
true, she is a strumpet. What's the news?   240

ROS. None, my lord, but that the world's grown
honest.

HAML. Then is Doomsday near. But your news is
not true. Let me question more in particular. What
have you, my good friends, deserved at the hands of
Fortune, that she sends you to prison hither?   247

GUIL. Prison, my lord!

HAML. Denmark's a prison.

ROS. Then is the world one.

HAML. A goodly one, in which there are many

---

162. loose: turn loose.   163. arras: tapestry hanging.   167. keep
. . . carters: i.e., turn country squire — like Justice Shallow.
See *II Hen IV*.   170. board: accost.   174. fishmonger: Hamlet is now in his "antic disposition," enjoying himself by
fooling Polonius.   181. sun . . . maggots: a general belief. Cf.
Ant & Cleo, II.vii.29–31.   182. god: Q2 and F1 read "good."
carrion: flesh.   202. hams: knee joints.

208. method: order, sense.   212. pregnant: apt, full of wit.
212. happiness: good turn of phrase.   228. My . . . friends: As
soon as Polonius has gone, Hamlet drops his assumed madness
and greets Rosencrantz and Guildenstern naturally.   231. indifferent: neither too great nor too little.   233. button: i.e., at
the top.   238. privates: with a pun on "private parts" and
"private," not concerned with politics.

confines,° wards,° and dungeons, Denmark being one o' the worst.

ROS. We think not so, my lord. 254

HAML. Why, then 'tis none to you, for there is nothing either good or bad but thinking makes it so. To me it is a prison.

ROS. Why, then your ambition° makes it one. 'Tis too narrow for your mind. 259

HAML. Oh, God, I could be bounded in a nutshell and count myself a king of infinite space were it not that I have bad dreams.

GUIL. Which dreams indeed are ambition, for the very substance of the ambitious° is merely the shadow of a dream. 265

HAML. A dream itself is but a shadow.

ROS. Truly, and I hold ambition of so airy and light a quality that it is but a shadow's shadow.

HAML. Then are our beggars bodies, and our monarchs and outstretched heroes the beggars' shadows.° Shall we to the Court? For, by my fay,° I cannot reason.° 272

ROS. & GUIL. We'll wait upon you.°

HAML. No such matter. I will not sort° you with the rest of my servants, for, to speak to you like an honest man, I am most dreadfully attended.° But in the beaten way of friendship, what make you at Elsinore? 278

ROS. To visit you, my lord, no other occasion.

HAML. Beggar that I am, I am even poor in thanks, but I thank you. And sure, dear friends, my thanks are too dear a halfpenny.° Were you not sent for? Is it your own inclining? Is it a free visitation?° Come, deal justly with me. Come, come. Nay, speak. 285

GUIL. What should we say, my lord?

HAML. Why, anything, but to the purpose.° You were sent for, and there is a kind of confession in your looks which your modesties have not craft enough to color.° I know the good King and Queen have sent for you.

ROS. To what end, my lord? 292

HAML. That you must teach me. But let me conjure° you, by the rights of our fellowship,° by the consonancy° of our youth, by the obligation of our ever preserved love, and by what more dear a better

proposer could charge you withal, be even° and direct with me, whether you were sent for, or no. 299

ROS. [Aside to GUILDENSTERN] What say you?

HAML. [Aside] Nay, then, I have an eye of you. — If you love me, hold not off.

GUIL. My lord, we were sent for. 303

HAML. I will tell you why. So shall my anticipation prevent your discovery, and your secrecy to the King and Queen molt no feather.° I have of late — but wherefore I know not — lost all my mirth, forgone all custom of exercises, and indeed it goes so heavily with my disposition that this goodly frame the earth seems to me a sterile promontory. 310 This most excellent canopy,° the air, look you, this brave o'erhanging firmament,° this majestical roof fretted° with golden fire — why, it appears no other thing to me than a foul and pestilent congregation of vapors. What a piece of work is a man! 315 How noble in reason! How infinite in faculty!° In form and moving° how express° and admirable! In action how like an angel! In apprehension how like a god! The beauty of the world! The paragon of animals! And yet, to me, what is this quintessence° of dust? Man delights not me — no, nor 320 woman neither, though by your smiling you seem to say so.

ROS. My lord, there was no such stuff in my thoughts.

HAML. Why did you laugh, then, when I said "Man delights not me"?

ROS. To think, my lord, if you delight not in man, what lenten entertainment° the players shall receive from you. We coted° them on the way, and hither are they coming to offer you service. 331

HAML. He that plays the King shall be welcome, His Majesty shall have tribute of me. The adventurous knight shall use his foil and target,° the lover shall not sigh gratis, the humorous man° shall end his part in peace, the clown shall make those laugh whose lungs are tickle o' the sere,° and the lady shall say her mind freely or the blank verse shall halt° for 't. What players are they? 340

ROS. Even those you were wont to take such delight in, the tragedians of the city.

HAML. How chances it they travel? Their resi-

252. confines: places of confinement. wards: cells. 258. your ambition: Rosencrantz is feeling after one possible cause of Hamlet's melancholy — thwarted ambition. 264. substance . . . ambitious: that on which an ambitious man feeds his fancies. 269–71. Then . . . shadows: i.e., by your reasoning beggars are the only men of substance, for kings and heroes are by nature ambitious and therefore "the shadows of a dream." outstretched: of exaggerated reputation. 271. fay: faith. 272. reason: argue. 273. wait . . . you: be your servants. 274. sort: class. 276. dreadfully attended: my attendants are a poor crowd. 282. too . . . halfpenny: not worth a halfpenny. 283. free visitation: voluntary visit. 287. anything . . . purpose: anything so long as it is not true. 290. color: conceal. 294. conjure: make solemn appeal to. fellowship: comradeship. 295. consonancy: concord.

298. even: straight. 304–06. So . . . feather: i.e., so by my telling you first you will not be obliged to betray the secrets of the King. prevent: forestall. molt no feather: be undisturbed. 311. canopy: covering. 312. firmament: sky. 313. fretted: ornamented. 316. faculty: power of the mind. 317. moving: movement. express: exact. 319. quintessence: perfection; the fifth essence, which would be left if the four elements were taken away. 329. lenten entertainment: fasting fare, meager welcome. 330. coted: overtook. 334. foil . . . target: rapier and small shield. 335. humorous man: the man who specializes in character parts; e.g., Jaques in As You Like It. 338. are . . . sere: explode at a touch. The sere is part of the trigger mechanism of a gun which if "ticklish" will go off at a touch. 340. halt: limp.

dence, both in reputation and profit, was better both ways.°   345

ROS. I° think their inhibition° comes by the means of the late innovation.°

HAML. Do they hold the same estimation they did when I was in the city? Are they so followed?

ROS. No, indeed are they not.   350

HAML. How comes it? Do they grow rusty?

ROS. Nay, their endeavor keeps in the wonted pace.° But there is, sir, an eyrie° of children, little eyases,° that cry out on the top of question° and are most tyrannically° clapped for 't. These are   355 now the fashion, and so berattle° the common stages° — so they call them — that many wearing rapiers are afraid of goose quills° and dare scarce come thither.   360

HAML. What, are they children? Who maintains 'em? How are they escoted?° Will they pursue the quality° no longer than they can sing? Will they not say afterward, if they should grow themselves to common players — as it is most like if their means are no better — their writers do them wrong to make them exclaim against their own succession?°   368

ROS. Faith, there has been much to-do on both sides, and the nation holds it no sin to tarre° them to controversy. There was for a while no money bid for argument° unless the poet and the player went to cuffs° in the question.   373

HAML. Is 't possible?

GUIL. Oh, there has been much throwing-about of brains.

HAML. Do the boys carry it away?

ROS. Aye, that they do, my lord, Hercules and his load° too.   379

HAML. It is not very strange, for my uncle is King of Denmark, and those that would make mows° at him while my father lived give twenty, forty, fifty, a hundred ducats apiece for his picture in little. 'Sblood,° there is something in this more than natural, if philosophy could find it out.   385

[Flourish of trumpets within.]

GUIL. There are the players.

HAML. Gentlemen, you are welcome to Elsinore. Your hands. Come then. The appurtenance of welcome is fashion and ceremony.° Let me comply° with you in this garb,° lest my extent° to the   390 players — which, I tell you, must show fairly outward — should more appear like entertainment° than yours. You are welcome. But my uncle-father and aunt-mother are deceived.

GUIL. In what, my dear lord?   395

HAML. I am but mad north-northwest.° When the wind is southerly,° I know a hawk from a handsaw.°

[Re-enter POLONIUS.*]*

POL. Well be with you, gentlemen!

HAML. Hark you, Guildenstern, and you too — at each ear a hearer. That great baby you see there is not yet out of his swaddling clouts.°   401

ROS. Happily he's the second time come to them, for they say an old man is twice a child.

HAML. I will prophesy he comes to tell me of the players, mark it. You say right, sir. O' Monday morning, 'twas so indeed.   407

POL. My lord, I have news to tell you.

HAML. My lord, I have news to tell you. When Roscius° was an actor in Rome ——

POL. The actors are come hither, my lord.

HAML. Buzz, buzz!°

POL. Upon my honor ——   413

HAML. Then came each actor on his ass ——

POL. The° best actors in the world, either for tragedy, comedy, history, pastoral, pastoral-comical, historical-pastoral, tragical-historical, tragical-comical-historical-pastoral, scene individable° or poem unlimited.° Seneca cannot be too heavy, nor Plautus° too light. For the law of writ° and the liberty,° these are the only men.   421

HAML. O Jephthah,° judge of Israel, what a treasure hadst thou!

343–45. Their . . . ways: i.e., if they stayed in the city, it would bring them more profit and fame. **346–79. I . . . too:** A reference to the "War of the Theaters," waged between the two Boys' Companies, which greatly excited playgoers in 1600 and 1601. **346. inhibition:** formal prohibition. **347. innovation:** riot. **352–53. endeavor . . . pace:** they try as hard as ever. **353. eyrie:** nest. **354. eyases:** young hawks. **354. cry . . . question:** either "cry in a shrill voice" or perhaps "cry out the latest detail of the dispute." **355. tyrannically:** outrageously. **356. berattle:** abuse. **357. common stages:** the professional players. The boys acted in "private" playhouses. **359. goose quills:** pens; i.e., of such as Ben Jonson. **362. escoted:** paid. **363. quality:** acting profession. **368. exclaim . . . succession:** abuse the profession to which they will afterward belong. **370. tarre:** urge on to fight; generally used of encouraging a dog. **372. argument:** plot of a play. See III.ii.242. **372–73. went to cuffs:** boxed each other's ears. **378–79. Hercules . . . load:** Hercules carrying the globe on his shoulders was the sign of the Globe Playhouse. **381. mows:** grimaces. **384. 'Sblood:** by God's blood.

388–89. appurtenance . . . ceremony: that which pertains to welcome is formal ceremony. **389. comply:** use the formality of welcome; i.e., shake hands with you. **390. garb:** fashion. **extent:** outward behavior. **392. entertainment:** welcome. **396. north-northwest:** i.e., 327° (out of 360°) of the compass. **397. wind is southerly:** The south wind was considered unhealthy. **396–97. hawk . . . handsaw:** Either "handsaw" is a corruption of "heronshaw," heron, or a hawk is a tool like a pickax. The phrase means "I'm not so mad as you think." **401. clouts:** clothes. **410. Roscius:** the most famous of Roman actors. **412. Buzz, buzz:** slang for "stale news." **415–21. The . . . men:** Polonius reads out the accomplishments of the actors from the license which they have presented him. Playing companies on tour carried a license permitting them to offer all kinds of dramatic entertainment. **418. scene individable:** i.e., a play preserving the unities. **418–19. poem unlimited:** i.e., a play which disregards the rules. **419–20. Seneca . . . Plautus:** the Roman writers of tragedy and comedy with whose plays every educated man was familiar. **420. law of writ:** the critical rules; i.e., classical plays. **liberty:** plays freely written; i.e., "modern" drama. **422. Jephthah:** The story of Jephthah is told in Judges, Chapter 11. He vowed that if successful against the Ammonites

POL. What a treasure had he, my lord?

HAML. Why,   425
    "One° fair daughter, and no more,
        The which he lovèd passing well."

POL. [*Aside*] Still° on my daughter.

HAML. Am I not i' the right, old Jephthah?

POL. If you call me Jephthah, my lord, I have a
daughter that I love passing well.   431

HAML. Nay, that follows not.

POL. What follows, then, my lord?

HAML. Why,
        "As by lot, God wot,"°   435
and then you know,
    "It came to pass, as most like it was — "
the first row° of the pious chanson° will show you
more, for look where my abridgement° comes.   439
[*Enter four or five* PLAYERS.] You are welcome, masters, welcome all. I am glad to see thee well. Welcome, good friends. Oh, my old friend!° Why, thy
face is valanced° since I saw thee last. Comest thou
to beard° me in Denmark? What, my young lady°
and mistress! By 'r Lady, your ladyship is nearer to
Heaven than when I saw you last, by the alti-   445
tude of a chopine.° Pray God your voice, like a piece
of uncurrent gold, be not cracked within the ring.°
Masters, you are all welcome. We'll e'en to 't like
French falconers,° fly at anything we see. We'll have
a speech straight. Come, give us a taste of your
quality° — come, a passionate speech.   452

I. PLAY. What speech, my good lord?

HAML. I heard thee speak me a speech once, but
it was never acted, or if it was, not above once; for
the play, I remember, pleased not the million, 'twas
caviar° to the general.° But it was — as I received
it, and others, whose judgments in such matters
cried in the top of mine° — an excellent play, well
digested° in the scenes, set down with as much   460
modesty° as cunning. I remember one said there
were no sallets° in the lines to make the matter
savory, nor no matter in the phrase that might indict the author of affection,° but called it an honest

method, as wholesome as sweet, and by very   465
much more handsome than fine.° One speech in it
I chiefly loved. 'Twas Aeneas' tale to Dido,° and
thereabout of it especially where he speaks of
Priam's° slaughter. If it live in your memory, begin
at this line — let me see, let me see —   471
    "The rugged Pyrrhus,° like th' Hyrcanian
        beast,° — "
It is not so. It begins with "Pyrrhus."
"The° rugged Pyrrhus, he whose sable° arms,
Black as his purpose, did the night resemble   475
When he lay couchèd in the ominous° horse,°
Hath now this dread and black complexion
    smeared
With heraldry° more dismal. Head to foot
Now is he total gules, horridly tricked   479
With blood of fathers, mothers, daughters, sons,
Baked and impasted° with the parching streets
That lend a tyrannous and a damnèd light
To their lord's murder. Roasted in wrath and
    fire,
And thus o'ersized with coagulate gore,°   484
With eyes like carbuncles, the hellish Pyrrhus
Old grandsire Priam seeks."
So, proceed you.

POL. 'Fore God, my lord, well spoken, with good
accent and good discretion.

I. PLAY.   "Anon he finds him   490
Striking too short at Greeks. His antique sword,
Rebellious to his arm, lies where it falls,
Repugnant to command.° Unequal matched,
Pyrrhus at Priam drives, in rage strikes wide,
But with the whiff and wind of his fell sword   495
The unnerved father falls. Then senseless Ilium,°
Seeming to feel this blow, with flaming top
Stoops to his base,° and with a hideous crash
Takes prisoner Pyrrhus' ear. For, lo! his sword,
Which was declining° on the milky° head   500
Of reverend Priam, seemed i' the air to stick.

affectation.   466. fine: subtle.   467. Aeneas' . . . Dido: the
story of the sack of Troy as told by Aeneas to Dido, Queen
of Carthage. The original is in Virgil's *Aeneid*. A similar
speech occurs in Marlowe's play *Dido, Queen of Carthage*.
469. Priam: the old King of Troy.   472. Pyrrhus: the son
of Achilles, one of the Greeks concealed in the Wooden
Horse.   473. Hyrcanian beast: the tiger.   474–541. The . . .
gods: The speech may be from some lost play of *Dido and
Aeneas*, but more likely it is Shakespeare's own invention. It is
written in the heavy elaborate style still popular in the dramas of
the Admiral's Men. The first player delivers it with excessive
gesture and emotion.   474. sable: black.   476. ominous: fateful. horse: the Wooden Horse by which a small Greek force
was enabled to make a secret entry into Troy.   478. heraldry:
painting. The image of heraldic painting is kept up in *gules* (the
heraldic term for red) and *tricked* (painted like a coat of arms).
481. impasted: turned into a crust by the heat of the burning
city.   484. o'ersized . . . gore: covered over with congealed
blood.   493. Repugnant to command: refusing to be used.
496. Ilium: the citadel of Troy.   498. stoops . . . base: col-
lapses.   500. declining: bending toward. milky: milk-white.

he would sacrifice the first creature to meet him on his return,
which was his daughter.   426–37. One . . . was: Quotation from
a ballad of Jephthah.   428. Still: always.   435. wot: knows.
438. row: line. pious chanson: godly poem.   439. abridgement:
entertainment. Cf. *MND*, V.i.39.   441. old friend: i.e., the leading player.   442. valanced: bearded. A valance is a fringe of
material hung round the sides and bottom of a bed.   443. beard:
dare, with a pun on "valanced." young lady: i.e., the boy who
takes the woman's parts.   446. chopine: lady's shoe with thick
cork sole.   447. cracked . . . ring: Before coins were milled on
the rim they were liable to crack. When the crack reached the ring
surrounding the device, the coin was no longer valid currency.
450. French falconers: They were famous for their skill in hawking.   452. quality: skill as an actor.   457. caviar: sturgeon's
roe, a Russian delicacy not then appreciated (or known) by any
but gourmets. general: common herd.   459. cried . . . mine:
surpassed mine.   460. digested: composed.   461. modesty: moderation.   462. sallets: tasty bits.   463–64. phrase . . . affection:
nothing in the language which could charge the author with

So as a painted tyrant° Pyrrhus stood,
And like a neutral to his will and matter,°
Did nothing.
But as we often see, against° some storm   505
A silence in the heavens, the rack° stand still,
The bold winds speechless and the orb° below
As hush as death, anon the dreadful thunder
Doth rend the region° — so after Pyrrhus' pause
Aroused vengeance sets him new awork.   510
And never did the Cyclops'° hammers fall
On Mars's armor, forged for proof eterne,°
With less remorse° than Pyrrhus' bleeding sword
Now falls on Priam.   514
Out, out, thou strumpet, Fortune! All you gods,
In general synod° take away her power,
Break all the spokes and fellies° from her wheel,
And bowl the round nave° down the hill of Heaven
As low as to the fiends! "

POL. This is too long.   520

HAML. It shall to the barber's, with your beard.
Prithee, say on. He's for a jig° or a tale of bawdry,
or he sleeps. Say on. Come to Hecuba.

I. PLAY. " But who, oh, who had seen the mobled°
    Queen — "

HAML. " The mobled Queen "?

POL. That's good, " mobled Queen " is good.

I. PLAY. " Run barefoot up and down, threatening
    the flames
With bisson rheum,° a clout° upon that head
Where late the diadem stood, and for a robe,   530
About her lank and all o'erteemèd° loins
A blanket, in the alarm of fear caught up.
Who this had seen, with tongue in venom steeped
'Gainst Fortune's state would treason have pro-
    nounced.°
But if the gods themselves did see her then,   535
When she saw Pyrrhus make malicious sport
In mincing with his sword her husband's limbs,
The instant burst of clamor that she made,
Unless things mortal move them not at all,
Would have made milch° the burning eyes of
    Heaven   540
And passion in the gods."

POL. Look whether he has not turned his color
and has tears in 's eyes. Prithee, no more.

HAML. 'Tis well; I'll have thee speak out the rest
of this soon. Good my lord, will you see the players
well bestowed?° Do you hear, let them be well used,
for they are the abstract and brief chronicles of the
time.° After your death you were better have a bad
epitaph than their ill report while you live.   551

POL. My lord, I will use them according to their
desert.°

HAML. God's bodykins,° man, much better. Use
every man after his desert and who shall 'scape
whipping? Use them after your own honor and dignity. The less they deserve, the more merit is in your
bounty. Take them in.

POL. Come, sirs.   559

HAML. Follow him, friends. We'll hear a play to-
morrow. [*Exit* POLONIUS *with all the* PLAYERS *but the*
FIRST.] Dost thou hear me, old friend? Can you play
The Murder of Gonzago?

I. PLAY. Aye, my lord.   564

HAML. We'll ha 't tomorrow night. You could, for
a need, study a speech of some dozen or sixteen lines
which I would set down and insert in 't, could you
not?

I. PLAY. Aye, my lord.   569

HAML. Very well. Follow that lord, and look you
mock him not. [*Exit* FIRST PLAYER.] My good
friends, I'll leave you till night. You are welcome to
Elsinore.

ROS. Good my lord!   574

HAML. Aye, so, God be wi' ye! [*Exeunt* ROSEN-
CRANTZ *and* GUILDENSTERN.] Now I am alone.
Oh, what a rogue and peasant slave am I!
Is it not monstrous that this player here,
But in a fiction, in a dream of passion,
Could force his soul so to his own conceit°   579
That from her working° all his visage wanned,°
Tears in his eyes, distraction° in 's aspect,°
A broken voice, and his whole function° suiting
With forms to his conceit? And all for nothing!
For Hecuba!
What's Hecuba to him or he to Hecuba,   585
That he should weep for her? What would he do
Had he the motive and the cue for passion
That I have? He would drown the stage with tears
And cleave the general ear° with horrid speech,
Make mad the guilty and appal the free,°   590

---

502. painted tyrant: as in the painting of a tyrant.   503. neutral ... matter: one midway (*neutral*) between his desire (*will*) and action (*matter*).   505. against: just before.   506. rack: the clouds in the upper air. Cf. *Ant & Cleo*, IV.xiv.10. 507. orb: world.   509. region: the country round.   511. Cyclops': of Titans, giants who aided Vulcan, the blacksmith god, to make armor for Mars, the war god.   512. proof eterne: everlasting protection.   513. remorse: pity.   516. synod: council.   517. fellies: the pieces forming the circumference of a wooden wheel.   518. nave: center of the wheel. 522. jig: pantomimic dance, usually bawdy.   525. mobled: muffled.   529. bisson rheum: blinding moisture. clout: rag. 531. o'erteemed: exhausted by bearing children; she had borne fifty-two.   533–34. Who ... pronounced: anyone who had seen this sight would with bitter words have uttered treason against the tyranny of Fortune.   540. milch: milky, i.e., dripping moisture.

548. bestowed: housed.   549–50. abstract ... time: they summarize and record the events of our time. Elizabethan players were often in trouble for too saucily commenting on their betters in plays dealing with history or contemporary events and persons and especially during the years 1597–1608.   552. desert: rank.   553. God's bodykins: by God's little body.   578. dream of passion: imaginary emotion. 579. conceit: imagination.   580. her working: i.e., the effect of imagination. wanned: went pale.   581. distraction: frenzy. aspect: countenance.   582. function: behavior.   589. general ear: ears of the audience.   590. free: innocent.

Confound the ignorant, and amaze indeed
The very faculties of eyes and ears.
Yet I,
A dull and muddy-mettled° rascal, peak,°   594
Like John-a-dreams,° unpregnant of my cause,°
And can say nothing — no, not for a King
Upon whose property° and most dear life
A damned defeat° was made. Am I a coward?
Who° calls me villain? Breaks my pate across?
Plucks off my beard and blows it in my face?   600
Tweaks me by the nose? Gives me the lie i' the
   throat
As deep as to the lungs? Who does me this?
Ha!
'Swounds,° I should take it. For it cannot be
But I am pigeon-livered° and lack gall°   605
To make oppression bitter, or ere this
I should have fatted all the region kites
With this slave's offal.° Bloody, bawdy villain!
Remorseless, treacherous, lecherous, kindless° vil-
   lain!
Oh, vengeance!   610
Why, what an ass am I! This is most brave,
That I, the son of a dear father murdered,
Prompted to my revenge by Heaven and Hell,
Must, like a whore, unpack my heart with words
And fall a-cursing like a very drab,°   615
A scullion!°
Fie upon 't! Foh! About, my brain! Hum, I have
   heard
That guilty creatures sitting at a play
Have by the very cunning of the scene
Been struck so to the soul that presently°   620
They have proclaimed their malefactions;°
For murder, though it have no tongue, will speak
With most miraculous organ. I'll have these players
Play something like the murder of my father
Before mine uncle. I'll observe his looks,   625
I'll tent° him to the quick. If he but blench,°
I know my course. The spirit that I have seen
May be the Devil, and the Devil hath power
To assume a pleasing shape. Yea, and perhaps
Out of my weakness and my melancholy,   630
As he is very potent with such spirits,
Abuses me to damn me.° I'll have grounds°

594. muddy-mettled: made of mud, not iron. peak: mope.
595. John-a-dreams: "Sleepy Sam." unpregnant . . . cause:
barren of plans for vengeance.   597. property: personality, life.
598. defeat: ruin.   599–602. Who . . . this: Hamlet runs through
all the insults which provoked a resolute man to mortal
combat. pate: head. lie . . . throat: the bitterest of insults.
604. 'Swounds: by God's wounds.   605. pigeon-livered: "as
gentle as a dove." gall: spirit.   606–08. ere . . . offal: before this
I would have fed this slave's (i.e., the King's) guts to the kites.
fatted: made fat.   609. kindless: unnatural.   615. drab:
"moll."   616. scullion: the lowest of the kitchen servants.
620. presently: immediately.   621. proclaimed . . . malefactions: shouted out their crimes.   626. tent: probe. See Cor,
I.ix.31. blench: flinch.   632. Abuses . . . me: i.e., deceives me
by thus assuming the appearance of my dead father so that I

More relative than this.° The play's the thing
Wherein I'll catch the conscience of the King.
   [Exit.]

Act III

SCENE I. *A room in the castle.*

[*Enter* KING, QUEEN, POLONIUS, OPHELIA,
   ROSENCRANTZ, *and* GUILDENSTERN.]

KING. And can you, by no drift of circumstance,°
Get from him why he puts on this confusion,
Grating° so harshly all his days of quiet
With turbulent and dangerous lunacy?   4
ROS. He does confess he feels himself distracted,
But from what cause he will by no means speak.
   GUIL. Nor do we find him forward to be
   sounded,°
But, with a crafty madness, keeps aloof
When we would bring him on to some confession
Of his true state.
   QUEEN.   Did he receive you well?   10
   ROS. Most like a gentleman.
   GUIL. But with much forcing of his disposition.°
   ROS. Niggard of question,° but of our demands
Most free in his reply.
   QUEEN.   Did you assay him
To any pastime?°   15
   ROS. Madam, it so fell out that certain players
We o'erraught° on the way. Of these we told him,
And there did seem in him a kind of joy
To hear of it. They are about the Court,
And, as I think, they have already order   20
This night to play before him.
   POL.   'Tis most true.
And he beseeched me to entreat your Majesties
To hear and see the matter.
   KING. With all my heart, and it doth much con-
   tent me
To hear him so inclined.   25
Good gentlemen, give him a further edge,°
And drive his purpose on to these delights.
   ROS. We shall, my lord.
       [*Exeunt* ROSENCRANTZ *and* GUILDENSTERN.]
   KING.   Sweet Gertrude, leave us too,
For we have closely° sent for Hamlet hither,
That he, as 'twere by accident, may here   30

may commit the sin of murder which will bring me to damnation.
grounds: reasons for action.   633. relative . . . this: i.e., more
convincing than the appearance of a ghost.

Act III, Sc. i: 1. drift of circumstance: circumstantial evidence, hint.   3. grating: disturbing.   7. forward . . . sounded:
eager to be questioned.   12. much . . . disposition: making a
great effort to be civil to us.   13. Niggard of question: not asking
many questions.   14–15. Did . . . pastime: did you try to interest him in any amusement.   17. o'erraught: overtook.
26. edge: encouragement.   29. closely: secretly.

Affront° Ophelia.
Her father and myself, lawful espials,°
Will so bestow ourselves that, seeing unseen,
We may of their encounter frankly judge
And gather by him, as he is behaved,°   35
If 't be the affliction of his love or no
That thus he suffers for.

QUEEN.   I shall obey you.
And for your part, Ophelia, I do wish
That your good beauties be the happy cause   39
Of Hamlet's wildness. So shall I hope your virtues
Will bring him to his wonted way° again,
To both your honors.

OPH..   Madam, I wish it may.   [*Exit* QUEEN.]
  POL. Ophelia, walk you here. Gracious,° so please
    you,
We will bestow ourselves. [*To* OPHELIA] Read on
    this book,°
That show of such an exercise may color   45
Your loneliness. We are oft to blame in this —
'Tis too much proved — that with devotion's
    visage°
And pious action we do sugar o'er
The Devil himself.

  KING. [*Aside*] Oh, 'tis too true!
How smart a lash that speech doth give my con-
    science!   50
The harlot's cheek, beautied with plastering art,
Is not more ugly to the thing that helps it°
Than is my deed to my most painted° word.
Oh, heavy burden!   54
  POL. I hear him coming. Let's withdraw, my lord.
            [*Exeunt* KING *and* POLONIUS.
            [*Enter* HAMLET.°]
  HAML. To be, or not to be — that is the question.
Whether 'tis nobler in the mind to suffer
The slings and arrows of outrageous° fortune,
Or to take arms against a sea° of troubles
And by opposing end them. To die, to sleep —   60
No more, and by a sleep to say we end
The heartache and the thousand natural shocks
That flesh is heir to. 'Tis a consummation°
Devoutly to be wished. To die, to sleep,
To sleep — perchance to dream. Aye, there's the
    rub,°   65
For in that sleep of death what dreams may come
When we have shuffled off this mortal coil°

Must give us pause. There's the respect°
That makes calamity of so long life.°   69
For who would bear the whips and scorns of time,
The oppressor's wrong, the proud man's contumely°
The pangs of déspised love, the law's delay,
The insolence of office° and the spurns
That patient merit of the unworthy takes,°
When he himself might his quietus° make   75
With a bare bodkin?° Who would fardels° bear,
To grunt and sweat under a weary life,
But that the dread of something after death,
The undiscovered country from whose bourn°
No traveler returns, puzzles the will,°   80
And makes us rather bear those ills we have
Than fly to others that we know not of?
Thus° conscience does make cowards of us all,
And thus the native hue° of resolution
Is sicklied o'er with the pale cast° of thought,   85
And enterprises of great pitch° and moment
With this regard their currents turn awry
And lose the name of action.° — Soft you now!
The fair Ophelia! Nymph, in thy orisons°
Be all my sins remembered.

  OPH.   Good my lord,   90
How does your Honor for this many a day?
  HAML. I humbly thank you — well, well, well.
  OPH. My lord, I have remembrances of yours
That I have longed long to redeliver.
I pray you now receive them.

  HAML.   No, not I.   95
I never gave you aught.
  OPH. My honored lord, you know right well you
    did,
And with them words of so sweet breath composed
As made the things more rich. Their perfume lost,
Take these again, for to the noble mind   100
Rich gifts wax poor when givers prove unkind.
There, my lord.
  HAML. Ha, ha! Are you honest?°
  OPH. My lord?
  HAML. Are you fair?   105
  OPH. What means your lordship?
  HAML. That if you be honest and fair, your hon-
esty should admit no discourse to your beauty.°

---

31. **Affront:** encounter.   32. **lawful espials:** who are justified in spying on him.   35. **by . . . behaved:** from his, from his behavior.   41. **wonted way:** normal state.   43. **Gracious:** your Majesty — addressed to the King.   44. **book:** i.e., of devotions.   47. **devotion's visage:** an outward appearance of religion.   52. **ugly . . . it:** i.e., lust, which is the cause of its artificial beauty.   53. **painted:** i.e., false.   55 s.d., **Enter Hamlet:** In Q1 the King draws attention to Hamlet's approach with the words "See where he comes poring upon a book." Hamlet is again reading, and is too much absorbed to notice Ophelia.   58. **outrageous:** cruel.   59. **sea:** i.e., an endless turmoil.   63. **consummation:** completion.   65. **rub:** impediment in the bowling green.   67. **shuffled . . . coil:** cast off this fuss of life.

68. **respect:** reason.   69. **makes . . . life:** makes it a calamity to have to live so long.   71. **contumely:** insulting behavior.   73. **insolence of office:** insolent behavior of government officials.   73–74. **spurns . . . takes:** insults which men of merit have patiently to endure from the unworthy.   75. **quietus:** discharge. See Sonnet 126.   76. **bodkin:** dagger. **fardels:** burdens, the coolie's pack.   79. **bourn:** boundary.   80. **will:** resolution, ability to act.   83–88. **Thus . . . action:** the religious fear that death may not be the end makes men shrink from heroic actions.   84. **native hue:** natural color.   85. **cast:** color.   86. **pitch:** height; used of the soaring flight of a hawk.   87–88. **With . . . action:** by continual brooding on this thought great enterprises are diverted from their course and fade away.   89. **orisons:** prayers.   103. **honest:** chaste.   107–08. **That . . . beauty:** if you are chaste and beautiful your chastity should have nothing to do with your beauty — because

OPH. Could beauty, my lord, have better commerce than with honesty?   110

HAML. Aye, truly, for the power of beauty will sooner transform honesty from what it is to a bawd° than the force of honesty can translate beauty into his likeness. This was sometime a paradox,° but now the time gives it proof. I did love you once.   116

OPH. Indeed, my lord, you made me believe so.

HAML. You should not have believed me, for virtue cannot so inoculate our old stock but we shall relish° of it. I loved you not.   120

OPH. I was the more deceived.

HAML. Get thee to a nunnery. Why wouldst thou be a breeder of sinners? I am myself indifferent honest,° but yet I could accuse me of such things that it were better my mother had not borne me. I am   125 very proud, revengeful, ambitious, with more offenses at my beck° than I have thoughts to put them in, imagination to give them shape, or time to act them in. What should such fellows as I do crawling between heaven and earth? We are arrant   130 knaves all. Believe none of us. Go thy ways to a nunnery.° Where's your father?

OPH. At home, my lord.

HAML. Let the doors be shut upon him, that he may play the fool nowhere but in 's own house. Farewell.   137

OPH. Oh, help him, you sweet Heavens!

HAML. If thou dost marry, I'll give thee this plague for thy dowry: Be thou as chaste as ice, as pure as snow — thou shalt not escape calumny.° Get thee to a nunnery, go. Farewell. Or if thou wilt needs marry, marry a fool, for wise men know well enough what monsters° you make of them. To a nunnery, go, and quickly too. Farewell.

OPH. O heavenly powers, restore him!   147

HAML. I have heard of your paintings° too, well enough. God hath given you one face and you make yourselves another. You jig,° you amble,° and you lisp,° and nickname God's creatures, and make your wantonness your ignorance.° Go to, I'll no more on 't — it hath made me mad. I say we will have no more marriages. Those that are married already, all but one, shall live; the rest shall keep as they   156 are. To a nunnery, go.   [Exit.]

OPH. Oh, what a noble mind is here o'erthrown! The courtier's, soldier's, scholar's, eye, tongue, sword —

The expectancy and rose° of the fair state,   160
The glass° of fashion and the mold of form,°
The observed of all observers — quite, quite down!
And I, of ladies most deject and wretched,
That sucked the honey of his music vows,
Now see that noble and most sovereign reason,   165
Like sweet bells jangled, out of tune and harsh,
That unmatched° form and feature of blown° youth
Blasted with ecstasy.° Oh, woe is me,
To have seen what I have seen, see what I see!   169
[*Re-enter* KING *and* POLONIUS.]

KING. Love! His affections° do not that way tend,
Nor what he spake, though it lacked form a little,
Was not like madness. There's something in his soul
O'er which his melancholy sits on brood,°
And I do doubt the hatch and the disclose°
Will be some danger. Which for to prevent,   175
I have in quick determination
Thus set it down: He shall with speed to England,
For the demand of our neglected tribute.
Haply° the seas and countries different
With variable objects° shall expel   180
This something-settled° matter in his heart
Whereon his brains still beating puts him thus
From fashion of himself.° What think you on 't?

POL. It shall do well. But yet do I believe
The origin and commencement of his grief   185
Sprung from neglected love. How now, Ophelia!
You need not tell us what Lord Hamlet said,
We heard it all. My lord, do as you please,
But, if you hold it fit, after the play
Let his Queen mother all alone entreat him   190
To show his grief. Let her be round° with him,
And I'll be placed, so please you, in the ear
Of all their conference. If she find him not,
To England send him, or confine him where
Your wisdom best shall think.

KING.   It shall be so.   195
Madness in great ones must not unwatched go.
[*Exeunt.*]

SCENE II. *A hall in the castle.*

[*Enter* HAMLET *and* PLAYERS.]
HAML. Speak the speech,° I pray you, as I pro-

(so Hamlet thinks in his bitterness) beautiful women are seldom chaste.   112. **bawd:** brothel-keeper.   115. **paradox:** statement contrary to accepted opinion.   120. **relish:** have some trace. 123–24. **indifferent honest:** moderately honorable.   127. **at . . . beck:** waiting to come when I beckon.   132. **nunnery:** i.e., a place where she will be removed from temptation.   141. **calumny:** slander.   145. **monsters:** horned beasts (deceived husbands). 148. **paintings:** using make-up.   150. **jig:** dance lecherously. **amble:** walk artificially.   151. **lisp:** talk affectedly.   152–53. **nickname . . . ignorance:** give things indecent names and pretend to be too simple to understand their meanings.

160. **expectancy . . . rose:** bright hope. The rose is used as a symbol for beauty and perfection. Cf. *I Hen IV*, I.iii.175.   161. **glass:** mirror. **mold of form:** perfect pattern of manly beauty. 167. **unmatched:** unmatchable. **blown:** perfect, like an open flower at its best.   168. **Blasted . . . ecstasy:** ruined by madness. 170. **affections:** state of mind.   173. **sits . . . brood:** sits hatching.   174. **doubt . . . disclose:** suspect the brood which will result.   179. **Haply:** perhaps.   180. **variable objects:** novel sights. 181. **something-settled:** somewhat settled; i.e., not yet incurable. 182–83. **puts . . . himself:** i.e., separates him from his normal self.   191. **round:** direct.
Sc. ii: 1. **the speech:** which he has written. See ll. 266–67. The whole passage which follows is Shakespeare's own comment

nounced it to you, trippingly° on the tongue. But if
you mouth° it, as many of your players do, I had as
lief° the town crier spoke my lines. Nor do not saw
the air too much with your hand, thus, but use   5
all gently. For in the very torrent, tempest, and, as I
may say, whirlwind of passion, you must acquire and
beget a temperance that may give it smoothness. Oh,
it offends me to the soul to hear a robustious° peri-
wig-pated° fellow tear a passion to tatters, to   10
very rags, to split the ears of the groundlings,° who
for the most part are capable of nothing but inexplicable dumb shows° and noise. I would have such
a fellow whipped for o'erdoing Termagant° — it
out-Herods Herod. Pray you, avoid it.   16

1. PLAY. I warrant your Honor.

HAML. Be not too tame neither, but let your own
discretion be your tutor. Suit the action to the word,
the word to the action, with this special observ-   20
ance, that you o'erstep not the modesty of nature.
For anything so overdone is from° the purpose of
playing, whose end, both at the first and now, was
and is to hold as 'twere the mirror up to Nature —
to show Virtue her own feature, scorn her own   25
image, and the very age and body of the time his
form and pressure.° Now this overdone or come
tardy off, though it make the unskillful laugh, cannot but make the judicious grieve, the censure of the
which one° must in your allowance o'erweigh a   30
whole theater of others. Oh, there be players° that I
have seen play, and heard others praise — and that
highly, not to speak it profanely — that neither having the accent of Christians nor the gait of Christian,
pagan, nor man, have so strutted and bellowed   35
that I have thought some of Nature's journeymen°
had made men, and not made them well, they imitated humanity so abominably.

1. PLAY. I hope we have reformed that indiffer-
ently° with us, sir.   41

HAML. Oh, reform it altogether. And let those that
play your clowns° speak no more than is set down

on the actor's art and states the creed and practice of his
company as contrasted with the more violent methods of
Edward Alleyn and his fellows at the Rose Playhouse. **2. trip-
pingly:** smoothly, easily. **3. mouth:** "ham" it. **4. lief:** soon.
9. robustious: ranting. **10. periwig-pated:** wearing a wig.
11. groundlings: the poorer spectators, who stood in the yard
of the playhouse. See Intro., p. 186. **14. dumb shows:** an
old-fashioned dramatic device, still being used by the Admiral's Men: before a tragedy, and sometimes before each act,
the characters mimed the action which was to follow. See later
l. 145. **15. Termagant:** God of the Saracens, who, like Herod,
was presented in early stage plays as a roaring tyrant. **22. from:**
contrary to. **26–27. very . . . pressure:** an exact reproduction of
the age. **form:** shape. **pressure:** imprint (of a seal). **30. the
. . . one:** i.e., the judicious spectator. **31. there . . . players:** An
obvious attack on Alleyn. **36. journeymen:** hired workmen, not
masters of the trade. **41. indifferently:** moderately. **42–43. those
. . . clowns:** A hit at Will Kempe, the former clown of Shakespeare's company. See Intro., pp. 186–87. Q1 adds the passage
"And then you have some again that keep one suit of jests, as a
man is known by one suit of apparel, and gentlemen quote his jests

for them. For there be of them that will themselves
laugh, to set on some quantity of barren spec-   45
tators to laugh too, though in the meantime some
necessary question of the play be then to be considered. That's villainous, and shows a most pitiful°
ambition in the fool that uses it. Go, make you   50
ready. [*Exeunt* PLAYERS. *Enter* POLONIUS, ROSEN-
CRANTZ, *and* GUILDENSTERN.] How now, my lord!
Will the King hear this piece of work?

POL. And the Queen too, and that presently.

HAML. Bid the players make haste. [*Exit* POLO-
NIUS.] Will you two help to hasten them?   55

ROS. & GUIL. We will, my lord.

[*Exeunt* ROSENCRANTZ *and* GUILDENSTERN.]

HAML. What ho! Horatio!

[*Enter* HORATIO.]

HOR. Here, sweet lord, at your service.

HAML. Horatio, thou art e'en as just a man
As e'er my conversation coped° withal.   60

HOR. Oh, my dear lord ——

HAML.   Nay, do not think I flatter,
For what advancement° may I hope from thee,
That no revénue hast but thy good spirits
To feed and clothe thee? Why should the poor be
    flattered?
No, let the candied° tongue lick absurd pomp   65
And crook the pregnant hinges of the knee
Where thrift may follow fawning.° Dost thou
    hear?
Since my dear soul was mistress of her choice
And could of men distinguish, her election
Hath sealed° thee for herself. For thou hast been   70
As one in suffering all that suffers nothing,
A man that fortune's buffets and rewards
Hast ta'en with equal thanks. And blest are those
Whose blood and judgment are so well commingled
That they are not a pipe° for fortune's finger   75
To sound what stop she please. Give me that man
That is not passion's slave, and I will wear him
In my heart's core — aye, in my heart of heart,
As I do thee. Something too much of this.
There is a play tonight before the King.   80
One scene of it comes near the circumstance
Which I have told thee of my father's death.
I prithee when thou seest that act afoot,
Even with the very comment° of thy soul
Observe my uncle. If his occulted° guilt   85

down in their tables before they come to the play, as thus: 'Cannot you stay till I eat my porridge?' and 'You owe me a quarter's
wages,' and 'My coat wants a cullison,' and 'Your beer is sour,'
and blabbering with his lips, and thus keeping in his cinquepace
of jests, when God knows the warm clown cannot make a jest unless by chance, as the blind man catcheth a hare. Masters tell
him of it." **49. pitiful:** contemptible. **60. coped:** met. **62. advancement:** promotion. **65. candied:** sugared over with hypocrisy. **66–67. crook . . . fawning:** bend the ready knees whenever
gain will follow flattery. **70. sealed:** set a mark on. **75. pipe:** an
instrument that varies its notes. **84. comment:** close observation. **85. occulted:** concealed.

Do not itself unkennel° in one speech
It is a damnèd ghost° that we have seen
And my imaginations are as foul
As Vulcan's° stithy.° Give him heedful note,°
For I mine eyes will rivet to his face,   90
And after we will both our judgments join
In censure of his seeming.°

HOR.   Well, my lord.
If he steal aught the whilst this play is playing,
And 'scape detecting, I will pay the theft.

HAML. They are coming to the play. I must be
idle.°   95
Get you a place.

[*Danish march. A flourish. Enter* KING, QUEEN,
POLONIUS, OPHELIA, ROSENCRANTZ, GUILDENSTERN,
and other LORDS *attendant, with the* GUARD
carrying torches.]

KING. How fares our cousin Hamlet?

HAML. Excellent, i' faith, of the chameleon's dish.
I eat the air, promise-crammed. You cannot feed capons so.°

KING. I have nothing with this answer,° Hamlet.
These words are not mine.

HAML. No, nor mine now.° [*To* POLONIUS] My
lord, you played once i' the university, you say?

POL. That did I, my lord, and was accounted a
good actor.   106

HAML. What did you enact?

POL. I did enact Julius Caesar. I was killed i' the
Capitol. Brutus killed me.

HAML. It was a brute part of him to kill so capital
a calf there. Be the players ready?   111

ROS. Aye, my lord, they stay upon your patience.°

QUEEN. Come hither, my dear Hamlet, sit by me.

HAML. No, good Mother, here's metal more attractive.   117

POL. [*To the* KING] Oh ho! Do you mark that?

HAML. Lady, shall I lie in your lap?

[*Lying down at* OPHELIA's *feet*]

OPH. No, my lord.   120

HAML. I mean, my head upon your lap?

OPH. Aye, my lord.

HAML. Do you think I meant country matters?°

OPH. I think nothing, my lord.

HAML. That's a fair thought to lie between maids'
legs.   126

OPH. What is, my lord?

HAML. Nothing.

OPH. You are merry, my lord.

HAML. Who, I?   130

OPH. Aye, my lord.

HAML. Oh God, your only jig-maker.° What
should a man do but be merry? For look you how
cheerfully my mother looks, and my father died
within 's two hours.   135

OPH. Nay, 'tis twice two months, my lord.

HAML. So long? Nay, then, let the Devil wear
black, for I'll have a suit of sables.° Oh heavens! Die
two months ago, and not forgotten yet? Then there's
hope a great man's memory may outlive his   140
life half a year. But, by 'r Lady, he must build
churches then, or else shall he suffer not thinking on,
with the hobbyhorse,° whose epitaph is "For, oh,
for oh, the hobbyhorse is forgot."   145

[*Hautboys° play. The dumb show enters.° Enter a*
KING *and a* QUEEN *very lovingly, the* QUEEN *embracing him and he her. She kneels, and makes show of
protestation unto him. He takes her up, and declines
his head upon her neck, lays him down upon a bank
of flowers. She, seeing him asleep, leaves him. Anon
comes in a fellow, takes off his crown, kisses it, and
pours poison in the* KING's *ears, and exit. The* QUEEN
returns, finds the KING *dead, and makes passionate
action. The Poisoner, with some two or three Mutes,
comes in again, seeming to lament with her. The
dead body is carried away. The Poisoner woos the*
QUEEN *with gifts. She seems loath and unwilling
awhile, but in the end accepts his love.   Exeunt.*]

OPH. What means this, my lord?

HAML. Marry, this is miching mallecho.° It means
mischief.

OPH. Belike this show imports the argument° of
the play.   150

[*Enter* PROLOGUE.]

HAML. We shall know by this fellow. The players
cannot keep counsel, they'll tell all.

OPH. Will he tell us what this show meant?

HAML. Aye, or any show that you'll show him. Be
not you ashamed to show, he'll not shame to tell you
what it means.   156

OPH. You are naught,° you are naught. I'll mark
the play.

---

86. **unkennel**: come to light; lit., force a fox from his hole.
87. **damned ghost**: See II.ii.627.   89. **Vulcan**: the blacksmith god. **stithy**: smithy. **heedful note**: careful observation.
92. **censure . . . seeming**: judgment on his looks.   95. **be idle**:
seem crazy.   98–100. **Excellent . . . so**: Hamlet takes "fare"
literally as "what food are you eating." The chameleon was supposed to feed on air. **promise-crammed**: stuffed, like a fattened
chicken (*capon*) — but with empty promises.   101. **I . . . answer**: I cannot make any sense of your answer.   103. **nor . . .
now**: i.e., once words have left the lips they cease to belong to
the speaker.   112. **stay . . . patience**: wait for you to be ready.
123. **country matters**: something indecent.

132. **jig-maker**: jigs were dances accompanied by songs.   138. **suit
of sables**: a quibble on "sable," black, and "sable" gown trimmed
with sable fur, worn by wealthy respectable old gentlemen.
144. **hobbyhorse**: imitation horse worn by performers in a
morris dance, an amusement much disapproved of by the severer Puritans.   145. s.d., **Hautboys**: oboes. **The dumb show
enters**: Critics have been disturbed because this dumb show
cannot be exactly paralleled in any other Elizabethan play, and
because the King is apparently not disturbed by it. Shakespeare's
intention, however, in presenting a play within a play is to produce something stagy and artificial compared with the play
proper. Moreover, as Hamlet has already complained, dumb
shows were often inexplicable.   147. **miching mallecho**: slinking
mischief.   149. **argument**: plot. She too is puzzled by the dumb
show.   157. **naught**: i.e., disgusting.

PRO.   For us, and for our tragedy,
      Here stooping to your clemency,   160
      We beg your hearing patiently.

HAML. Is this a prologue, or the posy of a ring?°
OPH. 'Tis brief, my lord.
HAML. As woman's love.

[*Enter two* PLAYERS, KING *and* QUEEN.]

P. KING. Full° thirty times hath Phoebus' cart°
    gone round   165
Neptune's° salt wash and Tellus'° orbèd ground,
And thirty dozen moons with borrowed sheen°
About the world have times twelve thirties been,
Since love our hearts and Hymen° did our hands
Unite commutual° in most sacred bands.   170

  P. QUEEN. So many journeys may the sun and
    moon
Make us again count o'er ere love be done!
But, woe is me, you are so sick of late,
So far from cheer and from your former state,
That I distrust° you. Yet, though I distrust,   175
Discomfort you, my lord, it nothing must.
For women's fear and love holds quantity°
In neither aught or in extremity.°
Now what my love is, proof hath made you know,
And as my love is sized, my fear is so.   180
Where love is great, the littlest doubts are fear,
Where little fears grow great, great love grows there.

  P. KING. Faith, I must leave thee,° love, and
    shortly too,
My operant powers° their functions leave to do.
And thou shalt live in this fair world behind,   185
Honored, beloved, and haply one as kind
For husband shalt thou ——

  P. QUEEN.   Oh, confound the rest!
Such love must needs be treason in my breast.
In second husband let me be accurst!
None wed the second but who killed the first.   190

  HAML. [*Aside*] Wormwood,° wormwood.

  P. QUEEN. The instances° that second marriage
    move
Are base respects of thrift,° but none of love.
A second time I kill my husband dead
When second husband kisses me in bed.   195

  P. KING. I do believe you think what now you
    speak,
But what we do determine oft we break.
Purpose is but the slave to memory,

Of violent birth but poor validity,
Which now, like fruit unripe, sticks on the tree   200
But fall unshaken when they mellow be.
Most necessary 'tis that we forget
To pay ourselves what to ourselves is debt.
What to ourselves in passion we propose,
The passion ending, doth the purpose lose.   205
The violence of either grief or joy
Their own enactures° with themselves destroy.
Where joy most revels, grief doth most lament,
Grief joys, joy grieves, on slender accident.   209
This world is not for aye,° nor 'tis not strange
That even our loves should with our fortunes
    change,
For 'tis a question left us yet to prove
Whether love lead fortune or else fortune love.
The great man down, you mark his favorite flies,
The poor advanced makes friends of enemies.   215
And hitherto doth love on fortune tend,
For who not needs shall never lack a friend,
And who in want a hollow friend doth try
Directly seasons° him his enemy.
But, orderly to end where I begun,   220
Our wills and fates do so contráry run
That our devices still are overthrown,
Our thoughts are ours, their ends none of our own.
So think thou wilt no second husband wed,   224
But die thy thoughts when thy first lord is dead.

  P. QUEEN. Nor earth to me give food nor Heaven
    light!
Sport and repose lock from me day and night!
To desperation turn my trust and hope!
An anchor's° cheer in prison be my scope!
Each opposite that blanks° the face of joy   230
Meet what I would have well and it destroy!
Both here and hence pursue me lasting strife
If, once a widow, ever I be wife!

  HAML. If she should break it now!

  P. KING. 'Tis deeply sworn. Sweet, leave me here
    a while.   235
My spirits grow dull, and fain I would beguile
The tedious day with sleep.   [*Sleeps.*]

  P. QUEEN.   Sleep rock thy brain,
And never come mischance between us twain!
                          [*Exit.*]

  HAML. Madam, how like you this play?
  QUEEN. The lady doth protest too much, methinks.
  HAML. Oh, but she'll keep her word.   241
  KING. Have you heard the argument?° Is there no
    offense in 't?
  HAML. No, no, they do but jest, poison in jest —
    no offense i' the world.   245
  KING. What do you call the play?

---

162. posy . . . ring: It was a pretty custom to inscribe rings with little mottoes or messages, which were necessarily brief. 165-238. Full . . . twain: The play is deliberately written in crude rhyming verse, full of ridiculous and bombastic phrases. 165. Phoebus' cart: the chariot of the sun. 166. Neptune: the sea god. Tellus: the earth goddess. 167. borrowed sheen: light borrowed from the sun. 169. Hymen: god of marriage. 170 commutual: mutually. 175. distrust: am anxious about. 177. quantity: proportion. 178. In . . . extremity: either nothing or too much. 183. leave thee: i.e., die. 184. operant powers: bodily strength. 191. Wormwood: bitterness. 192. instances: arguments. 193. respects of thrift: considerations of gain.

207. enactures: performances. 210. aye: ever. 219. seasons: ripens into. 229. anchor: anchorite, hermit. 230. blanks: makes pale. 242. argument: plot. When performances were given at Court it was sometimes customary to provide a written or printed synopsis of the story for the distinguished spectators.

HAML. *The Mousetrap.*° Marry, how? Tropically.° This play is the image of a murder done in Vienna. Gonzago is the Duke's name, his wife, Baptista. You shall see anon. 'Tis a knavish piece of 250 work, but what o' that? Your Majesty, and we that have free° souls, it touches us not. Let the galled jade wince, our withers are unwrung.°
[*Enter* LUCIANUS.] This is one Lucianus, nephew to the King.

OPH. You are as good as a chorus,° my lord. 255

HAML. I could interpret between you and your love, if I could see the puppets dallying.°

OPH. You are keen, my lord, you are keen.

HAML. It would cost you a groaning to take off my edge. 260

OPH. Still better, and worse.

HAML. So you must take your husbands.° Begin, murderer. Pox, leave thy damnable faces and begin. Come, the croaking raven doth bellow for revenge.

LUC. Thoughts black, hands apt, drugs fit, and time agreeing, 266
Confederate season, else no creature° seeing,
Thou mixture rank of midnight weeds collected,
With Hecate's ban° thrice blasted, thrice infected,
Thy natural magic and dire property° 270
On wholesome life usurp immediately.

[*Pours the poison into the sleeper's ear.*]

HAML. He poisons him i' the garden for his estate.° His name's Gonzago. The story is extant, and written in very choice Italian. You shall see anon how the murderer gets the love of Gonzago's wife.

OPH. The King rises. 276

HAML. What, frighted with false fire!°

QUEEN. How fares my lord?

POL. Give o'er the play.

KING. Give me some light. Away! 280

POL. Lights, lights, lights!

[*Exeunt all but* HAMLET *and* HORATIO.]

HAML. " Why, let the stricken deer go weep,
The hart ungallèd play,
For some must watch while some must sleep.
Thus runs the world away." 285
Would not this, sir, and a forest of feathers° — if the rest of my fortunes turn Turk° with me — with two Provincial roses° on my razed° shoes, get me a fellowship° in a cry° of players, sir?

HOR. Half a share. 290

HAML. A whole one, I.
" For thou dost know, O Damon° dear,
This realm dismantled° was
Of Jove himself, and now reigns here
A very, very — pajock."° 295

HOR. You might have rhymed.

HAML. O good Horatio, I'll take the ghost's word for a thousand pound. Didst perceive?

HOR. Very well, my lord.

HAML. Upon the talk of the poisoning? 300

HOR. I did very well note him.

HAML. Ah, ha! Come, some music! Come, the recorders!°
" For if the King like not the comedy,
Why then, belike, he likes it not, perdy."° 305
Come, some music!

[*Re-enter* ROSENCRANTZ *and* GUILDENSTERN.]

GUIL. Good my lord, vouchsafe me a word with you.

HAML. Sir, a whole history.

GUIL. The King, sir —— 310

HAML. Aye, sir, what of him?

GUIL. Is in his retirement marvelous distempered.°

HAML. With drink, sir?

GUIL. No, my lord, rather with choler.° 315

HAML. Your wisdom should show itself more richer to signify this to the doctor, for for me to put him to his purgation° would perhaps plunge him into far more choler. 319

GUIL. Good my lord, put your discourse into some frame,° and start not so wildly from my affair.

HAML. I am tame, sir. Pronounce.

GUIL. The Queen your mother, in most great affliction of spirit, hath sent me to you.

HAML. You are welcome. 325

GUIL. Nay, good my lord, this courtesy is not of the right breed. If it shall please you to make me a wholesome answer, I will do your mother's commandment. If not, your pardon and my return shall be the end of my business. 330

HAML. Sir, I cannot.

GUIL. What, my lord?

HAML. Make you a wholesome answer, my wit's

---

247. Mousetrap: The phrase was used of a device to entice a person to his own destruction (OED). **248. Tropically:** figuratively, with a pun on "trap." **252. free:** innocent. **252–53. galled . . . unwrung:** let a nag with a sore back flinch when the saddle is put on; our shoulders (being ungalled) feel no pain. **255. chorus:** the chorus sometimes introduced the characters and commented on what was to follow. See, for instance, the Chorus in *Hen V.* **257. puppets dallying:** Elizabethan puppets were crude marionettes, popular at fairs. While the figures were put through their motions, the puppet master explained what was happening. **262. So . . . husbands:** i.e., as the marriage service expresses it, "for better, for worse." **267. confederate . . . creature:** the opportunity conspiring with me, no other creature. **269. Hecate's ban:** the curse of Hecate, goddess of witchcraft. **270. property:** nature. **273. estate:** kingdom. **277. false fire:** a mere show. **286. forest of feathers:** set of plumes, much worn by players.

287. turn Turk: turn heathen, and treat me cruelly. **288. Provincial roses:** rosettes, worn on the shoes. **razed:** slashed, ornamented with cuts. **289. fellowship:** partnership, right to a full share. **cry:** pack. **292. Damon:** Damon and Pythias were types of perfect friends. **293. dismantled:** robbed. **295. pajock:** peacock, a strutting, lecherous bird. These verses, and the lines above, may have come from some ballad, otherwise lost. **303. recorders:** wooden pipes. **305. perdy:** by God. **312. distempered:** disturbed; but Hamlet takes the word in its other sense of "drunk." **315. choler:** anger, which Hamlet again pretends to understand as meaning "biliousness." **317–18. put . . . purgation:** "give him a dose of salts." **321. frame:** shape; i.e., "please talk sense."

diseased. But, sir, such answer as I can make you shall command, or rather, as you say, my mother. Therefore no more, but to the matter. My mother, you say —— 337

ROS. Then thus she says. Your behavior hath struck her into amazement and admiration.°

HAML. Oh, wonderful son that can so astonish a mother! But is there no sequel at the heels of this mother's admiration? Impart. 342

ROS. She desires to speak with you in her closet ere you go to bed.

HAML. We shall obey, were she ten times our mother. Have you any further trade with us?

ROS. My lord, you once did love me. 348

HAML. So I do still, by these pickers and stealers.°

ROS. Good my lord, what is your cause of distemper? You do surely bar the door upon your own liberty if you deny your griefs° to your friend.

HAML. Sir, I lack advancement.° 354

ROS. How can that be when you have the voice of the King himself for your succession in Denmark?

HAML. Aye, sir, but "While the grass grows"° — the proverb is something musty. [*Re-enter* 359 PLAYERS *with recorders.*] Oh, the recorders! Let me see one. To withdraw° with you —— why do you go about to recover the wind° of me, as if you would drive me into a toil?°

GUIL. O my lord, if my duty be too bold, my love is too unmannerly.° 365

HAML. I do not well understand that. Will you play upon this pipe?

GUIL. My lord, I cannot.

HAML. I pray you.

GUIL. Believe me, I cannot.

HAML. I do beseech you. 371

GUIL. I know no touch of it, my lord.

HAML. It is as easy as lying. Govern these ventages° with your fingers and thumb, give it breath with your mouth, and it will discourse most eloquent music. Look you, these are the stops. 376

GUIL. But these cannot I command to any utterance of harmony, I have not the skill.

HAML. Why, look you now, how unworthy a thing you make of me! You would play upon me, 380 you would seem to know my stops, you would pluck out the heart of my mystery, you would sound me

from my lowest note to the top of my compass — and there is much music, excellent voice, in this little organ — yet cannot you make it speak. 'Sblood, do you think I am easier to be played on than a pipe? Call me what instrument you will, though you can fret° me, you cannot play upon me. [*Re-enter* POLONIUS.] God bless you, sir! 390

POL. My lord, the Queen would speak with you, and presently.

HAML. Do you see yonder cloud that's almost in shape of a camel?

POL. By the mass, and 'tis like a camel indeed.

HAML. Methinks it is like a weasel. 396

POL. It is backed like a weasel.

HAML. Or like a whale?

POL. Very like a whale.

HAML. Then I will come to my mother by 400 and by. They fool me to the top of my bent.° I will come by and by.

POL. I will say so. [*Exit* POLONIUS.]

HAML. "By and by" is easily said. Leave me, friends. [*Exeunt all but* HAMLET.] 'Tis now the very witching time° of night, 406 When churchyards yawn and Hell itself breathes out Contagion° to this world. Now could I drink hot blood, And do such bitter business as the day 409 Would quake to look on. Soft! Now to my mother. O heart, lose not thy nature, let not ever The soul of Nero° enter this firm bosom. Let me be cruel, not unnatural. I will speak daggers to her, but use none. My tongue and soul in this be hypocrites, 415 How in my words soever she be shent,° To give them seals° never, my soul, consent! [*Exit.*]

SCENE III. *A room in the castle.*

[*Enter* KING, ROSENCRANTZ, *and* GUILDENSTERN.]

KING. I like him not, nor stands it safe with us To let his madness range.° Therefore prepare you. I your commission will forthwith dispatch, And he to England shall along with you. The terms of our estate° may not endure 5 Hazard so near us as doth hourly grow Out of his lunacies.

GUIL. We will ourselves provide.°

---

339. admiration: wonder. 349. pickers . . . stealers: i.e., hands — an echo from the Christian's duty in the catechism to keep his hands "from picking and stealing." 353. deny . . . griefs: refuse to tell your troubles. 354. advancement: promotion. Hamlet harks back to his previous interview with Rosencrantz and Guildenstern. See II.ii.258. 358. While . . . grows: the proverb ends "the steed starves." 361. withdraw: go aside. Hamlet leads Guildenstern to one side of the stage. 362. recover . . . wind: a hunting metaphor; approach me with the wind against you. 363. toil: net. 364–65. if . . . unmannerly: if I exceed my duty by asking these questions, then my affection for you shows lack of manners; i.e., please forgive me if I have been too impertinent. 374. ventages: holes, stops.

389. fret: annoy, with a pun on the frets or bars on stringed instruments by which the fingering is regulated. 401. top . . . bent: See II.ii.30,n. 406. witching time: deep night, when witches perform their foul rites. 408. Contagion: infection. 412. Nero: Nero killed his own mother. Hamlet is afraid that in the interview to come he will lose all self-control. 416. shent: rebuked. 417. give . . . seals: ratify words by actions, i.e., kill my mother.

Sc. iii:2. range: roam freely. 5. terms . . . estate: i.e., one in my position. 7. ourselves provide: make our preparations.

Most holy and religious fear° it is
To keep those many many bodies safe
That live and feed upon your Majesty.   10
    ROS. The single and peculiar° life is bound
With all the strength and armor of the mind
To keep itself from noyance,° but much more
That spirit upon whose weal° depends and rests
The lives of many. The cease of majesty°   15
Dies not alone, but like a gulf° doth draw
What's near it with it. It is a massy° wheel
Fixed on the summit of the highest mount,
To whose huge spokes ten thousand lesser things
Are mortised° and adjoined; which, when it falls,
Each small annexment, petty consequence,°   21
Attends° the boisterous ruin. Never alone
Did the King sigh but with a general groan.
    KING. Arm you, I pray you, to this speedy voyage,
For we will fetters put upon this fear,   25
Which now goes too free-footed.
    ROS. & GUIL.   We will haste us.
    [*Exeunt* ROSENCRANTZ *and* GUILDENSTERN.]
    [*Enter* POLONIUS.]
    POL. My lord, he's going to his mother's closet.
Behind the arras I'll convey myself
To hear the process.° I'll warrant she'll tax° him
    home.
And, as you said,° and wisely was it said,   30
'Tis meet that some more audience than a mother,
Since nature makes them partial, should o'erhear
The speech, of vantage.° Fare you well, my liege.
I'll call upon you ere you go to bed
And tell you what I know.
    KING.   Thanks, dear my lord. [*Exit* POLONIUS.]
Oh, my offense is rank,° it smells to Heaven.   36
It hath the primal eldest curse° upon 't,
A brother's murder. Pray can I not,
Though inclination be as sharp as will.°
My stronger guilt defeats my strong intent,   40
And like a man to double business bound,
I stand in pause where I shall first begin,
And both neglect. What if this cursèd hand
Were thicker than itself with brother's blood,
Is there not rain enough in the sweet heavens   45
To wash it white as snow? Whereto serves mercy
But to confront the visage of offense?°
And what's in prayer but this twofold force,
To be forestalled° ere we come to fall

Or pardoned being down? Then I'll look up,   50
My fault is past. But oh, what form of prayer
Can serve my turn? "Forgive me my foul mur-
    der"?
That cannot be, since I am still possessed
Of those effects° for which I did the murder —
My crown, mine own ambition, and my Queen.   55
May one be pardoned and retain the offense?°
In the corrupted currents° of this world
Offense's gilded hand may shove by justice,
And oft 'tis seen the wicked prize° itself
Buys out the law. But 'tis not so above.   60
There is no shuffling, there the action lies
In his true nature,° and we ourselves compelled
Even to the teeth and forehead° of our faults
To give in evidence. What then? What rests?
Try what repentance can. What can it not?   65
Yet what can it when one cannot repent?
Oh, wretched state! Oh, bosom black as death!
Oh, limèd° soul, that struggling to be free
Art more engaged!° Help, angels! Make assay!°
Bow, stubborn knees, and heart with strings of steel,
Be soft as sinews of the newborn babe!   71
All may be well.   [*Retires and kneels.*]
    [*Enter* HAMLET.]
    HAML. Now might I do it pat, now he is praying,
And now I'll do 't. And so he goes to Heaven,°
And so am I revenged. That would be scanned: 75
A villain kills my father, and for that
I, his sole son, do this same villain send
To Heaven.
Oh, this is hire and salary,° not revenge.
He took my father grossly,° full of bread,   80
With all his crimes broad blown, as flush° as May,
And how his audit° stands who knows save
    Heaven?
But in our circumstance and course of thought,°
'Tis heavy with him. And am I then revenged,
To take him in the purging of his soul,   85
When he is fit and seasoned,° for his passage?
No.
Up, sword, and know thou a more horrid hent.°
When he is drunk asleep, or in his rage,
Or in the incestuous pleasure of his bed —   90
At gaming, swearing, or about some act
That has no relish of salvation in 't —
Then trip him, that his heels may kick at Heaven
And that his soul may be as damned and black

---

8. fear: anxiety.   11. peculiar: individual.   13. noyance: injury.   14. weal: welfare.   15. cease of majesty: death of a king.   16. gulf: whirlpool.   17. massy: massive.   20. mortised: firmly fastened.   21. annexment . . . consequence: attachment, smallest thing connected with it.   22. Attends: waits on, is involved in.   29. process: proceeding. tax: censure.   30. as . . . said: Actually Polonius himself had said it (III.i.189–93).   33. of vantage: from a place of vantage; i.e., concealment.   36. rank: foul.   37. primal . . . curse: the curse laid upon Cain, the first murderer, who also slew his brother. 39. will: desire.   47. confront . . . offense: look crime in the face.   49. forestalled: prevented.

54. effects: advantages.   56. offense: i.e., that for which he has offended.   57. currents: courses, ways.   59. wicked prize: the proceeds of the crime.   61–62. there . . . nature: in Heaven the case is tried on its own merits.   63. teeth . . . forehead: i.e., face to face.   68. limed: caught as in birdlime.   69. engaged: stuck fast. assay: attempt.   74. And . . . Heaven: satisfactory vengeance demanded Hell.   79. hire . . . salary: i.e., a kind action deserving pay.   80. grossly: i.e., in a state of sin. See I.v.74–80.   81. broad . . . flush: in full blossom, as luxuriant. 82. audit: account.   83. circumstance . . . thought: as it appears to my mind.   86. seasoned: ripe.   88. hent: opportunity.

As Hell, whereto it goes. My mother stays.   95
This physic but prolongs thy sickly days.   *[Exit.]*
  KING. *[Rising]* My words fly up, my thoughts re-
  main below.
Words without thoughts never to Heaven go.
                                 [Exit.]

SCENE IV. *The* QUEEN's *closet.*

        [Enter QUEEN *and* POLONIUS.]

  POL. He will come straight. Look you lay home
to° him.
Tell him his pranks have been too broad° to bear
  with,
And that your grace hath screened and stood be-
  tween
Much heat and him. I'll sconce me° even here.
Pray you, be round with him.   5
  HAML. *[Within]* Mother, Mother, Mother!
  QUEEN.   I'll warrant you,
Fear me not. Withdraw, I hear him coming.
      *[*POLONIUS *hides behind the arras.]*
                [Enter HAMLET.]
  HAML. Now, Mother, what's the matter?
  QUEEN. Hamlet, thou hast thy father much of-
  fended.
  HAML. Mother, you have my father much of-
  fended.   10
  QUEEN. Come, come, you answer with an idle°
  tongue.
  HAML. Go, go, you question with a wicked
  tongue.
  QUEEN. Why, how now, Hamlet!
  HAML.   What's the matter now?
  QUEEN. Have you forgot me?
  HAML.   No, by the rood,° not so.   14
You are the Queen, your husband's brother's wife,
And — would it were not so! — you are my mother.
  QUEEN. Nay, then, I'll set those to you that can
  speak.
  HAML. Come, come, and sit you down. You shall
not budge,
You go not till I set you up a glass°
Where you may see the inmost part of you.   20
  QUEEN. What wilt thou do? Thou wilt not mur-
  der me?
Help, help, ho!
  POL. *[Behind]* What ho! Help, help, help!
  HAML. *[Drawing]* How now! A rat? Dead, for a
  ducat, dead! *[Makes a pass through the arras.]*
  POL. *[Behind]* Oh, I am slain! *[Falls and dies.]*
  QUEEN.   Oh me, what hast thou done?
  HAML. Nay, I know not. Is it the King?   26
  QUEEN. Oh, what a rash and bloody deed is this!

  HAML. A bloody deed! Almost as bad, good
  Mother,
As kill a king and marry with his brother.
  QUEEN. As kill a king!
  HAML.   Aye, lady, 'twas my word.   30
   [Lifts up the arras and discovers POLONIUS.]
Thou wretched, rash, intruding fool, farewell!
I took thee for thy better. Take thy fortune.
Thou find'st to be too busy is some danger.
Leave wringing of your hands. Peace! Sit you down,
And let me wring your heart. For so I shall   35
If it be made of penetrable stuff,
If damnèd custom have not brassed° it so
That it be proof and bulwark against sense.
  QUEEN. What have I done that thou darest wag
  thy tongue
In noise so rude against me?
  HAML.   Such an act   40
That blurs the grace and blush of modesty,
Calls virtue hypocrite, takes off the rose
From the fair forehead of an innocent love,
And sets a blister° there — makes marriage vows
As false as dicers' oaths. Oh, such a deed   45
As from the body of contraction° plucks
The very soul, and sweet religion makes
A rhapsody of words.° Heaven's face doth glow,
Yea, this solidity and compound mass,°
With tristful visage, as against the doom,°   50
Is thought-sick at the act.
  QUEEN.   Aye me, what act
That roars so loud and thunders in the index?°
  HAML. Look here upon this picture,° and on this,
The counterfeit presentment° of two brothers.
See what a grace was seated on this brow —   55
Hyperion's curls, the front° of Jove himself,
An eye like Mars, to threaten and command,
A station° like the herald Mercury°
New-lighted° on a heaven-kissing hill,
A combination° and a form indeed   60
Where every god did seem to set his seal°
To give the world assurance of a man.
This was your husband. Look you now what fol-
  lows.
Here is your husband, like a mildewed ear,
Blasting his wholesome brother. Have you eyes? 65
Could you on this fair mountain leave to feed

---

37. **brassed:** made brazen; i.e., impenetrable.   44. **sets a blister:** brands as a harlot.   46. **contraction:** the marriage contract.
48. **rhapsody of words:** string of meaningless words.   49. **solidity . . . mass:** i.e., solid earth.   50. **tristful . . . doom:** sorrowful
face, as in anticipation of Doomsday.   52. **in . . . index:** i.e., if
the beginning (*index,* i.e., table of contents) is so noisy, what
will follow?   53. **picture:** Modern producers usually interpret
the pictures as miniatures, Hamlet wearing one of his father,
Gertrude one of Claudius. In the eighteenth century, wall portraits were used.   54. **counterfeit presentment:** portrait.
56. **front:** forehead.   58. **station:** figure; lit., standing. **Mercury:**
messenger of the gods, and one of the most beautiful.   59. **New-
lighted:** newly alighted.   60. **combination:** i.e., of physical
qualities.   61. **set . . . seal:** guarantee as a perfect man.

Sc. iv: 1. **lay . . . to:** be strict with.   2. **broad:** unrestrained.
Polonius is thinking of the obvious insolence of the remarks about
second marriage in the play scene.   4. **sconce me:** hide myself.
11. **idle:** foolish.   14. **rood:** crucifix.   19. **glass:** looking-glass.

And batten° on this moor? Ha! Have you eyes?
You cannot call it love, for at your age
The heyday° in the blood is tame, it's humble,   69
And waits upon the judgment. And what judgment
Would step from this to this? Sense° sure you have,
Else could you not have motion.° But sure that sense
Is apoplexed;° for madness would not err,
Nor sense to ecstasy° was ne'er so thralled°
But it reserved some quantity of choice   75
To serve in such a difference.° What devil was 't
That thus hath cozened° you at hoodman-blind?°
Eyes without feeling, feeling without sight,
Ears without hands or eyes, smelling sans° all,
Or but a sickly part of one true sense   80
Could not so mope.°
Oh, shame! Where is thy blush? Rebellious° Hell,
If thou canst mutine° in a matron's bones,
To flaming youth let virtue be as wax
And melt in her own fire. Proclaim no shame   85
When the compulsive ardor° gives the charge,
Since frost itself as actively doth burn,
And reason panders° will.
    QUEEN.   O Hamlet, speak no more.
Thou turn'st mine eyes into my very soul,
And there I see such black and grainèd° spots   90
As will not leave their tinct.°
    HAML.   Nay, but to live
In the rank sweat of an enseamèd° bed,
Stewed in corruption, honeying and making love
Over the nasty sty ——
    QUEEN.   Oh, speak to me no more,
These words like daggers enter in my ears.   95
No more, sweet Hamlet!
    HAML.   A murderer and a villain,
A slave that is not twentieth part the tithe°
Of your precedent° lord, a vice of kings,°
A cutpurse° of the empire and the rule,
That from a shelf the precious diadem stole   100
And put it in his pocket!
    QUEEN.   No more!
    HAML. A king of shreds and patches ——
[Enter GHOST] Save me, and hover o'er me with
    your wings,
You heavenly guards! What would your gracious
    figure?

    QUEEN. Alas, he's mad!   105
    HAML. Do you not come your tardy son to chide
That, lapsed in time and passion, lets go by
The important acting of your dread command?°
Oh, say!
    GHOST. Do not forget. This visitation   110
Is but to whet thy almost blunted purpose.
But look, amazement on thy mother sits.
Oh, step between her and her fighting soul.
Conceit° in weakest bodies strongest works.
Speak to her, Hamlet.
    HAML.   How is it with you, lady?   115
    QUEEN. Alas, how is 't with you
That you do bend your eye on vacancy°
And with the incorporal° air do hold discourse?
Forth at your eyes your spirits wildly peep,
And as the sleeping soldiers in the alarm,   120
Your bedded° hairs, like life in excrements,°
Start up and stand an° end. O gentle son,
Upon the heat and flame of thy distemper°
Sprinkle cool patience. Whereon do you look?
    HAML. On him, on him! Look you how pale he
    glares!   125
His form and cause conjoined,° preaching to stones,
Would make them capable.° Do not look upon
    me,
Lest with this piteous action you convert
My stern effects.° Then what I have to do   129
Will want true color — tears perchance for blood.
    QUEEN. To whom do you speak this?
    HAML.   Do you see nothing there?
    QUEEN. Nothing at all, yet all that is I see.
    HAML. Nor did you nothing hear?
    QUEEN.   No, nothing but ourselves.
    HAML. Why, look you there! Look how it steals
    away!
My father, in his habit as he lived!   135
Look where he goes, even now, out at the portal!
                   [Exit GHOST.]
    QUEEN. This is the very coinage of your brain.
This bodiless creation ecstasy°
Is very cunning in.
    HAML.   Ecstasy!   139
My pulse, as yours, doth temperately keep time,
And makes as healthful music. It is not madness
That I have uttered. Bring me to the test
And I the matter will reword, which madness
Would gambol° from. Mother, for love of grace,

---

67. batten: glut yourself.   69. heyday: excitement.   71. Sense:
feeling.   72. motion: desire.   73. apoplexed: paralyzed.   74. ecstasy: excitement, passion. See II.i.102. thralled: enslaved.
76. serve . . . difference: to enable you to see the difference between your former and your present husband.   77. cozened:
cheated. hoodman-blind: blind-man's-buff.   79. sans: without.
81. mope: be dull.   82–88. Rebellious . . . will: i.e., if the passion
(Hell) of a woman of your age is uncontrollable (rebellious), youth
can have no restraints; there is no shame in a young man's lust
when the elderly are just as eager and their reason (which should
control desire) encourages them.   83. mutine: mutiny.   86. compulsive ardor: compelling lust.   88. panders: acts as go-between.
90. grained: dyed in the grain.   91. tinct: color.   92. enseamed:
greasy.   97. tithe: tenth part.   98. precedent: former. vice of
kings: caricature of a king.   99. cutpurse: thief.

107–08. That . . . command: who has allowed time to pass and
passion to cool, and neglects the urgent duty of obeying your
dread command.   114. Conceit: imagination.   117. vacancy:
empty space.   118. incorporal: bodiless.   121. bedded: evenly
laid. excrements: anything that grows out of the body, such as
hair or fingernails; here hair.   122. an: on.   123. distemper:
mental disturbance.   126. form . . . conjoined: his appearance
and the reason for his appearance joined.   127. capable: i.e., of
feeling.   128–29. convert . . . effects: change the stern action
which should follow.   138. ecstasy: madness.   144. gambol:
start away.

Lay not that flattering unction° to your soul,   145
That not your trespass but my madness speaks.
It will but skin and film the ulcerous place,
Whiles rank corruption, mining° all within,
Infects unseen. Confess yourself to Heaven,
Repent what's past, avoid what is to come,   150
And do not spread the compost° on the weeds
To make them ranker. Forgive me this my virtue,
For in the fatness° of these pursy° times
Virtue itself of vice must pardon beg —
Yea, curb° and woo for leave to do him good.   155
    QUEEN. O Hamlet, thou hast cleft my heart in
      twain.
    HAML. Oh, throw away the worser part of it,
And live the purer with the other half.
Good night. But go not to my uncle's bed.
Assume a virtue if you have it not.   160
That° monster, custom, who all sense doth eat,
Of habits devil,° is angel yet in this,
That to the use° of actions fair and good
He likewise gives a frock or livery
That aptly° is put on. Refrain tonight,   165
And that shall lend a kind of easiness
To the next abstinence, the next more easy.
For use almost can change the stamp° of nature,
And either the Devil,° or throw him out   169
With wondrous potency. Once more, good night.
And when you are desirous to be blest,
I'll blessing beg of you. For this same lord,
                 [*Pointing to* POLONIUS]
I do repent; but Heaven hath pleased it so,
To punish me with this, and this with me,
That I must be their scourge and minister.   175
I will bestow° him, and will answer well
The death I gave him. So again good night.
I must be cruel only to be kind.
Thus bad begins, and worse remains behind.
One word more, good lady.
    QUEEN.   What shall I do?   180
    HAML. Not this, by no means, that I bid you do.
Let the bloat° king tempt you again to bed,
Pinch wanton° on your cheek, call you his mouse,
And let him, for a pair of reechy° kisses   184
Or paddling in your neck with his damned fingers,
Make you to ravel° all this matter out,
That I essentially am not in madness,

But mad in craft. 'Twere good you let him know.
For who that's but a Queen, fair, sober, wise,
Would from a paddock,° from a bat, a gib,°   190
Such dear concernings° hide? Who would do so?
No, in despite° of sense and secrecy,
Unpeg the basket on the house's top,
Let the birds fly, and like the famous ape,°
To try conclusions,° in the basket creep   195
And break your own neck down.
    QUEEN. Be thou assured if words be made of
      breath
And breath of life, I have no life to breathe
What thou hast said to me.
    HAML. I must to England. You know that?
    QUEEN.   Alack,   200
I had forgot. 'Tis so concluded on.
    HAML. There's letters sealed, and my two school-
      fellows,
Whom I will trust as I will adders fanged,
They bear the mandate.° They must sweep my way,
And marshal me to knavery. Let it work,   205
For 'tis the sport to have the enginer°
Hoist with his own petar.° And 't shall go hard
But I will delve one yard below their mines
And blow them at the moon: Oh, 'tis most sweet
When in one line two crafts° directly meet.   210
This man shall set me packing.
I'll lug the guts into the neighbor room.
Mother, good night. Indeed this counselor
Is now most still, most secret, and most grave
Who was in life a foolish prating knave.   215
Come, sir, to draw toward an end with you.
Good night, Mother.   [*Exeunt severally,°*
         HAMLET *dragging in* POLONIUS.]

Act IV

SCENE I. *A room in the castle.*

[*Enter* KING, QUEEN, ROSENCRANTZ, *and*
         GUILDENSTERN.]
    KING. There's matter° in these sighs, these pro-
      found heaves,
You must translate. 'Tis fit we understand them.
Where is your son?

---

145. unction: healing ointment.   148. mining: undermining.
151. compost: manure.   153. fatness: grossness. pursy: bloated.
155. curb: bow low.   161–65. That . . . on: i.e., custom (bad
habits) like an evil monster destroys all sense of good and evil, but
yet can become an angel (good habits) when it makes us perform
good actions as mechanically as we put on our clothes.   162. devil:
This is the Q2 reading; the passage is omitted in F1. Probably the
word should be "evil."   163. use: practice.   165. aptly: readily.
168. stamp: impression.   169. either the Devil: some verb such
as "shame" or "curb" has been omitted.   176. bestow: get rid of.
182. bloat: bloated.   183. wanton: lewdly.   184. reechy: foul.
186. ravel: unravel, reveal.

190. paddock: toad. gib: tomcat.   191. dear concernings:
important matters.   192. despite: spite.   194. famous ape:
The story is not known, but evidently told of an ape that
let the birds out of their cage and, seeing them fly, crept
into the cage himself and jumped out, breaking his own
neck.   195. try conclusions: repeat the experiment.   204. mandate:
command.   206. enginer: engineer.   207. petar: petard, land
mine.   210. crafts: devices.   217 s.d., Exeunt severally: i.e.,
by separate exits. In F1 there is no break here. The King enters as soon as Hamlet has dragged the body away. Q2 marks the
break. The act division was first inserted in a quarto of 1676.
    Act IV, Sc. i: 1. matter: something serious.

QUEEN. Bestow this place° on us a little while.

[*Exeunt* ROSENCRANTZ *and* GUILDENSTERN.]

Ah, mine own lord, what have I seen tonight!   5

KING. What, Gertrude? How does Hamlet?

QUEEN. Mad as the sea and wind when both contend

Which is the mightier. In his lawless fit,

Behind the arras hearing something stir,

Whips out his rapier, cries " A rat, a rat! "   10

And in this brainish apprehension° kills

The unseen good old man.

KING.   Oh, heavy deed!

It had been so with us had we been there.

His liberty is full of threats to all,

To you yourself, to us, to everyone.   15

Alas, how shall this bloody deed be answered?

It will be laid to us, whose providence°

Should have kept short,° restrained and out of
haunt,°

This mad young man. But so much was our love

We would not understand what was most fit,   20

But, like the owner of a foul disease,

To keep it from divulging° let it feed

Even on the pith° of life. Where is he gone?

QUEEN. To draw apart the body he hath killed,

O'er whom his very madness, like some ore   25

Among a mineral of metals base,

Shows itself pure. He weeps for what is done.

KING. O Gertrude, come away!

The sun no sooner shall the mountains touch

But we will ship him hence. And this vile deed   30

We must, with all our majesty and skill,

Both countenance° and excuse. Ho, Guildenstern!

[*Re-enter* ROSENCRANTZ *and* GUILDENSTERN.]

Friends both, go join you with some further aid.

Hamlet in madness hath Polonius slain,   34

And from his mother's closet hath he dragged him.

Go seek him out, speak fair, and bring the body

Into the chapel. I pray you, haste in this.

[*Exeunt* ROSENCRANTZ *and* GUILDENSTERN.]

Come, Gertrude, we'll call up our wisest friends,

And let them know both what we mean to do

And what's untimely done,°   40

Whose whisper o'er the world's diameter

As level as the cannon to his blank°

Transports his poisoned shot, may miss our name

And hit the woundless air. Oh, come away!

My soul is full of discord and dismay.   [*Exeunt.*]

---

4. Bestow . . . place: give place, leave us.   11. brainish apprehension: mad imagination.   17. providence: foresight.
18. short: confined. out of haunt: away from others.   22. di-
vulging: becoming known.   23. pith: marrow.   32. countenance: take responsibility for.   40. done: A half-line has been
omitted. Some editors fill the gap with "So, haply slander."
42. blank: target.

SCENE II. *Another room in the castle.*

[*Enter* HAMLET.]

HAML. Safely stowed.

ROS. & GUIL. [*Within*] Hamlet! Lord Hamlet!

HAML. But soft, what noise? Who calls on Hamlet?

Oh, here they come.

[*Enter* ROSENCRANTZ *and* GUILDENSTERN.]

ROS. What have you done, my lord, with the dead
body?   5

HAML. Compounded it with dust, whereto 'tis kin.

ROS. Tell us where 'tis, that we may take it thence
And bear it to the chapel.

HAML. Do not believe it.

ROS. Believe what?   10

HAML. That I can keep your counsel and not mine
own. Besides, to be demanded of a sponge! What
replication° should be made by the son of a king?

ROS. Take you me for a sponge, my lord?   15

HAML. Aye, sir, that soaks up the King's countenance,° his rewards, his authorities. But such officers
do the King best service in the end. He keeps them,
like an ape, in the corner of his jaw, first mouthed,
to be last swallowed. When he needs what you have
gleaned, it is but squeezing you and, sponge, you
shall be dry again.   23

ROS. I understand you not, my lord.

HAML. I am glad of it. A knavish speech sleeps in
a foolish ear.°

ROS. My lord, you must tell us where the body is,
and go with us to the King.   28

HAML. The body is with the King, but the King
is not with the body.° The King is a thing ——

GUIL. A thing, my lord?

HAML. Of nothing. Bring me to him. Hide   32
fox, and all after.°   [*Exeunt.*]

SCENE III. *Another room in the castle.*

[*Enter* KING, *attended.*]

KING. I have sent to seek him, and to find the
body.

How dangerous is it that this man goes loose!

Yet must not we put the strong law on him.

He's loved of the distracted° multitude,

Who like not in their judgment but their eyes;°   5

And where 'tis so, the offender's scourge° is
weighed,

Sc. ii: 14. replication: answer.   17. countenance: favor.
25–26. A . . . ear: a fool never understands the point of a sinister
speech.   29–30. The . . . body: Hamlet deliberately bewilders
his companions.   32–33. Hide . . . after: a form of the game of
hide-and-seek. With these words Hamlet runs away from them.

Sc. iii: 4. distracted: bewildered.   5. like . . . eyes: whose
likings are swayed not by judgment but by looks.   6. scourge:
punishment.

But never the offense. To bear° all smooth and
    even,
This sudden sending him away must seem
Deliberate pause.° Diseases desperate grown
By desperate appliance are relieved,   10
Or not at all.
  [*Enter* ROSENCRANTZ.] How now! What hath be-
    fall'n?
ROS. Where the dead body is bestowed, my lord,
We cannot get from him.
  KING.   But where is he?
  ROS. Without, my lord, guarded, to know your
    pleasure.
  KING. Bring him before us.   15
  ROS. Ho, Guildenstern! Bring in my lord.
      [*Enter* HAMLET *and* GUILDENSTERN.]
  KING. Now, Hamlet, where's Polonius?
  HAML. At supper.
  KING. At supper! Where?   19
  HAML. Not where he eats, but where he is eaten.
A certain convocation of politic worms° are e'en at
him. Your worm is your only emperor for diet. We
fat all creatures else to fat us, and we fat ourselves
for maggots. Your fat king and your lean beggar is
but variable service,° two dishes, but to one table.
That's the end.   26
  KING. Alas, alas!
  HAML. A man may fish with the worm that hath
eat of a king, and eat of the fish that hath fed of that
worm.
  KING. What dost thou mean by this?
  HAML. Nothing but to show you how a king may
go a progress° through the guts of a beggar.
  KING. Where is Polonius?   34
  HAML. In Heaven—send thither to see. If your
messenger find him not there, seek him i' the other
place yourself. But indeed if you find him not with-
in this month, you shall nose him as you go up the
stairs into the lobby.   39
  KING. [*To some* ATTENDANTS] Go seek him there.
  HAML. He will stay till you come.
               [*Exeunt* ATTENDANTS.]
  KING. Hamlet, this deed, for thine especial safety,
Which we do tender,° as we dearly grieve
For that which thou hast done, must send thee
    hence
With fiery quickness. Therefore prepare thyself.   45
The bark is ready and the wind at help,°
The associates tend,° and every thing is bent°
For England.
  HAML.   For England?
  KING.   Aye, Hamlet.

  HAML.   Good.
  KING. So is it if thou knew'st our purposes.
  HAML. I see a cherub that sees them. But, come,
for England! Farewell, dear Mother.   51
  KING. Thy loving father, Hamlet.
  HAML. My mother. Father and mother is man and
wife, man and wife is one flesh, and so, my mother.
Come, for England!   [*Exit.*]
  KING. Follow him at foot,° tempt° him with
    speed aboard.   56
Delay it not, I'll have him hence tonight.
Away! For everything is sealed and done
That else leans on the affair. Pray you make haste.
      [*Exeunt* ROSENCRANTZ *and* GUILDENSTERN.]
And, England, if my love thou hold'st at aught—
As my great power thereof may give thee sense,   61
Since yet thy cicatrice° looks raw and red
After the Danish sword, and thy free awe°
Pays homage to us—thou mayst not coldly set
Our sovereign process,° which imports at full,   65
By letters congruing° to that effect,
The present° death of Hamlet. Do it, England,
For like the hectic° in my blood he rages,
And thou must cure me. Till I know 'tis done,
Howe'er my haps,° my joys were ne'er begun.   70
                      [*Exit.*]

SCENE IV. *A plain in Denmark.*

[*Enter* FORTINBRAS, *a* CAPTAIN *and* SOLDIERS,
      marching.]
  FOR. Go, Captain, from me greet the Danish
    King.
Tell him that by his license Fortinbras
Craves the conveyance of a promised march°
Over his kingdom. You know the rendezvous.
If that His Majesty would aught with us,   5
We shall express our duty in his eye,°
And let him know so.
  CAP.   I will do 't, my lord.
  FOR. Go softly on.
         [*Exeunt* FORTINBRAS *and* SOLDIERS.]
[*Enter* HAMLET, ROSENCRANTZ, GUILDENSTERN, *and*
      others.]
  HAML. Good sir, whose powers° are these?
  CAP. They are of Norway, sir.   10
  HAML. How purposed, sir, I pray you?
  CAP. Against some part of Poland.

---

7. **bear:** make.   9. **Deliberate pause:** the result of careful
planning.   21. **convocation . . . worms:** an assembly of political-
minded worms.   25. **variable service:** choice of alternatives.
33. **go a progress:** make a state journey.   43. **tender:** regard
highly.   46. **at help:** favorable.   47. **associates tend:** your
companions are waiting. **bent:** ready.

56. **at foot:** at his heels. **tempt:** entice.   62. **cicatrice:** scar.
There is nothing in the play to explain this incident.   63. **free
awe:** voluntary submission.   64–65. **coldly . . . process:** hesitate to carry out our royal command.   66. **congruing:** agreeing.
67. **present:** immediate.   68. **hectic:** fever.   70. **Howe'er my
haps:** whatever may happen to me.
  Sc. iv: 3. Craves . . . march: asks for permission to transport
his army, as had already been promised. See II.ii.76–82.   6. **in
. . . eye:** before his eyes; i.e., in person.   9. **powers:** forces.

HAML. Who commands them, sir?

CAP. The nephew to old Norway, Fortinbras.   14

HAML. Goes it against the main° of Poland, sir,
Or for some frontier?

CAP. Truly to speak, and with no addition,°
We go to gain a little patch of ground
That hath in it no profit but the name.
To pay five ducats, five, I would not farm it,   20
Nor will it yield to Norway or the Pole
A ranker° rate should it be sold in fee.°

HAML. Why, then the Polack never will defend it.

CAP. Yes, it is already garrisoned.

HAML. Two thousand souls and twenty thousand
  ducats   25
Will not debate the question of this straw.
This is the imposthume of° much wealth and peace,
That inward breaks, and shows no cause without
Why the man dies. I humbly thank you, sir.

CAP. God be wi' you, sir.   [Exit.]

ROS.   Will 't please you go, my lord?   30

HAML. I'll be with you straight. Go a little before.
                         [Exeunt all but HAMLET.]
How° all occasions do inform against° me
And spur my dull revenge! What is a man
If his chief good and market° of his time
Be but to sleep and feed? A beast, no more.   35
Sure, He that made us with such large discourse,
Looking before and after,° gave us not
That capability and godlike reason
To fust° in us unused. Now whether it be
Bestial oblivion, or some craven scruple   40
Of thinking too precisely on the event—
A thought which, quartered, hath but one part wis-
  dom
And ever three parts coward—I do not know
Why yet I live to say " This thing's to do,"   44
Sith I have cause, and will, and strength, and means
To do 't. Examples gross° as earth exhort me.
Witness this army, of such mass and charge,°
Led by a delicate and tender Prince
Whose spirit with divine ambition puffed
Makes mouths at the invisible event,°   50
Exposing what is mortal and unsure
To all that fortune, death, and danger dare,
Even for an eggshell.° Rightly to be great
Is not to stir without great argument,
But greatly to find quarrel in a straw   55
When honor's at the stake.° How stand I then,

That have a father killed, a mother stained,
Excitements of my reason and my blood,
And let all sleep while to my shame I see
The imminent death of twenty thousand men   60
That for a fantasy and trick° of fame
Go to their graves like beds, fight for a plot
Whereon the numbers cannot try the cause,°
Which is not tomb enough and continent°
To hide the slain? Oh, from this time forth,   65
My thoughts be bloody or be nothing worth!
                                        [Exit.]

SCENE V. *Elsinore. A room in the castle.*

[*Enter* QUEEN, HORATIO, *and a* GENTLEMAN.]

QUEEN. I will not speak with her.

GEN. She is importunate, indeed distract.°
Her mood will needs be pitied.

QUEEN   What would she have?

GEN. She speaks much of her father, says she hears
There's tricks° i' the world, and hems° and beats
  her heart,   5
Spurns enviously° at straws, speaks things in doubt
That carry but half-sense. Her speech is nothing,
Yet the unshaped use° of it doth move
The hearers to collection.° They aim° at it,   9
And botch° the words up fit to their own thoughts,
Which, as her winks and nods and gestures yield
  them,
Indeed would make one think there might be
  thought,
Though nothing sure, yet much unhappily.

HOR. 'Twere good she were spoken with, for she
  may strew
Dangerous conjectures in ill-breeding minds.   15

QUEEN. Let her come in.   [*Exit* GENTLEMAN.]
[*Aside*] To my sick soul, as sin's true nature is,
Each toy° seems prologue to some great amiss.°
So full of artless jealousy° is guilt,
It spills itself in fearing to be spilt.°   20
        [*Re-enter* GENTLEMAN, *with* OPHELIA.°]

OPH. Where is the beauteous Majesty of Denmark?

QUEEN. How now, Ophelia!

OPH. [*Sings.*]
  " How should I your truelove know
      From another one?

---

15. **main:** mainland.   17. **addition:** exaggeration.   22. **ranker:** richer. **in fee:** with possession as freehold.   27. **imposthume of:** inward swelling caused by.   32–66. **How . . . worth:** The soliloquy and all the dialogue after the exit of Fortinbras are omitted in F1.   32. **inform against:** accuse.   34. **market:** profit. **36–37. such . . . after:** intelligence that enables us to consider the future and the past.   39. **fust:** grow musty.   46. **gross:** iarge.   47. **charge:** expense.   50. **Makes . . . event:** mocks at the unseen risk.   53. **eggshell:** i.e., worthless trifle.   53–56. **Rightly . . . stake:** true greatness is a matter of fighting not for a mighty cause but for the merest trifle when honor is concerned.

61. **fantasy . . . trick:** illusion and whim.   63. **Whereon . . cause:** a piece of ground so small that it would not hold the combatants.   64. **continent:** large enough to contain.

Sc. v: 2. **distract:** out of her mind.   5. **tricks:** trickery. **hems:** makes significant noises.   6. **Spurns enviously:** kicks spitefully.   8. **unshaped use:** disorder.   9. **collection:** i.e., attempts to find a sinister meaning. **aim:** guess.   10. **botch:** patch.   18. **toy:** trifle. **amiss:** calamity.   19. **artless jealousy:** clumsy suspicion.   20. **It . . . spilt:** guilt reveals itself by its efforts at concealment.   20 **s.d.,** Re-enter . . . Ophelia: Q1 notes "Enter Ophelia playing on a lute, and her hair down, singing."

By his cockle hat° and staff   25
    And his sandal shoon."°

QUEEN. Alas, sweet lady, what imports this song?

OPH. Say you? nay, pray you, mark. [*Sings.*]
    "He is dead and gone, lady,
        He is dead and gone,   30
    At his head a grass-green turf,
        At his heels a stone."

Oh, oh!

QUEEN. Nay, but, Ophelia ——

OPH.   Pray you, mark. [*Sings.*]
"White his shroud as the mountain snow ——"   35
        [*Enter* KING.]

QUEEN. Alas, look here, my lord.

OPH. [*Sings.*]
    "Larded° with sweet flowers,
    Which bewept to the grave did go
        With truelove showers."°

KING. How do you, pretty lady?   40

OPH. Well, God 'ild° you! They say the owl was
a baker's daughter.° Lord, we know what we are
but know not what we may be. God be at your table!

KING. Conceit upon her father.   45

OPH. Pray you let's have no words of this, but
when they ask you what it means, say you this
[*Sings*]:
    "Tomorrow is Saint Valentine's day,°
        All in the morning betime,
    And I a maid at your window,   50
        To be your Valentine.

    "Then up he rose, and donned his clothes,
        And dupped° the chamber door,
    Let in the maid, that out a maid
        Never departed more."   55

KING. Pretty Ophelia!

OPH. Indeed, la, without an oath, I'll make an end
on 't. [*Sings.*]
    "By Gis° and by Saint Charity,
        Alack, and fie for shame!   60
    Young men will do 't, if they come to 't,
        By cock, they are to blame.
    Quoth she, before you tumbled me,
        You promised me to wed."

He answers:

    "So would I ha' done, by yonder sun,   65
        An thou hadst not come to my bed."

KING. How long hath she been thus?

OPH. I hope all will be well. We must be patient.
But I cannot choose but weep to think they should
lay him i' the cold ground. My brother shall   70
know of it. And so I thank you for your good counsel. Come, my coach! Good night, ladies, good night,
sweet ladies, good night, good night.   [*Exit.*]

KING. Follow her close,° give her good watch, I
pray you.   [*Exit* HORATIO.]
Oh, this is the poison of deep grief. It springs   76
All from her father's death. O Gertrude, Gertrude,
When sorrows come, they come not single spies,°
But in battalions! First, her father slain.
Next, your son gone, and he most violent author°
Of his own just remove. The people muddied,   81
Thick and unwholesome in their thoughts and
    whispers,
For good Polonius' death. And we have done but
    greenly°
In huggermugger° to inter him. Poor Ophelia
Divided from herself and her fair judgment,°   85
Without the which we are pictures,° or mere beasts.
Last, and as much containing as all these,
Her brother is in secret come from France,
Feeds on his wonder, keeps himself in clouds,
And wants not buzzers° to infect his ear   90
With pestilent speeches of his father's death,
Wherein necessity, of matter beggared,
Will nothing stick our person to arraign°
In ear and ear. O my dear Gertrude, this,
Like to a murdering piece,° in many places   95
Gives me superfluous death.   [*A noise within*]

QUEEN.   Alack, what noise is this?

KING. Where are my Switzers?° Let them guard
the door.
[*Enter another* GENTLEMAN.] What is the matter?

GEN.   Save yourself, my lord.
The ocean, overpeering of his list,°
Eats not the flats° with more impetuous haste   100
Than young Laertes, in a riotous head,°
O'erbears your officers. The rabble call him lord,
And as the world were now but to begin,
Antiquity forgot, custom not known,
The ratifiers and props of every word,°   105

---

25. cockle hat: a hat adorned with a cockleshell worn by pilgrims. 26. sandal shoon: sandals, the proper footwear of pilgrims. 37. Larded: garnished. 39. truelove showers: the tears
of his faithful love. 41. 'ild (yield): reward. 41–42. owl . . .
daughter: An allusion to a legend that Christ once went into a
baker's shop and asked for bread. The baker's wife gave him a
piece but was rebuked by her daughter for giving him too much.
Thereupon the daughter was turned into an owl. 48. Saint . . .
day: February 14, the day when birds are supposed to mate.
According to the old belief the first single man then seen by a
maid is destined to be her husband. 53. dupped: opened.
59–62. Gis . . . cock: for "Jesus" and "God," both words being
used instead of the sacred names, like the modern "Jeez" and
"Gee."

74. close: closely. 78. spies: scouts. 80. author: cause.
83. done) . . . greenly: shown immature judgment. 84. huggermugger: secret haste, "any which way." 85. Divided . . . judgment: no longer able to use her judgment. 86. pictures: lifeless
imitations. 90. buzzers: scandalmongers. 92–93. Wherein . . .
arraign: in which, knowing nothing of the true facts, he must
necessarily accuse us. 95. murdering piece: cannon loaded with
grapeshot. 97. Switzers: Swiss bodyguard. 99. overpeering
. . . list: looking over its boundary; i.e., flooding the mainland.
100. Eats . . . flats: floods not the flat country. 101. in . . .
head: with a force of rioters. 104–05. Antiquity . . . word: forgetting ancient rule and ignoring old custom, by which all promises must be maintained.

They cry " Choose we — Laertes shall be King! "
Caps, hands, and tongues applaud it to the clouds —
" Laertes shall be King, Laertes King! "
  QUEEN. How cheerfully on the false trail they cry!
Oh, this is counter,° you false Danish dogs!   110
                        [Noise within]
  KING. The doors are broke.
    [Enter LAERTES, *armed,* DANES *following.]*
  LAER. Where is this King? Sirs, stand you all
    without.
  DANES. No, let's come in.
  LAER.   I pray you, give me leave.
  DANES. We will, we will.
            [They retire without the door.]
  LAER. I thank you. Keep the door. O thou vile
    King,   115
Give me my father!
  QUEEN.   Calmly, good Laertes.
  LAER. That drop of blood that's calm proclaims
    me bastard,
Cries cuckold° to my father, brands the harlot°
Even here, between the chaste unsmirchèd brows
Of my true mother.
  KING.   What is the cause, Laertes,   120
That thy rebellion looks so giantlike?
Let him go, Gertrude. Do not fear° our person.
There's such divinity doth hedge a king°
That treason can but peep° to what it would,
Acts little of his will. Tell me, Laertes,   125
Why thou art thus incensed. Let him go, Gertrude.
Speak, man.
  LAER. Where is my father?
  KING.   Dead.
  QUEEN.   But not by him.
  KING. Let him demand his fill.
  LAER. How came he dead? I'll not be juggled
    with.   130
To Hell, allegiance! Vows, to the blackest devil!
Conscience and grace, to the profoundest pit!
I dare damnation. To this point I stand,
That both the worlds I give to negligence.°
Let come what comes, only I'll be revenged   135
Most throughly° for my father.
  KING.   Who shall stay you?
  LAER. My will, not all the world.
And for my means, I'll husband° them so well
They shall go far with little.
  KING.   Good Laertes,
If you desire to know the certainty   140
Of your dear father's death, is 't writ in your revenge

That, swoopstake,° you will draw both friend and
  foe,
Winner and loser?
  LAER. None but his enemies.
  KING.   Will you know them, then?
  LAER. To his good friends thus wide I'll ope my
    arms,   145
And like the kind life-rendering pelican,°
Repast° them with my blood.
  KING.   Why, now you speak
Like a good child and a true gentleman.
That I am guiltless of your father's death,
And am most sensibly° in grief for it,   150
It shall as level° to your judgment pierce
As day does to your eye.
  DANES.   *[Within]* Let her come in.
  LAER. How now! What noise is that?
[Re-enter OPHELIA.*]* O heat, dry up my brains! Tears
    seven times salt
Burn out the sense and virtue of mine eye!   155
By Heaven, thy madness shall be paid with weight
Till our scale turn the beam.° O rose of May!°
Dear maid, kind sister, sweet Ophelia!
Oh heavens! Is 't possible a young maid's wits
Should be as mortal as an old man's life?   160
Nature is fine in love, and where 'tis fine
It sends some precious instance of itself
After the thing it loves.°
  OPH. *[Sings.]*
    " They bore him barefaced on the bier,
      Hey non nonny, nonny, hey nonny,   165
    And in his grave rained many a tear —— "
Fare you well, my dove!
  LAER. Hadst thou thy wits and didst persuade re-
    venge,
It could not move thus.
  OPH. *[Sings.]*
    " You must sing down a-down   170
      An you call him a-down-a."
Oh, how the wheel° becomes it! It is the false stew-
ard, that stole his master's daughter.
  LAER. This nothing's more than matter.°   174
  OPH. There's° rosemary, that's for remembrance

110. **counter:** in the wrong direction of the scent.   118. **cuckold:** a husband deceived by his wife.   **brands . . . harlot:** Convicted harlots were branded with a hot iron. Cf. III.iv.44.
122. **fear:** fear for.   123. **divinity . . . king:** divine protection
surrounds a king as with a hedge.   124. **peep:** look over, not
break through.   134. **That . . . negligence:** I do not care what
happens to me in this world or the next.   136. **throughly:** thoroughly.   138. **husband:** use economically.

142. **swoopstake:** "sweeping the board."   146. **life-rendering
pelican:** The mother pelican was supposed to feed her young
with blood from her own breast.   147. **Repast:** feed.   150. **sensibly:** feelingly.   151. **level:** clearly.   157. **turn . . . beam:** weigh
down the beam of the scale. **rose of May:** perfection of young
beauty. See III.i.160.   161–63. **Nature . . . loves:** i.e., her love
for her father was so exquisite that she has sent her sanity
after him. Laertes, especially in moments of emotion, is
prone to use highly exaggerated speech.   172. **wheel:** explained
variously as the spinning wheel, Fortune's wheel, or the refrain.
The likeliest explanation is that she breaks into a little dance
at the words "You must sing," and that the *wheel* is the turn
as she circles round.   174. **This . . . matter:** this nonsense means
more than sense.   175–85. **There's . . . died:** In the language of
flowers, each has its peculiar meaning, and Ophelia distributes
them appropriately: for her brother rosemary (remembrance) and
pansies (thoughts); for the King fennel (flattery) and columbine

— pray you, love, remember. And there is pansies,
that's for thoughts.

LAER. A document° in madness, thoughts and remembrance fitted.   179

OPH. There's fennel for you, and columbines.
There's rue for you, and here's some for me — we
may call it herb of grace o' Sundays. Oh, you must
wear your rue with a difference. There's a daisy. I
would give you some violets, but they withered all
when my father died. They say a' made a good
end. [*Sings.*]   186
     "For bonny sweet Robin is all my joy."

LAER. Thought and affliction, passion, Hell itself,
She turns to favor° and to prettiness.

OPH. [*Sings.*]
     "And will a' not come again?   190
     And will a' not come again?
       No, no, he is dead,
       Go to thy deathbed,
     He never will come again.

     "His beard was as white as snow,   195
     All flaxen was his poll.°
       He is gone, he is gone,
       And we cast away moan.
     God ha' mercy on his soul!"

And of all Christian souls, I pray God. God be wi'
you.   [*Exit.*]

LAER. Do you see this, O God?   201

KING. Laertes, I must commune with your grief,·
Or you deny me right. Go but apart,
Make choice of whom your wisest friends you will,
And they shall hear and judge 'twixt you and me.
If by direct or by collateral° hand   206
They find us touched,° we will our kingdom give,
Our crown, our life, and all that we call ours,
To you in satisfaction. But if not,
Be you content to lend your patience to us   210
And we shall jointly labor with your soul
To give it due content.

LAER.   Let this be so.
His means of death, his obscure funeral,°
No trophy, sword, nor hatchment° o'er his bones,
No noble rite nor formal ostentation,°   215
Cry to be heard, as 'twere from Heaven to earth,
That I must call 't in question.

KING.   So you shall,
And where the offense is let the great ax fall.
I pray you, go with me.   [*Exeunt.*]

(thanklessness); for the Queen rue, called also herb o' grace
(sorrow), and daisy (light of love). Neither is worthy of violets
(faithfulness).   **178. document:** instruction.   **189. favor:**
charm.   **196. flaxen . . . poll:** white as flax was his head.
206. collateral: i.e., as an accessory.   **207. touched:** implicated.
213. obscure funeral: Men of rank were buried with much
ostentation. To bury Polonius "huggermugger" was thus an
insult to his memory and to his surviving family.   **214. hatch-**
ment: device of the coat of arms carried in a funeral and hung
up over the tomb.   **215. formal ostentation:** ceremony properly
ordered.

SCENE VI. *Another room in the castle.*

[*Enter* HORATIO *and a* SERVANT.]

HOR. What are they that would speak with me?

SER. Seafaring men, sir. They say they have letters
for you.

HOR. Let them come in.   [*Exit* SERVANT.]
I do not know from what part of the world
I should be greeted, if not from Lord Hamlet.   5

[*Enter* SAILORS.]

1. SAIL. God bless you, sir.

HOR. Let Him bless thee too.

1. SAIL. He shall, sir, an 't please Him. There's a
letter for you, sir. It comes from the ambassador that
was bound for England — if your name be Horatio,
as I am let to know it is.   11

HOR. [*Reads.*] "Horatio, when thou shalt have
overlooked° this, give these fellows some means° to
the King. They have letters for him. Ere we were
two days old at sea, a pirate of very warlike ap-   15
pointment° gave us chase. Finding ourselves too
slow of sail, we put on a compelled valor, and in the
grapple I boarded them. On the instant they got
clear of our ship, so I alone became their prisoner.
They have dealt with me like thieves of mercy;   20
but they knew what they did — I am to do a good
turn for them. Let the King have the letters I have
sent, and repair thou to me with as much speed as
thou wouldest fly death. I have words to speak in
thine ear will make thee dumb, yet are they   25
much too light for the bore of the matter.° These
good fellows will bring thee where I am. Rosencrantz and Guildenstern hold their course for England. Of them I have much to tell thee. Farewell.   30
     "He that thou knowest thine,
         "HAMLET"

Come, I will make you way for these your letters,
And do 't the speedier that you may direct me
To him from whom you brought them.   [*Exeunt.*]

SCENE VII. *Another room in the castle.*

[*Enter* KING *and* LAERTES.]

KING. Now must your conscience my acquittance
seal,°
And you must put me in your heart for friend,
Sith you have heard, and with a knowing ear,
That he which hath your noble father slain
Pursued my life.

LAER.   It well appears. But tell me   5
Why you proceeded not against these feats,°
So crimeful and so capital° in nature,

Sc. vi: 13. overlooked: read. **means:** access.   **16. appoint-**
ment: equipment.   **26. too . . . matter:** i.e., words fall short,
like a small shot fired from a cannon with too wide a bore.
     Sc. vii: 1. my . . . seal: acquit me.   **6. feats:** acts.   **7. capi-**
tal: deserving death.

As by your safety, wisdom, all things else,
You mainly were stirred up.

KING.   Oh, for two special reasons,
Which may to you perhaps seem much unsinewed,°
But yet to me they're strong. The Queen his mother
Lives almost by his looks, and for myself —   12
My virtue or my plague, be it either which —
She's so conjunctive° to my life and soul
That as the star moves not but° in his sphere,   15
I could not but by her. The other motive
Why to a public count° I might not go
Is the great love the general gender° bear him,
Who, dipping all his faults in their affection,°
Would, like the spring that turneth wood to stone,°
Convert his gyves to graces.° So that my arrows,   21
Too slightly timbered° for so loud a wind,
Would have reverted to my bow again
And not where I had aimed them.

LAER. And so have I a noble father lost,   25
A sister driven into desperate terms,°
Whose worth, if praises may go back again,°
Stood challenger on mount of all the age
For her perfections.° But my revenge will come.

KING. Break not your sleeps for that. You must
    not think
That we are made of stuff so flat and dull   31
That we can let our beard be shook with danger
And think it pastime. You shortly shall hear more.°
I loved your father, and we love ourself,
And that, I hope, will teach you to imagine——   35
[Enter a MESSENGER, with letters.] How now! What
    news?

MESS. Letters, my lord, from Hamlet.
This to your Majesty, this to the Queen.

KING. From Hamlet! Who brought them?

MESS. Sailors, my lord, they say — I saw them
    not.
They were given me by Claudio, he received them
Of him that brought them.   41

KING. Laertes, you shall hear them.
Leave us.   [Exit MESSENGER.]
[Reads] " High and Mighty, you shall know I am
set naked° on your kingdom. Tomorrow shall I beg
leave to see your kingly eyes, when I shall, first asking your pardon thereunto, recount the occasion of

my sudden and more strange return.
                            " HAMLET "
What should this mean? Are all the rest come
    back?
Or is it some abuse,° and no such thing?   50

LAER. Know you the hand?

KING. 'Tis Hamlet's character.° " Naked! "
And in a postscript here, he says " alone."
Can you advise me?

LAER. I'm lost in it, my lord. But let him come.
It warms the very sickness in my heart   56
That I shall live and tell him to his teeth
" Thus didest thou."

KING.   If it be so, Laertes —
As how should it be so, how otherwise? —
Will you be ruled by me?

LAER.   Aye, my lord,   60
So you will not o'errule° me to a peace.

KING. To thine own peace. If he be now returned,
As checking at° his voyage, and that he means
No more to undertake it, I will work him
To an exploit now ripe in my device,   65
Under the which he shall not choose but fall.
And for his death no wind of blame shall breathe,
But even his mother shall uncharge the practice°
And call it accident.

LAER.   My lord, I will be ruled,
The rather if you could devise it so   70
That I might be the organ.°

KING.   It falls right.
You have been talked of since your travel much,
And that in Hamlet's hearing, for a quality
Wherein they say you shine. Your sum of parts°
Did not together pluck such envy from him   75
As did that one, and that in my regard
Of the unworthiest siege.°

LAER.   What part is that, my lord?

KING. A very ribbon in the cap of youth,
Yet needful too; for youth no less becomes
The light and careless livery that it wears   80
Than settled age his sables and his weeds,°
Importing health and graveness. Two months since,
Here was a gentleman of Normandy.
I've seen myself, and served against, the French,
And they can well° on horseback; but this gallant
Had witchcraft in 't, he grew unto his seat,   86
And to such wondrous doing brought his horse
As had he been incorpsed and deminatured°
With the brave beast. So far he topped my thought°

---

10. unsinewed: weak, flabby.   14. conjunctive: joined inseparably.   15. but: only in. See Note A, p. 195.   17. count:
trial.   18. general gender: common people.   19. dipping
. . . affection: gilding his faults with their love.   20. like . . .
stone: In several places in England there are springs of water
so strongly impregnated with lime that they will quickly
cover with stone anything placed under them.   21. Convert
. . . graces: regard his fetters as honorable ornaments.   22. tim-
bered: shafted. A light arrow is caught by the wind and
blown back.   26. terms: condition.   27. if . . . again: if one may
praise her for what she used to be.   28–29. Stood . . . perfections:
i.e., her worth challenged the whole world to find one as perfect.
33. hear more: i.e., when news comes from England that Hamlet
is dead.   45. naked: destitute.

50. abuse: attempt to deceive.   52. character: handwriting.
61. o'errule: command.   63. checking at: swerving aside from,
like a hawk that leaves the pursuit of his prey.   68. uncharge
. . . practice: not suspect that his death was the result of the
plot.   71. organ: instrument.   74. sum of parts: accomplishments as a whole.   77. siege: seat, place.   81. sables . . .
weeds: dignified robes. See III.ii.138.   85. can well: can do
well.   88. incorpsed . . . deminatured: of one body.   89. topped
my thought: surpassed what I could imagine.

That I, in forgery of shapes and tricks,°   90
Come short of what he did.

LAER.   A Norman was 't?

KING. A Norman.

LAER. Upon my life, Lamond.

KING.   The very same.

LAER. I know him well. He is the brooch° indeed
And gem of all the nation.   95

KING. He made confession° of you,
And gave you such a masterly report
For art and exercise in your defense,
And for your rapier most especial,
That he cried out 'twould be a sight indeed   100
If one could match you. The scrimers° of their na-
tion,
He swore, had neither motion, guard, nor eye
If you opposed them. Sir, this report of his
Did Hamlet so envenom° with his envy
That he could nothing do but wish and beg   105
Your sudden coming o'er, to play with him.
Now, out of this ——

LAER.   What out of this, my lord?

KING. Laertes, was your father dear to you?
Or are you like the painting° of a sorrow,
A face without a heart?

LAER.   Why ask you this?   110

KING. Not that I think you did not love your
father,
But that I know love is begun by time,
And that I see, in passages of proof,°
Time qualifies° the spark and fire of it.
There lives within the very flame of love   115
A kind of wick or snuff° that will abate it.
And nothing is at a like goodness still,°
For goodness, growing to a pleurisy,°
Dies in his own too much. That we would do
We should do when we would; for this " would "
changes   120
And hath abatements and delays as many
As there are tongues, are hands, are accidents,
And then this " should " is like a spendthrift° sigh
That hurts by easing. But to the quick o' the ulcer.°
Hamlet comes back. What would you undertake
To show yourself your father's son in deed   126
More than in words?

LAER.   To cut his throat i' the church.°

KING. No place indeed should murder sanctuar-
ize,°
Revenge should have no bounds. But, good Laertes,
Will you do this, keep close within your chamber.
Hamlet returned shall know you are come home.
We'll put on those° shall praise your excellence   132
And set a double varnish on the fame
The Frenchman gave you, bring you in fine° to-
gether
And wager on your heads. He, being remiss,°   135
Most generous° and free from all contriving,°
Will not peruse the foils, so that with ease,
Or with a little shuffling, you may choose
A sword unbated,° and in a pass of practice°
Requite him for your father.

LAER.   I will do 't,   140
And for that purpose I'll anoint my sword.
I bought an unction° of a mountebank°
So mortal that but dip a knife in it,
Where it draws blood no cataplasm° so rare,
Collected from all simples° that have virtue   145
Under the moon,° can save the thing from death
That is but scratched withal. I'll touch my point
With this contagion, that if I gall° him slightly,
It may be death.

KING.   Let's further think of this,
Weigh what convenience both of time and means
May fit us to our shape.° If this should fail,   151
And that our drift look through our bad perform-
ance,°
'Twere better not assayed. Therefore this project
Should have a back or second, that might hold
If this did blast in proof.° Soft! Let me see ——   155
We'll make a solemn wager on your cunnings.
I ha 't.
When in your motion you are hot and dry —
As make your bouts° more violent to that end —
And that he calls for drink, I'll have prepared him
A chalice° for the nonce,° whereon but sipping,
If he by chance escape your venomed stuck,°   162
Our purpose may hold there. But stay, what noise?
[Enter QUEEN.] How now, sweet Queen!

QUEEN. One woe doth tread upon another's heel,
So fast they follow. Your sister's drowned, Laertes.

LAER. Drowned! Oh, where?   166

---

90. forgery . . . tricks: imagination of all kinds of fancy tricks. shapes: fancies.   94. brooch: ornament.   96. confession: report.   101. scrimers: fencers.   104. envenom: poison. 109. painting: i.e., imitation.   113. passages of proof: ex- periences which prove.   114. qualifies: diminishes.   116. snuff: Before the invention of self-consuming wicks for candles, the wick smoldered and formed a ball of soot which dimmed the light and gave out a foul smoke.   117. still: always. 118. pleurisy: fullness.   123. spendthrift: wasteful, because sighing was supposed to be bad for the blood.   124. quick . . . ulcer: i.e., to come to the real issue. quick: flesh, sensitive part.   127. cut . . . church: i.e., to commit murder in a holy place, which would bring Laertes in danger of everlasting damna- tion; no crime could be worse.

128. sanctuarize: give sanctuary to.   132. put . . . those: set on some.   134. fine: short.   135. remiss: careless.   136. gen- erous: noble. contriving: plotting.   139. unbated: not blunt- ed, with a sharp point. pass of practice: treacherous thrust. 142. unction: poison. mountebank: quack doctor.   144. cata- plasm: poultice.   145. simples: herbs.   146. Under . . . moon: herbs collected by moonlight were regarded as partic- ularly potent.   148. gall: break the skin.   150-51. Weigh . . . shape: consider the best time and method of carrying out our plan.   152. drift . . . performance: intention be revealed through bungling.   155. blast in proof: break in trial, like a cannon which bursts when being tested.   159. bouts: attacks, in the fencing match.   161. chalice: cup. nonce: occasion.   162. stuck: thrust.

QUEEN. There is a willow grows aslant a brook
That shows his hoar° leaves in the glassy stream.
There with fantastic garlands did she come
Of crowflowers, nettles, daisies, and long purples
That liberal° shepherds give a grosser name,   171
But our cold maids do dead-men's-fingers call them.
There on the pendent° boughs her coronet weeds°
Clambering to hang, an envious sliver° broke,
When down her weedy trophies and herself   175
Fell in the weeping brook. Her clothes spread wide,
And mermaidlike awhile they bore her up —
Which time she chanted snatches of old tunes,
As one incapable° of her own distress,
Or like a creature native and indued°   180
Unto that element. But long it could not be
Till that her garments, heavy with their drink,
Pulled the poor wretch from her melodious lay°
To muddy death.

LAER.   Alas, then, she is drowned!
QUEEN. Drowned, drowned.   185
LAER. Too much of water hast thou, poor Ophelia,
And therefore I forbid my tears. But yet
It is our trick° — Nature her custom holds,
Let shame say what it will. When these° are gone,
The woman will be out.° Adieu, my lord.   190
I have a speech of fire that fain° would blaze
But that this folly douts° it.   [Exit.]
KING.   Let's follow, Gertrude.
How much I had to do to calm his rage!
Now fear I this will give it start again,
Therefore let's follow.   [Exeunt.]

Act V

SCENE I. *A churchyard.*

[*Enter two* CLOWNS,° *with spades, etc.*]
1. CLO. Is she to be buried in Christian burial°
that willfully seeks her own salvation?

2. CLO. I tell thee she is, and therefore make her
grave straight.° The crowner° hath sat on her, and
finds it Christian burial.   5
1. CLO. How can that be, unless she drowned herself in her own defense?
2. CLO. Why, 'tis found so.
1. CLO. It must be " se offendendo,"° it cannot be
else. For here lies the point. If I drown myself   10
wittingly,° it argues an act, and an act hath three
branches — it is to act, to do, and to perform. Argal,°
she drowned herself wittingly.
2. CLO. Nay, but hear you, goodman delver.°   15
1. CLO. Give me leave. Here lies the water, good.
Here stands the man, good. If the man go to this
water and drown himself, it is will he, nill he° he
goes, mark you that; but if the water come to him
and drown him, he drowns not himself. Argal, he
that is not guilty of his own death shortens not his
own life.   22
2. CLO. But is this law?
1. CLO. Aye, marry, is 't, crowner's quest° law.
2. CLO. Will you ha' the truth on 't? If this had
not been a gentlewoman, she should have been
buried out o' Christian burial.   28
1. CLO. Why, there thou say'st. And the more pity
that great folks should have countenance° in this
world to drown or hang themselves more than their
even° Christian. Come, my spade. There is no ancient gentlemen but gardeners, ditchers, and   34
gravemakers. They hold up° Adam's profession.
2. CLO. Was he a gentleman?
1. CLO. A' was the first that ever bore arms.°
2. CLO. Why, he had none.   39
1. CLO. What, art a heathen? How dost thou understand the Scripture? The Scripture says Adam
digged. Could he dig without arms? I'll put another
question to thee. If thou answerest me not to the
purpose, confess thyself——
2. CLO. Go to.   45
1. CLO. What is he that builds stronger than either
the mason, the shipwright, or the carpenter?
2. CLO. The gallows-maker, for that frame outlives
a thousand tenants.   50
1. CLO. I like thy wit well, in good faith. The gallows does well, but how does it well? It does well to
those that do ill. Now thou dost ill to say the gallows
is built stronger than the church; argal, the gallows
may do well to thee. To 't again, come.   56
2. CLO. Who builds stronger than a mason, a shipwright, or a carpenter?

---

168. hoar: gray. The underside of the leaves of the willow
are silver-gray.   171. liberal: coarse-mouthed.   173. pendent:
hanging over the water. coronet weeds: wild flowers woven
into a crown.   174. envious sliver: malicious branch.
179. incapable: not realizing.   180. indued: endowed; i.e.,
a creature whose natural home is the water (*element*).
183. lay: song.   187–88. But . . . trick: it is our habit; i.e., to
break into tears at great sorrow.   189. these: i.e., my tears.
190. woman . . . out: I shall be a man again.   191. fain:
willingly.   192. douts: puts out.
Act V, Sc. i: s.d., Clowns: countrymen. See Intro., p. 186.
1. Christian burial: Suicides were not allowed burial in consecrated ground, but were buried at crossroads. The gravediggers and the priest are professionally scandalized that Ophelia
should be allowed Christian burial solely because she is a lady
of the Court.

4. straight: straightway. crowner: coroner who inquired into cases
of suicide.   9. se offendendo: for *defendendo*, in self-defense.
11. wittingly: with full knowledge.   12. Argal: for the Latin
ergo, therefore.   15. delver: digger.   18. will he, nill he:
willy-nilly, whether he wishes or not.   24. quest: inquest.
30. countenance: favor.   33. even: fellow.   35. hold up: support.   38. bore arms: had a coat of arms — the outward sign of
a gentleman.

1. CLO. Aye, tell me that, and unyoke.°

2. CLO. Marry, now I can tell.   60

1. CLO. To 't.

2. CLO. Mass,° I cannot tell.

[*Enter* HAMLET *and* HORATIO, *afar off.*]

1. CLO. Cudgel thy brains no more about it, for your dull ass will not mend his pace with beating, and when you are asked this question next, say " A gravemaker." The houses that he makes last till Doomsday. Go, get thee to Yaughan,° fetch me 67 a stoup° of liquor.   [*Exit* SECOND CLOWN.]

[FIRST CLOWN *digs, and sings.*]

" In youth,° when I did love, did love,
    Methought it was very sweet,
To contract; oh, the time, for-a my behoove,° 71
    Oh, methought, there-a was nothing-a meet."

HAML. Has this fellow no feeling of his business, that he sings at grave-making?

HOR. Custom hath made it in him a property of easiness.°

HAML. 'Tis e'en so. The hand of little employment hath the daintier sense.°   78

1. CLO. [*Sings.*] " But age, with his stealing steps,
    Hath clawed me in his clutch,
And hath shipped me intil the land°
    As if I had never been such."   82

[*Throws up a skull.*]

HAML. That skull had a tongue in it, and could sing once. How the knave jowls° it to the ground, as if it were Cain's jawbone, that did the first murder! It might be the pate of a politician which this ass now o'erreaches° — one that would circumvent° God, might it not?

HOR. It might, my lord.   89

HAML. Or of a courtier, which could say " Good morrow, sweet lord! How dost thou, good lord? " This might be my lord Such-a-one that praised my lord Such-a-one's horse when he meant to beg it, might it not?

HOR. Aye, my lord.   95

HAML. Why, e'en so. And now my Lady Worm's chapless,° and knocked about the mazzard° with a sexton's spade. Here's fine revolution, an we had the trick to see 't. Did these bones cost no more the breeding but to play at loggats° with 'em? Mine ache to think on 't.   101

1. CLO. [*Sings.*] " A pickax and a spade, a spade,
    For and a shrouding sheet —
Oh, a pit of clay for to be made
    For such a guest is meet."   105

[*Throws up another skull.*]

HAML. There's another. Why may not that be the skull of a lawyer?° Where be his quiddities now, his quillets, his cases, his tenures, and his tricks? Why does he suffer this rude knave now to knock him about the sconce° with a dirty shovel, and will 110 not tell him of his action of battery? Hum! This fellow might be in 's time a great buyer of land, with his statutes, his recognizances, his fines, his double vouchers, his recoveries. Is this the fine° of his fines and the recovery of his recoveries, to have his 115 fine pate full of fine dirt? Will his vouchers vouch him no more of his purchases, and double ones too, than the length and breadth of a pair of indentures? The very conveyances of his lands will hardly lie in this box,° and must the inheritor himself have no **120** more, ha?   121

HOR. Not a jot more, my lord.

HAML. Is not parchment made of sheepskins?

HOR. Aye, my lord, and of calfskins too.

HAML. They are sheep and calves which seek out assurance in that. I will speak to this fellow. Whose grave's this, sirrah?

1. CLO. Mine, sir. [*Sings.*]
" Oh, a pit of clay for to be made
    For such a guest is meet."   129

HAML. I think it be thine indeed, for thou liest in 't.

1. CLO. You lie out on 't, sir, and therefore 'tis not yours. For my part, I do not lie in 't, and yet it is mine.   135

HAML. Thou dost lie in 't, to be in 't and say it is thine. 'Tis for the dead, not for the quick, therefore thou liest.

1. CLO. 'Tis a quick lie, sir, 'twill away again, from me to you.   140

HAML. What man dost thou dig it for?

1. CLO. For no man, sir.

HAML. What woman, then?

1. CLO. For none, neither.

HAML. Who is to be buried in 't?   145

1. CLO. One that was a woman, sir, but, rest her soul, she's dead.

HAML. How absolute° the knave is! We must speak by the card,° or equivocation° will undo us.

---

59. unyoke: finish the job, unyoking the plow oxen being the end of the day's work.   **62. Mass:** by the mass. **67. Yaughan:** apparently the keeper of an inn near the Globe Theatre.   **68. stoup:** large pot.   **69–105. In youth . . . meet:** The song which the gravedigger sings without much care for accuracy or sense was first printed in *Tottel's Miscellany*, 1558. **71. behoove:** benefit.   **75–76. property of easiness:** careless habit.   **77–78. hand . . . sense:** those who have little to do are the most sensitive.   **81. shipped . . . land:** shoved me into the ground.   **84. jowls:** dashes.   **87. o'erreaches:** gets the better of. **circumvent:** get around.   **97. chapless:** without jaws. **mazzard:** head, a slang word; lit., drinking-bowl.   **100. loggats:** a game in which billets of wood or bones were stuck in the ground and knocked over by throwing at them.

107–18. lawyer . . . indentures: Hamlet strings out a number of the legal phrases loved by lawyers: *quiddities:* subtle arguments; *quillets:* quibbles; *tenures:* titles to property; *tricks:* knavery; *statutes:* bonds; *recognizances:* obligations; *fines:* conveyances; *vouchers:* guarantors; *recoveries:* transfers; *indentures:* legal agreements to purchase. **110. sconce:** head; lit., blockhouse.   **114. fine:** ending.   **120. box:** coffin. **148. absolute:** exact.   **149. by . . . card:** exactly. The card is the mariner's compass. **equivocation:** speaking with a double

By the Lord, Horatio, this three years I have taken note of it — the age is grown so picked° that the toe of the peasant comes so near the heel of the courtier, he galls his kibe.° How long hast thou been a grave-maker?   154

I. CLO. Of all the days i' the year, I came to 't that day that our last King Hamlet o'ercame Fortinbras.

HAML. How long is that since?

I. CLO. Cannot you tell that? Every fool can tell that. It was that very day that young Hamlet was born, he that is mad, and sent into England.   164

HAML. Aye, marry, why was he sent into England?

I. CLO. Why, because a' was mad. A' shall recover his wits there, or, if a' do not, 'tis no great matter there.

HAML. Why?

I. CLO. 'Twill not be seen in him there — there the men are as mad as he.   170

HAML. How came he mad?

I. CLO. Very strangely, they say.

HAML. How "strangely"?

I. CLO. Faith, e'en with losing his wits.

HAML. Upon what ground?

I. CLO. Why, here in Denmark. I have been sexton here, man and boy, thirty years.°

HAML. How long will a man lie i' the earth ere he rot?   179

I. CLO. I' faith, if a' be not rotten before a' die — as we have many pocky° corses nowadays that will scarce hold the laying in — a' will last you some eight year or nine year. A tanner will last you nine year.

HAML. Why he more than another?   185

I. CLO. Why, sir, his hide is so tanned with his trade that a' will keep out water a great while, and your water is a sore decayer of your whoreson° dead body. Here's a skull now. This skull has lain in the earth three and twenty years.   191

HAML. Whose was it?

I. CLO. A whoreson mad fellow's it was. Whose do you think it was?

HAML. Nay, I know not.   195

I. CLO. A pestilence on him for a mad rogue! A' poured a flagon of Rhenish on my head once. This same skull, sir, was Yorick's skull, the King's jester.

HAML. This?

I. CLO. E'en that.

HAML. Let me see. [Takes the skull.] Alas, poor Yorick! I knew him, Horatio — a fellow of infinite jest, of most excellent fancy. He hath borne me on his back a thousand times, and now how ab-   205 horred in my imagination it is! My gorge rises° at it. Here hung those lips that I have kissed I know not how oft. Where be your gibes now? Your gam-bols? Your songs? Your flashes of merriment that were wont to set the table on a roar? Not one   210 now, to mock your own grinning? Quite chop-fallen?° Now get you to my lady's chamber and tell her, let her paint an inch thick, to this favor° she must come — make her laugh at that. Prithee, Hora-tio, tell me one thing.

HOR. What's that, my lord?   217

HAML. Dost thou think Alexander looked o' this fashion i' the earth?

HOR. E'en so.

HAML. And smelt so? Pah!

[Puts down the skull.]

HOR. E'en so, my lord.

HAML. To what base uses we may return, Horatio! Why may not imagination trace the noble dust of Alexander till he find it stopping a bunghole?°

HOR. 'Twere to consider too curiously° to consider so.   228

HAML. No, faith, not a jot, but to follow him thither with modesty° enough and likelihood to lead it. As thus: Alexander died, Alexander was buried, Alexander returneth into dust; the dust is earth; of earth we make loam;° and why of that loam, whereto he was converted, might they not stop a beer barrel?   235

"Imperious Caesar, dead and turned to clay,
    Might stop a hole to keep the wind away.
Oh, that that earth which kept the world in awe
    Should patch a wall to expel the winter's flaw!"°

But soft! But soft! Aside — here comes the King.

[Enter PRIESTS,° etc., in procession; the corpse of
    Ophelia, LAERTES and MOURNERS following;
    KING, QUEEN, their trains, etc.]

The Queen, the courtiers — who is this they follow? And with such maimèd° rites? This doth betoken° The corse they follow did with desperate hand   243 Fordo° its own life. 'Twas of some estate.°

---

sense. The word was being much discussed when *Hamlet* was written.   151. picked: refined.   151–53. toe . . . kibe: i.e., the peasant follows the courtier so closely that he rubs the courtier's heel into a blister. From about 1598 onward, writers, especially dramatists, often satirized the practice of yeoman farmers grown rich from war profits in sending their awkward sons to London to learn gentlemanly manners. Ben Jonson portrays two specimens in Stephen in *Every Man in His Humour* and Sogliardo in *Every Man out of His Humour*.   177. thirty years: The Clown's chronology has puzzled critics, for the general im-pression is that Hamlet was much younger.   181. pocky: suffer-ing from the pox (venereal disease).   189. whoreson: bastard, "son of a bitch."

206. My . . . rises: I feel sick. gorge: throat.   212. chop-fallen: downcast, with a pun on "chapless," (see l. 97).   213. favor: appearance, especially in the face.   226. bunghole: the hole in a beer barrel.   227. curiously: precisely.   230. with modesty: without exaggeration.   233. loam: mixture of clay and sand, used in plastering walls.   239. flaw: blast.   240. s.d., Enter Priests. The stage directions in early texts are less elaborate. Q2 notes, curtly, Enter K.Q. Laertes and the corse. F1 has Enter King, Queen, Laertes, and a coffin, with Lords attendant. Q1 prints Enter King and Queen, Laertes and other lords, with a Priest after the coffin. This probably was how the scene was originally staged. The modern directions ignore the whole signif-icance of the "maimed rites" — Ophelia's funeral is insult-ingly simple.   242. maimed: curtailed. betoken: indicate.   244. Fordo: destroy. estate: high rank.

Couch° we awhile, and mark.

                    [Retiring with HORATIO.]

LAER. What ceremony else?

HAML. That is Laertes, a very noble youth. Mark.

LAER. What ceremony else?   248

1. PRIEST. Her obsequies have been as far enlarged
As we have warranty.° Her death was doubtful,
And but that great command o'ersways the order,°
She should in ground unsanctified have lodged
Till the last trumpet; for° charitable prayers,
Shards,° flints, and pebbles should be thrown on her.
Yet here she is allowed her virgin crants,°   255
Her maiden strewments° and the bringing home
Of bell and burial.

LAER. Must there no more be done?

1. PRIEST.   No more be done.
We should profane the service of the dead
To sing a requiem and such rest to her   260
As to peace-parted souls.°

LAER.   Lay her i' the earth.
And from her fair and unpolluted flesh
May violets spring! I tell thee, churlish priest,
A ministering angel shall my sister be
When thou liest howling.

HAML.   What, the fair Ophelia! 265

QUEEN. *[Scattering flowers]* Sweets to the sweet.
Farewell!
I hoped thou shouldst have been my Hamlet's wife,
I thought thy bride bed to have decked, sweet maid,
And not have strewed thy grave.

LAER.   Oh, treble woe
Fall ten times treble on that cursèd head   270
Whose wicked deed thy most ingenious sense°
Deprived thee of! Hold off the earth a while
Till I have caught her once more in mine arms.

                     [Leaps into the grave.]

Now pile your dust upon the quick° and dead
Till of this flat a mountain you have made   275
To o'ertop old Pelion° or the skyish° head
Of blue Olympus.

HAML. *[Advancing]* What is he whose grief
Bears such an emphasis? Whose phrase of sorrow
Conjures the wandering stars and makes them
     stand°
Like wonder-wounded hearers? This is I,   280
Hamlet the Dane.   *[Leaps into the grave.]*

---

245. Couch: lie down.   **249-50. Her . . . warranty:** the funeral rites have been as complete as may be allowed.   **251. but . . . order:** if the King's command had not overruled the proper procedure.   **253. for:** instead of.   **254. Shards:** pieces of broken crockery.   **255. crants:** wreaths of flowers — a sign that she had died unwed.   **256. maiden strewments:** the flowers strewn on the corpse of a maiden.   **261. peace-parted souls:** souls which departed in peace, fortified with the rites of the Church.   **271. most . . . sense:** lively intelligence.   **274. quick:** living.   **276. Pelion:** When the giants fought against the gods in order to reach Heaven, they tried to pile Mount Pelion and Mount Ossa on Mount Olympus, the highest mountain in Greece. **skyish:** reaching the sky.   **279. stand:** stand still.

LAER. The Devil take thy soul!

                    [Grappling with him]

HAML.   Thou pray'st not well.
I prithee, take thy fingers from my throat,
For though I am not splenitive° and rash,
Yet have I in me something dangerous,   285
Which let thy wisdom fear. Hold off thy hand.

KING. Pluck them asunder.

QUEEN.   Hamlet, Hamlet!

ALL.   Gentlemen ——

HOR. Good my lord, be quiet.

         [The ATTENDANTS *part them,
           and they come out of the grave.]*

HAML. Why, I will fight with him upon this
     theme
Until my eyelids will no longer wag.   290

QUEEN. O my son, what theme?

HAML. I loved Ophelia. Forty thousand brothers
Could not, with all their quantity of love,
Make up my sum. What wilt thou do for her?

KING. Oh, he is mad, Laertes.   295

QUEEN. For love of God, forbear him.°

HAML. 'Swounds,° show me what thou'lt do.
Woo 't weep? Woo 't fight? Woo 't fast? Woo 't tear
     thyself?
Woo 't drink up eisel?° Eat a crocodile?
I'll do 't. Dost thou come here to whine?   300
To outface° me with leaping in her grave?
Be buried quick with her, and so will I.
And if thou prate of mountains, let them throw
Millions of acres on us, till our ground,
Singeing his pate against the burning zone,   305
Make Ossa° like a wart! Nay, an thou 'lt mouth,
I'll rant as well as thou.

QUEEN.   This is mere madness.
And thus awhile the fit will work on him.
Anon, as patient as the female dove
When that her golden couplets° are disclosed,°   310
His silence will sit drooping.

HAML.   Hear you, sir.
What is the reason that you use me thus?
I loved you ever. But it is no matter,
Let Hercules himself do what he may,   314
The cat will mew and dog will have his day.° *[Exit.]*

KING. I pray thee, good Horatio, wait upon him.

                   [Exit HORATIO.]

[To LAERTES] Strengthen your patience in our last
     night's speech.
We'll put the matter to the present push.°

---

284. splenitive: hot-tempered.   **296. forbear him:** leave him alone.   **297-307. 'Swounds . . . thou:** Hamlet in his excitement cries out that if Laertes wishes to make extravagant boasts of what he will do to show his sorrow, he will be even more extravagant.   **299. eisel:** vinegar.   **301. outface:** browbeat.   **306. Ossa:** See l. 276, n.   **310. couplets:** eggs, of which the dove lays two only. **disclosed:** hatched.   **314-15. Let . . . day:** i.e., let this ranting hero have his turn; mine will come sometime.   **318. push:** test; lit., thrust of a pike.

Good Gertrude, set some watch over your son.
This grave shall have a living monument.°   320
An hour of quiet shortly shall we see,
Till then, in patience our proceeding be.   [*Exeunt.*]

SCENE II. *A hall in the castle.*

[*Enter* HAMLET *and* HORATIO.]
HAML. So much for this, sir. Now shall you see
the other.
You do remember all the circumstance?
HOR. Remember it, my lord!
HAML. Sir, in my heart there was a kind of fight-
ing
That would not let me sleep. Methought I lay   5
Worse than the mutines in the bilboes.° Rashly,
And praised be rashness for it, let us know,
Our indiscretion sometime serves us well
When our deep plots do pall.° And that should
    learn° us
There's a divinity that shapes our ends,   10
Roughhew them how we will.°
HOR.   That is most certain.
HAML. Up from my cabin,
My sea gown° scarfed° about me, in the dark
Groped I to find out them,° had my desire,
Fingered their packet, and in fine withdrew   15
To mine own room again, making so bold,
My fears forgetting manners, to unseal
Their grand commission where I found, Horatio —
Oh royal knavery! — an exact command,
Larded° with many several sorts of reasons,   20
Importing Denmark's health and England's too,
With, ho! such bugs° and goblins in my life°
That, on the supervise,° no leisure bated,°
No, not to stay the grinding of the ax,
My head should be struck off.
HOR.   Is 't possible?   25
HAML. Here's the commission. Read it at more
leisure
But wilt thou hear me how I did proceed?
HOR. I beseech you.
HAML. Being thus benetted round with vil-
lainies —
Ere I could make a prologue to my brains,   30
They had begun the play — I sat me down,
Devised a new commission, wrote it fair.
I once did hold it, as our statists° do,

320. living monument: with the double meaning of "lifelike
memorial" and "the death of Hamlet."
    Sc. ii: 6. mutines . . . bilboes: mutineers in the shackles used
on board ship.   9. pall: fail. learn: teach.   10-11. There's . . .
will: though we may make the rough beginning, God finishes our
designs.   13. sea gown: a thick coat with a high collar worn by
seamen. scarfed: wrapped.   14. them: i.e., Rosencrantz and
Guildenstern.   20. Larded: garnished.   22. bugs: bugbears.
in my life: so long as I was alive.   23. supervise: reading. bated:
allowed.   33. statists: statesmen. As scholars who have had to

A baseness to write fair, and labored much
How to forget that learning, but, sir, now   35
It did me yeoman's service.° Wilt thou know
The effect of what I wrote?
HOR.   Aye, good my lord.
HAML. An earnest conjuration from the King,
As England was his faithful tributary,
As love between them like the palm might flourish,
As peace should still her wheaten garland wear   41
And stand a comma 'tween their amities,°
And many suchlike " Ases "° of great charge,°
That, on the view and knowing of these contents,
Without debatement° further, more or less,   45
He should the bearers put to sudden death,
Not shriving time allowed.°
HOR.   How was this sealed?
HAML. Why, even in that was Heaven ordinant.°
I had my father's signet in my purse,
Which was the model° of that Danish seal —   50
Folded the writ° up in the form of the other,
Subscribed° it, gave 't the impression,° placed it
    safely,
The changeling° never known. Now the next day
Was our sea fight, and what to this was sequent°
Thou know'st already.   55
HOR. So Guildenstern and Rosencrantz go to 't.
HAML. Why, man, they did make love to this em-
ployment.
They are not near my conscience, their defeat°
Does by their own insinuation° grow.
'Tis dangerous when the baser nature comes   60
Between the pass and fell incensèd points
Of mighty opposites.°
HOR.   Why, what a King is this!
HAML. Does it not, think'st thee, stand me now
upon —
He that hath killed my King and whored my
    mother,
Popped in between the election and my hopes,°   65

read Elizabethan documents know, the more exalted the writer,
the worse his handwriting. As a girl Queen Elizabeth wrote a
beautiful script; as Queen her letters are as illegible as any. All
but the most confidential documents were copied out in a fair
hand by a secretary. 36. yeoman's service: faithful service.
The most reliable English soldiers were yeomen — farmers
and their men. 42. stand . . . amities: be a connecting
link of their friendship. 43. "Ases": Official documents
were written in flowery language full of metaphorical clauses
beginning with "As." Hamlet puns on "asses." great charge:
"great weight" and "heavy burden." 45. debatement:
argument. 47. Not . . . allowed: without giving them time
even to confess their sins. 48. ordinant: directing, in control. 50. model: copy. 51. writ: writing. 52. Subscribed:
signed. impression: of the seal. 53. changeling: lit., an ugly
child exchanged by the fairies for a fair one. 54. sequent: following. 58. defeat: destruction. 59. by . . . insinuation: because they insinuated themselves into this business. 60-62. 'Tis
. . . opposites: it is dangerous for inferior men to interfere in
a duel between mighty enemies. pass: thrust. fell: fierce.
65. Popped . . . hopes: As is from time to time shown in the play
the Danes chose their King by election.

Thrown out his angle° for my proper° life,
And with such cozenage° — is 't not perfect con-
　science,
To quit° him with this arm? And is 't not to be
　damned,
To let this canker° of our nature come
In further evil?　　　　　　　　　　　　　70
　　HOR. It must be shortly known to him from Eng-
　land
What is the issue of the business there.
　　HAML. It will be short. The interim° is mine,
And a man's life's no more than to say "One."
But I am very sorry, good Horatio,　　　　75
That to Laertes I forgot myself,
For by the image of my cause I see
The portraiture of his. I'll court his favors.
But, sure, the bravery° of his grief did put me
Into a towering passion.
　　HOR.　　　　　　　Peace! Who comes here? 80
　　　　　　[*Enter* OSRIC.°]
　　OSR. Your lordship is right welcome back to Den-
mark.
　　HAML. I humbly thank you, sir. Dost know this
water fly?°
　　HOR. No, my good lord.　　　　　　　　84
　　HAML. Thy state is the more gracious,° for 'tis a
vice to know him. He hath much land, and fertile.
Let a beast be lord of beasts and his crib shall stand
at the King's mess.° 'Tis a chough,° but, as I say,
spacious° in the possession of dirt.　　　　90
　　OSR. Sweet lord, if your lordship were at lei-
sure, I should impart a thing to you from His Majesty.
　　HAML. I will receive it, sir, with all diligence of
spirit. Put your bonnet to his right use,° 'tis for the
head.
　　OSR. I thank your lordship, it is very hot.　97
　　HAML. No, believe me, 'tis very cold. The wind is
northerly.
　　OSR. It is indifferent° cold, my lord, indeed.　100
　　HAML. But yet methinks it is very sultry and hot,
for my complexion ——
　　OSR. Exceedingly, my lord. It is very sultry, as
'twere — I cannot tell how. But, my lord, His Majes-

ty bade me signify to you that he has laid a great
wager on your head. Sir, this is the matter ——
　　HAML. I beseech you, remember ——　　　108
　　　　[HAMLET *moves him to put on his hat.*]
　　OSR. Nay, good my lord, for mine ease, in good
faith. Sir, here is newly come to Court Laertes — believe me, an absolute° gentleman, full of most excellent differences,° of very soft society° and great
showing.° Indeed, to speak feelingly° of him, he is
the card or calendar of gentry,° for you shall find in
him the continent of what part a gentleman would
see.°　　　　　　　　　　　　　　　116
　　HAML. Sir,° his definement suffers no perdition in
you, though I know to divide him inventorially
would dizzy the arithmetic of memory, and yet but
yaw neither, in respect of his quick sail. But in　120
the verity of extolment, I take him to be a soul of
great article, and his infusion of such dearth and
rareness as, to make true diction of him, his semblable is his mirror, and who else would trace him,
his umbrage — nothing more.　　　　　　125
　　OSR. Your lordship speaks most infallibly of
him.
　　HAML. The concernancy,° sir? Why do we wrap
the gentleman in our more rawer breath?°
　　OSR. Sir?°　　　　　　　　　　　　129
　　HOR. Is 't not possible to understand in another
tongue? You will do 't, sir, really.
　　HAML. What imports the nomination° of this
gentleman?
　　OSR. Of Laertes?
　　HOR. His purse is empty already, all's golden　135
words are spent.
　　HAML. Of him, sir.
　　OSR. I know you are not ignorant ——　　139
　　HAML. I would you did, sir. Yet, in faith, if you
did, it would not much approve° me. Well, sir?

---

66. **angle:** fishing rod and line. **proper:** own.　67. **cozenage:** cheating.　68. **quit:** pay back.　69. **canker:** maggot. See I.iii.39.　73. **in-
terim:** interval; between now and the news from England.
79. **bravery:** excessive show.　80 s.d., **Osric:** Osric is a specimen
of the fashionable, effeminate courtier. He dresses prettily and
talks the jargon of his class, which at this time affected elaborate
and allusive metaphors and at all costs avoided saying plain things
plainly.　83. **water fly:** a useless little creature that flits about.
85. **Thy . . . gracious:** you are in the better state.　88–89. **Let . . .
mess:** i.e., any man, however low, who has wealth enough will
find a good place at Court. **crib:** manger. **mess:** table.
89. **chough:** jackdaw.　90. **spacious:** wealthy.　95. **Put . . .
use:** i.e., put your hat on your head. Osric is so nice-mannered
that he cannot bring himself to wear his hat in the presence of
the Prince.　100. **indifferent:** moderately.

111. **absolute:** perfect.　112. **differences:** qualities peculiar to himself. **soft society:** gentle breeding.　112–13. **great showing:** distinguished appearance.　113. **feelingly:** with proper appreciation.
114. **card . . . gentry:** the very fashion plate of what a gentleman
should be.　115–16. **continent . . . see:** all the parts that should be
in a perfect gentleman.　117–25. **Sir . . . more:** Hamlet retorts in
similar but even more extravagant language. This is too much for
Osric (and for most modern readers). Hamlet's words may be paraphrased: "Sir, the description of this perfect gentleman loses
nothing in your account of him; though I realize that if one
were to try to enumerate his excellences, it would exhaust our
arithmetic, and yet" — here he changes the image to one of sailing — "we should still lag behind him as he outsails us. But in
the true vocabulary of praise, I take him to be a soul of the
greatest worth, and his perfume" — i.e., his personal essence —
"so scarce and rare that to speak truly of him, the only thing
like him is his own reflection in his mirror, and everyone else
who tries to follow him merely his shadow." **yaw:** fall off from
the course laid. **verity . . . extolment:** in true praise. **infusion:**
essence. **semblable:** resemblance. **trace:** follow. **umbrage:** shadow.
127. **concernancy:** i.e., what is all this talk about?　127–28. **Why
. . . breath:** why do we discuss the gentleman with our inadequate voices?　129. **Sir:** Osric is completely baffled.　133. **nomi-
nation:** naming.　141. **approve:** commend.

OSR. You are not ignorant of what excellence Laertes is ——   144

HAML. I dare not confess that, lest I should compare with him in excellence, but to know a man well were to know himself.

OSR. I mean, sir, for his weapon,° but in the imputation° laid on him by them, in his meed° he's unfellowed.°   150

HAML. What's his weapon?

OSR. Rapier and dagger.

HAML. That's two of his weapons, but, well.

OSR. The King, sir, hath wagered with him six Barbary horses, against the which he has im- 155 poned,° as I take it, six French rapiers and poniards, with their assigns,° as girdle, hanger,° and so — three of the carriages, in faith, are very dear to fancy,° very responsive to° the hilts, most delicate carriages, and of very liberal conceit.°   160

HAML. What call you the carriages?

HOR. I knew you must be edified by the margent° ere you had done.

OSR. The carriages, sir, are the hangers.   164

HAML. The phrase would be more germane° to the matter if we could carry a cannon by our sides. I would it might be hangers till then. But, on — six Barbary horses against six French swords, their assigns, and three liberal-conceited carriages. That's the French bet against the Danish. Why is this "imponed," as you call it?   171

OSR. The King, sir, hath laid, sir, that in a dozen passes between yourself and him, he shall not exceed you three hits. He hath laid on twelve for nine,° and it would come to immediate trial if your lordship would vouchsafe the answer.

HAML. How if I answer no?   177

OSR. I mean, my lord, the opposition of your person in trial.

HAML. Sir, I will walk here in the hall. If it please His Majesty, it is the breathing-time of day with me.° Let the foils be brought, the gentleman willing, and the King hold his purpose, I will win for him an I can. If not, I will gain nothing but my shame and the odd hits.   185

OSR. Shall I redeliver you e'en so?

HAML. To this effect, sir, after what flourish° your nature will.

OSR. I commend my duty to your lordship.   189

HAML. Yours, yours. [Exit OSRIC.] He does well to commend it himself, there are no tongues else for 's turn.

HOR. This lapwing° runs away with the shell on his head.

HAML. He did comply with his dug° before he sucked it. Thus has he — and many more of the same breed that I know the drossy° age dotes on — only got the tune of the time and outward habit of encounter,° a kind of yesty collection° which carries them through and through the most fond° and 200 winnowed° opinions — and do but blow them to their trial, the bubbles are out.°

[Enter a LORD.]

LORD. My lord, His Majesty commended him to you by young Osric, who brings back to him that you attend him in the hall. He sends to know if your pleasure hold to play with Laertes, or that you will take longer time.   207

HAML. I am constant to my purposes, they follow the King's pleasure. If his fitness speaks, mine is ready, now or whensoever, provided I be so able as now.   211

LORD. The King and Queen and all are coming down.

HAML. In happy time.°

LORD. The Queen desires you to use some gentle entertainment° to Laertes before you fall to play.

HAML. She well instructs me.   [Exit LORD.]

HOR. You will lose this wager, my lord.   219

HAML. I do not think so. Since he went into France I have been in continual practice, I shall win at the odds. But thou wouldst not think how ill all's here about my heart — but it is no matter.

HOR. Nay, good my lord ——   224

HAML. It is but foolery, but it is such a kind of gaingiving° as would perhaps trouble a woman.

HOR. If your mind dislike anything, obey it. I will forestall their repair hither and say you are not fit.

HAML. Not a whit, we defy augury.° There's 230 special providence in the fall of a sparrow.° If it be now, 'tis not to come; if it be not to come, it will be now; if it be not now, yet it will come. The read-

193. lapwing: a little bird so lively that it can run about the moment it is hatched.   195. did ... dug: was ceremonious with the nipple; i.e., behaved in this fantastic way from his infancy. See II.ii.389.   197. drossy: scummy, frivolous. 198-99. tune ... encounter: i.e., they sing the same tune as everyone else and have the same society manners.   199. yesty collection: frothy catchwords.   200. fond: foolish.   201. winnowed: light as chaff. Winnowing is the process of fanning the chaff from the grain.   201-02. do ... out: force them to make sense of their words and they are deflated, as Hamlet has just deflated Osric.   214. In ... time: at a good moment.   215-16. gentle entertainment: kindly treatment; i.e., be reconciled after the brawl in the churchyard.   226. gaingiving: misgiving.   230. augury: omens.   231. special ... sparrow: The idea comes from Matthew 10:29. "Are not two sparrows sold for a farthing? and one of them shall not fall to the ground without your Father."

148. his weapon: i.e., skill with his weapon.   149. imputation: reputation. meed: merit.   150. unfellowed: without an equal. 156. imponed: laid down as a stake.   157. assigns: that which goes with them. hanger: straps by which the scabbard was hung from the belt.   158-59. dear to fancy: of beautiful design. 159. responsive to: matching.   160. liberal conceit: elaborately artistic.   162. edified ... margent: informed by the notes. In Shakespeare's time the notes were often printed in the margin. 165. germane: related.   174-75. twelve ... nine: See Note C, p. 196.   181-82. breathing-time ... me: time when I take exercise.   187. flourish: fanfare, elaborate phrasing.

iness is all. Since no man has aught of what he leaves,
what is 't to leave betimes? Let be.   235
[*Enter* KING, QUEEN, LAERTES, *and* LORDS, OSRIC *and
other* ATTENDANTS *with foils; a table and flagons of
wine on it.*]
   KING. Come, Hamlet, come, and take this hand
     from me.
     [*The* KING *puts* LAERTES' *hand into* HAMLET'S.]
   HAML. Give me your pardon, sir. I've done you
     wrong,
But pardon 't, as you are a gentleman.
This presence° knows,
And you must needs have heard, how I am pun-
     ished   240
With sore distraction. What I have done
That might your nature, honor, and exception°
Roughly awake, I here proclaim was madness.
Was 't Hamlet wronged Laertes? Never Hamlet.
If Hamlet from himself be ta'en away,°   245
And when he's not himself does wrong Laertes,
Then Hamlet does it not, Hamlet denies it.
Who does it, then? His madness. If 't be so,
Hamlet is of the faction that is wronged,
His madness is poor Hamlet's enemy.   250
Sir, in this audience
Let my disclaiming from a purposed evil°
Free me so far in your most generous thoughts
That I have shot mine arrow o'er the house,
And hurt my brother.
   LAER.   I am satisfied in nature,   255
Whose motive, in this case, should stir me most
To my revenge. But in my terms of honor
I stand aloof, and will no reconcilement
Till by some elder masters of known honor
I have a voice and precedent of peace   260
To keep my name ungored.° But till that time
I do receive your offered love like love
And will not wrong it.
   HAML.   I embrace it freely,
And will this brother's wager frankly play.
Give us the foils. Come on.
   LAER.   Come, one for me.   265
   HAML. I'll be your foil,° Laertes. In mine ignor-
     ance
Your skill shall, like a star i' the darkest night,
Stick° fiery off indeed.
   LAER.   You mock me, sir.
   HAML. No, by this hand.

239. **presence:** the whole Court.   242. **exception:** resentment.
245. **If . . . away:** i.e., Hamlet mad is not Hamlet.   252. **Let . . .
evil:** let my declaration that I did not intend any harm.
255–61. **I . . . ungored:** I bear you no grudge so far as concerns
my personal feelings, which would most readily move me to vengeance: but as this matter touches my honor, I cannot accept
your apology until I have been assured by those expert in matters
of honor that I may so do without loss of reputation.   266. **foil:**
Hamlet puns on the other meaning of foil — tin foil set behind
a gem to give it luster.   268. **Stick . . . off:** Shine out.

   KING. Give them the foils, young Osric. Cousin
     Hamlet,   270
You know the wager?
   HAML.   Very well, my lord.
Your Grace has laid the odds o' the weaker side.
   KING. I do not fear it, I have seen you both.
But since he is bettered,° we have therefore odds.
   LAER. This is too heavy, let me see another.   275
   HAML. This likes° me well. These foils have all a
length?°   [*They prepare to play.*]
   OSR. Aye, my good lord.
   KING. Set me the stoups° of wine upon that table.
If Hamlet give the first or second hit,
Or quit° in answer of the third exchange,   280
Let all the battlements their ordnance fire.
The King shall drink to Hamlet's better breath,
And in the cup a union° shall he throw
Richer than that which four successive kings   284
In Denmark's crown have worn. Give me the cups,
And let the kettle° to the trumpet speak,
The trumpet to the cannoneer without,
The cannon to the Heavens, the Heaven to earth,
" Now the King drinks to Hamlet." Come, begin,
And you, the judges, bear a wary eye.   290
   HAML. Come on, sir.
   LAER.   Come, my lord.   [*They play.*]
   HAML.   One.
   LAER.   No.
   HAML.   Judgment.
   OSR. A hit, a very palpable° hit.
   LAER.   Well, again.
   KING. Stay, give me drink. Hamlet, this pearl is
     thine° —
Here's to thy health.
     [*Trumpets sound, and cannon shot off within.*]
            Give him the cup.   294
   HAML. I'll play this bout first. Set it by a while.
Come. [*They play.*] Another hit, what say you?
   LAER. A touch, a touch, I do confess.
   KING. Our son shall win.
   QUEEN.   He's fat° and scant of breath.
Here, Hamlet, take my napkin, rub thy brows.
The Queen carouses to thy fortune, Hamlet.   300
   HAML. Good madam!
   KING.   Gertrude, do not drink.
   QUEEN. I will, my lord, I pray you pardon me.
                   [*She drinks.*]
   KING. [*Aside*] It is the poisoned cup, it is too late.
   HAML. I dare not drink yet, madam — by and by.
   QUEEN. Come, let me wipe thy face.   305
   LAER. My lord, I'll hit him now.

274. **bettered:** considered your superior.   276. **likes:** pleases.
have . . . length: are all of equal length.   278. **stoups:** drinking-
vessels.   280. **quit:** strike back.   283. **union:** a large pearl.
286. **kettle:** kettledrum.   292. **palpable:** clear.   293. **this . . .
thine:** With these words the King drops the poisoned pearl
into the cup intended for Hamlet.   298. **fat:** out of condition.

KING.   I do not think 't.

LAER. *[Aside]* And yet 'tis almost against my
conscience.

HAML. Come, for the third, Laertes. You but
dally.°
I pray you pass with your best violence,
I am afeard you make a wanton of me.°   310

LAER. Say you so? Come on.   *[They play.]*

OSR. Nothing, neither way.

LAER. Have at you now!

*[LAERTES wounds HAMLET; then, in scuffling, they
change rapiers,° and HAMLET wounds LAERTES.]*

KING.   Part them, they are incensed.

HAML. Nay, come, again.   *[The QUEEN falls.]*

OSR.   Look to the Queen there, ho!

HOR. They bleed on both sides. How is it, my
lord?   315

OSR. How is 't, Laertes?

LAER. Why, as a woodcock to mine own springe,°
Osric,
I am justly killed with mine own treachery.

HAML. How does the Queen?

KING.   She swounds to see them bleed.

QUEEN. No, no, the drink, the drink! — O my dear
Hamlet —   320
The drink, the drink! I am poisoned.   *[Dies.]*

HAML. Oh, villainy! Ho! Let the door be locked.
Treachery! Seek it out.   *[LAERTES falls.]*

LAER. It is here, Hamlet. Hamlet, thou art slain.
No medicine in the world can do thee good,   325
In thee there is not half an hour of life.
The treacherous instrument is in thy hand,
Unbated and envenomed. The foul practice
Hath turned itself on me. Lo, here I lie
Never to rise again. Thy mother's poisoned.   330
I can no more. The King, the King's to blame.

HAML. The point envenomed too!
Then, venom, to thy work.   *[Stabs the KING.]*

ALL. Treason! Treason!
                                                  334

KING. Oh, yet defend me, friends, I am but hurt.

HAML. Here, thou incestuous, murderous,
damnèd Dane,
Drink off this potion. Is thy union° here?
Follow my mother.   *[KING dies.]*

LAER.   He is justly served.
It is a poison tempered° by himself.
Exchange forgiveness with me, noble Hamlet.   340
Mine and my father's death come not upon thee,°
Nor thine on me!   *[Dies.]*

HAML. Heaven make thee free of it!° I follow
thee.
I am dead, Horatio. Wretched Queen, adieu!

You that look pale and tremble at this chance, 345
That are but mutes or audience to this act,
Had I but time — as this fell° sergeant,° Death,
Is strict in his arrest — oh, I could tell you——
But let it be. Horatio, I am dead,
Thou livest. Report me and my cause aright   350
To the unsatisfied.°

HOR.   Never believe it.
I am more an antique Roman° than a Dane.
Here's yet some liquor left.

HAML.   As thou 'rt a man,
Give me the cup. Let go — by Heaven, I'll have 't.
O good Horatio, what a wounded name,   355
Things standing thus unknown, shall live behind
me!
If thou didst ever hold me in thy heart,
Absent thee from felicity a while,
And in this harsh world draw thy breath in pain
To tell my story. *[March afar off, and shot within]*
                    What warlike noise is this?   360

OSR. Young Fortinbras, with conquest come from
Poland,
To the ambassadors of England gives
This warlike volley.

HAML.   Oh, I die, Horatio,
The potent poison quite o'ercrows° my spirit.
I cannot live to hear the news from England,   365
But I do prophesy the election° lights
On Fortinbras. He has my dying voice.°
So tell him, with the occurrents, more and less,
Which have solicited.° The rest is silence.   *[Dies.]*

HOR. Now cracks a noble heart. Good night,
sweet Prince,   370
And flights of angels sing thee to thy rest!
                                      [March within.]
Why does the drum come hither?

*[Enter FORTINBRAS, and the ENGLISH AMBASSADORS,
with drum, colors, and ATTENDANTS.]*

FOR. Where is this sight?

HOR.   What is it you would see?
If aught of woe or wonder, cease your search.   374

FOR. This quarry cries on havoc.° O proud Death,
What feast is toward° in thine eternal cell
That thou so many princes at a shot
So bloodily hast struck?

I. AMB.   The sight is dismal,
And our affairs from England come too late.   379
The ears are senseless that should give us hearing,

---

308. dally: play.   310. make . . . me: treat me like a child by
letting me win.   313. s.d., they . . . rapiers: See Note C, p. 196.
317. springe: snare.   337. union: pearl, as in l. 283.   339. tempered: mixed.   341. come . . . thee: are not on your head.
343. Heaven . . . it: may God forgive you for it.

347. fell: dread. sergeant: the officer of the Court who made
arrests.   351. unsatisfied: who do not know the truth.
352. antique Roman: like Cato and Brutus, who killed themselves
rather than survive in a world which was unpleasing to them.
364. o'ercrows: overpowers.   366. election: as King of Denmark. See l. 65 above.   367. voice: support.   368–69. occurrents . . . solicited: events great and small which have caused
me to act.   375. quarry . . . havoc: heap of slain denotes a
pitiless slaughter. See *Caesar*, III.i.273.   376. toward: being
prepared.

To tell him his commandment is fulfilled,
That Rosencrantz and Guildenstern are dead.
Where should we have our thanks?
    HOR.   Not from his mouth
Had it the ability of life to thank you.
He never gave commandment for their death.   385
But since, so jump° upon this bloody question,°
You from the Polack wars, and you from England,
Are here arrived, give order that these bodies
High on a stage be placèd to the view,
And let me speak to the yet unknowing world   390
How these things came about. So shall you hear
Of carnal, bloody, and unnatural acts,
Of accidental judgments, casual slaughters,
Of deaths put on by cunning and forced cause,
And, in this upshot, purposes mistook   395
Fall'n on the inventors' heads.° All this can I
Truly deliver.
    FOR.   Let us haste to hear it,
And call the noblest to the audience.
For me, with sorrow I embrace my fortune.   399

I have some rights of memory° in this kingdom,
Which now to claim my vantage° doth invite me.
    HOR. Of that I shall have also cause to speak,
And from his mouth whose voice will draw on
    more.°
But let this same be presently performed,
Even while men's minds are wild, lest more mis-
    chance   405
On plots and errors happen.
    FOR.   Let four captains
Bear Hamlet, like a soldier, to the stage.
For he was likely, had he been put on,°
To have proved most royally. And for his passage
The soldiers' music and the rites of war   410
Speak loudly for him.
Take up the bodies. Such a sight as this
Becomes the field, but here shows much amiss.
Go, bid the soldiers shoot.
    [*A dead march. Exeunt, bearing off the bodies;
    after which a peal of ordnance is shot off.*]

---

386. jump: exactly. See I.i.65. question: matter. 392-96. carnal ... heads: These lines sum up the whole tragedy: Claudius' adultery with Gertrude, his murder of his brother, the death of Ophelia due to an accident, that of Polonius by casual chance, Hamlet's device which caused the deaths of Rosencrantz and Guildenstern, the plan which went awry and caused the deaths of Claudius and Laertes.

400. rights of memory: rights which will be remembered; i.e., with the disappearance of all the family of the original King Hamlet the situation reverts to what it was before the death of Fortinbras' father. See I.i.80-95. 401. vantage: i.e., my advantage, there being none to dispute my claim. 403. voice ... more: i.e., Hamlet's dying voice will strengthen your claim. 408. had ... on: had he become King.

THE TEMPEST

So far as is known *The Tempest* was Shakespeare's last comedy, and it contains some of his finest and maturest blank verse. It is a fairy tale, but Shakespeare has used it to illustrate the theme of reconciliation; wrongs committed in one generation are set right in the happiness of the next.

Shakespeare also achieved a remarkable feat of plot construction: he not only brings the two generations together, but actually preserves the unity of time: the action on the stage occurs within the time of real events, and almost in one place.

If a dramatist is to construct his play of two generations and at the same time keep the unity of time, he must either choose a story so well known to the audience that they need only be told at what point the play begins, or, if the story is new, quite early some explanation of past events must be given. Shakespeare begins with a stirring, noisy scene, a ship at sea in great peril. The ship runs aground. Then, in the quiet that follows, there enter an elderly man and his daughter. Here begins the glimpse into past history which is necessary before the story can move further. Critics differ in their opinions about the interpretation of this scene. To some, Prospero is yet another specimen of Shakespeare's somewhat overbearing, tyrannical fathers, like Capulet or Polonius. To others, he is a shy, gentle, melancholy student. The impression which the character will make on an audience depends on the interpretation of this scene. The common view is that, though technically excellent, the scene is inclined to be difficult. Prospero, as he tells his story, keeps interjecting: " Thou attend'st not. — Dost thou hear? " as if he were an incompetent schoolteacher trying to keep the attention of an undisciplined class. Miranda, too, seems a little lacking in politeness when she cannot at least pretend to be listening.

There is another and likelier interpretation. Hitherto, Miranda has known nothing of her father's past; now she must learn. As a duke Prospero has been a failure; he must now tell his daughter and be judged by her. It is a humiliating moment — a trial which at some time or other comes to all parents when for the first time their children look at them frankly and critically. When Prospero comes to tell his story, he lives again in the past and speaks musingly to himself more than to her. His ejaculations are in fact pleas to Miranda because he is so desperately anxious that she shall judge his case favorably and pass a merciful verdict. It is also

necessary, as a matter of mere stage technique, that a long speech shall be broken up, or it becomes tedious. Miranda says little not because she is inattentive or unsympathetic, but because she is amazed at this strange tale, not knowing what will come next.

The play is now ready to move. Miranda is asleep when Ariel — a spirit of the air — appears. Except to Prospero (and to the audience) Ariel, unless assuming a disguise, is always invisible to the other characters.

We are next introduced to Caliban, who in contrast with Ariel is a creature all earth. He is Shakespeare's portrait of the horrid savage. Caliban was greatly admired by critics of the eighteenth century as a marvelous effort of the imagination. Shakespeare seemed not to have shared the views of his contemporary Montaigne that savages are naturally gentle creatures, though it is perhaps unfair to judge by this specimen, whose mother was a witch and father a devil. With such heredity one hardly expects refinement. Yet Shakespeare is always fair to Caliban. He has his case and is allowed to state it. It is not surprising that he should be fascinated by Stephano and Trinculo, with their divine liquor.

The plot is now on the move, and hereafter Prospero makes his victims dance to his music. Ferdinand comes in, and at first glance, he and Miranda " change eyes." This to the Elizabethans was the ideal form of true love:

Who ever lived that loved not at first sight?

But Prospero, so that things may not be too easy for Ferdinand, pretends to be rough and terrifying, and from that moment Ferdinand becomes Miranda's slave.

After this idyllic scene, a very different and less ideal set of people are introduced. They are Prospero's wrongers, Alonso, the father of Ferdinand, and the wicked pair Sebastian and Antonio. Also in this party is Gonzalo, the old councilor, who is a sort of refined version of Polonius. The bold, bad men Sebastian and Antonio plot Alonso's murder so nicely and so grimly. Their conversation is admirably invented — neither of them quite likes to give plain words to a plain, dirty action. But this is a fairy tale, and no blood is to be shed; besides, Prospero and Ariel always have the situation well in hand. So Alonso is saved, and the party wander away to their predestined meeting place with Prospero.

Next, to clean the palate of the unpleasant taste of this scene, follows a passage of first-class low comedy. Trinculo, the jester, encounters the cowering Caliban. There is a kind of parody here of Miranda's first sight of a third human being. Then comes Stephano, the drunken butler, and finds Trinculo covered by Caliban's cloak, and all three go off inspired by liquor.

Shakespeare then repeats the pattern. Ferdinand and Miranda pass from love to courtship and a pledging of troth. To high romance the natural contrast is low comedy when Stephano, Trinculo, and Caliban re-enter, with Caliban the only man among them with a plan. He will murder Prospero. It is part of Caliban's simplicity that he mistakes the nature of Stephano, who has not the stuff in him to make a murderer.

Now Prospero has everything ready for the conversion of Alonso, and to crown Alonso's sorrow there comes the sudden, unexpected, overwhelming denunciation of Ariel. Thereafter Prospero, knowing that all is as he would have it, relents toward Ferdinand and accepts him, and in honor of the lovers presents a little wedding masque, which is suddenly broken off as he remembers the plot. It is the excuse for one of the most famous, oft-quoted, and finest of Shakespeare's speeches.

The play is now working toward an end. The three plotters, Caliban, Stephano, and Trinculo, are punished; they were poor plotters after all. A few gay cloths on a line easily turned them aside. Finally, all Prospero's enemies are brought before him and forgiven. To Alonso, his son is restored, and both old men are reconciled in the happiness of their children. *The Tempest* is a very simple story.

DATE AND SOURCE OF THE PLAY. *The Tempest* was performed at court on November 1, 1611, and was then probably a new play. It was again acted as one of fourteen plays performed for the wedding festivities of the Princess Elizabeth with the Elector Palatine on February 14, 1613. It was first printed in the first folio in 1623, and the text is good. There is no known source for the story, but the idea of the shipwreck was suggested by a disaster to Sir Thomas Gates's expedition to Virginia; Gates's flagship was wrecked in the Bermudas. Accounts describing the wreck were being printed in the autumn of 1610.

The Tempest

DRAMATIS PERSONAE

ALONSO, *King of Naples*
SEBASTIAN, *his brother*
PROSPERO, *the right Duke of Milan*
ANTONIO, *his brother, the usurping Duke of Milan*
FERDINAND, *son to the King of Naples*
GONZALO, *an honest old councilor*
ADRIAN ⎱ *lords*
FRANCISCO ⎰
CALIBAN, *a savage and deformed slave*
TRINCULO, *a jester*
STEPHANO, *a drunken butler*
MASTER *of a ship*
BOATSWAIN

MARINERS

MIRANDA, *daughter to Prospero*

ARIEL, *an airy spirit*

IRIS
CERES
JUNO ⎱ *presented by spirits*
NYMPHS
REAPERS ⎰

OTHER SPIRITS, *attending on Prospero*

SCENE — *A ship at sea: an uninhabited island.*

Act I

SCENE I. *On a ship at sea. A tempestuous noise of thunder and lightning heard.*°

[*Enter a* SHIPMASTER *and a* BOATSWAIN.]
MAST. Boatswain!
BOATS. Here, master. What cheer?
MAST. Good,° speak to the mariners. Fall to't yarely,° or we run ourselves aground. Bestir, bestir.
[*Exit.*]

[*Enter* MARINERS.]
BOATS. Heigh, my hearts! Cheerly, cheerly, my   6
hearts! Yare, yare! Take in the topsail.° Tend° to the master's whistle. Blow till thou burst thy wind, if room° enough!

[*Enter* ALONSO, SEBASTIAN, ANTONIO, FERDINAND, GONZALO, *and others.*]
ALON. Good boatswain, have care. Where's the master? Play the men.°   11
BOATS. I pray now, keep below.
ANT. Where is the master, boatswain?
BOATS. Do you not hear him? You mar our labor. Keep your cabins. You do assist the storm.   15
GON. Nay, good, be patient.
BOATS. When the sea is. Hence! What cares these roarers for the name of King? To cabin. Silence! Trouble us not.
GON. Good, yet remember whom thou hast aboard.   21

BOATS. None that I more love than myself. You are a councilor. If you can command these elements to silence, and work the peace of the present,° we will not hand a rope more. Use your authority. If you cannot, give thanks you have lived so long, and make yourself ready in your cabin for the mischance of the hour, if it so hap. Cheerly, good hearts!   29
Out of our way, I say.   [*Exit.*]
GON. I have great comfort from this fellow. Methinks he hath no drowning mark upon him, his complexion is perfect gallows.° Stand fast, good Fate, to his hanging. Make the rope of his destiny our cable, for our own doth little advantage. If   35
he be not born to be hanged, our case is miserable.
[*Exeunt.*]

[*Re-enter* BOATSWAIN.]
BOATS. Down with the topmast! Yare! Lower, lower! Bring her to try with main course.° [*A cry within.*] A plague upon this howling! They are louder than the weather or our office.°   40
[*Re-enter* SEBASTIAN, ANTONIO, *and* GONZALO.] Yet again! What do you here? Shall we give o'er, and drown? Have you a mind to sink?
SEB. A pox o' your throat, you bawling, blasphemous, incharitable dog!
BOATS. Work you, then.   45
ANT. Hang, cur! Hang, you whoreson,° insolent noisemaker. We are less afraid to be drowned than thou art.
GON. I'll warrant him for drowning,° though the

Act I, Sc. i: s.d., On . . . heard: When the scene opens the ship is in great danger. The wind is blowing hard from the sea; on the landward side lies the rocky island, and between there is too little sea room for her to sail past without being driven ashore by the drift.   3. Good: my good man.   4. yarely: quickly, smartly.   7. Take . . . topsail: i.e., to lessen the drift.   Tend: attend.   9. room: sea room.   11. Play . . . men: act like men.   24. work

. . . present: bring us peace at once.   32–33. hath . . . gallows: Gonzalo remembers the proverb "He that is born to be hanged will never be drowned," and the boatswain looks like a gallows bird.   38. try . . . course: i.e., use only the mainsail to heave her to.   course: sail.   40. office: business.   46. whoreson: bastard.   49. warrant . . . drowning: guarantee him against drowning.

ship were no stronger than a nutshell and as leaky as
an unstanched wench.   51
   BOATS. Lay her ahold,° ahold! Set her two
courses.° Off to sea again, lay her off.

              [*Enter* MARINERS *wet.*]
   MAR. All lost! To prayers, to prayers! All lost!   55
   BOATS. What, must our mouths be cold?°
   GON. The King and Prince at prayers! Let's assist
them,
For our case is as theirs.
   SEB.   I'm out of patience.
   ANT. We are merely cheated of our lives by
     drunkards.
This wide-chapped° rascal — would thou mightst lie
     drowning
The washing of ten tides!°
   GON.   He'll be hanged yet,   61
Though every drop of water swear against it
And gape at widest to glut° him.
       [*A confused noise within:* "Mercy on us!"
     — "We split, we split!" — "Farewell my
     wife and children!" — "Farewell, brother!"
     — "We split, we split, we split!"]
   ANT. Let's all sink with the King.
   SEB. Let's take leave of him.   68
        [*Exeunt* ANTONIO *and* SEBASTIAN.]
   GON. Now would I give a thousand furlongs of
sea for an acre of barren ground, long heath,° brown
furze,° anything. The wills above be done! But   72
I would fain die a dry death.   [*Exeunt.*]

SCENE II. *The island. Before* PROSPERO's *cell.*

        [*Enter* PROSPERO *and* MIRANDA.]
   MIRA. If by your art, my dearest father, you have
Put the wild waters in this roar, allay° them.
The sky, it seems, would pour down stinking pitch
But that the sea, mounting to the welkin's° cheek,
Dashes the fire out. Oh, I have suffered   5
With those that I saw suffer! A brave vessel,
Who had no doubt some noble creature in her,
Dashed all to pieces. Oh, the cry did knock
Against my very heart! Poor souls, they perished!
Had I been any god of power, I would   10
Have sunk the sea within the earth or ere
It should the good ship so have swallowed and
The fraughting° souls within her.
   PRO.   Be collected.°

52. **ahold:** close to the wind.   52–53. **two courses:** two sails; i.e.,
set the foresail as well. The maneuver of heaving-to has failed;
the boatswain now hopes to get the ship moving into the wind
enough to pass the island.   56. **mouths be cold:** Here the boatswain abandons hope and falls to drinking.   60. **wide-chapped:**
large-cheeked, because full of liquor.   61. **washing . . . tides:**
Pirates were hanged on the seashore and left until three high
tides had passed over them.   63. **glut:** swallow.   71. **long
heath:** rough grass.   72. **furze:** a prickly bushy shrub.
    Sc. ii: 2. **allay:** abate.   4. **welkin:** sky.   13. **fraughting:** lit.,
who were her freight. **collected:** calm.

No more amazement. Tell your piteous heart
There's no harm done.
   MIRA.   Oh, woe the day!
   PRO.   No harm.   15
I have done nothing but in care of thee,
Of thee, my dear one, thee, my daughter, who
Art ignorant of what thou art, naught knowing
Of whence I am, nor that I am more better
Than Prospero, master of a full° poor cell,   20
And thy no greater father.
   MIRA.   More to know
Did never meddle° with my thoughts.
   PRO.   'Tis time
I should inform thee farther. Lend thy hand,
And pluck my magic garment from me. — So.
            [*Lays down his mantle.*]
Lie there, my art. Wipe thou thine eyes, have com-
     fort.   25
The direful spectacle of the wreck, which touched
The very virtue of compassion in thee,
I have with such provision° in mine art
So safely ordered that there is no soul,
No, not so much perdition° as a hair,   30
Betid° to any creature in the vessel
Which thou heard'st cry, which thou saw'st sink. Sit
     down,
For thou must now know farther.
   MIRA.   You have often
Begun to tell me what I am, but stopped,
And left me to a bootless inquisition,°   35
Concluding "Stay, not yet."
   PRO.   The hour's now come,
The very minute bids thee ope thine ear.
Obey, and be attentive. Canst thou remember
A time before we came unto this cell?
I do not think thou canst, for then thou wast not   40
Out° three years old.
   MIRA.   Certainly, sir, I can.
   PRO. By what? By any other house or person?
Of anything the image tell me that
Hath kept with thy remembrance.
   MIRA.   'Tis far off,
And rather like a dream than an assurance   45
That my remembrance warrants. Had I not
Four or five women once that tended me?
   PRO. Thou hadst, and more, Miranda. But how
     is it
That this lives in thy mind? What seest thou else
In the dark backward and abysm of time?°   50
If thou remember'st aught ere thou camest here,
How thou camest here thou mayst.
   MIRA.   But that I do not.

20. **full:** exceedingly.   22. **meddle:** interfere; i.e., cause to be
curious.   28. **provision:** foresight.   30. **perdition:** loss.
31. **Betid:** befallen.   35. **bootless inquisition:** vain inquiry.
41. **Out:** more than.   50. **abysm of time:** i.e., the past, which is
like a dark abyss.

PRO. Twelve year since, Miranda, twelve year
  since,
Thy father was the Duke of Milan, and
A prince of power.
MIRA.   Sir, are not you my father?   55
PRO. Thy mother was a piece of virtue, and
She said thou wast my daughter, and thy father
Was Duke of Milan, and his only heir
A Princess, no worse issued.
MIRA.   Oh, the Heavens!
What foul play had we that we came from thence?
Or blessèd was't we did?
PRO.   Both, both, my girl.   61
By foul play, as thou say'st, were we heaved thence,
But blessedly holp° hither.
MIRA.   Oh, my heart bleeds
To think o' the teen° that I have turned you to,
Which is from my remembrance! Please you, far-
  ther.   65
PRO. My brother, and thy uncle, called Antonio —
I pray thee mark me — that a brother should
Be so perfidious! — he whom, next thyself,
Of all the world I loved, and to him put
The manage° of my state — as at that time   70
Through all the signories° it was the first,
And Prospero the prime° Duke, being so reputed
In dignity, and for the liberal arts°
Without a parallel, those being all my study —
The government I cast upon my brother,   75
And to my state grew stranger, being transported
And rapt in secret studies. Thy false uncle ——
Dost thou attend me?
MIRA.   Sir, most heedfully.
PRO. Being once perfected° how to grant suits,
How to deny them, who to advance, and who   80
To trash for overtopping,° new-created°
The creatures that were mine, I say, or changed 'em,
Or else new-formed 'em — having both the key°
Of officer and office, set all hearts i' the state
To what tune pleased his ear, that now he was   85
The ivy which had hid my princely trunk,
And sucked my verdure out on't. Thou attend'st
  not.
MIRA. Oh, good sir, I do.
PRO.   I pray thee, mark me.
I, thus neglecting worldly ends, all dedicated
To closeness° and the bettering of my mind   90
With that which, but by being so retired,°
O'erprized all popular rate,° in my false brother

Awaked an evil nature. And my trust,
Like a good parent, did beget of him
A falsehood in its contrary as great   95
As my trust was, which had indeed no limit,
A confidence sans° bound. He being thus lorded,
Not only with what my revenue yielded,
But what my power might else exact, like one
Who having into truth, by telling of it,   100
Made such a sinner of his memory,
To credit his own lie, he did believe
He was indeed the Duke° — out o' the substitution,
And executing the outward face of royalty,
With all prerogative.° — Hence his ambition grow-
  ing ——   105
Dost thou hear?
MIRA.   Your tale, sir, would cure deafness.
PRO. To have no screen between this part he
  played
And him he played it for, he needs will be
Absolute Milan.° Me, poor man, my library
Was dukedom large enough. Of temporal royalties°
He thinks me now incapable; confederates,°   111
So dry° he was for sway, wi' the King of Naples
To give him annual tribute, do him homage,
Subject his coronet to his crown,° and bend
The dukedom, yet unbowed — alas, poor Milan! —
To most ignoble stooping.
MIRA.   Oh, the Heavens!   116
PRO. Mark his condition, and the event,° then tell
  me
If this might be a brother.
MIRA.   I should sin
To think but nobly of my grandmother.
Good wombs have borne bad sons.
PRO.   Now the condition.   120
This King of Naples, being an enemy
To me inveterate, hearkens my brother's suit.
Which was that he, in lieu o' the premises,°
Of homage, and I know not how much tribute,
Should presently° extirpate° me and mine   125
Out of the dukedom, and confer fair Milan,
With all the honors, on my brother. Whereon,
A treacherous army levied, one midnight
Fated to the purpose did Antonio open
The gates of Milan, and, i' the dead of darkness   130
The ministers for the purpose hurried thence
Me and thy crying self.

63. holp: helped.   64. teen: sorrow.   70. manage: management.
71. signories: lordships.   72. prime: leading.   73. liberal arts:
academic learning.   79. perfected: become perfect by practice.
81. trash . . . overtopping: check for running ahead, a metaphor
from training a pack of hounds.   new-created: made them new
creatures — by tampering with their loyalty.   83. key: tool
used for tuning a stringed instrument.   90. closeness: privacy.
91. but . . . retired: except that it kept me away from state
affairs.   92. O'erprized . . . rate: was worth more than it is
commonly regarded.

97. sans: without.   97–103. He . . . Duke: he, getting such
greatness not only from my wealth but also by abusing my power,
began to believe as he had hitherto pretended, that he was in
truth the Duke.   103–05. out . . . prerogative: from being my
substitute and acting outwardly as Duke with all the rights of a
ruler.   109. Absolute Milan: Duke of Milan in fact.   110. temporal royalties: worldly power.   111. confederates: conspires.
112. dry: thirsty.   114. Subject . . . crown: i.e., pay homage as
to his overlord. The coronet was worn as a symbol by rulers of
lower rank than that of King.   117. event: sequel.   123. in . . .
premises: in return for these conditions.   125. presently: immediately.   extirpate: root out.

MIRA.   Alack, for pity!
I, not remembering how I cried out then,
Will cry it o'er again. It is a hint°
That wrings mine eyes to't.

PRO.   Hear a little further,   135
And then I'll bring thee to the present business
Which now's upon 's, without the which this story
Were most impertinent.

MIRA.   Wherefore did they not
That hour destroy us?

PRO.   Well demanded, wench.   139
My tale provokes that question. Dear, they durst not,
So dear the love my people bore me, nor set
A mark so bloody on the business, but
With colors fairer painted their foul ends.
In few,° they hurried us aboard a bark,   144
Bore us some leagues to sea, where they prepared
A rotten carcass of a butt,° not rigged,
Nor tackle, sail, nor mast. The very rats
Instinctively have quit it. There they hoist us,
To cry to the sea that roared to us, to sigh
To the winds, whose pity, sighing back again,   150
Did us but loving wrong.

MIRA.   Alack, what trouble
Was I then to you!

PRO.   Oh, a cherubin
Thou wast that did preserve me. Thou didst smile,
Infusèd with a fortitude from Heaven,   154
When I have decked the sea with drops full salt.
Under my burden groaned, which raised in me
An undergoing stomach° to bear up
Against what should ensue.

MIRA.   How came we ashore?
PRO. By Providence divine.
Some food we had, and some fresh water, that   160
A noble Neapolitan, Gonzalo,
Out of his charity, who being then appointed
Master of this design, did give us, with
Rich garments, linens, stuffs, and necessaries,
Which since have steaded much.° So, of his gentle-
    ness,   165
Knowing I loved my books, he furnished me
From mine own library with volumes that
I prize above my dukedom.

MIRA.   Would I might
But ever see that man!

PRO.   Now I arise. [*Resumes his mantle.*]
Sit still, and hear the last of our sea sorrow.   170
Here in this island we arrived, and here
Have I, thy schoolmaster, made thee more profit
Than other princes can that have more time
For vainer hours, and tutors not so careful.

MIRA. Heavens thank you for't! And now I pray
    you, sir,   175

134. hint: occasion.   144. In few: in a few words.   146. butt:
tub.   157. undergoing stomach: courage to endure, the stomach
being regarded as the seat of valor.   165. have . . . much: have
been of great benefit.

For still 'tis beating° in my mind, your reason
For raising this sea storm?

PRO.   Know thus far forth.°
By accident most strange, bountiful Fortune,
Now my dear lady,° hath mine enemies
Brought to this shore. And by my prescience°   180
I find my zenith° doth depend upon
A most auspicious star, whose influence
If now I court not,° but omit, my fortunes
Will ever after droop. Here cease more questions.
Thou art inclined to sleep, 'tis a good dullness,   185
And give it way. I know thou canst not choose.
                    [MIRANDA *sleeps.*]
Come away, servant, come. I am ready now.
Approach, my Ariel, come.
               [*Enter* ARIEL.]
ARI. All hail, great master! Grave sir, hail! I come
To answer thy best pleasure, be 't to fly,   190
To swim, to dive into the fire, to ride
On the curled clouds, to thy strong bidding task°
Ariel and all his quality.°

PRO.   Hast thou, spirit,
Performed to point° the tempest that I bade thee?
ARI. To every article.   195
I boarded the King's ship. Now on the beak,
Now in the waist,° the deck, in every cabin,
I flamed amazement.° Sometime I'd divide,
And burn in many places; on the topmast,   199
The yards and bowsprit, would I flame distinctly,
Then meet and join. Jove's lightnings, the precur-
    sors°
O' the dreadful thunderclaps, more momentary
And sight-outrunning were not. The fire and cracks
Of sulphurous roaring the most mighty Neptune
Seem to besiege, and make his bold waves tremble —
Yea, his dread trident shake.

PRO.   My brave spirit!   206
Who was so firm, so constant, that this coil°
Would not infect his reason?

ARI.   Not a soul
But felt a fever of the mad° and played
Some tricks of desperation.° All but mariners   210
Plunged in the foaming brine, and quit the vessel,
Then all afire with me. The King's son, Ferdinand,
With hair upstaring — then like reeds, not hair —
Was the first man that leaped, cried, " Hell is empty,

176. beating: throbbing.   177. Know . . . forth: i.e., I will now
tell you more.   179. Now . . . lady: Fortune (once my foe) is
now kind to me.   180. prescience: foreknowledge.   181. zenith:
the highest point of my fortunes.   183. court not: do not seek
to win.   192. task: impose a task on.   193. quality: ability.
194. to point: in all points, exactly.   197. waist: the middle part
of a large ship which lies between the forecastle and the poop.
198. flamed amazement: appeared in the form of fire which
caused amazement. This phenomenon, known as Saint Elmo's
fire or a corposant, is sometimes seen on ships during a storm.
201. precursors: forerunners.   207. coil: confusion.   209. fever
. . . mad: fever of madness.   210. tricks of desperation: desperate tricks.

And all the devils are here."

PRO.   Why, that's my spirit!   215
But was not this nigh shore?

ARI.   Close by, my master.

PRO. But are they, Ariel, safe?

ARI.   Not a hair perished,
On their sustaining° garments not a blemish,
But fresher than before. And, as thou badest me,
In troops I have dispersed them 'bout the isle.   220
The King's son have I landed by himself,
Whom I left cooling of the air with sighs
In an odd angle° of the isle, and sitting
His arms in this sad knot.°

PRO.   Of the King's ship,
The mariners, say how thou hast disposed,   225
And all the rest o' the fleet.

ARI.   Safely in harbor
Is the King's ship — in the deep nook where once
Thou call'dst me up at midnight to fetch dew
From the still-vexed Bermoothes,° there she's hid.
The mariners all under hatches stowed,   230
Who, with a charm joined to their suffered labor,°
I have left asleep. And for the rest o' the fleet,
Which I dispersed, they all have met again,
And are upon the Mediterranean flote,°
Bound sadly home for Naples,   235
Supposing that they saw the King's ship wrecked
And his great person perish.

PRO.   Ariel, thy charge
Exactly is performed. But there's more work.
What is the time o' the day?

ARI.   Past the midseason.

PRO. At least two glasses.° The time 'twixt six and
now   240
Must by us both be spent most preciously.

ARI. Is there more toil? Since thou dost give me
pains,°
Let me remember° thee what thou hast promisèd,
Which is not yet performed me.

PRO.   How now? Moody?
What is't thou canst demand?

ARI.   My liberty.   245

PRO. Before the time be out? No more!

ARI.   I prithee
Remember I have done thee worthy service,
Told thee no lies, made thee no mistakings, served
Without or grudge or grumblings. Thou didst
promise
To bate° me a full year.

PRO.   Dost thou forget   250
From what a torment I did free thee?

ARI.   No.

PRO. Thou dost, and think'st it much to tread the
ooze
Of the salt deep,
To run upon the sharp wind of the North,
To do me business in the veins o' the earth   255
When it is baked with frost.

ARI.   I do not, sir.

PRO. Thou liest, malignant thing! Hast thou forgot
The foul witch Sycorax, who with age and envy
Was grown into a hoop?° Hast thou forgot her?

ARI. No, sir.

PRO.   Thou hast. Where was she born?
Speak, tell me.°   260

ARI. Sir, in Argier.°

PRO.   Oh, was she so? I must
Once in a month recount what thou hast been,
Which thou forget'st. This damned witch Sycorax,
For mischiefs manifold and sorceries terrible
To enter human hearing,° from Argier,   265
Thou know'st, was banished. For one thing she did°
They would not take her life. Is not this true?

ARI. Aye, sir.

PRO. This blue-eyed° hag was hither brought
with child,
And here was left by the sailors. Thou, my slave,
As thou report'st thyself, wast then her servant.   271
And, for thou wast a spirit too delicate
To act her earthy and abhorred commands,
Refusing her grand hests,° she did confine thee,
By help of her more potent ministers   275
And in her most unmitigable° rage,
Into a cloven pine. Within which rift
Imprisoned thou didst painfully remain
A dozen years. Within which space she died,
And left thee there, where thou didst vent thy
groans   280
As fast as mill wheels strike.° Then was this is-
land —
Save for the son that she did litter here,
A freckled whelp hag-born° — not honored with
A human shape.

ARI.   Yes, Caliban her son.

PRO. Dull thing, I say so, he, that Caliban   285
Whom now I keep in service. Thou best know'st
What torment I did find thee in. Thy groans
Did make wolves howl and penetrate the breasts
Of ever-angry bears. It was a torment
To lay upon the damned, which Sycorax   290
Could not again undo. It was mine art,
When I arrived and heard thee, that made gape
The pine and let thee out.

ARI.   I thank thee, master.

218. sustaining: which bore them up.   223. angle: corner.
224. in . . . knot: sadly folded. Ariel imitates the posture.
229. still-vexed Bermoothes: ever stormy Bermudas.   231. joined
. . . labor: as well as the labor they had endured.   234. flote:
sea.   240. glasses: i.e., hours; turns of the hourglass.   242. pains:
toil.   243. remember: remind.   250. bate: abate, lessen.

259. grown . . . hoop: bent double.   261. Argier: Algiers.   265. To
. . . hearing: for a human being to hear.   266. one . . . did: This
good action is not recalled.   269. blue-eyed: with dark rings
under the eyes.   274. hests: commands.   276. unmitigable:
absolute.   281. mill . . . strike: i.e., the continuous clack of a
water mill.   283. hag-born: child of a hag.

PRO. If thou more murmur'st, I will rend an oak°
And peg thee in his knotty entrails till   295
Thou hast howled away twelve winters.

ARI.   Pardon, master.
I will be correspondent° to command,
And do my spiriting° gently.

PRO.   Do so, and after two days
I will discharge thee.

ARI.   That's my noble master!
What shall I do? Say what. What shall I do?   300

PRO. Go make thyself like a nymph o' the sea.
Be subject to no sight but thine and mine, invisible
To every eyeball else. Go take this shape,
And hither come in't. Go, hence with diligence!
                            [Exit ARIEL.]
Awake, dear heart, awake! Thou hast slept well.
Awake!

MIRA. The strangeness of your story put   306
Heaviness in me.

PRO.   Shake it off. Come on,
We'll visit Caliban my slave, who never
Yields us kind answer.

MIRA.   'Tis a villain, sir,
I do not love to look on.

PRO.   But, as 'tis,   310
We cannot miss° him. He does make our fire,
Fetch in our wood, and serves in offices
That profit us. What ho! Slave! Caliban!
Thou earth,° thou! Speak.

CAL. *[Within]*   There's wood enough within.

PRO. Come forth, I say! There's other business for
    thee.   315
Come, thou tortoise! When?

[Re-enter ARIEL *like a water nymph.*] Fine apparition! My quaint° Ariel,
Hark in thine ear.

ARI.   My lord, it shall be done. *[Exit.]*

PRO. Thou poisonous slave, got° by the Devil himself
Upon thy wicked dam,° come forth!   320
                  [Enter CALIBAN.]

CAL. As wicked dew as e'er my mother brushed
With raven's feather from unwholesome fen
Drop on you both! A southwest° blow on ye
And blister you all o'er!

PRO. For this, be sure, tonight thou shalt have
    cramps,   325
Side stitches that shall pen thy breath up. Urchins°
Shall, for that vast° of night that they may work,
All exercise on thee. Thou shalt be pinched
As thick as honeycomb, each pinch more stinging

Than bees that made 'em.

CAL.   I must eat my dinner.   330
This island's mine, by Sycorax my mother,
Which thou takest from me. When thou camest first,
Thou strokedst me, and madest much of me, wouldst
    give me
Water with berries in't.° And teach me how
To name the bigger light, and how the less,   335
That burn by day and night. And then I loved thee,
And showed thee all the qualities° o' th' isle,
The fresh springs, brine pits, barren place and fertile.
Cursèd be I that did so! All the charms
Of Sycorax, toads, beetles, bats, light on you!   340
For I am all the subjects that you have,
Which first was mine own king. And here you sty°
    me
In this hard rock whiles you do keep from me
The rest o' th' island.

PRO.   Thou most lying slave,
Whom stripes° may move, not kindness! I have used
    thee,   345
Filth as thou art, with human care, and lodged thee
In mine own cell till thou didst seek to violate
The honor of my child.

CAL. Oh ho, oh ho! Would 't had been done!
Thou didst prevent me. I had peopled else   350
This isle with Calibans.

PRO.   Abhorrèd slave,
Which any print° of goodness wilt not take,
Being capable of all ill! I pitied thee,
Took pains to make thee speak, taught thee each
    hour   354
One thing or other. When thou didst not, savage,
Know thine own meaning, but wouldst gabble like
A thing most brutish, I endowed thy purposes
With words that made them known. But thy vile
    race,
Though thou didst learn, had that in't which good
    natures
Could not abide to be with. Therefore wast thou
Deservedly confined into this rock,   361
Who hadst deserved more than a prison.

CAL. You taught me language, and my profit on't
Is I know how to curse. The red plague° rid° you
For learning° me your language!

PRO.   Hagseed,° hence!   365
Fetch us in fuel, and be quick, thou'rt best,
To answer other business. Shrug'st thou, malice?
If thou neglect'st, or dost unwillingly
What I command, I'll rack thee with old° cramps,

---

294. **rend an oak**: i.e., a far worse torment than imprisonment in a pine.   297. **correspondent**: agreeable, submissive.   298. **spiriting**: my work as a spirit.   311. **miss**: do without.   314. **earth**: lump of dirt.   317. **quaint**: elegant.   319. **got**: begotten. 320. **dam**: mother.   323. **southwest**: regarded as an unhealthy wind.   326. **Urchins**: goblins, or hedgehogs.   327. **vast**: desolate period.

334. **Water . . . in't**: Shakespeare apparently took this from William Strachey's account of the Bermuda shipwreck, which records that the castaways made a pleasant drink from cedar berries. 337. **qualities**: good spots.   342. **sty**: pen.   345. **stripes**: blows. 352. **print**: impression.   364. **red plague**: bubonic plague. **rid**: destroy.   365. **learning**: teaching. **Hagseed**: son of a hag. 369. **old**: abundant.

Fill all thy bones with achés,° make thee roar   370
That beasts shall tremble at thy din.

CAL.   No, pray thee.
[*Aside*] I must obey. His art is of such power
It would control my dam's god, Setebos,   373
And make a vassal° of him.

PRO.   So, slave. Hence!
                    [*Exit* CALIBAN.]
[*Re-enter* ARIEL, *invisible, playing and singing;*
      FERDINAND *following.*]
ARI. [*Sings.*]
   " Come unto these yellow sands,
      And then take hands.
   Curtsied when you have and kissed
      The wild waves whist,°
   Foot it featly° here and there,   380
   And, sweet sprites, the burden° bear."

BURDEN. [*Dispersedly*]° " Hark, hark! "
                      "Bowwow."

ARI. " The watchdogs bark."
BURDEN. [*Dispersedly*]   "Bowwow."
ARI. " Hark, hark! I hear
   The strain of strutting chanticleer   385
   Cry Cock-a-diddle-dow."

FER. Where should this music be? I' th' air or th'
earth?
It sounds no more, and, sure, it waits upon
Some god o' th' island. Sitting on a bank,
Weeping again the King my father's wreck,   390
This music crept by me upon the waters,
Allaying both their fury and my passion°
With its sweet air. Thence I have followed it,
Or it hath drawn me rather. But 'tis gone.   395
No, it begins again.
ARI. [*Sings.*]
   " Full fathom five thy father lies,
      Of his bones are coral made,
   Those are pearls that were his eyes.
      Nothing of him that doth fade   400
   But doth suffer a sea change
   Into something rich and strange.
   Sea nymphs hourly ring his knell."
BURDEN.   "Dingdong."
ARI. " Hark! Now I hear them. — Dingdong,
bell."   404
FER. The ditty does remember my drowned father.
This is no mortal business, nor no sound
That the earth owes.° — I hear it now above me.
PRO. The fringèd curtains of thine eye advance,°
And say what thou seest yond.
MIRA.   What is't? A spirit?
Lord, how it looks about! Believe me, sir,   410

It carries a brave form.° But 'tis a spirit.
PRO. No, wench, it eats and sleeps and hath such
senses
As we have, such. This gallant which thou seest
Was in the wreck, and but he's something stained
With grief, that's beauty's canker,° thou mightst
call him   415
A goodly person. He hath lost his fellows,
And strays about to find 'em.
MIRA.   I might call him
A thing divine, for nothing natural
I ever saw so noble.
PRO.   [*Aside*] It goes on,° I see,   419
As my soul prompts it. Spirit, fine spirit! I'll free thee
Within two days for this.
FER.   Most sure, the goddess
On whom these airs attend!° Vouchsafe my prayer
May know if you remain upon this island,°
And that you will some good instruction give
How I may bear me° here. My prime request,   425
Which I do last pronounce, is, O you wonder!
If you be maid or no?°
MIRA.   No wonder, sir,
But certainly ⌐ maid.
FER.   My language! Heavens!
I am the best of them° that speak this speech,
Were I but where 'tis spoken.
PRO.   How? The best?   430
What wert thou if the King of Naples heard thee?
FER. A single° thing, as I am now, that wonders
To hear thee speak of Naples. He does hear me,
And that he does I weep. Myself am Naples,
Who with mine eyes, never since at ebb,° beheld
The King my father wrecked.
MIRA.   Alack, for mercy!   436
FER. Yes, faith, and all his lords, the Duke of
Milan
And his brave son being twain.°
PRO.   [*Aside*] The Duke of Milan
And his more braver daughter could control thee,
If now 'twere fit to do't. At the first sight   440
They have changed eyes.° Delicate Ariel,
I'll set thee free for this. [*To* FERDINAND] A word,
good sir.
I fear you have done yourself some wrong. A word.
MIRA. Why speaks my father so ungently? This
Is the third man that e'er I saw, the first   445
That e'er I sighed for. Pity move my father
To be inclined my way!

---

370. **aches:** a two-syllable word, pronounced like "h's."
374. **vassal:** slave.   379. **whist:** silent.   380. **featly:** smartly.
381. **burden:** refrain.   382 s.d., Dispersedly: from different
sides.   392. **passion:** emotion, sorrow.   407. **owes:** owns, possesses.   408. **advance:** raise.

411. **brave form:** fine shape.   415. **canker:** maggot.   419. **It . . .
on:** i.e., Prospero's plan that Miranda and Ferdinand shall fall in
love.   422. **attend:** wait on.   422–23. **Vouchsafe . . . island:**
grant my prayer, which is to know whether you inhabit this
island.   425. **bear me:** behave myself.   427. **maid or no:** i.e., a
mortal or a goddess.   429. **best of them:** i.e., I am now King of
Naples since my father's death.   432. **single:** lonely.   435. **never
. . . ebb:** i.e., have not ceased to flow.   438. **twain:** i.e., two of
those drowned.   441. **changed eyes:** fallen in love.

FER.   Oh, if a virgin,
And your affection not gone forth,° I'll make you
The Queen of Naples.
    PRO.   Soft, sir! One word more.
[*Aside*] They are both in either's powers. But this
    swift business   450
I must uneasy make, lest too light winning
Make the prize light. [*To* FERDINAND] One word
    more. I charge thee
That thou attend me. Thou dost here usurp
The name thou owest not, and hast put thyself
Upon this island as a spy, to win it   455
From me, the lord on 't.
    FER.   No, as I am a man.
    MIRA. There's nothing ill can dwell in such a
    temple.°
If the ill spirit have so fair a house,
Good things will strive to dwell with 't.
    PRO.   Follow me.
Speak not you for him, he's a traitor. Come,   460
I'll manacle thy neck and feet together.
Sea water shalt thou drink, thy food shall be
The fresh-brook mussels, withered roots, and husks
Wherein the acorn cradled. Follow.
    FER.   No.
I will resist such entertainment till   465
Mine enemy has more power.
              [*Draws, and is charmed from moving.*]
    MIRA.   O dear Father,
Make not too rash a trial of him, for
He's gentle, and not fearful.°
    PRO.   What! I say,
My foot my tutor?° Put thy sword up, traitor,
Who makest a show but darest not strike, thy con-
    science   470
Is so possessed with guilt. Come from thy ward,°
For I can here disarm thee with this stick
And make thy weapon drop.
    MIRA.   Beseech you, Father.
    PRO. Hence! Hang not on my garments.
    MIRA.   Sir, have pity.
I'll be his surety.
    PRO.   Silence! One word more   475
Shall make me chide thee, if not hate thee. What!
An advocate for an impostor! Hush!
Thou think'st there is no more such shapes as he,
Having seen but him and Caliban. Foolish wench!
To the most of men this is a Caliban,   480
And they to him are angels.
    MIRA.   My affections
Are, then, most humble. I have no ambition
To see a goodlier man.

PRO.   Come on, obey.
Thy nerves° are in their infancy again,
And have no vigor in them.
    FER.   So they are.   485
My spirits, as in a dream, are all bound up.
My father's loss, the weakness which I feel,
The wreck of all my friends, nor this man's threats,
To whom I am subdued, are but light to me
Might I but through my prison once a day   490
Behold this maid. All corners else o' th' earth
Let liberty make use of, space enough
Have I in such a prison.
    PRO.   [*Aside*] It works.
              [*To* FERDINAND] Come on.
Thou hast done well, fine Ariel!
              [*To* FERDINAND] Follow me.   494
[*To* ARIEL] Hark what thou else shalt do me.
    MIRA.   Be of comfort.
My father's of a better nature, sir,
Than he appears by speech. This is unwonted°
Which now came from him.
    PRO.   Thou shalt be as free
As mountain winds. But then exactly do
All points of my command.
    ARI.   To the syllable.   500
    PRO. Come, follow. Speak not for him. [*Exeunt.*]

Act II

SCENE I. *Another part of the island.*

[*Enter* ALONSO, SEBASTIAN, ANTONIO, GONZALO,
        ADRIAN, FRANCISCO, *and others.*]
    GON. Beseech you, sir, be merry. You have cause,
So have we all, of joy, for our escape
Is much beyond our loss. Our hint° of woe
Is common. Every day some sailor's wife,   4
The masters of some merchant,° and the merchant,°
Have just our theme of woe. But for the miracle —
I mean our preservation — few in millions
Can speak like us. Then wisely, good sir, weigh
Our sorrow with our comfort.
    ALON.   Prithee, peace.
    SEB. He receives comfort like cold porridge.   10
    ANT. The visitor° will not give him o'er so.
    SEB. Look, he's winding up the watch of his wit.
By and by it will strike.
    GON. Sir ——

---

448. gone forth: i.e., been bestowed on someone else. 457. temple:
i.e., beautiful body. 468. fearful: to be feared. 469. My . . .
tutor: The head is the tutor to the body, but Miranda (who is by
nature subordinate and so the foot) is trying to tell her father
what he should do. 471. ward: position of defense.

484. nerves: sinews. 497. unwonted: unusual.
    Act II, Sc. i: 3. hint: occasion. See I.ii.134. 5. masters . . .
merchant: captains of merchant ships. the merchant: i.e., the
owner. 11. visitor: visiting minister. See *T Night*, IV.ii.25–26.
Sebastian means that Gonzalo will insist on having his say
whether Alonso wishes to hear it or not.

SEB. One. Tell.°   15

GON. When every grief is entertained° that's offered,

Comes to the entertainer ——

SEB. A dollar.

GON. Dolor comes to him, indeed. You have spoken truer than you purposed.   20

SEB. You have taken it wiselier than I meant you should.

GON. Therefore, my lord ——

ANT. Fie, what a spendthrift is he of his tongue!

ALON. I prithee, spare.   25

GON. Well, I have done. But yet ——

SEB. He will be talking.

ANT. Which, of he or Adrian, for a good wager, first begins to crow?

SEB. The old cock.   30

ANT. The cockerel.

SEB. Done. The wager?

ANT. A laughter.°

SEB. A match!

ADR. Though this island seem to be desert ——

SEB. Ha, ha, ha! — So, you're paid.°   36

ADR. Uninhabitable, and almost inaccessible ——

SEB. Yet ——

ADR. Yet ——

ANT. He could not miss 't.°   40

ADR. It must needs be of subtle, tender, and delicate temperance.

ANT. Temperance was a delicate wench.

SEB. Aye, and a subtle, as he most learnedly delivered.°   45

ADR. The air breathes upon us here most sweetly.

SEB. As if it had lungs, and rotten ones.

ANT. Or as 'twere perfumed by a fen.

GON. Here is everything advantageous to life.

ANT. True — save means to live.   50

SEB. Of that there's none, or little.

GON. How lush and lusty the grass looks! How green!

ANT. The ground indeed is tawny.

SEB. With an eye° of green in't.   55

ANT. He misses not much.

SEB. No, he doth but mistake the truth totally.

GON. But the rarity° of it is — which is indeed almost beyond credit° ——

SEB. As many vouched° rarities are.   60

GON. That our garments, being, as they were, drenched in the sea, hold notwithstanding their freshness and glosses, being rather new-dyed than stained with salt water.

ANT. If but one of his pockets could speak,° would it not say he lies?   66

SEB. Aye, or very falsely pocket up his report.

GON. Methinks our garments are now as fresh as when we put them on first in Afric, at the marriage of the King's fair daughter Claribel to the King of Tunis.   71

SEB. 'Twas a sweet marriage, and we prosper well in our return.

ADR. Tunis was never graced° before with such a paragon to° their Queen.   75

GON. Not since Widow Dido's° time.

ANT. Widow! A pox° o' that! How came that widow in?° Widow Dido!

SEB. What if he had said " Widower Aeneas " too? Good Lord, how you take it!   80

ADR. "Widow Dido," said you? You make me study of that. She was of Carthage, not of Tunis.

GON. This Tunis, sir, was Carthage.

ADR. Carthage?

GON. I assure you, Carthage.   85

ANT. His word is more than the miraculous harp.°

SEB. He hath raised the wall, and houses too.

ANT. What impossible matter will he make easy next?

SEB. I think he will carry this island home in his pocket, and give it his son for an apple.   91

ANT. And, sowing the kernels of it in the sea, bring forth more islands.

GON. Aye.

ANT. Why, in good time.   95

GON. Sir, we were talking that our garments seem now as fresh as when we were at Tunis at the marriage of your daughter, who is now Queen.

ANT. And the rarest that e'er came there.

SEB. Bate,° I beseech you, Widow Dido.   100

ANT. Oh, Widow Dido! Aye, Widow Dido.

GON. Is not, sir, my doublet° as fresh as the first day I wore it? I mean, in a sort.°

ANT. That sort was well fished for.°

GON. When I wore it at your daughter's marriage?   105

ALON. You cram these words into mine ears against

---

15. **Tell:** count.   16. **entertained:** received.   33. **A laughter:** the winner is to have the laugh on the loser, on the principle of the proverb "He laughs that wins." Cf. *Oth.*, IV.i.126. (Kittredge).   36. **Ha . . . paid:** F1 divides the speech: "*Sebastian:* Ha, ha, ha. *Antonio:* So, you're paid"; i.e., you've had your laugh as winner.   40. **He . . . miss 't:** i.e., if he begins the first clause with "though," he is sure to follow it up with a "yet."   45. **delivered:** declared.   55. **eye:** tinge.   58. **rarity:** strange thing.   59. **credit:** belief.   60. **vouched:** guaranteed.

65. **pockets . . . speak:** i.e., his pockets are still wet.   74. **graced:** honored.   75. **to:** for.   76. **Widow Dido:** Dido was the Queen of Carthage (near the modern Tunis) who entertained Aeneas on his way from Troy to Italy. She was a widow and had vowed eternal fidelity to the memory of her husand, but she fell in love with Aeneas. When he deserted her, she committed suicide.   77. **pox:** plague; lit., venereal disease.   77–78. **How . . . in:** why do you call her a widow?   86. **His . . . harp:** According to the legends told by Ovid, the walls of Thebes came together at the music of Amphion's harp. By a like miracle Gonzalo has erected a Carthage at Tunis.   100. **Bate:** except.   102. **doublet:** short, close-fitting jacket.   103. **in a sort:** after a fashion.   104. **That . . . for:** i.e., he had to add "after a fashion."

The stomach of my sense. Would I had never
Married my daughter there! For, coming thence,
My son is lost and, in my rate,° she too
Who is so far from Italy removed   110
I ne'er again shall see her. O thou mine heir
Of Naples and of Milan, what strange fish
Hath made his meal on thee?

FRAN.   Sir, he may live.
I saw him beat the surges° under him,
And ride upon their backs. He trod the water,   115
Whose enmity he flung aside, and breasted
The surge most swoln° that met him. His bold head
'Bove the contentious waves he kept, and oared
Himself with his good arms in lusty stroke
To the shore, that o'er his wave-worn basis bowed,°
As stooping to relieve him. I not doubt   121
He came alive to land.

ALON.   No, no, he's gone.

SEB. Sir, you may thank yourself for this great
     loss,
That would not bless our Europe with your
     daughter,
But rather lose her to an African,   125
Where she, at least, is banished from your eye
Who hath cause to wet° the grief on 't.

ALON.   Prithee, peace.

SEB. You were kneeled to, and importuned other-
wise,
By all of us, and the fair soul herself   129
Weighed° between loathness° and obedience, at
Which end o' the beam° should bow. We have lost
     your son,
I fear, forever. Milan and Naples have
Mo° widows in them of this business' making
Than we bring men to comfort them.
The fault's your own.

ALON.   So is the dear'st° o' the loss.   135

GON. My lord Sebastian,
The truth you speak doth lack some gentleness,
And time to speak it in. You rub the sore
When you should bring the plaster.

SEB.   Very well.

ANT. And most chirurgeonly.°   140

GON. It is foul weather in us all, good sir,
When you are cloudy.

SEB.   Foul weather?

ANT.   Very foul.

GON. Had I plantation° of this isle, my lord ——

ANT. He'd sow 't with nettle seed.

SEB.   Or docks, or mallows.°

GON. And were the King on 't, what would I do?

SEB. 'Scape being drunk for want of wine.   146

GON. I' the commonwealth° I would by con-
traries°
Execute all things, for no kind of traffic°
Would I admit, no name of magistrate.
Letters° should not be known; riches, poverty,   150
And use of service,° none; contract,° succession,°
Bourn,° bound° of land, tilth,° vineyard, none;
No use of metal,° corn, or wine, or oil;
No occupation° — all men idle, all;
And women too, but innocent and pure;   155
No sovereignty ——

SEB.   Yet he would be King on 't.

ANT. The latter end of his commonwealth forgets
the beginning.

GON. All things in common nature should pro-
duce
Without sweat or endeavor. Treason, felony,   160
Sword, pike, knife, gun, or need of any engine°
Would I not have. But Nature should bring
forth,
Of it° own kind, all foison,° all abundance,
To feed my innocent people.

SEB. No marrying 'mong his subjects?   165

ANT. None, man — all idle, whores and knaves.

GON. I would with such perfection govern, sir,
To excel the Golden Age.°

SEB.   'Save° His Majesty!

ANT. Long live Gonzalo!

GON.   And — do you mark me, sir?

ALON. Prithee, no more. Thou dost talk nothing to
me.   171

GON. I do well believe your Highness, and did it
to minister occasion° to these gentlemen, who are of
such sensible° and nimble lungs that they always use
to laugh at nothing.   175

ANT. 'Twas you we laughed at.

GON. Who in this kind of merry fooling am nothing to you. So you may continue and laugh at nothing still.

ANT. What a blow was there given!   180

SEB. An° it had not fallen flat-long.°

GON. You are gentlemen of brave mettle,° you
would lift the moon out of her sphere° if she would
continue in it five weeks without changing.

147. I' . . . commonwealth: This passage was taken from one of
Montaigne's *Essays*. by contraries: contrary to the usual plan.
148. traffic: trade.   150. Letters: learning.   151. use of service:
no one should have servants. contract: legal agreements. succession: right of inheritance.   152. Bourn: boundary. bound:
limit; i.e., private property rights. tilth: tillage.   153. use of
metal: i.e., exchange of money.   154. occupation: manual labor.
161. engine: instrument of warfare.   163. it: its. foison: plenty.
168. Golden Age: the days of perfect innocence at the beginning
of the world. 'Save: God save.   173. minister occasion: provide
opportunity.   174. sensible: sensitive.   181. An: if. flat-long:
on the flat side of the sword.   182. mettle: material, stuff.
183. sphere: course.

109. rate: estimation.   114. surges: waves.   117. swoln: swollen.   120. his . . . bowed: hung over its base, which had been
worn away by the sea.   127. wet: weep for.   130. Weighed:
balanced. loathness: reluctance.   131. end . . . beam: which
scale should sink.   133. Mo: more.   135. dear'st: most grievous.   140. chirurgeonly: like a good surgeon.   143. plantation:
colonization, but Antonio pretends to take it literally as "planting."   144. docks or mallows: common English weeds.

[Enter ARIEL *(invisible) playing solemn music.]*

SEB. We would so, and then go a-batfowling.°

ANT. Nay, good my lord, be not angry.   186

GON. No, I warrant you, I will not adventure my
discretion so weakly.° Will you laugh me asleep,
for I am very heavy?

ANT. Go sleep, and hear us.   190

[All sleep except ALONSO, SEBASTIAN, *and* ANTONIO.]

ALON. What, all so soon asleep! I wish mine eyes
Would, with themselves, shut up my thoughts. I find
They are inclined to do so.

SEB.   Please you, sir,
Do not omit the heavy offer° of it.
It seldom visits sorrow. When it doth,   195
It is a comforter.

ANT.   We two, my lord,
Will guard your person while you take your rest,
And watch your safety.

ALON.   Thank you. — Wondrous heavy.

*[*ALONSO *sleeps. Exit* ARIEL.]

SEB. What a strange drowsiness possesses them!

ANT. It is the quality° o' the climate.

SEB.   Why   200
Doth it not then our eyelids sink? I find not
Myself disposed to sleep.

ANT.   Nor I. My spirits are nimble.
They fell together all, as by consent,
They dropped as by a thunderstroke. What might,
Worthy Sebastian? — Oh, what might? — No
     more. —   205
And yet methinks I see it in thy face,
What thou shouldst be. The occasion speaks thee,°
     and
My strong imagination sees a crown
Dropping upon thy head.

SEB.   What, art thou waking?°

ANT. Do you not hear me speak?

SEB.   I do, and surely   210
It is a sleepy language, and thou speak'st
Out of thy sleep. What is it thou didst say?
This is a strange repose, to be asleep
With eyes wide-open — standing, speaking, moving,
And yet so fast asleep.

ANT.   Noble Sebastian,   215
Thou let'st thy fortune sleep — die, rather —
     wink'st
Whiles thou art waking.

SEB.   Thou dost snore distinctly.
There's meaning in thy snores.

ANT. I am more serious than my custom. You
Must be so too, if heed me,° which to do   220

Trebles thee o'er.°

SEB.   Well, I am standing water.°

ANT. I'll teach you how to flow.°

SEB.   Do so. To ebb
Hereditary sloth instructs me.

ANT.   Oh,
If you but knew how you the purpose cherish
Whiles thus you mock it! How, in stripping it,   225
You more invest it! Ebbing men, indeed,
Most often do so near the bottom run
By their own fear or sloth.°

SEB.   Prithee, say on.
The setting° of thine eye and cheek proclaim
A matter° from thee, and a birth, indeed,   230
Which throes thee much to yield.°

ANT.   Thus, sir.
Although this lord of weak remembrance, this,°
Who shall be of as little memory
When he is earthed, hath here almost persuaded —
For he's a spirit of persuasion, only   235
Professes to persuade — the King his son's alive,
'Tis as impossible that he's undrowned
As he that sleeps here swims.

SEB.   I have no hope
That he's undrowned.

ANT.   Oh, out of that " no hope "
What great hope have you! No hope that way is
Another way so high a hope that even   241
Ambition cannot pierce a wink beyond,
But doubt discovery there.° Will you grant with me
That Ferdinand is drowned?

SEB.   He's gone.

ANT.   Then tell me,
Who's the next heir of Naples?

SEB.   Claribel.   245

ANT. She that is Queen of Tunis, she that dwells
Ten leagues beyond man's life,° she that from
     Naples
Can have no note, unless the sun were post° —
The man i' the moon's too slow — till newborn
     chins
Be rough and razorable.° She that from whom   250
We all were sea-swallowed, though some cast° again,

---

185. **batfowling:** hunting for birds at night with the aid of torches
and sticks or bats. 187–88. **adventure . . . weakly:** risk my reputation as a discreet man so easily, by showing anger at such as
you. 194. **omit . . . offer:** do not lose this chance of sleeping.
200. **quality:** nature. 207. **occasion . . . thee:** opportunity calls
you. 209. **waking:** awake. 220. **if . . . me:** if you will listen
to me.

221. **Trebles . . . o'er:** makes you three times the man you are.
standing water: i.e., at the turning of the tide, which for a while
neither ebbs nor flows. 222. **flow:** advance (like the rising tide).
224–28. **If . . . sloth:** if you would only realize how much you are
moved by the prospect of becoming King, even while you mock it;
how in stripping it of its glamour you make it more attractive.
Ebbing men (i.e., the lazy and unambitious) often run aground
through fear or sloth. 229. **setting:** expression. 230. **matter:**
something serious. 231. **throes . . . yield:** is very painful to bring
forth. 232. **this . . . this:** i.e., Francisco. See ll. 113–22.
240–43. **No . . . there:** i.e., your certainty that the true heir is
drowned gives you a greater hope in another direction (i.e., of
being King yourself), where even your ambition cannot look
higher. 247. **Ten . . . life:** ten leagues farther than a man could
travel in his lifetime. 248. **post:** messenger. 249–50. **newborn
. . . razorable:** i.e., newborn children are grown men. 251. **cast:**
vomited up.

And by that destiny, to perform an act
Whereof what's past is prologue, what to come,
In yours and my discharge.°

   SEB.   What stuff is this! How say you?
'Tis true, my brother's daughter's Queen of Tunis,
So is she heir of Naples, 'twixt which regions 256
There is some space.

   ANT.   A space whose every cubit
Seems to cry out, "How shall that Claribel
Measure us° back to Naples? Keep° in Tunis,
And let Sebastian wake." Say this were death 260
That now hath seized them — why, they were no
    worse
Than now they are. There be that can rule Naples
As well as he that sleeps, lords that can prate
As amply and unnecessarily
As this Gonzalo. I myself could make   265
A chough of as deep chat.° Oh, that you bore
The mind that I do! What a sleep were this
For your advancement! Do you understand me?

   SEB. Methinks I do.

   ANT.   And how does your content
Tender your own good fortune?

   SEB.   I remember 270
You did supplant your brother Prospero.

   ANT.   True.
And look how well my garments sit upon me,
Much feater° than before. My brother's servants
Were then my fellows,° now they are my men.°

   SEB. But — for your conscience.   275

   ANT. Aye, sir, where lies that? If 'twere a kibe,
'Twould put me to my slipper.° But I feel not
This deity in my bosom. Twenty consciences,
That stand 'twixt me and Milan, candied be they,
And melt ere they molest!° Here lies your brother,
No better than the earth he lies upon   281
If he were that which now he's like, that's dead.
Whom I, with this obedient steel, three inches of it,
Can lay to bed forever whiles you, doing thus,
To the perpetual wink° for aye might put 285
This ancient morsel, this Sir Prudence who
Should not upbraid our course. For all the rest,
They'll take suggestion as a cat laps milk,
They'll tell the clock to° any business that
We say befits the hour.

   SEB.   Thy case, dear friend, 290
Shall be my precedent. As thou got'st Milan,
I'll come by Naples. Draw thy sword. One stroke

Shall free thee from the tribute which thou payest,
And I the King shall love thee.

   ANT.   Draw together,
And when I rear my hand, do you the like, 295
To fall° it on Gonzalo.

   SEB.   Oh, but one word. [*They talk apart.*]
                [*Re-enter* ARIEL, *invisible.*]

   ARI. My master through his art foresees the danger
That you, his friend, are in, and sends me forth —
For else his project dies — to keep them living.
              [*Sings in* GONZALO's *ear.*]
     " While you here do snoring lie,   300
       Open-eyed conspiracy
         His time° doth take.
      If of life you keep a care,
      Shake off slumber, and beware.
        Awake, awake! "   305

   ANT. Then let us both be sudden.

   GON.   Now, good angels
Preserve the King!   [*They wake.*]

   ALON. Why, how now? Ho, awake! — Why are
    you drawn?
Wherefore this ghastly looking?

   GON.   What's the matter?

   SEB. Whiles we stood here securing° your repose,
Even now, we heard a hollow burst of bellowing
Like bulls, or rather lions. Did 't not wake you? 312
It struck mine ear most terribly.

   ALON.   I heard nothing.

   ANT. Oh, 'twas a din to fright a monster's ear,
To make an earthquake! Sure, it was the roar 315
Of a whole herd of lions.

   ALON.   Heard you this, Gonzalo?

   GON. Upon mine honor, sir, I heard a humming,
And that a strange one too, which did awake me.
I shaked you, sir, and cried. As mine eyes opened
I saw their weapons drawn. — There was a noise,
That's verily.° 'Tis best we stand upon our guard,
Or that we quit this place. Let's draw our weapons.

   ALON. Lead off this ground, and let's make further
    search   32
For my poor son.

   GON.   Heavens keep him from these beasts!
For he is sure i' th' island.

   ALON.   Lead away.

   ARI. Prospero my lord shall know what I have
    done.
So, King, go safely on to seek thy son.   [*Exeunt.*]

SCENE II. *Another part of the island.*

[*Enter* CALIBAN *with a burden of wood. A noise of
thunder heard.*]

   CAL. All the infections that the sun sucks up
From bogs, fens, flats, on Prosper fall, and make him

---

254. discharge: task to be performed.   259. Measure us: retrace
her journey after us. Keep: let her remain.   266. chough . . .
chat: I could make a jackdaw (*chough*, rhyming with rough) talk
as profoundly as he does. 273. feater: more trimly. 274. fellows:
equals. men: servants. 276–77. kibe . . . slipper: a chilblain which
would make me wear a slipper. 278–80. Twenty . . . molest:
i.e., if twenty consciences had stood between me and the dukedom of Milan, I should have let them melt like candy before
they would have disturbed me. Other editors take "candied" to
mean "frozen." 285. perpetual wink: everlasting sleep. 289. tell
. . . to: say it is time for.

296. fall: let fall.   302. time: opportunity.   310. securing:
keeping safe.   321. verily: truth.

By inchmeal° a disease! His spirits hear me,
And yet I needs must curse. But they'll nor pinch,
Fright me with urchin shows,° pitch me i' the mire,
Nor lead me, like a firebrand,° in the dark   6
Out of my way, unless he bid 'em. But
For every trifle are they set upon me —
Sometime like apes, that mow° and chatter at me,
And after bite me; then like hedgehogs, which   10
Lie tumbling in my barefoot way and mount°
Their pricks at my footfall. Sometime am I
All wound with adders, who with cloven tongues
Do hiss me into madness.
    [*Enter* TRINCULO.] Lo, now, lo!
Here comes a spirit of his, and to torment me   15
For bringing wood in slowly. I'll fall flat.
Perchance he will not mind me.
    TRIN. Here's neither bush nor shrub to bear off
any weather at all, and another storm brewing, I
hear it sing i' the wind. Yond same black cloud,   20
yond huge one, looks like a foul bombard° that
would shed his liquor. If it should thunder as it did
before, I know not where to hide my head. Yond
same cloud cannot choose but fall by pailfuls. What
have we here? A man or a fish? Dead or alive?   25
A fish — he smells like a fish, a very ancient and fish-
like smell, a kind of not of the newest Poor John.° A
strange fish! Were I in England now, as once I was,
and had but this fish painted,° not a holiday fool
there but would give a piece of silver. There would
this monster make a man° — any strange beast   31
there makes a man. When they will not give a doit°
to relieve a lame beggar, they will lay out ten to see
a dead Indian. Legged like a man! And his fins like
arms! Warm, o' my troth! I do now let loose   35
my opinion, hold it no longer — this is no fish, but
an islander that hath lately suffered by a thunderbolt.
[*Thunder.*] Alas, the storm is come again! Best
way is to creep under his gaberdine,° there is no
other shelter hereabout. Misery acquaints a man   40
with strange bedfellows. I will here shroud° till the
dregs of the storm be past.
    [*Enter* STEPHANO, *singing, a bottle in his hand.*]
    STE.   " I shall no more to sea, to sea,
        Here shall I die ashore——"   45
This is a very scurvy° tune to sing at a man's funeral.
Well, here's my comfort.   [*Drinks. Sings.*]
" The master, the swabber, the boatswain, and I,
    The gunner, and his mate,
Loved Mall, Meg, and Marian, and Margery,   50
    But none of us cared for Kate.

For she had a tongue with a tang,°
    Would cry to a sailor, Go hang!
She loved not the savor° of tar nor of pitch,   54
Yet a tailor might scratch her where'er she did itch.
    Then, to sea, boys, and let her go hang! "
This is a scurvy tune too, but here's my comfort.
                         [*Drinks.*]
    CAL. Do not torment me. — Oh!   58
    STE. What's the matter? Have we devils here? Do
you put tricks upon 's with salvages° and men of
Ind,° ha? I have not 'scaped drowning to be afeard
now of your four legs, for it hath been said,   62
As proper° a man as ever went on four legs cannot
make him give ground. And it shall be said so again
while Stephano breathes at nostrils.
    CAL. The spirit torments me. — Oh!   66
    STE. This is some monster of the isle with four
legs, who hath got, as I take it, an ague.° Where the
devil should he learn our language? I will give him
some relief, if it be but for that. If I can recover°
him, and keep him tame, and get to Naples with
him, he's a present for any emperor that ever trod on
neat's leather.°   73
    CAL. Do not torment me, prithee, I'll bring my
wood home faster.
    STE. He's in his fit now, and does not talk after
the wisest. He shall taste of my bottle. If he have
never drunk wine afore, it will go near to remove his
fit. If I can recover him, and keep him tame, I will
not take too much for him.° He shall pay for him
that hath him, and that soundly.   81
    CAL. Thou dost me yet but little hurt, thou wilt
anon, I know it by thy trembling.° Now Prosper
works upon thee.   84
    STE. Come on your ways. Open your mouth, here
is that which will give language to you, cat. Open
your mouth, this will shake your shaking, I can tell
you, and that soundly. You cannot tell who's your
friend. Open your chaps° again.   89
    TRIN. I should know that voice. It should be —
but he is drowned, and these are devils. — Oh, defend me!   92
    STE. Four legs and two voices — a most delicate
monster! His forward voice, now, is to speak well of
his friend, his backward voice is to utter foul
speeches and to detract. If all the wine in my bottle
will recover him, I will help his ague. Come. —
Amen! I will pour some in thy other mouth.   99
    TRIN. Stephano!
    STE. Doth thy other mouth call me? Mercy, mercy!

Sc. ii: **3. inchmeal**: by inches.   **5. urchin shows**: the appearance of goblins. See I.ii.326.   **6. firebrand**: will-o'-the-wisp.
9. mow: make faces.   **11. mount**: raise.   **21. bombard**: large
black leathern jug for carrying liquor.   **27. Poor John**: dried salt
hake.   **29. had . . . painted**: had a poster of this fish painted.
31. make a man: i.e., his fortune.   **32. doit**: a small Dutch coin,
a cent.   **39. gaberdine**: cloak.   **41. shroud**: cover myself.
46. scurvy: "lousy."

52. tang: a sharp sound.   **54. savor**: taste.   **60. salvages**: savages.   **60–61. men of Ind**: natives of India.   **63. proper**: fine.
68. ague: fever, which makes him shiver.   **71. recover**: cure.
73. neat's leather: i.e., shoes.   **79–80. I . . . him**: I'll not take
even an excessive price.   **83. trembling**: Trinculo is the trembler,
for he believes that the voice of Stephano comes from a ghost.
Trinculo is a natural coward.   **89. chaps**: chops, jaws.

This is a devil and no monster. I will leave him, I
have no long spoon.°   103

TRIN. Stephano! If thou beest Stephano, touch me,
and speak to me, for I am Trinculo — be not afeard
— thy good friend Trinculo.

STE. If thou beest Trinculo, come forth. I'll pull
thee by the lesser legs. If any be Trinculo's legs, these
are they. Thou art very Trinculo indeed! How
camest thou to be the siege° of this mooncalf?° Can
he vent Trinculos?   111

TRIN. I look him to be killed with a thunderstroke. But art thou not drowned, Stephano? I hope,
now, thou art not drowned. Is the storm overblown?
I hid me under the dead mooncalf's gaberdine for
fear of the storm. And art thou living, Stephano? O
Stephano, two Neapolitans 'scaped!   117

STE. Prithee do not turn me about, my stomach is
not constant.°

CAL. [Aside] These be fine things, an if they be
not sprites.
That's a brave god, and bears celestial liquor.
I will kneel to him.   122

STE. How didst thou 'scape? How camest thou
hither? Swear, by this bottle, how thou camest
hither. I escaped upon a butt of sack,° which the
sailors heaved o'erboard, by this bottle, which I made
of the bark of a tree with mine own hands, since I
was cast ashore.   128

CAL. I'll swear upon that bottle to be thy true subject, for the liquor is not earthly.

STE. Here, swear, then, how thou escapedst.

TRIN. Swam ashore, man, like a duck. I can swim
like a duck, I'll be sworn.   133

STE. Here, kiss the book. Though thou canst swim
like a duck, thou art made like a goose.

TRIN. O Stephano, hast any more of this?

STE. The whole butt, man. My cellar is in a rock
by the seaside, where my wine is hid. How now,
mooncalf! How does thine ague?   139

CAL. Hast thou not dropped from Heaven?

STE. Out o' the moon, I do assure thee. I was the
man 'i the moon when time was.°   142

CAL. I have seen thee in her, and I do adore thee.
My mistress showed me thee, and thy dog, and thy
bush.°

STE. Come, swear to that, kiss the book. I will furnish it anon with new contents. Swear.   147

103. I . . . spoon: "He that sups with the Devil needs a long
spoon" — a proverb from the time when men dipped into a common dish. A long spoon was needed, as the Devil's claws were long
and sharp, and his table manners nasty.   110. siege: excrement.
mooncalf: misshapen monster, freak.   119. constant: steady.
Trinculo is pawing him all over, and turning him round in his
excitement.   125. sack: a dry wine from Spain. For Falstaff on
the merits of sack, see II Hen IV, IV.iii.102-35.   142. when
. . . was: once upon a time.   144-45. thee . . . bush: the man
in the moon had his dog and bush of thorns, as Quince knew.
See MND, III.i.60.

TRIN. By this good light, this is a very shallow
monster! I afeard of him! A very weak monster!
The man i' the moon! A most poor credulous monster! Well drawn,° monster, in good sooth!°   151

CAL. I'll show thee every fertile inch o' th' island,
And I will kiss thy foot. I prithee be my god.

TRIN. By this light, a most perfidious and drunken
monster! When's god's asleep, he'll rob his bottle.

CAL. I'll kiss thy foot, I'll swear myself thy subject.

STE. Come on, then, down, and swear.

TRIN. I shall laugh myself to death at this puppy-
headed monster. A most scurvy monster! I could find
in my heart to beat him ——   160

STE. Come, kiss.

TRIN. But that the poor monster's in drink. An
abominable monster!

CAL. I'll show thee the best springs, I'll pluck thee
     berries,
I'll fish for thee, and get thee wood enough.
A plague upon the tyrant that I serve!
I'll bear him no more sticks, but follow thee,
Thou wondrous man.   168

TRIN. A most ridiculous monster, to make a wonder of a poor drunkard!

CAL. I prithee let me bring thee where crabs°
     grow.   171
And I with my long nails will dig thee pignuts,°
Show thee a jay's nest, and instruct thee how
To snare the nimble marmoset.° I'll bring thee
To clustering filberts, and sometimes I'll get thee
Young scamels° from the rock. Wilt thou go with
     me?   176

STE. I prithee now, lead the way, without any
more talking. Trinculo, the King and all our company else being drowned, we will inherit here. Here,
bear my bottle, fellow Trinculo, we'll fill him by and
by again.   181

CAL. [Sings drunkenly.]
    " Farewell, master, farewell, farewell! "

TRIN. A howling monster, a drunken monster!

CAL. " No more dams I'll make for fish.
        Nor fetch in firing   185
        At requiring,
        Nor scrape trencher,° nor wash dish.
        'Ban, 'Ban, Cacaliban
        Has a new master. — Get a new man."
Freedom, heyday! Heyday, freedom! Freedom, heyday, freedom!   191

STE. O brave monster! Lead the way. [Exeunt.]

151. drawn: sucked. sooth: truth.   171. crabs: crab apples.
172. pignut: called also earthnut, a plant producing edible tubers.
174. marmoset: kind of small monkey.   176. scamels: a much-
discussed word which does not occur elsewhere and so has been
variously interpreted or emended, the likeliest guess being
seamel: sea gull.   187. trencher: wooden plate.

Act III

SCENE I. *Before* PROSPERO's *cell.*

[*Enter* FERDINAND, *bearing a log.*]
FER. There be some sports are painful, and their labor
Delight in them sets off.° Some kinds of baseness
Are nobly undergone, and most poor matters
Point° to rich ends. This my mean task
Would be as heavy to me as odious, but   5
The mistress which I serve quickens° what's dead
And makes my labors pleasures. Oh, she is
Ten times more gentle than her father's crabbèd,
And he's composed of harshness. I must remove
Some thousands of these logs, and pile them up,   10
Upon a sore injunction.° My sweet mistress
Weeps when she sees me work, and says such baseness
Had never like executor.° I forget.
But these sweet thoughts do even refresh my labors,
Most busy lest when I do it.°
[*Enter* MIRANDA, *and* PROSPERO *at a distance,*°
unseen.]
MIRA.   Alas, now, pray you   15
Work not so hard. I would the lightning had
Burned up those logs that you are enjoined to pile!
Pray set it down and rest you. When this burns,
'Twill weep° for having wearied you. My father
Is hard at study, pray now, rest yourself.   20
He's safe for these three hours.
FER.   O most dear mistress,
The sun will set before I shall discharge
What I must strive to do.
MIRA.   If you'll sit down,
I'll bear your logs the while. Pray give me that,
I'll carry it to the pile.
FER.   No, precious creature,   25
I had rather crack my sinews, break my back,
Than you should such dishonor undergo
While I sit lazy by.
MIRA.   It would become me
As well as it does you. And I should do it
With much more ease, for my goodwill is to it,   30
And yours it is against.
PRO.   Poor worm, thou art infected!

Act III, Sc. i: 1–2. their . . . off: the delight which they bring outweighs the fatigue.   4. Point: lead.   6. quickens: brings to life.   11. injunction: a command enforced with penalties against disobedience.   13. executor: performer.   15. Most . . . it: This line has been much discussed and may be corrupt. It means apparently "I am most busy when I am idle, for then I think so many sweet thoughts." lest: least. s.d., and . . . distance: F1 simply reads "Enter Miranda and Prospero." They obviously do not enter together, and on the Elizabethan stage probably Prospero entered on the balcony above, as later (III.iii.19). The balcony was a most convenient place for eavesdroppers.   19. weep: i.e., drip with sap when burning.

This visitation° shows it.
MIRA.   You look wearily.
FER. No, noble mistress, 'tis fresh morning with me
When you are by at night. I do beseech you —
Chiefly that I might set it in my prayers —   35
What is your name?
MIRA.   Miranda. — O my father,
I have broke your hest° to say so!
FER.   Admired Miranda!°
Indeed the top° of admiration! Worth
What's dearest to the world! Full many a lady
I have eyed with best regard, and many a time   40
The harmony of their tongues hath into bondage
Brought my too diligent ear. For several° virtues
Have I liked several women, never any
With so full soul but some defect in her
Did quarrel with the noblest grace she owed,   45
And put it to the foil.° But you, oh, you,
So perfect and so peerless, are created
Of every creature's best!
MIRA.   I do not know
One of my sex, no woman's face remember
Save, from my glass, mine own. Nor have I seen   50
More that I may call men than you, good friend,
And my dear father. How features are abroad,
I am skill-less of.° But, by my modesty,
The jewel in my dower, I would not wish
Any companion in the world but you,   55
Nor can imagination form a shape
Besides yourself to like of. But I prattle
Something too wildly, and my father's precepts
I therein do forget.
FER.   I am, in my condition,
A prince, Miranda, I do think, a king —   60
I would not so! — and would no more endure
This wooden slavery° than to suffer
The flesh fly blow° my mouth. Hear my soul speak.
The very instant that I saw you did
My heart fly to your service, there resides,   65
To make me slave to it, and for your sake
Am I this patient logman.
MIRA.   Do you love me?
FER. O Heaven, O earth, bear witness to this sound,
And crown what I profess with kind event°
If I speak true! If hollowly, invert   70
What best is boded° me to mischief! I,
Beyond all limit of what else i' the world,

---

32. visitation: visit.   37. hest: command. Admired Miranda: a play on her name, for *miranda* in Latin means "she who ought to be wondered at." "Admired" at this time had a stronger meaning than today.   38. top: summit.   42. several: separate, individual.   46. put . . . foil: bring it to disgrace.   52–53. features . . . of: I have no experience of how people look elsewhere.   62. wooden slavery: i.e., task of having to carry wood.   63. blow: lay its eggs on, foul.   69. event: result.   71. What . . . boded: the best fate that is prophesied.

Do love, prize, honor you.
    MIRA.   I am a fool
To weep at what I am glad of.
    PRO.   Fair encounter
Of two most rare affections! Heavens rain grace 75
On that which breeds between 'em!
    FER.   Wherefore weep you?
    MIRA. At mine unworthiness, that dare not offer
What I desire to give, and much less take
What I shall die to want.° But this is trifling,
And all the more it seeks to hide itself,   80
The bigger bulk it shows. Hence, bashful cunning!
And prompt me, plain and holy innocence!
I am your wife, if you will marry me.
If not, I'll die your maid. To be your fellow°
You may deny me, but I'll be your servant,   85
Whether you will or no.
    FER.   My mistress, dearest,
And I thus humble ever.
    MIRA.   My husband, then?
    FER. Aye, with a heart as willing°
As bondage e'er of freedom. Here's my hand.
    MIRA. And mine, with my heart in 't. And now
        farewell
Till half an hour hence.   90
    FER.   A thousand thousand!°
    [*Exeunt* FERDINAND *and* MIRANDA *severally.*°]
    PRO. So glad of this as they I cannot be,
Who° are surprised withal,° but my rejoicing
At nothing can be more. I'll to my book,
For yet ere suppertime must I perform   95
Much business appertaining.   [*Exit.*]

SCENE II. *Another part of the island.*

    [*Enter* CALIBAN, STEPHANO, *and* TRINCULO.]
    STE. Tell not me. — When the butt is out, we will
drink water, not a drop before. Therefore bear up,°
and board 'em. Servant-monster, drink to me.   4
    TRIN. Servant-monster! The folly of this island!°
They say there's but five upon this isle. We are three
of them. If th' other two be brained like us, the state
totters.
    STE. Drink, servant-monster, when I bid thee. Thy
eyes are almost set° in thy head.   10
    TRIN. Where should they be set else? He were a
brave monster indeed if they were set in his tail.
    STE. My man-monster hath drowned his tongue in
sack. For my part, the sea cannot drown me. I swam,

ere I could recover the shore, five-and-thirty leagues
off and on. By this light, thou shalt be my lieutenant,
monster, or my standard.°   17
    TRIN. Your lieutenant, if you list. He's no stand-
ard.
    STE. We'll not run, Monsieur Monster.
    TRIN. Nor go neither, but you'll lie, like dogs, and
yet say nothing neither.
    STE. Mooncalf, speak once in thy life, if thou beest
a good mooncalf.   25
    CAL. How does thy Honor? Let me lick thy shoe.
I'll not serve him, he is not valiant.
    TRIN. Thou liest, most ignorant monster. I am in
case° to jostle a constable. Why, thou deboshed° fish
thou, was there ever man a coward that hath drunk
so much sack as I today? Wilt thou tell a monstrous
lie, being but half a fish and half a monster?   33
    CAL. Lo, how he mocks me! Wilt thou let him,
my lord?
    TRIN. "Lord," quoth he! That a monster should
be such a natural!°
    CAL. Lo, lo, again! Bite him to death, I prithee.
    STE. Trinculo, keep a good tongue in your 40
head. If you prove a mutineer — the next tree! The
poor monster's my subject, and he shall not suffer
indignity.
    CAL. I thank my noble lord. Wilt thou be pleased
to hearken once again to the suit I made to thee? 45
    STE. Marry,° will I. Kneel and repeat it. I will
stand, and so shall Trinculo.
    [*Enter* ARIEL, *invisible.*]
    CAL. As I told thee before, I am subject to a tyrant,
a sorcerer, that by his cunning hath cheated me of
the island.   50
    ARI. Thou liest.
    CAL. Thou liest,° thou jesting monkey thou.
I would my valiant master would destroy thee!
I do not lie.
    STE. Trinculo, if you trouble him any more in 's
tale, by this hand, I will supplant° some of your
teeth.   57
    TRIN. Why, I said nothing.
    STE. Mum, then, and no more. Proceed.
    CAL. I say, by sorcery he got this isle.   60
From me he got it. If thy greatness will
Revenge it on him — for I know thou darest,
But this thing dare not——
    STE. That's most certain.
    CAL. Thou shalt be lord of it, and I'll serve thee.
    STE. How now shall this be compassed?° 66
Canst thou bring me to the party?

---

79. want: be without.   84. fellow: equal. See II.i.274.   88. willing: eager.   91. thousand thousand: i.e., farewells. s.d., severally: by different exits.   93. Who: i.e., Ferdinand and Miranda.
withal: therewith.

Sc. ii: 2. bear up: crowd on more sail.   5. The . . . island:
what a silly place this island is.   10. set: closed, dazed with
drink.

15. league: three miles.   17. standard: standard-bearer (or ensign), the junior officer in the company, the others being the
captain and the lieutenant. Caliban is now too unsteady to be a
satisfactory *standard.*   29. in case: in a condition. deboshed:
debauched.   38. natural: born fool.   46. Marry: Mary, by the
Virgin.   52. Thou liest: Caliban supposes the voice to be Trinculo's.   56. supplant: displace.   66. compassed: brought about.

CAL. Yea, yea, my lord. I'll yield him thee asleep,
Where thou mayst knock a nail into his head.

ARI. Thou liest, thou canst not.   70

CAL. What a pied ninny's° this! Thou scurvy
    patch!°
I do beseech thy greatness, give him blows,
And take his bottle from him. When that's gone,
He shall drink naught but brine, for I'll not show
    him
Where the quick freshes° are.   75

STE. Trinculo, run into no further danger. Interrupt the monster one word further and, by this
hand, I'll turn my mercy out o' doors and make a
stockfish° of thee.

TRIN. Why, what did I? I did nothing. I'll go
farther off.   81

STE. Didst thou not say he lied?

ARI. Thou liest.

STE. Do I so? Take thou that. [Beats him.] As
you like this, give me the lie° another time.   85

TRIN. I did not give the lie. Out o' your wits, and
hearing too? A pox o' your bottle! This can sack
and drinking do. A murrain° on your monster, and
the devil take your fingers!

CAL. Ha, ha, ha!   90

STE. Now, forward with your tale. — Prithee,
stand farther off.

CAL. Beat him enough. After a little time
I'll beat him too.

STE.   Stand farther. — Come, proceed.

CAL. Why, as I told thee, 'tis a custom with him
I' th' afternoon to sleep. There thou mayst brain
    him,   96
Having first seized his books, or with a log
Batter his skull, or paunch° him with a stake,
Or cut his weasand° with thy knife. Remember
First to possess his books, for without them   100
He's but a sot, as I am, nor hath not
One spirit to command. They all do hate him
As rootedly° as I. Burn but his books.
He has brave utensils° — for so he calls them —
Which, when he has a house, he'll deck withal.   105
And that most deeply to consider is
The beauty of his daughter. He himself
Calls her a nonpareil.° I never saw a woman
But only Sycorax my dam and she,
But she as far surpasseth Sycorax   110
As great'st does least.

STE.   Is it so brave a lass?

CAL. Aye, lord, she will become thy bed, I warrant,

And bring thee forth brave brood.

STE. Monster, I will kill this man. His daughter
and I will be King and Queen — save our Graces! —
and Trinculo and thyself shall be Viceroys. Dost
thou like the plot, Trinculo?   117

TRIN. Excellent.

STE. Give me thy hand. I am sorry I beat thee, but
while thou livest keep a good tongue in thy head.

CAL. Within this half-hour will he be asleep.
Wilt thou destroy him then?

STE.   Aye, on mine honor.

ARI. This will I tell my master.

CAL. Thou makest me merry, I am full of pleasure.
Let us be jocund. Will you troll° the catch°   126
You taught me but whilere?°

STE. At thy request, monster, I will do reason,°
any reason. — Come on, Trinculo, let us sing.
[Sings.]   "Flout° 'em and scout° 'em,
              And scout 'em and flout 'em.   131
              Thought is free."

CAL. That's not the tune.
    [ARIEL plays the tune on a tabor° and pipe.]

STE. What is this same?

TRIN. This is the tune of our catch, played by the
picture of Nobody.°   136

STE. If thou beest a man, show thyself in thy likeness. If thou beest a devil, take 't as thou list.

TRIN. Oh, forgive me my sins!

STE. He that dies pays all debts. I defy thee. Mercy
upon us!   141

CAL. Art thou afeard?

STE. No, monster, not I.

CAL. Be not afeard. The isle is full of noises,°
Sounds and sweet airs that give delight and hurt not.
Sometimes a thousand twangling instruments   146
Will hum about mine ears, and sometime voices
That, if I then had waked after long sleep,
Will make me sleep again. And then, in dreaming,
The clouds methought would open and show riches
Ready to drop upon me, that when I waked,   151
I cried to dream again.

STE. This will prove a brave kingdom to me,
where I shall have my music for nothing.

CAL. When Prospero is destroyed.   155

STE. That shall be by and by.° I remember the
story.

TRIN. The sound is going away. Let's follow it,
and after do our work.

STE. Lead, monster, we'll follow. I would I could
see this taborer, he lays it on.   161

TRIN. Wilt come? I'll follow, Stephano. [Exeunt.]

71. pied ninny: patched fool, because Trinculo as a jester wears
motley, the "patched" or particolored dress of his profession.
patch: fool.   75. quick freshes: running springs of fresh water.
79. stockfish: dried, salted cod, beaten to make it tender.
85. give . . . lie: call me a liar.   88. murrain: plague.   98. paunch:
stab him in the belly.   99. weasand: windpipe.   103. rootedly:
fixedly.   104. utensils: furnishings.   108. nonpareil: without
an equal.

126. troll: sing. catch: a noisy, rowdy part song.   127. whilere:
just now.   128. reason: anything within reason.   130. Flout:
mock. scout: deride.   133. s.d., tabor: small drum.   136. picture of Nobody: i.e., by an invisible player. There is a picture
of Nobody in a play called Nobody and Some-body, printed 1606.
It is all head and no body, like Humpty Dumpty.   144. noises:
music.   156. by . . . by: in the near future.

SCENE III. *Another part of the island.*

[*Enter* ALONSO, SEBASTIAN, ANTONIO, GONZALO,
ADRIAN, FRANCISCO, *and others.*]

GON. By'r Lakin,° I can go no further, sir,
My old bones ache. Here's a maze trod, indeed,
Through forthrights and meanders!° By your pa-
    tience,
I needs must rest me.

ALON.   Old lord, I cannot blame thee,
Who am myself attached with° weariness,   5
To the dulling of my spirits. Sit down and rest.
Even here I will put off my hope, and keep it
No longer for my flatterer. He is drowned
Whom thus we stray to find, and the sea mocks
Our frustrate° search on land. Well, let him go. 10

ANT. [*Aside to* SEBASTIAN] I am right glad that
he's so out of hope.
Do not, for one repulse, forgo the purpose
That you resolved to effect.

SEB. [*Aside to* ANTONIO] The next advantage
Will we take throughly.°

ANT. [*Aside to* SEBASTIAN] Let it be tonight,
For now they are oppressed with travel, they   15
Will not, nor cannot, use such vigilance
As when they are fresh.

SEB. [*Aside to* ANTONIO] I say tonight. No more.
                   [*Solemn and strange music.*]

ALON. What harmony is this? — My good friends,
hark!

GON. Marvelous sweet music!

[*Enter* PROSPERO *above, invisible. Enter several
strange Shapes, bringing in a banquet.° They dance
about it with gentle actions of salutation, and, inviting the King, etc., to eat, they depart.*]

ALON. Give us kind keepers, Heavens! — What
were these?   20

SEB. A living drollery.° Now° I will believe
That there are unicorns, that in Arabia
There is one tree, the phoenix'° throne, one phoenix
At this hour reigning there.

ANT.   I'll believe both,
And what does else want credit,° come to me   25
And I'll be sworn 'tis true. Travelers ne'er did lie,
Though fools at home condemn 'em.

GON.   If in Naples
I should report this now, would they believe me?

If I should say I saw such islanders —
For, certes,° these are people of the island —   30
Who, though they are of monstrous shape, yet note,
Their manners are more gentle-kind than of
Our human generation° you shall find
Many — nay, almost any.

PRO.   [*Aside*] Honest lord,   34
Thou hast said well, for some of you there present
Are worse than devils.

ALON.   I cannot too much muse°
Such shapes, such gesture, and such sound, express-
    ing —
Although they want the use of tongue — a kind
Of excellent dumb discourse.

PRO.   [*Aside*] Praise in departing.°

FRAN. They vanished strangely.

SEB.   No matter, since   40
They have left their viands behind, for we have
    stomachs. —
Will 't please you taste of what is here?

ALON.   Not I.

GON. Faith, sir, you need not fear. When we were
boys,
Who would believe that there were mountaineers
Dewlapped° like bulls, whose throats had hanging
    at 'em   45
Wallets of flesh? Or that there were such men
Whose heads stood in their breasts?° Which now
    we find
Each putter-out of five for one° will bring us
Good warrant of.

ALON.   I will stand to and feed,
Although my last. No matter, since I feel   50
The best is past. Brother, my lord the Duke,
Stand to, and do as we.

[*Thunder and lightning. Enter* ARIEL, *like a harpy,°
claps his wings upon the table, and, with a quaint
device,° the banquet vanishes.*]

ARI. You are three men of sin, whom Destiny —·
That hath to instrument this lower world

---

30. certes: certainly.   **33. generation:** breed.   **36. muse:** wonder at.   **39. Praise in departing:** a proverb meaning "Don't give
thanks for your entertainment until you see how it will end."
45. Dewlapped: having folds of loose skin hanging from the
throat.   **46–47. men ... breasts:** Sir Walter Raleigh in his account of Guiana (1595) noted "a nation of people whose heads appear not above their shoulders; which though it may be thought a
mere fable, yet for mine own part I am resolved it is true, because
every child in the provinces of Arromaia and Canuri affirms the
same. They are called Ewaipanoma. They are reported to have
their eyes in their shoulders, and their mouths in the middle of
their breasts, and that a long train of hair groweth backward between their shoulders."   **48. putter-out ... one:** In Shakespeare's time voyages to distant and strange ports were so risky
that the traveler sometimes left a sum of money with a merchant
at home on condition that he should receive five times the amount
if he returned; if he did not, the premium was forfeited.   **52 s.d.,
harpy:** a foul creature, half bird of prey, half woman. This episode
was suggested by an event in Virgil's *Aeneid* when the harpies
seize and foul the food of Aeneas and his followers. **quaint device:**
piece of ingenious stage machinery.

Sc. iii: 1. By'r Lakin: by Our Lady.   **2–3. Here's ... meanders:** we have wandered as in a maze by straight paths (*forthrights*) and winding paths (*meanders*).   **5. attached with:** overcome by; lit., arrested.   **10. frustrate:** vain.   **14. throughly:**
thoroughly.   **19 s.d., banquet:** light refreshments, such as fruit
and jellies.   **21. drollery:** puppet show.   **21–27. Now ... 'em:**
i.e., after this we can believe any fantastic traveler's yarn.
23. phoenix: a mythical bird. According to the legend only one
phoenix was alive at a time. It lived for five hundred years. Then
it built itself a nest of spices, which were set alight by the rapid
beating of its wings. From the ashes a new phoenix was born.
25. want credit: is not believed.

And what is in 't° — the never-surfeited° sea   55
Hath caused to belch up you. And on this island,
Where man doth not inhabit — you 'mongst men
Being most unfit to live. I have made you mad,
And even with suchlike valor men hang and drown
Their proper° selves.

    [ALONZO, SEBASTIAN, etc., draw their swords.]
               You fools! I and my fellows   60
Are ministers of Fate. The elements
Of whom your swords are tempered may as well
Wound the loud winds, or with bemocked-at stabs
Kill the still-closing° waters, as diminish
One dowle° that's in my plume.° My fellow minis-
    ters   65
Are like invulnerable. If you could hurt,
Your swords are now too massy° for your strengths,
And will not be uplifted. But remember —
For that's my business to you — that you three
From Milan did supplant good Prospero,   70
Exposed unto the sea, which hath requit° it,
Him and his innocent child. For which foul deed
The powers, delaying not forgetting, have
Incensed the seas and shores — yea, all the crea-
    tures —
Against your peace. Thee of thy son, Alonso,   75
They have bereft, and do pronounce by me
Lingering perdition° — worse than any death
Can be at once — shall step by step attend
You and your ways. Whose wraths to guard you
    from —
Which here, in this most desolate isle, else falls   80
Upon your heads — is nothing but° heart sorrow
And a clear° life ensuing.

[He vanishes in thunder; then, to soft music, enter
the Shapes again, and dance, with mocks° and
mows,° and carrying out the table.]

    PRO. Bravely the figure of this harpy hast thou
Performed, my Ariel, a grace it had, devouring.°
Of my instruction hast thou nothing bated°   85
In what thou hadst to say. So, with good life°
And observation° strange,° my meaner ministers°
Their several kinds° have done. My high charms
    work,
And these mine enemies are all knit up°
In their distractions.° They now are in my power,

And in these fits I leave them while I visit   91
Young Ferdinand — whom they suppose is
    drowned —
And his and mine loved darling.   [Exit above.]
    GON. I' the name of something holy, sir, why stand
    you
In this strange stare?
    ALON.   Oh, it is monstrous, monstrous!   95
Methought the billows spoke, and told me of it,
The winds did sing it to me, and the thunder,
That deep and dreadful organ pipe, pronounced
The name of Prosper. It did bass my trespass.°
Therefore my son i' th' ooze is bedded, and   100
I'll seek him deeper than e'er plummet° sounded,
And with him there lie mudded.   [Exit.]
    SEB.   But one fiend at a time,
I'll fight their legions o'er.
    ANT.   I'll be thy second.
    [Exeunt SEBASTIAN and ANTONIO.]
    GON. All three of them are desperate. Their great
    guilt,
Like poison given to work a great time after,   105
Now 'gins to bite the spirits. I do beseech you
That are of suppler joints, follow them swiftly,
And hinder them from what this ecstasy°
May now provoke them to.
    ADR.   Follow, I pray you.   [Exeunt.]

Act IV

SCENE I. Before PROSPERO's cell.

[Enter PROSPERO, FERDINAND, and MIRANDA.]
    PRO. If I have too austerely punished you,
Your compensation makes amends. For I
Have given you here a third° of mine own life,
Or that for which I live, who once again
I tender° to thy hand. All thy vexations   5
Were but my trials of thy love, and thou
Hast strangely° stood the test. Here, afore Heaven,
I ratify this my rich gift. O Ferdinand,
Do not smile at me that I boast her off,°
For thou shalt find she will outstrip all praise   10
And make it halt° behind her.
    FER.   I do believe it
Against an oracle.°

53-55. Destiny . . . in 't: Destiny (Providence), which uses this world below and its powers as its instrument.   55. never-surfeited: never overfull. A surfeit is an excess of food. Even the sea, which can retain most things, cannot stomach Alonso and his fellow sinners.   60. proper: own.   64. still-closing: always closing up; i.e., which cannot be wounded.   65. dowle: downy feather. plume: wing.   67. massy: heavy.   71. requit: paid back.   77. perdition: destruction.   81. is . . . but: i.e., only repentance will guard you from destruction.   82. clear: innocent.   s.d., mocks: mocking gestures. mows: grimaces.   84. grace . . . devouring: the action of devouring was splendidly (bravely) performed.   85. bated: abated, left out.   86. with . . . life: realistically.   87. observation: obedience. strange: unusual. meaner ministers: lesser servants.   88. several kinds: particular tasks.   89. knit up: entangled.   90. distractions: fits of madness.

99. bass my trespass: proclaim my sin in a deep note.   101. plummet: the lead weight at the end of a cord used by sailors to discover the depth of the water.   108. ecstasy: mad fit. See Haml, III.iv.137-44.
    Act IV, Sc. i: 3. third: i.e., a great part of.   5. tender: hand over.   7. strangely: exceptionally.   9. boast . . . off: boast about her.   11. halt: come limping; i.e., she will excel all praise.   12. Against an oracle: i.e., even if a god had said the contrary.

PRO. Then, as my gift, and thine own acquisition
Worthily purchased, take my daughter. But
If thou dost break her virgin knot before 15
All sanctimonious° ceremonies may
With full and holy rite be ministered,
No sweet aspersion° shall the Heavens let fall
To make this contract grow;° but barren hate,
Sour-eyed disdain, and discord shall bestrew 20
The union of your bed with weeds so loathly
That you shall hate it both. Therefore take heed,
As Hymen's° lamps shall light you.

FER.   As I hope
For quiet days, fair issue,° and long life,
With such love as 'tis now, the murkiest den, 25
The most opportune place, the strong'st suggestion°
Our worser genius° can, shall never melt
Mine honor into lust, to take away
The edge of that day's celebration
When I shall think or Phoebus' steeds are foundered,
Or Night kept chained below.°

PRO.   Fairly spoke. 31
Sit, then, and talk with her, she is thine own.
What, Ariel! My industrious servant, Ariel!

       [Enter ARIEL.]

ARI. What would my potent master? Here I am.
PRO. Thou and thy meaner fellows your last
       service 35
Did worthily perform, and I must use you
In such another trick. Go bring the rabble,
O'er whom I give thee power, here to this place.
Incite them to quick motion, for I must
Bestow upon the eyes of this young couple 40
Some vanity° of mine art. It is my promise,
And they expect it from me.

ARI.   Presently?°
PRO. Aye, with a twink.°
ARI. Before you can say, "come," and "go,"
And breathe twice and cry, "so, so," 45
Each one, tripping on his toe,
Will be here with mop° and mow.
Do you love me, master? No? 48
PRO. Dearly, my delicate Ariel. Do not approach
Till thou dost hear me call.

ARI.   Well, I conceive.° [Exit.]
PRO. Look thou be true. Do not give dalliance°
Too much the rein. The strongest oaths are straw
To the fire i' the blood. Be more abstemious,
Or else, good night your vow!

FER.   I warrant you, sir,

The white cold virgin snow upon my heart 55
Abates the ardor of my liver.°
PRO.   Well.
Now come, my Ariel! Bring a corollary°
Rather than want° a spirit. Appear, and pertly!°
No tongue! All eyes! Be silent. [Soft music.]
       [Enter IRIS.°]
IRIS. Ceres,° most bounteous lady, thy rich leas°
Of wheat, rye, barley, vetches, oats, and pease; 61
Thy turfy mountains, where live nibbling sheep,
And flat meads° thatched with stover,° them to
       keep;
Thy banks with pioned and twilled brims,°
Which spongy April at thy hest° betrims° 65
To make cold nymphs chaste crowns; and thy
       broom° groves,
Whose shadow the dismissed° bachelor loves,
Being lasslorn;° thy pole-clipped° vineyard;
And thy sea marge,° sterile and rocky-hard,
Where thou thyself dost air — the Queen o' the Sky,°
Whose watery arch° and messenger am I, 71
Bids thee leave these, and with her sovereign grace,
Here on this grassplot, in this very place,
To come and sport. — Her peacocks° fly amain.°
Approach, rich Ceres, her to entertain. 75
       [Enter CERES.]
CER. Hail, many-colored messenger, that ne'er
Dost disobey the wife of Jupiter;
Who, with thy saffron° wings, upon my flowers
Diffusest honey drops, refreshing showers,
And with each end of thy blue bow dost crown 80
My bosky° acres and my unshrubbed down,°
Rich scarf° to my proud earth. — Why hath thy
       Queen
Summoned me hither, to this short-grassed green?
IRIS. A contract of true love to celebrate,
And some donation° freely to estate° 85
On the blest lovers.
CER.   Tell me, heavenly bow,

16. sanctimonious: religious. 18. aspersion: blessing; lit., sprinkling. 19. grow: prosper. 23. Hymen: the god of marriage. 24. issue: children. 26. suggestion: temptation. 27. worser genius: evil angel. 30–31. or . . . below: either the horses of the Sun have fallen or Night has been imprisoned; i.e., my wedding day, when night seems never to come. 41. vanity: display. 42. Presently: at once. 43. twink: the twinkling of an eye. 47. mop: grimace. 50. conceive: understand. 51. dalliance: fondling.

56. liver: passion. The liver was regarded as the seat of passion. 57. corollary: excess; i.e., too many rather than too few. 58. want: be without. pertly: briskly. 59 s.d., Enter Iris: Prospero now produces a little wedding masque in honor not only of the lovers, Ferdinand and Miranda, but as a compliment to the Princess Elizabeth and her bridegroom before whom The Tempest was acted in 1613. Iris: the female messenger of the gods, also the personification of the rainbow. 60. Ceres: goddess of corn and plenty. leas: arable lands. 63. meads: meadows. thatched . . . stover: covered over with grass for fodder. 64. pioned . . . brims: a difficult phrase, much disputed and emended. The likeliest explanation is that pioned means dug, and twilled, heaped up; i.e., with high banks. 65. hest: command. betrims: trims with wild flowers, especially kingcups, a kind of buttercup that grows by streams. 66. broom: a shrub with yellow flowers. 67. dismissed: rejected. 68. lasslorn: without his girl. pole-clipped: poles embraced by vines. 69. sea marge: seashore. 70. Queen . . . Sky: the goddess Juno, wife of Jupiter. 71. watery arch: i.e., the rainbow. 74. peacocks: birds sacred to Juno. amain: swiftly. 78. saffron: yellow. 81. bosky: wooded. unshrubbed down: rolling open country, without shrubs. 82. scarf: adornment. 85. donation: present. estate: donate.

If Venus or her son, as thou dost know,
Do now attend the Queen? Since they did plot
The means that dusky Dis° my daughter got,
Her and her blind boy's° scandaled° company   90
I have forsworn.
IRIS.   Of her society
Be not afraid. I met Her Deity
Cutting the clouds towards Paphos,° and her son
Dove-drawn° with her. Here thought they to have
    done
Some wanton charm upon this man and maid,   95
Whose vows are, that no bedright shall be paid
Till Hymen's torch° be lighted. But in vain,
Mars's hot minion° is returned again.
Her waspish-headed° son has broke his arrows,
Swears he will shoot no more, but play with spar-
    rows,   100
And be a boy right out.
CER.   High'st Queen of state,
Great Juno, comes. I know her by her gait.
              [Enter JUNO.]
JUNO. How does my bounteous sister? Go with
    me
To bless this twain, that they may prosperous be,
And honored in their issue.   105
[They sing.]

JUNO.   "Honor, riches, marriage blessing,
         Long continuance, and increasing,
         Hourly joys be still° upon you!
         Juno sings her blessings on you."
CER.   "Earth's increase, foison° plenty,   110
         Barns and garners never empty,
         Vines with clustering bunches growing,
         Plants with goodly burden bowing,
         Spring come to you at the farthest
         In the very end of harvest!°   115
         Scarcity and want shall shun you,
         Ceres' blessing so is on you."

FER. This is a most majestic vision, and
Harmonious charmingly. May I be bold
To think these spirits?
PRO.   Spirits which by mine art 120
I have from their confines° called to enact
My present fancies.°
FER.   Let me live here ever.

So rare a wondered° father and a wise
Makes this place Paradise.
              [JUNO and CERES whisper, and send IRIS
                           on employment.]
PRO.   Sweet, now silence!
Juno and Ceres whisper seriously,   125
There's something else to do. Hush, and be mute,
Or else our spell is marred.
IRIS. You nymphs, called Naiads,° of the win-
    dring° brooks,
With your sedged° crowns and ever-harmless looks,
Leave your crisp° channels, and on this green land
Answer your summons. Juno does command.   131
Come, temperate° nymphs, and help to celebrate
A contract of true love. Be not too late.
              [Enter certain NYMPHS.]
You sunburned sicklemen,° of August weary,
Come hither from the furrow, and be merry.   135
Make holiday, your rye-straw hats put on,
And these fresh nymphs encounter every one
In country footing.°
[Enter certain REAPERS, properly habited. They join
with the NYMPHS in a graceful dance, towards the
end whereof PROSPERO starts suddenly, and speaks.
After which, to a strange, hollow, and confused
          noise, they heavily° vanish.]
PRO. [Aside] I had forgot that foul conspiracy
Of the beast Caliban and his confederates   140
Against my life. The minute of their plot
Is almost come. [To the SPIRITS] Well done! Avoid,°
    no more!
FER. This is strange. Your father's in some passion
That works him strongly.
MIRA.   Never till this day
Saw I him touched with anger so distempered.°
PRO. You do look, my son, in a movèd sort,°   146
As if you were dismayed. Be cheerful, sir.
Our revels now are ended. These our actors,
As I foretold you, were all spirits, and
Are melted into air, into thin air.   150
And, like the baseless fabric° of this vision,
The cloud-capped towers, the gorgeous palaces,
The solemn temples, the great globe itself —
Yea, all which it inherit — shall dissolve
And, like this insubstantial pageant faded,   155
Leave not a rack° behind. We are such stuff
As dreams are made on, and our little life
Is rounded° with a sleep. Sir, I am vexed.
Bear with my weakness, my old brain is troubled.

89. dusky Dis: Pluto, god of the underworld, and so dark. He
seized Ceres' daughter Persephone and carried her down to his
kingdom.   90. blind boy: Cupid. scandaled: scandalous.   93. Paphos: in Sicily, a town sacred to Venus.   94. Dove-drawn: in a
chariot drawn by doves.   97. Hymen's torch: The torches of the
wedding god were lit to escort bride and bridegroom to bed.
98. Mars's . . . minion: Mars' lusty darling; i.e., Venus.
99. waspish-headed: quick-tempered.   108. still: always.
110. foison: bounteous harvest.   114-15. Spring . . . harvest:
may spring follow autumn; i.e., may there be no bitterness of
winter in your lives. Cf. Ant & Cleo, V.ii.86-88 for a similar
image.   121. confines: places of confinement.   122. fancies:
devices of my imagination.

123. wondered: wonderful.   128. Naiads: water nymphs. win-
dring: wandering, winding.   129. sedged: covered with sedge, a
kind of water grass.   130. crisp: curled, rippling.   132. temperate:
chaste.   134. sicklemen: reapers, who cut the wheat with sickles.
138. footing: dancing. s.d., heavily: sorrowfully.   142. Avoid: be
gone.   145. distempered: disturbed.   146. moved sort: as if you
were distressed.   151. baseless fabric: unreal stuff.   156. rack:
cloud.   158. rounded: completed; i.e., life is but a moment of
consciousness in an everlasting sleep.

Be not disturbed with my infirmity.   160
If you be pleased, retire into my cell,
And there repose. A turn or two I'll walk,
To still my beating° mind.

FER. & MIRA.   We wish your peace. [*Exeunt.*]

PRO. Come with a thought. I thank thee, Ariel.
Come.

[*Enter* ARIEL.]

ARI. Thy thoughts I cleave to. What's thy pleasure?

PRO.   Spirit,   165
We must prepare to meet with Caliban.

ARI. Aye, my commander. When I presented°
Ceres,
I thought to have told thee of it, but I feared
Lest I might anger thee.

PRO. Say again, where didst thou leave these
varlets?°   170

ARI. I told you, sir, they were red-hot with drinking,
So full of valor that they smote the air
For breathing in their faces, beat the ground
For kissing of their feet, yet always bending°
Toward their project. Then I beat my tabor.   175
At which, like unbacked° colts, they pricked their
ears,
Advanced their eyelids, lifted up their noses
As° they smelt music. So I charmed their ears,
That, calflike, they my lowing followed through
Toothed briers, sharp furzes,° pricking goss,° and
thorns   180
Which entered their frail shins. At last I left them
I' the filthy-mantled° pool beyond your cell,
There dancing up to the chins, that the foul lake
O'erstunk their feet.

PRO.   This was well done, my bird.
Thy shape invisible retain thou still.   185
The trumpery° in my house, go bring it hither,
For stale° to catch these thieves.

ARI.   I go, I go. [*Exit.*]

PRO. A devil, a born devil, on whose nature
Nurture° can never stick, on whom my pains,
Humanely taken, all, all lost, quite lost.   190
And as with age his body uglier grows,
So his mind cankers.° I will plague them all,
Even to roaring.

[*Re-enter* ARIEL, *loaden with glistering° apparel,
etc.*]
Come, hang them on this line.°

[PROSPERO *and* ARIEL *remain, invisible. Enter*
CALIBAN, STEPHANO, *and* TRINCULO, *all wet.*]

CAL. Pray you, tread softly, that the blind mole
may not
Hear a footfall. We now are near his cell.   195

STE. Monster, your fairy, which you say is a harmless fairy, has done little better than played the jack°
with us.

TRIN. Monster, I do smell all horse piss, at which
my nose is in great indignation.   200

STE. So is mine. Do you hear, monster? If I should
take a displeasure against you, look you ——

TRIN. Thou wert but a lost monster.

CAL. Good my lord, give me thy favor still.
Be patient, for the prize I'll bring thee to   205
Shall hoodwink this mischance.° Therefore speak
softly.
All's hushed as midnight yet.

TRIN. Aye, but to lose our bottles in the pool ——

STE. There is not only disgrace and dishonor in
that, monster, but an infinite loss.   210

TRIN. That's more to me than my wetting. Yet
this is your harmless fairy, monster.

STE. I will fetch off° my bottle, though I be o'er
ears° for my labor.   214

CAL. Prithee, my King, be quiet. See'st thou here,
This is the mouth o' the cell. No noise, and enter.
Do that good mischief which may make this island
Thine own forever, and I, thy Caliban,
For aye thy footlicker.

STE. Give me thy hand. I do begin to have bloody
thoughts.   221

TRIN. O King Stephano!° O peer! O worthy
Stephano! Look what a wardrobe here is for thee!

CAL. Let it alone, thou fool, it is but trash.

TRIN. Oh ho, monster! We know what belongs to
a frippery.° O King Stephano!   226

STE. Put off that gown, Trinculo. By this hand,
I'll have that gown.

TRIN. Thy Grace shall have it.

CAL. The dropsy drown this fool! What do you
mean   230
To dote thus on such luggage?° Let 's alone,
And do the murder first. If he awake
From toe to crown he'll fill our skins with pinches,
Make us strange stuff.   234

STE. Be you quiet, monster. Mistress° line, is not
this my jerkin? Now is the jerkin under the line.
Now, jerkin, you are like to lose your hair and prove
a bald jerkin.

---

163. **beating**: throbbing. Cf. I.ii.176.   167. **presented**: either
introduced the masques or acted the part of Ceres. There is, however, very little time for a change of costume between Ariel's
exit at l. 50 and Ceres' entry at l. 75.   170. **varlets**: knaves.
174. **bending**: inclining.   176. **unbacked**: never saddled.
178. **As**: as if.   180. **furzes**: See I.i.72,n. **goss**: gorse.   182. **filthy-mantled**: covered with scum.   186. **trumpery**: cheap finery.
187. **stale**: bait.   189. **Nurture**: education.   192. **cankers**: grows
malignant.   193 s.d., **glistering**: glittering. **line**: lime tree.

197. **jack**: knave.   206. **hoodwink . . . mischance**: blindfold this
misfortune; i.e., make us forget it.   213. **fetch off**: rescue.
214. **o'er ears**: up to my ears in the pond.   222. **O . . . Stephano**:
The sight of all the clothes reminds Trinculo of the old ballad
"King Stephen was a worthy peer." See *Oth*, II.iii.92–99.
226. **frippery**: secondhand-clothes shop.   231. **luggage**: baggage,
which will hinder them.   235–40. **Mistress . . . Grace**: These
lines have mystified editors, and indeed elaborate Elizabethan

TRIN. **Do, do. We steal by line and** level, an 't like your Grace.   240

STE. I thank thee for that jest — here's a garment for 't. Wit shall not go unrewarded while I am King of this country. "Steal by line and level" is an excellent pass of pate° — there's another garment for 't.

TRIN. Monster, come, put some lime° upon   246 your fingers, and away with the rest.

CAL. I will have none on 't. We shall lose our time, And all be turned to barnacles,° or to apes With foreheads villainous low.   250

STE. Monster, lay to your fingers. Help to bear this away where my hogshead of wine is, or I'll turn you out of my kingdom. Go to, carry this.

TRIN. And this.

STE. Aye, and this.   255

[*A noise of hunters heard. Enter divers* SPIRITS, *in shape of dogs and hounds, hunting them about,* PROSPERO *and* ARIEL *setting them on.*]

PRO. Hey, Mountain, hey!

ARI. Silver! There it goes, Silver!

PRO. Fury, Fury! There, Tyrant,° there! Hark, hark!

[CALIBAN, STEPHANO, *and* TRINCULO *are driven out.*]

Go charge my goblins that they grind their joints With dry convulsions. Shorten up their sinews   260 With agèd cramps,° and more pinch-spotted make them

Then pard° or cat-o'-mountain.°

ARI.   Hark, they roar!

PRO. Let them be hunted soundly. At this hour Lie at my mercy all mine enemies.

Shortly shall all my labors end, and thou   265 Shalt have the air at freedom. For a little Follow, and do me service.   [*Exeunt.*]

jokes, especially when made by a half-drunk butler, are not always easy to follow. Stephano begins by addressing the lime tree as "Mistress Line" as if he were talking to the dealer in an old-clothes shop. He appeals to her to decide whether the jerkin is his or Trinculo's. Having taken the jerkin for himself, he then puns on "under the line" (i.e., south of the Equator), where the various skin diseases common to long voyages in the tropics caused hair to fall out. Trinculo caps the remark by a further pun on "line and level"; i.e., "on the square," lit., by the bricklayer's instruments for ensuring perpendicular and horizontal exactness. **245. pass of pate:** sally of wit.   **246. lime:** birdlime, to make them sticky, because Caliban disgustedly drops the garments. **249. barnacles:** tree geese. It was believed, even by serious botanists, that from the barnacles, which grow on rotten wood immersed in sea water, emerged creatures which grew into birds like geese.   **256–58. Mountain . . . Silver . . . Fury . . . Tyrant:** the names of the hounds.   **261. aged cramps:** the cramps which come with old age.   **262. pard:** leopard. **cat-o'-mountain:** mountain cat.

Act V

SCENE I. *Before the cell of* PROSPERO.

[*Enter* PROSPERO *in his magic robes, and* ARIEL.]

PRO. Now does my project gather to a head. My charms crack not,° my spirits obey, and Time Goes upright with his carriage.° How's the day?

ARI. On the sixth hour, at which time, my lord, You said our work should cease.

PRO.   I did say so   5 When first I raised the tempest. Say, my spirit, How fares the King and 's followers?

ARI.   Confined together In the same fashion as you gave in charge, Just as you left them — all prisoners, sir, In the line grove° which weather-fends° your cell. They cannot budge till your release. The King,   11 His brother, and yours abide all three distracted, And the remainder mourning over them, Brimful of sorrow and dismay. But chiefly Him that you termed, sir, "The good old lord, Gonzalo."   15 His tears run down his beard like winter's drops From eaves of reeds.° Your charm so strongly works 'em That if you now beheld them, your affections Would become tender.

PRO.   Dost thou think so, spirit?

ARI. Mine would, sir, were I human.

PRO.   And mine shall.   20 Hast thou, which art but air, a touch, a feeling Of their afflictions, and shall not myself, One of their kind, that relish° all as sharply, Passion° as they, be kindlier moved than thou art? Though with their high wrongs I am struck to the quick,   25 Yet with my nobler reason 'gainst my fury Do I take part. The rarer action is In virtue than in vengeance.° They being penitent, The sole drift° of my purpose doth extend Not a frown further. Go release them, Ariel.   30 My charms I'll break, their senses I'll restore, And they shall be themselves.

ARI.   I'll fetch them, sir. [*Exit.*]

PRO. Ye elves of hills, brooks, standing lakes, and groves, And ye that on the sands with printless foot° Do chase the ebbing Neptune° and do fly him   35

Act V, Sc. i: 2. crack not: do not break down.   **2–3. Time . . . carriage:** Time bears his burden without stooping, because it has now grown so light.   **10. line grove:** grove of lime trees. **weather-fends:** protects from the weather.   **17. eaves of reeds:** a thatched roof.   **23. relish:** feel.   **24. Passion:** suffer emotion. **27–28. rarer . . . vengeance:** it is a finer action to be self-controlled than to take vengeance.   **29. drift:** intention.   **34. printless foot:** without leaving a footprint.   **35. ebbing Neptune:** i.e., the outgoing tide.

When he comes back; you demipuppets° that
By moonshine do the green sour° ringlets° make,
Whereof the ewe not bites; and you whose pastime
Is to make midnight mushrooms° that rejoice
To hear the solemn curfew,° by whose aid —   40
Weak masters though ye be — I have bedimmed
The noontide sun, called forth the mutinous winds,
And 'twixt the green sea and the azured vault°
Set roaring war. To the dread rattling thunder
Have I given fire, and rifted° Jove's stout oak   45
With his own bolt. The strong-based promontory
Have I made shake, and by the spurs° plucked up
The pine and cedar. Graves at my command
Have waked their sleepers, oped, and let 'em forth
By my so potent art. But this rough magic   50
I here abjure, and when I have required
Some heavenly music — which even now I do —
To work mine end upon their senses, that
This airy charm is for, I'll break my staff,
Bury it certain fathoms in the earth,   55
And deeper than did ever plummet° sound
I'll drown my book.°   [*Solemn music.*]
[*Re-enter* ARIEL *before; then* ALONSO, *with a frantic gesture, attended by* GONZALO; SEBASTIAN *and* ANTONIO *in like manner, attended by* ADRIAN *and* FRANCISCO. *They all enter the circle which* PROSPERO *had made, and there stand charmed, which* PROSPERO *observing, speaks:*]
A solemn air,° and the best comforter
To an unsettled fancy, cure thy brains,
Now useless, boiled° within thy skull! There stand,
For you are spell-stopped.   61
Holy Gonzalo, honorable man,
Mine eyes, even sociable° to the show of thine,
Fall° fellowly° drops. The charm dissolves apace,°
And as the morning steals upon the night,   65
Melting the darkness, so their rising senses
Begin to chase the ignorant fumes° that mantle°
Their clearer reason. O good Gonzalo,
My true preserver, and a loyal sir
To him thou follow'st! I will pay thy graces   70
Home° both in word and deed. Most cruelly
Didst thou, Alonso, use me and my daughter.
Thy brother was a furtherer in the act.

Thou art pinched for 't now, Sebastian. Flesh and
   blood,
You, brother mine, that entertained ambition,   75
Expelled remorse° and nature, who with Sebas-
   tian —
Whose inward pinches therefore are most strong —
Would here have killed your King, I do forgive thee,
Unnatural though thou art. Their understanding
Begins to swell, and the approaching tide   80
Will shortly fill the reasonable shore°
That now lies foul and muddy. Not one of them
That yet looks on me, or would know me. Ariel,
Fetch me the hat and rapier in my cell.
I will disease° me, and myself present   85
As I was sometime Milan.° Quickly, spirit.
Thou shalt ere long be free.
   ARI. [*Sings and helps to attire him.*]
   " Where the bee sucks, there suck I.
     In a cowslip's bell I lie,
     There I couch° when owls do cry.   90
     On the bat's back I do fly
     After summer merrily.
   Merrily, merrily shall I live now
   Under the blossom that hangs on the bough."
   PRO. Why, that's my dainty Ariel! I shall miss
    thee,   95
But yet thou shalt have freedom. So, so, so.°
To the King's ship, invisible as thou art.
There shalt thou find the mariners asleep
Under the hatches. The master and the boatswain
Being awake, enforce them to this place,   100
And presently, I prithee.
   ARI. I drink the air before me, and return
Or ere your pulse twice beat.   [*Exit.*]
   GON. All torment, trouble, wonder, and amaze-
   ment
Inhabits here. Some heavenly power guide us   105
Out of this fearful country!
   PRO.   Behold, Sir King,
The wrongèd Duke of Milan, Prospero.
For more assurance that a living prince
Does now speak to thee, I embrace thy body,
And to thee and thy company I bid   110
A hearty welcome.
   ALON.   Whether thou be'st he or no,
Or some enchanted trifle° to abuse° me,
As late I have been, I not know. Thy pulse
Beats, as of° flesh and blood, and since I saw thee,
The affliction of my mind amends, with which,   115
I fear, a madness held me. This must crave —

---

36. demipuppets: tiny creatures, half the size of a puppet.
37. sour: i.e., unacceptable to the cattle. **ringlets:** fairy rings, circles of grass of a darker green often seen in English meadows, supposed to be caused by the fairies dancing in a ring. **39. midnight mushrooms:** As mushrooms grow in a single night, they were thought to be the work of fairies. **40. curfew:** rung at 9 P.M. to warn people to go indoors. Thereafter the fairies can work without interruption. **43. azured vault:** blue sky. **45. rifted:** split. **47. spurs:** roots. **56. plummet:** See III.iii.101,n. **57. book:** i.e., of magic spells. **58. air:** musical air. **60. boiled:** boiling. Cf. *MND*, V.i.4, "Lovers and madmen have such seething brains." **63. sociable:** of fellow feeling. **64. Fall:** let fall. **fellowly:** in sympathy. **apace:** quickly. **67. ignorant fumes:** mists of ignorance. **mantle:** cloak. **70–71. pay . . . Home:** reward your kind deeds fully.

76. remorse: pity. **81. reasonable shore:** shore of reason; i.e., sanity is beginning to flow back like the incoming tide. **85. disease:** remove my outer garment. Prospero is still in his magic robe and so not recognized by his former associates. **86. As . . . Milan:** as I was when I was Duke of Milan. **90. couch:** lie. **96. So, so, so:** "so," used thus, often indicates movement. Cf. *Lear*, III.vi.90. **112. enchanted trifle:** hallucination caused by enchantment. **abuse:** deceive. **114. as of:** as if composed of.

An if this be at all°—a most strange story.
Thy dukedom I resign, and do entreat
Thou pardon me my wrongs.°—But how should
    Prospero
Be living and be here?

PRO.   First, noble friend,   120
Let me embrace thine age, whose honor cannot
Be measured or confined.

GON.   Whether this be
Or be not, I'll not swear.

PRO.   You do yet taste
Some subtilties° o' the isle, that will not let you
Believe things certain. Welcome, my friends all!
[Aside to SEBASTIAN and ANTONIO] But you, my
    brace of lords, were I so minded,   126
I here could pluck His Highness' frown upon you,
And justify you traitors. At this time
I will tell no tales.

SEB.   [Aside] The Devil speaks in him.

PRO.   No.
For you, most wicked sir, whom to call brother   130
Would even infect my mouth, I do forgive
Thy rankest fault—all of them—and require
My dukedom of thee, which perforce I know
Thou must restore.

ALON.   If thou be'st Prospero,
Give us particulars of thy preservation—   135
How thou hast met us here, who three hours
    since
Were wrecked upon this shore, where I have lost—
How sharp the point of this remembrance is!—
My dear son Ferdinand.

PRO.   I am woe for't,° sir.

ALON. Irreparable is the loss, and Patience   140
Says it is past her cure.

PRO.   I rather think
You have not sought her help of whose soft grace
For the like loss I have her sovereign° aid,
And rest myself content.

ALON.   You the like loss!

PRO. As great to me as late, and, supportable   145
To make the dear loss, have I means much weaker
Than you may call to comfort you, for I
Have lost my daughter.

ALON.   A daughter?
O Heavens, that they were living both in Naples,
The King and Queen there! That they were, I wish
Myself were mudded in that oozy bed   151
Where my son lies. When did you lose your daugh-
    ter?

PRO. In this last tempest. I perceive these lords
At this encounter do so much admire°
That they devour their reason, and scarce think   155

Their eyes do offices of truth,° their words
Are natural breath. But howsoe'er you have
Been jostled from your senses, know for certain
That I am Prospero, and that very Duke
Which was thrust forth of Milan, who most strangely
Upon this shore where you were wrecked was
    landed,   161
To be the lord on 't. No more yet of this,
For 'tis a chronicle of day by day,
Not a relation for a breakfast, nor
Befitting this first meeting. Welcome, sir.   165
This cell's my Court. Here have I few attendants,
And subjects none abroad. Pray you look in.
My dukedom since you have given me again,
I will requite° you with as good a thing,
At least bring forth a wonder to content ye   170
As much as me my dukedom.
[Here PROSPERO discovers° FERDINAND and MIRANDA
            playing at chess.]

MIRA. Sweet lord, you play me false.

FER.   No, my dear'st love,
I would not for the world.

MIRA. Yes, for a score of kingdoms you should
    wrangle,
And I would call it fair play.

ALON.   If this prove   175
A vision of the island, one dear son
Shall I twice lose.

SEB.   A most high miracle!

FER. Though the seas threaten, they are merciful.
I have cursed them without cause.   [Kneels.]

ALON.   Now all the blessings
Of a glad father compass thee about!   180
Arise, and say how thou camest here.

MIRA.   Oh, wonder!
How many goodly creatures are there here!
How beauteous mankind is! Oh, brave new world,
That has such people in 't!

PRO.   'Tis new to thee.

ALON. What is this maid with whom thou wast at
    play?   185
Your eld'st° acquaintance cannot be three hours.
Is she the goddess that hath severed us,
And brought us thus together?

FER.   Sir, she is mortal,
But by immortal Providence she's mine.
I chose her when I could not ask my father   190
For his advice, nor thought I had one. She
Is daughter to this famous Duke of Milan,
Of whom so often I have heard renown
But never saw before, of whom I have
Received a second life, and second father   195
This lady makes him to me.

ALON.   I am hers.

117. An . . . all: if this is really true.   119. my wrongs: the
wrongs which I have committed.   123–24. You . . . subtilties:
you still have the taste of the magic nature.   139. woe for't: sorry
for it.   143. sovereign: all-powerful.   154. admire: wonder.

156. offices of truth: true service.   169. requite: pay back.
171 s.d., discovers: reveals by drawing back the curtain.
186. eld'st: longest.

But oh, how oddly will it sound that I
Must ask my child° forgiveness!

PRO.   There, sir, stop.
Let us not burden our remembrances with
A heaviness that's gone.

GON.   I have inly wept,   200
Or should have spoke ere this. Look down, you gods,
And on this couple drop a blessèd crown!
For it is you that have chalked forth° the way
Which brought us hither.

ALON.   I say Amen, Gonzalo!

GON. Was Milan thrust from Milan, that his issue
Should become Kings of Naples? Oh, rejoice   206
Beyond a common joy! And set it down
With gold on lasting pillars. In one voyage
Did Claribel her husband find at Tunis
And Ferdinand, her brother, found a wife   210
Where he himself was lost, Prospero his dukedom
In a poor isle, and all of us ourselves
When no man was his own.

ALON. [*To* FERDINAND *and* MIRANDA] Give me your
    hands.
Let grief and sorrow still embrace° his heart
That doth not wish you joy!

GON.   Be it so! Amen!   215
[*Re-enter* ARIEL, *with the* MASTER *and* BOATSWAIN
      amazedly° *following.*]
Oh, look, sir, look, sir! Here is more of us.
I prophesied if a gallows were on land,
This fellow could not drown.° Now, blasphemy,°
That swear'st grace o'erboard,° not an oath on
    shore?   219
Hast thou no mouth by land? What is the news?

BOATS. The best news is that we have safely found
Our King and company. The next, our ship —
Which, but three glasses since, we gave out split —
Is tight and yare and bravely rigged as when
We first put out to sea.

ARI. [*Aside to* PROSPERO] Sir, all this service   225
Have I done since I went.

PRO. [*Aside to* ARIEL] My tricksy° spirit!

ALON. These are not natural events, they
    strengthen
From strange to stranger. Say, how came you hither?

BOATS. If I did think, sir, I were well awake,
I'd strive to tell you. We were dead of sleep,   230
And — how we know not — all clapped° under
    hatches,
Where, but even now, with strange and several
    noises
Of roaring, shrieking, howling, jingling chains,

And mo diversity of sounds, all horrible,
We were awaked, straightway at liberty.   235
Where we, in all her trim, freshly beheld
Our royal, good, and gallant ship, our master
Capering° to eye her. — On a trice, so please you,
Even in a dream, were we divided from them,
And were brought moping hither.

ARI. [*Aside to* PROSPERO] Was 't well done?   240

PRO. [*Aside to* ARIEL] Bravely, my diligence. Thou
    shalt be free.

ALON. This is as strange a maze as e'er men trod,
And there is in this business more than nature
Was ever conduct of. Some oracle
Must rectify° our knowledge.

PRO.   Sir, my liege,   245
Do not infest your mind with beating on
The strangeness of this business. At picked leisure
Which shall be shortly, single° I'll resolve° you,
Which to you shall seem probable, of every
These happened accidents. Till when, be cheerful,
And think of each thing well. [*Aside to* ARIEL] Come
    hither, spirit.   251
Set Caliban and his companions free,
Untie the spell. [*Exit* ARIEL.] How fares my gracious
    sir?
There are yet missing of your company
Some few odd lads that you remember not.   255
[*Re-enter* ARIEL, *driving in* CALIBAN, STEPHANO, *and*
     TRINCULO, *in their stolen apparel.*]

STE. Every man shift for all the rest, and let no
man take care for himself, for all is but fortune. —
Coragio,° bully-monster, coragio!

TRIN. If these be true spies° which I wear in my
head, here's a goodly sight.   260

CAL. Oh, Setebos, these be brave spirits indeed!
How fine my master is! I am afraid
He will chastise me.

SEB.   Ha, ha!
What things are these, my lord Antonio?
Will money buy 'em?

ANT.   Very like. One of them   265
Is a plain fish, and no doubt marketable.

PRO. Mark but the badges° of these men, my
    lords,
Then say if they be true. This misshapen knave,
His mother was a witch, and one so strong   269
That could control the moon, make flows and ebbs,
And deal in her command,° without her power.°
These three have robbed me, and this demidevil —
For he's a bastard one — had plotted with them
To take my life. Two of these fellows you

Must know and own, this thing of darkness I   275
Acknowledge mine.

CAL.   I shall be pinched to death.

ALON. Is not this Stephano, my drunken butler?

SEB. He is drunk now. Where had he wine?

ALON. And Trinculo is reeling ripe. Where should
they   279
Find this grand liquor that hath gilded 'em?° —
How camest thou in this pickle?

TRIN. I have been in such a pickle since I saw you
last that I fear me will never out of my bones. I shall
not fear flyblowing.°

SEB. Why, how now, Stephano!   285

STE. Oh, touch me not. — I am not Stephano, but
a cramp.

PRO. You'd be King o' the isle, sirrah?

STE. I should have been a sore one, then.

ALON. This is a strange thing as e'er I looked on.
                              [*Pointing to* CALIBAN.]

PRO. He is as disproportioned in his manners°
As in his shape. Go, sirrah, to my cell.   291
Take with you your companions. As you look
To have my pardon, trim° it handsomely.

CAL. Aye, that I will, and I'll be wise hereafter,
And seek for grace.° What a thrice-double ass   295
Was I to take this drunkard for a god
And worship this dull fool!

PRO.   Go to, away!

ALON. Hence, and bestow your luggage where you
found it.

SEB. Or stole it, rather.   299
          [*Exeunt* CALIBAN, STEPHANO, *and* TRINCULO.]

PRO. Sir, I invite your Highness and your train
To my poor cell, where you shall take your rest
For this one night. Which, part of it, I'll waste
With such discourse as I not doubt shall make it
Go quick away — the story of my life,
And the particular accidents° gone by   305
Since I came to this isle. And in the morn
I'll bring you to your ship, and so to Naples,
Where I have hope to see the nuptial
Of these our dear-belovèd solemnized,

And thence retire me to my Milan, where   310
Every third thought shall be my grave.

ALON.   I long
To hear the story of your life, which must
Take the ear strangely.

PRO.   I'll deliver all,
And promise you calm seas, auspicious° gales,
And sail so expeditious that shall catch   315
Your royal fleet far off. [*Aside to* ARIEL] My Ariel,
chick,
That is thy charge. Then to the elements
Be free, and fare thou well! Please you, draw near.
                                           [*Exeunt.*]

EPILOGUE°

SPOKEN BY PROSPERO

Now my charms are all o'erthrown,
And what strength I have's mine own,
Which is most faint. Now, 'tis true,
I must be here confined by you,
Or sent to Naples. Let me not,   5
Since I have my dukedom got,
And pardoned the deceiver, dwell
In this bare island by your spell,
But release me from my bands°
With the help of your good hands.°   10
Gentle breath° of yours my sails
Must fill, or else my project fails,
Which was to please. Now I want°
Spirits to enforce, art to enchant,
And my ending is despair   15
Unless I be relieved by prayer
Which pierces so that it assaults
Mercy itself, and frees all faults.
As you from crimes would pardoned be,
Let your indulgence set me free.   20

314. auspicious: favorable.
   Epilogue: A concluding epilogue is fairly common in Elizabethan plays, especially those performed before a Courtly audience. It is usually a conventional apology for the inadequacies of
the performance, and an appeal for applause. Cf. the epilogues
in *MND, AYLI,* and *II Hen IV.*   9. bands: bonds.   10. good
hands: i.e., by clapping.   11. Gentle breath: kindly criticism.
13. want: lack.

280. gilded 'em: made them glow.   284. fear flyblowing: i.e.,
shall never go bad, for I have been so well pickled.   290. manners: behavior.   293. trim: make tidy.   295. grace: favor.
305. accidents: events.

Francis Bacon

1561–1626

FRANCIS BACON called himself "the trumpeter of the new age" (*buccinator novi temporis*), and it is as the herald of the modern or Faustian era of Western civilization that he still impresses us. For over three centuries he has remained a symbolical figure, revered thoughout Europe as the prophet of science and as a modern Solomon — even if, like his prototype, he combined universal wisdom with certain flaws of character. In his own century his vision of "Salomon's House" inspired the founders of the Royal Society; in the eighteenth century D'Alembert, in projecting the *Encyclopédie,* called him "the greatest, the most universal, the most eloquent of philosophers," and based his classification of the sciences on Bacon's. Shelley classed him among the "poets" in virtue of his prophetic insight, and all down the nineteenth century the chorus of praise went on, tempered only by regrets that such a man could be both "the wisest *and* the meanest of mankind," combining intellectual pre-eminence with corruption and the betrayal of his friend Essex. An examination of the facts of his career tends, I think, to blunt the edges of Pope's epigram, and to show Bacon as neither the wisest nor the meanest, but certainly one of the most distinguished of mankind.

Bacon was born in January, 1561, at York House, Strand, the London residence of his father, Sir Nicholas Bacon, Lord Keeper of the Great Seal. Through his mother (Anne Cooke) he was related to one of the greatest Elizabethan families, for her sister was the wife of William Cecil, Lord Burghley. Next to nothing is known

of his early boyhood, except that he seems to have divided his time between London and Gorhambury, his father's stately seat in Hertfordshire, to which Queen Elizabeth paid more than one visit.

His entry to Trinity College, Cambridge, at the age of twelve need not indicate any special precocity (the age of admission was then often absurdly low by our standards), though Rawley[1] records that the queen used to enjoy questioning the boy, and hearing his replies delivered "with that gravity and maturity above his years, that Her Majesty would often term him 'the young Lord Keeper.'" His precocity appears far more strikingly (if we may believe Rawley) in his alleged judgment on the Cambridge curriculum, for it contains already the essence of his contribution to modern thought:

Whilst he was commorant [living] at the University, about sixteen years of age (as his lordship hath been pleased to impart unto myself), he first fell into the dislike of the philosophy of Aristotle; not for the worthlessness of the author, to whom he would ever ascribe all high attributes, but for the unfruitfulness of the way; being a philosophy . . . only strong for disputations and contentions, but barren of the production of works for the benefit of the life of man. . . .

His father planned for him a career of diplomacy or politics, and, after entering him for legal training at Gray's Inn (1570) sent him to Paris

[1] William Rawley (1588?–1667), Bacon's chaplain, amenuensis, and first biographer. After Bacon's death Rawley edited his unpublished writings and translated his English works into Latin.

with Sir Amyas Paulet, the new ambassador to France. Two years later Sir Nicholas Bacon died, and the young Francis, now and for long afterwards thrown upon his own resources, took up residence at Gray's Inn to train as a barrister. Ambitious by nature, and conscious of his great gifts, he now began a long struggle for advancement. It was an uphill fight lasting over twenty years, in the course of which he acquired that knowledge of men and affairs which appears in the *Essays*. He tried to secure the patronage of his powerful uncle Lord Burghley, but the Cecils were perhaps jealous of their clever " poor " relation (by marriage), and the suit was a failure. Soon after being called to the bar (1582), he entered parliament as M.P. for Melcombe Regis, and long remained a prominent House of Commons man, serving on many important committees, and later representing various other constituencies including Taunton, Liverpool, Ipswich, Middlesex, and the University of Cambridge. His influence was always exerted on the side of moderation: the *via media* between royal prerogative and parliamentary privilege, and unity through toleration in religion. In his defense of parliamentary privilege, however, he had the misfortune to offend the queen, and this for many years stood in the way of his advancement — the Cecils meanwhile fanning the flame of her resentment.

He next attached himself to the ill-fated Earl of Essex, whose importunate zeal on his behalf seems to have annoyed the queen still more. Essex tried, without success, to get him appointed to the Mastership of the Rolls and the office of Attorney General, and finally, in his impulsive friendship, presented him with some land near Twickenham which brought him £1800. It must not be supposed that throughout all this period of intrigue for preferment Bacon had none but worldly ends in view. His was not a simple character. Hungry though he certainly was for wealth and ostentation, he was also a dreamer of dreams and a seer of visions; he had a vast idea to bring to fruition — nothing less than " the knowledge of causes and secret motions of things; and the enlarging of the bounds of human empire, to the effecting of all things possible." In the midst of his poverty and struggle he wrote to Burghley, " I have taken all knowledge for my province." One, at least, of his motives for

seeking wealth and honor was to gain leisure for pursuing this great aim. " My mind," he wrote to Elizabeth, " turneth upon other wheels than those of profit." The first fruits of his meditations were given to the world in 1597, when the slender first edition of the *Essays* was published (it contained only ten essays: " Of Studies," " Of Discourse," " Of Ceremonies and Respect," " Of Followers and Friends," " Of Suits " [" Suitors "], " Of Expense," " Of Regiment of Health," " Of Honor and Reputation," " Of Faction," and " Of Negotiating," all of them enlarged by 1625 into the form in which we now know them). Fine and characteristic as these are, they represent only the more immediate preoccupations of a man of affairs, not Bacon's whole mind in " the wide circuit of its musings."

The disgrace of Essex, following his disastrous campaign in Ireland (1599), involved Bacon in a maze of negotiations too intricate to unfold here. The part he played in the final trial and condemnation of his former friend and patron has left — not quite justly — a slur upon his name. Gardiner [1] the historian said, " That the course Bacon took indicates poverty of moral feeling cannot be denied." Yet it seems clear that in the earlier stages of Essex's downward course, when Bacon did not know the full story of his treasonable plot to seize the queen's person, he consistently tried to restore Essex to favor. Even at the time of his closest intimacy with the Earl, when acknowledging the gift of land at Twickenham, he had with modest dignity reminded him that his first duty was to the sovereign: " My lord, I see I must be your homager and hold land of your gift: but do you know the manner of doing homage in law? Always it is with a saving [reservation] of his faith to the king . . .: and therefore, my lord, I can be no more yours than I was, and it must be with the ancient savings." Later, then, when he discovered the full extent of Essex's treason, was it so blameworthy to carry out this principle of superior loyalty by accepting appointment as one of Essex's minor accusers? Let Gardiner speak again: " Our sentiment on the precedence of personal over political ties is based on our increased sense of politi-

---

[1] Samuel Rawson Gardiner (1829–1902), English historian, famous for his lengthy and elaborate histories of England in the seventeenth century (eighteen volumes published over a period of forty years).

cal security, and is hardly applicable to a state of things in which anarchy, with its attendant miseries, would inevitably have followed on the violent overthrow of the queen's right to select her ministers." We may shrink from the judicial coldness of Bacon's character (it is evident in his *Essays,* especially those on personal relationships), but as a public man he acted with probity, and his contemporaries — even Essex himself — did not censure him.

The accession of James I in 1603 brought no immediate improvement to Bacon's prospects (except a knighthood). Yet it is clear that Bacon had high hopes of benefit from the reign of this learned monarch; to see this it is enough to read the dedication of *The Advancement of Learning,* in which he fulsomely ascribes to James "the power and fortune of a king, and knowledge and illumination of a priest, and the learning and universality of a philosopher." In 1605 he published *The Advancement of Learning,* which he conceived as the first part of his grandiose but never fully completed design, the *Magna Instauratio* (the Great Renewal, or New Foundation). The *Instauratio* was really the name for Bacon's conception of his life's work: laying new and firmer foundations on which science could be securely built. All his philosophical works were, so to speak, fragments of the vast idea which, in its greater part, remained unfulfilled. It would have contained, for example, a survey of the present state of knowledge (realized in the *Advancement*); a method for investigating and interpreting nature (the *Novum Organum*); a huge tabulated list of the phenomena of the universe and of their operations; and an application of the new method to all these phenomena. The *Advancement* was later (1623) published (with important additions) in Latin, then the "universal language" of scholars, so that it might become accessible to learned readers throughout Europe.

Bacon's marriage (1606) at the age of forty-five to Alice Barnham, daughter of a London alderman, appears as only a minor episode in the main drama of his career. This indeed is what one would expect from the writer of the essay "Of Love," in which he says that "the stage is more beholding to love than the life of man," adds that "great spirits and great business do keep out this weak passion," and quotes with approval the saying "that it is impossible to love and to be wise." The wedding itself illustrated one side of Bacon's nature, his passion for display; Carleton[1] reports that "he was clad from top to toe in purple, and hath made himself and his wife such store of fine raiments of cloth of silver and gold that it draws deep into her portion." In the essay "Of Parents and Children" he wrote "the noblest works and foundations have proceeded from childless men, which have sought to express the images of their minds, where those of their bodies have failed" (see also "Of Marriage and Single Life," below); his own marriage was childless, and there was an estrangement in its later years.

The next ten years saw Bacon rising, first slowly and then with mounting rapidity, to the height of his worldly ambition. He became Solicitor General in 1607, Attorney General in 1613, Lord Keeper in 1617, Lord Chancellor and Baron Verulam in 1618, and Viscount St. Albans in 1621. Meanwhile he produced many writings, of which the best-known are the *De Sapientia Veterum* (Wisdom of the Ancients) (1609), the 1612 enlarged edition of the *Essays,* and his most important philosophical work, the *Novum Organum* (1620), which was the second part (dealing with scientific method) of the *Instauratio.*

Bacon's fall from his pinnacle of glory came with a suddenness unusual even in those days of swift reversals of fortune. It is indeed painfully disturbing to reflect that one so great and so nobly endowed should have been indicted for the sordid offense of taking bribes in the execution of the highest legal office in the country. There was a touch of greatness in his very confession of guilt, but his refusal to defend himself need not prevent his admirers from taking a more lenient view of his behavior. There are palliating considerations, which should not be overlooked. First, one must remember what he himself called the *vitia temporis,* the evil customs of the age; judges did accept gifts in those days. Secondly, he never allowed the gifts to pervert justice; even his accusers admitted that he decided against them in spite of the bribes. "I had no bribe or reward in my eye or thought

---

[1] Sir Dudley Carleton (1573–1632), afterwards Viscount Dorchester, ambassador at Venice and The Hague. His numerous letters and dispatches are a mine of information on contemporary affairs and personalities.

when I pronounced any sentence or order," he said. Thirdly, gifts received after a case was ended were universally considered to be legitimate. The only fault of which, after close self-examination, he could accuse himself, was that of neglecting to ascertain, when accepting a gift, whether a case were "fully at an end or no." One gets the impression of a luxury-loving man, willing enough to enjoy the full perquisites of office as then understood and condoned, yet essentially incorruptible at heart, and too much preoccupied with his inward life to trouble about observing those punctilios which might have made him safe from his enemies. His own verdict may stand: "I was the justest judge that was in England these fifty years; but it was the justest censure in Parliament that was these two hundred years." His sentence was drastically severe, including an immense fine, imprisonment, and loss of all office. Most of it was soon afterwards remitted, but he never held office again, and spent his few remaining years in retirement. He occupied his leisure in writing his *History of Henry VII* (1622), in the translation of the *Advancement,* in compiling installments of his natural history, and in putting the finishing touches to the final edition of the *Essays* (1625).

The *New Atlantis,* which was first published in 1627, was at one time regarded as a work of Bacon's last years, but it was more probably produced or sketched at least ten years before his death. Bacon had intended to depict here an ideal commonwealth or Utopia, but he got no further than describing (in Rawley's words) "a college instituted for the interpreting of nature and the producing of great and marvelous works for the benefit of men, under the name of Salomon's House." This imaginary college became to some extent a model and inspiration for the foundation of the Royal Society (1662).

The cause of his death has about it more pathos than dignity: it was a chill caught by stuffing a fowl with snow, on a cold spring day, to test its powers of refrigeration. Even in this slightly grotesque experiment there is evidence of a mind careless of outward things, and actively pursuing its own concerns to the last. We may end with Rawley's concluding words:

But howsoever his body was mortal, yet no doubt his memory and works will live, and will in all probability last as long as the world lasteth.

II

"The end of our foundation is the knowledge of causes and secret motions of things; and the enlarging of the bounds of human empire, to the effecting of all things possible" (*New Atlantis*).

"FRANCIS OF VERULAM THOUGHT THUS, AND SUCH IS THE METHOD WHICH HE DETERMINED WITHIN HIMSELF, AND WHICH HE THOUGHT IT CONCERNED THE LIVING AND POSTERITY TO KNOW:

Being convinced, by a careful observation, that the human understanding perplexes itself, or makes not a sober and advantageous use of the real helps within its reach, whence manifold ignorance and inconveniences arise, he was determined to employ his utmost endeavors towards restoring or cultivating a just and legitimate familiarity between the mind and things. . . .

The philosophy we principally received from the Greeks must be acknowledged puerile, or rather talkative than generative — as being fruitful in controversies, but barren of effects. . . .

Those, therefore, who determine not to conjecture and guess, but to find out and know; not to invent fables and romances of worlds, but to look into, and dissect the nature of this real world, must consult only things themselves."

(*The Great Instauration:*
Announcement, Preface, and
Distribution of the Work)

Bacon stands at the threshold of the seventeenth century as the prophet and chief propagandist of the greatest intellectual revolution of modern times — the scientific movement which changed the traditional world-picture. It was not that he made any of the significant discoveries; that was left to men like Copernicus, Kepler, Galileo, Gilbert, and Harvey. What Bacon did was to seize with fine insight, and proclaim with incomparable literary power, the principles by which alone any scientific advances could be made. Bacon belonged to an age of expansion and exuberant vitality, when unlimited possibilities seemed to be opening up on all sides. The Pillars of Hercules were no longer the boundary of the known world: beyond the Atlantic lay an unexploited America, and beyond the Cape the riches of the gorgeous East. Since the shattering of the medieval cosmography, the very universe had expanded to infinity, and this world, no longer its fixed center, might be but one of innumerable worlds.[1] Marlowe's Faustus spoke for his age when he exclaimed

> O what a world of profit and delight
> Is promised to the studious artisan!

The vision which had dawned upon Bacon, and which lends excitement to his writings, was a vision of power achieved through knowledge; of nature mastered and controlled in the interests of mankind; of progress and unheard-of glory for humanity. The dreams of the astrologer and the alchemist — dreams of control over fortune and over natural forces — might be realized after all, but only by those who were humble enough to consult Nature herself, not their own imagination or reason: in a word, by the experimental physicist and chemist.

It has been said that an age gets the sort of philosophy it deserves, or at any rate one which reflects its own deepest interests. Bacon's was an age of newly awakened national consciousness, in which the modern competition for wealth and power had just begun. As I have elsewhere said,[2]

Roger Bacon, who preached the same doctrines as Francis, only about three and a half centuries too soon, spent much of his life in prison as a sorcerer. Francis Bacon, more fortunate in the date of his nativity, preached just the doctrines his age most wanted to hear. Given the ends assumed as all-important in the modern world — material progress, power, wealth, success in competition and the like — then Bacon's advice was the only wise advice, his method the true method; hence his extraordinary prestige.

What, then, was this "advice," and what this "method"?

In Swift's *Battle of the Books* there is a well-known fable of the spider and the bee, which may suggest an answer. The spider and the bee each argues that he, and his own work, is the more important. The spider points with pride to the beauty, symmetry, and geometrical perfection of his web, and it is his special glory to have spun all this out of his own entrails. In reply, the bee asks what end it serves? For

catching flies. And what is it made of? Gossamer, mere cobweb. Now the bee for his part flies about the garden sucking nectar from flowers. Out of the mingling of sweet juices he makes honey and wax, substances useful to society because they yield, respectively, "sweetness and light." Bacon's advice to his age was to become bees instead of spiders. The ancients and the medieval Schoolmen had been too busy spinning "cobwebs of learning, admirable for the fineness of thread and work, but of no substance or profit" (*Advancement*, Book I. iv. 5, below); they had "withdrawn themselves too much from the contemplation of nature, and the observations of experience," and "tumbled up and down in their own reason and conceits" (*ibid.*, I. v. 6, below). Now was the time for the bee's task of going straight to Nature, and extracting her secrets by direct observation and experiment. To gain power over Nature we must know these secrets, and they must be sought in Nature herself and not in logic; there must be a transference of interest from abstract speculation to concrete observation.

The circumstances of Bacon's age were such that this part of his program necessarily assumed a theological cast. Among the obstacles which blocked the road for the new science were several beliefs or attitudes inherited from the past, of which one of the chief was the idea that natural science was the knowledge forbidden to Adam, its pursuit the re-enactment of the Fall, and its end damnation. This association of science with the Devil and all his works had been vividly expressed in the Faust legend (the first surviving quarto of Marlowe's *Dr. Faustus* was published only the year before the *Advancement*); behind it, too, lay St. Paul's warning against the wisdom of this world and the knowledge that puffeth up (see *Advancement*, I. i. 2 and 3, below). At the very outset, therefore, Bacon had to deal with this fundamental objection. He disposes of it by arguing, first, that God has declared himself to mankind by two kinds of revelation: by Scripture, the book of his word, and by Nature, the book of his works. It is no more impious, then, to study Nature than to read the Bible. The knowledge which caused the Fall was not natural science (symbolized by Adam's naming of the creatures); it was rather that of the Scholastic philosophers themselves: the speculative curiosity which presumes to read the

---

[1] See Donne's *Anatomy of the World*, especially ll. 205–18, below.
[2] In *Christianity Past and Present*, 1952, pp. 75–76.

mind of God, and know good and evil, and to make man independent of God. No amount of natural science will harm us, provided it be seasoned with the "corrective spice" of piety or charity; that is to say, it must be directed to "the glory of the Creator and the relief of man's estate." Nor will the study of natural laws (" second causes ") lead to atheism; a little learning may indeed be a dangerous thing, but deeper drafts will bring us back to God, the first of all causes. So long, then, as our knowledge is devoted " to charity, and not to swelling," " to use, and not to ostentation," we cannot be " too well studied . . . in the book of God's works." We must beware, however, not to confuse science and religion; if we do, the result will be a fabulous science on the one hand and a heretical religion on the other. Through Nature we can indeed ascend to God, but we learn there merely of his existence, power, and wisdom; to know his will for us, and how we may be saved, we must turn to revealed religion: " give to faith the things that are faith's."

Among the other hindrances to knowledge which Bacon enumerates are the study of words rather than of things, that is, excessive attention to philology, grammar, and rhetoric and not enough to " weight of matter "; vanity of the matter itself, as in the " subtle, idle, and . . . vermiculate questions " of the Schoolmen; and excessive reverence for antiquity and tradition, leading men to repeat ancient errors from century to century rather than take the trouble of going to Nature for the true answers.

But the deepest sources of error lie within the human mind itself, and it is in his exposure of these " idols " (as he afterwards called them) that Bacon shows his profoundest insight. The mind of man, by its very fabric and constitution, has within it certain radical tendencies to error, which must be recognized and corrected before it can interpret Nature aright. Bacon elaborated his critique on the " idols of the mind " more fully in the *Novum Organum* and the *De Augmentis,* but much of it is already sketched out in the *Advancement* (see II. xiv. 9, 10, and 11, below). First, there are the " false appearances that are imposed upon us by the general nature of the mind " — the " idols of the tribe." These spring from our habit of making man the measure of all things, and assuming that Nature must

necessarily behave according to our own sense of fitness. We " usually suppose and feign in nature a greater equality and uniformity than is in truth," and thus we distort nature instead of interpreting her. This was the typical fallacy of the ancient and medieval philosophers who, instead of noting how Nature actually behaved, tried to make her conform to preconceived notions. Thus the moon was a celestial body; it is the nature of celestial bodies to be perfect; the only perfect shape is a sphere; therefore the moon is spherical, and if Galileo's telescope reveals mountains and hollows on its surface, so much the worse for the telescope and for Galileo. Bacon's point is that God's ways are not our ways, neither are his thoughts our thoughts; " if that great workmaster had been of an human disposition, he would have cast the stars into some pleasant and beautiful works and orders, like the frets in the roofs of houses; whereas one can scarce find a posture in square, or triangle, or straight line, amongst such an infinite number; so differing an harmony there is between the spirit of man and the spirit of nature."

Next there are the " idols of the cave," errors arising, not from the general defectiveness of the human mind, but from the limitations of each man's individual upbringing or environment. We must come forth into the light of things, abandon the delusions of sect and coterie, and let Nature be our teacher.

Thirdly, there are the " idols of the market place," the " false appearances that are imposed upon us by words." We may try to think with the wise, but we have to speak with the vulgar — that is, make use of words whose " popular " meanings often conflict with the exact meaning intended. In all discussions we should begin by defining our terms; otherwise we shall find ourselves arguing at cross-purposes, and have to end where we should have begun.

In the *Novum Organum* Bacon added a fourth class of idols, those of the " theater " (i.e., the lecture theater); these are errors which have arisen from various systems of philosophy. There is the " sophistic," which takes certain common observations without reducing them to certainty, and relies for the rest upon meditation and activity of wit. Aristotle is the chief offender here; he decides the nature of things on insufficient evidence, and then " drags experiment along as a captive constrained to accommodate herself to his decisions." There is the "empiric," which does indeed make a few careful experiments, but produces a complete system prematurely, and on an inadequate basis. And there is the "superstitious" type, which mixes up theology with science, some even having tried to build a system of natural philosophy upon the first chapter of the Book of Genesis.

These, in fine, are the idols which must be abjured before the human mind can begin to interpret the divine mind as it is expressed in nature. "The understanding must be completely freed and cleared of them, so that the access to the kingdom of man, which is founded on the sciences, may resemble that to the kingdom of heaven, where no admission is conceded except to children" (*Novum Organum*, I. 68).

The last-quoted remark well illustrates the technique by which Bacon, while always distinguishing clearly between the spheres of religion and science, tries to give a religious sanction to his scientific propaganda. What he means, in this context, is that science, so far from leading to pride of intellect, can only be successfully pursued in that very same spirit of humility which is required of the Christian believer. There is no need to question Bacon's sincerity when, as constantly happens, he exalts revelation above reason, and places the *summum bonum* where religion places it — in salvation and heavenly joy. What is certain, however, is that the emphasis of his interest is steadily upon this world, upon the active rather than the contemplative life, upon becoming rather than upon being. The other world has for ages been sufficiently attended to; it is now this world's turn. This attitude comes out very clearly in the extract printed below (*Advancement*, II. vii. 1–7), where the topic is the inquiry into causes. What needs investigating, Bacon urges, are the inward atomic structures, which make things what they are (he calls them "forms" or "formal causes"), and the "efficient" causes, i.e., the physical forces which actually produce motions. But these are just what have been neglected. Men have contented themselves by explaining why or to what purpose things existed and behaved in such and such fashion (the "final causes"), and ignored the "how" almost entirely. The point is not, he characteristically adds, that these "final causes" are not true or not worth considering, but that "their excursions into the limits of physical causes hath bred a vastness and solitude in that tract."

Similarly in morality, the ultimate issues and sanctions lie within the sphere of religion, but there has been a neglect of the humbler details of daily living and the actual technique of self-discipline. The theoretical principles of ethics have been well discussed, and fair copies of the virtues held up for admiration, but the question of "how to attain these excellent marks" has been passed over in silence.

Bacon devotes a section of the *Advancement* to this practical wisdom, which he calls the "Georgics of the mind, concerning the husbandry and tillage thereof." But it is in his *Essays* that he goes farthest towards filling the gap, for they are the distillation of his experience of men and affairs. He himself aptly described them as "certain brief notes, set down rather significantly than curiously . . . of a nature whereof a man shall find much in experience, little in books." In the *Advancement* he had pleaded for rules of self-management, and for a science of psychological types whereby we could manage other men. In the *Essays* we get the wise guidance of an experienced sage on how to manage our own concerns — our health, our wealth, our affections, and our fortunes, on how to govern others, and on the methods of administering public affairs. There is no need to enlarge upon the pungency, the conciseness, the aphoristic brilliance, the vivid imagery, and (especially in the later essays and added passages) the eloquence which have made these *Essays* famous. A point worth remembering, however, is that, though Bacon is justly reputed the father of the English essay, it is the form of this genre, rather than its tone and temper, that we owe to him. The essay properly so called derives from Montaigne rather than from Bacon: it was Montaigne who taught such men as Browne, Cowley, Addison, Lamb, Hazlitt, and R. L. Stevenson how to exploit their own personalities in that intimate, that deliberately informal or carpet-slipper style, which we have come to regard as the essential note of this literary form. The essayists in this succession have mostly been whimsical individualists who preferred byways to highways, and cared little for the things most valued by the first-class passengers through life. Bacon, on the other hand, scorned to be found anywhere but at the metropolis of the world and of the mind; he writes like a lord chancellor, and his essays are the *sententiae* of a worldly-wise man. His advice is nowhere corrupt; its basis is in Christian ethics, but his values are those of the world rather than of the spirit.

An important group of the *Essays* (e.g., "Of Unity in Religion," "Of Great Place," "Of Seditions and Troubles," "Of Cunning," "Of Negotiating," etc.) deal with the technique of statecraft, and it is significant that in the *Advancement* Bacon has referred approvingly (though not uncritically) to Machiavelli: "we are much beholden to Machiavelli and others," he said, "that write what men do, and not what they ought to do." Bacon saw Machiavelli as the founder of the scientific method in political science. If you want a science of men in society, you must observe them scientifically, as you would observe any other part of nature, and to do this you must attempt the difficult task of seeing them as they really are, not as they ought to be or as you may think they are. Bacon (always anxious for religious support) here remembers that St. Paul has bidden us not only to be innocent as doves, but also wise as serpents. But, says he, "It is not possible to join serpentine wisdom with the columbine innocency, except men know exactly all the conditions of the serpent; his baseness and going on his belly, his volubility and lubricity, his envy and sting, and the rest, that is, all forms and natures of evil." There are numerous examples in the *Essays* of Bacon's application of this "serpentine wisdom" to the handling of men and the maintenance of the authority of princes. Thus in the essay "Of Cunning," after defining it in his inimitable way as "a sinister or crooked wisdom," he proceeds with evident relish to give a series of points of cunning — in short, rules of the game. Or again, in "Of Negotiating" he says:

If you would work any man, you must either know his nature and fashions, and so lead him; or his ends, and so persuade him; or his weaknesses and disadvantages, and so awe him; or those that have interest in him, and so govern him.

Bacon is perhaps most attractive to a modern reader when he writes of general topics such as truth, atheism, self-wisdom, death, adversity, building, or studies. He is not at his best in dealing with the personal relationships: marriage and single life, love, parents and children, even friendship; in these essays we may detect a certain chilliness, a touch of inhumanity, which seem to have been part of Bacon's own character. But they are not, in Blake's phrase, "good advice for Satan's Kingdom"; we shall value the essays most for such things as:

Certainly virtue is like precious odors, most fragrant when they are incensed or crushed: for prosperity doth best discover vice; but adversity doth best discover virtue ("Of Adversity").

Therefore, as atheism is in all respects hateful, so in this, that it depriveth human nature of the means to exalt itself above human frailty ("Of Atheism").

It is a poor center of a man's actions, himself. It is right earth. For that only stands fast upon his own center; whereas all things that have affinity with the heavens move upon the center of another, which they benefit ("Of Wisdom for a Man's Self").

Certainly, it is heaven upon earth, to have a man's mind move in charity, rest in Providence, and turn upon the poles of truth ("Of Truth").

Bacon is a prophet, not of the Kingdom of Heaven, but of the Kingdom of Man. What he would have us do is to exploit to the uttermost the brave new world, not to be lookers-on but active workers for the benefit of humanity; then death, when it comes, will come unnoticed:

He that dies in an earnest pursuit is like one that is wounded in hot blood; who, for the time, scarce feels the hurt ("Of Death").

Reading Suggestions

EDITIONS

James Spedding (with R. L. Ellis and D. D. Heath), *The Works of Francis Bacon*, 7 vols. (1857–59). The great Victorian edition.

Edward Arber, *A Harmony of the Essays* (1871), in the English Reprints Series. Gives all the editions in parallel columns, and contains Rawley's short *Life of Bacon*, the earliest biography.

Geoffrey Grigson, editor, *Bacon's Essays* (1937), with Introduction. World's Classics Edition. This edition of the 1625 volume reproduces also all the 1597 essays for purposes of comparison.

Bacon's Advancement of Learning (1951), in the World's Classics Edition. Contains a useful introduction by Thomas Case, and also *The New Atlantis*.

CRITICISM

T. B. Macaulay, "Essay on Bacon," in *Essays* (1837). A famous essay, now mainly of interest as a period piece.

James Spedding, *Life and Times of Francis Bacon* (1878). The main source of information.

R. W. Church, *Bacon* (1884), in the English Men of Letters Series. Readable and useful.

C. D. Broad, *The Philosophy of Francis Bacon* (1926). Brief, but very acute.

R. F. Jones, *Ancients and Moderns* (1936). Includes a full discussion of Bacon's scientific influence.

G. Bullough, "Bacon and the Defence of Learning," in *Seventeenth Century Studies Presented to Sir H. Grierson* (1938). Shows how necessary Bacon's apologia was.

ESSAYS OR COUNSELS

Civil and Moral

Bacon's *Essays* were first published in 1597. This volume contained only the following ten essays (the original titles are given here): "Of Studies," "Of Discourse," "Of Ceremonies and Respects," "Of Followers and Friends," "Of Suits," "Of Expense," "Of Regiment of Health," "Of Honor and Reputation," "Of Faction," and "Of Negotiating."

Revised and enlarged editions appeared in 1612 and 1625, the number of essays being increased to thirty-eight in 1612 and fifty-eight in 1625. In general, the successive revisions took the form of enrichment by added allusions and illustrations, but there was also some transference from one essay to another, and in some essays considerable rewriting.

The essays are given here in their final form of 1625. The date appended to each indicates when the essay first appeared; it does not mean (except where the essay first appeared in 1625) that its original version is here given. As a specimen of the 1597 volume, the essay "Of Studies" is reproduced as it appeared in that edition, as well as in its final form. Readers will thus be able to note the contrast between the concise, aphoristic style of the first essays and the richer, more developed manner of the later ones. A good notion of the development of Bacon's style can be gained by comparing Essay V, "Of Adversity" (1625), with the 1597 version of "Of Studies."

ESSAY I

OF TRUTH

What is truth? said jesting Pilate, and would not stay for an answer. Certainly there be that delight in giddiness, and count it a bondage to fix a belief; affecting free will in thinking, as well as in acting. And though the sects of philosophers of that kind be gone, yet there remain certain discoursing wits which are of the same veins, though there be not so much blood in them as was in those of the ancients. But it is not only the difficulty and labor which men take in finding out of truth, nor again that when it is found it imposeth upon men's thoughts, that doth bring lies in favor; but a natural though corrupt love of the lie itself. One of the later school of the Grecians [1] examineth the matter, and is at a stand to think what should be in it, that men should love lies; where neither they make for pleasure, as with poets; nor for advantage, as with the merchant; but for the lie's sake. But I cannot tell: this same truth is a naked and open daylight, that doth not show the masques and mummeries and triumphs of the world, half so stately and daintily as candlelights. Truth may perhaps come to the price of a pearl, that showeth best by day; but it will not rise to the price of a diamond or carbuncle, that showeth best in varied lights. A mixture of a lie doth ever add pleasure. Doth any man doubt, that if there were taken out of men's minds vain opinions, flattering hopes, false valuations, imaginations as one would, and the like, but it would leave the minds of a number of men poor shrunken things, full of melancholy and indisposition, and unpleasing to themselves? One of the fathers, in great severity, called poesy *vinum daemonum*,[2] because it filleth the imagination, and yet it is but with the shadow of a lie. But it is not the lie that passeth through the mind, but the lie that sinketh in and settleth in it, that doth the hurt, such as we spake of before. But howsoever these things are thus in men's depraved judgments and affections, yet truth, which only doth judge itself, teacheth that the inquiry of truth, which is the love-making or wooing of it, the knowledge of truth, which is the presence of it, and the belief of truth, which is the enjoying of it, is the sovereign good of human nature. The first creature of God, in the works of the days, was the light of the sense; the last was the light of reason; and his sabbath work, ever since, is the illumination of his Spirit. First he breathed light upon the face of the matter or chaos; then he breathed light into the face of man; and still he breatheth and inspireth

ESSAYS. 1. Grecians: probably Lucian, who in his *Philopseudes* has a character who asks why men love lying. 2. *vinum daemonum:* "the wine of evil spirits" (Jerome, Augustine, or Tertullian, early Fathers of the Christian Church).

light into the face of his chosen. The poet that beautified the sect [3] that was otherwise inferior to the rest, saith yet excellently well: *It is a pleasure to stand upon the shore, and to see ships tossed upon the sea: a pleasure to stand in the window of a castle, and to see a battle and the adventures thereof below: but no pleasure is comparable to the standing upon the vantage ground of truth* (a hill not to be commanded, and where the air is always clear and serene), *and to see the errors, and wanderings, and mists, and tempests, in the vale below:* [4] so always that this prospect be with pity, and not with swelling or pride. Certainly, it is heaven upon earth, to have a man's mind move in charity, rest in Providence, and turn upon the poles of truth.

To pass from theological and philosophical truth, to the truth of civil business: it will be acknowledged, even by those that practice it not, that clear and round dealing is the honor of man's nature; and that mixture of falsehood is like allay [5] in coin of gold and silver; which may make the metal work the better, but it embaseth it. For these winding and crooked courses are the goings of the serpent; which goeth basely upon the belly, and not upon the feet. There is no vice that doth so cover a man with shame as to be found false and perfidious. And therefore Mountaigny [6] saith prettily, when he inquired the reason, why the word of the lie should be such a disgrace and such an odious charge? saith he, *If it be well weighed, to say that a man lieth, is as much to say as that he is brave towards God and a coward towards men.* For a lie faces God, and shrinks from man. Surely the wickedness of falsehood and breach of faith cannot possibly be so highly expressed, as in that it shall be the last peal to call the judgments of God upon the generations of men; it being foretold, that when Christ cometh, *he shall not find faith upon the earth.*

1625

ESSAY II

OF DEATH

Men fear death, as children fear to go in the dark; and as that natural fear in children is increased with tales, so is the other. Certainly, the

contemplation of death, as the *wages of sin,* and passage to another world, is holy and religious; but the fear of it, as a tribute due unto nature, is weak. Yet in religious meditations there is sometimes mixture of vanity and of superstition. You shall read in some of the friars' books of mortification, that a man should think with himself what the pain is if he have but his finger's end pressed or tortured, and thereby imagine what the pains of death are, when the whole body is corrupted and dissolved: when many times death passeth with less pain than the torture of a limb; for the most vital parts are not the quickest of sense. And by him, that spake only as a philosopher and natural man,[7] it was well said, *Pompa mortis magis terret quam mors ipsa.*[8] Groans and convulsions, and a discolored face, and friends weeping, and blacks, and obsequies, and the like, show death terrible. It is worthy the observing, that there is no passion in the mind of man so weak, but it mates and masters the fear of death; and therefore death is no such terrible enemy, when a man hath so many attendants about him that can win the combat of him. Revenge triumphs over death; love slights it; honor aspireth to it; grief flieth to it; fear pre-occupateth [9] it; nay, we read, after Otho the emperor had slain himself, pity (which is the tenderest of affections) provoked many to die, out of mere compassion to their sovereign, and as the truest sort of followers. Nay, Seneca adds niceness [10] and satiety: *Cogita quam diu eadem feceris; mori velle, non tantum fortis, aut miser, sed etiam fastidiosus potest.*[11] A man would die, though he were neither valiant nor miserable, only upon a weariness to do the same thing so oft over and over. It is no less worthy to observe, how little alteration, in good spirits, the approaches of death make; for they appear to be the same men till the last instant. Augustus Caesar died in a compliment: *Livia, conjugii nostri memor, vive et vale.*[12] Tiberius in dissimulation, as Tacitus saith of him: *Jam Tiberium vires et corpus, non dissimulatio, deserebant.*[13] Vespasian in a jest, sitting upon the stool: *Ut puto Deus fio.*[14] Galba with a sen-

7. *him . . . man:* Seneca; "natural": pagan.   8. *Pompa . . . ipsa:* "The parade of death frightens more than death itself."   9. pre-occupateth: anticipates [i.e., by suicide].   10. niceness: fastidiousness.   11. *Cogita . . . potest:* "Consider how often you do the same things; a man may wish to die, not only because he is brave, or miserable, but even because he is disgusted with life."   12. *Livia . . . vale:* "Farewell, Livia, and remember our married life."   13. *Jam . . . deserebant:* "At length vitality and bodily strength were deserting Tiberius, not his duplicity."   14. *Ut . . . fio:* "As I think [a pun on *puto,* cleanse], I am becoming a god."

3. The poet . . . sect: Lucretius; the Epicureans.   4. *below:* The passage from *De Rerum Natura,* II. 1–10, is freely paraphrased.   5. allay: alloy.   6. Mountaigny: Michel de Montaigne (1533–92), French essayist.

tence: *Feri, si ex re sit populi Romani,*[15] holding forth his neck. Septimius Severus in dispatch: *Adeste si quid mihi restat agendum.*[16] And the like. Certainly the Stoics bestowed too much cost upon death, and by their great preparations made it appear more fearful. Better saith he, *Qui finem vitae extremum inter munera ponat Naturae.*[17] It is as natural to die as to be born; and to a little infant, perhaps, the one is as painful as the other. He that dies in an earnest pursuit is like one that is wounded in hot blood; who, for the time, scarce feels the hurt; and therefore a mind fixed and bent upon somewhat that is good doth avert the dolors of death. But above all, believe it, the sweetest canticle is *Nunc dimittis;* [18] when a man hath obtained worthy ends and expectations. Death hath this also, that it openeth the gate to good fame, and extinguisheth envy. *Extinctus amabitur idem.*[19]

1612

ESSAY V
OF ADVERSITY

It was an high speech of Seneca (after the manner of the Stoics): *That the good things which belong to prosperity are to be wished; but the good things that belong to adversity are to be admired. Bona rerum secundarum optabilia, adversarum mirabilia.* Certainly, if miracles be the command over nature, they appear most in adversity. It is yet a higher speech of his than the other (much too high for a heathen): *It is true greatness to have in one the frailty of a man, and the security of a god. Vere magnum, habere fragilitatem hominis, securitatem dei.* This would have done better in poesy, where transcendences are more allowed. And the poets indeed have been busy with it; for it is in effect the thing which is figured in that strange fiction of the ancient poets, which seemeth not to be without mystery; nay, and to have some approach to the state of a Christian: that *Hercules, when he went to unbind Prometheus* (by whom human nature is represented), *sailed the length of the great ocean in an earthen pot or pitcher:* lively describing Chris-

tian resolution, that saileth in the frail bark of the flesh through the waves of the world. But to speak in a mean.[20] The virtue of prosperity is temperance; the virtue of adversity is fortitude; which in morals is the more heroical virtue. Prosperity is the blessing of the Old Testament; adversity is the blessing of the New; which carrieth the greater benediction, and the clearer revelation of God's favor. Yet even in the Old Testament, if you listen to David's harp, you shall hear as many hearse-like airs as carols; and the pencil of the Holy Ghost hath labored more in describing the afflictions of Job than the felicities of Salomon. Prosperity is not without many fears and distastes; and adversity is not without comforts and hopes. We see in needleworks and embroideries, it is more pleasing to have a lively work upon a sad and solemn ground, than to have a dark and melancholy work upon a lightsome ground: judge therefore of the pleasure of the heart by the pleasure of the eye. Certainly virtue is like precious odors, most fragrant when they are incensed or crushed: for prosperity doth best discover vice; but adversity doth best discover virtue.

1625

ESSAY VIII
OF MARRIAGE AND SINGLE LIFE

He that hath wife and children hath given hostages to fortune; for they are impediments to great enterprises, either of virtue or mischief. Certainly, the best works, and of greatest merit for the public, have proceeded from the unmarried or childless men, which both in affection and means have married and endowed the public. Yet it were great reason that those that have children should have greatest care of future times; unto which they know they must transmit their dearest pledges. Some there are, who though they lead a single life, yet their thoughts do end with themselves, and account future times impertinences. Nay, there are some other that account wife and children but as bills of charges.[21] Nay more, there are some foolish rich covetous men that take a pride in having no children, because they may be thought so much the richer. For perhaps they have heard some talk, *Such an one is a great rich man,* and another except to it, *Yea, but he hath a great charge of chil-*

---

15. *Feri ... Romani:* "Strike, if it be in the interest of the Roman people."   **16.** *Adeste ... agendum:* "Come along, if anything remains for me to do."   **17.** *Qui ... Naturae:* "He who reckons the close of life among the boons of nature" (paraphrase of Juvenal).   **18.** *Nunc dimittis:* "(Lord) now lettest thou (thy servant) depart (in peace)" (Luke 2:29).   **19.** *Extinctus ... idem:* "The same [i.e., the envied] man will be beloved when he is dead."

20. mean: prosaic language, or level terms.   **21.** bills of charges: accounts to be paid.

dren; as if it were an abatement to his riches. But the most ordinary cause of a single life is liberty; especially in certain self-pleasing and humorous.[22] minds, which are so sensible of every restraint, as they will go near to think their girdles and garters to be bonds and shackles. Unmarried men are best friends, best masters, best servants; but not always best subjects; for they are light to run away; and almost all fugitives are of that condition. A single life doth well with churchmen; for charity will hardly water the ground where it must first fill a pool. It is indifferent for judges and magistrates; for if they be facile and corrupt, you shall have a servant five times worse than a wife. For soldiers, I find the generals commonly in their hortatives put men in mind of their wives and children; and I think the despising of marriage amongst the Turks maketh the vulgar soldier more base. Certainly wife and children are a kind of discipline of humanity; and single men, though they be many times more charitable, because their means are less exhaust, yet, on the other side, they are more cruel and hard-hearted (good to make severe inquisitors), because their tenderness is not so oft called upon. Grave natures, led by custom, and therefore constant, are commonly loving husbands; as was said of Ulysses, *Vetulam suam praetulit immortalitati.*[23] Chaste women are often proud and froward, as presuming upon the merit of their chastity. It is one of the best bonds both of chastity and obedience in the wife, if she think her husband wise; which she will never do if she find him jealous. Wives are young men's mistresses; companions for middle age; and old men's nurses. So as a man may have a quarrel[24] to marry when he will. But yet he was reputed one of the wise men, that made answer to the question, when a man should marry?[25] *A young man not yet, an elder man not at all.* It is often seen that bad husbands have very good wives; whether it be that it raiseth the price of their husband's kindness when it comes; or that the wives take a pride in their patience. But this never fails, if the bad husbands were of their own choosing, against their friends' consent; for then they will be sure to make good[26] their own folly.

1612

Men in great places are thrice servants: servants of the sovereign or state; servants of fame; and servants of business. So as they have no freedom, neither in their persons, nor in their actions, nor in their times. It is a strange desire, to seek power and to lose liberty; or to seek power over others and to lose power over a man's self. The rising unto place is laborious, and by pains men come to greater pains; and it is sometimes base, and by indignities men come to dignities. The standing is slippery; and the regress is either a downfall, or at least an eclipse, which is a melancholy thing. *Cum non sis qui fueris, non esse cur velis vivere.*[28] Nay, retire men cannot when they would; neither will they when it were reason; but are impatient of privateness,[29] even in age and sickness, which require the shadow: like old townsmen, that will be still sitting at their street door, though thereby they offer age to scorn. Certainly, great persons had need to borrow other men's opinions, to think themselves happy; for if they judge by their own feeling, they cannot find it: but if they think with themselves what other men think of them, and that other men would fain be as they are, then they are happy as it were by report, when perhaps they find the contrary within. For they are the first that find their own griefs, though they be the last that find their own faults. Certainly, men in great fortunes are strangers to themselves, and while they are in the puzzle of business they have no time to tend their health, either of body or mind. *Illi mors gravis incubat, qui notus nimis omnibus, ignotus moritur sibi.*[30] In place there is license to do good and evil; whereof the latter is a curse: for in evil the best condition is not to will, the second not to can. But power to do good is the true and lawful end of aspiring. For good thoughts (though God accept them) yet towards men are little better then good dreams, except they be put in act; and that cannot be without power and place, as the vantage and commanding ground. Merit and good works is the end of man's motion; and conscience of the same is the accomplishment of man's rest. For if a man can be partaker of God's theater,[31] he

22. humorous: whimsical.   23. *Vetulam . . . immortalitati:* "He preferred his little aged wife [Penelope] to immortality" (Cicero).   24. quarrel: excuse or pretext (to marry at any age).   25. he . . . marry: The ancient Greek philosopher Thales is said to have expressed this view about himself.   26. make good: justify.

27. Great Place: high office.   28. *Cum . . . vivere:* "When [or since] you are no longer what you were, there is no reason why you should wish to live" (Cicero).   29. are . . . privateness: cannot endure private life [retirement].   30. *Illi . . . sibi:* "Death lies heavily on the man who dies too well known to everyone but ignorant of himself" (Seneca).   31. God's theater: the world.

shall likewise be partaker of God's rest. *Et conversus Deus, ut aspiceret opera quae fecerunt manus suae, vidit quod omnia essent bona nimis;* [32] and then the Sabbath. In the discharge of thy place, set before thee the best examples; for imitation is a globe of precepts. And after a time set before thee thine own example; and examine thyself strictly, whether thou didst not best at first. [33] Neglect not also the examples of those that have carried themselves ill in the same place; not to set off thyself by taxing their memory, but to direct thyself what to avoid. Reform, therefore, without bravery [34] or scandal of former times and persons; but yet set it down to thyself as well to create good precedents as to follow them. Reduce things to the first institution, and observe wherein and how they have degenerate; but yet ask counsel of both times; of the ancient time, what is best; and of the latter time, what is fittest. Seek to make thy course regular, that men may know beforehand what they may expect; but be not too positive and peremptory; and express thyself well when thou digressest from thy rule. Preserve the right of thy place, but stir not questions of jurisdiction: [35] and rather assume thy right in silence and *de facto*, [36] than voice it with claims and challenges. Preserve likewise the rights of inferior places; and think it more honor to direct in chief than to be busy in all. Embrace and invite helps and advices touching the execution of thy place; and do not drive away such as bring thee information as meddlers, but accept of them in good part. The vices of authority are chiefly four: delays, corruption, roughness, and facility. [37] For delays, give easy access; keep times appointed; go through with that which is in hand; and interlace not business but of necessity. For corruption, do not only bind thine own hands or thy servants' hands from taking, but bind the hands of suitors also from offering. For integrity used doth the one; but integrity professed, and with a manifest detestation of bribery, doth the other. And avoid not only the fault, but the suspicion. Whosoever is found variable, and changeth manifestly without manifest cause, giveth suspicion of corruption. Therefore always when thou changest thine opinions of course,

profess it plainly and declare it, together with the reasons that move thee to change; and do not think to steal it. A servant or a favorite, if he be inward, [38] and no other apparent cause of esteem, is commonly thought but a byway to close [39] corruption. For roughness, it is a needless cause of discontent: severity breedeth fear, but roughness breedeth hate. Even reproofs from authority ought to be grave, and not taunting. As for facility, it is worse than bribery. For bribes come but now and then; but if importunity or idle respects lead a man, he shall never be without. As Salomon saith: "To respect persons is not good; for such a man will transgress for a piece of bread." [40] It is most true that was anciently spoken, *A place showeth the man:* and it showeth some to the better, and some to the worse. *Omnium consensu capax imperii, nisi imperasset,* [41] saith Tacitus of Galba; but of Vespasian he saith, *Solus imperantium Vespasianus mutatus in melius:* [42] though the one was meant of sufficiency, the other of manners and affection. It is an assured sign of a worthy and generous spirit, whom honor amends. For honor is, or should be, the place of virtue; and as in nature things move violently to their place, and calmly in their place; so virtue in ambition is violent, in authority settled and calm. All rising to great place is by a winding stair; and if there be factions, it is good to side a man's self whilst he is in the rising, and to balance himself when he is placed. Use the memory of thy predecessor fairly and tenderly; for if thou dost not, it is a debt will sure be paid when thou art gone. If thou have colleagues, respect them, and rather call them when they look not for it, than exclude them when they have reason to look to be called. Be not too sensible [43] or too remembering of thy place in conversation and private answers to suitors; but let it rather be said, *When he sits in place he is another man.*

1612

ESSAY XIII

OF GOODNESS, AND GOODNESS OF NATURE

I take goodness in this sense, the affecting [44] of the weal of men, which is that the Grecians call

---

32. *Et . . . nimis:* "And God turned to behold the works which his hands had made, and saw that all things were very good" (Gen. 1:31). **33. whether . . . first:** to see whether you did not begin better than you have gone on. **34. bravery:** flouting, defiance. **35. stir . . . jurisdiction:** Do not raise discussions about the powers of your office. **36. de facto:** as a matter of course. **37. facility:** being too easygoing, too easily influenced by others.

38. inward: intimate, in your confidence. **39. close:** secret. **40. "To . . . bread":** Prov. 28:21. **41. Omnium . . . imperasset:** "By universal consent he was fit to govern, if only he had not governed." **42. Solus . . . melius:** "Of all the emperors, Vespasian alone changed for the better" [i.e., after accession]. **43. sensible:** sensitive, or conscious. **44. affecting:** caring for.

philanthropia; and the word *humanity* (as it is used) is a little too light to express it. Goodness I call the habit, and goodness of nature the inclination. This, of all virtues and dignities of the mind, is the greatest, being the character of the Deity; and without it man is a busy, mischievous, wretched thing, no better than a kind of vermin. Goodness answers to the theological virtue charity, and admits no excess, but error. The desire of power in excess caused the angels to fall; the desire of knowledge in excess caused man to fall; but in charity there is no excess; neither can angel or man come in danger by it. The inclination to goodness is imprinted deeply in the nature of man; insomuch that if it issue not towards men, it will take unto other living creatures; as it is seen in the Turks, a cruel people, who nevertheless are kind to beasts, and give alms to dogs and birds; insomuch as Busbechius [45] reporteth, a Christian boy in Constantinople had like to have been stoned for gagging in a waggishness a long-billed fowl. Errors indeed in this virtue of goodness or charity may be committed. The Italians have an ungracious proverb, *Tanto buon che val niente: So good, that he is good for nothing.* And one of the doctors of Italy, Nicholas Machiavel, had the confidence to put in writing, almost in plain terms, *That the Christian faith had given up good men in prey to those that are tyrannical and unjust.* Which he spake, because indeed there was never law, or sect, or opinion, did so much magnify goodness as the Christian religion doth. Therefore, to avoid the scandal and the danger both, it is good to take knowledge of the errors of an habit so excellent. Seek the good of other men, but be not in bondage to their faces or fancies; for that is but facility or softness; which taketh an honest mind prisoner. Neither give thou Aesop's cock a gem, who would be better pleased and happier if he had had a barleycorn. The example of God teacheth the lesson truly: "He sendeth his rain, and maketh his sun to shine, upon the just and unjust "; but he doth not rain wealth, nor shine honor and virtues, upon men equally. Common benefits are to be communicate with all, but peculiar benefits with choice. And beware how in making the portraiture thou breakest the pattern; for divinity maketh the love of ourselves the pattern, the love of our neighbors but the portraiture. "Sell

all thou hast, and give it to the poor, and follow me"; but sell not all thou hast, except thou come and follow me; that is, except thou have a vocation wherein thou mayest do as much good with little means as with great; for otherwise in feeding the streams thou driest the fountain. Neither is there only a habit of goodness, directed by right reason; but there is in some men, even in nature, a disposition towards it; as on the other side there is a natural malignity. For there be that in their nature do not affect the good of others. The lighter sort of malignity turneth but to a crossness, or frowardness, or aptness to oppose, or difficilness, [46] or the like; but the deeper sort, to envy and mere mischief. Such men in other men's calamities are, as it were, in season, and are ever on the loading part; [47] not so good as the dogs that licked Lazarus' sores, but like flies that are still buzzing upon anything that is raw; *misanthropi,* that make it their practice to bring men to the bough, [48] and yet have never a tree for the purpose in their gardens, as Timon [49] had. Such dispositions are the very errors of human nature; and yet they are the fittest timber to make great politiques [50] of; like to knee timber, [51] that is good for ships that are ordained to be tossed, but not for building houses that shall stand firm. The parts and signs of goodness are many. If a man be gracious and courteous to strangers, it shows he is a citizen of the world, and that his heart is no island cut off from other lands, but a continent that joins to them. If he be compassionate towards the afflictions of others, it shows that his heart is like the noble tree, [52] that is wounded itself when it gives the balm. If he easily pardons and remits offenses, it shows that his mind is planted above injuries, so that he cannot be shot. If he be thankful for small benefits, it shows that he weighs men's minds, and not their trash. But above all, if he have St. Paul's perfection, that he would wish to be an

---

45. **Busbechius:** Augier de Ghislien, Seigneur de Busbecq (1522–92), German ambassador to Turkey.

46. **difficileness:** cantankerousness. (We still call a person *difficile* when he is always "making difficulties.") 47. **on . . . part:** increasing their burden; "piling it on." 48. **bring . . . bough:** i.e., to hang themselves. 49. **Timon:** Timon of Athens. Shakespeare paraphrases North's Plutarch thus: "I have a tree, which grows here in my garden,/That mine own use invites me to cut down,/And shortly must I fell it: tell my friends,/Tell Athens in the sequence of degree/From high to low throughout, that whoso please/To stop affliction, let him take his haste,/Come hither, ere my tree hath felt the axe,/And hang himself." (*Timon of Athens,* V. ii. 208–15.) 50. **politiques:** politicians. 51. **knee timber:** timber so cut that trunk and branch form a kneeshaped and flexible piece. 52. **noble tree:** one of the balsam trees, probably *Commiphora opobalsamum* which yielded "Mecca balsam" or the "balm of Gilead" mentioned in Scriptures.

anathema [53] from Christ for the salvation of his brethren, it shows much of a divine nature, and a kind of conformity with Christ himself.

1612

ESSAY XV
OF SEDITIONS AND TROUBLES

Shepherds of people had need know the kalendars of tempests [54] in state; which are commonly greatest when things grow to equality; as natural tempests are greatest about the *Aequinoctia.*[55] And as there are certain hollow blasts of wind and secret swelling of seas before a tempest, so are there in states:

> *Ille etiam caecos instare tumultus*
> *Saepe monet, fraudesque et operta tumescere bella.*[56]

Libels and licentious discourses against the state, when they are frequent and open; and in like sort, false news, often running up and down, to the disadvantage of the state, and hastily embraced; are amongst the signs of troubles. Virgil, giving the pedigree of Fame,[57] saith *she was sister to the Giants:*

Illam Terra parens, ira irritata Deorum,
Extremam (ut perhibent) Coeo Enceladoque soro-
*   rem*
Progenuit.[58]

As if fames were the relics of seditions past; but they are no less, indeed, the preludes of seditions to come. Howsoever, he noteth it right, that seditious tumults and seditious fames differ no more but as brother and sister, masculine and feminine; especially if it come to that, that the best actions of a state, and the most plausible, and which ought to give greatest contentment, are taken in ill sense, and traduced; for that shows the envy great, as Tacitus saith, *Conflata magna invidia, seu bene seu*

male gesta premunt.[59] Neither doth it follow, that because these fames are a sign of troubles, that the suppressing of them with too much severity should be a remedy of troubles. For the despising of them many times checks them best; and the going about to stop them doth but make a wonder long-lived. Also that kind of obedience, which Tacitus speaketh of, is to be held suspected: *Erant in officio, sed tamen qui mallent mandata imperantium interpretari, quam exequi:* [60] disputing, excusing, caviling upon mandates and directions, is a kind of shaking off the yoke, and assay of disobedience; especially if in those disputings they which are for the direction speak fearfully and tenderly, and those that are against it audaciously.

Also, as Machiavel noteth well, when princes, that ought to be common parents, make themselves as a party, and lean to a side, it is as a boat that is overthrown by uneven weight on the one side; as was well seen in the time of Henry the Third of France; for first himself entered league for the extirpation of the Protestants, and presently after the same league was turned upon himself. For when the authority of princes is made but an accessory to a cause, and that there be other bands that tie faster than the band of sovereignty, kings begin to be put almost out of possession.

Also, when discords and quarrels and factions are carried openly and audaciously, it is a sign the reverence of government is lost. For the motions of the greatest persons in a government ought to be as the motions of the planets under *primum mobile,*[61] according to the old opinion, which is, that every [62] of them is carried swiftly by the highest motion, and softly in their own motion. And therefore, when great ones in their own particular motion move violently, and, as Tacitus expresseth it well, *liberius quam ut imperantium meminissent,*[63] it is a sign the orbs are out of frame. For reverence is that wherewith princes are girt from God, who threateneth the dissolving thereof: *Solvam cingula regum.*[64]

So when any of the four pillars of government

---

53. *anathema:* originally a votive offering, then something "devoted" to evil, and so accursed. (See Rom. 9:3: "I could wish that myself were accursed from Christ for my brethren.") Christ himself was "devoted" to death for the redemption of man. 54. *kalendars of tempests:* anticipatory schedules of the phases of the moon, etc., with prophecies of the storms which were supposed to accompany them. 55. *Aequinoctia:* the equinoxes. 56. *Ille . . . bella:* "Often, too, he gives warning that secret revolts are impending, and that treachery and open wars are swelling up" (Virgil, *Georgics,* I. 465). 57. *Fame:* here used in its Latin sense of "rumor." 58. *Illam . . . Progenuit:* "Mother Earth, exasperated by the wrath of the gods, produced her (so men relate) as a final birth: sister to Coeus and Enceladus" (Virgil, *Aeneid,* IV. 179).

59. *Conflata . . . premunt:* "Once great ill will has been excited, all his deeds, whether good or bad, are resented" (Bacon paraphrases Tacitus). 60. *Erant . . . exequi:* "They did their duty, but in the spirit of men preferring to discuss the orders of their rulers rather than to carry them out." 61. *primum mobile:* first mover, the outermost or highest of the heavenly spheres, whose motion actuated that of all the planets. Cf. Donne's "Good Friday," ll. 7–8n. 62. *every:* each, or everyone. 63. *liberius . . . meminissent:* "too freely to be mindful of their rulers." 64. *Solvam . . . regum:* "I will unloose the girdles of kings" (Isa. 45:1).

are mainly shaken or weakened (which are religion, justice, counsel, and treasure), men had need to pray for fair weather. But let us pass from this part of predictions (concerning which, nevertheless, more light may be taken from that which followeth), and let us speak first of the materials of seditions; then of the motives of them; and thirdly of the remedies.

Concerning the materials of seditions. It is a thing well to be considered; for the surest way to prevent seditions (if the times do bear it) is to take away the matter of them. For if there be fuel prepared, it is hard to tell whence the spark shall come that shall set it on fire. The matter of seditions is of two kinds: much poverty and much discontentment. It is certain, so many overthrown estates, so many votes for troubles. Lucan noteth well the state of Rome before the civil war:

Hinc usura vorax, rapidumque in tempore foenus,
Hinc concussa fides, et multis utile bellum.[65]

This same *multis utile bellum* is an assured and infallible sign of a state disposed to seditions and troubles. And if this poverty and broken estate in the better sort be joined with a want and necessity in the mean people, the danger is imminent and great. For the rebellions of the belly are the worst. As for discontentments, they are in the politic body like to humors[66] in the natural, which are apt to gather a preternatural heat and to inflame. And let no prince measure the danger of them by this, whether they be just or unjust; for that were to imagine people to be too reasonable, who do often spurn at their own good: nor yet by this, whether the griefs whereupon they rise be in fact great or small; for they are the most dangerous discontentments where the fear is greater than the feeling. *Dolendi modus, timendi non item.*[67] Besides, in great oppressions, the same things that provoke patience, do withal mate[68] the courage; but in fears it is not so. Neither let any prince or state be secure[69] concerning discontentments, because they have been often, or have been long, and yet no peril hath ensued: for as it is true that every vapor or fume doth not turn into a storm; so it is nevertheless true that storms, though they blow over divers

times, yet may fall at last; and, as the Spanish proverb noteth well, *The cord breaketh at the last by the weakest pull.*

The causes and motives of seditions are: innovation in religion; taxes; alteration of laws and customs; breaking of privileges; general oppression; advancement of unworthy persons; strangers; dearths; disbanded soldiers; factions grown desperate; and whatsoever, in offending people, joineth and knitteth them in a common cause.

For the remedies, there may be some general preservatives, whereof we will speak; as for the just cure, it must answer to the particular disease, and so be left to counsel rather than rule.

The first remedy or prevention is to remove by all means possible that material cause of sedition whereof we spake; which is want and poverty in the estate. To which purpose serveth the opening and well-balancing of trade; the cherishing of manufactures; the banishing of idleness; the repressing of waste and excess by sumptuary laws; the improvement and husbanding of the soil; the regulating of prices of things vendible; the moderating of taxes and tributes; and the like. Generally, it is to be foreseen that the population of a kingdom (especially if it be not mown down by wars) do not exceed the stock of the kingdom which should maintain them. Neither is the population to be reckoned only by number; for a smaller number, that spend more and earn less, do wear out an estate sooner than a greater number, that live lower and gather more. Therefore the multiplying nobility and other degrees of quality, in an overproportion to the common people, doth speedily bring a state to necessity; and so doth likewise an overgrown clergy, for they bring nothing to the stock; and in like manner, when more are bred scholars than preferments can take off.

It is likewise to be remembered that, forasmuch as the increase of any estate must be upon the foreigner[70] (for whatsoever is somewhere gotten is somewhere lost), there be but three things which one nation selleth unto another: the commodity as nature yieldeth it; the manufacture; and the vecture or carriage. So that if these three wheels go, wealth will flow as in a spring tide. And it cometh many times to pass that *materiam superabit opus;*[71] that the work and carriage is more worth than the

---

65. *Hinc . . . bellum:* "Hence devouring usury, and interest mounting daily; hence shaken credit, and war profitable to many." 66. humors: the "four humors" in the body: blood, bile, phlegm, and choler. If one of these became too preponderant, it upset the balance of health. See Additional Note B, p. 196, above. 67. *Dolendi . . . item:* "To suffering there is a limit; to fearing, none." 68. mate: check. 69. secure: careless.

70. increase . . . foreigner: Increase in the wealth of one nation must be at the expense of another nation. 71. *materiam . . . opus:* "the workmanship will surpass the material" (Ovid, *Metamorphoses*, II. 5).

material, and enricheth a state more; as is notably seen in the Low Countrymen, who have the best mines above ground [72] in the world.

Above all things, good policy is to be used, that the treasure and monies in a state be not gathered into few hands. For otherwise a state may have a great stock, and yet starve. And money is like muck, not good except it be spread. This is done chiefly by suppressing, or at the least keeping a strait hand upon the devouring trades of usury, engrossing,[73] great pasturages, and the like.

For removing discontentments, or at least the danger of them. There is in every state (as we know) two portions of subjects, the noblesse and the commonalty. When one of these is discontent, the danger is not great; for common people are of slow motion, if they be not excited by the greater sort; and the greater sort are of small strength, except the multitude be apt and ready to move of themselves. Then is the danger, when the greater sort do but wait for the troubling of the waters amongst the meaner, that then they may declare themselves. The poets feign, that the rest of the gods would have bound Jupiter; which he hearing of, by the counsel of Pallas sent for Briareus, with his hundred hands, to come in to his aid. An emblem, no doubt, to show how safe it is for monarchs to make sure of the good will of common people.

To give moderate liberty for griefs and discontentments to evaporate (so it be without too great insolency or bravery) is a safe way. For he that turneth the humors back, and maketh the wound bleed inwards, endangereth malign ulcers and pernicious impostumations.

The part of Epimetheus might well become Prometheus,[74] in the case of discontentments; for there is not a better provision against them. Epimetheus, when griefs and evils flew abroad, at last shut the lid, and kept hope in the bottom of the vessel. Certainly, the politic and artificial nourishing and entertaining of hopes, and carrying men from hopes to hopes, is one of the best antidotes against the poison of discontentments. And it is a certain sign of a wise government and proceeding when it can hold men's hearts by hopes, when it cannot by satisfaction; and when it can handle things in such manner, as no evil shall appear so peremptory but that it hath some outlet of hope: which is the less hard to do, because both particular persons and factions are apt enough to flatter themselves, or at least to brave that which they believe not.

Also, the foresight and prevention, that there be no likely or fit head whereunto discontented persons may resort, and under whom they may join, is a known but an excellent point of caution. I understand a fit head to be one that hath greatness and reputation; that hath confidence with [75] the discontented party, and upon whom they turn their eyes; and that is thought discontented in his own particular: which kind of persons are either to be won and reconciled to the state, and that in a fast and true manner; or to be fronted with some other of the same party, that may oppose them, and so divide the reputation. Generally, the dividing and breaking of all factions and combinations that are adverse to the state, and setting them at distance or at least distrust amongst themselves, is not one of the worst remedies. For it is a desperate case, if those that hold with the proceeding of the state be full of discord and faction, and those that are against it be entire and united.

I have noted that some witty and sharp speeches which have fallen from princes have given fire to seditions. Caesar did himself infinite hurt in that speech, *Sylla nescivit litteras, non potuit dictare,*[76] for it did utterly cut off that hope which men had entertained, that he would at one time or other give over his dictatorship. Galba undid himself by that speech, *Legi a se militem, non emi,*[77] for it put the soldiers out of hope of the donative. Probus likewise, by that speech, *Si vixero, non opus erit amplius Romano imperio militibus,*[78] a speech of great despair for the soldiers. And many the like. Surely princes had need, in tender matters and ticklish times, to beware what they say; especially in these short speeches, which fly abroad like darts, and are thought to be shot out of their secret intentions. For as for large discourses, they are flat things, and not so much noted.

Lastly, let princes, against all events, not be with-

---

72. mines ... ground: source of riches not underground (i.e., the Dutch carrying trade).   **73. engrossing:** buying up to get a monopoly.   **74.** Epimetheus ("Afterthought") was brother to Prometheus ("Forethought"), and husband of Pandora. Prometheus, the friend of man in Greek mythology, had confined all the woes of men in a box, which Pandora opened. All the evils escaped but hope alone remained within when Epimetheus closed the lid.

75. confidence with: enjoys the confidence of.   **76. Sylla ... dictare:** "Sylla was illiterate, so could not dictate" (Suetonius). **77. Legi ... emi:** "That soldiers were levied by him, not bought" (Tacitus).   **78. Si ... militibus:** "If I live, the Roman Empire will need no more soldiers" (Flavius Vopiscus).

out some great person, one or rather more, of military valor, near unto them, for the repressing of seditions in their beginnings. For without that, there useth to be more trepidation in court upon the first breaking out of troubles than were fit. And the state runneth the danger of that which Tacitus saith: *Atque is habitus animorum fuit, ut pessimum facinus auderent pauci, plures vellent, omnes paterentur.*[79] But let such military persons be assured, and well reputed of, rather than factious and popular; holding also good correspondence with the other great men in the state; or else the remedy is worse than the disease.

1625

ESSAY XVI
OF ATHEISM

I had rather believe all the fables in the Legend,[80] and the Talmud,[81] and the Alcoran,[82] than that this universal frame is without a mind. And therefore God never wrought miracle to convince atheism, because his ordinary works convince it. It is true, that a little philosophy inclineth man's mind to atheism; but depth in philosophy bringeth men's minds about to religion: [83] for while the mind of man looketh upon second causes [84] scattered, it may sometimes rest in them, and go no further; but when it beholdeth the chain of them, confederate and linked together, it must needs fly to Providence and Deity. Nay, even that school which is most accused of atheism doth most demonstrate religion; that is, the school of Leucippus and Democritus and Epicurus.[85] For it is a thousand times more credible, that four mutable elements and one immutable fifth essence,[86] duly and eternally placed, need

no God, than that an army of infinite small portions or seeds unplaced should have produced this order and beauty without a divine marshal. The Scripture saith, "The fool hath said in his heart, there is no God": it is not said, "The fool hath thought in his heart": so as he rather saith it by rote to himself, as that he would have, than that he can throughly believe it, or be persuaded of it. For none deny there is a God but those for whom it maketh [87] that there were no God. It appeareth in nothing more, that atheism is rather in the lip than in the heart of man, than by this; that atheists will ever be talking of that their opinion, as if they fainted in it within themselves, and would be glad to be strengthened by the consent of others: nay more, you shall have atheists strive to get disciples, as it fareth with other sects: and, which is most of all, you shall have of them that will suffer for atheism, and not recant; whereas, if they did truly think that there were no such thing as God, why should they trouble themselves? Epicurus is charged that he did but dissemble for his credit's sake, when he affirmed there were blessed natures, but such as enjoyed themselves without having respect to the government of the world. Wherein they say he did temporize, though in secret he thought there was no God. But certainly he is traduced; for his words are noble and divine: *Non deos vulgi negare profanum, sed vulgi opiniones diis applicare profanum.*[88] Plato could have said no more. And although he had the confidence to deny the administration, he had not the power to deny the nature. The Indians of the West have names for their particular gods, though they have no name for God: as if the heathens should have had the names Jupiter, Apollo, Mars, etc., but not the word *Deus*: which shows that even those barbarous people have the notion, though they have not the latitude and extent of it. So that against atheists the very savages take part with the very subtlest philosophers. The contemplative atheist is rare; a Diagoras, a Bion, a Lucian [89] perhaps, and some others; and yet they seem to be more than they are; for that all that impugn a received religion, or superstition, are, by the adverse part, branded with the name of atheists. But the great atheists indeed are hypocrites; which

79. *Atque ... paterentur:* "And such was their frame of mind, that a few ventured on the worst villainy, more wished to do so, and all endured it [or tolerated it]."   80. **Legend:** probably *The Golden Legend* of Jacobus de Voragine (containing the story of St. George and the Dragon, etc.).   81. **Talmud:** the book of Jewish traditions and Rabbinical glosses on the Law.   82. **Alcoran:** the Koran, the sacred book of Islam.   83. **It ... religion:** Cf. Pope: "A little learning is a dangerous thing," etc. (See below, *Essay on Criticism*, ll. 215 ff.).   84. **second causes:** physical or natural causes (God being the "first cause"). Cf. *Advancement*, I. i. 2, and n. 6.   85. **Leucippus ... Epicurus:** the three ancient Greek "atomists," who taught that the world was formed from the motions of atoms in a void. Cf. *Advancement*, II. vii. 7, and n. 46.   86. **fifth essence:** quintessence, or spirit residing in all things in addition to the four elements (earth, water, air, fire). Bacon means that this alternative theory fits in better with atheism than that of the atomists. Cf. Donne's "Nocturnal upon St. Lucy's Day," l. 12–18n. and l. 29n.

87. **for ... maketh:** to whose interest it would be.   88. *Non ... profanum:* "It is not profane to deny the gods of the common people; what is profane is to apply the popular notions to the gods."   89. **Diagoras ... Lucian:** Diagoras of Melos, "the Atheist" (fifth century B.C.); Bion, a philosopher of the Cyrenaic School (third century B.C.); Lucian Greek satirist and wit (second century A.D.).

are ever handling holy things, but without feeling; so as they must needs be cauterized in the end. The causes of atheism are: divisions in religion, if they be many; for any one main division addeth zeal to both sides, but many divisions introduce atheism. Another is, scandal of priests; when it is come to that which St. Bernard saith: *Non est jam dicere, ut populus, sic sacerdos; quia nec sic populus, ut sacerdos.*[90] A third is, custom of profane scoffing in holy matters, which doth by little and little deface the reverence of religion. And lastly, learned times, especially with peace and prosperity; for troubles and adversities do more bow men's minds to religion. They that deny a God destroy man's nobility; for certainly man is of kin to the beasts by his body; and if he be not of kin to God by his spirit, he is a base and ignoble creature. It destroys likewise magnanimity, and the raising of human nature; for take an example of a dog, and mark what a generosity and courage he will put on when he finds himself maintained by a man, who to him is in stead of a god, or *melior natura;* [91] which courage is manifestly such as that creature, without that confidence of a better nature than his own, could never attain. So man, when he resteth and assureth himself upon divine protection and favor, gathereth a force and faith which human nature in itself could not obtain. Therefore, as atheism is in all respects hateful, so in this, that it depriveth human nature of the means to exalt itself above human frailty. As it is in particular persons, so it is in nations: never was there such a state for magnanimity as Rome: of this state hear what Cicero saith: *Quam volumus licet, patres conscripti, nos amemus, tamen nec numero Hispanos, nec robore Gallos, nec calliditate Poenos, nec artibus Graecos, nec denique hoc ipso hujus gentis et terrae domestico nativoque sensu Italos ipsos et Latinos; sed pietate, ac religione, atque hac una sapientia, quod Deorum immortalium numine omnia regi gubernarique perspeximus, omnes gentes nationesque superavimus.*[92]

1612

90. *Non . . . sacerdos:* "It cannot now be said 'like priest, like people,' for the people are not as bad as the priest."   91. *melior natura:* better nature.   92. *Quam . . . superavimus:* "We may admire ourselves as much as we like, conscript fathers, yet it is not in superior numbers that we have surpassed the Spaniards, nor in strength the Gauls, nor in cunning the Carthaginians, nor in arts the Greeks, nor, finally, in that native and inborn sense peculiar to this race and land, the Italians and Latins themselves; where we have excelled all nations and peoples is in devotion, in religion, and in this one wisdom — the recognition that all things are ruled and controlled by the power of the immortal gods."

ESSAY XVII
OF SUPERSTITION

It were better to have no opinion of God at all, than such an opinion as is unworthy of him: for the one is unbelief, the other is contumely: and certainly superstition is the reproach of the Deity. Plutarch saith well to that purpose: *Surely* (saith he) *I had rather a great deal men should say there was no such man at all as Plutarch, than that they should say that there was one Plutarch that would eat his children as soon as they were born;* as the poets speak of Saturn. And as the contumely is greater towards God, so the danger is greater towards men. Atheism leaves a man to sense, to philosophy, to natural piety, to laws, to reputation; all which may be guides to an outward moral virtue, though religion were not, but superstition dismounts all these, and erecteth an absolute monarchy in the minds of men. Therefore atheism did never perturb states; for it makes men wary of themselves, as looking no further: and we see the times inclined to atheism (as the time of Augustus Caesar) were civil times. But superstition hath been the confusion of many states, and bringeth in a new *primum mobile,* that ravisheth all the spheres of government. The master of superstition is the people; and in all superstition wise men follow fools; and arguments are fitted to practice, in a reversed order. It was gravely said by some of the prelates in the Council of Trent,[93] where the doctrine of the Schoolmen bare great sway, *that the Schoolmen were like astronomers, which did feign eccentrics and epicycles, and such engines of orbs, to save the phenomena,*[94] *though they knew there were no such things;* and in like manner, that the Schoolmen had framed a number of subtle and intricate axioms and theorems, to save the practice of the Church. The causes of superstition are: pleasing and sensual rites and ceremonies; excess of outward and pharisaical holiness; overgreat reverence of traditions, which cannot but load the Church; the stratagems of prelates for their own ambition and lucre; the favoring too much of good intentions, which openeth the gate to conceits and novelties; the taking an aim at divine matters by human, which

93. **Council of Trent:** 1545–63, convened to define Roman Catholic doctrine as against Protestantism.   94. *eccentrics . . . phenomena:* imaginary irregularities and secondary orbits (of the heavenly bodies) to account for astronomical facts. Cf. Donne's *Anatomy of the World,* l. 256n. An "epicycle" is a smaller circle whose center is on the circumference of a larger one.

cannot but breed mixture of imaginations; and lastly, barbarous times, especially joined with calamities and disasters. Superstition, without a veil, is a deformed thing; for, as it addeth deformity to an ape to be so like a man, so the similitude of superstition to religion makes it the more deformed. And as wholesome meat corrupteth to little worms, so good forms and orders corrupt into a number of petty observances. There is a superstition in avoiding superstition, when men think to do best if they go furthest from the superstition formerly received: therefore care would be had that (as it fareth in ill purgings) the good be not taken away with the bad; which commonly is done, when the the people is the reformer.

1612

ESSAY XVIII
OF TRAVEL

Travel, in the younger sort, is a part of education; in the elder, a part of experience. He that traveleth into a country before he hath some entrance into the language, goeth to school, and not to travel. That young men travel under some tutor, or grave servant, I allow well; so that he be such a one that hath the language and hath been in the country before; whereby he may be able to tell them what things are worthy to be seen in the country where they go; what acquaintances they are to seek; what exercises or discipline the place yieldeth. For else young men shall go hooded, and look abroad little. It is a strange thing that in sea voyages, where there is nothing to be seen but sky and sea, men should make diaries, but in land travel, wherein so much is to be observed, for the most part they omit it; as if chance were fitter to be registered than observation. Let diaries, therefore, be brought in use. The things to be seen and observed are: the courts of princes, specially when they give audience to ambassadors; the courts of justice, while they sit and hear causes, and so of consistories ecclesiastic; [95] the churches and monasteries, with the monuments which are therein extant; the walls and fortifications of cities and towns, and so the havens and harbors; antiquities and ruins; libraries; colleges, disputations, and

lectures, where any are; shipping and navies; houses and gardens of state and pleasure, near great cities; armories; arsenals; magazines; exchanges; burses; warehouses; exercises of horsemanship, fencing, training of soldiers, and the like; comedies, such whereunto the better sort of persons do resort, treasuries of jewels and robes; cabinets and rarities; and, to conclude, whatsoever is memorable in the places where they go. After all which the tutors or servants ought to make diligent inquiry. As for triumphs, [96] masques, feasts, weddings, funerals, capital executions, and such shows, men need not to be put in mind of them; yet are they not to be neglected. If you will have a young man to put his travel into a little room, and in short time to gather much, this you must do. First, as was said, he must have some entrance into the language, before he goeth. Then he must have such a servant, or tutor, as knoweth the country, as was likewise said. Let him carry with him also some card or book describing the country where he traveleth; which will be a good key to his inquiry. Let him keep also a diary. Let him not stay long in one city or town; more or less as the place deserveth, but not long: nay, when he stayeth in one city or town, let him change his lodging from one end and part of the town to another; which is a great adamant [97] of acquaintance. Let him sequester himself from the company of his countrymen, and diet in such places where there is good company of the nation where he traveleth. Let him, upon his removes from one place to another, procure recommendation to some person of quality residing in the place whither he removeth; that he may use his favor in those things he desireth to see or know. Thus he may abridge his travel with much profit. As for the acquaintance which is to be sought in travel, that which is most of all profitable is acquaintance with the secretaries and employed men of ambassadors; for so in traveling in one country he shall suck the experience of many. Let him also see and visit eminent persons in all kinds, which are of great name abroad; that he may be able to tell how the life agreeth with the fame. For quarrels, they are with care and discretion to be avoided: they are commonly for mistresses, healths, [98] place, and words. And let a man beware how he keepeth company with choleric and quarrelsome persons; for they will engage him into their own quarrels. When a traveler returneth home, let

95. **consistories ecclesiastic:** church convocations and courts.

96. **triumphs:** processions, pageants.   97. **adamant:** literally "loadstone"; hence, means of attracting.   98. **healths:** i.e., drinking toasts.

him not leave the countries where he hath traveled altogether behind him, but maintain a correspondence by letters with those of his acquaintance which are of most worth. And let his travel appear rather in his discourse than in his apparel or gesture; and in his discourse, let him be rather advised [99] in his answers than forwards to tell stories; and let it appear that he doth not change his country manners [1] for those of foreign parts, but only prick in some flowers of that he hath learned abroad into the customs of his own country.

1625

ESSAY XXII
OF CUNNING

We take cunning for a sinister or crooked wisdom. And certainly there is a great difference between a cunning man and a wise man; not only in point of honesty, but in point of ability. There be that can pack the cards, and yet cannot play well; so there are some that are good in canvasses and factions, that are otherwise weak men. Again, it is one thing to understand persons, and another thing to understand matters; for many are perfect in men's humors, that are not greatly capable of the real part of business; which is the constitution of one that hath studied men more than books. Such men are fitter for practice than for counsel; and they are good but in their own alley: turn them to new men, and they have lost their aim; so as the old rule to know a fool from a wise man, *Mitte ambos nudos ad ignotos et videbis,*[2] doth scarce hold for them. And because these cunning men are like haberdashers of small wares, it is not amiss to set forth their shop.

It is a point of cunning, to wait upon him with whom you speak, with your eye, as the Jesuits give it in precept; for there be many wise men that have secret hearts and transparent countenances. Yet this would be done with a demure abasing of your eye sometimes, as the Jesuits also do use.

Another is, that when you have anything to obtain of present dispatch, you entertain and amuse the party with whom you deal with some other discourse, that he be not too much awake to make objections. I knew a counselor and secretary, that never came to Queen Elizabeth of England with bills to sign, but he would always first put her into some discourse of estate, that she might the less mind the bills.

The like surprise may be made by moving things [3] when the party is in haste, and cannot stay to consider advisedly of that is moved.

If a man would cross a business that he doubts some other would handsomely and effectually move, let him pretend to wish it well, and move it himself in such sort as may foil it.

The breaking off in the midst of that one was about to say, as if he took himself up, breeds a greater appetite in him with whom you confer to know more.

And because it works better when anything seemeth to be gotten from you by question, than if you offer it of yourself, you may lay a bait for a question, by showing another visage and countenance than you are wont; to the end to give occasion for the party to ask what the matter is of the change? As Nehemias did: " And I had not before that time been sad before the king."

In things that are tender and unpleasing, it is good to break the ice by some whose words are of less weight, and to reserve the more weighty voice to come in as by chance, so that he may be asked the question upon the other's speech. As Narcissus did, in relating to Claudius the marriage of Messalina and Silius.

In things that a man would not be seen in himself, it is a point of cunning to borrow the name of the world; as to say, *The world says,* or, *There is a speech abroad.*

I knew one that, when he wrote a letter, he would put that which was most material in the postscript, as if it had been a by-matter.

I knew another that, when he came to have speech, he would pass over that that he intended most, and go forth, and come back again, and speak of it as of a thing that he had almost forgot.

Some procure themselves to be surprised at such times as it is like the party that they work upon will suddenly come upon them, and to be found with a letter in their hand, or doing somewhat which they are not accustomed; to the end they may be apposed of [4] those things which of themselves they are desirous to utter.

---

99. advised: well informed.   1. his . . . manners: the manners of his own country.   2. *Mitte . . . videbis:* "Send both naked amongst strangers, and you will see."

3. moving things: bringing up matters for discussion.   4. apposed of: questioned about.

It is a point of cunning, to let fall those words in a man's own name, which he would have another man learn and use, and thereupon take advantage. I knew two that were competitors for the secretary's place in Queen Elizabeth's time, and yet kept good quarter between themselves, and would confer one with another upon the business; and the one of them said, That to be a secretary in the *declination of a monarchy* was a ticklish thing, and that he did not affect it:[5] the other straight caught up those words, and discoursed with divers of his friends, that he had no reason to desire to be secretary in the *declination of a monarchy*. The first man took hold of it, and found means it was told the Queen; who, hearing of a *declination of a monarchy,* took it so ill, as she would never after hear of the other's suit.

There is a cunning, which we in England call *the turning of the cat in the pan;* which is, when that which a man says to another, he lays[6] it as if another had said it to him. And to say truth, it is not easy, when such a matter passed between two, to make it appear from which of them it first moved and began.

It is a way that some men have, to glance and dart at others by justifying themselves by negatives; as to say, *This I do not:* as Tigellinus did towards Burrhus; *Se non diversas spes, sed incolumitatem imperatoris simpliciter spectare.*[7]

Some have in readiness so many tales and stories, as there is nothing they would insinuate, but they can wrap it into a tale; which serveth both to keep themselves more in guard, and to make others carry it with more pleasure.

It is a good point of cunning, for a man to shape the answer he would have in his own words and propositions; for it makes the other party stick the less.

It is strange how long some men will lie in wait to speak somewhat they desire to say, and how far about they will fetch,[8] and how many other matters they will beat over, to come near it. It is a thing of great patience, but yet of much use.

A sudden, bold, and unexpected question doth many times surprise a man, and lay him open. Like to him, that having changed his name, and walking in Paul's,[9] another suddenly came behind him and called him by his true name, whereat straightways he looked back.

But these small wares and petty points of cunning are infinite; and it were a good deed to make a list of them; for that nothing doth more hurt in a state than that cunning men pass for wise.

But certainly some there are that know the resorts and falls[10] of business, that cannot sink into the main of it; like a house that hath convenient stairs and entries, but never a fair room. Therefore you shall see them find out pretty looses[11] in the conclusion, but are no ways able to examine or debate matters. And yet commonly they take advantage of their inability, and would be thought wits of direction. Some build rather upon the abusing of others, and (as we now say) *putting tricks upon them,* than upon soundness of their own proceedings. But Salomon saith: *Prudens advertit ad gressus suos: stultus divertit ad dolos.*[12]

1612

ESSAY XXIII
OF WISDOM FOR A MAN'S SELF

An ant is a wise creature for itself, but it is a shrewd[13] thing in an orchard or garden. And certainly men that are great lovers of themselves waste the public. Divide with reason between self-love and society; and be so true to thyself, as thou be not false to others, specially to thy king and country. It is a poor center of a man's actions, himself. It is right earth. For that only stands fast upon his own center; whereas all things that have affinity with the heavens move upon the center of another, which they benefit.[14] The referring of all to a man's self is more tolerable in a sovereign prince; because themselves are not only themselves, but their good and evil is at the peril of the public fortune. But it is a desperate evil in a servant to a prince, or a citizen in a republic. For whatsoever affairs pass such a man's hands, he crooketh them to his own ends; which must needs be often eccentric to[15] the ends of his master or state. Therefore let princes, or states, choose such servants as have not this mark; except they mean their service

---

5. affect it: care for, or favor it.   6. lays: represents.   7. *Se . . . spectare:* "That he did not entertain a variety of hopes [hinting that Burrhus did], but simply considered the safety of the emperor" (Tacitus).   8. how . . . fetch: what roundabout ways they will use.   9. Paul's: St. Paul's Cathedral in London.

10. resorts . . . falls: expedients and chances.   11. looses: weak points.   12. *Prudens . . . dolos:* "The wise man looks to his own footsteps: the fool turns aside into deceits [snares]" (Prov. 14:15).   13. shrewd: mischievous.   14. For . . . benefit: Bacon writes here as a believer in the pre-Copernican system (geocentric).   15. eccentric to: having a different center, hence divergent from.

should be made but the accessory. That which maketh the effect more pernicious is that all proportion is lost. It were disproportion enough for the servant's good to be preferred before the master's; but yet it is a greater extreme, when a little good of the servant shall carry things against a great good of the master's. And yet that is the case of bad officers, treasurers, ambassadors, generals, and other false and corrupt servants; which set a bias upon their bowl, of their own petty ends and envies, to the overthrow of their master's great and important affairs. And for the most part, the good such servants receive is after the model of their own fortune; but the hurt they sell for that good is after the model of their master's fortune. And certainly it is the nature of extreme self-lovers, as they will set an house on fire, and it were but to roast their eggs; and yet these men many times hold credit with their masters, because their study is but to please them and profit themselves; and for either respect they will abandon the good of their affairs.

Wisdom for a man's self is, in many branches thereof, a depraved thing. It is the wisdom of rats, that will be sure to leave a house somewhat before it fall. It is the wisdom of the fox, that thrusts out the badger, who digged and made room for him. It is the wisdom of crocodiles, that shed tears when they would devour. But that which is specially to be noted is, that those which (as Cicero says of Pompey) are *sui amantes sine rivali*,[16] are many times unfortunate. And whereas they have all their time sacrificed to themselves, they become in the end themselves sacrifices to the inconstancy of fortune, whose wings they thought by their self-wisdom to have pinioned.

1612

ESSAY XXXI

OF SUSPICION

Suspicions amongst thoughts are like bats amongst birds, they ever fly by twilight. Certainly they are to be repressed, or at the least well guarded: for they cloud the mind; they lose friends; and they check[17] with business, whereby business cannot go on currently and constantly. They dispose kings to tyranny, husbands to jealousy, wise men to irresolution and melancholy. They are defects, not

in the heart, but in the brain; for they take place in the stoutest natures: as in the example of Henry the Seventh of England: there was not a more suspicious man, nor a more stout. And in such a composition they do small hurt. For commonly they are not admitted but with examination, whether they be likely or no? But in fearful natures they gain ground too fast. There is nothing makes a man suspect much, more than to know little; and therefore men should remedy suspicion by procuring to know more, and not to keep their suspicions in smother. What would men have? Do they think those they employ and deal with are saints? Do they not think they will have their own ends, and be truer to themselves than to them? Therefore there is no better way to moderate suspicions, than to account upon such suspicions as true, and yet to bridle them as false. For so far a man ought to make use of suspicions, as to provide as, if that should be true that he suspects, yet it may do him no hurt. Suspicions, that the mind of itself gathers, are but buzzes;[18] but suspicions, that are artificially nourished and put into men's heads by the tales and whisperings of others, have stings. Certainly, the best mean to clear the way in this same wood of suspicions, is frankly to communicate them with the party that he suspects: for thereby he shall be sure to know more of the truth of them than he did before; and withal shall make that party more circumspect not to give further cause of suspicion. But this would not be done to men of base natures; for they, if they find themselves once suspected, will never be true. The Italian says, *Sospetto licentia fede;*[19] as if suspicion did give a passport to faith: but it ought rather to kindle it to discharge itself.

1625

ESSAY XXXII

OF DISCOURSE

Some in their discourse desire rather commendation of wit, in being able to hold all arguments, than of judgment, in discerning what is true; as if it were a praise to know what might be said, and not what should be thought. Some have certain commonplaces and themes wherein they are good, and want variety; which kind of poverty is for the

---

16. *sui . . . rivali:* "lovers of themselves without a rival."
17. check: interfere.

18. buzzes: buzzing beetles, without any sting.   19. *Sospetto . . . fede:* "Suspicion is the passport to faith."

most part tedious, and, when it is once perceived, ridiculous. The honorablest part of talk is to give the occasion; [20] and again to moderate and pass to somewhat else; for then a man leads the dance. It is good, in discourse, and speech of conversation, to vary and intermingle speech of the present occasion with arguments; tales with reasons; asking of questions with telling of opinions; and jest with earnest: for it is a dull thing to tire, and, as we say now, to jade anything too far. As for jest, there be certain things which ought to be privileged from it; namely, religion, matters of state, great persons, any man's present business of importance, and any case that deserveth pity. Yet there be some that think their wits have been asleep, except they dart out somewhat that is piquant and to the quick: that is a vein which would be bridled:

Parce, puer, stimulis, et fortius utere loris.[21]

And generally, men ought to find the difference between saltness and bitterness. Certainly, he that hath a satirical vein, as he maketh others afraid of his wit, so he had need be afraid of others' memory. He that questioneth much, shall learn much, and content much; but especially if he apply his questions to the skill of the persons whom he asketh: for he shall give them occasion to please themselves in speaking, and himself shall continually gather knowledge. But let his questions not be troublesome; for that is fit for a poser. And let him be sure to leave other men their turns to speak. Nay, if there be any that would reign and take up all the time, let him find means to take them off and to bring others on; as musicians use to do with those that dance too long galliards. If you dissemble sometimes your knowledge of that you are thought to know, you shall be thought another time to know that you know not. Speech of a man's self ought to be seldom, and well chosen. I knew one was wont to say in scorn, *He must needs be a wise man, he speaks so much of himself:* and there is but one case wherein a man may commend himself with good grace, and that is in commending virtue in another, especially if it be such a virtue whereunto himself pretendeth. Speech of touch [22] towards others should be sparingly used; for discourse ought to be as a field,[23] without coming home to any man.

I knew two noblemen, of the west part of England, whereof the one was given to scoff, but kept ever royal cheer in his house: the other would ask of those that had been at the other's table, *Tell truly, was there never a flout or dry blow* [24] *given?* to which the guest would answer, *Such and such a thing passed:* the lord would say, *I thought he would mar a good dinner.* Discretion of speech is more than eloquence; and to speak agreeably to him with whom we deal, is more than to speak in good words or in good order. A good continued speech,[25] without a good speech of interlocution, shows slowness; and a good reply or second speech, without a good settled speech, showeth shallowness and weakness. As we see in beasts, that those that are weakest in the course, are yet nimblest in the turn; as it is betwixt the greyhound and the hare. To use too many circumstances, ere one come to the matter, is wearisome; to use none at all, is blunt.

1597

ESSAY XXXIII
OF PLANTATIONS

" Plantation " means a settlement or colony in a new country. Bacon was personally interested in colonization, and after the failure of Sir Walter Ralegh's Virginian colony he was one of the new " adventurers " (along with his cousin the Earl of Salisbury, Captain John Smith, and others) in the London or South Virginia Company — chartered by King James I in 1606.

Plantations are amongst ancient, primitive, and heroical works. When the world was young, it begat more children; but now it is old, it begets fewer: for I may justly account new plantations to be the children of former kingdoms. I like a plantation in a pure soil; that is, where people are not displanted to the end to plant in others. For else it is rather an extirpation than a plantation. Planting of countries is like planting of woods; for you must make account to lose almost twenty years' profit, and expect your recompense in the end. For the principal thing that hath been the destruction of most plantations, hath been the base and hasty drawing of profit in the first years. It is true, speedy profit is not to be neglected, as far as may stand with the good of

---

20. give . . . occasion: start the subject.   21. *Parce . . . loris:* "Boy, spare the whip, and tightlier hold the reins" (Ovid, *Metamorphoses,* II. 127).   22. of touch: personal references which might give offense.   23. be . . . field: i.e., deal with general topics only.

24. *flout . . . blow:* an insult or sarcastic hit.   25. speech: It should be remembered that Bacon is using "speech" to mean "habit or way of speaking."

the plantation, but no further. It is a shameful and unblessed thing to take the scum of people, and wicked condemned men, to be the people with whom you plant: and not only so, but it spoileth the plantation; for they will ever live like rogues, and not fall to work, but be lazy, and do mischief, and spend victuals, and be quickly weary, and then certify [26] over to their country to the discredit of the plantation. The people wherewith you plant ought to be gardeners, plowmen, laborers, smiths, carpenters, joiners, fishermen, fowlers, with some few apothecaries, surgeons, cooks, and bakers. In a country of plantation, first look about, what kind of victual the country yields of itself to hand; as chestnuts, walnuts, pineapples, olives, dates, plums, cherries, wild honey, and the like; and make use of them. Then consider what victual or esculent things there are, which grow speedily, and within the year; as parsnips, carrots, turnips, onions, radish, artichokes of Jerusalem, maize, and the like. For wheat, barley, and oats, they ask too much labor; but with peas and beans you may begin, both because they ask less labor, and because they serve for meat as well as for bread. And of rice likewise cometh a great increase, and it is a kind of meat. Above all, there ought to be brought store of biscuit, oatmeal, flour, meal, and the like, in the beginning, till bread may be had. For beasts or birds, take chiefly such as are least subject to diseases, and multiply fastest; as swine, goats, cocks, hens, turkeys, geese, house doves, and the like. The victual in plantations ought to be expended almost as in a besieged town; that is, with certain allowance. And let the main part of the ground employed to gardens or corn be to a common stock; and to be laid in, and stored up, and then delivered out in proportion; besides some spots of ground that any particular person will manure for his own private. Consider likewise what commodities the soil where the plantation is doth naturally yield, that they may some way help to defray the charge of the plantation: so it be not, as was said, to the untimely prejudice of the main business; as it hath fared with tobacco in Virginia. Wood commonly aboundeth but too much; and therefore timber is fit to be one. If there be iron ore, and streams whereupon to set the mills, iron is a brave commodity where wood aboundeth. Making of bay salt,[27] if the climate be proper for it, would be put in experience. Growing silk likewise, if any be, is a likely commodity. Pitch and tar, where store of firs and pines are, will not fail. So drugs and sweet woods, where they are, cannot but yield great profit. Soap ashes likewise, and other things that may be thought of. But moil not too much under ground; for the hope of mines is very uncertain, and useth to make the planters lazy in other things. For government, let it be in the hands of one, assisted with some counsel; and let them have commission to exercise martial laws, with some limitation. And above all, let men make that profit of being in the wilderness, as they have God always, and his service, before their eyes. Let not the government of the plantation depend upon too many counselors and undertakers in the country that planteth, but upon a temperate number: and let those be rather noblemen and gentlemen, than merchants; for they look ever to the present gain. Let there be freedom from custom, till the plantation be of strength; and not only freedom from custom, but freedom to carry their commodities where they may make their best of them, except there be some special cause of caution. Cram not in people, by sending too fast company after company; but rather harken how they waste, and send supplies proportionably; but so as the number may live well in the plantation, and not by surcharge be in penury. It hath been a great endangering to the health of some plantations, that they have built along the sea and rivers, in marish [28] and unwholesome grounds. Therefore, though you begin there, to avoid carriage and other like discommodities, yet build still rather upwards from the streams than along. It concerneth likewise the health of the plantation that they have good store of salt with them, that they may use it in their victuals when it shall be necessary. If you plant where savages are, do not only entertain them with trifles and jingles; but use them justly and graciously, with sufficient guard nevertheless: and do not win their favor by helping them to invade their enemies, but for their defense it is not amiss. And send oft of them over to the country that plants, that they may see a better condition than their own, and commend it when they return. When the plantation grows to strength, then it is time to plant with women as well as with men; that the plantation may spread into generations, and not be ever pieced from without. It is the sin-

---

26. certify: testify, or send messages. **27. bay salt:** salt from evaporation of sea water.

28. marish: marshy.

fullest thing in the world to forsake or destitute a plantation once in forwardness: for besides the dishonor, it is the guiltiness of blood of many commiserable persons.

1625

ESSAY XXXVII
OF MASQUES AND TRIUMPHS

"Masques" were a popular form of entertainment at court and at noblemen's houses in Elizabethan and Jacobean times. They consisted mainly of dancing and acting in dumb show by performers who were masked and clad in elaborate costumes, often of an allegorical kind. In some of the later masques dialogue and music were added. "Triumphs" were solemn processions or pageants.

These things are but toys, to come amongst such serious observations. But yet, since princes will have such things, it is better they should be graced with elegancy, than daubed[29] with cost. Dancing to song is a thing of great state and pleasure. I understand it, that the song be in quire, placed aloft, and accompanied with some broken music;[30] and the ditty fitted to the device. Acting in song, especially in dialogues, hath an extreme good grace: I say acting, not dancing (for that is a mean and vulgar thing); and the voices of the dialogue would be strong and manly (a bass and a tenor, no treble); and the ditty high and tragical, not nice or dainty. Several quires, placed one over against another, and taking the voice by catches,[31] anthem-wise, give great pleasure. Turning dances into figure[32] is a childish curiosity. And generally, let it be noted, that those things which I here set down are such as do naturally take the sense, and not respect petty wonderments.[33] It is true, the alterations of scenes, so it be quietly and without noise, are things of great beauty and pleasure; for they feed and relieve the eye, before it be full of the same object. Let the scenes abound with light, specially colored and varied; and let the masquers, or any other, that are to come down from the scene, have some motions upon the scene itself before their coming down; for it draws the eye strangely, and makes it with great

pleasure to desire to see that it cannot perfectly discern. Let the songs be loud and cheerful, and not chirpings or pulings. Let the music likewise be sharp and loud and well placed. The colors that show best by candlelight are white, carnation, and a kind of sea-water green; and oes, or spangs,[34] as they are of no great cost, so they are of most glory. As for rich embroidery, it is lost and not discerned. Let the suits of the masquers be graceful, and such as become the person when the vizards are off: not after examples of known attires, Turks, soldiers, mariners, and the like. Let antimasques not be long; they have been commonly of fools, satyrs, baboons, wild men, antics,[35] beasts, sprites, witches, Ethiopes, pygmies, turquets,[36] nymphs, rustics, cupids, statues moving, and the like. As for angels, it is not comical enough to put them in antimasques; and anything that is hideous, as devils, giants, is on the other side as unfit. But chiefly, let the music of them be recreative, and with some strange changes. Some sweet odors, suddenly coming forth, without any drops falling, are, in such a company as there is steam and heat, things of great pleasure and refreshment. Double masques, one of men, another of ladies, addeth state and variety. But all is nothing, except the room be kept clear and neat.

For jousts, and tourneys, and barriers, the glories of them are chiefly in the chariots, wherein the challengers make their entry; especially if they be drawn with strange beasts, as lions, bears, camels, and the like; or in the devices[37] of their entrance; or in the bravery of their liveries; or in the goodly furniture of their horses and armor. But enough of these toys.

1625

ESSAY XLV
OF BUILDING

Houses are built to live in, and not to look on; therefore let use be preferred before uniformity, except where both may be had. Leave the goodly fabrics of houses, for beauty only, to the enchanted palaces of the poets, who build them with small cost. He that builds a fair house upon an ill seat, committeth himself to prison. Neither do I reckon it an ill seat only where the air is unwholesome,

---

29. **daubed:** bungled, clumsily handled.   30. **broken music:** music played by an ensemble ("consort") in which the instruments were of different kinds.   31. **catches:** rounds; part songs in which each singer enters successively, catching the tune from the previous singer.   32. **figure:** patterns of dancers (as in the more modern "lancers").   33. **take . . . wonderments:** things naturally pleasing to eye and ear, not crudely surprising effects.

34. **oes, or spangs:** glittering circles or spangles.   35. **antics:** clowns, grotesque figures.   36. **turquets:** players dressed up like Turks.   37. **devices:** heraldic emblems.

but likewise where the air is unequal; as you shall see many fine seats set upon a knap [38] of ground, environed with higher hills round about it; whereby the heat of the sun is pent in, and the wind gathereth as in troughs; so as you shall have, and that suddenly, as great diversity of heat and cold as if you dwelt in several places. Neither is it ill air only that maketh an ill seat, but ill ways, ill markets, and, if you will consult with Momus,[39] ill neighbors. I speak not of many more: want of water; want of wood, shade, and shelter; want of fruitfulness, and mixture of grounds of several natures; want of prospect; want of level grounds; want of places, at some near distance, for sports of hunting, hawking, and races; too near the sea, too remote; having the commodity of navigable rivers, or the discommodity of their overflowing; too far off from great cities, which may hinder business; or too near them, which lurcheth [40] all provisions, and maketh everything dear; where a man hath a great living laid together, and where he is scanted: all which as it is impossible perhaps to find together, so it is good to know them and think of them, that a man may take as many as he can; and if he have several dwellings, that he sort them so, that what he wanteth in the one he may find in the other. Lucullus answered Pompey well; who, when he saw his stately galleries and rooms so large and lightsome, in one of his houses, said: *Surely an excellent place for summer, but how do you in winter?* Lucullus answered: *Why, do you not think me as wise as some fowl are, that ever change their abode towards the winter?*

To pass from the seat to the house itself; we will do as Cicero doth in the orator's art, who writes books *De Oratore,* and a book he entitles *Orator;* whereof the former delivers the precepts of the art, and the latter the perfection. We will therefore describe a princely palace, making a brief model thereof. For it is strange to see, now in Europe, such huge buildings as the Vatican and Escorial and some others be, and yet scarce a very fair room in them.

First, therefore, I say, you cannot have a perfect palace, except you have two several sides; a side for the banquet, as is spoken of in the book of Esther, and a side for the household; the one for feasts and

triumphs, and the other for dwelling. I understand both these sides to be not only returns,[41] but parts of the front; and to be uniform without, though severally partitioned within; and to be on both sides of a great and stately tower in the midst of the front, that, as it were, joineth them together on either hand. I would have on the side of the banquet, in front, one only goodly room abovestairs, of some forty foot high; and under it, a room for a dressing or preparing place at times of triumphs. On the other side, which is the household side, I wish it divided at the first into a hall and a chapel (with a partition between), both of good state and bigness; and those not to go all the length, but to have at the further end a winter and a summer parlor, both fair. And under these rooms, a fair and large cellar, sunk underground; and likewise some privy kitchens, with butteries and pantries, and the like. As for the tower, I would have it two stories, of eighteen foot high apiece, above the two wings; and a goodly leads upon the top, railed with statues interposed; and the same tower to be divided into rooms, as shall be thought fit. The stairs likewise to the upper rooms, let them be upon a fair open newel,[42] and finely railed in with images of wood cast into a brass color; and a very fair landing place at the top. But this to be, if you do not point [43] any of the lower rooms for a dining place of servants. For otherwise you shall have the servants' dinner after your own: for the steam of it will come up as in a tunnel. And so much for the front. Only, I understand the height of the first stairs to be sixteen foot, which is the height of the lower room.

Beyond this front is there to be a fair court, but three sides of it of a far lower building than the front. And in all the four corners of that court, fair staircases, cast into turrets on the outside, and not within the row of buildings themselves. But those towers are not to be of the height of the front, but rather proportionable to the lower building. Let the court not be paved, for that striketh up a great heat in summer, and much cold in winter. But only some side alleys, with a cross, and the quarters to graze,[44] being kept shorn, but not too near shorn. The row of return, on the banquet side, let it be all stately galleries; in which galleries let there be three, or five, fine cupolas in the length of it, placed at equal distance; and fine colored windows of sev-

---

38. knap: knoll.   **39. Momus:** the god of mockery and fault-finding. Bacon has in mind Aesop's fable in which Momus criticizes Athena's house for having no wheels on which it could be rolled away from undesirable neighbors.   **40. lurcheth:** steals away.

41. returns: side wings; parts "returning" at right angles from the front portion.   **42. newel:** center pillar (or well) of a winding stair.   **43. point:** appoint, assign.   **44. to graze:** i.e., be turfed.

eral works. On the household side, chambers of presence [45] and ordinary entertainments, with some bedchambers; and let all three sides be a double house, without through lights on the sides, that you may have rooms from the sun, both for forenoon and afternoon. Cast it also that you may have rooms both for summer and winter; shady for summer, and warm for winter. You shall have sometimes fair houses so full of glass, that one cannot tell where to become to be out of the sun or cold. For inbowed [46] windows, I hold them of good use; (in cities, indeed, upright do better, in respect of the uniformity towards the street); for they be pretty retiring places for conference; and besides, they keep both the wind and sun off; for that which would strike almost through the room, doth scarce pass the window. But let them be but few, four in the court, on the sides only.

Beyond this court, let there be an inward court, of the same square and height; which is to be environed with the garden on all sides; and in the inside, cloistered on all sides, upon decent and beautiful arches, as high as the first story. On the under story, towards the garden, let it be turned to a grotto, or place of shade or estivation; [47] and only have opening and windows towards the garden; and be level upon the floor, no whit sunk underground, to avoid all dampishness. And let there be a fountain, or some fair work of statues, in the midst of this court; and to be paved as the other court was. These buildings to be for privy lodgings on both sides; and the end, for privy galleries. Whereof you must foresee that one of them be for an infirmary, if the prince or any special person should be sick, with chambers, bedchamber, antecamera,[48] and recamera,[49] joining to it. This upon the second story. Upon the ground story, a fair gallery, open, upon pillars; and upon the third story likewise, an open gallery upon pillars, to take the prospect and freshness of the garden. At both corners of the further side, by way of return, let there be two delicate or rich cabinets, daintily paved, richly hanged, glazed with crystalline glass, and a rich cupola in the midst; and all other elegancy that may be thought upon. In the upper gallery too, I wish that there may be, if the place will yield it, some fountains running in divers places from the wall, with some fine avoidances.[50] And thus much

for the model of the palace; save that you must have, before you come to the front, three courts. A green court plain, with a wall about it: a second court of the same, but more garnished, with little turrets, or rather embellishments, upon the wall: and a third court, to make a square with the front, but not to be built, nor yet enclosed with a naked wall, but enclosed with terraces leaded aloft, and fairly garnished, on the three sides; and cloistered on the inside, with pillars, and not with arches below. As for offices, let them stand at distance, with some low galleries, to pass from them to the palace itself.

1625

ESSAY L
OF STUDIES

Studies serve for delight, for ornament, and for ability. Their chief use for delight is in privateness and retiring; for ornament, is in discourse; and for ability, is in the judgment and disposition of business. For expert men can execute, and perhaps judge of particulars, one by one; but the general counsels, and the plots and marshaling of affairs, come best from those that are learned. To spend too much time in studies is sloth; to use them too much for ornament is affectation; to make judgment wholly by their rules is the humor of a scholar. They perfect nature, and are perfected by experience; for natural abilities are like natural plants, that need pruning by study; and studies themselves do give forth directions too much at large, except they be bounded in by experience. Crafty men contemn [51] studies; simple men admire [52] them; and wise men use them: for they teach not their own use; but that is a wisdom without them and above them, won by observation. Read not to contradict and confute; nor to believe and take for granted; nor to find talk and discourse; but to weigh and consider. Some books are to be tasted, others to be swallowed, and some few to be chewed and digested: that is, some books are to be read only in parts; others to be read, but not curiously; and some few to be read wholly, and with diligence and attention. Some books also may be read by deputy, and extracts made of them by others; but that would be only in the less important arguments, and the

45. chambers of presence: reception rooms.   46. inbowed: bow or bay windows.   47. estivation: spending the summer. 48. antecamera: anteroom.   49. recamera: withdrawing room. 50. avoidances: pipes or water channels.

51. contemn: despise.   52. admire: wonder at (with open mouths).

meaner sort of books; else distilled books are like common distilled waters, flashy[53] things. Reading maketh a full man; conference a ready man; and writing an exact man. And therefore, if a man write little, he had need have a great memory; if he confer little, he had need have a present wit; and if he read little, he had need have much cunning, to seem to know that he doth not. Histories make men wise; poets witty;[54] the mathematics subtle; natural philosophy deep; moral grave; logic and rhetoric able to contend. *Abeunt studia in mores.*[55] Nay, there is no stond[56] or impediment in the wit, but may be wrought out by fit studies: like as diseases of the body may have appropriate exercises. Bowling is good for the stone and reins;[57] shooting for the lungs and breast; gentle walking for the stomach; riding for the head; and the like. So if a man's wit be wandering, let him study the mathematics; for in demonstrations, if his wit be called away never so little, he must begin again: if his wit be not apt to distinguish or find differences, let him study the Schoolmen; for they are *cymini sectores:*[58] if he be not apt to beat over matters, and to call one thing to prove and illustrate another, let him study the lawyers' cases: so every defect of the mind may have a special receipt.[59]

1597

OF STUDIES (1597)

Here follows the essay " Of Studies " as it appeared in the 1597 volume. The original spelling and paragraphing are retained.

¶ Studies serue for pastimes, for ornaments & for abilities. The chiefe vse for pastime is in priuatenes and retiring; for ornamente is in discourse, and for abilitie is in iudgement. For expert men can execute, but learned men are fittest to iudge or censure.
¶ To spend too much time in them is slouth, to vse them too much for ornament is affectation: to make iudgement wholly by their rules, is the humour of a Scholler.
¶ They perfect *Nature,* and are perfected by experience.
¶ Craftie men contemne them, simple men admire them, wise men vse them: For they teach not their owne vse, but that is a wisedome without them: and aboue them wonne by obseruation.
¶ Reade not to contradict, nor to belieue, but to waigh and consider.
¶ Some bookes are to bee tasted, others to bee swallowed, and some few to bee chewed and disgested: That is, some bookes are to be read only in partes; others to be read, but cursorily, and some few to be read wholly and with diligence and attention.
¶ Reading maketh a full man, conference a readye man, and writing an exacte man. And therefore if a man write little, he had neede haue a great memorie, if he conferre little, he had neede haue a present wit, and if he reade little, he had neede haue much cunning, to seeme to know that he doth not.
¶ Histories make men wise, Poets wittie: the Mathematickes subtle, naturall Phylosophie deepe: Morall graue, Logicke and Rhetoricke able to contend.

THE ADVANCEMENT OF LEARNING

In this work, published in 1605, Bacon made (as it were) his first sketch map of the intellectual world, noting which territories had already been charted, and which were still insufficiently or wholly unexplored. It was later translated into Latin and published (1623) in a much expanded form as *De Augmentis Scientiarum.*

It should be explained that the extracts given below begin after the preliminary address to the king (James I), in which Bacon explains the purpose of the book. He has just said that his treatise will have two main parts, the first dealing with the true excellence and advancement of knowledge (see note 1), and the second with its previous history and present defects.

THE

FIRST BOOK OF FRANCIS BACON

OF THE PROFICIENCE AND

ADVANCEMENT OF LEARNING

DIVINE AND HUMAN

I. 1. In the entrance to the former of these,[1] to clear the way, and as it were to make silence, to have the true testimonies concerning the dignity of learning to be better heard, without the interruption of tacit objections; I think good to deliver it

---

53. flashy: insipid.   54. witty: full of nimble fancy.   55. *Abeunt . . . mores:* "Studies influence behavior" (Ovid, *Heroides,* XV. 83).   56. stond: stoppage.   57. reins: kidneys.   58. *cymini sectores:* "hairsplitters" (literally, "dividers of cumin seed").   59. receipt: prescription (in the medical sense), remedy.

ADVANCEMENT OF LEARNING.   1. former of these: i.e., "the excellency of learning and knowledge . . . and the . . . merit and true glory in the augmentation and propagation thereof."

from the discredits and disgraces which it hath received, all from ignorance; but ignorance severally [2] disguised; appearing sometimes in the zeal and jealousy of divines; sometimes in the severity and arrogancy of politiques,[3] and sometimes in the errors and imperfections of learned men themselves.

[The true dignity of learning vindicated against those who think that knowledge caused the Fall of Man, and that it leads to pride and atheism. Natural science was not the knowledge forbidden to Adam; moreover, through nature we arrive at a knowledge of God's existence and power.]

2. I hear the former sort say, that knowledge is of those things which are to be accepted of with great limitation and caution: that the aspiring to overmuch knowledge was the original temptation and sin whereupon ensued the Fall of Man: that knowledge hath in it somewhat of the serpent, and therefore where it entereth into a man it makes him swell; *Scientia inflat:* [4] that Salomon gives a censure, " That there is no end of making books, and that much reading is weariness of the flesh "; and again in another place, " That in spacious knowledge there is much contristation,[5] and that he that increaseth knowledge increaseth anxiety ": that St. Paul gives a caveat, " That we be not spoiled through vain philosophy ": that experience demonstrates how learned men have been archheretics, how learned times have been inclined to atheism, and how the contemplation of second causes [6] doth derogate from our dependence upon God, who is the first cause.[7]

3. To discover then the ignorance and error of this opinion, and the misunderstanding in the grounds thereof, it may well appear these men do not observe or consider that it was not the pure knowledge of nature and universality,[8] a knowledge by the light whereof man did give names unto other creatures in Paradise, as they were brought before him, according unto their proprieties,[9] which gave the occasion to the Fall: but it was the proud knowledge of good and evil, with an intent in man to give law unto himself, and to depend no more upon God's commandments, which was the form of the temptation. Neither is it any quantity of knowledge, how great soever, that can make the mind of man to swell: for nothing can fill, much less extend the soul of man, but God and the contemplation of God; . . .

If then such be the capacity and receipt of the mind of man, it is manifest that there is no danger at all in the proportion or quantity of knowledge, how large soever, lest it should make it swell or outcompass itself; no, but it is merely the quality of knowledge, which, be it in quantity more or less, if it be taken without the true corrective thereof, hath in it some nature of venom or malignity, and some effects of that venom, which is ventosity [10] or swelling. This corrective spice, the mixture whereof maketh knowledge so sovereign, is charity, which the Apostle immediately addeth to the former clause: for so he saith, " Knowledge bloweth up, but charity buildeth up "; not unlike unto that which he delivereth in another place: " If I spake," saith he, " with the tongues of men and angels, and had not charity, it were but as a tinkling cymbal "; not but that it is an excellent thing to speak with the tongues of men and angels, but because, if it be severed from charity, and not referred to the good of men and mankind, it hath rather a sounding and unworthy glory, than a meriting and substantial virtue. And as for that censure of Salomon, concerning the excess of writing and reading books, and the anxiety of spirit which redoundeth from knowledge, and that admonition of St. Paul, " That we be not seduced by vain philosophy "; let those places be rightly understood, and they do indeed excellently set forth the true bounds and limitations, whereby human knowledge is confined and circumscribed; and yet without any such contracting or coarctation,[11] but that it may comprehend all the universal nature of things; for these limitations are three: the first, That we do not so place our felicity in knowledge, as we forget our mortality: the second, That we make application of our knowledge, to give ourselves repose and contentment, and not distaste or repining: the third, That we do not presume by the contemplation of nature to attain to the mysteries of God. . . .

And as for the conceit that too much knowledge should incline a man to atheism, and that the ignorance of second causes should make a more de-

---

2. severally: in various ways.   3. politiques: politicians.
4. *Scientia inflat:* "Knowledge puffs up."   5. contristation: sadness.   6. second causes: natural laws or causes.   7. first cause: Cf. essay "Of Atheism," n. 84.   8. universality: general principles.   9. proprieties: particular natures.

10. ventosity: windiness.   11. coarctation: restriction.

vout dependence upon God, which is the first cause; first, it is good to ask the question which Job asked of his friends: "Will you lie for God, as one man will do for another, to gratify him?" For certain it is that God worketh nothing in nature but by second causes:[12] and if they would have it otherwise believed, it is mere imposture, as it were in favor towards God; and nothing else but to offer to the author of truth the unclean sacrifice of a lie. But further, it is an assured truth, and a conclusion of experience, that a little or superficial knowledge of philosophy may incline the mind of man to atheism, but a further proceeding therein doth bring the mind back again to religion. For in the entrance of philosophy,[13] when the second causes, which are next unto the senses, do offer themselves to the mind of man, if it dwell and stay there it may induce some oblivion of the highest cause; but when a man passeth on further, and seeth the dependence of causes, and the works of Providence, then, according to the allegory of the poets, he will easily believe that the highest link of nature's chain must needs be tied to the foot of Jupiter's chair. To conclude therefore, let no man upon a weak conceit of sobriety or an ill-applied moderation think or maintain, that a man can search too far, or be too well studied in the book of God's word, or in the book of God's works, divinity or philosophy; but rather let men endeavor an endless progress or proficience in both; only let men beware that they apply both to charity, and not to swelling; to use, and not to ostentation; and again, that they do not unwisely mingle or confound these learnings together.

[The "vanities" of learning: "vain" imaginations, disputes, and affectations. The "distempers" of learning: (a) studying words rather than things; (b) the degenerate learning of the Schoolmen.]

IV. 2. There be therefore chiefly three vanities in studies, whereby learning hath been most traduced: . . . the first, fantastical learning; the second, contentious learning; and the last, delicate[14] learning; vain imaginations, vain altercations, and vain affectations; and with the last I will begin. Martin Luther, conducted (no doubt) by an higher providence, but in discourse of reason, finding what a province he had undertaken against the bishop of

Rome and the degenerate traditions of the Church, and finding his own solitude, being no ways aided by the opinions of his own time, was enforced to awake all antiquity, and to call former times to his succors to make a party against the present time: so that the ancient authors, both in divinity and in humanity, which had long time slept in libraries, began generally to be read and revolved. This by consequence did draw on a necessity of a more exquisite travail in the languages original, wherein those authors did write, for the better understanding of those authors, and the better advantage of pressing and applying their words. And thereof grew again a delight in their manner of style and phrase, and an admiration of that kind of writing; which was much furthered and precipitated by the enmity and opposition that the propounders of those primitive but seeming new opinions had against the Schoolmen; who were generally of the contrary part, and whose writings were altogether in a different style and form; taking liberty to coin and frame new terms of art to express their own sense, and to avoid circuit of speech, without regard to the pureness, pleasantness, and (as I may call it) lawfulness of the phrase or word. And again, because the great labor then was with the people (of whom the Pharisees were wont to say, *Execrabilis ista turba, quae non novit legem*)[15] for the winning and persuading of them, there grew of necessity in chief price and request eloquence and variety of discourse, as the fittest and forciblest access into the capacity of the vulgar sort: so that these four causes concurring, the admiration of ancient authors, the hate of the Schoolmen, the exact study of languages, and the efficacy of preaching, did bring in an affectionate[16] study of eloquence and copie[17] of speech, which then began to flourish. This grew speedily to an excess; for men began to hunt more after words than matter; more after the choiceness of the phrase, and the round and clean composition of the sentence, and the sweet falling of the clauses, and the varying and illustration of their works with tropes and figures, than after the weight of matter, worth of subject, soundness of argument, life of invention, or depth of judgment. . . .

3. Here therefore is the first distemper of learning, when men study words and not matter; where-

12. God . . . causes: all God's operations in nature are carried out through natural laws. 13. philosophy: i.e., natural science. 14. delicate: affected.

15. *Execrabilis . . . legem:* "This multitude which knoweth not the law are accursed" (John 7:49). 16. affectionate: zealous. 17. copie: abundance.

of, though I have represented an example of late times, yet it hath been and will be *secundum majus et minus* [18] in all time. . . .

5. The second which followeth is in nature worse than the former: for as substance of matter is better than beauty of words, so contrariwise vain matter is worse than vain words: . . .

Surely, like as many substances in nature which are solid do putrefy and corrupt into worms; so it is the property of good and sound knowledge to putrefy and dissolve into a number of subtle, idle, unwholesome, and (as I may term them) vermiculate [19] questions, which have indeed a kind of quickness and life of spirit, but no soundness of matter or goodness of quality. This kind of degenerate learning did chiefly reign amongst the Schoolmen: who having sharp and strong wits, and abundance of leisure, and small variety of reading, but their wits being shut up in the cells of a few authors (chiefly Aristotle their dictator) as their persons were shut up in the cells of monasteries and colleges, and knowing little history, either of nature or time, did out of no great quantity of matter and infinite agitation of wit spin out unto us those laborious webs of learning which are extant in their books. For the wit and mind of man, if it work upon matter, which is the contemplation of the creatures of God, worketh according to the stuff and is limited thereby; but if it work upon itself, as the spider worketh his web, then it is endless, and brings forth indeed cobwebs of learning, admirable for the fineness of thread and work, but of no substance or profit. [20]

[The "distempers of learning" (continued): (c) excessive respect for traditional authority.]

V. 6. Another error hath proceeded from too great a reverence, and a kind of adoration of the mind and understanding of man; by means whereof, men have withdrawn themselves too much from the contemplation of nature, and the observations of experience, and have tumbled up and down, in their own reason and conceits. Upon these intellectualists, which are notwithstanding commonly taken for the most sublime and divine philosophers, Heraclitus gave a just censure, saying, " Men sought truth in their own little worlds, and not in the great and common world "; for they disdain to spell, and so by degrees to read in the volume of God's works: and contrariwise by continual meditation and agitation of wit do urge and as it were invoke their own spirits to divine and give oracles unto them, whereby they are deservedly deluded. . . .

[(d) Misconception of the true object of science, namely " the glory of the Creator and the relief of man's estate."]

11. But the greatest error of all the rest is the mistaking or misplacing of the last or furthest end of knowledge. For men have entered into a desire of learning and knowledge, sometimes upon a natural curiosity and inquisitive appetite; sometimes to entertain their minds with variety and delight; sometimes for ornament and reputation; and sometimes to enable them to victory of wit and contradiction; and most times for lucre and profession, [21] and seldom sincerely to give a true account of their gift of reason, to the benefit and use of men: as if there were sought in knowledge a couch whereupon to rest a searching and restless spirit; or a terrace for a wandering and variable mind to walk up and down with a fair prospect; or a tower of state for a proud mind to raise itself upon; or a fort or commanding ground for strife and contention; or a shop for profit or sale; and not a rich storehouse for the glory of the Creator and the relief of man's estate. But this is that which will indeed dignify and exalt knowledge, if contemplation and action may be more nearly and straitly conjoined and united together than they have been; a conjunction like unto that of the two highest plants, Saturn, the planet of rest and contemplation, and Jupiter, the planet of civil society and action. Howbeit, I do not mean, when I speak of use and action, that end beforementioned of the applying of knowledge to lucre and profession; for I am not ignorant how much that diverteth and interrupteth the prosecution and advancement of knowledge, like unto the golden ball thrown before Atalanta, which while she goeth aside and stoopeth to take up, the race is hindered,

Declinat cursus, aurumque volubile tollit. [22]

Neither is my meaning, as was spoken of Socrates, to call philosophy down from Heaven to converse

---

18. *secundum . . . minus:* in greater or lesser degree.   19. vermiculate: full of worms.   20. The third "vice" or "disease" in learning — not included here — is "deceit or untruth."

21. profession: livelihood.   22. *Declinat . . . tollit:* "deserts the race, and picks up the golden ball" (Ovid, *Metamorphoses*, X. 667).

upon the earth; that is, to leave natural philosophy aside, and to apply knowledge only to manners and policy.[23] But as both Heaven and earth do conspire and contribute to the use and benefit of man; so the end ought to be, from both philosophies to separate and reject vain speculations, and whatsoever is empty and void, and to preserve and augment whatsoever is solid and fruitful; that knowledge may not be as a courtesan, for pleasure and vanity only, or as a bondwoman, to acquire and gain to her master's use; but as a spouse, for generation, fruit, and comfort.

[Philosophy serves religion by manifesting God's glory in his own works.]

VI. 16. Wherefore to conclude this part, let it be observed, that there be two principal duties and services, besides ornament and illustration, which philosophy and human learning do perform to faith and religion. The one, because they are an effectual inducement to the exaltation of the glory of God. For as the Psalms and other Scriptures do often invite us to consider and magnify the great and wonderful works of God, so if we should rest only in the contemplation of the exterior of them as they first offer themselves to our senses, we should do a like injury unto the majesty of God, as if we should judge or construe of the store of some excellent jeweler, by that only which is set out toward the street in his shop. The other, because they minister a singular help and preservative against unbelief and error. For our Savior saith, " You err, not knowing the Scriptures, nor the power of God "; laying before us two books or volumes to study, if we will be secured from error; first the Scriptures, revealing the will of God, and then the creatures expressing his power; whereof the latter is a key unto the former: not only opening our understanding to conceive the true sense of the Scriptures, by the general notions of reason and rules of speech; but chiefly opening our belief, in drawing us into a due meditation of the omnipotency of God, which is chiefly signed and engraven upon his works. Thus much therefore for divine testimony and evidence concerning the true dignity and value of learning.

23. **manners ... policy:** practical affairs, social or political.

THE
SECOND BOOK OF FRANCIS BACON
OF THE PROFICIENCE AND
ADVANCEMENT OF LEARNING
DIVINE AND HUMAN
[Poetry as imaginary history.]

IV. 1. Poesy is a part of learning in measure of words for the most part restrained, but in all other points extremely licensed, and doth truly refer to the imagination; which, being not tied to the laws of matter, may at pleasure join that which nature hath severed, and sever that which nature hath joined; and so make unlawful matches and divorces of things; *Pictoribus atque poetis, etc.*[24] It is taken in two senses in respect of words or matter. In the first sense it is but a character of style, and belongeth to arts of speech, and is not pertinent for the present. In the latter it is (as hath been said) one of the principal portions of learning, and is nothing else but feigned history, which may be styled as well in prose as in verse.

2. The use of this feigned history hath been to give some shadow of satisfaction to the mind of man in those points wherein the nature of things doth deny it, the world being in proportion inferior to the soul; by reason whereof there is, agreeable to the spirit of man, a more ample greatness, a more exact goodness, and a more absolute variety, than can be found in the nature of things. Therefore, because the acts or events of true history have not that magnitude which satisfieth the mind of man, poesy feigneth acts and events greater and more heroical. Because true history propoundeth the successes and issues of actions not so agreeable to the merits of virtue and vice, therefore poesy feigns them more just in retribution, and more according to revealed providence. Because true history representeth actions and events more ordinary and less interchanged, therefore poesy endueth them with more rareness, and more unexpected and alternative variations. So as it appeareth that poesy serveth and conferreth to magnanimity, morality, and to delectation. And therefore it was ever thought to have some participation of divineness, because it doth raise and erect the mind, by submitting the shows of things to the desires of the mind; whereas reason doth buckle and bow the mind unto the

24. *Pictoribus ... poetis:* "Painters and poets [have been still allowed their pencils, and their fancies, unconfined]" (Horace, *Ars Poetica,* IX, Roscommon's translation).

nature of things. And we see that by these insinuations [25] and congruities with man's nature and pleasure, joined also with the agreement and consort it hath with music, it hath had access and estimation in rude times and barbarous regions, where other learning stood excluded.

[Religion and science must be kept separate.]

VI. 1. . . . And as concerning divine philosophy or natural theology, it is that knowledge or rudiment of knowledge concerning God, which may be obtained by the contemplation of his creatures; which knowledge may be truly termed divine in respect of the object, and natural in respect of the light. The bounds of this knowledge are, that it sufficeth to convince atheism, but not to inform religion: and therefore there was never miracle wrought by God to convert an atheist, because the light of nature might have led him to confess a God: but miracles have been wrought to convert idolaters and the superstitious, because no light of nature extendeth to declare the will and true worship of God. For as all works do show forth the power and skill of the workman, and not his image, so it is of the works of God, which do show the omnipotency and wisdom of the maker, but not his image. And therefore therein the heathen opinion differeth from the sacred truth; for they supposed the world to be the image of God, and man to be an extract [26] or compendious image of the world; but the Scriptures never vouchsafe to attribute to the world that honor, as to be the image of God, but only " the work of his hands "; neither do they speak of any other image of God, but man. Wherefore by the contemplation of nature to induce and enforce the acknowledgment of God, and to demonstrate his power, providence, and goodness, is an excellent argument, and hath been excellently handled by divers.[27] But on the other side, out of the contemplation of nature, or ground of human knowledges, to induce any verity or persuasion concerning the points of faith, is in my judgment not safe: *Da fidei quae fidei sunt.*[28] For the heathen themselves conclude as much in that excellent and divine fable of the golden chain: " That men and gods were not able to draw Jupiter down to the earth; but contrariwise Jupiter was able to draw them up to heaven." So as we ought not to attempt to draw down or to submit the mysteries of God to our reason; but contrariwise to raise and advance our reason to the divine truth. So as in this part of knowledge, touching divine philosophy, I am so far from noting any deficience, as I rather note an excess: whereunto I have digressed because of the extreme prejudice which both religion and philosophy hath received and may receive by being commixed together; as that which undoubtedly will make an heretical religion, and an imaginary and fabulous philosophy.

[Natural science divided into " physic," dealing with matter and motion, and " metaphysic," dealing with " formal and final causes," i.e., the inner principles of things and their ultimate purpose. Too much attention has been paid to " purposes " and not enough to investigating the inner natures (" forms ") of phenomena.]

VII. 1. Leaving therefore divine philosophy or natural theology (not divinity or inspired theology, which we reserve for the last of all as the haven and sabbath of all man's contemplations) we will now proceed to natural philosophy. . . .

2. Natural science or theory is divided into physic and metaphysic: wherein I desire it may be conceived that I use the word " metaphysic " in a differing sense from that that is received.[29] And in like manner, I doubt not but it will easily appear to men of judgment, that in this and other particulars, wheresoever my conception and notion may differ from the ancient, yet I am studious to keep the ancient terms. For hoping well to deliver myself from mistaking, by the order and perspicuous expressing of that I do propound; I am otherwise zealous and affectionate to recede as little from antiquity, either in terms or opinions, as may stand with truth and the proficience of knowledge. . . .

3. To return therefore to the use and acception of the term " metaphysic," as I do now understand the word: it appeareth, by that which hath been already said, that I intend *philosophia prima,*[30] summary [31] philosophy and metaphysic, which heretofore have been confounded as one, to be two distinct things. For the one I have made as a parent or common ancestor to all knowledge; and the other I have now brought in as a branch or descendant of natural science. It appeareth like-

---

25. **insinuations:** intertwinings (hence, close relationship). 26. **extract:** epitome; miniature reproduction (man as "microcosm"). 27. **divers:** various (writers). 28. *Da . . . sunt:* "Render unto faith the things that are faith's."

29. **received:** accepted or understood. 30. *philosophia prima:* first (primary) philosophy. 31. **summary:** highest (or "basic").

wise that I have assigned to summary philosophy the common principles and axioms which are promiscuous and indifferent [32] to several sciences: I have assigned unto it likewise the inquiry touching the operation of the relative and adventive characters of essences,[33] as quantity, similitude, diversity, possibility, and the rest: with this distinction and provision: that they be handled as they have efficacy in nature, and not logically. It appeareth likewise that natural theology, which heretofore hath been handled confusedly with metaphysic, I have enclosed and bounded by itself. It is therefore now a question what is left remaining for metaphysic; wherein I may without prejudice preserve thus much of the conceit of antiquity, that physic should contemplate that which is inherent in matter, and therefore transitory; and metaphysic that which is abstracted and fixed. And again, that physic should handle that which supposeth in nature only a being and moving; and metaphysic should handle that which supposeth further in nature a reason, understanding, and platform.[34] But the difference, perspicuously expressed, is most familiar and sensible. For as we divided natural philosophy in general into the inquiry of causes, and productions of effects: so that part which concerneth the inquiry of causes we do subdivide according to the received and sound division of causes. The one part, which is physic, inquireth and handleth the material and efficient causes; and the other, which is metaphysic, handleth the formal and final causes.[35]

5. For metaphysic, we have assigned unto it the inquiry of formal and final causes; which assignation, as to the former of them, may seem to be nugatory and void, because of the received and inveterate opinion, that the inquisition of man is not competent to find out essential forms or true differences: of which opinion we will take this

hold, that the invention [36] of forms is of all other parts of knowledge the worthiest to be sought, if it be possible to be found. As for the possibility, they are ill discoverers that think there is no land, when they can see nothing but sea. But it is manifest that Plato, in his opinion of ideas,[37] as one that had a wit of elevation situate as upon a cliff,[38] did descry *that forms were the true object of knowledge;* but lost the real fruit of his opinion, by considering of forms as absolutely abstracted from matter, and not confined and determined by matter; and so turning his opinion upon theology, wherewith all his natural philosophy is infected. But if any man shall keep a continual watchful and severe eye upon action, operation, and the use of knowledge, he may advise and take notice what are the forms, the disclosures whereof are fruitful and important to the state of man. For as to the forms of substances [39] (man only except, of whom it is said, *Formavit hominem de limo terrae, et spiravit in faciem eius spiraculum vitae,*[40] and not as of all other creatures, *Producant aquae, producat terra*),[41] the forms of substances I say (as they are now by compounding and transplanting multiplied) are so perplexed, as they are not to be inquired; no more than it were either possible or to purpose to seek in gross the forms of those sounds which make words, which by composition and transposition of letters are infinite. But on the other side to inquire the form of those sounds or voices which make simple letters is easily comprehensible; and being known induceth and manifesteth the forms of all words, which consist and are compounded of them. In the same manner to inquire the form of a lion, of an oak, of gold; nay, of water, of air, is a vain pursuit: but to inquire the forms of sense, of voluntary motion, of vegetation, of colors, of gravity and levity, of density, of tenuity, of heat, of cold, and all other natures and qualities, which, like an alphabet, are not many, and of which the essences (upheld by matter) of all creatures do consist; to inquire, I say, the true forms of these, is that part of metaphysic which we now define of. Not but that physic

32. **promiscuous . . . indifferent:** generally applicable. 33. **relative . . . essences:** the attributes of things when considered in their relationship with other things; thus, their "adventitious" qualities — qualities arising from outward relations. 34. **platform:** plan, or idea. 35. **material . . . causes:** This "division" of causes is Aristotle's (*Metaphysics*): (1) "material," the stuff which is acted upon; (2) "efficient," that which actuates; (3) "formal," the inner individuating principle (*raison d'être*) which makes a thing what it is: often called the "form" (see below); (4) "final," that for the sake of which a thing exists: its end or purpose. For example, take a stone: its "material" cause is simply the stuff it is made of; its "efficient" cause is the force which places it where it is; its "formal" cause is what makes it a particular kind of stone (e.g., flint or quartz) and not another; its "final" cause is the purpose for which it exists e.g., for throwing at somebody, for ornament.) Bacon's innovation is to assign "formal causes" in scientific inquiry.

36. **invention:** discovery. 37. **Plato . . . ideas:** Plato's theory of ideal forms existing in heaven, of which earthly things, qualities, etc., were imperfect or shadowy copies. 38. **as . . . cliff:** like a person viewing distant objects from a point of vantage. 39. **substances:** here used to mean complex created things, or creatures, e.g., animals and trees. 40. *Formavit . . . vitae:* "[God] formed man of the dust of the earth, and breathed into his nostrils the breath of life" (Gen. 2:7). 41. *Producant . . . terra:* "Let the waters bring forth, let the earth bring forth" (Gen. 1:20,24).

doth make inquiry and take consideration of the same natures: but how? Only as to the material and efficient causes of them, and not as to the forms. For example, if the cause of whiteness in snow or froth be inquired, and it be rendered thus, that the subtle intermixture of air and water is the cause, it is well rendered; but nevertheless is this the form of whiteness? No; but it is the efficient, which is ever but *vehiculum formae*.[42] This part of metaphysic I do not find labored and performed: whereat I marvel not: because I hold it not possible to be invented by that course of invention which hath been used; in regard that men (which is the root of all error) have made too untimely a departure and too remote recess from particulars.

7. The second part of metaphysic is the inquiry of final causes, which I am moved to report not as omitted but as misplaced. And yet if it were but a fault in order, I would not speak of it: for order is matter of illustration, but pertaineth not to the substance of sciences. But this misplacing hath caused a deficience, or at least a great improficience in the sciences themselves. For the handling of final causes, mixed with the rest in physical inquiries, hath intercepted the severe and diligent inquiry of all real and physical causes, and given men the occasion to stay upon these satisfactory and specious causes,[43] to the great arrest and prejudice of further discovery. For this I find done not only by Plato, who ever anchoreth upon that shore, but by Aristotle, Galen,[44] and others which do usually likewise fall upon these flats of discoursing causes. For to say that "the hairs of the eyelids are for a quickset and fence about the sight"; or that "the firmness of the skins and hides of living creatures is to defend them from the extremities of heat and cold"; or that "the bones are for the columns or beams, whereupon the frames of the bodies of living creatures are built"; or that "the leaves of trees are for protecting of the fruit"; or that "the clouds are for watering of the earth"; or that "the solidness of the earth is for the station and mansion of living creatures," and the like, is well inquired and collected in metaphysic, but in physic they are impertinent. Nay, they are indeed but *remoraes*[45] and

hindrances to stay and slug the ship from further sailing; and have brought this to pass, that the search of the physical causes hath been neglected and passed in silence. And therefore the natural philosophy of Democritus[46] and some others, who did not suppose a mind or reason in the frame of things, but attributed the form thereof able to maintain itself to infinite essays or proofs[47] of nature, which they term fortune, seemeth to me (as far as I can judge by the recital and fragments which remain unto us) in particularities of physical causes more real and better inquired than that of Aristotle and Plato; whereof both intermingled final causes, the one as a part of theology, and the other as a part of logic, which were the favorite studies, respectively, of both those persons. Not because those final causes are not true, and worthy to be inquired, being kept within their own province; but because their excursions into the limits of physical causes hath bred a vastness[48] and solitude in that tract. . . .

[The fallacies ("idols") imposed upon us by the human mind itself: (a) making man the measure of all things and assuming that nature must behave according to our own sense of fitness; (b) individual prejudices and delusions; (c) inexact use of words.]

XIV. 9. But lastly, there is yet a much more important and profound kind of fallacies in the mind of man, which I find not observed or inquired at all, and think good to place here, as that which of all others appertaineth most to rectify judgment: the force whereof is such, as it does not dazzle or snare the understanding in some particulars, but doth more generally and inwardly infect and corrupt the state thereof. For the mind of man is far from the nature of a clear and equal glass, wherein the beams of things should reflect according to their true incidence; nay, it is rather like an enchanted glass, full of superstition and imposture, if it be not delivered and reduced. For this purpose, let us consider the false appearances[49] that are imposed upon us by the general nature of the mind, beholding them in an example or two; as first, in that instance which is the root of all superstition, namely, that to the nature of the mind of all men it is consonant for the affirmative or active to affect more than the

---

42. *vehiculum formae*: vehicle of the form; that which carries within it the formal principle.   43. **stay . . . causes**: to be too soon contented with these plausible explanations (in terms of "end" or "purpose"), and so to neglect physical inquiries. 44. **Galen**: the most celebrated of ancient medical writers, born in Mysia about 130 A.D.   45. *remoraes*: remora, a fabulous fish said to adhere to the hull of a ship, and so impede its motion; thus, a hindrance.

46. **Democritus**: Greek philosopher who reduced nature to material atoms in a void. Cf. essay "Of Atheism," n. 85. 47. **proofs**: efforts or experiments.   48. **vastness**: empty wilderness.   49. **false appearances**: elsewhere called by Bacon "idols of the mind." This first type he calls the "idols of the tribe." See Intro., p. 322.

negative or privative. So that a few times hitting or presence, countervails ofttimes failing or absence; as was well answered by Diagoras to him that showed him in Neptune's temple the great number of pictures of such as had scaped shipwreck, and had paid their vows to Neptune, saying, "Advise now, you that think it folly to invocate Neptune in tempest." "Yea, but" (saith Diagoras) "where are they painted that are drowned?" [50] Let us behold it in another instance, namely, that the spirit of man, being of an equal and uniform substance, doth usually suppose and feign in nature a greater equality and uniformity than is in truth. Hence it cometh, that the mathematicians cannot satisfy themselves except they reduce the motions of the celestial bodies to perfect circles, rejecting spiral lines, and laboring to be discharged of eccentrics.[51] Hence it cometh, that whereas there are many things in nature, as it were *monodica, sui juris;* [52] yet the cogitations of man do feign unto them relatives, parallels, and conjugates,[53] whereas no such thing is; as they have feigned an element of fire, to keep square with earth, water, and air, and the like. Nay, it is not credible, till it be opened, what a number of fictions and fantasies the similitude of human actions and arts, together with the making of man *communis mensura,*[54] have brought into natural philosophy; not much better than the heresy of the Anthropomorphites,[55] bred in the cells of gross and solitary monks, and the opinion of Epicurus, answerable to the same in heathenism, who supposed the gods to be of human shape. And therefore Velleius the Epicurean needed not to have asked, why God should have adorned the heavens with stars, as if he had been an *aedilis,*[56] one that should have set forth some magnificent shows or plays. For if that great workmaster had been of an human disposition, he would have cast the stars into some pleasant and beautiful works and orders, like the frets in the roofs of houses; whereas one can scarce find a posture in square, or triangle, or straight line, amongst such an infinite number; so differing an harmony there is between the spirit of man and the spirit of nature.

10. Let us consider again the false appearances imposed upon us by every man's own individual nature and custom,[57] in that feigned supposition that Plato maketh of the cave: for certainly if a child were continued in a grot or cave under the earth until maturity of age, and came suddenly abroad, he would have strange and absurd imaginations. So in like manner, although our persons live in the view of heaven, yet our spirits are included in the caves of our own complexions and customs, which minister unto us infinite errors and vain opinions, if they be not recalled to examination. . . .

11. And lastly, let us consider the false appearances that are imposed upon us by words,[58] which are framed and applied according to the conceit and capacities of the vulgar sort: and although we think we govern our words, and prescribe it well, *Loquendum ut vulgus sentiendum ut sapientes;* [59] yet certain it is that words, as a Tartar's bow,[60] do shoot back upon the understanding of the wisest, and mightily entangle and pervert the judgment. So as it is almost necessary, in all controversies and disputations, to imitate the wisdom of the mathematicians, in setting down in the very beginning the definitions of our words and terms, that others may know how we accept and understand them, and whether they concur with us or no. For it cometh to pass, for want of this, that we are sure to end there where we ought to have begun, which is, in questions and differences about words. To conclude therefore, it must be confessed that it is not possible to divorce ourselves from these fallacies and false appearances, because they are inseparable from our nature and condition of life; so yet nevertheless the caution of them (for all *elenches,*[61] as was said, are but cautions) doth extremely import the true conduct of human judgment. The particular *elenches* or cautions against these three false appearances, I find altogether deficient.

[Morality. Philosophers have described the virtues and discussed the theory of ethics, but have not shown us how to attain the good.]

XX. 1. We proceed now to that knowledge

---

50. **drowned:** The story is told by Cicero (*De Natura Deorum*).
51. **eccentrics:** irregular orbits. Cf. essay "Of Superstition," n. 94.   52. *monodica . . . juris:* unique, obeying no law but their own.   53. **relatives . . . conjugates:** relationships, analogies and connections.   54. *communis mensura:* the common measure (of all things); the teaching of Protagoras.   55. **Anthropomorphites:** a branch of the Monophysite heretics, who held that God was of human shape.   56. *aedilis:* The Roman "aediles" were officers in charge of public decorations, etc.

57. **false . . . custom:** the "idols of the cave" (or den). Reference is to Plato's parable in the *Republic*. In Book VII Plato describes ordinary men as dwellers in a cave with their backs turned to the light, seeing only shadows on the wall and mistaking them for realities.   58. **false . . . words:** the "idols of the market place."   59. *Loquendum . . . sapientes:* "Speak like common folk but think like wise men."   60. **Tartar's bow:** The Tartars, or Parthians, were said to shoot backward in retreat.   61. *elenches:* self-contradictions, or logical refutations.

which considereth of the appetite and will of man: whereof Salomon saith, *Ante omnia, fili, custodi cor tuum; nam inde procedunt actiones vitae.*[62] In the handling of this science, those which have written seem to me to have done as if a man, that professed to teach to write, did only exhibit fair copies of alphabets and letters joined, without giving any precepts or directions for the carriage of the hand and framing of the letters. So have they made good and fair exemplars and copies, carrying the drafts and portraitures of good, virtue, duty, felicity; propounding them well described as the true objects and scopes of man's will and desires. But how to attain these excellent marks, and how to frame and subdue the will of man to become true and conformable to these pursuits, they pass it over altogether, or slightly and unprofitably. For it is not the disputing, that moral virtues are in the mind of man by habit and not by nature; or the distinguishing, that generous spirits are won by doctrines and persuasions, and the vulgar sort by reward and punishment;[63] and the like scattered glances and touches, that can excuse the absence of this part.

2. The reason of this omission I suppose to be that hidden rock whereupon both this and many other barks of knowledge have been cast away; which is, that men have despised to be conversant in ordinary and common matters, the judicious direction whereof nevertheless is the wisest doctrine (for life consisteth not in novelties nor subtleties), but contrariwise they have compounded sciences chiefly of a certain resplendent or lustrous mass of matter, chosen to give glory either to the subtlety of disputations, or to the eloquence of discourses. But Seneca giveth an excellent check to eloquence, *Nocet illis eloquentia, quibus non rerum cupiditatem facit, sed sui.*[64] Doctrine should be such as should make men in love with the lesson, and not with the teacher; being directed to the auditor's benefit, and not to the author's commendation. And therefore those are of the right kind which may be concluded as Demosthenes concludes his counsel, *Quae si feceritis, non oratorem duntaxat in praesentia laudabitis, sed vosmetipsos etiam non ita multo post statu rerum vestrarum meliore.*[65]

3. Neither needed men of so excellent parts to have despaired of a fortune, which the poet Virgil promised himself, and indeed obtained, who got as much glory of eloquence, wit, and learning in the expressing of the observations of husbandry, as of the heroical acts of Aeneas:

Nec sum animi dubius, verbis ea vincere magnum
Quam sit, et angustis his addere rebus honorem.[66]

And surely, if the purpose be in good earnest, not to write at leisure that which men may read at leisure, but really to instruct and suborn action and active life, these Georgics of the mind, concerning the husbandry and tillage thereof, are no less worthy than the heroical descriptions of virtue, duty, and felicity. Wherefore the main and primitive division of moral knowledge seemeth to be into the exemplar or platform [67] of good, and the regiment or culture of the mind: the one describing the nature of good, the other prescribing rules how to subdue, apply, and accommodate the will of man thereunto.

[The doctrines of the Christian religion are based on revelation, not on reason or the light of nature.]

XXV. 1. The prerogative of God extendeth as well to the reason as to the will of man; so that as we are to obey his law, though we find a reluctation [68] in our will, so we are to believe his word, though we find a reluctation in our reason. For if we believe only that which is agreeable to our sense, we give consent to the matter, and not to the author; which is no more than we would do towards a suspected and discredited witness; but that faith which was accounted to Abraham for righteousness was of such a point as whereat Sarah laughed,[69] who therein was an image of natural reason.

2. Howbeit (if we will truly consider of it) more worthy it is to believe than to know as we now know. For in knowledge man's mind suffereth from [70] sense; but in belief it suffereth from spirit, such one as it holdeth for more authorized than itself, and so suffereth from the worthier agent. Otherwise it is of the state of man glorified; for

62. *Ante . . . vitae:* "Before all, my son, keep thy heart with all diligence, for out of it are the issues of life" (Prov. 4:23). 63. *For . . . punishment:* topics in Aristotle. 64. *Nocet . . . sui:* "Eloquence harms those in whom it arouses love, not of the subject, but of itself." 65. *Quae . . . meliore:* "If you do these things, you shall not only praise the orator at the moment, but yourselves also soon after, when your state of affairs has improved." 66. *Nec . . . honorem:* "Well do I know how hard it is to bind words to such use, and add luster even to these mean affairs" (Virgil, *Georgics,* III. 289). 67. **exemplar or platform:** pattern or ground plan. 68. **reluctation:** refractoriness. 69. **Sarah laughed:** at the news that she should bear a son to Abraham, although "well stricken in age" (Gen. 18:11-12). 70. **suffereth from:** receives impressions from.

then faith shall cease, and we shall know as we are known.

3. Wherefore we conclude that sacred theology (which in our idiom we call divinity) is grounded only upon the word and oracle of God, and not upon the light of nature: for it is written, *Coeli enarrant gloriam Dei;* [71] but it is not written, *Coeli enarrant voluntatem Dei;* [72] but of that it is said, *Ad legem et testimonium: si non fecerint secundum verbum istud, etc.* [73] This holdeth not only in those points of faith which concern the great mysteries of the Deity, of the creation, of the redemption, but likewise those which concern the law moral truly interpreted: " Love your enemies: do good to them that hate you: Be like to your heavenly Father, that suffereth his rain to fall upon the just and unjust." To this it ought to be applauded, *Nec vox hominem sonat:* [74] it is a voice beyond the light of nature. So we see the heathen poets, when they fall upon a libertine passion, do still expostulate with laws and moralities, as if they were opposite and malignant to nature; *Et quod natura remittit, invida jura*

negant. [75] So said Dendamis the Indian unto Alexander's messengers, that he had heard somewhat of Pythagoras, and some other of the wise men of Grecia, and that he held them for excellent men: but that they had a fault, which was that they had in too great reverence and veneration a thing they called law and manners. So it must be confessed, that a great part of the law moral is of that perfection, whereunto the light of nature cannot aspire: how then is it that man is said to have by the light and law of nature, some notions and conceits of virtue and vice, justice and wrong, good and evil? Thus, because the light of nature is used in two several senses; the one, that which springeth from reason, sense, induction, argument, according to the laws of heaven and earth; the other, that which is imprinted upon the spirit of man by an inward instinct, according to the law of conscience, which is a sparkle of the purity of his first estate; [76] in which latter sense only he is participant of some light and discerning touching the perfection of the moral law: but how? sufficient to check the vice, but not to inform the duty. So then the doctrine of religion, as well moral as mystical, is not to be attained but by inspiration and revelation from God.

71. *Coeli . . . Dei:* "The heavens declare the glory of God" (Ps. 19:1).   72. *Coeli . . . Dei:* "The heavens declare the will of God."   73. *Ad . . . etc.:* "To the law and to the testimony: if they speak [act] not according to this word [it is because there is no light in them]" (Isa. 8:20).   74. *Nec . . . sonat:* "Nor does this voice sound [like that of] a man" (Virgil, *Aeneid*, I. 328).

75. *Et . . . negant:* "And that which nature allows, jealous laws forbid" (Ovid, *Metamorphoses*, X. 330).   76. first estate: i.e., in Eden before the Fall.

John Donne

1572-1631

JOHN DONNE is a fascinating figure, whether you think of him as a man, as a poet, or as a divine, and still more when you consider him in all three aspects together. His poetry "went to the head" of many readers and critics in the two decades following World War I, and ever since it has been more read and discussed than at any time since his death. He impressed his contemporaries, first by his wit, learning, and personal charm, and later by the passion and eloquence of his preaching.

One may think of his life as a process in which he gradually turned away from dissipation, cynicism, and worldly ambition and became a devout Christian and a great churchman. Donne was born in London, probably in the early part of 1572, of Roman Catholic parents. His father, a prosperous ironmonger, was a Welshman of high pedigree; his mother was descended from the family of Sir Thomas More. She, left a widow when Donne was an infant, brought up her children strictly as Roman Catholics — in those days a risky thing to do. One of Donne's brothers died in prison for harboring a priest, and he himself not only had to leave Oxford (and perhaps Cambridge as well) without a degree, but later went through agonies of study and inward conflict before he could decide which Church was Christ's true "spouse" (compare "Satire III" and "Holy Sonnet XVIII" below). After leaving the university about a year younger than most students now enter it, he began to study law, a subject which suited his precise and subtle mind and in which he afterwards became very proficient. But first he had to face the press-

ing problem of religion, and, in the words of his earliest biographer Isaak Walton,

About the nineteenth year of his age, he being then unresolved what religion to adhere to, and considering how much it concerned his soul to choose the most orthodox, did therefore . . . lay aside all study of the law . . . , and begun seriously to survey and consider the body of divinity, as it was then controverted between the reformed and the Roman church.

It was then that he wrote the oft-quoted lines ("Satire III," ll. 79-84):

> On a huge hill,
> Cragged, and steep, Truth stands, and he that will
> Reach her, about must, and about must go;
> And what the hill's suddenness resists, win so;
> Yet strive so, that before age, death's twilight,
> Thy soul rest, for none can work in that night.

But we must not allow Walton to romanticize Donne's turbulent youth for us unduly; he was no pensive Hamlet, no mere "wrestler for the truth" — or if he was, he was a great deal else besides. The Donne who wrote the lines above was also writing the other *Satires,* the *Elegies,* and the early *Songs and Sonnets,* poems coruscating with wit, insolence, cynicism, and sophistication. Walton's obituary piety must be balanced against the realism of Sir Richard Baker,[1] who describes the young Donne as "not dissolute, but very neat, a great visitor of ladies, a great frequenter of plays, a great writer of con-

[1] Sir Richard Baker (1568-1645), historian; Donne's contemporary and friend at Oxford.

ceited verses." No doubt Donne's religious struggle was both genuine and severe, and yet a correct choice concerned his worldly prospects as well as his soul. Walton, describing his final choice of the Reformed Church, complacently remarks that " Truth had too much light about her to be hid from so sharp an inquirer; and he had too much ingenuity not to acknowledge he had found her." We have no right to question Donne's sincerity, and yet we cannot forget that he was ambitious, and that in rejecting Rome he was shaking off a handicap which would have excluded him forever from all public employment, and condemned him to the life of obscurity and danger from which his family had long suffered. He certainly hoped at one time that his skill in theological dispute would win the favor of King James I, and so lead on to some showy and lucrative office like a secretaryship or an ambassadorship rather than — as actually happened — to holy orders.

But no sooner had he cleared the way to advancement by becoming a Protestant, than he condemned himself to years of poverty and struggle by a hasty and (in a worldly sense) imprudent marriage. After voyaging to Cadiz (1596) and the Azores (1597) with Essex (and traveling also, at some undetermined date, in Italy and Spain), he had become private secretary to Sir Thomas Egerton, Keeper of the Great Seal, later Lord Ellesmere and Lord Chancellor of England. This seemed a very promising start, for Egerton (according to Walton) was much impressed by Donne's " learning, languages, and other abilities " and intended the secretaryship to be an introduction to " some more weighty employment in the state; for which, his Lordship did often protest, he thought him very fit." " Nor," Walton adds, " did his Lordship . . . account him to be so much his servant, as to forget he was his friend; and to testify it, did always use him with much courtesy, appointing him a place at his own table, to which he esteemed his company and discourse to be a great ornament." Within a short time, however, Donne had fallen hopelessly in love with Lady Egerton's niece Anne More, who lived with her aunt's family; and she, captivated by his irresistible charm, agreed to a secret engagement. Her father, Sir George More, tried to nip this love affair in the bud by carrying his daughter off home (she was still under seven-

teen). But it was too late, and they were secretly married, Anne being seventeen and Donne twenty-nine.

" This was the remarkable error of his life," says Walton. But was it? It certainly aroused the fury of Anne's father, who not only forced Egerton to dismiss Donne but even had his son-in-law thrown into jail, together with the parson who had performed the wedding ceremony and the friend who had given away the bride. It is true that all this put an end to Donne's worldly advancement; he fell out of the race for promotion and sank into a dim and rather squalid routine of rural domesticity, varied only by constant appeals to this potential patron or that, and by the distracting noise and the sicknesses of an ever-increasing family (there were twelve children in all). When he felt most depressed about his prospects he sometimes allowed himself to ask Hamlet's question, and even wrote a book (*Biathanatos, c.* 1608) justifying suicide. Undoubtedly the marriage, judged by ordinary standards, had been rash. But it had been a love match, and through all the vicissitudes of family life — the ever-recurring cycle of births, illnesses, deaths, and poverty — Donne and his wife remained constant lovers until death parted them. This love steadied and purified Donne's nature (it had needed some purifying), and was a necessary stage in his spiritual progress. Had he not loved Anne so much, he might never have come (as he finally did) to love God still more. The actual dating of the individual *Songs and Sonnets* will probably always remain conjectural, but the contrast between the more outrageous " evaporations " (such as " The Flea," " The Indifferent," " Go and Catch a Falling Star," " Woman's Constancy," and several of the *Elegies*) and such passionate utterances as " The Good Morrow," " The Anniversary," " A Valediction Forbidding Mourning," " The Ecstasy," etc., is too striking to be without inward significance, and we must believe — with Grierson — that the poems " in which ardor is combined with elevation and delicacy of feeling were addressed to Anne More before and after their marriage."

Meanwhile Donne's destiny — or, as he himself afterwards believed, the guiding hand of Providence — was leading him steadily towards the Church. He helped Thomas Morton, then Dean of Gloucester and one of the King's chaplains, in a task the king had set his heart upon: the conversion of the English Roman Catholics. And the controversial skill and theological knowledge which he displayed (especially in his *Pseudo-Martyr,* 1610) convinced the king that Donne was marked for ordination. Donne hesitated at first, whether for worldly or for spiritual reasons, or for both; and when Morton offered him a living he declined it on the ground that "some irregularities of his past life" might disgrace the sacred calling. However, as Walton observes, "the heart of man is not in his own keeping, and he was destined to this sacred service by a higher hand: a hand so powerful [i.e., the king's], as at last forced him to a compliance."

And so, a few years later, he was ordained (1615), and in Walton's words "the English Church gained a second St. Augustine, for I think none was so like him before his conversion; none so like St. Ambrose after it; and if his youth had the infirmities of the one, his age had the excellences of the other; the learning and holiness of both." Two years after this, as if to wean him from all earthly affections, his wife was taken from him, and the whole force of his impassioned and tormented soul was now turned towards God. Four years after Anne's death, the king appointed him Dean of St. Paul's. To the duties of this responsible and conspicuous post, in spite of recurrent sickness and declining strength, Donne now devoted all the energies of his mind and heart. That personal magnetism which in his youth had won him friends and lovers as by "a strange kind of elegant irresistible art" now held his congregations spellbound.

His *Divine Poems, Devotions,* and *Sermons,* which include some of his finest work and rank high in the devotional literature of all time, show clearly that, although his faith burned strongly, it was seldom free from smoke. He never for long achieved the tranquil poise of one who is assured of salvation and whose conversation is in heaven. Contraries still met in him, and he had to wrestle daily with his God, beseeching him to

break, blow, burn and make me new.

Towards the close of his life, when he felt death approaching, he "prepared to leave the world before life left him." He had a portrait painted of himself in his winding sheet, and this, placed by his bedside, "became his hourly object until his death." A few days before the end, when he had "preached his own funeral sermon," he seems to have attained spiritual tranquillity. Looking back on his past life, he was able to say to an old friend:

I now plainly see that it was his [God's] will I should never settle or thrive till I entered into the ministry; in which I have now lived almost twenty years (I hope to his glory). . . . I cannot plead innocency of life, especially of my youth; but I am to be judged by a merciful God, who is not willing to see what I have done amiss. And though of myself I have nothing to present to him but sins and misery, yet I know he looks not upon me now as I am of myself, but as I am in my Saviour . . . : I am therefore full of inexpressible joy, and shall die in peace.

II

There are certain epochs in the history of poetry when a break has to be made with the past, and a new style devised to meet new needs. This happens when, as a result of complex historical causes — the rise of a new social class, a changed world picture, new scientific theories, religious, social, and economic developments, or a combination of these — a new kind of sensibility appears, which cannot be adequately expressed in the established forms.

Donne, as we shall see, was one of these innovators, the first in a series covering the past three hundred years. In him the intellectual curiosity of the Renaissance and the stimulus and strain of a new world view forced themselves into (nondramatic) verse and changed its quality. Donne is a representative figure in that he, like his age, had been trained along medieval lines and had then had to face the disturbing implications of the Copernican cosmography. Medieval and modern elements were mixed in him, and the result was the "Metaphysical" style, of which more anon.

Another break of this kind occurred after 1660, when the era of civil war and religious fanaticism seemed safely over, when the ideas of the Royal Society were in the ascendant, and men aspired above all to be civilized, rational, correct, clear, and classical. In the eyes of men like Dryden the Elizabethan and Metaphysical styles, though admittedly admirable in their own time and for their own purposes, appeared barbarous, pedantic, or "gothic." The heroic couplet, as shaped by Dryden and perfected by Pope, was the medium best suited to an age no longer in love with paradox and mystery, no longer bent upon imaginative or spiritual pioneering, but anxious instead to say as crisply, plainly, and effectively as possible what all reasonable men were thinking. Another such break occurred at the end of the eighteenth century, when Rousseau and the French Revolution had cracked the molds of the *ancien régime* and spread abroad new ferments of enthusiasm, nature worship, and humanitarian sentiment. The couplet, so expressive of fixity and finality in thought and in society, seemed no longer able to contain the new and heady wine, and Wordsworth wrote his Preface and the *Lyrical Ballads*. Another break came (after World War I) in the 1920's, when the tradition started by Wordsworth and developed by the Victorians seemed itself to have lost vitality, and Yeats, Eliot, D. H. Lawrence, and others struggled to free themselves from the nineteenth century in order to speak as men of their own time.

When these breaks and new starts take place, it generally happens that an earlier style or school, long out of favor, enjoys a renewed vogue. This is what happened to Donne in the 1920's. Everyone was then reading and discussing him, and the new poets were learning from him how to talk and argue in verse, how to be tough, subtle, and allusive. In that postwar decade there was a widespread revolt against something called "Victorianism," almost against the nineteenth century as such. The war seemed to have made nonsense of that century's hopes and ideals; accordingly, it was hastily assumed that the ideals had been bogus all the time, and that the whole period had been worm-eaten with sentimentality, progress worship, escapism, and hypocrisy. Those who felt that the world was much harsher, uglier, and more puzzling than their grandfathers had imagined turned with distaste from the whole Wordsworthian and Tennysonian tradition (often without understanding it) and found in Donne something much more to their taste. Here at least was a poet as inquisitive, as cynical, and as disenchanted as themselves, and one who could use his brains as well as his emotions. The very fact that Donne had been neglected for a couple of

centuries added zest to the new enthusiasm, and Professor Grierson and T. S. Eliot were at hand to give it support and interpretation. The feeling was very much like that expressed three centuries earlier by Thomas Carew in his "Elegy upon the Death of Dr. John Donne":

> The Muses' garden, with pedantic weeds
> O'erspread, was purged by thee; the lazy seeds
> Of servile imitation thrown away,
> And fresh invention planted. . . .
> Thou hast . . . opened us a mine
> Of rich and pregnant fancy, drawn a line
> Of masculine expression. . . .

These lines show that Donne was recognized in his own time as an innovator. Although his world picture is essentially Elizabethan, and although witty and "conceited" writing abounds in the poetry which precedes him, nevertheless it is right to think of him as one who deliberately broke with the tradition of the Petrarchan sonneteers and with the classical and pastoral conventions of the mellifluous song writers, and infused into lyric poetry new qualities of psychological realism and intellectual complexity. Instead of sighing or yearning or singing, he often scoffed, analyzed, or argued, and into everything that he wrote he packed a weight of close and clear thinking.

Donne's reputation has always had its ups and downs. His contemporary, Ben Jonson, said that "for not keeping of accent he deserved hanging," but he also "esteemed him the first poet in the world in some things" (he seems to have meant some of the early *Elegies* and *Epistles,* in which Donne's intellectual fireworks appear in their most exuberant and dazzling form). Dryden called him "the greatest wit, though not the greatest poet of our nation." It was Dryden (followed by Dr. Johnson [see his *Life of Cowley* in Vol. II]) who fixed upon Donne and his school the label "Metaphysical." "He affects the metaphysics," said Dryden, "and perplexes the minds of the fair sex with nice speculations of philosophy, when he should engage their hearts, and entertain them with the softnesses of love." Dryden meant that Donne appeared to him learned and obscure; he sensed in Donne that medieval-Scholastic cast of mind from which he and his generation were emancipating themselves. The term "Metaphysical" has stuck to Donne and his followers, and it is important to remember, when using it ourselves, that it does not mean simply "philosophical." There is philosophical poetry, poetry dealing with ultimate issues, or the nature of things, even with strictly metaphysical problems, which is not "Metaphysical" in this special sense (one thinks of Lucretius, Milton, Pope, Goethe, Wordsworth, Tennyson, and others). When we call Donne "Metaphysical" we are not classing him with such poets as these; he seldom writes from a purely philosophical impulse. What he does constantly do, however, is to use philosophical imagery to illustrate and define his emotional and intellectual adventures. And this imagery is mainly drawn from Scholastic sources of the medieval type: astronomy, astrology, alchemy, mathematics, the Aristotelian doctrines of form and matter, soul and body; and of course from the vast reservoir of Christian theology. It was precisely because so much of this was coming to seem obsolete in Dryden's time that Dryden broke with it and changed his notes to "heroic."

Dr. Johnson thought that poetry should deal in sublime or moving generalities, such as find an echo in every heart, and found the Metaphysicals too elaborate, too analytical, and too full of farfetched conceits. "Deficient in the sublime and the pathetic," he wrote, "they abounded in hyperbole, in unnatural thoughts, violent fictions, foolish conceits"; they "yoked heterogeneous ideas by violence together"; "to show their learning was their whole endeavor." He conceded that to write on their plan it was at least necessary to read and to think, but it is not surprising that Johnson, to whom Gray's "Elegy" was a touchstone of poetic excellence, should have found Donne neither "natural" nor "just."

The Romantics, on the whole, had little use for Donne. He was too purely intellectual, cared nothing for nature, and was deficient in color and music. Coleridge, who relished his wit and admired his sermons, wrote of him:

With Donne, whose Muse on dromedary trots,
Wreathe iron pokers into true-love knots;
Rhyme's sturdy cripple, fancy's maze and clue,
Wit's forge and fire-blast, meaning's press and
    screw.

And this was the general view of him until about 1920; he was like a fire choked with fuel and smoke, which only seldom flashed into pure flame — that is to say, into lines or images pleasing to a romantic taste.

To say that the poets, critics, and readers of the 1920's found in Donne a model and a stimulus is not to say that his vogue was a passing fashion. It is not likely that he will ever again be omitted, as Arnold omitted him,[1] from the muster roll of our great poets. We no longer instinctively judge poets by nineteenth-century standards; "great" poetry, we now see, can be conceived and composed in the "wits" as well as in what the Victorians meant by the "soul." The distinctive merit of Donne (though some other poets, not all of them of his school or period, have it also) is that he can be "witty" — that is, intellectually nimble and alert — without ceasing to be passionate. Sometimes, indeed, his brain seems to be doing all the work and his heart very little; he will at times draw out an argument, expand a metaphor, or exploit a paradox, in a spirit of sheer extravagance. But at his best he thinks and feels simultaneously; his brilliant intellect plays with glancing lights upon a stream of strong emotion. Moreover, he brought the language of lyric poetry much closer than his predecessors had done to that of speech, skillfully counterpointing speech rhythms with metrical patterns and introducing a new bluntness of tone and vocabulary. Coupled with this tone is a new directness of approach. In his love poetry Donne usually brushes convention aside and explores his feelings — sometimes with curiosity, irony, or cynicism, or again with ardent idealism or intense devotion, but always with subtlety and precision — never with mere profuseness or sentimentality. It is useless, in reading Donne, to sit passively and expect to be charmed, or lulled, or glutted with sound and color. To read him properly is a bracing experience; one's whole self, mind as well as soul, must be on the alert. There is in him no imprecise word or image, no vague suggestiveness; no phrase of his can be slurred over without loss of essential meaning. To read Donne is indeed an excellent preparation for reading "modern" poetry. For although he does not give us the abrupt transitions, the cinematograph technique of some living poets, he yet demands from us, by his high speed and his ever-shifting imagery, a similar kind of vigilance.

[1] See Arnold's essay, "Wordsworth," in Vol. II.

With all this in mind, let us consider a few examples of Donne's poetry. First, what about these "conceits" which Dr. Johnson condemned? What is a conceit? We might begin by calling it a farfetched comparison, a bringing together of thoughts or images usually considered to be very remote from each other. In the poem "A Valediction: Of Weeping," where Donne is bidding a tearful farewell to his lady, he first compares his tears to coins bearing her image, and thence deriving their value:

For thy face coins them, and thy stamp they bear,
And by this mintage they are something worth, . . .

But this does not satisfy him, and he passes on to a far more extravagant comparison:

On a round ball
A workman that hath copies by, can lay
An Europe, Afric, and an Asia,
And quickly make that, which was nothing. *All;*
So doth each tear,
Which thee doth wear,
A globe, yea world by that impression grow,
Till thy tears mixed with mine do overflow
This world, by waters sent from thee, my heaven
dissolvèd so.

The shape of the teardrop reminds him first of a globe; then he thinks of a globe on which a map of the world is depicted; the mapmaker has turned the round "O" of the globe — i.e., in another sense, "nothing" — into "everything," because the world is "all." Similarly, each teardrop which bears the lady's image becomes a whole world, because she is everything to him; and lastly, because she is his "heaven," *her* tears are like rain from "dissolving" clouds above, and mixed with his own will overflow the earth. The "world" image is a favorite one with Donne; he often uses it to symbolize the wholeness of perfect love. Thus the lovers in "The Sun Rising" are a world of themselves, and Donne tells the sun:

Thou sun art half as happy as we,
In that the world's contracted thus;
Thine age asks ease, and since thy duties be
To warm the world, that's done in warming us.

The same image or "conceit" appears again in a very different form and with a quite different meaning, in the "Hymn to God My God, in My Sickness," where his own prone figure, as he lies on his bed sick to death, becomes a map studied by his physicians. This thought at once suggests others: his death will be a "Southwest discovery"; it will be a passing through the straits of death into the Pacific of eternity. Moreover, just as in all flat maps east and west are one, though apparently so far apart, so his west (sunset, death) is really also his east (sunrise, resurrection) because it is the entrance into new life:

As west and east
In all flat maps (and I am one) are one,
So death doth touch the Resurrection.

The word "conceit" used to carry with it a flavor of disparagement; it implied a forced or unnatural comparison, and a poet who used many conceits was held to be "insincere" and artificial. T. S. Eliot, however, has taught us to think of the fusion of disparate images and attitudes as part of the very secret of poetic creation;[1] the poet, according to this view, is a man whose sensibility is inclusive enough to be aware of Spinoza, the sound of a typewriter, and the smell of cooking all at once. Undoubtedly the renewed sense of the puzzling complexity of life, of its manifold paradoxes, which has followed the decline of the nineteenth-century certainties, has brought conceits back into favor, and made them once again seem true to experience. Yet *some* conceits still strike us as frigid — in fact, as intellectual jugglery rather than poetry. This, I think, is true of Donne's comparison of the armlet of his mistress's hair, worn round the arm of his dead body, to the sinewy threads of his spinal cord; these last, descending from his brain, used to hold his body together in life; and the lady's hair, which grew upwards and from a better brain than his, can still better preserve his corpse from dissolution (see "The Funeral" below). The same is true of Crashaw's description of Mary Magdalene's eyes as "portable and compendious oceans," and of Butler's (deliberately funny) lines about the dawn:

And like a lobster boiled, the morn
From black to red began to turn.

It is true of Dryden's description, in an early poem written before he had escaped from the decadent "Metaphysical" manner, of Lord Hastings's smallpox:

[1] See Introduction to Eliot and his essay on the "Metaphysical Poets" in Vol. II.

Each little pimple had a tear in it,
To wail the fault its rising did commit.
("Elegy upon the Death of
the Lord Hastings," 1650)

It is true of the basic hyperbole (though not of all the component parts) of Donne's "Anatomy of the World: The First Anniversary" (below), in which he affects to consider that the death of the child Elizabeth Drury (whose father he then wished to flatter) had brought about the disintegration of the physical and moral worlds.

When is a conceit not a conceit (in the disparaging sense)? We may reply that a conceit is justified when the poet is genuinely moved or passionately alert, and when the conceit, after the first shock of surprise, leaves us with a growing sense of meaning—in a word, when it has the unifying power of the "imagination" as described by Coleridge. This happens in Donne's "A Valediction: Forbidding Mourning," in which the subject is the unity of two souls, persisting in spite of physical separation:

Our two souls therefore, which are one,
Though I must go, endure not yet
A breach, but an expansion,
Like gold to airy thinness beat.

If they be two, they are two so
As stiff twin compasses are two,
Thy soul the fixed foot, makes no show
To move, but doth, if th' other do.

And though it in the center sit,
Yet when the other far doth roam,
It leans, and hearkens after it,
And grows erect, as that comes home.

No poet after the middle of the seventeenth century until (say) 1920 would have brought a mathematical instrument into a love poem; this would indeed have been considered a defiance of poetic decorum, a harsh intermixture of incompatibles. Yet how apt and expressive the image is! Donne offers no profuse or gushing sentiment; he is feeling strongly, but this does not stop the working of his active brain.

Perhaps the most important source of Donne's conceits (and this applies also to other poets of his time and type, such as George Herbert and Crashaw) is his sense of underlying and all-embracing paradox:

Oh, to vex me, contraries meet in one . . .

This sense he owed chiefly to his training in Christian doctrine, which is based upon profound paradoxes. In the teaching of Christ himself there is a continual reversal of the world's values and expectations: the child, the prodigal son, the publicans and sinners are nearer the kingdom of Heaven than the self-righteous and the pharisaical; to gain your life you must lose it; the first shall be last, and the last first. But above all there are the most tremendous of all paradoxes—the union of God and man in the Incarnation, the Word becoming flesh and dwelling among us; and the paradox of the cross, where victory and redemption are snatched from death itself. The habit of mind which comes from continual dwelling upon these and other meaningful contradictions is responsible, I believe, for much that is distinctive of "Metaphysical" poetry (which, after all, was mostly written by clerics). Naturally, this union of contraries is most evident in Donne's religious poetry, that is to say, in that part of his work where his sincerity is quite unmistakable. Take, as an example, "Good Friday, 1613, Riding Westward." Here we first meet the clash of west and east: Donne's body is riding westward, but on Good Friday his inmost soul "bends towards the east." Next we get the paradox of rising and setting (accompanied by an implied play on the words "Sun" and "Son"): Christ, the sun of righteousness, eternal life, rises upon the cross and thereby dies (sets), but that sunset begets, not the night of sin, but everlasting day. Next is the paradox of life and death: God is life itself, yet to look upon his face means death:

"What a death were it then to see God die?"

Lastly, there is the greatest and most baffling paradox of all: the realization that this human figure, suffering the final ignominies of crucifixion, is the second person of the Trinity—the Word by whom all things were made:

Could I behold those hands which span the Poles
And turn all spheres at once, pierced with those holes?

Other fine examples occur in "Holy Sonnet XIV," where Donne is begging God to exert his redemptive force upon him:

That I may rise and stand, o'erthrow me, . . .
Take me to you, imprison me, for I

Except you enthrall me, never shall be free,
Nor ever chaste, except you ravish me.

To appreciate Donne we have to shed all romantic preconceptions; it is useless to go to him expecting beautiful pictures, musical diction, or sustained grandeur. If he mentions " beautiful " things such as a flower, or the moon, it is not to extract any romantic glamour from them, but make a point by analogy. He uses them as emblems or parables, as here in " The Ecstasy ":

A single violet transplant,
The strength, the color, and the size,
(All which before was poor and scant)
Redoubles still, and multiplies.

The violet is not there for its color or its spring associations, nor because it is sweeter than Cytherea's breath, but simply because it flourishes better when transplanted, and so illustrates Donne's argument about the transplanting of each lover's soul into the other's. Or if he refers to the moon (in " A Valediction: Of Weeping "):

O more than moon,
Draw not up seas to drown me in thy sphere,

it is with no thought of its magic. Donne's moon unlike Tennyson's throws no " long glories on the level lake"; it is there as a celestial body, which, like his mistress, has powers of gravitational attraction.

Donne can at times write musically in the lyric vein, though even then he does not stop thinking:

Sweetest love, I do not go,
For weariness of thee,
Nor in hope the world can show
A fitter love for me;
But since that I
Must die at last, 'tis best
To use myself in jest,
Thus by feigned deaths to die.

He can also *begin* to soar aloft on eagle wing, but the grandeur of his flight is usually broken up into circlings and eddyings of thought. Take the magnificent opening of " Holy Sonnet VII ":

At the round earth's imagined corners, blow
Your trumpets, angels, and arise, arise
From death, you numberless infinities
Of souls, and to your scattered bodies go,

All whom the flood did, and fire shall o'erthrow,
All whom war, dearth, age, agues, tyrannies,
Despair, law, chance, hath slain, and you whose eyes
Shall behold God, and never taste death's woe.

The pressure of emotion, which sweeps unbroken through the first four lines, is checked by the thudding monosyllables which follow. Donne can, however, use this sledge-hammer effect to express impassioned pleading with God, and at the same time to convey the very violence which he begs from the divine Blacksmith:

Batter my heart, three-personed God; for you
As yet but knock, breathe, shine, and seek to mend;
That I may rise and stand, o'erthrow me, and bend
Your force, to break, blow, burn, and make me
    new.

The best of Donne's prose is in his *Meditations* and *Sermons,* of which some specimens are given below. We saw above how powerfully his sermons affected his hearers, and it is possible to guess why this was so — although by our standards they are too long, and too heavily laden with Scholastic learning and ingenious analogies. But he evidently preached like a man possessed: possessed by the thoughts of God, of eternity, of Heaven, of sin, judgment, mercy, and redemption; and in his passionate yearning to save souls he constantly rose to a richly orchestrated eloquence, often varied, however, and made more telling by a familiar, everyday allusion. Donne's prose unit is the cumulative period (often of enormous length and intricacy), and no short passage can give a true impression of his style. The reader is referred to the extracts which follow; and when he has read these and the *Divine Poems,* and juxtaposed both with the earlier secular verse, he will perhaps begin to see more clearly why Carew ended his " Elegy upon Donne " with these words:

Here lies a King that ruled as he thought fit
The universal Monarchy of wit;
Here lie two Flamens, and both those the best,
Apollo's first, at last the true God's priest.

Reading Suggestions

EDITIONS

Sir H. J. C. Grierson, *The Poems of John Donne* (1912, reissued 1929). The standard, definitive edition. The introductory essay and notes are of the greatest value.
Sir H. J. C. Grierson, *Metaphysical Lyrics and Poems of the Seventeenth Century: Donne to Butler* (1921,

and several later reprints). Contains an important introductory essay.

John Hayward, editor, *The "Nonesuch" Donne* (1949). Contains all Donne's verse and ample selections from his prose, with useful headnotes.

Helen Gardner, *Donne: The Divine Poems* (1952). With an introductory essay on Donne as a religious poet, and a commentary relating these poems to his life and religious position.

CRITICISM

Izaak Walton, *Lives* (of Donne and others) (1640, enlarged 1658). Available in *Oxford World's Classics*, Vol. 303 (1927). The earliest biography, written with great charm by Donne's affectionate friend (author of *The Compleat Angler*). No reader of Donne should miss this, but the facts need to be corrected by the work of later scholars.

T. S. Eliot, "The Metaphysical Poets" (1921). Reprinted in *Selected Essays* (1932), and given in the present anthology (in Vol. II). This essay did more than anything, apart from Grierson's work, to establish the twentieth-century revaluation of the Metaphysical poets.

G. Williamson, *The Donne Tradition* (1930). This book (and Bald's below) analyzes the poetic influence of Donne in the seventeenth century.

Theodore Spencer, *A Garland for John Donne* (1931). This tercentenary volume contains essays by T. S. Eliot, E. M. Simpson, Mario Praz, John Hayward, Mary P. Ramsay, John Sparrow, George Williamson, and Theodore Spencer.

R. C. Bald, *Donne's Influence in English Literature* (1932).

Evelyn M. Simpson, *A Study of the Prose Works of John Donne* (2nd edition, 1948). The best general guide to Donne's prose and thought.

J. B. Leishman, *The Monarch of Wit* (1951). A penetrating analytical and comparative study of Donne's poetry.

---

from SONGS AND SONNETS

First published in 1633 (after Donne's death). It is not possible to date the composition of these poems exactly, but they were probably written before 1600 (Ben Jonson says "ere he was twenty-five years old"). It is usually supposed that the more cynical ones were written before 1598, and the more passionate and heartfelt after his meeting with Anne More in that year.

THE GOOD MORROW

I wonder by my troth, what thou and I
Did, till we loved? were we not weaned till then?
But sucked° on country pleasures, childishly?
Or snorted° we in the seven sleepers'° den?
'Twas so; but this, all pleasures fancies be.
If ever any beauty I did see,
Which I desired, and got, 'twas but a dream of thee.

And now good morrow to our waking souls,
Which watch not one another out of fear;
For love all love of other sights controls,   10
And makes one little room an everywhere.
Let sea-discoverers to new worlds have gone,
Let maps to other, worlds on worlds have shown,
Let us possess one world, each hath one, and is one.

My face in thine eye, thine in mine appears,
And true plain hearts do in the faces rest;
Where can we find two better hemispheres
Without sharp north, without declining west?

THE GOOD MORROW. **3. sucked:** suckled. **4. snorted:** snored.
seven sleepers: seven young men of Ephesus who (according to Gregory of Tours) were walled up in a cave by the persecuting Emperor Decius in 250 A.D., and slept there till they were found alive in 479 A.D.

Whatever dies, was not mixed equally;°
If our two loves be one, or thou and I   20
Love so alike that none do slacken, none can die.

SONG

Go, and catch a falling star,
    Get with child a mandrake° root,
Tell me, where all past years are,
    Or who cleft the devil's foot,
Teach me to hear mermaids singing,
Or to keep off envy's stinging,
        And find
        What wind
Serves to advance an honest mind.

If thou be'st born to strange sights,   10
    Things invisible to see,
Ride ten thousand days and nights,
    Till age snow white hairs on thee,
Thou, when thou return'st, wilt tell me
All strange wonders that befell thee,
        And swear
        Nowhere
Lives a woman true, and fair.

If thou find'st one, let me know,
    Such a pilgrimage were sweet;   20
Yet do not, I would not go,
    Though at next door we might meet,

19. not ... equally: not compounded of simple and similar elements, and therefore subject to corruption. Cf. Aquinas: "For there is no corruption save where there is contrariety." SONG. **2. mandrake:** the mandragora plant, with a forked root like the lower part of the human body. It was currently supposed to shriek when pulled up.

Though she were true, when you met her,
And last, till you write your letter,
    Yet she
    Will be
False, ere I come, to two, or three.

WOMAN'S CONSTANCY

Now thou hast loved me one whole day,
Tomorrow when thou leav'st, what wilt thou say?
Wilt thou then antedate some new-made vow?
    Or say that now
We are not just those persons, which we were?
Or, that oaths made in reverential fear
Of Love, and his wrath, any may forswear?
Or, as true deaths true marriages untie,
So lovers' contracts, images of those,
Bind but till sleep, death's image, them unloose?
    Or, your own end to justify,   11
For having purposed change, and falsehood, you
Can have no way but falsehood to be true?
Vain lunatic, against these 'scapes° I could
    Dispute, and conquer, if I would,
    Which I abstain to do,
For by tomorrow, I may think so too.

THE SUN RISING

    Busy old fool, unruly sun,
    Why dost thou thus,
Through windows, and through curtains call on
    us?
Must to thy motions lovers' seasons run?
    Saucy, pedantic wretch, go chide
    Late schoolboys, and sour prentices,
    Go tell court huntsmen, that the king will ride,
    Call country ants to harvest offices;
Love, all alike, no season knows, nor clime,
Nor hours, days, months, which are the rags of
    time.   10

    Thy beams, so reverend and strong
    Why shouldst thou think?
I could eclipse and cloud them with a wink,
But that I would not lose her sight so long:
    If her eyes have not blinded thine,
    Look, and tomorrow late, tell me,
Whether both th' Indias of spice and mine°
Be where thou left'st them, or lie here with
    me.
Ask for those kings whom thou saw'st yesterday,
And thou shalt hear, All here in one bed lay.   20

She's all states, and all princes, I,
    Nothing else is.
Princes do but play us; compared to this,
All honor's mimic; all wealth alchemy.
    Thou sun art half as happy as we,
    In that the world's contracted thus;
    Thine age asks ease, and since thy duties be
    To warm the world, that's done in warming us.
Shine here to us, and thou art everywhere;
This bed thy center is, these walls, thy sphere.   30

THE CANONIZATION

For God's sake hold your tongue, and let me
    love;
    Or chide my palsy, or my gout,
My five gray hairs, or ruined fortune flout;
    With wealth your state, your mind with arts im-
        prove,
        Take you a course, get you a place,
        Observe his Honor, or his Grace,
Or the king's real, or his stampèd face°
    Contemplate; what you will, approve,
    So you will let me love.

Alas, alas, who's injured by my love?   10
    What merchant's ships have my sighs drowned?
Who says my tears have overflowed his ground?
    When did my colds a forward spring remove?
        When did the heats which my veins fill
        Add one more to the plaguy bill?°
Soldiers find wars, and lawyers find out still
    Litigious men, which quarrels move,
    Though she and I do love.

Call us what you will, we are made such by love;
    Call her one, me another fly,   20
We're tapers too, and at our own cost die,°
    And we in us find th' eagle and the dove.°
        The Phoenix° riddle hath more wit
        By us; we two being one, are it.
So to one neutral thing both sexes fit,
    We die and rise the same, and prove
    Mysterious by this love.

We can die by it, if not live by love,
    And if unfit for tombs and hearse
Our legend be, it will be fit for verse;   30

WOMAN'S CONSTANCY. 14. 'scapes: excuses, evasions. THE
SUN RISING. 17. Indias . . . mine: i.e., the East Indies or Spice
Islands, and the West Indies, where there were mines of gold
and silver. Cf. *Anatomy of the World,* ll. 230–33.

THE CANONIZATION. 7. stamped face: i.e., on coins. 15. plaguy
bill: list of deaths from the plague (issued weekly during epi-
demics). A big epidemic of plague occurred in 1605. 20–
21. Call . . . die: "Call us each midges, which burn in a taper's
flame; we are also like the tapers, self-consumed." 22. Eagle
. . . dove: symbols of constancy and love. 23–27. Phoenix . . .
love: Only one of these fabulous birds ever existed at a time;
it died (like the taper) self-consumed in flame, but from its
ashes arose a new phoenix. Cf. *Anatomy of the World,* ll. 217–
18; also *The Tempest,* III.iii. 23n.

And if no piece of chronicle° we prove,
　　We'll build in sonnets pretty rooms;
　　As well a well-wrought urn becomes
The greatest ashes, as half-acre tombs,
　　And by these hymns, all shall approve
　　Us canonized for love;

And thus invoke us: "You whom reverend love
　　Made one another's hermitage;
You, to whom love was peace, that now is rage;
　　Who° did the whole world's soul contract, and
　　　　drove　　　　　　　　　　　　　　　40
　　　　Into the glasses of your eyes
　　　　(So made such mirrors, and such spies,
That they did all to you epitomize),
　　Countries, towns, courts: beg from above
　　A pattern of your love!"°

LOVERS' INFINITENESS

If yet I have not all thy love,
Dear, I shall never have it all,
I cannot breathe one other sigh, to move,
Nor can entreat one other tear to fall,
And all my treasure, which should purchase thee,
Sighs, tears, and oaths, and letters I have spent.
Yet no more can be due to me,
Than at the bargain made was meant.
If then thy gift of love were partial,
That some to me, some should to others fall,　10
　　Dear, I shall never have thee all.

Or if then thou gavest me all,
All was but all, which thou hadst then;°
But if in thy heart, since, there be or shall
New love created be, by other men,
Which have their stocks entire, and can in tears,
In sighs, in oaths, and letters outbid me,
This new love may beget new fears,
For, this love was not vowed by thee.
And yet it was, thy gift being general;　　20
The ground, thy heart, is mine; whatever shall
　　Grow there, dear, I should have it all.

Yet I would not have all yet,
He that hath all can have no more,
And since my love doth every day admit
New growth, thou shouldst have new rewards in
　　store;
Thou canst not every day give me thy heart,
If thou canst give it, then thou never gavest it:
Love's riddles are, that though thy heart depart,

It stays at home, and thou with losing savest it:　30
But we will have a way more liberal,
Than changing hearts, to join them, so we shall
　　Be one, and one another's all.

SONG

Sweetest love, I do not go,
　　For weariness of thee,
Nor in hope the world can show
　　A fitter love for me;
　　　　But since that I
Must die at last, 'tis best
To use myself in jest,
　　Thus by feigned deaths° to die.

Yesternight the sun went hence,
　　And yet is here today;　　　　　　　　10
He hath no desire nor sense,
　　Nor half so short a way:
　　　　Then fear not me,
But believe that I shall make
Speedier journeys, since I take
　　More wings and spurs than he.

O how feeble is man's power,
　　That° if good fortune fall,
Cannot add another hour,
　　Nor a lost hour recall!　　　　　　　　20
　　　　But come bad chance,
And we join to it our strength,
And we teach it art and length,
　　Itself o'er us to advance.

When thou sigh'st, thou sigh'st not wind,
　　But sigh'st° my soul away,
When thou weep'st, unkindly kind,
　　My life's blood doth decay.
　　　　It cannot be
That thou lov'st me, as thou say'st,　　　　30
If in thine my life thou waste,
　　That art the best of me.

Let not thy divining heart
　　Forethink me any ill,
Destiny may take thy part,
　　And may thy fears fulfill;
　　　　But think that we
Are but turned aside to sleep;
They who one another keep
　　Alive, ne'er parted be.　　　　　　　　40

---

31. chronicle: prose history or inscription.　40–44. Who . . .
courts: Cf. "The Good Morrow," l. 14, "Let us possess one
world, each hath one, and is one."　44–45. beg . . . love: The
canonized lovers are asked to pray Heaven for a pattern for
others to copy. LOVERS' INFINITENESS. 13. All . . . then:
That "all" was merely "all the love you had then."

SONG. 8. feigned deaths: imagined deaths (departure from his
mistress being considered as a form of "dying").　18–23. That
. . . length: "We can make ill luck seem worse and last longer,
though we cannot prolong or recover good fortune."　26. sigh'st:
Each sigh was supposed to consume a drop of the heart's blood.

AIR AND ANGELS

Twice or thrice had I loved thee,
Before I knew thy face or name;
So in a voice, so in a shapeless flame,
Angels affect us oft, and worshiped be;
　　Still when, to where thou wert, I came,
　　Some lovely glorious nothing I did see.
But since my soul, whose child love is,
Takes limbs of flesh, and else could nothing do,
　　More subtle than the parent is
Love must not be, but take a body too,　　10
　　And therefore what thou wert, and who,
　　　　I bid love ask, and now
That it assume thy body, I allow,
And fix itself in thy lip, eye, and brow.

Whilst thus to ballast love I thought,
And so more steadily to have gone,
With wares which would sink admiration
I saw, I had love's pinnace overfraught;
　　Every thy hair° for love to work upon
Is much too much, some fitter must be sought;
For, nor in nothing, nor in things　　21
Extreme, and scatt'ring° bright, can love inhere;
　　Then as an angel, face and wings
Of air, not pure as it, yet pure doth wear,°
　　So° thy love may be my love's sphere;
　　　　Just such disparity
As is 'twixt air and angels' purity,
'Twixt women's love and men's will ever be.

THE ANNIVERSARY

All kings, and all their favorites,
　　All glory of honors, beauties, wits,
The sun itself, which makes times,° as they pass,
Is elder by a year, now, than it was
When thou and I first one another saw:
All other things to their destruction draw,
　　Only our love hath no decay;
This, no tomorrow hath, nor yesterday,
Running it never runs from us away,
But truly keeps his first, last, everlasting day.　　10

Two graves must hide thine and my corse,
　　If one might, death were no divorce.
Alas, as well as other princes, we
(Who prince enough in one another be)
Must leave at last in death, these eyes, and ears,
Oft fed with true oaths, and with sweet salt tears;
　　But souls where nothing dwells but love
(All other thoughts being inmates°) then shall
　　　　prove
This, or a love increasèd there above,
When bodies to their graves, souls from their
　　　　graves remove.　　20

And then we shall be throughly blessed,
　　But we no more than all the rest;°
Here upon earth, we're kings, and none but we
Can be such kings, nor of such subjects be.
Who is so safe as we? where none can do
Treason to us, except one of us two.
　　True and false fears let us refrain,
Let us love nobly, and live, and add again
Years and years unto years, till we attain　　29
To write threescore: this is the second of our reign.

A VALEDICTION: OF MY NAME,
IN THE WINDOW

I

My name engraved herein°
Doth contribute my firmness to this glass,
　　Which, ever since that charm, hath been
　　As hard as that which graved it was;
Thine eye will give it price enough, to mock
　　The diamonds of either rock.°

II

'Tis much that glass should be
As all-confessing, and through-shine° as I,
　　'Tis more, that it shows thee to thee,
　　And clear reflects thee to thine eye.　　10
But all such rules, love's magic can undo,
　　Here you see me, and I am you.°

III

As° no one point, nor dash,
Which are but accessories to this name,
　　The showers and tempests can outwash,

18. **inmates**: transient lodgers (as distinct from the permanent dweller, love).　**22. But . . . rest**: In Heaven all are equally happy, whereas here on earth "none but we can be such kings." OF MY NAME, IN THE WINDOW.　**1. herein**: i.e., scratched (with a diamond) on the windowpane.　**6. either rock**: "Of the old, or the new rock" was then said of precious stones. Those from ancient mines were considered finer than those from more recent ones.　**8. through-shine**: transparent.　**12. Here . . . you**: "You see me, because my name is written there, but in seeing me you see yourself, because lovers are identical."　**13–18. As . . . still**: "As no storms can wash away the inscription, so likewise I shall remain unchanged. For you, with the pattern of my constancy before you, fidelity should be easier."

AIR AND ANGELS.　**19. Every . . . hair**: "each hair of yours."　**22. scatt'ring**: dazzling.　**23–24. Then . . . wear**: According to the Schoolmen, angels appeared to men by assuming a body of condensed air; this body, though pure, was less pure than the angel's own spiritual essence or self.　**25–28. So . . . be**: Donne assumes that woman's love is less spiritual than man's; thus, her love may be his love's "sphere" (or embodiment), and be to his what an angel's aerial body is to the angel.　THE ANNIVERSARY.　**3. times**: seasons.

So shall all times find me the same;
You this entireness better may fulfill,
    Who have the pattern with you still.

IV

Or if too hard and deep
This learning be, for a scratched name to teach,
    It, as a given death's head° keep,   21
    Lovers' mortality to preach,
Or think this ragged bony name to be
    My ruinous anatomy.°

V

Then, as all my souls° be
Emparadised in you (in whom alone
    I understand, and grow and see)
The rafters of my body, bone
Being still with you, the muscle, sinew, and
        vein,
    Which tile this house, will come again.   30

VI

Till my return, repair
And recompact my scattered body so.°
    As all the virtuous powers° which are
    Fixed in the stars, are said to flow
Into such characters, as gravèd be
    When these stars have supremacy:

VII

So, since this name was cut
When love and grief their exaltation had,
    No door 'gainst this name's influence shut;
    As much more loving, as more sad,   40
'Twill make thee; and thou shouldst, till I return,
    Since I die daily, daily mourn.

VIII

When thy inconsiderate hand
Flings ope this casement, with my trembling
        name,
    To look on one, whose wit or land,
    New battery to thy heart may frame,
Then think this name alive, and that thou thus
    In it offend'st my Genius.°

21. given . . . head: a skull, kept in view as a *memento mori* or reminder of mortality. 24. anatomy: skeleton. 25. all my souls: The soul was supposed to comprise three parts: the soul of growth (shared with the plants), the soul of sense (shared with the animals), and the rational soul (distinctively human); cf. "Countess of Bedford," ll. 34–35. 31–32. Till . . . so: She has with her all the elements needed to rebuild his body — the skeleton (the scratched name) and the three souls; he bids her put these together, and the rest will be added. 33. virtuous powers: efficacious influences. From ll. 33–39 Donne is using astrological language; the sense is: letters ("characters") inscribed ("graved") at a time when certain stars are in the ascendant ("have supremacy") absorb the influences of those stars; my name was cut when love and grief were in the ascendant ("exaltation had"), so do not oppose its influence. Cf. *Anatomy of the World*, ll. 391 ff. 48. Genius: guardian angel.

IX

And when thy melted maid,
Corrupted by thy lover's gold, and page,   50
    His letter at thy pillow hath laid,
    Disputed it, and tamed thy rage,
And thou begin'st to thaw towards him, for
        this,
    May my name step in, and hide his.

X

And if this treason go
To an overt act, and that thou write again;
    In superscribing,° this name flow
    Into thy fancy, from the pane.
So, in forgetting thou remmb'rest right,
    And unaware to me shalt write.   60

XI

But glass and lines must be
No means our firm substantial love to keep;
    Near death inflicts this lethargy,
    And this I murmur in my sleep;
Impute this idle talk to that I go,°
    For dying° men talk often so.

TWICKENHAM° GARDEN

Blasted with sighs, and surrounded° with tears,
    Hither I come to seek the spring,
    And at mine eyes, and at mine ears,
Receive such balms, as else cure everything;
    But O, self-traitor, I do bring
The spider° love, which transubstantiates° all,
    And can convert manna to gall,
And that this place may thoroughly be thought
    True Paradise, I have the serpent brought.

'Twere wholesomer for me, that winter did   10
    Benight the glory of this place,
    And that a grave frost did forbid
These trees to laugh, and mock me to my face;
    But that I may not this disgrace
Endure, nor yet leave loving, Love, let me
    Some senseless piece of this place be;
Make me a mandrake, so I may groan here,°
    Or a stone fountain weeping out my year.

Hither with crystal vials, lovers come,
    And take my tears, which are love's wine,   20

57. superscribing: writing the (lover's) name and address. 65. to . . . go: "to the fact that I am going away." 66. dying: to leave his mistress is to "die" (a frequent conceit with Donne). TWICKENHAM GARDEN. Twickenham: the residence of the Countess of Bedford, Donne's friend and patron. 1. surrounded: overflowed. 6. spider: supposed to infuse poison into food, etc. transubstantiates: i.e., changes the substance of everything. 17. mandrake . . . here: Grierson adopts the MS reading "groan" here (rather than the "grow" of the editions), although the mandrake plant was more usually said to "shriek" when pulled up. See "Song," p. 365, l. 2n.

And try your mistress' tears at home,
For all are false, that taste not just like mine;
  Alas, hearts do not in eyes shine,
Nor can you more judge woman's thoughts by
    tears,
Than by her shadow, what she wears.
O perverse sex, where none is true but she,
Who's therefore true, because her truth kills me.

LOVE'S GROWTH

I scarce believe my love to be so pure
    As I had thought it was,
    Because it doth endure
Vicissitude, and season, as the grass;
Methinks I lied all winter, when I swore
My love was infinite, if spring make it more.
But if this medicine, love, which cures all sorrow
With more, not only be no quintessence,°
But mixed of all stuffs, paining soul, or sense,
And of the sun his working vigor borrow,   10
Love's not so pure, and abstract, as they use
To say, which have no mistress but their Muse,
But as all else, being elemented° too,
Love sometimes would contemplate, sometimes do.

And yet no greater, but more eminent,°
    Love by the spring is grown;
    As, in the firmament,
Stars by the sun are not enlarged, but shown,°
Gentle love deeds, as blossoms on a bough,
From love's awakened root do bud out now.   20
If, as in water stirred more circles be
Produced by one, love such additions take,
Those like so many spheres, but one heaven make,
For they are all concentric unto thee.°
And though each spring do add to love new heat,
As princes do in times of action get
New taxes, and remit them not in peace,
No winter shall abate the spring's increase.

THE DREAM

Dear love, for nothing less than thee
Would I have broke this happy dream,
    It was a theme
For reason, much too strong for fantasy,
Therefore thou waked'st me wisely; yet
My dream thou brok'st not, but continued'st it;

LOVE'S GROWTH. 8. quintessence: (in ancient and medieval philosophy) the fifth essence, apart from the "four elements"; a refined extract supposed to have medicinal properties. See Bacon's *Essays*, p. 334, n. 86. 13. elemented: embodied in, or mixed with, material elements (earth, water, air, fire). 15. eminent: conspicuous. 18. shown: i.e., made to *seem* larger (said to be the case just before sunrise). 23–24. Those . . . thee: referring to the medieval world picture of concentric heavenly "spheres" surrounding the earth. See Additional Note A, p. 195.

Thou art so truth,° that thoughts of thee suffice
To make dreams truths, and fables histories;
Enter these arms, for since thou thought'st it best,
Not to dream all my dream, let's act the rest.   10

As lightning, or a taper's light,
Thine eyes, and not thy noise waked me;
    Yet I thought thee
(For thou lovest truth) an angel, at first sight,
But when I saw thou sawest my heart,
And knew'st my thoughts, beyond an angel's art,°
When thou knew'st what I dreamt, when thou
    knew'st when
Excess of joy would wake me, and cam'st then,
I must confess, it could not choose but be
Profane, to think thee anything but thee.   20

Coming and staying showed thee, thee,
But rising makes me doubt, that now,
    Thou art not thou.
That love is weak, where fear's as strong as he;
'Tis not all spirit, pure, and brave,
If mixture it of *Fear, Shame, Honor,* have.
Perchance as torches which must ready be,
Men light and put out, so thou deal'st with me,
Thou cam'st to kindle, goest to come; then I
Will dream that hope again, but else would die.   30

A VALEDICTION: OF WEEPING

    Let me pour forth
My tears before thy face, whilst I stay here,
For thy face coins them, and thy stamp they bear,°
And by this mintage they are something worth,
    For thus they be
    Pregnant of thee;
Fruits of much grief they are, emblems of more;
When a tear falls, that thou falls which it bore,°
So thou and I are nothing then, when on a diverse
    shore.

    On a round ball   10
A workman that hath copies by, can lay
An Europe, Afric, and an Asia,
And quickly make that, which was nothing, *All;*°
    So doth each tear,
    Which thee doth wear,
A globe, yea world by that impression grow,°

THE DREAM. 7. truth: She is Truth itself (like God himself), hence — 16. And . . . art: She can read his thoughts, which angels cannot do. A VALEDICTION: OF WEEPING. 3. For . . . bear: in general, because she causes them, but probably also because each (like a tiny mirror) reflects her face. 8. that . . . bore: "Thou" is probably a noun, thus: "With each tear that falls, there falls also that 'Thou' (image of thee) which it carried upon it." 10–13. On . . . All: A skilled geographer, with maps at hand, can soon turn a globe (shaped like "O," hence "nothing") into a representation of the world, i.e., "All." 14–16. So . . . grow: "In the same way each tear of mine, because it has your image in it, becomes a globe, indeed a whole world

Till thy tears mixed with mine do overflow
This world, by waters sent from thee, my heaven
   dissolvèd so.

      O more than moon,
Draw not up seas to drown me in thy sphere,   20
Weep me not dead, in thine arms, but forbear
To teach the sea, what it may do too soon;
      Let not the wind
      Example find,
To do me more harm, than it purposeth;
Since thou and I sigh one another's breath,
Whoe'er sighs most, is cruelest, and hastes the
   other's death.

THE MESSAGE

Send home my long strayed eyes to me,
Which O! too long have dwelt on thee;
Yet since there they have learned such ill,
      Such forced fashions,
      And false passions,
        That they be
        Made by thee
Fit for no good sight, keep them still.

Send home my harmless heart again,
Which no unworthy thought could stain;   10
But if it be taught by thine
      To make jestings
      Of protestings,
        And cross° both
        Word and oath,
Keep it, for then 'tis none of mine.

Yet send me back my heart and eyes,
That I may know, and see thy lies,
And may laugh and joy, when thou
      Art in anguish   20
      And dost languish
        For someone
        That will none,
Or prove as false as thou art now.

A NOCTURNAL
UPON ST. LUCY'S DAY

Being the Shortest Day

'Tis the year's midnight, and it is the day's,
Lucy's,° who scarce seven hours herself unmasks;
   The sun is spent, and now his flasks°

Send forth light squibs, no constant rays;
   The world's whole sap is sunk:
The general balm th' hydroptic earth hath drunk,°
Whither, as to the bed's feet, life is shrunk,
Dead and interred; yet all these seem to laugh,
Compared with me, who am their epitaph.

Study me then, you who shall lovers be   10
At the next world, that is, at the next spring:
   For° I am every dead thing,
   In whom love wrought new alchemy.
     For his art did express
A quintessence even from nothingness,
From dull privations, and lean emptiness:
He ruined me, and I am re-begot
Of absence, darkness, death; things which are not.

All° others, from all things, draw all that's good,
Life, soul, form, spirit, whence they being have;
   I, by love's limbeck am the grave   21
   Of all, that's nothing. Oft a flood
     Have we two wept, and so
Drowned the whole world, us two; oft did we grow
To be two Chaoses, when we did show
Care to aught else;° and often absences
Withdrew our souls, and made us carcasses.

But I am by her death (which word wrongs her)
Of the first nothing, the elixir° grown;
   Were I a man, that I were one   30
   I needs must know; I should prefer,
     If I were any beast,
Some ends, some means; yea plants, yea stones detest
And love;° all, all some properties invest;
If I an ordinary nothing were,
As shadow, a light, and body must be here.

But I am none; nor will my sun renew.
You lovers, for whose sake, the lesser sun
   At this time to the Goat° is run

6. The . . . drunk: The dropsical (hence thirsty) earth has drunk all the world's vital juices (sap sinks in winter). 12–18. For . . . not: The object of "alchemy" was to extract the "quintessence" of things. "From my former state of nothingness ('privations' and 'emptiness') love extracted this 'quintessence'; he ruined me (by her death?), and now I am rebegotten of further negations ('absence, darkness, death')." 19–22. All . . . nothing: "Other men draw life, etc., from everything, whereas I, distilled into nothingness by love's alembic ('limbeck'), have become the grave of all negations." ("Grave of all, that's nothing" might mean "grave of all things, that is to say — nothing.") 24–26. "We were a 'world' (cosmos) when united, but 'two Chaoses' (mere unordered matter) when distracted by other thoughts." 29. elixir: distilled essence, or quintessence. He is now the essence, not merely of nonentity, but of "the first nothing," i.e., that out of which God created all things. 33–34. yea . . . love: The very plants, and even inanimate things, have likes and dislikes (as a stem leans to the light, or iron moves to a loadstone). 39. Goat: Capricornus, zodiacal sign where the sun passes in spring.

(because you are all the world to me)." THE MESSAGE. 14. cross: cancel. ST. LUCY'S DAY. 2. Lucy's: St. Lucy's Day, according to the old style of reckoning, was on December 23, and was accounted the shortest day of the year. In more northern latitudes (e.g., in England) the shortest days are shorter than in the United States. 3. flasks: probably a metaphor from "powder flask," a container for gunpowder.

To fetch new lust, and give it you,   40
  Enjoy your summer all;
Since she enjoys her long night's festival,
Let me prepare towards her, and let me call
This hour her vigil, and her eve, since this
Both the year's, and the day's deep midnight is.

A VALEDICTION:
FORBIDDING MOURNING

As virtuous men pass mildly away,
  And whisper to their souls, to go,
Whilst some of their sad friends do say,
  The breath goes now, and some say, no:

So let us melt, and make no noise,
  No tear-floods, nor sigh-tempests move,
'Twere profanation of our joys
  To tell the laity our love.

Moving° of th' earth brings harms and fears,
  Men reckon what it did and meant,   10
But trepidation of the spheres,
  Though greater far, is innocent.

Dull sublunary lovers' love
  (Whose soul is sense) cannot admit
Absence, because it doth remove
  Those things which elemented it.°

But we by a love, so much refined,
  That ourselves know not what it is,
Interassurèd of the mind,
  Care less eyes, lips, and hands to miss.   20

Our two souls therefore, which are one,
  Though I must go, endure not yet
A breach, but an expansion,
  Like gold to airy thinness beat.

If they be two, they are two so
  As stiff twin compasses are two,
Thy soul the fixed foot, makes no show
  To move, but doth, if th' other do.

And though it in the center sit,
  Yet when the other far doth roam,   30
It leans, and hearkens after it,
  And grows erect, as that comes home.

Such wilt thou be to me, who must
  Like th' other foot, obliquely run;

Thy firmness makes my circle just,
  And makes me end, where I begun.

THE ECSTASY

Where, like a pillow on a bed,
  A pregnant bank swelled up, to rest
The violet's reclining head,
  Sat we two, one another's best.
Our hands were firmly cemented
  With a fast balm, which thence did spring,
Our eyebeams° twisted, and did thread
  Our eyes, upon one double string;
So t' intergraft our hands, as yet
  Was all the means to make us one,   10
And pictures in our eyes to get
  Was all our propagation.
As 'twixt two equal armies, Fate
  Suspends uncertain victory,
Our souls (which to advance their state
  Were gone out) hung 'twixt her and me.
And whilst our souls negotiate there,
  We like sepulchral statues lay;
All day, the same our postures were,
  And we said nothing, all the day.   20
If any, so by love refined,
  That he soul's language understood,
And by good love were grown all mind,
  Within convenient distance stood,
He (though he knew not which soul spake,
  Because both meant, both spake the same)
Might thence a new concoction° take,
  And part far purer than he came.
This° ecstasy doth unperplex
  (We said) and tell us what we love;   30
We see by this, it was not sex,
  We see, we saw not what did move:
But as all several souls contain
  Mixture of things, they know not what,
Love these mixed souls doth mix again,
  And makes both one, each this and that.
A single violet transplant,
  The strength, the color, and the size,
(All which before was poor and scant)
  Redoubles still, and multiplies.   40
When love, with one another so
  Interinanimates two souls,
That abler soul, which thence doth flow,
  Defects of loneliness controls.
We then, who are this new soul, know,
  Of what we are composed, and made,

VALEDICTION: FORBIDDING MOURNING. **9–12. Moving . . . innocent:** Earthquakes cause alarm and damage, but heavenly
movements (specifically the oscillation of the ecliptic or sun's
orbit, which was supposed to cause the precession of the equinoxes — continuous changes in the time of the equinoxes due
to slow change in the position of the earth's axis) are harmless.
16. which . . . it: in which it was embodied; or simply, which
composed it.

THE ECSTASY. **7. eyebeams:** invisible rays emitted by the eyes
(in Elizabethan theory), along which images of objects traveled
to the brain. **27. concoction:** compound of ingredients; hence,
here, frame of mind. **29–32. This . . . move:** "In the light of
this 'ecstasy' (detachment of soul from body) we now realize
that we had previously mistaken the true source of our emotion."

For th' atomies° of which we grow,
　　Are souls, whom no change can invade.
But O alas, so long, so far
　　Our bodies why do we forbear?　　　　50
They are ours, though they are not we: we are
　　The intelligences, they the sphere.°
We owe them thanks, because they thus,
　　Did us, to us, at first convey,
Yielded their forces,° sense, to us,
　　Nor are dross to us, but allay.°
On man heaven's influence works not so,
　　But that it first imprints the air:°
So soul into the soul may flow,
　　Though it to body first repair.　　　　60
As our blood labors to beget
　　Spirits,° as like souls as it can,
Because such fingers need to knit
　　That subtle knot, which makes us man:
So must pure lovers' souls descend
　　T' affections, and to faculties,
Which sense may reach and apprehend,
　　Else a great prince in prison lies.°
To our bodies turn we then, that so
　　Weak men on love revealed may look;　　70
Love's mysteries in souls do grow,
　　But yet the body is his book,
And if some lover, such as we,
　　Have heard this dialogue of one,
Let him still mark us, he shall see
　　Small change, when we're to bodies gone.

LOVE'S DEITY

I long to talk with some old lover's ghost,
　　Who died before the god of love was born:
I cannot think that he, who then loved most,
　　Sunk so low, as to love one which did scorn.
But since this god produced a destiny,
And that vice-nature,° custom, lets it be;
　　I must love her, that loves not me.

Sure, they which made him god, meant not so
　　much,
　　Nor he, in his young godhead practiced it.
But when an even flame two hearts did touch,　10
　　His office was indulgently to fit
Actives to passives. Correspondency

Only his subject was; it cannot be
　　Love, till I love her, that loves me.

But every modern° god will now extend
　　His vast prerogative, as far as Jove.
To rage, to lust, to write to, to commend,
　　All is the purlieu of the god of love.
Oh were we wakened by this tyranny
To ungod this child again, it could not be　　20
　　I should love her, who loves not me.

Rebel and atheist too, why murmur I,
　　As though I felt the worst that love could do?
Love might make me leave loving, or might try
　　A deeper plague, to make her love me too,
Which, since she loves before, I'm loth to see;
Falsehood is worse than hate; and that must be,
　　If she whom I love, should love me.

THE FUNERAL

Whoever comes to shroud me, do not harm
　　　　Nor question much
That subtle wreath of hair, which crowns my arm;
　　The mystery, the sign you must not touch,
　　　　For° 'tis my outward soul,
Viceroy to that, which then to heaven being gone,
　　　　Will leave this to control,
And keep these limbs, her provinces, from dissolu-
　　　　tion.

For° if the sinewy thread my brain lets fall
　　　　Through every part,　　　　　　　　10
Can tie those parts, and make me one of all;
These hairs which upward grew, and strength and
　　　　art
　　　　Have from a better brain,
Can better do't; except she meant that I
　　　　By this should know my pain,
As prisoners then are manacled, when they're con-
　　　　demned to die.

Whate'er she meant by it, bury it with me,
　　　　For since I am
Love's martyr, it might breed idolatry,
　　If into others' hands these reliques came;　　20
　　　　As 'twas humility
To afford° to it all that a soul can do,
　　　　So, 'tis some bravery,°
That since you would save none of me, I bury some
　　　　of you.

47. atomies: component parts.　51–52. we . . . sphere: The
heavenly bodies were guided and ruled by angelic spirits or
"intelligences"; so, "our bodies are the 'sphere' of our souls."
55. forces, sense: The body's contribution to the soul is sensation, which gives the soul material to work in and upon.
56. allay: alloy.　57–58. On . . . air: "The stars can only affect
us through the medium of the air."　62. Spirits: i.e., the
"natural," "vital," and "animal" spirits which acted as inter-
mediaries between body and soul. They were said to spring,
respectively, from brain, heart, and liver.　68. Else . . . lies:
"Just as the body generates 'spirits,' so the soul must descend
to the body, otherwise half our nature remains imprisoned."
LOVE'S DEITY.　6. vice-nature: Custom is "second nature,"
hence nature's deputy.

15. modern: ordinary, everyday, commonplace.　THE FUNERAL.
5–8. For . . . dissolution: "The soul is what keeps the body in-
tact; when mine has departed, the wreath of hair must act as
its external representative.　9–13. For . . . brain: "If the
spinal cord and nerves ('sinewy thread') descending from the
brain can unify my bodily parts, surely her hairs, which grew
'upward,' and from a better brain, can do it better still. See
Intro., p. 362.　22. afford: attribute.　23. some bravery: a
spirited act.

THE BLOSSOM

Little think'st thou, poor flower,
  Whom I have watched six or seven days,
And seen thy birth, and seen what every hour
Gave to thy growth, thee to this height to raise,
And now dost laugh and triumph on this bough:
    Little think'st thou
That it will freeze anon, and that I shall
Tomorrow find thee fall'n, or not at all.

Little think'st thou, poor heart,
  That labor'st yet to nestle thee,   10
And think'st by hovering here to get a part
In a forbidden or forbidding tree,
And hop'st her stiffness by long siege to bow:
    Little think'st thou
That thou tomorrow, ere that sun doth wake,
Must with this sun, and me a journey take.

But thou which lov'st to be
  Subtle to plague thyself, wilt say:
Alas, if you must go, what's that to me?
Here lies my business, and here I will stay;   20
You go to friends, whose love and means present
    Various content
To your eyes, ears, and tongue, and every part;
If then your body go, what need you a heart?

Well then, stay here; but know,
  When thou hast stayed and done thy most:
A naked thinking heart, that makes no show,
Is to a woman, but a kind of ghost;
How shall she know my heart; or having none,
    Know thee for one?   30
Practice may make her know some other part,
But take my word, she doth not know a heart.

Meet me at London, then,
  Twenty days hence, and thou shalt see
Me fresher, and more fat, by being with men,
Than if I had stayed still with her and thee.
For God's sake, if you can, be you so too:
    I would give you
There, to another friend, whom we shall find
As glad to have my body, as my mind.   40

THE RELIQUE

When my grave is broke up again
  Some second guest to entertain,
(For graves have learned that womanhead°
  To be to more than one a bed)
    And he that digs it, spies

A bracelet of bright hair about the bone,
  Will he not let us alone,
And think that there a loving couple lies,
Who thought that this device might be some way
To make their souls, at the last busy day,   10
Meet at this grave, and make a little stay?

If this fall in a time, or land,
  Where misdevotion° doth command,
Then, he that digs us up, will bring
Us, to the bishop, and the king,
    To make us reliques; then
Thou shalt be a Mary Magdalen,° and I
    A something else thereby;
All women shall adore us, and some men;
And since at such time, miracles are sought,   20
I would have that age by this paper taught
What miracles we harmless lovers wrought.

First, we loved well and faithfully,
  Yet knew not what we loved, nor why:
Difference of sex no more we knew,
  Than our guardian angels do;
    Coming and going, we
Perchance might kiss,° but not between those meals;
  Our hands ne'er touched the seals,
Which nature, injured by late law, sets free:°   30
These miracles we did; but now alas,
All measure, and all language, I should pass,
Should I tell what a miracle she was.

THE PROHIBITION

    Take heed of loving me,
At least remember, I forbade it thee;
Not that I shall repair my unthrifty waste
Of breath and blood, upon thy sighs, and tears,
By being to thee then what to me thou wast;
But so great joy our life at once outwears,
Then, lest thy love, by my death, frustrate be,
If thou love me, take heed of loving me.

    Take heed of hating me,
Or too much triumph in the victory.   10
Not that I shall be mine own officer,°
And hate with hate again retaliate;
But thou wilt lose the style° of conqueror,
If I, thy conquest, perish by thy hate.
Then, lest my being nothing lessen thee,
If thou hate me, take heed of hating me.

13. misdevotion: Donne means popery (the 1669 edition has
"mass-devotion").   17. Mary Magdalen: i.e., a reformed sinner, afterward canonized.   27–28. Coming . . . kiss: i.e., "the
kiss of salutation and parting" [Grierson].   29–30. Our . . .
free: i.e., "we never indulged in illicit love, though 'nature'
knows of no prohibition of 'free love.'"   THE PROHIBITION.
11. Not . . . officer: i.e., "not that I shall execute justice in my
own person."   13. style: title.

THE RELIQUE.   3. womanhead: i.e., feminine characteristic or
habit.

Yet, love and hate me too,
So, these extremes shall neither's office do;°
Love me, that I may die the gentler way;
Hate me, because thy love is too great for
    me;   20
Or let these two, themselves, not me decay;
So shall I, live, thy stage, not triumph be;
Lest thou thy love and hate and me undo,°
To let me live, O love and hate me too.

THE EXPIRATION

So, so, break off this last lamenting kiss,
  Which sucks two souls, and vapors both away;
Turn thou ghost that way, and let me turn this,
  And let ourselves benight our happiest day;
We asked none leave to love; nor will we owe
  Any so cheap a death, as saying, Go;°

Go; and if that word have not quite killed thee,
  Ease me with death, by bidding me go too.
Oh, if it have, let my word work on me,
  And a just office on a murderer do.   10
Except it be too late, to kill me so,
  Being double dead, going, and bidding, Go.

from the SATIRES

The *Satires* are also among Donne's earliest compositions, and show the youthful extravagance of his wit at its height. They may be assigned roughly to the last five or six years of the sixteenth century.

SATIRE III

No exact date can be given, but this satire reflects Donne's state of mind when he was trying to decide between Roman Catholicism and the various forms of Protestantism. It thus probably belongs to 1594–97.

Kind pity chokes my spleen; brave scorn forbids
Those tears to issue which swell my eyelids;
I must not laugh, nor weep sins, and be wise:
Can railing then cure these worn maladies?
Is not our mistress fair religion,
As worthy of all our soul's devotion,
As virtue was to the first blinded age?°

Are not heaven's joys as valiant to assuage
Lusts, as earth's honor was to them? Alas,
As we do them in means, shall they surpass   10
Us in the end, and shall thy father's spirit
Meet blind philosophers in heaven, whose
    merit
Of strict life may be imputed faith, and hear
Thee, whom he taught so easy ways and near
To follow, damned? O if thou dar'st, fear this;
This fear great courage, and high valor is.
Dar'st thou aid mutinous Dutch,° and dar'st thou
    lay   ,
Thee in ships' wooden sepulchers, a prey
To leaders' rage, to storms, to shot, to dearth?
Dar'st thou dive seas, and dungeons of the earth?
Hast thou courageous fire to thaw the ice   21
Of frozen north discoveries? and thrice
Colder than salamanders,° like divine
Children in th' oven,° fires of Spain,° and the line,°
Whose countries limbecks° to our bodies be,
Canst thou for gain bear? and must every he
Which cries not, Goddess, to thy mistress, draw,
Or eat thy poisonous words? courage of straw!
O desperate coward, wilt thou seem bold, and
To thy foes and his° (who made thee to stand   30
Sentinel in his world's garrison) thus yield,
And for the forbidden wars, leave th' appointed
    field?
Know thy foes:° the foul Devil (whom thou
Strivest to please) for hate, not love, would allow
Thee fain, his whole realm to be quit;° and as
The world's all parts wither away and pass,
So the world's self, thy other loved foe, is
In her decrepit wane, and thou loving this,
Dost love a withered and worn strumpet; last,
Flesh (itself's death)° and joys which flesh can
    taste,   40
Thou lovest; and thy fair goodly soul, which doth
Give this flesh power to taste joy, thou dost loathe.
Seek true religion. O where? Mirreus°
Thinking her unhoused here,° and fled from us,
Seeks her at Rome; there, because he doth know

18. So . . . do: In that way, neither of these extremes will perform its proper function. 22–23. So . . . undo: "Or let these two (love and hate) destroy, not me, but one another. In this way I shall live to show off — as on a stage — your daily victories, whereas if you 'triumphed' over me completely I should be dead." THE EXPIRATION. 5–6. We . . . Go: "We asked nobody's permission to love, nor will we owe to anyone else the death so cheaply bought by saying 'go.'" SATIRE III. 7. first . . . age: i.e., the worthies of pagan antiquity, whose eyes had not been opened by revelation, and who made virtue and earthly honor their aim, and not salvation ("heaven's joys").

17. aid . . . Dutch: fight for the Dutch against their Spanish rulers (as many Englishmen then did). Donne was still a Roman Catholic when he wrote this, hence the word "mutinous." 23. salamanders: lizard-like creatures, (wrongly) supposed by the ancients to be able to withstand fire. 23–24. divine . . . oven: Ananias, Azarias and Misael, thrown into the furnace by Nebuchadnezzar (see Old Testament Apocrypha, The Song of the Three Holy Children). 24. fires of Spain: the Spanish Inquisition's burnings of heretics (*autos-da-fé*). line: equator. 25. limbecks: alembics, retorts for distilling (hence, subjected to intense heat). 30. his: i.e., God's. 33. foes: Man's real foes are the Devil, the world, and the flesh; it is against these that true courage is to be shown. 35. quit: This seems to mean, "The Devil would gladly allow you the freedom of his whole kingdom." 40. itself's death: This may mean either that flesh is the cause of its own death (through sin), or it may be simply a statement: "flesh itself is death." 43. Mirreus: an imaginary name (cf. l. 49n.) for one who seeks true religion in Rome. 44. here: i.e., in England after the Reformation.

That she was there a thousand years ago;
He loves her rags so, as we here obey
The statecloth where the prince sate yesterday.
Crantz° to such brave loves will not be enthralled,
But loves her only, who at Geneva is called   50
Religion, plain, simple, sullen, young,
Contemptuous, yet unhandsome; as among
Lecherous humors, there is one that judges
No wenches wholesome, but coarse country
    drudges.
Graius stays still at home here, and because
Some preachers, vile ambitious bawds, and laws
Still new like fashions, bid him think that she
Which dwells with us, is only perfect, he
Embraceth her, whom his godfathers will
Tender to him, being tender, as wards still   60
Take such wives as their guardians offer, or
Pay values.° Careless Phrygius doth abhor
All, because all cannot be good, as one
Knowing some women whores, dares marry none.
Gracchus loves all as one, and thinks that so
As women do in divers countries go
In divers habits, yet are still one kind,
So doth, so is religion; and this blind-
ness too much light breeds; but unmoved thou
Of force must one, and forced but one allow;   70
And the right;° ask thy father which is she.
Let him ask his; though truth and falsehood be
Near twins, yet truth a little elder is;
Be busy to seek her, believe me this,
He's not of none, nor worst, that seeks the best.°
To adore, or scorn an image, or protest,
May all be bad; doubt wisely; in strange way
To stand inquiring right, is not to stray;
To sleep, or run wrong, is. On a huge hill,
Cragged, and steep, Truth stands, and he that will
Reach her, about must, and about must go;°   81
And what the hill's suddenness resists, win so;
Yet strive so, that before age, death's twilight,
Thy soul rest, for none can work in that night.
To will, implies delay, therefore now do:
Hard deeds, the body's pains; hard knowledge
    too
The mind's endeavors reach, and mysteries
Are like the sun, dazzling, yet plain to all eyes.
Keep the truth which thou hast found; men° do not
    stand
In so ill case here, that God hath with his hand

Signed kings blank charters to kill whom they
    hate,   91
Nor are they vicars, but hangmen to fate.
Fool and wretch, wilt thou let thy soul be tied
To man's laws, by which she shall not be tried
At the last day? Oh, will it then boot thee
To say a Philip, or a Gregory,
A Harry, or a Martin° taught thee this?
Is not this excuse for mere contraries,
Equally strong? cannot both sides say so?
That thou mayest rightly obey power, her bounds
    know;   100
Those passed,° her nature, and name is changed; to
    be
Then humble to her is idolatry.
As streams are, power is; those blest flowers that
    dwell
At the rough stream's calm head, thrive and do
    well,
But having left their roots, and themselves given
To the stream's tyrannous rage, alas are driven
Through mills, and rocks, and woods, and at last,
    almost
Consumed in going, in the sea are lost:
So perish souls, which more choose men's unjust
Power from God claimed, than God himself to
    trust.   110

SATIRE IV

Based on Horace's *Ibam forte via Sacra* (*Satires,* I.
9), but Donne's encounter with a bore leads on to an
exposure of court life and its vices. The reference to
the loss of Amiens (l. 114) makes it possible to date
the poem after March, 1597, when the town was re-
taken by France's Henry IV.
   The reader should compare this satire with Pope's
"The Fourth Satire of Dr. John Donne Versified"
(see below).

Well; I may now receive,° and die. My sin
Indeed is great, but I have been in
A purgatory,° such as feared hell is
A recreation to, and scarce° map of this.
My mind, neither with pride's itch, nor yet hath
    been
Poisoned with love to see, or to be seen.
I had no suit there, nor new suit to show,
Yet went to court; but as Glaze° which did go
To a Mass in jest, catched, was fain to disburse

49. Crantz: Donne may have given this character a Dutch
name because the Dutch were largely Genevan Calvinists.
62. Pay values: pay a money equivalent or fine.   **69–71. unmoved . . . right:** "Unaffected by all these opinions, you must
perforce accept one form of religion, and only one, and that the
right one."   **75. He's . . . best:** "The man who is seeking the
best religion neither lacks religion nor professes the worst one."
81. about . . . go: i.e., must climb by zigzag paths.   **89–
92. men . . . fate:** God has not authorized kings to damn
("kill") those they hate; kings are not deputies ("vicars") of
destiny, only its executioners.

96–97. Philip . . . Martin: Philip of Spain; Gregory — uncertain
which, but probably one of the post-Reformation popes (Gregory
XIII or XIV); Harry, Henry VIII; Martin, Luther.   SATIRE IV.
1. receive: i.e., extreme unction and absolution.   **3. purgatory:**
the court.   **4. scarce:** scanty, sketchy.   **8. Glaze:** another invented character. Cf. "Satire III," l. 43n., above.

The hundred marks, which is the statute's curse,°
Before he 'scaped, so it pleased my destiny 11
(Guilty of my sin of going), to think me
As prone to all ill, and of good as forget-
ful, as proud, as lustful, and as much in debt,
As vain, as witless, and as false as they
Which dwell at court, for once going that way.
Therefore I suffered this; towards me did run
A thing more strange than on Nile's slime the sun
E'er bred;° or all which into Noah's ark came;
A thing, which would have posed° Adam to name;
Stranger than seven antiquaries'° studies, 21
Than Afric's monsters, Guiana's rarities.°
Stranger than strangers;° one, who for a Dane,
In the Danes' massacre° had sure been slain,
If he had lived then; and without help dies,
When next the 'prentices 'gainst strangers rise.
One, whom the watch at noon lets scarce go by,
One, to whom, the examining Justice sure would
     cry,
"Sir, by your priesthood° tell me what you are."
His clothes were strange, though coarse; and black,
     though bare; 30
Sleeveless his jerkin was, and it had been
Velvet, but 'twas now (so much ground was seen)
Become tufftaffaty;° and our children shall
See it plain rash° awhile, then naught at all.
This thing hath traveled, and saith,° speaks all
     tongues
And only knoweth what to all states belongs.
Made of th' accents, and best phrase of all these,
He speaks no language;° if strange meats displease,
Art can deceive, or hunger force my taste,
But pedant's motley tongue, soldier's bombast, 40
Mountebank's drugtongue,° nor the terms of law
Are strong enough preparatives, to draw
Me to bear this: yet I must be content
With his tongue, in his tongue, called compliment:
In which he can win widows, and pay scores,
Make men speak treason, cozen° subtlest whores,
Outflatter favorites, or outlie either

Jovius, or Surius,° or both together.
He names me, and comes to me; I whisper, "God!
How have I sinned, that thy wrath's furious rod,
This fellow, chooseth me?" He saith, "Sir, 51
I love your judgment; whom do you prefer,
For the best linguist?" And I sillily°
Said, that I thought Calepine's Dictionary;°
"Nay but of men, most sweet sir"; Beza° then,
Some other Jesuits,° and two reverend men
Of our two academies,° I named. There
He stopped me, and said: "Nay, your Apostles
     were
Good pretty linguists,° and so Panurge° was;
Yet a poor gentleman, all these may pass 60
By travel."° Then, as if he would have sold
His tongue, he praised it, and such wonders told
That I was fain to say, "If you had lived, sir,
Time enough to have been interpreter
To Babel's bricklayers, sure the tower had stood."
He adds, "If of court life you knew the good,
You would leave loneness." I said, "Not alone
My loneness is,° but Spartan's fashion,
To teach by painting drunkards, doth not last 69
Now; Aretine's° pictures have made few chaste;
No more can princes' courts, though there be few
Better pictures of vice, teach me virtue";
He, like to a high-stretched lute-string squeaked,
     "O sir,
'Tis sweet to talk of kings." "At Westminster,"
Said I, "the man that keeps the Abbey tombs,
And for his price doth with whoever comes,
Of all our Harrys, and our Edwards talk,
From king to king and all their kin can walk:
Your ears shall hear naught, but kings; your eyes
     meet
Kings only; the way to it, is King Street."° 80
He smacked, and cried, "He's base, mechanic,
     coarse,
So are all your Englishmen in their discourse.
Are not your Frenchmen neat?" "Mine? as you
     see,

---

10. statute's curse: fine for being caught attending a mass. A statute prescribed a fine of 100 marks for being present at mass. 18–19. sun ... bred: It was an ancient belief that the sun's rays bred living creatures out of the Nile's mud. 20. posed: puzzled. 21. antiquaries: a hit at contemporary antiquarians, e.g., Stow. Cf. l. 97. 22. Guiana's rarities: Sir Walter Raleigh went up the Orinoco in 1595 in search of El Dorado, the fabled city of gold. 23. strangers: the current term for foreign refugees from persecution or religious wars. Cf. l. 26: London apprentices objected to their presence, and rose against them. 24. Danes' massacre: possibly a reference to the "Harrying of the North" by William the Conqueror, in which many Danes were slaughtered. 29. priesthood: The man looked liable to arrest as a disguised Jesuit. 33. tufftaffaty: thin glossy silk (taffeta). 34. rash: (Latin rasus, scraped) a smooth silk or worsted fabric. 35. saith: i.e., so he says. 37–38. Made .. language: His language, being made up of phrases from all tongues, is no real language. 41. drugtongue: jargon used by quacks in selling their medicines. 46. cozen: deceive.

48. Jovius, or Surius: Paolo Giovio and Laurentius Surius, sixteenth-century Catholic historians, notorious for inaccuracy. 53. sillily: in my innocence. 54. Calepine's Dictionary: a well-known polyglot dictionary (1502). 55. Beza: French Calvinist (1519–1605), editor of the New Testament and Greek professor. 56. other Jesuits: Beza was of course not a Jesuit, but Catholics hated him for his "jesuitical" casuistry. 57. academies: Oxford and Cambridge. 59. linguists: referring to the gift of tongues at Pentecost. Panurge: polyglot character in Rabelais' Pantagruel. 60–61. Yet ... travel: "Yet a poor gentleman may surpass all these linguists (i.e., the Apostles and Panurge) by travel." (Pope understood it thus, but Donne's spelling is "travaile," which might mean that he may excel them by hard work.") 67–68. Not ... is: "My solitude is not really loneliness." (He goes on: "But the Spartan method of teaching virtue by examples of vice is out of date now.") 70. Aretine: Pietro Aretino (1492–1556) wrote lascivious sonnets for Giulio Romano's pictures. 80. King Street: former road from Charing Cross to the king's palace at Westminster.

I have but one Frenchman,° look, he follows me."
"Certes they are neatly clothed; I of this mind am,
Your only wearing is your grogaram."°
"Not so, sir, I have more." Under this pitch°
He would not fly; I chaffed him; but as itch
Scratched into smart, and as blunt iron ground
Into an edge, hurts worse: so, I (fool) found,   90
Crossing hurt me; to fit my sullenness,
He to another key his style doth address,
And asks, what news? I tell him of new plays.
He takes my hand, and as a still, which stays
A semibreve 'twixt each drop, he niggardly,
As loth to enrich me, so tells many a lie.
More than ten Holinsheds, or Halls, or Stows,°
Of trivial household trash he knows; he knows
When the queen frowned, or smiled, and he knows
    what
A subtle statesman may gather of that;   100
He knows who loves whom; and who by poison
Hastes to an office's reversion;
He knows who hath sold his land, and now doth
    beg
A license, old iron, boots, shoes, and egg-
shells to transport; shortly boys shall not play
At span-counter,° or blowpoint,° but they pay
Toll to some courtier; and wiser than all us,
He knows what lady is not painted; thus
He with home meats tries me; I belch, spew, spit,
Look pale, and sickly, like a patient; yet   110
He thrusts on more; and as if he'd undertook
To say Gallo-Belgicus° without book
Speaks of all states, and deeds, that have been since
The Spaniards came, to the loss of Amiens.°
Like a big wife, at sight of loathèd meat,
Ready to travail, so I sigh, and sweat
To hear this macaron° talk: in vain, for yet,
Either my humor, or his own to fit,
He like a privileged spy, whom nothing can
Discredit, libels now 'gainst each great man.   120
He names a price for every office paid;
He saith, our wars thrive ill, because delayed;

That offices are entailed,° and that there are
Perpetuities° of them, lasting as far
As the last day; and that great officers,
Do with the pirates share, and Dunkirkers.°
Who wastes in meat, in clothes, in horse, he notes;
Who loves whores, who boys, and who goats.
I more amazed than Circe's prisoners, when
They felt themselves turn beasts, felt myself then
Becoming traitor, and methought I saw   131
One of our Giant Statutes ope his jaw
To suck me in; for hearing him, I found
That as burnt venom lechers do grow sound
By giving others their sores, I might grow
Guilty, and he free:° therefore I did show
All signs of loathing; but since I am in,
I must pay mine, and my forefathers' sin
To the last farthing. Therefore to my power
Toughly and stubbornly I bear this cross; but the
    hour   140
Of mercy now was come; he tries to bring
Me to pay a fine to 'scape his torturing,
And says, " Sir, can you spare me "; I said, " Wil-
    lingly ";
" Nay, sir, can you spare me a crown? " Thank-
    fully I
Gave it, as ransom; but as fiddlers, still,
Though they be paid to be gone, yet needs will
Thrust one more jig upon you: so did he
With his long complimental° thanks vex me.
But he is gone, thanks to his needy want,
And the prerogative of my crown: scant°   150
His thanks were ended, when I (which did see
All the court filled with more strange things than
    he),
Ran from thence with such or more haste, than one
Who fears more actions, doth make from prison.
At home in wholesome solitariness
My precious soul began the wretchedness
Of suitors at court to mourn, and a trance
Like his, who dreamt he saw hell,° did advance
Itself on me. Such men as he saw there,
I saw at court, and worse, and more. Low fear   160
Becomes the guilty, not the accuser; then,
Shall I, none's slave, of high-born or raised men
Fear frowns? And, my Mistress Truth, betray thee
To th' huffing braggart, puffed Nobility?
No, no, thou which since yesterday hast been
Almost about the whole world, hast thou seen,
O Sun, in all thy journey, vanity,

---

84. **Frenchman:** We know that Donne had a French servant.
86. **your grogaram:** grogram, coarse fabric of silk, mohair, and
wool. "Your" is used indefinitely (Elizabethan colloquialism,
familiar in Shakespeare), meaning "that well-known thing, you
know what," etc. Donne here pretends to take it literally, and
replies: "On the contrary, I have other clothes as well."
87. **pitch:** height to which a falcon soars before swooping.
97. **Holinsheds ... Stows:** the Tudor chroniclers, who often
mingle trivialities with their narrative of graver events.
106. **span-counter:** a game in which one player threw counters
so close to those of his opponent that the distance between
them could be "spanned" with the hand.   **blowpoint:** another
game; probably blowing an arrow through a tube at certain
numbers by way of lottery.   112. **Gallo-Belgicus:** *Mercurius
Gallo-Belgicus*, a news journal started at Cologne in 1598.
114. **The ... Amiens:** i.e., from 1588 to 1597.   117. **macaron:**
a buffoon or fop, especially one who affects foreign tastes and
phrases.

123. **entailed:** i.e., earmarked for succession from father to son.
124. **Perpetuities:** inalienable hereditary rights.   126. **Dunkirkers:** Dunkirk, on the coast of French Flanders, was then a
nest of pirates; hence, pirates or privateers.   135-36. **I ... free:**
"I should be convicted of treason; he would go free as a spy who
had spoken treason only to draw me out" [Grierson].   148. **com-
plimental:** courtly but insincere.   150. **scant:** scarcely.   158. **his
... hell:** referring to Dante's *Inferno*.

Such as swells the bladder of our court? I
Think he which made your waxen garden, and
Transported it from Italy° to stand   170
With us, at London, flouts our Presence, for
Just such gay painted things, which no sap, nor
Taste have in them, ours are; and natural
Some of the stocks are, their fruits, bastard all.
'Tis ten a-clock and past; all whom the mews,°
Baloon,° tennis, diet,° or the stews,°
Had all the morning held, now the second
Time made ready, that day, in flocks, are found
In the Presence, and I (God pardon me).
As fresh, and sweet their apparels be, as be   180
The fields they sold to buy them; for a king
Those hose are, cry the flatterers; and bring
Them next week to the theater to sell;
Wants reach all states; meseems they do as well
At stage, as court; all are players; whoe'er looks
(For themselves dare not go) o'er Cheapside
    books,°
Shall find their wardrobe's inventory. Now,
The ladies come. As pirates, which do know
That there came weak ships fraught with cutchan-
    nel,°
The men board them; and praise, as they think,
    well,   190
Their beauties; they the men's wits; both are
    bought.
Why good wits ne'er wear scarlet gowns, I thought
This cause: these men, men's wits for speeches buy,
And women buy all reds which scarlets dye.°
He called her beauty lime-twigs,° her hair net;
She fears her drugs ill laid, her hair loose set.
Would not Heraclitus° laugh to see Macrine,
From hat to shoe, himself at door refine,
As if the Presence were a Moschite,° and lift
His skirts and hose, and call his clothes to shrift,°
Making them confess not only mortal   201
Great stains and holes in them, but venial
Feathers and dust, wherewith they fornicate:
And then by Dürer's rules° survey the state
Of his each limb, and with strings the odds try

Of his neck to his leg, and waist to thigh.
So in immaculate clothes, and symmetry
Perfect as circles, with such nicety
As a young preacher at his first time goes
To preach, he enters, and a lady which owes   210
Him not so much as good will, he arrests,
And unto her protests, protests, protests,°
So much as at Rome would serve to have thrown
Ten cardinals into the Inquisition;
And whispered° by Jesu, so often, that a
Pursuivant° would have ravished him away
For saying of our Lady's psalter; but 'tis fit
That they each other plague, they merit it.
But here comes Glorius that will plague them both,
Who, in the other extreme, only doth   220
Call a rough carelessness, good fashion;
Whose cloak his spurs tear; whom he spits on
He cares not, his ill words do no harm
To him; he rusheth in, as if Arm, arm,
He meant to cry; and though his face be as ill
As theirs which in old hangings° whip Christ, still
He strives to look worse, he keeps all in awe;
Jests like a licensed fool, commands like law.
Tired, now I leave this place, and but pleased so
As men which from jails to execution go,   230
Go through the great chamber° (why is it hung°
With the seven deadly sins?). Being among
Those Ascaparts,° men big enough to throw
Charing Cross for a bar,° men that do know
No token of worth, but Queen's man,° and fine
Living, barrels of beef, flagons of wine;
I shook like a spied spy. Preachers which are
Seas of wit and arts, you can, then dare,
Drown the sins of this place, for, for me
Which am but a scarce° brook, it enough shall be
To wash the stains away; although I yet   241
With Maccabee's modesty,° the known merit
Of my work lessen: yet some wise man shall,
I hope, esteem my writs canonical.°

---

212. **protests:** an allusion to "Protestants," as the next lines
show.   215. **whispered:** The editions of 1635–69 read "whispers," which seems more in place here.   216. **Pursuivant:**
Grierson points out that three MSS read "Topcliffe" — "one
of the cruelest of the creatures employed to ferret out and . . .
torture Catholics."   226. **hangings:** tapestries (depicting the
scourging of Christ).   231. **great chamber:** where public audiences were held.   **hung:** i.e., with tapestries depicting the
seven deadly sins.   233. **Ascaparts:** Ascapart is a giant thirty
feet high who figures in the legend of Sir Bevis of Southampton.
The reference is to the queen's halberdiers or guards ("beef-
eaters").   233–34. **men . . . bar:** Throwing an iron bar (or
sledge hammer) was a proof of strength; these guards could have
thrown Charing Cross (stone monument) itself.   235. **Queen's
man:** i.e., the title of Queen's man.   240. **scarce:** scanty.
242. **Maccabee's modesty:** See Apocrypha, II Macc. 15:38:
"And if I have done well, and as is fitting the story, it is that
which I desired: but if slenderly and meanly, it is that which I
could attain unto."   244. **canonical:** i.e., belonging to the
canon of Scripture (unlike Maccabees, which is Apocryphal).

169–70. **he . . . Italy:** The reference is to artificial gardens in
wax exhibited apparently by Italian puppet or motion exhibitors.
175. **mews:** stables.   176. **Baloon:** (Donne spells it "Baloune")
a game played with a large windball or football struck to and
fro with the arm or foot.   **diet:** eating.   **stews:** brothels.
186. **Cheapside books:** account books of secondhand-clothes
shops in Cheapside, London.   189. **cutchannel:** cochineal (suggested by the ladies' painted faces).   192–94. **Why . . . dye:** Wit
and scarlet (i.e., scholars') gowns are never found together, because courtiers buy up all the wit, and women buy up all the materials for painting or dyeing things scarlet.   195. **lime-twigs:**
twigs smeared with sticky stuff to catch birds.   197. **Heraclitus:** "the Weeping Philosopher."   199. **Moschite:** mosque.
200. **shrift:** confession (i.e., to a priest); hence, to make his
clothes show up their faults.   204. **Dürer's rules:** Albrecht
Dürer (1471–1528) wrote a book on the proportions of the human
figure.

VERSE LETTER TO THE COUNTESS OF BEDFORD

Most of Donne's *Verse Letters* belong to 1596–97, but his acquaintance with Lady Bedford began about 1607–08. Although several of his Letters to her were written soon after this, the present one probably dates from 1611–12, and may have been composed to counteract the effect of his extravagant praise of Elizabeth Drury (see headnote to *An Anatomy of the World*, below).

Honor is so sublime perfection,
And so refined, that when God was alone
And creatureless at first, himself had none;

But as of the elements, these which we tread,°
Produce all things with which we're joyed or fed,
And those are barren both above our head:°

So from low persons doth all honor flow;
Kings, whom they would have honored, to us show,
And but *direct* our honor, not *bestow*.

For when from herbs the pure part must be won   10
From gross, by stilling,° this is better done
By despised dung,° than by the fire or sun.

Care not then, Madam, how low your praisers lie;
In laborers' ballads oft more piety
God finds, than in *Te Deums'* melody.

And, ordnance raised on towers, so many mile
Send not their voice, nor last so long a while
As fires from th' earth's low vaults in Sicil Isle.°

Should I say I lived darker than were true,
Your radiation can all clouds subdue;   20
But one,° 'tis best light to contemplate you.

You, for whose body God made better clay,
Or took soul's stuff such as shall late decay,
Or such as needs small change at the last day.

This, as an amber drop enwraps a bee,
Covering discovers your quick soul; that we
May in your through-shine° front your heart's thoughts see.

You teach (though we learn not) a thing unknown
To our late times, the use of specular stone,°
Through which all things within without were shown.   30

Of such were temples; so and of such you are;
Being and *seeming* is your equal care,
And virtue's whole sum is but *know* and *dare*.

But as our souls of growth and souls of sense
Have birthright of our reason's soul,° yet hence
They fly not from that, nor seek presidence:

Nature's first lesson, so, discretion,
Must not grudge zeal a place, nor yet keep none,
Not banish itself, nor religion.

Discretion is a wise man's soul,° and so   40
Religion is a Christian's, and you know
How these are one; her *yea,* is not her *no.*°

Nor may we hope to solder still and knit
These two, and dare to break them; nor must wit
Be colleague to religion, but be it.°

In those poor types of God (round circles) so
Religion's types,° the pieceless centers flow,
And are in all the lines which all ways go.°

If either° ever wrought in you alone
Or principally, then religion   50
Wrought your ends, and your ways discretion.

Go thither still, go the same way you went,
Who so° would change, do covet or repent;
Neither can reach you, great and innocent.

---

29. **specular stone:** mica, or transparent marble, of which Donne believed some heathen temples were built.   34–35. **But . . . soul:** The human soul contains three parts: vegetative, sensitive, and rational (see "Of My Name, in the Window," l. 25n.). The meaning of this and the next stanza is: "just as the two lower souls are first in order of time, yet neither shun reason nor seek precedence over it; so prudence, nature's first lesson, must allow a place for religion without banishing itself."   40. **Discretion . . . soul:** Prudence (the pagan virtue) is the soul of a wise man; religion, that of a Christian.   42. **How . . . no:** There is harmony between human wisdom and supernatural grace; the "yes" of one is not the "no" of the other.   43–45. **Nor . . . it:** probable sense: "Nor must we think to join them together in such a way that they may afterwards be separated; human reason must not be merely a colleague to religion, but actually be identified with it."   46–47. **In . . . types:** The circle is an ancient emblem of God and infinity (because its circumference has no beginning or end); it is thus also a "type" of religion.   47–48. **pieceless . . . go:** pieceless, i.e., having no parts, indivisible. The center of a circle is an indivisible point, present in all the radii of the circle.   49. **either:** i.e., religion or prudence.   53. **Who so:** best read as one word — "whosoever."

COUNTESS OF BEDFORD.   **4. elements . . . tread:** i.e., earth and water.   **6. those . . . head:** i.e., air and fire.   **11. stilling:** distilling.   **12. dung:** i.e., by the heat of a dunghill.   **18. Sicil isle:** referring to the volcano Etna, in Sicily.   **21. But one:** i.e., except for the divine light.   **27. through-shine:** transparent.

AN ANATOMY OF THE WORLD

WHEREIN,

BY OCCASION OF THE UNTIMELY DEATH OF
MISTRESS ELIZABETH DRURY, THE FRAILTY AND THE
DECAY OF THIS WHOLE WORLD IS REPRESENTED

This poem and its successor, *The Progress of the Soul: The Second Anniversary,* were the first of Donne's poems to be published in his lifetime (1611 and 1612). Its ostensible subject is the death of the fifteen-year-old Elizabeth Drury, daughter of Donne's patron, Sir Robert Drury. If it is read simply as an elegy on a dead child, its hyperbolical eulogies of the girl must seem ridiculous if not (as they appeared to Ben Jonson) "profane and full of blasphemies." Jonson said "if it had been written of the Virgin Mary it had been something," but Donne replied that he described "the idea of a woman," and not the child herself. But one can go further still, and say that the death of Elizabeth Drury (like that of Edward King for Milton) was only the occasion enabling him to express his actual thoughts and feelings about life and death, and particularly about the disintegrating effect of the "new philosophy" upon the older world picture. If we read the poem with this in mind, we see the force of Grierson's remark — that the disturbance of the accepted medieval cosmology affected Donne "much as the later geology [and the] doctrine of evolution absorbed and perturbed Tennyson when he wrote *In Memoriam.*"

The First Anniversary

When that rich soul which to her heaven   *The entry*
  is gone,   *into the*
Whom all do celebrate, who know they   *work.*
  have one,
(For who is sure he hath a soul, unless
It see, and judge, and follow worthiness,
And by deeds praise it? he who doth not this,
May lodge an inmate° soul, but 'tis not his.)
When that queen ended here her progress time,
And, as to her standing house, to heaven did climb,
Where loth to make the saints attend her long,
She's now a part both of the quire, and song,°   10
This world, in that great earthquake languishèd;
For in a common bath of tears it bled,
Which drew the strongest vital spirits out:
But succored then with a perplexèd doubt,
Whether the world did lose, or gain in this,
(Because since now no other way there is,
But goodness, to see her, whom all would see,
All must endeavor to be good as she)

This great consumption to a fever turned,   19
And so the world had fits; it joyed, it mourned;
And, as men think that agues physic are,°
And th'ague being spent, give over° care,
So thou sick world, mistak'st thyself to be
Well, when alas, thou'rt in a lethargy.
Her death did wound and tame thee then, and then
Thou might'st have better spared the sun, or man.
That wound was deep, but 'tis more misery,
That thou hast lost thy sense and memory.
'Twas heavy then to hear thy voice of moan,   29
But this is worse, that thou art speechless grown.
Thou hast forgot thy name, thou hadst;° thou wast
Nothing but she, and her thou hast o'erpast.
For as a child kept from the font, until
A prince, expected long, come to fulfill
The ceremonies, thou unnamed had'st laid,
Had not her coming, thee her palace made:
Her name defined thee, gave thee form, and frame,
And thou forget'st to celebrate thy name.
Some months she hath been dead (but being dead,
Measures of times are all determinèd)°   40
But long she hath been away, long, long, yet none
Offers to tell us who it is that's gone.
But as in states doubtful of future heirs,
When sickness without remedy impairs
The present prince, they're loth it should be said,
The prince doth languish, or the prince is dead:
So mankind feeling now a general thaw,
A strong example gone, equal to law,
The cement which did faithfully compact,   49
And glue all virtues, now resolved, and slacked,
Thought it some blasphemy to say she was dead,
Or that our weakness was discoverèd
In that confession; therefore spoke no more
Than tongues, the soul being gone, the loss deplore.
But though it be too late to succor thee,
Sick world, yea dead, yea putrefied, since she
Thy intrinsic balm,° and thy preservative,
Can never be renewed, thou never live,
I (since no man can make thee live) will try,
What we may gain by thy Anatomy.°   60
Her death hath taught us dearly, that thou art
Corrupt and mortal in thy purest part.
Let no man say, the world itself being dead,
'Tis labor lost to have discoverèd
The world's infirmities, since there is none
Alive to study this dissection;
For there's a kind of world remaining   *What life*
  still,   *the world*
Though she which did inanimate and   *hath still.*
  fill

ANATOMY OF THE WORLD: THE FIRST ANNIVERSARY. **6. inmate:** i.e., a soul, which is an outsider or lodger, not his own. **10. part . . . song:** She is now both a member of the choir of saints, and the subject of their song.

21. agues . . . are: i.e., they cure themselves. **22. give over:** cease, give up. **31. thy . . . hadst:** the name you had. **40. determined:** terminated, made meaningless. **57. intrinsic balm:** sap of life. **60. Anatomy:** analysis, dissection.

The world, be gone, yet in this last long night,
Her ghost doth walk; that is, a glimmering light,
A faint weak love of virtue, and of good,   71
Reflects from her, on them which understood
Her worth; and though she have shut in all day,
The twilight of her memory doth stay;
Which, from the carcass of the old world, free,
Creates a new world, and new creatures be
Produced: the matter and the stuff of this,
Her virtue, and the form our practice is:°
And though to be thus elemented,° arm
These creatures, from homeborn intrinsic harm,
(For all assumed unto this dignity,   81
So many weedless Paradises be,
Which of themselves produce no venomous sin,
Except some foreign serpent bring it in)
Yet, because outward storms the strongest break,
And strength itself by confidence grows weak,
This new world may be safer, being told
The dangers and diseases of the old: *The sick-*
For with due temper men do then forgo,   *nesses of*
Or covet things, when they their true   *the world.*
    worth know.   *Impossi-*
There is no health; physicians say that   *bility of*
    we,   *health.*
At best, enjoy but a neutrality.
And can there be worse sickness, than to know   93
That we are never well, nor can be so?
We are born ruinous: poor mothers cry,
That children come not right, nor orderly;
Except they headlong come and fall upon
An ominous precipitation.
How witty's° ruin! how importunate
Upon mankind! it labored to frustrate   100
Even God's purpose; and made woman, sent
For man's relief, cause of his languishment.
They were to good ends, and they are so still,
But accessory, and principal in ill;
For that first marriage was our funeral:
One woman at one blow, then killed us all,
And singly, one by one, they kill us now.
We do delightfully ourselves allow
To that consumption; and profusely blind,
We kill ourselves to propagate our kind.   110
And yet we do not that; we are not men:
There is not now that mankind, which was then,°
Whenas the sun and man did seem to strive,
(Joint tenants of the world) who   *Shortness*
    should survive;   *of life.*
When stag, and raven, and the long-lived tree,°

Compared with man, died in minority;
When, if a slow-paced star had stolen away
From the observer's marking, he might stay
Two or three hundred years to see it again,
And then make up his observation plain;   120
When, as the age was long, the size was great;°
Man's growth confessed, and recompensed the
    meat;
So spacious and large, that every soul
Did a fair kingdom, and large realm control:
And when the very stature, thus erect,
Did that soul a good way towards heaven direct.
Where is this mankind now? who lives to age,
Fit to be made *Methusalem* his page?°
Alas, we scarce live long enough to try
Whether a true-made clock run right, or lie.   130
Old grandsires talk of yesterday with sorrow,
And for our children we reserve tomorrow.
So short is life, that every peasant strives,
In a torn house, or field, to have three lives.
And as in lasting, so in length is man
Contracted to an inch, who was a span;   *Smallness*
For had a man at first in forests strayed,   *of stature.*
Or shipwrecked in the sea, one would have laid
A wager, that an elephant, or whale,
That met him, would not hastily assail   140
A thing so equal to him: now, alas,
The fairies, and the pygmies well may pass
As credible; mankind decays so soon,
We're scarce our fathers' shadows cast at noon:
Only death adds to our length: nor are we grown
In stature to be men, till we are none.
But this were light,° did our less volume hold
All the old text; or had we changed to gold
Their silver; or disposed into less glass
Spirits of virtue, which then scattered was.   150
But 'tis not so: we're not retired, but damped;
And as our bodies, so our minds are cramped:
'Tis shrinking, not close weaving that hath thus,
In mind, and body both bedwarfèd us.
We seem ambitious, God's whole work to undo;
Of nothing he made us, and we strive too,
To bring ourselves to nothing back; and we
Do what we can, to do't so soon as he.
With new diseases on ourselves we war,
And with new physic,° a worse engine° far.   160
Thus man, this world's vice-emperor, in whom
All faculties, all graces are at home;
And if in other creatures they appear,
They're but man's ministers, and legates there,
To work on their rebellions, and reduce
Them to civility, and to man's use:

77–78. matter . . . is: According to the Aristotelian philosophy
of the medieval Schoolmen, the world consists of matter and
"form"; "forms" are the individuating principles, i.e., the principles in matter which make one thing different from another.
79. elemented: constituted, made up.   99. witty: ingenious.
112. then: i.e., in the days of Methuselah.   115. stag . . . tree:
The raven and the stag were supposed to live long. The tree
might be the yew or the oak.

121. great: There were giants in those days.   128. his page:
i.e., Methusalem's page.   147. light: of little account.   160. new
physic: "the new mineral drugs of the Paracelsians" [Grierson].
engine: i.e., method or device (metaphor from weapons or "engines" of war).

This man, whom God did woo, and loth to attend
Till man came up, did down to man descend,
This man, so great, that all that is, is his,
Oh what a trifle, and poor thing he is!   170
If man were anything, he's nothing now:
Help, or at least some time to waste, allow
To his other wants, yet when he did depart
With her whom we lament, he lost his heart.
She, of whom th' ancients seemed to prophesy,
When they called virtues by the name of *she*;°
She in whom virtue was so much refined,
That for allay° unto so pure a mind
She took the weaker sex; she that could drive
The poisonous tincture, and the stain of *Eve*,   180
Out of her thoughts, and deeds; and purify
All, by a true religious alchemy;
She, she is dead; she's dead: when thou knowest
    this,
Thou knowest how poor a trifling thing man is.
And learn'st thus much by our Anatomy,
The heart being perished, no part can be free.
And that except thou feed (not banquet) on
The supernatural food, religion,
Thy better growth grows witherèd, and scant;°
Be more than man, or thou'rt less than an ant.
Then, as mankind, so is the world's whole frame
Quite out of joint, almost created lame: 192
For, before God had made up all the rest,
Corruption entered, and depraved the best.
It seized the angels, and then first of all
The world did in her cradle take a fall,
And turned her brains, and took a general maim,
Wronging each joint of th' universal frame.
The noblest part, man, felt it first; and   *Decay of*
    then   *nature in*
Both beasts and plants, cursed in the   *other parts.*
    curse of man.
So did the world from the first hour decay,   201
That evening was beginning of the day,
And now the springs and summers which we
    see,
Like sons of women after fifty be.
And new philosophy calls all in doubt,°
The element of fire is quite put out;°
The sun is lost, and th' earth,° and no man's wit
Can well direct him where to look for it.
And freely men confess that this world's spent,
When in the planets, and the firmament   210

They seek so many new;° then see that this
Is crumbled out again to his atomies.
'Tis all in pieces, all coherence gone;
All just supply, and all relation:
Prince, subject, father, son, are things forgot,°
For every man alone thinks he hath got
To be a phoenix, and that then can be
None of that kind, of which he is, but he.°
This is the world's condition now, and now
She that should all parts to reunion bow,   220
She that had all magnetic force alone,
To draw, and fasten sundered parts in one;
She whom wise nature had invented then
When she observed that every sort of men
Did in their voyage in this world's sea stray,
And needed a new compass for their way;
She that was best, and first original
Of all fair copies, and the general
Steward to fate; she whose rich eyes, and breast
Gilt° the West Indies, and perfumed the East;
Whose having breathed in this world, did
    bestow   231
Spice on those Isles, and bade them still smell so,
And that rich Indy which doth gold inter,
Is but as single money, coined from her:
She to whom this world must itself refer,
As suburbs, or the microcosm° of her,
She, she is dead; she's dead: when thou know'st
    this,
Thou know'st how lame a cripple this world is.
And learn'st thus much by our Anatomy,
That this world's general sickness doth not lie   240
In any humor, or one certain part;
But as thou sawest it rotten at the heart,
Thou seest a hectic fever hath got hold
Of the whole substance, not to be controlled,
And that thou hast but one way, not to admit
The world's infection, to be none of it.
For the world's subtlest immaterial parts
Feel this consuming wound, and age's darts.
For the world's beauty is decayed or   *Disformity*
    gone,   *of parts.*
Beauty, that's color, and proportion.
We think the heavens enjoy their spherical,°   251
Their round proportion embracing all;
But yet their various and perplexèd course,
Observed in divers ages, doth enforce
Men to find out so many eccentric parts,

---

176. *she:* i.e., feminine names.   178. allay: alloy.   187–89. And
... scant: "Unless you make a proper meal (and not merely
nibble snacks) of religion, all that is best in you withers away."
Banquet in Donne's time meant "light refreshments" such as
jellies.   205. new ... doubt: i.e., that of Copernicus, Kepler,
Galileo, etc., which had discredited the medieval cosmography.
Cf. Sermon LXXX, p. 397.   206. element ... out: Fire, the
purest of the "four elements," had been supposed to surround
the earth, above the air and below the moon.   207. sun ...
earth: the sun, because it no longer moves on its old path; the
earth, because it is no longer the fixed center of the universe.

211. seek ... new: i.e., through the telescope. (The new conception of infinite space implied the possibility of other worlds.)
215. Prince ... forgot: In bemoaning the breakdown of "degree" amongst men, Donne may have been thinking of the
religious and civil wars in Germany, France, the Low Countries,
etc.   217–18. phoenix ... he: There was never more than one
phoenix alive at a time. Cf. "The Canonization," ll. 23–27. It
is now "each man for himself."   230–33. Gilt ... inter: Cf.
"The Sun Rising," l. 17n.   236. microcosm: literally, "little
world"; a reproduction in miniature of a larger whole (usually
the universe).   251. spherical: i.e., are perfect spheres.

Such divers downright lines, such overthwarts,°
As disproportion that pure form: it tears
The firmament in eight and forty shares,°
And in these constellations then arise
New stars,° and old do vanish from our eyes: 260
As though heav'n suffered earthquakes, peace, or war,
When new towers rise, and old demolished are.
They have impaled within a zodiac
The freeborn sun, and keep twelve signs awake
To watch his steps; the Goat and Crab control,
And fright him back, who else to either pole
(Did not these tropics fetter him) might run:
For his course is not round; nor can the sun
Perfect a circle, or maintain his way
One inch direct; but where he rose today   270
He comes no more, but with a cozening° line,
Steals by that point, and so is serpentine:
And seeming weary with his reeling thus,
He means to sleep, being now fall'n nearer us.
So, of the stars, which boast that they do run
In circle still, none ends where he begun.
All their proportion's lame, it sinks, it swells.
For of meridians, and parallels,
Man hath weaved out a net, and this net thrown
Upon the heavens, and now they are his own.   280
Loth to go up the hill, or labor thus
To go to heaven, we make heaven come to us.
We spur, we rein the stars, and in their race
They're diversely content t' obey our pace.°
But keeps the earth her round proportion still?
Doth not a Teneriffe, or higher hill
Rise so high like a rock, that one might think
The floating moon would shipwreck there, and sink?
Seas are so deep, that whales being struck today,
Perchance tomorrow, scarce at middle way   290
Of their wished journey's end, the bottom, die.
And men, to sound depths, so much line untie,
As one might justly think that there would rise
At end thereof, one of th' Antipodes:
If under all, a vault infernal be,°
(Which sure is spacious, except that we
Invent another torment, that there must
Millions into a strait hot room be thrust)
Then solidness, and roundness have no place.
Are these but warts, and pockholes in the face   300
Of th' earth? Think so: but yet confess, in this
The world's proportion disfigured is:

That those two legs whereon it doth rely,
Reward and punishment, are bent awry.°   *Disorder in the world.*
And, oh, it can no more be questionèd,
That beauty's best, proportion, is dead,
Since even grief itself, which now alone
Is left us, is without proportion.
She by whose lines proportion should be
Examined, measure of all symmetry,   310
Whom had that ancient seen, who thought souls made
Of harmony,° he would at next have said
That harmony was she, and thence infer,
That souls were but resultances° from her,
And did from her into our bodies go,
As to our eyes, the forms from objects flow:
She, who if those great Doctors truly said
That the ark to man's proportions was made,°
Had been a type for that, as that might be
A type of her in this, that contrary   320
Both elements, and passions lived at peace
In her, who caused all civil war to cease;
She, after whom, what form soe'er we see,
Is discord, and rude incongruity;
She, she is dead; she's dead: when thou know'st this,
Thou know'st how ugly a monster this world is,
And learn'st thus much by our Anatomy,
That here is nothing to enamor thee:
And that, not only faults in inward parts,
Corruptions in our brains, or in our hearts,   330
Poisoning the fountains, whence our actions spring,
Endanger us: but that if everything
Be not done fitly and in proportion,
To satisfy wise, and good lookers-on,
(Since most men be such as most think they be)
They're loathsome too, by this deformity.
For good, and well, must in our actions meet;
Wicked is not much worse than indiscreet.
But beauty's other second element,
Color, and luster now, is as near spent.   340
And had the world his just proportion,
Were it a ring still, yet the stone is gone.
As° a compassionate turquoise which doth tell
By looking pale, the wearer is not well,
As gold falls sick being stung with mercury,
All the world's parts of such complexion be.
When nature was most busy, the first week,
Swaddling the newborn earth, God seemed to like
That she should sport herself sometimes, and play,

---

256. overthwarts: thrusts or displacements. (In ll. 251–58 Donne means that astronomers, to account for the phenomena, have turned the heavens into a maze of mathematical lines, sections, epicycles, etc. See Bacon's *Essays*, p. 335, n. 94.)   258. eight ... shares: according to Ptolemy, the stars were divided into forty-eight constellations.   260. New stars: One had appeared in 1572, and another in 1604.   271. cozening: beguiling.   284. They're ... pace: because their apparent motions are now ascribed to the earth's motion.   295. If ... be: Hell was supposed to be in the middle of the earth.

304. Reward ... awry: "The sudden transition from the physical to the moral sphere is very disconcerting" [Grierson].   311–12. ancient ... harmony: Aristoxenus, or perhaps Pythagoras. Cf. Simmias in Plato's *Phaedo*.   314. resultances: emanations.   317–18. Doctors ... made: e.g., St. Augustine, who said that the ark's length, breadth, and depth were in the same proportions as those of the human body, and that the ark was an emblem of the Church in its earthly pilgrimage.   343–46. As ... be: These prescientific beliefs explain themselves.

To mingle, and vary colors every day: 350
And then, as though she could not make enow,
Himself his various rainbow did allow.
Sight is the noblest sense of any one,
Yet sight hath only color to feed on,
And color is decayed: summer's robe grows
Dusky, and like an oft-dyed garment shows.
Our blushing red, which used in cheeks to spread,
Is inward sunk, and only our souls are red.
Perchance the world might have recoverèd,
If she whom we lament had not been dead: 360
But she, in whom all white, and red, and blue
(Beauty's ingredients) voluntary grew,
As in an unvexed Paradise; from whom
Did all things' verdure, and their luster come,
Whose composition was miraculous,
Being all color, all diaphanous,
(For air and fire but thick gross bodies were,
And liveliest stones but drowsy and pale to her),
She, she, is dead; she's dead: when thou know'st
    this,
Thou know'st how wan a ghost this our world
    is. 370
And learn'st thus much by our Anatomy,
That it should more affright, than pleasure thee.
And that, since all fair color then did sink,
'Tis now but wicked vanity, to think
To color vicious deeds with good pre- *Weakness*
    tense, *in the*
Or with bought colors to illude men's *want of*
    sense. *corre-*
Nor in aught more this world's decay *spond-*
    appears, *ence of*
Than that her influence the heav'n for- *heaven*
    bears, *and earth.*
Or that the elements do not feel this,
The father, or the mother barren is.° 380
The clouds conceive not rain, or do not pour,
In the due birthtime, down the balmy shower;
Th' air doth not motherly sit on the earth,
To hatch her seasons, and give all things birth;
Springtimes were common cradles, but are tombs;
And false conceptions fill the general wombs;
Th' air shows such meteors, as none can see,
Not only what they mean, but what they be;°
Earth such new worms,° as would have troubled
    much
Th' Aegyptian *Mages* to have made more
    such. 390
What artist° now dares boast that he can bring

Heaven hither, or constellate° anything,
So as the influence of those stars may be
Imprisoned in an herb, or charm, or tree,
And do by touch, all which those stars could do?
The art is lost, and correspondence too.
For heaven gives little, and the earth takes less,
And man least knows their trade and purposes.
If this commerce 'twixt heaven and earth were not
Embarred, and all this traffic quite forgot, 400
She, for whose loss we have lamented thus,
Would work more fully, and pow'rfully on us:
Since herbs, and roots, by dying lose not all,
But they, yea ashes too, are medicinal,
Death could not quench her virtue so, but that
It would be (if not followed) wondered at:
And all the world would be one dying swan,
To sing her funeral praise, and vanish then.
But as some serpents' poison hurteth not,
Except it be from the live serpent shot, 410
So doth her virtue need her here, to fit
That unto us; she working more than it.
But she, in whom to such maturity
Virtue was grown, past growth, that it must die;
She, from whose influence all impressions came,
But, by receivers' impotencies, lame,
Who, though she could not transubstantiate
All states to gold, yet gilded every state,
So that some princes have some temperance;
Some counselors some purpose to advance 420
The common profit; and some people have
Some stay,° no more than kings should give, to
    crave;
Some women have some taciturnity,
Some nunneries some grains of chastity;
She that did thus much, and much more could
    do,
But that our age was iron, and rusty too,
She, she is dead; she's dead; when thou know'st
    this,
Thou know'st how dry a cinder this world is.
And learn'st thus much by our Anatomy,
That 'tis in vain to dew, or mollify 430
It with thy tears, or sweat, or blood: nothing
Is worth our travail, grief, or perishing,
But those rich joys, which did possess her heart,
Of which she's now partaker, and a part.
But as in cutting up a man that's dead, *Con-*
The body will not last out, to have read° *clusion.*
On every part, and therefore men direct
Their speech to parts, that are of most effect;
So the world's carcass would not last, if I
Were punctual in this Anatomy; 440
Nor smells it well to hearers, if one tell

---

380. father . . . is: The "father" is the "heavens," the celestial
bodies whose influences and motions used to affect the earth
(the "mother"). Cf. Bacon, *Advancement*, II. xxi. 1: "The
heavens, which are the more worthy, are the agent; and the
earth, which is the less worthy, is the patient." 387-88.
Th' air . . . be: Meteors and monsters were regarded as portents of disaster. 389. new worms: new reptiles, as described
by recent travelers. 391. artist: e.g., astrologer.

392. constellate: (in astrology) to fashion anything under a
particular constellation so that it absorbs the power or "influence" of the stars. Cf. "Of My Name, in the Window," ll. 33–39,
and l. 33n. 422. stay: self-restraint. 436. read: lectured.

Them their disease, who fain would think they're
    well.
Here therefore be the end: and, blessed maid,
Of whom is meant whatever hath been said,
Or shall be spoken well by any tongue,
Whose name refines coarse lines, and makes prose
    song,
Accept this tribute, and his first year's rent,
Who till his dark short taper's end be spent,
As oft as thy feast sees this widowed earth,
Will yearly celebrate thy second birth,   450
That is, thy death; for though the soul of man
Be got when man is made, 'tis born but then
When man doth die; our body's as the womb,
And, as a midwife, death directs it home.
And you her creatures, whom she works upon,
And have your last, and best concoction°
From her example, and her virtue, if you
In reverence to her, do think it due,
That no one should her praises thus rehearse,
As matter fit for chronicle, not verse;   460
Vouchsafe to call to mind that God did make
A last, and lasting'st piece, a song.° He spake
To *Moses* to deliver unto all,
That song, because he knew they would let fall
The Law, the Prophets, and the History,
But keep the song still in their memory:
Such an opinion (in due measure)° made
Me this great office boldly to invade:
Nor could incomprehensibleness deter
Me, from thus trying to emprison her,   470
Which when I saw that a strict grave could do,
I saw not why verse might not do so too.
Verse hath a middle nature: heaven keeps souls,
The grave keeps bodies, verse the fame enrolls.

from HOLY SONNETS

The "Holy Sonnets" given here are taken from the
series of nineteen composed after the death of Donne's
wife, which occurred in 1617, two years after his ordination. These sonnets, and the last three (above all) of
the other *Divine Poems* printed below, show all the
force of Donne's passionate nature turned towards
God. His poetical powers are seen here at their height,
for, though his "wit" has not ceased to be active, it
is used, not for the sake of "conceit" but as a means
of expressing profound and sincere emotion.

I

Thou hast made me, and shall thy work decay?
Repair me now, for now mine end doth haste,
I run to death, and death meets me as fast,

And all my pleasures are like yesterday;
I dare not move my dim eyes any way,
Despair behind, and death before doth cast
Such terror, and my feeble flesh doth waste
By sin in it, which it towards hell doth weigh;
Only thou art above, and when towards thee
By thy leave I can look, I rise again;   10
But our old subtle foe so tempteth me,
That not one hour myself I can sustain;
Thy grace may wing me to prevent his art,
And thou like adamant° draw mine iron heart.

VII

At the round earth's imagined corners, blow
Your trumpets, angels, and arise, arise
From death, you numberless infinities
Of souls, and to your scattered bodies go,
All whom the flood did, and fire shall o'erthrow,
All whom war, dearth, age, agues, tyrannies,
Despair, law, chance, hath slain, and you whose
    eyes
Shall behold God, and never taste death's woe.°
But let them sleep, Lord, and me mourn a space,
For, if above all these, my sins abound,   10
'Tis late to ask abundance of thy grace,
When we are there; here on this lowly ground,
Teach me how to repent; for that's as good
As if thou hadst sealed my pardon, with thy blood.

X

Death be not proud, though some have callèd thee
Mighty and dreadful, for thou art not so,
For those whom thou think'st thou dost overthrow,
Die not, poor Death, nor yet canst thou kill me.
From rest and sleep, which but thy pictures be,
Much pleasure, then from thee, much more must
    flow,
And soonest our best men with thee do go,
Rest of their bones, and soul's delivery.
Thou art slave to fate, chance, kings, and desperate
    men,
And dost with poison, war, and sickness dwell,   10
And poppy, or charms can make us sleep as well,
And better than thy stroke; why swell'st thou then?
One short sleep past, we wake eternally,
And death shall be no more; Death, thou shalt die.

XIII

What if this present were the world's last night?
Mark in my heart, O Soul, where thou dost dwell,
The picture of Christ crucified, and tell
Whether that countenance can thee affright,
Tears in his eyes quench the amazing light,

---

456. concoction: composition or blending, with the added sense
of "maturity."   462. song: the Song of Moses in Deut. 32.
467. due measure: i.e., humanly speaking, or with due reverence:
"Donne finds that he is attributing to himself the same thoughts
as God" [Grierson].

HOLY SONNETS. I. 14. adamant: here used in the obsolete sense
of "loadstone."   VII. 7–8. you . . . woe: i.e., "you who will be
alive at the time of the Last Judgment."

Blood fills his frowns, which from his pierced head
    fell.
And can that tongue adjudge thee unto hell,
Which prayed forgiveness for his foes' fierce spite?
No, no; but as in my idolatry
I said to all my profane mistresses,   10
Beauty, of pity, foulness only is
A sign of rigor:° so I say to thee,
To wicked spirits are horrid shapes assigned,
This beauteous form assures a piteous mind.

XIV

Batter my heart, three-personed God; for, you
As yet but knock, breathe, shine, and seek to mend;
That I may rise and stand, o'erthrow me, and bend
Your force, to break, blow, burn, and make me
    new.
I, like an usurped town, to another due,
Labor to admit you, but oh, to no end,
Reason, your viceroy in me, me should defend,
But is captived, and proves weak or untrue.
Yet dearly I love you, and would be lovèd fain,
But am betrothed unto your enemy: 10
Divorce me, untie, or break that knot again,
Take me to you, imprison me, for I
Except you enthrall me, never shall be free,
Nor ever chaste, except you ravish me.

XVIII

Show me, dear Christ, thy spouse,° so bright and
    clear.
What! is it she,° which on the other shore
Goes richly painted? or which robbed and tore
Laments and mourns in Germany and here?°
Sleeps she a thousand, then peeps up one year?
Is she self truth and errs? now new, now outwore?
Doth she, and did she, and shall she evermore
On one, on seven, or on no hill° appear?
Dwells she with us, or like adventuring knights
First travail we to seek and then make love?   10
Betray, kind husband, thy spouse to our sights,
And let mine amorous soul court thy mild dove,
Who is most true, and pleasing to thee, then
When she is embraced and open to most men.

XIX

Oh, to vex me, contraries meet in one;
Inconstancy unnaturally hath begot
A constant habit; that when I would not
I change in vows, and in devotion.
As humorous° is my contrition

As my profane love, and as soon forgot:
As riddlingly distempered, cold and hot,
As praying, as mute; as infinite, as none.
I durst not view heaven yesterday; and today
In prayers, and flattering speeches I court God: 10
Tomorrow I quake with true fear of his rod.
So my devout fits come and go away
Like a fantastic ague: save that here
Those are my best days, when I shake with fear.

OTHER *DIVINE POEMS*

GOOD FRIDAY, 1613, RIDING WESTWARD

This poem contains its date in the title. It is thus
earlier than the "Holy Sonnets," but the traditional
order is preserved in the present extracts. Written two
years before Donne was ordained, this poem is less
intense in feeling; the poet is less deeply implicated,
and his wit, accordingly, plays with the paradoxes of
religion more objectively.

Let man's soul be a sphere, and then, in this,
The intelligence that moves,° devotion is,
And as the other° spheres, by being grown
Subject to foreign motions, lose their own,
And being by others hurried every day,
Scarce in a year their natural form obey:
Pleasure or business, so, our souls admit
For their first mover, and are whirled by it.°
Hence is't, that I am carried towards the west
This day, when my soul's form bends toward the
    east.   10
There I should see a Sun, by rising set,
And by that setting endless day beget;
But that° Christ on this cross, did rise and fall,
Sin had eternally benighted all.
Yet dare I almost be glad, I do not see
That spectacle of too much weight for me.
Who sees God's face, that is self life,° must die;
What a death were it then to see God die?
It made his own lieutenant, nature, shrink,
It made his footstool crack, and the sun wink.°   20
Could I behold those hands which span the Poles,
And turn all spheres at once, pierced with those
    holes?
Could I behold that endless height which is

GOOD FRIDAY, 1613, RIDING WESTWARD. 2. intelligence . . .
moves: Each of the heavenly "spheres" was moved and guided
by an angel or "intelligence"; so, if we regard the soul as a
sphere, its motive force should be religion ("devotion"). 3–
6. other . . . obey: The heavenly bodies are deflected from their
natural orbits by the motions of other bodies. 7–8. Pleasure
. . . it: Similarly our souls, whose "first mover" (*primum mobile*) should be religion, are in fact deflected by pleasure or
business. 13. But that: if he (Christ) had not. 17. self life:
life itself. 20. wink: Darkness covered the earth at the death
of Christ.

XIII. 11–12. Beauty . . . rigor: Beauty betokens a compassionate heart; ugliness betokens severity. XVIII. 1. spouse: i.e.,
the Church. 2. she: the Roman Catholic Church. 3–4. or . . .
here: the reformed Church in Germany and England. 8. one
. . . hill: Wittenberg, Rome, and Geneva. XIX. 5. humorous:
fickle, subject to changing "humors."

Zenith to us, and our antipodes,
Humbled below us? or that blood which is
The seat of all our souls, if not of his,
Made dirt of dust, or that flesh which was worn,
By God, for his apparel, ragged, and torn?
If on these things I durst not look, durst I
Upon his miserable mother cast mine eye,   30
Who was God's partner here, and furnished thus
Half of that sacrifice which ransomed us?
Though these things, as I ride, be from mine eye,
They're present yet unto my memory,
For that looks towards them; and thou look'st to-
      wards me,
O Saviour, as thou hang'st upon the tree;
I turn my back to thee, but to receive
Corrections, till thy mercies bid thee leave.°
O think me worth thine anger, punish me,
Burn off my rusts, and my deformity,   40
Restore thine image, so much, by thy grace,
That thou may'st know me, and I'll turn my face.

from THE LITANY

Referred to in a letter written by Donne in 1609 or
1611. These sections (XV and XVI — there are twenty-
eight in all) are given here because, like the "Letter
to the Countess of Bedford," they show Donne in a
remarkably balanced frame of mind. Just as, in the
"Letter," he holds the scales between nature and
grace, so here he is poised between the various extreme
views which are damaging to the spiritual life.

XV

From being anxious, or secure,
Dead clods of sadness, or light squibs of mirth,
From thinking that great courts immure
All, or no happiness, or that this earth
      Is only for our prison framed,
      Or that thou art covetous
To them thou lovest, or that they are maimed
From reaching this world's sweet, who seek thee
      thus,
With all their might, good Lord deliver us.

XVI

From needing danger, to be good,   10
From owing thee yesterday's tears today,
From trusting so much to thy blood,
That in that hope, we wound our soul away,
      From bribing thee with alms, to excuse
      Some sin more burdenous,
From light affecting, in religion, news,°
From thinking us all soul, neglecting thus
Our mutual duties, Lord deliver us.

38. leave: desist. LITANY. 16. From ... news: too easily
adopting new doctrines in religion.

A HYMN TO CHRIST

At the Author's Last Going into Germany

This journey was made in 1619, when Donne accompanied the Earl of Doncaster on an embassy to
Frederick and Elizabeth of Bohemia. Donne also
preached a valedictory sermon before this voyage (Lincoln's Inn, April 18, 1619).

In what torn ship soever I embark,
That ship shall be my emblem of thy ark;
What sea soever swallow me, that flood
Shall be to me an emblem of thy blood;
Though thou with clouds of anger do disguise
Thy face; yet through that mask I know those eyes,
      Which, though they turn away sometimes,
         They never will despise.

I sacrifice this island unto thee,
And all whom I loved there, and who loved me;
When I have put our seas 'twixt them and me,   11
Put thou thy sea betwixt my sins and thee.
As the tree's sap doth seek the root below
In winter, in my winter now I go,
      Where none but thee, th' eternal root
         Of true Love I may know.

Nor thou nor thy religion dost control,
The amorousness of an harmonious soul,
But thou would'st have that love thyself: as thou
Art jealous, Lord, so I am jealous now;   20
Thou lov'st not, till from loving more, thou free
My soul: whoever gives, takes liberty:
      O, if thou car'st not whom I love
         Alas, thou lov'st not me.

Seal then this bill of my divorce to all,
On whom those fainter beams of love did fall;
Marry those loves, which in youth scattered be
On fame, wit, hopes (false mistresses) to thee.
Churches are best for prayer, that have least light:
To see God only, I go out of sight: 30
      And to 'scape stormy days, I choose
         An everlasting night.

HYMN TO GOD MY GOD, IN MY SICKNESS

Written March 23, 1631, eight days before Donne's
death.

Since I am coming to that holy room,
      Where, with thy quire of Saints for evermore,
I shall be made thy music; as I come

I tune the instrument here at the door,
And what I must do then, think here before.

Whilst my physicians by their love are grown
  Cosmographers, and I their map, who lie
Flat on this bed, that by them may be shown
  That this is my Southwest discovery,°
  Per fretum febris,° by these straits to die,   10

I joy, that in these straits, I see my west;
  For, though their currents yield return to none,
What shall my west hurt me? As west and east
  In all flat maps (and I am one) are one,
  So death doth touch the Resurrection.

Is the Pacific Sea my home? Or are
  The eastern riches? Is *Jerusalem?*
Anyan,° and *Magellan,* and *Gibraltar,*
  All straits, and none but straits, are ways to them,
  Whether where *Japhet* dwelt, or *Cham,* or
    Shem.°   20

We think that *Paradise* and *Calvary,*
  Christ's cross, and *Adam's* tree, stood in one
    place;°
Look, Lord, and find both *Adams* met in me;
  As the first *Adam's* sweat surrounds my face,
  May the last *Adam's* blood my soul embrace.

So, in his purple wrapped receive me, Lord,
  By these his thorns give me his other crown;
And as to others' souls I preached thy word,
  Be this my text, my sermon to mine own,
  Therefore that he may raise the Lord throws
    down.   30

A HYMN TO GOD THE FATHER

No exact date is available, but this is clearly one of
Donne's last poems. Walton tells us that Donne had it
set to music, and often caused it to be sung in St. Paul's
Cathedral, especially at evensong. Walton reports
Donne as saying: "The words of this hymn have restored me to the same thoughts of joy that possessed
my soul in my sickness when I composed it. And, O
the power of church music! that harmony added to it
has raised the affections of my heart, and quickened
my graces of zeal and gratitude; and I observe that I
always return from paying this public duty of prayer
and praise to God, with an unexpressible tranquillity
of mind, and a willingness to leave the world."

HYMN TO GOD MY GOD, IN MY SICKNESS. 9. **Southwest discovery:**
the Straits of Magellan.   10. *Per . . . febris:* through the
"strait" of fever.   18. **Anyan:** Bering Strait.   20. *Japhet . . .
Shem:* According to ancient tradition the world was divided
between the sons of Noah thus: Japhet, Europe; Ham (*Cham*)
Africa; Shem, Asia.   22. **one place:** It was another ancient
belief that the tree of knowledge in Eden, and the cross of
Christ on Calvary, stood in one and the same place.

1

Wilt thou forgive that sin where I begun,
  Which is my sin, though it were done before?
Wilt thou forgive that sin, through which I run,
  And do run still: though still I do deplore?
    When thou hast done, thou hast not done,°
      For I have more.

2

Wilt thou forgive that sin by which I have won
  Others to sin? and made my sin their door?
Wilt thou forgive that sin which I did shun
  A year, or two: but wallowed in, a score?   10
    When thou hast done, thou hast not done,
      For I have more.

3

I have a sin of fear, that when I have spun
  My last thread, I shall perish on the shore;
Swear by thyself, that at my death thy son
  Shall shine as he shines now, and heretofore;
    And, having done that, thou hast done,
      I fear no more.

from DEVOTIONS UPON EMERGENT OCCASIONS

These meditations, suggested to Donne during a
serious illness by the various stages of the malady as
they arose or developed ("emergent occasions"), were
written in 1623 and published in 1624. They are
prayers, soliloquies, or reflections, and form a sequence
following the course of the disease. Death and sickness always fascinated Donne, and here we see him
extracting spiritual meanings even from his own pain
and grave danger.

The Latin mottoes mark each successive stage: the
onset of the illness, its effects, the coming of the physician, the final crisis, and the recovery; the English sentence opposite each epigraph is Donne's free translation of it. (Readers will understand that only a few
of these stages are represented in the following extracts.)

II

Actio Laesa.[1]   The strength, and the function of the
              senses, and other faculties change and
              fail.

The heavens are not the less constant because
they move continually, because they move continually one and the same way. The earth is not the
more constant because it lies still continually,[2] be-

HYMN TO GOD THE FATHER. 5. **done:** probably a pun on "Donne."
  DEVOTIONS. 1. *Actio Laesa:* "[Powers of] action stricken
down." 2. Donne here assumes the truth of the pre-Copernican
(geocentric) system.

cause continually it changes, and melts in all parts thereof. Man, who is the noblest part of the earth, melts so away, as if he were a statue, not of earth, but of snow. We see his own envy melts him, he grows lean with that; he will say, another's beauty melts him; but he feels that a fever doth not melt him like snow, but pour him out like lead, like iron, like brass melted in a furnace: it doth not only melt him, but calcine him, reduce him to atoms, and to ashes; not to water, but to lime. And how quickly? Sooner than thou canst receive an answer, sooner than thou canst conceive the question; earth is the center of my body, heaven is the center of my soul; these two are the natural places of those two; but those go not to these two in an equal pace: my body falls down without pushing, my soul does not go up without pulling: ascension is my soul's pace and measure, but precipitation my body's: and even angels, whose home is heaven, and who are winged too, yet had a ladder to go to heaven by steps. The sun who goes so many miles in a minute, the stars of the firmament, which go so very many more, go not so fast as my body to the earth. In the same instant that I feel the first attempt of the disease, I feel the victory; in the twinkling of an eye, I can scarce see, instantly the taste is insipid, and fatuous; instantly the appetite is dull and desireless; instantly the knees are sinking and strengthless; and in an instant, sleep, which is the picture, the copy of death, is taken away, that the original, death itself may succeed, and that so I might have death to the life. It was part of Adam's punishment, In the sweat of thy brows thou shalt eat thy bread:[3] it is multiplied to me, I have earned bread in the sweat of my brows, in the labor of my calling, and I have it; and I sweat again and again, from the brow to the sole of the foot, but I eat no bread, I taste no sustenance: miserable distribution of mankind, where one half lacks meat, and the other stomach.

III

Decubitus sequitur tandem.[4] The patient takes his bed.

We attribute but one privilege and advantage to man's body, above other moving creatures, that he is not as others, groveling, but of an erect, of an upright form, naturally built and disposed to the contemplation of heaven. Indeed it is a thankful form, and recompenses that soul which gives it, with carrying that soul so many foot higher towards heaven. Other creatures look to the earth; and even that is no unfit object, no unfit contemplation for man; for thither he must come; but because man is not to stay there, as other creatures are, man in his natural form is carried to the contemplation of that place which is his home, heaven. This is man's prerogative; but what state hath he in this dignity? A fever can fillip him down, a fever can depose him; a fever can bring that head, which yesterday carried a crown of gold five foot towards a crown of glory, as low as his own foot today. When God came to breathe into man the breath of life, he found him flat upon the ground; when he comes to withdraw that breath from him again, he prepares him to it, by laying him flat upon his bed. Scarce any prison so close, that affords not the prisoner two, or three steps. The anchorites[5] that barked themselves up in hollow trees, and immured themselves in hollow walls; that perverse man, that barreled himself in a tub,[6] all could stand, or sit, and enjoy some change of posture. A sick-bed is a grave; and all that the patient says there, is but a varying of his own epitaph. Every night's bed is a type of the grave: at night we tell our servants at what hour we will rise; here we cannot tell ourselves at what day, what week, what month. Here the head lies as low as the foot; the Head of the people, as low as they whom those feet trod upon; and that hand that signed pardons, is too weak to beg his own, if he might have it for lifting up that hand: strange fetters to the feet, strange manacles to the hands, when the feet and hands are bound so much the faster, by how much the cords are slacker; so much the less able to do their offices, by how much more the sinews and ligaments are the looser. In the grave I may speak through the stones in the voice of my friends, and in the accents of those words which their love may afford my memory; here I am mine own ghost, and rather affright my beholders than instruct them; they conceive the worst of me now, and yet fear worse; they give me for dead now, and yet wonder how I do, when they wake at midnight, and ask how I do tomorrow. Miserable and (though common to all) inhuman posture, where I must practice my lying in the grave by lying still, and not practice my resurrection by rising any more.

---

3. In . . . bread: Gen. 3:19.   4. *Decubitus . . . tandem:* At length he continues, lying in bed.

5. anchorites: hermits.   6. perverse . . . tub: Diogenes.

XVI

Et properare meum clamant,   From the bells of the
  è Turre propinqua,   church adjoining, I
Obstreperae Campanae aliorum   am daily remem-
  in funere, funus.[7]   bered of my burial
     in the funerals of
     others.

We have a convenient author, who writ a discourse of bells, when he was prisoner in Turkey.
How would he have enlarged himself if he had
been my fellow prisoner in this sick-bed, so near
to that steeple which never ceases, no more than
the harmony of the spheres, but is more heard.[8]
When the Turks took Constantinople, they melted
the bells into ordnance; I have heard both bells and
ordnance, but never been so much affected with
those, as with these bells. I have lain near a steeple,
in which there are said to be more than thirty bells;
and near another, where there is one so big as that
the clapper is said to weigh more than six hundred
pound, yet never so affected as here. Here the
bells can scarce solemnize the funeral of any person, but that I knew him, or knew that he was my
neighbor: we dwelt in houses near to one another
before, but now he is gone into that house, into
which I must follow him. There is a way of correcting the children of great persons, that other
children are corrected in their behalf, and in their
names, and this works upon them, who indeed had
more deserved it. And when these bells tell me that
now one and now another is buried, must not I
acknowledge that they have the correction due to
me, and paid the debt that I owe? There is a story
of a bell in a monastery which, when any of the
house was sick to death, rung always voluntarily,
and they knew the inevitableness of the danger by
that. It rung once, when no man was sick; but the
next day one of the house fell from the steeple and
died, and the bell held the reputation of a prophet
still. If these bells that warn to a funeral now, were
appropriated to none, may not I, by the hour of the
funeral, supply? How many men that stand at an
execution, if they would ask, for what dies that
man, should hear their own faults condemned, and
see themselves executed by attorney? We scarce
hear of any man preferred, but we think of our-

selves, that we might very well have been that
man; why might not I have been that man, that is
carried to his grave now? Could I fit myself to
stand or sit in any man's place, and not to lie in
any man's grave? I may lack much of the good
parts of the meanest, but I lack nothing of the mortality of the weakest; they may have acquired better
abilities than I, but I was born to as many infirmities as they. To be an incumbent [9] by lying down
in a grave, to be a doctor by teaching mortification [10] by example, by dying: though I may have
seniors, others may be elder than I, yet I have proceeded apace in a good university, and gone a great
way in a little time, by the furtherance of a vehement fever; and whomsoever these bells bring to
the ground today, if he and I had been compared
yesterday, perchance I should have been thought
likelier to come to this preferment, then, than he.
God hath kept the power of death in his own
hands, lest any man should bribe death. If man
knew the gain of death, the ease of death, he would
solicit, he would provoke death to assist him by
any hand which he might use. But as when men
see many of their own professions preferred, it ministers a hope that that [11] may light upon them; so
when these hourly bells tell me of so many funerals
of men like me, it presents, if not a desire that it
may, yet a comfort whensoever mine shall come.

XVII

Nunc lento sonitu dicunt,   Now, this bell tolling softly
  Morieris.[12]   for another, says to me,
     Thou must die.

Perchance he for whom this bell tolls, may be so
ill, as that he knows not it tolls for him; and perchance I may think myself so much better than I
am, as that they who are about me, and see my
state, may have caused it to toll for me, and I know
not that. The Church is Catholic, universal, so are
all her actions; all that she does belongs to all.
When she baptizes a child, that action concerns me;
for that child is thereby connected to that Head
which is my Head too, and engrafted into that
body, whereof I am a member. And when she buries
a man, that action concerns me: all mankind is of
one Author, and is one volume; when one man dies,

---

7. *Et . . . funus:* "And it is to hasten my burial that the noisy
bells toll from the neighboring tower at the funeral of others."
8. *spheres . . . heard:* The heavenly spheres, in their revolutions,
were thought to make harmonious sounds inaudible to our gross
ears. Cf. "ninefold harmony" in Milton's "Nativity," st. 13,
below.

9. **incumbent:** a beneficed clergyman (a play on the Latin
meaning of *incumbere,* to lie down). 10. **doctor . . . mortification:** probably a play on the medical and theological senses of
these words. 11. **that:** i.e., promotion or "preferment."
12. *Nunc . . . Morieris:* Donne's own (free) translation suffices.

one chapter is not torn out of the book, but translated into a better language; and every chapter must be so translated; God employs several translators; some pieces are translated by age, some by sickness, some by war, some by justice; but God's hand is in every translation; and his hand shall bind up all our scattered leaves again, for that Library where every book shall lie open to one another: As therefore the bell that rings to a sermon, calls not upon the preacher only, but upon the congregation to come; so this bell calls us all: but how much more me, who am brought so near the door by this sickness. There was a contention as far as a suit (in which both piety and dignity, religion and estimation,[13] were mingled), which of the religious orders should ring to prayers first in the morning; and it was determined, that they should ring first that rose earliest. If we understand aright the dignity of this bell that tolls for our evening prayer, we would be glad to make it ours, by rising early, in that application, that it might be ours, as well as his, whose indeed it is. The bell doth toll for him that thinks it doth; and though it intermit again, yet from that minute, that that occasion wrought upon him, he is united to God. Who casts not up his eye to the sun when it rises? but who takes off his eye from a comet when that breaks out?[14] Who bends not his ear to any bell, which upon any occasion rings? but who can remove it from that bell, which is passing a piece of himself out of this world? No man is an island, entire of itself; every man is a piece of the continent, a part of the main;[15] if a clod be washed away by the sea, Europe is the less, as well as if a promontory were, as well as if a manor of thy friends or of thine own were; any man's death diminishes me, because I am involved in mankind; and therefore never send to know for whom the bell tolls; it tolls for thee. Neither can we call this a begging of misery or a borrowing of misery, as though we were not miserable enough of ourselves, but must fetch in more from the next house, in taking upon us the misery of our neighbors. Truly it were an excusable covetousness if we did; for affliction is a treasure, and scarce any man hath enough of it. No man hath affliction enough that is not matured, and ripened by it, and made fit for God by that affliction. If a man carry treasure in bullion, or in a wedge of gold, and have none coined into current monies, his treasure will not defray him as he travels. Tribulation is treasure in

the nature of it, but it is not current money in the use of it, except we get nearer and nearer our home, Heaven, by it. Another man may be sick too, and sick to death, and this affliction may lie in his bowels, as gold in a mine, and be of no use to him; but this bell, that tells me of his affliction, digs out, and applies that gold to me; if by this consideration of another's danger I take mine own into contemplation, and so secure myself by making my recourse to my God, who is our only security.

XVIII

<table>
<tr><td>At inde</td><td>The bell rings out, and</td></tr>
<tr><td>Mortuus es, Sonitu celeri,</td><td>tells me in him, that I</td></tr>
<tr><td>pulsuque agitato.[16]</td><td>am dead.</td></tr>
</table>

The bell rings out; the pulse thereof is changed; the tolling was a faint and intermitting pulse, upon one side; this stronger, and argues more and better life. His soul is gone out; and as a man who had a lease of one thousand years after the expiration of a short one, or an inheritance after the life of a man in a consumption, he is now entered into the possession of his better estate. His soul is gone; whither? Who saw it come in, or who saw it go out? Nobody; yet everybody is sure he had one, and hath none. If I will ask mere philosophers what the soul is, I shall find amongst them that will tell me it is nothing but the temperament and harmony, and just and equal composition of the elements in the body, which produces all those faculties which we ascribe to the soul; and so in itself is nothing, no separable substance that overlives[17] the body. They see the soul is nothing else in other creatures, and they affect an impious humility, to think as low of man. But if my soul were no more than the soul of a beast, I could not think so; that soul that can reflect upon itself, consider itself, is more than so. If I will ask, not mere philosophers, but mixed men, philosophical divines, how the soul, being a separate substance, enters into the man, I shall find some that will tell me that it is by generation and procreation from parents, because they think it hard to charge the soul with the guiltiness of original sin, if the soul were infused into a body,[18] in which it must necessarily grow foul, and contract original sin, whether it will or no; and I shall find some that will tell me, that it is by immediate infusion

---

13. estimation: self-esteem.   14. comet ... out: comets were regarded as portents of disaster.   15. main: mainland.

16. At ... agitato: "Then lo! with rapid stroke and uneasy throb [it says], 'Thou art dead.'"   17. overlives: survives.   18. if ... body: i.e., as would be the case if the soul were directly infused by God.

from God, because they think it hard, to maintain an immortality in such a soul, as should be begotten, and derived with the body from mortal parents. If I will ask, not a few men, but almost whole bodies, whole Churches, what becomes of the souls of the righteous at the departing thereof from the body, I shall be told by some that they attend an expiation, a purification in a place of torment; by some, that they attend the fruition of the sight of God, in a place of rest but yet of expectation; by some, that they pass to an immediate possession of the presence of God. St. Augustine studied the nature of the soul as much as anything but the salvation of the soul; and he sent an express messenger to St. Jerome, to consult of some things concerning the soul: but he satisfies himself with this: let the departure of my soul to salvation be evident to my faith, and I care the less how dark the entrance of my soul into my body be to my reason. It is the going out, more than the coming in, that concerns us. This soul, this bell tells me, is gone out; whither? Who shall tell me that? I know not who it is; much less what he was; the condition of the man, and the course of his life, which should tell me whither he is gone, I know not. I was not there in his sickness, nor at his death; I saw not his way, nor his end, nor can ask them who did, thereby to conclude or argue whither he is gone. But yet I have one nearer me than all these: mine own charity; I ask that, and that tells me he is gone to everlasting rest, and joy, and glory: I owe him a good opinion; it is but thankful charity in me, because I received benefit and instruction from him when his bell tolled: and I, being made the fitter to pray, by that disposition wherein I was assisted by his occasion, did pray for him; and I pray not without faith; so I do charitably, so I do faithfully believe, that that soul is gone to everlasting rest, and joy, and glory. But for the body, how poor a wretched thing is

that? we cannot express it so fast, as it grows worse and worse. That body which scarce three minutes since was such a house, as that that soul, which made but one step from thence to heaven, was scarce thoroughly content to leave that for heaven: that body hath lost the name of a dwelling house, because none dwells in it, and is making haste to lose the name of a body, and dissolve to putrefaction. Who would not be affected, to see a clear and sweet river in the morning, grow a kennel of muddy land-water by noon, and condemned to the saltness of the sea by night? And how lame a picture, how faint a representation is that, of the precipitation of man's body to dissolution! Now all the parts built up, and knit by a lovely soul, now but a statue of clay, and now these limbs melted off, as if that clay were but snow; and now, the whole house is but a handful of sand, so much dust, and but a peck of rubbish, so much bone. If he who, as this bell tells me, is gone now, were some excellent artificer, who comes to him for a clock or for a garment now? or for counsel, if he were a lawyer? If a magistrate, for justice? Man, before he hath his immortal soul, hath a soul of sense, and a soul of vegetation before that: this immortal soul did not forbid other souls to be in us before,[19] but when this soul departs, it carries all with it; no more vegetation, no more sense: such a mother-in-law[20] is the earth, in respect of our natural mother; in her womb we grew; and when she was delivered of us, we were planted in some place, in some calling in the world; in the womb of the earth, we diminish, and when she is delivered of us, our grave opened for another, we are not transplanted, but transported, our dust blown away with profane dust, with every wind.

19. Man . . . before: for this doctrine of the three souls, see "Of my home, in the window," l. 25n.   20. mother-in-law: probably in the sense of "step-mother."

THE SERMONS

Donne's first surviving sermon dates from 1615; his last was preached at St. Paul's shortly before his death in 1631. The sermons were published posthumously, *LXXX Sermons* in 1640, *Fifty Sermons* in 1649, and *XXVI Sermons* in 1660.

"He preached the word," wrote Walton, "so as showed his own heart was possessed by those very thoughts that he labored to distill into others. A preacher in earnest, weeping sometimes for his auditors, sometimes with them; always preaching to himself like an angel from a cloud, but in none; carrying some, as St. Paul was, to heaven in holy raptures, and enticing others by a sacred art and courtship to amend their lives."

In these sermons we see the whole range of Donne's rhetorical power, from the homely illustration, through reasoned argument, up to impassioned utterance.

LXXX SERMONS, 1640

from SERMON II

St. Paul's. Christmas Day in the Evening. 1624

The text of the sermon is from Ps. 101:1: "I will sing of mercy and judgment."

The air is not so full of motes, of atoms, as the Church is of mercies; and as we can suck in no part of air, but we take in those motes, those atoms; so here in the congregation we cannot suck in a word from the preacher, we cannot speak, we cannot sigh a prayer to God, but that that whole breath and air is made of mercy. But we call not upon you from this text, to consider God's ordinary mercy, that which he exhibits to all in the ministry of his Church; nor his miraculous mercy, his extraordinary deliverances of states and churches; but we call upon particular consciences, by occasion of this text, to call to mind God's occasional mercies to them; such mercies as a regenerate man will call mercies, though a natural man[1] would call them accidents, or occurrences, or contingencies; a man wakes at midnight full of unclean thoughts, and he hears a passing bell; this is an occasional mercy, if he call that his own knell, and consider how unfit he was to be called out of the world then, how unready to receive that voice: *Fool, this night they shall fetch away thy soul*. The adulterer, whose eye waits for the twilight, goes forth, and

casts his eyes upon forbidden houses, and would enter, and sees a *Lord have mercy upon us* upon the door; this is an occasional mercy, if this bring him to know that they who lie sick of the plague within, pass through a furnace, but by God's grace, to heaven; and he without, carries his own furnace to hell, his lustful loins to everlasting perdition. What an occasional mercy had Balaam, when his ass catechized him:[2] what an occasional mercy had one thief, when the other catechized him so, "Art not thou afraid, being under the same condemnation?"[3] What an occasional mercy had all they that saw that, when the Devil himself fought for the name of Jesus, and wounded the sons of Sceva for exorcising in the name of Jesus, with that indignation, with that increpation,[4] "Jesus we know, and Paul we know, but who are ye?"[5] If I should declare what God hath done (done occasionally) for my soul, where he instructed me for fear of falling, where he raised me when I was fallen, perchance you would rather fix your thoughts upon my illness, and wonder at that, than at God's goodness, and glorify him in that; rather wonder at my sins, than at his mercies, rather consider how ill a man I was, than how good a God he is. If I should inquire upon what occasion God elected me, and writ my name in the Book of Life, I should sooner be afraid that it were not so, than find a reason why it should be so. God made sun and moon to distinguish seasons, and day, and night, and we cannot have the fruits of the earth but in their seasons: but God hath made no decree to distinguish the seasons of his mercies; in paradise, the fruits were ripe the first minute, and in heaven it is always autumn, his mercies are ever in their maturity. We ask *panem quotidianum,* our daily bread, and God never says you should have come yesterday, he never says you must again tomorrow, but *today if you will hear his voice,*[6] today he will hear you. If some king of the earth have so large an extent of dominion, in north and south, as that he hath winter and summer together in his dominions, so large an extent east and west, as that he hath day and night together in his dominions, much more hath God mercy and judgment together: he brought light out of darkness, not out of a lesser light; he can bring thy summer out of winter, though thou have no spring; though in the ways of fortune, or understanding, or conscience, thou have been benighted

---

SERMONS. **1. natural man:** a pagan, or any man unredeemed by supernatural grace.

2. Balaam . . . him: Num. 22:28.   **3. "Art . . . condemnation":** Luke 23:40.   **4. increpation:** cry of protest.   **5. Jesus . . . ye:** Acts 19:15.   **6. today . . . voice:** Ps. 95:7.

till now, wintered and frozen, clouded and eclipsed, damped and benumbed, smothered and stupefied till now, now God comes to thee, not as in the dawning of the day, not as in the bud of the spring, but as the sun at noon to illustrate [7] all shadows, as the sheaves in harvest, to fill all penuries: all occasions invite his mercies, and all times are his seasons.

from SERMON VII

St. Paul's. Christmas Day. 1629

2

What eye can fix itself upon east and west at once? And he must see more than east and west, that sees God, for God spreads infinitely beyond both: God alone is all; not only all that is, but all that is not, all that might be, if he would have it be. God is too large, too immense, and then man is too narrow, too little to be considered; for who can fix his eye upon an atom? and he must see a less thing than an atom, that sees man, for man is nothing. First, for the incomprehensibleness of God, the understanding of man, hath a limited, a determined latitude; it is an intelligence able to move that sphere [8] which it is fixed to, but could not move a greater: I can comprehend *naturam naturatam*,[9] created nature, but for that *natura naturans*,[10] God himself, the understanding of man cannot comprehend. I can see the sun in a looking glass, but the nature and the whole working of the sun I cannot see in that glass. I can see God in the creature, but the nature, the essence, the secret purposes of God, I cannot see there. There is *defatigatio in intellectualibus*,[11] says the saddest and soundest of the Hebrew Rabbins, the soul may be tired, as well as the body, and the understanding dazzled, as well as the eye.

3

Let man be something; how poor, and inconsiderable a rag of this world, is man! Man, whom Paracelsus [12] would have undertaken to have made, in a limbeck,[13] in a furnace: man, who, if they were altogether, all the men that ever were, and are, and shall be, would not have the power of one angel in them all, whereas all the angels (who, in the School [14] are conceived to be more in number, than, not only all the species, but all the individuals of this lower world) have not in them all, the power of one finger of God's hand: man, of whom when David had said (as the lowest diminution that he could put upon him), " I am a worm and no man," [15] he might have gone lower, and said, I am a man and no worm; for man is so much less than a worm, as that worms of his own production, shall feed upon his dead body in the grave, and an immortal worm [16] gnaw his conscience in the torments of hell.

from SERMON XV

At Whitehall. 1st Friday in Lent. March 8, 1621/2

Doth not man die even in his birth? The breaking of prison is death, and what is our birth, but a breaking of prison? As soon as we were clothed by God, our very apparel was an emblem of death. In the skins of dead beasts, he covered the skins of dying men. As soon as God set us on work, our very occupation was an emblem of death; it was to dig the earth; not to dig pitfalls for other men, but graves for ourselves. Hath any man here forgot today, that yesterday is dead? And the bell tolls for today, and will ring out anon; and for as much of every one of us as appertains to this day. *Quotidie morimur, et tamen nos esse aeternos putamus*,[17] says St. Jerome; we die every day, and we die all the day long; and because we are not absolutely dead, we call that an eternity, an eternity of dying: and is there comfort in that state? why, that is the state of hell itself, eternal dying, and not dead.

But for this there is enough said, by the moral man; [18] (that we may respite divine proofs, for divine points anon, for our several resurrections) for this death is merely natural, and it is enough that the moral man says, *Mors lex, tributum, officium mortalium*.[19] First it is *lex*, you were born under that law, upon that condition to die: so it is a rebellious thing not to be content to die; it opposes the law. Then it is *tributum*, an imposition which nature, the queen of this world, lays upon

---

7. illustrate: illumine.   8. intelligence . . . sphere: Cf. "Good Friday," ll. 1–2 and l. 2n.   9. *naturam naturatam*: literally "nature natured," i.e., the finished creation.   10. *natura naturans*: literally "nature naturing," i.e., the creative process of God, or God himself.   11. *defatigatio in intellectualibus*: "fatigue of the intellect."   12. Paracelsus: (c. 1490), German-Swiss mystical physician, who held that man's body is an extract of the ingredients of the creation, especially salt, sulfur, and mercury.   13. limbeck: alembic.

14. the School: i.e., amongst the Scholastic divines.   15. "I . . . man": Ps. 22:6.   16. immortal worm: Mark 9:44, 46, 48.   17. *Quotidie . . . putamus*: "We die daily, yet deem ourselves eternal."   18. moral man: i.e., Seneca, the Roman Stoic philosopher.   19. *Mors . . . mortalium*: "Death is the law, the tribute, and the function of mortals."

us, and which she will take, when and where she list; here a young man, there an old man, here a happy, there a miserable man; and so it is a seditious thing not to be content to die; it opposes the prerogative. And lastly, it is *officium,* men are to have their turns, to take their time, and then to give way by death to successors; and so it is *incivile, inofficiosum,*[20] not to be content to die; it opposes the frame and form of government. It comes equally to us all, and makes us all equal when it comes. The ashes of an oak in the chimney are no epitaph of that oak, to tell me how high or how large that was; it tells me not what flocks it sheltered while it stood, nor what men it hurt when it fell. The dust of great persons' graves is speechless too, it says nothing, it distinguishes nothing: as soon the dust of a wretch whom thou wouldest not, as of a prince whom thou couldest not look upon, will trouble thine eyes, if the wind blow it thither; and when a whirlwind hath blown the dust of the churchyard into the church, and the man sweeps out the dust of the church into the churchyard, who will undertake to sift those dusts again, and to pronounce: This is the patrician, this is the noble flour, and this the yeomanly, this the plebeian bran?

from SERMON LXVI

January 29, 1625/6

If you look upon this world in a map, you find two hemispheres, two half-worlds. If you crush heaven into a map, you may find two hemispheres too, two half-heavens; half will be joy, and half will be glory; for in these two, the joy of heaven, and the glory of heaven, is all heaven often represented unto us. And as of those two hemispheres of the world, the first hath been known long before, but the other (that of America, which is the richer in treasure), God reserved for later discoveries; so though he reserve that hemisphere of heaven, which is the glory thereof, to the resurrection, yet the other hemisphere, the joy of heaven, God opens to our discovery, and delivers for our habitation even whilst we dwell in this world. As God hath cast upon the unrepentant sinner two deaths, a temporal, and a spiritual death, so hath he breathed into us two lives; for so, as the word for death is doubled, *Morte morieris,* "Thou shalt die the death,"[21]

so is the word for life expressed in the plural, *Chaiim, vitarum,* "God breathed into his nostrils the breath of lives,"[22] of divers lives. Though our natural life were no life, but rather a continual dying, yet we have two lives besides that, an eternal life reserved for heaven, but yet a heavenly life too, a spiritual life, even in this world; and as God doth thus inflict two deaths, and infuse two lives, so doth he also pass two judgments upon man, or rather repeats the same judgment twice. For, that which Christ shall say to thy soul then at the Last Judgment, "Enter into thy Master's joy,"[23] he says to thy conscience now, "Enter into thy Master's joy." The everlastingness of the joy is the blessedness of the next life, but the entering, the inchoation is afforded here. . . .

Howling is the noise of hell, singing the voice of heaven; sadness the damp of hell, rejoicing the serenity of heaven. And he that hath not this joy here, lacks one of the best pieces of his evidence for the joys of heaven; and hath neglected or refused that earnest, by which God uses to bind his bargain, that true joy in this world shall flow into the joy of heaven, as a river flows into the sea; this joy shall not be put out in death, and a new joy kindled in me in heaven; but as my soul, as soon as it is out of my body, is in heaven, and does not stay for the possession of heaven, nor for the fruition of the sight of God, till it be ascended through air, and fire, and moon, and sun, and planets, and firmament, to that place which we conceive to be heaven, but without the thousandth part of a minute's stop, as soon as it issues, is in a glorious light, which is heaven (for all the way to heaven is heaven; and as those angels, which came from heaven hither, bring heaven with them, and are in heaven here, so that soul that goes to heaven, meets heaven here; and as those angels do not devest[24] heaven by coming, so these souls invest heaven in their going). As my soul shall not go towards heaven, but go by heaven to heaven, to the heaven of heavens, so the true joy of a good soul in this world is the very joy of heaven; and we go thither, not that being without joy, we might have joy infused into us, but that as Christ says, "our joy might be full,"[25] perfected, sealed with an everlastingness; for, as he promises that no man shall take our joy from us,[26] so neither shall death itself take it away, nor so much as interrupt it, or dis-

---

20. *incivile, inofficiosum:* "ungracious, undutiful."   21. "Thou . . . death": Gen. 2:17.

22. "God . . . lives": Gen. 2:7.   23. "Enter . . . joy": Matt. 25:23.   24. devest: divest, strip.   25. "our . . . full": John 16:24.   26. that . . . us: John 16:22.

continue it, but as in the face of death, when he lays hold upon me, and in the face of the Devil, when he attempts me, I shall see the face of God (for everything shall be a glass, to reflect God upon me), so in the agonies of death, in the anguish of that dissolution, in the sorrows of that valediction, in the irreversibleness of that transmigration, I shall have a joy which shall no more evaporate than my soul shall evaporate, a joy that shall pass up, and put on a more glorious garment above, and be joy superinvested [27] in glory. Amen.

from SERMON LXXX

Preached at the Funeral of Sir William Cokayne, Knight, Alderman of London.
December 12, 1626

But when we consider with a religious seriousness the manifold weaknesses of the strongest devotions in time of prayer, it is a sad consideration. I throw myself down in my chamber, and I call in and invite God and his angels thither, and when they are there, I neglect God and his angels, for the noise of a fly, for the rattling of a coach, for the whining of a door; I talk on, in the same posture of praying; eyes lifted up, knees bowed down, as though I prayed to God; and if God or his angels should ask me when I thought last of God in that prayer, I cannot tell: sometimes I find that I had forgot what I was about, but when I began to forget it, I cannot tell. A memory of yesterday's pleasures, a fear of tomorrow's dangers, a straw under my knee, a noise in mine ear, a light in mine eye, an anything, a nothing, a fancy, a chimera in my brain, troubles me in my prayer. So certainly is there nothing, nothing in spiritual things, perfect in this world. . . .

I need not call in new philosophy,[28] that denies a settledness, an acquiescence [29] in the very body of the earth, but makes the earth to move in that place, where we thought the sun had moved; I need not that help, that the earth itself is in motion, to prove this: that nothing upon earth is permanent; the assertion will stand of itself, till some man assign me some instance, something that a man may rely upon, and find permanent. Consider the greatest bodies upon earth, the monarchies, objects

which one would think destiny might stand and stare at, but not shake; consider the smallest bodies upon earth, the hairs of our head, objects which one would think destiny would not observe, or could not discern; and yet destiny (to speak to a natural man) and God (to speak to a Christian) is no more troubled to make a monarchy ruinous, than to make a hair gray. Nay, nothing needs be done to either, by God, or destiny; a monarchy will ruin, as a hair will grow gray, of itself. In the elements [30] themselves, of which all sub-elementary things are composed, there is no acquiescence, but a vicissitudinary [31] transmutation into one another; air condensed becomes water, a more solid body, and air rarefied becomes fire, a body more disputable, and inapparent. It is so in the conditions of men too; a merchant condensed, kneaded, and packed up in a great estate becomes a lord; and a merchant rarefied, blown up by a perfidious factor,[32] or by a riotous son, evaporates into air, into nothing, and is not seen. And if there were anything permanent and durable in this world, yet we got nothing by it, because howsoever that might last in itself, yet we could not last to enjoy it; if our goods were not amongst movables, yet we ourselves are; if they could stay with us, yet we cannot stay with them; which is another consideration in this part.

The world is a great volume, and man the index of that book; even in the body of man, you may turn to the whole world; [33] this body is an illustration of all nature; God's recapitulation of all that he had said before, in his *Fiat lux,* and *Fiat firmamentum,*[34] and in all the rest, said or done, in all the six days.[35] Propose this body to thy consideration in the highest exaltation thereof; as it is the temple of the Holy Ghost: [36] nay, not in a metaphor, or comparison of a temple, or any other similitudinary [37] thing, but as it was really and truly the very body of God, in the person of Christ, and yet this body must wither, must decay, must languish, must perish. When Goliath [38] had armed and fortified this body, and Jezebel [39] had painted

27. **superinvested:** clothed over again.   28. **new philosophy:** the Copernican system, which made the earth revolve round the sun. Cf. *Anatomy of the World,* ll. 205 ff., and l. 205n.   29. **acquiescence:** motionlessness, or stability.

30. **elements:** earth, water, air and fire; thought to be in constant warfare or interchange.   31. **vicissitudinary:** alternating.   32. **factor:** agent.   33. **body . . . world:** alluding to the belief that man is a little "world" (microcosm) corresponding in every particular with the great world (macrocosm). See *Anatomy of the World,* l. 236n.   34. *Fiat . . . firmamentum:* "Let there be light," "Let there be a firmament" (Gen. 1:3,6).   35. **six days:** i.e., of the creation.   36. **temple . . . Holy Ghost:** I Cor. 6:19.   37. **similitudinary:** thing to which it may be compared.   38. **Goliath:** I Sam. 17:4-58.   39. **Jezebel:** wife of Ahab, King of Israel (II Kings 9:30); a byword for wickedness in a queen.

and perfumed this body, and Dives [40] had pampered and larded this body, as God said to Ezekiel, when he brought him to the dry bones, *Fili hominis,* "son of man, dost thou think these bones can live?" [41] They said in their hearts to all the world, Can these bodies die? And they are dead, Jezebel's dust is not amber, nor Goliath's dust *Terra sigillata,* [42] medicinal; nor does the serpent, whose meat they are both, find any better relish in Dives's dust, than in Lazarus'.

L SERMONS, 1649

from SERMON XXXVI

St. Paul's. Christmas Day. 1621

It is but a slack opinion, it is not belief, that is not grounded upon reason. He that should come to a heathen man, a mere natural man, uncatechized, uninstructed in the rudiments of the Christian religion, and should at first, without any preparation, present him first with this necessity: "Thou shalt burn in fire and brimstone eternally, except thou believe a Trinity of persons, in an unity of one God, except thou believe the Incarnation of the second person of the Trinity, the Son of God, except thou believe that a Virgin had a Son, and the same Son that God had, and that God was Man too, and being the immortal God, yet died," he should be so far from working any spiritual cure upon this poor soul, as that he should rather bring Christian mysteries into scorn, than him to a belief. For that man, if you proceed so: "believe all, or you burn in hell," would find an easy, an obvious way to escape all; that is, first not to believe hell itself, and then nothing could bind him to believe the rest.

The reason therefore of man, must first be satisfied; but the way of such satisfaction must be this, to make him see that this world, a frame of so much harmony, so much concinnity [43] and conveniency, and such a correspondence, and subordination in the parts thereof, must necessarily have had a workman, for nothing can make itself: that no such workman would deliver over a frame and work, of so much majesty, to be governed by fortune, casually, but would still retain the administration thereof in his own hands: that if he do so, if he made the world, and sustain it still by his watchful providence, there belongeth a worship and service to him for doing so: that therefore he hath certainly revealed to man, what kind of worship and service shall be acceptable to him: that this manifestation of his will must be permanent, it must be written, there must be a Scripture, which is his word and his will: and that therefore, from that Scripture, from that word of God, all articles of our belief are to be drawn.

If then his reason confessing all this, ask farther proof, how he shall know that these Scriptures accepted by the Christian Church are the true Scriptures, let him bring any other book which pretendeth to be the word of God, into comparison with these; it is true we have not a demonstration; not such an evidence as that one and two are three, to prove these to be Scriptures of God; God hath not proceeded in that manner, to drive our reason into a pound, [44] and to force it by a peremptory necessity to accept these for Scriptures, for then here had been no exercise of our will and our assent, if we could not have resisted. . . .

Knowledge cannot save us, but we cannot be saved without knowledge; faith is not on this side knowledge, but beyond it; we must necessarily come to knowledge first, though we must not stay at it when we are come thither. For a regenerate Christian, being now a new creature, [45] hath also a new faculty of reason: and so believeth the mysteries of religion, out of another reason than as a mere natural man he believed natural and moral things. He believeth them for their own sake, by faith, though he take knowledge of them before by that common reason, and by those human arguments, which work upon other men in natural or moral things. Divers men may walk by the seaside, and the same beams of the sun giving light to them all, one gathereth by the benefit of that light pebbles, or speckled shells, for curious vanity, and another gathers precious pearl or medicinal amber by the same light. So the common light of reason illumines us all; but one employs this light upon the searching of impertinent vanities, another by a better use of the same light, finds out the mysteries of religion; and when

---

40. **Dives**: the rich man of the parable of Lazarus, Luke 16:19–31. 41. **as . . . live**: Ezek. 37:1–3. 42. *Terra sigillata*: "Bole" or "Lemnian earth," a claylike substance in ancient times of great repute medicinally. It was dug with ceremony once a year, mixed with goats' blood, and made into pellets which were sealed or stamped (*sigillata*) by the priests. 43. **concinnity**: fine workmanship, elegance.

44. **into a pound**: A pound is an enclosure or confined space (metaphor from collecting sheep for shearing). 45. **new creature**: II Cor. 5:17.

he hath found them, loves them, not for the light's sake, but for the natural and true worth of the thing itself. . . .

Thou shalt never envy the luster and glory of the great lights of worldly men, which are great by the infirmity of others, or by their own opinion great because others think them great, or because they think themselves so, but thou shalt find, that howsoever they magnify their lights, their wit, their learning, their industry, their fortune, their favor, and " sacrifice to their own nets," [46] yet thou shalt see that thou by thy small light hast gathered pearl and amber, and they by their great lights nothing but shells and pebbles; they have determined the light of nature upon [47] the book of nature, this world, and thou hast carried the light of nature

higher: thy natural reason, and even human arguments, have brought thee to read the Scriptures, and to that love, God hath set to the seal of faith. . . .

Before the sun was made, there was a light which did that office of distinguishing night and day; but when the sun was created, that did all the offices of the former light, and more. Reason is that first, and primogenial [48] light, and goes no farther in a natural man; but in a man regenerate by faith, that light does all that reason did, and more; and all his moral, and civil, and domestic, and indifferent actions, though they be never done without reason, yet their principal scope and mark is the glory of God, and though they seem but moral, or civil, or domestic, yet they have a deeper tincture, a heavenly nature, a relation to God, in them.

46. "sacrifice . . . nets": worship their own (human) powers (Hab. 1:16).   47 determined . . . upon: limited the light of nature to.

48. primogenial: first-born.

John Milton

1608-1674

I. BIOGRAPHICAL SKETCH

JOHN MILTON was born in London on December 9, 1608. Spenser had died nine years earlier; Shakespeare was soon to retire to Stratford; Bacon had published *The Advancement of Learning* and was pursuing both his philosophic aims and public office; and John Donne, in the unhappy middle phase of his career, had perhaps written his treatise on suicide. King James had been on the throne for nearly six years and had lost some of his initial popularity; he had shown his antagonism to two forces that were steadily rising in strength, Puritanism and the authority of parliament. But, as yet, England seemed to be enjoying an era of peace and prosperity.

Milton grew up in an ideal setting. John Milton senior, a well-to-do scrivener (that is, a notary, conveyancer, and private banker), was able and eager to give his talented son the best possible education, and the boy's ardent devotion to the humanities marked him out, in the minds of his elders and in his own mind, for the Church. Then the father was a composer, of some repute even in the richest period of English music, and the son, as many glowing allusions in his verse and prose testify, was a lover of music from youth to old age. And this intellectual and aesthetic cultivation was combined, in family life, with religious and moral training that was an active reality. Although, when the time came, Milton was too convinced of ecclesiastical corruption and tyranny to take holy orders, he always thought of the true poet as a priest.

Milton attended St. Paul's School in London and had additional instruction from tutors at home. From the age of twelve, he records, he hardly ever went to bed before midnight; and, if we think of him reading, by candlelight, the crabbed type of many old classical texts, we may share his opinion that such study was the first cause of his later blindness. In 1625 he went up to Christ's College, Cambridge. The one close friend of his youth and early manhood, Charles Diodati, had already gone to Oxford, and the two exchanged letters in Latin verse. Of Milton's many early Latin poems some of the best reveal elements in his nature that we might not infer from his early English verse, in particular an intense susceptibility to feminine beauty and to the intoxications of springtime. Milton's own feminine fairness of complexion gained him the college nickname "the Lady of Christ's," a nickname further borne out by his dislike of the coarser diversions of his fellows. At Christmas, 1629, when he was just twenty-one, he wrote his first great poem, "On the Morning of Christ's Nativity." "L'Allegro" and "Il Penseroso," which reflect complementary sides of his temperament, may perhaps be assigned to the long vacation of 1631.

Milton's intellectual and idealistic ardor showed itself in some of the Latin speeches that he gave as part of the curriculum: reacting against the academic tradition of scholastic logic, he held up, before himself and his audience, a fervent vision of a great awakening, of man's mastering all problems through humanistic and scientific inquiry. He was already both a Platonist and a Baconian (whether or not he had read Bacon).

Milton received his B.A. degree in 1629, his M.A. in 1632. Since he had decided against taking orders, he retired to his father's country place at Horton, near Windsor, and there set about giving himself the kind of liberal education he believed in — a strenuous and prolonged effort to digest all fruitful knowledge and thought, classical and modern. His state of mind, after some months of such labor, is recorded in Sonnet VII, "How Soon Hath Time," a sober dedication of his life and talents to whatever service God has in store for him. The chief early literary fruit of that self-consecration was the masque *Comus* (1634), a radiant expression of his Christian Platonism. Toward the end of the Horton period, when he had spent five years in studious obscurity preparing for the unknown future, and had so far, it seemed, accomplished little or nothing, the hint of self-doubt revealed in Sonnet VII became, in "Lycidas" (1637), a vehement questioning of his own destiny and of God's providence and justice — but that great poem will be discussed later.

During 1638–39 Milton spent some fifteen months abroad, chiefly in Italy, where he richly enjoyed association with Italian men of letters and where, as he says in *Areopagitica,* he visited Galileo in his confinement. On his homeward journey — which was hastened, though not unduly, by news of religious and political troubles in England — he learned of the death of his old friend Diodati, whom he later mourned in a heartfelt Latin elegy. Since he was not equipped for any profession, Milton rented a house in London and took in private pupils. The nature of his teaching may be judged from the small tract, *Of Education,* which he wrote in 1644; it is the last and, for English-speaking readers, the most famous of the many Renaissance expositions of the humanistic creed. At the same time Milton followed with close interest the conflicts that were leading toward civil war. He had already, like so many Renaissance poets, planned to write the great modern heroic poem, but he had even more than his share of the Renaissance humanist's sense of civic responsibility, along with a higher religious motive; and — as he explains in *The Reason of Church Government* — he felt obliged to put aside poetic ambition and take part in the struggle for liberty. St. Peter's speech in "Lycidas" had indicated Milton's view of the religious and ecclesiastical situation. The essence of the very complex problem was this: the Elizabethan settlement of the Church of England had been a compromise, a combination of Protestant doctrine with the traditional Catholic hierarchy and the Catholic ritual (this modified and in English), but a growing body of people inside the Church, and some who were splitting off, abhorred these relics of Romanism and insisted that the Reformation be carried on to its logical end, to the pure simplicity of the apostolic church. The majority of Puritans desired a Presbyterian system, while Archbishop Laud, supported by King Charles, insisted that the traditional discipline and hierarchy of the Church of England be rigorously maintained. When in 1641–42 the agitation against the bishops was at its height, Milton wrote five tracts in support of the Presbyterian position. But Presbyterianism, when it got the upper hand, showed itself to be no less uniformitarian and tyrannical than episcopacy had been, as Milton said in *Areopagitica* (1644), and he moved from Presbyterianism (the Right of the revolutionary party) to Independency (the Center), which was liberal, progressive, and tolerant.

In 1642, a couple of months before war broke out, Milton had married Mary Powell, the sixteen-year-old daughter of a somewhat down-at-heel Royalist squire. The marriage, as everyone knows, turned out unhappily; the bride of a few weeks, going home for a visit, declined to return. (The pair were reconciled in 1645, and Milton took her family into his house as well.) His four pamphlets on divorce (1643–45) were partly inspired by painful experience, but partly also by his prolonged concern with social and public questions. In pleading for divorce on the ground of incompatibility rather than adultery alone, Milton was setting up a high ideal of marriage and of woman as a true companion and helpmate of man.

Milton's greatest work in English prose, *Areopagitica,* one of the classic documents of our civilization, is no less clear than powerful in its eloquence, and only three general remarks on it are offered here. First, there is the principle of "Christian liberty" which Milton, like other men, inherited from the Reformation but which he made peculiarly his own. Whereas the Mosaic law was a largely external and ceremonial code imposed upon the relatively primitive Hebrews, by the Christian gospel man achieved Christian liberty and became, under God, a self-directing agent, free from constraint by any earthly power or institution. Obviously such a doctrine contained revolutionary dynamite, and it inspired Milton's battles for liberty on many fronts; it is one of the central doctrines of *Paradise Lost* (and is expounded in Book XII, ll. 285–306).

But for Milton liberty always presupposes wisdom, goodness, discipline, and responsibility, and *Areopagitica* is not a plea for complete freedom of speech and of the press. Like other Christian liberals of his time, Milton assumes that certain absolutes of religion and morality must be safeguarded; and, while he attacks censorship before publication, he allows for subsequent censorship of writings that endanger the public good.

Finally, we can measure the despair that Milton had later to overcome if we appreciate the boundless optimism that animates his early tracts in general and — in spite of parliament's effort to suppress free discussion — *Areopagitica* in particular. He sees a whole nation resuming its role as the standard-bearer of religious and civil liberty, a nation of Platonic philosopher-kings and Puritan saints; Christ's kingdom is being established on earth, and Milton himself is to have a share, as both pamphleteer and poet, in the great work. But, as time went on, the "unrealistic" idealist was to learn more and more of human inertia and corruption, to see the grand reformation fading into the light of common day.

While attacking the bishops, Milton had been a supporter of the monarchy, but his first political tract, *The Tenure of Kings and Magistrates* (1649), was an attempt to reconcile the public mind to the execution of Charles I. Shortly after the publication of that tract, he became Latin Secretary to Cromwell's Council of State. In addition to his regular work of drafting diplomatic correspondence, he wrote, among other things, two defenses of the English people (1651, 1654) in reply to Royalist attacks on the men who had executed the king; since these two works were addressed to all Europe, they were written in Latin. The first *Defense* cost Milton what remained of his failing eyesight (though he refused to slacken his labor on that account); his blindness became complete early in 1652, when he was only 43 and when the heroic poem was still unwritten. His last important tract in prose, *A Ready and Easy Way to Establish a Free Commonwealth,* was published — and republished — on the very eve of Charles II's restoration in 1660; it was a last and bold but despairing plea for a republic. When the new government took revenge on dead and living leaders of the Commonwealth, the defender of the regicides was in danger, and was indeed held in custody for a time, but he was spared, whether because of influential friends or because he was thought to be now harmless.

The Restoration, though it destroyed all that Milton had hoped and striven for during twenty years, did not make him a sullen or cynical defeatist. His hostility to the new regime flamed out at times in the major works of his later years, *Paradise Lost* (1667), *Paradise Regained* (1671), and *Samson Agonistes* (1671), but a more important effect of his profound disillusionment was a purer and even stronger religious and moral faith, a faith wholly independent of popular movements and founded only on God and the individual soul. If he had written his epic in the early 1640's, it would doubtless have embodied his triumphant confidence in immediate revolution and reformation; as it was, his later works contained a sadder and sterner reading of human experience. They were concerned with individual and inward temptations, defeats, and victories.

Mary Milton had died in 1652; Milton's second wife, Katherine Woodcock, died in 1658, a little more than a year after marriage, and was lamented in the last, and one of the greatest, of his sonnets; in 1663 he married an Elizabeth Minshull, who long outlived him. In his old age Milton suffered from blindness, from gout (not the result of high living), from trouble with his daughters, and from unhappy memories of "the Good Old Cause," but he had some compensations. His quiet routine began, John Aubrey records, at 4:30 in the morning, when a man came to read him the Hebrew Bible. In addition to hearing books read aloud, there was the dictating and revising of his own compositions. Otherwise, he passed his days in meditation, in walking in his garden ("he always had a garden where he lived," says Aubrey), in playing on the organ and singing, and in talking with friends, old and young, and with the English and foreign visitors who sought him out. It is pleasant to learn that, before going to bed, he took not only the ascetic refreshment of a glass of water but a pipe. He died in 1674.

II. THE MINOR POEMS

Milton has long held a secure place as, next to Shakespeare, the greatest of English poets, and, it might be added (with the same qualification), the greatest of European poets between Dante and Goethe. Like Dante, the voice of the Catholic Middle Ages, the Protestant Milton possessed, or was possessed by, a comprehensive religious and moral vision, and, as artist, was at once greatly traditional and greatly original. We can glance only briefly at some elements of that vision and that art; and what can be said is addressed to those who are reading a fair amount of Milton for the first time.

English poetry in the early seventeenth century flowed mainly in three channels associated with the names of Spenser, Donne, and Ben Jonson. These three poets — and Milton — all had much the same kind of classical education, which included training in rhetoric and logic, but their instincts and experience led them along partly different roads. Readers of this book will have already discovered the notably divergent qualities of Spenser and Donne. When the young Milton began to write, the heirs of Spenser were a minor group, and most rising poets were disciples of Donne or Jonson or, very often, of both. Milton was almost wholly untouched by the influence of Donne and his followers. As we might infer from lines 116–20 of " Il Penseroso " or the passage on romances in *An Apology for Smectymnuus,* he would be attracted by Spenser's fusion of romance with Christian and Platonic idealism, and his poetic manner was, and for all its originality remained, more or less in the Spenserian tradition; Dryden reported that in his old age Milton named Spenser as his master. But the young scholar-poet was attracted also by the disciplined classical art of Jonson, who prized organic symmetry, rational clarity of thought and image, and impersonal restraint In his

early poems Milton may be said to have begun as a Spenserian and then to have inclined in the Jonsonian direction. " On the Morning of Christ's Nativity " is akin to the work of some Spenserians in its Italianate quality (including its fanciful conceits) and its stanza forms, but it also displays Milton's own concern for symmetrical organization and firm texture, his verbal and rhythmical energy, his instinct for blending the classical and the Christian, and his large imagination that embraces time and space and links earth with heaven. Perhaps a year and a half later, in " L'Allegro " and " Il Penseroso," Milton writes in a very different manner appropriate for very different themes; and, apart from the deliberate extravagance of the ten-line preludes, it is a crisp, polished, and graceful manner that suggests Jonson. The young poet's classicism appears in the impersonal rendering of personal moods, the generalized — but evocative — images, the subordination of particulars to a dominant theme, and the urbane modulation of tone and rhythm. But the terms " Spenserian " and " Jonsonian " are only pointers; in the " Nativity " and the less ambitious but charming twin poems, Milton is already a master who knows the effects he wants and does not fumble.

In " Lycidas " — we are not here concerned with the elaborate and beautiful *Comus* — the poet, now nearly 29, is reacting to the first really dark shadow that has fallen across the bookish and happy serenity of his sheltered life; and, in its complexity and depth, " Lycidas " is his first completely mature poem. It has been called the greatest short poem in English, and, though such exclusive superlatives always provoke dispute, it well may be. But its real theme and its emotional intensity are under such firm artistic control, and are in fact conveyed so often obliquely, that the poem may not make a full immediate impact; some persons, after a too casual first reading, may, like Dr. Johnson,[1] resent both the absence of grief and the presence of the pastoral convention. There was, however, no apparent reason for Milton to feel keen personal sorrow; the drowning of Edward King evokes the poet's impassioned questioning of both his own past, present, and future and the religious meaning of life and death. In a world

[1] See Johnson's *Life of Milton* in Vol. II.

in which not a sparrow falls to the ground without God's will, and in which an exemplary and promising life is cut off on its threshold, what is to be thought of God's providence and justice, what is the use of man's self-discipline and high aspiration? But the poet's own involvement is barely touched. The pastoral convention becomes — as it had been for Theocritus and Virgil and others — an impersonal vehicle for the most personal utterance, a dramatic mask that enlarges rather than restricts the poet's freedom; and Milton's subtle interweaving of pagan and Christian images and ideas is a central element in his complexity of suggestion. The poem progresses through a series of marked contrasts in theme, imagery, language, tone, and sound which express or veil oscillations of feeling; and everywhere, even in the picture of Lycidas' reception into heaven, details are concrete and build up a solid whole. "Lycidas" is Milton's first attempt to assert Eternal Providence and justify the ways of God to men, but his acceptance of life is assured only after a struggle with dismay and fear, a struggle that goes on before our eyes and yet below the mainly smooth surface.

Milton's sonnets of 1642–58, the minor but massive by-products of the years given to prose and official duties, fall into two groups, personal and public (and are all very far from the Elizabethan sequences). The nine printed in this book represent both. Milton's personal sonnets range from the dignified geniality of addresses to friends to the exalted meditations on his blindness and his dead wife. In a number of public sonnets — which were to inspire Wordsworth to noble emulation — Milton contrasts the integrity and wisdom of Commonwealth leaders with the ignoble motives and conduct of the mass of men. The sonnets to friends and the heroic pieces remind us, in tone if not in form, of the convivial and the patriotic Horace. Milton's sonnets, in addition to their individual and intrinsic interest, show elements of the "grand style" of *Paradise Lost* (indeed from the "Nativity" onward, and notably in "Lycidas," an appropriate theme could evoke that grand style). The tremendous outburst on the massacre of the Piedmontese is one example. While Milton uses the Italian form, not the English, he is less concerned with the traditional division between the octave and sestet than with the mold-

ing of the sonnet as a total unit, as a verse paragraph.

Then, although the lines stand out as rhythmic units by virtue of their especially sonorous rhymes, the strong pauses at various points within lines set up another and irregular pattern of rhythmic units which begin in one line and run on into the next. In the matter of style many things might be noticed, such as the placing of adjectives before and after a noun (consider the effect of changing "Alpine mountains cold" into "cold Alpine mountains"), or the allusive periphrasis that heightens emotional response — "The triple tyrant," "the Babylonian woe."

III. "PARADISE LOST"

Only portions of *Paradise Lost* can be included in this book, and it may be hoped that readers will look up a complete edition and read the parts omitted, so that they can see the organic structure of the whole and our sections in the right perspective.

The story of the creation and of the fall of man had been told, in narrative or dramatic form, by many medieval and later writers in various European countries, and had also been the subject of much theological commentary, and Milton would know a number of works of both kinds. Like most earlier writers (and like most people for a long time afterward), he seems to have regarded the Biblical story of Adam and Eve as in essence historical, but the degree of the poet's belief in the truth of his fable has no real bearing on the present value of the poem; what matters is that the fable embodies elements of human experience that are true in all ages. Furthermore, Milton felt quite free to amplify the sacred material both with traditional embellishments and with his own inventions. Thus in his large and rigorous treatise on Christian doctrine — which now serves as a theological companion to the poem — Milton gave only a few lines to Satan and the war in heaven, as these were mentioned in the Bible; in *Paradise Lost* the proportions were reversed. Incidentally, while using the Bible as a final authority, Milton evolved some bold religious and metaphysical heresies, such as the anti-Trinitarian doctrine of the Son's inferiority to the Father; God's creation of the world from his own substance, not from nothing; and the essential goodness of matter and its oneness with spirit (this last appears in *Paradise Lost,* V. 468 f.).

In his beliefs and ideas Milton was the last and greatest poetic exemplar of the Christian humanism of the Renaissance. Modern historians have established a partly false antithesis between the Renaissance and the Reformation. For a multitude of Renaissance humanists, Catholic or Protestant, as for their medieval predecessors, there was no antithesis between classical wisdom and the Christian religion; the natural reason of the Greeks and Romans was the helpmate of Christian faith and morality, since reason itself was a divine gift to all men, and since some great ancient minds had gone far toward Christian righteousness. The principle is illustrated at the end of our extract from *An Apology for Smectymnuus* and is assumed in *Areopagitica.* And Milton's tract on education is a pedagogical example of the traditional view; the main materials of education are the classics, but these are subordinate to Christian faith and practice.

What we now call Christian humanism was a philosophy of order. Christian faith was of course the central foundation, but that does not need to be outlined: some other general ideas do. The doctrine of Christian liberty has been touched on already. Another and all-embracing set of doctrines we meet in many writers, because these doctrines formed the framework of thought and belief for centuries. The universe was conceived of as a great chain of being, from God the Creator down to plants and stones, in which every creature and thing had its appointed place and function.[1] Man, placed midway between the angels and the beasts, partakes of the character of both; his reason links him with the angels, his appetites and passions with the beasts. What God is in the universe, man's reason should be among the discordant elements of his nature. In the good man, reason informs the will and the will obeys reason. Man is, however, prone to sin, and he lives in a world, he is himself a little world, in which evil is at war with good; but he can be saved, here and hereafter, through faith in Christ and through the efficacy of divine grace. At this point the

[1] See also in this volume Pope's *Essay on Man.*

Christian humanist diverges from Luther and Calvin. Whereas they saw man as utterly corrupt and helpless without grace, the Christian humanist insisted on man's rational dignity and free will and power of choice; and Milton was bound to break away from his inherited Calvinism. We may remember that in the first book of *The Faerie Queene* the sinning hero is saved by grace (Arthur), while the hero of the second book is a representative of classical reason (though he too, in a crisis, is saved by Arthur). We may remember also that in *Areopagitica* Milton praised "our sage and serious poet Spenser" for putting temptation and choice before his hero of temperance. In *Paradise Lost* and his other late works, it should be added, Milton still exalts reason, but he lays even more stress upon faith, humility, obedience, and grace.

It may be said that today most of this is obsolete theology and ethics and metaphysics, that we have moved far beyond such notions of man and the world and God. One partial answer might be that this general creed was more or less shared by nearly all the writers of the English Renaissance whom we read, including Shakespeare. Milton, to be sure, was much more positively theological than Shakespeare, but the two were far closer to each other in belief and outlook than either is to the modern secular mind, though the imagination and insight of both, as of all great writers, transcend any particular limitations of time and place. What is most essential for a sympathetic reading of Milton, or of Shakespeare, is a conviction that religious and moral values exist and are supremely important, that good and evil are profound realities.

Furthermore, the modern consciousness of a spiritual vacuum, and the religious revival of recent years, have helped to create an atmosphere favorable to the understanding of religious poetry in general. Literary criticism has added to its vocabulary such unwonted terms as pride, humility, original sin, grace, redemption. And, if the new religious impulse has affected only a limited number of people, there is a large fact that weighs inescapably upon every individual: it is a cliché, but none the less a paralyzing reality, that man's pride, fortified by scientific power (which itself can be one manifestation of pride), has made our world a world of force and fear. How relevant *Paradise Lost* is to such a world we may try to see.

Milton's theme is the war between good and evil in the individual soul and in the world at large. The root of evil is pride, the pride that violates the law of love and righteousness in order to exalt the unregenerate self, to win power. Satan is, in Milton's presentation, a figure of heroic magnificence, one of the great creations of world literature, and it was almost inevitable that a character great in evil should, in dramatic force, overshadow Christ, the active agent of good; evil characters are always more vivid than good ones. But that should not lead us into misunderstanding of Milton's total design. If Satan's first great speech of defiance (ll. 84–124) wins our applause, except for its rhetorical power and intensity, then we are quite off the track and in a fair way to misapprehend the whole poem; for the speech is a passionately egoistic defiance of all goodness, love, reason, order, all the highest values we believe in.

Here we must take note of Milton's dramatic and ironic method, because the irony with which Satan is enveloped is the corrective to admiration for grandly heroic qualities (if any corrective be needed when those qualities are continually shown to be perverted and corrupt). The use of a story universally known was for Milton, as for the Greek dramatists, an asset rather than a liability, since the author could therefore use irony and ambiguity with much more certain effect. Also, Milton could rely upon all the beliefs, attitudes, and associations that ages of Christian teaching had made a central part of everyone's consciousness. Thus, at least for Milton's early readers, Satan's defiance of God and his heroic grandeur involved no risk of misunderstanding; it is mainly since the Romantic age that, for many readers, rebellion has appeared altogether laudable, regardless of what is rebelled against. Shakespeare also had his wicked characters, from Macbeth down to Iago, violate or blaspheme goodness, since he knew that he could rely upon the reaction of the audience (although, like Milton, he might guide that reaction as well). And in both poets such characters may avow their villainy in truthful soliloquies; thus in his great speech to the sun (IV. 32–113) Satan's condemnation of himself is as thorough as God's could have been,

and yet, in damnation and despair, he must pursue evil.

Apart from these soliloquies, Satan and his followers are treated throughout in terms of irony. Though the poem does embody a tragic reading of human life, its pattern is that of a "divine comedy"; evil can work evil, but it must in the end be overcome by good. (The aging poet no longer dreams, as he had dreamed in his early pamphlets, of a reformation here on earth; the vision of a new world is to be realized only after the day of judgment.) Meanwhile Satan — in his public harangues — and his followers are blind to the true nature of the conflict; they see themselves as temporarily defeated by a superior military force, and they seek victory or revenge. And they use such words as "free," "right," "order," with a false conception of their meaning. On the other hand, the innocent Adam and Eve are likewise enveloped in irony. We witness their first idyllic happiness knowing that it is not to last long, that Satan is already in Paradise, so that everything they say and do has tragic overtones.

In addition to Satan's defiances of Heaven, the modern reader's conditioning may lead him astray from the poet's design on two other points. One is very directly concerned with the main theme of pride. Satan bases his whole campaign against Eve and Adam on their being forbidden to eat the fruit of the tree of knowledge. He instills into Eve the desire to attain superhuman knowledge, to become a goddess, and it is to that motive that she succumbs. Before her fall, in Adam's and Raphael's discussion of the cosmos (Book VIII), the angel enforced the lesson that such remote subjects of inquiry as astronomy may distract man from religious humility and the practice of virtue. The importance in the poem of this principle is underlined by its reappearance at the very end (XII. 557–87). The modern mind may react violently against what perhaps seems to be a condemnation of the pursuit of knowledge (and a repudiation of *Areopagitica*), and may urge that without the pursuit of knowledge we would still be in a state of barbarism. That is true, no doubt, and yet a good many people, including some scientists, would reply that we are now in a state of barbarism, that human pride, with its scientific power, has in the last two decades committed barbaric crime and murder on a colossal scale, and that we are all contemplating the unimaginable horrors of the next war. At any rate Milton is not repudiating *Areopagitica,* where he was concerned with the knowledge that leads to wisdom and goodness, nor is he condemning science in itself; he is insisting that first things must be put first.

The other passage where the average modern reader may lose sympathy with the poet's attitude is that in which Adam declares his loyalty to the sinning Eve (IX. 906-16, 952-59). Adam's words are very moving, and we are intended to sympathize, up to a point; but it is again a question of the scale of values. Adam puts loyalty to his wife, which in itself is right, before loyalty to God and goodness, which has a higher claim. Gerard Manley Hopkins, sharing Milton's view, described Adam's behavior as sinfully chivalrous. If we are disposed to applaud Adam, we should think of the parallel political doctrine, " My country, right or wrong."

There was special need for the imaginative embellishment of the story Milton had to tell. Although, through the centuries, a good deal had been added to the simple brevity of Genesis, it was a story of God, Christ, Satan and other angels, and two earthly characters who were not ordinary human beings and who, in their paradisal garden, were remote from ordinary human life and interests. All this was very far from the solid concreteness of Homer and heroic narratives in general. At every turn Milton faced a problem that did not exist for Homer, though it did in some degree for Virgil — that is, the problem of rendering an abstract theme or idea through the concrete characters and action that the heroic poem required. In the several invocations of *Paradise Lost,* and most explicitly in that of Book IX, Milton speaks of his Christian poem as moving on a higher level than pagan fictions, but he was, as artist, proudly and humbly conscious of being in the succession of Homer and Virgil, and he followed both in many things large and small, re-creating what he borrowed for his own purposes, as Virgil had re-created what he took from Homer. While Milton was said to have known the Homeric poems almost by heart, and often echoed Homer, his main pattern was closer to the *Aeneid,* which was the great formal model for the Renaissance epic and which had,

moreover, some affinity with Milton's theme: Virgil's hero had been tempted into betrayal of his divinely appointed destiny, and the whole story of the fall of Troy and the founding of a new nation in the west was akin to the fall of man and his being brought to see the way of redemption for himself and his posterity.

The large epic conventions that Milton uses are supernatural agencies (though his assertion of Eternal Providence is of course a main theme, not a mere convention); the roll call and council of leaders; an inset narrative of events preceding that with which the poem opened; and a prophetic revelation of future history. In the first book Milton gives a roll call of the chief followers of Satan, based on the tradition that they became the gods of later heathenism and on details drawn mostly from the Old Testament; thus the leaders of what had been a nameless and nebulous throng emerge as individual characters. Some of these leaders take part in the great debate in the second book. Many earlier poets had presented an epic council, but Milton's has dwarfed them all, not merely in its full-dress elaboration but in its realistic stage management, in the persuasive power of the oratory, and in the subtle ways in which the style and tone as well as the ideas individualize the speakers and their various methods of working on the audience. The parts of *Paradise Lost* that exemplify the other large epic devices (recapitulation of the past and revelation of the future) could not — except for one passage — be included in our selections, but the summaries that are given in appropriate places indicate their significance in the pattern of the whole.

Along with those large devices that contribute to solidity and concreteness, there was epic simile and allusion, which Milton employed in original ways suited to the needs of his fable. For the substance he drew mainly upon the Old Testament, classical myth and history, and geography; and miscellaneous items range from the romances of Charlemagne to the Turkish sultan, from Shakespeare's English fairies to the lewd hirelings who climb into the English Church. Such similes and allusions — many of them among the richest jewels in the poem — have diverse and often complex effects. For one thing, apropos of the line we have been following, allusions to Biblical and classical history and to geography add elements of concreteness and relate the bare, primitive, remote fable to all subsequent human history. Even classical myth — which Milton, in his sacred context, so often labels as pagan fiction, even while his imagination is inspired by its beauty — had been regarded by many writers as only a corruption of authentic history (the flood of classical myth being identified with Noah's, and so on); and such myths were at any rate so familiar to everyone that even they were a sort of link with actuality.

Similes and allusions are very numerous in the first book, where Milton is setting the stage. Thus in the account of Satan's rising from the lake of fire and moving toward the shore, he is made a solid, grand, and gigantic figure partly through direct description, partly through allusions to the Giants and Titans, the Biblical Leviathan (and a realistic fisherman mistaking a whale for an island), an earthquake in Sicily and the volcano of Etna. A little later Satan's shield is likened to the spotty moon seen by Galileo through his telescope, his spear to a Norwegian pine-tree used for a flagship's mast. His followers are not only innumerable as fallen autumn leaves (a traditional epic simile), but as leaves in the brooks of the Italian Vallombrosa. And while that simile suggests great numbers of angels lying motionless where they fell, the effect of confused multitudinousness is added through the detailed picture of the Egyptians — God's enemies also — overwhelmed in the Red Sea. All these allusions heighten our visual and imaginative response and make Satan and his fellows more real. At the same time such allusions add ideas of immensity, of grandeur, of power, of beauty, of horror.

As the picture of the fallen angels is developed, other similes and allusions make Satan heroic in his defeat and in the setting of evil, while a sort of contrapuntal commentary from the poet keeps us aware that this heroic grandeur is corrupt and illusory. When Satan has made his courageous but truly diabolical journey through hell and Chaos and approaches God's newly created world and earth, the abode of goodness and perfection, his loss of grandeur, the emergence of his real self, is marked not only by comment and by his own truthful soliloquy (IV. 32–113) but by unheroic similes: he is compared to a vulture (III. 431), a prowling wolf, a burglar, a cormorant (IV. 183–96). Then, while we have Satan and all these images in our minds, we enter Paradise with him, and Milton calls up all the famous gardens and earthly paradises of myth and history to suggest the indescribable beauty, and also the actuality, of the home of innocence.

Another device that helps to give solidity to Milton's characters and scenes is what Keats, in his notes on *Paradise Lost,* called "stationing," that is, the placing of persons in relation to substantial objects. While this may be said to be a matter of course in any narrative, it is more than that in a narrative concerned with characters who are inevitably, or initially, somewhat shadowy. And *Paradise Lost* is full of pictures of this kind that stand out in our visual memory: Satan standing on the beach of the inflamed sea and calling to his legions, or standing in the open gate of hell and looking out upon Chaos; or Adam as first seen by Eve "Under a platan"; or Eve when Satan draws near, as she props up flowers,

> Herself, though fairest unsupported flower,
> From her best prop so far, and storm so nigh.

With all this concreteness, this "material sublime," that belongs to the epic is combined what is perhaps even more distinctive of Milton's imagination and art, namely vagueness of description. It is an element of technique that accords with the vast scene of the poem, and that is in marked contrast with the precise particularity of Dante's circumscribed world. Milton's world is not merely the so-called Ptolemaic universe of spheres and planets and fixed stars, with the earth at its center, for that large universe hangs from heaven by a golden chain, and all around is the infinite space of Chaos and far below is the huge prison of hell. (While Milton shows his knowledge of the Copernican doctrine, his use of the Ptolemaic world was justified by its traditional familiarity and by the fact that it kept the earth and man in the focal center; but the total universe, containing heaven, Chaos, hell, and the newly created Ptolemaic world, was in part the poet's invention.) We are never allowed to lose our consciousness of vast space. For instance, Satan voyages from the lake of hell to its gates, then through measureless Chaos to the top of the outer shell of the world, then down through the spheres to the sun and finally to the earth; when he is seeking an opportunity to confront Eve, he goes around and around the globe, following darkness and avoiding light. At the same time the vast space, though it reflects the infinite power and universal presence of God, is in a sense only the backdrop for the fateful drama that is enacted on a spot of earth in the souls of Adam and Eve. To come back to the technique of vagueness, the opening descriptions of hell are superlative examples; they afford no basis for any picture that one could draw, but they are richly suggestive to the imagination. Furthermore, if Milton were always vague, the result would be as nebulous as Shelley or Swinburne; it is the fusion and interplay of vagueness and concreteness that is so effective. And to think of Miltonic vagueness is to think of his use of darkness and light, as both physical phenomena and spiritual symbols; there are continual contrasts between the lurid darkness of hell on the one hand and the sunlight of earth and the radiance of heaven on the other. Indeed the whole poem is knit together by innumerable parallels and contrasts, large and minute, concrete and abstract, in scene and action and character — heaven and hell, goodness and evil, order and anarchy, reason and passion, humility and pride, love and hate, creation and destruction, nature and artifice, and so on.

The texture of Milton's style shows a similar blending of the ornate and the plain, the general and the relatively particular. We think, rightly enough, of elevated and generalized grandeur of style and tone as the dominant quality; in writing an epic, above all an epic on such a theme as his, Milton naturally wished to raise the reader's mind above mundane affairs, to create a world and an atmosphere befitting his divine and superhuman characters. In other words, *Paradise Lost* is highly stylized, as the *Iliad, Odyssey,* and *Aeneid* were. The theory and practice of much recent writing have enforced the doctrine that poetry must use the language and rhythms of common speech, but that is a wholly arbitrary dogma which is right for some kinds of poetry and wrong for others. And Milton's grand style is not monotonous because of the continual contrasts and variations (not to mention his unflagging energy) that are

possible, for him, within the stylization; examples are found on almost any page. Then Milton's elevation of style and generalizing habit have the effect of keeping action and scene and characters at a requisite aesthetic distance; everything must have a recognizable reality, but not too much. A realistic treatment of Adam and Eve would be quite fatal; as it is, they are both human and superhuman, and their home is both a garden and all ideal gardens — although, in the close-up drama of Book IX, Milton adopts a semidramatic manner. In earlier books Adam and Eve speak with the majestic courtesy and rhetorical amplitude that belong to their nature and situation, but, as temptation and sin reduce them to the ordinary human level, their utterance becomes more colloquial. We might compare, for instance, the beautiful speech (IV. 635-58) in which Eve declares her love for Adam, weaving and unweaving a chain of pastoral images, with the everyday naturalness of her soliloquy (IX. 795-833) after she has eaten the fruit, in which her words come out just as her thoughts occur to her. Finally — to cut short generalities which the reader must apply himself — the ornate splendor of *Paradise Lost* owes something to the many interwoven threads of simplicity (even if this is at times a sophisticated simplicity):

> where peace
> And rest can never dwell, hope never comes
> That comes to all.

> There rest, if any rest can harbor there.

> Thus with the year
> Seasons return; but not to me returns
> Day, or the sweet approach of even or morn,
> Or sight of vernal bloom, or summer's rose,
> Or flocks, or herds, or human face divine.

In the invocation to Light, from which these last lines come, Milton had created such an atmosphere, such quiet emotional intensity, that he can achieve the most poignant effect by a listing of familiar sights which those who have eyes take for granted; if we want to know what we mean when we talk of classical generality and classical restraint, this is it. And no lines are at once more simple and more complex than the last ones in the poem, where we see Adam and Eve departing from Paradise to begin life anew in the grim world of history; the lines seem to be only a succession of plain narrative statements, yet every phrase carries ambiguities that play off against one another.

The few lines just quoted remind us that, in all the varied emotional effects Milton creates, the rich complexities of his rhythms have a large share, from the grandiose glamor of sonorous proper names to the subtlest overtones of meaning. In all poetry (within the main tradition) the essence of rhythm is of course the blending of regularity and recurrence with variation and surprise. Milton's epic rhythm, like his language and syntax, was bound to be stylized; the writer of a long poem must strike a gait that will carry him to the end. But, as T. S. Eliot has said, Milton is never monotonous. While he sticks closely to the ten-syllable line, the number, weight, and position of stresses are open to an infinity of permutations and combinations. In connection with the sonnets we noticed some elements of Milton's technique, and these have much fuller scope in his blank verse — the molding of many lines into a long verse-paragraph, and the use of the line, with its internal variations, as a rhythmic unit, along with a secondary and even more variable system of units that flow from a pause in one line to a pause in another. For a random example we might take the opening lines (remembering that two signs are not at all adequate for showing differences of stress and tempo):

Ŏf mán's / fírst dĭs/ŏbéd/iĕnce, // ănd / thĕ frúit
Ŏf thát / fŏrbíd/dĕn trée, // whŏse mór/tăl táste
Bróught / déath / íntŏ / thĕ wórld, // ănd áll / ŏur
    wóe,
Wíth lóss / ŏf Éd/en, // tíll / ŏne gréat/ĕr Mán
Restóre / ŭs, // ănd / regáin / thĕ blíss/fŭl séat, . . .

Whatever particular changes in scansion other readers might make, it is clear that in the first five lines we have not reached the main verb of the sentence, that three of the five lines are run on, and that stresses, falling on important words, reinforce the sense. In the first phrase the consecutive heavy beats underline the heinousness of the sin. The relentless regularity of the

second line (the only regular one) leads into the positive action, and irregular accents, of "Brought death . . . world"; and the two final iambic feet, "and all our woe," with their prolonged monosyllabic stresses, their regularity in the midst of irregularity, and the ensuing pause, deepen the sense of irrevocable doom. In line 4, the weak ending of "Eden," coming at the caesura, contributes to the idea of loss, but the line ends with the strong accents of "one greater Man" that emphasize the note of hope and salvation, a note carried on in the alliterative strength of "Restore . . . regain." These and many other things are best discovered by the individual reader; the analysis of even a few lines will quicken and refine his perceptions and make it impossible to read with the eye alone. And Milton's orchestration is not something added to the text; it is an essential part of its life and meaning.

IV. "SAMSON AGONISTES"

Since we have glanced at metrics, we might follow that road into *Samson Agonistes,* where Milton displays still greater boldness than he had within the more conventional patterns. The bulk of the drama is in blank verse, although this goes beyond the dramatic parts of *Paradise Lost* in semicolloquial and rugged irregularity. A more distinct innovation, which comes closer still to dramatic speech, is the use, in choruses and some parts of the dialogue, of more or less short and irregular lines (much more irregular and less lyrical than those of "Lycidas"). These are not free verse but varied combinations of regular metrical feet. One characteristic principle — which Gerard Hopkins, with reference to this drama, called counterpoint — is the superimposing of one rhythm upon another. To take a simple instance, line 81 may be scanned thus:

Ĭrrĕcóv/ĕráb/lў dárk, // tótăl / éclípse.

The first part of the line is in rising rhythm, each foot ending with a stressed syllable (an anapaest and two iambs); the first foot after the caesura begins with one. Thus a falling (trochaic) rhythm disrupts the basic movement, and the effect — illustrated throughout in rich variety — is both colloquially "prosaic" and strongly emotive. For a somewhat less simple instance we might take lines 631–34:

Thence faint/ings, // swoon/ings of / despair,

And sense / of Heaven's / deser/tion.

I was / his nurs/ling once // and choice / delight,

His des/tined from / the womb, ...

Here one cannot miss the contrast in rhythm as well as sense between the first two and the second two lines. The irregularities of the first two, including weak endings, reflect the speaker's despair, while the last two, on his former greatness, are relatively regular, the caesura falling after a stressed syllable and most of the feet ending on strong accents.

Samson, with all its bareness, makes a greater or fuller impact on some readers than *Paradise Lost.* In addition to its obvious brevity, it is much less complex; its hero, except in his physical strength, is an ordinary human being and a sinner; and the theme of sin and regeneration, while religious, has no theological framework, so that the drama remains as universal as the Greek tragedies. *Samson* is indeed the only English drama on the Greek model that can be ranked with them.

Samson had been included in Milton's list of possible heroic subjects, compiled twenty years before the Restoration, so that it had dwelt in his mind a long time. (There have been some recent and, it may be thought, entirely unconvincing arguments that the drama was composed before 1660.) How far the elderly poet, now eyeless in London under Charles II, projected himself into his hero is a question. Certainly at some points (e.g., ll. 692–700) Milton is thinking of the Stuart government and his own situation; and some critics have found topical significance or wishful thinking in Samson's destruction of the Philistines and have even called up the unhappy ghost of Mary Powell. It is probably a mistake to scan these things too closely. We can say with some assurance that Milton felt a sufficient parallel between himself and England and Samson and Israel to be able to treat the subject with remarkable force and fire; but we must add, with even more assurance, that everything in the tragedy is dramatically relevant, and that Mil-

ton, whatever boiled up inside him, remained to the last the impersonal artist.

His preface sets forth his classical conception of tragedy and, as we should expect of a scholar-poet in the Renaissance tradition, he follows the formal pattern of classical and neoclassical dramas. But his genius, and his dynamic motives, were far too powerful to produce a tame imitation. While Milton has natural affinities with all three of the Greek tragic dramatists, two plays may have been especially in his mind, Aeschylus' *Prometheus Bound* and Sophocles' *Oedipus at Colonus.* One classical device that Milton exploits to the full is dramatic irony, the use of words and ideas that have one meaning for the speaker and persons addressed and another for the reader. Thus even in the title the Greek word *agonistes,* which means a contestant in public games, applies — both literally and ironically — to Samson's last acts in the Philistine temple and applies also to his spiritual wrestlings with himself. In addition to many such particular ambiguities, there is a larger irony in the effect Samson's successive visitors have upon him, an effect contrary to their and our expectation.

In the Bible Samson is a mere barbarian of strength; Milton greatly elevates his character and gives him a conscience wanting in the original. In fact Samson's agonized sense of his personal relation to God — which is partly similar to Job's — is the one, and a central, element in the drama that may be called un-Greek, though it is not altogether so. However, as befits an Old Testament story, no reference is made to specifically Christian doctrine. The chief thing for the reader to realize (as Dr. Johnson did not) is that the action is, until the end, purely psychological. Through a series of encounters with sympathetic or hostile visitors Samson rises from self-centered preoccupation with his miseries and wrongs to a new humility and faith. And he is isolated even from the sympathetic; neither the chorus nor Manoa understands the real depth of his inward struggles and inward victory.

What has been said here about Milton's life and character and writings gives at least, or at best, an indication of the greatness of his spirit and of his poetic art. The word " sublime " has dropped out of the modern critical vocabulary, but it has always, and rightly, been attached to

Milton, by virtue of both his themes and his poetic quality. Much of the most serious fiction of our day has been concerned with evil and with hell; one difference, no doubt an inevitable difference, between such fiction and Milton's poetry is suggested by one of those incidental sublimities struck out in his prose — "that as no man apprehends what vice is so well as he who is truly virtuous, no man knows hell like him who converses most in heaven."

The publishers of this book and the editor of the selections from Milton make grateful acknowledgment to the Viking Press for the use of the Milton text prepared by the same editor for *The Portable Milton*, 1949 (Viking, $2.50), which contains all the major poems, *Of Education,* and *Areopagitica,* most of the early poems, and selections from other prose works. In the present text many minute changes, chiefly in punctuation, have been made.

Reading Suggestions

Of the many editions and critical works this list names only a few that might interest users of this book; a number of them contain full bibliographies.

EDITIONS

F. A. Patterson, editor, *The Student's Milton* (revised edition, 1933). Contains complete poems, most of the prose, early biographies, and some apparatus.
A. W. Verity, editor, *Paradise Lost, Samson,* etc. (various volumes and editions). Full and valuable annotation.
M. Y. Hughes, editor, *Paradise Lost* and *Paradise Regained, the Minor Poems, and Samson Agonistes,* 2 vols. (1935–37). Full and much fresh annotation.
J. W. Hales, editor, *Areopagitica* (1878).
M. Y. Hughes, editor, *Prose Selections* (1947). Both fully annotated.

BIOGRAPHY

David Masson, *Life,* 6 vols. (1859–80; revised editions of first 3 vols., and Index, 1881–96). The big standard work, now subject to modification here and there.
James Holly Hanford, *John Milton, Englishman* (1949). A compendious up-to-date biography.

CRITICISM

J. H. Hanford, "The Youth of Milton," "*Samson Agonistes* and Milton in Old Age," in *Studies in Shakespeare, Milton and Donne,* by O. J. Campbell *et al.* (1925). Elaborate and important essays.
J. H. Hanford, *A Milton Handbook* (4th edition, revised, 1946). The standard compendium of information and criticism on all the works.
E. M. W. Tillyard, *The Miltonic Setting* (1938). Essays on the early twin poems, the epic tradition, and so forth.
C. S. Lewis, *A Preface to Paradise Lost* (1942). Provocative comment on Milton's epic theme and manner.
C. M. Bowra, *From Virgil to Milton* (1945). *Paradise Lost* in relation to the heroic tradition as represented by Virgil, Camoëns, and Tasso.
Douglas Bush, *Paradise Lost in Our Time* (1945). Lectures on Milton's religious outlook and epic method.
Douglas Bush, "Milton" chap. xii in *English Literature in the Earlier Seventeenth Century* (1945).
John S. Diekhoff, *Milton's Paradise Lost: A Commentary* (1946). A helpful exposition of the theme.
B. Rajan, *Paradise Lost and the Seventeenth Century Reader* (1947). Much illuminating analysis of matter and manner.
Tucker Brooke, chaps. xiii–xv in *A Literary History of England,* edited by A. C. Baugh (1948).
James Thorpe, editor, *Milton Criticism: Selections from Four Centuries* (1950). A very useful anthology, extending from Addison to T. S. Eliot, emphasizing recent criticism (Raleigh, Stoll, Ransom, Grierson, Charles Williams, and others, including a number listed above).
Cleanth Brooks and J. E. Hardy, editors, *Poems of Mr. John Milton with Essays in Analysis* (1951). Much suggestive analysis of language and imagery.
E. M. W. Tillyard, *Studies in Milton* (1951). Presents especially the author's revised view of the theme and pattern of *Paradise Lost.*
A. S. P. Woodhouse, "Pattern in *Paradise Lost,*" *University of Toronto Quarterly,* vol. xxii, pp. 109–27 (1953). An excellent brief study of the epic pattern and theme.

ON THE MORNING OF CHRIST'S NATIVITY

Milton's first great poem was written at Christmas time, 1629, shortly after his twenty-first birthday; it was printed in his *Poems* (1645). The "Hymn" develops three motifs: peace on earth; the angelic music which links earth and man with heaven (and the birth of Christ with the Creation and Judgment); and the flight of the pagan gods. The triumphant rhythm befits a celebration of divine love, order, and harmony.

1

This is the month, and this the happy morn,
Wherein the Son of Heaven's eternal King,
Of wedded Maid and Virgin Mother born,
Our great redemption from above did bring;
For so the holy sages° once did sing,
  That he our deadly forfeit° should release,
And with his Father work us a perpetual peace.

2

That glorious form, that light unsufferable,
And that far-beaming blaze of majesty,
Wherewith he wont° at Heaven's high council-
    table   10
To sit the midst of Trinal Unity,°
He laid aside; and here with us to be,
  Forsook the courts of everlasting day,
And chose with us a darksome house of mortal clay.

3

Say, Heavenly Muse, shall not thy sacred vein
Afford a present to the infant God?
Hast thou no verse, no hymn, or solemn strain,
To welcome him to this his new abode,
Now while the Heaven, by the sun's team untrod,
  Hath took no print of the approaching light,   20
And all the spangled host keep watch in squadrons
    bright?

4

See how from far upon the eastern road
The star-led wizards° haste with odors sweet!
O run, prevent° them with thy humble ode,
And lay it lowly at his blessed feet;
Have thou the honor first thy Lord to greet,
  And join thy voice unto the angel quire,
From out his secret altar touched with hallowed
    fire.

1

It was the winter wild
While the Heaven-born child   30
  All meanly wrapped in the rude manger lies;
Nature in awe to him
Had doffed her gaudy trim,
  With her great Master so to sympathize;
It was no season then for her
To wanton with the sun, her lusty paramour.

2

Only with speeches fair
She woos the gentle air
  To hide her guilty front° with innocent snow,
And on her naked shame,   40
Pollute with sinful blame,
  The saintly veil of maiden white to throw,
Confounded that her Maker's eyes
Should look so near upon her foul deformities.

3

But he her fears to cease,
Sent down the meek-eyed Peace;
  She, crowned with olive green, came softly slid-
    ing
Down through the turning sphere,°
His ready harbinger,
  With turtle° wing the amorous clouds dividing,
And waving wide her myrtle wand,   51
She strikes a universal peace through sea and land.

4

No war or battle's sound
Was heard the world around:
  The idle spear and shield were high uphung;
The hookèd° chariot stood
Unstained with hostile blood;
  The trumpet spake not to the armèd throng;
And kings sat still with awful° eye,
As if they surely knew their sovran° Lord was by.

5

But peaceful was the night   61
Wherein the Prince of Light
  His reign of peace upon the earth began:
The winds with wonder whist,°
Smoothly the waters kissed,
  Whispering new joys to the mild ocëan,
Who now hath quite forgot to rave,

ON THE MORNING OF CHRIST'S NATIVITY. **5. holy sages:** Old Testament prophets.   **6. deadly forfeit:** the penalty of death brought upon man by Adam's sin. Cf. *Paradise Lost*, XII. 395–410.   **10. wont:** was wont.   **11. Trinal Unity:** the Trinity.   **23. wizards:** the three Wise Men (Matt. 2:1–11).   **24. prevent:** anticipate.

39. front: face.   **48. turning sphere:** the whole globe of the stars which, in the old, more or less Ptolemaic, astronomy, turned daily about the earth.   **50. turtle:** turtledove (an emblem of peace and love).   **56. hooked:** armed with projecting blades.   **59. awful:** filled with awe.   **60. sovran:** sovereign.   **64. whist:** hushed.

While birds of calm° sit brooding on the charmèd
    wave.

6

The stars with deep amaze
Stand fixed in steadfast gaze,   70
  Bending one way their precious influence,°
And will not take their flight
For all the morning light,
  Or Lucifer° that often warned them thence;
But in their glimmering orbs did glow,
Until their Lord himself bespake, and bid them go.

7

And though the shady gloom
Had given day her room,
  The sun himself withheld his wonted speed,
And hid his head for shame,   80
As his inferior flame
  The new-enlightened world no more should
    need;
He saw a greater sun appear
Than his bright throne or burning axletree could
    bear.

8

The shepherds on the lawn,
Or ere° the point of dawn,
  Sat simply chatting in a rustic row;
Full little thought they than°
That the mighty Pan°
  Was kindly come to live with them below; 90
Perhaps their loves, or else their sheep,
Was all that did their silly° thoughts so busy keep.

9

When such music sweet
Their hearts and ears did greet,
  As never was by mortal finger strook,
Divinely warbled voice
Answering the stringèd noise,
  As all their souls in blissful rapture took;°
The air, such pleasure loth to lose,
With thousand echoes still prolongs each heavenly
    close.°   100

10

Nature that heard such sound
Beneath the hollow round

Of Cynthia's seat,° the airy region thrilling,
Now was almost won
To think her part was done,
  And that her reign had here its last fulfilling;
She knew such harmony alone
Could hold all Heaven and Earth in happier union.

11

At last surrounds their sight
A globe of circular light,   110
  That with long beams the shame-faced Night ar-
    rayed;
The helmèd Cherubim°
And sworded Seraphim°
  Are seen in glittering ranks with wings displayed,
Harping in loud and solemn quire,
With unexpressive° notes to Heaven's new-born
    Heir.

12

Such music (as 'tis said)
Before was never made,
  But when of old the sons of morning° sung,
While the Creator great   120
His constellations set,
  And the well-balanced world on hinges hung,
And cast the dark foundations deep,
And bid the weltering waves their oozy channel
    keep.

13

Ring out, ye crystal spheres,°
Once bless our human ears
  (If ye have power to touch our senses so),
And let your silver chime
Move in melodious time,
  And let the bass of Heaven's deep organ blow;
And with your ninefold harmony   131
Make up full consort° to the angelic symphony.

14

For if such holy song
Enwrap our fancy long,
  Time will run back and fetch the age of gold,°
And speckled Vanity
Will sicken soon and die,
  And leprous Sin will melt from earthly mold,

102–03. round . . . seat: sphere of the moon. 112–13. Cherubim, Seraphim: See *PL*, I.129n. 116. unexpressive: inexpressible. 119. sons of morning: See Job 38:6–7. 125. spheres:
the celestial spheres of old astronomy, here taken as nine in
number (l. 131); their movements made "the music of the
spheres." 132. consort: harmony. 135–48. age . . . hall:
Ancient poets nostalgically celebrated the golden age, a mythical
time of ideal goodness, peace, and abundance which was followed by progressive corruption. Milton has in mind Virgil's
fourth *Eclogue* and Ps. 85:10–11.

68. birds of calm: halcyons, whose nesting, at the winter solstice
(about December 22), was associated with calm at sea. 71. influence: in astrology, the power exerted over nature and man
by the celestial bodies. 74. Lucifer: the morning star, or the
sun. 86. Or ere: before. 88. than: a variant form of *then*.
89. Pan: the Greek god of shepherds; here Christ. 92. silly:
simple, innocent. 98. took: charmed. 100. close: cadence.

And Hell itself will pass away,
And leave her dolorous mansions to the peering°
day.   140

15

Yea, Truth and Justice then
Will down return to men,
    Orbed in a rainbow; and, like glories wearing,
Mercy will sit between,
Throned in celestial sheen,
    With radiant feet the tissued clouds down steer-
    ing;
And Heaven, as at some festival,
Will open wide the gates of her high palace hall.

16

But wisest Fate says no,
This must not yet be so;   150
    The Babe lies yet in smiling infancy,
That on the bitter cross
Must redeem our loss,
    So both himself and us to glorify;
Yet first to those ychained in sleep,
The wakeful trump of doom must thunder through
    the deep,

17

With such a horrid clang
As on Mount Sinai rang
    While the red fire and smoldering clouds out-
    brake;°
The aged Earth aghast   160
With terror of that blast
    Shall from the surface to the center shake,
When at the world's last session
The dreadful Judge in middle air° shall spread his
    throne.

18

And then at last our bliss
Full and perfect is,
    But now begins; for from this happy day
The old Dragon° under ground,
In straiter limits bound,
    Not half so far casts his usurpèd sway,   170
And, wroth to see his kingdom fail,
Swinges° the scaly horror of his folded tail.

19

The oracles are dumb,°
No voice or hideous hum

Runs through the archèd roof in words deceiv-
    ing.
Apollo from his shrine
Can no more divine,
    With hollow shriek the steep of Delphos° leav-
    ing.
No nightly trance or breathèd spell
Inspires the pale-eyed priest from the prophetic
    cell.   180

20

The lonely mountains o'er,
And the resounding shore,
    A voice of weeping heard, and loud lament;
From haunted spring and dale,
Edged with poplar pale,
    The parting Genius° is with sighing sent;
With flower-inwoven tresses torn
The nymphs in twilight shade of tangled thickets
    mourn.

21

In consecrated earth,
And on the holy hearth,   190
    The Lars° and Lemures° moan with midnight
    plaint;
In urns and altars round,
A drear and dying sound
    Affrights the flamens° at their service quaint;°
And the chill marble seems to sweat,
While each peculiar power forgoes his wonted seat.

22

Peor° and Baalim°
Forsake their temples dim,
    With that twice-battered god of Palestine;°
And moonèd Ashtaroth,°   200
Heaven's queen and mother both,
    Now sits not girt with tapers' holy shine;
The Libyc Hammon° shrinks his horn,
In vain the Tyrian maids their wounded Tham-
    muz° mourn.

23

And sullen Moloch,° fled,
Hath left in shadows dread
    His burning idol all of blackest hue;
In vain with cymbals' ring

They call the grisly king,
In dismal dance about the furnace blue;   210
The brutish gods of Nile as fast,
Isis° and Orus, and the dog Anubis,° haste.

24

Nor is Osiris° seen
In Memphian° grove or green,
   Trampling the unshowered grass with lowings
     loud;
Nor can he be at rest
Within his sacred chest,
   Nought but profoundest Hell can be his shroud;
In vain with timbreled° anthems dark
The sable-stolèd sorcerers bear his worshiped ark.

25

He feels from Juda's land   221
The dreaded Infant's hand,
   The rays of Bethlehem blind his dusky eyn;°
Nor all the gods beside
Longer dare abide,
   Not Typhon° huge ending in snaky twine:
Our Babe, to show his Godhead true,
Can in his swaddling bands control the damnèd
   crew.

26

So when the sun in bed,
Curtained with cloudy red,   230
   Pillows his chin upon an orient° wave,
The flocking shadows pale
Troop to the infernal jail;
   Each fettered ghost slips to his several grave,
And the yellow-skirted fays°
Fly after the night-steeds, leaving their moon-loved
   maze.

27

But see, the Virgin blest
Hath laid her Babe to rest.
   Time is our tedious song should here have end-
     ing;
Heaven's youngest-teemèd° star   240
Hath fixed her polished car,
   Her sleeping Lord with handmaid lamp attend-
     ing;
And all about the courtly stable
Bright-harnessed° angels sit in order serviceable.

---

212. **Isis:** sister and wife of Osiris, mother of Orus, a sun god. **Anubis:** identified with the Greek Hermes, represented with a jackal's head.   213. **Osiris:** the chief Egyptian god, worshiped as a bull.   214. **Memphian:** Egyptian (from the capital, Memphis).   219. **timbreled:** accompanied by tambourines.   223. **eyn:** old plural of *eye.*   226. **Typhon:** See *PL*, I. 197n.   231. **orient:** eastern.   235. **fays:** fairies.   240. **youngest-teemèd:** latest-born, the star that led the Wise Men to Bethlehem.   244. **Bright-harnessed:** in bright armor

L'ALLEGRO

"L'Allegro" and "Il Penseroso" were written probably in the long vacation of 1631, when Milton was 22;
they were published in the *Poems* of 1645. The twin
pieces, which describe ideal days (and nights) in the
life of a cheerful and of a contemplative man, are
linked by continual and contrasting parallels; the
cheerful man is, among other things, a lover of light
and the human scene; the thoughtful man loves darkness and solitude. The poems partake of various traditions — the pastoral, the prose "character" (a sketch of
an ethical or social type), the academic disputation.
There seem to be many echoes of other poets, for example, of Marlowe's lyric, "Come live with me and be
my love." The four-stressed lines vary between seven
and eight syllables and between trochaic and iambic
measures.

Hence, loathèd Melancholy,°
   Of Cerberus° and blackest Midnight born,
In Stygian° cave forlorn
   'Mongst horrid shapes, and shrieks, and sights
     unholy,
Find out some uncouth° cell,
   Where brooding darkness spreads his jealous
     wings,
And the night-raven sings;
   There under ebon° shades and low-browed rocks,
As ragged as thy locks,
   In dark Cimmerian desert ever dwell.   10
But come, thou Goddess fair and free,
In heaven yclept° Euphrosyne,
And by men, heart-easing Mirth,
Whom lovely Venus, at a birth,
With two sister Graces more,
To ivy-crownèd Bacchus bore;
Or whether (as some sager sing)
The frolic wind that breathes the spring,
Zephyr, with Aurora playing,
As he met her once a-Maying,   20
There on beds of violets blue,
And fresh-blown roses washed in dew,
Filled her with thee, a daughter fair,
So buxom,° blithe, and debonair.
Haste thee, Nymph, and bring with thee
Jest and youthful Jollity,
Quips and Cranks° and wanton Wiles,
Nods, and Becks, and wreathèd Smiles,
Such as hang on Hebe's cheek,

L'ALLEGRO. **1–10.** The melancholy here banished is a disease, not the contemplative mood celebrated in "Il Penseroso" (nor is the folly condemned at the beginning of the latter poem the innocent mirth of "L'Allegro").   **2. Cerberus:** in classical myth, the three-headed dog that guarded the entrance to Hades.   **3. Stygian:** relating to the Styx, a river of the mythological underworld; infernal.   **5. uncouth:** strange, desolate.   **8. ebon:** black.   **12. yclept:** called.   **24. buxom:** lively.   **27. Cranks:** odd turns of speech.

And love to live in dimple sleek;   30
Sport that wrinkled Care derides,
And Laughter holding both his sides.
Come, and trip it as ye go
On the light fantastic toe,
And in thy right hand lead with thee
The mountain nymph, sweet Liberty;
And if I give thee honor due,
Mirth, admit me of thy crew,
To live with her, and live with thee,
In unreprovèd° pleasures free;   40
To hear the lark begin his flight,
And singing startle the dull night,
From his watch-tower in the skies,
Till the dappled dawn doth rise;
Then to come,° in spite of sorrow,
And at my window bid good-morrow,
Through the sweet-briar, or the vine,
Or the twisted eglantine;
While the cock, with lively din,
Scatters the rear of darkness thin,   50
And to the stack or the barn door
Stoutly struts his dames before;
Oft listening how the hounds and horn
Cheerly rouse the slumbering morn,
From the side of some hoar hill,
Through the high wood echoing shrill:
Sometime walking, not unseen,
By hedgerow elms, on hillocks green,
Right against the eastern gate,
Where the great sun begins his state,°   60
Robed in flames and amber light,
The clouds in thousand liveries dight;
While the ploughman, near at hand,
Whistles o'er the furrowed land,
And the milkmaid singeth blithe,
And the mower whets his scythe,
And every shepherd tells his tale°
Under the hawthorn in the dale.
Straight mine eye hath caught new pleasures,
Whilst the lantskip° round it measures: 70
Russet lawns and fallows gray,
Where the nibbling flocks do stray,
Mountains on whose barren breast
The laboring clouds do often rest,
Meadows trim with daisies pied,
Shallow brooks and rivers wide;
Towers and battlements it sees
Bosomed high in tufted trees,
Where perhaps some beauty lies,
The cynosure of neighboring eyes.   80
Hard by, a cottage chimney smokes
From betwixt two aged oaks,

Where Corydon° and Thyrsis° met
Are at their savory dinner set
Of herbs and other country messes,
Which the neat-handed Phillis° dresses;
And then in haste her bower she leaves,
With Thestylis° to bind the sheaves;
Or if the earlier season lead,
To the tanned haycock in the mead.   90
Sometimes with secure° delight
The upland hamlets will invite,
When the merry bells ring round,
And the jocund rebecks° sound
To many a youth and many a maid
Dancing in the chequered shade;
And young and old come forth to play
On a sunshine holiday,
Till the livelong daylight fail:
Then to the spicy nut-brown ale,   100
With stories told of many a feat,
How fairy Mab the junkets eat;
She° was pinched and pulled, she said,
And he,° by friar's lantern° led,
Tells how the drudging goblin° sweat
To earn his cream-bowl duly set,
When in one night, ere glimpse of morn,
His shadowy flail hath threshed the corn
That ten day-laborers could not end;
Then lies him down the lubber fiend,°   110
And stretched out all the chimney's length,
Basks at the fire his hairy strength;
And crop-full out of doors he flings,
Ere the first cock his matin rings.
Thus done the tales, to bed they creep,
By whispering winds soon lulled asleep.
Towered cities please us then,
And the busy hum of men,
Where throngs of knights and barons bold
In weeds of peace high triumphs hold,   120
With store of ladies, whose bright eyes
Rain influence,° and judge the prize
Of wit or arms, while both contend
To win her grace whom all commend.
There let Hymen° oft appear
In saffron robe, with taper clear,
And pomp, and feast, and revelry,
With masque and antique pageantry;
Such sights as youthful poets dream
On summer eves by haunted stream.   130
Then to the well-trod stage anon,
If Jonson's learnèd sock° be on,
Or sweetest Shakespeare, Fancy's child,

83, 86, 88. Corydon, Thyrsis, Phillis, Thestylis: traditional names in pastoral literature.   91. secure: carefree.   94. rebecks: fiddles.   103-04. She, he: members of the story-telling group. 104. friar's lantern: will-o'-the-wisp.   105. goblin: Robin Goodfellow, Puck.   110. lubber fiend: drudging spirit.   122. influence: Cf. "Nativity," l. 71n.   125. Hymen: the classical god of marriage.   132. sock: the light shoe of ancient comic actors, a symbol of comedy.

40. unreproved: not deserving reproof.   45. to come: i.e., the poet comes to his window to greet the new day.   60. state: stately progress (compare this image of the sun with those in the "Nativity," st. 7 and 26).   67. tells his tale: counts the number (of his sheep).   70. lantskip: landscape.

Warble his native wood-notes wild;°
And ever against eating cares,
Lap me in soft Lydian° airs,
Married to immortal verse,
Such as the meeting soul may pierce
In notes with many a winding bout°
Of linkèd sweetness long drawn out,⠀⠀⠀140
With wanton heed and giddy cunning,
The melting voice through mazes running,
Untwisting all the chains that tie
The hidden soul of harmony;
That Orpheus' self may heave his head
From golden slumber on a bed
Of heaped Elysian flowers, and hear
Such strains as would have won the ear
Of Pluto, to have quite set free
His half-regained Eurydice.⠀⠀⠀150
These delights if thou canst give,
Mirth, with thee I mean to live.

IL PENSEROSO

Hence, vain deluding Joys,
⠀⠀The brood of Folly without father bred,
How little you bestead,
⠀⠀Or fill the fixèd mind with all your toys;°
Dwell in some idle brain,
⠀⠀And fancies fond° with gaudy shapes possess,
As thick and numberless
⠀⠀As the gay motes that people the sunbeams,
Or likest hovering dreams,
⠀⠀The fickle pensioners of Morpheus' train.⠀⠀10
But hail, thou Goddess sage and holy,
Hail, divinest Melancholy,
Whose saintly visage is too bright
To hit the sense of human sight,
And therefore to our weaker view
O'erlaid with black, staid Wisdom's hue;
Black, but such as in esteem
Prince Memnon's° sister might beseem,
Or that starred Ethiop queen° that strove
To set her beauty's praise above⠀⠀20
The sea nymphs, and their powers offended.
Yet thou art higher far descended:
Thee bright-haired Vesta° long of yore
To solitary Saturn° bore;

His daughter she (in Saturn's reign°
Such mixture was not held a stain).
Oft in glimmering bowers and glades
He met her, and in secret shades
Of woody Ida's° inmost grove,
While yet there was no fear of Jove.⠀⠀30
Come, pensive Nun, devout and pure,
Sober, steadfast, and demure,
All in a robe of darkest grain,
Flowing with majestic train,
And sable stole of cypress lawn
Over thy decent° shoulders drawn.
Come, but keep thy wonted state,°
With even step and musing gait,
And looks commercing° with the skies,
Thy rapt soul sitting in thine eyes;⠀⠀40
There held in holy passion still,
Forget thyself to marble, till
With a sad° leaden downward cast
Thou fix them on the earth as fast.
And join with thee calm Peace and Quiet,
Spare Fast, that oft with gods doth diet,
And hears the Muses in a ring
Aye round about Jove's altar sing;
And add to these retired Leisure,
That in trim gardens takes his pleasure;⠀⠀50
But first, and chiefest, with thee bring
Him that yon soars on golden wing,
Guiding the fiery-wheelèd throne,°
The Cherub Contemplation;
And the mute Silence hist° along,
'Less Philomel° will deign a song,
In her sweetest, saddest plight,
Smoothing the rugged brow of Night,
While Cynthia checks her dragon yoke
Gently o'er the accustomed oak.°⠀⠀60
Sweet bird, that shunn'st the noise of folly,
Most musical, most melancholy!
Thee, chauntress, oft the woods among
I woo to hear thy even-song;
And missing thee, I walk unseen
On the dry smooth-shaven green,
To behold the wandering moon,
Riding near her highest noon,
Like one that had been led astray
Through the Heaven's wide pathless way;⠀⠀70
And oft, as if her head she bowed,
Stooping through a fleecy cloud.
Oft on a plat° of rising ground

133–34. Shakespeare is characterized partly in contrast with the learned Jonson, partly in terms of the outdoor comedies which the mirthful man would like.⠀⠀136. Lydian: delicate, sensuous.⠀⠀139. bout: a musical "run," passage.⠀IL PENSEROSO.⠀4. toys: trifles.⠀6. fond: foolish.⠀18. Memnon was a handsome Ethiopian prince who fought in the Trojan War.⠀19. Ethiop queen: Cassiopeia boasted of her daughter Andromeda's beauty (not her own) and was changed into a constellation. Milton's version is that of some mythographers.⠀23. Vesta: goddess of the hearth, a symbol of purity.⠀24. Saturn: father of Jove, here an astrological symbol of contemplative melancholy. Cf. *saturnine*.

25. Saturn's reign: a golden age. See "Nativity," ll. 135–48n.⠀29. Ida: a mountain in Crete where Jove was born.⠀36. decent: comely.⠀37. state: dignity.⠀39. commercing: communing.⠀43. sad: serious.⠀53. fiery-wheeled throne: see Ezek. 10.⠀55. hist: summon silently.⠀56. Philomel: the nightingale.⠀59–60. While . . . oak: Cynthia (Diana, the moon), rising as usual over a particular tree, pauses to listen to the bird's song (the team of dragons was, in classical myth, associated with Diana in another of her threefold functions, as goddess of the underworld).⠀73. plat: plot.

I hear the far-off curfew sound
Over some wide-watered shore,
Swinging slow with sullen roar;
Or if the air will not permit,
Some still removèd place will fit,
Where glowing embers through the room
Teach light to counterfeit a gloom,   80
Far from all resort of mirth,
Save the cricket on the hearth,
Or the bellman's° drowsy charm,
To bless the doors from nightly harm.
Or let my lamp at midnight hour
Be seen in some high lonely tower,
Where I may oft outwatch the Bear,°
With thrice-great Hermes,° or unsphere°
The spirit of Plato to unfold
What worlds or what vast regions hold   90
The immortal mind that hath forsook
Her mansion in this fleshly nook;
And of those daemons that are found
In fire, air, flood, or under ground,
Whose power hath a true consent
With planet or with element.°
Sometime let gorgeous Tragedy
In sceptered pall come sweeping by,
Presenting Thebes,° or Pelops'° line,
Or the tale of Troy divine,   100
Or what (though rare) of later age
Ennobled hath the buskined° stage.
But, O sad Virgin, that thy power
Might raise Musaeus° from his bower,
Or bid the soul of Orpheus sing
Such notes as, warbled to the string,
Drew iron tears down Pluto's cheek,
And made Hell grant what love did seek;
Or° call up him that left half told
The story of Cambuscan bold,   110
Of Camball, and of Algarsife,
And who had Canace to wife,
That owned the virtuous° ring and glass,
And of the wondrous horse of brass,
On which the Tartar king did ride;
And if aught else great bards° beside
In sage and solemn tunes have sung,
Of tourneys and of trophies hung,

Of forests and enchantments drear,
Where more is meant than meets the ear.   120
Thus, Night, oft see me in thy pale career,
Till civil-suited Morn appear,
Not tricked° and frounced° as she was wont
With the Attic boy° to hunt,
But kerchieft in a comely cloud,
While rocking winds are piping loud,
Or ushered with a shower still,
When the gust hath blown his fill,
Ending on the rustling leaves,
With minute° drops from off the eaves.   130
And when the sun begins to fling
His flaring beams, me, Goddess, bring
To archèd walks of twilight groves,
And shadows brown that Sylvan° loves,
Of pine or monumental oak,
Where the rude axe with heavèd stroke
Was never heard the nymphs to daunt,
Or fright them from their hallowed haunt.
There in close covert by some brook,
Where no profaner eye may look,   140
Hide me from Day's garish eye,
While the bee with honied thigh,
That at her flowery work doth sing,
And the waters murmuring
With such consort° as they keep,
Entice the dewy-feathered Sleep;
And let some strange mysterious dream
Wave at his wings in airy stream
Of lively portraiture displayed,
Softly on my eyelids laid.   150
And as I wake, sweet music breathe
Above, about, or underneath,
Sent by some spirit to mortals good,
Or the unseen Genius of the wood.
But let my due feet never fail
To walk the studious cloister's pale,°
And love the high embowèd roof,
With antic° pillars massy proof,°
And storied windows richly dight,
Casting a dim religious light.   160
There let the pealing organ blow
To the full-voiced quire below,
In service high and anthems clear,
As may with sweetness, through mine ear,
Dissolve me into ecstasies,
And bring all Heaven before mine eyes.
And may at last my weary age
Find out the peaceful hermitage,
The hairy gown and mossy cell,

83. **bellman**: a watchman who cried the hours. 87. **outwatch...
Bear**: sit up all night (since the constellation of Great Bear
does not set). 88. **thrice-great Hermes**: Hermes Trismegistus,
supposed author of Neoplatonic writings of the third century
A.D. **unsphere**: call down from his sphere. 96. **element**: earth,
water, air, fire. Cf. *PL*, II. 275n. 99. **Thebes**: plays concerning
Oedipus and his family. **Pelops**: progenitor of Atreus, Agamemnon, and other Greek tragic figures. 102. **buskined**: tragic
(from the high boot worn by Greek tragic actors). 104. **Mu-
saeus**: a mythical Greek poet. 109–15. **Or . . . ride**: Chaucer's
unfinished Squire's Tale. 113. **virtuous**: magical. 116–20. **bards
. . . ear**: Milton is doubtless thinking especially of *The Faerie
Queene*.

123. **tricked**: adorned. **frounced**: with hair curled. 124. **Attic
boy**: Cephalus, the hunter loved by Aurora ("Morn")
130. **minute**: falling at intervals of a minute. 134. **Sylvan**:
Silvanus, an ancient rural divinity. 145. **consort**: harmony.
156. **pale**: enclosure. 158. **antic**: ornamented, or perhaps old
(antique). **massy proof**: massive and strong.

Where I may sit and rightly spell   170
Of every star that Heaven doth shew,
And every herb that sips the dew,
Till old experience do attain
To something like prophetic strain.
These pleasures, Melancholy, give,
And I with thee will choose to live.

SONNET VII. HOW SOON HATH TIME

This sonnet, written probably on Milton's twenty-fourth birthday (December 9, 1632), is a landmark in his personal and poetic development. He has left Cambridge and academic fame behind him and while contemporaries — like his close friend, Charles Diodati — forge ahead, he is studying, in the obscurity of his father's house at Horton, to fit himself for God's service, in the world if not in the Church (see Introduction, p. 402). It is characteristic that the Christian self-dedication of the sestet should include an echo of Pindar's fourth Nemean ode.

How soon hath Time, the subtle thief of youth,
    Stolen on his wing my three and twentieth
         year!°
My hasting days fly on with full career,
But my late spring no bud or blossom
      shew'th.
Perhaps my semblance might deceive the truth,
    That I to manhood am arrived so near,
    And inward ripeness doth much less appear,
    That some more timely-happy spirits endu'th.
Yet be it less or more, or soon or slow,
    It shall be still° in strictest measure even   10
    To that same lot, however mean or high,
Toward which Time leads me, and the will of
      Heaven;
    All is, if° I have grace to use it so,
    As ever in my great Task-Master's eye.

SONNET VII.   **2. three and twentieth year:** i.e., twenty-three years.   **10. still:** always.   **13. All is, if:** all depends on whether I am enabled by divine grace to use my talent.

LYCIDAS

"Lycidas," written in November, 1637, was Milton's contribution to a volume of elegies, published in 1638, in memory of a Cantabrigian, Edward King, who had drowned in a wreck in the Irish Sea. While King was apparently not a close friend of Milton's, he was a virtuous young cleric and, in a small way, a poet, and his death on the threshold of a fruitful life in the Church carried Milton far beyond the usual themes of a pastoral elegy (see Introduction, pp. 404–05). But his personal feeling is masked and controlled by the pastoral conventions: the lament of nature for the shepherd-poet, the procession of mourners, and — as in the Christianized pastoral tradition — the consolation of heavenly immortality. Irregularities of line and rhyme assist expressive flexibility; there are ten unrhymed lines. The text was somewhat revised in Milton's *Poems* of 1645, and the introductory note — printed just below — was added.

In this monody the author bewails a learned friend, unfortunately drowned in his passage from Chester on the Irish Seas, 1637. And by occasion foretells the ruin of our corrupted clergy, then in their height.

Yet once more, O ye laurels, and once more,
Ye myrtles brown, with ivy never sere,°
I come to pluck your berries harsh and crude,°
And with forced fingers rude
Shatter your leaves before the mellowing year.
Bitter constraint, and sad occasion dear,°
Compels me to disturb your season due;
For Lycidas° is dead, dead ere his prime,
Young Lycidas, and hath not left his peer.
Who would not sing for Lycidas? he knew°   10
Himself to sing, and build the lofty rhyme.
He must not float upon his watery bier
Unwept, and welter to the parching wind,
Without the meed of some melodious tear.
    Begin then, Sisters° of the sacred well
That from beneath the seat of Jove doth spring,
Begin, and somewhat loudly sweep the string.
Hence with denial vain, and coy° excuse;
So may some gentle Muse
With lucky words favor my destined urn,   20
And as he passes turn,
And bid fair peace be to my sable shroud.
For we were nursed upon the self-same hill,
Fed the same flock, by fountain, shade, and rill.
    Together both, ere the high lawns appeared

LYCIDAS.   **1–2.** Crowns of laurel, myrtle, and ivy were classical emblems of poetic achievement. Milton's last notable work had been *Comus* (1634).   **3. crude:** unripe.   **6. dear:** costly grievous.   **8. Lycidas:** a traditional pastoral name.   **10. knew** knew how.   **15. Sisters:** the Muses, who dance about the fountain of Aganippe ("the sacred well") and the altar of Zeus on Mount Helicon.   **18. coy:** modest, reluctant.

Under the opening eyelids of the morn,
We drove afield, and both together heard
What time the gray-fly winds her sultry horn,
Battening° our flocks with the fresh dews of night,
Oft till the star° that rose, at evening, bright   30
Toward Heaven's descent had sloped his westering
    wheel.
Meanwhile the rural ditties were not mute,
Tempered to the oaten flute;
Rough Satyrs danced, and Fauns with cloven heel
From the glad sound would not be absent long,
And old Damoetas° loved to hear our song.
    But O the heavy change, now thou art gone,
Now thou art gone, and never must return!
Thee, Shepherd, thee the woods and desert caves,
With wild thyme and the gadding vine o'ergrown,
And all their echoes mourn.   41
The willows and the hazel copses green
Shall now no more be seen
Fanning their joyous leaves to thy soft lays.
As killing as the canker to the rose,
Or taint-worm to the weanling herds that graze,
Or frost to flowers, that their gay wardrobe wear,
When first the white-thorn° blows;°
Such, Lycidas, thy loss to shepherd's ear.
    Where were ye, Nymphs, when the remorseless
    deep   50
Closed o'er the head of your loved Lycidas?
For neither were ye playing on the steep
Where your old bards, the famous Druids, lie,°
Nor on the shaggy top of Mona° high,
Nor yet where Deva° spreads her wizard stream.
Ay me, I fondly° dream,
Had ye been there! — for what could that have
    done?
What could the Muse herself that Orpheus° bore,
The Muse herself, for her enchanting son,
Whom universal Nature did lament,   60
When by the rout° that made the hideous roar
His gory visage down the stream was sent,
Down the swift Hebrus to the Lesbian shore?
    Alas! what boots° it with uncessant care
To tend the homely slighted shepherd's trade,
And strictly meditate the thankless Muse?
Were it not better done as others use,°
To sport with Amaryllis° in the shade,

Or with the tangles of Neaera's° hair?
Fame is the spur that the clear spirit doth raise   70
(That last infirmity of noble mind)
To scorn delights, and live laborious days;
But the fair guerdon when we hope to find,
And think to burst out into sudden blaze,
Comes the blind Fury° with the abhorrèd shears,
And slits the thin-spun life. "But not the praise,"
Phoebus° replied, and touched my trembling ears:
"Fame is no plant that grows on mortal soil,
Nor in the glistering foil°
Set off to the world, nor in broad rumor lies,   80
But lives and spreads aloft by those pure eyes
And perfect witness of all-judging Jove;
As he pronounces lastly on each deed,
Of so much fame in Heaven expect thy meed."
    O fountain Arethuse,° and thou honored flood,
Smooth-sliding Mincius,° crowned with vocal
    reeds,
That strain I heard was of a higher mood.
But now my oat° proceeds,
And listens to the Herald of the Sea,°
That came in Neptune's plea.   90
He asked the waves, and asked the felon winds,
What hard mishap hath doomed this gentle swain?
And questioned every gust of rugged wings
That blows from off each beakèd promontory;
They knew not of his story,
And sage Hippotades° their answer brings,
That not a blast was from his dungeon strayed;
The air was calm, and on the level brine
Sleek Panope° with all her sisters played.
It was that fatal and perfidious bark,   100
Built in the eclipse,° and rigged with curses dark,
That sunk so low that sacred head of thine.
    Next Camus,° reverend sire, went footing slow,
His mantle hairy, and his bonnet sedge,
Inwrought with figures dim, and on the edge
Like to that sanguine flower inscribed with woe.°
"Ah, who hath reft," quoth he, "my dearest
    pledge?"
Last came, and last did go,
The Pilot of the Galilean Lake;°
Two massy keys he bore of metals twain   110
(The golden opes, the iron shuts amain°).
He shook his mitered locks, and stern bespake:

---

29. **Battening:** feeding.   30. **star:** the evening star, Hesperus or Venus.   36. **Damoetas:** a pastoral name, presumably for some Cambridge don.   48. **white-thorn:** hawthorn. **blows:** blossoms.   52–53. **steep . . . lie:** a mountain in north Wales where the bardic priests of the early Britons were buried.   54. **Mona:** the Isle of Man off the Welsh coast.   55. **Deva:** the river Dee, which flows into the Irish Sea; its changes supposedly foretold good or ill for England and Wales.   56. **fondly:** foolishly.   58–63. Orpheus, son of the Muse Calliope, was torn to pieces by Thracian Bacchantes; his head was thrown into the river Hebrus and floated to Lesbos.   61. **rout:** disorderly band.   64. **boots:** profits.   67. **use:** are wont to do.   68–69. **Amaryllis, Neaera:** traditional names of pastoral maidens.

75. **Fury:** Atropos, that one of the Fates who cut the thread of life.   77. **Phoebus:** Apollo, god of poetry.   79. **glistering foil:** glittering setting (of a jewel).   85–86. **Arethuse, Mincius:** a Sicilian fountain and a north Italian river, associated with Theocritus and Virgil, respectively, as symbols of pastoral poetry.   88. **oat:** oaten pipe.   89. **Herald . . . Sea:** Triton.   96. **Hippotades:** Aeolus, god of the winds.   99. **Panope:** a sea nymph.   101. **eclipse:** of evil omen.   103. **Camus:** god of the river Cam, a symbol of Cambridge University.   106. **sanguine . . . woe:** the hyacinth, supposedly marked with the Greek cry of lamentation, "*aiai.*"   109 f. **Pilot . . . Lake:** St. Peter, the fisherman of Galilee, traditionally the first bishop ("mitered locks"), to whom Jesus gave the keys of Heaven.   111. **amain:** with force.

"How well could I have spared for thee, young
  swain,
Enow° of such as for their bellies' sake
Creep and intrude and climb into the fold!
Of other care they little reckoning make
Than how to scramble at the shearers' feast,
And shove away the worthy bidden guest.
Blind mouths! that scarce themselves know how
  to hold
A sheep-hook, or have learned aught else the least
That to the faithful herdman's art belongs!   121
What recks it° them? What need they? They are
  sped;°
And when they list,° their lean and flashy° songs
Grate on their scrannel° pipes of wretched straw;
The hungry sheep look up, and are not fed,
But swoln with wind and the rank mist they draw,
Rot inwardly, and foul contagion spread;
Besides what the grim wolf° with privy paw
Daily devours apace, and nothing said;
But that two-handed engine° at the door   130
Stands ready to smite once, and smite no more."
  Return, Alpheus,° the dread voice is past
That shrunk thy streams; return, Sicilian Muse,
And call the vales, and bid them hither cast
Their bells and flowerets of a thousand hues.
Ye valleys low where the mild whispers use
Of shades and wanton winds and gushing brooks,
On whose fresh lap the swart star° sparely looks,
Throw hither all your quaint° enameled eyes,
That on the green turf suck the honied showers,
And purple all the ground with vernal flowers.   141
Bring the rathe° primrose that forsaken dies,
The tufted crow-toe, and pale jessamine,
The white pink, and the pansy freaked° with
  jet,
The glowing violet,
The musk-rose, and the well-attired woodbine,
With cowslips wan that hang the pensive head,
And every flower that sad embroidery wears.
Bid amaranthus° all his beauty shed,
And daffadillies fill their cups with tears,   150
To strew the laureate hearse° where Lycid lies.
For so to interpose a little ease,
Let our frail thoughts dally with false surmise;
Ay me! whilst thee the shores and sounding seas
Wash far away, where'er thy bones are hurled,
Whether beyond the stormy Hebrides,°

Where thou perhaps under the whelming
  tide
Visit'st the bottom of the monstrous° world;
Or whether thou, to our moist vows denied,
Sleep'st by the fable of Bellerus° old,   160
Where the great Vision of the guarded mount°
Looks toward Namancos° and Bayona's hold;°
Look homeward, Angel,° now, and melt with
  ruth;°
And, O ye dolphins,° waft the hapless youth.
  Weep no more, woeful shepherds, weep no
  more,
For Lycidas, your sorrow, is not dead,
Sunk though he be beneath the watery floor;
So sinks the day-star° in the ocean bed,
And yet anon repairs his drooping head,
And tricks° his beams, and with new-spangled
  ore°
Flames in the forehead of the morning sky: 171
So Lycidas sunk low, but mounted high,
Through the dear might of him that walked the
  waves,
Where, other groves and other streams along,
With nectar pure his oozy locks he laves,
And hears the unexpressive nuptial song,°
In the blest kingdoms meek of joy and love.
There entertain him all the saints above,
In solemn troops and sweet societies
That sing, and singing in their glory move,   180
And wipe the tears for ever from his eyes.
Now, Lycidas, the shepherds weep no more;
Henceforth thou art the Genius° of the shore,
In thy large recompense, and shalt be good
To all that wander in that perilous flood.
  Thus sang the uncouth° swain to the oaks and
  rills,
While the still morn went out with sandals gray;
He touched the tender stops of various quills,
With eager thought warbling his Doric° lay.
And now the sun had stretched out all the hills,
And now was dropped into the western bay;   191
At last he rose, and twitched° his mantle blue:
To-morrow to fresh woods, and pastures new.

---

158. monstrous: inhabited by sea monsters. 160. Bellerus: a
fabled giant from whom Land's End (the tip of Cornwall)
supposedly got its Roman name, Bellerium. 161. Vision . . .
mount: St. Michael's Mount, off the Cornish coast. 162. Na-
mancos, Bayona: on the Spanish coast. 163. Angel: St.
Michael, who is asked to turn his gaze away from Spain to England and pity Lycidas. ruth: pity. 164. dolphins: a dolphin
had carried to shore the dead body of Melicertes, when his mother
Ino leaped with him into the sea; he became the sea god Palae-
mon, whom the Romans identified with Portunus, the protecting
god of harbors. 168. day-star: the sun. 170. tricks: dresses.
ore: gold. 176. unexpressive . . . song: the inexpressible or
mystical song for the marriage of the Lamb. See the end of the
extract from *Smectymnuus* below and n. 38 thereon. 183. Genius: local divinity. See l. 164n., above. 186. uncouth: rustic,
rude. 188. quills: the hollow reeds of pastoral pipes. 189. Doric:
pastoral. 192. twitched: pulled up.

114. Enow: enough. 122. recks it: does it matter to. sped:
well-established. 123. list: are inclined. flashy: tasteless.
124. scrannel: thin, harsh. 128. wolf: the Roman Catholic
Church. 130. two-handed engine: this much-discussed phrase
probably means the sword of God's avenging justice. 132. Alpheus: the river god who loved Arethusa; a symbol of pastoral
poetry. 138. swart star: Sirius, associated with the browned
herbage of late summer. 139. quaint: fanciful. 142. rathe:
early. 144. freaked: spotted. 149. amaranthus: an actual
flower and also an imaginary unfading one. 151. hearse: bier.
156. Hebrides: islands west of Scotland.

AUTOBIOGRAPHICAL EXTRACTS

In 1641–42 England was flooded with pamphlets on religious and political questions (see Introduction, p. 402). Milton, now settled in London, joined the Presbyterians in attacking episcopacy. Since he was already planning a heroic poem, it was not easy to set aside his poetic ambitions, but he felt obliged to obey the call of religious and civic duty. The tracts that are quoted from here were both published in 1642. In the first extract Milton, with a kind of sublime naïveté, takes his readers into his confidence about the poem he hopes to write; the whole passage gives a grand statement of his conception of poetry as the teacher of religion and virtue, a conception in accord with Renaissance and classical theory but heightened by Milton's special fervor. The second, a more intimate portrait of the artist, is a likewise fervent account of his youthful reading in relation to the growth of his Platonic and Christian idealism, and it provides the best possible introduction to his earlier poems. Since he is answering charges of immorality brought by controversial opponents, he naturally insists on his innocence.

from THE REASON OF CHURCH GOVERNMENT

. . . I must say, therefore, that after I had from my first years, by the ceaseless diligence and care of my father (whom God recompense), been exercised to the tongues and some sciences, as my age would suffer, by sundry masters and teachers both at home and at the schools, it was found that whether aught was imposed me by them that had the overlooking, or betaken to of mine own choice in English, or other tongue, prosing or versing, but chiefly this latter, the style, by certain vital signs it had, was likely to live. But much latelier, in the private academies of Italy,[1] whither I was favored to resort — perceiving that some trifles which I had in memory, composed at under twenty or thereabout (for the manner is that everyone must give some proof of his wit[2] and reading there), met with acceptance above what was looked for, and other things, which I had shifted in scarcity of books and conveniences to patch up amongst them, were received with written encomiums, which the Italian is not forward to bestow on men of this side the Alps — I began thus far to assent both to them and divers of my friends here at home, and not less to an inward prompting which now grew

daily upon me, that by labor and intent study (which I take to be my portion in this life) joined with the strong propensity of nature, I might perhaps leave something so written to aftertimes as they should not willingly let it die. These thoughts at once possessed me, and these other: that if I were certain to write as men buy leases, for three lives and downward, there ought no regard be sooner had than to God's glory, by the honor and instruction of my country. For which cause, and not only for that I knew it would be hard to arrive at the second rank among the Latins,[3] I applied myself to that resolution which Ariosto[4] followed against the persuasions of Bembo, to fix all the industry and art I could unite to the adorning of my native tongue; not to make verbal curiosities the end (that were a toilsome vanity), but to be an interpreter and relater of the best and sagest things among mine own citizens throughout this island in the mother dialect. That what the greatest and choicest wits of Athens, Rome, or modern Italy, and those Hebrews of old did for their country, I, in my proportion, with this over and above of being a Christian, might do for mine; not caring to be once named abroad, though perhaps I could attain to that, but content with these British islands as my world; whose fortune hath hitherto been that, if the Athenians, as some say, made their small deeds great and renowned by their eloquent writers, England hath had her noble achievements made small by the unskillful handling of monks and mechanics.

Time serves not now, and perhaps I might seem too profuse to give any certain account of what the mind at home, in the spacious circuits of her musing, hath liberty to propose to herself, though of highest hope and hardest attempting; whether that epic form whereof the two poems of Homer and those other two of Virgil and Tasso[5] are a diffuse, and the book of Job a brief, model: or whether the rules of Aristotle[6] herein are strictly to be kept, or nature to be followed, which, in them that know art and use judgment, is no transgression but an enriching of art; and lastly, what king or knight before the conquest might be

---

AUTOBIOGRAPHICAL EXTRACTS. 1. **Italy**: during Milton's foreign tour in 1638–39.   2. **wit**: imaginative and intellectual power.

3. **Latins**: modern writers of Latin verse.   4. Ludovico Ariosto (1474–1533), author of the romance, *Orlando Furioso:* Cardinal Bembo (d. 1547), a leader of literary taste.   5. Torquato Tasso (1544–95), author of *Jerusalem Delivered*, etc.   6. **rules of Aristotle**: The rediscovery of the *Poetics* had led Italian critics to discuss romances like Ariosto's in the light of Aristotle's principles (notably unity of action), and to codify those principles into rules for the epic and especially for tragedy. See Milton's preface to *Samson* and notes.

chosen in whom to lay the pattern of a Christian hero. And as Tasso gave to a prince of Italy his choice whether he would command him to write of Godfrey's [7] expedition against the infidels, or Belisarius [8] against the Goths, or Charlemain against the Lombards; [9] if to the instinct of nature and the emboldening of art aught may be trusted, and that there be nothing adverse in our climate or the fate of this age, it haply would be no rashness, from an equal diligence and inclination, to present the like offer in our own ancient stories; or whether those dramatic constitutions, wherein Sophocles and Euripides reign, shall be found more doctrinal and exemplary to a nation. The Scripture also affords us a divine pastoral drama in the Song of Solomon, consisting of two persons and a double chorus, as Origen rightly judges. And the Apocalypse [10] of St. John is the majestic image of a high and stately tragedy, shutting up and intermingling her solemn scenes and acts with a sevenfold chorus of hallelujahs and harping symphonies: and this my opinion the grave authority of Pareus,[11] commenting that book, is sufficient to confirm. Or if occasion shall lead, to imitate those magnific odes and hymns, wherein Pindarus and Callimachus [12] are in most things worthy, some others in their frame judicious, in their matter most an end [13] faulty. But those frequent songs throughout the law and prophets [14] beyond all these, not in their divine argument alone, but in the very critical art of composition, may be easily made appear over all the kinds of lyric poesy to be incomparable. These abilities, wheresoever they be found, are the inspired gift of God, rarely bestowed, but yet to some (though most abuse) in every nation; and are of power, beside the office of a pulpit, to inbreed and cherish in a great people the seeds of virtue and public civility, to allay the perturbations of the mind, and set the affections in right tune; to celebrate in glorious and lofty hymns the throne and equipage of God's almightiness, and what he works and what he suffers to be wrought with high providence in his church; to sing the victorious agonies of martyrs and saints, the deeds and triumphs of just and pious nations doing valiantly through faith against the enemies of Christ; to deplore the general relapses of kingdoms and states from justice and God's true worship. Lastly, whatsoever in religion is holy and sublime, in virtue amiable or grave, whatsoever hath passion or admiration in all the changes of that which is called fortune from without, or the wily subtleties and refluxes of man's thoughts from within, all these things with a solid and treatable smoothness to paint out and describe. Teaching over the whole book of sanctity and virtue through all the instances of example, with such a delight to those especially of soft and delicious temper, who will not so much as look upon truth herself unless they see her elegantly dressed, that whereas the paths of honesty and good life appear now rugged and difficult, though they be indeed easy and pleasant, they would then appear to all men both easy and pleasant, though they were rugged and difficult indeed. And what a benefit this would be to our youth and gentry may be soon guessed by what we know of the corruption and bane which they suck in daily from the writings and interludes of libidinous and ignorant poetasters, who, having scarce ever heard of that which is the main consistence of a true poem, the choice of such persons as they ought to introduce, and what is moral and decent to each one, do for the most part lap up vicious principles in sweet pills to be swallowed down, and make the taste of virtuous documents harsh and sour.

But because the spirit of man cannot demean [15] itself lively in this body without some recreating intermission of labor and serious things, it were happy for the commonwealth if our magistrates, as in those famous governments of old, would take into their care not only the deciding of our contentious law-cases and brawls, but the managing of our public sports and festival pastimes; that they might be, not such as were authorized a while since,[16] the provocations of drunkenness and lust, but such as may inure and harden our bodies by martial exercises to all warlike skill and performance; and may civilize, adorn, and make discreet our minds by the learned and affable meeting of frequent academies, and the procurement of wise and artful recitations sweetened with eloquent and graceful enticements to the love and practice of justice, temperance, and fortitude, instructing and bettering the nation at all opportunities, that the call of wisdom and virtue may be heard every-

7. Godfrey of Bouillon: French crusader and hero of Tasso's epic. 8. Belisarius: general of the Emperor Justinian. 9. Charlemain: Charlemagne conquered the Lombards of northern Italy in 774. 10. Origen: a Church Father (d. c. 254). Apocalypse: the Biblical book of Revelation. 11. David Pareus (d. 1622), a German theologian. 12. Pindar (518–438 B.C.), the Greek author of heroic odes: Callimachus (d. c. 240 B.C.), a Greek scholar-poet of Alexandria. 13. most an end: for the most part. 14. law . . . prophets: in the Old Testament.

15. demean: conduct. 16. The Declaration of Sports, issued by King James and again by Charles, which sanctioned sports on Sunday.

where, as Solomon saith: "She crieth without, she uttereth her voice in the streets, in the top of high places, in the chief concourse, and in the openings of the gates." [17] Whether this may not be, not only in pulpits but after another persuasive method, at set and solemn panegyries,[18] in theatres, porches, or what other place or way may win most upon the people to receive at once both recreation and instruction, let them in authority consult.

The thing which I had to say, and those intentions which have lived within me ever since I could conceive myself anything worth to my country, I return to crave excuse that urgent reason hath plucked from me by an abortive and foredated discovery. And the accomplishment of them lies not but in a power above man's to promise; but that none hath by more studious ways endeavored, and with more unwearied spirit that none shall, that I dare almost aver of myself, as far as life and free leisure will extend; and that the land had once enfranchised herself from this impertinent yoke of prelaty, under whose inquisitorious and tyrannical duncery no free and splendid wit can flourish. Neither do I think it shame to covenant with any knowing reader, that for some few years yet I may go on trust with him toward the payment of what I am now indebted, as being a work not to be raised from the heat of youth or the vapors of wine, like that which flows at waste from the pen of some vulgar amorist or the trencher fury of a rhyming parasite; nor to be obtained by the invocation of Dame Memory and her siren daughters;[19] but by devout prayer to that eternal Spirit who can enrich with all utterance and knowledge, and sends out his Seraphim, with the hallowed fire of his altar, to touch and purify the lips of whom he pleases:[20] to this must be added industrious and select reading, steady observation, insight into all seemly and generous arts and affairs; till which in some measure be compassed, at mine own peril and cost I refuse not to sustain this expectation from as many as are not loth to hazard so much credulity upon the best pledges that I can give them.

Although it nothing content me to have disclosed thus much beforehand, but that I trust hereby to make it manifest with what small willingness I endure to interrupt the pursuit of no less hopes

than these, and leave a calm and pleasing solitariness, fed with cheerful and confident thoughts, to embark in a troubled sea of noises and hoarse disputes, put from beholding the bright countenance of truth in the quiet and still air of delightful studies, to come into the dim reflection of hollow antiquities sold by the seeming bulk, and there be fain to club quotations with men whose learning and belief lies in marginal stuffings, who, when they have like good sumpters[21] laid ye down their horse-load of citations and fathers[22] at your door, with a rhapsody of who and who were bishops here or there, ye may take off their packsaddles, their day's work is done, and episcopacy, as they think, stoutly vindicated. Let any gentle apprehension, that can distinguish learned pains from unlearned drudgery, imagine what pleasure or profoundness can be in this, or what honor to deal against such adversaries. But were it the meanest under-service, if God by his secretary conscience enjoin it, it were sad for me if I should draw back; for me especially, now when all men offer their aid to help ease and lighten the difficult labors of the church, to whose service, by the intentions of my parents and friends, I was destined of a child, and in mine own resolutions: till coming to some maturity of years, and perceiving what tyranny had invaded the church — that he who would take orders must subscribe slave and take an oath withal, which, unless he took with a conscience that would retch, he must either straight perjure or split his faith — I thought it better to prefer a blameless silence before the sacred office of speaking, bought and begun with servitude and forswearing. Howsoever thus church-outed by the prelates, hence may appear the right I have to meddle in these matters, as before the necessity and constraint appeared.

from AN APOLOGY FOR SMECTYMNUUS [23]

. . . I had my time, readers, as others have who have good learning bestowed upon them, to be sent to those places where, the opinion was, it

---

17. Prov. 8:2–3.   18. **panegyries:** assemblies.   19. **invocation . . . daughters:** the classical poets' appeals to the Muses.   20. **prayer . . . pleases:** See Isa. 6:6–7, and Milton's "Nativity," l. 28.

21. **sumpters:** pack animals.   22. **fathers:** the Church Fathers, often cited by defenders of episcopal tradition.   23. **Smectymnuus:** a pseudonym formed from the initials of five Presbyterian divines, Stephen Marshall, Edmund Calamy, Thomas Young (Milton's boyhood tutor), Matthew Newcomen, and William Spurstowe.

might be soonest attained; and, as the manner is, was not unstudied in those authors which are most commended. Whereof some were grave orators and historians, whose matter methought I loved indeed, but as my age then was, so I understood them; others were the smooth elegiac poets,[24] whereof the schools are not scarce, whom both for the pleasing sound of their numerous [25] writing, which in imitation I found most easy and most agreeable to nature's part in me, and for their matter, which what it is, there be few who know not, I was so allured to read that no recreation came to me better welcome. For that it was then those years with me which are excused, though they be least severe, I may be saved the labor to remember ye. Whence having observed them to account it the chief glory of their wit,[26] in that they were ablest to judge, to praise, and by that could esteem themselves worthiest to love those high perfections which under one or other name they took to celebrate, I thought with myself by every instinct and presage of nature, which is not wont to be false, that what emboldened them to this task might, with such diligence as they used, embolden me; and that what judgment, wit, or elegance was my share, would herein best appear, and best value itself, by how much more wisely and with more love of virtue I should choose (let rude ears be absent) the object of not unlike praises. For albeit these thoughts to some will seem virtuous and commendable, to others only pardonable, to a third sort perhaps idle, yet the mentioning of them now will end in serious.

Nor blame it, readers, in those years to propose to themselves such a reward as the noblest dispositions above other things in this life have sometimes preferred: whereof not to be sensible, when good and fair in one person meet, argues both a gross and shallow judgment and withal an ungentle and swainish breast. For by the firm settling of these persuasions I became, to my best memory, so much a proficient that, if I found those authors [27] anywhere speaking unworthy things of themselves, or unchaste of those names which before they had extolled, this effect it wrought with me: from that time forward their art I still applauded, but the men I deplored; and above them all preferred the two famous renowners of Beatrice

and Laura,[28] who never write but honor of them to whom they devote their verse, displaying sublime and pure thoughts, without transgression. And long it was not after when I was confirmed in this opinion, that he who would not be frustrate of his hope to write well hereafter in laudable things, ought himself to be a true poem, that is, a composition and pattern of the best and honorablest things; [29] not presuming to sing high praises of heroic men or famous cities unless he have in himself the experience and the practice of all that which is praiseworthy. These reasonings, together with a certain niceness [30] of nature, an honest haughtiness, and self-esteem either of what I was or what I might be (which let envy call pride), and lastly that modesty, whereof, though not in the title-page, yet here I may be excused to make some beseeming profession — all these, uniting the supply of their natural aid together, kept me still above those low descents of mind beneath which he must deject and plunge himself that can agree to salable and unlawful prostitutions.

Next (for hear me out now, readers) that I may tell ye whither my younger feet wandered, I betook me among those lofty fables and romances which recount in solemn cantos the deeds of knighthood founded by our victorious kings, and from hence had in renown over all Christendom. There I read it in the oath of every knight, that he should defend to the expense of his best blood, or of his life if it so befell him, the honor and chastity of virgin or matron; from whence even then I learned what a noble virtue chastity sure must be, to the defense of which so many worthies, by such a dear [31] adventure of themselves, had sworn. And if I found in the story afterward, any of them, by word or deed, breaking that oath, I judged it the same fault of the poet as that which is attributed to Homer, to have written indecent things of the gods. Only this my mind gave me, that every free and gentle spirit, without that oath, ought to be born a knight, nor needed to expect the gilt spur, or the laying of a sword upon his shoulder, to stir him up both by his counsel and his arm to secure and protect the weakness of any attempted [32] chastity. So that even those books which to many others have been the fuel of wan-

---

24. smooth . . . poets: Ovid and other Roman love poets who used the elegiac meter. 25. numerous: metrical, rhythmical. 26. wit: genius. 27. those authors: the Roman love poets.

28. Beatrice, Laura: the women who are idealized by Dante and Petrarch. 29. that . . . things: a classical ideal revived in the Renaissance. 30. niceness: fastidiousness. 31. dear: costly. 32. attempted: assailed.

tonness and loose living, I cannot think how, unless by divine indulgence, proved to me so many incitements, as you have heard, to the love and steadfast observation of that virtue which abhors the society of bordellos.

Thus, from the laureate fraternity of poets, riper years and the ceaseless round of study and reading led me to the shady spaces of philosophy, but chiefly to the divine volumes of Plato and his equal,[33] Xenophon: where, if I should tell ye what I learnt of chastity and love, I mean that which is truly so, whose charming cup is only virtue, which she bears in her hand to those who are worthy (the rest are cheated with a thick intoxicating potion which a certain sorceress,[34] the abuser of love's name, carries about), and how the first and chiefest office of love begins and ends in the soul, producing those happy twins of her divine generation, knowledge and virtue — with such abstracted sublimities as these, it might be worth your listening, readers, as I may one day hope to have ye in a still time, when there shall be no chiding; not in these noises, the adversary, as ye know, barking at the door, or searching for me at the bordellos, where it may be he has lost himself, and raps up without pity the sage and rheumatic old prelatess, with all her young Corinthian laity,[35] to inquire for such a one.

Last of all, not in time, but as perfection is last, that care was ever had of me, with my earliest capacity, not to be negligently trained in the precepts of Christian religion: this that I have hitherto related hath been to show that, though Christianity had been but slightly taught me, yet a certain reservedness of natural disposition, and moral discipline learnt out of the noblest philosophy, was enough to keep me in disdain of far less incontinences than this of the bordello. But having had the doctrine of Holy Scripture, unfolding those chaste and high mysteries, with timeliest care infused, that "the body is for the Lord, and the Lord for the body,"[36] thus also I argued to myself: that if unchastity in a woman, whom St. Paul[37] terms the glory of man, be such a scandal and dishonor, then certainly in a man, who is both the image and glory of God, it must, though commonly not

so thought, be much more deflowering and dishonorable; in that he sins both against his own body, which is the perfecter sex, and his own glory, which is in the woman, and, that which is worst, against the image and glory of God, which is in himself. Nor did I slumber over that place[38] expressing such high rewards of ever accompanying the Lamb with those celestial songs to others inapprehensible, but not to those who were not defiled with women, which doubtless means fornication; for marriage must not be called a defilement.

Thus large I have purposely been, that if I have been justly taxed with this crime, it may come upon me, after all this my confession, with a tenfold shame.

AREOPAGITICA

A Speech for the Liberty of Unlicensed Printing, to the Parliament of England

From before Shakespeare's time books and pamphlets had to be registered with the Stationers' Company (the guild of London printers) and approved by the Archbishop of Canterbury or the Bishop of London (i.e., by their chaplains). In 1637 a Star Chamber decree reinforced the existing law and restricted printing to twenty printers, but this decree lapsed with the Long Parliament's abolition of that much-hated court in 1641. The years 1641–43 brought a flood of unlicensed pamphlets, Milton's among them, and in June, 1643, the mainly Presbyterian parliament, now more concerned to suppress opposition than to uphold liberty, re-established censorship of books before their publication. Milton's grand protest appeared in November, 1644. (Some comments on his ideas and attitudes are made in the Introduction, pp. 402–03.) The tract was not actually a speech, though it was composed in the form of a classical oration (see note 18 below). *Areopagitica* had little or no effect in its own time, partly perhaps because Milton's learning and manner were over the heads of many readers, partly because the main theme of pamphlet debate in 1644–45 was religious toleration (a topic that Milton only touches on in the course of his main argument against censorship).

This is true liberty, when free-born men,
Having to advise the public, may speak free,
Which he who can, and will, deserves high praise;
Who neither can, nor will, may hold his peace:
What can be juster in a state than this?

EURIPIDES, *Suppliants*

---

33. equal: contemporary. Xenophon (d. *c.* 354 B.C.), soldier and author of books on Socrates, etc.   34. sorceress: Circe, whose transformation of men into animals made her a traditional symbol of sensuality. With this Milton contrasts the Platonic conception of love, the ascent from the world of sense to contemplation of ideal beauty and goodness.   35. her . . . laity: prostitutes. 36. See I Cor. 6:13.   37. *Ibid.*, 11:7.

38. place: passage (Rev. 14:3–4, and 19:7–9). Cf. "Lycidas,' l. 176.

They who to states [1] and governors of the commonwealth direct their speech, High Court of Parliament, or, wanting such access in a private condition, write that which they foresee may advance the public good; I suppose them, as at the beginning of no mean endeavor, not a little altered [2] and moved inwardly in their minds: some with doubt of what will be the success,[3] others with fear of what will be the censure; [4] some with hope, others with confidence of what they have to speak. And me perhaps each of these dispositions, as the subject was whereon I entered, may have at other times variously affected; and likely might in these foremost expressions now also disclose which of them swayed most, but that the very attempt of this address thus made, and the thought of whom it hath recourse to, hath got the power within me to a passion far more welcome than incidental to a preface.

Which though I stay not to confess ere any ask, I shall be blameless, if it be no other than the joy and gratulation which it brings to all who wish and promote their country's liberty; whereof this whole discourse proposed will be a certain testimony, if not a trophy. For this is not the liberty which we can hope, that no grievance ever should arise in the commonwealth — that let no man in this world expect; but when complaints are freely heard, deeply considered, and speedily reformed, then is the utmost bound of civil liberty attained that wise men look for. To which if I now manifest, by the very sound of this which I shall utter, that we are already in good part arrived, and yet from such a steep disadvantage of tyranny and superstition grounded into our principles as was beyond the manhood of a Roman recovery,[5] it will be attributed first, as is most due, to the strong assistance of God our deliverer, next, to your faithful guidance and undaunted wisdom, Lords and Commons of England. Neither is it in God's esteem the diminution of his glory, when honorable things are spoken of good men and worthy magistrates; which if I now first should begin to do, after so fair a progress of your laudable deeds, and such a long obligement upon the whole realm to your indefatigable virtues, I might be justly reckoned among the tardiest and the unwillingest of them that praise ye.

Nevertheless there being three principal things, without which all praising is but courtship and flattery: first, when that only is praised which is solidly worth praise; next, when greatest likelihoods are brought that such things are truly and really in those persons to whom they are ascribed; the other,[6] when he who praises, by showing that such his actual persuasion is of whom he writes, can demonstrate that he flatters not; the former two of these I have heretofore endeavored, rescuing the employment from him [7] who went about to impair your merits with a trivial and malignant encomium; the latter,[8] as belonging chiefly to mine own aquittal, that whom I so extolled I did not flatter, hath been reserved opportunely to this occasion. For he who freely magnifies what hath been nobly done, and fears not to declare as freely what might be done better, gives ye the best covenant of his fidelity; and that his loyalest affection and his hope waits on your proceedings. His highest praising is not flattery, and his plainest advice is a kind of praising; for though I should affirm and hold by argument that it would fare better with truth, with learning, and the commonwealth, if one [9] of your published orders, which I should name, were called in; yet at the same time it could not but much redound to the luster of your mild and equal [10] government, whenas private persons are hereby animated to think ye better pleased with public advice than other statists [11] have been delighted heretofore with public flattery. And men will then see what difference there is between the magnanimity of a triennial parliament [12] and that jealous haughtiness of prelates and cabin [13] counselors that usurped of late, whenas they shall observe ye, in the midst of your victories and successes, more gently brooking written exceptions against a voted order than other courts, which had produced nothing worth memory but the weak ostentation of wealth, would have endured the least signified dislike at any sudden proclamation.

If I should thus far presume upon the meek demeanor of your civil [14] and gentle greatness, Lords and Commons, as what your published order hath directly said, that to gainsay, I might defend myself with ease, if any should accuse me of being new or insolent, [15] did they but know how much better I find ye esteem it to imitate the old and elegant hu-

---

6. **other:** third.   7. **him:** Joseph Hall (1574–1656), bishop and defender of the Church of England against the Presbyterians. 8. **latter:** third point.   9. **one:** the ordinance on printing, which Milton cites below.   10. **equal:** just.   11. **statists:** statesmen. 12. **triennial parliament:** an act of February, 1641, provided for a meeting at least once in three years.   13. **cabin:** cabinet. 14. **civil:** civilized.   15. **insolent:** the word meant both "unusual" and "presumptuous."

AREOPAGITICA.   1. **states:** public men.   2. **altered:** disturbed. 3. **success:** result.   4. **censure:** judgment.   5. **Roman recovery:** republican recovery from imperial rule.

manity [16] of Greece than the barbaric pride of a Hunnish and Norwegian stateliness. And out of those ages to whose polite wisdom and letters we owe that we are not yet [17] Goths and Jutlanders, I could name him [18] who from his private house wrote that discourse to the parliament of Athens, that persuades them to change the form of democracy which was then established. Such honor was done in those days to men who professed the study of wisdom and eloquence, not only in their own country but in other lands, that cities and seigniories heard them gladly and with great respect, if they had aught in public to admonish the state. Thus did Dion Prusaeus,[19] a stranger and a private orator, counsel the Rhodians against a former edict; and I abound with other like examples, which to set here would be superfluous. But if from the industry of a life wholly dedicated to studious labors, and those natural endowments haply not the worst for two and fifty degrees of northern latitude, so much must be derogated as to count me not equal to any of those who had this privilege, I would obtain to be thought not so inferior as yourselves are superior to the most of them who received their counsel; and how far you excel them, be assured, Lords and Commons, there can no greater testimony appear than when your prudent spirit acknowledges and obeys the voice of reason, from what quarter soever it be heard speaking; and renders ye as willing to repeal any act of your own setting forth as any set forth by your predecessors.

If ye be thus resolved, as it were injury to think ye were not, I know not what should withhold me from presenting ye with a fit instance wherein to show both that love of truth which ye eminently profess, and that uprightness of your judgment which is not wont to be partial to yourselves; by judging over again that order which ye have ordained *to regulate printing: that no book, pamphlet, or paper shall be henceforth printed, unless the same be first approved and licensed by such,* or at least one of such, as shall be thereto appointed. For that part which preserves justly every man's copy [20] to himself, or provides for the poor, I touch not; only wish they be not made pretenses to abuse and persecute honest and painful [21] men who offend not in either of these particulars. But that other clause of licensing books, which we thought had died

with his brother *quadragesimal* [22] and *matrimonial* [23] when the prelates expired,[24] I shall now attend with such a homily as shall lay before ye, first, the inventors of it to be those whom ye will be loth to own; next, what is to be thought in general of reading, whatever sort the books be; and that this order avails nothing to the suppressing of scandalous, seditious, and libelous books, which were mainly intended to be suppressed; last, that it will be primely to the discouragement of all learning, and the stop of truth, not only by disexercising and blunting our abilities in what we know already, but by hindering and cropping the discovery that might be yet further made both in religious and civil wisdom.

I deny not but that it is of greatest concernment in the church and commonwealth to have a vigilant eye how books demean [25] themselves, as well as men, and thereafter to confine, imprison, and do sharpest justice on them as malefactors. For books are not absolutely dead things, but do contain a potency of life in them to be as active as that soul was whose progeny they are; nay, they do preserve as in a vial the purest efficacy and extraction of that living intellect that bred them. I know they are as lively, and as vigorously productive, as those fabulous dragon's teeth; and being sown up and down, may chance to spring up armed men.[26] And yet, on the other hand, unless wariness be used, as good almost kill a man as kill a good book: who kills a man kills a reasonable creature, God's image; but he who destroys a good book, kills reason itself, kills the image of God, as it were, in the eye. Many a man lives a burden to the earth; but a good book is the precious life-blood of a master spirit, embalmed and treasured up on purpose to a life beyond life. 'Tis true, no age can restore a life, whereof perhaps there is no great loss; and revolutions of ages do not oft recover the loss of a rejected truth, for the want of which whole nations fare the worse. We should be wary, therefore, what persecution we raise against the living labors of public men, how we spill that seasoned life of man preserved and stored up in books; since we see a kind of homicide may be thus committed, sometimes a martyrdom; and if it extend to the whole impression, a kind of massacre, whereof the execution ends not in the slaying of an elemental life, but

---

16. **humanity:** humane culture.   17. **yet:** still.   18. **him:** Isocrates, the orator whose address to the Athenian Areopagus suggested Milton's title.   19. **Dion Prusaeus:** philosopher and orator (d. *c.* 115 A.D.).   20. **copy:** copyright.   21. **painful:** painstaking.

22. *quadragesimal:* pertaining to the church's Lenten restrictions on food.   23. *matrimonial:* Milton viewed marriage as a civil contract, not a sacrament.   24. **prelates expired:** lost their powers, through legislation of 1642–43.   25. **demean:** behave.   26. **dragon's . . . men:** as in the myths of Cadmus and Jason.

strikes at that ethereal and fifth essence,[27] the breath
of reason itself, slays an immortality rather than a
life. But lest I should be condemned of introducing
license, while I oppose licensing, I refuse not the
pains to be so much historical as will serve to show
what hath been done by ancient and famous commonwealths against this disorder, till the very time
that this project of licensing crept out of the Inquisition,[28] was catched up by our prelates, and hath
caught some of our presbyters.

In Athens, where books and wits were ever busier
than in any other part of Greece, I find but only
two sorts of writings which the magistrate cared
to take notice of, those either blasphemous and
atheistical, or libelous. Thus the books of Protagoras[29] were by the judges of Areopagus commanded to be burnt, and himself banished the territory, for a discourse begun with his confessing
not to know " whether there were gods, or whether
not." And against defaming, it was decreed that
none should be traduced by name, as was the manner of Vetus Comoedia,[30] whereby we may guess
how they censured libeling; and this course was
quick[31] enough, as Cicero writes,[32] to quell both
the desperate wits of other atheists and the open way
of defaming, as the event showed. Of other sects
and opinions, though tending to voluptuousness,
and the denying of divine Providence, they took no
heed. Therefore we do not read that either Epicurus,[33] or that libertine school of Cyrene,[34] or what
the Cynic[35] impudence uttered, was ever questioned
by the laws. Neither is it recorded that the writings
of those old comedians were suppressed, though the
acting of them were forbid; and that Plato commended the reading of Aristophanes,[36] the loosest
of them all, to his royal scholar Dionysius,[37] is commonly known, and may be excused, if holy Chrysostom,[38] as is reported, nightly studied so much the
same author, and had the art to cleanse a scurrilous
vehemence into the style of a rousing sermon.

That other leading city of Greece, Lacedaemon,
considering that Lycurgus their lawgiver was so addicted to elegant learning as to have been the first
that brought out of Ionia the scattered works of
Homer, and sent the poet Thales[39] from Crete to
prepare and mollify the Spartan surliness with his
smooth songs and odes, the better to plant among
them law and civility, it is to be wondered how
museless and unbookish they were, minding naught
but the feats of war. There needed no licensing of
books among them, for they disliked all but their
own laconic apothegms, and took a slight occasion
to chase Archilochus[40] out of their city, perhaps for
composing in a higher strain than their own soldier-
ly ballads and roundels could reach to; or if it were
for his broad verses, they were not therein so cautious, but they were as dissolute in their promiscuous conversing;[41] whence Euripides affirms, in
Andromache, that their women were all unchaste.
Thus much may give us light after what sort books
were prohibited among the Greeks.

The Romans also, for many ages trained up only
to a military roughness, resembling most the Lace-
daemonian guise, knew of learning little but what
their twelve tables[42] and the pontific college with
their augurs and flamens[43] taught them in religion
and law; so unacquainted with other learning that
when Carneades and Critolaus, with the Stoic
Diogenes,[44] coming ambassadors to Rome, took
thereby occasion to give the city a taste of their
philosophy, they were suspected for seducers by no
less a man than Cato the Censor,[45] who moved it in
the senate to dismiss them speedily, and to banish
all such Attic babblers out of Italy. But Scipio[46] and
others of the noblest senators withstood him and
his old Sabine austerity; honored and admired the
men; and the Censor himself at last, in his old age,
fell to the study of that whereof before he was so
scrupulous. And yet at the same time Naevius and
Plautus, the first Latin comedians, had filled the
city with all the borrowed scenes of Menander and
Philemon.[47] Then began to be considered there also
what was to be done to libelous books and authors;

<hr/>

27. **fifth essence:** quintessence, that substance, purer than the four elements, of which the heavenly bodies were made.   28. **Inquisition:** Roman Catholic tribunals, especially in Spain, for the extirpation of heretics.   29. **Protagoras:** Greek sophist (d. 411 B.C.).   30. **Vetus Comoedia:** the "Old Comedy" of Aristophanes and others, which satirized public affairs and public men.   31. **quick:** effective.   32. **Cicero writes:** in *De Natura Deorum,* I. 23.   33. **Epicurus:** the Greek philosopher (d. 270 B.C.), who taught, among other things, that the gods had no concern with man.   34. **Cyrene:** the philosophy of hedonism taught by Aristippus (fourth century B.C.).   35. **Cynic:** the philosophic school represented by Diogenes (d. c. 325 B.C.), who practiced a crabbed austerity.   36. **Aristophanes:** the great Athenian writer of comedy (d. 385? B.C.).   37. **Dionysius:** tyrant of Syracuse (d. 367 B.C.).   38. **Chrysostom:** the most famous Greek Father of the Church (d. 407).

39. **Thales:** a Cretan poet who settled in Sparta.   40. **Archilochus:** early poet and satirist (*fl.* 650 B.C.).   41. **conversing:** association.   42. **twelve tables:** the early code of Roman law, framed in 450 B.C.   43. **augurs and flamens:** Roman priests, augurs being concerned with omens, flamens with the service of special gods.   44. **Carneades, Critolaus, Diogenes** (of Babylonia): Athenian philosophers sent to Rome in 155 B.C. on a public mission.   45. **Cato:** the Roman official (d. 149 B.C.) a proverbial embodiment of "the old Sabine austerity.'   46. **Scipio:** the younger Scipio, conqueror of Carthage in 146 B.C., and patron of letters.   47. **Menander, Philemon:** Greek writers of the New Comedy of manners.

for Naevius was quickly cast into prison for his unbridled pen, and released by the tribunes upon his recantation: we read also that libels were burnt, and the makers punished, by Augustus. The like severity, no doubt, was used, if aught were impiously written against their esteemed gods. Except in these two points, how the world went in books, the magistrate kept no reckoning. And therefore Lucretius,[48] without impeachment, versifies his Epicurism to Memmius, and had the honor to be set forth the second time by Cicero, so great a father of the commonwealth; although himself disputes against that opinion in his own writings. Nor was the satirical sharpness or naked plainness of Lucilius,[49] or Catullus,[50] or Flaccus,[51] by any order prohibited. And for matters of state, the story of Titus Livius,[52] though it extolled that part which Pompey [53] held, was not therefore suppressed by Octavius Caesar [54] of the other faction. But that Naso [55] was by him banished in his old age, for the wanton poems of his youth, was but a mere covert of state over some secret cause; and besides, the books were neither banished nor called in. From hence we shall meet with little else but tyranny in the Roman empire, that we may not marvel if not so often bad as good books were silenced. I shall therefore deem to have been large enough in producing what among the ancients was punishable to write, save only which, all other arguments were free to treat on.

By this time the emperors were become Christians, whose discipline in this point I do not find to have been more severe than what was formerly in practice. The books of those whom they took to be grand heretics were examined, refuted, and condemned in the general councils; and not till then were prohibited, or burnt, by authority of the emperor. As for the writings of heathen authors, unless they were plain invectives against Christianity, as those of Porphyrius and Proclus,[56] they met with no interdict that can be cited, till about the year 400, in a Carthaginian council, wherein bishops themselves were forbid to read the books of Gentiles, but heresies they might read; while others long before them, on the contrary, scrupled more the books of heretics than of Gentiles. And that the primitive councils and bishops were wont only to declare what books were not commendable, passing no further, but leaving it to each one's conscience to read or to lay by, till after the year 800, is observed already by Padre Paolo,[57] the great unmasker of the Trentine council. After which time the popes of Rome, engrossing what they pleased of political rule into their own hands, extended their dominion over men's eyes, as they had before over their judgments, burning and prohibiting to be read what they fancied not; yet sparing in their censures, and the books not many which they so dealt with; till Martin V, by his bull, not only prohibited, but was the first that excommunicated, the reading of heretical books; for about that time Wycliffe [58] and Huss [59] growing terrible, were they who first drove the papal court to a stricter policy of prohibiting. Which course Leo X and his successors followed, until the Council of Trent and the Spanish Inquisition, engendering together, brought forth or perfected those catalogues and expurging indexes,[60] that rake through the entrails of many an old good author, with a violation worse than any could be offered to his tomb.

Nor did they stay in matters heretical, but any subject that was not to their palate, they either condemned in a prohibition, or had it straight into the new purgatory of an Index. To fill up the measure of encroachment, their last invention was to ordain that no book, pamphlet, or paper should be printed (as if St. Peter had bequeathed them the keys of the press also out of Paradise) unless it were approved and licensed under the hands of two or three glutton friars. For example:

Let the Chancellor Cini be pleased to see if in this present work be contained aught that may withstand the printing.

VINCENT RABATTA, *Vicar of Florence*

I have seen this present work, and find nothing athwart the Catholic faith and good manners: in witness whereof I have given, &c.

NICOLÒ CINI, *Chancellor of Florence*

48. Lucretius: author (d. 55 B.C.) of *De Rerum Natura*, in which he set forth Epicurean doctrines of the gods and the mortality of the soul.   49. Lucilius: the pioneer Roman satirist (d. *c.* 102 B.C.).   50. Catullus: the Roman lyrist and satirist (d. *c.* 54 B.C.).   51. Flaccus: the Roman poet Horace (d. 8 B.C.).   52. Livius: Livy (d. 17 A.D.), the historian of Rome.   53. Pompey: the Roman general, ally and later opponent of Julius Caesar.   54. Octavius Caesar: great-nephew of Julius Caesar, later the Emperor Augustus.   55. Naso: Ovid (d. 17/18 A.D.), a favorite poet of Milton's youth, author of love poems, the *Metamorphoses*, etc., who was banished by Augustus to the Crimea in 8 A.D.   56. Porphyrius, Proclus: Neoplatonic philosophers of the third and fifth centuries A.D.

57. Padre Paolo: Pietro Sarpi (d. 1623), historian of the Council of Trent (1545–63). The Council's program of reform was hampered by papal domination, and its main result was a partial restatement of Roman Catholic as opposed to Protestant doctrine. Sarpi, a Venetian, was hostile to the papal claim of secular authority.   58. Wycliffe: the English reformer of the church (d. 1384).   59. Huss: the Bohemian reformer who was burned at the stake in 1415.   60. indexes: lists of books and parts of books Catholics are forbidden to read.

Attending the precedent relation, it is allowed that this present work of Davanzati [61] may be printed.

VINCENT RABATTA, &c.

It may be printed, July 15.

FRIAR SIMON MOMPEI d'AMELIA,
Chancellor of the Holy Office in Florence

Sure they have a conceit, if he of the bottomless pit had not long since broke prison, that this quadruple exorcism would bar him down. I fear their next design will be to get into their custody the licensing of that which they say Claudius [62] intended, but went not through with. Vouchsafe to see another of their forms, the Roman stamp:

Imprimatur,[63] If it seem good to the reverend master of the Holy Palace.

BELCASTRO, *Vicegerent*
Imprimatur.

FRIAR SIMON MOMPEI d'AMELIA,
Master of the Holy Palace

Sometimes five Imprimaturs are seen together, dialogue-wise, in the piazza [64] of one title page, complimenting and ducking each to other with their shaven reverences, whether the author, who stands by in perplexity at the foot of his epistle, shall to the press or to the sponge.[65] These are the pretty responsories, these are the dear antiphonies,[66] that so bewitched of late our prelates and their chaplains with the goodly echo they made; and besotted us to the gay imitation of a lordly Imprimatur, one from Lambeth House,[67] another from the west end of Paul's,[68] so apishly Romanizing that the word of command still was set down in Latin, as if the learned grammatical pen that wrote it would cast no ink without Latin; or perhaps, as they thought, because no vulgar tongue was worthy to express the pure conceit [69] of an Imprimatur; but rather, as I hope, for that our English, the language of men ever famous and foremost in the achievements of liberty, will not easily find servile letters enow [70] to spell such a dictatory presumption English.

And thus ye have the inventors and the original of book-licensing ripped up and drawn as lineally

as any pedigree. We have it not, that can be heard of, from any ancient state, or polity, or church, nor by any statute left us by our ancestors elder or later; nor from the modern custom of any reformed city or church abroad; but from the most antichristian council and the most tyrannous Inquisition that ever inquired. Till then books were ever as freely admitted into the world as any other birth; the issue of the brain was no more stifled than the issue of the womb: no envious Juno [71] sat cross-legged over the nativity of any man's intellectual offspring; but if it proved a monster, who denies but that it was justly burnt, or sunk into the sea? But that a book, in worse condition than a peccant soul, should be to stand before a jury ere it be born to the world, and undergo yet in darkness the judgment of Radamanth [72] and his colleagues, ere it can pass the ferry backward into light, was never heard before, till that mysterious iniquity, provoked and troubled at the first entrance of reformation, sought out new limbos [73] and new hells wherein they might include our books also within the number of their damned. And this was the rare morsel so officiously snatched up, and so ill-favoredly imitated by our inquisiturient bishops and the attendant minorites,[74] their chaplains. That ye like not now these most certain authors of this licensing order, and that all sinister intention was far distant from your thoughts when ye were importuned the passing it, all men who know the integrity of your actions, and how ye honor truth, will clear ye readily.

But some will say, "What though the inventors were bad, the thing for all that may be good." It may so; yet if that thing be no such deep invention, but obvious and easy for any man to light on, and yet best and wisest commonwealths through all ages and occasions have forborne to use it, and falsest seducers and oppressors of men were the first who took it up, and to no other purpose but to obstruct and hinder the first approach of reformation, I am of those who believe it will be a harder alchemy [75] than Lullius [76] ever knew to sublimate [77] any good use out of such an invention. Yet this only is what I request to gain from this reason, that it may be held a dangerous and suspicious fruit, as certainly it deserves, for the tree that bore it, until I can dissect one by one the properties it

61. **Davanzati**: author of a history of the church in England before Henry VIII's break with Rome.   62. **Claudius**: emperor of Rome, 41–54 A.D. Milton's text has a Latin marginal note, from Suetonius' life (c. 32), on the granting of a pardon to those afflicted by intestinal disturbances at the table.   63. **Imprimatur**: "Let it be printed," the ecclesiastical formula.   64. **piazza**: square, market place.   65. **sponge**: i.e., be wiped out.   66. **responsories, antiphonies**: sung portions of the Catholic church service.   67. **Lambeth House**: the Archbishop of Canterbury's London residence.   68. **Paul's**: the Bishop of London's residence, near St. Paul's Church.   69. **conceit**: idea.   70. **enow**: enough.

71. **Juno**, jealous of Jove's intrigue with Alcmena, used charms to try to prevent her giving birth to Hercules.   72. **Radamanth**: Rhadamanthus, one of the judges in the classical underworld.   73. **limbos**: lesser hells.   74. **minorites**: Franciscan friars.   75. **alchemy**: task of alchemy.   76. **Lullius**: Raymond Lully (d. 1315), alchemist, philosopher, and missionary.   77. **sublimate**: extract (alchemy).

has. But I have first to finish, as was propounded, what is to be thought in general of reading books, whatever sort they be, and whether be more the benefit or the harm that thence proceeds.

Not to insist upon the examples of Moses, Daniel, and Paul, who were skillful in all the learning of the Egyptians, Chaldeans, and Greeks, which could not probably be without reading their books of all sorts (in Paul especially, who thought it no defilement to insert into Holy Scripture the sentences of three Greek poets, and one of them a tragedian [78]), the question was notwithstanding sometimes controverted among the primitive doctors, but with great odds on that side which affirmed it both lawful and profitable, as was then evidently perceived when Julian [79] the Apostate, and subtlest enemy to our faith, made a decree forbidding Christians the study of heathen learning; for, said he, they wound us with our own weapons, and with our own arts and sciences they overcome us. And indeed the Christians were put so to their shifts by this crafty means, and so much in danger to decline into all ignorance, that the two Apollinarii [80] were fain, as a man may say, to coin all the seven liberal sciences out of the Bible, reducing it into divers forms of orations, poems, dialogues, even to the calculating of a new Christian grammar. But, saith the historian Socrates,[81] the providence of God provided better than the industry of Apollinarius and his son, by taking away that illiterate law with the life of him who devised it. So great an injury they then held it to be deprived of Hellenic learning, and thought it a persecution more undermining, and secretly decaying the church, than the open cruelty of Decius or Diocletian.[82]

And perhaps it was the same politic drift that the devil whipped St. Jerome [83] in a Lenten dream, for reading Cicero; or else it was a phantasm bred by the fever which had then seized him. For had an angel been his discipliner, unless it were for dwelling too much upon Ciceronianisms, and had chastised the reading, not the vanity, it had been plainly partial, first, to correct him for grave Cicero and not for scurrile Plautus, whom he confesses to have been reading not long before; next, to correct him only, and let so many more ancient fathers wax old in those pleasant and florid studies without the lash of such a tutoring apparition; insomuch that Basil [84] teaches how some good use may be made of *Margites*,[85] a sportful poem, not now extant, writ by Homer; and why not then of *Morgante*,[86] an Italian romance much to the same purpose?

But if it be agreed we shall be tried by visions, there is a vision recorded by Eusebius,[87] far ancienter than this tale of Jerome to the nun Eustochium, and, besides, has nothing of a fever in it. Dionysius Alexandrinus was, about the year 240, a person of great name in the church for piety and learning, who had wont to avail himself much against heretics by being conversant in their books, until a certain presbyter laid it scrupulously to his conscience, how he durst venture himself among those defiling volumes. The worthy man, loth to give offence, fell into a new debate with himself what was to be thought; when suddenly a vision sent from God (it is his own epistle that so avers it) confirmed him in these words: "Read any books, whatever come to thy hands, for thou art sufficient both to judge aright and to examine each matter." To this revelation he assented the sooner, as he confesses, because it was answerable to that of the Apostle to the Thessalonians: "Prove all things, hold fast that which is good." [88] And he might have added another remarkable saying of the same author: "To the pure, all things are pure"; [89] not only meats and drinks, but all kind of knowledge, whether of good or evil: the knowledge cannot defile, nor consequently the books, if the will and conscience be not defiled. For books are as meats and viands are, some of good, some of evil substance; and yet God in that unapocryphal vision said, without exception, "Rise, Peter, kill and eat," [90] leaving the choice to each man's discretion. Wholesome meats to a vitiated stomach differ little or nothing from unwholesome, and best books to a naughty mind are not unappliable to occasions of evil. Bad meats will scarce breed good nourishment in the healthiest concoction; [91] but herein the difference is of bad books, that they to a discreet and judicious reader serve in many respects to discover, to confute, to forewarn, and to illustrate. Whereof what better

78. tragedian: Acts 17:28 (from Aratus); I Cor. 15:33 (from Euripides); Titus 1:12 (from Epimenides).   79. Julian: emperor of Rome, 361–63, who tried to restore paganism.   80. Apollinarii: a father and son who sought to circumvent Julian's decree by turning much of the Bible into secular literary forms.   81. Socrates: a fifth-century church historian.   82. Decius, Diocletian: Roman emperors (249–51, 284–305), who persecuted the Christians.   83. Jerome: one of the chief Fathers of the Church, author of the Vulgate translation of the Bible (d. 420).

84. Basil: bishop and scholar (d. 379).   85. *Margites*: a comic poem formerly attributed to Homer.   86. *Morgante*: the mockheroic romance of Luigi Pulci (d. 1487).   87. Eusebius: bishop and church historian (d. 340).   88. "Prove . . . good": I Thess. 5:21.   89. "To . . . pure": Titus 1:15.   90. "Rise . . . eat": Acts 10:9–16.   91. concoction: digestion.

witness can ye expect I should produce than one of your own now sitting in parliament, the chief of learned men reputed in this land, Mr. Selden,[92] whose volume of natural and national laws proves, not only by great authorities brought together, but by exquisite reasons and theorems almost mathematically demonstrative, that all opinions, yea, errors, known, read, and collated, are of main service and assistance toward the speedy attainment of what is truest.

I conceive, therefore, that when God did enlarge the universal diet of man's body, saving ever the rules of temperance, he then also, as before, left arbitrary the dieting and repasting of our minds; as wherein every mature man might have to exercise his own leading capacity. How great a virtue is temperance, how much of moment through the whole life of man! Yet God commits the managing so great a trust, without particular law or prescription, wholly to the demeanor [93] of every grown man. And therefore when he himself tabled the Jews from heaven, that omer,[94] which was every man's daily portion of manna, is computed to have been more than might have well sufficed the heartiest feeder thrice as many meals. For those actions which enter into a man, rather than issue out of him, and therefore defile not, God uses not to captivate under a perpetual childhood of prescription, but trusts him with the gift of reason to be his own chooser; there were but little work left for preaching, if law and compulsion should grow so fast upon those things which heretofore were governed only by exhortation. Solomon [95] informs us that much reading is a weariness to the flesh, but neither he nor other inspired author tells us that such or such reading is unlawful; yet certainly had God thought good to limit us herein, it had been much more expedient to have told us what was unlawful than what was wearisome. As for the burning of those Ephesian books by St. Paul's converts,[96] 'tis replied the books were magic, the Syriac so renders them. It was a private act, a voluntary act, and leaves us to a voluntary imitation: the men in remorse burnt those books which were their own; the magistrate by this example is not appointed; these men practiced the books, another might perhaps have read them in some sort usefully.

Good and evil we know in the field of this world grow up together almost inseparably; and the knowledge of good is so involved and interwoven with the knowledge of evil, and in so many cunning resemblances hardly to be discerned, that those confused seeds which were imposed on Psyche [97] as an incessant labor to cull out and sort asunder, were not more intermixed. It was from out the rind of one apple tasted that the knowledge of good and evil, as two twins cleaving together, leaped forth into the world. And perhaps this is that doom which Adam fell into of knowing good and evil, that is to say, of knowing good by evil. As therefore the state of man now is, what wisdom can there be to choose, what continence to forbear, without the knowledge of evil? He that can apprehend and consider vice with all her baits and seeming pleasures, and yet abstain, and yet distinguish, and yet prefer that which is truly better, he is the true warfaring Christian. I cannot praise a fugitive and cloistered virtue, unexercised and unbreathed, that never sallies out and sees her adversary, but slinks out of the race where that immortal garland is to be run for, not without dust and heat. Assuredly we bring not innocence into the world, we bring impurity much rather; that which purifies us is trial, and trial is by what is contrary. That virtue therefore which is but a youngling in the contemplation of evil, and knows not the utmost that vice promises to her followers, and rejects it, is but a blank virtue, not a pure; her whiteness is but an excremental [98] whiteness; which was the reason why our sage and serious poet Spenser,[99] whom I dare be known to think a better teacher than Scotus [1] or Aquinas, describing true temperance under the person of Guyon, brings him in with his palmer through the cave of Mammon and the bower of earthly bliss, that he might see and know, and yet abstain. Since therefore the knowledge and survey of vice is in this world so necessary to the constituting of human virtue, and the scanning of error to the confirmation of truth, how can we more safely, and with less danger, scout into the regions of sin and falsity than by reading all manner of tractates and hearing all manner of reason? And this is the benefit which may be had of books promiscuously read.

But of the harm that may result hence, three

92. **Selden:** John Selden (1584–1654), the great legal and historical scholar of the age.   93. **demeanor:** management.
94. **omer:** See Exod. 16:16.   95. **Solomon:** Eccles. 12:12.
96. **converts:** Acts 19:19.

97. **Psyche:** Apuleius, *The Golden Ass*, VI. Psyche, because she was loved by Venus' son Cupid, was given impossible tasks by Venus.   98. **excremental:** external.   99. **Spenser:** see *Faerie Queene*, II.vii,xii, above (the Palmer was not with Guyon in the cave of Mammon).   1. **Scotus:** Duns Scotus (d. 1308), Scholastic philosopher; Thomas Aquinas (d. 1274), the greatest of the Scholastics.

kinds are usually reckoned. First is feared the infection that may spread; but then all human learning and controversy in religious points must remove out of the world, yea, the Bible itself; for that ofttimes relates blasphemy not nicely, it describes the carnal sense of wicked men not unelegantly, it brings in holiest men passionately murmuring against Providence through all the arguments of Epicurus: in other great disputes it answers dubiously and darkly to the common reader; and ask a Talmudist [2] what ails the modesty of his marginal Keri,[3] that Moses and all the prophets cannot persuade him to pronounce the textual Chetiv. For these causes we all know the Bible itself put by the papist into the first rank of prohibited books. The ancientest fathers must be next removed, as Clement of Alexandria,[4] and that Eusebian book of evangelic preparation,[5] transmitting our ears through a hoard of heathenish obscenities to receive the gospel. Who finds not that Irenaeus, Epiphanius,[6] Jerome, and others discover [7] more heresies than they well confute, and that oft for heresy which is the truer opinion?

Nor boots it to say for these and all the heathen writers of greatest infection, if it must be thought so, with whom is bound up the life of human learning, that they writ in an unknown tongue, so long as we are sure those languages are known as well to the worst of men, who are both most able and most diligent to instil the poison they suck, first into the courts of princes, acquainting them with the choicest delights and criticisms [8] of sin. As perhaps did that Petronius [9] whom Nero called his arbiter, the master of his revels; and that notorious ribald of Arezzo,[10] dreaded and yet dear to the Italian courtiers. I name not him, for posterity's sake, whom Harry VIII named in merriment his vicar of hell.[11] By which compendious way all the contagion that foreign books can infuse will find a passage to the people far easier and shorter than an Indian voyage, though it could be sailed either by the north of Cataio [12] eastward, or of Canada westward, while our Spanish licensing gags the English press never so severely.

But, on the other side, that infection which is from books of controversy in religion is more doubtful and dangerous to the learned than to the ignorant; and yet those books must be permitted untouched by the licenser. It will be hard to instance where any ignorant man hath been ever seduced by papistical book in English, unless it were commended and expounded to him by some of that clergy; and indeed all such tractates, whether false or true, are as the prophecy of Isaiah was to the eunuch, not to be " understood without a guide." [13] But of our priests and doctors how many have been corrupted by studying the comments of Jesuits and Sorbonists,[14] and how fast they could transfuse that corruption into the people, our experience is both late and sad. It is not forgot, since the acute and distinct Arminius [15] was perverted merely by the perusing of a nameless discourse written at Delft, which at first he took in hand to confute.

Seeing therefore that those books, and those in great abundance, which are likeliest to taint both life and doctrine, cannot be suppressed without the fall of learning, and of all ability in disputation; and that these books of either sort are most and soonest catching to the learned (from whom to the common people whatever is heretical or dissolute may quickly be conveyed); and that evil manners are as perfectly learnt without books a thousand other ways which cannot be stopped; and evil doctrine not with books can propagate, except a teacher guide, which he might also do without writing, and so beyond prohibiting; I am not able to unfold how this cautelous [16] enterprise of licensing can be exempted from the number of vain and impossible attempts. And he who were pleasantly disposed could not well avoid to liken it to the exploit of that gallant man who thought to pound up the crows by shutting his park gate.

Besides another inconvenience, if learned men be the first receivers out of books and dispreaders both of vice and error, how shall the licensers themselves be confided in, unless we can confer upon them, or they assume to themselves above all others in the land, the grace of infallibility and uncorruptedness? And again, if it be true that a wise man, like a good refiner, can gather gold out of

---

2. Talmudist: an expert in Jewish oral traditions concerning Old Testament law.   3. Keri: in the Hebrew Old Testament, a gloss substituting what is to be read in place of a coarser term in the text ("Chetiv").   4. Clement of Alexandria: Christian theologian (*fl.* 200) who wrote against paganism.   5. preparation: Eusebius' collection of pagan writings designed to turn readers to Christianity.   6. Irenaeus, Epiphanius: early bishops who attacked heresies.   7. discover: uncover.   8. criticisms: refinements.   9. Petronius: author of the *Satyricon*, arbiter of taste at Nero's court.   10. Arezzo: Pietro Aretino (d. 1556), Italian satirist.   11. vicar of hell: Sir Francis Bryan, a courtier and cousin of Anne Boleyn.   12. Cataio: Cathay, China.

13. "understood . . . guide": Acts 8:28–35.   14. Sorbonists: members of the theological school of the University of Paris.   15. Arminius: Dutch opponent of Calvinistic predestination and founder of the liberal "Arminian" theology (d. 1609). Milton later held Arminian views.   16. cautelous: deceitful.

the drossiest volume, and that a fool will be a fool with the best book, yea, or without book, there is no reason that we should deprive a wise man of any advantage to his wisdom, while we seek to restrain from a fool that which, being restrained, will be no hindrance to his folly. For if there should be so much exactness always used to keep that from him which is unfit for his reading, we should, in the judgment of Aristotle [17] not only, but of Solomon [18] and of our Savior,[19] not vouchsafe him good precepts, and by consequence not willingly admit him to good books; as being certain that a wise man will make better use of an idle pamphlet than a fool will do of sacred Scripture.

'Tis next alleged we must not expose ourselves to temptations without necessity, and next to that, not employ our time in vain things. To both these objections one answer will serve, out of the grounds already laid, that to all men such books are not temptations nor vanities, but useful drugs and materials wherewith to temper and compose effective and strong medicines, which man's life cannot want.[20] The rest, as children and childish men, who have not the art to qualify and prepare these working minerals, well may be exhorted to forbear, but hindered forcibly they cannot be by all the licensing that sainted Inquisition could ever yet contrive. Which is what I promised to deliver next: that this order of licensing conduces nothing to the end for which it was framed; and hath almost prevented [21] me by being clear already while thus much hath been explaining. See the ingenuity [22] of truth, who, when she gets a free and willing hand, opens herself faster than the pace of method and discourse can overtake her.

It was the task which I began with, to show that no nation, or well instituted state, if they valued books at all, did ever use this way of licensing; and it might be answered that this is a piece of prudence lately discovered. To which I return that, as it was a thing slight and obvious to think on, so if it had been difficult to find out, there wanted not among them long since who suggested such a course; which they not following, leave us a pattern of their judgment that it was not the not knowing, but the not approving, which was the cause of their not using it. Plato, a man of high authority indeed, but least of all for his common-

wealth, in the book of his laws,[23] which no city ever yet received, fed his fancy with making many edicts to his airy burgomasters, which they who otherwise admire him wish had been rather buried and excused in the genial cups of an Academic [24] night-sitting. By which laws he seems to tolerate no kind of learning but by unalterable decree, consisting most of practical traditions, to the attainment whereof a library of smaller bulk than his own dialogues would be abundant. And there also enacts that no poet should so much as read to any private man what he had written, until the judges and lawkeepers had seen it and allowed it; but that Plato meant this law peculiarly to that commonwealth which he had imagined, and to no other, is evident. Why was he not else a lawgiver to himself, but a transgressor, and to be expelled by his own magistrates, both for the wanton epigrams and dialogues which he made, and his perpetual reading of Sophron Mimus [25] and Aristophanes, books of grossest infamy; and also for commending the latter of them, though he were the malicious libeler of his chief friends,[26] to be read by the tyrant Dionysius, who had little need of such trash to spend his time on? But that he knew this licensing of poems had reference and dependence to many other provisos there set down in his fancied republic, which in this world could have no place; and so neither he himself, nor any magistrate or city, ever imitated that course, which, taken apart from those other collateral injunctions, must needs be vain and fruitless.

For if they fell upon one kind of strictness, unless their care were equal to regulate all other things of like aptness to corrupt the mind, that single endeavor they knew would be but a fond [27] labor — to shut and fortify one gate against corruption and be necessitated to leave others round about wide open. If we think to regulate printing, thereby to rectify manners, we must regulate all recreations and pastimes, all that is delightful to man. No music must be heard, no song be set or sung, but what is grave and Doric.[28] There must be licensing dancers, that no gesture, motion, or deportment be taught our youth, but what by their allowance shall be thought honest; for such Plato was provided of. It will ask more than the work of twenty licensers to examine all the lutes, the vio-

---

17. Aristotle (*Nicomachean Ethics*, I. 3 and X. 9) admits that the discussion of ethics does not affect the mass of mankind. 18. Solomon: Prov. 17:2 and 23:9. 19. Savior: Matt. 7:6. 20. want: do without. 21. prevented: anticipated. 22. ingenuity: openness.

23. laws: *Laws*, VII. 800–02. 24. Academic: pertaining to Plato's Academy. 25. Sophron Mimus: author of mimes or dramatic sketches. 26. friends: Aristophanes satirized Socrates in *The Clouds*. 27. fond: foolish. 28. Doric: manly. Cf. Plato, *Republic*, III. 399.

lins, and the guitars in every house; they must not be suffered to prattle as they do, but must be licensed what they may say. And who shall silence all the airs and madrigals that whisper softness in chambers? The windows also, and the balconies, must be thought on; there are shrewd [29] books, with dangerous frontispieces, set to sale: who shall prohibit them, shall twenty licensers? The villages also must have their visitors [30] to inquire what lectures the bagpipe and the rebeck [31] reads, even to the ballatry [32] and the gamut [33] of every municipal fiddler; for these are the countryman's *Arcadias,* and his Montemayors.[34]

Next, what more national corruption, for which England hears ill [35] abroad, than household gluttony? Who shall be the rectors of our daily rioting? And what shall be done to inhibit the multitudes that frequent those houses where drunkenness is sold and harbored? Our garments also should be referred to the licensing of some more sober work-masters, to see them cut into a less wanton garb. Who shall regulate all the mixed conversation [36] of our youth, male and female together, as is the fashion of this country? Who shall still appoint what shall be discoursed, what presumed, and no further? Lastly, who shall forbid and separate all idle resort, all evil company? These things will be, and must be; but how they shall be least hurtful, how least enticing, herein consists the grave and governing wisdom of a state.

To sequester out of the world into Atlantic and Utopian polities,[37] which never can be drawn into use, will not mend our condition; but to ordain wisely as in this world of evil, in the midst whereof God hath placed us unavoidably. Nor is it Plato's licensing of books will do this, which necessarily pulls along with it so many other kinds of licensing as will make us all both ridiculous and weary, and yet frustrate; but those unwritten or at least unconstraining laws of virtuous education, religious and civil nurture, which Plato there mentions [38] as the bonds and ligaments of the commonwealth, the pillars and the sustainers of every written statute; these they be which will bear chief sway in such matters as these, when all licensing will be easily eluded. Impunity and remissness, for certain, are the bane of a commonwealth; but here the great art lies, to discern in what the law is to bid restraint and punishment, and in what things persuasion only is to work. If every action which is good or evil in man at ripe years were to be under pittance and prescription and compulsion, what were virtue but a name, what praise could be then due to well-doing, what gramercy [39] to be sober, just, or continent?

Many there be that complain of divine Providence for suffering Adam to transgress. Foolish tongues! when God gave him reason, he gave him freedom to choose, for reason is but choosing; he had been else a mere artificial Adam, such an Adam as he is in the motions.[40] We ourselves esteem not of that obedience, or love, or gift, which is of force; God therefore left him free, set before him a provoking object, ever almost in his eyes; herein consisted his merit, herein the right of his reward, the praise of his abstinence. Wherefore did he create passions within us, pleasures round about us, but that these, rightly tempered, are the very ingredients of virtue? They are not skillful considerers of human things who imagine to remove sin by removing the matter of sin; for, besides that it is a huge heap increasing under the very act of diminishing, though some part of it may for a time be withdrawn from some persons, it cannot from all, in such a universal thing as books are; and when this is done, yet the sin remains entire. Though ye take from a covetous man all his treasure, he has yet one jewel left — ye cannot bereave him of his covetousness. Banish all objects of lust, shut up all youth into the severest discipline that can be exercised in any hermitage, ye cannot make them chaste that came not thither so: such great care and wisdom is required to the right managing of this point.

Suppose we could expel sin by this means: look how much we thus expel of sin, so much we expel of virtue, for the matter of them both is the same; remove that, and ye remove them both alike. This justifies the high providence of God, who, though he command us temperance, justice, continence, yet pours out before us even to a profuseness all desirable things, and gives us minds that can wander beyond all limit and satiety. Why should we then affect a rigor contrary to the manner of God and of nature, by abridging or scanting those means, which books freely permitted are, both to

---

29. shrewd: mischievous.   **30. visitors:** a term recalling Laud's much-resented campaign for uniformity in the church.   **31. rebeck:** fiddle.   **32. ballatry:** balladry.   **33. gamut:** range of notes.   **34.** *Arcadias . . . Montemayors:* romances like Sidney's *Arcadia* and the Spanish Montemayor's *Diana.*   **35. hears ill:** is ill spoken of.   **36. conversation:** association.   **37. Atlantic . . . polities:** ideal states like Bacon's New Atlantis and More's *Utopia.*   **38. Plato . . . mentions:** *Republic,* IV. 424–33, *Laws,* I. 643.

39. gramercy: thanks.   **40. motions:** puppet shows.

the trial of virtue and the exercise of truth?

It would be better done to learn that the law must needs be frivolous which goes to restrain things uncertainly and yet equally working to good and to evil. And were I the chooser, a dram of well-doing should be preferred before many times as much the forcible hindrance of evil-doing. For God sure esteems the growth and completing of one virtuous person more than the restraint of ten vicious. And albeit whatever thing we hear or see, sitting, walking, traveling, or conversing, may be fitly called our book, and is of the same effect that writings are; yet grant the thing to be prohibited were only books, it appears that this order hitherto is far insufficient to the end which it intends. Do we not see, not once or oftener, but weekly, that continued court-libel [41] against the parliament and city printed, as the wet sheets can witness, and dispersed among us, for all that licensing can do? Yet this is the prime service, a man would think, wherein this order should give proof of itself. If it were executed, you'll say. But certain, if execution be remiss or blindfold now, and in this particular, what will it be hereafter and in other books?

If then the order shall not be vain and frustrate, behold a new labor, Lords and Commons: ye must repeal and proscribe all scandalous and unlicensed books already printed and divulged,[42] after ye have drawn them up into a list, that all may know which are condemned and which not; and ordain that no foreign books be delivered out of custody till they have been read over. This office will require the whole time of not a few overseers, and those no vulgar men. There be also books which are partly useful and excellent, partly culpable and pernicious; this work will ask as many more officials, to make expurgations and expunctions, that the common-wealth of learning be not damnified. In fine, when the multitude of books increase upon their hands, ye must be fain to catalogue all those printers who are found frequently offending, and forbid the importation of their whole suspected typography. In a word, that this your order may be exact and not deficient, ye must reform it perfectly according to the model of Trent and Seville,[43] which I know ye abhor to do.

Yet though ye should condescend to this, which God forbid, the order still would be but fruitless and defective to that end whereto ye meant it. If to prevent sects and schisms, who is so unread or so uncatechized in story that hath not heard of many sects refusing books as a hindrance, and preserving their doctrine unmixed for many ages, only by un-written traditions? The Christian faith (for that was once a schism) is not unknown to have spread all over Asia, ere any gospel or epistle was seen in writing. If the amendment of manners be aimed at, look into Italy and Spain, whether those places be one scruple the better, the honester, the wiser, the chaster, since all the inquisitional rigor that hath been executed upon books.

Another reason, whereby to make it plain that this order will miss the end it seeks, consider by the quality which ought to be in every licenser. It cannot be denied but that he who is made judge to sit upon the birth or death of books, whether they may be wafted into this world or not, had need to be a man above the common measure, both studious, learned, and judicious; there may be else no mean mistakes in the censure of what is passable or not, which is also no mean injury. If he be of such worth as behooves him, there cannot be a more tedious and unpleasing journeywork,[44] a greater loss of time levied upon his head, than to be made the perpetual reader of unchosen books and pamphlets, ofttimes huge volumes. There is no book that is acceptable unless at certain seasons; but to be en-joined the reading of that at all times, and in a hand scarce legible, whereof three pages would not down at any time in the fairest print, is an imposi-tion which I cannot believe how he that values time and his own studies, or is but of a sensible [45] nostril, should be able to endure. In this one thing I crave leave of the present licensers to be par-doned for so thinking; who doubtless took this office up, looking on it through their obedience to the parliament, whose command perhaps made all things seem easy and unlaborious to them; but that this short trial hath wearied them out already, their own expressions and excuses to them who make so many journeys to solicit their license, are testimony enough. Seeing, therefore, those who now possess the employment, by all evident signs wish themselves well rid of it, and that no man of worth, none that is not a plain unthrift of his own hours, is ever likely to succeed them, except he mean to put himself to the salary of a press-cor-rector, we may easily foresee what kind of licensers we are to expect hereafter, either ignorant, imperi-

---

41. court-libel: the royalist newspaper, *Mercurius Aulicus.*
42. divulged: distributed.   43. Trent and Seville: the Councii of Trent and the Spanish Inquisition.

44. journeywork: the work of a day laborer   45. sensible: sensitive.

ous, and remiss, or basely pecuniary. This is what I had to show, wherein this order cannot conduce to that end whereof it bears the intention.

I lastly proceed from the no good it can do, to the manifest hurt it causes, in being first the greatest discouragement and affront that can be offered to learning and to learned men. It was the complaint and lamentation of prelates, upon every least breath of a motion to remove pluralities [46] and distribute more equally church revenues, that then all learning would be for ever dashed and discouraged. But as for that opinion, I never found cause to think that the tenth part of learning stood or fell with the clergy; nor could I ever but hold it for a sordid and unworthy speech of any churchman who had a competency left him. If therefore ye be loth to dishearten utterly and discontent, not the mercenary crew of false pretenders to learning, but the free and ingenuous sort of such as evidently were born to study and love learning for itself, not for lucre or any other end but the service of God and of truth, and perhaps that lasting fame and perpetuity of praise which God and good men have consented shall be the reward of those whose published labors advance the good of mankind; then know, that so far to distrust the judgment and the honesty of one who hath but a common repute in learning, and never yet offended, as not to count him fit to print his mind without a tutor and examiner, lest he should drop a schism or something of corruption, is the greatest displeasure and indignity to a free and knowing spirit that can be put upon him.

What advantage is it to be a man over it is to be a boy at school, if we have only scaped the ferula [47] to come under the fescue [48] of an Imprimatur; if serious and elaborate writings, as if they were no more than the theme of a grammarlad under his pedagogue, must not be uttered without the cursory eyes of a temporizing and extemporizing licenser? He who is not trusted with his own actions, his drift not being known to be evil, and standing to the hazard of law and penalty, has no great argument to think himself reputed, in the commonwealth wherein he was born, for other than a fool or a foreigner. When a man writes to the world, he summons up all his reason and deliberation to assist him; he searches, meditates, is industrious, and likely consults and confers with his judicious friends; after all which done, he takes

himself to be informed in what he writes, as well as any that writ before him. If in this, the most consummate act of his fidelity and ripeness, no years, no industry, no former proof of his abilities can bring him to that state of maturity as not to be still mistrusted and suspected (unless he carry all his considerate diligence, all his midnight watchings and expense of Palladian [49] oil, to the hasty view of an unleisured licenser, perhaps much his younger, perhaps far his inferior in judgment, perhaps one who never knew the labor of book-writing), and if he be not repulsed or slighted, must appear in print like a puny [50] with his guardian, and his censor's hand on the back of his title to be his bail and surety that he is no idiot or seducer; it cannot be but a dishonor and derogation to the author, to the book, to the privilege and dignity of learning.

And what if the author shall be one so copious of fancy as to have many things, well worth the adding, come into his mind after licensing, while the book is yet under the press, which not seldom happens to the best and diligentest writers; and that perhaps a dozen times in one book. The printer dares not go beyond his licensed copy; so often then must the author trudge to his leave-giver, that those his new insertions may be viewed; and many a jaunt will be made ere that licenser (for it must be the same man) can either be found, or found at leisure; meanwhile either the press must stand still, which is no small damage, or the author lose his accuratest thoughts, and send the book forth worse than he had made it, which to a diligent writer is the greatest melancholy and vexation that can befall.

And how can a man teach with authority, which is the life of teaching, how can he be a doctor in his book, as he ought to be, or else had better be silent, whenas all he teaches, all he delivers, is but under the tuition, under the correction, of his patriarchal [51] licenser, to blot or alter what precisely accords not with the hidebound humor which he calls his judgment? When every acute reader, upon the first sight of a pedantic license, will be ready with these like words to ding [52] the book a quoit's distance from him: "I hate a pupil teacher, I endure not an instructor that comes to me under the wardship of an overseeing fist. I know nothing of the licenser, but that I have his own hand here for

---

46. pluralities: two or more livings held by one cleric.   **47. ferula:** a schoolmaster's rod.   **48. fescue:** pointer.

49. Palladian: pertaining to Pallas Athene, goddess of wisdom; the olive, which furnished oil for lamps, was sacred to her. **50. puny:** minor.   **51. patriarchal:** like an archbishop.   **52. ding:** throw.

his arrogance; who shall warrant me his judgment? " " The state, sir," replies the stationer,[53] but has a quick return: " The state shall be my governors, but not my critics; they may be mistaken in the choice of a licenser, as easily as this licenser may be mistaken in an author. This is some common stuff." And he might add from Sir Francis Bacon, that " such authorized books are but the language of the times." [54] For though a licenser should happen to be judicious more than ordinary (which will be a great jeopardy of the next succession), yet his very office and his commission enjoins him to let pass nothing but what is vulgarly [55] received already.

Nay, which is more lamentable, if the work of any deceased author, though never so famous in his lifetime and even to this day, come to their hands for license to be printed or reprinted, if there be found in his book one sentence of a venturous edge, uttered in the height of zeal (and who knows whether it might not be the dictate of a divine spirit?), yet not suiting with every low decrepit humor of their own, though it were Knox [56] himself, the reformer of a kingdom, that spake it, they will not pardon him their dash; [57] the sense of that great man shall to all posterity be lost, for the fearfulness or the presumptuous rashness of a perfunctory licenser. And to what an author this violence hath been lately done,[58] and in what book of greatest consequence to be faithfully published, I could now instance, but shall forbear till a more convenient season. Yet if these things be not resented seriously and timely by them who have the remedy in their power, but that such iron-molds [59] as these shall have authority to gnaw out the choicest periods of exquisitest books, and to commit such a treacherous fraud against the orphan remainders of worthiest men after death, the more sorrow will belong to that hapless race of men whose misfortune it is to have understanding. Henceforth let no man care to learn, or care to be more than worldly wise; for certainly in higher matters to be ignorant and slothful, to be a common steadfast dunce, will be the only pleasant life, and only in request.

And as it is a particular disesteem of every knowing person alive, and most injurious to the written labors and monuments of the dead, so to me it seems an undervaluing and vilifying of the whole nation. I cannot set so light by all the invention, the art, the wit,[60] the grave and solid judgment which is in England, as that it can be comprehended in any twenty capacities, how good soever; much less that it should not pass except their superintendence be over it, except it be sifted and strained with their strainers, that it should be uncurrent without their manual stamp. Truth and understanding are not such wares as to be monopolized and traded in by tickets and statutes and standards. We must not think to make a staple commodity of all the knowledge in the land, to mark and license it like our broadcloth and our woolpacks. What is it but a servitude like that imposed by the Philistines,[61] not to be allowed the sharpening of our own axes and colters,[62] but we must repair from all quarters to twenty licensing forges?

Had anyone written and divulged erroneous things and scandalous to honest life, misusing and forfeiting the esteem had of his reason among men, if after conviction this only censure were adjudged him, that he should never henceforth write but what were first examined by an appointed officer, whose hand should be annexed to pass his credit for him, that now he might be safely read, it could not be apprehended less than a disgraceful punishment. Whence to include the whole nation, and those that never yet thus offended, under such a diffident [63] and suspectful prohibition, may plainly be understood what a disparagement it is. So much the more whenas debtors and delinquents may walk abroad without a keeper, but unoffensive books must not stir forth without a visible jailer in their title. Nor is it to the common people less than a reproach; for if we be so jealous over them as that we dare not trust them with an English pamphlet, what do we but censure them for a giddy, vicious, and ungrounded people, in such a sick and weak estate of faith and discretion as to be able to take nothing down but through the pipe [64] of a licenser? That this is care or love of them we cannot pretend, whenas in those popish places where the laity are most hated and despised, the same strictness is used over them. Wisdom we cannot call it, because it stops but one breach of license, nor that neither, whenas those corruptions which it seeks to prevent, break in faster at other doors which cannot be shut.

---

53. stationer: printer or bookseller.   54. Bacon . . . times: See Bacon's *Advertisement Touching the Controversies of the Church of England.*   55. vulgarly: commonly.   56. Knox: John Knox (d. 1572), leader of the Scottish Reformation.   57. dash: deletion.   58. author . . . done: the reference is uncertain.   59. ironmolds: spots made by rust.

60. invention . . . wit: creative and intellectual powers.   61. Philistines: I Sam. 13:20.   62. colter: iron point of a plow.   63. diffident: distrustful.   64. pipe: medical tube.

And in conclusion, it reflects to the disrepute of our ministers also, of whose labors we should hope better, and of the proficiency which their flock reaps by them, than that after all this light of the gospel which is and is to be, and all this continual preaching, they should be still frequented with such an unprincipled, unedified, and laic [65] rabble, as that the whiff of every new pamphlet should stagger them out of their catechism and Christian walking. This may have much reason to discourage the ministers, when such a low conceit [66] is had of all their exhortations and the benefiting of their hearers, as that they are not thought fit to be turned loose to three sheets of paper without a licenser; that all the sermons, all the lectures preached, printed, vented in such numbers and such volumes as have now well-nigh made all other books unsalable, should not be armor enough against one single enchiridion,[67] without the castle of St. Angelo [68] of an Imprimatur.

And lest some should persuade ye, Lords and Commons, that these arguments of learned men's discouragement at this your order are mere flourishes and not real, I could recount what I have seen and heard in other countries where this kind of inquisition tyrannizes, when I have sat among their learned men (for that honor I had), and been counted happy to be born in such a place of philosophic freedom as they supposed England was, while themselves did nothing but bemoan the servile condition into which learning amongst them was brought; that this was it which had damped the glory of Italian wits; that nothing had been there written now these many years but flattery and fustian. There it was that I found and visited the famous Galileo,[69] grown old, a prisoner to the Inquisition, for thinking in astronomy otherwise than the Franciscan and Dominican licensers thought. And though I knew that England then was groaning loudest under the prelatical yoke, nevertheless I took it as a pledge of future happiness that other nations were so persuaded of her liberty.

Yet was it beyond my hope that those worthies were then breathing in her air, who should be her leaders to such a deliverance as shall never be forgotten by any revolution of time that this world hath to finish. When that was once begun, it was as little in my fear that what words of complaint I heard among learned men of other parts uttered

against the Inquisition, the same I should hear by as learned men at home uttered in time of parliament against an order of licensing; and that so generally, that when I had disclosed myself a companion of their discontent, I might say, if without envy, that he whom an honest quaestorship had endeared to the Sicilians was not more by them importuned against Verres,[70] than the favorable opinion which I had among many who honor ye, and are known and respected by ye, loaded me with entreaties and persuasions that I would not despair to lay together that which just reason should bring into my mind toward the removal of an undeserved thralldom upon learning.

That this is not therefore the disburdening of a particular fancy, but the common grievance of all those who had prepared their minds and studies above the vulgar pitch to advance truth in others, and from others to entertain it, thus much may satisfy. And in their name I shall for neither friend nor foe conceal what the general murmur is: that if it come to inquisitioning again, and licensing, and that we are so timorous of ourselves and so suspicious of all men as to fear each book and the shaking of every leaf, before we know what the contents are; if some, who but of late were little better than silenced from preaching, shall come now to silence us from reading, except what they please, it cannot be guessed what is intended by some but a second tyranny over learning; and will soon put it out of controversy that bishops and presbyters are the same to us, both name and thing.

That those evils of prelaty, which before from five or six and twenty sees were distributively charged upon the whole people, will now light wholly upon learning, is not obscure to us; whenas now the pastor of a small unlearned parish on the sudden shall be exalted archbishop over a large diocese of books, and yet not remove, but keep his other cure too, a mystical pluralist. He who but of late cried down the sole ordination of every novice Bachelor of Art, and denied sole jurisdiction over the simplest parishioner, shall now at home in his private chair assume both these over worthiest and excellentest books and ablest authors that write them. This is not, ye covenants [71] and protestations [72] that we have made, this is not to put down

---

65. **laic:** of the laity.   66. **conceit:** opinion.   67. **enchiridion:** handbook.   68. **St. Angelo:** the papal prison in Rome.   69. **Galileo:** the Italian scientist (d. 1642).

70. **he . . . Verres:** Cicero, as an official in Sicily in 75 B.C., inspired such confidence that the Sicilians urged him to prosecute the dishonest Verres.   71. **covenants:** such as the Scottish Covenant (1638), a general agreement to resist Charles' imposition of episcopacy, and the Solemn League and Covenant (1643), a treaty between the English parliament and the Scots.   72. **protestations:** parliamentary protests (e.g., in 1641) against Charles'

prelaty; this is but to chop [73] an episcopacy; this is but to translate the palace metropolitan [74] from one kind of dominion into another; this is but an old canonical sleight [75] of commuting our penance. To startle thus betimes at a mere unlicensed pamphlet will after a while be afraid of every conventicle, and a while after will make a conventicle of every Christian meeting.

But I am certain that a state governed by the rules of justice and fortitude, or a church built and founded upon the rock of faith and true knowledge, cannot be so pusillanimous. While things are yet not constituted in religion, that freedom of writing should be restrained by a discipline imitated from the prelates, and learnt by them from the Inquisition, to shut us up all again into the breast of a licenser, must needs give cause of doubt and discouragement to all learned and religious men. Who cannot but discern the fineness [76] of this politic drift, and who are the contrivers: that while bishops were to be baited down,[77] then all presses might be open — it was the people's birthright and privilege in time of parliament, it was the breaking forth of light? But now, the bishops abrogated and voided out of the church, as if our reformation sought no more but to make room for others into their seats under another name, the episcopal arts begin to bud again; the cruse [78] of truth must run no more oil; liberty of printing must be enthralled again, under a prelatical commission of twenty; the privilege of the people nullified; and, which is worse, the freedom of learning must groan again, and to her old fetters — all this the parliament yet sitting. Although their own late arguments and defenses against the prelates might remember them that this obstructing violence meets for the most part with an event utterly opposite to the end which it drives at: instead of suppressing sects and schisms, it raises them and invests them with a reputation. " The punishing of wits enhances their authority," saith the Viscount St. Albans, " and a forbidden writing is thought to be a certain spark of truth that flies up in the faces of them who seek to tread it out." This order, therefore, may prove a nursing mother to sects, but I shall easily show how it will be a stepdame [79] to truth: and first by disenabling us to the maintenance of what is known already.

Well knows he who uses to consider, that our faith and knowledge thrives by exercise, as well as our limbs and complexion.[80] Truth is compared in Scripture [81] to a streaming fountain; if her waters flow not in a perpetual progression, they sicken into a muddy pool of conformity and tradition. A man may be a heretic in the truth; and if he believe things only because his pastor says so, or the Assembly [82] so determines, without knowing other reason, though his belief be true, yet the very truth he holds becomes his heresy. There is not any burden that some would gladlier post off to another than the charge and care of their religion. There be — who knows not that there be? — of Protestants and professors [83] who live and die in as arrant an implicit faith as any lay papist of Loretto.[84]

A wealthy man, addicted to his pleasure and to his profits, finds religion to be a traffic so entangled, and of so many piddling accounts, that of all mysteries he cannot skill [85] to keep a stock going upon that trade. What should he do? Fain he would have the name to be religious, fain he would bear up with his neighbors in that. What does he, therefore, but resolves to give over toiling, and to find himself out some factor [86] to whose care and credit he may commit the whole managing of his religious affairs; some divine of note and estimation that must be. To him he adheres, resigns the whole warehouse of his religion, with all the locks and keys, into his custody; and indeed makes the very person of that man his religion; esteems his associating with him a sufficient evidence and commendatory of his own piety. So that a man may say his religion is now no more within himself, but is become a dividual [87] movable, and goes and comes near him, according as that good man frequents the house. He entertains him, gives him gifts, feasts him, lodges him; his religion comes home at night, prays, is liberally supped, and sumptuously laid to sleep; rises, is saluted, and after the malmsey,[88] or some well-spiced brewage, and better breakfasted than he whose morning appetite would have gladly fed on green figs between Bethany and Jerusalem,[89] his religion walks abroad

---

tyrannical acts. **73. chop:** exchange. **74. metropolitan:** of an archbishop. **75. canonical sleight:** a trick of canon law. **76. fineness:** cunning. **77. baited down:** from the sport of bearbaiting. **78. cruse:** like the widow's cruse or jar (I Kings 17:12–16). **79. stepdame:** stepmother, i.e., harsh.

80. complexion: constitution. **81. Truth . . . Scripture:** Ps. 85:11. **82. Assembly:** the mainly Presbyterian Westminster Assembly, convened in July, 1643, to discuss reorganization of the Church. **83. professors:** professing Christians, presumably Protestants and especially Puritans. **84. Loretto:** a noted Italian shrine. **85. skill:** manage. **86. factor:** agent. **87. dividual:** separable. **88. malmsey:** a sweet wine. **89. he . . . Jerusalem:** Jesus, when hungry, found no fruit on a fig tree (Matt. 21:18–21, Mark 11:12–24)

at eight, and leaves his kind entertainer in the shop trading all day without his religion.

Another sort there be, who, when they hear that all things shall be ordered, all things regulated and settled, nothing written but what passes through the customhouse of certain publicans [90] that have the tonnaging and the poundaging [91] of all free-spoken truth, will straight give themselves up into your hands, make 'em and cut 'em out what religion ye please; there be delights, there be recreations and jolly pastimes, that will fetch the day about from sun to sun, and rock the tedious year as in a delightful dream. What need they torture their heads with that which others have taken so strictly and so unalterably into their own purveying? These are the fruits which a dull ease and cessation of our knowledge will bring forth among the people. How goodly and how to be wished were such an obedient unanimity as this, what a fine conformity would it starch us all into! Doubtless a staunch and solid piece of framework as any January could freeze together.

Nor much better will be the consequence even among the clergy themselves. It is no new thing never heard of before, for a parochial minister, who has his reward and is at his Hercules' pillars [92] in a warm benefice, to be easily inclinable, if he have nothing else that may rouse up his studies, to finish his circuit in an English concordance and a topic folio, the gatherings and savings of a sober graduateship, a Harmony [93] and a Catena,[94] treading the constant round of certain common doctrinal heads, attended with their uses, motives, marks and means; out of which, as out of an alphabet or sol-fa,[95] by forming and transforming, joining and disjoining variously, a little bookcraft and two hours' meditation might furnish him unspeakably to the performance of more than a weekly charge of sermoning; not to reckon up the infinite helps of interlinearies, breviaries, synopses, and other loitering gear. But as for the multitude of sermons ready printed and piled up, on every text that is not difficult, our London trading St. Thomas in his vestry, and add to boot St. Martin and St. Hugh,[96] have not within their hallowed limits more vendible ware of all sorts ready made; so that penury he

never need fear of pulpit provision, having where so plenteously to refresh his magazine. But if his rear and flanks be not impaled,[97] if his back door be not secured by the rigid licenser, but that a bold book may now and then issue forth and give the assault to some of his old collections in their trenches, it will concern him then to keep waking, to stand in watch, to set good guards and sentinels about his received opinions, to walk the round and counterround with his fellow inspectors, fearing lest any of his flock be seduced, who also then would be better instructed, better exercised, and disciplined. And God send that the fear of this diligence, which must then be used, do not make us affect the laziness of a licensing church.

For if we be sure we are in the right, and do not hold the truth guiltily (which becomes not), if we ourselves condemn not our own weak and frivolous teaching, and the people for an untaught and irreligious gadding rout, what can be more fair than when a man judicious, learned, and of a conscience, for aught we know, as good as theirs that taught us what we know, shall not privily from house to house, which is more dangerous, but openly by writing, publish to the world what his opinion is, what his reasons, and wherefore that which is now thought cannot be sound? Christ urged it as wherewith to justify himself, that he preached in public; yet writing is more public than preaching, and more easy to refutation if need be, there being so many whose business and profession merely it is to be the champions of truth; which if they neglect, what can be imputed but their sloth or unability?

Thus much we are hindered and disinured [98] by this course of licensing toward the true knowledge of what we seem to know. For how much it hurts and hinders the licensers themselves in the calling of their ministry, more than any secular employment, if they will discharge that office as they ought, so that of necessity they must neglect either the one duty or the other, I insist not, because it is a particular, but leave it to their own conscience how they will decide it there.

There is yet behind of what I purposed to lay open, the incredible loss and detriment that this plot of licensing puts us to. More than if some enemy at sea should stop up all our havens and ports and creeks, it hinders and retards the importation of our richest merchandise, truth. Nay, it

---

90. publicans: tax collectors.   91. tonnaging ... poundaging: excise taxes that Charles had tried to impose without parliament's consent.   92. Hercules' pillars: Gibraltar, the western limit of the ancient world.   93. Harmony: a fusion of the gospel narratives.   94. Catena: a chain, a compilation of extracts. 95. sol-fa: musical scale.   96. St. Thomas ... St. Hugh: apparently landmarks of shopping districts.

97. impaled: enclosed.   98. disinured: put out of practice.

was first established and put in practice by anti-Christian malice and mystery, on set purpose to extinguish, if it were possible, the light of reformation, and to settle falsehood; little differing from that policy wherewith the Turk upholds his Alcoran,[99] by the prohibition of printing. 'Tis not denied, but gladly confessed, we are to send our thanks and vows to Heaven, louder than most of nations, for that great measure of truth which we enjoy, especially in those main points between us and the pope, with his appurtenances the prelates; but he who thinks we are to pitch our tent here, and have attained the utmost prospect of reformation that the mortal glass wherein we contemplate can show us, till we come to beatific vision,[1] that man by this very opinion declares that he is yet far short of truth.

Truth indeed came once into the world with her divine Master, and was a perfect shape most glorious to look on. But when he ascended, and his apostles after him were laid asleep, then straight arose a wicked race of deceivers, who (as that story goes of the Egyptian Typhon with his conspirators, how they dealt with the good Osiris[2]) took the virgin Truth, hewed her lovely form into a thousand pieces, and scattered them to the four winds. From that time ever since, the sad friends of Truth, such as durst appear, imitating the careful search that Isis made for the mangled body of Osiris, went up and down gathering up limb by limb still as they could find them. We have not yet found them all, Lords and Commons, nor ever shall do, till her Master's second coming; he shall bring together every joint and member, and shall mold them into an immortal feature of loveliness and perfection. Suffer not these licensing prohibitions to stand at every place of opportunity, forbidding and disturbing them that continue seeking, that continue to do our obsequies to the torn body of our martyred saint.

We boast our light; but if we look not wisely on the sun itself, it smites us into darkness. Who can discern those planets that are oft combust,[3] and those stars of brightest magnitude that rise and set with the sun, until the opposite motion of their orbs bring them to such a place in the firmament where they may be seen evening or morning? The light which we have gained was given us, not to be ever staring on, but by it to discover onward things more remote from our knowledge. It is not the unfrocking of a priest, the unmitering of a bishop, and the removing him from off the Presbyterian shoulders, that will make us a happy nation; no, if other things as great in the church, and in the rule of life both economical[4] and political, be not looked into and reformed, we have looked so long upon the blaze that Zuinglius[5] and Calvin hath beaconed up to us, that we are stark blind.

There be who perpetually complain of schisms and sects, and make it such a calamity that any man dissents from their maxims. 'Tis their own pride and ignorance which causes the disturbing, who neither will hear with meekness, nor can convince, yet all must be suppressed which is not found in their syntagma.[6] They are the troublers, they are the dividers of unity, who neglect and permit not others to unite those dissevered pieces which are yet wanting to the body of Truth. To be still searching what we know not by what we know, still closing up truth to truth as we find it (for all her body is homogeneal and proportional), this is the golden rule in theology as well as in arithmetic, and makes up the best harmony in a church; not the forced and outward union of cold and neutral and inwardly divided minds.

Lords and Commons of England, consider what nation it is whereof ye are, and whereof ye are the governors: a nation not slow and dull, but of a quick, ingenious, and piercing spirit, acute to invent, subtle and sinewy to discourse, not beneath the reach of any point the highest that human capacity can soar to. Therefore the studies of learning in her deepest sciences have been so ancient and so eminent among us, that writers of good antiquity and ablest judgment have been persuaded that even the school of Pythagoras[7] and the Persian wisdom took beginning from the old philosophy of this island. And that wise and civil Roman, Julius Agricola,[8] who governed once here for Caesar, preferred the natural wits of Britain before the labored studies of the French. Nor is it for nothing that the grave and frugal Transylvanian[9] sends out yearly from as far as the mountainous borders of Russia and beyond the Hercynian[10] wilderness, not their youth but their staid men, to learn our lan-

99. Alcoran: the Koran.   1. beatific vision: the sight of God in heaven.   2. Osiris: a myth from Plutarch's *Isis and Osiris*. 3. combust: burned up (an astrological term used of planets whose "influence" was nullified by nearness to the sun).

4. economical: domestic.   5. Zuinglius: Zwingli (d. 1531), the Swiss Protestant theologian.   6. syntagma: compilation. 7. Pythagoras: the early Greek philosopher whom legend made a visitor to Britain.   8. Agricola: Roman governor of Britain, 78–85 A.D.   9. Transylvania: a Protestant nation, later part of Hungary.   10. Hercynian: used of the mountainous regions of south and central Germany.

guage and our theologic arts. Yet that which is above all this, the favor and the love of Heaven, we have great argument to think in a peculiar manner propitious and propending [11] towards us. Why else was this nation chosen before any other, that out of her, as out of Sion, should be proclaimed and sounded forth the first tidings and trumpet of reformation to all Europe? And had it not been the obstinate perverseness of our prelates against the divine and admirable spirit of Wycliffe, to suppress him as a schismatic and innovator, perhaps neither the Bohemian Huss and Jerome, [12] no, nor the name of Luther or of Calvin had been ever known; the glory of reforming all our neighbors had been completely ours. But now, as our obdurate clergy have with violence demeaned [13] the matter, we are become hitherto the latest and the backwardest scholars of whom God offered to have made us the teachers.

Now once again by all concurrence of signs, and by the general instinct of holy and devout men, as they daily and solemnly express their thoughts, God is decreeing to begin some new and great period in his church, even to the reforming of reformation itself; what does he then but reveal himself to his servants and, as his manner is, first to his Englishmen? I say, as his manner is, first to us, though we mark not the method of his counsels, and are unworthy. Behold now this vast city, a city of refuge, the mansion-house of liberty, encompassed and surrounded with his protection; the shop of war hath not there more anvils and hammers waking to fashion out the plates [14] and instruments of armed justice in defense of beleaguered truth, than there be pens and heads there, sitting by their studious lamps, musing, searching, revolving new notions and ideas wherewith to present, as with their homage and their fealty, the approaching reformation; others as fast reading, trying all things, assenting to the force of reason and convincement.

What could a man require more from a nation so pliant and so prone to seek after knowledge? What wants there to such a towardly and pregnant soil but wise and faithful laborers, to make a knowing people, a nation of prophets, of sages, and of worthies? We reckon more than five months yet to harvest; there need not be five weeks, had we but eyes to lift up; the fields are white already.

Where there is much desire to learn, there of necessity will be much arguing, much writing, many opinions; for opinion in good men is but knowledge in the making. Under these fantastic terrors of sect and schism, we wrong the earnest and zealous thirst after knowledge and understanding which God hath stirred up in this city. What some lament of, we rather should rejoice at, should rather praise this pious forwardness among men to reassume the ill-deputed care of their religion into their own hands again. A little generous prudence, a little forbearance of one another, and some grain of charity might win all these diligences to join and unite into one general and brotherly search after truth, could we but forgo this prelatical tradition of crowding free consciences and Christian liberties into canons and precepts of men. I doubt not, if some great and worthy stranger should come among us, wise to discern the mold and temper of a people and how to govern it, observing the high hopes and aims, the diligent alacrity of our extended thoughts and reasonings in the pursuance of truth and freedom, but that he would cry out as Pyrrhus [15] did, admiring the Roman docility and courage, "If such were my Epirots, I would not despair the greatest design that could be attempted to make a church or kingdom happy."

Yet these are the men cried out against for schismatics and sectaries; as if, while the temple of the Lord was building, some cutting, some squaring the marble, others hewing the cedars, there should be a sort of irrational men who could not consider there must be many schisms and many dissections made in the quarry and in the timber ere the house of God can be built. And when every stone is laid artfully together, it cannot be united into a continuity, it can but be contiguous in this world; neither can every piece of the building be of one form; nay rather, the perfection consists in this, that out of many moderate varieties and brotherly dissimilitudes that are not vastly disproportional, arises the goodly and graceful symmetry that commends the whole pile and structure.

Let us therefore be more considerate builders, more wise in spiritual architecture, when great reformation is expected. For now the time seems come wherein Moses, the great prophet, may sit in heaven rejoicing to see that memorable and glorious wish of his fulfilled, when not only our seventy

---

11. **propending:** inclining.   12. **Jerome:** of Prague, a follower of Huss and also a martyr (d. 1416).   13. **demeaned:** handled.   14. **plates:** armor.

15. **Pyrrhus:** King of Epirus (d. 272 B.C.) who invaded Italy.

elders,[16] but all the Lord's people, are become prophets. No marvel then though some men, and some good men too perhaps, but young in goodness, as Joshua then was, envy them. They fret, and out of their own weakness are in agony, lest these divisions and subdivisions will undo us. The adversary again applauds, and waits the hour: when they have branched themselves out, saith he, small enough into parties and partitions, then will be our time. Fool! he sees not the firm root out of which we all grow, though into branches; nor will beware, until he see our small divided maniples [17] cutting through at every angle of his ill-united and unwieldy brigade. And that we are to hope better of all these supposed sects and schisms, and that we shall not need that solicitude, honest perhaps, though over-timorous, of them that vex in this behalf, but shall laugh in the end at those malicious applauders of our differences, I have these reasons to persuade me.

First, when a city shall be as it were besieged and blocked about, her navigable river infested, inroads and incursions round, defiance and battle oft rumored to be marching up even to her walls and suburb trenches; [18] that then the people, or the greater part, more than at other times, wholly taken up with the study of highest and most important matters to be reformed, should be disputing, reasoning, reading, inventing, discoursing, even to a rarity and admiration, things not before discoursed or written of, argues first a singular goodwill, contentedness, and confidence in your prudent foresight and safe government, Lords and Commons; and from thence derives itself to a gallant bravery and well-grounded contempt of their enemies, as if there were no small number of as great spirits among us, as his was who, when Rome was nigh besieged by Hannibal, being in the city, bought that piece of ground at no cheap rate whereon Hannibal himself encamped his own regiment.

Next, it is a lively and cheerful presage of our happy success and victory. For as in a body, when the blood is fresh, the spirits pure and vigorous not only to vital but to rational faculties, and those in the acutest and the pertest [19] operations of wit and subtlety, it argues in what good plight and constitution the body is; so when the cheerfulness of the people is so sprightly up, as that it has not only wherewith to guard well its own freedom and safety, but to spare, and to bestow upon the solidest and sublimest points of controversy and new invention, it betokens us not degenerated nor drooping to a fatal decay, but casting off the old and wrinkled skin of corruption to outlive these pangs and wax young again, entering the glorious ways of truth and prosperous virtue, destined to become great and honorable in these latter ages. Methinks I see in my mind a noble and puissant nation rousing herself like a strong man after sleep, and shaking her invincible locks: methinks I see her as an eagle mewing [20] her mighty youth, and kindling her undazzled eyes at the full midday beam, purging and unscaling her long-abused sight at the fountain itself of heavenly radiance; while the whole noise of timorous and flocking birds, with those also that love the twilight, flutter about, amazed at what she means, and in their envious gabble would prognosticate a year of sects and schisms.

What should ye do then, should ye suppress all this flowery crop of knowledge and new light sprung up and yet springing daily in this city? Should ye set an oligarchy of twenty engrossers [21] over it, to bring a famine upon our minds again, when we shall know nothing but what is measured to us by their bushel? Believe it, Lords and Commons, they who counsel ye to such a suppressing do as good as bid ye suppress yourselves; and I will soon show how. If it be desired to know the immediate cause of all this free writing and free speaking, there cannot be assigned a truer than your own mild and free and humane government; it is the liberty, Lords and Commons, which your own valorous and happy counsels have purchased us, liberty which is the nurse of all great wits. This is that which hath rarefied and enlightened our spirits like the influence of heaven; this is that which hath enfranchised, enlarged, and lifted up our apprehensions degrees above themselves. Ye cannot make us now less capable, less knowing, less eagerly pursuing of the truth, unless ye first make yourselves, that made us so, less the lovers, less the founders of our true liberty. We can grow ignorant again, brutish, formal, and slavish, as ye found us; but you then must first become that which ye cannot be, oppressive, arbitrary, and tyrannous, as they were from whom ye have freed us. That our hearts are now more capacious, our thoughts more erected

---

16. seventy elders: Moses assembled seventy elders who were inspired to prophecy, and rebuked young Joshua for urging him to silence two other prophets who had remained in camp (Num. 11:16–29). **17. maniples:** companies in a Roman legion. **18. trenches:** See Sonnet VIII, below, and ll. 10–12n., ll. 12–14n. **19. pertest:** liveliest. **20. mewing:** renewing by molting. **21. engrossers:** monopolists.

to the search and expectation of greatest and exactest things, is the issue of your own virtue propagated in us; ye cannot suppress that unless ye reinforce an abrogated and merciless law, that fathers may dispatch at will their own children. And who shall then stick closest to ye and excite others? Not he who takes up arms for coat and conduct,[22] and his four nobles of Danegelt.[23] Although I dispraise not the defense of just immunities, yet love my peace better, if that were all. Give me the liberty to know, to utter, and to argue freely according to conscience, above all liberties.

What would be best advised, then, if it be found so hurtful and so unequal[24] to suppress opinions for the newness, or the unsuitableness to a customary acceptance, will not be my task to say. I only shall repeat what I have learned from one of your own honorable number, a right noble and pious lord, who had he not sacrificed his life and fortunes to the church and commonwealth, we had not now missed and bewailed a worthy and undoubted patron of this argument. Ye know him, I am sure; yet I for honor's sake, and may it be eternal to him, shall name him, the Lord Brooke.[25] He, writing of episcopacy, and by the way treating of sects and schisms, left ye his vote, or rather now the last words of his dying charge (which I know will ever be of dear and honored regard with ye), so full of meekness and breathing charity that, next to his last testament who bequeathed love and peace to his disciples, I cannot call to mind where I have read or heard words more mild and peaceful. He there exhorts us to hear with patience and humility those, however they be miscalled, that desire to live purely, in such a use of God's ordinances as the best guidance of their conscience gives them, and to tolerate them, though in some disconformity to ourselves. The book itself will tell us more at large, being published to the world and dedicated to the parliament by him who, both for his life and for his death, deserves that what advice he left be not laid by without perusal.

And now the time in special is, by privilege to write and speak what may help to the further discussing of matters in agitation. The temple of Janus,[26] with his two controversial faces, might now

not unsignificantly be set open. And though all the winds of doctrine were let loose to play upon the earth, so truth be in the field, we do injuriously by licensing and prohibiting to misdoubt her strength. Let her and falsehood grapple; who ever knew truth put to the worse, in a free and open encounter? Her confuting is the best and surest suppressing. He who hears what praying there is for light and clearer knowledge to be sent down among us, would think of other matters to be constituted beyond the discipline of Geneva,[27] framed and fabricked already to our hands.

Yet when the new light which we beg for shines in upon us, there be who envy and oppose, if it come not first in at their casements. What a collusion is this, whenas we are exhorted by the wise man to use diligence, "to seek for wisdom as for hidden treasures"[28] early and late, that another order shall enjoin us to know nothing but by statute? When a man hath been laboring the hardest labor in the deep mines of knowledge, hath furnished out his findings in all their equipage, drawn forth his reasons as it were a battle ranged, scattered and defeated all objections in his way, calls out his adversary into the plain, offers him the advantage of wind and sun, if he please, only that he may try the matter by dint of argument; for his opponents then to skulk, to lay ambushments, to keep a narrow bridge of licensing where the challenger should pass, though it be valor enough in soldiership, is but weakness and cowardice in the wars of truth. For who knows not that truth is strong, next to the Almighty? She needs no policies, nor stratagems, nor licensings to make her victorious; those are the shifts and the defenses that error uses against her power. Give her but room, and do not bind her when she sleeps, for then she speaks not true, as the old Proteus[29] did, who spake oracles only when he was caught and bound, but then rather she turns herself into all shapes except her own, and perhaps tunes her voice according to the time, as Micaiah[30] did before Ahab, until she be adjured into her own likeness.

Yet is it not impossible that she may have more shapes than one. What else is all that rank of things indifferent,[31] wherein truth may be on this

---

22. coat . . . conduct: a military tax.   23. Danegelt: money raised to appease the early Danish invaders of England.   24. unequal: unjust.   25. Lord Brooke: parliamentary leader and writer, killed in the war (1643). The book cited is *A Discourse Opening the Nature of . . . Episcopacy.*   26. Janus: the Roman temple of Janus, the two-faced god of gates, had doors that were shut in time of peace, open in time of war.

27. Geneva: the uniformitarian system of Calvin which the Presbyterians wanted.   28. "to . . . treasures": Prov. 8:11, Matt. 13:44.   29. Proteus: the old man of the sea, who, when caught, assumed various shapes, but, if held firmly, foretold the future.   30. Micaiah: a good prophet who at first gave Ahab the same advice as the false prophets (I Kings 22:1–28).   31. indifferent: nonessential.

side, or on the other, without being unlike herself? What but a vain shadow else is the abolition of "those ordinances, that handwriting nailed to the cross"?[32] What great purchase is this Christian liberty which Paul[33] so often boasts of? His doctrine is that he who eats or eats not, regards a day or regards it not, may do either to the Lord. How many other things might be tolerated in peace and left to conscience, had we but charity, and were it not the chief stronghold of our hypocrisy to be ever judging one another? I fear yet this iron yoke of outward conformity hath left a slavish print upon our necks; the ghost of a linen decency[34] yet haunts us. We stumble and are impatient at the least dividing of one visible congregation from another, though it be not in fundamentals; and through our forwardness to suppress, and our backwardness to recover, any enthralled piece of truth out of the gripe of custom, we care not to keep truth separated from truth, which is the fiercest rent and disunion of all. We do not see that while we still affect by all means a rigid external formality, we may as soon fall again into a gross conforming stupidity, a stark and dead congealment of "wood and hay and stubble"[35] forced and frozen together, which is more to the sudden degenerating of a church than many subdichotomies of petty schisms.

Not that I can think well of every light separation; or that all in a church is to be expected "gold and silver and precious stones."[36] It is not possible for man to sever the wheat from the tares, the good fish from the other fry;[37] that must be the angels' ministry at the end of mortal things. Yet if all cannot be of one mind — as who looks they should be? — this doubtless is more wholesome, more prudent, and more Christian, that many be tolerated, rather than all compelled. I mean not tolerated popery[38] and open superstition, which as it extirpates all religions and civil supremacies, so itself should be extirpate, provided first that all charitable and compassionate means be used to win and regain the weak and the misled; that also which is impious or evil absolutely, either against faith or manners, no law can possibly permit that intends not to unlaw itself; but those neighboring differences, or rather indifferences, are what I speak

of, whether in some point of doctrine or of discipline, which though they may be many, yet need not interrupt "the unity of Spirit," if we could but find among us "the bond of peace."[39]

In the meanwhile, if anyone would write and bring his helpful hand to the slow-moving reformation which we labor under, if truth have spoken to him before others, or but seemed at least to speak, who hath so bejesuited us that we should trouble that man with asking license to do so worthy a deed; and not consider this, that if it come to prohibiting, there is not aught more likely to be prohibited than truth itself, whose first appearance, to our eyes bleared and dimmed with prejudice and custom, is more unsightly and unplausible than many errors, even as the person is of many a great man slight and contemptible to see to?[40] And what do they tell us vainly of new opinions, when this very opinion of theirs, that none must be heard but whom they like, is the worst and newest opinion of all others; and is the chief cause why sects and schisms do so much abound, and true knowledge is kept at distance from us; besides yet a greater danger which is in it. For when God shakes a kingdom with strong and healthful commotions to a general reforming, 'tis not untrue that many sectaries and false teachers are then busiest in seducing.

But yet more true it is that God then raises to his own work men of rare abilities and more than common industry, not only to look back and revise what hath been taught heretofore, but to gain further and go on some new enlightened steps in the discovery of truth. For such is the order of God's enlightening his church, to dispense and deal out by degrees his beam, so as our earthly eyes may best sustain it. Neither is God appointed and confined where and out of what place these his chosen shall be first heard to speak; for he sees not as man sees, chooses not as man chooses, lest we should devote ourselves again to set places and assemblies, and outward callings of men; planting our faith one while in the old Convocation house,[41] and another while in the Chapel[42] at Westminster; when all the faith and religion that shall be there canonized is not sufficient, without plain convincement and the charity of patient instruction, to supple the least bruise of conscience, to edify the meanest Christian

32. "those . . . cross": Col. 2:14.   33. Paul: See Rom. 6:18, Gal. 5:1.   34. linen decency: a satirical glance at the bishops' fine robes.   35. "wood . . . stubble": I Cor. 3:12.   36. "gold . . . stones": Rev. 18:12.   37. fry: Matt. 13:24-49.   38. popery: Milton, like other good liberals of his age, exempts Catholicism from toleration on political as well as religious grounds; everyone remembered the Gunpowder Plot (1605) and other conspiracies in which some Catholics had engaged.

39. "unity . . . peace": Eph. 4:3.   40. see to: look at.   41. Convocation house: the Chapter House at Westminster, where the Anglican clergy had held their assemblies.   42. Chapel: Henry VII's Chapel, the meeting place of the Westminster Assembly.

who desires to walk in the spirit and not in the let-ter of human trust, for all the number of voices that can be there made; no, though Harry VII himself there, with all his liege tombs about him, should lend them voices from the dead to swell their number.

And if the men be erroneous who appear to be the leading schismatics, what withholds us but our sloth, our self-will, and distrust in the right cause, that we do not give them gentle meetings and gentle dismissions, that we debate not and examine the matter thoroughly with liberal and frequent audi-ence, if not for their sakes yet for our own? Seeing no man who hath tasted learning but will confess the many ways of profiting by those who, not con-tented with stale receipts, are able to manage and set forth new positions to the world. And were they but as the dust and cinders of our feet, so long as in that notion they may yet serve to polish and brighten the armory of truth, even for that respect they were not utterly to be cast away. But if they be of those whom God hath fitted for the special use of these times with eminent and ample gifts — and those perhaps neither among the priests nor among the pharisees — and we, in the haste of a precipitant zeal, shall make no distinction, but re-solve to stop their mouths because we fear they come with new and dangerous opinions (as we commonly forejudge them ere we understand them), no less than woe to us while, thinking thus to defend the gospel, we are found the persecu-tors.

There have been not a few [43] since the beginning of this parliament,[44] both of the presbytery and others, who by their unlicensed books, to the con-tempt of an Imprimatur, first broke that triple ice clung about our hearts, and taught the people to see day. I hope that none of those were the per-suaders to renew upon us this bondage, which they themselves have wrought so much good by con-temning. But if neither the check that Moses gave to young Joshua, nor the countermand which our Saviour gave to young John,[45] who was so ready to prohibit those whom he thought unlicensed, be not enough to admonish our elders how unacceptable to God their testy mood of prohibiting is; if neither their own remembrance what evil hath abounded in the church by this let [46] of licensing, and what

good they themselves have begun by transgressing it, be not enough, but that they will persuade and execute the most Dominican part of the Inquisition over us, and are already with one foot in the stir-rup so active at suppressing, it would be no un-equal distribution in the first place to suppress the suppressors themselves, whom the change of their condition hath puffed up more than their late ex-perience of harder times hath made wise.

And as for regulating the press, let no man think to have the honor of advising ye better than your-selves have done in that order published next be-fore this,[47] "that no book be printed, unless the printer's and the author's name, or at least the printer's, be registered." Those which otherwise come forth, if they be found mischievous and libelous, the fire and the executioner will be the timeliest and the most effectual remedy that man's prevention can use. For this authentic Spanish pol-icy of licensing books, if I have said aught, will prove the most unlicensed book itself within a short while; and was the immediate image of a Star Chamber [48] decree to that purpose made in those very times when that court did the rest of those her pious works, for which she is now fallen from the stars with Lucifer.[49] Whereby ye may guess what kind of state prudence, what love of the people, what care of religion or good manners there was at the contriving, although with singular hypocrisy it pretended to bind books to their good behavior. And how it got the upper hand of your precedent orders so well constituted before, if we may believe those men whose profession gives them cause to inquire most, it may be doubted there was in it the fraud of some old patentees and monopolizers in the trade of bookselling; who, under pretense of the poor in their Company not to be defrauded, and the just retaining of each man his several copy (which God forbid should be gainsaid), brought divers glozing colors [50] to the House, which were indeed but colors, and serving to no end except it be to exercise a superiority over their neighbors; men who do not therefore labor in an honest pro-fession, to which learning is indebted, that they should be made other men's vassals. Another end is thought was aimed at by some of them in pro-curing by petition this order, that having power in

43. **not a few:** including Milton.   44. **this parliament:** the Long Parliament, which met in November, 1640, began with large reforms.   45. **John:** Jesus rebuked John for complaining of a man who had cast out devils in Jesus' name (Luke 9:50). 46. **let:** hindrance.

47. **order . . . this:** Milton means the order of January, 1642. 48. **Star Chamber:** this court, established by Henry VII, had become, notably during the regime of Charles and Laud, an agent and symbol of arbitrary power. See the introductory note to *Areopagitica*.   49. **Lucifer:** See *PL*, I. 84.   50. **glozing colors:** specious interpretations.

their hands, malignant [51] books might the easier scape abroad, as the event shows. But of these sophisms and elenchs [52] of merchandise I skill [53] not. This I know, that errors in a good government and in a bad are equally almost incident; for what magistrate may not be misinformed, and much the sooner, if liberty of printing be reduced into the power of a few? But to redress willingly and speedily what hath been erred, and in highest authority to esteem a plain advertisement [54] more than others have done a sumptuous bribe, is a virtue, honored Lords and Commons, answerable to your highest actions, and whereof none can participate but greatest and wisest men.

SONNETS

VIII. WHEN THE ASSAULT WAS INTENDED TO THE CITY

Written in November, 1642, when the Royalist army reached the outskirts of London. The Cambridge manuscript has two alternative titles, the one used here and "On His Door When the City Expected an Assault," the latter being scratched out. Milton presumably did not think of affixing the sonnet to his door; he was writing, with dramatic impersonality, on the poet and poetry in wartime.

Captain or colonel,° or knight in arms,
  Whose chance on these defenseless doors may
    seize,
  If deed of honor did thee ever please,
  Guard them, and him within protect from harms;
He can requite thee, for he knows the charms
  That call fame on such gentle acts as these,
  And he can spread thy name o'er lands and seas,
  Whatever clime the sun's bright circle warms.
Lift not thy spear against the Muses' bower:
  The great Emathian conqueror bid spare   10
  The house of Pindarus, when temple and tower
Went to the ground;° and the repeated air
  Of sad Electra's poet had the power
  To save the Athenian walls from ruin bare.°

51. malignant: a word applied to Royalists and Anglicans by parliamentarians and Puritans.   52. elenchs: sophistical arguments.   53. skill: have no part in.   54. advertisement: notification.

SONNET VIII. 1. colonel: the word has three syllables. 10–12. The . . . ground: the Macedonian (Emathian) Alexander the Great was said to have spared Pindar's house when he razed Thebes. 12–14. the repeated . . . bare: Plutarch (*Lysander*) tells how the victorious Spartans, in 404 B.C., were dissuaded from demolishing Athens when an officer among their allies recited a chorus from Euripides' *Electra*.

XII. I DID BUT PROMPT THE AGE TO QUIT THEIR CLOGS

Areopagitica showed Milton's disillusioned recognition that there was little to choose between Presbyterian and Laudian tyranny, that — to quote another sonnet — "New Presbyter is but old Priest writ large." The following sonnet is apparently a comment on the hostile reaction to his pleas for more liberal divorce. The last two tracts on divorce were published together in 1645 and, as W. R. Parker suggests, may be glanced at in "twin-born progeny."

I did but prompt the age to quit their clogs
  By the known rules of ancient liberty,
  When straight a barbarous noise environs me
  Of owls and cuckoos, asses, apes, and dogs;
As° when those hinds that were transformed to
    frogs
  Railed at Latona's twin-born progeny,
  Which after held the sun and moon in fee.°
But this is got by casting pearl to hogs,
That bawl for freedom in their senseless mood,
  And still revolt when truth would set them free.
License they mean when they cry liberty;   11
For who loves that must first be wise and good:
  But from that mark how far they rove we see,
  For all this waste of wealth and loss of blood.

XV. ON THE LORD GENERAL FAIRFAX AT THE SIEGE OF COLCHESTER

Sir Thomas Fairfax, the parliamentary general, won the decisive battle of Naseby (1645). Some later Royalist uprisings were ended with his siege and capture (August, 1648) of Colchester. Fairfax did not favor the king's execution (1649) and soon afterward withdrew largely from public affairs.

Fairfax, whose name in arms through Europe rings,
  Filling each mouth with envy or with praise,
  And all her jealous monarchs with amaze,
  And rumors loud that daunt remotest kings,
Thy firm unshaken virtue ever brings
  Victory home, though new rebellions raise
  Their Hydra° heads, and the false North° displays

SONNET XII. 5–7 As . . . fee: Latona, weary from carrying her twin children, Apollo and Diana, in her arms, sought a drink from a lake and was denied it by the local peasants (hinds), who were turned into frogs for their churlishness. 7. in fee: in full possession. SONNET XV. 7. Hydra: the monster that sprouted new heads for every one destroyed and that Hercules conquered. false North: in violation of the Solemn League and Covenant (1643), a Scottish force came to Charles' aid in 1648; it was defeated by Cromwell at Preston some days before Colchester was taken.

Her broken league to imp° their serpent wings.
O yet a nobler task awaits thy hand;
For what can war but endless war still breed,
Till truth and right from violence be freed,   11
And public faith cleared from the shameful brand
Of public fraud? In vain doth valor bleed
While avarice and rapine share the land.

XIX. WHEN I CONSIDER HOW MY LIGHT IS SPENT

This sonnet was probably composed early in 1652, when Milton's blindness became complete.

When I consider how my light is spent,
Ere half my days° in this dark world and wide,
And that one talent which is death to hide°
Lodged with me useless, though my soul more bent
To serve therewith my Maker, and present
My true account, lest he returning chide,
"Doth God exact day-labor, light denied?"
I fondly° ask. But Patience, to prevent
That murmur, soon replies, "God doth not need
Either man's work or his own gifts; who best
Bear his mild yoke, they serve him best. His state   11
Is kingly: thousands° at his bidding speed,
And post o'er land and ocean without rest;
They also serve who only stand and wait."

XVI. TO THE LORD GENERAL CROMWELL

*On the Proposals of Certain Ministers
at the Committee for Propagation of the Gospel*

The Committee referred to in the subtitle was considering proposals for clerical censorship of preaching, to which Milton (like Cromwell) was opposed. The sonnet was written in May, 1652.

Cromwell, our chief of men, who through a cloud
Not of war only, but detractions rude,
Guided by faith and matchless fortitude,
To peace and truth thy glorious way hast plowed,
And on the neck of crownèd Fortune proud
Hast reared God's trophies and his work pursued,
While Darwen stream,° with blood of Scots imbrued,
And Dunbar° field resounds thy praises loud,
And Worcester's° laureate wreath; yet much remains
To conquer still: peace hath her victories   10
No less renowned than war; new foes arise
Threatening to bind our souls with secular chains.
Help us to save free conscience from the paw
Of hireling wolves whose gospel is their maw.

XVIII. ON THE LATE MASSACRE IN PIEMONT

In April, 1655, members of the Protestant Vaudois or Waldensian sect, who had long inhabited the mountains of Piedmont, and had been granted freedom of worship, were massacred by Italian soldiers who had been billeted among them. Cromwell sent a protest (written by Milton as secretary) to the Duke of Savoy and addressed appeals (also written by Milton) to the leaders of continental Protestantism; a large fund was raised in England for the surviving refugees.

Avenge, O Lord, thy slaughtered saints, whose bones
Lie scattered on the Alpine mountains cold,
Even them who kept thy truth so pure of old
When all our fathers worshiped stocks and stones,°
Forget not; in thy book record their groans
Who were thy sheep, and in their ancient fold
Slain by the bloody Piemontese, that rolled
Mother with infant down the rocks. Their moans
The vales redoubled to the hills, and they   9
To heaven. Their martyred blood and ashes sow
O'er all the Italian fields, where still doth sway
The triple tyrant,° that from these may grow
A hundredfold, who, having learnt thy way,
Early may fly the Babylonian woe.°

8. imp: replace a falcon's broken feathers with new ones. SONNET XIX. 2. Ere . . . days: Milton is presumably thinking, not of his whole life span, but of his fruitful maturity. 3. talent . . . hide: See the parable of the talents (Matt. 25:14–30) and the early Sonnet VII above. 8. fondly: foolishly. 12. thousands: of angels.

7. Darwen stream: the scene of the battle of Preston. See l. 7n., Sonnet XV. 8. Dunbar: where Cromwell defeated the Scots on September 3, 1650. 9. Worcester: where Cromwell routed the Scots on September 3, 1651. Charles II, who was with the Scots, became a fugitive. SONNET XVIII. 3–4. who . . . stones: the Waldensian "heresy" arose in the twelfth century. 12. triple tyrant: the pope, as claiming authority on earth and in Heaven and Hell. 14. Babylonian woe: Protestant tradition (and such Catholics as Petrarch) saw an image of papal corruption in the Babylon of Rev. 14:8, 17:5, 18:2.

XX. LAWRENCE, OF VIRTUOUS FATHER
VIRTUOUS SON

Edward Lawrence (1633–57), the young man Milton addresses, was the eldest son of Henry Lawrence, Lord President of the Council under Cromwell. The sonnet was perhaps written in 1655.

Lawrence, of virtuous father virtuous son,
　Now that the fields are dank and ways are mire,
　Where shall we sometimes meet, and by the fire
　Help waste a sullen day, what may be won
From the hard season gaining? Time will run
　On smoother, till Favonius° reinspire
　The frozen earth, and clothe in fresh attire
　The lily and rose, that neither sowed nor spun.°
What neat repast shall feast us, light and choice,
　Of Attic taste,° with wine, whence we may rise
　To hear the lute well touched, or artful voice　11
Warble immortal notes and Tuscan° air?
　He who of those delights can judge, and spare°
　To interpose them oft, is not unwise.

XXII. TO MR. CYRIACK SKINNER
UPON HIS BLINDNESS

Skinner was a lawyer who had been Milton's pupil and remained his friend. The title, evidently not Milton's, was used by his nephew, Edward Phillips, when he printed the sonnet in 1694. It was probably written in 1655.

Cyriack, this three years' day° these eyes, though
　clear
　To outward view of blemish or of spot,
　Bereft of light their seeing have forgot;
　Nor to their idle orbs doth sight appear
Of sun or moon or star throughout the year,
　Or man or woman. Yet I argue not
　Against Heaven's hand or will, nor bate a jot

Of heart or hope, but still bear up° and steer
Right onward. What supports me, dost thou
　ask?
　The conscience,° friend, to have lost them over-
　plied　　　　　　　　　　　　　　　　10
In liberty's defense,° my noble task,
Of which all Europe talks from side to side.
　This thought might lead me through the world's
　vain masque,
　Content though blind, had I no better guide.°

XXIII. METHOUGHT I SAW MY LATE
ESPOUSÈD SAINT

Katherine Woodcock, at the age of 28, became Milton's second wife in November, 1656, and died in February, 1658, some four months after the birth of a child.

Methought I saw my late espousèd saint°
　Brought to me like Alcestis from the grave,
　Whom Jove's great son to her glad husband gave,
　Rescued from death by force, though pale and
　faint.°
Mine, as whom washed from spot of child-bed
　taint
　Purification in the Old Law did save,°
　And such as yet once more I trust to have
　Full sight of her in Heaven without restraint,
Came vested all in white, pure as her mind.
　Her face was veiled,° yet to my fancied sight　10
　Love, sweetness, goodness, in her person
　shined
So clear as in no face with more delight.
　But O as to embrace me she inclined,
　I waked, she fled, and day brought back my
　night.

8. bear up: turn the helm so as to put a vessel before the wind. **10. conscience:** consciousness. **11. liberty's defense:** See Intro., 402–03. **14. better guide:** God, his conscience. SONNET XXIII. **1. late . . . saint:** the woman I lately married, now a saint in Heaven. **2–4. Alcestis . . . faint:** In the myth dramatized by Euripides, Alcestis, King Admetus' wife, yielded herself to death as a substitute for her husband, but was brought back from Hades by Heracles (Hercules). **5–6.** In Hebrew law (Lev. 12) a woman underwent a ritual of purification after childbirth. **10. Her . . . veiled:** like Alcestis, and because apparently Milton had never seen her.

SONNET XX. **6. Favonius:** the west wind. **8. lily . . . spun:** See Matt. 6:28. **10. Of . . . taste:** as at Athenian banquets. **12. Tuscan:** Florentine, Italian. **13. spare:** the context perhaps favors "spare time," but Milton's usage — and perhaps his character — favor "forbear." SONNET XXII. **1. this . . . day:** these last three years.

PARADISE LOST

[General critical comments on *Paradise Lost* are made in the Introduction. Some factual data are given here.

As early as 1639 Milton had in mind an epic on King Arthur, the kind of subject that would have been in accord with classical and Renaissance tradition, but he shifted to a subject of higher and more universal significance. He shifted also, for a time, to the idea of dramatic treatment and made some outlines for a drama; he returned, however, to the epic plan. The actual composition of *Paradise Lost* apparently began some time during the years 1655–58; the latter part of the invocation to Book VII obviously belongs to the Restoration period. Day and night were much alike to the blind poet, and, as he says several times, he composed at night. The first edition (1667) contained ten books; in the second edition (1674) the seventh and tenth books were each split into two and some small revisions were made.

Only portions of the poem can be given in this volume, and gaps in the narrative are filled in, after a fashion, by brief editorial summaries. Milton's arguments to the individual books are given for those books reprinted in full (I, II, and IX) and for Book IV; otherwise they are omitted.]

THE VERSE

The measure is English heroic verse without rhyme, as that of Homer in Greek and of Virgil in Latin, rhyme being no necessary adjunct or true ornament of poem or good verse, in longer works especially, but the invention of a barbarous age, to set off wretched matter and lame meter — graced indeed since by the use of some famous modern poets, carried away by custom, but much to their own vexation, hindrance, and constraint to express many things otherwise, and for the most part worse, than else they would have expressed them. Not without cause, therefore, some both Italian and Spanish poets of prime note have rejected rhyme both in longer and shorter works, as have also long since our best English tragedies, as a thing of itself, to all judicious ears, trivial and of no true musical delight; which consists only in apt numbers, fit quantity of syllables, and the sense variously drawn out from one verse into another, not in the jingling sound of like endings, a fault avoided by the learned ancients both in poetry and all good oratory. This neglect then of rhyme so little is to be taken for a defect, though it may seem so perhaps to vulgar readers, that it rather is to be esteemed an example set, the first in English, of ancient liberty recovered to heroic poem from the troublesome and modern bondage of rhyming.

BOOK I

THE ARGUMENT

This first book proposes, first in brief, the whole subject, man's disobedience, and the loss thereupon of Paradise wherein he was placed: then touches the prime cause of his fall, the Serpent, or rather Satan in the Serpent; who, revolting from God, and drawing to his side many legions of angels, was by the command of God driven out of Heaven with all his crew into the great Deep. Which action passed over, the poem hastes into the midst of things, presenting Satan with his angels now fallen into Hell — described here, not in the center (for Heaven and Earth may be supposed as yet not made, certainly not yet accursed), but in a place of utter darkness, fitliest called Chaos. Here Satan with his angels lying on the burning lake, thunderstruck and astonished, after a certain space recovers, as from confusion; calls up him who, next in order and dignity, lay by him; they confer of their miserable fall. Satan awakens all his legions, who lay till then in the same manner confounded. They rise: their numbers, array of battle, their chief leaders named, according to the idols known afterwards in Canaan and the countries adjoining. To these Satan directs his speech, comforts them with hope yet of regaining Heaven, but tells them lastly of a new world and new kind of creature to be created, according to an ancient prophecy or report in Heaven; for that angels were long before this visible creation, was the opinion of many ancient Fathers. To find out the truth of this prophecy, and what to determine thereon, he refers to a full council. What his associates thence attempt. Pandemonium, the palace of Satan, rises, suddenly built out of the Deep; the infernal peers there sit in council.

Of man's first disobedience, and the fruit
Of that forbidden tree, whose mortal° taste
Brought death into the world, and all our woe,
With loss of Eden, till one greater Man°
Restore us, and regain the blissful seat,
Sing, Heavenly Muse,° that on the secret° top
Of Oreb, or of Sinai,° didst inspire
That shepherd, who first taught the chosen seed
In the beginning how the Heavens and Earth
Rose out of Chaos; or if Sion hill°   10
Delight thee more, and Siloa's brook that flowed
Fast by the oracle of God, I thence
Invoke thy aid to my adventurous song,
That with no middle flight intends to soar
Above the Aonian mount,° while it pursues
Things unattempted yet in prose or rhyme.

PARADISE LOST. Book I: 2. **mortal**: the word may combine the sense of "human" with that of "deadly." 4. **one ... Man**: Christ, traditionally thought of as "the second Adam." 6. **Heavenly Muse**: Milton's invocations are not mere imitations of Homer and Virgil but prayers. See his account, in the *Reason of Church Government*, above (pp. 424–26), of the inspiration he craved. Urania, the Muse of astronomy, became for Renaissance writers the Muse of sacred poetry, and Milton associates her with the divine spirit that illuminated Moses ("That shepherd"), the supposed author of the first five books of the Bible, and the later Hebrew prophets. 6. **secret**: remote, mysterious. 7. **Oreb ... Sinai**: alternative names for the mountain north of the Red Sea, where Moses received the law from God. 10. **Sion hill**: Zion, the hill of Jerusalem on which, later, stood the temple ("the oracle of God"). 15. **Aonian mount**: Helicon, in Boeotia, the haunt of the Muses. As a Christian poet, Milton can hope for more than classical inspiration.

And chiefly thou, O Spirit,° that dost prefer
Before all temples the upright heart and pure,
Instruct me, for thou know'st; thou from the
    first
Wast present, and with mighty wings outspread
Dove-like sat'st brooding on the vast abyss   21
And mad'st it pregnant: what in me is dark
Illumine, what is low raise and support;
That to the highth° of this great argument°
I may assert Eternal Providence,
And justify the ways of God to men.
    Say first, for Heaven hides nothing from thy
    view,
Nor the deep tract of Hell, say first what cause
Moved our grand° parents in that happy state,
Favored of Heaven so highly, to fall off   30
From their Creator, and transgress his will
For one restraint, lords of the world besides?
Who first seduced them to that foul revolt?
The infernal Serpent; he it was, whose guile,
Stirred up with envy and revenge, deceived
The mother of mankind, what time his pride°
Had cast him out from Heaven, with all his host
Of rebel angels, by whose aid aspiring
To set himself in glory above his peers,
He trusted to have equaled the Most High,   40
If he opposed; and with ambitious aim
Against the throne and monarchy of God,
Raised impious war in Heaven and battle proud
With vain attempt. Him the Almighty Power
Hurled headlong flaming from the ethereal sky
With hideous ruin° and combustion down
To bottomless perdition, there to dwell
In adamantine chains and penal fire,
Who durst defy the Omnipotent to arms.
Nine times the space that measures day and night°
To mortal men, he with his horrid crew   51
Lay vanquished, rolling in the fiery gulf,
Confounded though immortal. But his doom
Reserved him to more wrath; for now° the thought
Both of lost happiness and lasting pain
Torments him; round he throws his baleful eyes,
That witnessed huge affliction and dismay
Mixed with obdúrate pride and steadfast hate.
At once as far as angels ken° he views
The dismal situation waste and wild: 60
A dungeon horrible on all sides round
As one great furnace flamed, yet from those flames

No light,° but rather darkness visible
Served only to discover sights of woe,
Regions of sorrow, doleful shades, where peace
And rest can never dwell, hope never comes
That comes to all; but torture without end
Still urges,° and a fiery deluge, fed
With ever-burning sulphur unconsumed:
Such place Eternal Justice had prepared   70
For those rebellious, here their prison ordained
In utter° darkness, and their portion set
As far removed from God and light of Heaven
As from the center° thrice to the utmost pole.°
O how unlike the place from whence they fell!
There the companions of his fall, o'erwhelmed
With floods and whirlwinds of tempestuous fire,
He soon discerns, and weltering by his side
One next himself in power, and next in crime,
Long after known in Palestine, and named   80
Beëlzebub. To whom the Arch-Enemy,
And thence in Heaven called Satan,° with bold
    words
Breaking the horrid silence thus began:
    "If thou beest he — but O how fallen! how
    changed
From him,° who in the happy realms of light
Clothed with transcendent brightness didst outshine
Myriads though bright — if he whom mutual
    league,
United thoughts and counsels, equal hope
And hazard in the glorious enterprise,
Joined with me once, now misery hath joined   90
In equal ruin: into what pit thou seest
From what highth fallen! so much the stronger
    proved
He with his thunder; and till then who knew
The force of those dire arms? Yet not for those,
Nor what the potent Victor in his rage
Can else inflict, do I repent or change,
Though changed in outward luster, that fixed mind
And high disdain, from sense of injured merit,
That with the Mightiest raised me to contend,
And to the fierce contention brought along   100
Innumerable force of spirits armed
That durst dislike his reign, and, me preferring,
His utmost power with adverse power opposed
In dubious battle on the plains of Heaven,
And shook his throne. What though the field be
    lost?
All is not lost; the unconquerable will,

---

17 f. Spirit: the creative spirit of God that "moved upon the
face of the waters" (Gen. 1:2) and later inspired his prophets.
24. highth: Milton preferred this form of the word. argument:
theme.   29. grand: first.   36. pride: the traditional motive of
Satan, irreligious and unbridled self-sufficiency and ambition.
46 ruin: fall (the Latin sense).   50. Nine . . . night: In the
myth of the Titans' war on the gods, the defeated Titans, hurled
from heaven by Zeus, fell nine days and nights to earth, and
nine more to hell.   54. for now: the transition from the general
statement of the theme to the epic action, which begins in medias
res.   59. ken: probably a verb ("see"), perhaps a noun ("angel's ken").

62–63. yet . . . light: In traditional belief the fires of Hell gave
no light.   68. urges: drives, afflicts.   72. utter: outer.   74. center: earth. pole: either end of the axis of the Ptolemaïc universe, pointing toward Heaven and Hell.   82. Satan: the name
means "adversary."   84–85. how . . . him: These words (to cite
one of Milton's countless echoes) seem to combine Isa. 14:12:
"How art thou fallen from heaven, O Lucifer, son of the morning," and Virgil's picture of the dead Hector appearing to Aeneas,
"quantum mutatus ab illo Hectore," "how changed from that Hector . . ." (Aeneid, II. 274). Satan's unfinished phrases (ll. 84–94)
reflect his agitation.

And study of revenge, immortal hate,
And courage never to submit or yield:
And what is else not to be overcome?°
That glory never shall his wrath or might   110
Extort from me. To bow and sue for grace
With suppliant knee, and deify his power
Who from the terror of this arm so late
Doubted his empire, that were low indeed,
That were an ignominy° and shame beneath
This downfall; since by fate the strength of gods
And this empyreal substance° cannot fail,
Since through experience of this great event,
In arms not worse, in foresight much advanced,
We may with more successful hope resolve   120
To wage by force or guile eternal war
Irreconcilable to our grand Foe,
Who now triumphs, and in the excess of joy
Sole reigning holds the tyranny of Heaven."
    So spake the apostate Angel, though in pain,
Vaunting aloud, but racked with deep despair;
And him thus answered soon his bold compeer:°
    "O Prince, O Chief of many thronèd Powers,
That led the embattled Seraphim° to war
Under thy conduct, and in dreadful deeds   130
Fearless, endangered Heaven's perpetual King,
And put to proof his high supremacy,
Whether upheld by strength, or chance, or fate;
Too well I see and rue the dire event,°
That with sad overthrow and foul defeat
Hath lost us Heaven, and all this mighty host
In horrible destruction laid thus low,
As far as gods and heavenly essences°
Can perish: for the mind and spirit remains
Invincible, and vigor soon returns,   140
Though all our glory extinct, and happy state
Here swallowed up in endless misery.
But what if he our Conqueror (whom I now
Of force° believe almighty, since no less
Than such could have o'erpowered such force as
        ours)
Have left us this our spirit and strength entire
Strongly to suffer and support our pains,
That we may so suffice his vengeful ire,
Or do him mightier service as his thralls
By right of war, whate'er his business be,   150
Here in the heart of Hell to work in fire,
Or do his errands in the gloomy deep?
What can it then avail, though yet we feel
Strength undiminished, or eternal being
To° undergo eternal punishment?"

Whereto with speedy words the Arch-Fiend re-
        plied:
"Fallen Cherub, to be weak is miserable,
Doing or suffering: but of this be sure,
To do aught good never will be our task,
But ever to do ill our sole delight,   160
As being the contrary to his high will
Whom we resist. If° then his providence
Out of our evil seek to bring forth good,
Our labor must be to pervert that end,
And out of good still° to find means of evil;
Which ofttimes may succeed, so as perhaps
Shall grieve him, if I fail° not, and disturb
His inmost counsels from their destined aim.
But see the angry Victor hath recalled
His ministers of vengeance and pursuit   170
Back to the gates of Heaven; the sulphurous hail
Shot after us in storm, o'erblown hath laid
The fiery surge, that from the precipice
Of Heaven received us falling, and the thunder,
Winged with red lightning and impetuous rage,
Perhaps hath spent his shafts, and ceases now
To bellow through the vast and boundless deep.
Let us not slip° the occasion, whether scorn
Or satiate fury yield it from our Foe.
Seest thou yon dreary plain, forlorn and wild,   180
The seat of desolation, void of light,
Save what the glimmering of these livid flames
Casts pale and dreadful? Thither let us tend
From off the tossing of these fiery waves,
There rest, if any rest can harbor there,
And reassembling our afflicted powers,°
Consult how we may henceforth most offend
Our Enemy, our own loss how repair,
How overcome this dire calamity,
What reinforcement we may gain from hope,   190
If not, what resolution from despair."
    Thus Satan talking to his nearest mate
With head uplift above the wave, and eyes
That sparkling blazed; his other parts besides,
Prone on the flood, extended long and large,
Lay floating many a rood, in bulk as huge
As whom the fables name of monstrous size,°
Titanian or Earth-born, that warred on Jove,
Briareos° or Typhon,° whom the den
By ancient Tarsus held, or that sea-beast   200
Leviathan,° which God of all his works
Created hugest that swim the ocean stream:
Him haply slumbering on the Norway foam,°

109. And . . . overcome: How can we be said to be overcome if
we still cherish our revengeful hatred and courage?   115. ignominy: pronounced "ignomy."   117. empyreal substance:
Heaven, the empyrean, and its inhabitants were composed of an
indestructible substance superior to that of man's world and
man.   127. compeer: companion.   129. Seraphim: In medieval
angelology there were nine orders, which were, from the highest
downward: Seraphim, Cherubim, Thrones; Dominations, Virtues, Powers; Principalities, Archangels, Angels; but Milton uses
the terms loosely.   134. event: outcome.   138. heavenly essences: See l. 117n.   144. Of force: perforce.   155. To: so as to.

162–65. If . . . evil: one of Milton's many reminders of his
central theme.   165. still: always.   167. fail: mistake.
178. slip: lose.   186. afflicted powers: overthrown forces.
197 f. See l. 5on. The Titans and Giants ("Earth-born") were often confused. Briareos was a hundred-handed Giant who helped
Zeus (Jove) against the Titans. Typhon or Typhoeus, a son of
Earth, was a hundred-headed serpent-monster of Cilicia (near
Tarsus) who attacked heaven and was imprisoned by Zeus beneath Mount Etna.   201. Leviathan: sea monster or whale
(Isa. 27:1).   203 f. The story of seamen's mistaking a whale
for an island was widespread in medieval literature; the whale

The pilot of some small night-foundered° skiff,

The pilot of some small night-foundered° skiff,
Deeming some island, oft, as seamen tell,
With fixèd anchor in his scaly rind
Moors by his side under the lee, while night
Invests the sea, and wishèd morn delays:
So stretched out huge in length the Arch-Fiend lay
Chained on the burning lake; nor ever thence   210
Had risen or heaved his head, but that the will
And high permission of all-ruling Heaven
Left him at large to his own dark designs,
That with reiterated crimes he might
Heap on himself damnation, while he sought
Evil to others, and enraged might see
How all his malice served but to bring forth
Infinite goodness, grace and mercy shown
On man by him seduced, but on himself   219
Treble confusion, wrath and vengeance poured.
  Forthwith upright he rears from off the pool
His mighty stature; on each hand the flames
Driven backward slope their pointing spires, and
  rolled
In billows, leave in the midst a horrid vale.
Then with expanded wings he steers his flight
Aloft, incumbent on the dusky air
That felt unusual weight, till on dry land
He lights, if it were land that ever burned
With solid, as the lake with liquid fire;
And such appeared in hue,° as when the force   230
Of subterranean wind transports a hill
Torn from Pelorus,° or the shattered side
Of thundering Etna, whose combustible
And fueled entrails thence conceiving fire,
Sublimed° with mineral fury, aid the winds,
And leave a singèd bottom all involved
With stench and smoke: such resting found the
  sole
Of unblest feet. Him followed his next mate,
Both glorying to have scaped the Stygian flood
As gods, and by their own recovered strength,   240
Not by the sufferance of supernal power.
  "Is this the region, this the soil, the clime,"
Said then the lost Archangel, "this the seat
That we must change for Heaven, this mournful
  gloom
For that celestial light? Be it so, since he
Who now is sovran° can dispose and bid
What shall be right: farthest from him is best,
Whom reason hath equaled, force hath made su-
  preme
Above his equals. Farewell, happy fields,
Where joy for ever dwells! Hail, horrors! hail,   250
Infernal world! and thou, profoundest Hell,
Receive thy new possessor; one who brings
A mind not to be changed by place or time.

The mind is its° own place, and in itself
Can make a Heaven of Hell, a Hell of Heaven.
What matter where, if I be still the same,
And what I should be, all but less than° he
Whom thunder hath made greater? Here° at
  least
We shall be free; the Almighty hath not built
Here for his envy, will not drive us hence: 260
Here we may reign secure, and in my choice
To reign is worth ambition, though in Hell:
Better to reign in Hell than serve in Heaven.
But wherefore let we then our faithful friends,
The associates and copartners of our loss,
Lie thus astonished° on the oblivious° pool,
And call them not to share with us their part
In this unhappy mansion, or once more
With rallied arms to try what may be yet
Regained in Heaven, or what more lost in Hell?"
  So Satan spake, and him Beëlzebub   271
Thus answered: "Leader of those armies bright,
Which but the Omnipotent none could have foiled,
If once they hear that voice, their liveliest pledge
Of hope in fears and dangers, heard so oft
In worst extremes, and on the perilous edge
Of battle when it raged, in all assaults
Their surest signal, they will soon resume
New courage and revive, though now they lie
Groveling and prostrate on yon lake of fire,   280
As we erewhile, astounded and amazed;°
No wonder, fallen such a pernicious° highth!"
  He scarce had ceased when the superior Fiend
Was moving toward the shore; his ponderous
  shield,
Ethereal° temper, massy, large, and round,
Behind him cast; the broad circumference
Hung on his shoulders like the moon, whose orb
Through optic glass° the Tuscan artist° views
At evening from the top of Fesole,°
Or in Valdarno,° to descry new lands,   290
Rivers or mountains in her spotty globe.
His spear, to equal which the tallest pine
Hewn on Norwegian hills, to be the mast
Of some great ammiral,° were but a wand,
He walked with, to support uneasy steps
Over the burning marl,° not like those steps
On Heaven's azure; and the torrid clime
Smote on him sore besides, vaulted with fire.
Nathless° he so endured, till on the beach

254. its: one of the three places in Milton's verse (see "Nativity," l. 106, and *PL*, IV. 813) where he uses "its"; ordinarily he uses "her" or "his." Satan's boast in lines 254–55 he later finds to be untrue (cf. IV. 75). 257. all . . . than: almost equal to. 258–63. Here . . . Heaven: one of Satan's many revelations of his false conception of freedom. 266. astonished: dazed. oblivious: causing forgetfulness. 281. amazed: stupefied. 282. pernicious: destructive. 285. Ethereal: heavenly. 288. optic glass: telescope. Tuscan artist: Galileo (d. 1642). 289. Fesole: Fiesole, a hill town near Florence. 290. Valdarno: the valley of the Arno river, in which Florence is situated. 294. ammiral: flagship. 296. marl: soil. 299. Nathless: nevertheless.

was sometimes allegorized as Satan.   204. night-foundered: benighted.   230. hue: appearance.   232. Pelorus: a Sicilian promontory.   235. Sublimed: made incandescent (from alchemy).   246. sovran: sovereign.

Of that inflamèd sea he stood and called   300
His legions, angel forms, who lay entranced,
Thick as autumnal leaves that strow the brooks
In Vallombrosa,° where the Etrurian shades
High over-arched embower; or scattered sedge
Afloat, when with fierce winds Orion° armed
Hath vexed the Red Sea coast, whose waves o'er-
    threw
Busiris° and his Memphian° chivalry,
While with perfidious hatred they pursued
The sojourners of Goshen,° who beheld
From the safe shore their floating carcasses   310
And broken chariot wheels; so thick bestrown,
Abject° and lost lay these, covering the flood,
Under amazement of their hideous change.
He called so loud, that all the hollow deep
Of Hell resounded: " Princes, Potentates,
Warriors, the flower of Heaven, once yours, now
    lost,
If such astonishment as this can seize
Eternal spirits! or have ye chosen this place
After the toil of battle to repose
Your wearied virtue, for the ease you find   320
To slumber here, as in the vales of Heaven?
Or in this abject posture have ye sworn
To adore the Conqueror, who now beholds
Cherub and Seraph rolling in the flood
With scattered arms and ensigns, till anon
His swift pursuers from Heaven gates discern
The advantage, and descending tread us down
Thus drooping, or with linkèd thunderbolts
Transfix us to the bottom of this gulf?
Awake, arise, or be forever fallen! "   330
    They heard, and were abashed, and up they
        sprung
Upon the wing, as when men wont to watch
On duty, sleeping found by whom they dread,
Rouse and bestir themselves ere well awake.
Nor did they not perceive the evil plight
In which they were, or the fierce pains not feel;
Yet to their general's voice they soon obeyed
Innumerable. As when the potent rod
Of Amram's son° in Egypt's evil day
Waved round the coast, up called a pitchy° cloud
Of locusts, warping° on the eastern wind,   341
That o'er the realm of impious Pharaoh hung
Like night, and darkened all the land of Nile:
So numberless were those bad angels seen
Hovering on wing under the cope° of Hell

'Twixt upper, nether, and surrounding fires;
Till, as a signal given, the uplifted spear
Of their great Sultan° waving to direct
Their course, in even balance down they light
On the firm brimstone, and fill all the plain;   350
A multitude like which the populous North
Poured never from her frozen loins, to pass
Rhene or the Danaw,° when her barbarous sons
Came like a deluge on the South, and spread
Beneath Gibraltar to the Libyan sands.
Forthwith from every squadron and each band
The heads and leaders thither haste where stood
Their great commander; godlike shapes and forms
Excelling human, princely dignities,   359
And powers that erst in Heaven sat on thrones;
Though of their names in heavenly records now
Be no memorial, blotted out and rased°
By their rebellion from the Books of Life.
Nor had they yet among the sons of Eve°
Got them new names, till wandering o'er the
    Earth,
Through God's high sufferance for the trial of
    man,
By falsities and lies the greatest part
Of mankind they corrupted to forsake
God their Creator, and the invisible
Glory of him that made them to transform   370
Oft to the image of a brute, adorned
With gay religions° full of pomp and gold,
And devils to adore for deities:
Then were they known to men by various names,
And various idols through the heathen world.
    Say, Muse, their names then known, who first,
        who last,
Roused from the slumber on that fiery couch,
At their great emperor's call, as next in worth
Came singly where he stood on the bare strand,
While the promiscuous crowd stood yet aloof.   380
    The chief were those who from the pit of Hell,
Roaming to seek their prey on Earth, durst fix
Their seats long after next the seat of God,
Their altars by his altar, gods adored
Among the nations round, and durst abide
Jehovah thundering out of Sion, throned
Between the Cherubim; yea, often placed
Within his sanctuary itself their shrines,
Abominations; and with cursèd things
His holy rites and solemn feasts profaned,   390
And with their darkness durst affront his light.
First Moloch,° horrid king besmeared with blood
Of human sacrifice, and parents' tears,
Though for the noise of drums and timbrels loud

---

303. Vallombrosa: a "shady valley" (very different from the fires of Hell) eighteen miles from Florence.   305. Orion: a constellation associated with storms.   307-11. Busiris . . . wheels: for the destruction of the Egyptians who were pursuing the Israelites, see Exod. 14:26-31. The name Busiris for Pharaoh perhaps came (as D. C. Allen suggests) from a universal history by the German theologian Melanchthon.   Memphian: Egyptian (from the city of Memphis).   309. Goshen: the Egyptian home of the Israelites.   312. Abject: thrown down.   339. Amram's son: Moses (see Exod. 10:12-15).   340. pitchy: black as pitch.   341. warping: tacking, veering.   345. cope: vault.

348. Sultan: the word recalls the age-old European fear of the Turks.   353. Rhene . . . Danaw: Rhine, Danube; a reference to the barbarian invasions of the Roman empire.   362. rased: erased.   364 f. Milton follows the tradition that the fallen angels became the pagan gods.   372. religions: rites.   392. Moloch: the name means "king." For the human sacrifices see II

Their children's cries unheard, that passed through fire
To his grim idol. Him the Ammonite°
Worshiped in Rabba and her watery plain,
In Argob and in Basan, to the stream
Of utmost Arnon. Nor content with such
Audacious neighborhood, the wisest heart   400
Of Solomon he led by fraud to build
His temple right against the temple of God
On that opprobrious hill,° and made his grove
The pleasant valley of Hinnom,° Tophet thence
And black Gehenna called, the type of Hell.
Next Chemos,° the obscene dread of Moab's sons,
From Aroer to Nebo, and the wild
Of southmost Abarim;° in Hesebon
And Horonaim, Seon's° realm, beyond
The flowery dale of Sibma clad with vines,   410
And Elealè to the Asphaltic pool:
Peor his other name, when he enticed
Israel in Sittim on their march from Nile
To do him wanton rites, which cost them woe.
Yet thence his lustful orgies he enlarged
Even to that hill of scandal,° by the grove
Of Moloch homicide, lust hard by hate;
Till good Josiah° drove them thence to Hell.
With these came they, who from the bordering flood
Of old Euphrates° to the brook that parts   420
Egypt from Syrian ground, had general names
Of Baalim° and Ashtaroth,° those male,
These feminine. For spirits° when they please
Can either sex assume, or both; so soft
And uncompounded is their essence pure,
Not tied or manacled with joint or limb,
Nor founded on the brittle strength of bones,
Like cumbrous flesh; but in what shape they choose,
Dilated or condensed, bright or obscure,
Can execute their aery purposes,   430
And works of love or enmity fulfil.
For those the race of Israel oft forsook
Their Living Strength, and unfrequented left
His righteous altar, bowing lowly down
To bestial gods; for which their heads as low

Bowed down in battle, sunk before the spear
Of despicable foes. With these in troop
Came Astoreth,° whom the Phoenicians called
Astarte, queen of heaven, with crescent horns;
To whose bright image nightly by the moon   440
Sidonian° virgins paid their vows and songs;
In Sion also not unsung, where stood
Her temple on the offensive mountain,° built
By that uxorious king° whose heart though large,
Beguiled by fair idolatresses, fell
To idols foul. Thammuz° came next behind,
Whose annual wound in Lebanon allured
The Syrian damsels to lament his fate
In amorous ditties all a summer's day,
While smooth Adonis° from his native rock   450
Ran purple to the sea, supposed with blood
Of Thammuz yearly wounded: the love-tale
Infected Sion's daughters with like heat,
Whose wanton passions in the sacred porch
Ezekiel saw, when by the vision led
His eye surveyed the dark idolatries
Of alienated Judah.° Next came one°
Who mourned in earnest, when the captive ark
Maimed his brute image, head and hands lopped off
In his own temple, on the grunsel° edge,   460
Where he fell flat, and shamed his worshipers:
Dagon his name, sea monster, upward man
And downward fish; yet had his temple high
Reared in Azotus, dreaded through the coast
Of Palestine, in Gath and Ascalon,
And Accaron and Gaza's° frontier bounds.
Him followed Rimmon,° whose delightful seat
Was fair Damascus, on the fertile banks
Of Abbana and Pharphar, lucid streams.
He also against the house of God was bold: 470
A leper° once he lost and gained a king,
Ahaz° his sottish conqueror, whom he drew
God's altar to disparage and displace
For one of Syrian mode, whereon to burn
His odious offerings, and adore the gods
Whom he had vanquished. After these appeared
A crew who under names of old renown,

Kings 23:10, Jer. 7:31, 19:1-6. **396. Ammonite:** The Ammonites were a nation east of the Jordan; Rabba was their capital. **403. opprobrious hill:** the Mount of Olives, where Solomon built heathen shrines (I Kings 11:7, II Kings 23:13). **404. Hinnom:** a valley (in Greek, Gehenna) near Jerusalem, where human sacrifices were offered to Moloch and where later rubbish was burned (see Biblical references in l. 392n., above). **406. Chemos:** a Moabite god, otherwise Baal-Peor (l. 412). See Num. 25. Moab was east of the Dead Sea ("the Asphaltic pool"). **408. Abarim:** hills, including Mount Nebo, east of the Dead Sea. **409. Seon:** Sihon, king of the Amorites, conquered by the Israelites. **416. hill of scandal:** Mount of Olives. See l. 403n., above. **418. Josiah:** See II Kings 23. **420. Euphrates:** the eastern boundary of Palestine. **422. Baalim, Ashtaroth:** See "Nativity," ll. 197-200, and *PL*, I. 438n., below. **423-31. spirits . . . fulfil:** This power possessed by the angels is utilized at later points in the poem.

438. Astoreth: a Phoenician moon goddess (pl. Ashtaroth), identified with Aphrodite and Venus. **441. Sidonian:** Sidon was a city on the Phoenician coast. **443. offensive mountain:** See l. 403n. and l. 416n., above. **444. that . . . king:** Solomon (I Kings 11:1-8). **446. Thammuz:** the Phoenician Adonis, whose annual death was mourned in seasonal rites. **450. Adonis:** the Syrian river, which was reddened by mud in spring floods. **455-57. Ezekiel . . . Judah:** See Ezek. 8:14-15. **457-66: one . . . bounds:** Dagon, a Philistine god, whose image fell before the ark of the Lord, which the Philistines had captured and placed in Dagon's temple (I Sam. 5:1-5). **460. grunsel:** ground sill. **464-66. Azotus . . . Gaza's:** the five main Philistine cities. **467. Rimmon:** a Syrian god. **471-76. A leper . . . vanquished:** Naaman, the Syrian general, when cured of leprosy by Elisha in the water of Jordan, accepted Israel's God (II Kings 5:1-19). **472. Ahaz:** the Jewish king who adopted the Syrian religion (II Kings 16).

Osiris, Isis, Orus,° and their train,
With monstrous shapes and sorceries abused°
Fanatic Egypt and her priests, to seek   480
Their wandering gods disguised in brutish forms
Rather than human. Nor did Israel scape
The infection when their borrowed gold composed
The calf in Oreb;° and the rebel king
Doubled that sin in Bethel and in Dan,°
Likening his Maker to the grazèd ox —
Jehovah, who in one night when he passed
From Egypt marching, equaled with one stroke
Both her first-born and all her bleating gods.°
Belial° came last, than whom a spirit more lewd
Fell not from Heaven, or more gross to love   491
Vice for itself. To him no temple stood
Or altar smoked; yet who more oft than he
In temples and at altars, when the priest
Turns atheist, as did Eli's sons,° who filled
With lust and violence the house of God?
In courts and palaces he also reigns
And in luxurious° cities, where the noise
Of riot ascends above their loftiest towers,
And injury and outrage; and when night   500
Darkens the streets, then wander forth the sons
Of Belial,° flown° with insolence and wine.
Witness the streets of Sodom,° and that night
In Gibeah,° when the hospitable door
Exposed a matron to avoid worse rape.
These were the prime in order and in might;
The rest were long to tell, though far renowned,
The Ionian gods, of Javan's° issue held
Gods, yet confessed later than Heaven° and Earth,
Their boasted parents; Titan, Heaven's first-born,
With his enormous brood, and birthright seized
By younger Saturn; he from mightier Jove,   512
His own and Rhea's son, like measure found;
So Jove usurping reigned. These, first in Crete
And Ida° known, thence on the snowy top
Of cold Olympus ruled the middle air,°

478. Osiris ... Orus: See "Nativity," ll. 212–13n. 479. abused: deceived. 482–84. Nor ... Oreb: Aaron made a golden calf as an idol (Exod. 12:35–36, 32:4). 484–85. king ... Dan: Jereboam, leader of ten revolting tribes of Israel, set up two golden calves for worship (I Kings 12). 487–89. Jehovah ... gods: When the Israelites were not allowed to leave Egypt, the Lord smote the first-born of every Egyptian and of his beasts, and the Egyptian animal gods (Exod. 12:12). 490. Belial: not properly a god; the name is an abstract term meaning "worthlessness." 495. Eli's sons: See I Sam. 2:12–25. 498. luxurious: lewd. 500–02. "The sons of Eli were sons of Belial" (I Sam. 2:12). "Sons of Belial" had often been applied by Puritans to their Cavalier enemies; Milton is thinking of young roisterers in London. 502. flown: overflowing, swollen. 503–04. Sodom, Gibeah: See Gen. 19:4–11, Judg. 19:22–28. 508. Javan: son of Japheth or Japhet (Gen. 10:2), supposed progenitor of the Ionians or Greeks. 509–14. Heaven ... reigned: Heaven and Earth were the primordial Greek deities and parents of the Titans; in Milton's version, one, Titan, was dethroned by his brother Saturn, who in turn was dethroned by Jove, son of Saturn and Rhea. 515. Ida: Jove was born and reared on Mount Ida in Crete. 516. middle air: See "Nativity," l. 164n.

Their highest Heaven; or on the Delphian cliff,°
Or in Dodona,° and through all the bounds
Of Doric° land; or who with Saturn old
Fled over Adria to the Hesperian fields,°   520
And o'er the Celtic° roamed the utmost isles.°
    All these and more came flocking; but with looks
Downcast and damp, yet such wherein appeared
Obscure some glimpse of joy, to have found their
    Chief
Not in despair, to have found themselves not lost
In loss itself; which on his countenance cast
Like doubtful hue. But he, his wonted pride
Soon recollecting, with high words, that bore
Semblance of worth, not substance, gently raised
Their fainting courage, and dispelled their fears.
Then straight commands that, at the warlike sound
Of trumpets loud and clarions, be upreared   532
His mighty standard; that proud honor claimed
Azazel as his right, a Cherub tall;
Who forthwith from the glittering staff unfurled
The imperial ensign, which full high advanced
Shone like a meteor streaming to the wind,
With gems and golden luster rich emblazed,
Seraphic arms and trophies; all the while
Sonorous metal blowing martial sounds;   540
At which the universal host upsent
A shout that tore Hell's concave, and beyond
Frighted the reign° of Chaos° and old Night.°
All in a moment through the gloom were seen
Ten thousand banners rise into the air
With orient° colors waving; with them rose
A forest huge of spears; and thronging helms
Appeared, and serried° shields in thick array
Of depth immeasurable. Anon they move
In perfect phalanx to the Dorian° mood   550
Of flutes and soft recorders; such as raised
To highth of noblest temper heroes old
Arming to battle, and instead of rage
Deliberate valor breathed, firm and unmoved
With dread of death to flight or foul retreat,
Nor wanting power to mitigate and swage°
With solemn touches troubled thoughts, and chase
Anguish and doubt and fear and sorrow and pain
From mortal or immortal minds. Thus they,
Breathing united force with fixèd thought,   560
Moved on in silence to soft pipes that charmed
Their painful steps o'er the burnt soil; and now
Advanced in view they stand, a horrid° front

517–18. Delphian cliff, Dodona: the oracle of Apollo at Delphi on Mount Parnassus and that of Zeus (Jove) at Dodona in Epirus. 519. Doric: Greek (strictly the southern half of Greece). 519–20. Saturn ... fields: Saturn was said to have crossed the Adriatic Sea to Italy (the "Hesperian" or "western" fields), where his reign was a golden age. 521. Celtic: French. isles: British Isles. 543. reign: realm. Chaos: for this personification see PL, II. 894–95, 907–09, 959 ff. Night: a classical personification. 546. orient: bright. 548. serried: interlocked. 550. Dorian: Spartan, manly. Lines 549–60 seem to be based on Plutarch's account (Lycurgus) of the Spartans marching. 556. swage: assuage. 563. horrid: bristling.

Of dreadful length and dazzling arms, in guise
Of warriors old with ordered spear and shield,
Awaiting what command their mighty Chief
Had to impose. He through the armèd files
Darts his experienced eye, and soon traverse°
The whole battalion views, their order due,
Their visages and stature as of gods;   570
Their number last he sums. And now his heart
Distends with pride, and hardening in his strength
Glories; for never, since created man,°
Met such embodied force as named with these
Could merit more than that small infantry°
Warred on by cranes: though all the giant brood
Of Phlegra° with the heroic race were joined
That fought at Thebes and Ilium,° on each side
Mixed with auxiliar gods; and what resounds
In fable or romance of Uther's son°   580
Begirt with British and Armoric° knights;
And all who since, baptized or infidel,
Jousted in Aspramont or Montalban,°
Damasco, or Marocco, or Trebisond,°
Or whom Biserta° sent from Afric shore
When Charlemain with all his peerage fell°
By Fontarabbia.° Thus far these beyond
Compare of mortal prowess, yet observed°
Their dread commander. He above the rest
In shape and gesture proudly eminent   590
Stood like a tower; his form had yet not lost
All her° original brightness, nor appeared
Less than Archangel ruined, and the excess
Of glory obscured: as when the sun new risen
Looks through the horizontal misty air
Shorn of his beams, or from behind the moon
In dim eclipse disastrous twilight sheds
On half the nations, and with fear of change
Perplexes monarchs. Darkened so, yet shone
Above them all the Archangel; but his face   600
Deep scars of thunder had intrenched, and care
Sat on his faded cheek, but under brows
Of dauntless courage, and considerate° pride
Waiting revenge. Cruel his eye, but cast
Signs of remorse and passion to behold

The fellows of his crime, the followers rather
(Far other once beheld in bliss), condemned
For ever now to have their lot in pain,
Millions of spirits for his fault amerced°
Of Heaven, and from eternal splendors flung   610
For his revolt, yet faithful how they stood,
Their glory withered: as when Heaven's fire
Hath scathed° the forest oaks or mountain pines,
With singèd top their stately growth though bare
Stands on the blasted heath. He now prepared
To speak; whereat their doubled ranks they bend
From wing to wing, and half enclose him round
With all his peers: attention held them mute.
Thrice he assayed,° and thrice in spite of scorn,
Tears such as angels weep burst forth; at last 620
Words interwove with sighs found out their way:
"O myriads of immortal spirits, O Powers
Matchless, but with the Almighty, and that strife
Was not inglorious, though the event° was dire,
As this place testifies, and this dire change
Hateful to utter. But what power of mind
Foreseeing or presaging, from the depth
Of knowledge past or present, could have feared
How such united force of gods, how such
As stood like these, could ever know repulse? 630
For who can yet believe, though after loss,
That all these puissant legions, whose exile
Hath emptied Heaven, shall fail to re-ascend
Self-raised, and repossess their native seat?
For me, be witness all the host of Heaven,
If counsels different, or danger shunned
By me, have lost our hopes. But he who reigns
Monarch in Heaven, till then as one secure
Sat on his throne, upheld by old repute,
Consent or custom, and his regal state   640
Put forth at full, but still his strength concealed,
Which tempted our attempt, and wrought our fall.
Henceforth his might we know, and know our
    own,
So as not either to provoke, or dread
New war, provoked; our better part remains
To work° in close° design, by fraud or guile,
What force effected not; that he no less
At length from us may find, who overcomes
By force hath overcome but half his foe.   649
Space may produce new worlds; whereof so rife
There went a fame° in Heaven that he ere long
Intended to create, and therein plant
A generation, whom his choice regard
Should favor equal to the sons of Heaven.
Thither, if but to pry, shall be perhaps
Our first eruption, thither or elsewhere;
For this infernal pit shall never hold
Celestial spirits in bondage, nor the abyss

---

568. **traverse:** across.   573. **created man:** the creation of man
(a Latinism).   575. **small infantry:** the Pygmies, who were
warred on by cranes (*Iliad*, III. 3–6).   577. **Phlegra:** the scene,
in Macedonia, of the battle between the Olympian gods and the
Giants.   578. **Thebes, Ilium:** such warriors as the "seven" who
attacked Thebes and those who fought at Troy.   580. **Uther's
son:** King Arthur.   581. **Armoric:** of Brittany, a region important in Arthurian story.   583. **Aspramont, Montalban:**
places in southern France that figure in romances of Charlemagne (the two names carry transverse rhyme and assonance).
584. **Trebisond:** on the Black Sea.   585. **Biserta:** the Tunisian
seaport, where, in romance, Saracens assembled to attack
Charlemagne.   586. **Charlemain . . . fell:** was utterly defeated
(Charlemagne himself was not killed).   587. **Fontarabbia:** on
the French-Spanish border where, according to some writers,
the famous Roland was killed (the common tradition put his
death at Roncesvalles).   588. **observed:** paid reverence to.
592. **her:** See l 254n., above.   603. **considerate:** based on deliberation.

609. **amerced:** punished with the loss of.   613. **scathed:** damaged.   619. **assayed:** essayed, tried.   624. **event:** outcome.
646. **work:** achieve.   **close:** secret.   651. **fame:** rumor.

Long under darkness cover. But these thoughts
Full counsel must mature. Peace is despaired,° 660
For who can think submission? War then, war
Open or understood,° must be resolved."

He spake; and to confirm his words, out flew
Millions of flaming swords, drawn from the thighs
Of mighty Cherubim; the sudden blaze
Far round illumined Hell. Highly they raged
Against the Highest, and fierce with graspèd arms
Clashed on their sounding shields the din of war,
Hurling defiance toward the vault of Heaven.

There stood a hill not far, whose grisly top   670
Belched fire and rolling smoke; the rest entire
Shone with a glossy scurf, undoubted sign
That in his womb was hid metallic ore,
The work of sulphur.° Thither winged with speed
A numerous brígade hastened: as when bands
Of pioneers° with spade and pickaxe armed
Forerun the royal camp, to trench a field,
Or cast a rampart. Mammon° led them on,
Mammon, the least erected° spirit that fell
From Heaven, for even in Heaven his looks and
    thoughts   680
Were always downward bent, admiring more
The riches of Heaven's pavement, trodden gold,
Than aught divine or holy else enjoyed
In vision beatific. By him first
Men also, and by his suggestion taught,
Ransacked the center,° and with impious hands
Rifled the bowels of their mother Earth
For treasures better hid. Soon had his crew
Opened into the hill a spacious wound
And digged out ribs of gold. Let none admire°
That riches grow in Hell; that soil may best   691
Deserve the precious bane. And here let those
Who boast in mortal things, and wondering tell
Of Babel,° and the works of Memphian kings,°
Learn how their greatest monuments of fame,
And strength and art, are easily outdone
By spirits reprobate, and in an hour
What in an age they with incessant toil
And hands innumerable scarce perform.
Nigh on the plain in many cells prepared,   700
That underneath had veins of liquid fire
Sluiced from the lake, a second multitude
With wondrous art founded the massy ore,°
Severing each kind, and scummed the bullion dross.
A third as soon had formed within the ground
A various mold, and from the boiling cells
By strange conveyance filled each hollow nook,
As in an organ from one blast of wind

To many a row of pipes the sound-board breathes.
Anon out of the earth a fabric huge   710
Rose like an exhalation,° with the sound
Of dulcet symphonies and voices sweet,
Built like a temple, where pilasters round
Were set, and Doric pillars overlaid
With golden architrave; nor did there want
Cornice or frieze, with bossy° sculptures graven;
The roof was fretted gold.° Not Babylon,
Nor great Alcairo° such magnificence
Equaled in all their glories, to enshrine
Belus° or Serapis° their gods, or seat   720
Their kings, when Egypt with Assyria strove
In wealth and luxury. The ascending pile
Stood fixed her stately highth, and straight the
    doors
Opening their brazen folds discover, wide
Within, her ample spaces, o'er the smooth
And level pavement; from the archèd roof,
Pendent by subtle magic, many a row
Of starry lamps and blazing cressets,° fed
With naphtha and asphaltus, yielded light
As from a sky. The hasty multitude   730
Admiring entered, and the work some praise,
And some the architect: his hand was known
In Heaven by many a towered structure high,
Where sceptered angels held their residence,
And sat as princes, whom the supreme King
Exalted to such power, and gave to rule,
Each in his hierarchy, the orders bright.
Nor was his name unheard or unadored
In ancient Greece, and in Ausonian° land
Men called him Mulciber;° and how he fell   740
From Heaven, they fabled, thrown by angry Jove
Sheer o'er the crystal battlements: from morn
To noon he fell, from noon to dewy eve,
A summer's day; and with the setting sun
Dropped from the zenith like a falling star,
On Lemnos the Aegean isle. Thus they relate,
Erring; for he with this rebellious rout°
Fell long before; nor aught availed him now
To have built in Heaven high towers; nor did he
    scape
By all his engines,° but was headlong sent   750
With his industrious crew to build in Hell.

    Meanwhile the wingèd heralds by command
Of sovran power, with awful ceremony
And trumpet's sound, throughout the host proclaim
A solemn council forthwith to be held
At Pandemonium,° the high capitol

---

660. despaired: despaired of.   662. understood: by us in secret.
674. sulphur: In alchemy, metals were believed to be products of
sulphur and mercury.   676. pioneers: sappers.   678. Mammon: an abstract word meaning "riches" (Matt. 6:24), but
personified in medieval tradition.   679. erected: elevated.
686. center: earth.   690. admire: wonder.   694. Babel: See
Gen. 10:10, 11:1-9. works . . . kings: Egyptian pyramids.
703. founded . . . ore: extracted the heavy or solid metal.

711. exhalation: vapor.   716. bossy: embossed.   717. fretted
gold: gold wrought in designs.   718. Alcairo: Cairo (for Memphis, the old capital).   720. Belus: a Babylonian god (Baal).
Serapis: the Egyptian Osiris as god of the underworld.
728. cressets: hanging lamps.   739. Ausonian: Italian.
740. Mulciber: the Greek god Hephaestus (Vulcan), whom his
father Zeus threw out of heaven (Iliad, I. 590-94).   747. rout:
mob.   750. engines: contrivances.   756. Pandemonium:
"place of all the demons" (apparently a Miltonic coinage).

Of Satan and his peers; their summons called
From every band and squarèd regiment
By place or choice the worthiest; they anon
With hundreds and with thousands trooping came
Attended. All access was thronged, the gates   761
And porches wide, but chief the spacious hall
(Though like a covered field, where champions
          bold
Wont° ride in armed, and at the Soldan's chair
Defied the best of paynim chivalry
To mortal combat or career with lance)
Thick swarmed, both on the ground and in the air,
Brushed with the hiss of rustling wings. As bees
In springtime, when the sun with Taurus° rides,
Pour forth their populous youth about the hive
In clusters; they among fresh dews and flowers
Fly to and fro, or on the smoothèd plank,   772
The suburb of their straw-built citadel,
New rubbed with balm, expatiate° and confer°
Their state affairs. So thick the aery crowd
Swarmed and were straitened;° till the signal given,
Behold a wonder! they but now who seemed
In bigness to surpass Earth's giant sons,
Now less than smallest dwarfs, in narrow room
Throng numberless, like that Pygmean race   780
Beyond the Indian mount,° or fairy elves,°
Whose midnight revels, by a forest side
Or fountain, some belated peasant sees,
Or dreams he sees, while overhead the moon
Sits arbitress,° and nearer to the Earth
Wheels her pale course; they on their mirth and
          dance
Intent, with jocund music charm his ear;
At once with joy and fear his heart rebounds.
Thus incorporeal spirits to smallest forms
Reduced their shapes immense, and were at large,°
Though without number still, amidst the hall   791
Of that infernal court. But far within,
And in their own dimensions like themselves,
The great Seraphic Lords and Cherubim
In close recess and secret conclave sat,
A thousand demi-gods on golden seats,
Frequent° and full. After short silence then
And summons read, the great consult° began.

BOOK II

THE ARGUMENT

The consultation begun, Satan debates whether another battle be to be hazarded for the recovery of
Heaven: some advise it, others dissuade. A third pro-

posal is preferred, mentioned before by Satan, to search
the truth of that prophecy or tradition in Heaven concerning another world, and another kind of creature,
equal or not much inferior to themselves, about this
time to be created. Their doubt who shall be sent on
this difficult search; Satan, their chief, undertakes
alone the voyage; is honored and applauded. The council thus ended, the rest betake them several ways and
to several employments, as their inclinations lead them,
to entertain the time till Satan return. He passes on
his journey to Hell gates, finds them shut, and who
sat there to guard them; by whom at length they are
opened, and discover to him the great gulf between
Hell and Heaven; with what difficulty he passes
through, directed by Chaos, the Power of that place, to
the sight of this new world which he sought.

High on a throne of royal state,° which far
Outshone the wealth of Ormus° and of Ind,°
Or where the gorgeous East with richest hand
Showers on her kings barbaric pearl and gold,
Satan exalted sat, by merit raised
To that bad eminence; and from despair
Thus high uplifted beyond hope, aspires
Beyond thus high, insatiate to pursue
Vain war with Heaven, and by success° untaught,
His proud imaginations thus displayed: 10
     "Powers and Dominions, Deities of Heaven,
For since no deep within her gulf can hold
Immortal vigor, though oppressed and fallen,
I give° not Heaven for lost. From this descent
Celestial Virtues° rising will appear
More glorious and more dread than from no fall,
And trust themselves to fear no second fate.
Me though just right and the fixed laws of Heaven
Did first create your leader, next, free choice,
With what besides, in counsel or in fight,   20
Hath been achieved of merit, yet this loss,
Thus far at least recovered, hath much more
Established in a safe unenvied throne
Yielded with full consent. The happier state
In Heaven, which follows dignity,° might draw
Envy from each inferior; but who here
Will envy whom the highest place exposes
Foremost to stand against the Thunderer's° aim
Your bulwark, and condemns to greatest share
Of endless pain? Where there is then no good   30
For which to strive, no strife can grow up there
From faction; for none sure will claim in Hell
Precedence, none whose portion is so small
Of present pain, that with ambitious mind
Will covet more. With this advantage then
To union, and firm faith, and firm accord,

---

764. Wont: were wont to.   769. Taurus: the sun is in the zodiacal sign of Taurus the Bull in April and May.   774. expatiate:
walk abroad. confer: discuss.   776. straitened: crowded.
780-81. Pygmean . . . mount: the Pygmies were supposed to live
in central Asia.   781-88. fairy elves . . . rebounds: Milton is
recalling A Midsummer Night's Dream and Virgil, Aeneid,
VI. 450-55.   785. arbitress: witness.   790. at large: not
crowded.   797. Frequent: in a crowd.   798. consult: debate.

Book II: 1-4. Artificial luxury is, as usual, a symbol of evil.
2. Ormus: a famous trading port in the Persian Gulf.   Ind:
India.   9. success: outcome.   14. give: count.   15. Virtues:
the word has both a general and a special sense. See I.129n.
25. dignity: worth.   28. the Thunderer: the epithet, an echo of
the Roman poets' Jupiter Tonans, is a crude conception in
keeping with Satan's perverted view of God, "just right,"
"merit." etc.

More than can be in Heaven, we now return
To claim our just inheritance of old,
Surer to prosper than prosperity
Could have assured us; and by what best way,   40
Whether of open war or covert guile,
We now debate; who can advise, may speak."

He ceased, and next him Moloch, sceptered king,
Stood up, the strongest and the fiercest spirit
That fought in Heaven, now fiercer by despair.
His trust was with the Eternal to be deemed
Equal in strength, and rather than be less
Cared not to be at all; with that care lost
Went all his fear: of God, or Hell, or worse
He recked not, and these words thereafter spake:
"My sentence° is for open war. Of wiles,   51
More unexpert,° I boast not: them let those
Contrive who need, or when they need, not now.
For while they sit contriving, shall the rest,
Millions that stand in arms, and longing wait
The signal to ascend, sit lingering here,
Heaven's fugitives, and for their dwelling-place
Accept this dark opprobrious den of shame,
The prison of his tyranny who reigns
By our delay? No, let us rather choose,   60
Armed with Hell flames and fury, all at once
O'er Heaven's high towers to force resistless way,
Turning our tortures into horrid arms
Against the Torturer; when to meet the noise
Of his almighty engine° he shall hear
Infernal thunder, and for lightning see
Black fire and horror shot with equal rage
Among his angels, and his throne itself
Mixed° with Tartarean° sulphur and strange fire,
His own invented torments. But perhaps   70
The way seems difficult and steep to scale
With upright wing against a higher foe.°
Let such bethink them, if the sleepy drench°
Of that forgetful lake° benumb not still,
That in our proper motion we ascend
Up to our native seat; descent and fall
To us is adverse.° Who but felt of late,
When the fierce foe hung on our broken rear
Insulting, and pursued us through the deep,
With what compulsion and laborious flight   80
We sunk thus low? The ascent is easy then;
The event° is feared! Should we again provoke
Our stronger, some worse way his wrath may find
To our destruction, if there be in Hell
Fear to be worse destroyed: what can be worse
Than to dwell here, driven out from bliss, con-
    demned

In this abhorrèd deep to utter woe;
Where pain of unextinguishable fire
Must exercise° us without hope of end
The vassals of his anger, when the scourge   90
Inexorably, and the torturing hour,
Calls us to penance? More destroyed than thus,
We should be quite abolished and expire.
What fear we then? what° doubt we to incense
His utmost ire? which to the highth enraged,
Will either quite consume us, and reduce
To nothing this essential,° happier far
Than miserable to have eternal being;
Or if our substance be indeed divine,
And cannot cease to be, we are at worst   100
On this side nothing; and by proof we feel
Our power sufficient to disturb his Heaven,
And with perpetual inroads to alarm,
Though inaccessible, his fatal° throne;
Which if not victory is yet revenge."

He ended frowning, and his look denounced°
Desperate revenge, and battle dangerous
To less than gods. On the other side up rose
Belial, in act more graceful and humane;°
A fairer person lost not Heaven; he seemed   110
For dignity composed and high exploit:
But all was false and hollow, though his tongue
Dropped manna, and could make the worse appear
The better reason, to perplex and dash°
Maturest counsels: for his thoughts were low;
To vice industrious, but to nobler deeds
Timorous and slothful: yet he pleased the ear,
And with persuasive accent thus began:
"I should be much for open war, O Peers,
As not behind in hate, if what was urged   120
Main reason to persuade immediate war
Did not dissuade me most, and seem to cast
Ominous conjecture on the whole success:
When he who most excels in fact° of arms,
In what he counsels and in what excels
Mistrustful, grounds his courage on despair
And utter dissolution, as the scope
Of all his aim, after some dire revenge.
First, what revenge? The towers of Heaven are
    filled
With armèd watch, that render all access   130
Impregnable; oft on the bordering deep
Encamp their legions, or with obscure wing
Scout far and wide into the realm of Night,
Scorning surprise. Or could we break our way
By force, and at our heels all Hell should rise
With blackest insurrection, to confound
Heaven's purest light, yet our great Enemy
All incorruptible would on his throne
Sit unpolluted, and the ethereal mold°

---

51. sentence: vote.   52. unexpert: inexperienced.   65. engine:
thunderbolt.   69. Mixed: confounded.   Tartarean: Tartarus
was one of the classical names for hell.   70–72: But . . . foe:
Here, and in ll. 82–85, Moloch anticipates objections.   73. sleepy
drench: drink causing sleep.   74. forgetful lake: causing forgetfulness, like the mythological river Lethe. Cf. I. 266, II. 583.
77. adverse: contrary to our nature.   82. event: outcome.

89. exercise: torment.   94. what: why.   97. essential: essence.
104. fatal: upheld by fate.   106. denounced: threatened.
109. humane: urbane.   114. dash: frustrate.   124. fact: feat.
139. mold: substance.

Incapable of stain would soon expel   140
Her mischief, and purge off the baser fire,
Victorious. Thus repulsed, our final hope
Is flat despair; we must exasperate
The almighty Victor to spend all his rage,
And that must end us, that must be our cure,
To be no more. Sad cure! for who would lose,
Though full of pain, this intellectual being,
Those thoughts that wander through eternity,
To perish rather, swallowed up and lost
In the wide womb of uncreated Night,   150
Devoid of sense and motion? And who knows,
Let° this be good, whether our angry Foe
Can give it, or will ever? How he can
Is doubtful; that he never will is sure.
Will he, so wise, let loose at once his ire,
Belike° through impotence, or unaware,
To give his enemies their wish, and end
Them in his anger, whom his anger saves
To punish endless? ' Wherefore cease we then? '
Say they who counsel war; ' we are decreed,   160
Reserved, and destined to eternal woe;
Whatever doing, what can we suffer more,
What can we suffer worse? ' Is this then worst,
Thus sitting, thus consulting, thus in arms?
What when we fled amain,° pursued and strook
With Heaven's afflicting thunder, and besought
The deep to shelter us? this Hell then seemed
A refuge from those wounds. Or when we lay
Chained on the burning lake? that sure was worse.
What if the breath that kindled those grim fires,
Awaked, should blow them into sevenfold rage
And plunge us in the flames? or from above   172
Should intermitted vengeance arm again
His red right hand to plague us? What if all
Her stores were opened, and this firmament
Of Hell should spout her cataracts of fire,
Impendent horrors, threatening hideous fall
One day upon our heads; while we perhaps
Designing or exhorting glorious war,
Caught in a fiery tempest shall be hurled   180
Each on his rock transfixed, the sport and prey
Of racking° whirlwinds, or forever sunk
Under yon boiling ocean, wrapped in chains,
There to converse° with everlasting groans,
Unrespited, unpitied, unreprieved,
Ages of hopeless end? this would be worse.
War therefore, open or concealed, alike
My voice dissuades; for what can° force or guile
With him, or who deceive his mind, whose eye
Views all things at one view? He from Heaven's
    highth   190
All these our motions° vain, sees and derides;
Not more almighty to resist our might

Than wise to frustrate all our plots and wiles.
Shall we then live thus vile, the race of Heaven
Thus trampled, thus expelled to suffer here
Chains and these torments? Better these than
    worse,
By my advice; since fate inevitable
Subdues us, and omnipotent decree,
The Victor's will. To suffer, as to do,
Our strength is equal, nor the law unjust   200
That so ordains: this was at first resolved,
If we were wise, against so great a foe
Contending, and so doubtful what might fall.°
I laugh when those who at the spear are bold
And venturous, if that fail them, shrink and fear
What yet they know must follow, to endure
Exile, or ignominy,° or bonds, or pain,
The sentence of their Conqueror. This is now
Our doom; which if we can sustain and bear,
Our supreme Foe in time may much remit   210
His anger, and perhaps, thus far removed,
Not mind us not offending, satisfied
With what is punished; whence these raging fires
Will slacken, if his breath stir not their flames.
Our purer essence then will overcome
Their noxious vapor, or inured not feel,
Or changed at length, and to the place conformed
In temper and in nature, will receive
Familiar the fierce heat, and void of pain;
This horror will grow mild, this darkness light,
Besides what hope the never-ending flight   221
Of future days may bring, what chance, what
    change
Worth waiting, since our present lot appears
For happy° though but ill, for ill not worst,
If we procure not to ourselves more woe.
    Thus Belial with words clothed in reason's garb,
Counseled ignoble ease, and peaceful sloth,
Not peace; and after him thus Mammon spake:
" Either to disenthrone the King of Heaven
We war, if war be best, or to regain   230
Our own right lost. Him to unthrone we then
May hope, when everlasting Fate shall yield
To fickle Chance, and Chaos judge the strife:
The former,° vain to hope, argues as vain
The latter;° for what place can be for us
Within Heaven's bound, unless Heaven's Lord su-
    preme
We overpower? Suppose he should relent
And publish grace to all, on promise made
Of new subjection; with what eyes could we
Stand in his presence humble, and receive   240
Strict laws imposed, to celebrate his throne
With warbled hymns, and to his Godhead sing
Forced halleluiahs; while he lordly sits

---

152. Let: granted.   **156. Belike:** doubtless (ironical).
165. amain: with all speed.   **182. racking:** driving, torturing.
184. converse: live.   **188. can:** can achieve.   **191. motions:** schemes.

203. fall: befall.   **207. ignominy:** see I. 115n.   **224. For happy:** in comparison with happiness.   **234. The former:** to dethrone God.   **235. The latter:** to regain our rights.

Our envied Sovran, and his altar breathes
Ambrosial odors and ambrosial flowers,
Our servile offerings? This must be our task
In Heaven, this our delight; how wearisome
Eternity so spent in worship paid
To whom we hate. Let° us not then pursue,
By force impossible, by leave obtained   250
Unácceptable, though in Heaven, our state
Of splendid vassalage, but rather seek
Our own good from ourselves, and from our own
Live to ourselves, though in this vast recess,
Free, and to none accountable, preferring
Hard liberty before the easy yoke
Of servile pomp. Our greatness will appear
Then most conspicuous, when great things of
    small,
Useful of hurtful, prosperous of adverse
We can create, and in what place soe'er   260
Thrive under evil, and work ease out of pain
Through labor and endurance. This deep world
Of darkness do we dread? How oft amidst
Thick clouds and dark doth Heaven's all-ruling
    Sire
Choose to reside, his glory unobscured,
And with the majesty of darkness round
Covers his throne, from whence deep thunders roar,
Mustering their rage, and Heaven resembles Hell!
As he our darkness, cannot we his light
Imitate when we please? This desert soil   270
Wants° not her hidden luster, gems and gold;
Nor want we skill or art, from whence to raise
Magnificence; and what can Heaven show more?
Our torments also may in length of time
Become our elements,° these piercing fires
As soft as now severe, our temper changed
Into their temper; which must needs remove
The sensible° of pain. All things invite
To peaceful counsels, and the settled state
Of order, how in safety best we may   280
Compose our present evils, with regard
Of what we are and where, dismissing quite
All thoughts of war. Ye have what I advise."
    He scarce had finished, when such murmur filled
The assembly, as when hollow rocks retain
The sound of blustering winds, which all night
    long
Had roused the sea, now with hoarse cadence lull
Seafaring men o'erwatched,° whose bark by chance
Or pinnace anchors in a craggy bay
After the tempest. Such applause was heard   290
As Mammon ended, and his sentence pleased,

Advising peace; for such another field°
They dreaded worse than Hell: so much the fear
Of thunder and the sword of Michaël°
Wrought still within them; and no less desire
To found this nether empire, which might rise
By policy, and long process of time,
In emulation opposite to Heaven.
Which when Beëlzebub perceived, than whom,
Satan except, none higher sat, with grave   300
Aspect he rose, and in his rising seemed
A pillar of state; deep on his front° engraven
Deliberation sat and public care;
And princely counsel in his face yet shone,
Majestic though in ruin: sage he stood,
With Atlantean° shoulders fit to bear
The weight of mightiest monarchies; his look
Drew audience and attention still as night
Or summer's noontide air, while thus he spake:
    "Thrones and imperial Powers, offspring of
    Heaven,   310
Ethereal Virtues! or these titles now
Must we renounce, and changing style° be called
Princes of Hell? for so the popular vote
Inclines, here to continue, and build up here
A growing empire; doubtless! while we dream,
And know not that the King of Heaven hath
    doomed
This place our dungeon, not our safe retreat
Beyond his potent arm, to live exempt
From Heaven's high jurisdiction, in new league
Banded against his throne, but to remain   320
In strictest bondage, though thus far removed,
Under the inevitable curb, reserved
His captive multitude. For he, be sure,
In highth or depth, still first and last will reign
Sole king, and of his kingdom lose no part
By our revolt, but over Hell extend
His empire, and with iron scepter rule
Us here, as with his golden those in Heaven.
What° sit we then projecting peace and war?
War hath determined° us, and foiled with loss
Irreparable; terms of peace yet none   331
Vouchsafed or sought; for what peace will be given
To us enslaved, but custody severe,
And stripes, and arbitrary punishment
Inflicted? and what peace can we return,
But to° our power hostility and hate,
Untamed reluctance,° and revenge though slow,
Yet ever plotting how the Conqueror least
May reap his conquest, and may least rejoice
In doing what we most in suffering feel?   340
Nor will occasion want,° nor shall we need

249–52. Let . . . vassalage: Let us not seek to regain our state of splendid subservience in Heaven; we cannot regain it by force, and we could not bear to regain it by God's permission. **271. Wants:** lacks. **275. elements:** the four elements, earth, water, air, fire, with which devils were traditionally associated. **278. sensible:** sense, sensation. **288. o'erwatched:** weary with watching.

292. field: battle. **294. Michael:** the leader of God's angelic army. **302. front:** forehead. **306. Atlantean:** of Atlas, the Titan who held up the sky. **312. style:** title. **329. What:** why. **330. determined:** made an end of. **336. to:** to the utmost of. **337. reluctance:** resistance. **341. want:** be wanting.

With dangerous expedition to invade
Heaven, whose high walls fear no assault or siege,
Or ambush from the deep. What if we find
Some easier enterprise? There is a place
(If ancient and prophetic fame° in Heaven
Err not), another world, the happy seat
Of some new race called man, about this time
To be created like to us, though less
In power and excellence, but favored more   350
Of him who rules above; so was his will
Pronounced among the gods, and by an oath,
That shook Heaven's whole circumference, con-
     firmed.
Thither let us bend all our thoughts, to learn
What creatures there inhabit, of what mold
Or substance, how endued,° and what their power,
And where their weakness, how attempted° best,
By force or subtlety. Though Heaven be shut,
And Heaven's high Arbitrator sit secure
In his own strength, this place may lie exposed,
The utmost border of his kingdom, left   361
To their defense who hold it; here perhaps
Some advantageous act may be achieved
By sudden onset, either with Hell fire
To waste his whole creation, or possess
All as our own, and drive, as we were driven,
The puny habitants; or if not drive,
Seduce them to our party, that their God
May prove their foe, and with repenting hand
Abolish his own works. This would surpass   370
Common revenge, and interrupt his joy
In our confusion, and our joy upraise
In his disturbance; when his darling sons,
Hurled headlong to partake with us, shall curse
Their frail original,° and faded bliss,
Faded so soon. Advise° if this be worth
Attempting, or to sit in darkness here
Hatching vain empires." Thus Beëlzebub
Pleaded his devilish counsel, first devised
By Satan, and in part proposed; for whence,   380
But from the author of all ill, could spring
So deep a malice, to confound the race
Of mankind in one root, and Earth with Hell
To mingle and involve, done all to spite
The great Creator? But their spite still serves
His glory to augment. The bold design
Pleased highly those infernal States,° and joy
Sparkled in all their eyes; with full assent
They vote: whereat his speech he thus renews:
     "Well have ye judged, well ended long debate,
Synod of gods, and like to what ye are,   391
Great things resolved; which from the lowest deep
Will once more lift us up, in spite of Fate,
Nearer our ancient seat; perhaps in view

Of those bright confines, whence with neighboring
     arms
And opportune excursion we may chance
Re-enter Heaven; or else in some mild zone
Dwell not unvisited of Heaven's fair light
Secure, and at the brightening orient beam
Purge off this gloom; the soft delicious air,   400
To heal the scar of these corrosive fires,
Shall breathe her balm. But first whom shall we
     send
In search of this new world, whom shall we find
Sufficient? who shall tempt° with wandering feet
The dark unbottomed infinite abyss°
And through the palpable obscure° find out
His uncouth° way, or spread his aery flight
Upborne with indefatigable wings
Over the vast abrupt,° ere he arrive
The happy isle;° what strength, what art can then
Suffice, or what evasion bear him safe   411
Through the strict senteries° and stations thick
Of angels watching round? Here he had need
All circumspection, and we now no less
Choice in our suffrage;° for on whom we send,
The weight of all and our last hope relies."
     This said, he sat; and expectation held
His look suspense,° awaiting who appeared
To second, or oppose, or undertake
The perilous attempt: but all sat mute,   420
Pondering the danger with deep thoughts; and
     each
In other's countenance read his own dismay
Astonished.° None among the choice and prime
Of those Heaven-warring champions could be
     found
So hardy as to proffer or accept
Alone the dreadful voyage; till at last
Satan, whom now transcendent glory raised
Above his fellows, with monarchal pride
Conscious of highest worth, unmoved thus spake:
     "O Progeny of Heaven, empyreal° Thrones,
With reason hath deep silence and demur°   431
Seized us, though undismayed. Long is the way
And hard, that out of Hell leads up to light;°
Our prison strong, this huge convex° of fire,
Outrageous to devour, immures us round
Ninefold, and gates of burning adamant
Barred over us prohibit all egress.
These passed, if any pass, the void profound
Of unessential° Night receives him next
Wide gaping, and with utter loss of being   440

---

346. fame: rumor.   356. endued: endowed (in mind).   357. attempted: attacked.   375. original: progenitor, i.e., Adam.
376. Advise: consider.   387. States: peers.

404. tempt: attempt.   405. abyss: Chaos.   406. palpable obscure: darkness that can be felt (Exod. 10:21).   407. uncouth:
unknown.   409. abrupt: the space between Hell and Heaven,
Chaos.   410. isle: the created universe, in the "ocean" of
Chaos.   412. senteries: sentries.   415. Choice . . . suffrage:
care in our voting.   418. suspense: in suspense.   423. Astonished: dismayed.   430. empyreal: heavenly.   431. demur:
hesitation.   432–33. Long . . . light: See III. 19–21n.   434. convex: vault.   439. unessential: without substance.

Threatens him, plunged in that abortive° gulf.
If thence he scape into whatever world,
Or unknown region, what remains° him less
Than unknown dangers and as hard escape?
But I should ill become this throne, O Peers,
And this imperial sovranty, adorned
With splendor, armed with power, if aught pro-
    posed
And judged of public moment, in the shape
Of difficulty or danger could deter
Me from attempting. Wherefore do I assume   450
These royalties, and not refuse to reign,
Refusing° to accept as great a share
Of hazard as of honor, due alike
To him who reigns, and so much to him due
Of hazard more, as he above the rest
High honored sits? Go therefore, mighty Powers,
Terror of Heaven, though fallen; intend° at home,
While here shall be our home, what best may ease
The present misery, and render Hell
More tolerable, if there be cure or charm   460
To respite or deceive,° or slack the pain
Of this ill mansion; intermit no watch
Against a wakeful foe, while I abroad
Through all the coasts of dark destruction seek
Deliverance for us all: this enterprise
None shall partake with me." Thus saying rose
The Monarch, and prevented° all reply;
Prudent,° lest from his resolution raised°
Others among the chief might offer now
(Certain to be refused) what erst they feared;   470
And so refused might in opinion stand
His rivals, winning cheap the high repute
Which he through hazard huge must earn. But
    they
Dreaded not more the adventure than his voice
Forbidding, and at once with him they rose;
Their rising all at once was as the sound
Of thunder heard remote. Towards him they bend
With awful reverence prone; and as a god
Extol him equal to the Highest in Heaven.
Nor failed they to express how much they praised
That for the general safety he despised   481
His own: for° neither do the spirits damned
Lose all their virtue; lest bad men should boast
Their specious deeds on Earth, which glory excites,
Or close° ambition varnished o'er with zeal.
    Thus they their doubtful consultations dark
Ended rejoicing in their matchless Chief:
As when from mountain tops the dusky clouds
Ascending, while the north wind sleeps, o'erspread

Heaven's cheerful face, the louring element°   490
Scowls o'er the darkened lantskip° snow or shower;
If chance° the radiant sun with farewell sweet
Extend his evening beam, the fields revive,
The birds their notes renew, and bleating herds
Attest their joy, that hill and valley rings.
O shame to men! Devil with devil damned
Firm concord holds, men only disagree
Of creatures rational, though under hope
Of heavenly grace; and God proclaiming peace,
Yet live in hatred, enmity, and strife   500
Among themselves, and levy cruel wars,
Wasting the Earth, each other to destroy:
As if (which might induce us to accord)
Man had not hellish foes enow° besides,
That day and night for his destruction wait.
    The Stygian council thus dissolved; and forth
In order came the grand infernal Peers;
Midst came their mighty Paramount,° and seemed
Alone the antagonist of Heaven, nor less
Than Hell's dread Emperor, with pomp supreme,
And god-like imitated state; him round   511
A globe° of fiery Seraphim enclosed
With bright emblazonry and horrent° arms.
Then of their session ended they bid cry
With trumpet's regal sound the great result.
Toward the four winds four speedy Cherubim
Put to their mouths the sounding alchemy°
By herald's voice explained; the hollow abyss
Heard far and wide, and all the host of Hell
With deafening shout returned them loud acclaim.
Thence more at ease their minds and somewhat
    raised   521
By false presumptuous hope, the rangèd powers°
Disband, and wandering each his several way
Pursues, as inclination or sad choice
Leads him perplexed, where he may likeliest find
Truce to his restless thoughts, and entertain
The irksome hours, till his great Chief return.
Part° on the plain, or in the air sublime°
Upon the wing, or in swift race contend,
As at the Olympian° games or Pythian° fields;
Part curb their fiery steeds, or shun the goal   531
With rapid wheels,° or fronted° brígades form;
As when to warn proud cities war appears°
Waged in the troubled sky, and armies rush
To battle in the clouds; before each van°

441. **abortive:** monstrous, or destructive.   443. **remains:** awaits.
452. **Refusing:** if I refuse.   457. **intend:** consider.   461. **deceive:** beguile.   467. **prevented:** forestalled.   468. **Prudent:**
shrewd.   **raised:** made bolder.   482–85. **for . . . zeal:** Let not
bad men boast of seemingly noble deeds inspired by love of glory
and ambition, since even damned angels retain that degree of
virtue.   485. **close:** secret.

490. **element:** sky.   491. **lantskip:** landscape.   492. **If chance:**
if it chances that.   504. **enow:** enough.   508. **Paramount:** chief.
512. **globe:** solid troop.   513. **horrent:** bristling.   517. **sounding alchemy:** trumpets of material resembling gold.   522. **ranged
powers:** assembled armies.   528–38. **Part . . . burns:** Milton
here uses, in his own way, the epic convention of athletic games.
528. **sublime:** aloft.   530. **Olympian:** the Olympic Games held
at Olympia in southern Greece. **Pythian:** the similar games
held at Delphi.   531–32. **shun . . . wheels:** chariots turning
close around a mark.   532. **fronted:** in line.   533 f. Such visions
have been reported, throughout history, in times of crisis or war;
or the reference may be to phenomena like the Northern Lights.
535. **van:** vanguard.

Prick° forth the aery knights, and couch their
    spears,
Till thickest legions close; with feats of arms
From either end of Heaven the welkin burns.
Others with vast Typhoean° rage more fell
Rend up both rocks and hills, and ride the air   540
In whirlwind; Hell scarce holds the wild uproar;
As° when Alcides, from Oechalia crowned
With conquest, felt the envenomed robe, and tore
Through pain up by the roots Thessalian pines,
And Lichas from the top of Oeta threw
Into the Euboic sea. Others more mild,
Retreated in a silent valley, sing
With notes angelical to many a harp
Their own heroic deeds and hapless fall
By doom of battle; and complain that Fate   550
Free virtue should enthrall to force or chance.
Their song was partial,° but the harmony
(What could it less when spirits immortal sing?)
Suspended Hell, and took° with ravishment
The thronging audience. In discourse more sweet
(For eloquence the soul, song charms the sense)
Others apart sat on a hill retired,
In thoughts more elevate, and reasoned high
Of providence, foreknowledge, will, and fate,
Fixed fate, free will, foreknowledge absolute,   560
And found no end, in wandering mazes lost.
Of good and evil much they argued then,
Of happiness and final misery,
Passion and apathy,° and glory and shame,
Vain wisdom all, and false philosophy;
Yet with a pleasing sorcery could charm
Pain for a while or anguish, and excite
Fallacious hope, or arm the obdured° breast
With stubborn patience as with triple steel.
Another part, in squadrons and gross° bands,   570
On bold adventure to discover wide
That dismal world, if any clime perhaps
Might yield them easier habitation, bend
Four ways their flying march, along the banks
Of four infernal rivers° that disgorge
Into the burning lake their baleful streams:
Abhorrèd Styx, the flood of deadly hate;
Sad Acheron of sorrow, black and deep;
Cocytus, named of lamentation loud   579
Heard on the rueful stream; fierce Phlegethon,
Whose waves of torrent fire inflame with rage.

Far off from these a slow and silent stream,
Lethe, the river of oblivion, rolls
Her watery labyrinth, whereof who drinks
Forthwith his former state and being forgets,
Forgets both joy and grief, pleasure and pain.
Beyond this flood a frozen continent°
Lies dark and wild, beat with perpetual storms
Of whirlwind and dire hail, which on firm land
Thaws not, but gathers heap,° and ruin seems   590
Of ancient pile; all else deep snow and ice,
A gulf profound as that Serbonian bog°
Betwixt Damiata and Mount Casius old,
Where armies whole have sunk; the parching air
Burns frore,° and cold performs the effect of fire.
Thither by harpy-footed Furies° haled,
At certain revolutions° all the damned
Are brought; and feel by turns the bitter change
Of fierce extremes, extremes by change more fierce,
From beds of raging fire to starve° in ice   600
Their soft ethereal warmth, and there to pine
Immovable, infixed, and frozen round,
Periods of time; thence hurried back to fire.
They ferry over this Lethean sound
Both to and fro, their sorrow to augment,
And wish and struggle, as they pass, to reach
The tempting stream, with one small drop to lose
In sweet forgetfulness all pain and woe,
All in one moment, and so near the brink;
But Fate withstands, and to oppose the attempt
Medusa° with Gorgonian terror guards   611
The ford, and of itself the water flies
All taste of living wight, as once it fled
The lip of Tantalus.° Thus roving on
In confused march forlorn, the adventurous bands,
With shuddering horror pale, and eyes aghast,
Viewed first their lamentable lot, and found
No rest. Through many a dark and dreary vale
They passed, and many a region dolorous,
O'er many a frozen, many a fiery Alp,°   620
Rocks, caves, lakes, fens, bogs, dens, and shades of
    death,
A universe of death, which God by curse
Created evil, for evil only good,
Where all life dies, death lives, and Nature breeds,
Perverse, all monstrous, all prodigious things,
Abominable, inutterable, and worse
Than fables yet have feigned, or fear conceived,
Gorgons and Hydras,° and Chimeras° dire.

---

536. Prick: spur, ride.   **539. Typhoean:** See note on I. 197 f.
542–46. As . . . sea: Nessus, a centaur, dying at the hand of
Hercules (Alcides), told Hercules' wife, Deianira, that his blood
would preserve her husband's love. When Hercules, returning
from victory in Oechalia with the captive Iole, prepared to offer
sacrifice on Mount Oeta in Thessaly, he sent home for a fresh
robe. The robe, which Deianira steeped in Nessus' blood, tortured Hercules into frenzy, and he threw Lichas, who had
brought it, into the sea.   **552. partial:** prejudiced.   **554. took:**
captured, charmed.   **564. apathy:** a Stoic term for freedom
from passion.   **568 obdured:** hardened.   **570. gross:** compact.
575 f. The four underworld rivers of classical myth.

587 f. In medieval belief Hell contained a frozen as well as a
fiery region.   **590. gathers heap:** gathers in a heap.   **592. Serbonian bog:** Lake Serbonis on the east side of the Nile delta.
595. frore: frozen.   **596. harpy-footed Furies:** The Furies, the
avenging spirits of Greek myth, are here given the claws of the
foul bird-women called Harpies.   **597. revolutions:** i.e., of time.
600. starve: freeze.   **611. Medusa:** one of the three Gorgons,
whose face turned beholders to stone.   **614.** Tantalus was condemned by Zeus to stand in water which eluded his attempts to
drink.   **620. Alp:** any high mountain.   **628. Hydras:** see
Sonnet XV, l. 7n.   **Chimeras:** The Chimera was a fire-breathing

Meanwhile the Adversary of God and man,   629
Satan, with thoughts inflamed of highest design,
Puts on swift wings, and toward the gates of Hell
Explores his solitary flight; sometimes
He scours the right-hand coast, sometimes the left;
Now shaves with level wing the deep, then soars
Up to the fiery concave° towering high:
As when far off at sea a fleet descried
Hangs in the clouds, by equinoctial winds
Close sailing from Bengala,° or the isles
Of Ternate and Tidore,° whence merchants bring
Their spicy drugs: they on the trading flood,   640
Through the wide Ethiopian° to the Cape,°
Ply stemming nightly toward the pole.° So seemed
Far off the flying Fiend. At last appear
Hell bounds high reaching to the horrid roof,
And thrice threefold the gates; three folds were
    brass,
Three iron, three of adamantine rock,
Impenetrable, impaled° with circling fire,
Yet unconsumed. Before the gates there sat°
On either side a formidable shape;
The one seemed woman to the waist, and fair,
But ended foul in many a scaly fold   651
Voluminous and vast, a serpent armed
With mortal sting. About her middle round
A cry° of Hell-hounds never ceasing barked
With wide Cerberean mouths full loud, and rung
A hideous peal; yet, when they list,° would creep,
If aught disturbed their noise, into her womb,
And kennel there, yet there still barked and
    howled,
Within unseen. Far less abhorred than these
Vexed Scylla, bathing in the sea that parts   660
Calabria° from the hoarse Trinacrian° shore;
Nor uglier follow the night-hag,° when called
In secret, riding through the air she comes,
Lured with the smell of infant blood, to dance
With Lapland° witches, while the laboring° moon
Eclipses at their charms. The other shape —
If shape it might be called that shape had none
Distinguishable in member, joint, or limb,
Or substance might be called that shadow seemed,
For each seemed either — black it stood as Night,

Fierce as ten Furies, terrible as Hell,   671
And shook a dreadful dart; what seemed his head
The likeness of a kingly crown had on.
Satan was now at hand, and from his seat
The monster moving onward came as fast,
With horrid strides; Hell trembled as he strode.
The undaunted Fiend what this might be ad-
    mired,°
Admired, not feared; God and his Son except,
Created thing nought valued he nor shunned;
And with disdainful look thus first began: 680
"Whence and what art thou, execrable Shape,
That dar'st, though grim and terrible, advance
Thy miscreated front athwart my way
To yonder gates? Through them I mean to pass,
That be assured, without leave asked of thee.
Retire, or taste thy folly, and learn by proof,
Hell-born, not to contend with spirits of Heaven."
    To whom the goblin full of wrath replied:
"Art thou that traitor angel, art thou he,
Who first broke peace in Heaven and faith, till
    then   690
Unbroken, and in proud rebellious arms
Drew after him the third part of Heaven's sons
Conjured° against the Highest, for which both
    thou
And they, outcast from God, are here condemned
To waste eternal days in woe and pain?
And reckon'st thou thyself with spirits of Heaven,
Hell-doomed, and breath'st defiance here and scorn
Where I reign king, and to enrage thee more,
Thy king and lord? Back to thy punishment,
False fugitive, and to thy speed add wings,   700
Lest with a whip of scorpions I pursue
Thy lingering, or with one stroke of this dart
Strange horror seize thee, and pangs unfelt before."
    So spake the grisly terror, and in shape,
So speaking and so threatening, grew tenfold
More dreadful and deform.° On the other side,
Incensed° with indignation Satan stood
Unterrified, and like a comet burned,
That fires the length of Ophiuchus° huge
In the arctic sky, and from his horrid hair   710
Shakes pestilence and war. Each at the head
Leveled his deadly aim; their fatal hands
No second stroke intend; and such a frown
Each cast at the other, as when two black clouds,
With Heaven's artillery fraught, come rattling on
Over the Caspian, then stand front to front
Hovering a space, till winds the signal blow
To join their dark encounter in mid-air:
So frowned the mighty combatants, that Hell
Grew darker at their frown, so matched they
    stood;   720

monster killed by Bellerophon. The names are symbols of the
physical and mental hell of the fallen angels.   **635. concave:**
the vault of Hell.   **638. Bengala:** Bengal.   **639. Ternate,**
Tidore: islands of the Moluccas, south of the Philippines.
641. Ethiopian: the Indian Ocean.   **Cape:** Cape of Good Hope.
642. pole: the South Pole.   **647. impaled:** surrounded.
648 f. The allegory of Sin and Death is based on Jas. 1:15: "Then
when lust hath conceived, it bringeth forth sin: and sin, when it
is finished, bringeth forth death." Sin is modeled on Scylla
(l. 660; cf. l. 1020n., below) and similar monsters; Spenser's
Error (Faerie Queene, I. i) is one of the family.   **654. cry:** pack.
656 list: pleased.   **661. Calabria:** the "toe" of Italy.   **Trina-**
crian: Sicilian (see l. 1020n., below).   **662. night-hag:** Hecate,
the queen of witches (as in Macbeth).   **665. Lapland:** the northern part of Europe, in popular belief a notorious abode of
witches.   **laboring:** eclipsing.

677. admired: wondered.   **693. Conjured:** united by an oath.
706. deform: deformed.   **707. Incensed:** kindled.   **709. Ophiu-**
chus: a large constellation, "the Serpent-Bearer."

For never but once more was either like
To meet so great a foe.° And now great deeds
Had been achieved, whereof all Hell had rung,
Had not the snaky sorceress that sat
Fast by Hell gate, and kept the fatal key,
Risen, and with hideous outcry rushed between.
  "O father, what intends thy hand," she cried,
"Against thy only son?° What fury, O son,
Possesses thee to bend that mortal dart
Against thy father's head? and know'st for whom?
For him who sits above and laughs the while   731
At thee ordained his drudge, to execute
Whate'er his wrath, which he calls justice, bids,
His wrath which one day will destroy ye both."
  She spake, and at her words the hellish pest
Forbore; then these to her Satan returned:
  "So strange thy outcry, and thy words so strange
Thou interposest, that my sudden hand
Prevented spares to tell thee yet by deeds
What it intends; till first I know of thee,   740
What thing thou art, thus double-formed, and why
In this infernal vale first met thou call'st
Me father, and that phantasm call'st my son.
I know thee not, nor ever saw till now
Sight more detestable than him and thee."
  To whom thus the portress of Hell gate replied:
"Hast thou forgot me then, and do I seem
Now in thine eye so foul? once deemed so fair
In Heaven, when at the assembly, and in sight
Of all the Seraphim with thee combined   750
In bold conspiracy against Heaven's King,
All on a sudden miserable pain
Surprised thee; dim thine eyes, and dizzy swum
In darkness, while thy head flames thick and fast
Threw forth, till on the left side opening wide,
Likest to thee in shape and countenance bright,
Then shining heavenly fair, a goddess armed
Out of thy head I sprung.° Amazement seized
All the host of Heaven; back they recoiled afraid
At first, and called me *Sin,* and for a sign   760
Portentous held me; but familiar grown,
I pleased, and with attractive graces won
The most averse, thee chiefly, who full oft
Thyself in me thy perfect image viewing
Becam'st enamored; and such joy thou took'st
With me in secret, that my womb conceived
A growing burden. Meanwhile war arose,
And fields were fought in Heaven; wherein re-
    mained
(For what could else?) to our almighty Foe
Clear victory, to our part loss and rout   770
Through all the empyrean:° down they fell
Driven headlong from the pitch° of Heaven, down

Into this deep, and in the general fall
I also; at which time this powerful key
Into my hand was given, with charge to keep
These gates for ever shut, which none can pass
Without my opening. Pensive here I sat
Alone, but long I sat not, till my womb,
Pregnant by thee, and now excessive grown,
Prodigious motion felt and rueful throes.   780
At last this odious offspring whom thou seest,
Thine own begotten, breaking violent way
Tore through my entrails, that with fear and pain
Distorted, all my nether shape thus grew
Transformed; but he my inbred enemy
Forth issued, brandishing his fatal dart
Made to destroy. I fled, and cried out *Death!*
Hell trembled at the hideous name, and sighed
From all her caves, and back resounded *Death!*
I fled, but he pursued (though more, it seems,   790
Inflamed with lust than rage) and swifter far,
Me overtook, his mother, all dismayed,
And in embraces forcible and foul
Engendering with me, of that rape begot
These yelling monsters that with ceaseless cry
Surround me, as thou saw'st, hourly conceived
And hourly born, with sorrow infinite
To me; for when they list, into the womb
That bred them they return, and howl and gnaw
My bowels, their repast; then bursting forth   800
Afresh, with conscious terrors vex me round,
That rest or intermission none I find.
Before mine eyes in opposition sits
Grim Death my son and foe, who sets them on,
And me his parent would full soon devour
For want of other prey, but that he knows
His end with mine involved; and knows that I
Should prove a bitter morsel, and his bane,
Whenever that shall be; so Fate pronounced.
But thou, O father, I forewarn thee, shun   810
His deadly arrow; neither vainly hope
To be invulnerable in those bright arms,
Though tempered heavenly, for that mortal dint,
Save he who reigns above, none can resist."
  She finished, and the subtle Fiend his lore
Soon learned, now milder, and thus answered
    smooth:
"Dear daughter, since thou claim'st me for thy sire,
And my fair son here show'st me, the dear pledge
Of dalliance had with thee in Heaven, and joys
Then sweet, now sad to mention, through dire
    change   820
Befallen us unforeseen, unthought of, know
I come no enemy, but to set free
From out this dark and dismal house of pain
Both him and thee, and all the heavenly host
Of spirits that in our just pretenses° armed

---

722. **so . . . foe:** Christ.   728. **thy . . . son:** one of several details that make these characters profane counterparts of God
and the Son.   757–58. **goddess . . . sprung:** like Athene from
the head of Zeus.   771. **empyrean:** Heaven.   772. **pitch:** height.

825. **pretenses:** claims.

Fell with us from on high. From them I go
This uncouth errand sole, and one for all
Myself expose,° with lonely steps to tread
The unfounded° deep, and through the void immense
To search with wandering quest a place foretold
Should be, and, by concurring signs, ere now   831
Created vast and round, a place of bliss
In the purlieus of Heaven, and therein placed
A race of upstart creatures, to supply
Perhaps our vacant room, though more removed,
Lest Heaven surcharged with potent multitude
Might hap to move new broils.° Be this or aught
Than this more secret now designed, I haste
To know, and this once known, shall soon return,
And bring ye to the place where thou and Death
Shall dwell at ease, and up and down unseen   841
Wing silently the buxom° air, embalmed
With odors; there ye shall be fed and filled
Immeasurably; all things shall be your prey."
He ceased, for both seemed highly pleased, and Death
Grinned horrible a ghastly smile, to hear
His famine° should be filled, and blessed his maw
Destined to that good hour. No less rejoiced
His mother bad, and thus bespake her sire:
    "The key of this infernal pit, by due   850
And by command of Heaven's all-powerful King
I keep, by him forbidden to unlock
These adamantine gates; against all force
Death ready stands to interpose his dart,
Fearless to be o'ermatched by living might.
But what owe I to his commands above
Who hates me, and hath hither thrust me down
Into this gloom of Tartarus° profound,
To sit in hateful office here confined,
Inhabitant of Heaven and heavenly-born,   860
Here in perpetual agony and pain,
With terrors and with clamors compassed round
Of mine own brood, that on my bowels feed?
Thou art my father, thou my author, thou
My being gav'st me; whom should I obey
But thee, whom follow? Thou wilt bring me soon
To that new world of light and bliss, among
The gods who live at ease, where I shall reign
At thy right hand voluptuous,° as beseems
Thy daughter and thy darling, without end."   870
    Thus saying, from her side the fatal key,
Sad instrument of all our woe, she took;
And towards the gate rolling her bestial train,
Forthwith the huge portcullis high up drew,
Which but herself not all the Stygian powers

Could once have moved; then in the key-hole turns
The intricate wards, and every bolt and bar
Of massy iron or solid rock with ease
Unfastens. On a sudden open fly
With impetuous recoil and jarring sound   880
The infernal doors, and on their hinges grate
Harsh thunder, that the lowest bottom shook
Of Erebus.° She opened, but to shut
Excelled her power; the gates wide open stood,
That with extended wings a bannered host
Under spread ensigns marching might pass through
With horse and chariots ranked in loose array;
So wide they stood, and like a furnace mouth
Cast forth redounding° smoke and ruddy flame.
Before their eyes in sudden view appear°   890
The secrets of the hoary deep,° a dark
Illimitable ocean without bound,
Without dimension; where length, breadth, and highth,
And time and place are lost; where eldest Night
And Chaos, ancestors of Nature, hold
Eternal anarchy, amidst the noise
Of endless wars, and by confusion stand.
For Hot, Cold, Moist, and Dry, four champions fierce,°
Strive here for mastery, and to battle bring
Their embryon atoms; they around the flag   900
Of each his faction, in their several clans,
Light-armed or heavy, sharp, smooth, swift or slow,
Swarm populous, unnumbered as the sands
Of Barca or Cyrene's° torrid soil,
Levied° to side with warring winds, and poise
Their lighter wings.° To whom these most adhere,
He rules a moment; Chaos umpire sits,
And by decision more embroils the fray
By which he reigns; next him, high arbiter,
Chance governs all. Into this wild abyss,   910
The womb of Nature and perhaps her grave,
Of neither sea, nor shore, nor air, nor fire,
But all these in their pregnant causes mixed
Confusedly, and which thus must ever fight,
Unless the Almighty Maker them ordain
His dark materials to create more worlds,
Into this wild abyss the wary Fiend
Stood on the brink of Hell and looked a while,
Pondering his voyage; for no narrow frith
He had to cross. Nor was his ear less pealed°   920

827–28. one ... expose: a contrast with the Son's self-sacrifice. 829. unfounded: bottomless. 837. broils: disturbances, tumults. 842. buxom: yielding. 847. famine: hunger. 858. Tartarus: the classical Hades, or a hell below it. 868–69. where ... voluptuous: like the Son at the right hand of the Father, except for the shock of the final word

883. Erebus: a classical name for hell. 889. redounding: in rolling clouds. 890 ff. The nature of the Miltonic universe is touched upon in the Intro., pp. 409–10. 891. deep: Chaos. The name is used both for the chaotic sea of warring elements and for the name of their personified ruler. 898 ff. The strife of the four elements had been familiar since early Greek antiquity, especially through the opening lines of Ovid's *Metamorphoses*. 904. Barca, Cyrene: cities of Cyrenaica in northern Africa. 905. Levied: raised. 905–06. poise ... wings: give weight to the too light wings of the winds. 920. pealed: assailed by noise.

With noises loud and ruinous (to compare
Great things with small) than when Bellona°
    storms,
With all her battering engines bent to raze
Some capital city; or less than if this frame
Of Heaven were falling, and these elements
In mutiny had from her axle torn
The steadfast Earth. At last his sail-broad vans°
He spreads for flight, and in the surging smoke
Uplifted spurns the ground; thence many a league
As in a cloudy chair ascending rides   930
Audacious, but that seat soon failing, meets
A vast vacuity: all unawares
Fluttering his pennons vain plumb down he drops
Ten thousand fadom° deep, and to this hour
Down had been falling, had not by ill chance
The strong rebuff of some tumultuous cloud
Instinct° with fire and niter hurried him
As many miles aloft. That fury stayed,
Quenched in a boggy Syrtis,° neither sea,
Nor good dry land, nigh foundered on he fares,
Treading the crude consistence, half on foot,   941
Half flying; behoves him now both oar and sail.
As when a gryphon° through the wilderness
With wingèd course o'er hill or moory dale,
Pursues the Arimaspian, who by stealth
Had from his wakeful custody purloined
The guarded gold: so eagerly the Fiend
O'er bog or steep, through strait, rough, dense, or
    rare,
With head, hands, wings, or feet pursues his way,
And swims or sinks, or wades, or creeps, or flies.
At length a universal hubbub wild   951
Of stunning sounds and voices all confused,
Borne through the hollow dark, assaults his ear
With loudest vehemence; thither he plies,
Undaunted to meet there whatever power
Or spirit of the nethermost abyss
Might in that noise reside, of whom to ask
Which way the nearest coast of darkness lies
Bordering on light; when straight behold the
    throne
Of Chaos, and his dark pavilion spread   960
Wide on the wasteful deep; with him enthroned
Sat sable-vested Night, eldest of things,
The consort of his reign; and by them stood
Orcus and Ades,° and the dreaded name
Of Demogorgon;° Rumor next and Chance,
And Tumult and Confusion all embroiled,
And Discord with a thousand various mouths.

922. **Bellona**: the Roman goddess of war.   927. **vans**: wings.
934. **fadom**: fathoms.   937. **Instinct**: filled, charged.   939. **Syrtis**: two gulfs near Tripoli, notorious for quicksands.   943–
47. **gryphon . . . gold**: Gryphons were fabulous Scythian monsters whose gold the Arimaspians tried to steal.   964. **Orcus,
Ades**: Latin and Greek names for the underworld (Hades) or,
as here, its god.   964–65. **dreaded . . . Demogorgon**: i.e., Demogorgon of dreaded name, a mysterious (and postclassical)
infernal deity.

To whom Satan turning boldly, thus: "Ye pow-
    ers
And spirits of this nethermost abyss,
Chaos and ancient Night, I come no spy,   970
With purpose to explore or to disturb
The secrets of your realm, but by constraint
Wandering this darksome desert, as my way
Lies through your spacious empire up to light,
Alone, and without guide, half lost, I seek
What readiest path leads where your gloomy
    bounds
Confine° with Heaven; or if some other place
From your dominion won, the Ethereal° King
Possesses lately, thither to arrive
I travel this profound.° Direct my course;   980
Directed, no mean recompense it brings
To your behoof, if I that region lost,
All usurpation thence expelled, reduce
To her original darkness and your sway
(Which is° my present journey), and once more
Erect the standard there of ancient Night;
Yours be the advantage all, mine the revenge."

    Thus Satan; and him thus the Anarch° old,
With faltering speech and visage incomposed,°
Answered: "I know thee, stranger, who thou art,
That mighty leading angel, who of late   991
Made head against Heaven's King, though over-
    thrown.
I saw and heard, for such a numerous host
Fled not in silence through the frighted deep
With ruin upon ruin,° rout on rout,
Confusion worse confounded; and Heaven gates
Poured out by millions her victorious bands
Pursuing. I upon my frontiers here
Keep residence; if all I can will serve
That little which is left so to defend,   1000
Encroached on still through our intestine broils
Weakening the scepter of old Night: first Hell
Your dungeon stretching far and wide beneath;
Now lately Heaven and Earth, another world°
Hung o'er my realm, linked in a golden chain
To that side Heaven from whence your legions
    fell.
If that way be your walk, you have not far;
So much the nearer danger; go and speed;
Havoc and spoil and ruin are my gain."

    He ceased; and Satan stayed not to reply,   1010
But glad that now his sea should find a shore,
With fresh alacrity and force renewed
Springs upward like a pyramid of fire
Into the wild expanse, and through the shock
Of fighting elements, on all sides round

977. **Confine**: border.   978. **Ethereal**: heavenly.   980. **profound**: deep, abyss.   985. **is**: is the motive of.   988. **Anarch**:
Chaos (as personified in this passage).   989. **incomposed**: disturbed.   995. **ruin**: fall.   1004. **world**: the lately created universe comprising "Heaven" (the sky) and the earth. Cf. ll.
1051–52.

Environed, wins his way; harder beset
And more endangered, than when Argo° passed
Through Bosporus betwixt the justling rocks,
Or when Ulysses on the larboard shunned
Charybdis,° and by the other whirlpool steered.
So he with difficulty and labor hard   1021
Moved on, with difficulty and labor he;
But he once passed, soon after when man fell,
Strange alteration! Sin and Death amain
Following his track, such was the will of Heaven,
Paved after him a broad and beaten way°
Over the dark abyss, whose boiling gulf
Tamely endured a bridge of wondrous length
From Hell continued reaching the utmost orb°
Of this frail world; by which the spirits perverse
With easy intercourse pass to and fro   1031
To tempt or punish mortals, except whom
God and good angels guard by special grace.

But now at last the sacred influence
Of light appears, and from the walls of Heaven
Shoots far into the bosom of dim Night
A glimmering dawn; here Nature first begins
Her farthest verge,° and Chaos to retire
As from her° outmost works a broken foe,
With tumult less and with less hostile din,   1040
That° Satan with less toil, and now with ease
Wafts° on the calmer wave by dubious light,
And like a weather-beaten vessel holds°
Gladly the port, though shrouds and tackle torn;
Or in the emptier waste, resembling air,
Weighs his spread wings, at leisure to behold
Far off the empyreal° Heaven, extended wide
In circuit, undetermined° square or round,
With opal towers and battlements adorned
Of living sapphire,° once his native seat;   1050
And fast by hanging in a golden chain°
This pendent world,° in bigness as a star
Of smallest magnitude close by the moon.
Thither full fraught with mischievous revenge,
Accurst, and in a cursèd hour, he hies.

from BOOK III

[The invocation to Light, one of the greatest things in
Milton and in all poetry, has its immediate motive in the
change of scene from Hell and Chaos to Heaven. Milton's
lifelong preoccupation with light and its symbolism inspires
reflections, poignant but firmly controlled, on the contrast
between his physical blindness and his inward vision; personal feeling is merged in a dramatic picture of "the blind
poet."]

Hail, holy Light, offspring of Heaven first-born,°
Or° of the Eternal coeternal beam
May I express° thee unblamed? since God is light,
And never but in unapproachèd light
Dwelt from eternity, dwelt then in thee,
Bright effluence of bright essence increate.°
Or hear'st° thou rather pure ethereal stream,
Whose fountain who shall tell?° Before° the sun,
Before the Heavens thou wert, and at the voice
Of God, as with a mantle didst invest   10
The rising world of waters dark and deep,
Won from the void and formless infinite.
Thee I revisit now with bolder wing,
Escaped the Stygian pool, though long detained
In that obscure sojourn, while in my flight,
Through utter and through middle darkness°
    borne,
With other notes than to the Orphean lyre°
I sung of Chaos and eternal Night,
Taught by the Heavenly Muse to venture down
The dark descent, and up to reascend,   20
Though hard and rare.° Thee I revisit safe,
And feel thy sovran vital lamp; but thou
Revisit'st not these eyes, that roll in vain
To find thy piercing ray, and find no dawn;
So thick a drop serene° hath quenched their orbs,
Or dim suffusion veiled. Yet not the more
Cease I to wander° where the Muses haunt
Clear spring, or shady grove, or sunny hill,
Smit with the love of sacred song; but chief
Thee, Sion,° and the flowery brooks beneath   30

Book III: 1. first-born: The first of three theories of light:
that it was the first thing God created.   2–6. Or . . . increate:
the second theory, that it was not created but was co-eternal
with God, an emanation of his own essence.   3. express: call.
unblamed: without incurring blame for touching a divine mystery.   6. increate: uncreated.   7–8. Or . . . tell: the third
theory, that light is a divine thing to which man can assign no
origin.   7. hear'st: art called (a classicism).   8–12. Before . . .
infinite: a recollection of Gen. 1:1–5.   16. utter and . . . middle
darkness: Hell and Chaos.   17. Orphean lyre: The name of the
mythical bard, Orpheus, who had gone down to Hades in quest
of his wife, was linked with the mystical "Orphic Hymns,"
such as that to Night. Milton distinguishes his own Christian
inspiration from the pagan.   19–21. Taught . . . rare: an echo
of the sibyl's words to Aeneas before he visited the underworld
(*Aeneid*, VI. 126–29). Cf. II. 432–33.   25. drop serene: a medical
term (*gutta serena*).   26–27. Yet . . . wander: yet I wander
none the less. The declaration of attachment to the pagan classical poets (ll. 26–29) echoes Virgil, *Georgics*, II. 475–78, 485–89.
29–32. Sion: As elsewhere in his prose and verse, Milton ranks the
Bible far above the classics. See, e.g., the *Reason of Church
Government*, above.

1017. Argo: the ship in which Jason and his fellow Argonauts
sailed through the Bosporus (the strait between the Sea of
Marmara and the Black Sea).   1020. Charybdis: the whirlpool
in the strait between Italy and Sicily; Scylla ("the other whirlpool"), opposite, was the other great danger for mariners. The
two were referred to as both whirlpools and rocks (and monsters).
1026 f.: The building of the bridge is described in X. 282–324.
1029. utmost orb: the outermost sphere or shell enclosing the
universe.   1037–38. here . . . verge: Here Nature, the created,
ordered universe, meets the boundary of Chaos.   1039. her: Nature's.   1041. That: so that.   1042. Wafts: sails.   1043. holds:
makes for.   1047. empyreal: See I. 117n., above.   1048. undetermined: it could not be known whether.   1050. sapphire:
See Rev. 21:19.   1051. hanging . . . chain: This image, originally in the *Iliad*, VIII. 18–27, had been used by countless writers
in various symbolic senses.   1052. world: not merely the earth
but the whole Ptolemaic universe with the earth at its center
and outer spheres in which the planets revolved

That wash thy hallowed feet, and warbling flow,
Nightly I visit;° nor sometimes forget
Those° other two equaled with me in fate,
So were I equaled with them in renown,
Blind Thamyris and blind Maeonides,
And Tiresias and Phineus, prophets old:
Then feed on thoughts, that voluntary move
Harmonious numbers,° as the wakeful bird°
Sings darkling,° and in shadiest covert hid
Tunes her nocturnal note. Thus with the year   40
Seasons return; but not to me returns
Day, or the sweet approach of even or morn,
Or sight of vernal bloom, or summer's rose,
Or flocks, or herds, or human face divine;
But cloud instead, and ever-during dark
Surrounds me, from the cheerful ways of men
Cut off, and for the book of knowledge fair
Presented with a universal blank°
Of Nature's works to me expunged and rased,
And wisdom at one entrance quite shut out.   50
So much the rather thou, celestial Light,
Shine inward, and the mind through all her powers
Irradiate, there plant eyes, all mist from thence
Purge and disperse, that I may see and tell
Of things invisible to mortal sight.

[Book III has two parts, a council in Heaven and Satan's
continued journey. The council, a counterpart to the debate
in Hell, provides the theological exposition of the poem.
God declares that he has endowed man with reason, the
power of choice, and that this freedom carries with it the
power of sinful choice. God foresees but does not prede-
termine man's fall, and, since Milton is repudiating Calvinism, salvation shall be open to all believers; but first justice
must be satisfied for man's sin. The Son, the agent of love,
humility, and goodness (as Satan is of hate, pride, and evil),
volunteers to make atonement for man. All Heaven rejoices
in the ultimate victory of good and the prospect of an eternity of joy and love and truth.

In the rest of the book Satan, voyaging through Chaos,
alights on the outer shell of the universe, at a point where
he can look up to Heaven and down to earth and the
paradisal home of Adam and Eve; then he flies down to
the sun, and from the sun to the top of Mount Niphates in
Armenia.]

from BOOK IV

THE ARGUMENT

Satan, now in prospect of Eden, and nigh the place
where he must now attempt the bold enterprise which
he undertook alone against God and man, falls into
many doubts with himself, and many passions, fear,
envy, and despair; but at length confirms himself in

evil, journeys on to Paradise, whose outward prospect
and situation is described, overleaps the bounds, sits
in the shape of a cormorant on the Tree of Life, as
highest in the Garden, to look about him. The Garden
described; Satan's first sight of Adam and Eve; his
wonder at their excellent form and happy state, but
with resolution to work their fall; overhears their discourse; thence gathers that the Tree of Knowledge was
forbidden them to eat of, under penalty of death; and
thereon intends to found his temptation by seducing
them to transgress; then leaves them a while, to know
further of their state by some other means. Meanwhile
Uriel, descending on a sunbeam, warns Gabriel, who
had in charge the gate of Paradise, that some evil
spirit had escaped the deep, and passed at noon by his
sphere, in the shape of a good angel, down to Paradise;
discovered after by his furious gestures in the mount.
Gabriel promises to find him ere morning. Night coming on, Adam and Eve discourse of going to their rest:
their bower described; their evening worship. Gabriel,
drawing forth his bands of night-watch to walk the
round of Paradise, appoints two strong angels to
Adam's bower, lest the evil spirit should be there doing
some harm to Adam or Eve sleeping; there they find
him at the ear of Eve, tempting her in a dream, and
bring him, though unwilling, to Gabriel; by whom
questioned, he scornfully answers, prepares resistance,
but hindered by a sign from Heaven, flies out of Paradise.

O for that warning voice, which he° who saw
The Apocalypse heard cry in Heaven aloud,
Then when the Dragon,° put to second rout,
Came furious down to be revenged on men,
"Woe to the inhabitants on Earth!" that now,
While time was, our first parents had been warned
The coming of their secret foe, and scaped,
Haply so scaped, his mortal snare; for now
Satan, now first inflamed with rage, came down,
The tempter ere° the accuser of mankind,   10
To wreak on innocent frail man his loss
Of that first battle, and his flight to Hell:
Yet not rejoicing in his speed, though bold,
Far off and fearless, nor with cause to boast,
Begins his dire attempt, which nigh the birth
Now rolling, boils in his tumultuous breast,
And like a devilish engine° back recoils
Upon himself; horror and doubt distract
His troubled thoughts, and from the bottom stir
The Hell within him, for within him Hell   20
He brings, and round about him, nor from Hell
One step no more than from himself can fly
By change of place. Now conscience wakes despair
That slumbered, wakes the bitter memory
Of what he was, what is, and what must be
Worse; of worse deeds worse sufferings must en-
sue.

32. **Nightly I visit:** Milton composed chiefly at night and dictated the result. Cf. VII. 28–30, IX. 22–23.   33–36. In his blindness, though not in his degree of fame, Milton links himself
with two blind poets, Homer (Maeonides) and Thamyris (mentioned in the *Iliad,* II. 595–600), and two blind prophets, the
Theban Tiresias and the Thracian Phineus.   38. **numbers:**
verses.   **wakeful bird:** the nightingale.   39. **darkling:** in the
dark.   48. **blank:** the gray-white effect of light apparent to
Milton's blind eyes.

Book IV: 1. he: St. John, supposed author of the Apocalypse
(Revelation). Lines 1–5 are based on Rev. 12:7–12.   3. **the
Dragon:** the serpent, Satan (Rev. 12:9). Cf. "Nativity," l. 168.
10. **ere:** before he was. See Rev. 12:10.   17. **engine:** cannon.

Sometimes towards Eden which now in his view
Lay pleasant, his grieved look he fixes sad,
Sometimes towards Heaven and the full-blazing
    sun,
Which now sat high in his meridian tower.   30
Then much revolving, thus in sighs began:
    " O thou° that with surpassing glory crowned,
Look'st from thy sole dominion like the god
Of this new world; at whose sight all the stars
Hide their diminished heads; to thee I call,
But with no friendly voice, and add thy name,
O sun, to tell thee how I hate thy beams
That bring to my remembrance from what state
I fell, how glorious once above thy sphere;
Till pride and worse ambition threw me down,   40
Warring in Heaven against Heaven's matchless
    King.
Ah wherefore? He deserved no such return
From me, whom he created what I was
In that bright eminence, and with his good
Upbraided none; nor was his service hard.
What could be less than to afford him praise,
The easiest recompense, and pay him thanks,
How due! Yet all his good proved ill in me,
And wrought but malice; lifted up so high
I sdained° subjection, and thought one step higher
Would set me highest, and in a moment quit°   51
The debt immense of endless gratitude,
So burdensome still° paying, still° to owe;
Forgetful what from him I still° received,
And understood not that a grateful mind
By owing owes not, but still° pays, at once
Indebted and discharged; what burden then?
O had his powerful destiny ordained
Me some inferior angel, I had stood
Then happy; no unbounded hope had raised   60
Ambition. Yet why not? some other power
As great might have aspired, and me though mean
Drawn to his part; but other powers as great
Fell not, but stand unshaken, from within
Or from without, to all temptations armed.
Hadst thou the same free will and power to stand?
Thou hadst. Whom hast thou then or what to ac-
    cuse,
But Heaven's free love dealt equally to all?
Be then his love accurst, since love or hate,
To me alike, it deals eternal woe.   70
Nay cursed be thou, since against his thy will
Chose freely what it now so justly rues.
Me miserable! which way shall I fly
Infinite wrath, and infinite despair?
Which way I fly is Hell; myself am Hell;°

And in the lowest deep a lower deep
Still threatening to devour me opens wide,
To which the Hell I suffer seems a Heaven.
O then at last relent: is there no place
Left for repentance, none for pardon left?
None left but by submission; and that word
Disdain forbids me, and my dread of shame
Among the spirits beneath, whom I seduced
With other promises and other vaunts
Than to submit, boasting I could subdue
The Omnipotent. Ay me, they little know
How dearly I abide that boast so vain,
Under what torments inwardly I groan;
While they adore me on the throne of Hell,
With diadem and scepter high advanced,   90
The lower still I fall, only supreme
In misery; such joy ambition finds.
But say I could repent and could obtain
By act of grace° my former state; how soon
Would highth recall high thoughts, how soon un-
    say
What feigned submission swore: ease would recant
Vows made in pain, as violent° and void.
For never can true reconcilement grow
Where wounds of deadly hate have pierced so deep;
Which would but lead me to a worse relapse   100
And heavier fall: so should I purchase dear
Short intermission bought with double smart.
This knows my Punisher; therefore as far
From granting he, as I from begging peace.
All hope excluded thus, behold instead
Of us outcast, exiled, his new delight,
Mankind created, and for him this World.
So farewell hope, and with hope farewell fear,
Farewell remorse! All good to me is lost;
Evil, be thou my good; by thee at least   110
Divided empire with Heaven's King I hold,
By thee, and more than half perhaps will reign;°
As man ere long, and this new World shall know."
    Thus while he spake, each passion dimmed his
    face
Thrice changed with pale,° ire, envy, and despair,
Which marred his borrowed visage,° and betrayed
Him counterfeit, if any eye beheld.
For heavenly minds from such distempers foul
Are ever clear. Whereof he soon aware,
Each perturbation smoothed with outward calm,
Artificer of fraud; and was the first   121
That practiced falsehood under saintly show,
Deep malice to conceal, couched° with revenge:
Yet not enough had practiced to deceive
Uriel once warned, whose eye pursued him down

32-41. O . . . King: Milton's nephew tells us that these lines
were written as Lucifer's first speech in the drama that the
poet planned in the early 1640's.   50. sdained: disdained.
51. quit: settle.   53, 54, 56. still: always.   75. Which . . . Hell:
Cf. Satan's early boast, I, 254-55.

94. act of grace: pardon.   97. violent: made under duress and
hence void.   112. reign: rule.   115. pale: paleness.   116. borrowed visage: In III. 634-44, Satan had changed himself into
the likeness of a good angel to inquire his way from Uriel, one
of God's chief angels.   123. couched: joined in concealment.

The way he went, and on the Assyrian mount°
Saw him disfigured, more than could befall
Spirit of happy sort: his gestures fierce
He° marked and mad demeanor, then alone,
As he° supposed, all unobserved, unseen.   130
So on he fares, and to the border comes
Of Eden, where delicious Paradise,°
Now nearer, crowns with her enclosure green
As with a rural mound the champaign head°
Of a steep wilderness, whose hairy sides
With thicket overgrown, grotesque and wild,
Access denied; and overhead up grew
Insuperable highth of loftiest shade,
Cedar, and pine, and fir, and branching palm,
A sylvan scene, and as the ranks ascend   140
Shade above shade, a woody theater
Of stateliest view. Yet higher than their tops
The verdurous wall of Paradise up sprung;
Which to our general sire° gave prospect large
Into his nether empire neighboring round.
And higher than that wall a circling row
Of goodliest trees loaden with fairest fruit,
Blossoms and fruits at once of golden hue,
Appeared, with gay enameled colors mixed;
On which the sun more glad impressed his beams
Than in fair evening cloud, or humid bow,°   151
When God hath showered the earth; so lovely
        seemed
That lantskip.° And of pure° now purer air
Meets his approach, and to the heart inspires
Vernal delight and joy, able to drive
All sadness but despair; now gentle gales
Fanning their odoriferous wings dispense
Native perfúmes, and whisper whence they stole
Those balmy spoils. As when to them who sail
Beyond the Cape of Hope,° and now are past   160
Mozambic,° off at sea north-east winds blow
Sabaean odors from the spicy shore
Of Araby the Blest, with such delay
Well pleased they slack their course, and many a
        league
Cheered with the grateful smell old ocean smiles;
So entertained those odorous sweets the Fiend
Who came their bane, though with them better
        pleased
Than Asmodëus° with the fishy fume,

126. Assyrian mount: Niphates, where Satan had alighted on earth.   129. He: Uriel.   130. he: Satan.   132. Paradise: the "park" or "garden" which is the home of Adam and Eve, in the eastern part of Eden. See ll. 208–14.   134. champaign head: plateau.   144. our . . . sire: Adam.   151. humid bow: the rainbow.   153. lantskip: landscape. of pure: after pure.   160. Hope: Good Hope.   161. Mozambic: Mozambique, on the east coast of Africa.   162. Sabaean: of Saba (the Biblical Sheba) in Arabia.   168–71. Asmodëus . . . bound: In the Apocryphal Book of Tobit, Asmodëus, an evil spirit, loved a woman and destroyed her seven husbands; her eighth husband, Tobit's son, drove Asmodëus away with the smell of burning fish, as the angel Raphael had advised. Asmodëus "fled into the utmost parts of Egypt, and the angel bound him" (chap. 8).

That drove him, though enamored, from the spouse
Of Tobit's son, and with a vengeance sent   170
From Media post to Egypt, there fast bound.
    Now to the ascent of that steep savage hill
Satan had journeyed on, pensive and slow;
But further way found none, so thick entwined,
As one continued brake, the undergrowth
Of shrubs and tangling bushes had perplexed
All path of man or beast that passed that way.
One gate there only was, and that looked east
On the other side; which when the Arch-Felon
        saw,
Due entrance he disdained, and in contempt,   180
At one slight bound high overleaped all bound
Of hill or highest wall, and sheer within
Lights on his feet. As when a prowling wolf,
Whom hunger drives to seek new haunt for prey,
Watching where shepherds pen their flocks at eve
In hurdled cotes amid the field secure,
Leaps o'er the fence with ease into the fold;
Or as a thief bent to unhoard the cash
Of some rich burgher, whose substantial doors,
Cross-barred and bolted fast, fear no assault,   190
In at the window climbs, or o'er the tiles:
So clomb this first grand thief into God's fold;
So since into his church lewd° hirelings climb.
Thence up he flew, and on the Tree of Life,
The middle tree and highest there that grew,
Sat like a cormorant; yet not true life
Thereby regained, but sat devising death
To them who lived; nor on the virtue thought
Of that life-giving plant, but only used
For prospect,° what well used had been the pledge
Of immortality. So little knows   201
Any, but God alone, to value right
The good before him, but perverts best things
To worst abuse, or to their meanest use.
    Beneath him with new wonder now he views
To all delight of human sense exposed
In narrow room Nature's whole wealth, yea more,
A Heaven on Earth, for blissful Paradise
Of God the garden was, by him in the east
Of Eden planted; Eden stretched her line   210
From Auran° eastward to the royal towers
Of great Seleucia,° built by Grecian kings,
Or where the sons of Eden long before
Dwelt in Telassar.° In this pleasant° soil
His far more pleasant° garden God ordained;
Out of the fertile ground he caused to grow
All trees of noblest kind for sight, smell, taste;
And all amid them stood the Tree of Life,
High eminent, blooming ambrosial fruit

193. lewd: base.   200. For prospect: as a lookout.   211. Auran: probably Auranitis, on the Euphrates.   212. Seleucia: the capital, on the Tigris, of the kingdom founded by Alexander's general, Seleucus.   214. Telassar: a place in Eden, somewhere in Mesopotamia.   214–15. pleasant: The name Eden means "pleasure." Cf. ll 27–28.

Of vegetable gold; and next to life   220
Our death, the Tree of Knowledge, grew fast by,
Knowledge of good bought dear by knowing ill.
Southward through Eden went a river large,
Nor changed his course, but through the shaggy
        hill
Passed underneath ingulfed, for God had thrown
That mountain as his garden mold,° high raised
Upon the rapid current, which through veins
Of porous earth with kindly° thirst up drawn,
Rose a fresh fountain, and with many a rill
Watered the garden; thence united fell   230
Down the steep glade, and met the nether flood,
Which from his darksome passage now appears,
And now divided into four main streams,
Runs díverse, wandering° many a famous realm
And country whereof here needs no account;
But rather to tell how, if art could tell,
How from that sapphire fount the crispèd° brooks,
Rolling on orient pearl and sands of gold,
With mazy error° under pendent shades
Ran nectar, visiting each plant, and fed   240
Flowers worthy of Paradise, which not nice° art
In beds and curious knots, but Nature boon°
Poured forth profuse on hill and dale and plain,
Both where the morning sun first warmly smote
The open field, and where the unpierced shade
Imbrowned° the noontide bowers. Thus was this
        place,
A happy rural seat of various view;°
Groves whose rich trees wept odorous gums and
        balm,
Others whose fruit burnished with golden rind
Hung amiable,° Hesperian fables true,   250
If true, here only,° and of delicious taste.
Betwixt them lawns, or level downs, and flocks
Grazing the tender herb, were interposed,
Or palmy hillock, or the flowery lap
Of some irriguous° valley spread her store,
Flowers of all hue, and without thorn the rose.
Another side, umbrageous grots and caves
Of cool recess, o'er which the mantling vine
Lays forth her purple grape, and gently creeps
Luxuriant; meanwhile murmuring waters fall   260
Down the slope hills, dispersed, or in a lake,
That to the fringèd bank with myrtle crowned
Her crystal mirror holds, unite their streams.
The birds their quire apply;° airs, vernal airs,
Breathing the smell of field and grove, attune

The trembling leaves, while universal Pan,°
Knit with the Graces and the Hours in dance,
Led on the eternal spring. Not that fair field
Of Enna,° where Prosérpine gathering flowers,
Herself a fairer flower, by gloomy Dis   270
Was gathered, which cost Ceres all that pain
To seek her through the world; nor that sweet
        grove
Of Daphne by Orontes, and the inspired
Castalian spring,° might with this Paradise
Of Eden strive; nor that Nyseian isle,°
Girt with the river Triton, where old Cham,
Whom Gentiles° Ammon call and Libyan Jove,
Hid Amalthea and her florid° son,
Young Bacchus, from his stepdame Rhea's eye;
Nor where Abassin kings their issue guard,   280
Mount Amara,° though this by some supposed
True Paradise, under the Ethiop line°
By Nilus' head,° enclosed with shining rock,
A whole day's journey high, but wide remote
From this Assyrian garden,° where the Fiend
Saw undelighted all delight, all kind
Of living creatures new to sight and strange.
    Two of far nobler shape erect and tall,
God-like erect,° with native honor clad
In naked majesty seemed lords of all,   290
And worthy seemed, for in their looks divine
The image of their glorious Maker shone,
Truth, wisdom, sanctitude severe and pure,
Severe but in true filial freedom placed;
Whence true authority in men; though both
Not° equal, as their sex not equal seemed;
For contemplation he and valor formed,
For softness she and sweet attractive grace;
He for God only, she for God in him.
His fair large front° and eye sublime° declared
Absolute rule; and hyacinthine° locks   301

266. universal Pan: "the All," the god of universal nature.
269. Enna: in Sicily, where Pluto (Dis) carried off Ceres' daughter
to be his queen in Hades.   272–74. grove . . . spring: the gardens of Daphne on the river Orontes in Syria; they contained a
spring (named after the Castalian spring at Delphi) which,
through marks on leaves, gave oracular answers to questioners.
275–79. Nyseian isle . . . Rhea's eye: Nysa, an island in the
river Triton in Tunisia, where the Libyan King Ammon, husband of Rhea, hid his mistress Amalthea and their son Bacchus.
Ammon was identified with Cham (Noah's son Ham) and with
the Greek god Zeus Ammon and the Roman Jupiter Ammon.
Cf. "Nativity," l. 203 and note.   277. Gentiles: non-Jewish
peoples, the Greeks and Romans.   278. florid: flushed (Bacchus
being god of wine).   280–81. Abassin . . . Amara: Amara was
a hill with palaces in Abyssinia, where the native princes were
brought up in seclusion.   282. Ethiop line: the equator.
283. Nilus' head: the source of the Nile.   285. this . . . garden:
the home of Adam and Eve.   288–89. erect: Milton follows
tradition in emphasizing the posture that befits creatures endowed "With sanctity of reason" (VII. 508).   296–99. Not
equal . . . him: The idea of woman's inferiority was not a peculiarly Miltonic view; it was traditional orthodoxy and was bound
up with the whole conception of the great chain of being.
300. front: forehead. sublime: uplifted.   301. hyacinthine:
dark, brown (?) (a Homeric epithet).

226. garden mold: rich topsoil for a garden.   228. kindly:
natural.   234. wandering: traversing.   237. crisped: rippling.
239. error: wandering (the Latin sense).   241. nice: fastidious,
elegant. As elsewhere, Milton contrasts artifice with nature and
nature's fecundity.   242. boon: bounteous.   246. Imbrowned:
darkened.   247. view: appearance.   250. amiable: lovely.
250–51. Hesperian . . . only: like the golden apples of the
Hesperides, the myth being true only in Eden.   255. irriguous:
well-watered.   264. apply: contribute.

Round from his parted forelock manly hung
Clustering, but not beneath his shoulders broad:
She as a veil down to the slender waist
Her unadornèd golden tresses wore
Disheveled, but in wanton ringlets waved
As the vine curls her tendrils, which implied
Subjection, but required with gentle sway,
And by her yielded, by him best received,
Yielded with coy° submission, modest pride,   310
And sweet reluctant amorous delay.
Nor those mysterious parts were then concealed;
Then was not guilty shame; dishonest° shame
Of Nature's works, honor dishonorable,
Sin-bred, how have ye troubled all mankind
With shows instead, mere shows of seeming pure,
And banished from man's life his happiest life,
Simplicity and spotless innocence.°
So passed they naked on, nor shunned the sight
Of God or angel, for they thought no ill;   320
So hand in hand they passed, the loveliest pair
That ever since in love's embraces met,
Adam the goodliest man of men since born
His sons, the fairest of her daughters Eve.
Under a tuft of shade that on a green
Stood whispering soft, by a fresh fountain side
They sat them down; and after no more toil
Of their sweet gardening labor than sufficed
To recommend cool Zephyr,° and made ease
More easy, wholesome thirst and appetite   330
More grateful, to their supper fruits they fell,
Nectarine fruits which the compliant boughs
Yielded them, sidelong as they sat recline°
On the soft downy bank damasked° with flowers.
The savory pulp they chew, and in the rind
Still as they thirsted scoop the brimming stream;
Nor gentle purpose,° nor endearing smiles
Wanted,° nor youthful dalliance, as beseems
Fair couple linked in happy nuptial league,
Alone as they. About them frisking played   340
All beasts of the earth, since wild, and of all chase°
In wood or wilderness, forest or den;
Sporting the lion ramped,° and in his paw
Dandled the kid; bears, tigers, ounces,° pards,°
Gamboled before them; the unwieldy elephant
To make them mirth used all his might, and
    wreathed
His lithe proboscis; close the serpent sly
Insinuating,° wove with Gordian twine
His braided train,° and of his fatal guile

Gave proof unheeded; others on the grass   350
Couched, and now filled with pasture gazing sat,
Or bedward ruminating;° for the sun
Declined was hasting now with prone career
To the ocean isles,° and in the ascending scale
Of Heaven the stars that usher evening rose:
When Satan still in gaze, as first he stood,
Scarce thus at length failed speech° recovered sad:
    "O Hell! what do mine eyes with grief behold!
Into our room of bliss thus high advanced
Creatures of other mold,° earth-born perhaps,   360
Not spirits, yet to heavenly spirits bright
Little inferior; whom my thoughts pursue
With wonder, and could love, so lively shines
In them divine resemblance, and such grace
The hand that formed them on their shape hath
    poured.
Ah gentle pair, ye little think how nigh
Your change approaches, when all these delights
Will vanish and deliver ye to woe,
More woe, the more your taste is now of joy;
Happy, but for so happy ill secured   370
Long to continue, and this high seat your Heaven
Ill fenced for Heaven to keep out such a foe
As now is entered; yet no purposed foe
To you whom I could pity thus forlorn,
Though I unpitied. League° with you I seek,
And mutual amity so strait, so close,
That I with you must dwell, or you with me
Henceforth; my dwelling haply may not please,
Like this fair Paradise, your sense, yet such
Accept your Maker's work; he gave it me,   380
Which I as freely give; Hell shall unfold,
To entertain you two, her widest gates,
And send forth all her kings; there will be room,
Not like these narrow limits, to receive
Your numerous offspring; if no better place,
Thank him who puts me loth to this revenge
On you who wrong me not, for him who wronged.
And should I at your harmless innocence
Melt, as I do, yet public reason just,
Honor and empire with revenge enlarged   390
By conquering this new World, compels me now
To do what else though damned I should abhor."
    So spake the Fiend, and with necessity,
The tyrant's plea, excused his devilish deeds.
Then from his lofty stand on that high tree
Down he alights among the sportful herd
Of those four-footed kinds, himself now one,
Now other, as their shape served best his end
Nearer to view his prey, and unespied   399
To mark what of their state he more might learn
By word or action marked. About them round
A lion now he stalks with fiery glare;

310. coy: shy.   313. dishonest: impure.   317–18. banished
. . . innocence: Here and elsewhere Milton, for all his stress
on rational choice (Intro., p. 406), cannot subdue his nostalgic
vision of primal innocence.   329. recommend . . . Zephyr:
make the cool breeze pleasant.   333. recline: reclining.
334. damasked: richly variegated.   337. purpose: conversation.   338. Wanted: were lacking.   341. all chase: every
habitat.   343. ramped: reared up.   344. ounces: lynxes.
pards: leopards.   348. Insinuating: winding into folds.
349. train: body.

352. bedward ruminating: chewing the cud before sleeping.
354. ocean isles: the Azores. Cf. l. 592.   357. failed speech: speech
that had failed him.   360. mold: substance.   375–85. League . . .
offspring: Satan is enjoying his own sardonic irony.

Then as a tiger, who by chance hath spied
In some purlieu two gentle fawns at play,
Straight couches close, then rising, changes oft
His couchant watch, as one who chose his ground
Whence rushing he might surest seize them both
Gripped in each paw; when Adam first of men
To first of women, Eve, thus moving speech,
Turned him all ear to hear new utterance flow:
    "Sole partner and sole part of all these joys,   411
Dearer thyself than all, needs must the Power
That made us, and for us this ample World,
Be infinitely good, and of his good
As liberal and free as infinite,
That raised us from the dust and placed us here
In all this happiness, who at his hand
Have nothing merited, nor can perform
Aught whereof he hath need; he who requires
From us no other service than to keep   420
This one, this easy charge, of all the trees
In Paradise that bear delicious fruit
So various, not to taste that only Tree
Of Knowledge, planted by the Tree of Life,
So near grows death to life, whate'er death is,
Some dreadful thing no doubt; for well thou
        know'st
God hath pronounced it death to taste that Tree,
The only sign of our obedience left
Among so many signs of power and rule
Conferred upon us, and dominion given   430
Over all other creatures that possess
Earth, air, and sea. Then let us not think hard
One easy prohibition, who enjoy
Free leave so large to all things else, and choice
Unlimited of manifold delights;
But let us ever praise him, and extol
His bounty, following our delightful task
To prune these growing plants, and tend these
        flowers,
Which were it toilsome, yet with thee were sweet."
    To whom thus Eve replied: "O thou for whom
And from whom I was formed flesh of thy flesh,
And without whom am to no end, my guide   442
And head, what thou hast said is just and right.
For we to him indeed all praises owe,
And daily thanks, I chiefly who enjoy
So far the happier lot, enjoying thee
Pre-eminent by so much odds, while thou
Like consort to thyself canst nowhere find.
That day I oft remember, when from sleep
I first awaked, and found myself reposed   450
Under a shade on flowers, much wondering where
And what I was, whence thither brought, and how.
Not distant far from thence a murmuring sound
Of waters issued from a cave and spread
Into a liquid plain, then stood unmoved
Pure as the expanse of Heaven; I thither went
With unexperienced thought, and laid me down

On the green bank, to look into the clear
Smooth lake, that to me seemed another sky
As° I bent down to look, just opposite   460
A shape within the watery gleam appeared
Bending to look on me: I started back,
It started back, but pleased I soon returned,
Pleased it returned as soon with answering looks
Of sympathy and love; there I had fixed
Mine eyes till now, and pined with vain desire,
Had not a voice thus warned me: 'What thou seest,
What there thou seest, fair creature, is thyself,
With thee it came and goes; but follow me,
And I will bring thee where no shadow stays°   470
Thy coming, and thy soft embraces, he
Whose image thou art, him thou shalt enjoy
Inseparably thine; to him shalt bear
Multitudes like thyself, and thence be called
Mother of human race.' What could I do
But follow straight, invisibly thus led?
Till I espied thee, fair indeed and tall,
Under a platan; yet methought less fair,
Less winning soft, less amiably mild,   479
Than that smooth watery image; back I turned,
Thou following cried'st aloud, 'Return, fair Eve,
Whom fli'st thou?° whom thou fli'st, of him thou
        art,
His flesh, his bone; to give thee being I lent
Out of my side to thee, nearest my heart,
Substantial life, to have thee by my side
Henceforth an individual° solace dear.
Part of my soul I seek thee, and thee claim
My other half.' With that thy gentle hand
Seized mine, I yielded, and from that time see
How beauty is excelled by manly grace   490
And wisdom, which alone is truly fair."
    So spake our general mother, and with eyes
Of conjugal attraction unreproved,°
And meek surrender, half embracing leaned
On our first father; half her swelling breast
Naked met his under the flowing gold
Of her loose tresses hid. He in delight
Both of her beauty and submissive charms
Smiled with superior love, as Jupiter   499
On Juno° smiles, when he impregns° the clouds
That shed May flowers; and pressed her matron lip
With kisses pure. Aside the Devil turned
For envy, yet with jealous leer malign
Eyed them askance, and to himself thus plained:°

460–66. As . . . desire: Although Eve was at her creation,
and still is, quite innocent, Milton's use of the myth of Narcissus gives a first faint hint of the vanity that is to be her undoing.   470. stays: waits for.   481–82. Thou . . . thou: Both
the action and the language recall Ovid's tale of Apollo's pursuing Daphne, and, in a way parallel to the myth of Narcissus
above, this veiled allusion gives a hint of the extreme devotion
to Eve that is to be Adam's undoing.   486. individual: inseparable.   493. unreproved: not deserving reproof.   499–
500. Jupiter, Juno: here the sky and the air, respectively.
500. impregns: impregnates.   504. plained: complained.

" Sight hateful, sight tormenting! thus these two
Imparadised in one another's arms,
The happier Eden, shall enjoy their fill
Of bliss on bliss, while I to Hell am thrust,
Where neither joy nor love, but fierce desire,
Among our other torments not the least,   510
Still unfulfilled with pain of longing pines;°
Yet let me not forget what I have gained
From their own mouths. All is not theirs, it seems;
One fatal tree there stands, of Knowledge called,
Forbidden them to taste. Knowledge forbidden?
Suspicious, reasonless. Why should their Lord
Envy them that? can it be sin to know,
Can it be death? and do they only stand
By ignorance, is that their happy state,
The proof of their obedience and their faith?   520
O fair foundation laid whereon to build
Their ruin! Hence I will excite their minds
With more desire to know, and to reject
Envious commands, invented with design
To keep them low whom knowledge might exalt
Equal with gods. Aspiring to be such,
They taste and die; what likelier can ensue?
But first with narrow search I must walk round
This garden, and no corner leave unspied;   529
A chance but chance may lead where I may meet
Some wandering spirit of Heaven, by fountain side,
Or in thick shade retired, from him to draw
What further would be learnt. Live while ye may,
Yet happy pair; enjoy, till I return,
Short pleasures, for long woes are to succeed."
    So saying, his proud step he scornful turned,
But with sly circumspection, and began
Through wood, through waste, o'er hill, o'er dale,
        his roam.
Meanwhile in utmost longitude,° where Heaven
With Earth and Ocean meets, the setting sun   540
Slowly descended, and with right aspect°
Against the eastern gate of Paradise
Leveled his evening rays. It was a rock
Of alablaster,° piled up to the clouds,
Conspicuous far, winding with one ascent
Accessible from Earth, one entrance high;
The rest was craggy cliff, that overhung
Still as it rose, impossible to climb.
Betwixt these rocky pillars Gabriel sat,
Chief of the angelic guards, awaiting night;   550
About him exercised heroic games
The unarmed youth of Heaven, but nigh at hand
Celestial armory, shields, helms, and spears,
Hung high, with diamond flaming and with gold.
Thither came Uriel, gliding through the even
On a sunbeam, swift as a shooting star
In autumn thwarts° the night, when vapors fired°

Impress the air, and shows the mariner
From what point of his compass to beware
Impetuous winds. He thus began in haste: 560
    " Gabriel, to thee thy course by lot hath given
Charge and strict watch that to this happy place
No evil thing approach or enter in;
This° day at highth of noon came to my sphere
A spirit, zealous, as he seemed, to know
More of the Almighty's works, and chiefly man,
God's latest image. I described° his way
Bent all on speed, and marked his aery gait;°
But in the mount that lies from Eden north,   569
Where he first lighted, soon discerned his looks
Alien from Heaven, with passions foul obscured.
Mine eye pursued him still, but under shade
Lost sight of him; one of the banished crew,
I fear, hath ventured from the deep, to raise
New troubles; him thy care must be to find."
    To whom the wingèd warrior thus returned:
" Uriel, no wonder if thy perfect sight,
Amid the sun's bright circle where thou sitt'st,
See far and wide. In at this gate none pass
The vigilance° here placed, but such as come   580
Well known from Heaven; and since meridian
        hour
No creature thence. If spirit of other sort,
So minded, have o'erleaped these earthy bounds
On purpose, hard thou know'st it to exclude
Spiritual substance with corporeal bar.
But if within the circuit of these walks,
In whatsoever shape he lurk, of whom
Thou tell'st, by morrow dawning I shall know."
    So promised he, and Uriel to his charge
Returned on that bright beam, whose point now
        raised   590
Bore him slope downward to the sun now fallen
Beneath the Azores; whether the prime orb,
Incredible how swift, had thither rolled
Diurnal,° or this less volúble Earth,
By shorter flight to the east,° had left him there
Arraying with reflected purple and gold
The clouds that on his western throne attend.
    Now came still evening on, and twilight gray
Had in her sober livery all things clad;
Silence accompanied, for beast and bird,   600
They to their grassy couch, these to their nests
Were slunk, all but the wakeful nightingale;
She all night long her amorous descant sung;
Silence was pleased. Now glowed the firmament
With living sapphires; Hesperus° that led
The starry host rode brightest, till the moon,

511. pines: makes (me) pine.   539. utmost longitude: farthest
west.   541. right aspect: directly (so as to light up the inner
side of the rock).   544. alablaster: alabaster.   557. thwarts:
crosses.   vapors fired: heat lightning.

564–71. This . . . obscured: The incident occurred in III.
621–735.   567. described: descried. See ll. 114–30 and l. 116n.
568. aery gait: flight through the air.   580. vigilance: guards.
592–94. whether . . . Diurnal: if, as in old astronomy, the sun
had revolved to the west.   594–95. or . . . east: or, as in Copernican astronomy, the earth had made a much smaller rotation
to the east.   605. Hesperus: the evening star.

Rising in clouded majesty, at length
Apparent° queen unveiled her peerless light,
And o'er the dark her silver mantle threw;
　　When Adam thus to Eve: "Fair consort, the
　　　　hour   610
Of night, and all things now retired to rest
Mind us of like repose, since God hath set
Labor and rest, as day and night to men
Successive, and the timely dew of sleep
Now falling with soft slumbrous weight inclines
Our eyelids; other creatures all day long
Rove idle, unemployed, and less need rest;
Man hath his daily work of body or mind
Appointed, which declares his dignity,
And the regard of Heaven on all his ways;   620
While other animals unactive range,
And of their doings God takes no account.
To-morrow ere fresh morning streak the east
With first approach of light, we must be risen,
And at our pleasant labor, to reform
Yon flowery arbors, yonder alleys green,
Our walks at noon, with branches overgrown,
That mock our scant manuring,° and require
More hands than ours to lop their wanton growth.
Those blossoms also, and those dropping gums,
That lie bestrown unsightly and unsmooth,   631
Ask riddance, if we mean to tread with ease;
Meanwhile, as Nature wills, night bids us rest."
　　To whom thus Eve with perfect beauty adorned:
"My author° and disposer, what thou bidd'st
Unargued I obey; so God ordains.
God is thy law, thou mine; to know no more
Is woman's happiest knowledge and her praise.
With thee conversing° I forget all time,
All seasons° and their change, all please alike.
Sweet is the breath of morn, her rising sweet,   641
With charm° of earliest birds; pleasant the sun
When first on this delightful land he spreads
His orient beams, on herb, tree, fruit, and flower,
Glistering with dew; fragrant the fertile Earth
After soft showers; and sweet the coming on
Of grateful evening mild, then silent night
With this her solemn bird and this fair moon,
And these the gems of Heaven, her starry train:
But neither breath of morn when she ascends   650
With charm of earliest birds, nor rising sun
On this delightful land, nor herb, fruit, flower,
Glistering with dew, nor fragrance after showers,
Nor grateful evening mild, nor silent night
With this her solemn bird, nor walk by moon
Or glittering starlight, without thee is sweet.
But wherefore all night long shine these, for whom
This glorious sight, when sleep hath shut all eyes?"

　　To whom our general ancestor replied: 659
"Daughter of God and man, accomplished Eve,
Those have their course to finish, round the Earth,
By morrow evening, and from land to land
In order, though to nations yet unborn,
Ministering light prepared, they set and rise;
Lest total darkness° should by night regain
Her old possession, and extinguish life
In nature and all things; which these soft fires
Not only enlighten, but with kindly° heat
Of various influence° foment and warm,
Temper or nourish, or in part shed down   670
Their stellar virtue on all kinds that grow
On Earth, made hereby apter to receive
Perfection from the sun's more potent ray.
These then, though unbeheld in deep of night,
Shine not in vain, nor think, though men were
　　none,
That Heaven would want spectators, God want
　　praise;
Millions of spiritual creatures walk the Earth
Unseen, both when we wake, and when we sleep:
All these with ceaseless praise his works behold
Both day and night. How often from the steep
Of echoing hill or thicket have we heard   681
Celestial voices to the midnight air,
Sole, or responsive each to other's note,
Singing their great Creator; oft in bands
While they keep watch, or nightly rounding° walk,
With heavenly touch of instrumental sounds
In full harmonic number joined, their songs
Divide the night,° and lift our thoughts to
　　Heaven."
　　Thus talking, hand in hand alone they passed
On to their blissful bower; it was a place   690
Chosen by the sovran Planter, when he framed
All things to man's delightful use; the roof
Of thickest covert was inwoven shade,
Laurel and myrtle, and what higher grew
Of firm and fragrant leaf; on either side
Acanthus, and each odorous bushy shrub
Fenced up the verdant wall; each beauteous flower,
Iris all hues, roses, and jessamine
Reared high their flourished heads between, and
　　wrought
Mosaic; under foot the violet,   700
Crocus, and hyacinth with rich inlay
Broidered the ground, more colored than with stone
Of costliest emblem.° Other creature here,
Beast, bird, insect, or worm durst enter none;
Such was their awe of man. In shadier bower
More sacred and sequestered, though but feigned,°

665. total darkness: the darkness of Chaos.   668. kindly:
natural.   669–73. influence . . . ray: a limited recognition of
astrological influence.   685. rounding: making the rounds, as
sentries.   688. Divide . . . night: i.e., into watches (a Roman
military term).   703. emblem: inlaid work.   706. feigned:
poetical and pagan fictions.

608. Apparent: a manifest.   628. manuring: cultivating.
635. "My author": source of my being.   639. conversing:
living.   640. seasons: times of day (since Eden enjoys eternal
spring).   642. charm: song.

Pan or Silvanus° never slept, nor nymph
Nor Faunus° haunted. Here in close recess
With flowers, garlands, and sweet-smelling herbs
Espousèd Eve decked first her nuptial bed,   710
And heavenly quires the hymenean° sung,
What day the genial° angel to our sire
Brought her in naked beauty more adorned,
More lovely than Pandora,° whom the gods
Endowed with all their gifts, and O too like
In sad event, when to the unwiser son
Of Japhet brought by Hermes, she ensnared
Mankind with her fair looks, to be avenged
On him who had stole Jove's authentic fire.

    Thus at their shady lodge arrived, both stood,
Both turned, and under open sky adored   721
The God that made both sky, air, Earth, and
    Heaven,
Which they beheld, the moon's resplendent globe
And starry pole:° "Thou also mad'st the night,
Maker Omnipotent, and thou the day,
Which we in our appointed work employed
Have finished happy in our mutual help
And mutual love, the crown of all our bliss
Ordained by thee, and this delicious place
For us too large, where thy abundance wants   730
Partakers, and uncropped falls to the ground.
But thou hast promised from us two a race
To fill the Earth, who shall with us extol
Thy goodness infinite, both when we wake,
And when we seek, as now, thy gift of sleep."

    This said unanimous, and other rites
Observing none, but adoration pure
Which God likes best, into their inmost bower
Handed they went; and eased the putting off
These troublesome disguises which we wear,   740
Straight side by side were laid, nor turned, I ween,
Adam from his fair spouse, nor Eve the rites
Mysterious of connubial love refused;
Whatever hypocrites austerely talk
Of purity and place and innocence,
Defaming as impure what God declares
Pure, and commands to some, leaves free to all.
Our Maker bids increase;° who bids abstain
But our destroyer, foe to God and man?
Hail, wedded Love, mysterious law,° true source
Of human offspring, sole propriety°   751
In Paradise of all things common else.
By thee adulterous lust was driven from men

Among the bestial herds to range; by thee
Founded in reason, loyal, just, and pure,
Relations dear, and all the charities°
Of father, son, and brother first were known.
Far be it that I should write thee sin or blame,
Or think thee unbefitting holiest place,
Perpetual fountain of domestic sweets,   760
Whose bed is undefiled and chaste pronounced,
Present or past, as saints and patriarchs used.
Here Love his golden shafts employs, here lights
His constant lamp, and waves his purple wings,
Reigns here and revels;° not in the bought smile
Of harlots, loveless, joyless, unendeared,
Casual fruition; nor in court amours,
Mixed dance, or wanton mask, or midnight ball,
Or serenate,° which the starved° lover sings
To his proud fair, best quitted° with disdain.   770
These lulled by nightingales, embracing slept,
And on their naked limbs the flowery roof
Showered roses, which the morn repaired.° Sleep
    on,
Blest pair; and O yet happiest if ye seek
No happier state, and know to know no more.°

[The action of the rest of Book IV is summarized in Milton's prefatory Argument. The most important thing is Satan's embarking on his plan of campaign (see IV. 512–27) by tempting Eve in a dream.]

from BOOK V

[Eve, in great distress, tells Adam of a dream (of Satanic inspiration): she had been led to the forbidden Tree of Knowledge and had yielded to the solicitations of a seeming angel and eaten of the fruit, which, she was told, would make her a goddess. She is relieved that it was all a dream and is reassured by Adam. The two utter a grand canticle in praise of the Creation and the Creator and go about their daily work. Since temptation is near, God sends down Raphael to warn the pair of their responsibility. Adam wishes to know "Of things above his world," and Raphael begins (ll. 469 ff.) with an account of the great chain of being, an account which departs from orthodoxy in its monistic theory of matter and spirit. Then Raphael goes on to tell of the great example of pride and disobedience, Satan's revolt after God's proclamation of the Son as his vicegerent.]

    To whom the wingèd Hierarch° replied:
"O Adam, one° Almighty is, from whom
All things proceed, and up to him return,   470
If not depraved from good, created all
Such to perfection, one first matter all,
Endued with various forms, various degrees

707–08. Silvanus, Faunus: Roman divinities of field and woodland.   711. hymenean: marriage song.   712. genial: nuptial.
714–19. Pandora . . . fire: When Prometheus ("Forethought"), the son of Japhet, stole fire from Zeus to aid man, Zeus had Hephaestus make a woman, Pandora (so called because the gods endowed her with "all gifts"), who should be fatal to man. She was brought by Hermes to Prometheus' brother, Epimetheus ("Afterthought"), who married her. A box sent with her, opened, let loose all the evils of life.   724. pole: sky.   748. Our . . . increase: See Gen. 1:28.   750. mysterious law: See Eph. 5:32.   751. sole propriety: the one thing peculiar to Adam and Eve.

756. charities: affections.   763–65. Here . . . revels: Milton transfers to pure marital love the romantic, sensual Cupid of Ovid and other poets. Cupid's golden arrow inspired love, his leaden one repelled it.   769. serenate: serenade. starved: frozen (outside a mistress' door).   770. quitted: repaid.   773. repaired: replaced.   775. know . . . more: are wise enough not to seek further knowledge (of good and evil).   Book V: 468. the . . . Hierarch: The periphrasis is an apt preliminary to the account of hierarchical order in the universe.   469–79. one . . . kind: Milton is far from materialism, since all matter pro-

Of substance, and in things that live, of life;
But more refined, more spiritous, and pure,
As nearer to him placed or nearer tending,
Each in their several active spheres assigned,
Till body up to spirit work, in bounds
Proportioned to each kind. So from the root
Springs lighter the green stalk, from thence the
    leaves   480
More aery, last the bright consummate flower
Spirits odorous breathes: flowers and their fruit,
Man's nourishment, by gradual scale sublimed,°
To vital spirits aspire, to animal,
To intellectual;° give both life and sense,
Fancy and understanding, whence the soul
Reason° receives, and reason is her being,
Discursive, or intuitive; discourse
Is oftest yours, the latter most is ours,
Differing but in degree, of kind the same.   490
Wonder not then, what God for you saw good
If I refuse not, but convert, as you,
To proper° substance. Time may come when
    men
With angels may participate, and find
No inconvenient diet, nor too light fare;
And from these corporal nutriments perhaps
Your bodies may at last turn all to spirit,
Improved by tract of time, and winged ascend
Ethereal, as we, or may at choice
Here or in heavenly paradises dwell;   500
If ye be found obedient, and retain
Unalterably firm his love entire
Whose progeny you are. Meanwhile enjoy
Your fill what happiness this happy state
Can comprehend, incapable of more."
    To whom the patriarch of mankind replied:
" O favorable Spirit, propitious guest,
Well hast thou taught the way that might direct
Our knowledge, and the scale of Nature set

From center to circumference,° whereon   510
In contemplation of created things
By steps we may ascend to God. But say,
What meant that caution joined, *If ye be found
Obedient?* Can we want obedience then
To him, or possibly his love desert
Who formed us from the dust, and placed us here
Full to the utmost measure of what bliss
Human desires can seek or apprehend? "
    To whom the Angel: " Son of Heaven and
    Earth,
Attend: that thou art happy, owe to God;   520
That thou continu'st such, owe to thyself,
That is, to thy obedience; therein stand.
This was that caution given thee; be advised.
God° made thee perfect, not immutable;
And good he made thee, but to persevere
He left it in thy power, ordained thy will
By nature free, not over-ruled by fate
Inextricable, or strict necessity.
Our voluntary service he requires,
Not our necessitated; such with him   530
Finds no acceptance, nor can find, for how
Can hearts not free be tried whether they serve
Willing or no, who will but what they must
By destiny, and can no other choose?
Myself and all the angelic host that stand
In sight of God enthroned, our happy state
Hold, as you yours, while our obedience holds;
On other surety none; freely we serve,
Because we freely love, as in our will
To love or not; in this we stand or fall.   540
And some are fallen, to disobedience fallen,
And so from Heaven to deepest Hell; O fall
From what high state of bliss into what woe! "
    To whom our great progenitor: " Thy words
Attentive, and with more delighted ear,
Divine instructor, I have heard, than when
Cherubic songs by night from neighboring hills
Aerial music send.° Nor knew I not
To be both will and deed created free;
Yet that we never shall forget to love   550
Our Maker, and obey him whose command
Single is yet so just, my constant thoughts
Assured me, and still assure; though what thou
    tell'st
Hath passed in Heaven some doubt within me
    move,
But more desire to hear, if thou consent,
The full relation, which must needs be strange,
Worthy of sacred silence to be heard;

ceeds from and returns to God, and since, in various forms and degrees, it is in the process of becoming spirit. And, having such an origin and end, matter is not evil (as in some religions and philosophies), but intrinsically good. See Intro., pp. 405–06. **483. sublimed:** elevated, distilled. **484–85. vital . . . intellectual:** In traditional physiology and psychology, the soul operated on three levels: the vegetative soul is purely biological and is shared by plants, animals, and men; the sensitive soul, in animals and men, has the faculties of motion, perception, and feeling; the rational soul, in men only, has the higher and peculiarly human faculties. Corresponding to and nourishing these several powers are three kinds of "spirits," distilled from the blood, namely, natural, vital, and animal (this last pertaining to the soul, *anima*). **487–90. Reason . . . same:** Man's reason is discursive; i.e., it deliberates, while angelic reason has immediate apprehension. But human reason — for Milton and other men — comprehends more than the mere reasoning faculty; it is the whole rational self of man, the highest of creatures (next to the angels), made in the image of God and finding fulfillment in him. **491–93. Wonder . . . substance:** Adam had been hesitant about offering lunch to an angel, but Raphael had explained that angels require and digest food, and the topic of digestion had led on to the metaphysical account of the chain of being. **493. proper:** (my) own.

510. From . . . circumference: from the earth to the spheres around it. **524–34. God . . . choose:** Adam was endowed with "right reason" which was capable of ordering his life rightly in relation to God and Eve, but, as the event was to show, his will would not necessarily obey his reason. Free will, however, could not exist if overruled by fate or necessity; the condition of freedom is freedom to choose wrongly. **547–48. Cherubic . . . send:** Cf. IV. 680–88.

And we have yet large day, for scarce the sun
Hath finished half his journey, and scarce begins
His other half in the great zone of heaven."   560
  Thus Adam made request, and Raphael,
After short pause assenting, thus began:
  "High matter° thou enjoin'st me, O prime of
     men,
Sad task and hard, for how shall I relate
To human sense the invisible exploits
Of warring spirits; how without remorse°
The ruin of so many glorious once
And perfect while they stood; how last unfold
The secrets of another world, perhaps
Not lawful to reveal? Yet for thy good   570
This is dispensed,° and what surmounts the reach
Of human sense I shall delineate so,
By likening spiritual to corporal forms,
As may express them best, though what if Earth
Be but the shadow of Heaven, and things therein
Each to other like, more than on Earth is
     thought?°
  "As yet this World was not, and Chaos wild
Reigned where these Heavens° now roll, where
     Earth now rests
Upon her center poised, when on a day°
(For time, though in eternity, applied   580
To motion, measures all things durable
By present, past, and future), on such day
As Heaven's great year° brings forth, the empyreal
     host
Of angels by imperial summons called,
Innumerable before the Almighty's throne
Forthwith from all the ends of Heaven appeared
Under their hierarchs in orders bright.
Ten thousand thousand ensigns high advanced,
Standards and gonfalons 'twixt van and rear
Stream in the air, and for distinction serve   590
Of hierarchies, of orders, and degrees;
Or in their glittering tissues bear emblazed°
Holy memorials, acts of zeal and love
Recorded eminent. Thus when in orbs°
Of circuit inexpressible they stood,
Orb within orb, the Father Infinite,

By whom in bliss embosomed sat the Son,
Amidst as from a flaming mount, whose top
Brightness had made invisible, thus spake:
  "'Hear, all ye Angels, progeny of light,   600
Thrones, Dominations, Princedoms, Virtues, Pow-
     ers,°
Hear my decree, which unrevoked shall stand.
This day I have begot° whom I declare
My only Son, and on this holy hill
Him have anointed, whom ye now behold
At my right hand. Your head I him appoint;
And by myself have sworn to him shall bow
All knees in Heaven, and shall confess him Lord.
Under his great vicegerent reign abide
United as one individual° soul   610
Forever happy. Him who disobeys
Me disobeys, breaks union, and that day
Cast out from God and blessed vision,° falls
Into utter darkness, deep engulfed, his place
Ordained without redemption, without end.'
  "So spake the Omnipotent, and with his words
All seemed well pleased; all seemed, but were not
     all.
That day, as other solemn days, they spent
In song and dance about the sacred hill;
Mystical° dance, which yonder starry sphere   620
Of planets and of fixed° in all her wheels
Resembles nearest, mazes intricate,
Eccentric,° intervolved, yet regular
Then most, when most irregular they seem;
And in their motions harmony divine
So smooths her charming tones, that God's own ear
Listens delighted.° Evening now approached
(For we have also our evening and our morn,
We ours for change delectable, not need);
Forthwith from dance to sweet repast they turn
Desirous; all in circles as they stood,   631
Tables are set, and on a sudden piled
With angels' food, and rubied nectar flows
In pearl, in diamond, and massy gold,
Fruit of delicious vines, the growth of Heaven.

---

563 ff. High matter: Raphael's reference (ll. 541–43) to Satan's fall prompts Adam's query and the angel's long account
of preceding events, which fills the rest of this book and Books VI
and VII. Such a narrative corresponds, in the epic structure,
to Odysseus' story of his wanderings and Aeneas' story of the
fall of Troy and his wandering. Lines 563–76 are the first of
Raphael's—i.e., Milton's—several apologies for the attempt to
render spiritual things in comprehensible terms; thus the subsequent narrative is a mixture of the literal and the symbolic or
metaphorical.   566. remorse: pity.   571. dispensed: allowed.
574–76. though . . . thought: a Platonic idea.   577–79. As . . .
day: the chronological beginning of the events treated in the
poem.   578. these Heavens: the sky, not the heaven of God
and the angels.   583. Heaven's . . . year: an allusion to the
Platonic "great year," the long period between the times when
all the heavenly bodies returned to their original positions.
592. emblazed: emblazoned.   594. orbs: circles.

601. Thrones . . . Powers: See I. 129n.   603. begot: Milton
is echoing Ps. 2:6–7. The word is not used literally but means
God's designation of his Son as his vicegerent, as king and media-
tor between himself and the angels and man, as the active force
of good in the world.   610. individual: not to be divided.
613. blessed vision: the beatific vision, the sight of God in Heaven.
620–27. Mystical . . . delighted: the starry dance (the planetary
system and the music of the spheres) always arouses in the un-
mystical Milton a half-mystical sense of the beauty of divine
order and harmony.   621. fixed: the eighth sphere, containing
the fixed stars. The seven inner spheres or orbits (listed from
the earth outward) carried the moon, Mercury, Venus, the sun,
Mars, Jupiter, and Saturn; the ninth or crystalline sphere contained water; the tenth or Primum Mobile kept the inner spheres
in motion.   623. Eccentric: Technically, the word means the
center of a planetary orbit placed, not in the earth, but on a
line between the earth and the moving sun, so that the center
of the orbit described a circle around the earth.   625–27. harmony . . . delighted: the music of the spheres. Cf. "Nativity,"
ll. 125 ff.

On flowers reposed, and with fresh flowerets
    crowned,
They eat, they drink, and in communion sweet
Quaff immortality and joy, secure
Of surfeit where full measure only bounds
Excess, before the all-bounteous King, who show-   640
    ered
With copious hand, rejoicing in their joy.
Now when ambrosial° night, with clouds exhaled
From that high mount of God, whence light and
    shade
Spring both, the face of brightest Heaven had
    changed
To grateful twilight (for night comes not there
In darker veil) and roseate dews disposed
All but the unsleeping eyes of God to rest,
Wide over all the plain, and wider far
Than all this globous Earth in plain outspread
(Such are the courts of God), the angelic throng,
Dispersed in bands and files, their camp extend
By living streams among the trees of life,   652
Pavilions numberless and sudden reared,
Celestial tabernacles, where they slept
Fanned with cool winds, save those who in their
    course
Melodious hymns about the sovran throne
Alternate all night long. But not so waked
Satan° — so call him now, his former name
Is heard no more in Heaven; he of the first,
If not the first Archangel, great in power,   660
In favor, and pre-eminence, yet fraught
With envy against the Son of God, that day
Honored by his great Father, and proclaimed
Messiah,° King anointed, could not bear
Through pride that sight, and thought himself im-
    paired.
Deep malice thence conceiving and disdain,
Soon as midnight brought on the dusky hour
Friendliest to sleep and silence, he resolved
With all his legions to dislodge, and leave
Unworshiped, unobeyed, the throne supreme,   670
Contemptuous, and his next subordinate°
Awakening, thus to him in secret spake:
  " ' Sleep'st thou, companion dear, what sleep can
    close
Thy eyelids? and remember'st what decree
Of yesterday, so late hath passed the lips
Of Heaven's Almighty? Thou to me thy thoughts
Wast wont, I mine to thee was wont to impart;
Both waking we were one; how then can now
Thy sleep dissent? New laws thou seest imposed;

New laws from him who reigns, new minds may
    raise   680
In us who serve, new counsels, to debate
What doubtful may ensue. More in this place
To utter is not safe. Assemble thou
Of all those myriads which we lead the chief;
Tell them that by command, ere yet dim night
Her shadowy cloud withdraws, I am to haste,
And all who under me their banners wave,
Homeward with flying march where we possess
The quarters of the north,° there to prepare°
Fit entertainment to receive our King,   690
The great Messiah, and his new commands,
Who speedily through all the hierarchies
Intends to pass triumphant, and give laws.'
  " So spake the false Archangel, and infused
Bad influence into the unwary breast
Of his associate; he° together calls,
Or several one by one, the regent powers,
Under him regent, tells, as he was taught,
That the Most High commanding, now ere night,
Now ere dim night had disencumbered Heaven,
The great hierarchal standard was to move;   701
Tells the suggested cause, and casts between
Ambiguous words and jealousies, to sound
Or taint integrity; but all obeyed
The wonted signal, and superior voice
Of their great Potentate; for great indeed
His name, and high was his degree in Heaven;
His countenance, as the morning star° that guides
The starry flock, allured them, and with lies   709
Drew after him the third part of Heaven's host."°

[In the rest of the book Satan, in the north, rouses his
followers to rebellion. Abdiel alone denounces his wicked
course and, "Unshaken, unseduced, unterrified," leaves Satan's host to return to the mount of God.]

BOOK VI

[In Book VI Raphael tells Adam of the war in Heaven
between Satan and his followers and the army of God led
by Michael. The war begins, in Homeric fashion, with
verbal exchanges between Abdiel (who had been welcomed
with praise by God) and Satan: true freedom, Abdiel declares, is found within the divine order, whereas Satan, for
all his boasts, is a slave to himself. The combats between
the angelic hosts, with their mounting violence and havoc,
are an objectification of Satan's pride and passion; and at
the same time a note of tragicomic extravagance suggests
the ultimate futility of war against Good. On the third day
God ordains that the Son shall end the war, and the irresistible strength and splendor of Good are symbolized in
the picture of the Son:

      Forth rushed with whirlwind sound
    The chariot of Paternal Deity,
    Flashing thick flames. . . .

642. ambrosial: fragrant.   658-65. Satan . . . impaired: Milton
is not giving a philosophical explanation of the origin of evil;
he is, in imaginative terms, showing evil in action. Satan's
resentment at the Son's elevation is akin to Macbeth's over
Duncan's naming Malcolm as Prince of Cumberland, but
Satan's pride is irreligious self-assertion against divine order.
664. Messiah: the word means "anointed."   671. his . . .
subordinate: Beelzebub.

689. the north: See Isa. 14:13 (and folklore in general for the
north as the home of evil).   689-93. prepare . . . laws: Satan
gives a false account of his purpose.   696. he: Beelzebub.
708. morning star: Lucifer, "light-bearer." See Isa. 14:12,
quoted above in I. 84-85n.   710. third . . . host: Cf. II. 692
and Rev. 12:4.

Attended with ten thousand thousand saints,
He onward came, far off his coming shone. . . .

Satan and his fellows, overwhelmed, are driven through a gap in the wall of Heaven and fall through Chaos into Hell —the point in the action where the poem had begun. In concluding the story Raphael reminds Adam of the warning it contains for him.]

from BOOK VII

[The body of Book VII is an expansion of the first two chapters of Genesis, with details added from a multitude of sources. In its total effect the account of Creation is a hymn to the divine glory and wonder of nature and life. Raphael ends his narrative with a warning of the conditions of man's continued happiness.]

Descend from Heaven, Urania,° by that name
If rightly thou art called, whose voice divine
Following, above the Olympian hill I soar,°
Above the flight of Pegasean wing.°
The meaning, not the name I call; for thou
Nor of the Muses nine, nor on the top
Of old Olympus dwell'st, but heavenly born,
Before the hills appeared or fountain° flowed,
Thou with eternal Wisdom° didst converse,°
Wisdom thy sister, and with her didst play   10
In presence of the Almighty Father, pleased
With thy celestial song. Up led by thee
Into the Heaven of Heavens I have presumed,
An earthly guest, and drawn empyreal° air,°
Thy tempering;° with like safety guided down,
Return me to my native element,°
Lest° from this flying steed unreined (as once
Bellerophon, though from a lower clime)
Dismounted, on the Aleian field I fall,

Erroneous° there to wander and forlorn.   20
Half yet remains unsung, but narrower bound
Within the visible diurnal sphere;°
Standing on Earth, not rapt above the pole,°
More° safe I sing with mortal voice, unchanged
To hoarse or mute, though fallen on evil days,
On evil days though fallen, and evil tongues;°
In darkness, and with dangers compassed round,
And solitude; yet not alone, while thou
Visit'st my slumbers nightly,° or when morn
Purples the east. Still govern thou my song,   30
Urania, and fit audience find, though few.
But drive far off the barbarous dissonance
Of Bacchus and his revelers,° the race
Of that wild rout° that tore the Thracian bard
In Rhodope, where woods and rocks had ears
To rapture,° till the savage clamor drowned
Both harp and voice; nor could the Muse defend
Her son. So fail not thou who thee implores;
For thou art heavenly, she° an empty dream.

[Adam wishes to know of his own world, and Raphael, who is commissioned to satisfy his desire for knowledge "within bounds," tells the story of Creation, the great work of peace that follows the destructive chaos of the war in Heaven. The evil angels having been expelled, God ordains the creation of the world and a race of beings who in time may merit Heaven. The Son, Satan's mightier opposite, is God's active agent in the work of creation, and the description of his setting forth is a signal example of vague pictorial suggestion and of rhythms that powerfully reflect both tumultuous disorder and the imposition of order (ll. 205–21):

"Heaven opened wide
Her ever-during gates, harmonious sound
On golden hinges moving, to let forth
The King of Glory in his powerful Word
And Spirit coming to create new worlds.
On heavenly ground they stood, and from the shore
They viewed the vast immeasurable abyss
Outrageous as a sea, dark, wasteful, wild,
Up from the bottom turned by furious winds
And surging waves, as mountains to assault
Heaven's highth, and with the center mix the pole.
'Silence, ye troubled waves, and thou deep, peace,'
Said then the omnific Word, 'your discord end.'
Nor stayed, but on the wings of Cherubim
Uplifted, in paternal glory rode
Far into Chaos and the World unborn;
For Chaos heard his voice."]

Book VII: 1–39. The war in Heaven over, the poet is returning to earth, which is to be the chief scene of action in the latter half of the poem; this change, and arrival at the middle point, invite a new invocation of the poet's Heavenly Muse. 1–12. Urania . . . song: See I. 6n. As in I. 6–22 and III. 16–32, Milton distinguishes between the classical Muse and his own religious inspiration. 3. above . . . soar: Cf. I. 15, "Above the Aonian mount . . ." Olympus, like Helicon, was a home of the Muses. 4. Pegasean wing: The winged horse Pegasus (which was ridden by Bellerophon when he killed the Chimera) with a blow from his hoof started the fountain of Hippocrene, so that he, as well as the spring, was associated with poetic inspiration. 8. hills . . . fountain: Milton seems to be thinking both of the Muses' hills and fountains and of the Creation as described in Genesis and in Prov. 8:24–25. 9–12. Wisdom . . . song: Milton associates his Heavenly Muse with the Wisdom of Prov. 8:27–30 (who speaks of attending God at the Creation) and of the Apocryphal Book of Wisdom. 9. converse: live. 12–14. Up . . . air: In Books III, V, and VI Milton had described events in Heaven. 14. empyreal: See I. 117n. 15. Thy tempering: His Heavenly Muse had tempered celestial air so that a mortal might breathe it. 16. native element: the air of earth. 17–20. Lest . . . forlorn: Bellerophon, on Pegasus, had tried to reach the heaven of Zeus ("a lower clime" than the Christian Heaven) and, thrown off his horse by the offended god, had fallen down to the Aleian plain in Lycia, where he wandered miserably until he died.

20. Erroneous: in the Latin sense of "wandering" and probably also in the sense of "having erred." 21–22. narrower . . . sphere: a more limited scene, within man's universe. The "visible diurnal sphere" is the whole firmament which, in the old astronomy, revolved daily about the earth. 23. pole: the top of the axis of the created universe. See II. 1051–52 and I. 74n. 24–28. More . . . solitude: a poignant picture of the blind republican after the Restoration. Lines 25–26 are a great example of the Miltonic "turn," the use, with variations, of repeated phrases. 26. evil tongues: the public and private hostility of Royalists. 29. Visit'st . . . nightly: See the note on III. 32. 33. Bacchus . . . revelers: Charles II and his court. 34–38. rout . . . son: See "Lycidas," ll. 58–63n. 35–36. where . . . rapture: Orpheus' song could move stones and trees, if not his human pursuers. 39. she: Calliope, the classical Muse, mother of Orpheus.

BOOK VIII

[The first part of Book VIII carries on the theme of temperance in the pursuit of knowledge that does not further the true ends of life. The most obvious example is astronomical inquiry, which had since Copernicus become the most conspicuous branch of science, and which over the centuries had led to so much debate and confusion. Adam asks about the relation of the earth to the firmament around it, and Raphael outlines alternative geocentric and heliocentric theories of the universe and also raises old questions that had revived with the new astronomy, such as the possibility of other inhabited worlds. But the lesson he draws is Adam's need of humility and a right scale of values in his view of knowledge. The significance of the discussion is commented upon in the Introduction, p. 407.

In the rest of Book VIII Adam tells of his first experience of life, of his desire for a companion, and of the creation of Eve and their first union. His fervent tribute to Eve's beauty and her power over him draws from Raphael a rebuke that relates this episode to the astronomical discussion and to the occasion of Adam's fall. It is again a question of order and degree. Milton is not condemning Adam's true devotion or his happiness in physical relations (which, in Book IV, ll. 741–70, he goes out of his way to celebrate); he is saying that Adam, through both his senses and the affections of his heart, seems in danger of letting Eve, who is not only a human being but a being of inferior reason, come between himself and God — as he is to do in Book IX.]

BOOK IX

THE ARGUMENT

Satan, having compassed the Earth, with meditated guile returns as a mist by night into Paradise; enters into the Serpent sleeping. Adam and Eve in the morning go forth to their labors, which Eve proposes to divide in several places, each laboring apart: Adam consents not, alleging the danger lest that enemy, of whom they were forewarned, should attempt her found alone. Eve, loth to be thought not circumspect or firm enough, urges her going apart, the rather desirous to make trial of her strength; Adam at last yields. The Serpent finds her alone: his subtle approach, first gazing, then speaking, with much flattery extolling Eve above all other creatures. Eve, wondering to hear the Serpent speak, asks how he attained to human speech and such understanding, not till now; the Serpent answers that by tasting of a certain tree in the garden he attained both to speech and reason, till then void of both. Eve requires him to bring her to that tree, and finds it to be the Tree of Knowledge forbidden. The Serpent, now grown bolder, with many wiles and arguments induces her at length to eat; she, pleased with the taste, deliberates a while whether to impart thereof to Adam or not; at last brings him of the fruit; relates what persuaded her to eat thereof. Adam, at first amazed, but perceiving her lost, resolves through vehemence of love to perish with her, and, extenuating the trespass, eats also of the fruit. The effects thereof in them both; they seek to cover their nakedness; then fall to variance and accusation of one another.

No° more of talk where God or angel guest
With man, as with his friend, familiar used
To sit indulgent, and with him partake
Rural repast, permitting him the while
Venial discourse unblamed. I now must change
Those notes to tragic: foul distrust, and breach
Disloyal on the part of man, revolt,
And disobedience; on the part of Heaven
Now alienated, distance and distaste,
Anger and just rebuke, and judgment given,   10
That brought into this World a world of woe,
Sin and her shadow Death, and misery,°
Death's harbinger. Sad task, yet argument
Not less but more heroic than the wrath
Of stern Achilles on his foe pursued
Thrice fugitive about Troy wall;° or rage
Of Turnus for Lavinia disespoused;°
Or Neptune's ire° or Juno's,° that so long
Perplexed the Greek and Cytherea's son;
If answerable style I can obtain   20
Of my celestial patroness,° who deigns
Her nightly° visitation unimplored,
And dictates to me slumbering, or inspires
Easy my unpremeditated verse,
Since first this subject for heroic song
Pleased me, long choosing and beginning late;°
Not sedulous by nature to indite
Wars, hitherto the only argument
Heroic deemed, chief mastery° to dissect
With long and tedious havoc fabled knights°   30
In battles feigned (the better fortitude
Of patience and heroic martyrdom
Unsung), or to describe races and games,
Or tilting furniture,° emblazoned shields,
Impresses° quaint, caparisons and steeds,
Bases° and tinsel trappings, gorgeous knights
At joust and tournament; then marshaled feast
Served up in hall with sewers and seneschals;
The skill of artifice or office mean,

Book IX: 1–47. This proem — not, like its predecessors, a direct invocation of the Heavenly Muse — introduces the crucial theme of man's sin, a theme that invites comparison with the heroic tradition. In emphasizing the high truth and significance of his own subject Milton does not do justice to his love of Homer and Virgil and the later romances. Cf. his view of poetry in the *Reason of Church Government*, pp. 424–26, above. 1–5. No . . . unblamed: Raphael has returned to Heaven, and the stage is left to Adam and Eve and Satan.   12. misery: diseases.   14–16. wrath . . . wall: the subject of the *Iliad*.   16–17. rage . . . disespoused: the main story of the second half of the *Aeneid*.   18–19. Neptune's ire: the hostility of Neptune (Poseidon) toward Odysseus ("the Greek").   Juno: her enmity toward Aeneas, the son of Venus (Cytherea). These references to the classical epics contrast God's anger (l. 10) with the less significant anger of mythological gods and men.   21. celestial patroness: Urania, the Heavenly Muse.   22. nightly: Cf. III. 29–40, VII. 28–30. 25–26. Since . . . late: See the headnote to *PL* and IV. 32–41n. 29. chief mastery: the chief mastery being.   30–38. knights . . . seneschals: the medieval and later romances of chivalry. 34. tilting furniture: equipment for tournaments.   35. Impresses: heraldic devices on shields, etc.   36. Bases: the ornate housings of a horse.

Not that which justly gives heroic name   40
To person or to poem. Me of these
Nor skilled nor studious, higher argument
Remains, sufficient of itself to raise
That name, unless an age too late,° or cold
Climate,° or years damp my intended wing
Depressed, and much they may, if all be mine,
Not hers who brings it nightly to my ear.
  The sun was sunk, and after him the star
Of Hesperus, whose office is to bring
Twilight upon the Earth, short arbiter   50
'Twixt day and night, and now from end to end
Night's hemisphere had veiled the horizon round,
When Satan, who late fled° before the threats
Of Gabriel out of Eden, now improved
In meditated fraud and malice, bent
On man's destruction, maugre° what might hap
Of heavier on himself, fearless returned.
By night he fled, and at midnight returned
From compassing the Earth, cautious of day,
Since Uriel, regent of the sun, descried   60
His entrance, and forewarned the Cherubim
That kept their watch; thence full of anguish
        driven,
The space of seven continued nights he rode
With darkness, thrice the equinoctial line°
He circled, four times crossed the car of Night
From pole to pole, traversing each colure;°
On the eighth returned, and on the coast averse°
From entrance or cherubic watch, by stealth
Found unsuspected way. There was a place —
Now not, though sin, not time, first wrought the
        change —   70
Where Tigris at the foot of Paradise
Into a gulf shot under ground, till part
Rose up a fountain by the Tree of Life;
In with the river sunk, and with it rose
Satan, involved in rising mist, then sought
Where to lie hid; sea he had searched and land
From Eden over Pontus,° and the pool
Maeotis,° up beyond the river Ob;°
Downward as far antarctic; and in length
West from Orontes° to the ocean barred   80
At Darien,° thence to the land where flows
Ganges and Indus. Thus the orb° he roamed
With narrow° search, and with inspection deep

44. age . . . late: In the earlier seventeenth century there was a
widespread idea that all nature, including man, was in process
of decay—an idea Milton had opposed in some Cambridge
utterances.   44–45. cold Climate: Milton referred elsewhere
to the common belief that the cold north was unfavorable to
genius (although early biographers report that he composed
happily only from autumn to spring).   53. Satan . . . fled: at
the end of Book IV.   56. maugre: in spite of.   64. equinoctial
line: equator.   66. From . . . colure: from the north pole to the
south and back, following the colures (lines drawn around the
globe through the poles and the equinoctial and solstitial points).
67. coast averse: side opposite.   77. Pontus: the Black Sea.
77–78. pool Maeotis: Sea of Azov. Ob: in Siberia.   80. Orontes:
a Syrian river.   81. Darien: Isthmus of Panama.   82. orb:
globe.   83. narrow: close.

Considered every creature, which of all
Most opportune might serve his wiles, and found
The serpent subtlest beast of all the field.°
Him after long debate, irresolute
Of thoughts revolved,° his final sentence chose
Fit vessel, fittest imp° of fraud, in whom
To enter, and his dark suggestions hide   90
From sharpest sight; for in the wily snake,
Whatever sleights none would suspicious mark,
As from his wit and native subtlety
Proceeding, which, in other beasts observed,
Doubt° might beget of diabolic power
Active within beyond the sense of brute.
Thus he resolved, but first from inward grief
His bursting passion into plaints thus poured:
  "O Earth, how like to Heaven, if not preferred
More justly, seat worthier of gods, as built   100
With second thoughts, reforming what was old!
For what God after better worse would build?
Terrestrial Heaven, danced round by other Heavens
That shine, yet bear their bright officious° lamps,
Light above light, for thee alone, as seems,
In thee concentring all their precious beams
Of sacred influence!° As God in Heaven
Is center, yet extends to all, so thou
Centring receiv'st from all those orbs; in thee,
Not in themselves, all their known virtue appears
Productive in herb, plant, and nobler birth   111
Of creatures animate with gradual life
Of growth, sense, reason, all summed up in man.
With what delight could I have walked thee round,
If I could joy in aught, sweet interchange
Of hill and valley, rivers, woods, and plains,
Now land, now sea, and shores with forest crowned,
Rocks, dens, and caves; but I in none of these
Find place or refuge; and the more I see
Pleasures about me, so much more I feel   120
Torment within me, as from the hateful siege°
Of contraries; all good to me becomes
Bane, and in Heaven much worse would be my
        state.
But neither here seek I, no nor in Heaven
To dwell, unless by mastering Heaven's Supreme;
Nor hope to be myself less miserable
By what I seek, but others to make such
As I, though thereby worse to me redound.
For only in destroying I find ease
To my relentless thoughts; and him destroyed,   130
Or won to what may work his utter loss,
For whom all this° was made, all this will soon
Follow, as to him linked in weal or woe;
In woe then, that destruction wide may range.

86. serpent . . . field: See Gen. 3:1.   88. Of . . . revolved:
among thoughts considered.   89. imp: child.   95. Doubt:
suspicion.   104. officious: serviceable.   107–13. influence . . .
man: On the influence of the stars, see IV. 668–73; on the scale
of nature, see V. 484–85n.   121. siege: battle.   132. all this:
The world of nature (the result Satan predicts is described in X.
651–714).

To me shall be the glory sole among
The infernal Powers, in one day to have marred
What he, Almighty styled, six nights and days
Continued making, and who knows how long
Before had been contriving? though perhaps
Not longer than since I in one night freed   140
From servitude inglorious well-nigh half
The angelic name, and thinner left the throng
Of his adorers. He to be avenged,
And to repair his numbers thus impaired,
Whether such virtue spent of old now failed
More angels to create, if they at least
Are his created,° or to spite us more,
Determined to advance into our room
A creature formed of earth, and him endow,
Exalted from so base original,   150
With heavenly spoils, our spoils. What he decreed
He effected; man he made, and for him built
Magnificent this World, and Earth his seat,
Him lord pronounced, and, O indignity!
Subjected to his service angel wings,
And flaming ministers to watch and tend
Their earthy charge. Of these the vigilance
I dread, and to elude, thus wrapped in mist
Of midnight vapor glide obscure, and pry
In every bush and brake, where hap may find   160
The serpent sleeping, in whose mazy folds
To hide me, and the dark intent I bring.
O foul descent! that I, who erst contended
With Gods to sit the highest, am now constrained
Into a beast, and mixed with bestial slime,
This essence° to incarnate and imbrute,
That to the height of deity aspired;
But what will not ambition and revenge
Descend to? Who aspires must down as low
As high he soared, obnoxious° first or last   170
To basest things. Revenge, at first though sweet,
Bitter ere long back on itself recoils;
Let it; I reck not, so it light well aimed,
Since higher° I fall short, on him who next
Provokes my envy, this new favorite
Of Heaven, this man of clay, son of despite,
Whom us the more to spite his Maker raised
From dust: spite then with spite is best repaid."

So saying, through each thicket dank or dry,
Like a black mist low creeping, he held on   180
His midnight search, where soonest he might find
The serpent. Him fast sleeping soon he found
In labyrinth of many a round self-rolled,
His head the midst, well stored with subtle wiles;
Not yet in horrid shade or dismal den,
Nor nocent yet, but on the grassy herb
Fearless, unfeared, he slept. In at his mouth
The Devil entered, and his brutal sense,

In heart or head, possessing soon inspired
With act° intelligential, but his sleep   190
Disturbed not, waiting close° the approach of
     morn.
Now whenas sacred light began to dawn
In Eden on the humid flowers, that breathed
Their morning incense, when all things that breathe
From the Earth's great altar send up silent praise
To the Creator, and his nostrils fill
With grateful smell, forth came the human pair
And joined their vocal worship to the quire   198
Of creatures wanting voice; that done, partake
The season, prime for sweetest scents and airs;
Then cómmune how that day they best may ply
Their growing work; for much their work outgrew
The hands' dispatch of two gardening so wide.
And Eve first to her husband thus began:
"Adam, well may we labor still° to dress
This garden, still° to tend plant, herb, and flower,
Our pleasant task enjoined, but till more hands
Aid us, the work under our labor grows,
Luxurious by restraint; what we by day
Lop overgrown, or prune, or prop, or bind,   210
One night or two with wanton growth derides,
Tending to wild.° Thou therefore now advise
Or hear what to my mind first thoughts present:
Let us divide our labors, thou where choice
Leads thee, or where most needs, whether to wind
The woodbine round this arbor, or direct
The clasping ivy where to climb, while I
In yonder spring° of roses intermixed
With myrtle, find what to redress till noon.
For while so near each other thus all day   220
Our task we choose, what wonder if so near
Looks intervene and smiles, or object new
Casual discourse draw on, which intermits
Our day's work, brought to little, though begun
Early, and the hour of supper comes unearned."
To whom mild answer Adam thus returned:
"Sole Eve, associate sole, to me beyond
Compare above all living creatures dear,
Well hast thou motioned,° well thy thoughts em-
     ployed
How we might best fulfil the work which here
God hath assigned us, nor of me shalt pass   231
Unpraised; for nothing lovelier can be found
In woman, than to study household good,
And good works in her husband to promote.
Yet not so strictly hath our Lord imposed
Labor, as to debar us when we need
Refreshment, whether food, or talk between,
Food of the mind, or this sweet intercourse
Of looks and smiles, for smiles from reason flow,
To brute denied, and are of love the food,   240

146–47. if . . . created: Satan had acknowledged God's creation
of the angels in IV. 43.   166. This essence: See I. 117n. and
I. 138n.   170. obnoxious: liable.   174. higher: aiming higher
(against God).

190. act: activity.   191. close: hidden.   205, 206. still: always.
212. wild: wildness.   218. spring: clump.   229. motioned:
proposed.

Love not the lowest end of human life.
For not to irksome toil, but to delight
He made us, and delight to reason joined.
These paths and bowers doubt not but our joint
    hands
Will keep from wilderness° with ease, as wide
As we need walk, till younger hands ere long
Assist us. But if much converse perhaps
Thee satiate, to short absence I could yield.
For solitude sometimes is best society,
And short retirement urges sweet return.   250
But other doubt possesses me, lest harm
Befall thee severed from me; for thou know'st
What hath been warned us, what malicious foe,
Envying our happiness, and of his own
Despairing, seeks to work us woe and shame
By sly assault; and somewhere nigh at hand
Watches, no doubt, with greedy hope to find
His wish and best advantage, us asunder,
Hopeless to circumvent us joined, where each
To other speedy aid might lend at need;   260
Whether his first design be to withdraw
Our fealty from God, or to disturb
Conjugal love, than which perhaps no bliss
Enjoyed by us excites his envy more;
Or this, or worse,° leave not the faithful side
That gave thee being, still shades thee and protects.
The wife, where danger or dishonor lurks,
Safest and seemliest by her husband stays,
Who guards her, or with her the worst endures."
  To whom the virgin° majesty of Eve,   270
As one who loves, and some unkindness meets,
With sweet austere composure thus replied:
  "Offspring of Heaven and Earth, and all Earth's
    lord,
That such an enemy we have, who seeks
Our ruin, both by thee informed I learn,
And from the parting angel° overheard
As in a shady nook I stood behind,
Just then returned at shut of evening flowers.
But that thou shouldst my firmness therefore doubt
To God or thee, because we have a foe   280
May tempt it, I expected not to hear.°
His violence thou fear'st not, being such
As we, not capable of death or pain,
Can either not receive, or can repel.
His fraud is then thy fear, which plain infers
Thy equal fear that my firm faith and love
Can by his fraud be shaken or seduced;
Thoughts, which how found they harbor in thy
    breast,
Adam, misthought of her to thee so dear?"
  To whom with healing words Adam replied:

"Daughter of God and man, immortal Eve,   291
For such thou art, from sin and blame entire;°
Not diffident of thee do I dissuade
Thy absence from my sight, but to avoid
The attempt itself, intended by our foe.
For he who tempts, though in vain, at least
    asperses°
The tempted with dishonor foul, supposed
Not incorruptible of faith, not proof
Against temptation. Thou thyself with scorn
And anger wouldst resent the offered wrong,   300
Though ineffectual found. Misdeem not then,
If such affront I labor to avert
From thee alone, which on us both at once
The enemy, though bold, will hardly dare,
Or daring, first on me the assault shall light.
Nor thou his malice and false guile contemn;
Subtle he needs must be, who could seduce
Angels, nor think superfluous others' aid.
I from the influence of thy looks receive
Access in every virtue, in thy sight   310
More wise, more watchful, stronger, if need were
Of outward strength; while shame, thou looking
    on,
Shame to be overcome or overreached,
Would utmost vigor raise, and raised unite.°
Why shouldst not thou like sense° within thee feel
When I am present, and thy trial choose
With me, best witness of thy virtue tried?"
  So spake domestic° Adam in his care
And matrimonial love; but Eve, who thought
Less attribúted to her faith sincere,   320
Thus her reply with accent sweet renewed:
  "If this be our condition, thus to dwell
In narrow circuit straitened° by a foe,
Subtle or violent, we not endued
Single with like defense, wherever met,
How are we happy, still in fear of harm?
But harm precedes not sin: only our foe
Tempting affronts us with his foul esteem
Of our integrity; his foul esteem
Sticks no dishonor on our front,° but turns   330
Foul on himself; then wherefore shunned or feared
By us? who rather double honor gain
From his surmise proved false, find peace within,
Favor from Heaven, our witness, from the event.°
And what is faith, love, virtue, unassayed
Alone, without exterior help sustained?°

245. wilderness: wildness.   265. Or . . . worse: whether he
plans this or worse.   270. virgin: sinless, innocent.   276. angel:
Raphael (at the end of Book VIII).   279–81. But . . . hear:
the first note of something like earthly and feminine shrillness
in Eve's utterances.

292. entire: untouched by.   296. asperses: sprinkles, smears.
314. unite: unite the virtues just spoken of.   315. like sense:
a similar feeling.   318. domestic: devoted (with a hint of excess). Throughout this dramatic book, the epithets applied to
Adam and Eve are important indications of Milton's view of
their behavior.   323. straitened: confined.   330. front: forehead.   334. event: outcome.   335-36. unassayed . . . sustained: if not tested by themselves, without external help. Eve
has sometimes been said to express the spirit of *Areopagitica*,
but (as J. S. Diekhoff has shown) she does not. In the tract
Milton wrote of a world containing evil that must be met, while

Let us not then suspect our happy state
Left so imperfect by the Maker wise
As not secure to single or combined.°
Frail is our happiness, if this be so,   340
And Eden were no Eden° thus exposed."
    To whom thus Adam fervently replied:
"O woman, best are all things as the will
Of God ordained them; his creating hand
Nothing imperfect or deficient left
Of all that he created, much less man,
Or aught that might his happy state secure,
Secure from outward force: within himself
The danger lies, yet lies within his power;
Against his will he can receive no harm.   350
But God left free the will,° for what obeys
Reason is free, and reason he made right,
But bid her well beware, and still erect,°
Lest by some fair appearing good surprised
She dictate false, and misinform the will
To do what God expressly hath forbid.°
Not then mistrust, but tender love, enjoins
That I should mind° thee oft, and mind thou me.
Firm we subsist, yet possible to swerve,
Since reason not impossibly may meet   360
Some specious object by the foe suborned,°
And fall into deception unaware,
Not keeping strictest watch, as she was warned.
Seek not temptation then, which to avoid
Were better, and most likely if from me
Thou sever not; trial will come unsought.
Wouldst thou approve thy constancy, approve°
First thy obedience; the other who can know,
Not seeing thee attempted, who attest?
But if thou think trial unsought may find   370
Us both securer° than thus warned thou seem'st,
Go; for thy stay, not free, absents thee more;
Go in thy native innocence, rely
On what thou hast of virtue, summon all,
For God towards thee hath done his part, do
    thine."
    So spake the patriarch of mankind, but Eve
Persisted; yet submiss, though last, replied:°
    "With thy permission then, and thus forewarned,
Chiefly by what thy own last reasoning words
Touched only, that our trial, when least sought,
May find us both perhaps far less prepared,   381

Eve, in a world created perfect, is needlessly courting temptation; and, as Adam points out, she is criticizing God's creation
and not showing obedience. As Milton says in both *Areopagitica*
and *PL*, to know good by evil is a far less happy state than to
know good only.   **339. As . . . combined:** as not safe for us
either separate or together.   **341. Eden . . . Eden:** See IV. 214–
15n.   **351–53.** Adam repeats a central theme of the poem, already affirmed by God and by Raphael, the freedom of man's
will and his rational power of choice.   **353. still erect:** (be) always on the alert.   **354–56. Lest . . . forbid:** Adam anticipates
exactly what happens to Eve.   **358. mind:** remind.   **361. suborned:** employed for an evil purpose.   **367. approve:** prove.
371. securer: less careful. Cf. ll. 379–81.   **377. yet . . . replied:**
spoke, though submissively, the last word.

The willinger I go, nor much expect
A foe so proud will first the weaker seek;
So bent, the more shall shame him his repulse."
Thus saying, from her husband's hand her hand
Soft she withdrew, and like a wood-nymph light,
Oread or Dryad, or of Delia's° train,
Betook her to the groves, but Delia's self
In gait surpassed and goddess-like deport,°
Though not as she with bow and quiver armed,
But with such gardening tools as art yet rude,   391
Guiltless of fire, had formed, or angels brought.
To Pales,° or Pomona,° thus adorned,
Likest she seemed, Pomona when she fled
Vertumnus, or to Ceres in her prime,
Yet virgin of Proserpina from Jove.°
Her long with ardent look his eye pursued
Delighted, but desiring more her stay.
Oft he to her his charge of quick return
Repeated, she to him as oft engaged   400
To be returned by noon amid the bower,
And all things in best order to invite
Noontide repast, or afternoon's repose.
O much deceived, much failing, hapless Eve,
Of thy presumed return! event perverse!
Thou never from that hour in Paradise
Found'st either sweet repast or sound repose;
Such ambush, hid among sweet flowers and shades,
Waited with hellish rancor imminent
To intercept thy way, or send thee back   410
Despoiled of innocence, of faith, of bliss.
For now, and since first break of dawn the Fiend,
Mere° serpent in appearance, forth was come,
And on his quest, where likeliest he might find
The only two of mankind, but in them
The whole included race, his purposed prey.
In bower and field he sought, where any tuft
Of grove or garden-plot more pleasant lay,
Their tendance° or plantation for delight;
By fountain or by shady rivulet   420
He sought them both, but wished his hap might
    find
Eve separate; he wished, but not with hope
Of what so seldom chanced, when to his wish,
Beyond his hope, Eve separate he spies,
Veiled in a cloud of fragrance, where she stood,
Half spied, so thick the roses bushing round
About her glowed, oft stooping to support°
Each flower of slender stalk, whose head, though
    gay

387. Delia: Diana (from her birthplace, Delos).   **389. deport:**
bearing.   **393. Pales:** a Roman goddess of flocks and shepherds.
Pomona: a Roman goddess of fruit who was loved by Vertumnus, a god of fruit.   **395–96. Ceres . . . Jove:** young Ceres
before she became, by Jupiter, the mother of Proserpine.
413. Mere: pure. (Milton puts aside a tradition that made Satan
appear as part serpent, part angel.)   **419. Their tendance:**
which they tended.   **427–33. support . . . nigh:** a beautiful
variation on the simile of Proserpine (IV. 268–72).

Carnation, purple, azure, or specked with gold,
Hung drooping unsustained; them she upstays
Gently with myrtle band, mindless° the while,   431
Herself, though fairest unsupported flower,
From her best prop so far, and storm so nigh.
Nearer he drew, and many a walk traversed
Of stateliest covert, cedar, pine, or palm,
Then voluble° and bold, now hid, now seen
Among thick-woven arborets° and flowers
Imbordered° on each bank, the hand° of Eve:
Spot more delicious than those gardens feigned
Or° of revived Adonis,° or renowned   440
Alcinous,° host of old Laertes' son,
Or that, not mystic,° where the sapient king
Held dalliance with his fair Egyptian spouse.°
Much he the place admired, the person more.
As one who long in populous city pent,
Where houses thick and sewers annoy° the air,
Forth issuing on a summer's morn to breathe
Among the pleasant villages and farms
Adjoined, from each thing met conceives delight,
The smell of grain, or tedded° grass, or kine,   450
Or dairy, each rural sight, each rural sound;
If chance with nymph-like step fair virgin pass,
What pleasing seemed, for her° now pleases more,
She most, and in her look sums° all delight:
Such pleasure took the Serpent to behold
This flowery plat,° the sweet recess of Eve
Thus early, thus alone; her heavenly form
Angelic, but more soft and feminine,
Her graceful innocence, her every air
Of gesture or least action overawed   460
His malice, and with rapine sweet bereaved
His fierceness of the fierce intent it brought.
That space the Evil One abstracted stood
From his own evil, and for the time remained
Stupidly good,° of enmity disarmed,
Of guile, of hate, of envy, of revenge;
But the hot hell that always in him burns,
Though in mid Heaven, soon ended his delight,
And tortures him now more, the more he sees
Of pleasure not for him ordained; then soon   470
Fierce hate he recollects, and all his thoughts
Of mischief, gratulating,° thus excites:
  "Thoughts, whither have ye led me, with what
    sweet

Compulsion thus transported to forget
What hither brought us? hate, not love, nor hope
Of Paradise for Hell, hope here to taste
Of pleasure, but all pleasure to destroy,
Save what is in destroying; other joy
To me is lost. Then let me not let pass
Occasion which now smiles: behold alone   480
The woman, opportune to all attempts,
Her husband, for I view far round, not nigh,
Whose higher intellectual more I shun,
And strength, of courage haughty, and of limb
Heroic built, though of terrestrial mold,
Foe not informidable, exempt from wound,°
I not; so much hath Hell debased, and pain
Enfeebled me, to what I was in Heaven.
She fair, divinely fair, fit love for gods,
Not terrible, though terror be in love   490
And beauty,° not° approached by stronger hate,
Hate stronger, under show of love well feigned,
The way which to her ruin now I tend."
  So spake the Enemy of mankind, enclosed
In serpent, inmate bad, and toward Eve
Addressed his way, not with indented wave,
Prone on the ground, as since, but on his rear,
Circular base of rising folds, that towered
Fold above fold a surging maze; his head
Crested aloft, and carbuncle° his eyes;   500
With burnished neck of verdant gold, erect
Amidst his circling spires,° that on the grass
Floated redundant. Pleasing was his shape,
And lovely, never since of serpent kind
Lovelier; not those that in Illyria changed
Hermione and Cadmus,° or the god
In Epidaurus;° nor to which transformed
Ammonian Jove,° or Capitoline was seen,
He with Olympias, this with her who bore
Scipio, the highth of Rome.° With tract° oblique
At first, as one who sought access, but feared   511
To interrupt, sidelong he works his way.
As when a ship by skillful steersman wrought
Nigh river's mouth or foreland, where the wind
Veers oft, as oft so steers, and shifts her sail,
So varied he, and of his tortuous train
Curled many a wanton wreath in sight of Eve,
To lure her eye; she busied heard the sound

431. mindless: heedless.   436. voluble: rolling.   437. arborets: shrubs.   438. Imbordered: planted in the form of borders. hand: handiwork.   439-40. gardens . . . Adonis: Milton may be thinking of such descriptions as Spenser's (*Faerie Queene,* III. vi). Cf. *Comus,* 998 f.   440. Or: either.   441. Alcinous: king of Phaeacia, who entertained Odysseus and who had a miraculous garden (*Odyssey,* VII. 112 f.).   442. not mystic: actual, not mythical or allegorical like the preceding.   442-43. sapient king . . . spouse: Solomon married Pharaoh's daughter (I Kings 3:1; Song of Sol. 7:1).   446. annoy: pollute.   450. tedded: spread out to dry.   453. for her: because of her.   454. sums: comprises, completes.   456. plat: plot.   465. Stupidly good: Satan is incapable of positive good, but for the moment his evil nature is blunted.   472 gratulating: rejoicing.

486. exempt . . . wound: See l. 283.   490-91. though . . . beauty: Although put in the mouth of Satan, the idea is a potent indication of Milton's sensuous intensity.   491. not: if not, unless.   500. carbuncle: deep red.   502. spires: coils.   505-06. changed . . . Cadmus: those that Hermione (more commonly Harmonia) and Cadmus became, when metamorphosed at their own desire.   506-07. god . . . Epidaurus: Aesculapius, god of medicine, whose chief shrine was at Epidaurus and who appeared in serpent form.   508-09. Plutarch records the legend that Jupiter Ammon (see IV. 275-79n.) was the father of Alexander the Great by Olympias, the queen of Philip of Macedon.   508-10. Capitoline . . . Rome: according to the tale that Scipio Africanus, the conqueror of Hannibal, was the son of Sempronia and Jupiter (called Capitoline from his temple on the Capitoline hill).   510. tract: course.

Of rustling leaves, but minded not, as used
To such disport before her through the field   520
From every beast, more duteous at her call
Than at Circean call the herd disguised.°
He bolder now, uncalled before her stood,
But as in gaze admiring. Oft he bowed
His turret crest, and sleek enameled neck,
Fawning, and licked the ground whereon she trod.
His gentle dumb expression turned at length
The eye of Eve to mark his play; he glad
Of her attention gained, with serpent tongue
Organic, or impulse of vocal air,°   530
His fraudulent temptation thus began:
   "Wonder° not, sovran mistress, if perhaps
Thou canst, who art sole wonder, much less arm
Thy looks, the heaven of mildness, with disdain,
Displeased that I approach thee thus, and gaze
Insatiate, I thus single, nor have feared
Thy awful brow, more awful thus retired.
Fairest resemblance of thy Maker fair,
Thee all things living gaze on, all things thine
By gift, and thy celestial beauty adore,   540
With ravishment beheld, there best beheld
Where universally admired; but here
In this enclosure wild, these beasts among,
Beholders rude, and shallow to discern
Half what in thee is fair, one man except,
Who sees thee? (and what is one?) who shouldst be
   seen
A goddess among gods, adored and served
By angels numberless, thy daily train."
   So glozed° the Tempter, and his proem tuned;
Into the heart of Eve his words made way,   550
Though at the voice much marveling; at length
Not unamazed she thus in answer spake:
   "What may this mean? Language of man pro-
   nounced
By tongue of brute, and human sense expressed?
The first at least of these I thought denied
To beasts, whom God on their creation-day
Created mute to all articulate sound;
The latter I demur,° for in their looks
Much reason, and in their actions, oft appears.
Thee, Serpent, subtlest beast of all the field   560
I knew, but not with human voice endued;
Redouble then this miracle, and say,
How cam'st thou speakable of° mute, and how
To me so friendly grown above the rest
Of brutal kind, that daily are in sight?
Say, for such wonder claims attention due."
   To whom the guileful Tempter thus replied:

"Empress of this fair World, resplendent Eve,
Easy to me it is to tell thee all
What thou command'st, and right thou shouldst be
   obeyed.   570
I was at first as other beasts that graze
The trodden herb, of abject thoughts and low,
As was my food, nor aught but food discerned
Or sex, and apprehended nothing high:
Till on a day roving the field, I chanced
A goodly tree far distant to behold,
Loaden with fruit of fairest colors mixed,
Ruddy and gold. I nearer drew to gaze;
When from the boughs a savory odor blown,
Grateful to appetite, more pleased my sense   580
Than smell of sweetest fennel, or the teats
Of ewe or goat dropping with milk at even,°
Unsucked of lamb or kid, that tend their play.
To satisfy the sharp desire I had
Of tasting those fair apples, I resolved
Not to defer; hunger and thirst at once,
Powerful persuaders, quickened at the scent
Of that alluring fruit, urged me so keen.
About the mossy trunk I wound me soon,
For high from ground the branches would require
Thy utmost reach or Adam's: round the tree   591
All other beasts that saw, with like desire
Longing and envying stood, but could not reach.
Amid the tree now got, where plenty hung
Tempting so nigh, to pluck and eat my fill
I spared not, for such pleasure till that hour
At feed or fountain never had I found.
Sated at length, ere long I might perceive
Strange alteration in me, to degree
Of reason in my inward powers, and speech   600
Wanted not long, though to this shape retained.
Thenceforth to speculations high or deep
I turned my thoughts, and with capacious mind
Considered all things visible in Heaven,
Or Earth, or middle,° all things fair and good;
But all that fair and good in thy divine
Semblance, and in thy beauty's heavenly ray,
United I beheld; no fair° to thine
Equivalent or second, which compelled
Me thus, though importune perhaps, to come   610
And gaze, and worship thee of right declared
Sovran of creatures, universal dame."°
   So talked the spirited° sly Snake; and Eve
Yet more amazed unwary thus replied:
   "Serpent, thy overpraising leaves in doubt
The virtue of that fruit, in thee first proved.
But say, where grows the tree, from hence how far?
For many are the trees of God that grow
In Paradise, and various, yet unknown

521–22. more . . . disguised: more ready obedience than that of
the men Circe transformed into beasts.   530. Organic . . . air:
by the use of speech organs or producing the effect of speech
through vibration of the air.   532–48. Wonder . . . train: Satan,
in the manner of an amatory poet, appeals to Eve's vanity.
549. glozed: flattered.   558. The . . . demur: I am doubtful if
reason is denied to beasts.   563. of: from being.

581–82. fennel . . . even: In popular lore snakes were said to be
fond of fennel and to suck the teats of sheep and goats.
605. middle: the air.   608. fair: fairness, beauty.   612. dame:
mistress.   613. spirited: inspired (by Satan).

To us; in such abundance lies our choice   620
As leaves a greater store of fruit untouched,
Still hanging incorruptible, till men
Grow up to their provision,° and more hands
Help to disburden Nature of her birth."°
  To whom the wily Adder, blithe and glad:
"Empress, the way is ready, and not long,
Beyond a row of myrtles, on a flat,
Fast by a fountain, one small thicket past
Of blowing° myrrh and balm; if thou accept
My conduct, I can bring thee thither soon."   630
  "Lead then," said Eve. He leading swiftly rolled
In tangles, and made intricate seem straight,
To mischief swift. Hope elevates, and joy
Brightens his crest, as when a wandering fire,°
Compact of unctuous° vapor, which the night
Condenses, and the cold environs round,
Kindled through agitation to a flame,
Which oft, they say, some evil spirit attends,
Hovering and blazing with delusive light,   639
Misleads the amazed night-wanderer from his way
To bogs and mires, and oft through pond or pool,
There swallowed up and lost, from succor far.
So glistered the dire Snake, and into fraud
Led Eve our credulous mother, to the tree
Of prohibition, root of all our woe;
Which when she saw, thus to her guide she spake:
  "Serpent, we might have spared our coming
    hither,
Fruitless to me, though fruit be here to excess,
The credit of whose virtue rest with thee,
Wondrous indeed, if cause of such effects.   650
But of this tree we may not taste nor touch;
God so commanded, and left that command
Sole daughter of his voice; the rest,° we live
Law to ourselves, our reason is our law."
  To whom the Tempter guilefully replied:
"Indeed? Hath God then said that of the fruit
Of all these garden trees ye shall not eat,
Yet lords declared of all in Earth or air?"
  To whom thus Eve yet sinless: "Of the fruit
Of each tree in the garden we may eat,   660
But of the fruit of this fair tree amidst
The garden, God hath said, 'Ye shall not eat
Thereof, nor shall ye touch it, lest ye die.'"
  She scarce had said, though brief, when now
    more bold
The Tempter, but with show of zeal and love
To man, and indignation at his wrong,
New part puts on,° and as to passion moved,
Fluctuates disturbed, yet comely, and in act
Raised, as of some great matter to begin.

As when of old some orator renowned   670
In Athens or free Rome, where eloquence
Flourished, since mute, to some great cause ad-
    dressed,
Stood in himself collected, while each part,°
Motion, each act won audience° ere the tongue,
Sometimes in highth° began, as no delay
Of preface brooking through his zeal of right:
So standing, moving, or to highth upgrown,
The Tempter all impassioned thus began:
  "O sacred, wise, and wisdom-giving Plant,
Mother of science,° now I feel thy power   680
Within me clear, not only to discern
Things in their causes, but to trace the ways
Of highest agents, deemed however wise.
Queen of this universe, do not believe
Those rigid threats of death; ye shall not die:
How should ye? by the fruit? it gives you life
To° knowledge; by the Threatener? look on me,
Me who have touched and tasted, yet both live,
And life more perfect have attained than Fate
Meant me, by venturing higher than my lot.   690
Shall that be shut to man, which to the beast
Is open? or will God incense° his ire
For such a petty trespass, and not praise
Rather your dauntless virtue, whom the pain
Of death denounced,° whatever thing death be,
Deterred not from achieving what might lead
To happier life, knowledge of good and evil?
Of good, how just? of evil, if what is evil
Be real, why not known, since easier shunned?
God therefore cannot hurt ye, and be just;   700
Not just, not God; not feared then, nor obeyed:
Your fear itself of death removes the fear.
Why then was this forbid? Why but to awe,
Why but to keep ye low and ignorant,
His worshipers? he knows that in the day
Ye eat thereof, your eyes that seem so clear,
Yet are but dim, shall perfectly be then
Opened and cleared, and ye shall be as gods,°
Knowing both good and evil as they know.
That ye should be as gods, since I as man,   710
Internal man,° is but proportion meet,
I of brute human, ye of human gods.
So ye shall die perhaps, by putting off
Human, to put on gods,° death to be wished,
Though threatened, which no worse than this can
    bring.
And what are gods that man may not become
As they, participating godlike food?

623. Grow . . . provision: multiply in proportion to the fruit provided.   624. birth (spelled *bearth* by Milton): the fruit Nature bears.   629. blowing: blossoming.   634. wandering fire: will-o'-the-wisp.   635. Compact of unctuous: composed of oily.   653. the rest: with respect to the rest.   667. New . . . on: assumes a new role, that of sympathy with man.

673. part: of his body.   674. audience: attention.   675. highth: of the subject and of feeling.   680. science: knowledge.   687. To: as well as.   692. incense: kindle.   695. denounced: ordained, threatened.   708. ye . . . gods: Satan is carrying out his original plan. Cf. IV. 522–26, V. 70, IX. 547 (the first and last of these passages are in this book).   711. Internal man: a man in mental powers.   713–14. by . . . gods: rising from the human to a godlike state — a perverting of St. Paul's phrase for religious conversion, putting off the old man and putting on the new.

The gods are first, and that advantage use
On our belief, that all from them proceeds;
I question it, for this fair Earth I see,   720
Warmed by the sun, producing every kind,
Them nothing. If they° all things, who enclosed
Knowledge of good and evil in this tree,
That whoso eats thereof, forthwith attains
Wisdom without their leave? and wherein lies
The offense, that man should thus attain to know?
What can your knowledge hurt him, or this tree
Impart against his will, if all be his?
Or is it envy, and can envy dwell
In heavenly breasts?° These, these and many more
Causes import° your need of this fair fruit.   731
Goddess humane,° reach then, and freely taste!”
   He ended, and his words replete with guile
Into her heart too easy entrance won.
Fixed on the fruit she gazed, which to behold
Might tempt alone, and in her ears the sound
Yet rung of his persuasive words, impregned°
With reason, to her seeming, and with truth;
Meanwhile the hour of noon drew on, and waked
An eager appetite, raised by the smell   740
So savory of that fruit, which with desire,
Inclinable now grown to touch or taste,
Solicited her longing eye; yet first
Pausing a while, thus to herself she mused:
   “Great are thy virtues, doubtless, best of fruits,
Though kept from man, and worthy to be admired,
Whose taste, too long forborne, at first assay°
Gave elocution to the mute, and taught
The tongue not made for speech to speak thy praise.
Thy praise he also who forbids thy use   750
Conceals not from us, naming thee the Tree
Of Knowledge, knowledge both of good and evil;
Forbids us then to taste, but his forbidding
Commends thee more, while it infers° the good
By thee communicated, and our want;
For good unknown sure is not had, or had
And yet unknown, is as not had at all.
In plain° then, what forbids he but to know,
Forbids us good, forbids us to be wise?
Such prohibitions bind not. But if Death   760
Bind us with after-bands, what profits then
Our inward freedom? In the day we eat
Of this fair fruit, our doom is, we shall die.
How dies the Serpent? He hath eaten and lives,
And knows, and speaks, and reasons, and discerns,
Irrational till then. For us alone
Was death invented? or to us denied
This intellectual food, for beasts reserved?
For beasts it seems; yet that one beast which first
Hath tasted, envies not, but brings with joy   770

The good befallen him, author unsuspect,°
Friendly to man, far from deceit or guile.
What fear I then, rather what know to fear
Under this ignorance of good and evil,
Of God or death, of law or penalty?
Here grows the cure of all, this fruit divine,
Fair to the eye, inviting to the taste,
Of virtue to make wise; what hinders then
To reach, and feed at once both body and mind?”
   So saying, her rash hand in evil hour   780
Forth reaching to the fruit, she plucked, she eat.°
Earth felt the wound, and Nature from her seat
Sighing through all her works gave signs of woe,
That all was lost.° Back to the thicket slunk
The guilty Serpent, and well might, for Eve
Intent now wholly on her taste, nought else
Regarded; such delight till then, as seemed,
In fruit she never tasted, whether true
Or fancied so, through expectation high
Of knowledge, nor was Godhead° from her
      thought.   790
Greedily she engorged without restraint,
And knew not eating death.° Satiate at length,
And heightened as with wine, jocund and boon,°
Thus to herself she pleasingly began:
   “O sovran,° virtuous, precious of all trees
In Paradise, of operation blest
To sapience,° hitherto obscured, infamed,°
And thy fair fruit let hang, as to no end
Created; but henceforth my early care,
Not without song, each morning, and due praise,°
Shall tend thee, and the fertile burden ease   801
Of thy full branches offered free to all;
Till dieted by thee I grow mature
In knowledge, as the gods who all things know;
Though others° envy what they cannot give;
For had the gift been theirs, it had not here
Thus grown. Experience, next to thee I owe,
Best guide; not following thee, I had remained
In ignorance; thou open’st wisdom’s way,
And giv’st access, though secret she retire.   810
And I perhaps am secret; Heaven is high,
High and remote to see from thence distinct
Each thing on Earth; and other care perhaps
May have diverted from continual watch
Our great Forbidder, safe° with all his spies
About him. But to Adam in what sort

722. If they: if they produced.   729–30. can . . . breasts: Cf.
Virgil, Aeneid, I. 11.   731. import: prove.   732. humane: gracious.   737. impregned: impregnated.   747. assay: trial.
754. infers: implies.   758. In plain: in plain terms.

771. author unsuspect: the serpent, whose authority is not to be
doubted — a sample of the reasoning of the “unwary” Eve.
781. eat: the past tense (pronounced et).   782–84. Earth . . .
lost: The divine order of Nature has been violated.   790. Godhead: In this and later passages Milton suggests the Greek
tragic sin of hubris, infatuated, irreligious self-sufficiency and
pride.   792. knew . . . death: knew not that she was eating
death — in contrast with the angels who “Quaff immortality
and joy” (V. 638).   793. boon: blithe.   795. sovran: most
sovereign.   796–97. of . . . sapience: having the power to confer
wisdom.   797. infamed: defamed.   800. Not . . . praise: In
Eve’s mind the tree has replaced God. Cf. l. 835.   805. others:
gods (Eve is recalling Satan’s assertion in l. 718 f.).   815. safe:
not dangerous.

Shall I appear? Shall I to him make known
As yet my change, and give him to partake
Full happiness with me, or rather not,
But keep the odds of knowledge in my power   820
Without copartner? so to add what wants
In female sex, the more to draw his love,
And render me more equal, and perhaps,
A thing not undesirable, sometime
Superior; for inferior who is free?°
This may be well. But what if God have seen,
And death ensue? then I shall be no more,
And Adam wedded to another Eve,
Shall live with her enjoying, I extinct;
A death to think. Confirmed then I resolve,   830
Adam shall share with me in bliss or woe.
So dear I love him, that with him all deaths
I could endure, without him live no life."
   So saying, from the tree her step she turned,
But first low reverence done, as to the power
That dwelt within, whose presence had infused
Into the plant sciential° sap, derived
From nectar, drink of gods. Adam the while,
Waiting desirous her return, had wove
Of choicest flowers a garland to adorn   840
Her tresses, and her rural labors crown,
As reapers oft are wont their harvest queen.
Great joy he promised to his thoughts, and new
Solace in her return, so long delayed;
Yet oft his heart, divine of° something ill,
Misgave him; he the faltering measure° felt;
And forth to meet her went, the way she took
That morn when first they parted. By the Tree
Of Knowledge he must pass; there he her met,
Scarce from the tree returning; in her hand   850
A bough of fairest fruit that downy smiled,
New gathered, and ambrosial smell diffused.
To him she hasted; in her face excuse
Came prologue, and apology to prompt,°
Which with bland words at will she thus addressed:
   "Hast thou not wondered, Adam, at my stay?
Thee I have missed, and thought it long,° deprived
Thy presence, agony of love till now
Not felt, nor shall be twice, for never more
Mean I to try what rash untried I sought,°   860
The pain of absence from thy sight. But strange
Hath been the cause, and wonderful to hear:
This tree is not as we are told, a tree
Of danger tasted,° nor to evil unknown
Opening the way, but of divine effect
To open eyes, and make them gods who taste;
And hath been tasted° such. The Serpent wise,

Or not restrained as we, or not obeying,
Hath eaten of the fruit, and is become
Not dead, as we are threatened, but thenceforth
Endued with human voice and human sense,   871
Reasoning to° admiration, and with me
Persuasively hath so prevailed, that I
Have also tasted, and have also found
The effects to correspond, opener mine eyes,
Dim erst, dilated spirits, ampler heart,
And growing up to Godhead; which for thee
Chiefly I sought,° without thee can despise.
For bliss, as thou hast part, to me is bliss;
Tedious, unshared with thee, and odious soon.   880
Thou therefore also taste, that equal lot
May join us, equal joy, as equal love;
Lest thou not tasting, different degree
Disjoin us, and I then too late renounce°
Deity for thee, when Fate will not permit."
   Thus Eve with countenance blithe° her story
      told;
But in her cheek distemper flushing glowed.
On the other side, Adam, soon as he heard
The fatal trespass done by Eve, amazed,
Astonied° stood and blank, while horror chill   890
Ran through his veins, and all his joints relaxed;
From his slack hand the garland wreathed for Eve
Down dropped, and all the faded roses shed.
Speechless he stood and pale, till thus at length
First to himself he inward silence broke:
   "O fairest of creation, last and best
Of all God's works, creature in whom excelled
Whatever can to sight or thought be formed,
Holy, divine, good, amiable, or sweet!
How art thou lost, how on a sudden lost,   900
Defaced, deflowered, and now to death devote!°
Rather how hast thou yielded to transgress
The strict forbiddance, how to violate
The sacred fruit forbidden! Some cursèd fraud
Of enemy hath beguiled thee, yet unknown,
And me with thee hath ruined, for with thee
Certain my resolution is to die;
How can I live without thee, how forgo
Thy sweet converse and love so dearly joined,
To live again in these wild woods forlorn?°   910
Should God create another Eve, and I
Another rib afford, yet loss of thee
Would never from my heart; no, no! I feel
The link of nature draw me: flesh of flesh,
Bone of my bone thou art,° and from thy state
Mine never shall be parted, bliss or woe."
   So having said, as one from sad dismay

825. for . . . free: the corrupted Eve now holds Satan's false view of freedom.   837. sciential: conferring knowledge.
845. divine of: divining, foreseeing.   846. faltering measure: irregular beat.   853–54. in . . . prompt: Her expression was a prologue to the defense she was about to make.   857. Thee . . . long: Eve's new knowledge seems to be the art of lying.
860. what . . . sought: what, untried, I rashly sought.
864. tasted: if tasted.   867. tasted such: found such by tasting.

872. to: so as to arouse.   877–78. which . . . sought: another fib.   884. renounce: try to renounce.   886. blithe: an epithet that sums up Eve's terrible unawareness of what she has done.
890. Astonied: astounded.   901. devote: doomed.   908–10. How . . . forlorn: a poignant utterance, especially in the sudden vision of Paradise, without Eve, as "these wild woods forlorn."   914–15. flesh . . . art: See Gen. 2:23.

Recomforted, and after thoughts disturbed
Submitting to what seemed remediless,
Thus in calm mood his words to Eve he turned:
"Bold deed thou hast presumed, adventurous
    Eve,   921
And peril great provoked, who thus hast dared,
Had it been only coveting to eye
That sacred fruit, sacred to abstinence,
Much more to taste it under ban to touch.
But past who can recall, or done undo?
Not God omnipotent, nor Fate. Yet so
Perhaps thou shalt not die; perhaps the fact°
Is not so heinous now, foretasted fruit,°
Profaned first by the Serpent, by him first   930
Made common and unhallowed ere our taste,
Nor yet on him found deadly; he yet lives,
Lives, as thou saidst, and gains to live as man
Higher degree of life, inducement strong
To us, as likely, tasting, to attain
Proportional ascent, which cannot be
But to be gods, or angels, demi-gods.°
Nor can I think that God, Creator wise,
Though threatening, will in earnest so destroy
Us his prime creatures, dignified so high,   940
Set over all his works, which in our fall,
For us created, needs with us must fail,
Dependent made; so God shall uncreate,
Be frustrate, do, undo, and labor lose,
Not well conceived of God,° who though his power
Creation could repeat, yet would be loth
Us to abolish, lest the Adversary
Triumph and say: 'Fickle their state whom God
Most favors, who can please him long? Me first
He ruined, now mankind; whom will he next?'
Matter of scorn not to be given the Foe;   951
However, I with thee have fixed my lot,
Certain to undergo like doom: if death
Consort with thee, death is to me as life;
So forcible within my heart I feel
The bond of nature draw me to my own,
My own in thee, for what thou art is mine;
Our state cannot be severed; we are one,
One flesh; to lose thee were to lose myself."
    So Adam, and thus Eve to him replied: 960
"O glorious trial of exceeding love,°
Illustrious evidence, example high!
Engaging me to emulate, but short
Of thy perfection, how shall I attain,
Adam? from whose dear side I boast me sprung,
And gladly of our union hear thee speak,
One heart, one soul in both; whereof good proof
This day affords, declaring thee resolved,

Rather than death or aught than death more dread
Shall separate us, linked in love so dear,   970
To undergo with me one guilt, one crime,
If any be, of tasting this fair fruit,
Whose virtue (for of good still good proceeds,
Direct, or by occasion) hath presented
This happy trial of thy love, which else
So eminently never had been known.
Were it I thought death menaced would ensue
This my attempt, I would sustain alone
The worst, and not persuade thee, rather die
Deserted, than oblige° thee with a fact   980
Pernicious to thy peace, chiefly assured
Remarkably so late of thy so true,
So faithful love unequaled; but I feel
Far otherwise the event, not death, but life
Augmented, opened eyes, new hopes, new joys,
Taste so divine, that what of sweet before
Hath touched my sense, flat seems to this and harsh.
On my experience, Adam, freely taste,
And fear of death deliver to the winds."
    So saying, she embraced him, and for joy   990
Tenderly wept, much won that he his love
Had so ennobled, as of choice to incur
Divine displeasure for her sake, or death.
In recompense (for such compliance bad
Such recompense best merits) from the bough
She gave him of that fair enticing fruit
With liberal hand. He scrupled not to eat
Against his better knowledge, not deceived,
But fondly overcome with female charm.°
Earth trembled from her entrails, as again   1000
In pangs, and Nature gave a second groan;
Sky loured, and, muttering thunder, some sad drops
Wept at completing of the mortal sin
Original; while Adam took no thought,
Eating his fill, nor Eve to iterate
Her former trespass feared, the more to soothe
Him with her loved society, that now
As with new wine intoxicated both
They swim in mirth, and fancy that they feel
Divinity within them breeding wings   1010
Wherewith to scorn the Earth. But that false fruit
Far other operation first displayed,
Carnal desire inflaming: he on Eve
Began to cast lascivious eyes, she him
As wantonly repaid; in lust they burn,
Till Adam thus 'gan Eve to dalliance move:
    "Eve, now I see thou art exact° of taste,°
And elegant, of sapience no small part;
Since to each meaning savor we apply,
And palate call judicious; I the praise   1020

928. fact: deed.   929. foretasted fruit: the fruit having been
tasted already.   934-37. Higher . . . demi-gods: Adam now
shares the motive of pride.   945. Not . . . God: not a fitting
conception of God.   961. O . . . love: The words suggest
Christ's selfless love for man and hence an ironic contrast with
Eve's and Adam's inadequate conception of love.

980. oblige: involve.   998-99. Against . . . charm: Unlike Eve,
whose inferior reason was deceived, Adam knows what he is
doing, but his will is overswayed by his devotion to Eve. See
the summary of Book VIII, above.   1017. exact: refined.
1017-20. taste . . . judicious: Adam is playing on the double
meaning of "taste" and "savor" as applied to both the mind
and the palate (the Latin sapere means both).

Yield thee, so well this day thou hast purveyed.
Much pleasure we have lost, while we abstained
From this delightful fruit, nor known till now
True relish, tasting; if such pleasure be
In things to us forbidden, it might be wished
For this one tree had been forbidden ten.
But come, so well refreshed, now let us play,
As meet is, after such delicious fare;
For never did thy beauty since the day
I saw thee first and wedded thee, adorned   1030
With all perfections, so inflame my sense
With ardor to enjoy thee,° fairer now
Than ever, bounty of this virtuous tree."
    So said he, and forbore not glance or toy°
Of amorous intent, well understood
Of Eve, whose eye darted contagious fire.
Her hand he seized, and to a shady bank,
Thick overhead with verdant roof embowered,
He led her nothing loth; flowers were the couch,
Pansies, and violets, and asphodel,   1040
And hyacinth, Earth's freshest softest lap.
There they their fill of love and love's disport
Took largely, of their mutual guilt the seal,
The solace of their sin, till dewy sleep
Oppressed them, wearied with their amorous play.
Soon as the force of that fallacious fruit,
That with exhilarating vapor bland
About their spirits had played, and inmost powers
Made err, was now exhaled, and grosser sleep,
Bred of unkindly° fumes, with conscious dreams
Encumbered, now had left them, up they rose
As from unrest, and each the other viewing,   1052
Soon found their eyes how opened, and their minds
How darkened; innocence, that as a veil
Had shadowed them from knowing ill, was gone;
Just confidence, and native righteousness,
And honor from about them, naked left
To guilty Shame; he° covered, but his robe
Uncovered more. So rose the Danite° strong,
Herculean Samson, from the harlot-lap   1060
Of Philistean Dálilah, and waked
Shorn of his strength, they destitute and bare
Of all their virtue. Silent, and in face
Confounded, long they sat, as strucken mute,
Till Adam, though not less than Eve abashed,
At length gave utterance to these words constrained:
    "O Eve, in evil hour thou didst give ear
To that false worm,° of whomsoever taught
To counterfeit man's voice, true in our fall,
False in our promised rising; since our eyes   1070

Opened we find indeed, and find we know
Both good and evil, good lost and evil got,
Bad fruit of knowledge, if this be to know,
Which leaves us naked thus, of honor void,
Of innocence, of faith, of purity,
Our wonted ornaments now soiled and stained,
And in our faces evident the signs
Of foul concupiscence; whence evil store,°
Even shame, the last° of evils; of the first°
Be sure then. How shall I behold the face   1080
Henceforth of God or angel, erst with joy
And rapture so oft beheld? those heavenly shapes
Will dazzle now this earthly, with their blaze
Insufferably bright. O might I here
In solitude live savage, in some glade
Obscured, where highest woods impenetrable
To star or sunlight, spread their umbrage broad,
And brown° as evening! Cover me, ye pines,
Ye cedars, with innumerable boughs
Hide me, where I may never see them more.°
But let us now, as in bad plight, devise   1091
What best may for the present serve to hide
The parts of each from other that seem most
To shame obnoxious,° and unseemliest seen,
Some tree whose broad smooth leaves together
        sewed,
And girded on our loins, may cover round
Those middle parts, that this newcomer, Shame,
There sit not, and reproach us as unclean."
    So counseled he, and both together went   1099
Into the thickest wood; there soon they chose
The fig-tree,° not that kind for fruit renowned,
But such as at this day to Indians known
In Malabar° or Deccan° spreads her arms
Branching so broad and long, that in the ground
The bended twigs take root, and daughters grow
About the mother tree, a pillared shade
High overarched, and echoing walks between;
There oft the Indian herdsman shunning heat
Shelters in cool, and tends his pasturing herds
At loopholes cut through thickest shade. Those
        leaves   1110
They gathered, broad as Amazonian targe,°
And with what skill they had, together sewed,
To gird their waist, vain covering if to hide
Their guilt and dreaded shame, O° how unlike
To that first naked glory! Such of late
Columbus found the American, so girt
With feathered cincture, naked else and wild
Among the trees on isles and woody shores.

1029–32. For . . . thee: Adam's words recall two amorous scenes in the *Iliad*, between Paris and Helen (III. 441–47) and Zeus and Hera (XIV. 292–353). His horrible mixture of levity and lust is completed by such a phrase as "enjoy thee," which degrades both Eve and himself so far below their former state. 1034. toy: caress. 1050. unkindly: unnatural. 1058. he: Shame. 1059–62. Danite . . . strength: See Judg. 16:4–20 and Milton's *Samson*, ll. 710–996. 1068. worm: serpent.

1078. evil store: a store of evil. 1079. last: worst. first: lesser. 1088. brown: dark. 1088–90. Cover . . . more: See Rev. 6:16. 1094. obnoxious: liable. 1101. fig-tree: the banyan. 1103. Malabar: the southwestern coast of India. Deccan: the whole peninsula of India. 1111. Amazonian targe: the crescent-shaped shield of the Amazons, the warrior women of classical myth. 1114–18. O . . . shores: The allusions to India and America suggest that the king and queen of the earth have become primitive savages.

Thus fenced, and as they thought, their shame in
    part
Covered, but not at rest or ease of mind,   1120
They sat them down to weep; nor only tears
Rained at their eyes, but high winds worse within
Began to rise, high passions, anger, hate,
Mistrust, suspicion, discord, and shook sore
Their inward state of mind, calm region once
And full of peace, now tossed and turbulent;
For° understanding ruled not, and the will
Heard not her lore, both in subjection now
To sensual appetite, who from beneath
Usurping over sovran reason claimed   1130
Superior sway. From thus distempered breast,
Adam, estranged in look and altered style,
Speech intermitted thus to Eve renewed:
    " Would thou hadst hearkened to my words, and
    stayed
With me, as I besought thee, when that strange
Desire of wandering, this unhappy morn,
I know not whence possessed thee; we had then
Remained still happy, not as now, despoiled
Of all our good, shamed, naked, miserable.
Let none henceforth seek needless cause to ap-
    prove°   1140
The faith they owe;° when earnestly they seek
Such proof, conclude they then begin to fail."
    To whom, soon moved with touch of blame, thus
    Eve:
" What words have passed thy lips, Adam severe!
Imput'st thou that to my default, or will
Of wandering, as thou call'st it, which who knows
But might as ill have happened thou being by,
Or to thyself perhaps? Hadst thou been there,
Or here the attempt, thou couldst not have dis-
    cerned
Fraud in the Serpent, speaking as he spake;   1150
No ground of enmity between us known
Why he should mean me ill, or seek to harm.
Was I to have never parted from thy side?
As good have grown there still a lifeless rib.
Being as I am, why didst not thou, the head,°
Command me absolutely not to go,
Going into such danger as thou saidst?
Too facile then, thou didst not much gainsay,
Nay didst permit, approve, and fair dismiss.   1159
Hadst thou been firm and fixed in thy dissent,
Neither had I transgressed, nor thou with me."
    To whom then first incensed Adam replied:
" Is this the love, is this the recompense
Of mine to thee, ingrateful Eve, expressed
Immutable° when thou wert lost, not I,

Who might have lived and joyed immortal bliss,
Yet willingly chose rather death with thee?
And am I now upbraided, as the cause
Of thy transgressing? not enough severe,
It seems, in thy restraint. What could I more?
I warned thee, I admonished thee, foretold   1171
The danger, and the lurking enemy
That lay in wait; beyond this had been force,
And force upon free will hath here no place.
But confidence then bore thee on, secure°
Either to meet no danger, or to find
Matter of glorious trial; and perhaps
I also erred in overmuch admiring
What seemed in thee so perfect, that I thought
No evil durst attempt thee, but I rue   1180
That error now, which is become my crime,
And thou the accuser. Thus it shall befall
Him who to worth in women overtrusting
Lets her will rule; restraint she will not brook,
And left to herself, if evil thence ensue,
She first his weak indulgence will accuse."
    Thus they in mutual accusation spent
The fruitless hours, but neither self-condemning,
And of their vain contést appeared no end.

BOOK X

[The Son is sent down to pronounce judgment on the guilty pair. Sin and Death build a bridge from Hell to the new world and show it to Satan on his return to Hell. Satan reports to his followers his success, but, in the moment of applause, they all turn into hissing serpents. On earth, the eternal spring of Paradise gives place to heat and cold, and beasts prey on one another; the golden age is over. Adam, outstretched on the cold ground, in a long soliloquy reproaches God for setting impossible conditions, but finally blames himself, and longs for death. When Eve appears, he denounces her bitterly, but he is softened by her remorseful entreaty, and the two are reunited in unselfish love. Eve proposes that they blunt the judgment pronounced on their posterity either by refraining from having children or by killing themselves; but Adam feels that the only remedy is in penitent confession, in the hope of pardon from their compassionate judge. They confess their sin and pray for mercy.]

BOOK XI

[Although Adam and Eve have lost happiness and immortality, God declares that Heaven will still be open to them after a life of trial, and death; he sends Michael down to expel them from Paradise and to unfold to Adam the course of history. Adam and Eve, while feeling new peace and hope after their prayers, are stricken by the sentence Michael delivers. Michael assures them that God is everywhere and will compass them round with goodness and paternal love. Then — after the pattern of the *Aeneid* (Book VI) and stories of the Fall — Michael takes Adam to the top of a hill and shows him, in a series of visions, the history of his descendants, from Cain's murder of Abel to God's covenant with man after the flood. The theme of all these episodes is " supernal grace contending / With sinfulness of men."]

1127-31. For . . . sway: The natural order and sway of the superior faculties have been reversed.   1140. approve: prove, test (cf. ll. 335-36, 367).   1141. owe: own.   1155. head: Eve uses the word in a very different spirit from that of IV. 443. 1164-65. expressed Immutable: shown to be unchangeable (ll. 906-16, 952-59).

1175. secure: rashly confident.

from BOOK XII

[Michael continues his revelation of the future, now in
the form of narrative. The story of Moses leads to an exposition of the doctrine of "Christian liberty." Then
Michael tells of the birth and crucifixion of Christ, who
shall redeem man from the sin of Adam and thus defeat
Satan and Sin and Death, and who, at the end of the world,
shall return to judge mankind and receive the faithful into
bliss far happier than that of Eden.]

So spake the Archangel Michaël, then paused,
As at the World's great period;° and our sire
Replete with joy and wonder thus replied:
  "O goodness° infinite, goodness immense!
That all this good of evil shall produce,   470
And evil turn to good; more wonderful
Than that which by creation first brought forth
Light out of darkness! full of doubt I stand,
Whether I should repent me now of sin
By me done and occasioned, or rejoice
Much more, that much more good thereof shall
    spring,
To God more glory, more good will to men
From God, and over wrath grace shall abound.
But say, if our Deliverer up to Heaven
Must reascend, what will betide the few   480
His faithful, left among the unfaithful herd,
The enemies of truth; who then shall guide
His people, who defend? will they not deal
Worse with his followers than with him they
    dealt?"
  "Be sure they will," said the Angel; "but from
    Heaven
He to his own a Comforter° will send,
The promise of the Father, who shall dwell,
His Spirit, within them, and the law of faith
Working through love, upon their hearts shall
    write,
To guide them in all truth, and also arm   490
With spiritual armor, able to resist
Satan's assaults, and quench his fiery darts,°
What man can do against them, not afraid,
Though to the death, against such cruelties
With inward consolations recompensed,
And oft supported so as shall amaze
Their proudest persecutors. For the Spirit
Poured first on his Apostles, whom he sends
To evangelize the nations, then on all
Baptized, shall them with wondrous gifts endue
To speak all tongues, and do all miracles,   501
As did their Lord before them. Thus they win
Great numbers of each nation to receive

With joy the tidings brought from Heaven: at
    length
Their ministry performed, and race well run,
Their doctrine and their story written left,
They die; but in their room, as they forewarn,
Wolves shall succeed for teachers, grievous wolves,°
Who all the sacred mysteries of Heaven
To their own vile advantages shall turn   510
Of lucre and ambition, and the truth
With superstitions and traditions taint,
Left only in those written records pure,
Though not but by the Spirit understood.
Then shall they seek to avail themselves of names,
Places and titles, and with these to join
Secular power, though feigning still to act
By spiritual, to themselves appropriating
The Spirit of God, promised alike and given
To all believers; and from that pretense,   520
Spiritual laws by carnal power shall force
On every conscience; laws which none shall find
Left them enrolled, or what the Spirit within
Shall on the heart engrave. What will they then
But force the Spirit of Grace itself, and bind
His consort Liberty? what but unbuild
His living temples,° built by faith to stand,
Their own faith, not another's? for on Earth
Who against faith and conscience can be heard
Infallible? yet many will presume: 530
Whence heavy persecution shall arise
On all who in the worship persevere
Of Spirit and Truth; the rest, far greater part,
Will deem in outward rites and specious forms
Religion satisfied; Truth shall retire
Bestuck with slanderous darts, and works of faith
Rarely be found. So shall the World go on,
To good malignant, to bad men benign,
Under her own weight groaning, till the day
Appear of respiration° to the just,   540
And vengeance to the wicked, at return
Of him so lately promised to thy aid,
The Woman's Seed, obscurely then foretold,
Now amplier known thy Saviour and thy Lord,
Last in the clouds from Heaven to be revealed
In glory of the Father, to dissolve
Satan with his perverted World; then raise
From the conflagrant mass,° purged and refined,
New Heavens, new Earth, ages of endless date
Founded in righteousness and peace and love,   550
To bring forth fruits, joy and eternal bliss."
  He ended; and thus Adam last replied:
"How soon hath thy prediction, seer blest,

Book XII: 467. period: end. 469–78. goodness . . . abound:
The idea of Christ's redemption of man, of the goodness called
into action by evil (an idea repeatedly enunciated from the
beginning of the poem), is a traditional paradox of theology —
felix culpa, "the fortunate fall." 486. a Comforter: the Holy
Spirit (John 15:26). 491–92. armor . . . darts: The military
metaphor is from Eph. 6:11-17 (the text of the first book of
The Faerie Queene).

508. wolves: See Acts 20:29 (and "Lycidas," l. 128; Sonnet XVI, to
Cromwell). 527. His . . . temples: individual persons (1 Cor.
3:16-17, 6:19). 540. respiration: refreshing. 548. conflagrant
mass: the world consumed by fire at the last day. Lines 547-51
are the last of a number of passages (e.g., III. 333-41, VII. 157-
61, XI. 898-901) in which Milton's early hope of a speedy reformation on earth is put off to the end of the world.

Measured this transient World, the race of Time,
Till Time stand fixed: beyond is all abyss,
Eternity, whose end no eye can reach.
Greatly instructed I shall hence depart,
Greatly in peace of thought, and have my fill
Of knowledge,° what this vessel° can contain;
Beyond which was my folly to aspire.   560
Henceforth I learn that to obey is best,
And love with fear the only God, to walk
As in his presence, ever to observe
His providence, and on him sole depend,
Merciful over all his works, with good
Still overcoming evil, and by small
Accomplishing great things, by things deemed weak
Subverting worldly strong, and worldly wise
By simply meek; that suffering for truth's sake
Is fortitude to highest victory,   570
And to the faithful death the gate of life;
Taught this by his example whom I now
Acknowledge my Redeemer ever blest."
    To whom thus also the Angel last replied:
"This having learnt, thou hast attained the sum
Of wisdom; hope no higher, though all the stars
Thou knew'st by name, and all the ethereal powers,
All secrets of the deep, all Nature's works,
Or works of God in heaven, air, earth, or sea,
And all the riches of this world enjoy'dst,   580
And all the rule, one empire; only add
Deeds to thy knowledge answerable, add faith,
Add virtue, patience, temperance, add love,
By name to come called charity,° the soul
Of all the rest: then wilt thou not be loth
To leave this Paradise, but shalt possess
A Paradise within thee, happier far.
Let us descend now therefore from this top
Of speculation;° for the hour precise
Exacts our parting hence; and see the guards,   590
By me encamped on yonder hill, expect
Their motion, at whose front a flaming sword,
In signal of remove, waves fiercely round;
We may no longer stay: go, waken Eve;
Her also I with gentle dreams have calmed,
Portending good, and all her spirits composed
To meek submission: thou at season fit
Let her with thee partake what thou hast heard,
Chiefly what may concern her faith to know,
The great deliverance by her seed to come   600
(For by the Woman's Seed) on all mankind:
That ye may live, which will be many days,°

Both in one faith unanimous though sad,
With cause for evils past, yet much more cheered
With meditation on the happy end."
    He ended, and they both descend the hill;
Descended, Adam to the bower where Eve
Lay sleeping ran before, but found her waked;
And thus with words not sad she him received:
"Whence thou return'st, and whither went'st, I
        know;   610
For God is also in sleep, and dreams advise,
Which he hath sent propitious, some great good
Presaging, since with sorrow and heart's distress
Wearied I fell asleep. But now lead on;°
In me is no delay; with° thee to go,
Is to stay here; without thee here to stay,
Is to go hence unwilling; thou to me
Art all things under Heaven, all places thou,
Who for my willful crime art banished hence.
This further consolation yet secure   620
I carry hence; though all by me is lost,
Such favor I unworthy am vouchsafed,
By me the Promised Seed shall all restore."
    So spake our mother Eve, and Adam heard
Well pleased, but answered not; for now too nigh
The Archangel stood, and from the other hill
To their fixed station, all in bright array
The Cherubim descended; on the ground
Gliding meteorous, as evening mist
Risen from a river o'er the marish° glides,   630
And gathers ground fast at the laborer's heel
Homeward returning. High in front advanced,°
The brandished sword of God before them blazed
Fierce as a comet; which° with torrid heat,
And vapor° as the Libyan air adust,°
Began to parch that temperate clime; whereat
In either hand the hastening Angel caught
Our lingering parents, and to the eastern gate
Led them direct, and down the cliff as fast
To the subjected° plain; then disappeared.   640
They, looking back, all the eastern side beheld
Of Paradise, so late their happy seat,
Waved over by that flaming brand,° the gate
With dreadful faces thronged and fiery arms.
Some° natural tears they dropped, but wiped them
        soon;
The world was all before them, where to choose
Their place of rest, and Providence their guide.
They hand in hand with wandering steps and slow,
Through Eden took their solitary way.

559–79. knowledge . . . sea: Adam's declaration and Michael's reply are a final reiteration of the principle emphasized throughout the poem, in Satan's temptation of Eve and in Raphael's discussion of astronomy (Book VIII) — that is, the priority of the religious and righteous life over mere knowledge of nature (or wealth or power).   **559. vessel:** Adam.   **584. charity:** Milton anticipates the use of "charity" for "love" in translations of the Bible (I Cor. 13:1–8).   **588–89. top . . . speculation:** the hill they are on, from which they had surveyed the world   **602. many days:** Adam was to live 930 years (Gen. 5:5).

614. lead on: Contrast Eve's "Lead then" addressed to the serpent (IX. 631).   **615–18. with . . . thou:** After her tragic experience Eve can, with a new simplicity and depth of feeling, reaffirm the devotion she had expressed with lyrical richness in IV. 635–56.   **630. marish:** marsh.   **632. advanced:** raised aloft.   **634. which:** the sword.   **635. the sword.**   **637. vapor:** heat. **adust:** burnt.   **640. subjected:** lying below.   **643. brand:** sword.   **645–49. Some . . . way:** *PL*, like Milton's other long poems, ends quietly, but — to repeat what was said in the Introduction — no other ending invests such simple narrative statements with so much complexity of feeling

SAMSON AGONISTES

A Dramatic Poem

Some comment on this drama is made at the end of the Introduction, pp. 411-12.

OF THAT SORT OF DRAMATIC POEM WHICH IS CALLED TRAGEDY

Tragedy, as it was anciently composed, hath been ever held the gravest, moralest, and most profitable of all other poems: therefore said by Aristotle [1] to be of power, by raising pity and fear, or terror, to purge the mind of those and suchlike passions, that is, to temper and reduce them to just measure with a kind of delight, stirred up by reading or seeing those passions well imitated. Nor is Nature wanting in her own effects to make good his assertion; for so in physic, things of melancholic hue and quality are used against melancholy, sour against sour, salt to remove salt humors. Hence philosophers and other gravest writers, as Cicero, Plutarch, and others, frequently cite out of tragic poets, both to adorn and illustrate their discourse. The Apostle Paul [2] himself thought it not unworthy to insert a verse of Euripides into the text of Holy Scripture, I Cor. 15:33; and Pareus,[3] commenting on the Revelation, divides the whole book, as a tragedy, into acts distinguished each by a chorus of heavenly harpings and song between. Heretofore men in highest dignity have labored not a little to be thought able to compose a tragedy. Of that honor Dionysius the elder [4] was no less ambitious than before of his attaining to the tyranny. Augustus Caesar also had begun his *Ajax,* but, unable to please his own judgment with what he had begun, left it unfinished. Seneca [5] the philosopher is by some thought the author of those tragedies (at least the best of them) that go under that name. Gregory Nazianzen, a Father of the Church, thought it not unbeseeming the sanctity of his person to write a tragedy, which he entitled *Christ Suffering.*[6] This is mentioned to vindicate tragedy from the small esteem, or rather infamy, which in the account of many it undergoes at this day, with other common interludes; happening through the poet's error of intermixing comic stuff with tragic sadness and gravity, or introducing trivial and vulgar persons, which by all judicious hath been counted absurd, and brought in without discretion, corruptly to gratify the people. And though ancient tragedy use no prologue, yet using sometimes, in case of self-defense or explanation, that which Martial [7] calls an epistle; in behalf of this tragedy, coming forth after the ancient manner, much different from what among us passes for best, thus much

beforehand may be epistled: that chorus is here introduced after the Greek manner, not ancient only but modern, and still in use among the Italians. In the modeling therefore of this poem, with good reason, the ancients and Italians are rather followed, as of much more authority and fame. The measure of verse used in the chorus is of all sorts, called by the Greeks *monostrophic,*[8] or rather *apolelymenon,* without regard had to strophe, antistrophe, or epode, which were a kind of stanzas framed only for the music, then used with the chorus that sung; not essential to the poem, and therefore not material; or, being divided into stanzas or pauses, they may be called *allœostropha.* Division into act and scene, referring chiefly to the stage (to which this work never was intended), is here omitted.

It suffices if the whole drama be found not produced beyond the fifth act. Of the style and uniformity, and that commonly called the plot, whether intricate or explicit [9] — which is nothing indeed but such economy, or disposition of the fable, as may stand best with verisimilitude and decorum [10] — they only will best judge who are not unacquainted with Aeschylus, Sophocles, and Euripides, the three tragic poets unequaled yet by any, and the best rule to all who endeavor to write tragedy. The circumscription of time wherein the whole drama begins and ends is, according to ancient rule and best example, within the space of twenty-four hours.[11]

THE ARGUMENT

Samson, made captive, blind, and now in the prison at Gaza, there to labor as in a common workhouse, on a festival day, in the general cessation from labor, comes forth into the open air, to a place nigh, somewhat retired, there to sit a while and bemoan his condition. Where he happens at length to be visited by certain friends and equals [12] of his tribe, which make the chorus, who seek to comfort him what they can; then by his old father, Manoa, who endeavors the like, and withal tells him his purpose to procure his liberty by ransom; lastly, that this feast was proclaimed by the Philistines as a day of thanksgiving for their deliverance from the hands of Samson, which yet more troubles him. Manoa then departs to prosecute his endeavor with the Philistian lords for Samson's redemption; who in the meanwhile is visited by other persons; and lastly by a public officer to require his coming to the feast before the lords and people, to play or show his strength in their presence. He at first refuses, dismissing the public officer with absolute denial to come; at length persuaded inwardly that this was from God, he yields to go along with him, who came now the second time with great threatenings to fetch him. The chorus yet re-

---

SAMSON AGONISTES. **1. Aristotle**: Milton paraphrases Aristotle's definition of tragic catharsis (*Poetics,* VI). **2. Paul**: See *Areopagitica,* n. 78. **3. Pareus**: See *Reason of Church Government,* n. 11. **4. Dionysius**: the tyrant of Syracuse. **5.** Seneca's declamatory Latin tragedies had great influence on the Renaissance theater, notably in the development of the "revenge" type. In *Samson* Milton is concerned with Greek and Italian models. **6. Christ Suffering**: In attributing this drama to Gregory, Milton shared an error of his age. **7. Martial**: the Roman poet (first century A.D.).

8. monostrophic: The context sufficiently explains this and other technical terms: Milton's choric odes are continuous, not divided into parts. **9. intricate or explicit**: complex (in reversals of fortune) or simple. **10. decorum**: a key word for neoclassical art, meaning fitness and harmony in all the elements of a work. **11. twenty-four hours**: Aristotle had required only unity of action, but Greek tragedies, acted continuously on an uncurtained stage, were normally confined to one place and a brief period of time; out of such precept and practice Italian critics of the Renaissance codified "the three unities." **12. equals**: men of his own age.

maining on the place, Manoa returns full of joyful hope to procure ere long his son's deliverance; in the midst of which discourse an Hebrew comes in haste, confusedly at first, and afterward more distinctly, relating the catastrophe, what Samson had done to the Philistines, and by accident to himself; wherewith the tragedy ends.

THE PERSONS

SAMSON
MANOA, *the father of Samson*
DÁLILA, *his wife*
HARAPHA OF GATH
PUBLIC OFFICER
MESSENGER
CHORUS OF DANITES [13]

The Scene, before the Prison in Gaza

SAMSON. A little onward lend thy guiding hand°
To these dark steps, a little further on;
For yonder bank hath choice of sun or shade;
There I am wont to sit, when any chance
Relieves me from my task of servile toil,
Daily in the common prison else enjoined me,
Where I, a prisoner chained, scarce freely draw
The air imprisoned also, close and damp,
Unwholesome draught. But here I feel amends,
The breath of Heaven fresh-blowing, pure and
    sweet,   10
With day-spring° born; here leave me to respire.
This day a solemn feast the people hold
To Dagon° their sea-idol, and forbid
Laborious works; unwillingly this rest
Their superstition yields me; hence with leave
Retiring from the popular noise, I seek
This unfrequented place to find some ease,
Ease to the body some, none to the mind
From restless thoughts, that like a deadly swarm
Of hornets armed, no sooner found alone,   20
But rush upon me thronging, and present
Times past, what once I was, and what am now.
O wherefore was my birth from Heaven foretold°
Twice by an angel, who at last in sight
Of both my parents all in flames ascended
From off the altar, where an offering burned,
As in a fiery column charioting
His godlike presence, and from some great act
Or benefit revealed to Abraham's race?
Why was my breeding ordered and prescribed   30
As of a person separate to God,

13. **Danites:** members of the tribe of Dan, to which Manoa belonged.   1. **A ... hand:** This first line has its literal sense as addressed to the blind hero's attendant; it also suggests God's continued help of his chosen champion during the brief remainder of his life.   11. **day-spring:** dawn. Lines 10–11, along with the literal sense, carry a hint of divine inspiration and aid.   13. **Dagon:** See *PL*, I. 457–66n.   23. **foretold:** See Judg. 13:3–20.

Designed for great exploits, if I must die
Betrayed, captived, and both my eyes put out,
Made of my enemies the scorn and gaze,
To grind in brazen fetters under task
With this Heaven-gifted strength? O glorious
    strength,
Put to the labor of a beast, debased
Lower than bondslave! Promise was that I
Should Israel from Philistian yoke deliver;
Ask for this great deliverer now, and find him   40
Eyeless in Gaza at the mill with slaves,
Himself in bonds under Philistian yoke;
Yet stay, let me not rashly call in doubt
Divine prediction; what if all foretold
Had been fulfilled but through mine own default?
Whom have I to complain of but myself?
Who this high gift of strength committed to me,
In what part lodged, how easily bereft me,
Under the seal of silence could not keep,
But weakly to a woman must reveal it,   50
O'ercome with importunity and tears.
O impotence of mind, in body strong!
But what is strength without a double share
Of wisdom? vast, unwieldy, burdensome,
Proudly secure, yet liable to fall
By weakest subtleties; not made to rule,
But to subserve where wisdom bears command.
God, when he gave me strength, to show withal
How slight the gift was, hung it in my hair.
But peace! I must not quarrel with the will   60
Of highest dispensation, which herein
Haply had ends above my reach to know:
Suffices that to me strength is my bane,
And proves the source of all my miseries,
So many, and so huge, that each apart
Would ask a life to wail; but chief of all,
O loss of sight, of thee I most complain!
Blind among enemies, O worse than chains,
Dungeon, or beggary, or decrepit age!
Light, the prime work of God, to me is extinct,
And all her various objects of delight   71
Annulled, which might in part my grief have eased,
Inferior to the vilest now become
Of man or worm; the vilest here excel me,
They creep, yet see; I, dark in light, exposed
To daily fraud, contempt, abuse and wrong,
Within doors, or without, still° as a fool,
In power of others, never in my own;
Scarce half I seem to live, dead more than half.
O dark, dark, dark, amid the blaze of noon,   80
Irrecoverably dark, total eclipse
Without all° hope of day!
O first-created beam, and thou great Word,
" Let there be light, and light was over all ";°
Why am I thus bereaved thy prime decree?
The sun to me is dark

77. **still:** always.   82. **all:** any.   83–84. **O ... all:** See Gen. 1:3.

And silent° as the moon,
When she deserts the night,
Hid in her vacant interlunar cave.°
Since light so necessary is to life,   90
And almost life itself, if it be true
That light is in the soul,
She all in every part, why was the sight
To such a tender ball as the eye confined?
So obvious° and so easy to be quenched,
And not, as feeling, through all parts diffused,
That she might look at will through every pore?
Then had I not been thus exiled from light,
As in the land of darkness, yet in light,
To live a life half dead, a living death,   100
And buried; but O yet more miserable!
Myself my sepulcher, a moving grave,
Buried, yet not exempt
By privilege of death and burial
From worst of other evils, pains and wrongs,
But made hereby obnoxious° more
To all the miseries of life,
Life in captivity
Among inhuman foes.
But who are these? for with joint pace I hear   110
The tread of many feet steering this way;
Perhaps my enemies who come to stare
At my affliction, and perhaps to insult,
Their daily practice to afflict me more.
    CHORUS. This, this is he; softly a while;
Let us not break in upon him.
O change beyond report, thought, or belief!
See how he lies at random, carelessly diffused,°
With languished head unpropped,
As one past hope, abandoned,   120
And by himself given over;°
In slavish habit, ill-fitted weeds°
O'er-worn and soiled;
Or do my eyes misrepresent? Can this be he,
That heroic, that renowned,
Irresistible Samson? whom unarmed
No strength of man, or fiercest wild beast could
    withstand;
Who tore the lion as the lion tears the kid,
Ran on embattled armies clad in iron,
And, weaponless himself,°   130
Made arms ridiculous, useless the forgery°
Of brazen shield and spear, the hammered cuirass,
Chalybean°-tempered steel, and frock of mail

Adamantean proof;
But safest he who stood aloof,
When insupportably° his foot advanced,
In scorn of their proud arms and warlike tools,
Spurned them to death by troops. The bold
    Ascalonite°
Fled from his lion ramp,° old warriors turned
Their plated backs under his heel;   140
Or groveling soiled their crested helmets in the
    dust.
Then with what trivial weapon came to hand,
The jaw of a dead ass, his sword of bone,
A thousand foreskins fell, the flower of Palestine,
In Ramath-lechi, famous to this day;°
Then° by main force pulled up, and on his shoul-
    ders bore
The gates of Azza, post and massy bar,
Up to the hill by Hebron, seat of giants old,
No journey of a Sabbath day, and loaded so;
Like whom the Gentiles feign to bear up Heaven.°
Which shall I first bewail,   151
Thy bondage or lost sight,
Prison within prison
Inseparably dark?
Thou art become (O worst imprisonment!)
The dungeon of thyself; thy soul
(Which° men enjoying sight oft without cause
    complain)
Imprisoned now indeed,
In real darkness of the body dwells,
Shut up from outward light   160
To incorporate with gloomy night;
For inward light, alas,
Puts forth no visual beam.
O mirror of our fickle state,
Since man on earth unparalleled!
The° rarer thy example stands,
By how much from the top of wondrous glory,
Strongest of mortal men,
To lowest pitch of abject fortune thou art fallen.
For him I reckon not in high estate   170
Whom long descent of birth
Or the sphere of fortune raises;
But thee whose strength, while virtue was her mate,
Might have subdued the earth,
Universally crowned with highest praises.
    SAMS. I hear the sound of words; their sense the
    air
Dissolves unjointed ere it reach my ear.
    CHOR. He speaks; let us draw nigh. Matchless in
    might,
The glory late of Israel, now the grief!
We come, thy friends and neighbors not unknown,

---

87. **silent**: not performing its function, i.e., dark. Cf. Virgil, *Aeneid*, II. 255, Dante, *Inferno*, I. 60, V. 28.   **89. vacant . . . cave**: Milton is using the ancient notion that the moon, between her appearances, was hidden in a cave ("vacant" meaning "unoccupied"). Lines 86–99 may suggest to the reader that God, like the sun or moon, has only seemed to desert Samson and will return.   **95. obvious**: exposed.   **106. obnoxious**: liable.   **118. diffused**: stretched out.   **121. given over**: despaired of.   **122. habit, weeds**: clothes.   **130. weaponless himself**: as he is to be in his last action, in the drama.   **131. forgery**: forging.   **133. Chalybean**: The Chalybes on the Black Sea were famous for metalwork.

136. insupportably: irresistibly.   **138. Ascalonite**: See *PL*, I. 464–66n.   **139. ramp**: spring.   **142–45. Then . . . day**: See Judg. 15:15–17.   **146–49. Then . . . so**: See Judg. 16:3. Azza is another name for Gaza.   **150. Like . . . Heaven**: In a Hebrew context, an oblique allusion to the classical myth of Atlas.   **157. Which**: referring to lines 157–63.   **166–69. The . . . fallen**: a traditional definition of tragedy.

From Eshtaol and Zora's fruitful vale,   181
To visit or bewail thee, or if better,
Counsel or consolation we may bring,
Salve to thy sores; apt words have power to swage°
The tumors of a troubled mind,
And are as balm to festered wounds.
    SAMS. Your coming, friends, revives me, for I
      learn
Now of my own experience, not by talk,
How counterfeit a coin they are who " friends "
Bear in their superscription (of the most   190
I would be understood). In prosperous days
They swarm, but in adverse withdraw their head,
Not to be found, though sought. Ye see, O friends,
How many evils have enclosed me round;
Yet that which was the worst now least afflicts me,
Blindness, for had I sight, confused with shame,
How could I once look up, or heave the head,
Who like a foolish pilot have shipwracked
My vessel trusted to me from above,
Gloriously rigged; and for a word, a tear,   200
Fool, have divulged the secret gift of God
To a deceitful woman? Tell me, friends,
Am I not sung and proverbed for a fool
In every street, do they not say, " How well
Are come upon him his deserts "? Yet why?
Immeasurable strength they might behold
In me, of wisdom nothing more than mean;
This with the other should, at least, have paired;°
These two, proportioned ill, drove me transverse.°
    CHOR. Tax not divine disposal; wisest men   210
Have erred, and by bad women been deceived;
And shall again, pretend they ne'er so wise.
Deject not then so overmuch thyself,
Who hast of sorrow thy full load besides.
Yet° truth to say, I oft have heard men wonder
Why thou shouldst wed Philistian women rather
Than of thine own tribe fairer, or as fair,
At least of thy own nation, and as noble.
    SAMS. The first I saw at Timna, and she pleased
Me, not my parents, that I sought to wed,   220
The daughter of an infidel: they° knew not
That what I motioned was of God; I knew
From intimate impulse, and therefore urged
The marriage on; that by occasion hence
I might begin Israel's deliverance,
The work to which I was divinely called.
She proving false, the next I took to wife
(O that I never had! fond° wish too late!)
Was in the vale of Sorec, Dálila,
That specious monster, my accomplished snare.
I thought it lawful from my former act,   231
And the same end,° still watching to oppress

Israel's oppressors. Of what now I suffer
She was not the prime cause, but I myself,
Who, vanquished with a peal of words (O weak
    ness!),
Gave up my fort of silence to a woman.
    CHOR. In seeking just occasion to provoke
The Philistine, thy country's enemy,
Thou never wast remiss, I bear thee witness:
Yet Israel still serves° with all his sons.   240
    SAMS. That fault I take not on me, but transfer
On Israel's governors and heads of tribes,
Who, seeing those great acts which God had done
Singly by me against their conquerors,
Acknowledged not, or not at all considered,
Deliverance offered: I on the other side
Used no ambition° to commend my deeds;
The deeds themselves, though mute, spoke loud the
    doer;
But they persisted deaf, and would not seem   249
To count them things worth notice, till at length
Their lords the Philistines with gathered powers
Entered Judea seeking me, who then
Safe to the rock of Etham was retired,
Not flying, but forecasting in what place
To set upon them, what advantaged best;
Meanwhile° the men of Judah, to prevent
The harass of their land, beset me round;
I willingly on some conditions came
Into their hands, and they as gladly yield me
To the uncircumcised a welcome prey,   260
Bound with two cords; but cords to me were
    threads
Touched with the flame: on their whole host I flew
Unarmed, and with a trivial weapon felled
Their choicest youth; they only lived who fled.
Had Judah that day joined, or one whole tribe,
They had by this possessed the towers of Gath,
And lorded over them whom now they serve;
But° what more oft in nations grown corrupt,
And by their vices brought to servitude,
Than to love bondage more than liberty,   270
Bondage with ease than strenuous liberty;
And to despise, or envy, or suspect
Whom God hath of his special favor raised
As their deliverer; if he aught begin,
How frequent to desert him, and at last
To heap ingratitude on worthiest deeds?
    CHOR. Thy words to my remembrance bring
How Succoth and the fort of Penuel
Their great deliverer contemned,
The matchless Gideon° in pursuit   280
Of Madian and her vanquished kings:
And how ingrateful Ephraim

---

184. swage: assuage.   208. paired: made equal.   209. transverse: off the course.   215–18: Yet . . . noble: The chorus, like
Job's comforters, contrive to turn the knife in Samson's wound.
221–26. they . . . called: See Judg. 14:4.   228. fond: foolish.
231–32. I . . . end: This motive is not in Judg. 16:4.

240. serves: is in servitude.   247. ambition: canvassing for
support.   256–64. Meanwhile . . . fled: See Judg. 15:9–17.
268–71. But . . . liberty: a recurrent idea in Milton, exemplified
for him in the failure of the Puritan Revolution and England's
restoration of the monarchy.   280. Gideon: See Judg. 8:4–12.

Had dealt with Jephtha,° who by argument,
Not worse than by his shield and spear,
Defended Israel from the Ammonite,
Had not his prowess quelled their pride
In that sore battle when so many died
Without reprieve adjudged to death,
For want of well pronouncing *Shibboleth*.

   SAMS. Of such examples add me to the roll;   290
Me easily indeed mine° may neglect,
But God's proposed deliverance not so.

   CHOR. Just° are the ways of God,
And justifiable to men;
Unless there be who think not° God at all:
If any be, they walk obscure;
For of such doctrine never was there school,
But the heart of the fool,
And no man therein doctor but himself.

   Yet more there be who doubt his ways not just,
As to his own edicts, found contradicting,   301
Then give the reins to wandering thought,
Regardless of his glory's diminution;
Till by their own perplexities involved
They ravel° more, still less resolved,
But never find self-satisfying solution.

   As if they would confine the Interminable,°
And tie him to his own prescript,
Who made our laws to bind us, not himself,
And hath full right to exempt   310
Whomso it pleases him by choice
From national obstriction,° without taint
Of sin, or legal debt;
For with his own laws he can best dispense.

   He would not else, who never wanted means,
Nor in respect of the enemy just cause,
To set his people free,
Have prompted this heroic Nazarite,°
Against his vow of strictest purity,
To seek in marriage that fallacious bride,   320
Unclean,° unchaste.

   Down, Reason, then, at least vain reasonings
     down,
Though Reason here aver
That moral verdict quits° her of unclean:
Unchaste was subsequent; her stain, not his.

   But see, here comes thy reverend sire
With careful° step, locks white as down,
Old Manoa: advise°
Forthwith how thou ought'st to receive him.   329

   SAMS. Ay me, another inward grief, awaked

With mention of that name, renews the assault.

   MANOA. Brethren and men of Dan, for such ye
     seem,
Though in this uncouth° place; if old respect,
As I suppose, towards your once gloried friend,
My son now captive, hither hath informed°
Your younger feet, while mine cast back with age
Came lagging after; say if he be here.

   CHOR. As signal° now in low dejected state,
As erst in highest, behold him where he lies.

   MAN. O miserable change! is this the man,   340
That invincible Samson, far renowned,
The dread of Israel's foes, who with a strength
Equivalent to angels' walked their streets,
None offering fight; who, single combatant,
Dueled° their armies ranked in proud array,
Himself an army, now unequal match
To save himself against a coward armed
At one spear's length? O ever-failing trust
In mortal strength! and oh what not in man
Deceivable and vain! Nay, what thing good   350
Prayed for, but often proves our woe, our bane?
I prayed for children, and thought barrenness
In wedlock a reproach; I gained a son,
And such a son as° all men hailed me happy:
Who would be now a father in my stead?
O wherefore did God grant me my request,
And as a blessing with such pomp adorned?
Why are his gifts desirable, to tempt
Our earnest prayers, then, given with solemn hand
As graces, draw a scorpion's tail behind?   360
For this did the angel twice descend? for this
Ordained thy nurture holy, as of a plant;
Select and sacred, glorious for a while,
The miracle of men; then in an hour
Ensnared, assaulted, overcome, led bound,
Thy foes' derision, captive, poor, and blind,
Into a dungeon thrust, to work with slaves?
Alas, methinks whom God hath chosen once
To worthiest deeds, if he through frailty err,
He should not so o'erwhelm, and as a thrall   370
Subject him to so foul indignities,
Be it but for honor's sake of former deeds.

   SAMS. Appoint not heavenly disposition, father.
Nothing of all these evils hath befallen me
But justly; I myself have brought them on,
Sole author I, sole cause: if aught seem vile,
As vile hath been my folly, who have profaned
The mystery of God given me under pledge
Of vow, and have betrayed it to a woman,
A Canaanite,° my faithless enemy.   380
This well I knew, nor was at all surprised,
But warned by oft experience: did° not she

---

283. Jephtha: See Judg. 11:12–33.   **291. mine:** my nation.
293 f. : As ll. 315–25 show, the theme of the chorus is Samson's
marriages, which inspire their general reflections.   **295. think
not:** do not believe in.   **305. ravel:** become tangled.
307. Interminable: Infinite (God).   **312. national obstriction:**
Jewish law forbidding marriage with Gentiles.   **318. Nazarite:**
a person vowed to the special service of God, to abstinence from
wines and a razor, etc. (Num. 6).   **321. Unclean:** as being a
Gentile.   **324. quits:** acquits.   **327. careful:** full of care.
328. advise: consider.

333. uncouth: unfamiliar.   **335. informed:** led.   **338. signal:**
notable.   **345. Dueled:** fought singly.   **354. as:** that.   **380. Canaanite:** equivalent to Philistine, since the Philistines had held
Canaan, the coastal region of southern Palestine.   **382–87. did
. . . rivals:** See Judg. 14:11–18.

Of Timna first betray me, and reveal
The secret wrested from me in her highth
Of nuptial love professed, carrying it straight
To them who had corrupted her, my spies,
And rivals? In this other° was there found
More faith? who also in her prime of love,
Spousal embraces, vitiated with gold,
Though offered only, by the scent conceived   390
Her spurious first-born, treason against me.
Thrice she assayed° with flattering prayers and
    sighs,
And amorous reproaches, to win from me
My capital° secret, in what part my strength
Lay stored, in what part summed, that she might
    know:
Thrice I deluded her, and turned to sport
Her importunity, each time perceiving
How openly, and with what impudence,
She purposed to betray me, and (which was worse
Than undissembled hate) with what contempt
She sought to make me traitor to myself;   401
Yet the fourth time, when mustering all her wiles,
With blandished parleys, feminine assaults,
Tongue-batteries, she surceased° not day nor night
To storm me overwatched,° and wearied out:
At times when men seek most repose and rest,
I yielded, and unlocked her all my heart,°
Who with a grain of manhood well resolved
Might easily have shook off all her snares;
But° foul effeminacy held me yoked   410
Her bondslave; O indignity, O blot
To honor and religion! servile mind
Rewarded well with servile punishment!
The base degree to which I now am fallen,
These rags, this grinding, is not yet so base
As was my former servitude, ignoble,
Unmanly, ignominious, infamous,
True slavery, and that blindness worse than this,
That saw not how degenerately I served.   419
    MAN. I cannot praise thy marriage choices, son,
Rather approved them not; but thou didst plead
Divine impulsion prompting how thou might'st
Find some occasion to infest our foes.
I state not that; this I am sure, our foes
Found soon occasion thereby to make thee
Their captive, and their triumph; thou the sooner
Temptation found'st, or overpotent charms,
To violate the sacred trust of silence
Deposited within thee; which to have kept
Tacit was in thy power; true; and thou bear'st   430
Enough, and more, the burden of that fault;
Bitterly hast thou paid, and still art paying,

That rigid score.° A worse thing yet remains:
This day the Philistines a popular feast
Here celebrate in Gaza, and proclaim
Great pomp, and sacrifice, and praises loud
To Dagon, as their god who hath delivered
Thee, Samson, bound and blind, into their hands,
Them out of thine, who slew'st them° many a
    slain.°
So Dagon shall be magnified, and God,   440
Besides whom is no god, compared with idols,
Disglorified, blasphemed, and had in scorn
By the idolatrous rout amidst their wine;
Which to have come to pass by means of thee,
Samson, of all thy sufferings think the heaviest,
Of all reproach the most with shame that ever
Could have befallen thee and thy father's house.
    SAMS. Father,° I do acknowledge and confess
That I this honor, I this pomp, have brought
To Dagon, and advanced his praises high   450
Among the heathen round; to God have brought
Dishonor, obloquy, and oped the mouths
Of idolists and atheists; have brought scandal
To Israel, diffidence° of God, and doubt
In feeble hearts, propense° enough before
To waver, or fall off and join with idols:
Which is my chief affliction, shame and sorrow,
The anguish of my soul, that suffers not
Mine eye to harbor sleep, or thoughts to rest.
This only hope relieves me, that the strife   460
With me hath end; all the contést is now
'Twixt God and Dagon; Dagon hath presumed,
Me overthrown, to enter lists with God,
His deity comparing and preferring
Before the God of Abraham. He, be sure,
Will not connive,° or linger, thus provoked,
But will arise and his great name assert:
Dagon must stoop, and shall ere long receive
Such a discomfit, as shall quite despoil him
Of all these boasted trophies won on° me,   470
And with confusion blank° his worshipers.
    MAN. With cause this hope relieves thee, and
    these words
I as a prophecy receive; for God,
Nothing more certain, will not long defer
To vindicate the glory of his name
Against all competition, nor will long
Endure it doubtful whether God be Lord,
Or Dagon. But for thee what shall be done?
Thou must not in the meanwhile, here forgot,
Lie in this miserable loathsome plight   480

---

387. **this other:** Dalila.   392. **assayed:** essayed, tried.   394. **capital:** fatal (with a pun on *caput*, "head").   404. **surceased:** ceased.   405. **overwatched:** weary from keeping awake. 407. **I . . . heart:** See Judg. 16:5–21.   410–19. **But . . . served:** These lines, and the whole speech, show that Manoa's reproaching of God rouses Samson to condemn himself more strongly than before.

433. **score:** record of debts.   439. **slew'st . . . slain:** redundant, for emphasis.   **them:** for them, to their hurt.   448–71. Manoa's account of the glorification of Dagon enlarges the significance of Samson's fall and deepens his grief, not now for his personal plight but for the dishonor he has brought on the God of Israel. 454. **diffidence:** distrust.   455. **propense:** inclined.   466. **connive:** let pass, wink at.   470. **on:** over.   471. **blank:** confound. Lines 465–71 are one of a number of general premonitions that build toward the climax.

Neglected. I already have made way
To some Philistian lords, with whom to treat
About thy ransom: well they may by this
Have satisfied their utmost of revenge
By pains and slaveries, worse than death, inflicted
On thee, who now no more canst do them harm.
   SAMS. Spare that proposal, father, spare the
     trouble
Of that solicitation; let me here,
As I deserve, pay on my punishment,
And expiate, if possible, my crime,   490
Shameful garrulity. To have revealed
Secrets of men, the secrets of a friend,
How heinous had the fact° been, how deserving
Contempt, and scorn of all, to be excluded
All friendship, and avoided as a blab,
The mark of fool set on his front!
But I God's counsel have not kept, his holy secret
Presumptuously have published, impiously,
Weakly at least, and shamefully: a sin
That Gentiles in their parables condemn   500
To their abyss and horrid pains confined.°
   MAN. Be penitent and for thy fault contrite,
But act not in thy own affliction, son;
Repent the sin, but if the punishment
Thou canst avoid, self-preservation bids;
Or the execution leave to high disposal,
And let another hand, not thine, exact
Thy penal forfeit from thyself; perhaps
God will relent, and quit° thee all his debt;
Who ever more approves and more accepts   510
(Best pleased with humble and filial submission)
Him who imploring mercy sues for life,
Than who self-rigorous chooses death as due;
Which argues overjust, and self-displeased
For self-offense, more than for God offended.
Reject not then what offered means who knows
But God hath set before us, to return thee
Home to thy country and his sacred house,
Where thou mayst bring thy offerings, to avert
His further ire, with prayers and vows renewed.
   SAMS. His pardon I implore; but as for life,   521
To what end should I seek it?° When in strength
All mortals I excelled, and great in hopes
With youthful courage and magnanimous thoughts
Of birth from Heaven foretold and high exploits,
Full of divine instinct, after some proof
Of acts indeed heroic, far beyond
The sons of Anak,° famous now and blazed,
Fearless of danger, like a petty god
I walked about admired of° all and dreaded   530

On hostile ground, none daring my affront.°
Then swollen with pride, into the snare I
     fell
Of fair fallacious looks, venereal trains,°
Softened with pleasure and voluptuous life;
At length to lay my head and hallowed pledge
Of all my strength in the lascivious lap
Of a deceitful concubine, who shore me
Like a tame wether, all my precious fleece,
Then turned me out ridiculous, despoiled,
Shaven, and disarmed among my enemies.   540
   CHOR. Desire of wine and all delicious drinks,
Which many a famous warrior overturns,
Thou couldst repress, nor did the dancing ruby
Sparkling outpoured, the flavor, or the smell,
Or taste that cheers the heart of gods and men,
Allure thee from the cool crystálline stream.
   SAMS. Wherever fountain or fresh current flowed
Against the eastern ray, translucent, pure
With touch ethereal of Heaven's fiery rod,°
I drank, from the clear milky juice allaying   550
Thirst, and refreshed; nor envied them the grape
Whose heads that turbulent liquor fills with fumes.
   CHOR. O madness, to think use of strongest wines
And strongest drinks our chief support of health,
When God with these forbidden made choice to
     rear
His mighty champion, strong above compare,
Whose drink was only from the liquid brook.
   SAMS. But what availed this temperance, not com-
     plete
Against another object more enticing?
What boots° it at one gate to make defense,   560
And at another to let in the foe,
Effeminately vanquished? by which means,
Now blind, disheartened, shamed, dishonored,
     quelled,
To what can I be useful, wherein serve
My nation, and the work from Heaven imposed,
But to sit idle on the household hearth,
A burdenous drone? to visitants a gaze,
Or pitied object; these redundant° locks,
Robustious° to no purpose, clustering down,
Vain monument of strength; till length of years
And sedentary numbness craze° my limbs   571
To a contemptible old age obscure.
Here rather let me drudge and earn my bread,
Till vermin or the draff of servile food
Consume me, and oft-invocated death
Hasten the welcome end of all my pains.
   MAN. Wilt thou then serve the Philistines with
    that gift
Which was expressly given thee to annoy them?

---

493. fact: act.   500–01. Gentiles . . . confined: such as Tantalus, who was punished for betraying the secrets of the gods.
509. quit: cancel.   521–22. His . . . it: Samson's reaction, here
and earlier, to Manoa's plan for ransom marks another upward
step in his relations with himself and God. Cf. ll. 410–19, 448–71
and notes.   528. sons of Anak: See l. 1080n.   530. admired of:
wondered at by.

531. my affront: to meet me.   533. venereal trains: sensual
temptations.   549. fiery rod: rays of the sun.   560. boots:
avails.   568. redundant: luxuriantly flowing.   569. Robustious:
strong.   571. craze: weaken.

Better at home lie bed-rid, not only idle,
Inglorious, unemployed, with age outworn.   580
But God, who caused a fountain at thy prayer
From the dry ground to spring, thy thirst to allay
After the brunt of battle,° can as easy
Cause light again within thy eyes to spring,
Wherewith to serve him better than thou hast;
And I persuade me so; why else this strength
Miraculous yet remaining in those locks?
His might continues in thee not for nought,
Nor shall his wondrous gifts be frustrate thus.   589
  SAMS. All otherwise to me my thoughts portend,
That these dark orbs no more shall treat with light,
Nor the other light of life continue long,
But yield to double darkness nigh at hand:
So much I feel my genial° spirits droop,
My hopes all flat; Nature within me seems
In all her functions weary of herself;
My race of glory run, and race of shame,
And I shall shortly be with them that rest.
    MAN. Believe not these suggestions, which pro-
        ceed
From anguish of the mind and humors black,°
That mingle with thy fancy. I however   601
Must not omit a father's timely care
To prosecute the means of thy deliverance
By ransom or how else: meanwhile be calm,
And healing words from these thy friends admit.
  SAMS. O that torment should not be confined
To the body's wounds and sores,
With maladies innumerable
In heart, head, breast, and reins;°
But must secret passage find   610
To the inmost mind,
There exercise all his fierce accidents,°
And on her purest spirits prey,
As on entrails, joints, and limbs,
With answerable pains, but more intense,
Though void of corporal sense.
  My griefs not only pain me
As a lingering disease,
But finding no redress, ferment and rage,
Nor less than wounds immedicable   620
Rankle, and fester, and gangrene,
To black mortification.
Thoughts, my tormentors, armed with deadly stings
Mangle my apprehensive° tenderest parts,
Exasperate, exulcerate, and raise
Dire inflammation which no cooling herb
Or med'cinal liquor can assuage,
Nor breath of vernal air from snowy Alp.°
Sleep hath forsook and given me o'er

To death's benumbing opium as my only cure.
Thence faintings, swoonings of despair,   631
And sense of Heaven's desertion.
  I was his nursling once and choice delight,
His destined from the womb,
Promised by heavenly message° twice descending.
Under his special eye
Abstemious I grew up and thrived amain;
He led me on to mightiest deeds
Above the nerve° of mortal arm
Against the uncircumcised, our enemies.   640
But now hath cast me off as never known,
And to those cruel enemies,
Whom I by his appointment had provoked,
Left me all helpless with the irreparable loss
Of sight, reserved alive to be repeated°
The subject of their cruelty or scorn.
Nor am I in the list of them that hope;
Hopeless are all my evils, all remediless;
This one prayer yet remains, might I be heard,
No long petition — speedy death,   650
The close of all my miseries, and the balm.°
  CHOR. Many are the sayings of the wise
In ancient and in modern books enrolled,
Extolling patience as the truest fortitude;
And to the bearing well of all calamities,
All chances incident to man's frail life,
Consolatories writ
With studied argument, and much persuasion
        sought,
Lenient of° grief and anxious thought;
But with the afflicted in his pangs their sound   660
Little prevails, or rather seems a tune
Harsh and of dissonant mood from his complaint,
Unless he feel within
Some source of consolation from above,
Secret refreshings that repair his strength,
And fainting spirits uphold.
    God of our fathers, what is man!°
That thou towards him with hand so various —
Or might I say contrarious? —
Temper'st thy providence through his short course,
Not evenly, as thou rul'st   671
The angelic orders and inferior creatures mute,
Irrational and brute.
Nor do I name of men the common rout,
That wandering loose about
Grow up and perish, as the summer fly,
Heads without name, no more remembered;
But such as thou hast solemnly elected,

581–83. God . . . battle: See Judg. 15:18–19.   594. genial: of the
essential self.   600. humors black: black bile ("melancholy"),
one of the four humors of the body which, if in excess, altered
the constitution and character.   609. reins: kidneys.   612. accidents: technically, medical symptoms; here, torments.   624. apprehensive: sensitive.   628. Alp: any high mountain.

635. message: messenger (cf. ll. 23–24).   639. nerve: muscle.
645. repeated: made repeatedly.   651. Lines 590–98 and 606–51
mark the one relapse in Samson's upward progression; the chief
enemy he has now to conquer is despair.   659. Lenient of:
healing. In 652–62 Milton has in mind the essays of consolation
written by classical moralists, which are inadequate without
divine help.   667–86. In these and following lines the bold and
bitter questioning of God's justice brings out the parallel between
Samson's situation and Job's.

With gifts and graces eminently adorned
To some great work, thy glory,   680
And people's safety, which in part they effect;
Yet toward these thus dignified, thou oft
Amidst their highth of noon
Changest thy countenance and thy hand, with no
      regard
Of highest favors past
From thee on them, or them to thee of service.
   Nor only dost degrade them, or remit
To life obscured, which were a fair dismission,
But throw'st them lower than thou didst exalt them
      high,
Unseemly falls in human eye,   690
Too grievous for the trespass or omission;
Oft° leav'st them to the hostile sword
Of heathen and profane, their carcasses
To dogs and fowls a prey, or else captived,
Or to the unjust tribunals, under change of times,
And condemnation of the ingrateful multitude.
If° these they scape, perhaps in poverty
With sickness and disease thou bow'st them down,
Painful diseases and deformed,
In crude° old age;   700
Though not disordinate, yet causeless suffering
The punishment of dissolute days; in fine,
Just or unjust, alike seem miserable,
For oft alike, both come to evil end.
   So deal not with this once thy glorious cham-
      pion,
The image of thy strength, and mighty minister.
What do I beg? how hast thou dealt already?
Behold him in this state calamitous, and turn
His labors, for thou canst, to peaceful end.
   But who is this, what thing of sea or land?   710
Female of sex it seems,
That so bedecked, ornate, and gay,
Comes this way sailing
Like a stately ship
Of Tarsus,° bound for the isles
Of Javan° or Gadire,°
With all her bravery on, and tackle trim,
Sails filled, and streamers waving,
Courted by all the winds that hold them play,
An amber° scent of odorous perfume   720
Her harbinger, a damsel train behind;
Some rich Philistian matron she may seem,

692–96. Oft . . . multitude: the clearest topical reference in the
drama — the treatment of Commonwealth leaders by the Restoration government.   697–702. If . . . days: Milton could
hardly write these lines without thinking of his own career, his
reduced circumstances, and his suffering from gout, which could
afflict the temperate ("not disordinate") as well as the dissolute.
700. crude: premature.   715. Tarsus: a trading city near the
coast of Cilicia.   715–16. isles . . . Javan: isles of Greece.
See *PL*, I. 508n.   Gadire: Cadiz in Spain. The highly colored
picture of Dalila in her luxury — luxury gained through her
betrayal of Samson — is contrasted with the captive in his
squalor.   720. amber: ambergris.

And now at nearer view, no other certain
Than Dálila thy wife.
   SAMS. My wife, my traitress, let her not come near
      me.
   CHOR. Yet on she moves, now stands and eyes
      thee fixed,
About to have spoke; but now, with head declined
Like a fair flower surcharged with dew, she weeps,
And words addressed seem into tears dissolved,
Wetting the borders of her silken veil;   730
But now again she makes address to speak.
   DAL. With doubtful feet and wavering resolution
I came, still dreading thy displeasure, Samson,
Which to have merited, without excuse,
I cannot but acknowledge; yet if tears
May expiate (though the fact more evil drew
In the perverse event than I foresaw),
My penance hath not slackened, though my pardon
No way assured. But conjugal affection,
Prevailing over fear and timorous doubt,   740
Hath led me on, desirous to behold
Once more thy face, and know of thy estate;
If aught in my ability may serve
To lighten what thou suffer'st, and appease
Thy mind with what amends is in my power,
Though late, yet in some part to recompense
My rash but more unfortunate misdeed.
   SAMS. Out, out, hyena!° these are thy wonted arts,
And arts of every woman false like thee,
To break all faith, all vows, deceive, betray;   750
Then as repentant to submit, beseech,
And reconcilement move with feigned remorse,
Confess, and promise wonders in her change,
Not truly penitent, but chief to try
Her husband, how far urged his patience bears,
His virtue or weakness which way to assail;
Then with more cautious and instructed skill
Again transgresses, and again submits;
That wisest and best men, full oft beguiled,
With goodness principled° not to reject   760
The penitent, but ever to forgive,
Are drawn to wear out miserable days,
Entangled with a poisonous bosom snake,
If not by quick destruction soon cut off,
As I by thee, to ages an example.
   DAL. Yet hear me, Samson; not that I endeavor
To lessen or extenuate my offense,
But that on the other side if it be weighed
By itself, with aggravations not surcharged,
Or else with just allowance counterpoised,   770
I may, if possible, thy pardon find
The easier towards me, or thy hatred less.
First granting, as I do, it was a weakness
In me, but incident to all our sex,
Curiosity, inquisitive, importúne

748. hyena: The hyena was a traditional type of the wily deceiver.   760. With . . . principled: acting on the good principle.

Of secrets, then with like infirmity
To publish them, both common female faults;
Was it not weakness also to make known
For importunity, that is for nought,
Wherein consisted all thy strength and safety?   780
To what I did thou show'dst me first the way.
But I to enemies revealed, and should not!
Nor shouldst thou have trusted that to woman's
    frailty:
Ere I to thee, thou to thyself wast cruel.
Let weakness then with weakness come to parle,°
So near related, or the same of kind;
Thine forgive mine, that men may censure thine
The gentler, if severely thou exact not
More strength from me than in thyself was found.
And what if love, which thou interpret'st hate,
The jealousy of love, powerful of sway   791
In human hearts, nor less in mine towards thee,
Caused what I did? I saw thee mutable
Of fancy, feared lest one day thou wouldst leave
    me
As her at Timna, sought by all means therefore
How to endear, and hold thee to me firmest:
No better way I saw than by importuning
To learn thy secrets, get into my power
Thy key of strength and safety. Thou wilt say,
"Why then revealed?" I was assured by those   800
Who tempted me, that nothing was designed
Against thee but safe custody and hold:
That made for me;° I knew that liberty
Would draw thee forth to perilous enterprises,
While I at home sat full of cares and fears,
Wailing thy absence in my widowed bed;
Here I should still enjoy thee day and night,
Mine and love's prisoner, not the Philistines',
Whole to myself, unhazarded abroad,
Fearless at home of partners in my love.   810
These reasons in love's law have passed for good,
Though fond° and reasonless to some perhaps;
And love hath oft, well meaning, wrought much
    woe,
Yet always pity or pardon hath obtained.
Be not unlike all others, not austere
As thou art strong, inflexible as steel.
If thou in strength all mortals dost exceed,
In uncompassionate anger do not so.
    SAMS. How cunningly the sorceress displays   819
Her own transgressions, to upbraid me mine!°
That malice, not repentance, brought thee hither,
By this appears: I gave, thou say'st, the example,
I led the way — bitter reproach, but true;
I to myself was false ere thou to me;
Such pardon therefore as I give my folly,
Take to thy wicked deed; which when thou seest
Impartial, self-severe, inexorable,

785. parle: parley.   803. That . . . me: that favored my plan.
812. fond: foolish.   820. mine: with mine.

Thou wilt renounce thy seeking, and much rather
Confess it feigned. Weakness is thy excuse,
And I believe it, weakness to resist   830
Philistian gold; if weakness may excuse,
What murderer, what traitor, parricide,
Incestuous, sacrilegious, but may plead it?
All wickedness is weakness: that plea therefore
With God or man will gain thee no remission.
But love constrained thee! call it furious rage
To satisfy thy lust: love seeks to have love;
My love how couldst thou hope, who took'st the
    way
To raise in me inexpiable hate,
Knowing, as needs I must, by thee betrayed?   840
In vain thou striv'st to cover shame with shame,
Or by evasions thy crime uncover'st more.
    DAL. Since thou determin'st weakness for no
    plea
In man or woman, though to thy own condemning,
Hear what assaults I had, what snares besides,
What sieges girt me round, ere I consented;
Which might have awed the best-resolved of men,
The constantest, to have yielded without blame.
It was not gold, as to my charge thou layst,
That wrought with me: thou know'st the magis-
    trates   850
And princes of my country came in person,
Solicited, commanded, threatened, urged,
Adjured by all the bonds of civil duty
And of religion, pressed how just it was,
How honorable, how glorious to entrap
A common enemy, who had destroyed
Such numbers of our nation: and the priest
Was not behind, but ever at my ear,
Preaching how meritorious with the gods
It would be to ensnare an irreligious   860
Dishonorer of Dagon. What had I
To oppose against such powerful arguments?
Only my love of thee held long debate,
And combated in silence all these reasons
With hard contest. At length, that grounded
    maxim,
So rife and celebrated in the mouths
Of wisest men, that to the public good
Private respects must yield, with grave authority
Took full possession of me and prevailed;
Virtue, as I thought, truth, duty, so enjoining.
    SAMS. I thought where all thy circling wiles
    would end,   871
In feigned religion, smooth hypocrisy.
But had thy love, still odiously pretended,
Been, as it ought, sincere, it would have taught thee
Far other reasonings, brought forth other deeds.
I, before all the daughters of my tribe
And of my nation, chose thee from among
My enemies, loved thee, as too well thou knew'st,
Too well; unbosomed all my secrets to thee,

Not out of levity, but overpowered   880
By thy request, who could deny thee nothing;
Yet now am judged an enemy. Why then
Didst thou at first receive me for thy husband,
Then, as since then, thy country's foe professed?°
Being once a wife, for me thou wast to leave
Parents and country; nor was I their subject,
Nor under their protection, but my own;
Thou mine, not theirs. If aught against my life
Thy country sought of thee, it sought unjustly,
Against the law of nature, law of nations;   890
No more thy country, but an impious crew
Of men conspiring to uphold their state
By worse than hostile deeds, violating the ends
For which our country is a name so dear;
Not therefore to be obeyed. But zeal moved thee;
To please thy gods thou didst it; gods unable
To acquit themselves and prosecute their foes
But by ungodly deeds, the contradiction
Of their own deity, gods cannot be: 899
Less therefore to be pleased, obeyed, or feared.
These false pretexts and varnished colors failing,
Bare in thy guilt how foul must thou appear!
    DAL. In argument with men a woman ever
Goes by° the worse, whatever be her cause.
    SAMS. For want of words, no doubt, or lack of
        breath;
Witness when I was worried with thy peals.
    DAL. I was a fool, too rash, and quite mistaken
In what I thought would have succeeded best.
Let me obtain forgiveness of thee, Samson;
Afford me place to show what recompense   910
Towards thee I intend for what I have misdone,
Misguided; only what remains past cure
Bear not too sensibly,° nor still insist
To afflict thyself in vain. Though sight be lost,
Life yet hath many solaces, enjoyed
Where other senses want° not their delights,
At home in leisure and domestic ease,
Exempt from many a care and chance to which
Eyesight exposes daily men abroad.
I to the lords will intercede, not doubting   920
Their favorable ear, that I may fetch thee
From forth this loathsome prison-house, to abide
With me, where my redoubled love and care
With nursing diligence, to me glad office,
May ever tend about thee to old age
With all things grateful cheered, and so supplied,
That what by me thou hast lost thou least shall
        miss.
    SAMS. No, no, of my condition take no care;
It fits not; thou and I long since are twain;
Nor think me so unwary or accursed°   930

To bring my feet again into the snare
Where once I have been caught; I know thy
        trains,°
Though dearly to my cost, thy gins, and toils;°
Thy fair enchanted cup and warbling charms°
No more on me have power, their force is nulled;
So much of adder's wisdom° I have learned
To fence my ear against thy sorceries.
If in my flower of youth and strength, when all
        men
Loved, honored, feared me, thou alone could hate
        me,
Thy husband, slight me, sell me, and forgo me;
How wouldst thou use me now, blind, and
        thereby   941
Deceivable, in most things as a child
Helpless, thence easily contemned, and scorned,
And last neglected? How wouldst thou insult
When I must live uxorious to thy will
In perfect thraldom, how again betray me,
Bearing my words and doings to the lords
To gloss° upon, and censuring,° frown or smile?
This jail I count the house of liberty
To thine, whose doors my feet shall never enter.
    DAL. Let me approach at least, and touch thy
        hand.   951
    SAMS. Not for thy life, lest fierce remembrance
        wake
My sudden rage to tear thee joint by joint.°
At distance I forgive thee, go with that;
Bewail thy falsehood, and the pious works
It hath brought forth to make thee memorable
Among illustrious women, faithful wives;
Cherish thy hastened widowhood with the gold
Of matrimonial treason: so farewell.
    DAL. I see thou art implacable, more deaf   960
To prayers than winds and seas; yet winds to seas
Are reconciled at length, and sea to shore:
Thy anger, unappeasable, still rages,
Eternal tempest never to be calmed.
Why do I humble thus myself, and suing
For peace, reap nothing but repulse and hate?
Bid go with evil omen° and the brand
Of infamy upon my name denounced?
To mix with thy concernments I desist
Henceforth, nor too much disapprove my own.
Fame,° if not double-faced, is double-mouthed,   971
And with contrary blast proclaims most deeds;
On both his wings, one black, the other white,
Bears greatest names in his wild aery flight.
My name perhaps among the circumcised
In Dan, in Judah, and the bordering tribes,

---

884. professed: openly declared.   904 Goes by: comes off.
913. sensibly: keenly.   916. want: lack.   930. accursed: under
a curse.

932. trains: schemes.   933. gins, . . . toils: traps and nets.
934. Thy . . . charms: Milton is thinking of Circe.   935. adder's
wisdom: Adders were supposed to stop their ears and refuse to
hear a charmer.   948. gloss: comment. censuring: judging.
952–53. Not . . . joint: Dalila's pleas have included sensual hints
and Samson's fear of her touch provokes this violent outburst.
967. evil omen: Cf. ll. 955–59.   971. Fame: rumor, repute.

To all posterity may stand defamed,
With malediction mentioned, and the blot
Of falsehood most unconjugal traduced.
But in my country where I most desire,   980
In Ekron, Gaza, Asdod, and in Gath,
I shall be named among the famousest
Of women, sung at solemn festivals,
Living and dead recorded, who, to save
Her country from a fierce destroyer, chose
Above the faith of wedlock bands; my tomb
With odors° visited and annual flowers:
Not less renowned than in Mount Ephraim
Jael,° who with inhospitable guile
Smote Sisera sleeping, through the temples nailed.
Nor shall I count it heinous to enjoy   991
The public marks of honor and reward
Conferred upon me, for the piety
Which to my country I was judged to have shown.
At this whoever envies or repines,
I leave him to his lot, and like my own.
    CHOR. She's gone, a manifest serpent by her sting
Discovered in the end, till now concealed.
    SAMS. So let her go; God sent her to debase me,
And aggravate my folly who committed   1000
To such a viper his most sacred trust
Of secrecy, my safety, and my life.
    CHOR. Yet beauty, though injurious, hath strange
        power,
After offense returning, to regain
Love once possessed, nor can be easily
Repulsed, without much inward passion felt
And secret sting of amorous remorse.°
    SAMS. Love-quarrels oft in pleasing concord end,
Not wedlock-treachery endangering life.
    CHOR. It is not virtue, wisdom, valor, wit,   1010
Strength, comeliness of shape, or amplest merit
That woman's love can win or long inherit;°
But what it is, hard is to say,
Harder to hit,
(Which way soever men refer it),
Much like thy riddle,° Samson, in one day
Or seven, though one should musing sit;
    If any of these,° or all, the Timnian bride
Had not so soon preferred
Thy paranymph,° worthless to thee compared,
Successor in thy bed,   1021
Nor both so loosely disallied
Their nuptials, nor this last so treacherously
Had shorn the fatal harvest of thy head.
Is it for that° such outward ornament
Was lavished on their sex, that inward gifts

Were left for haste unfinished, judgment scant,
Capacity not raised to apprehend
Or value what is best
In choice, but oftest to affect° the wrong?   1030
Or was too much of self-love mixed,
Of constancy no root infixed,
That either they love nothing, or not long?
    Whate'er it be, to wisest men and best
Seeming at first all heavenly under virgin veil,
Soft, modest, meek, demure,
Once joined, the contrary she proves, a thorn
Intestine, far within defensive arms
A cleaving° mischief, in his way to virtue
Adverse and turbulent; or by her charms   1040
Draws him awry, enslaved
With dotage, and his sense depraved
To folly and shameful deeds, which ruin
    ends.
What pilot so expert but needs must wreck,
Embarked with such a steers-mate at the helm?
    Favored of Heaven who finds
One virtuous, rarely found,
That in domestic good combines:°
Happy that house! his way to peace is smooth;
But virtue which breaks through all opposition,
And all temptation can remove,   1051
Most shines and most is acceptable above.
    Therefore God's universal law
Gave to the man despotic power
Over his female in due awe,
Nor from that right to part an hour,
Smile she or lour:
So shall he least confusion draw
On his whole life, not swayed
By female usurpation, nor dismayed.   1060
    But had we best retire? I see a storm.
    SAMS. Fair days have oft contracted° wind and
        rain.
    CHOR. But this another kind of tempest brings.
    SAMS. Be less abtruse, my riddling days are past.
    CHOR. Look now for no enchanting voice, nor
        fear
The bait of honeyed words; a rougher tongue
Draws hitherward; I know him by his stride,
The giant Harapha of Gath, his look
Haughty, as is his pile° high-built and proud.
Comes he in peace? What wind hath blown him
    hither   1070
I less conjecture than when first I saw
The sumptuous Dálila floating this way;
His habit carries peace, his brow defiance.
    SAMS. Or peace or not, alike to me he comes.

---

987. odors: spices.   **989. Jael:** Sisera, defeated by the Hebrews, was lured into a tent by Jael, who drove a nail through his head while he slept (Judg. 4:17–21).   **1007. remorse:** pity. **1012. inherit:** possess.   **1016. thy riddle:** See Judg. 14:5–18. **1018. these:** the qualities listed in 1010–11.   **1020. paranymph:** "best man." Samson having neglected his bride, her father gave her to one of Samson's companions (Judg. 14:20, 15:1–2). **1025. for that:** because.

1030. affect: seek.   **1039. cleaving:** clinging; an allusion to Nessus' robe. See *PL*, II. 542–46n.   **1048. combines:** unites with her husband. This whole chorus, as usual a reflection on the preceding scene, is dramatically relevant and does not necessarily embody any special misogynistic view of Milton's, though he would, like other men, support a husband's authority. **1062. contracted:** brought along.   **1069. pile:** huge body.

CHOR. His fraught° we soon shall know, he now
    arrives.
HARAPHA. I come not, Samson, to condole thy
    chance,
As these° perhaps, yet wish it had not been,
Though for no friendly intent. I am of Gath;
Men call me Harapha, of stock renowned
As Og or Anak and the Emims° old   1080
That Kiriathaim held; thou know'st me now,
If thou at all art known. Much I have heard
Of thy prodigious might and feats performed,
Incredible to me, in this displeased,
That I was never present on the place
Of those encounters where we might have tried
Each other's force in camp° or listed° field:
And now am come to see of whom such noise
Hath walked about, and each limb to survey,
If thy appearance answer loud report.   1090
SAMS. The way to know were not to see, but taste.
HAR. Dost thou already single° me? I thought
Gyves and the mill had tamed thee. O that for-
    tune
Had brought me to the field where thou art famed
To have wrought such wonders with an ass's
    jaw;
I should have forced thee soon wish° other arms,
Or left thy carcass where the ass lay thrown:
So had the glory of prowess been recovered
To Palestine, won by a Philistine   1099
From the unforeskinned race, of whom thou bear'st
The highest name for valiant acts; that honor,
Certain to have won by mortal duel from thee,
I lose, prevented by thy eyes put out.
SAMS. Boast not of what thou wouldst have done,
    but do
What then thou wouldst; thou seest it in thy hand.°
HAR. To combat with a blind man I disdain,
And thou hast need much washing to be touched.
SAMS. Such usage as your honorable lords
Afford me, assassinated° and betrayed;
Who durst not with their whole united powers
In fight withstand me single and unarmed,   1111
Nor in the house with chamber ambushes
Close-banded durst attack me, no, not sleeping,
Till they had hired a woman with their gold,
Breaking her marriage faith, to circumvent me.
Therefore without feigned shifts, let be assigned
Some narrow place enclosed, where sight may give
    thee,
Or rather flight, no great advantage on me;
Then put on all thy gorgeous arms, thy helmet
And brigandine° of brass, thy broad habergeon,°

Vant-brace° and greaves, and gauntlet; add thy
    spear,   1121
A weaver's beam,° and seven-times-folded° shield;
I only with an oaken staff will meet thee,
And raise such outcries on thy clattered iron,
Which long shall not withhold me from thy head,
That in a little time, while breath remains thee,
Thou oft shalt wish thyself at Gath, to boast
Again in safety what thou wouldst have done
To Samson, but shalt never see Gath more.
HAR. Thou durst not thus disparage glorious
    arms,   1130
Which greatest heroes have in battle worn,
Their ornament and safety, had not spells
And black enchantments, some magician's art,
Armed thee or charmed thee strong, which thou
    from Heaven
Feign'dst at thy birth was given thee in thy hair,
Where strength can least abide, though all thy
    hairs
Were bristles ranged like those that ridge the back
Of chafed wild boars, or ruffled porcupines.
SAMS. I know no spells, use no forbidden arts;
My° trust is in the Living God who gave me   1140
At my nativity this strength, diffused
No less through all my sinews, joints and bones,
Than thine, while I preserved these locks unshorn,
The pledge of my unviolated vow.
For proof hereof, if Dagon be thy god,
Go to his temple, invocate his aid
With solemnest devotion, spread before him
How highly it concerns his glory now
To frustrate and dissolve these magic spells,
Which I to be the power of Israel's God   1150
Avow, and challenge Dagon to the test,
Offering to combat thee, his champion bold,
With the utmost of his godhead seconded:
Then thou shalt see, or rather to thy sorrow
Soon feel, whose God is strongest, thine or mine.
HAR. Presume not on thy God, whate'er he be;
Thee he regards not, owns not, hath cut off
Quite from his people, and delivered up
Into thy enemies' hand; permitted them
To put out both thine eyes, and fettered send thee
Into the common prison, there to grind   1161
Among the slaves and asses, thy comrades,
As good for nothing else, no better service
With those thy boisterous locks; no worthy match
For valor to assail, nor by the sword
Of noble warrior, so to stain his honor,
But by the barber's razor best subdued.
SAMS. All° these indignities, for such they are

1075. fraught: freight, purpose.   1077. these: the chorus.
1080. Og, Anak, Emims: giants referred to in Deut. 3:11, Num.
13:33, Deut. 2:10–11.   1087. camp: field of battle. listed: arranged for a tournament. 1092. single: challenge. 1096. wish:
to wish for. 1105. hand: power. 1109. assassinated: treacherously attacked.   1120. brigandine: armor-plated coat. habergeon: coat of mail.

1121. Vant-brace: armor for the arm. 1122. weaver's beam:
wooden roller in a loom. seven-times-folded: having seven
layers of hide. 1140–55. My . . . mine: Harapha's words
elicit an assertion of Samson's renewed faith; he has overcome
despair and can now again feel himself God's champion.
1168–77. All . . . adore: Samson's humble confession, made before such an enemy, is even better proof of his new state of mind.

From thine,° these evils I deserve and more,
Acknowledge them from God inflicted on me
Justly, yet despair not of his final pardon   1171
Whose ear is ever open, and his eye
Gracious to readmit the suppliant;
In confidence whereof I once again
Defy thee to the trial of mortal fight,
By combat to decide whose god is God,
Thine or whom I with Israel's sons adore.
    HAR. Fair honor that thou dost thy God, in trust-
ing
He will accept thee to defend his cause,
A murderer, a revolter, and a robber.   1180
    SAMS. Tongue-doughty giant, how dost thou
prove me these?
    HAR. Is not thy nation subject to our lords?
Their° magistrates confessed it, when they took
thee
As a league-breaker and delivered bound
Into our hands: for hadst thou not committed
Notorious murder on those thirty men
At Ascalon, who never did thee harm,
Then, like a robber, stripp'dst them of their robes?
The Philistines, when thou hadst broke the league,
Went up with armed powers thee only seeking,
To others did no violence nor spoil.   1191
    SAMS. Among the daughters of the Philistines
I chose a wife, which argued me no foe,
And in your city held my nuptial feast;
But your ill-meaning politician lords,
Under pretense of bridal friends and guests,
Appointed to await me thirty spies,
Who threatening cruel death constrained the bride
To wring from me and tell to them my secret,
That solved the riddle which I had proposed.   1200
When I perceived all set on enmity,
As on my enemies, wherever chanced,
I used hostility, and took their spoil
To pay my underminers in their coin.
My nation was subjected to your lords!
It was the force of conquest; force with force
Is well ejected when the conquered can.
But I a private person, whom my country
As a league-breaker gave up bound, presumed
Single rebellion and did hostile acts!   1210
I was no private but a person raised
With strength sufficient and command from
Heaven
To free my country; if their servile minds
Me, their deliverer sent, would not receive,
But to their masters gave me up for nought,
The unworthier they; whence to this day they
serve.
I was to do my part from Heaven assigned,
And had performed it if my known offense

Had not disabled me, not all your force.
These shifts° refuted, answer thy appellant,°   1220
Though by his blindness maimed for high at-
tempts,
Who now defies thee thrice to single fight,
As a petty enterprise of small enforce.°
    HAR. With thee, a man condemned, a slave en-
rolled,
Due by the law to capital punishment?
To fight with thee no man of arms will deign.
    SAMS. Cam'st thou for this, vain boaster, to survey
me,
To descant on my strength, and give thy verdict?
Come nearer, part not hence so slight informed;
But take good heed my hand survey not thee.   1230
    HAR. O Baal-zebub!° can my ears unused
Hear these dishonors, and not render death?
    SAMS. No man withholds thee, nothing from thy
hand
Fear I incurable; bring up thy van;°
My heels are fettered, but my fist is free.
    HAR. This insolence other kind of answer fits.
    SAMS. Go, baffled coward, lest I run upon thee,
Though in these chains, bulk without spirit vast,
And with one buffet lay thy structure low,   1239
Or swing thee in the air, then dash thee down
To the hazard of thy brains and shattered sides.
    HAR. By Astaroth,° ere long thou shalt lament
These braveries,° in irons loaden on thee.
    CHOR. His giantship is gone somewhat crestfallen,
Stalking with less unconscionable° strides,
And lower looks, but in a sultry chafe.
    SAMS. I dread him not, nor all his giant brood,
Though fame divulge him father of five sons,
All of gigantic size, Goliah chief.°
    CHOR. He will directly to the lords, I fear,   1250
And with malicious counsel stir them up
Some way or other yet further to afflict thee.
    SAMS. He must allege some cause, and offered
fight
Will not dare mention, lest a question rise
Whether he durst accept the offer or not,
And that he durst not plain enough appeared.
Much more affliction than already felt
They cannot well impose, nor I sustain,
If they intend advantage of my labors,
The work of many hands, which earns my keep-
ing   1260
With no small profit daily to my owners.
But come what will, my deadliest foe will prove
My speediest friend, by death to rid me hence,
The worst that he can give, to me the best.

1169. thine: thy people.   1183-1204. Their . . . coin: See Judg.
14:8-20, 15:9-15.

1220. shifts: excuses, tricks. appellant: challenger.   1223. enforce: effort.   1231. Baal-zebub: a particular title of the Philistine god Baal.   1234. van: vanguard (i.e., begin to fight).
1242. Astaroth: See PL, I. 438n.   1243. braveries: boasts.
1245. unconscionable: unreasonable (i.e., proud).   1248-
49. Though . . . chief: See II Sam. 21:19-22.

Yet so it may fall out, because their end
Is hate, not help to me, it may with mine
Draw their own ruin who attempt the deed.
  CHOR. Oh how comely it is and how reviving°
To the spirits of just men long oppressed,
When God into the hands of their deliverer 1270
Puts invincible might
To quell the mighty of the earth, the oppressor,
The brute and boisterous force of violent men,
Hardy and industrious to support
Tyrannic power, but raging to pursue
The righteous and all such as honor truth;
He all their ammunition
And feats of war defeats
With plain heroic magnitude of mind
And celestial vigor armed; 1280
Their armories and magazines contemns,
Renders them useless, while
With winged expedition
Swift as the lightning glance he executes
His errand on the wicked, who surprised
Lose their defense, distracted and amazed.
  But patience is more oft the exercise
Of saints, the trial of their fortitude,
Making them each his own deliverer,
And victor over all 1290
That tyranny or fortune can inflict;
Either of these is in thy lot,
Samson, with might endued
Above the sons of men; but sight bereaved
May chance to number thee with those
Whom patience finally must crown.°
  This Idol's day hath been to thee no day of rest,
Laboring thy mind
More than the working day thy hands;
And yet perhaps more trouble is behind. 1300
For I descry this way
Some other tending; in his hand
A scepter or quaint° staff he bears,
Comes on amain, speed in his look.
By his habit I discern him now
A public officer, and now at hand.
His message will be short and voluble.°
  OFF. Hebrews, the prisoner Samson here I seek.
  CHOR. His manacles remark° him; there he sits.
  OFF. Samson, to thee our lords thus bid me say:
This day to Dagon is a solemn feast, 1311
With sacrifices, triumph, pomp, and games;
Thy strength they know surpassing human rate,
And now some public proof thereof require
To honor this great feast, and great assembly;
Rise therefore with all speed and come along,
Where I will see thee heartened and fresh clad

To appear as fits before the illustrious lords.
  SAMS. Thou know'st I am an Hebrew, therefore tell them
Our Law forbids at their religious rites 1320
My presence; for that cause I cannot come.
  OFF. This answer, be assured, will not content them.
  SAMS. Have they not sword-players, and every sort
Of gymnic artists,° wrestlers, riders, runners,
Jugglers and dancers, antics,° mummers,° mimics,°
But they must pick me out, with shackles tired,
And overlabored at their public mill,
To make them sport with blind activity?
Do they not seek occasion of new quarrels,
On my refusal, to distress me more, 1330
Or make a game of my calamities?
Return the way thou cam'st; I will not come.
  OFF. Regard thyself; this will offend them highly.
  SAMS. Myself? my conscience and internal peace.°
Can they think me so broken, so debased
With corporal servitude, that my mind ever
Will condescend to such absurd commands?
Although their drudge, to be their fool or jester,
And in my midst of sorrow and heart-grief
To show them feats and play before their god,
The worst of all indignities, yet on me 1341
Joined° with extreme contempt? I will not come.
  OFF. My message was imposed on me with speed,
Brooks no delay; is this thy resolution?
  SAMS. So take it with what speed thy message needs.
  OFF. I am sorry what this stoutness will produce.
  SAMS. Perhaps thou shalt have cause to sorrow indeed.
  CHOR. Consider,° Samson; matters now are strained
Up to the highth, whether to hold or break;
He's gone, and who knows how he may report
Thy words by adding fuel to the flame? 1351
Expect another message, more imperious,
More lordly thundering than thou well wilt bear.
  SAMS. Shall I abuse this consecrated gift
Of strength, again returning with my hair
After my great transgression, so requite
Favor renewed, and a greater sin
By prostituting holy things to idols;
A Nazarite, in place abominable,
Vaunting° my strength in honor to their Dagon?
Besides, how vile, contemptible, ridiculous, 1361
What act more execrably unclean,° profane?

1268 f. The chorus underlines the effect of Harapha's visit, which has revived Samson's faith in himself (l. 1279) and in God's favor (l. 1280).   1294–96. but . . . crown: The chorus' forecast is of course wrong.   1303. quaint: decorated.   1307. voluble: rapid, pointed.   1309. remark: distinguish.

1324. gymnic artists: gymnasts.   1325. antics: clowns, buffoons. mummers: masqueraders. mimics: actors.   1334. Myself . . . peace: The distinction measures the distance Samson has come since his opening complaint.   1342. Joined: enjoined.   1348–53. Consider . . . bear: The chorus, representing average sentiment, advise submission; throughout they have no real understanding of Samson's inward struggles.   1360. Vaunting: displaying.   1362. unclean: See l. 321n.

CHOR. Yet with this strength thou serv'st the
    Philistines,
Idolatrous, uncircumcised, unclean.
    SAMS. Not in their idol-worship, but by labor
Honest and lawful to deserve my food
Of those who have me in their civil power.°
    CHOR. Where the heart joins not, outward acts
    defile not.
    SAMS. Where outward force constrains, the sen-
    tence° holds;   1369
But who constrains me to the temple of Dagon,
Not dragging? The Philistian lords command.
Commands are no constraints. If I obey them,
I do it freely, venturing to displease
God for the fear of man, and man prefer,
Set God behind; which in his jealousy
Shall never, unrepented, find forgiveness.
Yet that he may dispense with° me or thee,
Present in temples at idolatrous rites
For some important cause, thou need'st not doubt.
    CHOR. How thou wilt here come off surmounts
    my reach.   1380
    SAMS. Be of good courage; I begin to feel
Some rousing motions in me which dispose
To something extraordinary my thoughts.
I° with this messenger will go along,
Nothing to do, be sure, that may dishonor
Our Law, or stain my vow of Nazarite.
If there be aught of presage in the mind,
This day will be remarkable in my life
By some great act, or of my days the last.
    CHOR. In time thou hast resolved; the man re-
    turns.   1390
    OFF. Samson, this second message from our lords
To thee I am bid say: art thou our slave,
Our captive, at the public mill our drudge,
And dar'st thou at our sending and command
Dispute thy coming? Come without delay;
Or we shall find such engines to assail
And hamper thee, as thou shalt come of force,
Though thou wert firmlier fastened than a rock.
    SAMS. I could be well content to try their art,
Which to no few of them would prove pernicious.
Yet° knowing their advantages too many,   1401
Because° they shall not trail me through their
    streets
Like a wild beast, I am content to go.
Masters' commands come with a power resistless
To such as owe them absolute subjection;
And for a life who will not change his purpose?
(So mutable are all the ways of men.)

1365–67. Not ... power: an example of the sober reasonableness that is typical of Samson's later state of mind.
1369. sentence: saying.   1377. dispense with: grant a
special dispensation to.   1384. I ... along: Samson's altered
resolution, foreshortened in accordance with the necessities
of Greek drama, indicates that he feels a divine prompting.
1401–07. Yet ... men: Samson, his mind made up for other
reasons, pretends obedience.   1402. Because: so that.

Yet this be sure, in nothing to comply
Scandalous or forbidden in our Law.   1409
    OFF. I praise thy resolution; doff these links.
By this compliance thou wilt win the lords
To favor, and perhaps to set thee free.
    SAMS. Brethren, farewell; your company along
I will not wish, lest it perhaps offend them
To see me girt with friends; and how the sight
Of me as of a common enemy,
So dreaded once, may now exasperate them,
I know not. Lords are lordliest in their wine;
And the well-feasted priest then soonest fired
With zeal, if aught religion seem concerned;   1420
No less the people, on their holy-days,
Impetuous, insolent, unquenchable;
Happen what may, of me expect to hear
Nothing dishonorable, impure, unworthy
Our God, our Law, my nation, or myself;
The last of me or no I cannot warrant.
    CHOR. Go, and the Holy One
Of Israel be thy guide
To what may serve his glory best, and spread his
    name
Great among the heathen round;   1430
Send thee the angel° of thy birth, to stand
Fast by thy side, who from thy father's field
Rode up in flames after his message told
Of thy conception, and be now a shield
Of fire; that spirit that first rushed on thee
In the camp of Dan,°
Be efficacious in thee now at need.
For never was from Heaven imparted
Measure of strength so great to mortal seed,
As in thy wondrous actions hath been seen.   1440
But wherefore comes old Manoa in such haste
With youthful steps? Much livelier than erewhile
He seems: supposing here to find his son,
Or of him bringing to us some glad news?
    MAN. Peace with you, brethren; my inducement
    hither
Was not at present here to find my son,
By order of the lords new parted hence
To come and play before them at their feast.
I heard all as I came, the city rings,
And numbers thither flock; I had no will,   1450
Lest I should see him forced to things unseemly.
But that which moved my coming now was chiefly
To give ye part with me what hope I have
With good success to work his liberty.
    CHOR. That hope would much rejoice us to par-
    take
With thee; say, reverend sire; we thirst to hear.
    MAN. I have attempted one by one the lords,
Either at home, or through the high street passing,
With supplication prone and father's tears   1459

1431–34. the angel: Cf. ll. 24–28, 361, 635.   1435–36. spirit ...
Dan: See Judg. 13:25.

To accept of ransom for my son their prisoner.
Some° much averse I found and wondrous harsh,
Contemptuous, proud, set on revenge and spite;
That part most reverenced Dagon and his priests;
Others more moderate seeming, but their aim
Private reward, for which both God and State
They easily would set to sale; a third
More generous far and civil, who confessed
They had enough revenged, having reduced
Their foe to misery beneath their fears;
The rest was magnanimity to remit,   1470
If some convenient ransom were proposed.
What noise or shout was that? It tore the sky.
   CHOR. Doubtless the people shouting to behold
Their once great dread, captive and blind before
   them,
Or at some proof of strength before them shown.
   MAN. His ransom, if my whole inheritance
May compass it, shall willingly be paid
And numbered down; much rather I shall choose
To live the poorest in my tribe, than richest,
And he in that calamitous prison left.   1480
No, I am fixed not to part hence without him.
For his redemption all my patrimony,
If need be, I am ready to forgo
And quit; not wanting him, I shall want nothing.
   CHOR. Fathers are wont to lay up for their sons,
Thou for thy son art bent to lay out all;
Sons wont to nurse their parents in old age,
Thou in old age car'st how to nurse thy son,
Made older than thy age through eyesight lost.
   MAN. It° shall be my delight to tend his eyes,
And view him sitting in his house, ennobled
With all those high exploits by him achieved, 1492
And on his shoulders waving down those locks
That of a nation armed the strength contained.
And I persuade me God had not permitted
His strength again to grow up with his hair
Garrisoned round about him like a camp
Of faithful soldiery, were not his purpose
To use him further yet in some great service,
Not to sit idle with so great a gift   1500
Useless, and thence ridiculous, about him.
And since his strength with eyesight was not lost,
God will restore him eyesight to° his strength.
   CHOR. Thy hopes are not ill-founded, nor seem
   vain,
Of his delivery, and thy joy thereon
Conceived, agreeable to a father's love;
In both which we, as next,° participate.
   MAN. I know your friendly minds and — O what
   noise!

1461–71. Some . . . proposed: The details suggest that Milton
may be thinking of Restoration authorities' attitudes toward
his own defenders.   1490–1503. It . . . strength: Manoa's hope
of success is an ironical "false dawn" before the catastrophe.
1503. to: along with.   1507. as next: as members of the same
tribe.

Mercy of Heaven, what hideous noise was that!
Horribly loud, unlike the former shout.   1510
   CHOR. Noise call you it, or universal groan,
As if the whole inhabitation perished?
Blood, death, and deathful deeds are in that noise,
Ruin,° destruction at the utmost point.
   MAN. Of ruin indeed methought I heard the
   noise.
Oh it continues, they have slain my son.
   CHOR. Thy son is rather slaying them; that outcry
From slaughter of one foe could not ascend.
   MAN. Some dismal accident it needs must be;
What shall we do, stay here or run and see? 1520
   CHOR. Best keep together here, lest running
   thither
We unawares run into danger's mouth.
This evil on the Philistines is fallen;
From whom could else a general cry be heard?
The sufferers then will scarce molest us here;
From other hands we need not much to fear.
What if his eyesight (for to Israel's God
Nothing is hard) by miracle restored,
He now be dealing dole among his foes,   1529
And over heaps of slaughtered walk his way?
   MAN. That were a joy presumptuous to be
   thought.
   CHOR. Yet God hath wrought things as incredible
For his people of old; what hinders now?
   MAN. He can, I know, but doubt to think he will;
Yet hope would fain subscribe, and tempts belief.
A little stay will bring some notice hither.
   CHOR. Of good or bad so great, of bad the sooner;
For evil news rides post, while good news baits.°
And to our wish I see one hither speeding,
An Hebrew, as I guess, and of our tribe.   1540
   MESSENGER. O whither shall I run, or which way
   fly
The sight of this so horrid spectacle
Which erst° my eyes beheld and yet behold?
For dire imagination still pursues me.
But providence or instinct of nature seems,
Or reason, though disturbed and scarce consulted,
To have guided me aright, I know not how,
To thee first, reverend Manoa, and to these
My countrymen, whom here I knew remaining,
As at some distance from the place of horror, 1550
So in the sad event too much concerned.
   MAN. The accident was loud, and here before thee
With rueful cry, yet what it was we hear not;
No preface needs, thou seest we long to know.
   MESS. It would burst forth; but I recover breath
And sense distract, to know well what I utter.
   MAN. Tell us the sum, the circumstance defer.
   MESS. Gaza yet stands, but all her sons are fallen,
All in a moment overwhelmed and fallen.

1514, 1515. Ruin: downfall.   1538. baits: delays to take food.
1543. erst: a while ago.

MAN. Sad, but thou know'st to Israelites not saddest   1560
The desolation of a hostile city.

MESS. Feed on that first, there may in grief be
surfeit.

MAN. Relate by whom.

MESS.   By Samson.

MAN.   That still lessens
The sorrow, and converts it nigh to joy.

MESS. Ah, Manoa, I refrain too suddenly
To utter what will come at last too soon;
Lest evil tidings, with too rude irruption
Hitting thy aged ear, should pierce too deep.

MAN. Suspense in news is torture, speak them
out.

MESS. Then take the worst in brief: Samson is
dead.   1570

MAN. The worst indeed! O all my hope's de-
feated
To free him hence! but Death who sets all free
Hath paid his ransom now and full discharge.
What windy° joy this day had I conceived,
Hopeful of his delivery, which now proves
Abortive as the first-born bloom of spring
Nipped with the lagging rear of winter's frost.
Yet ere I give the reins to grief, say first,
How died he? death to life is crown or shame.
All by him fell, thou say'st; by whom fell he, 1580
What glorious hand gave Samson his death's
wound?

MESS. Unwounded of his enemies he fell.

MAN. Wearied with slaughter then, or how? explain.

MESS. By his own hands.

MAN.   Self-violence? What cause
Brought him so soon at variance with himself
Among his foes?

MESS.   Inevitable cause
At once both to destroy and be destroyed;
The edifice where all were met to see him,
Upon their heads and on his own he pulled.

MAN. O lastly overstrong against thyself!   1590
A dreadful way thou took'st to thy revenge.
More than enough we know; but while things
yet
Are in confusion, give us, if thou canst,
Eye-witness of what first or last was done,
Relation more particular and distinct.

MESS. Occasions drew me early to this city,
And, as the gates I entered with sunrise,
The morning trumpets festival proclaimed
Through each high street. Little° I had despatched
When all abroad was rumored that this day   1600
Samson should be brought forth to show the
people

Proof of his mighty strength in feats and games;
I sorrowed at his captive state, but minded
Not to be absent at that spectacle.
The building was a spacious theater
Half round on two main pillars vaulted high,
With seats where all the lords, and each degree
Of sort,° might sit in order to behold;
The other side was open, where the throng
On banks° and scaffolds under sky might stand;
I among these aloof obscurely stood.   1611
The feast and noon grew high, and sacrifice
Had filled their hearts with mirth, high cheer, and
wine,
When to their sports they turned. Immediately
Was Samson as a public servant brought,
In their state livery clad; before him pipes
And timbrels; on each side went armèd guards,
Both horse and foot before him and behind,
Archers, and slingers, cataphracts° and spears.°
At sight of him the people with a shout   1620
Rifted the air, clamoring their god with praise,
Who had made their dreadful enemy their thrall.
He, patient but undaunted, where they led him,
Came to the place; and what was set before him,
Which without help of eye might be assayed,°
To heave, pull, draw, or break, he still° performed,
All with incredible, stupendious° force,
None daring to appear antagonist.
At length for intermission sake they led him
Between the pillars; he his guide requested   1630
(For so from such as nearer stood we heard),
As overtired, to let him lean a while
With both his arms on those two massy pillars
That to the archèd roof gave main support.
He unsuspicious led him; which when Samson
Felt in his arms, with head a while inclined,
And eyes fast fixed he stood, as one who prayed,
Or some great matter in his mind revolved.
At last with head erect thus cried aloud:
"Hitherto, Lords, what your commands imposed
I have performed, as reason was,° obeying,   1641
Not without wonder or delight beheld.
Now of my own accord such other trial
I mean to show you of my strength, yet greater,
As with amaze shall strike° all who behold."
This uttered, straining all his nerves he bowed;
As with the force of winds and waters pent
When mountains tremble, those two massy pillars
With horrible convulsion to and fro
He tugged, he shook, till down they came and
drew   1650
The whole roof after them, with burst of thunder

1574. windy: empty.   1599. Little: little business.

1608. sort: rank.   1610. banks: benches.   1619. cataphracts:
armored men on armored horses.   spears: spearmen.   1625. assayed: attempted.   1626. still: always.   1627. stupendious:
stupendous.   1641. as reason was: See ll. 1365–67n.
1645. strike: Samson, who has moved far beyond personal concerns, and has conceived his plan, can indulge in a pun.

Upon the heads of all who sat beneath,
Lords, ladies, captains, counselors, or priests,
Their choice nobility and flower, not only
Of this but each Philistian city round,
Met from all parts to solemnize this feast.
Samson, with these immixed, inevitably
Pulled down the same destruction on himself;
The vulgar only scaped, who stood without.

CHOR. O dearly bought revenge, yet glorious!
Living or dying thou hast fulfilled   1661
The work for which thou wast foretold
To Israel, and now li'st victorious
Among thy slain self-killed,
Not willingly, but tangled in the fold
Of dire necessity,° whose law in death conjoined
Thee with thy slaughtered foes, in number more
Than all thy life had slain before.

SEMICHOR. While° their hearts were jocund and
     sublime,°
Drunk with idolatry, drunk with wine,   1670
And fat regorged° of bulls and goats,
Chanting their idol, and preferring
Before our living Dread who dwells
In Silo,° his bright sanctuary,
Among them he a spirit of frenzy sent,
Who hurt their minds,
And urged them on with mad desire
To call in haste for their destroyer;
They only set on sport and play
Unweetingly° importuned   1680
Their own destruction to come speedy upon
     them.
So fond are mortal men
Fallen into° wrath divine,
As their own ruin on themselves to invite,
Insensate left, or to sense reprobate,
And with blindness internal struck.

SEMICHOR. But he, though blind of sight,
Despised, and thought extinguished quite,
With inward eyes illuminated,
His fiery virtue roused   1690
From under ashes into sudden flame,
And as an evening dragon° came,
Assailant on the perchèd roosts
And nests in order ranged
Of tame villatic° fowl; but as an eagle
His cloudless thunder bolted° on their heads.
So virtue, given for° lost,

Depressed, and overthrown, as seemed,
Like that self-begotten bird°
In the Arabian woods embost,°   1700
That no second knows nor third,°
And lay erewhile a holocaust,°
From out her ashy womb now teemed,°
Revives, reflourishes, then vigorous most
When most unactive deemed,
And though her body die, her fame survives,
A secular° bird, ages of lives.

MAN. Come, come, no time for lamentation
     now,
Nor much more cause; Samson hath quit° himself
Like Samson, and heroicly hath finished   1710
A life heroic, on his enemies
Fully revenged; hath left them years of mourning,
And lamentation to the sons of Caphtor°
Through all Philistian bounds. To Israel
Honor hath left, and freedom — let but them
Find courage to lay hold on this occasion;
To himself and father's house eternal fame;
And, which is best and happiest yet, all this
With God not parted from him, as was feared,
But favoring and assisting to the end.   1720
Nothing is here for tears, nothing to wail
Or knock the breast, no weakness, no contempt,
Dispraise, or blame; nothing but well and fair,
And what may quiet us in a death so noble.°
Let us go find the body where it lies
Soaked in his enemies' blood, and from the
     stream
With lavers° pure and cleansing herbs wash off
The clotted gore. I with what speed the while
(Gaza is not in plight° to say us nay)
Will send for all my kindred, all my friends,   1730
To fetch him hence and solemnly attend,
With silent obsequy and funeral train,
Home to his father's house: there will I build
     him
A monument, and plant it round with shade
Of laurel ever green, and branching palm,
With all his trophies hung, and acts enrolled
In copious legend,° or sweet lyric song.
Thither shall all the valiant youth resort,
And from his memory inflame their breasts
To matchless valor and adventures high;   1740

1665–66. Not . . . necessity: Samson is exonerated from the sin of suicide.   1669–86. While . . . struck: The description suggests the Greek *hubris*, blind, infatuated confidence. Cf. *PL*, IX. 790–93.   1669. sublime: exalted.   1671. regorged: gorged to surfeit.   1674. Silo: Shiloh, where the Israelites set up their tabernacle (Josh. 18:1).   1680. Unweetingly: unwittingly.   1683. into: under.   1692. dragon: snake.   1695. villatic: belonging to a farmhouse.   1696. bolted: shot.   1697. given for: given up as.

1699. bird: the phoenix, the bird — in classical myth and Christian symbol — which, after five hundred years, builds a spicy nest, is burned, and rises to life again from its ashes.   1700. embost: hidden in the woods.   1701. That . . . third: there was only one phoenix in existence at a time.   1702. holocaust: a sacrifice burned whole.   1707. secular: living for ages (*saecula*).   1709. quit: acquitted.   1713. Caphtor: the Philistines' original home.   1721–24. Nothing . . . noble: In spite of this great eulogy, Manoa, like the chorus, sees only external evidence; he has not seen Samson's inward struggle and victory.   1727. lavers: basins of water.   1729. plight: condition.   1737. legend: inscription.

The virgins also shall on feastful days
Visit his tomb with flowers, only bewailing
His lot unfortunate in nuptial choice,
From whence captivity and loss of eyes.
    CHOR. All is best, though we oft doubt,
What the unsearchable dispose°
Of Highest Wisdom brings about,
And ever best found in the close.
Oft he seems to hide his face,
But unexpectedly returns,   1750

1746. dispose: disposal.

And to his faithful champion hath in place°
Bore witness gloriously; whence Gaza mourns,
And all that band them to resist
His uncontrollable intent:
His servants he, with new acquist°
Of true experience from this great event,
With peace and consolation hath dismissed,
And calm of mind, all passion° spent.

1751. in place: on the spot.   1755. acquist: acquisition
1758. passion: See the first sentence of Milton's Preface.

John Dryden

1631–1700

I. THE FIRST ENGLISH MAN OF LETTERS

JOHN DRYDEN, who without any rival dominated the literary scene of London during the last quarter of the seventeenth century, was so versatile a writer, and performed so ably in every role he tried, that he can be said to have established letters as a profession in his native country. Shakespeare had been a professional in the sense that he lived by writing plays, but Dryden gave a new meaning to the term, a meaning that survives best in the word " journalist." Dryden was a journalist in verse and prose; he turned his attention to whatever subject or form was current at the moment; he considered himself purely and simply a writer whose plain duty was to succeed with the assignments he undertook. If he was also a genius whose achievement in verse was to seem standard for a century and whose achievement in prose is still standard wherever English is written, that fact does not alter the impression he finally makes; rather, it reinforces it by reminding us of the dignity that letters as a profession may always have.

He was a generation younger than Milton, and as different from that great writer as anyone could be. The Northamptonshire family of Dridens into which he was born on August 9, 1631, was Puritan in its faith; both his father's and his mother's people had been for Parliament against the King in the great dispute that tore England apart in the middle of the century; but if Dryden himself was ever a Puritan at heart he utterly ceased to be so when the Stuarts

were restored in 1660. Beginning then, he was a confirmed Royalist until his death in 1700; in politics he was inveterately a Tory; and in religion he moved from the Church of England into the Roman Catholic fold. His instinct, or his prudence, kept him ever in tune with authority. The unimpeachable independence of Milton, who remained a Puritan until his death in 1674, had no counterpart in Dryden's temper. Nor did the wonderful rich weight of Milton's style survive in Dryden's. Both were learned poets, but Dryden lightened his style to conform with what he thought to be, and with what in fact was, modernity. Not only was it a lighter style than Milton's; it was a more rapid and racy one; and if it was also a more superficial one, as Milton clearly believed, at least it was proper to Dryden's career as he conceived it. It lent itself to professionalism, to versatility, and above all to success.

Dryden was educated at Westminster School in London and at Trinity College, Cambridge. He seems to have been a good student, especially of the Latin poets; but soon after receiving his bachelor's degree in 1654 he went to London and began his own career. His progress at first was slow, and may have involved hackwork of which no record exists. The few poems he had written in his school and college days, including one notably bad one, " Upon the Death of the Lord Hastings," had no sequel until 1658, when the death of Cromwell inspired (if that is the word) *Heroic Stanzas, Consecrated to the Glorious Memory of His Most Serene and Renowned Highness Oliver, Late Lord Protector of This Commonwealth.* The *Heroic Stanzas* are by no means bad; indeed, they are still impressive for their dignity, and for a certain clumsy grace they manage at their best moments; but it is hard to take their sentiments seriously in view of the fact that less than two years later, when Charles II was restored to the throne, Dryden celebrated the occasion with a poem which he called *Astraea Redux,* meaning in English "Justice Brought Back." The reference was to the Roman legend that the virgin goddess of justice had left earth for heaven but might return when signs were propitious. The Romans had decided that the installation of Augustus as emperor was such a sign; and so, Dryden's poem suggested, was the restoration of monarchy in England. He was to flatter two kings as Virgil and Horace flattered their emperor, and in doing so was to inaugurate a literary period still called Augustan. The period thought of itself as peaceful, civilized, and Roman; it even called itself classical; it valued order above all other things. Dryden, of course, had made a quick turnabout between his poems to Cromwell and to Charles; but so had the English people by and large; they had no stomach for another civil war.

Dryden in London went with the times, as three events in 1663 combined to make clear. He married Lady Elizabeth Howard, daughter of the Earl of Berkshire, and through her brother, Sir Robert Howard, widened his acquaintance with the loyalist nobility. He published a poem in honor of Dr. Walter Charleton, physician and antiquary, which praised the new spirit in science that soon was to produce brilliant results through the collective efforts of the Royal Society and through the individual efforts of such men of genius as Boyle and Newton; Dryden himself had become a member of the Royal Society in 1662, and was always to believe that "a man should be learned in several sciences, and should have a reasonable, philosophical, and in some measure a mathematical head, to be a complete and excellent poet." Thirdly, he wrote in this year the first of his twenty-eight plays. For the theaters, closed during the Civil War and the Commonwealth, had been restored with Charles and were the readiest outlet for any writer's energies.

Dryden's first reputation was made upon the stage, where he was the chief figure until his virtual retirement from it in 1681. He returned at intervals with further plays, some of them written in collaboration with others, but his primary impulse was spent within less than twenty years. It is doubtful that the impulse was ever strong or natural; he denied that it was himself, nor do his dramas now represent him as a poet at his best. He was proficient at the task, as he was proficient in all things; but his genius was not dramatic. Even his best play, *All for Love* (1677), a rewriting of Shakespeare's *Antony and Cleopatra,* lacks the kind of reality that matters, though its blank verse has many charms. It represented in his own mind an advance over what he had hitherto achieved, and he was right in thinking so. For the " heroic plays " which had made him famous — *The Indian Queen* (with Sir Robert Howard), *The Indian Emperor, Tyrannic Love, The Conquest of Granada,* and *Aureng-Zebe* — were bombastic at the best, and there could be no future for the form. They were written in rhyme, and Dryden's rhymes were a sort of triumph in themselves, plangent and rapid and exciting; yet nothing could redeem the absurd romantic plots he took no trouble to make real, and so the skill he developed in his verse was all but wasted — except, of course, that it furthered an art he eventually put to better use.

His *Essay of Dramatic Poesy,* written in 1666, had argued for rhyme in plays, and argued plausibly; Dryden, a critic from the beginning, was never at a loss for principles with which to defend his practice. His practice, however, changed when he read Thomas Rymer's *The Tragedies of the Last Age* (1677), a pedantic work which nevertheless called attention to the essentials of drama as the Greeks had understood it. Dryden, leaning also upon the classic tragedy of Racine in France, surely improved under such teaching; but even then he worked under the handicap of one for whom the stage was not a native habitat. His comedies, the best of which perhaps is *The Spanish Friar,* though *Marriage à la Mode* is a close competitor for this position, remain readable without convincing us that their gaiety is genuine; some of them, notably *Limberham, The Kind Keeper,* were thought even in their time to be coarse to the limits of indecency. *Troilus and Cressida* and *The Tempest,* the latter written in collaboration with Sir William Davenant, are further rewritings of Shakespeare, as their titles suggest. Dryden had announced in a famous paragraph of the *Essay of Dramatic Poesy* his admiration of England's greatest poet and playwright, and it is everywhere evident that he read him well; but little of Shakespeare survives his handling, as little of Milton comes through into *The State of Innocence,* an opera which Dryden based, it is said with Milton's contemptuous consent, upon *Paradise Lost.* A few passages of fine verse do not make up for such absurdities as that of Adam's first speech when he awakes to find himself created:

What am I? or from whence? For that I am
I know, because I think,

which is from Descartes rather than from Milton, and out of place at that.

It must have been a relief for Dryden to turn his talents toward satire, as he did in 1678 with *Mac Flecknoe* and in 1681 with *Absalom and Achitophel.* The object in the first case was literary and in the second case was political, but both times Dryden succeeded absolutely; he was in a deep vein at last. *Mac Flecknoe* was an attack upon Thomas Shadwell, a writer of comedies who had been a friend of Dryden but who then had offended him, probably in the dedication of one of his plays to the Duke of Buckingham, himself the author of a farce, *The Rehearsal,* which in 1671 had made unmerciful fun of Dryden's heroic tragedies. The literary manners of the time were rough; poets called one another names in public, and did not bother to prove their points. Whatever Shadwell's offense had been, Dryden repaid it with couplets so mordant and amusing that Shadwell's reputation, doubtless unjustly, now lies buried beneath them. Richard Flecknoe, a poor poet who had recently died, is put forth in the poem as a king of dullness who chooses Shadwell as the heir to his throne; Flecknoe was Irish, so Shadwell's name becomes Mac Flecknoe. The sâtire was not published until 1682, and then not with Dryden's consent; but its authorship was known before it saw the light. And in that same year Dryden returned to Shadwell in some even more ruthless rhymes which he contributed to *Absalom and Achitophel, Part II,* along with lines that found another victim in Elkanah Settle, a literary enemy of older date.

The first part of *Absalom and Achitophel,* appearing in 1681 at the height of a crisis in the politics of England, fixed Dryden's reputation forever. It is his best-known poem, and in many ways it is the most characteristic of all his works; at least it shows him at the top of his power. The occasion was the Popish Plot, or rather it was the political capital which the Earl of Shaftesbury was in process of making out of that dismal event. The Plot, allegedly one to massacre Protestants, burn London, and kill the king, had been mostly a fabrication of Titus Oates, the arch-informer whose name still lingers about any such national hysteria as then beset England. Shaftesbury, who may not have believed in the plot, nevertheless used it to promote the Whig contention that James, the Catholic Duke of York, brother and legitimate heir of Charles II, should be excluded from succession to the throne in favor of the Duke of Monmouth, Charles's illegitimate but Protestant son. The Tories were for the succession of the Duke of York, who in 1685 did actually become James II. But now there was great excitement in London. Pamphlets poured forth on both sides of the question; and *Absalom and Achitophel* itself was the most striking of these. It defended the Tories as it did the king, who wanted his brother to succeed him and who in secret was sympathetic with the Catholic party. Dryden's poem was not, however, so much for Catholicism as it was for peace; its author hated contention of all sorts. He had been made Poet Laureate in 1670, and as such was expected no doubt to write in the king's interest. Yet he might have done so in any case. Whatever his motive, he went to the Bible for his story: to II Sam. 13–20, where he found a comparable situation in the revolt of Absalom against David. In a day when every reader knew the Bible, Dryden counted on his parallel to be interesting and clear: David was Charles, Absalom was Monmouth, his counselor Achitophel was Shaftesbury, and the Jews were the English. The climax of the poem, an address by David to his people urging them to make peace with him, corresponded to the king's address at Oxford in the spring of 1681; Charles had gone there, as David had left Jerusalem, to escape the hostile atmosphere of his capital. English opinion did on the whole rally behind Charles; though Shaftesbury, sent to the Tower on a charge of high treason, could not be indicted because the grand jury which acted on his case had been appointed by Whig sheriffs. He was released, and his admirers circulated a medal in his honor — the occasion in 1682 for another satire by Dryden, *The Medal.*

Dryden at fifty, then, came into his own. Thereafter until his death he was the outstanding writer of all England. He was to have ups and downs of fortune, and he would continue to be various in his literary output; but nobody disputed his crown. Soon he engaged in another sort of public controversy, this time religious instead of political. Dryden was not a religious man as that term is ordinarily understood; but his century was never free of theological quarrels, and as a poet of affairs he himself could not avoid involvement with them. In his own country there were three centers about which controversy kept ever active: the puritanical or dissenting sects, for which John Milton and John Bunyan, in *Paradise Lost* and *The Pilgrim's Progress,* remain the principal spokesmen; the Church of England; and the Roman Catholic Church. These three held respectively the positions of Left, Center, and Right with respect to the issue of authority. For the dissenters authority resided in Scripture, of which the individual could be interpreter; for the Catholics it resided in the Church itself; for the Church of England it resided in both. Dryden had nothing but contempt for the extreme sects of the left, and so the issue for him was between the middle and right positions. He defended them both in turn: the Anglican position in *Religio Laici, or, A Layman's Faith,* and the Catholic position in *The Hind and the Panther* (1687), published two years after he himself had become a Catholic — the date coincided with the Duke of York's assumption of the throne as James II, and Dryden has been accused of self-seeking because of his conversion. The accusation may be just, yet there is less discrepancy between *Religio Laici* and *The Hind and the Panther* than might casually appear. And when William III restored Protestantism to the throne in 1688, Dryden did not change his faith again.

Both of his religious poems are concerned with the question of authority and its source, and both reveal a serious desire for something like a True Church; or rather, the first reveals this desire, and the second asserts that it has been satisfied. The opening lines of *Religio Laici* assert the primacy of faith over reason in matters pertaining to the ultimate truth:

> Dim as the borrowed beams of moon and stars
> To lonely, weary, wandering travelers,
> Is Reason to the soul: and, as on high
> Those rolling fires discover but the sky,
> Not light us here, so Reason's glimmering ray
> Was lent, not to assure our doubtful way,
> But guide us upward to a better day.
> And as those nightly tapers disappear,
> When day's bright lord ascends our hemisphere;
> So pale grows Reason at Religion's sight;
> So dies, and so dissolves in supernatural light.

From this beginning Dryden goes on to consider whether Scripture alone is a sufficient guide to revelation. He decides that it is not, for the higher criticism of Richard Simon, a French Catholic priest, had recently convinced him that the texts of the Bible are inconsistent with one another, incomplete, and therefore untrustworthy. It follows that an infallible Church would be desirable; but Dryden denies the existence of such a Church, and so escapes to the middle or Anglican position. But the Puritans, he concludes, are more dangerous than the Catholics; his poem is chiefly against what he considers the anarchy of individual interpretation.

All that is required of him then, if he is to argue in favor of the Catholic Church, is to affirm its infallibility. This he does in *The Hind and the Panther,* whose famous opening lines announce his new belief:

> A milk-white Hind, immortal and unchanged,
> Fed on the lawns, and in the forest ranged;
> Without unspotted, innocent within,
> She feared no danger, for she knew no sin.
> Yet had she oft been chased with horns and hounds
> And Scythian shafts; and many winged wounds
> Aimed at her heart; was often forced to fly,
> And doomed to death, though fated not to die.

The poem is argumentative, like *Religio Laici,* but the argument this time takes place between two animals: the Hind is the Catholic Church, the Panther is the English Church. The allegorical device may be absurd, but many fine verses derive from it; and in the two poems taken together Dryden earns his reputation of being the best ratiocinative poet in English.

The accession of William in 1688 meant that

Dryden lost his poet laureateship (to Thomas Shadwell, of all persons), along with the pension that made it profitable. Henceforward he had to make his own living, and he did so chiefly as a translator. It was not a new role for him. In 1680 he had turned three of Ovid's Epistles into English verse, contributing them to a volume printed for Jacob Tonson, thereafter Dryden's principal publisher. In 1684 and 1685 he had produced versions of Ovid, Theocritus, Lucretius, and Horace, playfully referring in a preface to "the disease (as I may call it) of translation" by which he seemed to be afflicted. The "disease" grew on him, and of course it was not a disease. Indeed the exercise of bringing his beloved Latin and Greek poets over into English was for him pure health and pleasure; and without his ever having exactly planned it, he was to become before his death one of the most valuable of English translators. His translations were in some sense his own poems; they were responsible to their originals, yet their style was Dryden's without a doubt, and they added to the one great effect which as an English poet he was making. In 1692 he translated five of Juvenal's satires and all of Persius, adding for good measure further pieces from Ovid. But his masterpiece of translation was his *Virgil,* which cost him three years of effort and was published by Tonson in a folio volume of 1697. All of his vigor is in this work, as Pope's is in his *Homer* — the two translations were standard until the nineteenth century, and Dryden's still is among the liveliest and best, as may be witnessed by the beginning of the first Georgic:

What makes a plenteous harvest, when to turn
The fruitful soil, and when to sow the corn;
The care of sheep, of oxen, and of kine,
And how to raise on elms the teeming vine;
The birth and genius of the frugal bee,
I sing, Maecenas, and I sing to thee.

Yet Dryden's *Fables, Ancient and Modern,* a folio published in his last year, 1700, may be the most popular of all his works today. It too is a volume of translations: from Chaucer, Ovid, Boccaccio, and Homer. It is a collection of tales in verse, as the title promises. It is a serene, spacious, and charming book; and the prose preface is Dryden's best piece of criticism unless the *Essay of Dramatic Poesy* is that. Between those two masterpieces he had written many other essays and prefaces, arguing literary methods and principles, and debating with his rivals. Now in this lordly preface he surveys his own dominion, smiling upon the fate that has made him its monarch. His tribute to Chaucer here balances his tribute in the *Essay* to Shakespeare. It was his keenest pleasure to praise his peers; more at home now in compliment than in censure, he writes with the same good nature that is said to have distinguished him in the last years of his life, when at Will's Coffee-House, in summer on the balcony, in winter by the fire, he received the addresses of younger writers, traded literary opinions with them, and sometimes assisted them with their compositions. He had never been a particularly sociable man; plump and unprepossessing, he avoided company and was noticeably reticent, not to say ineffectual, in his speech. This handicap he now seemed disposed to overcome; at least there is ample testimony concerning the kindly figure the aging poet cut. He remained a hard worker to the last. He never altogether relinquished his contact with the stage; he wrote some of his best epistles in this decade, for example the one to Congreve; and he reached only at the end his full stature as a lyric poet. His two odes for St. Cecilia's Day — the first written in 1687, about a year after his ode to Anne Killigrew, and the second in 1697 — are with "The Secular Masque" his happiest efforts in the kind. The St. Cecilia odes, occasional as so many of his poems were, he contributed to two annual celebrations by a musical society of the Feast of St. Cecilia, the patroness of music. "The Secular Masque" he contributed in 1700 to a performance of Fletcher's play, *The Pilgrim,* given that year as a benefit for him. Its closing chorus is a farewell to the seventeenth century which no subsequent century has forgotten:

All, all of a piece throughout:
Thy chase had a beast in view;
Thy wars brought nothing about;
Thy lovers were all untrue.
'Tis well an old age is out,
And time to begin a new.

The new age Dryden welcomed in these lines was to be in one sense not new at all. It would still be the Augustan Age that he himself had created, and Alexander Pope would be its little king. Even then, however, there would be differences; and eventually the eighteenth century was to take on, in Blake and Wordsworth, a complexion so altered from that of Dryden and Pope as to constitute an entirely new face for English literature.

II. DRYDEN'S VERSE

"The sweetness of English verse," says Eugenius in *An Essay of Dramatic Poesy,* "was never understood or practiced by our fathers." This statement may seem strange in view of the fact that the fathers included Chaucer, Spenser, and Shakespeare, each of whom must sound sweeter to any modern ear than Dryden and his school. The trouble is in the word "sweet." To Dryden it meant "smooth"; and even that word requires definition. It did not mean inane or flat, and certainly it did not mean monotonous or mechanical. What it did mean Dryden was at pains all of his life to expound. He went on in the *Essay* to remark that all who took part in the dialogue that day — for the *Essay* is a critical discussion among four friends — were "willing to acknowledge how much our poesy is improved by the happiness of some writers yet living; who first taught us how to mold our thoughts into easy and significant words — to retrench the superfluities of expression — and to make our rhyme so properly a part of the verse, that it should never mislead the sense, but itself be led and governed by it." By writers yet living Dryden meant chiefly Waller and Denham, two poets who now seem minor but who then were understood as having introduced a sweet new style that everyone must copy. "Easy" and "proper" are key words in this passage, comparable in importance to "soft" and "general," used elsewhere in the *Essay.* They might still be difficult to understand if one did not bring to them certain notions of the classical: the ordered, the urbane, the civil. And indeed it is necessary to remember that Dryden's time always thought of itself as a classic age. The barbarisms of civil war and the Middle Ages were put behind; peace and order now reigned as they would reign forever; letters and art had come at last into their own; the world had begun to be once more what it had ever been at its best; philosophy had arrived at its final resting place; civilization was here to stay, and this would be its

permanent form. We are in the habit of considering Dryden's period as merely one of many, each of which replaced the one before it. Not so with Dryden and his contemporaries. Theirs was the period of periods, and it had no forseeable end. They relaxed in this faith, and looked about them for literary devices with which to express their feeling of security. Language was best when it was "easy" because the sense of ease was necessary to any citizen of such a time. If to us all this suggests complacency, for them it had no connotation of the sort. There would always be hard work to do: the work of living, writing, and speaking well.

It is consistent with what has been said that "occasional" poetry flourished then. For any event in such a society, or for any situation, appropriate words could be found if one sought them in the vocabulary of knowing gentlemen. The society itself was quite as fascinating as anything that could be said about it; one did not wish to escape from London into fields and woods, or into the manners of savages and rustics. There were no transcendent subjects. Here was the very heart of the world; here was the proper hunting ground for men of sense and wit. Poetry itself went by the name of wit, as for that matter it had in the middle of the century; but now it had the special meaning of civil talk. Dryden's poetry is a speaking thing; it is one man speaking to many who he knows will understand every inflection of his voice, and who he hopes will smile at his allusions.

Dryden mastered the art of occasional verse in all of its branches. His complimentary addresses to Dr. Charleton, the Earl of Roscommon, John Oldham, Congreve, and Motteux are masterpieces of their kind; their couplets move gracefully through all the courts of praise, distributing felicities as they go. And they are very intelligent; Dryden is always saying something, even though his main interest seems to be in keeping decorum, in bowing well. He was so constituted that he could not write and say nothing. He might strain this or that point, but he was never without his point. His twenty-five lines "To the Memory of Mr. Oldham" could simply not be better than they are. John Oldham, a vehement satirist who was born later and who died sooner than Dryden, is addressed first of all in honor of that fact. The poem was prefatory to a volume of Oldham's "Remains," according to the custom of the time. The older poet praises the younger who has prematurely died; forgives him his roughness, which perhaps is better than the smoothness of his elder; and consigns him to the shades where all fine poets dwell.

But occasional poetry has still other mansions than this. There is the epigram, and there is the epitaph; Dryden wrote few such, yet his lines on Milton, Dundee, and Plutarch have the resonant authority which the form demands. And especially in his case there were the prologue and the epilogue: short poems delivered by actors before and after plays. Dryden was master in this field. The prologues and epilogues to his own plays are often better than the plays; and so successful did he become at supplying witty couplets for audiences to hear that he was sought after by other playwrights to perform the miracle for them; he often did so, in friendship or for a fee. Frequently the audience had the text before them, printed on a broadside; but even without this help the lines must always have seemed clear and good. Dryden's voice could be heard behind them, uttering phrases of the utmost naturalness and relevance, and sometimes saying rich things which only the wisest of those present would fully relish.

If *Annus Mirabilis, The Year of Wonders, 1666* was also an occasional poem, it belonged to a different and more ambitious order. Dryden called it "an historical poem"; its two subjects were the naval war with Holland and the Great Fire of London, which some thought to be judgments upon England, but which Dryden represents as trials imposed upon the great people of a great king. Its patriotism has not preserved it, and perhaps that patriotism was not pure, since Dryden may have believed he would gain by praising Charles, who indeed made him poet laureate not long after it was published. But its quatrains are often, like those of the *Heroic Stanzas,* quaintly impressive still.

Even satire is occasional, or at any rate in Dryden's case it was. He seldom took the large view of it that permitted him to write, in *Eleonora* (1692), a panegyric on the deceased Countess of Abingdon which the Earl had commissioned him to produce:

Let this suffice: nor thou, great saint, refuse
This humble tribute of no vulgar Muse;

Who, not by cares, or wants, or age depressed,
Stems a wild deluge with a dauntless breast;
And dares to sing thy praises in a clime
Where vice triumphs, and virtue is a crime;
Where even to draw a picture of thy mind
Is satire on the most of humankind.

The concluding couplet is one of Dryden's best, but it is in the service of a more general statement than his satirical genius normally inspired in him. For the most part he aimed at specific targets: a poet he despised, a politician of whom he disapproved. And the occasion too was specific: a preface by Shadwell, an intrigue by Shaftesbury. This again was journalism. The reference was current. And if at the moment there was the advantage of being in the news, in later times there would be the risk that what he talked about would never again be readily understood. Dryden does labor under such a disadvantage now; *Absalom and Achitophel* needs to be annotated, and so of course does *Mac Flecknoe.*

What saves such poems from unintelligibility, however, is their felicity, their dramatic structure, and their good nature. The last trait may seem inconsistent with their purpose, but it is present for anyone to recognize. It is Dryden's way of being humorous. Somewhere deep within him was that indispensable resource which, as Thomas Carlyle has said, every poet must have if he is ever to be great. Humor in poetry does not consist of jokes; the sign of it, rather, is largeness and good nature, is enjoyment of the world exactly as it presents itself to any unjaundiced eye; is the ability to see, as Carlyle went on to say, not only what is above us but what is around and beneath us too, and indeed to value anything for what it is. Humor by such a definition is profounder than wit; it is more personal, more easygoing, and ultimately more harmless.

It was Dryden's humor that gave him the freedom — from inarticulate rage, and from mere impotent malice — to make his satires first of all delightful in themselves. The man writing was less important than the artist. "If a poem have a genius," he said in the Preface to *Absalom and Achitophel,* "it will force its own reception in the world; for there's a sweetness in good verse, which tickles even while it hurts, and no man can be heartily angry with him who pleases him against his will. The commendation of adversaries is the greatest triumph of a writer, because it never comes unless extorted. . . . They who imagine I have done my worst, may be convinced at their own cost that I can write severely with more ease than I can gently. I have but laughed at some men's follies, when I could have declaimed against their vices." Dryden was still thinking this way when in 1692 he prefixed to his translation of Juvenal and Persius a "Discourse of Satire," in which he returned to the notion that it is nature to be severe, but art to be gentle. His subject at the moment was the fine art of etching characters in satire. Genius, he insisted, was necessary for this to be done well. " 'Tis not reading, 'tis not imitation of an author, which can produce this fineness; it must be inborn; it must proceed from a genius, and particular way of thinking, which is not to be taught. . . . How easy is it to call rogue and villain, and that wittily! But how hard to make a man appear a fool, a blockhead, or a knave, without using any of those opprobrious terms! . . . there is still a vast difference betwixt the slovenly butchering of a man, and the fineness of a stroke that separates the head from the body, and leaves it standing in its place. . . . The character of Zimri in my *Absalom* is, in my opinion, worth the whole poem: it is not bloody, but it is ridiculous enough; and he, for whom it was intended, was too witty to resent it as an injury. If I had railed, I might have suffered for it justly; but I managed my own work more happily, perhaps more dexterously. . . . It succeeded as I wished; the jest went round, and he was laughed at in his turn who began the frolic."

Zimri had been understood by everybody to be the Duke of Buckingham, whom Sir Walter Scott, the first editor of Dryden's complete works, called "the most lively, mercurial, ambitious, and licentious genius who ever lived." The "character" of Zimri — that is, the sketch of him — was drawn by Dryden in the same conviction; and, doubtless, in pique because Buckingham's wit had gone so straight to the weak spots in Dryden's heroic plays. But the pique did not get in Dryden's way as he settled to his task of engraving in Zimri the very image of waywardness and changeability: an image, incidentally, which has survived the occasion so that it may be used of other men. Lines 544–68 of *Absalom and Achitophel* have stepped out of

their frame and become a classic. And so have several other "characters" by Dryden, who excelled all of his contemporaries in the art; for it *was* an art, and the entire century had practiced it. Dryden, coming late in its history, merely consolidated its gains — and added what nobody could have taught him, since as he himself said there is no way to teach the final graces. One has them, or has not. Most books of "characters" in the seventeenth century had confined their attention to types: the pedant, the courtier, the student, the milkmaid, the zealot, the traitor, the fop, the fool. Dryden's contribution was the delineation of individuals; and the contribution was that of an artist. What he says about the art is applicable to the art of characterization generally, as every story-teller knows: it is not enough to claim that a character is wise or beautiful, it is necessary to show this in detail, in speech and action. Dryden's instinct as a satirist was to cast his material into narrative form, or at least to give it narrative, even dramatic interest. His reader always wants to know what will happen next; he is drawn on from line to line by curiosity which the poet has created. To this extent all successful poetry can be called dramatic — that is to say, very interesting.

The ratiocinative poems of Dryden, *Religio Laici* and *The Hind and the Panther,* are ostensibly not narrative at all, except to be sure in certain portions of the second poem that treat of the two animals as they meet to talk. The talk is what finally matters, as in *Religio Laici* the argument is. But argument too has its dramatic dimension, as exposition has. Some people talk more interestingly than others, and the reason has to do with their instinct for the dramatic development of ideas. This instinct was strong in Dryden. "They cannot be good poets," he once remarked, "who are not accustomed to argue well"; he admired nothing in Shakespeare more than the quarrel scene between Brutus and Cassius in *Julius Caesar.* Dr. Johnson said of him in the next century: "The favorite exercise of his mind was ratiocination." Even the Duke of Buckingham, ridiculing Dryden in *The Rehearsal,* had taken account of this propensity. Bayes, who stands for Dryden in that farce, suddenly breaks out: "Reasoning! I gad; I love reasoning in verse." The reference was to the heroic plays, in which ladies and heroes disputed interminably over points of love and honor. And application could have been made to Dryden's criticism, where the interest of the author is often in proving some other critic wrong. But the best application now is to the religious poems, where reasoning is conducted so well that no excerpt from either of them would do anything but injustice to the whole. As Thomas De Quincey says, the strength of these poems lies in their "sequaciousness," by which he means that no passage is without its links to neighboring passages: item follows item, as always in good argument. Argument for Dryden was not a thing that could happen only in prose, where to be sure we most regularly expect it. He did, as Buckingham made him say, love reasoning in verse; and he called the result poetry. His particular fondness for Lucretius was for a great poet who had argued well. And his translation of the immortal passage in which Lucretius argued against the fear of death becomes, quite naturally, one of his own best poems. As for the doubt of later generations that argument is proper to poetry, he would have made short work of that. To argue is human, he would have said, and nothing human is alien to poetry. He was so convinced of this that he molded his verse into new rhythms which would stand the strain; it was necessary that he do this, nor would he ever have called in question the importance of preparing himself to make argument beautiful.

Narrative talent, along with humor one of the best signs that a man is a poet, was possessed by Dryden in such abundance that he found use for it everywhere: not only in the satires and ratiocinative poems, and even in the lyrics which dot his plays, but also in many a piece that was narrative by definition. He got most relish out of it in his final work, the *Fables,* where he retold the stories of others but gave these stories his own style, and often embroidered them with flourishes of his own invention. The stories of Chaucer seemed to give him boundless delight. He says so in his preface, and nobody has ever forgotten those words; but it is equally evident from the happy, fresh way he sails into the task of translating his master. Or of modernizing him, if that is the more accurate term. Anyhow, the delight makes itself manifest at once. The beginnings of " The Cock and the Fox " and " The Wife of Bath, Her Tale " are among the most spontaneous and compelling passages in English verse. If Ovid's tale of Baucis and Philemon captures the same charm, the reason may be that Dryden had a special liking for what painters call genre scenes: Dutch interiors, as it were, with homely objects disposed in a pattern, or absence of pattern, that makes any human dwelling a natural subject for art. Even the dwelling of the gods, as Homer describes it at the end of the first book of the *Iliad,* appealed to the genre artist in Dryden:

> At Vulcan's homely mirth his mother smiled,
> And smiling took the cup the clown had filled.
> The reconciler bowl went round the board,
> Which, emptied, the rude skinker still restored.

So runs the piece of Homer that Dryden included in his *Fables.* He had once thought of translating Homer rather than Virgil. He would have succeeded in such passages as this.

His labor on Virgil, of course, was largely spent upon an epic — in Dryden's time, the most glorious enterprise that any poet could undertake. And many epics were undertaken, none of them with any fraction of the success Milton achieved in *Paradise Lost.* Dryden himself considered for a while the subject of the Black Prince in Spain. But he ended by putting another's epic into English, not in writing one of his own. Doubtless it was better that he did so, for the same limitation that kept him from being a true dramatist would almost certainly have marred his epic: he was not a master of what he called " the passions." He was a master only of verse. This is saying a great deal for any poet, but it is not saying that he has the original powers we worship in Homer and Shakespeare, and on a different level in Virgil. His job with Virgil, as he saw it, was to make the epic of Aeneas readable in English. He surely did that, even when he did not catch the subtle secrets of Virgil's style. He substituted his own style, and if it was more vigorous, more impetuous than Virgil's, the result at least is a magnificent English poem which moves rapidly and resoundingly to its close. He proceeded with Virgil as he proceeded with any poet he translated: he made him Dryden. Even Chaucer becomes Dryden in the *Fables,* as Juvenal does in the opening lines of the Sixth Satire, so strong, so sensational, so amusing.

Dryden's lyric poems have nothing in them of the dewy freshness we associate with Elizabethan song or of the grave, delicious, witty seriousness we look for and find in the best lyrics of the seventeenth century between Shakespeare and the Restoration. He is rapid and light, tuneful and efficient, without claiming much attention from the intellect of the reader. At least this is true of a typical song from any of his plays. Such a typical song is " Calm was the even, and clear was the sky," from *An Evening's Love*. These were the lyrics of Dryden which circulated in the anthologies of the period and were frequently sung. He had, to be sure, a weightier note, as for example in the song from *Secret Love, or The Maiden Queen* which begins: " I feed a flame within, which so torments me," or in the " Zambra Dance " from *The Conquest of Granada, Part II*, where the opening stanzas recall whatever had been most dignified in an older day:

> From the bright vision's head
> A careless veil of lawn was loosely spread:
> From her white temples fell her shaded hair,
> Like cloudy sunshine, not too brown nor fair.

But a more familiar pace announces itself in such beginnings as this:

> Wherever I am, and whatever I do,
> My Phyllis is still in my mind.

It is a pace that suggests sprinting rather than tripping; the time is easy, and the burden is light, so that instead of song we get singsong — an infectious commodity, but of no great worth.

Dryden, however, was ambitious enough on several occasions to try his hand at the ode, the elaborate lyric whose pedigree runs back as far as the great Greek poet Pindar. Such lyrics by tradition had complex subject matter as well as complex form. They tended to be serious; and their themes wound their way through a succession of intricate stanzas characterized by an ingenious variation in line-length. In Dryden's youth the master of the Pindaric ode in English was thought by everyone to be Abraham Cowley, whom Dryden too admired, and whom his own odes imitate. But whereas Cowley has ceased to exercise the charm he once unaccountably had, Dryden still represents the tradition at somewhere near its best. The reason in his case is the reason that operates every-

where with him: sheer metrical energy, and a magnificence of melody that takes over even when his imagination is failing to do first-rate work. The trouble with Cowley's odes was that they had lacked rhythmical organization; there was little or no drama in their succession of cadences. They were deficient, that is to say, in music. Now Dryden could miss greatness too, as he did for example in *Threnodia Augustalis, A Funeral-Pindaric Poem, Sacred to the Happy Memory of King Charles II*. The fact that this was an official poem, composed by the poet laureate upon the death of one king and the accession of another (James II), and that it was expected to flatter both, would not of necessity doom it to failure. The handicap was heavy, particularly if we remember the characters of Charles and James — characters scarcely suitable for celebration in religious language. Yet it might have been surmounted. It was not, and the *Threnodia* remains one of Dryden's works for which apology must be made. Not so, however, with the poem to Anne Killigrew and the two St. Cecilia odes. All three of these are ample evidence of Dryden's lyric power — a high power, if only here.

The poem to Anne Killigrew, a young poetess who died of smallpox in 1685 — before her time, as Oldham had — appeared in a posthumous volume of her works published a few months later. She had been the niece of Thomas and William Killigrew, dramatists whose reputations Dryden knew, and the daughter of a divine. She had also been interested in painting, which Dryden here assumes to be a " sister art " to poetry, as music was in his opinion and that of others in his age; in 1695 he was to translate a French treatise on painting, and to preface this with an essay on the " parallel " between painting and poetry. Furthermore, Anne Killigrew, dying a virgin (" Mrs." in the seventeenth century was used of unmarried as well as married women), suggested to Dryden how far his own plays, to name no other works of his, had fallen from the pedestal of purity. All of these things were in his mind as he wrote the ode. There is no knowing what he actually thought of Anne Killigrew's poems, or how much he knew about their writer; it was rather his own thoughts that engaged him, as was the case with Milton when he wrote *Lycidas* for Edward King, and as indeed is true for all the great elegies of the world — someone's death makes us think of ourselves, and inspires us to take stock of our own attainments. The subjects of the ode, that is to say, are real for Dryden; and this is all that matters now. The result is high harmony, and especially in the first, fourth, and tenth stanzas it is Pindaric splendor at its very best. The rhythms are mighty and inescapable; the rush of rhetoric alone is overwhelming and wonderful.

The St. Cecilia odes of 1687 and 1697 will be remembered as long as Dryden is remembered. The first one developed the conceit that music, which organizes the created world, will on the Day of Judgment, in the sound of the final trumpet, disorganize it too. The subject, in other words, is the power of music—an absolute thing, Dryden's own music tends to say. For the music of this poem is the remarkable thing about it; it is melody in meter, and perhaps no other English poet has ever succeeded at such a task so well. The middle stanzas, looking forward to the still grander ode of 1697, celebrate the specific powers of music over human moods: a favorite subject at the time, and one which every writer of a St. Cecilia poem was expected to develop. In "Alexander's Feast, or, The Power of Music" it is the only subject; and so richly is it set forth there that some critics put the poem highest among Dryden's works. Not long after its publication Dryden wrote to Tonson, who had published it: "I am glad to hear from all hands, that my Ode is esteemed the best of all my poetry, by all the town: I thought so myself when I wrote it; but being old, I mistrusted my own judgment." There is no way, of course, in which "Alexander's Feast" and Absalom and Achitophel may be sensibly compared, nor is there any strict necessity for the comparison. Perhaps the ode of 1687 is finer in certain lines, and subtler throughout. But if "Alexander's Feast" is indeed the triumph Dryden thought it was — and Handel too, since he composed music for it in 1736 — the reason could lie in the fact that it has a narrative frame: it is a story, with characters. Alexander the Great, sitting by the side of his Thais, is variously moved by the music of Timotheus to think of wine, of women, and of war. Nothing, says Dryden at the close, ever proved the power of music so clearly: nothing except the organ of St. Cecilia, which now enlarges the theme as heaven enlarges earth.

And yet it is in the heroic couplet, rather than in the swelling measures of the ode, that Dryden by and large reveals his resources as a poet.

Behold, where Dryden's less presumptuous car,
Wide o'er the fields of glory bear
Two coursers of ethereal race,
With necks in thunder clothed, and long-resounding pace.

These famous lines from Thomas Gray's Progress of Poesy sum up the eighteenth century's sense of what Dryden's achievement had been both generally as a writer of verse and specifically as a writer of iambic pentameter couplets. He did not invent the device, of course; it is as old as Chaucer, and virtually every poet before Dryden had used it. But Dryden took it for his own and made it march. It became his very voice, available on every occasion and variable according to the subject or the mood that might possess him. If to some modern readers he seems its slave, to his own time it seemed his slave: he was its master, as in a different way Pope was its master in the century to come. Dryden's way was perhaps the richer, more resonant, more musical and manly. Opinions vary as to this, but not as to the triumph both men accomplished. It is a forgotten triumph now, at least to the extent that the art of reading couplets has been lost. It is indeed an art, comparable to the art of writing them. For anyone whose ear is practiced, Dryden for one is never monotonous; his limits are narrow, but within them he does what he pleases, and says what he will. He thought he needed the "liberty" of triplets and alexandrines: three lines rhyming in a row, with an extra foot in the third one, as in lines 19–21 of the poem to Oldham. But he could have done without this liberty, because his own freedom was never bound. Sir Walter Scott called him "Glorious John," and the name has stuck.

III. DRYDEN'S PROSE

In one sense there is little to say about the prose of Dryden beyond what Matthew Arnold said when he called it "a prose such as we would all gladly use if we only knew how." It has never been surpassed for ease and grace, nor in two and a half centuries has any advance been made upon its art. The secret of it was

Dryden's from the beginning, and his alone. The *Essay of Dramatic Poesy,* written at thirty-six, showed it in full flower. The Preface to the *Fables* is the work of an older and riper man, but he writes no better than he had at first. He did not need to, and perhaps it was impossible. Dryden at one stroke, as it were, freed English prose from its past and indicated its future. In the past it had often been thick and harsh; it never again would have to be either of those things. We still write as Dryden did — when we are able to bend his bow. Matthew Arnold, who did not esteem him as a poet, thought him nevertheless supreme in what Dryden himself had called " the other harmony of prose." It is interesting and important that Dryden used the word " harmony " in that famous phrase from Aristotle. To him all words could be music; and those who hear in his couplets what Arnold evidently could not hear are content to have praise given to his prose at least, and for its melody. Nothing in it, says Dr. Johnson, " is cold or languid: the whole is airy, animated, and vigorous; what is little, is gay; what is great, is splendid. . . . Everything is excused by the play of images and the sprightliness of expression. Though all is easy, nothing is feeble; though all seems careless, there is nothing harsh; and though since his earlier works more than a century has passed, they have nothing yet uncouth or obsolete." The suggestion here is that Dryden's mind was at play in his prose, and therefore that it must have been completely natural for him to write it. The impression is one that nobody fails to have. To read Dryden's prose is to have an experience like that of listening to the most brilliant classical music: the next phrase, no sooner desired than delivered, is new and yet the same as the one before it. All belong, and each of them is alive.

Not that Dryden's prose is musical merely — sheer sound. One can even believe that he was unaware of the music, so bent was he upon saying whatever was in his mind. " The greatest possible merit of style," said Nathaniel Hawthorne, "is, of course, to make the words absolutely disappear into the thought." Dryden could have said this too, and nearly did on more than one occasion. The fact that he wanted his statements to be entertaining did not mean that he failed to take them seriously. He was always trying, for one thing, to be clear; he wanted to understand, and wanted his reader to understand, what was better or worse in writing, and why. His prose is largely in the service of literary criticism, which for him was little short of a way of life. " The criticism of Dryden," said Dr. Johnson, " is the criticism of a poet." He meant that it was professional, precise, and full of grace. The criticism of poets — Sidney, Ben Jonson, Milton, Dryden, Samuel Johnson, Wordsworth, Coleridge, Byron, Keats, Shelley, Matthew Arnold, T. S. Eliot — is on the whole the best we have, because it is the least disinterested. And most of it is delivered in excellent prose. The critics who argued with Dryden in public were sometimes infuriated by the very beauty of his words; they thought the readers of them had been bewitched. And they had; but at the same time they had been instructed. For Dryden was always doing his best to make distinctions, preferences, principles as explicit as he could. We may or may not care as much as he did about the relative merits of French and English drama, of new English drama and old, of prose and verse in the dialogue of plays; we may have entirely lost interest in the question of dramatic rules; but we do not miss the signs that he himself cares greatly. The chief sign is that he makes us understand and remember what he said, and hear it too in that chamber of our minds where prose no less than verse is harmony.

Reading Suggestions

EDITIONS

Sir Walter Scott and George Saintsbury, editors, *The Works of John Dryden,* 18 vols. (1882–93).

E. N. Hooker and H. T. Swedenberg, Jr., editors, *The Works of John Dryden* (1956—). In progress.

James Kinsley, editor, *The Poems of John Dryden,* 4 vols. (1958). The most correct and complete edition. In the Oxford English Texts series.

George R. Noyes, editor, *The Poetical Works of Dryden* (1909; revised, 1950). The best one-volume edition of the poems, and the Biographical Sketch is the best account of Dryden's life.

W. Bradford Gardner, editor, *Dryden's Prologues and Epilogues* (1951).

Cyrus Lawrence Day, editor, *The Songs of John Dryden* (1932).

Charles E. Ward, editor, *The Letters of John Dryden* (1942).

W. P. Ker, editor, *Essays of John Dryden,* 2 vols. (1900).

BIOGRAPHY

George Saintsbury, *Dryden* (1881). Friendly, sane, and eminently readable.

James M. Osborn, *John Dryden: Some Biographical Facts and Problems* (1940). Materials for the perfect biography when it shall be written.

CRITICISM

A. W. Verrall, *Lectures on Dryden* (1914).

Mark Van Doren, *The Poetry of John Dryden* (1920, 1931; revised in 1946 as *John Dryden: A Study of His Poetry*).

Louis I. Bredvold, *The Intellectual Milieu of John Dryden: Studies in Some Aspects of Seventeenth-Century Thought* (1934, 1956). Valuable on Dryden's subject matter.

T. S. Eliot, *Homage to John Dryden* (1924); *John Dryden: The Poet, the Dramatist, the Critic* (1932).

Frank L. Huntley, *On Dryden's Essay of Dramatic Poesy* (University of Michigan, Contributions in Modern Philology, No. 16, 1951).

TO MY HONORED FRIEND,

DR. CHARLETON

ON HIS LEARNED AND USEFUL WORKS; AND MORE PAR-
TICULARLY THIS OF STONEHENGE, BY HIM
RESTORED TO THE TRUE FOUNDERS

This poem, one of the earliest of those "complimentary addresses" in which Dryden excelled, was printed in Dr. Walter Charleton's *Chorea Gigantum,* 1663, written to prove that Stonehenge was not a ruined Roman temple, as the architect Inigo Jones had argued, but a Danish coronation seat for kings. The interest of the poem now lies not in that dispute, both parties to which were wrong, but in Dryden's tribute to the science of his century.

The longest tyranny that ever swayed
Was that wherein our ancestors betrayed
Their free-born reason to the Stagirite,°
And made his torch their universal light.
So truth, while only one supplied the state,
Grew scarce, and dear, and yet sophisticate;
Until 'twas bought, like empiric° wares, or charms,
Hard words sealed up with Aristotle's arms.
Columbus was the first that shook his throne,
And found a temperate in a torrid zone: 10
The feverish air fanned by a cooling breeze,
The fruitful vales set round with shady trees;
And guiltless men, who danced away their time,
Fresh as their groves, and happy as their clime.
Had we still paid that homage to a name,
Which only God and nature justly claim,
The western seas had been our utmost bound,
Where poets still might dream the sun was drowned:
And all the stars that shine in southern skies
Had been admired by none but salvage eyes.   20
    Among the asserters of free reason's claim,
The English are not the least in worth or fame.
The world to Bacon° does not only owe
Its present knowledge, but its future too.

Gilbert° shall live, till loadstones cease to draw,
Or British fleets the boundless ocean awe;
And noble Boyle,° not less in nature seen,
Than his great brother° read in states and men.
The circling streams, once thought but pools, of blood
(Whether life's fuel, or the body's food)   30
From dark oblivion Harvey's name° shall save;
While Ent° keeps all the honor that he gave.
Nor are *you,* learned friend, the least renowned;
Whose fame, not circumscribed with English ground,
Flies like the nimble journeys of the light;
And is, like that, unspent too in its flight.
Whatever truths have been, by art or chance,
Redeemed from error, or from ignorance,
Thin in their authors, like rich veins of ore,
Your works unite, and still discover more.   40
Such is the healing virtue of your pen,
To perfect cures on books, as well as men.
Nor is this work the least: you well may give
To men new vigor, who make stones to live.
Thro' you, the Danes, their short dominion lost,
A longer conquest than the Saxons boast.
Stonehenge, once thought a temple, you have found
A throne, where kings, our earthly gods, were crowned;
Where by their wondering subjects they were seen,
Joyed with their stature, and their princely mien.
Our sovereign here above the rest might stand,   51
And here be chose again to rule the land.
    These ruins sheltered once his sacred head,
Then when from Worcester's fatal field he fled;°
Watched by the genius of this royal place,
And mighty visions of the Danish race,
His refuge then was for a temple shown;
But, he restored, 'tis now become a throne.

25. **Gilbert:** William Gilbert (1540–1603), author of an important treatise on the magnet.   27. **Boyle:** Robert Boyle (1627–91), the great chemist.   28. **his . . . brother:** the Earl of Orrery (1627–79).   31. **Harvey's name:** William Harvey (1578–1657), discoverer of the circulation of the blood.   32. **Ent:** Dr. George Ent, who urged Harvey to publish.   54. **he fled:** Charles II visited Stonehenge after his defeat at Worcester (1651).

TO DR. CHARLETON.   3. **the Stagirite:** Aristotle.   7. **empiric:** quack.   23. **Bacon:** Sir Francis Bacon.

AN ESSAY
OF DRAMATIC POESY

Written in the country where Dryden had gone to escape the plague of 1665–66, which closed the London theaters, this critical dialogue (published in 1668) discusses, in addition to the issue referred to in Dryden's note "To the Reader," the relative excellence of (1) ancient and modern poetry (2) Elizabethan and Restoration plays; the value of dramatic "rules"; and the propriety of rhyme in drama. The persons of the dialogue were long thought to be identifiable thus: Eugenius as Charles Sackville, Lord Buckhurst, later Earl of Dorset; Crites as Sir Robert Howard, Dryden's brother-in-law; Lisideius as the poet Sir Charles Sedley; and Neander (Greek for "New Man") as Dryden himself. More recently it has been suggested that since these attributions do not fit many known opinions of the men named, it might be better to think of all the speakers as simply representative of positions Dryden wanted to compare. Dryden, as he confesses, plunders current criticism, French and English, for the material of his dialogue; but in the end he makes the whole his own, largely through its style. The text is that of the third edition, 1693.

To the Reader

The drift of the ensuing discourse was chiefly to vindicate the honor of our English writers, from the censure of those who unjustly prefer the French before them. This I intimate, lest any should think me so exceedingly vain as to teach others an art which they understand much better than myself. But if this incorrect *Essay,* written in the country without the help of books or advice of friends, shall find any acceptance in the world, I promise to myself a better success of the Second Part, wherein I shall more fully treat of the virtues and faults of the English poets, who have written either in this, the epic, or the lyric way.

It was that memorable day,[1] in the first summer of the late war, when our navy engaged the Dutch; a day wherein the two most mighty and best appointed fleets which any age had ever seen disputed the command of the greater half of the globe, the commerce of nations, and the riches of the universe: while these vast floating bodies, on either side, moved against each other in parallel lines, and our countrymen, under the happy conduct of his royal highness, went breaking, by little and little, into the line of the enemies; the noise of the cannon from both navies reached our ears about the city, so that all men being alarmed with it, and in a dreadful suspense of the event, which they knew was then deciding, everyone went following the sound as his fancy led him; and leaving the town almost empty, some took towards the park, some cross the river, others down it; all seeking the noise in the depth of silence.

Among the rest, it was the fortune of Eugenius, Crites, Lisideius, and Neander, to be in company together; three of them persons whom their wit and quality have made known to all the town; and whom I have chose to hide under these borrowed names, that they may not suffer by so ill a relation as I am going to make of their discourse.

Taking then a barge, which a servant of Lisideius had provided for them, they made haste to shoot the bridge, and left behind them that great fall of waters which hindered them from hearing what they desired: after which, having disengaged themselves from many vessels which rode at anchor in the Thames, and almost blocked up the passage towards Greenwich, they ordered the watermen to let fall their oars more gently; and then, everyone favoring his own curiosity with a strict silence, it was not long ere they perceived the air to break about them like the noise of distant thunder, or of swallows in a chimney: those little undulations of sound, though almost vanishing before they reached them, yet still seeming to retain somewhat of their first horror, which they had betwixt the fleets. After they had attentively listened till such time as the sound by little and little went from them, Eugenius, lifting up his head, and taking notice of it, was the first who congratulated to the rest that happy omen of our nation's victory: adding, that we had but this to desire in confirmation of it, that we might hear no more of that noise, which was now leaving the English coast. When the rest had concurred in the same opinion, Crites, a person of a sharp judgment, and somewhat too delicate a taste in wit, which the world have mistaken in him for ill-nature, said, smiling to us, that if the concernment of this battle had not been so exceeding great, he could scarce have wished the victory at the price he knew he must pay for it, in being subject to the reading and hearing of so many ill verses as he was sure would be made on that subject. Adding, that no argument could scape some of those eternal rhymers, who watch a battle with more diligence than the ravens and birds of prey; and the worst

AN ESSAY OF DRAMATIC POESY.   1. day: June 3, 1665.

of them surest to be first upon the quarry: while the better able, either out of modesty writ not at all, or set that due value upon their poems, as to let them be often desired and long expected. "There are some of those impertinent people of whom you speak," answered Lisideius, "who to my knowledge are already so provided, either way, that they can produce not only a panegyric upon the victory, but, if need be, a funeral elegy on the duke; wherein, after they have crowned his valor with many laurels, they will at last deplore the odds under which he fell, concluding that his courage deserved a better destiny." All the company smiled at the conceit of Lisideius; but Crites, more eager than before, began to make particular exceptions against some writers, and said the public magistrate ought to send betimes to forbid them; and that it concerned the peace and quiet of all honest people, that ill poets should be as well silenced as seditious preachers. "In my opinion," replied Eugenius, "you pursue your point too far; for as to my own particular, I am so great a lover of poesy, that I could wish them all rewarded who attempt but to do well; at least, I would not have them worse used than one of their brethren was by Sylla the Dictator: — *Quem in concione vidimus* (says Tully), *cum ei libellum malus poeta de populo subjecisset, quod epigramma in eum fecisset tantummodo alternis versibus longiusculis, statim ex iis rebus quas tunc vendebat jubere ei proemium tribui, sub ea conditione ne quid postea scriberet.*"[2] "I could wish with all my heart," replied Crites, "that many whom we know were as bountifully thanked upon the same condition,— that they would never trouble us again. For amongst others, I have a moral apprehension of two poets, whom this victory, with the help of both her wings, will never be able to escape." "'Tis easy to guess whom you intend," said Lisideius; "and without naming them, I ask you, if one of them does not perpetually pay us with clenches[3] upon words, and a certain clownish kind of raillery? if now and then he does not offer at a catachresis[4] or Clevelandism,[5] wresting and torturing a word into another meaning: in fine, if he be not one of those whom the French would call *un mauvais buffon;*[6] one who is so much a well-willer to the satire, that he intends at least to spare no man; and though he cannot strike a blow to hurt any, yet he ought to be punished for the malice of the action, as our witches are justly hanged, because they think themselves to be such; and suffer deservedly for believing they did mischief, because they meant it." "You have described him," said Crites, "so exactly, that I am afraid to come after you with my other extremity of poetry. He is one of those who, having had some advantage of education and converse, knows better than the other what a poet should be, but puts it into practice more unluckily than any man; his style and matter are everywhere alike: he is the most calm, peaceable writer you ever read: he never disquiets your passions with the least concernment, but still leaves you in as even a temper as he found you; he is a very leveller in poetry: he creeps along with ten little words in every line, and helps out his numbers with *For to,* and *Unto,* and all the pretty expletives he can find, till he drags them to the end of another line; while the sense is left tired half way behind it: he doubly starves all his verses, first for want of thought, and then of expression; his poetry neither has wit in it, nor seems to have it; like him in Martial:

Pauper videri Cinna vult, et est pauper.[7]

"He affects plainness, to cover his want of imagination: when he writes the serious way, the highest flight of his fancy is some miserable antithesis, or seeming contradiction; and in the comic he is still reaching at some thin conceit, the ghost of a jest, and that too flies before him, never to be caught; these swallows which we see before us on the Thames are the just resemblance of his wit: you may observe how near the water they stoop, how many proffers they make to dip, and yet how seldom they touch it; and when they do, it is but the surface: they skim over it but to catch a gnat, and then mount into the air and leave it."

"Well, gentlemen," said Eugenius, "you may speak your pleasure of these authors; but though I and some few more about the town may give you a peaceable hearing, yet assure yourselves, there are multitudes who would think you malicious and them injured: especially him whom you first described; he is the very Withers[8] of the city: they

---

2. *Quem . . . scriberet:* "Whom we have seen at the assembly, when a bad poet had submitted a complaint against him in longish couplets, order a reward to be paid him out of the goods he was selling, on condition that he never write again" (Cicero, *Pro Archia,* 25).   3. **clenches:** puns.   4. **catachresis:** defined in the following clause.   5. **Clevelandism:** John Cleveland (1613–58), a poet notorious for his difficulty, unjustified by his merit.

6. *un . . . buffon:* "an ill-tempered clown."   7. *Pauper . . . pauper:* "Cinna wishes to seem poor, and is."   8. **Withers:** George Withers (1588–1667).

have bought more editions of his works than would serve to lay under all their pies at the lord mayor's Christmas. When his famous poem first came out in the year 1660, I have seen them reading it in the midst of 'Change time; nay, so vehement they were at it, that they lost their bargain by the candles' ends;[9] but what will you say if he has been received amongst great persons? I can assure you this day he is the envy of one who is lord in the art of quibbling, and who does not take it well that any man should intrude so far into his province." " All I would wish," replied Crites, " is, that they who love his writings, may still admire him, and his fellow poet: *Qui Bavium non odit,* etc.,[10] is curse sufficient." " And farther," added Lisideius, " I believe there is no man who writes well, but would think he had hard measure, if their admirers should praise anything of his: *Nam quos contemnimus eorum quoque laudes contemnimus.*"[11] " There are so few who write well in this age," said Crites, " that methinks any praises should be welcome; they neither rise to the dignity of the last age, nor to any of the ancients: and we may cry out of the writers of this time, with more reason than Petronius of his, *Pace vestra liceat dixisse, primi omnium eloquentium perdidistis:*[12] you have debauched the true old poetry so far, that nature, which is the soul of it, is not in any of your writings."

" If your quarrel," said Eugenius, " to those who now write, be grounded only on your reverence to antiquity, there is no man more ready to adore those great Greeks and Romans than I am: but on the other side, I cannot think so contemptibly of the age in which I live, or so dishonorably of my own country, as not to judge we equal the ancients in most kinds of poesy, and in some surpass them; neither know I any reason why I may not be as zealous for the reputation of our age as we find the ancients themselves were in reference to those who lived before them. For you hear your Horace saying,

Indignor quidquam reprehendi, non quia crasse
Compositum, illepideve putetur, sed quia nuper.[13]

And after:

Si meliora dies, ut vina, poemata reddit,
Scire velim, pretim chartis quotus arroget annus?[14]

" But I see I am engaging in a wide dispute, where the arguments are not like to reach close on either side; for poesy is of so large an extent, and so many both of the ancients and moderns have done well in all kinds of it, that in citing one against the other, we shall take up more time this evening than each man's occasions will allow him: therefore I would ask Crites to what part of poesy he would confine his arguments, and whether he would defend the general cause of the ancients against the moderns, or oppose any age of the moderns against this of ours? "

Crites, a little while considering upon this demand, told Eugenius, that if he pleased, he would limit their dispute to Dramatic Poesy; in which he thought it not difficult to prove, either that the ancients were superior to the moderns, or the last age to this of ours.

Eugenius was somewhat surprised, when he heard Crites make choice of that subject. " For aught I see," said he, " I have undertaken a harder province than I imagined; for though I never judged the plays of the Greek or Roman poets comparable to ours, yet, on the other side, those we now see acted come short of many which were written in the last age: but my comfort is, if we are overcome, it will be only by our own countrymen: and if we yield to them in this one part of poesy, we may surpass them in all the other: for in the epic or lyric way, it will be hard for them to show us one such amongst them, as we have many now living, or who lately were: they can produce nothing so courtly writ, or which expresses so much the conversation of a gentleman, as Sir John Suckling; nothing so even, sweet, and flowing as Mr. Waller; nothing so majestic, so correct, as Sir John Denham; nothing so elevated, so copious, and full of spirit as Mr. Cowley; as for the Italian, French, and Spanish plays, I can make it evident, that those who now write surpass them; and that the drama is wholly ours."

All of them were thus far of Eugenius his opinion, that the sweetness of English verse was never understood or practised by our fathers; even Crites himself did not much oppose it; and everyone was

9. **candles' ends**: bids at auctions were heard until a candle burned out.   10. *Qui . . . odit:* "Who hates not living Bavius, let him be, Dead Maevius, damned to love thy works and thee!" (Virgil, *Eclogues,* III.90 [Dryden's translation]).   11. *Nam . . . contemnimus:* "For we despise the praises of those we despise."   12. *Pace . . . perdidistis:* "If I may say so, you were the first destroyer of eloquence" (*Satyricon,* 2).   13. *Indignor . . . nuper:* "I am indignant when a piece of writing is condemned not because it is bad but because it is new" (*Epistles,* II.i.76–77).

14. *Si . . . annus?:* "If time improves poetry as it does wine, I want to know how long it takes paper to become precious" (*Ibid.,* II.i.34–35).

willing to acknowledge how much our poesy is improved by the happiness of some writers yet living; who first taught us to mold our thoughts into easy and significant words,— to retrench the superfluities of expression,— and to make our rhyme so properly a part of the verse, that it should never mislead the sense, but itself be led and governed by it.

Eugenius was going to continue this discourse, when Lisideius told him that it was necessary, before they proceeded further, to take a standing measure of their controversy; for how was it possible to be decided who writ the best plays, before we know what a play should be? But, this once agreed on by both parties, each might have recourse to it, either to prove his own advantages, or to discover the failings of his adversary.

He had no sooner said this, but all desired the favor of him to give the definition of a play; and they were the more importunate, because neither Aristotle, nor Horace, nor any other, who had writ of that subject, had ever done it.

Lisideius, after some modest denials, at last confessed he had a rude notion of it; indeed, rather a description than a definition; but which served to guide him in his private thoughts, when he was to make a judgment of what others writ: that he conceived a play ought to be, *A just and lively image of human nature, representing its passions and humors, and the changes of fortune to which it is subject, for the delight and instruction of mankind.*

This definition, though Crites raised a logical objection against it — that it was only *a genere et fine*,[15] and so not altogether perfect, was yet well received by the rest; and after they had given order to the waterman to turn their barge, and row softly, that they might take the cool of the evening in their return, Crites, being desired by the company to begin, spoke on behalf of the ancients, in this manner:

"If confidence presage a victory, Eugenius, in his own opinion, has already triumphed over the ancients: nothing seems more easy to him than to overcome those whom it is our greatest praise to have imitated well; for we do not only build upon their foundations, but by their models. Dramatic Poesy had time enough, reckoning from Thespis (who first invented it) to Aristophanes, to be born, to grow up, and to flourish in maturity. It has been observed of arts and sciences, that in one and the same century they have arrived to great perfection;

and no wonder, since every age has a kind of universal genius, which inclines those that live in it to some particular studies: the work then, being pushed on by many hands, must of necessity go forward.

"Is it not evident, in these last hundred years, when the study of philosophy has been the business of all the Virtuosi in Christendom, that almost a new nature has been revealed to us? That more errors of the School [16] have been detected, more useful experiments in philosophy have been made, more noble secrets in optics, medicine, anatomy, astronomy, discovered, than in all those credulous and doting ages from Aristotle [17] to us? — so true it is, that nothing spreads more fast than science, when rightly and generally cultivated.

"Add to this, the more than common emulation that was in those times of writing well; which though it be found in all ages and all persons that pretend to the same reputation, yet poesy, being then in more esteem than now it is, had greater honors decreed to the professors of it, and consequently the rivalship was more high between them; they had judges ordained to decide their merit, and prizes to reward it; and historians have been diligent to record of Aeschylus, Euripides, Sophocles, Lycophron, and the rest of them, both who they were that vanquished in these wars of the theatre, and how often they were crowned: while the Asian kings and Grecian commonwealths scarce afforded them a nobler subject than the unmanly luxuries of a debauched court, or giddy intrigues of a factious city: — *Alit aemulatio ingenia* (saith Paterculus), *et nunc invidia, nunc admiratio incitationem accendit:* [18] Emulation is the spur of wit; and sometimes envy, sometimes admiration, quickens our endeavors.

"But now, since the rewards of honor are taken away, that virtuous emulation is turned into direct malice; yet so slothful, that it contents itself to condemn and cry down others, without attempting to do better: 'tis a reputation too unprofitable, to take the necessary pains for it; yet, wishing they had it, that desire is incitement enough to hinder others from it. And this, in short, Eugenius, is the reason why you have now so few good poets, and so many severe judges. Certainly, to imitate the ancients well, much labor and long study is required; which pains, I have already shown, our poets would want

---

15. *a . . . fine:* "by class and purpose."

16. **the School:** scholastic (medieval) philosophy.   17. **Aristotle:** Cf. "To Dr. Charleton," 3.   18. *Alit . . . accendit:* Dryden's paraphrase follows.

encouragement to take if yet they had ability to go through the work. Those ancients have been faithful imitators and wise observers of that nature which is so torn and ill represented in our plays; they have handed down to us a perfect resemblance of her; which we, like ill copiers, neglecting to look on, have rendered monstrous, and disfigured. But, that you may know how much you are indebted to those your masters, and be ashamed to have so ill requited them, I must remember you, that all the rules by which we practise the drama at this day (either such as relate to the justness and symmetry of the plot, or the episodical ornaments, such as descriptions, narrations, and other beauties, which are not essential to the play) were delivered to us from the observations which Aristotle made of those poets who either lived before him, or were his contemporaries: we have added nothing of our own, except we have the confidence to say our wit is better; of which, none boast in this our age, but such as understand not theirs. Of that book which Aristotle has left us, περὶ τῆς Ποιητικῆς,[19] Horace his *Art of Poetry* is an excellent comment, and, I believe, restores to us that second book of his concerning Comedy, which is wanting in him.

" Out of these two have been extracted the famous rules, which the French call *Des Trois Unités,* or, The Three Unities,[20] which ought to be observed in every regular play; namely, of Time, Place, and Action.

" The unity of time they comprehend in twenty-four hours, the compass of a natural day, or as near as it can be contrived; and the reason of it is obvious to everyone, — that the time of the feigned action, or fable of the play, should be proportioned as near as can be to the duration of that time in which it is represented: since, therefore, all plays are acted on the theatre in the space of time much within the compass of twenty-four hours, that play is to be thought the nearest imitation of nature, whose plot or action is confined within that time; and, by the same rule which concludes this general proportion of time, it follows, that all the parts of it are (as near as may be) to be equally subdivided; namely, that one act take not up the supposed time of half a day, which is out of proportion to the rest; since the other four are then to be straitened within the compass of the remaining half: for it is unnatural

that one act, which being spoke or written is not longer than the rest, should be supposed longer by the audience; it is therefore the poet's duty to take care that no act should be imagined to exceed the time in which it is represented on the stage; and that the intervals and inequalities of time be supposed to fall out between the acts.

" This rule of time, how well it has been observed by the ancients, most of their plays will witness; you see them in their tragedies (wherein to follow this rule is certainly most difficult), from the very beginning of their plays, falling close into that part of the story which they intend for the action or principal object of it, leaving the former part to be delivered by narration: so that they set the audience, as it were, at the post where the race is to be concluded; and, saving them the tedious expectation of seeing the poet set out and ride the beginning of the course, they suffer you not to behold him, till he is in sight of the goal, and just upon you.

" For the second unity, which is that of Place, the ancients meant by it, that the scene ought to be continued through the play, in the same place where it was laid in the beginning: for, the stage on which it is represented being but one and the same place, it is unnatural to conceive it many, — and those far distant from one another. I will not deny but, by the variation of painted scenes, the fancy, which in these cases will contribute to its own deceit, may sometimes imagine it several places, with some appearance of probability; yet it still carries the greater likelihood of truth if those places be supposed so near each other as in the same town or city; which may all be comprehended under the larger denominations of one place; for a greater distance will bear no proportion to the shortness of time which is allotted, in the acting, to pass from one of them to another; for the observation of this, next to the ancients, the French are to be most commended. They tie themselves so strictly to the unity of place that you never see in any of their plays a scene changed in the middle of an act: if the act begins in a garden, a street, or chamber, 'tis ended in the same place; and that you may know it to be the same, the stage is so supplied with persons, that it is never empty all the time: he who enters second, has business with him who was on before; and before the second quits the stage, a third appears who has business with him. This Corneille calls *la liaison des scènes,* the continuity or joining of the scenes; and 'tis a good mark of a well-contrived play, when all the persons

19. περὶ τῆς Ποιητικῆς: the *Poetics.*   20. The Unities: see pp. 98-103 in Vol. II.

are known to each other, and every one of them has some affairs with all the rest.

"As for the third unity, which is that of Action, the ancients meant no other by it than what the logicians do by their *finis,* the end or scope of any action; that which is the first in intention, and last in execution: now the poet is to aim at one great and complete action, to the carrying on of which all things in his play, even the very obstacles, are to be subservient; and the reason of this is as evident as any of the former. For two actions, equally labored and driven on by the writer, would destroy the unity of the poem; it would be no longer one play, but two: not but that there may be many actions in a play, as Ben Jonson has observed in his *Discoveries;* but they must be all subservient to the great one, which our language happily expresses in the name of *under-plots:* such as in Terence's *Eunuch* is the difference and reconcilement of Thais and Phaedria, which is not the chief business of the play, but promotes the marriage of Chaerea and Chremes's sister, principally intended by the poet. There ought to be but one action, says Corneille, that is, one complete action, which leaves the mind of the audience in a full repose; but this cannot be brought to pass but by many other imperfect actions, which conduce to it, and hold the audience in a delightful suspense of what will be.

"If by these rules (to omit many other drawn from the precepts and practice of the ancients) we should judge our modern plays, 'tis probable that few of them would endure the trial: that which should be the business of a day takes up in some of them an age; instead of one action, they are the epitomes of a man's life; and for one spot of ground, which the stage should represent, we are sometimes in more countries than the map can show us.

"But if we allow the ancients to have contrived well, we must acknowledge them to have written better. Questionless we are deprived of a great stock of wit in the loss of Menander among the Greek poets, and of Caecilius, Afranius, and Varius, among the Romans; we may guess at Menander's excellency by the plays of Terence, who translated some of his; and yet wanted so much of him, that he was called by C. Caesar the half-Menander; and may judge of Varius, by the testimonies of Horace, Martial, and Velleius Paterculus. 'Tis probable that these, could they be recovered, would decide the controversy; but so long as Aristophanes and Plautus are extant, while the tragedies of Euripides, Sophocles, and Seneca are in our hands, I can

never see one of these plays which are now written but it increases my admiration of the ancients. And yet I must acknowledge further, that to admire them as we ought, we should understand them better than we do. Doubtless many things appear flat to us, the wit of which depended on some custom or story, which never came to our knowledge; or perhaps on some criticism in their language, which being so long dead, and only remaining in their books, 'tis not possible they should make us understand perfectly. To read Macrobius, explaining the propriety and elegancy of many words in Virgil, which I had before passed over without consideration as common things, is enough to assure me that I ought to think the same of Terence; and that in the purity of his style (which Tully so much valued that he ever carried his works about him) there is yet left in him great room for admiration, if I knew but where to place it. In the meantime I must desire you to take notice that the greatest man of the last age, Ben Jonson, was willing to give place to them in all things: he was not only a professed imitator of Horace, but a learned plagiary of all the others; you track him everywhere in their snow: if Horace, Lucan, Petronius Arbiter, Seneca, and Juvenal had their own from him, there are few serious thoughts which are new in him: you will pardon me, therefore, if I presume he loved their fashion, when he wore their clothes. But since I have otherwise a great veneration for him, and you, Eugenius, prefer him above all other poets, I will use no farther arguments to you than his example: I will produce before you Father Ben, dressed in all the ornaments and colors of the ancients; you will need no other guide to our party, if you follow him; and whether you consider the bad plays of our age, or regard the good plays of the last, both the best and worst of the modern poets will equally instruct you to admire the ancients."

Crites had no sooner left speaking, but Eugenius, who had waited with some impatience for it, thus began:

"I have observed in your speech, that the former part of it is convincing as to what the moderns have profited by the rules of the ancients; but in the latter you are careful to conceal how much they have excelled them; we own all the helps we have from them, and want neither veneration nor gratitude, while we acknowledge that, to overcome them, we must make use of the advantages we have received from them: but to these assistances we have joined our own industry; for, had we sat down with a dull imitation of them, we might then have lost somewhat of the old perfection, but never acquired any that was new. We draw not therefore after their lines, but those of nature; and having the life before us, besides the experience of all they knew, it is no wonder if we hit some airs and features which they have missed. I deny not what you urge of arts and sciences, that they have flourished in some ages more than others; but your instance in philosophy makes for me: for if natural causes be more known now than in the time of Aristotle, because more studied, it follows that poesy and other arts may, with the same pains, arrive still nearer to perfection; and, that granted, it will rest for you to prove that they wrought more perfect images of human life than we; which seeing in your discourse you have avoided to make good, it shall now be my task to show you some part of their defects, and some few excellencies of the moderns. And I think there is none among us can imagine I do it enviously, or with purpose to detract from them; for what interest of fame or profit can the living lose by the reputation of the dead? On the other side, it is a great truth which Velleius Paterculus affirms: *Audita visis libentius laudamus; et proesentia invidia proeterita admiratione prosequimur; et his nos obrui, illis instrui credimus:* [21] that praise or censure is certainly the most sincere, which unbribed posterity shall give us.

"Be pleased then in the first place to take notice that the Greek poesy, which Crites has affirmed to have arrived to perfection in the reign of the old comedy, was so far from it that the distinction of it into acts was not known to them; or if it were, it is yet so darkly delivered to us that we cannot make it out.

"All we know of it is from the singing of their Chorus; and that too is so uncertain, that in some of their plays we have reason to conjecture they sung more than five times. Aristotle indeed divides the integral parts of a play into four. First, the *Protasis,* or entrance, which gives light only to the characters of the persons, and proceeds very little into any part of the action. Secondly, the *Epitasis,* or working up of the plot, where the play grows warmer; the design or action of it is drawing on, and you see something promising that it will come to pass. Thirdly, the *Catastasis,* called by the Romans, *Status,* the height and full growth of the play: we may call it properly the counter-turn, which destroys that expectation, embroils the action in new difficulties, and leaves you far distant from that hope in which it found you; as you may have observed in a violent stream resisted by a narrow passage — it runs round to an eddy, and carries back the waters with more swiftness than it brought them on. Lastly, the *Catastrophe,* which the Grecians called λύσις,[22] the French *le dénouement,* and we the discovery, or unravelling of the plot: there you see all things settling again upon their first foundations; and, the obstacles which hindered the design or action of the play once removed, it ends with that resemblance of truth and nature that the audience are satisfied with the conduct of it. Thus this great man delivered to us the image of a play; and I must confess it is so lively, that from thence much light has been derived to the forming it more perfectly into acts and scenes: but what poet first limited to five the number of the acts, I know not; only we see it so firmly established in the time of Horace, that he gives it for a rule in comedy — *Neu brevior quinto, neu sit productior actu.*[23] So that you see the Grecians cannot be said to have consummated this art; writing rather by entrances than by acts, and having rather a general indigested notion of a play, than knowing how and where to bestow the particular graces of it.

"But since the Spaniards at this day allow but three acts, which they call *Jornadas,* to a play, and the Italians in many of theirs follow them, when I condemn the ancients, I declare it is not altogether because they have not five acts to every play, but because they have not confined themselves to one certain number: 'tis building an house without a model; and when they succeeded in such undertakings, they ought to have sacrificed to Fortune, not to the Muses.

"Next, for the plot, which Aristotle called τό μῦθος, and often τῶν πραγμάτων σύνθεσις,[24] and from him the Romans *Fabula;* it has already been judiciously observed by a late writer, that in their tragedies it was only some tale derived from Thebes or Troy, or at least something that happened in those two ages; which was worn so threadbare by the pens of all the epic poets, and

---

21. *Audita . . . credimus:* "We would rather praise things heard than seen; we envy present but admire past things; we think we are eclipsed by the former, but instructed by the latter."

22. λύσις: "untying."   23. *Neu . . . actu:* "Let it be neither shorter nor longer than five acts" (*Ars Poetica,* 189).   24. τό μῦθος: "the mythos"; τῶν . . . σύνθεσις: "the management of events."

even by tradition itself of the talkative Greeklings (as Ben Jonson calls them), that before it came upon the stage it was already known to all the audience: and the people, so soon as ever they heard the name of Oedipus, knew as well as the poet, that he had killed his father by a mistake, and committed incest with his mother, before the play; that they were now to hear of a great plague, an oracle, and the ghost of Laius: so that they sat with a yawning kind of expectation, till he was to come with his eyes pulled out, and speak a hundred or more verses in a tragic tone, in complaint of his misfortunes. But one Oedipus, Hercules, or Medea, had been tolerable: poor people, they escaped not so good cheap; they had still the *chapon bouillé* [25] set before them, till their appetites were cloyed with the same dish, and, the novelty being gone, the pleasure vanished; so that one main end of Dramatic Poesy in its definition, which was to cause delight, was of consequence destroyed.

"In their comedies, the Romans generally borrowed their plots from the Greek poets; and theirs was commonly a little girl stolen or wandered from her parents, brought back unknown to the city, there got with child by some young fellow, who, by the help of his servant, cheats his father; and when her time comes, to cry, *Juno Lucina, fer opem,*[26] one or other sees a little box or cabinet which was carried away with her, and so discovers her to her friends, if some god do not prevent it, by coming down in a machine, and taking the thanks of it to himself.

"By the plot you may guess much of the characters of the persons. An old father, who would willingly, before he dies, see his son well married; his debauched son, kind in his nature to his mistress, but miserably in want of money; a servant or slave, who has so much wit to strike in with him, and help to dupe his father; a braggadocio captain, a parasite, and a lady of pleasure.

"As for the poor honest maid, on whom the story is built, and who ought to be one of the principal actors in the play, she is commonly a mute in it: she has the breeding of the old Elizabeth way, which was for maids to be seen and not to be heard; and it is enough you know she is willing to be married when the fifth act requires it.

"These are plots built after the Italian mode of houses — you see through them all at once: the

characters are indeed the imitation of nature, but so narrow, as if they had imitated only an eye or an hand, and did not dare to venture on the lines of a face, or the proportion of a body.

"But in how strait a compass soever they have bounded their plots and characters, we will pass it by, if they have regularly pursued them, and perfectly observed those three unities of time, place, and action; the knowledge of which you say is derived to us from them. But in the first place give me leave to tell you, that the unity of place, however it might be practised by them, was never any of their rules: we neither find it in Aristotle, Horace, or any who have written of it, till in our age the French poets first made it a precept of the stage. The unity of time, even Terence himself, who was the best and most regular of them, has neglected: his *Heautontimorumenos,* or *Self-Punisher,* takes up visibly two days, says Scaliger; the two first acts concluding the first day, the three last acts the day ensuing; and Euripides, in tying himself to one day, has committed an absurdity never to be forgiven him; for in one of his tragedies[27] he has made Theseus go from Athens to Thebes, which was about forty English miles, under the walls of it to give battle, and appear victorious in the next act; and yet, from the time of his departure to the return of the Nuntius, who gives the relation of his victory, Aethra and the Chorus have but thirty-six verses; which is not for every mile a verse.

"The like error is as evident in Terence his *Eunuch,* when Laches, the old man, enters by mistake into the house of Thais; where, betwixt his exit and the entrance of Pythias, who comes to give an ample relation of the disorders he has raised within, Parmeno, who was left upon the stage, has not above five lines to speak. *C'est bien employer un temps si court,*[28] says the French poet, who furnished me with one of the observations: and almost all their tragedies will afford us examples of the like nature.

"'Tis true, they have kept the continuity, or, as you called it, *liaison des scènes,* somewhat better: two do not perpetually come in together, talk, and go out together; and other two succeed them, and do the same throughout the act, which the English call by the name of single scenes; but the reason is, because they have seldom above two or three

---

25. *chapon bouillé:* "warmed-over stew."   26. *Juno . . . opem:* "Juno, goddess of childbirth, bring help."

27. one . . . tragedies: *The Suppliants.*   28. *C'est . . . court:* "It is well to use so little time."

scenes, properly so called, in every act; for it is to be accounted a new scene, not only every time the stage is empty, but every person who enters, though to others, makes it so; because he introduces a new business. Now the plots of their plays being narrow, and the persons few, one of their acts was written in a less compass than one of our well-wrought scenes; and yet they are often deficient even in this. To go no further than Terence; you find in the *Eunuch,* Antipho entering single in the midst of the third act, after Chremes and Pythias were gone off; in the same play you have likewise Dorias beginning the fourth act alone; and after she had made a relation of what was done at the Soldiers' entertainment (which by the way was very inartificial, because she was presumed to speak directly to the audience, and to acquaint them with what was necessary to be known, but yet should have been so contrived by the poet as to have been told by persons of the drama to one another, and so by them to have come to the knowledge of the people), she quits the stage, and Phaedria enters next, alone likewise: he also gives you an account of himself, and of his returning from the country, in monologue; to which unnatural way of narration Terence is subject in all his plays. In his *Adelphi,* or *Brothers,* Syrus and Demea enter after the scene was broken by the departure of Sostrata, Geta, and Canthara; and indeed you can scarce look unto any of his comedies where you will not presently discover the same interruption.

" But as they have failed both in laying of their plots, and in the management, swerving from the rules of their own art by misrepresenting nature to us, in which they have ill satisfied one intention of a play, which was delight; so in the instructive part they have erred worse: instead of punishing vice and rewarding virtue, they have often shown a prosperous wickedness, and an unhappy piety: they have set before us a bloody image of revenge in Medea, and given her dragons to convey her safe from punishment; a Priam and Astyanax murdered, and Cassandra ravished, and the lust and murder ending in the victory of him who acted them: in short, there is no indecorum in any of our modern plays, which if I would excuse, I could not shadow with some authority from the ancients.

" And one farther note of them let me leave you: tragedies and comedies were not writ then as they are now, promiscuously, by the same person; but he who found his genius bending to the one, never attempted the other way. This is so plain

that I need not instance to you, that Aristophanes, Plautus, Terence, never any of them writ a tragedy; Aeschylus, Euripides, Sophocles, and Seneca never meddled with comedy: the sock and buskin [29] were not worn by the same poet. Having then so much care to excel in one kind, very little is to be pardoned them if they miscarried in it; and this would lead me to the consideration of their wit, had not Crites given me sufficient warning not to be too bold in my judgment of it; because, the languages being dead, and many of the customs and little accidents on which it depended lost to us, we are not competent judges of it. But though I grant that here and there we may miss the application of a proverb or a custom, yet a thing well said will be wit in all languages; and though it may lose something in the translation, yet to him who reads it in the original, 'tis still the same: he has an idea of its excellency, though it cannot pass from his mind into any other expression or words than those in which he finds it. When Phaedria, in the *Eunuch,* had a command from his mistress to be absent two days, and, encouraging himself to go through with it, said, *Tandem ego non illa caream, si sit opus, vel totum triduum?* [30] — Parmeno, to mock the softness of his master, lifting up his hands and eyes, cries out, as it were in admiration, *Hui! universum triduum!* [31] the elegancy of which *universum,* though it cannot be rendered in our language, yet leaves an impression on our souls: but this happens seldom in him; in Plautus oftener, who is infinitely too bold in his metaphors and coining words, out of which many times his wit is nothing; which questionless was one reason why Horace falls upon him so severely in those verses:

Sed proavi nostri Plautinos et numeros et
Laudavere sales, nimium patienter utrumque,
Ne dicam stolidè.[32]

For Horace himself was cautious to obtrude a new word on his readers, and makes custom and common use the best measure of receiving it into our writings:

Multa renascentur quae nunc cecidere, cadentque
Quae nunc sunt in honore vocabula, si volet usus,
Quem penes arbitrium est, et jus, et norma loquendi.[33]

29. sock and buskin: a low shoe and a high boot, worn respectively by comic and tragic actors in the Greek theater; hence, symbols of comedy and tragedy.   **30. *Tandem . . . triduum?:*** "Shall I not do without her, if necessary, for three whole days?"   **31. *Hui! . . . triduum:*** "What! Three *entire* days?"   **32. *Sed . . . stolidè:*** "But our ancestors praised the verse and the wit of Plautus submissively—I may even say stupidly" (*Ars Poetica,* 189).   **33. *Multa . . . loquendi:*** "Many words now obsolete

" The not observing this rule is that which the world has blamed in our satirist, Cleveland: to express a thing hard and unnaturally, in his new way of elocution. 'Tis true, no poet but may sometimes use a catachresis: Virgil does it —

Mistaque ridenti colocasia fundet acantho — [34]

in his eclogue of Pollio; and in his seventh *Aeneid:*

> *mirantur et undae,*
> *Miratur nemus insuetum fulgentia longe*
> *Scuta virum fluvio pictasque innare carinas.*[35]

And Ovid once so modestly, that he asks leave to do it:

> *quem, si verbo audacia detur,*
> *Haud metuam summi dixisse Palatia coeli.*[36]

calling the court of Jupiter by the name of Augustus his palace; though in another place he is more bold, where he says, — *et longas visent Capitolia pompas.*[37] But to do this always, and never be able to write a line without it, though it may be admired by some few pedants, will not pass upon those who know that wit is best conveyed to us in the most easy language; and is most to be admired when a great thought comes dressed in words so commonly received, that it is understood by the meanest apprehensions, as the best meat is the most easily digested: but we cannot read a verse of Cleveland's without making a face at it, as if every word were a pill to swallow: he gives us many times a hard nut to break our teeth, without a kernel for our pains. So that there is this difference betwixt his Satires and Doctor Donne's; that the one gives us deep thoughts in common language, though rough cadence; the other gives us common thoughts in abstruse words: 'tis true, in some places his wit is independent of his words, as in that of the rebel Scot:

Had Cain been Scot, God would have changed his doom;
Not forced him wander, but confined him home.

" *Si sic omnia dixisset!* [38] This is wit in all lan-

guages: it is like Mercury, never to be lost or killed: — and so that other —

For beauty, like white powder, makes no noise,
And yet the silent hypocrite destroys.

You see the last line is highly metaphorical, but it is so soft and general, that it does not shock us as we read it.

" But, to return from whence I have digressed, to the consideration of the ancients' writing, and their wit (of which by this time you will grant us in some measure to be fit judges). Though I see many excellent thoughts in Seneca, yet he of them who had a genius most proper for the stage, was Ovid; he had a way of writing so fit to stir up a pleasing admiration and concernment, which are the objects of a tragedy, and to show the various movements of a soul combating betwixt two different passions, that, had he lived in our age, or in his own could have writ with our advantages, no man but must have yielded to him; and therefore I am confident the *Medea* is none of his: for, though I esteem it for the gravity and sententiousness of it, which he himself concludes to be suitable to a tragedy — *Omne genus scripti gravitate tragoedia vincit* [39] — yet it moves not my soul enough to judge that he, who in the epic way wrote things so near the drama as the story of Myrrha, of Caunus and Biblis, and the rest, should stir up no more concernment where he most endeavored it. The masterpiece of Seneca I hold to be that scene in the *Troades,* where Ulysses is seeking for Astyanax to kill him: there you see the tenderness of a mother so represented in Andromache, that it raises compassion to a high degree in the reader, and bears the nearest resemblance of anything in the tragedies of the ancients to the excellent scenes of passion in Shakespeare, or in Fletcher: for love-scenes, you will find few among them; their tragic poets dealt not with that soft passion, but with lust, cruelty, revenge, ambition, and those bloody actions they produced; which were more capable of raising horror than compassion in an audience: leaving love untouched, whose gentleness would have tempered them; which is the most frequent of all the passions, and which, being the private concernment of every person, is soothed by viewing its own image in a public entertainment.

" Among their comedies, we find a scene or two of tenderness, and that where you would least ex-

---

will be reborn, and many now in honor will go down, if usage pleases, which has right and law on its side" (*Ibid.,* 70–72). **34.** *Mistaque . . . acantho:* "The earth profusely will yield marsh-lilies and acanthus" (*Eclogues,* IV.20). **35.** *mirantur . . . carinas:* "the woods and waves wonder at the strange sight of shields shining over the water, and of ships floating there" (*Aeneid,* VIII.91). **36.** *quem . . . coeli:* "which, if I may be so bold, I shall call the Palace of highest heaven" (*Metamorphoses,* I.175). **37.** *et . . . pompas:* "and the Capitol shall see long processions" (*Ibid.,* I.561). **38.** *Si . . . dixisset!:* "If he had said all things thus!"

39. *Omne . . . vincit:* "Tragedy surpasses all kinds of writing in dignity."

pect it, in Plautus; but to speak generally, their lovers say little, when they see each other, but *anima mea, vita mea;* [40] Ζωὴ καὶ ψυχῆ,[41] as the women in Juvenal's time used to cry out in the fury of their kindness. Any sudden gust of passion (as an ecstasy of love in an unexpected meeting) cannot better be expressed than in a word and a sigh, breaking one another. Nature is dumb on such occasions; and to make her speak would be to represent her unlike herself. But there are a thousand other concernments of lovers, as iealousies, complaints, contrivances, and the like, where not to open their minds at large to each other were to be wanting to their own love, and to the expectation of the audience; who watch the movements of their minds, as much as the changes of their fortunes. For the imaging of the first is properly the work of a poet; the latter he borrows from the historian."

Eugenius was proceeding in that part of his discourse, when Crites interrupted him. " I see," said he, " Eugenius and I are never like to have this question decided betwixt us; for he maintains the moderns have acquired a new perfection in writing; I can only grant they have altered the mode of it. Homer described his heroes men of great appetites, lovers of beef broiled upon the coals, and good fellows; contrary to the practice of the French Romances, whose heroes neither eat, nor drink, nor sleep, for love. Virgil makes Aeneas a bold avower of his own virtues:

Sum pius Aeneas, fama super aethera notus; [42]

which, in the civility of our poets is the character of a fanfaron or Hector: [43] for with us the knight takes occasion to walk out, or sleep, to avoid the vanity of telling his own story, which the trusty 'squire is ever to perform for him. So in their love-scenes, of which Eugenius spoke last, the ancients were more hearty, were more talkative: they writ love as it was then the mode to make it; and I will grant thus much to Eugenius, that perhaps one of their poets, had he lived in our age, *si foret hoc nostrum fato delapsus in aevum* [44] (as Horace says of Lucilius), he had altered many things; not that they were not natural before, but that he might accommodate himself to the age in which he lived. Yet in the meantime, we are not to conclude any-

thing rashly against those great men, but preserve to them the dignity of masters, and give that honor to their memories, *quos Libitina sacravit,* [45] part of which we expect may be paid to us in future times."

This moderation of Crites, as it was pleasing to all the company, so it put an end to that dispute; which Eugenius, who seemed to have the better of the argument, would urge no farther: but Lisideius, after he had acknowledge himself of Eugenius his opinion concerning the ancients, yet told him, he had forborne, till his discourse were ended, to ask him why he preferred the English plays above those of other nations? and whether we ought not to submit our stage to the exactness of our next neighbors?

"Though," said Eugenius, "I am at all times ready to defend the honor of my country against the French, and to maintain we are as well able to vanquish them with our pens, as our ancestors have been with their swords; yet, if you please," added he, looking upon Neander, " I will commit this cause to my friend's management; his opinion of our plays is the same with mine, and besides, there is no reason, that Crites and I, who have now left the stage, should re-enter so suddenly upon it; which is against the laws of comedy."

"If the question had been stated," replied Lisideius, "who had writ best, the French or English, forty years ago, I should have been of your opinion, and adjudged the honor to our own nation; but since that time " (said he, turning towards Neander), "we have been so long together bad Englishmen that we had not leisure to be good poets. Beaumont, Fletcher, and Jonson (who were only capable of bringing us to that degree of perfection which we have) were just then leaving the world; as if in an age of so much horror, wit and those milder studies of humanity had no farther business among us. But the Muses, who ever follow peace, went to plant in another country: it was then that the great Cardinal of Richelieu began to take them into his protection; and that, by his encouragement, Corneille, and some other Frenchmen, reformed their theatre (which before was as much below ours, as it now surpasses it and the rest of Europe). But because Crites in his discourse for the ancients has prevented me, by observing many rules of the stage which the moderns have borrowed from them, I shall only, in short, demand of you, whether you are not convinced that of all

---

40. *anima . . . mea:* "my soul, my life."   41. Ζωὴ καὶ ψυχῆ: "Life and soul."   42. *Sum . . . notus:* "I am the excellent Aeneas, famous beyond the skies" (*Aeneid*, I.378-79).   43. Hector: braggart.   44. *si . . . aevum:* "if fate had brought him down to our time."

45. *quos . . . sacravit:* "whom the goddess of death has sanctified."

nations the French have best observed them? In the unity of time you find them so scrupulous that it yet remains a dispute among their poets, whether the artificial day of twelve hours, more or less, be not meant by Aristotle, rather than the natural one of twenty-four; and consequently, whether all plays ought not to be reduced into that compass. This I can testify, that in all their dramas writ within these last twenty years and upwards, I have not observed any that have extended the time to thirty hours: in the unity of place they are full as scrupulous; for many of their critics limit it to that very spot of ground where the play is supposed to begin; none of them exceed the compass of the same town or city. The unity of action in all their plays is yet more conspicuous; for they do not burden them with under-plots, as the English do: which is the reason why many scenes of our tragi-comedies carry on a design that is nothing of kin to the main plot; and that we see two distinct webs in a play, like those in ill-wrought stuffs; and two actions, that is, two plays, carried on together, to the confounding of the audience; who, before they are warm in their concernments for one part, are diverted to another; and by that means espouse the interest of neither. From hence likewise it arises that the one half of our actors are not known to the other. They keep their distances, as if they were Montagues and Capulets, and seldom begin an acquaintance till the last scene of the fifth act, when they are all to meet upon the stage. There is no theatre in the world has anything so absurd as the English tragi-comedy; 'tis a drama of our own invention, and the fashion of it is enough to proclaim it so; here a course of mirth, there another of sadness and passion, and a third of honor and a duel: thus, in two hours and a half, we run through all the fits of Bedlam. The French affords you as much variety on the same day, but they do it not so unseasonably, or *mal à propos*,[46] as we: our poets present you the play and the farce together; and our stages still retain somewhat of the original civility of the Red Bull: [47]

Atque ursum et pugiles media inter carmina poscunt.[48]

The end of tragedies or serious plays, says Aristotle, is to beget admiration, compassion, or concernment; but are not mirth and compassion things incompatible? and is it not evident that the poet must of

necessity destroy the former by intermingling of the latter? that is, he must ruin the sole end and object of his tragedy, to introduce somewhat that is forced into it, and is not of the body of it. Would you not think that physician mad, who, having prescribed a purge, should immediately order you to take restringents?

"But to leave our plays, and return to theirs. I have noted one great advantage they have had in the plotting of their tragedies; that is, they are always grounded upon some known history: according to that of Horace, *Ex noto fictum carmen sequar;* [49] and in that they have so imitated the ancients that they have surpassed them. For the ancients, as was observed before, took for the foundation of their plays some poetical fiction, such as under that consideration could move but little concernment in the audience, because they already knew the event of it. But the French goes farther:

Atque ita mentitur, sic veris falsa remiscet
Primo ne medium, medio ne discrepet imum.[50]

He so interweaves truth with probable fiction that he puts a pleasing fallacy upon us; mends the intrigues of fate, and dispenses with the severity of history, to reward that virtue which has been rendered to us there unfortunate. Sometimes the story has left the success so doubtful that the writer is free, by the privilege of a poet, to take that which of two or more relations will best suit with his design: as for example, in the death of Cyrus, whom Justin and some others report to have perished in the Scythian war, but Xenophon affirms to have died in his bed of extreme old age. Nay, more, when the event is past dispute, even then we are willing to be deceived, and the poet, if he contrives it with appearance of truth, has all the audience of his party; at least during the time his play is acting: so naturally we are kind to virtue, when our own interest is not in question, that we take it up as the general concernment of mankind. On the other side, if you consider the historical plays of Shakespeare, they are rather so many chronicles of kings, or the business many times of thirty or forty years, cramped into a representation of two hours and a half; which is not to imitate or paint nature, but rather to draw her in miniature, to take her in little; to look upon her through the wrong end of

---

46. *mal à propos:* "inappropriately."   47. **Red Bull:** a popular theater, dedicated to many diversions.   48. *Atque . . . poscunt:* "And in the middle of the play they call for a bear, and boxers" (Horace, *Epistles*, II.i.185).

49. *Ex . . . sequar:* "I will make my poetry out of familiar materials" (*Ars Poetica*, 240).   50. *Atque . . . imum:* "And he so tells his story, mingling false with true, that neither the middle is inconsistent with the beginning, nor the end with the middle" (*Ibid.*, 151–52).

a perspective,[51] and receive her images not only much less, but infinitely more imperfect than the life: this, instead of making a play delightful, renders it ridiculous:

Quodcunque ostendis mihi sic, incredulus odi.[52]

For the spirit of man cannot be satisfied but with truth, or at least verisimility; and a poem is to contain, if not τὰ ἔτυμα,[53] yet ἐτύμοισιν ὁμοῖα,[54] as one of the Greek poets has expressed it.

"Another thing in which the French differ from us and from the Spaniards, is that they do not embarrass, or cumber themselves with too much plot; they only represent so much of a story as will constitute one whole and great action sufficient for a play; we, who undertake more, do but multiply adventures which, not being produced from one another, as effects from causes, but rarely following, constitute many actions in the drama, and consequently make it many plays.

"But by pursuing closely one argument, which is not cloyed with many turns, the French have gained more liberty for verse, in which they write; they have leisure to dwell on a subject which deserves it; and to represent the passions (which we have acknowledged to be the poet's work), without being hurried from one thing to another, as we are in the plays of Calderón, which we have seen lately upon our theatres under the name of Spanish plots. I have taken notice but of one tragedy of ours whose plot has that uniformity and unity of design in it which I have commended in the French; and that is *Rollo*,[55] or rather, under the name of *Rollo*, or the story of Bassianus and Geta in Herodian: there indeed the plot is neither large nor intricate, but just enough to fill the minds of the audience, not to cloy them. Besides, you see it founded upon the truth of history — only the time of the action is not reducible to the strictness of the rules; and you see in some places a little farce mingled, which is below the dignity of the other parts, and in this all our poets are extremely peccant: even Ben Jonson himself, in *Sejanus* and *Catiline,* has given us this oleo[56] of a play, this unnatural mixture of comedy and tragedy; which to me sounds just as ridiculously as the history of David with the merry humors of

Golia's. In *Sejanus* you may take notice of the scene betwixt Livia and the physician which is a pleasant satire upon the artificial helps of beauty: in *Catiline* you may see the parliament of women; the little envies of them to one another; and all that passes betwixt Curio and Fulvia: scenes admirable in their kind, but of an ill mingle with the rest.

"But I return again to the French writers, who, as I have said, do not burden themselves too much with plot, which has been reproached to them by an ingenious person of our nation as a fault; for, he says, they commonly make but one person considerable in a play; they dwell on him, and his concernments, while the rest of the persons are only subservient to set him off. If he intends this by it — that there is one person in the play who is of greater dignity than the rest, he must tax, not only theirs, but those of the ancients, and which he would be loth to do, the best of ours; for it is impossible but that one person must be more conspicuous in it than any other, and consequently the greatest share in the action must devolve on him. We see it so in the management of all affairs; even in the most equal aristocracy, the balance cannot be so justly poised but some one will be superior to the rest, either in parts, fortune, interest, or the consideration of some glorious exploit; which will reduce the greatest part of business into his hands.

"But, if he would have us to imagine, that in exalting one character the rest of them are neglected, and that all of them have not some share or other in the action of the play, I desire him to produce any of Corneille's tragedies, wherein every person, like so many servants in a well-governed family, has not some employment, and who is not necessary to the carrying on of the plot, or at least to your understanding it.

"There are indeed some protatic[57] persons in the ancients, whom they make use of in their plays, either to hear or to give the relation: but the French avoid this with great address, making their narrations only to, or by such, who are some way interested in the main design. And now I am speaking of relations, I cannot take a fitter opportunity to add this in favor of the French, that they often use them with better judgment and more *à propos* than the English do. Not that I commend narrations in general — but there are two sorts of them. One of those things which are antecedent to the play, and are related to make the conduct of it

51. perspective: telescope.   52. *Quodcunque . . . odi:* "Incredulous, I loathe what you thus present to me" (*Ibid.,* 188). 53. τὰ ἔτυμα: "the truth."   54. ἐτύμοισιν ὁμοῖα: "things like the truth."   55. Rollo: John Fletcher's *The Bloody Brother or Rollo, Duke of Normandy.*   56. oleo: hash.

57. protatic: introductory.

more clear to us. But 'tis a fault to choose such subjects for the stage as will force us on that rock because we see they are seldom listened to by the audience, and that is many times the ruin of the play; for, being once let pass without attention, the audience can never recover themselves to understand the plot: and indeed it is somewhat unreasonable that they should be put to so much trouble, as that, to comprehend what passes in their sight, they must have recourse to what was done, perhaps, ten or twenty years ago.

"But there is another sort of relations, that is, of things happening in the action of the play, and supposed to be done behind the scenes; and this is many times both convenient and beautiful; for by it the French avoid the tumult to which we are subject in England, by representing duels, battles, and the like; which renders our stage too like the theatres where they fight for prizes. For what is more ridiculous than to represent an army with a drum and five men behind it; all which the hero of the other side is to drive in before him; or to see a duel fought, and one slain with two or three thrusts of the foils, which we know are so blunted that we might give a man an hour to kill another in good earnest with them.

"I have observed that in all our tragedies, the audience cannot forbear laughing when the actors are to die; it is the most comic part of the whole play. All *passions* may be lively represented on the stage, if to the well-writing of them the actor supplies a good commanded voice, and limbs that move easily, and without stiffness; but there are many *actions* which can never be imitated to a just height: dying especially is a thing which none but a Roman gladiator could naturally perform on the stage, when he did not imitate or represent, but do it; and therefore it is better to omit the representation of it.

"The words of a good writer, which describe it lively, will make a deeper impression of belief in us than all the actor can insinuate into us, when he seems to fall dead before us; as a poet in the description of a beautiful garden, or a meadow, will please our imagination more than the place itself can please our sight. When we see death represented, we are convinced it is but fiction; but when we hear it related, our eyes, the strongest witnesses, are wanting, which might have undeceived us; and we are all willing to favor the sleight, when the poet does not too grossly impose on us. They therefore who imagine these relations would make no

concernment in the audience, are deceived, by confounding them with the other, which are of things antecedent to the play: those are made often in cold blood, as I may say, to the audience; but these are warmed with our concernments, which were before awakened in the play. What the philosophers say of motion, that, when it is once begun, it continues of itself, and will do so to eternity, without some stop put to it, is clearly true on this occasion: the soul being already moved with the characters and fortunes of those imaginary persons, continues going of its own accord; and we are no more weary to hear what becomes of them when they are not on the stage, than we are to listen to the news of an absent mistress. But it is objected, that if one part of the play may be related, then why not all? I answer, some parts of the action are more fit to be represented, some to be related. Corneille says judiciously that the poet is not obliged to expose to view all particular actions which conduce to the principal: he ought to select such of them to be seen, which will appear with the greatest beauty, either by the magnificence of the show or the vehemence of the passions they produce, or some other charm which they have in them; and let the rest arrive to the audience by narration. 'Tis a great mistake in us to believe the French present no part of the action on the stage; every alteration or crossing of a design, every new-sprung passion, and turn of it, is a part of the action, and much the noblest, except we conceive nothing to be action till the players come to blows; as if the painting of the hero's mind were not more properly the poet's work than the strength of his body. Nor does this anything contradict the opinion of Horace, where he tells us,

Segnius irritant animos demissa per aurem,
Quam quae sunt oculis subjecta fidelibus.[58]

For he says immediately after,

Non tamen intus
Digna geri promes in scenam; multaque; tolles
Ex oculis, quae mox narret facundia praesens.[59]

Among which many he recounts some:

Nec pueros coram populo Medea trucidet,
Aut in avem Progne mutetur, Cadmus in anguem,[60] etc.

---

58. *Segnius . . . fidelibus:* "What we hear sinks in more slowly than what we see, for we believe our eyes" (*Ibid.*, 180–81). **59.** *Non . . . praesens:* "You will not show things that ought to happen off the stage, and you will conceal things a witness can narrate." **60.** *Nec . . . anguem:* "Nor should Medea kill her children in public, nor Procne be changed to a bird, nor Cadmus to a serpent" (*Ibid.*, 185–87).

That is, those actions which by reason of their cruelty will cause aversion in us, or by reason of their impossibility, unbelief, ought either wholly to be avoided by a poet, or only delivered by narration. To which we may have leave to add, such as, to avoid tumult (as was before hinted), or to reduce the plot into a more reasonable compass of time, or for defect of beauty in them, are rather to be related than presented to the eye. Examples of all these kinds are frequent, not only among all the ancients, but in the best received of our English poets. We find Ben Jonson using them in his *Magnetic Lady,* where one comes out from dinner, and relates the quarrels and disorders of it, to save the undecent appearance of them on the stage, and to abbreviate the story; and this in express imitation of Terence, who had done the same before him in his *Eunuch,* where Pythias makes the like relation of what happened within at the soldiers' entertainment. The relations likewise of Sejanus's death, and the prodigies before it, are remarkable; the one of which was hid from sight, to avoid the horror and tumult of the representation; the other, to shun the introducing of things impossible to be believed. In that excellent play, *The King and No King,* Fletcher goes yet farther; for the whole unraveling of the plot is done by narration in the fifth act, after the manner of the ancients; and it moves great concernment in the audience, though it be only a relation of what was done many years before the play. I could multiply other instances, but these are sufficient to prove that there is no error in choosing a subject which requires this sort of narrations; in the ill management of them, there may.

"But I find I have been too long in this discourse, since the French have many other excellencies not common to us; as that you never see any of their plays end with a conversion, or simple change of will, which is the ordinary way which our poets use to end theirs. It shows little art in the conclusion of a dramatic poem, when they who have hindered the felicity during the four acts, desist from it in the fifth, without some powerful cause to take them off their design; and though I deny not but such reasons may be found, yet it is a path that is cautiously to be trod, and the poet is to be sure he convinces the audience that the motive is strong enough. As for example, the conversion of the Usurer in *The Scornful Lady* seems to me a little forced; for, being an Usurer, which implies a lover of money to the highest degree of

covetousness,—and such the poet has represented him,—the account he gives for the sudden change is, that he has been duped by the wild young fellow; which in reason might render him more wary another time, and make him punish himself with harder fare and coarser clothes, to get up again what he had lost: but that he should look on it as a judgment, and so repent, we may expect to hear in a sermon, but I should never endure it in a play.

"I pass by this; neither will I insist on the care they take that no person after his first entrance shall ever appear but the business which brings him upon the stage shall be evident; which rule, if observed, must needs render all the events in the play more natural; for there you see the probability of every accident, in the cause that produced it; and that which appears chance in the play will seem so reasonable to you, that you will there find it almost necessary: so that in the exit of the actor you have a clear account of his purpose and design in the next entrance (though, if the scene be well wrought, the event will commonly deceive you); for there is nothing so absurd, says Corneille, as for an actor to leave the stage only because he has no more to say.

"I should now speak of the beauty of their rhyme, and the just reason I have to prefer that way of writing in tragedies before ours in blank verse; but because it is partly received by us, and therefore not altogether peculiar to them, I will say no more of it in relation to their plays. For our own, I doubt not but it will exceedingly beautify them; and I can see but one reason why it should not generally obtain, that is, because our poets write so ill in it. This indeed may prove a more prevailing argument than all others which are used to destroy it, and therefore I am only troubled when great and judicious poets, and those who are acknowledged such, have writ or spoke against it: as for others, they are to be answered by that one sentence of an ancient author: — *Sed ut primo ad consequendos eos quos priores ducimus, accendimur, ita ubi aut praeteriri, aut aequari eos posse desperavimus, studium cum spe senescit: quod, scilicet, assequi non potest, sequi desinit; . . . praeteritoque eo in quo eminere non possumus, aliquid in quo nitamur, conquirimus."* [61]

61. *Sed . . . conquirimus:* "But as at first we strive to equal those who are beyond us, so, when we despair of either equaling or surpassing them, our zeal dies with our hope, and, giving up what we cannot attain, we develop other ambitions" (Velleius Paterculus, I.17).

Lisideius concluded in this manner; and Neander, after a little pause, thus answered him:

"I shall grant Lisideius, without much dispute, a great part of what he has urged against us; for I acknowledge that the French contrive their plots more regularly, and observe the laws of comedy and decorum of the stage (to speak generally) with more exactness than the English. Farther, I deny not but he has taxed us justly in some irregularities of ours, which he has mentioned; yet, after all, I am of opinion that neither our faults nor their virtues are considerable enough to place them above us.

"For the lively imitation of nature being in the definition of a play, those which best fulfil that law ought to be esteemed superior to the others. 'Tis true, those beauties of the French poesy are such as will raise perfection higher where it is, but are not sufficient to give it where it is not: they are indeed the beauties of a statue, but not of a man, because not animated with the soul of poesy, which is imitation of humor [62] and passions: and this Lisideius himself, or any other, however biased to their party, cannot but acknowledge, if he will either compare the humors of our comedies, or the characters of our serious plays, with theirs. He who will look upon theirs which have been written till these last ten years, or thereabouts, will find it a hard matter to pick out two or three passable humors amongst them. Corneille himself, their arch-poet, what has he produced except *The Liar*, and you know how it was cried up in France; but when it came upon the English stage, though well translated, and that part of Durant acted to so much advantage as I am confident never received in its own country, the most favorable to it would not put it in competition with many of Fletcher's or Ben Jonson's. In the rest of Corneille's comedies you have little humor; he tells you himself his way is first to show two lovers in good intelligence with each other; in the working up of the play to embroil them by some mistake, and in the latter end to clear it and reconcile them.

"But of late years Molière, the younger Corneille, Quinault, and some others, have been imitating afar off the quick turns and graces of the English stage. They have mixed their serious plays with mirth, like our tragi-comedies, since the death of Cardinal Richelieu; which Lisideius and many others not observing, have commended that in them

for a virtue which they themselves no longer practise. Most of their new plays are, like some of ours, derived from the Spanish novels. There is scarce one of them without a veil, and a trusty Diego, who drolls much after the rate of the *Adventures*. But their humors, if I may grace them with that name, are so thin-sown, that never above one of them comes up in any play. I dare take upon me to find more variety of them in some one play of Ben Jonson's than in all theirs together; as he who has seen *The Alchemist, The Silent Woman,* or *Bartholomew Fair,* cannot but acknowledge with me.

"I grant the French have performed what was possible on the ground-work of the Spanish plays; what was pleasant before, they have made regular: but there is not above one good play to be writ on all those plots; they are too much alike to please often; which we need not the experience of our own stage to justify. As for their new way of mingling mirth with serious plot, I do not, with Lisideius, condemn the thing, though I cannot approve of their manner of doing it. He tells us, we cannot so speedily recollect ourselves after a scene of great passion and concernment, as to pass to another of mirth and humor, and to enjoy it with any relish: but why should he imagine the soul of man more heavy than his senses? Does not the eye pass from an unpleasant object to a pleasant in a much shorter time than is required to this? and does not the unpleasantness of the first commend the beauty of the latter? The old rule of logic might have convinced him, that contraries, when placed near, set off each other. A continued gravity keeps the spirit too much bent; we must refresh it sometimes, as we bait in a journey that we may go on with greater ease. A scene of mirth, mixed with tragedy, has the same effect upon us which our music has betwixt the acts; which we find a relief to us from the best plots and language of the stage, if the discourses have been long. I must therefore have stronger arguments, ere I am convinced that compassion and mirth in the same subject destroy each other; and in the meantime cannot but conclude, to the honor of our nation, that we have invented, increased, and perfected a more pleasant way of writing for the stage, than was ever known to the ancients or moderns of any nation, which is tragi-comedy.

"And this leads me to wonder why Lisideius and many others should cry up the barrenness of the French plots above the variety and copiousness

---

62. humor: Cf. p. 195 above.

of the English. Their plots are single; they carry on one design, which is pushed forward by all the actors, every scene in the play contributing and moving towards it. Our plays, besides the main design, have under-plots or by-concernments, of less considerable persons and intrigues, which are carried on with the motion of the main plot; as they say the orb of the fixed stars, and those of the planets, though they have motions of their own, are whirled about by the motion of the *primum mobile;* [63] in which they are contained. That similitude expresses much of the English stage; for if contrary motions may be found in nature to agree; if a planet can got east and west at the same time; — one way by virtue of his own motion, the other by the force of the first mover; — it will not be difficult to imagine how the under-plot, which is only different, not contrary to the great design, may naturally be conducted along with it.

"Eugenius has already shown us, from the confessions of the French poets, that the unity of action is sufficiently preserved, if all the imperfect actions of the play are conducing to the main design; but when those petty intrigues of a play are so ill ordered that they have no coherence with the other, I must grant that Lisideius has reason to tax that want of due connection; for co-ordination in a play is as dangerous and unnatural as in a state. In the meantime he must acknowledge, our variety, if well ordered, will afford a greater pleasure to the audience.

"As for his other argument, that by pursuing one single theme they gain an advantage to express and work up the passions, I wish any example he could bring from them would make it good; for I confess their verses are to me the coldest I have ever read. Neither, indeed, is it possible for them, in the way they take, so to express passion, as that the effects of it should appear in the concernment of an audience, their speeches being so many declamations, which tire us with their length; so that instead of persuading us to grieve for their imaginary heroes, we are concerned for our own trouble, as we are in tedious visits of bad company; we are in pain till they are gone. When the French stage came to be reformed by Cardinal Richelieu, those long harangues were introduced to comply with the gravity of a churchman. Look upon the *Cinna* and the *Pompey;* they are not so properly to be called plays, as long discourses of reason of state; and *Polieucte* in matters of religion is as solemn as the long stops upon our organs. Since that time it is grown into a custom, and their actors speak by the hour-glass, like our parsons; nay, they account it the grace of their parts, and think themselves disparaged by the poet, if they may not twice or thrice in a play entertain the audience with a speech of an hundred lines. I deny not but this may suit well enough with the French; for as we, who are a more sullen people, come to be diverted at our plays, so they, who are of an airy and gay temper, come thither to make themselves more serious: and this I conceive to be one reason why comedies are more pleasing to us, and tragedies to them. But to speak generally: it cannot be denied that short speeches and replies are more apt to move the passions and beget concernment in us, than the other; for it is unnatural for anyone in a gust of passion to speak long together, or for another in the same condition to suffer him, without interruption. Grief and passion are like floods raised in little brooks by a sudden rain; they are quickly up; and if the concernment be poured unexpectedly in upon us, it overflows us: but a long sober shower gives them leisure to run out as they came in, without troubling the ordinary current. As for comedy, repartee is one of its chiefest graces; the greatest pleasure of the audience is a chase of wit, kept up on both sides, and swiftly managed. And this our forefathers, if not we, have had in Fletcher's plays, to a much higher degree of perfection than the French poets can reasonably hope to reach.

"There is another part of Lisideius his discourse, in which he rather excused our neighbors than commended them; that is, for aiming only to make one person considerable in their plays. 'Tis very true what he has urged, that one character in all plays, even without the poet's care, will have advantage of all the others; and that the design of the whole drama will chiefly depend on it. But this hinders not that there may be more shining characters in the play: many persons of a second magnitude, nay, some so very near, so almost equal to the first, that greatness may be opposed to greatness, and all the persons be made considerable, not only by their quality, but their action. 'Tis evident that the more the persons are, the greater will be the variety of the plot. If then the parts are managed so regularly, that the beauty of the whole be kept entire, and that the variety become not a perplexed and confused mass of accidents, you will

63. *primum mobile:* the first or outermost sphere, that moves all the others.

find it infinitely pleasing to be led in a labyrinth of design, where you see some of your way before you, yet discern not the end till you arrive at it. And that all this is practicable, I can produce for examples many of our English plays: as *The Maid's Tragedy, The Alchemist, The Silent Woman.* I was going to have named *The Fox,* but that the unity of design seems not exactly observed in it; for there appear two actions in the play; the first naturally ending with the fourth act; the second forced from it in the fifth; which yet is the less to be condemned in him, because the disguise of Volpone, though it suited not with his character as a crafty or covetous person, agreed well enough with that of a voluptuary; and by it the poet gained the end at which he aimed, the punishment of vice, and the reward of virtue, both which that disguise produced. So that to judge equally of it, it was an excellent fifth act, but not so naturally proceeding from the former.

"But to leave this, and pass to the latter part of Lisideius his discourse, which concerns relations: I must acknowledge with him, that the French have reason to hide that part of the action which would occasion too much tumult on the stage, and to choose rather to have it made known by narration to the audience. Farther, I think it very convenient, for the reasons he has given, that all incredible actions were removed; but whether custom has so insinuated itself into our countrymen, or nature has so formed them to fierceness, I know not; but they will scarcely suffer combats and other objects of horror to be taken from them. And indeed, the indecency of tumults is all which can be objected against fighting: for why may not our imagination as well suffer itself to be deluded with the probability of it, as with any other thing in the play? For my part, I can with as great ease persuade myself that the blows are given in good earnest, as I can that they who strike them are kings or princes, or those persons which they represent. For objects of incredibility,—I would be satisfied from Lisideius, whether we have any so removed from all appearance of truth, as are those of Corneille's *Andromede;* a play which has been frequented the most of any he has writ. If the Perseus, or the son of a heathen god, the Pegasus, and the Monster, were not capable to choke a strong belief, let him blame any representation of ours hereafter. Those indeed were objects of delight; yet the reason is the same as to the probability: for he makes it not a ballet or masque, but a play, which is to resemble truth. But for death, that it ought not to be represented, I have, besides the arguments alleged by Lisideius, the authority of Ben Jonson, who has forborne it in his tragedies; for both the death of Sejanus and Catiline are related: though in the latter I cannot but observe one irregularity of that great poet; he has removed the scene in the same act from Rome to Catiline's army, and from thence again to Rome; and besides, has allowed a very inconsiderable time, after Catiline's speech, for the striking of the battle, and the return of Petreius, who is to relate the event of it to the senate: which I should not animadvert on him, who was otherwise a painful observer of τὸ πρέπον, or the *decorum* of the stage, if he had not used extreme severity in his judgment on the incomparable Shakespeare for the same fault. — To conclude on this subject of relations; if we are to be blamed for showing too much of the action, the French are as faulty for discovering too little of it: a mean betwixt both should be observed by every judicious writer, so as the audience may neither be left unsatisfied by not seeing what is beautiful, or shocked by beholding what is either incredible or undecent.

"I hope I have already proved in this discourse, that though we are not altogether so punctual as the French in observing the laws of comedy, yet our errors are so few, and little, and those things wherein we excel them so considerable, that we ought of right to be preferred before them. But what will Lisideius say, if they themselves acknowledge they are too strictly bounded by those laws, for breaking which he has blamed the English? I will allege Corneille's words, as I find them in the end of his *Discourse of the Three Unities: Il est facile aux spéculatifs d'estre sévères,* etc. ' 'Tis easy for speculative persons to judge severely; but if they would produce to public view ten or twelve pieces of this nature, they would perhaps give more latitude to the rules than I have done, when by experience they had known how much we are limited and constrained by them, and how many beauties of the stage they banished from it.' To illustrate a little what he has said: By their servile observations of the unities of time and place, and integrity of scenes, they have brought on themselves that dearth of plot, and narrowness of imagination, which may be observed in all their plays. How many beautiful accidents might naturally happen in two or three days, which cannot arrive with any probability in the compass of twenty-four hours? There is time to be allowed also for maturity of design, which, amongst great and prudent persons, such as are often represented in tragedy, cannot, with any likelihood of truth, be brought to pass at so short a warning. Farther; by tying themselves strictly to the unity of place, and unbroken scenes, they are forced many times to omit some beauties which cannot be shown where the act began; but might, if the scene were interrupted, and the stage cleared for the persons to enter in another place; and therefore the French poets are often forced upon absurdities; for if the act begins in a chamber, all the persons in the play must have some business or other to come thither, or else they are not to be shown that act; and sometimes their characters are very unfitting to appear there: as, suppose it were the king's bed-chamber; yet the meanest man in the tragedy must come and dispatch his business there, rather than in the lobby or courtyard (which is fitter for him), for fear the stage should be cleared, and the scenes broken. Many times they fall by it in a greater inconvenience; for they keep their scenes unbroken, and yet change the place; as in one of their newest plays, where the act begins in the street. There a gentleman is to meet his friend; he sees him with his man, coming out from his father's house; they talk together, and the first goes out: the second, who is a lover, has made an appointment with his mistress; she appears at the window, and then we are to imagine the scene lies under it. This gentleman is called away, and leaves his servant with his mistress; presently her father is heard from within; the young lady is afraid the serving-man should be discovered, and thrusts him into a place of safety, which is supposed to be her closet. After this, the father enters to the daughter, and now the scene is in a house; for he is seeking from one room to another for this poor Philipin, or French Diego, who is heard from within, drolling and breaking many a miserable conceit on the subject of his sad condition. In this ridiculous manner the play goes forward, the stage being never empty all the while: so that the street, the window, the houses, and the closet, are made to walk about, and the persons to stand still. Now what, I beseech you, is more easy than to write a regular French play, or more difficult than to write an irregular English one, like those of Fletcher, or of Shakespeare?

"If they content themselves, as Corneille did, with some flat design, which, like an ill riddle, is found out ere it be half proposed, such plots we can make every way regular, as easily as they; but

whenever they endeavor to rise to any quick turns and counterturns of plot, as some of them have attempted, since Corneille's plays have been less in vogue, you see they write as irregularly as we, though they cover it more speciously. Hence the reason is perspicuous why no French plays, when translated, have, or ever can succeed on the English stage. For, if you consider the plots, our own are fuller of variety; if the writing, ours are more quick and fuller of spirit; and therefore 'tis a strange mistake in those who decry the way of writing plays in verse, as if the English therein imitated the French. We have borrowed nothing from them; our plots are weaved in English looms: we endeavor therein to follow the variety and greatness of characters which are derived to us from Shakespeare and Fletcher; the copiousness and well-knitting of the intrigues we have from Jonson; and for the verse itself we have English precedents of elder date than any of Corneille's plays. Not to name our old comedies before Shakespeare, which were all writ in verse of six feet, or Alexandrines, such as the French now use — I can show in Shakespeare many scenes of rhyme together, and the like in Ben Jonson's tragedies: in *Catiline* and *Sejanus* sometimes thirty or forty lines — I mean besides the Chorus, or the monologues; which, by the way, showed Ben no enemy to this way of writing, especially if you read his *Sad Shepherd,* which goes sometimes on rhyme, sometimes on blank verse, like an horse who eases himself on trot and amble. You find him likewise commending Fletcher's pastoral of *The Faithful Shepherdess,* which is for the most part in rhyme, though not refined to that purity to which it hath since been brought. And these examples are enough to clear us from a servile imitation of the French.

"But to return whence I have digressed: I dare boldly affirm these two things of the English drama; — First, that we have many plays of ours as regular as any of theirs, and which, besides, have more variety of plot and characters; and secondly, that in most of the irregular plays of Shakespeare or Fletcher (for Ben Jonson's are for the most part regular), there is a more masculine fancy and greater spirit in the writing than there is in any of the French. I could produce, even in Shakespeare's and Fletcher's works, some plays which are almost exactly formed; as *The Merry Wives of Windsor,* and *The Scornful Lady:* but because (generally speaking) Shakespeare, who writ first, did not perfectly observe the laws of comedy, and

Fletcher, who came nearer to perfection, yet through carelessness made many faults; I will take the pattern of a perfect play from Ben Jonson, who was a careful and learned observer of the dramatic laws, and from all his comedies I shall select *The Silent Woman;* of which I will make a short examen,[64] according to those rules which the French observe."

As Neander was beginning to examine *The Silent Woman,* Eugenius, earnestly regarding him; "I beseech you, Neander," said he, "gratify the company, and me in particular, so far, as before you speak of the play, to give us a character of the author; and tell us frankly your opinion, whether you do not think all writers, both French and English, ought to give place to him."

"I fear," replied Neander, "that in obeying your commands I shall draw some envy on myself. Besides, in performing them, it will be first necessary to speak somewhat of Shakespeare and Fletcher, his rivals in poesy; and one of them, in my opinion, at least his equal, perhaps his superior.

"To begin, then, with Shakespeare. He was the man who of all modern, and perhaps ancient poets, had the largest and most comprehensive soul. All the images of nature were still present to him, and he drew them, not laboriously, but luckily; when he describes anything, you more than see it, you feel it too. Those who accuse him to have wanted learning give him the greater commendation: he was naturally learned; he needed not the spectacles of books to read nature; he looked inwards, and found her there. I cannot say he is everywhere alike; were he so, I should do him injury to compare him with the greatest of mankind. He is many times flat, insipid; his comic wit degenerating into clenches, his serious swelling into bombast. But he is always great when some great occasion is presented to him; no man can say he ever had a fit subject for his wit and did not then raise himself as high above the rest of poets,

Quantum lenta solent inter viburna cupressi.[65]

The consideration of this made Mr. Hales[66] of Eaton say, that there is no subject of which any poet ever writ, but he would produce it much better done in Shakespeare; and however others are now generally preferred before him, yet the age wherein he lived, which had contemporaries with him

Fletcher and Jonson, never equalled them to him in their esteem: and in the last king's court, when Ben's reputation was at highest, Sir John Suckling, and with him the greater part of the courtiers, set our Shakespeare far above him.

"Beaumont and Fletcher, of whom I am next to speak, had, with the advantage of Shakespeare's wit, which was their precedent, great natural gifts, improved by study: Beaumont especially being so accurate a judge of plays, that Ben Jonson, while he lived, submitted all his writings to his censure, and, 'tis thought, used his judgment in correcting, if not contriving, all his plots. What value he had for him, appears by the verses he writ to him; and therefore I need speak no farther of it. The first play that brought Fletcher and him in esteem was their *Philaster:* for before that, they had written two or three very unsuccessfully, as the like is reported of Ben Jonson, before he writ *Every Man in His Humor.* Their plots were generally more regular than Shakespeare's, especially those which were made before Beaumont's death; and they understood and imitated the conversation of gentlemen much better; whose wild debaucheries, and quickness of wit in repartees, no poet before them could paint as they have done. Humor, which Ben Jonson derived from particular persons, they made it not their business to describe: they represented all the passions very lively, but above all, love. I am apt to believe the English language in them arrived to its highest perfection: what words have since been taken in, are rather superfluous than ornamental. Their plays are now the most pleasant and frequent entertainments of the stage; two of theirs being acted through the year for one of Shakespeare's or Jonson's: the reason is, because there is a certain gaiety in their comedies, and pathos in their more serious plays, which suit generally with all men's humors. Shakespeare's language is likewise a little obsolete, and Ben Jonson's wit comes short of theirs.

"As for Jonson, to whose character I am now arrived, if we look upon him while he was himself (for his last plays were but his dotage), I think him the most learned and judicious writer which any theatre ever had. He was a most severe judge of himself, as well as others. One cannot say he wanted wit, but rather that he was frugal of it. In his works you find little to retrench or alter. Wit, and language, and humor also in some measure we had before him; but something of art was wanting to the drama till he came. He managed

64. **examen:** analysis.   65. *Quantum . . . cupressi:* "As cypresses are taller than viburnums" (Virgil, *Eclogues,* I.26). 66. **Mr. Hales:** John Hales (d. 1656).

his strength to more advantage than any who preceded him. You seldom find him making love in any of his scenes, or endeavoring to move the passions; his genius was too sullen and saturnine to do it gracefully, especially when he knew he came after those who had performed both to such an height. Humor was his proper sphere; and in that he delighted most to represent mechanic people. He was deeply conversant in the ancients, both Greek and Latin, and he borrowed boldly from them: there is scarce a poet or historian among the Roman authors of those times whom he has not translated in *Sejanus* and *Catiline*. But he has done his robberies so openly, that one may see he fears not to be taxed by any law. He invades authors like a monarch; and what would be theft in other poets is only victory in him. With the spoils of these writers he so represents old Rome to us, in its rites, ceremonies, and customs, that if one of their poets had written either of his tragedies, we had seen less of it than in him. If there was any fault in his language, 'twas that he weaved it too closely and laboriously, in his comedies especially: perhaps, too, he did a little too much Romanize our tongue, leaving the words which he translated almost as much Latin as he found them: wherein, though he learnedly followed their language, he did not enough comply with the idiom of ours. If I would compare him with Shakespeare, I must acknowledge him the more correct poet, but Shakespeare the greater wit. Shakespeare was the Homer, or father of our dramatic poets; Jonson was the Virgil, the pattern of elaborate writing; I admire him, but I love Shakespeare. To conclude of him; as he has given us the most correct plays, so in the precepts which he has laid down in his *Discoveries,* we have as many and profitable rules for perfecting the stage, as any wherewith the French can furnish us.

"Having thus spoken of the author, I proceed to the examination of his comedy, *The Silent Woman.*

EXAMEN OF "THE SILENT WOMAN"

"To begin first with the length of the action; it is so far from exceeding the compass of a natural day, that it takes not up an artificial one. 'Tis all included in the limits of three hours and a half, which is no more than is required for the presentment on the stage: a beauty perhaps not much observed; if it had, we should not have looked on the Spanish translation of *Five Hours* with so much wonder. The scene of it is laid in London; the latitude of place is almost as little as you can imagine; for it lies all within the compass of two houses, and after the first act, in one. The continuity of scenes is observed more than in any of our plays, except his own *Fox* and *Alchemist.* They are not broken above twice or thrice at most in the whole comedy; and in the two best of Corneille's plays, the *Cid* and *Cinna,* they are interrupted once. The action of the play is entirely one; the end or aim of which is the settling Morose's estate on Dauphine. The intrigue of it is the greatest and most noble of any pure unmixed comedy in any language; you see in it many persons of various characters and humors, and all delightful. As first, Morose, or an old man, to whom all noise but his own talking is offensive. Some who would be thought critics, say this humor of his is forced: but to remove that objection, we may consider him first to be naturally of a delicate hearing, as many are, to whom all sharp sounds are unpleasant; and secondly, we may attribute much of it to the peevishness of his age, or the wayward authority of an old man in his own house, where he may make himself obeyed; and to this the poet seems to allude in his name Morose. Besides this, I am assured from divers persons, that Ben Jonson was actually acquainted with such a man, one altogether as ridiculous as he is here represented. Others say, it is not enough to find one man of such an humor; it must be common to more, and the more common the more natural. To prove this, they instance in the best of comical characters, Falstaff. There are many men resembling him; old, fat, merry, cowardly, drunken, amorous, vain, and lying. But to convince these people, I need but tell them that humor is the ridiculous extravagance of conversation, wherein one man differs from all others. If then it be common, or communicated to many, how differs it from other men's? or what indeed causes it to be ridiculous so much as the singularity of it? As for Falstaff, he is not properly one humor, but a miscellany of humors or images, drawn from so many several men: that wherein he is singular is his wit, or those things he says *praeter expectatum,*[67] unexpected by the audience; his quick evasions, when you imagine him surprised, which, as they are extremely diverting of themselves, so receive a great addition from his person; for the very

67. *praeter expectatum:* "contrary to the expected."

sight of such an unwieldy old debauched fellow is a comedy alone. And here, having a place so proper for it, I cannot but enlarge somewhat upon this subject of humor into which I am fallen. The ancients had little of it in their comedies; for the τὸ γελοῖον [68] of the old comedy, of which Aristophanes was chief, was not so much to imitate a man, as to make the people laugh at some odd conceit, which had commonly somewhat of unnatural or obscene in it. Thus, when you see Socrates brought upon the stage, you are not to imagine him made ridiculous by the imitation of his actions, but rather by making him perform something very unlike himself; something so childish and absurd, as by comparing it with the gravity of the true Socrates, makes a ridiculous object for the spectators. In their new comedy which succeeded, the poets sought indeed to express the ἦθος, as in their tragedies the πάθος [69] of mankind. But this ἦθος contained only the general characters of men and manners; as old men, lovers, serving-men, courtezans, parasites, and such other persons as we see in their comedies; all which they made alike: that is, one old man or father, one lover, one courtezan, so like another, as if the first of them had begot the rest of every sort: *Ex homine hunc natum dicas.*[70] The same custom they observed likewise in their tragedies. As for the French, though they have the word *humeur* among them, yet they have small use of it in their comedies or farces; they being but ill imitations of the *ridiculum,* or that which stirred up laughter in the old comedy. But among the English 'tis otherwise: where by humor is meant some extravagant habit, passion, or affection, particular (as I have said before) to some one person, by the oddness of which, he is immediately distinguished from the rest of men; which being lively and naturally represented, most frequently begets that malicious pleasure in the audience which is testified by laughter; as all things which are deviations from customs are ever the aptest to produce it: though by the way this laughter is only accidental, as the person represented is fantastic or bizarre; but pleasure is essential to it, as the imitation of what is natural. The description of these humors, drawn from the knowledge and observation of particular persons, was the peculiar genius and talent of Ben Jonson; to whose play I now return.

" Besides Morose, there are at least nine or ten different characters and humors in *The Silent Woman;* all which persons have several concernments of their own, yet are all used by the poet to the conducting of the main design to perfection. I shall not waste time in commending the writing of this play; but I will give you my opinion, that there is more wit and acuteness of fancy in it than in any of Ben Jonson's. Besides that he has here described the conversation of gentlemen in the persons of True-Wit, and his friends, with more gaiety, air, and freedom, than in the rest of his comedies. For the contrivance of the plot, 'tis extreme, elaborate, and yet withal easy; for the λύσις, or untying of it, 'tis so admirable, that when it is done, no one of the audience would think the poet could have missed it; and yet it was concealed so much before the last scene, that any other way would sooner have entered into your thoughts. But I dare not take upon me to commend the fabric of it, because it is altogether so full of art, that I must unravel every scene in it to commend it as I ought. And this excellent contrivance is still the more to be admired, because 'tis comedy, where the persons are only of common rank, and their business private, not elevated by passions or high concernments, as in serious plays. Here everyone is a proper judge of all he sees, nothing is represented but that with which he daily converses: so that by consequence all faults lie open to discovery, and few are pardonable. 'Tis this which Horace has judiciously observed:

Creditur, ex medio quia res arcessit, habere
Sudoris minimum; sed habet Comedia tanto
Plus oneris, quanto veniae minus.[71]

" But our poet who was not ignorant of these difficulties has made use of all advantages; as he who designs a large leap takes his rise from the highest ground. One of these advantages is that which Corneille has laid down as the greatest which can arrive to any poem, and which he himself could never compass above thrice in all his plays; *viz.,* the making choice of some signal and long-expected day, whereon the action of the play is to depend. This day was that designed by Dauphine for the settling of his uncle's estate upon him; which to compass, he contrives to marry him. That the marriage had been plotted by him long before-

---

68. τὸ γελοῖον: "the ridiculous."   69. ἦθος: "character"; πάθος: "experience."   70. *Ex . . . dicas:* "You could say he was born of a human being."

71. *Creditur . . . minus:* "Comedy is thought to be easier because it takes its stuff from ordinary life; but it is harder, because fewer allowances are made for it" (*Epistles,* II.i.168).

hand, is made evident by what he tells True-Wit in the second act, that in one moment he had destroyed what he had been raising many months.

"There is another artifice of the poet, which I cannot here omit, because by the frequent practice of it in his comedies he has left it to us almost as a rule; that is, when he has any character or humor wherein he would show a *coup de maistre,* or his highest skill, he recommends it to your observation by a pleasant description of it before the person first appears. Thus, in *Bartholomew Fair* he gives you the pictures of Numps and Cokes, and in this those of Daw, Lafoole, Morose, and the Collegiate Ladies; all which you hear described before you see them. So that before they come upon the stage, you have a longing expectation of them, which prepares you to receive them favorably; and when they are there, even from their first appearance you are so far acquainted with them, that nothing of their humor is lost to you.

"I will observe yet one thing further of this admirable plot; the business of it rises in every act. The second is greater than the first; the third than the second; and so forward to the fifth. There too you see, till the very last scene, new difficulties arising to obstruct the action of the play; and when the audience is brought into despair that the business can naturally be effected, then, and not before, the discovery is made. But that the poet might entertain you with more variety all this while, he reserves some new characters to show you, which he opens not till the second and third act; in the second Morose, Daw, the Barber, and Otter; in the third the Collegiate Ladies: all which he moves afterwards in by-walks, or under-plots, as diversions to the main design, lest it should grow tedious, though they are still naturally joined with it, and somewhere or other subservient to it. Thus, like a skilful chess-player, by little and little he draws out his men, and makes his pawns of use to his greater persons.

"If this comedy and some others of his were translated into French prose (which would now be no wonder to them, since Molière has lately given them plays out of verse, which have not displeased them), I believe the controversy would soon be decided betwixt the two nations, even making them the judges. But we need not call our heroes to our aid. Be it spoken to the honor of the English, our nation can never want in any age such who are able to dispute the empire of wit with any people in the universe. And though the fury of a civil war, and

power for twenty years together abandoned to a barbarous race of men, enemies of all good learning, had buried the muses under the ruins of monarchy; yet, with the restoration of our happiness, we see revived poesy lifting up its head, and already shaking off the rubbish which lay so heavy on it. We have seen since his Majesty's return, many dramatic poems which yield not to those of any foreign nation, and which deserve all laurels but the English. I will set aside flattery and envy: it cannot be denied but we have had some little blemish either in the plot or writing of all those plays which have been made within these seven years; (and perhaps there is no nation in the world so quick to discern them, or so difficult to pardon them, as ours:) yet if we can persuade ourselves to use the candor of that poet, who, though the most severe of critics, has left us this caution by which to moderate our censures —

ubi plura nitent in carmine, non ego paucis
Offendar maculis; — [72]

if, in consideration of their many and great beauties, we can wink at some and little imperfections, if we, I say, can be thus equal to ourselves, I ask no favor from the French. And if I do not venture upon any particular judgment of our late plays, 'tis out of the consideration which an ancient writer gives me: *vivorum ut magna admiratio, ita censura difficilis:* [73] betwixt the extremes of admiration and malice, 'tis hard to judge uprightly of the living. Only I think it may be permitted me to say, that as it is no lessening to us to yield to some plays, and those not many, of our own nation in the last age, so can it be no addition to pronounce of our present poets, that they have far surpassed all the ancients, and the modern writers of other countries."

This was the substance of what was then spoken on that occasion; and Lisideius, I think, was going to reply, when he was prevented thus by Crites: "I am confident," said he, "that the most material things that can be said have been already urged on either side; if they have not, I must beg of Lisideius that he will defer his answer till another time: for I confess I have a joint quarrel to you both, because you have concluded, without any reason given for it, that rhyme is proper for the stage. I

72. *ubi . . . maculis:* "when there are many excellences in a poem, I shall not be offended by a few faults" (Horace, *Ars Poetica,* 351–52). 73. *vivorum . . . difficilis:* "living writers, being highly admired, are hard to judge" (Velleius Paterculus, II.36).

will not dispute how ancient it hath been among us to write this way; perhaps our ancestors knew no better till Shakespeare's time. I will grant it was not altogether left by him, and that Fletcher and Ben Jonson used it frequently in their Pastorals, and sometimes in other plays. Farther, — I will not argue whether we received it originally from our countrymen, or from the French; for that is an inquiry of as little benefit, as theirs who, in the midst of the great plague, were not so solicitous to provide against it, as to know whether we had it from the malignity of our own air, or by transportation from Holland. I have therefore only to affirm, that it is not allowable in serious plays; for comedies, I find you already concluding with me. To prove this, I might satisfy myself to tell you, how much in vain it is for you to strive against the stream of the people's inclination; the greatest part of which are prepossessed so much with those excellent plays of Shakespeare, Fletcher, and Ben Jonson, which have been written out of rhyme, that except you could bring them such as were written better in it, and those too by persons of equal reputation with them, it will be impossible for you to gain your cause with them, who will still be judges. This it is to which, in fine, all your reasons must submit. The unanimous consent of an audience is so powerful, that even Julius Caesar (as Macrobius reports of him), when he was perpetual dictator, was not able to balance it on the other side; but when Laberius, a Roman Knight, at his request contended in the Mime with another poet, he was forced to cry out, *Etiam favente me victus es, Laberi.*[74] But I will not on this occasion take the advantage of the greater number, but only urge such reasons against rhyme, as I find in the writings of those who have argued for the other way. First, then, I am of opinion that rhyme is unnatural in a play, because dialogue there is presented as the effect of sudden thought: for a play is the imitation of nature; and since no man, without premeditation, speaks in rhyme, neither ought he to do it on the stage. This hinders not but the fancy may be there elevated to an higher pitch of thought than it is in ordinary discourse; for there is a probability that men of excellent and quick parts may speak noble things *extempore:* but those thoughts are never fettered with the numbers or sound of verse without study, therefore it cannot be but unnatural to present the most free way of speak-

ing in that which is the most constrained. For this reason, says Aristotle, 'tis best to write tragedy in that kind of verse which is the least such, or which is nearest prose: and this amongst the ancients was the Iambic, and with us is blank verse, or the measure of verse kept exactly without rhyme. These numbers therefore are fittest for a play; the others for a paper of verses, or a poem; blank verse being as much below them as rhyme is improper for the drama. And if it be objected that neither are blank verses made *extempore,* yet, as nearest nature, they are still to be preferred. — But there are two particular exceptions, which many besides myself have had to verse; by which it will appear yet more plainly how improper it is in plays. And the first of them is grounded on that very reason for which some have commended rhyme; they say, the quickness of repartees in argumentative scenes receives an ornament from verse. Now what is more unreasonable than to imagine that a man should not only light upon the wit, but the rhyme too, upon the sudden? This nicking of him who spoke before both in sound and measure, is so great an happiness, that you must at least suppose the persons of your play to be born poets: *Arcades omnes, et cantare pares, et respondere parati:*[75] they must have arrived to the degree of *quicquid conabar dicere;*[76] — to make verses almost whether they will or no. If they are anything below this, it will look rather like the design of two, than the answer of one: it will appear that your actors hold intelligence together; that they perform their tricks like fortune-tellers, by confederacy. The hand of art will be too visible in it, against that maxim of all professions — *Ars est celare artem;*[77] that it is the greatest perfection of art to keep itself undiscovered. Nor will it serve you to object, that however you manage it, 'tis still known to be a play; and, consequently, the dialogue of two persons understood to be the labor of one poet. For a play is still an imitation of nature; we know we are to be deceived, and we desire to be so; but no man ever was deceived but with a probability of truth; for who will suffer a gross lie to be fastened on him? Thus we sufficiently understand that the scenes which represent cities and countries to us are not really such, but only painted on boards and canvas; but shall that excuse the ill painture or de-

---

74. *Etiam . . . Laberi:* "Even with my support you are beaten, Laberius."

75. *Arcades . . . parati:* "We are all Arcadians, ready to sing and to respond" (Virgil, *Eclogues,* VII.4).   76. *quicquid . . . dicere:* "Whatever I said, I sang."   77. *Ars . . . artem:* "The art is to conceal the art."

signment of them? Nay, rather ought they not be labored with so much the more diligence and exactness, to help the imagination? since the mind of man does naturally tend to truth; and therefore the nearer anything comes to the imitation of it, the more it pleases.

"Thus, you see, your rhyme is incapable of expressing the greatest thoughts naturally, and the lowest it cannot with any grace: for what is more unbefitting the majesty of verse, than to call a servant, or bid a door be shut in rhyme? and yet you are often forced on this miserable necessity. But verse, you say, circumscribes a quick and luxuriant fancy, which would extend itself too far on every subject, did not the labor which is required to well-turned and polished rhyme set bounds to it. Yet this argument, if granted, would only prove that we may write better in verse, but not more naturally. Neither is it able to evince that; for he who wants judgment to confine his fancy in blank verse, may want it as much in rhyme: and he who has it will avoid errors in both kinds. Latin verse was as great a confinement to the imagination of those poets as rhyme to ours; and yet you find Ovid saying too much on every subject. *Nescivit* (says Seneca) *quod bene cessit relinquere:*[78] of which he gives you one famous instance in his description of the deluge:

Omnia pontus erat, deerant quoque litora ponto.
Now all was sea, nor had that sea a shore.

Thus Ovid's fancy was not limited by verse, and Virgil needed not verse to have bounded his.

"In our own language we see Ben Jonson confining himself to what ought to be said, even in the liberty of blank verse; and yet Corneille, the most judicious of the French poets, is still varying the same sense an hundred ways, and dwelling eternally on the same subject, though confined by rhyme. Some other exceptions I have to verse; but since these I have named are for the most part already public, I conceive it reasonable they should first be answered."

"It concerns me less than any," said Neander (seeing he had ended), "to reply to this discourse; because when I should have proved that verse may be natural in plays, yet I should always be ready to confess, that those which I have written in this kind come short of that perfection which is required. Yet since you are pleased I should under-take this province, I will do it, though with all imaginable respect and deference, both to that person[79] from whom you have borrowed your strongest arguments, and to whose judgment, when I have said all, I finally submit. But before I proceed to answer your objections, I must first remember you, that I exclude all comedy from my defence; and next that I deny not but blank verse may be also used; and content myself only to assert, that in serious plays where the subject and characters are great, and the plot unmixed with mirth, which might allay or divert these concernments which are produced, rhyme is there as natural and more effectual than blank verse.

"And now having laid down this as a foundation — to begin with Crites — I must crave leave to tell him, that some of his arguments against rhyme reach no farther than, from the faults and defects of ill rhyme, to conclude against the use of it in general. May not I conclude against blank verse by the same reason? If the words of some poets who write in it are either ill chosen, or ill placed, which makes not only rhyme, but all kind of verse in any language unnatural, shall I, for their vicious affectation, condemn those excellent lines of Fletcher, which are written in that kind? Is there anything in rhyme more constrained than this line in blank verse? — *I heaven invoke, and strong resistance make;* where you see both the clauses are placed unnaturally, that is, contrary to the common way of speaking, and that without the excuse of a rhyme to cause it: yet you would think me very ridiculous, if I should accuse the stubbornness of blank verse for this, and not rather the stiffness of the poet. Therefore, Crites, you must either prove that words, though well chosen, and duly placed, yet render not rhyme natural in itself; or that, however natural and easy the rhyme may be, yet it is not proper for a play. If you insist on the former part, I would ask you, what other conditions are required to make rhyme natural in itself, besides an election of apt words, and a right disposition of them? For the due choice of your words expresses your sense naturally, and the due placing them adapts the rhyme to it. If you object that one verse may be made for the sake of another, though both the words and rhyme be apt, I answer, it cannot possibly so fall out; for either there is a dependence of sense betwixt the first line and the second, or there is none: if there be that connec-

---

78. *Nescivit . . . relinquere:* "He did not know how to leave well enough alone."

79. that person: Aristotle.

tion, then in the natural position of the words the latter line must of necessity flow from the former; if there be no dependence, yet still the due ordering of words makes the last line as natural in itself as the other: so that the necessity of a rhyme never forces any but bad or lazy writers to say what they would not otherwise. 'Tis true, there is both care and art required to write in verse. A good poet never establishes the first line till he has sought out such a rhyme as may fit the sense, already prepared to heighten the second: many times the close of the sense falls into the middle of the next verse, or farther off, and he may often prevail himself of the same advantages in English which Virgil had in Latin — he may break off in the hemistich,[80] and begin another line. Indeed, the not observing these two last things makes plays which are writ in verse so tedious: for though, most commonly, the sense is to be confined to the couplet, yet nothing that does *perpetuo tenore fluere,* run in the same channel, can please always. 'Tis like the murmuring of a stream, which not varying in the fall, causes at first attention, at last drowsiness. Variety of cadences is the best rule; the greatest help to the actors, and refreshment to the audience.

"If then verse may be made natural in itself, how becomes it unnatural in a play? You say the stage is the representation of nature, and no man in ordinary conversation speaks in rhyme. But you foresaw when you said this, that it might be answered — neither does any man speak in blank verse, or in measure without rhyme. Therefore you concluded, that which is nearest nature is still to be preferred. But you took no notice that rhyme might be made as natural as blank verse, by the well placing of the words, etc. All the difference between them, when they are both correct, is, the sound in one, which the other wants; and if so, the sweetness of it, and all the advantage resulting from it, which are handled in the Preface to *The Rival Ladies,* will yet stand good. As for that place of Aristotle, where he says, plays should be writ in that kind of verse which is nearest prose, it makes little for you; blank verse being properly but measured prose. Now measure alone, in any modern language, does not constitute verse; those of the ancients in Greek and Latin consisted in quantity of words, and a determinate number of feet. But when, by the inundation of the Goths and Vandals into Italy, new languages were introduced, and

barbarously mingled with the Latin, of which the Italian, Spanish, French, and ours (made out of them and the Teutonic) are dialects, a new way of poesy was practised; new, I say, in those countries, for in all probability it was that of the conquerors in their own nations: at least we are able to prove, that the eastern people have used it from all antiquity (*vide* Daniel his *Defence of Rhyme*). This new way consisted in measure or number of feet, and rhyme; the sweetness of rhyme, and observation of accent, supplying the place of quantity in words, which could neither exactly be observed by those barbarians, who knew not the rules of it, neither was it suitable to their tongues, as it had been to the Greek and Latin. No man is tied in modern poesy to observe any farther rule in the feet of his verse, but that they be dissyllables; whether Spondee, Trochee, or Iambic, it matters not; only he is obliged to rhyme: neither do the Spanish, French, Italian, or Germans, acknowledge at all, or very rarely, any such kind of poesy as blank verse amongst them. Therefore, at most 'tis but a poetic prose, a *sermo pedestris;*[81] and as such, most fit for comedies, where I acknowledge rhyme to be improper. — Farther; as to that quotation of Aristotle, our couplet verses may be rendered as near prose as blank verse itself, by using those advantages I lately named — as breaks in an hemistich, or running the sense into another line — thereby making art and order appear as loose and free as nature: or not tying ourselves to couplets strictly, we may use the benefit of the Pindaric way practised in *The Siege of Rhodes;* where the numbers vary, and the rhyme is disposed carelessly, and far from often chiming. Neither is that other advantage of the ancients to be despised, of changing the kind of verse when they please, with the change of the scene, or some new entrance; for they confine not themselves always to iambics, but extend their liberty to all lyric numbers, and sometimes even to hexameter. But I need not go so far as to prove that rhyme, as it succeeds to all other offices of Greek and Latin verse, so especially to this of plays, since the custom of nations at this day confirms it; the French, Italian, and Spanish tragedies are generally writ in it; and sure the universal consent of the most civilized parts of the world ought in this, as it doth in other customs, to include the rest.

"But perhaps you may tell me, I have proposed

---

80. **hemistich:** half-line (Cf. *Absalom and Achitophel,* 87).

81. *sermo pedestris:* "prose disquisition."

such a way to make rhyme natural, and consequently proper to plays, as is unpracticable; and that I shall scarce find six or eight lines together in any play, where the words are so placed and chosen as is required to make it natural. I answer, no poet need constrain himself at all times to it. It is enough he makes it his general rule; for I deny not but sometimes there may be a greatness in placing the words otherwise; and sometimes they may sound better; sometimes also the variety itself is excuse enough. But if, for the most part, the words be placed as they are in the negligence of prose, it is sufficient to denominate the way practicable; for we esteem that to be such, which in the trial oftener succeeds than misses. And thus far you may find the practice made good in many plays: where you do not, remember still, that if you cannot find six natural rhymes together, it will be as hard for you to produce as many lines in blank verse, even among the greatest of our poets, against which I cannot make some reasonable exception.

"And this, Sir, calls to my remembrance the beginning of your discourse, where you told us we should never find the audience favorable to this kind of writing, till we could produce as good plays in rhyme as Ben Jonson, Fletcher, and Shakespeare had writ out of it. But it is to raise envy to the living, to compare them with the dead. They are honored, and almost adored by us, as they deserve; neither do I know any so presumptuous of themselves as to contend with them. Yet give me leave to say thus much, without injury to their ashes; that not only we shall never equal them, but they could never equal themselves, were they to rise and write again. We acknowledge them our fathers in wit; but they have ruined their estates themselves, before they came to their children's hands. There is scarce an humor, a character, or any kind of plot, which they have not used. All comes sullied or wasted to us: and were they to entertain this age, they could not now make so plenteous treatments out of such decayed fortunes. This therefore will be a good argument to us, either not to write at all, or to attempt some other way. There is no bays to be expected in their walks: *tentanda via est, qua me quoque possum tollere humo.*[82]

"This way of writing in verse they have only left free to us; our age is arrived to a perfection in it, which they never knew; and which (if we

may guess by what of theirs we have seen in verse, as *The Faithful Shepherdess,* and *Sad Shepherd*) 'tis probable they never could have reached. For the genius of every age is different; and though ours excel in this, I deny not but to imitate nature in that perfection which they did in prose, is a greater commendation than to write in verse exactly. As for what you have added — that the people are not generally inclined to like this way, — if it were true, it would be no wonder, that betwixt the shaking off of an old habit, and the introducing of a new, there should be difficulty. Do we not see them stick to Hopkins' and Sternhold's[83] psalms, and forsake those of David, I mean Sandys[84] his translation of them? If by the people you understand the multitude, the οἱ πολλοί,[85] 'tis no matter what they think; they are sometimes in the right, sometimes in the wrong: their judgment is a mere lottery. *Est ubi plebs recte putat, est ubi peccat.*[86] Horace says it of the vulgar, judging poesy. But if you mean the mixed audience of the populace and the noblesse, I dare confidently affirm that a great part of the latter sort are already favorable to verse; and that no serious plays written since the king's return have been more kindly received by them than *The Siege of Rhodes, The Mustapha, The Indian Queen,* and *Indian Emperor.*

"But I come now to the inference of your first argument. You said that the dialogue of plays is presented as the effect of sudden thought, but no man speaks suddenly, or *extempore,* in rhyme; and you inferred from thence, that rhyme, which you acknowledge to be proper to epic poesy, cannot equally be proper to dramatic, unless we could suppose all men born so much more than poets, that verses should be made in them, not by them.

"It has been formerly urged by you, and confessed by me, that since no man spoke any kind of verse *extempore,* that which was nearest nature was to be preferred. I answer you, therefore, by distinguishing betwixt what is nearest to the nature of comedy, which is the imitation of common persons and ordinary speaking, and what is nearest the nature of a serious play: this last is indeed the representation of nature, but 'tis nature wrought up to a higher pitch. The plot, the characters, the wit, the passions, the descriptions, are all exalted above the level of common converse, as high as the imagi-

---

82. *tentanda . . . humo:* "A way must be sought that will let me leave the ground" (Virgil, *Georgics,* III.8).

83. **Hopkins' and Sternhold's:** John Hopkins and Thomas Sternhold, Elizabethan versifiers of the Psalms.   84. **Sandys:** George Sandys, seventeenth-century translator of the Psalms.   85. οἱ πολλοί: "the many."   86. *Est . . . peccat:* "The people are sometimes right, sometimes wrong."

nation of the poet can carry them, with proportion to verisimilitude. Tragedy, we know, is wont to image to us the minds and fortunes of noble persons, and to portray these exactly; heroic rhyme is nearest nature, as being the noblest kind of modern verse.

*Indignatur enim privatis et prope socco
Dignis carminibus narrari coena Thyestae,*[87]

says Horace: and in another place,

Effutire leves indigna tragoedia versus.[88]

Blank verse is acknowledged to be too low for a poem, nay more, for a paper of verses; but if too low for an ordinary sonnet, how much more for tragedy, which is by Aristotle, in the dispute betwixt the epic poesy and the dramatic, for many reasons he there alleges, ranked above it?

"But setting this defence aside, your argument is almost as strong against the use of rhyme in poems as in plays; for the epic way is everywhere interlaced with dialogue, or discoursive scenes; and therefore you must either grant rhyme to be improper there, which is contrary to your assertion, or admit it into plays by the same title which you have given it to poems. For though tragedy be justly preferred above the other, yet there is a great affinity between them, as may easily be discovered in that definition of a play which Lisideius gave us. The *genus* of them is the same — a just and lively image of human nature, in its actions, passions, and traverses of fortune: so is the end — namely, for the delight and benefit of mankind. The characters and persons are still the same, *viz.,* the greatest of both sorts; only the manner of acquainting us with those actions, passions, and fortunes, is different. Tragedy performs it *viva voce,* or by action, in dialogue; wherein it excels the epic poem, which does it chiefly by narration, and therefore is not so lively an image of human nature. However, the agreement betwixt them is such, that if rhyme be proper for one, it must be for the other. Verse, 'tis true, is not the effect of sudden thought; but this hinders not that sudden thought may be represented in verse, since those thoughts are such as must be higher than nature can raise them without premeditation, especially to a continuance of them, even out of verse; and consequently you cannot imagine them to have been

sudden either in the poet or in the actors. A play, as I have said, to be like nature, is to be set above it; as statues which are placed on high are made greater than the life, that they may descend to the sight in their just proportion.

"Perhaps I have insisted too long on this objection; but the clearing of it will make my stay shorter on the rest. You tell us, Crites, that rhyme appears most unnatural in repartees, or short replies: when he who answers (it being presumed he knew not what the other would say, yet) makes up that part of the verse which was left incomplete, and supplies both the sound and measure of it. This, you say, looks rather like the confederacy of two, than the answer of one.

"This, I confess, is an objection which is in every man's mouth, who loves not rhyme: but suppose, I beseech you, the repartee were made only in blank verse, might not part of the same argument be turned against you? for the measure is as often supplied there as it is in rhyme; the latter half of the hemistich as commonly made up, or a second line subjoined as a reply to the former; which any one leaf in Jonson's plays will sufficiently clear to you. You will often find in the Greek tragedians, and in Seneca, that when a scene grows up into the warmth of repartees, which is the close fighting of it, the latter part of the trimeter is supplied by him who answers; and yet it was never observed as a fault in them by any of the ancient or modern critics. The case is the same in our verse, as it was in theirs; rhyme to us being in lieu of quantity to them. But if no latitude is to be allowed a poet, you take from him not only his license of *quidlibet audendi,*[89] but you tie him up in a straiter compass than you would a philosopher. This is indeed *Musas colere severiores.*[90] You would have him follow nature, but he must follow her on foot: you have dismounted him from his Pegasus. But you tell us, this supplying the last half of a verse, or adjoining a whole second to the former, looks more like the design of two, than the answer of one. Suppose we acknowledge it: how comes this confederacy to be more displeasing to you, than in a dance which is well contrived? You see there the united design of many persons to make up one figure: after they have separated themselves in many petty divisions, they rejoin one by one into a gross: the confederacy is plain amongst them, for chance could never produce

---

87. *Indignatur . . . Thyestae:* "The story of Thyestes' banquet cannot be told in verses suitable to comedy" (*Ars Poetica,* 90-91). 88. *Effutire . . . versus:* "Tragedy is unsuited to light lines" (*Ibid.,* 231).

89. *quidlibet audendi:* "trying anything he pleases." 90. *Musas . . . severiores:* "to cultivate the stricter Muses."

anything so beautiful; and yet there is nothing in it that shocks your sight. I acknowledge the hand of art appears in repartee, as of necessity it must in all kinds of verse. But there is also the quick and poignant brevity of it (which is an high imitation of nature in those sudden gusts of passion) to mingle with it; and this, joined with the cadency and sweetness of the rhyme, leaves nothing in the soul of the hearer to desire. 'Tis an art which appears; but it appears only like the shadowings of painture, which being to cause the rounding of it, cannot be absent; but while that is considered, they are lost: so while we attend to the other beauties of the matter, the care and labor of the rhyme is carried from us, or at least drowned in its own sweetness, as bees are sometimes buried in their honey. When a poet has found the repartee, the last perfection he can add to it, is to put it into verse. However good the thought may be, however apt the words in which 'tis couched, yet he finds himself at a little unrest, while rhyme is wanting: he cannot leave it till that comes naturally, and then is at ease, and sits down contented.

"From replies, which are the most elevated thoughts of verse, you pass to those which are most mean, and which are common with the lowest of household conversation. In these, you say, the majesty of verse suffers. You instance in the calling of a servant, or commanding a door to be shut, in rhyme. This, Crites, is a good observation of yours, but no argument: for it proves no more but that such thoughts should be waived, as often as may be, by the address of the poet. But suppose they are necessary in the places where he uses them, yet there is no need to put them into rhyme. He may place them in the beginning of a verse, and break it off, as unfit, when so debased, for any other use: or granting the worst — that they require more room than the hemistich will allow, yet still there is a choice to be made of the best words, and least vulgar (provided they be apt), to express such thoughts. Many have blamed rhyme in general, for this fault, when the poet with a little care might have redressed it. But they do it with no more justice than if English poesy should be made ridiculous for the sake of the Water-poet's [91] rhymes. Our language is noble, full, and significant; and I know not why he who is master of it may not clothe ordinary things in it as decently as the Latin, if he use the same diligence in his choice of words:

delectus verborum origo est eloquentiae.[92] It was the saying of Julius Caesar, one so curious in his, that none of them can be changed but for a worse. One would think, *unlock the door,* was a thing as vulgar as could be spoken; and yet Seneca could make it sound high and lofty in his Latin:

> *Reserate clusos regii postes laris.*
> Set wide the palace gates.

"But I turn from this conception, both because it happens not above twice or thrice in any play that those vulgar thoughts are used; and then too (were there no other apology to be made, yet), the necessity of them, which is alike in all kinds of writing, may excuse them. For if they are little and mean in rhyme, they are of consequence such in blank verse. Besides that the great eagerness and precipitation with which they are spoken, makes us rather mind the substance than the dress; that for which they are spoken, rather than what is spoken. For they are always the effect of some hasty concernment, and something of consequence depends on them.

"Thus, Crites, I have endeavored to answer your objections; it remains only that I should vindicate an argument for verse, which you have gone about to overthrow. It had formerly been said that the easiness of blank verse renders the poet too luxuriant, but that the labor of rhyme bounds and circumscribes an over-fruitful fancy; the sense there being commonly confined to the couplet, and the words so ordered that the rhyme naturally follows them, not they the rhyme. To this you answered, that it was no argument to the question in hand; for the dispute was not which way a man may write best, but which is most proper for the subject on which he writes.

"First, give me leave, Sir, to remember you that the argument against which you raised this objection was only secondary: it was built on this hypothesis — that to write in verse was proper for serious plays. Which supposition being granted (as it was briefly made out in that discourse, by showing how verse might be made natural), it asserted, that this way of writing was an help to the poet's judgment, by putting bounds to a wild overflowing fancy. I think, therefore, it will not be hard for me to make good what it was to prove on that supposition. But you add, that were this let pass, yet he who wants judgment in the liberty of his fancy,

---

91. **Water-poet:** John Taylor (1580–1653), a Thames waterman so called.

92. *delectus . . . eloquentiae:* "choice of words is the beginning of eloquence."

may as well show the defect of it when he is confined to verse; for he who has judgment will avoid errors, and he who has it not will commit them in all kinds of writing.

"This argument, as you have taken it from a most acute person,[93] so I confess it carries much weight in it: but by using the word judgment here indefinitely, you seem to have put a fallacy upon us. I grant, he who has judgment, that is, so profound, so strong, or rather so infallible a judgment, that he needs no helps to keep it always poised and upright, will commit no faults either in rhyme or out of it. And on the other extreme, he who has a judgment so weak and crazed that no helps can correct or amend it, shall write scurvily out of rhyme, and worse in it. But the first of these judgments is nowhere to be found, and the latter is not fit to write at all. To speak therefore of judgment as it is in the best poets; they who have the greatest proportion of it, want other helps than from it, within. As for example, you would be loth to say that he who is endued with a sound judgment has no need of history, geography, or moral philosophy, to write correctly. Judgment is indeed the masterworkman in a play; but he requires many subordinate hands, many tools to his assistance. And verse I affirm to be one of these; 'tis a rule and line by which he keeps his building compact and even, which otherwise lawless imagination would raise either irregularly or loosely; at least, if the poet commits errors with this help, he would make greater and more without it: 'tis, in short, a slow and painful, but the surest kind of working. Ovid, whom you accuse for luxuriancy in verse, had perhaps been farther guilty of it, had he writ in prose. And for your instance of Ben Jonson, who, you say, writ exactly without the help of rhyme; you are to remember, 'tis only an aid to a luxuriant fancy, which his was not: as he did not want imagination, so none ever said he had much to spare. Neither was verse then refined so much, to be an help to that age, as it is to ours. Thus then, the second thoughts being usually the best, as receiving the maturest digestion from judgment, and the last and most mature product of those thoughts being artful and labored verse, it may well be inferred, that verse is a great help to a luxuriant fancy; and this is what that argument which you opposed was to evince."

Neander was pursuing this discourse so eagerly that Eugenius had called to him twice or thrice,

93. person: Seneca.

ere he took notice that the barge stood still, and that they were at the foot of Somerset-stairs, where they had appointed it to land. The company were all sorry to separate so soon, though a great part of the evening was already spent; and stood awhile looking back on the water, upon which the moonbeams played, and made it appear like floating quicksilver: at last they went up through a crowd of French people, who were merrily dancing in the open air, and nothing concerned for the noise of guns which had alarmed the town that afternoon. Walking thence together to the Piazze, they parted there; Eugenius and Lisideius to some pleasant appointment they had made, and Crites and Neander to their several lodgings.

from SECRET LOVE

OR, THE MAIDEN QUEEN

Secret Love, Dryden's fifth play, was produced in 1667. In the first of its two prologues, the only one printed here, Dryden grants that observance of the "rules" will be no guaranty of a play's success; the final test is its power to please the audience.

PROLOGUE

I

He who writ this, not without pains and thought
From French and English theaters has brought
The exactest rules by which a play is wrought:

II

The unities of action, place, and time;
The scenes unbroken; and a mingled chime
Of Jonson's humor° with Corneille's rhyme.°

III

But while dead colors he with care did lay,
He fears his wit or plot he did not weigh,
Which are the living beauties of a play.

IV

Plays are like towns, which, howe'er fortified   10
By engineers, have still some weaker side
By the o'er-seen defendant unespied.

V

And with that art you make approaches now;
Such skilful fury in assaults you show,
That every poet without shame may bow.

PROLOGUE TO SECRET LOVE. 6. humor: comedy of humors. Corneille's rhyme: Pierre Corneille (1606–84), whose French tragedies in rhyme Dryden much admired at this period.

VI

Ours therefore humbly would attend your doom,
If, soldier-like, he may have terms to come
With flying colors and with beat of drum. . . .

SONG

I

I feed a flame within, which so torments me,
That it both pains my heart, and yet contents me:
'Tis such a pleasing smart, and I so love it,
That I had rather die than once remove it.

II

Yet he for whom I grieve shall never know it;
My tongue does not betray, nor my eyes show it:
Not a sigh, nor a tear, my pain discloses,
But they fall silently, like dew on roses.

III

Thus to prevent my love from being cruel,
My heart's the sacrifice, as 'tis the fuel: 10
And while I suffer this, to give him quiet,
My faith rewards my love, tho' he deny it.

IV

On his eyes will I gaze, and there delight me;
Where I conceal my love, no frown can fright me:
To be more happy, I dare not aspire;
Nor can I fall more low, mounting no higher.

from THE TEMPEST

PROLOGUE

The Tempest (1667) was by Dryden and Sir William
Davenant. Dryden's prologue makes it clear that he
does not consider it worthy of its source, *The Tempest*
of Shakespeare.

As, when a tree's cut down, the secret root
Lives under ground, and thence new branches
    shoot;
So from old Shakespeare's honored dust, this day
Springs up and buds a new reviving play:
Shakespeare, who (taught by none) did first impart
To Fletcher° wit, to laboring Jonson art.
He, monarch-like, gave those, his subjects, law;
And is that nature which they paint and draw.
Fletcher reached that which on his heights did
    grow,
Whilst Jonson crept, and gathered all below.   10
This did his love, and this his mirth digest:

One imitates him most, the other best.
If they have since outwrit all other men,
'Tis with the drops which fell from Shakespeare's
    pen.
The storm which vanished on the neighboring
    shore,
Was taught by Shakespeare's *Tempest* first to roar.
That innocence and beauty which did smile
In Fletcher, grew on this *Enchanted Isle*.°
But Shakespeare's magic could not copied be;
Within that circle none durst walk but he.   20
I must confess 'twas bold, nor would you now
That liberty to vulgar wits allow,
Which works by magic supernatural things;
But Shakespeare's power is sacred as a king's.
Those legends from old priesthood were received,
And he then writ, as people then believed.
But if for Shakespeare we your grace implore,
We for our theater shall want it more:
Who by our dearth of youths are forced to employ
One of our women to present a boy;   30
And that's a transformation, you will say,
Exceeding all the magic in the play.
Let none expect in the last act to find
Her sex transformed from man to womankind.
Whate'er she was before the play began,
All you shall see of her is perfect man.
Or if your fancy will be farther led
To find her woman, it must be abed.

from AN EVENING'S LOVE

SONG

One of four songs from Dryden's comedy of 1668.

I

Calm was the even, and clear was the sky,
    And the new-budding flowers did spring,
When all alone went Amyntas and I
    To hear the sweet nightingal sing.
I sate, and he laid him down by me,
    But scarcely his breath he could draw;
For when with a fear, he began to draw near,
    He was dashed with: " A ha ha ha ha! "

II

He blushed to himself, and lay still for a while,
    And his modesty curbed his desire;   10
But straight I convinced all his fear with a smile,
    Which added new flames to his fire.
" O Sylvia," said he, " you are cruel,
    To keep your poor lover in awe; "
Then once more he pressed with his hand to my
    breast,
    But was dashed with: " A ha ha ha ha! "

PROLOGUE TO THE TEMPEST.   6. Fletcher: John Fletcher (1579–
1625), collaborator with Francis Beaumont.

18. *Enchanted Isle:* subtitle of this play.

III

I knew 'twas his passion that caused all his fears,
  And therefore I pitied his case;
I whispered him softly: "There's nobody near,"
  And laid my cheek close to his face: 20
But as he grew bolder and bolder,
  A shepherd came by us and saw,
And just as our bliss we began with a kiss,
  He laughed out with: "A ha ha ha ha!"

from TYRANNIC LOVE
EPILOGUE

SPOKEN BY MRS. ELLEN, WHEN SHE WAS TO BE
CARRIED OFF DEAD BY THE BEARERS

"Mrs. Ellen" is Nell Gwyn, the famous actress who
became the mistress of Charles II.

[*To the Bearer.*] Hold, are you mad? you damned
    confounded dog,
I am to rise, and speak the epilogue.
[*To the Audience.*] I come, kind gentlemen,
    strange news to tell ye,
I am the ghost of poor departed Nelly.
Sweet ladies, be not frighted, I'll be civil;
I'm what I was, a little harmless devil:
For after death, we sprites have just such natures
We had for all the world, when human creatures;
And therefore, I that was an actress here,
Play all my tricks in hell, a goblin there.   10
Gallants, look to't, you say there are no sprites;
But I'll come dance about your beds at nights.
And faith you'll be in a sweet kind of taking,
When I surprise you between sleep and waking.
To tell you true, I walk because I die
Out of my calling in a tragedy.
O poet, damned dull poet, who could prove
So senseless! to make Nelly die for love!
Nay, what's yet worse, to kill me in the prime
Of Easter term, in tart and cheese-cake time!   20
I'll fit the fop, for I'll not one word say
To excuse his godly out-of-fashion play:
A play, which if you dare but twice sit out,
You'll all be slandered, and be thought devout.
But farewell, gentlemen, make haste to me;
I'm sure ere long to have your company.
As for my epitaph, when I am gone,
I'll trust no poet, but will write my own:

Here Nelly lies, who, tho' she lived a slattern,
Yet died a princess, acting in St. Cathar'n.°   30

EPILOGUE TO TYRANNIC LOVE.   **30. St. Cathar'n:** heroine of
this play.

from THE CONQUEST OF GRANADA, II

In this epilogue from Dryden's most famous heroic
play (1670–71) he considers again the relative merits
of Elizabethan and Restoration drama.

EPILOGUE

They who have best succeeded on the stage
Have still conformed their genius to their age.
Thus Jonson did mechanic humor show,
When men were dull, and conversation low.
Then comedy was faultless, but 'twas coarse:
Cob's tankard° was a jest, and Otter's horse.°
And, as their comedy, their love was mean;
Except, by chance, in some one labored scene
Which must atone for an ill-written play.
They rose, but at their height could seldom stay.   10
Fame then was cheap, and the first comer sped;
And they have kept it since, by being dead.
But, were they now to write, when critics weigh
Each line, and every word, throughout a play,
None of 'em, no, not Jonson in his height,
Could pass, without allowing grains for weight.
Think it not envy, that these truths are told;
Our poet's not malicious, tho' he's bold.
'Tis not to brand 'em, that their faults are shown,
But, by their errors, to excuse his own.   20
If love and honor now are higher raised,
'Tis not the poet, but the age is praised.
Wit's now arrived to a more high degree;
Our native language more refined and free.
Our ladies and our men now speak more wit
In conversation, than those poets writ.
Then, one of these is, consequently, true;
That what this poet writes comes short of you,
And imitates you ill, (which most he fears,)
Or else his writing is not worse than theirs.   30
Yet, tho' you judge (as sure the critics will)
That some before him writ with greater skill,
In this one praise he has their fame surpassed,
To please an age more gallant than the last.

THE ZAMBRA DANCE

I

Beneath a myrtle shade,
Which love for none but happy lovers made,
I slept; and straight my love before me brought
Phyllis, the object of my waking thought.
Undressed she came my flames to meet,

EPILOGUE TO THE CONQUEST OF GRANADA, II.   **6. Cob's tankard:**
Cob was a water-bearer in Ben Jonson's *Every Man in His
Humor.*   **Otter's horse:** Captain Otter, in Jonson's *Silent
Woman,* christened one of his drinking-cups "Horse."

While love strowed flow'rs beneath her feet;
Flow'rs which, so pressed by her, became more
    sweet.

II

From the bright vision's head
A careless veil of lawn was loosely spread:
From her white temples fell her shaded hair,   10
Like cloudy sunshine, not too brown nor fair;
Her hands, her lips, did love inspire;
Her every grace my heart did fire:
But most her eyes, which languished with desire.

III

"Ah, charming fair," said I,
"How long can you my bliss and yours deny?
By nature and by love this lonely shade
Was for revenge of suffering lovers made.
Silence and shades with love agree;
Both shelter you and favor me: 20
You cannot blush, because I cannot see."

IV

"No, let me die," she said,
"Rather than lose the spotless name of maid!"
Faintly, methought, she spoke; for all the while
She bid me not believe her, with a smile.
"Then die," said I: she still denied;
"And is it thus, thus, thus," she cried,
"You use a harmless maid?"— and so she died!

V

I waked, and straight I knew,
I loved so well, it made my dream prove true: 30
Fancy, the kinder mistress of the two,
Fancy had done what Phyllis would not do!
Ah, cruel nymph, cease your disdain,
While I can dream, you scorn in vain —
Asleep or waking, you must ease my pain.

from MARRIAGE À LA MODE

PROLOGUE

This prologue (1672) refers to the current naval war
with the Dutch, and incidentally provides an intimate
view of the Restoration theater as a social institution.

Lord, how reformed and quiet are we grown,
Since all our braves and all our wits are gone!
Fop-corner° now is free from civil war,
White-wig and vizard° make no longer jar.

France,° and the fleet, have swept the town so clear
That we can act in peace, and you can hear.
Those that durst fight are gone to get renown,
And those that durst not, blush to stand in town.
'Twas a sad sight, before they marched from home,
To see our warriors in red waistcoats come,   10
With hair tucked up, into our tiring-room.
But 'twas more sad to hear their last adieu:
The women sobbed, and swore they would be true;
And so they were, as long as e'er they could,
But powerful guinea cannot be withstood,
And they were made of playhouse flesh and blood.
Fate did their friends for double use ordain;
In wars abroad they grinning honor° gain,
And mistresses for all that stay maintain.
Now they are gone, 'tis dead vacation here,   20
For neither friends nor enemies appear.
Poor pensive punk now peeps ere plays begin,
Sees the bare bench, and dares not venture in;
But manages her last half-crown with care,
And trudges to the Mall,° on foot, for air.
Our city friends so far will hardly come,
They can take up with pleasures nearer home;
And see gay shows and gaudy scenes elsewhere;
For we presume they seldom come to hear.
But they have now ta'en up a glorious trade,   30
And cutting Morecraft° struts in masquerade.
There's all our hope, for we shall show to-day
A masking ball, to recommend our play;
Nay, to endear 'em more, and let 'em see
We scorn to come behind in courtesy,
We'll follow the new mode which they begin,
And treat 'em with a room, and couch within:
For that's one way, howe'er the play fall short,
T'oblige the town, the city, and the court.

SONG

I

Why should a foolish marriage vow,
  Which long ago was made,
Oblige us to each other now,
  When passion is decayed?
We loved, and we loved, as long as we could,
  Till our love was loved out in us both;
But our marriage is dead, when the pleasure is fled:
  'Twas pleasure first made it an oath.

II

If I have pleasures for a friend,
  And farther love in store,   10
What wrong has he whose joys did end,

PROLOGUE TO MARRIAGE À LA MODE.   **3. Fop-corner:** gathering-
place of dandies.   **4. White-wig and vizard:** wigs and masks,
worn respectively by fops and prostitutes in the Restoration
theater.

5. France: now allied with England against Holland.   **18. grinning honor:** Cf. Shakespeare, *I Henry IV*. V.iii.62.   **25. the
Mall:** a walk in St. James's Park.   **31. cutting Morecraft:** a
character in Beaumont and Fletcher's *The Scornful Lady*.

And who could give no more?
'Tis a madness that he should be jealous of me,
Or that I should bar him of another:
For all we can gain is to give ourselves pain,
When neither can hinder the other.

EPILOGUE TO
THE UNIVERSITY OF OXFORD, 1674

One of several prologues and epilogues written by
Dryden when his players were at Oxford. In a letter
to the Earl of Rochester he once remarked, "How
easy 'tis to pass any thing upon an university, and
how gross flattery the learned will endure."

Oft has our poet wished, this happy seat
Might prove his fading Muse's last retreat:
I wondered at his wish, but now I find
He here sought quiet, and content of mind;
Which noiseful towns and courts can never know,
And only in the shades like laurels grow.
Youth, ere it sees the world, here studies rest,
And age returning thence concludes it best.
What wonder if we court that happiness
Yearly to share, which hourly you possess,   10
Teaching even you, while the vexed world we show,
Your peace to value more, and better know?
'Tis all we can return for favors past,
Whose holy memory shall ever last,
For patronage from him whose care presides
O'er every noble art, and every science guides:
Bathurst,° a name the learn'd with reverence know,
And scarcely more to his own Virgil owe;
Whose age enjoys but what his youth deserved,
To rule those Muses whom before he served.   20
His learning, and untainted manners too,
We find, Athenians, are derived to you:
Such ancient hospitality there rests
In yours, as dwelt in the first Grecian breasts,
Where kindness was religion to their guests.
Such modesty did to our sex appear,
As, had there been no laws, we need not fear,
Since each of you was our protector here.
Converse so chaste, and so strict virtue shown,
As might Apollo with the Muses own.   30
Till our return, we must despair to find
Judges so just, so knowing, and so kind.

from AURENG-ZEBE
PROLOGUE

Here, in the prologue to his last heroic play (1675),
Dryden repudiates that form and admits the superiority
of Shakespeare.

EPILOGUE TO OXFORD, 1674.   17. **Bathurst:** Ralph Bathurst
(1620–1704), vice chancellor of Oxford, proficient in Latin verse.

Our author, by experience, finds it true,
'Tis much more hard to please himself than you;
And out of no feigned modesty, this day
Damns his laborious trifle of a play:
Not that it's worse than what before he writ,
But he has now another taste of wit;
And, to confess a truth, (tho' out of time,)
Grows weary of his long-loved mistress, Rhyme.
Passion's too fierce to be in fetters bound,
And nature flies him like enchanted ground.   10
What verse can do, he has performed in this,
Which he presumes the most correct of his;
But spite of all his pride, a secret shame
Invades his breast at Shakespeare's sacred name:
Awed when he hears his godlike Romans rage,
He, in a just despair, would quit the stage;
And to an age less polished, more unskilled,
Does, with disdain, the foremost honors yield.
As with the greater dead he dares not strive,
He would not match his verse with those who live:
Let him retire, betwixt two ages cast,   21
The first of this, and hindmost of the last.
A losing gamester, let him sneak away;
He bears no ready money from the play.
The fate which governs poets thought it fit
He should not raise his fortunes by his wit.
The clergy thrive, and the litigious bar;
Dull heroes fatten with the spoils of war:
All southern vices, Heaven be praised, are here;
But wit's a luxury you think too dear.   30
When you to cultivate the plant are loth,
'Tis a shrewd sign 'twas never of your growth;
And wit in northern climates will not blow,
Except, like orange trees, 'tis housed from snow.
There needs no care to put a playhouse down,
'Tis the most desart place of all the town:
We and our neighbors, to speak proudly, are,
Like monarchs, ruined with expensive war;
While, like wise English, unconcerned you sit,
And see us play the tragedy of wit.   40

PROLOGUE TO
THE UNIVERSITY OF OXFORD, 1676

If the last four lines are gross flattery, Oxford may
be pardoned for having endured it.

Tho' actors cannot much of learning boast,
Of all who want it, we admire it most:
We love the praises of a learnèd pit,
As we remotely are allied to wit.
We speak our poet's wit, and trade in ore,
Like those who touch upon the golden shore:
Betwixt our judges can distinction make,
Discern how much, and why, our poems take:
Mark if the fools, or men of sense, rejoice;
Whether the applause be only sound or voice.   10

When our fop gallants, or our city folly
Clap over-loud, it makes us melancholy;
We doubt that scene which does their wonder raise,
And, for their ignorance, contemn their praise.
Judge then, if we who act, and they who write,
Should not be proud of giving you delight.
London likes grossly; but this nicer pit
Examines, fathoms all the depths of wit;
The ready finger lays on every blot;
Knows what should justly please, and what should not.   20
Nature herself lies open to your view;
You judge by her, what draught of her is true,
Where outlines false, and colors seem too faint,
Where bunglers daub, and where true poets paint.
But, by the sacred genius of this place,
By every Muse, by each domestic grace,
Be kind to wit, which but endeavors well,
And, where you judge, presumes not to excel.
Our poets hither for adoption come,
As nations sued to be made free of Rome: 30
Not in the suffragating° tribes to stand,
But in your utmost, last, provincial band.
If his ambition may those hopes pursue,
Who with religion loves your arts and you,
Oxford to him a dearer name shall be,
Than his own mother-university.
Thebes° did his green, unknowing youth ingage;
He chooses Athens° in his riper age.

from TROILUS AND CRESSIDA

PROLOGUE

SPOKEN BY MR. BETTERTON, REPRESENTING THE GHOST
OF SHAKESPEARE

In this prologue to Dryden's adaptation from Shakespeare's *Troilus and Cressida* (1679) Dryden lets
Shakespeare himself comment upon the difference between his theater and that of the Restoration.

See, my loved Britons, see your Shakespeare rise,
An awful ghost confessed to human eyes!
Unnamed, methinks, distinguished I had been
From other shades, by this eternal green,
About whose wreaths the vulgar poets strive,
And with a touch their withered bays revive.
Untaught, unpracticed, in a barbarous age,
I found not, but created first the stage;
And, if I drained no Greek or Latin store,
'Twas that my own abundance gave me more.   10
On foreign trade I needed not rely,
Like fruitful Britain, rich without supply.

PROLOGUE TO OXFORD, 1676.   31. suffragating: having the
right of suffrage.   37. Thebes: Cambridge.   38. Athens:
Oxford.

In this my rough-drawn play you shall behold
Some master-strokes, so manly and so bold,
That he who meant to alter, found 'em such,
He shook, and thought it sacrilege to touch.
Now, where are the successors to my name?
What bring they to fill out a poet's fame?
Weak, short-lived issues of a feeble age;
Scarce living to be christened on the stage!   20
For humor farce, for love they rhyme dispense,
That tolls the knell for their departed sense.
Dulness might thrive in any trade but this:
'Twould recommend to some fat benefice.
Dulness, that in a playhouse meets disgrace,
Might meet with reverence in its proper place.
The fulsome clench,° that nauseates the town,
Would from a judge or alderman go down,
Such virtue is there in a robe and gown!
And that insipid stuff which here you hate,   30
Might somewhere else be called a grave debate;
Dulness is decent in the Church and State.
But I forget that still 'tis understood
Bad plays are best decried by showing good.
Sit silent then, that my pleased soul may see
A judging audience once, and worthy me;
My faithful scene from true records shall tell
How Trojan valor did the Greek excel;
Your great forefathers shall their fame regain,
And Homer's angry ghost repine in vain.   40

from THE SPANISH FRIAR

The Spanish Friar (1680) is one of Dryden's best
comedies, and some think it his best play.

SONG

I

Farewell, ungrateful traitor!
    Farewell, my perjured swain!
Let never injured creature
    Believe a man again.
The pleasure of possessing
Surpasses all expressing,
But 'tis too short a blessing,
    And love too long a pain.

II

'Tis easy to deceive us,
    In pity of your pain;   10
But when we love, you leave us
    To rail at you in vain.
Before we have descried it,
There is no bliss beside it;
But she that once has tried it,
    Will never love again.

PROLOGUE TO TROILUS AND CRESSIDA.   27. clench: pun.

III

The passion you pretended,
　　Was only to obtain;
But when the charm is ended,
　　The charmer you disdain.　　20
Your love by ours we measure,
Till we have lost our treasure;
But dying is a pleasure,
　　When living is a pain.

from AMPHITRYON

MERCURY'S SONG TO PHAEDRA

Amphitryon is a late play (1690), but this song from it, and the two songs that follow, belong here among Dryden's lyric efforts in the minor mode.

I

Fair Iris I love, and hourly I die,
But not for a lip, nor a languishing eye:
She's fickle and false, and there we agree,
For I am as false and as fickle as she.
We neither believe what either can say;
And, neither believing, we neither betray.

II

'Tis civil to swear, and say things of course;
We mean not the taking for better for worse.
When present, we love; when absent, agree:
I think not of Iris, nor Iris of me.　　10
The legend of love no couple can find,
So easy to part, or so equally joined.

THE LADY'S SONG

It has always been assumed that this song refers to the banishment of James II and his queen in the Revolution of 1688.

I

A choir of bright beauties in spring did appear,
To choose a May-lady to govern the year;
All the nymphs were in white, and the shepherds
　　in green;
The garland was given, and Phyllis was queen:
But Phyllis refused it, and sighing did say:
"I'll not wear a garland while Pan is away."

II

While Pan and fair Syrinx are fled from our shore,
The Graces are banished, and Love is no more:
The soft god of pleasure, that warmed our desires,
Has broken his bow, and extinguished his fires;　　10
And vows that himself and his mother will mourn,
Till Pan and fair Syrinx in triumph return.

III

Forbear your addresses, and court us no more,
For we will perform what the deity swore;
But if you dare think of deserving our charms,
Away with your sheephooks, and take to your arms:
Then laurels and myrtles your brows shall adorn,
When Pan, and his son, and fair Syrinx return.

SONG TO A FAIR YOUNG LADY

GOING OUT OF THE TOWN IN THE SPRING

This song, contributed to *Examen Poeticum,* a "miscellany" of 1693, cannot be otherwise dated.

I

Ask not the cause, why sullen Spring
　　So long delays her flowers to bear;
Why warbling birds forget to sing,
　　And winter storms invert the year.
Chloris is gone, and fate provides
To make it spring where she resides.

II

Chloris is gone, the cruel fair:
　　She cast not back a pitying eye;
But left her lover in despair,
　　To sigh, to languish, and to die.　　10
Ah, how can those fair eyes endure
To give the wounds they will not cure!

III

Great God of Love, why hast thou made
　　A face that can all hearts command,
That all religions can invade,
　　And change the laws of every land?
Where thou hadst placed such power before,
Thou shouldst have made her mercy more.

IV

When Chloris to the temple comes,
　　Adoring crowds before her fall:　　20
She can restore the dead from tombs,
　　And every life but mine recall.
I only am by Love designed
To be the victim for mankind.

MAC FLECKNOE

OR, A SATIRE UPON THE TRUE-BLUE-PROTESTANT POET, T. S.

Dryden's first satire, written in 1678, was not published until 1682, and then not by his authority. He published a better text in 1684, but without signing his name; he did not acknowledge authorship until 1692 (see Introduction, p. 525, on the circumstances that produced the satire). Shadwell and Flecknoe are its subject; but so is London, which is presented realistically as opposed to the mock-heroic vein in which the poet-victims are ridiculed. The subtitle, apparently not Dryden's, refers to a name the Whigs had given themselves: True Protestants, as distinguished from the false Protestants, or Tories, who were thus accused of being papists.

All human things are subject to decay,
And when fate summons, monarchs must obey.
This Flecknoe° found, who, like Augustus, young
Was called to empire, and had governed long;
In prose and verse, was owned, without dispute,
Thro' all the realms of *Nonsense,* absolute.
This aged prince, now flourishing in peace,
And blest with issue of a large increase;
Worn out with business, did at length debate
To settle the succession of the State;   10
And, pondering which of all his sons was fit
To reign, and wage immortal war with wit,
Cried: "'Tis resolved; for nature pleads, that he
Should only rule, who most resembles me.
Sh——° alone my perfect image bears,
Mature in dulness from his tender years:
Sh—— alone, of all my sons, is he
Who stands confirmed in full stupidity.
The rest to some faint meaning make pretense,
But Sh—— never deviates into sense.   20
Some beams of wit on other souls may fall,
Strike thro', and make a lucid interval;
But Sh——'s genuine night admits no ray,
His rising fogs prevail upon the day.
Besides, his goodly fabric fills the eye,
And seems designed for thoughtless majesty;
Thoughtless as monarch oaks that shade the plain,
And, spread in solemn state, supinely reign.
Heywood and Shirley° were but types of thee,
Thou last great prophet of tautology.   30
Even I, a dunce of more renown than they,
Was sent before but to prepare thy way;
And, coarsely clad in Norwich drugget,° came
To teach the nations in thy greater name.
My warbling lute, the lute I whilom strung,
When to King John of Portugal° I sung,
Was but the prelude to that glorious day,
When thou on silver Thames didst cut thy way,
With well-timed oars before the royal barge,
Swelled with the pride of thy celestial charge;   40
And big with hymn, commander of a host,
The like was ne'er in Epsom blankets° tossed.
Methinks I see the new Arion° sail,

MAC FLECKNOE.   3. Flecknoe: Richard Flecknoe, a poet and
playwright born in Ireland, had recently died.   15. Sh——:
Thomas Shadwell, and so throughout.   29. Heywood and
Shirley: Thomas Heywood and James Shirley, early seventeenth-
century dramatists, better than suggested.   33. Norwich drugget: cheap woolen clothing, once worn by Dryden himself.
36. King John of Portugal: Flecknoe had boasted of visiting him.
42. Epsom blankets: Shadwell wrote a play called *Epsom Wells.*
43. Arion: Greek musician, saved by dolphins.

The lute still trembling underneath thy nail.
At thy well-sharpened thumb from shore to shore
The treble squeaks for fear, the basses roar;
Echoes from Pissing Alley° Sh—— call,
And Sh—— they resound from Aston Hall.°
About thy boat the little fishes throng,
As at the morning toast that floats along.   50
Sometimes, as prince of thy harmonious band,
Thou wield'st thy papers in thy threshing hand.
St. André's feet° ne'er kept more equal time,
Not even the feet of thy own *Psyche's* rhyme;°
Tho' they in number as in sense excel:
So just, so like tautology, they fell,
That, pale with envy, Singleton° forswore
The lute and sword, which he in triumph bore,
And vowed he ne'er would act Villerius° more."
Here stopped the good old sire, and wept for joy   60
In silent raptures of the hopeful boy.
All arguments, but most his plays, persuade,
That for anointed dulness he was made.
   Close to the walls which fair Augusta° bind,
(The fair Augusta much to fears inclined,)
An ancient fabric raised to inform the sight,
There stood of yore, and Barbican° it hight:
A watchtower once; but now, so fate ordains,
Of all the pile an empty name remains.
From its old ruins brothel-houses rise,   70
Scenes of lewd loves, and of polluted joys,
Where their vast courts the mother-strumpets keep,
And, undisturbed by watch, in silence sleep.
Near these a Nursery° erects its head,
Where queens are formed, and future heroes bred;
Where unfledged actors learn to laugh and cry,
Where infant punks their tender voices try,
And little Maximins° the gods defy.
Great Fletcher never treads in buskins here,
Nor greater Jonson dares in socks appear;   80
But gentle Simkin° just reception finds
Amidst this monument of vanished minds:
Pure clinches° the suburbian Muse affords,
And Panton° waging harmless war with words.
Here Flecknoe, as a place to fame well known,
Ambitiously designed his Sh——'s throne;
For ancient Dekker° prophesied long since,
That in this pile should reign a mighty prince,
Born for a scourge of wit, and flail of sense;   89
To whom true dulness should some *Psyches* owe,
But worlds of *Misers* from his pen should flow;
Humorists and *Hypocrites* it should produce,

47. Pissing Alley: in London, near the Strand.   48. Aston
Hall: unidentified.   53. St. André: a dancing master.   54.
Psyche: an opera by Shadwell.   57. Singleton: a contemporary
musician.   59. Villerius: in a play by Davenant.   64. Augusta: London.   67. Barbican: a London street.   74. Nursery: a theater where young actors were trained.   78. Maximin:
hero of Dryden's *Tyrannic Love.*   81. Simkin: a clown.
83. clinches: puns.   84. Panton: a famous punster.   87. Dekker: Thomas Dekker, an Elizabethan playwright, better than
suggested.

Whole Raymond families, and tribes of Bruce.°
　Now Empress Fame had published the renown
Of Sh——'s coronation thro' the town.
Roused by report of Fame, the nations meet,
From near Bunhill, and distant Watling Street.
No Persian carpets spread the imperial way,
But scattered limbs of mangled poets lay;
From dusty shops neglected authors come,　　100
Martyrs of pies,° and relics of the bum.
Much Heywood, Shirley, Ogleby° there lay,
But loads of Sh—— almost choked the way.
Bilked stationers for yeomen stood prepared,
And Herringman° was captain of the guard.
The hoary prince in majesty appeared,
High on a throne of his own labors reared.
At his right hand our young Ascanius° sate,
Rome's other hope, and pillar of the State.
His brows thick fogs, instead of glories, grace,　110
And lambent dulness played around his face.
As Hannibal° did to the altars come,
Sworn by his sire a mortal foe to Rome;
So Sh—— swore, nor should his vow be vain,
That he till death true dulness would maintain;
And, in his father's right, and realm's defense,
Ne'er to have peace with wit, nor truce with sense.
The king himself the sacred unction made,
As king by office, and as priest by trade.
In his sinister hand, instead of ball,　　120
He placed a mighty mug of potent ale;
Love's Kingdom° to his right he did convey,
At once his scepter, and his rule of sway;
Whose righteous lore the prince had practiced young,
And from whose loins recorded *Psyche* sprung.
His temples, last, with poppies° were o'erspread,
That nodding seemed to consecrate his head.
Just at that point of time, if fame not lie,
On his left hand twelve reverend owls did fly.
So Romulus, 'tis sung, by Tiber's brook,　　130
Presage of sway from twice six vultures took.
The admiring throng loud acclamations make,
And omens of his future empire take.
The sire then shook the honors of his head,
And from his brows damps of oblivion shed
Full on the filial dulness: long he stood,
Repelling from his breast the raging god;
At length burst out in this prophetic mood:
　"Heavens bless my son, from Ireland let him
　　reign
To far Barbadoes on the western main;　　140

Of his dominion may no end be known,
And greater than his father's be his throne;
Beyond *Love's Kingdom* let him stretch his pen!"
He paused, and all the people cried, "Amen."
Then thus continued he: "My son, advance
Still in new impudence, new ignorance.
Success let others teach, learn thou from me
Pangs without birth, and fruitless industry.
Let *Virtuosos*° in five years be writ;
Yet not one thought accuse thy toil of wit.　　150
Let gentle George° in triumph tread the stage,
Make Dorimant° betray, and Loveit° rage;
Let Cully,° Cockwood,° Fopling,° charm the pit,
And in their folly shew the writer's wit.
Yet still thy fools shall stand in thy defense,
And justify their author's want of sense.
Let 'em be all by thy own model made
Of dulness, and desire no foreign aid;
That they to future ages may be known,
Not copies drawn, but issue of thy own.　　160
Nay, let thy men of wit too be the same,
All full of thee, and differing but in name.
But let no alien S—dl—y interpose,
To lard with wit thy hungry *Epsom* prose.°
And when false flowers of rhetoric thou wouldst
　　cull,
Trust nature, do not labor to be dull;
But write thy best, and top; and, in each line,
Sir Formal's° oratory will be thine:
Sir Formal, tho' unsought, attends thy quill,
And does thy northern dedications° fill.　　170
Nor let false friends seduce thy mind to fame,
By arrogating Jonson's hostile name.
Let father Flecknoe fire thy mind with praise,
And uncle Ogleby thy envy raise.
Thou art my blood, where Jonson has no part:
What share have we in nature, or in art?
Where did his wit on learning fix a brand,
And rail at arts he did not understand?
Where made he love in Prince Nicander's° vein,
Or swept the dust in *Psyche's* humble strain?　　180
Where sold he bargains, 'whip-stitch, kiss my
　　arse,'°
Promis'd a play and dwindled to a farce?
When did his Muse from Fletcher scenes purloin,
As thou whole Etherege dost transfuse to thine?
But so transfused, as oil on water's flow,
His always floats above, thine sinks below.

91–93. *Misers* . . . *Humorists* . . . *Hypocrites* . . . *Raymond* . . . *Bruce*: plays by Shadwell, and characters in them.　101. Martyrs of pies: pages of books, torn out and sacrificed in the oven, under meat pies.　102. Ogleby: John Ogleby (Ogilby), poet and translator despised by Dryden.　105. Herringman: Henry Herringman, Dryden's first publisher.　108. Ascanius: son of Aeneas.　112. Hannibal: Hannibal was required by his father to swear eternal hatred to Rome.　122. *Love's Kingdom*: a play by Flecknoe.　126. poppies: Shadwell was believed to take opium.

149. *Virtuosos*: Shadwell wrote *The Virtuoso*, a satire on the Royal Society.　151. gentle George: Sir George Etherege, a playwright admired by Dryden.　152-53. Dorimant . . . Loveit . . . Cully, Cockwood, Fopling: characters in Etherege's plays.　163-64. S-dl-y . . . prose: Sir Charles Sedley, poet and friend of Dryden, had helped Shadwell write *Epsom Wells*.　168. Sir Formal: in Shadwell's *The Virtuoso*.　170. northern dedications: Shadwell often dedicated plays to the Duke of Newcastle, in the North of England.　179. Prince Nicander: in Shadwell's *Psyche*.　181. whip-stitch . . . arse: line spoken by Sir Samuel Hearty in Shadwell's *The Virtuoso*.

This is thy province, this thy wondrous way,
New humors to invent for each new play:
This is that boasted bias of thy mind,
By which one way, to dulness, 'tis inclined;   190
Which makes thy writings lean on one side still,
And, in all changes, that way bends thy will.°
Nor let thy mountain-belly make pretense
Of likeness; thine's a tympany of sense.
A tun of man in thy large bulk is writ,
But sure thou'rt but a kilderkin of wit.
Like mine, thy gentle numbers feebly creep;
Thy tragic Muse gives smiles, thy comic sleep.
With whate'er gall thou sett'st thyself to write,
Thy inoffensive satires never bite.   200
In thy felonious heart tho' venom lies,
It does but touch thy Irish pen,° and dies.
Thy genius calls thee not to purchase fame
In keen iambics, but mild anagram.
Leave writing plays, and choose for thy command
Some peaceful province in acrostic land.
There thou may'st wings display and altars raise,
And torture one poor word ten thousand ways.°
Or, if thou wouldst thy different talents suit,
Set thy own songs, and sing them to thy lute."   210
   He said: but his last words were scarcely heard;
For Bruce and Longvil° had a trap prepared,
And down they sent the yet declaiming bard.
Sinking he left his drugget robe behind,
Borne upwards by a subterranean wind.
The mantle fell to the young prophet's part,
With double portion of his father's art.

ABSALOM AND ACHITOPHEL

   The best preparation for understanding *Absalom
and Achitophel* is to read with care the two books of
Samuel in the Bible, which contain the biography of
David; but particularly II Sam. 13–20, which tells of
Absalom and his revolt, and of his counselor Achitophel.
The political situation in England to which Dryden
applied the tale is outlined in the Introduction (pp.
525–26). The parallel to contemporary persons and
events was surprisingly close, and this added not a
little to the cleverness of the satire. The Duke of Monmouth (Absalom), eldest of Charles's illegitimate sons,
claimed to be legitimate; and the Earl of Shaftesbury
(Achitophel), though Dryden grants him great merits
in another connection, deserves more or less the character here given him. Dryden's poem was published
anonymously in 1681, but his authorship was soon
known, and in spite of the fact that he did not acknowledge the poem until 1692, and never put his

name to it in his lifetime, it was basic to his contemporary reputation. Its largeness of manner and its
generosity of view — given Dryden's bias in favor of
Charles and the Tories — worked to make most of its
judgments as just as any that have been passed upon
this important crisis in the history of the English
people, who in 1688 were to see the second great revolution of their century.

In pious times, ere priestcraft did begin,
Before polygamy was made a sin;
When man on many multiplied his kind,
Ere one to one was cursedly confined;
When nature prompted, and no law denied
Promiscuous use of concubine and bride;
Then Israel's monarch after Heaven's own heart,
His vigorous warmth did variously impart
To wives and slaves; and, wide as his command,
Scattered his Maker's image thro' the land.°   10
Michal,° of royal blood, the crown did wear;
A soil ungrateful to the tiller's care:
Not so the rest; for several mothers bore
To godlike David several sons before.
But since like slaves his bed they did ascend,
No true succession could their seed attend.
Of all this numerous progeny was none
So beautiful, so brave, as Absalon:°
Whether, inspired by some diviner lust,
His father got him with a greater gust;   20
Or that his conscious destiny made way,
By manly beauty, to imperial sway.
Early in foreign fields he won renown,
With kings and states allied to Israel's crown:
In peace the thoughts of war he could remove,
And seemed as he were only born for love.
Whate'er he did, was done with so much ease,
In him alone 'twas natural to please:
His motions all accompanied with grace;
And paradise was opened in his face.   30
With secret joy indulgent David viewed
His youthful image in his son renewed:
To all his wishes nothing he denied;
And made the charming Annabel° his bride.
What faults he had, (for who from faults is free?)
His father could not, or he would not see.
Some warm excesses which the law forbore,
Were construed youth that purged by boiling o'er,
And Amnon's murther,° by a specious name,
Was called a just revenge for injured fame.   40
Thus praised and loved the noble youth remained,
While David, undisturbed, in Sion° reigned.

189-92. This . . . will: a parody of four lines by Shadwell in
The Humorists.   202. Irish pen: Shadwell was not Irish,
though Flecknoe was.   206-08. acrostic . . . ways: a reference to a seventeenth-century custom of printing poems in the
shape of wings, altars, crosses, etc.   212. Bruce and Longvil:
in Shadwell's *Virtuoso*.

ABSALOM AND ACHITOPHEL.   1-10. In . . . land: Charles II,
like David, had many concubines who bore him many children.
11. Michal: Queen Catherine had no children by Charles II, as
Michal had none by David.   18. Absalon: the Duke of Monmouth, son of Charles II by Lucy Walters.   34. Annabel:
Anne Scott, Monmouth's wife.   39. Amnon's murther: no
parallel is known for Absalom's murder of Amnon, his brother,
because he had violated Tamar, their sister.   42. Sion: London.

But life can never be sincerely blest;
Heaven punishes the bad, and proves the best.
The Jews,° a headstrong, moody, murmuring race,
As ever tried the extent and stretch of grace;
God's pampered people, whom, debauched with ease,
No king could govern, nor no God could please;
(Gods they had tried of every shape and size,
That god-smiths could produce, or priests devise:)
These Adam-wits, too fortunately free,   51
Began to dream they wanted liberty;
And when no rule, no precedent was found,
Of men by laws less circumscribed and bound;
They led their wild desires to woods and caves,
And thought that all but savages were slaves.
They who, when Saul° was dead, without a blow,
Made foolish Ishbosheth° the crown forego;
Who banished David did from Hebron° bring,
And with a general shout proclaimed him king: 60
Those very Jews, who, at their very best,
Their humor more than loyalty expressed,
Now wondered why so long they had obeyed
An idol monarch, which their hands had made;
Thought they might ruin him they could create,
Or melt him to that golden calf, a State.°
But these were random bolts; no formed design,
Nor interest made the factious crowd to join:
The sober part of Israel, free from stain,
Well knew the value of a peaceful reign;   70
And, looking backward with a wise affright,
Saw seams of wounds, dishonest to the sight:
In contemplation of whose ugly scars
They cursed the memory of civil wars.
The moderate sort of men, thus qualified,
Inclined the balance to the better side;
And David's mildness managed it so well,
The bad found no occasion to rebel.
But when to sin our biased nature leans,
The careful Devil is still at hand with means;   80
And providently pimps for ill desires.
The Good Old Cause° revived, a plot requires:
Plots, true or false, are necessary things,
To raise up commonwealths, and ruin kings.
    The inhabitants of old Jerusalem°
Were Jebusites;° the town so called from them;
And theirs the native right——
But when the chosen people° grew more strong,
The rightful cause at length became the wrong;
And every loss the men of Jebus bore,   90
They still were thought God's enemies the more.
Thus worn and weakened, well or ill content,

Submit they must to David's government:
Impoverished and deprived of all command,
Their taxes doubled as they lost their land;
And, what was harder yet to flesh and blood,
Their gods disgraced, and burnt like common wood.
This set the heathen priesthood in a flame;
For priests of all religions are the same:
Of whatsoe'er descent their godhead be,   100
Stock, stone, or other homely pedigree,
In his defense his servants are as bold,
As if he had been born of beaten gold.
The Jewish rabbins,° tho' their enemies,
In this conclude them honest men and wise:
For 'twas their duty, all the learnèd think,
T'espouse his cause, by whom they eat and drink.
From hence began that Plot,° the nation's curse,
Bad in itself, but represented worse;
Raised in extremes, and in extremes decried;   110
With oaths affirmed, with dying vows denied;
Not weighed or winnowed by the multitude;
But swallowed in the mass, unchewed and crude.
Some truth there was, but dashed and brewed with lies,
To please the fools, and puzzle all the wise.
Succeeding times did equal folly call,
Believing nothing, or believing all.
The Egyptian° rites the Jebusites embraced;
Where gods were recommended by their taste.
Such savory deities must needs be good,   120
As served at once for worship and for food.°
By force they could not introduce these gods,
For ten to one in former days was odds;
So fraud was used (the sacrificer's trade):
Fools are more hard to conquer than persuade.
Their busy teachers mingled with the Jews,
And raked for converts even the court and stews:
Which Hebrew priests° the more unkindly took,
Because the fleece accompanies the flock.
Some thought they God's anointed° meant to slay
By guns, invented since full many a day: 131
Our author swears it not; but who can know
How far the Devil and Jebusites may go?
This Plot, which failed for want of common sense,
Had yet a deep and dangerous consequence:
For, as when raging fevers boil the blood,
The standing lake soon floats into a flood,
And every hostile humor, which before
Slept quiet in its channels, bubbles o'er;
So several factions from this first ferment   140
Work up to foam, and threat the government.
Some by their friends, more by themselves thought wise,

---

45. The Jews: the English.   57. Saul: Oliver Cromwell.
58. Ishbosheth: Richard Cromwell.   59. Hebron: Scotland.
66. a State: a republic.   82. The . . . Cause: the Commonwealth, the government of England by Cromwell and Parliament, 1649–60.   85. Jerusalem: London.   86. Jebusites:
Roman Catholics.   88. chosen people: Protestants.

104. Jewish rabbins: Anglican theologians.   108. Plot: the
alleged Popish Plot (1678), first "exposed" by the informer
Titus Oates.   118. Egyptian: French.   121. for worship . . .
food: the doctrine of transubstantiation.   128. Hebrew priests:
Anglican clergymen.   130. God's anointed: Charles II.

Opposed the power to which they could not rise.
Some had in courts been great, and thrown from
    thence,
Like fiends were hardened in impenitence.
Some, by their monarch's fatal mercy, grown
From pardoned rebels kinsmen to the throne,
Were raised in power and public office high;
Strong bands, if bands ungrateful men could tie.
  Of these the false Achitophel° was first;   150
A name to all succeeding ages curst:
For close designs and crooked counsels fit;
Sagacious, bold, and turbulent of wit;
Restless, unfixed in principles and place;
In power unpleased, impatient of disgrace:
A fiery soul, which, working out its way,
Fretted the pigmy body° to decay,
And o'er-informed the tenement of clay.
A daring pilot in extremity;
Pleased with the danger, when the waves went high,
He sought the storms; but, for a calm unfit,   161
Would steer too nigh the sands, to boast his wit.
Great wits are sure to madness near allied,
And thin partitions do their bounds divide;
Else why should he, with wealth and honor blest,
Refuse his age the needful hours of rest?
Punish a body which he could not please;
Bankrupt of life, yet prodigal of ease?
And all to leave what with his toil he won,
To that unfeathered two-legged thing, a son;   170
Got, while his soul did huddled notions try;
And born a shapeless lump, like anarchy.
In friendship false, implacable in hate;
Resolved to ruin or to rule the State.
To compass this the triple bond° he broke;
The pillars of the public safety shook;
And fitted Israel for a foreign° yoke:
Then seized with fear, yet still affecting fame,
Usurped a patriot's all-atoning name.
So easy still it proves in factious times,   180
With public zeal to cancel private crimes.
How safe is treason, and how sacred ill,
Where none can sin against the people's will!
Where crowds can wink, and no offense be known,
Since in another's guilt they find their own!
Yet fame deserved no enemy can grudge;
The statesman we abhor, but praise the judge.
In Israel's courts ne'er sat an Abbethdin°
With more discerning eyes, or hands more clean;
Unbribed, unsought, the wretched to redress;   190
Swift of dispatch, and easy of access.
O, had he been content to serve the crown,

150. **Achitophel:** the Earl of Shaftesbury (1621–83), whose distinguished career does not wholly justify this portrait, though
he was cynical in the use he made of the Popish Plot.   157.
pigmy body: Shaftesbury's body was too small for his soul,
which burst its bounds.   175. **triple bond:** alliance between
England, Sweden, and Holland.   177. **foreign:** French.
188. **Abbethdin:** Hebrew judge; Shaftesbury was Lord Chancellor.

With virtues only proper to the gown;
Or had the rankness of the soil been freed
From cockle, that oppressed the noble seed;
David for him his tuneful harp had strung,
And Heaven had wanted one immortal song.
But wild Ambition loves to slide, not stand,
And Fortune's ice prefers to Virtue's land.
Achitophel, grown weary to possess   200
A lawful fame, and lazy happiness,
Disdained the golden fruit to gather free,
And lent the crowd his arm to shake the tree.
Now, manifest of crimes contrived long since,
He stood at bold defiance with his prince;
Held up the buckler of the people's cause
Against the crown, and skulked behind the laws.
The wished occasion of the Plot he takes;
Some circumstances finds, but more he makes.
By buzzing emissaries fills the ears   210
Of listening crowds with jealousies and fears
Of arbitrary counsels brought to light,
And proves the king himself a Jebusite.
Weak arguments! which yet he knew full well
Were strong with people easy to rebel.
For, governed by the moon, the giddy Jews
Tread the same track when she the prime renews;
And once in twenty years, their scribes record,
By natural instinct they change their lord.
Achitophel still wants a chief, and none   220
Was found so fit as warlike Absalon:
Not that he wished his greatness to create,
(For politicians neither love nor hate,)
But, for he knew his title not allowed,
Would keep him still depending on the crowd:
That kingly power, thus ebbing out, might be
Drawn to the dregs of a democracy.
Him he attempts with studied arts to please,
And sheds his venom in such words as these:
  "Auspicious prince, at whose nativity   230
Some royal planet ruled the southern sky;
Thy longing country's darling and desire;
Their cloudy pillar and their guardian fire:
Their second Moses, whose extended wand
Divides the seas, and shews the promised land;
Whose dawning day in every distant age
Has exercised the sacred prophets' rage:
The people's prayer, the glad diviners' theme,
The young men's vision, and the old men's dream!
Thee, Savior, thee, the nation's vows confess,   240
And, never satisfied with seeing, bless:
Swift unbespoken pomps thy steps proclaim,
And stammering babes are taught to lisp thy name.
How long wilt thou the general joy detain,
Starve and defraud the people of thy reign?
Content ingloriously to pass thy days
Like one of Virtue's fools that feeds on praise;
Till thy fresh glories, which now shine so bright,
Grow stale and tarnish with our daily sight.

Believe me, royal youth, thy fruit must be   250
Or gathered ripe, or rot upon the tree.
Heaven has to all allotted, soon or late,
Some lucky revolution of their fate;
Whose motions if we watch and guide with skill,
(For human good depends on human will,)
Our Fortune rolls as from a smooth descent,
And from the first impression takes the bent:
But, if unseized, she glides away like wind,
And leaves repenting Folly far behind.
Now, now she meets you with a glorious prize,   260
And spreads her locks before her as she flies.
Had thus old David, from whose loins you spring,
Not dared, when Fortune called him, to be king,
At Gath° an exile he might still remain,
And Heaven's anointing oil had been in vain.
Let his successful youth your hopes engage;
But shun the example of declining age:
Behold him setting in his western skies,
The shadows lengthening as the vapors rise.
He is not now, as when on Jordan's sand°   270
The joyful people thronged to see him land,
Covering the beach, and blackening all the strand;
But, like the Prince of Angels, from his height
Comes tumbling downward with diminished light;
Betrayed by one poor plot to public scorn,
(Our only blessing since his curst return;)
Those heaps of people which one sheaf did bind,
Blown off and scattered by a puff of wind.
What strength can he to your designs oppose,
Naked of friends, and round beset with foes?   280
If Pharaoh's° doubtful succor he should use,
A foreign aid would more incense the Jews:
Proud Egypt° would dissembled friendship bring;
Foment the war, but not support the king:
Nor would the royal party e'er unite
With Pharaoh's arms to assist the Jebusite;
Or if they should, their interest soon would break,
And with such odious aid make David weak.
All sorts of men by my successful arts,
Abhorring kings, estrange their altered hearts 290
From David's rule: and 'tis the general cry,
'Religion, commonwealth, and liberty.'
If you, as champion of the public good,
Add to their arms a chief of royal blood,
What may not Israel hope, and what applause
Might such a general gain by such a cause?
Not barren praise alone, that gaudy flower
Fair only to the sight, but solid power;
And nobler is a limited command,
Given by the love of all your native land,   300
Than a successive title, long and dark,
Drawn from the moldy rolls of Noah's ark."
    What cannot praise effect in mighty minds,

When flattery soothes, and when ambition blinds!
Desire of power, on earth a vicious weed,
Yet, sprung from high, is of celestial seed:
In God 'tis glory; and when men aspire,
'Tis but a spark too much of heavenly fire.
The ambitious youth, too covetous of fame,
Too full of angels' metal in his frame,   310
Unwarily was led from virtue's ways,
Made drunk with honor, and debauched with
    praise.
Half loth, and half consenting to the ill,
(For loyal blood within him struggled still,)
He thus replied: "And what pretense have I
To take up arms for public liberty?
My father governs with unquestioned right;
The faith's defender, and mankind's delight;
Good, gracious, just, observant of the laws:
And Heaven by wonders has espoused his
    cause.   320
Whom has he wronged in all his peaceful reign?
Who sues for justice to his throne in vain?
What millions has he pardoned of his foes,
Whom just revenge did to his wrath expose?
Mild, easy, humble, studious of our good;
Enclined to mercy, and averse from blood;
If mildness ill with stubborn Israel suit,
His crime is God's beloved attribute.
What could he gain, his people to betray,
Or change his right for arbitrary sway?   330
Let haughty Pharaoh curse with such a reign
His fruitful Nile, and yoke a servile train.
If David's rule Jerusalem displease,
The Dog-star heats their brains to this disease.
Why then should I, encouraging the bad,
Turn rebel and run popularly mad?
Were he a tyrant, who, by lawless might
Oppressed the Jews, and raised the Jebusite,
Well might I mourn; but nature's holy bands
Would curb my spirits and restrain my hands: 340
The people might assert their liberty;
But what was right in them were crime in me.
His favor leaves me nothing to require,
Prevents my wishes, and outruns desire.
What more can I expect while David lives?
All but his kingly diadem he gives:
And that "— But there he paused; then sighing,
    said —
"Is justly destined for a worthier head.
For when my father from his toils shall rest,
And late augment the number of the blest,   350
His lawful issue shall the throne ascend,
Or the *collateral* line, where that shall end.
His brother,° tho' oppressed with vulgar spite,
Yet dauntless, and secure of native right,

---

264. Gath: Brussels.   270. Jordan's sand: the cliffs of Dover.
281. Pharaoh: Louis XIV of France.   283. Egypt: France.

353. His brother: James, Duke of York, later James II.

Of every royal virtue stands possessed;
Still dear to all the bravest and the best.
His courage foes, his friends his truth proclaim;
His loyalty the king, the world his fame.
His mercy even the offending crowd will find;
For sure he comes of a forgiving kind.   360
Why should I then repine at Heaven's decree,
Which gives me no pretense to royalty?
Yet O that fate, propitiously inclined,
Had raised my birth, or had debased my mind;
To my large soul not all her treasure lent,
And then betrayed it to a mean descent!
I find, I find my mounting spirits bold,
And David's part disdains my mother's mold.
Why am I scanted by a niggard birth?
My soul disclaims the kindred of her earth;   370
And, made for empire, whispers me within,
'Desire of greatness is a godlike sin.'"
    Him staggering so when hell's dire agent found,
While fainting Virtue scarce maintained her
        ground,
He pours fresh forces in, and thus replies:
    "The eternal God, supremely good and wise,
Imparts not these prodigious gifts in vain:
What wonders are reserved to bless your reign!
Against your will, your arguments have shown,
Such virtue's only given to guide a throne.   380
Not that your father's mildness I contemn;
But manly force becomes the diadem.
'Tis true he grants the people all they crave;
And more, perhaps, than subjects ought to have:
For lavish grants suppose a monarch tame,
And more his goodness than his wit proclaim.
But when should people strive their bonds to break,
If not when kings are negligent or weak?
Let him give on till he can give no more,
The thrifty Sanhedrin° shall keep him poor;   390
And every shekel which he can receive,
Shall cost a limb of his prerogative.
To ply him with new plots shall be my care;
Or plunge him deep in some expensive war;
Which when his treasure can no more supply,
He must, with the remains of kingship, buy.
His faithful friends, our jealousies and fears
Call Jebusites, and Pharaoh's pensioners;
Whom when our fury from his aid has torn,
He shall be naked left to public scorn.   400
The next successor, whom I fear and hate,
My arts have made obnoxious to the State;
Turned all his virtues to his overthrow,
And gained our elders to pronounce a foe.
His right, for sums of necessary gold,
Shall first be pawned, and afterwards be sold;
Till time shall ever-wanting David draw,
To pass your doubtful title into law:

390. **Sanhedrin**: Parliament.

If not, the people have a right supreme
To make their kings; for kings are made for
        them.   410
All empire is no more than power in trust,
Which, when resumed, can be no longer just.
Succession, for the general good designed,
In its own wrong a nation cannot bind;
If altering that the people can relieve,
Better one suffer than a nation grieve.
The Jews well know their power: ere Saul they
        chose,
God was their king, and God they durst depose.
Urge now your piety, your filial name,
A father's right, and fear of future fame;   420
The public good, that universal call,
To which even Heaven submitted, answers all.
Nor let his love enchant your generous mind;
'Tis Nature's trick to propagate her kind.
Our fond begetters, who would never die,
Love but themselves in their posterity.
Or let his kindness by the effects be tried,
Or let him lay his vain pretense aside.
God said he loved your father; could he bring
A better proof, than to anoint him king?   430
It surely shewed he loved the shepherd well,
Who gave so fair a flock as Israel.
Would David have you thought his darling son?
What means he then, to alienate the crown?
The name of godly he may blush to bear:
'Tis after God's own heart to cheat his heir.
He to his brother gives supreme command,
To you a legacy of barren land:
Perhaps the old harp, on which he thrums his lays,
Or some dull Hebrew ballad in your praise.   440
Then the next heir, a prince severe and wise,
Already looks on you with jealous eyes;
Sees thro' the thin disguises of your arts,
And marks your progress in the people's hearts.
Tho' now his mighty soul its grief contains,
He meditates revenge who least complains;
And, like a lion, slumbering in the way,
Or sleep dissembling, while he waits his prey,
His fearless foes within his distance draws,
Constrains his roaring, and contracts his paws; 450
Till at the last, his time for fury found,
He shoots with sudden vengeance from the ground;
The prostrate vulgar passes o'er and spares,
But with a lordly rage his hunters tears.
Your case no tame expedients will afford:
Resolve on death, or conquest by the sword,
Which for no less a stake than life you draw;
And self-defense is nature's eldest law.
Leave the warm people no considering time;
For then rebellion may be thought a crime.   460
Prevail yourself of what occasion gives,
But try your title while your father lives;

And that your arms may have a fair pretense,
Proclaim you take them in the king's defense;
Whose sacred life each minute would expose
To plots, from seeming friends, and secret foes.
And who can sound the depth of David's soul?
Perhaps his fear his kindness may control.
He fears his brother, tho' he loves his son,
For plighted vows too late to be undone.   470
If so, by force he wishes to be gained;
Like women's lechery, to seem constrained.
Doubt not: but, when he most affects the frown,
Commit a pleasing rape upon the crown.
Secure his person to secure your cause:
They who possess the prince, possess the laws."
  He said, and this advice above the rest,
With Absalom's mild nature suited best:
Unblamed of life, (ambition set aside,)
Not stained with cruelty, nor puffed with
    pride;   480
How happy had he been, if destiny
Had higher placed his birth, or not so high!
His kingly virtues might have claimed a throne,
And blest all other countries but his own.
But charming greatness since so few refuse,
'Tis juster to lament him than accuse.
Strong were his hopes a rival to remove,
With blandishments to gain the public love;
To head the faction while their zeal was hot,
And popularly prosecute the Plot.   490
To farther this, Achitophel unites
The malcontents of all the Israelites;
Whose differing parties he could wisely join,
For several ends, to serve the same design:
The best, (and of the princes some were such,)
Who thought the power of monarchy too much;
Mistaken men, and patriots in their hearts;
Not wicked, but seduced by impious arts.
By these the springs of property were bent,
And wound so high, they cracked the gov-
    ernment.   500
The next for interest sought to embroil the State,
To sell their duty at a dearer rate;
And make their Jewish markets of the throne,
Pretending public good, to serve their own.
Others thought kings an useless heavy load,
Who cost too much, and did too little good.
These were for laying honest David by,
On principles of pure good husbandry.
With them joined all the haranguers of the throng,
That thought to get preferment by the tongue.   510
Who follow next, a double danger bring,
Not only hating David, but the king:
The Solymaean rout,° well-versed of old
In godly faction, and in treason bold;
Cowering and quaking at a conqueror's sword;

513. Solymaean rout: London mob.

But lofty to a lawful prince restored;
Saw with disdain an Ethnic° plot begun,
And scorned by Jebusites to be outdone.
Hot Levites° headed these; who, pulled before
From the ark, which in the Judges' days they
    bore,   520
Resumed their cant, and with a zealous cry
Pursued their old beloved Theocracy:
Where Sanhedrin and priest enslaved the nation,
And justified their spoils by inspiration:
For who so fit for reign as Aaron's race,°
If once dominion they could found in grace.
These led the pack; tho' not of surest scent,
Yet deepest mouthed against the government.
A numerous host of dreaming saints succeed,
Of the true old enthusiastic breed: 530
'Gainst form and order they their power imploy,
Nothing to build, and all things to destroy.
But far more numerous was the herd of such,
Who think too little, and who talk too much.
These, out of mere instinct, they knew not why,
Adored their fathers' God and property;
And, by the same blind benefit of fate,
The Devil and the Jebusite did hate:
Born to be saved,° even in their own despite,
Because they could not help believing right.   540
Such were the tools; but a whole Hydra more
Remains, of sprouting heads too long to score.
Some of their chiefs were princes of the land:
In the first rank of these did Zimri° stand;
A man so various, that he seemed to be
Not one, but all mankind's epitome:
Stiff in opinions, always in the wrong;
Was everything by starts, and nothing long;
But, in the course of one revolving moon,
Was chymist, fiddler, statesman, and buffoon: 550
Then all for women, painting, rhyming, drinking,
Besides ten thousand freaks that died in thinking.
Blest madman, who could every hour employ,
With something new to wish, or to enjoy!
Railing and praising were his usual themes;
And both (to shew his judgment) in extremes:
So over-violent, or over-civil,
That every man, with him, was God or Devil.
In squandering wealth was his peculiar art:
Nothing went unrewarded but desert.   560
Beggared by fools, whom still he found too late,
He had his jest, and they had his estate.
He laughed himself from court; then sought relief
By forming parties, but could ne'er be chief;
For, spite of him, the weight of business fell
On Absalom and wise Achitophel:

517. Ethnic: Greek for Gentile, meaning Popish here.   519. Hot
Levites: Presbyterian clergymen.   525. Aaron's race: the
clergy.   539. born . . . saved: Calvinist doctrine of election.
544. Zimri: the Duke of Buckingham, author of *The Rehearsal*
and hence a literary enemy of Dryden.

Thus, wicked but in will, of means bereft,
He left not faction, but of that was left.
   Titles and names 'twere tedious to rehearse
Of lords, below the dignity of verse.   570
Wits, warriors, Commonwealth's-men, were the
    best;
Kind husbands, and mere nobles, all the rest.
And therefore, in the name of dulness, be
The well-hung Balaam° and cold Caleb,° free;
And canting Nadab° let oblivion damn,
Who made new porridge for the paschal lamb.
Let friendship's holy band some names assure;
Some their own worth, and some let scorn secure.
Nor shall the rascal rabble here have place,
Whom kings no titles gave, and God no grace: 580
Not bull-faced Jonas,° who could statutes draw
To mean rebellion, and make treason law.
But he, tho' bad, is followed by a worse,
The wretch who Heaven's anointed dared to curse:
Shimei,° whose youth did early promise bring
Of zeal to God and hatred to his king,
Did wisely from expensive sins refrain,
And never broke the Sabbath, but for gain;
Nor ever was he known an oath to vent,
Or curse, unless against the government.   590
Thus heaping wealth, by the most ready way
Among the Jews, which was to cheat and pray,
The city, to reward his pious hate
Against his master, chose him magistrate.
His hand a vare° of justice did uphold;
His neck was loaded with a chain of gold.
During his office, treason was no crime;
The sons of Belial° had a glorious time;
For Shimei, tho' not prodigal of pelf,
Yet loved his wicked neighbor as himself.   600
When two or three were gathered to declaim
Against the monarch of Jerusalem,
Shimei was always in the midst of them;
And if they cursed the king when he was by,
Would rather curse than break good company.
If any durst his factious friends accuse,
He packed a jury of dissenting Jews;
Whose fellow-feeling in the godly cause
Would free the suffering saint from human laws.
For laws are only made to punish those   610
Who serve the king, and to protect his foes.
If any leisure time he had from power,
(Because 'tis sin to misimploy an hour,)
His business was, by writing, to persuade

That kings were useless, and a clog to trade;
And, that his noble style he might refine,
No Rechabite° more shunned the fumes of wine
Chaste were his cellars, and his shrieval° board
The grossness of a city feast abhorred:
His cooks, with long disuse, their trade forgot;   620
Cool was his kitchen, tho' his brains were hot.
Such frugal virtue malice may accuse,
But sure 'twas necessary to the Jews;
For towns once burnt such magistrates require
As dare not tempt God's providence by fire.
With spiritual food he fed his servants well,
But free from flesh that made the Jews rebel;
And Moses' laws he held in more account,
For forty days of fasting in the mount.
   To speak the rest, who better are forgot,   630
Would tire a well-breathed witness of the Plot.
Yet, Corah,° thou shalt from oblivion pass:
Erect thyself, thou monumental brass,
High as the serpent° of thy metal made,
While nations stand secure beneath thy shade.
What tho' his birth were base, yet comets rise
From earthy vapors, ere they shine in skies.
Prodigious actions may as well be done
By weaver's issue, as by prince's son.
This arch-attestor for the public good   640
By that one deed ennobles all his blood.
Who ever asked the witnesses' high race,
Whose oath with martyrdom did Stephen grace?
Ours was a Levite, and as times went then,
His tribe were God Almighty's gentlemen.
Sunk were his eyes, his voice was harsh and loud,
Sure signs he neither choleric was nor proud:
His long chin proved his wit; his saintlike grace
A church vermilion, and a Moses' face.
His memory, miraculously great,   650
Could plots, exceeding man's belief, repeat;
Which therefore cannot be accounted lies,
For human wit could never such devise.
Some future truths are mingled in his book;
But where the witness failed, the prophet spoke:
Some things like visionary flights appear;
The spirit caught him up, the Lord knows where;
And gave him his rabbinical degree,
Unknown to foreign university.
His judgment yet his memory did excel;   660
Which pieced his wondrous evidence so well,
And suited to the temper of the times,
Then groaning under Jebusitic crimes.
Let Israel's foes suspect his heavenly call,
And rashly judge his writ apocryphal;
Our laws for such affronts have forfeits made:
He takes his life, who takes away his trade.

---

574. Balaam: the Earl of Huntingdon.   **Caleb:** Lord Grey.
575. Nadab: Lord Howard of Escrick, who in the Tower of
London attoned for treason by receiving the sacrament, but his
communion consisted of "lamb's wool," or ale poured over roasted
apples and sugar.   **581. Jonas:** Sir William Jones, prosecutor
in the Popish Plot.   **585. Shimei:** Slingsby Bethel, Whig
sheriff of London.   **595. vare:** wand.   **598. Belial:** wickedness personified, or Satan.

617. Rechabite: in the Bible, one who drinks no wine.   **618.
shrieval:** sheriff's.   **632. Corah:** Titus Oates (1649–1705) (see
p. 575*n*.).   **634. the serpent:** the brazen serpent of Moses.

Were I myself in witness Corah's place,
The wretch who did me such a dire disgrace,
Should whet my memory, tho' once forgot,   670
To make him an appendix of my plot.
His zeal to Heaven made him his prince despise,
And load his person with indignities;
But zeal peculiar privilege affords,
Indulging latitude to deeds and words;
And Corah might for Agag's murther° call,
In terms as coarse as Samuel used to Saul.°
What others in his evidence did join,
(The best that could be had for love or coin,)
In Corah's own predicament will fall;   680
For *witness* is a common name to all.
    Surrounded thus with friends of every sort,
Deluded Absalom forsakes the court;
Impatient of high hopes, urged with renown,
And fired with near possession of a crown.
The admiring crowd are dazzled with surprise,
And on his goodly person feed their eyes.
His joy concealed, he sets himself to show,
On each side bowing popularly low;
His looks, his gestures, and his words he
        frames,   690
And with familiar ease repeats their names.
Thus formed by nature, furnished out with arts,
He glides unfelt into their secret hearts.
Then, with a kind compassionating look,
And sighs, bespeaking pity ere he spoke,
Few words he said; but easy those and fit,
More slow than Hybla-drops,° and far more sweet.
    "I mourn, my countrymen, your lost estate;
Tho' far unable to prevent your fate:
Behold a banished man, for your dear cause   700
Exposed a prey to arbitrary laws!
Yet O! that I alone could be undone,
Cut off from empire, and no more a son!
Now all your liberties a spoil are made;
Egypt and Tyrus° intercept your trade,
And Jebusites your sacred rites invade.
My father, whom with reverence yet I name,
Charmed into ease, is careless of his fame;
And, bribed with petty sums of foreign gold,
Is grown in Bathsheba's° embraces old;   710
Exalts his enemies, his friends destroys;
And all his power against himself imploys.
He gives, and let him give, my right away;
But why should he his own and yours betray?
He, only he, can make the nation bleed,
And he alone from my revenge is freed.
Take then my tears, (with that he wiped his eyes,)

'Tis all the aid my present power supplies:
No court-informer can these arms accuse;
These arms may sons against their fathers use: 720
And 'tis my wish, the next successor's reign
May make no other Israelite complain."
    Youth, beauty, graceful action seldom fail;
But common interest always will prevail;
And pity never ceases to be shown
To him who makes the people's wrongs his own.
The crowd, that still believe their kings oppress,
With lifted hands their young Messiah bless:
Who now begins his progress to ordain
With chariots, horsemen, and a numerous
        train;   730
From east to west his glories he displays,
And, like the sun, the promised land surveys.
Fame runs before him as the morning star,
And shouts of joy salute him from afar:
Each house receives him as a guardian god,
And consecrates the place of his abode.
But hospitable treats did most commend
Wise Issachar,° his wealthy western friend.
This moving court, that caught the people's eyes,
And seemed but pomp, did other ends dis-
        guise: 740
Achitophel had formed it, with intent
To sound the depths, and fathom, where it went,
The people's hearts; distinguish friends from foes,
And try their strength, before they came to blows.
Yet all was colored with a smooth pretense
Of specious love, and duty to their prince.
Religion, and redress of grievances,
Two names that always cheat and always please,
Are often urged; and good King David's life
Endangered by a brother and a wife.°   750
Thus in a pageant shew a plot is made,
And peace itself is war in masquerade.
O foolish Israel! never warned by ill!
Still the same bait, and circumvented still!
Did ever men forsake their present ease,
In midst of health imagine a disease;
Take pains contingent mischiefs to foresee,
Make heirs for monarchs, and for God decree?
What shall we think! Can people give away,
Both for themselves and sons, their native
        sway?   760
Then they are left defenseless to the sword
Of each unbounded, arbitrary lord:
And laws are vain, by which we right enjoy,
If kings unquestioned can those laws destroy.
Yet if the crowd be judge of fit and just,
And kings are only officers in trust,
Then this resuming covenant was declared
When kings were made, or is for ever barred.

---

676. **Agag's murther**: the murder of Sir Edmund Berry Godfrey,
the magistrate before whom Oates had made his depositions in
the Popish Plot.   677. **Samuel . . . Saul**: Cf. I Sam. 15.
697. **Hybla-drops**: of honey.   705. **Egypt and Tyrus**: France
and Holland.   710. **Bathsheba**: the Duchess of Portsmouth,
mistress of Charles II.

738. **Issachar**: Thomas Thynne of Wiltshire.   750. **a brother
. . . wife**: the Duke of York and Queen Catherine.

If those who gave the scepter could not tie
By their own deed their own posterity,   770
How then could Adam bind his future race?
How could his forfeit on mankind take place?
Or how could heavenly justice damn us all,
Who ne'er consented to our father's fall?
Then kings are slaves to those whom they com-
    mand,
And tenants to their people's pleasure stand.
Add, that the power for property allowed
Is mischievously seated in the crowd;
For who can be secure of private right,
If sovereign sway may be dissolved by might?   780
Nor is the people's judgment always true:
The most may err as grossly as the few.
And faultless kings run down, by common cry,
For vice, oppression, and for tyranny.
What standard is there in a fickle rout,
Which, flowing to the mark, runs faster out?
Nor only crowds, but Sanhedrins may be
Infected with this public lunacy,
And share the madness of rebellious times,
To murther monarchs for imagined crimes.   790
If they may give and take whene'er they please,
Not kings alone, (the Godhead's images,)
But government itself at length must fall
To nature's state, where all have right to all.
Yet, grant our lords the people kings can make,
What prudent men a settled throne would shake?
For whatsoe'er their sufferings were before,
That change they covet makes them suffer more.
All other errors but disturb a state,
But innovation is the blow of fate.   800
If ancient fabrics nod, and threat to fall,
To patch the flaws, and buttress up the wall,
Thus far 'tis duty: but here fix the mark;
For all beyond it is to touch our ark.°
To change foundations, cast the frame anew,
Is work for rebels, who base ends pursue,
At once divine and human laws control,
And mend the parts by ruin of the whole.
The tampering world is subject to this curse,
To physic their disease into a worse.   810
    Now what relief can righteous David bring?
How fatal 'tis to be too good a king!
Friends he has few, so high the madness grows:
Who dare be such, must be the people's foes.
Yet some there were, even in the worst of days;
Some let me name, and naming is to praise.
    In this short file Barzillai° first appears;
Barzillai, crowned with honor and with years.
Long since, the rising rebels he withstood
In regions waste, beyond the Jordan's flood: 820
Unfortunately brave to buoy the State;

But sinking underneath his master's fate:
In exile with his godlike prince he mourned;
For him he suffered, and with him returned.
The court he practiced, not the courtier's art:
Large was his wealth, but larger was his heart,
Which well the noblest objects knew to choose,
The fighting warrior, and recording Muse.
His bed could once a fruitful issue boast;
Now more than half a father's name is lost.   830
His eldest hope,° with every grace adorned,
By me (so Heaven will have it) always mourned,
And always honored, snatched in manhood's prime
By unequal fates, and Providence's crime;
Yet not before the goal of honor won,
All parts fulfilled of subject and of son:
Swift was the race, but short the time to run.
O narrow circle, but of power divine,
Scanted in space, but perfect in thy line!
By sea, by land, thy matchless worth was
    known,   840
Arms thy delight, and war was all thy own:
Thy force, infused, the fainting Tyrians propped;
And haughty Pharaoh found his fortune stopped.
O ancient honor! O unconquered hand,
Whom foes unpunished never could withstand!
But Israel was unworthy of thy name;
Short is the date of all immoderate fame.
It looks as Heaven our ruin had designed,
And durst not trust thy fortune and thy mind.
Now, free from earth, thy disencumbered soul   850
Mounts up, and leaves behind the clouds and starry
    pole:
From thence thy kindred legions mayst thou bring,
To aid the guardian angel of thy king.
Here stop, my Muse, here cease thy painful flight;
No pinions can pursue immortal height:
Tell good Barzillai thou canst sing no more,
And tell thy soul she should have fled before.
Or fled she with his life, and left this verse
To hang on her departed patron's hearse?
Now take thy steepy flight from heaven, and
    see   860
If thou canst find on earth another *he*:
Another *he* would be too hard to find;
See then whom thou canst see not far behind.
Zadoc° the priest, whom, shunning power and
    place,
His lowly mind advanced to David's grace.
With him the Sagan of Jerusalem,°
Of hospitable soul, and noble stem;
Him of the western dome,° whose weighty sense
Flows in fit words and heavenly eloquence.
The prophets' sons, by such example led,   870

804. touch our ark: commit sacrilege.   817. Barzillai: the
Duke of Ormond, benefactor of Charles II.

831. His . . . hope: the Earl of Ossory.   864. Zadoc: William
Sancroft, Archbishop of Canterbury.   866. the . . . Jerusalem: the Bishop of London.   868. Him . . . dome: the Dean
of Westminster.

To learning and to loyalty were bred:
For colleges on bounteous kings depend,
And never rebel was to arts a friend.
To these succeed the pillars of the laws;
Who best could plead, and best can judge a cause.
Next them a train of loyal peers ascend;
Sharp-judging Adriel,° the Muses' friend;
Himself a Muse — in Sanhedrin's debate
True to his prince, but not a slave of state:
Whom David's love with honors did adorn,   880
That from his disobedient son were torn.
Jotham° of piercing wit, and pregnant thought;
Endued by nature, and by learning taught
To move assemblies, who but only tried
The worse a while, then chose the better side:
Nor chose alone, but turned the balance too;
So much the weight of one brave man can do.
Hushai,° the friend of David in distress;
In public storms, of manly steadfastness:
By foreign treaties he informed his youth,   890
And joined experience to his native truth.
His frugal care supplied the wanting throne;
Frugal for that, but bounteous of his own:
'Tis easy conduct when exchequers flow,
But hard the task to manage well the low;
For sovereign power is too depressed or high,
When kings are forced to sell, or crowds to buy.
Indulge one labor more, my weary Muse,
For Amiel:° who can Amiel's praise refuse?
Of ancient race by birth, but nobler yet   900
In his own worth, and without title great:
The Sanhedrin long time as chief he ruled,
Their reason guided, and their passion cooled:
So dextrous was he in the crown's defense,
So formed to speak a loyal nation's sense,
That, as their band was Israel's tribes in small,
So fit was he to represent them all.
Now rasher charioteers the seat ascend,
Whose loose careers his steady skill commend:
They, like the unequal ruler of the day,   910
Misguide the seasons, and mistake the way;
While he withdrawn at their mad labor smiles,
And safe enjoys the sabbath of his toils.
   These were the chief, a small but faithful band
Of worthies, in the breach who dared to stand,
And tempt the united fury of the land.
With grief they viewed such powerful engines bent,
To batter down the lawful government:
A numerous faction, with pretended frights,
In Sanhedrins to plume the regal rights;   920
The true successor from the court removed;
The Plot, by hireling witnesses, improved.
These ills they saw, and, as their duty bound,

877. **Adriel:** the Earl of Mulgrave, patron and friend of Dryden.
882. **Jotham:** the Marquis of Halifax.   888. **Hushai:** Viscount
Hyde.   899. **Amiel:** Edward Seymour, Speaker of the House
of Commons.

They shewed the king the danger of the wound;
That no concessions from the throne would please,
But lenitives fomented the disease;
That Absalom, ambitious of the crown,
Was made the lure to draw the people down;
That false Achitophel's pernicious hate
Had turned the Plot to ruin Church and State;   930
The council violent, the rabble worse;
That Shimei taught Jerusalem to curse.
   With all these loads of injuries oppressed,
And long revolving in his careful breast
The event of things, at last, his patience tired,
Thus from his royal throne, by Heaven inspired,
The godlike David spoke: with awful fear
His train their Maker in their master hear.
   " Thus long have I, by native mercy swayed,
My wrongs dissembled, my revenge delayed: 940
So willing to forgive the offending age;
So much the father did the king assuage.
But now so far my clemency they slight,
The offenders question my forgiving right.
That one was made for many, they contend;
But 'tis to rule; for that's a monarch's end.
They call my tenderness of blood, my fear;
Tho' manly tempers can the longest bear.
Yet, since they will divert my native course,
'Tis time to shew I am not good by force.   950
Those heaped affronts that haughty subjects bring,
Are burthens for a camel, not a king.
Kings are the public pillars of the State,
Born to sustain and prop the nation's weight;
If my young Samson will pretend a call
To shake the column, let him share the fall:
But O that yet he would repent and live!
How easy 'tis for parents to forgive!
With how few tears a pardon might be won
From nature, pleading for a darling son!   960
Poor pitied youth, by my paternal care
Raised up to all the height his frame could bear!
Had God ordained his fate for empire born,
He would have given his soul another turn:
Gulled with a patriot's name, whose modern sense
Is one that would by law supplant his prince;
The people's brave, the politician's tool;
Never was patriot yet, but was a fool.
Whence comes it that religion and the laws
Should more be Absalom's than David's cause?   970
His old instructor, ere he lost his place,
Was never thought indued with so much grace.
Good heavens, how faction can a patriot paint!
My rebel ever proves my people's saint.
Would *they* impose an heir upon the throne?
Let Sanhedrins be taught to give their own.
A king's at least a part of government,
And mine as requisite as their consent;
Without my leave a future king to choose,

Infers a right the present to depose.   980
True, they petition me to approve their choice;
But Esau's hands suit ill with Jacob's voice.
My pious subjects for my safety pray;
Which to secure, they take my power away.
From plots and treasons Heaven preserve my years,
But save me most from my petitioners!
Unsatiate as the barren womb or grave;
God cannot grant so much as they can crave.
What then is left, but with a jealous eye
To guard the small remains of royalty?   990
The law shall still direct my peaceful sway,
And the same law teach rebels to obey:
Votes shall no more established power control —
Such votes as make a part exceed the whole:
No groundless clamors shall my friends remove,
Nor crowds have power to punish ere they prove;
For gods and godlike kings their care express,
Still to defend their servants in distress.
O that my power to saving were confined!
Why am I forced, like Heaven, against my
       mind,   1000
To make examples of another kind?
Must I at length the sword of justice draw?
O curst effects of necessary law!
How ill my fear they by my mercy scan!
Beware the fury of a patient man.
Law they require, let Law then shew her face;
They could not be content to look on Grace,
Her hinder parts, but with a daring eye
To tempt the terror of her front and die.°
By their own arts, 'tis righteously decreed,   1010
Those dire artificers of death shall bleed.
Against themselves their witnesses will swear,
Till viper-like their mother Plot they tear;
And suck for nutriment that bloody gore,
Which was their principle of life before.
Their Belial with their Belzebub will fight;
Thus on my foes, my foes shall do me right.
Nor doubt the event; for factious crowds engage,
In their first onset, all their brutal rage.
Then let 'em take an unresisted course;   1020
Retire, and traverse, and delude their force;
But, when they stand all breathless, urge the fight,
And rise upon 'em with redoubled might;
For lawful power is still superior found;
When long driven back, at length it stands the
       ground."
   He said. The Almighty, nodding, gave consent;
And peals of thunder shook the firmament.
Henceforth a series of new time began,
The mighty years in long procession ran:
Once more the godlike David was restored,   1030
And willing nations knew their lawful lord.

1006-09. Law . . . die: Cf. Exod. 33:20-23.

from ABSALOM AND ACHITOPHEL, Part II

The sequel to *Absalom and Achitophel* (1682) was written, according to Dryden's publisher Jacob Tonson, by Nahum Tate (1652–1715), at Dryden's suggestion and with his help. Tonson specifically says that Dryden contributed a section of some 200 lines containing the "characters" of Doeg (Elkanah Settle) and Og (Thomas Shadwell), the two poets with whom he was most often at war. Their Biblical names here have no special pertinence.

And hasten Og and Doeg to rehearse,
Two fools that crutch their feeble sense on verse;
Who, by my Muse, to all succeeding times   410
Shall live, in spite of their own doggerel rhymes.
   Doeg,° tho' without knowing how or why,
Made still a blundering kind of melody;
Spurred boldly on, and dashed thro' thick and thin,
Thro' sense and nonsense, never out nor in;
Free from all meaning, whether good or bad,
And, in one word, heroically mad:
He was too warm on picking-work to dwell,
But fagoted his notions as they fell,
And if they rhymed and rattled, all was well.   420
Spiteful he is not, tho' he wrote a satire,
For still there goes some *thinking* to ill-nature:
He needs no more than birds and beasts to think;
All his occasions are to eat and drink.
If he call rogue and rascal from a garret,
He means you no more mischief than a parrot;
The words for friend and foe alike were made,
To fetter 'em in verse is all his trade.
For almonds he'll cry whore to his own mother;
And call young Absalom King David's brother.   430
Let him be gallows-free by my consent,
And nothing suffer, since he nothing meant;
Hanging supposes human soul and reason,
This animal's below committing treason.
Shall he be hanged who never could rebel?
That's a preferment for Achitophel.
The woman that committed buggary,
Was rightly sentenced by the law to die;
But 'twas hard fate that to the gallows led
The dog that never heard the statute read.   440
Railing in other men may be a crime,
But ought to pass for mere instinct in him:
Instinct he follows, and no farther knows,
For to write verse with him is to *transprose*.°
'Twere pity treason at his door to lay,
Who *makes heaven's gate a lock to its own key*:°
Let him rail on, let his invective Muse

ABSALOM AND ACHITOPHEL II.   412. Doeg: Elkanah Settle.
444. transprose: the reference is to a phrase in Settle, but also to one in Buckingham's *The Rehearsal*, suggesting that Dryden turned verse into prose.   446. makes . . . key: a quotation from Settle.

Have four and twenty letters° to abuse,
Which if he jumbles to one line of sense,
Indict him of a capital offense.   450
In fireworks give him leave to vent his spite,
Those are the only serpents he can write;
The height of his ambition is, we know,
But to be master of a puppet show:
On that one stage his works may yet appear,
And a month's harvest keeps him all the year.
    Now stop your noses, readers, all and some,
For here's a tun of midnight work to come,
Og,° from a treason-tavern rolling home.
Round as a globe, and liquored every chink,   460
Goodly and great he sails behind his link.
With all this bulk there's nothing lost in Og,
For every inch that is not fool is rogue:
A monstrous mass of foul corrupted matter,
As all the devils had spewed to make the batter.
When wine has given him courage to blaspheme,
He curses God, but God before cursed him;
And if man could have reason, none has more,
That made his paunch so rich, and him so poor.
With wealth he was not trusted, for Heaven
      knew   470
What 'twas of old to pamper up a Jew;
To what would he on quail and pheasant swell,
That even on tripe and carrion could rebel?
But tho' Heaven made him poor, (with reverence
      speaking,)
He never was a poet of God's making.
The midwife laid her hand on his thick skull,
With this prophetic blessing: *Be thou dull;*
Drink, swear, and roar, forbear no lewd delight
Fit for thy bulk, do anything but write:
Thou art of lasting make, like thoughtless men, 480
A strong nativity — but for the pen;
Eat opium, mingle arsenic in thy drink,
Still thou mayst live, avoiding pen and ink.
I see, I see, 'tis counsel given in vain,
For treason botched in rhyme will be thy bane;
Rhyme is the rock on which thou art to wreck,
'Tis fatal to thy fame and to thy neck:
Why should thy meter good King David blast?
A psalm of his will surely be thy last.
Dar'st thou presume in verse to meet thy foes,   490
Thou whom the penny pamphlet foiled in prose?
Doeg, whom God for mankind's mirth has made,
O'ertops thy talent in thy very trade;
Doeg to thee, thy paintings are so coarse,
A poet is, tho' he's the poets' horse.
A double noose thou on thy neck dost pull,
For writing treason, and for writing dull;
To die for faction is a common evil,

But to be hanged for nonsense is the devil.
Hadst thou the glories of thy king expressed,   500
Thy praises had been satire at the best;
But thou in clumsy verse, unlicked, unpointed,
Hast shamefully defied the Lord's anointed:
I will not rake the dunghill of thy crimes,
For who would read thy life that reads thy rhymes?
But of King David's foes, be this the doom,
May all be like the young man Absalom;
And for my foes may this their blessing be,
To talk like Doeg, and to write like thee. . . .

EPIGRAM ON PLUTARCH

    This is a translation of the Greek epigram on Plu-
tarch, by Agathias, with which Dryden concludes his
Life of Plutarch, written for the first volume (1683)
of Tonson's edition of that author's *Lives*.

Chaeronean° Plutarch, to thy deathless praise
Does martial Rome this grateful statue raise,
Because both Greece and she thy fame have shared
(Their heroes written and their lives compared);
But thou thyself couldst never write thy own:
Their lives have parallels, but thine has none.

TO THE MEMORY OF MR. OLDHAM

    John Oldham, author of *Satires upon the Jesuits*
and other vigorous, not to say savage, poems, died in
1683 at the age of thirty. Dryden's lines in praise of
him, the best he wrote in their kind, appeared the next
year in Oldham's *Remains in Prose and Verse*. The
literary references are to Virgil's *Aeneid*. Nisus and
Euryalus, an old man and a boy, ran together in the
funeral games for Anchises (V.373–441). Marcellus
was the young nephew of Augustus, dead at twenty,
whom Virgil celebrated in VI.1188–226. The lines
cited are those of Dryden's translation of the *Aeneid*.

Farewell, too little, and too lately known,
Whom I began to think and call my own:
For sure our souls were near allied, and thine
Cast in the same poetic mold with mine.
One common note on either lyre did strike,
And knaves and fools we both abhorred alike.
To the same goal did both our studies drive;
The last set out the soonest did arrive.
Thus Nisus fell upon the slippery place,
While his young friend performed and won the
      race.   10
O early ripe! to thy abundant store
What could advancing age have added more?
It might (what nature never gives the young)
Have taught the numbers of thy native tongue.

---

448. four . . . letters: *i* and *j* were counted as one letter, and
so were *u* and *v*.   459. Og: Thomas Shadwell.

EPIGRAM ON PLUTARCH.   1. Chaeronean: Plutarch was born in
Chaeronia.

But satire needs not those, and wit will shine
Thro' the harsh cadence of a rugged line:
A noble error, and but seldom made,
When poets are by too much force betrayed.
Thy generous fruits, tho' gathered ere their prime,
Still shewed a quickness; and maturing time   20
But mellows what we write to the dull sweets of
    rhyme.
Once more, hail and farewell; farewell, thou young,
But ah too short, Marcellus of our tongue;
Thy brows with ivy, and with laurels bound;
But fate and gloomy night encompass thee around.

from SYLVAE

Sylvae was the title of a "Poetical Miscellany"
published by Jacob Tonson in 1685. Dryden contributed, besides a Preface, translations of Horace, Theocritus, and Lucretius (the *De Rerum Natura,* or *On
the Nature of Things*).

HORACE

THE NINTH ODE OF THE FIRST BOOK

I

Behold yon mountain's hoary height,
   Made higher with new mounts of snow;
Again behold the winter's weight
   Oppress the laboring woods below;
And streams, with icy fetters bound,
Benumbed and cramped to solid ground.

II

With well-heaped logs dissolve the cold,
   And feed the genial hearth with fires;
Produce the wine, that makes us bold,
   And sprightly wit and love inspires: 10
For what hereafter shall betide,
God, if 'tis worth his care, provide.

III

Let him alone, with what he made,
   To toss and turn the world below;
At his command the storms invade;
   The winds by his commission blow;
Till with a nod he bids 'em cease,
And then the calm returns, and all is peace.

IV

To-morrow and her works defy,
   Lay hold upon the present hour,   20
And snatch the pleasures passing by,
   To put them out of Fortune's power:
Nor love, nor love's delights disdain;
Whate'er thou gett'st to-day is gain.

V

Secure those golden early joys
   That youth unsoured with sorrow bears,
Ere withering time the taste destroys,
   With sickness and unwieldy years.
For active sports, for pleasing rest,
This is the time to be possessed;   30
The best is but in season best.

VI

The pointed hour of promised bliss,
   The pleasing whisper in the dark,
The half-unwilling willing kiss,
   The laugh that guides thee to the mark,
When the kind nymph would coyness feign,
And hides but to be found again;
These, these are joys the gods for youth ordain.

HORACE

THE TWENTY-NINTH ODE OF THE THIRD BOOK
PARAPHRASED IN PINDARIC VERSE

I

Descended of an ancient line,
   That long the Tuscan scepter swayed,
Make haste to meet the generous wine,
   Whose piercing is for thee delayed:
The rosy wreath is ready made;
   And artful hands prepare
The fragrant Syrian oil, that shall perfume thy hair.

II

When the wine sparkles from afar,
   And the well-natured friend cries, "Come
    away!"
Make haste, and leave thy business and thy care;   10
   No mortal interest can be worth thy stay.

III

Leave for a while thy costly country seat;
   And, to be great indeed, forget
The nauseous pleasures of the great:
   Make haste and come;
Come, and forsake thy cloying store;
   Thy turret that surveys, from high,
The smoke, and wealth, and noise of Rome;
   And all the busy pageantry
That wise men scorn, and fools adore: 20
Come, give thy soul a loose, and taste the pleasures
   of the poor.

IV

Sometimes 'tis grateful to the rich to try
A short vicissitude, and fit of poverty:
   A savory dish, a homely treat,
   Where all is plain, where all is neat,

Without the stately spacious room,
The Persian carpet, or the Tyrian loom,
Clear up the cloudy foreheads of the great.

V

The sun is in the Lion mounted high;
   The Syrian star°   30
   Barks from afar,
And with his sultry breath infects the sky;
The ground below is parched, the heavens above
   us fry.
The shepherd drives his fainting flock
   Beneath the covert of a rock,
   And seeks refreshing rivulets nigh:
The *sylvans* to their shades retire,
Those very shades and streams new shades and
   streams require,
And want a cooling breeze of wind to fan the rag-
   ing fire.

VI

Thou, what befits the new Lord Mayor,   40
And what the city faction dare,
And what the Gallic arms will do,
And what the quiver-bearing foe,
Art anxiously inquisitive to know;
But God has, wisely, hid from human sight
   The dark decrees of future fate,
   And sown their seeds in depth of night:
He laughs at all the giddy turns of state,
When mortals search too soon, and fear too late.

VII

Enjoy the present smiling hour,   50
And put it out of Fortune's power;
The tide of business, like the running stream,
   Is sometimes high, and sometimes low,
   A quiet ebb, or a tempestuous flow,
      And always in extreme.
Now with a noiseless gentle course
   It keeps within the middle bed;
   Anon it lifts aloft the head,
And bears down all before it with impetuous force;
   And trunks of trees come rolling down,   60
   Sheep and their folds together drown:
Both house and homestead into seas are borne;
And rocks are from their old foundations torn,
And woods, made thin with winds, their scattered
   honors mourn.

VIII

Happy the man, and happy he alone,
   He, who can call to-day his own;
   He who, secure within, can say:
"To-morrow do thy worst, for I have lived to-day.

HORACE TWENTY-NINTH ODE.   **30. Syrian star:** Sirius, the Dog
Star.

Be fair, or foul, or rain, or shine,
The joys I have possessed, in spite of fate,
   are mine.   70
Not Heaven itself upon the past has power;
But what has been, has been, and I have had my
   hour."

IX

Fortune, that with malicious joy
   Does man her slave oppress,
   Proud of her office to destroy,
     Is seldom pleased to bless:
Still various, and unconstant still,
But with an inclination to be ill,
Promotes, degrades, delights in strife,
   And makes a lottery of life.   80
I can enjoy her while she's kind;
But when she dances in the wind,
And shakes her wings, and will not stay,
   I puff the prostitute away:
The little or the much she gave is quietly resigned;
   Content with poverty, my soul I arm;
And virtue, tho' in rags, will keep me warm.

X

     What is't to me,
Who never sail in her unfaithful sea,
   If storms arise, and clouds grow black;   90
   If the mast split, and threaten wreck?
Then let the greedy merchant fear
   For his ill-gotten gain;
And pray to gods that will not hear,
While the debating winds and billows bear
   His wealth into the main.
For me, secure from Fortune's blows,
(Secure of what I cannot lose,)
In my small pinnace I can sail,
Contemning all the blustering roar;   100
   And running with a merry gale,
With friendly stars my safety seek,
   Within some little winding creek;
   And see the storm ashore.

LUCRETIUS

THE LATTER PART OF THE THIRD BOOK
AGAINST THE FEAR OF DEATH

In the preface to *Sylvae* Dryden dismissed as "absurd" the arguments of Lucretius against immortality,
but as arguments he admired them, and in general he
admired this Roman poet whose heroes were the Greek
materialist philosophers, Democritus and Epicurus.
The passage is in Dryden's best forensic manner.

What has this bugbear death to frighten man,
If souls can die, as well as bodies can?

For, as before our birth we felt no pain,
When Punic arms infested land and main,
When heaven and earth were in confusion hurled,
For the debated empire of the world,
Which awed with dreadful expectation lay,
Sure to be slaves, uncertain who should sway:
So, when our mortal frame shall be disjoined,
The lifeless lump uncoupled from the mind,   10
From sense of grief and pain we shall be free;
We shall not feel, because we shall not *be*.
Tho' earth in seas, and seas in heaven were lost,
We should not move, we only should be tossed.
Nay, even suppose when we have suffered fate,
The soul could feel in her divided state,
What's that to us? for we are only we
While souls and bodies in one frame agree.
Nay, tho' our atoms should revolve by chance,
And matter leap into the former dance;   20
Tho' time our life and motion could restore,
And make our bodies what they were before,
What gain to us would all this bustle bring?
The new-made man would be another thing.
When once an interrupting pause is made,
That individual being is decayed.
We, who are dead and gone, shall bear no part
In all the pleasures, nor shall feel the smart
Which to that other mortal shall accrue,
Whom of our matter time shall mold anew.   30
For backward if you look on that long space
Of ages past, and view the changing face
Of matter, tossed and variously combined
In sundry shapes, 'tis easy for the mind
From thence to infer, that seeds of things have
    been
In the same order as they now are seen:
Which yet our dark remembrance cannot trace,
Because a pause of life, a gaping space,
Has come betwixt, where memory lies dead,
And all the wandering motions from the sense are
    fled.   40
For whosoe'er shall in misfortunes live,
Must *be*, when those misfortunes shall arrive;
And since the man who *is* not, feels not woe,
(For death exempts him, and wards off the blow,
Which we, the living, only feel and bear,)
What is there left for us in death to fear?
When once that pause of life has come between,
'Tis just the same as we had never been.
    And therefore if a man bemoan his lot,
That after death his moldering limbs shall rot,   50
Or flames, or jaws of beasts devour his mass,
Know, he's an unsincere, unthinking ass.
A secret sting remains within his mind;
The fool is to his own cast offals kind.
He boasts no sense can after death remain,
Yet makes himself a part of life again,

As if some other He could feel the pain.
If, while he live, this thought molest his head,
What wolf or vulture shall devour me dead?
He wastes his days in idle grief, nor can   60
Distinguish 'twixt the body and the man;
But thinks himself can still himself survive;
And, what when dead he feels not, feels alive.
Then he repines that he was born to die,
Nor knows in death there is no other He,
No living He remains his grief to vent,
And o'er his senseless carcass to lament.
If after death 'tis painful to be torn
By birds, and beasts, then why not so to burn;
Or, drenched in floods of honey, to be soaked;   70
Imbalmed, to be at once preserved and choked;
Or on an airy mountain's top to lie,
Exposed to cold and heaven's inclemency;
Or crowded in a tomb to be oppressed
With monumental marble on thy breast?
    But to be snatched from all thy household joys,
From thy chaste wife, and thy dear prattling boys,
Whose little arms about thy legs are cast,
And climbing for a kiss prevent their mother's haste,
Inspiring secret pleasure thro' thy breast —   80
All these shall be no more: thy friends oppressed
Thy care and courage now no more shall free;
" Ah! wretch! " thou cry'st, " ah! miserable me!
One woful day sweeps children, friends, and wife,
And all the brittle blessings of my life! "
Add one thing more, and all thou say'st is true;
Thy want and wish of them is vanished too:
Which, well considered, were a quick relief
To all thy vain imaginary grief.
For thou shalt sleep, and never wake again,   90
And, quitting life, shalt quit thy living pain.
But we, thy friends, shall all those sorrows find,
Which in forgetful death thou leav'st behind;
No time shall dry our tears, nor drive thee from
    our mind.
The worst that can befall thee, measured right,
Is a sound slumber, and a long good-night.
Yet thus the fools, that would be thought the wits,
Disturb their mirth with melancholy fits:
When healths go round, and kindly brimmers flow,
Till the fresh garlands on their foreheads glow,   100
They whine, and cry: " Let us make haste to live.
Short are the joys that human life can give."
Eternal preachers, that corrupt the draught,
And pall the god, that never thinks, with thought;
Idiots with all that thought, to whom the worst
Of death is want of drink, and endless thirst,
Or any fond desire as vain as these.
For even in sleep, the body, wrapped in ease,
Supinely lies, as in the peaceful grave;
And, wanting nothing, nothing can it crave.   110
Were that sound sleep eternal, it were death;

Yet the first atoms then, the seeds of breath,
Are moving near to sense; we do but shake
And rouse that sense, and straight we are awake.
Then death to us, and death's anxiety,
Is less than nothing, if a less could be.
For then our atoms, which in order lay,
Are scattered from their heap, and puffed away,
And never can return into their place,   119
When once the pause of life has left an empty space.
    And last, suppose great Nature's voice should call
To thee, or me, or any of us all:
"What dost thou mean, ungrateful wretch, thou
    vain,
Thou mortal thing, thus idly to complain,
And sigh and sob that thou shalt be no more?
For if thy life were pleasant heretofore,
If all the bounteous blessings, I could give,
Thou hast enjoyed; if thou hast known to live,
And pleasure not leaked thro' thee like a sieve;
Why dost thou not give thanks as at a plenteous
    feast,   130
Crammed to the throat with life, and rise and take
    thy rest?
But if my blessings thou hast thrown away,
If indigested joys passed thro', and would not stay,
Why dost thou wish for more to squander still?
If life be grown a load, a real ill,
And I would all thy cares and labors end,
Lay down thy burden, fool, and know thy friend.
To please thee, I have emptied all my store;
I can invent and can supply no more,
But run the round again, the round I ran be-
    fore.   140
Suppose thou art not broken yet with years,
Yet still the selfsame scene of things appears,
And would be ever, couldst thou ever live;
For life is still but life, there's nothing new to give."
What can we plead against so just a bill?
We stand convicted, and our cause goes ill.
    But if a wretch, a man oppressed by fate,
Should beg of Nature to prolong his date,
She speaks aloud to him with more disdain:
"Be still, thou martyr fool, thou covetous of
    pain."   150
But if an old decrepit sot lament;
"What, thou," she cries, "who hast outlived con-
    tent!
Dost thou complain, who hast enjoyed my store?
But this is still the effect of wishing more.
Unsatisfied with all that Nature brings;
Loathing the present, liking absent things;
From hence it comes, thy vain desires, at strife
Within themselves, have tantalized thy life;
And ghastly death appeared before thy sight,
Ere thou hadst gorged thy soul and senses
    with delight.   160

Now leave those joys, unsuiting to thy age,
To a fresh comer, and resign the stage."
    Is Nature to be blamed if thus she chide?
No, sure; for 'tis her business to provide,
Against this ever-changing frame's decay,
New things to come, and old to pass away.
One being, worn, another being makes;
Changed, but not lost; for Nature gives and takes:
New matter must be found for things to come,
And these must waste like those, and follow
    Nature's doom.   170
All things, like thee, have time to rise and rot;
And from each other's ruin are begot:
For life is not confined to him or thee;
'Tis given to all for use, to none for property.
    Consider former ages past and gone,
Whose circles ended long ere thine begun,
Then tell me, fool, what part in them thou hast.
Thus may'st thou judge the future by the past.
What horror see'st thou in that quiet state?
What bugbear dreams to fright thee after fate?
No ghost, no goblins, that still passage keep;   181
But all is there serene, in that eternal sleep.
For all the dismal tales that poets tell
Are verified on earth, and not in hell.
No Tantalus looks up with fearful eye,
Or dreads the impending rock to crush him from
    on high;
But fear of chance on earth disturbs our easy hours,
Or vain imagined wrath of vain imagined powers.
No Tityus° torn by vultures lies in hell;
Nor could the lobes of his rank liver swell   190
To that prodigious mass for their eternal meal:
Not tho' his monstrous bulk had covered o'er
Nine spreading acres, or nine thousand more;
Not tho' the globe of earth had been the giant's
    floor:
Nor in eternal torments could he lie,
Nor could his corpse sufficient food supply.
But he's the Tityus, who by love oppressed,
Or tyrant passion preying on his breast,
And ever-anxious thoughts, is robbed of rest.
The Sisyphus is he, whom noise and strife   200
Seduce from all the soft retreats of life,
To vex the government, disturb the laws:
Drunk with the fumes of popular applause,
He courts the giddy crowd to make him great,
And sweats and toils in vain, to mount the sov-
    ereign seat.
For still to aim at power, and still to fail,
Ever to strive, and never to prevail,
What is it, but, in reason's true account,
To heave the stone against the rising mount?

LUCRETIUS.   189. Tityus: a giant slain by Apollo and Artemis.
His liver was devoured eternally by vultures in Tartarus, where
his body covered nine acres.

Which urged, and labored, and forced up
   with pain,   210
Recoils, and rolls impetuous down, and smokes
   along the plain.
Then still to treat thy ever-craving mind
With every blessing, and of every kind,
Yet never fill thy ravening appetite;
Tho' years and seasons vary thy delight,
Yet nothing to be seen of all the store,
But still the wolf within thee barks for more;
This is the fable's moral, which they tell
Of fifty foolish virgins damned in hell
To leaky vessels, which the liquor spill;   220
To vessels of their sex, which none could ever fill.
As for the Dog,° the Furies, and their snakes,
The gloomy caverns, and the burning lakes,
And all the vain infernal trumpery,
They neither are, nor were, nor e'er can be.
But here on earth the guilty have in view
The mighty pains to mighty mischiefs due;
Racks, prisons, poisons, the Tarpeian rock,°
Stripes, hangmen, pitch, and suffocating smoke;
And last, and most, if these were cast behind, 230
The avenging horror of a conscious mind,
Whose deadly fear anticipates the blow,
And sees no end of punishment and woe;
But looks for more, at the last gasp of breath:
This makes a hell on earth, and life a death.
   Meantime, when thoughts of death disturb thy
   head;
Consider, Ancus, great and good, is dead;
Ancus, thy better far, was born to die;
And thou, dost thou bewail mortality?
So many monarchs with their mighty state,
Who ruled the world, were overruled by fate. 241
That haughty king,° who lorded o'er the main,
And whose stupendous bridge did the wild waves
   restrain,
(In vain they foamed, in vain they threatened
   wreck,
While his proud legions marched upon their back,)
Him death, a greater monarch, overcame;
Nor spared his guards the more, for their immortal
   name.
The Roman chief, the Carthaginian dread,
Scipio, the thunderbolt of war, is dead,
And, like a common slave, by fate in triumph
   led.   250
The founders of invented arts are lost;
And wits, who made eternity their boast.
Where now is Homer, who possessed the throne?
The immortal work remains, the mortal author's
   gone.

222. the **Dog**: Cerberus, guardian of Hades.   **228. Tarpeian**
rock: whence Roman traitors were thrown.   **242. haughty**
king: Xerxes, who built a bridge of ships across the Hellespont.

Democritus, perceiving age invade,
His body weakened, and his mind decayed,
Obeyed the summons with a cheerful face;
Made haste to welcome death, and met him half
   the race.
That stroke even Epicurus could not bar,
Tho' he in wit surpassed mankind, as far   260
As does the midday sun the midnight star.
And thou, dost thou disdain to yield thy breath,
Whose very life is little more than death?
More than one half by lazy sleep possessed;
And when awake, thy soul but nods at best,
Day-dreams and sickly thoughts revolving in thy
   breast.
Eternal troubles haunt thy anxious mind,
Whose cause and cure thou never hop'st to find;
But still uncertain, with thyself at strife,
Thou wander'st in the labyrinth of life.   270
   O, if the foolish race of man, who find
A weight of cares still pressing on their mind,
Could find as well the cause of this unrest,
And all this burden lodged within the breast;
Sure they would change their course, nor live as
   now,
Uncertain what to wish or what to vow.
Uneasy both in country and in town,
They search a place to lay their burden down.
One, restless in his palace, walks abroad,
And vainly thinks to leave behind the load; 280
But straight returns, for he's as restless there,
And finds there's no relief in open air.
Another to his villa would retire,
And spurs as hard as if it were on fire;
No sooner entered at his country door,
But he begins to stretch, and yawn, and snore;
Or seeks the city which he left before.
Thus every man o'erworks his weary will,
To shun himself, and to shake off his ill;
The shaking fit returns, and hangs upon him
   still.   290
No prospect of repose, nor hope of ease;
The wretch is ignorant of his disease;
Which known would all his fruitless trouble spare,
For he would know the world not worth his care;
Then would he search more deeply for the cause;
And study nature well, and nature's laws:
For in this moment lies not the debate,
But on our future, fixed, eternal state;
That never-changing state, which all must keep,
Whom death has doomed to everlasting sleep. 300
   Why are we then so fond of mortal life,
Beset with dangers, and maintained with strife?
A life which all our care can never save;
One fate attends us, and one common grave.
Besides, we tread but a perpetual round;
We ne'er strike out, but beat the former ground,

And the same mawkish joys in the same track are
    found.
For still we think an absent blessing best,
Which cloys, and is no blessing when possessed;
A new arising wish expels it from the breast.   310
The feverish thirst of life increases still;
We call for more and more, and never have our fill,
Yet know not what to-morrow we shall try,
What dregs of life in the last draught may lie:
Nor, by the longest life we can attain,
One moment from the length of death we gain;
For all behind belongs to his eternal reign.
When once the Fates have cut the mortal thread,
The man as much to all intents is dead,
Who dies to-day, and will as long be so,   320
As he who died a thousand years ago.

TO THE PIOUS MEMORY

OF THE ACCOMPLISHED YOUNG LADY,

MRS. ANNE KILLIGREW

EXCELLENT IN THE TWO SISTER-ARTS OF POESY AND
PAINTING, AN ODE

On the circumstances and nature of this ode (1685)
see Introduction, pp. 532–33. Orinda, in line 162, is Mrs.
Katherine Philips, another young poetess much praised
in her day. She died in 1664, also of smallpox.

I

Thou youngest virgin-daughter of the skies,
Made in the last promotion of the blest;
Whose palms, new plucked from paradise,
In spreading branches more sublimely rise,
Rich with immortal green above the rest:
Whether, adopted to some neighboring star,
Thou roll'st above us, in thy wandering race,
   Or, in procession fixed and regular,
   Moved with the heavens' majestic pace;
   Or, called to more superior bliss,   10
Thou tread'st, with seraphims, the vast abyss:
Whatever happy region is thy place,
Cease thy celestial song a little space;
(Thou wilt have time enough for hymns divine,
   Since heaven's eternal year is thine.)
Hear then a mortal Muse thy praise rehearse,
   In no ignoble verse;
But such as thy own voice did practice here,
When thy first fruits of poesy were given,
To make thyself a welcome inmate there;   20
   While yet a young probationer,
   And candidate of heaven.

II

If by traduction° came thy mind,
Our wonder is the less to find

TO ANNE KILLIGREW.   **23. traduction:** inheritance.

A soul so charming from a stock so good;
Thy father was transfused into thy blood:
So wert thou born into the tuneful strain,
(An early, rich, and inexhausted vein.)
   But if thy preëxisting soul
   Was formed, at first, with myriads more,   30
It did thro' all the mighty poets roll,
   Who Greek or Latin laurels wore,
And was that Sappho last, which once it was before.
If so, then cease thy flight, *O heaven-born mind!*
Thou hast no dross to purge from thy rich ore;
Nor can thy soul a fairer mansion find,
Than was the beauteous frame she left behind:
Return, to fill or mend the choir of thy celestial
   kind.

III

May we presume to say, that at thy birth
New joy was sprung in heaven, as well as here on
   earth?   40
For sure the milder planets did combine
On thy auspicious horoscope to shine,
And even the most malicious were in trine.°
Thy brother-angels at thy birth
   Strung each his lyre, and tuned it high,
   That all the people of the sky
Might know a poetess was born on earth.
   And then, if ever, mortal ears
   Had heard the music of the spheres!
   And if no clustering swarm of bees°   50
On thy sweet mouth distilled their golden dew,
   'Twas that such vulgar miracles
   Heaven had no leisure to renew:
For all the blest fraternity of love
Solemnized there thy birth, and kept thy holiday
   above.

IV

O gracious God! how far have we
Profaned thy heavenly gift of poesy!
Made prostitute and profligate the Muse,
Debased to each obscene and impious use,
Whose harmony was first ordained above   60
For tongues of angels, and for hymns of love!
O wretched we! why were we hurried down
   This lubric° and adulterate age,
(Nay, added fat pollutions of our own,)
   To increase the steaming ordures of the stage?
What can we say to excuse our *second fall?*
Let this thy *vestal,* Heaven, atone for all:
Her Arethusian stream° remains unsoiled,

43. in trine: two planets distant from each other 120 degrees (one
third of the zodiac); a benign influence in astrology.   **50. bees:**
bees were supposed to have lit on the lips of Plato when a child.
63. lubric: lewd.   **68. Arethusian stream:** an ancient fountain
sacred to poetry.

Unmixed with foreign filth, and undefiled;
Her wit was more than man, her innocence a
    child!   70

V

Art she had none, yet wanted none;
  For nature did that want supply:
  So rich in treasures of her own,
  She might our boasted stores defy:
Such noble vigor did her verse adorn
That it seemed borrowed, where 'twas only born.
Her morals too were in her bosom bred,
  By great examples daily fed,
What in the best of books, her father's life, she read.
And to be read herself she need not fear;   80
Each test, and every light, her Muse will bear,
Tho' Epictetus° with his lamp were there.
Even love (for love sometimes her Muse expressed)
Was but a *lambent flame* which played about her
    breast,
Light as the vapors of a morning dream:
So cold herself, whilst she such warmth expressed,
'Twas Cupid bathing in Diana's stream.

VI

Born to the spacious empire of the Nine,°
One would have thought she should have been
    content
To manage well that mighty government;   90
But what can young ambitious souls confine?
  To the next realm she stretched her sway,
  For *painture* near adjoining lay,
A plenteous province, and alluring prey.
A chamber of dependences was framed,
(As conquerors will never want pretense,
  When armed, to justify the offense,)
And the whole fief in right of poetry she claimed.
The country open lay without defense;
For poets frequent inroads there had made,   100
  And perfectly could represent
  The shape, the face, with every lineament;
And all the large demains° which the *Dumb Sis-
  ter*° swayed,
  All bowed beneath her government;
  Received in triumph wheresoe'er she went.
Her pencil drew whate'er her soul designed,
And oft the happy draught surpassed the image in
    her mind.
  The *sylvan* scenes of herds and flocks,
  And fruitful plains and barren rocks,
  Of shallow brooks that flowed so clear   110
  The bottom did the top appear;

Of deeper too and ampler floods,
Which, as in mirrors, shewed the woods;
Of lofty trees, with sacred shades,
And perspectives of pleasant glades,
Where nymphs of brightest form appear,
And shaggy satyrs standing near,
Which them at once admire and fear:
The ruins too of some majestic piece,
Boasting the power of ancient Rome, or
    Greece,   120
Whose statues, friezes, columns broken lie,
And, tho' defaced, the wonder of the eye:
What nature, art, bold fiction, e'er durst frame,
Her forming hand gave feature to the name.
So strange a concourse ne'er was seen before,
But when the peopled ark the whole creation bore.

VII

The scene then changed: with bold erected look
Our martial king the sight with reverence strook;
For, not content to express his outward part,
Her hand called out the image of his heart: 130
His warlike mind, his soul devoid of fear,
His high-designing thoughts were figured there,
As when, by magic, ghosts are made appear.
Our Phoenix queen° was portrayed too so bright,
Beauty alone could beauty take so right:
Her dress, her shape, her matchless grace,
Were all observed, as well as heavenly face.
With such a peerless majesty she stands,
As in that day she took the crown from sacred
    hands;
Before a train of heroines was seen,   140
In beauty foremost, as in rank the queen.
Thus nothing to her *genius* was denied,
  But like a ball of fire the further thrown,
  Still with a greater blaze she shone,
And her bright soul broke out on every side.
What next she had designed, Heaven only knows;
To such immoderate growth her conquest rose
That fate alone its progress could oppose.

VIII

Now all those charms, that blooming grace,
The well-proportioned shape, and beauteous
    face,   150
Shall never more be seen by mortal eyes:
In earth the much-lamented virgin lies!
  Not wit, nor piety could fate prevent;
  Nor was the cruel Destiny content
  To finish all the murder at a blow,
  To sweep at once her life and beauty too;
But, like a hardened felon, took a pride
  To work more mischievously slow,

---

82. **Epictetus:** a mistake for Diogenes, who went about with a
lantern in daylight, looking for an honest man.   **88. the Nine:**
the nine Muses.   **103. demains:** demesnes, domains. *Dumb
Sister:* Painting.

134. **Our Phoenix Queen:** Mary of Este, Queen of James II.

And plundered first, and then destroyed.
O double sacrilege on things divine,   160
To rob the relic, and deface the shrine!°
    But thus Orinda° died:
Heaven, by the same disease, did both translate;
As equal were their souls, so equal was their fate.

IX

Meantime her warlike brother° on the seas
His waving streamers to the winds displays,
And vows for his return, with vain devotion, pays.
    Ah, generous youth, that wish forbear,
    The winds too soon will waft thee here!
    Slack all thy sails, and fear to come,   170
Alas, thou know'st not, thou art wrecked at home!
No more shalt thou behold thy sister's face,
Thou hast already had her last embrace.
But look aloft, and if thou kenn'st from far
Among the Pleiads a new kindled star;
If any sparkles than the rest more bright,
'Tis she that shines in that propitious light.

X

When in mid-air the golden trump shall sound,
    To raise the nations under ground;
    When in the Valley of Jehosaphat°   180
The judging God shall close the book of fate,
    And there the last assizes keep
    For those who wake and those who sleep;
    When rattling bones together fly
    From the four corners of the sky;
When sinews o'er the skeletons are spread,
Those clothed with flesh, and life inspires the dead;
The sacred poets first shall hear the sound,
And foremost from the tomb shall bound,
For they are covered with the lightest ground;   190
And straight, with inborn vigor, on the wing,
Like mounting larks, to the new morning sing.
There thou, sweet saint, before the choir shalt go,
As harbinger of heaven, the way to show,
The way which thou so well hast learned below.

A SONG FOR ST. CECILIA'S DAY, 1687

The second stanza may have inspired the beginning
lines of Edgar Allan Poe's *Israfel.*

I

From harmony, from heavenly harmony
    This universal frame began:
    When Nature underneath a heap

161. **deface the shrine**: ravage with smallpox. 162. **Orinda**:
Katherine Philips, "The Matchless Orinda." 165. **her warlike
brother**: Henry Killigrew, a captain in the navy. 180. **Jehosa-
phat**: Cf. Joel 3:2.

    Of jarring atoms lay,
    And could not heave her head,
The tuneful voice was heard from high:
    "Arise, ye more than dead."
Then cold, and hot, and moist, and dry,
    In order to their stations leap,
    And Music's power obey.   10
From harmony, from heavenly harmony
    This universal frame began:
    From harmony to harmony
Thro' all the compass of the notes it ran,
The diapason closing full in Man.

II

What passion cannot Music raise and quell!
    When Jubal° struck the corded shell,
    His listening brethren stood around,
    And, wondering, on their faces fell
    To worship that celestial sound.   20
Less than a god they thought there could not dwell
    Within the hollow of that shell
    That spoke so sweetly and so well.
What passion cannot Music raise and quell!

III

    The Trumpet's loud clangor
        Excites us to arms,
    With shrill notes of anger,
        And mortal alarms.
    The double double double beat
        Of the thundering Drum   30
Cries: "Hark! the foes come;
Charge, charge, 'tis too late to retreat."

IV

    The soft complaining Flute
    In dying notes discovers
    The woes of hopeless lovers,
Whose dirge is whispered by the warbling Lute.

V

    Sharp Violins proclaim
Their jealous pangs, and desperation,
Fury, frantic indignation,
Depth of pains, and height of passion,   40
    For the fair, disdainful dame.

VI

    But O! what art can teach,
    What human voice can reach,
    The sacred Organ's praise?
    Notes inspiring holy love,
Notes that wing their heavenly ways
    To mend the choirs above.

SONG FOR ST. CECILIA'S DAY.   17. **Jubal**: Cf. Gen. 4:21 ("Jubal:
he was the father of all such as handle the harp and organ").

VII

Orpheus could lead the savage race;
And trees unrooted left their place,
    Sequacious of the lyre;   50
But bright Cecilia raised the wonder higher:
When to her Organ vocal breath was given,
An angel heard, and straight appeared,
    Mistaking earth for heaven.

GRAND CHORUS

As from the power of sacred lays
    The spheres began to move,
And sung the great Creator's praise
    To all the blest above;
So, when the last and dreadful hour
This crumbling pageant shall devour,   60
The Trumpet shall be heard on high,
The dead shall live, the living die,
And Music shall untune the sky.

EPIGRAM ON MILTON

Dryden contributed this epigram to Tonson's edition
of *Paradise Lost* in 1688. The three poets, clearly, are
Homer, Virgil, and Milton.

Three poets, in three distant ages born,
Greece, Italy, and England did adorn.
The first in loftiness of thought surpassed,
The next in majesty, in both the last:
The force of Nature could no farther go;
To make a third, she joined the former two.

EPITAPH ON JOHN GRAHAM OF CLAVERHOUSE, VISCOUNT DUNDEE

The subject of this translated epitaph was the famous
Scottish Jacobite leader who died at Killicrankie in
1689. Dryden's lines are a free version of eight in
Latin by Dr. Archibald Pitcairne.

O last and best of Scots! who didst maintain
Thy country's freedom from a foreign reign;
New people fill the land now thou art gone,
New gods the temples, and new kings the throne.
Scotland and thou did each in other live;
Thou wouldst not her, nor could she thee survive.
Farewell, who living didst support the State,
And couldst not fall but with thy country's fate.

JUVENAL

FROM THE SIXTH SATIRE

The *Satires* of Juvenal and Persius, translated by
Dryden and others, were published in 1692, with a
prefatory discourse by Dryden on "The Original and

Progress of Satire." The opening lines of his Juvenal VI
are completely characteristic of him.

In Saturn's reign, at Nature's early birth,
There was that thing called chastity on earth;
When in a narrow cave, their common shade,
The sheep, the shepherds, and their gods were laid:
When reeds, and leaves, and hides of beasts were
    spread
By mountain huswifes for their homely bed,
And mossy pillows raised, for the rude husband's
    head.
Unlike the niceness of our modern dames,
(Affected nymphs with new affected names,)
The Cynthias and the Lesbias of our years,   10
Who for a sparrow's death dissolve in tears;
Those first unpolished matrons, big and bold,
Gave suck to infants of gigantic mold;
Rough as their savage lords who ranged the wood,
And fat with acorns belched their windy food.
For when the world was buxom, fresh, and young,
Her sons were undebauched and therefore strong;
And whether born in kindly beds of earth,
Or struggling from the teeming oaks to birth,
Or from what other atoms they begun,   20
No sires they had, or, if a sire, the sun. . . .

TO MY DEAR FRIEND MR. CONGREVE,

ON HIS COMEDY CALLED THE DOUBLE-DEALER

Dryden contributed this fine poem to the first edition of William Congreve's comedy *The Double-Dealer*
(1694). He wrote it out of affection for the author,
and out of a conviction that Congreve at last had
won the victory over the "wits" of the Elizabethan
age which Dryden had all his life been waiting for.

Well then, the promised hour is come at last;
The present age of wit obscures the past:
Strong were our sires, and as they fought they writ,
Conquering with force of arms, and dint of wit;
Theirs was the giant race, before the flood;
And thus, when Charles returned,° our empire
    stood.
Like Janus° he the stubborn soil manured,
With rules of husbandry the rankness cured;
Tamed us to manners, when the stage was rude;
And boisterous English wit with art indued.   10
Our age was cultivated thus at length,
But what we gained in skill we lost in strength.
Our builders were with want of genius curst;
The second temple was not like the first:
Till you, the best Vitruvius,° come at length;
Our beauties equal, but excel our strength.
Firm Doric pillars found your solid base;

TO MR. CONGREVE.   **6. when Charles returned**: the Restoration
of Charles II, 1660.   **7. Janus**: legendary Roman king.   **15.**
Vitruvius: Roman writer on architecture.

The fair Corinthian crowns the higher space:
Thus all below is strength, and all above is grace.
In easy dialogue is Fletcher's praise;   20
He moved the mind, but had not power to raise.
Great Jonson did by strength of judgment please;
Yet, doubling Fletcher's force, he wants his ease.
In differing talents both adorned their age;
One for the study, t'other for the stage:
But both to Congreve justly shall submit,
One matched in judgment, both o'ermatched in wit.
In him all beauties of this age we see,
Etherege° his courtship, Southerne's° purity,
The satire, wit, and strength of Manly Wycher-
    ley.°   30
All this in blooming youth you have achieved,
Nor are your foiled contemporaries grieved.
So much the sweetness of your manners move,
We cannot envy you, because we love.
Fabius might joy in Scipio,° when he saw
A beardless consul made against the law;
And join his suffrage to the votes of Rome,
Tho' he with Hannibal was overcome.
Thus old Romano° bowed to Raphael's fame,
And scholar to the youth he taught became.   40
    O that your brows my laurel had sustained;
Well had I been deposed, if you had reigned!
The father had descended for the son;
For only you are lineal to the throne.
Thus, when the state one Edward did depose,
A greater Edward° in his room arose.
But now, not I, but poetry is curst;
For Tom the Second° reigns like Tom the First.°
But let 'em not mistake my patron's° part,
Nor call his charity their own desert.   50
Yet this I prophesy: thou shalt be seen
(Tho' with some short parenthesis between)
High on the throne of wit; and, seated there,
Not mine—that's little—but thy laurel wear.
Thy first attempt an early promise made;
That early promise this has more than paid.
So bold, yet so judiciously you dare,
That your least praise is to be regular.
Time, place, and action, may with pains be
    wrought;
But genius must be born, and never can be
    taught.   60

29. Etherege: Sir George Etherege.   Southerne: Thomas
Southerne, another playwright.   30. Manly Wycherley: William Wycherley, the hero of whose contemporary comedy, *The
Plain Dealer*, is Manly.   35. Fabius . . . Scipio: Fabius, who
disapproved of Scipio's policies, might have liked them in a
young man as charming as Congreve.   39. Romano: Raphael's
pupil, not his master (a mistake by Dryden).   45-46. Edward
. . . Edward: Edward II and Edward III of England.   48.
Tom the Second: Thomas Rymer, who now had Dryden's old
office of Historiographer Royal.   Tom the First: Thomas
Shadwell, who was given the poet laureateship when Dryden
lost it in the Revolution of 1688.   49. my patron: the Earl of
Dorset.

This is your portion; this your native store;
Heaven, that but once was prodigal before,
To Shakespeare gave as much; she could not give
    him more.
    Maintain your post: that's all the fame you need;
For 'tis impossible you should proceed.
Already I am worn with cares and age,
And just abandoning the ungrateful stage;
Unprofitably kept at Heaven's expense,
I live a rent-charge on his providence:
But you, whom every Muse and Grace adorn,   70
Whom I foresee to better fortune born,
Be kind to my remains;° and O defend,
Against your judgment, your departed friend!
Let not the insulting foe my fame pursue,
But shade those laurels which descend to you;
And take for tribute what these lines express:
You merit more; nor could my love do less.

ALEXANDER'S FEAST

OR, THE POWER OF MUSIC; AN ODE IN HONOR OF
ST. CECILIA'S DAY

In Robert Burton's *Anatomy of Melancholy* there is
a sentence Dryden could have seen: "Timotheus the
musician compelled Alexander to skip up and down and
leave his dinner." And other writers of the seventeenth century had alluded to the power Timotheus wielded
over the conqueror of the world (see Introduction,
p. 533, for a further discussion of this ode).

I

'Twas at the royal feast, for Persia won
    By Philip's warlike son:°
    Aloft in awful state
    The godlike hero sate
        On his imperial throne:
    His valiant peers were placed around;
Their brows with roses and with myrtles bound:
    (So should desert in arms be crowned.)
The lovely Thais, by his side,
Sate like a blooming Eastern bride   10
In flower of youth and beauty's pride.
    Happy, happy, happy pair!
    None but the brave,
    None but the brave,
    None but the brave deserves the fair.

CHORUS

Happy, happy, happy pair!
None but the brave,
None but the brave,
None but the brave deserves the fair.

72. my remains: Congreve edited Dryden's plays in 1717.
ALEXANDER'S FEAST.   2. Philip's warlike son: Alexander the
Great.

II

Timotheus, placed on high   20
    Amid the tuneful choir,
    With flying fingers touched the lyre:
The trembling notes ascend the sky,
                            And heavenly joys inspire.
The song began from Jove,
Who left his blissful seats above,
(Such is the power of mighty love.)
A dragon's fiery form belied the god:
Sublime on radiant spires he rode,
        When he to fair Olympia° pressed;   30
        And while he sought her snowy breast:
Then, round her slender waist he curled,
And stamped an image of himself, a sovereign of
        the world.
The listening crowd admire the lofty sound;
" A present deity," they shout around;
" A present deity," the vaulted roofs rebound:
        With ravished ears
        The monarch hears,
        Assumes the god,
        Affects to nod,   40
And seems to shake the spheres.

CHORUS

With ravished ears
The monarch hears,
Assumes the god,
Affects to nod,
And seems to shake the spheres.

III

The praise of Bacchus then the sweet musician
        sung,
Of Bacchus ever fair and ever young:
    " The jolly god in triumph comes;
    Sound the trumpets; beat the drums;   50
        Flushed with a purple grace
        He shews his honest face:
Now give the hautboys breath; he comes, he comes.
    Bacchus, ever fair and young,
        Drinking joys did first ordain;
    Bacchus' blessings are a treasure,
    Drinking is the soldier's pleasure:
        Rich the treasure,
        Sweet the pleasure,
        Sweet is pleasure after pain."   60

CHORUS

Bacchus' blessings are a treasure,
Drinking is the soldier's pleasure:
    Rich the treasure,
    Sweet the pleasure,
    Sweet is pleasure after pain.

30. **Olympia**: Olympias, Alexander's mother.

IV

Soothed with the sound, the king grew vain;
    Fought all his battles o'er again;
And thrice he routed all his foes; and thrice he slew
        the slain.
The master saw the madness rise;
His glowing cheeks, his ardent eyes;   70
And, while he heaven and earth defied,
Changed his hand, and checked his pride.
        He chose a mournful Muse,
            Soft pity to infuse:
He sung Darius° great and good,
            By too severe a fate,
Fallen, fallen, fallen, fallen,
            Fallen from his high estate,
                And weltering in his blood;
Deserted, at his utmost need,   80
By those his former bounty fed;
On the bare earth exposed he lies,
With not a friend to close his eyes.

With downcast looks the joyless victor sate,
    Revolving in his altered soul
        The various turns of chance below;
    And, now and then, a sigh he stole;
    And tears began to flow.

CHORUS

Revolving in his altered soul
    The various turns of chance below;   90
And, now and then, a sigh he stole;
    And tears began to flow.

V

The mighty master smiled, to see
That love was in the next degree:
'Twas but a kindred sound to move,
For pity melts the mind to love.
    Softly sweet, in Lydian measures,
    Soon he soothed his soul to pleasures.
    " War," he sung, " is toil and trouble;
    Honor, but an empty bubble;   100
        Never ending, still beginning,
    Fighting still, and still destroying:
        If the world be worth thy winning,
    Think, O think it worth enjoying;
        Lovely Thais sits beside thee,
        Take the good the gods provide thee."
The many rend the skies with loud applause;
So Love was crowned, but Music won the cause.
    The prince, unable to conceal his pain,
            Gazed on the fair   110
        Who caused his care,
    And sighed° and looked, sighed and looked,
Sighed and looked, and sighed again:

75. **Darius**: Darius III of Persia, defeated by Alexander.

At length, with love and wine at once oppressed,
The vanquished victor sunk upon her breast.

CHORUS

The prince, unable to conceal his pain,
  Gazed on the fair
  Who caused his care,
And sighed and looked, sighed and looked,
Sighed and looked, and sighed again: 120
At length, with love and wine at once oppressed,
The vanquished victor sunk upon her breast.

VI

Now strike the golden lyre again:
A louder yet, and yet a louder strain.
Break his bands of sleep asunder,
And rouse him, like a rattling peal of thunder.
  Hark, hark, the horrid sound
  Has raised up his head:
  As awaked from the dead,
  And amazed, he stares around.   130
"Revenge, revenge!" Timotheus cries,
  "See the Furies arise!
  See the snakes that they rear,
  How they hiss in their hair,
And the sparkles that flash from their eyes!
  Behold a ghastly band,
  Each a torch in his hand!
Those are Grecian ghosts, that in battle were slain,
  And unburied remain
    Inglorious on the plain: 140
  Give the vengeance due
  To the valiant crew.
Behold how they toss their torches on high,
  How they point to the Persian abodes,
And glittering temples of their hostile gods!"
The princes applaud, with a furious joy;
And the king seized a flambeau with zeal to destroy;
  Thais led the way,
  To light him to his prey,
And, like another Helen, fired another Troy.   150

CHORUS

And the king seized a flambeau with zeal to destroy;
  Thais led the way,
  To light him to his prey,
And, like another Helen, fired another Troy.

VII

  Thus, long ago,
  Ere heaving bellows learned to blow,
  While organs yet were mute;
  Timotheus, to his breathing flute,
    And sounding lyre,
Could swell the soul to rage, or kindle soft de-
  sire.   160

  At last, divine Cecilia came,
  Inventress of the vocal frame;
The sweet enthusiast, from her sacred store,
  Enlarged the former narrow bounds,
  And added length to solemn sounds,
With nature's mother wit, and arts unknown be-
  fore.
  Let old Timotheus yield the prize,
  Or both divide the crown;
  He raised a mortal to the skies;
  She drew an angel down.   170

GRAND CHORUS

  At last, divine Cecilia came,
  Inventress of the vocal frame;
The sweet enthusiast, from her sacred store,
  Enlarged the former narrow bounds,
  And added length to solemn sounds,
With nature's mother wit, and arts unknown be-
  fore.
  Let old Timotheus yield the prize,
  Or both divide the crown;
  He raised a mortal to the skies;
  She drew an angel down.   180

TO MY FRIEND MR. MOTTEUX

Peter Anthony Motteux, the translator of Rabelais
and Cervantes, was a French Huguenot who came to
England after 1685 and wrote among other things a
tragedy, *Beauty in Distress,* to an edition of which in
1698 Dryden prefixed this poem. Dryden returns here,
after some remarks on Jeremy Collier's campaign
against the immorality of the stage, to one of his
favorite critical themes: the difference between English and French dramatic poetry.

'Tis hard, my friend, to write in such an age,
As damns not only poets, but the stage.
That sacred art, by heaven itself infused,
Which Moses, David, Solomon have used,
Is now to be no more: the Muses' foes
Would sink their Maker's praises into prose.
Were they content to prune the lavish vine
Of straggling branches, and improve the wine,
Who but a madman would his faults defend?
All would submit; for all but fools will mend.   10
But when to common sense they give the lie,
And turn distorted words to blasphemy,
They give the scandal; and the wise discern,
Their glosses teach an age too apt to learn.
What I have loosely or profanely writ,
Let them to fires, (their due desert,) commit;
Nor, when accused by me, let *them* complain:
Their faults and not their function I arraign.
Rebellion, worse than witchcraft, they pursued;
The pulpit preached the crime, the people rued.   20

The stage was silenced; for the saints would see
In fields performed their plotted tragedy.
But let us first reform, and then so live,
That we may teach our teachers to forgive.
Our desk be placed below their lofty chairs;
Ours be the practice, as the precept theirs.
The moral part at least we may divide,
Humility reward, and punish pride;
Ambition, interest, avarice accuse:
These are the province of the Tragic Muse.
These hast thou chosen; and the public voice   31
Has equaled thy performance with thy choice.
Time, action, place, are so preserved by thee,
That even Corneille might with envy see
The alliance of his tripled unity.
Thy incidents, perhaps, too thick are sown;
But too much plenty is thy fault alone:
At least but two can that good crime commit,
Thou in design, and Wycherley in wit.
Let thy own Gauls condemn thee, if they dare;   40
Contented to be thinly regular.
Born there, but not for them, our fruitful soil
With more increase rewards thy happy toil.
Their tongue, infeebled, is refined so much,
That, like pure gold, it bends at every touch;
Our sturdy Teuton yet will art obey,
More fit for manly thought, and strengthened with
    allay.
But whence art thou inspired, and thou alone,
To flourish in an idiom not thine own?
It moves our wonder, that a foreign guest
Should overmatch the most, and match the best.   51
In underpraising, thy deserts I wrong;
Here, find the first deficience of our tongue:
Words, once my stock, are wanting, to commend
So great a poet and so good a friend.

EPIGRAM ON TONSON

Dryden is said to have taken a pencil and written
these three lines under a portrait of his publisher
painted by Godfrey Kneller. They are his shortest
"character."

With leering look, bull faced and freckled fair,
With frowsy pores poisoning the ambient air,
With two left leggs and Judas coloured hair.

from FABLES, ANCIENT AND MODERN

PREFACE

In this last of Dryden's great critical pieces he discourses with practiced ease upon a variety of subjects,
including Homer, Ovid, Boccaccio, and Chaucer. His

praise of Chaucer helped to establish that poet's permanent reputation; Dryden could not have known that
Chaucer, far from being a rude versifier, was a master
of "numbers," yet in spite of this handicap he penetrated to Chaucer's central virtue, his understanding
of life and his power to describe it. Another subject
he treats is the charge of obscenity brought against him
and others by Jeremy Collier, whose *Short View of
the Immorality and Profaneness of the English Stage*
he accuses of exaggeration without denying its application to himself. At the end he takes a final witty
fling at two of his literary enemies: Luke Milbourne,
who had attacked his *Virgil,* and Sir Richard Blackmore, a writer of dull epics who had attacked his
character.

'Tis with a poet, as with a man who designs to
build, and is very exact as he supposes, in casting
up the cost beforehand; but, generally speaking,
he is mistaken in his account, and reckons short
of the expense he first intended. He alters his mind
as the work proceeds, and will have this or that
convenience more, of which he had not thought
when he began. So has it happened to me; I have
built a house, where I intended but a lodge; yet
with better success than a certain nobleman,[1] who,
beginning with a dog-kennel, never lived to finish
the palace he had contrived.

From translating the first of Homer's *Iliads*
(which I intended as an essay to the whole work),
I proceeded to the translation of the twelfth book
of Ovid's *Metamorphoses,* because it contains,
among other things, the causes, the beginning, and
ending of the Trojan war. Here I ought in reason
to have stopped; but the speeches of Ajax and
Ulysses lying next in my way, I could not balk 'em.
When I had compassed them, I was so taken with
the former part of the fifteenth book (which is the
masterpiece of the whole *Metamorphoses*), that I
enjoined myself the pleasing task of rendering it
into English. And now I found by the number of
my verses, that they began to swell into a little
volume; which gave me an occasion of looking
backward on some beauties of my author, in his
former books; there occurred to me the "Hunting of the Boar," "Cinyras and Myrrha," the good-
natured story of "Baucis and Philemon," with the
rest, which I hope I have translated closely enough,
and given them the same turn of verse which they
had in the original; and this, I may say, without
vanity, is not the talent of every poet. He who has
arrived the nearest to it, is the ingenious and

PREFACE.   1. nobleman: the Duke of Buckingham (Zimri in
Absalom and Achitophel).

learned Sandys,[2] the best versifier of the former age; if I may properly call it by that name, which was the former part of this concluding century. For Spenser and Fairfax [3] both flourished in the reign of Queen Elizabeth; great masters in our language, and who saw much further into the beauties of our numbers than those who immediately followed them. Milton was the poetical son of Spenser, and Mr. Waller of Fairfax; for we have our lineal descents and clans as well as other families. Spenser more than once insinuates that the soul of Chaucer was transfused into his body; and that he was begotten by him two hundred years after his decease. Milton has acknowledged to me that Spenser was his original; and many besides myself have heard our famous Waller own that he derived the harmony of his numbers from the *Godfrey of Bulloign*,[4] which was turned into English by Mr. Fairfax.

But to return: having done with Ovid for this time, it came into my mind, that our old English poet, Chaucer, in many things resembled him, and that with no disadvantage on the side of the modern author, as I shall endeavor to prove when I compare them; and as I am, and always have been, studious to promote the honor of my native country, so I soon resolved to put their merits to the trial, by turning some of the *Canterbury Tales* into our language, as it is now refined; for by this means, both the poets being set in the same light, and dressed in the same English habit, story to be compared with story, a certain judgment may be made betwixt them by the reader, without obtruding my opinion on him. Or, if I seem partial to my countryman and predecessor in the laurel, the friends of antiquity are not few; and, besides many of the learned, Ovid has almost all the beaux, and the whole fair sex, his declared patrons. Perhaps I have assumed somewhat more to myself than they allow me, because I have adventured to sum up the evidence; but the readers are the jury, and their privilege remains entire, to decide according to the merits of the cause; or, if they please, to bring it to another hearing before some other court. In the meantime, to follow the thread of my discourse (as thoughts, according to Mr. Hobbes,[5] have always some connection), so from Chaucer I was led to think on Boccace, who was not only his

contemporary, but also pursued the same studies; wrote novels in prose, and many works in verse; particularly is said to have invented the octave rhyme, or stanza of eight lines, which ever since has been maintained by the practice of all Italian writers who are, or at least assume the title of, heroic poets. He and Chaucer, among other things, had this in common, that they refined their mother-tongues; but with this difference, that Dante had begun to file their language, at least in verse, before the time of Boccace, who likewise received no little help from his master Petrarch; but the reformation of their prose was wholly owing to Boccace himself, who is yet the standard of purity in the Italian tongue, though many of his phrases are become obsolete, as in process of time it must needs happen. Chaucer (as you have formerly been told by our learned Mr. Rymer [6]) first adorned and amplified our barren tongue from the Provençal, which was then the most polished of all the modern languages; but this subject has been copiously treated by that great critic, who deserves no little commendation from us his countrymen. For these reasons of time, and resemblance of genius, in Chaucer and Boccace, I resolved to join them in my present work; to which I have added some original papers of my own, which whether they are equal or inferior to my other poems, an author is the most improper judge; and therefore I leave them wholly to the mercy of the reader. I will hope the best, that they will not be condemned; but if they should, I have the excuse of an old gentleman, who, mounting on horseback before some ladies, when I was present, got up somewhat heavily, but desired of the fair spectators, that they would count fourscore and eight before they judged him. By the mercy of God, I am already come within twenty years of his number; a cripple in my limbs, but what decays are in my mind the reader must determine. I think myself as vigorous as ever in the faculties of my soul, excepting only my memory, which is not impaired to any great degree: and if I lose not more of it, I have no great reason to complain. What judgment I had, increases rather than diminishes; and thoughts, such as they are, come crowding in so fast upon me, that my only difficulty is to choose or to reject, to run them into verse, or to give them the other harmony of prose; I have so long studied and practised both, that they are grown into a habit, and become familiar to me.

---

2. **Sandys:** George Sandys (1578–1644), whose translation of Ovid's *Metamorphoses* appeared in 1626.   3. **Fairfax:** Edward Fairfax, d. 1635.   4. **Godfrey of Bulloign:** Tasso's *Jerusalem Delivered*.   5. **Mr. Hobbes:** the author of *Leviathan*.

6. **Mr. Rymer:** Thomas Rymer, whose *Short View of Tragedy* set Chaucer above Shakespeare.

In short, though I may lawfully plead some part of the old gentleman's excuse, yet I will reserve it till I think I have greater need, and ask no grains of allowance for the faults of this my present work, but those which are given of course to human frailty. I will not trouble my reader with the shortness of time in which I writ it, or the several intervals of sickness. They who think too well of their own performances are apt to boast in their prefaces how little time their works have cost them, and what other business of more importance interfered; but the reader will be as apt to ask the question, why they allowed not a longer time to make their work more perfect? and why they had so despicable an opinion of their judges as to thrust their indigested stuff upon them, as if they deserved no better?

With this account of my present undertaking, I conclude the first part of this discourse; in the second part, as at a second sitting, though I alter not the draft, I must touch the same features over again, and change the dead-coloring of the whole. In general I will only say, that I have written nothing which savors of immorality or profaneness; at least, I am not conscious to myself of any such intention. If there happen to be found an irreverent expression, or a thought too wanton, they are crept into my verses through my inadvertency; if the searchers find any in the cargo, let them be staved[7] or forfeited, like counter-banded goods; at least, let their authors be answerable for them, as being but imported merchandise, and not of my own manufacture. On the other side, I have endeavored to choose such fables, both ancient and modern, as contain in each of them some instructive moral; which I could prove by induction, but the way is tedious, and they leap foremost into sight without the reader's trouble of looking after them. I wish I could affirm, with a safe conscience, that I had taken the same care in all my former writings; for it must be owned, that supposing verses are never so beautiful or pleasing, yet, if they contain anything which shocks religion or good manners, they are at best what Horace says of good numbers without good sense, *Versus inopes rerum, nugaeque canorae*.[8] Thus far, I hope, I am right in court, without renouncing to my other right of self-defence, where I have been wrongfully accused, and my sense wire-drawn into blasphemy or baw-

dry, as it has often been by a religious lawyer,[9] in a late pleading against the stage; in which he mixes truth with falsehood, and has not forgotten the old rule of calumniating strongly, that something may remain.

I resume the thread of my discourse with the first of my translations, which was the first *Iliad* of Homer. If it shall please God to give me longer life, and moderate health, my intentions are to translate the whole *Ilias;* provided still that I meet with those encouragements from the public, which may enable me to proceed in my undertaking with some cheerfulness. And this I dare assure the world beforehand, that I have found, by trial, Homer a more pleasing task than Virgil, though I say not the translation will be less laborious; for the Grecian is more according to my genius than the Latin poet. In the works of the two authors we may read their manners, and natural inclinations, which are wholly different. Virgil was of a quiet, sedate temper; Homer was violent, impetuous, and full of fire. The chief talent of Virgil was propriety of thoughts, and ornament of words; Homer was rapid in his thoughts, and took all the liberties, both of numbers and of expressions, which his language, and the age in which he lived, allowed him. Homer's invention was more copious, Virgil's more confined; so that if Homer had not led the way, it was not in Virgil to have begun heroic poetry; for nothing can be more evident than that the Roman poem is but the second part of the *Ilias;* a continuation of the same story, and the persons already formed. The manners of Aeneas are those of Hector, superadded to those which Homer gave him. The adventures of Ulysses in the *Odysseis* are imitated in the first six books of Virgil's *Aeneis;* and though the accidents are not the same (which would have argued him of a servile copying, and total barrenness of invention), yet the seas were the same in which both the heroes wandered; and Dido cannot be denied to be the poetical daughter of Calypso. The six latter books of Virgil's poem are the four-and-twenty *Iliads* contracted; a quarrel occasioned by a lady, a single combat, battles fought, and a town besieged. I say not this in derogation to Virgil, neither do I contradict anything which I have formerly said in his just praise; for his episodes are almost wholly of his own invention, and the form which he has

---

7. **staved**: broken up.   8. *Versus . . . canorae:* "verses empty of content, tuneful trifles."

9. **lawyer**: Jeremy Collier, whose *Short View of the Immorality and Profaneness of the English Stage* had appeared in 1698.

given to the telling makes the tale his own, even though the original story had been the same. But this proves, however, that Homer taught Virgil to design; and if invention be the first virtue of an epic poet, then the Latin poem can only be allowed a second place. Mr. Hobbes, in the preface to his own bald translation of the *Ilias* (studying poetry as he did mathematics, when it was too late), Mr. Hobbes, I say, begins the praise of Homer where he should have ended it. He tells us, that the first beauty of an epic poem consists in diction; that is, in the choice of words, and harmony of numbers. Now the words are the coloring of the work, which, in the order of nature, is last to be considered. The design, the disposition, the manners, and the thoughts, are all before it; where any of those are wanting or imperfect, so much wants or is imperfect in the imitation of human life, which is in the very definition of a poem. Words, indeed, like glaring colors, are the first beauties that arise and strike the sight; but, if the draft be false or lame, the figures ill disposed, the manners obscure or inconsistent, or the thoughts unnatural, then the finest colors are but daubing, and the piece is a beautiful monster at the best. Neither Virgil nor Homer were deficient in any of the former beauties; but in this last, which is expression, the Roman poet is at least equal to the Grecian, as I have said elsewhere; supplying the poverty of his language by his musical ear, and by his diligence.

But to return; our two great poets being so different in their tempers, one choleric and sanguine, the other phlegmatic and melancholic; that which makes them excel in their several ways is, that each of them has followed his own natural inclination, as well in forming the design, as in the execution of it. The very heroes show their authors: Achilles is hot, impatient, revengeful —

Impiger, iracundus, inexorabilis, acer, etc.[10]

Aeneas patient, considerate, careful of his people, and merciful to his enemies; ever submissive to the will of heaven —

. . . quo fata trahunt retrahuntque, sequamur.[11]

I could please myself with enlarging on this subject, but am forced to defer it to a fitter time. From all I have said, I will only draw this inference, that the action of Homer, being more full of vigor

than that of Virgil, according to the temper of the writer, is of consequence more pleasing to the reader. One warms you by degrees; the other sets you on fire all at once, and never intermits his heat. 'Tis the same difference which Longinus [12] makes betwixt the effects of eloquence in Demosthenes and Tully. One persuades, the other commands. You never cool while you read Homer, even not in the second book (a graceful flattery to his countrymen); but he hastens from the ships, and concludes not that book till he has made you an amends by the violent playing of a new machine. From thence he hurries on his action with variety of events, and ends it in less compass than two months. This vehemence of his, I confess, is more suitable to my temper; and, therefore, I have translated his first book with greater pleasure than any part of Virgil; but it was not a pleasure without pains. The continual agitations of the spirits must needs be a weakening of any constitution, especially in age; and many pauses are required for refreshment betwixt the heats; the *Iliad* of itself being a third part longer than all Virgil's works together.

This is what I thought needful in this place to say of Homer. I proceed to Ovid and Chaucer, considering the former only in relation to the latter. With Ovid ended the Golden Age of the Roman tongue; from Chaucer the purity of the English tongue began. The manners of the poets were not unlike. Both of them were well-bred, well-natured, amorous, and libertine, at least in their writings; it may be also in their lives. Their studies were the same, philosophy and philology. Both of them were knowing in astronomy; of which Ovid's books of *The Roman Feasts,* and Chaucer's *Treatise of the Astrolabe,* are sufficient witnesses. But Chaucer was likewise an astrologer, as were Virgil, Horace, Persius, and Manilius. Both writ with wonderful facility and clearness; neither were great inventors: for Ovid only copied the Grecian fables, and most of Chaucer's stories [13] were taken from his Italian contemporaries, or their predecessors. Boccace his *Decameron* was first published, and from thence [14] our Englishman has borrowed many of his *Canterbury Tales;* yet that of "Palamon and Arcite" was written, in all probability, by some Italian wit,[15] in a former age, as I shall prove hereafter.

12. **Longinus:** famous Greek critic, reputedly author of *On the Sublime.* 13. **Chaucer's stories:** Dryden is wrong in most of the following information. For example, Chaucer was not the author of *Piers Plowman.* 14. **from thence:** Chaucer probably did not know the *Decameron.* 15. **Italian wit:** Boccaccio's *Teseide.*

10. *Impiger . . . acer:* "Furious, wrathful, stubborn, vehement" Horace, *Ars Poetica,* 121). 11. *quo . . . sequamur:* "wherever fate pulls or pushes us, let us follow" (Virgil, *Aeneid,* V.709).

The tale of "Griselda" was the invention of Petrarch;[16] by him sent to Boccace, from whom it came to Chaucer. *Troilus and Criseyde* was also written by a Lombard author,[17] but much amplified by our English translator, as well as beautified; the genius of our countrymen, in general, being rather to improve an invention than to invent themselves, as is evident not only in our poetry, but in many of our manufactures. I find I have anticipated already, and taken up from Boccace before I come to him; but there is so much less behind; and I am of the temper of most kings, who love to be in debt, are all for present money, no matter how they pay it afterwards; besides, the nature of a preface is rambling, never wholly out of the way, nor in it. This I have learned from the practice of honest Montaigne, and return at my pleasure to Ovid and Chaucer, of whom I have little more to say.

Both of them built on the inventions of other men; yet since Chaucer had something of his own, as "The Wife of Bath's Tale," "The Cock and the Fox,"[18] which I have translated, and some others, I may justly give our countryman the precedence in that part; since I can remember nothing of Ovid which was wholly his. Both of them understood the manners, under which name I comprehend the passions, and, in a larger sense, the descriptions of persons, and their very habits. For an example, I see Baucis and Philemon as perfectly before me, as if some ancient painter had drawn them; and all the pilgrims in the *Canterbury Tales,* their humors, their features, and the very dress, as distinctly as if I had supped with them at the Tabard in Southwark. Yet even there, too, the figures of Chaucer are much more lively, and set in a better light; which though I have not time to prove, yet I appeal to the reader, and am sure he will clear me from partiality. The thoughts and words remain to be considered in the comparison of the two poets, and I have saved myself one half of that labor, by owning that Ovid lived when the Roman tongue was in its meridian; Chaucer, in the dawning of our language; therefore that part of the comparison stands not on an equal foot, any more than the diction of Ennius and Ovid, or of Chaucer and our present English. The words are given up, as a post not to be defended in our poet, because he wanted the modern art of fortifying.

The thoughts remain to be considered; and they are to be measured only by their propriety; that is, as they flow more or less naturally from the persons described, on such and such occasions. The vulgar judges, which are nine parts in ten of all nations, who call conceits and jingles wit, who see Ovid full of them, and Chaucer altogether without them, will think me little less than mad for preferring the Englishman to the Roman. Yet, with their leave, I must presume to say, that the things they admire are only glittering trifles, and so far from being witty, that in a serious poem they are nauseous, because they are unnatural. Would any man who is ready to die for love describe his passion like Narcissus? Would he think of *inopem me copia fecit*,[19] and a dozen more of such expressions, poured on the neck of one another, and signifying all the same thing? If this were wit, was this a time to be witty, when the poor wretch was in the agony of death? This is just John Littlewit, in *Bartholomew Fair*,[20] who had a conceit (as he tells you) left him in his misery; a miserable conceit. On these occasions the poet should endeavor to raise pity; but, instead of this, Ovid is tickling you to laugh. Virgil never made use of such machines when he was moving you to commiserate the death of Dido: he would not destroy what he was building. Chaucer makes Arcite violent in his love, and unjust in the pursuit of it; yet when he came to die, he made him think more reasonably; he repents not of his love, for that had altered his character; but acknowledges the injustice of his proceedings, and resigns Emilia to Palamon. What would Ovid have done on this occasion? He would certainly have made Arcite witty on his deathbed; he had complained he was further off from possession, by being so near, and a thousand such boyisms, which Chaucer rejected as below the dignity of the subject. They who think otherwise, would, by the same reason, prefer Lucan and Ovid to Homer and Virgil, and Martial to all four of them. As for the turn of words, in which Ovid particularly excels all poets, they are sometimes a fault, and sometimes a beauty, as they are used properly or improperly; but in strong passions always to be shunned, because passions are serious, and will admit no playing. The French have a high value for them; and, I confess, they are often what they call delicate, when they are introduced

---

16. **Petrarch:** who took it from Boccaccio.   17. **a Lombard author:** Boccaccio's *Il Filostrato.*   18. **The . . . Fox:** both tales were at least traditional, and hence not "his own."

19. *inopem . . . fecit:* "my abundance has made me poor" (Ovid, *Metamorphoses,* III.466).   20. *Bartholomew Fair:* by Ben Jonson.

with judgment; but Chaucer writ with more simplicity, and followed nature more closely than to use them. I have thus far, to the best of my knowledge, been an upright judge betwixt the parties in competition, not meddling with the design nor the disposition of it; because the design was not their own; and in the disposing of it they were equal. It remains that I say somewhat of Chaucer in particular.

In the first place, as he is the father of English poetry, so I hold him in the same degree of veneration as the Grecians held Homer, or the Romans Virgil. He is a perpetual fountain of good sense; learned in all sciences; and, therefore, speaks properly on all subjects. As he knew what to say, so he knows also when to leave off; a continence which is practised by few writers, and scarcely by any of the ancients, excepting Virgil and Horace. One of our late great poets [21] is sunk in his reputation, because he could never forgive any conceit which came in his way; but swept like a drag-net, great and small. There was plenty enough, but the dishes were ill sorted; whole pyramids of sweet-meats for boys and women, but little of solid meat for men. All this proceeded not from any want of knowledge, but of judgment. Neither did he want that in discerning the beauties and faults of other poets, but only indulged himself in the luxury of writing; and perhaps knew it was a fault, but hoped the reader would not find it. For this reason, though he must always be thought a great poet, he is no longer esteemed a good writer; and for ten impressions which his works have had in so many successive years, yet at present a hundred books are scarcely purchased once a twelve-month; for, as my last Lord Rochester [22] said, though somewhat profanely, Not being of God, he could not stand.

Chaucer followed nature everywhere, but was never so bold to go beyond her; and there is a great difference of being *poeta* and *nimis poeta*,[23] if we may believe Catullus,[24] as much as betwixt a modest behavior and affectation. The verse of Chaucer, I confess, is not harmonious to us; but 'tis like the eloquence of one whom Tacitus commends, it was *auribus istius temporis accommodata:* [25] they who lived with him, and some time after him, thought it musical; and it continues so, even in our judgment, if compared with the numbers of Lidgate

and Gower, his contemporaries; there is the rude sweetness of a Scotch tune in it, which is natural and pleasing, though not perfect. 'Tis true, I cannot go so far as he who published the last edition of him; [26] for he would make us believe the fault is in our ears, and that there were really ten syllables in a verse where we find but nine; but this opinion is not worth confuting; 'tis so gross and obvious an error, that common sense (which is a rule in everything but matters of faith and revelation) must convince the reader, that equality of numbers, in every verse which we call heroic, was either not known, or not always practised, in Chaucer's age. It were an easy matter to produce some thousands of his verses, which are lame for want of half a foot, and sometimes a whole one, and which no pronunciation can make otherwise. We can only say, that he lived in the infancy of our poetry, and that nothing is brought to perfection at the first. We must be children before we grow men. There was an Ennius, and in process of time a Lucilius, and a Lucretius before Virgil and Horace; even after Chaucer there was a Spenser, a Harington,[27] a Fairfax, before Waller and Denham were in being; and our numbers were in their nonage till these last appeared. I need say [28] little of his parentage, life, and fortunes; they are to be found at large in all the editions of his works. He was employed abroad, and favored, by Edward the Third, Richard the Second, and Henry the Fourth, and was poet, as I suppose, to all three of them. In Richard's time, I doubt, he was a little dipped in the rebellion of the Commons; and being brother-in-law to John of Gaunt, it was no wonder if he followed the fortunes of that family; and was well with Henry the Fourth when he had deposed his predecessor. Neither is it to be admired,[29] that Henry, who was a wise as well as a valiant prince, who claimed by succession, and was sensible that his title was not sound, but was rightfully in Mortimer, who had married the heir of York; it was not to be admired, I say, if that great politician should be pleased to have the greatest wit of those times in his interests, and to be the trumpet of his praises. Augustus had given him the example, by the advice of Maecenas, who recommended Virgil and Horace to him; whose praises helped to make

---

21. **poets:** Abraham Cowley.   22. **Rochester:** the Earl of Rochester (d. 1680).   23. **nimis poeta:** "too much the poet." 24. **Catullus:** a mistake for Martial.   25. **auribus . . . accommodata:** "accommodated to the ears of that generation."

26. **last . . . him:** by Thomas Speght (1687). Dryden never understood that Chaucer, because of his final *e*, was a perfect metrist.   27. **Harington:** Sir John Harington, translator of Ariosto's *Orlando Furioso* (1591).   28. **need say:** most of what follows is inaccurate.   29. **admired:** wondered at.

him popular while he was alive, and after his death have made him precious to posterity. As for the religion of our poet, he seems to have some little bias towards the opinions of Wycliffe, after John of Gaunt his patron; somewhat of which appears in the tale of *Piers Plowman;* yet I cannot blame him for inveighing so sharply against the vices of the clergy in his age; their pride, their ambition, their pomp, their avarice, their worldly interest, deserved the lashes which he gave them, both in that, and in most of his *Canterbury Tales.* Neither has his contemporary Boccace spared them: yet both those poets lived in much esteem with good and holy men in orders; for the scandal which is given by particular priests reflects not on the sacred function. Chaucer's Monk, his Canon, and his Friar, took not from the character of his Good Parson. A satirical poet is the check of the laymen on bad priests. We are only to take care that we involve not the innocent with the guilty in the same condemnation. The good cannot be too much honored, nor the bad too coarsely used; for the corruption of the best becomes the worst. When a clergyman is whipped, his gown is first taken off, by which the dignity of his order is secured. If he be wrongfully accused, he has his action of slander; and 'tis at the poet's peril if he transgress the law. But they will tell us, that all kind of satire, though never so well deserved by particular priests, yet brings the whole order into contempt. Is then the peerage of England anything dishonored when a peer suffers for his treason? If he be libelled, or any way defamed, he has his *scandalum magnatum* [30] to punish the offender. They who use this kind of argument, seem to be conscious to themselves of somewhat which has deserved the poet's lash, and are less concerned for their public capacity than for their private; at least there is pride at the bottom of their reasoning. If the faults of men in orders are only to be judged among themselves, they are all in some sort parties; for, since they say the honor of their order is concerned in every member of it, how can we be sure that they will be impartial judges? How far I may be allowed to speak my opinion in this case, I know not; but I am sure a dispute of this nature caused mischief in abundance betwixt a King of England and an Archbishop of Canterbury; [31] one standing up for the laws of his land, and the other for the honor (as he called it)

of God's church; which ended in the murder of the prelate, and in the whipping of his Majesty from post to pillar for his penance. The learned and ingenious Dr. Drake [32] has saved me the labor of inquiring into the esteem and reverence which the priests have had of old; and I would rather extend than diminish any part of it; yet I must needs say, that when a priest provokes me without any occasion given him, I have no reason, unless it be the charity of a Christian, to forgive him: *prior laesit* [33] is justification sufficient in the civil law. If I answer him in his own language, self-defence I am sure must be allowed me; and if I carry it further, even to a sharp recrimination, somewhat may be indulged to human frailty. Yet my resentment has not wrought so far but that I have followed Chaucer in his character of a holy man, and have enlarged on that subject with some pleasure; reserving to myself the right, if I shall think fit hereafter, to describe another sort of priests, such as are more easily to be found than the Good Parson; such as have given the last blow to Christianity in this age by a practice so contrary to their doctrine. But this will keep cold till another time. In the meanwhile, I take up Chaucer where I left him.

He must have been a man of a most wonderful comprehensive nature, because, as it has been truly observed of him, he has taken into the compass of his Canterbury Tales the various manners and humors (as we now call them) of the whole English nation, in his age. Not a single character has escaped him. All his pilgrims are severally distinguished from each other; and not only in their inclinations but in their very physiognomies and persons. Baptista Porta [34] could not have described their natures better, than by the marks which the poet gives them. The matter and manner of their tales, and of their telling, are so suited to their different educations, humors, and callings, that each of them would be improper in any other mouth. Even the grave and serious characters are distinguished by their several sorts of gravity: their discourses are such as belong to their age, their calling, and their breeding; such as are becoming of them, and of them only. Some of his persons are vicious, and some virtuous; some are unlearned, or (as Chaucer calls them) lewd, and some are learned. Even the ribaldry of the low characters is different:

---

30. *scandalum magnatum:* "slander magnified," i.e., when a peer or other great person is libeled.   **31. King . . . Canterbury:** Henry II and Thomas à Becket.   **32. Dr. Drake:** Dr. James Drake published an answer to Jeremy Collier in 1699.   **33.** *prior laesit:* "he offended first."   **34. Porta:** a Neopolitan writer on physiognomy.

the Reeve, the Miller, and the Cook, are several
men, and distinguished from each other as much
as the mincing Lady-Prioress and the broad-speak-
ing, gap-toothed Wife of Bath. But enough of this;
there is such a variety of game springing up before
me, that I am distracted in my choice, and know
not which to follow. 'Tis sufficient to say, according to the proverb, that here is God's plenty. We
have our forefathers and great-grand-dames all before us, as they were in Chaucer's days: their general characters are still remaining in mankind,
and even in England, though they are called by
other names than those of monks, and friars, and
canons, and lady-abbesses, and nuns; for mankind
is ever the same, and nothing lost out of nature,
though everything is altered. May I have leave to
do myself the justice (since my enemies will do me
none, and are so far from granting me to be a
good poet, that they will not allow me so much
as to be a Christian, or a moral man), may I have
leave, I say, to inform my reader, that I have confined my choice to such tales of Chaucer as savor
nothing of immodesty. If I had desired more to
please than to instruct, the Reeve, the Miller, the
Shipman, the Merchant, the Sumner, and, above
all, the Wife of Bath, in the prologue to her tale,
would have procured me as many friends and
readers as there are beaux and ladies of pleasure in
the town. But I will no more offend against good
manners: I am sensible as I ought to be of the
scandal I have given by my loose writings; and
make what reparation I am able, by this public
acknowledgment. If anything of this nature, or
of profaneness be crept into these poems, I am so
far from defending it, that I disown it. *Totum hoc
indictum volo.*[35] Chaucer makes another manner
of apology for his broad speaking, and Boccace
makes the like, but I will follow neither of them.
Our countryman, in the end of his *Characters*, before the *Canterbury Tales,* thus excuses the ribaldry,
which is very gross in many of his novels —

> But firste, I pray you, of your courtesy,
> That ye ne arrete it not my villany,
> Though that I plainly speak in this mattere,
> To tellen you her words, and eke her chere;
> Ne though I speak her words properly,
> For this ye knowen as well as I,
> Who shall tellen a tale after a man,
> He mote rehearse as nye as ever he can:
> Everich word of it ben in his charge,
> All speke he, never so rudely, ne large:

> Or else he mote tellen his tale untrue,
> Or feine things, or find words new:
> He may not spare, altho he were his brother,
> He mote as wel say o word as another.
> Crist spake himself full broad in holy Writ
> And well I wote no villany is it,
> Eke Plato saith, who so can him rede,
> The words mote been cousin to the dede.

Yet if a man should have enquired of Boccace
or of Chaucer, what need they had of introducing
such characters, where obscene words were proper
in their mouths, but very indecent to be heard, I
know not what answer they could have made; for
that reason, such tales shall be left untold by me.
You have here a specimen of Chaucer's language,
which is so obsolete that his sense is scarce to be
understood; and you have likewise more than one
example of his unequal numbers, which were mentioned before. Yet many of his verses consist of ten
syllables, and the words not much behind our present English; as for example, these two lines, in the
description of the Carpenter's young wife —

> Wincing she was, as is a jolly colt,
> Long as a mast, and upright as a bolt.[36]

I have almost done with Chaucer, when I have
answered some objections relating to my present
work. I find some people are offended that I have
turned these tales into modern English; because
they think them unworthy of my pains, and look
on Chaucer as a dry, old-fashioned wit, not worth
reviving. I have often heard the late Earl of Leicester say, that Mr. Cowley himself was of that opinion; who, having read him over at my lord's request, declared he had no taste of him. I dare not
advance my opinion against the judgment of so
great an author; but I think it fair, however, to
leave the decision to the public. Mr. Cowley was
too modest to set up for a dictator, and being
shocked perhaps with his old style, never examined
into the depth of his good sense. Chaucer, I confess, is a rough diamond, and must first be polished,
ere he shines. I deny not likewise, that, living in
our early days of poetry, he writes not always of a
piece; but sometimes mingles trivial things with
those of greater moment. Sometimes also, though
not often, he runs riot, like Ovid, and knows not
when he has said enough. But there are more great
wits besides Chaucer whose fault is their excess of
conceits, and those ill sorted. An author is not to
write all he can, but only all he ought. Having

---

35. *Totum . . . volo:* "I wish it all unsaid."   **36. Wincing . . . bolt:** *The Miller's Tale,* 77–78.

observed this redundancy in Chaucer (as it is an easy matter for a man of ordinary parts to find a fault in one of greater), I have not tied myself to a literal translation; but have often omitted what I judged unnecessary, or not of dignity enough to appear in the company of better thoughts. I have presumed further, in some places, and added somewhat of my own where I thought my author was deficient, and had not given his thoughts their true lustre, for want of words in the beginning of our language. And to this I was the more emboldened, because (if I may be permitted to say it myself) I found I had a soul congenial to his, and that I had been conversant in the same studies. Another poet, in another age, may take the same liberty with my writings; if at least they live long enough to deserve correction. It was also necessary sometimes to restore the sense of Chaucer, which was lost or mangled in the errors of the press. Let this example suffice at present; in the story of " Palamon and Arcite," where the temple of Diana is described, you find these verses, in all the editions of our author:

There saw I Danè turned unto a tree,
I mean not the goddess Diane,
But Venus daughter, which that hight Danè.

Which, after a little consideration, I knew was to be reformed into this sense, that Daphne, the daughter of Peneus, was turned into a tree. I durst not make thus bold with Ovid, lest some future Milbourne [37] should arise, and say, I varied from my author, because I understood him not.

But there are other judges, who think I ought not to have translated Chaucer into English, out of a quite contrary notion; they suppose there is a certain veneration due to his old language; and that it is little less than profanation and sacrilege to alter it. They are farther of opinion, that somewhat of his good sense will suffer in this transfusion, and much of the beauty of his thoughts will infallibly be lost, which appear with more grace in their old habit. Of this opinion was that excellent person, whom I mentioned, the late Earl of Leicester, who valued Chaucer as much as Mr. Cowley despised him. My lord dissuaded me from this attempt (for I was thinking of it for some years before his death), and his authority prevailed so far with me, as to defer my undertaking while he lived, in deference to him: yet my reason was not convinced with what he urged against it. If the first end of a writer be to be understood, then, as his language grows obsolete, his thoughts must grow obscure:

Multa renascentur, quae nunc cecidere; cadentque
Quae nunc sunt in honore vocabula, si volet usus,
Quem penes arbitrium est et jus et norma loquendi. [38]

When an ancient word, for its sound and significancy, deserves to be revived, I have that reasonable veneration for antiquity to restore it. All beyond this is superstition. Words are not like landmarks, so sacred as never to be removed; customs are changed, and even statutes are silently repealed, when the reason ceases for which they were enacted. As for the other part of the argument, that his thoughts will lose of their original beauty by the innovation of words; in the first place, not only their beauty, but their being is lost, where they are no longer understood, which is the present case. I grant that something must be lost in all transfusion, that is, in all translations; but the sense will remain, which would otherwise be lost, or at least be maimed, when it is scarce intelligible, and that but to a few. How few are there who can read Chaucer, so as to understand him perfectly! And if imperfectly, then with less profit, and no pleasure. 'Tis not for the use of some old Saxon friends,[39] that I have taken these pains with him: let them neglect my version, because they have no need of it. I made it for their sakes who understand sense and poetry as well as they, when that poetry and sense is put into words which they understand. I will go farther, and dare to add, that what beauties I lose in some places, I give to others which had them not originally: but in this I may be partial to myself; let the reader judge, and I submit to his decision. Yet I think I have just occasion to complain of them, who because they understand Chaucer, would deprive the greater part of their countrymen of the same advantage, and hoard him up, as misers do their grandam gold, only to look on it themselves, and hinder others from making use of it. In sum I seriously protest, that no man ever had, or can have, a greater veneration for Chaucer than myself. I have translated some part of his works, only that I might perpetuate his memory, or at least refresh it, amongst my countrymen. If I have altered him anywhere for the better, I must at the same time acknowledge,

37. **Milbourne:** Luke Milbourne, who had attacked Dryden's *Virgil*.

38. *Multa . . . loquendi:* Cf. *An Essay of Dramatic Poesy*, n. 33.
39. **Saxon friends:** students of Old English.

that I could have done nothing without him. *Facile est inventis addere* [40] is no great commendation; and I am not so vain to think I deserved a greater. I will conclude what I have to say of him singly, with this one remark: a lady of my acquaintance who keeps a kind of correspondence with some authors of the fair sex in France, has been informed by them, that Mademoiselle de Scudery, [41] who is as old as Sibyl, and inspired like her by the same God of Poetry, is at this time translating Chaucer into modern French. From which I gather, that he has been formerly translated into the old Provençal; for how she should come to understand Old English, I know not. But the matter of fact being true, it makes me think that there is something in it like fatality; that, after certain periods of time, the fame and memory of great wits should be renewed, as Chaucer is both in France and England. If this be wholly chance, 'tis extraordinary; and I dare not call it more, for fear of being taxed with superstition.

Boccace comes last to be considered, who, living in the same age with Chaucer, had the same genius, and followed the same studies. Both writ novels, and each of them cultivated his mother-tongue. But the greatest resemblance of our two modern authors being in their familiar style, and pleasing way of relating comical adventures, I may pass it over, because I have translated nothing from Boccace of that nature. In the serious part of poetry, the advantage is wholly on Chaucer's side; for though the Englishman has borrowed many tales from the Italian, yet it appears that those of Boccace were not generally of his own making, but taken from authors of former ages, and by him modelled; so that what there was of invention, in either of them, may be judged equal. But Chaucer has refined on Boccace, and has mended the stories which he has borrowed, in his way of telling; though prose allows more liberty of thought, and the expression is more easy when unconfined by numbers. Our countryman carries weight, and yet wins the race at disadvantage. I desire not the reader should take my word; and, therefore, I will set two of their discourses, on the same subject, in the same light, for every man to judge betwixt them. I translated Chaucer first, and, amongst the rest, pitched on "The Wife of Bath's Tale"; not

daring, as I have said, to adventure on her Prologue, because 'tis too licentious. There Chaucer introduces an old woman, of mean parentage, whom a youthful knight, of noble blood, was forced to marry, and consequently loathed her. The crone being in bed with him on the wedding-night and finding his aversion, endeavors to win his affection by reason, and speaks a good word for herself (as who could blame her?) in hope to mollify the sullen bridegroom. She takes her topics from the benefits of poverty, the advantages of old age and ugliness, the vanity of youth, and the silly pride of ancestry and titles, without inherent virtue, which is the true nobility. When I had closed Chaucer, I returned to Ovid, and translated some more of his fables; and, by this time, had so far forgotten "The Wife of Bath's Tale," that, when I took up Boccace unawares I fell on the same argument, of preferring virtue to nobility of blood and titles, in the story of Sigismonda; which I had certainly avoided, for the resemblance of the two discourses, if my memory had not failed me. Let the reader weigh them both; and, if he thinks me partial to Chaucer, 'tis in him to right Boccace.

I prefer, in our countryman, far above all his other stories, the noble poem of "Palamon and Arcite," [42] which is of the epic kind, and perhaps not much inferior to the *Ilias* or the *Aeneis*. The story is more pleasing than either of them, the manners as perfect, the diction as poetical, the learning as deep and various, and the disposition full as artful; only it includes a greater length of time, as taking up seven years at least; but Aristotle has left undecided the duration of the action; which yet is easily reduced into the compass of a year by a narration of what preceded the return of Palamon to Athens. I had thought, for the honor of our narration, and more particularly for his, whose laurel, though unworthy, I have worn after him, that this story was of English growth, and Chaucer's own; but I was undeceived by Boccace; for, casually looking on the end of his seventh *Giornata,* I found Dioneo (under which name he shadows himself), and Fiametta (who represents his mistress, the natural daughter of Robert, King of Naples), of whom these words are spoken: *Dioneo e Fiametta gran pezzo cantarono insieme d'Arcita, e di Palemone;* [43] by which it appears, that this story was

---

40. *Facile . . . addere:* "It is easy to supplement another's discoveries." 41. de Scudery: authoress of popular French romances (1607–1701).

42. **Palamon and Arcite:** *The Knight's Tale.* 43. *Dioneo . . . Palemone:* "Dioneo and Fiametta sang together much of the tale of Arcite and Palamon."

written before the time of Boccace but the name of its author [44] being wholly lost, Chaucer is now become an original; and I question not but the poem has received many beauties by passing through his noble hands. Besides this tale there is another of his own invention, after the manner of the Provençals, called " The Flower and the Leaf," [45] with which I was so particularly pleased, both for the invention and the moral, that I cannot hinder myself from recommending it to the reader.

As a corollary to this preface, in which I have done justice to others, I owe somewhat to myself; not that I think it worth my time to enter the lists with one M——,[46] or one B——,[47] but barely to take notice, that such men there are, who have written scurrilously against me, without any provocation. M——, who is in orders, pretends, amongst the rest, this quarrel to me, that I have fallen foul on priesthood: if I have, I am only to ask pardon of good priests, and am afraid his part of the reparation will come to little. Let him be satisfied, that he shall not be able to force himself upon me for an adversary. I contemn him too much to enter into competition with him. His own translations of Virgil have answered his criticisms on mine. If (as they say he has declared in print) he prefers the version of Ogilby [48] to mine, the world has made him the same compliment; for 'tis agreed, on all hands, that he writes even below Ogilby. That, you will say, is not easily to be done; but what cannot M—— bring about? I am satisfied, however, that, while he and I live together, I shall not be thought the worst poet of the age. It looks as if I had desired him underhand to write so ill against me; but upon my honest word I have not bribed him to do me this service, and am wholly guiltless of his pamphlet. 'Tis true, I should be glad if I could persuade him to continue his good offices, and write such another critique on anything of mine; for I find, by experience, he has a great stroke with the reader, when he condemns any of my poems, to make the world have a better opinion of them. He has taken some pains with my poetry; but nobody will be persuaded to take the same with his. If I had taken to the church, as he affirms, but which was never in my thoughts, I should have had more sense, if not more grace, than to have turned myself out of my benefice by writing libels

on my parishioners. But his account of my manners and my principles are of a piece with his cavils and his poetry; and so I have done with him for ever.

As for the city bard, or knight physician, I hear his quarrel to me is, that I was the author of *Absalom and Achitophel,* which, he thinks, is a little hard on his fanatic patrons [49] in London.

But I will deal the more civilly with his two poems, because nothing ill is to be spoken of the dead; and therefore peace be to the *manes* of his *Arthurs.*[50] I will only say, that it was not for this noble knight that I drew the plan of an epic poem on King Arthur, in my preface to the translation of Juvenal. The guardian angels of kingdoms were machines too ponderous for him to manage; and therefore he rejected them, as Dares did the whirlbats of Eryx when they were thrown before him by Entellus: [51] yet from that preface, he plainly took his hint; for he began immediately upon the story, though he had the baseness not to acknowledge his benefactor, but instead of it, to traduce me in a libel.

I shall say the less of Mr. Collier,[52] because in many things he has taxed me justly; and I have pleaded guilty to all thoughts and expressions of mine which can be truly argued of obscenity, profaneness, or immorality, and retract them. If he be my enemy, let him triumph; if he be my friend, as I have given him no personal occasion to be otherwise, he will be glad of my repentance. It becomes me not to draw my pen in the defence of a bad cause, when I have so often drawn it for a good one. Yet it were not difficult to prove, that in many places he has perverted my meaning by his glosses, and interpreted my words into blasphemy and bawdry, of which they were not guilty. Besides that, he is too much given to horse-play in his raillery, and comes to battle like a dictator from the plow. I will not say, " The zeal of God's house has eaten him up " ; [53] but I am sure it has devoured some part of his good manners and civility. It might also be doubted, whether it were altogether zeal which prompted him to this rough manner of proceeding; perhaps it became not one of his functions to rake into the rubbish of ancient and modern plays: a divine might have employed

---

44. its author: Boccaccio himself, in his *Teseide*.   45. The . . . Leaf: not written by Chaucer.   46. M——: Luke Milbourne.   47. B——: Sir Richard Blackmore.   48. version of Ogilby: 1654.

49. fanatic patrons: the middle-class Puritans of London.   50. his Arthurs: one of Blackmore's epics was *Prince Arthur* (1695).   51. Dares . . . Entellus: Cf. Virgil, *Aeneid*, V.533–59 (Dryden's translation).   52. Mr. Collier: Jeremy Collier.   53. "has . . up": Cf. Ps. 69:9.

his pains to better purpose, than in the nastiness of Plautus and Aristophanes, whose examples, as they excuse not me, so it might be possibly supposed that he read them not without some pleasure. They who have written commentaries on those poets, or on Horace, Juvenal, and Martial, have explained some vices which, without their interpretation, had been unknown to modern times. Neither has he judged impartially betwixt the former age and us. There is more bawdry in one play of Fletcher's called *The Custom of the Country,* than in all ours together. Yet this has been often acted on the stage in my remembrance. Are the times so much more reformed now than they were five-and-twenty years ago? If they are, I congratulate the amendment of our morals. But I am not to prejudice the cause of my fellow poets, though I abandon my own defence: they have some of them answered for themselves; and neither they nor I can think Mr. Collier so formidable an enemy that we should shun him. He has lost ground, at the latter end of the day, by pursuing his point too far, like the Prince of Condé, at the battle of Senneph: [54] from immoral plays to no plays, *ab abusu ad usum, non valet consequentia.*[55] But, being a party, I am not to erect myself into a judge. As for the rest of those who have written against me, they are such scoundrels, that they deserve not the least notice to be taken of them. B—— and M—— are only distinguished from the crowd by being remembered to their infamy:

> . . . *Demetri, teque, Tigelli,*
> *Discipulorum inter jubeo plorare cathedras.*[56]

TO MY HONORED KINSMAN, JOHN DRIDEN,

OF CHESTERTON, IN THE COUNTY OF HUNTINGDON, ESQUIRE

Dryden's complimentary poem to his cousin is crusty, as befits the age of its writer and (doubtless) the character of its subject, but the effect of its praise is noble.

How blest is he, who leads a country life,
Unvexed with anxious cares, and void of strife!
Who, studying peace and shunning civil rage,
Enjoyed his youth, and now enjoys his age:
All who deserve his love, he makes his own;

And, to be loved himself, needs only to be known.
Just, good, and wise, contending neighbors come,
From your award to wait their final doom;
And, foes before, return in friendship home.
Without their cost, you terminate the cause,   10
And save the expense of long litigious laws:
Where suits are traversed,° and so little won,
That he who conquers is but last undone.
Such are not your decrees; but so designed,
The sanction leaves a lasting peace behind:
Like your own soul, serene; a pattern of your mind.
Promoting concord, and composing strife,
Lord of yourself, uncumbered with a wife;
Where, for a year, a month, perhaps a night,
Long penitence succeeds a short delight: 20
Minds are so hardly matched, that even the first,
Tho' paired by Heaven, in Paradise were curst.
For man and woman, tho' in one they grow,
Yet, first or last, return again to two.
He to God's image, she to his was made;
So, farther from the fount, the stream at random strayed.
How could he stand, when, put to double pain,
He must a weaker than himself sustain!
Each might have stood perhaps, but each alone;
Two wrestlers help to pull each other down.   30
Not that my verse would blemish all the fair;
But yet if *some* be bad, 'tis wisdom to beware;
And better shun the bait than struggle in the snare.
Thus have you shunned, and shun, the married state,
Trusting as little as you can to fate.
No porter guards the passage of your door,
To admit the wealthy, and exclude the poor;
For God, who gave the riches, gave the heart,
To sanctify the whole, by giving part.
Heaven, who foresaw the will, the means has wrought,   40
And to the second son a blessing brought;
The first-begotten° had his father's share,
But you, like Jacob, are Rebecca's heir.
So may your stores and fruitful fields increase;
And ever be you blest, who live to bless.
As Ceres sowed, where'er her chariot flew;
As Heaven in desarts rained the bread of dew;
So free to many, to relations most,
You feed with manna your own Israel host.
With crowds attended of your ancient race,   50
You seek the champian° sports or sylvan chase;
With well-breathed beagles you surround the wood,
Even then industrious of the common good,
And often have you brought the wily fox
To suffer for the firstlings of the flocks;

---

54. battle of Senneph: in Flanders (1674).   **55. ab . . . consequentia:** "use is not invalidated by abuse."   **56. Demetri . . . cathedras:** "I bid you, Demetrius and Tigellius, go howl among the seats of your pupils" (Horace, *Satires,* I.x.90–91).

TO JOHN DRIDEN.   **12. traversed:** opposed.   **42. The first-begotten:** Sir Robert Dryden.   **51. champian:** of the champaign, or open country.

Chased even amid the folds, and made to bleed,
Like felons, where they did the murderous deed.
This fiery game your active youth maintained,
Not yet by years extinguished, tho' restrained:
You season still with sports your serious hours;   60
For age but tastes of pleasures, youth devours.
The hare in pastures or in plains is found,
Emblem of human life, who runs the round;
And after all his wandering ways are done,
His circle fills and ends where he begun,
Just as the setting meets the rising sun.

Thus princes ease their cares; but happier he
Who seeks not pleasure thro' necessity,
Than such as once on slippery thrones were placed;
And chasing, sigh to think themselves are
    chased.   70

So lived our sires, ere doctors learned to kill,
And multiplied with theirs the weekly bill.
The first physicians by debauch were made;
Excess began, and sloth sustains the trade.
Pity° the generous kind their cares bestow
To search forbidden truths; (a sin to know:)
To which if human science could attain,
The doom of death, pronounced by God, were vain.
In vain the leech° would interpose delay;
Fate fastens first, and vindicates the prey.   80
What help from art's endeavors can we have?
Gibbons° but guesses, nor is sure to save;
But Maurus° sweeps whole parishes, and peoples
    every grave;
And no more mercy to mankind will use,
Than when he robbed and murdered Maro's
    Muse.°
Wouldst thou be soon dispatched, and perish
    whole?
Trust Maurus with thy life, and M-lb-rne° with
    thy soul.

By chase our long-lived fathers earned their food;
Toil strung the nerves and purified the blood:
But we, their sons, a pampered race of men,   90
Are dwindled down to threescore years and ten.
Better to hunt in fields for health unbought
Than fee the doctor for a nauseous draught.
The wise for cure on exercise depend;
God never made his work for man to mend.

The tree of knowledge, once in Eden placed,
Was easy found, but was forbid the taste:
O had our grandsire walked without his wife,
He first had sought the better plant of life!
Now, both are lost; yet, wandering in the dark,

Physicians, for the tree, have found the bark.   101
They, laboring for relief of humankind,
With sharpened sight some remedies may find;
The apothecary train is wholly blind.
From files a random recipe they take,
And many deaths of one prescription make.
Garth,° generous as his Muse, prescribes and gives;
The shopman sells, and by destruction lives:
Ungrateful tribe! who, like the viper's brood,
From medicine issuing, suck their mother's
    blood!   110
Let these obey, and let the learn'd prescribe,
That men may die without a double bribe:
Let them but under their superiors kill,
When doctors first have signed the bloody bill;
He scapes the best, who, nature to repair,
Draws physic from the fields, in draughts of vital
    air.

You hoard not health for your own private use,
But on the public spend the rich produce;
When, often urged, unwilling to be great,
Your country calls you from your loved re-
    treat,   120
And sends to senates, charged with common care,
Which none more shuns, and none can better bear.
Where could they find another formed so fit,
To poise with solid sense a sprightly wit?
Were these both wanting, (as they both abound,)
Where could so firm integrity be found?

Well-born, and wealthy, wanting no support,
You steer betwixt the country and the court;
Nor gratify whate'er the great desire,
Nor grudging give what public needs require.   130
Part must be left, a fund when foes invade;
And part employed to roll the watery trade:
Even Canaan's happy land, when worn with toil,
Required a sabbath year to mend the meager soil.

Good senators (and such are you) so give,
That kings may be supplied, the people thrive.
And he, when want requires, is truly wise,
Who slights not foreign aids, nor overbuys,
But on our native strength, in time of need, relies.
Munster° was bought, we boast not the suc-
    cess;   140
Who fights for gain, for greater makes his peace.

Our foes, compelled by need, have peace° em-
    braced;
The peace both parties want is like to last:
Which if secure, securely we may trade;
Or, not secure, should never have been made.

75. Pity: a pity that.   **79. leech:** physician.   **82. Gibbons:** Dr. William Gibbons, Dryden's physician.   **83. Maurus:** Sir Richard Blackmore, the poet whom Dryden so thoroughly despised, was also a physician.   **85. Maro's Muse:** Virgil. Dryden may be thinking here of Luke Milbourne.   **87. M-lb-rne:** Luke Milbourne, discussed above in the Preface to the *Fables*.

107. Garth: Sir Samuel Garth (1661–1719), author of *The Dispensary*, a humorous poem; his free clinic for poor patients was disapproved of by the apothecaries (druggists) and by some doctors.   **140. Munster:** the Bishop of Münster was paid by Charles II to attack Holland in the naval war of 1666, but retired when France joined the Dutch.   **142. peace:** the Peace of Ryswick (1697).

Safe in ourselves, while on ourselves we stand,
The sea is ours, and that defends the land.
Be, then, the naval stores the nation's care,
New ships to build, and battered to repair.

   Observe the war, in every annual course;   150
What has been done was done with British force:
Namur° subdued is England's palm alone;
The rest besieged, but we constrained the town:
We saw the event that followed our success;
France, tho' pretending arms, pursued the peace;
Obliged, by one sole treaty, to restore
What twenty years of war had won before.
Enough for Europe has our Albion fought:
Let us enjoy the peace our blood has bought.
When once the Persian king was put to flight, 160
The weary Macedons refused to fight,
Themselves their own mortality confessed,
And left the son of Jove° to quarrel for the rest.

   Even victors are by victories undone;
Thus Hannibal, with foreign laurels won,
To Carthage was recalled, too late to keep his own.
While sore of battle, while our wounds are green,
Why should we tempt the doubtful die again?
In wars renewed, uncertain of success;
Sure of a share, as umpires of the peace.   170

   A patriot both the king and country serves;
Prerogative and privilege preserves:
Of each our laws the certain limit show;
One must not ebb, nor t'other overflow.
Betwixt the prince and parliament we stand;
The barriers of the state on either hand:
May neither overflow, for then they drown the
    land!
When both are full, they feed our blest abode;
Like those that watered once the paradise of God.

   Some overpoise of sway by turns they share;   180
In peace the people, and the prince in war:
Consuls of moderate power in calms were made;
When the Gauls came, one sole dictator swayed.

   Patriots, in peace, assert the people's right;
With noble stubbornness resisting might:
No lawless mandates from the court receive,
Nor lend by force, but in a body give.
Such was your generous grandsire; free to grant
In parliaments that weighed their prince's want:
But so tenacious of the common cause,   190
As not to lend the king against his laws;
And, in a loathsome dungeon doomed to lie,
In bonds retained his birthright liberty,
And shamed oppression, till it set him free.

   O true descendant of a patriot line,
Who, while thou shar'st their luster, lend'st 'em
    thine,
Vouchsafe this picture of thy soul to see;

'Tis so far good, as it resembles thee.
The beauties to the original I owe;
Which when I miss, my own defects I show: 200
Nor think the kindred Muses thy disgrace;
A poet is not born in every race.
Two of a house few ages can afford;
One to perform, another to record.
Praiseworthy actions are by thee embraced;
And 'tis my praise, to make thy praises last.
For even when death dissolves our human frame,
The soul returns to heaven, from whence it came;
Earth keeps the body, verse preserves the fame.

BAUCIS AND PHILEMON

OUT OF THE EIGHTH BOOK OF OVID'S "METAMORPHOSES"

Then Lelex° rose, an old experienced man,   11
And thus with sober gravity began:
"Heaven's power is infinite; earth, air, and sea,
The manufactured mass, the making power obey.
By proof to clear your doubt: in Phrygian ground
Two neighboring trees, with walls encompassed
    round,
Stand on a moderate rise, with wonder shown,
One a hard oak, a softer linden one:
I saw the place and them, by Pittheus sent
To Phrygian realms, my grandsire's govern-
    ment.   20
Not far from thence is seen a lake, the haunt
Of coots, and of the fishing cormorant:
Here Jove with Hermes came; but in disguise
Of mortal men concealed their deities:
One laid aside his thunder, one his rod;
And many toilsome steps together trod:
For harbor at a thousand doors they knocked —
Not one of all the thousand but was locked.
At last an hospitable house they found,
A homely shed; the roof, not far from ground,   30
Was thatched with reeds and straw together bound.
There Baucis and Philemon lived, and there
Had lived long married and a happy pair:
Now old in love; tho' little was their store,
Inured to want, their poverty they bore,
Nor aimed at wealth, professing to be poor.
For master or for servant here to call,
Was all alike, where only two were all.
Command was none, where equal love was paid,
Or rather both commanded, both obeyed.   40
   "From lofty roofs the gods repulsed before,

---

152. **Namur:** Namur, Belgium, captured by William III (1695).
163. **son of Jove:** Alexander the Great.

BAUCIS AND PHILEMON.   11. **Lelex:** In Ovid, the tale is preceded by a debate between friends concerning the power of the
gods to metamorphose people. Lelex, taking part in the debate,
cites the events that follow to prove that they have the power.

Now, stooping, entered thro' the little door;
The man (their hearty welcome first expressed)
A common settle drew for either guest,
Inviting each his weary limbs to rest.
But ere they sat, officious° Baucis lays
Two cushions stuffed with straw, the seat to raise;
Coarse, but the best she had; then rakes the load
Of ashes from the hearth, and spreads abroad
The living coals, and, lest they should expire,   50
With leaves and barks she feeds her infant fire:
It smokes, and then with trembling breath she blows,
Till in a cheerful blaze the flames arose.
With brushwood and with chips she strengthens these,
And adds at last the boughs of rotten trees.
The fire thus formed, she sets the kettle on —
Like burnished gold the little seether shone —
Next took the coleworts which her husband got
From his own ground (a small well-watered spot);
She stripped the stalks of all their leaves; the best   60
She culled, and then with handy care she dressed.
High o'er the hearth a chine of bacon hung:
Good old Philemon seized it with a prong,
And from the sooty rafter drew it down;
Then cut a slice, but scarce enough for one;
Yet a large portion of a little store,
Which for their sakes alone he wished were more.
This in the pot he plunged without delay,
To tame the flesh and drain the salt away.
The time between, before the fire they sat,   70
And shortened the delay by pleasing chat.
 "A beam there was, on which a beechen pail
Hung by the handle, on a driven nail:
This filled with water, gently warmed, they set
Before their guests; in this they bathed their feet,
And after with clean towels dried their sweat.
This done, the host produced the genial bed,
Sallow the feet, the borders, and the stead,
Which with no costly coverlet they spread,
But coarse old garments; yet such robes as these   80
They laid alone, at feasts, on holidays.
The good old housewife, tucking up her gown,
The table sets; the invited gods lie down.
The trivet° table of a foot was lame —
A blot which prudent Baucis overcame,
Who thrusts beneath the limping leg a sherd;
So was the mended board exactly reared:
Then rubbed it o'er with newly gathered mint,
A wholesome herb, that breathed a grateful scent.
Pallas began the feast, where first was seen   90
The party-colored olive, black and green;
Autumnal cornels next in order served,

In lees of wine well pickled and preserved;
A garden salad was the third supply,
Of endive, radishes, and succory;
Then curds and cream, the flower of country fare,
And new-laid eggs, which Baucis' busy care
Turned by a gentle fire, and roasted rear.°
All these in earthenware were served to board;
And, next in place, an earthen pitcher, stored   100
With liquor of the best the cottage could afford.
This was the table's ornament and pride,
With figures wrought: like pages at his side
Stood beechen bowls; and these were shining clean,
Vernished° with wax without, and lined within.
By this the boiling kettle had prepared
And to the table sent the smoking lard,
On which with eager appetite they dine,
A savory bit, that served to relish wine;
The wine itself was suiting to the rest,   110
Still working in the must, and lately pressed.
The second course succeeds like that before;
Plums, apples, nuts, and, of their wintry store,
Dry figs and grapes, and wrinkled dates were set
In canisters, to enlarge the little treat.
All these a milk-white honeycomb surround,
Which in the midst the country banquet crowned
But the kind hosts their entertainment grace
With hearty welcome, and an open face:
In all they did you might discern with ease   120
A willing mind, and a desire to please.
 "Meantime the beechen bowls went round, and still,
Tho' often emptied, were observed to fill;
Filled without hands, and of their own accord
Ran without feet, and danced about the board.
Devotion seized the pair, to see the feast
With wine, and of no common grape, increased;
And up they held their hands, and fell to prayer,
Excusing, as they could, their country fare.
 "One goose they had, ('twas all they could al low,)   130
A wakeful sentry, and on duty now,
Whom to the gods for sacrifice they vow:
Her, with malicious zeal, the couple viewed;
She ran for life, and, limping, they pursued.
Full well the fowl perceived their bad intent,
And would not make her masters' compliment;
But, persecuted, to the powers she flies,
And close between the legs of Jove she lies.
He, with a gracious ear, the suppliant heard,
And saved her life; then what he was declared,   140
And owned the god. 'The neighborhood,' said he,
'Shall justly perish for impiety:
You stand alone exempted; but obey
With speed, and follow where we lead the way;

Leave these accurst, and to the mountain's height
Ascend, nor once look backward in your flight.'
  "They haste, and what their tardy feet denied,
The trusty staff (their better leg) supplied.
An arrow's flight they wanted to the top,
And there secure, but spent with travel, stop;   150
Then turn their now no more forbidden eyes:
Lost in a lake the floated level lies;
A watery desart covers all the plains;
Their cot alone, as in an isle, remains;
Wondering with weeping eyes, while they deplore
Their neighbors' fate, and country now no more,
Their little shed, scarce large enough for two,
Seems, from the ground increased, in height and
    bulk to grow.
A stately temple shoots within the skies;
The crotches° of their cot in columns rise;   160
The pavement polished marble they behold,
The gates with sculpture graced, the spires and tiles
    of gold.
  "Then thus the Sire of Gods, with look serene:
'Speak thy desire, thou only just of men;
And thou, O woman, only worthy found
To be with such a man in marriage bound.'
  "A while they whisper; then, to Jove addressed,
Philemon thus prefers their joint request:
'We crave to serve before your sacred shrine,
And offer at your altars rites divine;   170
And since not any action of our life
Has been polluted with domestic strife,
We beg one hour of death; that neither she
With widow's tears may live to bury me,
Nor weeping I, with withered arms, may bear
My breathless Baucis to the sepulcher.'
  "The godheads sign their suit. They run their
    race
In the same tenor all the appointed space;
Then, when their hour was come, while they relate
These past adventures at the temple gate,   180
Old Baucis is by old Philemon seen
Sprouting with sudden leaves of sprightly green;
Old Baucis looked where old Philemon stood,
And saw his lengthened arms a sprouting wood.
New roots their fastened feet begin to bind,
Their bodies stiffen in a rising rind:
Then, ere the bark above their shoulders grew,
They give and take at once their last adieu,
At once: 'Farewell, O faithful spouse,' they said;
At once the incroaching rinds their closing lips
    invade.   190
Even yet, an ancient Tyanaean shows
A spreading oak, that near a linden grows;
The neighborhood confirm the prodigy,
Grave men, not vain of tongue, or like to lie.

160. crotches: poles with forked tops.

I saw myself the garlands on their boughs,
And tablets hung for gifts of granted vows;
And offering fresher up, with pious prayer,
'The good,' said I, 'are God's peculiar care,
And such as honor Heaven, shall heavenly honor
    share.' "

CHAUCER

from THE COCK AND THE FOX

OR, THE TALE OF THE NUN'S PRIEST

The opening lines of this translation, like those of
the one that follows, are offered here as specimens of
Dryden's verse at its ripest and most charming. (Cf.
pp. 82–90 above).

There lived, as authors tell, in days of yore,
A widow somewhat old, and very poor:
Deep in a dell her cottage lonely stood,
Well thatched, and under covert of a wood.
  This dowager, on whom my tale I found,
Since last she laid her husband in the ground,
A simple sober life in patience led,
And had but just enough to buy her bread:
But huswifing the little Heaven had lent,
She duly paid a groat for quarter rent;   10
And pinched her belly, with her daughters two,
To bring the year about with much ado.
  The cattle in her homestead were three sows,
An ewe called Mally, and three brinded° cows;
Her parlor window stuck with herbs around,
Of savory smell; and rushes strewed the ground.
A maple dresser in her hall she had,
On which full many a slender meal she made:
For no delicious morsel passed her throat;
According to her cloth she cut her coat.   20
No poynant° sauce she knew, no costly treat;
Her hunger gave a relish to her meat:
A sparing diet did her health assure;
Or sick, a pepper posset was her cure.
Before the day was done, her work she sped,
And never went by candlelight to bed.
With exercise she sweat ill humors out;
Her dancing was not hindered by the gout.
Her poverty was glad, her heart content,
Nor knew she what the spleen or vapors meant.   30
  Of wine she never tasted thro' the year,
But white and black was all her homely cheer:
Brown bread, and milk, (but first she skimmed her
    bowls,)
And rashers of singed bacon on the coals.
On holidays an egg, or two at most;
But her ambition never reached to roast. . . .

THE COCK AND THE FOX.   14. brinded: brindled.   21. poy-
nant: poignant, sharp.

from THE WIFE OF BATH, HER TALE

In days of old, when Arthur filled the throne,
Whose acts and fame to foreign lands were blown,
The king of elfs and little fairy queen
Gamboled on heaths, and danced on every green;
And where the jolly troop had led the round,
The grass unbidden rose, and marked the ground:
Nor darkling did they dance; the silver light
Of Phoebe served to guide their steps aright,
And, with their tripping pleased, prolonged the
    night.
Her beams they followed, where at full she played,
Nor longer than she shed her horns they stayed, 11
From thence with airy flight to foreign lands con-
    veyed.
Above the rest our Britain held they dear;
More solemnly they kept their sabbaths here,
And made more spacious rings, and reveled half the
    year.
  I speak of ancient times, for now the swain
Returning late may pass the woods in vain,
And never hope to see the nightly train;
In vain the dairy now with mints is dressed,
The dairymaid expects no fairy guest,   20
To skim the bowls, and after pay the feast.
She sighs, and shakes her empty shoes in vain,
No silver penny to reward her pain:
For priests with prayers, and other godly gear,
Have made the merry goblins disappear;
And where they played their merry pranks before,
Have sprinkled holy water on the floor;
And friars that thro' the wealthy regions run,
Thick as the motes that twinkle in the sun,
Resort to farmers rich, and bless their halls, 30
And exorcise the beds, and cross the walls:
This makes the fairy choirs forsake the place,
When once 'tis hallowed with the rites of grace.
But in the walks where wicked elves have been,
The learning of the parish now is seen,
The midnight parson, posting o'er the green,
With gown tucked up, to wakes, for Sunday next
With humming ale encouraging his text;
Nor wants the holy leer to country girl betwixt.
From fiends and imps he sets the village free, 40
There haunts not any incubus but he.
The maids and women need no danger fear
To walk by night, and sanctity so near:
For by some haycock, or some shady thorn,
He bids his beads both evensong and morn. . . .

THE SECULAR MASQUE

When John Fletcher's old play *The Pilgrim* was
revived in the spring of 1700 as a benefit for Dryden,
he contributed to the occasion a prologue and epilogue,
a song, and this masque to celebrate the end of a century. Sir Walter Scott observes: "By the introduction
of the deities of the chase, of war, and of love, as
governing the various changes of the seventeenth century, the poet alludes to the sylvan sports of James I,
the bloody wars of his son, and the licentious gallantry
which reigned in the courts of Charles II and James,
his successor."

[*Enter* JANUS.]

JANUS.°   Chronos, Chronos, mend thy pace;
               An hundred times the rolling sun
               Around the radiant belt has run
           In his revolving race.
           Behold, behold, the goal in sight;
           Spread thy fans, and wing thy flight.
[*Enter* CHRONOS, *with a scythe in his hand, and a*
great globe on his back, which he sets down at
his entrance.]
CHRONOS.° Weary, weary of my weight,
           Let me, let me drop my freight,
               And leave the world behind.
           I could not bear   10
           Another year
               The load of humankind.
           [*Enter* MOMUS, *laughing.*]
MOMUS.°   Ha! ha! ha! ha! ha! ha! well hast thou
               done
               To lay down thy pack,
               And lighten thy back;
           The world was a fool, e'er since it begun,
           And since neither Janus, nor Chronos,
               nor I
               Can hinder the crimes,
               Or mend the bad times,
           'Tis better to laugh than to cry.   20
CHORUS OF ALL THREE.
           'Tis better to laugh than to cry.
JANUS.   Since Momus comes to laugh below,
               Old Time, begin the show,
           That he may see, in every scene,
           What changes in this age have been.
CHRONOS.   Then, goddess of the silver bow, begin.
           [*Horns, or hunting music within.*]
               [*Enter* DIANA.]
DIANA.°   With horns and with hounds I waken
               the day,
           And hie to my woodland walks away;
           I tuck up my robe, and am buskined
               soon,
           And tie to my forehead a wexing°
               moon.   30
           I course the fleet stag, unkennel the fox,

THE SECULAR MASQUE.   1. Janus: god of beginnings.   7.
Chronos: god of time.   13. Momus: Mockery.   27. Diana:
goddess of the hunt.   30. wexing: waxing.

And chase the wild goats o'er summits
    of rocks;
With shouting and hooting we pierce
    thro' the sky,
And Echo turns hunter, and doubles the
    cry.

CHORUS OF ALL.
With shouting and hooting we pierce
    thro' the sky,
And Echo turns hunter, and doubles the
    cry.

JANUS. Then our age was in its prime:
CHRONOS. Free from rage:
DIANA.   And free from crime:
MOMUS. A very merry, dancing, drinking,
Laughing, quaffing, and unthinking
    time.   40

CHORUS OF ALL.
Then our age was in its prime,
Free from rage, and free from crime;
A very merry, dancing, drinking,
Laughing, quaffing, and unthinking
    time.
[*Dance of* DIANA's *attendants.*]
[*Enter* MARS.]

MARS.° Inspire the vocal brass, inspire;
The world is past its infant age:
    Arms and honor,
    Arms and honor,
Set the martial mind on fire,
And kindle manly rage.   50
Mars has looked the sky to red;
And Peace, the lazy good, is fled.
Plenty, Peace, and Pleasure fly;
    The sprightly green
    In woodland walks no more is seen;
The sprightly green has drunk the
    Tyrian dye.

CHORUS OF ALL.
Plenty, Peace, &c.

MARS. Sound the trumpet, beat the drum;
    Thro' all the world around,
    Sound a reveille, sound, sound,   60
The warrior god is come.

CHORUS OF ALL.
Sound the trumpet, &c.

45. **Mars**: god of war.

MOMUS. Thy sword within the scabbard keep,
    And let mankind agree;
Better the world were fast asleep,
    Than kept awake by thee.
The fools are only thinner,
    With all our cost and care;
But neither side a winner,
    For things are as they were.   70

CHORUS OF ALL.
The fools are only, &c.
[*Enter* VENUS.]

VENUS.° Calms appear when storms are past,
Love will have his hour at last:
Nature is my kindly care;
Mars destroys, and I repair;
Take me, take me, while you may;
Venus comes not every day.

CHORUS OF ALL.
Take her, take her, &c.

CHRONOS. The world was then so light,
    I scarcely felt the weight;   80
Joy ruled the day, and Love the
    night.
But since the Queen of Pleasure left the
    ground,
    I faint, I lag,
    And feebly drag
The ponderous orb around.

MOMUS. All, all of a piece throughout:
    [*Pointing to* DIANA.]
Thy chase had a beast in view;
    [*To* MARS.]
Thy wars brought nothing about;
    [*To* VENUS.]
Thy lovers were all untrue.

JANUS. 'Tis well an old age is out: 90
CHRONOS. And time to begin a new.

CHORUS OF ALL.
All, all of a piece throughout:
Thy chase had a beast in view;
Thy wars brought nothing about;
Thy lovers were all untrue.
'Tis well an old age is out,
And time to begin a new.
[*Dance of huntsmen, nymphs, warriors, and lovers.*]

72. **Venus**: goddess of love.

Jonathan Swift

1667–1745

SWIFT himself is in part responsible for the impression that has survived of him as a powerful but frustrated being, who in spite of many triumphs was always ultimately cheated or disappointed. He liked to represent himself as one who, lacking money and titles, had been forced to make his way in the world by using his intelligence and his wit; and as one who had indeed succeeded in making a reputation and gaining the friendship of the outstanding men of his generation. Nevertheless, as he looked back on his life when he was over sixty, he wrote: " I remember when I was a little boy I felt a great fish at the end of my line which I drew up almost on the ground, but it dropped in, . . . it was the type of all my future disappointments."

First he reckoned he had been cheated in the place of his birth. His parents were English and he was proud of his grandfather Swift, a Tory parson who had been passionately devoted to the Royalist cause in the Civil War; but he was born in Dublin in late November, 1667, when his mother had just been left a poor widow and was unable to provide for him. He resented being indebted to the charity of his uncle for his upbringing and his education, though he was sent to the best school in the country, at Kilkenny, and at the age of fourteen went to Trinity College, Dublin, where he stayed for about seven years.

At length, when he was a little more than twenty-one, through his family's influence he was able to go to England and join the household of Sir William Temple. It seemed likely at the time that the new king, William of Orange, who had known and trusted Temple when he was ambassador to Holland, would bring him out of his retirement into public life again. But if Swift had counted on this he was to be disappointed, for Temple refused to do more than offer his advice to William on certain occasions; and a few years later Swift decided to return to Ireland and take orders in the Church there. After a short time in a country parish, however, he was easily persuaded to return to be secretary to Temple, and remained with him until his death in 1699. But the only tangible results of the long service were the legacy of whatever honor and profit he might obtain from the publication of Temple's *Letters* and *Memoirs,* and the slight connection which he had established with the king and some of the leaders of the Whig party. His hopes for political advancement were shattered by the unexpected death of the king in 1702, and he returned to Ireland to wait for preferment in the Church; but in this also he was for a long time disappointed.

Nevertheless, the years that he spent in seclusion with Temple were of the greatest importance in his own development. He read hard, and lived in a ferment of ideas, stimulated by all the controversies that were raging in the literary world, arising out of the clash between the new ideas and the old in philosophy and religion and science and the arts. He emulated Cowley, the successful poet and best-seller of the seventeenth century, by trying his hand at Pindaric odes. But then he turned with disgust from the Muse who had cheated him with dreams and romantic notions, and determined to open his eyes and clear his gaze, and rid himself of all the conventions of the Schools, while being equally cautious and careful not to become a victim of the follies and absurdities of the new enthusiasts, the virtuosos and collectors and projectors who were to be found among the scientists and in the Royal Society.

Swift turned to satire, and amused himself making fun of everybody; parodying the great Mr. Dryden, the acknowledged master in the last years of the century, whether as poet, critic, or playwright; ridiculing Bentley, the greatest classical scholar England had produced, then Master of Trinity College, Cambridge; harrying the freethinkers, with their new enlightened ideas; but, more daring still, satirizing in the boldest fashion the superstitions of the Roman Church and the fanaticism of the Protestant sects. He wrote and tore up, he says, an enormous amount; but he kept enough for a volume, though it was not in any shape to be published, consisting of stories, parodies, critical stuff, and fragmentary jottings. He must have put this material aside until he had finished off his editing of Temple's *Letters,* Volumes I and II appearing in 1700 and Volume III in 1703. He also published in 1701 a very original and dignified paper, *A Discourse of the Contests and Dissensions Between the Nobles and the Commons in Athens and Rome,* which purported to be a discussion of certain matters in classical history, but which bore on the particular political crisis of the moment; in this he hoped to establish, and did establish, a reputation as a promising journalist, who might prove of great use to his party.

But nothing happened; he was still only an Irish parson with a small living, and no way of staying permanently in London and making a place for himself in the literary world.[1] It was probably then that he decided to take a risk, and publish some of the satires he had written; it would be a mad book, but a book whose wit and genius would astonish and mystify the world. He would not of course put his name to it, would just throw it out on the waters, like the tub that he had read whalers throw out to distract the attention of those dangerous leviathans who turn on the ship; he would just call it *A Tale of a Tub*. It was a satire on all the extravagances of the fanatical sects and of the superstitious practices of the Roman Church, with digressions on the follies of the academic and literary world. It was followed by *The Battle of the Books,* dealing with the controversy between the Ancients and the Moderns, and *A Discourse Concerning the Mechanical Operation of the Spirit,* which made dangerous play with the whole idea of divine inspiration.

The *Tale* made even more of a splash than Swift had expected. It established his position, among those who knew, as the leading wit and genius of the age; and, lacking the reticence expected of a clergyman's writing, it ruined forever his chance of a bishopric in the English Church. That was in 1704. In the next year or two he continued to write in verse and prose, and showed his astonishing versatility of wit and humor, so that when Steele and Addison started their adventures in journalism with the founding of the *Tatler,* Swift had a hand in it, too. But these pleasant friendships were soon to be disturbed by the bitterness of party politics when in 1710 Swift became the leading party writer for the new ministry — the moderate Tory ministry — which was to give him considerable power in public life and a vast acquaintance among the nobility and gentry who were prominent in town society during these last years of Queen Anne's reign.

He started by running the government's weekly newspaper, the *Examiner,* in which he professed to give a sensible moderate view of the political situation, attacked extremists on both sides, undermined the power of Marlborough, the great general, and prepared the public for coming to terms with France and bringing an end to the War of the Spanish Succession, which had been going on since the beginning of the century in an effort to maintain the balance of power in Europe. When, in the summer of 1711, the paper was well launched, Swift turned it over to others and began to work on a very important review of the conduct of the war to justify the negotiations the ministry had already begun with the enemy and were determined to carry on, whatever the attitude of their allies. And when the Peace of Utrecht was finally signed in 1713, Swift set to work to write a history of the whole affair to justify the terms that

---

[1] He seems to have spent the summers of 1701 and 1702 in England and managed to return to London again in November, 1703, for another six months.

had been accepted. He had access to the official papers and provided what was then recognized as an admirable account of the negotiations; but his characterizations of the ministers and their opponents and his comments on the state of affairs and the government's difficulties led them to decide not to print it.[1] Swift was, however, rewarded for all his efforts by being made Dean of St. Patrick's, Dublin, in 1713. He went to Ireland to be installed in June, but was soon recalled to England and remained there during the last months of the queen's reign, entering into a violent controversy with his friend Sir Richard Steele, who had accused the queen and her ministers of wishing to set aside the Protestant succession in favor of her Catholic brother, the so-called Pretender.

On the death of the queen, Swift saw that all his friends would be out of power, and that the new king George I would choose his ministers entirely from among the Whigs. He therefore retired to his deanery in Dublin and for five or six years continued to perform his duties and to work over his memoirs, without taking any part in public life. At first it seemed as if he were living in exile, after his exciting years in London, his friendships with the leading men of his day, and his connections with the great, whom he had deigned to treat as his equals, if he found them worthy of his notice.

But in Dublin he returned to the companionship of Esther Johnson, better known as Stella, who had been a child of eight when he first saw her in the household of Sir William Temple. At the time of his second stay, she was a girl of fifteen, and Swift enjoyed her companionship for the next three years. At Temple's death she was left some property in Ireland and a small legacy. Two years later, when Swift was returning to his parish in Ireland in September, 1701, he suggested that she and her elderly companion, Mrs. Dingley, should accompany him and settle in Dublin, where their small income would go further than in England. They were soon established among the circle of his friends, who came to admire and respect Stella for her wit and good sense and her humor. When Swift was away in London from 1710 to 1713, he wrote long detailed letters, addressed to both Stella

and Mrs. Dingley, giving the most intimate account of his doings from day to day; these were published after his death and are now generally known as the *Journal to Stella*. Among manuscripts which have recently come to light are passages of his memoirs and copies of his poems in the handwriting of Stella; they are proof of the close companionship between them, after he had been made Dean. Though the story of their secret marriage in 1716 cannot be accepted, there is no doubt of the depth and fullness of their friendship, in spite of the rigorous conventions he established between them. In his letters to her, in the verses regularly composed for her birthdays in Dublin, and above all in the account of her which he set down at the moment of her death, he revealed completely his tenderness and devotion and his anguish for her loss.

Yet even this friendship — the greatest solace of his life — was disturbed for a time by the demands made upon him by Hester Vanhomrigh (or Vanessa, as he called her in verse), who as a girl had fallen in love with him, a grave divine of twice her age, a regular visitor to her mother's home in London. Mrs. Vanhomrigh was the widow of a former Commissary-General of Ireland, and Vanessa had been born in Dublin. In 1714, she followed Swift there, and settled in a house that belonged to her at Celbridge a few miles away, craving his sympathy and demanding his help through her remaining years of illness until her early death in 1723. That story may also now be read in their letters and in a long poem called *Cadenus and Vanessa,* in which he tried to turn it into a comedy:

> But what success Vanessa met,
> Is to the world a secret yet:
> Whether the nymph, to please her swain,
> Talks in a high romantic strain:
> Or whether he at last descends
> To like with less seraphic ends;
> Or, to compound the business, whether
> They temper love and books together;
> Must never to mankind be told,
> Nor shall the conscious Muse unfold.

In the meantime his restless spirit had not been content with the affairs of the cathedral and visits to his friends in the country and the writing of occasional verses, but had driven him to interest himself in the affairs of Ireland. Disgust at the miseries of the tradesmen and coun-

---

[1] It was printed in 1758 as *The History of the Four Last Years of the Queen,* but its authenticity was doubted until in 1935 Sir Harold Williams found a manuscript copy of it in the Royal Library at Windsor.

tryfolk led him to enter the struggle against Ireland's complete political and economic subjugation to the power of England, and brought him the satisfaction of opposing again his old enemies, Walpole and the Whigs. He taught the Irish the use of a formidable weapon, the boycott, that is to say, the refusal to accept English imported goods that competed with their own industries; and he went so far in his letters to the people of Ireland, written under the assumed name of a Dublin draper, as to challenge the authority of the parliament of England to interfere at all in the affairs of Ireland. As a result of his triumph, in 1725 he was acclaimed as the " Hibernian Patriot," the acknowledged champion of the Irish cause, and for ten years more he continued to exercise a powerful influence in Dublin.

But Swift's final achievement was to overshadow these local successes and place him among the few who have been able to write a book so wide in its appeal that it has become known throughout the world. For he had quietly gathered up all his experience of the ways of the world, of kings and ministers and courts, all his observation of men and women, and had put these together into a book of travels, a sort of parody on the currently popular books of voyages and accounts of marvels in newly discovered lands.

In the spring of 1726, after some hesitation, not being quite sure how he would be received by the English government, he went to London to finish *Gulliver's Travels* and to arrange for it to be published. It came out in November after his return to Dublin, and was an immediate success; everyone was amused by the story and could not help being intrigued by the topical allusions and witty strokes of satire. So, for the last time, at the height of his fame, Swift spent the summer of 1727 in London, at the moment when there seemed to be some chance that his Tory friends might be in power again under George II, who had just come to the throne, and when there was talk once more of his getting an English preferment. But this was to be another disappointment.

He returned finally to Ireland in the autumn of 1727, at the age of sixty, to assume again his role as champion of the oppressed and to attack in verse and prose those whom he held responsible for the miserable state of the people: the

court and ministers in London, the members of the Irish parliament in Dublin, the absentee landlords, and the dishonest tradesmen who were themselves to blame for the failure of the campaign to encourage the use of their own manufactures. He sums up his case against these people and shows the depths of his bitterness in his own *Modest Proposal* to solve all the troubles of the poor people of Ireland; and in his final gesture, when he leaves a bequest to found a hospital for the insane (see below, " Verses on the Death of Dr. Swift," ll. 479–82):

> He gave the little wealth he had,
> To build a house for fools and mad:
> And showed by one satiric touch,
> No nation wanted it so much: . . .

Throughout these years Swift carried on a long struggle for health against the fits of deafness and giddiness which afflicted him, caused as we now know by what is called Menière's disease; until finally, when he was seventy-five, he suffered the loss of all his powers, and was condemned to live on without his reason for three more years, dying in a corner of the deanery " like a rat in a hole."

Yet, in spite of the disappointments and the sufferings which the years brought him, it should not be forgotten that he had seemed to Addison, who knew him well and was a rare observer and spectator of English life in the early eighteenth century, to be " the most agreeable companion, the truest friend, and the greatest genius of his age."

THE GREATEST GENIUS OF HIS AGE

Swift takes his place among the greatest masters of English literature not only because he has given to the world a book which has been continually read in English and in translation for over two hundred years, but for two other reasons. He has never been surpassed by any English writer in the power of his satire, especially when he uses irony; and he created an English prose which, depending on the virtue of simplicity, claims only to be clear and concise in order to be easily understood. These are the qualities of his work which he was himself most sure of. He speaks of them in his " Verses on the Death of Dr. Swift ": his " own humorous biting way " of satire; the irony which he " was born to introduce," " refined " first, " and showed its use "; and the power of his prose for purposes of controversy — to " maul a minister of state."

If now we try to analyze what accounts for the particular quality of all his writings, what gave such power to his work, we cannot do better than begin with the fact that Swift was always concerned above all to see clearly. He set himself to observe and find out what human beings were really like, to penetrate beneath the surface, to look at the inside as well as the outside, the unpleasant as well as the pleasant. He tried to make himself an impartial examiner who would make reasonable judgments on all that he observed.

In his own experience as a young writer, when he tried his hand at the kind of poetry which brought success to others, and hoped for inspiration from the Muse, he found instead that his vision had become clouded by romantic notions, which prevented him from seeing things as they were; and he boasted that he had found out the secret that the poetic Muse was only a " wild form dependent on the brain ":

> Troubling the crystal fountain of the sight
> Which darts on poets' eyes a trembling light;
> Kindled while reason sleeps, but quickly flies,
> Like antic shapes in dreams, from waking eyes.[1]

And so he decided to renounce that visionary power and break away from all such delusions. He became distrustful of all excess, whether in the world of learning or in religion. He began to discover, as soon as his eyes were opened, all sorts of fakes and follies and absurdities which would provide pleasant topics for wit and satire. He noticed the shallowness of modern wits and the pedantries of modern scholars:

We of this age have discovered a shorter and more prudent method to become scholars and wits without the fatigue of reading or thinking. The most accomplished way of using books at present is twofold: either first, to serve them as some men do lords, learn their titles exactly, and then brag of their acquaintance. Or secondly, which is indeed the choicer, the profounder, and politer method, to get a thorough insight into the index, by which the whole book is governed and turned, like fishes by the tail. For, to enter the palace of learning by the great gate, requires an expense of time and forms;

[1] *Poems* (H. Williams, editor), vol. i, p. 54.

therefore men of much haste and little ceremony are content to get in by the back door. (sect. vii)

He observed and described very fully the ways of modern critics, concluding pleasantly with three satirical maxims, by which a true modern critic can be distinguished from a pretender:

The first is, that *criticism,* contrary to all other faculties of the intellect, is ever held the truest and best when it is the very first result of the critic's mind: as fowlers reckon the first aim for the surest, and seldom fail of missing the mark, if they stay for a second.

Secondly, the *true critics* are known by their talent of swarming about the noblest writers, to which they are carried merely by instinct, as a rat to the best cheese, or a wasp to the fairest fruit. . . .

Lastly, a *true critic,* in the perusal of a book, is like a dog at a feast, whose thoughts and stomach are wholly set upon what the guests fling away, and consequently is apt to snarl most, when there are the fewest bones. (sect. iii)

He distrusted even more the new schools of philosophy and the freethinkers, who were carried away by their new-fangled notions, like the fanatical preachers and founders of new sects:

When a man's fancy gets astride on his reason, when imagination is at cuffs with the senses, and common understanding, as well as common sense, is kicked out of doors, the first proselyte he makes is himself, and when that is once compassed, the difficulty is not so great in bringing over others; a strong delusion operating from without, as vigorously as from within. (sect. ix)

I quote these passages from *A Tale of a Tub,* partly because it was not possible to include a sample from it in the selections, and also because it is more important to see exactly how Swift responds to the intellectual fashions then in vogue than it is merely to describe the characteristic ideas of the period of the Enlightenment which seem to influence his work.

Swift had learned a good deal from Bacon and from Hobbes, and he belonged to the same generation as John Locke. But he was neither a scientist nor a philosopher. He was too much of a skeptic and too much of a wit. As he began to look around him, as his vision cleared and things stood out in the bright light of his intelligence with a fresh startling clarity, his first impression was that they were amusing, and could be made the subject of witty observation.

As he gazed upon that turbulent eighteenth-century scene, with its strife of parties in religion and politics and all the petty jealousies and bickerings in the literary world, he felt both the desire of the moralist to try to bring a little order and decency into human society and the itch of the satirist to expose and deride the follies and absurdities of his fellows.

Others would share his views and be amused by his satire; and to those he would address himself. But if he was not to be bored himself and if he was to succeed in amusing this superior audience, he must avoid all dullness or pedantry; he must be clear and witty and gay, in his own humorous biting way; or he must be sharp and terrifying in his sardonic comments, ruthless in his invective, perfectly balanced and thus effective to the utmost in his irony. This was the problem he set himself as a literary artist; and it was in shaping a prose style which would serve all the variety of his purposes that he showed himself as the greatest genius of his age.

But even a satirist may be his own dupe unless he can protect himself against any foolish notions that he can ever really reach his victims or have any effect upon them. Swift is therefore careful to make it clear at the very start that he is aware of this. In the opening sentence of his Preface to *The Battle of the Books,* he says,

Satire is a sort of glass, wherein beholders do generally discover everybody's face but their own; which is the chief reason for that kind of reception it meets in the world, and that so very few are offended with it.

Nor will he allow himself to be taken in by trusting too much to wit; for he knows how shallow it can be if it is not based on knowledge, " a sort of cream, which gathers in a night to the top, and by a skillful hand may be soon whipped into froth; but once scummed away, what appears underneath will be fit for nothing, but to be thrown to the hogs." Further, he claims to have stripped himself of as many prejudices as he could by some thinking and much conversation in the world.

He needed more freedom than he could have allowed himself if he appeared as an Irish clergyman, or even as the editor of Sir William Temple's *Letters* and *Memoirs;* and so he presents himself as " a young gentleman much in the world," "his invention at the height, and his reading fresh in his head," who "wrote to the taste of those who were like himself." This role served him well, and enabled him to develop a sure tone and style well fitted for his purpose. But in his first appearance as " the author of *A Tale of a Tub* " he is inclined to be consciously literary, and even to show off his knowledge. As Dr. Johnson noted, Swift's writing at this time " exhibits a vehemence and rapidity of mind, a copiousness of images, and vivacity of diction, such as he afterwards never possessed, or never exerted." But Johnson, in making this criticism, gave too little heed to Swift's warning that he had allowed himself to indulge in parodies, to personate the style and manner of other writers, whom he had a mind to expose. *A Tale of a Tub* was intended to be partly a caricature of the heroics and extravagances of seventeenth-century art and thought, and the style is therefore naturally influenced by the reflections, appearing in Swift's mirror, of the century's solemnities and enthusiasms.

The ease and perfection of Swift's early style, the gaiety of his humor and the variety of his invention, and his skill in the use of irony are well shown in his *Argument Against Abolishing Christianity*. Here also he writes as a man of the world, who is fully aware that the great majority have of course no use for religion, and that the argument he is going to put forward must seem to them absurdly paradoxical. He fully realizes what a singular position he has taken, and promises to pay the utmost deference to all the arguments that can be brought against him. First he makes clear that he is not such a fool as to stand up in the defense of real Christianity as it is said to have existed in the earliest times; he will argue only in favor of preserving some sort of nominal Christianity, and try to prove that the abolishing of that might be attended with some inconveniences, or at least might not produce all the good effects which some people hope for. This is a novel way to uphold the need for a national church. But it is not only intended to show how witty and amusing he can be on such a dull subject; it is a device to make the gentlemen of wit and pleasure pay attention to him, to startle them by dropping the usual conventional tone in which such matters are discussed, and then, having drawn them around him, to indulge in some shrewd hits at their expense.

Even when he sets out to advise the younger clergy how to write their sermons, he chooses to write not as a Dean, but as a layman, an educated man of the world, who is concerned to give sensible advice on how to speak and write clearly and simply. Thus the *Letter to a Young Gentleman* becomes an important document on how to write by a master of prose. It does not reveal all the secrets of Swift's art. It only refers to a particular kind of composition, addressed to an audience of ordinary unlearned people, and therefore demanding the virtues of clarity and simplicity. It is concerned with writing not as the expression of a personality, but as a means of communication, exactly calculated to have a particular effect on those to whom it is addressed. This is the prose of a man speaking to men, not the voice of the prophet declaring the word of the Lord. It is a prose to be used for the practical needs of man in society; the prose of the lawyer pleading a case, the prose of political debate, for attack and for defense; it is good for plain statement, for narrative; and it is essential for satire and for irony.

If we ask how we are to achieve this perfection of simplicity and directness, we are told that " Proper words in proper places, makes the true definition of a style," and are warned of a few common faults which may easily be remedied. The most important are to avoid the use of obscure or unnecessarily technical words, to beware of all affectation of learning or knowledge of the world, and to distrust all rhetoric and emotional appeal. Our aim must be to attain "that simplicity without which no human performance can arrive at any great perfection."

He is repeating here what he had written ten years before in a letter addressed to the *Tatler* (Number 230), urging that it was the responsibility of that paper to reform "the great depravity of our taste and the corruption of our style; . . . and to be the instrument of introducing into our style that simplicity, which is the best and truest ornament of most things in human life, which the politer ages always aimed at in their building and dress (*simplex munditiis*) as well as their productions of wit."

In setting up these standards Swift exercised an incalculable influence on English writing, not only in the narrower world of polite letters, but in the world of scholarship and learning, as well as in the world of politics, in law, and in the church. He has taught us to suspect all sort of pedantry and pretension and ostentation. He has even warned us against too much wit, preferring modesty and good sense:

Fine sense and exalted sense are not half so useful as common sense: there are forty men of wit for one man of sense: and he that will carry about with him nothing but gold, will be every day at a loss for want of readier change.

Or again:

Modesty, if it were to be recommended for nothing else, this were enough, that the pretending to little leaves a man at ease, whereas boasting requires a perpetual labor to appear what he is not. If we have sense, modesty best proves it to others; if we have none, it best hides our want of it.

The lack of any kind of pretension in language — that is the secret of power. Simplicity and conciseness and order, which are the fruits of modesty and good sense, by removing all obscurity allow the full effect of all that is there to be perceived and felt.

It may be objected that an exclusive concern with plainness and simplicity limits the possibilities of variety in writing, confines the imagination and checks the fancy; or leads us into the worse dangers of a dull and drab uniformity. Indeed, Swift himself does not always escape. In his sermons, where he follows very closely the advice that he gives to the young clergyman, we may sometimes feel that in spite of their directness and force, and even though they are not wholly without humor and irony, their scope is limited and their pattern conventional. But it must in fairness be remembered that Swift himself did not think much of them, and probably did not intend that they should be printed. Yet the limited range of those sermons that have survived only serves to emphasize the extraordinary variety of the rest of his work.

It is particularly important to emphasize this fact here, since in these brief selections there is no room to illustrate properly the extent of his work. It is necessary also to stress the wide range of color and tone to be found in his work and the great variety of subjects that engage his attention, because too often his biographers and critics, to protect themselves against his satire and to take the sting out of the worst things he has to say about life and love, have treated him as one whose comments can be disregarded because of his abnormal condition and the frustrations and disappointments of his career. Such observers too often forget the richness of his personality, the gaiety as well as the somberness, the fancy as well as the intelligence, the charm as well as the roughness, the long and undisturbed friendships as well as the feuds; they forget the restless energy of his spirit, the boundless interest he shows in the whole human scene, fascinated like Hogarth or Fielding by every detail of it, watching it to get the full humor of it as well as to make exact observations with a view to its ultimate improvement.

That of course is the reason for our interest in his *Journal to Stella,* in which he sets down the same day the little things that have happened to him as well as the reports of his grand doings among the great, and records vivid, highly colored impressions of what he sees as he takes his walks through the city or moves about in his lodgings; so that we know all about his meals, the cost of things, the discomforts of the winter, where he hides his purse for fear of burglars, and the shortcomings of his drunken servant Patrick. That is why we still read his occasional verse, which was tossed off in an easy conversational tone for the amusement of his friends, describing the sights and smells of the city streets during a sudden heavy shower, or making fun of the squalor or the squabbles in the houses of some of his Irish friends or the domestic comedy in which he himself took a part during long summer visits in the country.

For many years Swift kept by him two works, to which he constantly made additions from his experience and which he finally published for the improvement of society — one dealing with all the petty misdeeds of the whole race of servants, who had such an important place in supporting the very complicated structure of eighteenth-century society, and the other exposing all the absurdities of the talk at fashionable tea tables and card parties in a parody which gathers up in a conversation piece every hackneyed joke and all the stale clichés of a hundred years. These later became known as *Directions to Servants* and *A Complete Collection of Genteel and Ingenious Conversation.*

If we compare Swift with his friends, the leading men and the greatest writers of the day, Congreve and Addison, Pope and Gay, we detect a difference which is due to other things than the quality of style. We get an impression that he is bigger than any of them. He has a wider experience of humanity, touching life at all levels, and he leaves out nothing that is an essential part of human nature. He is not afraid to look at everything and, however unpleasant or disturbing it is, to try to see it clearly. You can trust him not to hide or dodge the issue.

He is not concerned with speculative truth, not much interested in the discussions of philosophers, whether of the old or new variety, whether they are looking for metaphysical or scientific verities.

But as for me, who ne'er could clamber high
To understand Malebranche or Cambray;
Who send my mind (as I believe) less
Than others do, on errands sleeveless;
Can listen to a tale humdrum
And, with attention, read Tom Thumb;
My spirits with my body progging,
Both hand in hand together jogging;
Sunk over head and ears in matter,
Nor can of metaphysics smatter;
Am more diverted with a quibble
Than dreams of worlds intelligible;
And think all notions too abstracted
Are like the ravings of a cracked head; [1]

He is interested only in morality and virtue, and the Roman qualities of decency and order; he wishes to preserve the best that man has so far been able to achieve in society. He is distrustful of the new developments in banking and commerce and the power of the " moneyed man." He does not represent the advancing tip of human consciousness; he is rather a little behind the times, an old-fashioned Tory and churchman, unwilling to be drawn into extremes in politics or religion, with a firm footing in the midst of change, a solid vantage point from which to make his observations. He has been accused of changing his political position; but though he was forced to adjust to the shifting situation of parties, his political views remained unmodified from the time that he began to be occupied with public affairs. There was indeed, as has often been remarked, little development in his ideas or in his attitude from the time that he first began to write. He seemed to have all his powers at their full strength in *A*

[1] *Poems*, vol. iii, p. 400.

Tale of a Tub, which was the first important book he published. His active literary career was to continue for another thirty-five years, yet in some ways he never surpassed that first book. He had attained at once his full stature and the mastery of his art, and he continued to use his powers for different purposes and in many different ways. He liked to put on many disguises; though he was a strong character, with a marked individuality, he rarely wrote over his own name, even when there was no necessity for anonymity. Some of his controversial and political pamphlets could not have been acknowledged for obvious reasons; but he continued throughout his life to refuse to put his name on a title page of anything he had written, though he knew that the London booksellers would therefore take the liberty of selling all sorts of rubbish by attributing it to him. This matter of anonymity must have been of great importance to him, for it led him violently to oppose a proposal brought before parliament in 1713 "that the Author's name and place of abode should be set to every printed book, pamphlet or paper" with the strange argument that all persons of true genius or knowledge are prevented by an invincible modesty and suspicion of themselves from ever publishing at all on these terms, which would be only acceptable to the dull or superficial and those who are void of all taste and judgment.

But the real reason why he could not put his own name to many volumes of his works was because there was another name there already — Bickerstaff, the Examiner, the Drapier, Lemuel Gulliver. These are the names under which he was best known among his contemporaries; these are the titles with which Pope addressed him, when he dedicated to him the *Dunciad*:

> O thou, whatever title please thine ear,
> Dean, Drapier, Bickerstaff or Gulliver.

This is what gives his work such variety, for he is constantly appearing in some new role. He seems to have needed to dramatize himself, or rather to create a sort of puppet show with a whole box of properties and a group of actors, whose different voices he assumes as he manipulates his figures. If we are to understand the full quality of his work, and especially the power of his dramatic irony, it is necessary to have a look at all the puppets he makes use of, and see how he works them for different purposes.

Sometimes it is just for fun, as for instance when he uses the figure of a lady's waiting woman, and one or two other stock figures from the household of one of the Lord Justices of Ireland, imitating exactly the little movements that he has observed and speaking with the exact tone and with the very patter of Mrs. Francis Harris as she complains of the loss of her purse:

> Now you must know, because my trunk has a very
>   bad lock,
> Therefore all the money I have, which, God knows,
>   is a very small stock,
> I keep in a pocket tied about my middle, next my
>   smock.[1]

And the little comedy is played out with her complaints and her quarrels with the valet and the steward, and her suspicions of the footman's wife, and the unkindness of the chaplain who was supposed to be her lover.

This poem is the first indication of Swift's interest in and keen observation of the inhabitants of the servants' hall and the kitchen, which was to bear fruit thirty years later in the *Directions to Servants,* already mentioned. For it he chooses the role of "a footman of seven years' experience, who then foolishly demeaned himself by accepting an employment in the Custom House." He can thus assume the tone of one who had learned the game and remembered with satisfaction all the tricks he had played on his master; or he can bring in stories of the experiences of some of his friends when he was in service, and even give instructions to his fellow footmen on the proper behavior to be observed when going to be hanged.

On another occasion Swift actually impersonated the famous criminal Ebenezor Elliston, who was executed in Dublin on May 2, 1722, writing and printing in the usual form his last speech and dying words for the purpose of discouraging the other rogues of Dublin. In this case, he adopted the role and dressed himself up in the part, but produced his effect by playing it in a style and manner most like himself, leaving in the minds of some of his readers the fear that the repentant robber had indeed provided the Dean with information enough to hang them, too, if they continued their robberies.

There was the same play in his more famous role as M.B., a linen draper of Dublin, whom he impersonated in his campaign in 1724 to boy-

[1] *Poems,* vol. i, p. 69.

cott the copper coinage which under the royal patent was to be manufactured in England by William Wood and introduced into Ireland. In his first *Letter* he warned his fellow tradesmen and the farmers and common people of Ireland that if these coins were brought in they would debase the value of the whole currency; and at the same time he showed that the new money could not legally be forced upon them if they would only refuse to take it.

Swift probably chose the disguise of the Dublin draper because the Dean of St. Patrick's was still not altogether a popular figure, and he had had some very hard things to say about the tradesmen of Dublin; he would also have been regarded by the leaders in the Church, the parliament, and the city at this time as a rather doubtful ally. So it was better for the purposes of the campaign, where unity was essential, that he should not appear too obviously in the struggle. But once he has put on his disguise, he makes the fullest use of it. He talks in the language of a tradesman to his fellow tradesmen. He tells them what he will do in his shop:

I have a pretty good shop of Irish stuffs and silks, and instead of taking Mr. Wood's bad copper, I intend to truck with my neighbors the butchers and bakers and brewers, and the rest, goods for goods; and the little gold and silver I have, I will keep by me, like my heart's blood, until better times, . . .

If he wants to be able to speak with more authority, he has only to call in the lawyers:

Having said thus much, I will now go on to tell you the judgments of some great lawyers in this matter, whom I fee'd on purpose for your sakes, and got their opinions under their hands, that I might be sure I went upon good grounds.

or else he quotes in a very simple fashion some story he has heard scholars talk of, just enough of it to make a very effective finish:

I have heard scholars talk of a man who told the king, that he had invented a way to torment people by putting them into a bull of brass with fire under it: but the prince put the projector first into his own brazen bull, to make the experiment. This very much resembles the project of Mr. Wood; and the like of this may possibly be Mr. Wood's fate; that the brass he contrived to torment this kingdom with, may prove his own torment, and his destruction at last.

Even when he finds it necessary to answer the Report of the Privy Council on the matter of the coinage, he still preserves his character, only changing his tone to make it suitable for a letter to be addressed this time to the nobility and gentry of Ireland, who had been attacked in the Report because of the opposition they had raised in the Houses of Lords and Commons in Ireland. He apologizes for what may seem a strange way of discoursing in an illiterate shopkeeper, unskilled in law, but will try what can be done by plain reason unassisted by art, cunning, or eloquence. He even turns to account the acknowledgment of aid provided by "an eminent person" whose suggestions he has probably spoiled by not being competent to manage them properly. And then a splendid image occurs to him and he compares himself to David, "who could not move in the armor of Saul," and his opponent Wood to Goliath, whom he resembled in many circumstances applicable to his purpose:

For Goliath had a helmet of brass upon his head, and he was armed with a coat of mail, and the weight of the coat was five thousand shekels of brass, and he had greaves of brass upon his legs, and a target of brass between his shoulders. In short he was like Mr. Wood, all over brass; and he defied the armies of the living God. Goliath's conditions of combat were likewise the same with those of Wood: if he prevail against us then shall we be his servants. But if it happen that I prevail over him, I renounce the other part of the conditions; he shall never be a servant of mine; for I do not think him fit to be trusted in any *honest* man's shop.

By this time indeed Swift had been accepted by the Dublin populace, who were gathered around to applaud and support him in this conflict with the Philistine, Wood. Probably everyone now knew who was writing these letters. Nevertheless, in the fourth *Letter* when he stands forth as the champion of Ireland, claiming that her people are equal with the people of England, as subjects of the same crown, he is still content to declare what is meant by the king's prerogative "as far as a tradesman can be thought capable of explaining it," though we may wonder how this tradesman came to be able to quote my Lord Bacon so aptly and to know so much about the precedents from the practice of the Crown in earlier reigns; or how he came to be so familiar with the ways of courts and ministers that he is able to warn his readers against their trickery and hypocrisy. But, just as we are in danger of forgetting the tradesman of Dublin altogether, at the very height of his argument in his challenge of the whole authority of the English government to interfere in the affairs of Ireland, the draper himself steps forward, a heroic figure, symbolizing the united and indomitable power of a whole country in revolt.

Let whoever think otherwise, I *M. B., Drapier,* desire to be excepted. For I declare, next under God, I *depend* only on the King my sovereign, and on the laws of my own country, and I am so far from *depending* upon the people of *England,* that, if they should ever *rebel* against my sovereign (which God forbid) I would be ready at the first command from his Majesty to take arms against them. . . .

The genius of Swift is never more clearly shown than in the way he uses to the utmost the dramatic possibilities of the characters he creates for himself. They are never allowed to cramp or shackle his freedom, because they never remain mere disguises or even masks. They become living symbols, which grow and develop under his hands. In the campaign against the copper coinage the Drapier enters the conflict very modestly, but finds himself carried forward by the forces he has unleashed, like a revolutionary leader, who is created by the situation. So also Bickerstaff was at first just a name associated with a practical joke at the expense of a quack almanac maker, but he grew to be the symbol of the wit, whose task was to expose all the fakes and nonsense and pedantries of the literary world. The Examiner had been at first only the writer of an ordinary weekly Tory paper, but before long he assumed the right to examine the whole state of the nation's affairs, the conduct of the war at home and abroad, in order to change the mind of the nation so that it could be brought to accept the negotiations for peace.

But it was as Gulliver that Swift showed the fullness of his power to take a character and create a part. Swift conceived Gulliver at first because he wanted to write in the form of the popular travel books of the day and needed an appropriate mouthpiece. Gulliver is an honest and experienced ship's surgeon who has acquired some knowledge of navigation. Even when he gets a ship of his own, he remains an unaffected seaman. But in the course of his strange travels, he learns so much that his eyes are opened to the true state of the world; and as he goes on with the stories of his voyages one after the other, we notice his growth in wisdom and sense, in his understanding of what is good and what is evil, and in his ability to distinguish between that which is and that which is not.

In these selections it has not been possible to include the third of the voyages; but the rest is complete, and for the reader today the narrative may even gain somewhat in unity and intensity without that section, which contains so many varied and unrelated incidents that it does not quite fit into the obvious and simple framework of the book. Swift and his friends recognized at the time that it was not as good as the rest. It is probable that some of the incidents there satirizing the new science may have been taken from fragments of earlier work; other incidents seem to refer to matters so very recent that they must have been added during the summer of 1726 when Swift was in London immediately before the book appeared. And other parts of this third voyage probably arose out of Swift's experiences just before in Ireland. Perhaps for these reasons we are less aware of the figure of Gulliver. Swift himself seems almost to forget him sometimes and introduces asides and comments which break down our belief that we are listening to the story as narrated by Gulliver.

But in the other three voyages, Gulliver fits every purpose that Swift has in mind. In narrative style, in the simple framework of each part, with the short paragraphs at the beginning and end describing the voyage out and the return, with the references to actual ships and captains familiar to the readers of contemporary voyages, he is able to convince us of the reality, the simple truth, of his tale. Some of the popular travel books of course contain all sorts of extravagant stories and wild seamen's yarns, but in a short preface, " The Publisher to the Reader," we are given by a supposed editor, Richard Sympson, an intimate friend of the author, a certificate of Mr. Lemuel Gulliver's reliability:

There is an air of truth apparent through the whole; and indeed the author was so distinguished for his veracity, that it became a sort of proverb among his neighbors at Redriff, when any one affirmed a thing, to say it was as true as if Mr. Gulliver had spoke it.

And in a very short sketch of his life before these adventures begin, we are told that Gulliver was a man of considerable reading and had developed a great facility in learning foreign languages. He shows himself in his dealing with the Lilliputians to be a man of a mild and generous disposition, ready to try to win their good opinion by his patience and discreet behavior. He is rather taken by surprise and shocked when he learns of the plots of his Lilliput enemies to bring about his destruction, of the articles of impeachment against him in spite of his heroic exploits in capturing the whole fleet of their Blefuscudian enemies, and of the final decision whereby through the leniency of the emperor, he was only condemned to the loss of his eyes:

Yet, as to myself, I must confess, having never been designed for a courtier either by my birth or education, I was so ill a judge of things, that I could not discover the *lenity* and favor of this sentence, but conceived it (perhaps erroneously) rather to be rigorous than gentle.

Here (Part I, Chapter 7) Swift uses the innocence of Gulliver, his inexperience of the ways of courts and ministers, as a mean of expressing ironically his own feelings of horror at the way in which his friends, the ministers of the Crown in the last years of Queen Anne's reign, had been treated by their opponents the Whigs as soon as the Whigs had established their power in the new Hanoverian regime. And he gets a further effect by making Gulliver explain, when he comes later to write the story, that he now realizes — after more experience in the ways of courts — how rash he was not to "have submitted to so easy a punishment with great alacrity and readiness!"

It must not be forgotten that Gulliver is never a mere pseudonym, adopted simply as a disguise to protect the real author, should the book bring him into trouble. He is essential as a character whose eyes are opened to reality as a result of his experiences, whose whole standard of values is gradually changed under the influence first of the simple moral grandeur of the Brobdingnagians, and then finally by the benignant effect of his happy sojourn in the land of those perfectly rational and kindly beings, the Houyhnhnms.

For instance, on several occasions Gulliver tried his best to give the king of the Brobdingnagians a favorable account of the history of his own country, and, as he said, made every effort to " hide the frailties and deformities of his political mother and place her virtues and beauties in the most advantageous light," and to use his opportunity to impress his Majesty with the glories of Western civilization. Nevertheless, while listening to Gulliver's panegyrics (II.6) the king's horror and astonishment grew until finally —

he taking me into his hands, and stroking me gently, delivered himself in these words, which I shall never forget, nor the manner he spoke them in. " My little friend Grildrig, you have made a most admirable panegyric upon your country. . . . But, by what I have gathered from your own relation, and the answers I have with much pains wringed and extorted from you, I cannot but conclude the bulk of your natives to be the most pernicious race of little odious vermin that nature ever suffered to crawl upon the surface of the earth."

Gulliver confessed that he was so shocked and puzzled by this that he would have liked to omit all account of it from his story, if it had not been for his extreme love of truth. Notice that while he is living among the giants and so often suffering indignities because of his smallness he is still trying to maintain his belief in the superiority of his own race. In spite of the kindness shown him, and his position at court, and the favor of the king and queen, he felt that " it was upon such a foot as ill became the dignity of human kind." And so he tried to vindicate himself by placing at the disposal of his Majesty all his superior political skill and knowledge of the ways of civilized nations and their methods of gaining power and extending their influence over the world, and by revealing to him the secret of gunpowder, which would make him master of the world. But once again (II.7) Gulliver found that he had made a mistake, and had only succeeded in bringing forth another surprising outburst:

He was amazed how so impotent and groveling an insect as I (these were his expressions) could entertain such inhuman ideas, and in so familiar a manner as to appear wholly unmoved at all the scenes of blood and desolation, which I had painted as the common effects of those destructive machines, . . . he would rather lose half his kingdom than be privy to such a secret, which he commanded me, as I valued my life, never to mention any more.

Swift carries the irony even further, by describing how puzzled Gulliver was to explain such narrow principles and short views. He had the utmost admiration for his Majesty, his wisdom and his talents for government, and was worried at discovering such a defect in him, as to be hindered by " nice unnecessary scruples " from making himself absolute master of the lives, liberties, and fortunes of his people. He could only conclude that it was due to the general state of ignorance of the Brobdingnagians, who had not " reduced politics into a science, as the more acute wits of Europe have done."

But it was the experiences of his last voyage which completed the education of Gulliver, for among those admirable Houyhnhnms he could live in the contemplation and practice of every virtue, and be entirely without any incitement to lie. Swift does not leave us in any doubt about this. He explains how it was that Gulliver was no longer concerned about the dignity of human kind, though in what he said of his countrymen he still tried to extenuate their faults as much as he dared and give as favorable a turn as the matter would bear (IV.7).

But I must freely confess, that the many virtues of those excellent quadrupeds placed in opposite view to human corruptions, had so far opened my eyes and enlarged my understanding, that I began to view the actions and passions of man in a very different light, and to think the honor of my own kind not worth managing; . . . I had likewise learned from his example an utter detestation of all falsehood or disguise; and truth appeared so amiable to me, that I determined upon sacrificing everything to it.

Gulliver indeed soon began to plan never to return to his own country, and when he was finally forced to leave, " his heart quite sunk with grief." The account of his return and of the horrors that he endured when he found himself again among his own race, with its dreadful resemblance to the Yahoos, occupies the last chapters of the book. And here (IV.12) Gulliver is allowed to speak, as it were, in the fullness of his enlightenment, of his attempt to reconcile himself again to the Yahoo-kind.

[It] might not be so difficult, if they would be content with those vices and follies only which nature hath entitled them to. . . . but when I behold a lump of deformity, and diseases both in body and

mind, smitten with *pride,* it immediately breaks all the measures of my patience; . . .

When the book first appeared, the editor or publisher, Richard Sympson, explained that he had the author's permission to take the advice of " several worthy persons " who recommended that he should venture to send the *Travels* forth into the world in the hope that they would be " a better entertainment to our young noblemen, than the common scribbles of politics and party." When Swift was revising the book for the collected edition of his *Works,* in 1735, and restoring passages which the first printer had changed because he was afraid they might cause trouble, he decided to give us a little further information about Gulliver. This took the form of a prefatory letter from Captain Gulliver to his cousin Sympson, in which after complaining of the liberties taken with his original manuscript, he went on to express his regrets that he had ever allowed the book to be printed:

Pray bring to your mind how often I desired you to consider, when you insisted on the motive of *public good;* that the *Yahoos* were a species of animals utterly incapable of amendment by precepts or examples: and so it hath proved; for instead of seeing a full stop put to all abuses and corruptions, at least in this little island, as I had reason to expect: behold, after above six months' warning, I cannot learn that my book hath produced one single effect according to my intentions: . . .

Instead of the reformation he expected, Gulliver's book has produced nothing but doubts upon his veracity, all sorts of Keys and Reflections and Memoirs, in which he is attacked for degrading human nature and abusing the female sex. Some have even gone so far as to suggest that his book is a mere fiction. Finally, Gulliver confesses that since his return some corruptions of his Yahoo nature have revived in him; " else I should never have attempted so absurd a project as that of reforming the *Yahoo* race in this kingdom; but, I have now done with all such visionary schemes for ever."

But although, like Gulliver, Swift gave up all hope of reforming mankind, he continued to write in verse and in prose, and to give vent to his indignation and his bitterness. Faced by the miserable state of Ireland, he could still indulge in the luxury of satire, and find an escape from unprofitable political activity in pure irony. And so he comes forward once more among those who are putting out all kinds of schemes and projects with a *Modest Proposal,* of his own, something "wholly new," of "no expense and little trouble," *for preventing the children of poor people, . . . from being a burden to their parents or country; and for making them beneficial to the public.*

It is a very simple plan, and he is able to work out the economic and business details of the proposed new industry in a way which demonstrates very clearly that it would be profitable for all concerned. It would provide a new commodity for the rich and a modest living for the poor. It would cost only about two shillings to rear a child to the age of twelve months, and the carcass should then weigh about twenty-eight pounds, and should sell for about ten shillings. Infants' flesh would be always in season, and would make a "most delicious, nourishing, and wholesome food." It would be particularly "*proper for landlords,* who, as they have already devoured most of the parents, seem to have the best title to the children."[1] The *Proposal* is a kind of terrible parody of his own earlier proposals for improving the state of Ireland. He has learned now that he has no longer any power to influence the government or rouse the people. But he can still challenge the conscience of his readers to face a desperate situation and to force them, if they have no better alternative to suggest, to share in his passionate protest and his fierce indignation.

In this and his other later Irish pamphlets, though he did not put his name on the title page, Swift assumes no disguise; he speaks di-

rectly, in his own person, as the unnamed champion of the people of Ireland, with the experience of the Dean, the Drapier, and Lemuel Gulliver behind him. He shows the fullness of his power as a master of irony and a writer who has attained to the perfection of simplicity in the art of prose.

Reading Suggestions

The best way to understand an author is to read more of his work. I give first therefore a list of standard editions of Swift's writings, in verse or prose, and of his correspondence, with a few very fully annotated critical editions of the more important works.

STANDARD EDITIONS

Harold Williams, editor, *Poems* (1937).
Herbert Davis, editor, *Prose Works* (1939–   ).
Elrington Ball, editor, *Correspondence* (1914).
D. Nichol Smith, editor, *Letters to Ford* (1935).

SEPARATE CRITICAL EDITIONS

A. C. Guthkelch and D. Nichol Smith, editors, *Tale of a Tub* (1920).
Herbert Davis, editor, *Drapier's Letters* (1935).
Harold Williams, editor, *Journal to Stella,* 2 vols. (1948).

BIOGRAPHY AND CRITICISM

All important articles on Swift can be found by referring to *A List of Critical Studies Published from 1895 to 1945* by Louis Landa and James Tobin (1945), but the following five titles are recommended, the first containing full biographical information and the others commenting on the chief qualities of Swift's work and art.

Sir Henry Craik, *Life of Jonathan Swift,* 2 vols. (1894).
Carl Van Doren, *Swift* (1930).
Ricardo Quintana, *The Mind and Art of Jonathan Swift* (1936).
Herbert Davis, *The Satire of Jonathan Swift* (1947).
Maurice Johnson, *The Son of Wit* (1951). A study of Swift's verse.

---

[1] See below p. 645.

AN ARGUMENT

TO PROVE THAT THE ABOLISHING OF CHRIS-
TIANITY IN ENGLAND MAY, AS THINGS NOW
STAND, BE ATTENDED WITH SOME INCON-
VENIENCES, AND PERHAPS NOT PRODUCE
THOSE MANY GOOD EFFECTS PROPOSED
THEREBY

Probably written in 1708 as a reply to the attacks
that were being made upon the Church of England,
and the very idea of a national, state-supported church.
Instead of entering into the particular controversies
which were raging at the time, Swift chose to make
fun of the whole body of the deists and freethinkers
in such a fashion that they and their supporters would
be sure to read his Argument.

It was seriously intended as a warning to the Whig
leaders of the dangers that would follow upon any
attempt to weaken the position of the Church of England. At the same time it is the earliest example of the
way in which Swift could use all his wit and humor
for his particular purpose, and shows his already perfect mastery of that "irony which he was born to introduce." First printed in the *Miscellanies,* 1711.

I am very sensible what a weakness and presumption it is, to reason against the general humor and
disposition of the world. I remember it was with
great justice, and a due regard to the freedom both
of the public and the press, forbidden upon severe
penalties to write or discourse, or lay wagers
against the Union,[1] even before it was confirmed
by parliament; because that was looked upon as a
design, to oppose the current of the people, which,
besides the folly of it, is a manifest breach of the
fundamental law that makes this majority of opinion the voice of God. In like manner, and for the
very same reasons, it may perhaps be neither safe
nor prudent to argue against the abolishing of
Christianity, at a juncture when all parties appear
so unanimously determined upon the point; as we
cannot but allow from their actions, their discourses, and their writings. However, I know not
how, whether from the affectation of singularity,
or the perverseness of human nature, but so it unhappily falls out, that I cannot be entirely of this
opinion. Nay, although I were sure an order were
issued for my immediate prosecution by the Attorney General, I should still confess that in the present
posture of our affairs at home or abroad, I do not
yet see the absolute necessity of extirpating the
Christian religion from among us.

This perhaps may appear too great a paradox
even for our wise and paradoxical age to endure;
therefore I shall handle it with all tenderness, and
with the utmost deference to that great and profound majority which is of another sentiment.

And yet the curious may please to observe, how
much the genius of a nation is liable to alter in
half an age. I have heard it affirmed for certain
by some very old people, that the contrary opinion
was even in their memories as much in vogue as
the other is now; and, that a project for the abolishing of Christianity would then have appeared as
singular, and been thought as absurd, as it would
be at this time to write or discourse in its defense.

Therefore I freely own that all appearances are
against me. The system of the Gospel, after the
fate of other systems, is generally antiquated and
exploded; and the mass or body of the common
people, among whom it seems to have had its latest
credit, are now grown as much ashamed of it as
their betters; opinions, like fashions, always descending from those of quality to the middle sort,
and thence to the vulgar, where at length they are
dropped and vanish.

But here I would not be mistaken, and must
therefore be so bold as to borrow a distinction from
the writers on the other side, when they make a
difference between nominal and real Trinitarians.
I hope no reader imagines me so weak to stand up
in the defense of *real* Christianity, such as used in
primitive times (if we may believe the authors of
those ages) to have an influence upon men's belief
and actions. To offer at the restoring of that would
indeed be a wild project; it would be to dig up
foundations; to destroy at one blow *all* the wit, and
half the learning of the kingdom; to break the entire frame and constitution of things; to ruin trade,
extinguish arts and sciences with the professors of
them; in short, to turn our courts, exchanges, and
shops into deserts; and would be full as absurd as
the proposal of Horace,[2] where he advises the Romans all in a body to leave their city, and seek a
new seat in some remote part of the world, by way
of cure for the corruption of their manners.

Therefore I think this caution was in itself altogether unnecessary (which I have inserted only to
prevent all possibility of caviling), since every
candid reader will easily understand my discourse
to be intended only in defense of *nominal* Chris-

ARGUMENT AGAINST ABOLISHING CHRISTIANITY. 1. **penalties**
. . . **Union**: referring to the opposition in Scotland to the union
with England, in 1707, and the severe measures against the
Jacobites.

2. **proposal of Horace**: in the sixteenth *Epode*, where he recommends that they should sail away to the "islands of the blest"
to avoid tyranny.

tianity; the other having been for some time wholly laid aside by general consent, as utterly inconsistent with our present schemes of wealth and power.

But why we should therefore cast off the name and title of Christians, although the general opinion and resolution be so violent for it, I confess I cannot (with submission) apprehend the consequence necessary. However, since the undertakers propose such wonderful advantages to the nation by this project, and advance many plausible objections against the system of Christianity, I shall briefly consider the strength of both, fairly allow them their greatest weight, and offer such answers as I think most reasonable. After which I will beg leave to show what inconveniences may possibly happen by such an innovation, in the present posture of our affairs.

First, One great advantage proposed by the abolishing of Christianity is, that it would very much enlarge and establish liberty of conscience, that great bulwark of our nation, and of the Protestant religion, which is still too much limited by priestcraft, notwithstanding all the good intentions of the legislature, as we have lately found by a severe instance. For it is confidently reported, that two young gentlemen of real hopes, bright wit, and profound judgment, who upon a thorough examination of causes and effects, and by the mere force of natural abilities, without the least tincture of learning, having made a discovery, that there was no God, and generously communicating their thoughts for the good of the public, were some time ago, by an unparalleled severity, and upon I know not what *obsolete* law, broke *only* for *blasphemy*. And as it hath been wisely observed, if persecution once begins, no man alive knows how far it may reach, or where it will end.

In answer to all which, with deference to wiser judgments, I think this rather shows the necessity of a *nominal* religion among us. Great wits love to be free with the highest objects; and if they cannot be allowed a *God* to revile or renounce, they will *speak evil of dignities,* abuse the government, and reflect upon the ministry; which I am sure few will deny to be of much more pernicious consequence, according to the saying of Tiberius,[3] *Deorum offensa diis curae.*

As to the particular fact related, I think it is not fair to argue from one instance, perhaps another

cannot be produced; yet (to the comfort of all those who may be apprehensive of persecution) blasphemy we know is freely spoken a million of times in every coffeehouse and tavern, or wherever else *good company* meet. It must be allowed indeed, that to break an *English freeborn* officer only for blasphemy, was, to speak the gentlest of such an action, a very high strain of absolute power. Little can be said in excuse for the general; perhaps he was afraid it might give offense to the allies, among whom, for aught I know, it may be the custom of the country to believe a God. But if he argued, as some have done, upon a mistaken principle, that an officer who is guilty of speaking blasphemy, may some time or other proceed so far as to raise a mutiny, the consequence is by no means to be admitted; for, surely the commander of an *English* army is likely to be but ill obeyed, whose soldiers fear and reverence him as little as they do a deity.

It is further objected against the Gospel system, that it obliges men to the belief of things too difficult for freethinkers, and such who have shaken off the prejudices that usually cling to a confined education. To which I answer, that men should be cautious how they raise objections which reflect upon the wisdom of the nation. Is not everybody freely allowed to believe whatever he pleases, and to publish his belief to the world whenever he thinks fit, especially if it serves to strengthen the party which is in the right? Would any indifferent foreigner, who should read the trumpery lately written by Asgil, Tindal, Toland, Coward,[4] and forty more, imagine the Gospel to be our rule of faith, and confirmed by parliaments? Does any man either believe, or say he believes, or desire to have it thought that he says he believes one syllable of the matter? And is any man worse received upon that score, or does he find his want of *nominal* faith a disadvantage to him in the pursuit of any civil or military employment? What if there be an old dormant statute or two against him, are they not now obsolete, to a degree, that Empson and Dudley[5] themselves if they were now alive, would find it impossible to put them in execution?

It is likewise urged, that there are, by computation, in this kingdom, above ten thousand parsons, whose revenues added to those of my lords the

3. saying of Tiberius: misquoted from Tacitus, *Annals,* I. 63. Meaning, as Swift fully explains it elsewhere: "If there be a God, he is able enough to revenge any injuries done to himself, without expecting the civil power to interpose."

4. Asgill, Tindal, etc.: Deists, whose writings had been recently condemned. Swift himself replied to Tindal's *Rights of the Christian Church* and Collins' *Discourse on Freethinking.*
5. Empson . . . Dudley: notorious for their exaction of taxes and Crown fines under Henry VII; executed for treason by Henry VIII.

bishops, would suffice to maintain at least two hundred young gentlemen of wit and pleasure, and freethinking, enemies to priestcraft, narrow principles, pedantry, and prejudices; who might be an ornament to the court and town. And then, again, so great a number of able (bodied) divines might be a recruit to our fleet and armies. This indeed appears to be a consideration of some weight. But then, on the other side, several things deserve to be considered likewise: As, first, whether it may not be thought necessary that in certain tracts of country, like what we call parishes, there should be *one* man at least of abilities to read and write. Then it seems a wrong computation, that the revenues of the Church throughout this island would be large enough to maintain two hundred young gentlemen, or even half that number, after the present refined way of living; that is, to allow each of them such a rent, as in the modern form of speech, would make them *easy*. But still there is in this project a greater mischief behind; and we ought to beware of the woman's folly, who killed the hen that every morning laid her a golden egg. For, pray what would become of the race of men in the next age, if we had nothing to trust to beside the scrofulous, consumptive productions, furnished by our men of wit and pleasure, when, having squandered away their vigor, health, and estates, they are forced by some disagreeable marriage to piece up their broken fortunes and entail rottenness and politeness on their posterity? Now, here are ten thousand persons reduced by the wise regulations of Henry the Eighth,[6] to the necessity of a low diet, and moderate exercise, who are the only great restorers of our breed, without which the nation would in an age or two become but one great hospital.

Another advantage proposed by the abolishing of Christianity, is the clear gain of one day in seven, which is now entirely lost, and consequently the kingdom one-seventh less considerable in trade, business, and pleasure; beside the loss to the public of so many stately structures now in the hands of the clergy, which might be converted into theaters, exchanges, market houses, common dormitories, and other public edifices.

I hope I shall be forgiven a hard word, if I call this a perfect cavil. I readily own there has been an old custom time out of mind, for people to assemble in the churches every Sunday, and that shops are still frequently shut, in order as it is conceived, to

6. regulations . . . Eighth: his seizure of the revenues of the Church.

preserve the memory of that ancient practice; but how this can prove a hindrance to business or pleasure, is hard to imagine. What if the men of pleasure are forced one day in the week, to game at home instead of the chocolate house? Are not the taverns and coffeehouses open? Can there be a more convenient season for taking a dose of physic? Are fewer claps got upon Sundays than other days? Is not that the chief day for traders to sum up the accounts of the week, and for lawyers to prepare their briefs? But I would fain know how it can be pretended that the churches are misapplied? Where are more appointments and rendezvous of gallantry? Where more care to appear in the foremost box with greater advantage of dress? Where more meetings for business? Where more bargains driven of all sorts? And where so many conveniences or incitements to sleep?

There is one advantage greater than any of the foregoing, proposed by the abolishing of Christianity: that it will utterly extinguish parties among us, by removing those factious distinctions of High and Low Church, of Whig and Tory, Presbyterian and Church of England, which are now so many grievous clogs upon public proceedings, and dispose men to prefer the gratifying themselves, or depressing their adversaries, before the most important interest of the state.

I confess, if it were certain that so great an advantage would redound to the nation by this expedient, I would submit and be silent. But will any man say, that if the words *whoring, drinking, cheating, lying, stealing,* were by act of parliament ejected out of the English tongue and dictionaries, we should all awake next morning chaste and temperate, honest and just, and lovers of truth? Is this a fair consequence? Or, if the physicians would forbid us to pronounce the words *pox, gout, rheumatism,* and *stone,* would that expedient serve like so many talismans to destroy the diseases themselves? Are party and faction rooted in men's hearts no deeper than phrases borrowed from religion, or founded upon no firmer principles? And is our language so poor that we cannot find other terms to express them? Are envy, pride, avarice, and ambition such ill nomenclators, that they cannot furnish appellations for their owners? Will not *heydukes* and *mamalukes, mandarins* and *potshaws,* or any other words formed at pleasure, serve to distinguish those who are in the ministry from others who *would be in it if they could?* What, for instance, is easier than to vary the form of speech, and instead of the word *Church,* make it a question in politics, whether the *Monument* be in danger? Because religion was nearest at hand to furnish a few convenient phrases, is our invention so barren, we can find no others? Suppose, for argument sake, that the Tories favored Margarita,[7] the Whigs Mrs. Tofts, and the Trimmers [8] Valentini, would not *Margaritians, Toftians,* and *Valentinians* be very tolerable marks of distinction? The *Prasini* and *Veneti,*[9] two most virulent factions in Italy, began (if I remember right) by a distinction of colors in ribbons, which we might do, with as good a grace, about the dignity of the *Blue* and the *Green;* and would serve as properly to divide the court, the parliament, and the kingdom between them, as any terms of art whatsoever, borrowed from religion. Therefore, I think there is little force in this objection against Christianity, or prospect of so great an advantage as is proposed in the abolishing of it.

It is again objected, as a very absurd, ridiculous custom, that a set of men should be suffered, much less employed and hired, to bawl one day in seven against the lawfulness of those methods most in use toward the pursuit of greatness, riches, and pleasure, which are the constant practice of all men alive on the other six. But this objection is, I think, a little unworthy so refined an age as ours. Let us argue this matter calmly. I appeal to the breast of any polite freethinker, whether in the pursuit of gratifying a predominant passion, he hath not always felt a wonderful incitement, by reflecting it was a thing forbidden; and therefore we see, in order to cultivate this taste, the wisdom of the nation hath taken special care, that the ladies should be furnished with prohibited silks, and the men with prohibited wine. And indeed it were to be wished, that some other prohibitions were promoted, in order to improve the pleasures of the town; which, for want of such expedients, begin already, as I am told, to flag and grow languid, giving way daily to cruel inroads from the spleen.

It is likewise proposed as a great advantage to the public, that if we once discard the system of the Gospel, all religion will of course be banished forever; and consequently, along with it, those grievous prejudices of education, which under the names of virtue, conscience, honor, justice, and the like,

are so apt to disturb the peace of human minds; and the notions whereof are so hard to be eradicated by right reason or freethinking, sometimes during the whole course of our lives.

Here first, I observe how difficult it is to get rid of a phrase, which the world is once grown fond of, although the occasion that first produced it, be entirely taken away. For several years past, if a man had but an ill-favored nose, the deep thinkers of the age would some way or other contrive to impute the cause to the prejudice of his education. From this fountain are said to be derived all our foolish notions of justice, piety, love of our country; all our opinions of God, or a future state, Heaven, hell, and the like. And there might formerly perhaps have been some pretense for this charge. But so effectual care has been taken to remove those prejudices, by an entire change in the methods of education, that (with honor I mention it to our polite innovators) the young gentlemen who are now on the scene, seem to have not the least tincture left of those infusions, or string of those weeds; and, by consequence, the reason for abolishing *nominal* Christianity upon that pretext, is wholly ceased.

For the rest, it may perhaps admit a controversy, whether the banishing all notions of religion whatsoever, would be convenient for the vulgar. Not that I am in the least of opinion with those who hold religion to have been the invention of politicians, to keep the lower part of the world in awe by the fear of invisible powers; unless mankind were then very different from what it is now. For I look upon the mass or body of our people here in England, to be as freethinkers, that is to say, as staunch unbelievers, as any of the highest rank. But I conceive some scattered notions about a superior power to be of singular use for the common people, as furnishing excellent materials to keep children quiet when they grow peevish and providing topics of amusement in a tedious winter night.

Lastly, it is proposed as a singular advantage, that the abolishing of Christianity will very much contribute to the uniting of Protestants, by enlarging the terms of communion so as to take in all sorts of dissenters, who are now shut out of the pale upon account of a few ceremonies which all sides confess to be things indifferent: That this alone will effectually answer the great ends of a scheme for comprehension, by opening a large noble gate, at which all bodies may enter; whereas

---

7. **Margarita, etc.:** "Italian singers then in vogue" [Swift's note]. Actually Mrs. Tofts was English, but sang in Italian operas. 8. **Trimmers:** A name given to those who wished to compromise between the supporters of James II and those who stood for the Protestant succession.   9. **Prasini . . . Veneti:** the chief parties in the civil war under Justinian.

the chaffering with dissenters, and dodging about this or the other ceremony, is but like opening a few wickets, and leaving them ajar, by which no more than one can get in at a time, and that, not without stooping, and sidling, and squeezing his body.

To all this I answer; that there is one darling inclination of mankind, which usually affects to be a retainer to religion, though she be neither its parent, its godmother, or its friend; I mean the spirit of opposition, that lived long before Christianity, and can easily subsist without it. Let us, for instance, examine wherein the opposition of sectaries among us consists, we shall find Christianity to have no share in it at all. Does the Gospel anywhere prescribe a starched, squeezed countenance, a stiff, formal gait, a singularity of manners and habit, or any affected modes of speech different from the reasonable part of mankind? Yet, if Christianity did not lend its name to stand in the gap, and to employ or divert these humors, they must of necessity be spent in contraventions to the laws of the land, and disturbance of the public peace. There is a portion of enthusiasm assigned to every nation, which, if it hath not proper objects to work on, will burst out, and set all in a flame. If the quiet of a state can be bought by only flinging men a few ceremonies to devour, it is a purchase no wise man would refuse. Let the mastiffs amuse themselves about a sheepskin stuffed with hay, provided it will keep them from worrying the flock. The institution of convents abroad, seems in one point a strain of great wisdom, there being few irregularities in human passions, which may not have recourse to vent themselves in some of those orders, which are so many retreats for the speculative, the melancholy, the proud, the silent, the politic, and the morose, to spend themselves, and evaporate the noxious particles; for each of whom we in this island are forced to provide a several sect of religion, to keep them quiet: And whenever Christianity shall be abolished, the legislature must find some other expedient to employ and entertain them. For what imports it how large a gate you open, if there will be always left a number who place a pride and a merit in refusing to enter?

Having thus considered the most important objections against Christianity, and the chief advantages proposed by the abolishing thereof, I shall now with equal deference and submission to wiser judgments as before, proceed to mention a few inconveniences that may happen, if the Gospel should be repealed; which perhaps the projectors may not have sufficiently considered.

And first, I am very sensible how much the gentlemen of wit and pleasure are apt to murmur, and be shocked at the sight of so many draggled-tail parsons, who happen to fall in their way, and offend their eyes; but at the same time, these wise reformers do not consider what an advantage and felicity it is, for great wits to be always provided with objects of scorn and contempt, in order to exercise and improve their talents, and divert their spleen from falling on each other or on themselves; especially when all this may be done without the least imaginable *danger to their persons.*

And to urge another argument of a parallel nature: If Christianity were once abolished, how would the freethinkers, the strong reasoners, and the men of profound learning, be able to find another subject so calculated in all points whereon to display their abilities? What wonderful productions of wit should we be deprived of, from those whose genius by continual practice hath been wholly turned upon raillery and invectives against religion, and would therefore never be able to shine or distinguish themselves upon any other subject! We are daily complaining of the great decline of wit among us, and would we take away the greatest, perhaps the only topic we have left? Who would ever have suspected Asgil for a wit, or Toland for a philosopher, if the inexhaustible stock of Christianity had not been at hand to provide them with materials? What other subject, through all art or nature, could have produced Tindal for a profound author, or furnished him with readers? It is the wise choice of the subject that alone adorns and distinguishes the writer. For, had a hundred such pens as these been employed on the side of religion, they would have immediately sunk into silence and oblivion.

Nor do I think it wholly groundless, or my fears altogether imaginary, that the abolishing of Christianity may perhaps bring the Church into danger, or at least put the senate to the trouble of another securing vote. I desire I may not be mistaken; I am far from presuming to affirm or think that the Church is in danger at present, or as things now stand; but we know not how soon it may be so when the Christian religion is repealed. As plausible as this project seems, there may a dangerous design lurk under it. Nothing can be more notorious, than that the atheists, deists, Socinians, anti-Trinitarians, and other subdivisions of free-thinkers, are persons of little zeal for the present ecclesiastical establishment: Their declared opinion is for repealing the Sacramental Test; [10] they are very indifferent with regard to ceremonies; nor do they hold the *jus divinum* [11] of Episcopacy. Therefore this may be intended as one politic step toward altering the constitution of the Church established, and setting up Presbytery in the stead, which I leave to be further considered by those at the helm.

In the last place, I think nothing can be more plain, than that by this expedient, we shall run into the evil we chiefly pretend to avoid; and that the abolishment of the Christian religion will be the readiest course we can take to introduce popery. And I am the more inclined to this opinion, because we know it has been the constant practice of the Jesuits to send over emissaries, with instructions to personate themselves members of the several prevailing sects among us. So it is recorded, that they have at sundry times appeared in the guise of Presbyterians, Anabaptists, Independents, and Quakers, according as any of these were most in credit; so, since the fashion hath been taken up of exploding religion, the popish missionaries have not been wanting to mix with the freethinkers; among whom, Toland the great oracle of the anti-Christians is an Irish priest, the son of an Irish priest; and the most learned and ingenious author of a book called *The Rights of the Christian Church* [12] was in a proper juncture reconciled to the Romish faith, whose true son, as appears by a hundred passages in his treatise, he still continues. Perhaps I could add some others to the number; but the fact is beyond dispute, and the reasoning they proceed by is right; for, supposing Christianity to be extinguished, the people will never be at ease until they find out some other method of worship; which will as infallibly produce superstition, as this will end in popery.

And therefore, if notwithstanding all I have said, it shall still be thought necessary to have a bill brought in for repealing Christianity,[13] I would humbly offer an amendment; that instead of the word *Christianity,* may be put *Religion* in general; which I conceive will much better answer all the good ends proposed by the projectors of it. For, as

long as we leave in being a God and his providence, with all the necessary consequences which curious and inquisitive men will be apt to draw from such premises, we do not strike at the root of the evil, although we should ever so effectually annihilate the present scheme of the Gospel. For, of what use is freedom of thought, if it will not produce freedom of action, which is the sole end, how remote soever in appearance, of all objections against Christianity? And therefore, the freethinkers consider it as a sort of edifice, wherein all the parts have such a mutual dependence on each other, that if you happen to pull out one single nail, the whole fabric must fall to the ground. This was happily expressed by him who had heard of a text brought for proof of the Trinity, which in an ancient manuscript was differently read; he thereupon immediately took the hint, and by a sudden deduction of a long sorites, most logically concluded: "Why, if it be as you say, I may safely whore and drink on, and defy the parson." From which, and many the like instances easy to be produced, I think nothing can be more manifest, than that the quarrel is not against any particular points of hard digestion in the Christian system, but against religion in general; which, by laying restraints on human nature, is supposed the great enemy to the freedom of thought and action.

Upon the whole, if it shall still be thought for the benefit of Church and state, that Christianity be abolished; I conceive however, it may be more convenient to defer the execution to a time of peace, and not venture in this conjuncture to disoblige our allies, who, as it falls out, are all Christians, and many of them, by the prejudices of their education, so bigoted, as to place a sort of pride in the appellation. If upon being rejected by them, we are to trust to an alliance with the Turk, we shall find ourselves much deceived: For, as he is too remote, and generally engaged in war with the Persian emperor, so his people would be more scandalized at our infidelity, than our Christian neighbors. Because the Turks are not only strict observers of religious worship, but, what is worse, believe a God; which is more than is required of us, even while we preserve the name of Christians.

To conclude: Whatever some may think of the great advantages to trade by this favorite scheme, I do very much apprehend, that in six months' time after the act is passed for the extirpation of the Gospel, the Bank and East India stock may fall, at least, one *per cent.* And, since that is fifty times more than ever the wisdom of our age thought fit to venture for the *preservation* of Christianity, there is no reason we should be at so great a loss, merely for the sake of *destroying* it.

from A LETTER TO A YOUNG GENTLEMAN

LATELY ENTERED INTO HOLY ORDERS

By a Person of QUALITY

Originally printed in Dublin as *A Letter from a Lay Patron to a Gentleman Designing for Holy Orders,* it was probably never addressed by Swift to a particular person, but intended to give advice to the young clergy in a manner different from the usual books on the subject of writing sermons. Its chief value is that it provides a statement of Swift's views on composition and prose style, just at the time when he had begun to write his *Travels.* (Only the section of the *Letter* that deals with the art of writing is given here.)

January 9, 1720

Sir,

Although it was against my knowledge or advice, that you entered into holy orders, under the present dispositions of mankind toward the Church, yet since it is now supposed too late to recede (at least according to the general practice and opinion), I cannot forbear offering my thoughts to you upon this new condition of life you are engaged in.

I could heartily wish that the circumstances of your fortune had enabled you to have continued some years longer in the university, at least until you were ten years' standing; to have laid in a competent stock of human learning, and some knowledge in divinity, before you attempted to appear in the world: for I cannot but lament the common course, which at least nine in ten of those who enter into the ministry are obliged to run. When they have taken a degree, and are consequently grown a burden to their friends, who now think themselves fully discharged, they get into orders as soon as they can (upon which I shall make no remarks), first solicit a readership, and if they be very fortunate, arrive in time to a curacy here in town; or else are sent to be assistants in the country, where they probably continue several years (many of them their whole lives), with thirty or forty pounds a year for their support, until some bishop, who happens to be not overstocked with relations, or attached to favorites, or is content to

supply his diocese without colonies from England, bestows upon them some inconsiderable benefice, when it is odds they are already encumbered with a numerous family. I would be glad to know what intervals of life such persons can possibly set apart for improvement of their minds; or which way they could be furnished with books, the library they brought with them from their college being usually not the most numerous, or judiciously chosen. If such gentlemen arrive to be great scholars, it must, I think, be either by means supernatural, or by a method altogether out of any road yet known to the learned. But I conceive the fact directly otherwise, and that many of them lose the greatest part of the small pittance they received at the university.

I take it for granted, that you intend to pursue the beaten track, and are already desirous to be seen in a pulpit; only I hope you will think it proper to pass your quarantine among some of the desolate churches five miles round this town, where you may at least learn to *read* and to *speak* before you venture to expose your parts in a city congregation; not that these are better judges, but because, if a man must needs expose his folly, it is more safe and discreet to do so before few witnesses, and in a scattered neighborhood. And you will do well if you can prevail upon some intimate and judicious friend to be your constant hearer, and allow him with the utmost freedom to give you notice of whatever he shall find amiss either in your voice or gesture; for want of which early warning, many clergymen continue defective, and sometimes ridiculous, to the end of their lives; neither is it rare to observe among excellent and learned divines, a certain ungracious manner, or an unhappy tone of voice, which they never have been able to shake off.

I could likewise have been glad, if you had applied yourself a little more to the study of the English language, than I fear you have done; the neglect whereof is one of the most general defects among the scholars of this kingdom, who seem to have not the least conception of a style, but run on in a flat kind of phraseology, often mingled with barbarous terms and expressions, peculiar to the nation. Neither do I perceive that any person either finds or acknowledges his wants upon this head, or in the least desires to have them supplied. Proper words in proper places, makes the true definition of a style. But this would require too ample a disquisition to be now dwelt on: however, I shall venture to name one or two faults, which are easy to be remedied, with a very small portion of abilities.

The first is the frequent use of obscure terms, which by the women are called *hard words,* and by the better sort of vulgar, *fine language;* than which I do not know a more universal, inexcusable, and unnecessary mistake, among the clergy of all distinctions, but especially the younger practitioners. I have been curious enough to take a list of several hundred words in a sermon of a new beginner, which not one of his hearers among a hundred could possibly understand; neither can I easily call to mind any clergyman of my own acquaintance who is wholly exempt from this error, although many of them agree with me in the dislike of the thing. But I am apt to put myself in the place of the vulgar, and think many words difficult or obscure, which the preacher will not allow to be so, because those words are obvious to scholars. I believe the method observed by the famous Lord Falkland [1] in some of his writings, would not be an ill one for young divines: I was assured by an old person of quality who knew him well, that when he doubted whether a word was perfectly intelligible or no, he used to consult one of his lady's chambermaids (not the waiting woman, because it was possible she might be conversant in romances), and by her judgment was guided whether to receive or reject it. And if that great person thought such a caution necessary in treatises offered to the learned world, it will be sure at least as proper in sermons, where the meanest hearer is supposed to be concerned, and where very often a lady's chambermaid may be allowed to equal half the congregation, both as to quality and understanding. But I know not how it comes to pass, that professors in most arts and sciences are generally the worst qualified to explain their meanings to those who are not of their tribe. A common farmer shall make you understand in three words, *that his foot is out of joint, or his collarbone broken,* wherein a surgeon, after a hundred terms of art, if you are not a scholar, shall leave you to seek. It is frequently the same case in law, physic, and even many of the meaner arts.

And upon this account it is, that among *hard words,* I number likewise those which are peculiar to divinity as it is a science; because I have observed several clergymen, otherwise little fond of obscure terms, yet in their sermons very liberal of those which they find in ecclesiastical writers, as if it were our duty to understand them; which I am sure it is not. And I defy the greatest divine to produce any law either of God or man, which obliges me to comprehend the meaning of *omniscience, omnipresence, ubiquity, attribute, beatific vision,* with a thousand others so frequent in pulpits, any more than that of *eccentric, idiosyncracy, entity,* and the like. I believe I may venture to insist further, that many terms used in Holy Writ, particularly by St. Paul, might with more discretion be changed into plainer speech, except when they are introduced as part of a quotation.

I am the more earnest in this matter, because it is a general complaint, and the justest in the world. For a divine has nothing to say to the wisest congregation of any parish in this kingdom, which he may not express in a manner to be understood by the meanest among them. And this assertion must be true, or else God requires from us more than we are able to perform. However, not to contend whether a logician might possibly put a case that would serve for an exception, I will appeal to any man of letters, whether at least nineteen in twenty of those perplexing words might not be changed into easy ones, such as naturally first occur to ordinary men, and probably did so at first to those very gentlemen who are so fond of the former.

We are often reproved by divines from the pulpits, on account of our ignorance in things sacred, and perhaps with justice enough. However, it is not very reasonable for them to expect, that *common men* should understand expressions which are never made use of in *common life.* No gentleman thinks it safe or prudent to send a servant with a message, without repeating it more than once, and endeavoring to put it into terms brought down to the capacity of the bearer. Yet after all this care, it is frequent for servants to mistake, and sometimes to occasion misunderstandings between friends, although the common domestics in some gentlemen's families may have more opportunities of improving their minds than the ordinary sort of tradesmen.

It is usual for clergymen who are taxed with this learned defect, to quote Dr. Tillotson,[2] and other

---

LETTER TO A YOUNG GENTLEMAN. **1. Lord Falkland:** Lucius Cary, 2nd Viscount Falkland, killed at the age of thirty-three in the Civil War, 1643, but already famous among the wits and scholars of his day for his learning and nobility of character, and a poet among the "sons of Ben"; but Swift is presumably referring here to his philosophical prose writings.

2. **Dr. Tillotson:** Archbishop of Canterbury, who died in 1694, so that Swift would remember him as one of the great preachers at the time when he first arrived in England.

famous divines, in their defense, without considering the difference between elaborate discourses upon important occasions, delivered to princes or parliaments, written with a view of being made public, and a plain sermon intended for the middle or lower size of people. Neither do they seem to remember the many alterations, additions, and expungings, made by great authors in those treatises which they prepare for the public. Besides, that excellent prelate above-mentioned, was known to preach after a much more popular manner in the city congregations: and if in those parts of his works he be anywhere too obscure for the understandings of many who may be supposed to have been his hearers, it ought to be numbered among his omissions.

The fear of being thought pedants hath been of pernicious consequence to young divines. This hath wholly taken many of them off from their severer studies in the university, which they have exchanged for plays, poems, and pamphlets, in order to qualify them for tea tables and coffeehouses. This they usually call *polite conversation; knowing the world;* and *reading men instead of books.* These accomplishments when applied in the pulpit, appear by a quaint, terse, florid style, rounded into periods and cadences, commonly without either propriety or meaning. I have listened with my utmost attention for half an hour to an orator of this species, without being able to understand, much less to carry away one single sentence out of a whole sermon. Others, to show that their studies have not been confined to sciences, or ancient authors, will talk in the style of a gaming ordinary,[3] and Whitefriars,[4] where I suppose the hearers can be little edified by the terms of *palming, shuffling, biting, bamboozling,* and the like, if they have not been sometimes conversant among pickpockets and sharpers. And truly, as they say, a man is known by his company, so it should seem that a man's company may be known by his manner of expressing himself, either in public assemblies, or private conversation.

It would be endless to run over the several defects of style among us; I shall therefore say nothing of the *mean* and *paltry* (which are usually attended by the *fustian*), much less of the *slovenly* or *indecent.* Two things I will just warn you against: the first is the frequency of flat unnecessary epithets; and the other is the folly of using old threadbare phrases, which will often make you go out of your way to find and apply them, are nauseous to rational hearers, and will seldom express your meaning as well as your own natural words.

Although, as I have already observed, our English tongue is too little cultivated in this kingdom, yet the faults are nine in ten owing to affectation, and not to the want of understanding. When a man's thoughts are clear, the properest words will generally offer themselves first, and his own judgment will direct him in what order to place them, so as they may be best understood. Where men err against this method, it is usually on purpose, and to show their learning, their oratory, their politeness, or their knowledge of the world. In short, that simplicity without which no human performance can arrive to any great perfection, is nowhere more eminently useful than in this. . . .

THE FIRST DRAPIER LETTER

The first of a series of Letters written by Swift in 1724 to prevent the importation into Ireland of a large amount of copper coinage, which had been manufactured in England and was suspected of being debased currency. This is the simplest and the most direct appeal to the tradesmen and farmers and country people to boycott the new money, written in language fitting a shopkeeper, and easy enough to be understood by everybody; yet at the same time, as he intended, allowing them to recognize beneath the disguise the tone and authority of the Dean and the force of the once feared Tory Examiner, now returning to the attack against his old enemies. This letter shows Swift willing to exaggerate the dangers of the project in order to stir up popular fury against it, because he believed it was better for Ireland to be inconvenienced by lack of small change than to accept a coinage of which all the profits would go to England.

TO THE TRADESMEN, SHOPKEEPERS, FARMERS,
AND COUNTRY PEOPLE IN GENERAL,
OF THE KINGDOM OF IRELAND,

CONCERNING THE BRASS HALFPENCE COINED
BY ONE WILLIAM WOOD, HARDWAREMAN,
WITH A DESIGN TO HAVE THEM PASS
IN THIS KINGDOM:

Wherein is shown the power of his Patent, the value of the Halfpence, and how far every person may be obliged to take the same in payments, and

---

3. **gaming ordinary:** tavern for card playing. 4. **Whitefriars:** a district in the city of London which had become the resort of cardsharpers.

*how to behave himself, in case such an attempt
should be made by Wood, or any other person.*

(VERY PROPER TO BE KEPT IN EVERY FAMILY)

By M. B., DRAPIER. 1724

Brethren, Friends, Countrymen,
    and Fellow Subjects,
What I intend now to say to you, is, next to your
duty to God, and the care of your salvation, of the
greatest concern to yourselves and your children;
your bread and clothing, and every common necessary of life, entirely depend upon it. Therefore I do
most earnestly exhort you, as men, as Christians,
as parents, and as lovers of your country, to read
this paper with the utmost attention, or get it read
to you by others; which that you may do at the
less expense, I have ordered the printer to sell it
at the lowest rate.[1]

It is a great fault among you, that when a person writes with no other intention than to do you
good, you will not be at the pains to read his advices: One copy of this paper may serve a dozen
of you, which will be less than a farthing apiece.
It is your folly, that you have no common or general interest in your view, not even the wisest
among you; neither do you know, or inquire, or
care who are your friends, or who are your enemies.

About four years ago a little book was written,
to advise all people to wear the *manufactures of
this our own dear country*. It had no other design,
said nothing against the king or parliament, or any
person whatsoever; yet the poor printer was prosecuted two years with the utmost violence, and even
some weavers themselves (for whose sake it was
written) being upon the jury, found him guilty.
This would be enough to discourage any man from
endeavoring to do you good, when you will either
neglect him, or fly in his face for his pains; and
when he must expect only danger to himself, and
to be fined and imprisoned, perhaps to his ruin.

However, I cannot but warn you once more of
the manifest destruction before your eyes, if you
do not behave yourselves as you ought.

I will therefore first tell you the *plain story of
the fact;* and then I will lay before you how you
ought to act, in common prudence, according to the
laws of your country.

The fact is thus: It having been many years since
copper halfpence or farthings were last coined in
this kingdom, they have been for some time very
scarce,[2] and many counterfeits passed about under
the name of raps:[3] several applications were
made to England, that we might have liberty to
coin new *ones,* as in former times we did; but
they did not succeed. At last one Mr. Wood,[4] *a
mean ordinary man, a hardware dealer,* procured a
patent[5] under his Majesty's broad seal to coin
£108,000 in *copper* for this kingdom; which patent, however, did not oblige anyone here to take
them, unless they pleased. Now you must know,
that the halfpence and farthings in England pass
for very little more than they are worth; and if you
should beat them to pieces, and sell them to the
brasier, you would not lose much above a penny
in a shilling. But Mr. Wood made his halfpence of
such base metal, and so much smaller than the English ones, that the brasier would not give you above
a penny of good money for a shilling of his; so
that this sum of £108,000 in good gold and silver,
must be given for trash, that will not be worth
above eight or nine thousand pounds real value.
But this is not the worst; for Mr. Wood, when he
pleases, may by stealth send over another £108,000
and buy all our goods for eleven parts in twelve
under the value. For example, if a hatter sells a
dozen of hats for five shillings apiece, which
amounts to three pounds, and receives the payment
in Mr. Wood's coin, he really receives only the
value of five shillings.

Perhaps you will wonder how such an *ordinary
fellow* as this Mr. Wood could have so much interest as to get his Majesty's broad seal for so great
a sum of bad money to be sent to this poor country; and that all the nobility and gentry here
could not obtain the same favor, and let us make
our own halfpence, as we used to do. Now I will
make that matter very plain: We are at a great distance from the king's court, and have nobody there
to solicit for us, although a great number of lords
and squires, whose estates are here, and are our
countrymen, spend all their lives and fortunes
there; but this same Mr. Wood was able to attend
constantly for his own interest; he is an Englishman,
and had great friends; and, it seems, knew very

FIRST DRAPIER LETTER. **1. sell . . . rate:** advertised at three
dozen for two English shillings.

2. farthings . . . scarce: said to have been carried off by traders
to New England and the West Indies, some years before. Swift
admitted that £10,000 worth was needed.   3. raps: perhaps
from Dutch *rapper*, a farthing of mixed metal.   4. Mr. Wood:
at this time one of the largest iron manufacturers in the country,
and said to have really produced excellent copper coins.   5. patent: This was carefully drawn up, but it was reported to have
been obtained by the Duchess of Kendal, the king's mistress,
who sold it to Wood for £10,000.

well where to give money to those that would speak to others, that could speak to the king, and would tell a fair story. And his Majesty, and perhaps the great lord or lords who advised him, might think it was for our country's good; and so, as the lawyers express it, "the king was deceived in his grant," which often happens in all reigns. And I am sure if his Majesty knew that such a patent, if it should take effect according to the desire of Mr. Wood, would utterly ruin this kingdom, which has given such great proofs of its loyalty, he would immediately recall it, and perhaps show his displeasure to somebody or other: but a word to the wise is enough. Most of you must have heard with what anger our honorable House of Commons received an account of this Wood's patent. There were several fine speeches made upon it, and plain proofs, that it was all a wicked cheat from the bottom to the top; and several smart votes [6] were printed, which that same Wood had the assurance to answer likewise in print; and in so confident a way, as if he were a better man than our whole parliament put together.

This Wood, as soon as his patent was passed, or soon after, sends over a great many barrels of those halfpence to Cork, and other seaport towns; and to get them off, offered a hundred pounds in his coin, for seventy or eighty in silver: but the collectors of the king's customs very honestly refused to take them,[7] and so did almost everybody else. And since the parliament has condemned them, and desired the king that they might be stopped, all the kingdom do abominate them.

But Wood is still working underhand [8] to force his halfpence upon us; and if he can, by help of his friends in England, prevail so far as to get an order, that the commissioners and collectors of the king's money shall receive them, and that the army is to be paid with them, then he thinks his work shall be done. And this is the difficulty you will be under in such a case; for the common soldier, when he goes to the market or alehouse, will offer this money; and if it be refused, perhaps he will swagger and hector, and threaten to beat the butcher or alewife, or take the goods by force and throw them the bad halfpence. In this and the like cases, the shopkeeper or victualer, or any other

tradesman, has no more to do, than to demand ten times the price of his goods, if it is to be paid in Wood's money: for example, twenty pence of that money for a quart of ale, and so in all things else, and not part with his goods till he gets the money.

For, suppose you go to an alehouse with that base money, and the landlord gives you a quart for four of these halfpence, what must the victualer do? His brewer will not be paid in that coin; or, if the brewer should be such a fool, the farmers will not take it from them for their bere,[9] because they are bound, by their leases, to pay their rents in good and lawful money of England; which this is not, nor of Ireland neither; and the squire, their landlord, will never be so bewitched to take such trash for his land; so that it must certainly stop somewhere or other; and wherever it stops, it is the same thing, and we are all undone.

The common weight of these halfpence is between four and five to an ounce; suppose five, then three shillings and fourpence will weigh a pound, and consequently twenty shillings will weigh six pounds butter weight. Now there are many hundred farmers, who pay two hundred pounds a year rent; therefore, when one of these farmers comes with his half-year's rent, which is one hundred pounds, it will be at least six hundred pounds weight, which is three horses' load.

If a squire has a mind to come to town to buy clothes, and wine, and spices for himself and family, or perhaps to pass the winter here, he must bring with him five or six horses loaded with sacks, as the farmers bring their corn; and when his lady comes in her coach to our shops, it must be followed by a car loaded with Mr. Wood's money. And I hope we shall have the grace to take it for no more than it is worth.

They say Squire Conolly [10] has sixteen thousand pounds a year; now, if he sends for his rent to town, as it is likely he does, he must have two hundred and fifty horses to bring up his half-year's rent, and two or three great cellars in his house for stowage. But what the bankers will do, I cannot tell; for I am assured, that some great bankers keep by them forty thousand pounds in ready cash, to answer all payments; which sum, in Mr. Wood's money, would require twelve hundred horses to carry it.

6. smart votes: addresses to the King against the patent presented by both houses of parliament in Ireland.   7. collectors . . . them: Legally, custom duties had to be paid in current English money, and these halfpence were not current in England. 8. Wood . . . underhand: But he had in fact offered to forbear coining until the objections to the patent had been satisfied.

9. bere: a sort of barley in Ireland.   10. Squire Conolly: Speaker of the House of Commons in Ireland, devoted to the English interest, and trying to overcome the opposition to the coinage.

For my own part, I am already resolved what to do: I have a pretty good shop of Irish stuffs and silks, and instead of taking Mr. Wood's bad copper, I intend to truck with my neighbors the butchers and bakers and brewers, and the rest, goods for goods; and the little gold and silver I have, I will keep by me, like my heart's blood, till better times, or until I am just ready to starve; and then I will buy Mr. Wood's money, as my father did the brass money[11] in King James's time, who could buy ten pounds of it with a guinea; and I hope to get as much for a pistole, and so purchase bread from those who will be such fools as to sell it me.

These halfpence, if they once pass, will soon be counterfeited, because it may be cheaply done, the stuff is so base. The Dutch likewise will probably do the same thing, and send them over to us to pay for our goods; and Mr. Wood will never be at rest, but coin on: so that in some years we shall have at least five times £108,000 of this lumber. Now the current money of this kingdom is not reckoned to be above four hundred thousand pounds in all; and while there is a silver sixpence left, these bloodsuckers will never be quiet.

When once the kingdom is reduced to such a condition, I will tell you what must be the end: the gentlemen of estates will all turn off their tenants for want of payment; because, as I told you before, the tenants are obliged by their leases to pay sterling, which is lawful current money of England: then they will turn their own farmers, as too many of them do already; run all into sheep,[12] where they can, keeping only such other cattle as are necessary; then they will be their own merchants, and send their wool, and butter, and hides, and linen beyond sea, for ready money, and wine, and spices, and silks. They will keep only a few miserable cottagers:[13] the farmers must rob, or beg, or leave their country; the shopkeepers in this, and every other town, must break and starve; for it is the landed man that maintains the merchant, and shopkeeper and handicraftsman.

But when the squire turns farmer and merchant himself, all the good money he gets from abroad, he will hoard up to send for England, and keep some poor tailor or weaver, and the like, in his own house, who will be glad to get bread at any rate.

I should never have done, if I were to tell you all the miseries that we shall undergo, if we be so foolish and wicked as to take this cursed coin. It would be very hard, if all Ireland should be put into one scale, and this sorry fellow Wood into the other; that Mr. Wood should weigh down this whole kingdom, by which England gets above a million of good money every year clear into their pockets: and that is more than the English do by all the world besides.

But your great comfort is, that as his Majesty's patent does not oblige you to take this money, so the laws have not given the Crown a power of forcing the subject to take what money the king pleases; for then, by the same reason, we might be bound to take pebblestones, or cockleshells, or stamped leather, for current coin, if ever we should happen to live under an ill prince; who might likewise, by the same power make a guinea pass for ten pounds, a shilling for twenty shillings, and so on; by which he would, in a short time, get all the silver and gold of the kingdom into his own hands, and leave us nothing but brass or leather, or what he pleased. Neither is anything reckoned more cruel and oppressive in the French government,[14] than their common practice of calling in all their money, after they have sunk it very low, and then coining it anew at a much higher value; which, however, is not the thousandth part so wicked as this abominable project of Mr. Wood. For, the French give their subjects silver for silver, and gold for gold; but this fellow will not so much as give us good brass or copper for our gold and silver, nor even a twelfth part of their worth.

Having said thus much, I will now go on to tell you the judgments of some great lawyers in this matter, whom I fee'd on purpose for your sakes, and got their opinions under their hands, that I might be sure I went upon good grounds.

A famous lawbook,[15] called *The Mirror of Justice,* discoursing of the charters (or laws) ordained by our ancient kings, declares the law to be as follows: " It was ordained that no king of this realm should change or impair the money, or make any other money than of gold or silver, without the

---

11. **brass money:** debased coinage issued by James II, the circulation of which was forbidden by William III in February, 1691.
12. **run . . . sheep:** turn farms worked by tenants into sheep pasture.   13. **cottagers:** "Poor wretches who think themselves blessed, if they can obtain a hut worse than the squire's dog kennel, and an acre of ground for a potato plantation, on condition of being as very slaves as any in America" (*Mist's Weekly Journal,* Sept. 30, 1721).

14. **cruel . . . government:** Between September, 1719, and December, 1720, the value of money in France was altered twenty-eight times for gold and thirty-five times for silver.   15. **famous lawbook:** the *Mirror of Justice,* actually of little value "as evidence concerning the early jurisprudence of Anglo-Saxon England."

assent of all the counties "; that is, as my Lord Coke [16] says, without the assent of parliament.

This book is very ancient, and of great authority for the time in which it was written, and with that character is often quoted by that great lawyer my Lord Coke. By the laws of England the several metals are divided into lawful or true metal,[17] and unlawful or false metal: the former comprehends silver or gold, the latter all baser metals. That the former is only to pass in payments, appears by an act of parliament made the twentieth year of Edward the First, called the *Statute Concerning the Passing of Pence;* which I give you here as I got it translated into English; for some of our laws at that time were, as I am told, written in Latin: " Whoever, in buying or selling, presumeth to refuse a halfpenny or farthing of lawful money, bearing the stamp which it ought to have, let him be seized on as a contemner of the king's majesty, and cast into prison."

By this statute, no person is to be reckoned a contemner of the king's Majesty, and for that crime to be committed to prison, but he who refuseth to accept the king's coin made of lawful metal; by which, as I observed before, silver and gold only are intended.

That this is the true construction of the act, appears not only from the plain meaning of the words, but from my Lord Coke's observation upon it. " By this act," says he " it appears, that no subject can be forced to take, in buying, or selling, or other payments, any money made but of lawful metal; that is, of silver or gold."

The law of England gives the king all mines of gold and silver; but not the mines of other metals: the reason of which prerogative or power, as it is given by my Lord Coke, is, because money can be made of gold and silver; but not of other metals.

Pursuant to this opinion, halfpence and farthings were anciently made of silver, which is evident from the act of parliament of Henry the Fourth, chap. 4, whereby it is enacted as follows: " Item, for the great scarcity that is at present within the realm of England of halfpence and farthings of silver, it is ordained and established, that the third part of all the money of silver plate which shall be brought to the bullion, shall be made in halfpence and farthings." This shows that by the

words " halfpenny and farthing of lawful money," in that statute concerning the passing of pence, is meant a small coin in halfpence and farthings of silver.

This is farther manifest from the statute of the ninth year of Edward the Third, chap. 3, which enacts " that no sterling halfpenny or farthing be molten for to make vessels, or any other thing, by the goldsmiths, nor others, upon forfeiture of the money so molten " (or melted).

By another act in this king's reign, *black money* [18] was not to be current in England. And by an act made in the eleventh year of his reign, chap. 5, *galley halfpence* [19] were not to pass. What kind of coin these were, I do not know; but I presume they were made of base metal. And these acts were no new laws, but further declarations of the old laws relating to the coin.

Thus the law stands in relation to coin. Nor is there any example to the contrary, except one in Davis's Reports,[20] who tells us " that in the time of Tyrone's rebellion,[21] Queen Elizabeth ordered money of mixed metal to be coined in the Tower of London, and sent over hither for the payment of the army, obliging all people to receive it; and commanding that all silver money should be taken only as bullion "; that is, for as much as it weighed. Davis tells us several particulars in this matter, too long here to trouble you with, and " that the privy council of this kingdom obliged a merchant in England to receive this mixed money for goods transmitted hither."

But this proceeding is rejected by all the best lawyers, as contrary to law, the privy council here having no such legal power. And besides, it is to be considered, that the queen was then under great difficulties by a rebellion in this kingdom, assisted from Spain. And whatever is done in great exigencies and dangerous times, should never be an example to proceed by in seasons of peace and quietness.

I will now, my dear friends, to save you the trouble, set before you, in short, what the law obliges you to do; and what it does not oblige you to.

---

16. Lord Coke: Sir Edward Coke, famous as a judge and upholder of the common law against James I and Charles I, and author of the *Institutes of the Lawes of England,* here quoted. 17. lawful . . . metal: i.e., gold or silver, worth by weight what it denotes, not token money like our paper.

18. *black money:* money not made of silver or gold.   19. *galley halfpence:* smaller silver coin, said to have been brought to London in the fifteenth century by sailors from the Mediterranean galleys.   20. Davis's Reports: published in Ireland in 1615, when Sir John Davis was Attorney General. Swift is careful to deal with this case to prevent its being used as a precedent against him.   21. Tyrone's rebellion: Hugh O'Neill, Earl of Tyrone, who with the help of Spain tried to throw off the English yoke in the last years of Queen Elizabeth's reign.

First, You are obliged to take all money in payments which is coined by the king, and is of the English standard or weight, provided it be of gold or silver.

Secondly, You are not obliged to take any money which is not of gold or silver; not only the halfpence or farthings of England, but of any other country. And it is merely for convenience, or ease, that you are content to take them; because the custom of coining silver halfpence and farthings hath long been left off; I suppose on account of their being subject to be lost.

Thirdly, Much less are you obliged to take those vile halfpence of that same Wood, by which you must lose almost eleven pence in every shilling.

Therefore, my friends, stand to it one and all: refuse this filthy trash. It is no treason to rebel against Mr. Wood. His Majesty in his patent, obliges nobody to take these halfpence: our gracious prince hath no such ill advisers about him; or, if he had, yet you see the laws have not left it in the king's power to force us to take any coin but what is lawful, of right standard, gold and silver. Therefore you have nothing to fear.

And let me in the next place apply myself particularly to you who are the poorer sort of tradesmen. Perhaps you may think you will not be so great losers as the rich, if these halfpence should pass; because you seldom see any silver, and your customers come to your shops or stalls with nothing but brass, which you likewise find hard to be got. But you may take my word, whenever this money gains footing among you, you will be utterly undone. If you carry these halfpence to a shop for tobacco or brandy, or any other thing that you want, the shopkeeper will advance his goods accordingly, or else he must break, and leave the key under the door. "Do you think I will sell you a

yard of tenpenny stuff for twenty of Mr. Wood's halfpence? No, not under two hundred at least; neither will I be at the trouble of counting, but weigh them in a lump." I will tell you one thing further, that if Mr. Wood's project should take, it will ruin even our beggars; for when I give a beggar a halfpenny, it will quench his thirst, or go a good way to fill his belly; but the twelfth part of a halfpenny will do him no more service than if I should give him three pins out of my sleeve.

In short, these halfpence are like " the accursed thing," which " as the Scripture tells us, " the children of Israel were forbidden to touch." They will run about like the plague, and destroy everyone who lays his hands upon them. I have heard scholars talk of a man who told the king, that he had invented a way to torment people by putting them into a bull of brass [22] with fire under it: but the prince put the projector first into his own brazen bull, to make the experiment. This very much resembles the project of Mr. Wood; and the like of this may possibly be Mr. Wood's fate; that the brass he contrived to torment this kingdom with, may prove his own torment, and his destruction at last.

N.B. The author of this paper is informed by persons, who have made it their business to be exact in their observations on the true value of these halfpence,[23] that any person may expect to get a quart of twopenny ale for thirty-six of them.

I desire that all families may keep this paper carefully by them, to refresh their memories whenever they shall have farther notice of Mr. Wood's halfpence, or any other the like imposture.

22. bull of brass: a story from the *Letters of Phalaris*, very familiar to Swift because of the controversy they caused between Sir William Temple and Dr. Bentley, to which he had contributed his *Battle of the Books*.   23. true . . . halfpence: Swift's wild exaggeration here is partly due to the fear that the new coins could be easily counterfeited and the value thus further debased.

GULLIVER'S TRAVELS

Swift first speaks of being at work on his *Travels* in April, 1721; and he sounds as if he were then well under way. They were for the most part finished before he went to England in 1726, though it is possible that some additions were made to the Third Voyage at the suggestion of his friends in London, who seem to have provided him with some very recent examples of the kind of scientific experiments he was making fun of. The Four Voyages were published in two volumes before the end of the year, and were an immediate success. Swift may have set out to "vex the world," but he succeeded in amusing it. He had imitated the manner of the stories of the Discoverers, which were the best-sellers of the day. In the First Voyage to Lilliput there are many references to political figures and happenings which would be familiar to his first readers; but even here, though he likes to make fun of his old enemies, his attitude is not that of the party writer but of the moralist, whose business is to reveal the frailties and vices of human life as they are displayed among courtiers and politicians. In the Second and Fourth Voyages he allows himself more scope for dramatic irony by placing Gulliver as a pygmy among the giants and as a Yahoo among the Houyhnhnms (best pronounced "Whinnims"), where he is much at a disadvantage in trying to uphold the dignity of his race and to explain the glories of Western civilization. Some of the comments which Swift had permitted himself indeed were too much for his first publisher, who omitted and altered so greatly that Swift was careful to have the book printed under his own supervision in 1735 for the Dublin edition of his collected *Works*, with the full text as he intended it, adding the following letter from Captain Gulliver to his Cousin Sympson.

TRAVELS INTO SEVERAL REMOTE NATIONS OF THE WORLD

By Lemuel Gulliver, first a Surgeon, and then a Captain of several Ships

---

A LETTER FROM CAPTAIN GULLIVER TO HIS COUSIN SYMPSON [1]

I hope you will be ready to own publicly, whenever you shall be called to it, that by your great and frequent urgency you prevailed on me to publish a very loose and uncorrect account of my travels; with direction to hire some young gentlemen of either university to put them in order, and correct the style, as my cousin Dampier [2] did by my advice, in his book called *A Voyage Round the World*. But I do not remember I gave you power to consent, that anything should be omitted, and much less that anything should be inserted: therefore, as to the latter, I do here renounce everything of that kind; particularly a paragraph about her Majesty the late Queen Anne, of most pious and glorious memory; although I did reverence and esteem her more than any of human species. But you, or your interpolator, ought to have considered, that as it was not my inclination, so was it not decent to praise any animal of our composition before my master *Houyhnhnm:* and besides, the fact was altogether false; for to my knowledge, being in England during some part of her Majesty's reign, she did govern by a chief minister; nay, even by two successively; the first whereof was the Lord of Godolphin, and the second the Lord of Oxford; [3] so that you have made me *say the thing that was not.*[4] Likewise, in the account of the Academy of Projectors, and several passages of my discourse to my master *Houyhnhnm,* you have either omitted some material circumstances, or minced or changed them in such a manner, that I do hardly know my own work. When I formerly hinted to you something of this in a letter, you were pleased to answer that you were afraid of giving offense; that people in power were very watchful over the press, and apt not only to interpret, but to punish everything

GULLIVER'S TRAVELS. **Prefaces.   1. Letter . . . Sympson:** In spite of the date given, it was certainly written by Swift for the Dublin edition of 1735, in which he restored passages which had been omitted or modified in the first edition owing to the fears of the publisher. **2. Dampier:** Swift here draws attention to the famous account of the real voyages of this great explorer, William Dampier, which he had taken as a model for his own fiction.

3. Godolphin . . . Oxford: Lord Treasurer, i.e., first minister under Queen Anne until 1710, when replaced by Robert Harley, who was made Earl of Oxford.   **4. say . . . not:** a phrase coined by Gulliver's Houyhnhnm master to translate the word "lying," for which there was no term in their language.

which looked like an *innuendo* (as I think you called it). But pray, how could that which I spoke so many years ago, and at about five thousand leagues distance, in another reign, be applied to any of the *Yahoos,* who now are said to govern the herd,[5] especially, at a time when I little thought on or feared the unhappiness of living under them? Have not I the most reason to complain, when I see these very *Yahoos* carried by *Houyhnhnms* in a vehicle, as if these were brutes, and those the rational creatures? And indeed, to avoid so monstrous and destestable a sight, was one principal motive of my retirement hither.

Thus much I thought proper to tell you in relation to yourself, and to the trust I reposed in you.

I do in the next place complain of my own great want of judgment, in being prevailed upon by the entreaties and false reasonings of you and some others, very much against my own opinion, to suffer my travels to be published. Pray bring to your mind how often I desired you to consider, when you insisted on the motive of *public good;* that the *Yahoos* were a species of animals utterly incapable of amendment by precepts or examples: and so it hath proved; for instead of seeing a full stop put to all abuses and corruptions, at least in this little island, as I had reason to expect: behold, after above six months' warning, I cannot learn that my book hath produced one single effect according to my intentions: I desired you would let me know by a letter, when party and faction were extinguished; judges learned and upright; pleaders honest and modest, with some tincture of common sense; and Smithfield[6] blazing with pyramids of lawbooks; the young nobility's education entirely changed; the physicians banished; the female *Yahoos* abounding in virtue, honor, truth, and good sense; courts and levees of great ministers thoroughly weeded and swept; wit, merit, and learning rewarded; all disgracers of the press in prose and verse, condemned to eat nothing but their own cotton,[7] and quench their thirst with their own ink. These, and a thousand other reformations, I firmly counted upon by your encouragement; as indeed they were plainly deducible from the precepts delivered in my book. And, it must be owned, that seven months[8] were a sufficient time to correct every vice and folly to which *Yahoos* are subject; if their natures had been capable of the least disposition to virtue or wisdom: yet so far have you been from answering my expectation in any of your letters; that on the contrary, you are loading our carrier every week with libels, and keys, and reflections, and memoirs, and second parts,[9] wherein I see myself accused of reflecting upon great statesfolk; of degrading human nature (for so they have still the confidence to style it), and of abusing the female sex. I find likewise that the writers of those bundles are not agreed among themselves; for some of them will not allow me to be author of my own travels; and others make me author of books to which I am wholly a stranger.

I find likewise, that your printer hath been so careless as to confound the times, and mistake the dates of my several voyages and returns; neither assigning the true year, or the true month, or day of the month: and I hear the original manuscript is all destroyed, since the publication of my book. Neither have I any copy left: however, I have sent you some corrections, which you may insert, if ever there should be a second edition: and yet I cannot stand to them, but shall leave that matter to my judicious and candid readers, to adjust it as they please.

I hear some of our sea *Yahoos* find fault with my sea language, as not proper in many parts, nor now in use. I cannot help it. In my first voyages, while I was young, I was instructed by the oldest mariners,[10] and learned to speak as they did. But I have since found that the sea *Yahoos* are apt, like the land ones, to become newfangled in their words; which the latter change every year; insomuch, as I remember upon each return to my own country, their old dialect was so altered, that I could hardly understand the new. And I observe, when any *Yahoo* comes from London out of curiosity to visit me at my own house, we neither of us are able to deliver our conceptions in a manner intelligible to the other.

If the censure of *Yahoos* could any way affect me, I should have great reason to complain, that some of them are so bold as to think my book of travels a mere fiction out of my own brain; and have gone so far as to drop hints, that the *Houyhnhnms* and *Yahoos* have no more existence than the inhabitants of Utopia.[11]

---

5. *Yahoos* . . . herd: the court and government of George I. 6. Smithfield: a market place outside the walls of the city of London, where persons and books condemned for heresy used to be burned. 7. cotton: rag paper. 8. seven months: actually only five months before the supposed date of the letter.

9. libels . . . parts: The book was so popular that rubbishy *Keys* and imitations were quickly printed in the hope of an easy sale. 10. oldest mariners: Swift had borrowed some of the sea terms from Sturmy's *Compleat Mariner,* 1669; they were thus a little old-fashioned. 11. Utopia: Sir Thomas More's ideal commonwealth.

Indeed I must confess, that as to the people of *Lilliput, Brobdingrag* [12] (for so the word should have been spelt, and not erroneously *Brobdingnag*), and *Laputa;* I have never yet heard of any *Yahoo* so presumptuous as to dispute their being, or the facts I have related concerning them; because the truth immediately strikes every reader with conviction. And is there less probability in my account of the *Houyhnhnms* or *Yahoos,* when it is manifest as to the latter, there are so many thousands even in this city, who only differ from their brother brutes in *Houyhnhnm-land,* because they use a sort of a jabber, and do not go naked? I wrote for their amendment, and not their approbation. The united praise of the whole race would be of less consequence to me, than the neighing of those two degenerate *Houyhnhnms* I keep in my stable; because, from these, degenerate as they are, I still improve in some virtues, without any mixture of vice.

Do these miserable animals presume to think that I am so far degenerated as to defend my veracity? *Yahoo* as I am, it is well known through all *Houyhnhnm-land,* that by the instructions and example of my illustrious master, I was able in the compass of two years (although I confess with the utmost difficulty) to remove that infernal habit of lying, shuffling, deceiving, and equivocating, so deeply rooted in the very souls of all my species; especially the Europeans.

I have other complaints to make upon this vexatious occasion; but I forbear troubling myself or you any further. I must freely confess, that since my last return, some corruptions of my *Yahoo* nature have revived in me by conversing with a few of your species, and particularly those of my own family, by an unavoidable necessity; else I should never have attempted so absurd a project as that of reforming the *Yahoo* race in this kingdom; but I have now done with all such visionary schemes for ever.

April 2, 1727

THE PUBLISHER TO THE READER

The author of these Travels, Mr. Lemuel Gulliver, is my ancient and intimate friend; there is likewise some relation between us by the mother's side. About three years ago, Mr. Gulliver growing weary of the concourse of curious people coming to him at his house in Redriff, made a small purchase of land, with a convenient house, near Newark, in Nottinghamshire, his native country; where he now lives retired, yet in good esteem among his neighbors.

Although Mr. Gulliver was born in Nottinghamshire, where his father dwelt, yet I have heard him say his family came from Oxfordshire; to confirm which, I have observed in the churchyard at Banbury,[13] in that county, several tombs and monuments of the Gullivers.

Before he quitted Redriff,[14] he left the custody of the following papers in my hands, with the liberty to dispose of them as I should think fit. I have carefully perused them three times: the style is very plain and simple; and the only fault I find is, that the author, after the manner of travelers, is a little too circumstantial. There is an air of truth apparent through the whole; and indeed the author was so distinguished for his veracity, that it became a sort of proverb among his neighbors at Redriff, when any one affirmed a thing, to say it was as true as if Mr. Gulliver had spoke it.

By the advice of several worthy persons, to whom, with the author's permission, I communicated these papers, I now venture to send them into the world, hoping they may be at least, for some time, a better entertainment to our young noblemen, than the common scribbles of politics and party.

This volume would have been at least twice as large, if I had not made bold to strike out innumerable passages relating to the winds and tides, as well as to the variations and bearings in the several voyages; together with the minute descriptions of the management of the ship in storms, in the style of sailors: likewise the account of longitudes and latitudes; wherein I have reason to apprehend that Mr. Gulliver may be a little dissatisfied: but I was resolved to fit the work as much as possible to the general capacity of readers. However, if my own ignorance in sea affairs shall have led me to commit some mistakes, I alone am answerable for them: and if any traveler hath a curiosity to see the whole work at large, as it came from the hand of the author, I will be ready to gratify him.

As for any further particulars relating to the author, the reader will receive satisfaction from the first pages of the book.

RICHARD SYMPSON [15]

12. *Brobdingrag:* The correction of course is a trick to make the name sound more real.

13. **Banbury:** market town in Oxfordshire, which Swift must have often ridden through on his way from Ireland to London; the family name "Gulliver" is still known there.   14. **Redriff:** or Rotherhithe, a seafaring place near London on the south bank of the Thames.   15. **Richard Sympson:** Gulliver's imaginary cousin and editor, possibly suggested by William Sympson, from *A New Voyage to the East Indies,* 1715.

PART I
A Voyage to Lilliput

CHAPTER I

The Author gives some account of himself and family;
his first inducements to travel. He is shipwrecked,
and swims for his life, gets safe on shore in the coun-
try of Lilliput,[1] *is made a prisoner, and carried up*
the country.

My father had a small estate in Nottinghamshire; I was the third of five sons. He sent me to
Emmanuel College in Cambridge, at fourteen years [2]
old, where I resided three years, and applied myself
close to my studies; but the charge of maintaining
me (although I had a very scanty allowance) being
too great for a narrow fortune, I was bound apprentice to Mr. James Bates, an eminent surgeon
in London, with whom I continued four years; and
my father now and then sending me small sums
of money, I laid them out in learning navigation,
and other parts of the mathematics, useful to those
who intend to travel, as I always believed it would
be some time or other my fortune to do. When I
left Mr. Bates, I went down to my father; where,
by the assistance of him and my uncle John, and
some other relations, I got forty pounds, and a
promise of thirty pounds a year to maintain me at
Leyden;[3] there I studied physic two years and
seven months, knowing it would be useful in long
voyages.

Soon after my return from Leyden, I was recommended by my good master, Mr. Bates, to be surgeon to the *Swallow,* Captain Abraham Pannell,
Commander; with whom I continued three years
and a half, making a voyage or two into the Levant,[4] and some other parts. When I came back, I
resolved to settle in London, to which Mr. Bates,
my master, encouraged me, and by him I was recommended to several patients. I took part of a
small house in the Old Jury;[5] and being advised
to alter my condition, I married Mrs. Mary [6] Burton, second daughter to Mr. Edmund Burton, ho-

sier, in Newgate Street, with whom I received four
hundred pounds for a portion.

But, my good master Bates dying in two years
after, and I having few friends, my business began to fail; for my conscience would not suffer me
to imitate the bad practice of too many among my
brethren. Having therefore consulted with my wife,
and some of my acquaintance, I determined to go
again to sea. I was surgeon successively in two
ships, and made several voyages, for six years, to
the East and West Indies, by which I got some
addition to my fortune. My hours of leisure I spent
in reading the best authors, ancient and modern,
being always provided with a good number of
books; and when I was ashore in observing the
manners and dispositions of the people, as well as
learning their language, wherein I had a great facility by the strength of my memory.

The last of these voyages not proving very fortunate, I grew weary of the sea, and intended to
stay at home with my wife and family. I removed
from the Old Jury to Fetter Lane, and from thence
to Wapping, hoping to get business among the
sailors; but it would not turn to account. After
three years' expectation that things would mend, I
accepted an advantageous offer from Captain William Prichard, master of the *Antelope,* who was
making a voyage to the South Sea. We set sail
from Bristol, May 4, 1699, and our voyage at first
was very prosperous.

It would not be proper, for some reasons, to
trouble the reader with the particulars of our adventures in those seas: let it suffice to inform him,
that in our passage from thence to the East Indies,
we were driven by a violent storm to the northwest of Van Diemen's Land.[7] By an observation,
we found ourselves in the latitude of thirty degrees
two minutes south. Twelve of our crew were dead
by immoderate labor, and ill food; the rest were in a
very weak condition. On the fifth of November,
which was the beginning of summer in those parts,
the weather being very hazy, the seamen spied a
rock, within half a cable's length of the ship; but
the wind was so strong, that we were driven directly upon it, and immediately split. Six of the crew,
of whom I was one, having let down the boat into
the sea, made a shift to get clear of the ship, and
the rock. We rowed, by my computation, about
three leagues, till we were able to work no longer,
being already spent with labor while we were in

A Voyage to Lilliput.   1. Lilliput: Swift successfully invented
suitable-sounding names for the countries visited, and it is not
very profitable to attempt to give their derivations.   2. at . . .
years: Swift himself had entered Trinity College, Dublin, at
fourteen.   3. Leyden: the center of medical studies then in
Holland.   4. Levant: eastern part of Mediterranean.   5. Old
Jury: or Jewry, on the north of Cheapside, which had been the
medieval Jewish quarter of the city of London.   6. Mrs. Mary:
In Swift's day, "Miss" was used only of young girls, "Mrs." of

all adult women.   7. Van Diemen's Land: earlier name for Tas-
mania, then thought to be a part of the mainland of Australia.

the ship. We therefore trusted ourselves to the mercy of the waves, and in about half an hour the boat was overset by a sudden flurry from the north. What became of my companions in the boat, as well as of those who escaped on the rock, or were left in the vessel, I cannot tell; but conclude they were all lost.

For my own part, I swam as fortune directed me, and was pushed forward by wind and tide. I often let my legs drop, and could feel no bottom: but when I was almost gone, and able to struggle no longer, I found myself within my depth; and by this time the storm was much abated. The declivity was so small, that I walked near a mile before I got to the shore, which I conjectured was about eight o'clock in the evening. I then advanced forward near half a mile, but could not discover any sign of houses or inhabitants; at least I was in so weak a condition, that I did not observe them. I was extremely tired, and with that, and the heat of the weather, and about half a pint of brandy that I drank as I left the ship, I found myself much inclined to sleep. I lay down on the grass, which was very short and soft, where I slept sounder than ever I remember to have done in my life, and, as I reckoned, above nine hours; for when I awaked, it was just daylight. I attempted to rise, but was not able to stir: for as I happened to lie on my back, I found my arms and legs were strongly fastened on each side to the ground; and my hair, which was long and thick, tied down in the same manner. I likewise felt several slender ligatures across my body, from my armpits to my thighs. I could only look upwards; the sun began to grow hot, and the light offended my eyes. I heard a confused noise about me, but in the posture I lay, could see nothing except the sky.

In a little time I felt something alive moving on my left leg, which advancing gently forward over my breast, came almost up to my chin; when bending my eyes downwards as much as I could, I perceived it to be a human creature not six inches high,[8] with a bow and arrow in his hands, and a quiver at his back. In the meantime, I felt at least forty more of the same kind (as I conjectured) following the first. I was in the utmost astonishment, and roared so loud, that they all ran back in a fright; and some of them, as I was afterwards told, were hurt with the falls they got by leaping from my sides upon the ground. However, they soon re-

turned, and one of them, who ventured so far as to get a full sight of my face, lifting up his hands and eyes by way of admiration, cried out in a shrill, but distinct voice, *Hekinah degul:* the others repeated the same words several times, but then I knew not what they meant. I lay all this while, as the reader may believe, in great uneasiness: at length, struggling to get loose, I had the fortune to break the strings, and wrench out the pegs that fastened my left arm to the ground; for, by lifting it up to my face, I discovered the methods they had taken to bind me, and at the same time with a violent pull, which gave me excessive pain, I a little loosened the strings that tied down my hair on the left side, so that I was just able to turn my head about two inches. But the creatures ran off a second time, before I could seize them; whereupon there was a great shout in a very shrill accent, and after it ceased, I heard one of them cry aloud, *Tolgo phonac;* when in an instant I felt above an hundred arrows discharged on my left hand, which pricked me like so many needles; and besides, they shot another flight into the air, as we do bombs in Europe, whereof many, I suppose, fell on my body (though I felt them not), and some on my face, which I immediately covered with my left hand. When this shower of arrows was over, I fell a groaning with grief and pain, and then striving again to get loose, they discharged another volley larger than the first, and some of them attempted with spears to stick me in the sides; but, by good luck, I had on me a buff jerkin,[9] which they could not pierce. I thought it the most prudent method to lie still, and my design was to continue so till night, when, my left hand being already loose, I could easily free myself: and as for the inhabitants, I had reason to believe I might be a match for the greatest armies they could bring against me, if they were all of the same size with him that I saw. But fortune disposed otherwise of me.

When the people observed I was quiet, they discharged no more arrows; but, by the noise increasing, I knew their numbers were greater; and about four yards from me, over against my right ear, I heard a knocking for above an hour, like that of people at work; when turning my head that way, as well as the pegs and strings would permit me, I saw a stage erected, about a foot and a half from the ground, capable of holding four of the inhabitants, with two or three ladders to mount it: from whence one of them, who seemed to be a person of

---

8. **six . . . high:** In Lilliput Swift reduces everything roughly to a twelfth, and increases it by the same amount in Brobdingnag.

9. **buff jerkin:** heavy hide waistcoat.

quality, made me a long speech, whereof I understood not one syllable. But I should have mentioned, that before the principal person began his oration, he cried out three times, *Langro dehul san:* (these words and the former were afterwards repeated and explained to me). Whereupon immediately about fifty of the inhabitants came and cut the strings that fastened the left side of my head, which gave me the liberty of turning it to the right, and of observing the person and gesture of him who was to speak. He appeared to be of a middle age, and taller than any of the other three who attended him, whereof one was a page who held up his train, and seemed to be somewhat longer than my middle finger; the other two stood one on each side to support him. He acted every part of an orator, and I could observe many periods of threatenings, and others of promises, pity, and kindness.

I answered in a few words, but in the most submissive manner, lifting up my left hand, and both my eyes to the sun, as calling him for a witness; and being almost famished with hunger, having not eaten a morsel for some hours before I left the ship. I found the demands of nature so strong upon me, that I could not forbear showing my impatience (perhaps against the strict rules of decency) by putting my finger frequently on my mouth, to signify that I wanted food. The *Hurgo* (for so they call a great lord, as I afterwards learnt) understood me very well. He descended from the stage, and commanded that several ladders should be applied to my sides, on which above an hundred of the inhabitants mounted and walked towards my mouth, laden with baskets full of meat, which had been provided and sent thither by the King's orders, upon the first intelligence he received of me. I observed there was the flesh of several animals, but could not distinguish them by the taste. There were shoulders, legs, and loins, shaped like those of mutton, and very well dressed, but smaller than the wings of a lark. I eat them by two or three at a mouthful, and took three loaves at a time, about the bigness of musket bullets. They supplied me as fast as they could, showing a thousand marks of wonder and astonishment at my bulk and appetite.

I then made another sign that I wanted drink. They found by my eating, that a small quantity would not suffice me; and being a most ingenious people, they slung up with great dexterity one of their largest hogsheads, then rolled it towards my hand, and beat out the top; I drank it off at a draught, which I might well do, for it hardly held half a pint, and tasted like a small wine of Burgundy, but much more delicious. They brought me a second hogshead, which I drank in the same manner, and made signs for more, but they had none to give me. When I had performed these wonders, they shouted for joy, and danced upon my breast, repeating several times as they did at first, *Hekinah degul.*[10] They made me a sign that I should throw down the two hogsheads, but first warned the people below to stand out of the way, crying aloud, *Borach mivola,* and when they saw the vessels in the air, there was an universal shout of *Hekinah degul.* I confess I was often tempted, while they were passing backwards and forwards on my body, to seize forty or fifty of the first that came in my reach, and dash them against the ground. But the remembrance of what I had felt, which probably might not be the worst they could do, and the promise of honor I made them, for so I interpreted my submissive behavior, soon drove out those imaginations. Besides, I now considered myself as bound by the laws of hospitality to a people who had treated me with so much expense and magnificence. However, in my thoughts, I could not sufficiently wonder at the intrepidity of these diminutive mortals, who durst venture to mount and walk on my body, while one of my hands was at liberty, without trembling at the very sight of so prodigious a creature as I must appear to them.

After some time, when they observed that I made no more demands for meat, there appeared before me a person of high rank from his Imperial Majesty. His Excellency, having mounted on the small of my right leg, advanced forwards up to my face, with about a dozen of his retinue. And producing his credentials under the Signet Royal, which he applied close to my eyes, spoke about ten minutes, without any signs of anger, but with a kind of determinate resolution; often pointing forwards, which, as I afterwards found, was towards the capital city, about half a mile distant, whither it was agreed by his Majesty in council that I must be conveyed. I answered in few words, but to no purpose, and made a sign with my hand that was loose, putting it to the other (but over his Excellency's head for fear of hurting him or his train) and then to my own head and body, to signify that

10. *Hekinah degul:* possibly imitating Rabelais' method of coining names, or sheer inventions anticipating James Joyce.

I desired my liberty. It appeared that he understood me well enough, for he shook his head by way of disapprobation, and held his hand in a posture to show that I must be carried as a prisoner. However, he made other signs to let me understand that I should have meat and drink enough, and very good treatment. Whereupon I once more thought of attempting to break my bonds; but again, when I felt the smart of their arrows, upon my face and hands, which were all in blisters, and many of the darts still sticking in them, and observing likewise that the number of my enemies increased, I gave tokens to let them know that they might do with me what they pleased. Upon this, the *Hurgo* and his train withdrew, with much civility and cheerful countenances.

Soon after I heard a general shout, with frequent repetitions of the words, *Peplom selan,* and I felt great numbers of people on my left side relaxing the cords to such a degree, that I was able to turn upon my right, and to ease myself with making water; which I very plentifully did, to the great astonishment of the people, who conjecturing by my motions what I was going to do, immediately opened to the right and left on that side, to avoid the torrent which fell with such noise and violence from me. But before this, they had daubed my face and both my hands with a sort of ointment very pleasant to the smell, which in a few minutes removed all the smart of their arrows. These circumstances, added to the refreshment I had received by their victuals and drink, which were very nourishing, disposed me to sleep. I slept about eight hours, as I was afterwards assured; and it was no wonder, for the physicians, by the Emperor's order, had mingled a sleeping potion in the hogsheads of wine.

It seems that upon the first moment I was discovered sleeping on the ground after my landing, the Emperor had early notice of it by an express; and determined in council that I should be tied in the manner I have related (which was done in the night while I slept), that plenty of meat and drink should be sent me, and a machine prepared to carry me to the capital city.

This resolution perhaps may appear very bold and dangerous, and I am confident would not be imitated by any prince in Europe on the like occasion; however, in my opinion, it was extremely prudent, as well as generous: for supposing these people had endeavored to kill me with their spears and arrows while I was asleep, I should certainly have awaked with the first sense of smart, which might so far have roused my rage and strength, as to enable me to break the strings wherewith I was tied; after which, as they were not able to make resistance, so they could expect no mercy.

These people are most excellent mathematicians, and arrived to a great perfection in mechanics, by the countenance and encouragement of the Emperor, who is a renowned patron of learning. This prince hath several machines fixed on wheels, for the carriage of trees and other great weights. He often builds his largest men-of-war, whereof some are nine foot long, in the woods where the timber grows, and has them carried on these engines three or four hundred yards to the sea. Five hundred carpenters and engineers were immediately set at work to prepare the greatest engine they had. It was a frame of wood raised three inches from the ground, about seven foot long and four wide, moving upon twenty-two wheels. The shout I heard was upon the arrival of this engine, which it seems set out in four hours after my landing. It was brought parallel to me as I lay. But the principal difficulty was to raise and place me in this vehicle. Eighty poles, each of one foot high, were erected for this purpose, and very strong cords of the bigness of pack thread were fastened by hooks to many bandages, which the workmen had girt round my neck, my hands, my body, and my legs. Nine hundred of the strongest men were employed to draw up these cords by many pulleys fastened on the poles, and thus, in less than three hours, I was raised and slung into the engine, and there tied fast. All this I was told, for, while the whole operation was performing, I lay in a profound sleep, by the force of that soporiferous medicine infused into my liquor. Fifteen hundred of the Emperor's largest horses, each about four inches and a half high, were employed to draw me towards the metropolis, which, as I said, was half a mile distant.

About four hours after we began our journey, I awaked by a very ridiculous accident; for the carriage being stopped a while to adjust something that was out of order, two or three of the young natives had the curiosity to see how I looked when I was asleep; they climbed up into the engine, and advancing very softly to my face, one of them, an officer in the guards, put the sharp end of his half-pike a good way up into my left nostril, which tickled my nose like a straw, and made me sneeze violently: whereupon they stole off unperceived, and it was three weeks before I knew the cause of my awaking so suddenly. We made a long march the remaining part of the day, and rested at night with five hundred guards on each side of me, half with torches, and half with bows and arrows, ready to shoot me if I should offer to stir. The next morning at sunrise we continued our march, and arrived within two hundred yards of the city gates about noon. The Emperor, and all his court, came out to meet us; but his great officers would by no means suffer his Majesty to endanger his person by mounting on my body.

At the place where the carriage stopped, there stood an ancient temple,[11] esteemed to be the largest in the whole kingdom; which, having been polluted some years before by an unnatural murder, was, according to the zeal of those people, looked upon as profane, and therefore had been applied to common uses, and all the ornaments and furniture carried away. In this edifice it was determined I should lodge. The great gate fronting to the north was about four foot high, and almost two foot wide, through which I could easily creep. On each side of the gate was a small window not above six inches from the ground: into that on the left side, the King's smiths conveyed fourscore and eleven chains, like those that hang to a lady's watch in Europe, and almost as large, which were locked to my left leg with six and thirty padlocks.[12] Over against this temple, on the other side of the great highway, at twenty foot distance, there was a turret at least five foot high. Here the Emperor ascended, with many principal lords of his court, to have an opportunity of viewing me, as I was told, for I could not see them. It was reckoned that above an hundred thousand inhabitants came out of the town upon the same errand; and, in spite of my guards, I believe there could not be fewer than ten thousand at several times, who mounted my body by the help of ladders. But a proclamation was soon issued to forbid it upon pain of death. When the workmen found it was impossible for me to break loose, they cut all the strings that bound me; whereupon I rose up, with as melancholy a disposition as ever I had in my life. But the noise and astonishment of the people at seeing me rise and walk, are not to be expressed. The chains that held my left leg were about two

yards long, and gave me not only the liberty of walking backwards and forwards in a semicircle; but, being fixed within four inches of the gate, allowed me to creep in, and lie at my full length in the temple.

CHAPTER 2

The Emperor of Lilliput, attended by several of the nobility, comes to see the Author in his confinement. The Emperor's person and habit described. Learned men appointed to teach the Author their language. He gains favor by his mild disposition. His pockets are searched, and his sword and pistols taken from him.

When I found myself on my feet, I looked about me, and must confess I never beheld a more entertaining prospect. The country round appeared like a continued garden, and the enclosed fields, which were generally forty foot square, resembled so many beds of flowers. These fields were intermingled with woods of half a stang,[13] and the tallest trees, as I could judge, appeared to be seven foot high. I viewed the town on my left hand, which looked like the painted scene of a city in a theater.

I had been for some hours extremely pressed by the necessities of nature; which was no wonder, it being almost two days since I had last disburthened myself. I was under great difficulties between urgency and shame. The best expedient I could think on, was to creep into my house, which I accordingly did; and shutting the gate after me, I went as far as the length of my chain would suffer, and discharged my body of that uneasy load. But this was the only time I was ever guilty of so uncleanly an action; for which I cannot but hope the candid reader will give some allowance, after he hath maturely and impartially considered my case, and the distress I was in. From this time my constant practice was, as soon as I rose, to perform that business in open air, at the full extent of my chain, and due care was taken every morning before company came, that the offensive matter should be carried off in wheelbarrows, by two servants appointed for that purpose. I would not have dwelt so long upon a circumstance, that perhaps at first sight may appear not very momentous, if I had not thought it necessary to justify my character in point of cleanliness to the world;[14]

11. ancient temple: The description suggests Westminster Hall, where Charles I had been tried.   12. fourscore . . . padlocks: a curious echo of the numbers in *A Tale of a Tub* — fourscore and eleven pamphlets for six and thirty factions.

13. a stang: obsolete form of rood, about a quarter of an acre.
14. justify . . . world: This is, I believe, Swift's best reply to those

which I am told some of my maligners have been pleased, upon this and other occasions, to call in question.

When this adventure was at an end, I came back out of my house, having occasion for fresh air. The Emperor was already descended from the tower, and advancing on horseback towards me, which had like to have cost him dear; for the beast, though very well trained, yet wholly unused to such a sight, which appeared as if a mountain moved before him, reared up on his hinder feet: but that prince, who is an excellent horseman, kept his seat, until his attendants ran in, and held the bridle, while his Majesty had time to dismount. When he alighted, he surveyed me round with great admiration, but kept beyond the length of my chains. He ordered his cooks and butlers, who were already prepared, to give me victuals and drink, which they pushed forward in a sort of vehicles upon wheels, until I could reach them. I took these vehicles, and soon emptied them all; twenty of them were filled with meat, and ten with liquor; each of the former afforded me two or three good mouthfuls, and I emptied the liquor of ten vessels, which was contained in earthen vials, into one vehicle, drinking it off at a draught; and so I did with the rest.

The Empress, and young Princes of the blood of both sexes, attended by many ladies, sat at some distance in their chairs; but upon the accident that happened to the Emperor's horse, they alighted, and came near his person, which I am now going to describe. He is taller by almost the breadth of my nail, than any of his court; which alone is enough to strike an awe into the beholders. His features are strong and masculine, with an Austrian lip [15] and arched nose, his complexion olive, his countenance erect, his body and limbs well proportioned, all his motions graceful, and his deportment majestic. He was then past his prime, being twenty-eight years and three-quarters old, of which he had reigned about seven, in great felicity, and generally victorious. For the better convenience of beholding him, I lay on my side, so that my face was parallel to his, and he stood but three yards off: however, I have had him since many times in my

modern critics who find evidence of abnormality in what Aldous Huxley called "the almost insane violence of his 'hatred of bowels.' " It is odd that some squeamish editors have actually omitted this paragraph. Swift was unusually sensitive to personal cleanliness; and he never hesitated to describe in revolting detail the indecencies of contemporary manners, which disgusted him. **15. Austrian lip:** A thick lower lip was characteristic of the Hapsburgs. The Emperor's appearance is very unlike that of George I.

hand, and therefore cannot be deceived in the description. His dress was very plain and simple, the fashion of it between the Asiatic and the European: but he had on his head a light helmet of gold, adorned with jewels, and a plume on the crest. He held his sword drawn in his hand, to defend himself, if I should happen to break loose; it was almost three inches long; the hilt and scabbard were gold enriched with diamonds. His voice was shrill, but very clear and articulate, and I could distinctly hear it when I stood up. The ladies and courtiers were all most magnificently clad, so that the spot they stood upon seemed to resemble a petticoat spread on the ground, embroidered with figures of gold and silver. His Imperial Majesty spoke often to me, and I returned answers, but neither of us could understand a syllable. There were several of his priests and lawyers present (as I conjectured by their habits) who were commanded to address themselves to me, and I spoke to them in as many languages as I had the least smattering of, which were High and Low Dutch,[16] Latin, French, Spanish, Italian, and Lingua Franca;[17] but all to no purpose.

After about two hours the court retired, and I was left with a strong guard, to prevent the impertinence, and probably the malice, of the rabble, who were very impatient to crowd about me as near as they durst, and some of them had the impudence to shoot their arrows at me as I sat on the ground by the door of my house, whereof one very narrowly missed my left eye. But the colonel ordered six of the ringleaders to be seized, and thought no punishment so proper as to deliver them bound into my hands, which some of his soldiers accordingly did, pushing them forwards with the butt ends of their pikes into my reach; I took them all in my right hand, put five of them into my coat pocket, and as to the sixth, I made a countenance as if I would eat him alive. The poor man squalled terribly, and the colonel and his officers were in much pain, especially when they saw me take out my penknife: but I soon put them out of fear: for, looking mildly, and immediately cutting the strings he was bound with, I set him gently on the ground, and away he ran. I treated the rest in the same manner, taking them one by one out of my pocket, and I observed both the soldiers and people were highly obliged at this mark of my clemency, which was

16. High . . . Dutch: i.e., German and Dutch.   **17. Lingua Franca:** a pidgin French or Italian, used by traders in the Mediterranean.

represented very much to my advantage at court.

Towards night I got with some difficulty into my house, where I lay on the ground, and continued to do so about a fortnight; during which time the Emperor gave orders to have a bed prepared for me. Six hundred beds of the common measure were brought in carriages, and worked up in my house; an hundred and fifty of their beds sewn together made up the breadth and length, and these were four double, which, however, kept me but very indifferently from the hardness of the floor, that was of smooth stone. By the same computation they provided me with sheets, blankets, and coverlets, tolerable enough for one who had been so long inured to hardships as I.

As the news of my arrival spread through the kingdom, it brought prodigious numbers of rich, idle, and curious people to see me; so that the villages were almost emptied, and great neglect of tillage and household affairs must have ensued, if his Imperial Majesty had not provided, by several proclamations and orders of state, against this inconveniency. He directed that those who had already beheld me should return home, and not presume to come within fifty yards of my house without license from court; whereby the secretaries of state got considerable fees.

In the meantime, the Emperor held frequent councils to debate what course should be taken with me; and I was afterwards assured by a particular friend, a person of great quality, who was as much in the secret as any, that the court was under many difficulties concerning me. They apprehended my breaking loose, that my diet would be very expensive, and might cause a famine. Sometimes they determined to starve me, or at least to shoot me in the face and hands with poisoned arrows, which would soon dispatch me; but again they considered, that the stench of so large a carcass might produce a plague in the metropolis, and probably spread through the whole kingdom.

In the midst of these consultations, several officers of the army went to the door of the great council chamber; and two of them being admitted, gave an account of my behavior to the six criminals above mentioned, which made so favorable an impression in the breast of his Majesty and the whole board, in my behalf, that an imperial commission was issued out, obliging all the villages nine hundred yards round the city, to deliver in every morning six beeves, forty sheep, and other victuals for my sustenance; together with a pro-portionable quantity of bread, and wine, and other liquors; for the due payment of which his Majesty gave assignments upon his treasury. For this prince lives chiefly upon his own demesnes, seldom, except upon great occasions, raising any subsidies upon his subjects, who are bound to attend him in his wars at their own expense. An establishment was also made of six hundred persons to be my domestics, who had board wages allowed for their maintenance, and tents built for them very conveniently on each side of my door. It was likewise ordered, that three hundred tailors should make me a suit of clothes after the fashion of the country: that six of his Majesty's greatest scholars should be employed to instruct me in their language: and, lastly, that the Emperor's horses, and those of the nobility, and troops of guards, should be exercised in my sight, to accustom themselves to me.

All these orders were duly put in execution, and in about three weeks I made a great progress in learning their language; during which time, the Emperor frequently honored me with his visits, and was pleased to assist my masters in teaching me. We began already to converse together in some sort; and the first words I learnt were to express my desire that he would please give me my liberty, which I every day repeated on my knees. His answer, as I could apprehend, was, that this must be a work of time, not to be thought on without the advice of his council, and that first I must *Lumos kelmin pesso desmar lon Emposo;* that is, swear a peace with him and his kingdom. However, that I should be used with all kindness; and he advised me to acquire, by my patience and discreet behavior, the good opinion of himself and his subjects. He desired I would not take it ill, if he gave orders to certain proper officers to search me; for probably I might carry about me several weapons, which must needs be dangerous things, if they answered the bulk of so prodigious a person. I said, his Majesty should be satisfied, for I was ready to strip myself, and turn up my pockets before him. This I delivered part in words, and part in signs. He replied, that by the laws of the kingdom I must be searched by two of his officers; that he knew this could not be done without my consent and assistance; that he had so good an opinion of my generosity and justice, as to trust their persons in my hands: that whatever they took from me should be returned when I left the country, or paid for at the rate which I would set upon them. I took up the two officers in my hands, put them first into my coat pockets, and then into every other pocket about me, except my two fobs, and another secret pocket which I had no mind should be searched, wherein I had some little necessaries of no consequence to any but myself. In one of my fobs there was a silver watch, and in the other a small quantity of gold in a purse. These gentlemen, having pen, ink, and paper about them, made an exact inventory of everything they saw; and when they had done, desired I would set them down, that they might deliver it to the Emperor. This inventory I afterwards translated into English, and is word for word as follows:

Imprimis, In the right coat pocket of the Great Man-Mountain (for so I interpret the words *Quinbus Flestrin*), after the strictest search, we found only one great piece of coarse cloth, large enough to be a footcloth for your Majesty's chief room of state. In the left pocket we saw a huge silver chest, with a cover of the same metal, which we, the searchers, were not able to lift. We desired it should be opened, and one of us stepping into it, found himself up to the midleg in a sort of dust, some part whereof flying up to our faces, set us both a sneezing for several times together. In his right waistcoat pocket we found a prodigious bundle of white thin substances, folded one over another, about the bigness of three men, tied with a strong cable, and marked with black figures; which we humbly conceive to be writings, every letter almost half as large as the palm of our hands. In the left there was a sort of engine, from the back of which were extended twenty long poles, resembling the pallisados before your Majesty's court; wherewith we conjecture the Man-Mountain combs his head; for we did not always trouble him with questions, because we found it a great difficulty to make him understand us. In the large pocket on the right side of his middle cover (so I translate the word *ranfu-lo,* by which they meant my breeches), we saw a hollow pillar of iron, about the length of a man, fastened to a strong piece of timber, larger than the pillar; and upon one side of the pillar were huge pieces of iron sticking out, cut into strange figures, which we know not what to make of. In the left pocket, another engine of the same kind. In the smaller pocket, on the right side, were several round flat pieces of white and red metal, of different bulk; some of the white, which seemed to be silver, were so large and heavy, that my comrade and I could hardly lift them. In the left pocket were two black pillars irregularly shaped: we could not, without difficulty, reach the top of them as we stood at the bottom of his pocket. One of them was covered,

and seemed all of a piece; but at the upper end of the other, there appeared a white round substance, about twice the bigness of our heads. Within each of these was enclosed a prodigious plate of steel; which, by our orders, we obliged him to show us, because we apprehended they might be dangerous engines. He took them out of their cases, and told us, that in his own country his practice was to shave his beard with one of these, and to cut his meat with the other.

There were two pockets which we could not enter: these he called his fobs; they were two large slits cut into the top of his middle cover, but squeezed close by the pressure of his belly. Out of the right fob hung a great silver chain, with a wonderful kind of engine at the bottom. We directed him to draw out whatever was at the end of that chain; which appeared to be a globe,[18] half silver, and half of some transparent metal; for, on the transparent side, we saw certain strange figures circularly drawn, and thought we could touch them, until we found our fingers stopped with that lucid substance. He put this engine to our ears, which made an incessant noise like that of a water mill. And we conjecture it is either some unknown animal, or the god that he worships; but we are more inclined to the latter opinion, because he assured us (if we understood him right, for he expressed himself very imperfectly), that he seldom did anything without consulting it. He called it his oracle, and said it pointed out the time for every action of his life. From the left fob he took out a net almost large enough for a fisherman, but contrived to open and shut like a purse, and served him for the same use: we found therein several massy pieces of yellow metal, which, if they be of real gold, must be of immense value.

Having thus, in obedience to your majesty's commands, diligently searched all his pockets, we observed a girdle about his waist made of the hide of some prodigious animal; from which, on the left side, hung a sword of the length of five men; and on the right, a bag or pouch divided into two cells, each cell capable of holding three of your Majesty's subjects. In one of these cells were several globes or balls of a most ponderous metal, about the bigness of our heads, and requiring a strong hand to lift them: the other cell contained a heap of certain black grains, but of no great bulk or weight, for we could hold above fifty of them in the palms of our hands.

This is an exact inventory[19] of what we found about the body of the Man-Mountain, who used us

18. a globe: the high convex glass of the old-fashioned watch.
19. inventory: satirizes the government investigations of those suspected of Jacobite intrigues at the beginning of George I's reign.

with great civility, and due respect to your Majesty's Commission. Signed and sealed on the fourth day of the eighty-ninth moon of your Majesty's auspicious reign.

CLEFRIN FRELOCK, MARSI FRELOCK

When this inventory was read over to the Emperor, he directed me, although in very gentle terms, to deliver up the several particulars. He first called for my scimitar, which I took out, scabbard and all. In the meantime he ordered three thousand of his choicest troops (who then attended him) to surround me at a distance, with their bows and arrows just ready to discharge: but I did not observe it, for my eyes were wholly fixed upon his Majesty. He then desired me to draw my scimitar, which, although it had got some rust by the sea water, was in most parts exceeding bright. I did so, and immediately all the troops gave a shout between terror and surprise; for the sun shone clear, and the reflection dazzled their eyes, as I waved the scimitar to and fro in my hand. His Majesty, who is a most magnanimous prince, was less daunted than I could expect; he ordered me to return it into the scabbard, and cast it on the ground as gently as I could, about six foot from the end of my chain. The next thing he demanded was one of the hollow iron pillars, by which he meant my pocket pistols. I drew it out, and at his desire, as well as I could, expressed to him the use of it; and charging it only with powder, which, by the closeness of my pouch, happened to escape wetting in the sea (an inconvenience that all prudent mariners take special care to provide against), I first cautioned the Emperor not to be afraid, and then I let it off in the air. The astonishment here was much greater than at the sight of my scimitar. Hundreds fell down as if they had been struck dead; and even the Emperor, although he stood his ground, could not recover himself in some time. I delivered up both my pistols in the same manner as I had done my scimitar, and then my pouch of powder and bullets; begging him that the former might be kept from fire, for it would kindle with the smallest spark, and blow up his imperial palace into the air. I likewise delivered up my watch, which the Emperor was very curious to see, and commanded two of his tallest yeomen of the guards to bear it on a pole upon their shoulders, as draymen in England do a barrel of ale. He was amazed at the continual noise it made, and the motion of the minute hand, which he could easily discern; for their sight is much more acute

than ours: he asked the opinions of his learned men about him, which were various and remote, as the reader may well imagine without my repeating; although, indeed, I could not very perfectly understand them. I then gave up my silver and copper money, my purse, with nine large pieces of gold, and some smaller ones; my knife and razor, my comb and silver snuffbox, my handkerchief and journal book. My scimitar, pistols, and pouch, were conveyed in carriages to his Majesty's stores; but the rest of my goods were returned to me.

I had, as I before observed, one private pocket which escaped their search, wherein there was a pair of spectacles (which I sometimes use for the weakness of my eyes), a pocket perspective, and several other little conveniences; which being of no consequence to the Emperor, I did not think myself bound in honor to discover, and I apprehended they might be lost or spoiled if I ventured them out of my possession.

CHAPTER 3

The Author diverts the Emperor, and his nobility of both sexes, in a very uncommon manner. The diversions of the court of Lilliput described. The Author has his liberty granted him upon certain conditions.

My gentleness and good behavior had gained so far on the Emperor and his court, and indeed upon the army and people in general, that I began to conceive hopes of getting my liberty in a short time. I took all possible methods to cultivate this favorable disposition. The natives came by degrees to be less apprehensive of any danger from me. I would sometimes lie down, and let five or six of them dance on my hand. And at last the boys and girls would venture to come and play at hide-and-seek in my hair. I had now made a good progress in understanding and speaking their language. The Emperor had a mind one day to entertain me with several of the country shows, wherein they exceed all nations I have known, both for dexterity and magnificence. I was diverted with none so much as that of the rope dancers, performed upon a slender white thread, extended about two foot, and twelve inches from the ground. Upon which I shall desire liberty, with the reader's patience, to enlarge a little.

This diversion is only practiced by those persons who are candidates for great employments, and high favor, at court. They are trained in this art from their youth, and are not always of noble birth, or liberal education. When a great office is vacant, either by death or disgrace (which often happens), five or six of those candidates petition the Emperor to entertain his Majesty and the court with a dance on the rope, and whoever jumps the highest without falling, succeeds in the office. Very often the chief ministers themselves are commanded to show their skill, and to convince the Emperor that they have not lost their faculty. Flimnap, the Treasurer,[20] is allowed to cut a caper on the straight rope, at least an inch higher than any other lord in the whole empire. I have seen him do the summerset several times together upon a trencher fixed on the rope, which is no thicker than a common pack thread in England. My friend Reldresal,[21] principal Secretary for Private Affairs, is, in my opinion, if I am not partial, the second after the Treasurer; the rest of the great officers are much upon a par.

These diversions are often attended with fatal accidents, whereof great numbers are on record. I myself have seen two or three candidates break a limb. But the danger is much greater when the ministers themselves are commanded to show their dexterity; for, by contending to excel themselves and their fellows, they strain so far, that there is hardly one of them who hath not received a fall, and some of them two or three. I was assured that a year or two before my arrival, Flimnap would have infallibly broke his neck, if one of the King's cushions,[22] that accidentally lay on the ground, had not weakened the force of his fall.

There is likewise another diversion, which is only shown before the Emperor and Empress, and first minister, upon particular occasions. The Emperor lays on the table three fine silken threads of six inches long. One is blue, the other red, and the third green.[23] These threads are proposed as prizes for those persons whom the Emperor hath a mind to distinguish by a peculiar mark of his favor. The ceremony is performed in his Majesty's great chamber of state, where the candidates are to undergo a trial of dexterity very different from the former, and such as I have not observed the least resemblance of in any other country of the Old or the New World. The Emperor holds a stick in his hands, both ends parallel to the horizon, while the candidates advancing one by one, sometimes leap over the stick, sometimes creep under it backwards and forwards several times, according as the stick is advanced or depressed. Sometimes the Emperor holds one end of the stick, and his first minister the other; sometimes the minister has it entirely to himself. Whoever performs his part with most agility, and holds out the longest in leaping and creeping, is rewarded with the blue-colored silk; the red is given to the next, and the green to the third, which they all wear girt twice round about the middle; and you see few great persons about this court, who are not adorned with one of these girdles.

The horses of the army, and those of the royal stables, having been daily led before me, were no longer shy, but would come up to my very feet without starting. The riders would leap them over my hand as I held it on the ground, and one of the Emperor's huntsmen, upon a large courser, took my foot, shoe and all; which was indeed a prodigious leap. I had the good fortune to divert the Emperor one day after a very extraordinary manner. I desired he would order several sticks of two foot high, and the thickness of an ordinary cane, to be brought me; whereupon his Majesty commanded the master of his woods to give directions accordingly; and the next morning six woodmen arrived with as many carriages, drawn by eight horses to each. I took nine of these sticks, and fixing them firmly in the ground in a quadrangular figure, two foot and a half square; I took four other sticks, and tied them parallel at each corner, about two foot from the ground; then I fastened my handkerchief to the nine sticks that stood erect, and extended it on all sides, till it was as tight as the top of a drum; and the four parallel sticks rising about five inches higher than the handkerchief, served as ledges on each side. When I had finished my work, I desired the Emperor to let a troop of his best horse, twenty-four in number, come and exercise upon this plain. His Majesty approved of the proposal, and I took them up, one by one, in my hands, ready mounted and armed, with the proper officers to exercise them. As soon as they got into order, they divided into two parties, performed mock skirmishes, discharged blunt arrows, drew their swords, fled and pursued, attacked and retired, and in short discovered the best military discipline I ever beheld. The parallel sticks secured them and their horses from falling over

20. Flimnap . . . Treasurer: The name suggests a cheat, and is applied to Walpole, who was not unwilling to maintain his power by bribery.   21. Reldresal: possibly Walpole's chief ally, Lord Townshend.   22. one . . . cushions: Duchess of Kendal, mistress of the king.   23. three . . . green: the colors of the orders of the Garter, Bath, and Thistle.

the stage; and the Emperor was so much delighted, that he ordered this entertainment to be repeated several days, and once was pleased to be lifted up and give the word of command; and, with great difficulty, persuaded even the Empress herself to let me hold her in her close chair within two yards of the stage, from whence she was able to take a full view of the whole performance. It was my good fortune that no ill accident happened in these entertainments, only once a fiery horse, that belonged to one of the captains, pawing with his hoof, struck a hole in my handkerchief, and his foot slipping, he overthrew his rider and himself; but I immediately relieved them both: for covering the hole with one hand, I set down the troop with the other, in the same manner as I took them up. The horse that fell was strained in the left shoulder, but the rider got no hurt, and I repaired my handkerchief as well as I could: however, I would not trust to the strength of it any more in such dangerous enterprises.

About two or three days before I was set at liberty, as I was entertaining the court with these kinds of feats, there arrived an express to inform his Majesty, that some of his subjects riding near the place where I was first taken up, had seen a great black substance lying on the ground, very oddly shaped, extending its edges round as wide as his Majesty's bedchamber, and rising up in the middle as high as a man; that it was no living creature, as they at first apprehended, for it lay on the grass without motion, and some of them had walked round it several times: that by mounting upon each other's shoulders, they had got to the top, which was flat and even, and stamping upon it they found it was hollow within; that they humbly conceived it might be something belonging to the Man-Mountain; and if his Majesty pleased, they would undertake to bring it with only five horses. I presently knew what they meant, and was glad at heart to receive this intelligence. It seems upon my first reaching the shore after our shipwreck, I was in such confusion, that before I came to the place where I went to sleep, my hat, which I had fastened with a string to my head while I was rowing, and had stuck on all the time I was swimming, fell off after I came to land; the string, as I conjecture, breaking by some accident which I never observed, but thought my hat had been lost at sea. I entreated his Imperial Majesty to give orders it might be brought to me as soon as possible, describing to him the use and the nature of it: and the next day

the wagoners arrived with it, but not in a very good condition; they had bored two holes in the brim, within an inch and a half of the edge, and fastened two hooks in the holes; these hooks were tied by a long cord to the harness, and thus my hat was dragged along for above half an English mile; but the ground in that country being extremely smooth and level, it received less damage than I expected.

Two days after this adventure, the Emperor having ordered that part of his army which quarters in and about his metropolis to be in readiness, took a fancy of diverting himself in a very singular manner. He desired I would stand like a colossus, with my legs as far asunder as I conveniently could. He then commanded his General (who was an old experienced leader, and a great patron of mine) to draw up the troops in close order, and march them under me; the foot by twenty-four in a breast, and the horse by sixteen, with drums beating, colors flying, and pikes advanced. This body consisted of three thousand foot, and a thousand horse. His Majesty gave orders, upon pain of death, that every soldier in his march should observe the strictest decency with regard to my person; which, however, could not prevent some of the younger officers from turning up their eyes as they passed under me. And, to confess the truth, my breeches were at that time in so ill a condition, that they afforded some opportunities for laughter and admiration.

I had sent so many memorials and petitions for my liberty, that his Majesty at length mentioned the matter, first in the cabinet, and then in a full council; where it was opposed by none, except Skyresh Bolgolam,[24] who was pleased, without any provocation, to be my mortal enemy. But it was carried against him by the whole board, and confirmed by the Emperor. That minister was *Galbet,* or Admiral of the Realm, very much in his master's confidence, and a person well versed in affairs, but of a morose and sour complexion. However, he was at length persuaded to comply; but prevailed that the articles and conditions upon which I should be set free, and to which I must swear, should be drawn up by himself. These articles were brought to me by Skyresh Bolgolam in person, attended by two undersecretaries, and several persons of distinction. After they were read, I was demanded to swear to the performance of them; first in the manner of my own country, and afterwards in the

24. **Skyresh Bolgolam:** the Earl of Nottingham, a Tory, often lampooned by Swift as "Dismal."

method prescribed by their laws; which was to hold my right foot in my left hand, to place the middle finger of my right hand on the crown of my head, and my thumb on the tip of my right ear. But because the reader may perhaps be curious to have some idea of the style and manner of expression peculiar to that people, as well as to know the articles upon which I recovered my liberty, I have made a translation of the whole instrument word for word, as near as I was able, which I here offer to the public.

Golbasto [25] Momarem Evlame Gurdilo Shefin Mully Ully Gue, most mighty Emperor of Lilliput, delight and terror of the universe, whose dominions extend five thousand *blustrugs* (about twelve miles in circumference) to the extremities of the globe; monarch of all monarchs, taller than the sons of men; whose feet press down to the center, and whose head strikes against the sun; at whose nod the princes of the earth shake their knees; pleasant as the spring, comfortable as the summer, fruitful as autumn, dreadful as winter. His most sublime Majesty proposeth to the Man-Mountain, lately arrived at our celestial dominions, the following articles, which by a solemn oath he shall be obliged to perform.

First, The Man-Mountain shall not depart from our dominions, without our license under our great seal.

Secondly, He shall not presume to come into our metropolis, without our express order; at which time, the inhabitants shall have two hours warning to keep within their doors.

Thirdly, The said Man-Mountain shall confine his walks to our principal high roads, and not offer to walk or lie down in a meadow or field of corn.

Fourthly, As he walks the said roads, he shall take the utmost care not to trample upon the bodies of any of our loving subjects, their horses, or carriages, nor take any of our subjects into his hands, without their own consent.

Fifthly, If an express requires extraordinary dispatch, the Man-Mountain shall be obliged to carry in his pocket the messenger and horse a six days' journey once in every moon, and return the said messenger back (if so required) safe to our Imperial Presence.

Sixthly, He shall be our ally against our enemies in the Island of Blefuscu, and do his utmost to destroy their fleet, which is now preparing to invade us.

Seventhly, That the said Man-Mountain shall, at his times of leisure, be aiding and assisting to our workmen, in helping to raise certain great stones, towards covering the wall of the principal park, and other our royal buildings.

Eighthly, That the said Man-Mountain shall, in two moons time, deliver in an exact survey of the circumference of our dominions by a computation of his own paces round the coast.

Lastly, That upon his solemn oath to observe all the above articles, the said Man-Mountain shall have a daily allowance of meat and drink sufficient for the support of 1728 of our subjects, with free access to our Royal Person, and other marks of our favor. Given at our Palace at Belfaborac the twelfth day of the ninety-first moon of our reign.

I swore and subscribed to these articles with great cheerfulness and content, although some of them were not so honorable as I could have wished; which proceeded wholly from the malice of Skyresh Bolgolam, the High Admiral: whereupon my chains were immediately unlocked, and I was at full liberty; the Emperor himself in person did me the honor to be by at the whole ceremony. I made my acknowledgments by prostrating myself at his Majesty's feet: but he commanded me to rise; and after many gracious expressions, which, to avoid the censure of vanity, I shall not repeat, he added, that he hoped I should prove a useful servant, and well deserve all the favors he had already conferred upon me, or might do for the future.

The reader may please to observe, that in the last article for the recovery of my liberty, the Emperor stipulates to allow me a quantity of meat and drink sufficient for the support of 1728 Lilliputians. Some time after, asking a friend at court how they came to fix on that determinate number, he told me that his Majesty's mathematicians, having taken the height of my body by the help of a quadrant, and finding it to exceed theirs in the proportion of twelve to one, they concluded from the similarity of their bodies, that mine must contain at least 1728 of theirs, and consequently would require as much food as was necessary to support that number of Lilliputians. By which, the reader may conceive an idea of the ingenuity of that people, as well as the prudent and exact economy of so great a prince.

CHAPTER 4

Mildendo, *the metropolis of* Lilliput, *described, together with the Emperor's palace. A conversation between the Author and a principal Secretary, concerning the*

---

25. Golbasto: This paragraph is a parody of the oriental style found in the popular travel books.

affairs of that empire. The Author's offers to serve the Emperor in his wars.

The first request I made, after I had obtained my liberty, was, that I might have license to see Mildendo, the metropolis; which the Emperor easily granted me, but with a special charge to do no hurt either to the inhabitants or their houses. The people had notice by proclamation of my design to visit the town. The wall which encompassed it, is two foot and an half high, and at least eleven inches broad, so that a coach and horses may be driven very safely round it; and it is flanked with strong towers at ten foot distance. I stepped over the great Western Gate, and passed very gently, and sideling through the two principal streets, only in my short waistcoat, for fear of damaging the roofs and eaves of the houses with the skirts of my coat. I walked with the utmost circumspection, to avoid treading on any stragglers, who might remain in the streets, although the orders were very strict, that all people should keep in their houses, at their own peril. The garret windows and tops of houses were so crowded with spectators, that I thought in all my travels I had not seen a more populous place. The city is an exact square, each side of the wall being five hundred foot long. The two great streets, which run cross and divide it into four quarters, are five foot wide. The lanes and alleys, which I could not enter, but only viewed them as I passed, are from twelve to eighteen inches. The town is capable of holding five hundred thousand souls. The houses are from three to five stories. The shops and markets well provided.

The Emperor's palace is in the center of the city, where the two great streets meet. It is enclosed by a wall of two foot high, and twenty foot distant from the buildings. I had his Majesty's permission to step over this wall; and the space being so wide between that and the palace, I could easily view it on every side. The outward court is a square of forty foot, and includes two other courts: in the inmost are the royal apartments, which I was very desirous to see, but found it extremely difficult; for the great gates, from one square into another, were but eighteen inches high, and seven inches wide. Now the buildings of the outer court were at least five foot high, and it was impossible for me to stride over them without infinite damage to the pile, though the walls were strongly built of hewn stone, and four inches thick. At the same time the Emperor had a great desire that I should see the magnificence of his palace; but this

I was not able to do till three days after, which I spent in cutting down with my knife some of the largest trees in the royal park, about an hundred yards distant from the city. Of these trees I made two stools, each about three foot high, and strong enough to bear my weight. The people having received notice a second time, I went again through the city to the palace, with my two stools in my hands. When I came to the side of the outer court, I stood upon one stool, and took the other in my hand: this I lifted over the roof, and gently set it down on the space between the first and second court, which was eight foot wide. I then stepped over the buildings very conveniently from one stool to the other, and drew up the first after me with a hooked stick. By this contrivance I got into the inmost court; and lying down upon my side, I applied my face to the windows of the middle stories, which were left open on purpose, and discovered the most splendid apartments that can be imagined. There I saw the Empress and the young Princes, in their several lodgings, with their chief attendants about them. Her Imperial Majesty was pleased to smile very graciously upon me, and gave me out of the window her hand to kiss.

But I shall not anticipate the reader with farther descriptions of this kind, because I reserve them for a greater work, which is now almost ready for the press, containing a general description of this empire, from its first erection, through a long series of princes, with a particular account of their wars and politics, laws, learning, and religion: their plants and animals, their peculiar manners and customs, with other matters very curious and useful; my chief design at present being only to relate such events and transactions as happened to the public, or to myself, during a residence of about nine months in that empire.

One morning, about a fortnight after I had obtained my liberty, Reldresal, principal Secretary (as they style him) of Private Affairs, came to my house attended only by one servant. He ordered his coach to wait at a distance, and desired I would give him an hour's audience; which I readily consented to, on account of his quality and personal merits, as well as of the many good offices he had done me during my solicitations at court. I offered to lie down, that he might the more conveniently reach my ear; but he chose rather to let me hold him in my hand during our conversation. He began with compliments on my liberty: said he might pretend to some merit in it: but, however, added, that if it had not been for the present situation of things at court, perhaps I might not have obtained it so soon. "For," said he, "as flourishing a condition as we appear to be in to foreigners, we labor under two mighty evils: a violent faction at home, and the danger of an invasion by a most potent enemy from abroad. As to the first, you are to understand, that for about seventy moons [26] past there have been two struggling parties [27] in this empire, under the names of *Tramecksan* and *Slamecksan,* from the high and low heels on their shoes, by which they distinguish themselves. It is alleged indeed, that the high heels are most agreeable to our ancient constitution: but however this be, his Majesty hath determined to make use of only low heels in the administration of the government, and all offices in the gift of the Crown, as you cannot but observe; and particularly, that his Majesty's Imperial heels are lower [28] at least by a *drurr* than any of his court; (*drurr* is a measure about the fourteenth part of an inch). The animosities between these two parties run so high, that they will neither eat nor drink, nor talk with each other. We compute the *Tramecksan,* or High-Heels, to exceed us in number; but the power is wholly on our side. We apprehend his Imperial Highness, the Heir to the Crown, to have some tendency towards the High-Heels; at least we can plainly discover one of his heels higher than the other, which gives him a hobble [29] in his gait. Now, in the midst of these intestine disquiets, we are threatened with an invasion from the Island of Blefuscu,[30] which is the other great empire of the universe, almost as large and powerful as this of his Majesty. For as to what we have heard you affirm, that there are other kingdoms and states in the world inhabited by human creatures as large as yourself, our philosophers are in much doubt, and would rather conjecture that you dropped from the moon, or one of the stars; because it is certain, that an hundred mortals of your bulk would, in a short time, destroy all the fruits and cattle of his Majesty's dominions. Besides, our histories of six thousand moons make no mention of any other regions, than the two great empires of Lilliput and Blefuscu. Which two mighty powers have, as I was going to tell you, been engaged in a most obstinate war for six and thirty moons [31] past. It began upon the following occasion. It is allowed on all hands, that the primitive way of breaking eggs before we eat them, was upon the larger end: but his present Majesty's grandfather, while he was a boy, going to eat an egg, and breaking it according to the ancient practice, happened to cut one of his fingers. Whereupon the Emperor his father published an edict, commanding all his subjects, upon great penalties, to break the smaller end of their eggs. The people so highly resented this law, that our histories tell us there have been six rebellions raised on that account; wherein one Emperor lost his life, and another his crown. These civil commotions were constantly fomented by the monarchs of Blefuscu; and when they were quelled, the exiles always fled for refuge to that empire. It is computed, that eleven thousand persons have, at several times, suffered death, rather than submit to break their eggs at the smaller end. Many hundred large volumes have been published upon this controversy: but the books of the Big-Endians have been long forbidden,[32] and the whole party rendered incapable by law of holding employments.[33] During the course of these troubles, the Emperors of Blefuscu did frequently expostulate by their ambassadors, accusing us of making a schism in religion, by offending against a fundamental doctrine of our great prophet Lustrog, in the fifty-fourth chapter of the Blundrecal (which is their Alcoran).[34] This, however, is thought to be a mere strain upon the text: for the words are these: *That all true believers shall break their eggs at the convenient end:* and which is the convenient end, seems, in my humble opinion, to be left to every man's conscience, or at least in the power of the chief magistrate to determine. Now the Big-Endian exiles have found so much credit in the Emperor of Blefuscu's court, and so much private assistance and encouragement from their party here at home, that a bloody war has been carried on between the two empires for six and thirty moons with various success; during

---

26. seventy moons: As Gulliver is supposed to have arrived in Lilliput at the end of 1699, this may be taken as a reference to 1629, when the troubles began which led to the Civil War. 27. two . . . parties: High Church and Low Church, or Tory and Whig. 28. Majesty's . . . lower: George I, a Lutheran himself, and a supporter of the Whigs. 29. a hobble: By his intrigues with the Tory opposition, the Prince of Wales had made it doubtful which party he would favor. 30. Blefuscu: Fran

31. six . . . moons: The dates and incidents here do not fit the history of the religious struggles since Henry VIII, but they seem intended to refer to Henry VIII's break with the Pope, and to the fate of Charles I and James II resulting from these struggles. The Big-Endians are the Roman Catholics, and the Little-Endians the Protestants. 32. long forbidden: since the reign of Edward VI. 33. incapable . . . employments: by the Test Acts, after the Restoration. 34. Alcoran: or Koran. the Mohammedan scriptures

which time we have lost forty capital ships, and a much greater number of smaller vessels, together with thirty thousand of our best seamen and soldiers; and the damage received by the enemy is reckoned to be somewhat greater than ours. However, they have now equipped a numerous fleet, and are just preparing to make a descent upon us; and his Imperial Majesty, placing great confidence in your valor and strength, has commanded me to lay this account of his affairs before you."

I desired the Secretary to present my humble duty to the Emperor, and to let him know, that I thought it would not become me, who was a foreigner, to interfere with parties; but I was ready, with the hazard of my life, to defend his person and state against all invaders.

CHAPTER 5

The Author, by an extraordinary stratagem, prevents an invasion. A high title of honor is conferred upon him. Ambassadors arrive from the Emperor of Blefuscu, and sue for peace. The Empress's apartment on fire by an accident; the Author instrumental in saving the rest of the palace.

The Empire of Blefuscu is an island situated to the north northeast side of Lilliput, from whence it is parted only by a channel of eight hundred yards wide. I had not yet seen it, and upon this notice of an intended invasion, I avoided appearing on that side of the coast, for fear of being discovered by some of the enemy's ships, who had received no intelligence of me, all intercourse between the two empires having been strictly forbidden during the war, upon pain of death, and an embargo laid by our Emperor upon all vessels whatsoever. I communicated to his Majesty a project I had formed of seizing the enemy's whole fleet: which, as our scouts assured us, lay at anchor in the harbor ready to sail with the first fair wind. I consulted the most experienced seamen, upon the depth of the channel, which they had often plumbed, who told me, that in the middle at high water it was seventy *glumgluffs* deep, which is about six foot of European measure; and the rest of it fifty *glumgluffs* at most. I walked to the northeast coast over against Blefuscu; where, lying down behind a hillock, I took out my small pocket perspective glass, and viewed the enemy's fleet at anchor, consisting of about fifty men-of-war, and a great number of transports: I then came back to my house, and gave order (for which I had a war-

rant) for a great quantity of the strongest cable and bars of iron. The cable was about as thick as pack thread, and the bars of the length and size of a knitting needle. I trebled the cable to make it stronger, and for the same reason I twisted three of the iron bars together, binding the extremities into a hook. Having thus fixed fifty hooks to as many cables, I went back to the northeast coast, and putting off my coat, shoes, and stockings, walked into the sea in my leathern jerkin, about half an hour before high water. I waded with what haste I could, and swam in the middle about thirty yards till I felt ground; I arrived at the fleet in less than half an hour. The enemy was so frighted when they saw me, that they leaped out of their ships, and swam to shore, where there could not be fewer than thirty thousand souls. I then took my tackling, and fastening a hook to the hole at the prow of each, I tied all the cords together at the end. While I was thus employed, the enemy discharged several thousand arrows, many of which stuck in my hands and face; and besides the excessive smart, gave me much disturbance in my work. My greatest apprehension was for my eyes, which I should have infallibly lost, if I had not suddenly thought of an expedient. I kept among other little necessaries a pair of spectacles in a private pocket, which, as I observed before, had escaped the Emperor's searchers. These I took out and fastened as strongly as I could upon my nose, and thus armed went on boldly with my work in spite of the enemy's arrows, many of which struck against the glasses of my spectacles, but without any other effect, further than a little to discompose them. I had now fastened all the hooks, and taking the knot in my hand, began to pull; but not a ship would stir, for they were all too fast held by their anchors, so that the boldest part of my enterprise remained. I therefore let go the cord, and leaving the hooks fixed to the ships, I resolutely cut with my knife the cables that fastened the anchors, receiving above two hundred shots in my face and hands; then I took up the knotted end of the cables, to which my hooks were tied, and with great ease drew fifty of the enemy's largest men-of-war after me.

The Blefuscudians, who had not the least imagination of what I intended, were at first confounded with astonishment. They had seen me cut the cables, and thought my design was only to let the ships run adrift, or fall foul on each other: but when they perceived the whole fleet moving in order, and saw me pulling at the end, they set up such a scream of grief and despair, that it is almost impossible to describe or conceive. When I had got out of danger, I stopped awhile to pick out the arrows that stuck in my hands and face; and rubbed on some of the same ointment that was given me at my first arrival, as I have formerly mentioned. I then took off my spectacles, and waiting about an hour, till the tide was a little fallen, I waded through the middle with my cargo, and arrived safe at the royal port of Lilliput.

The Emperor and his whole court stood on the shore, expecting the issue of this great adventure. They saw the ships move forward in a large half-moon, but could not discern me, who was up to my breast in water. When I advanced to the middle of the channel, they were yet more in pain, because I was under water to my neck. The Emperor concluded me to be drowned, and that the enemy's fleet was approaching in a hostile manner: but he was soon eased of his fears, for the channel growing shallower every step I made, I came in a short time within hearing, and holding up the end of the cable by which the fleet was fastened, I cried in a loud voice, *Long live the most puissant Emperor of Lilliput!* This great prince received me at my landing with all possible encomiums, and created me a *Nardac* upon the spot, which is the highest title of honor among them.

His Majesty desired I would take some other opportunity of bringing all the rest of his enemy's ships into his ports. And so unmeasurable is the ambition of princes, that he seemed to think of nothing less than reducing the whole empire of Blefuscu into a province, and governing it by a viceroy; of destroying the Big-Endian exiles, and compelling that people to break the smaller end of their eggs, by which he would remain sole monarch of the whole world. But I endeavored to divert him from this design, by many arguments drawn from the topics of policy as well as justice; and I plainly protested, that I would never be an instrument of bringing a free and brave people into slavery. And when the matter was debated in council, the wisest part of the ministry were of my opinion.

This open bold declaration of mine was so opposite to the schemes and politics of his Imperial Majesty, that he could never forgive me; he mentioned it in a very artful manner at council, where I was told that some of the wisest appeared, at least by their silence, to be of my opinion; but

others, who were my secret enemies, could not forbear some expressions, which by a side wind[35] reflected on me. And from this time began an intrigue between his Majesty and a junto[36] of ministers maliciously bent against me, which broke out in less than two months, and had like to have ended in my utter destruction. Of so little weight are the greatest services to princes, when put into the balance with a refusal to gratify their passions.

About three weeks after this exploit, there arrived a solemn embassy from Blefuscu, with humble offers of a peace;[37] which was soon concluded upon conditions very advantageous to our Emperor, wherewith I shall not trouble the reader. There were six ambassadors, with a train of about five hundred persons, and their entry was very magnificent, suitable to the grandeur of their master, and the importance of their business. When their treaty was finished, wherein I did them several good offices by the credit I now had, or at least appeared to have at court, their Excellencies, who were privately told how much I had been their friend, made me a visit in form. They began with many compliments upon my valor and generosity, invited me to that kingdom in the Emperor their master's name, and desired me to show them some proofs of my prodigious strength, of which they had heard so many wonders; wherein I readily obliged them, but shall not interrupt the reader with the particulars.

When I had for some time entertained their Excellencies, to their infinite satisfaction and surprise, I desired they would do me the honor to present my most humble respects to the Emperor their master, the renown of whose virtues had so justly filled the whole world with admiration, and whose royal person I resolved to attend before I returned to my own country: accordingly, the next time I had the honor to see our Emperor, I desired his general license to wait on the Blefuscudian monarch, which he was pleased to grant me, as I could plainly perceive, in a very cold manner; but could not guess the reason, till I had a whisper from a certain person, that Flimnap and Bolgolam had represented my intercourse with those ambassadors as a mark of disaffection, from which I am sure my heart was wholly free. And this was the first time I began to conceive some

35. by . . . wind: indirectly.   36. junto: a political group, first applied to the leaders of the Whigs after the Revolution of 1688. 37. a peace: In all this passage Swift has in mind the negotiations for the Treaty of Utrecht, and the criticisms of the arrangements for the peace.

imperfect idea of courts and ministers.

It is to be observed, that these ambassadors spoke to me by an interpreter, the languages of both empires differing as much from each other as any two in Europe, and each nation priding itself upon the antiquity, beauty, and energy of their own tongues, with an avowed contempt for that of their neighbor; yet our Emperor, standing upon the advantage he had got by the seizure of their fleet, obliged them to deliver their credentials, and make their speech in the Lilliputian tongue. And it must be confessed, that from the great intercourse of trade and commerce between both realms, from the continual reception of exiles, which is mutual among them, and from the custom in each empire to send their young nobility and richer gentry to the other, in order to polish themselves by seeing the world, and understanding men and manners; there are few persons of distinction, or merchants, or seamen, who dwell in the maritime parts, but what can hold conversation in both tongues; as I found some weeks after, when I went to pay my respects to the Emperor of Blefuscu, which in the midst of great misfortunes, through the malice of my enemies, proved a very happy adventure to me, as I shall relate in its proper place.

The reader may remember, that when I signed those articles upon which I recovered my liberty, there were some which I disliked upon account of their being too servile, neither could anything but an extreme necessity have forced me to submit. But being now a *Nardac* of the highest rank in that empire, such offices were looked upon as below my dignity, and the Emperor (to do him justice) never once mentioned them to me. However, it was not long before I had an opportunity of doing his Majesty, at least, as I then thought, a most signal service. I was alarmed at midnight with the cries of many hundred people at my door; by which being suddenly awaked, I was in some kind of terror. I heard the word *burglum* repeated incessantly: several of the Emperor's court, making their way through the crowd, entreated me to come immediately to the palace, where her Imperial Majesty's apartment was on fire, by the carelessness of a maid of honor, who fell asleep while she was reading a romance. I got up in an instant; and orders being given to clear the way before me, and it being likewise a moonshine night, I made a shift to get to the palace without trampling on any of the people. I found they had already applied ladders to the walls of the apart-ment, and were well provided with buckets, but the water was at some distance. These buckets were about the size of a large thimble, and the poor people supplied me with them as fast as they could; but the flame was so violent that they did little good. I might easily have stifled it with my coat, which I unfortunately left behind me for haste, and came away only in my leathern jerkin. The case seemed wholly desperate and deplorable; and this magnificent palace would have infallibly been burnt down to the ground, if, by a presence of mind, unusual to me, I had not suddenly thought of an expedient. I had the evening before drunk plentifully of a most delicious wine, called *glimigrim* (the Blefuscudians call it *flunec,* but ours is esteemed the better sort), which is very diuretic. By the luckiest chance in the world, I had not discharged myself of any part of it. The heat I had contracted by coming very near the flames, and by laboring to quench them, made the wine begin to operate by urine; which I voided in such a quantity, and applied so well to the proper places, that in three minutes the fire was wholly extinguished, and the rest of that noble pile, which had cost so many ages in erecting, preserved from destruction.

It was now daylight, and I returned to my house without waiting to congratulate with the Emperor: because, although I had done a very eminent piece of service, yet I could not tell how his Majesty might resent the manner by which I had performed it: for, by the fundamental laws of the realm, it is capital in any person, of what quality soever, to make water within the precincts of the palace. But I was a little comforted by a message from his Majesty, that he would give orders to the Grand Justiciary for passing my pardon in form; which, however, I could not obtain. And I was privately assured, that the Empress, conceiving the greatest abhorrence of what I had done, removed to the most distant side of the court, firmly resolved that those buildings should never be repaired for her use: and, in the presence of her chief confidants could not forbear vowing revenge.[38]

CHAPTER 6

Of the inhabitants of Lilliput; *their learning, laws, and customs. The manner of educating their children.*

38. abhorrence . . . revenge: The Queen's resentment has been understood as a reference to her dislike of the coarseness of Swift's satire and her unwillingness that he should be made a bishop.

The Author's way of living in that country. His vindication of a great lady.

Although I intend to leave the description of this empire to a particular treatise, yet in the meantime I am content to gratify the curious reader with some general ideas. As the common size of the natives is somewhat under six inches, so there is an exact proportion in all other animals, as well as plants and trees: for instance, the tallest horses and oxen are between four and five inches in height, the sheep [39] an inch and a half, more or less: their geese about the bigness of a sparrow, and so the several gradations downwards till you come to the smallest, which, to my sight, were almost invisible; but nature hath adapted the eyes of the Lilliputians to all objects proper for their view: they see with great exactness, but at no great distance. And to show the sharpness of their sight towards objects that are near, I have been much pleased with observing a cook pulling a lark, which was not so large as a common fly; and a young girl threading an invisible needle with invisible silk. Their tallest trees are about seven foot high: I mean some of those in the great royal park, the tops whereof I could but just reach with my fist clinched. The other vegetables are in the same proportion; but this I leave to the reader's imagination.

I shall say but little at present of their learning, which for many ages hath flourished in all its branches among them: but their manner of writing [40] is very peculiar, being neither from the left to the right, like the Europeans; nor from the right to the left, like the Arabians; nor from up to down, like the Chinese; nor from down to up, like the Cascagians; but aslant from one corner of the paper to the other, like ladies in England.

They bury their dead with their heads directly downwards, because they hold an opinion, that in eleven thousand moons they are all to rise again, in which period the earth (which they conceive to be flat) will turn upside down, and by this means they shall, at their resurrection, be found ready standing on their feet. The learned among them confess the absurdity of this doctrine, but the practice still continues, in compliance to the vulgar.

There are some laws and customs in this empire very peculiar; and if they were not so directly contrary to those of my own dear country, I should be tempted to say a little in their justification. It is only to be wished that they were as well executed. The first I shall mention, relates to informers. All crimes against the state are punished here with the utmost severity; but if the person accused make his innocence plainly to appear upon his trial, the accuser is immediately put to an ignominious death; and out of his goods or lands, the innocent person is quadruply recompensed for the loss of his time, for the danger he underwent, for the hardship of his imprisonment, and for all the charges he hath been at in making his defense. Or, if that fund be deficient, it is largely supplied by the Crown. The Emperor does also confer on him some public mark of his favor, and proclamation is made of his innocence through the whole city.

They look upon fraud as a greater crime than theft, and therefore seldom fail to punish it with death; for they allege, that care and vigilance, with a very common understanding, may preserve a man's goods from thieves, but honesty has no fence against superior cunning; and since it is necessary that there should be a perpetual intercourse of buying and selling, and dealing upon credit, where fraud is permitted and connived at, or hath no law to punish it, the honest dealer is always undone, and the knave gets the advantage. I remember when I was once interceding with the Emperor for a criminal who had wronged his master of a great sum of money, which he had received by order, and ran away with; and happening to tell his Majesty, by way of extenuation, that it was only a breach of trust; the Emperor thought it monstrous in me to offer, as a defense, the greatest aggravation of the crime: and truly I had little to say in return, farther than the common answer, that different nations had different customs; for, I confess, I was heartily ashamed.

Although we usually call reward and punishment the two hinges upon which all government turns, yet I could never observe this maxim to be put in practice by any nation except that of Lilliput. Whoever can there bring sufficient proof that he hath strictly observed the laws of his country for seventy-three moons, hath a claim to certain privileges, according to his quality and condition of life, with a proportionable sum of money out of a fund appropriated for that use: he likewise acquires the title of *Snilpall,* or Legal, which is added to his name, but does not descend to his

---

39. the sheep: It must be remembered that the average size of sheep in Swift's time was about a quarter of the present size.
40. manner of writing: Swift is here parodying a paragraph from William Sympson's *New Voyage to the East Indies*, adding his own invention of the Cascagians.

posterity. And these people thought it a prodigious defect of policy among us, when I told them that our laws were enforced only by penalties, without any mention of reward. It is upon this account that the image of Justice, in their courts of judicature, is formed with six eyes, two before, as many behind, and on each side one, to signify circumspection; with a bag of gold open in her right hand, and a sword sheathed in her left, to show she is more disposed to reward than to punish.

In choosing persons for all employments, they have more regard to good morals than to great abilities; for, since government is necessary to mankind, they believe that the common size of human understandings is fitted to some station or other, and that Providence never intended to make the management of public affairs a mystery, to be comprehended only by a few persons of sublime genius, of which there seldom are three born in an age: but they suppose truth, justice, temperance, and the like, to be in every man's power; the practice of which virtues, assisted by experience and a good intention, would qualify any man for the service of his country, except where a course of study is required. But they thought the want of moral virtues was so far from being supplied by superior endowments of the mind, that employments could never be put into such dangerous hands as those of persons so qualified; and at least, that the mistakes committed by ignorance in a virtuous disposition, would never be of such fatal consequence to the public weal,[41] as the practices of a man whose inclinations led him to be corrupt, and had great abilities to manage, to multiply, and defend his corruptions.

In like manner, the disbelief of a divine Providence renders a man uncapable of holding any public station; for, since kings avow themselves to be the deputies of Providence, the Lilliputians think nothing can be more absurd than for a prince to employ such men as disown the authority under which he acts.

In relating these and the following laws, I would only be understood to mean the original institutions, and not the most scandalous corruptions into which these people are fallen by the degenerate nature of man. For as to that infamous practice of acquiring great employments by dancing on the ropes, or badges of favor and distinction by leaping over sticks and creeping under them, the reader

is to observe, that they were first introduced by the grandfather of the Emperor now reigning, and grew to the present height,[42] by the gradual increase of party and faction.

Ingratitude is among them a capital crime, as we read it to have been in some other countries: for they reason thus, that whoever makes ill returns to his benefactor, must needs be a common enemy to the rest of mankind, from whom he hath received no obligation, and therefore such a man is not fit to live.

Their notions relating to the duties of parents and children differ extremely from ours. For, since the conjunction of male and female is founded upon the great law of nature, in order to propagate and continue the species, the Lilliputians will needs have it, that men and women are joined together like other animals, by the motives of concupiscence; and that their tenderness towards their young proceeds from the like natural principle: for which reason they will never allow, that a child is under any obligation to his father for begetting him, or to his mother for bringing him into the world, which, considering the miseries of human life, was neither a benefit in itself, nor intended so by his parents, whose thoughts in their love encounters were otherwise employed. Upon these, and the like reasonings, their opinion is, that parents are the last of all others to be trusted with the education of their own children; and therefore they have in every town public nurseries, where all parents, except cottagers and laborers, are obliged to send their infants of both sexes to be reared and educated when they come to the age of twenty moons, at which time they are supposed to have some rudiments of docility. These schools are of several kinds, suited to different qualities, and to both sexes. They have certain professors well skilled in preparing children for such a condition of life as befits the rank of their parents, and their own capacities as well as inclinations. I shall first say something of the male nurseries, and then of the female.

The nurseries for males of noble or eminent birth, are provided with grave and learned professors, and their several deputies. The clothes and food of the children are plain and simple. They are bred up in

41. **weal:** well-being.

42. **present height:** The Order of the Bath had just been revived by George I in 1725 as a means of rewarding his loyal supporters. Cf. Swift's verses on "Reviving the Order of the Bath":

Quoth King Robin, our Ribbands I see are too few
Of St. Andrew's the Green, and St. George's the Blue
I must have another of Color more gay
That will make all my Subjects with Pride to obey.

the principles of honor, justice, courage, modesty, clemency, religion and love of their country; they are always employed in some business, except in the times of eating and sleeping, which are very short, and two hours for diversions, consisting of bodily exercises. They are dressed by men till four years of age, and then are obliged to dress themselves, although their quality be ever so great; and the women attendants, who are aged proportionably to ours at fifty, perform only the most menial offices. They are never suffered to converse with servants, but go together in small or greater numbers to take their diversions, and always in the presence of a professor, or one of his deputies; whereby they avoid those early bad impressions of folly and vice to which our children are subject. Their parents are suffered to see them only twice a year; the visit is not to last above an hour. They are allowed to kiss the child at meeting and parting; but a professor, who always stands by on those occasions, will not suffer them to whisper, or use any fondling expressions, or bring any presents of toys, sweetmeats, and the like.

The pension from each family for the education and entertainment of a child, upon failure of due payment, is levied by the Emperor's officers.

The nurseries for children of ordinary gentlemen, merchants, traders, and handicrafts, are managed proportionably after the same manner; only those designed for trades, are put out apprentices at seven years old, whereas those of persons of quality continue in their exercises till fifteen, which answers to one and twenty with us: but the confinement is gradually lessened for the last three years.

In the female nurseries, the young girls of quality are educated much like the males, only they are dressed by orderly servants of their own sex; but always in the presence of a professor or deputy, till they come to dress themselves, which is at five years old. And if it be found that these nurses ever presume to entertain the girls with frightful or foolish stories, or the common follies practiced by chambermaids among us, they are publicly whipped thrice about the city, imprisoned for a year, and banished for life to the most desolate part of the country. Thus the young ladies there are as much ashamed of being cowards and fools, as the men, and despise all personal ornaments beyond decency and cleanliness: neither did I perceive any difference in their education, made by their difference of sex, only that the exercises of the females were

not altogether so robust; and that some rules were given them relating to domestic life, and a smaller compass of learning was enjoined them: for their maxim is, that among people of quality, a wife should be always a reasonable and agreeable companion, because she cannot always be young. When the girls are twelve years old, which among them is the marriageable age, their parents or guardians take them home, with great expressions of gratitude to the professors, and seldom without tears of the young lady and her companions.

In the nurseries of females of the meaner sort, the children are instructed in all kinds of works proper for their sex, and their several degrees: those intended for apprentices, are dismissed at seven years old, the rest are kept to eleven.

The meaner families who have children at these nurseries, are obliged, besides their annual pension, which is as low as possible, to return to the steward of the nursery a small monthly share of their gettings, to be a portion for the child; and therefore all parents are limited in their expenses by the law. For the Lilliputians think nothing can be more unjust, than that people, in subservience to their own appetites, should bring children into the world, and leave the burthen of supporting them on the public. As to persons of quality, they give security to appropriate a certain sum for each child, suitable to their condition; and these funds are always managed with good husbandry, and the most exact justice.

The cottagers and laborers keep their children at home, their business being only to till and cultivate the earth, and therefore their education is of little consequence to the public; but the old and diseased among them are supported by hospitals: for begging is a trade unknown in this empire.

And here it may perhaps divert the curious reader, to give some account of my domestic, and my manner of living in this country, during a residence of nine months and thirteen days. Having a head mechanically turned, and being likewise forced by necessity, I had made for myself a table and chair convenient enough, out of the largest trees in the royal park. Two hundred sempstresses were employed to make me shirts, and linen for my bed and table, all of the strongest and coarsest kind they could get; which, however, they were forced to quilt together in several folds, for the thickest was some degrees finer than lawn. Their linen is usually three inches wide, and three foot make a piece. The sempstresses took my measure as I lay on the ground, one standing at my neck, and another at my midleg, with a strong cord extended, that each held by the end, while the third measured the length of the cord with a rule of an inch long. Then they measured my right thumb, and desired no more; for by a mathematical computation, that twice round the thumb [43] is once round the wrist, and so on to the neck and the waist, and by the help of my old shirt, which I displayed on the ground before them for a pattern, they fitted me exactly. Three hundred tailors were employed in the same manner to make me clothes; but they had another contrivance for taking my measure. I kneeled down, and they raised a ladder from the ground to my neck; upon this ladder one of them mounted, and let fall a plumb line from my collar to the floor, which just answered the length of my coat: but my waist and arms I measured myself. When my clothes were finished, which was done in my house (for the largest of theirs would not have been able to hold them), they looked like the patchwork made by the ladies in England, only that mine were all of a color.

I had three hundred cooks to dress my victuals, in little convenient huts built about my house, where they and their families lived, and prepared me two dishes apiece. I took up twenty waiters in my hand, and placed them on the table: an hundred more attended below on the ground, some with dishes of meat, and some with barrels of wine, and other liquors, slung on their shoulders; all which the waiters above drew up as I wanted, in a very ingenious manner, by certain cords, as we draw the bucket up a well in Europe. A dish of their meat was a good mouthful, and a barrel of their liquor a reasonable draught. Their mutton yields to ours, but their beef is excellent. I have had a sirloin so large, that I have been forced to make three bits [44] of it; but this is rare. My servants were astonished to see me eat it bones and all, as in our country we do the leg of a lark. Their geese and turkeys I usually eat at a mouthful, and I must confess they far exceed ours. Of their smaller fowl I could take up twenty or thirty at the end of my knife.

One day his Imperial Majesty, being informed of my way of living, desired that himself and his Royal Consort, with the young Princes of the blood of both sexes, might have the happiness (as he was pleased to call it) of dining with me. They came accordingly, and I placed them in chairs of state

on my table, just over against me, with their guards about them, Flimnap, the Lord High Treasurer, attended there likewise with his white staff, [45] and I observed he often looked on me with a sour countenance, which I would not seem to regard, but eat more than usual, in honor to my dear country, as well as to fill the court with admiration. I have some private reasons to believe, that this visit from his Majesty gave Flimnap an opportunity of doing me ill offices to his master. That minister had always been my secret enemy, although he outwardly caressed me more than was usual to the moroseness of his nature. He represented to the Emperor the low condition of his treasury; that he was forced to take up money at great discount; that exchequer bills [46] would not circulate under nine *per cent.* below par; that I had cost his Majesty above a million and a half of *sprugs* (their greatest gold coin, about the bigness of a spangle); and upon the whole, that it would be advisable in the Emperor to take the first occasion of dismissing me.

I am here obliged to vindicate the reputation of an excellent lady, who was an innocent sufferer upon my account. The Treasurer took a fancy to be jealous of his wife, [47] from the malice of some evil tongues, who informed him that her Grace had taken a violent affection for my person; and the court scandal ran for some time, that she once came privately to my lodging. This I solemnly declare to be a most infamous falsehood, without any grounds, farther than that her Grace was pleased to treat me with all innocent marks of freedom and friendship. I own she came often to my house, but always publicly, nor ever without three more in the coach, who were usually her sister and young daughter, and some particular acquaintance; but this was common to many other ladies of the court. And I still appeal to my servants round, whether they at any time saw a coach at my door without knowing what persons were in it. On those occasions, when a servant had given me notice, my custom was to go immediately to the door; and, after paying my respects, to take up the coach and two horses very carefully in my hands (for, if there were six horses, the postillion always unharnessed four) and place them on a table, where I had fixed a movable rim quite round, of five inches high, to prevent accidents. And I have often had four coaches

43. **thumb:** a "rule of thumb," a rough calculation among tailors and dressmakers.   44. **bits:** bites.

45. **white staff:** the symbol of office of the Treasurer in England. 46. **exchequer bills:** first issued by the Chancellor of the Exchequer in 1696, when he called in the depreciated currency. Swift disliked such Whig methods of public finance.   47. **his wife:** probably a little joke at Walpole's expense.

and horses at once on my table full of company, while I sat in my chair leaning my face towards them; and when I was engaged with one set, the coachmen would gently drive the others round my table. I have passed many an afternoon very agreeably in these conversations. But I defy the Treasurer, or his two informers (I will name them, and let them make their best of it) Clustril and Drunlo, to prove that any person ever came to me *incognito,*[48] except the secretary Reldresal, who was sent by express command of his Imperial Majesty, as I have before related. I should not have dwelt so long upon this particular, if it had not been a point wherein the reputation of a great lady is so nearly concerned, to say nothing of my own; although I had the honor to be a *Nardac,* which the Treasurer himself is not; for all the world knows he is only a *clumglum,* a title inferior by one degree, as that of a Marquis is to a Duke in England; yet I allow he preceded me in right of his post. These false informations, which I afterwards came to the knowledge of, by an accident not proper to mention, made the Treasurer show his lady for some time an ill countenance, and me a worse; for although he were at last undeceived and reconciled to her, yet I lost all credit with him, and found my interest decline very fast with the Emperor himself, who was indeed too much governed by that favorite.

CHAPTER 7

The Author, being informed of a design to accuse him of high treason, makes his escape to Blefuscu. His reception there.

Before I proceed to give an account of my leaving this kingdom, it may be proper to inform the reader of a private intrigue which had been for two months forming against me.

I had been hitherto all my life a stranger to courts, for which I was unqualified by the meanness of my condition. I had indeed heard and read enough of the dispositions of great princes and ministers; but never expected to have found such terrible effects of them in so remote a country, governed, as I thought, by very different maxims from those in Europe.

When I was just preparing to pay my attendance on the Emperor of Blefuscu, a considerable person at court (to whom I had been very serviceable at a time when he lay under the highest displeasure of his Imperial Majesty) came to my house very privately at night in a close chair, and without sending his name, desired admittance. The chairmen were dismissed; I put the chair, with his Lordship in it, into my coat pocket: and giving orders to a trusty servant to say I was indisposed and gone to sleep, I fastened the door of my house, placed the chair on the table, according to my usual custom, and sat down by it. After the common salutations were over, observing his Lordship's countenance full of concern, and inquiring into the reason, he desired I would hear him with patience in a matter that highly concerned my honor and my life. His speech was to the following effect, for I took notes of it as soon as he left me.

"You are to know," said he, "that several Committees of Council [49] have been lately called in the most private manner on your account; and it but two days since his Majesty came to a full resolution.

"You are very sensible that Skyris Bolgolam (*Galbet,* or High Admiral) hath been your mortal enemy almost ever since your arrival. His original reasons I know not; but his hatred is much increased since your great success against Blefuscu, by which his glory, as Admiral, is obscured. This Lord, in conjunction with Flimnap the High Treasurer, whose enmity against you is notorious on account of his lady, Limtoc the General, Lalcon the Chamberlain, and Balmuff the Grand Justiciary, have prepared articles of impeachment against you, for treason, and other capital crimes."

This preface made me so impatient, being conscious of my own merits and innocence, that I was going to interrupt; when he entreated me to be silent, and thus proceeded.

"Out of gratitude for the favors you have done me, I procured information of the whole proceedings, and a copy of the articles, wherein I venture my head for your service."

ARTICLES OF IMPEACHMENT AGAINST QUINBUS FLESTRIN (THE MAN-MOUNTAIN)

ARTICLE I

Whereas, by a statute made in the reign of his Imperial Majesty Calin Deffar Plune, it is enacted,

---

48. came . . . *incognito:* Perhaps this refers to incidents in the trial of Bishop Atterbury for Jacobite intrigue.

49. Committees . . . Council: referring to the committee appointed in 1715 to investigate the activities of the Tory ministers, who had been turned out of office on the death of the queen. The impeachments of Oxford and Bolingbroke followed, and are here satirized in the Articles of Impeachment brought against Gulliver.

that whoever shall make water within the precincts of the royal palace, shall be liable to the pains and penalties of high treason; nothwithstanding, the said Quinbus Flestrin, in open breach of the said law, under color of extinguishing the fire kindled in the apartment of his Majesty's most dear Imperial Consort, did maliciously, traitorously, and devilishly, by discharge of his urine, put out the said fire kindled in the said apartment, lying and being within the precincts of the said royal palace, against the statute in that case provided, *etc.* against the duty, *etc.*

ARTICLE II

That the said Quinbus Flestrin having brought the imperial fleet of Blefuscu into the royal port, and being afterwards commanded by his Imperial Majesty to seize all the other ships of the said empire of Blefuscu, and reduce that empire to a province, to be governed by a viceroy from hence, and to destroy and put to death not only all the Big-Endian exiles, but likewise all the people of that empire, who would not immediately forsake the Big-Endian heresy: He, the said Flestrin, like a false traitor against his most Auspicious, Serene, Imperial Majesty, did petition to be excused from the said service, upon pretense of unwillingness to force the consciences, or destroy the liberties and lives of an innocent people.

ARTICLE III

That, whereas certain ambassadors arrived from the court of Blefuscu, to sue for peace in his Majesty's court: He, the said Flestrin, did, like a false traitor, aid, abet, comfort and divert the said ambassadors, although he knew them to be servants to a prince who was lately an open enemy to his Imperial Majesty, and in open war against his said Majesty.

ARTICLE IV

That the said Quinbus Flestrin, contrary to the duty of a faithful subject, is now preparing to make a voyage to the court and empire of Blefuscu, for which he hath received only verbal license from his Imperial Majesty; and under color of the said license, doth falsely and traitorously intend to take the said voyage, and thereby to aid, comfort, and abet the Emperor of Blefuscu, so late an enemy, and in open war with his Imperial Majesty aforesaid.

" There are some other articles, but these are the the most important, of which I have read you an abstract.

" In the several debates upon this impeachment, it must be confessed that his Majesty gave many marks of his great lenity, often urging the serv-

ices you had done him, and endeavoring to extenuate your crimes. The Treasurer and Admiral insisted that you should be put to the most painful and ignominious death, by setting fire on your house at night, and the General was to attend with twenty thousand men armed with poisoned arrows to shoot you on the face and hands. Some of your servants were to have private orders to strew a poisonous juice on your shirts and sheets, which would soon make you tear your own flesh, and die in the utmost torture. The General came into the same opinion; so that for a long time there was a majority against you. But his Majesty resolving, if possible, to spare your life, at last brought off the Chamberlain.

" Upon this incident, Reldresal, principal Secretary for Private Affairs, who always approved himself your true friend, was commanded by the Emperor to deliver his opinion, which he accordingly did; and therein justified the good thoughts you have of him. He allowed your crimes to be great, but that still there was room for mercy, the most commendable virtue in a prince, and for which his Majesty was so justly celebrated. He said, the friendship between you and him was so well known to the world, that perhaps the most honorable board might think him partial: however, in obedience to the command he had received, he would freely offer his sentiments. That if his Majesty, in consideration of your services, and pursuant to his own merciful disposition, would please to spare your life, and only give orders to put out both your eyes,[50] he humbly conceived, that by this expedient, justice might in some measure be satisfied, and all the world would applaud the lenity of the Emperor, as well as the fair and generous proceedings of those who have the honor to be his counselors. That the loss of your eyes would be no impediment to your bodily strength, by which you might still be useful to his Majesty. That blindness is an addition to courage, by concealing dangers from us; that the fear you had for your eyes was the greatest difficulty in bringing over the enemy's fleet, and it would be sufficient for you to see by the eyes of the ministers, since the greatest princes do no more.

" This proposal was received with the utmost disapprobation by the whole board. Bolgolam, the Admiral, could not preserve his temper; but rising up in fury, said, he wondered how the Secretary durst presume to give his opinion for preserv-

---

50. would . . . eyes: Some had proposed that it would be enough to deprive Oxford and Bolingbroke of their titles and estates.

ing the life of a traitor: that the services you had performed, were, by all true reasons of state, the great aggravation of your crimes; that you, who were able to extinguish the fire, by discharge of urine in her Majesty's apartment (which he mentioned with horror), might, at another time, raise an inundation by the same means, to drown the whole palace; and the same strength which enabled you to bring over the enemy's fleet, might serve, upon the first discontent, to carry it back: that he had good reasons to think you were a Big-Endian in your heart; and as treason begins in the heart, before it appears in overt acts, so he accused you as a traitor on that account, and therefore insisted you should be put to death.[51]

"The Treasurer was of the same opinion; he showed to what straits his Majesty's revenue was reduced by the charge of maintaining you, which would soon grow insupportable: that the Secretary's expedient of putting out your eyes was so far from being a remedy against this evil, that it would probably increase it, as it is manifest from the common practice of blinding some kind of fowl, after which they fed the faster, and grew sooner fat: that his sacred Majesty and the Council, who are your judges, were in their own consciences fully convinced of your guilt, which was a sufficient argument to condemn you to death, without the *formal proofs required by the strict letter of the law*.

"But his Imperial Majesty, fully determined against capital punishment, was graciously pleased to say, that since the Council thought the loss of your eyes too easy a censure, some other may be inflicted hereafter. And your friend the Secretary humbly desiring to be heard again, in answer to what the Treasurer had objected concerning the great charge his Majesty was at in maintaining you, said, that his Excellency, who had the sole disposal of the Emperor's revenue, might easily provide against the evil, by gradually lessening your establishment; by which, for want of sufficient food, you would grow weak and faint, and lose your appetite, and consequently decay and consume in a few months; neither would the stench of your carcass be then so dangerous, when it should become more than half diminished; and immediately upon your death, five or six thousand of his Majesty's subjects might, in two or three days, cut your flesh

from your bones, take it away by cartloads, and bury it in distant parts to prevent infection, leaving the skeleton as a monument of admiration to posterity.

"Thus by the great friendship of the Secretary, the whole affair was compromised. It was strictly enjoined, that the project of starving you by degrees should be kept a secret, but the sentence of putting out your eyes was entered on the books; none dissenting except Bolgolam the Admiral, who, being a creature of the Empress, was perpetually instigated by her Majesty to insist upon your death, she having borne perpetual malice against you, on account of that infamous and illegal method you took to extinguish the fire in her apartment.

"In three days your friend the Secretary will be directed to come to your house, and read before you the articles of impeachment; and then to signify the great lenity and favor of his Majesty and Council, whereby you are only condemned to the loss of your eyes, which his Majesty doth not question you will gratefully and humbly submit to; and twenty of his Majesty's surgeons will attend, in order to see the operation well performed, by discharging very sharp-pointed arrows into the balls of your eyes, as you lie on the ground.

"I leave to your prudence what measures you will take; and to avoid suspicion, I must immediately return in as private a manner as I came."

His Lordship did so, and I remained alone, under many doubts and perplexities of mind.

It was a custom introduced by this prince and his ministry (very different, as I have been assured, from the practices of former times), that after the court had decreed any cruel execution, either to gratify the monarch's resentment, or the malice of a favorite, the Emperor always made a speech to his whole Council, expressing his *great lenity* [52] *and tenderness, as qualities known and confessed by all the world*. This speech was immediately published through the kingdom; nor did anything terrify the people so much as those encomiums on his Majesty's mercy; because it was observed, that the more these praises were enlarged and insisted on, the more *inhuman* was the punishment, and the *sufferer more innocent*. Yet, as to myself, I must confess, having never been designed for a courtier either by my birth or education, I was so ill a judge of things, that I could not discover the *lenity* and

51. death: Swift had in mind the violence of party hatred against his friends, the Tory leaders, whose loyalty he had constantly upheld, but the details of Gulliver's experience do not need to be given an historical interpretation.

52. great lenity: perhaps a reference to the Address of the House of Lords, praising his Majesty's "endearing tenderness and clemency" about the time of the execution of the rebels of 1715.

favor of this sentence, but conceived it (perhaps erroneously) rather to be rigorous than gentle. I sometimes thought of standing my trial; for although I could not deny the facts alleged in the several articles, yet I hoped they would admit of some extenuations. But having in my life perused many state trials, which I ever observed to terminate as the judges thought fit to direct, I durst not rely on so dangerous a decision, in so critical a juncture, and against such powerful enemies. Once I was strongly bent upon resistance, for while I had liberty, the whole strength of that empire could hardly subdue me, and I might easily with stones pelt the metropolis to pieces; but I soon rejected that project with horror, by remembering the oath I had made to the Emperor, the favors I received from him, and the high title of *Nardac* he conferred upon me. Neither had I so soon learned the gratitude of courtiers, to persuade myself that his Majesty's *present severities acquitted me of all past obligations.*

At last I fixed upon a resolution, for which it is probable I may incur some censure, and not unjustly; for I confess I owe the preserving my eyes, and consequently my liberty, to my own great rashness and want of experience: because if I had then known the nature of princes and ministers, which I have since observed in many other courts, and their methods of treating criminals less obnoxious than myself, I should with great alacrity and readiness have submitted to so *easy* a punishment. But hurried on by the precipitancy of youth, and having his Imperial Majesty's license to pay my attendance upon the Emperor of Blefuscu, I took this opportunity, before the three days were elapsed, to send a letter to my friend the Secretary, signifying my resolution of setting out that morning for Blefuscu pursuant to the leave I had got; and without waiting for an answer, I went to that side of the island where our fleet lay. I seized a large man-of-war, tied a cable to the prow, and, lifting up the anchors, I stripped myself, put my clothes (together with my coverlet, which I carried under my arm) into the vessel, and drawing it after me between wading and swimming, arrived at the royal port of Blefuscu, where the people had long expected me: they lent me two guides to direct me to the capital city, which is of the same name. I held them in my hands till I came within two hundred yards of the gate, and desired them to signify my arrival to one of the secretaries, and let him know, I there waited his Majesty's commands. I had an answer

in about an hour, that his Majesty, attended by the Royal Family, and great officers of the court, was coming out to receive me. I advanced a hundred yards. The Emperor and his train alighted from their horses, the Empress and ladies from their coaches, and I did not perceive they were in any fright or concern. I lay on the ground to kiss his Majesty's and the Empress's hands. I told his Majesty, that I was come according to my promise, and with the license of the Emperor my master, to have the honor of seeing so mighty a monarch, and to offer him any service in my power, consistent with my duty to my own prince; not mentioning a word of my disgrace, because I had hitherto no regular information of it, and might suppose myself wholly ignorant of any such design; neither could I reasonably conceive that the Emperor would discover the secret while I was out of his power: wherein, however, it soon appeared I was deceived.

I shall not trouble the reader with the particular account of my reception at this court, which was suitable to the generosity of so great a prince; nor of the difficulties I was in for want of a house and bed, being forced to lie on the ground, wrapped up in my coverlet.

CHAPTER 8

The Author, by a lucky accident, finds means to leave Blefuscu; and, after some difficulties, returns safe to his native country.

Three days after my arrival, walking out of curiosity to the northeast coast of the island, I observed, about half a league off, in the sea, somewhat that looked like a boat overturned. I pulled off my shoes and stockings, and wading two or three hundred yards, I found the object to approach nearer by force of the tide; and then plainly saw it to be a real boat, which I supposed might, by some tempest, have been driven from a ship; whereupon I returned immediately towards the city, and desired his Imperial Majesty to lend me twenty of the tallest vessels he had left after the loss of his fleet, and three thousand seamen under the command of his Vice-Admiral. This fleet sailed round, while I went back the shortest way to the coast where I first discovered the boat; I found the tide had driven it still nearer. The seamen were all provided with cordage, which I had beforehand twisted to a sufficient strength. When the ships came up, I stripped myself, and waded till I came within an hundred yards of the boat, after which

I was forced to swim till I got up to it. The seamen threw me the end of the cord, which I fastened to a hole in the forepart of the boat, and the other end to a man-of-war; but I found all my labor to little purpose; for being out of my depth, I was not able to work. In this necessity, I was forced to swim behind, and push the boat forwards as often as I could, with one of my hands; and the tide favoring me, I advanced so far, that I could just hold up my chin and feel the ground. I rested two or three minutes, and then gave the boat another shove, and so on till the sea was no higher than my armpits; and now the most laborious part being over, I took out my other cables, which were stowed in one of the ships, and fastening them first to the boat, and then to nine of the vessels which attended me; the wind being favorable, the seamen towed, and I shoved till we arrived within forty yards of the shore; and waiting till the tide was out, I got dry to the boat, and by the assistance of two thousand men, with ropes and engines, I made a shift to turn it on its bottom, and found it was but little damaged.

I shall not trouble the reader with the difficulties I was under by the help of certain paddles, which cost me ten days making, to get my boat to the royal port of Blefuscu, where a mighty concourse of people appeared upon my arrival, full of wonder at the sight of so prodigious a vessel. I told the Emperor that my good fortune had thrown this boat in my way, to carry me to some place from whence I might return into my native country, and begged his Majesty's orders for getting materials to fit it up, together with his license to depart; which, after some kind of expostulations, he was pleased to grant.

I did very much wonder, in all this time, not to have heard of any express relating to me from our Emperor to the court of Blefuscu. But I was afterwards given privately to understand, that his Imperial Majesty, never imagining I had the least notice of his designs, believed I was only gone to Blefuscu in performance of my promise, according to the license he had given me, which was well known at our court, and would return in a few days when that ceremony was ended. But he was at last in pain at my long absence; and after consulting with the Treasurer, and the rest of that cabal, a person of quality was dispatched with the copy of the articles against me. This envoy [53] had

instructions to represent to the monarch of Blefuscu, the great lenity of his master, who was content to punish me no farther than with the loss of my eyes; that I had fled from justice, and if I did not return in two hours, I should be deprived of my title of *Nardac,* and declared a traitor. The envoy further added, that in order to maintain the peace and amity between both empires, his master expected, that his brother of Blefuscu would give orders to have me sent back to Lilliput, bound hand and foot, to be punished as a traitor.

The Emperor of Blefuscu having taken three days to consult, returned an answer consisting of many civilities and excuses. He said, that as for sending me bound, his brother knew it was impossible; that although I had deprived him of his fleet, yet he owed great obligations to me for many good offices I had done him in making the peace. That however both their Majesties would soon be made easy; for I had found a prodigious vessel on the shore, able to carry me on the sea, which he had given order to fit up with my own assistance and direction; and he hoped in a few weeks both empires would be freed from so insupportable an encumbrance.

With this answer the envoy returned to Lilliput, and the monarch of Blefuscu related to me all that had passed; offering me at the same time (but under the strictest confidence) his gracious protection, if I would continue in his service; wherein although I believed him sincere, yet I resolved never more to put any confidence in princes or ministers, where I could possibly avoid it; and therefore, with all due acknowledgments for his favorable intentions, I humbly begged to be excused. I told him, that since fortune, whether good or evil, had thrown a vessel in my way, I was resolved to venture myself in the ocean, rather than be an occasion of difference between two such mighty monarchs. Neither did I find the Emperor at all displeased; and I discovered by a certain accident, that he was very glad of my resolution, and so were most of his ministers.

These considerations moved me to hasten my departure somewhat sooner than I intended; to which the court, impatient to have me gone, very readily contributed. Five hundred workmen were employed to make two sails to my boat, according to my directions, by quilting thirteenfold of their strongest linen together. I was at the pains of making ropes and cables, by twisting ten, twenty or thirty of the thickest and strongest of theirs. A great stone that I happened to find, after a long search,

53. **This envoy:** Frequent protests had been sent to the French government on account of its protection of Jacobites.

by the seashore, served me for an anchor. I had the tallow of three hundred cows for greasing my boat, and other uses. I was at incredible pains in cutting down some of the largest timber-trees for oars and masts, wherein I was, however, much assisted by his Majesty's ship carpenters, who helped me in smoothing them, after I had done the rough work.

In about a month, when all was prepared, I sent to receive his Majesty's commands, and to take my leave. The Emperor and Royal Family came out of the palace; I lay down on my face to kiss his hand, which he very graciously gave me: so did the Empress and young Princes of the blood. His Majesty presented me with fifty purses of two hundred *sprugs* apiece, together with his picture at full length, which I put immediately into one of my gloves, to keep it from being hurt. The ceremonies at my departure were too many to trouble the reader with at this time.

I stored the boat with the carcases of an hundred oxen, and three hundred sheep, with bread and drink proportionable, and as much meat ready dressed as four hundred cooks could provide. I took with me six cows and two bulls alive, with as many ewes and rams, intending to carry them into my own country, and propagate the breed. And to feed them on board, I had a good bundle of hay, and a bag of corn. I would gladly have taken a dozen of the natives, but this was a thing the Emperor would by no means permit; and besides a diligent search into my pockets, his Majesty engaged my honor not to carry away any of his subjects, although with their own consent and desire.

Having thus prepared all things as well as I was able, I set sail on the 24th day of September, 1701, at six in the morning; and when I had gone about four leagues to the northward, the wind being at southeast, at six in the evening I descried a small island about half a league to the northwest. I advanced forward, and cast anchor on the lee side of the island, which seemed to be uninhabited. I then took some refreshment, and went to my rest. I slept well, and as I conjecture at least six hours, for I found the day broke in two hours after I awaked. It was a clear night. I eat my breakfast before the sun was up; and heaving anchor, the wind being favorable, I steered the same course that I had done the day before, wherein I was directed by my pocket compass. My intention was to reach, if possible, one of those islands, which I had reason to believe lay to the northeast of Van Diemen's Land. I discovered nothing all that day; but upon

the next, about three in the afternoon, when I had by my computation made twenty-four leagues from Blefuscu, I descried a sail steering to the southeast; my course was due east. I hailed her, but could get no answer; yet I found I gained upon her, for the wind slackened. I made all the sail I could, and in half an hour she spied me, then hung out her ancient, and discharged a gun. It is not easy to express the joy I was in upon the unexpected hope of once more seeing my beloved country, and the dear pledges I had left in it. The ship slackened her sails, and I came up with her between five and six in the evening, September 26; but my heart leaped within me to see her English colors. I put my cows and sheep into my coat pockets, and got on board with all my little cargo of provisions. The vessel was an English merchantman, returning from Japan by the North and South Seas; [54] the Captain, Mr. John Biddel of Deptford, a very civil man, and an excellent sailor. We were now in the latitude of thirty degrees south; there were about fifty men in the ship; and here I met an old comrade of mine, one Peter Williams, who gave me a good character to the Captain. This gentleman treated me with kindness, and desired I would let him know what place I came from last, and whither I was bound; which I did in a few words, but he thought I was raving, and that the dangers I underwent had disturbed my head; whereupon I took my black cattle and sheep out of my pocket, which, after great astonishment, clearly convinced him of my veracity. I then showed him the gold given me by the Emperor of Blefuscu, together with his Majesty's picture at full length, and some other rarities of that country. I gave him two purses of two hundred *sprugs* each, and promised, when we arrived in England, to make him a present of a cow and a sheep big with young.

I shall not trouble the reader with a particular account of this voyage, which was very prosperous for the most part. We arrived in the Downs [55] on the 13th of April, 1702. I had only one misfortune, that the rats on board carried away one of my sheep; I found her bones in a hole, picked clean from the flesh. The rest of my cattle I got safe on shore, and set them a grazing in a bowling green at Greenwich, where the fineness of the grass made them feed very heartily, though I had always feared the contrary: neither could I possibly have pre-

54. North . . . Seas: North and South Pacific.   55. Downs: a roadstead in the English Channel between the Goodwin Sands and the Kent coast, opposite the North Downs.

served them in so long a voyage, if the Captain had not allowed me some of his best biscuit, which, rubbed to powder, and mingled with water, was their constant food. The short time I continued in England, I made a considerable profit by showing my cattle to many persons of quality, and others: and before I began my second voyage, I sold them for six hundred pounds. Since my last return, I find the breed is considerably increased, especially the sheep; which I hope will prove much to the advantage of the woolen manufacture, by the fineness of the fleeces.

I stayed but two months with my wife and family; for my insatiable desire of seeing foreign countries would suffer me to continue no longer. I left fifteen hundred pounds with my wife, and fixed her in a good house at Redriff. My remaining stock I carried with me, part in money, and part in goods, in hopes to improve my fortunes. My eldest uncle John had left me an estate in land, near Epping, of about thirty pounds a year; and I had a long lease of the Black Bull in Fetter Lane, which yielded me as much more; so that I was not in any danger of leaving my family upon the parish. My son Johnny, named so after his uncle, was at the Grammar School, and a towardly [56] child. My daughter Betty (who is now married, and has children) was then at her needlework. I took leave of my wife, and boy and girl, with tears on both sides, and went on board the *Adventure,* a merchant ship of three hundred tons, bound for Surat,[57] Captain John Nicholas, of Liverpool, Commander. But my account of this voyage must be referred to the second part of my *Travels.*

THE END OF THE FIRST PART

PART II
A Voyage to Brobdingnag [1]

CHAPTER I

A great storm described. The longboat sent to fetch water, the Author goes with it to discover the country. He is left on shore, is seized by one of the natives, and carried to a farmer's house. His reception there, with several accidents that happened there. A description of the inhabitants.

Having been condemned by nature and fortune to an active and restless life, in two months after my return, I again left my native country, and took shipping in the Downs on the 20th day of June, 1702, in the *Adventure,* Captain John Nicholas, a Cornish man, Commander, bound for Surat. We had a very prosperous gale till we arrived at the Cape of Good Hope, where we landed for fresh water, but discovering a leak we unshipped our goods and wintered there; for the Captain falling sick of an ague, we could not leave the Cape till the end of March. We then set sail, and had a good voyage till we passed the Straits of Madagascar; but having got northward of that island, and to about five degrees south latitude, the winds, which in those seas are observed to blow a constant equal gale between the north and west from the beginning of December to the beginning of May, on the 19th of April began to blow with much greater violence, and more westerly than usual, continuing so for twenty days together, during which time we were driven a little to the east of the Molucca Islands, and about three degrees northward of the Line, as our Captain found by an observation he took the 2nd of May, at which time the wind ceased, and it was a perfect calm, whereat I was not a little rejoiced. But he, being a man well experienced in the navigation of those seas, bid us all prepare against a storm, which accordingly happened the day following: for a southern wind, called the southern monsoon, began to set in.

Finding it was likely to overblow,[2] we took in our spritsail, and stood by to hand the foresail; but making foul weather we looked the guns were all fast, and handed the mizzen. The ship lay very broad off, so we thought it better spooning before the sea, than trying or hulling. We reefed the foresail and set him, we hauled aft the foresheet; the helm was hard aweather. The ship wore bravely. We belayed the fore-down-haul; but the sail was split, and we hauled down the yard, and got the sail into the ship, and unbound all the things clear of it. It was a very fierce storm; the sea broke strange and dangerous. We hauled off upon the lanyard of the whipstaff, and helped the man at helm. We would not get down our topmast, but let all stand, because she scudded before the sea very well, and we knew that the topmast being aloft, the ship was the wholesomer, and made better way through

56. **towardly:** promising.   57. **Surat:** an important seaport north of Bombay. **A Voyage to Brobdingnag: 1. Brobdingnag:** It is described as a great island or continent, jutting out into the Pacific from the northwest coast of North America, a region then little known.

2. to overblow: This paragraph is a parody of the use of seamen's technical terms in the popular accounts of voyages; it is stolen from Sturmy's *Compleat Mariner,* 1669.

the sea, seeing we had sea room. When the storm was over, we set foresail and mainsail, and brought the ship to. Then we set the mizzen, main topsail, and the fore topsail. Our course was east northeast, the wind was at southwest. We got the starboard tack aboard, we cast off our weather braces and lifts; we set in the lee braces, and hauled forward by the weather bowlines, and hauled them tight, and belayed them, and hauled over the mizzen tack to windward, and kept her full and by as near as she would lie.

During this storm, which was followed by a strong wind west southwest, we were carried by my computation about five hundred leagues to the east, so that the oldest sailor on board could not tell in what part of the world we were. Our provisions held out well, our ship was staunch, and our crew all in good health; but we lay in the utmost distress for water. We thought it best to hold on the same course, rather than turn more northerly, which might have brought us to the northwest parts of Great Tartary, and into the frozen sea.[3]

On the 16th day of June, 1703, a boy on the topmast discovered land. On the 17th we came in full view of a great island or continent (for we knew not whether) on the south side whereof was a small neck of land jutting out into the sea, and a creek too shallow to hold a ship of above one hundred tons. We cast anchor within a league of this creek, and our Captain sent a dozen of his men well armed in the longboat, with vessels for water if any could be found. I desired his leave to go with them, that I might see the country, and make what discoveries I could. When we came to land we saw no river or spring, nor any sign of inhabitants. Our men therefore wandered on the shore to find out some fresh water near the sea, and I walked alone about a mile on the other side, where I observed the country all barren and rocky. I now began to be weary, and seeing nothing to entertain my curiosity, I returned gently down towards the creek; and the sea being full in my view, I saw our men already got into the boat, and rowing for life to the ship. I was going to hollow after them, although it had been to little purpose, when I observed a huge creature walking after them in the sea, as fast as he could: he waded not much deeper than his knees, and took prodigious strides: but our men had the start of him

half a league, and the sea thereabouts being full of sharp-pointed rocks, the monster was not able to overtake the boat. This I was afterwards told, for I durst not stay to see the issue of that adventure; but ran as fast as I could the way I first went, and then climbed up a steep hill, which gave me some prospect of the country. I found it fully cultivated; but that which first surprised me was the length of the grass, which in those grounds that seemed to be kept for hay, was above twenty foot high.[4]

I fell into a highroad, for so I took it to be, though it served to the inhabitants only as a footpath through a field of barley. Here I walked on for some time, but could see little on either side, it being now near harvest, and the corn rising at least forty foot. I was an hour walking to the end of this field, which was fenced in with a hedge of at least one hundred and twenty foot high, and the trees so lofty that I could make no computation of their altitude. There was a stile to pass from this field into the next. It had four steps, and a stone to cross over when you came to the uppermost. It was impossible for me to climb this stile, because every step was six foot high, and the upper stone above twenty. I was endeavoring to find some gap in the hedge, when I discovered one of the inhabitants in the next field, advancing towards the stile, of the same size with him whom I saw in the sea pursuing our boat. He appeared as tall as an ordinary spire steeple, and took about ten yards at every stride, as near as I could guess. I was struck with the utmost fear and astonishment, and ran to hide myself in the corn, from whence I saw him at the top of the stile, looking back into the next field on the right hand, and heard him call in a voice many degrees louder than a speaking trumpet: but the noise was so high in the air, that at first I certainly thought it was thunder. Whereupon seven monsters like himself came towards him with reaping hooks in their hands, each hook about the largeness of six scythes. These people were not so well clad as the first, whose servants or laborers they seemed to be: for, upon some words he spoke, they went to reap the corn in the field where I lay. I kept from them at as great a distance as I could, but was forced to move with extreme difficulty, for the stalks of the corn were sometimes not above a foot distant, so that I could hardly squeeze my

3. **northwest . . . sea:** a curious way of describing the coast of Siberia and the Arctic Ocean.

4. **twenty . . . high:** The scale is not so carefully calculated as in Lilliput, but Swift uses a similar method by increasing sizes twelve times.

body betwixt them. However, I made a shift to go forward till I came to a part of the field where the corn had been laid by the rain and wind. Here it was impossible for me to advance a step; for the stalks were so interwoven that I could not creep through, and the beards of the fallen ears so strong and pointed that they pierced through my clothes into my flesh. At the same time I heard the reapers not above an hundred yards behind me. Being quite dispirited with toil, and wholly overcome by grief and despair, I lay down between two ridges, and heartily wished I might there end my days. I bemoaned my desolate widow, and fatherless children. I lamented my own folly and willfulness in attempting a second voyage against the advice of all my friends and relations. In this terrible agitation of mind I could not forbear thinking of Lilliput, whose inhabitants looked upon me as the greatest prodigy that ever appeared in the world; where I was able to draw an Imperial Fleet in my hand, and perform those other actions which will be recorded forever in the chronicles of that empire, while posterity shall hardly believe them, although attested by millions. I reflected what a mortification it must prove to me to appear as inconsiderable in this nation as one single Lilliputian would be among us. But this I conceived was to be the least of my misfortunes: for, as human creatures are observed to be more savage and cruel in proportion to their bulk, what could I expect but to be a morsel in the mouth of the first among these enormous barbarians who should happen to seize me? Undoubtedly philosophers are in the right when they tell us, that nothing is great or little otherwise than by comparison. It might have pleased fortune to let the Lilliputians find some nation, where the people were as diminutive with respect to them, as they were to me.[5] And who knows but that even this prodigious race of mortals might be equally overmatched in some distant part of the world, whereof we have yet no discovery?

Scared and confounded as I was, I could not forbear going on with these reflections, when one of the reapers approaching within ten yards of the ridge where I lay, made me apprehend that with the next step I should be squashed to death under his foot, or cut in two with his reaping hook. And

therefore when he was again about to move, I screamed as loud as fear could make me. Whereupon the huge creature trod short, and looking round about under him for some time, at last espied me as I lay on the ground. He considered a while with the caution of one who endeavors to lay hold on a small dangerous animal in such a manner that it shall not be able either to scratch or bite him, as I myself have sometimes done with a weasel in England. At length he ventured to take me up behind by the middle between his forefinger and thumb, and brought me within three yards of his eyes, that he might behold my shape more perfectly. I guessed his meaning, and my good fortune gave me so much presence of mind, that I resolved not to struggle in the least as he held me in the air about sixty foot from the ground, although he grievously pinched my sides, for fear I should slip through his fingers. All I ventured was to raise my eyes towards the sun, and place my hands together in a supplicating posture, and to speak some words in an humble melancholy tone, suitable to the condition I then was in. For I apprehended every moment that he would dash me against the ground, as we usually do any little hateful animal which we have a mind to destroy. But my good star would have it, that he appeared pleased with my voice and gestures, and began to look upon me as a curiosity, much wondering to hear me pronounce articulate words, although he could not understand them. In the meantime I was not able to forbear groaning and shedding tears, and turning my head towards my sides; letting him know, as well as I could, how cruelly I was hurt by the pressure of his thumb and finger. He seemed to apprehend my meaning; for, lifting up the lappet of his coat, he put me gently into it, and immediately ran along with me to his master, who was a substantial farmer, and the same person I had first seen in the field.

The farmer having (as I supposed by their talk) received such an account of me as his servant could give him, took a piece of a small straw, about the size of a walking staff, and therewith lifted up the lappets of my coat; which it seems he thought to be some kind of covering that nature had given me. He blew my hairs aside to take a better view of my face. He called his hinds about him, and asked them (as I afterwards learned) whether they had ever seen in the fields any little creature that resembled me. He then placed me softly on the ground upon all fours, but I got immediately up,

5. **diminutive . . . me**: or, as Swift expresses it in verse —

> So, Nat'ralists observe, a Flea
> Hath smaller fleas that on him prey,
> And these have smaller fleas to bite 'em,
> And so proceed *ad infinitum;* . . .

and walked slowly backwards and forwards, to let those people see I had no intent to run away. They all sat down in a circle about me, the better to observe my motions. I pulled off my hat, and made a low bow towards the farmer. I fell on my knees, and lifted up my hands and eyes, and spoke several words as loud as I could: I took a purse of gold out of my pocket, and humbly presented it to him. He received it on the palm of his hand, then applied it close to his eye, to see what it was, and afterwards turned it several times with the point of a pin (which he took out of his sleeve), but could make nothing of it. Whereupon I made a sign that he should place his hand on the ground. I then took the purse, and opening it, poured all the gold into his palm. There were six Spanish pieces of four pistoles [6] each, beside twenty or thirty smaller coins. I saw him wet the tip of his little finger upon his tongue, and take up one of my largest pieces, and then another, but he seemed to be wholly ignorant what they were. He made me a sign to put them again into my purse, and the purse again into my pocket, which after offering to him several times, I thought it best to do.

The farmer by this time was convinced I must be a rational creature. He spoke often to me, but the sound of his voice pierced my ears like that of a water mill, yet his words were articulate enough. I answered as loud as I could, in several languages, and he often laid his ear within two yards of me, but all in vain, for we were wholly unintelligible to each other. He then sent his servants to their work, and taking his handkerchief out of his pocket, he doubled and spread it on his hand, which he placed flat on the ground, with the palm upwards, making me a sign to step into it, as I could easily do, for it was not above a foot in thickness. I thought it my part to obey, and for fear of falling, laid myself at full length upon the handkerchief, with the remainder of which he lapped me up to the head for further security, and in this manner carried me home to his house. There he called his wife, and showed me to her; but she screamed and ran back, as women in England do at the sight of a toad or a spider. However, when she had a while seen my behavior, and how well I observed the signs her husband made, she was soon reconciled, and by degrees grew extremely tender of me.

It was about twelve at noon, and a servant brought in dinner. It was only one substantial dish

of meat (fit for the plain condition of an husbandman) in a dish of about four-and-twenty foot diameter. The company were the farmer and his wife, three children, and an old grandmother. When they were sat down, the farmer placed me at some distance from him on the table, which was thirty foot high from the floor. I was in a terrible fright, and kept as far as I could from the edge for fear of falling. The wife minced a bit of meat, then crumbled some bread on a trencher, and placed it before me. I made her a low bow, took out my knife and fork, and fell to eat, which gave them exceeding delight. The mistress sent her maid for a small dram cup, which held about two gallons, and filled it with drink; I took up the vessel with much difficulty in both hands, and in a most respectful manner drank to her ladyship's health, expressing the words as loud as I could in English, which made the company laugh so heartily that I was almost deafened with the noise. This liquor tasted like a small cider, and was not unpleasant. Then the master made me a sign to come to his trencher side; but as I walked on the table, being in great surprise all the time, as the indulgent reader will easily conceive and excuse, I happened to stumble against a crust, and fell flat on my face, but received no hurt. I got up immediately, and observing the good people to be in much concern, I took my hat (which I held under my arm out of good manners) and waving it over my head, made three huzzas, to show I had got no mischief by the fall. But advancing forwards toward my master (as I shall henceforth call him), his youngest son who sat next him, an arch boy of about ten years old, took me up by the legs, and held me so high in the air, that I trembled every limb; but his father snatched me from him, and at the same time gave him such a box on the left ear, as would have felled an European troop of horse to the earth, ordering him to be taken from the table. But being afraid the boy might owe me a spite, and well remembering how mischievous all children among us naturally are to sparrows, rabbits, young kittens, and puppy dogs, I fell on my knees, and pointing to the boy, made my master understand, as well as I could, that I desired his son might be pardoned. The father complied, and the lad took his seat again; whereupon I went to him and kissed his hand, which my master took, and made him stroke me gently with it.

In the midst of dinner, my mistress's favorite cat leapt into her lap. I heard a noise behind me like

6. **four pistoles:** the largest gold coins, worth between three and four pounds.

that of a dozen stocking weavers at work; and turning my head, I found it proceeded from the purring of this animal, who seemed to be three times larger than an ox, as I computed by the view of her head, and one of her paws, while her mistress was feeding and stroking her. The fierceness of this creature's countenance altogether discomposed me; though I stood at the farther end of the table, above fifty foot off; and although my mistress held her fast for fear she might give a spring, and seize me in her talons. But it happened there was no danger; for the cat took not the least notice of me when my master placed me within three yards of her. And as I have been always told, and found true by experience in my travels, that flying, or discovering fear before a fierce animal, is a certain way to make it pursue or attack you, so I resolved in this dangerous juncture to show no manner of concern. I walked with intrepidity five or six times before the very head of the cat, and came within half a yard of her; whereupon she drew herself back, as if she were more afraid of me: I had less apprehension concerning the dogs, whereof three or four came into the room, as it is usual in farmers' houses; one of which was a mastiff, equal in bulk to four elephants, and a greyhound, somewhat taller than the mastiff, but not so large.

When dinner was almost done, the nurse came in with a child of a year old in her arms, who immediately spied me, and began a squall that you might have heard from London Bridge to Chelsea, after the usual oratory of infants, to get me for a plaything. The mother out of pure indulgence took me up, and put me towards the child, who presently seized me by the middle, and got my head in his mouth, where I roared so loud that the urchin was frighted, and let me drop; and I should infallibly have broke my neck if the mother had not held her apron under me. The nurse to quiet her babe made use of a rattle, which was a kind of hollow vessel filled with great stones, and fastened by a cable to the child's waist: but all in vain, so that she was forced to apply the last remedy by giving it suck. I must confess no object ever disgusted me so much as the sight of her monstrous breast, which I cannot tell what to compare with, so as to give the curious reader an idea of its bulk, shape and color. It stood prominent six foot, and could not be less than sixteen in circumference. The nipple was about half the bigness of my head, and the hue both of that and the dug so varified with spots, pimples, and freckles, that nothing could appear more nauseous: for I had a near sight of her, she sitting down the more conveniently to give suck, and I standing on the table. This made me reflect upon the fair skins of our English ladies, who appear so beautiful to us, only because they are of our own size, and their defects not to be seen but through a magnifying glass, where we find by experiment that the smoothest and whitest skins look rough and coarse, and ill colored.

I remember when I was at Lilliput, the complexion of those diminutive people appeared to me the fairest in the world; and talking upon this subject with a person of learning there, who was an intimate friend of mine, he said that my face appeared much fairer and smoother when he looked on me from the ground, than it did upon a nearer view when I took him up in my hand and brought him close, which he confessed was at first a very shocking sight. He said he could discover great holes in my skin; that the stumps of my beard were ten times stronger than the bristles of a boar, and my complexion made up of several colors altogether disagreeable: although I must beg leave to say for myself, that I am as fair as most of my sex and country, and very little sunburnt by all my travels. On the other side, discoursing of the ladies in that Emperor's court, he used to tell me, one had freckles, another too wide a mouth, a third too large a nose, nothing of which I was able to distinguish. I confess this reflection was obvious enough; which, however, I could not forbear, lest the reader might think those vast creatures were actually deformed: for I must do them justice to say they are a comely race of people; and particularly the features of my master's countenance, although he were but a farmer, when I beheld him from the height of sixty foot, appeared very well proportioned.

When dinner was done, my master went out to his laborers, and as I could discover by his voice and gesture, gave his wife a strict charge to take care of me. I was very much tired, and disposed to sleep, which my mistress perceiving, she put me on her own bed, and covered me with a clean white handkerchief, but larger and coarser than the mainsail of a man-of-war.

I slept about two hours, and dreamed I was at home with my wife and children, which aggravated my sorrows when I awaked and found myself alone in a vast room, between two and three hundred foot wide, and above two hundred high, lying in a bed twenty yards wide. My mistress was gone about her household affairs, and had locked me in. The bed was eight yards from the floor. Some natural necessities required me to get down; I durst not presume to call, and if I had, it would have been in vain, with such a voice as mine, at so great a distance from the room where I lay to the kitchen where the family kept. While I was under these circumstances, two rats crept up the curtains, and ran smelling backwards and forwards on the bed. One of them came up almost to my face, whereupon I rose in a fright, and drew out my hanger [7] to defend myself. These horrible animals had the boldness to attack me on both sides, and one of them held his forefeet at my collar; but I had the good fortune to rip up his belly before he could do me any mischief. He fell down at my feet, and the other seeing the fate of his comrade, made his escape, but not without one good wound on the back, which I gave him as he fled, and made the blood run trickling from him. After this exploit, I walked gently to and fro on the bed, to recover my breath and loss of spirits. These creatures were of the size of a large mastiff, but infinitely more nimble and fierce, so that if I had taken off my belt before I went to sleep, I must have infallibly been torn to pieces and devoured. I measured the tail of the dead rat, and found it to be two yards long, wanting an inch; but it went against my stomach to drag the carcass off the bed, where it lay still bleeding; I observed it had yet some life, but with a strong slash across the neck, I thoroughly dispatched it.

Soon after my mistress came into the room, who seeing me all bloody, ran and took me up in her hand. I pointed to the dead rat, smiling and making other signs to show I was not hurt, whereat she was extremely rejoiced, calling the maid to take up the dead rat with a pair of tongs, and throw it out of the window. Then she set me on a table, where I showed her my hanger all bloody, and wiping it on the lappet of my coat, returned it to the scabbard. I was pressed to do more than one thing, which another could not do for me, and therefore endeavored to make my mistress understand that I desired to be set down on the floor; which after she had done, my bashfulness would not suffer me to express myself farther than by pointing to the door, and bowing several times. The good woman with much difficulty at last perceived what I would be at, and taking me up again in her hand, walked into the garden, where she set me down. I went on one side about two hundred yards, and beckoning to her not to look or to follow me, I hid myself between two leaves of sorrel, and there discharged the necessities of nature.

I hope the gentle reader will excuse me for dwelling on these and the like particulars, which however insignificant they may appear to groveling vulgar minds, yet will certainly help a philosopher to enlarge his thoughts and imagination, and apply them to the benefit of public as well as private life, which was my sole design in presenting this and other accounts of my travels to the world; wherein I have been chiefly studious of truth, without affecting any ornaments of learning or of style. But the whole scene of this voyage made so strong an impression on my mind, and is so deeply fixed in my memory, that in committing it to paper I did not omit one material circumstance: however, upon a strict review, I blotted out several passages of less moment which were in my first copy, for fear of being censured as tedious and trifling, whereof travelers are often, perhaps not without justice, accused.

CHAPTER 2

A description of the farmer's daughter. The Author carried to a market town, and then to the metropolis. The particulars of his journey.

My mistress had a daughter of nine years old, a child of towardly parts for her age, very dexterous at her needle, and skillful in dressing her baby.[8] Her mother and she contrived to fit up the baby's cradle for me against night: the cradle was put into a small drawer of a cabinet, and the drawer placed upon a hanging shelf for fear of the rats. This was my bed all the time I stayed with those people, although made more convenient by degrees, as I began to learn their language, and make my wants known. This young girl was so handy, that after I had once or twice pulled off my clothes before her, she was able to dress and undress me, although I never gave her that trouble when she would let me do either myself. She made me seven shirts, and some other linen, of as fine cloth as could be got, which indeed was coarser than sackcloth; and these she constantly washed for me with her own hands. She was likewise my schoolmistress to teach me the language: when I pointed

---

7. **hanger:** short sword.

8. **baby:** doll.

to anything she told me the name of it in her own tongue, so that in a few days I was able to call for whatever I had a mind to. She was very good-natured, and not above forty foot high, being little for her age. She gave me the name of *Grildrig,* which the family took up, and afterwards the whole kingdom. The word imports what the Latins call *nanunculus,* the Italians *homunceletino,*[9] and the English *mannikin.* To her I chiefly owe my preservation in that country: we never parted while I was there; I called her my *Glumdalclitch,* or little nurse: and I should be guilty of great ingratitude, if I omitted this honorable mention of her care and affection towards me, which I heartily wish it lay in my power to requite as she deserves, instead of being the innocent but unhappy instrument of her disgrace, as I have too much reason to fear.

It now began to be known and talked of in the neighborhood, that my master had found a strange animal in the field, about the bigness of a *splack-nuck,* but exactly shaped in every part like a human creature; which it likewise imitated in all its actions; seemed to speak in a little language of its own, had already learned several words of theirs, went erect upon two legs, was tame and gentle, would come when it was called, do whatever it was bid, had the finest limbs in the world, and a complexion fairer than a nobleman's daughter of three years old. Another farmer who lived hard by, and was a particular friend of my master, came on a visit on purpose to inquire into the truth of this story. I was immediately produced, and placed upon a table, where I walked as I was commanded, drew my hanger, put it up again, made my reverence to my master's guest, asked him in his own language how he did, and told him he was welcome, just as my little nurse had instructed me. This man who was old and dimsighted, put on his spectacles to behold me better, at which I could not forbear laughing very heartily, for his eyes appeared like the full moon shining into a chamber at two windows. Our people, who discovered the cause of my mirth, bore me company in laughing, at which the old fellow was fool enough to be angry and out of countenance. He had the character of a great miser, and to my misfortune he well deserved it, by the cursed advice he gave my master to show me as a sight upon a market day in the next town, which was half an hour's riding, about two and twenty miles from our house. I guessed there was some

mischief contriving, when I observed my master and his friend whispering long together, sometimes pointing at me; and my fears made me fancy that I overheard and understood some of their words. But the next morning Glumdalclitch, my little nurse, told me the whole matter, which she had cunningly picked out from her mother. The poor girl laid me on her bosom, and fell a weeping with shame and grief. She apprehended some mischief would happen to me from rude vulgar folks, who might squeeze me to death, or break one of my limbs by taking me in their hands. She had also observed how modest I was in my nature, how nicely I regarded my honor, and what an indignity I should conceive it to be exposed for money as a public spectacle to the meanest of the people. She said, her papa and mamma had promised that Grildrig should be hers, but now she found they meant to serve her as they did last year, when they pretended to give her a lamb, and yet, as soon as it was fat, sold it to a butcher. For my own part, I may truly affirm that I was less concerned than my nurse. I had a strong hope, which never left me, that I should one day recover my liberty; and as to the ignominy of being carried about for a monster, I considered myself to be a perfect stranger in the country, and that such a misfortune could never be charged upon me as a reproach, if ever I should return to England; since the King of Great Britain himself, in my condition, must have undergone the same distress.

My master, pursuant to the advice of his friend, carried me in a box the next market day to the neighboring town, and took along with him his little daughter, my nurse, upon a pillion behind him. The box was close on every side, with a little door for me to go in and out, and a few gimlet holes to let in air. The girl had been so careful to put the quilt of her baby's bed into it, for me to lie down on. However, I was terribly shaken and discomposed in this journey, though it were but of half an hour. For the horse went about forty foot at every step, and trotted so high, that the agitation was equal to the rising and falling of a ship in a great storm, but much more frequent. Our journey was somewhat further than from London to St. Albans.[10] My master alighted at an inn which he used to frequent; and after consulting a while with the innkeeper, and making some necessary preparations, he hired the *Grultrud,* or crier, to give notice through the town of a strange creature to be seen

9. *nanunculus . . . homunceletino:* coined words perhaps to ridicule such pedantries.

10. St. Albans: about twenty miles from London.

at the Sign of the Green Eagle, not so big as a *splacknuck* (an animal in that country very finely shaped, about six foot long), and in every part of the body resembling an human creature, could speak several words, and perform an hundred diverting tricks.

I was placed upon a table in the largest room of the inn, which might be near three hundred foot square. My little nurse stood on a low stool close to the table, to take care of me, and direct what I should do. My master, to avoid a crowd, would suffer only thirty people at a time to see me. I walked about on the table as the girl commanded: she asked me questions as far as she knew my understanding of the language reached, and I answered them as loud as I could. I turned about several times to the company, paid my humble respects, said they were welcome, and used some other speeches I had been taught. I took up a thimble filled with liquor, which Glumdalclitch had given me for a cup, and drank their health. I drew out my hanger, and flourished with it after the manner of fencers in England. My nurse gave me part of a straw, which I exercised as a pike, having learned the art in my youth. I was that day shown to twelve sets of company, and as often forced to go over again with the same fopperies, till I was half dead with weariness and vexation. For those who had seen me made such wonderful reports, that the people were ready to break down the doors to come in. My master for his own interest would not suffer anyone to touch me except my nurse; and, to prevent danger, benches were set round the table at such a distance as put me out of everybody's reach. However, an unlucky schoolboy aimed a hazelnut directly at my head, which very narrowly missed me; otherwise, it came with so much violence, that it would have infallibly knocked out my brains, for it was almost as large as a small pumpion: [11] but I had the satisfaction to see the young rogue well beaten, and turned out of the room.

My master gave public notice, that he would show me again the next market day, and in the meantime he prepared a more convenient vehicle for me, which he had reason enough to do; for I was so tired with my first journey, and with entertaining company eight hours together, that I could hardly stand upon my legs, or speak a word. It was at least three days before I recovered my strength; and that I might have no rest at home,

11. **pumpion:** pumpkin.

all the neighboring gentlemen from an hundred miles round, hearing of my fame, came to see me at my master's own house. There could not be fewer than thirty persons with their wives and children (for the country is very populous); and my master demanded the rate of a full room whenever he showed me at home, although it were only to a single family; so that for some time I had but little ease every day of the week (except Wednesday, which is their Sabbath) although I were not carried to the town.

My master finding how profitable I was like to be, resolved to carry me to the most considerable cities of the kingdom. Having therefore provided himself with all things necessary for a long journey, and settled his affairs at home, he took leave of his wife, and upon the 17th of August, 1703, about two months after my arrival, we set out for the metropolis, situated near the middle of that empire, and about three thousand miles distance from our house. My master made his daughter Glumdalclitch ride behind him. She carried me on her lap in a box tied about her waist. The girl had lined it on all sides with the softest cloth she could get, well quilted underneath, furnished it with her baby's bed, provided me with linen and other necessaries, and made everything as convenient as she could. We had no other company but a boy of the house, who rode after us with the luggage.

My master's design was to show me in all the towns by the way, and to step out of the road for fifty or an hundred miles, to any village or person of quality's house where he might expect custom. We made easy journeys of not above seven or eight score miles a day: for Glumdalclitch, on purpose to spare me, complained she was tired with the trotting of the horse. She often took me out of my box, at my own desire, to give me air, and show me the country, but always held me fast by leading strings. We passed over five or six rivers many degrees broader and deeper than the Nile or the Ganges; and there was hardly a rivulet so small as the Thames at London Bridge. We were ten weeks in our journey, and I was shown in eighteen large towns besides many villages and private families.

On the 26th day of October, we arrived at the metropolis, called in their language *Lorbrulgrud,* or Pride of the Universe. My master took a lodging in the principal street of the city, not far from the royal palace, and put out bills in the usual form, containing an exact description of my person and parts. He hired a large room between three and four hundred foot wide. He provided a table sixty foot in diameter, upon which I was to act my part, and pallisadoed it round three foot from the edge, and as many high, to prevent my falling over. I was shown ten times a day to the wonder and satisfaction of all people. I could now speak the language tolerably well, and perfectly understood every word that was spoken to me. Besides, I had learnt their alphabet, and could make a shift to explain a sentence here and there; for Glumdalclitch had been my instructor while we were at home, and at leisure hours during our journey. She carried a little book in her pocket, not much larger than a Sanson's Atlas; [12] it was a common treatise for the use of young girls, giving a short account of their religion: out of this she taught me my letters, and interpreted the words.

CHAPTER 3

The Author sent for to court. The Queen buys him of his master the farmer, and presents him to the King. He disputes with his Majesty's great scholars. An apartment at court provided for the Author. He is in high favor with the Queen. He stands up for the honor of his own country. His quarrels with the Queen's dwarf.

The frequent labors I underwent every day made in a few weeks a very considerable change in my health: the more my master got by me, the more insatiable he grew. I had quite lost my stomach, and was almost reduced to a skeleton. The farmer observed it, and concluding I soon must die, resolved to make as good a hand of me as he could. While he was thus reasoning and resolving with himself, a *Slardral,* or Gentleman Usher, came from court, commanding my master to bring me immediately thither for the diversion of the Queen and her ladies. Some of the latter had already been to see me, and reported strange things of my beauty, behavior, and good sense. Her Majesty and those who attended her were beyond measure delighted with my demeanor. I fell on my knees, and begged the honor of kissing her Imperial foot; but this gracious princess held out her little finger towards me (after I was set on a table), which I embraced in both my arms, and put the tip of it, with the utmost respect, to my lip. She made me some general questions about my country and my travels, which I answered as distinctly and in as few words as I could. She asked whether I would be content to live at court. I bowed down to the board of the table, and humbly answered, that I was my master's slave, but if I were at my own disposal, I should be proud to devote my life to her Majesty's service. She then asked my master whether he were willing to sell me at a good price. He, who apprehended I could not live a month, was ready enough to part with me, and demanded a thousand pieces of gold, which were ordered him on the spot, each piece being about the bigness of eight hundred moidores; but, allowing for the proportion of all things between that country and Europe, and the high price of gold among them, was hardly so great a sum as a thousand guineas would be in England. I then said to the Queen, since I was now her Majesty's most humble creature and vassal, I must beg the favor, that Glumdalclitch, who had always tended me with so much care and kindness, and understood to do it so well, might be admitted into her service, and continue to be my nurse and instructor. Her Majesty agreed to my petition, and easily got the farmer's consent, who was glad enough to have his daughter preferred at court: and the poor girl herself was not able to hide her joy. My late master withdrew, bidding me farewell, and saying he had left me in a good service; to which I replied not a word, only making him a slight bow.

The Queen observed my coldness, and when the farmer was gone out of the apartment, asked me the reason. I made bold to tell her Majesty that I owed no other obligation to my late master, than his not dashing out the brains of a poor harmless creature found by chance in his field; which obligation was amply recompensed by the gain he had made in showing me through half the kingdom, and the price he had now sold me for. That the life I had since led, was laborious enough to kill an animal of ten times my strength. That my health was much impaired by the continual drudgery of entertaining the rabble every hour of the day, and that if my master had not thought my life in danger, her Majesty perhaps would not have got so cheap a bargain. But as I was out of all fear of being ill treated under the protection of so great and good an Empress, the Ornament of Nature, the Darling of the World, the Delight of her Subjects, the Phoenix [13] of the Creation; so I hoped my late master's apprehensions would appear to be groundless, for I already found my spirits to revive by the influence of her most august presence.

12. **Sanson's Atlas:** a large folio, measuring 25 by 20 inches.

13. **Phoenix:** here used in the sense of "paragon."

This was the sum of my speech, delivered with great improprieties and hesitation; the latter part was altogether framed in the style peculiar to that people, whereof I learned some phrases from Glumdalclitch, while she was carrying me to court.

The Queen giving great allowance for my defectiveness in speaking, was however surprised at so much wit and good sense in so diminutive an animal. She took me in her own hand, and carried me to the King, who was then retired to his cabinet. His Majesty, a prince of much gravity, and austere countenance, not well observing my shape at first view, asked the Queen after a cold manner, how long it was since she grew fond of a *splacknuck;* for such it seems he took me to be, as I lay upon my breast in her Majesty's right hand. But this princess, who hath an infinite deal of wit and humor, set me gently on my feet upon the scrutore,[14] and commanded me to give his Majesty an account of myself, which I did in a very few words; and Glumdalclitch, who attended at the cabinet door, and could not endure I should be out of her sight, being admitted, confirmed all that had passed from my arrival at her father's house.

The King, although he be as learned a person as any in his dominions, and had been educated in the study of philosophy, and particularly mathematics; yet when he observed my shape exactly, and saw me walk erect, before I began to speak, conceived I might be a piece of clockwork (which is in that country arrived to a very great perfection), contrived by some ingenious artist. But when he heard my voice, and found what I delivered to be regular and rational, he could not conceal his astonishment. He was by no means satisfied with the relation I gave him of the manner I came into his kingdom, but thought it a story concerted between Glumdalclitch and her father, who had taught me a set of words to make me sell at a higher price. Upon this imagination he put several other questions to me, and still received rational answers, no otherwise defective than by a foreign accent, and an imperfect knowledge in the language, with some rustic phrases which I had learned at the farmer's house, and did not suit the polite style of a court.

His Majesty sent for three great scholars who were then in their weekly waiting, according to the custom in that country. These gentlemen, after they had a while examined my shape with much nicety, were of different opinions concerning me. They all agreed that I could not be produced ac-

cording to the regular laws of nature, because I was not framed with a capacity of preserving my life, either by swiftness, or climbing of trees, or digging holes in the earth. They observed by my teeth, which they viewed with great exactness, that I was a carnivorous animal; yet most quadrupeds being an overmatch for me, and field mice, with some others, too nimble, they could not imagine how I should be able to support myself, unless I fed upon snails and other insects, which they offered, by many learned arguments, to evince that I could not possibly do. One of them seemed to think that I might be an embryo, or abortive birth. But this opinion was rejected by the other two, who observed my limbs to be perfect and finished, and that I had lived several years, as it was manifested from my beard, the stumps whereof they plainly discovered through a magnifying glass. They would not allow me to be a dwarf, because my littleness was beyond all degrees of comparison; for the Queen's favorite dwarf, the smallest ever known in that kingdom, was near thirty foot high. After much debate, they concluded unanimously that I was only *relplum scalcath,* which is interpreted literally, *lusus naturae;* [15] a determination exactly agreeable to the modern philosophy [16] of Europe, whose professors, disdaining the old evasion of *occult causes,* whereby the followers of Aristotle endeavor in vain to disguise their ignorance, have invented this wonderful solution of all difficulties, to the unspeakable advancement of human knowledge.

After this decisive conclusion, I entreated to be heard a word or two. I applied myself to the King, and assured his Majesty, that I came from a country which abounded with several millions of both sexes, and of my own stature; where the animals, trees, and houses were all in proportion, and where by consequence I might be as able to defend myself, and to find sustenance, as any of his Majesty's subjects could do here; which I took for a full answer to those gentlemen's arguments. To this they only replied with a smile of contempt, saying, that the farmer had instructed me very well in my lesson. The King, who had a much better understanding, dismissing his learned men, sent for the farmer, who by good fortune was not yet gone out of town. Having therefore first examined him privately, and then confronted him with

---

14. **scrutore:** escritoire.

15. *lusus naturae:* a freak of nature.   16. **modern philosophy:** the new science, with its own special jargon to hide its ignorance.

me and the young girl, his Majesty began to think that what we told him might possibly be true. He desired the Queen to order that a particular care should be taken of me, and was of opinion that Glumdalclitch should still continue in her office of tending me, because he observed we had a great affection for each other. A convenient apartment was provided for her at court: she had a sort of governess appointed to take care of her education, a maid to dress her, and two other servants for menial offices; but the care of me was wholly appropriated to herself. The Queen commanded her own cabinetmaker to contrive a box that might serve me for a bedchamber, after the model that Glumdalclitch and I should agree upon. This man was a most ingenious artist, and according to my directions, in three weeks finished for me a wooden chamber of sixteen foot square, and twelve high, with sash windows, a door, and two closets, like a London bedchamber. The board that made the ceiling was to be lifted up and down by two hinges, to put in a bed ready furnished by her Majesty's upholsterer, which Glumdalclitch took out every day to air, made it with her own hands, and letting it down at night, locked up the roof over me. A nice workman, who was famous for little curiosities, undertook to make me two chairs, with backs and frames, of a substance not unlike ivory, and two tables, with a cabinet to put my things in. The room was quilted on all sides, as well as the floor and the ceiling, to prevent any accident from the carelessness of those who carried me, and to break the force of a jolt when I went in a coach. I desired a lock for my door, to prevent rats and mice from coming in: the smith, after several attempts, made the smallest that was ever seen among them, for I have known a larger at the gate of a gentleman's house in England. I made a shift to keep the key in a pocket of my own, fearing Glumdalclitch might lose it. The Queen likewise ordered the thinnest silks that could be gotten, to make me clothes, not much thicker than an English blanket, very cumbersome till I was accustomed to them. They were after the fashion of the kingdom, partly resembling the Persian, and partly the Chinese, and are a very grave, decent habit.

The Queen became so fond of my company, that she could not dine without me. I had a table placed upon the same at which her Majesty eat, just at her left elbow, and a chair to sit on. Glumdalclitch stood upon a stool on the floor, near my table, to assist and take care of me. I had an entire set of silver dishes and plates, and other necessaries, which, in proportion to those of the Queen, were not much bigger than what I have seen in a London toyshop, for the furniture of a baby-house: these my little nurse kept in her pocket, in a silver box, and gave me at meals as I wanted them, always cleaning them herself. No person dined with the Queen but the two Princesses Royal, the elder sixteen years old, and the younger at that time thirteen and a month. Her Majesty used to put a bit of meat upon one of my dishes, out of which I carved for myself, and her diversion was to see me eat in miniature. For the Queen (who had indeed but a weak stomach) took up at one mouthful, as much as a dozen English farmers could eat at a meal, which to me was for some time a very nauseous sight. She would craunch the wing of a lark, bones and all, between her teeth, although it were nine times as large as that of a full-grown turkey; and put a bit of bread into her mouth, as big as two twelve-penny loaves. She drank out of a golden cup, above a hogshead at a draught. Her knives were twice as long as a scythe set straight upon the handle. The spoons, forks, and other instruments were all in the same proportion. I remember when Glumdalclitch carried me out of curiosity to see some of the tables at court, where ten or a dozen of these enormous knives and forks were lifted up together, I thought I had never till then beheld so terrible a sight.

It is the custom that every Wednesday (which, as I have before observed, was their Sabbath) the King and Queen, with the royal issue of both sexes, dine together in the apartment of his Majesty, to whom I was now become a favorite; and at these times my little chair and table were placed at his left hand, before one of the saltcellars. This prince took a pleasure in conversing with me, inquiring into the manners, religion, laws, government, and learning of Europe; wherein I gave him the best account I was able. His apprehension was so clear, and his judgment so exact, that he made very wise reflections and observations upon all I said. But, I confess, that after I had been a little too copious in talking of my own beloved country, of our trade, and wars by sea and land, of our schisms in religion, and parties in the state; the prejudices of his education prevailed so far, that he could not forbear taking me up in his right hand, and stroking me gently with the other, after an hearty fit of laughing, asked me, whether I were a Whig or a Tory. Then turning to his first minister, who waited behind him with a white staff, near as tall as the mainmast of the *Royal Sovereign*,[17] he observed how contemptible a thing was human grandeur, which could be mimicked by such diminutive insects as I. "And yet," said he, "I dare engage, those creatures have their titles and distinctions of honor, they contrive little nests and burrows, that they call houses and cities; they make a figure in dress and equipage; they love, they fight, they dispute, they cheat, they betray." And thus he continued on, while my color came and went several times, with indignation to hear our noble country, the mistress of arts and arms, the scourge of France, the arbitress of Europe, the seat of virtue, piety, honor, and truth, the pride and envy of the world, so contemptuously treated.

But as I was not in a condition to resent injuries, so, upon mature thoughts, I began to doubt whether I were injured or no. For, after having been accustomed several months to the sight and converse of this people, and observed every object upon which I cast my eyes, to be of proportionable magnitude, the horror I had first conceived from their bulk and aspect was so far worn off, that if I had then beheld a company of English lords and ladies in their finery and birthday clothes, acting their several parts in the most courtly manner, of strutting, and bowing, and prating; to say the truth, I should have been strongly tempted to laugh as much at them as this King and his grandees did at me. Neither indeed could I forbear smiling at myself, when the Queen used to place me upon her hand towards a looking glass, by which both our persons appeared before me in full view together; and there could be nothing more ridiculous than the comparison; so that I really began to imagine myself dwindled many degrees below my usual size.

Nothing angered and mortified me so much as the Queen's dwarf, who being of the lowest stature that was ever in that country (for I verily think he was not full thirty foot high) became so insolent at seeing a creature so much beneath him, that he would always affect to swagger and look big as he passed by me in the Queen's antechamber, while I was standing on some table talking with the lords or ladies of the court, and he seldom failed of a smart word or two upon my littleness; against which I could only revenge myself by

calling him brother, challenging him to wrestle, and such repartees as are usual in the mouths of court pages. One day at dinner this malicious little cub was so nettled with something I had said to him, that raising himself upon the frame of her Majesty's chair, he took me up by the middle, as I was sitting down, not thinking any harm, and let me drop into a large silver bowl of cream, and then ran away as fast as he could. I fell over head and ears, and if I had not been a good swimmer, it might have gone very hard with me; for Glumdalclitch in that instant happened to be at the other end of the room, and the Queen was in such a fright that she wanted presence of mind to assist me. But my little nurse ran to my relief, and took me out, after I had swallowed above a quart of cream. I was put to bed; however, I received no other damage than the loss of a suit of clothes, which was utterly spoiled. The dwarf was soundly whipped, and as a farther punishment, forced to drink up the bowl of cream, into which he had thrown me: neither was he ever restored to favor: for, soon after the Queen bestowed him on a lady of high quality, so that I saw him no more, to my very great satisfaction; for I could not tell to what extremity such a malicious urchin might have carried his resentment.

He had before served me a scurvy trick, which set the Queen a laughing, although at the same time she was heartily vexed, and would have immediately cashiered him, if I had not been so generous as to intercede. Her Majesty had taken a marrow bone upon her plate, and after knocking out the marrow, placed the bone again in the dish erect as it stood before; the dwarf watching his opportunity, while Glumdalclitch was gone to the sideboard, mounted the stool that she stood on to take care of me at meals, took me up in both hands, and squeezing my legs together, wedged them into the marrow bone above my waist, where I stuck for some time, and made a very ridiculous figure. I believe it was near a minute before anyone knew what was become of me, for I thought it below me to cry out. But, as princes seldom get their meat hot, my legs were not scalded, only my stockings and breeches in a sad condition. The dwarf, at my entreaty, had no other punishment than a sound whipping.

I was frequently rallied by the Queen upon account of my fearfulness, and she used to ask me whether the people of my country were as great

---

17. *Royal Sovereign:* one of the largest ships in the British navy, launched in 1637, burned 1696.

cowards as myself. The occasion was this: the kingdom is much pestered with flies in summer; and these odious insects, each of them as big as a Dunstable lark, hardly gave me any rest while I sat at dinner, with their continual humming and buzzing about my ears. They would sometimes alight upon my victuals, and leave their loathsome excrement or spawn behind, which to me was very visible, though not to the natives of that country, whose large optics were not so acute as mine in viewing smaller objects. Sometimes they would fix upon my nose or forehead, where they stung me to the quick, smelling very offensively, and I could easily trace that viscous matter, which our naturalists tell us enables those creatures to walk with their feet upwards upon a ceiling. I had much ado to defend myself against these detestable animals, and could not forbear starting when they came on my face. It was the common practice of the dwarf to catch a number of these insects in his hand, as schoolboys do among us, and let them out suddenly under my nose, on purpose to frighten me, and divert the Queen. My remedy was to cut them in pieces with my knife as they flew in the air, wherein my dexterity was much admired.

I remember one morning when Glumdalclitch had set me in my box upon a window, as she usually did in fair days to give me air (for I durst not venture to let the box be hung on a nail out of the window, as we do with cages in England), after I had lifted up one of my sashes, and sat down at my table to eat a piece of sweet cake for my breakfast, above twenty wasps, allured by the smell, came flying into the room, humming louder than the drones of as many bagpipes. Some of them seized my cake, and carried it piecemeal away, others flew about my head and face, confounding me with the noise, and putting me in the utmost terror of their stings. However I had the courage to rise and draw my hanger, and attack them in the air. I dispatched four of them, but the rest got away, and I presently shut my window. These insects were as large as partridges: I took out their stings, found them an inch and a half long, and as sharp as needles. I carefully preserved them all, and having since shown them with some other curiosities in several parts of Europe; upon my return to England I gave three of them to Gresham College,[18] and kept the fourth for myself.

18. Gresham College: the home of the Royal Society.

CHAPTER 4

The country described. A proposal for correcting modern maps. The King's palace, and some account of the metropolis. The Author's way of traveling. The chief temple described.

I now intend to give the reader a short description of this country, as far as I traveled in it, which was not above two thousand miles round Lorbrulgrud the metropolis. For the Queen, whom I always attended, never went further when she accompanied the King in his progresses, and there stayed till his Majesty returned from viewing his frontiers. The whole extent of this prince's dominions reacheth about six thousand miles in length, and from three to five in breadth. From whence I cannot but conclude that our geographers of Europe are in a great error, by supposing nothing but sea between Japan and California; for it was ever my opinion, that there must be a balance of earth to counterpoise the great continent of Tartary; and therefore they ought to correct their maps and charts, by joining this vast tract of land to the northwest parts of America, wherein I shall be ready to lend them my assistance.

The kingdom is a peninsula, terminated to the northeast by a ridge of mountains thirty miles high, which are altogether impassable by reason of the volcanoes upon the tops. Neither do the most learned know what sort of mortals inhabit beyond those mountains, or whether they be inhabited at all. On the three other sides it is bounded by the ocean. There is not one seaport in the whole kingdom, and those parts of the coasts into which the rivers issue are so full of pointed rocks, and the sea generally so rough, that there is no venturing with the smallest of their boats, so that these people are wholly excluded from any commerce with the rest of the world. But the large rivers are full of vessels, and abound with excellent fish, for they seldom get any from the sea, because the sea fish are of the same size with those in Europe, and consequently not worth catching; whereby it is manifest, that nature, in the production of plants and animals of so extraordinary a bulk, is wholly confined to this continent, of which I leave the reasons to be determined by philosophers. However, now and then they take a whale that happens to be dashed against the rocks, which the common people feed on heartily. These whales I have known so large that a man could hardly carry one upon his shoulders; and sometimes for curiosity they are brought in hampers to Lorbrulgrud: I saw one of them in a dish at the King's table, which passed for a rarity, but I did not observe he was fond of it; for I think indeed the bigness disgusted him, although I have seen one somewhat larger in Greenland.

The country is well inhabited, for it contains fifty-one cities, near an hundred walled towns, and a great number of villages. To satisfy my curious reader, it may be sufficient to describe Lorbrulgrud. This city stands upon almost two equal parts on each side the river that passes through. It contains above eighty thousand houses, and about six hundred thousand inhabitants. It is in length three *glonglungs* (which make about fifty-four English miles) and two and a half in breadth, as I measured it myself in the royal map made by the King's order, which was laid on the ground on purpose for me, and extended an hundred feet: I paced the diameter and circumference several times barefoot, and computing by the scale, measured it pretty exactly.

The King's palace is no regular edifice, but an heap of buildings about seven miles round: the chief rooms are generally two hundred and forty foot high, and broad and long in proportion. A coach was allowed to Glumdalclitch and me, wherein her governess frequently took her out to see the town, or go among the shops; and I was always of the party, carried in my box; although the girl at my own desire would often take me out, and hold me in her hand, that I might more conveniently view the houses and the people, as we passed along the streets. I reckoned our coach to be about a square of Westminster Hall,[19] but not altogether so high; however, I cannot be very exact. One day the governess ordered our coachman to stop at several shops, where the beggars, watching their opportunity, crowded to the sides of the coach, and gave me the most horrible spectacles that ever an European eye beheld. There was a woman with a cancer in her breast, swelled to a monstrous size, full of holes, in two or three of which I could have easily crept, and covered my whole body. There was a fellow with a wen in his neck, larger than five woolpacks, and another with a couple of wooden legs, each about twenty foot high. But the most hateful sight of all was the lice crawling on their clothes. I could see distinctly the

limbs of these vermin with my naked eye, much better than those of an European louse through a microscope, and their snouts with which they rooted like swine. They were the first I had ever beheld, and I should have been curious enough to dissect one of them, if I had proper instruments (which I unluckily left behind me in the ship), although indeed the sight was so nauseous, that it perfectly turned my stomach.

Besides the large box in which I was usually carried, the Queen ordered a smaller one to be made for me, of about twelve foot square, and ten high, for the convenience of traveling, because the other was somewhat too large for Glumdalclitch's lap, and cumbersome in the coach; it was made by the same artist, whom I directed in the whole contrivance. This traveling closet was an exact square with a window in the middle of three of the squares, and each window was latticed with iron wire on the outside, to prevent accidents in long journeys. On the fourth side, which had no window, two strong staples were fixed, through which the person that carried me, when I had a mind to be on horseback, put in a leathern belt, and buckled it about his waist. This was always the office of some grave trusty servant in whom I could confide, whether I attended the King and Queen in their progresses, or were disposed to see the gardens, or pay a visit to some great lady or minister of state in the court, when Glumdalclitch happened to be out of order: for I soon began to be known and esteemed among the greatest officers, I suppose more upon account of their Majesties' favor, than any merit of my own. In journeys, when I was weary of the coach, a servant on horseback would buckle my box, and place it on a cushion before him; and there I had a full prospect of the country on three sides from my three windows. I had in this closet a field bed and a hammock hung from the ceiling, two chairs and a table, neatly screwed to the floor, to prevent being tossed about by the agitation of the horse or the coach. And having been long used to sea voyages, those motions, although sometimes very violent, did not much discompose me.

Whenever I had a mind to see the town, it was always in my traveling closet, which Glumdalclitch held in her lap in a kind of open sedan, after the fashion of the country, borne by four men, and attended by two others in the Queen's livery. The people who had often heard of me, were very curious to crowd about the sedan, and the girl was

19. **Westminster Hall:** probably means a square of the breadth, i.e., 68 feet; it was 85 feet high.

complaisant enough to make the bearers stop, and to take me in her hand that I might be more conveniently seen.

I was very desirous to see the chief temple, and particularly the tower belonging to it, which is reckoned the highest in the kingdom. Accordingly one day my nurse carried me thither, but I may truly say I came back disappointed; for the height is not above three thousand foot, reckoning from the ground to the highest pinnacle top; which allowing for the difference between the size of those people, and us in Europe, is no great matter for admiration, nor at all equal in proportion (if I rightly remember) to Salisbury steeple.[20] But, not to detract from a nation to which during my life I shall acknowledge myself extremely obliged, it must be allowed, that whatever this famous tower wants in height is amply made up in beauty and strength. For the walls are near an hundred foot thick, built of hewn stone, whereof each is about forty foot square, and adorned on all sides with statues of gods and emperors cut in marble larger than the life, placed in their several niches. I measured a little finger which had fallen down from one of these statues, and lay unperceived among some rubbish, and found it exactly four foot and an inch in length. Glumdalclitch wrapped it up in a handkerchief, and carried it home in her pocket to keep among other trinkets, of which the girl was very fond, as children at her age usually are.

The King's kitchen is indeed a noble building, vaulted at top, and about six hundred foot high. The great oven is not so wide by ten paces as the cupola at St. Paul's:[21] for I measured the latter on purpose after my return. But if I should describe the kitchen grate, the prodigious pots and kettles, the joints of meat turning on the spits, with many other particulars, perhaps I should be hardly believed; at least a severe critic would be apt to think I enlarged a little, as travelers are often suspected to do. To avoid which censure, I fear I have run too much into the other extreme; and that if this treatise should happen to be translated into the language of Brobdingnag (which is the general name of that kingdom) and transmitted thither, the King and his people would have reason to complain that I had done them an injury by a false and diminutive representation.

His Majesty seldom keeps above six hundred horses in his stables: they are generally from fifty-four to sixty foot high. But when he goes abroad on solemn days, he is attended for state by a militia guard of five hundred horse, which indeed I thought was the most splendid sight that could be ever beheld, till I saw part of his army in battalia, whereof I shall find another occasion to speak.

CHAPTER 5

Several adventures that happened to the Author. The execution of a criminal. The Author shows his skill in navigation.

I should have lived happy enough in that country, if my littleness had not exposed me to several ridiculous and troublesome accidents: some of which I shall venture to relate. Glumdalclitch often carried me into the gardens of the court in my smaller box, and would sometimes take me out of it and hold me in her hand, or set me down to walk. I remember, before the dwarf left the Queen, he followed us one day into those gardens, and my nurse having set me down, he and I being close together, near some dwarf apple trees, I must needs show my wit by a silly allusion between him and the trees, which happens to hold in their language as it doth in ours. Whereupon, the malicious rogue watching his opportunity, when I was walking under one of them, shook it directly over my head, by which a dozen apples, each of them near as large as a Bristol barrel, came tumbling about my ears; one of them hit me on the back as I chanced to stoop, and knocked me down flat on my face, but I received no other hurt, and the dwarf was pardoned at my desire, because I had given the provocation.

Another day Glumdalclitch left me on a smooth grassplot to divert myself while she walked at some distance with her governess. In the meantime there suddenly fell such a violent shower of hail, that I was immediately by the force of it struck to the ground: and when I was down, the hailstones gave me such cruel bangs all over the body, as if I had been pelted with tennis balls;[22] however, I made a shift to creep on all four, and shelter myself by lying flat on my face on the lee side of a border of lemon thyme, but so bruised from head to foot that I could not go abroad in ten days. Neither is this at all to be wondered at, because nature in that country observing the same proportion through

---

20. **Salisbury steeple:** about 400 feet high.   21. **cupola . . . St. Paul's:** 122 feet in diameter.

22. **tennis balls:** the hard balls used in the original game of court tennis.

all her operations, a hailstone is near eighteen hundred times as large as one in Europe, which I can assert upon experience, having been so curious to weigh and measure them.

But a more dangerous accident happened to me in the same garden, when my little nurse believing she had put me in a secure place, which I often entreated her to do, that I might enjoy my own thoughts, and having left my box at home to avoid the trouble of carrying it, went to another part of the garden with her governess and some ladies of her acquaintance. While she was absent, and out of hearing, a small white spaniel belonging to one of the chief gardeners, having got by accident into the garden, happened to range near the place where I lay. The dog following the scent, came directly up, and taking me in his mouth, ran straight to his master, wagging his tail, and set me gently on the ground. By good fortune he had been so well taught, that I was carried between his teeth without the least hurt, or even tearing my clothes. But the poor gardener, who knew me well, and had a great kindness for me, was in a terrible fright. He gently took me up in both his hands, and asked me how I did; but I was so amazed and out of breath, that I could not speak a word. In a few minutes I came to myself, and he carried me safe to my little nurse, who by this time had returned to the place where she left me, and was in cruel agonies when I did not appear, nor answer when she called: she severely reprimanded the gardener on account of his dog. But the thing was hushed up, and never known at court; for the girl was afraid of the Queen's anger, and truly as to myself, I thought it would not be for my reputation that such a story should go about.

This accident absolutely determined Glumdalclitch never to trust me abroad for the future out of her sight. I had been long afraid of this resolution, and therefore concealed from her some little unlucky adventures that happened in those times when I was left by myself. Once a kite hovering over the garden made a stoop [23] at me, and if I had not resolutely drawn my hanger, and run under a thick espalier, he would have certainly carried me away in his talons. Another time walking to the top of a fresh molehill, I fell to my neck in the hole through which that animal had cast up the earth, and coined some lie, not worth remembering, to excuse myself for spoiling my clothes. I likewise broke my right shin against the shell of a snail, which I happened to stumble over, as I was walking alone, and thinking on poor England.

I cannot tell whether I were more pleased or mortified, to observe in those solitary walks, that the smaller birds did not appear to be at all afraid of me, but would hop about within a yard distance, looking for worms, and other food, with as much indifference and security, as if no creature at all were near them. I remember, a thrush had the confidence to snatch out of my hand, with his bill, a piece of cake that Glumdalclitch had just given me for my breakfast. When I attempted to catch any of these birds, they would boldly turn against me, endeavoring to pick my fingers, which I durst not venture within their reach; and then they would hop back unconcerned, to hunt for worms or snails, as they did before. But one day I took a thick cudgel, and threw it with all my strength so luckily at a linnet, that I knocked him down, and seizing him by the neck with both my hands, ran with him in triumph to my nurse. However, the bird, who had only been stunned, recovering himself, gave me so many boxes with his wings on both sides of my head and body, although I held him at arm's length, and was out of the reach of his claws, that I was twenty times thinking to let him go. But I was soon relieved by one of our servants, who wrung off the bird's neck, and I had him next day for dinner, by the Queen's command. This linnet, as near as I can remember, seemed to be somewhat larger than an English swan.

The maids of honor often invited Glumdalclitch to their apartments, and desired she would bring me along with her, on purpose to have the pleasure of seeing and touching me. They would often strip me naked from top to toe, and lay me at full length in their bosoms; wherewith I was much disgusted; because, to say the truth, a very offensive smell came from their skins; which I do not mention or intend to the disadvantage of those excellent ladies, for whom I have all manner of respect; but I conceive that my sense was more acute in proportion to my littleness, and that those illustrious persons were no more disagreeable to their lovers, or to each other, than people of the same quality are with us in England. And, after all, I found their natural smell was much more supportable than when they used perfumes, under which

---

23. a stoop: the swoop downward of a bird of prey.

I immediately swooned away. I cannot forget that an intimate friend of mine in Lilliput took the freedom in a warm day, when I had used a good deal of exercise, to complain of a strong smell about me, although I am as little faulty that way as most of my sex: but I suppose his faculty of smelling was as nice with regard to me, as mine was to that of this people. Upon this point, I cannot forbear doing justice to the Queen my mistress, and Glumdalclitch my nurse, whose persons were as sweet as those of any lady in England.

That which gave me most uneasiness among these maids of honor (when my nurse carried me to visit them) was to see them use me without any manner of ceremony, like a creature who had no sort of consequence. For they would strip themselves to the skin, and put on their smocks in my presence, while I was placed on their toilet directly before their naked bodies, which, I am sure, to me was very far from being a tempting sight, or from giving me any other emotions than those of horror and disgust. Their skins appeared so coarse and uneven, so variously colored, when I saw them near, with a mole here and there as broad as a trencher, and hairs hanging from it thicker than pack threads, to say nothing further concerning the rest of their persons. Neither did they at all scruple, while I was by, to discharge what they had drunk, to the quantity of at least two hogsheads, in a vessel that held above three tuns. The handsomest among these maids of honor, a pleasant frolicsome girl of sixteen, would sometimes set me astride upon one of her nipples, with many other tricks, wherein the reader will excuse me for not being over particular. But I was so much displeased, that I entreated Glumdalclitch to contrive some excuse for not seeing that young lady any more.

One day a young gentleman, who was nephew to my nurse's governess, came and pressed them both to see an execution. It was of a man who had murdered one of that gentleman's intimate acquaintance. Glumdalclitch was prevailed on to be of the company, very much against her inclination, for she was naturally tender-hearted: and as for myself, although I abhorred such kind of spectacles, yet my curiosity tempted me to see something that I thought must be extraordinary. The malefactor was fixed in a chair upon a scaffold erected for the purpose, and his head cut off at one blow with a sword of about forty foot long.

The veins and arteries spouted up such a prodigious quantity of blood, and so high in the air, that the great *jet d'eau* [24] at Versailles was not equal for the time it lasted; and the head, when it fell on the scaffold floor, gave such a bounce, as made me start, although I were at least an English mile distant.

The Queen, who often used to hear me talk of my sea voyages, and took all occasions to divert me when I was melancholy, asked me whether I understood how to handle a sail, or an oar, and whether a little exercise of rowing might not be convenient for my health. I answered, that I understood both very well: for although my proper employment had been to be surgeon or doctor to the ship, yet often, upon a pinch, I was forced to work like a common mariner. But I could not see how this could be done in their country, where the smallest wherry was equal to a first-rate man-of-war among us, and such a boat as I could manage would never live in any of their rivers. Her Majesty said, if I would contrive a boat, her own joiner should make it, and she would provide a place for me to sail in. The fellow was an ingenious workman, and, by my instructions, in ten days finished a pleasure boat, with all its tackling, able conveniently to hold eight Europeans. When it was finished, the Queen was so delighted, that she ran with it in her lap to the King, who ordered it to be put in a cistern full of water, with me in it, by way of trial; where I could not manage my two sculls, or little oars, for want of room. But the Queen had before contrived another project. She ordered the joiner to make a wooden trough of three hundred foot long, fifty broad, and eight deep; which being well pitched to prevent leaking, was placed on the floor along the wall, in an outer room of the palace. It had a cock near the bottom to let out the water when it began to grow stale, and two servants could easily fill it in half an hour. Here I often used to row for my diversion, as well as that of the Queen and her ladies, who thought themselves agreeably entertained with my skill and agility. Sometimes I would put up my sail, and then my business was only to steer, while the ladies gave me a gale with their fans; and when they were weary, some of the pages would blow my sail forward with their breath, while I showed my art by steering starboard or

24. *jet d'eau:* The largest fountain at Versailles rose over 70 feet in the air.

larboard as I pleased. When I had done, Glumdalclitch always carried my boat into her closet, and hung it on a nail to dry.

In this exercise I once met an accident which had like to have cost me my life: for, one of the pages having put my boat into the trough, the governess, who attended Glumdalclitch, very officiously lifted me up to place me in the boat, but I happened to slip through her fingers, and should have infallibly fallen down forty feet upon the floor, if by the luckiest chance in the world, I had not been stopped by a corking pin [25] that stuck in the good gentlewoman's stomacher; the head of the pin passed between my shirt and the waistband of my breeches, and thus I was held by the middle in the air till Glumdalclitch ran to my relief.

Another time, one of the servants, whose office it was to fill my trough every third day with fresh water, was so careless to let a huge frog (not perceiving it) slip out of his pail. The frog lay concealed till I was put into my boat, but then seeing a resting place, climbed up, and made it lean so much on one side, that I was forced to balance it with all my weight on the other, to prevent overturning. When the frog was got in, it hopped at once half the length of the boat, and then over my head, backwards and forwards, daubing my face and clothes with its odious slime. The largeness of its features made it appear the most deformed animal that can be conceived. However, I desired Glumdalclitch to let me deal with it alone. I banged it a good while with one of my sculls, and at last forced it to leap out of the boat.

But the greatest danger I ever underwent in that kingdom, was from a monkey, who belonged to one of the clerks of the kitchen. Glumdalclitch had locked me up in her closet, while she went somewhere upon business, or a visit. The weather being very warm, the closet window was left open, as well as the windows and the door of my bigger box, in which I usually lived, because of its largeness and conveniency. As I sat quietly meditating at my table, I heard something bounce in at the closet window, and skip about from one side to the other; whereat, although I were much alarmed, yet I ventured to look out, but not stirring from my seat; and then I saw this frolicsome animal, frisking and leaping up and down, till at last he came to my box, which he seemed to view with great pleasure and curiosity, peeping in at the door

and every window. I retreated to the farther corner of my room, or box, but the monkey looking in at every side, put me into such a fright, that I wanted presence of mind to conceal myself under the bed, as I might easily have done. After some time spent in peeping, grinning, and chattering, he at last espied me, and reaching one of his paws in at the door, as a cat does when she plays with a mouse, although I often shifted place to avoid him, he at length seized the lappet of my coat (which being made of that country silk, was very thick and strong) and dragged me out. He took me up in his right forefoot, and held me as a nurse does a child she is going to suckle, just as I have seen the same sort of creature do with a kitten in Europe: and when I offered to struggle, he squeezed me so hard, that I thought it more prudent to submit. I have good reason to believe that he took me for a young one of his own species, by his often stroking my face very gently with his other paw. In these diversions he was interrupted by a noise at the closet door, as if somebody were opening it; whereupon he suddenly leaped up to the window, at which he had come in, and thence upon the leads and gutters, walking upon three legs, and holding me in the fourth, till he clambered up to a roof that was next to ours. I heard Glumdalclitch give a shriek at the moment he was carrying me out. The poor girl was almost distracted: that quarter of the palace was all in an uproar; the servants ran for ladders; the monkey was seen by hundreds in the court, sitting upon the ridge of a building, holding me like a baby in one of his forepaws, and feeding me with the other, by cramming into my mouth some victuals he had squeezed out of the bag on one side of his chaps, and patting me when I would not eat; whereat many of the rabble below could not forbear laughing; neither do I think they justly ought to be blamed, for without question the sight was ridiculous enough to everybody but myself. Some of the people threw up stones, hoping to drive the monkey down; but this was strictly forbidden, or else very probably my brains had been dashed out.

The ladders were now applied, and mounted by several men, which the monkey observing, and finding himself almost encompassed; not being able to make speed enough with his three legs, let me drop on a ridge tile, and made his escape. Here I sat for some time, five hundred yards from the ground, expecting every moment to be blown down by the wind, or to fall by my own giddiness, and

---

25. **corking pin:** or *calkin*, a pin of double the usual size.

come tumbling over and over from the ridge to the eaves; but an honest lad, one of my nurse's footmen, climbed up, and putting me into his breeches pocket, brought me down safe.

I was almost choked with the filthy stuff the monkey had crammed down my throat: but my dear little nurse picked it out of my mouth with a small needle, and then I fell a vomiting, which gave me great relief. Yet I was so weak and bruised in the sides with the squeezes given me by this odious animal, that I was forced to keep my bed a fortnight. The King, Queen, and all the court, sent every day to inquire after my health, and her Majesty made me several visits during my sickness. The monkey was killed, and an order made that no such animal should be kept about the palace.

When I attended the King after my recovery, to return him thanks for his favors, he was pleased to rally me a good deal upon this adventure. He asked me what my thoughts and speculations were while I lay in the monkey's paw; how I liked the victuals he gave me; his manner of feeding; and whether the fresh air on the roof had sharpened my stomach. He desired to know what I would have done upon such an occasion in my own country. I told his Majesty, that in Europe we had no monkeys, except such as were brought for curiosities from other places, and so small, that I could deal with a dozen of them together, if they presumed to attack me. And as for that monstrous animal with whom I was so lately engaged (it was indeed as large as an elephant), if my fears had suffered me to think so far as to make use of my hanger (looking fiercely and clapping my hand upon the hilt as I spoke), when he poked his paw into my chamber, perhaps I should have given him such a wound, as would have made him glad to withdraw it with more haste than he put it in. This I delivered in a firm tone, like a person who was jealous lest his courage should be called in question. However, my speech produced nothing else besides a loud laughter, which all the respect due to his Majesty from those about him could not make them contain. This made me reflect how vain an attempt it is for a man to endeavor doing himself honor among those who are out of all degree of equality or comparison with him. And yet I have seen the moral of my own behavior very frequent in England since my return, where a little contemptible varlet, without the least title to birth, person, wit, or common sense, shall presume to look with importance, and put himself upon a foot with the greatest persons of the kingdom.

I was every day furnishing the court with some ridiculous story: and Glumdalclitch, although she loved me to excess, yet was arch enough to inform the Queen, whenever I committed any folly that she thought would be diverting to her Majesty. The girl, who had been out of order, was carried by her governess to take the air about an hour's distance, or thirty miles from town. They alighted out of the coach near a small footpath in a field, and Glumdalclitch setting down my traveling box, I went out of it to walk. There was a cow dung in the path, and I must needs try my activity by attempting to leap over it. I took a run, but unfortunately jumped short, and found myself just in the middle up to my knees. I waded through with some difficulty, and one of the footmen wiped me as clean as he could with his handkerchief; for I was filthily bemired, and my nurse confined me to my box till we returned home; where the Queen was soon informed of what had passed, and the footmen spread it about the court: so that all the mirth, for some days, was at my expense.

CHAPTER 6

Several contrivances of the Author to please the King and Queen. He shows his skill in music. The King inquires into the state of Europe, which the Author relates to him. The King's observation thereon.

I used to attend the King's levee once or twice a week, and had often seen him under the barber's hand, which indeed was at first very terrible to behold: for the razor was almost twice as long as an ordinary scythe. His Majesty, according to the custom of the country, was only shaved twice a week. I once prevailed on the barber to give me some of the suds or lather, out of which I picked forty or fifty of the strongest stumps of hair. I then took a piece of fine wood, and cut it like the back of a comb, making several holes in it at equal distance with as small a needle as I could get from Glumdalclitch. I fixed in the stumps so artificially, scraping and sloping them with my knife toward the points, that I made a very tolerable comb; which was a seasonable supply, my own being so much broken in the teeth, that it was almost useless: neither did I know any artist in that country so nice and exact, as would undertake to make me another.

And this puts me in mind of an amusement wherein I spent many of my leisure hours. I desired the Queen's woman to save for me the combings of her Majesty's hair, whereof in time I got a good quantity, and consulting with my friend the cabinetmaker, who had received general orders to do little jobs for me, I directed him to make two chair frames, no larger than those I had in my box, and then to bore little holes with a fine awl round those parts where I designed the backs and seats; through these holes I wove the strongest hairs I could pick out, just after the manner of cane chairs in England. When they were finished, I made a present of them to her Majesty, who kept them in her cabinet, and used to show them for curiosities, as indeed they were the wonder of every one who beheld them. The Queen would have had me sit upon one of these chairs, but I absolutely refused to obey her, protesting I would rather die a thousand deaths than place a dishonorable part of my body on those precious hairs that once adorned her Majesty's head. Of these hairs (as I had always a mechanical genius) I likewise made a neat little purse about five foot long, with her Majesty's name deciphered in gold letters, which I gave to Glumdalclitch, by the Queen's consent. To say the truth, it was more for show than use, being not of strength to bear the weight of the larger coins, and therefore she kept nothing in it but some little toys that girls are fond of.

The King, who delighted in music, had frequent consorts [26] at court, to which I was sometimes carried, and set in my box on a table to hear them: but the noise was so great, that I could hardly distinguish the tunes. I am confident that all the drums and trumpets of a royal army, beating and sounding together just at your ears, could not equal it. My practice was to have my box removed from the places where the performers sat, as far as I could, then to shut the doors and windows of it, and draw the window curtains; after which I found their music not disagreeable.

I had learned in my youth to play a little upon the spinet. Glumdalclitch kept one in her chamber, and a master attended twice a week to teach her: I call it a spinet, because it somewhat resembled that instrument, and was played upon in the same manner. A fancy came into my head that I would entertain the King and Queen with an English tune upon this instrument. But this appeared extremely difficult: for the spinet was near sixty

26. consorts: musical entertainments.

foot long, each key being almost a foot wide, so that, with my arms extended, I could not reach to above five keys, and to press them down required a good smart stroke with my fist, which would be too great a labor, and to no purpose. The method I contrived was this. I prepared two round sticks about the bigness of common cudgels; they were thicker at one end than the other, and I covered the thicker end with a piece of a mouse's skin, that by rapping on them I might neither damage the tops of the keys, nor interrupt the sound. Before the spinet a bench was placed, about four foot below the keys, and I was put upon the bench. I ran sideling upon it that way and this, as fast as I could, banging the proper keys with my two sticks, and made a shift to play a jig, to the great satisfaction of both their Majesties: but it was the most violent exercise I ever underwent, and yet I could not strike above sixteen keys, nor, consequently, play the bass and treble together, as other artists do; which was a great disadvantage to my performance.

The King, who, as I before observed, was a prince of excellent understanding, would frequently order that I should be brought in my box, and set upon the table in his closet. He would then command me to bring one of my chairs out of the box, and sit down within three yards distance upon the top of the cabinet, which brought me almost to a level with his face. In this manner I had several conversations with him. I one day took the freedom to tell his Majesty, that the contempt he discovered towards Europe, and the rest of the world, did not seem answerable to those excellent qualities of mind that he was master of. That reason did not extend itself with the bulk of the body: on the contrary, we observed in our country, that the tallest persons were usually least provided with it. That among other animals, bees and ants had the reputation of more industry, art and sagacity, than many of the larger kinds. And that, as inconsiderable as he took me to be, I hoped I might live to do his Majesty some signal service. The King heard me with attention, and began to conceive a much better opinion of me than he had ever before. He desired I would give him as exact an account of the government of England as I possibly could; because, as fond as princes commonly are of their own customs (for so he conjectured of other monarchs, by my former discourses), he should be glad to hear of anything that might deserve imitation.

Imagine with thyself, courteous reader, how often I then wished for the tongue of Demosthenes or Cicero, that might have enabled me to celebrate the praise of my own dear native country in a style equal to its merits and felicity.

I began my discourse by informing his Majesty, that our dominions consisted of two islands, which composed three mighty kingdoms under one sovereign, beside our plantations in America. I dwelt long upon the fertility of our soil, and the temperature [27] of our climate. I then spoke at large upon the constitution of an English parliament, partly made up of an illustrious body called the House of Peers, persons of the noblest blood, and of the most ancient and ample patrimonies. I described that extraordinary care always taken of their education in arts and arms, to qualify them for being counselors born to the king and kingdom; to have a share in the legislature; to be members of the highest court of judicature, from whence there could be no appeal; and to be champions always ready for the defense of their prince and country, by their valor, conduct, and fidelity. That these were the ornament and bulwark of the kingdom, worthy followers of their most renowned ancestors, whose honor had been the reward of their virtue, from which their posterity were never once known to degenerate. To these were joined several holy persons, as part of that assembly, under the title of bishops, whose peculiar business it is to take care of religion, and of those who instruct the people therein. These were searched and sought out through the whole nation, by the prince and wisest counselors, among such of the priesthood as were most deservedly distinguished by the sanctity of their lives, and the depth of their erudition; who were indeed the spiritual fathers of the clergy and the people.

That the other part of the parliament consisted of an assembly called the House of Commons, who were all principal gentlemen, freely picked and culled out by the people themselves, for their great abilities and love of their country, to represent the wisdom of the whole nation. And these two bodies make up the most august assembly in Europe, to whom, in conjunction with the prince, the whole legislature is committed.

I then descended to the courts of justice, over which the judges, those venerable sages and interpreters of the law, presided, for determining the disputed rights and properties of men, as well as for the punishment of vice, and protection of innocence. I mentioned the prudent management of our treasury; the valor and achievements of our forces by sea and land. I computed the number of our people, by reckoning how many millions there might be of each religious sect, or political party among us. I did not omit even our sports and pastimes, or any other particular which I thought might redound to the honor of my country. And I finished all with a brief historical account of affairs and events in England for about an hundred years past.

This conversation was not ended under five audiences, each of several hours, and the King heard the whole with great attention, frequently taking notes of what I spoke, as well as memorandums of what questions he intended to ask me.

When I had put an end to these long discourses, his Majesty in a sixth audience consulting his notes, proposed many doubts, queries, and objections, upon every article. He asked what methods were used to cultivate the minds and bodies of our young nobility, and in what kind of business they commonly spent the first and teachable part of their lives. What course was taken to supply that assembly when any noble family became extinct. What qualifications were necessary in those who are to be created new lords: whether the humor of the prince, a sum of money to a court lady, or a prime minister, or a design of strengthening a party opposite to the public interest, ever happened to be motives in those advancements. What share of knowledge these lords had in the laws of their country, and how they came by it, so as to enable them to decide the properties of their fellow subjects in the last resort. Whether they were always so free from avarice, partialities, or want, that a bribe, or some other sinister view, could have no place among them. Whether those holy lords I spoke of were constantly promoted to that rank upon account of their knowledge in religious matters, and the sanctity of their lives, had never been compliers with the times, while they were common priests, or slavish prostitute chaplains to some nobleman, whose opinions they continued servilely to follow after they were admitted into that assembly.[28]

He then desired to know what arts were practiced in electing those whom I called commoners:

27. temperature: temperate quality. N.B. This simple comment on the climate gives the reader no warning of the change of tone in the ironic passage immediately following.

28. that assembly: aimed at the Low Church bishops appointed by the Whigs under George I.

whether a stranger with a strong purse might not influence the vulgar voters to choose him before their own landlord, or the most considerable gentleman in the neighborhood. How it came to pass, that people were so violently bent upon getting into this assembly, which I allowed to be a great trouble and expense, often to the ruin of their families, without any salary or pension: because this appeared such an exalted strain of virtue and public spirit, that his Majesty seemed to doubt it might possibly not be always sincere: and he desired to know whether such zealous gentlemen could have any views of refunding themselves for the charges and trouble they were at, by sacrificing the public good to the designs of a weak and vicious prince in conjunction with a corrupted ministry. He multiplied his questions, and sifted me thoroughly upon every part of this head, proposing numberless inquiries and objections, which I think it not prudent or convenient to repeat.

Upon what I said in relation to our courts of justice, his Majesty desired to be satisfied in several points: and this I was the better able to do, having been formerly almost ruined by a long suit in chancery,[29] which was decreed for me with costs. He asked, what time was usually spent in determining between right and wrong, and what degree of expense. Whether advocates and orators had liberty to plead in causes manifestly known to be unjust, vexatious, or oppressive. Whether party in religion or politics were observed to be of any weight in the scale of justice. Whether those pleading orators were persons educated in the general knowledge of equity, or only in provincial, national, and other local customs. Whether they or their judges had any part in penning those laws which they assumed the liberty of interpreting and glossing upon at their pleasure. Whether they had ever at different times pleaded for and against the same cause, and cited precedents to prove contrary opinions. Whether they were a rich or a poor corporation. Whether they received any pecuniary reward for pleading or delivering their opinions. And particularly, whether they were ever admitted as members in the lower senate.

He fell next upon the management of our treasury; and said, he thought my memory had failed me, because I computed our taxes at about five or six millions a year, and when I came to mention the issues, he found they sometimes amounted to more than double; for the notes he had taken were very particular in this point, because he hoped, as he told me, that the knowledge of our conduct might be useful to him, and he could not be deceived in his calculations. But, if what I told him were true, he was still at a loss how a kingdom could run out of its estate[30] like a private person. He asked me, who were our creditors; and where we found money to pay them. He wondered to hear me talk of such chargeable and extensive wars; that certainly we must be a quarrelsome people, or live among very bad neighbors, and that our generals must needs be richer than our kings.[31] He asked what business we had out of our own islands, unless upon the score of trade or treaty, or to defend the coasts with our fleet. Above all, he was amazed to hear me talk of a mercenary standing army[32] in the midst of peace, and among a free people. He said, if we were governed by our own consent in the persons of our representatives, he could not imagine of whom we were afraid, or against whom we were to fight; and would hear my opinion, whether a private man's house might not better be defended by himself, his children, and family, than by half a dozen rascals picked up at a venture in the streets, for small wages, who might get an hundred times more by cutting their throats.

He laughed at my odd kind of arithmetic (as he was pleased to call it) in reckoning the numbers of our people by a computation drawn from the several sects among us in religion and politics. He said, he knew no reason, why those who entertain opinions prejudicial to the public, should be obliged to change, or should not be obliged to conceal them. And as it was tyranny in any government to require the first, so it was weakness not to enforce the second: for a man may be allowed to keep poisons in his closet, but not to vend them about as cordials.

He observed, that among the diversions of our nobility and gentry, I had mentioned gaming. He desired to know at what age this entertainment was usually taken up, and when it was laid down; how much of their time it employed; whether it ever went so high as to affect their fortunes; whether mean vicious people, by their dexterity in that art, might not arrive at great riches, and sometimes keep our very nobles in dependence, as well

---

29. **suit in chancery:** The Court of Chancery was notorious for delays and expense.

30. **its estate:** Swift held that a nation could not afford to pile up an enormous national debt to pay for foreign wars. 31. **generals . . . kings:** a reference to the fortune Marlborough had made out of the war. 32. **standing army:** constantly opposed by the Tories.

as habituate them to vile companions, wholly take them from the improvement of their minds, and force them, by the losses they received, to learn and practice that infamous dexterity upon others.

He was perfectly astonished with the historical account I gave him of our affairs during the last century, protesting it was only an heap of conspiracies, rebellions, murders, massacres, revolutions, banishments; the very worst effects that avarice, faction, hypocrisy, perfidiousness, cruelty, rage, madness, hatred, envy, lust, malice, and ambition, could produce.

His Majesty, in another audience, was at the pains to recapitulate the sum of all I had spoken; compared the questions he made with the answers I had given; then taking me into his hands, and stroking me gently, delivered himself in these words, which I shall never forget, nor the manner he spoke them in. " My little friend Grildrig, you have made a most admirable panegyric upon your country. You have clearly proved that ignorance, idleness, and vice, are the proper ingredients for qualifying a legislator: that laws are best explained, interpreted, and applied by those whose interest and abilities lie in perverting, confounding, and eluding them. I observe among you some lines of an institution, which in its original might have been tolerable, but these half erased, and the rest wholly blurred and blotted by corruptions. It doth not appear from all you have said, how any one perfection is required towards the procurement of any one station among you; much less that men are ennobled on account of their virtue, that priests are advanced for their piety or learning, soldiers for their conduct or valor, judges for their integrity, senators for the love of their country, or counselors for their wisdom. As for yourself (continued the King), who have spent the greatest part of your life in traveling, I am well disposed to hope you may hitherto have escaped many vices of your country. But by what I have gathered from your own relation, and the answers I have with much pains wringed and extorted from you, I cannot but conclude the bulk of your natives to be the most pernicious race of little odious vermin that nature ever suffered to crawl upon the surface of the earth."

CHAPTER 7

The Author's love of his country. He makes a proposal of much advantage to the King, which is rejected. The King's great ignorance in politics. The learning

of that country very imperfect and confined. Their laws, and military affairs, and parties in the State.

Nothing but an extreme love of truth could have hindered me from concealing this part of my story. It was in vain to discover my resentments, which were always turned into ridicule; and I was forced to rest with patience while my noble and most beloved country was so injuriously treated. I am heartily sorry as any of my readers can possibly be, that such an occasion was given: but this prince happened to be so curious and inquisitive upon every particular, that it could not consist either with gratitude or good manners to refuse giving him what satisfaction I was able. Yet thus much I may be allowed to say in my own vindication, that I artfully eluded many of his questions, and gave to every point a more favorable turn by many degrees than the strictness of truth would allow. For I have always borne that laudable partiality to my own country, which Dionysius Halicarnassensis [33] with so much justice recommends to an historian: I would hide the frailties and deformities of my political mother, and place her virtues and beauties in the most advantageous light. This was my sincere endeavor in those many discourses I had with that mighty monarch, although it unfortunately failed of success.

But great allowances should be given to a King who lives wholly secluded from the rest of the world, and must therefore be altogether unacquainted with the manners and customs that most prevail in other nations: the want of which knowledge will ever produce many prejudices, and a certain narrowness of thinking, from which we and the politer countries of Europe are wholly exempted. And it would be hard indeed, if so remote a prince's notions of virtue and vice were to be offered as a standard for all mankind.

To confirm what I have now said, and further, to show the miserable effects of a confined education, I shall here insert a passage which will hardly obtain belief. In hopes to ingratiate myself farther into his Majesty's favor, I told him of an invention discovered between three and four hundred years ago, to make a certain powder, into an heap of which the smallest spark of fire falling, would kindle the whole in a moment, although it were as big as a mountain, and make it all fly up in the air together, with a noise and agitation greater

33. **Dionysius Halicarnassensis:** (54?–7? B.C.) or Halicarnassus, a Greek writer living in Rome under Augustus who upheld the virtues of the Romans and vindicated the power of their empire.

than thunder. That a proper quantity of this powder rammed into an hollow tube of brass or iron, according to its bigness, would drive a ball of iron or lead with such violence and speed, as nothing was able to sustain its force. That the largest balls thus discharged, would not only destroy whole ranks of an army at once, but batter the strongest walls to the ground, sink down ships, with a thousand men in each, to the bottom of the sea; and, when linked together by a chain, would cut through masts and rigging, divide hundreds of bodies in the middle, and lay all waste before them. That we often put this powder into large hollow balls of iron, and discharged them by an engine into some city we were besieging, which would rip up the pavement, tear the houses to pieces, burst and throw splinters on every side, dashing out the brains of all who came near. That I knew the ingredients very well, which were cheap, and common; I understood the manner of compounding them, and could direct his workmen how to make those tubes, of a size proportionable to all other things in his Majesty's kingdom, and the largest need not be above two hundred foot long; twenty or thirty of which tubes, charged with the proper quantity of powder and balls, would batter down the walls of the strongest town in his dominions in a few hours, or destroy the whole metropolis, if ever it should pretend to dispute his absolute commands. This I humbly offered to his Majesty, as a small tribute of acknowledgment in return of so many marks that I had received of his royal favor and protection.

The King was struck with horror at the description I had given of those terrible engines, and the proposal I had made. He was amazed how so impotent and groveling an insect as I (these were his expressions) could entertain such inhuman ideas, and in so familiar a manner as to appear wholly unmoved at all the scenes of blood and desolation, which I had painted as the common effects of those destructive machines, whereof he said, some evil genius, enemy to mankind, must have been the first contriver. As for himself, he protested, that although few things delighted him so much as new discoveries in art or in nature, yet he would rather lose half his kingdom than be privy to such a secret, which he commanded me, as I valued my life, never to mention any more.

A strange effect of *narrow principles* and *short views!* that a prince possessed of every quality which procures veneration, love, and esteem; of strong parts, great wisdom, and profound learning, endued with admirable talents for government, and almost adored by his subjects, should from a *nice unnecessary scruple,* whereof in Europe we can have no conception, let slip an opportunity put into his hands, that would have made him absolute master of the lives, the liberties, and the fortunes of his people. Neither do I say this with the least intention to detract from the many virtues of that excellent King, whose character I am sensible will on this account be very much lessened in the opinion of an English reader: but I take this defect among them to have risen from their ignorance, by not having hitherto reduced politics into a science, as the more acute wits of Europe have done. For, I remember very well, in a discourse one day with the King, when I happened to say there were several thousand books among us written upon the art of government, it gave him (directly contrary to my intention) a very mean opinion of our understandings. He professed both to abominate and despise all *mystery, refinement,* and *intrigue,* either in a prince or a minister. He could not tell what I meant by *secrets of state,* where an enemy or some rival nation were not in the case. He confined the knowledge of governing within very *narrow bounds;* to common sense and reason, to justice and lenity, to the speedy determination of civil and criminal causes; with some other obvious topics, which are not worth considering. And he gave it for his opinion, that whoever could make two ears of corn, or two blades of grass to grow upon a spot of ground where only one grew before, would deserve better of mankind, and do more essential service to his country, than the whole race of politicians put together.

The learning of this people is very defective, consisting only in morality, history, poetry, and mathematics, wherein they must be allowed to excel. But the last of these is wholly applied to what may be useful in life, to the improvement of agriculture, and all mechanical arts; so that among us it would be little esteemed. And as to ideas, entities, abstractions, and transcendentals,[34] I could never drive the least conception into their heads.

No law of that country must exceed in words the number of letters in their alphabet, which consists only of two and twenty. But, indeed, few of them extend even to that length. They are expressed in the most plain and simple terms, wherein those people are not mercurial enough to discover above

34. ideas . . . transcendentals: terms of the medieval Schoolmen.

one interpretation: and to write a comment upon any law is a capital crime. As to the decision of civil causes, or proceedings against criminals, their precedents are so few, that they have little reason to boast of any extraordinary skill in either.

They have had the art of printing, as well as the Chinese, time out of mind: but their libraries are not very large; for that of the King's, which is reckoned the largest, doth not amount to above a thousand volumes, placed in a gallery of twelve hundred foot long, from whence I had liberty to borrow what books I pleased. The Queen's joiner had contrived in one of Glumdalclitch's rooms a kind of wooden machine five and twenty foot high, formed like a standing ladder; the steps were each fifty foot long. It was indeed a movable pair of stairs, the lowest end placed at ten foot distance from the wall of the chamber. The book I had a mind to read was put up leaning against the wall. I first mounted to the upper step of the ladder, and turning my face towards the book, began at the top of the page, and so walking to the right and left about eight or ten paces, according to the length of the lines, till I had gotten a little below the level of my eyes, and then descending gradually till I came to the bottom: after which I mounted again, and began the other page in the same manner, and so turned over the leaf, which I could easily do with both my hands, for it was as thick and stiff as a pasteboard, and in the largest folios not above eighteen or twenty foot long.

Their style is clear, masculine, and smooth, but not florid; for they avoid nothing more than multiplying unnecessary words, or using various expressions. I have perused many of their books, especially those in history and morality. Among the latter, I was much diverted with a little old treatise, which always lay in Glumdalclitch's bedchamber, and belonged to her governess, a grave elderly gentlewoman, who dealt in writings of morality and devotion. The book treats of the weakness of human kind, and is in little esteem, except among women and the vulgar. However, I was curious to see what an author of that country could say upon such a subject. This writer went through all the usual topics of European moralists, showing how diminutive, contemptible, and helpless an animal was man in his own nature; how unable to defend himself from the inclemencies of the air, or the fury of wild beasts: how much he was excelled by one creature in strength, by another in speed, by a third in foresight, by a fourth in indus-

try. He added, that nature was degenerated in these latter declining ages of the world, and could now produce only small abortive births in comparison of those in ancient times. He said, it was very reasonable to think, not only that the species of man were originally much larger, but also, that there must have been giants in former ages, which, as it is asserted by history and tradition, so it hath been confirmed by huge bones and skulls casually dug up in several parts of the kingdom, far exceeding the common dwindled race of man in our days. He argued, that the very laws of nature absolutely required we should have been made in the beginning, of a size more large and robust, not so liable to destruction from every little accident of a tile falling from a house, or a stone cast from the hand of a boy, or of being drowned in a little brook. From this way of reasoning the author drew several moral applications useful in the conduct of life, but needless here to repeat. For my own part, I could not avoid reflecting how universally this talent was spread, of drawing lectures in morality, or indeed rather matter of discontent and repining, from the quarrels we raise with nature. And I believe, upon a strict inquiry, those quarrels might be shown as ill grounded among us, as they are among that people.

As to their military affairs, they boast that the King's army consists of an hundred and seventy-six thousand foot, and thirty-two thousand horse: if that may be called an army which is made up of tradesmen in the several cities, and farmers in the country, whose commanders are only the nobility and gentry, without pay or reward. They are indeed perfect enough in their exercises, and under very good discipline, wherein I saw no great merit; for how should it be otherwise, where every farmer is under the command of his own landlord, and every citizen under that of the principal men in his own city, chosen after the manner of Venice by ballot? [35]

I have often seen the militia of Lorbrulgrud drawn out to exercise in a great field near the city of twenty miles square. They were in all not above twenty-five thousand foot, and six thousand horse; but it was impossible for me to compute their number, considering the space of ground they took up. A cavalier mounted on a large steed, might be about ninety foot high. I have seen this whole

---

35. by ballot: the method of secret voting, introduced in Venice, of dropping a *ballotta*, or little ball, into one of the divisions of a box.

body of horse, upon the word of command, draw their swords at once, and brandish them in the air. Imagination can figure nothing so grand, so surprising, and so astonishing! It looked as if ten thousand flashes of lightning were darting at the same time from every quarter of the sky.

I was curious to know how this prince, to whose dominions there is no access from any other country, came to think of armies, or to teach his people the practice of military discipline. But I was soon informed, both by conversation, and reading their histories. For, in the course of many ages they have been troubled with the same disease to which the whole race of mankind is subject; the nobility often contending for power, the people for liberty, and the King for absolute dominion. All which, however happily tempered by the laws of that kingdom, have been sometimes violated by each of the three parties, and have more than once occasioned civil wars, the last whereof was happily put an end to by this prince's grandfather in a general composition; and the militia, then settled with common consent, hath been ever since kept in the strictest duty.

CHAPTER 8

The King and Queen make a progress to the frontiers. The Author attends them. The manner in which he leaves the country very particularly related. He returns to England.

I had always a strong impulse that I should some time recover my liberty, although it was impossible to conjecture by what means, or to form any project with the least hope of succeeding. The ship in which I sailed was the first ever known to be driven within sight of that coast, and the King had given strict orders, that if at any time another appeared, it should be taken ashore, and with all its crew and passengers brought in a tumbril [36] to Lorbrulgrud. He was strongly bent to get me a woman of my own size, by whom I might propagate the breed: but I think I should rather have died than undergone the disgrace of leaving a posterity to be kept in cages like tame canary birds, and perhaps, in time, sold about the kingdom to persons of quality for curiosities. I was, indeed, treated with much kindness: I was the favorite of a great King and Queen, and the delight of the whole court, but it was upon such a foot as ill became the dignity of human kind. I could never forget those domestic pledges I had left behind me. I wanted to be among people with whom I could converse upon even terms, and walk about the streets and fields without fear of being trod to death like a frog or young puppy. But my deliverance came sooner than I expected, and in a manner not very common: the whole story and circumstances of which I shall faithfully relate.

I had now been two years in this country; and about the beginning of the third, Glumdalclitch and I attended the King and Queen in a progress to the south coast of the kingdom. I was carried, as usual, in my traveling box, which, as I have already described, was a very convenient closet of twelve foot wide. I had ordered a hammock to be fixed by silken ropes from the four corners at the top, to break the jolts, when a servant carried me before him on horseback, as I sometimes desired, and would often sleep in my hammock while we were upon the road. On the roof of my closet, set not directly over the middle of the hammock, I ordered the joiner to cut out a hole of a foot square, to give me air in hot weather, as I slept; which hole I shut at pleasure with a board that drew backwards and forwards through a groove.

When we came to our journey's end, the King thought proper to pass a few days at a palace he hath near Flanflasnic, a city within eighteen English miles of the seaside. Glumdalclitch and I were much fatigued; I had gotten a small cold, but the poor girl was so ill as to be confined to her chamber. I longed to see the ocean, which must be the only scene of my escape, if ever it should happen. I pretended to be worse than I really was, and desired leave to take the fresh air of the sea, with a page whom I was very fond of, and who had sometimes been trusted with me. I shall never forget with what unwillingness Glumdalclitch consented, nor the strict charge she gave the page to be careful of me, bursting at the same time into a flood of tears, as if she had some foreboding of what was to happen. The boy took me out in my box about half an hour's walk from the palace, towards the rocks on the seashore. I ordered him to set me down, and lifting up one of my sashes, cast many a wistful melancholy look towards the sea. I found myself not very well, and told the page that I had a mind to take a nap in my hammock, which I hoped would do me good. I got in, and the boy shut the window close down to keep out the cold. I soon fell asleep, and all I can con-

36. tumbril: a tipcart, or dungcart.

jecture is, that while I slept, the page, thinking no danger could happen, went among the rocks to look for birds' eggs, having before observed him from my window searching about, and picking up one or two in the clefts. Be that as it will, I found myself suddenly awaked with a violent pull upon the ring which was fastened at the top of my box for the conveniency of carriage. I felt the box raised very high in the air, and then borne forward with prodigious speed. The first jolt had like to have shaken me out of my hammock, but afterwards the motion was easy enough. I called out several times, as loud as I could raise my voice, but all to no purpose. I looked towards my windows, and could see nothing but the clouds and sky. I heard a noise just over my head like the clapping of wings, and then began to perceive the woeful condition I was in; that some eagle had got the ring of my box in his beak, with an intent to let it fall on a rock like a tortoise in a shell, and then pick out my body, and devour it. For the sagacity and smell of this bird enable him to discover his quarry at a great distance, though better concealed than I could be within a two-inch board.

In a little time I observed the noise and flutter of wings to increase very fast, and my box was tossed up and down, like a signpost in a windy day. I heard several bangs or buffets, as I thought, given to the eagle (for such I am certain it must have been that held the ring of my box in his beak), and then all on a sudden felt myself falling perpendicularly down for above a minute, but with such incredible swiftness that I almost lost my breath. My fall was stopped by a terrible squash, that sounded louder to my ears than the cataract of Niagara; after which I was quite in the dark for another minute, and then my box began to rise so high that I could see light from the tops of my windows. I now perceived that I was fallen into the sea. My box, by the weight of my body, the goods that were in, and the broad plates of iron fixed for strength at the four corners of the top and bottom, floated about five foot deep in water. I did then, and do now suppose that the eagle which flew away with my box was pursued by two or three others, and forced to let me drop while he was defending himself against the rest, who hoped to share in the prey. The plates of iron fastened at the bottom of the box (for those were the strongest) preserved the balance while it fell, and hindered it from being broken on the surface of the water. Every joint of it was well grooved, and the door

did not move on hinges, but up and down like a sash, which kept my closet so tight that very little water came in. I got with much difficulty out of my hammock, having first ventured to draw back the slip board on the roof already mentioned, contrived on purpose to let in air, for want of which I found myself almost stifled.

How often did I then wish myself with my dear Glumdalclitch, from whom one single hour had so far divided me! And I may say with truth, that in the midst of my own misfortune I could not forbear lamenting my poor nurse, the grief she would suffer for my loss, the displeasure of the Queen, and the ruin of her fortune. Perhaps many travelers have not been under greater difficulties and distress than I was at this juncture, expecting every moment to see my box dashed in pieces, or at least overset by the first violent blast, or a rising wave. A breach in one single pane of glass would have been immediate death: nor could anything have preserved the windows, but the strong lattice wires placed on the outside against accidents in traveling. I saw the water ooze in at several crannies, although the leaks were not considerable, and I endeavored to stop them as well as I could. I was not able to lift up the roof of my closet, which otherwise I certainly should have done, and sat on the top of it, where I might at least preserve myself from being shut up, as I may call it, in the hold. Or, if I escaped these dangers for a day or two, what could I expect but a miserable death of cold and hunger! I was four hours under these circumstances, expecting and indeed wishing every moment to be my last.

I have already told the reader, that there were two strong staples fixed upon the side of my box which had no window, and into which the servant who used to carry me on horseback would put a leathern belt, and buckle it about his waist. Being in this disconsolate state, I heard or at least thought I heard some kind of grating noise on that side of my box where the staples were fixed, and soon after I began to fancy that the box was pulled or towed along in the sea; for I now and then felt a sort of tugging, which made the waves rise near the tops of my windows, leaving me almost in the dark. This gave me some faint hopes of relief, although I was not able to imagine how it could be brought about. I ventured to unscrew one of my chairs, which were always fastened to the floor; and having made a hard shift to screw it down again directly under the slipping board that I had lately opened, I mounted on the chair, and putting my mouth as near as I could to the hole, I called for help in a loud voice, and in all the languages I understood. I then fastened my handkerchief to a stick I usually carried, and thrusting it up the hole, waved it several times in the air, that if any boat or ship were near, the seamen might conjecture some unhappy mortal to be shut up in the box.

I found no effect from all I could do, but plainly perceived my closet to be moved along; and in the space of an hour, or better, that side of the box where the staples were, and had no window, struck against something that was hard. I apprehended it to be a rock, and found myself tossed more than ever. I plainly heard a noise upon the cover of my closet, like that of a cable, and the grating of it as it passed through the ring. I then found myself hoisted up by degrees at least three foot higher than I was before. Whereupon I again thrust up my stick and handkerchief, calling for help till I was almost hoarse. In return to which, I heard a great shout repeated three times, giving me such transports of joy, as are not to be conceived but by those who feel them. I now heard a trampling over my head, and somebody calling through the hole with a loud voice in the English tongue, If there be anybody below, let them speak. I answered, I was an Englishman, drawn by ill fortune into the greatest calamity that ever any creature underwent, and begged, by all that was moving, to be delivered out of the dungeon I was in. The voice replied, I was safe, for my box was fastened to their ship; and the carpenter should immediately come and saw an hole in the cover, large enough to pull me out. I answered, that was needless, and would take up too much time, for there was no more to be done, but let one of the crew put his finger into the ring, and take the box out of the sea into the ship, and so into the captain's cabin. Some of them upon hearing me talk so wildly thought I was mad; others laughed; for indeed it never came into my head that I was now got among people of my own stature and strength. The carpenter came, and in a few minutes sawed a passage about four foot square, then let down a small ladder, upon which I mounted, and from thence was taken into the ship in a very weak condition.

The sailors were all in amazement, and asked me a thousand questions, which I had no inclination to answer. I was equally confounded at the sight of so many pygmies, for such I took them to be, after having so long accustomed my eyes to the monstrous objects I had left. But the Captain, Mr. Thomas Wilcocks, an honest worthy Shropshire man, observing I was ready to faint, took me into his cabin, gave me a cordial to comfort me, and made me turn in upon his own bed, advising me to take a little rest of which I had great need. Before I went to sleep, I gave him to understand that I had some valuable furniture in my box, too good to be lost; a fine hammock, an handsome field bed, two chairs, a table, and a cabinet: that my closet was hung on all sides, or rather quilted, with silk and cotton: that if he would let one of the crew bring my closet into his cabin, I would open it there before him, and show him my goods. The Captain hearing me utter these absurdities, concluded I was raving: however (I suppose to pacify me), he promised to give order as I desired, and going upon deck sent some of his men down into my closet, from whence (as I afterwards found) they drew up all my goods, and stripped off the quilting; but the chairs, cabinet, and bedstead, being screwed to the floor, were much damaged by the ignorance of the seamen, who tore them up by force. Then they knocked off some of the boards for the use of the ship, and when they had got all they had a mind for, let the hulk drop into the sea, which by reason of many breaches made in the bottom and sides, sunk to rights. And indeed I was glad not to have been a spectator of the havoc they made; because I am confident it would have sensibly touched me, by bringing former passages into my mind, which I had rather forget.

I slept some hours, but perpetually disturbed with dreams of the place I had left, and the dangers I had escaped. However, upon waking I found myself much recovered. It was now about eight o'clock at night, and the Captain ordered supper immediately, thinking I had already fasted too long. He entertained me with great kindness, observing me not to look wildly, or talk inconsistently: and when we were left alone, desired I would give him a relation of my travels, and by what accident I came to be set adrift in that monstrous wooden chest. He said, that about twelve o'clock at noon, as he was looking through his glass, he spied it at a distance, and thought it was a sail, which he had a mind to make, being not much out of his course, in hopes of buying some biscuit, his own beginning to fall short. That upon coming nearer, and finding his error, he sent out his longboat to discover what I was; that his men came back in a fright, swearing they had seen a swimming house. That he laughed at their folly, and went himself in the boat, ordering his men to take a strong cable along with them. That the weather being calm, he rowed round me several times, observed my windows, and the wire lattices that defended them. That he discovered two staples upon one side, which was all of boards, without any passage for light. He then commanded his men to row up to that side, and fastening a cable to one of the staples, ordered them to tow my chest (as he called it) towards the ship. When it was there, he gave directions to fasten another cable to the ring fixed in the cover, and to raise up my chest with pulleys, which all the sailors were not able to do above two or three foot. He said, they saw my stick and handkerchief thrust out of the hole, and concluded that some unhappy man must be shut up in the cavity. I asked whether he or the crew had seen any prodigious birds in the air about the time he first discovered me. To which he answered, that discoursing this matter with the sailors while I was asleep, one of them said he had observed three eagles flying towards the north, but remarked nothing of their being larger than the usual size, which I suppose must be imputed to the great height they were at; and he could not guess the reason of my question. I then asked the Captain how far he reckoned we might be from land; he said, by the best computation he could make, we were at least an hundred leagues. I assured him, that he must be mistaken by almost half, for I had not left the country from whence I came above two hours before I dropped into the sea. Whereupon he began again to think that my brain was disturbed, of which he gave me a hint, and advised me to go to bed in a cabin he had provided. I assured him I was well refreshed with his good entertainment and company, and as much in my senses as ever I was in my life. He then grew serious, and desired to ask me freely whether I were not troubled in mind by the consciousness of some enormous crime, for which I was punished at the command of some prince, by exposing me in that chest, as great criminals in other countries have been forced to sea in a leaky vessel without provisions: for, although he should be sorry to have taken so ill a man into his ship, yet he would engage his word to set me safe on shore in the first port where we arrived. He added, that his suspicions were much increased by some very absurd speeches I had delivered at first to the sailors, and

afterwards to himself, in relation to my closet or chest, as well as by my odd looks and behavior while I was at supper.

I begged his patience to hear me tell my story, which I faithfully did from the last time I left England to the moment he first discovered me. And, as truth always forceth its way into rational minds, so this honest worthy gentleman, who had some tincture of learning, and very good sense, was immediately convinced of my candor and veracity. But further to confirm all I had said, I entreated him to give order that my cabinet should be brought, of which I kept the key in my pocket (for he had already informed me how the seamen disposed of my closet). I opened it in his presence, and showed him the small collection of rarities I made in the country from whence I had been so strangely delivered. There was the comb I had contrived out of the stumps of the King's beard, and another of the same materials, but fixed into a paring of her Majesty's thumbnail, which served for the back. There was a collection of needles and pins from a foot to half a yard long; four wasp stings, like joiners' tacks; some combings of the Queen's hair; a gold ring which one day she made me a present of in a most obliging manner, taking it from her little finger, and throwing it over my head like a collar. I desired the Captain would please to accept this ring in return of his civilities; which he absolutely refused. I showed him a corn that I had cut off with my own hand, from a maid of honor's toe; it was about the bigness of a Kentish pippin, and grown so hard that when I returned to England, I got it hollowed into a cup, and set in silver. Lastly, I desired him to see the breeches I had then on, which were made of a mouse's skin.

I could force nothing on him but a footman's tooth, which I observed him to examine with great curiosity, and found he had a fancy for it. He received it with abundance of thanks, more than such a trifle could deserve. It was drawn by an unskillful surgeon, in a mistake, from one of Glumdalclitch's men, who was afflicted with the toothache, but it was as sound as any in his head. I got it cleaned, and put it into my cabinet. It was about a foot long, and four inches in diameter.

The Captain was very well satisfied with this plain relation I had given him, and said, he hoped when we returned to England, I would oblige the world by putting it in paper, and making it public. My answer was, that I thought we were already overstocked with books of travels: that nothing could now pass which was not extraordinary; wherein I doubted some authors less consulted truth than their own vanity, or interest, or the diversion of ignorant readers. That my story could contain little besides common events, without those ornamental descriptions of strange plants, trees, birds, and other animals, or the barbarous customs and idolatry of savage people, with which most writers abound. However, I thanked him for his good opinion, and promised to take the matter into my thoughts.

He said he wondered at one thing very much, which was, to hear me speak so loud, asking me whether the King or Queen of that country were thick of hearing. I told him, it was what I had been used to for above two years past; and that I admired as much at the voices of him and his men, who seemed to me only to whisper, and yet I could hear them well enough. But when I spoke in that country, it was like a man talking in the street to another looking out from the top of a steeple, unless when I was placed on a table, or held in any person's hand. I told him, I had likewise observed another thing, that when I first got into the ship, and the sailors stood all about me, I thought they were the most little contemptible creatures I had ever beheld. For, indeed, while I was in that prince's country, I could never endure to look in a glass after my eyes had been accustomed to such prodigious objects, because the comparison gave me so despicable a conceit of myself. The Captain said, that while we were at supper, he observed me to look at everything with a sort of wonder, and that I often seemed hardly able to contain my laughter, which he knew not well how to take, but imputed it to some disorder in my brain. I answered, it was very true; and I wondered how I could forbear, when I saw his dishes of the size of a silver threepence, a leg of pork hardly a mouthful, a cup not so big as a nutshell; and so I went on, describing the rest of his household stuff and provisions after the same manner. For, although the Queen had ordered a little equipage of all things necessary for me while I was in her service, yet my ideas were wholly taken up with what I saw on every side of me, and I winked at my own littleness as people do at their own faults. The Captain understood my raillery very well, and merrily replied with the old English proverb, that he doubted my eyes were bigger than my belly, for he did not observe my stomach so good, although I had fasted all day; and continuing in his mirth, protested he would have gladly given an hundred pounds to have seen my closet in the eagle's bill, and afterwards in its fall from so great an height into the sea; which would certainly have been a most astonishing object, worthy to have the description of it transmitted to future ages: and the comparison of Phaeton was so obvious, that he could not forbear applying it, although I did not much admire the conceit.[37]

The Captain having been at Tonquin,[38] was in his return to England driven northeastward to the latitude of forty-four degrees, and of longitude one hundred and forty-three. But meeting a trade wind two days after I came on board him, we sailed southward a long time, and coasting New Holland[39] kept our course west-southwest, and then south-southwest till we doubled the Cape of Good Hope. Our voyage was very prosperous, but I shall not trouble the reader with a journal of it. The Captain called in at one or two ports, and sent in his longboat for provisions and fresh water, but I never went out of the ship till we came into the Downs, which was on the 3rd day of June, 1706, about nine months after my escape. I offered to leave my goods in security for payment of my freight:[40] but the Captain protested he would not receive one farthing. We took kind leave of each other, and I made him promise he would come to see me at my house in Redriff. I hired a horse and guide for five shillings, which I borrowed of the Captain.

As I was on the road, observing the littleness of the houses, the trees, the cattle, and the people, I began to think myself in Lilliput. I was afraid of trampling on every traveler I met, and often called aloud to have them stand out of the way, so that I had like to have gotten one or two broken heads for my impertinence.

When I came to my own house, for which I was forced to inquire, one of the servants opening the door, I bent down to go in (like a goose under a gate) for fear of striking my head. My wife ran out to embrace me, but I stooped lower than her knees, thinking she could otherwise never be able to reach my mouth. My daughter kneeled to ask my blessing, but I could not see her till she arose, having been so long used to stand with my head and eyes erect to above sixty foot; and then I went

---

37. **conceit:** The stale comparison with the fall of Phaëthon is dragged in to ridicule the unnecessary use of classical tags. 38. **Tonquin:** in French Indochina.   39. **New Holland:** the west coast of Australia.   40. **freight:** passage.

to take her up with one hand, by the waist. I looked down upon the servants and one or two friends who were in the house, as if they had been pygmies, and I a giant. I told my wife, she had been too thrifty, for I found she had starved herself and her daughter to nothing. In short, I behaved myself so unaccountably, that they were all of the Captain's opinion when he first saw me, and concluded I had lost my wits. This I mention as an instance of the great power of habit and prejudice.

In a little time I and my family and friends came to a right understanding: but my wife protested I should never go to sea any more; although my evil destiny so ordered that she had not power to hinder me, as the reader may know hereafter. In the meantime I here conclude the second part of my unfortunate voyages.

THE END OF THE SECOND PART

PART IV

A Voyage to the Country of the Houyhnhnms

CHAPTER I

The Author sets out as Captain of a ship. His men conspire against him, confine him a long time to his cabin, set him on shore in an unknown land. He travels up into the country. The Yahoos, a strange sort of animal, described. The Author meets two Houyhnhnms.

I continued at home with my wife and children about five months in a very happy condition, if I could have learned the lesson of knowing when I was well. I left my poor wife big with child, and accepted an advantageous offer made me to be Captain of the *Adventurer,* a stout merchantman of 350 tons: for I understood navigation well, and being grown weary of a surgeon's employment at sea, which however I could exercise upon occasion, I took a skillful young man of that calling, one Robert Purefoy, into my ship. We set sail from Portsmouth upon the 7th day of September, 1710; on the 14th we met with Captain Pocock of Bristol, at Teneriffe,[1] who was going to the Bay of Campechy,[2] to cut logwood. On the 16th, he

was parted from us by a storm; I heard since my return, that his ship foundered, and none escaped but one cabin boy. He was an honest man, and a good sailor, but a little too positive in his own opinions, which was the cause of his destruction, as it hath been of several others. For if he had followed my advice, he might at this time have been safe at home with his family, as well as myself.

I had several men died in my ship of calentures,[3] so that I was forced to get recruits out of Barbados, and the Leeward Islands, where I touched by the direction of the merchants who employed me, which I had soon too much cause to repent: for I found afterwards that most of them had been buccaneers. I had fifty hands on board, and my orders were, that I should trade with the Indians in the South Sea,[4] and make what discoveries I could. These rogues whom I had picked up debauched my other men, and they all formed a conspiracy to seize the ship and secure me; which they did one morning, rushing into my cabin, and binding me hand and foot, threatening to throw me overboard, if I offered to stir. I told them, I was their prisoner, and would submit. This they made me swear to do, and then unbound me, only fastening one of my legs with a chain near my bed, and placed a sentry at my door with his piece charged, who was commanded to shoot me dead, if I attempted my liberty. They sent me down victuals and drink, and took the government of the ship to themselves. Their design was to turn pirates, and plunder the Spaniards, which they could not do, till they got more men. But first they resolved to sell the goods in the ship, and then go to Madagascar[5] for recruits, several among them having died since my confinement. They sailed many weeks, and traded with the Indians, but I knew not what course they took, being kept close prisoner in my cabin, and expecting nothing less than to be murdered, as they often threatened me.

Upon the 9th day of May, 1711, one James Welch came down to my cabin; and said he had orders from the Captain to get me ashore. I expostulated with him, but in vain; neither would he so much as tell me who their new Captain was. They forced me into the longboat, letting me put on my best suit of clothes, which were as good as new, and a small bundle of linen, but no arms ex-

---

A Voyage to the Country of the Houyhnhnms: **1. Teneriffe:** the largest of the Canary Islands. **2. Campechy:** in the Gulf of Mexico where the best quality logwood was obtained for making dyes.

3. calentures: tropical fevers. **4. South Sea:** There was great interest in exploring the South Pacific when the South Sea Company got its monopoly in 1711. **5. Madagascar:** at the time a favorite haunt of pirates.

cept my hanger; and they were so civil as not to search my pockets, into which I conveyed what money I had, with some other little necessaries. They rowed about a league, and then set me down on a strand. I desired them to tell me what country it was. They all swore, they knew no more than myself, but said, that the Captain (as they called him) was resolved, after they had sold the lading, to get rid of me in the first place where they discovered land. They pushed off immediately, advising me to make haste, for fear of being overtaken by the tide, and bade me farewell.

In this desolate condition I advanced forward, and soon got upon firm ground, where I sat down on a bank to rest myself, and consider what I had best to do. When I was a little refreshed, I went up into the country, resolving so deliver myself to the first savages I should meet, and purchase my life from them by some bracelets, glass rings, and other toys which sailors usually provide themselves with in those voyages, and whereof I had some about me. The land was divided by long rows of trees, not regularly planted, but naturally growing; there was great plenty of grass, and several fields of oats. I walked very circumspectly for fear of being surprised, or suddenly shot with an arrow from behind or on either side. I fell into a beaten road, where I saw many tracks of human feet, and some of cows, but most of horses. At last I beheld several animals in a field, and one or two of the same kind sitting in trees. Their shape was very singular, and deformed, which a little discomposed me, so that I lay down behind a thicket to observe them better. Some of them coming forward near the place where I lay, gave me an opportunity of distinctly marking their form. Their heads and breasts were covered with a thick hair, some frizzled and others lank; they had beards like goats, and a long ridge of hair down their backs and the foreparts of their legs and feet, but the rest of their bodies were bare, so that I might see their skins, which were of a brown buff color. They had no tails, nor any hair at all on their buttocks, except about the anus; which, I presume, nature had placed there to defend them as they sat on the ground; for this posture they used, as well as lying down, and often stood on their hind feet. They climbed high trees, as nimbly as a squirrel, for they had strong extended claws before and behind, terminating in sharp points, hooked. They would often spring, and bound, and leap with prodigious agility. The females were not so large as the males;

they had long lank hair on their heads, and only a sort of down on the rest of their bodies, except about the anus, and pudenda. Their dugs hung between their forefeet, and often reached almost to the ground as they walked. The hair of both sexes was of several colors, brown, red, black, and yellow. Upon the whole, I never beheld in all my travels so disagreeable an animal, nor one against which I naturally conceived so strong an antipathy. So that thinking I had seen enough, full of contempt and aversion, I got up and pursued the beaten road, hoping it might direct me to the cabin of some Indian. I had not got far when I met one of these creatures full in my way, and coming up directly to me. The ugly monster, when he saw me, distorted several ways every feature of his visage, and stared as at an object he had never seen before; then approaching nearer, lifted up his forepaw, whether out of curiosity or mischief, I could not tell. But I drew my hanger, and gave him a good blow with the flat side of it, for I durst not strike with the edge, fearing the inhabitants might be provoked against me, if they should come to know, that I had killed or mained any of their cattle. When the beast felt the smart, he drew back, and roared so loud, that a herd of at least forty came flocking about me from the next field, howling and making odious faces; but I ran to the body of a tree, and leaning my back against it, kept them off by waving my hanger. Several of this cursed brood getting hold of the branches behind, leapt up into the tree, from whence they began to discharge their excrements on my head; however, I escaped pretty well, by sticking close to the stem of the tree, but was almost stifled with the filth, which fell about me on every side.

In the midst of this distress, I observed them all to run away on a sudden as fast as they could, at which I ventured to leave the tree, and pursue the road, wondering what it was that could put them into this fright. But looking on my left hand, I saw a horse walking softly in the field; which my persecutors having sooner discovered, was the cause of their flight. The horse started a little when he came near me, but soon recovering himself, looked full in my face with manifest tokens of wonder: he viewed my hands and feet, walking round me several times. I would have pursued my journey, but he placed himself directly in the way, yet looking with a very mild aspect, never offering the least violence. We stood gazing at each other for some time; at last I took the boldness to reach my hand towards his neck, with a design to stroke it, using the common style and whistle of jockeys when they are going to handle a strange horse. But this animal seeming to receive my civilities with disdain, shook his head, and bent his brows, softly raising up his left forefoot to remove my hand. Then he neighed three or four times, but in so different a cadence, that I almost began to think he was speaking to himself in some language of his own.

While he and I were thus employed, another horse came up; who applying himself to the first in a very formal manner, they gently struck each other's right hoof before, neighing several times by turns, and varying the sound, which seemed to be almost articulate. They went some paces off, as if it were to confer together, walking side by side, backward and forward, like persons deliberating upon some affair of weight, but often turning their eyes towards me, as it were to watch that I might not escape. I was amazed to see such actions and behavior in brute beasts, and concluded with myself, that if the inhabitants of this country were endued with a proportionable degree of reason, they must needs be the wisest people upon earth. This thought gave me so much comfort, that I resolved to go forward until I could discover some house or village, or meet with any of the natives, leaving the two horses to discourse together as they pleased. But the first, who was a dapple gray, observing me to steal off, neighed after me in so expressive a tone, that I fancied myself to understand what he meant; whereupon I turned back, and came near him, to expect his farther commands: but concealing my fear as much as I could, for I began to be in some pain, how this adventure might terminate; and the reader will easily believe I did not much like my present situation.

The two horses came up close to me, looking with great earnestness upon my face and hands. The gray steed rubbed my hat all round with his right forehoof, and discomposed it so much that I was forced to adjust it better, by taking it off, and settling it again; whereat both he and his companion (who was a brown bay) appeared to be much surprised: the latter felt the lappet of my coat, and finding it to hang loose about me, they both looked with new signs of wonder. He stroked my right hand, seeming to admire the softness and color; but he squeezed it so hard between his hoof and his pastern, that I was forced to roar; after which they both touched me with all possible tenderness. They were under great perplexity about my shoes and stockings, which they felt very often, neighing to each other, and using various gestures, not unlike those of a philosopher, when he would attempt to solve some new and difficult phenomenon.

Upon the whole, the behavior of these animals was so orderly and rational, so acute and judicious, that I at last concluded, they must needs be magicians, who had thus metamorphosed themselves upon some design, and seeing a stranger in the way, were resolved to divert themselves with him; or perhaps were really amazed at the sight of a man so very different in habit, feature, and complexion from those who might probably live in so remote a climate. Upon the strength of this reasoning, I ventured to address them in the following manner: " Gentlemen, if you be conjurers, as I have good cause to believe, you can understand any language; therefore I make bold to let your worships know, that I am a poor distressed Englishman, driven by his misfortunes upon your coast, and I entreat one of you, to let me ride upon his back, as if he were a real horse, to some house or village, where I can be relieved. In return of which favor, I will make you a present of this knife and bracelet " (taking them out of my pocket). The two creatures stood silent while I spoke, seeming to listen with great attention; and when I had ended, they neighed frequently towards each other, as if they were engaged in serious conversation. I plainly observed, that their language expressed the passions very well, and the words might with little pains be resolved into an alphabet more easily than the Chinese.

I could frequently distinguish the word *Yahoo,* which was repeated by each of them several times; and although it was impossible for me to conjecture what it meant, yet while the two horses were busy in conversation, I endeavored to practice this word upon my tongue; and as soon as they were silent, I boldly pronounced *Yahoo* in a loud voice, imitating, at the same time, as near as I could, the neighing of a horse; at which they were both visibly surprised, and the gray repeated the same word twice, as if he meant to teach me the right accent, wherein I spoke after him as well as I could, and found myself perceivably to improve every time, though very far from any degree of perfection. Then the bay tried me with a second word, much harder to be pronounced; but reducing it to the English orthography, may be spelt thus,

Houyhnhnm. I did not succeed in this so well as the former, but after two or three farther trials, I had better fortune; and they both appeared amazed at my capacity.

After some further discourse, which I then conjectured might relate to me, the two friends took their leaves, with the same compliment of striking each other's hoof; and the gray made me signs that I should walk before him, wherein I thought it prudent to comply, till I could find a better director. When I offered to slacken my pace, he would cry, *Hhuun, Hhuun;* I guessed his meaning, and gave him to understand, as well as I could, that I was weary, and not able to walk faster; upon which, he would stand a while to let me rest.

CHAPTER 2

The Author conducted by a Houyhnhnm *to his house. The house described. The Author's reception. The food of the* Houyhnhnms. *The Author in distress for want of meat, is at last relieved. His manner of feeding in that country.*

Having traveled about three miles, we came to a long kind of building, made of timber, stuck in the ground, and wattled across; the roof was low, and covered with straw. I now began to be a little comforted, and took out some toys, which travelers usually carry for presents to the savage Indians of America and other parts, in hopes the people of the house would be thereby encouraged to receive me kindly. The horse made me a sign to go in first; it was a large room with a smooth clay floor, and a rack and manger extending the whole length on one side. There were three nags, and two mares, not eating, but some of them sitting down upon their hams, which I very much wondered at; but wondered more to see the rest employed in domestic business. The last seemed but ordinary cattle; however, this confirmed my first opinion, that a people who could so far civilize brute animals, must needs excel in wisdom all the nations of the world. The gray came in just after, and thereby prevented any ill treatment, which the others might have given me. He neighed to them several times in a style of authority, and received answers.

Beyond this room there were three others, reaching the length of the house, to which you passed through three doors, opposite to each other, in the manner of a vista; we went through the second room towards the third; here the gray walked in

first, beckoning me to attend: I waited in the second room, and got ready my presents for the master and mistress of the house: they were two knives, three bracelets of false pearl, a small looking glass, and a bead necklace. The horse neighed three or four times, and I waited to hear some answers in a human voice, but I heard no other returns, than in the same dialect, only one or two a little shriller than his. I began to think that this house must belong to some person of great note among them, because there appeared so much ceremony before I could gain admittance. But, that a man of quality should be served all by horses, was beyond my comprehension. I feared my brain was disturbed by my sufferings and misfortunes: I roused myself, and looked about me in the room where I was left alone; this was furnished as the first, only after a more elegant manner. I rubbed my eyes often, but the same objects still occurred. I pinched my arms and sides, to awake myself, hoping I might be in a dream. I then absolutely concluded, that all these appearances could be nothing else but necromancy and magic. But I had no time to pursue these reflections; for the gray horse came to the door, and made me a sign to follow him into the third room, where I saw a very comely mare, together with a colt and foal, sitting on their haunches, upon mats of straw, not unartfully made, and perfectly neat and clean.

The mare soon after my entrance, rose from her mat, and coming up close, after having nicely observed my hands and face, gave me a most contemptuous look; then turning to the horse, I heard the word *Yahoo* often repeated betwixt them; the meaning of which word I could not then comprehend, although it were the first I had learned to pronounce; but I was soon better informed, to my everlasting mortification: for the horse beckoning to me with his head, and repeating the word *Hhuun, Hhuun,* as he did upon the road, which I understood was to attend him, led me out into a kind of court, where was another building at some distance from the house. Here we entered, and I saw three of those detestable creatures, which I first met after my landing, feeding upon roots, and the flesh of some animals, which I afterwards found to be that of asses and dogs, and now and then a cow dead by accident or disease. They were all tied by the neck with strong withes,[6] fastened to a beam; they held their food between the claws

6. withes: a halter made of flexible twigs.

of their forefeet, and tore it with their teeth.

The master horse ordered a sorrel nag, one of his servants, to untie the largest of these animals, and take him into the yard. The beast and I were brought close together, and our countenances diligently compared, both by master and servant, who thereupon repeated several times the word *Yahoo*. My horror and astonishment are not to be described, when I observed, in this abominable animal, a perfect human figure: the face of it indeed was flat and broad, the nose depressed, the lips large, and the mouth wide. But these differences are common to all savage nations, where the lineaments of the countenance are distorted by the natives suffering their infants to lie groveling on the earth, or by carrying them on their backs, nuzzling with their face against the mother's shoulders. The forefeet of the *Yahoo* differed from my hands in nothing else but the length of the nails, the coarseness and brownness of the palms, and the hairiness on the backs. There was the same resemblance between our feet, with the same differences, which I knew very well, although the horses did not, because of my shoes and stockings; the same in every part of our bodies, except as to hairiness and color, which I have already described.

The great difficulty that seemed to stick with the two horses, was, to see the rest of my body so very different from that of a *Yahoo,* for which I was obliged to my clothes, whereof they had no conception. The sorrel nag offered me a root, which he held (after their manner, as we shall describe in its proper place) between his hoof and pastern; I took it in my hand, and having smelt it, returned it to him again as civilly as I could. He brought out of the *Yahoo's* kennel a piece of ass's flesh, but it smelt so offensively that I turned from it with loathing: he then threw it to the *Yahoo,* by whom it was greedily devoured. He afterwards showed me a wisp of hay, and a fetlock full of oats; but I shook my head, to signify, that neither of these were food for me. And indeed, I now apprehended that I must absolutely starve, if I did not get to some of my own species; for as to those filthy *Yahoos,* although there were few greater lovers of mankind, at that time, than myself, yet I confess I never saw any sensitive being so detestable on all accounts; and the more I came near them, the more hateful they grew, while I stayed in that country. This the master horse observed by my behavior, and therefore sent the *Yahoo* back to his kennel. He then put his forehoof to his mouth, at which I

was much surprised, although he did it with ease, and with a motion that appeared perfectly natural, and made other signs to know what I would eat; but I could not return him such an answer as he was able to apprehend; and if he had understood me, I did not see how it was possible to contrive any way for finding myself nourishment. While we were thus engaged, I observed a cow passing by, whereupon I pointed to her, and expressed a desire to let me go and milk her. This had its effect; for he led me back into the house, and ordered a mare-servant to open a room, where a good store of milk lay in earthen and wooden vessels, after a very orderly and cleanly manner. She gave me a large bowl full, of which I drank very heartily, and found myself well refreshed.

About noon I saw coming towards the house a kind of vehicle, drawn like a sledge by four *Yahoos*. There was in it an old steed, who seemed to be of quality; he alighted with his hindfeet forward, having by accident got a hurt in his left forefoot. He came to dine with our horse, who received him with great civility. They dined in the best room, and had oats boiled in milk for the second course, which the old horse eat warm, but the rest cold. Their mangers were placed circular in the middle of the room, and divided into several partitions, round which they sat on their haunches upon bosses of straw. In the middle was a large rack with angles answering to every partition of the manger; so that each horse and mare eat their own hay, and their own mash of oats and milk, with much decency and regularity. The behavior of the young colt and foal appeared very modest, and that of the master and mistress extremely cheerful and complaisant to their guest. The gray ordered me to stand by him, and much discourse passed between him and his friend concerning me, as I found by the stranger's often looking on me, and the frequent repetition of the word *Yahoo*.

I happened to wear my gloves, which the master gray observing, seemed perplexed, discovering signs of wonder what I had done to my forefeet; he put his hoof three or four times to them, as if he would signify, that I should reduce them to their former shape, which I presently did, pulling off both my gloves, and putting them into my pocket. This occasioned farther talk, and I saw the company was pleased with my behavior, whereof I soon found the good effects. I was ordered to speak the few words I understood, and while they were at dinner, the master taught me the names for oats, milk, fire, water, and some others; which I could readily pronounce after him, having from my youth a great facility in learning languages.

When dinner was done, the master horse took me aside, and by signs and words made me understand the concern he was in, that I had nothing to eat. Oats in their tongue are called *hlunnh*. This word I pronounced two or three times; for although I had refused them at first, yet upon second thoughts, I considered that I could contrive to make of them a kind of bread, which might be sufficient with milk to keep me alive, till I could make my escape to some other country, and to creatures of my own species. The horse immediately ordered a white mare-servant of his family to bring me a good quantity of oats in a sort of wooden tray. These I heated before the fire as well as I could, and rubbed them till the husks came off, which I made a shift to winnow from the grain; I ground and beat them between two stones, then took water, and made them into a paste or cake, which I toasted at the fire, and ate warm with milk. It was at first a very insipid diet, though common enough in many parts of Europe, but grew tolerable by time; and having been often reduced to hard fare in my life, this was not the first experiment I had made how easily nature is satisfied. And I cannot but observe, that I never had one hour's sickness, while I stayed in this island. 'Tis true, I sometimes made a shift to catch a rabbit, or bird, by springes [7] made of *Yahoos'* hairs; and I often gathered wholesome herbs, which I boiled, and eat as salads with my bread, and now and then, for a rarity, I made a little butter, and drank the whey. I was at first at a great loss for salt; but custom soon reconciled the want of it; and I am confident that the frequent use of salt among us is an effect of luxury, and was first introduced only as a provocative to drink; except where it is necessary for preserving of flesh in long voyages, or in places remote from great markets. For we observe no animal to be fond of it but man: [8] and as to myself, when I left this country, it was a great while before I could endure the taste of it in anything that I eat.

This is enough to say upon the subject of my diet, wherewith other travelers fill their books, as if the readers were personally concerned whether we fare well or ill. However, it was necessary to mention this matter, lest the world should think it impossible that I could find sustenance for three years in such a country, and among such inhabitants.

When it grew towards evening, the master horse ordered a place for me to lodge in; it was but six yards from the house, and separated from the stable of the *Yahoos*. Here I got some straw, and covering myself with my own clothes, slept very sound. But I was in a short time better accommodated, as the reader shall know hereafter, when I come to treat more particularly about my way of living.

CHAPTER 3

The Author studious to learn the language, the Houyhnhnm *his master assists in teaching him. The language described. Several* Houyhnhnms *of quality come out of curiosity to see the Author. He gives his master a short account of his voyage.*

My principal endeavor was to learn the language, which my master (for so I shall henceforth call him), and his children, and every servant of his house, were desirous to teach me. For they looked upon it as a prodigy that a brute animal should discover such marks of a rational creature. I pointed to everything, and inquired the name of it, which I wrote down in my journal book when I was alone, and corrected my bad accent by desiring those of the family to pronounce it often. In this employment, a sorrel nag, one of the underservants, was very ready to assist me.

In speaking, they pronounce through the nose and throat, and their language approaches nearest to the High Dutch, or German, of any I know in Europe; but is much more graceful and significant. The Emperor Charles V made almost the same observation, when he said, that if he were to speak to his horse, it should be in High Dutch. [9]

The curiosity and impatience of my master were so great, that he spent many hours of his leisure to instruct me. He was convinced (as he afterwards told me) that I must be a *Yahoo,* but my teachableness, civility, and cleanliness, astonished him; which were qualities altogether so opposite to those animals. He was most perplexed about my clothes, reasoning sometimes with himself, whether they were a part of my body: for I never pulled them

---

7. **springes:** snares.   8. **no . . . man:** a strange comment, since horses as well as cattle are extremely fond of salt.

9. **Charles V:** What he is supposed to have said was that he would speak to God in Spanish, to his mistress in Italian, and to his horse in German.

off till the family were asleep, and got them on before they waked in the morning. My master was eager to learn from whence I came, how I acquired those appearances of reason, which I discovered in all my actions, and to know my story from my own mouth, which he hoped he should soon do by the great proficiency I made in learning and pronouncing their words and sentences. To help my memory, I formed all I learned into the English alphabet, and writ the words down with the translations. This last, after some time, I ventured to do in my master's presence. It cost me much trouble to explain to him what I was doing; for the inhabitants have not the least idea of books or literature.

In about ten weeks' time I was able to understand most of his questions, and in three months could give him some tolerable answers. He was extremely curious to know from what part of the country I came, and how I was taught to imitate a rational creature, because the Yahoos (whom he saw I exactly resembled in my head, hands, and face, that were only visible), with some appearance of cunning, and the strongest disposition to mischief, were observed to be the most unteachable of all brutes. I answered, that I came over the sea from a far place, with many others of my own kind, in a great hollow vessel made of the bodies of trees. That my companions forced me to land on this coast, and then left me to shift for myself. It was with some difficulty, and by the help of many signs, that I brought him to understand me. He replied, that I must needs be mistaken, or that I *said the thing which was not.* (For they have no word in their language to express lying or falsehood.) He knew it was impossible that there could be a country beyond the sea, or that a parcel of brutes could move a wooden vessel whither they pleased upon water. He was sure no Houyhnhnm alive could make such a vessel, nor would trust Yahoos to manage it.

The word Houyhnhnm, in their tongue, signifies a *horse,* and in its etymology, *the perfection of nature.* I told my master, that I was at a loss for expression, but would improve as fast as I could; and hoped in a short time I should be able to tell him wonders: he was pleased to direct his own mare, his colt and foal, and the servants of the family, to take all opportunities of instructing me, and every day for two or three hours, he was at the same pains himself. Several horses and mares of quality in the neighborhood came often to our house upon the report spread of a wonderful Yahoo, that could speak like a Houyhnhnm, and seemed in his words and actions to discover some glimmerings of reason. These delighted to converse with me: they put many questions, and received such answers as I was able to return. By all which advantages, I made so great a progress, that in five months from my arrival I understood whatever was spoke, and could express myself tolerably well.

The Houyhnhnms who came to visit my master, out of a design of seeing and talking with me, could hardly believe me to be a right Yahoo, because my body had a different covering from others of my kind. They were astonished to observe me without the usual hair or skin, except on my head, face, and hands; but I discovered that secret to my master, upon an accident, which happened about a fortnight before.

I have already told the reader, that every night when the family were gone to bed, it was my custom to strip and cover myself with my clothes: it happened one morning early, that my master sent for me, by the sorrel nag, who was his valet; when he came, I was fast asleep, my clothes fallen off on' one side and my shirt above my waist. I awaked at the noise he made, and observed him to deliver his message in some disorder; after which he went to my master, and in a great fright gave him a very confused account of what he had seen. This I presently discovered; for going as soon as I was dressed, to pay my attendance upon his Honor, he asked me the meaning of what his servant had reported, that I was not the same thing when I slept as I appeared to be at other times; that his valet assured him, some part of me was white, some yellow, at least not so white, and some brown.

I had hitherto concealed the secret of my dress, in order to distinguish myself, as much as possible, from that cursed race of Yahoos; but now I found it in vain to do so any longer. Besides, I considered that my clothes and shoes would soon wear out, which already were in a declining condition, and must be supplied by some contrivance from the hides of Yahoos or other brutes; whereby the whole secret would be known. I therefore told my master, that in the country from whence I came, those of my kind always covered their bodies with the hairs of certain animals prepared by art, as well for decency as to avoid the inclemencies of air, both hot and cold; of which, as to my own person, I would give him immediate conviction, if he pleased to command me: only desiring his excuse, if I did not expose those parts that nature taught us to conceal. He said my discourse was all very strange, but especially the last part; for he could not understand why nature should teach us to conceal what nature had given. That neither himself nor family were ashamed of any parts of their bodies; but however I might do as I pleased. Whereupon, I first unbuttoned my coat, and pulled it off. I did the same with my waistcoat; I drew off my shoes, stockings, and breeches. I let my shirt down to my waist, and drew up the bottom, fastening it like a girdle about my middle to hide my nakedness.

My master observed the whole performance with great signs of curiosity and admiration. He took up all my clothes in his pastern, one piece after another, and examined them diligently; he then stroked my body very gently, and looked round me several times, after which he said, it was plain I must be a perfect *Yahoo;* but that I differed very much from the rest of my species, in the whiteness, and smoothness of my skin, my want of hair in several parts of my body, the shape and shortness of my claws behind and before, and my affectation of walking continually on my two hinder feet. He desired to see no more, and gave me leave to put on my clothes again, for I was shuddering with cold.

I expressed my uneasiness at his giving me so often the appellation of *Yahoo,* an odious animal, for which I had so utter a hatred and contempt. I begged he would forbear applying that word to me, and take the same order in his family, and among his friends whom he suffered to see me. I requested likewise, that the secret of my having a false covering to my body might be known to none but himself, at least as long as my present clothing should last; for as to what the sorrel nag his valet had observed, his Honor might command him to conceal it.

All this my master very graciously consented to, and thus the secret was kept till my clothes began to wear out, which I was forced to supply by several contrivances, that shall hereafter be mentioned. In the meantime, he desired I would go on with my utmost diligence to learn their language, because he was more astonished at my capacity for speech and reason, than at the figure of my body, whether it were covered or no; adding, that he waited with some impatience to hear the wonders which I promised to tell him.

From thenceforward he doubled the pains he had been at to instruct me; he brought me into all company, and made them treat me with civility, because, as he told them privately, this would put me into good humor, and make me more diverting.

Every day when I waited on him, beside the trouble he was at in teaching, he would ask me several questions concerning myself, which I answered as well as I could; and by those means he had already received some general ideas, though very imperfect. It would be tedious to relate the several steps by which I advanced to a more regular conversation: but the first account I gave of myself in any order and length, was to this purpose:

That I came from a very far country, as I already had attempted to tell him, with about fifty more of my own species; that we traveled upon the seas, in a great hollow vessel made of wood, and larger than his Honor's house. I described the ship to him in the best terms I could, and explained by the help of my handkerchief displayed, how it was driven forward by the wind. That upon a quarrel among us, I was set on shore on this coast, where I walked forward without knowing whither, till he delivered me from the persecution of those execrable *Yahoos.* He asked me, who made the ship, and how it was possible that the *Houyhnhnms* of my country would leave it to the management of brutes? My answer was, that I durst proceed no further in my relation, unless he would give me his word and honor that he would not be offended, and then I would tell him the wonders I had so often promised. He agreed; and I went on by assuring him, that the ship was made by creatures like myself, who in all the countries I had traveled, as well as in my own, were the only governing, rational animals; and that upon my arrival hither, I was as much astonished to see the *Houyhnhnms* act like rational beings, as he or his friends could be in finding some marks of reason in a creature he was pleased to call a *Yahoo,* to which I owned my resemblance in every part, but could not account for their degenerate and brutal nature. I said farther, that if good fortune ever restored me to my native country, to relate my travels hither, as I resolved to do, everybody would believe that I *said the thing which was not;* that I invented the story out of my own head; and with all possible respect to himself, his family and friends, and under his promise of not being offended, our countrymen would hardly think it probable, that a *Houyhnhnm* should be the presiding creature of a nation, and a *Yahoo* the brute.

CHAPTER 4

The Houyhnhnm's notion of truth and falsehood. The Author's discourse disapproved by his master. The Author gives a more particular account of himself, and the accidents of his voyage.

My master heard me with great appearances of uneasiness in his countenance, because *doubting, or not believing,* are so little known in this country, that the inhabitants cannot tell how to behave themselves under such circumstances. And I remember in frequent discourses with my master concerning the nature of manhood, in other parts of the world, having occasion to talk of *lying* and *false representation,* it was with much difficulty that he comprehended what I meant, although he had otherwise a most acute judgment. For he argued thus: that the use of speech was to make us understand one another, and to receive information of facts; now if anyone *said the thing which was not,* these ends were defeated; because I cannot properly be said to understand him; and I am so far from receiving information, that he leaves me worse than in ignorance, for I am led to believe a thing black when it is white, and short when it is long. And these were all the notions he had concerning that faculty of *lying,* so perfectly well understood, and so universally practiced, among human creatures.

To return from this digression; when I asserted that the *Yahoos* were the only governing animals in my country, which my master said was altogether past his conception; he desired to know, whether we had *Houyhnhnms* among us, and what was their employment: I told him, we had great numbers, that in summer they grazed in the fields, and in winter were kept in houses, with hay and oats, where *Yahoo* servants were employed to rub their skins smooth, comb their manes, pick their feet, serve them with food, and make their beds. I understand you well, said my master, it is now very plain, from all you have spoken, that whatever share of reason the *Yahoos* pretend to, the *Houyhnhnms* are your masters; I heartily wish our *Yahoos* would be so tractable. I begged his Honor would please to excuse me from proceeding any farther, because I was very certain that the account he expected from me would be highly displeasing. But he insisted in commanding me to let him know the best and the worst: I told him, he should be obeyed. I owned, that the *Houyhnhnms* among us, whom we called horses, were the most generous and comely animals we had, that they excelled in strength and swiftness; and when they belonged to persons of quality, employed in traveling, racing, and drawing chariots, they were treated with much kindness and care till they fell into diseases, or became foundered in the feet; but then they were sold, and used to all kind of drudgery till they died; after which their skins were stripped and sold for what they were worth, and their bodies left to be devoured by dogs and birds of prey. But the common race of horses had not so good fortune, being kept by farmers and carriers, and other mean people, who put them to greater labor, and fed them worse. I described, as well as I could, our way of riding, the shape and use of a bridle, a saddle, a spur, and a whip, of harness and wheels. I added, that we fastened plates of a certain hard substance called iron at the bottom of their feet, to preserve their hoofs from being broken by the stony ways on which we often traveled.

My master, after some expressions of great indignation, wondered how we dared to venture upon a *Houyhnhnm's* back, for he was sure, that the meanest servant in his house would be able to shake off the strongest *Yahoo,* or by lying down, and rolling on his back, squeeze the brute to death. I answered, that our horses were trained up from three or four years old to the several uses we intended them for; that if any of them proved intolerably vicious, they were employed for carriages; that they were severely beaten while they were young for any mischievous tricks; that the males, designed for the common use of riding or draught, were generally castrated about two years after their birth, to take down their spirits, and make them more tame and gentle; that they were indeed sensible of rewards and punishments; but his Honor would please to consider, that they had not the least tincture of reason any more than the *Yahoos* in this country.

It put me to the pains of many circumlocutions to give my master a right idea of what I spoke; for their language doth not abound in variety of words, because their wants and passions are fewer than among us. But it is impossible to express his noble resentment at our savage treatment of the *Houyhnhnm* race, particularly after I had explained the manner and use of castrating horses among us, to hinder them from propagating their kind, and to render them more servile. He said, if it were possible there could be any country where *Yahoos* alone were endued with reason, they certainly must be the governing animal, because reason will in time always prevail against brutal strength. But, considering the frame of our bodies, and especially of mine, he thought no creature of equal bulk was so ill contrived, for employing that reason in the common offices of life; whereupon he desired to know whether those among whom I lived resembled me or the *Yahoos* of his country. I assured him, that I was as well shaped as most of my age; but the younger and the females were much more soft and tender, and the skins of the latter generally as white as milk. He said, I differed indeed from other *Yahoos,* being much more cleanly, and not altogether so deformed, but, in point of real advantage, he thought I differed for the worse. That my nails were of no use either to my fore or hinder feet; as to my forefeet, he could not properly call them by that name, for he never observed me to walk upon them; that they were too soft to bear the ground; that I generally went with them uncovered, neither was the covering I sometimes wore on them, of the same shape, or so strong as that on my feet behind. That I could not walk with any security, for if either of my hinder feet slipped, I must inevitably fall. He then began to find fault with other parts of my body, the flatness of my face, the prominence of my nose, my eyes placed directly in front, so that I could not look on either side without turning my head: that I was not able to feed myself, without lifting one of my forefeet to my mouth: and therefore nature had placed those joints to answer that necessity. He knew not what could be the use of those several clefts and divisions in my feet behind; these were too soft to bear the hardness and sharpness of stones without a covering made from the skin of some other brute; that my whole body wanted a fence against heat and cold, which I was forced to put on and off every day with tediousness and trouble. And lastly, that he observed every animal in this country naturally to abhor the *Yahoos,* whom the weaker avoided, and the stronger drove from them. So that supposing us to have the gift of reason, he could not see how it were possible to cure that natural antipathy which every creature discovered against us; nor consequently, how we could tame and render them serviceable. However, he would (as he said) debate the matter no farther, because he was more desirous to know my own story, the country where I was born, and the several actions and events of my life before I came hither.

I assured him, how extremely desirous I was that he should be satisfied in every point; but I doubted much, whether it would be possible for me to explain myself on several subjects whereof his Honor could have no conception, because I saw nothing in his country to which I could resemble them. That, however, I would do my best, and strive to express myself by similitudes, humbly desiring his assistance when I wanted proper words; which he was pleased to promise me.

I said, my birth was of honest parents in an island called England, which was remote from this country, as many days' journey as the strongest of his Honor's servants could travel in the annual course of the sun. That I was bred a surgeon, whose trade is to cure wounds and hurts in the body, got by accident or violence; that my country was governed by a female man, whom we called Queen. That I left it to get riches, whereby I might maintain myself and family when I should return. That, in my last voyage, I was commander of the ship, and had about fifty *Yahoos* under me, many of which died at sea, and I was forced to supply them by others picked out from several nations. That our ship was twice in danger of being sunk; the first time by a great storm, and the second, by striking against a rock. Here my master interposed, by asking me, how I could persuade strangers out of different countries to venture with me, after the losses I had sustained, and the hazards I had run. I said, they were fellows of desperate fortunes, forced to fly from the places of their birth, on account of their poverty or their crimes. Some were undone by lawsuits; others spent all they had in drinking, whoring, and gaming; others fled for treason; many for murder, theft, poisoning, robbery, perjury, forgery, coining false money; for committing rapes or sodomy; for flying from their colors, or deserting to the enemy; and most of them had broken prison. None of these durst return to their native countries for fear of being hanged, or of starving in a jail; and therefore were under the necessity of seeking a livelihood in other places.

During this discourse, my master was pleased often to interrupt me. I had made use of many circumlocutions in describing to him the nature of the several crimes for which most of our crew had been forced to fly their country. This labor took up several days' conversation, before he was able to comprehend me. He was wholly at a loss to know what could be the use or necessity of practicing those vices. To clear up which I endeavored to give some ideas of the desire of power and riches, of the terrible effects of lust, intemperance, malice, and envy. All this I was forced to define and describe by putting of cases, and making suppositions. After which, like one whose imagination was struck with something never seen or heard of before, he would lift up his eyes with amazement and indignation. Power, government, war, law, punishment, and a thousand other things had no terms, wherein that language could express them, which made the difficulty almost insuperable to give my master any conception of what I meant. But being of an excellent understanding, much improved by contemplation and converse, he at last arrived at a competent knowledge of what human nature in our parts of the world is capable to perform, and desired I would give him some particular account of that land which we call Europe, especially of my own country.

CHAPTER 5

The Author, at his master's commands, informs him of the state of England. *The causes of war among the princes of* Europe. *The Author begins to explain the* English *constitution.*

The reader may please to observe, that the following extract of many conversations I had with my master, contains a summary of the most material points, which were discoursed at several times for above two years; his Honor often desiring fuller satisfaction as I farther improved in the *Houyhnhnm* tongue. I laid before him, as well as I could, the whole state of Europe; I discoursed of trade and manufactures; of arts and sciences; and the answers I gave to all the questions he made, as they arose upon several subjects, were a fund of conversation not to be exhausted. But I shall here only set down the substance of what passed between us concerning my own country, reducing it into order as well as I can, without any regard to time or other circumstances, while I strictly adhere to truth. My only concern is, that I shall hardly be able to do justice to my master's arguments and expressions, which must needs suffer by my want of capacity, as well as by a translation into our barbarous English.

In obedience, therefore, to his Honor's commands, I related to him the Revolution under the Prince of Orange; the long war with France [10] en-

tered into by the said prince, and renewed by his successor, the present Queen, wherein the greatest powers of Christendom were engaged, and which still continued: I computed at his request, that about a million of *Yahoos* might have been killed in the whole progress of it; and perhaps a hundred or more cities taken, and five times as many ships burnt or sunk.

He asked me what were the usual causes or motives that made one country go to war with another. I answered they were innumerable; but I should only mention a few of the chief. Sometimes the ambition of princes, who never think they have land or people enough to govern; sometimes the corruption of ministers, who engage their master in a war in order to stifle or divert the clamor of the subjects against their evil administration. Difference in opinions [11] hath cost many millions of lives: for instance, whether flesh be bread, or bread be flesh; whether the juice of a certain berry be blood or wine; whether whistling be a vice or a virtue; whether it be better to kiss a post, or throw it into the fire; what is the best color for a coat, whether black, white, red, or gray; and whether it should be long or short, narrow or wide, dirty or clean; with many more. Neither are any wars so furious and bloody, or of so long continuance, as those occasioned by difference in opinion, especially if it be in things indifferent.

Sometimes the quarrel between two princes is to decide which of them shall dispossess a third of his dominions, where neither of them pretend to any right. Sometimes one prince quarreleth with another, for fear the other should quarrel with him. Sometimes a war is entered upon, because the enemy is too strong, and sometimes because he is too weak. Sometimes our neighbors want the things which we have, or have the things which we want; and we both fight, till they take ours or give us theirs. It is a very justifiable cause of war to invade a country after the people have been wasted by famine, destroyed by pestilence, or embroiled by factions among themselves. It is justifiable to enter into a war against our nearest ally, when one of his towns lies convenient for us, or a territory of land, that would render our dominions round and compact. If a prince sends forces into a nation, where the people are poor and ignorant, he may lawfully put half of them to death, and make slaves

---

10. war . . . France: from 1689–97 during the reign of William III, and from 1702–13 during the reign of Queen Anne.

11. Difference . . . opinions: referring to the controversies about transubstantiation, the use of music in churches, veneration of the crucifix, and ecclesiastical vestments.

of the rest, in order to civilize and reduce them from their barbarous way of living. It is a very kingly, honorable, and frequent practice, when one prince desires the assistance of another to secure him against an invasion, that the assistant, when he hath driven out the invader, should seize on the dominions himself, and kill, imprison, or banish the prince he came to relieve. Alliance by blood or marriage is a sufficient cause of war between princes; and the nearer the kindred is, the greater is their disposition to quarrel: poor nations are hungry, and rich nations are proud; and pride and hunger will ever be at variance. For these reasons, the trade of a soldier is held the most honorable of all others; because a soldier is a *Yahoo* hired to kill in cold blood as many of his own species, who have never offended him, as possibly he can.

There is likewise a kind of beggarly princes in Europe, not able to make war by themselves, who hire out their troops to richer nations, for so much a day to each man; of which they keep three-fourths to themselves, and it is the best part of their maintenance; such are those in many northern parts of Europe.

What you have told me (said my master), upon the subject of war, does indeed discover most admirably the effects of that reason you pretend to: however, it is happy that the shame is greater than the danger; and that nature hath left you utterly uncapable of doing much mischief.

For your mouths lying flat with your faces, you can hardly bite each other to any purpose, unless by consent. Then as to the claws upon your feet before and behind, they are so short and tender, that one of our *Yahoos* would drive a dozen of yours before him. And therefore in recounting the numbers of those who have been killed in battle, I cannot but think that you have *said the thing which is not*.

I could not forbear shaking my head, and smiling a little at his ignorance. And being no stranger to the art of war, I gave him a description of cannons, culverins, muskets, carabines, pistols, bullets, powder, swords, bayonets, sieges, retreats, attacks, undermines, countermines, bombardments, sea fights; ships sunk with a thousand men, twenty thousand killed on each side; dying groans, limbs flying in the air, smoke, noise, confusion, trampling to death under horses' feet; flight, pursuit, victory; fields strewed with carcasses left for food to dogs, and wolves, and birds of prey; plundering, stripping, ravishing, burning and destroying. And to set forth the valor of my own dear countrymen, I assured him, that I had seen them blow up a hundred enemies at once in a siege, and as many in a ship, and beheld the dead bodies drop down in pieces from the clouds, to the great diversion of all the spectators.

I was going on to more particulars, when my master commanded me silence. He said, whoever understood the nature of *Yahoos* might easily believe it possible for so vile an animal to be capable of every action I had named, if their strength and cunning equaled their malice. But as my discourse had increased his abhorrence of the whole species, so he found it gave him a disturbance in his mind, to which he was wholly a stranger before. He thought his ears being used to such abominable words, might by degrees admit them with less detestation. That although he hated the *Yahoos* of this country, yet he no more blamed them for their odious qualities, than he did a *gnnayh* (a bird of prey) for its cruelty, or a sharp stone for cutting his hoof. But when a creature pretending to reason could be capable of such enormities, he dreaded lest the corruption of that faculty might be worse than brutality itself. He seemed therefore confident, that instead of reason, we were only possessed of some quality fitted to increase our natural vices; as the reflection from a troubled stream returns the image of an ill-shapen body, not only larger, but more distorted.

He added, that he had heard too much upon the subject of war, both in this, and some former discourses. There was another point which a little perplexed him at present. I had said, that some of our crew left their country on account of being ruined by *Law;* that I had already explained the meaning of the word; but he was at a loss how it should come to pass, that the law which was intended for every man's preservation, should be any man's ruin. Therefore he desired to be farther satisfied what I meant by law, and the dispensers thereof, according to the present practice in my own country; because he thought nature and reason were sufficient guides for a reasonable animal, as we pretended to be, in showing us what we ought to do, and what to avoid.

I assured his Honor, that law was a science wherein I had not much conversed, further than by employing advocates, in vain, upon some injustices that had been done me: however, I would give him all the satisfaction I was able.

I said, there was a society of men among us,

bred up from their youth in the art of proving by words multiplied for the purpose, that white is black, and black is white, according as they are paid. To this society all the rest of the people are slaves. For example, if my neighbor hath a mind to my cow, he hires a lawyer to prove that he ought to have my cow from me. I must then hire another to defend my right, it being against all rules of law that any man should be allowed to speak for himself. Now in this case, I, who am the right owner, lie under two great disadvantages. First, my lawyer, being practiced almost from his cradle in defending falsehood, is quite out of his element when he would be an advocate for justice, which as an office unnatural, he always attempts with great awkwardness, if not with ill will. The second disadvantage is, that my lawyer must proceed with great caution, or else he will be reprimanded by the judges, and abhorred by his brethren, as one who would lessen the practice of the law. And therefore I have but two methods to preserve my cow. The first is, to gain over my adversary's lawyer with a double fee; who will then betray his client, by insinuating that he hath justice on his side. The second way is for my lawyer to make my cause appear as unjust as he can, by allowing the cow to belong to my adversary: and this, if it be skillfully done, will certainly bespeak the favor of the bench.

"Now, your Honor is to know, that these judges are persons appointed to decide all controversies of property, as well as for the trial of criminals, and picked out from the most dexterous lawyers, who are grown old or lazy, and having been biased all their lives against truth and equity, lie under such a fatal necessity of favoring fraud, perjury, and oppression, that I have known some of them to have refused a large bribe from the side where justice lay, rather than injure the faculty,[12] by doing any thing unbecoming their nature or their office.

"It is a maxim among these lawyers, that whatever hath been done before, may legally be done again: and therefore they take special care to record all the decisions formerly made against common justice, and the general reason of mankind. These, under the name of *precedents,* they produce as authorities, to justify the most iniquitous opinions; and the judges never fail of directing accordingly.

"In pleading, they studiously avoid entering into the merits of the cause; but are loud, violent, and

tedious in dwelling upon all circumstances which are not to the purpose. For instance, in the case already mentioned: they never desire to know what claim or title my adversary hath to my cow; but whether the said cow were red or black; her horns long or short; whether the field I graze her in be round or square; whether she were milked at home or abroad; what diseases she is subject to, and the like; after which they consult precedents, adjourn the cause from time to time, and in ten, twenty, or thirty years, come to an issue.

"It is likewise to be observed, that this society hath a peculiar cant and jargon of their own, that no other mortal can understand, and wherein all their laws are written, which they take special care to multiply; whereby they have wholly confounded the very essence of truth and falsehood, of right and wrong; so that it will take thirty years to decide whether the field left me by my ancestors for six generations belong to me, or to a stranger three hundred miles off.

"In the trial of persons accused for crimes against the state, the method is much more short and commendable: the judge first sends to sound the disposition of those in power, after which he can easily hang or save the criminal, strictly preserving all the forms of law." [13]

Here my master interposing, said it was a pity, that creatures endowed with such prodigious abilities of mind as these lawyers, by the description I gave of them, must certainly be, were not rather encouraged to be instructors of others in wisdom and knowledge. In answer to which, I assured his Honor, that in all points out of their own trade, they were usually the most ignorant and stupid generation among us, the most despicable in common conversation, avowed enemies to all knowledge and learning, and equally disposed to pervert the general reason of mankind in every other subject of discourse, as in that of their own profession.

CHAPTER 6

A continuation of the state of England *under Queen Anne. The character of a first minister of state in the courts of* Europe.

12. **faculty:** profession.

13. **strictly . . . law:** Swift was particularly bitter against judges as a result of the attempt to convict the Drapier in the Irish Courts. See below, "*Verses on the Death of Dr. Swift,*" ll.415 ff. The whole of this passage had been much altered by the publisher in the first edition, as he feared it would prejudice his case if legal action were taken against the book.

My master was yet wholly at a loss to understand what motives could incite this race of lawyers to perplex, disquiet, and weary themselves, engaging in a confederacy of injustice, merely for the sake of injuring their fellow animals; neither could he comprehend what I meant in saying they did it for hire. Whereupon I was at much pains to describe to him the use of money, the materials it was made of, and the value of the metals; that when a *Yahoo* had got a great store of this precious substance, he was able to purchase whatever he had a mind to; the finest clothing, the noblest houses, great tracts of land, the most costly meats and drinks, and have his choice of the most beautiful females. Therefore since money alone was able to perform all these feats, our *Yahoos* thought they could never have enough of it to spend or to save, as they found themselves inclined from their natural bent either to profusion or avarice. That the rich man enjoyed the fruit of the poor man's labor, and the latter were a thousand to one in proportion to the former. That the bulk of our people was forced to live miserably, by laboring every day for small wages to make a few live plentifully. I enlarged myself much on these and many other particulars to the same purpose; but his Honor was still to seek; [14] for he went upon a supposition that all animals had a title to their share in the productions of the earth, and especially those who presided over the rest. Therefore he desired I would let him know, what these costly meats were, and how any of us happened to want them. Whereupon I enumerated as many sorts as came into my head, with the various methods of dressing them, which could not be done without sending vessels by sea to every part of the world, as well for liquors to drink, as for sauces, and innumerable other conveniences. I assured him, that this whole globe of earth must be at least three times gone round, before one of our better female *Yahoos* could get her breakfast, or a cup to put it in. He said, that must needs be a miserable country which cannot furnish food for its own inhabitants. But what he chiefly wondered at, was how such vast tracts of ground as I described should be wholly without fresh water, and the people put to the necessity of sending over the sea for drink. I replied, that England (the dear place of my nativity) was computed to produce three times the quantity of food, more than its inhabitants are able to consume, as well as liquors extracted from

14. **to seek:** at a loss.

grain, or pressed out of the fruit of certain trees, which made excellent drink, and the same proportion in every other convenience of life. But, in order to feed the luxury and intemperance of the males, and the vanity of the females, we sent away the greatest part of our necessary things to other countries, from whence in return we brought the materials of diseases, folly, and vice, to spend among ourselves. Hence it follows of necessity, that vast numbers of our people are compelled to seek their livelihood by begging, robbing, stealing, cheating, pimping, forswearing, flattering, suborning, forging, gaming, lying, fawning, hectoring, voting, scribbling, stargazing, poisoning, whoring, canting, libeling, freethinking, and the like occupations: every one of which terms, I was at much pains to make him understand.

That wine was not imported among us from foreign countries, to supply the want of water or other drinks, but because it was a sort of liquid which made us merry, by putting us out of our senses; diverted all melancholy thoughts, begat wild extravagant imaginations in the brain, raised our hopes, and banished our fears, suspended every office of reason for a time, and deprived us of the use of our limbs, until we fell into a profound sleep; although it must be confessed, that we always awaked sick and dispirited, and that the use of this liquor filled us with diseases, which made our lives uncomfortable and short.

But beside all this, the bulk of our people supported themselves by furnishing the necessities or conveniences of life to the rich, and to each other. For instance, when I am at home and dressed as I ought to be, I carry on my body the workmanship of an hundred tradesmen; the building and furniture of my house employ as many more, and five times the number to adorn my wife.

I was going on to tell him of another sort of people, who get their livelihood by attending the sick, having upon some occasions informed his Honor that many of my crew had died of diseases. But here it was with the utmost difficulty, that I brought him to apprehend what I meant. He could easily conceive, that a *Houyhnhnm* grew weak and heavy a few days before his death, or by some accident might hurt a limb. But that nature, who worketh all things to perfection, should suffer any pains to breed in our bodies, he thought impossible, and desired to know the reason of so unaccountable an evil. I told him, we fed on a thousand things which operated contrary to each other; that we eat when we were not hungry, and drank without the provocation of thirst; that we sat whole nights drinking strong liquors without eating a bit, which disposed us to sloth, inflamed our bodies, and precipitated or prevented digestion. That prostitute female *Yahoos* acquired a certain malady, which bred rottenness in the bones of those who fell into their embraces; that this and many other diseases were propagated from father to son, so that great numbers come into the world with complicated maladies upon them; that it would be endless to give him a catalogue of all diseases incident to human bodies; for they could not be fewer than five or six hundred, spread over every limb and joint; in short, every part, external and intestine, having diseases appropriated to each. To remedy which, there was a sort of people bred up among us, in the profession or pretense of curing the sick. And because I had some skill in the faculty, I would in gratitude to his Honor, let him know the whole mystery and method by which they proceed.

Their fundamental is, that all diseases arise from repletion, from whence they conclude, that a great evacuation of the body is necessary, either through the natural passage, or upwards at the mouth. Their next business is, from herbs, minerals, gums, oils, shells, salts, juices, seaweed, excrements, barks of trees, serpents, toads, frogs, spiders, dead men's flesh and bones, birds, beasts, and fishes, to form a composition for smell and taste the most abominable, nauseous, and detestable, they can possibly contrive, which the stomach immediately rejects with loathing; and this they call a vomit; or else from the same storehouse, with some other poisonous additions, they command us to take in at the orifice above or below (just as the physician then happens to be disposed) a medicine equally annoying and disgustful to the bowels; which relaxing the belly, drives down all before it, and this they call a purge, or a clyster. For nature (as the physicians allege) having intended the superior anterior orifice only for the intromission of solids and liquids, and the inferior posterior for ejection, these artists ingeniously considering that in all diseases nature is forced out of her seat, therefore to replace her in it, the body must be treated in a manner directly contrary, by interchanging the use of each orifice; forcing solids and liquids in at the anus, and making evacuations at the mouth.

But, besides real diseases, we are subject to many that are only imaginary, for which the physicians have invented imaginary cures; these have their several names, and so have the drugs that are proper for them, and with these our female *Yahoos* are always infested.

One great excellency in this tribe is their skill at prognostics, wherein they seldom fail; their predictions in real diseases, when they rise to any degree of malignity, generally portending death, which is always in their power, when recovery is not: and therefore, upon any unexpected signs of amendment, after they have pronounced their sentence, rather than be accused as false prophets, they know how to approve their sagacity to the world by a seasonable dose.

They are likewise of special use to husbands and wives, who are grown weary of their mates; to eldest sons, to great ministers of state, and often to princes.

I had formerly upon occasion discoursed with my master upon the nature of government in general, and particularly of our own excellent constitution, deservedly the wonder and envy of the whole world. But having here accidentally mentioned a minister of state, he commanded me some time after to inform him, what species of *Yahoo* I particularly meant by that appellation.

I told him, that a first or chief minister [15] of state, whom I intended to describe, was a creature wholly exempt from joy and grief, love and hatred, pity and anger; at least makes use of no other passions but a violent desire of wealth, power, and titles; that he applies his words to all uses, except to the indication of his mind; that he never tells a truth, but with an intent that you should take it for a lie; nor a lie, but with a design that you should take it for a truth; that those he speaks worst of behind their backs, are in the surest way to preferment; and whenever he begins to praise you to others or to yourself, you are from that day forlorn. The worst mark you can receive is a promise, especially when it is confirmed with an oath; after which every wise man retires, and gives over all hopes.

There are three methods by which a man may rise to be chief minister: the first is, by knowing how with prudence to dispose of a wife, a daughter, or a sister: the second, by betraying or undermining his predecessor: and the third is, by a furious zeal in public assemblies against the corruptions of the court. But a wise prince would rather choose to employ those who practice the last of

15. first . . . minister: This passage was also much modified when first printed.

these methods; because such zealots prove always the most obsequious and subservient to the will and passions of their master. That these ministers having all employments at their disposal, preserve themselves in power, by bribing the majority of a senate or great council; and at last, by an expedient called an Act of Indemnity [16] (whereof I described the nature to him) they secure themselves from after-reckonings, and retire from the public, laden with the spoils of the nation.

The palace of a chief minister is a seminary to breed up others in his own trade: the pages, lackeys, and porter, by imitating their master, become ministers of state in their several districts, and learn to excel in the three principal ingredients, of insolence, lying, and bribery. Accordingly, they have a subaltern court paid to them by persons of the best rank, and sometimes by the force of dexterity and impudence, arrive through several gradations to be successors to their lord.

He is usually governed by a decayed wench, or favorite footman, who are the tunnels through which all graces are conveyed, and may properly be called, in the last resort, the governors of the kingdom.

One day, my master, having heard me mention the nobility of my country, was pleased to make me a compliment which I could not pretend to deserve: that he was sure I must have been born of some noble family, because I far exceeded in shape, color, and cleanliness, all the *Yahoos* of his nation, although I seemed to fail in strength and agility, which must be imputed to my different way of living from those other brutes; and besides, I was not only endowed with the faculty of speech, but likewise with some rudiments of reason, to a degree, that with all his acquaintance I passed for a prodigy.

He made me observe, that among the *Houyhnhnms,* the white, the sorrel, and the iron-gray, were not so exactly shaped as the bay, the dapple-gray, and the black; nor born with equal talents of mind, or a capacity to improve them; and therefore continued always in the condition of servants, without ever aspiring to match out of their own race, which in that country would be reckoned monstrous and unnatural.

I made his Honor my most humble acknowledgments for the good opinion he was pleased to conceive of me; but assured him at the same time,

16. **Act of Indemnity:** granting exemption from the penalties arising from any unconstitutional or illegal proceeding.

that my birth was of the lower sort, having been born of plain honest parents, who were just able to give me a tolerable education; that nobility among us was altogether a different thing from the idea he had of it; that our young noblemen are bred from their childhood in idleness and luxury; that as soon as years will permit, they consume their vigor, and contract odious diseases among lewd females; and when their fortunes are almost ruined, they marry some woman of mean birth, disagreeable person, and unsound constitution, merely for the sake of money, whom they hate and despise. That the productions of such marriages are generally scrofulous, rickety, or deformed children; by which means the family seldom continues above three generations, unless the wife takes care to provide a healthy father among her neighbors or domestics, in order to improve and continue the breed. That a weak diseased body, a meager countenance, and sallow complexion, are the true marks of noble blood; and a healthy robust appearance is so disgraceful in a man of quality, that the world concludes his real father to have been a groom or a coachman. The imperfections of his mind run parallel with those of his body, being a composition of spleen, dullness, ignorance, caprice, sensuality, and pride.

Without the consent of this illustrious body, no law can be enacted, repealed, or altered; and these nobles have likewise the decision of all our possessions without appeal.

CHAPTER 7

The Author's great love of his native country. His master's observations upon the constitution and administration of England, *as described by the Author, with parallel cases and comparisons. His master's observations upon human nature.*

The reader may be disposed to wonder how I could prevail on myself to give so free a representation of my own species, among a race of mortals who were already too apt to conceive the vilest opinion of human kind, from that entire congruity betwixt me and their *Yahoos.* But I must freely confess, that the many virtues of those excellent quadrupeds placed in opposite view to human corruptions, had so far opened my eyes and enlarged my understanding, that I began to view the actions and passions of man in a very different light, and to think the honor of my own kind not worth managing;[17] which, besides, it was impossible for me to do before a person of so acute a judgment as my master, who daily convinced me of a thousand faults in myself, whereof I had not the least perception before, and which with us would never be numbered even among human infirmities. I had likewise learned from his example an utter detestation of all falsehood or disguise; and truth appeared so amiable to me, that I determined upon sacrificing everything to it.

Let me deal so candidly with the reader, as to confess, that there was yet a much stronger motive for the freedom I took in my representation of things. I had not been a year in this country, before I contracted such a love and veneration for the inhabitants, that I entered on a firm resolution never to return to human kind, but to pass the rest of my life among these admirable *Houyhnhnms* in the contemplation and practice of every virtue; where I could have no example or incitement to vice. But it was decreed by fortune, my perpetual enemy, that so great a felicity should not fall to my share. However, it is now some comfort to reflect, that in what I said of my countrymen, I *extenuated* their faults as much as I durst before so strict an examiner, and upon every article gave as *favorable* a turn as the matter would bear. For, indeed, who is there alive that will not be swayed by his bias and partiality to the place of his birth?

I have related the substance of several conversations I had with my master, during the greatest part of the time I had the honor to be in his service, but have indeed for brevity sake omitted much more than is here set down.

When I had answered all his questions, and his curiosity seemed to be fully satisfied, he sent for me one morning early, and commanding me to sit down at some distance (an honor which he had never before conferred upon me), he said, he had been very seriously considering my whole story, as far as it related both to myself and my country; that he looked upon us as a sort of animals to whose share, by what accident he could not conjecture, some small pittance of reason had fallen, whereof we made no other use than by its assistance to aggravate our natural corruptions, and to acquire new ones, which nature had not given us. That we disarmed ourselves of the few abilities she had bestowed, had been very successful in multiplying our original wants, and seemed to spend our whole

lives in vain endeavors to supply them by our own inventions. That as to myself, it was manifest I had neither the strength or agility of a common *Yahoo;* that I walked infirmly on my hinder feet; had found out a contrivance to make my claws of no use or defense, and to remove the hair from my chin, which was intended as a shelter from the sun and the weather. Lastly, that I could neither run with speed, nor climb trees like my brethren (as he called them) the *Yahoos* in this country.

That our institutions of government and law were plainly owing to our gross defects in reason, and by consequence, in virtue; because reason alone is sufficient to govern a rational creature; which was therefore a character we had no pretense to challenge, even from the account I had given of my own people; although he manifestly perceived, that in order to favor them, I had concealed many particulars, and often *said the thing which was not.*

He was the more confirmed in this opinion, because he observed, that as I agreed in every feature of my body with other *Yahoos,* except where it was to my real disadvantage in point of strength, speed and activity, the shortness of my claws, and some other particulars where nature had no part; so from the representation I had given him of our lives, our manners, and our actions, he found as near a resemblance in the disposition of our minds. He said the *Yahoos* were known to hate one another more than they did any different species of animals; and the reason usually assigned was the odiousness of their own shapes, which all could see in the rest, but not in themselves. He had therefore begun to think it not unwise in us to cover our bodies, and by that invention conceal many of our deformities from each other, which would else be hardly supportable. But he now found he had been mistaken, and that the dissensions of those brutes in his country were owing to the same cause with ours, as I had described them. For if (said he) you throw among five *Yahoos* as much food as would be sufficient for fifty, they will, instead of eating peaceably, fall together by the ears, each single one impatient to *have all to itself;* and therefore a servant was usually employed to stand by while they were feeding abroad, and those kept at home were tied at a distance from each other. That if a cow died of age or accident, before a *Houyhnhnm* could secure it for his own *Yahoos,* those in the neighborhood would come in herds to seize it, and then would ensue such a battle as I had described, with terrible wounds made by their claws on both sides,

---

17. managing: treating with discretion.

although they seldom were able to kill one another, for want of such convenient instruments of death as we had invented. At other times the like battles have been fought between the *Yahoos* of several neighborhoods without any visible cause; those of one district watching all opportunities to surprise the next before they are prepared. But if they find their project hath miscarried, they return home, and, for want of enemies, engage in what I call a civil war among themselves.

That in some fields of his country, there are certain *shining stones* of several colors, whereof the *Yahoos* are violently fond, and when part of these stones are fixed in the earth, as it sometimes happeneth, they will dig with their claws for whole days to get them out, and carry them away, and hide them by heaps in their kennels; but still looking round with great caution, for fear their comrades should find out their treasure. My master said, he could never discover the reason of this unnatural appetite, or how these stones could be of any use to a *Yahoo;* but now he believed it might proceed from the same principle of avarice which I had ascribed to mankind: that he had once, by way of experiment, privately removed a heap of these stones from the place where one of his *Yahoos* had buried it: whereupon, the sordid animal missing his treasure, by his loud lamenting brought the whole herd to the place, there miserably howled, then fell to biting and tearing the rest; began to pine away, would neither eat, nor sleep, nor work, till he ordered a servant privately to convey the stones into the same hole, and hide them as before; which when his *Yahoo* had found, he presently recovered his spirits and good humor, but took care to remove them to a better hiding place, and hath ever since been a very serviceable brute.

My master farther assured me, which I also observed myself, that in the fields where these *shining stones* abound, the fiercest and most frequent battles are fought, occasioned by perpetual inroads of the neighboring *Yahoos.*

He said, it was common when two *Yahoos* discovered such a stone in a field, and were contending which of them should be the proprietor, a third would take the advantage, and carry it away from them both; which my master would needs contend to have some resemblance with our suits at law; wherein I thought it for our credit not to undeceive him; since the decision he mentioned was much more equitable than many decrees among us; because the plaintiff and defendant there lost nothing beside the stone they contended for, whereas our courts of equity would never have dismissed the cause while either of them had anything left.

My master continuing his discourse, said, there was nothing that rendered the *Yahoos* more odious than their undistinguishing appetite to devour everything that came in their way, whether herbs, roots, berries, corrupted flesh of animals, or all mingled together: and it was peculiar in their temper, that they were fonder of what they could get by rapine or stealth at a greater distance, than much better food provided for them at home. If their prey held out, they would eat till they were ready to burst, after which nature had pointed out to them a certain root that gave them a general evacuation.

There was also another kind of root very juicy, but somewhat rare and difficult to be found, which the *Yahoos* sought for with much eagerness, and would suck it with great delight; it produced the same effects that wine hath upon us. It would make them sometimes hug, and sometimes tear one another; they would howl and grin, and chatter, and roll, and tumble, and then fall asleep in the mud.

I did indeed observe, that the *Yahoos* were the only animals in this country subject to any diseases; which, however, were much fewer than horses have among us, and contracted not by any ill treatment they meet with, but by the nastiness and greediness of that sordid brute. Neither has their language any more than a general appellation for those maladies, which is borrowed from the name of the beast, and called *Hnea-Yahoo,* or the *Yahoo's evil,* and the cure prescribed is a mixture of their own dung and urine forcibly put down the *Yahoo's* throat. This I have since often known to have been taken with success: and do here freely recommend it to my countrymen, for the public good, as an admirable specific against all diseases produced by repletion.

As to learning, government, arts, manufactures, and the like, my master confessed he could find little or no resemblance between the *Yahoos* of that country and those in ours. For he only meant to observe what parity there was in our natures. He had heard indeed some curious *Houyhnhnms* observe, that in most herds there was a sort of ruling *Yahoo* (as among us there is generally some leading or principal stag in a park), who was always more deformed in body, and mischievous in disposition, than any of the rest. That this leader had usually a favorite as like himself as he could get, whose employment was to lick his master's feet and posteriors, and drive the female *Yahoos* to his kennel; for which he was now and then rewarded with a piece of ass's flesh. This favorite is hated by the whole herd, and therefore to protect himself, keeps always near the person of his leader. He usually continues in office till a worse can be found; but the very moment he is discarded, his successor, at the head of all the *Yahoos* in that district, young and old, male and female, come in a body, and discharge their excrements upon him from head to foot. But how far this might be applicable to our courts and favorites, and ministers of state, my master said I could best determine.

I durst make no return to this malicious insinuation, which debased human understanding below the sagacity of a common hound, who has judgment enough to distinguish and follow the cry of the ablest dog in the pack, without being ever mistaken.

My master told me, there were some qualities remarkable in the *Yahoos*, which he had not observed me to mention, or at least very slightly, in the accounts I had given him of human kind. He said, those animals, like other brutes, had their females in common; but in this they differed, that the she-*Yahoo* would admit the male while she was pregnant; and that the hes would quarrel and fight with the females as fiercely as with each other. Both which practices were such degrees of infamous brutality, that no other sensitive creature ever arrived at.

Another thing he wondered at in the *Yahoos*, was their strange disposition to nastiness and dirt, whereas there appears to be a natural love of cleanliness in all other animals. As to the two former accusations, I was glad to let them pass without any reply, because I had not a word to offer upon them in defense of my species, which otherwise I certainly had done from my own inclinations. But I could have easily vindicated human kind from the imputation of singularity upon the last article, if there had been any swine in that country (as unluckily for me there were not), which although it may be a sweeter quadruped than a *Yahoo*, cannot I humbly conceive in justice pretend to more cleanliness; and so his Honor himself must have owned, if he had seen their filthy way of feeding, and their custom of wallowing and sleeping in the mud.

My master likewise mentioned another quality which his servants had discovered in several *Yahoos*, and to him was wholly unaccountable. He said, a fancy would sometimes take a *Yahoo* to retire into a corner, to lie down and howl, and groan, and spurn away all that came near him, although he were young and fat, wanted neither food nor water; nor did the servants imagine what could possibly ail him. And the only remedy they found was to set him to hard work, after which he would infallibly come to himself. To this I was silent out of partiality to my own kind; yet here I could plainly discover the true seeds of spleen, which only seizeth on the lazy, the luxurious, and the rich; who, if they were forced to undergo the same regimen, I would undertake for the cure.

His Honor had further observed, that a female *Yahoo* would often stand behind a bank or a bush, to gaze on the young males passing by, and then appear, and hide, using many antic gestures and grimaces, at which time it was observed, that she had a most offensive smell; and when any of the males advanced, would slowly retire, looking often back, and with a counterfeit show of fear, run off into some convenient place where she knew the male would follow her.

At other times if a female stranger came among them, three or four of her own sex would get about her, and stare and chatter, and grin, and smell her all over; and then turn off with gestures that seemed to express contempt and disdain.

Perhaps my master might refine a little in these speculations, which he had drawn from what he observed himself, or had been told him by others; however, I could not reflect without some amazement, and much sorrow, that the rudiments of lewdness, coquetry, censure, and scandal, should have place by instinct in womankind.

I expected every moment, that my master would accuse the *Yahoos* of those unnatural appetites in both sexes, so common among us. But nature, it seems, hath not been so expert a schoolmistress; and these politer pleasures are entirely the productions of art and reason, on our side of the globe.

CHAPTER 8

The Author relates several particulars of the Yahoos. *The great virtues of the Houyhnhnms. The education and exercise of their youth. Their general assembly.*

As I ought to have understood human nature much better than I supposed it possible for my master to do, so it was easy to apply the character he gave of the *Yahoos* to myself and my countrymen; and I believed I could yet make farther discoveries from my own observation. I therefore often begged his Honor to let me go among the herds of *Yahoos* in the neighborhood, to which he always very graciously consented, being perfectly convinced that the hatred I bore those brutes would never suffer me to be corrupted by them; and his Honor ordered one of his servants, a strong sorrel nag, very honest and good-natured, to be my guard, without whose protection I durst not undertake such adventures. For I have already told the reader how much I was pestered by those odious animals upon my first arrival. And I afterwards failed very narrowly three or four times of falling into their clutches, when I happened to stray at any distance without my hanger. And I have reason to believe they had some imagination that I was of their own species, which I often assisted myself, by stripping up my sleeves, and showing my naked arms and breast in their sight, when my protector was with me. At which times they would approach as near as they durst, and imitate my actions after the manner of monkeys, but ever with great signs of hatred; as a tame jackdaw with cap and stockings is always persecuted by the wild ones, when he happens to be got among them.

They are prodigiously nimble from their infancy; however, I once caught a young male of three years old, and endeavored by all marks of tenderness to make it quiet; but the little imp fell a squalling, and scratching, and biting with such violence, that I was forced to let it go; and it was high time, for a whole troop of old ones came about us at the noise, but finding the cub was safe (for away it ran), and my sorrel nag being by, they durst not venture near us. I observed the young animal's flesh to smell very rank, and the stink was somewhat between a weasel and a fox, but much more disagreeable. I forgot another circumstance (and perhaps I might have the reader's pardon if it were wholly omitted), that while I held the odious vermin in my hands, it voided its filthy excrements of a yellow liquid substance, all over my clothes; but by good fortune there was a small brook hard by, where I washed myself as clean as I could; although I durst not come into my master's presence, until I were sufficiently aired.

By what I could discover, the *Yahoos* appear to be the most unteachable of all animals, their capacities never reaching higher than to draw or carry burdens. Yet I am of opinion, this defect ariseth chiefly from a perverse, restive disposition. For they are cunning, malicious, treacherous, and revengeful. They are strong and hardy, but of a cowardly spirit, and by consequence, insolent, abject, and cruel. It is observed, that the red-haired of both sexes are more libidinous and mischievous than the rest, whom yet they much exceed in strength and activity.

The *Houyhnhnms* keep the *Yahoos* for present use in huts not far from the house; but the rest are sent abroad to certain fields, where they dig up roots, eat several kinds of herbs, and search about for carrion, or sometimes catch weasels and *luhimuhs* (a sort of wild rat), which they greedily devour. Nature hath taught them to dig deep holes with their nails on the side of a rising ground, wherein they lie by themselves; only the kennels of the females are larger, sufficient to hold two or three cubs.

They swim from their infancy like frogs, and are able to continue long under water, where they often take fish, which the females carry home to their young. And upon this occasion, I hope the reader will pardon my relating an odd adventure.

Being one day abroad with my protector the sorrel nag, and the weather exceeding hot, I entreated him to let me bathe in a river that was near. He consented, and I immediately stripped myself stark naked, and went down softly into the stream. It happened that a young female *Yahoo,* standing behind a bank, saw the whole proceeding, and inflamed by desire, as the nag and I conjectured, came running with all speed, and leaped into the water, within five yards of the place where I bathed. I was never in my life so terribly frighted; the nag was grazing at some distance, not suspecting any harm. She embraced me after a most fulsome manner; I roared as loud as I could, and the nag came galloping towards me, whereupon she quitted her grasp, with the utmost reluctancy, and leaped upon the opposite bank, where she stood gazing and howling all the time I was putting on my clothes.

This was matter of diversion to my master and his family, as well as of mortification to myself. For now I could no longer deny that I was a real *Yahoo* in every limb and feature, since the females had a natural propensity to me, as one of their own species. Neither was the hair of this brute of a red color (which might have been some excuse for an appetite a little irregular), but black as a sloe, and her countenance did not make an appearance altogether so hideous as the rest of the kind; for, I think, she could not be above eleven years old.

Having already lived three years in this country, the reader I suppose will expect, that I should, like other travelers, give him some account of the manners and customs of its inhabitants, which it was indeed my principal study to learn.

As these noble *Houyhnhnms* are endowed by nature with a general disposition to all virtues, and have no conceptions or ideas of what is evil in a rational creature, so their grand maxim is, to cultivate reason, and to be wholly governed by it. Neither is reason among them a point problematical as with us, where men can argue with plausibility on both sides of a question; but strikes you with immediate conviction; as it must needs do where it is not mingled, obscured, or discolored by passion and interest. I remember it was with extreme difficulty that I could bring my master to understand the meaning of the word *opinion,* or how a point could be disputable; because reason taught us to affirm or deny only where we are certain; and beyond our knowledge we cannot do either. So that controversies, wranglings, disputes, and positiveness in false or dubious propositions, are evils unknown among the *Houyhnhnms.* In the like manner when I used to explain to him our several systems of natural philosophy, he would laugh that a creature pretending to reason, should value itself upon the knowledge of other people's conjectures, and in things, where that knowledge, if it were certain, could be of no use. Wherein he agreed entirely with the sentiments of Socrates, as Plato [18] delivers them; which I mention as the highest honor I can do that prince of philosophers. I have often since reflected what destruction such a doctrine would make in the libraries of Europe; and how many paths to fame would be then shut up in the learned world.

Friendship and benevolence are the two principal virtues among the *Houyhnhnms;* and these not confined to particular objects, but universal to the whole race. For a stranger from the remotest part is equally treated with the nearest neighbor, and wherever he goes, looks upon himself as at home. They preserve decency and civility in the highest degrees, but are altogether ignorant of ceremony. They have no fondness for their colts or foals, but the care they take in educating them proceeds entirely from the dictates of reason. And I observed my master to show the same affection to his neighbor's issue that he had for his own. They will have it that nature teaches them to love the whole species, and it is reason only that maketh a distinction of persons, where there is a superior degree of virtue.

When the matron *Houyhnhnms* have produced one of each sex, they no longer accompany with their consorts, except they lose one of their issue by some casualty, which very seldom happens; but in such a case they meet again, or when the like accident befalls a person whose wife is past bearing, some other couple bestows on him one of their own colts, and then go together a second time until the mother be pregnant. This caution is necessary to prevent the country from being overburthened with numbers. But the race of inferior *Houyhnhnms* bred up to be servants is not so strictly limited upon this article; these are allowed to produce three of each sex, to be domestics in the noble families.

In their marriages they are exactly careful to choose such colors as will not make any disagreeable mixture in the breed. Strength is chiefly valued in the male, and comeliness in the female; not upon the account of love, but to preserve the race from degenerating; for where a female happens to excel in strength, a consort is chosen with regard to comeliness. Courtship, love, presents, jointures, settlements, have no place in their thoughts; or terms whereby to express them in their language. The young couple meet and are joined, merely because it is the determination of their parents and friends: it is what they see done every day, and they look upon it as one of the necessary actions of a reasonable being. But the violation of marriage, or any other unchastity, was never heard of: and the married pair pass their lives with the same friendship, and mutual benevolence that they bear to all others of the same species, who come in their way; without jealousy, fondness, quarreling, or discontent.

In educating the youth of both sexes, their method is admirable, and highly deserves our imitation. These are not suffered to taste a grain of oats, except upon certain days, till eighteen years old; nor milk, but very rarely; and in summer they graze two hours in the morning, and as many in the evening, which their parents likewise observe; but the servants are not allowed above half that time, and a great part of their grass is brought home, which they eat at the most convenient hours, when they can be best spared from work.

18. **Plato:** in the fifth book of the *Republic,* where he makes a distinction between opinion or conjecture and real knowledge.

Temperance, industry, exercise, and cleanliness, are the lessons equally enjoined to the young ones of both sexes: and my master thought it monstrous in us to give the females a different kind of education from the males, except in some articles of domestic management; whereby as he truly observed, one-half of our natives were good for nothing but bringing children into the world: and to trust the care of their children to such useless animals, he said, was yet a greater instance of brutality.

But the *Houyhnhnms* train up their youth to strength, speed, and hardiness, by exercising them in running races up and down steep hills, and over hard stony grounds; and when they are all in a sweat, they are ordered to leap over head and ears into a pond or a river. Four times a year the youth of certain districts meet to show their proficiency in running and leaping, and other feats of strength or agility; where the victor is rewarded with a song made in his or her praise. On this festival the servants drive a herd of *Yahoos* into the field, laden with hay, and oats, and milk, for a repast to the *Houyhnhnms;* after which, these brutes are immediately driven back again, for fear of being noisome to the assembly.

Every fourth year, at the vernal equinox, there is a representative council of the whole nation, which meets in a plain about twenty miles from our house, and continues about five or six days. Here they inquire into the state and condition of the several districts; whether they abound or be deficient in hay or oats, or cows or *Yahoos*. And wherever there is any want (which is but seldom), it is immediately supplied by unanimous consent and contribution. Here likewise the regulation of children is settled: as for instance, if a *Houyhnhnm* hath two males, he changeth one of them with another who hath two females; and when a child hath been lost by any casualty, where the mother is past breeding, it is determined what family shall breed another to supply the loss.

CHAPTER 9

A grand debate at the general assembly of the Houyhnhnms, *and how it was determined. The learning of the* Houyhnhnms. *Their buildings. Their manner of burials. The defectiveness of their language.*

One of these grand assemblies was held in my time, about three months before my departure, whither my master went as the representative of our district. In this council was resumed their old debate, and indeed, the only debate that ever happened in their country; whereof my master after his return gave me a very particular account.

The question to be debated was, whether the *Yahoos* should be exterminated from the face of the earth. One of the members for the affirmative offered several arguments of great strength and weight, alleging, that as the *Yahoos* were the most filthy, noisome, and deformed animal which nature ever produced, so they were the most restive and indocible, mischievous and malicious: they would privately suck the teats of the *Houyhnhnms'* cows, kill and devour their cats, trample down their oats and grass, if they were not continually watched, and commit a thousand other extravagancies. He took notice of a general tradition, that *Yahoos* had not been always in their country; but, that many ages ago, two of these brutes appeared together upon a mountain; whether produced by the heat of the sun upon corrupted mud and slime, or from the ooze and froth of the sea, was never known. That these *Yahoos* engendered, and their brood in a short time grew so numerous as to overrun and infest the whole nation. That the *Houyhnhnms* to get rid of this evil, made a general hunting, and at last enclosed the whole herd; and destroying the older, every *Houyhnhnm* kept two young ones in a kennel, and brought them to such a degree of tameness, as an animal so savage by nature can be capable of acquiring; using them for draught and carriage. That there seemed to be much truth in this tradition, and that those creatures could not be *Ylnhniamshy* (or *aborigines* of the land), because of the violent hatred the *Houyhnhnms,* as well as all other animals, bore them; which although their evil disposition sufficiently deserved, could never have arrived at so high a degree, if they had been aborigines, or else they would have long since been rooted out. That the inhabitants taking a fancy to use the service of the *Yahoos,* had very imprudently neglected to cultivate the breed of asses, which were a comely animal, easily kept, more tame and orderly, without any offensive smell, strong enough for labor, although they yield to the other in agility of body; and if their braying be no agreeable sound, it is far preferable to the horrible howlings of the *Yahoos.*

Several others declared their sentiments to the same purpose, when my master proposed an expedient to the assembly, whereof he had indeed borrowed the hint from me. He approved of the tradition mentioned by the honorable member, who spoke before, and affirmed, that the two *Yahoos* said to be first seen among them, had been driven thither over the sea; that coming to land, and being forsaken by their companions, they retired to the mountains, and degenerating by degrees, became in process of time, much more savage than those of their own species in the country from whence these two originals came. The reason of his assertion was, that he had now in his possession a certain wonderful *Yahoo* (meaning myself), which most of them had heard of, and many of them had seen. He then related to them, how he first found me; that my body was all covered with an artificial composure of the skins and hairs of other animals; that I spoke in a language of my own, and had thoroughly learned theirs: that I had related to him the accidents which brought me thither: that when he saw me without my covering, I was an exact *Yahoo* in every part, only of a whiter color, less hairy, and with shorter claws. He added, how I had endeavored to persuade him, that in my own and other countries the *Yahoos* acted as the governing, rational animal, and held the *Houyhnhnms* in servitude: that he observed in me all the qualities of a *Yahoo,* only a little more civilized by some tincture of reason, which however was in a degree as far inferior to the *Houyhnhnm* race, as the *Yahoos* of their country were to me: that, among other things, I mentioned a custom we had of castrating *Houyhnhnms* when they were young, in order to render them tame; that the operation was easy and safe; that it was no shame to learn wisdom from brutes, as industry is taught by the ant, and building by the swallow. (For so I translate the word *lyhannh,* although it be a much larger fowl.) That this invention might be practiced upon the younger *Yahoos* here, which, besides rendering them tractable and fitter for use, would in an age put an end to the whole species without destroying life. That in the meantime the *Houyhnhnms* should be exhorted to cultivate the breed of asses, which, as they are in all respects more valuable brutes, so they have this advantage, to be fit for service at five years old, which the others are not till twelve.

This was all my master thought fit to tell me at that time, of what passed in the grand council. But he was pleased to conceal one particular, which related personally to myself, whereof I soon felt the unhappy effect, as the reader will know in its proper place, and from whence I date all the succeeding misfortunes of my life.

The *Houyhnhnms* have no letters, and consequently their knowledge is all traditional. But there happening few events of any moment among a people so well united, naturally disposed to every virtue, wholly governed by reason, and cut off from all commerce with other nations, the historical part is easily preserved without burthening their memories. I have already observed, that they are subject to no diseases, and therefore can have no need of physicians. However, they have excellent medicines composed of herbs, to cure accidental bruises and cuts in the pastern or frog of the foot by sharp stones, as well as other maims and hurts in the several parts of the body.

They calculate the year by the revolution of the sun and moon, but use no subdivision into weeks. They are well enough acquainted with the motions of those two luminaries, and understand the nature of eclipses; and this is the utmost progress of their astronomy.

In poetry they must be allowed to excel all other mortals; wherein the justness of their similes, and the minuteness, as well as exactness of their descriptions, are indeed inimitable. Their verses abound very much in both of these, and usually contain either some exalted notions of friendship and benevolence, or the praises of those who were victors in races, and other bodily exercises. Their buildings, although very rude and simple, are not inconvenient, but well contrived to defend them from all injuries of cold and heat. They have a kind of tree, which at forty years old loosens in the root, and falls with the first storm: it grows very straight, and being pointed like stakes with a sharp stone (for the *Houyhnhnms* know not the use of iron), they stick them erect in the ground about ten inches asunder, and then weave in oat-straw, or sometimes wattles betwixt them. The roof is made after the same manner, and so are the doors.

The *Houyhnhnms* use the hollow part between the pastern and the hoof of their forefeet, as we do our hands, and this with greater dexterity than I could at first imagine. I have seen a white mare of our family thread a needle (which I lent her on purpose) with that joint. They milk their cows, reap their oats, and do all the work which requires hands, in the same manner. They have a kind of hard flints, which by grinding against other stones, they form into instruments, that serve instead of wedges, axes, and hammers. With tools made of these flints, they likewise cut their hay, and reap their oats, which there groweth naturally in several fields: the *Yahoos* draw home the sheaves in carriages, and the servants tread them in certain covered huts, to get out the grain, which is kept in stores. They make a rude kind of earthen and wooden vessels, and bake the former in the sun.

If they can avoid casualties, they die only of old age, and are buried in the obscurest places that can be found, their friends and relations expressing neither joy nor grief at their departure; nor does the dying person discover the least regret that he is leaving the world, any more than if he were upon returning home from a visit to one of his neighbors. I remember my master having once made an appointment with a friend and his family to come to his house upon some affair of importance; on the day fixed, the mistress and her two children came very late; she made two excuses, first for her husband, who, as she said, happened that very morning to *Lhnuwnh*. The word is strongly expressive in their language, but not easily rendered into English; it signifies, *to retire to his first mother*. Her excuse for not coming sooner was, that her husband dying late in the morning, she was a good while consulting her servants about a convenient place where his body should be laid; and I observed she behaved herself at our house as cheerfully as the rest. She died about three months after.

They live generally to seventy or seventy-five years, very seldom to fourscore: some weeks before their death they feel a gradual decay, but without pain. During this time they are much visited by their friends, because they cannot go abroad with their usual ease and satisfaction. However, about ten days before their death, which they seldom fail in computing, they return the visits that have been made them by those who are nearest in the neighborhood, being carried in a convenient sledge drawn by *Yahoos;* which vehicle they use, not only upon this occasion, but when they grow old, upon long journeys, or when they are lamed by any accident. And therefore when the dying *Houyhnhnms* return those visits, they take a solemn leave of their friends, as if they were going to some remote part of the country, where they designed to pass the rest of their lives.

I know not whether it may be worth observing, that the *Houyhnhnms* have no word in their language to express any thing that is evil, except what they borrow from the deformities or ill qualities of the *Yahoos*. Thus they denote the folly of a servant, an omission of a child, a stone that cuts their feet, a

continuance of foul or unseasonable weather, and the like, by adding to each the epithet of *Yahoo*. For instance, *Hhnm Yahoo, Whnaholm Yahoo, Ynlhmnawihlma Yahoo,* and an ill-contrived house *Ynholmhnmrohlnw Yahoo.*

I could with great pleasure enlarge farther upon the manners and virtues of this excellent people; but intending in a short time to publish a volume by itself expressly upon that subject, I refer the reader thither. And in the meantime, proceed to relate my own sad catastrophe.

CHAPTER 10

The Author's economy, and happy life among the Houyhnhnms. *His great improvement in virtue, by conversing with them. Their conversations. The Author has notice given him by his master that he must depart from the country. He falls into a swoon for grief, but submits. He contrives and finishes a canoe, by the help of a fellow-servant, and puts to sea at a venture.*

I had settled my little economy to my own heart's content. My master had ordered a room to be made for me after their manner, about six yards from the house; the sides and floors of which I plastered with clay, and covered with rush mats of my own contriving; I had beaten hemp, which there grows wild, and made of it a sort of ticking: this I filled with the feathers of several birds I had taken with springes made of *Yahoos'* hairs, and were excellent food. I had worked two chairs with my knife, the sorrel nag helping me in the grosser and more laborious part. When my clothes were worn to rags, I made myself others with the skins of rabbits, and of a certain beautiful animal about the same size, called *nnuhnoh,* the skin of which is covered with a fine down. Of these I likewise made very tolerable stockings. I soled my shoes with wood which I cut from a tree, and fitted to the upper leather, and when this was worn out, I supplied it with the skins of *Yahoos* dried in the sun. I often got honey out of hollow trees, which I mingled with water, or eat it with my bread. No man could more verify the truth of these two maxims, *That nature is very easily satisfied;* and *That necessity is the mother of invention.* I enjoyed perfect health of body, and tranquillity of mind; I did not feel the treachery or inconstancy of a friend, nor the injuries of a secret or open enemy. I had no occasion of bribing, flattering, or pimping, to procure the favor of any great man or of his minion.

I wanted no fence against fraud or oppression; here was neither physician to destroy my body, nor lawyer to ruin my fortune; no informer to watch my words and actions, or forge accusations against me for hire; here were no gibers, censurers, backbiters, pickpockets, highwaymen, housebreakers, attorneys, bawds, buffoons, gamesters, politicians, wits, splenetics, tedious talkers, controvertists, ravishers, murderers, robbers, virtuosos; no leaders or followers of party and faction; no encouragers to vice, by seducement or examples; no dungeon, axes, gibbets, whipping posts, or pillories; no cheating shopkeepers or mechanics; no pride, vanity, or affectation; no fops, bullies, drunkards, strolling whores, or poxes; no ranting, lewd, expensive wives; no stupid, proud pedants; no importunate, overbearing, quarrelsome, noisy, roaring, empty, conceited, swearing companions; no scoundrels, raised from the dust upon the merit of their vices, or nobility thrown into it on account of their virtues; no lords, fiddlers, judges or dancing masters.

I had the favor of being admitted to several *Houyhnhnms*, who came to visit or dine with my master; where his Honor graciously suffered me to wait in the room, and listen to their discourse. Both he and his company would often descend to ask me questions, and receive my answers. I had also sometimes the honor of attending my master in his visits to others. I never presumed to speak, except in answer to a question; and then I did it with inward regret, because it was a loss of so much time for improving myself: but I was infinitely delighted with the station of an humble auditor in such conversations, where nothing passed but what was useful, expressed in the fewest and most significant words; where (as I have already said) the greatest decency was observed, without the least degree of ceremony; where no person spoke without being pleased himself, and pleasing his companions; where there was no interruption, tediousness, heat, or difference of sentiments. They have a notion, that when people are met together, a short silence doth much improve conversation: this I found to be true; for during those little intermissions of talk, new ideas would arise in their minds, which very much enlivened the discourse. Their subjects are generally on friendship and benevolence, on order and economy; sometimes upon the visible operations of nature, or ancient traditions; upon the bounds and limits of virtue; upon the unerring rules of reason, or upon some determinations to be taken at the next great assembly; and often upon the various excellencies of poetry. I may add, without vanity, that my presence often gave them sufficient matter for discourse, because it afforded my master an occasion of letting his friends into the history of me and my country, upon which they were all pleased to descant in a manner not very advantageous to human kind; and for that reason I shall not repeat what they said: only I may be allowed to observe, that his Honor, to my great admiration, appeared to understand the nature of *Yahoos* much better than myself. He went through all our vices and follies, and discovered many which I had never mentioned to him, by only supposing what qualities a *Yahoo* of their country, with a small proportion of reason, might be capable of exerting; and concluded, with too much probability, how vile as well as miserable such a creature must be.

I freely confess, that all the little knowledge I have of any value, was acquired by the lectures I received from my master, and from hearing the discourses of him and his friends; to which I should be prouder to listen, than to dictate to the greatest and wisest assembly in Europe. I admired the strength, comeliness, and speed of the inhabitants; and such a constellation of virtues in such amiable persons produced in me the highest veneration. At first, indeed, I did not feel that natural awe which the *Yahoos* and all other animals bear towards them; but it grew upon me by degrees, much sooner than I imagined, and was mingled with a respectful love and gratitude, that they would condescend to distinguish me from the rest of my species.

When I thought of my family, my friends, my countrymen, or human race in general, I considered them as they really were, *Yahoos* in shape and disposition, perhaps a little more civilized, and qualified with the gift of speech, but making no other use of reason, than to improve and multiply those vices, whereof their brethren in this country had only the share that nature allotted them. When I happened to behold the reflection of my own form in a lake or fountain, I turned away my face in horror and detestation of myself, and could better endure the sight of a common *Yahoo*, than of my own person. By conversing with the *Houyhnhnms*, and looking upon them with delight, I fell to imitate their gait and gesture, which is now grown into a habit, and my friends often tell me in a blunt way, that *I trot like a horse;* which, however, I take for a great compliment. Neither shall I disown, that in speaking I am apt to fall into the voice and manner of the *Houyhnhnms,* and hear myself ridiculed on that account without the least mortification.

In the midst of all this happiness, and when I looked upon myself to be fully settled for life, my master sent for me one morning a little earlier than his usual hour. I observed by his countenance that he was in some perplexity, and at a loss how to begin what he had to speak. After a short silence, he told me, he did not know how I would take what he was going to say; that in the last general assembly, when the affair of the *Yahoos* was entered upon, the representatives had taken offense at his keeping a *Yahoo* (meaning myself) in his family more like a *Houyhnhnm* than a brute animal. That he was known frequently to converse with me, as if he could receive some advantage or pleasure in my company; that such a practice was not agreeable to reason or nature, or a thing ever heard of before among them. The assembly did therefore exhort him, either to employ me like the rest of my species, or command me to swim back to the place from whence I came. That the first of these expedients was utterly rejected by all the *Houyhnhnms* who had ever seen me at his house or their own: for they alleged, that because I had some rudiments of reason, added to the natural pravity of those animals, it was to be feared, I might be able to seduce them into the woody and mountainous parts of the country, and bring them in troops by night to destroy the *Houyhnhnms'* cattle, as being naturally of the ravenous kind, and averse from labor.

My master added, that he was daily pressed by the *Houyhnhnms* of the neighborhood to have the assembly's exhortation executed, which he could not put off much longer. He doubted it would be impossible for me to swim to another country, and therefore wished I would contrive some sort of vehicle resembling those I had described to him, that might carry me on the sea; in which work I should have the assistance of his own servants, as well as those of his neighbors. He concluded, that for his own part, he could have been content to keep me in his service as long as I lived; because he found I had cured myself of some bad habits and dispositions, by endeavoring, as far as my inferior nature was capable, to imitate the *Houyhnhnms.*

I should here observe to the reader, that a decree of the general assembly in this country is expressed by the word *hnhloayn,* which signifies an exhortation, as near as I can render it; for they have no conception how a rational creature can be compelled, but only advised, or exhorted; because no person can disobey reason, without giving up his claim to be a rational creature.

I was struck with the utmost grief and despair at my master's discourse; and being unable to support the agonies I was under, I fell into a swoon at his feet: when I came to myself, he told me, that he concluded I had been dead (for these people are subject to no such imbecilities of nature). I answered, in a faint voice, that death would have been too great an happiness; that although I could not blame the assembly's exhortation, or the urgency of his friends; yet, in my weak and corrupt judgment, I thought it might consist with reason to have been less rigorous. That I could not swim a league, and probably the nearest land to theirs might be distant above an hundred: that many materials, necessary for making a small vessel to carry me off, were wholly wanting in this country, which, however, I would attempt in obedience and gratitude to his Honor, although I concluded the thing to be impossible, and therefore looked on myself as already devoted to destruction. That the certain prospect of an unnatural death was the least of my evils: for, supposing I should escape with life by some strange adventure; how could I think with temper [19] of passing my days among *Yahoos,* and relapsing into my old corruptions, for want of examples to lead and keep me within the paths of virtue. That I knew too well upon what solid reasons all the determinations of the wise *Houyhnhnms* were founded, not to be shaken by arguments of mine, a miserable *Yahoo;* and therefore, after presenting him with my humble thanks for the offer of his servants' assistance in making a vessel, and desiring a reasonable time for so difficult a work, I told him I would endeavor to preserve a wretched being; and, if ever I returned to England, was not without hopes of being useful to my own species, by celebrating the praises of the renowned *Houyhnhnms,* and proposing their virtues to the imitation of mankind.

My master in a few words made me a very gracious reply, allowed me the space of two months to finish my boat; and ordered the sorrel nag, my fellow-servant (for so at this distance I may presume to call him) to follow my instructions, because I

---

19. temper: calmness of mind.

told my master, that his help would be sufficient; and I knew he had a tenderness for me.

In his company my first business was to go to that part of the coast where my rebellious crew had ordered me to be set on shore. I got upon a height, and looking on every side into the sea, fancied I saw a small island, towards the northeast: I took out my pocket glass, and could then clearly distinguish it about five leagues off, as I computed; but it appeared to the sorrel nag to be only a blue cloud: for, as he had no conception of any country beside his own, so he could not be as expert in distinguishing remote objects at sea, as we who so much converse in that element.

After I had discovered this island, I considered no farther; but resolved it should, if possible, be the first place of my banishment, leaving the consequence to fortune.

I returned home, and consulting with the sorrel nag, we went into a copse at some distance, where I with my knife, and he with a sharp flint fastened very artificially,[20] after their manner, to a wooden handle, cut down several oak wattles about the thickness of a walking staff, and some larger pieces. But I shall not trouble the reader with a particular description of my own mechanics; let it suffice to say, that in six weeks' time, with the help of the sorrel nag, who performed the parts that required most labor, I finished a sort of Indian canoe, but much larger, covering it with the skins of *Yahoos* well stitched together, with hempen threads of my own making. My sail was likewise composed of the skins of the same animal; but I made use of the youngest I could get, the older being too tough and thick; and I likewise provided myself with four paddles. I laid in a stock of boiled flesh, of rabbits and fowls, and took with me two vessels, one filled with milk, and the other with water.

I tried my canoe in a large pond near my master's house, and then corrected in it what was amiss; stopping all the chinks with *Yahoos'* tallow, till I found it staunch, and able to bear me, and my freight. And when it was as complete as I could possibly make it, I had it drawn on a carriage very gently by *Yahoos* to the seaside, under the conduct of the sorrel nag, and another servant.

When all was ready, and the day came for my departure, I took leave of my master and lady, and the whole family, my eyes flowing with tears,

20. artificially: ingeniously.

and my heart quite sunk with grief. But his Honor, out of curiosity, and, perhaps (if I may speak it without vanity) partly out of kindness, was determined to see me in my canoe, and got several of his neighboring friends to accompany him. I was forced to wait above an hour for the tide, and then observing the wind very fortunately bearing towards the island, to which I intended to steer my course, I took a second leave of my master: but as I was going to prostrate myself to kiss his hoof, he did me the honor to raise it gently to my mouth. I am not ignorant how much I have been censured for mentioning this last particular. For my detractors are pleased to think it improbable, that so illustrious a person should descend to give so great a mark of distinction to a creature so inferior as I. Neither have I forgot, how apt some travelers are to boast of extraordinary favors they have received. But if these censurers were better acquainted with the noble and courteous disposition of the *Houyhnhnms,* they would soon change their opinion.

I paid my respects to the rest of the *Houyhnhnms* in his Honor's company; then getting into my canoe, I pushed off from shore.

CHAPTER II

The Author's dangerous voyage. He arrives at New Holland, *hoping to settle there. Is wounded with an arrow by one of the natives. Is seized and carried by force into a* Portuguese *ship. The great civilities of the Captain. The Author arrives at* England.

I began this desperate voyage on February 15, 1714–15, at nine o'clock in the morning. The wind was very favorable; however, I made use at first only of my paddles; but considering I should soon be weary, and that the wind might probably chop about, I ventured to set up my little sail; and thus, with the help of the tide, I went at the rate of a league and a half an hour, as near as I could guess. My master and his friends continued on the shore, till I was almost out of sight; and I often heard the sorrel nag (who always loved me) crying out, *Hnuy illa nyha majah Yahoo,* Take care of thyself, gentle *Yahoo.*

My design was, if possible, to discover some small island uninhabited, yet sufficient by my labor to furnish me with necessaries of life, which I would have thought a greater happiness than to be first minister in the politest court of Europe; so horrible was the idea I conceived of returning to live in the society and under the government of *Yahoos*. For in such a solitude as I desired, I could at least enjoy my own thoughts, and reflect with delight on the virtues of those inimitable *Houyhnhnms*, without any opportunity of degenerating into the vices and corruptions of my own species.

The reader may remember what I related when my crew conspired against me, and confined me to my cabin. How I continued there several weeks, without knowing what course we took; and when I was put ashore in the longboat, how the sailors told me with oaths, whether true or false, that they knew not in what part of the world we were. However, I did then believe us to be about ten degrees southward of the Cape of Good Hope, or about forty-five degrees southern latitude, as I gathered from some general words I overheard among them, being I supposed to the southeast in their intended voyage to Madagascar. And although this were little better than conjecture, yet I resolved to steer my course eastward, hoping to reach the southwest coast of New Holland, and perhaps some such island as I desired, lying westward of it. The wind was full west, and by six in the evening I computed I had gone eastward at least eighteen leagues, when I spied a very small island about half a league off, which I soon reached. It was nothing but a rock with one creek, naturally arched by the force of tempests. Here I put in my canoe, and climbing up a part of the rock, I could plainly discover land to the east, extending from south to north. I lay all night in my canoe; and repeating my voyage early in the morning, I arrived in seven hours to the southeast point of New Holland.[21] This confirmed me in the opinion I have long entertained, that the maps and charts place this country at least three degrees more to the east than it really is; which thought I communicated many years ago to my worthy friend Mr. Herman Moll,[22] and gave him my reasons for it, although he hath rather chosen to follow other authors.

I saw no inhabitants in the place where I landed, and being unarmed, I was afraid of venturing far into the country. I found some shellfish on the shore, and eat them raw, not daring to kindle a fire, for fear of being discovered by the natives. I continued three days feeding on oysters and limpets,

to save my own provisions; and I fortunately found a brook of excellent water, which gave me great relief.

On the fourth day, venturing out early a little too far, I saw twenty or thirty natives upon a height, not above five hundred yards from me. They were stark naked, men, women, and children round a fire, as I could discover by the smoke. One of them spied me, and gave notice to the rest; five of them advanced towards me, leaving the women and children at the fire. I made what haste I could to the shore, and getting into my canoe, shoved off: the savages observing me retreat, ran after me; and before I could get far enough into the sea, discharged an arrow, which wounded me deeply on the inside of my left knee (I shall carry the mark to my grave). I apprehended the arrow might be poisoned, and paddling out of the reach of their darts (being a calm day), I made a shift to suck the wound, and dress it as well as I could.

I was at a loss what to do, for I durst not return to the same landing place, but stood to the north, and was forced to paddle; for the wind, though very gentle, was against me, blowing northwest. As I was looking about for a secure landing place, I saw a sail to the north-northeast, which appearing every minute more visible, I was in some doubt whether I should wait for them or no; but at last my detestation of the *Yahoo* race prevailed, and turning my canoe, I sailed and paddled together to the south, and got into the same creek from whence I set out in the morning, choosing rather to trust myself among these barbarians, than live with European *Yahoos*. I drew up my canoe as close as I could to the shore, and hid myself behind a stone by the little brook, which, as I have already said, was excellent water.

The ship came within half a league of this creek, and sent her longboat with vessels to take in fresh water (for the place it seems was very well known), but I did not observe it until the boat was almost on shore, and it was too late to seek another hiding place. The seamen at their landing observed my canoe, and rummaging it all over, easily conjectured that the owner could not be far off. Four of them well armed searched every cranny and lurking hole, until at last they found me flat on my face behind the stone. They gazed awhile in admiration at my strange uncouth dress; my coat made of skins, my wooden-soled shoes, and my furred stockings; from whence, however, they concluded I was not a native of the place, who all go

---

21. New Holland: The apparent confusion between the "southwest coast" and "southeast point" can be cleared up by reference to the very simple map Swift provided, in which the land of the Houyhnhnms is shown as a large island, west of the coast of Australia, which runs from the northwest to the southeast. 22. Hermann Moll: a famous Dutch mapmaker, who settled in London in 1698.

naked. One of the seamen in Portuguese bid me rise, and asked who I was. I understood that language very well, and getting upon my feet, said, I was a poor *Yahoo,* banished from the *Houyhnhnms,* and desired they would please to let me depart. They admired to hear me answer them in their own tongue, and saw by my complexion I must be an European; but were at a loss to know what I meant by *Yahoos* and *Houyhnhnms,* and at the same time fell a laughing at my strange tone in speaking, which resembled the neighing of a horse. I trembled all the while betwixt fear and hatred. I again desired leave to depart, and was gently moving to my canoe; but they laid hold on me, desiring to know, what country I was of? whence I came? with many other questions. I told them, I was born in England, from whence I came about five years ago, and then their country and ours were at peace. I therefore hoped they would not treat me as an enemy, since I meant them no harm, but was a poor *Yahoo,* seeking some desolate place where to pass the remainder of his unfortunate life.

When they began to talk, I thought I never heard or saw anything so unnatural; for it appeared to me as monstrous as if a dog or a cow should speak in England, or a *Yahoo* in *Houyhnhnm-land.* The honest Portuguese were equally amazed at my strange dress, and the odd manner of delivering my words, which however they understood very well. They spoke to me with great humanity, and said they were sure their Captain would carry me *gratis* to Lisbon, from whence I might return to my own country; that two of the seamen would go back to the ship, to inform the Captain of what they had seen, and receive his orders; in the meantime, unless I would give my solemn oath not to fly, they would secure me by force. I thought it best to comply with their proposal. They were very curious to know my story, but I gave them very little satisfaction; and they all conjectured that my misfortunes had impaired my reason. In two hours the boat, which went loaden with vessels of water, returned with the Captain's commands to fetch me on board. I fell on my knees to preserve my liberty; but all was in vain, and the men having tied me with cords, heaved me into the boat, from whence I was taken into the ship, and from thence into the Captain's cabin.

His name was Pedro de Mendez; he was a very courteous and generous person; he entreated me to give some account of myself, and desired to know what I would eat or drink; said, I should be used as well as himself, and spoke so many obliging things, that I wondered to find such civilities from a *Yahoo.* However, I remained silent and sullen; I was ready to faint at the very smell of him and his men. At last I desired something to eat out of my own canoe; but he ordered me a chicken and some excellent wine, and then directed that I should be put to bed in a very clean cabin. I would not undress myself, but lay on the bedclothes, and in half an hour stole out, when I thought the crew was at dinner, and getting to the side of the ship was going to leap into the sea, and swim for my life, rather than continue among *Yahoos.* But one of the seamen prevented me, and having informed the Captain, I was chained to my cabin.

After dinner Don Pedro came to me, and desired to know my reason for so desperate an attempt; assured me he only meant to do me all the service he was able; and spoke so very movingly, that at last I descended to treat him like an animal which had some little portion of reason. I gave him a very short relation of my voyage; of the conspiracy against me by my own men; of the country where they set me on shore, and of my five years' residence there. All which he looked upon as if it were a dream or a vision; whereat I took great offense; for I had quite forgot the faculty of lying, so peculiar to *Yahoos* in all countries where they preside, and, consequently the disposition of suspecting truth in others of their own species. I asked him, whether it were the custom of his country to *say the thing that was not?* I assured him I had almost forgot what he meant by falsehood, and if I had lived a thousand years in *Houyhnhnm-land,* I should never have heard a lie from the meanest servant; that I was altogether indifferent whether he believed me or no; but however, in return for his favors, I would give so much allowance to the corruption of his nature, as to answer any objection he would please to make; and he might easily discover the truth.

The Captain, a wise man, after many endeavors to catch me tripping in some part of my story, at last began to have a better opinion of my veracity. But he added, that since I professed so inviolable an attachment to truth, I must give him my word of honor to bear him company in this voyage, without attempting anything against my life, or else he would continue me a prisoner until we arrived at Lisbon. I gave him the promise he required; but at the same time protested that I would suffer the greatest hardships rather than return to live among *Yahoos.*

Our voyage passed without any considerable accident. In gratitude to the Captain I sometimes sat with him at his earnest request, and strove to conceal my antipathy against human kind, although it often broke out, which he suffered to pass without observation. But the greatest part of the day, I confined myself to my cabin, to avoid seeing any of the crew. The Captain had often entreated me to strip myself of my savage dress, and offered to lend me the best suit of clothes he had. This I would not be prevailed on to accept, abhorring to cover myself with anything that had been on the back of a *Yahoo.* I only desired he would lend me two clean shirts, which having been washed since he wore them, I believed would not so much defile me. These I changed every second day, and washed them myself.

We arrived at Lisbon, Nov. 5, 1715. At our landing the Captain forced me to cover myself with his cloak, to prevent the rabble from crowding about me. I was conveyed to his own house, and at my earnest request, he led me up to the highest room backwards.[23] I conjured him to conceal from all persons what I had told him of the *Houyhnhnms,* because the least hint of such a story would not only draw numbers of people to see me, but probably put me in danger of being imprisoned, or burnt by the Inquisition. The Captain persuaded me to accept a suit of clothes newly made; but I would not suffer the tailor to take my measure; however, Don Pedro being almost my size, they fitted me well enough. He accoutered me with other necessaries all new, which I aired for twenty-four hours before I would use them.

The Captain had no wife, nor above three servants, none of which were suffered to attend at meals, and his whole deportment was so obliging, added to very good *human* understanding, that I really began to tolerate his company. He gained so far upon me, that I ventured to look out of the back window. By degrees I was brought into another room, from whence I peeped into the street, but drew my head back in a fright. In a week's time he seduced me down to the door. I found my terror gradually lessened, but my hatred and contempt seemed to increase. I was at last bold enough to walk the street in his company, but kept my nose well stopped with rue, or sometimes with tobacco.

In ten days, Don Pedro, to whom I had given some account of my domestic affairs, put it upon me as a point of honor and conscience, that I ought to return to my native country, and live at home with my wife and children. He told me, there was an English ship in the port just ready to sail, and he would furnish me with all things necessary. It would be tedious to repeat his arguments, and my contradictions. He said it was altogether impossible to find such a solitary island as I had desired to live in; but I might command in my own house, and pass my time in a manner as recluse as I pleased.

I complied at last, finding I could not do better. I left Lisbon the 24th day of November, in an English merchantman, but who was the master I never inquired. Don Pedro accompanied me to the ship, and lent me twenty pounds. He took kind leave of me, and embraced me at parting, which I bore as well as I could. During this last voyage I had no commerce with the master or any of his men; but pretending I was sick, kept close in my cabin. On the 5th of December, 1715, we cast anchor in the Downs about nine in the morning, and at three in the afternoon I got safe to my house at Redriff.

My wife and family received me with great surprise and joy, because they concluded me certainly dead; but I must freely confess the sight of them filled me only with hatred, disgust, and contempt, and the more by reflecting on the near alliance I had to them. For, although since my unfortunate exile from the *Houyhnhnm* country, I had compelled myself to tolerate the sight of *Yahoos,* and to converse with Don Pedro de Mendez; yet my memory and imagination were perpetually filled with the virtues and ideas of those exalted *Houyhnhnms.* And when I began to consider, that by copulating with one of the *Yahoo* species I had become a parent of more, it struck me with the utmost shame, confusion, and horror.

As soon as I entered the house, my wife took me in her arms, and kissed me; at which, having not been used to the touch of that odious animal for so many years, I fell in a swoon for almost an hour. At the time I am writing it is five years [24] since my last return to England: during the first year, I could not endure my wife or children in my presence, the very smell of them was intolerable; much less could I suffer them to eat in the same room.

23. backwards: at the rear of the house.

24. five years: i.e., the beginning of 1721. The first reference Swift makes to "writing a history of my Travels" is in a letter of April, 1721.

To this hour they dare not presume to touch my bread, or drink out of the same cup, neither was I ever able to let one of them take me by the hand. The first money I laid out was to buy two young stone-horses, which I keep in a good stable, and next to them the groom is my greatest favorite; for I feel my spirits revived by the smell he contracts in the stable. My horses understand me tolerably well; I converse with them at least four hours every day. They are strangers to bridle or saddle; they live in great amity with me, and friendship to each other.

CHAPTER 12

The Author's veracity. His design in publishing this work. His censure of those travelers who swerve from the truth. The Author clears himself from any sinister ends in writing. An objection answered. The method of planting colonies. His native country commended. The right of the Crown to those countries described by the Author is justified. The difficulty of conquering them. The Author takes his last leave of the reader; proposeth his manner of living for the future; gives good advice, and concludes.

Thus, gentle reader, I have given thee a faithful history of my travels for sixteen years and above seven months; wherein I have not been so studious of ornament as of truth. I could perhaps like others have astonished thee with strange improbable tales; but I rather chose to relate plain matter of fact in the simplest manner and style; because my principal design was to inform, and not to amuse thee.

It is easy for us who travel into remote countries, which are seldom visited by Englishmen or other Europeans, to form descriptions of wonderful animals both at sea and land. Whereas a traveler's chief aim should be to make men wiser and better, and to improve their minds by the bad as well as good example of what they deliver concerning foreign places.

I could heartily wish a law were enacted, that every traveler, before he were permitted to publish his voyages, should be obliged to make oath before the Lord High Chancellor that all he intended to print was absolutely true to the best of his knowledge; for then the world would no longer be deceived as it usually is, while some writers, to make their works pass the better upon the public, impose the grossest falsities on the unwary reader. I have perused several books of travels with great delight in my younger days; but having since gone over most parts of the globe, and been able to con-

tradict many fabulous accounts from my own observation, it hath given me a great disgust against this part of reading, and some indignation to see the credulity of mankind so impudently abused. Therefore, since my acquaintance were pleased to think my poor endeavors might not be unacceptable to my country, I imposed on myself as a maxim, never to be swerved from, that I would *strictly adhere to truth;* neither indeed can I be ever under the least temptation to vary from it, while I retain in my mind the lectures and example of my noble master, and the other illustrious *Houyhnhnms,* of whom I had so long the honor to be an humble hearer.

Nec si miserum Fortuna Sinonem
Finxit, vanum etiam, mendacemque improba
finget.[25]

I know very well how little reputation is to be got by writings which require neither genius nor learning, nor indeed any other talent, except a good memory, or an exact journal. I know likewise, that writers of travels, like dictionary makers, are sunk into oblivion by the weight and bulk of those who come last, and therefore lie uppermost. And it is highly probable, that such travelers who shall hereafter visit the countries described in this work of mine, may, by detecting my errors (if there be any), and adding many new discoveries of their own, jostle me out of vogue, and stand in my place, making the world forget that I was ever an author. This indeed would be too great a mortification if I wrote for fame: but, as my sole intention was the PUBLIC GOOD, I cannot be altogether disappointed. For who can read of the virtues I have mentioned in the glorious *Houyhnhnms,* without being ashamed of his own vices, when he considers himself as the reasoning, governing animal of his country? I shall say nothing of those remote nations where *Yahoos* preside; amongst which the least corrupted are the *Brobdingnagians,* whose wise maxims in morality and government it would be our happiness to observe. But I forbear descanting further, and rather leave the judicious reader to his own remarks and applications.

I am not a little pleased that this work of mine can possibly meet with no censurers: for what objections can be made against a writer who relates only plain facts that happened in such distant countries, where we have not the least interest with

25. *Nec . . . finget:* "Though Fortune has made Sinon wretched, she shall not for all her malice make him a cheat and a liar."

respect either to trade or negotiations? I have carefully avoided every fault with which common writers of travels are often too justly charged. Besides, I meddle not the least with any party, but write without passion, prejudice, or ill will against any man or number of men whatsoever. I write for the noblest end, to inform and instruct mankind, over whom I may, without breach of modesty, pretend to some superiority, from the advantages I received by conversing so long among the most accomplished *Houyhnhnms.* I write without any view towards profit [26] or praise. I never suffer a word to pass that may look like reflection, or possibly give the least offense even to those who are most ready to take it. So that I hope I may with justice pronounce myself an author perfectly blameless, against whom the tribes of answerers, considerers, observers, reflecters, detecters, remarkers, will never be able to find matter for exercising their talents.

I confess, it was whispered to me, that I was bound in duty as a subject of England, to have given in a memorial to a secretary of state, at my first coming over; because, whatever lands are discovered by a subject, belong to the Crown. But I doubt whether our conquests in the countries I treat of, would be as easy as those of Ferdinando Cortes [27] over the naked Americans. The *Lilliputians* I think, are hardly worth the charge of a fleet and army to reduce them; and I question whether it might be prudent or safe to attempt the *Brobdingnagians;* or whether an English army would be much at their ease with the Flying Island [28] over their heads. The *Houyhnhnms,* indeed, appear not to be so well prepared for war, a science to which they are perfect strangers, and especially against missive weapons. However, supposing myself to be a minister of state, I could never give my advice for invading them. Their prudence, unanimity, unacquaintedness with fear, and their love of their country, would amply supply all defects in the military art. Imagine twenty thousand of them breaking into the midst of an European army, confounding the ranks, overturning the carriages, battering the warriors' faces into mummy by terrible yerks from their hinder hoofs; for they would well deserve the character given to Augustus: *Recalcitrat undique tutus.*[29] But instead of proposals for con-

26. **profit:** Swift sold the book for £200.   27. **Cortes:** who subdued the Mexicans with only a handful of Spanish troops.
28. **Flying Island:** one of the episodes of Book III, here omitted.
29. *Recalcitrat . . . tutus:* An odd way to bring in Horace's warning against approaching the Emperor Augustus at the wrong moment, when, like a restive horse, "he will kick himself clear on all sides" (*Satires,* II.i.20).

quering that magnanimous nation, I rather wish they were in a capacity or disposition to send a sufficient number of their inhabitants for civilizing Europe, by teaching us the first principles of honor, justice, truth, temperance, public spirit, fortitude, chastity, friendship, benevolence, and fidelity. The names of all which virtues are still retained among us in most languages and are to be met with in modern as well as ancient authors; which I am able to assert from my own small reading.

But I had another reason which made me less forward to enlarge his Majesty's dominions by my discoveries. To say the truth, I had conceived a few scruples with relation to the distributive justice of princes upon those occasions. For instance, a crew of pirates are driven by a storm they know not whither; at length a boy discovers land from the topmast; they go on shore to rob and plunder; they see an harmless people, are entertained with kindness, they give the country a new name, they take formal possession of it for the king, they set up a rotten plank or a stone for a memorial, they murder two or three dozen of the natives, bring away a couple more by force for a sample, return home, and get their pardon. Here commences a new dominion acquired with a title by *divine right.* Ships are sent with the first opportunity; the natives driven out or destroyed, their princes tortured to discover their gold; a free license given to all acts of inhumanity and lust; the earth reeking with the blood of its inhabitants: and this execrable crew of butchers employed in so pious an expedition, is a *modern colony* sent to convert and civilize an idolatrous and barbarous people.

But this description, I confess, doth by no means affect the British nation, who may be an example to the whole world for their wisdom, care, and justice in planting colonies; their liberal endowments for the advancement of religion and learning; their choice of devout and able pastors to propagate Christianity; their caution in stocking their provinces with people of sober lives and conversations from this the mother kingdom; their strict regard to the distribution of justice, in supplying the civil administration through all their colonies with officers of the greatest abilities, utter strangers to corruption; and to crown all, by sending the most vigilant and virtuous governors, who have no other views than the happiness of the people over whom they preside, and the honor of the King their master.

But, as those countries which I have described

do not appear to have a desire of being conquered, and enslaved, murdered or driven out by colonies; nor abound either in gold, silver, sugar, or tobacco; I did humbly conceive, they were by no means proper objects of our zeal, our valor, or our interest. However, if those whom it may concern think fit to be of another opinion, I am ready to depose, when I shall be lawfully called, that no European did ever visit these countries before me. I mean, if the inhabitants ought to be believed. . . .

But, as to the formality of taking possession in my Sovereign's name, it never came once into my thoughts; and if it had, yet as my affairs then stood, I should perhaps in point of prudence and self-preservation, have put it off to a better opportunity.

Having thus answered the *only* objection that can ever be raised against me as a traveler, I here take a final leave of my courteous readers, and return to enjoy my own speculations in my little garden at Redriff; to apply those excellent lessons of virtue which I learned among the *Houyhnhnms;* to instruct the *Yahoos* of my own family as far as I shall find them docible animals; to behold my figure often in a glass, and thus if possible habituate myself by time to tolerate the sight of a human creature: to lament the brutality of *Houyhnhnms* in my own country, but always treat their persons with respect, for the sake of my noble master, his family, his friends, and the whole *Houyhnhnm* race, whom these of ours have the honor to resemble in all their lineaments, however their intellectuals came to degenerate.

I began last week to permit my wife to sit at dinner with me, at the farthest end of a long table; and to answer (but with the utmost brevity) the few questions I asked her. Yet the smell of a *Yahoo* continuing very offensive, I always keep my nose well stopped with rue, lavender, or tobacco leaves. And although it be hard for a man late in life to remove old habits, I am not altogether out of hopes in some time to suffer a neighbor *Yahoo* in my company, without the apprehensions I am yet under of his teeth or his claws.

My reconcilement to the *Yahoo*-kind in general might not be so difficult, if they would be content with those vices and follies only which nature hath entitled them to. I am not in the least provoked at the sight of a lawyer, a pickpocket, a colonel, a fool, a lord, a gamester, a politician, a whore-monger, a physician, an evidence, a suborner, an attorney, a traitor, or the like; this is all according to the due course of things: but when I behold a lump of deformity, and diseases both in body and mind, smitten with *pride*,[30] it immediately breaks all the measures of my patience; neither shall I be ever able to comprehend how such an animal and such a vice could tally together. The wise and virtuous *Houyhnhnms,* who abound in all excellencies that can adorn a rational creature, have no name for this vice in their language, which hath no terms to express anything that is evil, except those whereby they describe the detestable qualities of their *Yahoos,* among which they were not able to distinguish this of pride, for want of thoroughly understanding human nature, as it showeth itself in other countries, where that animal presides. But I, who had more experience, could plainly observe some rudiments of it among the wild *Yahoos.*

But the *Houyhnhnms,* who live under the government of reason, are no more proud of the good qualities they possess, than I should be for not wanting a leg or an arm, which no man in his wits would boast of, although he must be miserable without them. I dwell the longer upon this subject from the desire I have to make the society of an English *Yahoo* by any means not insupportable; and therefore I here entreat those who have any tincture of this absurd vice, that they will not presume to appear in my sight.

Finis

A MODEST PROPOSAL

FOR PREVENTING THE CHILDREN OF POOR PEOPLE IN IRELAND, FROM BEING A BURDEN TO THEIR PARENTS OR COUNTRY; AND FOR MAKING THEM BENEFICIAL TO THE PUBLIC

Written in the late summer of 1729, while Swift was staying with friends in the country. His mood at the time is shown in a letter to Pope written on August 11:

As to this country, there have been three terrible years' dearth of corn, and every place strewed with beggars; but dearths are common in better climates, and our evils here lie much deeper. Imagine a nation the two-thirds of whose revenues are spent out of it, and who are not permitted to trade with the other third, and where the pride of women will not suffer them to wear their own manufactures, even where

---

30. *pride:* which the moralists represent as the chief error of mankind. Cf. Pope's *Essay on Man,* "In pride, in reasoning pride, our error lies," which the Church regarded as the deadliest of the seven deadly sins, and which was the cause of the fall of Satan, the great rebel against God.

they excel what come from abroad. This is the true state of Ireland in a very few words. These evils operate more every day, and the kingdom is absolutely undone, as I have been telling often in print these ten years past.

Published in Dublin in October, 1729, and reprinted seven times within a year, this has remained the most widely known of all Swift's papers about Ireland.

He writes as one who is utterly wearied by the foolish proposals that were being constantly suggested for the betterment of Ireland, and driven at last to put forward a proposal of his own which would really meet the desperate situation of the country. It is a perfect example of his use of irony to shock his readers into an awareness of the miseries of the poor people of Ireland, which had roused him to such fierce indignation.

It is a melancholy object to those who walk through this great town, or travel in the country, when they see the streets, the roads, and cabin doors crowded with beggars [1] of the female sex, followed by three, four or six children, *all in rags,* and importuning every passenger for an alms. These mothers, instead of being able to work for their honest livelihood, are forced to employ all their time in strolling, to beg sustenance for their helpless infants, who, as they grow up, either turn thieves for want of work, or leave their dear native country to fight for the Pretender in Spain,[2] or sell themselves to the Barbados.[3]

I think it is agreed by all parties that this prodigious number of children in the arms, or on the backs, or at the heels of their mothers, and frequently of their fathers, is in the present deplorable state of the kingdom a very great additional grievance; and therefore whoever could find out a fair, cheap, and easy method of making these children sound and useful members of the commonwealth would deserve so well of the public as to have his statue set up for a preserver of the nation.

But my intention is very far from being confined to provide only for the children of professed beggars; it is of a much greater extent, and shall take in the whole number of infants at a certain age who are born of parents in effect as little able to support them as those who demand our charity in the streets.

As to my own part, having turned my thoughts,

A MODEST PROPOSAL. 1. crowded . . . beggars: It was estimated that there were nearly 35,000 strolling beggars in Ireland at this time.   2. fight . . . Spain: Cardinal Alberoni had equipped an expedition to fight for the Pretender in 1718. 3. Barbados: rapidly settled in the previous century, it offered opportunities for emigrants. The Irish Privy Council in 1729 complained of the number of Protestants seduced out of the kingdom.

for many years, upon this important subject, and maturely weighed the several schemes of other projectors, I have always found them grossly mistaken in their computation. It is true a child, just dropped from its dam, may be supported by her milk for a solar year with little other nourishment, at most not above the value of two shillings, which the mother may certainly get, or the value in scraps, by her lawful occupation of begging: and it is exactly at one year old that I propose to provide for them, in such a manner as, instead of being a charge upon their parents, or the parish, or wanting food and raiment for the rest of their lives, they shall, on the contrary, contribute to the feeding and partly to the clothing of many thousands.

There is likewise another great advantage in my scheme, that it will prevent those voluntary abortions, and that horrid practice of women murdering their bastard children, alas, too frequent among us; sacrificing the poor innocent babes, I doubt, more to avoid the expense than the shame; which would move tears and pity in the most savage and inhuman breast.

The number of souls in Ireland being usually reckoned one million and a half, of these I calculate there may be about two hundred thousand couples whose wives are breeders; from which number I subtract thirty thousand couples who are able to maintain their own children, although I apprehend there cannot be so many under the present distresses of the kingdom; but this being granted, there will remain an hundred and seventy thousand breeders. I again substract fifty thousand for those women who miscarry, or whose children die by accident or disease within the year. There only remain an hundred and twenty thousand children of poor parents, annually born: The question therefore is, how this number shall be reared, and provided for; which, as I have already said, under the present situation of affairs, is utterly impossible by all the methods hitherto proposed: for we can neither employ them in handicraft, or agriculture; we neither build houses (I mean in the country), nor cultivate land: they can very seldom pick up a livelihood by stealing until they arrive at six years old, except where they are of towardly parts; although, I confess they learn the rudiments much earlier, during which time they can however be properly looked upon only as *probationers*; as I have been informed by a principal gentleman in the County of Cavan,[4] who

4. County of Cavan: where Swift used to stay with his friend Sheridan.

protested to me that he never knew above one or two instances under the age of six, even in a part of the kingdom so renowned for the quickest proficiency in that art.

I am assured by our merchants that a boy or a girl, before twelve years old, is no saleable commodity, and even when they come to this age, they will not yield above three pounds, or three pounds and half a crown at most on the Exchange; which cannot turn to account either to the parents or kingdom, the charge of nutriment and rags having been at least four times that value.

I shall now therefore humbly propose my own thoughts, which I hope will not be liable to the least objection.

I have been assured by a very knowing American of my acquaintance in London, that a young healthy child well nursed is at a year old a most delicious, nourishing, and wholesome food, whether stewed, roasted, baked, or boiled; and I make no doubt that it will equally serve in a fricassee or a ragout.

I do therefore humbly offer it to public consideration, that of the hundred and twenty thousand children already computed, twenty thousand may be reserved for breed, whereof only one-fourth part to be males; which is more than we allow to sheep, black cattle, or swine; and my reason is that these children are seldom the fruits of marriage, a circumstance not much regarded by our savages, therefore one male will be sufficient to serve four females. That the remaining hundred thousand may at a year old be offered in sale to the persons of quality, and fortune, through the kingdom; always advising the mother to let them suck plentifully in the last month, so as to render them plump, and fat for a good table. A child will make two dishes at an entertainment for friends; and when the family dines alone, the fore- or hindquarter will make a reasonable dish, and seasoned with a little pepper or salt will be very good boiled on the fourth day, especially in winter.

I have reckoned upon a medium, that a child just born will weigh twelve pounds, and in a solar year if tolerably nursed increases to twenty-eight pounds.

I grant this food will be somewhat dear, and therefore very *proper for landlords,* who, as they have already devoured most of the parents, seem to have the best title to the children.

Infants' flesh will be in season throughout the year, but more plentiful in March, and a little before and after: for we are told by a grave au-

thor,[5] an eminent French physician, that fish being a prolific diet, there are more children born in Roman Catholic countries about nine months after Lent than at any other season; therefore reckoning a year after Lent, the markets will be more glutted than usual, because the number of Popish infants is at least three to one in this kingdom; and therefore it will have one other collateral advantage by lessening the number of Papists among us.

I have already computed the charge of nursing a beggar's child (in which list I reckon all cottagers, laborers, and four-fifths of the farmers) to be about two shillings *per annum,* rags included; and I believe no gentleman would repine to give ten shillings for the carcass of a good fat child, which, as I have said, will make four dishes of excellent nutritive meat, when he hath only some particular friend or his own family to dine with him. Thus the squire will learn to be a good landlord, and grow popular among his tenants, the mother will have eight shillings net profit, and be fit for work until she produces another child.

Those who are more thrifty (*as I must confess the times require*) may flay the carcass; the skin of which, artificially dressed, will make admirable gloves for ladies, and summer boots for fine gentlemen.

As to our City of Dublin, shambles may be appointed for this purpose, in the most convenient parts of it; and butchers we may be assured will not be wanting, although I rather recommend buying the children alive, and dressing them hot from the knife, as we do roasting pigs.

A very worthy person, a true lover of his country, and whose virtues I highly esteem, was lately pleased, in discoursing on this matter, to offer a refinement upon my scheme. He said that many gentlemen of this kingdom, having of late destroyed their deer, he conceived that the want of venison might be well supplied by the bodies of young lads and maidens, not exceeding fourteen years of age, nor under twelve; so great a number of both sexes in every country being now ready to starve, for want of work and service: and these to be disposed of by their parents if alive, or otherwise by their nearest relations. But with due deference to so excellent a friend, and so deserving a patriot, I cannot be altogether in his sentiments. For as to the males, my American acquaintance assured me from frequent experience that their flesh was generally tough and

---

5. **grave author:** a reference to Rabelais, whose grave humor Swift much admired.

lean, like that of our schoolboys, by continual exercise, and their taste disagreeable, and to fatten them would not answer the charge. Then as to the females, it would, I think with humble submission, be a loss to the public, because they soon would become breeders themselves: And besides, it is not improbable that some scrupulous people might be apt to censure such a practice (although indeed very unjustly) as a little bordering upon cruelty; which, I confess, hath always been with me the strongest objection against any project, how well soever intended.

But in order to justify my friend, he confessed that this expedient was put into his head by the famous Psalmanazar,[6] a native of the island Formosa, who came from thence to London, above twenty years ago, and in conversation told my friend that in his country when any young person happened to be put to death, the executioner sold the carcass to persons of quality, as a prime dainty; and that, in his time, the body of a plump girl of fifteen, who was crucified for an attempt to poison the emperor, was sold to his Imperial Majesty's Prime Minister of State, and other great mandarins of the court, in joints from the gibbet, at four hundred crowns. Neither indeed can I deny that if the same use were made of several plump young girls in this town, who, without one single groat to their fortunes, cannot stir abroad without a chair, and appear at a playhouse, and assemblies in foreign fineries, which they never will pay for, the kingdom would not be the worse.

Some persons of a desponding spirit are in great concern about that vast number of poor people, who are aged, diseased, or maimed; and I have been desired to employ my thoughts what course may be taken to ease the nation of so grievous an encumbrance. But I am not in the least pain upon that matter, because it is very well known that they are every day dying, and rotting, by cold, and famine, and filth, and vermin, as fast as can be reasonably expected. And as to the younger laborers they are now in almost as hopeful a condition. They cannot get work, and consequently pine away for want of nourishment, to a degree, that if at any time they are accidentally hired to common labor, they have not strength to perform it; and thus the country and themselves are in a fair way of being soon delivered from the evils to come.

I have too long digressed, and therefore shall return to my subject. I think the advantages by the proposal which I have made are obvious and many, as well as of the highest importance.

For first, as I have already observed, it would greatly lessen the number of Papists, with whom we are yearly overrun, being the principal breeders of the nation, as well as our most dangerous enemies; and who stay at home on purpose with a design to deliver the kingdom to the Pretender; hoping to take their advantage by the absence of so many good Protestants, who have chosen rather to leave their country than stay at home, and pay tithes against their conscience to an idolatrous Episcopal curate.

Secondly, The poorer tenants will have something valuable of their own, which by law may be made liable to distress,[7] and help to pay their landlord's rent, their corn and cattle being already seized, and *money a thing unknown.*

Thirdly, Whereas the maintenance of an hundred thousand children, from two years old, and upwards, cannot be computed at less than ten shillings apiece *per annum,* the nation's stock will be thereby increased fifty thousand pounds *per annum;* besides the profit of a new dish, introduced to the tables of all gentlemen of fortune in the kingdom, who have any refinement in taste; and the money will circulate among ourselves, the goods being entirely of our own growth and manufacture.

Fourthly, The constant breeders, besides the gain of eight shillings sterling *per annum,* by the sale of their children, will be rid of the charge of maintaining them after the first year.

Fifthly, This food would likewise bring great custom to taverns, where the vintners will certainly be so prudent as to procure the best receipts for dressing it to perfection, and consequently have their houses frequented by all the fine gentlemen, who justly value themselves upon their knowledge in good eating; and a skillful cook, who understands how to oblige his guests, will contrive to make it as expensive as they please.

Sixthly, This would be a great inducement to marriage, which all wise nations have either encouraged by rewards, or enforced by laws and penalties. It would increase the care and tenderness of mothers toward their children, when they were sure of a settlement for life, to the poor babes, provided in some sort by the public to their annual

---

6. **Psalmanazar:** a French adventurer, who posed as a Japanese convert, settled in London, and published fictitious works about Formosa.

7. **to distress:** to seizure for payment of debt

profit instead of expense. We should see an honest emulation among the married women, *which of them could bring the fattest child to the market.* Men would become as fond of their wives, during the time of their pregnancy, as they are now of their mares in foal, their cows in calf, or sows when they are ready to farrow; nor offer to beat or kick them (as it is too frequent a practice) for fear of a miscarriage.

Many other advantages might be enumerated. For instance, the addition of some thousand carcasses in our exportation of barreled beef; the propagation of swine's flesh, and improvement in the art of making good bacon, so much wanted among us by the great destruction of pigs, too frequent at our tables, and are no way comparable in taste or magnificence to a well-grown, fat yearling child, which roasted whole will make a considerable figure at a Lord Mayor's feast, or any other public entertainment. But this and many others I omit, being studious of brevity.

Supposing that one thousand families in this city would be constant customers for infants' flesh, besides others who might have it at merrymeetings, particularly at weddings and christenings, I compute that Dublin would take off annually about twenty thousand carcasses, and the rest of the kingdom (where probably they will be sold somewhat cheaper) the remaining eighty thousand.

I can think of no one objection that will possibly be raised against this proposal, unless it should be urged that the number of people will be thereby much lessened in the kingdom. This I freely own, and it was indeed one principal design in offering it to the world. I desire the reader will observe, that I calculate my remedy *for this one individual Kingdom of Ireland, and for no other that ever was, is, or, I think, ever can be upon earth.* Therefore let no man talk to me of other expedients: *Of taxing our absentees at five shillings a pound: Of using neither clothes, nor household furniture, except what is of our own growth and manufacture: Of utterly rejecting the materials and instruments that promote foreign luxury: Of curing the expensiveness of pride, vanity, idleness, and gaming in our women: Of introducing a vein of parsimony, prudence, and temperance: Of learning to love our Country, wherein we differ even from* LAPLANDERS, *and the inhabitants of* TOPINAMBOO:[8] *Of quitting our animosities and factions, nor act any longer like the Jews, who were murdering one another at the very moment their city was taken:*[9] *Of being a little cautious not to sell our country and consciences for nothing: Of teaching landlords to have at least one degree of mercy toward their tenants.* Lastly, *of putting a spirit of honesty, industry, and skill into our shopkeepers, who, if a resolution could now be taken to buy only our native goods, would immediately unite to cheat and exact upon us in the price, the measure, and the goodness; nor could ever yet be brought to make one fair proposal of just dealing, though often and earnestly invited to it.*

Therefore I repeat, let no man talk to me of these and the like expedients;[10] until he hath at least a glimpse of hope that there will ever be some hearty and sincere attempt to put them in practice.

But as to myself, having been wearied out for many years with offering vain, idle, visionary thoughts, and at length utterly despairing of success, I fortunately fell upon this proposal, which as it is wholly new, so it hath something *solid* and *real,* of no expense and little trouble, full in our own power, and whereby we can incur no danger in *disobliging* ENGLAND. For this kind of commodity will not bear exportation, the flesh being of too tender a consistence to admit a long continuance in salt; *although perhaps I could name a country which would be glad to eat up our whole nation without it.*

After all I am not so violently bent upon my own opinion as to reject any offer, proposed by wise men, which shall be found equally innocent, cheap, easy, and effectual. But before something of that kind shall be advanced in contradiction to my scheme, and offering a better, I desire the author, or authors, will be pleased maturely to consider two points. First, as things now stand, how they will be able to find food and raiment for an hundred thousand useless mouths and backs. And secondly, there being a round million of creatures in human figure, throughout this kingdom, whose whole subsistence put into a common stock would leave them in debt two millions of pounds sterling; adding those, who are beggars by profession, to

---

8. LAPLANDERS . . . TOPINAMBOO: Even the nomads in the frozen wastes of the Arctic and the most primitive tribes living on the equator in Brazil have more love for their country than the Irish.

9. *city . . . taken:* During the siege of Jerusalem in 70 A.D. a number of prominent men were put to death, falsely charged with being on the side of the Romans.   10. like expedients: For ten years Swift himself had been involved in schemes for the benefit of Ireland, but in spite of his popularity and influence he had found that little could be effected.

the bulk of farmers, cottagers, and laborers with their wives and children, who are beggars in effect; I desire those politicians, who dislike my overture, and may perhaps be so bold to attempt an answer, that they will first ask the parents of these mortals whether they would not at this day think it a great happiness to have been sold for food at a year old, in the manner I prescribe, and thereby have avoided such a perpetual scene of misfortunes as they have since gone through; by the oppression of landlords; the impossibility of paying rent without money or trade; the want of common sustenance, with neither house nor clothes to cover them from the inclemencies of the weather; and the most inevitable prospect of entailing the like, or greater miseries upon their breed forever.

I profess in the sincerity of my heart that I have not the least personal interest in endeavoring to promote this necessary work, having no other motive than the *public good of my country, by advancing our trade, providing for infants, relieving the poor, and giving some pleasure to the rich.* I have no children by which I can propose to get a single penny; the youngest being nine years old, and my wife past childbearing.

VERSES ON THE DEATH
OF DR. SWIFT

Occasioned by Reading a Maxim in Rochefoucault

Swift first refers to this in a letter to Gay, December 1, 1731: "I have been several months writing near five hundred lines on a pleasant subject, only to tell what my friends and enemies will say on me after I am dead. I shall finish it soon, for I add two lines every week, and blot out four and alter eight." The poem was finished and Swift was working through the notes in May, 1732. A version edited and much shortened by Pope was printed in London in 1739; and even the Dublin edition appeared with names and whole passages omitted.

Swift had started to write an autobiography in prose, but he did not get far with it. This poem, written in his characteristic familiar, easy verse, with the notes which he added to it, is a sort of humorous farewell to friends and enemies alike, in which he is able to set down indirectly among his comments on his friends and enemies the impression of himself and his work that he wished to leave behind him. This is given in the last third of the poem, where

> One quite indifferent in the cause,
> My character impartial draws;

and whether or not it is quite impartial, there is perhaps no better introduction to a knowledge of the Dean and an understanding of his writings.

Swift's own notes are retained in the following pages.

Dans l'adversité de nos meilleurs amis nous trouvons quelque chose, qui ne nous deplait pas.

[In the adversity of our best friends, we find something that doth not displease us.]

As *Rochefoucault* his maxims drew
From nature, I believe 'em true:
They argue no corrupted mind
In him; the fault is in mankind.

This maxim more than all the rest
Is thought too base for human breast;
" In all distresses of our friends
We first consult our private ends,
While nature, kindly bent to ease us,
Points out some circumstance to please us."   10

If this perhaps your patience move
Let reason and experience prove.

We all behold with envious eyes,
Our *Equal* raised above our *Size;*
Who would not at a crowded show,
Stand high himself, keep others low?
I love my friend as well as you,
But would not have him stop my view;
Then let me have the higher post;
I ask but for an inch at most.   20

If in a battle you should find,
One, whom you love of all mankind,
Had some heroic action done,
A champion killed, or trophy won;
Rather than thus be overtopped,
Would you not wish his laurels cropped?

Dear honest *Ned* is in the gout,
Lies racked with pain, and you without:
How patiently you hear him groan!
How glad the case is not your own!   30

What poet would not grieve to see,
His brethren write as well as he?
But rather than they should excel,
He'd wish his rivals all in hell.

Her end when Emulation misses,
She turns to Envy, stings and hisses:
The strongest friendship yields to Pride,
Unless the odds be on our side.

Vain human kind! fantastic race!
Thy various follies, who can trace? 40
Self-love, Ambition, Envy, Pride,
Their empire in our hearts divide:
Give others riches, power, and station,
'Tis all on me an usurpation.
I have no title to aspire;
Yet, when you sink, I seem the higher.
In *Pope,* I cannot read a line,
But with a sigh, I wish it mine:
When he can in one couplet fix
More sense than I can do in six: 50
It gives me such a jealous fit,
I cry, Pox take him, and his wit.

Why must I be outdone by *Gay,*
In my own hum'rous biting way?

Arbuthnot is no more my friend,
Who dares to irony pretend;
Which I was born to introduce,
Refined it first, and showed its use.

St. John, as well as *Pultney* knows,
That I had some repute for prose; 60
And till they drove me out of date,
Could maul a minister of state:
If they have mortified my pride,
And made me throw my pen aside;
If with such talents Heaven hath blessed 'em
Have I not reason to detest 'em?

To all my foes, dear Fortune, send
Thy gifts, but never to my Friend:
I tamely can endure the first,
But, this with envy makes me burst. 70

Thus much may serve by way of proem,
Proceed we therefore to our poem.

The time is not remote, when I
Must by the course of nature die:
When I foresee my special friends,
Will try to find their private ends:
Tho' it is hardly understood,
Which way my death can do them good,
Yet, thus methinks, I hear 'em speak;
"See, how the Dean begins to break: 80
Poor gentleman, he droops apace,
You plainly find it in his face:
That old vertigo in his head,
Will never leave him, till he's dead:
Besides, his memory decays,
He recollects not what he says;
He cannot call his friends to mind;
Forgets the place where last he dined:
Plies you with stories o'er and o'er,
He told them fifty times before. 90

How does he fancy we can sit,
To hear his out-of-fashioned wit?
But he takes up with younger folks,
Who for his wine will bear his jokes:
Faith, he must make his stories shorter,
Or change his comrades once a quarter:
In half the time, he talks them round;
There must another set be found.

"For poetry, he's past his prime,
He takes an hour to find a rhyme: 100
His fire is out, his wit decayed,
His fancy sunk, his Muse a jade.
I'd have him throw away his pen;
But there's no talking to some men."

And, then their tenderness appears
By adding largely to my years:
"He's older than he would be reckoned,
And well remembers *Charles* the Second.

"He hardly drinks a pint of wine;
And that, I doubt, is no good sign. 110
His stomach too begins to fail:
Last year we thought him strong and hale;
But now, he's quite another thing;
I wish he may hold out till Spring."

Then hug themselves, and reason thus:
"It is not yet so bad with us."

In such a case they talk in tropes,
And, by their fears express their hopes,
Some great misfortune to portend,
No enemy can match a friend. 120
With all the kindness they profess,
The merit of a lucky guess
(When daily Howd'y's come of course,
And servants answer: *Worse and worse*)
Would please 'em better than to tell,
That, *God* be praised, the Dean is well.
Then he who prophesied the best,
Approves his foresight to the rest:
"You know, I always feared the worst,
And often told you so at first": 130
He'd rather choose, that I should die,
Than his prediction prove a lie.
Not one foretells I shall recover;
But, all agree, to give me over.

Yet should some neighbor feel a pain,
Just in the parts, where I complain;
How many a message would he send?
What hearty prayers that I should mend?
Inquire what regimen I kept;
What gave me ease, and how I slept? 140
And more lament, when I was dead,
Than all the snivelers round my bed.

My good companions, never fear,
For though you may mistake a year;
Though your prognostics run too fast,
They must be verified at last.

Behold the fatal day arrive!
" How is the Dean? " " He's just alive."
Now the departing prayer is read:
" He hardly breathes. The Dean is dead."   150
Before the passing bell begun,
The news thro' half the town has run.
" O, may we all for death prepare!

What has he left? And who's his heir? "
" I know no more than what the news is,
'Tis all bequeathed to public uses."
" To public use! A perfect whim!
What had the public done for him!
Mere Envy, Avarice, and Pride!
He gave it all: — But first he died,   160
And had the Dean, in all the nation,
No worthy friend, no poor relation?
So ready to do strangers good,
Forgetting his own flesh and blood? "

Now Grub Street wits are all employed,
With elegies, the town is cloyed;
Some paragraph in ev'ry paper,
To *curse* the *Dean,* or *bless* the Drapier.°

The doctors tender of their fame,
Wisely on me lay all the blame: 170
" We must confess his case was nice;
But he would never take advice:
Had he been ruled, for aught appears,
He might have lived these twenty years:
For when we opened him we found,
That all his vital parts were sound."

From *Dublin* soon to *London* spread,
'Tis told at court, the Dean is dead.°

Kind Lady *Suffolk*° in the spleen,
Runs laughing up to tell the Queen,   180

The Queen so gracious, mild, and good,
Cries, " Is he gone? 'Tis time he should.
He's dead you say; Why, let him rot;
I'm glad the medals were forgot.°
I promised them, I own; but when?
I only was the Princess then;
But now as consort of the King
You know 'tis quite a different thing."

Now, *Chartres*° at Sir *Robert's* levee,
Tells, with a sneer, the tidings heavy: 190
" Why, is he dead without his shoes? "
(Cries *Bob*°) " I'm sorry for the news;
Oh, were the wretch but living still,
And, in his place my good friend *Will;*°
Or, had a miter on his head
Provided *Bolingbroke*° were dead."
Now, *Curll*° his shop from rubbish drains;
Three genuine tomes of *Swift's* Remains.
And then, to make them pass the glibber,
Revised by *Tibbalds, Moore,* and *Cibber.*°   200

her with a present worth ten pounds, which she promised before he should return to Ireland, but on his taking leave, the medals were not ready.   **184.** The medals were to be sent to the Dean in four months, but she forgot them, or thought them too dear. The Dean being in Ireland sent Mrs. Howard a piece of Indian plaid made in that kingdom, which the Queen seeing took from her and wore it herself, and sent to the Dean for as much as would clothe herself and children, desiring he would send the charge of it. He did the former. It cost £35, but he said he would have nothing except the medals. He was the summer following in England, was treated as usual, and she being then Queen, the Dean was promised a settlement in England, but returned as he went, and instead of favor or medals, hath been ever since under her Majesty's displeasure.   **189.** Chartres is a most infamous, vile scoundrel, grown from a footboy, or worse, to a prodigious fortune both in England and Scotland. He had a way of insinuating himself into all Ministers under every change, either as pimp, flatterer, or informer. He was tried at seventy for a rape, and came off by sacrificing a great part of his fortune (he is since dead, but this poem still preserves the scene and time it was writ in).   **192.** Sir Robert Walpole, Chief Minister of State, treated the Dean in 1726 with great distinction, invited him to dinner at Chelsea, with the Dean's friends chosen on purpose; appointed an hour to talk with him of Ireland, to which kingdom and people the Dean found him no great friend; for he defended Wood's project of halfpence, etc. The Dean would see him no more; and upon his next year's return to England, Sir Robert, on an accidental meeting, only made a civil compliment, and never invited him again.   **194.** Mr. William Pulteney, from being Mr. Walpole's intimate friend, detesting his administration, opposed his measures, and joined with my Lord Bolingbroke, to represent his conduct in an excellent paper, called the *Craftsman,* which is still continued.   **196.** Henry St. John, Lord Viscount Bolingbroke, Secretary of State to Queen Anne of blessed memory. He is reckoned the most universal genius in Europe; Walpole, dreading his abilities, treated him most injuriously, working with King George, who forgot his promise of restoring the said lord, upon the restless importunity of Walpole.   **197.** Curll hath been the most infamous bookseller of any age or country. His character in part may be found in Mr. Pope's *Dunciad.* He published three volumes all charged on the Dean, who never writ three pages of them. He hath used many of the Dean's friends in almost as vile a manner.   **200.** Three stupid verse writers in London, the

DEATH OF DR. SWIFT.   **168.** [Swift's notes] The author imagines, that the scribblers of the prevailing party, which he always opposed, will libel him after his death; but that others will remember him with gratitude, who consider the service he had done to Ireland, under the name of M. B., Drapier, by utterly defeating the destructive project of Wood's halfpence, in five letters to the people of Ireland, at that time read universally, and convincing every reader.   **178.** The Dean supposeth himself to die in Ireland.   **179.** Mrs. Howard, afterwards Countess of Suffolk, then of the Bedchamber to the Queen, professed much friendship for the Dean. The Queen then Princess, sent a dozen times to the Dean (then in London) with her command to attend her; which at last he did, by advice of all his friends. She often sent for him afterwards, and always treated him very graciously. He taxed

He'll treat me as he does my betters.
Publish my Will, my Life, my Letters.°
Revive the libels born to die;
Which *Pope* must bear, as well as I.

Here shift the scene, to represent
How those I love, my death lament.
Poor *Pope* will grieve a month; and *Gay*
A week; and *Arbuthnot* a day.

St. *John* himself will scarce forbear,
To bite his pen, and drop a tear.   210
The rest will give a shrug and cry,
I'm sorry; but we all must die.
Indifference clad in Wisdom's guise,
All fortitude of mind supplies:
For how can stony bowels melt,
In those who never pity felt;
When *We* are lashed, *They* kiss the rod;
Resigning to the will of God.

The fools, my juniors by a year,
Are tortured with suspense and fear.   220
Who wisely thought my age a screen,
When death approached, to stand between:
The screen removed, their hearts are trembling,
They mourn for me without dissembling.

My female friends, whose tender hearts,
Have better learned to act their parts,
Receive the news in *doleful dumps,*
" The Dean is dead (*and what is trumps?*)
Then Lord have mercy on his soul.
(Ladies I'll venture for the *Vole.*)   230
Six Deans they say must bear the pall.
(I wish I knew what *King* to call.)
Madam, your husband will attend
The funeral of so good a friend.
No madam, 'tis a shocking sight,
And he's engaged tomorrow night!
My Lady *Club* would take it ill,
If he should fail her at *Quadrill.*
He loved the Dean. (*I lead a Heart.*)
But dearest friends, they say, must part.   240

His time was come, he ran his race;
We hope he's in a better place."

Why do we grieve that friends should die?
No loss more easy to supply.
One year is past; a different scene;
No further mention of the Dean;
Who now, alas, no more is missed,
Than, if he never did exist.
Where's now this fav'rite of *Apollo?*
Departed; *and his Works must follow:*   250
Must undergo the common fate;
His kind of wit is out of date.
Some country squire to *Lintot*° goes,
Inquires for *Swift* in Verse and Prose:
Says *Lintot,* " I have heard the Name:
He died a year ago." The same.
He searcheth all his shop in vain;
" Sir, you may find them in *Duck Lane:*°
I sent them with a load of books,
Last *Monday,* to the pastry cooks.   260
To fancy they could live a year!
I find you're but a stranger here.
The Dean was famous in his time;
And had a kind of knack at rhyme:
His way of writing now is past;
The town hath got a better taste:
I keep no antiquated stuff;
But, spick and span I have enough.
Pray, do but give me leave to shew 'em,
Here's *Colley Cibber's* Birthday Poem.   270
This Ode you never yet have seen,
By *Stephen Duck,* upon the Queen.
Then, here's a Letter finely penned
Against the *Craftsman* and his friend;
It clearly shows that all reflection
On ministers, is disaffection.
Next, here's Sir *Robert's* Vindication,°
And Mr. *Henley's* last Oration:°
The hawkers have not got 'em yet,
Your Honor please to buy a set?   280
Here's *Wolston's*° Tracts, the twelfth edition;
'Tis read by every politician:

253. Bernard Lintot, a bookseller in London. *Vide* Mr. Pope's *Dunciad.*   258. A place in London where old books are sold. 277. Walpole hires a set of Party Scribblers, who do nothing else but write in his defense.   278. Henley is a clergyman who, wanting both merit and luck to get preferment, or even to keep his curacy in the Established Church, formed a new conventicle, which he calls an Oratory. There, at set times, he delivereth strange speeches compiled by himself and his associates, who share the profit with him. Every hearer pays a shilling each day for admittance. He is an absolute dunce, but generally reputed crazy.   281. Wolston was a clergyman, but for want of bread, hath in several treatises, in the most blasphemous manner, attempted to turn our Saviour and his miracles into ridicule. He is much caressed by many great courtiers, and by all the infidels, and his books read generally by the court ladies.

last to the shame of the court, and the highest disgrace to wit and learning, was made laureate. Moore, commonly called Jemmy Moore, son of Arthur Moore, whose father was jailer of Monaghan in Ireland. See the character of Jemmy Moore, and Tibalds, Theobald, in the *Dunciad.*   202. Curll is notoriously infamous for publishing the lives, letters, and last wills and testaments of the nobility and ministers of the state, as well as of all the rogues who are hanged at Tyburn. He hath been in custody of the House of Lords for publishing or forging the letters of many peers; which made the lords enter a resolution in their journal book, that no life or writings of any lord should be published without the consent of the next heir at law, or license from their House.

The country members, when in town,
To all their boroughs send them down:
You never met a thing so smart;
The courtiers have them all by heart:
Those maids of honor (who can read)
Are taught to use them for their creed.
The rev'rend author's good intention,
Hath been rewarded with a pension: 290
He doth an honor to his gown,
By bravely running *priestcraft* down:
He shews, as sure as *God's in Gloc'ster,*
That *Jesus* was a grand impostor:
That all his miracles were cheats,
Performed as jugglers do their feats:
The Church had never such a writer:
A shame, he hath not got a miter! "

Suppose me dead; and then suppose
A club assembled at the *Rose;*   300
Where from discourse of this and that,
I grow the subject of their chat:
And, while they toss my name about,
With favor some, and some without;
One quite indiff'rent in the cause,
My character impartial draws.

" The Dean, if we believe report,
Was never ill received at court:
As for his Works in verse and prose,
I own myself no judge of those: 310
Nor, can I tell what critics thought 'em;
But, this I know, all people bought 'em;
As with a moral view designed
To cure the vices of mankind:
His vein, ironically grave,
Exposed the fool, and lashed the knave:
To steal a hint was never known,
But what he writ was all his own.

" He never thought an honor done him,
Because a Duke was proud to own him: 320
Would rather slip aside, and choose
To talk with wits in dirty shoes:
Despised the fools with stars and garters,
So often seen caressing *Chartres:*°
He never courted men in station,
Nor persons had in admiration;
Of no man's greatness was afraid,
Because he sought for no man's aid.
Though trusted long in great affairs,
He gave himself no haughty airs: 330
Without regarding private ends,
Spent all his credit for his friends:

324. See the notes before on Chartres [l. 189n.].

And, only chose the wise and good;
No flatt'rers; no allies in blood;
But succored virtue in distress,
And seldom failed of good success;
As numbers in their hearts must own,
Who, but for him, had been unknown.

" With princes kept a due decorum,
But never stood in awe before 'em: 340
He followed *David's* lesson just,
In princes never put thy trust.
And, would you make him truly sour,
Provoke him with a *slave in power:*
The *Irish* Senate, if you named,
With what impatience he declaimed!
Fair *liberty* was all his cry;
For her he stood prepared to die;
For her he boldly stood alone;
For her he oft exposed his own.   350
Two kingdoms,° just as faction led,
Had set a price upon his head;
But, not a traitor could be found,
To sell him for six hundred pound.

" Had he but spared his tongue and pen,
He might have rose like other men:
But, power was never in his thought;
And, wealth he valued not a groat:
Ingratitude he often found,
And pitied those who meant the wound: 360
But, kept the tenor of his mind,
To merit well of human kind:
Nor made a sacrifice of those
Who still were true, to please his foes.
He labored many a fruitless hour
To reconcile his friends in power;°
Saw mischief by a faction brewing,
While they pursued each other's ruin.
But, finding vain was all his care,
He left the Court in mere despair.   370

351. In the year 1713, the late Queen was prevailed with by an address of the House of Lords in England, to publish a proclamation, promising three hundred pounds to whatever person would discover the author of a pamphlet called *The Public Spirit of the Whigs;* and in Ireland, in the year 1724, my Lord Carteret at his first coming into the government, was prevailed on to issue a proclamation for promising the like reward of three hundred pounds, to any person who could discover the author of a pamphlet called *The Drapier's Fourth Letter,* etc., writ against that destructive project of coining halfpence for Ireland; but in neither kingdoms was the Dean discovered.   366. Queen Anne's ministry fell to variance from the first year after their ministry began. Harcourt the Chancellor, and Lord Bolingbroke the Secretary, were discontented with the Treasurer Oxford, for his too much mildness to the Whig party; this quarrel grew higher every day until the Queen's death. The Dean, who was the only person that endeavored to reconcile them, found it impossible; and thereupon retired to the country about ten weeks before that fatal event,

"And, oh! how short are human schemes!
Here ended all our golden dreams.
What *St. John's* skill in state affairs,
What *Ormond's* valor, *Oxford's* cares,
To save their sinking country lent,
Was all destroyed by one event.
Too soon that precious life was ended,°
On which alone, our weal depended.
"When up a dangerous faction starts,°
With wrath and vengeance in their hearts;   380
By solemn League and Cov'nant bound,
To ruin, slaughter, and confound;
To turn religion to a fable,
And make the government a *Babel:*
Pervert the law, disgrace the gown,
Corrupt the Senate, rob the Crown;
To sacrifice old England's glory,
And make her infamous in story.
When such a tempest shook the land,
How could unguarded virtue stand?   390

"With horror, grief, despair the Dean
Beheld the dire destructive scene:
His friends in exile, or the Tower,
Himself within the frown of power;°
Pursued by base envenomed pens,
Far to the land of slaves and fens; °
A servile race in folly nursed,
Who truckle most, when treated worst.

"By innocence and resolution,
He bore continual persecution;   400
While numbers to preferment rose;
Whose merits were, to be his foes.
When *ev'n his own familiar friends*
Intent upon their private ends;
Like renegadoes now he feels,
Against him lifting up their heels.

"The Dean did by his pen defeat
An infamous destructive cheat.°

Taught fools their int'rest how to know;
And gave them arms to ward the blow.   410
Envy hath owned it was his doing,
To save that helpless land from ruin;
While they who at the steerage stood,
And reaped the profit, sought his blood.

"To save them from their evil fate,
In him was held a crime of state.
A wicked monster on the bench,°
Whose fury blood could never quench;
As vile and profligate a villain,
As modern *Scroggs,* or old *Tressilian;*°   420
Who long all justice had discarded,
Nor feared he GOD, nor Man regarded;
Vowed on the Dean his rage to vent,
And make him of his zeal repent;
But Heaven his innocence defends,
The grateful people stand his friends:
Not strains of law, nor judges' frown,
Nor topics brought to please the crown,
Nor witness hired, nor jury picked,
Prevail to bring him in convict.   430

"In exile° with a steady heart,
He spent his life's declining part;
Where folly, pride, and faction sway,
Remote from *St. John,*° Pope, and *Gay.*

"His friendship there to few confined,°
Were always of the middling kind:
No fools of rank, a mongrel breed,
Who fain would pass for Lords indeed;
Where titles give no right or power,
And peerage is a withered flower,°   440

upon which he returned to his deanery in Dublin, where for many years he was worried by the new people in power, and had hundreds of libels writ against him in England.   **377.** In the height of the quarrel between the ministers, the Queen died. **379.** Upon Queen Anne's death the Whig faction was restored to power, which they exercised with the utmost rage and revenge; impeached and banished the chief leaders of the Church party; and stripped all their adherents of what employments they had, after which England was never known to make so mean a figure in Europe. The greatest preferments in the Church in both kingdoms were given to the most ignorant men; fanatics were publicly caressed; Ireland utterly ruined and enslaved; only great ministers heaping up millions; and so affairs continue until this present 3rd of May, 1732, and are likely to remain so.   **394.** Upon the Queen's death, the Dean returned to live in Dublin, at his deanery house. Numberless libels were writ against him in England, as a Jacobite; he was insulted in the street, and at nights he was forced to be attended by his servants armed. **396.** The land of slaves and fens is Ireland.   **408.** One Wood, a

hardware man from England, had a patent for coining copper halfpence in Ireland, to the sum of £108,000, which in the consequence, must leave that kingdom without gold or silver. [See *Drapier Letter.*]   **417.** One Whitshed was then Chief Justice. He had some years before prosecuted a printer for a pamphlet writ by the Dean, to persuade the people of Ireland to wear their own manufactures. Whitshed sent the jury down eleven times, and kept them nine hours, until they were forced to bring in a special verdict. He sat as judge afterwards on the trial of the printer of the Drapier's *Fourth Letter;* but the jury, against all he could say or swear, threw out the bill. All the kingdom took the Drapier's part, except the courtiers, or those who expected places. The Drapier was celebrated in many poems and pamphlets: his sign was set up in most streets of Dublin (where many of them still continue) and in several country towns. **420.** Scroggs was Chief Justice under King Charles the Second. His judgment always varied in state trials, according to directions from court. Tressilian was a wicked judge, hanged above three hundred years ago.   **431.** In Ireland, which he had reason to call a place of exile; to which country nothing could have driven him but the Queen's death, who had determined to fix him in England, in spite of the Duchess of Somerset, etc.   **434.** Henry St. John, Lord Viscount Bolingbroke, mentioned before. **435.** In Ireland the Dean was not acquainted with one single lord spiritual or temporal. He only conversed with private gentlemen of the clergy or laity, and but a small number of either.   **440.** The

He would have held it a disgrace,
If such a wretch had known his face.
On rural squires, that kingdom's bane,
He vented oft his wrath in vain:
Biennial squires, to market brought;°
Who sell their souls and votes for naught;
The nation stripped go joyful back,
To rob the Church, their tenants rack,
Go snacks with rogues and rapparees°
And, keep the peace, to pick up fees: 450
In every job to have a share,
A jail or barrack to repair;°
And turn the tax for public roads
Commodious to their own abodes.

" Perhaps I may allow, the Dean
Had too much satire in his vein;
And seemed determined not to starve it,
Because no age could more deserve it.

peers of Ireland lost their jurisdiction by one single Act, and
tamely submitted to this infamous mark of slavery without the
least resentment or remonstrance.   445. The parliament, as
they call it, in Ireland meet but once in two years, and after
having given five times more than they can afford, return home
to reimburse themselves by all country jobs and oppressions, of
which some few only are here mentioned.   449. The highwaymen in Ireland, are, since the late wars there, usually called
rapparees, which was a name given to those Irish soldiers who in
small parties used at that time to plunder the Protestants.
452. The army in Ireland is lodged in barracks, the building and
repairing whereof and other charges have cost a prodigious sum
to that unhappy kingdom.

Yet, malice never was his aim;
He lashed the vice, but spared the name.   460
No individual could resent,
Where thousands equally were meant.
His satire points at no defect,
But what all mortals may correct:
For he abhorred that senseless tribe,
Who call it humor when they gibe:
He spared a hump, or crooked nose,
Whose owners set not up for beaux.
True genuine dullness moved his pity,
Unless it offered to be witty.   470
Those, who their ignorance confessed,
He ne'er offended with a jest;
But laughed to hear an idiot quote,
A verse from *Horace,* learned by rote.

" He knew an hundred pleasant stories,
With all the turns of *Whigs* and *Tories:*
Was cheerful to his dying day,
And friends would let him have his way.

" He gave the little wealth he had,
To build a house for fools and mad: 480
And showed by one satiric touch,
No nation wanted it so much:
That Kingdom° he hath left his debtor,
I wish it soon may have a better."

483. Meaning Ireland, where he now lives, and probably may
die.

Alexander Pope

1688–1744

ALEXANDER POPE was born on the twenty-first of May, 1688, into the modest Roman Catholic household of a London linen tradesman and his second wife.[1] To be an English Catholic in Pope's day, and especially after the expulsion of the Catholic king, James II, in the year of the poet's birth, was to be in some important respects an alien in one's native land. Though the anti-Catholic laws were seldom rigidly enforced, Catholics were legally prohibited from practicing their religion openly, from taking degrees at public school or university, from entering several of the learned professions, from sitting in parliament or holding office. During much of Pope's lifetime, Catholics were also subject to double taxes and to restrictions that forbade their "taking any lands by purchase" or residing within ten miles of London.

These discriminations may have influenced Pope's eventual preference for the Tory party as against the Whig, since the latter embraced the most intolerant anti-Catholic groups in England, the commercial middle classes. But they cannot be said to have determined his career. It had been plain from earliest boyhood that his inclinations lay toward poetry, a study not easily impaired by legislation, and this interest was undoubtedly confirmed by the increasing delicacy of his constitution, manifested by the time he was fully grown in a crippling curvature of the

spine, and later in chronic headaches, asthma, and all the other disorders which made up what he calls in the *Epistle to Dr. Arbuthnot* "this long disease, my life."

Pope's literary career begins at Binfield in Windsor Forest, where his parents went to live when he was twelve, apparently in compliance with the ten-mile law. His education, which had been conducted up to this point not very efficiently by family priests and at two or three small Catholic schools, he now took under his own direction. He taught himself Homer's Greek, went up to London to learn Italian and French, pored over the Latin and English poets while he tried on for size a good many of their subjects and styles, and composed before he was sixteen a "kind of play," a tragedy, and a fragmentary epic which have happily not survived.

Even as a youth, however, Pope had too keen an interest in life and people to confine himself to books. He took long rambles on horseback in the Windsor countryside, pausing, as we may observe from his poem on the subject, to catch in the clear azure gleam of the Loddon the reflection of "the headlong mountains and the downward skies," or to watch, with the mixed feelings which that poem also records, the stag fleeing from the hounds, the struck pheasant fluttering in his blood. Later, as he grew on to manhood, he laughed and flirted in the gardens of nearby Mapledurham with the Blount sisters, "the fair-haired Martha and Teresa brown," young ladies who seemed sometimes encouragingly to forget, in their pleasure at his witty sallies, that he was only four feet six, known

[1] This introduction draws at some points on ideas I have presented more fully in "Wit and Poetry and Pope: Some Observations on His Imagery" in *Pope and His Contemporaries* (ed. by J. L. Clifford and L. A. Landa), 1950; in "The Muse of Satire" in *Studies in the Literature of the Augustan Age* (ed. by R. C. Boys), 1952; and in an essay on satire and society as yet unpublished.

even to those who loved him as "little Pope," and to himself as "little Alexander that the women laugh at." Warm friendships were struck up, too, with men: with old Sir William Trumbull, a scholarly retired statesman, who watched with avuncular enthusiasm the progress of Pope's first memorable poems, the *Pastorals,* and suggested to him the writing of *Windsor Forest* and the translating of Homer; with John Caryll, who became his lifelong friend and correspondent, and whose concern a little later about a misunderstanding between the Petre and Fermor families supplied the germ of the *Rape of the Lock;* and with Wycherley the dramatist, a nodding ruin left over from the Restoration, through whose influence he began to come to the attention of the literary world.

When the *Pastorals* were published in 1709, Pope entered on the first of the two miraculous decades in his creative life. During the next eleven years, he wrote, apart from minor work, the *Essay on Criticism* (1711), both versions of the *Rape of the Lock* (1712, 1714), *Windsor Forest* (1713), the *Temple of Fame* (1715), *Eloïsa to Abelard* (1717), and the entire six volumes of his translation of the *Iliad* (1715-20) — an output not to be matched in English poetry for a hundred years. In the early part of the decade, he met often with a little group of Tory boon companions, who before the fall of their party on the queen's death in 1714 were gathered around the ministry of Lords Oxford and Bolingbroke — Swift, Arbuthnot, Atterbury, Parnell. With these kindred spirits and his new friend John Gay, he helped found the so-called Scriblerus Club, a festive and vinous organization whose lucubrations on the pedantries of the age, taking shape around a learned blockhead named Martinus Scriblerus, left their mark years after on both *Gulliver's Travels* and the *Dunciad.* Though this association saw the beginning of some of Pope's most lasting friendships, it was itself unhappily short-lived. On the accession of the Hanoverians, Oxford was disgraced, Bolingbroke had to flee for his life to France, and Swift, his hopes of preferment in England forever dashed by the ascendancy of the Whigs, went back to his Irish deanery. From this exile, he was to return only twice to England, before passing in 1740 into the stonelike silence of the deaf and mad.

During these same early years, Pope was also courted by Steele and Addison on behalf of the Whig literary circles, which they dominated. This was the crucial period of transition to party government in English politics, when party leaders kept strings of writers as noblemen kept horses, and Pope was judged a likely prize by either side. But the friendship with Addison was doomed before it began. Even if Pope had had it in him to become a Whig, he did not have it in him to be a follower, and Addison could bear no brother near the throne. Pope was warm, impulsive, mischievous, sensitive as a snail's horn to criticism, and could be surreptitious and guileful when need required. Addison, by contrast, was prim, jealous, consciously exemplary, and always busy, like Pope himself at a later period, seeming more exemplary than he was. Pope had been guilty of some cruel horseplay in punishing one of Addison's enemies, which was likely to impugn the latter's reputation for imperturbable uprightness. Addison may have been guilty of first encouraging Pope in his translation of Homer and then transferring his support and praise to a rival version, which there is reason to believe he helped inspire. When the inevitable explosion came, it produced the famous lines on Atticus, written and sent to Addison possibly in 1716, but subsequently incorporated in the *Epistle to Dr. Arbuthnot.* It also terminated Pope's brief flirtation with the Whigs.

By 1716 Pope's literary affairs, which were multiplying with his fame, required a residence nearer London. Accordingly, the house in the forest was given up, and after an interlude of two years at Chiswick, where his father died, Pope in 1718 moved with his mother to Twickenham, a village on the Thames convenient to the capital but outside the forbidden limit. Here he leased a small dwelling with some five acres of ground about it, and set to work building, gardening, landscaping, till the place was gradually transformed. The result was not quite a Roman villa, though it had a temple of sorts, and a vineyard, and, after his mother's death in 1733, a small obelisk in her memory; nor quite a model in miniature of a great peer's estate, though by his example at Twickenham as well as by his influence with noble friends, Pope exercised a liberalizing influence on English landscaping. It was something betwixt and between — and, though he can hardly have intended it so, a residence well suited to the imagination that had already grasped in one grotesque yet thrilling vision Belinda's dressing table and the windy plains of Troy, and was soon to do likewise, in the satires of the second miraculous decade (inaugurated by the *Dunciad* of 1728-29), for the England of George Augustus II of Hanover and the imperium of Augustan Rome.

Pope lived at Twickenham, in this modern Tusculum, until his death in 1744. During the '20's, for the most part, his imagination lay fallow. He wrote little original poetry, busying himself instead with a collaborative translation of the *Odyssey* (1725-26), an edition of Shakespeare (1725), and his grotto. This last was a cavelike underpass which he caused to be constructed beneath a highway dividing his property. From its doors — so he wrote Edward Blount — you look "thro' a sloping arcade of trees and see the sails on the river passing suddenly and vanishing," and when you close the doors, "it becomes on the instant, from a luminous room, a *camera obscura*," on the walls of which, inset with bits of looking glass, "all objects of the river, hills, woods, and boats are forming a moving picture in their visible radiations." For Pope's imagination, this place of retirement and meditation became increasingly a symbol of the philosophic life and mind. It was a refuge that could be posed against the ways and motives of the materialism he saw around him, yet a refuge where these ways and motives could be flashed at will upon the screen of poetry, like the ever moving picture on the wall.

With Bolingbroke's return from exile in 1725 and Swift's two visits to Twickenham in 1726 and 1727, Pope's poetic powers rekindled. Swift brought memories of Martinus Scriblerus, and snatched from Pope's fireplace, the story goes, an about-to-be-discarded satire on bad poets which grew thereafter rapidly into the *Dunciad* of 1728 and the *Dunciad Variorum* of 1729, while Bolingbroke, as everybody knows, generated in Pope the philosophical enthusiasm, though not necessarily the philosophy itself, which eventuated in the *Moral Essays* (1731-35) and the *Essay on Man* (1733-34). Through Bolingbroke, too, in the '30's, Pope's Muse took a political turn. The house and grotto at Twickenham became one of the meeting places of the Patriots, as they liked to call themselves — leaders both Whig and Tory of the parliamentary opposition to Walpole — and their views of the general disintegration of the nation under that "Great Man," while not always disinterested, unquestionably affected the poet's outlook, stiffening the accents of his satire after 1735 and deepening the "darkness visible" of the fourth book of the *Dunciad* in 1742.

By this time, and indeed well before it, "Mr. Pope" had become something very like a national institution. His financial independence had long been secured by the success of his Homer, establishing him as the first English man of letters since Shakespeare to make his fortune by his pen. He was loved by many, hated and feared by many, known to everyone. Through his house and garden for three decades passed an almost unending procession of friends, visitors, and acquaintances from every level of the realm: Bathurst, Burlington, Bolingbroke, Cobham, Chesterfield, Peterborough, Queensbury, Oxford, Marchmont, Lyttelton, Frederick, Prince of Wales, and many another — his friends among the great; the eminent physicians Mead and Cheselden; the lawyer Fortescue, Master of the Rolls, and the lawyer Murray, later Lord Chief Justice; the painters Kneller, Jervas, Richardson, Van Loo; the sculptor Roubiliac; the architects and landscapists Kent and Bridgman; the philosopher George Berkeley; the poet's intimates among the writers, Gay, Garth, Congreve, Arbuthnot, Swift; and his plain friends Bethell, Caryll, Ralph Allen, and Martha Blount. Here came Voltaire in 1726 to pay his respects to the British Homer. Here came often young Joseph Spence of Oxford, whose jottings might have made him the poet's Boswell if he had had a share of Boswell's dramatic instinct. Here regularly, fresh with news of Grub Street, came the derelict poet Richard Savage, Johnson's friend, to whose support Pope contributed. And always, as we do not need the *Epistle to Dr. Arbuthnot* to tell us, there was the choir of apprentices and crackpots which buzzes about the head of every successful writer, demanding "my friendship, and a prologue, and ten pound."

In these last days, contemporary reports inform us, there was likely to be an awed whisper of "Mr. Pope, Mr. Pope," when the poet entered a public gathering. Hands reached out to touch him, including the hand of Joshua Reynolds, then a boy. His voice, we are told, was "naturally musical"; his manners, "delicate, easy, and engaging"; in his house at Twickenham, "pleasure dwelt" and "elegance presided." But elegance did not preside alone. His body was by this time "very humpbacked and deformed." His cheek muscles were distended by frequent pain, "like small cords." He was so sensible of cold that he wore "a kind of fur doublet under a shirt of very warm coarse linen," and when he rose, was "invested in bodices made of stiff canvas, being scarcely able to hold himself erect till they were laced." His legs indeed were "so slender that he enlarged their bulk with three pairs of stockings drawn on and off by the maid, for he was not able to dress or undress himself."

The paraplegic who could objectify all this in humor:

There are, who to my person pay their court:
I cough like Horace, and, though lean, am short,
Ammon's great son one shoulder had too high,
Such Ovid's nose, and "Sir! you have an eye" —

or could dissolve his own pain in whimsical tenderness for the decay of things in general:

Years following years, steal something every day,
At last they steal us from ourselves away;
In one our frolics, one amusements end,
In one a mistress drops, in one a friend:
This subtle thief of life, this paltry Time,
What will it leave me, if it snatch my rhyme?

is a man whose inner fortitude and magnanimity entitle him to our respect, even though he was on all too many occasions (as some of the notes and headnotes to the poems that follow will illustrate) devious, testy, vain, and unforgiving, like the rest of us.

POPE'S POETRY

I

Pope is a great poet because he has the gift of turning history into symbol, the miscellany of experience into meaning. This is the gift of all the great poets, but it is striking in Pope because the aspects of experience he works with are so transparently mundane. He makes his poetry

out of the litter on a prom girl's dressing table —"Puffs, powders, patches, Bibles, billets-doux"; amorous trophies hanging from mirrors in bachelor rooms — "three garters, half a pair of gloves"; elderly dowagers who "die, and endow a college or a cat"; beat-up heroines of café society — "Still round and round the ghosts of beauty glide, / And haunt the places where their honor died"; or long weekends with dull relatives in the country, where there is nothing to do but "muse, and spill [one's] solitary tea, / Or o'er cold coffee trifle with the spoon."

These quotations are but a way of emphasizing that Pope is predominantly a social poet. His subject is human nature as it appears when viewed against all the paraphernalia of its communal life, its ephemera as well as its deeper concerns, its dignities, duties, pleasures, crimes. For this reason, his poems have much to say, either directly or by implication, about politics and economics, about education and public taste, about literature and the other arts, and, above all, about morals. Pope, Byron said, is "the moral poet of all civilization"; and by this we must assume he meant not that Pope's poetry is moral, since all poetry has its moral aspect, but that it is a poetry which frankly stands guard over *morals*: the systematic value codes of civilized behavior. The men and women in Pope's poetry, we may note in this connection, are usually seen, and see themselves, as the community sees them, either in their social stations as duchesses and serving-maids, or in their social functions as doctors, lawyers, tradesmen, journalists, poets; and they are regularly measured, with a few exceptions like Eloïsa, in terms of their contribution to the common stock of good or ill: they are sages and fools, philanthropists and misers, connoisseurs and Philistines, good citizens and scoundrels.

Pope's language too is social. In most of his poems, it is the speech of the coffeehouse, the street corner, the drawing room, though he has a selected language from which vulgarisms have been removed when he translates Homer, and sometimes, when he writes about nature, he has a second selected language, designed to bring out the moral significance of objects — "The fox *obscene* to gaping tombs retires" — rather than their sensory qualities; or else their place and rank in a universe which is conceived like civil state as a hierarchy of reconciled differences, from "the green myriads in the peopled grass" to the "rapt seraph that adores and burns." Even the well-known lines on the dying pheasant in *Windsor Forest,* which remind us that Pope was an amateur painter and brought a subtler palette of color to English poetry than had appeared in it before, are perhaps less a description of "nature" in the Romantic sense than a moral *exemplum,* less about the beauty of pheasants than the transience of all beauty: "Ah, what avail his glossy, varying dyes, / His purple crest, and scarlet-circled eyes . . . ?" The order of feeling in these lines is much closer to the order of feeling in such seventeenth-century poetry as "The glories of our blood and state / Are shadows not substantial things, / There is no armor against Fate . . ." than to anything written by the Romantic poets. When Wordsworth complained that the poets of Pope's day seldom wrote with their eye on the object, by which he meant with an eye for Romantic interpretation of nature, he was perfectly right. They had their eye on a different object.

II

But though primarily a moral and social poet in this larger perennial sense, Pope inherits certain characteristics from the Augustan age which are not always sufficiently understood by modern readers. Some of the qualities of his style, for instance, reflect the widespread intellectual effort of the period to bring the multiplicities and heterogeneities of observed reality under rational control, which for the Augustans usually meant the control of a general rule. The achievement of Newton in reducing the phenomena of motion to a single comprehensive formula was simply the greatest triumph, and the apparent confirmation, of a method universally applied. Hobbes had sought such a unifying principle for the phenomena of the state in egoism. Locke sought it for the mind in the operation of sensation and reflection. The deists sought it for religion in a generic creed — what would be left if the idiosyncrasies of existing creeds were distilled away. The critics sought it in a comprehensive "art" of poetry, based on the "rules" of individual genres. Even such unlikely bedfellows as the newly invented calculus of the mathematicians, the *carte du tendre* of the seventeenth-century lover, the courtier's *point*

d'honneur, or, closer home, Pope's hypothesis of a ruling passion in men, all bear witness to the overwhelming desire of the age to master a multiplicity of particulars by inducing from them, or deducing them from, a general rule.

Expressed in the stylistic features of Augustan writing, this concern made itself felt in a variety of devices for reducing the complicated to the simple. The maxim was one of these: "A little learning is a dangerous thing." The aphorism was another: "And die of nothing but a rage to live." The portrait of a type was still another: Atossa, Chloe, Atticus, Sporus; Sir Roger de Coverly, Squire Western, Pamela Andrews. And for poetry, the closed couplet with its neat lengths of thought set out in (usually) end-stopped lines was the groundwork of them all. Just here, however, we touch on one of the fundamental sources of strength in the Augustan style. For the habitual strategy of the great masters of this style is to play off against the apparent simplicity of their formulas, whether verbal like the couplet or psychological like the portrait, the real complexities of what is formulated. In this respect, Pope's achievement in the couplet, holding, as Miss Sitwell aptly says, "all the waves, and the towers and the gulfs of the world" in a narrow cage of twenty syllables, has obvious relations to Swift's achievement in *Gulliver,* where other waves, towers, and gulfs are held in the naïve formula of a shipman's tale and in a prose so transparent that it is intelligible in the nursery. Both achievements spring ultimately from the habit of mind that brought the mathematical functions under the law of the calculus, and the motions of bodies under the law of gravitation.

An equally prominent influence on Pope's style and thought was exercised by the Augustan metaphor of tension. This was in origin a very ancient metaphor, going back at least to Heraclitus' image for the world — "As with the bow and the lyre, so with the world: it is the tension of opposing forces that makes the structure one"; and to Cicero's for the state — "So the state achieves harmony by the agreement of unlike individuals, when there is a wise blending of the highest, the lowest, and the intervening middle classes, in the manner of tones; for what musicians call harmony in song is concord in a state." But in the age which had invented the spring-and-balance mechanism of the watch, explained the solar system by pitting the inertia of the planets against the attraction of the sun, formulated the concept of "balance" of power in international relations, the theory of "checks and counterchecks" in "mixed" government, the interpretation of experience in terms of tension seemed to have universal relevance. Thus when Pope has occasion to think about the universe, he thinks at once of opposing forces in equilibrium, sustained by "elemental strife." When he thinks of government, he thinks of "jarring interests," blended in "th' according music of a well-mixed state." When he thinks of human nature, he thinks of the passions whose "well-accorded strife" makes and maintains "the balance" of the mind; or perhaps he thinks of self-love, "the spring of motion," and reason's "comparing balance," as in a watch; or else of man's double duty to himself and society as twin Newtonian motions, whirling the planet-like individual simultaneously around his own axis and around the social sun. Even when he looks at the Windsor countryside, he sees instinctively a scene "harmoniously confused": "Here hills and vales, the woodland and the plain, / Here earth and water seem to *strive* again."

This way of thought is particularly noticeable in Pope's view of the structure of a work of art, and, accordingly, in his own poetic practice. The ideal garden for Pope is one so planted that "strength of shade contends with strength of light"; the ideal painting is one where darker and lighter colorings "invade" each other; the ideal building is "bold" but at the same time "regular"; the ideal poet-critic is one who, like Horace, "judged with coolness, though he sung with fire." For the same reasons, the ideal poem, if we try to define it from Pope's practice, is one in which maximum tension has resulted from a struggle of contraries of many kinds. The contraries may lie in style—the simile of the Alps *vs.* the anecdote of Don Quixote, in the *Essay on Criticism*. Or in theme—the life of Grace *vs.* the life of Nature, in *Eloïsa*. Or in tone—"Atticus" *vs.* "Sporus," in the *Epistle to Dr. Arbuthnot*. Or in matter *vs.* manner—in any of the mock heroic poems. Or in overt *vs.* implicit meaning—in the *Epistle to Augustus,* and the device of irony generally. Or in the subtlety of the thing said *vs.* the simplicity of the formula for saying it, as noted earlier. Here once

more, so far as poetry is concerned, the closed couplet with its movement by thesis and antithesis is the groundwork of all.

This aspect of Augustan writing is one that modern readers must be especially careful not to misapprehend. The Augustans did not write antithetically simply because they liked symmetry and point, though they did like these qualities, as all their arts show. They wrote antithetically partly because the function of literature in their view was to break apart the canned responses and the moral muddles by which man as a social being disguises from himself the real nature of his activities. And the most dramatic way they knew of doing this, whether in prose or verse, was through the explosive mixture of contending attitudes that the structure of thesis and antithesis affords: "The bookful blockhead, ignorantly read"; "And wretches hang that jurymen may dine"; "I am not in the least pain upon that matter, because it is very well known that they are every day dying, and rotting, by cold, and famine, and filth, and vermin, as fast as can be reasonably expected."

Finally, Pope shares with his age the habit of viewing contemporary reality in the light of traditional norms, usually norms derived from classical literature and civilization. This was a habit that could serve in two ways. On the one hand, it offered a means of taking imaginative hold of the vigorous but new and crude mercantile society that lay around him and had produced him; enabled him to distance and humanize it by imposing on it certain orders of value drawn from the English and European past: the massive paradigm of Rome in the satires; the heroic conventions of Homer in the *Rape of the Lock,* the medieval cosmic ladder of degree in the *Essay on Man,* the themes of *Paradise Lost* in the *Dunciad,* the moral implications of British history in *Windsor Forest,* and many more. All these, it is worth pausing to reflect, were mainly social orders of value, therapeutics for the intense individualism that Pope felt working centrifugally in the age. Similarly, in our own day, Mr. Eliot can be said to have helped distance and humanize the raw facts of an industrial culture, through the invocation of Grail mysteries, Greek myths, Dante's *Divine Comedy*, Catholic liturgy, and the contemplative ladder of the mystics—in this case, mainly individualist orders of value, correctives for the collectivist and totalitarian disposition of our century. Both poets have thus worked consciously or unconsciously to " redeem the time." A city crowd can never be the senseless arbitrary fact it was, once it has been seen through Mr. Eliot's eyes by way of Dante: " A crowd flowed over London Bridge, so many, / I had not thought death had undone so many." Nor could the then recently invented paper currency of a mercantilist society be quite the same, after it had been seen through Pope's eyes by way of Virgil: " A leaf, like Sibyl's, scatter[s] to and fro / Our fates and fortunes, as the winds shall blow."

The other utility of traditional norms for Pope was critical. If they helped him redeem the time, they also helped him measure it. They permitted him to place Belinda's world beside Homer's, the dunces beside Aeneas, George II beside Augustus Caesar, Sir Balaam beside Job, and to make all those other confrontations of the paltry and heroic that are a distinctive feature of his work. More especially, in the satires, they supplied him with his poles of value. For the structure of any of Pope's formal satires, it must be noticed, is a structure of debate between a way of life philosophically conditioned, based on classical precedents and the pursuit of " virtue," by which Pope usually means a sense of community responsibility, and another way of life economically conditioned, based on self-interest and the pursuit of gain. On one side of the argument stand the Hanoverian king, who has abdicated his function of moral and cultural leadership: " How shall the Muse, from such a monarch, steal / An hour, and not defraud the public weal? "; the court, with its flattering placemen of Walpole like Sporus: " Beauty that shocks you, parts that none will trust, / Wit that can creep, and pride that licks the dust "; and the trading City, many of its members infected, in Pope's view, with the *laissez-faire* philosophy of the new capitalism and hence indifferent, he feels, to communal obligation: " The grave Sir Gilbert holds it for a rule, / That 'every man in want is knave or fool.' "

On the other side stand the representatives of virtue. To this group belong men like the poet's father, who " walked innoxious thro' his age "; or like the Man of Ross, who is a kind of minor Moses of the Wye and Severn: " From the dry rock, who bade the waters flow? "; or like the Bathursts, Burlingtons, Cobhams, Oxfords, on whose hospitable estates, " English bounty yet awhile may stand, / And honor linger ere it leaves the land." What is particularly characteristic of Pope's use of traditional norms in these poems is that the men of virtue, however urbane they may be in actual life, are endowed in the poetry with the rugged independence of the English countryman, and presented, more often than not, in country settings: Pelham in " Esher's peaceful grove," Burlington among his " cheerful tenants," Peterborough forming quincunxes and ranking vines, the satirist himself in his secluded villa at Twickenham, living frugally " on broccoli and mutton, round the year."

In this alignment of values, it is clearly Pope the Tory who speaks; for the Tories, the country or landed interest, saw in the money power of the Whigs a threat to their way of life. But it is also Pope the poet who speaks. Like his predecessors, Spenser, Shakespeare, and Milton, he was haunted throughout his life (as a study of poems as far apart in time and spirit as *Windsor Forest* and the *Dunciad* makes clear) by a vision of England as the ideal commonwealth to be realized on earth — a Prospero's island, House of Temperance, Garden of Alcinoüs, and demi-Eden, all rolled in one. Pope knows that the vision is only a vision, but it is a cherished vision, and its enemies are real, looming far above the local frictions of Whig and Tory. It is for this reason that he dares invoke beside Cibber in his laureate's chair — emblem of a court's corrupted taste — the great shadow of Milton's Satan on his throne in hell; or beside the dapper Sporus — emblem of a court's corrupted morals — the shadow of the original Tempter, " at the ear of Eve, familiar toad." To Pope's satires, in this sense, we may apply what Miss Marianne Moore has finely said of poems generally: that they are " imaginary gardens, with real toads in them."

III

The enjoyment of Pope, like the enjoyment of the other poets in these volumes, depends to a large extent on bringing to his poetry appropriate expectations. Spenser, as the reader has found already, is not Chaucer, and Milton is not Donne; nor will Browning be like Wordsworth, or Arnold like Yeats. In Pope's case, the expectancies most helpful to a reader coming to his work for the first time can be summarized as follows. First, the experiences which Pope records, though they spring inevitably from his own subjective sensibility, are always reformulated in his poetry in representative terms; to do this is indeed the aim of poetry in Pope's view of it: "What oft was thought, but ne'er so well expressed." Second, Pope's relationship to his audience is invariably dramatic, like Chaucer's. Even when it seems most confessional and confidential, it is fully conscious, the performance of an accomplished public speaker or an actor on the stage. Third, Pope is in no sense a poet of supreme moments, whether of tragic agonies *de profundis* or of soaring exaltations. He is a poet of the long diurnal haul. This is his limitation, but it is also his strength. His poetry neither laments the limits of the human situation nor seeks to transcend or challenge them. It simply accepts them wryly, with a smile.

Perhaps the best way to grasp the representativeness of Pope is to compare his work with Donne's. Donne's poetry, if we may oversimplify to make the point, is intimate. Even if the poem was meant for publication, which is infrequently the case with Donne, the emphasis is on the privacy of the poetic situation. The poet is close-closeted with his mistress, or, in absence, addressing her ear only, or apostrophizing blossoms, or a flea, or that busy old fool, the unruly sun, or talking to his God, or performing any of the other verbal acts which presuppose that the speaker of a poem is "alone," and that the fiction to be maintained in poetry is that of a mind in the actual processes of thought, emotion, speech. Pope's poetry, on the other hand, is public. It is acutely conscious of the social audience beyond the immediate addressee. Its tacit assumption is that the social audience is the real audience, no matter whom the speaker professes to be addressing; and therefore its characteristic fiction is not that of a man undergoing an experience, but that of a man who has already undergone the experience and is now conveying what is representative in it, what is socially viable, to his peers. Donne's typical poem, in other words, and Pope's, are dramatizations

of different stages in the intellective process. The one strives to reproduce the insight, the illumination, the moment of conflict, in all its original flash and drama; the other, to present it after it has been digested — "normalized" — for general use.

This difference can be seen with exceptional clarity in the two poets' management of the couplet. Pope, to be sure, has a virtuosity in the use of this particular medium that was simply not available to poets a century earlier; but this is not the decisive factor. To read in quick succession Donne's fourth satire and Pope's paraphrase of it is to realize that Donne has taken pains to convey the illusion of thought tumbling immediately from the mind, tearing out with it, so to speak, lumps of apparently unpremeditated syntax and haphazard rhyme:

> Well, I may now receive, and die. My sin
> Indeed is great, but yet I have been in
> A purgatory, such as feared hell is
> A recreation to, and scant map of this.

Pope, we discover, has been at equal pains to stress the organization of thought, its articulations into principal and subordinate, prior and posterior, cause and effect; and his opening metaphor is significantly a reference to the stage:

> Well, if it be my time to quit the stage,
> Adieu to all the follies of the age!
> I die in charity with fool and knave,
> Secure of peace at least beyond the grave.
> I've had my Purgatory here betimes,
> And paid for all my satires, all my rhymes.
> The poet's Hell, its tortures, fiends, and flames,
> To this were trifles, toys, and empty names.

Each way of writing, though conditioned in part by the gifts of the man and the age, is essentially an artifice, and each has its triumphs. There is nothing in Pope comparable to Donne's *Anniversaries;* there is nothing in Donne comparable to *Dunciad,* Book IV.

To understand the sense in which Pope's poetry is dramatic, it is helpful, on the other hand, to compare him with the Romantics. Here there are several differences of importance. In the first place, Pope is reticent about revealing his inner self in poetry, as the Romantics are not. There were moments in Pope's life, we know, beset by illness and often by brutal attacks on his deformity, when he could have longed like Keats to fly far above "the weariness, the fever, and the fret, / Here, where men sit and hear each other groan"; but it would have been unthinkable to Pope to make such disclosures in verse. Nor, though he was surely subject to occasional self-pity like other men, could he ever have brought himself to cry out in poetry with Shelley: "I fall upon the thorns of life, I bleed." Pope's afflictions and frustrations, if they enter his poetry at all, must be handled with the humor and self-discipline that we expect of a man who is conscious of a public: "Weak though I am of limb, and short of sight, / Far from a lynx, and not a giant quite. . . ."

Pope's poetry is also dramatic in that he speaks with so many other accents than his own. There is the flatulent inanity of Sir Plume:

> "My Lord, why, what the devil?
> Zounds! damn the lock! 'fore Gad, you must be
>   civil!
> Plague on 't! 'tis past a jest — nay, prithee, pox!
> Give her the hair" — .

There is Papillia, the fashionable cliché-expert: "How charming is a park!" — "Oh, odious, odious trees!" There is the cockney climber, Balaam, into whose description, without direct quotation, Pope fits the idiom that reveals him:

> Sir Balaam now, he lives like other folks,
> He takes his chirping pint, and cracks his jokes.

> My good old Lady catched a cold, and died.

Pope is particularly fond of this device as a way of telescoping the actual motives of a character with the motives which the character likes to believe are his. Thus Cotta, in the *Epistle to Bathurst,* presents his niggardliness to himself as philosophical vegetarianism — "the use of barbarous spits forgot"; choosing to see in his inhospitable English manor a house of spiritual austerities — "some lone Chartreux," and in his penny-pinching habits "no more / Than Brahmins, saints, and sages did before." Just so his spendthrift son sees his prodigality as sacrificial patriotism: "'Tis George and Liberty that crowns the cup, / And zeal for that great House which eats him up."

Even when Pope speaks with his own idiom in his poems, it is a dramatic idiom, changing markedly from poem to poem in accordance with the theme. The easy ingratiation of the *Epistle to Dr. Arbuthnot* is quite a different thing from the imperious homiletics of the *Essay on Man;* and the ostensibly respectful ironist of the epistle to Augustus is not at all the same man as the animated portraitist of the epistle *On the Characters of Women,* tossing off specimens of his ability as he talks. Furthermore, and this is a point that especially distinguishes Pope from the Romantic poets, we are never safe in identifying the speaker in his poems with the actual Alexander Pope. We may call him Pope for purposes of convenience, but always with the recognition that he reveals himself as an actor in a drama, not as a man confiding in us. The distinction is apparent if we think of Wordsworth's use of the word "young" in a famous passage of the *Prelude* about the early days of the French Revolution: "Bliss was it in that dawn to be alive, / And to be young was very heaven" — and then compare it with the remark put into the mouth of the friend with whom Pope professes to converse in his imitation of the first satire of Horace's second book: "Alas, young man! your days can ne'er be long." Wordsworth's *young* is determined by conditions outside the poem, something true, in the years to which the poet refers, of himself in real life. But in real life, when Pope wrote his imitation, he was all but forty-five; his *young* is true only of the satiric speaker of the poem, who is, as always, an assumed identity.

"To the Middle Ages and the Elizabethans," the modern poet Sidney Keyes once noted in his diary, "Death was the leveler; to the seventeenth century, a metaphysical problem; to the eighteenth century, the end of life." This comment, though too sweeping, points directly at the unruffled acceptance of the human situation which has already been mentioned as the limitation of eighteenth-century literature and its strength. If the Augustan age produced little poetry of the rebellious inner man, it was partly because its mode was social, and one does not wear the tumults of the soul before the world; but it was also because the Augustan writer believed profoundly that man is limited, life inexorable. Much of the deepest feeling in Augustan literature is summed up in Johnson's powerful lines paraphrasing the proverb, " Go to the ant, thou sluggard":

Amidst the drowsy charms of dull delight,
Year chases year, with unremitted flight,
Till Want, now following fraudulent and slow,
Shall spring to seize thee like an ambushed foe.

Wordsworth, it is useful to remember, called these lines " a hubbub of words." His disapproval professed to be aimed at Johnson's " poetic diction"; but when one looks at the mood of this passage carefully and then at the mood of Wordsworth's own best work, it is difficult to believe that Johnson's view of the human predicament, governed by irremeable laws of decay, want, and folly leading to eventual defeat, or at best to a sustained cold war between the human will and the human lot, played no part in the Romantic poet's distaste. For the strength of the Romantic spirit is transcendental. In the words of a very famous passage from *The Prelude,*

whether we be young or old,
Our destiny, our being's heart and home,
Is with infinitude, and only there;
With hope it is, hope that can never die,
Effort, and expectation, and desire,
And something evermore about to be.

The Romantic spirit inclines to be impatient with the limited Here and Now, restless for the unlimited There and Then. Its gaze is typically away from this sphere of our sorrow, usually on some higher and happier state of being, which it symbolizes in the lark, the nightingale, the daffodil, the Grecian urn, the west wind, the poet's childhood. And the structure of its poems is not infrequently a kind of soaring flight — a curve of increasing psychical approach — to this ideal world, which at last it touches in an ecstasy, followed, as the moment crumbles, by what Browning finely calls " the pain / Of finite hearts that yearn." Augustan poetry has neither this capacity nor this desire. Soaring, like creeping, is for the Augustan poet a mode of motion inappropriate to man, whose place is firmly fixed, and upright, on the earth.

Donne, too, differs from the Augustans in this respect, though he is no less unlike the Romantics. In the typical poem of Donne, a conflict is stated and then by a witty dialectic taken to an apparent resolution, dramatizing not transcend-

ence but defiant conquest of the world, the mind's ability to find or create out of its own ingenuities a momentary reconciling view. The view is momentary in that the lovers are still apart at the poem's end (" A Valediction Forbidding Mourning "), the sick woman still has her fever (" The Fever "), death is not dead (" Death, Be Not Proud "). But the moment while it lasts becomes the poem, extracted out of time like Mr. Eliot's Chinese jar in " Burnt Norton," a stilled point in a turning world.

The typical Augustan poem realizes something quite remote from this. Here the effort is not to reconcile the conflicting opposites, but to recognize their opposition as part of the settled constitution of things — as in *Windsor Forest* the view of all the hunters is one thing, the view of all the hunted is another, and the poet's sympathy flows to both. The method in this poetry is not that of ingenious thrust and parry, holding a world at bay, but that of a poised, and ironic, elucidation of life's conditions. And the spirit behind it is very different from what has been called, in Donne's case, the mystical individualism of the Renaissance. This is a frame of mind that assimilates all experience to the self, amplifying the psyche and the microcosmic world till it swallows up the macrocosm: " What merchant's ships have my sighs drowned? " " She's all states, and all princes, I." " All women shall adore us, and some men." " I, by love's limbeck am the grave / Of all, that's nothing." " Think then, my soul, that Death is but a groom." In Augustan poetry, the ego has been socially conditioned: " Blessed with each talent and each art to please." It does not challenge life, but threads its way through the mighty maze, amplifying not the psyche but the macrocosm to which the psyche must adjust: " Know thy own point: This kind, this due degree / Of blindness, weakness, Heaven bestows on thee." And it therefore finds the decisive standard of behavior in a " path " or " way " — a radical image of the Augustan age, as defiance or challenge is of the Renaissance and soaring is of the Romantic — usually a middle way.

All of this is particularly evident in Pope, from whom indeed the two last quotations above are drawn. Pope was schooled both by his age and his bitter experience as a hunchback in the art of coming to terms with life. " Blessed are those who expect nothing," he was fond of saying, " for they will never be disappointed "; and the punning remark by which he liked to account for his having constructed a grotto beneath the highway running through his grounds carries the same tone of whimsical resignation: " What we cannot overcome, we must undergo."

For Pope's world is a world of controlled endurance. Homer's poetry for this reason struck such responsive chords in him that it is often impossible to tell in reading the English *Iliad* when Pope is translating Homer's outlook and when his own. " To mourn avails not, man was born to bear." " What must be, must be. Bear thy lot." " The happiest taste not happiness sincere." These sound like Homer, but in fact are Pope. Pope's world is also one of relentless transience. A world where " Years following years, steal something every day," where " Estates have wings, and hang in fortune's power," where " locks, curled or uncurled, *will* turn to gray," where language changes and betrays the poet, colors fade and betray the painter; where, even if (which is too much to hope) immortality should attend on human works, " Alas, how little from the grave we claim! Thou but preserv'st a face, and I a name."

But especially, as earlier suggested, Pope's world is a world of limits. Love has limits: even an Eloïsa has finally to acknowledge, " What dust we dote on, when 'tis man we love." Death too has limits; being, as Keyes says, simply the end of life, so much to be taken for granted that it can be dismissed in a parenthesis: " (. . . since life can little more supply / Than just to look about us and to die)," or compared like passing beauty to the passing sun: " When those fair suns shall set, as set they must." Grief itself has limits for the Augustans. They know that, even if some men do better than the friends of the Unfortunate Lady, who " grieve for an hour, . . . then ' mourn ' a year," no passion burns forever in so frail a lamp as man; and Swift consciously pays Pope's friendship the highest compliment one man can pay another, when he writes in his *Verses on the Death of Dr. Swift:*

> Poor Pope will grieve a month; and Gay
> A week; and Arbuthnot a day.

This is the kind of statement, the English critic Charles Williams reminds us, that sees life tenderly, yet steadily and whole: " for let us be quite honest and ask for which of our friends we should come anywhere near anything that could be called grieving, for anything like a month? And which of them for us? "

Finally, in Pope's world, ideals are strictly limited to what the human vessel can attain. " An honest man's the noblest work of God," Pope says in one place. " Ah! friend! to dazzle let the vain design," he says in another, " To raise the thought, and touch the heart be thine! " " What then remains but well our power to use, / And keep good humor still whate'er we lose," he says in a third. And in a fourth, remembering his father's kindly life and painless death: " O grant me thus to live, and thus to die." There is a certain fine excess missing from such ideals. They seem strangely shrunken, strangely modern, when we recall the towering aspirations of Shakespeare's heroes, or Spenser's knight-at-arms, girt with all the twelve Aristotelian virtues. Yet they have the compensatory strength that comes from being unpretentious, from being available to Everyman as well as knights and heroes; and they require an unsensational but continuing heroism of their own. Indeed, Pope's world, for the very reason that it is less " poetic " than some others, assumes a disturbing familiarity as we live with it. In its noonday hubbub, its humdrum practicality, its muted passions that nevertheless gleam like diamonds in the compression of a phrase; in its crowds and chandeliers and coffee spoons; in its Belindas, Balaams, Bentleys, Bubos, doctors, dunces, swindlers, statesmen; in its happy blends of gravity and gaiety, sympathy and anger, imagination and common sense — it may not be the highest world that English poetry offers us, but it is the one we know the best.

Reading Suggestions

EDITION

The Poems of Alexander Pope (1938–   ), Twickenham Edition. The indispensable edition of Pope's poetry, with full historical introductions, explanatory notes, and a record of Pope's revisions. Volumes ii–v have so far been published, containing all the poems in the present collection except *An Essay on Criticism, Windsor Forest,* " Ode on Solitude," and " To a Young Lady on Her Leaving the Town after the Coronation."

BIOGRAPHY

W. J. Courthope, *Life of Pope,* in the Elwin-Courthope Edition of Pope's *Works* 10 vols. (1871–89), vol. v. The best biography for the general reader, but unreliable on many points about which fuller information is now available.

George Sherburn, *The Early Career of Alexander Pope* (1934). A model work of scholarship, which unfortunately stops at 1727 and may contain more detail than the beginning student can absorb.

CRITICISM

R. K. Root, *The Poetical Career of Alexander Pope* (1938). A blend of criticism and biography, useful for the student new to Pope.

F. R. Leavis, "Pope," and "The Line of Wit," in *Revaluation* (1936). Two first-rate pioneering essays on the poetry of wit and Pope's relation to it.

Geoffrey Tillotson, *The Poetry of Pope* (1938, 1950). The best full-length critical study of Pope's poetry.

J. E. Tobin, *Alexander Pope, 1744–1944* (1945). Invaluable guide through the maze of modern writing about Pope.

Cleanth Brooks, "The Case of Miss Arabella Fermor," in *The Well-Wrought Urn* (1949). Perceptive comment on *The Rape of the Lock* by a distinguished modern critic.

Austin Warren, "The Mask of Pope," in *Rage for Order* (1948). A provocative essay on the cleavage between Augustan poetic theory and practice.

W. K. Wimsatt, "Rhetoric and Poems: The Example of Pope," in *English Institute Essays* (1949). Astute analysis of Pope's rhetorical devices.

L. I. Bredvold, "The Gloom of the Tory Satirists," in *Pope and His Contemporaries,* edited by J. L. Clifford and L. A. Landa (1950). Excellent discussion of the temper of the Augustan age as its satirists saw it.

Ian Jack, *Augustan Satire: Intention and Idiom in English Poetry, 1660–1750* (1952). Valuable comment on the many modes of Augustan satire in verse.

ESSAY ON CRITICISM

The *Essay on Criticism* seems to have been in progress from about 1708, when we know that Pope discussed an early sketch of it with his friend, William Walsh, to 1711, when he published the completed poem at the age of twenty-three. The work belongs to a type of poetry exemplified in ancient literature by Horace's *Ars Poetica,* in the Renaissance by Vida's *De Re Poetica,* and in the Augustan age by Boileau's *Art poétique.*

The question the poem faces up to is one that has to be met by artist and critic in every generation. How can the individual "judgment" or the individual "wit" (a term that signifies equally the creative imagination and the work produced by it) escape from the vicious circle of subjectivism? This question Pope seeks to answer in Part I, the theoretical portion of the *Essay,* through the three terms, Nature, the Ancients, and the Rules.

Nature for Augustan writers is a kind of normalizing principle in the world and man, making for stability and permanence beneath the shifting face of things. To this Nature, therefore, from whose "clear, unchanged, and universal light" our little lights are fed, we must constantly refer our subjective wit and judgment, and rectify them by it as we rectify our differing watches by the true time of the sun. In doing this, study of the great works of the past becomes essential (the Ancients), since these incarnate, as their long survival shows, the very principles of stability and permanence that we mean by Nature: Nature and they are in fact "the same." Correspondingly, the Rules, being nothing more than the fundamentals of effective writing which critics have derived from the great works of the past, are also incarnate Nature: they are "Nature still, but Nature methodized."

Part II of the *Essay* then takes up some of the pitfalls of practical criticism, the aberrations into which those fall who do not rectify their watches but simply trust them. And Part III follows this with a description of ideal critical behavior. The development of the poem as a whole is thus from what the critic or artist is supposed to know, to what he is supposed to do (and especially, not to do), to the aim and manner with and in which he is supposed to do it.

Introduction. That 'tis as great a fault to judge ill, as to write ill, and a more dangerous one to the public. That a *true taste* is as rare as to be found, as a *true genius.* That most men are born with some taste, but spoiled by false *education.* The multitude of *critics,* and causes of them. That we are to study our own *taste,* and know the *limits* of it. *Nature* the best guide of judgment. Improved by *art* and *rules,* which are but *methodized* Nature. Rules derived from the practice of the *ancient poets.* That therefore the *ancients* are necessary to be studied by a critic, particularly *Homer* and *Virgil.* Of *licenses,* and the use of them by the ancients. Reverence due to the *ancients,* and praise of them.

'Tis hard to say, if greater want of skill
Appear in writing or in judging ill;
But, of the two, less dangerous is th' offense
To tire our patience, than mislead our sense.
Some few in that, but numbers err in this,
Ten censure wrong for one who writes amiss;
A fool might once himself alone expose,
Now one in verse makes many more in prose.
'Tis with our judgments as our watches, none
Go just-alike, yet each believes his own.   10
In poets as true genius is but rare,
True taste as seldom is the critic's share;
Both must alike from Heaven derive their light,
These born to judge, as well as those to write.
Let such teach others who themselves excel,
And censure freely who have written well.
Authors are partial to their wit, 'tis true,
But are not critics to their judgment too?

Yet if we look more closely, we shall find
Most have the seeds of judgment in their mind:
Nature affords at least a glimmering light;   21
The lines, though touched but faintly, are drawn
     right.
But as the slightest sketch, if justly traced,
Is by ill coloring but the more disgraced,
So by false learning is good sense defaced:
Some are bewildered in the maze of schools,°
And some made coxcombs° Nature meant but
     fools.
In search of wit these lose their common sense,
And then turn critics in their own defense:
Each burns alike, who can, or cannot write,   30
Or with a rival's, or an eunuch's spite.
All fools have still an itching to deride,
And fain would be upon the laughing side.
If Maevius° scribble in Apollo's spite,
There are who judge still worse than he can write.
   Some have at first for wits, then poets passed,
Turned Critics next, and proved plain fools at last.
Some neither can for wits nor critics pass,
As heavy mules are neither horse nor ass.   39
Those half-learned witlings, numerous in our isle,
As half-formed insects on the banks of Nile;°
Unfinished things, one knows not what to call,
Their generation's so equivocal:
To tell° 'em, would a hundred tongues require,
Or one vain wit's, that might a hundred tire.
   But you who seek to give and merit fame,
And justly bear a critic's noble name,
Be sure yourself and your own reach to know,
How far your genius, taste, and learning go;
Launch not beyond your depth, but be discreet,   50
And mark that point where sense and dulness
     meet.
   Nature to all things fixed the limits fit,
And wisely curbed proud man's pretending wit.
As on the land while here the ocean gains,
In other parts it leaves wide sandy plains,
Thus° in the soul while memory prevails,
The solid power of understanding fails;
Where beams of warm imagination play,
The memory's soft figures melt away.
One science° only will one genius fit;   60
So vast is art, so narrow human wit:
Not only bounded to peculiar° arts,
But oft in those confined to single parts.
Like kings we lose the conquests gained before,
By vain ambition still to make them more;

Each might his several province well command,
Would all but stoop to what they understand.
   First follow Nature, and your judgment frame
By her just standard, which is still° the same:
Unerring Nature, still divinely bright,   70
One clear, unchanged, and universal light,
Life, force, and beauty must to all impart,
At once the source, and end, and test of art.
Art from that fund each just supply provides,
Works without show, and without pomp presides:
In some fair body thus th' informing soul
With spirits° feeds, with vigor fills the whole,
Each motion guides, and every nerve sustains;
Itself unseen, but in th' effects, remains.
Some, to whom Heaven in wit has been profuse,
Want as much more, to turn it to its use;   81
For wit and judgment often are at strife,
Tho' meant each other's aid, like man and wife.
'Tis more to guide, than spur the Muse's steed;
Restrain his fury, than provoke his speed;
The wingèd courser, like a generous° horse,
Shows most true mettle when you check his course.
   Those rules° of old discovered, not devised,
Are Nature still, but Nature methodized;
Nature, like liberty, is but restrained   90
By the same laws which first herself ordained.
   Hear how learn'd Greece her useful rules indites,
When to repress, and when indulge our flights:
High on Parnassus' top her sons she showed,
And pointed out those arduous paths they trod;
Held from afar, aloft, th' immortal prize,
And urged the rest by equal steps to rise.
Just precepts thus from great examples given,
She drew from them what they derived from
     Heaven.
The generous critic fanned the poet's fire,   100
And taught the world with reason to admire.
Then Criticism the Muse's handmaid proved,
To dress her charms, and make her more beloved:
But following wits from that intention strayed,
Who could not win the mistress, wooed the maid;
Against the poets their own arms they turned,
Sure to hate most the men from whom they
     learned.
So modern 'pothecaries, taught the art
By doctor's bills° to play the doctor's part,
Bold in the practice of mistaken° rules,   110
Prescribe, apply, and call their masters fools.
Some on the leaves of ancient authors prey,
Nor time nor moths e'er spoiled so much as they.
Some dryly plain, without invention's aid,
Write dull receipts how poems may be made.

ESSAY ON CRITICISM. **26. schools:** i.e., of criticism.   **27. cox-combs:** those who *affect* to have wit and judgment.   **34. Maevius:** type name for a poet without talent.   **41. As . . . Nile:** Insects were believed to spring from the Nile mud by spontaneous generation.   **44. tell:** number.   **56–60. Thus . . . fit:** Renaissance psychology held that strength in one of the mind's faculties was balanced by weakness in others.   **60. One science:** one branch of knowledge.   **62. peculiar:** individual.

69. still: always.   **77. spirits:** Renaissance physiology held that the blood and organs were permeated by subtle substances of three sorts, natural, animal, and vital.   **86. generous:** highbred.   **88. rules:** principles of composition (especially for drama and epic).   **109. bills:** prescriptions.   **110. mistaken:** misinterpreted.

These leave the sense, their learning to display,
And those explain the meaning quite away.
   You then whose judgment the right course would
      steer,
Know well each ancient's proper° character;
His fable,° subject, scope° in every page;   120
Religion, country, genius of his age:
Without all these at once before your eyes,
Cavil you may, but never criticize.
Be Homer's works your study and delight,
Read them by day, and meditate by night;
Thence form your judgment, thence your maxims
      bring,
And trace the Muses upward to their spring.°
Still with itself compared, his text peruse;
And let your comment be the Mantuan Muse.°
   When first young Maro° in his boundless mind
A work t' outlast immortal Rome designed,   131
Perhaps he seemed above the critic's law,
And but from Nature's fountains scorned to draw:
But when t' examine every part he came,
Nature and Homer were, he found, the same.
Convinced, amazed, he checks the bold design;
And rules as strict his labored work confine,
As if the Stagirite° o'erlooked each line.
Learn hence for ancient rules a just esteem;
To copy Nature is to copy them.   140
   Some beauties yet no precepts can declare,°
For there's a happiness as well as care.
Music resembles poetry, in each
Are nameless graces which no methods teach,
And which a master hand alone can reach.
If, where the rules not far enough extend,
(Since rules were made but to promote their end)
Some lucky license answer to the full
Th' intent proposed, that license is a rule.
Thus Pegasus, a nearer way to take,   150
May boldly deviate from the common track:
Great wits sometimes may gloriously offend,
And rise to faults true critics dare not mend,
From vulgar bounds with brave disorder part,
And snatch a grace beyond the reach of art,
Which, without passing through the judgment,
      gains
The heart, and all its end at once attains.
In prospects, thus, some objects please our eyes,
Which out of Nature's common order rise,
The shapeless rock, or hanging precipice.   160
But though the ancients thus their rules invade,
(As kings dispense with laws themselves have
      made)

Moderns, beware! or if you must offend
Against the precept, ne'er transgress its end;
Let it be seldom, and compelled by need;
And have, at least, their precedent to plead.
The critic else proceeds without remorse,
Seizes your fame, and puts his laws in force.
   I know there are, to whose presumptuous
      thoughts   169
Those freer beauties, even in them, seem faults.°
Some figures monstrous and misshaped appear,
Considered singly, or beheld too near,
Which, but proportioned to their light, or
      place,
Due distance reconciles to form and grace.
A prudent chief not always must display
His powers in equal ranks and fair array,
But with th' occasion and the place comply,
Conceal his force, nay seem sometimes to fly.
Those oft are stratagems which errors seem,
Nor is it Homer nods, but we that dream.°   180
   Still green with bays each ancient altar stands,
Above the reach of sacrilegious hands;
Secure from flames, from envy's fiercer rage,
Destructive war, and all-involving age.
See, from each clime the learn'd their incense
      bring!
Hear, in all tongues consenting° paeans ring!
In praise so just let every voice be joined,°
And fill the general chorus of mankind.
Hail, bards triumphant! born in happier days;
Immortal heirs of universal praise!   190
Whose honors with increase of ages grow,
As streams roll down, enlarging as they flow;
Nations unborn your mighty names shall sound,
And worlds applaud that must not yet be found!
Oh may some spark of your celestial fire,
The last, the meanest of your sons inspire,
(That on weak wings, from far, pursues your
      flights;
Glows while he reads, but trembles as he writes)
To teach vain wits a science little known,   199
T' admire superior sense, and doubt their own!

II

Causes hindering a *true judgment*. 1. *Pride*. 2. *Imperfect learning*. 3. Judging by *parts*, and not by the whole. Critics in *wit, language, versification* only. 4. Being too hard to please, or too apt to admire. 5. *Partiality* — too much to a *sect* — to the *ancients* or *moderns*. 6. *Prejudice* or *prevention*. 7. *Singularity*. 8. *Inconstancy*. 9. *Party spirit*. 10. *Envy*. Against envy, and in praise of good nature. When severity is chiefly to be used by critics.

---

119. proper: distinctive.   120. fable: plot.   scope: aim.
127. spring: with punning reference to the Pierian spring, haunt of the Muses.   129. let . . . Muse: i.e., as gloss on Homer's epics, study Virgil's epic (Mantua is Virgil's birthplace).
130. Maro: Virgil.   138. the Stagirite: Aristotle (born at Stagyra), whose *Poetics* contains the most influential of all discussions of epic.   141. declare: elucidate.

170. faults: pronounced to rhyme with *thoughts* in Pope's day.
180. Nor . . . dream: Cf. Horace's remark (*Ars Poetica*, l. 359) that Homer sometimes nods.   186. consenting: harmonizing.
187. joined: pronounced to rhyme with *kind* in Pope's day.

Of all the causes which conspire to blind
Man's erring judgment, and misguide the mind,
What the weak head with strongest bias rules,
Is pride, the never-failing vice of fools.
Whatever Nature has in worth denied,
She gives in large recruits° of needful pride;
For as in bodies, thus in souls, we find
What wants° in blood and spirits,° swelled with
     wind:
Pride, where wit fails, steps in to our defense,
And fills up all the mighty void of sense.   210
If once right reason drives that cloud away,
Truth breaks upon us with resistless day.
Trust not yourself; but your defects to know,
Make use of every friend — and every foe.
  A little learning is a dangerous thing;
Drink deep, or taste not the Pierian° spring:
There shallow draughts intoxicate the brain,
And drinking largely sobers us again.
Fired at first sight with what the Muse imparts,
In fearless youth we tempt° the heights of arts,
While from the bounded level of our mind,   221
Short views we take, nor see the lengths behind;
But more advanced, behold with strange surprise
New distant scenes of endless science° rise!
So pleased at first the towering Alps we try,
Mount o'er the vales, and seem to tread the sky,
Th' eternal snows appear already passed,
And the first clouds and mountains seem the last;
But, those attained, we tremble to survey
The growing labors of the lengthened way,   230
Th' increasing prospect tires our wandering eyes,
Hills peep o'er hills, and Alps on Alps arise!
  A perfect judge will read each work of wit°
With the same spirit that its author writ:
Survey the whole, nor seek slight faults to find
Where Nature moves, and rapture warms the
     mind;
Nor lose, for that malignant dull delight,
The generous pleasure to be charmed with wit.
But in such lays as neither ebb, nor flow,
Correctly cold, and regularly low,°   240
That shunning faults, one quiet tenor keep;
We cannot blame indeed — but we may sleep.
In wit, as Nature, what affects our hearts
Is not th' exactness of peculiar° parts;
'Tis not a lip, or eye, we beauty call,
But the joint force and full result of all.
Thus when we view some well-proportioned dome,°
(The world's just wonder, and even thine, O
     Rome!)

No single parts unequally surprise,
All comes united to th' admiring eyes;   250
No monstrous height, or breadth, or length appear;
The whole at once is bold, and regular.
  Whoever thinks a faultless piece to see,
Thinks what ne'er was, nor is, nor e'er shall be.
In every work regard the writer's end,
Since none can compass more than they intend;
And if the means be just, the conduct° true,
Applause, in spite of trivial faults, is due.
As men of breeding, sometimes men of wit,
T' avoid great errors, must the less commit: 260
Neglect the rules each verbal critic° lays,
For not to know some trifles, is a praise.
Most critics, fond of some subservient art,
Still make the whole depend upon a part:
They talk of principles, but notions° prize,
And all to one loved folly sacrifice.
  Once° on a time, La Mancha's knight, they say,
A certain bard encountering on the way,
Discoursed in terms as just, with looks as sage,
As e'er could Dennis° of the Grecian stage;   270
Concluding all were desperate sots and fools,
Who durst depart from Aristotle's rules.
Our author, happy in a judge so nice,
Produced his play, and begged the knight's advice;
Made him observe the subject, and the plot,
The manners, passions, unities; what not?
All which, exact to rule, were brought about,
Were but a combat in the lists left out.
"What! leave the combat out?" exclaims the
     knight;
Yes, or we must renounce the Stagirite.   280
"Not so, by Heaven" (he answers in a rage)
"Knights, squires, and steeds, must enter on the
     stage."
So vast a throng the stage can ne'er contain.
"Then build a new, or act it in a plain."
  Thus critics, of less judgment than caprice,
Curious° not knowing, not exact but nice,°
Form short ideas; and offend in arts
(As most in manners) by a love to parts.
Some to conceit° alone their taste confine,   289
And glittering thoughts struck out at every line;
Pleased with a work where nothing's just or fit;
One glaring chaos and wild heap of wit.
Poets like painters, thus, unskilled to trace
The naked nature and the living grace,
With gold and jewels cover every part,
And hide with ornaments their want of art.
True wit is Nature to advantage dressed,
What oft was thought, but ne'er so well expressed;

206. recruits: reinforcements. 208. wants: lacks. spirits: Cf.
l. 77n. 216. Pierian: Cf. l. 127n. 220. tempt: attempt.
224. science: knowledge. 233. work of wit: i.e., work of literary imagination. 240. regularly low: conforming to the rules
(regular), but uninspired. 244. peculiar: Cf. l. 62n. 247. dome:
any building (but here possibly a domed building like the Pan-
theon or St. Peter's).

257. conduct: arrangement of parts. 261. verbal critic: one
excessively concerned with niceties. 265. notions: whims.
267–84. Once . . . plain: The story is found in the spurious sequel to Cervantes' Don Quixote. The knight is of course Don
Quixote himself. 270. Dennis: Cf. l. 585n. 286. Curious:
"fussy." nice: punctilious. 289. conceit: farfetched expression.

Something, whose truth convinced at sight we find,
That gives us back the image of our mind.   300
As shades more sweetly recommend the light,
So modest plainness sets off sprightly wit.
For works may have more wit than does 'em good,
As bodies perish through excess of blood.

Others for language all their care express,
And value books, as women men, for dress:
Their praise is still — the style is excellent:
The sense, they humbly take upon content.°
Words are like leaves; and where they most abound,
Much fruit of sense beneath is rarely found.   310
False eloquence, like the prismatic glass,
Its gaudy colors spreads on every place;°
The face of Nature we no more survey,
All glares alike, without distinction gay:
But true expression, like th' unchanging sun,
Clears, and improves whate'er it shines upon,
It gilds all objects, but it alters none.
Expression is the dress of thought, and still
Appears more decent,° as more suitable;
A vile conceit in pompous words expressed,   320
Is like a clown° in regal purple dressed:
For different styles with different subjects sort,
As several garbs with country, town, and court.
Some by old words to fame have made pretense,
Ancients in phrase, mere moderns in their sense;
Such labored nothings, in so strange a style,
Amaze th' unlearn'd, and make the learnèd smile.
Unlucky, as Fungoso in the play,°
These sparks with awkward vanity display
What the fine gentleman wore yesterday;   330
And but so mimic ancient wits at best,
As apes our grandsires, in their doublets dressed.
In words, as fashions, the same rule will hold;
Alike fantastic, if too new, or old:
Be not the first by whom the new are tried,
Nor yet the last to lay the old aside.

But most by numbers° judge a poet's song;
And smooth or rough, with them is right or wrong:
In the bright Muse, though thousand charms conspire,
Her voice is all these tuneful fools admire;   340
Who haunt Parnassus but to please their ear,
Not mend their minds; as some to church repair,
Not for the doctrine, but the music there.
These equal syllables alone require,
Tho' oft the ear the open vowels tire;
While expletives their feeble aid do join;
And ten low words oft creep in one dull line;°

While they ring round the same unvaried chimes,
With sure returns of still expected rhymes.   349
Where'er you find " the cooling western breeze,"
In the next line, it " whispers thro' the trees ":
If crystal streams " with pleasing murmurs creep,"
The reader's threatened (not in vain) with
    " sleep ":
Then, at the last and only couplet fraught
With some unmeaning thing they call a thought,
A needless alexandrine ends the song,
That, like a wounded snake, drags its slow length
    along.°
Leave such to tune their own dull rhymes, and
    know
What's roundly smooth, or languishingly slow;
And praise the easy vigor of a line,   360
Where Denham's strength, and Waller's sweetness°
    join.
True ease in writing comes from art, not chance,
As those move easiest who have learned to dance.
'Tis not enough no harshness gives offense,
The sound must seem an echo to the sense:
Soft° is the strain when Zephyr gently blows,
And the smooth stream in smoother numbers flows;
But when loud surges lash the sounding shore,
The hoarse, rough verse should like the torrent
    roar:
When Ajax strives some rock's vast weight to
    throw,   370
The line too labors, and the words move slow;
Not so, when swift Camilla scours the plain,
Flies o'er th' unbending corn, and skims along the
    main.
Hear how Timotheus'° varied lays surprise,
And bid alternate passions fall and rise!
While, at each change, the son of Libyan Jove°
Now burns with glory, and then melts with love;
Now his fierce eyes with sparkling fury glow,
Now sighs steal out, and tears begin to flow: 379
Persians and Greeks like turns of Nature° found,
And the world's victor stood subdued by sound!
The power of music all our hearts allow,
And what Timotheus was, is Dryden now.

Avoid extremes; and shun the fault of such,
Who still are pleased too little or too much.
At every trifle scorn to take offense,
That always shows great pride, or little sense;

---

308. content: trust (with a pun).   312. colors . . . place: Pope alludes punningly to the "colors" of classical rhetoric (i.e., ornaments of style) and to the "places" of traditional logic (i.e., topics or themes).   319. decent: attractive.   321. clown: rustic.   328. play: Ben Jonson's *Every Man out of His Humour.*   337. numbers: versification (especially the concord of sounds).   345–47. Tho' . . . line: Pope illustrates the faults in *tho' oft, the ear, the open;* in *do join;* and in the monosyllables of l. 347.

357. like . . . along: Pope illustrates again.   361. strength, sweetness: qualities that Sir John Denham (1615–69) and Edmund Waller (1606–87) were reputed to have brought to the closed couplet.   366–73. Soft . . . main: Pope illustrates the mating of sound and sense in his own verses while alluding to episodes in the *Iliad,* VII.268 ff., XII.380 ff., and *Aeneid,* VII.808 ff., where such mating also occurs.   374. Timotheus: Alexander the Great's musician, the varying effects of whose music are described (and, Pope adds, equaled) in Dryden's ode, *Alexander's Feast, or The Power of Music.*   376. son . . . Jove: Alexander's title as pretended son to Ammon, the Libyan Zeus.   380. turns of Nature: feelings.

Those heads, as stomachs, are not sure the best,
Which nauseate all, and nothing can digest.
Yet let not each gay turn thy rapture move;   390
For fools admire,° but men of sense approve:°
As things seem large which we through mists
    descry,
Dulness is ever apt to magnify.
  Some foreign writers, some our own despise;
The ancients only, or the moderns prize.
Thus wit, like faith, by each man is applied
To one small sect, and all are damned beside.
Meanly they seek the blessing to confine,
And force that sun but on a part to shine,
Which not alone the southern wit sublimes,°   400
But ripens spirits in cold northern climes;
Which from the first has shone on ages past,
Enlights the present, and shall warm the last;
Tho' each may feel increases and decays,
And see now clearer and now darker days.
Regard not then if wit be old or new,
But blame the false, and value still the true.
  Some ne'er advance a judgment of their own,
But catch the spreading notion of the town;
They reason and conclude by precedent,   410
And own stale nonsense which they ne'er invent.
Some judge of authors' names, not works, and then
Nor praise nor blame the writings, but the men.
Of all this servile herd, the worst is he
That in proud dulness joins with quality.°
A constant critic at the great man's board,
To fetch and carry nonsense for my lord.
What woeful stuff this madrigal would be,
In some starved hackney sonneteer, or me?
But let a lord once own the happy lines,   420
How the wit brightens! how the style refines!
Before his sacred name flies every fault,
And each exalted stanza teems with thought!
  The vulgar thus through imitation err;
As oft the learn'd by being singular;
So much they scorn the crowd, that if the throng
By chance go right, they purposely go wrong:
So schismatics the plain believers quit,
And are but damned for having too much wit.
Some praise at morning what they blame at night;
But always think the last opinion right.   431
A Muse by these is like a mistress used,
This hour she's idolized, the next abused;
While their weak heads like towns unfortified,
Twixt sense and nonsense daily change their side.
Ask them the cause; they're wiser still, they say;
And still° tomorrow's wiser than today.
We think our fathers fools, so wise we grow;
Our wiser sons, no doubt, will think us so.   439

Once school divines° this zealous isle o'erspread;
Who knew most sentences,° was deepest read;
Faith, Gospel, all, seemed made to be disputed,
And none had sense enough to be confuted:
Scotists and Thomists,° now, in peace remain,
Amidst their kindred cobwebs in Duck Lane.°
If faith itself has different dresses worn,
What wonder modes in wit should take their turn?
Oft, leaving what is natural and fit,
The current folly proves the ready wit;
And authors think their reputation safe,   450
Which lives as long as fools are pleased to laugh.°
  Some valuing those of their own side, or mind,
Still make themselves the measure of mankind:
Fondly° we think we honor merit then,
When we but praise ourselves in other men.
Parties in wit attend on those of state,°
And public faction doubles private hate.
Pride, malice, folly, against Dryden rose,
In various shapes of parsons, critics, beaux;   459
But sense survived, when merry jests were past;
For rising merit will buoy up at last.
Might he return, and bless once more our eyes,
New Blackmores and new Milbourns° must arise:
Nay, should great Homer lift his awful head,
Zoilus° again would start up from the dead.
Envy will merit, as its shade, pursue;
But like a shadow, proves the substance true;
For envied wit, like Sol eclipsed, makes known
Th' opposing body's grossness, not its own.   469
When first that sun too powerful beams displays,
It draws up vapors which obscure its rays;
But even those clouds at last adorn its way,
Reflect new glories, and augment the day.
  Be thou the first true merit to befriend;
His praise is lost, who stays till all commend.
Short is the date, alas, of modern rhymes,
And 'tis but just to let them live betimes.
No longer now that golden age appears,
When patriarch wits survived a thousand years:
Now length of fame (our second life) is lost,   480
And bare threescore is all even that can boast;
Our sons their fathers' failing language see,
And such as Chaucer is, shall Dryden be.°
So when the faithful pencil has designed

440. school divines: Scholastic theologians.   441. sentences:
theological maxims.   444. Scotists, Thomists: adherents of
Duns Scotus and St. Thomas Aquinas.   445. Duck Lane:
where dealers in old books had their shops.   450–51. safe,
laugh: by this time probably an eye rhyme only.   454. Fondly:
foolishly.   456. Parties . . . state: i.e., approval of a writer depends on approval of his politics as Whig or Tory.   463. Blackmores, Milbourns: Among the *parsons, critics, beaux* (cf. l. 459)
were the critic and poet Sir Richard Blackmore, famed for
bombast, and the clergyman Luke Milbourn.   465. Zoilus:
an ancient grammarian whose strictures on Homer made him
notorious for pedantry.   483. And . . . be: Pope mistakenly
anticipates linguistic changes as radical and rapid as those that
had made Chaucer's English obsolete.

391. admire: stand agape.   approve: test.   400. Which . . .
sublimes: The eminence of classical culture was sometimes laid
to the influence of the warm Mediterranean climate.   415. quality: the aristocracy.   437. still: always.

Some bright idea° of the master's mind,
Where a new world leaps out at his command,
And ready Nature waits upon his hand;
When the ripe colors soften and unite,
And sweetly melt into just shade and light;   489
When mellowing years their full perfection give,
And each bold figure just begins to live;
The treacherous colors the fair art betray,
And all the bright creation fades away!

Unhappy wit, like most mistaken things,
Atones not for that envy which it brings.
In youth alone its empty praise we boast,
But soon the short-lived vanity is lost:
Like some fair flower the early spring supplies,
That gaily blooms, but even in blooming dies.
What is this wit, which must our cares employ?
The owner's wife, that other men enjoy;   501
Then most our trouble still when most admired,
And still the more we give, the more required;
Whose fame with pains we guard, but lose with
     ease,
Sure some to vex, but never all to please;
'Tis what the vicious fear, the virtuous shun,
By fools 'tis hated, and by knaves undone!

If wit so much from ignorance undergo,
Ah, let not learning too commence its foe!
Of old, those met rewards who could excel,   510
And such were praised who but endeavored well:
Tho' triumphs were to generals only due,
Crowns were reserved to grace the soldiers too.
Now, they who reach Parnassus' lofty crown,
Employ their pains to spurn some others down;
And while self-love each jealous writer rules,
Contending wits become the sport of fools.
But still the worst with most regret commend,
For each ill author is as bad a friend.
To what base ends, and by what abject ways,   520
Are mortals urged through sacred° lust of praise!
Ah ne'er so dire a thirst of glory boast,
Nor in the critic let the man be lost.
Good nature and good sense must ever join;
To err is human, to forgive, divine.

But if in noble minds some dregs remain
Not yet purged off, of spleen and sour disdain;
Discharge that rage on more provoking crimes,
Nor fear a dearth in these flagitious times.
No pardon vile obscenity should find,   530
Tho' wit and art conspire to move your mind;
But dulness with obscenity must prove
As shameful sure as impotence in love.
In the fat age° of pleasure, wealth, and ease,
Sprung the rank weed, and thrived with large in-
     crease:
When love was all an easy monarch's care;

Seldom at council, never in a war:
Jilts ruled the state, and statesmen farces writ;
Nay, wits had pensions, and young lords had wit:
The Fair sat panting at a courtier's play,   540
And not a mask° went unimproved away:
The modest fan was lifted up no more,
And virgins smiled at what they blushed before.
The following license of a foreign reign°
Did all the dregs of bold Socinus° drain;
Then unbelieving priests reformed the nation,
And taught more pleasant methods of salvation;
Where Heaven's free subjects might their rights
     dispute,
Lest God himself should seem too absolute:
Pulpits their sacred satire learned to spare,   550
And Vice admired to find a flatterer there!
Encouraged thus, wit's Titans braved° the skies,
And the press groaned with licensed° blasphemies.
These monsters, critics! with your darts engage,
Here point your thunder, and exhaust your rage!
Yet shun their fault, who, scandalously nice,
Will needs mistake an author into vice;
All seems infected that th' infected spy,
As all looks yellow to the jaundiced eye.

III

Rules for the conduct of manners in a critic. 1. Candor. Modesty. Good breeding. Sincerity, and freedom of advice. 2. When one's counsel is to be restrained. Character of an incorrigible poet. And of an impertinent critic. Character of a good critic. The history of criticism, and characters of the best critics: Aristotle. Horace. Dionysius. Petronius. Quintilian. Longinus. Of the decay of criticism, and its revival. Erasmus. Vida. Boileau. Lord Roscommon, etc. Conclusion.

Learn then what morals critics ought to show,
For 'tis but half a judge's task, to know.   561
'Tis not enough, taste, judgment, learning, join;
In all you speak, let truth and candor shine:
That not alone what to your sense is due
All may allow; but seek your friendship too.

Be silent always when you doubt your sense;
And speak, though sure, with seeming diffidence:
Some positive, persisting fops we know,
Who, if once wrong, will needs be always so;
But you, with pleasure own your errors past,   570
And make each day a critic° on the last.

'Tis not enough, your counsel still be true;
Blunt truths more mischief than nice falsehoods
     do;

---

485. idea: Cf. *Rape of the Lock,* I.83.   521. *Sacred* also means accursed (from Virgil's *auri sacra fames, Aeneid,* III.57). 534. age: i.e., of Charles II.

541. mask: Restoration gentlewomen were masked when attending the theater.   544. foreign reign: that of William III, a Hollander.   545. Socinus: founder of Unitarian tenets. 552. braved: defied (as did the Titans in revolting against Zeus). 553. licensed: alluding to King William's Licensing Act. 571. critic: critique.

Men must be taught as if you taught them not,
And things unknown proposed as things forgot.
Without good breeding, truth is disapproved;
That only makes superior sense beloved.
　Be niggards of advice on no pretense;
For the worst avarice is that of sense.
With mean complacence° ne'er betray your trust,
Nor be so civil as to prove unjust.　　　581
Fear not the anger of the wise to raise;
Those best can bear reproof, who merit praise.
'Twere well might critics still this freedom take,
But Appius° reddens at each word you speak,
And stares, tremendous, with a threatening eye,
Like some fierce tyrant in old tapestry.
Fear most to tax an honorable° fool,
Whose right it is, uncensured, to be dull;
Such, without wit, are poets when they please,
As without learning they can take degrees.°　591
Leave dangerous truths to unsuccessful satires,°
And flattery to fulsome dedicators,
Whom, when they praise, the world believes no
　　more,
Than when they promise to give scribbling o'er.
'Tis best sometimes your censure to restrain,
And charitably let the dull be vain:
Your silence there is better than your spite,
For who can rail so long as they can write?　599
Still humming on, their drowsy course they keep,
And lashed so long, like tops, are lashed asleep.°
False steps but help them to renew the race,
As, after stumbling, jades will mend their pace.
What crowds of these, impenitently bold,
In sounds and jingling syllables grown old,
Still run on poets, in a raging vein,
Even to the dregs and squeezings of the brain,
Strain out the last dull droppings of their sense,
And rhyme with all the rage of impotence.
　Such shameless bards we have; and yet 'tis true,
There are as mad abandoned critics too.　　611
The bookful blockhead, ignorantly read,
With loads of learnèd lumber in his head,
With his own tongue still edifies his ears,
And always listening to himself appears.
All books he reads, and all he reads assails,
From Dryden's Fables down to Durfey's Tales.°
With him, most authors steal their works, or buy;

Garth did not write his own Dispensary.°
Name a new play, and he's the poet's friend,　620
Nay, showed his faults — but when would poets
　　mend?
No place so sacred from such fops is barred,
Nor is Paul's° church more safe than Paul's church-
　　yard:
Nay, fly to altars; there they'll talk you dead:
For fools rush in where angels fear to tread.
Distrustful sense with modest caution speaks,
It still looks home, and short excursions makes;
But rattling nonsense in full volleys breaks,
And never shocked,° and never turned aside,
Bursts out, resistless, with a thundering tide.　630
　But where's the man, who counsel can bestow,
Still pleased to teach, and yet not proud to know?
Unbiased, or by favor, or by spite;
Not dully prepossessed, nor blindly right;
Tho' learn'd, well-bred; and though well-bred,
　　sincere;
Modestly bold, and humanly severe:
Who to a friend his faults can freely show,
And gladly praise the merit of a foe?
Blest with a taste exact, yet unconfined;
A knowledge both of books and human kind;　640
Generous converse; a soul exempt from pride;
And love to praise, with reason on his side?
　Such once were critics; such the happy few,
Athens and Rome in better ages knew.
The mighty Stagirite first left the shore,
Spread all his sails, and durst the deeps explore;
He steered securely, and discovered far,
Led by the light of the Maeonian Star.°
Poets, a race long unconfined, and free,
Still fond and proud of savage liberty,　　650
Received his laws; and stood convinced 'twas fit,
Who conquered Nature,° should preside o'er wit.
　Horace still charms with graceful negligence,
And without method talks us into sense,
Will, like a friend, familiarly convey
The truest notions in the easiest way.
He, who supreme in judgment, as in wit,
Might boldly censure, as he boldly writ,
Yet judged with coolness, though he sung with
　　fire;
His precepts teach but what his works inspire.　660
Our critics take a contrary extreme,
They judge with fury, but they write with fle'me:°
Nor suffers Horace more in wrong translations

580. complacence: desire to please.　585. Appius: John Dennis,
a critic of merit, but a vain and irascible man, whose tragedy
Appius and Virginia had failed in 1709, and whose favorite
expression seems to have been *tremendous* (l. 586). As a result
of this allusion and later personal embroilments, he pursued
Pope's writings with incredible violence for the rest of his life.
588. honorable: i.e., of rank.　591. As . . . degrees: English
universities admitted any nobleman to an unearned M.A.
592. satires: often pronounced *satyrs* in Pope's day.　601. asleep:
When a top turns so fast its motion is imperceptible, it is said
to sleep.　617. From . . . Tales: Pope refers to stories from
Chaucer and Boccaccio versified in modern English by Dryden,
and to some scurrilous verse tales by Thomas D'Urfey (1653–
1723).

619. Dispensary: a mock-epic forerunner of the *Rape of the Lock*
by Pope's friend Dr. Samuel Garth, treating of a quarrel between London doctors and apothecaries (cf. ll. 108–11).
623. Paul's: St. Paul's and its environs were a general social
and commercial rendezvous. Paul's churchyard was surrounded
by bookshops.　629. shocked: stopped.　648. Maeonian Star:
Homer (thought to have been born in Maeonia).　652. Who
. . . Nature: referring to Aristotle's work in science.　662. with
fle'me: with phlegm, i.e., coldly, heavily.

By wits, than critics in as wrong quotations.°
  See Dionysius° Homer's thoughts refine,
And call new beauties forth from every line!
  Fancy and art in gay Petronius° please,
The scholar's learning, with the courtier's ease.
  In grave Quintilian's° copious work, we find
The justest rules, and clearest method joined: 670
Thus useful arms in magazines we place,
All ranged in order, and disposed with grace,
But less to please the eye, than arm the hand,
Still fit for use, and ready at command.
  Thee, bold Longinus!° all the Nine inspire,
And bless their critic with a poet's fire.
An ardent judge, who zealous in his trust,
With warmth gives sentence, yet is always just;
Whose own example strengthens all his laws;
And is himself that great sublime he draws.   680
  Thus long succeeding critics justly reigned,
License repressed, and useful laws ordained.
Learning and Rome alike in empire grew;
And arts still followed where her eagles flew;
From the same foes, at last, both felt their doom,
And the same age saw learning fall, and Rome.
With tyranny, then superstition joined,
As that the body, this enslaved the mind;
Much was believed, but little understood,
And to be dull was construed to be good;   690
A second deluge learning thus o'errun,
And the monks finished what the Goths begun.
  At length Erasmus, that great injured name,
(The glory of the priesthood, and the shame!)°
Stemmed the wild torrent of a barbarous age,
And drove those holy Vandals off the stage.
  But see each Muse, in Leo's° golden days,
Starts from her trance, and trims her withered bays!
Rome's ancient Genius, o'er its ruins spread,   699
Shakes off the dust, and rears his reverend head.
Then Sculpture and her sister arts revive;
Stones leaped to form, and rocks began to live;°
With sweeter notes each rising temple rung;
A Raphael painted, and a Vida° sung.
Immortal Vida: on whose honored brow
The poet's bays and critic's ivy grow:
Cremona now shall ever boast thy name,

As next in place to Mantua,° next in fame!
  But soon by impious arms from Latium chased,°
Their ancient bounds the banished Muses passed;
Thence arts o'er all the northern world advance,
But critic learning flourished most in France: 712
The rules, a nation born to serve, obeys;
And Boileau° still in right of Horace sways.
But we, brave Britons, foreign laws despised,
And kept unconquered, and uncivilized;
Fierce for the liberties of wit, and bold,
We still defied the Romans, as of old.
Yet some there were, among the sounder few
Of those who less presumed, and better knew,   720
Who durst assert the juster ancient cause,
And here restored wit's fundamental laws.
Such was the Muse,° whose rules and practice tell,
"Nature's chief masterpiece is writing well."
Such was Roscommon,° not more learn'd than
    good,
With manners generous as his noble blood;
To him the wit of Greece and Rome was known,
And every author's merit, but his own.
Such late was Walsh° — the Muse's judge and
    friend,
Who justly knew to blame or to commend;   730
To failings mild, but zealous for desert;
The clearest head, and the sincerest heart.
This humble praise, lamented shade! receive,
This praise at least a grateful Muse may give:
The Muse, whose early voice you taught to sing,
Prescribed her heights, and pruned her tender wing,
(Her guide now lost) no more attempts to rise,
But in low numbers short excursions tries:
Content, if hence th' unlearn'd their wants may
    view,
The learn'd reflect on what before they knew: 740
Careless of censure, nor too fond of fame;
Still pleased to praise, yet not afraid to blame;
Averse alike to flatter, or offend;
Not free from faults, nor yet too vain to mend.

WINDSOR FOREST

  Though the idea of writing a pastoral poem on this
subject was suggested to Pope by Sir William Trumbull, *Windsor Forest* was a natural outgrowth of the
poet's long residence in the Windsor countryside. The
first 290 lines were written early, perhaps as early as
1704–06. The remainder were added — and the whole

663–64. Nor . . . quotations: i.e., Horace suffers no more from
poets' mistaken translations of his poetry than from critics'
mistaken interpretations of his criticism.   665. Dionysius:
Dionysius of Halicarnassus, Greek critic and historian.   667. Petronius: Roman author, whose *Satyricon* has astute though
scattered remarks on poetry.   669. Quintilian: most influential
and schematic of the Roman critics.   675. Longinus: supposed
author of a Greek treatise on "elevated" style, which has come
to be known as *On the Sublime*.   694. The . . . shame: Erasmus
is said to be the priesthood's *glory* because of his liberalism and
learning, its *shame* because he (1) exposed church abuses,
(2) was persecuted by the church.   697. Leo: Pope Leo X,
member of the great Medici family and patron of the arts.
702. Stones . . . live: This was the age of Michelangelo and his
peers.   704. Vida: Italian poet, whose Latin verse essay on
poetics Pope occasionally echoes in this poem.

707–08. Cremona, Mantua: birthplaces of Vida and Virgil.
709. But . . . chased: In 1527 the French armies sacked Rome.
714. Boileau: French critic and poet, author of *L'Art poëtique*
(1673) in the manner of Horace's *Ars Poetica*.   723. the Muse:
John Sheffield, Duke of Buckinghamshire, friend of Pope and
author of an *Essay on Poetry* (1682), from which the next line
is taken.   725. Roscommon: Wentworth Dillon, Earl of Roscommon, author of a verse *Essay on Translated Verse* (1684).
729. Walsh: William Walsh, Pope's critical mentor during his
early career.

poem, one may feel confident, was revamped — when the statesman and minor poet George Granville, Baron Lansdowne, asked Pope in 1712(?) to turn it into a celebration of the Peace of Utrecht. The poem was published in 1713.

Perhaps the best way to grasp the themes of *Windsor Forest* is to observe that near its center stands the episode of Lodona (ll. 171–218). This extends the situation of the hunter and hunted to the relations of male and female, as it has earlier been extended to those of war, establishing the fact of conflict as a fundamental article of life. On either side of this passage are two passages of myth (ll. 165–70, 219–34), which, together with the Lodona episode, itself an extended myth, indicate the extent to which the poet aims to mythologize the world of the forest. Outside these mythological passages stand two which, though both deal with the retired life, stress respectively its active and contemplative poles, hunting and poetry (ll. 93–164, 235–98). This is an opposition that also runs through the entire poem, since, as its opening lines announce and much of its subject matter illustrates, Windsor has always been identified with " the Monarch " on the one hand and " the Muse " on the other. The next two encompassing passages are passages of history, one relating history to the theme of hunting (ll. 43–92), and the other, to the theme of poetry (ll. 299–328). In both, the elemental urge of conflict is seen as anarchic when it takes the form of civil war. Finally, there are two passages about peace and prosperity. The first (ll. 7–42) deals with England as a present demi-Eden under a Stuart queen, whose realm, with its treasure from East and West, its blessings from the several gods, and even its varieties of landscape, exemplifies the harmony out of differences, the *concors discordia rerum,* on which the universe itself depends: "Where order in variety we see, / And where, tho' all things differ, all agree." The second passage (329–422) deals with the future Eden, which under the Peace of Utrecht and the *Pax Britannica,* also a type of concord out of conflict, is now to be restored for all the world.

To the Right Honorable
George, Lord Lansdowne

Non injussa cano: Te nostrae, Vare, myricae,
Te Nemus omne canet; nec Phoebo gratior ulla
   est,
Quam sibi quae Vari praescripsit pagina nomen.
       (Virgil [*Eclogues,* VI. 9, 10–12])

[The songs I sing are not unbidden: Of you, Varus, our tamarisks and every grove shall sing; for nothing is more grateful to Phoebus than a page bearing Varus' name.]

Thy forests, Windsor! and thy green retreats,
At once the monarch's and the Muse's seats,°
Invite my lays. Be present, sylvan maids!

WINDSOR FOREST. **2. At . . . seats:** the *monarch's* seat because of Windsor palace; the Muse's, for the reasons given in ll. 279–98.

Unlock your springs, and open all your shades.
Granville commands; your aid, O Muses, bring!
What Muse for Granville can refuse to sing?
  The groves of Eden, vanished now so long,
Live in description, and look green in song:
These, were my breast inspired with equal flame,
Like them in beauty, should be like in fame   10
Here hills and vales, the woodland and the plain,
Here earth and water seem to strive again;
Not chaos-like together crushed and bruised,
But,° as the world, harmoniously confused:
Where order in variety we see,
And where, tho' all things differ, all agree.
Here waving groves a checkered scene display,
And part admit, and part exclude the day;
As some coy nymph her lover's warm address
Nor quite indulges, nor can quite repress.   20
There, interspersed in lawns and opening glades,
Thin trees arise that shun each other's shades.
Here in full light the russet plains extend:
There wrapped in clouds the bluish hills ascend.
Even the wild heath displays her purple dyes,
And midst the desert fruitful fields arise,
That crowned with tufted trees and springing corn,
Like verdant isles the sable waste adorn.
Let° India boast her plants, nor envy we
The weeping amber or the balmy tree,   30
While by our oaks the precious loads are borne,
And realms commanded which those trees adorn.
Not proud Olympus yields a nobler sight,
Though gods assembled grace his towering height,
Than what more humble mountains offer here,
Where, in their blessings, all those gods appear.
See Pan with flocks, with fruits Pomona crowned,
Here blushing Flora paints th' enameled ground,
Here Ceres' gifts in waving prospect stand,
And nodding tempt the joyful reaper's hand;   40
Rich Industry sits smiling on the plains,
And peace and plenty tell, a Stuart° reigns.
  Not° thus the land appeared in ages past,
A dreary desert, and a gloomy waste,
To savage beasts and savage laws a prey,
And kings more furious and severe than they;
Who claimed the skies, dispeopled air and floods,
The lonely lords of empty wilds and woods:
Cities laid waste, they stormed the dens and caves,
(For wiser brutes were backward to be slaves)   50
What could be free, when lawless beasts obeyed,
And even the elements a tyrant swayed?
In vain kind seasons swelled the teeming grain,

14–42. Windsor Forest is depicted as a world in miniature, embodying the same principle of reconciled opposites, unity within variety, that was supposed in old accounts of Creation to have brought a cosmos out of chaos. **29–32. Let . . . adorn:** England's dominion of the East through her shipping. **42. a Stuart:** Queen Anne (1702–14). **43–84.** Alluding to the despotic rule of the first Norman kings, especially William I's segregation of large areas (the New Forest) for royal game preserves.

Soft showers distilled, and suns grew warm in vain;
The swain with tears his frustrate labor yields,
And famished dies amidst his ripened fields.
What wonder then, a beast or subject slain
Were equal crimes in a despotic reign?
Both doomed alike for sportive tyrants bled,
But while the subject starved, the beast was fed.
Proud Nimrod° first the bloody chase began,   61
A mighty hunter, and his prey was man:
Our haughty Norman boasts that barbarous name,
And makes his trembling slaves the royal game.
The fields are ravished from th' industrious swains,
From men their cities, and from gods their fanes:
The leveled towns with weeds lie covered o'er;
The hollow winds through naked temples roar;
Round broken columns clasping ivy twined;
O'er heaps of ruin stalked the stately hind;   70
The fox obscene to gaping tombs retires,
And savage howlings fill the sacred choirs.
Awed by his nobles, by his commons cursed,
Th' oppressor ruled tyrannic where he durst,
Stretched o'er the poor and church his iron rod,
And served alike his vassals and his God.
Whom even the Saxon spared and bloody Dane,°
The wanton victims of his sport remain.
But see, the man who spacious regions gave
A waste for beasts, himself denied a grave!°   80
Stretched° on the lawn his second hope survey,
At once the chaser, and at once the prey:
Lo, Rufus, tugging at the deadly dart,
Bleeds in the forest like a wounded hart.
Succeeding monarchs heard the subjects' cries,
Nor saw displeased the peaceful cottage rise.
Then gathering flocks on unknown mountains fed,
O'er sandy wilds were yellow harvests spread,
The forests wondered at th' unusual grain,
And secret transport touched the conscious swain.
Fair Liberty, Britannia's goddess, rears   91
Her cheerful head, and leads the golden years.
   Ye vigorous swains! while youth ferments your blood,
And purer spirits° swell the sprightly flood,
Now range the hills, the gameful woods beset,
Wind the shrill horn, or spread the waving net.
When milder autumn summer's heat succeeds,
And in the new-shorn field the partridge feeds,

Before his lord the ready spaniel bounds,   99
Panting with hope he tries the furrowed grounds,
But when the tainted gales the game betray,
Couched close he lies, and meditates° the prey:
Secure they trust th' unfaithful field, beset,
Till hovering o'er 'em sweeps the swelling net.
Thus (if small things we may with great compare)
When Albion° sends her eager sons to war,
Some thoughtless town, with ease and plenty blessed,
Near, and more near, the closing lines invest;
Sudden they seize th' amazed, defenseless prize,
And high in air Britannia's standard flies.   110
   See! from the brake the whirring pheasant springs,
And mounts exulting on triumphant wings:
Short is his joy; he feels the fiery wound,
Flutters in blood, and panting beats the ground.
Ah! what avail his glossy, varying dyes,
His purple crest, and scarlet-circled eyes,
The vivid green his shining plumes unfold,
His painted wings, and breast that flames with gold?
   Nor yet, when moist Arcturus clouds the sky,
The woods and fields their pleasing toils deny.
To plains with well-breathed° beagles we repair,
And trace the mazes of the circling hare: 122
(Beasts, urged by us, their fellow beasts pursue,
And learn of man each other to undo.)
With slaughtering guns th' unwearied fowler roves,
When frosts have whitened all the naked groves;
Where doves in flocks the leafless trees o'ershade,
And lonely woodcocks haunt the watery glade.
He lifts the tube,° and levels with his eye;
Straight a short thunder breaks the frozen sky.
Oft, as in airy rings they skim the heath,   131
The clamorous lapwings feel the leaden death:
Oft, as the mounting larks their notes prepare,
They fall, and leave their little lives in air.
   In genial spring, beneath the quivering shade,
Where cooling vapors breathe along the mead,
The patient fisher takes his silent stand,
Intent, his angle trembling in his hand:
With looks unmoved, he hopes the scaly breed,
And eyes the dancing cork, and bending reed.   140
Our plenteous streams a various race supply,
The bright-eyed perch with fins of Tyrian dye,
The silver eel, in shining volumes° rolled,
The yellow carp, in scales bedropped with gold,
Swift trouts, diversified with crimson stains,
And pikes, the tyrants° of the watery plains.
   Now Cancer glows with Phoebus' fiery car:°
The youth rush eager to the sylvan war,

---

61. Nimrod: reputed the first hunter of beasts and (consequently) the first warmaker and tyrant (cf. Gen.10:9; *Paradise Lost,* XII.24–37).   **77. Saxon, Dane:** earlier invaders.   **79–80. But . . . grave:** It is said that when William I was about to be buried (at Caen), the spot was at first refused him as being the property of another. The poetic justice implied by Pope's phrasing is that, as William had misused the earth in life, it denied him room in death.   **81–84. Stretched . . . hart:** Two other examples of poetic justice: Richard, William's second son, was slain by a stag in the New Forest, and Rufus, his third son and successor, was also slain there, by an arrow from an unknown source.   **94. spirits:** Cf. *E. on Crit.*, l. 77n.

102. meditates: lies in wait for.   **106. Albion:** England.   **121. well-breathed:** strong of wind.   **129. tube:** gun barrel.   **143. volumes:** folds.   **146. tyrants:** so-called because devourers of their own kind (cf. l. 61n.).   **147. Cancer . . . car:** The sun enters Cancer on June 21.

Swarm o'er the lawns, the forest walks surround,
Rouse the fleet hart, and cheer the opening° hound.
Th' impatient courser pants in every vein,   151
And, pawing, seems to beat the distant plain:
Hills, vales, and floods appear already crossed,
And ere he starts, a thousand steps are lost.
See the bold youth strain up the threatening steep,
Rush through the thickets, down the valleys sweep,
Hang o'er their coursers' heads with eager speed,
And earth rolls back beneath the flying steed.
Let old Arcadia boast her ample plain,
Th' immortal huntress, and her virgin train;   160
Nor envy, Windsor! since thy shades have seen
As bright a goddess, and as chaste a queen;
Whose care, like hers, protects the sylvan reign,
The earth's fair light, and empress of the main.
    Here too, 'tis sung, of old Diana strayed,
And Cynthus'° top forsook for Windsor shade;
Here was she seen o'er airy wastes to rove,
Seek the clear spring, or haunt the pathless grove;
Here armed with silver bows, in early dawn,
Her buskined virgins traced the dewy lawn.   170
Above° the rest a rural nymph was famed,
Thy offspring, Thames! the fair Lodona named;
(Lodona's fate, in long oblivion cast,
The Muse shall sing, and what she sings shall last.)
Scarce could the goddess from her nymph be
    known,
But by the crescent and the golden zone.°
She scorned the praise of beauty, and the care;
A belt her waist, a fillet binds her hair;
A painted quiver on her shoulder sounds,
And with her dart the flying deer she wounds.   180
It chanced, as eager of the chase, the maid
Beyond the forest's verdant limits strayed,
Pan saw and loved, and, burning with desire,
Pursued her flight; her flight increased his fire.
Not half so swift the trembling doves can fly,
When the fierce eagle cleaves the liquid sky;
Not half so swiftly the fierce eagle moves,
When through the clouds he drives the trembling
    doves;
As from the god she flew with furious pace,
Or as the god, more furious, urged the chase.   190
Now fainting, sinking, pale, the nymph appears;
Now close behind, his sounding steps she hears;
And now his shadow reached her as she run,
His shadow lengthened by the setting sun;
And now his shorter breath, with sultry air,
Pants on her neck, and fans her parting hair.
In vain on father Thames she calls for aid,
Nor could Diana help her injured maid.

Faint, breathless, thus she prayed, nor prayed in
    vain;
"Ah, Cynthia! ah — though banished from thy
    train,   200
Let me, O let me, to the shades repair,
My native shades — there weep, and murmur
    there."
She said, and melting as in tears she lay,
In a soft, silver stream dissolved away.
The silver stream her virgin coldness keeps,
Forever murmurs, and forever weeps;
Still bears the name the hapless virgin bore,
And bathes the forest where she ranged before.
In her chaste current oft the goddess laves,
And with celestial tears augments the waves.   210
Oft in her glass the musing shepherd spies
The headlong mountains and the downward skies,
The watery landscape of the pendent woods,
And absent trees that tremble in the floods;
In the clear azure gleam the flocks are seen,
And floating forests paint the waves with green,
Through the fair scene roll slow the lingering
    streams,
Then foaming pour along, and rush into the
    Thames.°
    Thou, too, great father of the British floods!
With joyful pride surveyst our lofty woods;   220
Where towering oaks their growing honors° rear,
And future navies on thy shores appear.
Not Neptune's self from all his streams receives
A wealthier tribute than to thine he gives.
No seas so rich, so gay no banks appear,
No lake so gentle, and no spring so clear.
Nor Po° so swells the fabling poet's lays,
While led along the skies his current strays,
As thine, which visits Windsor's famed abodes,
To grace the mansion of our earthly gods: 230
Nor all his stars above a luster show,
Like the bright beauties on thy banks below;
Where Jove, subdued by mortal passion still,
Might change Olympus for a nobler hill.
    Happy the man whom this bright court approves,
His sovereign favors, and his country loves:
Happy next him, who to these shades retires,
Whom Nature charms, and whom the Muse in-
    spires:
Whom humbler joys of home-felt quiet please,
Successive study, exercise, and ease.   240
He gathers health from herbs the forest yields,
And of their fragrant physic spoils the fields:
With chymic art exalts the mineral powers,
And draws° the aromatic souls of flowers:

---

150. opening: hunting term for giving tongue.   166. Cynthus:
Diana's birthplace.   171–218. Pope gives an Ovidian metamorphosis, to account for the presence in the forest of the Loddon, a tributary of the Thames.   176. crescent ... zone:
Diana's emblems are a crescent moon and belt of gold.

217–18. streams, Thames: still a perfect rhyme in Pope's lifetime.   221. honors: beauties, i.e., leaves (in women, hair).
227. Po: The Po came to be identified with the river Eridanus
of myth and so with the river-shaped constellation called Eri-
dani.   243–44. exalts, draws: terms from the old chemistry
for processes of distilling.

Now marks the course of rolling orbs on high;
O'er figured worlds° now travels with his eye;
Of ancient writ unlocks the learnèd store,
Consults the dead, and lives past ages o'er:
Or wandering thoughtful in the silent wood,
Attends the duties of the wise and good,   250
T' observe a mean, be to himself a friend,
To follow Nature, and regard his end;
Or looks on Heaven with more than mortal eyes,
Bids his free soul expatiate in the skies,
Amid her kindred stars° familiar roam,
Survey the region, and confess her home!
Such was the life great Scipio once admired;
Thus Atticus, and Trumbull thus retired.°
    Ye sacred Nine! that all my soul possess,
Whose raptures fire me, and whose visions bless,
Bear me, oh bear me to sequestered scenes,   261
The bowery mazes, and surrounding greens:
To Thames's banks, which fragrant breezes fill,
Or where ye Muses sport on Cooper's Hill.
(On Cooper's Hill eternal wreaths shall grow,
While lasts the mountain, or while Thames shall
    flow.)°
I seem through consecrated walks to rove,
I hear soft music die along the grove:
Led by the sound, I roam from shade to shade,
By godlike poets venerable made: 270
Here his first lays majestic Denham sung;
There the last numbers flowed from Cowley's
    tongue.
O early lost! what tears the river shed,
When the sad pomp along his banks was led?°
His° drooping swans on every note expire,
And on his willows hung each Muse's lyre.°
    Since fate relentless stopped their heavenly voice,
No more the forests ring, or groves rejoice;
Who now shall charm the shades, where Cowley
    strung
His living harp, and lofty Denham sung?   280
But hark! the groves rejoice, the forest rings!
Are these revived? or is it Granville sings?
'Tis yours, my lord, to bless our soft retreats,
And call the Muses to their ancient seats;
To paint anew the flowery sylvan scenes,
To crown the forests with immortal greens,
Make Windsor hills in lofty numbers rise,
And lift her turrets nearer to the skies;
To sing those honors you deserve to wear,

And add new luster to her silver star.°   290
    Here noble Surrey felt the sacred rage,
Surrey,° the Granville of a former age:
Matchless his pen, victorious was his lance,
Bold in the lists, and graceful in the dance:
In the same shades the cupids tuned his lyre,
To the same notes, of love, and soft desire:
Fair Geraldine, bright object of his vow,
Then filled the groves, as heavenly Mira° now.
    Oh, wouldst thou sing what heroes Windsor bore,
What kings first breathed upon her winding shore,
Or raise old warriors, whose adored remains   301
In weeping vaults her hallowed earth contains!
With Edward's° acts adorn the shining page,
Stretch his long triumphs down through every age,
Draw monarchs chained, and Cressi's glorious field,
The lilies blazing on the regal shield:
Then, from her roofs when Verrio's° colors fall,
And leave inanimate the naked wall,
Still in thy song should vanquished France appear,
And bleed forever under Britain's spear.   310
    Let softer strains ill-fated Henry mourn,
And palms eternal flourish round his urn.°
Here o'er the martyr king the marble weeps,°
And, fast beside him, once-feared Edward° sleeps:
Whom not th' extended Albion could contain,
From old Belerium° to the northern main,
The grave unites; where even the great find rest,
And blended lie th' oppressor and th' oppressed!
    Make sacred Charles's tomb forever known
(Obscure the place, and uninscribed the stone),°
Oh,° fact accurst! what tears has Albion shed,
Heavens, what new wounds! and how her old
    have bled!   322
She saw her sons with purple deaths expire,
Her sacred domes° involved in rolling fire,
A dreadful series of intestine wars,
Inglorious triumphs and dishonest scars.
At length great Anna said — "Let discord cease! "
She said! the world obeyed, and all was peace!°

290. star: badge of the knights of the Garter, who were installed at Windsor palace and whose founder, Edward III, rebuilt it. 292. Surrey: Windsor figures prominently in the poems of Henry Howard, Earl of Surrey, whose love poems are addressed to a certain Fair Geraldine (l. 297). 298. Mira: fictitious name of the lady addressed in Lansdowne's love poems. 303–06. Edward's . . . shield: Edward III was born at Windsor. Claiming the French crown through his mother, he quartered the fleur-de-lis on his shield, beat the French at Crécy (Cressi, l. 305) in 1346, and at various times held captive the kings of Scotland and France. 307. Verrio: seventeenth-century Neapolitan painter, whose murals adorn much of the palace. 311–12. Let . . . urn: Henry VI's reign ended in his murder. 313. weeps: Cf. Eloïsa to Abelard, l. 22n. 314. Edward: Edward IV, Henry VI's rival and successor. 316. Belerium: Land's End in Cornwall (cf. Milton's "Lycidas," l. 160, above). 320. Obscure . . . stone: Charles I was buried in St. George's Chapel, Windsor, but the exact location was not known until 1813. 321–26. Oh . . . scars: It was widely felt that the Great Plague and the Fire of London, as well as later civil dissensions, were a judgment on England for executing the sacred person of a king. 324. domes: Cf. E. on Crit., l. 247n. 327–28. At . . . peace: Cf. Rape of the Lock, III.46n.

246. figured worlds: maps (of skies or earth).   255. kindred stars: Many ancients believed that the soul was of one substance with the stars and native to them.   257–58. Such . . . retired: Scipio, Atticus (Cicero's great friend), and Pope's friend Sir William Trumbull are all statesmen who withdrew from public life.   264–66. Or . . . flow: Cooper's Hill is the title of a poem of the same genre as W. Forest, by Sir John Denham (cf. E. on Crit., l. 361n.).   272–74. There . . . led: Abraham Cowley died in 1667 at Chertsey on the Forest's edge, and was thence conveyed by an elaborate funeral procession to burial in Westminster Abbey.   275. His: the Thames's.   276. on . . . lyre: Cf. Ps. 137:1–2.

In that blest moment from his oozy bed 329
Old father Thames advanced his reverend head.
His tresses dropped with dews, and o'er the stream
His shining horns° diffused a golden gleam:
Graved on his urn appeared the moon, that guides
His swelling waters, and altérnate tides;
The figured streams in waves of silver rolled,
And on their banks Augusta° rose in gold.
Around his throne the sea-born brothers stood,
Who swell with tributary urns his flood;
First the famed authors of his ancient name,°
The winding Isis and the fruitful Thame: 340
The Kennet swift, for silver eels renowned;
The Loddon slow, with verdant alders crowned;
Cole, whose dark streams his flowery islands lave;
And chalky Wey, that rolls a milky wave:
The blue, transparent Vandalis appears;
The gulfy Lee his sedgy tresses rears;
And sullen Mole, that hides his diving flood;°
And silent Darent, stained with Danish° blood.

High in the midst, upon his urn reclined
(His sea-green mantle waving with the wind),
The god appeared: he turned his azure eyes 351
Where Windsor domes and pompous turrets rise;
Then bowed and spoke; the winds forget to roar,
And the hushed waves glide softly to the shore.

"Hail, sacred peace! hail, long-expected days,
That Thames's glory to the stars shall raise!
Tho' Tiber's streams immortal Rome behold,
Tho'° foaming Hermus° swells with tides of
gold,
From Heaven itself tho' sevenfold Nilus flows,°
And harvests on a hundred realms bestows; 360
These now no more shall be the Muse's themes,
Lost in my fame, as in the sea their streams.
Let Volga's banks with iron squadrons shine,
And groves of lances glitter on the Rhine,
Let barbarous Ganges arm a servile train;
Be mine the blessings of a peaceful reign.
No more my sons shall dye with British blood
Red Iber's sands, or Ister's foaming flood:°
Safe on my shore each unmolested swain
Shall tend the flocks, or reap the bearded grain;
The shady empire shall retain no trace 371
Of war or blood, but in the sylvan chase;

The trumpet sleep, while cheerful horns are blown,
And arms employed on birds and beasts alone.
Behold!° th' ascending villas on my side,
Project long shadows o'er the crystal tide.
Behold! Augusta's glittering spires increase,
And temples rise, the beauteous works of peace.
I see, I see, where two fair cities° bend
Their ample bow, a new Whitehall ascend! 380
There mighty nations shall inquire their doom,
The world's great oracle in times to come;
There kings shall sue, and suppliant states be seen
Once more to bend before a British queen.°

Thy trees, fair Windsor! now shall leave their
woods,
And half thy forests rush into thy floods,
Bear Britain's thunder, and her cross° display,
To the bright regions of the rising day;
Tempt icy seas, where scarce the waters roll,
Where clearer flames glow round the frozen pole;
Or under southern skies exalt their sails, 391
Led by new stars, and borne by spicy gales!
For me the balm shall bleed, and amber flow,
The coral redden, and the ruby glow,
The pearly shell its lucid globe infold,
And Phoebus warm the ripening ore to gold.°
The time shall come, when free as seas or wind
Unbounded° Thames shall flow for all mankind,
Whole nations enter with each swelling tide,
And seas but join the regions they divide; 400
Earth's distant ends our glory shall behold,
And the new world launch forth to seek the old.
Then ships of uncouth form shall stem the tide,
And feathered people crowd my wealthy side,
And naked youths and painted chiefs admire
Our speech, our color, and our strange attire!
O stretch thy reign, fair Peace! from shore to shore,
Till conquest cease, and slavery be no more;
Till the freed Indians in their native groves
Reap their own fruits, and woo their sable loves,
Peru once more a race of kings behold, 411
And other Mexicos be roofed with gold.
Exiled by thee from earth to deepest hell,
In brazen bonds, shall barbarous Discord dwell;
Gigantic Pride, pale Terror, gloomy Care,
And mad Ambition shall attend her there:
There purple Vengeance bathed in gore retires,
Her weapons blunted, and extinct her fires:
There hateful Envy her own snakes shall feel,
And Persecution morn her broken wheel: 420

332. horns: traditional insignia (like the *urn*) of river gods. **336. Augusta:** Roman name for London. **339. name:** Thames's *ancient name* was Tamesis, popularly supposed to have been formed by joining the names of two tributary rivers, *Thame* and *Isis*. **347. that . . . flood:** The Mole in some spots has a subterranean channel. **348. Danish:** It was apparently not the Danes but the Saxons who were repulsed at the Darent. **358–412.** Here the same principle of variety in unity, concord built from discord, is presented as at the poem's opening; but it is to be realized now in the Pax Britannica for the whole world. **358. Hermus:** a river in Aeolis said by the ancients to be "cloudy with gold" (Virgil, *Georgics,* II.135). **359. From . . . flows:** In antiquity, the as yet undiscovered sources of the Nile (*sevenfold* for its seven mouths) were placed in heaven. **367–68. No . . . flood:** In the war about to be closed by the peace that Pope celebrates, Englishmen had fought on the Ebro (*Iber*) in Spain and the Danube (*Ister*).

375–80. Behold . . . ascend: alluding to the rebuilding of London after the Great Fire (1666), including Christopher Wren's fifty-two churches and Inigo Jones's plans (never executed) for the enlargement of Whitehall. **379. cities:** London and Westminster. **384. Once . . . queen:** i.e., as under Elizabeth I. **387. cross:** the Union Jack. **396. Phoebus . . . gold:** Minerals were formerly supposed to be formed by the sun's rays. **398–434.** "A wish," Pope says in a note, "that London may be made a free port" — but transformed by his echoings of Isa. 60–66 and Virgil's fourth *Eclogue* into a vision of a New Jerusalem, or restored golden age.

There Faction roar, Rebellion bite her chain,
And gasping Furies thirst for blood in vain."
    Here cease thy flight, nor with unhallowed lays
Touch the fair fame of Albion's golden days:
The thoughts of gods let Granville's verse recite,
And bring the scenes of opening fate to light.
My humble Muse, in unambitious strains,
Paints the green forests and the flowery plains,
Where Peace descending bids her olives spring,
And scatters blessings from her dovelike wing.
Even I more sweetly pass my careless days,   431
Pleased in the silent shade with empty praise;
Enough for me, that to the listening swains
First in these fields I sung the sylvan strains.

THE RAPE OF THE LOCK

In the summer of 1711, Pope's friend Caryll asked
him to toss off a jesting little poem to help heal the
temporary ill feeling that had sprung up between the
Petre and Fermor families (to whom Caryll was connected by friendship and marriage), after Robert Lord
Petre had cut off a lock of Arabella Fermor's hair. The
result was *The Rape of the Lock*.

The first version of the *Rape*, in two cantos and 334
lines, was composed in about two weeks in the fall of
1711, and published in May, 1712. The present version
appeared two years later, Pope having added in the
meantime the "celestial machinery" of the sylphs, and
with it some of the happiest episodes in the poem:
Belinda's dream, her toilet, her voyage up the Thames,
Ariel's address to his fellows, the game of ombre, the
Cave of Spleen. The only subsequent addition of importance was Clarissa's speech, introduced in 1717,
Pope tells us (with what is probably his usual irony)
"to open more clearly the moral of the poem."

Though first and foremost a mock epic, as the reader who comes to it fresh from Milton will have no
difficulty in reminding himself, the *Rape* supplies also
an unforgettable picture of Augustan high life, with its
sedan chairs, coaches, cosmetics, curling irons, tweezer
cases, men, monkeys, lap dogs, parrots, politicians; and
and equally unforgettable criticism of that life, held
pinned and wriggling against the heroic backgrounds
of the *Iliad*, the *Aeneid*, and *Paradise Lost*.

Nolueram, Belinda, tuos violare capillos,
Sed juvat hoc precibus me tribuisse tuis.
                    (Martial [*Epigrams*, XII. 84])

[I thought it a pity, Belinda, to violate your locks,
but am happy to have granted *this* to your prayers.]

CANTO I

What dire offense from amorous causes springs,
What mighty contests rise from trivial things,
I sing — This verse to Caryll, Muse! is due:
This, even Belinda may vouchsafe to view:
Slight is the subject, but not so the praise,

If she inspire, and he approve my lays.
    Say what strange motive, goddess! could compel
A well-bred lord t' assault a gentle belle?
O say what stranger cause, yet unexplored,
Could make a gentle belle reject a lord?   10
In tasks so bold, can little men engage,
And in soft bosoms dwells such mighty rage?
    Sol through white curtains shot a timorous ray,
And oped those eyes that must eclipse the day:
Now lapdogs give themselves the rousing shake,
And sleepless lovers, just at twelve, awake:
Thrice rung the bell, the slipper knocked the
        ground,°
And the pressed watch° returned a silver sound.
Belinda still her downy pillow pressed,
Her guardian Sylph prolonged the balmy rest: 20
'Twas he had summoned to her silent bed
The morning dream that hovered o'er her head;
A youth more glittering than a birthnight beau,°
(That even in slumber caused her cheek to glow)
Seemed to her ear his winning lips to lay,
And thus in whispers said, or seemed to say:
    "Fairest of mortals, thou distinguished care
Of thousand bright inhabitants of air!°
If e'er one vision touched thy infant thought,
Of all the nurse and all the priest have taught;   30
Of airy elves by moonlight shadows seen,
The silver token,° and the circled green,
Or virgins visited by angel powers,
With golden crowns and wreaths of heavenly flow-
        ers;
Hear and believe! thy own importance know,
Nor bound thy narrow views to things below.
Some secret truths, from learnèd pride concealed,
To maids alone and children are revealed:
What though no credit doubting wits may give?
The fair and innocent shall still believe.   40
Know, then, unnumbered spirits round thee fly,
The light militia of the lower sky:
These, though unseen, are ever on the wing,
Hang o'er the box,° and hover round the Ring.°
Think what an equipage thou hast in air,
And view with scorn two pages and a chair.°
As now your own, our beings were of old,
And once enclosed in woman's beauteous mold;
Thence, by a soft transition, we repair
From earthly vehicles° to these of air,   50

RAPE OF THE LOCK. Canto I: **17. Thrice . . . ground:** Belinda's summons to her maid.   **18. pressed watch:** Such watches
when pressed sounded the hour and quarter-hour just past,
thus giving the time when it was too dark to see.   **23. birthnight beau:** i.e., adorned as for a royal birthday fete.   **27–
28. Fairest . . . air:** Epic protagonists are always under the
guardianship of higher powers (cf. *Paradise Lost*).   **32. silver
token:** Fairies were supposed to leave a sixpence in the shoe of
maids whom they approved.   **44. box:** theater box.   **Ring:**
a circular drive in Hyde Park, frequented by the coaches of
ladies of fashion.   **46. chair:** sedan chair.   **50. vehicles:** bodies
(with punning reference to *equipage* and *chair*).

Think not, when woman's transient breath is fled,
That all her vanities at once are dead;
Succeeding vanities she still regards,
And though she plays no more, o'erlooks the cards.
Her joy in gilded chariots,° when alive,
And love of ombre,° after death survive.
For° when the fair in all their pride expire,
To their first elements their souls retire:
The sprites of fiery termagants in flame
Mount up, and take a Salamander's° name.   60
Soft yielding minds to water glide away,
And sip, with Nymphs, their elemental tea.°
The graver prude sinks downward to a Gnome,
In search of mischief still on earth to roam.
The light coquettes in Sylphs aloft repair,
And sport and flutter in the fields of air.
  Know further yet; whoever fair and chaste
Rejects mankind, is by some Sylph embraced:
For spirits, freed from mortal laws, with ease
Assume what sexes and what shapes they please.°
What guards the purity of melting maids,   71
In courtly balls, and midnight masquerades,
Safe from the treacherous friend, the daring spark,°
The glance by day, the whisper in the dark,
When kind occasion prompts their warm desires,
When music softens, and when dancing fires?
'Tis but their Sylph, the wise celestials know,
Though honor is the word with men below.
  Some nymphs there are, too conscious of their
      face,
For life predestined to the Gnomes' embrace.   80
These swell their prospects and exalt their pride,
When offers are disdained, and love denied:
Then gay ideas° crowd the vacant brain,
While peers, and dukes, and all their sweeping
      train,
And garters, stars, and coronets appear,
And in soft sounds, ' your Grace ' salutes their ear.
'Tis these that early taint the female soul,
Instruct the eyes of young coquettes to roll,
Teach infant cheeks a bidden blush° to know,
And little hearts to flutter at a beau.   90
  Oft, when the world imagine women stray,
The Sylphs through mystic mazes guide their
      way,
Thro' all the giddy circle they pursue,
And old impertinence° expel by new.
What tender maid but must a victim fall
To one man's treat, but for another's ball?

When Florio speaks, what virgin could withstand,
If gentle Damon did not squeeze her hand?
With varying vanities, from every part,
They shift the moving toyshop of their heart;   100
Where wigs with wigs, with sword knots° sword
      knots strive,
Beaux banish beaux, and coaches coaches drive.
This erring mortals levity may call;
Oh blind to truth! the Sylphs contrive it all.
  Of these am I, who thy protection claim,
A watchful sprite, and Ariel is my name.
Late, as I ranged the crystal wilds of air,
In the clear mirror of thy ruling star
I saw, alas! some dread event impend,
Ere to the main this morning sun descend,   110
But heaven reveals not what, or how, or where:
Warned by the Sylph, oh pious maid, beware!
This to disclose is all thy guardian can:
Beware of all, but most beware of man! "
  He said; when Shock, who thought she slept too
      long,
Leaped up, and waked his mistress with his tongue.
'Twas then, Belinda, if report say true,
Thy eyes first opened on a billet-doux;
Wounds, charms, and ardors° were no sooner
      read,
But all the vision vanished from thy head.   120
  And now, unveiled, the toilet stands displayed,
Each silver vase in mystic order laid.
First, robed in white, the nymph intent adores,
With head uncovered, the cosmetic powers.
A° heavenly image in the glass appears,
To that she bends, to that her eyes she rears;
Th' inferior priestess, at her altar's side,
Trembling, begins the sacred rites of pride.
Unnumbered treasures ope at once, and here
The various offerings of the world appear;   130
From each she nicely culls with curious toil,
And decks the goddess with the glittering spoil.
This casket India's glowing gems unlocks,
And all Arabia breathes from yonder box.
The tortoise here and elephant unite,
Transformed to combs, the speckled, and the white.
Here files of pins extend their shining rows,
Puffs, powders, patches,° Bibles, billets-doux.
Now awful Beauty puts on all its arms;
The fair each moment rises in her charms,   140
Repairs her smiles, awakens every grace,
And calls forth all the wonders of her face;
Sees by degrees a purer blush arise,
And keener lightnings quicken in her eyes.
The busy Sylphs surround their darling care,

---

55. **chariots:** a kind of carriage (but used here for its epic appropriateness).   56. **ombre:** Cf. III.27 ff.   57–66. The thought in these lines is based on the theory of the four elements (earth, water, air, fire) and the supposed dominance of one of these in every temperament.   60. **Salamander:** so called because salamanders were reputed to inhabit fire.   61–62. **away, tea:** a perfect rhyme in Pope's lifetime (pronounced ā).   70. **Assume . . . please:** Cf. the angels in *Paradise Lost*.   73. **spark:** beau.   83. **ideas:** images (the usual older sense).   89. **a . . . blush:** i.e., by rouge.   94. **impertinence:** folly.

101. **sword knots:** decorative tassels tied to the hilt.   119. **Wounds . . . ardors:** i.e., the exaggerated expressions of the billet-doux.   125–32. **A . . . spoil:** Belinda has the role of chief priestess, her maid that of *inferior priestess*, and the manifestation of *the goddess* is Belinda's *image in the glass*.   138. **patches:** beauty patches.

These set the head, and those divide the hair,
Some fold the sleeve, whilst others plait the gown;
And Betty's° praised for labors not her own.

CANTO II

Not with more glories, in th' ethereal plain,
The sun first rises o'er the purpled main,
Than, issuing forth, the rival of his beams
Launched on the bosom of the silver Thames.
Fair nymphs, and well-dressed youths around her shone,
But every eye was fixed on her alone.
On her white breast a sparkling cross she wore,
Which Jews might kiss, and infidels adore.
Her lively looks a sprightly mind disclose,
Quick as her eyes, and as unfixed as those: 10
Favors to none, to all she smiles extends;
Oft she rejects, but never once offends.
Bright as the sun, her eyes the gazers strike,
And, like the sun, they shine on all alike.
Yet graceful ease, and sweetness void of pride,
Might hide her faults, if belles had faults to hide:
If to her share some female errors fall,
Look on her face, and you'll forget 'em all.
    This nymph, to the destruction of mankind,
Nourished two locks, which graceful hung behind
In equal curls, and well conspired to deck   21
With shining ringlets the smooth ivory neck.
Love in these labyrinths his slaves detains,
And mighty hearts are held in slender chains.
With hairy springes° we the birds betray,
Slight lines of hair surprise the finny prey,
Fair tresses man's imperial race ensnare,
And beauty draws us with a single hair.
    Th' adventurous Baron the bright locks admired;
He saw, he wished, and to the prize aspired.   30
Resolved to win, he meditates the way,
By force to ravish, or by fraud betray;
For when success a lover's toil attends,
Few ask, if fraud or force attained his ends.
    For this, ere Phoebus rose, he had implored
Propitious heaven, and every power adored,
But chiefly Love — to Love an altar built,
Of twelve vast French romances, neatly gilt.
There lay three garters, half a pair of gloves;
And all the trophies of his former loves;   40
With tender billets-doux he lights the pyre,
And breathes three amorous sighs to raise the fire.
Then prostrate falls, and begs with ardent eyes
Soon to obtain, and long possess the prize:
The powers gave ear, and granted half his prayer,
The rest, the winds dispersed in empty air.°

But now secure the painted vessel° glides,
The sunbeams trembling on the floating tides:
While melting music steals upon the sky,
And softened sounds along the waters die;   50
Smooth flow the waves, the zephyrs gently play,
Belinda smiled, and all the world was gay.
All but the Sylph — with careful thoughts oppressed,
Th' impending woe sat heavy on his breast.
He summons strait his denizens of air;
The lucid squadrons round the sails repair:
Soft o'er the shrouds aërial whispers breathe,
That seemed but zephyrs to the train beneath.
Some to the sun their insect wings unfold,
Waft on the breeze, or sink in clouds of gold;   60
Transparent forms, too fine for mortal sight,
Their fluid bodies half dissolved in light.
Loose to the wind their airy garments flew,
Thin glittering textures of the filmy dew,
Dipped in the richest tincture of the skies,
Where light disports in ever-mingling dyes,
While every beam new transient colors flings,
Colors that change whene'er they wave their wings.
Amid the circle, on the gilded mast,
Superior by the head,° was Ariel placed;   70
His purple pinions opening to the sun,
He raised his azure wand, and thus begun.
    " Ye Sylphs and Sylphids, to your chief give ear!
Fays, Fairies, Genii, Elves, and Daemons, hear!°
Ye know the spheres and various tasks assigned
By laws eternal to th' aërial kind.
Some° in the fields of purest aether play,
And bask and whiten in the blaze of day.
Some guide the course of wandering orbs on high,
Or roll the planets through the boundless sky.   80
Some less refined, beneath the moon's pale light
Pursue the stars that shoot athwart the night,
Or suck the mists in grosser air below,
Or dip their pinions in the painted bow,
Or brew fierce tempests on the wintry main,
Or o'er the glebe distill the kindly rain.
Others on earth o'er human race preside,
Watch all their ways, and all their actions guide:
Of these the chief the care of nations own,
And guard with arms divine the British throne.   90
    " Our humbler province is to tend the fair,
Not a less pleasing, though less glorious care;
To save the powder from too rude a gale,
Nor let th' imprisoned essences exhale;
To draw fresh colors from the vernal flowers;

---

148. Betty: the maid.   Canto II: 25. springes: snares.   45–
46. powers . . . air: a common mishap in epic.

47. painted vessel: the boat of the Thames waterman who is conveying Belinda and her friends to Hampton Court.   70. Superior . . . head: taller than the rest (as the epic hero always is).   73–74. Ye . . . hear: Cf. the various angelic salutations in *Paradise Lost.*   77–86. Some . . . rain: i.e., some in superlunar regions (supposed to be pure, immutable, ethereal), some in sublunar regions (tumultuous and gross, the home of change).

To steal from rainbows e'er they drop in showers
A brighter wash;° to curl their waving hairs,
Assist their blushes, and inspire their airs;
Nay oft, in dreams, invention we bestow,
To change a flounce, or add a furbelow.   100
"This day, black omens threat the brightest fair
That e'er deserved a watchful spirit's care;
Some dire disaster, or by force, or slight;
But what, or where, the fates have wrapped in
     night.
Whether the nymph shall break Diana's law,°
Or some frail china jar receive a flaw;
Or stain her honor, or her new brocade;
Forget her prayers, or miss a masquerade;
Or lose her heart, or necklace, at a ball;
Or whether Heaven has doomed that Shock must
     fall.   110
Haste, then, ye spirits! to your charge repair:
The fluttering fan be Zephyretta's° care;
The drops to thee, Brillante, we consign;
And, Momentilla, let the watch be thine;
Do thou, Crispissa, tend her favorite lock;
Ariel himself shall be the guard of Shock.
"To fifty chosen Sylphs, of special note,
We trust th' important charge, the petticoat:
Oft have we known that sevenfold fence to fail,
Though stiff with hoops, and armed with ribs of
     whale.   120
Form a strong line about the silver bound,
And guard the wide circumference around.
"Whatever spirit, careless of his charge,
His post neglects, or leaves the fair at large,
Shall feel sharp vengeance soon o'ertake his sins,
Be stopped in vials, or transfixed with pins;
Or plunged in lakes of bitter washes lie,
Or wedged whole ages in a bodkin's eye:
Gums and pomatums° shall his flight restrain,
While clogged he beats his silken wings in vain;
Or alum styptics with contracting power   131
Shrink his thin essence like a riveled° flower:
Or, as Ixion fixed, the wretch shall feel
The giddy motion of the whirling mill,°
In fumes of burning chocolate shall glow,
And tremble at the sea that froths below!"
He spoke; the spirits from the sails descend;
Some, orb in orb,° around the nymph extend;
Some thrid the mazy ringlets of her hair;
Some hang upon the pendants of her ear;   140
With beating hearts the dire event they wait,
Anxious, and trembling for the birth of fate.

97. wash: lotion.   **105. Diana's law:** chastity.   **112–16.** The
sylphs' names are suited to their functions in guarding the fan,
the diamond earrings, the watch, and the curls.   **129. poma-
tums:** pomades.   **132. riveled:** shriveled.   **133–34.** Or . . .
mill: Ixion was punished in Hades by being turned endlessly on
a wheel.   **mill:** the beater used to stir the chocolate.   **138. orb
in orb:** i.e., like the angels in *Paradise Lost*, V.596, above.

CANTO III

Close by those meads, forever crowned with flowers,
Where Thames with pride surveys his rising towers,
There stands a structure° of majestic frame,
Which from the neighboring Hampton takes its
     name.
Here Britain's statesmen oft the fall foredoom
Of foreign tyrants, and of nymphs at home;
Here thou, great Anna! whom three realms obey,
Dost sometimes counsel take—and sometimes tea.
Hither the heroes and the nymphs resort,
To taste awhile the pleasures of a court;   10
In various talk th' instructive hours they passed,
Who gave the ball, or paid the visit last;
One speaks the glory of the British queen,
And one describes a charming Indian screen;
A third interprets motions, looks, and eyes;
At every word a reputation dies.
Snuff, or the fan, supply each pause of chat,
With singing, laughing, ogling, and all that.
Meanwhile, declining from the noon of day,
The sun obliquely shoots his burning ray;   20
The hungry judges soon the sentence sign,
And wretches hang that jurymen may dine;
The merchant from th' Exchange returns in peace,
And the long labors of the toilet cease.
Belinda now, whom thirst of fame invites,
Burns to encounter two adventurous knights,
At ombre° singly to decide their doom;
And swells her breast with conquests yet to come.
Straight the three bands prepare in arms to join,
Each band the number of the sacred nine.   30
Soon as she spreads her hand, th' aërial guard
Descend, and sit on each important card:
First Ariel perched upon a Matador,
Then each, according to the rank they bore;
For Sylphs, yet mindful of their ancient race,
Are, as when women, wondrous fond of place.
Behold,° four Kings in majesty revered,
With hoary whiskers and a forky beard;
And four fair Queens whose hands sustain a flower,
Th' expressive emblem of their softer power;   40
Four Knaves in garbs succinct, a trusty band,
Caps on their heads, and halberds in their hand;
And particolored troops, a shining train,

Canto III: 3. structure: Hampton Court Palace.   **27–100.** Ombre is played with ordinary cards after removing the 10's, 9's,
and 8's. The remaining 40 cards are dealt to three players
(9 each) and a stock (13). The high bidder is called the ombre
(Spanish: *hombre*, man), names the trumps, and has to win more
tricks than his opponents combined. Failure to do so is codille.
The order of values in the hand described, once Belinda has
named trumps, is: Spadillio, ace of spades, always highest card
in ombre; Manillio, deuce of spades, second highest when spades
are trumps; Basto, ace of clubs, always third highest (these are
the *sable Matadors*); and king, queen, knave, 7, 6, 5, 4, 3, of
spades.   **37–42.** Here, and below, Pope describes the face cards
as depicted in his time.

Draw forth to combat on the velvet plain.
The skillful nymph reviews her force with care:
"Let Spades be trumps!" she said, and trumps they
were.°
Now move to war her sable Matadors,
In show like leaders of the swarthy Moors.
Spadillio first, unconquerable lord!
Led off two captive trumps, and swept the board.
As many more Manillio forced to yield,   51
And marched a victor from the verdant field.
Him Basto followed, but his fate more hard
Gained but one trump and one plebeian card.
With his broad saber next, a chief in years,
The hoary Majesty of Spades appears,
Puts forth one manly leg, to sight revealed,
The rest, his many-colored robe concealed.
The rebel Knave, who dares his prince engage,
Proves the just victim of his royal rage.   60
Even mighty Pam,° that Kings and Queens o'er-
threw
And mowed down armies in the fights of loo,
Sad chance of war! now destitute of aid,
Falls undistinguished by the victor Spade!
Thus far both armies to Belinda yield;
Now to the Baron fate inclines the field.
His warlike Amazon her host invades,
Th' imperial consort of the crown of Spades.
The Club's black tyrant first her victim died,
Spite of his haughty mien, and barbarous pride:
What boots the regal circle on his head,   71
His giant limbs, in state unwieldy spread;
That long behind he trails his pompous robe,
And, of all monarchs, only grasps the globe?
The Baron now his Diamonds pours apace;
Th' embroidered King who shows but half his face,
And his refulgent Queen, with powers combined,
Of broken troops an easy conquest find.
Clubs, Diamonds, Hearts, in wild disorder seen,
With throngs promiscuous strew the level green.
Thus when dispersed a routed army runs,   81
Of Asia's troops, and Afric's sable sons,
With like confusion different nations fly,
Of various habit, and of various dye,
The pierced battalions disunited fall,
In heaps on heaps; one fate o'erwhelms them all.
The Knave of Diamonds tries his wily arts,
And wins (oh shameful chance!) the Queen of
Hearts.
At this, the blood the virgin's cheek forsook,
A livid paleness spreads o'er all her look;   90
She sees, and trembles at th' approaching ill,
Just in the jaws of ruin, and codille.
And now (as oft in some distempered State)
On one nice trick depends the general fate.

An Ace of Hearts steps forth: The King unseen
Lurked in her hand, and mourned his captive
Queen:
He springs to vengeance with an eager pace,
And falls like thunder on the prostrate Ace.
The nymph exulting fills with shouts the sky;
The walls, the woods, and long canals reply.   100
Oh thoughtless mortals! ever blind to fate,
Too soon dejected and too soon elate.
Sudden, these honors shall be snatched away,
And cursed forever this victorious day.
For lo! the board with cups and spoons is
crowned,
The berries° crackle, and the mill° turns round;
On shining altars of Japan° they raise
The silver lamp; the fiery spirits blaze:
From silver spouts the grateful liquors glide,
While China's earth receives the smoking tide:°
At once they gratify their scent and taste,   111
And frequent cups prolong the rich repast.
Straight hover round the fair her airy band;
Some, as she sipped, the fuming liquor fanned,
Some o'er her lap their careful plumes displayed,
Trembling, and conscious of the rich brocade.
Coffee (which makes the politician wise,
And see through all things with his half-shut eyes)
Sent up in vapors to the Baron's brain
New stratagems, the radiant lock to gain.   120
Ah cease, rash youth! desist ere 'tis too late,
Fear the just gods, and think of Scylla's fate!
Changed to a bird, and sent to flit in air,
She dearly pays for Nisus' injured hair!°
But when to mischief mortals bend their will,
How soon they find fit instruments of ill!
Just then, Clarissa drew with tempting grace
A two-edged weapon from her shining case:
So ladies in romance assist their knight,
Present the spear, and arm him for the fight.   130
He takes the gift with reverence, and extends
The little engine on his fingers' ends;
This just behind Belinda's neck he spread,
As o'er the fragrant steams she bends her head.
Swift to the lock a thousand sprites repair,
A thousand wings, by turns, blow back the hair;
And thrice they twitched the diamond in her ear;
Thrice she looked back, and thrice the foe drew
near.
Just in that instant, anxious Ariel sought
The close recesses of the virgin's thought;   140

106. **berries:** coffee berries. **mill:** coffee mill. 107. **altars of Japan:** japanned tables, called altars to bring to mind the sacrifices accompanying feasts in epic. 110. **China's . . . tide:** alluding to the china cups, but also to the libations poured on the earth in classical epic. 122–24. **Scylla's . . . hair:** Scylla, daughter of Nisus, plucked from his head a hair on which his life depended and gave it to his enemy Minos. When Minos punished this treachery by drowning Scylla, she was changed to a small sea bird ever pursued by her father in the shape of a sea eagle.

46. **Let . . . were:** Cf. Gen. 1:3: "And God said, 'Let there be light' and there was light." 61. **Pam:** knave of clubs, high card in the game of loo.

As on the nosegay in her breast reclined,
He watched th' ideas rising in her mind,
Sudden he viewed, in spite of all her art,
An earthly lover lurking at her heart.
Amazed, confused, he found his power expired,°
Resigned to fate, and with a sigh retired.

The peer now spreads the glittering forfex° wide,
T' enclose the lock; now joins it, to divide.
Even then, before the fatal engine closed,
A wretched Sylph too fondly interposed;   150
Fate urged the shears, and cut the Sylph in twain,
(But airy substance soon unites again)°
The meeting points the sacred hair dissever
From the fair head, forever, and forever!

Then flashed the living lightning from her eyes,
And screams of horror rend th' affrighted skies.
Not louder shrieks to pitying Heaven are cast,
When husbands, or when lapdogs breathe their
     last;
Or when rich china vessels fallen from high,
In glittering dust, and painted fragments lie! 160

Let wreaths of triumph now my temples twine,
(The victor cried) the glorious prize is mine!
While fish in streams, or birds delight in air,
Or in a coach and six the British fair,
As long as Atalantis° shall be read,
Or the small pillow grace a lady's bed,
While visits shall be paid on solemn days,
When numerous wax-lights in bright order blaze,
While nymphs take treats, or assignations give,
So long my honor, name, and praise shall live! 170
What time would spare, from steel receives its date,
And monuments, like men, submit to fate!
Steel could the labor of the gods destroy,
And strike to dust th' imperial towers of Troy;
Steel could the works of mortal pride confound,
And hew triumphal arches to the ground.
What wonder then, fair nymph! thy hairs should
     feel,
The conquering force of unresisted steel?

CANTO IV

But anxious cares the pensive nymph oppressed,
And secret passions labored in her breast.
Not youthful kings in battle seized alive,
Not scornful virgins who their charms survive,
Not ardent lovers robbed of all their bliss,
Not ancient ladies when refused a kiss,
Not tyrants fierce that unrepenting die,
Not Cynthia when her manteau's pinned awry,
E'er felt such rage, resentment, and despair,
As thou sad virgin! for thy ravished hair.   10

For, that sad moment, when the Sylphs with-
     drew,
And Ariel weeping from Belinda flew,
Umbriel, a dusky, melancholy sprite
As ever sullied the fair face of light,
Down to the central earth, his proper scene,
Repaired to search the gloomy cave of Spleen.°

Swift on his sooty pinions flits the Gnome,°
And in a vapor° reached the dismal dome.°
No cheerful breeze this sullen region knows,
The dreaded East° is all the wind that blows. 20
Here in a grotto, sheltered close from air,
And screened in shades from day's detested glare,
She sighs forever on her pensive bed,
Pain at her side, and Megrim at her head.°

Two handmaids wait the throne: alike in place,
But differing far in figure and in face.
Here stood Ill Nature like an ancient maid,
Her wrinkled form in black and white arrayed;
With store of prayers, for mornings, nights, and
     noons,
Her hand is filled; her bosom with lampoons.   30

There Affectation, with a sickly mien,
Shows in her cheek the roses of eighteen,
Practiced to lisp, and hang the head aside,
Faints into airs, and languishes with pride;
On the rich quilt sinks with becoming woe,
Wrapped in a gown, for sickness, and for show.
The fair ones feel such maladies as these,
When each new nightdress gives a new disease.

A constant vapor o'er the palace flies;
Strange phantoms rising as the mists arise;   40
Dreadful, as hermit's dreams in haunted shades,
Or bright, as visions of expiring maids.
Now glaring fiends, and snakes on rolling spires,
Pale specters, gaping tombs, and purple fires:
Now lakes of liquid gold, Elysian scenes,
And crystal domes, and angels in machines.

Unnumbered throngs on every side are seen,
Of bodies changed to various forms by Spleen.
Here° living teapots stand, one arm held out,
One bent; the handle this, and that the spout: 50
A pipkin there, like Homer's tripod walks;
Here sighs a jar, and there a goose pie talks;
Men prove with child, as powerful fancy works,
And maids turned bottles, call aloud for corks.

Safe passed the Gnome thro' this fantastic band,
A branch of healing spleenwort in his hand.

Canto IV: **16. Spleen:** a name widely and vaguely applied, but usually, as here, to neurotic ailments.   **17. Gnome:** Belinda is no longer under the guardianship of former coquettes but former prudes (cf. I.63–66), and her behavior alters accordingly.   **18. vapor:** used to mean both mist and peevishness. **dome:** Cf. *E. on Crit.*, l. 247n.   **20. East:** Wind supposed to cause the spleen.   **24. Pain . . . head:** Pain and Megrim (migraine) are stationed where the discomforts of spleen were oftenest felt, in the side and head.   **49–54. Here . . . corks:** delusions attributed to the spleen.

---

145. Amazed . . . expired: Cf. I.67–68.   **147. forfex:** Latin (and therefore a heightened "heroic" term like *engine*) for scissors. **152. But . . . again:** as in *Paradise Lost*, VI.327 ff.   **165. Atalantis:** a scandalous novel of the period.

Then thus addressed the power: " Hail, wayward
   queen!
Who rule the sex to fifty from fifteen:
Parent of vapors and of female wit,
Who give th' hysteric, or poetic fit,   60
On various tempers act by various ways,
Make some take physic, others scribble plays;
Who cause the proud their visits to delay,
And send the godly in a pet to pray.
A nymph there is, that all thy power disdains,
And thousands more in equal mirth maintains.
But oh! if e'er thy Gnome could spoil a grace,
Or raise a pimple on a beauteous face,
Like citron waters° matrons cheeks inflame,
Or change complexions at a losing game;°   70
If e'er with airy horns I planted heads,°
Or rumpled petticoats, or tumbled beds,
Or caused suspicion when no soul was rude,
Or discomposed the headdress of a prude,
Or e'er to costive lap dog gave disease,
Which not the tears of brightest eyes could ease:
Hear me, and touch Belinda with chagrin;
That single act gives half the world the spleen."
    The goddess with a discontented air   79
Seems to reject him, tho' she grants his prayer.
A wondrous bag with both her hands she binds,
Like that where once Ulysses held the winds;°
There she collects the force of female lungs,
Sighs, sobs, and passions, and the war of tongues.
A vial next she fills with fainting fears,
Soft sorrows, melting griefs, and flowing tears.
The Gnome rejoicing bears her gifts away,
Spreads his black wings, and slowly mounts to day.
    Sunk in Thalestris' arms the nymph he found,
Her eyes dejected and her hair unbound.   90
Full o'er their heads the swelling bag he rent,
And all the Furies issued at the vent.
Belinda burns with more than mortal ire,
And fierce Thalestris fans the rising fire.
" O wretched maid! " she spread her hands, and
   cried,
(While Hampton's echoes, " Wretched maid! " re-
   plied)°
" Was it for this you took such constant care
The bodkin,° comb, and essence to prepare?
For this your locks in paper durance° bound,
For this with torturing irons wreathed around?
For this with fillets strained your tender head,   101
And bravely bore the double loads of lead?
Gods! shall the ravisher display your hair,
While the fops envy, and the ladies stare!
Honor forbid! at whose unrivaled shrine

Ease, pleasure, virtue, all, our sex resign.
Methinks already I your tears survey,
Already hear the horrid things they say,
Already see you a degraded toast,
And all your honor in a whisper lost!   110
How shall I, then, your helpless fame defend?
'Twill then be infamy to seem your friend!
And shall this prize, th' inestimable prize,
Exposed thro' crystal to the gazing eyes,
And heightened by the diamond's circling rays,°
On that rapacious hand forever blaze?
Sooner shall grass in Hyde Park Circus° grow,
And wits take lodgings in the sound of Bow;°
Sooner let earth, air, sea, to chaos fall,
Men, monkeys, lap dogs, parrots, perish all! "   120
    She said; then raging to Sir Plume repairs,
And bids her beau demand the precious hairs:
(Sir Plume of amber snuffbox justly vain,
And the nice conduct of a clouded° cane)
With earnest eyes, and round unthinking face,
He first the snuffbox opened, then the case,
And thus broke out — " My Lord, why, what the
   devil?
Zounds! damn the lock! 'fore Gad, you must be
   civil!
Plague on't! 'tis past a jest — nay prithee, pox!
Give her the hair " — he spoke, and rapped his
   box.   130
" It grieves me much " (replied the peer again)
" Who speaks so well should ever speak in vain.
But by this lock, this sacred lock I swear,
(Which never more shall join its parted hair;
Which never more its honors shall renew,
Clipped from the lovely head where late it grew)
That while my nostrils draw the vital air,
This hand, which won it, shall forever wear."
He spoke, and speaking, in proud triumph spread
The long-contended honors° of her head.   140
    But Umbriel, hateful Gnome! forbears not so;
He breaks the vial whence the sorrows flow.
Then see! the nymph in beauteous grief appears,
Her eyes half languishing, half drowned in tears;
On her heaved bosom hung her drooping head,
Which, with a sigh, she raised; and thus she said.
    " Forever cursed be this detested day,
Which snatched my best, my favorite curl away!
Happy! ah ten times happy had I been,
If Hampton Court these eyes had never seen!   150
Yet am not I the first mistaken maid,
By love of courts to numerous ills betrayed.
Oh had I rather unadmired remained
In some lone isle, or distant northern land;
Where the gilt chariot never marks the way,

---

69. **citron waters:** brandy flavored with lemon peel.   **70. Or . . .**
game: Cf. III.89.   **71. heads:** i.e., of those reputed to be
cuckolds.   **82. Ulysses . . . winds:** Cf. *Odyssey*, X.19 ff.
96. Pope's echo of III.100 stresses the Aristotelian reversal (from
exultation to suffering) that has occurred.   **98. bodkin:** hairpin
(as at V.95).   **99. paper durance:** i.e., curlers.

114–15. **Exposed . . . rays:** The baron will wear the lock made
up in a ring.   **117. Circus:** Cf. I.44n.   **118. Bow:** the church
of St. Mary-le-Bow, situated in London's unfashionable mercantile section.   **124. clouded:** mottled.   **140. honors:** Cf. *W.
Forest*, l. 221n.

Where none learn ombre, none e'er taste bohea!°
There kept my charms concealed from mortal eye,
Like roses, that in deserts bloom and die.
What moved my mind with youthful lords to
    roam?
Oh had I stayed, and said my prayers at home!
'Twas this, the morning omens seemed to tell, 161
Thrice from my trembling hand the patch-box fell;
The tottering china shook without a wind,
Nay, Poll sat mute, and Shock was most unkind!
A Sylph too warned me of the threats of fate,
In mystic visions, now believed too late!
See the poor remnants of these slighted hairs!
My hands shall rend what even thy rapine spares:
These, in two sable ringlets taught to break,
Once gave new beauties to the snowy neck; 170
The sister lock now sits uncouth, alone,
And in its fellow's fate foresees its own;
Uncurled it hangs, the fatal shears demands,
And tempts once more thy sacrilegious hands.
Oh hadst thou, cruel! been content to seize
Hairs less in sight, or any hairs but these!"

CANTO V

She said: the pitying audience melt in tears.
But Fate and Jove had stopped the Baron's ears.
In vain Thalestris with reproach assails,
For who can move when fair Belinda fails?
Not half so fixed the Trojan could remain,
While Anna begged and Dido raged in vain.°
Then grave Clarissa graceful waved her fan;
Silence ensued, and thus the nymph began.
  "Say° why are beauties praised and honored
    most,
The wise man's passion, and the vain man's toast?
Why decked with all that land and sea afford, 11
Why angels called, and angel-like adored?
Why round our coaches crowd the white-gloved
    beaux,
Why bows the side box from its inmost rows;
How vain are all these glories, all our pains,
Unless good sense preserve what beauty gains:
That men may say, when we the front box grace,
'Behold the first in virtue as in face!'
Oh! if to dance all night, and dress all day,
Charmed the smallpox, or chased old age away;
Who would not scorn what housewife's cares pro-
    duce, 21
Or who would learn one earthly thing of use?
To patch, nay ogle, might become a saint,
Nor could it sure be such a sin to paint.
But since, alas! frail beauty must decay,
Curled or uncurled, since locks will turn to gray;
Since painted, or not painted, all shall fade,

And she who scorns a man, must die a maid;
What then remains but well our power to use,
And keep good humor still whate'er we lose? 30
And trust me, dear! good humor can prevail,
When airs, and flights, and screams, and scolding
    fail.
Beauties in vain their pretty eyes may roll;
Charms strike the sight, but merit wins the soul."
  So spoke the dame, but no applause ensued;
Belinda frowned, Thalestris called her prude.
"To arms, to arms!" the fierce virago cries,
And swift as lightning to the combat flies.
All side in parties, and begin th' attack;
Fans clap, silks rustle, and tough whalebones crack;
Heroes' and heroines' shouts confus'dly rise, 41
And bass and treble voices strike the skies.
No common weapons in their hands are found,
Like gods they fight, nor dread a mortal wound.
  So when bold Homer makes the gods engage,
And heavenly breasts with human passions rage;
'Gainst Pallas, Mars; Latona, Hermes arms;
And all Olympus rings with loud alarms:
Jove's thunder roars, Heaven trembles all around,
Blue Neptune storms, the bellowing deeps resound:
Earth shakes her nodding towers, the ground gives
    way, 51
And the pale ghosts start at the flash of day!
  Triumphant Umbriel on a sconce's height
Clapped his glad wings, and sat to view the fight:
Propped on their bodkin spears, the sprites survey
The growing combat, or assist the fray.
  While thro' the press enraged Thalestris flies,
And scatters death around from both her eyes,
A beau and witling perished in the throng,
One died in metaphor, and one in song. 60
"O cruel nymph! a living death I bear,"
Cried Dapperwit, and sunk beside his chair.
A mournful glance Sir Fopling° upwards cast,
"Those eyes are made so killing"—was his last.
Thus on Maeander's flowery margin lies
Th' expiring swan, and as he sings he dies.
  When bold Sir Plume had drawn Clarissa down,
Chloe stepped in, and killed him with a frown;
She smiled to see the doughty hero slain,
But, at her smile, the beau revived again. 70
  Now° Jove suspends his golden scales in air,
Weighs the men's wits against the lady's hair;
The doubtful beam long nods from side to side;
At length the wits mount up, the hairs subside.
  See, fierce Belinda on the Baron flies,
With more than usual lightning in her eyes:
Nor feared the chief th' unequal fight to try,
Who sought no more than on his foe to die.
But this bold lord with manly strength endued,
She with one finger and a thumb subdued: 80

156. bohea: tea.   Canto V: 5–6. Not . . . vain: In *Aeneid*, IV,
Dido and her sister Anna plead with Aeneas to stay in Carthage.
9–34. Based on the most stirring speech in ancient epic, Sarpe-
don's address to Glaucus in *Iliad*, XII.

62–63. Dapperwit, Fopling: social types suggestive of Restoration
comedies.   71–74. Now . . . subside: Cf. *Paradise Lost*, IV.
996 ff.

Just where the breath of life his nostrils drew,
A charge of snuff the wily virgin threw;
The Gnomes direct, to every atom just,
The pungent grains of titillating dust.
Sudden with starting tears each eye o'erflows,
And the high dome re-echoes to his nose.

" Now meet thy fate," incensed Belinda cried,
And drew a deadly bodkin from her side.
(The same, his ancient personage to deck,
Her great-great-grandsire wore about his neck,　90
In three seal rings; which after, melted down,
Formed a vast buckle for his widow's gown:
Her infant grandame's whistle next it grew,
The bells she jingled, and the whistle blew;
Then in a bodkin graced her mother's hairs,
Which long she wore, and now Belinda wears.)
" Boast not my fall " (he cried) "insulting foe!
Thou by some other shalt be laid as low.
Nor think, to die dejects my lofty mind:
All that I dread is leaving you behind!　100
Rather than so, ah let me still survive,
And burn in Cupid's flames — but burn alive."
" Restore the lock!" she cries; and all around
" Restore the lock!" the vaulted roofs rebound.
Not fierce Othello in so loud a strain
Roared for the handkerchief that caused his pain.°
But see how oft ambitious aims are crossed,
And chiefs contend till all the prize is lost!
The lock, obtained with guilt, and kept with pain,
In every place is sought, but sought in vain:　110
With such a prize no mortal must be blessed,
So Heaven decrees! with Heaven who can contest?
Some° thought it mounted to the lunar sphere,
Since all things lost on earth are treasured there.
There heroes' wits are kept in ponderous vases,
And beaux' in snuffboxes and tweezer cases.
There broken vows and deathbed alms are found,
And lovers' hearts with ends of riband bound,
The courtier's promises, and sick man's prayers,
The smiles of harlots, and the tears of heirs,　120
Cages for gnats, and chains to yoke a flea,
Dried butterflies, and tomes of casuistry.
But trust the Muse — she saw it upward rise,
Though marked by none but quick, poetic eyes:
(So Rome's great founder to the heavens withdrew,
To Proculus alone confessed in view)°
A sudden star, it shot thro' liquid air,
And drew behind a radiant trail of hair.
Not Berenice's locks first rose so bright,
The heavens bespangling with disheveled light.°
The Sylphs behold it kindling as it flies,　131

And pleased pursue its progress thro' the skies.
This the beau monde shall from the Mall° survey,
And hail with music its propitious ray.
This the blest lover shall for Venus take,
And send up vows from Rosamonda's lake.°
This Partridge° soon shall view in cloudless skies,
When next he looks thro' Galileo's eyes;
And hence th' egregious wizard shall foredoom
The fate of Louis,° and the fall of Rome.　140
Then cease, bright nymph! to mourn thy ravished hair,
Which adds new glory to the shining sphere!
Not all the tresses that fair head can boast,
Shall draw such envy as the lock you lost.
For, after all the murders of your eye,
When, after millions slain, yourself shall die;
When those fair suns shall set, as set they must,
And all those tresses shall be laid in dust,
This lock, the Muse shall consecrate to fame,
And midst the stars inscribe Belinda's name.　150

ODE ON SOLITUDE

Pope says he wrote "On Solitude" at twelve, but it was surely much polished before its publication in 1717, and it was further revised for the edition of 1736, the version here given. Horatian in tone and movement, the poem stands in particular relation to Horace's second epode, whose opening line it paraphrases: (*Beatus ille qui procul negotiis* — "Happy the man who far from business cares. . . ."), and embodies the classical idyll of a life philosophically based that Pope was to set up often in his satires as a foil to the scramble for riches. (See Introduction, p. 754.) A useful comparison of the sensibilities of two different ages at work on a similar theme may be made by placing this poem beside Wordsworth's "The World Is Too Much with Us."

Happy the man whose wish and care
　A few paternal acres bound,
Content to breathe his native air,
　　　In his own ground.

Whose herds with milk, whose fields with bread,
　Whose flocks supply him with attire,
Whose trees in summer yield him shade,
　　　In winter fire.

Blest, who can unconcern'dly find
　Hours, days, and years slide soft away,　10

105–06. Othello . . . pain: see *Othello*, IV.i.　113–16. Some . . . cases: In Ariosto's *Orlando Furioso*, XXXIV, the hero's lost wits are recovered from the moon.　125–26. So . . . view: Romulus was translated to heaven in the sight of the Roman senator, Proculus.　129–30. Not . . . light: The hair dedicated by Berenice, queen of Ptolemy II, to insure her husband's safe return from battle, became the constellation Coma Berenices.

133. Mall: promenade in St. James's Park.　136. Rosamonda's lake: pond in St. James's Park named for Fair Rosamond, supposed mistress of Henry II, whose queen (according to story) forced her to take poison.　137. Partridge: contemporary maker of almanacs which purported to predict the future.　140. Louis: Louis XIV, with whom England had long been at war.

In health of body, peace of mind,
    Quiet by day,

Sound sleep by night; study and ease,
    Together mixed; sweet recreation;
And innocence, which most does please
    With meditation.

Thus let me live, unseen, unknown,
    Thus unlamented let me die,
Steal from the world, and not a stone
    Tell where I lie.   20

EPISTLE X

TO A YOUNG LADY
ON HER LEAVING THE TOWN
AFTER THE CORONATION

Pope evidently wrote this poem soon after the coronation of George I on October 20, 1714, though it was not published until 1717. The young lady addressed, "Zephalinda," is Teresa Blount, with whom Pope sometimes fancied himself in love at this period, while "Parthenia" (l. 46) is her sister Martha, the two pseudonyms being taken from a playfully gallant correspondence that the Blount sisters were currently conducting with a young neighbor named Moore. In its tone of teasing tenderness, in its vividly realized everyday world, where the encroachments of reality on the high dream of love are frankly and humorously acknowledged, and especially, perhaps, in its depiction of woman as a not-at-all-impossible she, whom one is obliged neither to reproach for "cruelty," nor to "worship" item by item, the poem illustrates clearly the changes that had taken place in literary conventions about love, as well as, to some extent, in the actual relations of men and women, since the time of Spenser and Donne.

As some fond virgin, whom her mother's care
Drags from the town to wholesome country air,
Just when she learns to roll a melting eye,
And hear a spark, yet think no danger nigh;
From the dear man unwilling she must sever,
Yet takes one kiss before she parts forever:
Thus from the world fair Zephalinda° flew,
Saw others happy, and with sighs withdrew;
Not that their pleasures caused her discontent,   9
She sighed not that they stayed, but that she went.
    She went to plain work,° and to purling brooks,
Old-fashioned halls, dull aunts, and croaking
    rooks;
She went from opera, park, assembly, play,

To morning walks, and prayers three hours a day;
To part her time 'twixt reading and bohea,°
To muse, and spill her solitary tea,
Or o'er cold coffee trifle with the spoon,
Count the slow clock, and dine exact at noon;
Divert her eyes with pictures in the fire,
Hum half a tune, tell stories to the squire;   20
Up to her godly garret after seven,
There starve and pray, for that's the way to Heaven.
    Some squire, perhaps, you take delight to rack,°
Whose game is whisk,° whose treat a toast in sack;
Who visits with a gun, presents you birds,
Then gives a smacking buss, and cries — No words!
Or with his hounds comes hallowing from the
    stable,
Makes love with nods and knees beneath a table:
Whose laughs are hearty, tho' his jests are coarse,
And loves you best of all things — but his horse.
    In some fair evening, on your elbow laid,   31
You dream of triumphs in the rural shade;
In pensive thought recall the fancied scene,
See coronations rise on every green;
Before you pass the imaginary sights
Of lords, and earls, and dukes, and gartered
    knights,
While the spread fan o'ershades your closing eyes;
Then give one flirt,° and all the vision flies.
Thus vanish scepters, coronets, and balls,
And leave you in lone woods or empty walls.   40
    So when your slave,° at some dear idle time,
(Not plagued with headaches,° or the want of
    rhyme)
Stands in the streets, abstracted from the crew,
And while he seems to study, thinks of you;
Just when his fancy points your sprightly eyes,
Or sees the blush of soft Parthenia rise,
Gay° pats my shoulder, and you vanish quite;
Streets, chairs, and coxcombs rush upon my sight;
Vexed to be still in town, I knit my brow,
Look sour, and hum a tune — as you may now.

ELEGY TO THE MEMORY OF
AN UNFORTUNATE LADY

By 1717, when this poem was published, Pope had known at least two unfortunate ladies, whose distresses — and in one case, troubles with a guardian — he had tried to relieve with sympathy and money. But neither

---

TO A YOUNG LADY. **7. Zephalinda:** Assumed names were habitually employed in gallantries. **11. plain work:** i.e., not embroidery or fancywork.

15. **bohea:** Cf. *Rape of the Lock,* IV.156n. 23. **rack:** torture.
24. **whisk:** whist (which, instead of ombre, would be the diversion in the unfashionable country). 38. **flirt:** i.e., of the fan.
41. **your slave:** i.e., the poet. 42. **headaches:** Pope was afflicted with violent headaches. 47. **Gay:** Pope's friend and fellow poet, John Gay.

story corresponds to that of the heroine of the poem, who is best taken, like Wordsworth's Lucy, as a useful fiction. Unfortunate ladies abounded in the ballads, plays, and romances of Pope's time, as they do in popular literature always; he was steeped in the classical elegies of Ovid, Tibullus, Propertius; and he knew at first hand, in his incapacity as a cripple, the pangs of hopeless love and misprized merit. Out of these three elements the poem is built.

What beckoning° ghost, along the moonlight shade
Invites my steps, and points to yonder glade?
'Tis she! — but why that bleeding bosom gored,
Why dimly gleams the visionary sword?°
Oh ever beauteous, ever friendly! tell,
Is it, in Heaven, a crime to love too well?
To bear too tender, or too firm a heart,
To act a lover's or a Roman's part?°
Is there no bright reversion in the sky,
For those who greatly think, or bravely die?　10
　　Why bade ye else, ye Powers! her soul aspire
Above the vulgar flight of low desire?
Ambition first sprung from your blest abodes;
The glorious fault of angels and of gods:
Thence to their images on earth it flows,
And in the breasts of kings and heroes glows.
Most souls, 'tis true, but peep out once an age,
Dull sullen prisoners in the body's cage:
Dim lights of life, that burn a length of years
Useless, unseen, as lamps in sepulchers;　20
Like Eastern kings a lazy state they keep,
And close confined to their own palace, sleep.
　　From these perhaps (ere Nature bade her die)
Fate snatched her early to the pitying sky.
As into air the purer spirits flow,
And separate from their kindred dregs below;°
So flew the soul to its congenial° place,
Nor left one virtue to redeem her race.°
　　But thou, false guardian of a charge too good,
Thou, mean deserter of thy brother's blood!　30
See on these ruby lips the trembling breath,
These cheeks, now fading at the blast of death;
Cold is that breast which warmed the world before,
And those love-darting eyes must roll no more.
Thus, if Eternal Justice rules the ball,
Thus shall your wives, and thus your children fall:
On all the line a sudden vengeance waits,
And frequent hearses shall besiege your gates.
There passengers shall stand, and pointing say,
(While the long funerals blacken all the way)　40
Lo, these were they, whose souls the Furies steeled,
And cursed with hearts unknowing how to yield.

Thus unlamented pass the proud away,
The gaze of fools, and pageant of a day!
So perish all, whose breast ne'er learned to glow
For others' good, or melt at others' woe.
　　What can atone (oh ever-injured shade!)
Thy fate unpitied, and thy rites unpaid?
No friend's complaint, no kind domestic tear
Pleased thy pale ghost, or graced thy mournful bier.
By foreign hands thy dying eyes were closed,　51
By foreign hands thy decent limbs composed,
By foreign hands thy humble grave adorned,
By strangers honored, and by strangers mourned!
What tho' no friends in sable weeds appear,
Grieve for an hour, perhaps, then mourn a year,
And bear about the mockery of woe
To midnight dances, and the public show?
What tho' no weeping Loves thy ashes grace,
Nor polished marble emulate thy face?　60
What tho' no sacred earth allow thee room,°
Nor hallowed dirge be muttered o'er thy tomb?
Yet shall thy grave with rising flowers be dressed,
And the green turf lie lightly on thy breast:
There shall the morn her earliest tears bestow,
There the first roses of the year shall blow;
While angels with their silver wings o'ershade
The ground, now sacred by thy reliques made.
　　So peaceful rests, without a stone, a name,
What once had beauty, titles, wealth, and fame.
How loved, how honored once, avails thee not,　71
To whom related, or by whom begot;
A heap of dust alone remains of thee,
'Tis all thou art, and all the proud° shall be!
　　Poets themselves must fall, like those they sung,
Deaf the praised ear, and mute the tuneful tongue.
Even he, whose soul now melts in mournful lays,
Shall shortly want the generous tear he pays;
Then from his closing eyes thy form shall part,
And the last pang shall tear thee from his heart,
Life's idle business at one gasp be o'er,　81
The Muse forgot, and thou belov'd no more!

ELOÏSA TO ABELARD

The Latin texts of the letters of Héloïse and Abélard were published in 1616; a French rendering of them, highly romanticized, was published by Roger de Rabutin, Comte de Bussy, in 1697, and an English translation from the French by John Hughes in 1713. Pope's epistle, drawing heavily on Hughes, must have been written at some time between the latter date and 1717, when it was published.

The poem belongs to a genre exemplified in Latin literature by Ovid's *Heroides*. These were widely imi-

ELEGY TO AN UNFORTUNATE LADY. 1. beckoning: i.e., because having something to impart. 4. sword: instrument of her suicide. 8. Roman's part: i.e., in taking one's own life. 25–26. As . . . below: i.e., in chemical sublimation. 27. congenial: (1) kindred, (2) natal. 28. race: lineage.

61. What . . . room: i.e., because a suicide. 74. the proud: i.e., the lady's kin (cf. l. 43).

tated by seventeenth-century poets, notably by Drayton, and one of them, Sappho's letter to Phaon, Pope had already translated before 1709. In the form as Ovid practiced it, the speaker is always a woman who has been forsaken by a man, the situation is always "heroic" in that it involves illustrious personages and exalted sentiments, and the passions expressed are intended to be generic rather than particular. That is, as one critic very well puts it, the heroines represent first of all "sorrowing or rebellious love," and only secondarily particular instances, or the poet's individual ideas, of such love. The persons, facts, and emotions being thus "given," the job of the poet is to furnish an interpretation, like the composer working with a known theme, or the painter with the fixed elements of a Pietà.

In achieving his interpretation of Eloïsa, Pope has assimilated a wide field of antecedents. There is the struggle of "honor"—in Eloïsa's case, religious honor—with passion, after the manner of the *drame psychologique* of French classical tragedy. There is an amatory idiom drawn from the new vocabulary of sentiment set abroad by the gallants of the salons and the mystical writers of the Counter-Reformation: "beauteous," "melting," "musing," "pensive," "sad," "dear," "warm," "lambent," "celestial," "pale-eyed," "pitying"—a vocabulary pictorialized in baroque religious painting. There is the psychological landscape of Milton's minor poems, especially *Comus:* "grots and caverns shagged with horrid thorn." And there is, especially, the adaptation to Eloïsa's situation of the structure of the religious exercise: the meditation on the crown, on the cross, on the holy name; only here, being applied to symbols of Nature rather than of Grace, it intensifies the pathos of Eloïsa's passion and its blasphemy. From these materials, Pope makes a poem which, if grasped frankly as an achievement in genre and not as an exercise of the free sensibility, reveals itself as the finest specimen of its kind in English.

ARGUMENT

Abelard and Eloïsa flourished in the twelfth century; they were two of the most distinguished persons of their age in learning and beauty, but for nothing more famous than for their unfortunate passion. After a long course of calamities, they retired each to a several convent, and consecrated the remainder of their days to religion. It was many years after this separation, that a letter of Abelard's to a friend, which contained the history of this misfortune, fell into the hands of Eloïsa. This awakening all her tenderness, occasioned those celebrated letters (out of which the following is partly extracted) which give so lively a picture of the struggles of grace and nature, virtue and passion.

In these deep solitudes and awful cells,
Where heavenly-pensive contemplation dwells,
And ever-musing melancholy reigns;
What means this tumult in a vestal's veins?
Why rove my thoughts beyond this last retreat?

Why feels my heart its long-forgotten heat?
Yet, yet I love!—From Abelard it came,
And Eloïsa yet must kiss the name.
Dear fatal name! rest ever unrevealed,
Nor pass these lips in holy silence sealed: 10
Hide it, my heart, within that close disguise,
Where mixed with God's, his loved idea° lies:
O write it not my hand—the name appears
Already written—wash it out, my tears!
In vain lost Eloïsa weeps and prays,
Her heart still dictates, and her hand obeys.
Relentless walls! whose darksome round contains
Repentant sighs, and voluntary pains: 18
Ye rugged rocks! which holy knees have worn;
Ye grots and caverns shagged with horrid thorn!
Shrines! where their vigils pale-eyed virgins keep,
And pitying saints, whose statues learn to weep!°
   Tho' cold like you, unmoved and silent
      grown,
I have not yet forgot myself to stone.
All is not Heaven's while Abelard has part,
Still rebel nature holds out half my heart;
Nor prayers nor fasts its stubborn pulse restrain,
Nor tears for ages taught to flow in vain.
   Soon as thy letters trembling I unclose,
That well-known name awakens all my woes.   30
Oh name forever sad! forever dear!
Still breathed in sighs, still ushered with a tear.
I tremble too, where'er my own I find,
Some dire misfortune follows close behind.°
Line after line my gushing eyes o'erflow,
Led thro' a sad variety of woe:
Now warm in love, now withering in thy bloom,
Lost in a convent's solitary gloom!
There stern religion quenched th' unwilling flame,
There died the best of passions, love and fame.°   40
   Yet write, oh write me all, that I may join
Griefs to thy griefs, and echo sighs to thine.
Nor foes nor fortune take this power away;
And is my Abelard less kind than they?
Tears still are mine, and those I need not spare,
Love but demands what else were shed in prayer;
No happier task these faded eyes pursue;
To read and weep is all they now can do.
   Then share thy pain, allow that sad relief;
Ah, more than share it, give me all thy grief.   50
Heaven first taught letters for some wretch's aid,
Some banished lover, or some captive maid;
They live, they speak, they breathe what love inspires,
Warm from the soul, and faithful to its fires,

ELOÏSA TO ABELARD. 12. idea: Cf. *Rape of the Lock*, I.83n. 22. statues . . . weep: alluding to the condensation of moisture on the cold stone. 33–34. where'er . . . behind: i.e., in the letter of Abelard's which has fallen into Eloïsa's hands, wherever her name is mentioned it is part of an account of some misfortune to their love. 40. fame: Abelard's retirement in disgrace had prevented his rise to high ecclesiastical office.

The virgin's wish without her fears impart,
Excuse the blush, and pour out all the heart,
Speed the soft intercourse from soul to soul,
And waft a sigh from Indus to the pole.

Thou knowst how guiltless first I met thy flame,
When love approached me under friendship's
    name;°   60
My fancy formed thee of angelic kind,
Some emanation of th' all-beauteous Mind.
Those smiling eyes, attempering every ray,
Shone sweetly lambent with celestial day.
Guiltless I gazed; Heaven listened while you
    sung;
And truths divine came mended from that tongue.
From lips like those what precept failed to move?
Too soon they taught me 'twas no sin to love:
Back thro' the paths of pleasing sense I ran,
Nor wished an angel whom I loved a man.   70
Dim and remote the joys of saints I see;
Nor envy them that heaven I lose for thee.

How oft, when pressed to marriage,° have I said,
Curse on all laws but those which love has made?
Love, free as air, at sight of human ties,
Spreads his light wings, and in a moment flies.
Let wealth, let honor, wait the wedded dame,
August her deed, and sacred be her fame;
Before true passion all those views remove,
Fame, wealth, and honor! what are you to Love?
The jealous god, when we profane his fires,   81
Those restless passions in revenge inspires,
And bids them make mistaken mortals groan,
Who seek in love for aught but love alone.
Should at my feet the world's great master fall,
Himself, his throne, his world, I'd scorn 'em all:
Not Caesar's empress would I deign to prove;
No, make me mistress to the man I love;
If there be yet another name more free,
More fond than mistress, make me that to thee!
Oh! happy state! when souls each other draw,   91
When love is liberty, and nature, law:
All then is full, possessing, and possessed,
No craving void left aching in the breast:
Even thought meets thought ere from the lips it
    part,
And each warm wish springs mutual from the
    heart.
This sure is bliss (if bliss on earth there be)
And once the lot of Abelard and me.

Alas, how changed! what sudden horrors rise!
A naked lover bound and bleeding lies!°   100
Where, where was Eloïse? her voice, her hand,
Her poniard, had opposed the dire command.
Barbarian, stay! that bloody stroke restrain;

The crime was common, common be the pain.°
I can no more; by shame, by rage suppressed,
Let tears, and burning blushes speak the rest.

Canst thou forget that sad, that solemn day,°
When victims at yon altar's foot we lay?
Canst thou forget what tears that moment fell,
When, warm in youth, I bade the world farewell?
As with cold lips I kissed the sacred veil,   111
The shrines all trembled, and the lamps grew pale:
Heaven scarce believed the conquest it surveyed,
And saints with wonder heard the vows I made.
Yet then, to those dread altars as I drew,
Not on the cross my eyes were fixed, but you:
Not grace, or zeal, love only was my call,
And if I lose thy love, I lose my all.
Come! with thy looks, thy words, relieve my woe,
Those still at least are left thee to bestow.   120
Still on that breast enamored let me lie,
Still drink delicious poison from thy eye,
Pant on thy lip, and to thy heart be pressed;
Give all thou canst—and let me dream the rest.
Ah no! instruct me other joys to prize,
With other beauties charm my partial eyes,
Full in my view set all the bright abode,
And make my soul quit Abelard for God.

Ah,° think at least thy flock deserves thy care,
Plants of thy hand, and children of thy prayer.   130
From the false world in early youth they fled,
By thee to mountains, wilds, and deserts led.
You raised these hallowed walls; the desert smiled,
And Paradise was opened in the wild.
No weeping orphan saw his father's stores
Our shrines irradiate, or emblaze the floors;
No silver saints, by dying misers given,
Here bribed the rage of ill-requited heaven:
But such plain roofs as piety could raise,
And only vocal with the Maker's praise.   140
In these lone walls (their day's eternal bound)
These moss-grown domes° with spiry turrets
    crowned,
Where awful arches make a noonday night,
And the dim windows shed a solemn light;
Thy eyes diffused a reconciling ray,
And gleams of glory brightened all the day.
But now no face divine contentment wears,
'Tis all blank sadness, or continual tears.
See how the force of others' prayers I try,
(O pious fraud of amorous charity!)   150
But why should I on others' prayers depend?
Come thou, my father, brother,° husband, friend!
Ah let thy handmaid, sister, daughter move,

---

60. When . . . name: It was while he was her tutor that Abelard fell in love with her.   73. marriage: Eloïsa refused Abelard's offer of marriage.   100. A . . . lies: Abelard was castrated by enraged members of Eloïsa's family.

104. pain: (1) penalty, (2) pain.   107. day: i.e., the day of Eloïsa's profession as a religious, at which Abelard was present. 129-46. Eloïsa speaks as from the Paraclete, a retreat in the wilderness built by Abelard and his students, where on his retirement to Brittany he had installed Eloïsa and her nuns. 142. domes: Cf. E. on Crit., l. 247n.   152. father, brother: i.e., as her spiritual director and fellow religious.

And all those tender names in one, thy love!
The darksome pines that o'er yon rocks reclined
Wave high, and murmur to the hollow wind,
The wandering streams that shine between the hills,
The grots that echo to the tinkling rills,
The dying gales that pant upon the trees,
The lakes that quiver to the curling breeze;   160
No more these scenes my meditation aid,
Or lull to rest the visionary maid:
But o'er the twilight groves and dusky caves,
Long-sounding aisles, and intermingled graves,
Black Melancholy sits, and round her throws
A deathlike silence, and a dread repose:
Her gloomy presence saddens all the scene,
Shades every flower, and darkens every green,
Deepens the murmur of the falling floods,
And breathes a browner horror on the woods.   170
  Yet here for ever, ever must I stay;
Sad proof how well a lover can obey!
Death, only death, can break the lasting chain;
And here, even then, shall my cold dust remain,
Here all its frailties, all its flames resign,
And wait till 'tis no sin to mix with thine.
  Ah wretch! believed the spouse of God in vain,
Confessed within the slave of love and man.
Assist me, Heaven! but whence arose that prayer?
Sprung it from piety, or from despair?   180
Even here, where frozen chastity retires,
Love finds an altar for forbidden fires.
I ought to grieve, but cannot what I ought;
I mourn the lover, not lament the fault;°
I view my crime, but kindle at the view,
Repent old pleasures, and solicit new;
Now turned to Heaven, I weep my past offense,
Now think of thee, and curse my innocence.
Of all affliction taught a lover yet,
'Tis sure the hardest science to forget!   190
How shall I lose the sin, yet keep the sense,
And love th' offender, yet detest th' offense?
How the dear object from the crime remove,
Or how distinguish penitence from love?
Unequal task! a passion to resign,
For hearts so touched, so pierced, so lost as mine.
Ere such a soul regains its peaceful state,
How often must it love, how often hate!
How often hope, despair, resent, regret,
Conceal, disdain — do all things but forget.   200
But let Heaven seize it, all at once 'tis fired;
Not touched, but rapt; not wakened, but inspired!
Oh come! oh teach me Nature to subdue,
Renounce my love, my life, myself — and you.
Fill my fond heart with God alone, for he
Alone can rival, can succeed to thee.
  How happy is the blameless vestal's lot!
The world forgetting, by the world forgot:
Eternal sunshine of the spotless mind!

184. fault: Cf *E. on Crit* , l. 170n.

Each prayer accepted, and each wish resigned;   210
Labor and rest, that equal periods keep;
"Obedient slumbers that can wake and weep";°
Desires composed, affections ever even;
Tears that delight, and sighs that waft to Heaven.
Grace shines around her with serenest beams,
And whispering angels prompt her golden dreams.
For her th' unfading rose of Eden blooms,
And wings of seraphs shed divine perfumes,
For her the Spouse prepares the bridal ring,
For her white virgins hymeneals sing,   220
To sounds of heavenly harps she dies away,
And melts in visions of eternal day.
  Far other dreams my erring soul employ,
Far other raptures, of unholy joy:
When at the close of each sad, sorrowing day,
Fancy restores what vengeance snatched away,
Then conscience sleeps, and leaving nature free,
All my loose soul unbounded springs to thee.
Oh cursed, dear horrors of all-conscious° night!
How glowing guilt exalts the keen delight!   230
Provoking Daemons all restraint remove,
And stir within me every source of love.
I hear thee, view thee, gaze o'er all thy charms,
And round thy phantom glue my clasping arms.
I wake: — no more I hear, no more I view,
The phantom flies me, as unkind as you.
I call aloud; it hears not what I say:
I stretch my empty arms; it glides away.
To dream once more I close my willing eyes;
Ye soft illusions, dear deceits, arise!   240
Alas, no more! methinks we wandering go
Thro' dreary wastes, and weep each other's woe,
Where round some moldering tower pale ivy
     creeps,
And low-browed rocks hang nodding o'er the deeps.
Sudden you mount, you beckon from the skies;
Clouds interpose, waves roar, and winds arise.
I shriek, start up, the same sad prospect find,
And wake to all the griefs I left behind.
  For thee the fates, severely kind, ordain
A cool suspense from pleasure and from pain;   250
Thy life a long dead calm of fixed repose;
No pulse that riots, and no blood that glows.
Still as the sea, ere winds were taught to blow,
Or moving spirit bade the waters flow;°
Soft as the slumbers of a saint forgiven,
And mild as opening gleams of promised heaven.
  Come, Abelard! for what hast thou to dread?
The torch of Venus burns not for the dead.
Nature stands checked; Religion disapproves;

212. "Obedient . . . weep": Pope quotes from Crashaw's poem, "Description of a Religious House," l. 16. **229. all-conscious:** The phrase combines its usual sense of intense awareness with its Latinate sense of sharing a (usually guilty) secret. **254. Or . . . flow:** Abelard's *dead calm* (l. 251) is like that which existed before "the Spirit of God moved upon the face of the waters" (Gen.1:2).

Even thou art cold — yet Eloïsa loves. 260
Ah hopeless, lasting flames! like those that burn
To light the dead, and warm th' unfruitful urn.°
　　What scenes appear where'er I turn my view?
The dear ideas, where I fly, pursue,
Rise in the grove, before the altar rise,
Stain all my soul, and wanton in my eyes.
I waste the matin lamp in sighs for thee,
Thy image steals between my God and me,
Thy voice I seem in every hymn to hear,
With every bead I drop too soft° a tear. 270
When from the censer clouds of fragrance roll,
And swelling organs lift the rising soul,
One thought of these puts all the pomp to flight,
Priests, tapers, temples, swim before my sight:
In seas of flame my plunging soul is drowned,
While altars blaze, and angels tremble round.
　　While prostrate here in humble grief I lie,
Kind, virtuous drops just gathering in my eye,
While praying, trembling, in the dust I roll,
And dawning grace is opening on my soul: 280
Come, if thou dar'st, all charming as thou art!
Oppose thyself to Heaven; dispute my heart;
Come, with one glance of those deluding eyes
Blot out each bright idea of the skies;
Take back that grace, those sorrows, and those
　　　　tears;
Take back my fruitless penitence and prayers;
Snatch me, just mounting, from the blest abode;
Assist the fiends, and tear me from my God!
　　No, fly me, fly me, far as pole from pole;
Rise Alps between us! and whole oceans roll! 290
Ah, come not, write not, think not once of me,
Nor share one pang of all I felt for thee.
Thy oaths I quit, thy memory resign;
Forget, renounce me, hate whate'er was mine.
Fair eyes, and tempting looks (which yet I view!)
Long loved, adored ideas, all adieu!
Oh grace serene! oh virtue heavenly fair!
Divine oblivion of low-thoughted care!
Fresh blooming hope, gay daughter of the sky!
And faith, our early immortality! 300
Enter, each mild, each amicable guest;
Receive, and wrap me in eternal rest!
　　See in her cell sad Eloïsa spread,
Propped on some tomb, a neighbor of the dead.
In each low wind methinks a spirit calls,
And more than echoes talk along the walls.
Here, as I watched the dying lamps around,
From yonder shrine I heard a hollow sound.
"Come, sister, come!" (it said, or seemed to say)
"Thy place is here, sad sister, come away! 310
Once like thyself, I trembled, wept, and prayed,
Love's victim then, tho' now a sainted maid:
But all is calm in this eternal sleep;

Here grief forgets to groan, and love to weep,
Even superstition loses every fear:
For God, not man, absolves our frailties here."
　　I come, I come! prepare your roseate bowers,
Celestial palms, and ever-blooming flowers.
Thither, where sinners may have rest, I go,
Where flames refined in breasts seraphic glow:°
Thou, Abelard! the last sad office pay, 321
And smooth my passage to the realms of day:
See my lips tremble, and my eyeballs roll,
Suck my last breath, and catch my flying soul!
Ah no — in sacred vestments mayst thou stand,
The hallowed taper trembling in thy hand,
Present the cross before my lifted eye,
Teach me at once, and learn of me to die.
Ah then, thy once-loved Eloïsa see!
It will be then no crime to gaze on me. 330
See from my cheek the transient roses fly!
See the last sparkle languish in my eye!
Till every motion, pulse, and breath be o'er;
And even my Abelard belov'd no more.
O Death all-eloquent! you only prove
What dust we dote on, when 'tis man we love.
　　Then too, when fate shall thy fair frame destroy,
(That cause of all my guilt, and all my joy)
In trance ecstatic may thy pangs be drowned,
Bright clouds descend, and angels watch thee
　　　　round, 340
From opening skies may streaming glories shine,
And saints embrace thee with a love like mine.
　　May one kind grave unite each hapless name,
And graft my love immortal on thy fame!
Then, ages hence, when all my woes are o'er,
When this rebellious heart shall beat no more;
If ever chance two wandering lovers brings
To Paraclete's white walls and silver springs,
O'er the pale marble shall they join their heads,
And drink the falling tears each other sheds; 350
Then sadly say, with mutual pity moved,
"Oh may we never love as these have loved!"
From the full choir when loud hosannas rise,
And swell the pomp of dreadful sacrifice,
Amid that scene if some relenting eye
Glance on the stone where our cold relics lie,
Devotion's self shall steal a thought from Heaven,
One human tear shall drop, and be forgiven.
And sure, if fate some future bard shall join
In sad similitude of griefs to mine, 360
Condemned whole years in absence to deplore,
And image charms he must behold no more;
Such if there be, who loves so long, so well;
Let him our sad, our tender story tell;
The well-sung woes will soothe my pensive ghost;
He best can paint 'em who shall feel 'em most.

261–62. like . . . urn: alluding to the lamps that the ancients kept perpetually alive in tombs. 270. too soft: because springing from love, not repentance.

320. Where . . . glow: alluding to the traditional association of seraphs with fire, and to the circumstance that in Heaven *flames* of love are *refined* to love of God.

ESSAY ON MAN

Stimulated to philosophical speculation by Boling-broke on his return from exile in 1723, Pope planned a large ethical work in four books on "Man," "Knowledge and its limits," "Government, both ec-clesiastical and civil," and "Morality, in eight or nine of the most concerning branches of it, four of which would have been the extremes to each of the Cardinal Virtues." Some of the materials garnered up for this scheme eventually made their way into the four so-called *Moral Essays,* or *Epistles to Several Persons,* of which the three addressed to Burlington, to Bathurst, and to a Lady are included in this collection; into the fourth book of the *Dunciad;* and possibly into the Horatian satires. Only the first book was completed as designed, and this was the *Essay on Man.* Pope worked steadily on the project between 1729 and 1733, and by August, 1731, had finished the first three epistles of the *Essay on Man.* These he published in the spring of 1733, and the fourth epistle in January, 1734.

Since the *Essay* is an effort almost unique in English literature to engage the realms of philosophy and poetry without the mediation of any sort of poetic fiction, the degree of Pope's success has always been controversial and is still a matter for debate. Experience shows, however, that the debate is more profitable if carried on unclouded by certain recurrent misunderstandings:

(1) The philosophical doctrines of the *Essay* are not original with Pope. Like the *Essay on Criticism,* and in accord with his views of literature generally, the poem aims to set down "what oft was thought, but ne'er so well expressed." The arguments by which Pope accounts for evil in the world belong to a tradition that goes back through Hooker and Aquinas to St. Augustine and the Stoics, Plato and Plotinus. If we find them unacceptable today, it is not because, given the premise of a divine Providence, we have better ones to offer. Evil remains a mystery, and one of the strengths of the ancient arguments Pope uses is that they do not pretend otherwise. They affirm that the world is rational, has a meaning. They do not affirm that it has a meaning which, in its entirety, can be grasped by men.

(2) The *Essay* does not deny the reality of evil. It does not say that what accords with the good of the whole is for that reason good for men, i.e., that uni-versal good equals partial good. The evils that men experience are real enough, only they must not be assumed to spring from any moral fault in God. Men must have faith that what they know as evil is good in relation to a larger scheme enclosing them, which they cannot comprehend, i.e., that partial evil equals uni-versal good. In this sense, and this only, "whatever is, is right," or as Milton puts it at the close of *Samson:* "All is best, though we oft doubt / What the un-searchable dispose / Of Highest Wisdom brings about." This assertion is made in some form by every theism in the history of the West.

(3) The style of the poem is deliberately abstract. Pope may have erred in giving it this characteristic, but it was not an oversight. The aspect of objects that he felt to be relevant to his theme in the *Essay* was their relation to, their place in, a cosmic order. Thus "the spider's touch," the "nice bee," the "flowery lawn," "man's imperial race," etc., are limited to their generic qualities in a poetic world of "kinds" for the same reason that everything else in the poem is spoken of as "assigned," "measured," "proportioned," "placed": Pope's subject is not the visible universe, but the intel-ligible universe manifested in the visible; the concrete-ness he is concerned with is not of objects as individ-uals, but of conceptual wholes in which objects are ar-ranged.

EPISTLE I

ARGUMENT

Of the nature and state of man with respect to the universe

Of *man* in the abstract. I. That we can judge only with regard to our *own system,* being ignorant of the *relations* of systems and things. II. That man is not to be deemed *imperfect,* but a being suited to his *place* and *rank* in the creation, agreeable to the *general order* of things, and conformable to *ends* and *relations* to him unknown. III. That it is partly upon his *ignorance* of *future* events, and partly upon the *hope* of a *future* state, that all his happiness in the present depends. IV. The *pride* of aiming at more knowledge, and pre-tending to more perfection, the cause of man's error and misery. The *impiety* of putting himself in the place of *God,* and judging of the fitness or unfitness, perfection or imperfection, justice or injustice of his dispensations. V. The *absurdity* of conceiting himself the *final cause* of the creation, or expecting that perfec-tion in the *moral* world, which is not in the *natural.* VI. The *unreasonableness* of his complaints against *Providence,* while on the one hand he demands the perfections of the angels, and on the other the bodily qualifications of the brutes; though, to possess any of the *sensitive faculties* in a higher degree, would render him miserable. VII. That throughout the whole visible world, an universal *order* and *gradation* in the sensual and mental faculties is observed, which causes a *sub-ordination* of creature to creature, and of all creatures to man. The gradations of *sense, instinct, thought, re-flection, reason;* that reason alone countervails all the other faculties. VIII. How much further this *order* and *subordination* of living creatures may extend, above and below us; were any part of which broken, not that part only, but the whole connected *creation* must be destroyed. IX. The *extravagance, madness,* and *pride* of such a desire. X. The consequence of all, the *abso-lute submission* due to Providence, both as to our *present* and *future* state.

Awake, my St. John! leave all meaner things
To low ambition, and the pride of kings.
Let° us (since life can little more supply
Than just to look about us and to die)
Expatiate free o'er all this scene of man;

ESSAY ON MAN.   **Epistle I:**   **3 ff.** The study of man is pre-sented as a tour of a gentleman's estate, or a hunt.

A mighty maze! but not without a plan;
A wild, where weeds and flowers promiscuous
    shoot;
Or garden, tempting with forbidden fruit.
Together let us beat this ample field,
Try what the open, what the covert yield;   10
The latent tracts,° the giddy heights, explore
Of all who blindly creep, or sightless soar;
Eye Nature's walks, shoot folly as it flies,
And catch the manners living as they rise;
Laugh where we must, be candid° where we can;
But vindicate the ways of God to man.
    I. Say first, of God above, or man below,
What can we reason, but from what we know?
Of man, what see we but his station here,
From which to reason, or to which refer?   20
Thro' worlds unnumbered tho' the God be
    known,
'Tis ours to trace him only in our own.
He, who thro' vast immensity can pierce,
See worlds on worlds compose one universe,
Observe how system into system runs,
What other planets circle other suns,
What varied being peoples every star,
May tell why Heaven has made us as we are.
But of this frame the bearings, and the ties,
The strong connections, nice dependencies,   30
Gradations just, has thy pervading soul
Looked thro'? or can a part contain the whole?
    Is the great chain,° that draws all to agree,
And drawn supports, upheld by God, or thee?
    II. Presumptuous man! the reason wouldst thou
    find,
Why formed so weak, so little, and so blind?
First, if thou canst, the harder reason guess,
Why formed no weaker, blinder, and no less?
Ask of thy mother earth, why oaks are made
Taller or stronger than the weeds they shade?   40
Or ask of yonder argent fields above,
Why Jove's satellites° are less than Jove?
    Of° systems possible, if 'tis confessed
That Wisdom Infinite must form the best,
Where all must full or not coherent be,
And all that rises, rise in due degree;
Then, in the scale of reasoning life, 'tis plain,
There must be, somewhere, such a rank as man:°
And all the question (wrangle e'er so long)

Is only this, if God has placed him wrong?   50
    Respecting° man, whatever wrong we call,
May, must be right, as relative to all.
In human works, though labored on with pain,
A thousand movements scarce one purpose gain;
In God's, one single can its end produce;
Yet serves to second too some other use.
So man, who here seems principal alone,
Perhaps acts second to some sphere unknown,
Touches some wheel, or verges to some goal;
'Tis but a part we see, and not a whole.   60
    When° the proud steed shall know why man re-
    strains
His fiery course, or drives him o'er the plains;
When the dull ox, why now he breaks the clod,
Is now a victim, and now Egypt's god:
Then shall man's pride and dulness comprehend
His actions', passions', being's, use and end;
Why doing, suffering, checked, impelled; and why
This hour a slave, the next a deity.
    Then say not man's imperfect, Heaven in fault;
Say rather, man's as perfect as he ought: 70
His knowledge measured to his state and place;
His time a moment, and a point his space.
If to be perfect in a certain sphere,°
What matter, soon or late, or here or there?
The blest today is as completely so,
As who began a thousand years ago.°
    III. Heaven from all creatures hides the book of
    fate,
All but the page prescribed, their present state:
From brutes what men, from men what spirits
    know:
Or who could suffer being here below?   80
The lamb thy riot dooms to bleed today,
Had he thy reason, would he skip and play?
Pleased to the last, he crops the flowery food,
And licks the hand just raised to shed his blood.
Oh blindness to the future! kindly given,
That each may fill the circle marked by Heaven:
Who° sees with equal eye, as God of all,
A hero perish, or a sparrow fall,
Atoms or systems into ruin hurled,
And now a bubble burst, and now a world.   90
    Hope humbly then; with trembling pinions soar;

---

11. **tracts:** regions, but also tracks. 15. **candid:** kindly disposed.
33. **chain:** Cf. I.207–41, and *Paradise Lost*, V.469–90, above.
42. **satellites:** Jupiter's moons (pronounced satéllités). 43–
46. **Of . . . degree:** Common assumptions of traditional cos-
mologies: that God in his goodness would choose to create only
the best world *possible;* that the best world would be a *full* one,
containing the maximum number of kinds of being; and that
the chain or ladder in which these kinds are organized rises by
even steps, *due degree.* 47–48. **Then . . . man:** i.e., in that
part of the ladder (*scale*) containing rational creatures, there
must be a rank combining the rational with the animal — as
man does.

51. **Respecting:** with respect to. 51 ff. Here begin the two
main arguments of this epistle: (1) that man's qualities and
defects are what they should be with respect to his function in
the whole scheme of things, which is known only to God (ll. 51–
172); and (2) that these qualities and defects are also what they
should be with respect to himself, since they constitute his well-
being (ll. 173–232). 61–68. **When . . . deity:** i.e., just as animals serve human purposes unintelligible to them, so man may
be serving divine purposes unintelligible to him. 73. **in . . .
sphere:** in an afterlife. 75–76. **The . . . ago:** i.e., beatitude
is not something one has more of by beginning to have it sooner.
87–90. **Who . . . world:** Cf. Matt. 10:29–31: "Are not two sparrows sold for a farthing? and one of them shall not fall on the
ground without your Father. . . . Fear ye not therefore, ye are
of more value than many sparrows."

Wait the great teacher Death; and God adore.
What future bliss, he gives not thee to know,
But gives that hope to be thy blessing now.
Hope springs eternal in the human breast:
Man never is, but always to be blest:
The soul, uneasy and confined from home,
Rests and expatiates in a life to come.

Lo,° the poor Indian! whose untutored mind   100
Sees God in clouds, or hears him in the wind;
His soul, proud science never taught to stray
Far as the solar walk, or milky way;
Yet simple Nature to his hope has given,
Behind the cloud-topped hill, an humbler Heaven;
Some safer world in depth of woods embraced,
Some happier island in the watery waste,
Where slaves once more their native land behold,
No fiends torment, no Christians thirst for gold.
To be, contents his natural desire,
He asks no angel's wing, no seraph's fire;   110
But thinks, admitted to that equal sky,
His faithful dog shall bear him company.

IV. Go, wiser thou! and, in thy scale of sense,
Weigh thy opinion against Providence;
Call imperfection what thou fanciest such,
Say, here he° gives too little, there too much;
Destroy all creatures for thy sport or gust,°
Yet cry, if man's unhappy, God's unjust;
If man alone engross not Heaven's high care,
Alone made perfect here, immortal there: 120
Snatch from his hand the balance and the rod,
Rejudge his justice, be the God of God.

In pride, in reasoning pride, our error lies;
All quit their sphere, and rush into the skies.
Pride still is aiming at the blest abodes,
Men would be angels, angels would be gods.
Aspiring to be gods, if angels fell,
Aspiring to be angels, men rebel:
And who but wishes to invert the laws
Of order, sins against th' Eternal Cause.   130

V. Ask° for what end the heavenly bodies shine,
Earth for whose use? Pride answers, " 'Tis for
    mine:
For me kind Nature wakes her genial power,
Suckles each herb, and spreads out every flower;
Annual for me, the grape, the rose renew
The juice nectareous, and the balmy dew;
For me, the mine a thousand treasures brings;
For me, health gushes from a thousand springs;
Seas roll to waft me, suns to light me rise;
My footstool earth, my canopy the skies."   140

But errs not Nature from this gracious end,
From burning suns when livid deaths descend,

When earthquakes swallow, or when tempests
    sweep
Towns to one grave, whole nations to the deep?
"No" ('tis replied) "the first Almighty Cause
Acts not by partial, but by general laws;
Th' exceptions few; some change° since all began:
And what created perfect? "° — Why then man?
If the great end be human happiness,
Then Nature deviates; and can man do less?   150
As much that end a constant course requires
Of showers and sunshine, as of man's desires;
As much eternal springs and cloudless skies,
As men forever temperate, calm, and wise.
If plagues or earthquakes break not Heaven's de-
    sign,
Why then a Borgia, or a Catiline?°
Who knows but He, whose hand the lightning
    forms,
Who heaves old ocean, and who wings the storms,
Pours fierce ambition in a Caesar's mind,
Or turns young Ammon° loose to scourge man-
    kind?   160
From pride, from pride, our very reasoning springs;
Account for moral, as for natural things:
Why charge we Heaven in those, in these acquit?
In both, to reason right is to submit.

Better for us, perhaps, it might appear,
Were there all harmony, all virtue here;
That never air or ocean felt the wind;
That never passion discomposed the mind.
But ALL subsists by elemental strife;
And passions are the elements of life.   170
The general order, since the whole began,
Is kept in Nature, and is kept in man.

VI. What° would this man? Now upward will
    he soar,
And little less than angel, would be more;
Now looking downwards, just as grieved appears
To want the strength of bulls, the fur of bears.
Made for his use all creatures if he call,
Say what their use, had he the powers of all?
Nature to these, without profusion, kind,
The proper organs, proper powers assigned;   180
Each seeming want compensated° of course,
Here with degrees of swiftness, there of force;
All in exact proportion to the state;

99-112. Lo . . . company: Cf. IV.177-78.   116. he: God.
117. gust: individual taste.   131-72. Man's "Pride" argues
that the universe was made for him exclusively; but just as
certain natural phenomena like earthquakes and tempests contradict this, so do certain moral phenomena — viz., man's
passions and his capacity through them to choose evil.

147. change: referring to Newton's belief that irregularities
were accumulating in the cosmic system, or to the deteriorations
traditionally laid to the Fall (cf. *Paradise Lost*, X.651 ff.)
148. "And . . . perfect?": i.e., every created thing is by definition imperfect, God alone being perfect.   156. Borgia, Catiline:
Pope alludes to the crimes associated with the Borgia family in
Renaissance Italy and to the conspiracies of Lucius Sergius
Catiline against the Roman republic.   160. young Ammon:
Cf. *E. on Crit.*, l. 376n.   173 ff. Having dealt with the complaint that man has been poorly treated in comparison with the
ranks above him, Pope turns to the complaint that he has been
poorly treated even in comparison with the ranks below.
181. compensated: pronounced compénsatéd.

Nothing to add, and nothing to abate.
Each beast, each insect, happy in its own:
Is Heaven unkind to man, and man alone?
Shall he alone, whom rational we call,
Be pleased with nothing, if not blessed with all?
　　The bliss of man (could pride that blessing find)
Is not to act or think beyond mankind;　　190
No powers of body or of soul to share,
But what his nature and his state can bear.
Why has not man a microscopic eye?
For this plain reason, man is not a fly.
Say what the use, were finer optics given,
T' inspect a mite, not comprehend the heaven?
Or touch, if tremblingly alive all o'er,
To smart and agonize at every pore?
Or quick effluvia darting through the brain,
Die of a rose in aromatic pain?　　200
If nature thundered in his opening ears,
And stunned him with the music of the spheres,
How would he wish that Heaven had left him
　　still
The whispering zephyr, and the purling rill?
Who finds not Providence all good and wise,
Alike in what it gives, and what denies?
　　VII. Far as creation's ample range extends,
The scale of sensual, mental powers ascends:
Mark how it mounts, to man's imperial race,
From the green myriads in the peopled grass:　　210
What modes of sight betwixt each wide extreme,
The mole's dim curtain, and the lynx's beam:°
Of smell, the headlong lioness between,
And hound sagacious° on the tainted green:
Of hearing, from the life that fills the flood,
To that which warbles thro' the vernal wood:
The spider's touch, how exquisitely fine!
Feels at each thread, and lives along the line:
In the nice bee, what sense so subtly true
From poisonous herbs extracts the healing dew?
How instinct varies in the groveling swine,　　221
Compared, half-reasoning elephant, with thine!
'Twixt that,° and reason, what a nice barrier,°
Forever separate, yet forever near!
Remembrance and reflection° how allied;
What thin partitions sense from thought divide:
And middle natures,° how they long to join,
Yet never pass th' insuperable line!
Without this just gradation, could they be
Subjected, these to those, or all to thee?　　230
The powers of all subdued by thee alone,
Is not thy reason all these powers in one?

212. beam: Sight was formerly believed to depend on rays
emitted by the eye.　214. sagacious: quick-scented.　223. that:
i.e., instinct (the animals' highest faculty, as reason is man's).
barrier: sometimes accented on the last syllable in Pope's time.
225. Remembrance, reflection: the animals' power of simple
memory; man's power of looking before and after, drawing
conclusions, making plans.　227. middle natures: those whose
qualities bridge two classes, like bats.

　　VIII. See, thro' this air, this ocean, and this
　　earth,
All matter quick, and bursting into birth.
Above, how high progressive life may go!
Around, how wide! how deep extend below!
Vast chain of being! which from God began,
Natures ethereal, human, angel, man,
Beast, bird, fish, insect, what no eye can see,
No glass can reach; from Infinite to thee,　　240
From thee to nothing. — On superior powers
Were we to press, inferior might on ours:
Or in the full creation leave a void,
Where, one step broken, the great scale's destroyed:
From Nature's chain whatever link you strike,
Tenth or ten thousandth, breaks the chain alike.
　　And, if each system in gradation roll
Alike essential to th' amazing whole,
The least confusion but in one, not all
That system only, but the whole must fall.　　250
Let earth unbalanced from her orbit fly,
Planets and suns run lawless thro' the sky;
Let ruling angels from their spheres be hurled,
Being on being wrecked, and world on world;
Heaven's whole foundations to their center nod,
And Nature tremble to the throne of God.
All this dread order break — for whom? for thee?
Vile worm! — Oh madness! pride! impiety!
　　IX. What° if the foot, ordained the dust to tread,
Or hand, to toil, aspired to be the head?　　260
What if the head, the eye, or ear repined
To serve mere engines to the ruling mind?
Just as absurd for any part to claim
To be another, in this general frame:
Just as absurd, to mourn the tasks or pains,
The great directing Mind of All ordains.
　　All are but parts of one stupendous whole,
Whose body Nature is, and God the soul;
That, changed thro' all, and yet in all the same;
Great in the earth, as in th' ethereal frame;　　270
Warms in the sun, refreshes in the breeze,
Glows in the stars, and blossoms in the trees,
Lives thro' all life, extends thro' all extent,
Spreads undivided, operates unspent;
Breathes in our soul, informs our mortal part,
As full, as perfect, in a hair as heart;
As full, as perfect, in vile man that mourns,
As the rapt seraph that adores and burns:
To him no high, no low, no great, no small;
He fills, he bounds, connects, and equals° all.　　280
　　X. Cease then, nor order imperfection name:
Our proper bliss depends on what we blame.
Know thy own point: This kind, this due degree
Of blindness, weakness, Heaven bestows on thee.
Submit. — In this, or any other sphere,

259 ff. Pope applies to unity in the cosmos the familiar analogy
of body-and-members that St. Paul applies to unity in the spirit
(I Cor. 12).　280. equals: makes all equal.

Secure to be as blest as thou canst bear:
Safe in the hand of one disposing Power,
Or in the natal, or the mortal hour.
All Nature is but art, unknown to thee;
All chance, direction, which thou canst not see;
All discord, harmony not understood;   291
All partial evil, universal good:
And, spite of pride, in erring reason's spite,
One truth is clear, Whatever is, is right.

EPISTLE II

ARGUMENT

Of the nature and state of *man* with respect to *himself*,
as an individual

I. *The* business of man not to pry into *God,* but to
study *himself.* His *middle nature;* his powers and frailties. The limits of his *capacity.* II. The two principles
of man, *self-love* and *reason,* both necessary. *Self-love*
the stronger, and why. Their end the same. III. The
passions and their use. The *predominant passion,* and
its force. Its necessity, in directing men to different
purposes. Its providential use, in fixing our principle,
and ascertaining our virtue. IV. *Virtue* and *vice* joined
in our *mixed nature;* the limits near, yet the things
separate and *evident:* What is the office of *reason.* V.
How odious *vice* in itself, and how we deceive ourselves
into it. VI. That, however, the *ends* of *Providence* and
general good are answered in our passions and imperfections. How usefully these are distributed to all *orders
of men.* How useful they are to *society.* And to the *individuals.* In every *state,* and every *age* of life.

I. Know then thyself, presume not God to scan;°
The proper study of mankind is man.
Placed on this isthmus of a middle state,
A being darkly wise, and rudely great:
With too much knowledge for the skeptic side,
With too much weakness for the Stoic's pride,°
He hangs between; in doubt to act, or rest;
In doubt to deem himself a god, or beast;
In doubt his mind or body to prefer;
Born but to die, and reasoning but to err;   10
Alike in ignorance, his reason such,
Whether he thinks too little, or too much:
Chaos of thought and passion, all confused;
Still by himself abused, or disabused;
Created half to rise, and half to fall;
Great lord of all things, yet a prey to all;
Sole judge of truth, in endless error hurled:
The glory, jest, and riddle of the world!
    Go,° wondrous creature! mount where science
      guides,

Go, measure earth, weigh air, and state the tides;
Instruct the planets in what orbs to run,   21
Correct old time, and regulate the sun;
Go, soar with Plato to th' empyreal sphere,
To the first good, first perfect, and first fair;
Or tread the mazy round his followers trod,
And quitting sense° call imitating God;
As Eastern priests in giddy circles run,
And turn their heads to imitate the sun.°
Go, teach Eternal Wisdom how to rule —
Then drop into thyself, and be a fool!   30
    Superior beings, when of late they saw
A mortal man unfold all Nature's law,
Admired such wisdom in an earthly shape,
And showed a Newton as we show an ape.
    Could he, whose rules the rapid comet bind,°
Describe or fix one movement of his mind?
Who saw its fires here rise, and there descend,
Explain his own beginning, or his end?
Alas what wonder! man's superior part
Unchecked may rise, and climb from art to art;   40
But when his own great work is but begun,
What reason weaves, by passion is undone.
Trace science then, with modesty thy guide;
First strip off all her equipage of pride;
Deduct what is but vanity, or dress,
Or learning's luxury, or idleness;
Or tricks to show the stretch of human brain,
Mere curious pleasure, or ingenious pain;
Expunge the whole, or lop th' excrescent parts
Of all our vices have created arts;   50
Then see how little the remaining sum,
Which served the past, and must the times to
      come!
    II. Two principles in human nature reign;
Self-love,° to urge, and reason, to restrain;
Nor this a good, nor that a bad we call,
Each works its end, to move or govern all:
And to their proper operation still,
Ascribe all good; to their improper, ill.
    Self-love, the spring of motion, acts° the soul;
Reason's comparing balance° rules the whole.   60
Man, but for that, no action could attend,
And but for this, were active to no end:
Fixed like a plant on his peculiar° spot,

is not physics or metaphysics, but ethics (cf. *Paradise Lost,*
VIII.172–87) — to know himself and learn how to live with his
dual nature, which is partly rational like the angels, partly
passional like the animals.   **26. quitting sense:** quitting not
only common sense, but also the body (in the soul's mystical
ascents to the *first fair*).   **28. turn . . . sun:** Certain Mohammedan devotees were credited with rotating the head in order to
imitate the motion of celestial bodies.   **35. rules . . . bind:**
Newton's *Principia* offered calculations of the trajectory of
comets.   **54. Self-love:** the name in Pope's time for the ap-
petitive elements in human nature — i.e., self-fulfillment, not
selfishness.   **59. acts:** actuates.   **60. balance:** Pope compares
the role of reason to that of the recently invented balance wheel
in the escapement mechanism of watches.   **63. peculiar:** individual.

Epistle II: 1. scan: i.e., pry into and judge by the limited standard of human reason (cf. *Paradise Lost,* VIII.71–75).   **6.** The
Stoic's pride is the notion that man can eradicate passion and
become a wholly intellectual being.   **19 ff.** i.e., man's main task

To draw nutrition, propagate, and rot;
Or, meteor-like, flame lawless thro' the void,
Destroying others, by himself destroyed.
    Most strength the moving principle requires;
Active its task, it prompts, impels, inspires.
Sedate and quiet the comparing lies,
Formed but to check, deliberate, and advise.   70
Self-love still stronger, as its objects nigh;
Reason's at distance, and in prospect lie:
That sees immediate good by present sense;
Reason, the future and the consequence.
Thicker than arguments, temptations throng,
At best more watchful this, but that more strong.
The action of the stronger to suspend,
Reason still use, to reason still attend.
Attention, habit and experience gains;
Each strengthens reason, and self-love restrains. 80
    Let subtle schoolmen teach these friends to fight,
More studious to divide than to unite;
And grace and virtue,° sense and reason split,
With all the rash dexterity of wit.
Wits, just like fools, at war about a name,
Have full as oft no meaning, or the same.
Self-love and reason to one end aspire,
Pain their aversion, pleasure their desire;
But greedy That, its object would devour,
This taste the honey, and not wound the flower:
Pleasure, or wrong or rightly understood,   91
Our greatest evil, or our greatest good.
    III. Modes of self-love the passions we may call:
'Tis real good, or seeming, moves them all:
But since not every good we can divide,
And reason bids us for our own provide;
Passions, tho' selfish, if their means be fair,
List° under reason, and deserve her care;
Those, that imparted,° court a nobler aim,
Exalt their kind, and take some virtue's name. 100
    In lazy apathy° let Stoics boast
Their virtue fixed; 'tis fixed as in a frost;
Contracted all, retiring to the breast;
But strength of mind is exercise, not rest:
The rising tempest puts in act the soul,
Parts it may ravage, but preserves the whole.
On life's vast ocean diversely we sail,
Reason the card,° but passion is the gale;
Nor God alone in the still calm we find,   109
He mounts the storm, and walks upon the wind.°
    Passions,° like elements, though born to fight,

Yet, mixed and softened, in his work unite:
These 'tis enough to temper and employ;
But what composes man, can man destroy?
Suffice that reason keep to Nature's road,
Subject, compound them, follow her and God.
Love, Hope, and Joy, fair Pleasure's smiling train,
Hate, Fear, and Grief, the family of Pain,
These mixed with art, and to due bounds confined,
Make and maintain the balance of the mind: 120
The lights and shades, whose well-accorded strife
Gives all the strength and color of our life.
    Pleasures are ever in our hands or eyes;
And when in act they cease, in prospect, rise:
Present to grasp, and future still to find,
The whole employ of body and of mind.
All spread their charms, but charm not all alike;
On different senses different objects strike;
Hence different passions more or less inflame,
As strong or weak, the organs of the frame;   130
And hence one master passion in the breast,
Like Aaron's serpent,° swallows up the rest.
    As man, perhaps, the moment of his breath,
Receives the lurking principle of death;
The young disease, that must subdue at length,
Grows with his growth, and strengthens with his
    strength:
So, cast and mingled with his very frame,
The mind's disease, its ruling passion came;
Each vital humor which should feed the whole,
Soon flows to this, in body and in soul: 140
Whatever warms the heart, or fills the head,°
As the mind opens, and its functions spread,
Imagination plies her dangerous art,
And pours it all upon the peccant part.
    Nature its mother, habit is its nurse;
Wit, spirit, faculties, but make it worse;
Reason itself but gives it edge and power;
As Heaven's blest beam turns vinegar more sour.°
    We, wretched subjects, tho' to lawful sway,
In this weak queen some favorite still obey;   150
Ah! if she lend not arms, as well as rules,
What can she more than tell us we are fools?
Teach us to mourn our nature, not to mend,
A sharp accuser, but a helpless friend!
Or from a judge turn pleader, to persuade
The choice we make, or justify it made;
Proud of an easy conquest all along,
She but removes weak passions for the strong:
So, when small humors gather to a gout,
The doctor fancies he has driven them out.   160

---

83. grace . . . virtue: Pope refers to the theological controversy whether man is saved by God's grace alone or contributes to his salvation by his works. **98. List:** enlist. **99. that imparted:** i.e., after reason has been imparted to them. **101. apathy:** technical Stoic term for the ideal passionless state. **108. card:** mariner's map, or, possibly, the card on which are marked the 32 points in a mariner's compass. **109–10. Nor . . . wind:** Thus God is revealed as a "still small voice" in I Kings 19:11–12, but as moving on "wings of the wind" in Ps. 18:10. **111 ff.** i.e., as God created a cosmic order from the chaos of the elements (*Paradise Lost*, II.890 ff., above, and VII.232 ff.), so man must

create an ethical order from the chaos of the passions — all of which, including the ruling passion, are divine in origin. **132. Aaron's serpent:** In Jehovah's contest with the Egyptian gods (Exod. 7:10–12), the rods of Pharaoh's magicians became serpents, but Aaron's rod became a bigger serpent that devoured the rest. **141. heart, head:** Vital spirits (cf. *E. on Crit.*, l. 77n.) were made in the heart, animal spirits in the head. **148. beam . . . sour:** To make an especially sour vinegar, wine was set out in the midday sun.

Yes,° Nature's road must ever be preferred;
Reason is here no guide, but still a guard:
'Tis hers to rectify, not overthrow,
And treat this passion more as friend than foe:
A mightier Power the strong direction sends,
And several men impels to several ends:
Like varying winds, by other passions tossed,
This drives them constant to a certain coast.
Let power or knowledge, gold or glory, please,
Or (oft more strong than all) the love of ease; 170
Thro' life 'tis followed, even at life's expense;
The merchant's toil, the sage's indolence,
The monk's humility, the hero's pride,
All, all alike, find reason on their side.

Th'° Eternal Art educing good from ill,
Grafts on this passion our best principle:
'Tis thus the mercury of man° is fixed,
Strong grows the virtue with his nature mixed;
The dross cements what else were too refined,
And in one interest body acts with mind. 180

As fruits, ungrateful to the planter's care,
On savage stocks inserted, learn to bear;
The surest virtues thus from passions shoot,
Wild nature's vigor working at the root.
What° crops of wit and honesty appear
From spleen, from obstinacy, hate, or fear!
See anger, zeal and fortitude supply;
Even avarice, prudence; sloth, philosophy;
Lust, thro' some certain strainers well refined,
Is gentle love, and charms all womankind; 190
Envy, to which th' ignoble mind's a slave,
Is emulation in the learn'd or brave;
Nor virtue, male or female, can we name,
But what will grow on pride, or grow on shame.

Thus Nature gives us (let it check our pride)°
The virtue nearest to our vice allied:
Reason the bias turns to good from ill,
And Nero reigns a Titus,° if he will.
The fiery soul abhorred in Catiline,
In Decius charms, in Curtius° is divine: 200
The same ambition can destroy or save,
And makes a patriot as it makes a knave.

IV. This light and darkness in our chaos joined,
What shall divide? The God within the mind.°

Extremes in Nature equal ends produce,°
In man they join to some mysterious use;
Tho' each by turns the other's bound invade,
As, in some well-wrought picture, light and shade,
And oft so mix, the difference is too nice
Where ends the virtue, or begins the vice. 210

Fools! who from hence into the notion fall,
That vice or virtue there is none at all.
If white and black blend, soften, and unite
A thousand ways, is there no black or white?
Ask your own heart, and nothing is so plain;
'Tis to mistake them, costs the time and pain.

V. Vice is a monster of so frightful mien,
As, to be hated, needs but to be seen;
Yet seen too oft, familiar with her face,
We first endure, then pity, then embrace. 220
But where th' extreme of vice, was ne'er agreed:
Ask where's the north? at York, 'tis on the Tweed;
In Scotland, at the Orcades; and there,
At Greenland, Zembla,° or the Lord knows where.
No creature owns it in the first degree,
But thinks his neighbor farther gone than he;
Even those who dwell beneath its very zone,
Or never feel the rage, or never own;
What happier natures shrink at with affright,
The hard inhabitant contends is right. 230

VI. Virtuous and vicious every man must be,
Few in th' extreme, but all in the degree;
The rogue and fool by fits is fair and wise;
And even the best, by fits, what they despise.
'Tis but by parts we follow good or ill;
For, vice or virtue, self directs it still;
Each individual seeks a several goal;
But Heaven's great view is one, and that the whole.
That counterworks each folly and caprice;
That disappoints th' effect of every vice; 240
That, happy frailties to all ranks applied;
Shame to the virgin, to the matron pride,
Fear to the statesman, rashness to the chief,
To kings presumption, and to crowds belief:
That, virtue's ends from vanity can raise,
Which seeks no interest, no reward but praise;
And build on wants, and on defects of mind,
The joy, the peace, the glory of mankind.

Heaven forming each on other to depend,
A master, or a servant, or a friend, 250
Bids each on other for assistance call,
Till one man's weakness grows the strength of all.
Wants, frailties, passions, closer still ally
The common interest, or endear the tie.
To these we owe true friendship, love sincere,

161-74. i.e., ruling passions are valuable in directing different men to different purposes and in keeping each man consistent to his own purpose. 175 ff. i.e., the strength of our virtues comes from their having the vigor of our passional nature behind them. 177. mercury of man: i.e., human character, as shifting and capricious as quicksilver. 185-94. Examples of virtues springing from passional forces. 195. pride: i.e., the Stoic pride of supposing that man attains virtue by eradicating the passional part of his nature; on the contrary, Pope argues, this is what gives him his characteristic virtue (though it may give him his characteristic vice if he leaves it unregulated by reason). 198. Titus: the Roman emperor who sighed to see a day pass without its good deed. 200. Decius, Curtius: legendary Romans who gave their lives for Rome's welfare. 203-04. This ... mind: alluding to the creative act of God (Gen. 1:4),

which man must imitate by distinguishing the virtue implicit in his passional self from the vice (cf. II.13, 111 ff.). 205. Extremes ... produce: meaning either that in nature opposites co-operate — as rain and drought for harvest; or that opposites have similar effects — as when extreme cold or extreme heat are applied to human flesh. 224. Zembla: Novaya Zemlya (formerly spelled Nova Zembla), a group of Arctic islands.

Each home-felt joy that life inherits here;
Yet from the same we learn, in its decline,
Those joys, those loves, those interests to resign;
Taught half by reason, half by mere decay,
To welcome death, and calmly pass away.   260
  Whate'er the passion, knowledge, fame, or pelf,
Not one will change his neighbor with himself.
The learn'd is happy Nature to explore,
The fool is happy that he knows no more;
The rich is happy in the plenty given,
The poor contents him with the care of Heaven.
See the blind beggar dance, the cripple sing,
The sot a hero, lunatic a king;
The starving chemist° in his golden views
Supremely blest, the poet in his Muse.   270
  See some strange comfort every state attend,
And pride bestowed on all, a common friend;
See some fit passion every age supply,
Hope travels thro', nor quits us when we die.
  Behold the child, by Nature's kindly law,
Pleased with a rattle, tickled with a straw:
Some livelier plaything gives his youth delight,
A little louder, but as empty quite:
Scarfs, garters,° gold, amuse his riper stage,
And beads° and prayer-books are the toys of age:
Pleased with this bauble still, as that before;   281
Till tired he sleeps, and life's poor play is o'er.°
  Meanwhile Opinion gilds with varying rays
Those painted clouds that beautify our days;
Each want of happiness by hope supplied,
And each vacuity of sense by pride:
These build as fast as knowledge can destroy;
In Folly's cup still laughs the bubble,° joy;
One prospect lost, another still we gain;
And not a vanity is given in vain;   290
Even mean self-love becomes, by force divine,
The scale to measure others' wants by thine.
See! and confess, one comfort still must rise,
'Tis this, Tho' man's a fool, yet God is wise.

EPISTLE III

ARGUMENT

Of the nature and state of *man* with respect to society

  I. The whole universe one system of society. Nothing made wholly for *itself,* nor yet wholly for *another.* The happiness of *animals* mutual. II. *Reason* or *instinct* operate alike to the good of each individual. *Reason* or *instinct* operate also to society, in all animals. III. How far *society* carried by instinct. How much farther by reason. IV. Of that which is called the *State of Nature.* Reason instructed by instinct in the invention of *arts,* and in the forms of *society.* V. Origin of political societies. Origin of monarchy. Patriarchal government.

VI. Origin of true religion and government, from the same principle, of love. Origin of superstition and tyranny, from the same principle, of fear. The influence of self-love operating to the *social* and *public* good. Restoration of true religion and government on their first principle. Mixed government. Various forms of each, and the true end of all.

Here then we rest: " The Universal Cause
Acts to one end, but acts by various laws."
In all the madness of superfluous health,
The trim of pride, the impudence of wealth,
Let this great truth be present night and day;
But most be present, if we preach or pray.
  I. Look round our world; behold the chain of
    love°
Combining all below and all above.
See plastic Nature° working to this end,
The single atoms each to other tend,   10
Attract, attracted to, the next in place
Formed and impelled its neighbor to embrace.
See matter next, with various life endued,
Press to one center still, the general good.
See dying vegetables life sustain,
See life dissolving vegetate again:
All forms that perish other forms supply,
(By turns we catch the vital breath, and die)
Like bubbles on the sea of matter born,
They rise, they break, and to that sea return.   20
Nothing is foreign: parts relate to whole;
One all-extending, all-preserving Soul
Connects each being, greatest with the least;
Made beast in aid of man, and man of beast;
All served, all serving: nothing stands alone;
The chain holds on, and where it ends, unknown.
  Has° God, thou fool! worked solely for thy good,
Thy joy, thy pastime, thy attire, thy food?
Who for thy table feeds the wanton fawn,
For him as kindly spread the flowery lawn.°   30
Is it for thee the lark ascends and sings?
Joy tunes his voice, joy elevates his wings.
Is it for thee the linnet pours his throat?
Loves of his own and raptures swell the note.
The bounding steed you pompously bestride,
Shares with his lord the pleasure and the pride.
Is thine alone the seed that strews the plain?
The birds of heaven shall vindicate their grain.
Thine the full harvest of the golden year?
Part pays, and justly, the deserving steer: 40
The hog, that plows not nor obeys thy call,

---

269. chemist: alchemist.   279. Scarfs, garters: badges of church (doctors of divinity) and state (knights of the Garter). 280. beads: rosaries.   282. life's . . . play: Cf. *Macbeth,* V.v.25. 288. bubble: (1) dupe, (2) deceptive show.

Epistle III: 7. The chain of love is a traditional conception like that of the chain of being, but stresses relationship (the love of each order of beings for those above and below it) rather than rank — in accord with the theme of this epistle.   9. plastic Nature: divine power as expressed in nature.   27–42. i.e., the lower orders are made not simply for man's delight but also for their own, and he not simply for his but also for theirs. 30. lawn: (1) meadow, (2) table linen.

Lives on the labors of this lord of all.

Know, Nature's children all divide her care;
The fur that warms a monarch, warmed a bear.
While man exclaims, " See all things for my use!"
" See man for mine! " replies a pampered goose:
And just as short of reason he must fall,
Who thinks all made for one, not one for all.

Grant that the powerful still the weak control;
Be man the wit° and tyrant of the whole: 50
Nature that tyrant checks; he only knows,
And helps, another creature's wants and woes.
Say, will the falcon, stooping from above,
Smit with her varying plumage, spare the dove?
Admires the jay the insect's gilded wings?
Or hears the hawk when Philomela° sings?
Man cares for all: to birds he gives his woods,
To beasts his pastures, and to fish his floods;
For some his interest prompts him to provide,
For more his pleasure, yet for more his pride: 60
All feed on one vain patron, and enjoy
Th' extensive blessing of his luxury.
That very life his learnèd hunger craves,
He saves from famine, from the savage° saves;
Nay, feasts the animal he dooms his feast,
And, till he ends the being, makes it blest;
Which sees no more the stroke, or feels the pain,
Than favored man by touch ethereal slain.°
The creature had his feast of life before;
Thou too must perish, when thy feast is o'er!   70

To each unthinking being, Heaven a friend,
Gives not the useless knowledge of its end:
To man imparts it; but with such a view
As, while he dreads it, makes him hope it too:
The hour concealed, and so remote the fear,
Death still draws nearer, never seeming near.
Great standing miracle! that Heaven assigned
Its only thinking thing this turn of mind.

II. Whether with reason, or with instinct blest,°
Know, all enjoy that power which suits them best;
To bliss alike by that direction tend,   81
And find the means proportioned to their end.
Say, where full instinct is th' unerring guide,
What pope or council can they need beside?°
Reason, however able, cool at best,
Cares not for service, or but serves when pressed,
Stays till we call, and then not often near;
But honest Instinct comes a volunteer,
Sure never to o'ershoot, but just to hit;
While still too wide or short is human wit;   90
Sure by quick Nature happiness to gain,
Which heavier reason labors at in vain,

This too serves always, reason never long;
One must go right, the other may go wrong.
See then the acting and comparing powers
One in their nature, which are two in ours;
And reason raise o'er instinct as you can,
In this 'tis God directs, in that 'tis man.

Who taught the nations of the field and wood
To shun their poison, and to choose their food?
Prescient, the tides or tempests to withstand,   101
Build on the wave,° or arch beneath the sand?°
Who made the spider parallels design,
Sure as Demoivre,° without rule or line?
Who bid the stork, Columbus-like, explore
Heavens not his own, and worlds unknown before?
Who calls the council, states the certain day,
Who forms the phalanx, and who points the way?

III. God in the nature of each being founds
Its proper bliss, and sets its proper bounds: 110
But as he framed a whole, the whole to bless,
On mutual wants built mutual happiness:
So from the first, eternal order ran,
And creature linked to creature, man to man.
Whate'er of life all-quickening aether° keeps,
Or breathes thro' air, or shoots beneath the deeps,
Or pours profuse on earth, one nature feeds
The vital flame, and swells the genial° seeds.
Not man alone, but all that roam the wood,
Or wing the sky, or roll along the flood,   120
Each loves itself, but not itself alone,
Each sex desires alike, till two are one.
Nor ends the pleasure with the fierce embrace;
They love themselves, a third time, in their race.
Thus beast and bird their common charge attend,
The mothers nurse it, and the sires defend;
The young dismissed to wander earth or air,
There stops the instinct, and there ends the care;
The link dissolves, each seeks a fresh embrace,
Another love succeeds, another race.   130
A longer care man's helpless kind demands;
That longer care contracts more lasting bands:
Reflection, reason, still the ties improve,°
At once extend the interest, and the love;
With choice we fix, with sympathy we burn;
Each virtue in each passion takes its turn;°
And still new needs, new helps, new habits rise,
That graft benevolence on charities.°

102. Build . . . wave: the supposed nesting habit of the halcyon.
arch . . . sand: actual nesting habit of the kingfisher, with which
the legendary halcyon is usually identified.   104. Demoivre:
French mathematician living in London at this time.   115.
aether: a fiery generative element originating above the moon.
118. genial: procreative.   133. Reflection . . . improve: Cf.
I.225n. Here, *reflection* is man's power to look back and acknowledge his debt to parents; *reason*, his power to look ahead and
realize that he too will need the care that they need now.   135–
36. With . . . turn: i.e., on marriage are founded all the characteristic human affections which ramify into the human virtues (cf.
Paradise Lost, IV.754–57, above).   138. That . . . charities: i.e.,
a general disposition to love and virtue becomes founded on the
particular affections and virtues required by familial relationships.

50. wit: i.e., the only rational being on earth.   56. Philomela:
the nightingale.   64. the savage: the wild beast.   68. Than
. . . slain: In some parts of the world, men slain by lightning
were held sacred.   79. Whether . . . blest: i.e., whether man or
animal.   84. What . . . beside: alluding to the infallibility
claimed for the Pope and the great councils of the Roman Church
like that of Trent.

Still as one brood, and as another rose,
These natural love maintained, habitual those:
The last, scarce ripened into perfect man,   141
Saw helpless him from whom their life began:
Memory and forecast just returns engage,
That pointed back to youth, this on to age;
While pleasure, gratitude, and hope, combined,
Still spread the interest, and preserved the kind.
  IV. Nor° think, in Nature's state they blindly
    trod;
The state of Nature was the reign of God:
Self-love and social at her birth began,
Union the bond of all things, and of man.   150
Pride then was not; nor arts, that pride to aid;
Man walked with beast, joint tenant of the shade;
The same his table, and the same his bed;
No murder clothed him, and no murder fed.
In the same temple, the resounding wood,
All vocal beings hymned their equal God:
The shrine with gore unstained,° with gold un-
    dressed,
Unbribed, unbloody, stood the blameless priest:
Heaven's attribute was universal care,
And man's prerogative to rule, but spare.   160
Ah!° how unlike the man of times to come!
Of half that live the butcher and the tomb;
Who, foe to Nature, hears the general groan,
Murders their species, and betrays his own.
But just disease to luxury succeeds,
And every death its own avenger breeds;
The fury-passions from that blood began,
And turned on man a fiercer savage, man.
  See° him from Nature rising slow to art!
To copy instinct then was reason's part;   170
Thus then to man the voice of Nature spake —
" Go, from the creatures thy instructions take:
Learn from the birds what food the thickets yield;°
Learn from the beasts the physic° of the field;
Thy arts of building from the bee receive;°
Learn of the mole to plow, the worm to weave;
Learn of the little nautilus to sail,°
Spread the thin oar, and catch the driving gale.
Here too all forms of social union find,
And hence let reason, late, instruct mankind: 180
Here subterranean works and cities see;

There towns aërial on the waving tree.
Learn each small people's genius, policies,
The ant's republic, and the realm of bees;
How those in common all their wealth bestow,
And anarchy without confusion know;
And these forever, tho' a monarch reign,
Their separate cells and properties maintain.
Mark what unvaried laws preserve each state,
Laws wise as Nature, and as fixed as fate.   190
In vain thy reason finer webs shall draw,
Entangle justice in her net of law,
And right, too rigid, harden into wrong;
Still for the strong too weak, the weak too strong.
Yet go! and thus o'er all the creatures sway,
Thus let the wiser make the rest obey;
And, for those arts mere instinct could afford,
Be crowned as monarchs, or as gods adored."°
  V. Great° Nature spoke; observant men obeyed;
Cities were built, societies were made: 200
Here rose one little state; another near
Grew by like means, and joined, thro' love or
    fear.
Did here the trees with ruddier burdens bend,
And there the streams in purer rills descend?
What war could ravish, commerce could bestow,
And he returned a friend, who came a foe.
Converse and love mankind might strongly
    draw,
When love was liberty, and Nature law.
Thus states were formed; the name of king un-
    known,
Till common interest placed the sway in one.   210
'Twas virtue only (or in arts or arms,
Diffusing blessings, or averting harms)
The same which in a sire the sons obeyed,
A prince the father of a people made.
  VI. Till then, by Nature crowned, each patriarch
    sate,
King, priest, and parent of his growing state;
On him, their second Providence, they hung,
Their law his eye, their oracle his tongue.
He from the wondering furrow called the food,
Taught to command the fire, control the flood,   220
Draw forth the monsters of th' abyss profound,
Or fetch th' aërial eagle to the ground.
Till drooping, sickening, dying they began
Whom they revered as God to mourn as man:
Then,° looking up from sire to sire, explored
One great first father, and that first adored.
Or plain tradition that this ALL begun,
Conveyed unbroken faith from sire to son;

147 ff. A picturing of the state of nature based on classical conceptions of the golden age, and opposing the view that man's
natural condition is anarchy (Lucretius) or a war of all on all
(Hobbes).   157. unstained: because in the golden age there
was no animal sacrifice.   161–68. Ah . . . man: After the golden
age (or the Fall), man becomes a carnivore, his killing of beasts
leading him on to kill men.   169 ff. i.e., the very arts on account
of which proud man presumes himself superior to nature and
the other creatures are rooted in nature.   173. Learn . . . yield:
e.g., as explorers used to distinguish edible fruits and berries by
watching what birds ate.   174. physic: the herbs animals seek
out when sick.   175. Thy . . . receive: The architecture of the
beehive had been admired since classical times.   177. nautilus
to sail: The "paper nautilus" was supposed to sail by raising
two of its arms with a membrane spread between.

198. as . . . adored: A common way of accounting for the origin
of the pagan gods was to suppose them deified benefactors of
mankind.   199–214. Political societies now develop out of
natural ones.   225–28. Then . . . son: Common explanations
of divine worship were (1) that the existence of a First Cause is
an inevitable inference of reason, (2) that a tradition of the
Creation had descended from the first man.

The worker from the work distinct was known,°
And simple reason never sought but one: 230
Ere wit oblique had broke that steady light,°
Man, like his Maker, saw that all was right;
To virtue, in the paths of pleasure, trod,°
And owned a Father when he owned a God.
Love all the faith, and all th' allegiance then;
For Nature knew no right divine in men,
No ill could fear in God: and understood
A sovereign being but a sovereign good.
True faith, true policy, united ran,
That was but love of God, and this of man.   240
    Who first taught souls enslaved, and realms un-
        done,
Th' enormous faith° of many made for one;
That proud exception to all Nature's laws,
T' invert the world, and counterwork its Cause?°
Force first made conquest, and that conquest, law;°
Till Superstition taught the tyrant awe,
Then shared the tyranny, then lent it aid,
And gods of conquerors, slaves of subjects made:
She, midst the lightning's blaze, and thunder's
        sound,
When rocked the mountains, and when groaned
        the ground,   250
She taught the weak to bend, the proud to pray,
To Power unseen, and mightier far than they:
She, from the rending earth and bursting skies,
Saw gods descend, and fiends infernal rise:
Here fixed the dreadful, there the blest abodes;
Fear made her devils, and weak hope° her gods;
Gods partial, changeful, passionate, unjust,
Whose attributes were rage, revenge, or lust;
Such as the souls of cowards might conceive,
And, formed like tyrants, tyrants would believe.
Zeal° then, not charity, became the guide;   261
And hell was built on spite,° and heaven on pride.
Then sacred seemed th' ethereal vault no more;
Altars grew marble then, and reeked with gore:
Then first the flamen tasted living food;°
Next his grim idol smeared with human blood;
With Heaven's own thunders shook the world be-
        low,
And played the god an engine on his foe.°
    So drives self-love, thro' just and thro' un-
        just,
To one man's power, ambition, lucre, lust: 270

The same self-love, in all, becomes the cause
Of what restrains him, government and laws.
For, what one likes if others like as well,
What serves one will, when many wills rebel?
How shall he keep, what, sleeping or awake,
A weaker may surprise, a stronger take?
His safety must his liberty restrain:
All join to guard what each desires to gain.
Forced into virtue thus by self-defense,
Even kings learned justice and benevolence: 280
Self-love forsook the path it first pursued,
And found the private in the public good.
    'Twas° then, the studious head or generous mind,
Follower of God or friend of humankind,
Poet or patriot, rose but to restore
The faith and moral, Nature gave before;
Relumed her ancient light, not kindled new;
If not God's image, yet his shadow drew:
Taught° power's due use to people and to kings,
Taught nor to slack, nor strain its tender strings,
The less, or greater, set so justly true,   291
That touching one must strike° the other too;
Till jarring interests of themselves create
Th' according music of a well-mixed state.
Such is the world's great harmony, that springs
From order, union, full consent of things:
Where small and great, where weak and mighty,
        made
To serve, not suffer, strengthen, not invade;
More powerful each as needful to the rest,
And, in proportion as it blesses, blest;   300
Draw to one point, and to one center bring
Beast, man, or angel, servant, lord, or king.
    For forms of government let fools contest;
Whate'er is best administered is best:°
For modes of faith let graceless° zealots fight;
His can't be wrong whose life is in the right:
In faith and hope the world will disagree,
But all mankind's concern is charity:°
All must be false that thwart this one great end;
And all of God, that bless mankind or mend.   310
    Man,° like the generous vine, supported lives;
The strength he gains is from th' embrace he gives.
On their own axis as the planets run,
Yet make at once their circle round the sun;

229. The . . . known: i.e., God was known to be transcendent as
well as immanent.   231. light: i.e., of the natural reason.
233. To . . . trod: i.e., as described in III.135 ff.   242. enormous
faith: monstrous creed.   244. T' invert . . . Cause: i.e., all creatures being in fact created for each other, the tyrant's contrary
assumption inverts fact and opposes the Creator's will.   245. that
. . . law: i.e., as described in III.271 ff.   256. weak hope: insufficient belief in God's ultimate goodness.   261. Zeal: sectar-
ian passion.   262. hell . . . spite: i.e., all were damned who
disagreed.   265. Then . . . food: Animal sacrifice was instituted.   268. played . . . foe: i.e., God was used as if he were
one's private instrument of vengeance.

283–86. 'Twas . . . before: alluding to the reforms of men like
Solon and Lycurgus.   289 ff. The metaphor of harmonized discords (cf. W. Forest, ll. 14–42n.), applied in Epistle I to the
universe, in Epistle II to man's nature, is applied here to society.
292. strike: cause to sound.   304. is . . . best: As Pope later
explained in an MS note, this does not mean that no one form
of government is better than another, but that even the best
form is corruptible by vicious administration and the worst
redeemable by virtuous administration.   305. graceless:
(1) ungracious, (2) wanting the divine grace they suppose they
have.   307–08. In . . . charity: Cf. I Cor. 13:13: "And now
abideth faith, hope, charity, these three; but the greatest of
these is charity."   311–18. Images of the mutual "love" that
binds the universe — that of the vine and elm (traditional in
this connection), and that of Newtonian gravitation.

So two consistent motions act the soul;
And one regards itself, and one the whole.
    Thus God and Nature linked the general frame,
And bade self-love and social be the same.

EPISTLE IV

ARGUMENT

Of the nature and state of *man* with respect to
happiness

    I. False notions of happiness, philosophical and popu-
lar, answered. II. It is the end of all men, and attainable
by all. God intends happiness to be *equal;* and to be so,
it must be *social,* since all particular happiness depends
on general, and since he governs by *general,* not *particular* laws. As it is necessary for *order,* and the peace
and welfare of *society,* that *external goods* should be
unequal, happiness is not made to consist in these. But,
notwithstanding that inequality, the *balance* of happiness among *mankind* is kept even by Providence, by
the two passions of *hope* and *fear.* III. What the happiness of *individuals* is, as far as is consistent with the
constitution of this world; and that the *good man* has
here the advantage. The error of imputing to *virtue*
what are only the calamities of *Nature,* or of *fortune.*
IV. The folly of expecting that God should alter his
general laws in favor of particulars. V. That we are
not judges who are good; but that, whoever they are,
they must be happiest. VI. That *external goods* are not
the proper rewards, but often inconsistent with, or destructive of virtue. That even these can make no man
happy without virtue: instanced in *riches; honors; nobility; greatness; fame; superior talents.* With pictures
of human infelicity in men possessed of them all. VII.
That *virtue only* constitutes a happiness, whose object
is *universal,* and whose prospect *eternal.* That the *perfection* of *virtue* and *happiness* consists in a *conformity*
to the *order* of Providence here, and a *resignation* to
it here and hereafter.

Oh happiness! our being's end and aim!
Good, pleasure, ease, content! whate'er thy name:
That something still which prompts th' eternal
    sigh,
For which we bear to live, or dare to die,
Which still so near us, yet beyond us lies,
O'erlooked, seen double, by the fool, and wise.
Plant of celestial seed! if dropped below,
Say, in what mortal soil thou deignst to grow?
Fair opening to some court's propitious shine,
Or deep with diamonds in the flaming mine? 10
Twined with the wreaths Parnassian laurels yield,
Or reaped in iron harvests of the field?
Where grows? — where grows it not? If vain our
    toil,
We ought to blame the culture, not the soil:
Fixed to no spot is happiness sincere,°

'Tis nowhere to be found, or everywhere;
'Tis never to be bought, but always free,
And fled from monarchs, St. John! dwells with thee.
    I. Ask of the learn'd the way? The learn'd are
    blind;
This° bids to serve, and that to shun mankind; 20
Some place the bliss in action, some in ease,
Those call it pleasure, and contentment these;
Some sunk to beasts, find pleasure end in pain;
Some swelled to gods, confess even virtue vain;
Or indolent, to each extreme they fall,
To trust in everything, or doubt of all.°
    Who thus define it, say they more or less
Than this, that happiness is happiness?
    II. Take Nature's path, and mad Opinion's leave;
All states can reach it, and all heads conceive; 30
Obvious her goods, in no extreme they dwell;
There needs but thinking right, and meaning well;
And mourn our various portions as we please,
Equal is common sense, and common ease.
    Remember, man, "the Universal Cause
Acts not by partial, but by general laws";
And makes what happiness we justly call
Subsist not in the good of one, but all.
There's not a blessing individuals find,
But some way leans and hearkens to the kind: 40
No bandit fierce, no tyrant mad with pride,
No caverned hermit, rests self-satisfied:
Who most to shun or hate mankind pretend,
Seek an admirer, or would fix a friend:
Abstract what others feel, what others think,
All pleasures sicken, and all glories sink:
Each has his share; and who would more obtain,
Shall find, the pleasure pays not half the pain.
    Order is Heaven's first law; and this confessed,
Some are, and must be, greater than the rest, 50
More rich, more wise; but who infers from hence
That such are happier, shocks all common sense.
Heaven to mankind impartial we confess,
If all are equal in their happiness:
But mutual wants this happiness increase;
All Nature's difference keeps all Nature's peace.
Condition, circumstance is not the thing;
Bliss is the same in subject or in king,
In who obtain defense, or who defend,
In him who is, or him who finds a friend: 60
Heaven breathes thro' every member of the
    whole
One common blessing, as one common soul.
But fortune's gifts if each alike possessed,
And each were equal, must not all contest?
If then to all men happiness was meant,
God in externals could not place content.
    Fortune her gifts may variously dispose,
And these be happy called, unhappy those;

But Heaven's just balance equal will appear,
While those are placed in hope, and these in fear:
Nor present good or ill, the joy or curse, 71
But future views of better, or of worse.

Oh° sons of earth! attempt ye still to rise,
By mountains piled on mountains, to the skies?
Heaven still with laughter the vain toil surveys,
And buries madmen in the heaps they raise.

III. Know, all the good that individuals find,
Or God and Nature meant to mere mankind,
Reason's whole pleasure, all the joys of sense,
Lie in three words, health, peace, and competence.°
But health consists with temperance alone; 81
And peace, oh Virtue! peace is all thy own.
The good or bad the gifts of fortune gain;
But these less taste them, as they worse obtain.
Say, in pursuit of profit or delight,
Who risk the most, that take wrong means, or
 right?
Of Vice or Virtue, whether blest or curst,°
Which meets contempt, or which compassion first?
Count all th' advantage prosperous Vice attains,
'Tis but what Virtue flies from and disdains: 90
And grant the bad what happiness they would,
One they must want, which is, to pass for good.

Oh blind to truth, and God's whole scheme be-
 low,
Who fancy bliss to vice, to virtue woe!
Who sees and follows that great scheme the best,
Best knows the blessing, and will most be blest.
But fools the good alone unhappy call,
For ills or accidents that chance to all.
See° Falkland dies, the virtuous and the just!
See godlike Turenne prostrate on the dust! 100
See Sidney bleeds amid the martial strife!
Was this their virtue, or contempt of life?
Say,° was it virtue, more tho' Heaven ne'er
 gave,
Lamented Digby! sunk thee to the grave?
Tell me, if virtue made the son expire,
Why, full of days and honor, lives the sire?
Why drew Marseilles' good bishop purer breath,
When Nature sickened, and each gale was death?

Or why so long (in life if long can be)
Lent Heaven a parent to the poor and me? 110
 What makes all physical or moral ill?
There deviates Nature, and here wanders Will.
God sends not ill; if rightly understood,
Or partial ill is universal good,
Or change° admits, or Nature lets it fall;
Short, and but rare, till man improved it all.
We just as wisely might of Heaven complain
That righteous Abel was destroyed by Cain,
As that the virtuous son is ill at ease
When his lewd father gave the dire disease. 120
Think we, like some weak prince, th' Eternal
 Cause,
Prone for his favorites to reverse his laws?

IV. Shall burning Etna, if a sage requires,
Forget to thunder, and recall her fires?°
On air or sea new motions be impressed,
Oh, blameless Bethel! to relieve thy breast?°
When the loose mountain trembles from on high,
Shall gravitation cease, if you go by?
Or some old temple, nodding to its fall, 129
For Chartres'° head reserve the hanging wall?

V. But still this world (so fitted for the knave)
Contents us not. A better shall we have?
A kingdom of the just then let it be:
But first consider how those just agree.
The good must merit God's peculiar care;
But who, but God, can tell us who they are?
One thinks on Calvin Heaven's own spirit fell;
Another deems him instrument of hell;
If Calvin feel Heaven's blessing, or its rod,
This cries there is, and that, there is no God. 140
What shocks one part will edify the rest,
Nor with one system can they all be blest.
The very best will variously incline,
And what rewards your virtue, punish mine.
Whatever is, is right. — This world, 'tis true,
Was made for Caesar — but for Titus° too:
And which more blest? who chained his country,
 say,
Or he whose virtue sighed to lose a day?
"But sometimes Virtue starves, while Vice is
 fed."
What then? Is the reward of Virtue bread? 150
That, Vice may merit; 'tis the price of toil;
The knave deserves it, when he tills the soil,
The knave deserves it, when he tempts the main,
Where Folly fights for kings, or dives for gain.
The good man may be weak, be indolent;
Nor is his claim to plenty, but content.
But grant him riches, your demand is o'er?

73–76. Oh . . . raise: i.e., materialists become buried by their possessions, as the Titans were buried under mountains they heaped up in their effort to reach the throne of Zeus. Pope thus associates the pride of ethical materialism with rebellion against God — like the pride of anthropocentrism in Epistle I, of hyper-intellectualism in Epistle II, of human isolationism in Epistle III. 80. competence: the goods necessary to support life. 87. whether . . . curst: i.e., with worldly success. 99–102. See . . . life: i.e., good men may die but not *because* they are good (instanced in Viscount Falkland, killed in 1643 in the civil wars; Turenne, killed at Sassbach in 1675; and Sidney, killed at Zutphen in 1586). 103–10. i.e., goodness has no bearing on length of life (instanced in Pope's friend, Robert Digby, who died at forty; his father, who was still alive at seventy-four; Bishop Belsunce, who tended plague victims at Marseilles in 1720 without contracting the disease; and Pope's mother, here praised for her charities to the poor, who had just died aged ninety-one.

---

115. change: Cf. I.147n. 123–24. Shall . . . fires: The Greek scientist Empedocles was reputed to have lost his life while studying an eruption of Etna. 125–26. Pope's close friend, Hugh Bethel, suffered from asthma. 130. Chartres: Cf. *Ep. to Bathurst*, l. 20n. 146. Titus: Cf. II.198n.

"No — shall the good want health, the good want
    power?"
Add health, and power, and every earthly thing,
"Why bounded power? why private? why no
    king?"   160
Nay, why external for internal given?
Why is not man a god, and earth a Heaven?
Who ask and reason thus, will scarce conceive
God gives enough, while he has more to give:
Immense the power, immense were the demand;
Say, at what part of Nature will they stand?
    VI. What nothing earthly gives, or can destroy,
The soul's calm sunshine, and the heartfelt joy,
Is Virtue's prize: A better would you fix?
Then give Humility a coach and six,   170
Justice a conqueror's sword, or Truth a gown,°
Or Public Spirit its great cure, a crown.
Weak, foolish man! will Heaven reward us there
With the same trash mad mortals wish for here?
The boy and man an individual makes,
Yet sighst thou now for apples and for cakes?
Go, like the Indian, in another life
Except thy dog, thy bottle, and thy wife:°
As well as dream such trifles are assigned,
As toys and empires, for a godlike mind.   180
Rewards, that either would to Virtue bring
No joy, or be destructive of the thing:
How oft by these at sixty are undone
The virtues of a saint at twenty-one!
    To whom can riches give repute, or trust,
Content, or pleasure, but the good and just?
Judges and senates have been bought for gold,
Esteem and love were never to be sold.
Oh fool! to think God hates the worthy mind,
The lover and the love of humankind,   190
Whose life is healthful, and whose conscience clear,
Because he wants a thousand pounds a year.
    Honor and shame from no condition° rise;
Act well your part, there all the honor lies.
Fortune in men has some small difference made,
One flaunts in rags, one flutters in brocade;
The cobbler aproned, and the parson gowned,
The friar hooded, and the monarch crowned.
"What differ more" (you cry) "than crown and
    cowl?"
I'll tell you, friend! a wise man and a fool.   200
You'll find, if once the monarch acts the monk,
Or, cobbler-like, the parson will be drunk,
Worth makes the man, and want of it, the fellow;
The rest is all but leather or prunella.°
    Stuck o'er with titles and hung round with
    strings,
That thou mayst be by kings, or whores of kings.
Boast the pure blood of an illustrious race,

In quiet flow from Lucrece° to Lucrece:
But by your fathers' worth if yours you rate,
Count me those only who were good and great.
Go! if your ancient, but ignoble blood   211
Has crept thro' scoundrels ever since the flood,
Go! and pretend your family is young;
Nor own, your fathers have been fools so long.
What can ennoble sots, or slaves, or cowards?
Alas! not all the blood of all the Howards.°
    Look next on greatness; say where greatness lies?
"Where, but among the heroes and the wise?"
Heroes are much the same, the point's agreed,
From Macedonia's madman to the Swede;°   220
The whole strange purpose of their lives, to find
Or make, an enemy of all mankind!
Not one looks backward, onward still he goes,
Yet ne'er looks forward farther than his nose.
No less alike the politic and wise;
All sly slow things, with circumspective eyes:
Men in their loose unguarded hours they take,
Not that themselves are wise, but others weak.
But grant that those can conquer, these can cheat;
'Tis phrase absurd to call a villain great: 230
Who wickedly is wise, or madly brave,
Is but the more a fool, the more a knave.
Who noble ends by noble means obtains,
Or failing, smiles in exile or in chains,
Like good Aurelius° let him reign, or bleed
Like Socrates, that man is great indeed.
    What's fame? a fancied life in others' breath,
A thing beyond us, even before our death.
Just what you hear, you have, and what's unknown
The same (my Lord) if Tully's,° or your own.
All that we feel of it begins and ends   241
In the small circle of our foes or friends;
To all beside as much an empty shade
An Eugene° living, as a Caesar dead;
Alike or when, or where, they shone, or shine,
Or on the Rubicon, or on the Rhine.
A wit's a feather, and a chief a rod;
An honest man's the noblest work of God.
Fame but from death a villain's name can save,
As Justice tears his body from the grave;   250
When what t' oblivion better were resigned,
Is hung on high, to poison half mankind.
All fame is foreign, but of true desert;
Plays round the head, but comes not to the heart:
One self-approving hour whole years outweighs
Of stupid starers, and of loud huzzas;
And more true joy Marcellus exiled feels,

171. gown: either clerical (cf. l. 197) or academic.   177–
78. Go . . . wife: Cf. I.99 ff.   193. condition: rank.   204. leather
or prunella: the materials of the cobbler's apron, the cleric's
gown.

208. Lucrece: the Roman matron Lucretia, who by suicide preserved her chastity (and her family's line purity).   216. Howards: one of the most distinguished lines in the peerage.   220.
From . . . Swede: i.e., from Alexander the Great to Charles XII of
Sweden, who had lately dazzled all Europe with his career of
conquest.   235. Aurelius: Marcus Aurelius Antoninus, Roman
emperor whose Meditations are one of the great moral documents of antiquity.   240. Tully: Cicero.   244. Eugene: Prince
Eugene of Savoy, one of the great eighteenth-century generals.

Than Caesar with a senate at his heels.°
  In parts superior what advantage lies?
Tell (for You° can) what is it to be wise?   260
'Tis but to know how little can be known;
To see all others' faults, and feel our own:
Condemned in business or in arts to drudge,
Without a second, or without a judge:
Truths would you teach, or save a sinking land?
All fear, none aid you, and few understand.
Painful pre-eminence! yourself to view
Above life's weakness, and its comforts too.
  Bring then these blessings to a strict account;
Make fair deductions; see to what they mount:
How much of other each is sure to cost;   271
How each for other oft is wholly lost;
How inconsistent greater goods with these;
How sometimes life is risked, and always ease:
Think, and if still the things thy envy call,
Say, wouldst thou be the man to whom they fall?
To sigh for ribbons if thou art so silly,
Mark how they grace Lord Umbra,° or Sir Billy:°
Is yellow dirt the passion of thy life?
Look but on Gripus,° or on Gripus' wife: 280
If parts allure thee, think how Bacon shined,
The wisest, brightest, meanest° of mankind:
Or ravished with the whistling of a name,
See Cromwell, damned to everlasting fame!°
If all, united, thy ambition call,
From ancient story learn to scorn them all.
There, in the rich, the honored, famed, and great,
See the false scale of happiness complete!
In hearts of kings, or arms of queens who lay,
How happy! those to ruin, these betray.°   290
Mark by what wretched steps their glory grows,
From dirt and seaweed as proud Venice rose;
In each how guilt and greatness equal ran,
And all that raised the hero, sunk the man:
Now Europe's laurels on their brows behold,
But stained with blood, or ill exchanged for gold:
Then see them broke with toils, or sunk in ease,
Or infamous for plundered provinces.
Oh wealth ill-fated! which no act of fame
E'er taught to shine, or sanctified from shame!   300
What greater bliss attends their close of life?
Some greedy minion, or imperious wife,
The trophied arches, storied halls invade
And haunt their slumbers in the pompous shade.
Alas! not dazzled with their noontide ray,
Compute the morn and evening to the day,
The whole amount of that enormous° fame,

A tale,° that blends their glory with their shame!
  VII. Know then this truth (enough for man to
    know)
"Virtue° alone is happiness below."   310
The only point where human bliss stands still,°
And tastes the good without the fall to ill;
Where only Merit constant pay receives,
Is blest in what it takes, and what it gives;
The joy unequaled, if its end° it gain,
And if it lose, attended with no pain:
Without satiety, tho' e'er so blessed,
And but more relished as the more distressed:
The broadest mirth unfeeling Folly wears,
Less pleasing far than Virtue's very tears: 320
Good, from each object, from each place acquired,
Forever exercised, yet never tired;
Never elated, while one man's oppressed;
Never dejected, while another's blessed;
And where no wants, no wishes can remain,
Since but to wish more virtue, is to gain.
  See the sole bliss Heaven could on all bestow!
Which who but feels can taste, but thinks can
    know:
Yet poor with fortune, and with learning blind,
The bad must miss; the good, untaught, will find;
Slave to no sect, who takes no private road,   331
But looks thro' Nature up to Nature's God;
Pursues that chain which links the immense de-
    sign,
Joins heaven and earth, and mortal and divine;
Sees, that no being any bliss can know,
But touches some above, and some below;
Learns, from this union of the rising whole,
The first, last purpose of the human soul;
And knows, where faith, law, morals, all began,
All end, in love of God, and love of man.   340
  For him alone, hope leads from goal to goal,
And opens still, and opens on his soul;
Till lengthened on to faith, and unconfined,
It pours the bliss that fills up all the mind.
He sees, why Nature plants in man alone
Hope of known bliss, and faith in bliss unknown:
(Nature, whose dictates to no other kind
Are given in vain, but what they seek they find)
Wise is her present; she connects in this
His greatest virtue with his greatest bliss;   350
At once his own bright prospect to be blest,
And strongest motive to assist the rest.
  Self-love thus pushed to social, to divine,
Gives thee to make thy neighbor's blessing thine.
Is this too little for the boundless heart?
Extend it, let thy enemies have part:
Grasp the whole worlds of reason, life, and sense,

257–58. And . . . heels: Marcellus was exiled by Caesar for his
loyalty to Pompey. **260. You:** Bolingbroke. **278. Umbra:**
from *umbra*, Latin for shadow, i.e., emptiness. **Sir Billy:** any
silly gentleman of minor rank. **280. Gripus:** "Gripe," i.e., a
miser. **282. meanest:** because dismissed from the chancelor-
ship for corruption. (See p. 319.) **284. damned . . . fame:** because of his leadership in executing Charles I. **290. these . . .
betray:** i.e., to ruin the kings, betray the queens. **307. enormous:** Cf. III.242n.

308. tale: (1) story, (2) tally or count. **310.** *Virtue* in this
epistle usually means charity, i.e., love. **311. The . . . still:**
Cf. I Cor. 13:8, where St. Paul says that though all else passes,
"charity never faileth." **315. end:** eternal life.

In one close system of benevolence:
Happier as kinder, in whate'er degree,
And height of bliss but height of charity.   360
   God loves from whole to parts: but human soul
Must rise from individual to the whole.
Self-love but serves the virtuous mind to wake,
As the small pebble stirs the peaceful lake;
The center moved, a circle straight succeeds,
Another still, and still another spreads;
Friend, parent, neighbor, first it will embrace;
His country next; and next all human race;
Wide and more wide, th' o'erflowings of the mind
Take every creature in, of every kind;   370
Earth smiles around, with boundless bounty blest,
And Heaven beholds its image in his breast.
Come then, my Friend! my Genius!° come along;
Oh master of the poet, and the song!
And while the Muse now stoops, or now ascends,
To man's low passions, or their glorious ends,
Teach me, like thee, in various nature wise,
To fall with dignity, with temper rise;°
Formed by thy converse, happily to steer
From grave to gay, from lively to severe;   380
Correct with spirit, eloquent with ease,
Intent to reason, or polite to please.
Oh! while along the stream of time thy name
Expanded flies, and gathers all its fame,
Say, shall my little bark attendant sail,
Pursue the triumph, and partake the gale?
When statesmen, heroes, kings, in dust repose,
Whose sons shall blush their fathers were thy foes,°
Shall then this verse to future age pretend°
Thou wert my guide, philosopher, and friend?
That urged by thee, I turned the tuneful art   391
From sounds to things, from fancy to the heart;
For wit's false mirror held up Nature's light;
Showed° erring pride, Whatever is, is right;
That Reason, Passion, answer one great aim;
That true Self-Love and Social are the same;
That Virtue only makes our bliss below;
And all our knowledge is, OURSELVES TO KNOW.

373. **Genius:** guardian spirit, i.e., Bolingbroke.   378. **To . . . rise:** alluding to Bolingbroke's fall on the accession of George I, his political recovery under George II.   388. **foes:** As leader of the opposition, Bolingbroke was seeking to unseat Walpole. 389. **pretend:** proclaim.   394-98. summary of the arguments of Epistles I–IV.

from EPISTLES TO SEVERAL PERSONS

EPISTLE IV
TO RICHARD BOYLE, EARL OF BURLINGTON

Of the Use of Riches

   This poem, finished in April, 1731, and published that December, was originally entitled *An Epistle to the Right Honorable Richard Earl of Burlington, Occasioned by his Publishing Palladio's Designs of the Baths, Arches, and Theaters of Ancient Rome.* Its half-title read *Of Taste,* which was corrected in the next edition to *Of False Taste.* And when the epistle was absorbed into Pope's collected works in 1735, it was retitled *Of the Use of Riches.* Each of these titles throws light on the poem's purposes.

   The original title refers to the fact that Pope's friend Burlington had brought out in 1730 a magnificent first volume of designs of ancient Roman buildings by the sixteenth-century Italian architect Palladio, and was contemplating a second volume in which, had it been issued, Pope's poem was to appear. But Burlington was himself an amateur architect of some attainments, whose influence pointed away from the baroque style toward something closer to the antique Roman in its combination of utility with grandeur, and his estate at Chiswick was an object lesson in the new utilitarian gardening — where "rising forests, not for pride or show, / But future buildings, future navies, grow." In these senses, therefore, the poem is about Burlington and "taste." Since, however, in Pope's opinion, the achievements of men like Burlington, Bathurst, and Cobham, whom he compliments in the poem, were abundantly offset by the rituals of conspicuous waste through which the Timons, Virros, and Bubos sought prestige, the poem is also about ostentation, "false taste." Finally, the poem is about the "use of riches," not simply in the obvious sense which relates to vulgar exhibitionism, but in a sense which exemplifies one of the aspects of Pope's projected ethical work (see the headnote to the *Essay on Man*), treating "the extremes to each of the Cardinal Virtues." The extreme in this case is the vice of prodigality, which, says one of the poet's preliminary jottings, "scatters abroad money that may turn out to be useful in other hands." To use the language of the *Essay on Man,* Heaven "counterworks each folly and caprice; / [And] disappoints th' effect of every vice." It does this by balancing prodigality against its opposite, avarice, the extreme that Pope pictures in the epistle to Bathurst; and also by balancing result against intention. For though Timon's expeditures are all self-centered, yet "what his hard heart denies, / His charitable vanity supplies"; and though they violate nature, there is a quiet power in things that will defeat them: deep harvests will "bury all his pride has planned, / And laughing Ceres reassume the land."

   This epistle created a tremendous scandal because it was alleged by Pope's enemies that in Timon and his villa he was attacking the Duke of Chandos (despite the fact that the Duke had once befriended Pope with a gift of £1,000) and that the Duke refused to accept Pope's assertions that he was not the man intended. This led to charges of ingratitude and malignity, blandly accepted by Johnson in his life of Pope, which have haunted the poet's reputation ever since. Actually, we now know, Chandos had given no money to Pope, whom he barely knew; he assured Pope in a letter that he did not take Timon to be a representation of himself; the portrait is a composite based on dozens of wealthy offenders.

ARGUMENT

The vanity of expense in people of wealth and quality. The abuse of the word *taste*. That the first principle and foundation, in this as in everything else, is *good sense*. The chief proof of it is to *follow Nature,* even in works of mere luxury and elegance. Instanced in *architecture* and *gardening,* where all must be adapted to the *genius* and *use* of the *place,* and the beauties not forced into it, but resulting from it. How men are disappointed in their most expensive undertakings, for want of this true foundation, without which nothing can please *long,* if *at all;* and the best *examples* and *rules* will but be perverted into something *burdensome* or ridiculous. A description of the *false taste of magnificence;* the first grand error of which is to imagine that *greatness* consists in the *size* and *dimension,* instead of the *proportion* and *harmony* of the *whole,* and the second, either in joining together *parts incoherent,* or too *minutely resembling,* or in the *repetition* of the *same* too frequently. A word or two of false taste in *books,* in *music,* in *painting,* even in *preaching* and *prayer,* and lastly in *entertainments.* Yet Providence is justified in giving wealth to be squandered in this manner, since it is dispersed to the poor and laborious part of mankind (recurring to what is laid down in the first book [the *Essay on Man*], Epistle II, and in the Epistle [to Bathurst] preceding this). What are the *proper objects* of magnificence, and a proper field for the expense of *great men,* and finally, the great and public works which become a *prince.*

'Tis strange, the miser should his cares employ
To gain those riches he can ne'er enjoy:
Is it less strange, the prodigal should waste
His wealth, to purchase what he ne'er can taste?
Not for himself he sees, or hears, or eats;
Artists must choose his pictures, music, meats:
He buys for Topham,° drawings and designs,
For Pembroke, statues, dirty gods, and coins;
Rare monkish manuscripts for Hearne alone,
And books for Mead, and butterflies for Sloane.
Think we all these are for himself! no more   11
Than his fine wife, alas! or finer whore.
For what has Virro° painted, built, and planted?

EPISTLE TO BURLINGTON.   7-10. Richard Topham; Thomas Herbert, eighth Earl of Pembroke; Thomas Hearne; Drs. Richard Mead and Hans Sloane — eminent collectors and connoisseurs in the fields indicated.   13. Virro: The point of the name is uncertain.

Only to show, how many tastes he wanted.°
What brought Sir Visto's° ill-got wealth to waste?
Some daemon whispered, " Visto! have a taste."
Heaven visits with a taste the wealthy fool,
And needs no rod but Ripley° with a rule.
See! sportive fate, to punish awkward pride,
Bids Bubo° build, and sends him such a guide: 20
A standing sermon, at each year's expense,
That never coxcomb reached magnificence!
You° show us, Rome was glorious, not profuse,
And pompous buildings once were things of use.
Yet shall (my Lord) your just, your noble rules
Fill half the land with imitating fools;
Who random drawings from your sheets shall take,
And of one beauty many blunders make;
Load some vain church with old theatric state,
Turn arcs of triumph to a garden gate;   30
Reverse your ornaments, and hang them all
On some patched doghole eked with ends of wall,
Then clap four slices of pilaster on't,
That, laced with bits of rustic,° makes a front;
Or call the winds thro' long arcades to roar,
Proud to catch cold at a Venetian door;
Conscious they act a true Palladian part,
And, if they starve, they starve by rules of art.
Oft have you hinted to your brother peer,°
A certain truth, which many buy too dear: 40
Something there is more needful than expense,
And something previous even to taste — 'tis sense:
Good sense, which only is the gift of Heaven,
And tho' no science, fairly worth the seven:
A light, which in yourself you must perceive;
Jones and Le Nôtre° have it not to give.
To° build, to plant, whatever you intend,
To rear the column, or the arch to bend,
To swell the terrace, or to sink the grot;
In all, let Nature never be forgot.   50
But treat the goddess like a modest fair,
Nor overdress, nor leave her wholly bare;
Let not each beauty everywhere be spied,
Where half the skill is decently to hide.
He gains all points, who pleasingly confounds,
Surprises, varies, and conceals the bounds.
Consult the genius of the place in all;
That tells the waters or to rise, or fall;

14. wanted: (1) desired, (2) lacked.   15. Visto: An alternative form of *vista,* the name suggests one who devotes himself to gardening and building on his estate.   18. Ripley: Thomas Ripley, an architect, whom Pope thought a mere carpenter *with a rule.*   20. Bubo: Latin for *owl,* with a glance at *booby.* Pope usually applies the name to Bubb Dodington, a minor Whig politician, who fancied himself a patron of arts.   23–28. You . . . make: Cf. headnote.   34. rustic: i.e., having an artificially roughened surface.   39. brother peer: The allusion is general, not specific.   46. Jones: Inigo Jones. See *W. Forest,* ll. 375–80n. Burlington had published some of Jones's drawings. Le Nôtre: designer of the prim gardens at Versailles and Fontainebleau. 47 ff. Pope took the lead in England in challenging the symmetrical French style of gardening, and through his own garden at Twickenham and those of his friends exercised considerable influence toward a more "natural" style and the blending of the garden with the landscape.

Or helps th' ambitious hill the heavens to scale,
Or scoops in circling theaters the vale;   60
Calls in the country, catches opening glades,
Joins willing woods, and varies shades from shades;
Now breaks, or now directs, th' intending lines;
Paints as you plant, and, as you work, designs.
    Still follow sense, of every art the soul,
Parts answering parts shall slide into a whole,
Spontaneous beauties all around advance,
Start even from difficulty, strike from chance;
Nature shall join you; time shall make it grow
A work to wonder at — perhaps a Stowe.°   70
    Without it, proud Versailles! thy glory falls;
And Nero's terraces desert their walls:°
The vast parterres a thousand hands shall make,
Lo! Cobham comes, and floats° them with a lake:
Or cut wide views thro' mountains to the plain,
You'll wish your hill or sheltered seat again.
Even in an ornament its place remark,
Nor in an Hermitage set Dr. Clarke.°
    Behold Villario's° ten years' toil complete;
His quincunx° darkens, his espaliers meet;   80
The wood supports the plain, the parts unite,
And strength of shade contends with strength of
        light;
A waving glow the bloomy beds display,
Blushing in bright diversities of day,
With silver-quivering rills meandered o'er —
Enjoy them, you! Villario can no more;
Tired of the scene parterres and fountains yield,
He finds at last he better likes a field.
    Thro' his young woods how pleased Sabinus°
        strayed,
Or sat delighted in the thickening shade,   90
With annual joy the reddening shoots to greet,
Or see the stretching branches long to meet!
His son's fine taste an opener vista loves,
Foe to the dryads of his father's groves;
One boundless green, or flourished carpet views,
With all the mournful family of yews;°
The thriving plants ignoble broomsticks made,
Now sweep those alleys they were born to shade.
    At Timon's° villa let us pass a day,

70. Stowe: the estate of Pope's friend, Richard Temple, Lord
Cobham, where the new style was being practiced.   72. Nero's
. . . walls: According to Suetonius, Nero's vast palace (the
Golden House) housed fields, vineyards, pastures, woods.
74. floats: floods.   78. Hermitage . . . Clarke: A bust of Dr.
Samuel Clarke had been placed by Queen Caroline, with busts
of other English philosophers, in the Hermitage, her grotto at
Richmond. All were incongruous in that environment, especially
Clarke's, who was neither an illustrious man nor, because of his
heterodoxy, suited to a hermitage.   79. Villario: The name is an
adaptation from villa.   80. quincunx: five trees, four set in a
square, with one in the midst.   89. Sabinus: The contemporary
allusion is not clear, but the classical allusion is perhaps to
"father Sabinus, planter of the vine" (Aeneid, VII.178-79).
95-96. One . . . yews: Three landscaping blunders — monoto-
nously unbroken lawn; lawn too broken; sacrifice of large trees
to ranks of yew.   99. Timon: a prodigal Athenian — here, Pope's
symbol of aristocratic pride, extravagance, and bad taste.

Where all cry out, "What sums are thrown away!"
So proud, so grand; of that stupendous air,   101
Soft and agreeable come never there.
Greatness, with Timon, dwells in such a draught
As brings all Brobdingnag before your thought.
To compass this, his building is a town,
His pond an ocean, his parterre a down:
Who but must laugh, the master when he sees,
A puny insect, shivering at a breeze!
Lo, what huge heaps of littleness around!
The whole, a labored quarry above ground.   110
Two Cupids squirt before: a lake behind
Improves the keenness of the northern wind.
His gardens next your admiration call,
On every side you look, behold the wall!
No pleasing intricacies intervene,
No artful wildness to perplex the scene;
Grove nods at grove, each alley has a brother,
And half the platform° just reflects the other.
The suffering eye inverted Nature sees,
Trees cut to statues, statues thick as trees;   120
With here a fountain, never to be played;
And there a summerhouse, that knows no shade;
Here Amphitrite° sails thro' myrtle bowers;
There gladiators fight, or die, in flowers;
Unwatered see the drooping sea horse mourn,
And swallows roost in Nilus' dusty urn.°
    My lord advances with majestic mien,
Smit with the mighty pleasure, to be seen:
But soft — by regular approach — not yet —
First thro' the length of yon hot terrace sweat;   130
And when up ten steep slopes you've dragged your
        thighs,
Just at his study door he'll bless your eyes.
    His study! with what authors is it stored?
In books, not authors, curious is my lord;
To all their dated backs he turns you round:
These Aldus printed, those Du Suëil° has bound.
Lo, some are vellum, and the rest as good
For all his lordship knows, but they are wood.°
For Locke° or Milton 'tis in vain to look,
These shelves admit not any modern book.   140
    And now the chapel's silver bell you hear,
That summons you to all the pride of prayer:
Light quirks of music, broken and uneven,
Make the soul dance upon a jig to Heaven.
On painted ceilings you devoutly stare,
Where sprawl the saints of Verrio° or Laguerre,°
On gilded clouds in fair expansion lie,
And bring all Paradise before your eye.

118. platform: terrace.   123. Amphitrite: a sea nymph.
126. urn: Cf. W. Forest, ll. 311-12n.   136. Aldus, Du Suëil:
Aldus Manutius was a Renaissance Venetian printer of Greek
texts; the Abbé du Suëil, a celebrated eighteenth-century book-
binder.   138. wood: i.e., fashioned and lettered to look like
books.   139. Locke: Cf. Ep. to a Lady, l. 23n.   146. Verrio:
Cf. W. Forest, l. 307n.   Laguerre: Louis Laguerre (1663-1721),
French muralist.

To rest, the cushion and soft dean invite,
Who never mentions hell to ears polite.   150
    But hark! the chiming clocks to dinner call;
A hundred footsteps scrape the marble hall:
The rich buffet well-colored serpents grace,
And gaping Tritons° spew to wash your face.
Is this a dinner? this a genial room?
No, 'tis a temple, and a hecatomb.°
A solemn sacrifice, performed in state,
You drink by measure, and to minutes eat.
So quick retires each flying course, you'd swear
Sancho's dread doctor and his wand were there.°
Between each act the trembling salvers ring,   161
From soup to sweet wine, and God bless the King.
In plenty starving, tantalized in state,
And complaisantly helped to all I hate,
Treated, caressed, and tired, I take my leave,
Sick of his civil pride from morn to eve;
I curse such lavish cost, and little skill,
And swear no day was ever passed so ill.
    Yet hence the poor are clothed, the hungry fed;
Health to himself, and to his infants bread   170
The laborer bears: What his hard heart denies,
His charitable vanity supplies.
    Another age shall see the golden ear
Embrown the slope, and nod on the parterre,
Deep harvests bury all his pride has planned,
And laughing Ceres° reassume the land.
    Who then shall grace, or who improve the soil?
Who plants like Bathurst, or who builds like
    Boyle.°
'Tis use alone that sanctifies expense,
And splendor borrows all her rays from sense.   180
    His father's acres who enjoys in peace,
Or makes his neighbors glad, if he increase:
Whose cheerful tenants bless their yearly toil,
Yet to their lord owe more than to the soil;
Whose ample lawns are not ashamed to feed
The milky heifer and deserving steed;
Whose rising forests, not for pride or show,
But future buildings, future navies, grow:
Let his plantations stretch from down to down,
First shade a country, and then raise a town.   190
    You too proceed! make falling arts your care,
Erect new wonders, and the old repair;
Jones and Palladio to themselves restore,
And be whate'er Vitruvius° was before:
Till kings call forth th' ideas of your mind,
(Proud to accomplish what such hands designed),
Bid° harbors open, public ways extend,

Bid temples, worthier of the God, ascend;
Bid the broad arch the dangerous flood contain,
The mole projected break the roaring main;   200
Back to his bounds their subject sea command,
And roll obedient rivers thro' the land:
These honors, peace to happy Britain brings,
These are imperial works, and worthy kings.

EPISTLE III

TO ALLEN, LORD BATHURST

Of the Use of Riches

Though Pope eventually placed this poem third among his *Epistles to Several Persons,* it was finished in late 1731 or early 1732, after the epistle to Burlington, and published in January, 1733. It is a pendant and counterpart to the earlier poem both in treating the opposite vice, avarice, and in being as heavily devoted to the money-grubbing vices of middle-class capitalism, as *Burlington* is to aristocratic waste. See the headnotes to *Burlington* and to the *Essay on Man.*

ARGUMENT

That it [the use of riches] is known to few, most falling into one of the extremes, avarice or profusion. The point discussed, whether the invention of money has been more commodious or pernicious to mankind. That riches, either to the avaricious or the prodigal, cannot afford happiness, scarcely necessaries. That avarice is an absolute frenzy, without an end or purpose. Conjectures about the motives of avaricious men. That the conduct of men, with respect to riches, can only be accounted for by the order of Providence, which works the general good out of extremes, and brings all to its great end by perpetual revolutions. How a miser acts upon principles which appear to him reasonable. How a prodigal does the same. The due medium, and true use of riches. The Man of Ross. The fate of the profuse and the covetous, in two examples; both miserable in life and in death. The story of Sir Balaam.

Who shall decide, when doctors disagree,
And soundest casuists doubt, like you and me?
You hold the word, from Jove to Momus° given,
That man was made the standing° jest of Heaven;
And gold but sent to keep the fools in play,
For some to keep, and some to throw away.
    But I, who think more highly of our kind
(And surely, Heaven and I are of a mind),
Opine, that Nature, as in duty bound,
Deep hid the shining mischief underground: 10
But when by man's audacious labor won,

153–54. serpents, Tritons: incongruous ornaments in this setting. 156. hecatomb: a sacrifice of a hundred oxen. 160. Sancho . . . there: Cf. *Don Quixote,* II.47. As Sancho is about to eat, the physician charged with his health touches each tempting dish with a wand, causing it to be whisked away. 176. Ceres: the harvest goddess. 178. Bathurst is Pope's friend Allen, Lord Bathurst; Boyle is the dedicatee of this poem. 194. Vitruvius: Latin author of *De Architectura.* 197–204. Pope alludes to the

corrupt turnpike system; the new churches in London (cf. *W. Forest,* ll. 375–80n.), some of which were sinking because they had been built on marshy land; the delays in going forward with the construction of Westminster Bridge; and other defects in the performance of the Walpole government. EP. TO BATHURST. 3. Momus: Derision, here personified. 4. standing: with a pun.

Flamed forth this rival to its sire, the sun,°
Then careful Heaven supplied two sorts of men,
To squander these, and those to hide again.
　Like doctors° thus, when much dispute has
　　passed,
We find our tenets just the same at last.
Both fairly owning riches, in effect,
No grace of Heaven or token of th' elect:
Given to the fool, the mad, the vain, the evil,　19
To Ward,° to Waters,° Chartres,° and the Devil.
　" What Nature wants, commodious gold bestows,
'Tis thus we eat the bread another sows."°
　But how unequal it bestows, observe,
'Tis thus we riot, while who sow it starve:
What Nature wants (a phrase I much distrust)
Extends to luxury, extends to lust:
Useful, I grant, it serves what life requires,
But, dreadful too, the dark assassin hires.
　" Trade it may help, society extend."
　" But lures the pirate, and corrupts the friend."
　" It raises armies in a nation's aid."　31
　" But bribes a senate, and the land's betrayed."
In vain may heroes fight, and patriots rave,
If secret gold sap on from knave to knave.
Once,° we confess, beneath the patriot's cloak,
From the cracked bag the dropping guinea spoke,
And jingling down the back stairs, told the crew,
" Old Cato° is as great a rogue as you."
Blest paper credit! last and best supply!
That lends corruption lighter wings to fly!　40
Gold imped° by thee, can compass hardest things,
Can pocket states, can fetch or carry kings;
A single leaf shall waft an army o'er,
Or ship off senates to a distant shore;°
A leaf, like Sibyl's,° scatter to and fro
Our fates and fortunes, as the winds shall blow:
Pregnant with thousands flits the scrap unseen,
And silent sells a king, or buys a queen.
　Oh! that such bulky bribes as all might see,
Still, as of old, encumbered villainy!　50

Could France or Rome divert our brave designs,
With all their brandies or with all their wines?
What could they more than knights and squires
　　confound,
Or water all the Quorum° ten miles round?
A statesman's slumbers how this speech would
　　spoil!
" Sir, Spain has sent a thousand jars of oil;
Huge bales of British cloth blockade the door;
A hundred oxen at your levee roar."
　Poor Avarice one torment more would find;
Nor could Profusion squander all, in kind.　60
Astride his cheese Sir Morgan° might we meet;
And Worldly crying coals from street to street,°
Whom with a wig so wild, and mien so mazed,
Pity mistakes for some poor tradesman crazed.
Had Colepepper's° whole wealth been hops and
　　hogs,
Could he himself have sent it to the dogs?
His Grace° will game: to White's° a bull be led,
With spurning heels and with a butting head.
To White's be carried, as to ancient games,
Fair coursers, vases, and alluring dames.　70
Shall then Uxorio,° if the stakes he sweep,
Bear home six whores, and make his Lady weep!
Or soft Adonis,° so perfumed and fine,
Drive to St. James's a whole herd of swine?
Oh filthy check on all industrious skill,
To spoil the nation's last great trade, quadrille!°
Since then, my lord, on such a world we fall,
What say you? " Say? Why take it, gold and all."
　What riches give us let us then inquire:
Meat, fire, and clothes. " What more? " Meat,
　　clothes, and fire.　80
Is this too little? would you more than live?
Alas! 'tis more than Turner° finds they give.
Alas! 'tis more than (all his visions past)
Unhappy Wharton,° waking, found at last!
What can they give? to dying Hopkins,° heirs?
To Chartres, vigor? Japhet,° nose and ears?
Can they in gems bid pallid Hippia° glow,

---

12. its . . . sun: Cf. *W. Forest*, l. 396n.　**15. doctors:** scholars.
20. Ward: John Ward of Hackney, M.P. One of the new "money
class," like most of those named in this epistle, he was convicted
in 1726 of frauds and forgeries and expelled from the House.
Waters: Peter Walter or Waters, M.P. for Bridport, a rapacious
usurer, original of Fielding's Peter Pounce.　**Chartres:** Francis
Chartres (d. 1732), the most notorious gambler, debauchee
(twice convicted of rapes), and swindler of the age. At his funeral,
Pope says in a note, the populace "almost tore the body out of
the coffin, and cast dead dogs, etc., into the grave along with it."
22. "'Tis . . . sows": Cf. Isa. 65:22.　**35–38. Once . . . you:**
a story told of Sir Christopher Musgrave, leader of the Tory
opposition under William III, who is said by Gilbert Burnet to
have received £12,000 for conniving at a vote of large funds for
the king's Civil List.　**38. Cato:** name of the incorruptible Roman republican, often applied to any patriot.　**41. imped:** To
imp a falcon's wing is to increase his power of flight by inserting
new feathers.　**44. Or . . . shore:** e.g., as the Paris *parlement*
was banished to Pontoise in 1720 for opposing the unsound
financial schemes of William Law, the Mississippi speculator.
45. leaf . . . Sibyl: cf. the leaves by which Virgil's sibyl foretells
destiny, *Aeneid*, VI.116.

54. Quorum: justices of the peace.　**61. Sir Morgan:** any knight
from Wales, famed for cheeses.　**62.** Pope's note tells us this
refers to a collusion among mineowners to keep up the price,
"till one of them taking advantage of underselling the rest, defeated the design." *Worldly* may refer to the second name of
Edward Wortley Montagu, Lady Mary Montagu's miserly husband.　**65. Colepepper:** Sir William Colepepper, a baronet who
is said to have squandered his estate in gambling.　**67. His
Grace:** any duke.　**White's:** a gaming house.　**71. Uxorio:** any
uxorious husband.　**73. Adonis:** any court dandy.　**76. quadrille:** a variety of ombre. Cf. *Rape of the Lock*, III.27–100.
82. Turner: Richard Turner, shipping merchant, so penurious he
was said to have given up his coach (though he was worth
£300,000) when interest was reduced from 5 to 4 per cent.
84. Wharton: Philip Duke of Wharton (d. 1731), who crowded
dissoluteness and religious fervor, inspired parliamentary service,
and treason, into an extravagant life of thirty-three years.
85. Hopkins: John Hopkins, a rich miser, popularly called
"Vulture" Hopkins, whose heir predeceased him.　**86. Japhet:**
Japhet Crook was punished for forgeries in 1731 by having his
ears cropped, his nose slit.　**87. Hippia:** unidentified.

In Fulvia's° buckle ease the throbs° below;
Or heal, old Narses,° thy obscener ail,
With all the embroidery plastered at thy tail?   90
They might (were Harpax° not too wise to spend)
Give Harpax self the blessing of a friend;
Or find some doctor that would save the life
Of wretched Shylock, spite of Shylock's wife:°
But thousands die, without or this or that,
Die, and endow a college or a cat.°
To some indeed, Heaven grants the happier fate,
T' enrich a bastard, or a son they hate.

  Perhaps you think the poor might have their
    part?
Bond° damns the poor, and hates them from his
    heart: 100
The grave Sir Gilbert° holds it for a rule,
That "every man in want is knave or fool":
"God cannot love" (says Blunt,° with tearless
    eyes)
"The wretch he starves" — and piously denies:
But the good bishop,° with a meeker air,
Admits, and leaves them, Providence's care.

  Yet, to be just to these poor men of pelf,
Each does but hate his neighbor as himself:°
Damned to the mines, an equal fate betides
The slave that digs it, and the slave that hides.

  Who suffer thus, mere charity should own,   111
Must act on motives powerful, tho' unknown.
Some war, some plague, or famine they foresee,
Some Revelation hid from you and me.
Why Shylock wants a meal, the cause is found,
He thinks a loaf will rise to fifty pound.
What made directors cheat in South Sea year?°
To live on venison when it sold so dear.
Ask you why Phryne the whole auction buys?

Phryne foresees a general excise°   120
Why she and Sappho° raise that monstrous
    sum?
Alas! they fear a man will cost a plum.°
  Wise Peter° sees the world's respect for gold,
And therefore hopes this nation may be sold:
Glorious ambition! Peter, swell thy store.
And be what Rome's great Didius° was before.

  The Crown of Poland, venal twice an age,°
To just three millions stinted modest Gage.°
But nobler scenes Maria's dreams unfold,
Hereditary realms, and worlds of gold.   130
Congenial souls! whose life one avarice joins,
And one fate buries in th' Asturian mines.

  Much injured Blunt! why bears he Britain's
    hate?
A wizard told him in these words our fate:
"At length Corruption, like a general flood,
(So long by watchful ministers withstood)
Shall deluge all; and Avarice, creeping on,
Spread like a low-born° mist, and blot the sun;
Statesman and Patriot° ply alike the stocks,
Peeress and butler share alike the box,°   140
And judges job,° and bishops bite the town,
And mighty dukes pack cards for half a crown.
See Britain sunk in lucre's sordid charms,
And France revenged of Anne's and Edward's°
    arms!"
'Twas no court badge, great scrivener!° fired thy
    brain,
Nor lordly luxury, nor City gain:
No, 'twas thy righteous end, ashamed to see
Senates degenerate, patriots disagree,
And, nobly wishing party rage to cease,   149
To buy both sides,° and give thy country peace.
  "All this is madness," cries a sober sage;
But who, my friend, has reason in his rage?
"The ruling passion, be it what it will,

---

88. **Fulvia:** Mark Antony's haughty wife is the best-known Roman Fulvia, but the contemporary application is lost.   **throbs:** i.e., of venereal disease.   89. **Narses:** Justinian's plebeian general, used here probably of Cadogan, one of Marlborough's generals.   91. **Harpax:** Greek for robber; used here of any sharper and miser.   94. **Shylock . . . wife:** any miserly pair, but sometimes identified as Mr. Wortley Montagu and Lady Mary. 96. **cat:** Frances Stuart, Duchess of Richmond, is said in Pope's note to have left legacies to her cats, but there is no worse evidence of this in her will.   100. **Bond:** Dennis Bond, M.P., was expelled from the House in 1732 for swindling from one of the confiscated Jacobite estates. He was also a director of the Charitable Corporation, a government fund set up to lend money to the poor; but "Mr. Bond said . . . 'Damn the poor! let us go into the City, where we may get money,'" i.e., a higher rate of interest (*Hist. Reg.*, 1732, vol. xvii).   101. **Sir Gilbert:** Sir Gilbert Heathcote, director of the Bank of England, reputed the richest commoner in England.   103. **Blunt:** Sir John Blunt (d. 1733), a canting dissenter who professed great piety. A director of the South Sea Company, he used every device of fraud to prevent the recapture by parliament of his ill-gotten gains.   105. **bishop:** not specific.   108. **Each . . . himself:** Cf. Matt. 22:39. 117. **South Sea year:** Stock of the South Sea Company, the great speculative venture of Pope's age, fell from £1000 in August, 1720, to £300 in September, and shortly after so low that it beggared thousands of families.   119-20. **Ask . . . excise:** Pope alludes to Walpole's Excise Bill of 1733. Phryne was a wealthy Athenian courtesan. The contemporary reference may be to Walpole's mistress Maria Skerritt.

121. **Sappho:** Cf. *Ep. to Arb.*, ll. 376-77n.   122. **plum:** slang for £100,000 (gained by graft).   123. **Peter:** Cf. l. 20n.   126. **Didius:** Didius Salvius Julianus, who bought the Roman empire when it was put up for sale by the Praetorian Guard in 193 A.D. 127. **venal . . . age:** The Polish throne was elective and the electors purchasable. It had been available in 1707 and 1709. 128-32. **Gage:** Joseph Gage, in 1719, is said to have offered the then king of Poland three million pounds for his crown, out of his paper profits in Mississippi stock. In 1727 he was granted the right to work all the gold mines in Spain. There he seems to have met and married Lady Mary Herbert, who earlier, having also made a killing in Mississippi stock, was said to have refused an offer of marriage from the Duke of Bouillon, being determined to marry at least a prince (*hereditary realms*).   138. **low-born:** punning reference to the humble origins of many in the new money class.   139. **Statesman . . . Patriot:** i.e., members of administration and opposition.   140. **Peeress . . . box:** i.e., both having prospered through speculation.   141. **job:** graft. 144. **Edward:** Cf. *W. Forest*, ll. 303-06n.   145. **scrivener:** Blunt began life as a scrivener, i.e., moneylender.   150. **To . . . sides:** As the leading spirit of the South Sea Company, which in early 1720 offered to buy out the entire national debt, and thus greatly enhanced its sales of stock to investors of both parties, Blunt could be said to have bought both sides.

The ruling passion conquers reason still."
Less mad the wildest whimsey we can frame,
Than even that passion, if it has no aim;
For tho' such motives folly you may call,
'The folly's greater to have none at all.
   Hear° then the truth: " 'Tis Heaven each passion
     sends,
And different men directs to different ends.   160
Extremes in nature equal good produce,
Extremes in man concur to general use."
Ask we what makes one keep, and one bestow?
That Power who bids the ocean ebb and flow,
Bids seedtime, harvest, equal course maintain,
Thro' reconciled extremes of drought and rain,°
Builds life on death, on change duration founds,
And gives th' eternal wheels to know their rounds.
   Riches, like insects, when concealed they lie,
Wait but for wings, and in their season fly.°   170
Who sees pale Mammon pine amidst his store,
Sees but a backward steward for the poor;
This year a reservoir, to keep and spare;
The next, a fountain, spouting thro' his heir,
In lavish streams to quench a country's thirst,
And men and dogs shall drink him till they burst.
   Old Cotta° shamed his fortune and his birth,
Yet was not Cotta void of wit or worth:
What tho' (the use of barbarous spits forgot)
His kitchen vied in coolness with his grot?   180
His court with nettles, moats with cresses stored,
With soups unbought and salads blessed his board?
If Cotta lived on pulse, it was no more
Than Brahmins, saints, and sages did before;
To cram the rich was prodigal expense,
And who would take the poor from Providence?
Like some lone Chartreux° stands the good old
     hall,
Silence without, and fasts within the wall;
No raftered roofs with dance and tabor sound,
No noontide bell invites the country round;   190
Tenants with sighs the smokeless towers survey,
And turn th' unwilling steeds another way;
Benighted wanderers, the forest o'er,
Curse the saved candle, and unopening door;
While the gaunt mastiff growling at the gate,
Affrights the beggar whom he longs to eat.
   Not so his son; he marked this oversight,
And then mistook reverse of wrong for right.
(For what to shun will no great knowledge need;
But what to follow, is a task indeed.)   200
Yet sure, of qualities deserving praise,

More go to ruin fortunes, than to raise.
What slaughtered hecatombs, what floods of wine,
Fill the capacious squire, and deep divine!
Yet no mean motive this profusion draws,
His oxen perish in his country's cause;
'Tis George and Liberty that crowns the cup,
And Zeal for that great House° which eats him up.
The woods recede around the naked seat;   209
The sylvans° groan — no matter — for the fleet;
Next goes his wool — to clothe our valiant bands;°
Last, for his country's love, he sells his lands.
To town he comes, completes the nation's hope,
And heads the bold train bands, and burns a pope.°
And shall not Britain now reward his toils,
Britain, that pays her patriots with her spoils?
In vain at court the bankrupt pleads his cause,
His thankless country leaves him to her laws.
   The sense to value riches, with the art
T' enjoy them, and the virtue to impart,   220
Not meanly, nor ambitiously pursued,
Not sunk by sloth, nor raised by servitude;
To balance fortune by a just expense,
Join with economy, magnificence;
With splendor, charity; with plenty, health;
O teach us, Bathurst! yet unspoiled by wealth!
That secret rare, between th' extremes to move
Of mad good nature, and of mean self-love.
   To worth or want well-weighed, be bounty given,
And ease, or emulate, the care of Heaven;   230
Whose° measure full o'erflows on human race
Mend Fortune's fault, and justify her grace.
Wealth in the gross is death, but life diffused;
As poison heals, in just proportion used:
In heaps, like ambergris, a stink it lies,
But well-dispersed, is incense to the skies.
   Who starves by nobles, or with nobles eats?
The wretch that trusts them, and the rogue that
     cheats.
Is there a lord, who knows a cheerful noon
Without a fiddler, flatterer, or buffoon?   240
Whose table, Wit, or modest Merit share,
Unelbowed by a gamester, pimp, or play'r!
Who copies yours or Oxford's° better part,
To ease th' oppressed, and raise the sinking heart?
Where'er he shines, oh Fortune, gild the scene,
And angels guard him in the golden mean!
There, English bounty yet awhile may stand,
And honor linger ere it leaves the land.
   But all our praises why should Lords engross?
Rise, honest Muse! and sing the Man of Ross:°

159–62. Cf. *E. on Man*, II. 165–66, 205–06. 165–66. Bids . .
rain: Cf. Gen. 8:22: "While the earth remaineth, seedtime and
harvest, and cold and heat, and summer and winter, and day
and night shall not cease." 169–70. Riches . . . fly: Cf. Prov.
23:5: ". . . for riches certainly make themselves wings; they fly
away as an eagle toward heaven." 177. Cotta: No wholly
satisfactory contemporary applications for Cotta and his son
have been found. 187. Chartreux: monastery of the Car-
thusian order, noted for austerity.

208. House: the House of Hanover; cf. Ps. 69:9. 210. sylvans:
the dryads of his groves, which he cuts to pay for his extravagances (disguised as patriotism). 211. bands: the *train bands*
of l. 214, a citizen soldiery. 214. burns a pope: i.e., in effigy.
Londoners were demonstratively Protestant. 231. Whose:
those whose. 243. Oxford: Edward Harley, Earl of Oxford,
son of Queen Anne's Tory minister. 250. the . . . Ross: John
Kyrle of Ross in Herefordshire, whose achievements Pope has
only slightly exaggerated.

Pleased Vaga° echoes thro' her winding bounds,
And rapid Severn hoarse applause resounds.   252
Who hung with woods yon mountain's sultry
      brow?
From the dry rock, who bade the waters flow?
Not to the skies in useless columns tossed,
Or in proud falls magnificently lost,
But clear and artless, pouring thro' the plain
Health to the sick, and solace to the swain.
Whose causeway parts the vale with shady rows?
Whose seats the weary traveler repose?   260
Who taught that Heaven-directed spire to rise?
"The Man of Ross," each lisping babe replies.
Behold the market place with poor o'erspread!
The Man of Ross divides the weekly bread;
He feeds yon almshouse, neat, but void of state,
Where Age and Want sit smiling at the gate;
Him portioned maids, apprenticed orphans blessed,
The young who labor, and the old who rest.
Is any sick? the Man of Ross relieves,
Prescribes, attends, the med'cine makes, and gives.
Is there a variance? enter but his door,   271
Balked are the courts, and contest is no more.
Despairing quacks with curses fled the place,
And vile attorneys, now an useless race.
   "Thrice happy man! enabled to pursue
What all so wish, but want the power to do!
Oh say, what sums that generous hand supply?
What mines, to swell that boundless charity?"
   Of debts, and taxes, wife and children clear,
This man possessed — five hundred pounds a year.
Blush, Grandeur, blush! proud courts, withdraw
      your blaze!   281
Ye little Stars!° hide your diminished rays.
   "And what? no monument, inscription, stone?
His race, his form, his name almost unknown?"
   Who builds a church to God, and not to fame,
Will never mark the marble with his name:
Go, search it there,° where to be born and die,
Of rich and poor makes all the history;
Enough, that virtue filled the space between;
Proved, by the ends of being, to have been.   290
When Hopkins° dies, a thousand lights attend
The wretch, who living saved a candle's end:
Shouldering God's altar a vile image stands,
Belies his features, nay extends his hands;
That livelong wig which Gorgon's° self might own,
Eternal buckle takes in Parian stone.
Behold what blessings wealth to life can lend:
And see, what comfort it affords our end.
   In° the worst inn's worst room, with mat half-
      hung,

The floors of plaster, and the walls of dung,   300
On once a flockbed, but repaired with straw,
With tape-tied curtains, never meant to draw,
The George and Garter dangling from that bed
Where tawdry yellow strove with dirty red,
Great Villiers lies — alas! how changed from him,°
That life of pleasure, and that soul of whim!
Gallant and gay, in Cliveden's° proud alcove,
The bower of wanton Shrewsbury° and love;
Or just as gay, at council, in a ring   309
Of mimicked statesmen, and their merry king.°
No wit to flatter left of all his store!
No fool to laugh at, which he valued more.
There, victor of his health, of fortune, friends,
And fame, this lord of useless thousands ends.
   His Grace's fate sage Cutler° could foresee,
And well (he thought) advised him, "Live like
      me."
As well his Grace replied, "Like you, Sir John?
That I can do, when all I have is gone."
Resolve me, Reason, which of these is worse,
Want with a full, or with an empty purse?   320
Thy life more wretched, Cutler, was confessed,
Arise, and tell me, was thy death more blest?
Cutler saw tenants break, and houses fall,
For very want; he could not build a wall.
His only daughter in a stranger's power,
For very want; he could not pay a dower.
A few gray hairs his reverend temples crowned,
'Twas very want that sold them for two pound.
What even denied a cordial at his end,
Banished the doctor, and expelled the friend?   330
What but a want, which you perhaps think mad,
Yet numbers feel, the want of what he had!
Cutler and Brutus,° dying, both exclaim,
"Virtue! and wealth! what are ye but a name!"
   Say, for such worth are other worlds prepared?
Or are they both, in this, their own reward?
A knotty point! to which we now proceed.
But you are tired — I'll tell a tale — "Agreed."
   Where London's column,° pointing at the skies,
Like a tall bully, lifts the head, and lies;   340
There° dwelt a citizen of sober fame,

---

305. how ... him: The allusion to *Paradise Lost* is suggestive
(I.84–85): "But O how fallen! how changed/From him ..."
307. Cliveden: Villiers' estate.   308. Shrewsbury: the Countess
of Shrewsbury, whose lover Villiers was and whose husband he
killed while she, according to report, held his horse in the guise
of a page.   310. king: Charles II.   315. Cutler: Sir John Cutler
(d. 1693), about whose parsimony a store of legends had accumulated by Pope's time, some of which he here records.
333. Brutus: Cf. the account of Brutus' death in Dion Cassius,
XLVII.49.   339. column: a monument whose inscription charged
the Catholics with setting the fire of London and plotting against
English liberty.   341 ff. A generalized portrait of the new
Puritan and Whig capitalist (as Pope saw him), pious in private
life, materialistic and quite unscrupulous sometimes in his dealings with the community. Some of Pope's details were perhaps
suggested by the career of Thomas Pitt, who acquired a diamond
while at Madras for £20,400 (cf. ll. 361–64) and later sold it
for more than £120,000.

---

251. Vaga: Latin name of the Wye.   282. Stars: punning
reference to wearers of the star and garter, i.e., the rich who
ought to do what the Man of Ross has done.   287. there: in
the parish register.   291. Hopkins: Cf. l. 85n.   295. Gorgon:
i.e., Medusa, famed for snaky locks.   299–314. Pope gives the
story of Villiers' death current in his time, though it is now
known he died neither in an inn nor in poverty. Villiers is
George Villiers, Duke of Buckingham, Dryden's Zimri.

A plain good man, and Balaam was his name;
Religious, punctual, frugal, and so forth;
His word would pass for more than he was worth.
One solid dish his weekday meal affords,
An added pudding solemnized the Lord's:
Constant at church, and Change;° his gains were
        sure,
His givings rare, save farthings to the poor.
    The Devil was piqued such saintship to behold,
And longed to tempt him like good Job of old:
But Satan now is wiser than of yore,   351
And tempts by making rich, not making poor.
    Roused by the Prince of Air,° the whirlwinds
        sweep
The surge, and plunge his father in the deep;
Then full against his Cornish lands they roar,
And two rich shipwrecks bless the lucky shore.
    Sir Balaam now, he lives like other folks,
He takes his chirping pint, and cracks his jokes:
"Live like yourself," was soon my Lady's word;
And lo! two puddings smoked upon the board.
    Asleep and naked as an Indian lay,   361
An honest factor° stole a gem away:
He pledged it to the knight; the knight had wit,
So kept the diamond, and the rogue was bit.
Some scruple rose, but thus he eased his thought,
"I'll now give sixpence where I gave a groat;
Where once I went to church, I'll now go twice —
And am so clear too of all other vice."
    The Tempter saw his time; the work he plied;
Stocks and subscriptions pour on every side,   370
Till all the Demon makes his full descent
In one abundant shower of cent per cent,
Sinks deep within him, and possesses whole,°
Then dubs director, and secures his soul.
    Behold Sir Balaam, now a man of spirit,
Ascribes his gettings to his parts and merit;
What late he called a blessing, now was wit,
And God's good Providence, a lucky hit.
Things change their titles, as our manners turn;
His counting-house employed the Sunday morn;
Seldom at church ('twas such a busy life)   381
But duly sent his family and wife.
There (so the Devil ordained) one Christmas tide,
My good old Lady catched a cold, and died.
    A nymph of quality admires our knight;
He marries, bows at court, and grows polite:
Leaves the dull Cits,° and joins (to please the fair)
The well-bred cuckolds in St. James's air:
First, for his son, a gay commission buys,   389
Who drinks, whores, fights, and in a duel dies:
His daughter flaunts, a viscount's tawdry wife;
She bears a coronet and p — x for life.

In Britain's senate he a seat obtains,
And one more pensioner St. Stephen gains.°
My lady falls to play; so bad her chance,
He must repair it; takes a bribe from France;
The House impeach him; Coningsby° harangues;
The court forsake him, and Sir Balaam hangs:
Wife, son, and daughter, Satan! are thy own,
His wealth, yet dearer, forfeit to the Crown: 400
The Devil and the King divide the prize,
And sad Sir Balaam curses God° and dies.

from IMITATIONS OF HORACE

THE FIRST SATIRE OF THE SECOND BOOK

To Mr. Fortescue°

This, the first of Pope's surviving Imitations of
Horace, was written in January, 1733. Pope was ill, he
tells us, and Bolingbroke, visiting him, picked up a
copy of Horace from his table, and falling upon the
first satire of the second book as he thumbed it through,
remarked how well it would fit Pope's case if he were
to imitate it in English. "After he was gone, I read it
over; translated it in a morning or two, and sent it to
the press in a week or fortnight after. And this was the
occasion of my imitating some other of the satires and
epistles afterwards." This must not, of course, be taken
to mean that the Horatian imitations were the result
of a lucky accident. Pope had been a translator, adapter,
and parodist of the classics all his life, and his success
with the new enterprise was due to the fact that it
corresponded perfectly with the view of the poetic function which he shared with his age: that wit "doth not
consist so much in advancing things that are new, as
in giving things that are known an agreeable turn."
Horace's satire hit Pope's case because, having just
published in this same month the Epistle to Bathurst,
he anticipated an outcry even greater than that which
had greeted the Epistle to Burlington the year before.
What Pope needed at this point was what every satirist must have: an authoritative ethos — that is to say,
a "public character" as a man of tolerance and virtue
who challenges the doings of other men, not whenever
he happens to feel vindictive, but whenever they deserve it. Horace, the great Roman, who had also spoken
out on *his* Augustan age, supplied this perfectly. By
speaking through him, Pope could identify himself
with one of the most urbane and agreeable personalities in literary history; and by imitating this particular
satire, he could make it very clear that his motive was
not malice but zeal for the common good: "To Virtue
only and her friends a friend."

347. Change: the Royal Exchange   353. Prince of Air: Satan.
362. factor: agent.   372–73. In . . . whole: Pope wittily adapts
the myth of Danae, into whose lap Jove descended in a shower
of gold.   387. Cits: the commercial classes.

394. pensioner . . . gains: i.e., he sells out to Walpole.
397. Coningsby: Thomas, Earl Coningsby, the Whig who moved
the impeachment of Lord Oxford in 1715.   402. curses God:
what the Biblical Job refused to do (Job 2:9).   IMIT. HORACE.
Satire II.i: Mr. Fortescue: Pope's friend William Fortescue,
lawyer and Whig M.P.

P. There are (I scarce can think it, but am told),
There are, to whom my satire seems too bold:
Scarce to wise Peter complaisant enough,
And something said of Chartres° much too rough.
The lines are weak, another's pleased to say,
Lord Fanny° spins a thousand such a day.
Timorous by nature, of the rich in awe,
I come to council learnèd in the law:
You'll give me, like a friend, both sage and free,
Advice; and (as you use) without a fee.   10
F. I'd write no more.
P.   Not write? but then I think,
And for my soul I cannot sleep a wink.
I nod in company, I wake at night,
Fools rush into my head, and so I write.
F. You could not do a worse thing for your life.
Why, if the nights seem tedious, take a wife:
Or rather truly, if your point be rest,
Lettuce and cowslip wine;° *Probatum est.*°
But talk with Celsus,° Celsus will advise   19
Hartshorn,° or something that shall close your eyes.
Or, if you needs must write, write Caesar's° praise,
You'll gain at least a *knighthood,* or the *bays.*
P. What?° like Sir Richard, rumbling, rough,
      and fierce,
With Arms, and George, and Brunswick crowd the
      verse,
Rend with tremendous sound your ears asunder,
With gun, drum, trumpet, blunderbuss, and thun-
      der?
Or nobly wild, with Budgell's fire and force,
Paint angels trembling round his *falling horse?*°
F. Then all your Muse's softer art display,
Let Carolina smooth the tuneful lay,   30
Lull with Amelia's° liquid name the Nine,
And sweetly flow thro' all the royal line.
P. Alas! few verses touch their nicer ear;
They scarce can bear their *laureate* twice a year;°
And justly Caesar scorns the poet's lays,
It is to *history*° he trusts for praise.
F. Better be Cibber, I'll maintain it still,
Than ridicule all taste, blaspheme quadrille,°
Abuse the City's best good men° in meter,   39
And laugh at peers that put their trust in Peter.

Even those you touch not, hate you.
P.   What should ail 'em?
F. A hundred smart in Timon and in Balaam:°
The fewer still you name, you wound the more;
Bond° is but one, but Harpax° is a score.
P. Each mortal has his pleasure: none deny
Scarsdale his bottle, Darty his ham pie;°
Ridotta° sips and dances, till she see
The doubling lusters° dance as fast as she;
F—— loves the Senate, Hockley Hole his brother,°
Like in all else, as one egg to another.   50
I love to pour out all myself, as plain
As downright Shippen,° or as old Montaigne:
In them, as certain to be loved as seen,
The soul stood forth, nor kept a thought within;
In me what spots (for spots I have) appear,
Will prove at least the medium must be clear.
In this impartial glass, my Muse intends
Fair to expose myself, my foes, my friends;
Publish the present age; but where my text
Is vice too high, reserve it for the next: 60
My foes shall wish my life a longer date,
And every friend the less lament my fate.
My head and heart thus flowing through my quill,
Verse man or prose man, term me which you will,
Papist or Protestant, or both between,
Like good Erasmus in an honest mean,
In moderation placing all my glory,
While Tories call me Whig, and Whigs a Tory.
Satire's my weapon, but I'm too discreet
To run amuck, and tilt at all I meet;   70
I only wear it in a land of hectors,°
Thieves, supercargoes,° sharpers, and directors.
Save but our *army!* and let Jove encrust
Swords, pikes, and guns, with everlasting rust!°
Peace is my dear delight — not Fleury's° more:
But touch me, and no minister so sore.
Whoe'er offends, at some unlucky time
Slides into verse, and hitches in a rhyme,
Sacred to ridicule his whole life long,
And the sad burden of some merry song.   80
Slander or poison dread from Delia's° rage,
Hard words or hanging, if your judge be Page.°

3–4. Peter, Chartres: Cf. *Ep. to Bathurst,* l. 20n.   6. Lord Fanny:
See *Ep. to Arb.,* headnote, l. 149, l. 305n.   18. Lettuce . . . wine:
a reputed anaphrodisiac and soporific.   *Probatum est:* "It is
proved" — often subjoined to recipes for cures.   19. Celsus:
Roman medical writer.   20. Hartshorn: another reputed soporific.   21. Caesar: George II.   23–26. What . . . thunder: Cf. *E.
on Crit.,* l. 463n. Pope's lines parody Blackmore's bombast.
27–28. Or . . . horse: alluding to a fatuous poem by Budgell (cf.
Ep. to Arb., l. 378–79n.) on the horse shot out from under
George II at Oudenarde, in Belgium, scene of Marlborough's
victory over the French in 1708. There may also be a glance
at the "falling evil," a distemper of nags.   31. Amelia: second
daughter of George II and Queen Caroline.   33–34. Alas . . .
year: Cf. *Ep. to Arb.,* l. 222n.   36. history: i.e., the royal
historiographer.   38. quadrille: Cf. *Ep. to Bathurst,* l. 76n.
39. the . . . men: i.e., the "cits," the moneyed class satirized in
Ep. to Bathurst.

42. Timon . . . Balaam: Cf. *Ep. to Burlington,* ll. 99 ff., and *Ep.
to Bathurst,* ll. 341 ff.   44. Bond: Cf. *Ep. to Bathurst,* l. 100n.
Harpax: Cf. *Ep. to Bathurst,* l. 91n.   46. Scarsdale, pie: Nicholas
Leke, fourth Earl of Scarsdale, connoisseur of wines, and Charles
Dartineuf, celebrated gourmet.   47. Ridotta: type name for a
lighthearted woman (from Italian *ridotto,* a music-and-dancing
party).   48. lusters: prismatic glass pendants on chandeliers.
49. brother: i.e., Stephen Fox's taste is for parliament, Henry
Fox's for gaming.   52. Shippen: William Shippen, outspoken and
incorruptible leader of the Jacobites in parliament.   71. hectors:
rowdies.   72. supercargoes: cargo officers aboard merchantmen
(who got rich fast and not always honestly).   73–74. let . . . rust:
Walpole's maintenance of a standing army was thought by Tories
a menace to liberty.   75. Fleury: Louis XV's chief minister.
81. Delia: Mary Howard, Countess of Delorain, mistress of
George II, credited with a jealous attempt to poison a maid of
honor.   82. Page: Sir Francis Page, whose "usual insolence
and severity" is noted in Johnson's *Life of Savage.*

From furious Sappho° scarce a milder fate,
P-xed by her love, or libeled by her hate.
Its proper power to hurt, each creature feels;
Bulls aim their horns, and asses lift their heels;
'Tis a bear's talent not to kick, but hug;
And no man wonders he's not stung by Pug.°
So drink with Walters,° or with Chartres eat,
They'll never poison you, they'll only cheat.   90

   Then, learned sir! (to cut the matter short)
Whate'er my fate, or well or ill at court,
Whether old age, with faint but cheerful ray,
Attends to gild the evening of my day,
Or Death's black wing already be displayed,
To wrap me in the universal shade;
Whether the darkened room° to Muse invite,
Or whitened wall provoke the skewer to write:
In durance, exile, Bedlam, or the Mint,°   99
Like Lee° or Budgell,° I will rhyme and print.

   F. Alas, young man! your days can ne'er be long,
In flower of age you perish for a song!
Plums° and directors, Shylock and his wife,°
Will club their testers,° now, to take your life!

   P. What? armed for Virtue when I point the pen,
Brand the bold front of shameless guilty men;
Dash the proud gamester in his gilded car;
Bare the mean heart that lurks beneath a *star;*°
Can there be wanting, to defend her cause,   109
Lights of the church, or guardians of the laws?
Could pensioned Boileau° lash in honest strain
Flatterers and bigots even in Louis' reign?
Could laureate Dryden pimp and friar engage,
Yet neither Charles nor James be in a rage?
And I not strip the gilding off a knave,
Unplaced, unpensioned, no man's heir, or slave?°
I will, or perish in the generous cause:
Hear this, and tremble! you who 'scape the laws.
Yes, while I live, no rich or noble knave
Shall walk the world, in credit, to his grave.   120
To VIRTUE ONLY AND HER FRIENDS A FRIEND,
The world beside may murmur, or commend.
Know, all the distant din that world can keep,
Rolls o'er my grotto, and but soothes my sleep.°
There, my retreat the best companions grace,
Chiefs out of war, and statesmen out of place.
There St. John° mingles with my friendly bowl

The feast of reason and the flow of soul:
And he,° whose lightning pierced th' Iberian lines,
Now forms my quincunx,° and now ranks my vines,   130
Or tames the genius of the stubborn plain,
Almost as quickly as he conquered Spain.

   Envy must own, I live among the great,
No pimp of pleasure, and no spy of state,
With eyes that pry not, tongue that ne'er repeats,
Fond to spread friendships, but to cover heats;
To help who want, to forward who excel;
This, all who know me, know; who love me, tell;
And who unknown defame me, let them be
Scribblers or peers, alike are *mob* to me.   140
This is my plea, on this I rest my cause —
What saith my counsel, learnèd in the laws?

   F. Your plea is good; but still I say, beware!
Laws are explained by men — so have a care.
It stands on record, that in Richard's times
A man was hanged for very honest rhymes.°
Consult the statute: *quart.* I think, it is,
Edwardi Sext, or *prim. et quint. Eliz.*°
See *Libels, Satires* — here you have it — read.

   P. *Libels and satires!* lawless things indeed!   150
But grave *Epistles,* bringing vice to light,
Such as a king might read, a bishop write,
Such as Sir Robert° would approve —

   F.   Indeed?
The case is altered — you may then proceed;
In such a cause the plaintiff will be hissed,
My lords the judges laugh, and you're dismissed.

from IMITATIONS OF DONNE

THE FOURTH SATIRE
OF DR. JOHN DONNE,
DEAN OF ST. PAUL'S, VERSIFIED

   As part of his youthful self-education in the art of poetry, Pope composed imitations of a number of English poets. His imitations of Donne, the second and fourth of Donne's five satires, seem to have been prompted by the suggestion of Lord Oxford while he was Lord Treasurer, which is to say, between 1711 and 1714. But a surviving manuscript of the imitated second satire shows that it was thoroughly revised before publication, and as much may be said of the fourth, both from the maturity of the verse and a number of late topical references. The poem was published in the fall of 1733.

   Pope admired Donne greatly, and, as the last practitioner before the twentieth century of a poetry found-

---

83. Sappho: Cf. *Ep. to Arb.,* ll. 101, 369, ll. 376–77n.; *Ep. to a Lady,* ll. 24–26n.   88. Pug: name often given to pet monkeys; also the name of a Cornish boxer.   89. Walters: Cf. *Ep. to Bathurst,* l. 20n.   97. darkened room: a treatment for the mad.   99. Mint: Cf. *Ep. to Arb.,* l. 13n.   100. Lee: Nathaniel Lee, mad Restoration playwright.   Budgell: Cf. *Ep. to Arb.,* ll. 378–79n. Budgell was believed mad, and eventually committed suicide.   103. Plums: grafters worth £100,000 (dishonestly acquired).   Shylock . . . wife: Cf. *Ep. to Bathurst,* l. 94n.   104. testers: sixpences.   108. star: Cf. *W. Forest,* l. 290n.   111. Boileau: Cf. *E. on Crit.,* l. 714n.   116. Unplaced . . . slave: As a Roman Catholic, Pope could not hold government *place,* and had twice refused *pensions.*   124. grotto . . . sleep: Cf. Intro., p. 751.   127. St. John: Bolingbroke.

129. he: alluding to the Spanish campaigns in 1705–06 of Charles Mordaunt, Earl of Peterborough.   130. quincunx: Cf. *Ep. to Burlington,* l. 8on.   145–46. It . . . rhymes: the fate of the poet Collingbourne under Richard III for writing, "The cat, the rat, and Lovel our dog/Do rule all England under a hog."   147–48. Statutes dealing with libel.   153. Sir Robert: Walpole.   IMIT. DONNE. Satire IV. See Donne's "Satire IV," above.

ed in "wit," has a good deal in common with Donne, notably the habit of yoking together heterogeneous ideas and objects, though in Pope's case only in satirical passages and without much use of the extended Metaphysical conceit. One aspect of Donne's poetry that Pope and his age did not admire, however, was its management of the rhymed couplet. (See Introduction, p. 662.) "Would not Donne's satires," Dryden had asked, "which abound with so much wit, appear more charming, if he had taken care of his words, and of his numbers?" To "take care" of Donne's words and numbers is what Pope has clearly proposed to himself in the imitation below.

Quid vetat, ut nosmet Lucili scripta legentes
Quaerere, num illius, num rerum dura negarit
Versiculos natura magis factos, et euntes
Mollius?

(Horace [*Satires*, I.x.56–59])

["And so (since *he* criticized *his* predecessors) what forbids us to inquire as we read Lucilius whether it was his own fault or that of his subject matter which prevented his verses from being well made and running more smoothly? . . ."]

Well, if it be my time to quit the stage,
Adieu to all the follies of the age!
I die in charity with fool and knave,
Secure of peace at least beyond the grave.
I've had my Purgatory here betimes,
And paid for all my satires, all my rhymes.
The poet's Hell, its tortures, fiends, and flames,
To this were trifles, toys, and empty names.
    With foolish pride my heart was never fired,
Nor the vain itch t' admire, or be admired;   10
I hoped for no commission from his Grace;
I bought no benefice, I begged no place;
Had no new verses, nor new suit to show;
Yet went to court! — the Devil would have it so.
But, as the fool that in reforming days
Would go to Mass in jest (as story says)
Could not but think, to pay his fine was odd,
Since 'twas no formed design of serving God;
So was I punished, as if full as proud,
As prone to ill, as negligent of good,   20
As deep in debt, without a thought to pay,
As vain, as idle, and as false, as they
Who live at court, for going once that way!
    Scarce was I entered, when, behold! there came
A thing which Adam had been posed° to name;
Noah had refused it lodging in his ark,
Where all the race of reptiles might embark:
A verier monster, than on Afric's shore
The sun e'er got, or slimy Nilus° bore,
Or Sloane° or Woodward's° wondrous shelves contain,   30

25. posed: perplexed.   29. Nilus: Cf. *E. on Crit.*, l. 41n.
30. Sloane: *Cf. Ep. to Burlington*, ll. 7–10n.   Woodward:
Dr. John Woodward, a collector of curiosities.

Nay, all that lying travelers can feign.
The watch would hardly let him pass at noon,
At night, would swear him dropped out of the
    moon.
One whom the mob, when next we find or make°
A popish plot, shall for a Jesuit take,
And the wise justice starting from his chair
Cry: "By your priesthood tell me what you are?"
    Such was the wight: Th' apparel on his back
Tho' coarse, was reveren'd, and tho' bare, was
    black.
The suit, if by the fashion one might guess,   40
Was velvet in the youth of good Queen *Bess,*
But mere tuff-taffety° what now remained;
So time, that changes all things, had ordained!
Our sons shall see it leisurely decay,
First turn plain rash,° then vanish quite away.
    This thing has traveled, speaks each language too,
And knows what's fit for every state to do;
Of whose best phrase and courtly accent joined,
He forms one tongue, exotic and refined.
Talkers I've learned to bear; Motteux° I knew,   50
Henley° himself I've heard, and Budgell° too.
The Doctor's wormwood style,° the hash of tongue
A pedant makes, the storm of Gonson's° lungs,
The whole artillery of the terms of war,
And (all those plagues in one) the bawling bar:
These I could bear; but not a rogue so civil,
Whose tongue will compliment you to the Devil.
A tongue, that can cheat widows, cancel scores,
Make Scots speak treason,° cozen subtlest whores,
With royal favorites in flattery vie,   60
And Oldmixon and Burnet° both outlie.
    He spies me out. I whisper: "Gracious God!
What sin of mine could merit such a rod?
That all the shot of dulness now must be
From this thy blunderbuss discharged on me!"
"Permit" (he cries) "no stranger to your fame
To crave your sentiment, if —'s your name.
What *Speech* esteem you most?" "The *King's,*"°
    said I.
"But the best *words?*" — "O Sir, the *dictionary.*"
"You miss my aim; I mean the most acute   70
And perfect *Speaker?*" — "Onslow,° past dispute."

34. make: The Popish Plot of 1678 was in part contrived by enemies of the Roman Catholics.   42. tuff-taffety: a taffeta having its pile in tufts.   45. rash: i.e., lose its pile entirely (*rash* is a smooth fabric).   50. Motteux: Peter Motteux, miscellaneous writer and tedious companion.   51. Henley: Cf. *Ep. to Arb.*, l. 98n.   Budgell: Cf. *ibid.*, ll. 378–79n.; *Imit. Horace*, Sat. II.i.27–28n., 100n.   52. The . . . style: i.e., the scholar's scolding style.   53. Gonson: Sir John Gonson, J.P., whose charges to juries were orotund.   59. Make . . . treason: i.e., despite their native canniness.   61. John Oldmixon had been a historian in Whig pay; Gilbert Burnet, Bishop of Salisbury, was a strongly Whiggish and anti-Catholic writer.   68. "The *King's*": a play on "the King's English," with a slur on George II's German accent.   71. Onslow: Arthur Onslow, eloquent Speaker of the House of Commons.

"But, sir, of writers?" "Swift, for closer style,
But Ho——y° for a period° of a mile."
"Why, yes, 'tis granted, these indeed may pass:
Good common linguists, and so Panurge was;°
Nay troth, th' Apostles (tho' perhaps too rough)
Had once a pretty gift° of tongues enough:
Yet these were all poor gentlemen! I dare
Affirm, 'twas travel made them what they were."
   Thus others' talents having nicely shown,   80
He came by sure transition to his own:
Till I cried out: "You prove yourself so able,
Pity! you was not druggerman° at Babel;
For had they found a linguist half so good,
I make no question but the tower had stood."
   "Obliging Sir! for courts you sure were made:
Why then forever buried in the shade?
Spirits like you, should see and should be seen,
The King would smile on you — at least the
    Queen."
"Ah gentle sir! you courtiers so cajole us —   90
But Tully has it, *Nunquam minus solus:*°
And as for courts, forgive me, if I say
No lessons now are taught the Spartan way:
Tho' in his pictures lust be full displayed,
Few are the converts Aretine has made;°
And tho' the court show vice exceeding clear,
None should, by my advice, learn virtue there."
   At this entranced, he lifts his hands and eyes,
Squeaks like a high-stretched lutestring, and re-
    plies:
"Oh, 'tis the sweetest of all earthly things   100
To gaze on princes, and to talk of kings!"
"Then,° happy man who shows the tombs!"
    said I,
"He dwells amidst the royal family:
He every day, from king to king can walk,
Of all our Harrys, all our Edwards talk,
And get by speaking truth of monarchs dead,
What few can of the living, ease and bread."
"Lord, sir, a mere mechanic! strangely low,
And coarse of phrase, — your English all are so.
How elegant your Frenchman!" "Mine, d'ye
    mean?   110
I have but one, I hope the fellow's clean."°
"Oh! sir, politely so! nay, let me die,
Your only wearing is your paduasoy."°
"Not, sir, my only, I have better still,

And this you see is but my dishabille — "
Wild to get loose, his patience I provoke,
Mistake, confound, object at all he spoke.
But as coarse iron, sharpened, mangles more,
And itch most hurts when angered to a sore;
So when you plague a fool, 'tis still the curse,   120
You only make the matter worse and worse.
   He passed it o'er; affects an easy smile
At all my peevishness, and turns his style.
He asks, "What news?" I tell him of new plays,
New eunuchs,° harlequins, and operas.
He hears, and as a still with simples in it
Between each drop it gives, stays half a minute,
Loth to enrich me with too quick replies,
By little and by little, drops his lies.
Mere household trash! of birthnights,° balls, and
    shows,   130
More than ten Holinsheds, or Halls, or Stowes.°
When the *Queen* frowned, or smiled, he knows;
    and what
A subtle minister may make of that:
Who sins with whom: who got his pension rug,°
Or quickened a reversion by a drug:
Whose place is quartered out, three parts in four,
And whether to a bishop, or a whore:
Who having lost his credit, pawned his rent,
Is therefore fit to have a government:°
Who in the secret, deals in stocks secure,   140
And cheats th' unknowing widow and the poor:
Who makes a trust or charity a job,°
And gets an Act of Parliament to rob:°
Why turnpikes° rise, and now no cit nor clown
Can gratis see the country, or the town:
Shortly no lad shall chuck,° or lady vole,°
But some excising courtier will have toll.
He tells what strumpet places sells for life,
What squire his lands, what citizen his wife:
And last (which proves him wiser still than all)
What lady's face is not a whited wall.°   151
   As one of Woodward's patients, sick, and sore,
I puke, I nauseate, — yet he thrusts in more:°
Trims Europe's balance, tops the statesman's part,
And talks Gazettes and Postboys° o'er by heart.
Like a big° wife at sight of loathsome meat

73. Ho——y: Bishop Hoadley, notorious for long sentences.
period: sentence. **75. linguists . . . was:** For Panurge's linguistic prowess, cf. Rabelais, II.9. Panurge there addresses
Pantagruel in ten known languages and three of his own invention. **77. gift:** the gift described in I Cor. 14. **83. drugger-
man:** dragoman, i.e., interpreter. **91.** Cf. Cicero's *De Officiis,*
III.1: "Never less alone" than when alone. **94–95.** Pope alludes
to Pietro Aretino's erotic sonnets, written to accompany lewd
drawings by Giulio Caccini. **102–07. "Then . . . bread":**
alluding to the attendant who shows the royal tombs in Westminster. **110–11. How . . . clean:** The poet annoys the bore
by understanding him to mean a French servant in livery.
113. paduasoy: corded silk.

125. eunuchs: Italian *castrati* singing in opera. **130. birthnights:** Cf. *Rape of the Lock,* I.23n. **131.** Pope refers to the
element of legend and hearsay in these sixteenth-century English
chroniclers. **134. rug:** safe. **139. government:** political post.
142. job: i.e., graft. **143. And . . . rob:** i.e., as had the swindling directors of the Charitable Corporation; cf. *Ep. to Bathurst,*
l. 100n. **144. turnpikes:** toll roads, also used for private gain
(cf. *Ep. to Burlington,* ll. 197–204n.). **146. chuck:** play at
pitch penny. **vole:** bid a grand slam at ombre or quadrille.
151. What . . . wall: alluding to venereal disease, but also to
Matt. 23:27: "Woe unto you, scribes and Pharisees, hypocrites!
for ye are like unto whited sepulchers, which indeed appear
beautiful outward, but are within full of dead men's bones, and
of all uncleanness." **152–53. As . . . more:** Woodward had a
fondness for prescribing emetics. **155. Gazettes, Postboys:** i.e.,
political news. **156. big:** pregnant.

Ready to cast, I yawn, I sigh, and sweat.
Then as a licensed spy, whom nothing can
Silence or hurt, he libels the Great Man;°
Swears every place entailed for years to come,
In sure succession to the day of doom: 161
He names the price for every office paid,°
And says our wars thrive ill, because delayed:
Nay hints, 'tis by connivance of the court,
That Spain robs on, and Dunkirk's still a port.°
Not more amazement seized on Circe's guests,
To see themselves fall endlong into beasts,
Than mine, to find a subject staid and wise
Already half turned traitor by surprise.
I felt th' infection slide from him to me,   170
As in the pox, some give it to get free;
And quick to swallow me, methought I saw
One of our giant statutes ope its jaw.

In that nice moment, as another lie
Stood just atilt, the minister came by.
To him he flies, and bows, and bows again,
Then, close as Umbra,° joins the dirty train,
Not Fannius' self more impudently near,
When half his nose is in his prince's ear.°
I quaked at heart; and still afraid, to see   180
All the court filled with stranger things than he,
Ran out as fast, as one that pays his bail
And dreads more actions, hurries from a jail.

Bear me, some God! oh, quickly bear me hence
To wholesome Solitude, the nurse of sense:
Where Contemplation prunes her ruffled wings,
And the free soul looks down to pity kings!
There sober thought pursued th' amusing theme,
Till fancy colored it, and formed a dream.
A vision hermits can to Hell transport,   190
And force even me to see the damned at court.
Not Dante dreaming all th' infernal state,
Beheld such scenes of envy, sin, and hate.
Base fear becomes the guilty, not the free;
Suits tyrants, plunderers, but suits not me:
Shall I, the terror of this sinful town,
Care, if a liveried lord or smile or frown?
Who cannot flatter, and detest who can,
Tremble before a noble serving-man?
Oh my fair mistress, Truth! shall I quit thee   200
For huffing, braggart, puffed Nobility?
Thou, who since yesterday hast rolled o'er all
The busy, idle blockheads of the ball,
Hast thou, oh Sun! beheld an emptier sort,
Than such as swell this bladder of a court?
Now pox on those who show a *court in wax!*°
It ought to bring all courtiers on their backs:

Such painted puppets! such a varnished race
Of hollow gewgaws, only dress and face!
Such waxen noses, stately staring things —   210
No wonder some folks bow, and think them
      kings.

See! where the British youth, engaged no more
At Fig's, at White's,° with felons, or a whore,
Pay their last duty to the court, and come
All fresh and fragrant, to the drawing room;
In hues as gay, and odors as divine,
As the fair fields they sold to look so fine.
"That's velvet for a king!" the flatterer swears;
'Tis true, for ten days hence 'twill be King Lear's.°
Our court may justly to our stage give rules,   220
That helps it both to fools-coats and to fools.
And why not players strut in courtiers' clothes?
For these are actors too, as well as those:
Wants reach all states; they beg but better dressed,
And all is *splendid poverty* at best.

Painted for sight, and essenced for the smell,
Like frigates fraught with spice and cochinel,°
Sail in the ladies: how each pirate eyes
So weak a vessel, and so rich a prize!
Topgallant he, and she in all her trim,   230
He boarding her, she striking sail to him:
"Dear Countess! you have charms all hearts to
      hit!"
And "Sweet Sir Fopling! you have so much
      wit!"
Such wits and beauties are not praised for nought,
For both the beauty and the wit are bought.
'Twould burst even Heraclitus with the spleen,°
To see those antics, Fopling and Courtine:
The Presence° seems, with things so richly odd,
The mosque of Mahound,° or some queer pagod.°
See them survey their limbs by Dürer's rules,°
Of all beau-kind the best-proportioned fools!   241
Adjust° their clothes, and to confession draw
Those venial sins, an atom, or a straw;
But oh! what terrors must distract the soul
Convicted of that mortal crime, a hole;
Or should one pound of powder less bespread
Those monkey tails that wag behind their head.
Thus finished, and corrected to a hair,
They march, to prate their hour before the Fair.
So first to preach a white-gloved chaplain goes,
With band of lily, and with cheek of rose,°   251
Sweeter than Sharon,° in immaculate trim,
Neatness itself impertinent in him.

159. the . . . Man: Walpole.   160–62. Swears . . . paid: Walpole's government rested on systematic bribery.   165. That . . . port: alluding to Spanish seizures of English shipping, and to the French failure to defortify Dunkirk (promised in the Treaty of Utrecht).   177. Umbra: Cf. *E. on Man*, IV.278n.   178–79. Not . . . ear: Cf. *Ep. to Arb.*, ll. 319, 357.   206. *court in wax:* The French court, in waxwork, was exhibited in London in 1731.

213. Fig's, White's: a prizefighters' school, and a gaming house·   219. i.e., given or sold cheap to an actor.   227. cochinel: cochineal, a red dye.   236. burst . . . spleen: i.e., it would make even Heraclitus ("the weeping philosopher") burst into laughter.   238. Presence: royal presence chamber.   239. Mahound: Mohammed; pagod: idol.   240. rules: i.e., in his treatise on the proportions of the human figure.   242–45. Adjust . . . hole: i.e., They are as concerned with the state of their dress as one should be with the state of one's soul.   251. band . . . rose: i.e., with his clerical band all fresh and his cheeks rouged.   252. Sharon: rose of Sharon (cf. Song of Sol. 2:1).

Let but the ladies smile, and they are blest:
Prodigious! how the things *protest, protest:*°
Peace, fools, or Gonson will for Papists seize you,
If once he catch you at your *Jesu! Jesu!*°

Nature made every fop to plague his brother,
Just as one beauty mortifies another.   259
But here's the Captain that will plague them
        both,
Whose air cries, "Arm!" whose very look's an
        oath:
The Captain's honest, sirs, and that's enuff,°
Tho' his soul's bullet, and his body buff.°
He spits foreright; his haughty chest before,
Like battering-rams, beats open every door:
And with a face as red, and as awry,
As Herod's hangdogs° in old tapestry,
Scarecrow to boys, the breeding woman's curse,°
Has yet a strange ambition to look worse;
Confounds the civil, keeps the rude in awe,   270
Jests like a licensed fool, commands like law.

Frighted, I quit the room, but leave it so
As men from jails to execution go;
For hung with deadly sins I see the wall,°
And lined with giants deadlier than 'em all:°
Each man an *Ascapart,*° of strength to toss
For quoits, both Temple Bar and Charing Cross.
Scared at the grisly forms, I sweat, I fly,
And shake all o'er, like a discovered spy.   279

Courts are too much for wits so weak as mine:
Charge them with Heaven's artillery, bold Divine!
From such alone the Great rebukes endure,
Whose satire's sacred, and whose rage secure:
'Tis mine to wash a few light stains, but theirs
To deluge sin, and drown a court in tears.
Howe'er, what's now *Apocrypha,* my wit,
In time to come, may pass for holy writ.

AN EPISTLE
TO DR. ARBUTHNOT

The *Epistle to Dr. Arbuthnot* was written in the late
summer of 1734 and published in January, 1735. Arbuthnot, Pope's lifelong friend since Scriblerus days,
feeling that his end was near (he died within a few
weeks after the poem's publication), had written to

255, 257. protest, Jesu: Pope echoes their affected palaver.
262. enuff: Pope parodies the captain's bluster throughout this
passage.   263. Tho' .. buff: i.e., though his soul's as hard as a
bullet, and his body like buff leather.   267. hangdogs: executioners.   268. the ... curse: Ugly faces were reputed to be
upsetting to pregnant women.   274. hung ... wall: Tapestries
representing the seven deadly sins hung in the anteroom to the
presence chamber at Hampton Court.   275. giants ... all:
a reference to the stature of the guardsmen.   276. Ascapart:
a giant who appears in several romances.

Pope urging him to continue his disdain of vice in his
poetry. On Pope's replying that he would do so indeed,
with examples made of particular persons, Arbuthnot
feared for Pope's safety and cautioned him against making enemies. This exchange led to the epistle, "written,"
Pope tells Arbuthnot, "by piecemeal many years, wherein the question is stated, what were, and are my motives
in writing, the objections to them, and my answers."
In "written by piecemeal," Pope apparently refers to
the fact that the poem incorporates revisions of certain
passages that we know were composed earlier: the portrait of Atticus (ll. 151–56, 193–214, in 1716; ll. 151–214
in 1727), the lines on his mother (ll. 406–19) in 1731,
the passage on slander (ll. 289–304) in 1733. Possibly it
incorporates other earlier passages that have not been
identified.

Despite his apologia for satire in the imitation of
Horace's first satire of the second book, Pope felt the
need of bringing this issue before the public again in
1734–35, for reasons that concerned both his personal
feelings and his ethos as a satirist. He had made a
glancing allusion in the earlier poem to one "Lord
Fanny," which Lord Hervey, vice-chamberlain to
George II and confidant to Queen Caroline, had chosen
to take to himself — as Pope probably intended, though
the title could apply equally to several court poetasters.
He had also made a cutting reference to one "Sappho,"
intended, we know, for Lady Mary Wortley Montagu,
though again there was a sufficiency of disreputable
poetesses to generalize the attribution. With Hervey's
aid, Lady Mary replied in *Verses Addressed to the Imitator of Horace* (1733), a savage onslaught on Pope's
family, deformity, character, life, and work. Coming
from persons so highly placed, one of them in constant
contact with the throne itself, this was an impugnment
of his ethos that Pope dared not ignore had he wished
to. Accordingly, he not only paid off Hervey as
"Sporus" in the *Epistle to Dr. Arbuthnot,* but offered,
in the interests of ethos, a spirited vindication of his
whole career, from the first attacks on his works when
his subjects were still "a painted mistress, or a purling stream," to the current attacks on his character
now that he had turned satirist and "moralized his
song."

The first part of the poem (though, strictly speaking, the subject matter is indivisible) tends to be literary in atmosphere, and stresses the exasperations to
which the poet is subject from pesterings of crackpots,
pedantries of critics, and envy of rivals, summing up
much of this in the lines on Atticus. The second part
tends to be moral in atmosphere, and stresses the in-
famies to which the poet is subjected when he applies
his art to the service of the commonweal and faces up
to evil in high places, even "at the ear of Eve." The
portrait of Sporus, though it is biographically about
Hervey, is poetically about Evil, as the references to
Satan make clear. Because the lines associate Sporus
with Evil in this larger sense, his portrait can be the
ladder by which Pope mounts, in the evolution of the
poem as a whole, from the studiedly personal impatience of the opening lines: "Shut, shut the door, good
John! fatigued I said," to the impersonal trumpet tones
of the public defender on the walls of *Civitas Dei:*
"Welcome for thee, fair Virtue! all the past."

Shut, shut the door, good John!° fatigued, I said,
Tie up the knocker, say I'm sick, I'm dead.
The Dog Star° rages! nay 'tis past a doubt,
All Bedlam, or Parnassus, is let out:
Fire in each eye, and papers in each hand,
They rave, recite, and madden round the land.

    What walls can guard me, or what shades can
      hide?
They pierce my thickets, thro' my grot° they glide;
By land, by water, they renew the charge;
They stop the chariot, and they board the barge.°
No place is sacred, not the church is free;   11
Even Sunday shines no Sabbath day to me:
Then from the Mint° walks forth the man of
    rhyme,
Happy! to catch me just at dinner time.

    Is there a parson, much bemused in beer,
A maudlin poetess, a rhyming peer,
A clerk, foredoomed his father's soul to cross,
Who pens a stanza, when he should engross?°
Is there, who, locked from ink and paper, scrawls
With desperate charcoal round his darkened walls?
All fly to Twitnam, and in humble strain   21
Apply to me, to keep them mad or vain.
Arthur,° whose giddy son neglects the laws,
Imputes to me and my damned works the cause:
Poor Cornus° sees his frantic wife elope,
And curses wit, and poetry, and Pope.

    Friend to my life! (which did not you prolong,
The world had wanted many an idle song)
What drop° or nostrum can this plague remove?
Or which must end me, a fool's wrath or love?   30
A dire dilemma! either way I'm sped,
If foes, they write, if friends, they read me dead.
Seized and tied down to judge, how wretched I!
Who can't be silent, and who will not lie:
To laugh, were want of goodness and of grace,
And to be grave, exceeds all power of face.
I sit with sad civility, I read
With honest anguish, and an aching head;
And drop at last, but in unwilling ears,
This saving counsel, "Keep your piece nine
    years."°   40

    "Nine years!" cries he, who high° in Drury
    Lane,
Lulled by soft zephyrs thro' the broken pane,
Rhymes ere he wakes, and prints before Term°
    ends,
Obliged by hunger, and request of friends:°
"The piece, you think, is incorrect? why, take it,
I'm all submission, what you'd have it, make it"

    Three things another's modest wishes bound,
My friendship, and a prologue, and ten pound.

    Pitholeon° sends to me: "You know his Grace,
I want a patron; ask him for a place."   50
Pitholeon libeled me — "but here's a letter
Informs you, sir, 'twas when he knew no better.
Dare you refuse him? Curll° invites to dine,
He'll write a Journal,° or he'll turn divine."°

    Bless me! a packet. — "'Tis a stranger sues,
A virgin tragedy, an orphan Muse."
If I dislike it, "Furies, death and rage!"
If I approve, "Commend it to the stage."
There (thank my stars) my whole commission
    ends,
The players and I are, luckily, no friends.   60
Fired that the house reject him, "'Sdeath I'll print
    it,
And shame the fools — Your interest, sir, with
    Lintot."°
Lintot, dull rogue! will think your price too much:
"Not, sir, if you revise it, and retouch."
All my demurs but double his attacks;
At last he whispers, "Do; and we go snacks."°
Glad of a quarrel, straight I clap the door,
"Sir, let me see your works and you no more."

    'Tis sung, when Midas'° ears began to spring,
(Midas, a sacred person and a king)   70
His very minister who spied them first,
(Some say his queen) was forced to speak, or burst.
And is not mine, my friend, a sorer case,
When every coxcomb perks them in my face?

    "Good friend, forbear! you deal in dangerous
    things.
I'd never name queens, ministers, or kings;
Keep close to ears, and those let asses prick;
'Tis nothing" — Nothing? if they bite and kick?
Out with it, Dunciad! let the secret pass,

EP. TO ARBUTHNOT. **1. John:** Pope's servant, John Serle. **3. Dog Star:** Sirius, whose rising in August associates it with maddening heat, and also with August rehearsals of poetry in Juvenal's Rome. **8. grot:** Pope's grotto. See Intro., p. 657. **10. barge:** Pope kept a waterman to convey him up and down the Thames. **13. Mint:** refuge of debtors (so called from Henry VIII's mint there), who were not liable to arrest on Sundays. **18. engross:** write out accounts in legal form. **23. Arthur:** Arthur Moore, a politician, whose son James Moore Smythe had taken up writing and got into trouble with Pope for using some of Pope's verses in a play. Later young Smythe collaborated in a poem attacking Pope (cf. l. 385). He is said to have been a leader in English freemasonry (cf. l. 98). **25. Cornus:** Latin for *horn*, i.e., any cuckold. **29. drop:** quack remedy (an especially famous one was sold by Dr. Joshua Ward; cf. *To Augustus*, l. 182). **40. "Keep . . . years":** Horace's advice in *Ars Poetica*, ll. 386–89.

41. high: i.e., living in an attic. **43. Term:** the law-court terms, which were also the publishing seasons. **44. request of friends:** a reason often advanced in the prefaces of bad writers. **49. Pitholeon,** Codrus (l. 85), Bavius (ll. 99, 250), and Balbus (l. 276) are traditional names for bad poets. **53. Curll:** Edmund Curll, unsavory publisher and Pope's enemy, whose dinner might induce Pitholeon to write another libel against Pope. **54. write a Journal:** i.e., abuse Pope in the newspapers. **turn divine:** This reference is not clear, unless Pope means that Pitholeon will write against the doctrine of the *Essay on Man*. **62. Lintot:** Pope's publisher early in his career. **66. go snacks:** "go shares." **69. Midas:** Midas, king of Phrygia (the same whose touch turned everything to gold), was given asses' ears by Apollo for awarding the victory in a musical contest to Apollo's rival, Pan. Cf. Chaucer's Wife of Bath's Tale, ll. 145–72, above.

That secret to each fool, that he's an ass: 80
The truth once told (and wherefore should we lie?)
The queen of Midas slept, and so may I.
　　You think this cruel? take it for a rule,
No creature smarts so little as a fool.
Let peals of laughter, Codrus! round thee break,
Thou unconcerned canst hear the mighty crack:
Pit, box, and gallery in convulsions hurled,
Thou standst unshook amidst a bursting world.
Who shames a scribbler? break one cobweb thro',
He spins the slight, self-pleasing thread anew: 90
Destroy his fib or sophistry; in vain,
The creature's at his dirty work again,
Throned in the center of his thin designs,
Proud of a vast extent of flimsy lines!
Whom have I hurt? has poet yet, or peer,
Lost the arched eyebrow, or Parnassian sneer?
And has not Colley° still his lord, and whore?
His butchers Henley,° his Freemasons Moore?°
Does not one table Bavius still admit?
Still to one bishop Philips° seem a wit?   100
Still Sappho° — "Hold! for God's sake — you'll
　　offend,
No names — be calm — learn prudence of a friend:
I too could write, and I am twice as tall;
But foes like these — " One flatterer's worse than
　　all.
Of all mad creatures, if the learn'd are right,
It is the slaver kills, and not the bite.
A fool quite angry is quite innocent:
Alas! 'tis ten times worse when they repent.
　　One dedicates in high heroic prose,
And ridicules beyond a hundred foes: 110
One from all Grub Street° will my fame defend,
And, more abusive, calls himself my friend.
This prints my *Letters*,° that expects a bribe,
And others roar aloud, " Subscribe,° subscribe."
　　There are, who to my person pay their court:
I cough like Horace, and, tho' lean, am short,
Ammon's great son° one shoulder had too high,
Such Ovid's nose, and " Sir! you have an eye " —
Go on, obliging creatures, make me see
All that disgraced my betters, met in me.   120
Say for my comfort, languishing in bed,
" Just so immortal Maro° held his head ":
And when I die, be sure you let me know
Great Homer died three thousand years ago.
　　Why did I write? what sin to me unknown

Dipped me in ink, my parents', or my own?°
As yet a child, nor yet a fool to fame,
I lisped in numbers, for the numbers came.
I left no calling for this idle trade,
No duty broke, no father disobeyed.   130
The Muse but served to ease some friend, not wife,
To help me thro' this long disease, my life,
To second, Arbuthnot! thy art and care,
And teach the being you preserved, to bear.°
　　But why then publish? Granville° the polite,
And knowing Walsh, would tell me I could write;
Well-natured Garth inflamed with early praise;
And Congreve loved, and Swift endured my lays;
The courtly Talbot, Somers, Sheffield read,
Even mitered Rochester would nod the head,   140
And St. John's self (great Dryden's friends before)
With open arms received one poet more.
Happy my studies, when by these approved!
Happier their author, when by these beloved!
From these the world will judge of men and books,
Not from the Burnets, Oldmixons, and Cookes.
　　Soft were my numbers; who could take offense
While pure description held the place of sense?
Like gentle Fanny's° was my flowery theme,
A painted mistress, or a purling stream.   150
Yet then did Gildon° draw his venal quill;
I wished the man a dinner, and sat still.
Yet then did Dennis° rave in furious fret;
I never answered — I was not in debt.
If want provoked, or madness made them print,
I waged no war with Bedlam or the Mint.
　　Did some more sober critic come abroad;
If wrong, I smiled; if right, I kissed the rod.
Pains, reading, study, are their just pretense,
And all they want is spirit, taste, and sense.   160
Commas and points they set exactly right,
And 'twere a sin to rob them of their mite.
Yet ne'er one sprig of laurel graced these ribalds,
From slashing Bentley down to piddling Tibalds:°
Each wight, who reads not, and but scans and spells,
Each word-catcher, that lives on syllables,
Even such small critics some regard may claim,
Preserved in Milton's or in Shakespeare's name.
Pretty! in amber to observe the forms   169
Of hairs, or straws, or dirt, or grubs, or worms!

125–26. what . . . own: Cf. John 9:2: ". . . who did sin, this man or his parents, that he was born blind?"   **134. bear:** (1) endure, (2) bear fruit (in poetry).   **135–46.** Writers, critics, and peers who had approved the poet's work, set against the hacks who did not.   **149. Fanny:** any insipid poet (but cf. l. 305n.).   **151. Gildon:** Charles Gildon the critic, who (Pope believed) had been instigated to write against him.   **153. Dennis:** Cf. *E. on Crit.*, l. 585n.   **164. Bentley, Tibalds:** Richard Bentley, a great classical scholar, had depreciated Pope's translation of Homer, as had Lewis Theobald Pope's edition of Shakespeare; but the two men are indicted here for their lack of *spirit, taste,* and *sense,* a lack which Bentley had handsomely evinced in his *slashing* treatment of the text of *Paradise Lost* (1732), and Theobald, despite some memorable exceptions, in a pedantically *piddling* treatment of the text of Shakespeare. Cf. *Dunciad* IV, headnote.

97. Colley: Cf. l. 222n., and *Dunciad*, IV, headnote.   **98. Henley:** John Henley, eccentric preacher, who had celebrated the trade of butcher in one of his open-air sermons.   **Moore:** Cf. l. 23n.   **100. Philips:** Ambrose Philips, secretary for some years to Hugh Boulter, Archbishop of Armagh.   **101. Sappho:** Cf. ll. 376–77n.; *Ep. to a Lady*, ll. 24–26n.   **111. Grub Street:** section inhabited by hack writers.   **113. This . . . Letters:** Curll had published some of Pope's letters without his permission in 1726.   **114. Subscribe:** i.e., to their writings.   **117. Ammon's . . . son:** Cf. *E. on Crit.*, l. 376n.   **122. Maro:** Virgil. Cf. *ibid.*, l. 130.

The things, we know, are neither rich nor rare,
But wonder how the devil they got there.
  Were others angry: I excused them too;
Well might they rage, I gave them but their due.
A man's true merit 'tis not hard to find;
But each man's secret standard in his mind,
That casting weight° pride adds to emptiness,
This, who can gratify? for who can guess?
The bard° whom pilfered pastorals renown,
Who turns a Persian tale for half a crown,   180
Just writes to make his barrenness appear,
And strains, from hard-bound brains, eight lines a
      year;
He,° who still wanting, tho' he lives on theft,
Steals much, spends little, yet has nothing left:
And he, who now to sense, now nonsense leaning,
Means not, but blunders round about a meaning:
And he, whose fustian's so sublimely bad,
It is not poetry, but prose run mad:
All these, my modest satire bade translate,°
And owned that nine such poets made a Tate.°
How did they fume, and stamp, and roar, and
      chafe!   191
And swear, not Addison himself was safe.
  Peace to all such! but were there one whose
    fires
True genius kindles, and fair fame inspires;
Blest with each talent and each art to please,
And born to write, converse, and live with ease:
Should such a man, too fond to rule alone,
Bear, like the Turk, no brother near the throne,°
View him with scornful, yet with jealous eyes,
And hate for arts that caused himself to rise;   200
Damn with faint praise, assent with civil leer,
And without sneering, teach the rest to sneer;
Willing to wound, and yet afraid to strike,
Just hint a fault, and hesitate dislike;
Alike reserved to blame, or to commend,
A timorous foe, and a suspicious friend;
Dreading even fools, by flatterers besieged,
And so obliging, that he ne'er obliged;
Like Cato, give his little senate laws,
And sit attentive to his own applause;°   210
While wits and Templars° every sentence raise,
And wonder with a foolish face of praise —
Who but must laugh, if such a man there be?

Who would not weep, if Atticus° were he?
  What tho' my name stood rubric° on the walls,
Or plastered posts, with claps,° in capitals?
Or smoking forth, a hundred hawkers' load,
On wings of wind came flying all abroad?
I sought no homage from the race that write;
I kept, like Asian monarchs, from their sight: 220
Poems I heeded (now berhymed so long)
No more than thou, great George! a birthday
      song.°
I ne'er with wits or witlings passed my days,
To spread about the itch of verse and praise;
Nor like a puppy daggled through the town,
To fetch and carry singsong up and down;
Nor at rehearsals sweat, and mouthed, and cried,
With handkerchief and orange at my side;
But sick of fops, and poetry, and prate,
To Bufo left the whole Castalian state.   230
  Proud as Apollo on his forkèd hill,°
Sat full-blown Bufo,° puffed by every quill;
Fed with soft dedication all day long,
Horace and he went hand in hand in song.
His library (where busts of poets dead
And a true Pindar stood without a head)
Received of wits an undistinguished race,
Who first his judgment asked, and then a place:
Much they extolled his pictures, much his seat,
And flattered every day, and some days eat: 240
Till grown more frugal in his riper days,
He paid some bards with port, and some with
      praise;
To some a dry rehearsal was assigned,
And others (harder still) he paid in kind.°
Dryden alone (what wonder?) came not nigh,
Dryden alone escaped this judging eye:
But still the Great have kindness in reserve,
He helped to bury whom he helped to starve.
  May some choice patron bless each gray goose
    quill!
May every Bavius have his Bufo still!   250
So, when a statesman wants a day's defense,
Or envy holds a whole week's war with sense,
Or simple pride for flattery makes demands,
May dunce by dunce be whistled off my hands!
Blest be the Great! for those they take away,
And those they left me;° for they left me Gay;°
Left me to see neglected genius bloom,

177. **casting weight:** the added weight that turns the scale.
179–82. **bard . . . year:** Ambrose Philips (cf. l. 100n.) had written some derivative pastorals and Persian tales. The reference is general, as in ll. 185 and 187. 183. **He:** The reference is general, as in ll. 185 and 187. 189. **translate:** (1) turn their limited talents to the field of translation, (2) transform themselves into men of real talent (advice given ironically). 190. **Tate:** Nahum Tate (1652–1715), minor versifier best known for his translations. 198. **Bear . . . throne:** Sultans had a reputation for murdering their kinsmen to prevent usurpation. 209–10. **Like . . . applause:** Pope alludes to Addison's tragedy about Cato the Elder, leader of the Roman Senate. 211. **Templars:** i.e., lawyers — the name being applied to those who had law chambers in the Inner or Middle Temple and who were often amateurs of literature.

214. **Atticus:** the name of Cicero's cultivated friend, chosen both to suggest Addison and to indicate his better qualities. 215. **rubric:** displayed in red. 216. **claps:** placards. 222. A glance at the laureate, Colley Cibber, whose odes for the royal birthdays were execrable; and at the king, who was too unliterary to *heed* them if they had been good. 231. **forked hill:** Parnassus. 232. **Bufo:** a composite portrait of a literary patron, with some details drawn from Bubb Dodington (cf. *Ep. to Burlington,* l. 20n.). 244. **in kind:** with his own writings. 255–56. **Blest . . . me:** alluding ironically to Job's submission to *his* Lord: "The Lord gave, and the Lord hath taken away; blessed be the name of the Lord" (Job 1:21). 256. **Gay:** Pope's friend, the poet John Gay, who died in 1732.

Neglected die, and tell it on his tomb:
Of all thy blameless life the sole return
My verse, and Queensbury weeping o'er thy urn!°
   Oh let me live my own! and die so too!   261
" To live and die is all I have to do "°:
Maintain a poet's dignity and ease,
And see what friends, and read what books I please:
Above a patron, tho' I condescend
Sometimes to call a minister my friend.
I was not born for courts or great affairs;
I pay my debts, believe, and say my prayers;
Can sleep without a poem in my head,
Nor know, if Dennis be alive or dead.   270
   Why am I asked what next shall see the light?
Heavens! was I born for nothing but to write?
Has life no joys for me? or (to be grave)
Have I no friend to serve, no soul to save?
" I found him close with Swift " — " Indeed? no
   doubt "
(Cries prating Balbus) " something will come out."
'Tis all in vain, deny it as I will.
" No, such a genius never can lie still ";
And then for mine obligingly mistakes
The first Lampoon Sir Will.° or Bubo° makes.
Poor guiltless I! and can I choose but smile,   281
When every coxcomb knows me by my *style*?
   Curst be the verse, how well soe'er it flow,
That tends to make one worthy man my foe,
Give virtue scandal, innocence a fear,
Or from the soft-eyed virgin steal a tear!
But he who hurts a harmless neighbor's peace,
Insults fallen worth, or beauty in distress,
Who loves a lie, lame slander helps about,
Who writes a libel, or who copies out: 290
That fop, whose pride affects a patron's name,
Yet absent, wounds an author's honest fame:
Who can your merit selfishly approve,
And show the sense of it without the love;
Who has the vanity to call you friend,
Yet wants the honor, injured, to defend;
Who tells whate'er you think, whate'er you say,
And, if he lie not, must at least betray:
Who to the *Dean,* and *silver bell* can swear,
And sees at Cannons what was never there;°   300
Who reads, but with a lust to misapply,
Make satire a lampoon, and fiction, lie.
A lash like mine no honest man shall dread,
But all such babbling blockheads in his stead.
   Let Sporus° tremble — " What? that thing of
   silk,

260. The Duke of Queensbury had befriended Gay, and Pope
had written his epitaph.   262. Pope quotes Denham's "Of
Prudence," ll. 93–94.   280. Sir Will.: customarily identified as
Sir William Yonge, who enjoyed a wide reputation as a saphead.
Bubo: cf. *Ep. to Burlington,* l. 20n.   299–300. Who . . . there:
Cf. *ibid.,* l. 141 ff. Pope's enemies had charged that Timon's
villa was Cannons, the estate of his acquaintance the Duke
of Chandos.   305. Sporus: a homosexual favorite of Nero's.
The contemporary application is to Lord Hervey (whom Pope

Sporus, that mere white curd of ass's milk?
Satire or sense, alas! can Sporus feel?
Who breaks a butterfly upon a wheel? "
   Yet let me flap this bug with gilded wings,
This painted child of dirt, that stinks and stings;
Whose buzz the witty and the fair annoys,   311
Yet wit ne'er tastes, and beauty ne'er enjoys:
So well-bred spaniels civilly delight
In mumbling of the game they dare not bite.
Eternal smiles his emptiness betray,
As shallow streams run dimpling all the way.
Whether in florid impotence he speaks,
And, as the prompter breathes, the puppet squeaks;
Or at the ear of Eve,° familiar toad,
Half froth, half venom, spits himself abroad,   320
In puns, or politics, or tales, or lies,
Or spite, or smut, or rhymes, or blasphemies.
His wit all seesaw, between *that* and *this,*
Now high, now low, now Master up, now Miss,
And he himself one vile antithesis.
Amphibious thing! that acting either part,
The trifling head, or the corrupted heart,
Fop at the toilet, flatterer at the board,
Now trips a lady, and now struts a lord.
Eve's tempter thus the rabbins° have expressed,
A cherub's face, a reptile all the rest;   331
Beauty that shocks you, parts that none will trust,
Wit that can creep, and pride that licks the dust.
   Not fortune's worshiper, nor fashion's fool,
Not lucre's madman, nor ambition's tool,
Not proud, nor servile, be one poet's praise
That, if he pleased, he pleased by manly ways:
That flattery, even to kings, he held a shame,
And thought a lie in verse or prose the same.
That not in fancy's maze he wandered long,   340
But stooped to truth and moralized his song:
That not for fame, but virtue's better end,
He stood the furious foe, the timid friend,
The damning critic, half-approving wit,
The coxcomb hit, or fearing to be hit;
Laughed at the loss of friends he never had,
The dull, the proud, the wicked, and the mad;
The distant threats of vengeance on his head,
The blow unfelt, the tear he never shed;
The tale revived, the lie so oft o'erthrown,   350
Th' imputed trash, and dulness not his own;
The morals blackened when the writings 'scape,
The libeled person, and the pictured shape;
Abuse, on all he loved, or loved him, spread,
A friend in exile, or a father, dead;°
The whisper that to greatness still too near,
Perhaps, yet vibrates on his sovereign's ear —°

usually calls Lord Fanny), court Vice Chamberlain and intimate
of Queen Caroline. He was well known for his trifling verses,
effeminacy, profligacy, and tittle-tattle.   319. ear of Eve: i.e.,
Queen Caroline's ear (cf. *Paradise Lost,* IV.800).   330. rabbins:
rabbis.   355. Pope's exiled friend Atterbury had died in 1732,
Pope's father in 1717.   357. Cf. l. 319.

Welcome for thee, fair Virtue! all the past:
For thee, fair Virtue! welcome even the *last!*
" But why insult the poor, affront the great? "
A knave's a knave, to me, in every state: 361
Alike my scorn, if he succeed or fail,
Sporus at court, or Japhet° in a jail,
A hireling scribbler, or a hireling peer,
Knight of the Post° corrupt, or of the shire;
If on a pillory, or near a throne,
He gain his prince's ear, or lose his own.
    Yet soft by nature, more a dupe than wit,
Sappho can tell you how this man was bit:°
This dreaded satirist Dennis will confess   370
Foe to his pride, but friend to his distress:°
So humble, he has knocked at Tibbald's door,
Has drunk with Cibber, nay, has rhymed for
    Moore.°
Full ten years slandered, did he once reply?
Three thousand suns went down on Welsted's°
    lie.
To please a mistress one aspersed his life;
He lashed him not, but let her be his wife:°
Let Budgell charge low Grub Street on his quill,
And write whate'er he pleased, except his will;°
Let the two Curlls° of town and court, abuse   380
His father, mother, body, soul, and Muse.
Yet why? that father held it for a rule,
It was a sin to call our neighbor fool:
That harmless mother thought no wife a whore:
Hear this, and spare his family, James Moore!°
Unspotted names, and memorable long!
If there be force in virtue, or in song.
    Of gentle blood (part shed in honor's cause,
While yet in Britain honor had applause)
Each parent sprung—" What fortune, pray? "—
    Their own,   390
And better got, than Bestia's° from the throne.
Born to no pride, inheriting no strife,
Nor marrying discord in a noble wife,
Stranger to civil and religious rage,
The good man walked innoxious thro' his age.

No courts he saw, no suits would ever try,
Nor dared an oath, nor hazarded a lie.°
Unlearn'd, he knew no schoolman's subtle art,
No language, but the language of the heart.
By nature honest, by experience wise,   400
Healthy by temperance, and by exercise;
His life, tho' long, to sickness passed unknown,
His death was instant, and without a groan.
O grant me thus to live, and thus to die!
Who sprung from kings shall know less joy than I.
    O friend! may each domestic bliss be thine!
Be no unpleasing melancholy mine:
Me, let the tender office long engage,
To rock the cradle of reposing age,
With lenient arts extend a mother's breath,   410
Make languor smile, and smooth the bed of death,
Explore the thought, explain the asking eye,
And keep a while one parent from the sky!°
On cares like these if length of days attend,
May Heaven, to bless those days, preserve my
    friend,
Preserve him social, cheerful, and serene,
And just as rich as when he served a queen.
Whether that blessing be denied or given,
Thus far was right, the rest belongs to Heaven.

from EPISTLES TO SEVERAL PERSONS

EPISTLE II
TO A LADY

Of the Characters of Women

This poem was completed in January, 1733. As first published in February, 1735, it lacked the characters of Philomedé (ll. 69–86), Atossa (ll. 115–50), Chloe (ll. 157–80), and the back-handed salute to Queen Caroline (ll. 181–98). These passages were first printed with the poem just before Pope's death in 1744, though " Chloe " had been published separately in 1738. There is evidence that some or all made up part of the original text and were withheld because they had to do with real persons still alive in 1735. This plainly could have been the case with the lines on the queen, who did not die till 1737, and with Atossa, based on the notorious Duchess of Buckingham, who did not die till 1743.

The poem derives ultimately from Juvenal's famed sixth satire on women, and Boileau's tenth, but in delicacy of handling as well as psychological penetration it outshines its predecessors. Its relation to the large ethical work Pope planned (see the headnote to the *Essay on Man*), though it draws casually on the theory of the ruling passion, is nominal. It is primarily a portrait

---

363. Japhet: Cf. *Ep. to Bathurst*, l. 86n.   365. Knight . . . Post: one who gives false evidence for hire.   369. Sappho . . . bit: Pope alludes to some betrayal by Lady Mary Wortley Montagu, formerly his friend.   371. friend . . . distress: Pope had solicited aid for Dennis from influential noblemen in 1731, and contributed to the success of the benefit held for him in 1733.   373. Moore: Cf. l. 23n.   375. Welsted: Leonard Welsted, minor poet, had helped circulate several slanders about Pope.   376–77. Pope probably alludes to William Wyndham, co-author (with Lady Mary and Lord Hervey) of the attack mentioned in the headnote, who had lately taken to wife Lady Delorain, the probable original of Pope's poisoning Delia (cf. *Imit. Horace*, Sat. II.i.81n.). 378–79. Let . . . will: The poet has let Budgell charge him with operating a hack newspaper called the *Grub Street Journal* — has let him, in fact, write whatever he pleased, except Pope's will (a reference to the charge that Budgell had forged a friend's will in order to obtain his property for himself).   380. two Curlls: the publisher (l. 53n.) and Lord Hervey.   385. Moore: Cf. l. 23n. 391. Bestia: a Roman bribe taker.

397. English Roman Catholics were still required to take certain oaths — which they could not take without a *lie* — or be deprived of most of their civil rights. Pope's father and Pope himself chose deprivation.   413. keep . . . sky: Cf. *E. on Man*, IV.110.

gallery, and it is worth noting how the metaphor of painting which runs through it is gradually deepened from a pleasant way of imaging the transient variegations of the female temperament to a very profound image for what is the matter with this world, which lives like painting, like the woman of the opening lines, who is merely a succession of "paintings," in appearances, in surfaces, in pose.

ARGUMENT

Of the characters of women (considered only as contradistinguished from the other sex). That these are yet more inconsistent and incomprehensible than those of men, of which instances are given even from such characters as are plainest, and most strongly marked: as in the affected, the soft-natured, the cunning, the whimsical, the wits and refiners, the stupid and silly. How contrarieties run through them all.

But though the particular characters of this sex are more various than those of men, the general characteristic, as to the ruling passion, is more uniform and confined. In what that lies, and whence it proceeds. Men are best known in public life, women in private. What are the aims, and the fate of the sex, both as to power and pleasure. Advice for their true interest. The picture of an estimable woman, made up of the best kind of contrarieties.

Nothing so true as what you once let fall,
"Most women have no characters at all."
Matter too soft a lasting mark to bear,
And best distinguished by black, brown, or fair.
    How many pictures of one nymph we view,
All how unlike each other, all how true!
Arcadia's countess,° here, in ermined pride,
Is, there, Pastora by a fountainside.
Here Fannia, leering on her own good man,
And there, a naked Leda with a swan.   10
Let then the fair one beautifully cry,
In Magdalen's loose hair and lifted eye,
Or dressed in smiles of sweet Cecilia shine,
With simpering angels, palms, and harps divine;
Whether the charmer sinner it, or saint it,
If folly grow romantic, I must paint it.
    Come then, the colors and the ground° prepare!
Dip in the rainbow, trick her off in air;
Choose a firm cloud, before it fall, and in it   19
Catch, ere she change, the Cynthia° of this minute.
    Rufa,° whose eye quick-glancing o'er the park,
Attracts each light gay meteor of a spark,°
Agrees as ill with Rufa studying Locke,°

EPISTLE TO A LADY. 7–14. Attitudes in which a fashionable lady might be painted: as Arcadian countess, shepherdess, matron, Leda (seduced by Zeus in the form of a swan), Mary Magdalene, and St. Cecilia (patroness of music). 17. ground: background. 20. Cynthia: one of the moon's names, symbolic of woman's changefulness. 21. Rufa: "Redhead." 22. spark: Cf. Rape of the Lock, I.73n. 23. Locke: John Locke, author of the influential Essay Concerning Human Understanding (1690).

As Sappho's diamonds with her dirty smock;
Or Sappho at her toilet's greasy task,
With Sappho fragrant at an evening masque:°
So morning insects that in muck begun,
Shine, buzz, and flyblow in the setting sun.
    How soft is Silia!° fearful to offend;
The frail one's advocate, the weak one's friend:
To her, Calista° proved her conduct nice;   31
And good Simplicius° asks of her advice.
Sudden, she storms! she raves! You tip the wink,
But spare your censure; Silia does not drink.
All eyes may see from what the change arose,
All eyes may see — a pimple on her nose.
    Papillia,° wedded to her amorous spark,
Sighs for the shades — "How charming is a park!"
A park is purchased, but the fair he sees
All bathed in tears — "Oh, odious, odious trees!"
    Ladies, like variegated tulips, show;   41
'Tis to their changes half their charms we owe;
Fine by defect, and delicately weak,
Their happy spots the nice admirer take,
'Twas thus Calypso° once each heart alarmed,
Awed without virtue, without beauty charmed;
Her tongue bewitched as oddly as her eyes,
Less wit than mimic, more a wit than wise;
Strange graces still, and stranger flights she had,
Was just not ugly, and was just not mad;   50
Yet ne'er so sure our passion to create,
As when she touched the brink of all we hate.
    Narcissa's° nature, tolerably mild,
To make a wash,° would hardly stew a child;
Has even been proved to grant a lover's prayer,
And paid a tradesman once to make him stare;
Gave alms at Easter, in a Christian trim,
And made a widow happy, for a whim.
Why then declare good nature is her scorn,
When 'tis by that alone she can be borne?   60
Why pique all mortals, yet affect a name?
A fool to pleasure, yet a slave to fame:
Now deep in Taylor and the Book of Martyrs,°
Now drinking citron with his Grace° and Chartres:°
Now conscience chills her, and now passion burns;
And atheism and religion take their turns;
A very heathen in the carnal part,

24–26. Sappho: any slovenly poetess (but the customary identification is Lady Mary Wortley Montagu, a notoriously unkempt woman). 29. Silia: The meaning of this name remains uncertain. 31. Calista: "Fairest" (but with implications from Calisto, an Arcadian nymph seduced by Zeus, and from the guilty Calista of Rowe's play, The Fair Penitent, 1703). 32. Simplicius: "Simple-mind." 37. Papilla: "Butterfly." 45. Calypso: The name means "one who conceals something." 53. Narcissa: "Self-love" (from the story of Narcissus). 54. wash: lotion. Cf. Rape of the Lock, II.97. 63. Taylor . . . Martyrs: i.e., immersed in devotional readings, such as Jeremy Taylor's works and Foxe's Book of Martyrs. 64. his Grace: any duke. Chartres: Cf. Ep. to Bathurst, l. 20n.

Yet still a sad, good Christian at her heart.
   See Sin in state, majestically drunk;
Proud as a peeress, prouder as a punk;   70
Chaste to her husband, frank to all beside,
A teeming mistress, but a barren bride.
What then? let blood and body bear the fault,
Her head's untouched, that noble seat of thought:
Such this day's doctrine — in another fit
She sins with poets thro' pure love of wit.
What has not fired her bosom or her brain?
Caesar and Tallboy, Charles and Charlemagne.°
As Helluo,° late dictator of the feast,
The nose of hautgout,° and the tip of taste,   80
Critiqued your wine, and analyzed your meat,
Yet on plain pudding deigned at home to eat;
So Philomedé,° lecturing all mankind
On the soft passion, and the taste refined,
Th' address, the delicacy — stoops at once,
And makes her hearty meal upon a dunce.
   Flavia's° a wit, has too much sense to pray;
To toast our wants and wishes, is her way;
Nor asks of God, but of her stars, to give
The mighty blessing, "while we live, to live."   90
Then all for death, that opiate of the soul!
Lucretia's° dagger, Rosamonda's° bowl.
Say, what can cause such impotence of mind?
A spark too fickle, or a spouse too kind.
Wise wretch! with pleasures too refined to please;
With too much spirit to be e'er at ease;
With too much quickness ever to be taught;
With too much thinking to have common thought:
You purchase pain with all that joy can give,
And die of nothing but a rage to live.   100
   Turn then from wits; and look on Simo's° mate,
No ass so meek, no ass so obstinate.
Or her, that owns her faults, but never mends,
Because she's honest, and the best of friends.
Or her, whose life the Church and scandal share,
Forever in a passion, or a prayer.
Or her, who laughs at Hell, but (like her Grace°)
Cries, "Ah! how charming if there's no such
    place!"
Or who in sweet vicissitude appears
Of mirth and opium, ratafie° and tears,   110
The daily anodyne, and nightly draught,
To kill those foes to fair ones, time and thought.
Woman and fool are two hard things to hit;
For true no-meaning puzzles more than wit.
   But what are these to great Atossa's° mind?

Scarce once herself, by turns all womankind!
Who, with herself, or others, from her birth
Finds all her life one warfare upon earth:
Shines, in exposing knaves, and painting fools,
Yet is, whate'er she hates and ridicules.   120
No thought advances, but her eddy brain
Whisks it about, and down it goes again.
Full sixty years the world has been her trade,
The wisest fool much time has ever made.
From loveless youth to unrespected age,
No passion gratified except her rage.
So much the fury still outran the wit,
The pleasure missed her, and the scandal hit.
Who breaks with her, provokes revenge from Hell,
But he's a bolder man who dares be well.°   130
Her every turn with violence pursued,
Nor more a storm her hate than gratitude:
To that each passion turns, or soon or late;
Love, if it makes her yield, must make her hate:
Superiors? death! and equals? what a curse!
But an inferior not dependent? worse.
Offend her, and she knows not to forgive;
Oblige her, and she'll hate you while you live:
But die, and she'll adore you — Then the bust
And temple rise — then fall again to dust.   140
Last night, her lord was all that's good and great;
A knave this morning, and his will a cheat.
Strange! by the means defeated of the ends,
By spirit robbed of power, by warmth of friends,
By wealth of followers! without one distress
Sick of herself thro' very selfishness!
Atossa, curst with every granted prayer,
Childless with all her children, wants an heir.
To heirs unknown descends th' unguarded store,
Or wanders, Heaven-directed, to the poor.   150
   Pictures like these, dear madam, to design,
Asks no firm hand, and no unerring line;
Some wandering touches, some reflected light,
Some flying stroke alone can hit 'em right:
For how should equal° colors do the knack?°
Chameleons who can paint in white and black?
   "Yet Chloe° sure was formed without a spot" —
Nature in her then erred not, but forgot.
"With every pleasing, every prudent part,   159
Say, what can Chloe want?" — She wants a heart.
She speaks, behaves, and acts just as she ought;
But never, never, reached one generous thought.
Virtue she finds too painful an endeavor,
Content to dwell in decencies° forever.
So very reasonable, so unmoved,
As never yet to love, or to be loved.
She, while her lover pants upon her breast,

78. i.e., any man will do. Tallboy is a booby lover in Richard Brome's *Jovial Crew* (1641); Charles is a type name for servant. 79. Helluo: "Glutton." 80. hautgout: anything with a strong scent. Pronounced ō'-gōō. 83. Philomede: "Laughter-loving." 87. Flavia: "Blonde." 92. Lucretia: Cf. *E. on Man*, l. 208n. Rosamonda: Cf. *Rape of the Lock*, V.136n. 101. Simo: "Old Man" (from elderly characters in Terence's *Andria* and Plautus's *Mostellaria*). 107. her Grace: an unnamed duchess. 110. ratafie: a liqueur. 115. Atossa: a Persian queen, daughter of Cyrus, sister to Cambyses. The contemporary application is

general, but the portrait is based upon Katherine, Duchess of Buckinghamshire, an arrogant, quarrelsome eccentric, who was natural daughter of James II and thus (half) sister to the Old Pretender. 130. well: in her good graces. 155. equal: uniform. knack: trick. 157. Chloe: another portrait of a type (possibly based in one or two respects on the Countess of Suffolk, George II's mistress). 164. decencies: proprieties.

Can mark the figures on an Indian chest;
And when she sees her friend in deep despair,
Observes how much a chintz exceeds mohair.   170
Forbid it Heaven, a favor or a debt
She e'er should cancel — but she may forget.
Safe is your secret still in Chloe's ear;
But none of Chloe's shall you ever hear.
Of all her dears she never slandered one,
But cares not if a thousand are undone.
Would Chloe know if you're alive or dead?
She bids her footman put it in her head.
Chloe is prudent — Would you too be wise?
Then never break your heart when Chloe dies.

One certain portrait may (I grant) be seen,   181
Which Heaven has varnished out, and made a
    Queen:°
The same forever! and described by all
With truth and goodness, as with crown and ball.
Poets heap virtues, painters gems at will,
And show their zeal, and hide their want of
    skill.
'Tis well — but, artists! who can paint or write,
To draw the naked is your true delight.
That robe of quality so struts and swells,
None see what parts of nature it conceals: 190
Th' exactest traits of body or of mind,
We owe to models of an humble kind.
If Queensbury° to strip there's no compelling,
'Tis from a handmaid we must take a Helen.
From peer or bishop 'tis no easy thing
To draw the man who loves his God, or king:
Alas! I copy (or my draught would fail)
From honest Mah'met° or plain Parson Hale.°

But grant, in public men sometimes are shown,
A woman's seen in private life alone: 200
Our bolder talents in full light displayed;
Your virtues open fairest in the shade.
Bred to disguise, in public 'tis you hide;
There, none distinguish 'twixt your shame or pride,
Weakness or delicacy; all so nice,
That each may seem a virtue, or a vice.

In men, we various ruling passions find;
In women, two almost divide the kind;
Those, only fixed, they first or last obey,
The love of pleasure, and the love of sway.   210

That, Nature gives; and where the lesson taught
Is but to please, can pleasure seem a fault?°
Experience, this; by man's oppression cursed,
They seek the second not to lose the first.

Men, some to business, some to pleasure take;
But every woman is at heart a rake:
Men, some to quiet, some to public strife;

But every lady would be queen for life.

Yet mark the fate of a whole sex of queens!°
Power all their end, but beauty all the means: 220
In youth they conquer, with so wild a rage,
As leaves them scarce a subject in their age:
For foreign glory, foreign joy, they roam;
No thought of peace or happiness at home.
But wisdom's triumph is well-timed retreat,
As hard a science to the fair as great!
Beauties, like tyrants, old and friendless grown,
Yet hate repose, and dread to be alone,
Worn out in public, weary every eye,
Nor leave one sigh behind them when they die.

Pleasures the sex, as children birds, pursue,   231
Still out of reach, yet never out of view;
Sure, if they catch, to spoil the toy at most,
To covet flying, and regret when lost:
At last, to follies youth could scarce defend,
It grows their age's prudence to pretend;
Ashamed to own they gave delight before,
Reduced to feign it, when they give no more:
As hags hold sabbaths, less for joy than spite,
So these their merry, miserable night;   240
Still round and round the ghosts of beauty glide,
And haunt the places where their honor died.

See how the world its veterans rewards!
A youth of frolics, an old age of cards;
Fair to no purpose, artful to no end,
Young without lovers, old without a friend;
A fop their passion, but their prize a sot;
Alive, ridiculous, and dead, forgot!

Ah friend! to dazzle let the vain design;
To raise the thought, and touch the heart be thine!
That charm shall grow, while what fatigues the
    Ring,°   251
Flaunts and goes down, an unregarded thing:
So when the sun's broad beam has tired the sight,
All mild ascends the moon's more sober light,
Serene in virgin modesty she shines,
And unobserved the glaring orb declines.

Oh! blest with temper, whose unclouded ray
Can make tomorrow cheerful as today;
She, who can love a sister's charms, or hear
Sighs for a daughter with unwounded ear;   260
She, who ne'er answers till a husband cools,
Or, if she rules him, never shows she rules;
Charms by accepting, by submitting sways,
Yet has her humor most, when she obeys;
Lets fops or fortune fly which way they will;
Disdains all loss of tickets,° or codille;°
Spleen, vapors, or smallpox, above them all,
And mistress of herself, though China° fall.

And yet, believe me, good as well as ill,
Woman's at best a contradiction still.   270
Heaven, when it strives to polish all it can

182. Queen: Queen Caroline.   193. Queensbury: Kitty Hyde, Duchess of Queensbury, one of the most beautiful women of her time.   198. Mah'met: a Turk named Mahomet, servant to George I.   Parson Hale: Pope's friend Dr. Stephen Hales, clergyman and pioneer physiologist.   212. fault: Cf. E. on Crit., l. 170n.

219. queens: with a pun on queans.   251. Ring: Cf. Rape of the Lock, I.44n.   266. tickets: lottery tickets.   codille: Cf. Rape of the Lock, III.27–100n.   268. China: with a pun.

Its last best work, but forms a softer man;
Picks from each sex, to make the favorite blest,
Your love of pleasure, our desire of rest:
Blends, in exception to all general rules,
Your taste of follies, with our scorn of fools:
Reserve with frankness, art with truth allied,
Courage with softness, modesty with pride;
Fixed principles, with fancy ever new;
Shakes all together, and produces — you.   280
  Be this a woman's fame: with this unblest,
Toasts live a scorn, and queens may die a jest.
This Phoebus promised (I forget the year)
When those blue eyes first opened on the sphere;
Ascendant Phoebus watched that hour with care,
Averted half your parents' simple prayer;
And gave you beauty, but denied the pelf
That buys your sex a tyrant° o'er itself.
The generous god, who wit and gold refines,
And ripens spirits as he ripens mines,°   290
Kept dross for duchesses, the world shall know it,
To you gave sense, good humor, and a poet.

from IMITATIONS OF HORACE

THE FIRST EPISTLE
OF THE SECOND BOOK

TO AUGUSTUS

Pope's imitation of the first epistle of the second book
of Horace, usually called the *Epistle to Augustus,* was
written in 1736 and published in May, 1737. The poem
is partly an apology for poetry, following the argument of the original, in which, as Pope says in his
"Advertisement," Horace pleads the cause of the living Roman poets, "first against the taste of the town,
whose humor it was to magnify the authors of the preceding age; secondly against the court and the nobility,
who encouraged only the writers for the theaters; and
lastly against the emperor himself, who had conceived
them [poets] of little use to the government." But from
behind this apology as a stalking horse, Pope directs a
withering attack upon the court, and upon the Whigs
as the court party, through the central symbol of both,
George II.

Horace's Augustus might doubt the use of poets to
the government, but he had stood at the center of a
great classical civilization in what was generally regarded as its finest age, an emperor of wide attainments, munificent through his minister Maecenas to
learning and all the arts of life. George Augustus of
Hanover was another breed of cat. As Lord Hervey
put it in his *Memoirs,* struck with the same grotesque
contrast that Pope makes in the epistle, "not that there
was any similitude between the two princes who presided in the Roman and English Augustan ages besides
their names, for George Augustus neither loved learn-

ing nor encouraged men of letters, nor were there any
Maecenases about him. There was another very material difference too between these two Augustuses. For
as personal courage was the only quality necessary to
form a great prince which the one was suspected to
want, so I fear it was the only one the other was ever
thought to possess."

Conspicuous for a thirst of glory that the pacific policies of Walpole forbade him to indulge (except in the
"arms abroad" of his Hanoverian mistress, Mme.
Walmoden); blinded by his self-importance from realizing that the royal power was actually wielded by his
queen; completely indifferent to the culture of his
adopted country — George II made an ideal ironic recipient for a poem which bristles with allusions to great
leaders of the past, whose central content is a review of
English art and literature, and whose implicit theme
is that the indifferent values of current English civilization reflect the indifferent value of the current monarch. Pope had never heard of T. S. Eliot's Fisher-
King, whose land is impotent because he is maimed,
but he knew perfectly well that in the long poetic tradition of "praise of majesty" the point of the panegyric
was always the relation of the king's health-in-virtue
to the health-in-virtue of the polity. The epistle to Augustus is therefore a political poem in the broadest
sense. Though it expresses the poet's personal disapproval of the Whig government and court, its fundamental subject is the polity of England, which is what
it is (the poem claims) because the king is what he is.
And this is also the force of the comparison, *via* Horace,
to the polity of Rome. The English past can be aligned
with Rome's, as the poem shows, but in the English
present the only "Augustus" is a name.

While you, great patron of mankind! sustain
The balanced world, and open all the main;
Your country, chief, in arms abroad defend,°
At home, with morals, arts, and laws amend;
How shall the Muse, from such a monarch, steal
An hour, and not defraud the public weal?
  Edward and Henry,° now the boast of fame,
And virtuous Alfred, a more sacred name,
After a life of generous toils endured,
The Gaul° subdued, or property secured,   10
Ambition humbled, mighty cities stormed,
Or laws established, and the world reformed;
Closed their long glories with a sigh, to find
Th' unwilling gratitude of base mankind!
All human virtue, to its latest breath,
Finds Envy never conquered, but by death.
The great Alcides,° every labor past,
Had still this monster to subdue at last.
Sure fate of all, beneath whose rising ray
Each star of meaner merit fades away!   20

288. tyrant: i.e., husband.   289–90. The . . . mines: As god of
poetry, Apollo refines wit; as god of the sun (supposed to ripen
mines), he refines gold.

TO AUGUSTUS. 3. Your . . . defend: Cf. *Imit. Horace,* Sat.
II.i.27–28n. Pope hints also at the government's unpopular
peace policy, and at the arms of Mme. Walmoden (cf. headnote).
7. Edward, Henry: Edward III (cf. *W. Forest,* ll. 303–06n.)
and Henry V, England's warrior kings.   10. The Gaul: France.
17. Alcides: Hercules.

Oppressed we feel the beam directly beat,
Those suns of glory please not till they set.
   To thee, the world its present homage pays,
The harvest early, but mature the praise:
Great friend of liberty!° in *kings* a name
Above all Greek, above all Roman fame:
Whose word is truth, as sacred and revered,
As Heaven's own oracles from altars heard.
Wonder of kings! like whom, to mortal eyes
None e'er has risen, and none e'er shall rise.   30
   Just in one instance, be it yet confessed
Your people, sir, are partial in the rest:
Foes to all living worth except your own,
And advocates for folly dead and gone.
Authors, like coins, grow dear as they grow old;
It is the rust we value, not the gold.
Chaucer's worst ribaldry is learned by rote,
And beastly Skelton° heads of houses quote:
One likes no language but the Faery Queen;
A Scot will fight for Christ's Kirk o' the Green;°   40
And each true Briton is to Ben° so civil,
He swears the Muses met him at the Devil.°
Tho' justly Greece her eldest sons admires,
Why should not we be wiser than our sires?
In every public virtue we excel;
We build, we paint, we sing, we dance as well,
And learnèd Athens to our art must stoop,
Could she behold us tumbling thro' a hoop.°
   If time improve our wit as well as wine,
Say at what age a poet grows divine?   50
Shall we, or shall we not, account him so,
Who died, perhaps, an hundred years ago?
End all dispute; and fix the year precise
When British bards begin t' immortalize?
"Who lasts a century can have no flaw,
I hold that wit a classic, good in law."
Suppose he wants a year, will you compound?
And shall we deem him ancient, right and sound,
Or damn to all eternity at once,
At ninety-nine, a modern and a dunce?   60
   "We shall not quarrel for a year or two;
By courtesy of England, he may do."
   Then by the rule that made the horsetail bare,°
I pluck out year by year, as hair by hair,
And melt down ancients like a heap of snow:
While you, to measure merits, look in Stowe,°
And estimating authors by the year,
Bestow a garland only on a bier.
   Shakespeare (whom you and every playhouse bill

Style the divine, the matchless, what you will)   70
For gain, not glory, winged his roving flight,
And grew immortal in his own despite.
Ben, old and poor, as little seemed to heed
The life to come, in every poet's creed.
Who now reads Cowley? if he pleases yet,
His moral pleases, not his pointed wit;
Forgot his epic, nay pindaric art,°
But still I love the language of his heart.
   "Yet surely, surely, these were famous men!
What boy but hears the sayings of old Ben?   80
In all debates where critics bear a part,
Not one but nods, and talks of Jonson's art,
Of° Shakespeare's nature, and of Cowley's wit;
How Beaumont's judgment checked what Fletcher
      writ;
How Shadwell hasty, Wycherley was slow;
But, for the passions, Southerne sure and Rowe.°
These, only these, support the crowded stage,
From eldest Heywood° down to Cibber's° age."
   All this may be; the people's voice is odd,
It is, and it is not, the voice of God.   90
To *Gammer Gurton*° if it give the bays,
And yet deny the *Careless Husband*° praise,
Or say our fathers never broke a rule;
Why then, I say, the public is a fool.
But let them own, that greater faults than we
They had, and greater virtues, I'll agree.
Spenser himself affects the obsolete,
And Sidney's verse halts ill on Roman feet:
Milton's strong pinion now not Heaven can bound,
Now serpent-like, in prose he sweeps the
      ground,   100
In quibbles, angel and archangel join,
And God the Father turns a school divine.°
Not that I'd lop the beauties from his book,
Like slashing Bentley with his desperate hook,°
Or damn all Shakespeare, like th' affected fool
At court, who hates whate'er he read at school.°
   But for the wits of either Charles's days,
The mob of gentlemen who wrote with ease;
Sprat, Carew, Sedley,° and a hundred more,
(Like twinkling stars the *Miscellanies* o'er)   110

75–77. **Cowley ... art:** Cowley (cf. *W. Forest*, ll. 272–74n.) had written odes based on the style of Pindar, and a religious epic based on the life of King David. 83–86. Pope parodies the clichés of critical chitchat. 85–86. **Shadwell ... Rowe:** dramatists, the first two of comedies, and the last two of sentimental tragedies. 88. **Heywood:** John Heywood, pre-Shakespearean dramatist. **Cibber:** Cf. *Dunciad*, IV, headnote. 91. *Gammer Gurton:* in Pope's time, thought to be the first English comedy. 92. *Careless Husband:* a comedy by Cibber. 101–02. **In ... divine:** Cf. *Paradise Lost*, VI.609–28, III.80–134. 104. **hook:** Cf. *Ep. to Arb.*, l. 164n. A *hook* is (1) a pruning tool, (2) the square bracket Bentley used to indicate passages he thought spurious in *Paradise Lost*. 105–06. **Or ... school:** Pope refers to some lines of self-confession in Lord Hervey's *Epistle from a Nobleman to a Doctor of Divinity* (1733). 109. Thomas Sprat, Thomas Carew (pron. Carey), and Sir Charles Sedley were seventeenth-century gentlemen-poets (not professional men of letters like Pope).

25. **liberty:** i.e., what the Tories felt was being lost under George II. 38. **Skelton:** John Skelton, laureate under Henry VIII. 40. **Christ's ... Green:** a Scots ballad variously attributed to James I or James V. 41. **Ben:** Ben Jonson. 42. **the Devil:** with a pun on the name of Jonson's haunt, the Devil Tavern. 48. **tumbling ... hoop:** Cf. l. 309n. 63. **rule ... bare:** This is the logical puzzle called *sorites:* at what point does subtraction, one grain at a time, ever make that not a heap which was still a heap one grain before? 66. **Stowe:** Cf. *Imit. Donne*, Sat. IV.131n.

One simile, that solitary shines
In the dry desert of a thousand lines,
Or lengthened thought that gleams thro' many a
    page,
Has sanctified whole poems for an age.
I lose my patience, and I own it too,
When works are censured, not as bad but new;
While if our elders break all reason's laws,
These fools demand not pardon, but applause.
    On Avon's bank, where flowers eternal blow,
If I but ask if any weed can grow?   120
One tragic sentence if I dare deride,
Which Betterton's° grave action dignified,
Or well-mouthed Booth° with emphasis proclaims
(Tho' but, perhaps, a muster roll of names),
How will our fathers rise up in a rage,
And swear, all shame is lost in George's age!
You'd think no fools disgraced the former reign,
Did not some grave examples yet remain,
Who scorn a lad should teach his father skill,
And, having once been wrong, will be so still.   130
He who to seem more deep than you or I,
Extols old bards, or Merlin's Prophecy,°
Mistake him not; he envies, not admires,
And to debase the sons, exalts the sires.
Had ancient times conspired to disallow
What then was new, what had been ancient now?
Or what remained, so worthy to be read
By learnèd critics, of the mighty dead?
    In days of ease, when now the weary sword
Was sheathed, and *luxury* with *Charles*°
    restored;   140
In every taste of foreign courts improved,
" All, by the king's example, lived and loved."°
Then peers grew proud in horsemanship t' excel,°
Newmarket's° glory rose, as Britain's fell;
The soldier breathed the gallantries of France,
And every flowery courtier writ romance.°
Then° marble, softened into life, grew warm,
And yielding metal flowed to human form:
Lely on animated canvas stole
The sleepy eye, that spoke the melting soul.   150
No wonder then, when all was love and sport,
The willing Muses were debauched at court:
On each enervate string they taught the note
To pant or tremble thro' an eunuch's throat.°

But Britain, changeful as a child at play,
Now calls in princes, and now turns away.°
Now Whig, now Tory, what we loved we hate;
Now all for pleasure, now for Church and state;
Now for prerogative,° and now for laws;
Effects unhappy! from a noble cause.   160
    Time was, a sober Englishman would knock
His servants up, and rise by five o'clock,
Instruct his family in every rule,
And send his wife to church, his son to school.
To worship like his fathers was his care;
To teach their frugal virtues to his heir;
To prove that luxury could never hold;
And place, on good security, his gold.
Now times are changed, and one poetic itch
Has seized the court and city, poor and rich: 170
Sons, sires, and grandsires, all will wear the bays,
Our wives read Milton, and our daughters plays,
To theaters, and to rehearsals throng,
And all our grace at table is a song.
I, who so oft renounce the Muses, lie,
Not ———'s self e'er tells more *fibs* than I;
When sick of Muse, our follies we deplore,
And promise our best friends to rhyme no more;
We wake next morning in a raging fit,
And call for pen and ink to show our wit.   180
    He served a prenticeship, who sets up shop;
Ward tried on puppies, and the poor, his drop;°
Even Radcliffe's doctors travel first to France,
Nor dare to practice till they've learned to dance.°
Who builds a bridge that never drove a pile?
(Should Ripley° venture, all the world would
    smile)
But those who cannot write, and those who can,
All rhyme, and scrawl, and scribble, to a man.
    Yet,° sir, reflect, the mischief is not great;
These madmen never hurt the Church or state:
Sometimes the folly benefits mankind;   191
And rarely avarice taints the tuneful mind.
Allow him but his plaything of a pen,
He ne'er rebels, or plots, like other men:
Flight of cashiers, or mobs,° he'll never mind;
And knows no losses while the Muse is kind.

122. **Betterton:** Pope's friend Thomas Betterton, outstanding tragic actor of the Restoration.   123. **Booth:** Barton Booth, also a tragic actor, famed for his musical voice.   132. **Merlin's Prophecy:** in Geoffrey of Monmouth's *History*, VII.   140. *Charles:* Charles II.   142. **"All . . . loved":** Pope quotes from Granville's "Progress of Beauty."   143. **t' excel:** The Duke of Newcastle had written two books on horsemanship (1658, 1667).   144. **Newmarket:** a race track frequented by Charles II.   146. **romance:** the genre of elaborate love story exemplified in the Earl of Orrery's *Parthenissa* (1654).   147–50. **Then . . . soul:** alluding to the soft languor of Restoration sculptures and of the portraits by Sir Peter Lely.   152–54. **The . . . throat:** i.e., opera made its appearance in England (in Sir William Davenant's *Siege of Rhodes*).

156. **calls . . . away:** England had *turned away* Charles I by beheading him (1649), had *called in* Charles II from exile (1660), had *turned away* James II (1688) and *called in* William of Orange to replace him, and in 1714, on the death of Anne, had finally *called in* the Hanoverians. Pope perhaps hints to George II that another *turning away* might be in order.   159. **prerogative:** the royal prerogative, an area of authority not defined by *laws*.   182. **drop:** Cf. *Ep. to Arb.*, l. 29n.   183–84. **Radcliffe . . . dance:** Pope alludes to the medical traveling fellowships established by Dr. John Radcliffe, and to the attainments physicians were thought most likely to acquire by them.   186. **Ripley:** Cf. *Ep. to Burlington*, l. 18n.   189–240. Pope's "defense of poetry" — ironically, for its "practical" values (such as might be supposed to appeal to George II), actually for its moral values (which Pope illustrates by satirizing the court and praising Swift).   195. **Flight . . . mobs:** alluding to embezzlements in the South Sea Company, which had cost many their savings.

To cheat a friend, or Ward, he leaves to Peter;°
The good man heaps up nothing but mere meter,
Enjoys his garden and his book in quiet;
And then — a perfect hermit in his diet.   200
 Of little use the man you may suppose,
Who says in verse what others say in prose;
Yet let me show, a poet's of some weight,
And (tho' no soldier) useful to the state.
What will a child learn sooner than a song?
What better teach a foreigner the tongue?
What's long or short, each accent where to place,
And speak in public with some sort of grace.°
I scarce can think him such a worthless thing,
Unless he praise some monster of a king;   210
Or virtue, or religion turn to sport,
To please a lewd, or unbelieving court.
Unhappy Dryden!° — In all Charles's days,
Roscommon° only boasts unspotted bays;
And in our own (excuse some courtly stains)
No whiter page than Addison remains.
He, from the taste obscene reclaims our youth,
And sets the passions on the side of truth,
Forms the soft bosom with the gentlest art,°
And pours each human virtue in the heart.   220
Let° Ireland tell, how wit upheld her cause,
Her trade supported, and supplied° her laws;
And leave on Swift this grateful verse engraved,
"The rights a court attacked, a poet saved."
Behold the hand that wrought a nation's cure,
Stretched to relieve the idiot and the poor,
Proud Vice to brand, or injured Worth adorn,
And stretch the ray to ages yet unborn.
Not but there are, who merit other palms;
Hopkins and Sternhold glad the heart with
     Psalms:°   230
The boys and girls whom charity maintains,
Implore your help in these pathetic strains:
How could devotion touch the country pews,
Unless the gods bestowed a proper Muse?
Verse cheers their leisure, verse assists their work,
Verse prays for peace, or sings down Pope and
     Turk.°
The silenced preacher yields to potent strain,
And feels that grace his prayer besought in vain;
The blessing thrills thro' all the laboring throng,

And Heaven is won by violence of song.°   240
 Our rural ancestors, with little blessed,
Patient of labor when the end was rest,
Indulged the day that housed their annual grain,
With feasts, and offerings, and a thankful strain:
The joy their wives, their sons, and servants
     share,
Ease of their toil, and partners of their care:
The laugh, the jest, attendants on the bowl,
Smoothed every brow, and opened every soul:
With growing years the pleasing license grew,
And taunts alternate innocently flew.   250
But times corrupt, and nature, ill-inclined,
Produced the point that left a sting behind;
Till friend with friend, and families at strife,
Triumphant malice raged through private life.
Who felt the wrong, or feared it, took th' alarm,
Appealed to law, and Justice lent her arm.
At length, by wholesome dread of statutes bound,
The poets learned to please, and not to wound:
Most warped to flattery's side; but some, more nice,
Preserved the freedom, and forbore the vice.   260
Hence satire rose, that just the medium hit,
And heals with morals what it hurts with wit.
 We conquered France, but felt our captive's
     charms;
Her arts victorious triumphed o'er our arms;
Britain to soft refinements less a foe,
Wit grew polite, and numbers learned to flow.
Waller° was smooth; but Dryden taught to join
The varying verse, the full-resounding line,
The long majestic march, and energy divine.
Tho' still some traces of our rustic vein   270
And splayfoot verse remained, and will remain.
Late, very late, correctness grew our care,
When the tired nation breathed from civil war.
Exact Racine, and Corneille's noble fire,
Showed us that France had something to admire.
Not but the tragic spirit was our own,
And full in Shakespeare, fair in Otway° shone:
But Otway failed to polish or refine,
And fluent Shakespeare scarce effaced a line.°
Even copious Dryden wanted, or forgot,   280
The last and greatest art, the art to blot.
 Some doubt, if equal pains, or equal fire
The humbler Muse of comedy require.
But in known images of life, I guess

197. Peter: Cf. *Ep. to Bathurst*, l. 20n.   **206–08. What . . .
grace:** Cf. *Imit. Donne*, Sat. IV.68n.   **213. Unhappy Dryden:**
By shifting suddenly to Dryden, Pope makes the indictment in
ll. 210–12 *seem* to apply to Charles II.   **214. Roscommon:** Cf.
E. on Crit., l. 725n.   **219. Forms . . . art:** e.g., as in the *Tatlers*
and *Spectators* directed to the ladies.   **221–27.** Pope refers to
Swift's efforts for improvement of the Irish economy; to his attacks (in the guise of a Dublin draper: see p. 545) on a court-
approved project that would have debased the Irish monetary
system (l. 224); to his founding a hospital for the feeble-minded
and a fund for aiding the poor; and to his satires on the vicious,
praises of the good (l. 227).   **222. supplied:** made up for the
defects in.   **230. Psalms:** alluding to a naïve sixteenth-century
metrical version of the Psalms.   **236. or . . . Turk:** A prayer at
the close of the Sternhold-Hopkins version has the line, "From
Pope and Turk defend us, Lord."

240. Hymn-singing was especially associated with dissenters, who
were violently anti-Catholic. Hence Pope qualifies his sympathy
with a glance at Matt. 11:12: "And from the days of John the
Baptist until now, the kingdom of heaven suffereth violence,
and the violent take it by force."   **267.** Waller (cf. *E. on
Crit.*, l. 361n.) was looked on as a pioneer of the Augustan style,
because in his verse were worked out some of the principles on
which effective use of the closed couplet depends.   **277. Otway:**
Thomas Otway, Restoration tragic dramatist.   **279. fluent . . .
line:** alluding to Ben Jonson's comment that though it might be
said in praise of Shakespeare that he never blotted a line,
"would he had blotted a thousand."

The labor greater, as th' indulgence less.
Observe how seldom even the best succeed:
Tell me if Congreve's fools are fools indeed?
What pert, low dialogue has Farquhar writ!
How Van wants grace, who never wanted wit!
The stage how loosely does Astraea tread,°   290
Who fairly puts all characters to bed!
And idle Cibber, how he breaks the laws,
To make poor Pinky eat with vast applause!°
But fill their purse, our poet's work is done,
Alike to them, by pathos or by pun.

O you!° whom vanity's light bark conveys
On fame's mad voyage by the wind of praise,
With what a shifting gale your course you ply,
Forever sunk too low, or borne too high!
Who pants for glory finds but short repose,   300
A breath revives him, or a breath o'erthrows.
Farewell the stage! if just as thrives the play,
The silly bard grows fat, or falls away.

There still remains, to mortify a wit,
The many-headed monster of the Pit:
A senseless, worthless, and unhonored crowd;
Who, to disturb their betters mighty proud,
Clattering their sticks before ten lines are spoke,
Call for the farce, the bear, or the Black Joke.°
What dear delight to Britons farce affords!   310
Ever the taste of mobs, but now of lords;
(Taste, that eternal wanderer, which flies
From heads to ears, and now from ears to eyes°)
The play stands still; damn action and discourse,
Back fly the scenes,° and enter foot and horse;
Pageants on pageants, in long order drawn,
Peers, heralds, bishops, ermine, gold, and lawn;
The champion too! and, to complete the jest,
Old Edward's armor beams on Cibber's breast.°
With laughter sure Democritus° had died,   320
Had he beheld an audience gape so wide.
Let bear or elephant be e'er so white,
The people, sure, the people are the sight!
Ah luckless poet! stretch thy lungs and roar,
That bear or elephant shall heed thee more;
While all its throats the gallery extends,
And all the thunder of the Pit ascends!
Loud as the wolves, on Orcas'° stormy steep;
Howl to the roarings of the northern deep.

Such is the shout, the long-applauding note,   330
At Quin's high plume, or Oldfield's° petticoat;
Or when from court a birthday suit bestowed,
Sinks the lost actor in the tawdry load.°
Booth enters — hark! the universal peal!
" But has he spoken? " Not a syllable.
What shook the stage, and made the people stare?
Cato's long wig, flowered gown, and lacquered
      chair.°
Yet lest you think I rally more than teach,
Or praise malignly arts I cannot reach,
Let me for once presume t' instruct the times,   340
To know the poet° from the man of rhymes:
'Tis he, who gives my breast a thousand pains,
Can make me feel each passion that he feigns;
Enrage, compose, with more than magic art,
With pity, and with terror, tear my heart;
And snatch me, o'er the earth, or thro' the air,
To Thebes, to Athens, when he will, and where.

But not this part of the poetic state
Alone, deserves the favor of the Great:
Think of those authors, sir, who would rely   350
More on a reader's sense, than gazer's eye.
Or who shall wander where the Muses sing?
Who climb their mountain, or who taste their
      spring?
How shall we fill a library with wit,
When Merlin's Cave is half unfurnished yet?°

My liege! why writers little claim your thought,
I guess; and, with their leave, will tell the fault:
We poets are (upon a poet's word)
Of all mankind, the creatures most absurd:
The season, when to come, and when to go,   360
To sing, or cease to sing, we never know;
And if we will recite nine hours in ten,
You lose your patience, just like other men.
Then too we hurt ourselves, when to defend
A single verse, we quarrel with a friend;
Repeat unasked; lament, the wit's too fine
For vulgar eyes, and point out every line.
But most, when straining with too weak a wing,
We needs will write Epistles to the king;
And from the moment we oblige the town,   370
Expect a place, or pension from the Crown;
Or dubbed historians° by express command,
T' enroll your triumphs o'er the seas and land,
Be called to court to plan some work divine,
As once for Louis, Boileau, and Racine.°

288-90. What . . . tread: George Farquhar, Sir John Vanbrugh, and Mrs. Aphra Behn (pseudonym, Astraea) were all authors of comedies — Mrs. Behn, of several bawdy ones.   293. Pinky . . . applause: In his role in Cibber's *Love Makes a Man*, the actor William Pinkethman ate two chickens on stage.   296. you: playwrights.   309. Black Joke: To draw crowds, theater managers companioned their performances of serious plays with pantomimes, farces, spectacles (ll. 315 ff.), acrobatics (l. 48), and ballads. *The Black Joke* is an indecent ballad.   313. From . . . eyes: i.e., from drama to opera, from opera to pantomime.   315. s᷎enes: equivalents of the modern curtain.   319. armor . . . breast: Edward III's armor is said to have been borrowed from the Tower of London for one of these spectacles.   320. Democritus: "the laughing philosopher" of Greece.   328. Orcas: the northernmost tip of Scotland.

331. James Quin and Anne Oldfield, actors.   332-33. Or . . . load: Cf. *Rape of the Lock*, I.23n.; *Imit. Donne*, Sat. IV. 219n.   337. Cato . . . chair: i.e., in performances of Addison's *Cato*.   341. poet: i.e., dramatic poet.   354-55. How . . . yet: The Roman Augustus had ordered the building of the great Palatine Library; Queen Caroline, in contrast, had ordered a nondescript structure for her garden at Richmond, which she stocked with wax figures (Merlin among them) and a few books.   372-75. Under Charles II and Louis XIV, poets had been the royal historiographers.   375. Louis . . . Racine: Pope contrasts with George II, the French king Louis XIV, who supported art and

Yet think, great sir! (so many virtues shown)
Ah think, what poet best may make them
  known?
Or choose at least some minister of grace,
Fit to bestow the laureate's° weighty place.

  Charles,° to late times to be transmitted fair,   380
Assigned his figure to Bernini's care;
And great Nassau to Kneller's hand decreed
To fix him graceful on the bounding steed;
So well in paint and stone they judged of merit:
But kings in wit may want discerning spirit.
The hero William, and the martyr Charles,
One knighted Blackmore, and one pensioned
  Quarles;
Which made old Ben, and surly Dennis swear,
" No Lord's anointed, but a Russian bear."°

  Not with such majesty, such bold relief,   390
The forms august, of king, or conquering chief,
E'er swelled on marble; as in verse have shined
(In polished verse) the manners and the mind.
Oh, could I mount on the Maeonian° wing,
Your arms, your actions, your repose to sing!
What seas you traversed, and what fields you
  fought!
Your country's peace, how oft, how dearly bought!
How barbarous rage subsided at your word,
And nations wondered while they dropped the
  sword!
How, when you nodded, o'er the land and deep,
Peace stole her wing, and wrapped the world in
  sleep;   401
Till earth's extremes your mediation own,
And Asia's tyrants tremble at your throne —
But verse, alas! your majesty disdains;
And I'm not used to panegyric strains:
The zeal of fools offends at any time,
But most of all, the zeal of fools in rhyme.
Besides, a fate attends on all I write,
That when I aim at praise, they say I bite.
A vile encomium doubly ridicules: 410
There's nothing blackens like the ink of fools.
If true, a woeful likeness; and if lies,
" Praise undeserved is scandal in disguise ":°
Well may he blush, who gives it, or receives;°
And when I flatter, let my dirty leaves
(Like Journals, odes,° and such forgotten things

learning, and made the poet Boileau and the playwright Racine
his royal historiographers.   **379.** The laureate had not been a
poet of talent since 1688.   **380–84. Charles . . . steed:** alluding
to Bernini's bust of Charles I; Kneller's equestrian portrait of
William III.   **387–89.** Blackmore (cf. *E. on Crit.*, l. 463n. and
Imit. Horace, Sat. II.i.23–26n.) was a physician by profession
and had been knighted for his services; Quarles was a minor
versifier of Charles I's time, but nothing is known of his pension
or of the opinion of royal taste attributed to both Ben Jonson
and Dennis.   **394. Maeonian:** Cf. *E. on Crit.*, l. 648n.
413. Pope quotes an anonymous poem of 1709, "The Celebrated
Beauties."   **414.** i.e., both George and his laureate Cibber.
416. Journals, odes: Cf. *Ep. to Arb.*, l. 54n., l. 222n.

As Eusden, Philips, Settle,° writ of kings)
Clothe spice, line trunks, or fluttering in a row,
Befringe the rails of Bedlam and Soho.°

from THE DUNCIAD

BOOK IV

The *Dunciad,* and, within the *Dunciad,* Book IV, is
Pope's masterpiece. The poem began to take shape after
the spring of 1726, when, as noted in the Introduction,
Swift visited Pope and apparently snatched from the
discard an early sketch of it. It was first published in
1728, complete in three books, and then enlarged a year
later by the addition of " Proeme, Prolegomena, Testi-
monia Scriptorum, Index Authorum, and Notes Variorum " into the *Dunciad Variorum.* The additions purported to be from the pen of that old discovery of the
Scriblerus Club, the learned blockhead Martinus Scriblerus, and they added to the poem's satire on bad
poets and critics a further level of satire on pedantic
scholarship.

In the *Dunciad* of 1728–29, the first book dealt with
the discovery and proclamation of a new ruler for the
Empire of Dulness, as in Dryden's mock poem *Mac
Flecknoe;* the second, with heroic games held in his
honor, based on the heroic games in the *Iliad* and
Aeneid; and the third, with a Pisgah vision, resembling
Adam's in *Paradise Lost,* in which the new monarch is
shown by Dulness the promised land of the future,
when all England shall be his. To complete this structure, Pope published separately in 1742 the *New Dunciad,* a fourth book wherein the prophecies of Book III
were finally fulfilled, and the results of twenty years
of Walpole's administration (as Pope interpreted them)
exposed: " He shows the Goddess coming in her majesty " — like an anti-Messiah at the Last Day — " to
destroy Order and Science, and to substitute the Kingdom of the Dull upon earth."

Up through this point, the hero of the poem, the
king dunce, was Lewis Theobald. Theobald had embarrassed Pope by publishing in 1726 a work entitled
*Shakespeare Restored, or a Specimen of the Many Errors
as well Committed, as Unamended, by Mr. Pope in his
Late Edition of This Poet.* In this respect, his position
in the poem was owing to a personal grievance. But
Theobald also made an appropriate king dunce. The
poem at this stage was still concerned with degeneration in learning and the arts; and, though Theobald
had a fine grasp of Elizabethan learning and a better
command than Pope of editorial principles (some of
his emendations to Shakespeare's text rank among the
best ever made), both his *Shakespeare Restored* and his
subsequent edition (1728) were clogged with learned
lumber and hilarious pedantries.

After the addition of the fourth book, however, extending the degeneration of English life into the fields

417. For Philips, cf. *Ep. to Arb.*, l. 100n., ll. 179–82n.; Laurence
Eusden was poet laureate, 1718–30; Elkanah Settle had written
birthday odes to George I.   **419. Bedlam, Soho:** centers for
old books.

of religion, education, and morals, and tracing it to what Pope believed were its ultimate social and political causes, a more versatile hero was clearly called for. Pope found him in Colley Cibber. With Cibber, as with Theobald, Pope had a personal score to settle; but Pope rarely elevated a man to duncehood who had not won it on his merits, and Cibber's qualifications were perfectly splendid. As George II's incapable poet laureate, he was an obvious instance of that monarch's cultural irresponsibility. As an appointee of Walpole, he exemplified Walpole's interest in men who, whether or not their powers were suited to a government post, would do as they were told. And as a nationally famous coxcomb, shrewd, shallow, impudent (though not without talent as dramatist and actor), Cibber offered a handsome specimen of the type of moral and artistic opportunism which was making good in the reign of Walpole and George Augustus. In 1743, therefore, Pope revised the original *Dunciad*, incorporated the *New Dunciad*, and brought out *The Dunciad, in Four Books*, with Cibber throned in Theobald's place.

The themes of the *Dunciad*, and especially of its fourth book, have a profundity that this account of origins and personalities should not be permitted to obscure. The poem is about a world with which the twentieth century is painfully familiar — a world teeming with energy and activity, but without a spiritual center, splintering in fractured atoms. "Turning and turning in the widening gyre," says Yeats in "The Second Coming" (Vol. II), "The falcon cannot hear the falconer; / Things fall apart; the center cannot hold; / Mere anarchy is loosed upon the world."

Dunciad IV is about the preliminaries to this situation which Pope believed he saw around him in the Augustan age. The classical and Renaissance ideal of the "compleat man" was splitting at the seams. The dunces — and this is the reason that in the larger meanings of the poem they are dunces — were exalting their partial disciplines into shabby substitutes for a whole. Education, it seemed to Pope, had become entangled in "the pale of words"; scholarship dealt in "fragments, not a meal"; criticism expended itself in minutiae, indifferent "how parts relate to parts, or they to whole"; the Grand Tour had shriveled into tourism. Moreover, the new sciences, with their well-known slogan, "I meddle only in my sphere," were taking on, Pope felt, the attributes of the narrow objects they pursued: "It fled, I followed; now in hope, now pain; / It stopped, I stopped; it moved, I moved again." The new creeds were thrusting "some mechanic cause" into the Creator's place, or abandoning Him altogether to "make God man's image, man the final Cause." We need not agree with the poet's evaluation of these developments, some of which held future benefits he could not foresee, to understand the relevance of the poem's thesis equally to Pope's time and our own: that without a center, activity is only mobility without direction; that without a One, the Many fall apart; that without a Word, a Logos, some constant standard of respective values, men are divided not united, blinded not illuminated, by their private, atomistic, uncreating words:

Lo! thy dread empire, CHAOS! is restored;
Light dies before thy uncreating word:

Thy hand, great Anarch! lets the curtain fall;
And Universal Darkness buries all.

ARGUMENT

The poet being, in this book, to declare the *completion* of the *prophecies* mentioned at the end of the former, makes a new *Invocation;* as the greater poets are wont, when some high and worthy matter is to be sung. He shows the Goddess coming in her majesty, to destroy *Order* and *Science,* and to substitute the *Kingdom of the Dull* upon earth. How she leads captive the *Sciences,* and silenceth the *Muses,* and *what* they be who succeed in their stead. All her children, by a wonderful attraction, are drawn about her; and bear along with them divers others, who promote her empire by connivance, weak resistance, or discouragement of arts; such as half-wits, tasteless admirers, vain pretenders, the flatterers of dunces, or the patrons of them. All these crowd round her; one of them offering to approach her is driven back by a rival, but she commends and encourages both. The first who speak in form are the *Geniuses* of the *Schools,* who assure her of their care to advance her cause, by confining youth to *words,* and keeping them out of the way of real knowledge. Their address, and her gracious answer; with her charge to them and the Universities. The *Universities* appear by their proper deputies, and assure her that the same method is observed in the progress of *Education.* The speech of *Aristarchus* on this subject. They are driven off by a band of young Gentlemen returned from *travel* with their *tutors;* one of whom delivers to the Goddess, in a polite oration, an account of the whole conduct and fruits of their *travels:* presenting to her at the same time a young Nobleman perfectly accomplished. She receives him graciously, and endues him with the happy quality of *Want of Shame.* She sees loitering about her a number of *Indolent Persons* abandoning all business and duty, and dying with laziness: To these approaches the antiquary *Annius,* entreating her to make them *Virtuosos,* and assign them over to him: But *Mummius,* another antiquary, complaining of his fraudulent proceeding, she finds a method to reconcile their difference. Then enter a Troop of people fantastically adorned, offering her strange and exotic presents: Amongst them, one stands forth and demands justice on another, who had deprived him of one of the greatest curiosities in Nature: but he justifies himself so well, that the Goddess gives them both her approbation. She recommends to them to find proper employment for the *Indolents* before-mentioned, in the study of *butterflies, shells, birds' nests, moss, etc.,* but with particular caution, not to proceed beyond *trifles,* to any useful or extensive views of Nature, or of the Author of Nature. Against the last of these apprehensions, she is secured by a hearty address from the *Minute Philosophers* and *Freethinkers,* one of whom speaks in the name of the rest. The Youth, thus instructed and principled, are delivered to her in a body, by the hands of *Silenus,* and then admitted to taste the cup of the *Magus,* her High Priest, which causes a total oblivion of all obligations, divine, civil, moral, or rational. To these her Adepts she sends *Priests, Attend-*

ants, and *Comforters,* of various kinds; confers on them *Orders* and *Degrees;* and then dismissing them with a speech, confirming to each his *Privileges,* and telling what she expects from each, concludes with a *yawn* of extraordinary virtue: The Progress and Effects whereof on all Orders of men, and the consummation of all, in the restoration of *Night* and *Chaos,* conclude the poem.

Yet, yet a moment, one dim ray of light
Indulge, dread Chaos, and eternal Night!
Of darkness visible° so much be lent,
As half to show, half veil, the deep intent.
Ye Powers! whose mysteries restored I sing,
To whom Time bears me on his rapid wing,
Suspend a while your force inertly strong,
Then take at once the poet and the song.
   Now flamed the Dog Star's° unpropitious ray,
Smote every brain, and withered every bay;°   10
Sick was the sun, the owl forsook his bower,
The moon-struck prophet felt the madding hour:
Then rose the Seed of Chaos, and of Night,
To blot out Order, and extinguish Light,
Of dull and venal a new world to mold,
And bring Saturnian days of lead and gold.°
   She mounts the throne: her head a cloud concealed,
In broad effulgence all below revealed;
('Tis thus aspiring Dulness ever shines)
Soft on her lap her laureate son reclines.°   20
   Beneath° her footstool, *Science* groans in chains,
And *Wit* dreads exile, penalties, and pains.
There foamed rebellious *Logic,* gagged and bound,
There, stripped, fair *Rhetoric* languished on the ground;
His blunted arms by *Sophistry* are borne,
And shameless *Billingsgate°* her robes adorn.
Morality, by her false guardians drawn,
Chicane in furs, and *Casuistry* in lawn,°
Gasps, as they straiten at each end the cord,
And dies, when Dulness gives her Page the word.
Mad *Máthesis°* alone was unconfined,   31
Too mad for mere material chains to bind,
Now to pure space lifts her ecstatic stare,
Now running round the circle finds it square.
But held in tenfold bonds the *Muses* lie,°
Watched both by Envy's and by Flattery's eye:
There to her heart sad Tragedy addressed

The dagger wont to pierce the tyrant's breast;
But sober History restrained her rage,
And promised vengeance on a barbarous age.   40
There sunk Thalia,° nerveless, cold, and dead,
Had not her sister Satire held her head:
Nor couldst thou, Chesterfield! a tear refuse,
Thou weptst, and with thee wept each gentle Muse.°
   When lo! a harlot form° soft sliding by,
With mincing step, small voice, and languid eye:
Foreign her air, her robe's discordant pride
In patchwork fluttering, and her head aside:
By singing peers upheld on either hand,
She tripped and laughed, too pretty much to stand;   50
Cast on the prostrate Nine a scornful look,
Then thus in quaint recitativo spoke.
   "O *Cara! Cara!* silence all that train:°
Joy to great Chaos! let Division° reign:
Chromatic tortures° soon shall drive them hence,
Break all their nerves, and fritter all their sense:
One trill shall harmonize joy, grief, and rage,
Wake the dull Church, and lull the ranting Stage;
To the same notes thy sons shall hum, or snore,
And all thy yawning daughters cry, *encore.*   60
Another Phoebus,° thy own Phoebus, reigns,
Joys in my jigs, and dances in my chains.
But soon, ah soon, Rebellion will commence,
If Music meanly borrows aid from Sense.°
Strong in new arms, lo! Giant Handel stands,
Like bold Briareus,° with a hundred hands;
To stir, to rouse, to shake the soul he comes,
And Jove's own thunders follow Mars's drums.
Arrest him, Empress; or you sleep no more —"
She heard, and drove him to th' Hibernian shore.°   70
   And now had Fame's posterior trumpet blown,
And all the nations summoned to the throne.
The° young, the old, who feel her inward sway,
One instinct seizes, and transports away.

controls, e.g., the act of 1737 requiring plays to be licensed. **41. Thalia:** the Muse of comedy. **43–44. Chesterfield . . . Muse:** Lord Chesterfield had opposed the licensing act. **45. harlot form:** i.e., Opera. Pope describes her in terms that express his view of the debilitating effects of current Italian operas on English musical and dramatic taste. **53. that train:** i.e., the Muses. **54. Division:** used in its musical senses of (1) variation on a theme, (2) discord, as well as in the sense of anarchy, chaos. **55. Chromatic tortures:** probably with a pun on rheumatic, and another on the Latin sense of *torture,* to twist, pervert. **61. Another Phoebus:** i.e., a different Phoebus from the one who was god of light and of the arts (with a pun on *phébus,* French for bombast). Pope's line echoes one in which Virgil was believed to have announced the birth of the Messiah (*Eclogue,* IV); for Opera is announcing the Anti-Messiah. **64. Music . . . Sense:** i.e., as it was doing in Handel's oratorios, which Pope compliments in ll. 65–68. **66. Briareus:** the hundred-headed giant of Greek myth. **70. Hibernian shore:** Ireland, where Handel was enjoying great success after neglect in London. **73–78. The . . . around:** The metaphor is of Newtonian gravitation.

DUNCIAD, IV. **3. darkness visible:** Pope borrows Milton's characterization of hell (*Paradise Lost,* I.63) to suggest the graver implications of his theme. **9. Dog Star:** Cf. *Ep. to Arb.,* l. 3n. **10. bay:** laurel, i.e., art. **16.** Saturn's reign was the legendary golden age, but Saturn is also the alchemical name for lead. The new Saturnian age, Pope implies, is golden in its love of lucre, leaden in its love of dulness. **20. laureate . . . reclines:** Likened to Anti-Christ in the developing theme of the poem, Cibber is here shown in a modern Adoration. **21 ff.** The scene suggests an inverted Last Judgment. **26. Billingsgate:** abusive language. **28. furs, lawn:** i.e., law (the judge's furred gown) and church (the bishop's linen sleeves). **31. Máthesis:** i.e., mathematics. **35. bonds . . . lie:** Pope refers to governmental

None need a guide, by sure attraction led,
And strong impulsive gravity of head:
None want a place, for all their center found,
Hung to the Goddess, and cohered around.
Not closer, orb in orb,° conglobed are seen
The buzzing bees about their dusky queen.   80

The gathering number, as it moves along,
Involves a vast involuntary throng,
Who gently drawn, and struggling less and less,
Roll in her vortex,° and her power confess.
Not those alone who passive own her laws,
But who, weak rebels, more advance her cause.
Whate'er of dunce in college or in town
Sneers at another, in toupee or gown;
Whate'er of mongrel no one class admits,
A wit with dunces, and a dunce with wits.   90

Nor absent they, no members of her state,
Who pay her homage in her sons, the Great;
Who, false to Phoebus, bow the knee to Baal;°
Or, impious, preach his Word without a call.°
Patrons, who sneak from living worth to dead,
Withhold the pension, and set up the head;°
Or vest dull Flattery in the sacred gown;
Or give from fool to fool the laurel crown.
And (last and worst) with all the cant of wit,
Without the soul, the Muse's hypocrite.°   100

There° marched the bard and blockhead, side by
     side,
Who rhymed for hire, and patronized for pride.
Narcissus, praised with all a parson's power,
Looked a white lily sunk beneath a shower.
There moved Montalto with superior air;
His stretched-out arm displayed a volume fair;
Courtiers and Patriots in two ranks divide,
Thro' both he passed, and bowed from side to
     side:
But as in graceful act, with awful eye
Composed he stood, bold Benson thrust him
     by: 110
On two unequal crutches propped he came,
Milton's on this, on that one Johnston's name.
The decent knight retired with sober rage,
Withdrew his hand, and closed the pompous
     page.

But° (happy for him as the times went then)
Appeared Apollo's mayor and aldermen,
On whom three hundred gold-capped youths await,
To lug the ponderous volume off in state.

When Dulness, smiling — " Thus revive the wits!
But murder first, and mince them all to bits;   120
As erst Medea (cruel, so to save!)
A new edition of old Aeson gave;°
Let standard° authors, thus, like trophies born,
Appear more glorious as more hacked and torn.
And you, my critics! in the checkered shade,
Admire new light thro' holes yourselves have
     made.
" Leave not a foot of verse, a foot of stone,
A page, a grave, that they° can call their own;
But spread, my sons, your glory thin or thick,
On passive paper, or on solid brick,   130
So by each bard an alderman shall sit,
A heavy lord shall hang at every wit,
And while on Fame's triumphal car they ride,
Some slave of mine be pinioned to their side."

Now crowds on crowds around the Goddess
     press,
Each eager to present the first Address.°
Dunce scorning dunce beholds the next advance,
But fop shows fop superior complaisance,
When lo! a specter° rose, whose index hand
Held forth the virtue of the dreadful wand;   140
His beavered° brow a birchen garland° wears,
Dropping with infant's blood, and mother's tears.
O'er every vein a shuddering horror runs;
Eton and Winton° shake thro' all their Sons.
All flesh is humbled, Westminster's bold race
Shrink, and confess the Genius of the place:
The pale boy senator° yet tingling stands.
And holds his breeches close with both his hands.

Then thus: " Since man from beast by words is
     known,
Words are man's province, words we teach
     alone.   150
When reason doubtful, like the Samian letter,°
Points him two ways, the narrower is the better.
Placed at the door of learning, youth to guide,
We never suffer it to stand too wide.
To ask, to guess, to know, as they commence,

As fancy opens the quick springs of sense,
We ply the memory, we load the brain,
Bind rebel wit, and double chain on chain;
Confine the thought, to exercise the breath;
And keep them in the pale° of words till death.
Whate'er the talents, or howe'er designed,   161
We hang one jingling padlock on the mind:°
A poet the first day he dips his quill;
And what the last? A very poet still.
Pity! the charm works only in our wall,
Lost, lost too soon in yonder House or Hall.°
There° truant Wyndham every Muse gave o'er,
There Talbot sunk, and was a wit no more!
How sweet an Ovid, Murray was our boast!
How many Martials were in Pulteney lost!   170
Else sure some bard, to our eternal praise,
In twice ten thousand rhyming nights and days,
Had reached the work, the all that mortal can;
And South beheld that Masterpiece of Man."
  " Oh " (cried the Goddess) " for some pedant
    reign!
Some gentle James,° to bless the land again;
To stick the doctor's chair into the throne,
Give law to words, or war with words alone,
Senates and courts with Greek and Latin rule,
And turn the council to a grammar school!   180
For sure, if Dulness sees a grateful day,
'Tis in the shade of arbitrary sway.°
O! if my sons may learn one earthly thing,
Teach but that one, sufficient for a king;
That which my priests, and mine alone, maintain,
Which as it dies, or lives, we fall, or reign:
May you, may Cam and Isis, preach it long!
' The right divine of kings to govern wrong.'"
  Prompt° at the call, around the Goddess roll
Broad hats, and hoods, and caps, a sable shoal: 190
Thick and more thick the black blockade extends,
A hundred head of Aristotle's friends.
Nor wert thou, Isis!° wanting to the day,
[Though Christ Church long kept prudishly
    away.]°
Each stanch polemic, stubborn as a rock,
Each fierce logician, still expelling Locke,
Came whip and spur, and dashed thro' thin and
    thick

On German Crousaz, and Dutch Burgersdyck.°
As many quit the streams that murmuring fall
To lull the sons of Margaret and Clare Hall,°   200
Where Bentley° late tempestuous wont° to sport
In troubled waters, but now sleeps in port.
Before them marched that awful Aristarch;
Plowed was his front with many a deep remark:°
His hat, which never vailed to human pride,
Walker° with reverence took, and laid aside.
Low bowed the rest: He, kingly, did but nod;
So upright° Quakers please both man and God.
" Mistress! dismiss that rabble from your throne:
Avaunt — is Aristarchus yet unknown?   210
Thy mighty scholiast,° whose unwearied pains
Made Horace dull, and humbled Milton's strains.
Turn what they will to verse, their toil is vain,
Critics like me shall make it prose again.
Roman° and Greek grammarians! know your
    better:
Author of something yet more great than letter;
While towering o'er your alphabet, like Saul,
Stands our digamma, and o'ertops them all.
'Tis true, on words is still our whole debate,
Disputes of *Me* or *Te*, of *aut* or *at*,   220
To sound or sink in *cano*, O or A,
Or give up Cicero to C or K.°
Let Freind affect to speak as Terence spoke,
And Alsop° never but like Horace joke:
For° me, what Virgil, Pliny may deny,
Manilius or Solinus shall supply:
For Attic phrase in Plato let them seek,
I poach in Suidas for unlicensed Greek.
In ancient sense if any needs will deal,
Be sure I give them fragments, not a meal;   230
What Gellius or Stobaeus hashed before,
Or chewed by blind old scholiasts o'er and o'er.
The critic eye, that microscope of wit,
Sees hairs and pores, examines bit by bit:

---

160. pale: confine.   **162.** jingling . . . mind: alluding to the role of versifying in the old classical education.   **166.** House, Hall: House of Commons; Westminster Hall (location of the law courts).   **167–70.** The dunce as schoolmaster laments (naming four distinguished young M.P.'s) that his pupils don't carry on with versifying in political life; for if they did, one of them might reach what Robert South declared to be the apex of human achievement — a perfect epigram. Pope is satirizing what he feels to be purely verbal education.   **176.** James: James I, renowned for his pedantic learning.   **182.** arbitrary sway: James was a learned proponent of the divine right of kings (cf. l. 188).   **189 ff.** Following the schoolmasters, the professors pay *their* respects to Dulness.   **193.** Isis: Oxford.   **194.** Christ . . . away: Pope felt that Christ Church contained the most enlightened scholars in Oxford.

198. Crousaz, Burgersdyck: a Swiss and a Dutch logician.   **200.** Margaret, Clare Hall: Cambridge colleges.   **201 ff.** On Bentley, cf. *Ep. to Arb.*, l. 164n. He was master of Trinity College, Cambridge, *tempestuous* in quarreling with his Fellows, fond of *port.* He is called Aristarchus (the name of an ancient textual critic and editor like himself) because Pope is presenting him as a type: "the dunce as scholar."   **201.** wont: was accustomed.   **204.** many . . . remark: i.e., critical and editorial "remarks."   **206.** Walker: Bentley's vice-master at Trinity.   **208.** upright: alluding (with a pun) to the fact that Quakers do not bow while worshiping.   **211.** scholiast: commentator.   **215–18.** Roman . . . all: Bentley was the first to grasp fully the significance of the Greek letter diagamma — which, being shaped like one gamma resting on another was *yet more great than* other letters, and overtopped them, as the Biblical Saul "was higher than any of the people" (I Sam. 9:2).   **220–22.** Disputes . . . K: Examples of trifling academic disputes.   **223–24.** Freind, Alsop: Dr. Robert Freind and Antony Alsop, two well-known Latinists.   **225 ff.** Pope's point is that the dunce as scholar chooses to work over writers of small literary value: Manilius not Virgil, Solinus not Pliny, Suidas not Plato — or over mere fragmentary quotations from ancient literature preserved by such writers as the Roman Aulus Gellius or the Greek Stobaeus. Pope advocates the study of literature as an art and a repository of wisdom.

How parts relate to parts, or they to whole,
The body's harmony, the beaming soul,
Are things which Kuster, Burman, Wasse shall
    see,°
When man's whole frame is obvious to a *flea*.
    "Ah, think not, Mistress! more true Dulness lies
In Folly's cap, than Wisdom's grave disguise. 240
Like buoys, that never sink into the flood,
On learning's surface we but lie and nod.
Thine is the genuine head of many a house,°
And much divinity without a *Noûs*.°
Nor could a Barrow work on every block,°
Nor has one Atterbury° spoiled the flock.
See! still thy own, the heavy canon° roll,
And metaphysic smokes involve the pole.°
For thee we dim the eyes, and stuff the head
With all such reading as was never read: 250
For thee explain a thing till all men doubt it,
And write about it, Goddess, and about it:
So spins the silkworm small its slender store,
And labors till it clouds itself all o'er.
    "What tho' we let some better sort of fool
Thrid every science, run thro' every school?
Never by tumbler thro' the hoops was shown
Such skill in passing all, and touching none.
He may indeed (if sober all this time)
Plague with dispute, or persecute with rhyme. 260
We only furnish what he cannot use,
Or wed to what he must divorce, a Muse:°
Full in the midst of Euclid dip at once,
And petrify a genius to a dunce:
Or set on metaphysic ground to prance,
Show all his paces, not a step advance.
With the same cement,° ever sure to bind,
We bring to one dead level every mind.
Then take him to develop, if you can,
And hew the block off, and get out the man.°   270
But wherefore waste I words? I see advance
Whore, pupil, and laced governor from France.
Walker! our hat"— nor more he deigned to say,
But, stern as Ajax' specter,° strode away.
    In° flowed at once a gay embroidered race,
And tittering pushed the pedants off the place:
Some would have spoken, but the voice was
    drowned
By the French horn, or by the opening° hound.
The first came forwards, with as easy mien,

As if he saw St. James's and the Queen.   280
When thus th' attendant orator begun:
    "Receive, great Empress! thy accomplished
        son:
Thine from the birth, and sacred from the rod,
A dauntless infant! never scared with God.
The sire saw, one by one, his virtues wake:
The mother begged the blessing of a rake.
Thou gav'st that ripeness, which so soon began,
And ceased so soon, he ne'er was boy, nor man.
Thro' school and college, thy kind cloud o'ercast,
Safe and unseen the young Aeneas passed:°   290
Thence bursting glorious, all at once let down,
Stunned with his giddy larum half the town.
Intrepid then, o'er seas and lands he flew:
Europe he saw, and Europe saw him too.
There all thy gifts and graces we display,
Thou, only thou, directing all our way!
To° where the Seine, obsequious as she runs,
Pours at great Bourbon's feet her silken sons;
Or Tiber, now no longer Roman, rolls,
Vain of Italian arts, Italian souls: 300
To happy convents, bosomed deep in vines,
Where slumber abbots, purple as their wines:
To isles of fragrance, lily-silvered vales,
Diffusing languor in the panting gales:
To lands of singing or of dancing slaves,
Love-whispering woods, and lute-resounding waves.
But° chief her shrine where naked Venus keeps,
And Cupids ride the Lion° of the Deeps;
Where, eased of fleets, the Adriatic main   309
Wafts the smooth eunuch and enamored swain.
Led by my hand, he sauntered Europe round,
And gathered every vice on Christian ground;
Saw every court, heard every king declare
His royal sense, of operas or the fair;
The stews° and palace equally explored,
Intrigued with glory, and with spirit whored;
Tried all *hors d'oeuvres,* all *liqueurs* defined,
Judicious drank, and greatly daring dined;
Dropped the dull lumber of the Latin store,
Spoiled his own language, and acquired no
    more;   320
All classic learning lost on classic ground;
And last turned *Air,°* the echo of a sound!
See now, half-cured, and perfectly well-bred,
With nothing but a solo in his head;
As much estate, and principle, and wit,
As Jansen, Fleetwood,° Cibber shall think fit;
Stolen from a duel, followed by a nun,

237. Kuster . . . see: three more instances of the scholar as dunce.
243. house: i.e., college.   244. i.e., thine is many a teacher (the
university scholars belonged to the clergy) whose system of
divinity forgets the Divine Mind — the Logos.   245–46. Barrow, Atterbury: two clergyman-scholars whom Pope exempts
because they were interested in humane learning in general.
245. block: (1) block to be sculptured, (2) blockhead.
247. canon: with a pun.   248. pole: also with a pun — on pole
(sky) and poll (head).   262. wed . . . Muse: Cf. ll. 167–70n.
267. cement: pronounced cément in Pope's time.   270. Cf.
l. 245n.   274. stern . . . specter: In the underworld, Ajax
turns sullenly away from Odysseus, who had defeated him on
earth.   275 ff. Pope turns now to a different form of education,
the Grand Tour.   278. opening: Cf *W. Forest,* l. 150n.

290. Thus Virgil's Aeneas is shielded by his mother's cloud
(*Aeneid,* I.411–14).   297 ff. i.e., the great France of the seventeenth century is now deteriorating, as Rome did long ago,
Venice more recently — and it is only their deteriorations that
we seek out and imitate.   307–10. Venice was regarded at this
time as the brothel of Europe.   308. the Lion: emblem of
Venice.   315. stews: brothels.   322. And . . . Air: i.e., had
nothing to show except a knowledge of opera tunes (*arias*).
326. Jansen, Fleetwood: notorious gamblers, as was Cibber.

And, if a borough choose him not,° undone;
See, to my country happy I restore
This glorious youth, and add one Venus° more.
Her too receive (for her my soul adores)   331
So may the sons of sons of sons of whores,
Prop thine, O Empress! like each neighbor throne,
And make a long posterity thy own."
    Pleased, she accepts the hero and the dame
Wraps in her veil, and frees from sense of shame.
    Then° looked, and saw a lazy, lolling sort,
Unseen at church, at senate, or at court,
Of ever-listless loiterers, that attend
No cause, no trust, no duty, and no friend.   340
Thee too, my Paridel!° she marked thee there,
Stretched on the rack of a too easy chair,
And heard thy everlasting yawn confess
The pains and penalties of idleness.
She pitied! but her pity only shed
Benigner influence on thy nodding head.
    But Annius,° crafty seer, with ebon wand,
And well-dissembled emerald on his hand,
False as his gems, and cankered as his coins,
Came, crammed with capon, from where Pollio°
    dines.   350
Soft, as the wily fox is seen to creep,
Where bask on sunny banks the simple sheep,
Walk round and round, now prying here, now
    there,
So he; but pious, whispered first his prayer.
    "Grant, gracious Goddess! grant me still to cheat,
O may thy cloud still cover the deceit!
Thy choicer mists on this assembly shed,
But pour them thickest on the noble head.
So shall each youth, assisted by our eyes,
See other Caesars, other Homers rise;   360
Thro' twilight ages hunt th' Athenian fowl,
Which Chalcis gods, and mortals call an owl,°
Now see an Attys, now a Cecrops° clear,°
Nay, Máhomet! the pigeon at thine ear;°
Be rich in ancient brass, tho' not in gold,
And keep his Lares, tho' his house be sold;
To headless Phoebe his fair bride postpone,°

328. choose . . . not: i.e., for parliament.   330. Venus: i.e.,
the youth's mistress.   337 ff. Pope turns now to collectors of
the relics of a culture that they do not trouble to understand —
the amateurs of coins, gems, and other antiquities.   341. Paridel: name of a wandering squire in *The Faerie Queene*, III.ix
(the contemporary application is uncertain).   347. Annius:
name of a monk famed for his forgeries of antiquities (the contemporary application is again uncertain).   350. Pollio: a
Roman patron of the arts (the contemporary reference is uncertain).   361–63. Thro' . . . clear: alluding to the designs on
ancient coins (in this case, forged).   362. It is a convention of
epic that gods and men differ in their names for things.
363. Attys, Cecrops: princes of legend only and therefore not
likely to be found on genuine coins.   364. Mahomet . . . ear:
i.e., even such an imposture as Mahomet's, who is said to have
claimed that a pigeon he had taught to take grain from his ear
was the angel Gabriel.   366–67. Lares . . . postpone: i.e., the
collector will sell his house to pay for (Roman) household gods,
and defer his marriage to pay for a mutilated statue of (Phoebe,
the goddess of) chastity.

Honor a Syrian prince above his own;
Lord of an Otho, if I vouch it true;
Blest in one Niger,° till he knows of two."   370
    Mummius° o'erheard him; Mummius, fool-
    renowned,
Who like his Cheops° stinks above the ground,
Fierce as a startled adder, swelled, and said,
Rattling an ancient sistrum° at his head:
    "Speakst thou of Syrian princes? Traitor base!
Mine, Goddess! mine is all the hornèd race.°
True, he° had wit, to make their value rise;
From foolish Greeks to steal them, was as wise;
More glorious yet, from barbarous hands to keep,
When Sallee Rovers° chased him on the deep.   380
Then taught by Hermes,° and divinely bold,
Down his own throat he risked the Grecian gold,
Received each Demigod, with pious care,
Deep in his entrails — I revered them there,
I bought them, shrouded in that living shrine,
And, at their second birth, they issue mine."²
    "Witness, great Ammon! by whose horns I
    swore,"
(Replied soft Annius) "this our paunch before
Still bears them, faithful; and that thus I eat,
Is to refund° the medals with the meat.   390
To prove me, Goddess! clear of all design,
Bid me with Pollio sup, as well as dine:
There all the learn'd shall at the labor stand,
And Douglas° lend his soft obstetric hand."
    The Goddess smiling seemed to give consent;
So back to Pollio, hand in hand, they went.
    Then° thick as locusts blackening all the ground,
A tribe, with weeds and shells fantastic crowned,
Each with some wondrous gift approached the
    Power,
A nest, a toad, a fungus, or a flower.   400
But far the foremost, two, with earnest zeal,
And aspect ardent to the throne appeal.
    The first thus opened: "Hear thy suppliant's call,
Great Queen, and common mother of us all!
Fair from its humble bed I reared this flower,
Suckled, and cheered, with air, and sun, and
    shower.
Soft on the paper ruff its leaves I spread,
Bright with the gilded button tipped its head;
Then throned in glass, and named it Caroline.°

369–70. Otho, Niger: rare coins.   371. Mummius: another collector, especially of mummies.   372. Cheops: i.e., King Cheops'
mummy.   374. sistrum: Egyptian musical instrument.
376. horned race: The heads of Syrian kings were depicted with
the horns of Jupiter Ammon, whose sons they professed to be.
377. he: Annius.   380. Sallee Rovers: Moorish pirates.
381. Hermes: patron of travelers and thieves.   384–86. Deep
. . . mine: Pope chooses his imagery to accord with the Anti-
Christ theme of the poem.   390. refund: with a pun on funda-
ment.   394. Douglas: James Douglas, an obstetrician.
397 ff. Pope now turns to the dabblers in science.   407–
09. Soft . . . Caroline: alluding to the efforts of contemporary
horticulturists to produce the perfect carnation.   409. Caroline: i.e., for the Queen.

Each maid cried, Charming! and each youth,
    Divine!   410
Did Nature's pencil ever blend such rays,
Such varied light in one promiscuous blaze?
Now prostrate! dead! behold that Caroline:
No maid cries, Charming! and no youth, Divine!
And lo the wretch! whose vile, whose insect lust
Laid this gay daughter of the spring in dust.
Oh punish him, or to th' Elysian shades
Dismiss my soul, where no carnation fades!"
He ceased, and wept. With innocence of mien,
Th' accused stood forth, and thus addressed the
    Queen.   420
  "Of all th' enameled race,° whose silvery
    wing
Waves to the tepid zephyrs of the spring,
Or swims along the fluid atmosphere,
Once brightest shined this child of heat and air.
I saw, and started from its vernal bower,
The rising game, and chased from flower to flower.
It fled, I followed; now in hope, now pain;
It stopped, I stopped; it moved, I moved again.°
At last it fixed, 'twas on what plant it pleased,
And where it fixed, the beauteous bird I seized:
Rose or carnation was below my care;   431
I meddle, Goddess! only in my sphere.
I tell the naked fact without disguise,
And, to excuse it, need but show the prize;
Whose spoils this paper offers to your eye,
Fair even in death! this peerless *butterfly.*"
  "My sons!" (she answered) "both have done
    your parts:
Live happy both, and long promote our arts!
But hear a mother, when she recommends
To your fraternal care our sleeping friends.°   440
The common soul, of Heaven's more frugal make,
Serves but to keep fools pert, and knaves awake:
A drowsy watchman, that just gives a knock,
And breaks our rest, to tell us what's a-clock.
Yet by some object every brain is stirred;
The dull may waken to a hummingbird;
The most recluse, discreetly opened,° find
Congenial matter in the cockle kind;
The mind, in metaphysics at a loss,
May wander in a wilderness of moss;   450
The head that turns at superlunar things,
Poised with a tail, may steer on Wilkins' wings.°
  "O!° would the sons of men once think their
    eyes
And reason given them but to study *flies!*

See Nature in some partial narrow shape,
And let the Author of the Whole escape:
Learn but to trifle; or, who most observe,
To wonder at their Maker, not to serve!"
  "Be° that my task" (replies a gloomy clerk,
Sworn foe to mystery, yet divinely dark;   460
Whose pious hope aspires to see the day
When moral evidence° shall quite decay,
And damns implicit faith,° and holy lies,
Prompt to impose, and fond to dogmatize):
"Let others creep by timid steps, and slow,
On plain experience lay foundations low,
By common sense to common knowledge bred,
And last, to Nature's Cause through Nature led.
All-seeing in thy mists, we want no guide,
Mother of Arrogance, and Source of Pride!   470
We nobly take the high priori° road,
And reason downward, till we doubt of God:
Make Nature still encroach upon his plan;
And shove him off as far as e'er we can:
Thrust some mechanic cause into his place;
Or bind in matter, or diffuse in space.
Or, at one bound o'erleaping all his laws,
Make God man's image, man the final Cause,
Find virtue local,° all relation scorn,
See all in *self,* and but for self be born: 480
Of naught so certain as our *reason* still,
Of naught so doubtful as of *soul* and *will.*
Oh hide the God still more! and make us see
Such as Lucretius drew, a god like thee:°
Wrapped up in self, a god without a thought,
Regardless of our merit or default.
Or° that bright image to our fancy draw,
Which Theocles in raptured vision saw,
While thro' poetic scenes the Genius roves,
Or wanders wild in academic groves;   490
That Nature our society adores,
Where Tindal dictates, and Silenus° snores."
  Roused at his name, up rose the bousy° sire,
And shook from out his pipe the seeds of fire;
Then snapped his box, and stroked his belly down:
Rosy and reverend, tho' without a gown.°
Bland and familiar to the throne he came,
Led up the youth, and called the Goddess *Dame.*

---

421. th' . . . race: butterflies.   427–28. Pope echoes Milton's lines on Eve admiring her reflection (*Paradise Lost,* IV.462–65, above), perhaps with an implication of a like narcissistic relationship in this case (cf. l. 447 n.).   440. our . . . friends: Cf. ll. 345–46. 447. opened: Pope suggests a similarity between the collector and the collected.   452. wings: John Wilkins had suggested man might fly by attaching wings to his body.   453–58. Pope protests against study of Nature that does not include regard for its Creator.

459 ff. Pope refers to deistical clergymen, who sought to rationalize the element of mystery (i.e., revelation) out of Christianity. Earlier, Pope had been more sympathetic to deism (cf. *E. on Man*).   462. moral evidence: i.e., the argument from probability that the Christian narrative is true.   463. implicit faith: faith resting on the authority of the church.   471. high priori: with a pun on *a priori.*   479. local: i.e., relative to man and his particular societies, not founded in eternal relations established by God.   484. Lucretius pictures the gods as having no thought for men.   487–90. Or . . . groves: In Shaftesbury's dialogue *The Moralists,* the chief speaker Theocles rhapsodizes about "Nature" as if Nature were God.   492. Tindal, Silenus: Matthew Tindal was a well-known deist; Silenus is a fat drunken god, symbol here of the Epicurean creed.   493. bousy: boozy. 496. gown: clerical gown.

Then thus: "From priestcraft happily set free,
Lo! every finished son returns to thee: 500
First slave to words, then vassal to a name,
Then dupe to party; child and man the same;
Bounded by Nature, narrowed still by art,
A trifling head, and a contracted heart.
Thus bred, thus taught, how many have I seen,
Smiling on all, and smiled on by a queen?
Marked out for honors, honored for their birth,
To thee the most rebellious things on earth:
Now to thy gentle shadow all are shrunk,
All melted down, in pension, or in punk!°   510
So K——, so B——° sneaked into the grave,
A monarch's half, and half a harlot's slave.
Poor W——° nipped in folly's broadest bloom,
Who praises now? his chaplain on his tomb.
Then take them all, oh take them to thy breast!
Thy *Magus,*° Goddess! shall perform the rest."
With that, a wizard old his *cup*° extends;
Which whoso tastes, forgets his former friends,
Sire, ancestors, himself. One° casts his eyes
Up to a *Star,* and like Endymion dies: 520
A *Feather,* shooting from another's head,
Extracts his brain, and principle is fled;
Lost is his God, his country, everything;
And nothing left but homage to a king!
The vulgar herd turn off to roll with hogs,
To run with horses, or to hunt with dogs;
But, sad example! never to escape
Their infamy, still keep the human shape.
But she, good Goddess, sent to every child
Firm Impudence, or Stupefaction mild;   530
And straight succeeded, leaving shame no room,
Cibberian° forehead, or Cimmerian° gloom.
Kind Self-conceit to some her glass applies,
Which no one looks in with another's eyes:
But as the flatterer or dependent paint,
Beholds himself a patriot, chief, or saint.
On others Interest her gay livery flings,
Interest that waves on parti-colored wings:
Turned to the sun, she casts a thousand dyes,
And, as she turns, the colors fall or rise.   540
Others the Siren Sisters° warble round,
And empty heads console with empty sound.
No more, alas! the voice of Fame they hear,
The balm of Dulness trickling in their ear.

Great C——, H——, P——, R——, K——,°
Why all your toils? your sons have learned to sing.
How quick Ambition hastes to ridicule!
The sire is made a peer, the son a fool.
On° some, a priest succinct in amice white
Attends; all flesh is nothing in his sight!   550
Beeves, at his touch, at once to jelly turn,
And the huge boar is shrunk into an urn:
The board with specious miracles he loads,
Turns hares to larks, and pigeons into toads.
Another (for in all what one can shine?)
Explains the *sève* and *verdeur*° of the vine.
What cannot copious sacrifice atone?
Thy truffles, Perigord! thy hams, Bayonne!
With French libation, and Italian strain,
Wash Bladen white, and expiate Hays's stain.   560
Knight lifts the head, for what are crowds undone,°
To three essential partridges in one?
Gone every blush, and silent all reproach,
Contending princes mount them in their coach.
Next, bidding all draw near on bended knees,
The Queen confers her *Titles* and *Degrees.*
Her children first of more distinguished sort,
Who study Shakespeare at the Inns of Court,°
Impale a glowworm, or vertú° profess,
Shine in the dignity of F. R. S.°   570
Some, deep Freemasons, join the silent race
Worthy to fill Pythagoras's° place:
Some botanists, or florists at the least,
Or issue members of an annual feast.°
Nor passed the meanest unregarded, one
Rose a Gregorian, one a Gormogon.°
The last, not least in honor or applause,
Isis and Cam made Doctors of her° Laws.
Then, blessing all, "Go, children of my care!
To practice now from theory repair.   580
All my commands are easy, short, and full:
My sons! be proud, be selfish, and be dull.
Guard my prerogative, assert my throne:
This nod confirms each privilege your own.
The° cap and switch be sacred to his Grace;

510. melted . . . punk: i.e., they have become enslaved either to the court (which pays them) or to a mistress.   511. K——, B—: Possibly the Duke of Kent and the Earl of Berkeley, with the implication that they were placemen and owed their places to a royal mistress.   513. W—: Perhaps the young Earl of Warwick, d. 1721.   516. *Magus:* wizard.   517. *cup:* i.e., Walpole's payroll (with reference to Circe's transforming cup; cf. ll. 525–26).   519–24. One . . . king: i.e., aspiring to the badges of the orders of knighthood (*Star, Feather*), men let their political independence die (as Endymion died for love of the moon), or lose their principles.   532. Cibberian: i.e., like Cibber's (impudent).   Cimmerian: The Cimmerians were reputed to live in caves.   541. Siren Sisters: the operatic Muses (or prima donnas).

545. Probably Lords Cowper, Harcourt, Parker, Raymond, King, men of standing, whose offspring did not amount to much.   549 ff. Through religious terms applied to cookery, Pope suggests the completed secularization of a society where the Anti-Messiah is about to reign.   556. *sève, verdeur:* terms signifying flavor and piquancy.   560–61. Bladen was a gambler; Knight, an embezzler; Hays is unknown.   568. Who . . . Court: i.e., the lawyers who dabbled in Shakespearean studies.   569. vertu: a taste for the arts.   570. F.R.S.: Fellow of the Royal Society.   572. Pythagoras was said not to have permitted his pupils to speak to him till they had studied for several years.   574. an . . . feast: annual banquet of a learned society.   576. Gregorians and Gormogons were organizations burlesquing the Freemasons.   578. her: Dulness's.   585–96. A description of the several careers for which Dulness qualifies her devotees: horse racing (l. 585), foot racing (l. 586), stagecoaching (with a pun on the theatrical stage), drawing butterflies (l. 589), weaving with spider's webs (a feat seriously attempted), legal revels (l. 591), cricket, cookery (ll. 593–96).

With staff and pumps the Marquis lead the race;
From stage to stage the licensed Earl may run,
Paired with his fellow charioteer the sun;
The learned Baron butterflies design,
Or draw to silk Arachne's subtle line; 590
The Judge to dance his brother Sergeant call;
The Senator at cricket urge the ball;
The Bishop stow (pontific luxury!)
An hundred souls of turkeys in a pie;
The sturdy Squire to Gallic masters stoop,
And drown his lands and manors in a *soupe.*
Others import yet nobler arts from France,
Teach kings to fiddle, and make senates dance.
Perhaps more high some daring son° may soar,
Proud to my list to add one monarch more; 600
And nobly conscious, princes are but things
Born for first ministers, as slaves for kings,
Tyrant supreme! shall three Estates command,
And MAKE ONE MIGHTY DUNCIAD OF THE LAND! "
    More she had spoke, but yawned — All Nature
        nods:°
What mortal can resist the yawn of gods?
Churches and chapels instantly it reached;
(St. James's first, for leaden G——° preached)
Then catched the schools; the Hall scarce kept
        awake; 609
The Convocation° gaped, but could not speak:
Lost was the Nation's Sense, nor could be found,
While the long solemn unison° went round:
Wide, and more wide, it spread o'er all the realm;
Even Palinurus° nodded at the helm:
The vapor mild o'er each committee crept;
Unfinished treaties in each office slept;
And chiefless armies dozed out the campaign;
And navies yawned for orders on the main.
    O Muse! relate (for you can tell alone,
Wits have short memories, and dunces none), 620

599. son: probably Walpole.   605. yawned, nods: Both are
puns.   608. G—: John Gilbert, later Archbishop of York.
610. Convocation: House of Convocation, an assembly of ec-
clesiastics.   612. unison: monotone.   614. Palinurus: i.e.,
Walpole, pilot of the state (from Aeneas pilot, who fell into
the sea).

Relate, who first, who last resigned to rest;
Whose heads she partly, whose completely blessed;
What charms could Faction, what Ambition lull,
The venal quiet, and entrance the dull;
Till drowned was sense, and shame, and right, and
        wrong —
O sing, and hush the nations with thy Song!

  .   .   .   .

    In vain, in vain — the all-composing hour
Resistless falls: The Muse obeys the Power.
She comes! she comes! the sable throne behold
Of *Night* primeval, and of *Chaos* old! 630
Before her, *Fancy's* gilded clouds decay,
And all its varying rainbows die away.
Wit shoots in vain its momentary fires,
The meteor drops, and in a flash expires.
As one by one, at dread Medea's strain,
The sickening stars fade off th' ethereal plain;°
As Argus' eyes by Hermes' wand oppressed,
Closed one by one to everlasting rest;°
Thus at her felt approach, and secret might,
Art after *art* goes out, and all is Night. 640
See skulking *Truth* to her old cavern fled,
Mountains of casuistry heaped o'er her head!
Philosophy, that leaned on Heaven before,
Shrinks to her second cause, and is no more.
Physic of *Metaphysic* begs defense,
And *Metaphysic* calls for aid on *Sense!*
See *Mystery* to *Mathematics* fly!
In vain! they gaze, turn giddy, rave, and die.
Religion blushing veils her sacred fires,
And unawares *Morality* expires. 650
For *public* flame, nor *private,* dares to shine;
Nor *human* spark is left, nor glimpse *divine!*
Lo! thy dread empire, CHAOS! is restored;
Light dies before thy uncreating word:°
Thy hand, great Anarch! lets the curtain fall;
And universal darkness buries All.

635–36. dread . . . plain: Cf. Ovid, *Metamorphoses,* VII.192 ff.,
where Medea invokes her magic powers.   637–38. Argus, hun-
dred-eyed giant set to guard Io by Hera, fell victim to Hermes.
654. word: alluding to the Word (the Logos), whose antithesis
this is.

BERTRAND H. BRONSON, *Editor*

Samuel Johnson 1709-1784

& James Boswell

1740-1795

That a close personal attachment could be established between two men so different as Johnson and Boswell in character and experience would hardly have been predicted. Johnson's early impressions were of poverty and insecurity; Boswell's were of social position and established comfort. Johnson knew, long before he came of age, that success in life for him would depend mainly on his own personal effort and proof of merit. Boswell had reason to expect his way to be cleared by his father's distinction and the inheritance of an estate that had been in the family for generations. Johnson had an unprepossessing and craggy appearance, a reserved and defensive and odd bearing, which fenced him like a moat. Boswell had an outgoing good humor, an eager curiosity and readiness of sympathetic address that made him welcome in nearly any company, and invited friendship from all ages, types, and occupations. Johnson thought the world a place where much was to be endured and little to be enjoyed; Boswell thought it an inexhaustible banquet of varied delights, at which the chief call upon endurance was in keeping the appetite poignant and unjaded. Johnson saw suffering as normal; Boswell saw it as mostly avoidable, given a little judgment and moderate good luck. Johnson was a stern moralist, in precept and practice, and, if forgiving to others, relentless toward himself. Boswell greatly admired moral strength but found it easier to be a man of pleasure. Johnson had a mind of extraordinary vigor, range, and logical resource, as well as a startling breadth of learning and an incomparably ready recollection. Boswell's mind was a weathercock so variable that he had to write down his impressions to convince himself of his own continuity. The staple of Boswell's journals, when they are — as is usual — concerned with his own progress, is the fascinated and indulgent register of his changes of feeling and attitude; Johnson's diaries, sparingly kept and reluctantly written, are full of self-accusation over supposed departures from a charted course or failures to make headway in it. When the two first met, Boswell was a twenty-two-year-old of no personal importance nor even (except in his own eyes) of much promise; Johnson was two and a half times his age, and famous as a poet (*The Vanity of Human Wishes*), moral essayist (The *Rambler*), biographer (*Life of Savage*), novelist (*Rasselas*), lexicographer, and personality. Yet, in spite of all this disparity, which could be illustrated without end, these men were in vital ways ideal counterparts, needing only to be brought into sympathetic contact in order to take up their complementary roles. How the event came about has been memorably recorded by Boswell in the first of the extracts that follow from his *Life of Johnson.*

I

Johnson was born on September 18, 1709, a moment when the literary world now known as the Augustan Age was close to its zenith. The brilliant circle of Queen Anne "Wits" was just entering upon the years of its most character- istic and memorable expression. Johnson him- self would one day give a masterly summing up of the achievement of these writers, from the van- tage point of one who, sympathetic but unwor- shiping, had spent his mature working life in a London steeped in the familiar memory of their physical presence. But Johnson was not a native Londoner; he was born in the quiet ca- thedral town of Lichfield, a small country com- munity where manners and society changed but slowly and where one could tell whether one's neighbor took after a maternal grandparent or a father's cross-grained uncle. Johnson's roots were in the tangled and unstirred compost of this provincial society, and he never, in spite of his love of London, where he felt "the full tide of human existence," denied his anchorage in the place of his birth. The pull of the tide is best felt by one whose anchor does not drag.

Johnson's father, Michael, was a respectable member of the Lichfield community, but his business as bookseller, while it kept him in touch with people of education, seldom put him much above the level of bare subsistence. If his stock did not move rapidly from his shelves, there was the more time for his son to satisfy a desultory but omnivorous curiosity about a wider variety of books than would ordinarily be collected in a private library. Johnson had, besides, the benefit of a reasonably good school- ing in the Lichfield and Stourbridge grammar schools; and when he was by some temporary turn of good fortune enabled to enter Pembroke College, Oxford, he came there better prepared than most of his fellows to carry on the classical studies that then formed the main business of a university education. But regularity was by this time decidedly repugnant to him. He flouted the rules and neglected the college exercises;

his studies were fitful and self-indulgent, and his amusements idle and troublesome to author- ity. *Mad, violent,* and *bitter* were the terms he later found to describe his conduct and state of mind at this time. "I was miserably poor, and I thought to fight my way by my literature and my wit; so I disregarded all power and all authority." In that era, if not in ours, a uni- versity student could go far along the road of inattention to work, and Johnson was not ex- pelled. But, whether from despondency or from a failure of funds, he left college at the Christ- mas holidays of his second year and returned home in a state of utmost dejection, entirely un- settled as to his future course. Two years later, and before he had found any regular occupa- tion, his father died, leaving him a meager por- tion of twenty pounds. Johnson meanwhile had been making, and continued to make, abortive efforts to get established as a schoolteacher and to secure literary work of one kind or another.

While he was still in this nadir of gloomy un- certainty, he married in the summer of 1735 a widow of forty-six with three children, aged ten, eighteen, and nineteen, and a fortune of seven or eight hundred pounds. He was twenty years her junior, nearly penniless, with no set- tled prospects, and in appearance (according to contemporary testimony) gaunt and rawboned to an unpleasant degree, his face scarred with scrofula that had also permanently affected his eyesight; he was given besides to convulsive twitches and oddities of gesture that made peo- ple stare. In spite of these formidable handicaps, Elizabeth Porter had had the inspired perspi- cacity to discern in him the "most sensible" man she had ever known; and for her, certainly, the risks were vastly greater than for him. It is not surprising that her older son, already eighteen, never forgave his mother for her folly. But at any rate, it is more than probable that by this supreme compliment of trust and belief in his human worth she saved Johnson from de- spair and even madness. In return, eighteen years after her death, he could confide to his private journal: "My grief for her departure is not abated; and I have less pleasure in any good that befalls me, because she does not partake it."

The years of Johnson's marriage were the most crucial years of his life. Until now, he had scarcely been able to force himself, such was his apathy and inertia, to complete the translation of a travel book to which he was committed, and which was already partly set up in print. He had as yet never made a sustained effort to finish any considerable task. He and his wife were well aware of the universal disapproval of their marriage, among their acquaintances and friends; and Johnson could see that the burden of proving its rightness rested squarely on him. We know next to nothing about the character and personality of Mrs. Johnson. But it is certain that in one way and another, with her at his side, he was gradually enabled to loosen and throw off the fetters that had immobilized his will. His sense of obligation and responsibility, his personal pride, his dignity as a man, his ambition and hope, were kindled by the challenge of her presence, her faith in his powers, her affectionate respect and her justifiable need to have her judgment vindicated, to be made proud of her choice; and these elements together combined to forge in him a determined purpose not to fail. The springs of his creative life began to unlock. One by one, in the ensuing years of marriage, most of the works that were to give him his commanding position in his age appeared or were planned and projected. There is not a particle of evidence, nor anywhere a suggestion, that his wife ever tried to obstruct or deflect a single one of Johnson's more serious purposes, however laborious or time-consuming or careless of quick returns it might be. He once in all sincerity assured his cynical young friend Beauclerk that his marriage was a love match on both sides. Clearly, it also rested on a foundation of mutual respect and understanding. Save possibly from her husband, Elizabeth Johnson has never received her due for the part she played in Johnson's achievement.

The couple's first venture was to try to establish a boarding school, at Edial near Lichfield. They rented a large, solid brick house, and Mrs. Johnson put a good deal of money into furnishing and readying it for use. By the efforts of friends, a few pupils were enrolled from the neighborhood, including David Garrick, soon to be famous, and his younger brother, but advertisement farther afield brought no result, and the total number of scholars never rose above eight. The school languished for about a year and expired.

It would be natural if the Johnsons began to grow restive under the coldly appraising eyes of their Lichfield neighbors, and to feel that less constant scrutiny would be a relief. Years later Johnson wrote that in a small country town " every human being is a spy." The couple commenced to think about the possibilities of London. Johnson had been working on a play, a classical tragedy, that he thought one of the London theater managers might be willing to produce; and in the spring of 1737 he and his pupil Garrick went up to see if they could gain a foothold and find a way of life in the city. Garrick was to study law, and Johnson would find work among the booksellers while he finished his play. Thanks largely to Edward Cave, the founder and proprietor of the *Gentleman's Magazine,* he did glimpse the possibility of a livelihood. Consequently, although the play made little progress, Johnson returned home in the summer with an optimistic report, and toward the end of the year the Johnsons packed up and moved to the decent obscurity of London.

For a long while the going was rocky indeed, but little by little Johnson began to establish himself, to get miscellaneous literary assignments with less of an effort than before, and to win time for more ambitious and independent performances. As early as the spring of 1739, his first important creative work, the poem *London,* brought him significant acclaim and went into four editions within a year. He was given the important and continuing job of writing up for the *Gentleman's Magazine* fictionalized reports — since factual reporting was then virtually illegal — of the parliamentary debates: really a major creative effort on the slenderest factual material, but read by the general public as a truthful record. The *Life of Richard Savage* (1744), the *Drury Lane Prologue* (1747), *Irene* (1749), *The Vanity of Human Wishes* (1749), the *Rambler* (1750–52), and the Dictionary (1755) followed in due course — the last, unhappily, appearing three years after his wife's death, to which he poignantly alluded in the immortal last sentence of his Preface. The *Idler* and *Rasselas* followed toward the end of the same decade (1758–59), while he was engaged on his great edition of Shakespeare. The *Shakespeare* finally appeared in 1765, but meanwhile three things of greatest moment had occurred to affect the course of Johnson's history. The first was the granting of a royal pension in the spring of 1762. The second was his meeting with Boswell, on May 16, 1763. The third was his acquaintance with the Henry Thrales, in 1764 or 1765, who were to make a second home for him during most of the last twenty years of his life, and to whom he was consequently indebted for much comfort and happiness. And we may add a fourth of equal consequence to us: the establishing of the Literary Club — that brilliant constellation of talents — in 1764.

The last two decades of Johnson's life were passed in a blaze of celebrity, but his conversation, rather than any biographical events or literary publications, was the chief agent of his increasing fame. Apart from some political pamphlets, written (albeit with much hard-headed good sense) on the negative side of historical progress, his most important work thereafter was the generalized digest of his trip to the Scottish Highlands and islands with Boswell, and his Prefaces to the poets, now called *Lives,* the ripe fruit of a life spent on letters and literary values and their place in the diapason of man's experience. These were published in 1779 and 1781. Three years later he died, on December 13, 1784.

II

The last quarter of Johnson's life was lived, we have noted, in the full glare of public attention, and also under the anatomizing lens of Boswell's probing curiosity, which has brought him closer to posterity than any other figure in literary history (save Boswell himself, as we are lately discovering).

The immediacy of Boswell's record introduces a danger not ordinarily to be reckoned with, but a danger that carries within it such opportunities of deeper insight that we willingly run the concomitant risk. There is a pitfall for the unwary in the often noticeable disparity between Johnson's writing and Boswell's record of his talk. To put the matter abruptly, Johnson often talked for immediate victory, but he almost always wrote upon oath. There is a considered and formal finality about most of his writing that demands an answering sincerity in the reader. His talk, however, is always subject to correction by the spirit of the occasion that evoked it. He cannot, therefore, be quoted indifferently from the written or spoken record, as

if both had an equal claim to be accepted as his conviction. For a hundred years, indeed, under the powerful influence of Macaulay's mischievous simplifications, readers were virtually persuaded to ignore Johnson's writing as mere hieroglyphics, and to look for the true Johnson in his conversation. There is enough truth in this position to make it a most pernicious falsehood. Johnson's published writing is, in the main, the unrefracted image of his deepest nature, and should be taken at its face value. It is true that the man Johnson is to be found equally in his talk as in his writing, and that the revelation of character and personality which abides in contradiction and overstatement, in the impulsive expression of prejudice, or thrusting for advantage at the risk of inconsistency, is more evident in Boswell's reports than anywhere else. And of course this is a precious and revealing kind of truth. But, although we recognize, when we consult our own experience, that the conversation of ourselves and our acquaintances is always a distorted and imperfect representation of the truth that is in us — something that requires always to be corrected in the light of fuller knowledge — yet we are here liable to forget this obvious fact, because so full a record as Boswell's of actual conversation, so authentic and so vivid, is unique except in fiction and drama. His record is neither of these, as we know; and reading it as history we are easily misled into granting it an authority and weight in particular utterances that the original participants would be quick to deny if they could. Boswell knew this, and continually does his best to provide the friendly correctives so necessary to a true reading. But again, a school of readers who despised him tried to trim away as much of Boswell as possible in order, as they thought, to do Johnson the service of letting him stand out clear. They were misguided; for Boswell is essential to the right interpretation of his subject. Furthermore, the better we know Boswell and the more we learn about what went into his book and how it took tangible form, the better chance we shall have of reading it with genuine comprehension. Thanks to the all but incredible recoveries, in the last quarter-century, of the vast bulk of Boswell's journals and collectanea (still to be edited and published in their entirety), we already know more about him and his gathering and treatment of source material than anyone but himself hitherto could have known. The fascinating tale of these recoveries, possibly the most remarkable literary news of our century, has been published in newspapers and magazines everywhere, and will be recalled by every reader. In consequence of it, Boswell has suddenly become a twentieth-century "best seller."

III

Boswell in person is such a collection of assets and liabilities, of genius and imbecility, kindliness and malice, loyalty and betrayal, boundless vanity and abject humility, high spirits and bottomless depressions, lofty resolutions and headlong plunges, intellectual hunger and sensual debauchery, love of cloud castles and passion for factual truth, that his account is very difficult to cast up. He himself, indeed, found the prospect quite bewildering. " My life," he wrote to his friend Temple, " is one of the most romantic that I believe either you or I really know of; and yet I am a very sensible, good sort of man. What is the meaning of this? "

Boswell came of an ancient and very respectable Scottish family. He boasted that the blood of Robert the Bruce flowed in his veins. There is no reason to doubt his claim, but there might be some question whether he could carry it without spilling; the pride of it, he declared, " was his predominant passion." He was an eldest son, and heir to the estate of Auchinleck in Ayrshire. His father was a judge of the Court of Sessions, a strict and dour but humorous Presbyterian; and the regard in which he was generally held opened doors for Boswell and Johnson when they traveled in the Highlands. The father was steady and self-controlled, and found his son's mercurial temper more than he could usually bear. He was in such dread of some new folly that he bribed Boswell, upon the latter's coming of age, into signing himself into perpetual guardianship — a documentary club to bring Boswell to terms if he became too outrageous. But Lord Auchinleck was ready to be kind, even generously indulgent, if only the son would conform to his wishes — which he could never do — and live the sober, settled kind of life appropriate to a " laird." Boswell admired his father and really wished to please him, but inner compul-

sions were always overmastering his soberer purposes. Respect it as he might, his father's staid pattern of life was not for him; when he tried it, he sank into speechless gloom, from which he would break out into the wildest extravagance. He longed to be an army officer, for the typical peacetime reasons; but a commission required patronage as well as money; and after nearly a year of unsuccessful solicitation in London, he succumbed to his father's desire that he should go to Holland as Auchinleck himself had done, and study Roman law. After the exhilaration of London, where he had made friends with Johnson and many other notables, Utrecht bored him almost to distraction, but he tried hard to hold himself to a regular course, and for nearly a year was not altogether unsuccessful. Then, however, fortune favored him with his father's permission to depart under most lucky auspices to Berlin — in company with Lord Keith, Earl Marischal of Scotland, friend of Frederick the Great, Voltaire, and Rousseau. He was thus fairly launched upon a career of celebrity chasing. Thereafter his orbit widened; he proceeded to Switzerland, where he " collected " the two notable *philosophes* just mentioned. Then he moved south into Italy, and added the reprobate, libertine, and popular hero, John Wilkes, to his belt; he had first met him in London a year previously. Next, he doubled over to present Rousseau's introduction to the Corsican patriot, Paoli, collecting the materials for his first important literary work, *The Journal of a Tour to Corsica; and Memoirs of Pascal Paoli,* published with *An Account of Corsica,* early in 1768.

In the Preface to this work, Boswell confessed to a hunger for literary fame. The book was at once translated into several foreign tongues, and in the third English edition he was able to announce that his desire had been gratified. He became at once a notable figure, and even succeeded in rousing his countrymen to quite a pitch of enthusiasm for the Corsicans and their heroic leader. After Corsica was ceded to France in the following year and Paoli escaped to England, Paoli's London residence became Boswell's headquarters in town, and the friendship between the two was never broken.

Meanwhile, Boswell had been admitted to the Scottish bar (July 29, 1766), and began a professional practice for which he found less and less time as the years went by. Until his death on May 19, 1795, it is singular, in a life so crammed (as we now realize) with trivial incident, how few important dates occurred, apart from those associated with Johnson. On November 25, 1769, he was married to his cousin, Margaret Montgomerie. In the summer of 1773 he made the extended tour through the north of Scotland with Johnson, of which his memorable record was published late in 1785. The great *Life* was published in May, 1791. There were his visits to London, to Oxford, to Ashbourne in Derbyshire to meet Johnson, and to Ireland. There were the births of his children, Veronica, Euphemia, Elizabeth, Alexander, and James. There was his father's death in 1782, and his own succession to the estate of Auchinleck; and the death of his wife, on June 4, 1789 — the last a calamity in the wake of which his own life rapidly deteriorated.

IV

Throughout all these years, however, Boswell was projecting new careers and adventures, pursuing celebrities new and old, vainly scheming to get into parliament, writing political pamphlets, throwing off articles for magazines and newspapers, and above all writing his diaries and journals. The last was felt as an absolute duty, possibly his supreme duty in life. It is hardly too much to say that his existence was one never-ending correspondence course with himself. When he awoke in the morning, he jotted down instructions and admonitions for the day's proceedings. For example, on the day when, unknown to him, he was to meet Johnson for the first time, he wrote to himself before rising:

Send breeches mend by barber's boy. You are now on good plan. Breakfast neat today, toast, rolls, and butter, easily and not too laughable. Then Love's and get money, or first finish journal. Keep plan in mind and be earnest. Keep in this fine frame, and be directed by Temple. At night see Pringle. Go to Piazza and take some negus ere you go; or go cool and take letter and bid him [i.e., Pringle] settle all, but not too fast.

And when he retired at night, it was his custom to report — if possible — to himself in writing, in similar brief fashion, what the day had brought forth, and to tell himself what he thought of his conduct in it. As, for instance:

Received a letter from Mr. Johnson treating you with esteem and kindness; nobly elated by it, and resolved to maintain the dignity of yourself.

(Private Papers, VII.60)

Or, again,

You resolved to be yourself, to break free from slavery [to the current mistress]. What strength of mind you have had this winter, to go through so much business and at the same time have so violent a Passion! . . . You wavered and knew not how to determine. You saw yourself gone. . . . Was stunned, but resolved to be firm. To bed quite agitated.

(Private Papers, VII.114–115)

Or, once more,

You was in great vigor of genius, and in the library you dictated *Dorando*. You thought it excellent.

(Private Papers, VII.120 [4/15/1767])

These memoranda were full enough to prompt his memory and provide the basis for an informal regular journal, which he strove to keep up to date. This was written in the first, not as before, in the second, person; it was the completed report which he transmitted to himself — and, as it ultimately turned out, to posterity — of what on each day was done and said, seen and heard and felt, by him, or by others in his presence; and submitted for future examination and comparison with other scenes, past or to come. He could use it for enjoyment, or as source material for the books and essays he would write when time should serve, or as a private manual of instruction. "As a lady," he declared, "adjusts her dress before a mirror, a man adjusts his character by looking at his journal." He came to feel secretly guilty when he failed in his task of journalizing, like one who, instead of decanting and sealing up the elixir of life, betrays his essential being by pouring the precious stuff on the ground, to be forever lost.

Boswell had tentatively begun such a record of his life by the time he was eighteen, and already foresaw what a treasury of experience it could prove to him if he could keep it up. In spite of his consuming egoism and *amour-propre*, he had deep within his nature a haunting sense of his own insufficiency, a desperate need for all the props and supports he could find — for particular advice and general wisdom, for the caveats of friends who knew his besetting weaknesses and for the encouraging example of stronger characters who stood firm against the temptations that he found irresistible. One of the valuable uses of his journals was in the amassing and hoarding of intellectual and spiritual stiffening against the devil and mischance. It was in significant part for his own immediate profit that he went to the trouble of preserving the wisdom and counsel that he extracted from his elders and betters.

The lack of sympathetic rapport between Boswell and his father is an important factor in the shaping of his life and accomplishment. Had Lord Auchinleck, like the father of Charles James Fox, been able to initiate his son into the ways of the world, constituting himself the cynical but sagacious mentor and companion of youth, it is likely that Johnson would have remained to Boswell no more than a celebrated name. This was a role the father was incapable of playing: from every point of view it was unthinkable. Never did a son stand in more constant need of sympathetic and understanding guidance; never was an adolescent more susceptible to influence; never was a boy less able to emulate a father's virtues. The two natures were mutually repellent. " I write to him with warmth," Boswell pathetically complains, " but my letters shock him." But Boswell had to pattern himself on others: he was formed to follow, not to lead. He spent much of his life in pursuit of notable personalities, but he was not a toady, not a sycophant. He had to find, outside, the strength that his own nature lacked. If his father could not accept him, a substitute must somewhere be found. In the long list of his friends and companions, the men of his own age are relatively unimportant. The clergyman, Temple, who was to him like a father-confessor, to whom especially he confided his sensual lapses ("Admonish me, but forgive me "), was the only contemporary who in the long run meant much in his life. His most valued friendships were with those of his father's generation. " I really," he once wrote in his journal, " feel myself happier in the company of those of whom I stand in awe than in any other company. [Such society] composes the uneasy tumult of my spirits, and gives me the pleasure of contemplating something at least comparatively great." This attitude of mind is very forcibly illustrated in his *Tour to Corsica*, in what he has to say about Paoli:

The contemplation of such a character really existing was of more service to me than all I had been able to draw from books, from conversation, or from the exertions of my own mind. . . . It was impossible for me . . . to have a little opinion of human nature in him. . . . I ventured to reason like a libertine, that I might be confirmed in virtuous principles by so illustrious a preceptor. . . . I took leave of Paoli with regret and agitation. . . . From having known intimately so exalted a character, my sentiments of human nature were raised, while, by a sort of contagion, I felt an honest ardor to distinguish myself, and be useful, as far as my situation and abilities would allow.

V

When Boswell came up to London in 1762, he came as fully determined to see Johnson as he was to visit St. Paul's or any other public monument. He was already familiar with his writings, and knew from the *Rambler* that here was a man from whom his own nature could draw the sustenance for which it hungered. He had heard from their mutual friend Thomas Sheridan, and others, wonderful things of his talk, and he was impatient to experience such wisdom and wit. The wit would be an additional delight and give zest to the discourse, but it was the wisdom, and more especially the moral instruction, that Boswell most wanted.

Boswell's mode of existence from day to day, during the spring in which he first saw his polestar, has latterly become the notorious object of sniggering allusion, and it may at first seem paradoxical that so libidinous a puppy should be so keen for virtue. The paradox is superficial. These are opposite but equally valid demonstrations of Boswell's radical insecurity. In both directions he is trying, somewhat feverishly, to assure himself of his manhood, to become a force whose positive impact on his world will be beyond dispute. Either way he aggrandizes his stature in his own eyes. The testimony of the pulses is the easiest and most immediate kind of reassurance, and the level on which Boswell was willing to acquire it proves how desperate was his need to be reassured. But, again, he was bright enough to see that such a course in the long run did not tend to develop the sort of character to which the world paid tribute. He was a sensualist from weakness, not from principle: fundamentally he was religiously moral, and this was the side of his nature that Johnson was to love and nourish. Boswell wished above all things to acquire a character to win the respect of those whom he himself most admired. In Johnson he very soon discovered a talisman, from whose presence he could not but feel that moral strength emanated. After surviving the shock of their first meeting, which for less resilient — that is, more crystallized — natures than his would have been the last, Boswell continued to seek him out, and at the fourth meeting made explicit acknowledgment of his purpose:

Finding him in a placid humor, and wishing to avail myself of the opportunity which I fortunately had of consulting a sage, to hear whose wisdom, I conceived . . . , men filled with a noble enthusiasm for intellectual improvement would gladly have resorted from distant lands, I opened my mind to him ingenuously, and gave him a little sketch of my life, to which he was pleased to listen with great attention. . . . Being at all times a curious examiner of the human mind, and pleased with an undisguised display of what had passed in it, he called to me with warmth, " Give me your hand; I have taken a liking to you." [And after their subsequent conversation, which Boswell reports:] " Sir, I am glad we have met. I hope we shall pass many evenings and mornings, too, together." We finished a couple of bottles of port, and sat till between one and two in the morning.

(*Life,* I.404, 410)

Not two months from that date, Johnson was traveling all the way to Harwich to see his new young friend off to Holland. Why? Among the motives leading to so benevolent a gesture, we may be sure that on Johnson's part there was, as well as a spontaneous response to good nature and to the flattery of youth's sincere deference to age, a recognition of Boswell's human need for strengthening and support, a sense that he himself had something to give that Boswell sorely lacked. Boswell interrupts his narrative of the interview quoted above to introduce a paragraph of more general comment:

I appeal to every impartial reader whether this faithful detail of his frankness, complacency, and kindness to a young man, a stranger and a Scotchman, does not refute the unjust opinion of the harshness of his general demeanor. His occasional reproofs of folly, impudence, or impiety, and even the sudden sallies of his constitutional irritability of temper, which have been preserved for the

poignancy of their wit, have produced that opinion among those who have not considered that such instances . . . were, in fact, scattered through a long series of years: years, in which his time was chiefly spent in instructing and delighting mankind by his writings and conversation, in acts of piety to God, and good will to men.

VI

There is no reason to presume that Johnson was in the least mistaken in his general estimate of Boswell's worth. It has been variously suggested that their relation subsisted on a big-and-little-brother basis; that Johnson tolerated Boswell because he fed him unbounded adulation, and Johnson could browbeat and bully him without protest; that Johnson cherished the lesser man in order to ensure that his biography should be written with a proper stock of materials and with due recording of Johnson's conversational prowess; and that Johnson kept Boswell about for a priming device, to develop the situations and ask the questions that would set him off to most effect in company. The truth is that Johnson never developed any kind of dependency on Boswell, and that Boswell's dependency on Johnson was a valid tribute which did them both honor. Boswell was no " slave " and no " idolater," as Macaulay would have him. He came — whatever Macaulay might suppose — with the laudable desire to be improved, and he venerated his mentor and frequented his society — though by no means so assiduously as is generally supposed — because Johnson seldom disappointed his hopes of improvement. Johnson, for his part, took Boswell as he found him, enjoyed his good humor, was engaged by his busy curiosity, and was moved to reminiscence, to ripe reflection, to critical comment, to witty retort, by his flow of questions and observations. Johnson responded with instinctive sympathy to his filial need, and was glad, from the almost inexhaustible stores of his own knowledge of men, his wide learning, his profound and humane wisdom, to give and go on giving so long as he was asked. He would have been grateful to anyone who would sit with him and by converse keep the black dog outside. Boswell not only performed this service but gave him the additional satisfaction of knowing that he was doing active good. Soon after their acquaintance began, Boswell wrote to another friend, " The conversation of that great and good man has formed me to manly virtue, and kindled in my mind a generous ardor which I trust shall never be extinguished." And, however he might fail in performance, the flame never did go out. Perhaps no greater service can be rendered by one human being to another than the all but involuntary service here exemplified. It was the kind of benefit so memorably praised by Thoreau, " not a partial and transitory act, but a constant superfluity," which came from Johnson like warmth from the sun. Johnson's whole life and all that he wrote were, in Heaven's eye, in the service of moral purpose; but he was not a reformer: he did not think to cure the world's stomach-ache by warning it against eating green apples. The apple, he thought, had been eaten already, and there was little enough to be done about it but endure the pain with as little whining as possible.

VII

Boswell's total debt to Johnson was in the long run incalculably great. What in the eyes of posterity he might have amounted to, had they never come together, is an interesting question and one to which, even today, more than a century and a half after his death, only tentative answers can be given. So much fresh knowledge about him has come to light in our own time, and is still being disclosed, that we cannot yet assess all the evidence. It may fairly be said that a number of his important writings are still in manuscript, though we need not suppose that what is unprinted will be different in kind from what we already have, or that his personal or literary reputation will be much altered by what is yet to come. There is no doubt that the new discoveries have occurred at a historical moment more favorable to their tolerant reception than he could ever have expected. His wife, who execrated his journalizing, predicted that it would leave him " embroweled " to posterity. But the possibility did not greatly disturb him, who confessed to a strange feeling of not really wanting anything about himself to be concealed. The temper of the present age is so accustomed and friendly to the clinical revelation of intimate detail, in both historical and imaginary biography — the novel — that Boswell's frank self-disclosure is generally accepted with tolerant

amusement rather than consternation or disgust. In a curious way, with the upsurge of psychological investigation and the subsiding of Christianity, the old Christian truisms about the beast in man have again become *news,* and all genuine confirmation of the animal side of human nature is welcomed with eager curiosity and even delight.

The nineteenth century, when it thought about Boswell apart from Johnson — which it seldom did — was inclined to regard him as a zany. It admired his two masterpieces, but it gave him little credit for them and was content to seek no farther. It now seems probable that the verdict of the twentieth century will do him justice as a writer. The present age is ready to acknowledge that a man who has written a work universally regarded not only as the greatest of its species, but also as possessing unique originality, must himself have had genius; and, proceeding from that assumption, it will analyze and explore the character and quality of his art. The current popular excitement about Boswell is, however, too much affected by the prevailing breezes to be acceptable as an objective judgment. The unstudied achievement of the *London Journal,* published in 1950, seems, it is true, to display an innate sense of narrative art beyond what we could have inferred from the works earlier known, but except in single episodes it is a question how much is due to artistic control and how much to favoring circumstance or to Boswell's besetting desire to live in such a way that his life would make a good story. His power of invention and his shaping hand operate on events themselves and not primarily on the literary product. His imagination and creative energy are often responsible for the living narrative that he records. But the structure of life is inevitably episodic, and Boswell seldom labored at the realization of a larger unity than life was ready to offer. The great arches of character development and fulfillment, the slow elaboration of purpose and act and result, he neither planned nor often attempted, in life or in art. He preferred the given framework of journey or biographical fact. His best achievements have a unity for which he is only indirectly responsible. The *London Journal,* the *Corsica* episode, the account of his visits to Voltaire and Rousseau, the *Tour to the Hebrides,* and the *Life of Johnson* have the kind of coherency and completeness that sufficed him: a unity comprised of chronological sequences or scenes, beginning and ending at fixed moments of historical time and connected by a personal identity.

In our present view, Boswell's miscellaneous writing — his letters, his periodical essays, his pamphlets with a political purpose, his magazine articles written to persuade or impress, his *jeux d'esprit* in verse or prose — will not in sum total set him high in the ranks of literature. His journals, *apart* from the record they contain of Johnson's conversation and deportment, will certainly give him a leading place among the diarists of all time, not so much on literary as on psychological grounds. But because they do contain the Johnson record, they possess a high degree of literary importance. They are the indispensable preliminary sketches of the most remarkable parts of Boswell's two great literary achievements.

We may say, then, that without Johnson, Boswell's literary accomplishment would have given him at best a second- or third-rate place in the annals of eighteenth-century literature. Johnson gave him the subject matter and the impulse for his two masterpieces, and without Johnson he did not — it may be unfair to say, *could* not — achieve the front rank. The effect of Johnson's personality on Boswell's was galvanic. Johnson aroused Boswell to such a pitch of admiration and absorbed attention that the unusual combination of faculties composing his latent genius was rendered incandescent.

Boswell, we have said, with his adolescent capacity for hero worship, was predisposed to imitation. The need to imitate made it natural for him to project himself imaginatively into another personality and catch instinctively the tone of voice, turn of phrase, physical mannerisms, the characteristic habit and attitude of the object of his attention and admiration. This native faculty of mimicry facilitated and co-operated with a gift of memory for certain kinds of experience — a gift rare if not unique, and amounting almost to total recall. We can readily see how all these elements of Boswell's personality would come into play in their greatest intensity in Johnson's presence, to subserve the ends of biography through conversation.

It is, then, the conversations in the *Tour* and the *Life* that give these works their unique distinction. It is because Johnson was a *great* talker

that Boswell wished to preserve as much of his talk as possible, and went to the enormous, wearying, effort of writing it down. And it is mainly because Johnson's conversation was so truly valuable that the books which preserve so much of it are themselves not merely interesting and curious, but great and memorable.

VIII

All the characteristic features of Boswell's genius at work with spontaneous and happy art upon congenial material are displayed in possibly the most famous and brilliant scene in the *Life,* the account of Johnson's first meeting with John Wilkes at the dinner of the brothers Dilly, in May, 1776. There was hardly a man of note in England whom Johnson more abominated than Wilkes. Wilkes was a notorious offender against the values Johnson most prized. He was a libertine in private life, a member of the Medmenham Abbey brotherhood, who turned the forms of religion into Rabelaisian license; and for his obscene verses on Woman he had been duly reprobated in the House of Lords. He was a rabble-rouser, who had done his utmost to weaken the King's authority by his cool and calculated ridicule and defiance of a House of Commons subservient to the Crown. The kind of liberty that was meant by those who cried "Wilkes and Liberty" was in Johnson's mind nothing more than license. And of such patriotism he declared that it was the last refuge of a scoundrel. He had directed his most pungent political tract, *The False Alarm,* specifically against Wilkes and his claim to be readmitted to parliament. "It will not be easily found," he had written, "why, among the innumerable wrongs of which a great part of mankind are hourly complaining, the whole care of the public should be transferred to Mr. Wilkes and the freeholders of Middlesex, who might all sink into nonexistence, without any other effect, than that there would be room made for a new rabble, and a new retailer of sedition and obscenity." Wilkes, besides, had fled the country for several years and had been outlawed for failure to reappear to answer the charges against him; had eventually surrendered and been sentenced to twelve months in jail. Persons rioting in his behalf had lost their lives.

Boswell, being familiar with the whole history of the violent and mutual hostility between Johnson and Wilkes, conceived, as he declares, an "irresistible wish" to bring them together. He opens his narrative with deliberation, conscious that it was "a very curious incident" and willing to take due credit for his part in it — which was in fact that of its only begetter. No one else would have dreamed of it, much less tried to bring it to pass. "How to manage it," he admits, "was a nice and difficult matter." He first overcomes the objections of his host, Edward Dilly, to including Johnson when Wilkes is to be among the dinner guests; he does this by offering to take full responsibility. But to persuade Johnson even to enter a room with Wilkes will, he realizes, be a feat in itself. In a sentence that reveals in successive steps, and with ironic understatement, the complexity of his own attitude toward Johnson, he confides in the reader: "Notwithstanding the high veneration which I entertained for Dr. Johnson, I was sensible that he was sometimes a little actuated by the spirit of contradiction, and by means of that I hoped I should gain my point." With perfect knowledge and practiced skill he proceeds to draw out Leviathan with an hook, and the monster is unaware that he is caught. "I therefore," says Boswell, "while we were sitting quietly by ourselves at his house in an evening, took occasion to open my plan thus: 'Mr. Dilly, sir, sends his respectful compliments to you, and would be happy if you would do him the honor to dine with him on Wednesday next along with me, as I must soon go to Scotland.' JOHNSON: 'Sir, I am obliged to Mr. Dilly. I will wait upon him —' BOSWELL: 'Provided, sir, I suppose, that the company which he is to have, is agreeable to you.' JOHNSON: 'What do you mean, sir? What do you take me for? Do you think I am so ignorant of the world, . . . that I am to prescribe to a gentleman what company he is to have at his table?'" There might be people very obnoxious at that table, hints Boswell, whipping the water into foam. "Well, sir, and what then?" Johnson exclaims, ". . . as if I could not meet any company whatever, occasionally." "Pray forgive me, sir," replies Boswell meekly, "I meant well. But you shall meet whoever comes, for me." "*Thus I secured him.*" The inimitable page that follows exhibits Boswell disposing with equal mastery of an unforeseen obstacle that arises on the very evening,

half an hour before the dinner, from Johnson's forgetfully having ordered dinner at home with Mrs. Williams, Johnson's blind lodger. It is filled with vivid pictorial and dramatic detail: Boswell's consternation to find the Doctor covered with dust and "buffeting his books"; his vehement entreaties, first to Johnson, then to Mrs. Williams. "'Yes, sir,' said she, pretty peevishly, 'Dr. Johnson is to dine at home.' . . . She gradually softened to my solicitations, . . . I flew back to him, still in dust, . . . he roared, 'Frank, a clean shirt,' and was very soon dressed. When I had him fairly seated in a hackney coach with me, I exulted as much as a fortune hunter who has got an heiress into a post chaise with him to set out for Gretna Green." The sequel is in every respect worthy of this wonderful prologue, and must be read entire. The drama is superb, the persons display their essential selves, the conversation is witty, mischievously anecdotical, and classic. While Boswell keeps himself "snug and silent," watching what may ensue, Wilkes and Johnson join in good-natured fun at the expense of Boswell and the Scotch, and one of Johnson's best-known mots is elicited. (The dinner, we should recall, took place in the second year of our American Revolution.) "Amidst some patriotic groans, . . ." writes Boswell, "somebody said, 'Poor old England is lost.' JOHNSON: 'Sir, it is not so much to be lamented that old England is lost, as that the Scotch have found it.'" There is nothing in the pages of the comic dramatists, and nothing in the greatest masters of the social novel, that surpasses this scene in conveying the sense of living and breathing reality. And it is all true; for a brief while, by virtue of Boswell's unparalleled talent, we are transported through time and space and rendered actually present in an eighteenth-century London dining-room, No. 22 the Poultry, Wednesday, May 15, 1776. Boswell's dual accomplishment on this occasion, as creative dramatist and ideal recorder, constitutes a double charge on our gratitude which we can never sufficiently acknowledge.

IX

And now, if it has become evident that Johnson was all-important in fructifying Boswell's latent genius, making possible the full realization of his potentialities as an author, it is proper to ask in return what Boswell did for his "venerable friend" and mentor. The first and most immediate service is inferential. Evidence in the *Life* points to many hours of solace gained from agreeable companionship by one who dreaded to be left alone. "When we had left Mr. Scott's, he said, 'Will you go home with me?' 'Sir,' said I, 'it is late; but I'll go with you for three minutes.' JOHNSON: 'Or *four*.'" (It was during this unpremeditated call that Johnson defied Boswell to take down in shorthand a passage of prose. "It was found that I had it very imperfectly," Boswell ruefully confesses — thereby disposing of the common misconception that he took down the great conversations at the time. He did nothing of the sort; *he remembered them*.) Johnson's occasional outbursts of impatience at Boswell's perpetual questioning are often recalled ("I will not be baited with *what,* and *why;* why is a cow's tail long? why is a fox's tail bushy?") — and recalled to the exclusion of his expressions of pleasure in Boswell's society. But there can be no doubt of his fondness; his letters carry — together with plenty of admonition and reproof — abundant demonstration of his unforced love. "My dear Boswell," he ends a letter of 1777, "do not neglect to write to me; for your kindness is one of the pleasures of my life which I should be sorry to lose." And again, "I set a very high value upon your friendship, and count your kindness as one of the chief felicities of my life." This sort of thing could be multiplied. But when he felt that Boswell was trying to tease or force such expressions out of him, he could be very forthright: "You always seem to call for tenderness. Know then, that in the first month of the present year [he is writing on January 24, 1778] I very highly esteem and very cordially love you. I hope to tell you this at the beginning of every year as long as we live; and why should we trouble ourselves to tell or hear it oftener?"

Besides the alleviation of loneliness, Johnson owed to Boswell a variety of new acquaintances and new experiences. Wilkes is a signal example of the former; and the trip to the Hebrides is the most outstanding instance of the latter. It was the greatest *adventure* of his life — and indeed to take to the road in rough and wild country, subject to every vicissitude of bad lodging, food, and transportation, sometimes on horseback and sometimes tossed about on a high sea in an open boat, is no slight undertaking for a city dweller at any age, let alone one in his sixties, lethargic from corpulence and ill health. But Johnson's intrepid spirit was evident in his having anticipated even the probability that he would be called upon to defend himself against physical attack: he had brought north with him two pistols with sufficient powder and ball. He never ceased to look back on this expedition with satisfaction keener than that aroused by any other of his journeys, whether to Wales or Paris with the Thrales, or to any of the nearer places he visited. Three years later, he could write Boswell: "The expedition to the Hebrides was the most pleasant journey that I ever made. Such an effort annually would give the world a little diversification." And again, two years before the end: "Shall we ever have another frolic like our journey to the Hebrides?" Could they have contrived the ways and means, he and Boswell would certainly have gone on other frolics; they discoursed with avidity of a trip through the Baltic to visit Catherine of Russia, and even of going to see the Great Wall of China! "He talked," writes Boswell, "with an uncommon animation of traveling into distant countries; that the mind was enlarged by it, and that an acquisition of dignity of character was derived from it."

Certain it is that without Boswell Johnson would never have been brought to make this journey to the Hebrides. And thus it came about that in addition to the pleasure of it, Johnson owed to Boswell the inspiration for one of his most characteristic and entertaining works, his *Journey to the Western Islands of Scotland,* a book full of alert curiosity, of attention to natural and social phenomena, informative and wisely reflective, and rising to the memorable eloquence of the passage on the ancient Christian settlement of Iona.

Whatever withdraws us from the power of our senses, whatever makes the past, the distant, or the future predominate over the present, advances us in the dignity of thinking beings. Far from me and from my friends be such frigid philosophy as may conduct us indifferent and unmoved over any ground which has been dignified by wisdom, bravery, or virtue. That man is little to be envied whose patriotism would not gain force upon the plain of Marathon or whose piety would not grow warmer among the ruins of Iona!

Before such dignity of utterance, Scott's famous lines, "Breathes there a man with soul so dead," sound like the noisy declamation of a jingo. Had Boswell been nothing more to Johnson than the indirect instigator of this one work, he would still have been greatly useful.

But of course he did much more: he wrote his own incomparable account of the journey, in which Johnson himself holds the center of attention and proves a more absorbing object of contemplation than anything the Highlands could show. Here for the first time the complementary talents of the two men are seen in complete and harmonious fusion; and here for the first time emerges to full view the three-dimensional, solid, and indestructible figure of Johnson, taking up, at once and forever, his indisputable place as the friend and companion of the generations to come.

X

Boswell preserves and manages to convey with incomparable vividness the very habit of Johnson's conversation: its pursuit of underlying principles, its characteristic thrust toward the positions that command the area of debate, and its sinewy athletic challenge. We can see the man matching the play of ideas with a similar expenditure of physical force, using far more lung power than the occasion requires, and blowing out his breath in gusts after making a good point, like the picture of Boreas on an old map. This violence and muscularity is central in Johnson's nature: he was not a temperate man. He could be rigidly abstemious, as Boswell tells us, but not moderate. Moderation lies in an equipoise between opposite tensions: it is the classical ideal of virtue, to be so perfectly balanced that one is effortlessly at rest. Johnson, on the contrary, needed always to be proving his strength; effort and living were for him synonymous terms. "To strive with difficulties and to conquer them," he once wrote, "is the highest human felicity; the next is, to strive, and deserve to conquer; but he whose life has passed without a contest, and who can boast neither success nor merit, can survey himself only as a useless filler of existence; and if he is content with his own character, must owe his satisfaction to insensibility." This conviction, radically Christian, but also felt in the blood, that life on earth is no place for rest, that we are here to fight for the good, permeates every aspect of Johnson's being. It is this that lends a

dark and terrifying weight of guilt to his paradoxically inveterate habits of indolence and procrastination, causing him to load his private meditations with an urgency of self-condemnation that to some readers is merely ludicrous. In him, sloth contained more of disease than of vice; but by temperament and conviction he found himself incapable of distinguishing in his own case. His heart and his mind were united to the end in proclaiming, "I will be conquered: I will not capitulate." Knowing the fathomless subtlety of self-love, could one ever safely feel exonerated from blame? At what point was one freed from the moral imperative of "dogged" effort?

Certainly, Johnson was most essentially himself in combat with ideas. From his earliest years he displayed an unwillingness to take things on trust, to fall into step at command. What in the young is frequently called — and no doubt often is — sheer obstinacy, may develop in the mature man, given judgment, into strength of character, a habit of resistance to adventitious pressures. Young or old, Johnson was all his life temperamentally disposed to gainsay. In his youth, he told Boswell, he always chose the wrong side of a debate. And in later years, well knowing how interwoven are truth and falsehood, he would allow himself, in the heat of contest, to try how much of lesser or immediate truth could be found in the opposite camp. "A man," he once wrote, "heated in talk, and eager of victory, takes advantage of the mistakes or ignorance of his adversary, lays hold of concessions to which he knows he has no right, and urges proofs likely to prevail on his opponent, though he knows himself that they have no force." Once, hearing that a man with whom he had carried on a long argument had afterwards expressed elsewhere his thankfulness because Johnson had convinced him "that an opinion which he had embraced as a settled truth was no better than a vulgar error: 'Nay,' said Johnson, 'do not let him be thankful, for he was right, and I was wrong.'"

This negative habit was strikingly evident in a trick he had of commencing or summarizing a position with "No," before any of his hearers had signified an intention to contradict. "No, sir, he was irresistible." It was as if he were merely opening the door on a debate that had already been proceeding in the closed chamber of his own thoughts. And, indeed, conversation was for him but the audible part of a perpetual discussion, the ultimate goal of which was the discovery and defense of truth, not by guess, not by instinct, intuition, nor even by revelation (unless all else failed), but by rational means. Essentially, Johnson was dedicated to reclaiming as much as possible of human life from the rush-lights and snares of irrationality and the "dangerous prevalence of imagination." In this incessant dialogue, he was, ideally, the devoted antagonist of falsehood and obfuscation. He feared the enemy, because he saw that the possibility of defeat was always imminent, from within or from without, whether from man's natural though corrupt love of the lie, as Bacon said, or from mere human liability to error. Therefore he entered every contest with a determination to win. At times, when he felt himself hard pressed, he was blustering and overbearing and willing to settle for the shadow, not the substance, of victory. Not to give ground in battle was essential. At the worst, to be exercising the mental faculties in a rational, discursive way was preferable to any sort of capitulation. On a wider ground, surrender in solitude to reverie, to uncontrolled imagination, to the "chasing of airy good," was abjectly to give away advantage. Therefore, the idling motor must always be thrown as soon as possible into gear. Johnson hated to be alone with his thoughts because the surrender to vacancy was then so much harder to resist. He dreaded the mild insanity of sleepless nights; they were a frightening reminder of how thin was the partition between the rational and irrational. So he clung to his companions far into the small hours, in the hope of wearying himself into slumber when retirement could no longer be postponed.

XI

The aggressive habit of his mind continued to the very end of his life. It is indicative that his last work, the *Lives of the Poets,* is his most unconstrained, most athletic and vigorous, most various and self-assured expression of his views on literature and the literary life. Not for nothing had he spent a great part of the last quarter-century in conversational debate, constantly exercising his intellectual muscle in that arena of impromptu challenge and defense against all comers. However it might be with the heavy body, there was evident no lethargy of the mind. Nor was there any wavering or unsteadiness in his estimates of the great figures on whom he pronounces. It is very striking how he refuses to be seduced by his own enthusiasms or prejudices. Shakespeare, Dryden, and Pope were probably his best-loved authors. Yet, although he praises them all magnificently, his praise always discriminates: he tells where their special excellences lie, and, without abating any of the force of his admiration, turns his level judgment on their weaknesses, whether of character or of achievement, in order to reach a verdict that shall be dispassionate and just. His discussion of Shakespeare's and Dryden's faults of neglect or carelessness, and of Pope's affectation and self-deception in life as in letters, is a model for all hero-worshiping critics, showing the true height of praise that can offset shortcomings so considerable and so clearly discerned. And on the contrary, in the face of his antipathy to Milton the man and the republican, his noble, whole-hearted tribute to Milton's towering grandeur is unshaded by the least hint of grudging reservation or disparagement. His judgment and his magnanimity are perfectly matched, and there is no trace of meanness anywhere, either in blame or praise. The critic himself is great, and without awe or false humility or pride salutes the greatness of the poet.

It has been customary to regard Johnson as the epitome of conservatism, as the last of the great Augustans, or rather, as a belated Augustan, the final bulwark to be borne down by the flood of the new Romanticism. Conservative he doubtless was, in politics, in religion, in literature, in precept, and, at least by intention, in practice. But we must be careful not to take his conservatism too simply, as a mere desire to preserve the *status quo,* a dislike of change. Principles apart, a temperament so dynamic as Johnson's could not be apathetic. His nature was passionate, and he held his principles passionately. "Everything about his character and manners," wrote Boswell, "was forcible and violent." When we call him conservative, we must think of a strenuous conservatism. But conservatism, of course, like any other attitude, becomes strenuous not while it is dominant and taken for granted but when it is confronting serious challenge. Johnson's age, however tamely some observers would picture it, was only superficially stable. The generally placid surface which we see from afar belies the truth that the actual state of affairs is just sim-

mering to a boil. Everywhere accepted values
were being undermined; the common core of
agreement was dissolving. On the Continent the
ferment of ideas was leading directly to the
French Revolution. In England the Industrial
Revolution had already begun, and the whole social pattern was being more and more rapidly
altered by its impact. Around these great cycles
of change were revolving many epicycles, religious, artistic, and literary. The forces at work
were far too powerful to be successfully opposed;
and, as always, the battle line was not clearly
drawn on any wide front. Things gave way
piecemeal, here and there, and bit by bit; and
most of Johnson's generation display traits both
new and old, both forward-looking and retro-
spective. The past itself becomes an avenue to
the future: to cast an eye down its long vistas is
to be lured away from the familiar present.

Johnson himself exhibits some of the complexities of his day. Anticlassical by temperament, he declared that there was always open
an appeal from critical theory to nature, which
in his case meant that he refused ultimately to
be bound by any formal rule. For him there is
only one final authority, and that is not literary,
it is divine. Nevertheless, on a lower level he
took his stand, by and large, in opposition to the
powerfully disintegrating tendencies of his day.
And since these tendencies have not even yet
spent themselves, but bear us forward upon the
same current, he seems perhaps to speak to us
over a great distance. It requires of us some effort of will and sympathetic imagination to recover his critical position.

XII

The basis of it, clearly, is religious. It rests
squarely upon the radically democratic assumption, uncongenial to the prepossessions of our
time, that we are all moral beings with a common stake in the working out on earth of our
personal salvation. Democratic, because under
the infinite overarching heaven our differences,
comparatively, are insignificant. Democratic, because we all face the same impartial, inescapable
examination:

There is no shuffling; there the action lies
In his true nature, and we ourselves compelled,
Even to the teeth and forehead of our faults,
To give in evidence.

In this view, the grounds of agreement are
compelling and far-reaching. The human predicament remains fundamentally the same in
all times and places. Man's nature has not been,
in the measurable past, and in the measurable
future is unlikely to be, significantly modified
by either science or philosophy.

Some truths, Johnson believed, are too important to be new. The most important truths have
been known for a very long time. They require
always to be restated. And because, as he says,
of themselves " they raise no unaccustomed emotion in the mind," one of the paramount uses of
literature is to restate them in fresh and varied
ways, so that they may be vividly and meaning-
fully re-experienced. " Men more frequently require to be reminded than informed." The literary ideal, therefore, would be to convey the most
important sentiments in the most effective manner to the widest possible audience. The pleasure
of novelty, absent from the great and familiar
verities, is restored to them by the felicity, or
convincing power, with which they are presented — " what oft was thought, but ne'er so
well expressed." It is this power for which Johnson especially admired Milton: his ability to give
a different appearance to known truths, " with
pregnancy and vigor of mind peculiar to himself. Whoever considers the few radical positions which the Scriptures afforded him will
wonder by what energetic operation he expanded them to such extent and ramified them to so
much variety."

The same ideal makes it natural to set a high
value on generalization, the depersonalizing of
experience, the distilling of particular instances
into a statement comprehending the class as a
whole. Johnson and his older contemporaries responded with a keen delight to " the grandeur
of generality " — an emotion peculiarly antipathetic or, rather, all but unknown, to the modern sensibility. Yet, upon occasion, Johnson himself manages to combine generality with intensely personal statement, in an amalgam of which
he alone had the secret, and which carries a lofty
dignity about it that defies familiar approach, as
if he were in intimate converse with the Spirit
of History. The Preface to the Dictionary contains striking examples of such writing. Thus:

But these [i.e., his first ideal intentions] were the
dreams of a poet doomed at last to wake a lexi-

cographer. I soon found that it is too late to look for instruments, when the work calls for execution, and that whatever abilities I had brought to my task, with those I must finally perform it. To deliberate whenever I doubted, to inquire whenever I was ignorant, would have protracted the undertaking without end and, perhaps, without much improvement; for I did not find by my first experiments, that what I had not of my own was easily to be obtained; I saw that one inquiry only gave occasion to another, that book referred to book, that to search was not always to find, and to find was not always to be informed; and that thus to pursue perfection was, like the first inhabitants of Arcadia, to chase the sun, which, when they had reached the hill where he seemed to rest, was still beheld at the same distance from them.

I then contracted my design, determining to confide in myself, and no longer to solicit auxiliaries which produced more encumbrance than assistance; by this I obtained at least one advantage, that I set limits to my work, which would in time be ended, though not completed.

Characteristically, Johnson aimed at generalized statement in his writing, and approved, in his critical comment on the work of others, that which was inattentive to the disguises of local customs and manners, and particular instances. "Great thoughts," he declares, "are always general, and consist in positions not limited by exceptions, and in descriptions not descending to minuteness." And in obedience to this prescription, he will describe the downfall of a beautiful girl in the abstract manner that follows:

What care, what rules your heedless charms shall save,
Each nymph your rival, and each youth your slave?
Against your fame with fondness hate combines,
The rival batters, and the lover mines.
With distant voice neglected Virtue calls,
Less heard and less, the faint remonstrance falls. . . .
In crowd at once, where none the pass defend,
The harmless Freedom, and the private Friend. . . .
Now beauty falls betrayed, despised, distressed,
And hissing Infamy proclaims the rest.

Johnson's ideal had already begun to be displaced in his own lifetime by a greater liking for the individual instance, picturesquely or vividly described; by an increasing distrust of the grand generalization, consequent upon the weakening of religious conviction and the fragmentation of agreement as to the purpose and destiny of man. Sensibility was increasingly cultivated

as a virtue in and of itself; and the verbal celebration of fine feeling was audible between inarticulate sobs and floods of tears. Self-consciousness and egocentricity became more and more the order of the day, and feelings came to be prized rather for their claims to the distinction of rarity than for their purchase on another heart.

To an age prone to believe that salvation lies in the perfection of a " space ship," and that human perfectibility proceeds in a one-to-one ratio with the multiplication of " gadgets " that increase a man's accessibility to conflicting claims on his attention, Johnson offers a loud and tonic, " Why, no, sir! " If we will consent to listen to him, he will offer us, instead of panaceas applied from without, a variety of arguments and his personal example to convince us that we might profit by self-scrutiny. He will assure us that luck is not the measure of success, and that if success comes without being paid for in advance by unremitting effort, we shall either lose it, or be destroyed by it, or earn the right to keep it by paying off the debt. He will urge us to clear our minds of cant. He will warn us that we cannot ultimately evade the responsibility for our own acts and will enjoin us therefore to give the best that is in us. He will teach us that the cost of such a discharge of responsibility is nothing less than all we have, that the battle is incessant, and that our effort is of supreme importance. He will show us the sense of self-fulfillment and exhilaration that comes of acquitting oneself as best one can in the never-ending combat for the true and the good. " The certainty," he will tell us, " that life cannot be long, and the probability that it will be much shorter than nature allows, ought to awaken every man to the active prosecution of whatever he is desirous to perform. It is true that no diligence can ascertain success; death may intercept the swiftest career; but he who is cut off in the execution of an honest undertaking, has at least the honor of falling in his rank, and has fought the battle, though he missed the victory." Johnson, in a word, can add a cubit to our human stature, and make us proud that we belong to the same order of being.

Reading Suggestions

George Birkbeck Hill, editor, *Boswell's Life of Johnson Together with Boswell's Journal of a Tour to the*

Hebrides and Johnson's Diary of a Journey into North Wales. Revised and enlarged edition by L. F. Powell. 6 vols. (1934–50). The indispensable edition, with a very full critical apparatus, notes that reflect the accumulated knowledge of a century and a half, many appendixes on special topics, identifications of persons unnamed in Boswell's text, and an index so detailed as to fill the whole last volume. An eighteenth-century library in itself.

George Birkbeck Hill, editor, *Johnsonian Miscellanies*, 2 vols. (1897). Contains the most important non-Boswellian authorities and references dating from Johnson's own era, among them Mrs. Thrale-Piozzi's *Anecdotes of Johnson*, extracts from Sir John Hawkins's *Life of Johnson*, Johnson's autobiographical notes, prayers, and meditations, Arthur Murphy's "Essay on the Life and Genius of Johnson," and anecdotes and reminiscences from many other sources. Spectacular evidence of how notable a personality Johnson seemed to all sorts of men and women, his contemporaries.

Walter Alexander Raleigh, *Six Essays on Johnson* (1910). The real turning point in the reappraisal of Johnson by the twentieth century. On the whole, the finest writing yet on Johnson as author and man.

Chauncey Brewster Tinker, editor, *Dr. Johnson and Fanny Burney: Being the Johnsonian Passages from the Works of Mme. d'Arblay* (1912). Delightful and vivid reporting of Johnson's lighter social side as seen through the eyes of a young woman of whom he was especially fond.

Joseph Wood Krutch, *Samuel Johnson* (1944). The best modern critical biography; especially valuable chapters on the major works.

There is no recent, nor any critical, edition of Johnson's collected works. The standard complete edition is that in eleven volumes, printed in Oxford in 1825, the Oxford English Classics Edition. Separate works have been authoritatively edited, most notably:

George Birkbeck Hill, editor, *History of Rasselas Prince of Abyssinia*, with introduction and notes (1887 and subsequently reprinted).

George Birkbeck Hill, editor, *Lives of the English Poets*, 3 vols. (1905).

R. W. Chapman, collector and editor, *The Letters of Samuel Johnson*, 3 vols. (1952).

Three convenient annotated one-volume anthologies of Johnson's own writings:

Charles Grosvenor Osgood, editor, *Selections from the Works of Samuel Johnson*, with an introduction and notes (1909 and subsequently reprinted). Contains, among other things, the *Life of Savage* and *Addison*.

C. H. Conley, editor, *The Reader's Johnson* (1940). Contains *Rasselas*, the *Life of Pope*, and much of *Savage*.

Bertrand H. Bronson, editor, *Samuel Johnson: Selected Prose and Poetry* (1952). Contains the *Life of Pope*, *Philips*, *Prior*, *Gray*.

James L. Clifford, *Johnsonian Studies, 1887–1950: A Survey and Bibliography* (1951). A most useful classified guide to the work of sixty years on Johnson.

Chauncey Brewster Tinker, editor and collector, *Letters of James Boswell*, 2 vols. (1924). These are often as vivid and dramatic as anything in the *Journals*, and provide a general biographical outline until the definitive *Life* appears.

A. S. Turberville, editor, *Johnson's England*, 2 vols. (1933). A most valuable collection of essays, each by a different specialist but intended for the general reader, on various aspects of eighteenth-century life, in town and country, in the professions and crafts, in the sciences and the arts; with bibliographical aids to further reading in each of the fields treated, and with scores of illustrations.

Frederick A. Pottle and Charles H. Bennett, editors, *Boswell's Journal of a Tour to the Hebrides with Samuel Johnson, LL.D.*, with preface and notes (1936). Now first published from the original manuscript. Contains some informalities and details lacking in the version published by Boswell, a comparison with which is an instructive lesson in Boswell's standards of propriety.

Frederick A. Pottle, editor, *Boswell's London Journal, 1762–1763*, with introduction and notes (1950). Now first published from the original manuscript. Contains the original account of the first meeting with Johnson, and a very striking picture of Boswell's daily existence in town at the age of twenty-two. The first volume of the Yale Edition of the Private Papers of James Boswell.

Frederick A. Pottle, editor, *Boswell on the Grand Tour: Germany and Switzerland, 1764*, with introduction and notes (1953). The diary of Boswell's travels into these countries, and of his visits to Voltaire and Rousseau. The fourth volume of the Yale Edition of Boswell's Private Papers.

---

from THE JOURNAL OF A TOUR TO THE HEBRIDES

The tour that was immortalized in Boswell's record and in Johnson's own characteristic account occupied the late summer and autumn of 1773. The two were together just over three months. Johnson arrived in Edinburgh on the 14th of August and departed thence on November 22. They traveled up along the eastern coast of Scotland to Inverness, down along Loch Ness, at the foot of which they struck west and crossed to the island of Skye. They then made the somewhat hazardous passage to Coll and Mull, and from Oban came down into Ayrshire, where Boswell's father received them at the ancestral estate of Auchinleck; and so back to Edinburgh. Boswell faithfully wrote up his account from day to day in a diary which Johnson read in large part as it was written, and which has survived to find its ultimate resting place in the library of Yale

University. Needless to say, the Doctor never expected so intimate a journal to be published as it stood; and its indiscretions, even apart from what is written of Johnson, and after revision, nearly involved the author in a duel. With the encouragement of the Shakespearean critic, Edmund Malone, Boswell revised his original manuscript and brought it to publication on October 1, 1785. It was an immediate success and went into its third edition in a year. The original journal was unearthed so recently as 1930, and was edited and published by F. A. Pottle and C. H. Bennett in 1936. The following text is the one Boswell chose to present to the world.

. . . Dr. Samuel Johnson's character, religious, moral, political, and literary, nay his figure and manner, are, I believe, more generally known than those of almost any man; yet it may not be superfluous here to attempt a sketch of him. Let my readers then remember that he was a sincere and zealous Christian, of High Church of England and monarchical principles, which he would not tamely suffer to be questioned; steady and inflexible in maintaining the obligations of piety and virtue, both from a regard to the order of society, and from a veneration for the Great Source of all order; correct, nay stern, in his taste; hard to please, and easily offended; impetuous and irritable in his temper, but of a most humane and benevolent heart; having a mind stored with a vast and various collection of learning and knowledge, which he communicated with peculiar perspicuity and force, in rich and choice expression. He united a most logical head with a most fertile imagination, which gave him an extraordinary advantage in arguing; for he could reason close or wide, as he saw best for the moment. He could, when he chose it, be the greatest sophist that ever wielded a weapon in the schools of declamation, but he indulged this only in conversation, for he owned he sometimes talked for victory; he was too conscientious to make error permanent and pernicious, by deliberately writing it. He was conscious of his superiority. He loved praise when it was brought to him, but was too proud to seek for it. He was somewhat susceptible of flattery. His mind was so full of imagery, that he might have been perpetually a poet. It has been often remarked, that in his poetical pieces, which it is to be regretted are so few, because so excellent, his style is easier than in his prose. There is deception in this: it is not easier, but better suited to the dignity of verse; as one may dance with grace, whose motions, in ordinary walking — in the common step — are awkward. He had a con-

stitutional melancholy, the clouds of which darkened the brightness of his fancy and gave a gloomy cast to his whole course of thinking; yet, though grave and awful in his deportment, when he thought it necessary or proper, he frequently indulged himself in pleasantry and sportive sallies. He was prone to superstition, but not to credulity. Though his imagination might incline him to a belief of the marvelous, and the mysterious, his vigorous reason examined the evidence with jealousy. He had a loud voice, and a slow deliberate utterance, which no doubt gave some additional weight to the sterling metal of his conversation. Lord Pembroke said once to me at Wilton, with a happy pleasantry, and some truth, that "Dr. Johnson's sayings would not appear so extraordinary, were it not for his *bow-wow way*"; but I admit the truth of this only on some occasions. *The Messiah*, played upon the *Canterbury organ*, is more sublime than when played upon an inferior instrument, but very slight music will seem grand when conveyed to the ear through that majestic medium. *While therefore Dr. Johnson's sayings are read, let his manner be taken along with them.* Let it however be observed, that the sayings themselves are generally great; that, though he might be an ordinary composer at times, he was for the most part a Handel. His person was large, robust, I may say approaching to the gigantic, and grown unwieldy from corpulency. His countenance was naturally of the cast of an ancient statue, but somewhat disfigured by the scars of that *evil*, which, it was formerly imagined, the *royal touch* could cure.[1] He was now in his sixty-fourth year, and was become a little dull of hearing. His sight had always been somewhat weak, yet, so much does mind govern, and even supply the deficiency of organs, that his perceptions were uncommonly quick and accurate. His head, and sometimes also his body, shook with a kind of motion like the effect of a palsy; he appeared to be frequently disturbed by cramps, or convulsive contractions,[2] of the nature of that dis-

TOUR. **1. royal . . . cure**: It was believed that the divinity residing in the royal person could miraculously cure scrofula. Johnson himself was "touched" for this purpose, when an infant, by Queen Anne. **2. contractions**: "Such they appeared to me, but since the first edition, Sir Joshua Reynolds has observed to me, 'that Dr. Johnson's extraordinary gestures were only habits, in which he indulged himself at certain times. When in company, where he was not free, or when engaged earnestly in conversation, he never gave way to such habits, which proves that they were not involuntary.' I still however think, that these gestures were involuntary; for surely had not that been the case, he would have restrained them in the public streets" [Boswell's note].

temper called *St. Vitus's* dance. He wore a full suit of plain brown clothes, with twisted hair buttons of the same color, a large bushy grayish wig, a plain shirt, black worsted stockings, and silver buckles. Upon this tour, when journeying, he wore boots, and a very wide brown cloth great-coat, with pockets which might have almost held the two volumes of his folio dictionary; and he carried in his hand a large English oak stick. . . .

Monday, 30th August

We might have taken a chaise to Fort Augustus, but, had we not hired horses at Inverness, we should not have found them afterwards: so we resolved to begin here to ride. We had three horses, for Dr. Johnson, myself, and Joseph, and one which carried our portmanteaus, and two Highlanders who walked along with us, John Hay and Lauchland Vass, whom Dr. Johnson has remembered with credit in his *Journey,*[3] though he has omitted their names. Dr. Johnson rode very well.

About three miles beyond Inverness, we saw, just by the road, a very complete specimen of what is called a druid's temple. There was a double circle, one of very large, the other of smaller, stones. Dr. Johnson justly observed, that, "To go and see one druidical temple is only to see that it is nothing, for there is neither art nor power in it; and seeing one is quite enough."

It was a delightful day. Loch Ness, and the road upon the side of it, shaded with birch trees, and the hills above it, pleased us much. The scene was as sequestered and agreeably wild as could be desired, and for a time engrossed all our attention.

To see Dr. Johnson in any new situation is always an interesting object to me; and, as I saw him now for the first time on horseback, jaunting about at his ease in quest of pleasure and novelty, the very different occupations of his former laborious life, his admirable productions, his *London,* his *Rambler,* etc., etc., immediately presented themselves to my mind, and the contrast made a strong impression on my imagination.

When we had advanced a good way by the side of Loch Ness, I perceived a little hut, with an old-looking woman at the door of it. I thought here might be a scene that would amuse Dr. Johnson; so I mentioned it to him. "Let's go in," said he. We dismounted, and we and our guides entered the hut. It was a wretched little hovel of earth only, I think, and for a window had only a small hole, which was stopped with a piece of turf, that was taken out occasionally to let in light. In the middle of the room or space which we entered, was a fire of peat, the smoke going out at a hole in the roof. She had a pot upon it, with goat's flesh, boiling. There was at one end under the same roof, but divided by a kind of partition made of wattles, a pen or fold in which we saw a good many kids.

Dr. Johnson was curious to know where she slept. I asked one of the guides, who questioned her in Erse. She answered with a tone of emotion, saying (as he told us) she was afraid we wanted to go to bed to her. This *coquetry,* or whatever it may be called, of so wretched a being, was truly ludicrous. Dr. Johnson and I afterwards were merry upon it. I said, it was he who alarmed the poor woman's virtue. "No, sir," said he, "she'll say, 'There came a wicked young fellow, a wild dog, who I believe would have ravished me, had there not been with him a grave old gentleman, who repressed him, but when he gets out of the sight of his tutor, I'll warrant you he'll spare no woman he meets, young or old.'" — "No, sir," I replied, "she'll say, 'There was a terrible ruffian who would have forced me, had it not been for a civil decent young man who, I take it, was an angel sent from Heaven to protect me.'"

Dr. Johnson would not hurt her delicacy by insisting on "seeing her bedchamber," like *Archer* in the *Beaux' Stratagem.*[4] But my curiosity was more ardent; I lighted a piece of paper, and went into the place where the bed was. There was a little partition of wicker, rather more neatly done than that for the fold, and close by the wall was a kind of bedstead of wood with heath upon it by way of bed; at the foot of which I saw some sort of blankets or covering rolled up in a heap. The woman's name was Fraser; so was her husband's. He was a man of eighty. Mr. Fraser of Balnain allows him to live in this hut, and keep sixty goats, for taking care of his woods, where he then was. They had five children, the eldest only thirteen. Two were gone to Inverness to buy meal; the rest were looking after the goats. This contented family had four stacks of barley, twenty-four sheaves in each. They had a few fowls. We were informed that they lived all the spring without meal, upon

---

3. *Journey:* The book that Johnson himself wrote about the present tour: *A Journey to the Western Islands of Scotland* (1775).

4. *Beaux' Stratagem:* The last and best comedy of George Farquhar, produced in 1707, at the theater in the Haymarket, London.

milk and curds and whey alone. What they get for their goats, kids, and fowls, maintains them during the rest of the year.

She asked us to sit down and take a dram. I saw one chair. She said she was as happy as any woman in Scotland. She could hardly speak any English except a few detached words. Dr. Johnson was pleased at seeing, for the first time, such a state of human life. She asked for snuff. It is her luxury, and she uses a great deal. We had none, but gave her sixpence apiece. She then brought out her whisky bottle. I tasted it, as did Joseph and our guides, so I gave her sixpence more. She sent us away with many prayers in Erse. . . .

Tuesday, 31st August

Between twelve and one we set out, and traveled eleven miles, through a wild country, till we came to a house in Glen Moriston, called *Anoch,* kept by a M'Queen.[5] Our landlord was a sensible fellow; he had learnt his grammar, and Dr. Johnson justly observed, that " A man is the better for that as long as he lives." There were some books here: a treatise against drunkenness, translated from the French; a volume of the *Spectator;* a volume of Prideaux's *Connection,* and *Cyrus's Travels.*[6] M'Queen said he had more volumes; and his pride seemed to be much piqued that we were surprised at his having books.

Near to this place we had passed a party of soldiers, under a sergeant's command, at work upon the road. We gave them two shillings to drink. They came to our inn, and made merry in the barn. We went and paid them a visit, Dr. Johnson saying, " Come, let's go and give 'em another shilling apiece." We did so; and he was saluted " My lord " by all of them. He is really generous, loves influence, and has the way of gaining it. He said, " I am quite feudal, sir." Here I agree with him. I said, I regretted I was not the head of a clan; however, though not possessed of such an hereditary advantage, I would always endeavor to make my tenants follow me. I could not be a *patriarchal* chief, but I would be a *feudal* chief.

The poor soldiers got too much liquor. Some of them fought, and left blood upon the spot, and cursed whisky next morning. The house here was built of thick turfs, and thatched with thinner turfs and heath. It had three rooms in length, and a little room which projected. Where we sat, the side walls were *wainscoted,* as Dr. Johnson said, with wicker, very neatly plaited. Our landlord had made the whole with his own hands.

After dinner, M'Queen sat by us awhile, and talked with us. He said, all the Laird of Glen Moriston's people would bleed for him, if they were well used, but that seventy men had gone out of the glen to America. That he himself intended to go next year, for that the rent of his farm, which twenty years ago was only five pounds, was now raised to twenty pounds. That he could pay ten pounds, and live; but no more. Dr. Johnson said, he wished M'Queen laird of Glen Moriston, and the laird to go to America. M'Queen very generously answered, he should be sorry for it; for the laird could not shift for himself in America as he could do.

I talked of the officers whom we had left today; how much service they had seen, and how little they got for it, even of fame. JOHNSON: " Sir, a soldier gets as little as any man can get." BOSWELL: " Goldsmith has acquired more fame than all the officers last war, who were not generals." JOHNSON: " Why, sir, you will find ten thousand fit to do what they did, before you find one who does what Goldsmith has done. You must consider, that a thing is valued according to its rarity. A pebble that paves the street is in itself more useful than the diamond upon a lady's finger." I wish our friend Goldsmith had heard this.

I yesterday expressed my wonder that John Hay, one of our guides, who had been pressed aboard a man-of-war, did not choose to continue in it longer than nine months, after which time he got off. JOHNSON: " Why, sir, no man will be a sailor, who has contrivance enough to get himself into a jail; for being in a ship is being in a jail, with the chance of being drowned."

We had tea in the afternoon, and our landlord's daughter, a modest civil girl, very neatly dressed, made it for us. She told us, she had been a year at Inverness, and learned reading and writing, sewing, knotting, working lace, and pastry. Dr. John-

5. M'Queen: " *A* M'Queen is a Highland mode of expression. An Englishman would say *one* M'Queen. But where there are *clans* or *tribes* of men, distinguished by *patronymic* surnames, the individuals of each are considered as if they were of different species, at least as much as nations are distinguished: so that a *M'Queen,* a *M'Donald,* a *M'Lean,* is said, as we say a Frenchman, an Italian, a Spaniard" [B]. 6. Prideaux's . . . *Travels:* Humphrey Prideaux, *The Old and New Testament Connected, in the History of the Jews and Neighboring Nations* (1716–18); and Andrew Michael Ramsay, *Les Voyages de Cyrus* (1727). The latter was translated in the year of publication and frequently republished: its author was tutor to Charles Edward, " Bonnie Prince Charlie."

son made her a present of a book which he had bought at Inverness.[7]

The room had some deals laid across the joists, as a kind of ceiling. There were two beds in the room, and a woman's gown was hung on a rope to make a curtain of separation between them. Joseph had sheets, which my wife had sent with us, laid on them. We had much hesitation, whether to undress, or lie down with our clothes on. I said at last, "I'll plunge in! There will be less harbor for vermin about me, when I am stripped!" Dr. Johnson said, he was like one hesitating to go into the cold bath. At last he resolved, too. I observed, he might serve a campaign. JOHNSON: "I could do all that can be done by patience; whether I should have strength enough, I know not." He was in excellent humor. To see the Rambler as I saw him tonight was really an amusement. I yesterday told him, I was thinking of writing a poetical letter to him, *on his return from Scotland,* in the style of Swift's humorous epistle in the character of Mary Gulliver to her husband, Captain Lemuel Gulliver, on his return to England from the country of the *Houyhnhnms:*

At early morn I to the market haste,
Studious in ev'rything to please thy taste.
A curious *fowl* and *sparagrass* I chose
(For I remember you were fond of those);
Three shillings cost the first, the last sev'n groats;
Sullen you turn from both, and call for oats.

He laughed, and asked in whose name I would write it. I said, in Mrs. Thrale's. He was angry. "Sir, if you have any sense of decency or delicacy, you won't do that!" BOSWELL: "Then let it be in Cole's, the landlord of the Mitre Tavern, where we have so often sat together." JOHNSON: "Ay, that may do."

7. book . . . Inverness: "This book has given rise to much inquiry, which has ended in ludicrous surprise. Several ladies, wishing to learn the kind of reading which the great and good Dr. Johnson esteemed most fit for a young woman, desired to know what book he had selected for this Highland nymph. 'They never adverted,' said he, 'that I had no *choice* in the matter. I have said that I presented her with a book which I *happened* to have about me.' And what was this book? My readers, prepare your features for merriment. It was *Cocker's Arithmetic!* Wherever this was mentioned, there was a loud laugh, at which Dr. Johnson, when present, used sometimes to be a little angry. One day, when we were dining at General Oglethorpe's, where we had many a valuable day, I ventured to interrogate him, 'But, sir, is it not somewhat singular that you should *happen* to have *Cocker's Arithmetic* about you on your journey? What made you buy such a book at Inverness?' He gave me a very sufficient answer. 'Why, sir, if you are to have but one book with you upon a journey, let it be a book of science. When you have read through a book of entertainment, you know it, and it can do no more for you; but a book of science is inexhaustible'" [B].

After we had offered up our private devotions, and had chatted a little from our beds, Dr. Johnson said, "GOD bless us both, for Jesus Christ's sake! Good night!" I pronounced *"Amen."* He fell asleep immediately. I was not so fortunate for a long time. I fancied myself bit by innumerable vermin under the clothes, and that a spider was traveling from the *wainscot* towards my mouth. At last I fell into insensibility.

Wednesday, 1st September

We passed through Glen Shiel, with prodigious mountains on each side. We saw where the battle was fought in the year 1719. Dr. Johnson owned he was now in a scene of as wild nature as he could see, but he corrected me sometimes in my inaccurate observations. "There," said I, "is a mountain like a cone." JOHNSON: "No, sir. It would be called so in a book, and when a man comes to look at it, he sees it is not so. It is indeed pointed at the top, but one side of it is larger than the other." Another mountain I called immense. JOHNSON: "No; it is no more than a considerable protuberance."

We came to a rich green valley, comparatively speaking, and stopped awhile to let our horses rest and eat grass.[8] We soon afterwards came to Auchnashiel, a kind of rural village, a number of cottages being built together, as we saw all along in the Highlands. We passed many miles this day without seeing a house, but only little summer huts, called *shielings.* Evan Campbell, servant to Mr. Murchison, factor to the Laird of Macleod in Glenelg, ran along with us today. He was a very obliging fellow. At Auchnashiel, we sat down on a green turf seat at the end of a house; they brought us out two wooden dishes of milk, which we tasted. One of them was frothed like a syllabub. I saw a woman preparing it with such a stick as is used for chocolate, and in the same manner. We had a considerable circle about us, men, women, and children, all M'Craas, Lord Seaforth's people. Not one of them could speak English. I observed to Dr. Johnson, it was much the same as being with a tribe of Indians. JOHNSON: "Yes, sir, but not

8. We . . . grass: "Dr. Johnson, in his *Journey,* thus beautifully describes his situation here: 'I sat down on a bank, such as a writer of romance might have delighted to feign. I had, indeed, no trees to whisper over my head, but a clear rivulet streamed at my feet. The day was calm, the air soft, and all was rudeness, silence, and solitude. Before me, and on either side, were high hills, which, by hindering the eye from ranging, forced the mind to find entertainment for itself. Whether I spent the hour well, I know not; for here I first conceived the thought of this narration'" [B].

so terrifying." I gave all who chose it, snuff and tobacco. Governor Trapaud had made us buy a quantity at Fort Augustus, and put them up in small parcels. I also gave each person a bit of wheat bread, which they had never tasted before. I then gave a penny apiece to each child. I told Dr. Johnson of this, upon which he called to Joseph and our guides, for change for a shilling, and declared that he would distribute among the children. Upon this being announced in Erse, there was a great stir; not only did some children come running down from neighboring huts, but I observed one black-haired man, who had been with us all along, had gone off, and returned, bringing a very young child. My fellow traveler then ordered the children to be drawn up in a row, and he dealt about his copper, and made them and their parents all happy. The poor M'Craas, whatever may be their present state, were of considerable estimation in the year 1715, when there was a line in a song,

And aw the brave M'Craas are coming.

There was great diversity in the faces of the circle around us. Some were as black and wild in their appearance as any American savages whatever. One woman was as comely almost as the figure of Sappho, as we see it painted. We asked the old woman, the mistress of the house where we had the milk (which by the by, Dr. Johnson told me, for I did not observe it myself, was built not of turf, but of stone), what we should pay. She said, what we pleased. One of our guides asked her, in Erse, if a shilling was enough. She said, "Yes." But some of the men bade her ask more. This vexed me, because it showed a desire to impose upon strangers, as they knew that even a shilling was high payment. The woman, however, honestly persisted in her first price, so I gave her half a crown. Thus we had one good scene of life uncommon to us. The people were very much pleased, gave us many blessings, and said they had not had such a day since the old Laird of Macleod's time.

Dr. Johnson was much refreshed by this repast. He was pleased when I told him he would make a good chief. He said, " Were I a chief, I would dress my servants better than myself, and knock a fellow down if he looked saucy to a Macdonald in rags, but I would not treat men as brutes. I would let them know why all of my clan were to have attention paid to them. I would tell my upper servants why, and make them tell the others."

We rode on well, till we came to the high mountain called the Rattakin, by which time both Dr. Johnson and the horses were a good deal fatigued. It is a terrible steep to climb, notwithstanding the road is formed slanting along it; however, we made it out. On the top of it we met Captain M'Leod of Balmenoch (a Dutch officer who had come from Skye) riding with his sword slung across him. He asked, "Is this Mr. Boswell?" which was a proof that we were expected. Going down the hill on the other side was no easy task. As Dr. Johnson was a great weight, the two guides agreed that he should ride the horses alternately. Hay's were the two best, and the Doctor would not ride but upon one or other of them, a black or a brown. But, as Hay complained much after ascending the *Rattakin,* the Doctor was prevailed with to mount one of Vass's grays. As he rode upon it downhill, it did not go well; and he grumbled. I walked on a little before, but was excessively entertained with the method taken to keep him in good humor. Hay led the horse's head, talking to Dr. Johnson as much as he could; and (having heard him, in the forenoon, express a pastoral pleasure on seeing the goats browsing) just when the Doctor was uttering his displeasure, the fellow cried, with a very Highland accent, " See such pretty goats! " Then he whistled, *" Whu! "* and made them jump. Little did he conceive what Doctor Johnson was. Here now was a common ignorant Highland clown imagining that he could divert, as one does a child, *Dr. Samuel Johnson!* The ludicrousness, absurdity, and extraordinary contrast between what the fellow fancied, and the reality, was truly comic.

It grew dusky, and we had a very tedious ride for what was called five miles, but I am sure would measure ten. We had no conversation. I was riding forward to the inn at Glenelg, on the shore opposite to Skye, that I might take proper measures, before Dr. Johnson, who was now advancing in dreary silence, Hay leading his horse, should arrive. Vass also walked by the side of his horse, and Joseph followed behind: as therefore he was thus attended, and seemed to be in deep meditation, I thought there could be no harm in leaving him for a little while. He called me back with a tremendous shout, and was really in a passion with me for leaving him. I told him my intentions, but he was not satisfied, and said, "Do you know, I should as soon have thought of picking a pocket, as doing so." BOSWELL: "I am diverted with you, sir." JOHNSON: " Sir, I could never be diverted with incivility. Doing such a thing, makes one lose confidence in him who has done it, as one cannot tell what he may do next." His extraordinary warmth confounded me so much, that I justified myself but lamely to him; yet my intentions were not improper. I wished to get on, to see how we were to be lodged, and how we were to get a boat; all which I thought I could best settle myself, without his having any trouble. To apply his great mind to minute particulars, is wrong; it is like taking an immense balance, such as is kept on quays for weighing cargoes of ships, to weigh a guinea. I knew I had neat little scales, which would do better, and that his attention to everything which falls in his way, and his uncommon desire to be always in the right, would make him weigh, if he knew of the particulars; it was right therefore for me to weigh them, and let him have them only in effect. I however continued to ride by him, finding he wished I should do so.

As we passed the barracks at Bernera, I looked at them wishfully, as soldiers have always everything in the best order, but there was only a sergeant and a few men there. We came on to the inn at Glenelg. There was no provender for our horses, so they were sent to grass, with a man to watch them. A maid showed us upstairs into a room damp and dirty, with bare walls, a variety of bad smells, a coarse black greasy fir table, and forms of the same kind; and out of a wretched bed started a fellow from his sleep, like Edgar in *King Lear,* "*Poor Tom's a cold.*" [9]

This inn was furnished with not a single article that we could either eat or drink, but Mr. Murchison, factor to the Laird of Macleod in Glenelg, sent us a bottle of rum and some sugar, with a polite message, to acquaint us, that he was very sorry that he did not hear of us till we had passed his house, otherwise he should have insisted on our sleeping there that night; and that, if he were not obliged to set out for Inverness early next morning, he would have waited upon us. Such extraordinary attention from this gentleman, to entire strangers, deserves the most honorable commemoration.

Our bad accommodation here made me uneasy, and almost fretful. Dr. Johnson was calm. I said, he was so from vanity. JOHNSON: "No, sir, it is from philosophy." It pleased me to see that the *Rambler* could practice so well his own lessons.

I resumed the subject of my leaving him on the road, and endeavored to defend it better. He was still violent upon that head, and said, "Sir, had you gone on, I was thinking that I should have returned with you to Edinburgh, and then have parted from you, and never spoken to you more."

I sent for fresh hay, with which we made beds for ourselves, each in a room equally miserable. Like Wolfe, we had a "*choice of difficulties.*" [10] Dr. Johnson made things easier by comparison. At M'Queens, last night, he observed, that few were so well lodged in a ship. Tonight he said, we were better than if we had been upon the hill. He lay down buttoned up in his greatcoat. I had my sheets spread on the hay, and my clothes and greatcoat laid over me, by way of blankets.

Wednesday, 8th September

When I waked, the rain was much heavier than yesterday, but the wind had abated. By breakfast, the day was better, and in a little while it was calm and clear. I felt my spirits much elated. The propriety of the expression, "*the sunshine of the breast,*" [11] now struck me with peculiar force; for the brilliant rays penetrated into my very soul. We were all in better humor than before. Mrs. M'Kinnon, with unaffected hospitality and politeness, expressed her happiness in having such company in her house, and appeared to understand and relish Dr. Johnson's conversation, as indeed all the company seemed to do. When I knew she was old Kingsburgh's daughter, I did not wonder at the good appearance which she made.

She talked as if her husband and family would emigrate, rather than be oppressed by their landlord, and said, "How agreeable would it be, if these gentlemen should come in upon us when we are in America." Somebody observed that Sir Alexander Macdonald was always frightened at sea. JOHNSON: "*He* is frightened at sea; and his tenants are frightened when he comes to land."

We resolved to set out directly after breakfast. We had about two miles to ride to the seaside, and there we expected to get one of the boats belonging to the fleet of bounty herring-busses [12] then on the coast, or at least a good country fishingboat. But while we were preparing to set out, there arrived

9. "*Poor . . . cold*": "It is amusing to observe the different images which this being presented to Dr. Johnson and me. The Doctor, in his *Journey,* compares him to a Cyclops" [B]. See *King Lear,* III.iv.

10. "*choice of difficulties*": The allusion is to General Wolfe's alternatives before the battle of Quebec, September, 1759. 11. "*the . . . breast*": See Gray's "Ode on a Distant Prospect of Eton College." Had Boswell's elation contradicted the weather, the allusion would have had more point. 12. bounty herring-busses: fishing vessels operating for the sake of the government bounty of thirty shillings a ton for white herring.

a man with the following card from the Rev. Mr. Donald M'Queen:

Mr. M'Queen's compliments to Mr. Boswell, and begs leave to acquaint him that, fearing the want of a proper boat, as much as the rain of yesterday, might have caused a stop, he is now at Skianwden with Macgillichallum's [13] carriage, to convey him and Dr. Johnson to Raasay, where they will meet with a most hearty welcome, and where Macleod, being on a visit, now attends their motions.

Wednesday forenoon

This card was most agreeable; it was a prologue to that hospitable and truly polite reception which we found at Raasay. In a little while arrived Mr. Donald M'Queen himself; a decent minister, an elderly man with his own black hair, courteous, and rather slow of speech, but candid, sensible, and well informed, nay learned. Along with him came, as our pilot, a gentleman whom I had a great desire to see, Mr. Malcolm Macleod, one of the Raasay family, celebrated in the year 1745–46.[14] He was now sixty-two years of age, hale, and well proportioned, with a manly countenance, tanned by the weather, yet having a ruddiness in his cheeks, over a great part of which his rough beard extended. His eye was quick and lively, yet his look was not fierce, but he appeared at once firm and good-humored. He wore a pair of brogues, Tartan hose which came up only near to his knees and left them bare, a purple camlet kilt, a black waistcoat, a short green cloth coat bound with gold cord, a yellowish bushy wig, a large blue bonnet with a gold thread button. I never saw a figure that gave a more perfect representation of a Highland gentleman. I wished much to have a picture of him just as he was. I found him frank and *polite,* in the true sense of the word.

The good family at Corrichatachin said, they hoped to see us on our return. We rode down to the shore, but Malcolm walked with graceful agility.

We got into Raasay's *carriage,* which was a good strong open boat made in Norway. The wind had now risen pretty high, and was against us; but we had four stout rowers, particularly a Macleod, a robust, black-haired fellow, half-naked, and bare-headed, something between a wild Indian and an English tar. Dr. Johnson sat high on the stern, like

a magnificent Triton. Malcolm sung an Erse song, the chorus of which was "*Hatyin foam foam eri,*" [15] with words of his own. The tune resembled "*Owr the muir amang the heather.*" The boatmen and Mr. M'Queen chorused, and all went well. At length Malcolm himself took an oar, and rowed vigorously. We sailed along the coast of Scalpay, a rugged island, about four miles in length. Dr. Johnson proposed that he and I should buy it, and found a good school, and an Episcopal church (Malcolm said, he would come to it) and have a printing press, where he would print all the Erse that could be found.

Here I was strongly struck with our long-projected scheme of visiting the Hebrides being realized. I called to him, "We are contending with seas," which I think were the words of one of his letters to me. "Not much," said he; and though the wind made the sea lash considerably upon us, he was not discomposed. After we were out of the shelter of Scalpay, and in the sound between it and Raasay, which extended about a league, the wind made the sea very rough. I did not like it. JOHNSON: "This now is the Atlantic. If I should tell at a tea table in London, that I have crossed the Atlantic in an open boat, how they'd shudder, and what a fool they'd think me to expose myself to such danger!" He then repeated Horace's ode,

Otium Divos rogat in patenti
Prensus Aegaeo —— .[16]

In the confusion and hurry of this boisterous sail, Dr. Johnson's spurs, of which Joseph had charge, were carried overboard into the sea, and lost. This was the first misfortune that had befallen us. Dr. Johnson was a little angry at first, observing that "there was something wild in letting a pair of spurs be carried into the sea out of a boat"; but then he remarked, "that, as Janes the naturalist had said upon losing his pocketbook, it was rather an inconvenience than a loss." He told us, he now recollected that he dreamed the night before, that he put his staff into a river, and chanced to let it go, and it was carried down the stream and lost. "So now you see," said he, "that I have lost my spurs; and this story is better than many of those which we have concerning second sight and dreams." Mr. M'Queen said he did not believe the second sight;

---

13. **Macgillichallum:** the Highland expression for Laird of Raasay. 14. 1745–46: Alluding to the vain attempt to restore the House of Stuart, in the person of Charles Edward, "Bonnie Prince Charlie," to the British throne, in 1745.   15. "*Hatyin . . . eri*": More correctly, *Tha Tighinn fotham eirigh:* "I intend to arise" — here, presumably, to defend Prince Charles. The tune Boswell mentions may be found in J. C. Dick, *The Songs of Robert Burns* (1903), p. 344.   16. Horace, *Odes,* II.xvi.1: "Caught in the stormy Aegean, he begs the gods for ease."

that he never met with any well-attested instances; and if he should, he should impute them to chance, because all who pretend to that quality often fail in their predictions, though they take a great scope, and sometimes interpret literally, sometimes figuratively, so as to suit the events. He told us that, since he came to be minister of the parish where he now is, the belief of witchcraft, or charms, was very common, insomuch that he had many prosecutions before his *session* (the parochial ecclesiastical court) against women, for having by these means carried off the milk from people's cows. He disregarded them, and there is not now the least vestige of that superstition. He preached against it, and in order to give a strong proof to the people that there was nothing in it, he said from the pulpit, that every woman in the parish was welcome to take the milk from his cows, provided she did not touch them.

Dr. Johnson asked him as to Fingal.[17] He said he could repeat some passages in the original; that he heard his grandfather had a copy of it; but that he could not affirm that Ossian composed all that poem as it is now published. This came pretty much to what Dr. Johnson had maintained, though he goes farther, and contends that it is no better than such an epic poem as he could make from the song of Robin Hood, that is to say, that, except a few passages, there is nothing truly ancient but the names and some vague traditions. Mr. M'Queen alleged that Homer was made up of detached fragments. Dr. Johnson denied this, observing that it had been one work originally, and that you could not put a book of the *Iliad* out of its place; and he believed the same might be said of the *Odyssey*.

The approach to Raasay was very pleasing. We saw before us a beautiful bay, well defended by a rocky coast; a good family mansion; a fine verdure about it — with a considerable number of trees — and beyond it hills and mountains in gradation of wildness. Our boatmen sung with great spirit. Dr. Johnson observed, that naval music was very ancient. As we came near the shore, the singing of

our rowers was succeeded by that of reapers, who were busy at work, and who seemed to shout as much as to sing, while they worked with a bounding activity. Just as we landed, I observed a cross, or rather the ruins of one, upon a rock, which had to me a pleasing vestige of religion. I perceived a large company coming out from the house. We met them as we walked up. There were Raasay himself; his brother Dr. Macleod; his nephew the Laird of M'Kinnon; the Laird of Macleod; Colonel Macleod of Talisker, an officer in the Dutch service, a very genteel man, and a faithful branch of the family; Mr. Macleod of Muiravenside, best known by the name of Sandie Macleod, who was long in exile on account of the part which he took in 1745; and several other persons. We were welcomed upon the green, and conducted into the house, where we were introduced to Lady Raasay, who was surrounded by a numerous family, consisting of three sons and ten daughters. The laird of Raasay is a sensible, polite, and most hospitable gentleman. I was told that his island of Raasay, and that of Rona (from which the eldest son of the family has his title) and a considerable extent of land which he has in Skye, do not altogether yield him a very large revenue: and yet he lives in great splendor; and so far is he from distressing his people that, in the present rage for emigration, not a man has left his estate.

It was past six o'clock when we arrived. Some excellent brandy was served round immediately, according to the custom of the Highlands, where a dram is generally taken every day. They call it a *scalch*. On a sideboard was placed for us, who had come off the sea, a substantial dinner, and a variety of wines. Then we had coffee and tea. I observed in the room several elegantly bound books, and other marks of improved life. Soon afterwards a fiddler appeared, and a little ball began. Raasay himself danced with as much spirit as any man, and Malcolm bounded like a roe. Sandie Macleod, who has at times an excessive flow of spirits, and had it now, was, in his days of absconding, known by the name of *M'Cruslick,* which it seems was the designation of a kind of wild man in the Highlands, something between Proteus and Don Quixote; and so he was called here. He made much jovial noise. Dr. Johnson was so delighted with this scene that he said, "I know not how we shall get away." It entertained me to observe him sitting by, while we danced, sometimes in deep meditation — sometimes smiling complacently — sometimes looking

---

17. **Fingal:** The first of the so-called "epic" poems "discovered" (really composed) by James Macpherson, and based in small part upon Gaelic legend. It had a hero of the same name, and was in six "books" of cadenced prose. The legend was that Ossian, the bardic author, was Fingal's son, and that his poems had been preserved in oral tradition since the early centuries of the Christian era. Fingal was king of the Gaels, and defended his country against invasion from abroad. Macpherson stood on his own bare word, and "scorned" to produce documentary evidence in support.

upon Hooke's *Roman History* — and sometimes talking a little, amidst the noise of the ball, to Mr. Donald M'Queen, who anxiously gathered knowledge from him. He was pleased with M'Queen, and said to me, "This is a critical man, sir. There must be great vigor of mind to make him cultivate learning so much in the Isle of Skye, where he might do without it. It is wonderful how many of the new publications he has. There must be a snatch of every opportunity." Mr. M'Queen told me that his brother (who is the fourth generation of the family following each other as ministers of the parish of Snizort) and he joined together, and bought from time to time such books as had reputation. Soon after we came in, a black cock and gray hen, which had been shot, were shown, with their feathers on, to Dr. Johnson, who had never seen that species of bird before. We had a company of thirty at supper, and all was good humor and gaiety, without intemperance.

Thursday, 16th September

Last night much care was taken of Dr. Johnson, who was still distressed by his cold. He had hitherto most strangely slept without a nightcap. Miss M'Leod made him a large flannel one, and he was prevailed with to drink a little brandy when he was going to bed. He has great virtue, in not drinking wine or any fermented liquor, because, as he acknowledged to us, he could not do it in moderation. Lady M'Leod would hardly believe him, and said, "I am sure, sir, you would not carry it too far." JOHNSON: "Nay, madam, it carried me. I took the opportunity of a long illness to leave it off. It was then prescribed to me not to drink wine; and having broken off the habit, I have never returned to it."

In the argument on Tuesday night, about natural goodness, Dr. Johnson denied that any child was better than another, but by difference of instruction; though, in consequence of greater attention being paid to instruction by one child than another, and of a variety of imperceptible causes, such as instruction being counteracted by servants, a notion was conceived, that of two children, equally well educated, one was naturally much worse than another. He owned, this morning, that one might have a greater aptitude to learn than another, and that we inherit dispositions from our parents. "I inherited," said he, "a vile melancholy from my father, which has made me mad

all my life, at least not sober." Lady M'Leod wondered he should tell this. "Madam," said I, "he knows that with that madness he is superior to other men."

I have often been astonished with what exactness and perspicuity he will explain the process of any art. He this morning explained to us all the operation of coining, and, at night, all the operation of brewing, so very clearly, that Mr. M'Queen said, when he heard the first, he thought he had been bred in the Mint; when he heard the second, that he had been bred a brewer.

I was elated by the thought of having been able to entice such a man to this remote part of the world. A ludicrous, yet just, image presented itself to my mind, which I expressed to the company. I compared myself to a dog who has got hold of a large piece of meat, and runs away with it to a corner, where he may devour it in peace, without any fear of others taking it from him. "In London, Reynolds, Beauclerk, and all of them, are contending who shall enjoy Dr. Johnson's conversation. We are feasting upon it, undisturbed, at Dunvegan."

It was still a storm of wind and rain. Dr. Johnson, however, walked out with M'Leod, and saw Rorie More's cascade in full perfection. Colonel M'Leod, instead of being all life and gaiety, as I have seen him, was at present grave, and somewhat depressed by his anxious concern about M'Leod's affairs, and by finding some gentlemen of the clan by no means disposed to act a generous or affectionate part to their chief in his distress, but bargaining with him as with a stranger. However, he was agreeable and polite, and Dr. Johnson said, he was a very pleasing man. My fellow traveler and I talked of going to Sweden; and, while we were settling our plan, I expressed a pleasure in the prospect of seeing the king. JOHNSON: "I doubt, sir, if he would speak to us." Colonel M'Leod said, "I am sure Mr. Boswell would speak to *him*." But, seeing me a little disconcerted by his remark, he politely added, "And with great propriety." Here let me offer a short defense of that propensity in my disposition, to which this gentleman alluded. It has procured me much happiness. I hope it does not deserve so hard a name as either forwardness or impudence. If I know myself, it is nothing more than an eagerness to share the society of men distinguished either by their rank or their talents, and a diligence to attain what I desire. If a man is praised for seeking knowledge, though mountains and seas are in his way, may he not be pardoned, whose ardor, in the pursuit of the same object, leads him to encounter difficulties as great, though of a different kind?

After the ladies were gone from table, we talked of the Highlanders not having sheets; and this led us to consider the advantage of wearing linen. JOHNSON: "All animal substances are less cleanly than vegetables. Wool, of which flannel is made, is an animal substance; flannel therefore is not so cleanly as linen. I remember I used to think tar dirty, but when I knew it to be only a preparation of the juice of the pine, I thought so no longer. It is not disagreeable to have the gum that oozes from a plum tree upon your fingers, because it is vegetable; but if you have any candle grease, any tallow upon your fingers, you are uneasy till you rub it off. I have often thought that, if I kept a seraglio, the ladies should all wear linen gowns, or cotton; I mean stuffs made of vegetable substances. I would have no silk; you cannot tell when it is clean. It will be very nasty before it is perceived to be so. Linen detects its own dirtiness."

To hear the grave Dr. Samuel Johnson, "that majestic teacher of moral and religious wisdom," while sitting solemn in an armchair in the Isle of Skye, talk, *ex cathedra,* of his keeping a seraglio, and acknowledge that the supposition had *often* been in his thoughts, struck me so forcibly with ludicrous contrast, that I could not but laugh immoderately. He was too proud to submit, even for a moment, to be the object of ridicule, and instantly retaliated with such keen sarcastic wit, and such a variety of degrading images, of every one of which I was the object, that, though I can bear such attacks as well as most men, I yet found myself so much the sport of all the company, that I would gladly expunge from my mind every trace of this severe retort. . . .

Sunday, 3d October

While we were chatting in the indolent style of men who were to stay here all this day at least, we were suddenly roused by being told that the wind was fair, that a little fleet of herring-busses was passing by for Mull, and that Mr. Simpson's vessel was about to sail. Hugh M'Donald, the skipper, came to us, and was impatient that we should get ready, which we soon did. Dr. Johnson, with composure and solemnity, repeated the observation of Epictetus, that "As man has the voyage of death before him, whatever may be his employ-

ment, he should be ready at the master's call; and an old man should never be far from the shore, lest he should not be able to get himself ready." He rode, and I and the other gentlemen walked, about an English mile to the shore, where the vessel lay. Dr. Johnson said, he should never forget Skye, and returned thanks for all civilities. We were carried to the vessel in a small boat which she had, and we set sail very briskly about one o'clock. I was much pleased with the motion for many hours. Dr. Johnson grew sick, and retired under cover, as it rained a good deal. I kept above, that I might have fresh air, and finding myself not affected by the motion of the vessel, I exulted in being a stout seaman, while Dr. Johnson was quite in a state of annihilation. But I was soon humbled, for after imagining that I could go with ease to America or the East Indies, I became very sick, but kept aboveboard, though it rained hard.

As we had been detained so long in Skye by bad weather, we gave up the scheme that Coll [18] had planned for us of visiting several islands, and contented ourselves with the prospect of seeing Mull, and Icolmkill and Inch Kenneth, which lie near to it.

Mr. Simpson was sanguine in his hopes for a while, the wind being fair for us. He said, he would land us at Icolmkill that night. But when the wind failed, it was resolved we should make for the Sound of Mull, and land in the harbor of Tobermory. We kept near the five herring vessels for some time, but afterwards four of them got before us, and one little wherry fell behind us. When we got in full view of the point of Ardnamurchan, the wind changed, and was directly against our getting into the sound. We were then obliged to tack, and get forward in that tedious manner. As we advanced, the storm grew greater, and the sea very rough. Coll then began to talk of making for Eigg, or Canna, or his own island. Our skipper said, he would get us into the Sound. Having struggled for this a good while in vain, he said, he would push forward till we were near the land of Mull, where we might cast anchor, and lie till the morning; for although, before this, there had been a good moon, and I had pretty distinctly seen not only the land of Mull, but up the Sound, and the country of Morven as at one end of it, the night was now grown very dark. Our crew consisted of one M'Donald, our skipper,

18. Coll: The young laird of the island of Coll, Donald Maclean, who was only a year later to meet death by drowning.

and two sailors, one of whom had but one eye; Mr. Simpson himself, Coll, and Hugh M'Donald his servant, all helped. Simpson said, he would willingly go for Coll, if young Coll or his servant would undertake to pilot us to a harbor; but, as the island is low land, it was dangerous to run upon it in the dark. Coll and his servant appeared a little dubious. The scheme of running for Canna seemed then to be embraced; but Canna was ten leagues off, all out of our way; and they were afraid to attempt the harbor of Eigg. All these different plans were successively in agitation. The old skipper still tried to make for the land of Mull, but then it was considered that there was no place there where we could anchor in safety. Much time was lost in striving against the storm. At last it became so rough, and threatened to be so much worse, that Coll and his servant took more courage, and said they would undertake to hit one of the harbors in Coll. "Then let us run for it in God's name," said the skipper; and instantly we turned towards it. The little wherry which had fallen behind us, had hard work. The master begged that, if we made for Coll, we should put out a light to him. Accordingly one of the sailors waved a glowing peat for some time. The various difficulties that were started, gave me a good deal of apprehension, from which I was relieved, when I found we were to run for a harbor before the wind. But my relief was but of short duration, for I soon heard that our sails were very bad, and were in danger of being torn in pieces, in which case we should be driven upon the rocky shore of Coll. It was very dark, and there was a heavy and incessant rain. The sparks of the burning peat flew so much about, that I dreaded the vessel might take fire. Then, as Coll was a sportsman, and had powder on board, I figured that we might be blown up. Simpson and he appeared a little frightened, which made me more so; and the perpetual talking, or rather shouting, which was carried on in Erse, alarmed me still more. A man is always suspicious of what is saying in an unknown tongue; and, if fear be his passion at the time, he grows more afraid. Our vessel often lay so much on one side, that I trembled lest she should be overset; and indeed they told me afterwards, that they had run her sometimes to within an inch of the water, so anxious were they to make what haste they could before the night should be worse. I now saw what I never saw before, a prodigious sea, with immense billows coming upon a vessel, so as that it seemed hardly possible to escape. There was something grandly horrible in the sight. I am glad I have seen it once. Amidst all these terrifying circumstances, I endeavored to compose my mind. It was not easy to do it, for all the stories that I had heard of the dangerous sailing among the Hebrides, which is proverbial, came full upon my recollection. When I thought of those who were dearest to me, and would suffer severely, should I be lost, I upbraided myself, as not having a sufficient cause for putting myself in such danger. Piety afforded me comfort, yet I was disturbed by the objections that have been made against a particular Providence, and by the arguments of those who maintain that it is in vain to hope that the petitions of an individual, or even of congregations, can have any influence with the Deity — objections which have been often made, and which Dr. Hawkesworth has lately revived, in his Preface to the *Voyages to the South Seas* [19] — but Dr. Ogden's excellent doctrine on the efficacy of intercession prevailed.

It was half an hour after eleven before we set ourselves in the course for Coll. As I saw them all busy doing something, I asked Coll, with much earnestness, what I could do. He, with a happy readiness, put into my hand a rope, which was fixed to the top of one of the masts, and told me to hold it till he bade me pull. If I had considered the matter, I might have seen that this could not be of the least service; but his object was to keep me out of the way of those who were busy working the vessel, and at the same time to divert my fear, by employing me, and making me think that I was of use. Thus did I stand firm to my post, while the wind and rain beat upon me, always expecting a call to pull my rope.

The man with one eye steered; old M'Donald, and Coll and his servant, lay upon the forecastle, looking sharp out for the harbor. It was necessary to carry much *cloth,* as they termed it, that is to say, much sail, in order to keep the vessel off the shore of Coll. This made violent plunging in a rough sea. At last they spied the harbor of Lochiern, and Coll cried, "Thank GOD, we are safe!" We ran up till we were opposite to it, and soon afterwards we got into it, and cast anchor.

Dr. Johnson had all this time been quiet and unconcerned. He had lain down on one of the beds,

19. *Voyages . . . Seas:* Dr. John Hawkesworth edited the accounts of Captain Cook's first voyage, in three volumes, 1773.

and having got free from sickness, was satisfied. The truth is, he knew nothing of the danger we were in, but, fearless and unconcerned, might have said, in the words which he has chosen for the motto to his *Rambler,*

Quo me cunque rapit tempestas, deferor hospes.[20]

Once, during the doubtful consultations, he asked whither we were going; and upon being told that it was not certain whether to Mull or Coll, he cried, "Coll for my money!" I now went down, with Coll and Mr. Simpson, to visit him. He was lying in philosophic tranquillity, with a greyhound of Coll's at his back, keeping him warm. . . .

from THE LIFE OF SAMUEL JOHNSON

Not much about the *Life of Johnson* need be added here to what has been already said in the Introduction. After the success of the *Tour* — really a segment of the *Life* — Boswell saw that he could not evade the longer task. He was irresolute, however, from the mere bulk of his collected materials, and was also distracted by his desire to get into politics and become a member of parliament. Supported again by Malone, he set to work in the summer of 1786 to weave together in a connected narrative the biographical facts, the letters of Johnson, and the conversational episodes that originally formed portions of his own sprawling autobiographical record, but were now to find their proper places in a new configuration. As Geoffrey Scott, the brilliant editor of Boswell's journals, who died in 1929, has remarked, there was in the task so much of the mere drudgery of transcription, and so much of troublesome verification of historical fact, that the exhilaration of creative effort could play only a relatively small part in the act of composition. Boswell often sank under the burden of it. But he managed to keep faith with his responsibility and, at last, after nearly five years of toil, brought it to completion. During this period his wife died, but, although she had been a steadying influence, it is unlikely that with her conventional ideas of propriety, she could have given him in this work very much support or encouragement. The *Life* was published on May 16, 1791, and, in a little more than a year, the first edition had been sold off with a profit to Boswell of nearly the exact amount that Johnson received for the Dictionary. In celebration, he gave a little dinner to his bookseller, his friends, and children. He records: " I got into a pretty good state of joviality, though still dreary at bottom." The immediate satisfactions were relatively inconsiderable; his true rewards were posthumous.

20. "For as the tempest drives, I shape my way" (Francis). Horace, *Epistles*, I.i.15.

1763

This is to me a memorable year, for in it I had the happiness to obtain the acquaintance of that extraordinary man whose memoirs I am now writing, an acquaintance which I shall ever esteem as one of the most fortunate circumstances in my life. Though then but two-and-twenty, I had for several years read his works with delight and instruction, and had the highest reverence for their author, which had grown up in my fancy into a kind of mysterious veneration, by figuring to myself a state of solemn elevated abstraction, in which I supposed him to live in the immense metropolis of London. Mr. Gentleman, a native of Ireland, who passed some years in Scotland as a player, and as an instructor in the English language, a man whose talents and worth were depressed by misfortunes, had given me a representation of the figure and manner of " Dictionary Johnson," as he was then generally called; and during my first visit to London, which was for three months in 1760, Mr. Derrick the poet, who was Gentleman's friend and countryman, flattered me with hopes that he would introduce me to Johnson, an honor of which I was very ambitious. But he never found an opportunity, which made me doubt that he had promised to do what was not in his power; till Johnson some years afterwards told me, " Derrick, sir, might very well have introduced you. I had a kindness for Derrick, and am sorry he is dead."

In the summer of 1761 Mr. Thomas Sheridan[1] was at Edinburgh, and delivered lectures upon the English language and public speaking to large and respectable audiences. I was often in his company, and heard him frequently expatiate upon Johnson's extraordinary knowledge, talents, and virtues, repeat his pointed sayings, describe his particularities, and boast of his being his guest sometimes till two or three in the morning. At his house I hoped to have many opportunities of seeing the sage, as Mr. Sheridan obligingly assured me I should not be disappointed.

When I returned to London in the end of 1762, to my surprise and regret I found an irreconcilable difference had taken place between Johnson and Sheridan. A pension of two hundred pounds a year had been given to Sheridan. Johnson, who, as has

LIFE OF JOHNSON.   1. Sheridan: son of a famous father, and father of a more famous son: the former was the close friend of Swift; the latter was the dramatist, Richard Brinsley Sheridan. Thomas was himself an actor and author, as well as a lecturer on elocution.

been already mentioned, thought slightingly of Sheridan's art, upon hearing that he was also pensioned, exclaimed, "What! have they given *him* a pension? Then it is time for me to give up mine." Whether this proceeded from a momentary indignation, as if it were an affront to his exalted merit that a player should be rewarded in the same manner with him, or was the sudden effect of a fit of peevishness, it was unluckily said, and, indeed, cannot be justified. Mr. Sheridan's pension was granted to him not as a player but as a sufferer in the cause of government, when he was manager of the Theatre Royal in Ireland, when parties ran high in 1753. And it must also be allowed that he was a man of literature, and had considerably improved the arts of reading and speaking with distinctness and propriety. . . .

Johnson complained that a man who disliked him repeated his sarcasm to Mr. Sheridan, without telling him what followed, which was, that after a pause he added, "However, I am glad that Mr. Sheridan has a pension, for he is a very good man." Sheridan could never forgive this hasty contemptuous expression. It rankled in his mind; and though I informed him of all that Johnson said, and that he would be very glad to meet him amicably, he positively declined repeated offers which I made, and once went off abruptly from a house where he and I were engaged to dine, because he was told that Dr. Johnson was to be there. I have no sympathetic feeling with such persevering resentment. It is painful when there is a breach between those who have lived together socially and cordially; and I wonder that there is not, in all such cases, a mutual wish that it should be healed. I could perceive that Mr. Sheridan was by no means satisfied with Johnson's acknowledging him to be a good man. That could not soothe his injured vanity. I could not but smile, at the same time that I was offended, to observe Sheridan, in the *Life of Swift* which he afterwards published, attempting, in the writhings of his resentment, to depreciate Johnson, by characterizing him as "A writer of gigantic fame in these days of little men"; that very Johnson whom he once so highly admired and venerated.

This rupture with Sheridan deprived Johnson of one of his most agreeable resources for amusement in his lonely evenings, for Sheridan's well-informed, animated, and bustling mind never suffered conversation to stagnate, and Mrs. Sheridan was a most agreeable companion to an intellectual man. She was sensible, ingenious, unassuming, yet communicative. I recollect, with satisfaction, many pleasing hours which I passed with her under the hospitable roof of her husband, who was to me a very kind friend. Her novel, entitled *Memoirs of Miss Sydney Biddulph,* contains an excellent moral, while it inculcates a future state of retribution; and what it teaches is impressed upon the mind by a series of as deep distress as can affect humanity, in the amiable and pious heroine who goes to her grave unrelieved, but resigned, and full of hope of "Heaven's mercy." Johnson paid her this high compliment upon it: "I know not, madam, that you have a right, upon moral principles, to make your readers suffer so much."

Mr. Thomas Davies the actor, who then kept a bookseller's shop in Russell Street, Covent Garden, told me that Johnson was very much his friend, and came frequently to his house, where he more than once invited me to meet him; but by some unlucky accident or other he was prevented from coming to us.

Mr. Thomas Davies was a man of good understanding and talents, with the advantage of a liberal education. Though somewhat pompous, he was an entertaining companion; and his literary performances have no inconsiderable share of merit. He was a friendly and very hospitable man. Both he and his wife (who has been celebrated for her beauty), though upon the stage for many years, maintained an uniform decency of character; and Johnson esteemed them, and lived in as easy an intimacy with them as with any family which he used to visit. Mr. Davies recollected several of Johnson's remarkable sayings, and was one of the best of the many imitators of his voice and manner, while relating them. He increased my impatience more and more to see the extraordinary man whose works I highly valued, and whose conversation was reported to be so peculiarly excellent.

At last, on Monday the 16th of May, when I was sitting in Mr. Davies's back parlor, after having drunk tea with him and Mrs. Davies, Johnson unexpectedly came into the shop; and Mr. Davies having perceived him through the glass door in the room in which we were sitting, advancing towards us, he announced his awful approach to me, somewhat in the manner of an actor in the part of Horatio, when he addresses Hamlet on the appearance of his father's ghost, "Look, my lord, it comes." I found that I had a very perfect idea of Johnson's figure, from the portrait of him painted by Sir Joshua Reynolds soon after he had published his Dictionary, in the attitude of sitting in his easy chair in deep meditation; which was the first picture his friend did for him, which Sir Joshua very kindly presented to me, and from which an engraving has been made for this work. Mr. Davies mentioned my name, and respectfully introduced me to him. I was much agitated, and recollecting his prejudice against the Scotch, of which I had heard much, I said to Davies, "Don't tell where I come from." "From Scotland," cried Davies, roguishly. "Mr. Johnson," said I, "I do indeed come from Scotland, but I cannot help it." I am willing to flatter myself that I meant this as light pleasantry to soothe and conciliate him, and not as an humiliating abasement at the expense of my country. But however that might be, this speech was somewhat unlucky; for with that quickness of wit for which he was so remarkable, he seized the expression "come from Scotland," which I used in the sense of being of that country; and, as if I had said that I had come away from it, or left it, retorted, "That, sir, I find, is what a very great many of your countrymen cannot help." This stroke stunned me a good deal; and when we had sat down, I felt myself not a little embarrassed, and apprehensive of what might come next. He then addressed himself to Davies: "What do you think of Garrick? He has refused me an order for the play for Miss Williams,[2] because he knows the house will be full, and that an order would be worth three shillings." Eager to take any opening to get into conversation with him, I ventured to say, "O, sir, I cannot think Mr. Garrick would grudge such a trifle to you." "Sir," said he, with a stern look, "I have known David Garrick longer than you have done: and I know no right you have to talk to me on the subject." Perhaps I deserved this check, for it was rather presumptuous in me, an entire stranger, to express any doubt of the justice of his animadversion upon his old acquaintance and pupil.[3] I now felt myself much mortified, and began to think that the hope which I had long indulged of obtaining his acquaintance was blasted. And, in truth, had not my ardor been uncommonly strong, and my resolution uncommonly persevering, so rough a reception might have deterred me forever from making any further attempts. Fortunately, however, I remained upon the field not wholly discomfited, and was soon rewarded by hearing some of his conversation, of which I preserved the following short minute, without marking the questions and observations by which it was produced.

"People," he remarked, "may be taken in once, who imagine that an author is greater in private life than other men. Uncommon parts require uncommon opportunities for their exertion.

"In barbarous society, superiority of parts is of real consequence. Great strength or great wisdom is of much value to an individual. But in more polished times there are people to do everything for money; and then there are a number of other superiorities, such as those of birth and fortune, and rank, that dissipate men's attention, and leave no extraordinary share of respect for personal and intellectual superiority. This is wisely ordered by Providence, to preserve some equality among mankind."

"Sir, this book (*The Elements of Criticism*,[4] which he had taken up) is a pretty essay, and deserves to be held in some estimation, though much of it is chimerical."

Speaking of one who with more than ordinary boldness attacked public measures and the royal family, he said, "I think he is safe from the law, but he is an abusive scoundrel; and instead of applying to my Lord Chief Justice to punish him, I would send half a dozen footmen and have him well ducked."

"The notion of liberty amuses the people of England, and helps to keep off the *taedium vitae*. When a butcher tells you that *his heart bleeds for his country,* he has, in fact, no uneasy feeling."

"Sheridan will not succeed at Bath with his oratory. Ridicule has gone down before him, and, I doubt, Derrick is his enemy."[5]

"Derrick may do very well, as long as he can outrun his character, but the moment his character gets up with him, it is all over."

2. **Miss Williams:** Anna Williams was a blind lady who lived mostly under Johnson's hospitable roof from 1752 until her death in 1783. She was a peevish inmate, but Johnson gave her credit for "universal curiosity and comprehensive knowledge." She had literary ambitions, and he helped her to publish *Miscellanies in Prose and Verse* in 1766.   3. "That this was a momentary sally against Garrick there can be no doubt; for at Johnson's desire he had, some years before, given a benefit night at his theater to this very person, by which he had got two hundred pounds. Johnson, indeed, upon all other occasions, when I was in his company, praised the very liberal charity of Garrick. I once mentioned to him, 'It is observed, sir, that you attack Garrick yourself, but will suffer nobody else to do it.' Johnson (smiling): 'Why, sir, that is true'" [B].

4. *Elements of Criticism:* by Henry Home, Lord Kames (1762 and later dates).   5. "Mr. Sheridan was then reading lectures upon oratory at Bath, where Derrick was master of the ceremonies, or, as the phrase is, King" [B].

It is, however, but just to record, that some years afterwards, when I reminded him of this sarcasm, he said, "Well, but Derrick has now got a character that he need not run away from."

I was highly pleased with the extraordinary vigor of his conversation, and regretted that I was drawn away from it by an engagement at another place. I had, for a part of the evening, been left alone with him, and had ventured to make an observation now and then, which he received very civilly; so that I was satisfied that though there was a roughness in his manner, there was no ill nature in his disposition. Davies followed me to the door, and when I complained to him a little of the hard blows which the great man had given me, he kindly took upon him to console me by saying, "Don't be uneasy. I can see he likes you very well."

A few days afterwards I called on Davies, and asked him if he thought I might take the liberty of waiting on Mr. Johnson at his chambers in the Temple.[6] He said I certainly might, and that Mr. Johnson would take it as a compliment. So upon Tuesday the 24th of May, after having been enlivened by the witty sallies of Messrs. Thornton, Wilkes, Churchill, and Lloyd,[7] with whom I had passed the morning, I boldly repaired to Johnson. His chambers were on the first floor of No. 1, Inner Temple Lane, and I entered them with an impression given me by the Rev. Dr. Blair,[8] of Edinburgh, who had been introduced to him not long before, and described his having "found the Giant in his den," an expression which, when I came to be pretty well acquainted with Johnson, I repeated to him, and he was diverted at this picturesque account of himself. Dr. Blair had been presented to him by Dr. James Fordyce. At this time the controversy concerning the pieces published by Mr. James Macpherson, as translations of Ossian, was at its height. Johnson had all along denied their authenticity, and, what was still more provoking to their admirers, maintained that they had no merit. The subject having been introduced by Dr. Fordyce, Dr. Blair, relying on the internal evidence of their antiquity, asked Dr. Johnson whether

he thought any man of a modern age could have written such poems? Johnson replied, "Yes, sir, many men, many women, and many children." Johnson, at this time, did not know that Dr. Blair had just published a dissertation, not only defending their authenticity, but seriously ranking them with the poems of Homer and Virgil; and when he was afterwards informed of this circumstance, he expressed some displeasure at Dr. Fordyce's having suggested the topic, and said, "I am not sorry that they got thus much for their pains. Sir, it was like leading one to talk of a book, when the author is concealed behind the door."

He received me very courteously, but it must be confessed that his apartment and furniture and morning dress were sufficiently uncouth. His brown suit of clothes looked very rusty; he had on a little old shriveled unpowdered wig, which was too small for his head; his shirt-neck and knees of his breeches were loose; his black worsted stockings ill drawn up; and he had a pair of unbuckled shoes by way of slippers. But all these slovenly particularities were forgotten the moment that he began to talk. Some gentlemen, whom I do not recollect, were sitting with him; and when they went away, I also rose; but he said to me, "Nay, don't go." "Sir," said I, "I am afraid that I intrude upon you. It is benevolent to allow me to sit and hear you." He seemed pleased with this compliment, which I sincerely paid him, and answered, "Sir, I am obliged to any man who visits me." I have preserved the following short minute of what passed this day.

"Madness frequently discovers itself merely by unnecessary deviation from the usual modes of the world. My poor friend Smart showed the disturbance of his mind by falling upon his knees and saying his prayers in the street, or in any other unusual place. Now although, rationally speaking, it is greater madness not to pray at all than to pray as Smart did, I am afraid there are so many who do not pray, that their understanding is not called in question."

Concerning this unfortunate poet, Christopher Smart, who was confined in a madhouse, he had, at another time, the following conversation with Dr. Burney.[9] BURNEY: "How does poor Smart do, sir; is he likely to recover?" JOHNSON: "It seems as if his mind had ceased to struggle with the disease; for he grows fat upon it." BURNEY: "Perhaps, sir, that may be from want of exercise."

6. Temple: one of the Law Societies, or "Inns of Court." There are four of these residential colleges, dating from medieval times: Lincoln's Inn, Gray's Inn, and the Inner and Middle Temple. They have the sole right of admitting to the English bar.   7. Thornton . . . Lloyd: Bonnell Thornton and Robert Lloyd were minor literary figures at this time. For the demagogue John Wilkes, see Intro., pp. 852–53. Wilkes was assisted by the satirist Charles Churchill in his attacks on the government in the antiministerial journal, the North Briton, for the forty-fifth number of which he was expelled from parliament.   8. Dr. Blair: Hugh Blair was the author of admired sermons and lectures on literary subjects.

9. Dr. Burney: Dr. Charles Burney was a well-known musician, historian of music, and father of the novelist, Fanny Burney.

JOHNSON: " No, sir; he has partly as much exercise as he used to have, for he digs in the garden. Indeed, before his confinement, he used for exercise to walk to the alehouse, but he was *carried* back again. I did not think he ought to be shut up. His infirmities were not noxious to society. He insisted on people praying with him; and I'd as lief pray with Kit Smart as anyone else. Another charge was, that he did not love clean linen; and I have no passion for it."

Johnson continued. " Mankind have a great aversion to intellectual labor, but even supposing knowledge to be easily attainable, more people would be content to be ignorant than would take even a little trouble to acquire it."

" The morality of an action depends on the motive from which we act. If I fling half a crown to a beggar with intention to break his head, and he picks it up and buys victuals with it, the physical effect is good; but, with respect to me, the action is very wrong. So, religious exercises, if not performed with an intention to please God, avail us nothing. As our Savior says of those who perform them from other motives, ' Verily they have their reward.' "

" The Christian religion has very strong evidences. It, indeed, appears in some degree strange to reason; but in history we have undoubted facts, against which, in reasoning *à priori,* we have more arguments than we have for them; but then, testimony has great weight, and casts the balance. I would recommend to every man whose faith is yet unsettled, Grotius — Dr. Pearson — and Dr. Clarke." [10]

Talking of Garrick, he said, " He is the first man in the world for sprightly conversation."

When I rose a second time, he again pressed me to stay, which I did.

He told me that he generally went abroad at four in the afternoon, and seldom came home till two in the morning. I took the liberty to ask if he did not think it wrong to live thus, and not make more use of his great talents. He owned it was a bad habit. On reviewing, at the distance of many years, my journal of this period, I wonder how, at my first visit, I ventured to talk to him so freely, and that he bore it with so much indulgence.

Before we parted, he was so good as to promise

to favor me with his company one evening at my lodgings; and, as I took my leave, shook me cordially by the hand. It is almost needless to add that I felt no little elation at having now so happily established an acquaintance of which I had been so long ambitious.

My readers will, I trust, excuse me for being thus minutely circumstantial, when it is considered that the acquaintance of Dr. Johnson was to me a most valuable acquisition, and laid the foundation of whatever instruction and entertainment they may receive from my collections concerning the great subject of the work which they are now perusing.

I did not visit him again till Monday, June 13, at which time I recollect no part of his conversation, except that when I told him I had been to see Johnson ride upon three horses, he said, " Such a man, sir, should be encouraged, for his performances show the extent of the human powers in one instance, and thus tend to raise our opinion of the faculties of man. He shows what may be attained by persevering application; so that every man may hope, that by giving as much application, although perhaps he may never ride three horses at a time, or dance upon a wire, yet he may be equally expert in whatever profession he has chosen to pursue."

He again shook me by the hand at parting, and asked me why I did not come oftener to him. Trusting that I was now in his good graces, I answered, that he had not given me much encouragement, and reminded him of the check I had received from him at our first interview. " Poh, poh! " said he, with a complacent smile, " never mind these things. Come to me as often as you can. I shall be glad to see you."

I had learned that his place of frequent resort was the Mitre Tavern in Fleet Street, where he loved to sit up late, and I begged I might be allowed to pass an evening with him there soon, which he promised I should. A few days afterwards I met him near Temple Bar, about one o'clock in the morning, and asked if he would then go to the Mitre. " Sir," said he, " it is too late; they won't let us in. But I'll go with you another night with all my heart."

A revolution of some importance in my plan of life had just taken place; for instead of procuring a commission in the foot guards, which was my own inclination, I had, in compliance with my father's wishes, agreed to study the law, and was soon to set out for Utrecht, to hear the lectures

10. Grotius . . . Clarke: These were all famous seventeenth-century writers on divinity. Grotius was a great Dutch jurist as well.

of an excellent civilian in that university, and then to proceed on my travels. Though very desirous of obtaining Dr. Johnson's advice and instructions on the mode of pursuing my studies, I was at this time so occupied, shall I call it? or so dissipated, by the amusements of London, that our next meeting was not till Saturday, June 25, when, happening to dine at Clifton's eating house, in Butcher Row, I was surprised to perceive Johnson come in and take his seat at another table. The mode of dining, or rather being fed, at such houses in London, is well known to many to be particularly unsocial, as there is no ordinary, or united company, but each person has his own mess, and is under no obligation to hold any intercourse with anyone. A liberal and full-minded man, however, who loves to talk, will break through this churlish and unsocial restraint. Johnson and an Irish gentleman got into a dispute concerning the cause of some part of mankind being black. "Why, sir," said Johnson, "it has been accounted for in three ways: either by supposing that they are the posterity of Ham, who was cursed; or that God at first created two kinds of men, one black and another white; or that by the heat of the sun the skin is scorched, and so acquires a sooty hue. This matter has been much canvassed among naturalists, but has never been brought to any certain issue." What the Irishman said is totally obliterated from my mind, but I remember that he became very warm and intemperate in his expressions, upon which Johnson rose, and quietly walked away. When he had retired, his antagonist took his revenge, as he thought, by saying, "He has a most ungainly figure, and an affectation of pomposity, unworthy of a man of genius."

Johnson had not observed that I was in the room. I followed him, however, and he agreed to meet me in the evening at the Mitre. I called on him, and we went thither at nine. We had a good supper, and port wine, of which he then sometimes drank a bottle. The orthodox High Church sound of the Mitre, the figure and manner of the celebrated Samuel Johnson, the extraordinary power and precision of his conversation, and the pride arising from finding myself admitted as his companion, produced a variety of sensations, and a pleasing elevation of mind beyond what I had ever before experienced. I find in my journal the following minute of our conversation, which, **though it will give but a very faint notion of what**

passed, is, in some degree, a valuable record; and it will be curious in this view, as showing how habitual to his mind were some opinions which appear in his works.

"Colley Cibber,[11] sir, was by no means a blockhead, but by arrogating to himself too much, he was in danger of losing that degree of estimation to which he was entitled. His friends gave out that he *intended* his birthday odes should be bad, but that was not the case, sir; for he kept them many months by him, and a few years before he died he showed me one of them, with great solicitude to render it as perfect as might be, and I made some corrections, to which he was not very willing to submit. I remember the following couplet in allusion to the king and himself:

> Perched on the eagle's soaring wing,
> The lowly linnet loves to sing.

Sir, he had heard something of the fabulous tale of the wren sitting upon the eagle's wing, and he had applied it to a linnet. Cibber's familiar style, however, was better than that which Whitehead[12] has assumed. *Grand* nonsense is insupportable. Whitehead is but a little man to inscribe verses to players."

I did not presume to controvert this censure, which was tinctured with his prejudice against players but I could not help thinking that a dramatic poet might with propriety pay a compliment to an eminent performer, as Whitehead has very happily done in his verses to Mr. Garrick.

"Sir, I do not think Gray a first-rate poet. He has not a bold imagination, nor much command of words. The obscurity in which he has involved himself will not persuade us that he is sublime. His 'Elegy in a Churchyard' has a happy selection of images, but I don't like what are called his great things. His Ode[13] which begins

> Ruin seize thee, ruthless King,
> Confusion on thy banners wait!

has been celebrated for its abruptness, and plunging into the subject all at once. But such arts as these have no merit, unless when they are original. We admire them only once; and this abruptness has nothing new in it. We have had it often before.

11. Cibber (1671–1757): poet laureate, actor, and playwright, whose *Apology* for his life (1740) came in for much ridicule, and who was raised to the throne of Dulness in Pope's revised *Dunciad*. See pp. 832–41, above. 12. **Whitehead**: William Whitehead also became poet laureate, and wrote plays and poems. 13. **Ode**: "The Bard," published in 1757.

Nay, we have it in the old song of 'Johnny Armstrong';

Is there ever a man in all Scotland,
From the highest estate to the lowest degree, etc.

And then, sir,

Yes, there is a man in Westmoreland
And Johnny Armstrong they do him call.

There, now, you plunge at once into the subject. You have no previous narration to lead you to it. The two next lines in that Ode are, I think, very good:

Though fanned by conquest's crimson wing,
They mock the air with idle state."

Here let it be observed, that although his opinion of Gray's poetry was widely different from mine, and I believe from that of most men of taste, by whom it is with justice highly admired, there is certainly much absurdity in the clamor which has been raised, as if he had been culpably injurious to the merit of that bard, and had been actuated by envy. Alas! ye little short-sighted critics, could Johnson be envious of the talents of any of his contemporaries? That his opinion on this subject was what in private and in public he uniformly expressed, regardless of what others might think, we may wonder, and perhaps regret; but it is shallow and unjust to charge him with expressing what he did not think.

Finding him in a placid humor, and wishing to avail myself of the opportunity which I fortunately had of consulting a sage, to hear whose wisdom, I conceived, in the ardor of youthful imagination, that men filled with a noble enthusiasm for intellectual improvement would gladly have resorted from distant lands, I opened my mind to him ingenuously, and gave him a little sketch of my life, to which he was pleased to listen with great attention.

I acknowledged that, though educated very strictly in the principles of religion, I had for some time been misled into a certain degree of infidelity; but that I was come now to a better way of thinking, and was fully satisfied of the truth of the Christian revelation, though I was not clear as to every point considered to be orthodox. Being at all times a curious examiner of the human mind, and pleased with an undisguised display of what had passed in it, he called to me with warmth, "Give me your hand; I have taken a liking to you." He then began to descant upon the force of testimony, and the little we could know of final causes; so that the objections of, why was it so? or why was it not so? ought not to disturb us; adding that he himself had at one period been guilty of a temporary neglect of religion, but that it was not the result of argument, but mere absence of thought.

After having given credit to reports of his bigotry, I was agreeably surprised when he expressed the following very liberal sentiment, which has the additional value of obviating an objection to our holy religion, founded upon the discordant tenets of Christians themselves: "For my part, sir, I think all Christians, whether Papists or Protestants, agree in the essential articles, and that their differences are trivial, and rather political than religious."

We talked of belief in ghosts. He said, "Sir, I make a distinction between what a man may experience by the mere strength of his imagination, and what imagination cannot possibly produce. Thus, suppose I should think that I saw a form, and heard a voice cry, 'Johnson, you are a very wicked fellow, and unless you repent you will certainly be punished'; my own unworthiness is so deeply impressed upon my mind, that I might *imagine* I thus saw and heard, and therefore I should not believe that an external communication had been made to me. But if a form should appear, and a voice should tell me that a particular man had died at a particular place, and a particular hour, a fact which I had no apprehension of, nor any means of knowing, and this fact, with all its circumstances, should afterwards be unquestionably proved, I should, in that case, be persuaded that I had supernatural intelligence imparted to me."

Here it is proper, once for all, to give a true and fair statement of Johnson's way of thinking upon the question, whether departed spirits are ever permitted to appear in this world, or in any way to operate upon human life. He has been ignorantly misrepresented as weakly credulous upon that subject; and, therefore, though I feel an inclination to disdain and treat with silent contempt so foolish a notion concerning my illustrious friend, yet as I find it has gained ground, it is necessary to refute it. The real fact then is, that Johnson had a very philosophical mind, and such a rational respect for testimony, as to make him submit his understanding to what was authentically proved, though he could not comprehend why it was so. Being thus disposed, he was willing to inquire into the truth of any relation of supernatural agency, a general belief of which has prevailed in all nations and ages. But so far was he from being the dupe of implicit faith, that he examined the matter with a jealous attention, and no man was more ready to refute its falsehood when he had discovered it. Churchill, in his poem entitled "The Ghost," availed himself of the absurd credulity imputed to Johnson, and drew a caricature of him under the name of "Pomposo," representing him as one of the believers of the story of a ghost in Cock Lane, which, in the year 1762, had gained very general credit in London. Many of my readers, I am convinced, are to this hour under an impression that Johnson was thus foolishly deceived. It will therefore surprise them a good deal when they are informed upon undoubted authority that Johnson was one of those by whom the imposture was detected. The story had become so popular that he thought it should be investigated; and in this research he was assisted by the Rev. Dr. Douglas, now Bishop of Salisbury, the great detector of impostures, who informs me that after the gentlemen who went and examined into the evidence were satisfied of its falsity, Johnson wrote in their presence an account of it, which was published in the newspapers and *Gentleman's Magazine,* and undeceived the world.

Our conversation proceeded. "Sir," said he, "I am a friend to subordination, as most conducive to the happiness of society. There is a reciprocal pleasure in governing and being governed."

"Dr. Goldsmith is one of the first men we now have as an author, and he is a very worthy man too. He has been loose in his principles, but he is coming right."

I mentioned Mallet's tragedy of *Elvira,* which had been acted the preceding winter at Drury Lane, and that the Hon. Andrew Erskine, Mr. Dempster,[14] and myself, had joined in writing a pamphlet, entitled *Critical Strictures,* against it. That the mildness of Dempster's disposition had, however, relented; and he had candidly said, "We have hardly a right to abuse this tragedy; for bad as it is, how vain should either of us be to write one not near so good." JOHNSON: "Why no, sir;

this is not just reasoning. You *may* abuse a tragedy, though you cannot write one. You may scold a carpenter who has made you a bad table, though you cannot make a table. It is not your trade to make tables."

When I talked to him of the paternal estate to which I was heir, he said, "Sir, let me tell you, that to be a Scotch landlord, where you have a number of families dependent upon you, and attached to you, is, perhaps, as high a situation as humanity can arrive at. A merchant upon the 'Change of London, with a hundred thousand pounds, is nothing; an English duke, with an immense fortune, is nothing; he has no tenants who consider themselves as under his patriarchal care, and who will follow him to the field upon any emergency."

His notion of the dignity of a Scotch landlord had been formed upon what he had heard of the Highland chiefs; for it is long since a Lowland landlord has been so curtailed in his feudal authority, that he has little more influence over his tenants than an English landlord; and of late years most of the Highland chiefs have destroyed, by means too well known, the princely power which they once enjoyed.

He proceeded: "Your going abroad, sir, and breaking off idle habits, may be of great importance to you. I would go where there are courts and learned men. There is a good deal of Spain that has not been perambulated. I would have you go thither. A man of inferior talents to yours may furnish us with useful observations upon that country." His supposing me, at that period of life, capable of writing an account of my travels that would deserve to be read, elated me not a little.

I appeal to every impartial reader whether this faithful detail of his frankness, complacency, and kindness to a young man, a stranger and a Scotchman, does not refute the unjust opinion of the harshness of his general demeanor. His occasional reproofs of folly, impudence, or impiety, and even the sudden sallies of his constitutional irritability of temper, which have been preserved for the poignancy of their wit, have produced that opinion among those who have not considered that such instances, though collected by Mrs. Piozzi into a small volume,[15] and read over in a few hours, were,

---

14. **Mallet . . . Dempster:** Erskine and Dempster were Edinburgh cronies of Boswell's. David Mallet (Malloch) had alienated himself from his fellow Scots by changing his name and attempting to blur his northern origin. He was a poet, playwright, and the editor of Bolingbroke's works, which Johnson considered impious.

15. **Mrs. Piozzi . . . volume:** Mrs. Piozzi, earlier Hester Lynch Thrale, had been a rival of Boswell's for Johnson's affection, but after twenty years of intimate friendship had broken with him on the subject of her second marriage. Her *Anecdotes of the Late Samuel Johnson* (1786) had a great success, and are not so spiteful as Boswell implies.

in fact, scattered through a long series of years: years, in which his time was chiefly spent in instructing and delighting mankind by his writings and conversation, in acts of piety to God, and good-will to men.

I complained to him that I had not yet acquired much knowledge, and asked his advice as to my studies. He said, " Don't talk of study now. I will give you a plan; but it will require some time to consider of it." " It is very good in you," I replied, " to allow me to be with you thus. Had it been foretold to me some years ago that I should pass an evening with the author of the *Rambler,* how should I have exulted! " What I then expressed was sincerely from the heart. He was satisfied that it was, and cordially answered, " Sir, I am glad we have met. I hope we shall pass many evenings and mornings, too, together." We finished a couple of bottles of port, and sat till between one and two in the morning.

He wrote this year in the *Critical Review* the account of " Telemachus, a Mask," by the Rev. George Graham, of Eton College. The subject of this beautiful poem was particularly interesting to Johnson, who had much experience of " the conflict of opposite principles," which he describes as " The contention between pleasure and virtue, a struggle which will always be continued while the present system of nature shall subsist; nor can history or poetry exhibit more than pleasure triumphing over virtue, and virtue subjugating pleasure."

As Dr. Oliver Goldsmith will frequently appear in this narrative, I shall endeavor to make my readers in some degree acquainted with his singular character. He was a native of Ireland, and a contemporary with Mr. Burke, at Trinity College, Dublin, but did not then give much promise of future celebrity. He, however, observed to Mr. Malone, that " though he made no great figure in mathematics, which was a study in much repute there, he could turn an ode of Horace into English better than any of them." He afterwards studied physic at Edinburgh, and upon the Continent and, I have been informed, was enabled to pursue his travels on foot, partly by demanding at universities to enter the lists as a disputant, by which, according to the custom of many of them, he was entitled to the premium of a crown, when luckily for him his challenge was not accepted; so that, as I once observed to Dr. Johnson, he *disputed* his passage through Europe. He then came to England,

and was employed successively in the capacities of an usher to an academy, a corrector of the press, a reviewer, and a writer for a newspaper. He had sagacity enough to cultivate assiduously the acquaintance of Johnson, and his faculties were gradually enlarged by the contemplation of such a model. To me and many others it appeared that he studiously copied the manner of Johnson, though, indeed, upon a smaller scale.

At this time I think he had published nothing with his name, though it was pretty generally known that *one Dr. Goldsmith* was the author of *An Enquiry into the Present State of Polite Learning in Europe,* and of *The Citizen of the World,* a series of letters supposed to be written from London by a Chinese. No man had the art of displaying with more advantage as a writer, whatever literary acquisitions he made. *" Nihil quod tetigit non ornavit."* [16] His mind resembled a fertile, but thin soil. There was a quick, but not a strong vegetation, of whatever chanced to be thrown upon it. No deep root could be struck. The oak of the forest did not grow there, but the elegant shrubbery and the fragrant parterre appeared in gay succession. It has been generally circulated and believed that he was a mere fool in conversation; [17] but, in truth, this has been greatly exaggerated. He had, no doubt, a more than common share of that hurry of ideas which we often find in his countrymen, and which sometimes produces a laughable confusion in expressing them. He was very much what the French call *un étourdi,* [18] and from vanity and an eager desire of being conspicuous wherever he was, he frequently talked carelessly without knowledge of the subject, or even without thought. His person was short, his countenance coarse and vulgar, his deportment that of a scholar awkwardly affecting the easy gentleman.

---

16. *" Nihil . . . ornavit":* The Latin is part of the epitaph Johnson wrote on his friend for the memorial in Westminster Abbey: "He gave luster to every sort of writing he touched."   17. "In allusion to this, Mr. Horace Walpole, who admired his writings, said he was 'an inspired idiot'; and Garrick described him as one 'for shortness called Noll, / Who wrote like an angel, and talked like poor Poll.' Sir Joshua Reynolds mentioned to me that he frequently heard Goldsmith talk warmly of the pleasure of being liked, and observe how hard it would be if literary excellence should preclude a man from that satisfaction, which he perceived it often did, from the envy which attended it; and therefore Sir Joshua was convinced that he was intentionally more absurd, in order to lessen himself in social intercourse, trusting that his character would be sufficiently supported by his work. If it indeed was his intention to appear absurd in company, he was often very successful. But with due deference to Sir Joshua's ingenuity I think the conjecture too refined" [B].   18. *un étourdi:* "a giddy fellow."

Those who were in any way distinguished excited envy in him to so ridiculous an excess, that the instances of it are hardly credible. When accompanying two beautiful young ladies with their mother on a tour in France, he was seriously angry that more attention was paid to them than to him; and once at the exhibition of the *Fantoccini* in London, when those who sat next him observed with what dexterity a puppet was made to toss a pike, he could not bear that it should have such praise, and exclaimed with some warmth, "Pshaw! I can do it better myself." [19]

He, I am afraid, had no settled system of any sort, so that his conduct must not be strictly scrutinized; but his affections were social and generous, and when he had money he gave it away very liberally. His desire of imaginary consequence predominated over his attention to truth. When he began to rise into notice, he said he had a brother who was Dean of Durham, [20] a fiction so easily detected, that it is wonderful how he should have been so inconsiderate as to hazard it. He boasted to me at this time of the power of his pen in commanding money, which I believe was true in a certain degree, though in the instance he gave he was by no means correct. He told me that he had sold a novel for four hundred pounds. This was his *Vicar of Wakefield*. But Johnson informed me, that he had made the bargain for Goldsmith, and the price was sixty pounds. "And, sir," said he, "a sufficient price, too, when it was sold; for then the fame of Goldsmith had not been elevated, as it afterwards was, by his *Traveler,* and the bookseller had such faint hopes of profit by his bargain, that he kept the manuscript by him a long time, and did not publish it till after the *Traveler* had appeared. Then, to be sure, it was accidentally worth more money."

Mrs. Piozzi and Sir John Hawkins [21] have strangely misstated the history of Goldsmith's situation and Johnson's friendly interference, when this novel was sold. I shall give it authentically from Johnson's own exact narration:

"I received one morning a message from poor Goldsmith that he was in great distress, and, as it was not in his power to come to me, begging that I would come to him as soon as possible. I sent him a guinea, and promised to come to him directly. I accordingly went as soon as I was dressed, and found that his landlady had arrested him for his rent, at which he was in a violent passion. I perceived that he had already changed my guinea, and had got a bottle of Madeira and a glass before him. I put the cork into the bottle, desired he would be calm, and began to talk to him of the means by which he might be extricated. He then told me that he had a novel ready for the press, which he produced to me. I looked into it, and saw its merit; told the landlady I should soon return, and having gone to a bookseller, sold it for sixty pounds. I brought Goldsmith the money, and he discharged his rent, not without rating his landlady in a high tone for having used him so ill."

My next meeting with Johnson was on Friday the 1st of July, when he and I and Dr. Goldsmith supped together at the Mitre. I was before this time pretty well acquainted with Goldsmith, who was one of the brightest ornaments of the Johnsonian school. Goldsmith's respectful attachment to Johnson was then at its height, for his own literary reputation had not yet distinguished him so much as to excite a vain desire of competition with his great master. He had increased my admiration of the goodness of Johnson's heart, by incidental remarks in the course of conversation, such as, when I mentioned Mr. Levet, [22] whom he entertained under his roof, "He is poor and honest, which is recommendation enough to Johnson"; and when I wondered that he was very kind to a man of whom I had heard a very bad character, "He is now become miserable, and that insures the protection of Johnson."

Goldsmith attempting this evening to maintain, I suppose from an affectation of paradox, "that knowledge was not desirable on its own account, for it often was a source of unhappiness." JOHNSON: "Why, sir, that knowledge may in some cases produce unhappiness, I allow. But, upon the whole, knowledge, per se, is certainly an object which every man would wish to attain, although, perhaps, he may not take the trouble necessary for attaining it."

Dr. John Campbell, the celebrated political and

---

19. "He went home with Mr. Burke to supper; and broke his shin by attempting to exhibit to the company how much better he could jump over a stick than the puppets" [B].   **20. Dean of Durham:** "I am willing to hope that there may have been some mistake as to this anecdote, though I had it from a dignitary of the Church. Dr. Isaac Goldsmith, his near relation, was Dean of Cloyne, in 1747" [B].   **21. Hawkins:** Sir John Hawkins, an old friend, had anticipated Boswell in writing Johnson's life: it appeared four times in 1787. Boswell was mentioned in it once, in a footnote.

22. Levet: Dr. Levet, without any proper medical schooling, was a practicing physician among the very poor. At his death, in 1782, Johnson celebrated his "single talent" in one of his finest poems.

biographical writer, being mentioned, Johnson said, "Campbell is a man of much knowledge, and has a good share of imagination. His *Hermippus Redivivus* is very entertaining, as an account of the Hermetic philosophy, and as furnishing a curious history of the extravagances of the human mind. If it were merely imaginary, it would be nothing at all. Campbell is not always rigidly careful of truth in his conversation, but I do not believe there is anything of this carelessness in his books. Campbell is a good man, a pious man. I am afraid he has not been in the inside of a church for many years, but he never passes a church without pulling off his hat. This shows that he has good principles. I used to go pretty often to Campbell's on a Sunday evening, till I began to consider that the shoals of Scotchmen who flocked about him might probably say, when anything of mine was well done, 'Ay, ay, he has learnt this of Cawmell!'"

He talked very contemptuously of Churchill's poetry, observing, that "it had a temporary currency, only from its audacity of abuse, and being filled with living names, that it would sink into oblivion." I ventured to hint that he was not quite a fair judge, as Churchill had attacked him violently. JOHNSON: "Nay, sir, I am a very fair judge. He did not attack me violently till he found I did not like his poetry; and his attack on me shall not prevent me from continuing to say what I think of him, from an apprehension that it may be ascribed to resentment. No, sir, I called the fellow a blockhead at first, and I will call him a blockhead still. However, I will acknowledge that I have a better opinion of him now, than I once had; for he has shown more fertility than I expected. To be sure, he is a tree that cannot produce good fruit: he only bears crabs.[23] But, sir, a tree that produces a great many crabs is better than a tree which produces only a few."

In this depreciation of Churchill's poetry I could not agree with him. It is very true that the greatest part of it is upon the topics of the day, on which account, as it brought him great fame and profit at the time, it must proportionally slide out of the public attention as other occasional objects succeed. But Churchill had extraordinary vigor both of thought and expression. His portraits of the players will ever be valuable to the true lovers of

the drama; and his strong caricatures of several eminent men of his age will not be forgotten by the curious. Let me add, that there are in his works many passages which are of a general nature; and his "Prophecy of Famine" is a poem of no ordinary merit. It is, indeed, falsely injurious to Scotland, but therefore may be allowed a greater share of invention.

Bonnell Thornton had just published a burlesque "Ode on St. Cecilia's Day, adapted to the ancient British music, viz. the salt-box, the jew's-harp, the marrowbones and cleaver, the humstrum or hurdy-gurdy, etc." Johnson praised its humor, and seemed much diverted with it. He repeated the following passage:

In strains more exalted the salt box shall join,
And clattering and battering and clapping combine;
With a rap and a tap, while the hollow side sounds,
Up and down leaps the flap, and with rattling re-
     bounds.

I mentioned the periodical paper called the *Connoisseur*. He said it wanted matter. No doubt it has not the deep thinking of Johnson's writings. But surely it has just views of the surface of life, and a very sprightly manner. His opinion of the *World* was not much higher than of the *Connoisseur*.[24]

Let me here apologize for the imperfect manner in which I am obliged to exhibit Johnson's conversation at this period. In the early part of my acquaintance with him, I was so wrapped in admiration of his extraordinary colloquial talents, and so little accustomed to his peculiar mode of expression, that I found it extremely difficult to recollect and record his conversation with its genuine vigor and vivacity. In progress of time, when my mind was, as it were, *strongly impregnated with the Johnsonian aether,* I could, with much more facility and exactness, carry in my memory and commit to paper the exuberant variety of his wisdom and wit.

At this time *Miss* Williams,[25] as she was then called, though she did not reside with him in the Temple under his roof, but had lodgings in Bolt Court, Fleet Street, had so much of his attention,

23. Charles Churchill attacked Johnson in "The Ghost," 1762. See above, n. 7. He turned out his poems with surprising speed, and in the space of four years established his position as the greatest satirical poet of the second half of the century.

24. *World, Connoisseur:* Both these papers were in the tradition established by Steele and Addison. They ran between the years 1753 and 1756. Lord Chesterfield had contributed to the *World* the two papers on Johnson's Dictionary that evoked the famous letter. See the letter, below, and the headnote to the letters. 25. For Miss Williams, see above, n. 2. She was eminently respectable, and no breath of scandal attached to her connection with Johnson.

that he every night drank tea with her before he went home, however late it might be, and she always sat up for him. This, it may be fairly conjectured, was not alone a proof of his regard for *her,* but of his own unwillingness to go into solitude, before that unseasonable hour at which he had habituated himself to expect the oblivion of repose. Dr. Goldsmith, being a privileged man, went with him this night, strutting away, and calling to me with an air of superiority, like that of an esoteric over an exoteric disciple of a sage of antiquity, " I go to Miss Williams." I confess, I then envied him this mighty privilege, of which he seemed so proud, but it was not long before I obtained the same mark of distinction.

On Tuesday the 5th of July, I again visited Johnson. He told me he had looked into the poems of a pretty voluminous writer, Mr. (now Dr.) John Ogilvie, one of the Presbyterian ministers of Scotland, which had lately come out, but could find no thinking in them. BOSWELL: " Is there not imagination in them, sir? " JOHNSON: " Why, sir, there is in them what *was* imagination, but it is no more imagination in *him,* than sound is sound in the echo. And his diction too is not his own. We have long ago seen *white-robed innocence,* and *flower-bespangled meads."*

Talking of London, he observed, " Sir, if you wish to have a just notion of the magnitude of this city, you must not be satisfied with seeing its great streets and squares, but must survey the innumerable little lanes and courts. It is not in the showy evolutions of buildings, but in the multiplicity of human habitations which are crowded together, that the wonderful immensity of London consists." I have often amused myself with thinking how different a place London is to different people. They, whose narrow minds are contracted to the consideration of some one particular pursuit, view it only through that medium. A politician thinks of it merely as the seat of government in its different departments; a grazier, as a vast market for cattle; a mercantile man, as a place where a prodigious deal of business is done upon 'Change; a dramatic enthusiast, as the grand scene of theatrical entertainments; a man of pleasure, as an assemblage of taverns, and the great emporium for ladies of easy virtue. But the intellectual man is struck with it, as comprehending the whole of human life in all its variety, the contemplation of which is inexhaustible.

On Wednesday, July 6, he was engaged to sup with me at my lodgings in Downing Street, Westminster. But on the preceding night my landlord having behaved very rudely to me and some company who were with me, I had resolved not to remain another night in his house. I was exceedingly uneasy at the awkward appearance I supposed I should make to Johnson and the other gentlemen whom I had invited, not being able to receive them at home, and being obliged to order supper at the Mitre. I went to Johnson in the morning, and talked of it as of a serious distress. He laughed, and said, " Consider, sir, how insignificant this will appear a twelvemonth hence." Were this consideration to be applied to most of the little vexatious incidents of life, by which our quiet is too often disturbed, it would prevent many painful sensations. I have tried it frequently, with good effect. " There is nothing," continued he, " in this mighty misfortune; nay, we shall be better at the Mitre." I told him that I had been at Sir John Fielding's office,[26] complaining of my landlord, and had been informed, that though I had taken my lodgings for a year, I might, upon proof of his bad behavior, quit them when I pleased, without being under an obligation to pay rent for any longer time than while I possessed them. The fertility of Johnson's mind could show itself even upon so small a matter as this. " Why, sir," said he, " I suppose this must be the law, since you have been told so in Bow Street. But, if your landlord could hold you to your bargain, and the lodgings should be yours for a year, you may certainly use them as you think fit. So, sir, you may quarter two life guardmen upon him; or you may send the greatest scoundrel you can find into your apartments; or you may say that you want to make some experiments in natural philosophy, and may burn a large quantity of asafetida in his house."

I had as my guests this evening at the Mitre Tavern, Dr. Johnson, Dr. Goldsmith, Mr. Thomas Davies, Mr. Eccles, an Irish gentleman, for whose agreeable company I was obliged to Mr. Davies, and the Rev. Mr. John Ogilvie, who was desirous of being in company with my illustrious friend, while I, in my turn, was proud to have the honor of showing one of my countrymen upon what easy terms Johnson permitted me to live with him.

26. **Fielding's office:** Sir John Fielding succeeded his half-brother, Henry, as a London magistrate. The main police court of London was — and is — situated in Bow Street, near Covent Garden. Here the Fieldings presided.

Goldsmith, as usual, endeavored, with too much eagerness, to *shine,* and disputed very warmly with Johnson against the well-known maxim of the British constitution, "the king can do no wrong," affirming that "what was morally false could not be politically true; and as the king might, in the exercise of his regal power, command and cause the doing of what was wrong, it certainly might be said, in sense and in reason, that he could do wrong." JOHNSON: "Sir, you are to consider, that in our constitution, according to its true principles, the king is the head; he is supreme; he is above everything; and there is no power by which he can be tried. Therefore it is, sir, that we hold the king can do no wrong; that whatever may happen to be wrong in government may not be above our reach, by being ascribed to Majesty. Redress is always to be had against oppression, by punishing the immediate agents. The king, though he should command, cannot force a judge to condemn a man unjustly; therefore it is the judge whom we prosecute and punish. Political institutions are formed upon the consideration of what will most frequently tend to the good of the whole, although now and then exceptions may occur. Thus it is better in general that a nation should have a supreme legislative power, although it may at times be abused. And then, sir, there is this consideration, that *if the abuse be enormous, Nature will rise up and, claiming her original rights, overturn a corrupt political system."* I mark this animated sentence with peculiar pleasure, as a noble instance of that truly dignified spirit of freedom which ever glowed in his heart, though he was charged with slavish tenets by superficial observers; because he was at all times indignant against that false patriotism, that pretended love of freedom, that unruly restlessness which is inconsistent with the stable authority of any good government.

This generous sentiment, which he uttered with great fervor, struck me exceedingly, and stirred my blood to that pitch of fancied resistance, the possibility of which I am glad to keep in mind, but to which I trust I never shall be forced.

"Great abilities," said he, "are not requisite for an historian; for in historical composition, all the greatest powers of the human mind are quiescent. He has facts ready to his hand; so there is no exercise of invention. Imagination is not required in any high degree, only about as much as is used in the lower kinds of poetry. Some penetration, accuracy, and coloring will fit a man for the task, if he can give the application which is necessary."

"Bayle's Dictionary is a very useful work for those to consult who love the biographical part of literature, which is what I love most."

Talking of the eminent writers in Queen Anne's reign, he observed, "I think Dr. Arbuthnot the first man among them. He was the most universal genius, being an excellent physician, a man of deep learning, and a man of much humor. Mr. Addison was, to be sure, a great man; his learning was not profound; but his morality, his humor, and his elegance of writing, set him very high."

Mr. Ogilvie was unlucky enough to choose for the topic of his conversation the praises of his native country. He began with saying that there was very rich land around Edinburgh. Goldsmith, who had studied physic there, contradicted this, very untruly, with a sneering laugh. Disconcerted a little by this, Mr. Ogilvie then took new ground, where, I suppose, he thought himself perfectly safe; for he observed, that Scotland had a great many noble wild prospects. JOHNSON: "I believe, sir, you have a great many. Norway, too, has noble wild prospects; and Lapland is remarkable for prodigious noble wild prospects. But, sir, let me tell you, the noblest prospect which a Scotchman ever sees, is the high road that leads him to England!" This unexpected and pointed sally produced a roar of applause. After all, however, those who admire the rude grandeur of nature, cannot deny it to Caledonia.

On Saturday, July 9, I found Johnson surrounded with a numerous levee, but have not preserved any part of his conversation. On the 14th we had another evening by ourselves at the Mitre. It happening to be a very rainy night, I made some commonplace observations on the relaxation of nerves and depression of spirits which such weather occasioned, adding, however, that it was good for the vegetable creation. Johnson, who, as we have already seen, denied that the temperature of the air had any influence on the human frame, answered, with a smile of ridicule, "Why, yes, sir, it is good for vegetables, and for the animals who eat those vegetables, and for the animals who eat those animals." This observation of his aptly enough introduced a good supper; and I soon forgot, in Johnson's company, the influence of a moist atmosphere.

Feeling myself now quite at ease as his companion, though I had all possible reverence for him, I expressed a regret that I could not be so easy with my father, though he was not much older than Johnson, and certainly however respectable had not more learning and greater abilities to depress me. I asked him the reason of this. JOHNSON: "Why, sir, I am a man of the world. I live in the world, and I take, in some degree, the color of the world as it moves along. Your father is a judge in a remote part of the island, and all his notions are taken from the old world. Besides, sir, there must always be a struggle between a father and son, while one aims at power and the other at independence." I said, I was afraid my father would force me to be a lawyer. JOHNSON: "Sir, you need not be afraid of his forcing you to be a laborious practicing lawyer; that is not in his power. For as the proverb says, 'One man may lead a horse to the water, but twenty cannot make him drink.' He may be displeased that you are not what he wishes you to be, but that displeasure will not go far. If he insists only on your having as much law as is necessary for a man of property, and then endeavors to get you into parliament, he is quite in the right."

He enlarged very convincingly upon the excellence of rhyme over blank verse in English poetry. I mentioned to him that Dr. Adam Smith, in his lectures upon composition, when I studied under him in the College of Glasgow, had maintained the same opinion strenuously, and I repeated some of his arguments. JOHNSON: "Sir, I was once in company with Smith, and we did not take to each other; but had I known that he loved rhyme as much as you tell me he does, I should have *hugged* him."

Talking of those who denied the truth of Christianity, he said, "It is always easy to be on the negative side. If a man were now to deny that there is salt upon the table, you could not reduce him to an absurdity. Come, let us try this a little further. I deny that Canada is taken, and I can support my denial by pretty good arguments. The French are a much more numerous people than we; and it is not likely that they would allow us to take it. 'But the ministry have assured us, in all the formality of the *Gazette,* that it is taken.' Very true. But the ministry have put us to an enormous expense by the war in America, and it is their interest to persuade us that we have got something for our money. 'But the fact is confirmed by thousands of men who were at the taking of it.' Ay, but

these men have still more interest in deceiving us. They don't want that you should think the French have beat them, but that they have beat the French. Now suppose you should go over and find that it is really taken, that would only satisfy yourself; for when you come home, we will not believe you. We will say you have been bribed. Yet, sir, notwithstanding all these plausible objections, we have no doubt that Canada is really ours. Such is the weight of common testimony. How much stronger are the evidences of the Christian religion?"

"Idleness is a disease which must be combated, but I would not advise a rigid adherence to a particular plan of study. I myself have never persisted in any plan for two days together. A man ought to read just as inclination leads him; for what he reads as a task will do him little good. A young man should read five hours in a day, and so may acquire a great deal of knowledge."

To a man of vigorous intellect and ardent curiosity like his own, reading without a regular plan may be beneficial; though even such a man must submit to it, if he would attain a full understanding of any of the sciences.

To such a degree of unrestrained frankness had he now accustomed me, that in the course of this evening I talked of the numerous reflections which had been thrown out against him on account of his having accepted a pension from his present Majesty. "Why, sir," said he, with a hearty laugh, "it is a mighty foolish noise that they make.[27] I have accepted of a pension as a reward which has been thought due to my literary merit; and now that I have this pension, I am the same man in every respect that I have ever been; I retain the same principles. It is true, that I cannot now curse (smiling) the House of Hanover; nor would it be decent for me to drink King James's health in the wine that King George gives me money to pay for. But, sir, I think that the pleasure of cursing the House of Hanover, and drinking King James's health, are amply overbalanced by three hundred pounds a year."

There was here, most certainly, an affectation of more Jacobitism than he really had; and indeed an intention of admitting, for the moment, in a much greater extent than it really existed, the charge of disaffection imputed to him by the world, merely

27. "When I mentioned the same idle clamor to him several years afterwards, he said, with a smile, 'I wish my pension were twice as large, that they might make twice as much noise'" [B].

for the purpose of showing how dexterously he could repel an attack, even though he were placed in the most disadvantageous position; for I have heard him declare, that if holding up his right hand would have secured victory at Culloden to Prince Charles's army, he was not sure he would have held it up, so little confidence had he in the right claimed by the House of Stuart, and so fearful was he of the consequences of another revolution on the throne of Great Britain; and Mr. Topham Beauclerk assured me, he had heard him say this before he had his pension. At another time he said to Mr. Langton, "Nothing has ever offered, that has made it worth my while to consider the question fully." He, however, also said to the same gentleman, talking of King James II, "It was become impossible for him to reign any longer in this country." He no doubt had an early attachment to the House of Stuart, but his zeal had cooled as his reason strengthened. Indeed, I heard him once say that "after the death of a violent Whig, with whom he used to contend with great eagerness, he felt his Toryism much abated." I suppose he meant Mr. Walmsley.

Yet there is no doubt that at earlier periods he was wont often to exercise both his pleasantry and ingenuity in talking Jacobitism. My much respected friend, Dr. Douglas, now Bishop of Salisbury, has favored me with the following admirable instance from his Lordship's own recollection. One day when dining at old Mr. Langton's, where Miss Roberts, his niece, was one of the company, Johnson, with his usual complacent attention to the fair sex, took her by the hand and said, "My dear, I hope you are a Jacobite." Old Mr. Langton, who, though a high and steady Tory, was attached to the present royal family, seemed offended, and asked Johnson, with great warmth, what he could mean by putting such a question to his niece! "Why, sir," said Johnson, "I meant no offense to your niece, I meant her a great compliment. A Jacobite, sir, believes in the divine right of kings. He that believes in the divine right of kings believes in a divinity. A Jacobite believes in the divine right of bishops. He that believes in the divine right of bishops believes in the divine authority of the Christian religion. Therefore, sir, a Jacobite is neither an atheist nor a deist. That cannot be said of a Whig; for *Whiggism is a negation of all principle.*"

He advised me, when abroad, to be as much as I could with the professors in the universities, and with the clergy; for from their conversation I might expect the best accounts of everything in whatever country I should be, with the additional advantage of keeping my learning alive.

It will be observed that, when giving me advice as to my travels, Dr. Johnson did not dwell upon cities and palaces and pictures and shows and Arcadian scenes. He was of Lord Essex's opinion, who advises his kinsman Roger Earl of Rutland, "rather to go an hundred miles to speak with one wise man, than five miles to see a fair town."

I described to him an impudent fellow [28] from Scotland, who affected to be a savage, and railed at all established systems. JOHNSON: "There is nothing surprising in this, sir. He wants to make himself conspicuous. He would tumble in a hogsty, as long as you looked at him and called to him to come out. But let him alone, never mind him, and he'll soon give it over."

I added that the same person maintained that there was no distinction between virtue and vice. JOHNSON: "Why, sir, if the fellow does not think as he speaks, he is lying; and I see not what honor he can propose to himself from having the character of a liar. But if he does really think that there is no distinction between virtue and vice, why, sir, when he leaves our houses let us count our spoons."

Sir David Dalrymple, now one of the judges of Scotland by the title of Lord Hailes, had contributed much to increase my high opinion of Johnson, on account of his writings, long before I attained to a personal acquaintance with him; I, in return, had informed Johnson of Sir David's eminent character for learning and religion; and Johnson was so much pleased, that at one of our evening meetings he gave him for his toast. I at this time kept up a very frequent correspondence with Sir David, and I read to Dr. Johnson tonight the following passage from the letter which I had last received from him:

"It gives me pleasure to think that you have obtained the friendship of Mr. Samuel Johnson. He is one of the best moral writers which England has produced. At the same time, I envy you the free and undisguised converse with such a man. May I beg you to present my best respects to him, and to assure him of the veneration which I entertain for the author of the *Rambler* and of *Rasselas?* Let me recommend this last work to you; with the *Rambler* you certainly are acquainted. In *Rasselas* you will

28. **fellow:** Boswell elsewhere identifies this man as James Macpherson, author of the poems attributed to Ossian. See *Tour,* n. 17, above.

see a tender-hearted operator, who probes the wound only to heal it. Swift, on the contrary, mangles human nature. He cuts and slashes, as if he took pleasure in the operation, like the tyrant who said, ' *Ita feri ut se sentiat emori.*' " [29] Johnson seemed to be much gratified by this just and well-turned compliment.

He recommended to me to keep a journal of my life, full and unreserved. He said it would be a very good exercise, and would yield me great satisfaction when the particulars were faded from my remembrance. I was uncommonly fortunate in having had a previous coincidence of opinion with him upon this subject, for I had kept such a journal for some time; and it was no small pleasure to me to have this to tell him, and to receive his approbation. He counseled me to keep it private, and said I might surely have a friend who would burn it in case of my death.[30] From this habit I have been enabled to give the world so many anecdotes, which would otherwise have been lost to posterity. I mentioned that I was afraid I put into my journal too many little incidents. JOHNSON: "There is nothing, sir, too little for so little a creature as man. It is by studying little things that we attain the great art of having as little misery and as much happiness as possible."

Next morning Mr. Dempster happened to call on me, and was so much struck even with the imperfect account which I gave him of Dr. Johnson's conversation, that to his honor be it recorded, when I complained that drinking port and sitting up late with him, affected my nerves for some time after,[31] he said, "One had better be palsied at eighteen than not keep company with such a man."

On Tuesday, July 18, I found tall Sir Thomas Robinson sitting with Johnson. Sir Thomas said, that the King of Prussia valued himself upon three things: upon being a hero, a musician, and an author. JOHNSON: "Pretty well, sir, for one man. As to his being an author, I have not looked at his poetry; but his prose is poor stuff. He writes just as you might suppose Voltaire's footboy to do, who has been his amanuensis. He has such parts as the

valet might have, and about as much of the coloring of the style as might be got by transcribing his works." When I was at Ferney, I repeated this to Voltaire, in order to reconcile him somewhat to Johnson, whom he, in affecting the English mode of expression, had previously characterized as " a superstitious dog," but after hearing such a criticism on Frederick the Great, with whom he was then on bad terms, he exclaimed, " An honest fellow! "

But I think the criticism much too severe; for the *Memoirs of the House of Brandenburg* are written as well as many works of that kind. His poetry, for the style of which he himself makes a frank apology, " *Jargonnant un français barbare,*" [32] though fraught with pernicious ravings of infidelity, has, in many places, great animation, and in some a pathetic tenderness.

Upon this contemptuous animadversion on the King of Prussia, I observed to Johnson, "It would seem then, sir, that much less parts are necessary to make a king, than to make an author: for the King of Prussia is confessedly the greatest king now in Europe, yet you think he makes a very poor figure as an author."

Mr. Levet [33] this day showed me Dr. Johnson's library, which was contained in two garrets over his chambers, where Lintot, son of the celebrated bookseller of that name, had formerly his warehouse. I found a number of good books, but very dusty and in great confusion. The floor was strewed with manuscript leaves, in Johnson's own handwriting, which I beheld with a degree of veneration, supposing they perhaps might contain portions of the *Rambler,* or of *Rasselas.* I observed an apparatus for chemical experiments, of which Johnson was all his life very fond. The place seemed to be very favorable for retirement and meditation. Johnson told me, that he went up thither without mentioning it to his servant when he wanted to study secure from interruption, for he would not allow his servant to say he was not at home when he really was. "A servant's strict regard for truth," said he, "must be weakened by such a practice. A philosopher may know that it is merely a form of denial, but few servants are such nice distinguishers. If I accustom a servant to tell a lie for *me,* have I not reason to apprehend that he will tell many lies for *himself?*" I am, however, satisfied that ev-

29. '*Ita . . . emori*': Suetonius quotes Caligula to this effect, in his *Lives of the Caesars*, Chapter 30: "Do it in such a way that he may feel the approach of death."   30. With regard to his private records, this was Johnson's own intention and desire. Boswell's instincts were quite the opposite, and he did his best to preserve Johnson's diaries, as well as his own. The contrast epitomizes the difference between the neoclassic and modern attitudes.   31. Reminding Johnson of such occasions many years later, Boswell received the reply, "Nay, sir, it was not the *wine* that made your head ache, but the *sense* that I put into it."

32. "*Jargonnant . . . barbare*": "Jabbering vile French." 33. **Levet:** Robert Levet was another "pensioner" of Johnson's household; see above, n. 22. He is said to have acquired his knowledge by serving as a waiter in a coffeehouse frequented by physicians, and listening to their conversation.

ery servant, of any degree of intelligence, understands saying his master is not at home, not at all as the affirmation of a fact, but as the customary words, intimating that his master wishes not to be seen; so that there can be no bad effect from it.

Mr. Temple, now vicar of St. Gluvias, Cornwall, who had been my intimate friend for many years, had at this time chambers in Farrar's buildings, at the bottom of Inner Temple Lane, which he kindly lent me upon my quitting my lodgings, he being to return to Trinity Hall, Cambridge. I found them particularly convenient for me, as they were so near Dr. Johnson's.

On Wednesday, July 20, Dr. Johnson, Mr. Dempster, and my uncle Dr. Boswell, who happened to be now in London, supped with me at these chambers. JOHNSON: " Pity is not natural to man. Children are always cruel. Savages are always cruel. Pity is acquired and improved by the cultivation of reason. We may have uneasy sensations for seeing a creature in distress, without pity; for we have not pity unless we wish to relieve them. When I am on my way to dine with a friend, and, finding it late, have bid the coachman make haste, if I happen to attend when he whips his horses, I may feel unpleasantly that the animals are put to pain, but I do not wish him to desist. No, sir, I wish him to drive on."

Mr. Alexander Donaldson, bookseller, of Edinburgh, had for some time opened a shop in London, and sold his cheap editions of the most popular English books, in defiance of the supposed common-law right of *literary property*. Johnson, though he concurred in the opinion which was afterwards sanctioned by a judgment of the House of Lords, that there was no such right, was at this time very angry that the booksellers of London, for whom he uniformly professed much regard, should suffer from an invasion of what they had ever considered to be secure; and he was loud and violent against Mr. Donaldson. " He is a fellow who takes advantage of the law to injure his brethren; for, notwithstanding that the statute secures only fourteen years of exclusive right, it has always been understood by the *trade* that he, who buys the copyright of a book from the author, obtains a perpetual property; and upon that belief, numberless bargains are made to transfer that property after the expiration of the statutory term. Now Donaldson, I say, takes advantage here, of people who have really an equitable title from usage; and if we consider how few of the books of which they buy the property suc-

ceed so well as to bring profit, we should be of opinion that the term of fourteen years is too short; it should be sixty years." DEMPSTER: " Donaldson, sir, is anxious for the encouragement of literature. He reduces the price of books, so that poor students may buy them." JOHNSON (laughing): " Well, sir, allowing that to be his motive, he is no better than Robin Hood, who robbed the rich in order to give to the poor."

It is remarkable that when the great question concerning literary property came to be ultimately tried before the supreme tribunal of this country, in consequence of the very spirited exertions of Mr. Donaldson, Dr. Johnson was zealous against a perpetuity, but he thought that the term of the exclusive right of authors should be considerably enlarged. He was then for granting a hundred years.

The conversation now turned upon Mr. David Hume's style. JOHNSON: " Why, sir, his style is not English; the structure of his sentences is French. Now the French structure and the English structure may, in the nature of things, be equally good. But if you allow that the English language is established, he is wrong. My name might originally have been Nicholson, as well as Johnson; but were you to call me Nicholson now, you would call me very absurdly."

Rousseau's treatise on the inequality of mankind [34] was at this time a fashionable topic. It gave rise to an observation by Mr. Dempster, that the advantages of fortune and rank were nothing to a wise man, who ought to value only merit. JOHNSON: " If man were a savage, living in the woods by himself, this might be true; but in civilized society we all depend upon each other, and our happiness is very much owing to the good opinion of mankind. Now, sir, in civilized society, external advantages make us more respected. A man with a good coat upon his back meets with a better reception than he who has a bad one. Sir, you may analyze this, and say what is there in it? But that will avail you nothing, for it is a part of a general system. Pound St. Paul's Church into atoms, and consider any single atom; it is, to be sure, good for nothing; but, put all these atoms together, and you have St. Paul's Church. So it is with human felicity, which is made up of many ingredients, each of which may be shown to be very insignificant. In civilized society, personal merit will not serve you so much as money will. Sir, you may make the ex-

34. treatise . . . mankind: *Discours sur l'origine et les fondements de l'inégalité parmi les hommes* (1755).

periment. Go into the street, and give one man a lecture on morality, and another a shilling, and see which will respect you most. If you wish only to support nature, Sir William Petty [35] fixes your allowance at three pounds a year, but, as times are much altered, let us call it six pounds. This sum will fill your belly, shelter you from the weather, and even get you a strong lasting coat, supposing it to be made of good bull's hide. Now, sir, all beyond this is artificial, and is desired in order to obtain a greater degree of respect from our fellow creatures. And, sir, if six hundred pounds a year procure a man more consequence and, of course, more happiness than six pounds a year, the same proportion will hold as to six thousand, and so on as far as opulence can be carried. Perhaps he who has a large fortune may not be so happy as he who has a small one; but that must proceed from other causes than from his having the large fortune; for, *caeteris paribus,*[36] he who is rich in a civilized society, must be happier than he who is poor, as riches, if properly used (and it is a man's own fault if they are not) must be productive of the highest advantages. Money, to be sure, of itself is of no use, for its only use is to part with it. Rousseau, and all those who deal in paradoxes, are led away by a childish desire of novelty. When I was a boy, I used always to choose the wrong side of a debate, because most ingenious things, that is to say, most new things, could be said upon it. Sir, there is nothing for which you may not muster up more plausible arguments, than those which are urged against wealth and other external advantages. Why, now, there is stealing; why should it be thought a crime? When we consider by what unjust methods property has been often acquired, and that what was unjustly got it must be unjust to keep, where is the harm in one man's taking the property of another from him? Besides, sir, when we consider the bad use that many people make of their property, and how much better use the thief may make of it, it may be defended as a very allowable practice. Yet, sir, the experience of mankind has discovered stealing to be so very bad a thing that they make no scruple to hang a man for it. When I was running about this town a very poor fellow, I was a great arguer for the advantages of poverty, but I was, at the same time, very sorry to be poor. Sir, all the arguments which are brought to represent poverty as no evil, show it to be evidently a great evil. You never find people laboring to convince you that you may live very happily upon a plentiful fortune. So you hear people talking how miserable a king must be, and yet they all wish to be in his place."

It was suggested that kings must be unhappy, because they are deprived of the greatest of all satisfactions, easy and unreserved society. JOHNSON: "That is an ill-founded notion. Being a king does not exclude a man from such society. Great kings have always been social. The King of Prussia, the only great king at present, is very social. Charles II, the last king of England who was a man of parts, was social; and our Henrys and Edwards were all social."

Mr. Dempster having endeavored to maintain that intrinsic merit *ought* to make the only distinction amongst mankind. JOHNSON: "Why, sir, mankind have found that this cannot be. How shall we determine the proportion of intrinsic merit? Were that to be the only distinction amongst mankind, we should soon quarrel about the degrees of it. Were all distinctions abolished, the strongest would not long acquiesce, but would endeavor to obtain a superiority by their bodily strength. But, sir, as subordination is very necessary for society, and contentions for superiority very dangerous, mankind, that is to say, all civilized nations, have settled it upon a plain invariable principle. A man is born to hereditary rank, or his being appointed to certain offices gives him a certain rank. Subordination tends greatly to human happiness. Were we all upon an equality, we should have no other enjoyment than mere animal pleasure."

I said, I considered distinction of rank to be of so much importance in civilized society, that if I were asked on the same day to dine with the first duke in England, and with the first man in Britain for genius, I should hesitate which to prefer. JOHNSON: "To be sure, sir, if you were to dine only once, and it were never to be known where you dined, you would choose rather to dine with the first man for genius; but to gain most respect, you should dine with the first duke in England. For nine people in ten that you meet with, would have a higher opinion of you for having dined with a duke; and the great genius himself would receive you better, because you had been with the great duke."

He took care to guard himself against any possible suspicion that his settled principles of rever-

---

35. **Petty:** an esteemed political economist of the previous century, author of *Political Arithmetick* (1690), and other treatises.
36. *caeteris paribus:* "supposing the rest equal."

ence for rank and respect for wealth were at all owing to mean or interested motives, for he asserted his own independence as a literary man. "No man," said he, "who ever lived by literature, has lived more independently than I have done." He said he had taken longer time than he needed to have done in composing his Dictionary. He received our compliments upon that great work with complacency, and told us that the Academy *della Crusca* [37] could scarcely believe that it was done by one man.

Next morning I found him alone, and have preserved the following fragments of his conversation. Of a gentleman [38] who was mentioned, he said, "I have not met with any man for a long time who has given me such general displeasure. He is totally unfixed in his principles, and wants to puzzle other people." I said, his principles had been poisoned by a noted infidel writer, but that he was, nevertheless, a benevolent, good man. JOHNSON: "We can have no dependence upon that instinctive, that constitutional goodness which is not founded upon principle. I grant you that such a man may be a very amiable member of society. I can conceive him placed in such a situation that he is not much tempted to deviate from what is right; and as every man prefers virtue, when there is not some strong incitement to transgress its precepts, I can conceive him doing nothing wrong. But if such a man stood in need of money, I should not like to trust him; and I should certainly not trust him with young ladies, for *there* there is always temptation. Hume, and other skeptical innovators, are vain men, and will gratify themselves at any expense. Truth will not afford sufficient food to their vanity; so they have betaken themselves to error. Truth, sir, is a cow that will yield such people no more milk, and so they are gone to milk the bull. If I could have allowed myself to gratify my vanity at the expense of truth, what fame might I have acquired. Everything which Hume has advanced against Christianity had passed through my mind long before he wrote. Always remember this, that after a system is well settled upon positive evidence, a few partial objections ought not to shake it. The human mind is so limited, that it cannot take in all the parts of a subject, so that there may be objections raised against anything. There are objections against a *plenum,* and objections against a *vacuum;* yet one of them must certainly be true." [39]

I mentioned Hume's argument against the belief of miracles, that it is more probable that the witnesses to the truth of them are mistaken, or speak falsely, than that the miracles should be true. JOHNSON: "Why, sir, the great difficulty of proving miracles should make us very cautious in believing them. But let us consider: although God has made nature to operate by certain fixed laws, yet it is not unreasonable to think that he may suspend those laws, in order to establish a system highly advantageous to mankind. Now the Christian religion is a most beneficial system, as it gives us light and certainty where we were before in darkness and doubt. The miracles which prove it are attested by men who had no interest in deceiving us, but who, on the contrary, were told that they should suffer persecution, and did actually lay down their lives in confirmation of the truth of the facts which they asserted. Indeed, for some centuries the heathens did not pretend to deny the miracles, but said they were performed by the aid of evil spirits. This is a circumstance of great weight. Then, sir, when we take the proofs derived from prophecies which have been so exactly fulfilled, we have most satisfactory evidence. Supposing a miracle possible, as to which, in my opinion, there can be no doubt, we have as strong evidence for the miracles in support of Christianity, as the nature of the thing admits."

At night, Mr. Johnson and I supped in a private room at the Turk's Head Coffeehouse, in the Strand. "I encourage this house," said he, "for the mistress of it is a good civil woman, and has not much business."

"Sir, I love the acquaintance of young people, because, in the first place, I don't like to think myself growing old. In the next place, young acquaintances must last longest, if they do last; and then, sir, young men have more virtue than old men; they have more generous sentiments in every respect. I love the young dogs of this age: they have more wit and humor and knowledge of life than we had; but then the dogs are not so good scholars. Sir, in my early years I read very hard. It is a sad reflection, but a true one, that I knew almost as much at eighteen as I do now. My judg-

---

37. *della Crusca:* the Florentine academy of learning, established to purify the Italian language, and responsible for an authoritative dictionary.   38. **gentleman:** probably Dempster. See above, n. 14.

39. **There . . . true:** i.e., either all space is occupied, or some of it is empty; but neither alternative is entirely acceptable.

ment, to be sure, was not so good; but I had all the facts. I remember very well, when I was at Oxford, an old gentleman said to me, 'Young man, ply your book diligently now, and acquire a stock of knowledge; for when years come upon you, you will find that poring upon books will be but an irksome task.'"

This account of his reading, given by himself in plain words, sufficiently confirms what I have already advanced upon the disputed question as to his application. It reconciles any seeming inconsistency in his way of talking upon it at different times; and shows that idleness and reading hard were with him relative terms, the import of which, as used by him, must be gathered from a comparison with what scholars of different degrees of ardor and assiduity have been known to do. And let it be remembered, that he was now talking spontaneously, and expressing his genuine sentiments, whereas at other times he might be induced, from his spirit of contradiction, or more properly from his love of argumentative contest, to speak lightly of his own application to study. It is pleasing to consider that the old gentleman's gloomy prophecy as to the irksomeness of books to men of an advanced age, which is too often fulfilled, was so far from being verified in Johnson, that his ardor for literature never failed, and his last writings had more ease and vivacity than any of his earlier productions.

He mentioned to me now, for the first time, that he had been distressed by melancholy, and for that reason had been obliged to fly from study and meditation, to the dissipating variety of life. Against melancholy he recommended constant occupation of mind, a great deal of exercise, moderation in eating and drinking, and especially to shun drinking at night. He said melancholy people were apt to fly to intemperance for relief, but that it sunk them much deeper in misery. He observed that laboring men who work hard, and live sparingly, are seldom or never troubled with low spirits.

He again insisted on the duty of maintaining subordination of rank. "Sir, I would no more deprive a nobleman of his respect, than of his money. I consider myself as acting a part in the great system of society, and I do to others as I would have them to do to me. I would behave to a nobleman as I should expect he would behave to me, were I a nobleman and he Sam. Johnson. Sir,

there is one Mrs. Macaulay [40] in this town, a great republican. One day when I was at her house, I put on a very grave countenance, and said to her, 'Madam, I am now become a convert to your way of thinking. I am convinced that all mankind are upon an equal footing, and to give you an unquestionable proof, madam, that I am in earnest, here is a very sensible, civil, well-behaved fellow citizen, your footman; I desire that he may be allowed to sit down and dine with us.' I thus, sir, showed her the absurdity of the leveling doctrine. She has never liked me since. Sir, your levelers wish to level *down* as far as themselves; but they cannot bear leveling *up* to themselves. They would all have some people under them; why not then have some people above them?" I mentioned a certain author who disgusted me by his forwardness, and by showing no deference to noblemen into whose company he was admitted. JOHNSON: "Suppose a shoemaker should claim an equality with him, as he does with a lord; how he would stare. 'Why, sir, do you stare?' says the shoemaker. 'I do great service to society. 'Tis true, I am paid for doing it, but so are you, sir, and I am sorry to say it, paid better than I am, for doing something not so necessary. For mankind could do better without your books, than without my shoes.' Thus, sir, there would be a perpetual struggle for precedence, were there no fixed invariable rules for the distinction of rank, which creates no jealousy, as it is allowed to be accidental."

He said, Dr. Joseph Warton was a very agreeable man, and his *Essay on the Genius and Writings of Pope* a very pleasing book. I wondered that he delayed so long to give us the continuation of it.[41] JOHNSON: "Why, sir, I suppose he finds himself a little disappointed, in not having been able to persuade the world to be of his opinion as to Pope."

We have now been favored with the concluding volume, in which, to use a parliamentary expression, he has *explained,* so as not to appear quite so adverse to the opinion of the world, concerning Pope, as was at first thought; and we must all agree that his work is a most valuable accession to English literature.

A writer of deserved eminence being mentioned, Johnson said, "Why, sir, he is a man of good parts, but being originally poor, he has got a love of

---

40. **Mrs. Macaulay:** Catherine Macaulay (1731–91), authoress on political subjects and education.   41. **continuation of it:** Part I was first published in 1756; Part II not until 1782.

mean company and low jocularity, a very bad thing, sir. To laugh is good, and to talk is good. But you ought no more to think it enough if you laugh, than you are to think it enough if you talk. You may laugh in as many ways as you talk, and surely *every* way of talking that is practiced cannot be esteemed."

I spoke of Sir James Macdonald as a young man of most distinguished merit,[42] who united the highest reputation at Eton and Oxford, with the patriarchal spirit of a great Highland chieftain. I mentioned that Sir James had said to me, that he had never seen Mr. Johnson, but he had a great respect for him, though at the same time it was mixed with some degree of terror. JOHNSON: " Sir, if he were to be acquainted with me, it might lessen both."

The mention of this gentleman led us to talk of the Western Islands of Scotland, to visit which he expressed a wish that then appeared to me a very romantic fancy, which I little thought would be afterwards realized. He told me, that his father had put Martin's account[43] of those islands into his hands when he was very young, and that he was highly pleased with it; that he was particularly struck with the St. Kilda man's notion that the high church of Glasgow had been hollowed out of a rock, a circumstance to which old Mr. Johnson had directed his attention. He said, he would go to the Hebrides with me, when I returned from my travels, unless some very good companion should offer when I was absent, which he did not think probable, adding, " There are few people whom I take so much to, as you." And when I talked of my leaving England, he said, with a very affectionate air, " My dear Boswell, I should be very unhappy at parting, did I think we were not to meet again." I cannot too often remind my readers, that, although such instances of his kindness are doubtless very flattering to me, yet I hope my recording them will be ascribed to a better motive than to vanity, for they afford unquestionable evidence of his tenderness and complacency, which some, while they were forced to acknowledge his great powers, have been so strenuous to deny.

He maintained that a boy at school was the happiest of human beings. I supported a different opinion, from which I have never yet varied, that

a man is happier; and I enlarged upon the anxiety and sufferings which are endured at school. JOHNSON: " Ah! Sir, a boy's being flogged is not so severe as a man's having the hiss of the world against him. Men have a solicitude about fame; and the greater share they have of it, the more afraid they are of losing it." I silently asked myself, " Is it possible that the great Samuel Johnson really entertains any such apprehension, and is not confident that his exalted fame is established upon a foundation never to be shaken? "

He this evening drank a bumper to Sir David Dalrymple, " as a man of worth, a scholar, and a wit." " I have," said he, " never heard of him except from you; but let him know my opinion of him, for as he does not show himself much in the world, he should have the praise of the few who hear of him."

On Tuesday, July 26, I found Mr. Johnson alone. It was a very wet day, and I again complained of the disagreeable effects of such weather. JOHNSON: " Sir, this is all imagination, which physicians encourage; for man lives in air, as a fish lives in water, so that if the atmosphere press heavy from above, there is an equal resistance from below. To be sure, bad weather is hard upon people who are obliged to be abroad; and men cannot labor so well in the open air in bad weather, as in good, but, sir, a smith or a tailor, whose work is within doors, will surely do as much in rainy weather, as in fair. Some very delicate frames, indeed, may be affected by wet weather, but not common constitutions."

We talked of the education of children, and I asked him what he thought was best to teach them first. JOHNSON: " Sir, it is no matter what you teach them first, any more than what leg you shall put into your breeches first. Sir, you may stand disputing which is best to put in first, but in the meantime your breech is bare. Sir, while you are considering which of two things you should teach your child first, another boy has learned them both."

On Thursday, July 28, we again supped in private at the Turk's Head Coffeehouse. JOHNSON: " Swift has a higher reputation than he deserves. His excellence is strong sense; for his humor, though very well, is not remarkably good. I doubt whether the *Tale of a Tub* be his; for he never owned it, and it is much above his usual manner."

" Thomson,[44] I think, had as much of the poet

---

42. Macdonald . . . merit: The hopes of all in this young Scot were terminated by his early death in Rome in 1766.   43. account: Martin Martin, *A Voyage to St. Kilda* (1698) and *A Description of the Western Islands of Scotland* (1703).

44. Thomson: This is James Thomson (d. 1748), the author of *The Seasons* and *The Castle of Indolence*.

about him as most writers. Everything appeared to him through the medium of his favorite pursuit. He could not have viewed those two candles burning but with a poetical eye."

"Has not —— [45] a great deal of wit, sir?" JOHNSON: "I do not think so, sir. He is, indeed, continually attempting wit, but he fails. And I have no more pleasure in hearing a man attempting wit and failing, than in seeing a man trying to leap over a ditch and tumbling into it."

He laughed heartily when I mentioned to him a saying of his concerning Mr. Thomas Sheridan, which Foote took a wicked pleasure to circulate. "Why, sir, Sherry is dull, naturally dull, but it must have taken him a great deal of pains to become what we now see him. Such an excess of stupidity, sir, is not in nature." "So," said he, "I allowed him all his own merit."

He now added, "Sheridan cannot bear me. I bring his declamation to a point. I ask him a plain question, 'What do you mean to teach?' Besides, sir, what influence can Mr. Sheridan have upon the language of this great country, by his narrow exertions? Sir, it is burning a farthing candle at Dover, to show light at Calais."

Talking of a young man [46] who was uneasy from thinking that he was very deficient in learning and knowledge, he said, "A man has no reason to complain who holds a middle place, and has many below him; and perhaps he has not six of his years above him; perhaps not one. Though he may not know anything perfectly, the general mass of knowledge that he has acquired is considerable. Time will do for him all that is wanting."

The conversation then took a philosophical turn. JOHNSON: "Human experience, which is constantly contradicting theory, is the great test of truth. A system, built upon the discoveries of a great many minds, is always of more strength, than what is produced by the mere workings of any one mind, which, of itself, can do little. There is not so poor a book in the world that would not be a prodigious effort were it wrought out entirely by a single mind, without the aid of prior investigators. The French writers are superficial, because they are not scholars, and so proceed upon the mere power of their own minds; and we see how very little power they have."

"As to the Christian religion, sir, besides the strong evidence which we have for it, there is a balance in its favor from the number of great men who have been convinced of its truth, after a serious consideration of the question. Grotius was an acute man, a lawyer, a man accustomed to examine evidence, and he was convinced. Grotius was not a recluse, but a man of the world, who certainly had no bias to the side of religion. Sir Isaac Newton set out an infidel, and came to be a very firm believer."

He this evening again recommended to me to perambulate Spain. I said it would amuse him to get a letter from me dated at Salamanca. JOHNSON: "I love the University of Salamanca; for when the Spaniards were in doubt as to the lawfulness of their conquering America, the University of Salamanca gave it as their opinion that it was not lawful." He spoke this with great emotion, and with that generous warmth which dictated the lines in his London, against Spanish encroachment.

I expressed my opinion of my friend Derrick as but a poor writer. JOHNSON: "To be sure, sir, he is, but you are to consider that his being a literary man has got for him all that he has. It has made him King of Bath.[47] Sir, he has nothing to say for himself but that he is a writer. Had he not been a writer, he must have been sweeping the crossings in the streets, and asking halfpence from everybody that passed."

In justice, however, to the memory of Mr. Derrick, who was my first tutor in the ways of London, and showed me the town in all its variety of departments, both literary and sportive, the particulars of which Dr. Johnson advised me to put in writing, it is proper to mention what Johnson, at a subsequent period, said of him both as a writer and an editor: "Sir, I have often said, that if Derrick's letters had been written by one of a more established name, they would have been thought very pretty letters." And, "I sent Derrick to Dryden's relations to gather materials for his life; and I believe he got all that I myself should have got."

Poor Derrick! I remember him with kindness. . . .

Johnson said once to me, "Sir, I honor Derrick for his presence of mind. One night, when Floyd, another poor author, was wandering about the streets in the night, he found Derrick fast asleep

---

45. Edmund Burke is conjectured to have been the subject of this question.   46. man: probably Boswell himself.

47. King of Bath: master of ceremonies in the city of Bath, an office long held by Richard "Beau" Nash, who died in 1761.

upon a bulk; [48] upon being suddenly waked, Derrick started up, 'My dear Floyd, I am sorry to see you in this destitute state; will you go home with me to *my lodgings?*'"

I again begged his advice as to my method of study at Utrecht. "Come," said he, "let us make a day of it. Let us go down to Greenwich and dine, and talk of it there." The following Saturday was fixed for this excursion.

As we walked along the Strand tonight, arm in arm, a woman of the town accosted us, in the usual enticing manner. "No, no, my girl," said Johnson, "it won't do." He, however, did not treat her with harshness; and we talked of the wretched life of such women, and agreed that much more misery than happiness, upon the whole, is produced by illicit commerce between the sexes.

On Saturday, July 30, Dr. Johnson and I took a sculler at the Temple Stairs, and set out for Greenwich. I asked him if he really thought a knowledge of the Greek and Latin languages an essential requisite to a good education. JOHNSON: "Most certainly, sir; for those who know them have a very great advantage over those who do not. Nay, sir, it is wonderful what a difference learning makes upon people even in the common intercourse of life, which does not appear to be much connected with it." "And yet," said I, "people go through the world very well, and carry on the business of life to good advantage, without learning." JOHNSON: "Why, sir, that may be true in cases where learning cannot possibly be of any use; for instance, this boy rows us as well without learning, as if he could sing the song of Orpheus to the Argonauts, who were the first sailors." He then called to the boy, "What would you give, my lad, to know about the Argonauts?" "Sir," said the boy, "I would give what I have." Johnson was much pleased with his answer, and we gave him a double fare. Dr. Johnson then turning to me, "Sir," said he, "a desire of knowledge is the natural feeling of mankind; and every human being, whose mind is not debauched, will be willing to give all that he has, to get knowledge."

We landed at the Old Swan, and walked to Billingsgate, where we took oars and moved smoothly along the silver Thames. It was a very fine day. We were entertained with the immense number and variety of ships that were lying at anchor, and with the beautiful country on each side of the river.

I talked of preaching, and of the great success which those called Methodist have. JOHNSON: "Sir, it is owing to their expressing themselves in a plain and familiar manner, which is the only way to do good to the common people, and which clergymen of genius and learning ought to do from a principle of duty, when it is suited to their congregations; a practice, for which they will be praised by men of sense. To insist against drunkenness as a crime, because it debases reason, the noblest faculty of man, would be of no service to the common people, but to tell them that they may die in a fit of drunkenness, and show them how dreadful that would be, cannot fail to make a deep impression. Sir, when your Scotch clergy give up their homely manner, religion will soon decay in that country." Let this observation, as Johnson meant it, be ever remembered.

I was much pleased to find myself with Johnson at Greenwich, which he celebrates in his *London* as a favorite scene. I had the poem in my pocket, and read the lines aloud with enthusiasm:

On Thames's banks in silent thought we stood,
Where Greenwich smiles upon the silver flood:
Pleased with the seat which gave Eliza [49] birth,
We kneel, and kiss the consecrated earth.

He remarked that the structure of Greenwich hospital was too magnificent for a place of charity, and that its parts were too much detached, to make one great whole.

Buchanan,[50] he said, was a very fine poet; and observed that he was the first who complimented a lady, by ascribing to her the different perfections of the heathen goddesses, but that Johnston improved upon this, by making his lady, at the same time, free from their defects.

He dwelt upon Buchanan's elegant verses to Mary, Queen of Scots, *Nympha Caledoniae,* &c. and spoke with enthusiasm of the beauty of Latin verse. "All the modern languages," said he, "cannot furnish so melodious a line as

Formosam resonare doces Amarillida silvas.[51]

---

48. bulk: a stall or projecting part of a building.

49. Eliza: Queen Elizabeth, of course, is meant. The royal palace of "Nonesuch" was pulled down by Charles II, and a marine hospital erected on the site.   50. Buchanan: George Buchanan (1506–82), a Scottish poet who wrote in Latin. So also did Arthur Johnston (1587–1641).   51. Virgil, *Eclogues,* I.5: "You teach the woods to echo lovely Amaryllis' name."

Afterwards he entered upon the business of the day, which was to give me his advice as to a course of study. And here I am to mention with much regret, that my record of what he said is miserably scanty. I recollect with admiration an animating blaze of eloquence, which roused every intellectual power in me to the highest pitch, but must have dazzled me so much that my memory could not preserve the substance of his discourse; for the note which I find of it is no more than this: "He ran over the grand scale of human knowledge; advised me to select some particular branch to excel in, but to acquire a little of every kind." The defect of my minutes will be fully supplied by a long letter upon the subject, which he favored me with, after I had been some time at Utrecht, and which my readers will have the pleasure to peruse in its proper place.

We walked in the evening in Greenwich Park. He asked me, I suppose, by way of trying my disposition, "Is not this very fine?" Having no exquisite relish of the beauties of nature, and being more delighted with "the busy hum of men," [52] I answered, "Yes, sir, but not equal to Fleet Street." JOHNSON: "You are right, sir."

I am aware that many of my readers may censure my want of taste. Let me, however, shelter myself under the authority of a very fashionable baronet [53] in the brilliant world, who, on his attention being called to the fragrance of a May evening in the country, observed, "This may be very well; but for my part, I prefer the smell of a flambeau at the playhouse."

We stayed so long at Greenwich, that our sail up the river, in our return to London, was by no means so pleasant as in the morning; for the night air was so cold that it made me shiver. I was the more sensible of it from having sat up all the night before recollecting and writing in my journal what I thought worthy of preservation, an exertion which, during the first part of my acquaintance with Johnson, I frequently made. I remember having sat up four nights in one week, without being much incommoded in the daytime.

Johnson, whose robust frame was not in the least affected by the cold, scolded me, as if my shivering had been a paltry effeminacy, saying, "Why do you shiver?" Sir William Scott, of the Commons,[54] told me that, when he complained of a headache in the post chaise, as they were traveling together to Scotland, Johnson treated him in the same manner: "At your age, sir, I had no headache." It is not easy to make allowance for sensations in others, which we ourselves have not at the time. We must all have experienced how very differently we are affected by the complaints of our neighbors, when we are well and when we are ill. In full health, we can scarcely believe that they suffer much, so faint is the image of pain upon our imagination; when softened by sickness, we readily sympathize with the sufferings of others.

We concluded the day at the Turk's Head Coffeehouse very socially. He was pleased to listen to a particular account which I gave him of my family, and of its hereditary estate, as to the extent and population of which he asked questions, and made calculations, recommending, at the same time, a liberal kindness to the tenantry, as people over whom the proprietor was placed by Providence. He took delight in hearing my description of the romantic seat of my ancestors. "I must be there, sir," said he, "and we will live in the old castle; and if there is not a room in it remaining, we will build one." I was highly flattered, but could scarcely indulge a hope that Auchinleck would indeed be honored by his presence, and celebrated by a description, as it afterwards was, in his *Journey to the Western Islands.*

After we had again talked of my setting out for Holland, he said, "I must see thee out of England; I will accompany you to Harwich." I could not find words to express what I felt upon this unexpected and very great mark of his affectionate regard.

Next day, Sunday, July 31, I told him I had been that morning at a meeting of the people called Quakers, where I had heard a woman preach. JOHNSON: "Sir, a woman's preaching is like a dog's walking on his hinder legs. It is not done well; but you are surprised to find it done at all."

On Tuesday, August 2 (the day of my departure from London having been fixed for the 5th), Dr. Johnson did me the honor to pass a part of the morning with me at my chambers. He said

---

52. "the . . . men": See Milton's "L'Allegro," l. 118, p. 418, above.   53. baronet: "My friend Sir Michael Le Fleming. This gentleman, with all his experience of sprightly and elegant life, inherits, with the beautiful family domain, no inconsiderable share of that love of literature which distinguished his venerable grandfather, the bishop of Carlisle. He one day observed to me, of Dr. Johnson, in a felicity of phrase, 'There is a blunt dignity about him on every occasion'" [B].

54. Commons: that is, Doctors' Commons, whose members' practice of law was confined to the ecclesiastical courts and the Court of the Admiralty.

that " he always felt an inclination to do nothing." I observed that it was strange to think that the most indolent man in Britain had written the most laborious work, the English Dictionary.

I mentioned an imprudent publication, by a certain friend of his, at an early period of life, and asked him if he thought it would hurt him. JOHNSON: " No, sir, not much. It may, perhaps, be mentioned at an election."

I had now made good my title to be a privileged man, and was carried by him in the evening to drink tea with Miss Williams, whom, though under the misfortune of having lost her sight, I found to be agreeable in conversation, for she had a variety of literature, and expressed herself well; but her peculiar value was the intimacy in which she had long lived with Johnson, by which she was well acquainted with his habits, and knew how to lead him on to talk.

After tea he carried me to what he called his walk, which was a long narrow paved court in the neighborhood, overshadowed by some trees. There we sauntered a considerable time; and I complained to him that my love of London and of his company was such, that I shrunk almost from the thought of going away even to travel, which is generally so much desired by young men. He roused me by manly and spirited conversation. He advised me, when settled in any place abroad, to study with an eagerness after knowledge, and to apply to Greek an hour every day; and when I was moving about, to read diligently the great book of mankind.

On Wednesday, August 3, we had our last social evening at the Turk's Head Coffeehouse, before my setting out for foreign parts. I had the misfortune, before we parted, to irritate him unintentionally. I mentioned to him how common it was in the world to tell absurd stories of him, and to ascribe to him very strange sayings. JOHNSON: " What do they make me say, sir? " BOSWELL: " Why, sir, as an instance very strange indeed (laughing heartily as I spoke), David Hume told me, you said that you would stand before a battery of cannon to restore the Convocation [55] to its full powers." Little did I apprehend that he had actually said this, but I was soon convinced of my error; for, with a determined look, he thundered out, " And would I not, sir? Shall the Presbyterian Kirk of Scotland

have its General Assembly, and the Church of England be denied its Convocation? " He was walking up and down the room while I told him the anecdote, but when he uttered this explosion of High Church zeal, he had come close to my chair, and his eyes flashed with indignation. I bowed to the storm, and diverted the force of it, by leading him to expatiate on the influence which religion derived from maintaining the Church with great external respectability.

I must not omit to mention that he this year wrote *The Life of Ascham,* and the dedication to the Earl of Shaftesbury, prefixed to the edition of that writer's [56] English works, published by Mr. Bennet.

On Friday, August 5, we set out early in the morning in the Harwich stagecoach. A fat elderly gentlewoman, and a young Dutchman, seemed the most inclined among us to conversation. At the inn where we dined, the gentlewoman said that she had done her best to educate her children, and, particularly, that she had never suffered them to be a moment idle. JOHNSON: " I wish, madam, you would educate me, too; for I have been an idle fellow all my life." " I am sure, sir," said she, " you have not been idle." JOHNSON: " Nay, madam, it is very true; and that gentleman there (pointing to me) has been idle. He was idle at Edinburgh. His father sent him to Glasgow, where he continued to be idle. He then came to London, where he has been very idle; and now he is going to Utrecht, where he will be as idle as ever." I asked him privately how he could expose me so. JOHNSON: " Poh, poh! " said he, " they knew nothing about you, and will think of it no more." In the afternoon the gentlewoman talked violently against the Roman Catholics, and of the horrors of the Inquisition. To the utter astonishment of all the passengers but myself, who knew that he could talk upon any side of a question, he defended the Inquisition, and maintained that " false doctrine should be checked on its first appearance; that the civil power should unite with the Church in punishing those who dared to attack the established religion, and that such only were punished by the Inquisition." He had in his pocket *Pomponius Mela de Situ Orbis,*[57] in which he read occasionally, and seemed very intent upon ancient

---

55. **Convocation:** a formal gathering of clergy of the English Church, coincident with the meetings of parliament. Since 1717 it had been discontinued.

56. Besides writing the Life and the Dedication, there is reason to think that Johnson was the actual, though not the nominal, editor of this edition of Roger Ascham, and that he allowed Bennet the credit of it. 57. *Pomponius . . . Orbis:* This work of Mela's was the first known geography of the ancient world to be written in Latin. Mela lived in the first century A.D.

geography. Though by no means niggardly, his attention to what was generally right was so minute, that having observed at one of the stages that I ostentatiously gave a shilling to the coachman, when the custom was for each passenger to give only sixpence, he took me aside and scolded me, saying that what I had done would make the coachman dissatisfied with all the rest of the passengers, who gave him no more than his due. This was a just reprimand; for in whatever way a man may indulge his generosity or his vanity in spending his money, for the sake of others he ought not to raise the price of any article for which there is a constant demand.

He talked of Mr. Blacklock's poetry, so far as it was descriptive of visible objects, and observed, that "as its author had the misfortune to be blind, we may be absolutely sure that such passages are combinations of what he has remembered of the works of other writers who could see. That foolish fellow, Spence,[58] has labored to explain philosophically how Blacklock may have done, by means of his own faculties, what it is impossible he should do. The solution, as I have given it, is plain. Suppose I know a man to be so lame that he is absolutely incapable to move himself, and I find him in a different room from that in which I left him; shall I puzzle myself with idle conjectures, that, perhaps, his nerves have by some unknown change all at once become effective? No, sir; it is clear how he got into a different room: he was *carried*."

Having stopped a night at Colchester, Johnson talked of that town with veneration, for having stood a siege for Charles I. The Dutchman alone now remained with us. He spoke English tolerably well; and thinking to recommend himself to us by expatiating on the superiority of the criminal jurisprudence of this country over that of Holland, he inveighed against the barbarity of putting an accused person to the torture, in order to force a confession. But Johnson was as ready for this as for the Inquisition. "Why, sir, you do not, I find, understand the law of your own country. The torture in Holland is considered as a favor to an accused person, for no man is put to the torture there, unless there is as much evidence against him as would amount to conviction in England. An accused person among you, therefore, has one chance more to escape punishment, than those who are tried among us."

At supper this night he talked of good eating with uncommon satisfaction. "Some people," said he, "have a foolish way of not minding, or pretending not to mind, what they eat. For my part, I mind my belly very studiously, and very carefully; for I look upon it, that he who does not mind his belly, will hardly mind anything else." He now appeared to me *Jean Bull philosophe,*[59] and he was, for the moment, not only serious, but vehement. Yet I have heard him, upon other occasions, talk with great contempt of people who were anxious to gratify their palates; and the 206th number of his *Rambler* is a masterly essay against gulosity.[60] His practice, indeed, I must acknowledge, may be considered as casting the balance of his different opinions upon this subject; for I never knew any man who relished good eating more than he did. When at table, he was totally absorbed in the business of the moment; his looks seemed riveted to his plate; nor would he, unless when in very high company, say one word, or even pay the least attention to what was said by others, till he had satisfied his appetite, which was so fierce, and indulged with such intenseness, that while in the act of eating, the veins of his forehead swelled, and generally a strong perspiration was visible. To those whose sensations were delicate, this could not but be disgusting; and it was doubtless not very suitable to the character of a philosopher, who should be distinguished by self-command. But it must be owned, that Johnson, though he could be rigidly *abstemious,* was not a *temperate* man either in eating or drinking. He could refrain, but he could not use moderately. He told me, that he had fasted two days without inconvenience, and that he had never been hungry but once. They who beheld with wonder how much he eat upon all occasions when his dinner was to his taste, could not easily conceive what he must have meant by hunger; and not only was he remarkable for the extraordinary quantity which he eat, but he was, or affected to be, a man of very nice discernment in the science of cookery. He used to descant critically on the dishes which had been at table where he had dined or supped, and to recollect very minutely what he had liked. I remember, when he was in Scotland, his praising "*Gordon's palates*" (a dish of palates[61] at the Hon. Alexander Gordon's) with a warmth of expression which might have done

58. Spence: Joseph Spence, *An Account of the Life, Character, and Poems of Mr. Blacklock* (1754).

59. *Jean . . . philosophe:* "John Bull turned philosopher." 60. gulosity: gluttony.   61. palates: Cows' palates were formerly thought a delicacy.

honor to more important subjects. "As for Maclaurin's imitation of a *made dish,* it was a wretched attempt. He about the same time was so much displeased with the performances of a nobleman's French cook, that he exclaimed with vehemence, "I'd throw such a rascal into the river"; and he then proceeded to alarm a lady at whose house he was to sup, by the following manifesto of his skill: "I, madam, who live at a variety of good tables, am a much better judge of cookery, than any person who has a very tolerable cook, but lives much at home, for his palate is gradually adapted to the taste of his cook; whereas, Madam, in trying by a wider range, I can more exquisitely judge." When invited to dine, even with an intimate friend, he was not pleased if something better than a plain dinner was not prepared for him. I have heard him say on such an occasion, "This was a good dinner enough, to be sure; but it was not a dinner to *ask* a man to." On the other hand, he was wont to express, with great glee, his satisfaction when he had been entertained quite to his mind. One day when we had dined with his neighbor and landlord, in Bolt Court, Mr. Allen, the printer, whose old housekeeper had studied his taste in everything, he pronounced this eulogy: "Sir, we could not have had a better dinner, had there been a *synod of cooks.*"

While we were left by ourselves, after the Dutchman had gone to bed, Dr. Johnson talked of that studied behavior which many have recommended and practiced. He disapproved of it, and said, "I never considered whether I should be a grave man, or a merry man, but just let inclination, for the time, have its course."

He flattered me with some hopes that he would, in the course of the following summer, come over to Holland, and accompany me in a tour through the Netherlands.

I teased him with fanciful apprehensions of unhappiness. A moth having fluttered round the candle, and burned itself, he laid hold of this little incident to admonish me, saying, with a sly look and in a solemn but quiet tone, "That creature was its own tormentor, and I believe its name was Boswell."

Next day we got to Harwich, to dinner, and my passage in the packet boat to Helvoetsluys being secured and my baggage put on board, we dined at our inn by ourselves. I happened to say, it would be terrible if he should not find a speedy opportunity of returning to London, and be con-

fined in so dull a place. JOHNSON: "Don't, sir, accustom yourself to use big words for little matters. It would *not* be *terrible,* though I *were* to be detained some time here." The practice of using words of disproportionate magnitude is, no doubt, too frequent everywhere, but, I think, most remarkable among the French, of which all who have traveled in France must have been struck with innumerable instances.

We went and looked at the church, and, having gone into it and walked up to the altar, Johnson, whose piety was constant and fervent, sent me to my knees, saying, "Now that you are going to leave your native country, recommend yourself to the protection of your Creator and Redeemer."

After we came out of the church, we stood talking for some time together of Bishop Berkeley's ingenious sophistry to prove the nonexistence of matter, and that everything in the universe is merely ideal. I observed, that though we are satisfied his doctrine is not true, it is impossible to refute it. I never shall forget the alacrity with which Johnson answered, striking his foot with mighty force against a large stone, till he rebounded from it, "I refute it *thus.*" This was a stout exemplification of the *first truths* of Père Buffier,[62] or the *original principles* of Reid and of Beattie, without admitting which, we can no more argue in metaphysics, than we can argue in mathematics without axioms. To me it is not conceivable how Berkeley can be answered by pure reasoning, but I know that the nice and difficult task was to have been undertaken by one of the most luminous minds [63] of the present age, had not politics "turned him from calm philosophy aside." What an admirable display of subtlety, united with brilliance, might his contending with Berkeley have afforded us! How must we, when we reflect on the loss of such an intellectual feast, regret that he should be characterized as the man,

Who born for the universe narrowed his mind,
And to party gave up what was meant for mankind? [64]

My revered friend walked down with me to the beach, where we embraced and parted with tender-

62. **Père Buffier:** The reference is to Claude Buffier (1661–1737), *Traité des vérités premières et de la source de nos jugements* ("Treatise on first truths and on the source of our judgments"). Thomas Reid was one of the leaders of the contemporary school of Scottish philosophers. James Beattie won more distinction as a poet and divine than as a philosopher.   63. **minds:** Edmund Burke is meant. The phrase here is inexactly quoted from Pope's *Satires,* II.ii.5.   64. From Goldsmith's spirited *Retaliation.*

ness, and engaged to correspond by letters. I said, "I hope, sir, you will not forget me in my absence." JOHNSON: "Nay, sir, it is more likely you should forget me, than that I should forget you." As the vessel put out to sea, I kept my eyes upon him for a considerable time, while he remained rolling his majestic frame in his usual manner; and at last I perceived him walk back into the town, and he disappeared. . . .

1769

He honored me with his company at dinner on the 16th of October, at my lodgings in Old Bond Street, with Sir Joshua Reynolds, Mr. Garrick, Dr. Goldsmith, Mr. Murphy, Mr. Bickerstaffe,[65] and Mr. Thomas Davies. Garrick played round him with a fond vivacity, taking hold of the breasts of his coat, and, looking up in his face with a lively archness, complimented him on the good health which he seemed then to enjoy; while the sage, shaking his head, beheld him with a gentle complacency. One of the company not being come at the appointed hour, I proposed, as usual upon such occasions, to order dinner to be served, adding, "Ought six people to be kept waiting for one?" "Why, yes," answered Johnson, with a delicate humanity, "if the one will suffer more by your sitting down, than the six will do by waiting." Goldsmith, to divert the tedious minutes, strutted about, bragging of his dress, and I believe was seriously vain of it, for his mind was wonderfully prone to such impressions. "Come, come," said Garrick, "talk no more of that. You are, perhaps, the worst—eh, eh!"—Goldsmith was eagerly attempting to interrupt him, when Garrick went on, laughing ironically, "Nay, you will always *look* like a gentleman, but I am talking of being well or *ill dressed.*" "Well, let me tell you," said Goldsmith, "when my tailor brought home my bloom-colored coat, he said, 'Sir, I have a favor to beg of you. When anybody asks you who made your clothes, be pleased to mention John Filby, at the Harrow, in Water Lane.'" JOHNSON: "Why, sir, that was because he knew the strange color would attract crowds to gaze at it, and thus they might hear of him, and see how well he could make a coat even of so absurd a color."

After dinner our conversation first turned upon Pope. Johnson said his characters of men were admirably drawn, those of women not so well. He repeated to us, in his forcible, melodious manner, the concluding lines of the *Dunciad.* While he was talking loudly in praise of those lines, one of the company [66] ventured to say, "Too fine for such a poem—a poem on what?" JOHNSON (with a disdainful look): "Why, on *dunces.* It was worth while being a dunce then. Ah, sir, hadst *thou* lived in those days! It is not worth while being a dunce now, when there are no wits." Bickerstaffe observed, as a peculiar circumstance, that Pope's fame was higher when he was alive than it was then. Johnson said, his *Pastorals* were poor things, though the versification was fine. He told us, with high satisfaction, the anecdote of Pope's inquiring who was the author of his *London,* and saying, he will be soon *déterré.*[67] He observed, that in Dryden's poetry there were passages drawn from a profundity which Pope could never reach. He repeated some fine lines on love, by the former (which I have now forgotten), and gave great applause to the character of Zimri.[68] Goldsmith said that Pope's character of Addison [69] showed a deep knowledge of the human heart. Johnson said that the description of the temple, in *The Mourning Bride,*[70] was the finest poetical passage he had ever read; he recollected none in Shakespeare equal to it. "But," said Garrick, all alarmed for "the God of his idolatry," "we know not the extent and variety of his powers. We are to suppose there are such passages in his works. Shakespeare must not suffer from the badness of our memories." Johnson, diverted by this enthusiastic jealousy, went on with great ardor: "No, sir; Congreve has *nature*" (smiling on the tragic eagerness of Garrick), but composing himself, he added, "Sir, this is not comparing Congreve on the whole with Shakespeare on the whole; but only maintaining that Congreve has one finer passage than any that can be found in Shakespeare. Sir, a man may have no more than ten guineas in the world, but he may have those ten guineas in one piece; and so may have a finer piece than a man who has ten thousand pounds; but then he has only one ten-guinea piece. What I mean is, that you can show me no passage where there is simply a description of material objects, without any intermixture of moral notions, which produces such an effect." Mr. Murphy mentioned Shakespeare's description of the night before the battle

65. Murphy, Bickerstaffe: Arthur Murphy and Isaac Bickerstaffe were popular playwrights.

66. one . . . company: doubtless Boswell himself.   67. *déterré:* "unearthed."   68. Zimri: in Dryden's *Absalom and Achitophel,* a character standing for the Duke of Buckingham.   69. Addison: in *An Epistle to Dr. Arbuthnot,* ll. 193 ff. See p. 821 above.   70. *The . . . Bride:* by William Congreve, II.i.

of Agincourt, but it was observed it had *men* in it. Mr. Davies suggested the speech of Juliet, in which she figures herself awaking in the tomb of her ancestors. Someone mentioned the description of Dover Cliff.[71] JOHNSON: "No, sir; it should be all precipice, all vacuum. The crows impede your fall. The diminished appearance of the boats, and other circumstances, are all very good description, but do not impress the mind at once with the horrible idea of immense height. The impression is divided; you pass on by computation, from one stage of the tremendous space to another. Had the girl in *The Mourning Bride* said she could not cast her shoe to the top of one of the pillars in the temple, it would not have aided the idea, but weakened it."

Talking of a barrister who had a bad utterance, someone (to rouse Johnson) wickedly said that he was unfortunate in not having been taught oratory by Sheridan. JOHNSON: "Nay, sir, if he had been taught by Sheridan, he would have cleared the room." GARRICK: "Sheridan has too much vanity to be a good man." We shall now see Johnson's mode of *defending* a man; taking him into his own hands, and discriminating. JOHNSON: "No, sir. There is, to be sure, in Sheridan, something to reprehend, and everything to laugh at; but, sir, he is not a bad man. No, sir, were mankind to be divided into good and bad, he would stand considerably within the ranks of good. And, sir, it must be allowed that Sheridan excels in plain declamation, though he can exhibit no character."

I should, perhaps, have suppressed this disquisition concerning a person of whose merit and worth I think with respect, had he not attacked Johnson so outrageously in his *Life of Swift,* and, at the same time, treated us his admirers as a set of pygmies. He who has provoked the lash of wit cannot complain that he smarts from it.

Mrs. Montagu,[72] a lady distinguished for having written an essay on Shakespeare, being mentioned, REYNOLDS: "I think that essay does her honor." JOHNSON: "Yes, sir, it does *her* honor, but it would do nobody else honor. I have, indeed, not read it all. But when I take up the end of a web, and find it pack thread, I do not expect, by looking further, to find embroidery. Sir, I will venture to say, there is not one sentence of true criticism in her book." GARRICK: "But, sir, surely it shows how much Voltaire has mistaken Shakespeare, which nobody

else has done." JOHNSON: "Sir, nobody else has thought it worth while. And what merit is there in that? You may as well praise a schoolmaster for whipping a boy who has construed ill. No, sir, there is no real criticism in it: none showing the beauty of thought, as formed on the workings of the human heart."

The admirers of this essay may be offended at the slighting manner in which Johnson spoke of it; but let it be remembered, that he gave his honest opinion unbiased by any prejudice, or any proud jealousy of a woman intruding herself into the chair of criticism; for Sir Joshua Reynolds has told me, that when the essay first came out, and it was not known who had written it, Johnson wondered how Sir Joshua could like it. At this time Sir Joshua himself had received no information concerning the author, except being assured by one of our most eminent literati that it was clear its author did not know the Greek tragedies in the original. One day at Sir Joshua's table, when it was related that Mrs. Montagu, in an excess of compliment to the author of a modern tragedy, had exclaimed, "I tremble for Shakespeare," Johnson said, "When Shakespeare has got —— for his rival, and Mrs. Montagu for his defender, he is in a poor state indeed."

Johnson proceeded: "The Scotchman [73] has taken the right method in his *Elements of Criticism.* I do not mean that he has taught us anything, but he has told us old things in a new way." MURPHY: "He seems to have read a great deal of French criticism, and wants to make it his own; as if he had been for years anatomizing the heart of man, and peeping into every cranny of it." GOLDSMITH: "It is easier to write that book than to read it." JOHNSON: "We have an example of true criticism in Burke's *Essay on the Sublime and Beautiful,*[74] and, if I recollect, there is also Du Bos; and Bouhours, who shows all beauty to depend on truth. There is no great merit in telling how many plays have ghosts in them, and how this ghost is better than that. You must show how terror is impressed on the human heart. In the description of night in *Macbeth,*[75] the beetle and the bat detract from the general idea of darkness, — inspissated [76] gloom."

Politics being mentioned, he said, "This petitioning is a new mode of distressing government, and

---

71. Dover Cliff: See *King Lear,* IV.vi.17 ff.   72. Mrs. Montagu: Elizabeth Montagu, "Queen" of the Bluestockings, defended Shakespeare's reputation against the attacks of Voltaire.

73. Scotchman: Henry Home, Lord Kames. See n. 4, above. 74. Burke's *Essay:* first published 1757 and often thereafter. The two Frenchmen here mentioned were names of great influence in critical theory of the Neoclassical school.   75. *Macbeth:* III.ii.40 ff.   76. inspissated: thickened or condensed.

a mighty easy one. I will undertake to get petitions either against quarter-guineas or half-guineas, with the help of a little hot wine. There must be no yielding to encourage this. The object is not important enough. We are not to blow up half a dozen palaces, because one cottage is burning."

The conversation then took another turn. JOHNSON: "It is amazing what ignorance of certain points one sometimes finds in men of eminence. A wit about town, who wrote Latin bawdy verses, asked me, how it happened that England and Scotland, which were once two kingdoms, were now one: — and Sir Fletcher Norton [77] did not seem to know that there were such publications as the *Reviews*."

"The ballad of Hardyknute [78] has no great merit, if it be really ancient. People talk of nature. But mere obvious nature may be exhibited with very little power of mind."

On Thursday, October 19, I passed the evening with him at his house. He advised me to complete a dictionary of words peculiar to Scotland, of which I showed him a specimen. "Sir," said he, "Ray has made a collection of North Country words. By collecting those of your country, you will do a useful thing towards the history of the language." He bade me also go on with collections which I was making upon the antiquities of Scotland. "Make a large book, a folio." BOSWELL: "But of what use will it be, sir?" JOHNSON: "Never mind the use; do it."

I complained that he had not mentioned Garrick in his Preface to Shakespeare, and asked him if he did not admire him. JOHNSON: "Yes, as 'a poor player, who frets and struts his hour upon the stage' [79] — as a shadow." BOSWELL: "But has he not brought Shakespeare into notice?" JOHNSON: "Sir, to allow that, would be to lampoon the age. Many of Shakespeare's plays are the worse for being acted: Macbeth, for instance." BOSWELL: "What, sir, is nothing gained by decoration and action? Indeed, I do wish that you had mentioned Garrick." JOHNSON: "My dear sir, had I mentioned him, I must have mentioned many more: Mrs. Pritchard, Mrs. Cibber — nay, and Mr. Cibber, too; he too altered Shakespeare." BOSWELL: "You

have read his apology,[80] sir?" JOHNSON: "Yes, it is very entertaining. But as for Cibber himself, taking from his conversation all that he ought not to have said, he was a poor creature. I remember when he brought me one of his odes to have my opinion of it, I could not bear such nonsense, and would not let him read it to the end; so little respect had I for *that great man!* (laughing). Yet I remember Richardson wondering that I could treat him with familiarity."

I mentioned to him that I had seen the execution of several convicts at Tyburn, two days before, and that none of them seemed to be under any concern. JOHNSON: "Most of them, sir, have never thought at all." BOSWELL: "But is not the fear of death natural to man?" JOHNSON: "So much so, sir, that the whole of life is but keeping away the thoughts of it." He then, in a low and earnest tone, talked of his meditating upon the awful hour of his own dissolution, and in what manner he should conduct himself upon that occasion: "I know not," said he, "whether I should wish to have a friend by me, or have it all between God and myself."

Talking of our feeling for the distresses of others, JOHNSON: "Why, sir, there is much noise made about it, but it is greatly exaggerated. No, sir, we have a certain degree of feeling to prompt us to do good; more than that, Providence does not intend. It would be misery to no purpose." BOSWELL: "But suppose now, sir, that one of your intimate friends were apprehended for an offense for which he might be hanged." JOHNSON: "I should do what I could to bail him, and give him any other assistance; but if he were once fairly hanged, I should not suffer." BOSWELL: "Would you eat your dinner that day, sir?" JOHNSON: "Yes, sir; and eat it as if he were eating it with me. Why, there's Baretti,[81] who is to be tried for his life tomorrow; friends have risen up for him on every side; yet if he should be hanged, none of them will eat a slice of plum pudding the less. Sir, that sympathetic feeling goes a very little way in depressing the mind."

I told him that I had dined lately at Foote's, who showed me a letter which he had received from Tom Davies, telling him that he had not been able to sleep from the concern he felt on account of "*This sad affair of Baretti,*" begging of him to try

77. **Norton:** This man, who was often unfavorably noticed, was none the less Speaker of the House of Commons.   78. **Hardyknute:** "Hardyknute" was attributed to Elizabeth Halket, Lady Wardlaw. But many in Johnson's day believed it an ancient traditional ballad, and admired it the more for being old. Johnson thought ill of it in either case.   79. *Macbeth,* V.v.24–25.

80. **apology:** See n. 11, above.   81. Giuseppe Baretti, an educated Italian who lived in terms of some intimacy with the London literary circle, and who had been engaged by the Thrales to tutor their children. See p. 901, below, under date October 20.

if he could suggest anything that might be of service; and, at the same time, recommending to him an industrious young man who kept a pickle shop. JOHNSON: "Ay, sir, here you have a specimen of human sympathy: a friend hanged, and a cucumber pickled. We know not whether Baretti or the pickle man has kept Davies from sleep; nor does he know himself. And as to his not sleeping, sir, Tom Davies is a very great man; Tom has been upon the stage and knows how to do those things: I have not been upon the stage, and cannot do those things." BOSWELL: "I have often blamed myself, sir, for not feeling for others as sensibly as many say they do." JOHNSON: "Sir, don't be duped by them any more. You will find these very feeling people are not very ready to do you good. They *pay* you by *feeling*."

BOSWELL: "Foote has a great deal of humor." JOHNSON: "Yes, sir." BOSWELL: "He has a singular talent of exhibiting character." JOHNSON: "Sir, it is not a talent; it is a vice; it is what others abstain from. It is not comedy, which exhibits the character of a species, as that of a miser gathered from many misers: it is a farce which exhibits individuals." BOSWELL: "Did not he think of exhibiting you, sir?" JOHNSON: "Sir, fear restrained him; he knew I would have broken his bones. I would have saved him the trouble of cutting off a leg; I would not have left him a leg to cut off." BOSWELL: "Pray, sir, is not Foote an infidel?" JOHNSON: "I do not know, sir, that the fellow is an infidel; but if he be an infidel, he is an infidel as a dog is an infidel; that is to say, he has never thought upon the subject." [82] BOSWELL: "I suppose, sir, he has thought superficially, and seized the first notions which occurred to his mind." JOHNSON: "Why, then, sir, still he is like a dog, that snatches the piece next him. Did you never observe that dogs have not the power of comparing? A dog will take a small bit of meat as readily as a large, when both are before him."

"Buchanan," he observed, "has fewer *centos* [83] than any modern Latin poet. He not only had great knowledge of the Latin language, but was a great poetical genius. Both the Scaligers praise him."

He again talked of the passage in Congreve with high commendation, and said, "Shakespeare never has six lines together without a fault. Perhaps you may find seven, but this does not refute my general assertion. If I come to an orchard, and say there's no fruit here, and then comes a poring man, who finds two apples and three pears, and tells me, 'Sir, you are mistaken, I have found both apples and pears,' I should laugh at him; what would that be to the purpose?"

BOSWELL: "What do you think of Dr. Young's *Night Thoughts*,[84] sir?" JOHNSON: "Why, sir, there are very fine things in them." BOSWELL: "Is there not less religion in the nation now, sir, than there was formerly?" JOHNSON: "I don't know, sir, that there is." BOSWELL: "For instance, there used to be a chaplain in every great family, which we do not find now." JOHNSON: "Neither do you find any of the state servants which great families used formerly to have. There is a change of modes in the whole department of life."

Next day, October 20, he appeared, for the only time I suppose in his life, as a witness in a court of justice, being called to give evidence to the character of Mr. Baretti, who having stabbed a man in the street, was arraigned at the Old Bailey for murder. Never did such a constellation of genius enlighten the awful Sessions House, emphatically called Justice Hall: Mr. Burke, Mr. Garrick, Mr. Beauclerk, and Dr. Johnson; and undoubtedly their favorable testimony had due weight with the court and jury. Johnson gave his evidence in a slow, deliberate, and distinct manner, which was uncommonly impressive. It is well known that Mr. Baretti was acquitted.

On the 26th of October, we dined together at the Mitre Tavern. I found fault with Foote for indulging his talent of ridicule at the expense of his visitors, which I colloquially termed making fools of his company. JOHNSON: "Why, sir, when you go to see Foote, you do not go to see a saint: you

82. "When Mr. Foote was at Edinburgh, he thought fit to entertain a numerous Scotch company with a great deal of coarse jocularity, at the expense of Dr. Johnson, imagining it would be acceptable. I felt this as not civil to me; but sat very patiently till he had exhausted his merriment on that subject; and then observed, that surely Johnson must be allowed to have some sterling wit, and that I had heard him say a very good thing of Mr. Foote himself. 'Ah, my old friend Sam,' cried Foote, 'no man says better things: do let us have it.' Upon which I told the above story, which produced a very loud laugh from the company. But I never saw Foote so disconcerted. He looked grave and angry, and entered into a serious refutation of the justice of the remark. 'What, sir,' said he, 'talk thus of a man of liberal education — a man who for years was at the University of Oxford — a man who has added sixteen new characters to the English drama of his country!'" [B] Samuel Foote (1720–77) was a not very respectable actor and dramatist, whose chief skill lay in mimicking his contemporaries. He wrote many farces, based as a rule upon topics of the day.

83. *centos:* scraps pieced together from older authors.   84. *Night Thoughts:* the best-known work of the poet and playwright, Edward Young. It was gradually enlarged to nine books in blank verse (1742–45) and was enormously popular for more than a century.

go to see a man who will be entertained at your house, and then bring you on a public stage; who will entertain you at his house, for the very purpose of bringing you on a public stage. Sir, he does not make fools of his company; they whom he exposes are fools already; he only brings them into action."

Talking of trade, he observed, " It is a mistaken notion that a vast deal of money is brought into a nation by trade. It is not so. Commodities come from commodities; but trade produces no capital accession of wealth. However, though there should be little profit in money, there is a considerable profit in pleasure, as it gives to one nation the productions of another; as we have wines and fruits, and many other foreign articles, brought to us." BOSWELL: " Yes, sir, and there is a profit in pleasure, by its furnishing occupation to such numbers of mankind." JOHNSON: " Why, sir, you cannot call that pleasure to which all are averse, and which none begin but with the hope of leaving off; a thing which men dislike before they have tried it, and when they have tried it." BOSWELL: " But, sir, the mind must be employed, and we grow weary when idle." JOHNSON: " That is, sir, because, others being busy, we want company; but if we were all idle, there would be no growing weary; we should all entertain one another. There is indeed, this in trade: it gives men an opportunity of improving their situation. If there were no trade, many who are poor would always remain poor. But no man loves labor for itself." BOSWELL: " Yes, sir, I know a person who does. He is a very laborious judge, and he loves the labor." JOHNSON: " Sir, that is because he loves respect and distinction. Could he have them without labor, he would like it less." BOSWELL: " He tells me he likes it for itself." " Why, sir, he fancies so because he is not accustomed to abstract."

We went home to his house to tea. Mrs. Williams made it with sufficient dexterity, notwithstanding her blindness, though her manner of satisfying herself that the cups were full enough appeared to me a little awkward; for I fancied she put her finger down a certain way, till she felt the tea touch it.[85] In my first elation at being allowed the privilege of attending Dr. Johnson at his late visits to this lady, which was like being è secretioribus

consiliis,[86] I willingly drank cup after cup, as if it had been the Heliconian spring. But as the charm of novelty went off, I grew more fastidious; and besides, I discovered that she was of a peevish temper.

There was a pretty large circle this evening. Dr. Johnson was in very good humor, lively, and ready to talk upon all subjects. Mr. Fergusson, the self-taught philosopher, told him of a new invented machine which went without horses: a man who sat in it turned a handle, which worked a spring that drove it forward. " Then, sir," said Johnson, " what is gained is, the man has his choice whether he will move himself alone, or himself and the machine too." Dominicetti[87] being mentioned, he would not allow him any merit. " There is nothing in all this boasted system. No, sir; medicated baths can be no better than warm water: their only effect can be that of tepid moisture." One of the company took the other side, maintaining that medicines of various sorts, and some too of most powerful effect, are introduced into the human frame by the medium of the pores, and, therefore, when warm water is impregnated with salutiferous substances, it may produce great effects as a bath. This appeared to me very satisfactory. Johnson did not answer it, but talking for victory, and determined to be master of the field, he had recourse to the device which Goldsmith imputed to him in the witty words of one of Cibber's comedies: " There is no arguing with Johnson; for when his pistol misses fire, he knocks you down with the butt end of it." He turned to the gentleman,[88] " Well, sir, go to Dominicetti, and get thyself fumigated, but be sure that the steam be directed to thy *head*, for *that* is the *peccant part*." This produced a triumphant roar of laughter from the motley assembly of philosophers, printers, and dependants, male and female.

I know not how so whimsical a thought came into my mind, but I asked, " If, sir, you were shut up in a castle, and a newborn child with you, what would you do? " JOHNSON: " Why, sir, I should not much like my company." BOSWELL: " But would you take the trouble of rearing it? " He seemed, as may well be supposed, unwilling to pursue the subject, but, upon my persevering in my question, replied, " Why yes, sir, I would; but I must have

---

85. "I have since had reason to think that I was mistaken; for I have been informed by a lady, who was long intimate with her, and likely to be a more accurate observer of such matters, that she had acquired such a niceness of touch, as to know, by the feeling on the outside of the cup, how near it was to being full" [B].

86. è . . . *consiliis:* "a member of the inner cabinet."   87. **Do-minicetti:** an Italian pretender to science, who had established in Chelsea a place for medicated hot bathing.   88. **gentleman:** Boswell was probably again the butt of this jest.

all conveniences. If I had no garden, I would make a shed on the roof, and take it there for fresh air. I should feed it, and wash it much, and with warm water to please it, not with cold water to give it pain." BOSWELL: "But, sir, does not heat relax?" JOHNSON: "Sir, you are not to imagine the water is to be very hot. I would not *coddle* the child. No, sir, the hardy method of treating children does no good. I'll take you five children from London, who shall cuff five Highland children. Sir, a man bred in London will carry a burthen, or run, or wrestle, as well as a man brought up in the hardiest manner in the country." BOSWELL: "Good living, I suppose, makes the Londoners strong." JOHNSON: "Why, sir, I don't know that it does. Our chairmen [89] from Ireland, who are as strong men as any, have been brought up upon potatoes. Quantity makes up for quality." BOSWELL: "Would you teach this child that I have furnished you with, anything?" JOHNSON: "No, I should not be apt to teach it." BOSWELL: "Would not you have a pleasure in teaching it?" JOHNSON. "No, sir, I should *not* have a pleasure in teaching it." BOSWELL: "Have you not a pleasure in teaching men? *There* I have you. You have the same pleasure in teaching men that I should have in teaching children." JOHNSON: "Why, something about that."

BOSWELL. "Do you think, sir, that what is called natural affection is born with us? It seems to me to be the effect of habit, or of gratitude for kindness. No child has it for a parent whom it has not seen." JOHNSON: "Why, sir, I think there is an instinctive natural affection in parents towards their children."

Russia being mentioned as likely to become a great empire, by the rapid increase of population, JOHNSON: "Why, sir, I see no prospect of their propagating more. They can have no more children than they can get. I know of no way to make them breed more than they do. It is not from reason and prudence that people marry, but from inclination. A man is poor; he thinks, 'I cannot be worse, and so I'll e'en take Peggy.'" BOSWELL: "But have not nations been more populous at one period than another?" JOHNSON: "Yes, sir, but that has been owing to the people being less thinned at one period than another, whether by emigrations, war, or pestilence, not by their being more or less prolific. Births at all times bear the same proportion to the same number of people." BOSWELL: "But, to consider the state of our own country — does not

throwing a number of farms into one hand hurt population?" JOHNSON: "Why, no, sir; the same quantity of food being produced will be consumed by the same number of mouths, though the people may be disposed of in different ways. We see, if corn be dear, and butchers' meat cheap, the farmers all apply themselves to the raising of corn, till it becomes plentiful and cheap, and then butchers' meat becomes dear; so that an equality is always preserved. No, sir, let fanciful men do as they will, depend upon it, it is difficult to disturb the system of life.". . .

May 7, 1773

He did not give me full credit when I mentioned that I had carried on a short conversation by signs with some Esquimaux, who were then in London, particularly with one of them who was a priest. He thought I could not make them understand me. No man was more incredulous as to particular facts, which were at all extraordinary; and therefore no man was more scrupulously inquisitive, in order to discover the truth.

I dined with him this day at the house of my friends, Messrs. Edward and Charles Dilly, booksellers in the Poultry; there were present their elder brother Mr. Dilly of Bedfordshire, Dr. Goldsmith, Mr. Langton, Mr. Claxton, Rev. Dr. Mayo, a dissenting minister, the Rev. Mr. Toplady, [90] and my friend the Rev. Mr. Temple.

Hawkesworth's compilation of the voyages to the South Sea being mentioned, JOHNSON: "Sir, if you talk of it as a subject of commerce, it will be gainful; if as a book that is to increase human knowledge, I believe there will not be much of that. Hawkesworth can tell only what the voyagers have told him; and they have found very little, only one new animal, I think." BOSWELL: "But many insects, sir." JOHNSON: "Why, sir, as to insects, Ray reckons of British insects twenty thousand species. They might have stayed at home and discovered enough in that way."

Talking of birds, I mentioned Mr. Daines Barrington's [91] ingenious essay against the received notion of their migration. JOHNSON: "I think we have as good evidence for the migration of woodcocks as can be desired. We find they disappear at a certain time of the year, and appear again at a certain time of the year; and some of them, when

90. Toplady: the author of the favorite hymn, "Rock of Ages."
91. Barrington: amateur naturalist and correspondent of Gilbert White of Selborne, more than half of whose letters in *The Natural History of Selborne* are addressed to him.

weary in their flight, have been known to alight on the rigging of ships far out at sea." One of the company observed that there had been instances of some of them found in summer in Essex. JOHNSON: "Sir, that strengthens our argument. *Exceptio probat regulam.*[92] Some being found shows that, if all remained, many would be found. A few sick or lame ones may be found." GOLDSMITH: "There is a partial migration of the swallows; the stronger ones migrate, the others do not."

BOSWELL: "I am well assured that the people of Otaheite,[93] who have the bread tree, the fruit of which serves them for bread, laughed heartily when they were informed of the tedious process necessary with us to have bread — plowing, sowing, harrowing, reaping, threshing, grinding, baking." JOHNSON: "Why, sir, all ignorant savages will laugh when they are told of the advantages of the civilized life. Were you to tell men who live without houses how we pile brick upon brick, and rafter upon rafter, and that after a house is raised to a certain height, a man tumbles off a scaffold, and breaks his neck, [they] would laugh heartily at our folly in building; but it does not follow that men are better without houses. No, sir (holding up a slice of a good loaf), this is better than the bread tree."

He repeated an argument, which is to be found in his *Rambler,* against the notion that the brute creation is endowed with the faculty of reason: "Birds build by instinct; they never improve; they build their first nest as well as any one they ever build."[94] GOLDSMITH: "Yet we see if you take away a bird's nest with the eggs in it, she will make a slighter nest and lay again." JOHNSON: "Sir, that is because at first she has full time and makes her nest deliberately. In the case you mention she is pressed to lay, and must therefore make her nest quickly, and consequently it will be slight." GOLDSMITH: "The nidification[95] of birds is what is least known in natural history, though one of the most curious things in it."

I introduced the subject of toleration. JOHNSON: "Every society has a right to preserve public peace and order, and therefore has a good right to prohibit the propagation of opinions which have a dangerous tendency. To say the *magistrate* has this right, is using an inadequate word: it is the *society* for which the magistrate is agent. He may be morally or theologically wrong in restraining the propa-

gation of opinions which he thinks dangerous, but he is politically right." MAYO: "I am of opinion, sir, that every man is entitled to liberty of conscience in religion, and that the magistrate cannot restrain that right." JOHNSON: "Sir, I agree with you. Every man has a right to liberty of conscience, and with that the magistrate cannot interfere. People confound liberty of thinking with liberty of talking, nay, with liberty of preaching. Every man has a physical right to think as he pleases, for it cannot be discovered how he thinks. He has not a moral right, for he ought to inform himself, and think justly. But, sir, no member of a society has a right to *teach* any doctrine contrary to what the society holds to be true. The magistrate, I say, may be wrong in what he thinks, but, while he thinks himself right, he may and ought to enforce what he thinks." MAYO: "Then, sir, we are to remain always in error, and truth never can prevail, and the magistrate was right in persecuting the first Christians." JOHNSON: "Sir, the only method by which religious truth can be established is by martyrdom. The magistrate has a right to enforce what he thinks, and he who is conscious of the truth has a right to suffer. I am afraid there is no other way of ascertaining the truth, but by persecution on the one hand and enduring it on the other." GOLDSMITH: "But how is a man to act, sir? Though firmly convinced of the truth of his doctrine, may he not think it wrong to expose himself to persecution? Has he a right to do so? Is it not, as it were, committing voluntary suicide?" JOHNSON: "Sir, as to voluntary suicide, as you call it, there are twenty thousand men in an army who will go without scruple to be shot at, and mount a breach for fivepence a day." GOLDSMITH: "But have they a moral right to do this?" JOHNSON: "Nay, sir, if you will not take the universal opinion of mankind, I have nothing to say. If mankind cannot defend their own way of thinking, I cannot defend it. Sir, if a man is in doubt whether it would be better for him to expose himself to martyrdom or not, he should not do it. He must be convinced that he has a delegation from Heaven." GOLDSMITH: "I would consider whether there is the greater chance of good or evil upon the whole. If I see a man who has fallen into a well, I would wish to help him out, but if there is a greater probability that he shall pull me in, than that I shall pull him out, I would not attempt it. So were I to go to Turkey, I might wish to convert the grand Signor to the Christian faith; but when I considered that I should probably

92. *Exceptio . . . regulam:* "The exception proves the rule." 93. Otaheite: now called Tahiti. 94. *Rambler,* No. 41. 95. nidification: nestmaking.

be put to death without effectuating my purpose in any degree, I should keep myself quiet." JOHNSON: " Sir, you must consider that we have perfect and imperfect obligations. Perfect obligations, which are generally not to do something, are clear and positive, as, 'thou shalt not kill.' But charity, for instance, is not definable by limits. It is a duty to give to the poor, but no man can say how much another should give to the poor, or when a man has given too little to save his soul. In the same manner, it is a duty to instruct the ignorant, and of consequence to convert infidels to Christianity, but no man in the common course of things is obliged to carry this to such a degree as to incur the danger of martyrdom, as no man is obliged to strip himself to the shirt in order to give charity. I have said that a man must be persuaded that he has a particular delegation from Heaven." GOLDSMITH: " How is this to be known? Our first reformers, who were burned for not believing bread and wine to be Christ — " JOHNSON (interrupting him): " Sir, they were not burned for not believing bread and wine to be Christ, but for insulting those who did believe it. And, sir, when the first reformers began, they did not intend to be martyred; as many of them ran away as could." BOSWELL: " But, sir, there was your countryman,[96] Elwal, who you told me challenged King George with his black guards, and his red guards." JOHNSON: " My countryman, Elwal, sir, should have been put in the stocks, a proper pulpit for him; and he'd have had a numerous audience. A man who preaches in the stocks will always have hearers enough." BOSWELL: " But Elwal thought himself in the right." JOHNSON: " We are not providing for mad people; there are places for them in the neighborhood " (meaning Moorfields). MAYO: " But, sir, is it not very hard that I should not be allowed to teach my children what I really believe to be the truth? " JOHNSON: " Why, sir, you might contrive to teach your children *extra scandalum,* but, sir, the magistrate, if he knows it, has a right to restrain you. Suppose you teach your children to be thieves? " MAYO: " This is making a joke of the subject." JOHNSON: " Nay, sir, take it thus — that you teach them the community of goods, for which there are as many plausible arguments as for most erroneous doctrines. You teach them that all things at first were in common, and that no man had a right to anything but as he laid his hands upon it; and that this still is, or ought to

be, the rule amongst mankind. Here, sir, you sap a great principle in society — property. And don't you think the magistrate would have a right to prevent you? Or suppose you should teach your children the notion of the Adamites, and they should run naked into the streets, would not the magistrate have a right to flog 'em into their doublets? " MAYO: " I think the magistrate has no right to interfere till there is some overt act." BOSWELL: " So, sir, though he sees an enemy to the state charging a blunderbuss, he is not to interfere till it is fired off? " MAYO: " He must be sure of its direction against the state." JOHNSON: " The magistrate is to judge of that. He has no right to restrain your thinking, because the evil centers in yourself. If a man were sitting at this table, and chopping off his fingers, the magistrate, as guardian of the community, has no authority to restrain him, however he might do it from kindness as a parent. Though, indeed, upon more consideration, I think he may, as it is probable that he who is chopping off his own fingers may soon proceed to chop off those of other people. If I think it right to steal Mr. Dilly's plate, I am a bad man, but he can say nothing to me. If I make an open declaration that I think so, he will keep me out of his house. If I put forth my hand, I shall be sent to Newgate. This is the gradation of thinking, preaching, and acting: if a man thinks erroneously, he may keep his thoughts to himself, and nobody will trouble him; if he preaches erroneous doctrine, society may expel him; if he acts in consequence of it, the law takes place, and he is hanged." MAYO: " But, sir, ought not Christians to have liberty of conscience? " JOHNSON: " I have already told you so, sir. You are coming back to where you were." BOSWELL: " Dr. Mayo is always taking a return post chaise, and going the stage over again. He has it at half price." JOHNSON: " Dr. Mayo, like other champions for unlimited toleration, has got a set of words.[97] Sir, it is no matter, politically, whether the magistrate be right or wrong. Suppose a club were to be formed, to drink confusion to King George III, and a happy restoration to Charles III; this would be very bad with respect to the state, but every member of that club must either conform to its rules, or be turned

---

96. **countryman:** Elwall came from the same *county* as Johnson.

97. "Dr. Mayo's calm temper and steady perseverance rendered him an admirable subject for the exercise of Dr. Johnson's powerful abilities. He never flinched, but after reiterated blows remained seemingly unmoved as at the first. The scintillations of Johnson's genius flashed every time he was struck, without his receiving any injury. Hence he obtained the epithet of 'The Literary Anvil'" [B].

out of it. Old Baxter, I remember, maintains that the magistrate should 'tolerate all things that are tolerable.' This is no good definition of toleration upon any principle, but it shows that he thought some things were not tolerable." TOPLADY: " Sir, you have untwisted this difficult subject with great dexterity."

During this argument, Goldsmith sat in restless agitation, from a wish to get in and *shine*. Finding himself excluded, he had taken his hat to go away but remained for some time with it in his hand, like a gamester who, at the close of a long night, lingers for a little while, to see if he can have a favorable opening to finish with success. Once when he was beginning to speak, he found himself overpowered by the loud voice of Johnson, who was at the opposite end of the table and did not perceive Goldsmith's attempt. Thus disappointed of his wish to obtain the attention of the company, Goldsmith in a passion threw down his hat, looking angrily at Johnson, and exclaimed in a bitter tone, *"Take it."* When Toplady was going to speak, Johnson uttered some sound, which led Goldsmith to think that he was beginning again, and taking the words from Toplady. Upon which, he seized this opportunity of venting his own envy and spleen, under the pretext of supporting another person: " Sir," said he to Johnson, " the gentleman has heard you patiently for an hour; pray allow us now to hear him." JOHNSON (sternly): " Sir, I was not interrupting the gentleman. I was only giving him a signal of my attention. Sir, you are impertinent." Goldsmith made no reply, but continued in the company for some time.

A gentleman present ventured to ask Dr. Johnson if there was not a material difference as to toleration of opinions which lead to action, and opinions merely speculative; for instance, would it be wrong in the magistrate to tolerate those who preach against the doctrine of the Trinity? Johnson was highly offended and said, " I wonder, sir, how a gentleman of your piety can introduce this subject in a mixed company." He told me afterwards that the impropriety was that perhaps some of the company might have talked on the subject in such terms as would have shocked him, or he might have been forced to appear in their eyes a narrow-minded man. The gentleman, with submissive deference, said he had only hinted at the question from a desire to hear Dr. Johnson's opinion upon it. JOHNSON: " Why, then, sir, I think that permitting men to preach any opinion contrary to the doctrine of the established church tends, in a certain degree, to lessen the authority of the church, and, consequently, to lessen the influence of religion." " It may be considered," said the gentleman, " whether it would not be politic to tolerate in such a case." JOHNSON: " Sir, we have been talking of *right*; this is another question. *I* think it is *not* politic to tolerate in such a case."

Though he did not think it fit that so awful a subject should be introduced in a mixed company, and therefore at this time waived the theological question, yet his own orthodox belief in the sacred mystery of the Trinity is evinced beyond doubt by the following passage in his private devotions: " O Lord, hear my prayer, for Jesus Christ's sake, to whom with thee and the Holy Ghost, *three persons and one* God, be all honor and glory, world without end, Amen."

BOSWELL: " Pray, Mr. Dilly, how does Dr. Leland's *History of Ireland* sell? " JOHNSON (bursting forth with a generous indignation): " The Irish are in a most unnatural state, for we see there the minority prevailing over the majority. There is no instance, even in the ten persecutions, of such severity as that which the Protestants of Ireland have exercised against the Catholics. Did we tell them we have conquered them, it would be aboveboard; to punish them by confiscation and other penalties, as rebels, was monstrous injustice. King William was not their lawful sovereign; he had not been acknowledged by the parliament of Ireland, when they appeared in arms against him."

I here suggested something favorable of the Roman Catholics. TOPLADY: " Does not their invocation of saints suppose omnipresence in the saints? " JOHNSON: " No, sir, it supposes only pluripresence; and when spirits are divested of matter, it seems probable that they should see with more extent than when in an embodied state. There is, therefore, no approach to an invasion of any of the divine attributes, in the invocation of saints. But I think it is will-worship, and presumption. I see no command for it, and therefore think it is safer not to practice it."

He and Mr. Langton and I went together to the Club, where we found Mr. Burke, Mr. Garrick, and some other members, and amongst them our friend Goldsmith, who sat silently brooding over Johnson's reprimand to him after dinner. Johnson perceived this, and said aside to some of us, " I'll make Goldsmith forgive me," and then called to him in a loud voice, " Dr. Goldsmith — something passed today where you and I dined; I ask your pardon." Goldsmith answered placidly, "It must be much from you, sir, that I take ill." And so at once the difference was over, and they were on as easy terms as ever, and Goldsmith rattled away as usual.

In our way to the club tonight, when I regretted that Goldsmith would, upon every occasion, endeavor to shine, by which he often exposed himself, Mr. Langton observed that he was not like Addison, who was content with the fame of his writings and did not aim also at excellency in conversation, for which he found himself unfit; and that he said to a lady who complained of his having talked little in company, "Madam, I have but ninepence in ready money, but I can draw for a thousand pounds." I observed that Goldsmith had a great deal of gold in his cabinet but, not content with that, was always taking out his purse. JOHNSON: "Yes, sir, and that so often an empty purse!"

Goldsmith's incessant desire of being conspicuous in company was the occasion of his sometimes appearing to such disadvantage as one should hardly have supposed possible in a man of his genius. When his literary reputation had risen deservedly high, and his society was much courted, he became very jealous of the extraordinary attention which was everywhere paid to Johnson. One evening, in a circle of wits, he found fault with me for talking of Johnson as entitled to the honor of unquestionable superiority. "Sir," said he, "you are for making a monarchy of what should be a republic."

He was still more mortified, when talking in a company with fluent vivacity and, as he flattered himself, to the admiration of all who were present; a German who sat next him, and perceived Johnson rolling himself, as if about to speak, suddenly stopped him, saying, "Stay, stay — Toctor Shonson is going to say something." This was, no doubt, very provoking, especially to one so irritable as Goldsmith, who frequently mentioned it with strong expressions of indignation.

It may also be observed, that Goldsmith was sometimes content to be treated with an easy familiarity, but, upon occasions, would be consequential and important. An instance of this occurred in a small particular. Johnson had a way of contracting the names of his friends: as Beauclerk, Beau; Boswell, Bozzy; Langton, Lanky; Murphy, Mur; Sheridan, Sherry. I remember one day, when Tom Davies was telling that Dr. Johnson said, "We are all in labor for a name to Goldy's play," Goldsmith seemed displeased that such a liberty should be taken with his name, and said, "I have often desired him not to call me Goldy." Tom was remarkably attentive to the most minute circumstance about Johnson. I recollect his telling me once, on my arrival in London, "Sir, our great friend has made an improvement on his appellation of old Mr. Sheridan. He calls him now Sherry derry."

May, 1776

I am now to record a very curious incident in Dr. Johnson's life, which fell under my own observation; of which pars magna fui,[98] and which I am persuaded will, with the liberal-minded, be much to his credit.

My desire of being acquainted with celebrated men of every description had made me, much about the same time, obtain an introduction to Dr. Samuel Johnson and to John Wilkes, Esq. Two men more different could perhaps not be selected out of all mankind. They had even attacked one another with some asperity in their writings; yet I lived in habits of friendship with both. I could fully relish the excellence of each, for I have ever delighted in that intellectual chemistry, which can separate good qualities from evil in the same person.

Sir John Pringle,[99] "mine own friend and my father's friend," between whom and Dr. Johnson I in vain wished to establish an acquaintance, as I respected and lived in intimacy with both of them, observed to me once, very ingeniously, "It is not in friendship as in mathematics, where two things, each equal to a third, are equal between themselves. You agree with Johnson as a middle quality, and you agree with me as a middle quality; but Johnson and I should not agree." Sir John was not sufficiently flexible, so I desisted, knowing, indeed, that the repulsion was equally strong on the part of Johnson, who, I know not from what cause, unless his being a Scotchman, had formed a very erroneous opinion of Sir John. But I conceived an irresistible wish, if possible, to bring Dr. Johnson and Mr. Wilkes together. How to manage it, was a nice and difficult matter.

My worthy booksellers and friends, Messrs. Dilly in the Poultry, at whose hospitable and well-covered table I have seen a greater number of literary men than at any other, except that of Sir Joshua Reynolds, had invited me to meet Mr. Wilkes and some more gentlemen, on Wednesday, May 15.

98. pars . . . fui: i.e., "for which I was mainly responsible."
99. Pringle: a friend, also, of Benjamin Franklin, and president of the Royal Society.

"Pray," said I, "let us have Dr. Johnson." "What, with Mr. Wilkes? not for the world," said Mr. Edward Dilly. "Dr. Johnson would never forgive me." "Come," said I, "if you'll let me negotiate for you, I will be answerable that all shall go well." DILLY: "Nay, if you will take it upon you, I am sure I shall be very happy to see them both here."

Notwithstanding the high veneration which I entertained for Dr. Johnson, I was sensible that he was sometimes a little actuated by the spirit of contradiction, and by means of that I hoped I should gain my point. I was persuaded that if I had come upon him with a direct proposal, "Sir, will you dine in company with Jack Wilkes?" he would have flown into a passion, and would probably have answered, "Dine with Jack Wilkes, sir! I'd as soon dine with Jack Ketch."[1] I therefore, while we were sitting quietly by ourselves at his house in an evening, took occasion to open my plan thus: "Mr. Dilly, sir, sends his respectful compliments to you, and would be happy if you would do him the honor to dine with him on Wednesday next along with me, as I must soon go to Scotland." JOHNSON: "Sir, I am obliged to Mr. Dilly. I will wait upon him —" BOSWELL: "Provided, sir, I suppose, that the company which he is to have, is agreeable to you." JOHNSON: "What do you mean, sir? What do you take me for? Do you think I am so ignorant of the world, as to imagine that I am to prescribe to a gentleman what company he is to have at his table?" BOSWELL: "I beg your pardon, sir, for wishing to prevent you from meeting people whom you might not like. Perhaps he may have some of what he calls his patriotic friends with him." JOHNSON: "Well, sir, and what then? What care *I* for his *patriotic friends*? Poh!" BOSWELL: "I should not be surprised to find Jack Wilkes there." JOHNSON: "And if Jack Wilkes *should* be there, what is that to *me,* sir? My dear friend, let us have no more of this. I am sorry to be angry with you, but really it is treating me strangely to talk to me as if I could not meet any company whatever, occasionally." BOSWELL: "Pray forgive me, sir; I meant well. But you shall meet whoever comes, for me." Thus I secured him, and told Dilly that he would find him very well pleased to be one of his guests on the day appointed.

Upon the much expected Wednesday, I called on him about half an hour before dinner, as I often

did when we were to dine out together, to see that he was ready in time, and to accompany him. I found him buffeting his books, as upon a former occasion, covered with dust, and making no preparation for going abroad. "How is this, sir?" said I. "Don't you recollect that you are to dine at Mr. Dilly's?" JOHNSON: "Sir, I did not think of going to Dilly's; it went out of my head. I have ordered dinner at home with Mrs. Williams." BOSWELL: "But, my dear sir, you know you were engaged to Mr. Dilly, and I told him so. He will expect you, and will be much disappointed if you don't come." JOHNSON: "You must talk to Mrs. Williams about this."

Here was a sad dilemma. I feared that what I was so confident I had secured would yet be frustrated. He had accustomed himself to show Mrs. Williams such a degree of humane attention, as frequently imposed some restraint upon him; and I knew that if she should be obstinate, he would not stir. I hastened downstairs to the blind lady's room, and told her I was in great uneasiness, for Dr. Johnson had engaged to me to dine this day at Mr. Dilly's, but that he had told me he had forgotten his engagement and had ordered dinner at home. "Yes, sir," said she, pretty peevishly, "Dr. Johnson is to dine at home." "Madam," said I, "his respect for you is such, that I know he will not leave you, unless you absolutely desire it. But as you have so much of his company, I hope you will be good enough to forgo it for a day, as Mr. Dilly is a very worthy man, has frequently had agreeable parties at his house for Dr. Johnson, and will be vexed if the Doctor neglects him today. And then, madam, be pleased to consider my situation: I carried the message, and I assured Mr. Dilly that Dr. Johnson was to come, and no doubt he has made a dinner, and invited a company, and boasted of the honor he expected to have. I shall be quite disgraced if the Doctor is not there." She gradually softened to my solicitations, which were certainly as earnest as most entreaties to ladies upon any occasion, and was graciously pleased to empower me to tell Dr. Johnson "That all things considered, she thought he should certainly go." I flew back to him, still in dust, and careless of what should be the event, "indifferent in his choice to go or stay,"[2] but as soon as I had announced to him Mrs. Williams' consent, he roared, "Frank, a clean shirt," and was very soon dressed. When I had him fairly seated in a hackney coach with me, I exulted as much as

1. **Jack Ketch:** generic name for the official executioner. The original Jack Ketch labored in his vocation under Charles II.

2. **"indifferent . . . stay":** adapted from Addison's *Cato,* V.i.

a fortune hunter who has got an heiress into a post chaise with him to set out for Gretna Green.

When we entered Mr. Dilly's drawing room, he found himself in the midst of a company he did not know. I kept myself snug and silent, watching how he would conduct himself. I observed him whispering to Mr. Dilly, " Who is that gentleman, sir? " " Mr. Arthur Lee." JOHNSON: " Too, too, too " (under his breath), which was one of his habitual mutterings. Mr. Arthur Lee could not but be very obnoxious to Johnson, for he was not only a *patriot,* but an *American.* He was afterwards minister from the United States at the court of Madrid. " And who is the gentleman in lace? " " Mr. Wilkes, sir." This information confounded him still more; he had some difficulty to restrain himself and, taking up a book, sat down upon a window seat and read, or at least kept his eye upon it intently for some time, till he composed himself. His feelings, I dare say, were awkward enough. But he no doubt recollected his having rated me for supposing that he could be at all disconcerted by any company, and he, therefore, resolutely set himself to behave quite as an easy man of the world, who could adapt himself at once to the disposition and manners of those whom he might chance to meet.

The cheering sound of " Dinner is upon the table " dissolved his reverie, and we *all* sat down without any symptom of ill humor. There were present, beside Mr. Wilkes, and Mr. Arthur Lee, who was an old companion of mine when he studied physic at Edinburgh, Mr. (now Sir John) Miller, Dr. Lettsom, and Mr. Slater, the druggist. Mr. Wilkes placed himself next to Dr. Johnson, and behaved to him with so much attention and politeness that he gained upon him insensibly. No man eat more heartily than Johnson, or loved better what was nice and delicate. Mr. Wilkes was very assiduous in helping him to some fine veal. " Pray give me leave, sir — It is better here — A little of the brown — Some fat, sir — A little of the stuffing — Some gravy — Let me have the pleasure of giving you some butter — Allow me to recommend a squeeze of this orange — or the lemon, perhaps, may have more zest." " Sir, sir, I am obliged to you, sir," cried Johnson, bowing and turning his head to him with a look for some time of " surly virtue "[3] but, in a short while, of complacency.

Foote being mentioned, Johnson said, " He is not a good mimic." One of the company added, " A merry Andrew, a buffoon." JOHNSON: " But he has wit, too, and is not deficient in ideas, or in fertility and variety of imagery, and not empty of reading; he has knowledge enough to fill up his part. One species of wit he has in an eminent degree, that of escape. You drive him into a corner with both hands, but he's gone, sir, when you think you have got him — like an animal that jumps over your head. Then he has a great range for his wit; he never lets truth stand between him and a jest, and he is sometimes mighty coarse. Garrick is under many restraints from which Foote is free." WILKES: " Garrick's wit is more like Lord Chesterfield's." JOHNSON: " The first time I was in company with Foote was at Fitzherbert's. Having no good opinion of the fellow, I was resolved not to be pleased; and it is very difficult to please a man against his will. I went on eating my dinner pretty sullenly, affecting not to mind him. But the dog was so very comical, that I was obliged to lay down my knife and fork, throw myself back upon my chair, and fairly laugh it out. No, sir, he was irresistible. He upon one occasion experienced, in an extraordinary degree, the efficacy of his powers of entertaining. Amongst the many and various modes which he tried of getting money, he became a partner with a small-beer brewer, and he was to have a share of the profits for procuring customers amongst his numerous acquaintance. Fitzherbert was one who took his small beer, but it was so bad that the servants resolved not to drink it. They were at some loss how to notify their resolution, being afraid of offending their master, who they knew liked Foote much as a companion. At last they fixed upon a little black boy, who was rather a favorite, to be their deputy, and deliver their remonstrance; and having invested him with the whole authority of the kitchen, he was to inform Mr. Fitzherbert, in all their names, upon a certain day, that they would drink Foote's small beer no longer. On that day Foote happened to dine at Fitzherbert's, and this boy served at table; he was so delighted with Foote's stories and merriment and grimace that, when he went downstairs, he told them, ' This is the finest man I have ever seen. I will not deliver your message. I will drink his small beer.' "

Somebody observed that Garrick could not have done this. WILKES: " Garrick would have made the small beer still smaller. He is now leaving the stage, but he will play *Scrub*[4] all his life." I knew that

---

3. " surly virtue ": " Johnson's *London, a Poem,* v.145" [B].

4. *Scrub:* a servant in Farquhar's *The Beaux' Stratagem,* III.iii.

Johnson would let nobody attack Garrick but himself, as Garrick once said to me, and I had heard him praise his liberality; so to bring out his commendation of his celebrated pupil, I said, loudly, "I have heard Garrick is liberal." JOHNSON: "Yes, sir, I know that Garrick has given away more money than any man in England that I am acquainted with, and that not from ostentatious views. Garrick was very poor when he began life, so when he came to have money, he probably was very unskillful in giving away, and saved when he should not. But Garrick began to be liberal as soon as he could; and I am of opinion, the reputation of avarice which he has had, has been very lucky for him, and prevented his having many enemies. You despise a man for avarice, but do not hate him. Garrick might have been much better attacked for living with more splendor than is suitable to a player; if they had had the wit to have assaulted him in that quarter, they might have galled him more. But they have kept clamoring about his avarice, which has rescued him from much obloquy and envy."

Talking of the great difficulty of obtaining authentic information for biography, Johnson told us, "When I was a young fellow, I wanted to write the life of Dryden, and in order to get materials, I applied to the only two persons then alive who had seen him; these were old Swinney,[5] and old Cibber. Swinney's information was no more than this, 'that at Will's Coffeehouse Dryden had a particular chair for himself, which was set by the fire in winter, and was then called his winter chair; and that it was carried out for him to the balcony in summer, and was then called his summer chair.' Cibber could tell no more but 'that he remembered him a decent old man, arbiter of critical disputes at Will's.' You are to consider that Cibber was then at a great distance from Dryden, had perhaps one leg only in the room, and durst not draw in the other." BOSWELL: "Yet Cibber was a man of observation?" JOHNSON: "I think not." BOSWELL: "You will allow his *Apology* to be well done." JOHNSON: "Very well done, to be sure, sir. That book is a striking proof of the justice of Pope's remark:

Each might his several province well command,
Would all but stoop to what they understand.[6]

5. **Swinney:** "Owen McSwinney, who died in 1754, and bequeathed his fortune to Mrs. Woffington, the actress. He had been a Manager of Drury Lane Theater, and afterwards of the Queen's Theater in the Haymarket" (Malone).   6. Pope, *Essay on Criticism*, I.66–67. See p. 761, above.

BOSWELL: "And his plays are good." JOHNSON: "Yes, but that was his trade; *l'esprit du corps;* he had been all his life among players and playwriters. I wondered that he had so little to say in conversation, for he had kept the best company, and learned all that can be got by the ear. He abused Pindar to me, and then showed me an ode of his own, with an absurd couplet, making a linnet soar on an eagle's wing. I told him that when the ancients made a simile, they always made it like something real."

Mr. Wilkes remarked that "among all the bold flights of Shakespeare's imagination, the boldest was making Birnam Wood march to Dunsinane, creating a wood where there never was a shrub; a wood in Scotland! ha! ha! ha!" And he also observed that "the clannish slavery of the Highlands of Scotland was the single exception to Milton's remark of 'The mountain nymph, sweet Liberty,'[7] being worshipped in all hilly countries." "When I was at Inverary," said he, "on a visit to my old friend Archibald, Duke of Argyle, his dependents congratulated me on being such a favorite of his Grace. I said, 'It is then, gentlemen, truly lucky for me; for if I had displeased the Duke, and he had wished it, there is not a Campbell among you but would have been ready to bring John Wilkes's head to him in a charger. It would have been only

Off with his head! so much for *Aylesbury.*

I was then member for Aylesbury."

Dr. Johnson and Mr. Wilkes talked of the contested passage in Horace's *Art of Poetry*, "*Difficile est proprie communia dicere.*"[8] Mr. Wilkes, according to my note, gave the interpretation thus: "It is difficult to speak with propriety of common things, as, if a poet had to speak of Queen Caroline drinking tea, he must endeavor to avoid the vulgarity of cups and saucers." But upon reading my note, he tells me that he meant to say that "the word *communia,* being a Roman law term, signifies here things *communis juris,* that is to say, what have never yet been treated by anybody, and this appears clearly from what followed:

— *Tuque*
Rectius Iliacum carmen deducis in actus
Quam si proferres ignota indictaque primus.[9]

7. **'The ... Liberty':** "L'Allegro," l. 36. See p. 418, above.   8. **"Difficile . . . dicere":** *Ars Poetica*, ll. 128 ff. The meaning is still debated.   9. The passage is thus translated by Fairclough (Loeb Library): "It is hard to treat in your own way what is common; and you are doing better in spinning into acts a song of Troy

You will easier make a tragedy out of the *Iliad* than on any subject not handled before." JOHNSON: " He means that it is difficult to appropriate to particular persons qualities which are common to all mankind, as Homer has done."

WILKES: "We have no city poet now; that is an office which has gone into disuse. The last was Elkanah Settle.[10] There is something in *names* which one cannot help feeling. Now *Elkanah Settle* sounds so *queer,* who can expect much from that name? We should have no hesitation to give it for John Dryden, in preference to Elkanah Settle, from the names only, without knowing their different merits. JOHNSON: " I suppose sir, Settle did as well for aldermen in his time as John Home could do now. Where did Beckford and Trecothick learn English?"[11]

Mr. Arthur Lee mentioned some Scotch who had taken possession of a barren part of America, and wondered why they should choose it. JOHNSON: "Why, sir, all barrenness is comparative. The *Scotch* would not know it to be barren." BOSWELL: " Come, come, he is flattering the English. You have now been in Scotland, sir, and say if you did not see meat and drink enough there." JOHNSON: "Why, yes, sir, meat and drink enough to give the inhabitants sufficient strength to run away from home." All these quick and lively sallies were said sportively, quite in jest, and with a smile, which showed that he meant only wit. Upon this topic he and Mr. Wilkes could perfectly assimilate; here was a bond of union between them, and I was conscious that, as both of them had visited Caledonia, both were fully satisfied of the strange narrow ignorance of those who imagine that it is a land of famine. But they amused themselves with persevering in the old jokes. When I claimed a superiority for Scotland over England in one respect, that no man can be arrested there for a debt merely because another swears it against him, but there must first be the judgment of a court of law ascertaining its justice; and that a seizure of the person, before judgment is obtained, can take place only if his creditor should swear that he is about to fly from the country or, as it is technically expressed, is *in meditatione fugae.* WILKES: " That, I should think, may be safely sworn of all the

Scotch nation." JOHNSON (to Mr. Wilkes): " You must know, sir, I lately took my friend Boswell, and showed him genuine civilized life in an English provincial town. I turned him loose at Lichfield, my native city, that he might see for once real civility, for you know he lives among savages in Scotland, and among rakes in London." WILKES: " Except when he is with grave, sober, decent people, like you and me." JOHNSON (smiling): " And we ashamed of him."

They were quite frank and easy. Johnson told the story of his asking Mrs. Macaulay[12] to allow her footman to sit down with them, to prove the ridiculousness of the arguments for the equality of mankind; and he said to me afterwards, with a nod of satisfaction, " You saw Mr. Wilkes acquiesced." Wilkes talked with all imaginable freedom of the ludicrous title given to the Attorney General, *Diabolus Regis,*[13] adding, " I have reason to know something about that officer, for I was prosecuted for a libel."[14] Johnson, who many people would have supposed must have been furiously angry at hearing this talked of so lightly, said not a word. He was now, *indeed,* " a good-humored fellow."[15]

After dinner we had an accession of Mrs. Knowles, the Quaker lady, well known for her various talents, and of Mr. Alderman Lee. Amidst some patriotic groans, somebody (I think the alderman) said, " Poor old England is lost." JOHNSON: " Sir, it is not so much to be lamented that old England is lost, as that the Scotch have found it." WILKES: " Had Lord Bute governed Scotland only, I should not have taken the trouble to write his eulogy, and dedicate *Mortimer* to him."[16]

Mr. Wilkes held a candle to show a fine print of a beautiful female figure which hung in the room, and pointed out the elegant contour of the bosom with the finger of an arch connoisseur. He afterwards in a conversation with me waggishly insisted that all the time Johnson showed visible

than if, for the first time, you were giving the world a theme unknown and unsung."   10. Settle: a contemporary of Dryden's and the object of his satire, as Doeg in *Absalom and Achitophel.* 11. Where . . . English?: London aldermen, neither remarkable for polished speech. Johnson implies that they learned English in the American colonies.

12. Mrs. Macaulay: See n. 40, p. 890.   13. *Diabolus Regis:* i.e., the King's Devil, with a latent reference to *Advocatus Diaboli,* the Devil's Advocate.   14. libel: Wilkes is referring to the most notorious episode of his career, the protracted legal actions against him, instigated by the Crown, consequent upon his forty-fifth number of the *North Briton.* See n. 7, p. 874.   15. good-humored fellow: When Johnson had once called himself so in a conversation with Boswell, the latter objected, saying that he was good-natured rather than good-humored.   16. This play, *The Fall of Mortimer,* was an old play republished in 1763 at Wilkes's instigation as a political weapon against the prime minister, Lord Bute, a Scot. There was an implied analogy between the relationship of Bute to George III (and his mother) and of Roger Mortimer to Edward III (and Queen Isabella, his mother).

signs of a fervent admiration of the corresponding charms of the fair Quaker.

This record, though by no means so perfect as I could wish, will serve to give a notion of a very curious interview, which was not only pleasing at the time, but had the agreeable and benignant effect of reconciling any animosity, and sweetening any acidity which, in the various bustle of political contest, had been produced in the minds of two men, who, though widely different, had so many things in common — classical learning, modern literature, wit, and humor, and ready repartee — that it would have been much to be regretted if they had been forever at a distance from each other.

Mr. Burke gave me much credit for this successful *negotiation,* and pleasantly said, that " there was nothing equal to it in the whole history of the *Corps Diplomatique."*

I attended Dr. Johnson home, and had the satisfaction to hear him tell Mrs. Williams how much he had been pleased with Mr. Wilkes's company, and what an agreeable day he had passed.

I talked a good deal to him of the celebrated Margaret Caroline Rudd,[17] whom I had visited, induced by the fame of her talents, address, and irresistible power of fascination. To a lady who disapproved of my visiting her, he said on a former occasion, " Nay, madam, Boswell is in the right; I should have visited her myself, were it not that they have now a trick of putting everything into the newspapers." This evening he exclaimed, " I envy him his acquaintance with Mrs. Rudd."

I mentioned a scheme which I had of making a tour to the Isle of Man, and giving a full account of it, and that Mr. Burke had playfully suggested as a motto,

The proper study of mankind is Man.[18]

JOHNSON: " Sir, you will get more by the book than the jaunt will cost you; so you will have your diversion for nothing, and add to your reputation."

On the evening of the next day I took leave of him, being to set out for Scotland. I thanked him with great warmth for all his kindness. " Sir," said he, " you are very welcome. Nobody repays it with more."

How very false is the notion that has gone round

the world of the rough and passionate and harsh manners of this great and good man. That he had occasional sallies of heat of temper, and that he was sometimes, perhaps, " too easily provoked " by absurdity and folly, and sometimes too desirous of triumph in colloquial contest, must be allowed. The quickness both of his perception and sensibility disposed him to sudden explosions of satire, to which his extraordinary readiness of wit was a strong and almost irresistible incitement. To adopt one of the finest images in Mr. Home's *Douglas,*

> On each glance of thought
> Decision followed, as the thunderbolt
> Pursues the flash!

I admit that the beadle within him was often so eager to apply the lash that the judge had not time to consider the case with sufficient deliberation.

That he was occasionally remarkable for violence of temper may be granted, but let us ascertain the degree, and not let it be supposed that he was in a perpetual rage, and never without a club in his hand to knock down everyone who approached him. On the contrary, the truth is, that by much the greatest part of his time he was civil, obliging, nay, polite in the true sense of the word; so much so that many gentlemen who were long acquainted with him never received, or even heard a strong expression from him.

LETTERS

Johnson's personal relations with his correspondents always determine the content and character of his letters. He is not one of those who cultivate the epistolary art for its own sake, or with a view to a posthumous collection. Nevertheless, his letters contain some of his most characteristic and even moving writing. The celebrated letter to Lord Chesterfield has brought him more credit than perhaps the circumstances of its composition entitle him to, although judged as one would judge a work of art it can never be too much admired. The known facts are that he made an insincere gesture (as he himself admitted to Boswell) by addressing his Proposals for the Dictionary to Lord Chesterfield; was accorded as much initial encouragement as a relatively unknown petitioner for financial support has a right to expect from a man often thus approached; was possibly treated rather like one of a number of patients in a doctor's waiting room, on some subsequent visit, and thereafter waited aloof and haughtily for the patron to exchange roles and seek him in turn; and finally chose to resent Chesterfield's not unfriendly, if too flippant, advance press notices in his behalf. If Chesterfield's two papers in the *World* were an indirect bid

---

17. Margaret . . . Rudd: Mrs. Rudd was tried for forgery, and acquitted, while her two companions, the brothers Perreau, were convicted and hanged. Boswell made himself very agreeable to her.   18. Pope, *Essay on Man,* II.2. See p. 793, above.

for a dedication, we may at least acknowledge that they were not a belated money bribe, and that Johnson had already as much as publicly signified his intention, seven years earlier, to dedicate the work to Chesterfield; and perhaps an uneasy consciousness that he would not be fulfilling a tacit commitment drove him into self-justification. All this does not derogate from the proud dignity of the letter, which was indubitably sincere and deeply felt.

The letter to Mrs. Montagu shows Johnson outdoing Chesterfield in courtliness, in a generous cause. The letter to George Strahan, his publisher's son, is an endearing example of Johnson's anxiety to help and instruct young people, and was written just after he had begun to interest himself in Boswell's welfare. The letter to Mrs. Boswell was written four years after Johnson had first offended that lady by holding her tapers upside down to make a brighter light, while the wax dripped onto her rugs. Her reservations about him were due not only to the Doctor's uncouthness but also to the fact that he encouraged her husband's passion for London, where, as she well knew, wasting time was but the most innocent of Boswell's self-indulgences. The letters to Mrs. Thrale, in their variety of mood, reveal some phases of a relationship which, after that with his wife, meant more to Johnson than any other. For twenty years he was treated like a member of the Thrale family; but when the letter of 1783 was written, Henry Thrale had died and Mrs. Thrale had signified her desire to marry an Italian musician, Gabriele Piozzi, a connection that Johnson joined with the rest of the world in disapproving. This caused an irreparable breach between the two friends.

The letter to Macpherson was a consequence of that author's efforts to cow Johnson into suppressing or retracting his expressions of disbelief in the antiquity of the poems of Ossian. Macpherson first tried to bring pressure through Johnson's publisher, to make him cancel a passage on Ossian in the *Journey to the Western Islands*. Next, he had the form of an apology brought to Johnson, which the latter was to publish. Thereafter, Macpherson seems to have threatened to administer a beating, and perhaps even challenged him to a duel. The story goes that after this exchange Johnson went abroad armed with a stout oak staff that had a head as big as a grapefruit.

I. To THE RIGHT HONORABLE THE EARL OF CHESTERFIELD

February 7, 1755.

My Lord:

I have been lately informed, by the proprietor of the *World*,[1] that two papers, in which my Dictionary is recommended to the public, were written by your lordship. To be so distinguished is an honor which, being very little accustomed to favors from the great, I know not well how to receive, or in what terms to acknowledge.

When, upon some slight encouragement, I first visited your lordship, I was overpowered, like the rest of mankind, by the enchantment of your address; and could not forbear to wish that I might boast myself *le vainqueur du vainqueur de la terre;*[2] — that I might obtain that regard for which I saw the world contending; but I found my attendance so little encouraged, that neither pride nor modesty would suffer me to continue it. When I had once addressed your lordship in public, I had exhausted all the art of pleasing which a retired and uncourtly scholar can possess. I had done all that I could; and no man is well pleased to have his all neglected, be it ever so little.

Seven years, my Lord, have now passed, since I waited in your outward rooms, or was repulsed from your door, during which time I have been pushing on my work through difficulties of which it is useless to complain, and have brought it, at last, to the verge of publication, without one act of assistance, one word of encouragement, or one smile of favor. Such treatment I did not expect, for I never had a patron before.

The shepherd in Virgil grew at last acquainted with Love, and found him a native of the rocks.[3]

Is not a patron, my Lord, one who looks with unconcern on a man struggling for life in the water, and, when he has reached ground, encumbers him with help? The notice which you have been pleased to take of my labors, had it been early, had been kind; but it has been delayed till I am indifferent, and cannot enjoy it; till I am solitary, and cannot impart it; till I am known, and do not want it. I hope it is no very cynical asperity not to confess obligations where no benefit has been received, or to be unwilling that the public should consider me as owing that to a patron, which Providence has enabled me to do for myself.

Having carried on my work thus far with so little obligation to any favorer of learning, I shall not be disappointed though I should conclude it, if less be possible, with less; for I have been long wakened from that dream of hope, in which I once boasted myself with so much exultation, my Lord,

your lordship's most humble,
most obedient servant,

Sam: Johnson.

LETTERS. 1. *World*: See *Life*, n. 24, p. 881, above. Chesterfield's essays in this periodical were Nos. 100 and 101.

2. *le . . . terre:* "the conqueror of the conqueror of the earth."
3. The . . . rocks: The reference is to *Eclogue*, I.43 ff.

II. To MRS. MONTAGU [4]

Gray's Inn, Dec. 17, 1759.

Madam:

Goodness so conspicuous as yours will be often solicited, and perhaps sometimes solicited by those who have little pretension to your favor. It is now my turn to introduce a petitioner, but such as I have reason to believe you will think worthy of your notice. Mrs. Ogle, who kept the music room in Soho Square, a woman who struggles with great industry for the support of eight children, hopes by a benefit concert to set herself free from a few debts, which she cannot otherwise discharge. She has, I know not why, so high an opinion of me as to believe that you will pay less regard to her application than to mine. You know, madam, I am sure you know, how hard it is to deny, and therefore would not wonder at my compliance, though I were to suppress a motive which you know not, the vanity of being supposed to be of any importance to Mrs. Montagu. But though I may be willing to see the world deceived for my advantage, I am not deceived myself, for I know that Mrs. Ogle will owe whatever favors she shall receive from the patronage which we humbly entreat on this occasion, much more to your compassion for honesty in distress, than to the request of,

Madam,

Your most obedient and most humble servant,

Sam: Johnson.

III. To GEORGE STRAHAN [5]

Dear George:

To give pain ought always to be painful, and I am sorry that I have been the occasion of any uneasiness to you, to whom I hope never to do anything but for your benefit or your pleasure. Your uneasiness was without any reason on your part, as you had written with sufficient frequency to me, and I had only neglected to answer then, because as nothing new had been proposed to your study, no new direction or incitement could be offered you. But if it had happened that you had omitted what you did not omit, and that I had for an hour, or a week, or a much longer time, thought myself put out of your mind by something to which presence gave that prevalence, which presence will sometimes give even where there is the most prudence and experience, you are not to imagine that my friendship is light enough to be blown away by the first cross blast, or that my regard or kindness hangs by so slender a hair as to be broken off by the unfelt weight of a petty offense. I love you, and hope to love you long. You have hitherto done nothing to diminish my good will, and though you had done much more than you have supposed imputed to you, my good will would not have been diminished.

I write thus largely on this suspicion which you have suffered to enter your mind, because in youth we are apt to be too rigorous in our expectations, and to suppose that the duties of life are to be performed with unfailing exactness and regularity; but in our progress through life we are forced to abate much of our demands, and to take friends such as we can find them, not as we would make them.

These concessions every wise man is more ready to make to others, as he knows that he shall often want them for himself; and when he remembers how often he fails in the observance or cultivation of his best friends, is willing to suppose that his friends may in their turn neglect him, without any intention to offend him.

When therefore it shall happen, as happen it will, that you or I have disappointed the expectation of the other, you are not to suppose that you have lost me, or that I intended to lose you; nothing will remain but to repair the fault, and to go on as if it never had been committed.

I am, sir,

Your affectionate servant,

Sam: Johnson.

Thursday, July 14, 1763.

IV. To JAMES MACPHERSON [6]

Mr. James Macpherson —

I received your foolish and impudent note. Whatever insult is offered me I will do my best to repel, and what I cannot do for myself, the law will do for me. I will not desist from detecting what I think a cheat, from any fear of the menaces of a ruffian.

4. Elizabeth Montagu (1720–1800), a wealthy widow, authoress, and Queen of the Bluestockings. See *Life*, n. 72, p. 899.
5. **Strahan:** George Strahan (1744–1824), son of Johnson's friend and printer, William Strahan; preparing for the Church, and subsequently editor of Johnson's *Prayers and Meditations* (1785). See below.

6. **Macpherson:** For Macpherson (1736–96), see headnote, above, and *Tour*, n. 17.

You want me to retract. What shall I retract? I thought your book an imposture from the beginning. I think it upon yet surer reasons an imposture still. For this opinion I give the public my reasons which I here dare you to refute.

But however I may despise you, I reverence truth, and if you can prove the genuineness of the work I will confess it. Your rage I defy, your abilities since your Homer [7] are not so formidable, and what I have heard of your morals disposes me to pay regard not to what you shall say, but to what you can prove.

You may print this if you will.

Sam: Johnson.

Jan. 20, 1775

V. To MRS. BOSWELL [8]

Madam:

Though I am well enough pleased with the taste of sweetmeats, very little of the pleasure which I received at the arrival of your jar of marmalade arose from eating it. I received it as a token of friendship, as a proof of reconciliation, things much sweeter than sweetmeats, and upon this consideration I return you, dear madam, my sincerest thanks. By having your kindness I think I have a double security for the continuance of Mr. Boswell's, which it is not to be expected that any man can long keep when the influence of a lady so highly and so justly valued operates against him. Mr. Boswell will tell you that I was always faithful to your interest, and always endeavored to exalt you in his estimation. You must now do the same for me. We must all help one another, and you must now consider me, as

Dear madam, your most obliged,
and most humble servant,

Sam: Johnson.

July 22, 1777.

VI. To MRS. THRALE
Ashbourne, October 6, 1777.

Dear Madam:

You are glad that I am absent; and I am glad that you are sick.[9] When you went away, what did you do with your aunt? I am glad she liked my Susy;

I was always a Susy, when nobody else was a Susy. How have you managed at your new place? Could you all get lodgings in one house, and meat at one table? Let me hear the whole series of misery; for, as Dr. Young says, *I love horror.*[10]

Methinks you are now a great way off; and if I come, I have a great way to come to you; and then the sea is so cold, and the rooms are so dull; yet I do love to hear the sea roar and my mistress talk — For when she talks, ye gods! how she will talk.[11] I wish I were with you, but we are now near half the length of England asunder. It is frightful to think how much time must pass between writing this letter and receiving an answer, if any answer were necessary.

Taylor [12] is now going to have a ram; and then, after Aries and Taurus, we shall have Gemini. His oats are now in the wet; here is a deal of rain. Mr. Langdon bought, at Nottingham Fair, fifteen tun of cheese, which, at an ounce apiece, will suffice after dinner for four hundred and eighty thousand men. This is all the news that the place affords. I purpose soon to be at Lichfield, but know not just when, having been defeated of my first design. When I come to town, I am to be very busy about my *Lives.*[13] — Could not you do some of them for me?

I am glad Master huspelled you, and run you all on rucks,[14] and drove you about, and made you stir. Never be cross about it. Quiet and calmness you have enough of — a little hurry stirs life — and

Brushing o'er, adds motion to the pool.[15]

Now *pool* brings my master's excavations into my head. I wonder how I shall like them; I should like not to see them, till we all see them together. He will have no waterfall to roar like the Doctor's. I sat by it yesterday, and read Erasmus' *Militis Christiani Enchiridion.*[16] Have you got that book?

member of the Thrale household. He was now visiting his lifelong friend, Dr. John Taylor, in Derbyshire. The Thrales were at the seaside, in Brighton. Mrs. Thrale was expecting another child, and hoping for a son. Susy was a younger daughter toward whom Johnson was partial.   10. *I . . . horror:* Edward Young's *The Revenge* (1721) opens on this note.   11. *For . . . talk:* Johnson playfully called Henry Thrale his "Master" and Mrs. Thrale his "Mistress." He is here quoting Nathaniel Lee's *The Rival Queens,* I.i.375.   12. *Taylor:* Dr. Taylor spent much time and money on fine livestock. He owned a prize bull, and Johnson is amusing himself with astronomical analogies.   13. *my Lives:* He means, with the writing of his biographical prefaces later known as *Lives of the Poets,* published 1779–81.   14. *huspelled . . . rucks:* that is, "shook you up and jolted you into ruts (or ditches)."   15. Quoted from Dryden's *Cymon and Iphigenia,* l. 30.   16. *Militis . . . Enchiridion:* i.e., *The Christian Soldier's Handbook.*

7. **Homer:** Macpherson published a prose translation of the *Iliad* in 1773.   8. **Mrs. Boswell:** See headnote, above.   9. **sick:** Johnson, after nearly fifteen years of intimacy, was virtually a

Make my compliments to dear Queeney.[17] I suppose she will dance at the Rooms, and your heart will go one knows not how.

I am, dearest, and dearest lady,
Your most humble servant,
Sam: Johnson.

VII. To MRS. THRALE

Lichfield, October 27, 1777.

Dear Madam:

You talk of writing and writing, as if you had all the writing to yourself. If our correspondence were printed, I am sure posterity, for posterity is always the author's favorite, would say that I am a good writer, too. — *Anch'io sono pittore.*[18] To sit down so often with nothing to say, to say something so often, almost without consciousness of saying, and without any remembrance of having said, is a power of which I will not violate my modesty by boasting, but I do not believe that everybody has it.

Some, when they write to their friends, are all affection; some are wise and sententious; some strain their powers for efforts of gaiety; some write news; and some write secrets; but to make a letter without affection, without wisdom, without gaiety, without news, and without a secret, is, doubtless, the great epistolic art.

In a man's letters, you know, madam, his soul lies naked, his letters are only the mirror of his breast; whatever passes within him is shown undisguised in its natural process; nothing is inverted, nothing distorted; you see systems in their elements; you discover actions in their motives.

Of this great truth, sounded by the knowing to the ignorant, and so echoed by the ignorant to the knowing, what evidence have you now before you! Is not my soul laid open in these veracious pages? Do not you see me reduced to my first principles? This is the pleasure of corresponding with a friend, where doubt and distrust have no place, and everything is said as it is thought. The original idea is laid down in its simple purity, and all the supervenient conceptions are spread over it *stratum super stratum,* as they happen to be formed. These are the letters by which souls are united, and by which minds naturally in unison move each

other as they are moved themselves. I know, dearest lady, that in the perusal of this, such is the consanguinity of our intellects, you will be touched as I am touched. I have indeed concealed nothing from you, nor do I expect ever to repent of having thus opened my heart.

I am, Madam,
Your most humble servant,
Sam: Johnson.

VIII. To MRS. THRALE

Bolt Court, Fleet Street,
June 19, 1783.

Dear Madam:

I am sitting down in no cheerful solitude to write a narrative which would once [19] have affected you with tenderness and sorrow, but which you will perhaps pass over now with the careless glance of frigid indifference. For this diminution of regard, however, I know not whether I ought to blame you, who may have reasons which I cannot know, and I do not blame myself, who have for a great part of human life done you what good I could, and have never done you evil.

I had been disordered in the usual way, and had been relieved by the usual methods, by opium and cathartics, but had rather lessened my dose of opium.

On Monday the 16th I sat for my picture, and walked a considerable way with little inconvenience. In the afternoon and evening I felt myself light and easy, and began to plan schemes of life. Thus I went to bed, and in a short time waked and sat up, as has been long my custom, when I felt a confusion and indistinctness in my head, which lasted, I suppose, about half a minute. I was alarmed, and prayed God that, however he might afflict my body, he would spare my understanding. This prayer, that I might try the integrity of my faculties, I made in Latin verse. The lines were not very good, but I knew them not to be very good; I made them easily, and concluded myself to be unimpaired in my faculties.

Soon after, I perceived that I had suffered a paralytic stroke, and that my speech was taken from me. I had no pain, and so little dejection in this dreadful state, that I wondered at my own apathy, and considered that perhaps death itself when it

---

17. **Queeney:** the Thrales' eldest daughter, just being introduced to society at Brighton and Bath.   18. *Anch'io . . . pittore:* a saying attributed to Correggio, when he saw Raphael's painting: "I too am a painter."

19. **once:** Henry Thrale had died, and a rift had opened between Mrs. Thrale and Johnson on account of her desire to remarry. See headnote, above.

should come would excite less horror than seems now to attend it.

In order to rouse the vocal organs I took two drams. Wine has been celebrated for the production of eloquence. I put myself into violent motion, and I think repeated it; but all was vain. I then went to bed, and, strange as it may seem, I think, slept. When I saw light, it was time to contrive what I should do. Though God stopped my speech, he left me my hand. I enjoyed a mercy which was not granted to my dear friend Lawrence,[20] who now perhaps overlooks me as I am writing, and rejoices that I have what he wanted. My first note was necessarily to my servant, who came in talking, and could not immediately comprehend why he should read what I put into his hands.

I then wrote a card to Mr. Allen,[21] that I might have a discreet friend at hand to act as occasion should require. In penning this note I had some difficulty: my hand, I knew not how nor why, made wrong letters. I then wrote to Dr. Taylor to come to me, and bring Dr. Heberden, and I sent to Dr. Brocklesby, who is my neighbor. My physicians are very friendly and very disinterested, and give me great hopes, but you may imagine my situation. I have so far recovered my vocal powers, as to repeat the Lord's Prayer with no very imperfect articulation. My memory, I hope, yet remains as it was, but such an attack produces solicitude for the safety of every faculty.

How this will be received by you I know not. I hope you will sympathize with me; but perhaps

> My mistress gracious, mild, and good,
> Cries, "Is he dumb? 'Tis time he should." [22]

But can this be possible? I hope it cannot. I hope that what, when I could speak, I spoke of you, and to you, will be in a sober and serious hour remembered by you; and surely it cannot be remembered but with some degree of kindness. I have loved you with virtuous affection; I have honored you with sincere esteem. Let not all our endearment be forgotten, but let me have in this great distress your pity and your prayers. You see I yet turn to you with my complaints as a settled and unalienable friend; do not, do not drive me from you, for I have not deserved either neglect or hatred.

To the girls, who do not write often, for Susy has written only once, and Miss Thrale owes me a letter, I earnestly recommend, as their guardian and friend, that they remember their Creator in the days of their youth.

I suppose you may wish to know how my disease is treated by the physicians. They put a blister upon my back, and two from my ear to my throat, one on a side. The blister on the back has done little, and those on the throat have not risen. I bullied and bounced (it sticks to our last sand) [23] and compelled the apothecary to make his salve according to the Edinburgh Dispensatory, that it might adhere better. I have two on now of my own prescription. They likewise give me salt of hartshorn, which I take with no great confidence, but am satisfied that what can be done is done for me.

O God! give me comfort and confidence in Thee; forgive my sins; and if it be Thy good pleasure, relieve my diseases for Jesus Christ's sake. Amen.

I am almost ashamed of this querulous letter, but now it is written, let it go.

> I am, Madam,
> Your most humble servant,
> Sam: Johnson.

A SHORT SONG OF CONGRATULATION

Johnson sent the "Short Song" to Mrs. Thrale in August of 1780, with an amusing comment: "It is odd that it should come into anybody's head . . . it is, I believe, one of the author's first essays in that way of writing, and a beginner is always to be treated with tenderness." It has recently been asserted that A. E. Housman owned his obligation to this poem in fixing the style of his *Shropshire Lad.*

> Long-expected one and twenty,
>   Ling'ring year, at last is flown.
> Pomp and pleasure, pride and plenty,
>   Great Sir John, are all your own.
>
> Loosened from the minor's tether,
>   Free to mortgage or to sell,
> Wild as wind, and light as feather,
>   Bid the slaves of thrift farewell.

---

23. **it . . . sand:** quoted from Pope, *Moral Essays,* I.225.
 SONG OF CONGRATULATION. 4. **Sir John:** Sir John Lade was Henry Thrale's sister's son. These uncomplimentary verses were sent privately to Mrs. Thrale and were not published till after Johnson's death. Sir John is said to have approximated Johnson's predictions in his course of life.

20. **Lawrence:** Johnson's physician for many years; he had just died.   21. **Mr. Allen:** Edmund Allen, printer, a friend and neighbor of Johnson's.   22. The quotation is adapted from Swift's "Verses on the Death of Dr. Swift," ll. 181–82. See p. 744, above.

Call the Bettys, Kates, and Jennys,
 Every name that laughs at care: 10
Lavish of your grandsire's guineas,
 Show the spirit of an heir.

All that prey on vice and folly
 Joy to see their quarry fly,
Here the gamester light and jolly,
 There the lender grave and sly.

Wealth, Sir John, was made to wander,
 Let it wander as it will;
See the jockey, see the pander,
 Bid them come, and take their fill. 20

When the bonny blade carouses,
 Pockets full, and spirits high,
What are acres? What are houses?
 Only dirt, or wet or dry.

If the guardian or the mother
 Tell the woes of willful waste,
Scorn their counsel and their pother,
 You can hang or drown at last.

PROLOGUE

*Spoken by Mr. Garrick, at the Opening
of the Theater in Drury Lane, 1747*

The "Prologue" was written for Garrick's inaugura-
tion as manager of Drury Lane Theater, September 15,
1747. It remained a popular speaking prologue throughout Johnson's lifetime, and was also very frequently
reprinted.

When Learning's triumph o'er her barb'rous foes
First reared the stage, immortal Shakespeare rose;
Each change of many-colored life he drew,
Exhausted worlds, and then imagined new.
Existence saw him spurn her bounded reign,
And panting time toiled after him in vain;
His powerful strokes presiding truth impressed,
And unresisted passion stormed the breast.
 Then Jonson came, instructed from the School,
To please in method, and invent by rule; 10
His studious patience, and laborious art,
By regular approach essayed the heart;
Cold approbation gave the ling'ring bays,
For those who durst not censure, scarce could
 praise.
A mortal born, he met the general doom,
But left, like Egypt's kings, a lasting tomb.

PROLOGUE FOR DRURY LANE THEATER. **9. Jonson:** Ben Jonson
(1572–1637), most learned of Elizabethan dramatists.

The wits of Charles found easier ways to
 fame,
Nor wished for Jonson's art, or Shakespeare's
 flame;
Themselves they studied; as they felt, they writ;
Intrigue was plot, obscenity was wit. 20
Vice always found a sympathetic friend;
They pleased their age, and did not aim to mend.
Yet bards like these aspired to lasting praise,
And proudly hoped to pimp in future days.
Their cause was gen'ral, their supports were strong,
Their slaves were willing, and their reign was
 long;
Till shame regained the post that sense betrayed,
And virtue called oblivion to her aid.
 Then, crushed by rules, and weakened as re-
 fined,
For years the power of tragedy declined; 30
From bard to bard, the frigid caution crept,
Till declamation roared, while passion slept.
Yet still did virtue deign the stage to tread,
Philosophy remained, though nature fled.
But, forced at length her ancient reign to quit,
She saw great Faustus lay the ghost of wit:
Exulting folly hailed the joyful day,
And pantomime, and song, confirmed her sway.
 But who the coming changes can presage,
And mark the future periods of the stage? — 40
Perhaps if skill could distant times explore,
New Behns, new Durfeys, yet remain in store.
Perhaps, where Lear has raved and Hamlet died,
On flying cars new sorcerers may ride.
Perhaps, for who can guess th' effects of chance?
Here Hunt may box, or Mahomet may dance.
 Hard is his lot, that here by fortune placed,
Must watch the wild vicissitudes of taste;
With ev'ry meteor of caprice must play,
And chase the new-blown bubbles of the day. 50
Ah! let not censure term our fate our choice;
The stage but echoes back the public voice.
The drama's laws the drama's patrons give,
For we that live to please must please to live.
 Then prompt no more the follies you decry,
As tyrants doom their tools of guilt to die;
'Tis yours this night to bid the reign commence
Of rescued nature, and reviving sense;
To chase the charms of sound, the pomp of show,
For useful mirth, and salutary woe; 60
Bid scenic virtue form the rising age,
And truth diffuse her radiance from the stage.

17. The . . . Charles: the playwrights of the Restoration.
36. Faustus: Faustus was a favorite subject of eighteenth-century
farce. **42. Behns, Durfeys:** Aphra Behn (1640–89) and Thomas
D'Urfey (1653–1723), prolific authors of comedies of intrigue.
44. flying . . . ride: As stage machinery became more elaborate,
spectacles and variety shows tended to encroach on regular
drama. **46. Hunt, Mahomet:** Hunt and Mahomet were,
respectively, a pugilist and a rope dancer much in evidence in the
1740's.

from the RAMBLER

The *Rambler* appeared on Tuesdays and Saturdays, from March 20, 1750, to March 14, 1752. Of the 208 numbers, Johnson wrote all but four. These periodical essays, following in the tradition of the *Spectator* papers, cover a considerable range of topics, literary and moral, and everywhere bear the seal of Johnson's somber and penetrating observation of human motivation and conduct. Their eloquence reflects the attention that the author at this time was devoting to the uses of words: he was midway in the compilation of the Dictionary, and probably nowhere else is his language so especially "Johnsonian" as in these essays.

No. 25. Tuesday, June 12, 1750

> *Possunt quia posse videntur.*
> (Virgil [*Aeneid*, V.231])
>
> [For they can conquer who believe they can.]
> (Dryden)

There are some vices and errors which, though often fatal to those in whom they are found, have yet, by the universal consent of mankind, been considered as entitled to some degree of respect, or have, at least, been exempted from contemptuous infamy, and condemned by the severest moralists with pity rather than detestation.

A constant and invariable example of this general partiality will be found in the different regard which has always been shown to rashness and cowardice, two vices, of which, though they may be conceived equally distant from the middle point where true fortitude is placed, and may equally injure any public or private interest, yet the one is never mentioned without some kind of veneration, and the other always considered as a topic of unlimited and licentious censure, on which all the virulence of reproach may be lawfully exerted.

The same distinction is made, by the common suffrage, between profusion and avarice, and, perhaps, between many other opposite vices; and, as I have found reason to pay great regard to the voice of the people, in cases where knowledge has been forced upon them by experience, without long deductions or deep researches, I am inclined to believe that this distribution of respect is not without some agreement with the nature of things, and that in the faults which are thus invested with extraordinary privileges there are generally some latent principles of merit, some possibilities of future virtue, which may, by degrees, break from

obstruction, and by time and opportunity be brought into act.

It may be laid down as an axiom, that it is more easy to take away superfluities than to supply defects, and, therefore, he that is culpable, because he has passed the middle point of virtue, is always accounted a fairer object of hope, than he who fails by falling short. The one has all that perfection requires, and more, but the excess may be easily retrenched; the other wants the qualities requisite to excellence, and who can tell how he shall obtain them? We are certain that the horse may be taught to keep pace with his fellows, whose fault is that he leaves them behind. We know that a few strokes of the axe will lop a cedar; but what arts of cultivation can elevate a shrub?

To walk with circumspection and steadiness in the right path, at an equal distance between the extremes of error, ought to be the constant endeavor of every reasonable being; nor can I think those teachers of moral wisdom much to be honored as benefactors to mankind, who are always enlarging upon the difficulty of our duties, and providing rather excuses for vice, than incentives to virtue.

But, since to most it will happen often, and to all sometimes, that there will be a deviation towards one side or the other, we ought always to employ our vigilance with most attention on that enemy from which there is greatest danger, and to stray, if we must stray, towards those parts from whence we may quickly and easily return.

Among other opposite qualities of the mind which may become dangerous, though in different degrees, I have often had occasion to consider the contrary effects of presumption and despondency; of heady confidence, which promises victory without contest, and heartless pusillanimity, which shrinks back from the thought of great undertakings, confounds difficulty with impossibility, and considers all advancement towards any new attainment as irreversibly prohibited.

Presumption will be easily corrected. Every experiment will teach caution, and miscarriages will hourly show that attempts are not always rewarded with success. The most precipitate ardor will in time be taught the necessity of methodical gradation and preparatory measures; and the most daring confidence be convinced that neither merit nor abilities can command events.

It is the advantage of vehemence and activity, that they are always hastening to their own reformation, because they incite us to try whether our expectations are well grounded, and therefore detect the deceits which they are apt to occasion. But timidity is a disease of the mind more obstinate and fatal; for a man once persuaded that any impediment is insuperable has given it, with respect to himself, that strength and weight which it had not before. He can scarcely strive with vigor and perseverance, when he has no hope of gaining the victory; and, since he never will try his strength, can never discover the unreasonableness of his fears.

There is often to be found in men devoted to literature a kind of intellectual cowardice, which whoever converses much among them may observe frequently to depress the alacrity of enterprise, and, by consequence, to retard the improvement of science. They have annexed to every species of knowledge some chimerical character of terror and inhibition, which they transmit, without much reflection, from one to another; they first fright themselves and then propagate the panic to their scholars and acquaintance. One study is inconsistent with a lively imagination, another with a solid judgment; one is improper in the early parts of life, another requires so much time that it is not to be attempted at an advanced age; one is dry and contracts the sentiments, another is diffuse and overburdens the memory; one is insufferable to taste and delicacy, and another wears out life in the study of words, and is useless to a wise man, who desires only the knowledge of things.

But of all the bugbears by which the *Infantes barbati*,[1] boys both young and old, have been hitherto frighted from digressing into new tracts of learning, none has been more mischievously efficacious than an opinion that every kind of knowledge requires a peculiar genius, or mental constitution, framed for the reception of some ideas and the exclusion of others; and that to him whose genius is not adapted to the study which he prosecutes, all labor shall be vain and fruitless, vain as an endeavor to mingle oil and water or, in the language of chemistry, to amalgamate bodies of heterogeneous principles.

This opinion we may reasonably suspect to have been propagated, by vanity, beyond the truth. It is natural for those who have raised a reputation by any science, to exalt themselves as endowed by Heaven with peculiar powers, or marked out by an extraordinary designation for their profession;

RAMBLER.   1. *Infantes barbati:* "bearded children."

and to fright competitors away by representing the difficulties with which they must contend, and the necessity of qualities which are supposed to be not generally conferred, and which no man can know, but by experience, whether he enjoys.

To this discouragement it may be possibly answered that since a genius, whatever it be, is like fire in the flint, only to be produced by collision with a proper subject, it is the business of every man to try whether his faculties may not happily co-operate with his desires; and since they whose proficiency he admires knew their own force only by the event, he needs but engage in the same undertaking with equal spirit, and may reasonably hope for equal success.

There is another species of false intelligence, given by those who profess to show the way to the summit of knowledge, of equal tendency to depress the mind with false distrust of itself, and weaken it by needless solicitude and dejection. When a scholar whom they desire to animate consults them at his entrance on some new study, it is common to make flattering representations of its pleasantness and facility. Thus they generally attain one of two ends almost equally desirable: they either incite his industry by elevating his hopes, or produce a high opinion of their own abilities, since they are supposed to relate only what they have found, and to have proceeded with no less ease than they promise to their followers.

The student, inflamed by this encouragement, sets forward in the new path, and proceeds a few steps with great alacrity, but he soon finds asperities and intricacies of which he has not been forewarned, and, imagining that none ever were so entangled or fatigued before him, sinks suddenly into despair, and desists as from an expedition in which fate opposes him. Thus his terrors are multiplied by his hopes, and he is defeated without resistance, because he had no expectation of an enemy.

Of these treacherous instructors, the one destroys industry, by declaring that industry is vain, the other by representing it as needless; the one cuts away the root of hope, the other raises it only to be blasted. The one confines his pupil to the shore by telling him that his wreck is certain; the other sends him to sea without preparing him for tempests.

False hopes and false terrors are equally to be avoided. Every man who proposes to grow eminent by learning should carry in his mind at once the difficulty of excellence and the force of industry, and remember that fame is not conferred but as the recompense of labor, and that labor, vigorously continued, has not often failed of its reward.

No. 154. Saturday, September 7, 1751

— Tibi res antiquae laudis et artis
Aggredior, sanctos ausus recludere fontes.
(Virgil [*Georgics*, II.174])

[For thee my tuneful accents will I raise,
And treat of arts disclos'd in ancient days;
Once more unlock for thee the sacred spring.]
(Dryden)

The direction of Aristotle to those that study politics is first to examine and understand what has been written by the ancients upon government; then to cast their eyes round upon the world, and consider by what causes the prosperity of communities is visibly influenced, and why some are worse, and others better, administered.

The same method must be pursued by him who hopes to become eminent in any other part of knowledge. The first task is to search books, the next to contemplate nature. He must first possess himself of the intellectual treasures which the diligence of former ages has accumulated, and then endeavor to increase them by his own collections.

The mental disease of the present generation is impatience of study, contempt of the great masters of ancient wisdom, and a disposition to rely wholly upon unassisted genius and natural sagacity. The wits of these happy days have discovered a way to fame, which the dull caution of our laborious ancestors durst never attempt; they cut the knots of sophistry which it was formerly the business of years to untie, solve difficulties by sudden irradiations of intelligence, and comprehend long processes of argument by immediate intuition.

Men who have flattered themselves into this opinion of their own abilities look down on all who waste their lives over books, as a race of inferior beings condemned by nature to perpetual pupilage, and fruitlessly endeavoring to remedy their barrenness by incessant cultivation, or succor their feebleness by subsidiary strength. They presume that none would be more industrious than they, if they were not more sensible of deficiencies, and readily conclude that he who places no confidence in his own powers, owes his modesty only to his weakness.

It is, however, certain that no estimate is more in danger of erroneous calculations than those by which a man computes the force of his own genius. It generally happens at our entrance into the world that, by the natural attraction of similitude, we associate with men like ourselves young, sprightly, and ignorant, and rate our accomplishments by comparison with theirs; when we have once obtained an acknowledged superiority over our acquaintances, imagination and desire easily extend it over the rest of mankind, and if no accident forces us into new emulations, we grow old, and die in admiration of ourselves.

Vanity, thus confirmed in her dominion, readily listens to the voice of idleness, and soothes the slumber of life with continual dreams of excellence and greatness. A man elated by confidence in his natural vigor of fancy and sagacity of conjecture soon concludes that he already possesses whatever toil and inquiry can confer. He then listens with eagerness to the wild objections which folly has raised against the common means of improvement; talks of the dark chaos of indigested knowledge; describes the mischievous effects of heterogeneous sciences fermenting in the mind; relates the blunders of lettered ignorance; expatiates on the heroic merit of those who deviate from prescription, or shake off authority; and gives vent to the inflations of his heart by declaring that he owes nothing to pedants and universities.

All these pretensions, however confident, are very often vain. The laurels which superficial acuteness gains in triumphs over ignorance unsupported by vivacity are observed by Locke [2] to be lost whenever real learning and rational diligence appear against her; the sallies of gaiety are soon repressed by calm confidence, and the artifices of subtlety are readily detected by those who, having carefully studied the question, are not easily confounded or surprised.

But though the contemner of books had neither been deceived by others nor himself, and was really born with a genius surpassing the ordinary abilities of mankind, yet surely such gifts of Providence may be more properly urged as incitements to labor than encouragements to negligence. He that neglects the culture of ground naturally fertile is more shamefully culpable than he whose field would scarcely recompense his husbandry.

Cicero remarks that not to know what has been transacted in former times is to continue always a

2. **Locke:** John Locke, in *Some Thoughts Concerning Education* (1693 and later dates), writes to this effect in Section 70.

child. If no use is made of the labors of past ages, the world must remain always in the infancy of knowledge. The discoveries of every man must terminate in his own advantage, and the studies of every age be employed on questions which the past generation had discussed and determined. We may with as little reproach borrow science as manufactures from our ancestors; and it is as rational to live in caves till our own hands have erected a palace, as to reject all knowledge of architecture which our understandings will not supply.

To the strongest and quickest mind it is far easier to learn than to invent. The principles of arithmetic and geometry may be comprehended by a close attention in a few days; yet who can flatter himself that the study of a long life would have enabled him to discover them, when he sees them yet unknown to so many nations whom he cannot suppose less liberally endowed with natural reason than the Grecians or Egyptians?

Every science was thus far advanced towards perfection by the emulous diligence of contemporary students and the gradual discoveries of one age improving on another. Sometimes unexpected flashes of instruction were struck out by the fortuitous collision of happy incidents, or an involuntary concurrence of ideas, in which the philosopher to whom they happened had no other merit than that of knowing their value and transmitting unclouded to posterity that light which had been kindled by causes out of his power. The happiness of these casual illuminations no man can promise to himself, because no endeavors can procure them; and therefore, whatever be our abilities or application, we must submit to learn from others what perhaps would have lain hid forever from human penetration, had not some remote inquiry brought it to view; as treasures are thrown up by the plowman and the digger in the rude exercise of their common occupations.

The man whose genius qualifies him for great undertakings must at least be content to learn from books the present state of human knowledge; that he may not ascribe to himself the invention of arts generally known; weary his attention with experiments of which the event has been long registered; and waste, in attempts which have already succeeded or miscarried, that time which might have been spent with usefulness and honor upon new undertakings.

But though the study of books is necessary, it is not sufficient to constitute literary eminence. He

that wishes to be counted among the benefactors of posterity must add by his own toil to the acquisitions of his ancestors, and secure his memory from neglect by some valuable improvement. This can only be effected by looking out upon the wastes of the intellectual world, and extending the power of learning over regions yet undisciplined and barbarous; or by surveying more exactly her ancient dominions, and driving ignorance from the fortresses and retreats where she skulks undetected and undisturbed. Every science has its difficulties which yet call for solution before we attempt new systems of knowledge, as every country has its forests and marshes, which it would be wise to cultivate and drain, before distant colonies are projected as a necessary discharge of the exuberance of inhabitants.

No man ever yet became great by imitation. Whatever hopes for the veneration of mankind must have invention in the design or the execution; either the effect must itself be new, or the means by which it is produced. Either truths hitherto unknown must be discovered, or those which are already known enforced by stronger evidence, facilitated by clearer method, or elucidated by brighter illustrations.

Fame cannot spread wide or endure long that is not rooted in nature, and manured by art. That which hopes to resist the blast of malignity, and stand firm against the attacks of time, must contain in itself some original principle of growth. The reputation which arises from the detail or transposition of borrowed sentiments may spread for a while, like ivy on the rind of antiquity, but will be torn away by accident or contempt, and suffered to rot unheeded on the ground.

No. 155. Tuesday, September 10, 1751

> *Steriles transmisimus annos,*
> *Haec aevi mihi prima dies, haec limina vitae.*
> (Statius [*Thebaid*, I.362])

> [Our barren years are past;
> Be this of life the first, of sloth the last.]
> (Elphinston)

No weakness of the human mind has more frequently incurred animadversion than the negligence with which men overlook their own faults, however flagrant, and the easiness with which they pardon them, however frequently repeated.

It seems generally believed that, as the eye cannot see itself, the mind has no faculties by which it can contemplate its own state, and that therefore we have not means of becoming acquainted with our real characters; an opinion which, like innumerable other postulates, an inquirer finds himself inclined to admit upon very little evidence, because it affords a ready solution of many difficulties. It will explain why the greatest abilities frequently fail to promote the happiness of those who possess them; why those who can distinguish with the utmost nicety the boundaries of vice and virtue, suffer them to be confounded in their own conduct; why the active and vigilant resign their affairs implicitly to the management of others; and why the cautious and fearful make hourly approaches towards ruin, without one sigh of solicitude or struggle for escape.

When a position teems thus with commodious consequences, who can without regret confess it to be false? Yet it is certain that declaimers have indulged a disposition to describe the dominion of the passions as extended beyond the limits that nature assigned. Self-love is often rather arrogant than blind; it does not hide our faults from ourselves, but persuades us that they escape the notice of others, and disposes us to resent censures lest we should confess them to be just. We are secretly conscious of defects and vices which we hope to conceal from the public eye, and please ourselves with innumerable impostures by which, in reality, nobody is deceived.

In proof of the dimness of our internal sight, or the general inability of man to determine rightly concerning his own character, it is common to urge the success of the most absurd and incredible flattery, and the resentment always raised by advice, however soft, benevolent, and reasonable. But flattery, if its operation be nearly examined, will be found to owe its acceptance not to our ignorance but knowledge of our failures, and to delight us rather as it consoles our wants than displays our possessions. He that shall solicit the favor of his patron by praising him for qualities which he can find in himself will be defeated by the more daring panegyrist who enriches him with adscititious [3] excellence. Just praise is only a debt, but flattery is a present. The acknowledgment of those virtues on which conscience congratulates us is a tribute that we can at any time exact with confidence, but the celebration of those which we only feign, or desire without any vigorous endeavors to attain them, is

received as a confession of sovereignty over regions never conquered, as a favorable decision of disputable claims, and is more welcome as it is more gratuitous.

Advice is offensive, not because it lays us open to unexpected regret, or convicts us of any fault which had escaped our notice, but because it shows us that we are known to others as well as to ourselves; and the officious monitor is persecuted with hatred, not because his accusation is false, but because he assumes that superiority which we are not willing to grant him, and has dared to detect what we desired to conceal.

For this reason advice is commonly ineffectual. If those who follow the call of their desires, without inquiry whither they are going, had deviated ignorantly from the paths of wisdom and were rushing upon dangers unforeseen, they would readily listen to information that recalls them from their errors, and catch the first alarm by which destruction or infamy is denounced. Few that wander in the wrong way mistake it for the right; they only find it more smooth and flowery, and indulge their own choice rather than approve it; therefore few are persuaded to quit it by admonition or reproof, since it impresses no new conviction, nor confers any powers of action or resistance. He that is gravely informed how soon profusion will annihilate his fortune hears with little advantage what he knew before, and catches at the next occasion of expense, because advice has no force to suppress his vanity. He that is told how certainly intemperance will hurry him to the grave runs with his usual speed to a new course of luxury, because his reason is not invigorated, nor his appetite weakened.

The mischief of flattery is, not that it persuades any man that he is what he is not, but that it suppresses the influence of honest ambition, by raising an opinion that honor may be gained without the toil of merit; and the benefit of advice arises commonly, not from any new light imparted to the mind, but from the discovery which it affords of the public suffrages. He that could withstand conscience is frighted at infamy, and shame prevails when reason was defeated.

As we all know our own faults, and know them commonly with many aggravations which human perspicacity cannot discover, there is, perhaps, no man, however hardened by impudence or dissipated by levity, sheltered by hypocrisy, or blasted by disgrace, who does not intend some time to review his conduct, and to regulate the remainder of

3. adscititious: adopted from without.

his life by the laws of virtue. New temptations indeed attack him, new invitations are offered by pleasure and interest, and the hour of reformation is always delayed; every delay gives vice another opportunity of fortifying itself by habit; and the change of manners, though sincerely intended and rationally planned, is referred to the time when some craving passion shall be fully gratified, or some powerful allurement cease its importunity.

Thus procrastination is accumulated on procrastination, and one impediment succeeds another, till age shatters our resolution, or death intercepts the project of amendment. Such is often the end of salutary purposes, after they have long delighted the imagination, and appeased that disquiet which every mind feels from known misconduct, when the attention is not diverted by business or by pleasure.

Nothing surely can be more unworthy of a reasonable nature than to continue in a state so opposite to real happiness, as that all the peace of solitude and felicity of meditation must arise from resolutions of forsaking it. Yet the world will often afford examples of men who pass months and years in a continual war with their own convictions, and are daily dragged by habit or betrayed by passion into practices which they closed and opened their eyes with purposes to avoid, purposes which, though settled on conviction, the first impulse of momentary desire totally overthrows.

The influence of custom is indeed such that to conquer it will require the utmost efforts of fortitude and virtue, nor can I think any man more worthy of veneration and renown than those who have burst the shackles of habitual vice. This victory, however, has different degrees of glory, as of difficulty; it is more heroic as the objects of guilty gratification are more familiar, and the recurrence of solicitation more frequent. He that from experience of the folly of ambition resigns his offices may set himself free at once from temptation to squander his life in courts, because he cannot regain his former station. He who is enslaved by an amorous passion may quit his tyrant in disgust, and absence will without the help of reason overcome by degrees the desire of returning. But those appetites to which every place affords their proper object, and which require no preparatory measures or gradual advances, are more tenaciously adhesive; the wish is so near the enjoyment that compliance often precedes consideration, and before the powers of reason can be summoned the time for employing them is past.

Indolence is therefore one of the vices from which those whom it once infects are seldom reformed. Every other species of luxury operates upon some appetite that is quickly satiated, and requires some concurrence of art or accident which every place will not supply; but the desire of ease acts equally at all hours, and the longer it is indulged is the more increased. To do nothing is in every man's power; we can never want an opportunity of omitting duties. The lapse to indolence is soft and imperceptible, because it is only a mere cessation of activity; but the return to diligence is difficult, because it implies a change from rest to motion, from privation to reality.

Facilis descensus Averni:
Noctes atque dies patet atri janua Ditis:
Sed revocare gradum, superasque evadere ad auras,
Hoc opus, hic labor est.
(Virgil [*Aeneid*, VI.126])

[The gates of Hell are open night and day;
Smooth the descent, and easy is the way:
But to return, and view the cheerful skies;
In this, the task and mighty labor lies.]
(Dryden)

Of this vice, as of all others, every man who indulges it is conscious; we all know our own state, if we could be induced to consider it; and it might perhaps be useful to the conquest of all these ensnarers of the mind, if at certain stated days life was reviewed. Many things necessary are omitted because we vainly imagine that they may be always performed, and what cannot be done without pain will forever be delayed if the time of doing it be left unsettled. No corruption is great but by long negligence, which can scarcely prevail in a mind regularly and frequently awakened by periodical remorse. He that thus breaks his life into parts will find in himself a desire to distinguish every stage of his existence by some improvement, and delight himself with the approach of the day of recollection, as of the time which is to begin a new series of virtue and felicity.

from the IDLER

The *Idler* ran in the *Universal Chronicle* from April 25, 1758, until April 5, 1760, appearing every Saturday. Johnson wrote 92 of the 104 numbers. The essays are shorter and lighter in tone than those of the earlier series, but the topics, on the whole, are similar in kind.

No. 32. Saturday, November 25, 1758

Among the innumerable mortifications that waylay human arrogance on every side, may well be reckoned our ignorance of the most common objects and effects, a defect of which we become more sensible by every attempt to supply it. Vulgar and inactive minds confound familiarity with knowledge, and conceive themselves informed of the whole nature of things when they are shown their form or told their use; but the speculatist who is not content with superficial views, harasses himself with fruitless curiosity, and still as he inquires more perceives only that he knows less.

Sleep is a state in which a great part of every life is passed. No animal has been yet discovered whose existence is not varied with intervals of insensibility; and some late philosophers have extended the empire of Sleep over the vegetable world.

Yet of this change so frequent, so great, so general, and so necessary, no searcher has yet found either the efficient or final cause, or can tell by what power the mind and body are thus chained down in irresistible stupefaction, or what benefits the animal receives from this alternate suspension of its active powers.

Whatever may be the multiplicity or contrariety of opinions upon this subject, nature has taken sufficient care that theory shall have little influence on practice. The most diligent inquirer is not able long to keep his eyes open; the most eager disputant will begin about midnight to desert his argument; and once in four and twenty hours the gay and the gloomy, the witty and the dull, the clamorous and the silent, the busy and the idle are all overpowered by the gentle tyrant, and all lie down in the equality of sleep.

Philosophy has often attempted to repress insolence by asserting that all conditions are leveled by death, a position which, however it may deject the happy, will seldom afford much comfort to the wretched. It is far more pleasing to consider that sleep is equally a leveler with death; that the time is never at a great distance when the balm of rest shall be effused alike upon every head, when the diversities of life shall stop their operation, and the high and the low shall lie down together.

It is somewhere recorded of Alexander, that in the pride of conquests and intoxication of flattery, he declared that he only perceived himself to be a man by the necessity of sleep. Whether he considered sleep as necessary to his mind or body, it was indeed a sufficient evidence of human infirmity: the body which required such frequency of renovation gave but faint promises of immortality; and the mind which, from time to time, sunk gladly into insensibility, had made no very near approaches to the felicity of the supreme and self-sufficient Nature.

I know not what can tend more to repress all the passions that disturb the peace of the world, than the consideration that there is no height of happiness or honor from which man does not eagerly descend to a state of unconscious repose; that the best condition of life is such that we contentedly quit its good to be disentangled from its evils; that in a few hours splendor fades before the eye, and praise itself deadens in the ear; the senses withdraw from their objects, and reason favors the retreat.

What then are the hopes and prospects of covetousness, ambition, and rapacity? Let him that desires most have all his desires gratified, he never shall attain a state which he can, for a day and a night, contemplate with satisfaction, or from which, if he had the power of perpetual vigilance, he would not long for periodical separations.

All envy would be extinguished if it were universally known that there are none to be envied, and surely none can be much envied who are not pleased with themselves. There is reason to suspect that the distinctions of mankind have more show than value, when it is found that all agree to be weary alike of pleasures and of cares; that the powerful and the weak, the celebrated and obscure, join in one common wish, and implore from Nature's hand the nectar of oblivion.

Such is our desire of abstraction from ourselves, that very few are satisfied with the quantity of stupefaction which the needs of the body force upon the mind. Alexander himself added intemperance to sleep, and solaced with the fumes of wine the sovereignty of the world; and almost every man has some art by which he steals his thoughts away from his present state.

It is not much of life that is spent in close attention to any important duty. Many hours of every day are suffered to fly away without any traces left upon the intellects. We suffer phantoms to rise up before us, and amuse ourselves with the dance of airy images, which after a time we dismiss forever, and know not how we have been busied.

Many have no happier moments than those that they pass in solitude, abandoned to their own imagination, which sometimes puts scepters in their hands or miters on their heads, shifts the scene of pleasure with endless variety, bids all the forms of beauty sparkle before them, and gluts them with every change of visionary luxury.

It is easy in these semi-slumbers to collect all the possibilities of happiness, to alter the course of the sun, to bring back the past, and anticipate the future, to unite all the beauties of all seasons and all the blessings of all climates, to receive and bestow felicity, and forget that misery is the lot of man. All this is a voluntary dream, a temporary recession from the realities of life to airy fictions, and habitual subjection of reason to fancy.

Others are afraid to be alone, and amuse themselves by a perpetual succession of companions; but the difference is not great: in solitude we have our dreams to ourselves, and in company we agree to dream in concert. The end sought in both is forgetfulness of ourselves.

No. 60. Saturday, June 9, 1759

Criticism is a study by which men grow important and formidable at a very small expense. The power of invention has been conferred by nature upon few, and the labor of learning those sciences which may by mere labor be obtained is too great to be willingly endured; but every man can exert such judgment as he has upon the works of others; and he whom nature has made weak, and idleness keeps ignorant, may yet support his vanity by the name of a critic.

I hope it will give comfort to great numbers who are passing through the world in obscurity, when I inform them how easily distinction may be obtained. All the other powers of literature are coy and haughty; they must be long courted, and at last are not always gained; but Criticism is a goddess easy of access and forward of advance, who will meet the slow and encourage the timorous; the want of meaning she supplies with words, and the want of spirit she recompenses with malignity.

This profession has one recommendation peculiar to itself, that it gives vent to malignity without real mischief. No genius was ever blasted by the breath of critics. The poison which, if confined, would have burst the heart, fumes away in empty hisses, and malice is set at ease with very little danger to merit. The critic is the only man whose triumph is without another's pain, and whose greatness does not rise upon another's ruin.

To a study at once so easy and so reputable, so malicious and so harmless, it cannot be necessary to invite my readers by a long or labored exhortation; it is sufficient, since all would be critics if they could, to show by one eminent example that all can be critics if they will.

Dick Minim, after the common course of puerile studies, in which he was no great proficient, was put apprentice to a brewer, with whom he had lived two years, when his uncle died in the city, and left him a large fortune in the stocks. Dick had for six months before used the company of the lower players, of whom he had learned to scorn a trade, and being now at liberty to follow his genius, he resolved to be a man of wit and humor.[1] That he might be properly initiated in his new character, he frequented the coffeehouses near the theaters, where he listened very diligently, day after day, to those who talked of language and sentiments, and unities and catastrophes, till by slow degrees he began to think that he understood something of the stage, and hoped in time to talk himself.

But he did not trust so much to natural sagacity as wholly to neglect the help of books. When the theaters were shut, he retired to Richmond with a few select writers, whose opinions he impressed upon his memory by unwearied diligence, and when he returned with other wits to the town, was able to tell, in very proper phrases, that the chief business of art is to copy nature; that a perfect writer is not to be expected, because genius decays as judgment increases; that the great art is the art of blotting; and that, according to the rule of Horace, every piece should be kept nine years.[2]

Of the great authors he now began to display the characters, laying down as an universal position that all had beauties and defects. His opinion was that Shakespeare, committing himself wholly to the impulse of nature, wanted that correctness which learning would have given him; and that Jonson, trusting to learning, did not sufficiently cast his eye on nature. He blamed the stanza of Spenser, and could not bear the hexameters of Sidney. Denham and Waller he held the first reformers of English numbers, and thought that if Waller could have obtained the strength of Denham, or Denham the sweetness of Waller, there had been nothing wanting to complete a Poet.[3] He often expressed his commiseration of Dryden's poverty, and his in-

IDLER. 1. humor: temperament, caprice. 2. every . . . years: *Ars Poetica*, l. 388. 3. Denham . . . Poet: Cf. Pope, *Essay on Criticism*, l. 361, p. 764, above.

dignation at the age which suffered him to write for bread; he repeated with rapture the first lines of *All for Love*,[4] but wondered at the corruption of taste which could bear anything so unnatural as rhyming tragedies. In Otway he found uncommon powers of moving the passions, but was disgusted by his general negligence, and blamed him for making a conspirator his hero; and never concluded his disquisition without remarking how happily the sound of the clock is made to alarm the audience. Southerne [5] would have been his favorite, but that he mixes comic with tragic scenes, intercepts the natural course of the passions, and fills the mind with a wild confusion of mirth and melancholy. The versification of Rowe he thought too melodious for the stage, and too little varied in different passions. He made it the great fault of Congreve that all his persons were wits, and that he always wrote with more art than nature. He considered *Cato* [6] rather as a poem than a play, and allowed Addison to be the complete master of allegory and grave humor, but paid no great deference to him as a critic. He thought the chief merit of Prior was in his easy tales and lighter poems, though he allowed that his *Solomon* had many noble sentiments elegantly expressed. In Swift he discovered an inimitable vein of irony, and an easiness which all would hope and few would attain. Pope he was inclined to degrade from a poet to a versifier, and thought his numbers rather luscious than sweet. He often lamented the neglect of *Phaedra and Hippolytus*,[7] and wished to see the stage under better regulations.

These assertions passed commonly uncontradicted; [8] and if now and then an opponent started up, he was quickly repressed by the suffrages of the company, and Minim went away from every dispute with elation of heart and increase of confidence.

He now grew conscious of his abilities, and began to talk of the present state of dramatic poetry; wondered what was become of the comic genius which supplied our ancestors with wit and pleasantry, and why no writer could be found that durst now venture beyond a farce. He saw no reason for thinking that the vein of humor was exhausted, since we live in a country where liberty suffers every character to spread itself to its utmost bulk, and which therefore produces more originals than all the rest of the world together. Of tragedy he concluded business to be the soul, and yet often hinted that love predominates too much upon the modern stage.

He was now an acknowledged critic, and had his own seat in a coffeehouse, and headed a party in the pit. Minim has more vanity than ill-nature, and seldom desires to do much mischief; he will perhaps murmur a little in the ear of him that sits next him, but endeavors to influence the audience to favor by clapping when an actor exclaims *ye Gods,* or laments the misery of his country.

By degrees he was admitted to rehearsals, and many of his friends are of opinion that our present poets are indebted to him for their happiest thoughts: by his contrivance the bell was rung twice in *Barbarossa,* and by his persuasion the author of *Cleone* [9] concluded his play without a couplet; for what can be more absurd, said Minim, than that part of a play should be rhymed, and part written in blank verse? and by what acquisition of faculties is the speaker who never could find rhymes before enabled to rhyme at the conclusion of an act?

He is the great investigator of hidden beauties, and is particularly delighted when he finds *the sound an echo to the sense.*[10] He has read all our poets with particular attention to this delicacy of versification, and wonders at the supineness with which their works have been hitherto perused, so that no man has found the sound of a drum in this distich:

> When Pulpit, drum ecclesiastic,
> Was beat with fist instead of a stick; [11]

and that the wonderful lines upon honor and a bubble have hitherto passed without notice:

> Honor is like the glassy bubble,
> Which costs philosophers such trouble;
> Where, one part cracked, the whole does fly,
> And wits are cracked to find out why.[12]

In these verses, says Minim, we have two striking accommodations of the sound to the sense. It

---

4. Dryden's *All for Love*, based on Shakespeare's *Antony and Cleopatra*, abandons heroic couplets for blank verse.   **5. Southerne:** Although most of Thomas Southerne's plays are contemporary with Dryden's and Otway's, he lived almost to the midpoint of the next century. Nicholas Rowe, who died in 1718, is a more typical eighteenth-century figure.   **6.** *Cato:* Addison's *Cato* (1713) was a tragedy much admired by his contemporaries.   **7.** *Phaedra . . . Hippolytus:* a play by Addison's friend, Edmund Smith, published in 1707.   **8. uncontradicted:** The point is, of course, that Minim never ventures an opinion that transcends platitude.   **9.** *Barbarossa* (1754) by Dr. John Brown; *Cleone* (1758) by Robert Dodsley.   **10.** *the . . . sense:* Pope, *Essay on Criticism*, l. 365, p. 764, above.   **11.** Samuel Butler, *Hudibras*, I.i.11–12.   **12.** *Hudibras*, II.ii.385–88.

is impossible to utter the [first] two lines emphatically without an act like that which they describe, *bubble* and *trouble* causing a momentary inflation of the cheeks by the retention of the breath, which is afterwards forcibly emitted, as in the practice of blowing bubbles. But the greatest excellence is in the third line, which is *cracked* in the middle to express a crack, and then shivers into monosyllables. Yet has this diamond lain neglected with common stones, and among the innumerable admirers of *Hudibras* the observation of this superlative passage has been reserved for the sagacity of Minim.

from the PREFACE TO
A DICTIONARY OF
THE ENGLISH LANGUAGE

How long Johnson had been thinking about the principles and method of his Dictionary before he drew up his Plan in 1747 is not known. Robert Dodsley, one of its publishers, was instrumental in its inception and in the decision to address the project to Lord Chesterfield. The outline of procedure in the Plan was closely followed in the work itself, and, by and large, the Preface is a restatement of the Plan on a grander scale, and with the necessary change of tense. Johnson agreed on the sum of £1575 with the contracting publishers, and during the years of labor was advanced the whole sum in installments. He had the assistance of six copyists in transcribing, five of whom, as Boswell takes pains to point out, were Scots. The great work first appeared in two folio volumes, on April 15, 1755. Johnson had so clearly foreseen the requirements of his task that all subsequent dictionaries have proceeded along the same systematic lines. His held the field unrivaled for a hundred years.

It is the fate of those who toil at the lower employments of life to be rather driven by the fear of evil, than attracted by the prospect of good; to be exposed to censure, without hope of praise; to be disgraced by miscarriage, or punished for neglect, where success would have been without applause, and diligence without reward.

Among these unhappy mortals is the writer of dictionaries, whom mankind have considered, not as the pupil, but the slave of science, the pioneer [1] of literature, doomed only to remove rubbish and clear obstructions from the paths through which Learning and Genius press forward to conquest

and glory, without bestowing a smile on the humble drudge that facilitates their progress. Every other author may aspire to praise; the lexicographer can only hope to escape reproach, and even this negative recompense has been yet granted to very few.

I have, notwithstanding this discouragement, attempted a dictionary of the English language, which, while it was employed in the cultivation of every species of literature, has itself been hitherto neglected; suffered to spread, under the direction of chance, into wild exuberance; resigned to the tyranny of time and fashion; and exposed to the corruptions of ignorance and caprices of innovation.

When I took the first survey of my undertaking, I found our speech copious without order, and energetic without rules: wherever I turned my view, there was perplexity to be disentangled and confusion to be regulated; choice was to be made out of boundless variety, without any established principle of selection; adulterations were to be detected, without a settled test of purity; and modes of expression to be rejected or received, without the suffrages of any writers of classical reputation or acknowledged authority.

Having therefore no assistance but from general grammar, I applied myself to the perusal of our writers; and, noting whatever might be of use to ascertain or illustrate any word or phrase, accumulated in time the materials of a dictionary, which, by degrees, I reduced to method, establishing to myself, in the progress of the work, such rules as experience and analogy suggested to me; experience, which practice and observation were continually increasing; and analogy, which, though in some words obscure, was evident in others.

In adjusting the ORTHOGRAPHY, which has been to this time unsettled and fortuitous, I found it necessary to distinguish those irregularities that are inherent in our tongue, and perhaps coeval with it, from others which the ignorance or negligence of later writers has produced. Every language has its anomalies, which, though inconvenient, and in themselves once unnecessary, must be tolerated among the imperfections of human things, and which require only to be registered, that they may not be increased, and ascertained, that they may not be confounded; but every language has likewise its improprieties and absurdities, which it is the duty of the lexicographer to correct or proscribe.

As language was at its beginning merely oral, all words of necessary or common use were spoken

---

PREFACE TO DICTIONARY.   1. **pioneer**: in a military sense, one of a corps of engineers, whose job is to dig mines, "remove obstructions," and level the road for the main force that follows.

before they were written, and while they were unfixed by any visible signs, must have been spoken with great diversity, as we now observe those who cannot read catch sounds imperfectly, and utter them negligently. When this wild and barbarous jargon was first reduced to an alphabet, every penman endeavored to express, as he could, the sounds which he was accustomed to pronounce or to receive, and vitiated in writing such words as were already vitiated in speech. The powers of the letters, when they were applied to a new language, must have been vague and unsettled, and therefore different hands would exhibit the same sound by different combinations.

From this uncertain pronunciation arise in a great part the various dialects of the same country, which will always be observed to grow fewer, and less different, as books are multiplied; and from this arbitrary representation of sounds by letters proceeds that diversity of spelling observable in the Saxon remains, and I suppose in the first books of every nation, which perplexes or destroys analogy, and produces anomalous formations that, being once incorporated, can never be afterward dismissed or reformed.

Of this kind are the derivatives *length* from *long*, *strength* from *strong*, *darling* from *dear*, *breadth* from *broad*, from *dry*, *drought*, and from *high*, *height*, which Milton, in zeal for analogy, writes *highth*; *Quid te exempta juvat spinis de pluribus una*; [2] to change all would be too much, and to change one is nothing.

This uncertainty is most frequent in the vowels, which are so capriciously pronounced, and so differently modified, by accident or affectation, not only in every province, but in every mouth, that to them, as is well known to etymologists, little regard is to be shown in the deduction of one language from another.

Such defects are not errors in orthography, but spots of barbarity impressed so deep in the English language that criticism can never wash them away; these, therefore, must be permitted to remain untouched, but many words have likewise been altered by accident, or depraved by ignorance, as the pronunciation of the vulgar has been weakly followed; and some still continue to be variously written, as authors differ in their care or skill; of these it was proper to inquire the true orthography, which I have always considered as depending on their derivation, and have therefore referred them to their original languages. Thus I write *enchant, enchantment, enchanter*, after the French, and *incantation* after the Latin; thus *entire* is chosen rather than *intire*, because it passed to us not from the Latin *integer*, but from the French *entier*.

Of many words it is difficult to say whether they were immediately received from the Latin or the French, since at the time when we had dominions in France, we had Latin service in our churches. It is, however, my opinion, that the French generally supplied us, for we have few Latin words, among the terms of domestic use, which are not French; but many French which are very remote from Latin.

Even in words of which the derivation is apparent, I have been often obliged to sacrifice uniformity to custom; thus I write, in compliance with a numberless majority, *convey* and *inveigh*, *deceit* and *receipt, fancy* and *phantom;* sometimes the derivative varies from the primitive, as *explain* and *explanation, repeat,* and *repetition.*

Some combinations of letters having the same power are used indifferently without any discoverable reason of choice, as in *choak, choke; soap, sope; fewel, fuel,* and many others, which I have sometimes inserted twice, that those who search for them under either form may not search in vain.

In examining the orthography of any doubtful word, the mode of spelling by which it is inserted in the series of the dictionary is to be considered as that to which I give, perhaps not often rashly, the preference. I have left, in the examples, to every author his own practice unmolested, that the reader may balance suffrages, and judge between us; but this question is not always to be determined by reputed or by real learning; some men, intent upon greater things, have thought little on sounds and derivations; some, knowing in the ancient tongues, have neglected those in which our words are commonly to be sought. Thus Hammond writes *fecibleness* for *feasibleness,* because, I suppose, he imagined it derived immediately from the Latin; and some words, such as *dependant, dependent; dependance, dependence,* vary their final syllable, as one or another language is present to the writer.

In this part of the work, where caprice has long wantoned without control, and vanity sought praise by petty reformation, I have endeavored to proceed with a scholar's reverence for antiquity, and a grammarian's regard to the genius of our tongue. I have attempted few alterations, and among those few

---

2. *Quid . . . una:* "What good does it do you to pull out one thorn among so very many?" Horace, *Epistles,* II.ii.212.

perhaps the greater part is from the modern to the ancient practice; and I hope I may be allowed to recommend to those whose thoughts have been perhaps employed too anxiously on verbal singularities, not to disturb, upon narrow views, or for minute propriety, the orthography of their fathers. It has been asserted that for the law to be *known,* is of more importance than to be *right.* Change, says Hooker, is not made without inconvenience, even from worse to better.[3] There is in constancy and stability a general and lasting advantage, which will always overbalance the slow improvements of gradual correction. Much less ought our written language to comply with the corruptions of oral utterance, or copy that which every variation of time or place makes different from itself, and imitate those changes which will again be changed while imitation is employed in observing them.

This recommendation of steadiness and uniformity does not proceed from an opinion that particular combinations of letters have much influence on human happiness, or that truth may not be successfully taught by modes of spelling fanciful and erroneous; I am not yet so lost in lexicography as to forget that *words are the daughters of earth, and that things are the sons of heaven.* Language is only the instrument of science, and words are but the signs of ideas; I wish, however, that the instrument might be less apt to decay, and that signs might be permanent, like the things which they denote. . . .[4]

That part of my work on which I expect malignity most frequently to fasten is the EXPLANATION; in which I cannot hope to satisfy those who are perhaps not inclined to be pleased, since I have not always been able to satisfy myself. To interpret a language by itself is very difficult: many words cannot be explained by synonyms, because the idea signified by them has not more than one appellation; nor by paraphrase, because simple ideas cannot be described. When the nature of things is unknown, or the notion unsettled and indefinite, and various in various minds, the words by which such notions are conveyed, or such things denoted, will be ambiguous and perplexed. And such is the fate of hapless lexicography, that not only darkness, but light, impedes and distresses it; things may be not only too little, but too much known, to be happily illustrated. To explain, requires the use of terms less abstruse than that which is to be explained, and such terms cannot always be found; for as nothing can be proved but by supposing something intuitively known and evident without proof, so nothing can be defined but by the use of words too plain to admit a definition.

Other words there are, of which the sense is too subtle and evanescent to be fixed in a paraphrase; such are all those which are by the grammarians termed *expletives,* and, in dead languages, are suffered to pass for empty sounds, of no other use than to fill a verse, or to modulate a period, but which are easily perceived in living tongues to have power and emphasis, though it be sometimes such as no other form of expression can convey.

My labor has likewise been much increased by a class of verbs too frequent in the English language, of which the signification is so loose and general, the use so vague and indeterminate, and the senses detorted[5] so widely from the first idea, that it is hard to trace them through the maze of variation, to catch them on the brink of utter inanity, to circumscribe them by any limitations, or interpret them by any words of distinct and settled meaning; such are *bear, break, come, cast, full, get, give, do, put, set, go, run, make, take, turn, throw.* If of these the whole power is not accurately delivered, it must be remembered that while our language is yet living, and variable by the caprice of everyone that speaks it, these words are hourly shifting their relations, and can no more be ascertained in a dictionary, than a grove, in the agitation of a storm, can be accurately delineated from its picture in the water.

The particles[6] are among all nations applied with so great latitude, that they are not easily reducible under any regular scheme of explication; this difficulty is not less, nor perhaps greater, in English than in other languages. I have labored them with diligence, I hope with success; such at least as can be expected in a task which no man, however learned or sagacious, has yet been able to perform.

Some words there are which I cannot explain, because I do not understand them. These might have been omitted very often with little inconvenience, but I would not so far indulge my vanity as to decline this confession; for when Tully owns

---

3. change . . . better: Richard Hooker, *Of the Laws of Ecclesiastical Polity* (1594), IV.xiv.   4. Some paragraphs on etymology, and on classes of words admitted or excluded, are here omitted.

5. detorted: perverted, "twisted away."   6. particles: uninflected and subordinate elements of speech (e.g., preposition, conjunction, affix).

himself ignorant whether *lessus,* in the twelve tables,[7] means a *funeral song* or *mourning garment;* [8] and Aristotle doubts whether οὐρεὺς in the *Iliad* signifies a *mule* or *muleteer,*[9] I may surely, without shame, leave some obscurities to happier industry, or future information.

The rigor of interpretative lexicography requires that *the explanation, and the word explained, should be always reciprocal;* this I have always endeavored but could not always attain. Words are seldom exactly synonymous; a new term was not introduced, but because the former was thought inadequate; names, therefore, have often many ideas, but few ideas have many names. It was then necessary to use the proximate word, for the deficiency of single terms can very seldom be supplied by circumlocution; nor is the inconvenience great of such mutilated interpretations, because the sense may be easily be collected entire from the examples.

In every word of extensive use, it was requisite to mark the progress of its meaning, and show by what gradations of intermediate sense it has passed from its primitive to its remote and accidental signification; so that every foregoing explanation should tend to that which follows, and the series be regularly concatenated from the first notion to the last.

This is specious, but not always practicable; kindred senses may be so interwoven that the perplexity cannot be disentangled, nor any reason be assigned why one should be ranged before the other. When the radical idea branches out into parallel ramifications, how can a consecutive series be formed of senses in their nature collateral? The shades of meaning sometimes pass imperceptibly into each other, so that though on one side they apparently differ, yet it is impossible to mark the point of contact. Ideas of the same race, though not exactly alike, are sometimes so little different, that no words can express the dissimilitude, though the mind easily perceives it when they are exhibited together; and sometimes there is such a confusion of acceptations, that discernment is wearied, and distinction puzzled, and perseverance herself hurries to an end, by crowding together what she cannot separate.

These complaints of difficulty will, by those that have never considered words beyond their popular use, be thought only the jargon of a man willing to magnify his labors, and procure veneration to his studies by involution and obscurity. But every art is obscure to those that have not learned it; this uncertainty of terms, and commixture of ideas, is well known to those who have joined philosophy with grammar; and if I have not expressed them very clearly, it must be remembered that I am speaking of that which words are insufficient to explain.

The original sense of words is often driven out of use by their metaphorical acceptations, yet must be inserted for the sake of a regular origination. Thus I know not whether *ardor* is used for *material heat,* or whether *flagrant,* in English, ever signifies the same with *burning;* yet such are the primitive ideas of these words, which are therefore set first, though without examples, that the figurative senses may be commodiously deduced.

Such is the exuberance of signification which many words have obtained, that it was scarcely possible to collect all their senses; sometimes the meaning of derivatives must be sought in the mother term, and sometimes deficient explanations of the primitive may be supplied in the train of derivation. In any case of doubt or difficulty, it will be always proper to examine all the words of the same race; for some words are slightly passed over to avoid repetition, some admitted easier and clearer explanation than others, and all will be better understood, as they are considered in greater variety of structures and relations.

All the interpretations of words are not written with the same skill, or the same happiness; things equally easy in themselves are not all equally easy to any single mind. Every writer of a long work commits errors, where there appears neither ambiguity to mislead, nor obscurity to confound him; and in a search like this, many felicities of expression will be casually overlooked, many convenient parallels will be forgotten, and many particulars will admit improvement from a mind utterly unequal to the whole performance.

But many seeming faults are to be imputed rather to the nature of the undertaking, than the negligence of the performer. Thus some explanations are unavoidably reciprocal or circular, as *hind, the female of the stag; stag, the male of the hind;* sometimes easier words are changed into harder, as *burial* into *sepulture* or *interment, drier* into *desiccative, dryness* into *siccity* or *aridity, fit* into *paroxysm;* for the easiest word, whatever it be, can never be translated into one more easy. But easiness and

---

7. The "twelve tables" refer to the revered code of Roman law drawn up by the commission of Decemviri and published 451–50 B.C.   8. Tully ... *garment:* Cicero, *Laws,* II.xxiii.59.
9. Aristotle ... *muleteer:* Aristotle, *Poetics,* XXV.9.

difficulty are merely relative, and if the present prevalence of our language should invite foreigners to this dictionary, many will be assisted by those words which now seem only to increase or produce obscurity. For this reason I have endeavored frequently to join a Teutonic and Roman interpretation, as to CHEER, to *gladden,* or *exhilarate,* that every learner of English may be assisted by his own tongue.

The solution of all difficulties, and the supply of all defects, must be sought in the examples, subjoined to the various senses of each word, and ranged according to the time of their authors.

When first I collected these authorities, I was desirous that every quotation should be useful to some other end than the illustration of a word; I therefore extracted from philosophers principles of science; from historians remarkable facts; from chemists complete processes; from divines striking exhortations; and from poets beautiful descriptions. Such is design, while it is yet at a distance from execution. When the time called upon me to range this accumulation of elegance and wisdom into an alphabetical series, I soon discovered that the bulk of my volumes would fright away the student, and was forced to depart from my scheme of including all that was pleasing or useful in English literature, and reduce my transcripts very often to clusters of words in which scarcely any meaning is retained; thus, to the weariness of copying I was condemned to add the vexation of expunging. Some passages I have yet spared, which may relieve the labor of verbal searches, and intersperse with verdure and flowers the dusty deserts of barren philology.

The examples, thus mutilated, are no longer to be considered as conveying the sentiments or doctrine of their authors; the word for the sake of which they are inserted, with all its appendant clauses, has been carefully preserved; but it may sometimes happen, by hasty detruncation, that the general tendency of the sentence may be changed: the divine may desert his tenets, or the philosopher his system.

Some of the examples have been taken from writers who were never mentioned as masters of elegance or models of style; but words must be sought where they are used, and in what pages, eminent for purity, can terms of manufacture or agriculture be found? Many quotations serve no other purpose than that of proving the bare existence of words, and are therefore selected with less scrupulousness than those which are to teach their structures and relations.

My purpose was to admit no testimony of living authors, that I might not be misled by partiality, and that none of my contemporaries might have reason to complain; nor have I departed from this resolution, but when some performance of uncommon excellence excited my veneration, when my memory supplied me, from late books, with an example that was wanting, or when my heart, in the tenderness of friendship, solicited admission for a favorite name.

So far have I been from any care to grace my pages with modern decorations, that I have studiously endeavored to collect examples and authorities from the writers before the Restoration, whose works I regard as *the wells of English undefiled,*[10] as the pure sources of genuine diction. Our language, for almost a century, has, by the concurrence of many causes, been gradually departing from its original Teutonic character and deviating towards a Gallic structure and phraseology, from which it ought to be our endeavor to recall it, by making our ancient volumes the groundwork of style, admitting among the additions of later times only such as may supply real deficiencies, such as are readily adopted by the genius of our tongue, and incorporate easily with our native idioms.

But as every language has a time of rudeness antecedent to perfection, as well as of false refinement and declension, I have been cautious lest my zeal for antiquity might drive me into times too remote, and crowd my book with words now no longer understood. I have fixed Sidney's work for the boundary beyond which I make few excursions. From the authors which rose in the time of Elizabeth, a speech might be formed adequate to all the purposes of use and elegance. If the language of theology were extracted from Hooker and the translation of the Bible; the terms of natural knowledge from Bacon; the phrases of policy, war, and navigation from Raleigh; the dialect of poetry and fiction from Spenser and Sidney; and the diction of common life from Shakespeare, few ideas would be lost to mankind for want of English words in which they might be expressed.

It is not sufficient that a word is found, unless it be so combined as that its meaning is apparently determined by the tract and tenor of the sentence. Such passages I have therefore chosen, and when it happened that any author gave a definition of a term, or such an explanation as is equivalent to a

---

10. *the . . . undefiled:* Spenser, *Faerie Queene,* IV.ii.33.

definition, I have placed his authority as a supplement to my own, without regard to the chronological order that is otherwise observed.

Some words, indeed, stand unsupported by any authority, but they are commonly derivative nouns or adverbs formed from their primitives by regular and constant analogy, or names of things seldom occurring in books, or words of which I have reason to doubt the existence.

There is more danger of censure from the multiplicity than paucity of examples; authorities will sometimes seem to have been accumulated without necessity or use, and perhaps some will be found which might, without loss, have been omitted. But a work of this kind is not hastily to be charged with superfluities; those quotations which to careless or unskillful perusers appear only to repeat the same sense will often exhibit, to a more accurate examiner, diversities of signification or, at least, afford different shades of the same meaning. One will show the word applied to persons, another to things; one will express an ill, another a good, and a third a neutral sense; one will prove the expression genuine from an ancient author; another will show it elegant from a modern; a doubtful authority is corroborated by another of more credit; an ambiguous sentence is ascertained by a passage clear and determinate; the word, how often soever repeated, appears with new associates and in different combinations, and every quotation contributes something to the stability or enlargement of the language.

When words are used equivocally, I receive them in either sense; when they are metaphorical, I adopt them in their primitive acceptation.

I have sometimes, though rarely, yielded to the temptation of exhibiting a genealogy of sentiments, by showing how one author copied the thoughts and diction of another; such quotations are indeed little more than repetitions, which might justly be censured, did they not gratify the mind by affording a kind of intellectual history.

The various syntactical structures occurring in the examples have been carefully noted; the license or negligence with which many words have been hitherto used has made our style capricious and indeterminate; when the different combinations of the same word are exhibited together, the preference is readily given to propriety, and I have often endeavored to direct the choice.

Thus have I labored, by settling the orthography, displaying the analogy, regulating the structures,

and ascertaining the signification of English words, to perform all the parts of a faithful lexicographer; but I have not always executed my own scheme, or satisfied my own expectations. The work, whatever proofs of diligence and attention it may exhibit, is yet capable of many improvements: the orthography which I recommend is still controvertible; the etymology which I adopt is uncertain, and perhaps frequently erroneous; the explanations are sometimes too much contracted, and sometimes too much diffused; the significations are distinguished rather with subtlety than skill; and the attention is harassed with unnecessary minuteness.

The examples are too often injudiciously truncated, and perhaps sometimes, I hope very rarely, alleged in a mistaken sense; for in making this collection I trusted more to memory than, in a state of disquiet and embarrassment, memory can contain, and purposed to supply at the review what was left incomplete in the first transcription.

Many terms appropriated to particular occupations, though necessary and significant, are undoubtedly omitted; and of the words most studiously considered and exemplified, many senses have escaped observation.

Yet these failures, however frequent, may admit extenuation and apology. To have attempted much is always laudable, even when the enterprise is above the strength that undertakes it. To rest below his own aim is incident to everyone whose fancy is active and whose views are comprehensive; nor is any man satisfied with himself because he has done much, but because he can conceive little. When first I engaged in this work, I resolved to leave neither words nor things unexamined, and pleased myself with a prospect of the hours which I should revel away in feasts of literature; with the obscure recesses of northern learning [11] which I should enter and ransack; the treasures with which I expected every search into those neglected mines to reward my labor; and the triumph with which I should display my acquisitions to mankind. When I had thus inquired into the original of words, I resolved to show likewise my attention to things; to pierce deep into every science, to inquire the nature of every substance of which I inserted the name, to limit every idea by a definition strictly logical, and exhibit every production of art or nature in an accurate description, that my book might

11. northern learning: i.e., of northern Europe, as distinguished from Mediterranean, or classical, culture.

be in place of all other dictionaries whether appellative or technical. But these were the dreams of a poet doomed at last to wake a lexicographer. I soon found that it is too late to look for instruments when the work calls for execution, and that whatever abilities I had brought to my task, with those I must finally perform it. To deliberate whenever I doubted, to inquire whenever I was ignorant, would have protracted the undertaking without end and, perhaps, without much improvement; for I did not find by my first experiments, that what I had not of my own was easily to be obtained; I saw that one inquiry only gave occasion to another, that book referred to book, that to search was not always to find, and to find was not always to be informed; and that thus to pursue perfection was, like the first inhabitants of Arcadia, to chase the sun, which, when they had reached the hill where he seemed to rest, was still beheld at the same distance from them.

I then contracted my design, determining to confide in myself and no longer to solicit auxiliaries, which produced more encumbrance than assistance; by this I obtained at least one advantage, that I set limits to my work, which would in time be ended, though not completed.

Despondency has never so far prevailed as to depress me to negligence; some faults will at last appear to be the effects of anxious diligence and persevering activity. The nice and subtle ramifications of meaning were not easily avoided by a mind intent upon accuracy and convinced of the necessity of disentangling combinations, and separating similitudes. Many of the distinctions which to common readers appear useless and idle will be found real and important by men versed in the school philosophy, without which no dictionary shall ever be accurately compiled, or skillfully examined.

Some senses however there are which, though not the same, are yet so nearly allied that they are often confounded. Most men think indistinctly, and therefore cannot speak with exactness; and consequently some examples might be indifferently put to either signification; this uncertainty is not to be imputed to me, who do not form, but register the language; who do not teach men how they should think, but relate how they have hitherto expressed their thoughts.

The imperfect sense of some examples I lamented but could not remedy, and hope they will be compensated by innumerable passages selected with propriety and preserved with exactness; some shining with sparks of imagination, and some replete with treasures of wisdom.

The orthography and etymology, though imperfect, are not imperfect for want of care, but because care will not always be successful, and recollection or information come too late for use.

That many terms of art and manufacture are omitted must be frankly acknowledged, but for this defect I may boldly allege that it was unavoidable: I could not visit caverns to learn the miner's language, nor take a voyage to perfect my skill in the dialect of navigation, nor visit the warehouses of merchants, and shops of artificers, to gain the names of wares, tools, and operations, of which no mention is found in books. What favorable accident, or easy inquiry, brought within my reach has not been neglected; but it had been a hopeless labor to glean up words, by courting living information, and contesting with the sullenness of one, and the roughness of another.

To furnish the academicians *della Crusca* with words of this kind, a series of comedies called *La Fiera,* or *The Fair,* was professedly written by *Buonarotti,*[12] but I had no such assistant, and therefore was content to want what they must have wanted likewise, had they not luckily been so supplied.

Nor are all words which are not found in the vocabulary to be lamented as omissions. Of the laborious and mercantile part of the people, the diction is in a great measure casual and mutable; many of their terms are formed for some temporary or local convenience and, though current at certain times and places, are in others utterly unknown. This fugitive cant, which is always in a state of increase or decay, cannot be regarded as any part of the durable materials of a language, and therefore must be suffered to perish with other things unworthy of preservation.

Care will sometimes betray to the appearance of negligence. He that is catching opportunities which seldom occur, will suffer those to pass by unregarded, which he expects hourly to return; he that is searching for rare and remote things, will neglect those that are obvious and familiar; thus many of the most common and cursory words have been inserted with little illustration, because in gathering the authorities, I forbore to copy those which I thought likely to occur whenever they were wanted.

---

12. **Buonarotti:** the nephew of Michelangelo. His comedies deliberately introduced characters from various industries, for the sake of the special words they employed.

It is remarkable that, in reviewing my collection, I found the word *sea* unexemplified.

Thus it happens, that in things difficult there is danger from ignorance, and in things easy from confidence; the mind, afraid of greatness, and disdainful of littleness, hastily withdraws herself from painful searches, and passes with scornful rapidity over tasks not adequate to her powers, sometimes too secure for caution, and again too anxious for vigorous effort; sometimes idle in a plain path, and sometimes distracted in labyrinths, and dissipated by different intentions.

A large work is difficult because it is large, even though all its parts might singly be performed with facility; where there are many things to be done, each must be allowed its share of time and labor, in the proportion only which it bears to the whole; nor can it be expected that the stones which form the dome of a temple should be squared and polished like the diamond of a ring.

Of the event of this work, for which, having labored it with so much application, I cannot but have some degree of parental fondness, it is natural to form conjectures. Those who have been persuaded to think well of my design will require that it should fix our language, and put a stop to those alterations which time and chance have hitherto been suffered to make in it without opposition. With this consequence I will confess that I flattered myself for a while, but now begin to fear that I have indulged expectation which neither reason nor experience can justify. When we see men grow old and die at a certain time one after another, from century to century, we laugh at the elixir that promises to prolong life to a thousand years; and with equal justice may the lexicographer be derided, who, being able to produce no example of a nation that has preserved their words and phrases from mutability, shall imagine that his dictionary can embalm his language, and secure it from corruption and decay, that it is in his power to change sublunary nature, and clear the world at once from folly, vanity, and affectation.

With this hope, however, academies have been instituted, to guard the avenues of their languages, to retain fugitives, and repulse intruders; but their vigilance and activity have hitherto been vain; sounds are too volatile and subtle for legal restraints; to enchain syllables, and to lash the wind, are equally the undertakings of pride, unwilling to measure its desires by its strength. The French language has visibly changed under the inspection of the academy;[13] the style of Amelot's translation of Father Paul[14] is observed by *Le Courayer* to be *un peu passé;* and no Italian will maintain that the diction of any modern writer is not perceptibly different from that of *Boccace, Machiavel,* or *Caro.*[15]

Total and sudden transformations of a language seldom happen; conquests and migrations are now very rare; but there are other causes of change which, though slow in their operation and invisible in their progress, are perhaps as much superior to human resistance as the revolutions of the sky or intumescence of the tide. Commerce, however necessary, however lucrative, as it depraves the manners, corrupts the language; they that have frequent intercourse with strangers, to whom they endeavor to accommodate themselves, must in time learn a mingled dialect, like the jargon which serves the traffickers on the Mediterranean and Indian coasts. This will not always be confined to the exchange, the warehouse, or the port, but will be communicated by degrees to other ranks of the people, and be at last incorporated with the current speech.

There are likewise internal causes equally forcible. The language most likely to continue long without alteration would be that of a nation raised a little, and but a little, above barbarity, secluded from strangers, and totally employed in procuring the conveniences of life, either without books or, like some of the Mahometan countries, with very few; men thus busied and unlearned, having only such words as common use requires, would perhaps long continue to express the same notions by the same signs. But no such constancy can be expected in a people polished by arts, and classed by subordination, where one part of the community is sustained and accommodated by the labor of the other. Those who have much leisure to think will always be enlarging the stock of ideas, and every increase of knowledge, whether real or fancied, will produce new words, or combinations of words. When the mind is unchained from necessity, it will range after convenience; when it is left at large in the fields of speculation, it will shift opinions; as any custom is disused, the words that expressed it must perish with it; as any opinion grows popular,

13. **academy:** the Académie Française, established in 1635 by Cardinal Richelieu to preside over the French literary world. 14. **Father Paul:** Paolo Sarpi, *History of the Council of Trent* (1619); translated from Italian into French by Amelot (1683); and by Courayer (1736), because Amelot's French was "a little out of date." 15. **Boccace . . . Caro:** Boccaccio died in 1375; Machiavelli died in 1527; Annibal Caro, a poet who translated the *Aeneid,* died about 1566.

it will innovate speech in the same proportion as it alters practice.

As by the cultivation of various sciences, a language is amplified, it will be more furnished with words deflected from original sense; the geometrician will talk of a courtier's zenith, or the eccentric virtue of a wild hero; and the physician, of sanguine expectations and phlegmatic delays. Copiousness of speech will give opportunities to capricious choice, by which some words will be preferred, and others degraded; vicissitudes of fashion will enforce the use of new, or extend the signification of known, terms. The tropes of poetry will make hourly encroachments, and the metaphorical will become the current sense; pronunciation will be varied by levity or ignorance, and the pen must at length comply with the tongue; illiterate writers will at one time or other, by public infatuation, rise into renown, who, not knowing the original import of words, will use them with colloquial licentiousness, confound distinction, and forget propriety. As politeness increases, some expressions will be considered as too gross and vulgar for the delicate, others as too formal and ceremonious for the gay and airy; new phrases are therefore adopted, which must, for the same reasons, be in time dismissed. Swift, in his petty treatise on the English language,[16] alows that new words must sometimes be introduced, but proposes that none should be suffered to become obsolete. But what makes a word obsolete, more than general agreement to forbear it? and how shall it be continued, when it conveys an offensive idea, or recalled again into the mouths of mankind, when it has once become unfamiliar by disuse and unpleasing by unfamiliarity?

There is another cause of alteration more prevalent than any other, which yet in the present state of the world cannot be obviated. A mixture of two languages will produce a third distinct from both, and they will always be mixed, where the chief part of education, and the most conspicuous accomplishment, is skill in ancient or in foreign tongues. He that has long cultivated another language will find its words and combinations crowd upon his memory; and haste and negligence, refinement and affectation, will obtrude borrowed terms and exotic expressions.

The great pest of speech is frequency of translation. No book was ever turned from one language into another without imparting something of its native idiom. This is the most mischievous and comprehensive innovation; single words may enter by thousands, and the fabric of the tongue continue the same, but new phraseology changes much at once; it alters not the single stones of the building, but the order of the columns. If an academy should be established for the cultivation of our style, which I, who can never wish to see dependence multiplied, hope the spirit of English liberty will hinder or destroy, let them, instead of compiling grammars and dictionaries, endeavor, with all their influence, to stop the license of translators, whose idleness and ignorance, if it be suffered to proceed, will reduce us to babble a dialect of France.

If the changes that we fear be thus irresistible, what remains but to acquiesce with silence, as in the other insurmountable distresses of humanity? It remains that we retard what we cannot repel, that we palliate what we cannot cure. Life may be lengthened by care, though death cannot be ultimately defeated; tongues, like governments, have a natural tendency to degeneration; we have long preserved our constitution, let us make some struggles for our language.

In hope of giving longevity to that which its own nature forbids to be immortal, I have devoted this book, the labor of years, to the honor of my country, that we may no longer yield the palm of philology, without a contest, to the nations of the Continent. The chief glory of every people arises from its authors; whether I shall add anything by my own writings to the reputation of English literature must be left to time; much of my life has been lost under the pressures of disease, much has been trifled away, and much has always been spent in provision for the day that was passing over me; but I shall not think my employment useless or ignoble, if by my assistance foreign nations, and distant ages, gain access to the propagators of knowledge, and understand the teachers of truth; if my labors afford light to the repositories of science, and add celebrity to *Bacon,* to *Hooker,* to *Milton,* and to *Boyle.*

When I am animated by this wish, I look with pleasure on my book, however defective, and deliver it to the world with the spirit of a man that has endeavored well. That it will immediately become popular I have not promised to myself: a few wild blunders, and risible absurdities, from which no work of such multiplicity was ever free, may for a time furnish folly with laughter, and harden ignorance in contempt; but useful diligence will

16. Swift . . . language: *A Proposal for Correcting, Improving, and Ascertaining the English Tongue* (1712).

at last prevail, and there never can be wanting some who distinguish desert; who will consider that no dictionary of a living tongue ever can be perfect, since while it is hastening to publication, some words are budding, and some falling away; that a whole life cannot be spent upon syntax and etymology, and that even a whole life would not be sufficient; that he, whose design includes whatever language can express, must often speak of what he does not understand; that a writer will sometimes be hurried by eagerness to the end, and sometimes faint with weariness under a task, which *Scaliger* compares [17] to the labors of the anvil and the mine; that what is obvious is not always known, and what is known is not always present; that sudden fits of inadvertency will surprise vigilance, slight avocations will seduce attention, and casual eclipses of the mind will darken learning; and that the writer shall often in vain trace his memory at the moment of need, for that which yesterday he knew with intuitive readiness, and which will come uncalled into his thoughts tomorrow.

In this work, when it shall be found that much is omitted, let it not be forgotten that much likewise is performed, and, though no book was ever spared out of tenderness to the author, and the world is little solicitous to know whence proceeded the faults of that which it condemns, yet it may gratify curiosity to inform it, that the *English Dictionary* was written with little assistance of the learned, and without any patronage of the great; not in the soft obscurities of retirement, or under the shelter of academic bowers, but amidst inconvenience and distraction, in sickness and in sorrow. It may repress the triumph of malignant criticism to observe that, if our language is not here fully displayed, I have only failed in an attempt which no human powers have hitherto completed. If the lexicons of ancient tongues, now immutably fixed, and comprised in a few volumes, be yet, after the toil of successive ages, inadequate and delusive; if the aggregated knowledge, and co-operating diligence of the Italian academicians, did not secure them from the censure of Beni; [18] if the embodied critics of France,[19] when fifty years had been spent upon their work, were obliged to change its econ-

omy, and give their second edition another form, I may surely be contented without the praise of perfection, which, if I could obtain, in this gloom of solitude, what would it avail me? I have protracted my work till most of those whom I wished to please have sunk into the grave, and success and miscarriage are empty sounds; I therefore dismiss it with frigid tranquillity, having little to fear or hope from censure or from praise.

from the PREFACE TO SHAKESPEARE

Johnson had the intention to edit Shakespeare even before he undertook the Dictionary, and attached Proposals for a ten-volume duodecimo edition to his *Miscellaneous Observations on the Tragedy of Macbeth,* published in 1745. The Dictionary prevented his proceeding in this enterprise, but, when that was off his hands, he again issued Proposals in the late spring of 1756 for an edition to be completed before the end of 1757. He was dilatory in performance, however, and the work did not appear until 1765, before which time it was being charged that he had accepted subscriptions without intending to fulfill his obligation. The satirist Charles Churchill wrote:

> He for subscribers baits his hook,
> And takes their cash; but where's the book?
> No matter where; wise fear, we know,
> Forbids the robbing of a foe;
> But what, to serve our private ends,
> Forbids the cheating of our friends?

The taunt is credited with having stung Johnson into quickening his pace. In his *Life of Pope* he writes of such delays: " Perhaps no extensive and multifarious performance was ever effected within the term originally fixed in the undertaker's mind. He that runs against Time, has an antagonist not subject to casualties."

By modern editorial standards, Johnson's collation of the early readings was negligent and far from exhaustive. What makes his edition memorable and still a potent element in our understanding of Shakespeare is the amount of lucid interpretation it contains of obscure passages other editors had either stumbled over or given up to conjectural emendation. Johnson deliberately denied himself the vanity of ingenious conjecture. His powerfully ratiocinative mind always made sense of a passage if any sense remained to be made. His notes, also, contain many penetrating observations of wider bearing than the immediate occasion requires — interpreting character, commenting on the mores of the Elizabethan age and on Shakespeare's practice, throwing out obiter dicta on a great variety of topics. They abound with illustrations of Johnson's critical views, pungent personality, and ripe wisdom. At the end of each play he customarily adds a " short stric-

---

17. *Scaliger* compares: J. C. Scaliger, *In Lexicorum Compilatores,* in his collected poems (ed. 1868), p. 38. He and his son, J. J. Scaliger, were two very famous Renaissance scholars. **18. Beni:** He complained that the Tuscan dialect had been made regulative and controlling. **19. critics of France:** The French Academy had undertaken their dictionary in 1639; it was published in 1694.

ture" on the play as a whole, but these are usually loose and casual, not balanced summaries.

The greatest of the component parts of this edition is the Preface — greatest of all prefaces to Shakespeare and by itself sufficient to establish Johnson among the first half-dozen English literary critics of all time. To the reader of today there may not at first, apart from its sturdily independent and unawed tone, seem to be anything very new or very striking in this preface. It contains no psychological subtleties; its defense of Shakespeare for disregarding the unities of time and place seems not very daring to a generation that has never known respect for them; its survey of Shakespeare's learning has been superseded by a multiplicity of special studies; its review of preceding editors, then recent but now familiar only to the specialist, cannot excite attention. But what Johnson said of Dryden and Addison may now be quoted in his own support: "A writer who obtains his full purpose loses himself in his own luster. Of an opinion which is no longer doubted, the evidence ceases to be examined. Of an art universally practiced, the first teacher is forgotten. Learning once made popular is no longer learning: it has the appearance of something which we have bestowed upon ourselves, as the dew appears to rise from the field which it refreshes." And again: "It is not uncommon for those who have grown wise by the labor of others to add a little of their own, and overlook their masters. Addison is now despised by some who perhaps would never have seen his defects, but by the lights which he afforded them."

Johnson's criticism in the Preface to Shakespeare is of this broad and general kind. It is remarkable in that its emphases still appear true and unexceptionable; that its critical positions almost all strike with immediate conviction; that its occasional prejudices always provoke us to examine our own; and that every idea is expressed with such eloquent sufficiency that we despair of saying it so well again, and turn away to other types, and another scale, of investigation.

One caveat may be offered in conclusion. It is easy to simplify Johnson's comparison of Shakespearean comedy and tragedy into a value-judgment favoring the comedies. But this he does not mean. He did not think that any comedy was *greater* than *Lear,* or *Hamlet,* or *Othello.* He *does* say that Shakespeare's natural disposition led him to comedy; that "in comedy he seems to repose, or luxuriate, as in a mode of thinking congenial to his nature."

That praises are without reason lavished on the dead, and that the honors due only to excellence are paid to antiquity, is a complaint likely to be always continued by those who, being able to add nothing to truth, hope for eminence from the heresies of paradox; or those who, being forced by disappointment upon consolatory expedients, are willing to hope from posterity what the present age refuses, and flatter themselves that the regard which is yet denied by envy will be at last bestowed by time.

Antiquity, like every other quality that attracts the notice of mankind, has undoubtedly votaries that reverence it, not from reason, but from prejudice. Some seem to admire indiscriminately whatever has been long preserved, without considering that time has sometimes co-operated with chance; all perhaps are more willing to honor past than present excellence; and the mind contemplates genius through the shades of age, as the eye surveys the sun through artificial opacity. The great contention of criticism is to find the faults of the moderns, and the beauties of the ancients. While an author is yet living we estimate his powers by his worst performance, and when he is dead we rate them by his best.

To works, however, of which the excellence is not absolute and definite, but gradual and comparative; to works not raised upon principles demonstrative and scientific, but appealing wholly to observation and experience, no other test can be applied than length of duration and continuance of esteem. What mankind have long possessed they have often examined and compared, and if they persist to value the possession, it is because frequent comparisons have confirmed opinion in its favor. As among the works of nature no man can properly call a river deep or a mountain high, without the knowledge of many mountains and many rivers; so in the productions of genius, nothing can be styled excellent till it has been compared with other works of the same kind. Demonstration immediately displays its power, and has nothing to hope or fear from the flux of years, but works tentative and experimental must be estimated by their proportion to the general and collective ability of man, as it is discovered in a long succession of endeavors. Of the first building that was raised, it might be with certainty determined that it was round or square, but whether it was spacious or lofty must have been referred to time. The Pythagorean scale of numbers was at once discovered to be perfect,[1] but the poems of Homer we yet know not to transcend the common limits of human intelligence, but by remarking, that nation after nation, and century after century, has

PREFACE TO SHAKESPEARE.   1. **The . . . perfect:** See Aristotle, *Metaphysics,* I.v. What Johnson means by the "scale" is not exactly clear. The multiplication table may be meant. Pythagoras attached mystical significance to odd and even numbers, and deduced all the principles of the cosmos from this balance or opposition.

been able to do little more than transpose his incidents, new-name his characters, and paraphrase his sentiments.

The reverence due to writings that have long subsisted arises therefore not from any credulous confidence in the superior wisdom of past ages, or gloomy persuasion of the degeneracy of mankind, but is the consequence of acknowledged and indubitable positions, that what has been longest known has been most considered, and what is most considered is best understood.

The poet of whose works I have undertaken the revision may now begin to assume the dignity of an ancient, and claim the privilege of established fame and prescriptive veneration. He has long outlived his century, the term commonly fixed as the test of literary merit. Whatever advantages he might once derive from personal allusions, local customs, or temporary opinions have for many years been lost; and every topic of merriment or motive of sorrow, which the modes of artificial life afforded him, now only obscure the scenes which they once illuminated. The effects of favor and competition are at an end; the tradition of his friendships and his enmities has perished; his works support no opinion with arguments, nor supply any faction with invectives; they can neither indulge vanity nor gratify malignity, but are read without any other reason than the desire of pleasure, and are therefore praised only as pleasure is obtained; yet, thus unassisted by interest or passion, they have passed through variations of taste and changes of manners and, as they devolved from one generation to another, have received new honors at every transmission.

But because human judgment, though it be gradually gaining upon certainty, never becomes infallible, and approbation, though long continued, may yet be only the approbation of prejudice or fashion, it is proper to inquire by what peculiarities of excellence Shakespeare has gained and kept the favor of his countrymen.

Nothing can please many, and please long, but just representations of general nature. Particular manners can be known to few, and therefore few only can judge how nearly they are copied. The irregular combinations of fanciful invention may delight awhile, by that novelty of which the common satiety of life sends us all in quest; but the pleasures of sudden wonder are soon exhausted, and the mind can only repose on the stability of truth.

Shakespeare is, above all writers, at least above all modern writers, the poet of nature; the poet that holds up to his readers a faithful mirror of manners and of life. His characters are not modified by the customs of particular places, unpracticed by the rest of the world; by the peculiarities of studies or professions, which can operate but upon small numbers; or by the accidents of transient fashions or temporary opinions; they are the genuine progeny of common humanity, such as the world will always supply, and observation will always find. His persons act and speak by the influence of those general passions and principles by which all minds are agitated and the whole system of life is continued in motion. In the writings of other poets a character is too often an individual; in those of Shakespeare it is commonly a species.

It is from this wide extension of design that so much instruction is derived. It is this which fills the plays of Shakespeare with practical axioms and domestic wisdom. It was said of Euripides, that every verse was a precept; [2] and it may be said of Shakespeare, that from his works may be collected a system of civil and economical prudence. Yet his real power is not shown in the splendor of particular passages, but by the progress of his fable and the tenor of his dialogue; and he that tries to recommend him by select quotations will succeed like the pedant in Hierocles, [3] who, when he offered his house to sale, carried a brick in his pocket as a specimen.

It will not easily be imagined how much Shakespeare excels in accommodating his sentiments to real life, but by comparing him with other authors. It was observed of the ancient schools of declamation, that the more diligently they were frequented, the more was the student disqualified for the world, because he found nothing there which he should ever meet in any other place. The same remark may be applied to every stage but that of Shakespeare. The theater, when it is under any other direction, is peopled by such characters as were never seen, conversing in a language which was never heard, upon topics which will never arise in the commerce of mankind. But the dialogue of this author is often so evidently determined by the incident which produces it, and is pursued with so much ease and simplicity, that it seems scarcely to claim the merit of fiction, but to have been gleaned by diligent selection out of common conversation, and common occurrences.

2. It . . . precept: by Cicero, *Familiar Epistles*, XVI.8
3. Hierocles: *Commentary on the Golden Verses.*

Upon every other stage the universal agent is love, by whose power all good and evil is distributed, and every action quickened or retarded. To bring a lover, a lady, and a rival into the fable; to entangle them in contradictory obligations, perplex them with oppositions of interest, and harass them with violence of desires inconsistent with each other; to make them meet in rapture and part in agony; to fill their mouths with hyperbolical joy and outrageous sorrow; to distress them as nothing human ever was distressed; to deliver them as nothing human ever was delivered: is the business of a modern dramatist. For this probability is violated, life is misrepresented, and language is depraved. But love is only one of many passions, and, as it has no great influence upon the sum of life, it has little operation in the dramas of a poet, who caught his ideas from the living world, and exhibited only what he saw before him. He knew that any other passion, as it was regular or exorbitant, was a cause of happiness or calamity.

Characters thus ample and general were not easily discriminated and preserved, yet perhaps no poet ever kept his personages more distinct from each other. I will not say with Pope, that every speech may be assigned to the proper speaker,[4] because many speeches there are which have nothing characteristical; but, perhaps, though some may be equally adapted to every person, it will be difficult to find any that can be properly transferred from the present possessor to another claimant. The choice is right, when there is reason for choice.

Other dramatists can only gain attention by hyperbolical or aggravated characters, by fabulous and unexampled excellence or depravity, as the writers of barbarous romances invigorated the reader by a giant and a dwarf; and he that should form his expectations of human affairs from the play, or from the tale, would be equally deceived. Shakespeare has no heroes; his scenes are occupied only by men who act and speak as the reader thinks that he should himself have spoken or acted on the same occasion. Even where the agency is supernatural the dialogue is level with life. Other writers disguise the most natural passions and most frequent incidents, so that he who contemplates them in the book will not know them in the world. Shakespeare approximates the remote, and familiarizes the wonderful; the event which he represents will not happen, but if it were possible, its effects would be probably such as he has assigned; and it may be said that he has not only shown human nature as it acts in real exigences, but as it would be found in trials to which it cannot be exposed.

This therefore is the praise of Shakespeare, that his drama is the mirror of life; that he who has mazed his imagination in following the phantoms which other writers raise up before him may here be cured of his delirious ecstasies, by reading human sentiments in human language, by scenes from which a hermit may estimate the transactions of the world, and a confessor predict the progress of the passions.

His adherence to general nature has exposed him to the censure of critics who form their judgments upon narrower principles. Dennis and Rymer think his Romans not sufficiently Roman; and Voltaire censures his kings as not completely royal. Dennis is offended, that Menenius, a senator of Rome, should play the buffoon;[5] and Voltaire perhaps thinks decency violated when the Danish usurper is represented as a drunkard.[6] But Shakespeare always makes nature predominate over accident, and, if he preserves the essential character, is not very careful of distinctions superinduced and adventitious. His story requires Romans or kings, but he thinks only on men. He knew that Rome, like every other city, had men of all dispositions, and, wanting a buffoon, he went into the senate house for that which the senate house would certainly have afforded him. He was inclined to show an usurper and a murderer not only odious but despicable; he therefore added drunkenness to his other qualities, knowing that kings love wine like other men, and that wine exerts its natural power upon kings. These are the petty cavils of petty minds; a poet overlooks the casual distinction of country and condition, as a painter, satisfied with the figure, neglects the drapery.

The censure which he has incurred by mixing comic and tragic scenes, as it extends to all his works, deserves more consideration. Let the fact be the first stated, and then examined.

Shakespeare's plays are not in the rigorous and critical sense either tragedies or comedies, but compositions of a distinct kind, exhibiting the real state of sublunary nature, which partakes of

---

4. Pope . . . speaker: Pope's Preface to Shakespeare, para. 4.

5. buffoon: John Dennis, *Essay on the Genius and Writings of Shakespeare* (1712), in Dennis's *Critical Works* (ed. Hooker, 1943), II.v. See Shakespeare's *Coriolanus*.   6. drunkard: Voltaire, *Du Théâtre Anglais, par Jerome Carré* (1761).

good and evil, joy and sorrow, mingled with endless variety of proportion and innumerable modes of combination; and expressing the course of the world, in which the loss of one is the gain of another, in which, at the same time, the reveler is hasting to his wine, and the mourner burying his friend; in which the malignity of one is sometimes defeated by the frolic of another; and many mischiefs and many benefits are done and hindered without design.

Out of this chaos of mingled purposes and casualties, the ancient poets, according to the laws which custom had prescribed, selected some the crimes of men, and some their absurdities; some the momentous vicissitudes of life, and some the lighter occurrences; some the terrors of distress, and some the gaieties of prosperity. Thus rose the two modes of imitation, known by the names of *tragedy* and *comedy,* compositions intended to promote different ends by contrary means, and considered as so little allied, that I do not recollect among the Greeks or Romans a single writer who attempted both.

Shakespeare has united the powers of exciting laughter and sorrow not only in one mind, but in one composition. Almost all his plays are divided between serious and ludicrous characters, and, in the successive evolutions of the design, sometimes produce seriousness and sorrow, and sometimes levity and laughter.

That this is a practice contrary to the rules of criticism will be readily allowed, but there is always an appeal open from criticism to nature. The end of writing is to instruct; the end of poetry is to instruct by pleasing. That the mingled drama may convey all the instruction of tragedy or comedy cannot be denied, because it includes both in its alternations of exhibition, and approaches nearer than either to the appearance of life, by showing how great machinations and slender designs may promote or obviate one another, and the high and the low cooperate in the general system by unavoidable concatenation.

It is objected that by this change of scenes the passions are interrupted in their progression, and that the principal event, being not advanced by a due gradation of preparatory incidents, wants at last the power to move, which constitutes the perfection of dramatic poetry. This reasoning is so specious that it is received as true even by those who in daily experience feel it to be false. The interchanges of mingled scenes seldom fail to pro-

duce the intended vicissitudes of passion. Fiction cannot move so much, but that the attention may be easily transferred; and though it must be allowed that pleasing melancholy be sometimes interrupted by unwelcome levity, yet let it be considered likewise, that melancholy is often not pleasing, and that the disturbance of one man may be the relief of another; that different auditors have different habitudes; and that, upon the whole, all pleasure consists in variety.

The players, who in their edition [7] divided our author's works into comedies, histories, and tragedies, seem not to have distinguished the three kinds by any very exact or definite ideas.

An action which ended happily to the principal persons, however serious or distressful through its intermediate incidents, in their opinion constituted a comedy. This idea of a comedy continued long amongst us, and plays were written which, by changing the catastrophe, were tragedies today and comedies tomorrow.

Tragedy was not in those times a poem of more general dignity or elevation than comedy; it required only a calamitous conclusion, with which the common criticism of that age was satisfied, whatever lighter pleasure it afforded in its progress.

History was a series of actions, with no other than chronological succession, independent of each other, and without any tendency to introduce or regulate the conclusion. It is not always very nicely distinguished from tragedy. There is not much nearer approach to unity of action in the tragedy of *Antony and Cleopatra* than in the history of *Richard the Second*. But a history might be continued through many plays; as it had no plan, it had no limits.

Through all these denominations of the drama, Shakespeare's mode of composition is the same; an interchange of seriousness and merriment, by which the mind is softened at one time, and exhilarated at another. But whatever be his purpose, whether to gladden or depress, or to conduct the story, without vehemence or emotion, through tracts of easy and familiar dialogue, he never fails to attain his purpose; as he commands us, we laugh or mourn, or sit silent with quiet expectation, in tranquillity without indifference.

When Shakespeare's plan is understood, most of

---

7. **players . . . edition:** that is, John Heming and Henry Condell, members of Shakespeare's company and his first editors (1623).

the criticisms of Rymer [8] and Voltaire vanish away. The play of *Hamlet* is opened, without impropriety, by two sentinels; Iago bellows at Brabantio's window, without injury to the scheme of the play, though in terms which a modern audience would not easily endure; the character of Polonius is seasonable and useful; and the Gravediggers themselves may be heard with applause.

Shakespeare engaged in dramatic poetry with the world open before him; the rules of the ancients were yet known to few; the public judgment was unformed; he had no example of such fame as might force him upon imitation, nor critics of such authority as might restrain his extravagance. He therefore indulged his natural disposition, and his disposition, as Rymer has remarked, led him to comedy. In tragedy he often writes with great appearance of toil and study what is written at last with little felicity; but in his comic scenes he seems to produce without labor what no labor can improve. In tragedy he is always struggling after some occasion to be comic, but in comedy he seems to repose, or to luxuriate, as in a mode of thinking congenial to his nature. In his tragic scenes there is always something wanting, but his comedy often surpasses expectation or desire. His comedy pleases by the thoughts and the language, and his tragedy for the greater part by incident and action. His tragedy seems to be skill, his comedy to be instinct.

The force of his comic scenes has suffered little diminution from the changes made by a century and a half, in manners or in words. As his personages act upon principles arising from genuine passion, very little modified by particular forms, their pleasures and vexations are communicable to all times and to all places; they are natural, and therefore durable; the adventitious peculiarities of personal habits are only superficial dyes, bright and pleasing for a little while, yet soon fading to a dim tinct, without any remains of former luster; but the discriminations of true passion are the colors of nature; they pervade the whole mass, and can only perish with the body that exhibits them. The accidental compositions of heterogeneous modes are dissolved by the chance which combined them, but the uniform simplicity of primitive qualities neither admits increase, nor suffers decay. The sand heaped by one flood is scattered by another, but the rock always contin-

8. See Thomas Rymer, *A Short View of Tragedy* (1693), Chapters 7 and 5.

ues in its place. The stream of time, which is continually washing the dissoluble fabrics of other poets, passes without injury by the adamant of Shakespeare.

If there be, what I believe there is, in every nation, a style which never becomes obsolete, a certain mode of phraseology so consonant and congenial to the analogy and principles of its respective language as to remain settled and unaltered, this style is probably to be sought in the common intercourse of life, among those who speak only to be understood, without ambition of elegance. The polite are always catching modish innovations, and the learned depart from established forms of speech, in hope of finding or making better; those who wish for distinction forsake the vulgar, when the vulgar is right; but there is a conversation above grossness and below refinement, where propriety resides, and where this poet seems to have gathered his comic dialogue. He is therefore more agreeable to the ears of the present age than any other author equally remote, and among his other excellences deserves to be studied as one of the original masters of our language.

These observations are to be considered not as unexceptionably constant, but as containing general and predominant truth. Shakespeare's familiar dialogue is affirmed to be smooth and clear, yet not wholly without ruggedness or difficulty, as a country may be eminently fruitful, though it has spots unfit for cultivation. His characters are praised as natural, though their sentiments are sometimes forced and their actions improbable; as the earth upon the whole is spherical, though its surface is varied with protuberances and cavities.

Shakespeare with his excellences has likewise faults, and faults sufficient to obscure and overwhelm any other merit. I shall show them in the proportion in which they appear to me, without envious malignity or superstitious veneration. No question can be more innocently discussed than a dead poet's pretensions to renown; and little regard is due to that bigotry which sets candor higher than truth.

His first defect is that to which may be imputed most of the evil in books or in men. He sacrifices virtue to convenience, and is so much more careful to please than to instruct, that he seems to write without any moral purpose. From his writings indeed a system of social duty may be selected, for he that thinks reasonably must think morally; but his precepts and axioms drop casually from him; he makes no just distribution of good or evil, nor is always careful to show in the virtuous a disapprobation of the wicked; he carries his persons indifferently through right and wrong, and at the close dismisses them without further care, and leaves their examples to operate by chance. This fault the barbarity of his age cannot extenuate, for it is always a writer's duty to make the world better, and justice is a virtue independent on time or place.

The plots are often so loosely formed, that a very slight consideration may improve them, and so carelessly pursued, that he seems not always fully to comprehend his own design. He omits opportunities of instructing or delighting which the train of his story seems to force upon him, and apparently rejects those exhibitions which would be more affecting, for the sake of those which are more easy.

It may be observed that in many of his plays the latter part is evidently neglected. When he found himself near the end of his work and in view of his reward, he shortened the labor, to snatch the profit. He therefore remits his efforts where he should most vigorously exert them, and his catastrophe is improbably produced or imperfectly represented.

He had no regard to distinction of time or place, but gives to one age or nation, without scruple, the customs, institutions, and opinions of another, at the expense not only of likelihood but of possibility. These faults Pope has endeavored, with more zeal than judgment, to transfer to his imagined interpolators. We need not wonder to find Hector quoting Aristotle, when we see the loves of Theseus and Hippolyta combined with the Gothic mythology of fairies. Shakespeare, indeed, was not the only violator of chronology, for in the same age Sidney, who wanted not the advantages of learning, has, in his *Arcadia,* confounded the pastoral with the feudal times, the days of innocence, quiet, and security with those of turbulence, violence, and adventure.

In his comic scenes he is seldom very successful, when he engages his characters in reciprocations of smartness and contest of sarcasm; their jests are commonly gross, and their pleasantry licentious; neither his gentlemen nor his ladies have much delicacy, nor are sufficiently distinguished from his clowns by any appearance of refined manners. Whether he represented the real conversation of his time is not easy to determine; the reign of

Elizabeth is commonly supposed to have been a time of stateliness, formality, and reserve; yet perhaps the relaxations of that severity were not very elegant. There must, however, have been always some modes of gaiety preferable to others, and a writer ought to choose the best.

In tragedy his performance seems constantly to be worse, as his labor is more. The effusions of passion which exigence forces out are for the most part striking and energetic; but whenever he solicits his invention, or strains his faculties, the offspring of his throes is tumor, meanness, tediousness, and obscurity.

In narration he affects a disproportionate pomp of diction and a wearisome train of circumlocution, and tells the incident imperfectly in many words, which might have been more plainly delivered in few. Narration in dramatic poetry is naturally tedious, as it is unanimated and inactive and obstructs the progress of the action; it should therefore always be rapid, and enlivened by frequent interruption. Shakespeare found it an encumbrance, and instead of lightening it by brevity, endeavored to recommend it by dignity and splendor.

His declamations or set speeches are commonly cold and weak, for his power was the power of nature; when he endeavored, like other tragic writers, to catch opportunities of amplification, and instead of inquiring what the occasion demanded, to show how much his stores of knowledge could supply, he seldom escapes without the pity or resentment of his reader.

It is incident to him to be now and then entangled with an unwieldy sentiment which he cannot well express, and will not reject; he struggles with it awhile and, if it continues stubborn, comprises it in words such as occur, and leaves it to be disentangled and evolved by those who have more leisure to bestow upon it.

Not that always where the language is intricate the thought is subtle, or the image always great where the line is bulky; the equality of words to things is very often neglected, and trivial sentiments and vulgar ideas disappoint the attention to which they are recommended by sonorous epithets and swelling figures.

But the admirers of this great poet have most reason to complain when he approaches nearest to his highest excellence, and seems fully resolved to sink them in dejection, and mollify them with tender emotions by the fall of greatness, the danger of innocence, or the crosses of love. What he does best, he soon ceases to do. He is not long soft and pathetic without some idle conceit, or contemptible equivocation. He no sooner begins to move than he counteracts himself; and terror and pity, as they are rising in the mind, are checked and blasted by sudden frigidity.

A quibble is to Shakespeare what luminous vapors are to the traveler; he follows it at all adventures; it is sure to lead him out of his way, and sure to engulf him in the mire. It has some malignant power over his mind, and its fascinations are irresistible. Whatever be the dignity or profundity of his disquisition, whether he be enlarging knowledge or exalting affection, whether he be amusing attention with incidents, or enchaining it in suspense, let but a quibble spring up before him, and he leaves his work unfinished. A quibble is the golden apple for which he will always turn aside from his career, or stoop from his elevation. A quibble, poor and barren as it is, gave him such delight that he was content to purchase it by the sacrifice of reason, propriety, and truth. A quibble was to him the fatal Cleopatra for which he lost the world, and was content to lose it.

It will be thought strange that, in enumerating the defects of this writer, I have not yet mentioned his neglect of the unities, his violation of those laws which have been instituted and established by the joint authority of poets and of critics.

For his other deviations from the art of writing, I resign him to critical justice, without making any other demand in his favor, than that which must be indulged to all human excellence; that his virtues be rated with his failings. But, from the censure which this irregularity may bring upon him, I shall, with due reverence to that learning which I must oppose, adventure to try how I can defend him.

His histories, being neither tragedies nor comedies, are not subject to any of their laws; nothing more is necessary to all the praise which they expect than that the changes of action be so prepared as to be understood, that the incidents be various and affecting, and the characters consistent, natural, and distinct. No other unity is intended, and therefore none is to be sought.

In his other works he has well enough preserved the unity of action. He has not, indeed, an intrigue regularly perplexed and regularly unraveled; he does not endeavor to hide his design only to discover it, for this is seldom the order of real events, and Shakespeare is the poet of nature. But his plan has commonly what Aristotle requires, a beginning, a middle, and an end; one event is concatenated with another, and the conclusion follows by easy consequence. There are perhaps some incidents that might be spared, as in other poets there is much talk that only fills up time upon the stage; but the general system makes gradual advances, and the end of the play is the end of expectation.

To the unities of time and place he has shown no regard; and perhaps a nearer view of the principles on which they stand will diminish their value, and withdraw from them the veneration which, from the time of Corneille, they have very generally received, by discovering that they have given more trouble to the poet than pleasure to the auditor.

The necessity of observing the unities of time and place arises from the supposed necessity of making the drama credible. The critics hold it impossible that an action of months or years can be possibly believed to pass in three hours; or that the spectator can suppose himself to sit in the theater while ambassadors go and return between distant kings, while armies are levied and towns besieged, while an exile wanders and returns, or till he whom they saw courting his mistress, shall lament the untimely fall of his son. The mind revolts from evident falsehood, and fiction loses its force when it departs from the resemblance of reality.

From the narrow limitation of time necessarily arises the contraction of place. The spectator, who knows that he saw the first act at Alexandria, cannot suppose that he sees the next at Rome, at a distance to which not the dragons of Medea could, in so short a time, have transported him; he knows with certainty that he has not changed his place; and he knows that place cannot change itself; that what was a house cannot become a plain; that what was Thebes can never be Persepolis.

Such is the triumphant language with which a critic exults over the misery of an irregular poet, and exults commonly without resistance or reply. It is time therefore to tell him, by the authority of Shakespeare, that he assumes, as an unquestionable principle, a position which, while his breath is forming it into words, his understanding pronounces to be false. It is false, that any representation is mistaken for reality; that any dramatic fable in its materiality was ever credible or, for a single moment, was ever credited.

The objection arising from the impossibility of

passing the first hour at Alexandria and the next at Rome supposes that, when the play opens the spectator really imagines himself at Alexandria, and believes that his walk to the theater has been a voyage to Egypt, and that he lives in the days of Antony and Cleopatra. Surely he that imagines this may imagine more. He that can take the stage at one time for the palace of the Ptolemies may take it in half an hour for the promontory of Actium. Delusion, if delusion be admitted, has no certain limitation; if the spectator can be once persuaded that his old acquaintance are Alexander and Caesar, that a room illuminated with candles is the plain of Pharsalia, or the bank of Granicus, he is in a state of elevation above the reach of reason or of truth, and from the heights of empyrean poetry may despise the circumscriptions of terrestrial nature. There is no reason why a mind thus wandering in ecstasy should count the clock, or why an hour should not be a century in that calenture of the brains that can make the stage a field.

The truth is that the spectators are always in their senses and know, from the first act to the last, that the stage is only a stage, and that the players are only players. They come to hear a certain number of lines recited with just gesture and elegant modulation. The lines relate to some action, and an action must be in some place; but the different actions that complete a story may be in places very remote from each other; and where is the absurdity of allowing that space to represent first Athens, and then Sicily, which was always known to be neither Sicily nor Athens but a modern theater?

By supposition, as place is introduced, time may be extended. The time required by the fable elapses for the most part between the acts; for, of so much of the action as is represented, the real and poetical duration is the same. If, in the first act, preparations for war against Mithridates are represented to be made in Rome, the event of the war may without absurdity be represented, in the catastrophe, as happening in Pontus; we know that there is neither war, nor preparation for war; we know that we are neither in Rome nor Pontus; that neither Mithridates nor Lucullus are before us. The drama exhibits successive imitations of successive actions; and why may not the second imitation represent an action that happened years after the first, if it be so connected with it that nothing but time can be supposed to intervene? Time is, of all modes of existence, most obsequious to the imagination; a lapse of years is as easily conceived as a passage of hours. In contemplation we easily contract the time of real actions, and therefore willingly permit it to be contracted when we only see their imitation.

It will be asked how the drama moves, if it is not credited. It is credited with all the credit due to a drama. It is credited, whenever it moves, as a just picture of a real original; as representing to the auditor what he would himself feel, if he were to do or suffer what is there feigned to be suffered or to be done. The reflection that strikes the heart is not that the evils before us are real evils, but that they are evils to which we ourselves may be exposed. If there be any fallacy, it is not that we fancy the players, but that we fancy ourselves, unhappy for a moment; but we rather lament the possibility than suppose the presence of misery, as a mother weeps over her babe when she remembers that death may take it from her. The delight of tragedy proceeds from our consciousness of fiction; if we thought murders and treasons real, they would please no more.

Imitations produce pain or pleasure not because they are mistaken for realities, but because they bring realities to mind. When the imagination is recreated by a painted landscape, the trees are not supposed capable to give us shade, or the fountains coolness; but we consider how we should be pleased with such fountains playing beside us, and such woods waving over us. We are agitated in reading the history of *Henry the Fifth,* yet no man takes his book for the field of Agincourt. A dramatic exhibition is a book recited with concomitants that increase or diminish its effect. Familiar comedy is often more powerful on the theater than in the page; imperial tragedy is always less. The humor of Petruchio may be heightened by grimace, but what voice or what gesture can hope to add dignity or force to the soliloquy of Cato? [9]

A play read affects the mind like a play acted. It is therefore evident that the action is not supposed to be real, and it follows that between the acts a longer or shorter time may be allowed to pass, and that no more account of space or duration is to be taken by the auditor of a drama than by the reader of a narrative, before whom may pass in an hour the life of a hero, or the revolutions of an empire.

9. soliloquy of Cato: Cato's soliloquy is the most famous passage in Addison's tragedy of *Cato,* V.i; in it Cato reasons on death, suicide, and immortality.

Whether Shakespeare knew the unities and rejected them by design, or deviated from them by happy ignorance, it is, I think, impossible to decide and useless to inquire. We may reasonably suppose that, when he rose to notice, he did not want [10] the counsels and admonitions of scholars and critics, and that he at last deliberately persisted in a practice which he might have begun by chance. As nothing is essential to the fable but unity of action, and as the unities of time and place arise evidently from false assumptions and, by circumscribing the extent of the drama, lessen its variety, I cannot think it much to be lamented that they were not known by him, or not observed. Nor, if such another poet could arise, should I very vehemently reproach him, that his first act passed at Venice, and his next in Cyprus. Such violations of rules merely positive become the comprehensive genius of Shakespeare, and such censures are suitable to the minute and slender criticism of Voltaire:

> Non usque adeo permiscuit imis
> Longus summa dies, ut non, si voce Metelli
> Serventur leges, malint a Caesare tolli. [11]

Yet when I speak thus slightly of dramatic rules, I cannot but recollect how much wit and learning may be produced against me. Before such authorities I am afraid to stand, not that I think the present question one of those that are to be decided by mere authority, but because it is to be suspected that these precepts have not been so easily received but for better reasons than I have yet been able to find. The result of my inquiries, in which it would be ludicrous to boast of impartiality, is that the unities of time and place are not essential to a just drama, that though they may sometimes conduce to pleasure, they are always to be sacrificed to the nobler beauties of variety and instruction; and that a play, written with nice observation of critical rules, is to be contemplated as an elaborate curiosity, as the product of superfluous and ostentatious art, by which is shown rather what is possible, than what is necessary.

He that without diminution of any other excellence shall preserve all the unities unbroken deserves the like applause with the architect, who shall display all the orders of architecture in a cita-del, without any deduction from its strength; but the principal beauty of a citadel is to exclude the enemy, and the greatest graces of a play are to copy nature and instruct life.

Perhaps what I have here not dogmatically but deliberatively written, may recall the principles of the drama to a new examination. I am almost frighted at my own temerity and, when I estimate the fame and the strength of those that maintain the contrary opinion, am ready to sink down in reverential silence, as Aeneas withdrew from the defense of Troy when he saw Neptune shaking the wall and Juno heading the besiegers. [12]

Those whom my arguments cannot persuade to give their approbation to the judgment of Shakespeare will easily, if they consider the condition of his life, make some allowance for his ignorance.

Every man's performances, to be rightly estimated, must be compared with the state of the age in which he lived, and with his own particular opportunities; and though to the reader a book be not worse or better for the circumstances of the author, yet as there is always a silent reference of human works to human abilities, and as the inquiry, how far man may extend his designs, or how high he may rate his native force, is of far greater dignity than in what rank we shall place any particular performance, curiosity is always busy to discover the instruments, as well as to survey the workmanship, to know how much is to be ascribed to original powers, and how much to casual and adventitious help. The palaces of Peru or Mexico were certainly mean and incommodious habitations, if compared to the houses of European monarchs; yet who could forbear to view them with astonishment, who remembered that they were built without the use of iron? . . . [13]

The part of criticism in which the whole succession of editors has labored with the greatest diligence, which has occasioned the most arrogant ostentation and excited the keenest acrimony, is the emendation of corrupted passages, to which the public attention, having been first drawn by the violence of contention between Pope and Theobald, [14] has been continued by the persecution which,

---

10. **want:** lack.   11. Lucan, *Pharsalia*, III.138–40, translated as follows by J. D. Duff: "The course of time has not wrought such confusion that the laws would not rather be trampled on by Caesar than saved by Metellus."   12. **as . . . besiegers:** *Aeneid*, II.610.   13. A discussion of Shakespeare's sources, learning, and editors is here omitted, together with some remarks on textual annotation.   14. **Pope . . . Theobald:** Pope's edition of Shakespeare (1721) was scornfully attacked by Theobald in a pamphlet, *Shakespeare Restored* (1726), in return for which Pope made Theobald the hero of *The Dunciad* (1728). See *Pope*, n. 50, below.

with a kind of conspiracy, has been since raised against all the publishers of Shakespeare. . . .

Conjecture, though it be sometimes unavoidable, I have not wantonly nor licentiously indulged. It has been my settled principle, that the reading of the ancient books is probably true, and therefore is not to be disturbed for the sake of elegance, perspicuity, or mere improvement of the sense. For though much credit is not due to the fidelity, nor any to the judgment of the first publishers, yet they who had the copy before their eyes were more likely to read it right, than we who only read it by imagination. But it is evident that they have often made strange mistakes by ignorance or negligence, and that therefore something may be properly attempted by criticism, keeping the middle way between presumption and timidity.

Such criticism I have attempted to practice, and where any passage appeared inextricably perplexed, have endeavored to discover how it may be recalled to sense, with least violence. But my first labor is always to turn the old text on every side, and try if there be any interstice through which light can find its way; nor would Huetius [15] himself condemn me, as refusing the trouble of research, for the ambition of alteration. In this modest industry I have not been unsuccessful. I have rescued many lines from the violations of temerity, and secured many scenes from the inroads of correction. I have adopted the Roman sentiment that it is more honorable to save a citizen than to kill an enemy, and have been more careful to protect than to attack.

I have preserved the common distribution of the plays into acts, though I believe it to be in almost all the plays void of authority. Some of those which are divided in the later editions have no division in the first folio, and some that are divided in the folio have no division in the preceding copies. The settled mode of the theater requires four intervals in the play, but few, if any, of our author's compositions can be properly distributed in that manner. An act is so much of the drama as passes without intervention of time or change of place. A pause makes a new act. In every real, and therefore in every imitative, action the intervals may be more or fewer, the restriction of five acts being accidental and arbitrary. This Shakespeare knew, and this he practiced; his plays were written, and at first printed, in one unbroken continuity, and ought now to be exhibited with short pauses, interposed as often as the scene is changed, or any considerable time is required to pass. This method would at once quell a thousand absurdities. . . .

As I practiced conjecture more, I learned to trust it less; and after I had printed a few plays, resolved to insert none of my own readings in the text. Upon this caution I now congratulate myself, for every day increases my doubt of my emendations.

Since I have confined my imagination to the margin, it must not be considered as very reprehensible if I have suffered it to play some freaks in its own dominion. There is no danger in conjecture, if it be proposed as conjecture; and while the text remains uninjured, those changes may be safely offered which are not considered even by him that offers them as necessary or safe.

If my readings are of little value, they have not been ostentatiously displayed or importunately obtruded. I could have written longer notes, for the art of writing notes is not of difficult attainment. The work is performed, first by railing at the stupidity, negligence, ignorance, and asinine tastelessness of the former editors, and showing, from all that goes before and all that follows, the inelegance and absurdity of the old reading; then by proposing something which to superficial readers would seem specious, but which the editor rejects with indignation; then by producing the true reading, with a long paraphrase, and concluding with loud acclamations on the discovery, and a sober wish for the advancement and prosperity of genuine criticism.

All this may be done, and perhaps done sometimes without impropriety. But I have always suspected that the reading is right which requires many words to prove it wrong; and the emendation wrong that cannot without so much labor appear to be right. The justness of a happy restoration strikes at once, and the moral precept may be well applied to criticism, *quod dubitas ne feceris*.[16]

To dread the shore which he sees spread with wrecks is natural to the sailor. I had before my eye so many critical adventures ended in miscarriage,

---

15. Huetius: Pierre Huet, *De Interpretatione Libri Duo* ("two books [i.e., Books I and II] on the subject of critical exegesis") (1661). In his comments on the best kind of interpretation, Huet blamed those who preferred the easy path of emendation to the difficult one of explaining the given text.

16. quod . . . feceris: i.e., "if you aren't sure yourself, refrain (from emendation)"; literally, "abstain from an action of which you doubt whether it be good or ill."

that caution was forced upon me. I encountered in every page Wit struggling with its own sophistry, and Learning confused by the multiplicity of its views. I was forced to censure those whom I admired, and could not but reflect, while I was dispossessing their emendations, how soon the same fate might happen to my own, and how many of the readings which I have corrected may be by some other editor defended and established.

Critics I saw that others' names efface,
And fix their own, with labor, in the place;
Their own, like others, soon their place resigned,
Or disappeared, and left the first behind.[17]

(Pope)

That a conjectural critic should often be mistaken cannot be wonderful, either to others or himself, if it be considered that in his art there is no system, no principal and axiomatical truth that regulates subordinate positions. His chance of error is renewed at every attempt; an oblique view of the passage, a slight misapprehension of a phrase, a casual inattention to the parts connected, is sufficient to make him not only fail, but fail ridiculously; and when he succeeds best, he produces perhaps but one reading of many probable, and he that suggests another will always be able to dispute his claims.

It is an unhappy state, in which danger is hid under pleasure. The allurements of emendation are scarcely resistible. Conjecture has all the joy and all the pride of invention, and he that has once started a happy change is too much delighted to consider what objections may rise against it.

Yet conjectural criticism has been of great use in the learned world; nor is it my intention to depreciate a study that has exercised so many mighty minds, from the revival of learning to our own age, from the Bishop of Aleria[18] to English Bentley. The critics on ancient authors have, in the exercise of their sagacity, many assistances which the editor of Shakespeare is condemned to want. They are employed upon grammatical and settled languages, whose construction contributes so much to perspicuity that Homer has fewer passages unintelligible than Chaucer. The words have not only a known regimen, but invariable quantities, which direct and confine the choice. There are commonly

more manuscripts than one; and they do not often conspire in the same mistakes. Yet Scaliger could confess to Salmasius how little satisfaction his emendations gave him: "*Illudunt nobis conjecturae nostrae, quarum nos pudet, posteaquam in meliores codices incidimus.*"[19] And Lipsius could complain that critics were making faults by trying to remove them: "*Ut olim vitiis, ita nunc remediis laboratur.*"[20] And indeed, where mere conjecture is to be used, the emendations of Scaliger and Lipsius, notwithstanding their wonderful sagacity and erudition, are often vague and disputable, like mine or Theobald's.

Perhaps I may not be more censured for doing wrong than for doing little; for raising in the public expectations which at last I have not answered. The expectation of ignorance is indefinite, and that of knowledge is often tyrannical. It is hard to satisfy those who know not what to demand, or those who demand by design what they think impossible to be done. I have indeed disappointed no opinion more than my own; yet I have endeavored to perform my task with no slight solicitude. Not a single passage in the whole work has appeared to me corrupt, which I have not attempted to restore; or obscure, which I have not endeavored to illustrate. In many I have failed like others; and from many, after all my efforts, I have retreated, and confessed the repulse. I have not passed over, with affected superiority, what is equally difficult to the reader and to myself, but where I could not instruct him, have owned my ignorance. I might easily have accumulated a mass of seeming learning upon easy scenes, but it ought not to be imputed to negligence that, where nothing was necessary, nothing has been done, or that, where others have said enough, I have said no more.

Notes are often necessary, but they are necessary evils. Let him that is yet unacquainted with the powers of Shakespeare, and who desires to feel the highest pleasure that the drama can give, read every play from the first scene to the last, with utter negligence of all his commentators. When his fancy is once on the wing, let it not stoop at correction or explanation. When his attention is strongly engaged, let it disdain alike to turn aside to the name of Theobald and of Pope. Let him

---

17. *The Temple of Fame*, ll. 37–40.   18. Bishop of Aleria: the librarian of Pope Sixtus IV: a great classical editor named Joannes Andreas (1417–80). Richard Bentley was one of the greatest of English classical scholars (1662–1742).

19. *Illudunt . . . incidimus:* "Our conjectures make us ridiculous and shame us when later we come across better manuscripts." 20. *Ut . . . laboratur:* "Whereas before we were toiling over corruptions, now it is emendations that give us the trouble."

read on through brightness and obscurity, through integrity and corruption; let him preserve his comprehension of the dialogue and his interest in the fable. And when the pleasures of novelty have ceased, let him attempt exactness, and read the commentators.

Particular passages are cleared by notes, but the general effect of the work is weakened. The mind is refrigerated by interruption; the thoughts are diverted from the principal subject; the reader is weary, he suspects not why; and at last throws away the book, which he has too diligently studied.

Parts are not to be examined till the whole has been surveyed; there is a kind of intellectual remoteness necessary for the comprehension of any great work in its full design and its true proportions; a close approach shows the smaller niceties, but the beauty of the whole is discerned no longer.

It is not very grateful to consider how little the succession of editors has added to this author's power of pleasing. He was read, admired, studied, and imitated, while he was yet deformed with all the improprieties which ignorance and neglect could accumulate upon him; while the reading was yet not rectified, nor his allusions understood; yet then did Dryden pronounce "that Shakespeare was the man who, of all modern and perhaps ancient poets, had the largest and most comprehensive soul. All the images of nature were still present to him, and he drew them not laboriously, but luckily. When he describes anything, you more than see it, you feel it, too. Those who accuse him to have wanted learning, give him the greater commendation: he was naturally learned: he needed not the spectacles of books to read Nature; he looked inwards, and found her there. I cannot say he is everywhere alike; were he so, I should do him injury to compare him with the greatest of mankind. He is many times flat and insipid, his comic wit degenerating into clenches, his serious swelling into bombast. But he is always great, when some great occasion is presented to him: no man can say, he ever had a fit subject for his wit, and did not then raise himself as high above the rest of poets,

Quantum lenta solent inter viburna cupressi." [21]

Justus Lipsius (1547–1606), a Flemish humanist, preceded Scaliger as professor at the University of Leyden. 21. *Quantum . . . cupressi:* Dryden, "An Essay of Dramatic Poesy," p. 555, above. The Latin is from Virgil, *Eclogue,* I.25: "as cypresses tower above the bending osiers."

It is to be lamented that such a writer should want a commentary, that his language should become obsolete or his sentiments obscure. But it is vain to carry wishes beyond the condition of human things; that which must happen to all has happened to Shakespeare, by accident and time; and more than has been suffered by any other writer since the use of types has been suffered by him through his own negligence of fame, or perhaps by that superiority of mind which despised its own performances, when it compared them with its powers, and judged those works unworthy to be preserved which the critics of following ages were to contend for the fame of restoring and explaining.

Among these candidates of inferior fame, I am now to stand the judgment of the public; and wish that I could confidently produce my commentary as equal to the encouragement which I have had the honor of receiving. Every work of this kind is by its nature deficient, and I should feel little solicitude about the sentence were it to be pronounced only by the skillful and the learned.

ON HENRY IV

None of Shakespeare's plays are more read than the first and second parts of *Henry the Fourth.* Perhaps no author has ever in two plays afforded so much delight. The great events are interesting, for the fate of kingdoms depends upon them; the slighter occurrences are diverting and, except one or two, sufficiently probable; the incidents are multiplied with wonderful fertility of invention, and the characters diversified with the utmost nicety of discernment, and the profoundest skill in the nature of man.

The prince, who is the hero both of the comic and tragic part, is a young man of great abilities and violent passions, whose sentiments are right, though his actions are wrong; whose virtues are obscured by negligence, and whose understanding is dissipated by levity. In his idle hours he is rather loose than wicked, and when the occasion forces out his latent qualities, he is great without effort, and brave without tumult. The trifler is roused into a hero, and the hero again reposes in the trifler. This character is great, original, and just.

Percy is a rugged soldier, choleric and quarrelsome, and has only the soldier's virtues, generosity and courage.

But Falstaff unimitated, unimitable Falstaff, how shall I describe thee? Thou compound of sense and vice; of sense which may be admired but not esteemed, of vice which may be despised, but hardly detested. Falstaff is a character loaded with faults, and with those faults which naturally produce contempt. He is a thief and a glutton, a coward and a boaster, always ready to cheat the weak and prey upon the poor; to terrify the timorous and insult the defenseless. At once obsequious and malignant, he satirizes in their absence those whom he lives by flattering. He is familiar with the prince only as an agent of vice, but of this familiarity he is so proud as not only to be supercilious and haughty with common men, but to think his interest of importance to the Duke of Lancaster. Yet the man thus corrupt, thus despicable, makes himself necessary to the prince that despises him, by the most pleasing of all qualities, perpetual gaiety, by an unfailing power of exciting laughter, which is the more freely indulged, as his wit is not of the splendid or ambitious kind, but consists in easy escapes and sallies of levity, which make sport but raise no envy. It must be observed that he is stained with no enormous or sanguinary crimes, so that his licentiousness is not so offensive but that it may be borne for his mirth.

The moral to be drawn from this representation is that no man is more dangerous than he that with a will to corrupt hath the power to please; and that neither wit nor honesty ought to think themselves safe with such a companion when they see Henry seduced by Falstaff.

ON POLONIUS

Polonius is a man bred in courts, exercised in business, stored with observation, confident of his knowledge, proud of his eloquence, and declining into dotage. His mode of oratory is truly represented as designed to ridicule the practice of those times, of prefaces that made no introduction, and of method that embarrassed rather than explained. This part of his character is accidental, the rest is natural. Such a man is positive and confident because he knows that his mind was once strong, and knows not that it is become weak. Such a man excels in general principles, but fails in the particular application. He is knowing in retrospect, and ignorant in foresight. While he depends upon his memory, and can draw from his repositories

of knowledge, he utters weighty sentences and gives useful counsel; but as the mind in its enfeebled state cannot be kept long busy and intent, the old man is subject to sudden dereliction of his faculties; he loses the order of his ideas, and entangles himself in his own thoughts, till he recovers the leading principle, and falls again into his former train. This idea of dotage encroaching upon wisdom, will solve all the phenomena of the character of Polonius.

THE LIVES OF THE POETS

In the spring of 1777, Johnson was asked to supply concise biographical prefaces to a collective edition of the more considerable English poets. The idea was congenial, and he undertook it, apparently, without scrutinizing any list of authors. He neither decided the names to be included nor urged the dropping of any already chosen — except that four or five minor poets seem to have been added at his suggestion. Johnson labored at his task during four years, "dilatorily and hastily," as he described it: "unwilling to work and working with vigor and haste." Not all were published at the same time. The first four volumes, containing twenty-two prefaces (seventeen of them in volume iv), appeared in 1779. Six more volumes, with the remaining thirty prefaces, were published in 1781. In this series Cowley and Waller shared a volume, as did also Milton and Butler, while Dryden and Pope had each a volume to himself. The works of the poets were published separate from the prefaces, in fifty-six following volumes, and concluded with a two-volume index. The earliest poet included was Cowley; Collins and Gray were two of the latest.

The inequality of length among the prefaces had not been anticipated, and was due to the fact that on the most interesting or congenial figures Johnson was moved to write detailed biographies and a serial examination of the works. He kept to the original scale where he was not particularly engaged by his subject. The *Cowley,* the first considerable departure from the norm, is known to have been in the press by July, 1778. It is important today, not so much for its account of Cowley himself, as for the memorable discussion of wit and the Metaphysical school of poets, a name to which Johnson gave general currency, although he was not the first to use it. The essay on Milton is a magnificent tribute but was resented by Milton worshipers on its first appearance. It was written in six weeks, at the beginning of the year 1779. The *Dryden,* which Johnson wrote *con amore* out of a lifelong familiarity with that favorite poet, also belonged to the first series, published in 1779. Few things in evaluative criticism excel the judicial summing up of Dryden's debits and credits, his strengths and weaknesses, and the critic's registering of confident opinion about Dryden's habits of learning and of work. "Of all this, however," writes Johnson, "if the proof be demanded I will not undertake to give it; the atoms of probability, of which my opinion has been formed, lie scattered over all his works." The memorable passage beginning, "Of him that knows much it is natural to suppose that he has read with diligence," deserves to be, and has often been, memorized: no brief characterization of a poet's mind will ever surpass it, nor has anything so good of Dryden since been written.

The *Pope* was written last of all. It is the longest and (with the possible exception of the *Savage*), the finest, most subtly discriminating, of all the *Lives*. It is a tripartite essay, unfortunately too extensive for full inclusion here. The first part is a chronological account of Pope's life; the second, a character analysis rising out of, and transcending, the biographical evidence; and the last, a judicial review of the series of Pope's published writings. It is both a literary history and a psychological study. The complexity of Pope's nature and the greatness of his genius evoke the fullest exercise of Johnson's capacity for blending justice and mercy; for the impartial detection of motive, level judgment of conduct, and compassion for human weakness; and for magnanimous acknowledgment, with no self-protective reservations, of genuinely great achievement.

from MILTON

Milton has the reputation of having been in his youth eminently beautiful, so as to have been called the Lady of his college. His hair, which was of a light brown, parted at the foretop, and hung down upon his shoulders, according to the picture which he has given of Adam. He was, however, not of the heroic stature, but rather below the middle size, according to Mr. Richardson, who mentions him as having narrowly escaped from being "short and thick."[1] He was vigorous and active, and delighted in the exercise of the sword, in which he is related to have been eminently skillful. His weapon was, I believe, not the rapier, but the backsword, of which he recommends the use in his book on education.[2]

His eyes are said never to have been bright; but, if he was a dexterous fencer, they must have been once quick.

His domestic habits, so far as they are known, were those of a severe student. He drank little strong drink of any kind, and fed without excess in quantity, and in his earlier years without delicacy of choice. In his youth he studied late at night; but afterwards changed his hours, and rested in bed from nine to four in the summer, and five in winter. The course of his day was best known after he was blind. When he first rose he heard a chapter in the Hebrew Bible, and then studied till twelve; then took some exercise for an hour; then dined; then played on the organ and sung, or heard another sing; then studied to six; then entertained his visitors till eight; then supped and, after a pipe of tobacco and a glass of water, went to bed.

So is his life described; but this even tenor appears attainable only in colleges. He that lives in the world will sometimes have the succession of his practice broken and confused. Visitors, of whom Milton is represented to have had great numbers, will come and stay unseasonably; business, of which every man has some, must be done when others will do it.

When he did not care to rise early he had something read to him by his bedside; perhaps at this time his daughters were employed. He composed much in the morning and dictated in the day, sitting obliquely in an elbow chair, with his leg thrown over the arm.

Fortune appears not to have had much of his care. In the civil wars he lent his personal estate to the parliament, but when, after the contest was decided, he solicited repayment, he met not only with neglect but "sharp rebuke"; and, having tired both himself and his friends, was given up to poverty and hopeless indignation, till he showed how able he was to do greater service. He was then made Latin secretary, with two hundred pounds a year, and had a thousand pounds for his *Defense of the People*. His widow, who after his death retired to Namptwich in Cheshire, and died about 1729, is said to have reported that he lost two thousand pounds by entrusting it to a scrivener; and that, in the general depredation upon the Church, he had grasped an estate of about sixty pounds a year belonging to Westminster Abbey, which, like other sharers of the plunder of rebellion, he was afterwards obliged to return. Two thousand pounds which he had placed in the Excise Office were also lost. There is yet no reason to believe that he was ever reduced to indigence; his wants being few were competently supplied. He sold his library before his death, and left his family fifteen hundred pounds; on which his widow laid hold, and only gave one hundred to each of his daughters.

His literature was unquestionably great. He read all the languages which are considered either as

LIFE OF MILTON.   1. "short . . . thick": Jonathan Richardson, *Explanatory Notes and Remarks on Paradise Lost* (1734), p. 2.   2. book on education: *Of Education: To Master Samuel Hartlib* (1644), final section.

learned or polite: Hebrew, with its two dialects, Greek, Latin, Italian, French, and Spanish. In Latin his skill was such as places him in the first rank of writers and critics; and he appears to have cultivated Italian with uncommon diligence. The books in which his daughter, who used to read to him, represented him as most delighting, after Homer, which he could almost repeat, were Ovid's *Metamorphoses* and Euripides. His Euripides is, by Mr. Cradock's kindness, now in my hands; the margin is sometimes noted, but I have found nothing remarkable.

Of the English poets he set most value upon Spenser, Shakespeare, and Cowley. Spenser was apparently his favorite; Shakespeare he may easily be supposed to like, with every other skillful reader, but I should not have expected that Cowley, whose ideas of excellence were different from his own, would have had much of his approbation. His character of Dryden, who sometimes visited him, was that he was a good rhymist, but no poet.

His theological opinions are said to have been first Calvinistical and afterwards, perhaps when he began to hate the Presbyterians, to have extended towards Arminianism. In the mixed questions of theology and government he never thinks that he can recede far enough from popery or prelacy, but what Baudius says of Erasmus seems applicable to him: "*magis habuit quod fugeret, quam quod sequeretur.*"[3] He had determined rather what to condemn than what to approve. He has not associated himself with any denomination of Protestants; we know rather what he was not, than what he was. He was not of the Church of Rome; he was not of the Church of England.

To be of no church is dangerous. Religion, of which the rewards are distant and which is animated only by faith and hope, will glide by degrees out of the mind unless it be invigorated and reimpressed by external ordinances, by stated calls to worship, and the salutary influence of example. Milton, who appears to have had full conviction of the truth of Christianity, and to have regarded the Holy Scriptures with the profoundest veneration, to have been untainted by any heretical peculiarity of opinion, and to have lived in a confirmed belief of the immediate and occasional agency of Providence, yet grew old without any visible worship. In the distribution of his hours, there was

no hour of prayer, either solitary or with his household; omitting public prayers, he omitted all.

Of this omission the reason has been sought, upon a supposition which ought never to be made, that men live with their own approbation, and justify their conduct to themselves. Prayer certainly was not thought superfluous by him, who represents our first parents as praying acceptably in the state of innocence, and efficaciously after their fall. That he lived without prayer can hardly be affirmed; his studies and meditations were an habitual prayer. The neglect of it in his family was probably a fault for which he condemned himself, and which he intended to correct, but that death, as too often happens, intercepted his reformation.

His political notions were those of an acrimonious and surly republican, for which it is not known that he gave any better reason than that "a popular government was the most frugal; for the trappings of a monarchy would set up an ordinary commonwealth."[4] It is surely very shallow policy that supposes money to be the chief good; and even this without considering that the support and expense of a court is for the most part only a particular kind of traffic, by which money is circulated without any national impoverishment.

Milton's republicanism was, I am afraid, founded in an envious hatred of greatness, and a sullen desire of independence; in petulance impatient of control, and pride disdainful of superiority. He hated monarchs in the state and prelates in the church; for he hated all whom he was required to obey. It is to be suspected that his predominant desire was to destroy rather than establish, and that he felt not so much the love of liberty as repugnance to authority.

It has been observed that they who most loudly clamor for liberty do not most liberally grant it. What we know of Milton's character in domestic relations is that he was severe and arbitrary. His family consisted of women; and there appears in his books something like a Turkish contempt of females, as subordinate and inferior beings. That his own daughters might not break the ranks, he suffered them to be depressed by a mean and penurious education. He thought woman made only for obedience, and man only for rebellion. . . .

One of the poems on which much praise has been bestowed is "Lycidas"; of which the diction

3. "*magis . . . sequeretur*": Dominic Baudius, *Epistolae*, II, letter 27. Johnson gives the sense of the Latin.

4. "a . . . commonwealth": quoted from John Toland's *Life of Milton* (1698), p. 139.

is harsh, the rhymes uncertain, and the numbers unpleasing. What beauty there is, we must therefore seek in the sentiments and images. It is not to be considered as the effusion of real passion, for passion runs not after remote allusions and obscure opinions. Passion plucks no berries from the myrtle and ivy, nor calls upon Arethuse and Mincius, nor tells of " rough satyrs and fauns with cloven heel." Where there is leisure for fiction there is little grief.

In this poem there is no nature, for there is no truth; there is no art, for there is nothing new. Its form is that of a pastoral, easy, vulgar, and therefore disgusting; whatever images it can supply are long ago exhausted, and its inherent improbability always forces dissatisfaction on the mind. When Cowley tells of Hervey [5] that they studied together, it is easy to suppose how much he must miss the companion of his labors and the partner of his discoveries; but what image of tenderness can be excited by these lines!

We drove afield, and both together heard
What time the grey-fly winds her sultry horn,
Battening our flocks with the fresh dews of
    night.

We know that they never drove afield, and that they had no flocks to batten; and though it be allowed that the representation may be allegorical, the true meaning is so uncertain and remote that it is never sought because it cannot be known when it is found.

Among the flocks and copses and flowers appear the heathen deities, Jove and Phoebus, Neptune and Aeolus, with a long train of mythological imagery, such as a college easily supplies. Nothing can less display knowledge or less exercise invention than to tell how a shepherd has lost his companion and must now feed his flocks alone, without any judge of his skill in piping; and how one god asks another god what is become of Lycidas, and how neither god can tell. He who thus grieves will excite no sympathy; he who thus praises will confer no honor.

This poem has yet a grosser fault. With these trifling fictions are mingled the most awful and sacred truths, such as ought never to be polluted with such irreverent combinations. The shepherd likewise is now a feeder of sheep, and afterwards an ecclesiastical pastor, a superintendent of a Christian flock. Such equivocations are always unskillful,

5. Cowley . . . Hervey: Abraham Cowley, "On the Death of Mr. William Hervey," in *Miscellanies* (1656).

but here they are indecent, and at least approach to impiety, of which, however, I believe the writer not to have been conscious.

Such is the power of reputation justly acquired that its blaze drives away the eye from nice examination. Surely no man could have fancied that he read " Lycidas " with pleasure had he not known its author.

Of the two pieces, " L'Allegro " and " Il Penseroso," I believe opinion is uniform; every man tha reads them, reads them with pleasure. The author's design is not, what Theobald has remarked, merely to show how objects derived their colors from the mind, by representing the operation of the same things upon the gay and the melancholy temper, or upon the same man as he is differently disposed; but rather how, among the successive variety of appearances, every disposition of mind takes hold on those by which it may be gratified.

The *cheerful* man hears the lark in the morning; the *pensive* man hears the nightingale in the evening. The *cheerful* man sees the cock strut, and hears the horn and hounds echo in the wood; then walks " not unseen " to observe the glory of the rising sun or listen to the singing milkmaid, and view the labors of the plowman and the mower; then casts his eyes about him over scenes of smiling plenty, and looks up to the distant tower, the residence of some fair inhabitant; thus he pursues rural gaiety through a day of labor or of play, and delights himself at night with the fanciful narratives of superstitious ignorance.

The *pensive* man at one time walks " unseen " to muse at midnight, and at another hears the sullen curfew. If the weather drives him home he sits in a room lighted only by " glowing embers "; or by a lonely lamp outwatches the North Star to discover the habitation of separate souls, and varies the shades of meditation by contemplating the magnificent or pathetic scenes of tragic and epic poetry. When the morning comes, a morning gloomy with rain and wind, he walks into the dark trackless woods, falls asleep by some murmuring water, and with melancholy enthusiasm expects some dream of prognostication or some music played by aerial performers.

Both Mirth and Melancholy are solitary, silent inhabitants of the breast that neither receive nor transmit communication; no mention is therefore made of a philosophical friend or a pleasant companion. The seriousness does not arise from any participation of calamity, nor the gaiety from the pleasures of the bottle.

The man of *cheerfulness* having exhausted the country tries what "towered cities" will afford, and mingles with scenes of splendor, gay assemblies, and nuptial festivities; but he mingles a mere spectator as, when the learned comedies of Jonson or the wild dramas of Shakespeare are exhibited, he attends the theater.

The *pensive* man never loses himself in crowds, but walks the cloister or frequents the cathedral. Milton probably had not yet forsaken the Church.

Both his characters delight in music; but he seems to think that cheerful notes would have obtained from Pluto a complete dismission of Eurydice, of whom solemn sounds only procured a conditional release.

For the old age of Cheerfulness he makes no provision, but Melancholy he conducts with great dignity to the close of life. His Cheerfulness is without levity, and his Pensiveness without asperity.

Through these two poems the images are properly selected and nicely distinguished, but the colors of the diction seem not sufficiently discriminated. I know not whether the characters are kept sufficiently apart. No mirth can, indeed, be found in his melancholy; but I am afraid that I always meet some melancholy in his mirth. They are two noble efforts of imagination. . . .

Those little pieces may be dispatched without much anxiety; a greater work calls for greater care. I am now to examine *Paradise Lost,* a poem which, considered with respect to design, may claim the first place, and with respect to performance the second, among the productions of the human mind.

By the general consent of critics the first praise of genius is due to the writer of an epic poem, as it requires an assemblage of all the powers which are singly sufficient for other compositions. Poetry is the art of uniting pleasure with truth, by calling imagination to the help of reason. Epic poetry undertakes to teach the most important truths by the most pleasing precepts, and therefore relates some great event in the most affecting manner. History must supply the writer with the rudiments of narration, which he must improve and exalt by a nobler art, must animate by dramatic energy, and diversify by retrospection and anticipation; morality must teach him the exact bounds and different shades of vice and virtue; from policy and the practice of life he has to learn the discriminations of character and the tendency of the passions, either single or combined; and physiology must supply him with illustrations and images. To put these materials to poetical use is required an imagination capable of painting nature and realizing fiction. Nor is he yet a poet till he has attained the whole extension of his language, distinguished all the delicacies of phrase and all the colors of words, and learned to adjust their different sounds to all the varieties of metrical modulation.

Bossu is of opinion that the poet's first work is to find a *moral,* which his fable is afterwards to illustrate and establish.[6] This seems to have been the process only of Milton: the moral of other poems is incidental and consequent; in Milton's only it is essential and intrinsic. His purpose was the most useful and the most arduous: "to vindicate the ways of God to man"; to show the reasonableness of religion, and the necessity of obedience to the Divine Law.

To convey this moral there must be a *fable,* a narration artfully constructed so as to excite curiosity and surprise expectation. In this part of his work Milton must be confessed to have equaled every other poet. He has involved in his account of the fall of man the events which preceded, and those that were to follow it; he has interwoven the whole system of theology with such propriety that every part appears to be necessary, and scarcely any recital is wished shorter for the sake of quickening the progress of the main action.

The subject of an epic poem is naturally an event of great importance. That of Milton is not the destruction of a city, the conduct of a colony, or the foundation of an empire. His subject is the fate of worlds, the revolutions of heaven and of earth; rebellion against the Supreme King raised by the highest order of created beings; the overthrow of their host and the punishment of their crime; the creation of a new race of reasonable creatures; their original happiness and innocence, their forfeiture of immortality, and their restoration to hope and peace.

Great events can be hastened or retarded only by persons of elevated dignity. Before the greatness displayed in Milton's poem all other greatness shrinks away. The weakest of his agents are the highest and noblest of human beings, the original parents of mankind; with whose actions the elements consented; on whose rectitude or deviation

6. **Bossu . . . establish:** Le Bossu, *Traité du Poème Épique,* I.7.

of will depended the state of terrestrial nature and the condition of all the future inhabitants of the globe.

Of the other agents in the poem, the chief are such as it is irreverence to name on slight occasions. The rest were lower powers,

> of which the least could wield
> Those elements, and arm him with the force
> Of all their regions; [7]

powers which only the control of Omnipotence restrains from laying creation waste, and filling the vast expanse of space with ruin and confusion. To display the motives and actions of beings thus superior, so far as human reason can examine them or human imagination represent them, is the task which this mighty poet has undertaken and performed.

In the examination of epic poems much speculation is commonly employed upon the *characters*. The characters in the *Paradise Lost* which admit of examination are those of angels and of man; of angels good and evil, of man in his innocent and sinful state.

Among the angels the virtue of Raphael is mild and placid, of easy condescension and free communication; that of Michael is regal and lofty, and, as may seem, attentive to the dignity of his own nature. Abdiel and Gabriel appear occasionally, and act as every incident requires; the solitary fidelity of Abdiel is very amiably painted.[8]

Of the evil angels the characters are more diversified. To Satan, as Addison observes, such sentiments are given as suit "the most exalted and most depraved being." [9] Milton has been censured by Clarke for the impiety which sometimes breaks from Satan's mouth. For there are thoughts, as he justly remarks, which no observation of character can justify, because no good man would willingly permit them to pass, however transiently, through his own mind.[10] To make Satan speak as a rebel, without any such expressions as might taint the reader's imagination, was indeed one of the great difficulties in Milton's undertaking, and I cannot but think that he has extricated himself with great happiness. There is in Satan's speeches little that can give pain to a pious ear. The language of rebellion cannot be the same with that

of obedience. The malignity of Satan foams in haughtiness and obstinacy; but his expressions are commonly general, and no otherwise offensive than as they are wicked.

The other chiefs of the celestial rebellion are very judiciously discriminated in the first and second books; and the ferocious character of Moloch appears, both in the battle and the council, with exact consistency.

To Adam and to Eve are given during their innocence such sentiments as innocence can generate and utter. Their love is pure benevolence and mutual veneration; their repasts are without luxury and their diligence without toil. Their addresses to their Maker have little more than the voice of admiration and gratitude. Fruition left them nothing to ask, and Innocence left them nothing to fear.

But with guilt enter distrust and discord, mutual accusation, and stubborn self-defense; they regard each other with alienated minds, and dread their Creator as the avenger of their transgression. At last they seek shelter in his mercy, soften to repentance, and melt in supplication. Both before and after the Fall the superiority of Adam is diligently sustained.

Of the *probable* and the *marvelous,* two parts of a vulgar epic poem which immerge the critic in deep consideration, the *Paradise Lost* requires little to be said. It contains the history of a miracle, of creation and redemption; it displays the power and the mercy of the Supreme Being; the probable therefore is marvelous, and the marvelous is probable. The substance of the narrative is truth; and, as truth allows no choice, it is, like necessity, superior to rule. To the accidental or adventitious parts, as to everything human, some slight exceptions may be made. But the main fabric is immovably supported.

It is justly remarked by Addison [11] that this poem has, by the nature of its subject, the advantage above all others, that it is universally and perpetually interesting. All mankind will, through all ages, bear the same relation to Adam and to Eve, and must partake of that good and evil which extend to themselves.

Of the *machinery,* so called from θεὸς ἀπὸ μηχανῆς,[12] by which is meant the occasional interposition of supernatural power, another fertile topic of critical remarks, here is no room to speak,

---

7. *Paradise Lost*, VI.221. Many of the following quotations from *Paradise Lost* may be found on pp. 454–502, above.   8. *Paradise Lost*, V.802 ff.   9. "the . . . being": *Spectator*, No. 303. 10. Clarke . . . mind: John Clarke, *Essay upon Study* (1731), p. 204.

11. Addison: *Spectator*, No. 273.   12. θεὸς . . . μηχανῆς: Aristotle, *Poetics*, XV.10: "*Deus ex machina.*"

because everything is done under the immediate and visible direction of Heaven; but the rule is so far observed that no part of the action could have been accomplished by any other means.

Of *episodes* I think there are only two, contained in Raphael's relation of the war in heaven and Michael's prophetic account of the changes to happen in this world.[13] Both are closely connected with the great action; one was necessary to Adam as a warning, the other as a consolation.

To the completeness or *integrity* of the design nothing can be objected; it has distinctly and clearly what Aristotle requires, a beginning, a middle, and an end. There is perhaps no poem of the same length from which so little can be taken without apparent mutilation. Here are no funeral games, nor is there any long description of a shield.[14] The short digressions at the beginning of the third, seventh, and ninth books might doubtless be spared; but superfluities so beautiful who would take away? or who does not wish that the author of the *Iliad* had gratified succeeding ages with a little knowledge of himself? Perhaps no passages are more frequently or more attentively read than those extrinsic paragraphs; and, since the end of poetry is pleasure, that cannot be unpoetical with which all are pleased.

The questions, whether the action of the poem be strictly *one,* whether the poem can be properly termed *heroic,* and who is the hero, are raised by such readers as draw their principles of judgment rather from books than from reason. Milton, though he entitled *Paradise Lost* only a " poem," yet calls it himself " heroic song." [15] Dryden, petulantly and indecently, denies the heroism of Adam because he was overcome, but there is no reason why the hero should not be unfortunate except established practice, since success and virtue do not go necessarily together. Cato is the hero of Lucan, but Lucan's authority will not be suffered by Quintilian to decide.[16] However, if success be necessary, Adam's deceiver was at last crushed; Adam was restored to his Maker's favor, and therefore may securely resume his human rank.

After the scheme and fabric of the poem must be considered its component parts, the sentiments, and the diction.

The *sentiments,* as expressive of manners or appropriated to characters, are for the greater part unexceptionably just.

Splendid passages containing lessons of morality or precepts of prudence occur seldom. Such is the original formation of this poem that as it admits no human manners till the Fall, it can give little assistance to human conduct. Its end is to raise the thoughts above sublunary cares or pleasures. Yet the praise of that fortitude, with which Abdiel maintained his singularity of virtue against the scorn of multitudes, may be accommodated to all times; and Raphael's reproof of Adam's curiosity after the planetary motions, with the answer returned by Adam, may be confidently opposed to any rule of life which any poet has delivered.[17]

The thoughts which are occasionally called forth in the progress are such as could only be produced by an imagination in the highest degree fervid and active, to which materials were supplied by incessant study and unlimited curiosity. The heat of Milton's mind might be said to sublimate his learning, to throw off into his work the spirit of science, unmingled with its grosser parts.

He had considered creation in its whole extent, and his descriptions are therefore learned. He had accustomed his imagination to unrestrained indulgence, and his conceptions therefore were extensive. The characteristic quality of his poem is sublimity. He sometimes descends to the elegant, but his element is the great. He can occasionally invest himself with grace, but his natural port is gigantic loftiness. He can please when pleasure is required, but it is his peculiar power to astonish.

He seems to have been well acquainted with his own genius, and to know what it was that Nature had bestowed upon him more bountifully than upon others: the power of displaying the vast, illuminating the splendid, enforcing the awful, darkening the gloomy, and aggravating the dreadful; he therefore chose a subject on which too much could not be said, on which he might tire his fancy without the censure of extravagance.

The appearances of nature and the occurrences of life did not satiate his appetite of greatness. To paint things as they are requires a minute attention, and employs the memory rather than the fancy. Milton's delight was to sport in the wide regions of possibility; reality was a scene too narrow for his mind. He sent his faculties out upon

13. Raphael's . . . world: *Paradise Lost,* V.577 ff., XI.334 ff. 14. funeral . . . shield: The references here are to Books XVIII and XXIII of the *Iliad.* 15. "heroic song": *Paradise Lost,* IX.25. 16. but . . . decide: i.e., Quintilian does not regard Lucan as beyond challenge. Of the *Pharsalia,* he declared it fitter to be studied by orators than by poets.

17. Raphael's . . . delivered: *Paradise Lost,* VIII.66 ff.

discovery, into worlds where only imagination can travel, and delighted to form new modes of existence, and furnish sentiment and action to superior beings, to trace the counsels of hell, or accompany the choirs of heaven.

But he could not be always in other worlds; he must sometimes revisit earth, and tell of things visible and known. When he cannot raise wonder by the sublimity of his mind he gives delight by its fertility.

Whatever be his subject he never fails to fill the imagination. But his images and descriptions of the scenes or operations of Nature do not seem to be always copied from original form, nor to have the freshness, raciness, and energy of immediate observation. He saw Nature, as Dryden expresses it, "through the spectacles of books"; [18] and on most occasions calls learning to his assistance. The garden of Eden brings to his mind the vale of Enna, where Proserpine was gathering flowers. Satan makes his way through fighting elements, like Argo between the Cyanean rocks or Ulysses between the two *Sicilian* whirlpools, when he shunned Charybdis "on the larboard." The mythological allusions have been justly censured,[19] as not being always used with notice of their vanity; but they contribute variety to the narration, and produce an alternate exercise of the memory and the fancy.

His similes are less numerous and more various than those of his predecessors. But he does not confine himself within the limits of rigorous comparison; his great excellence is amplitude, and he expands the adventitious image beyond the dimensions which the occasion required. Thus, comparing the shield of Satan to the orb of the moon, he crowds the imagination with the discovery of the telescope and all the wonders which the telescope discovers.

Of his moral sentiments it is hardly praise to affirm that they excel those of all other poets; for this superiority he was indebted to his acquaintance with the sacred writings. The ancient epic poets, wanting the light of revelation, were very unskillful teachers of virtue; their principal characters may be great, but they are not amiable. The reader may rise from their works with a greater degree of active or passive fortitude, and sometimes of prudence; but he will be able to carry away few precepts of justice, and none of mercy.

From the Italian writers it appears that the advantages of even Christian knowledge may be possessed in vain. Ariosto's pravity is generally known; and, though the *Deliverance of Jerusalem* may be considered as a sacred subject, the poet [20] has been very sparing of moral instruction.

In Milton every line breathes sanctity of thought and purity of manners, except when the train of the narration requires the introduction of the rebellious spirits; and even they are compelled to acknowledge their subjection to God in such a manner as excites reverence and confirms piety.

Of human beings there are but two; but those two are the parents of mankind, venerable before their fall for dignity and innocence, and amiable after it for repentance and submission. In their first state their affection is tender without weakness, and their piety sublime without presumption. When they have sinned they show how discord begins in mutual frailty, and how it ought to cease in mutual forbearance; how confidence of the divine favor is forfeited by sin, and how hope of pardon may be obtained by penitence and prayer. A state of innocence we can only conceive, if indeed in our present misery it be possible to conceive it; but the sentiments and worship proper to a fallen and offending being we have all to learn, as we have all to practice.

The poet whatever be done is always great. Our progenitors in their first state conversed with angels; even when folly and sin had degraded them they had not in their humiliation "the port of mean suitors"; [21] and they rise again to reverential regard when we find that their prayers were heard.

As human passions did not enter the world before the Fall, there is in the *Paradise Lost* little opportunity for the pathetic; but what little there is has not been lost. That passion which is peculiar to rational nature, the anguish arising from the consciousness of transgression and the horrors attending the sense of the divine displeasure, are very justly described and forcibly impressed. But the passions are moved only on one occasion; sublimity is the general and prevailing quality in this poem — sublimity variously modified, sometimes descriptive, sometimes argumentative.

18. "through . . . books": *Essays* (ed. Ker), I.80, where Dryden says this is *not* true of Shakespeare.   19. censured: by Addison, *Spectator*, No. 297.

20. poet: Torquato Tasso (1544–95). Ariosto's "pravity" is exemplified by wild flights of imaginary adventure in a poem (the *Orlando Furioso*), grounded on the defense of Christendom against the Saracens.   21. "the . . . suitors": *Paradise Lost*, XI.8.

The defects and faults of *Paradise Lost,* for faults and defects every work of man must have, it is the business of impartial criticism to discover. As in displaying the excellence of Milton I have not made long quotations, because of selecting beauties there had been no end, I shall in the same general manner mention that which seems to deserve censure; for what Englishman can take delight in transcribing passages which, if they lessen the reputation of Milton, diminish in some degree the honor of our country?

The generality of my scheme does not admit the frequent notice of verbal inaccuracies which Bentley,[22] perhaps better skilled in grammar than in poetry, has often found, though he sometimes made them, and which he imputed to the obtrusions of a reviser whom the author's blindness obliged him to employ. A supposition rash and groundless, if he thought it true; and vile and pernicious if, as is said, he in private allowed it to be false.

The plan of *Paradise Lost* has this inconvenience, that it comprises neither human actions nor human manners. The man and woman who act and suffer are in a state which no other man or woman can ever know. The reader finds no transaction in which he can be engaged, beholds no condition in which he can by any effort of imagination place himself; he has, therefore, little natural curiosity or sympathy.

We all, indeed, feel the effects of Adam's disobedience; we all sin like Adam, and like him must all bewail our offenses; we have restless and insidious enemies in the fallen angels, and in the blessed spirits we have guardians and friends; in the redemption of mankind we hope to be included: in the description of heaven and hell we are surely interested, as we are all to reside hereafter either in the regions of horror or of bliss.

But these truths are too important to be new; they have been taught to our infancy; they have mingled with our solitary thoughts and familiar conversation, and are habitually interwoven with the whole texture of life. Being therefore not new they raise no unaccustomed emotion in the mind; what we knew before we cannot learn; what is not unexpected cannot surprise.

Of the ideas suggested by these awful scenes, from some we recede with reverence, except when stated hours require their association; and from others we shrink with horror, or admit them only as salutary inflictions, as counterpoises to our interests and passions. Such images rather obstruct the career of fancy than incite it.

Pleasure and terror are indeed the genuine sources of poetry; but poetical pleasure must be such as human imagination can at least conceive, and poetical terror such as human strength and fortitude may combat. The good and evil of eternity are too ponderous for the wings of wit; the mind sinks under them in passive helplessness, content with calm belief and humble adoration.

Known truths however may take a different appearance, and be conveyed to the mind by a new train of intermediate images. This Milton has undertaken, and performed with pregnancy and vigor of mind peculiar to himself. Whoever considers the few radical positions which the Scriptures afforded him will wonder by what energetic operation he expanded them to such extent and ramified them to so much variety, restrained as he was by religious reverence from licentiousness of fiction.

Here is a full display of the united force of study and genius; of a great accumulation of materials, with judgment to digest and fancy to combine them; Milton was able to select from nature or from story, from ancient fable or from modern science, whatever could illustrate or adorn his thoughts. An accumulation of knowledge impregnated his mind, fermented by study and exalted by imagination.

It has been therefore said without an indecent hyperbole by one of his encomiasts, that in reading *Paradise Lost* we read a book of universal knowledge.

But original deficience cannot be supplied. The want of human interest is always felt. *Paradise Lost* is one of the books which the reader admires and lays down, and forgets to take up again. None ever wished it longer than it is. Its perusal is a duty rather than a pleasure. We read Milton for instruction, retire harassed and overburdened, and look elsewhere for recreation; we desert our master, and seek for companions.

Another inconvenience of Milton's design is that it requires the description of what cannot be described, the agency of spirits. He saw that immateriality supplied no images, and that he could not show angels acting but by instruments of action; he therefore invested them with form and matter. This being necessary was therefore defensible; and

22. **Bentley:** Richard Bentley, in the Preface to his edition of the poem (1732), suggests that Paradise was twice lost by the corruptions introduced by Milton's intermediary.

he should have secured the consistency of his system by keeping immateriality out of sight, and enticing his reader to drop it from his thoughts. But he has unhappily perplexed his poetry with his philosophy. His infernal and celestial powers are sometimes pure spirit and sometimes animated body. When Satan walks with his lance upon the "burning marl" he has a body; when in his passage between hell and the new world he is in danger of sinking in the vacuity and is supported by a gust of rising vapors he has a body; when he animates the toad he seems to be mere spirit that can penetrate matter at pleasure; when he "starts up in his own shape," he has at least a determined form; and when he is brought before Gabriel he has "a spear and a shield," which he had the power of hiding in the toad, though the arms of the contending angels are evidently material.[23]

The vulgar inhabitants of Pandæmonium, being "incorporeal spirits," are "at large though without number" in a limited space, yet in the battle when they were overwhelmed by mountains their armor hurt them, "crushed in upon their substance, now grown gross by sinning." This likewise happened to the uncorrupted angels, who were overthrown "the sooner for their arms, for unarmed they might easily as spirits have evaded by contraction or remove." Even as spirits they are hardly spiritual, for "contraction" and "remove" are images of matter; but if they could have escaped without their armor, they might have escaped from it and left only the empty cover to be battered. Uriel, when he rides on a sunbeam, is material; Satan is material when he is afraid of the prowess of Adam.[24]

The confusion of spirit and matter which pervades the whole narration of the war of heaven fills it with incongruity; and the book in which it is related is, I believe, the favorite of children, and gradually neglected as knowledge is increased.

After the operation of immaterial agents which cannot be explained may be considered that of allegorical persons, which have no real existence. To exalt causes into agents, to invest abstract ideas with form, and animate them with activity has always been the right of poetry. But such airy beings are for the most part suffered only to do their natural office, and retire. Thus Fame tells a tale and

Victory hovers over a general or perches on a standard, but Fame and Victory can do no more. To give them any real employment or ascribe to them any material agency is to make them allegorical no longer, but to shock the mind by ascribing effects to nonentity. In the *Prometheus* of Aeschylus we see Violence and Strength, and in the *Alcestis* of Euripides we see Death, brought upon the stage, all as active persons of the drama; but no precedents can justify absurdity.

Milton's allegory of Sin and Death is undoubtedly faulty. Sin is indeed the mother of Death, and may be allowed to be the portress of hell; but when they stop the journey of Satan, a journey described as real, and when Death offers him battle, the allegory is broken. That Sin and Death should have shown the way to hell might have been allowed; but they cannot facilitate the passage by building a bridge, because the difficulty of Satan's passage is described as real and sensible, and the bridge ought to be only figurative. The hell assigned to the rebellious spirits is described as not less local than the residence of man. It is placed in some distant part of space, separated from the regions of harmony and order by a chaotic waste and an unoccupied vacuity; but Sin and Death worked up a "mole of aggregated soil," cemented with asphaltus, a work too bulky for ideal architects.[25]

This unskillful allegory appears to me one of the greatest faults of the poem, and to this there was no temptation but the author's opinion of its beauty.

To the conduct of the narrative some objections may be made. Satan is with great expectation brought before Gabriel in paradise, and is suffered to go away unmolested. The creation of man is represented as the consequence of the vacuity left in heaven by the expulsion of the rebels; yet Satan mentions it as a report "rife in heaven" before his departure.[26]

To find sentiments for the state of innocence was very difficult; and something of anticipation perhaps is now and then discovered. Adam's discourse of dreams seems not to be the speculation of a new-created being. I know not whether his answer to the angel's reproof for curiosity does not want something of propriety; it is the speech of a man acquainted with many other men. Some philosophical notions, especially when the philosophy is false,

---

23. See, for the allusions above, *Paradise Lost*, I.296; II.931; IV.800, 819, 990.   24. For the above, *Paradise Lost*, I.789; VI.651, 595 (in that order); IV.555, 590; IX.480 ff.

25. See *Paradise Lost*, II.648 ff.; X.283 ff.   26. See *Paradise Lost*, IV.874; VII.150; and I.650.

might have been better omitted. The angel in a comparison speaks of "timorous deer," before deer were yet timorous, and before Adam could understand the comparison.[27]

Dryden remarks that Milton has some flats among his elevations.[28] This is only to say that all the parts are not equal. In every work one part must be for the sake of others; a palace must have passages, a poem must have transitions. It is no more to be required that wit should always be blazing than that the sun should always stand at noon. In a great work there is a vicissitude of luminous and opaque parts, as there is in the world a succession of day and night. Milton, when he has expatiated in the sky, may be allowed sometimes to revisit earth; for what other author ever soared so high or sustained his flight so long?

Milton, being well versed in the Italian poets, appears to have borrowed often from them; and, as every man catches something from his companions, his desire of imitating Ariosto's levity has disgraced his work with the "Paradise of Fools," a fiction not in itself ill-imagined, but too ludicrous for its place.[29]

His play on words, in which he delights too often; his equivocations, which Bentley endeavors to defend by the example of the ancients; his unnecessary and ungraceful use of terms of art it is not necessary to mention, because they are easily remarked and generally censured, and at last bear so little proportion to the whole that they scarcely deserve the attention of a critic.

Such are the faults of that wonderful performance *Paradise Lost,* which he who can put in balance with its beauties must be considered not as nice but as dull, as less to be censured for want of candor than pitied for want of sensibility. . . .

"Rhyme," he says, and says truly, "is no necessary adjunct of true poetry."[30] But perhaps of poetry as a mental operation meter or music is no necessary adjunct; it is, however, by the music of meter that poetry has been discriminated in all languages, and in languages melodiously constructed with a due proportion of long and short syllables meter is sufficient. But one language cannot communicate its rules to another; where meter is scanty and imperfect some help is necessary. The music of

the English heroic line strikes the ear so faintly that it is easily lost, unless all the syllables of every line co-operate together; this co-operation can be only obtained by the preservation of every verse unmingled with another as a distinct system of sounds, and this distinctness is obtained and preserved by the artifice of rhyme. The variety of pauses, so much boasted by the lovers of blank verse, changes the measures of an English poet to the periods of a declaimer; and there are only a few skillful and happy readers of Milton who enable their audience to perceive where the lines end or begin. "Blank verse," said an ingenious critic, "seems to be verse only to the eye."[31]

Poetry may subsist without rhyme, but English poetry will not often please; nor can rhyme ever be safely spared but where the subject is able to support itself. Blank verse makes some approach to that which is called the "lapidary style";[32] has neither the easiness of prose nor the melody of numbers, and therefore tires by long continuance. Of the Italian writers without rhyme, whom Milton alleges as precedents, not one is popular; what reason could urge in its defense has been confuted by the ear.

But whatever be the advantage of rhyme I cannot prevail on myself to wish that Milton had been a rhymer, for I cannot wish his work to be other than it is; yet like other heroes he is to be admired rather than imitated. He that thinks himself capable of astonishing may write blank verse, but those that hope only to please must condescend to rhyme.

The highest praise of genius is original invention. Milton cannot be said to have contrived the structure of an epic poem, and therefore owes reverence to that vigor and amplitude of mind to which all generations must be indebted for the art of poetical narration, for the texture of the fable, the variation of incidents, the interposition of dialogue, and all the stratagems that surprise and enchain attention. But of all the borrowers from Homer, Milton is perhaps the least indebted. He was naturally a thinker for himself, confident of his own abilities and disdainful of help or hindrance; he did not refuse admission to the thoughts or images of his predecessors, but he did not seek them. From his contemporaries he neither courted nor received support; there is in his writings nothing by which the pride of other authors might be

---

27. See *Paradise Lost,* V.100; VIII.179; and VI.857.   28. Dryden . . . elevations: Dryden, Preface to *Sylvae,* in *Essays* (ed. Ker), I.268.   29. *Paradise Lost,* III.444 ff.   30. "Rhyme . . . poetry": Preface to *Paradise Lost.*

31. "Blank . . . verse": William Locke; see Boswell's *Johnson.* (ed. Hill-Powell), IV.43.   32. "lapidary style": i.e., the style of pompous inscription.

gratified or favor gained, no exchange of praise or solicitation of support. His great works were performed under discountenance and in blindness, but difficulties vanished at his touch; he was born for whatever is arduous; and his work is not the greatest of heroic poems, only because it is not the first.

from COWLEY

Wit, like all other things subject by their nature to the choice of man, has its changes and fashions, and at different times takes different forms. About the beginning of the seventeenth century appeared a race of writers that may be termed the Metaphysical poets, of whom in a criticism on the works of Cowley it is not improper to give some account.

The Metaphysical poets were men of learning, and to show their learning was their whole endeavor; but, unluckily resolving to show it in rhyme, instead of writing poetry they only wrote verses, and very often such verses as stood the trial of the finger better than of the ear; for the modulation was so imperfect that they were only found to be verses by counting the syllables.

If the father of criticism has rightly denominated poetry τέχνη μιμητική, an imitative art,[1] these writers will without great wrong lose their right to the name of poets, for they cannot be said to have imitated anything: they neither copied nature nor life; neither painted the forms of matter nor represented the operations of intellect.

Those, however, who deny them to be poets allow them to be wits. Dryden confesses of himself and his contemporaries that they fall below Donne in wit, but maintains that they surpass him in poetry.[2]

If wit be well described by Pope as being " that which has been often thought, but was never before so well expressed," [3] they certainly never attained nor ever sought it, for they endeavored to be singular in their thoughts, and were careless of their diction. But Pope's account of wit is undoubtedly erroneous; he depresses it below its natural dignity, and reduces it from strength of thought to happiness of language.

If by a more noble and more adequate conception that be considered as wit which is at once natural and new, that which though not obvious is, upon its first production, acknowledged to be just; if it be that, which he that never found it, wonders how he missed; to wit of this kind the Metaphysical poets have seldom risen. Their thoughts are often new, but seldom natural; they are not obvious, but neither are they just; and the reader, far from wondering that he missed them, wonders more frequently by what perverseness of industry they were ever found.

But wit, abstracted from its effects upon the hearer, may be more rigorously and philosophically considered as a kind of *discordia concors,* a combination of dissimilar images, or discovery of occult resemblances in things apparently unlike. Of wit, thus defined, they have more than enough. The most heterogeneous ideas are yoked by violence together; nature and art are ransacked for illustrations, comparisons, and allusions; their learning instructs, and their subtlety surprises; but the reader commonly thinks his improvement dearly bought, and, though he sometimes admires, is seldom pleased.

From this account of their compositions it will be readily inferred that they were not successful in representing or moving the affections. As they were wholly employed on something unexpected and surprising they had no regard to that uniformity of sentiment which enables us to conceive and to excite the pains and the pleasure of other minds: they never inquired what on any occasion they should have said or done, but wrote rather as beholders than partakers of human nature; as beings looking upon good and evil, impassive and at leisure; as Epicurean deities making remarks on the actions of men and the vicissitudes of life, without interest and without emotion. Their courtship was void of fondness, and their lamentation of sorrow. Their wish was only to say what they hoped had been never said before.

Nor was the sublime more within their reach than the pathetic; for they never attempted that comprehension and expanse of thought which at once fills the whole mind, and of which the first effect is sudden astonishment, and the second rational admiration. Sublimity is produced by aggregation, and littleness by dispersion. Great thoughts are always general, and consist in positions not limited by exceptions, and in descriptions not descending to minuteness. It is with great propriety that subtlety, which in its original import means exility [4] of particles, is taken in its metaphorical

LIFE OF COWLEY. **1.** *imitative art:* Aristotle, *Poetics,* I,V,VI, but without using the exact phrase. **2.** Dryden . . . poetry: Dryden, *Essays* (ed. Ker), II.102. **3.** "that . . . expressed": *Essay on Criticism,* ll. 297–98, p. 766, above.

4. exility: thinness.

meaning for nicety of distinction. Those writers who lay on the watch for novelty could have little hope of greatness; for great things cannot have escaped former observation. Their attempts were always analytic: they broke every image into fragments, and could no more represent by their slender conceits and labored particularities the prospects of nature or the scenes of life, than he who dissects a sunbeam with a prism can exhibit the wide effulgence of a summer noon.

What they wanted, however, of the sublime they endeavored to supply by hyperbole; their amplification had no limits; they left not only reason but fancy behind them, and produced combinations of confused magnificence that not only could not be credited, but could not be imagined.

Yet great labor directed by great abilities is never wholly lost; if they frequently threw away their wit upon false conceits, they likewise sometimes struck out unexpected truth; if their conceits were far-fetched, they were often worth the carriage. To write on their plan it is at least necessary to read and think. No man could be born a Metaphysical poet, nor assume the dignity of a writer by descriptions copied from descriptions, by imitations borrowed from imitations, by traditional imagery and hereditary similes, by readiness of rhyme and volubility of syllables.

In perusing the works of this race of authors the mind is exercised either by recollection or inquiry; either something already learned is to be retrieved, or something new is to be examined. If their greatness seldom elevates, their acuteness often surprises; if the imagination is not always gratified, at least the powers of reflection and comparison are employed; and in the mass of materials, which ingenious absurdity has thrown together, genuine wit and useful knowledge may be sometimes found, buried perhaps in grossness of expression, but useful to those who know their value, and such as, when they are expanded to perspicuity and polished to elegance, may give luster to works which have more propriety though less copiousness of sentiment.

from DRYDEN

Dryden may be properly considered as the father of English criticism, as the writer who first taught us to determine upon principles the merit of composition. Of our former poets, the greatest dramatist wrote without rules, conducted through life

and nature by a genius that rarely misled, and rarely deserted him. Of the rest, those who knew the laws of propriety had neglected to teach them.

Two *Arts of English Poetry* were written in the days of Elizabeth by Webb and Puttenham,[1] from which something might be learned, and a few hints had been given by Jonson and Cowley;[2] but Dryden's *Essay on Dramatic Poetry* was the first regular and valuable treatise on the art of writing.

He who, having formed his opinions in the present age of English literature, turns back to peruse this dialogue, will not perhaps find much increase of knowledge or much novelty of instruction; but he is to remember that critical principles were then in the hands of a few, who had gathered them partly from the ancients, and partly from the Italians and French. The structure of dramatic poems was not then generally understood. Audiences applauded by instinct, and poets perhaps often pleased by chance.

A writer who obtains his full purpose loses himself in his own luster. Of an opinion which is no longer doubted, the evidence ceases to be examined. Of an art universally practiced, the first teacher is forgotten. Learning once made popular is no longer learning; it has the appearance of something which we have bestowed upon ourselves, as the dew appears to rise from the field which it refreshes.

To judge rightly of an author we must transport ourselves to his time and examine what were the wants of his contemporaries, and what were his means of supplying them. That which is easy at one time was difficult at another. Dryden at least imported his science, and gave his country what it wanted before; or rather, he imported only the materials, and manufactured them by his own skill.

The Dialogue on the Drama was one of his first essays of criticism, written when he was yet a timorous candidate for reputation, and therefore labored with that diligence which he might allow himself somewhat to remit when his name gave sanction to his positions, and his awe of the public was abated, partly by custom, and partly by success. It will not be easy to find in all the opulence of our language a treatise so artfully variegated with successive representations of opposite probabilities, so enlivened with imagery, so brightened with illustrations. His portraits of the English dramatists are

LIFE OF DRYDEN.   1. Webb . . . Puttenham: William Webbe, *A Discourse of English Poetrie* (1586); Richard Puttenham, *The Arte of English Poesie* (1589).   2. Jonson . . . Cowley: Ben Jonson, *Timber* (1640); Abraham Cowley, in his Prefaces.

wrought with great spirit and diligence. The account of Shakespeare may stand as a perpetual model of encomiastic criticism;[3] exact without minuteness, and lofty without exaggeration. The praise lavished by Longinus, on the attestation of the heroes of Marathon by Demosthenes, fades away before it.[4] In a few lines is exhibited a character, so extensive in its comprehension and so curious in its limitations, that nothing can be added, diminished, or reformed; nor can the editors and admirers of Shakespeare, in all their emulation of reverence, boast of much more than of having diffused and paraphrased this epitome of excellence, of having changed Dryden's gold for baser metal, of lower value though of greater bulk.

In this, and in all his other essays on the same subject, the criticism of Dryden is the criticism of a poet; not a dull collection of theorems, nor a rude detection of faults, which perhaps the censor was not able to have committed; but a gay and vigorous dissertation, where delight is mingled with instruction, and where the author proves his right of judgment by his power of performance. . . .

As he had studied with great diligence the art of poetry, and enlarged or rectified his notions by experience perpetually increasing, he had his mind stored with principles and observations; he poured out his knowledge with little labor; for of labor, notwithstanding the multiplicity of his productions, there is sufficient reason to suspect that he was not a lover. To write *con amore,* with fondness for the employment, with perpetual touches and retouches, with unwillingness to take leave of his own idea, and an unwearied pursuit of unattainable perfection, was, I think, no part of his character.

His criticism may be considered as general or occasional. In his general precepts, which depend upon the nature of things and the structure of the human mind, he may doubtless be safely recommended to the confidence of the reader; but his occasional and particular positions were sometimes interested, sometimes negligent, and sometimes capricious. . . .

His literature, though not always free from ostentation, will be commonly found either obvious, and made his own by the art of dressing it; or superficial, which by what he gives shows what he want-

ed; or erroneous, hastily collected, and negligently scattered.

Yet it cannot be said that his genius is ever unprovided of matter, or that his fancy languishes in penury of ideas. His works abound with knowledge and sparkle with illustrations. There is scarcely any science or faculty that does not supply him with occasional images and lucky similitudes; every page discovers a mind very widely acquainted both with art and nature, and in full possession of great stores of intellectual wealth. Of him that knows much it is natural to suppose that he has read with diligence; yet I rather believe that the knowledge of Dryden was gleaned from accidental intelligence and various conversation; by a quick apprehension, a judicious selection, and a happy memory, a keen appetite of knowledge, and a powerful digestion; by vigilance that permitted nothing to pass without notice, and a habit of reflection that suffered nothing useful to be lost. A mind like Dryden's, always curious, always active, to which every understanding was proud to be associated, and of which everyone solicited the regard by an ambitious display of himself, had a more pleasant, perhaps a nearer, way to knowledge than by the silent progress of solitary reading. I do not suppose that he despised books or intentionally neglected them, but that he was carried out by the impetuosity of his genius to more vivid and speedy instructors, and that his studies were rather desultory and fortuitous than constant and systematical. . . .

Of all this, however, if the proof be demanded I will not undertake to give it; the atoms of probability, of which my opinion has been formed, lie scattered over all his works: and by him who thinks the question worth his notice his works must be perused with very close attention.

Criticism, either didactic or defensive, occupies almost all his prose, except those pages which he has devoted to his patrons; but none of his prefaces were ever thought tedious. They have not the formality of a settled style, in which the first half of the sentence betrays the other. The clauses are never balanced, nor the periods modeled; every word seems to drop by chance, though it falls into its proper place. Nothing is cold or languid; the whole is airy, animated, and vigorous: what is little is gay; what is great is splendid. He may be thought to mention himself too frequently, but, while he forces himself upon our esteem, we cannot refuse him to stand high in his own. Every

3. **criticism:** See above, p. 107, where it is quoted in Johnson's own Preface to Shakespeare.   4. **The . . . it:** Longinus, *On the Sublime,* XVI; Demosthenes, *On the Crown,* CCLXIII,xi.

thing is excused by the play of images and the spriteliness of expression. Though all is easy, nothing is feeble; though all seems careless, there is nothing harsh; and though since his earlier works more than a century has passed they have nothing yet uncouth or obsolete. . . .

From his prose, however, Dryden derives only his accidental and secondary praise; the veneration with which his name is pronounced by every cultivator of English literature is paid to him as he refined the language, improved the sentiments, and tuned the numbers of English poetry. . . .

In a general survey of Dryden's labors he appears to have had a mind very comprehensive by nature, and much enriched with acquired knowledge. His compositions are the effects of a vigorous genius operating upon large materials.

The power that predominated in his intellectual operations was rather strong reason than quick sensibility. Upon all occasions that were presented he studied rather than felt, and produced sentiments not such as Nature enforces, but meditation supplies. With the simple and elemental passions, as they spring separate in the mind, he seems not much acquainted, and seldom describes them but as they are complicated by the various relations of society and confused in the tumults and agitations of life. . . .

The favorite exercise of his mind was ratiocination; and, that argument might not be too soon at an end, he delighted to talk of liberty and necessity, destiny and contingence; these he discusses in the language of the school with so much profundity that the terms which he uses are not always understood. It is indeed learning, but learning out of place.

When once he had engaged himself in disputation, thoughts flowed in on either side: he was now no longer at a loss; he had always objections and solutions at command: " *verbaque provisam rem* " [5] — give him matter for his verse, and he finds without difficulty verse for his matter.

In comedy, for which he professes himself not naturally qualified, the mirth which he excites will perhaps not be found so much to arise from any original humor or peculiarity of character nicely distinguished and diligently pursued, as from incidents and circumstances, artifices and surprises;

from jests of action rather than of sentiment. What he had of humorous or passionate, he seems to have had not from nature, but from other poets; if not always as a plagiary, at least as an imitator.

Next to argument, his delight was in wild and daring sallies of sentiment, in the irregular and eccentric violence of wit. He delighted to tread upon the brink of meaning, where light and darkness begin to mingle; to approach the precipice of absurdity, and hover over the abyss of unideal vacancy. . . .

Of Dryden's works it was said by Pope, that " he could select from them better specimens of every mode of poetry than any other English writer could supply." Perhaps no nation ever produced a writer that enriched his language with such variety of models. To him we owe the improvement, perhaps the completion, of our meter, the refinement of our language, and much of the correctness of our sentiments. By him we were taught " *sapere et fari*," to think naturally and express forcibly. Though Davies [6] has reasoned in rhyme before him, it may be perhaps maintained that he was the first who joined argument with poetry. He showed us the true bounds of a translator's liberty. What was said of Rome, adorned by Augustus, may be applied by an easy metaphor to English poetry embellished by Dryden, " *lateritiam invenit, marmoream reliquit*," [7] he found it brick, and he left it marble.

from ADDISON

Addison is now to be considered as a critic, a name which the present generation is scarcely willing to allow him. His criticism is condemned as tentative or experimental rather than scientific, and he is considered as deciding by taste rather than by principles.

It is not uncommon for those who have grown wise by the labor of others to add a little of their own, and overlook their masters. Addison is now despised by some who perhaps would never have seen his defects, but by the lights which he afforded them. That he always wrote as he would think it necessary to write now cannot be affirmed; his instructions were such as the character of his readers made proper. That general knowledge which now

5. " *verbaque . . . rem*": Horace, *Ars Poetica*, l. 311; Johnson paraphrases the Latin.

6. **Davies:** Sir John Davies (1570–1626), author of *Orchestra* (1596) and *Nosce Teipsum* (1599).   7. " *lateritiam . . . reliquit*": Suetonius, *Augustus*, XXIX.

circulates in common talk was in his time rarely to be found. Men not professing learning were not ashamed of ignorance; and in the female world any acquaintance with books was distinguished only to be censured. His purpose was to infuse literary curiosity by gentle and unsuspected conveyance into the gay, the idle, and the wealthy; he therefore presented knowledge in the most alluring form, not lofty and austere, but accessible and familiar. When he showed them their defects, he showed them likewise that they might be easily supplied. His attempt succeeded; enquiry was awakened, and comprehension expanded. An emulation of intellectual elegance was excited, and, from his time to our own, life has been gradually exalted, and conversation purified and enlarged.

Dryden had not many years before scattered criticism over his *Prefaces* with very little parsimony; but, though he sometimes condescended to be somewhat familiar, his manner was in general too scholastic for those who had yet their rudiments to learn, and found it not easy to understand their master. His observations were framed rather for those that were learning to write, than for those that read only to talk.

An instructor like Addison was now wanting, whose remarks, being superficial, might be easily understood, and being just, might prepare the mind for more attainments. Had he presented *Paradise Lost* to the public with all the pomp of system and severity of science, the criticism would perhaps have been admired, and the poem still have been neglected; but by the blandishments of gentleness and facility he has made Milton an universal favorite, with whom readers of every class think it necessary to be pleased.

He descended now and then to lower disquisitions; and by a serious display of the beauties of *Chevy Chase* [1] exposed himself to the ridicule of "Wagstaff," who bestowed a like pompous character on *Tom Thumb;* and to the contempt of Dennis, who, considering the fundamental position of his criticism, that *Chevy Chase* pleases, and ought to please, because it is natural, observes that "there is a way of deviating from nature, by bombast or tumor, which soars above nature, and enlarges images beyond their real bulk; by affectation, which forsakes nature in quest of something unsuitable; and by imbecility, which degrades nature by faintness and diminution, by obscuring its appearances, and weakening its effects." [2] In *Chevy Chase* there is not much of either bombast or affectation; but there is chill and lifeless imbecility. The story cannot possibly be told in a manner that shall make less impression on the mind.

Before the profound observers of the present race repose too securely on the consciousness of their superiority to Addison, let them consider his "Remarks on Ovid," in which may be found specimens of criticism sufficiently subtle and refined; let them peruse likewise his "Essays on Wit," [3] and on "The Pleasures of Imagination," [4] in which he founds art on the base of nature, and draws the principles of invention from dispositions inherent in the mind of man with skill and elegance, such as his contemners will not easily attain.

As a describer of life and manners he must be allowed to stand perhaps the first of the first rank. His humor, which, as Steele observes, is peculiar to himself, is so happily diffused as to give the grace of novelty to domestic scenes and daily occurrences. He never "outsteps the modesty of nature," nor raises merriment or wonder by the violation of truth. His figures neither divert by distortion nor amaze by aggravation. He copies life with so much fidelity that he can be hardly said to invent; yet his exhibitions have an air so much original that it is difficult to suppose them not merely the product of imagination.

As a teacher of wisdom he may be confidently followed. His religion has nothing in it enthusiastic or superstitious: he appears neither weakly credulous nor wantonly sceptical; his morality is neither dangerously lax nor impracticably rigid. All the enchantment of fancy and all the cogency of argument are employed to recommend to the reader his real interest, the care of pleasing the Author of his being. Truth is shown sometimes as the phantom of a vision, sometimes appears half-veiled in an allegory, sometimes attracts regard in the robes of fancy, and sometimes steps forth in the confidence of reason. She wears a thousand dresses, and in all is pleasing.

Mille habet ornatus, mille decenter habet. [5]

His prose is the model of the middle style; on grave subjects not formal, on light occasions not groveling; pure without scrupulosity, and exact

LIFE OF ADDISON. 1. *Chevy Chase:* Cf. *Spectator*, Nos. 70 and 74.

2. "there . . . effects": Dennis, *Critical Works* (ed. Hooker), II.29–42. 3. "Essays on Wit": *Spectator*, Nos. 58–63. 4. "The . . . Imagination": *Spectator*, Nos. 411–21. 5. Tibullus, *Elegies*, IV.ii.14, paraphrased above by Johnson.

without apparent elaboration; always equable and always easy, without glowing words or pointed sentences. Addison never deviates from his track to snatch a grace; he seeks no ambitious ornaments, and tries no hazardous innovations. His page is always luminous, but never blazes in unexpected splendor.

It was apparently his principal endeavor to avoid all harshness and severity of diction; he is therefore sometimes verbose in his transitions and connections, and sometimes descends too much to the language of conversation: yet if his language had been less idiomatical it might have lost somewhat of its genuine Anglicism. What he attempted, he performed; he is never feeble, and he did not wish to be energetic; he is never rapid, and he never stagnates. His sentences have neither studied amplitude nor affected brevity; his periods, though not diligently rounded, are voluble and easy. Whoever wishes to attain an English style, familiar but not coarse, and elegant but not ostentatious, must give his days and nights to the volumes of Addison.

from POPE

The person of Pope is well known not to have been formed by the nicest model. He has, in his account of the "Little Club,"[1] compared himself to a spider, and by another is described as protuberant behind and before. He is said to have been beautiful in his infancy, but he was of a constitution originally feeble and weak, and, as bodies of a tender frame are easily distorted, his deformity was probably in part the effect of his application. His stature was so low that, to bring him to a level with common tables, it was necessary to raise his seat. But his face was not displeasing, and his eyes were animated and vivid.

By natural deformity or accidental distortion his vital functions were so much disordered that his life was a "long disease."[2] His most frequent assailant was the headache, which he used to relieve by inhaling the steam of coffee, which he very frequently required.

Most of what can be told concerning his petty peculiarities was communicated by a female domestic of the Earl of Oxford, who knew him per-

haps after the middle of life. He was then so weak as to stand in perpetual need of female attendance; extremely sensible of cold, so that he wore a kind of fur doublet under a shirt of very coarse warm linen with fine sleeves. When he rose he was invested in bodice made of stiff canvas, being scarce able to hold himself erect till they were laced, and he then put on a flannel waistcoat. One side was contracted. His legs were so slender that he enlarged their bulk with three pair of stockings, which were drawn on and off by the maid; for he was not able to dress or undress himself, and neither went to bed nor rose without help. His weakness made it very difficult for him to be clean.

His hair had fallen almost all away, and he used to dine sometimes with Lord Oxford, privately, in a velvet cap. His dress of ceremony was black, with a tie wig and a little sword.

The indulgence and accommodation which his sickness required had taught him all the unpleasing and unsocial qualities of a valetudinary man. He expected that everything should give way to his ease or humor, as a child whose parents will not hear her cry has an unresisted dominion in the nursery.

C'est que l'enfant toujours est homme,
C'est que l'homme est toujours enfant.[3]

When he wanted to sleep he "nodded in company,"[4] and once slumbered at his own table while the Prince of Wales was talking of poetry.

The reputation which his friendship gave procured him many invitations, but he was a very troublesome inmate. He brought no servant, and had so many wants that a numerous attendance was scarcely able to supply them. Wherever he was he left no room for another, because he exacted the attention and employed the activity of the whole family. His errands were so frequent and frivolous that the footmen in time avoided and neglected him, and the Earl of Oxford discharged some of the servants for their resolute refusal of his messages. The maids, when they had neglected their business, alleged that they had been employed by Mr. Pope. One of his constant demands was of coffee in the night, and to the woman that waited on him in his chamber he was very burdensome, but he was careful to recompense her want of sleep, and Lord Oxford's servant declared that in a house

LIFE OF POPE. 1. "Little Club": This imaginary club is described in the *Guardian*, No. 92, a periodical, like the *Spectator*, which ran from March to October, 1713. 2. "long disease": Pope's words in his *Epistle to Dr. Arbuthnot*, l. 131. Most of the following quotations from Pope may be found on pp. 760–841, above.

3. "The child is always the grown-up, the adult forever a child." 4. "nodded in company": Pope, *Imitations of Horace, Satires*, II.i.13, p. 813, above.

where her business was to answer his call she would not ask for wages.

He had another fault, easily incident to those who suffering much pain think themselves entitled to whatever pleasures they can snatch. He was too indulgent to his appetite: he loved meat highly seasoned and of strong taste, and, at the intervals of the table, amused himself with biscuits and dry conserves. If he sat down to a variety of dishes he would oppress his stomach with repletion, and though he seemed angry when a dram was offered him, did not forbear to drink it. His friends, who knew the avenues to his heart, pampered him with presents of luxury, which he did not suffer to stand neglected. The death of great men is not always proportioned to the luster of their lives. Hannibal, says Juvenal,[5] did not perish by a javelin or a sword; the slaughters of Cannae were revenged by a ring. The death of Pope was imputed by some of his friends to a silver saucepan, in which it was his delight to heat potted lampreys.

That he loved too well to eat is certain; but that his sensuality shortened his life will not be hastily concluded when it is remembered that a conformation so irregular lasted six and fifty years, notwithstanding such pertinacious diligence of study and meditation.

In all his intercourse with mankind he had great delight in artifice, and endeavored to attain all his purposes by indirect and unsuspected methods. " He hardly drank tea without a stratagem."[6] If at the house of his friends he wanted any accommodation he was not willing to ask for it in plain terms, but would mention it remotely as something convenient; though, when it was procured, he soon made it appear for whose sake it had been recommended. Thus he teased Lord Orrery till he obtained a screen. He practiced his arts on such small occasions that Lady Bolingbroke used to say, in a French phrase, that " he played the politician about cabbages and turnips." His unjustifiable impression of *The Patriot King*,[7] as it can be imputed to no particular motive, must have proceeded from his general habit of secrecy and cunning: he caught an opportunity

of a sly trick, and pleased himself with the thought of outwitting Bolingbroke.

In familiar or convivial conversation it does not appear that he excelled. He may be said to have resembled Dryden, as being not one that was distinguished by vivacity in company. It is remarkable that, so near his time, so much should be known of what he has written, and so little of what he has said; traditional memory retains no sallies of raillery nor sentences of observation, nothing either pointed or solid, either wise or merry. One apothegm only stands upon record. When an objection raised against his inscription for Shakespeare was defended by the authority of Patrick,[8] he replied — *horresco referens* — that " he would allow the publisher of a dictionary to know the meaning of a single word, but not of two words put together."

He was fretful and easily displeased, and allowed himself to be capriciously resentful. He would sometimes leave Lord Oxford silently, no one could tell why, and was to be courted back by more letters and messages than the footmen were willing to carry. The table was indeed infested by Lady Mary Wortley,[9] who was the friend of Lady Oxford and who, knowing his peevishness, could by no entreaties be restrained from contradicting him, till their disputes were sharpened to such asperity that one or the other quitted the house.

He sometimes condescended to be jocular with servants or inferiors, but by no merriment, either of others or his own, was he ever seen excited to laughter.

Of his domestic character frugality was a part eminently remarkable. Having determined not to be dependent he determined not to be in want, and therefore wisely and magnanimously rejected all temptations to expense unsuitable to his fortune. This general care must be universally approved, but it sometimes appeared in petty artifices of parsimony, such as the practice of writing his compositions on the back of letters, as may be seen in the remaining copy of the *Iliad,* by which perhaps in five years five shillings were saved; or in a niggardly reception of his friends and scantiness of entertainment, as when he had two guests in his house he would set at supper a single pint upon the table and, having himself taken two small

5. Juvenal: *Satires*, X.163–66. Hannibal committed suicide, when a suppliant at the court of Bithynia, by taking poison which had been contained in a ring (183 B.C.)   6. " He . . . stratagem ": Edward Young, *Satires*, VI.188.   7. His . . . *King:* Johnson described the incident earlier in his essay: Pope, intrusted with Lord Bolingbroke's MS for the purpose of getting a few copies of it printed, secretly ordered an edition of 1500 copies. These remained unknown to their author until after Pope's death. They were then delivered to him by the printer and promptly burned with indignation for Pope's perfidy.

8. Patrick: Samuel Patrick was responsible for a Latin dictionary. Johnson " shudders " with mock horror " to bring up the anecdote," being himself a maker of a dictionary. The phrase is in *Aeneid,* II.204.   9. Wortley: Lady Mary Wortley Montagu (d. 1762) was a brilliant letter writer and amateur poet with whom Pope, after a close attachment, had fallen out. See p. 818, above.

glasses would retire and say, "Gentlemen, I leave you to your wine." Yet he tells his friends that "he has a heart for all, a house for all, and, whatever they may think, a fortune for all." [10]

He sometimes, however, made a splendid dinner, and is said to have wanted no part of the skill or elegance which such performances require. That this magnificence should be often displayed, that obstinate prudence with which he conducted his affairs would not permit; for his revenue, certain and casual, amounted only to about eight hundred pounds a year, of which, however, he declares himself able to assign one hundred to charity.

Of this fortune, which, as it arose from public approbation, was very honorably obtained, his imagination seems to have been too full; it would be hard to find a man so well entitled to notice by his wit, that ever delighted so much in talking of his money. In his Letters and in his Poems, his garden and his grotto, his quincunx and his vines, or some hints of his opulence, are always to be found. The great topic of his ridicule is poverty: the crimes with which he reproaches his antagonists are their debts, their habitation in the Mint,[11] and their want of a dinner. He seems to be of an opinion, not very uncommon in the world, that to want money is to want everything.

Next to the pleasure of contemplating his possessions seems to be that of enumerating the men of high rank with whom he was acquainted, and whose notice he loudly proclaims not to have been obtained by any practices of meanness or servility, a boast which was never denied to be true, and to which very few poets have ever aspired. Pope never set genius to sale: he never flattered those whom he did not love, or praised those whom he did not esteem. Savage, however, remarked that he began a little to relax his dignity when he wrote a distich for "his Highness's dog." [12]

His admiration of the great seems to have increased in the advance of life. He passed over peers and statesmen to inscribe his *Iliad* to Congreve, with a magnanimity of which the praise had been complete, had his friend's virtue been equal to his wit. Why he was chosen for so great an honor it is not now possible to know; there is no trace in literary history of any particular intimacy between them. The name of Congreve appears in the Letters among those of his other friends, but without any observable distinction or consequence.

To his latter works, however, he took care to annex names dignified with titles, but was not very happy in his choice, for, except Lord Bathurst, none of his noble friends were such as that a good man would wish to have his intimacy with them known to posterity; he can derive little honor from the notice of Cobham, Burlington, or Bolingbroke.

Of his social qualities, if an estimate be made from his Letters, an opinion too favorable cannot easily be formed; they exhibit a perpetual and unclouded effulgence of general benevolence and particular fondness. There is nothing but liberality, gratitude, constancy, and tenderness. It has been so long said as to be commonly believed that the true characters of men may be found in their letters, and that he who writes to his friend lays his heart open before him.[13] But the truth is that such were the simple friendships of the Golden Age, and are now the friendships only of children. Very few can boast of hearts which they dare lay open to themselves and of which, by whatever accident exposed, they do not shun a distinct and continued view; and certainly what we hide from ourselves we do not show to our friends. There is, indeed, no transaction which offers stronger temptations to fallacy and sophistication than epistolary intercourse. In the eagerness of conversation the first emotions of the mind often burst out before they are considered; in the tumult of business interest and passion have their genuine effect; but a friendly letter is a calm and deliberate performance in the cool of leisure, in the stillness of solitude, and surely no man sits down to depreciate by design his own character.

Friendship has no tendency to secure veracity, for by whom can a man so much wish to be thought better than he is as by him whose kindness he desires to gain or keep? Even in writing to the world there is less constraint: the author is not confronted with his reader, and takes his chance of approbation among the different dispositions of mankind; but a letter is addressed to a single mind of which the prejudices and partialities are known, and must therefore please, if not by favoring them, by forbearing to oppose them.

To charge those favorable representations which

---

10. "he . . . all": Pope to Swift, March 23, 1736/37.   11. Mint: a part of London infested by fugitives from the law, and the refuge of debtors in hiding.   12. "his . . . dog": Richard Savage, Johnson's friend and a poet himself, died in 1743. Johnson wrote and published his life in 1744; the account was afterwards included among the *Lives of the Poets*. Pope's verses on his Highness's dog at Kew are in all editions of his work.

13. It . . . him: See above, Johnson's letter to Mrs. Thrale, Oct. 27, 1777.

men give of their own minds, with the guilt of hypocritical falsehood, would show more severity than knowledge. The writer commonly believes himself. Almost every man's thoughts, while they are general, are right; and most hearts are pure while temptation is away. It is easy to awaken generous sentiments in privacy, to despise death when there is no danger, to glow with benevolence when there is nothing to be given. While such ideas are formed they are felt, and self-love does not suspect the gleam of virtue to be the meteor of fancy.

If the letters of Pope are considered merely as compositions, they seem to be premeditated and artificial. It is one thing to write because there is something which the mind wishes to discharge, and another to solicit the imagination because ceremony or vanity requires something to be written. Pope confesses his early letters to be vitiated with "affectation and ambition"; [14] to know whether he disentangled himself from these perverters of epistolary integrity his book and his life must be set in comparison.

One of his favorite topics is contempt of his own poetry. For this, if it had been real, he would deserve no commendation, and in this he was certainly not sincere; for his high value of himself was sufficiently observed, and of what could he be proud but of his poetry? He writes, he says, when "he has just nothing else to do," [15] yet Swift complains that he was never at leisure for conversation because he "had always some poetical scheme in his head." It was punctually required that his writing box should be set upon his bed before he rose; and Lord Oxford's domestic related that, in the dreadful winter of '40, she was called from her bed by him four times in one night to supply him with paper, lest he should lose a thought.

He pretends insensibility to censure and criticism, though it was observed by all who knew him that every pamphlet disturbed his quiet, and that his extreme irritability laid him open to perpetual vexation; but he wished to despise his critics, and therefore hoped that he did despise them.

As he happened to live in two reigns when the court paid little attention to poetry he nursed in his mind a foolish disesteem of kings, and proclaims that "he never sees courts." [16] Yet a little

regard shown him by the Prince of Wales melted his obduracy, and he had not much to say when he was asked by his Royal Highness "how he could love a prince while he disliked kings." [17]

He very frequently professes contempt of the world, and represents himself as looking on mankind, sometimes with gay indifference, as on emmets [18] of a hillock below his serious attention, and sometimes with gloomy indignation, as on monsters more worthy of hatred than of pity. These were dispositions apparently counterfeited. How could he despise those whom he lived by pleasing, and on whose approbation his esteem of himself was superstructed? Why should he hate those to whose favor he owed his honor and his ease? Of things that terminate in human life the world is the proper judge: to despise its sentence, if it were possible, is not just; and if it were just is not possible. Pope was far enough from this unreasonable temper; he was sufficiently "a fool to Fame," [19] and his fault was that he pretended to neglect it. His levity and his sullenness were only in his letters; he passed through common life, sometimes vexed and sometimes pleased, with the natural emotions of common men.

His scorn of the great is repeated too often to be real; no man thinks much of that which he despises; and as falsehood is always in danger of inconsistency, he makes it his boast at another time that he lives among them.

It is evident that his own importance swells often in his mind. He is afraid of writing lest the clerks of the post office should know his secrets; he has many enemies; he considers himself as surrounded by universal jealousy; "after many deaths, and many dispersions, two or three of us," says he, "may still be brought together, not to plot, but to divert ourselves, and the world, too, if it pleases"; and they can live together, and "show what friends wits may be, in spite of all the fools in the world." [20] All this while it was likely that the clerks did not know his hand; he certainly had no more enemies than a public character like his inevitably excites, and with what degree of friendship the wits might live very few were so much fools as ever to inquire.

Some part of this pretended discontent he learned from Swift, and expresses it, I think, most

---

14. "affectation ... ambition": Pope's Preface to his Letters (1737).   15. "he ... do": Swift, *Works* (ed. 1883), XVIII.138.   16. "he ... courts": Pope to Swift: Pope's *Works* (ed. Elwin and Courthope), VII.111, Jan., 1727/28.

17. "how ... kings": O. Ruffhead, *Life of Pope* (1769), p. 535.   18. emmets: ants.   19. "a ... Fame": Pope, *Epistle to Dr. Arbuthnot*, l. 127, p. 820, above.   20. "after ... world": Pope to Swift, letters of Sept. 14, 1725, and March 23, 1736/37.

frequently in his correspondence with him. Swift's resentment was unreasonable, but it was sincere; Pope's was the mere mimicry of his friend, a fictitious part which he began to play before it became him. When he was only twenty-five years old he related that "a glut of study and retirement had thrown him on the world," and that there was danger lest "a glut of the world should throw him back upon study and retirement." [21] To this Swift answered with great propriety that Pope had not yet either acted or suffered enough in the world to have become weary of it. And, indeed, it must be some very powerful reason that can drive back to solitude him who has once enjoyed the pleasures of society.

In the letters both of Swift and Pope there appears such narrowness of mind as makes them insensible of any excellence that has not some affinity with their own, and confines their esteem and approbation to so small a number, that whoever should form his opinion of the age from their representation would suppose them to have lived amidst ignorance and barbarity, unable to find among their contemporaries either virtue or intelligence, and persecuted by those that could not understand them.

When Pope murmurs at the world, when he professes contempt of fame, when he speaks of riches and poverty, of success and disappointment, with negligent indifference, he certainly does not express his habitual and settled sentiments, but either willfully disguises his own character or, what is more likely, invests himself with temporary qualities, and sallies out in the colors of the present moment. His hopes and fears, his joys and sorrows, acted strongly upon his mind, and if he differed from others it was not by carelessness. He was irritable and resentful; his malignity to Philips,[22] whom he had first made ridiculous, and then hated for being angry, continued too long. Of his vain desire to make Bentley contemptible, I never heard any adequate reason. He was sometimes wanton in his attacks, and before Chandos, Lady Wortley, and Hill,[23] was mean in his retreat.

The virtues which seem to have had most of his affection were liberality and fidelity of friendship, in which it does not appear that he was other than he describes himself. His fortune did not suffer his charity to be splendid and conspicuous, but he assisted Dodsley [24] with a hundred pounds that he might open a shop; and of the subscription of forty pounds a year that he raised for Savage twenty were paid by himself. He was accused of loving money, but his love was eagerness to gain, not solicitude to keep it.

In the duties of friendship he was zealous and constant; his early maturity of mind commonly united him with men older than himself, and therefore, without attaining any considerable length of life, he saw many companions of his youth sink into the grave; but it does not appear that he lost a single friend by coldness or by injury: those who loved him once continued their kindness. His ungrateful mention of Allen [25] in his will was the effect of his adherence to one whom he had known much longer, and whom he naturally loved with greater fondness. His violation of the trust reposed in him by Bolingbroke [26] could have no motive inconsistent with the warmest affection; he either thought the action so near to indifference that he forgot it, or so laudable that he expected his friend to approve it.

It was reported, with such confidence as almost to enforce belief, that in the papers entrusted to his executors was found a defamatory *Life of Swift*, which he had prepared as an instrument of vengeance to be used, if any provocation should be ever given. About this I inquired of the Earl of Marchmont, who assured me that no such piece was among his remains.

The religion in which he lived and died was that of the Church of Rome, to which in his correspondence with Racine [27] he professes himself a sincere adherent. That he was not scrupulously pious in some part of his life is known by many idle and indecent applications of sentences taken from the Scriptures, a mode of merriment which a good man dreads for its profaneness, and a witty

---

21. 'a ... retirement": *Works* (ed. Elwin and Courthope), VII.37, Aug., 1723.   22. **Philips:** Ambrose Philips (d. 1749), belittled by Pope for his *Pastorals* (1710).   23. **Chandos ... Hill:** Pope is thought to have satirized the Duke of Chandos under the name of "Timon" in Epistle IV of *Moral Essays*, Lady Mary as "Sappho" in Epistle II, Aaron Hill as one of the divers in the Fleet Ditch contest (*Dunciad*, II.295). With these Pope tried to insinuate that he was unintentionally guilty of offense.

24. **Dodsley:** Robert Dodsley (1703–64), bookseller, publisher, poet, playwright, and editor.   25. **Allen:** Ralph Allen (1694–1764), a generous friend to needy authors and deserving causes; built Prior Park, near Bath, and made it a seat of hospitality. Pope became estranged from him, and in his will left Allen a sum represented to be the total amount of the benefits he had received. Johnson tells that it was £150, and adds that Allen gave it to the Bath Hospital, saying that Pope was always a bad accountant, and that ten times the sum would have been nearer the truth.   26. **Bolingbroke:** See n. 7, above.   27. **Racine:** i.e., Louis, son of the great dramatist J. B. Racine. He attacked Pope as impious, in *La Religion* (1742).

man disdains for its easiness and vulgarity. But to whatever levities he has been betrayed, it does not appear that his principles were ever corrupted, or that he ever lost his belief of revelation. The positions which he transmitted from Bolingbroke he seems not to have understood, and was pleased with an interpretation that made them orthodox.

A man of such exalted superiority and so little moderation would naturally have all his delinquencies observed and aggravated; those who could not deny that he was excellent would rejoice to find that he was not perfect.

Perhaps it may be imputed to the unwillingness with which the same man is allowed to possess many advantages that his learning has been depreciated. He certainly was in his early life a man of great literary curiosity, and when he wrote his *Essay on Criticism* had for his age a very wide acquaintance with books. When he entered into the living world it seems to have happened to him as to many others that he was less attentive to dead masters; he studied in the academy of Paracelsus,[28] and made the universe his favorite volume. He gathered his notions fresh from reality, not from the copies of authors, but the originals of nature. Yet there is no reason to believe that literature ever lost his esteem; he always professed to love reading, and Dobson,[29] who spent some time at his house translating his *Essay on Man,* when I asked him what learning he found him to possess, answered, "More than I expected." His frequent references to history, his allusions to various kinds of knowledge, and his images selected from art and nature, with his observations on the operations of the mind and the modes of life, show an intelligence perpetually on the wing, excursive, vigorous, and diligent, eager to pursue knowledge and attentive to retain it.

From this curiosity arose the desire of traveling, to which he alludes in his verses to Jervas,[30] and which, though he never found an opportunity to gratify it, did not leave him till his life declined.

Of his intellectual character the constituent and fundamental principle was good sense, a prompt and intuitive perception of consonance and propriety. He saw immediately, of his own conceptions, what was to be chosen and what to be rejected; and, in the works of others, what was to be shunned and what was to be copied.

But good sense alone is a sedate and quiescent quality, which manages its possessions well but does not increase them; it collects few materials for its own operations, and preserves safety but never gains supremacy. Pope had likewise genius; a mind active, ambitious, and adventurous, always investigating, always aspiring; in its widest searches still longing to go forward, in its highest flights still wishing to be higher; always imagining something greater than it knows, always endeavoring more than it can do.

To assist these powers he is said to have had great strength and exactness of memory. That which he had heard or read was not easily lost; and he had before him not only what his own meditation suggested, but what he had found in other writers that might be accommodated to his present purpose.

These benefits of nature he improved by incessant and unwearied diligence; he had recourse to every source of intelligence, and lost no opportunity of information; he consulted the living as well as the dead; he read his compositions to his friends, and was never content with mediocrity when excellence could be attained. He considered poetry as the business of his life, and, however he might seem to lament his occupation, he followed it with constancy; to make verses was his first labor, and to mend them was his last.

From his attention to poetry he was never diverted. If conversation offered anything that could be improved he committed it to paper; if a thought, or perhaps an expression more happy than was common, rose to his mind, he was careful to write it; an independent distich was preserved for an opportunity of insertion, and some little fragments have been found containing lines, or parts of lines, to be wrought upon at some other time.

He was one of those few whose labor is their pleasure; he was never elevated to negligence, nor wearied to impatience; he never passed a fault unamended by indifference, nor quitted it by despair. He labored his works first to gain reputation, and afterwards to keep it.

Of composition there are different methods. Some employ at once memory and invention and, with little intermediate use of the pen, form and polish large masses by continued meditation, and write their productions only when, in their own

---

28. Paracelsus (1493–1541) wandered about the world, a learned adventurer, regarded with suspicion by established scholars. His academy was nowhere.   29. **Dobson:** William Dobson practiced the vanishing art of translation into Latin poetry; Prior's *Solomon* was so embalmed by him.   30. **Jervas:** Charles Jervas published a translation of *Don Quixote* in 1742.

opinion, they have completed them. It is related of Virgil that his custom was to pour out a great number of verses in the morning, and pass the day in retrenching exuberances and correcting inaccuracies. The method of Pope, as may be collected from his translation, was to write his first thoughts in his first words, and gradually to amplify, decorate, rectify, and refine them.

With such faculties and such dispositions he excelled every other writer in *poetical prudence;* he wrote in such a manner as might expose him to few hazards. He used almost always the same fabric of verse; and, indeed, by those few essays which he made of any other, he did not enlarge his reputation. Of this uniformity the certain consequence was readiness and dexterity. By perpetual practice language had in his mind a systematical arrangement; having always the same use for words, he had words so selected and combined as to be ready at his call. This increase of facility he confessed himself to have perceived in the progress of his translation.

But what was yet of more importance, his effusions were always voluntary, and his subjects chosen by himself. His independence secured him from drudging at a task, and laboring upon a barren topic; he never exchanged praise for money, nor opened a shop of condolence or congratulation. His poems, therefore, were scarce ever temporary. He suffered coronations and royal marriages to pass without a song, and derived no opportunities from recent events, nor any popularity from the accidental disposition of his readers. He was never reduced to the necessity of soliciting the sun to shine upon a birthday, of calling the Graces and Virtues to a wedding, or of saying what multitudes have said before him. When he could produce nothing new, he was at liberty to be silent.

His publications were for the same reason never hasty. He is said to have sent nothing to the press till it had lain two years under his inspection; it is at least certain that he ventured nothing without nice examination. He suffered the tumult of imagination to subside, and the novelties of invention to grow familiar. He knew that the mind is always enamored of its own productions, and did not trust his first fondness. He consulted his friends, and listened with great willingness to criticism; and, what was of more importance, he consulted himself, and let nothing pass against his own judgment.

He professed to have learned his poetry from Dryden, whom, whenever an opportunity was presented, he praised through his whole life with unvaried liberality; and perhaps his character may receive some illustration if he be compared with his master.

Integrity of understanding and nicety of discernment were not allotted in a less proportion to Dryden than to Pope. The rectitude of Dryden's mind was sufficiently shown by the dismission of his poetical prejudices, and the rejection of unnatural thoughts and rugged numbers. But Dryden never desired to apply all the judgment that he had. He wrote, and professed to write, merely for the people; and when he pleased others, he contented himself. He spent no time in struggles to rouse latent powers; he never attempted to make that better which was already good, nor often to mend what he must have known to be faulty. He wrote, as he tells us, with very little consideration; when occasion or necessity called upon him, he poured out what the present moment happened to supply, and, when once it had passed the press, ejected it from his mind; for when he had no pecuniary interest, he had no further solicitude.

Pope was not content to satisfy; he desired to excel, and therefore always endeavored to do his best; he did not court the candor, but dared the judgment, of his reader and, expecting no indulgence from others, he showed none to himself. He examined lines and words with minute and punctilious observation, and retouched every part with indefatigable diligence, till he had left nothing to be forgiven.

For this reason he kept his pieces very long in his hands, while he considered and reconsidered them. The only poems which can be supposed to have been written with such regard to the times as might hasten their publication were the two satires of "Thirty-Eight," of which Dodsley told me that they were brought to him by the author, that they might be fairly copied. "Almost every line," he said, "was then written twice over; I gave him a clean transcript, which he sent sometime afterwards to me for the press, with almost every line written twice over a second time."

His declaration that his care for his works ceased at their publication was not strictly true. His parental attention never abandoned them; what he found amiss in the first edition, he silently corrected in those that followed. He appears to have revised the *Iliad,* and freed it from some of its imperfections; and the *Essay on Criticism* received many improvements after its first appearance. It will seldom be found that he altered without adding clearness, elegance, or vigor. Pope had perhaps the judgment of Dryden; but Dryden certainly wanted the diligence of Pope.

In acquired knowledge the superiority must be allowed to Dryden, whose education was more scholastic, and who before he became an author had been allowed more time for study, with better means of information. His mind has a larger range, and he collects his images and illustrations from a more extensive circumference of science. Dryden knew more of man in his general nature, and Pope in his local manners. The notions of Dryden were formed by comprehensive speculation, and those of Pope by minute attention. There is more dignity in the knowledge of Dryden, and more certainty in that of Pope.

Poetry was not the sole praise of either, for both excelled likewise in prose; but Pope did not borrow his prose from his predecessor. The style of Dryden is capricious and varied, that of Pope is cautious and uniform; Dryden obeys the motions of his own mind, Pope constrains his mind to his own rules of composition. Dryden is sometimes vehement and rapid; Pope is always smooth, uniform, and gentle. Dryden's page is a natural field, rising into inequalities, and diversified by the varied exuberance of abundant vegetation; Pope's is a velvet lawn, shaven by the scythe, and leveled by the roller.

Of genius, that power which constitutes a poet, that quality without which judgment is cold and knowledge is inert, that energy which collects, combines, amplifies, and animates — the superiority must, with some hesitation, be allowed to Dryden. It is not to be inferred that of this poetical vigor Pope had only a little, because Dryden had more, for every other writer since Milton must give place to Pope; and even of Dryden it must be said that if he has brighter paragraphs, he has not better poems. Dryden's performances were always hasty, either excited by some external occasion or extorted by domestic necessity; he composed without consideration, and published without correction. What his mind could supply at call, or gather in one excursion, was all that he sought, and all that he gave. The dilatory caution of Pope enabled him to condense his sentiments, to multiply his images, and to accumulate all that study might produce or chance might supply. If the flights of Dryden therefore are higher, Pope continues longer on the

wing. If of Dryden's fire the blaze is brighter, of Pope's the heat is more regular and constant. Dryden often surpasses expectation, and Pope never falls below it. Dryden is read with frequent astonishment, and Pope with perpetual delight.

This parallel will, I hope, when it is well considered, be found just; and if the reader should suspect me, as I suspect myself, of some partial fondness for the memory of Dryden, let him not too hastily condemn me; for meditation and inquiry may, perhaps, show him the reasonableness of my determination.

The works of Pope are now to be distinctly examined, not so much with attention to slight faults or petty beauties, as to the general character and effect of each performance. . . .

The design of *Windsor Forest* is evidently derived from *Cooper's Hill*,[31] with some attention to Waller's poem on *The Park;* but Pope cannot be denied to excel his masters in variety and elegance, and the art of interchanging description, narrative, and morality. The objection made by Dennis is the want of plan, of a regular subordination of parts terminating in the principal and original design.[32] There is this want in most descriptive poems, because as the scenes, which they must exhibit successively, are all subsisting at the same time, the order in which they are shown must by necessity be arbitrary, and more is not to be expected from the last part than from the first. The attention, therefore, which cannot be detained by suspense, must be excited by diversity, such as his poem offers to its reader.

But the desire of diversity may be too much indulged; the parts of *Windsor Forest* which deserve least praise are those which were added to enliven the stillness of the scene, the appearance of Father Thames, and the transformation of Lodona. Addison had in his *Campaign* derided the "Rivers" that "rise from their oozy beds" to tell stories of heroes,[33] and it is therefore strange that Pope should adopt a fiction not only unnatural but lately censured. The story of Lodona[34] is told with sweetness, but a new metamorphosis is a ready and puerile expedient: nothing is easier than to tell how a flower was once a blooming virgin, or a rock an obdurate tyrant. . . .

31. *Cooper's Hill:* by Sir John Denham (1642).   32. The . . . design: Dennis, "Remarks on Pope's Homer," *Critical Works* (ed. Hooker), II.136.   33. stories of heroes: Addison, *The Campaign*, l. 470.   34. See *Windsor Forest*, ll. 171 ff., p. 677, above.

The "Verses on the Unfortunate Lady" have drawn much attention by the illaudable singularity of treating suicide with respect, and they must be allowed to be written in some parts with vigorous animation, and in others with gentle tenderness; nor has Pope produced any poem in which the sense predominates more over the diction. But the tale is not skillfully told: it is not easy to discover the character of either the lady or her guardian. History relates that she was about to disparage herself by a marriage with an inferior; Pope praises her for the dignity of ambition, and yet condemns the uncle to detestation for his pride; the ambitious love of a niece may be opposed by the interest, malice, or envy of an uncle, but never by his pride. On such an occasion a poet may be allowed to be obscure, but inconsistency never can be right. . . .

One of his greatest though of his earliest works is the *Essay on Criticism,* which if he had written nothing else would have placed him among the first critics and the first poets, as it exhibits every mode of excellence that can embellish or dignify didactic composition: selection of matter, novelty of arrangement, justness of precept, splendor of illustration, and propriety of digression. I know not whether it be pleasing to consider that he produced this piece at twenty, and never afterwards excelled it; he that delights himself with observing that such powers may be so soon attained cannot but grieve to think that life was ever after at a stand.

To mention the particular beauties of the *Essay* would be unprofitably tedious, but I cannot forbear to observe that the comparison of a student's progress in the sciences with the journey of a traveler in the Alps [35] is perhaps the best that English poetry can show. A simile, to be perfect, must both illustrate and ennoble the subject; must show it to the understanding in a clearer view, and display it to the fancy with greater dignity; but either of these qualities may be sufficient to recommend it. In didactic poetry, of which the great purpose is instruction, a simile may be praised which illustrates, though it does not ennoble; in heroics, that may be admitted which ennobles, though it does not illustrate. That it may be complete it is required to exhibit, independently of its references, a pleasing image; for a simile is said to be a short episode. To this antiquity was so attentive that circumstances were sometimes added which, having no parallels, served only to fill the imagination, and produced what Perrault ludicrously called "comparisons with a long tail." [36] In their similes the greatest writers have sometimes failed: the ship race, compared with the chariot race, is neither illustrated nor aggrandized; [37] land and water make all the difference; when Apollo running after Daphne is likened to a greyhound chasing a hare, [38] there is nothing gained; the ideas of pursuit and flight are too plain to be made plainer, and a god and the daughter of a god are not represented much to their advantage by a hare and dog. The simile of the Alps has no useless parts, yet affords a striking picture by itself: it makes the foregoing position better understood, and enables it to take faster hold on the attention; it assists the apprehension, and elevates the fancy.

Let me likewise dwell a little on the celebrated paragraph,[39] in which it is directed that "the sound should seem an echo to the sense," a precept which Pope is allowed to have observed beyond any other English poet.

This notion of representative meter, and the desire of discovering frequent adaptations of the sound to the sense, have produced, in my opinion, many wild conceits and imaginary beauties. All that can furnish this representation are the sounds of the words considered singly, and the time in which they are pronounced. Every language has some words framed to exhibit the noises which they express, as *thump, rattle, growl, hiss.* These, however, are but few, and the poet cannot make them more, nor can they be of any use but when sound is to be mentioned. The time of pronunciation was in the dactylic measures of the learned languages capable of considerable variety; but that variety could be accommodated only to motion or duration, and different degrees of motion were perhaps expressed by verses rapid or slow, without much attention of the writer, when the image had full possession of his fancy; but our language having little flexibility, our verses can differ very little in their cadence. The fancied resemblances, I fear, arise sometimes merely from the ambiguity of words; there is supposed to be some relation between a *soft* line and a *soft* couch, or between *hard* syllables and *hard* fortune.

Motion, however, may be in some sort exempli-

35. Alps: *Essay on Criticism*, ll. 219 ff., p. 669, above.

36. Perrault . . . tail: Charles Perrault (d. 1703), defender of the Moderns in the quarrel over their superiority or inferiority to the Ancients. Addison mentions his phrase in *Spectator*, No. 303. 37. ship . . . aggrandized: *Aeneid*, V.144–47. 38. Apollo . . . hare: Ovid, *Metamorphoses*, I.533 ff. 39. *Essay on Criti-*

fied; and yet it may be suspected that even in such resemblances the mind often governs the ear, and the sounds are estimated by their meaning. One of the most successful attempts has been to describe the labor of Sisyphus:

With many a weary step, and many a groan,
Up a high hill he heaves a huge round stone;
The huge round stone, resulting with a bound,
Thunders impetuous down, and smokes along the
    ground.⁴⁰

Who does not perceive the stone to move slowly upward, and roll violently back? But set the same numbers to another sense:

While many a merry tale, and many a song,
Cheered the rough road, we wished the rough road
    long.
The rough road then, returning in a round,
Mocked our impatient steps, for all was fairy
    ground.

We have now surely lost much of the delay, and much of the rapidity.

But to show how little the greatest master of numbers can fix the principles of representative harmony, it will be sufficient to remark that the poet, who tells us that

When Ajax strives some rock's vast weight to
    throw,
The line too labors, and the words move slow;
Not so when swift Camilla scours the plain,
Flies o'er th' unbending corn, and skims along the
    main,⁴¹

when he had enjoyed for about thirty years the praise of Camilla's lightness of foot, tried another experiment upon *sound* and *time,* and produced this memorable triplet:

Waller was smooth; but Dryden taught to join ⎫
The varying verse, the full resounding line,   ⎬
The long majestic march, and energy divine.⁴² ⎭

Here are the swiftness of the rapid race and the march of slow-paced majesty exhibited by the same poet in the same sequence of syllables, except that the exact prosodist will find the line of *swiftness* by one time longer than that of *tardiness.*

Beauties of this kind are commonly fancied, and when real are technical and nugatory, not to be rejected and not to be solicited.

To the praises which have been accumulated on *The Rape of the Lock* by readers of every class, from the critic to the waiting maid, it is difficult to make any addition. Of that which is universally allowed to be the most attractive of all ludicrous compositions, let it rather be now inquired from what sources the power of pleasing is derived.

Dr. Warburton, who excelled in critical perspicacity, has remarked that the preternatural agents are very happily adapted to the purposes of the poem.⁴³ The heathen deities can no longer gain attention: we should have turned away from a contest between Venus and Diana. The employment of allegorical persons always excites conviction of its own absurdity: they may produce effects, but cannot conduct actions; when the phantom is put in motion, it dissolves; thus Discord may raise a mutiny, but Discord cannot conduct a march nor besiege a town. Pope brought into view a new race of beings, with powers and passions proportionate to their operation. The sylphs and gnomes act at the toilet and the tea table, what more terrific and more powerful phantoms perform on the stormy ocean or the field of battle; they give their proper help, and do their proper mischief.

Pope is said by an objector not to have been the inventor of this petty nation, a charge which might with more justice have been brought against the author of the *Iliad,* who doubtless adopted the religious system of his country; for what is there but the names of his agents which Pope has not invented? Has he not assigned them characters and operations never heard of before? Has he not, at least, given them their first poetical existence? If this is not sufficient to denominate his work original, nothing original ever can be written.

In this work are exhibited in a very high degree the two most engaging powers of an author: new things are made familiar, and familiar things are made new. A race of aerial people never heard of before is presented to us in a manner so clear and easy that the reader seeks for no further information, but immediately mingles with his new acquaintance, adopts their interests, and attends their pursuits, loves a sylph and detests a gnome.

That familiar things are made new every paragraph will prove. The subject of the poem is an event below the common incidents of common life; nothing real is introduced that is not seen so

---

cism, ll. 337–83, pp. 766–67, above.   40. Pope, *Odyssey,* XI.735–38.   41. *Essay on Criticism,* ll. 370–73, p. 766, above.   42. *Imitations of Horace,* Epistles II.i.267–69.

43. poem: William Warburton (d. 1779) was Pope's authorized editor. His comment occurs in his introductory remarks, 1751.

often as to be no longer regarded, yet the whole detail of a female day is here brought before us invested with so much art of decoration that, though nothing is disguised, everything is striking, and we feel all the appetite of curiosity for that from which we have a thousand times turned fastidiously away.

The purpose of the poet is, as he tells us, to laugh at "the little unguarded follies of the female sex." It is therefore without justice that Dennis charges *The Rape of the Lock* with the want of a moral,[44] and for that reason sets it below *The Lutrin,* which exposes the pride and discord of the clergy. Perhaps neither Pope nor Boileau has made the world much better than he found it, but if they had both succeeded, it were easy to tell who would have deserved most from public gratitude. The freaks, and humors, and spleen, and vanity of women, as they embroil families in discord and fill houses with disquiet, do more to obstruct the happiness of life in a year than the ambition of the clergy in many centuries. It has been well observed that the misery of man proceeds not from any single crush of overwhelming evil, but from small vexations continually repeated.

It is remarked by Dennis likewise that the machinery is superfluous;[45] that by all the bustle of preternatural operation the main event is neither hastened nor retarded. To this charge an efficacious answer is not easily made. The sylphs cannot be said to help or to oppose, and it must be allowed to imply some want of art that their power has not been sufficiently intermingled with the action. Other parts may likewise be charged with want of connection; the game at *ombre* might be spared, but if the lady had lost her hair while she was intent upon her cards, it might have been inferred that those who are too fond of play will be in danger of neglecting more important interests. Those perhaps are faults, but what are such faults to so much excellence!

The Epistle of Eloïsa to Abelard is one of the most happy productions of human wit: the subject is so judiciously chosen that it would be difficult, in turning over the annals of the world, to find another which so many circumstances concur to recommend. We regularly interest ourselves most in the fortune of those who most deserve our no-

tice. Abelard and Eloïsa were conspicuous in their days for eminence of merit. The heart naturally loves truth. The adventures and misfortunes of this illustrious pair are known from undisputed history. Their fate does not leave the mind in hopeless dejection, for they both found quiet and consolation in retirement and piety. So new and so affecting is their story that it supersedes invention, and imagination ranges at full liberty without straggling into scenes of fable.

The story thus skillfully adopted has been diligently improved. Pope has left nothing behind him which seems more the effect of studious perseverance and laborious revisal. Here is particularly observable the "curiosa felicitas," a fruitful soil, and careful cultivation. Here is no crudeness of sense, nor asperity of language.

The sources from which sentiments which have so much vigor and efficacy have been drawn are shown to be the mystic writers by the learned author of the *Essay on the Life and Writings of Pope,*[46] a book which teaches how the brow of criticism may be smoothed, and how she may be enabled, with all her severity, to attract and to delight.

The train of my disquisition has now conducted me to that poetical wonder, the translation of the *Iliad,* a performance which no age or nation can pretend to equal. To the Greeks translation was almost unknown; it was totally unknown to the inhabitants of Greece. They had no recourse to the barbarians for poetical beauties, but sought for everything in Homer, where, indeed, there is but little which they might not find.

The Italians have been very diligent translators, but I can hear of no version, unless perhaps Anguillara's *Ovid*[47] may be excepted, which is read with eagerness. The *Iliad*[48] of Salvini every reader may discover to be punctiliously exact; but it seems to be the work of a linguist skillfully pedantic, and his countrymen, the proper judges of its power to please, reject it with disgust.

Their predecessors the Romans have left some specimens of translation behind them, and that employment must have had some credit in which Tully and Germanicus engaged; but unless we suppose, what is perhaps true, that the plays of Terence were versions of Menander,[49] nothing

---

44. **Dennis . . . moral:** Dennis, *Critical Works* (ed. Hooker), II.330–31. Boileau's *Lutrin* (i.e., *The Lectern*) was translated by Nicholas Rowe in 1708, and by others about that date. 45. **Dennis . . . superfluous:** *Critical Works,* II.328.

46. **author . . . Pope:** Joseph Warton, *An Essay on the Genius and Writings of Pope* (1756–82).   47. **Anguillara's Ovid:** This translation, in ottava rima, was published in 1584.   48. *Iliad:* The date of Salvini's *Iliad* was 1723.   49. **plays . . . Menander:** It is now generally accepted that such is the fact.

translated seems ever to have risen to high reputation. The French, in the meridian hour of their learning, were very laudably industrious to enrich their own language with the wisdom of the ancients, but found themselves reduced, by whatever necessity, to turn the Greek and Roman poetry into prose. Whoever could read an author could translate him. From such rivals little can be feared.

The chief help of Pope in this arduous undertaking was drawn from the versions of Dryden. Virgil had borrowed much of his imagery from Homer, and part of the debt was now paid by his translator. Pope searched the pages of Dryden for happy combinations of heroic diction, but it will not be denied that he added much to what he found. He cultivated our language with so much diligence and art that he has left in his *Homer* a treasure of poetical elegances to posterity. His version may be said to have tuned the English tongue, for since its appearance no writer, however deficient in other powers, has wanted melody. Such a series of lines so elaborately corrected and so sweetly modulated took possession of the public ear; the vulgar was enamored of the poem, and the learned wondered at the translation.

But in the most general applause discordant voices will always be heard. It has been objected by some, who wish to be numbered among the sons of learning, that Pope's version of Homer is not Homerical; that it exhibits no resemblance of the original and characteristic manner of the Father of Poetry, as it wants his awful simplicity, his artless grandeur, his unaffected majesty. This cannot be totally denied, but it must be remembered that *necessitas quod cogit defendit,* that may be lawfully done which cannot be forborne. Time and place will always enforce regard. In estimating this translation consideration must be had of the nature of our language, the form of our meter, and, above all, of the change which two thousand years have made in the modes of life and the habits of thought. Virgil wrote in a language of the same general fabric with that of Homer, in verses of the same measure, and in an age nearer to Homer's time by eighteen hundred years; yet he found even then the state of the world so much altered, and the demand for elegance so much increased, that mere nature would be endured no longer; and perhaps, in the multitude of borrowed passages, very few can be shown which he has not embellished.

There is a time when nations emerging from barbarity, and falling into regular subordination, gain leisure to grow wise, and feel the shame of ignorance and the craving pain of unsatisfied curiosity. To this hunger of the mind plain sense is grateful; that which fills the void removes uneasiness, and to be free from pain for a while is pleasure; but repletion generates fastidiousness, a saturated intellect soon becomes luxurious, and knowledge finds no willing reception till it is recommended by artificial diction. Thus it will be found in the progress of learning that in all nations the first writers are simple, and that every age improves in elegance. One refinement always makes way for another, and what was expedient to Virgil was necessary to Pope.

I suppose many readers of the English *Iliad,* when they have been touched with some unexpected beauty of the lighter kind, have tried to enjoy it in the original, where, alas! it was not to be found. Homer doubtless owes to his translator many Ovidian graces not exactly suitable to his character, but to have added can be no great crime if nothing be taken away. Elegance is surely to be desired if it be not gained at the expense of dignity. A hero would wish to be loved as well as to be reverenced.

To a thousand cavils one answer is sufficient; the purpose of a writer is to be read, and the criticism which would destroy the power of pleasing must be blown aside. Pope wrote for his own age and his own nation; he knew that it was necessary to color the images and point the sentiments of his author; he therefore made him graceful, but lost him some of his sublimity.

The copious notes with which the version is accompanied and by which it is recommended to many readers, though they were undoubtedly written to swell the volumes, ought not to pass without praise: commentaries which attract the reader by the pleasure of perusal have not often appeared; the notes of others are read to clear difficulties, those of Pope to vary entertainment.

It has, however, been objected with sufficient reason that there is in the commentary too much of unseasonable levity and affected gaiety; that too many appeals are made to the ladies, and the ease which is so carefully preserved is sometimes the ease of a trifler. Every art has its terms and every kind of instruction its proper style; the gravity of common critics may be tedious, but is less despicable than childish merriment.

Of the *Odyssey* nothing remains to be observed;

the same general praise may be given to both translations, and a particular examination of either would require a large volume. The notes were written by Broome, who endeavored not unsuccessfully to imitate his master.

Of the *Dunciad* the hint is confessedly taken from Dryden's "Mac Flecknoe," but the plan is so enlarged and diversified as justly to claim the praise of an original, and affords perhaps the best specimen that has yet appeared of personal satire ludicrously pompous.

That the design was moral, whatever the author might tell either his readers or himself, I am not convinced. The first motive was the desire of revenging the contempt with which Theobald [50] had treated his *Shakespeare,* and regaining the honor which he had lost, by crushing his opponent. Theobald was not of bulk enough to fill a poem, and therefore it was necessary to find other enemies with other names, at whose expense he might divert the public.

In this design there was petulance and malignity enough, but I cannot think it very criminal. An author places himself uncalled before the tribunal of criticism, and solicits fame at the hazard of disgrace. Dullness or deformity are not culpable in themselves, but may be very justly reproached when they pretend to the honor of wit or the influence of beauty. If bad writers were to pass without reprehension, what should restrain them? *impune diem consumpserit ingens Telephus;* [51] and upon bad writers only will censure have much effect. The satire which brought Theobald and Moore [52] into contempt dropped impotent from Bentley, like the javelin of Priam. [53]

All truth is valuable, and satirical criticism may be considered as useful when it rectifies error and improves judgment: he that refines the public taste is a public benefactor.

The beauties of this poem are well known; its chief fault is the grossness of its images. Pope and Swift had an unnatural delight in ideas physically impure, such as every other tongue utters with unwillingness, and of which every ear shrinks from the mention.

But even this fault, offensive as it is, may be forgiven for the excellence of other passages, such as the formation and dissolution of Moore, the account of the Traveler, [54] the misfortune of the Florist, [55] and the crowded thoughts and stately numbers which dignify the concluding paragraph.

The alterations which have been made in the *Dunciad,* not always for the better, require that it should be published, as in the last collection, with all its variations.

The *Essay on Man* was a work of great labor and long consideration, but certainly not the happiest of Pope's performances. The subject is perhaps not very proper for poetry, and the poet was not sufficiently master of his subject; metaphysical morality was to him a new study; he was proud of his acquisitions and, supposing himself master of great secrets, was in haste to teach what he had not learned. Thus he tells us, in the first Epistle, that from the nature of the Supreme Being may be deduced an order of beings such as mankind, because Infinite Excellence can do only what is best. He finds out that these beings must be "somewhere," and that "all the question is whether man be in a wrong place." Surely if, according to the poet's Leibnitian reasoning, [56] we may infer that man ought to be only because he is, we may allow that his place is the right place, because he has it. Supreme Wisdom is not less infallible in disposing than in creating. But what is meant by "somewhere" and "place" and "wrong place" it had been vain to ask Pope, who probably had never asked himself.

Having exalted himself into the chair of wisdom he tells us much that every man knows, and much that he does not know himself; that we see but little, and that the order of the universe is beyond our comprehension, an opinion not very uncommon; and that there is a chain of subordinate beings "from infinite to nothing," of which himself and his readers are equally ignorant. But he gives us one comfort which, without his help, he supposes unattainable, in the position "that though we are fools, yet God is wise."

This *Essay* affords an egregious instance of the predominance of genius, the dazzling splendor of imagery, and the seductive powers of eloquence. Never were penury of knowledge and vulgarity

---

50. Theobald: Lewis Theobald (pronounced Tibbald) attacked Pope's edition in *Shakespeare Restored, or, a Specimen of the Many Errors as Well Committed, as Unamended, by Mr. Pope, in His Late Edition of This Poet* (1726). See *Dunciad* headnote, p. 832, above.   **51. impune . . . Telephus:** "Shall a vast *Telephus* take up the whole day without punishment?" Juvenal, *Satires,* I.5.   **52. Moore:** James Moore Smythe, or "More," is ridiculed in *Dunciad,* II.35–46.   **53. javelin of Priam:** *Aeneid,* II.544. Priam's spear, hurled by the old man with feeble force, recoiled from his enemy Pyrrhus without doing any harm.

54. Traveler: *Dunciad,* IV.293–336, pp. 837–38, above.   **55. Florist:** *Dunciad,* IV.403–36, pp. 838–39, above.   **56. Leibnitian reasoning:** i.e., patterned after the thinking of Leibnitz (1646–1716), who argued a harmonious system in which spirit and matter were reconciled by God's supreme intention.

of sentiment so happily disguised. The reader feels his mind full, though he learns nothing; and when he meets it in its new array no longer knows the talk of his mother and his nurse. When these wonder-working sounds sink into sense and the doctrine of the *Essay,* disrobed of its ornaments, is left to the powers of its naked excellence, what shall we discover? That we are, in comparison with our Creator, very weak and ignorant; that we do not uphold the chain of existence; and that we could not make one another with more skill than we are made. We may learn yet more: that the arts of human life were copied from the instinctive operations of other animals; that if the world be made for man, it may be said that man was made for geese. To these profound principles of natural knowledge are added some moral instructions equally new: that self-interest well understood will produce social concord; that men are mutual gainers by mutual benefits; that evil is sometimes balanced by good; that human advantages are unstable and fallacious, of uncertain duration and doubtful effect; that our true honor is not to have a great part, but to act it well; that virtue only is our own; and that happiness is always in our power.

Surely a man of no very comprehensive search may venture to say that he has heard all this before, but it was never till now recommended by such a blaze of embellishment or such sweetness of melody. The vigorous contraction of some thoughts, the luxuriant amplification of others, the incidental illustrations, and sometimes the dignity, sometimes the softness of the verses, enchain philosophy, suspend criticism, and oppress judgment by overpowering pleasure.

This is true of many paragraphs; yet if I had undertaken to exemplify Pope's felicity of composition before a rigid critic I should not select the *Essay on Man,* for it contains more lines unsuccessfully labored, more harshness of diction, more thoughts imperfectly expressed, more levity without elegance, and more heaviness without strength, than will easily be found in all his other works.

The "Characters of Men and Women" are the product of diligent speculation upon human life; much labor has been bestowed upon them, and Pope very seldom labored in vain. That his excellence may be properly estimated I recommend a comparison of his "Characters of Women" with Boileau's *Satire;* it will then be seen with how much more perspicacity female nature is investi-

gated and female excellence selected; and he surely is no mean writer to whom Boileau shall be found inferior. The "Characters of Men," however, are written with more, if not with deeper, thought, and exhibit many passages exquisitely beautiful. "The Gem and the Flower" will not easily be equaled.[57] In the women's part are some defects: the character of Atossa is not so neatly finished as that of Clodio,[58] and some of the female characters may be found perhaps more frequently among men; what is said of Philomede[59] was true of Prior.

In the *Epistles to Lord Bathurst* and *Lord Burlington* Dr. Warburton has endeavored to find a train of thought which was never in the writer's head and, to support his hypothesis, has printed that first which was published last. In one the most valuable passage is perhaps the elogy on good sense,[60] and the other the end of the Duke of Buckingham.[61]

The *Epistle to Arbuthnot,* now arbitrarily called the *Prologue to the Satires,* is a performance consisting, as it seems, of many fragments wrought into one design, which by this union of scattered beauties contains more striking paragraphs than could probably have been brought together into an occasional work. As there is no stronger motive to exertion than self-defense, no part has more elegance, spirit, or dignity than the poet's vindication of his own character.[62] The meanest passage is the satire upon Sporus.[63] . . .

The *Imitations of Horace* seem to have been written as relaxations of his genius. This employment became his favorite by its facility; the plan was ready to his hand, and nothing was required but to accommodate as he could the sentiments of an old author to recent facts or familiar images; but what is easy is seldom excellent: such imitations cannot give pleasure to common readers. The man of learning may be sometimes surprised and delighted by an unexpected parallel, but the comparison requires knowledge of the original, which will likewise often detect strained applications. Between Roman images and English manners there will be an irreconcilable dissimilitude, and the work will be generally uncouth and parti-colored;

---

57. Gem . . . equaled: *Moral Essays,* I.141–48.   58. Atossa, Clodio: *Dunciad,* II.115 ff. and I.179 ff. (Wharton later substituted for "Clodio").   59. Philomede: *Dunciad,* II.83 ff.   60. elogy . . . sense: *Dunciad,* IV.39 ff., p. 834, above.   61. Buckingham: *Dunciad,* III.299 ff.   62. character: *Epistle to Dr. Arbuthnot,* ll. 334 ff., p. 822, above.   63. Sporus: *Epistle to Dr. Arbuthnot,* ll. 305 ff., p. 822, above.

neither original nor translated, neither ancient nor modern.

Pope had, in proportions very nicely adjusted to each other, all the qualities that constitute genius. He had invention, by which new trains of events are formed and new scenes of imagery displayed, as in *The Rape of the Lock,* and by which extrinsic and adventitious embellishments and illustrations are connected with a known subject, as in the *Essay on Criticism;* he had imagination, which strongly impresses on the writer's mind and enables him to convey to the reader the various forms of nature, incidents of life, and energies of passion, as in his *Eloïsa, Windsor Forest,* and the *Ethic Epistles;* he had judgment, which selects from life or nature what the present purpose requires and, by separating the essence of things from its concomitants, often makes the representation more powerful than the reality; and he had colors of language always before him ready to decorate his matter with every grace of elegant expression, as when he accommodates his diction to the wonderful multiplicity of Homer's sentiments and descriptions.

Poetical expression includes sound as well as meaning. "Music," says Dryden, "is inarticulate poetry";[64] among the excellences of Pope, therefore, must be mentioned the melody of his meter. By perusing the works of Dryden he discovered the most perfect fabric of English verse, and habituated himself to that only which he found the best; in consequence of which restraint his poetry has been censured as too uniformly musical, and as glutting the ear with unvaried sweetness. I suspect this objection to be the cant of those who judge by principles rather than perception; and who would even themselves have less pleasure in his works if he had tried to relieve attention by studied discords, or affected to break his lines and vary his pauses.

But though he was thus careful of his versification he did not oppress his powers with superfluous rigor. He seems to have thought with Boileau that the practice of writing might be refined till the difficulty should overbalance the advantage. The construction of his language is not always strictly grammatical; with those rhymes which prescription had conjoined he contented himself, without regard to Swift's remonstrances,[65] though there was no striking consonance; nor was he very careful to vary his terminations or to refuse admission at a small distance to the same rhymes.

To Swift's edict for the exclusion of alexandrines and triplets he paid little regard; he admitted them, but, in the opinion of Fenton,[66] too rarely: he uses them more liberally in his translation than his poems.

He has a few double rhymes, and always, I think, unsuccessfully, except once in *The Rape of the Lock.*

Expletives he very early ejected from his verses; but he now and then admits an epithet rather commodious than important. Each of the six first lines of the *Iliad* might lose two syllables with very little diminution of the meaning; and sometimes, after all his art and labor, one verse seems to be made for the sake of another. In his latter productions the diction is sometimes vitiated by French idioms, with which Bolingbroke had perhaps infected him.

I have been told that the couplet by which he declared his own ear to be most gratified was this:

Lo, where Maeotis sleeps, and hardly flows
The freezing Tanais thro' a waste of snows.[67]

But the reason of this preference I cannot discover.

It is remarked by Watts[68] that there is scarcely a happy combination of words or a phrase poetically elegant in the English language which Pope has not inserted into his version of Homer. How he obtained possession of so many beauties of speech it were desirable to know. That he gleaned from authors, obscure as well as eminent, what he thought brilliant or useful, and preserved it all in a regular collection, is not unlikely. When, in his last years, Hall's *Satires*[69] were shown him, he wished that he had seen them sooner.

New sentiments and new images others may produce, but to attempt any further improvement of versification will be dangerous. Art and diligence have now done their best, and what shall be added will be the effort of tedious toil and needless curiosity.

After all this it is surely superfluous to answer the question that has once been asked, whether Pope was a poet? otherwise than by asking in return, if Pope be not a poet, where is poetry to be found? To circumscribe poetry by a definition will only show the narrowness of the definer, though a

---

64. "Music . . . poetry": Preface to *Tyrannick Love* (1670). 65. remonstrances: Swift to Pope, June 28, 1715. See Boileau, *L'Art Poétique,* I.64–68.

66. Fenton: Elijah Fenton was one of Pope's assistants in the translation of Homer.   67. *Dunciad,* III.87–88.   68. Watts: Isaac Watts, *The Improvement of the Mind* (1741), I.xx.36. "Few books," Johnson wrote in his *Life of Watts,* "have been perused by me with greater pleasure."   69. Hall's *Satires:* Joseph Hall, *Virgidemiarum* (1597–98). Hall's six books of satires treat of contemporary abuses and persons, with Juvenalian invective, and thus would have provided Pope with analogies.

definition which shall exclude Pope will not easily be made. Let us look round upon the present time, and back upon the past; let us inquire to whom the voice of mankind has decreed the wreath of poetry; let their productions be examined and their claims stated, and the pretensions of Pope will be no more disputed. Had he given the world only his version the name of poet must have been allowed him; if the writer of the *Iliad* were to class his successors he would assign a very high place to his translator, without requiring any other evidence of genius.

THOUGHTS DURING AND AFTER THE WRITING OF *THE LIVES OF THE POETS*

March 30, 1777. Easter Day, 1ma mane [earliest morning]

The day is now come again, in which by a custom which since the death of my wife I have by the divine assistance always observed, I am to renew the great covenant with my Maker and my Judge. I humbly hope to perform it better. I hope for more efficacy of resolution, and more diligence of endeavor. When I survey my past life, I discover nothing but a barren waste of time, with some disorders of body, and disturbances of the mind very near to madness, which I hope He that made me will suffer to extenuate many faults and excuse many deficiencies. Yet much remains to be repented and reformed. I hope that I refer more to God than in former times, and consider more what submission is due to his dispensations. But I have very little reformed my practical life; and the time in which I can struggle with habits cannot be now expected to be long. Grant, O God, that I may no longer resolve in vain, or dream away the life which thy indulgence gives me, in vacancy and uselessness.

THOUGHTS. These extracts are from the posthumous volume, *Prayers and Meditations* (1785), published by the Reverend George Strahan, the son of Johnson's old printer, from papers entrusted to him not long before Johnson died. Johnson thought that something might be salvaged from these loose and disconnected fragments, to make a little book the proceeds of which might be put to charitable uses; but he can hardly have re-examined the contents with any attention or remembered how intimately personal the journal entries and occasional memoranda often were. Such passages, doubtless, he would have expected the editor to withhold and destroy, but Strahan seems not to have felt at liberty to do so. For evidence on the nature of their earlier connection, see Johnson's letter to Strahan of July 15, 1763, on p. 914, above.

April 6, 1777

At the beginning of the year I proposed to myself a scheme of life, and a plan of study; but neither life has been rectified nor study followed. Days and months pass in a dream; and I am afraid that my memory grows less tenacious, and my observation less attentive. If I am decaying, it is time to make haste. My nights are restless and tedious, and my days drowsy.

April 20, 1778

After a good night, as I am forced to reckon, I rose seasonably, and prayed, using the Collect for yesterday.

In reviewing my time from Easter, 1777, I find a very melancholy and shameful blank. So little has been done, that days and months are without any trace. My health has, indeed, been very much interrupted. My nights have been commonly not only restless but painful and fatiguing. My respiration was once so difficult that an asthma was suspected. I could not walk, but with great difficulty, from Stowhill to Greenhill. Some relaxation of my breast has been procured, I think, by opium, which, though it never gives me sleep, frees my breast from spasms.

I have written a little of the *Lives of the Poets*. I think with all my usual vigor. I have made sermons, perhaps as readily as formerly. My memory is less faithful in retaining names and, I am afraid, in retaining occurrences. Of this vacillation and vagrancy of mind, I impute a great part to a fortuitous and unsettled life, and therefore purpose to spend my time with more method.

This year, the 28th of March passed away without memorial. Poor Tetty,[1] whatever were our faults and failings, we loved each other. I did not forget thee yesterday. Couldest thou have lived! — I am now, with the help of God, to begin a new life.

April 2, 1779. Good Friday, 11 P.M.

I am now to review the last year, and find little but dismal vacuity, neither business nor pleasure; much intended, and little done. My health is much broken; my nights afford me little rest. I have tried opium, but its help is counterbalanced with great disturbance; it prevents the spasms, but it hinders sleep. O God, have mercy on me.

Last week I published [the first part of] the *Lives of the Poets,* written, I hope, in such a manner as may tend to the promotion of piety.

1. **Tetty:** Johnson's wife, who had died in 1752.

In this last year I have made little acquisition; I have scarcely read anything. I maintain Mrs. [Desmoulins] and her daughter. Other good of myself I know not where to find, except a little charity.

But I am now in my seventieth year; what can be done, ought not to be delayed.

April 3, 1779. Easter Eve, 11 P.M.

This is the time of my annual review, and annual resolution. The review is comfortless, little done. Part of the *Life of Dryden* and the *Life of Milton* have been written; but my mind has neither been improved nor enlarged. I have read little, almost nothing. And I am not conscious that I have gained any good, or quitted any evil, habits.

Of resolutions I have made so many, with so little effect, that I am almost weary, but, by the help of God, am not yet hopeless. Good resolutions must be made and kept. I am almost seventy years old, and have no time to lose. The distressful restlessness of my nights makes it difficult to settle the course of my days. Something, however, let me do.

September 18, 1780

I am now beginning the seventy-second year of my life, with more strength of body and greater vigor of mind than I think is common at that age. But though the convulsions in my breast are relieved, my sleep is seldom long. My nights are wakeful and therefore I am sometimes sleepy in the day. I have been attentive to my diet, and have diminished the bulk of my body. I have not at all studied nor written diligently. I have *Swift* and *Pope* yet to write; *Swift* is just begun.

I have forgotten or neglected my resolutions or purposes, which I now humbly and timorously renew. Surely I shall not spend my whole life with my own total disapprobation. Perhaps God may grant me now to begin a wiser and a better life.

Almighty God, my Creator and Preserver, who hast permitted me to begin another year, look with mercy upon my wretchedness and frailty. Rectify my thoughts, relieve my perplexities, strengthen my purposes, and reform my doings. Let increase of years bring increase of faith, hope, and charity. Grant me diligence in whatever work thy providence shall appoint me. Take not from me thy Holy Spirit, but let me pass the remainder of the days which Thou shalt yet allow me, in thy fear and to thy glory; and when it shall be thy good pleasure to call me hence, grant me, O Lord, forgiveness of my sins, and receive me to everlasting happiness, for the sake of Jesus Christ our Lord. Amen.

April 13, 1781. Good Friday

I forgot my prayer and resolutions, till two days ago I found this paper.

Some time in March I finished the *Lives of the Poets,* which I wrote in my usual way, dilatorily and hastily, unwilling to work, and working with vigor and haste.

On Wednesday 11 was buried my dear friend Thrale, who died on Wednesday 4; and with him were buried many of my hopes and pleasures. About five, I think, on Wednesday morning he expired; I felt almost the last flutter of his pulse, and looked for the last time upon the face that for fifteen years had never been turned upon me but with respect or benignity. Farewell. May God, that delighteth in mercy, have had mercy on thee.

September 18, 1781

This is my seventy-third birthday, an awful day. I said a preparatory prayer last night, and waking early made use, in the dark, as I sat up in bed, of the prayer [beginning of this year]. I rose, breakfasted, and gave thanks at church for my creation, preservation, and redemption. As I came home, I thought I had never begun any period of life so placidly. . . . I have always been accustomed to let this day pass unnoticed, but it came this time into my mind that some little festivity was not improper. I had a dinner, and invited Allen and Levet.

The following prayer was composed and used by Doctor Johnson previous to his receiving the sacrament of the Lord's Supper, on Sunday, December 5, 1784. He died on December 13.

Almighty and most merciful Father, I am now, as to human eyes it seems, about to commemorate, for the last time, the death of thy Son Jesus Christ, our Saviour and Redeemer. Grant, O Lord, that my whole hope and confidence may be in his merits, and thy mercy; enforce and accept my imperfect repentance; make this commemoration available to the confirmation of my faith, the establishment of my hope, and the enlargement of my charity; and make the death of thy Son Jesus Christ effectual to my redemption. Have mercy upon me, and pardon the multitude of my offenses. Bless my friends; have mercy upon all men. Support me, by the grace of thy Holy Spirit, in the days of weakness, and at the hour of death; and receive me, at my death, to everlasting happiness, for the sake of Jesus Christ. Amen.

Author-Title Index

This is a combined index for both volumes of *Major British Writers*. The appropriate volume number is indicated by a roman numeral after each entry. Author's names are in boldface type, and the page numbers of the introductions to their writings are in italics.

Index of First Lines by Volume

VOLUME I

VOLUME II